THE NEW FONTANA DICTIONARY OF MODERN THOUGHT

THE NEW FONTANA DICTIONARY OF MODERN THOUGHT

Edited by Alan Bullock & Stephen Trombley
Assistant editor: Alf Lawrie

HarperCollins*Publishers*

HarperCollins*Publishers*
77–85 Fulham Palace Road
Hammersmith, London W6 8JB

First published in Great Britain by
Fontana Press 1977

Second edition published by Fontana Press 1988
Reprinted eleven times

Third edition published by HarperCollins*Publishers* 1999
1 3 5 7 9 8 6 4 2

A catalogue record for this book
is available from the British Library

ISBN 0 00 255871 8

Set in Postscript Linotype Times by
Rowland Phototypesetting Ltd
Bury St Edmunds, Sufffolk
Printed and bound in Great Britain by
Caledonian International Book Manufacturing Ltd, Glasgow

Introduction

This third edition of the *Fontana Dictionary of Modern Thought* is the result of more than twenty-five years of work. It contains 3,764 entries by 326 contributors; 711 entries were deleted from the second edition; 984 entries are wholly new to this edition, and the majority of those that remain have been recommissioned or revised to reflect the changes that have occurred over a quarter-century. Though many of the ideas and concepts of the original edition have survived, very few have escaped substantial revision. These include not only the basic foundations of the twentieth-century intellectual climate (Darwinism, Marxism, psychoanalysis, etc.), but even old and well-established subjects as diverse as mathematics and theology. In the decade that has passed since the second edition, the pace of change has been enormous. Much of that change has been the result of technologies that have greatly influenced the way we live. Ten years ago, it would have been unthinkable that the entire text of this book could be generated on a personal computer via a combination of databases and word-processing software, and delivered to the publisher in a matter of seconds via twenty-six e-mail attachments. In the last edition of this book, random access memory and central processing units were entries; today they require no explanation that cannot be found in an ordinary dictionary. We now live in a world of hypertext, virtual reality and fuzzy logic. Biotechnologies have brought about a different order of change. Today (and tomorrow) ideas such as gene therapy and cloning are realities which pose fresh challenges in law and human rights, and have led to new disciplines such as bioethics to help meet those challenges.

But most change has by no means been technology-driven. Movements like feminism have now matured into full-blown disciplines with a history that is already long and complex, complete with schools, factions, revisionists and a vanguard that continues not only to explore concepts but to exert powerful influence on our social structures. The same is true in the area of environmental studies, a subject that has been much expanded in the present edition. Identity politics – whether of race, gender or sexual identity – has become, in the past decade, a cornerstone of the new Western academic tradition. These disciplines not only embrace and challenge the foundations on which twentieth-century thought is based but have had an immense impact on both the political culture and the wider social attitudes of Western democracies.

The question of what to include, what to omit, and what to delete is one that has vexed us for a quarter of a century, and has been perhaps most difficult in the preparation of the present edition. In the end, as editors whose intellectual and cultural experiences are quite different, but which embrace most of the twentieth century and two continents, we have followed our own counsel in deciding upon the contents of this book, and on our choices of contributors. It is unthinkable that we can satisfy all readers; but we hope we have satisfied the majority of most readers' enquiries.

Finally: throughout the book we have used the third person pronoun 'he' and its possessive 'his'. We recognise that in many hundreds of instances 'she' and 'her' are equally applicable. But to use 'she/he' and 'her/his' would have put a strain on the pages allotted to us. In submitting to these constraints, we wish to make clear that we imply no preference as to gender.

Alan Bullock
Stephen Trombley

Acknowledgements

In the preparation of the third edition, the editors have benefited greatly from the labours of Alf Lawrie, assistant editor, whose broad learning and wide-ranging curiosity proved invaluable. We are also grateful for his able execution of the enormous volume of administrative work that goes into an enterprise such as this.

We would also like to thank Ingaret Eden for her careful copy-editing and inputting of text. We are grateful to Bruce Eadie, assistant editor of the second edition, who made himself available to answer many queries from the editors.

A large debt of thanks is due to our agent, Andrew Best. He has been present from the start, when he was with Curtis Brown, not only by introducing the editors of this book but also in offering a keen critical and publishing intelligence which has helped to shape the first and subsequent editions. Thanks are also due to Jonathan Lloyd, Managing Director, Curtis Brown, London, and to John F. Thornton of the Spieler Agency, New York, for their support.

We would like to thank our publishers for their continuing faith in this project. In their days at Fontana, Helen Fraser and Simon King nurtured the previous edition through the press. At HarperCollins, Stuart Proffitt and Toby Mundy have been active collaborators, and they are ably succeeded by Michael Fishwick and Richard Johnson. We wish also to thank Ian Paten, whose careful reading of the text led to many improvements. We are fortunate to have W. W. Norton as our American publishers, and we are grateful to Donald S. Lamm and Angela von der Lippe for their commitment to this new edition.

Our main thanks go to our contributors. Over the past twenty-five years we have had the privilege of working with men and women of outstanding ability who have invariably risen to the difficult task of communicating their specialist knowledge to a general reader. While the editors have made every effort to supply information about the contributors that is correct at the time of going to press, certain contributors whose entries have survived from previous editions have proved impossible to trace. The editors and publishers would be grateful to receive information which will enable them to put matters right where necessary in future printings.

How to Use This Book

The arrangement of this book should be largely self-explanatory, and the best general rule is: follow your nose. Words and phrases should always, in the first instance, be sought directly, not under some more comprehensive term; this is a dictionary rather than an encyclopaedia. The term sought *may*, of course, prove to be explained under some other heading; if so, there will always be a cross-reference. Thus, a reader wishing to learn the meaning of 'acquired characteristics' will find **acquired characteristics**, see under LAMARCKISM.

Alphabetical arrangement. This is on the word-by-word principle – meaning, for example, that phrases beginning with the word 'art' – '***art autre***', '**art history**', '***art nouveau***', and so on – precede terms such as '**artificial intelligence**' (which, on the letter-by-letter principle, would come before '***art nouveau***'). Acronyms are treated as if they were words, so that, for example, '**ABC art**' comes between '**Abbaye de Créteil**' and '**abduction**'.

Phrases. These are mostly to be found under the first word of the phrase. For example, '**abstract expressionism**' is found under the letter '**A**'. In certain cases, however, the phrase has been inverted because the important word is not the first (for example, '**science, sociology of**', *not* 'sociology of science').

Full or abbreviated heading. Entries on organizations or concepts commonly known by their initials (**UN, ESP**) will be found under their initials, and *not* the full name, which in many cases (such as **KGB**) might be known only to specialists. However, where the abbreviation tends to be confined to professionals addressing other professionals (such as 'AI' for '**artificial intelligence**'), or where the full term is very well known (such as '**Exchange Rate Mechanism**' for '**ERM**'), then the full term has been adopted.

Cross-references. Cross-references within the dictionary are indicated by SMALL CAPITALS, and most entries contain one or more references to other entries in the book. However, the cross-reference will have been included only if it seems genuinely relevant to the context.

In many cases, the cross-references in small capitals are to a slightly different form of the word or phrase thus given. Singulars and plurals are regarded as interchangeable, as are the terminations -ISM and -IST: for example, a reader following up an allusion to 'MARXIST thought' will find the entry not under 'marxist' but under '**marxism**'.

List of Contributors

A.A.L. Alf Lawrie, writer and television researcher

A.B. Albert Bandura, David Starr Jordan Professor of Social Science in Psychology, Stanford University

A.B.E. A. B. Eadie, Managing Director, Worldview Pictures, London

A.B.S. A. Babington Smith, consultant, management training; formerly Senior Lecturer in Experimental Psychology, University of Oxford

A.BEN. Andy Bennet, Lecturer in Sociology, University of Glasgow

A.BR. Alex Brummer, Financial Editor of the *Guardian*

A.C. the late Sir Alec Cairncross, FBA, formerly Master of St Peter's College, Oxford; Economic Adviser to the British government

A.C.G. A. C. Grayling, Lecturer in Philosophy, Birkbeck College, University of London

A.CL. Angus Clarke, Reader in Clinical Genetics, University of Wales, College of Medicine

A.D.M. A. D. Mendelow, Professor of Neurosurgery and consultant neurosurgeon, Newcastle General Hospital

A.E. Amitai Etzioni, PhD, writer and director and founder, The Communitarian Network

A.E.B. A. E. Bender, Emeritus Professor of Nutrition, University of London

A.EH. Anoushiravan Ehteshami, Reader in International Relations, Centre for Middle Eastern and Islamic Studies, University of Durham

A.F.B. the late Alastair Buchan, formerly Professor of International Relations, University of Oxford, and Director of the Institute of Strategic Studies

A.G. Anna Grimshaw, author and editor

A.GH. Ali Gheissari, Adjunct Professor of History and Religious Studies, University of San Diego

A.H. Antony Hopkins, composer, conductor and broadcaster on music; formerly Lecturer and Piano Professor, Royal College of Music, London

A.J.H.R. Anthony J. Harding Rains, Editor, *Journal of the Royal Society of Medicine*; formerly Professor of Surgery, Charing Cross Hospital, London, and Assistant Director of the

British Post Graduate Medical Federation

A.J.M. Andrew Milner, Associate Professor in Comparative Literature and Cultural Studies, Monash University

A.J.M.W. Andrew Wheatcroft, formerly at the Department of History, University of Edinburgh

A.J.W. A. J. Wing, formerly Consultant Physician, St Thomas' Hospital, London

A.K. Alexander Knapp, formerly Visiting Lecturer in Music, Goldsmiths' College, London

A.K.S. Amartya Sen, Master of Trinity College, Cambridge

A.K.W. Angela K. Westwater, art gallery proprietor and director; formerly Managing Editor, *Artforum*

A.KU. Annette Kuhn, teacher and cultural critic

A.L. Andrew Lumsden, formerly Associate Editor, *New Statesman*

A.L.C.B. Alan (Lord) Bullock, FBA, Fellow and Founding Master of St Catherine's College, Oxford; formerly Vice-Chancellor of the University of Oxford

A.L.L. Ann Loades, Professor of Divinity, University of Durham

A.P. Andrew Pomiankowski, formerly Research Student, Wellcome Institute for the History of Medicine, London

A.P.H. Anthony Hall, civilian consultant physician to the Ministry of Defence

A.P.HI. Anne Hill, Lecturer in Media Studies, West Kent College

A.Q. Anthony (Lord) Quinton, FBA, formerly Chairman of the British Library Board; formerly President of Trinity College, University of Oxford

A.R. Alan Ryan, Professor of Politics, Princeton University

A.R.H. A. R. Hoelzel, Reader in Molecular Ecology, Department of Biological Sciences, University of Durham

A.R.T. Alan Templeton, Professor of Biology and Genetics, Washington University

A.S. Aaron Sloman, Professor of Cognitive Science and Artificial Intelligence, School of Computer Science, University of Birmingham

A.S.G. Andrew Goudie, Professor of Geography, University of Oxford

A.SA. Alex Sakula, consultant physician, formerly at Redhill General Hospital, Surrey

A.V.D.B. Annette Van den Bosch, art historian, Director of Graduate Programmes in Art Administration, National Centre for Australian Studies, Monash University

A.W. Andrew Williams, Reader in International Relations, University of Kent at Canterbury

B.A.F. B. A. Farrell, Emeritus Fellow, Corpus Christi College, formerly Wilde Reader in Mental Philosophy, University of Oxford

LIST OF CONTRIBUTORS

B.BE. Bice Benevenuto, psychoanalyst; founder of the Cultural Centre for Freudian Studies and Research, London

B.BU. Bernard Burgoyne, Senior Lecturer in Sociology and Director of the Psychoanalytic Study Group, University of Middlesex

B.C. Barry Cunliffe, FBA, Fellow of Keble College; Professor of European Archaeology and Director of the Institute of Archaeology, University of Oxford

B.CO. Billy Cowie, Senior Lecturer in Music, University of Brighton

B.D.A. Barry Adam, Professor of Sociology, University of Windsor, Canada

B.D.S. Barrie D. Sherman, author of *State of the Unions*

B.E.L. Bill Lawson, Professor of African Studies, Michigan State University

B.F. Brian Fender, Vice-Chancellor, University of Keele; formerly Director, Institut Laue-Langevin, Grenoble

B.H.K. Bernard Knight, MD, barrister; Professor of Forensic Pathology, University of Wales College of Medicine, Cardiff

B.K. Bernard Keeffe, conductor and broadcaster

B.L.B. Barbara L. Baer, writer on dance

B.M. Barry MacDonald, Professor of Education and Director of the Centre for Applied Research in Education, University of East Anglia

B.M.-H. Ben Martin-Hoogewerf, Lecturer in Communications, Uxbridge Technical College

B.R. Boris Rubinsky, Chancellor's Professor, Biomedical Engineering, University of California at Berkeley

C.C. Colin Crowder, Lecturer in Theology, Durham University

C.C.B. Conor Cruise O'Brien, writer and journalist

C.C.N. Christopher Norris, Distinguished Research Professor in Philosophy, University of Wales, Cardiff

C.E.D. Collins English Dictionary, Second Edition, London and Glasgow, 1986

C.G. Clara Greed, Reader in the Built Environment, University of the West of England

C.J. Christine Jones, District Physiotherapist, Waltham Forest Health Authority

C.L.-H. Christopher Longuet-Higgins, FRS, Emeritus Royal Society Research Professor, University of Sussex

C.M.B. Chris M. Bishop, Senior Researcher, Microsoft Research, Cambridge; Professor of Computer Science, University of Edinburgh

C.O. the late Christopher Ounstead, formerly Medical Director, Park Hospital for Children, University of Oxford

C.P. Chris Philo, formerly at the Department of Geography,

University of Cambridge
C.S. the late Christopher Strachey, formerly Professor of Computation, University of Oxford
C.T. Carl Talbot, Lecturer in Philosophy, University of Wales, Cardiff
D.A.P. D. A. Pyke, formerly Physician-in-Charge, Diabetic Department, King's College Hospital, London
D.B. the late Daniel Bell, Professor Emeritus, Harvard University
D.BR. David Brown, formerly Assistant Keeper, Modern Collection, Tate Gallery, London
D.C. David Crystal, OBE, Honorary Professor of Linguistics, University of Wales, Bangor
D.C.M.Y. D. C. M. Yardley, Chairman, Commission for Local Administration in England
D.C.W. Donald Cameron Watt, Stevenson Professor of International History, London School of Economics
D.D. David Doyle, Consultant Rheumatologist, Whipps Cross and St Bartholomew's Hospitals, London
D.E. Douglas Evans, author and lecturer
D.E.B. the late Donald Broadbent, FRS, external staff, Medical Research Council, University of Oxford
D.F. Dominique Florin, Honorary Lecturer in Public Health Medicine, London School of Hygiene and Tropical Medicine
D.H. David Hartley, formerly Lecturer in Psychology, University of Strathclyde
D.H.G. D. H. Gath, Emeritus Clinical Reader in Psychiatry, University of Oxford; and Honorary Consultant Psychiatrist, the Warneford Hospital, Oxford
D.H.M.W. the late D. Woollam, formerly Fellow of Emmanuel College, Cambridge
D.J.E. D. J. Enright, poet, novelist, critic, editor and publisher
D.J.W. D. J. Wood, Professor of Psychology, University of Nottingham
D.L. Darian Leader, Founder of the Cultural Centre for Freudian Studies and Research, London
D.L.E. David Edwards, formerly Provost of Southwark Cathedral, London
D.L.W. Douglas L. Woolf, Honorary Consultant Rheumatologist, Forest Health Care; Trustee, Arthritis Care; formerly Consultant Rheumatologist; Medical Director, Horder Centre for Arthritis
D.M. David Morris, Consultant Paediatrician Emeritus
D.P. David Papineau, Lecturer in History and Philosophy of Science, University of Cambridge
D.P.M. Daniel Patrick Moynihan, United States Senator, Washington, DC

LIST OF CONTRIBUTORS

D.PR. David Priestland, Tutor in Modern History, St Edmund Hall, University of Oxford

D.S. David Souden, writer and television producer; formerly Fellow of Emmanuel College, Cambridge

D.T.M. David McLellan, Professor of Political Theory, University of Kent at Canterbury

D.V. Deryck Viney, formerly Czechoslovak Programme Organizer, BBC External Services

D.W. Don White, advertising executive

D.W.R. D. W. Ryan, Consultant in Intensive Care, Freeman Hospital, Newcastle-upon-Tyne

E.A.R. Adam Roberts, FBA, Montague Burton Professor of International Relations, University of Oxford

E.B.B. Edmund Blair Bolles, author

E.E. E. Ernst, Haemorheology Research Laboratory, Clinic for Physical Medicine, University of Munich

E.G. E. Gerbenik, formerly Principal, Civil Service College, and Joint Editor, *Population Studies*

E.H. Edward Higginbottom, FRCO, Tutor in Music and Fellow of New College, University of Oxford

E.H.P.B. Sir Henry Phelps Brown, FBA, Professor Emeritus of Economics of Labour, University of London

E.J.L. E. John Lowe, Professor of Philosophy, University of Durham

E.L.-S. Erika Lueders-Salmon, formerly Research Officer, Inner London Education Authority

E.O.W. Edward O. Wilson, F. B. Baird Professor of Science, Harvard University

E.R.L. E. R. Laithwaite, formerly Professor of Heavy Electrical Engineering, Imperial College of Science and Technology, London

E.V.B. Eileen Barker, Professor of Sociology with special reference to the study of religion, London School of Economics

E.W.N. Wayne Nafziger, Commerce Bank Distinguished Graduate Faculty and Professor of Economics, Kansas State University

G.B. George Butterworth, Professor of Psychology, University of Stirling

G.B.R. George Richardson, Honorary Fellow, St John's College, University of Oxford

G.D.R. Graham Richards, part-time Principal Lecturer in Psychology, Staffordshire University

G.H.P. George Henry Peters, Research Professor in Agricultural Economics, University of Oxford

G.M. Gordon Mangan, Senior Research Fellow, Department of Psychology, University of Auckland

G.N. Garet Newell, teacher of the Feldenkrais Method
G.P.W. G. Wagner, Professor and Chair, Department of Ecology and Evolutionary Biology, Yale University
G.R.S. Graham Smith, Department of Geography, University of Cambridge
G.S. the late G. Stuvel, Emeritus Fellow of All Souls College; formerly University Lecturer in Economic Statistics, University of Oxford
GE.S. Geoff Smith, writer and broadcaster on music
H.G. Howard Gardner, Professor of Education, Graduate School of Education, Harvard University
H.L. Hope Liebersohn, formerly Lecturer in Linguistics, Hatfield Polytechnic
H.L.A.H. the late Herbert Hart, FBA, formerly Principal of Brasenose College, University of Oxford
H.L'E. the late Hugh L'Etang, Editor, *Travel Medicine International*; Consultant Medical Editor, *The Physician*
H.M. Howard McGary, Professor of Philosophy, Rutgers, the State University of New Jersey
H.M.R. the late H. M. Rosenberg, Reader in Physics, Clarendon Laboratory, University of Oxford
H.TA. the late Henry Tajfel, formerly Professor of Social Psychology, University of Bristol
H.TH. Howard Thomas, formerly Director of the Decisions Analysis Unit, London Graduate School of Business Studies
H.W. Helen Wilkinson, writer and Project Director at DEMOS; Research Associate at the Families and Work Institute in New York; 1997–98 Commonwealth Fund Harkness Fellow
I.K. Irma Kurtz, writer and broadcaster
I.L.W. Isobel Wollaston, Lecturer in Theology, University of Birmingham
I.M.D.L. Ian Little, FBA, formerly Professor of the Economics of Underdeveloped Countries, University of Oxford, and Special Adviser to the World Bank
I.M.L.H. Ian M. L. Hunter, Professor Emeritus of Psychology, University of Keele
I.P.R. Ian Roberts, Lecturer in Sociology, University of Durham
J.A.A.S. J. Stockwin, Nissan Professor of Modern Japanese Studies and Director of the Nissan Institute of Japanese Studies, University of Oxford
J.A.G. Jeffrey A. Gray, Professor of Psychology, Institute of Psychiatry, University of London
J.A.M. Sir J. A. Mirrlees, FBA, Emeritus Professor of Nuffield College, University of Oxford
J.D. the late John Davy, formerly Assistant Principal, Emerson

College, Forest Row

J.D.B. John Barrow, Professor of Astronomy, Astronomy Centre, University of Sussex

J.D.N. John North, Professor of the History of Philosophy, University of Groningen

J.D.O. J. D. Oriel, formerly Consultant Physician in Genito-Urinary Medicine, University College Hospital, London

J.E. John Erickson, Professor Emeritus, Defence Studies, University of Edinburgh

J.E.O. James Ourie, lawyer

J.E.S. J. E. Stoy, Vice-Master of Balliol College and Tutor in Computation, University of Oxford

J.F.T. John Thornton, author and literary agent

J.G. Jean Gottman, FBA, Emeritus Professor of Geography, University of Oxford

J.G.R. Julian Rushton, formerly Lecturer in Music, University of Cambridge

J.G.W. John Weightman, Professor Emeritus, University of London

J.H. Janet Husband, Professor of Radiology, Royal Marsden Hospital, Surrey

J.H.G. John H. Goldthorpe, FBA, Official Fellow of Nuffield College, University of Cambridge

J.H.H. J. H. Humphrey, Professor Emeritus of Immunology, University of London

J.I. John Izbicki, Chief Paris Correspondent, formerly Education Editor, *Daily Telegraph*, London

J.J.J. John J. Joughin, Senior Lecturer in Cultural and Critical Theory at the Department of Cultural Studies, University of Central Lancashire

J.K. John Keegan, military historian and Defence Correspondent for the *Daily Telegraph*

J.L.M.L. J. L. M. Lambert, freelance writer and part-time academic; formerly Museum Lecturer, Geological Museum, London

J.L.V. Julian Verbov, Consultant Dermatologist, Liverpool Health Authority; Clinical Lecturer in Dermatology, University of Liverpool

J.M. James Montaldi, Professor of Mathematics, University of Nice

J.M.C. J. M. Cullen, Department of Zoology, Monash University

J.M.M. Jeffrey Masson, writer and Research Associate, University of California at Berkeley

J.M.S. J. Maynard Smith, FRS, Professor of Biology, University of Sussex

J.ME. Jeremy Melvin, journalist

J.N.B. J. N. Buxton, Professor of Information Technology, King's College, London

J.N.W. Sir John Walton, Warden of Green College, Oxford; formerly Professor of Neurology, University of Newcastle-upon-Tyne

J.P. John Pierson, Lecturer in Economics, University of Kent at Canterbury; and Director of the Kent Energy Economic Research Group

J.P.G. Joshua Gamson, Assistant Professor of Sociology, Yale University

J.R. Jonathan Raban, writer and journalist

J.R.T. John Torrance, Emeritus Fellow of Hertford College, University of Oxford

J.R.W. John Wilmoth, Associate Professor of Demography, University of California Berkeley

J.R.Y. J. R. Yarnold, Consultant in Radiotherapy and Oncology, Royal Marsden Hospital, London

J.S. Jack Schofield, Computer Editor of the *Guardian*

J.S.B. Jerome Bruner, Research Professor of Psychology and Senior Research Fellow in Law, New York University

J.S.F. J. S. Fleming, formerly Economic Adviser to the Governor of the Bank of England

J.T. James Thorpe, Director, Huntingdon Library, Art Gallery and Botanical Gardens, San Marino, California

J.T.M. Toby Mundy, writer and publisher

J.V.D. Sir John Dacie, FRS, Emeritus Professor of Haematology, Royal Postgraduate Medical School, Hammersmith Hospital, University of London

J.V.H.K. J. V. Harvey Kemble, Consultant Plastic Surgeon, St Bartholomew's Hospital, London, and North-East Thames Regional Plastic Surgery Centre, St Andrew's Hospital, Billericay, Essex

J.W. John Willett, formerly Assistant Editor, *Times Literary Supplement*; writer and critic

J.WI. John Winstanley, Consulting Ophthalmic Surgeon, St Thomas' Hospital, London

J.Z. John Michael Ziman, FRS, Chairman of the Science Policy Support Group; Visiting Professor, Imperial College, London; formerly Professor of Physics, University of Bristol

K.A. the late Kingsley Amis, writer

K.A.A. Karen Armstrong, historian of religion

K.D. Katherina Dalton, Consultant Gynaecological Endocrinologist, London

K.E.H. the late K. E. Hunt, formerly Director, Institute of Agricultural Economics, University of Oxford

K.H. Keith Hope, Professor of Sociology, Southern Illinois University

K.K. Krishan Kumar, Professor of Sociology, University of Virginia
K.M. Kenneth Mellanby, writer; formerly Honorary Professor of Biology, Cardiff University College
K.M.D. Keith Dowding, Reader in Public Choice and Public Administration, London School of Economics
K.W. Kwasi Wiredu, Professor of Philosophy, University of South Florida
L.A. Liz Aggiss, Senior Lecturer on Dance, University of Brighton
L.J.F. Leisa Freeman, Honorary Lecturer and Associate Specialist in Cardiology, Norfolk and Norwich Health Care Trust, Norfolk
L.L. Leopold Labedz, Editor, *Survey*; formerly Professor of Politics, Stanford University
L.M. Lynda Morris, writer on art
L.R.G. Lewis Gordon, Professor of Afro-American Studies, Contemporary Religious Thought, and Modern Culture and Media, Brown University; Faculty Member of the Center for the Study of Race and Ethnicity in America
L.T. Lionel Trippett, CND Information and Education Worker
M.A. Michael Anderson, Professor of Drama, University College of North Wales
M.A.H.D. M. A. H. Dempster, Professor of Mathematics, Dalhousie University, New Brunswick
M.A.P. Marcelo Pollack, DPhil, Research Associate, Institute for European-Latin American Relations, Madrid
M.B. Michele Barrett, Professor of Sociology, the City University
M.BE. Marion Bernstein, District Psychologist, West Lambeth Health Authority, London
M.BI. Michael Billington, drama critic, the *Guardian*
M.BR. Michael Brawne, practising architect; Professor Emeritus, University of Bath
M.C. Mary Chamot, formerly Assistant Keeper, Tate Gallery, London
M.D. Mark Dery, cultural critic and writer
M.D.B. Michael D. Biddiss, Professor of History, University of Reading
M.D.H. Martin Holborn, Lecturer in Sociology, Preston College, and freelance writer
M.D.L. Manfred Laubichler, Program in History of Science, Princeton University
M.E. Maria Enzensberger, writer and translator
M.E.A.B. the late Marian Bowley, formerly Professor Emeritus of Political Economy, University College, London
M.F. the late Maurice Freedman, formerly Professor of Social Anthropology, University of Oxford

M.F.G.S. M. F. G. Scott, Emeritus Fellow of Nuffield College, University of Oxford

M.F.H. Mark Hussey, Professor of English, Pace University, New York

M.G.A. Michael Archer, art critic and lecturer, Chelsea College of Art & Design

M.H. Mark Harris, Researcher in anthropology, University of Manchester

M.H.A.B. Michel Blanc, Emeritus Reader in Applied Linguistics and Bilingualism, University of London

M.J. Medwyn Jones, lawyer

M.J.C. M. J. Crowe, Consultant Psychiatrist, Maudsley Hospital, London

M.JA. Mo Jamshidi, AT & T Professor and Director, NASA Center for Autonomous Control Engineering, University of New Mexico

M.K. M. Kinsbourne, Associate Professor of Pediatrics and Neurology, Duke University Medical Center

M.L. Mary Lambert, formerly geography teacher, Highworth School, Ashford, Kent

M.LO. Michelle Lowe, formerly at the Department of Geography, University of Cambridge

M.R. Mark Ridley, Lecturer in biology, Somerville College, Oxford

M.S. the late Michael Shephard, formerly Professor of Epidemiological Psychiatry, Institute of Psychiatry, University of London

M.S.-S. the late Martin Seymour-Smith, formerly Visiting Professor of English, University of Wisconsin; author of *A Guide to Modern World Literature*

M.S.B. the late M. S. Bartlett, FRS, formerly Emeritus Professor of Biomathematics, University of Oxford

M.S.BR. Malcolm Bradbury, novelist, critic and Professor Emeritus of American Studies, University of East Anglia

M.S.E. Mary Evans, Professor of Women's Studies, the University of Kent at Canterbury

M.S.P. Michael Piraino, Executive Assistant to the President and College Council, Allegheny College, Meadville, Pennsylvania

M.V.B. Sir Michael Berry, FRS, Professor of Physics, University of Bristol

M.V.P. Michael Posner, formerly Economic Director, National Economic Development Office, London

M.W. Michael Walters, formerly postgraduate at the University of Kent at Canterbury

N.A.R. Norman Routledge, PhD, formerly Fellow of King's College,

University of Cambridge, and mathematics master at Eton College

N.G. N. Glazer, Graduate School of Education, Harvard University

N.H.H. Nigel H. Harris, Honorary Consultant Orthopaedic Surgeon, St Mary's Hospital and Medical School, London

N.M. Nicola Miller, Lecturer in Latin American History, University College, London

N.O. Nicholas Owen, Praelector and University Lecturer in Politics, Queen's College, Oxford

N.S. Nigel South, Professor of Sociology, University of Essex

N.SM. Ninian Smart, J. F. Rowny Professor of Comparative Religion, University of California, Santa Barbara; and President of the American Academy of Religion

N.T. the late Niko Tinbergen, FRS, Emeritus Professor of Animal Behaviour, University of Oxford; Nobel Laureate in Physiology

O.S. the late Oliver Stallybrass, Joint Editor of the first edition of *The Fontana Dictionary of Modern Thought*

O.Y.E. O. Y. Elagab, Reader in Law, City University, London

P.A.D.S. Peter Singer, Center for Human Bioethics, Monash University, New Zealand

P.A.L. Paul Lombardo, Associate Professor of Law, Institute of Law, Psychiatry and Public Policy, University of Virginia

P.B. Peter Burke, Fellow of Emmanuel College, University of Cambridge

P.C. Patrick Conner, Associate, Martyn Gregory Gallery, London

P.C.B. Philip Ball, Associate Editor of *Nature*

P.C.P. Patrick C. Pietroni, Senior Lecturer in General Practice, St Mary's Hospital Medical School, London

P.E.B. Peter Elwood Bryant, Watts Professor of Psychology, University of Oxford

P.G.B. Paul G. Bahn, freelance writer; Contributing Editor, *Archaeology* magazine, New York

P.G.F.N. Peter Nixon, formerly Consultant Cardiologist, Charing Cross Hospital, London

P.H. Peter Haggett, Professor of Urban and Regional Geography, University of Bristol

P.J. Peter Jay, Editor, *Banking World*; broadcaster; formerly British Ambassador to the USA

P.J.B. Peter Bowler, Professor of History and Philosophy of Science, Queen's University, Belfast

P.J.D. Paul Davies, Senior Lecturer in Architecture at South Bank University, London

P.J.S. Peter J. Smith, Reader in Earth Sciences, the Open University; Scientific Editor, *Geology Today*

P.J.W. Paul Weindling, Reader in the History of Medicine, University of Oxford

P.L. Peter Lentini, lecturer in Politics, Monash University, New Zealand

P.L.H. Paul L. Harris, Vice-President of St John's College, University of Oxford

P.LE. Peter Levine, Research Scholar, Institute for Philosophy and Public Policy, University of Maryland

P.M. the late Sir Peter Medawar, OM, FRS, Member of the Scientific Staff, Medical Research Council; Nobel Laureate in Medicine

P.M.K. P. M. Kelly, Assistant Director, Climatic Research Unit, University of East Anglia

P.M.O. Peter M. Oppenheimer, Student of Christ Church, University of Oxford

P.N. Peter Newmark, Publishing Director and Editor, *Current Biology*

P.O.M. Peter Muller, Professor of Geography, University of Miami

P.S.L. Peter S. Leuner, Chairman, Division of Social Sciences, Richmond College, Surrey

P.T. Peter B. Townsend, Emeritus Professor of Social Policy, University of Bristol

P.W. Paul Wilkinson, Professor of International Relations, University of Aberdeen

Q.B. the late Quentin Bell, formerly Emeritus Professor of Fine Art, University of Sussex

R.A.H. R. A. Hodgkin, formerly Lecturer in Education

R.B. Ronald Butt, political columnist, *The Times*; formerly Assistant Editor, *Sunday Times*

R.C. Robert Conquest, writer; author of *The Great Terror*

R.C.O.M. R. C. O. Matthews, FBA, Master of Clare College and Professor of Political Economy, University of Chicago

R.D. R. D'Amico, Graduate Co-ordinator, Department of Philosophy, University of Florida

R.F. the late Ronald Fletcher, formerly Professor Emeritus of Sociology, University of Reading

R.F.H. Robin F. Hendry, Lecturer in Philosophy, University of Durham

R.G. the late Robin Gandy, Emeritus Reader in Mathematical Logic, University of Oxford

R.G.T. Robert Twycross, Senior Research Fellow, St Peter's College, Oxford; Director, WHO Collaborating Centre for Palliative Cancer Care, Oxford

R.GI. Raanan Gillon, Professor of Medical Ethics, Imperial College School of Medicine, University of London

R.H. the late Roy Harrod, FBA, formerly Tutor of Christ Church, Oxford

R.H.H. Roger Higgs, MBE, FRCP, FRCGP, Professor of General Practice and Primary Care, King's College School of Medicine, London

R.H.S. R. H. Salter, Clinical Tutor, Cumberland Infirmary, Carlisle

R.HE. Robert Heilbroner, Professor Emeritus, New School for Social Research, New York City

R.I.T. R. I. Tricker, Professor of Finance and Accounting, University of Hong Kong

R.K.H. Kyle Hughes, journalist

R.L. Robert Lekachman, Distinguished Professor of Economics, City University of New York

R.L.G. Richard L. Gregory, Professor of Neuropsychology and Head of the Brain and Perception Laboratory, University of Bristol

R.M.H.L. Robert Lefever, Director of the PROMIS Recovery Centres in London and Kent

R.M.J. R. M. Jameson, formerly Consultant Urologist, Royal Liverpool Hospital

R.M.N. R. M. Needham, FRS, Pro Vice-Chancellor of the Computer Science Department, University of Cambridge

R.P. Roy Porter, Senior Lecturer in the Social History of Medicine, Wellcome Institute for the History of Medicine, London

R.P.S. Renée Paton-Saltzberg, Senior Lecturer in Psychology, Oxford Brookes University

R.PO. Roger Poole, Professor of English, University of Nottingham

R.R. Richard Rosencrance, Professor of International and Comparative Politics, Cornell University

R.S.C. Richard Crouch, formerly Research Assistant, Computer Laboratory, University of Cambridge

R.SI. Robin Sibson, Vice-Chancellor, University of Kent

R.ST. the late Sir Richard Stone, FBA, formerly P. D. Leake Professor of Finance and Accounting, University of Cambridge

R.V.D. Richard Denenberg, writer and former Lecturer in Political Theory and Government, University of Wales

R.W.S. R. W. Sharples, Head of the Department of Greek and Latin, University College, London

S.A. Stanislav Andreski, Professor of Sociology, University of Reading

S.B. Shaun Breslin, Research Student, East Asia Centre, University of Newcastle-upon-Tyne

S.BA. Sara Baase, Professor of Computer Science, San Diego State University

S.BE. Stafford Beer, Visiting Professor of Cybernetics, University of Manchester; Adjunct Professor of Social Systems

Sciences, University of Pennsylvania

S.BR. Samuel Brittan, Assistant Editor, *Financial Times*; Visiting Fellow, Nuffield College, Oxford

S.E.G.L. Stephen Lea, Professor of Psychology, University of Exeter

S.F. Steve Fuller, FRSA, Professor of Social Policy and Sociology, University of Durham

S.H. Susan Haack, Professor of Philosophy, University of Miami

S.J.B. Stephen Ball, Professor of the Sociology of Education and Director of the Centre for Public Policy Research at King's College, London

S.J.F. Stephen Frosh, Professor of Psychology, Birkbeck College, University of London; and Consultant Clinical Psychologist, Tavistock Clinic, London

S.J.G. Julius Gould, Professor Emeritus of Sociology, University of Nottingham

S.J.S. S. J. Steele, Honorary Consultant, UCL Hospital and the Great Ormond Street Children's Hospital; Reader Emeritus in Obstetrics and Gynaecology, University of London

S.L. Sutherland Lyall, journalist

S.M. Sonia Mazey, formerly Senior Lecturer in Politics, University of North London

S.R. Steve Reilly, Lecturer in Politics and Government, University of Kent at Canterbury

S.T. Stephen Trombley, writer and film producer at Worldview Pictures, London

S.T.S.B. Sherry Bates, architect and writer

S.W.L. Stephen Law, Lecturer in Philosophy, Heythrop College, University of London

T.C.C.M. Tom Milne, film critic and film historian

T.G. Tony Gould, writer

T.M. Terence Morris, Professor of Social Institutions, University of London

T.S. Tim Steele, Chairman, Self Direct Ltd

T.T. Trevor Turner, Psychiatric Consultant, Homerton Hospital, London

T.Z.C. Thomas Z. Cassel, Faculties of Human Development, Wayne State University and the Merrill-Palmer Institute

V.A.B. Valerie Bryson, Senior Lecturer in Politics, University of Huddersfield

V.A.M. Victor McKusick, University Professor of Medical Genetics, Johns Hopkins University, Baltimore

V.L. Valerio Lintner, Principal Lecturer, London Guildhall University

W.A.C.S. the late W. A. C. Stewart, formerly Vice-Chancellor and Professor of Education, University of Keele

W.B. Wilfred Beckerman, Fellow of Balliol College, Oxford;

formerly Professor of Political Economy, University of London, and Head of Department of Political Economy, University College, London

W.D.M.P. the late W. D. M. Paton, FRS, Emeritus Professor of Pharmacology, University of Oxford

W.E.C.G. Bill Gillham, Senior Lecturer in Psychology, University of Strathclyde

W.G.R. Walter Rosen, PhD, science policy consultant

W.K. Wilfred Knapp, Emeritus Professor of St Catherine's College, University of Oxford

W.R.L. W. R. Lee, Emeritus Professor of Occupational Health, University of Manchester

W.R.T. W. R. Tyldesley, former Director of Dental Education, University of Liverpool

W.Z. Wendy Zerin, formerly Research Assistant, Department of Experimental Psychology, University of Oxford

A

a posteriori, a priori. Knowledge is *a posteriori* (literally: after experience) when it depends for its justification or authority upon the evidence of experience. *A priori* knowledge, conversely, is not in this way dependent upon experience. Our knowledge of the location of a pen on the table or that Paris is the capital of France is *a posteriori* knowledge. On the other hand, our knowledge that 5 + 7 = 12, or that a vixen is a female fox, is (arguably) *a priori*. It has often been supposed that *a priori* knowledge is restricted to what is necessary and *a posteriori* knowledge to what is contingent (see CONTINGENCY). The above examples obviously conform to this rule. However, the American philosopher Saul Kripke has argued persuasively that there are both contingent truths which can be known *a priori* and NECESSARY TRUTHS that are only establishable *a posteriori*. S.W.L.

Abbaye de Créteil. An early 20th-century experiment in COMMUNITY living, called after the utopian (see UTOPIANISM) Abbaye de Thélème imagined by Rabelais. In 1906 a group of young French writers, artists, and musicians, of whom Georges Duhamel was to become the most famous, settled in a house at Créteil, near Paris, and tried, while pursuing their artistic vocations, to support themselves by growing their own vegetables and working a printing-press. During this period Jules Romains, an associate member of the group, evolved the short-lived literary theory known as *l'unanimisme*, which tried to draw rather facile humanistic (see HUMANISM) reassurance from the fact that all the individuals in a given social group tend to be interdependent and to react on each other. The experiment ended after 14 months, because of disagreements and lack of money. In 1937 Duhamel gave a rather melancholy transposition of it in his novel *Le Désert de Bièvres*. J.G.W.

ABC art, see MINIMAL ART.

abduction. A term popularized by the American pragmatist philosopher C. S. Peirce (1839–1914) as part of an attempt to redefine the relations between facts and theories. Peirce denied the plausibility of INDUCTION, i.e. the doctrine that generalizations emerged almost automatically from the piling up of data. Against this Peirce argued that theorizing was, and should be, a creative process, and that theories should have a validity in their own right, to some degree independent of the data already available which they explained. Not least, he claimed, theories possessed an important predictive function, enabling the formulation of hypotheses which could later be tested experimentally. Good theories should also embody other rational characteristics, such as being simple or readily modified when confronted with counter-factual evidence. Peirce's 'abduction' represents one of many ways in which traditional induction, POSITIVISM and EMPIRICISM began to appear shallow and arid to 20th-century philosophy. For further reading: J. Losee, *An Historical Introduction to the Philosophy of Science* (1980). R.P.

Abell clusters, see under GALAXY CLUSTERS.

ABM (anti-ballistic missiles). An ABM system consists of missiles, radar and other equipment designed to intercept incoming ballistic missiles. A ballistic missile is one which, although initially powered by rockets, completes its trajectory in free-fall. Although in theory it is possible to predict the flight-path of a ballistic missile, in practice it has proved impossible to design an ABM system that works. Nevertheless, the idea has had great appeal for public and politicians alike. Hence President Reagan's STRATEGIC DEFENCE INITIATIVE (SDI, popularly known as Star Wars). This was not much more than a very expensive exercise in science fiction and was abandoned by his successor.

Even at a more modest level, consistent missile interception has proved impossible to achieve. Contrary to the publicity at the time, it is accepted that the US Patriot missiles fired at Iraqi Scud missiles during the Gulf War almost always missed. Nonetheless, the ABM idea is revived at intervals, although such programmes are inevitably seen as hostile by other states, since a state with an effective ABM system might feel it could use its own weapons, knowing it could not be hit in return. For further reading: A. Karp, *Ballistic Missile Proliferation* (1996). L.T.

abnormal psychology. The branch of PSYCHOLOGY concerned with the abnormal behaviour and functioning of organisms. The organisms may be human or infrahuman; but the many psychologists investigating the conditions that produce abnormalities of animal behaviour (e.g. by the use of drugs, by surgical methods, by the design of conflict-producing situations) would not naturally be described as working in the field of abnormal psychology unless their studies were also designed to throw light on the abnormalities of human functioning. The expression is further restricted to functioning that is abnormal in ways which make life difficult for the people concerned, and which may lead them to require special help. Thus, studies of men who are 6 feet 6 inches tall, or who have an intelligence quotient of over 140, would not usually and naturally be called studies of abnormal psychology; whereas similar studies of dwarfs, or of people with IQs (see INTELLIGENCE of under 60, would be so classified (see also MENTAL RETARDATION). The expression is applied, in particular, and most importantly, to phenomena that are abnormal in that they are regarded as 'morbid' in character, i.e. as evidence that the person concerned is in an unhealthy condition. In consequence of the growth, over the last century, of a whole array of therapeutic procedures for the relief of people suffering from mental morbidities, workers in abnormal psychology have also been involved in studying the effectiveness of different methods of therapy.

Because a psychologist working in this field is characteristically concerned with people who are in difficulties or suffering from mental ill-health, he meets them (typically) as patients in a psychiatric and therefore medical context. Whereas the psychiatrist (see PSYCHIATRY) is the medical specialist concerned with the diagnosis and treatment of these patients, the psychologist is solely concerned with the scientific study of their condition, or of the therapy being given them; and he conducts his enquiries with the permission and cooperation (often very active) of the psychiatrist in charge of the patients.

In this century, work in abnormal psychology has contributed to raise standards of precision and caution in the whole field of abnormal mental functioning. It has also uncovered much that was new, e.g. about the constitutional correlates of abnormal functioning, the variables of personality involved (see PERSONALITY TYPES), the environmental conditions that adversely affect the development of personality, and the difficulties of establishing that a therapeutic method is really effective. For further reading: G. Davison, *Abnormal Psychology* (1997). B.A.F.

abolitionism.

(1) Historically, a term associated with the movement for the abolition of slavery and leading abolitionists such as William Wilberforce (1759–1833).

(2) A term in CRIMINOLOGY regarding opposition to the use of prisons and imprisonment, literally calling for their abolition. This may follow a period of phasing out of imprisonment, and embrace new forms of dispute resolution, community sanctions and alternative forms of atonement by rule breakers.

(3) The movement to abolish CAPITAL PUNISHMENT. N.S.

abortion. The death and expulsion of a foetus or embryo before it is viable (between the 20th and 24th week of gestation). Abortion is a medical phenomenon when it occurs naturally (miscarriage). It is also a medical procedure about which there is much ethical debate; and, in the USA, it is a political issue which has been crucial in state and federal elections since the 1970s. The foetus may be removed by a range of methods which include suction, scraping, inducing labour with saline or prostaglandins and, since the 1990s, by taking the artificial steroid mifepristone (RU 486).

Abortion is strictly forbidden for Roman Catholics and Muslims (see CATHOLICISM; ISLAM), and in the USA Christian fundamentalists (see RELIGIOUS RIGHT) are vehement opponents of it (see FUNDAMENTALISM). Abortion became legal in the UK in 1967 and in the whole of the USA in 1973, largely owing to the demands of supporters of 'a woman's right to choose', and because illegal so-called 'back-street' abortions by unqualified operators were frequent, and often fatal or harmful to the mother.

Supporters of the 'right to choose' are opposed by so-called 'right to life' advocates, who tend to be Christian fundamentalists or Roman Catholics. Pro-choice advocates tend to be liberal or left-leaning politically, while their 'right to life' opponents identify with the political right. Opponents of abortion consider it murder; supporters argue that the foetus is not a person. The pro-choice movement grew out of first-wave feminists' (see FEMINISM) demand for control over their own bodies, and their view of abortion as an aspect of reproductive rights.

During the 1980s in the USA, 'right to life' campaigners became militant (a trend that continues). They regularly picket abortion clinics, and often verbally assault both patients and staff. 'Right to life' militancy increased with the fire-bombing of abortion clinics and the murder by activists of doctors who work at them, a tactic that escalated alarmingly during the 1990s. In American elections, politicians must routinely defend their stance as 'pro-choice' or 'pro-life', just as they must address the issue of the death penalty (see CAPITAL PUNISHMENT (it is seen as a deep irony by many critics of American culture that the great majority of 'right to life' advocates also support executions). For further reading: R. B. Edwards, *New Essays on Abortion and Bioethics* (1997). S.T.

abreaction. In PSYCHOTHERAPY, a term used most usefully, and perhaps most frequently, for the actual release of emotion into CONSCIOUSNESS in which the process of CATHARSIS (sense 3) culminates. It is, however, also used synonymously with 'catharsis'. B.A.F.

absolute liability, see under STRICT LIABILITY.

absolute poverty. The state of existing below the income that secures the bare essentials of food, clothing, and shelter. World Bank (see BRETTON WOODS) economists, who assume a population with a 'normal' distribution by age and GENDER, define the absolute poverty line as the income ($1 daily at 1985 international prices) needed to attain basic nutrition, that is, 2,250 calories per person daily. Using the World Bank line, 30 per cent, or 1.4 billion people, in DEVELOPING COUNTRIES, and 25 per cent of the world, were poor in 1996, only a modest percentage reduction from the previous decade. For further reading: E. W. Nafziger, *The Economics of Developing Countries* (1997). E.W.N.

absolute space and time. The laws of mechanics finally formulated by Isaac Newton presupposed that uniform motion would continue indefinitely in straight lines unless impeded by other objects or forces. Such a view demanded conceptions of space and time as abstract, infinitely extendible grids within which movement over time could be comprehended. Such concepts of space and time as independent of mundane, transient objects gained plausibility during the Scientific Revolution because the New Astronomy suggested that the universe did indeed extend infinitely, and cosmogony was to open up the prospect of an infinitely old cosmos. CLASSICAL PHYSICS (see also PHYSICS) flowered after Newton within a concept of the independence of space from time which was to be fundamentally challenged by Minkowski's formulation in 1908 of the notion of SPACE-TIME (i.e. their interdependence as dimensions) and the exploitation by Einstein of this idea in his theory of general RELATIVITY. Many important cultural movements of the 20th century have rejected objective notions of space and time, substituting instead subjective concepts based on human experience. Important in this respect was the philosophy of Bergson. For further reading: S. Hawking, *A Brief History of Time* (1988). R.P.

absolute threshold, see under THRESHOLD.

absolute zero. The temperature of −273.15°C, which is the lowest possible according to the well-established theories of THERMODYNAMICS and STATISTICAL MECHANICS. At the absolute zero, the random heat motion of the constituents of matter is at a minimum, and structural order is at a maximum. This means that thermal noise in measuring instruments is greatly reduced at low temperatures, enabling very weak signals to be detected, e.g. faint radio emissions from distant GALAXIES and stars. Near the absolute zero, two dramatic effects of QUANTUM MECHANICS occur: SUPERCONDUCTIVITY, which is the total vanishing of electrical resistance in some metals, and superfluidity, which is the total vanishing of flow resistance in liquid helium. Temperatures within 1/1000 of a degree above absolute zero can be attained by modern CRYOGENIC techniques, but the absolute zero itself remains an unattainable limit. See also BROWNIAN MOTION; ZERO POINT ENERGY. M.V.B.

absorption cost, see under MARGINAL COSTING.

abstract art. Paintings and sculpture making no identifiable reference to the visible world. Such works, which must have some claim to exist in their own right if they are to be distinguished from ornament or decoration, are often considered analogous to works of music. They have become increasingly common in Western art (and CULTURES influenced by it) since *c.* 1910, when a number of scattered experimenters influenced by SYMBOLISM and/or CUBISM began producing art with no recognizable 'subject' in the traditional sense. Among these were the German Adolf Hoelzel, the Russians Wassily Kandinsky, Kasimir Malevich, Michel Larionov, and Sonia Delaunay-Terk, the Lithuanian M. K. Čiurlionis, the Czech František Kupka, and the Dutchman Piet Mondrian. The term itself, whose use only became common after 1918, appears to derive from Wilhelm Worringer's *Abstraktion und Einfühlung* (1907), though Kandinsky's *Über das Geistige in der Kunst* (1912) is the classic exposition from a symbolist, quasi-musical point of view.

The first abstract films, by the DADA artists Hans Richter and Viking Eggeling, were shown in Germany in 1921. The first exhibition of abstract art in Paris, in 1930, led to the formation in 1931 of the Abstraction-Création group, consisting mainly of non-French artists. This became the main stream of the movement during the 1930s when abstract art was condemned in Germany and Russia for (respectively) DEGENERACY and FORMALISM. After World War II this condemnation made it seem an embodiment of Western values, particularly after the emergence in the 1950s of ABSTRACT EXPRESSIONISM in the USA. Hence it has developed into an established, academically respectable form of art, with many overlapping versions, e.g. (1) such early branches as Malevich's SUPREMATISM (1915), Alexander Rodchenko's NON-OBJECTIVISM (*c.* 1920), and Theo van Doesburg's CONCRETE ART (1930); (2) general sub-categories like 'geometric' and BIOMORPHIC art (two basic divisions often adopted by critics), or, more recently, HARD-EDGE; (3) alternative names for the whole trend, such as 'non-figurative', 'non-representational', or 'non-objective'; (4) genuinely distinct recent branches like KINETIC ART and OP ART; finally (5) critics' and dealers' labels which give a deceptive air of novelty, for instance '*art autre*', MINIMAL ART, and '*réalités nouvelles*'. Other movements more or less involved with abstract art are ORPHISM, CONSTRUCTIVISM, *De Stijl* (see STIJL, DE) and Larionov's RAYONISM, while even SURREALISM has a link with it in the biomorphic abstractions of Joan Miró and Hans Arp. J.W.

abstract expressionism. A term first used in 1919, in Germany and Russia, to describe the painting of Wassily Kandinsky, and again in that context in 1929 by Alfred Barr, director of the Museum of Modern Art, New York. It was subsequently applied by the *New Yorker* critic Robert Coates in 1946 to the emerging post-World War II American painting, both abstract (see ABSTRACT ART) and figurative. Stylistically, the term implies loose, rapid paint-handling, indistinct shapes, large rhythms, broken colour, uneven saturation of the canvas, and pronounced brushwork, as found in the work of de Kooning, Pollock, Kline, and Gorky; it also includes more reductive painters (e.g. Barnett Newman, Mark Rothko, and Ad Reinhardt) who focus on single, centralized images expressed in terms of large areas or fields of colour – hence the term *colour field painting* subsequently applied to such painters. The term has been extended to cover several sculptors stylistically related to the painters. See also ACTION PAINTING; COBRA; NEW YORK SCHOOL. A.K.W.

absurd, theatre of the, see THEATRE OF THE ABSURD.

accelerator.

(1) In PHYSICS, a device for accelerating sub-atomic particles of matter to high energy (see PARTICLE COLLIDER; ELEMENTARY PARTICLES). Particle accelerators collide particles at the highest obtainable energies in order to investigate the internal

structure of the colliding particles which disintegrate in the collision process. Most research in elementary particles is carried out by this method at very large purpose-built facilities. These are often funded by international collaboration (as in the case of CERN in Geneva). The acceleration of particles can be achieved by electric fields alone, as in the VAN DE GRAAF GENERATOR and the LINEAR ACCELERATOR, or in conjunction with magnetic fields which deflect particles into space-saving circular paths, as in the *cyclotron, synchrotron, synchrocyclotron* and Bevatron. Most particle accelerators accelerate charged particles (ELECTRONS, POSITRONS OF PROTONS). The latest accelerator to be constructed is the LARGE HADRON COLLIDER at CERN in Switzerland. For further reading: L. Lederman and D. Teresi, *The God Particle* (1993). J.D.B.

(2) In ECONOMICS, the accelerator principle states that the level of INVESTMENT depends on the expected change in output. For an expected increase in output, it is necessary for investment to increase in order to have sufficient capacity to produce the expected level of output. The expected increase in output refers to a permanent rather than a temporary increase. Sophisticated versions of the principle allow for the depreciation of the capital stock, replacement investment and the impossibility of having negative gross investment. The accelerator and multiplier principles form the basis of simple MODELS of the TRADE CYCLE and ECONOMIC GROWTH. J.P.

accessible environments. Environments which enable full access and mobility for everyone experiencing any form of mobility difficulties, permanent or temporary, including disabled people, the elderly, and those accompanied by babies and small children. The disabled are not a unitary group, geographically located in one particular area, but are found throughout the range of socio-economic classes and urban localities. Pressure groups have argued that 'accessible environments' should be created, both in terms of individual building access design, and in enabling the disabled to move around more freely in the CITY, as an integral part of mainstream PLANNING. Measures are likely to include *inter alia* public toilet provision, accessible public transport, crèches, and provision of ramps, handrails, and auditory and visual signage to facilitate access. A series of legislative measures has grown up, alongside, and often separate from, planning policy, such as the Americans with Disabilities Act (1989) and the 1995 Disability Discrimination Act in Britain, which it should be stressed is not retrospective. For further reading: L. Davies, 'Equality and Planning: gender and disability', in C. Greed (ed.), *Implementing Town Planning* (1996). C.G.

accommodation. In DEVELOPMENTAL PSYCHOLOGY, a PIAGETIAN term for the adjustment of an organized schema of action to fit new situations. More generally, the subordination of activity to the requirements of external reality, as in imitation. Along with ASSIMILATION, it is one of the main organizing concepts of Piaget's PSYCHOLOGY. P.L.H.

accretion (as power source). Massive objects in space attract material by the force of gravity (see GRAVITATION). For many objects the rate of capture of extraneous material by the accretion process is negligible. For example, the Milky Way GALAXY gains a mass equal to about the mass of the sun each year, but its total mass is 100 billion times greater than this. In other astronomical sites the accreted material can be very significant. When two stars are in close orbit, then if one is sufficiently large it can lose its loosely bound outer material to its companion. This material may then orbit the capturing star in a disc-like configuration – an accretion disc. Very large amounts of energy can be radiated by material as it is accreted by a strong gravitational field. This process is believed to be responsible for the energy output from QUASARS and other active galaxies, and in these cases it is believed that the accretion is taking place on to a BLACK HOLE. The material in the accretion disc of orbiting material is slowly captured by the central source of gravitational attraction. When a black hole occurs in close orbit around an ordinary star it will very readily accrete material from the outer layers of the star which will fall into an accretion disc and radiate large quantities of X-radiation (see X-RAY ASTRONOMY). This distinctive combination of large X-ray emission from a binary system, with one member of the system the unseen source of the

X-rays, is therefore regarded as the signature of a black hole by astronomers. The strongest candidate for a black hole of this sort is the unseen companion in the binary X-ray source Cygnus X-1. J.D.B.

accretion disc, see under ACCRETION.

acculturation (US term; in the UK, *culture contact*). A kind of CULTURE change that emerges from the interaction of two or more societies or groups with different cultural traditions. Acculturation theory was slow to emerge in ANTHROPOLOGY, which was dominated, up to the 1930s, by an historical approach that concentrated on EVOLUTION and DIFFUSION of cultural traits. Following the efforts of Malinowski and Fortes in England, and Redfield and Linton in the USA, to formulate a more consciously FUNCTIONALIST approach – which saw culture as a system rather than a collection of disparate traits – culture contact theory became more important as a means of analysing social change. The earlier contact theories tended to assume that the normal outcome of acculturation was cultural fusion or assimilation; the dominant (because of superior TECHNOLOGY or political power) culture became the melting-pot for the weaker one. Later theories have tended to be more pluralist, i.e. to show how new and creative mixtures often result from the interaction of diverse cultural traditions and groups. D.B.

accumulation theory, see under SOLAR SYSTEM.

acephalous. 'Headless'. In ANTHROPOLOGY, a term applied to societies without centralized political organization or a recognized head. The term was developed by Evans-Pritchard and Fortes (*African Political Systems*, 1940) as part of a TYPOLOGY of political systems. They made a distinction between societies with centralized authority and judicial institutions (primitive states) and those without (stateless, acephalous societies). The question raised by acephalous societies was to understand how order was maintained in the absence of centralized authority. The Nuer of East Africa were cited as the classic example of an acephalous society. The basis of Nuer political organization was the segmentary LINEAGE. Other acephalous societies include hunter-gathering communities (see HUNTER-GATHERERS) and those organized on the basis of AGE-SET SYSTEMS. A.G.

achievement orientation, see under PATTERN VARIABLES.

Achille Lauro. The name of an Italian cruise ship hijacked in 1985 off Port Said, Egypt, by Palestinian terrorists who shot American passenger Leon Klinghoffer, 69, and threw his body and wheelchair into the Mediterranean. The terrorists, led by a rogue PLO operative named Mohammed (Abul) Abbas, released their hostages three days later in Egypt, then boarded a plane for Tunis. US Navy fighter jets forced the plane down in Sicily, where Italian authorities ignored US extradition requests, prevented Abbas's capture, and allowed him to fly to Yugoslavia, where he disappeared. Abbas, who was sentenced *in absentia* to life in prison by an Italian court, resurfaced in the Gaza Strip in April 1996 to show support for Yasser Arafat and the peace accord. 'The killing of the passenger was a mistake. . . . we are sorry,' he said. R.K.H.

acid jazz. An attempt in the early 1990s to relieve the electromechanical tedium of DISCO dance music by adding some of the instrumental colours of JAZZ. The results were somewhat reminiscent of jazz-rock FUSION, but the relentlessly electronic essence of the hybrid limited the jazz output to little more than a flavouring. GE.S.

acid rain. All rain is slightly acid because of the carbon dioxide that it absorbs from the atmosphere, but it is made much more acidic by the release into the atmosphere of sulphates, nitrates and chlorine from industrial processes, which results in the formation of sulphuric, nitric and hydrochloric acid. The death of vast expanses of forest has been attributed to acid rain, often caused by industrial processes many hundreds or thousands of miles away. For example, high-sulphur coal or oil burned in factories of the United States Midwest have caused acid rain to fall in the north-east USA and in Canada, a consequence of the prevailing wind patterns. Similar patterns of long-range transport of acid rain are found in Europe and elsewhere. Man-made structures are also harmed by acid rain, which has accelerated the decay of classic structures such as the Acropolis in Athens. Preventing emission of the chemicals which cause acid rain is costly, especially for DEVELOPING COUNTRIES such as China, where an abundance of cheap high-sulphur fuels provides a tempting alternative to stringent emission controls. A long-term solution will depend on developing clean alternatives to fossil fuels, such as solar energy techniques. For further reading: D. Botkin and E. Keller, *Environmental Science* (1995). W.G.R.

acmeism (from Greek *acme*: 'zenith, blossoming, ripening'). A movement in Russian poetry which grew out of SYMBOLISM as a reaction against its MYSTICISM and excessive allusiveness. The Acmeists wanted to restore concreteness and immediacy to poetic language, 'to admire a rose because it is beautiful, not because it is a symbol of purity'. Their refined lyrical verse combined poetic archaisms with simple everyday language.

The first Acmeist group, the 'Guild of Poets', was founded in St Petersburg in 1912 by Gumilev, the movement's main theoretician. Acmeism produced three outstanding poets: Gumilev, Anna Akhmatova, and Mandelstam. Its main publication was *Apollon* (1909–17). It was suppressed in the early 1920s, stamped as 'decadent' and 'individualist'. Gumilev was executed in 1921 for his association with a counter-revolutionary plot, Mandelstam perished in the purges of the 1930s (see YEZHOVSHCHINA), Akhmatova remained silent. During World War II she published patriotic poetry. In 1946 she was severely criticized (see ZHDANOVSHCHINA), but after the thaw she re-emerged on the literary scene and published several volumes of poetry. M.E.

acquired characteristics, see under LAMARCKISM.

action painting. A phrase coined by the critic Harold Rosenberg in 1952 to define the abstract (see ABSTRACT ART), GESTURAL painting then prevalent. Rosenberg referred particularly to Willem de Kooning, although later the phrase came to be popularly associated with the name of Jackson Pollock, and with the splashing or squirting of paint on canvas; it has also been used synonymously with ABSTRACT EXPRESSIONISM and with *tachisme*, a French term for much the same thing. According to Rosenberg, the canvas had become 'an arena in which to act', the scene of an encounter between the artist and his materials – an encounter possessing a psychological as well as a physical dimension. The term has been rejected by many artists and critics because of Rosenberg's linkage of the artist's psyche to European EXISTENTIALIST thought, and because of the FORMALIST criticism of, notably, Clement Greenberg. See also NEW YORK SCHOOL. A.K.W.

action systems, see under PARSONIAN.

active galaxies, see under QUASAR.

activism. Two main senses can be distinguished:

(1) In its German form *Aktivismus*, a term used at the end of World War I to signify the principle of active political engagement by INTELLECTUALS; hence a subdivision of EXPRESSIONISM, whose political wing was strong at that time. It was associated particularly with Kurt Hiller, organizer of the *Neuer Club* of early expressionist poets, and with Franz Pfemfert, whose magazine *Die Aktion*, founded in 1911, was the more politically engaged rival of *Der Sturm* (see STURM, DER).

(2) More widely, an especially vigorous attitude towards political action, an attitude resulting in particularly zestful political practice. It implies a special role for *activists* who form the active core of political parties. It is notable in revolutionary movements (see REVOLUTION) and particularly important in radical party politics (see RADICALISM). In its extreme form it is held to justify DIRECT ACTION and/or the use of force for political ends. In LEFT-WING politics *militant* is sometimes used, substantivally, in the same sense as *activist*, but the first refers properly to the degree of radicalism in a person's politics, the second to the degree of his involvement in politics; though usually correlated, the two are clearly distinguishable. Activists of all parties are as a rule more concerned with the purity of the party's creed than are their fellow members; this is particularly true of COMMUNIST parties, at least before they come to power, after which the role of the apparat becomes paramount. L.L.

Actors' Studio, see under METHOD, THE.

acupuncture. An approach to treatment based on the Chinese model of health and disease. The Chinese believe that in addition to a circulatory and nervous system the body possesses an energy system which flows in channels called meridians. This energy, *chi*, is seen to have two opposing forces, *yin* and *yang*. Disease occurs when the energy flow for whatever reason is blocked. Needles are placed in different parts of the body along meridians to help 'unblock' energy channels. The placing of needles is only one aspect of acupuncture, and a physician trained in traditional Chinese medicine will take a very long time to arrive at his diagnosis and will pay particular attention to diet, and emotional and environmental factors. Although Western science has been unable accurately to locate the existence of either 'energy flow' or meridians, there is good scientific evidence that acupuncture causes the release of brain chemicals (endorphins) which act as an internal analgesic. In the West acupuncture has largely been used for muscular and arthritic conditions to relieve pain. It has also been used as an anaesthetic, and there are several reports of operations being conducted solely with the use of acupuncture. Chinese medicine as practised in China, of which acupuncture is only a part, is practised in this country mostly by non-doctors. They generally accept and treat a much wider range of disorders than conventional medical practitioners. For further reading: H. Macpherson *et al*, *Acupuncture in Practice: Case History Insights from the West* (1997).
P.C.P.

adaptable theatre, see under OPEN STAGE.

adaptation.

(1) In general BIOLOGY, the process by which an organism becomes fitted to its ENVIRONMENT, or the characteristic that renders it fit.

(2) In BACTERIOLOGY, a change in a bacterial population which makes it possible, after a certain interval, for bacteria to use a new foodstuff or avoid the action of a new ANTIBIOTIC.

(3) In sensory PHYSIOLOGY, the process by which an end organ ceases to respond to some uniformly applied stimulus – e.g. the adaptation of the nose to a uniform pervasive smell. In vision, adaptations are prevented from occurring by tiny wandering or scanning movements of the eye. P.M.

adaptive mutation. A genetic change (see GENETICS/GENOMICS) that improves the quality of the organism. In BIOLOGY, adaptation refers to how well the organism is designed for, or adjusted to, the environment it is living in. The neo-Darwinian theory of EVOLUTION holds that mutation is not adaptive, and it is one of the deepest features of NEO-DARWINISM that the direction of mutation is uncoupled from the direction of evolution. In most alternatives to neo-Darwinism, such as LAMARCKISM and ORTHOGENESIS, the direction of MUTATION is the same as, and the cause of, evolution. These alternatives to neo-Darwinism are generally thought to be factually erroneous. In neo-Darwinism, the direction of mutation is accidental and adaptation evolves by NATURAL SELECTION among the mutations. Such is still widely held to be the correct theory of adaptive evolution.

However, in 1988 John Cairns and colleagues carried out an experiment with bacteria, and seemed to find that mutations were disproportionately arising in an adaptive direction, to a new environment that the experimenters had imposed on the bacteria. The result stimulated many further experiments. Two possible interpretations are that (i) the genetic changes in the experiments are not purely due to mutation, but natural selection is also operating and is the real cause of the directionality. In the experiments, it is essential to prevent selection from operating among the bacteria and biologists differ as to how effectively this has been achieved. Alternatively, (ii) the genetic changes in the experiment may be due to the switching on of previously unobserved genes – genes that are held in reserve for when the bacteria encounters the experimental environment. The changes are then not mutations, but the DNA (see NUCLEIC ACID) of the bacteria is behaving in a sense intelligently, able to switch on appropriate genes when they are needed. The issue remains open, and research continues. M.R.

adaptive radiation. The exploitation by the members of an animal or plant group of a wide variety of different HABITATS or habits of life to each of which the ORGANISMS are appropriately adapted. Thus the higher (placental) mammals show a high degree of adaptive radiation as exemplified by terrestrial carnivores, whales, moles, bats, and chimpanzees. The marsupial mammals have undergone an adaptive radiation of their own curiously similar in many ways to that of the terrestrial higher mammals. In this context the word 'radiation' is of course figurative and refers to a fanning out of evolutionary lines; and adaptive radiation calls for no special explanations that do not apply equally to the remainder of EVOLUTION.

P.M.

addiction. Perhaps the most useful definition of an addiction is 'the inability to predict further use or abstinence in any day after the first use of an addictive substance or process' (Dr Richard Heilman). However, there are as many definitions of addiction as there are addicts and therapeutic approaches. For addicts any definition excludes themselves. This denial is the basic psychopathology: the nature of the condition is that it 'tells' them, through disordered perception, that they have not got it. Addicts generally seek help only when they are in pain from the consequences of use of addictive substances or processes. Enabling (relieving their pain) can therefore be counter-productive.

From a psychological perspective, Dr Jim Orford describes *Excessive Appetites* (1985) for drinking, gambling, drug taking, eating and sex. Professor Ernest Noble attributes excessive appetites for alcohol, nicotine, cocaine, caffeine and sugar to genetic defects in the 11th chromosome affecting the number of dopamine receptors in the mood centres of the brain.

Excessive use of addictive substances often underlies major killing diseases such as cancer, strokes, heart attacks and arterial disease, gastrointestinal disturbances and obesity. Addictive behaviour is therefore more widespread and devastating than is commonly perceived.

Genetic and environmental factors and the mood-altering capacity of specific substances and processes all play a part in the addictive process, although there has been considerable resistance to the implication of genetic impairment leading to individual powerlessness over the process of addiction, even while still being responsible for behaviour towards others. Prevention has tended to focus upon educating drinkers to stay within sensible limits, smokers to cut down or quit, and others (especially children) to 'say no to drugs'. These strategies may be generally effective but a significant minority, perhaps 10 to 15 per cent of the population, fail, possibly as a result of genetic predisposition as well as environmental influences.

The therapeutic strategy of harm-minimization aims to protect established drug users from the risks of contaminated drugs or needles leading to septicaemia, hepatitis B and C, AIDS and other damaging consequences; the supervised prescription of oral Methadone in place of black-market heroin and other drugs is intended to stabilize the individual addict and reduce the dependency upon crime for supply. However, there is increasing concern that Methadone itself has a black market and also leads to significant morbidity and mortality. The precedent that heroin was introduced to the pharmacopoeia as a non-addictive alternative to morphia is not encouraging. Nor has been the reluctance (until very recently) to accept the addictive nature of various prescription medications such as tranquillizers, painkillers and sleeping tablets. The debate continues on anti-depressants, currently seen by some as a panacea and by others as just another addictive substance.

Further debates on the relative risks of 'hard' or 'soft' drugs and whether some should be legalized or decriminalized may underestimate the individual risk from genetic predisposition. The full structural analysis of the HUMAN GENOME PROJECT, anticipated by the year 2005, will present enormous challenges to current ideas and clinical practices on the treatment of addiction.

The concept of addictive disease affecting some people but not others is central to the Minnesota method of treatment, based upon the principles of Alcoholics Anonymous (see ALCOHOLISM). Some people are said to be powerless over the use of some or all mood-altering substances and processes and therefore total abstinence is advisable, combined with regular attendance at an appropriate anonymous fellowship as a continuing substitute mood-altering process. The requirement that sufferers should have a

God or Higher Power than self is highly contentious and is discussed extensively in *Not God* by Ernest Kurtz.

The comprehensive 'matching study' funded by the National Institute for Alcoholism and Alcohol Abuse in the USA (1997) found the therapeutic approach of Alcoholics Anonymous to be more effective than motivational enhancement or cognitive behavioural approaches that attempt to build upon the sufferer's own resources.

The mirror-image of addiction (in which the addict needs to be 'fixed' in some way) is 'compulsive helping', the need to be needed. Compulsive helping is also progressive and destructive and is also treated with a continuing twelve-step programme of an anonymous fellowship. R.M.H.L.

Adelphi, The, see under CRITERION, THE.

adelphic polyandry, see under POLYANDRY.

adequacy. A term used in GENERATIVE GRAMMAR as a CRITERION of the extent to which the goals of linguistic theory have been achieved. Three *levels of adequacy*, or stages of achievement, are recognized.

Observational adequacy is achieved when a grammar gives a correct description of a corpus of data, but does not make generalizations based on this. *Descriptive* adequacy is achieved to the extent that a grammar gives a correct account of a speaker's COMPETENCE, his intuitive knowledge of a language. *Explanatory* adequacy is achieved to the extent that a linguistic theory provides principles for determining which of a number of descriptively adequate grammars is the best (see EVALUATION PROCEDURE). Structural LINGUISTICS was criticized by Chomsky as being too preoccupied with observational adequacy. Very little headway has been made in the study of explanatory adequacy. D.C.

adhocracy. An organization in which there is no rigid organizational structure and in which people work in teams on individual projects. The teams often change their personnel, their shape and relationship to one another. Managers, experts and support staff are brought together to work on specific projects on an *ad hoc* basis, and teams are disbanded and new teams reformed once projects are complete. Adhocracies are held to be less hierarchical than bureaucracies and more suited to operating in a POST-FORDIST world in which markets are constantly changing and organizations need to be flexible to react rapidly to changing conditions. For further reading: H. Mintzberg, *Structures in Fives: Designing Effective Organizations* (1983). M.D.H.

Adlerian. Adjective applied to a school of PSYCHOANALYSIS originating in the work of Alfred Adler (Vienna, 1870–1937); also a substantive, meaning a member of that school. In the course of an early, close association with Freud (see FREUDIAN), Adler began to develop his own INDIVIDUAL PSYCHOLOGY, in which he came to reject Freud's LIBIDO theory, together with his views of infantile sexuality and of sexuality as the root source of NEUROSIS; and finally (1912) he severed relations with Freud. Adler's fundamental notion was the helplessness of the infant, with its feelings of inferiority. The infant has an urge to overcome and compensate for all this. The key conditions that determine how he achieves this compensation are the inter-personal relations in the family. The upshot is that the child acquires his own LIFESTYLE, or way of dealing with his situation. Where this fails, the person may retain an uncompensated feeling of inferiority (an INFERIORITY COMPLEX), and this can lead to a neurotic style of behaviour (see NEUROSIS). Adler's influence, though to some extent indirect and unacknowledged, has been considerable, especially in the USA. For further reading: A. Adler, *The Practice and Theory of Individual Psychology* (1924); B. Handlbauer, *The Freud–Adler Controversy* (1997). B.A.F.

admass. Term coined by J. B. Priestley in 1955 (*Journey Down a Rainbow*) for an economic, cultural and social order dominated and saturated by the drive reflecting the illusory world of the ADVERTISING copywriter's 'ad', and obsessively promoted through the mass media. Admass leads to the creation and purveying of LIFESTYLES in the context of a glittering CONSUMER SOCIETY which, it is claimed, stifles creativity and individuality, and distorts human feelings, needs, and emotions (see MASS CULTURE; MASS SOCIETY). P.S.L.

adult education (continuing education). Part-time education for adults, irrespective of their previous educational attainment. In Britain, it is a tradition developed and maintained by the Workers' Educational Association (WEA), whose original purpose was to teach liberal arts subjects to persons in full employment who may have left school at a young age; but WEA courses became popular with a broad section of the population, and anyone is welcome to attend them. It is an idea also promoted by local education authorities, who offer evening courses in schools. In Britain and in Europe adult education can also include the idea of *continuing professional development*, in which managers, technicians and professionals attend courses, often paid for by their employer, in order to keep up with the latest developments in their field. Britain's OPEN UNIVERSITY, where adults may take university degrees by correspondence, is a significant adult education institute.

In the USA, adult education is modelled more closely on the university or college system, where students are offered courses for which they receive 'credits' (often transferrable) which may be accumulated over time and which count towards a college degree. S.T.

adventurism, see under DEVIATIONISM.

advertising. The earliest advertisement extant can be found in the ruins of Ephesus. It is for a brothel. Advertising thinking has not advanced a great deal since then. Prior to World War II, advertising was sloganeering: 'Guinness is good for you', 'Friday night is Amami night'. With the advent of commercial television it became big business. Thinking now originated with marketing directors and brand managers (clients); agency reps and bag carriers (account executives) assumed a new importance as 'custodians of the brand', with the consumer represented by a curious mixture of researcher and strategy creator (planners). Their findings were passed to the copywriter and art director whose job it became to translate the strategy into a memorable and effective television, press or poster advertisement, the key word being creativity. Creativity, to be noticed by the TV viewer, newspaper or magazine reader, or poster observer, necessarily means instant attention-getting, resulting in a glibness or lateral cleverness, not to be confused with creativity in, say, film, literature or art, and frequently is exposed as a new form of prewar sloganeering ('Heineken refreshes the parts other beers cannot reach', 'Drinka pinta milka day', 'Hello Tosh gotta Toshiba'). Concern that such creativity has hidden shallows has resulted in a plethora of self-aggrandizing award festivals, locally and internationally, at which 'creatives' award each other glittering prizes to celebrate the quality of their creative thinking. D.W.

advocacy planning. In TOWN PLANNING, professional advice and representation for COMMUNITY groups and individuals in challenging and providing alternative inputs to proposed development proposals. Many socially motivated planners would argue that the planning process must incorporate and reflect the views of all members of the community, especially under-represented groups such as ethnic minorities, women, youth groups and the elderly. In particular, there are demands for greater acknowledgement of the contribution of black people and businesses to urban society and the economy in the development of planning policy. Concern has been expressed on both sides of the Atlantic at what has been seen as the discriminatory application of planning controls, zoning ordinances and public health regulations in respect of ethnic minority restaurants, taxi services and businesses. For further reading: M. Cross and M. Keith (eds), *Racism, the City and the State* (1993). C.G.

aerobes, see under BACTERIOLOGY.

aesthetic distance. In drama and other forms of art, a critic's phrase intended to remind the spectator (reader, etc.) that a work of art is not to be confused with reality, and its conventions must be fully respected: there is little point in warning the hero that the villain is creeping up behind him with a knife. The process whereby the artist seeks to establish the aesthetic distance is known as *distancing*, or in BRECHTIAN parlance ALIENATION (*Verfremdung*). Distancing should not preclude some degree of 'identification' on the spectator's part. D.J.E.

aestheticism. Either

(1) the view that works of art should be judged by strictly aesthetic criteria (see AESTHETICS; CRITERION) and that their value has nothing to do with their moral, political, or religious utility; or

(2) the more extreme view that in life and action as a whole aesthetic values should take precedence over values of other kinds. Gautier's slogan 'art for art's sake' expresses the more moderate view. The theory of life expounded in the conclusion to Pater's *Renaissance* and practised by Oscar Wilde is closer to the more extreme one. It has seldom been chosen as a label by those who are held to adhere to it and has a mildly derogatory flavour. A.Q.

aesthetics. The philosophical study of art, and also of nature to the extent that we take the same attitude to it as we do to art. The notion of any aesthetic attitude is thus of central importance. It is commonly held to be a style of PERCEPTION concerned neither with the factual information to be gained from the things perceived, nor with their practical uses, but rather with the immediate qualities of the contemplative experience itself. Works of art are human productions designed to reward this kind of attention. But it can also be given to natural objects such as scenery, flowers, human bodies. Aesthetics aims to define the CONCEPT of the aesthetic attitude and of the work of art which is its primary object. It asks to what extent works of art should be representative, and to what extent they should express the emotions of their creators. It aims to identify the characteristic value (which few would now call beauty) of aesthetically satisfying objects. It considers the problem of the nature of a work of art's existence (is it a pattern of words or sounds or patches of colour, or is it a physical thing?), and that of the relation between aesthetic and moral value. For further reading: G. Graham, *Philosophy of the Arts: An Introduction to Aesthetics* (1997). A.Q.

aetiology (*or* **etiology**), see under EPIDEMIOLOGY.

affective fallacy. Term invented by literary critics W. K. Wimsatt and Monroe C. Beardsley to describe the supposed fallacy of reading a work in terms of its 'results in the mind of its audience'. The CONCEPT is useful but limited: part of reading a work is indeed the study of it as an independent structure; but it would not, in practical terms, be worth study if it had no emotional effect. In fact, works have an 'effect' on Wimsatt and Beardsley, and whenever they discuss them they too are guilty of their own fallacy, even if in terms which only initially appear to be 'non-affective': these critics prefer one, 'dry', kind of emotion over another 'wet' one, and that is what the critical debate was really about. Egregious though the 'affective fallacy' may be in terms of the humanity of literature, however, it has been of stimulative value. For further reading: W. K. Wimsatt, *The Verbal Icon* (1970). M.S.-S.

affectivity, see under PATTERN VARIABLES.

affine geometry, see under GEOMETRY.

affirmative action. Term which describes attempts, usually through government policy, to correct the effects of past or present discrimination against particular groups (usually racial MINORITIES or women) by securing them access to e.g. education and employment, by such means as demographic quotas and differential entry requirements. The idea has been most developed and applied in the USA since the mid-1960s, has been a constant and growing source of political conflict, and now seems to have passed its zenith. The idea has never sat comfortably in the traditions of a nation which prefers individual rather than group conceptions of rights. It has long been attacked as 'positive discrimination', harming non-minority members who are not responsible for the broad forces of past and current prejudice. Despite the creation of a new black middle class which arguably owes much of its existence to affirmative action, the concept is also increasingly criticized as cumbersome, ineffective, and decreasingly relevant to a society which, some feel, is increasingly free of sexual and racial discrimination (see RACISM) and in need of new approaches to questions of disadvantage. For further reading: S. Cahn (ed.), *The Affirmative Action Debate* (1995). S.R.

affluent society. Term made famous by

John Kenneth Galbraith with his book *The Affluent Society* (1958), in which the first and still most complete exposition of its popular meaning is given. An affluent society is one where the widespread poverty and want that have been the lot of mankind through the ages have been replaced by sufficient abundance to enable the population as a whole to enjoy conventional notions of a reasonably comfortable standard of living (see POVERTY). In such a society the 'conventional wisdom' of economic theory, designed as it is for dealing with the problems of scarcity, is no longer a useful tool of economic analysis. For the priority traditionally given to increasing production in the PRIVATE SECTOR of the economy is no longer rational. It leads to a neglect of the supply of PUBLIC GOODS, e.g. roads and the police force. This situation is aggravated by the artificial stimulation of consumer DEMAND through ADVERTISING, and the excessive expansion of consumer credit provisions. The imbalance between private and public sector output, and other effects of the conventional economic goals, means that although national income may rise, human welfare may decline. W.B.; J.P.

afforestation, see under DEFORESTATION.

Afghanistan. In the 1980s, Afghanistan was the scene of a protracted and ultimately unsuccessful attempt at invasion by the Soviet Union, starting in December 1979 and ending in February 1989 with the withdrawal of the last Soviet troops by Mikhail Gorbachev, an episode often compared to America's similarly inglorious campaign in Vietnam. The Soviet Union had invaded Afghanistan on political grounds, attempting to install a MARXIST government which would be sympathetic to Soviet interests. Opposition to the invasion was mobilized by various groups whose collective name was the Mujahedin, and although there was a vast exodus of refugees to neighbouring Islamic countries, the resistance fighters continued to harry the Soviet Army throughout the 1980s. As countries such as the US, the UK and China began to supply the Mujahedin with better technology, the latter were able to cause increasing damage, and eventually political will in the Soviet Union ran out. Since the Soviet Union withdrew, the country has remained extremely unstable, divided on religious and ethnic grounds. At present, most of the country is controlled by the Taliban, a group of Islamic fundamentalists who have been criticized by human rights organizations for imposing a very strict interpretation of Islamic law – floggings and amputations are carried out for certain crimes, and Afghan women are no longer allowed to be educated in schools. A.A.L.

African National Congress (ANC). A leading force in the political struggle against APARTHEID, the ANC evolved from the South African Native National Congress and acquired its current name in 1923. Initially a small organization of moderate tenor which espoused constitutional approaches to reform, it developed a more militant character in the 1940s. It was captured by its own radical Congress Youth League, developed links with the South African Communist Party, and in 1949 issued a Programme of Action which produced the 1952 Defiance Campaign of non-violent protest. This drew a great increase in membership from a few thousand to nearly 100,000, and encouraged contact with other political groups, who joined in the adoption in 1955 of the Freedom Charter. Throughout the 1950s the state was hostile to the ANC and banned it and its splinter group, the Pan-African Congress, after the Sharpeville episode of April 1960 in which schoolchildren were killed by police. The movement was forced underground and revised its strategy and methods. In 1961 it formed a military wing, Umkhonto we Sizwe (Spear of the Nation), under the command of Nelson Mandela, who with other ANC leaders was arrested and sentenced to life in prison.

During the 1960s the ANC developed increasing links with other African liberation movements, the USSR and other SOCIALIST states. Its vocabulary became more thoroughly MARXIST and strategy more comprehensive. Despite continued attempts by the state to destroy it, the ANC survived and benefited from the upsurge of black militancy in the 1970s (see BLACK CONSCIOUSNESS). It pursued a combined strategy of mass mobilization and GUERRILLA actions, generally against state property. As the regime's stability was threatened, the ANC came to be internationally regarded as an organization vital to prospects of a relatively orderly reconstruction of the South African state. Nelson Mandela was released from prison in 1990 and formed the first government based on universal suffrage. For further reading: H. Holland, *The Struggle: A History of the African National Congress* (1990). S.R.

African philosophy. The philosophical thought embedded in the oral traditions of the peoples of Africa and the written philosophies of modern Africans (see ORAL HISTORY; ORAL TRADITION). Some scholars trace the written tradition of African PHILOSOPHY to Pharoic Egypt. And through the work of Professor Claude Sumner we know that Ethiopia has a long tradition of written philosophy with Zar'a Ya'eqob (1599–1692) as its most remarkable thinker.

The oral tradition, containing both communal thought and the reflections of individual sages, is a rich source of philosophical conceptions which are now under active study by contemporary African philosophers. Interestingly different from the Christian (see CHRISTIANITY) conception of GOD as creator of the world out of nothing, for example, is the notion of the supreme being as a fashioner of the world order from some presumably indeterminate antecedent stuff. There are other such contrasts in the traditional thought of various African peoples, including the conception of a person as, ontologically, consisting of the BODY and other constituents that are only relatively less material and, socially, entailing conformity with basic communal norms and ideals (see ONTOLOGY; BELIEF). Frequently associated with this is a concept of MIND as a capacity rather than an entity, spiritual or otherwise. The widespread COMMUNALISM of Africa is reflected, in moral thought, in the conception of ETHICS as a quest for the adjustment of the interests of the individual with that of others in society and, in politics, in the concept of consensus as the ideal basis of political decision making.

Modern African philosophers, though historically influenced by Western philosophy, have usually drawn on their traditional roots in their interpretations of the world and proposals for changing it. This is best illustrated in the philosophies of social reconstruction propounded by African political leaders in the immediate post-independence period (see POST-COLONIALISM). Though some of them were quite impressed with MARXISM, virtually in every case they appealed to African communalism as their starting point. More recently, the academic philosophers of Africa have intensely debated the question of the African IDENTITY of their discipline in the face of the impact of the West. For further reading: T. Serequeberhan, *African Philosophy: The Essential Readings* (1991). K.W.

African religions. The RELIGIONS of sub-Saharan Africa plus the diaspora (mainly South American, Caribbean and African-American). In addition to classical African religions there are African forms of ISLAM, CATHOLICISM and PROTESTANTISM, as well as new independent churches which blend the CHRISTIANITY preached by the missionaries with African themes. For instance, healing is important in traditional African societies, and a large theme in the gospels, and they combine well. Likewise, prophetism occurs both in the Old Testament and in the African context. But probably the main motive for independent churches was the desire to control the organizations, rather than have their religion ruled by white missionaries, as was normal. Of course, with the crumbling of colonial rule (see POST-COLONIALISM), Africans came to dominate the regular churches. There were similar movements, though fewer, among Muslims. For further reading: H. W. Turner, *African Traditions* (1980). N.SM.

African socialism. Collective name for the systems of SOCIALISM propounded by several of the immediate post-independence leaders of Africa in the 1960s (see POST-COLONIALISM). Some of these, such as Nkrumah of Ghana, Sékou Touré of Guinea and, less substantially, Senghor of Senegal, were under the influence of MARXISM, while others, such as Nyerere of Tanzania and Kaunda of Zambia, were not. But all of them were united in citing pristine African COMMUNALISM as their inspiration and foundation. Moreover, the Marxist group were at various points keen to dissociate themselves from certain components of Marxist doctrine that they considered un-African, such as its ATHEISM and commitment to the class struggle. Additionally, they seemed to make room for considerable private participation in the economy, though in some cases this may have been conceived as a transitional phenomenon. In this last respect, indeed, Nyerere's version of African socialism with its massive programme of resettlements (see UJAMAA) was in many cases more thoroughgoing in the state control of the economy than the neo-Marxist variety. K.W.

afrocentricity. According to one of its most celebrated proponents, Molefi Asante, afrocentricity is first and foremost a state of mind. It is a state of consciousness that is achieved when a person who has been victimized by a system of racial oppression, which includes a dehumanizing self-definition, is changed by an active engagement in his mental liberation (see RACISM).

This process of self-liberation involves a critical assessment of certain key questions and issues. The most fundamental question on the ontological level (see ONTOLOGY) is 'What does it mean to be a African?' Questions on the next level involve an interaction between ethical precepts (see ETHICS) and ontological claims. Such questions include: 'Do people of African descent have special duties and obligations to members of their group?' Then the examination moves to the teleological level (see TELEOLOGY). Questions here involve the ends and goals that should be pursued by people who have achieved an afrocentric consciousness. Finally, there are epistemological concerns (see EPISTEMOLOGY) like: What are the criteria for knowing? Are these criteria universally applicable? Do unique cultural and ethnic experiences warrant special or privileged ways of knowing?

Besides the epistemological, ethical and ontological concerns, there is also a political agenda. According to Asante in *The Afrocentric Idea* (1998), afrocentricism is 'a critique that propounds a cultural theory of society by the very act of criticism'. Afrocentrists have a political agenda of re-establishing the centrality of the ancient Kemetic civilization as a point of reference for people of African descent. H.M.

Afro-Cuban. JAZZ has always been receptive to Latin rhythms, even from its early days: the St Louis Blues, for instance, sported a habanera section. This 'Spanish tinge' came into its own in the 1940s, spearheaded by BEBOP trumpeter Dizzy Gillespie, who hired the conga drummer Chano Pozo to play with his BIG BAND. Pozo's intoxicating pulse and colourful accents set the style for what was dubbed Afro-Cuban, and many bands adopted one or even more Latin percussion players. The exotic fad was less adaptable to small groups and faded somewhat as the big bands declined. Nonetheless, the tinge has remained an effective part of the jazz vocabulary, and has sometimes become a dominant hue of its own, as in the BOSSA NOVA craze of the early 1960s and the heady SALSA form of the 1980s. GE.S.

after-image. In PERCEPTION, the visual after-effect produced by focusing on an object and then looking at a blank surface. It usually appears in a colour complementary to the original and obeys *Emmert's Law* to the effect that its apparent size varies in direct proportion to the apparent distance of the surface against which it is cast. J.S.B.

age-and-area hypothesis. Anthropological hypothesis that CULTURE traits tend to diffuse from single or multiple centres rather like ripples on a pond after a stone is thrown. Consequently cultures on the periphery may show traits which were characteristic of the centre in an earlier period. There is considerable dispute as to the reliability of the MODEL in reconstructing any given culture history. See also DIFFUSION (3). P.H.

age-grade, see under AGE-SET SYSTEM.

age-set system. A form of social organization in which males become members of groups through the process of initiation (see RITE DE PASSAGE). The system divides males into different groups and ranks them in a hierarchy based upon seniority. Age-set systems are commonly found among societies in East Africa: for example among the Masai, Jie and Turkana. All young men born within a certain number of years are initiated at the same time into an age-set. They remain members of this set throughout their lives, but the members of the set move collectively through a series of age-grades – from junior warriorhood to senior warriorhood to junior elderhood to senior elderhood. An age-set system establishes a series of roles through which individuals pass in an ordered and socially recognized way. It also frequently provides the basis for the exercise of political authority (see ACEPHALOUS; RITE DE PASSAGE). A.G.

agency shop, see under CLOSED SHOP.

Agent Orange. A selective weedkiller that was used by American forces during the VIETNAM War to defoliate forests and woodland. The intention was to eliminate ground cover for opposing troops. There was a considerable degree of international outcry because of the possible long-term environmental and human health implications. Dioxins, a family of highly toxic chlorinated organic compounds, were present in Agent Orange. A.S.G.

aggiornamento. Italian word meaning 'bringing up to date'; it usually refers to the renewal of Roman CATHOLICISM begun while John XXIII was Pope (1958–63) and in large measure authorized by VATICAN COUNCIL II. The Mass has been made a more corporate act of worship, and the use of Latin has almost ceased (see LITURGICAL MOVEMENT). More responsibility has been attributed to the laity, instead of to the clergy; and to all the bishops, instead of a papal monopoly of power. There has been more emphasis on the Christian's involvement in the modern world, sustained by simpler prayer. An intellectually active and free THEOLOGY, in its inspiration biblical, has begun to emerge. More acknowledgement of other Christian Churches, and more cooperation with them in the ECUMENICAL MOVEMENT, have been encouraged. Some Roman Catholics have reacted conservatively, suspecting MODERNISM. Others have felt that the officially tolerated pace of change has been too slow and have left either the priesthood or the Church. The election of Karol Wojtyla as Pope John Paul II in 1978 ended the period when the papacy itself had seemed to be involved in this uncertainty. Essentially conservative, as befitted a bishop who had experienced the popularity of a conservative Catholicism in Poland, this masterful leader was no blind reactionary. He advocated the renewal of the Church in the form of CONCILIARITY. D.L.E.

agglomeration. A geographical term denoting a significant concentration of people and/or activities. In ECONOMIC GEOGRAPHY, the term is frequently used to describe the economies or savings achieved by clustering manufacturing and office facilities, mostly within metropolitan areas already possessing locational and scale advantages by virtue of their superior transport accessibility and large concentrations of skilled labour, producer services, and venture CAPITAL (see ENTREPRENEUR). In urban geography, the term is most often used to describe the distribution of population and activities within a metropolitan region (see POPULATION GEOGRAPHY). Whereas both were historically dominated by a steady increase in density from the suburban edge of the metropolis towards a peak at the core of the central CITY, urban development today is changing from a single-centred to a multicentred metropolitan structure. Led by the US, where decades of massive, automobile-based SUBURBANIZATION have turned most cities inside out, this trend is now spreading throughout the world's higher-income countries. The prototype example of this latest, 'edge city' form of agglomeration, an increasingly important landscape feature of the newly globalized economy, is the *La Défense* business complex just west of Paris, which has already developed its own vast network of direct international linkages. P.O.M.

agglutinating (or **agglutinative).** In comparative LINGUISTICS, terms applied to languages such as Turkish, Finnish and Japanese in which words typically consist of long sequences of affixes and roots, each element usually having a clear identity and separate meaning. English shows little tendency to agglutinate: humorous constructs such as *antidisestablishmentarianism* are exceptional. The term is one of three used in the approach to linguistic typology proposed by August von Schlegel (1767–1845), the others being ISOLATING and INFLECTING. D.C.

aggregate demand. The value of total planned expenditures on domestically produced output, i.e. public and private consumption and investment, plus exports minus imports. In a one-sector KEYNESIAN economic MODEL, aggregate demand depends mainly on the level of NATIONAL INCOME and the exchange rate – the latter affects exports and imports. The EQUI-

LIBRIUM level of national income is that income which is equal to aggregate demand, i.e. income is equal to planned expenditure. Keynesian economic theory proposes that certain markets, particularly the labour market, may fail to move towards equilibrium and involuntarily UNEMPLOYMENT occurs. The demand of the involuntarily unemployed is ineffective, as it is not backed by income. A possible lack of effective demand lies behind the view that national income is the major determinant of effective aggregate demand. In MONETARIST economic theory, it is assumed that all markets adjust towards equilibrium, in which case the interactions of supplies and demands for products and inputs of production would eventually determine an equilibrium in which there is no excess demand or supply for anything and, in particular, there is no involuntary unemployment. In an economic model which has markets for money, labour and a single good, aggregate demand is a relation between the price level and output, which gives equilibrium in the money and the goods markets. In this economic model, AGGREGATE SUPPLY and demand determine total output and employment. J.P.

aggregate supply. The total value of output that the economy wishes to supply at each price level. AGGREGATE DEMAND and supply together determine NATIONAL INCOME. See KEYNESIAN and MONETARISM. J.P.

aggregation.

(1) In STATISTICS, ECONOMETRICS and ECONOMICS, the grouping of similar variables together, i.e. into aggregates, to simplify the description or modelling of complex phenomena. For example, NATIONAL INCOME is not described by recording the output of each product, but is represented by the sum of the level of each output multiplied by its price; and, in modelling the effects of INFLATION, the increases in prices of different goods may be represented by a single index. Condensation of different variables into a single aggregate involves a loss of information. The cost of this loss should be balanced against the benefits that are gained from conciseness. See INDEX NUMBER. J.P.

(2) In BIOLOGY, a grouping or crowding together of separate ORGANISMS. The term is used also to describe the movement of tentacles and tendrils to a point which is stimulated, as for instance in sea anemones. The gregarious habit, producing aggregations of animals, is considered to be a primitive form of social behaviour. It implies a temporary grouping of individuals, usually of the same age and in the same state of development (e.g. caterpillars on a food plant, mosquitoes over a pond). Mating may occur when aggregations exist, but the pairs usually separate soon afterwards. K.M.

aggression. Animal or human behaviour which is provoked by another individual and which has deterrent or aversive effects on that individual: it leads him to withdraw, either by moving away or by ceasing to dispute some object which is the occasion of the aggression. The charge of a ram in rut, the measured display of two male Siamese fighting fish, and the malicious remark made by a man about a professional colleague may all represent examples of aggression in these SPECIES.

Animal aggression is extremely widespread, and appears to evolve whenever a species needs some kind of deterrent behaviour to secure access to some commodity in short supply. Thus there may be fighting over TERRITORY, food, females, sleeping places, or nesting burrows, or for social precedence as a determinant of access to any of these. The hunting behaviour of predators shares some of the features of aggression but is essentially different in that the goal is to eat the other animal rather than simply to drive it away. It may, however, provoke aggression in the form of defensive reactions. Such reactions against predators and against prey should be distinguished from social aggression directed at members of the same species. In the latter, while there is usually the ultimate sanction of physical violence, more often the fight consists of a graduated series of escalating displays which indicate to each combatant how ready the opponent is to continue the struggle. The fight ends when one combatant either runs away or assumes some special posture of appeasement which tends to ensure safety from attack. If, however, space to flee is restricted, e.g. in captivity, the attack on the defeated animal may continue and it may be killed.

The relation between aggression in animals and in man has been much disputed. This is especially true of the last decade, with the development of the specialized study of SOCIOBIOLOGY, which has reaffirmed the continuity between animal and human behaviour within the Darwinian framework (see DARWINISM) of adaptive evolutionism (see EVOLUTION). Postulating some kind of putative genetic (see GENETICS/GENOMICS) underpinning, sociobiologists have contended that apparently dysfunctional human attributes (such as mass aggression) may mark not cultural backwardness but necessary survival strategies. A more complex approach argues that sociocultural requirements and genetic programming have here become out of step. Certainly, however, the view outlined above suggests that the matter should be examined in the light of the lifestyles and needs of each species. The complexity of human society involves infinitely complex social, psychological and biological needs, and many of these goals are achieved through aggressive behaviour, often largely verbal. Such behaviour seems to correspond to animal threat signals in that it is designed to gain access to special facilities, and if unsuccessful may lead to more violent forms of aggression. The expression of individual aggression in man can take almost any form and be associated with a great number of motivational factors, frustration of some goal-directed behaviour being a common one. In man too there is WAR, which operates as aggression at the level of society, but in which the motives of the combatants may be very different from the anger of a private dispute. For further reading: S. Feshbach and J. Zagrodzka (eds) *Aggression: Biological, Developmental and Social Perspectives* (1997). J.M.C.; R.P.

agnosia, see under NEUROPSYCHOLOGY.

agnosticism. The philosophical position which claims that it is impossible in principle (or at least in practice) to know whether GOD exists or not. The term itself was coined in 1869 by the biologist and essayist T. H. Huxley, and was designed to distinguish his position from that of THEISM and ATHEISM, which, from an agnostic point of view, make claims that cannot possibly be justified. The phenomenon it names, however, is much older, and is in effect the application of philosophical scepticism to the question of the existence of God. Huxley's agnosticism is related to Kant's critique, a century before, of 'speculative' theism and atheism, on the grounds that there can be no knowledge of that which transcends all possible experience; but Huxley's agnosticism perhaps owes less to Kant (who thought that faith remained rational as a postulate of the ethical life) than to English EMPIRICISM, which had long emphasized the duty to proportion one's belief to the available evidence (see EVIDENTIALISM). The even-handedness of Huxley's position has proved unsustainable, as understandings of agnosticism have proliferated, except, ironically, in the popular (mis)interpretation of agnosticism as a kind of 'don't know' option in the great metaphysical opinion poll of life. C.C.

agrarian history. The history of farming techniques and peasant customs. The term came into general use about 1950, and covers two rather different approaches:

(1) that of economic historians interested in a particular industry, agriculture; this approach is dominant in England (the 'Leicester school') and the Netherlands (the 'Wageningen school', led by B. H. Slicher van Bath);

(2) that of social historians interested in a particular social group, the peasants; this is the French approach, associated in particular with Marc Bloch and Emmanuel Le Roy Ladurie, and perhaps better described as *rural history*. For further reading: J. Thirsk (series ed.), *The Agrarian History of England and Wales* (1972–). P.B.

agribusiness. The sum total of all operations involved in (1) the manufacture and distribution of products used for production purposes on farms; (2) production on farms; and (3) the storage, processing and distribution of commodities produced on farms and items made from them. For the situation in most developed countries in the mid-20th century the term can be regarded as covering those activities which were carried out on family farms before draught animals were displaced by tractors and before the growth of the artificial fertilizer and specialist animal feeding-stuffs industries and the highly organized processing and distribution industries for food and natural fibres. Interest in the subject usually centres on the means of securing co-ordination between the various stages. K.E.H.

agricultural policy. A set of official measures, of widely varying type, used to influence the agricultural sector, often with the aim of increasing incomes. In Britain after a long period of laissez-faire through the later 19th century and some intervention in 1914–21, specific instruments (notably the formation of marketing boards and the introduction of some DEFICIENCY PAYMENTS) were adopted as a response to the 1930s depression and continued after war-time control under the 1947 Agriculture Act. Prices of products paid to farmers were raised by deficiency payments and imports were subsidized through production grants. This phase ended with accession to the EEC (see EUROPEAN UNION) and the gradual adoption of the markedly different frontier protection, intervention purchase and export subsidization characteristic of the CAP. The US also adopted wide-ranging price support measures in the 1930s (the loan rate scheme) and has continued to do so, bolstering their effect with other devices such as land set-aside schemes and deficiency payments. Some attempt to reorientate American agriculture to market forces was made in the 1985 Farm Bill. Centrally planned economies frequently, though not exclusively, base their policy on forms of collectivization. In the THIRD WORLD there is emphasis on promoting development through LAND REFORM, the use of GREEN REVOLUTION technology, and irrigation, though pricing policy is common. The emphasis sometimes switches towards FOOD POLICY.

Influential opinion, best expressed by the World Bank (see BRETTON WOODS), is that many developed countries have been over-protectionist, thus misallocating resources and forgoing the benefits of increasing trade. The laudable aims of increasing the stability of a sector, notoriously subject to fluctuating prices and sometimes in need of STRUCTURAL REFORM, have been under-emphasized. It is also not uncommon in developing countries for micro- and macro-economic policies (see ECONOMICS) to inhibit agriculture (through overvalued EXCHANGE RATES, protection of domestic manufactures providing inputs, and TAXATION of exportable and import competing crops), though this is not universal. G.H.P.

agrology, see under SOIL SCIENCE.

AI, see ARTIFICIAL INTELLIGENCE.

AID, see under ARTIFICIAL INSEMINATION.

AIDS. Acronym for the acquired immune deficiency syndrome, an end result of infection by the human immunodeficiency virus (HIV). AIDS is a disease complex of opportunistic infections and malignant disease which occurs because defence mechanisms have been irreparably damaged by the virus, and is almost invariably fatal. Common manifestations are severe weight loss, intractable diarrhoea, pneumonia and cerebral disease. The first documented case is from 1959, from a man who lived in the Belgian Congo (now the Democratic Republic of the Congo). This makes it likely that the first such infections occurred in humans in the late 1940s or early 1950s.

The incubation period between infection by HIV and the appearance of AIDS is uncertain. In most cases, it is several years. However, some have lived with HIV for well over a decade without showing any signs of developing AIDS; and if it is the case that they are somehow immune to the disease, their genetic make-up may hold a clue to a possible cure. During the incubation period, the victim feels well, but is nonetheless infectious to others.

The disease is sexually transmissible, and can spread through exposure to blood, semen and genital secretions, and breast milk. The chances of infection are particularly increased in unprotected oral or anal sex. However, it cannot be transmitted through saliva, routine physical contact, or coughing or sneezing. In the US and UK the disease has principally affected homosexuals; and also intravenous drug abusers who share needles and syringes. This fact meant that when HIV first caught the attention of the general public in the 1980s, many regarded it as a kind of retribution for an immoral lifestyle, and there was little sympathy from movements like the New Christian Right (see RELIGIOUS RIGHT).

In recent years, however, there has been much less intolerance, due to the growing realization that the disease is not confined to any particular sections of society. In fact, it is heterosexual intercourse that accounts for 70 per cent of the worldwide cases of HIV, currently estimated at 23 million. The disease has particularly afflicted DEVELOPING COUNTRIES, and in some parts of Africa nearly one in three people is infected. More than six million people across the world have died of AIDS.

At present, the only way to control the spread of AIDS is by health education to encourage safer sexual practices, since there is neither a cure nor a preventative vaccine. A blood test which detects exposure to HIV (but not AIDS) is available, which can allow partners to ensure they are both free of the disease before they have unprotected sex. At present, doctors can only slow the onset of AIDS, using a combination of three powerful drugs – the 'triple-drug therapy' – which have strong, unpleasant side-effects. J.D.O.; A.A.L.

AIH, see under ARTIFICIAL INSEMINATION.

AIM, see AMERICAN INDIAN MOVEMENT.

Aktion, Die, see under ACTIVISM; EXPRESSIONISM.

Alawites, see under ISLAM.

alcoholism. Before the 19th century excessive habitual consumption of alcoholic drinks was chiefly seen as a vice or a sin. From the time of Thomas Trotter and Benjamin Rush at the beginning of the 19th century, the weakness was increasingly called a disease by medical men and temperance reformers alike, on the grounds that a biochemically based dependence was created, withdrawal produced illness symptoms, and psychiatric disturbance followed. This MEDICALIZATION of alcoholism reached its high point with Jellinek's 1960 book, *The Disease Concept of Alcoholism*. The anti-addictive organization, Alcoholics Anonymous, set up in 1935, also subscribed to the disease theory, partly because it reduced stigmatization. Today's therapists are deeply divided as to whether the DISEASE MODEL is either accurate or helpful. BEHAVIOUR THERAPIES have recently found preference over drug and aversion therapies, and supportive groups are commonly used. It is nowadays stressed that the motivation and co-operation of the patient are requisite to overcome this increasing social scourge (see ADDICTION). R.P.

aleatory (*or, less commonly,* **aleatoric).** Adjective (derived from Latin *alea*, a game using dice) applied to several of the arts, and indicating that the artist or writer or composer allows some element of chance to be involved.

In art, the deliberate exploitation of chance goes back to the blot drawings of Alexander Cozens in the late 18th century. In the 20th century the practice began with the 'found objects' (see OBJET TROUVÉ) of the SURREALISTS and, in the 1940s, the accidental drip technique of Jackson Pollock (see ACTION PAINTING). In KINETIC ART effects are regarded as aleatory in so far as they are achieved with the aid of unpredictable natural forces such as air, water, fire, magnetism, or chemical action. A more mathematical use of random selection can be seen in many forms of COMPUTER art (e.g. computer graphics) and in the permutation of symbols in CONCRETE POETRY.

In literature, the 'cut-out' and 'fold-in' method of William Burroughs involved the random stringing together of sentences (his own and other people's) in whose combination some mystical significance is assumed; other writers (e.g. B. S. Johnson in *Trawl*) allow the reader to assemble pages *ad lib*.

In music, an aleatory element is introduced if the order in which sections of a composition are performed is decided by the throwing of a dice, or if there is improvisation by the performers, usually on patterns suggested in the score. J.W.; P.C.; A.H.

Alexander Technique. A movement awareness technique created by Frederick Matthias Alexander (1869–1945), which focuses on conscious participation, correcting and re-educating habitual movement patterns. Alexander lessons are conducted on a one-to-one basis in which the student is guided through simple everyday actions, e.g. walking, getting up from a chair, writing. The key to postural realignment in Alexander Technique is that of initiating movement from the head in a forward and upward motion concentrating on the process of the action rather than the end product.

The application of Alexander Technique can also have a therapeutic value and create a sense of physical and psychological relaxation by preventing habitual overreactions to everyday stimuli. Traditionally the Alexander Technique has been used by musicians and actors to relieve themselves from the tensions and postural problems related to their acts, but is now increasingly studied by a wide range of individuals. Dancers, and particularly those involved in NEW DANCE, often study Alexander Technique alongside other awareness-through-movement techniques (see FELDENKRAIS METHOD; RELEASE DANCE; CONTACT IMPROVISATION). L.A.

algebra. From the Arabic *Al-jabra* (in a book title *c.* AD 800). It dealt with the manipulation of expressions involving letters (e.g. $3x^2 + 4xy$). By the 19th century it was possible to handle expressions of great complexity but attention focused more and more on the rules – or axioms (see AXIOMATIC METHOD) – governing these manipulations. In particular mathematicians have investigated what happens if you change some of these rules.

By selecting different axioms (new and old) we get a variety of algebraic systems: group theory, lattice theory, homological algebra, BOOLEAN ALGEBRA, category theory, linear algebra, etc. N.A.R.

algedonic. Pertaining to REGULATION in a non-analytic mode. The word derives from the Greek words for pain and pleasure, and expresses the fact that some regulators operate within a system (see SYSTEMS) from CRITERIA that exist only in a METASYSTEM. For example, people may be trained to perform a task by explaining the system in which that task plays a part, analysing the 'why' and the 'how' of the job. But they may also be trained algedonically by a series of rewards and punishments which offer no such explanations. The metasystem making these awards constrains the system by regulating outcomes and not by direct intervention. For example, a failsafe device switches off an entire system because some output of the system has reached a level regarded as dangerous to the whole: it may take days to discover later what actually went wrong. S.BE.

Algerian War of Independence. France annexed Algeria in 1834, systematically colonizing the country and creating a strong sense of IDENTITY among the colonists. The Muslim (see ISLAM) majority were left, however, in an underprivileged position, and after World War II, the Front de Libération Nationale (FLN) was formed under the leadership of Ahmed Ben Bela, waging a GUERRILLA war against the French, who responded with bloody repression. A state of hostility continued until 1959, precipitating a political crisis in France and the return to power of General de Gaulle as the only statesman who could end the war and preserve 'Algérie Française'. De Gaulle then proposed to give Algerians the choice of whether or not to remain part of France, to the dismay of nationalists, who attempted to overthrow him in 1960 and 1961. A ceasefire was eventually agreed in March 1962 and the following July the Algerians voted overwhelmingly for independence.

The National Liberation Front (FLN) took power, and turned Algeria into a SOCIALIST economy, with no DEMOCRACY. However, popular unrest in 1988 forced them to allow multiparty elections. When Islamic fundamentalists (see FUNDAMENTALISM, ISLAMIC looked as though they would win the most seats in the 1991 elections, the government used military force to retain power. This led to TERRORISM by Islamic groups, and by 1995 Algeria had become embroiled in a bloody civil war. V.L.

algorithm. (From al-Kwarizmi, Muhammad ibn Musa, *c.* AD 800, an early writer on arithmetic and ALGEBRA). A procedure for solving a problem or, nowadays, a description of a computer program (see COMPUTING). For a basic operation such as sorting numbers (see NUMBER) into increasing order, or sorting names into alphabetical order, there are a variety of algorithms (such as heap sort, bucket sort, etc.). Some work faster than others (and we may hope to find an algorithm that runs in polynomial time, rather than the much slower exponential time).

The methods some of us learned at school for long multiplication and division are, of course, algorithms. N.A.R.

alias transformation, see under TRANSFORMATION.

alienation. For about a century (*c.* 1840–1940) the term was used to denote either the transfer of ownership or title of a piece of property, or a quality of mental derangement or insanity. Then a set of new and different meanings began to appear: a sense of estrangement from society, a feeling of powerlessness to affect social change, or a depersonalization of the individual in a large and bureaucratic (see BUREAUCRACY) society. By the 1950s the new meanings had become widely established and alienation had become a central term of contemporary SOCIOLOGY.

Reasons for these developments included the evident disorientations of the Western world in the upheaval of society following World War II; the expansion of an intelligentsia (see INTELLECTUAL) which found its own ROLE and STATUS problematic; the growing influence of German sociological writers (notably Georg Simmel and Max Weber) who stressed bureaucratization and the helplessness of the individual; the theological writings of Paul Tillich with his emphasis on the depersonalization of the individual in modern society; and – the most direct and important influence – the discovery of some early writings of Marx which had used alienation as a key CONCEPT in the analysis of CAPITALISM (see also MARXISM; REIFICATION). These were the so-called Economic and Philosophical Manuscripts written in 1844, and published only in 1932 in the abortive *Marx-Engels Gesamtausgabe*. They reflect the strong influence on Marx's thinking of Hegel, for whom alienation is the central process in the growing self-consciousness of man. As Hegel traces the idea in his *Phenomenology of Mind*, CONSCIOUSNESS 'divides' itself into subject and object, and alienation is the process whereby mind 'objectifies' itself in thought – a positive step in the development of self-consciousness. Marx concentrates on the alienation of labour and emphasizes the invidious aspects. He uses three terms, all of which have confusingly been translated as 'alienation': *Vergegenstandlichung*, or objectification, whose English equivalent in the philosophical sense is reification; *Entfremdung* or estrangement (Hegel had used principally *Selbstentfremdung* – 'self-estrangement'); and *Entäusserung*, or the sale of one's self as a commodity. In effect, Marx is saying that in the condition of alienation a worker loses control over the *processes* of work, over the product of his labour, and becomes a *thing*. Later, as Marx focused his attention on social organization and CLASS relations, this cluster of terms disappeared from his vocabulary, and was replaced by the specific analytical concept of *Ausbeutung* or exploitation. The resurrection of the term 'alienation' in the late 1940s and 1950s was part of the effort of NEO-MARXISTS to reinstate a broader, more HUMANIST version of Marx's thought.

Within academic sociology, alienation was given a social-psychological emphasis (see SOCIAL PSYCHOLOGY) and, for a time, mingled with the concept of ANOMIE. Social psychologists sought to develop 'scales' of alienation to measure the degree of 'powerlessness', 'normlessness', 'meaninglessness', and 'social isolation' felt by individuals, and further efforts were made to correlate these psychological states with conformity, political apathy, cynicism, suicide, and a host of similar phenomena. Most of these efforts had evaporated by the end of the 1960s. Within MARXISM, an onslaught against the concept of alienation as central to Marx was mounted by the French COMMUNIST philosopher Louis Althusser, who contended that Marx had discarded the earlier Hegelian influences and had come to what Althusser calls a STRUCTURALIST interpretation of society. For these reasons, plus the rise of a mood of revolutionary (see REVOLUTION) ACTIVISM by students in the late 1960s, the concept of alienation had by the close of the decade begun to lose much of its resonance in LEFT-wing thinking. For further reading: R. Schacht, *Alienation* (1970). D.B.

all people's state. Formula used in Soviet IDEOLOGY to describe the nature of the STATE in the Soviet Union. Marx and Lenin considered that once class conflict had ended the state would wither away. Stalin explained the growth of state power under the dictatorship of the proletariat even after SOCIALISM had officially been achieved by citing the need to oppose hostile forces abroad and class enemies within. The concept of the all people's state, first used in the early 1960s and enshrined in the 1977 Constitution, explained why the state was strengthened once those internal and external threats had diminished. The idea stressed the unity of Soviet society, particularly in a new stage of MATURE/DEVELOPED SOCIALISM, which rendered the notion of the state as the instrument of dictatorship by the working class redundant. Instead the state's duty, while still defending its territory, was increasingly directed towards WELFARE provision and the administration of the economy. Because of the increasing complexity of these functions, the responsibilities of the state would necessarily grow rather than decrease. D.PR.

Alldeutscher verband, see under PAN-GERMANISM.

allo-. A prefix used widely in linguistics to refer to any variation in the form of a linguistic unit which does not affect that unit's functional identity in the language. The formal variation is not linguistically distinctive, and results in no change in meaning. For example, different graphic shapes of the letter *A* (a, *a*, etc.) can be said to be *allographs* (i.e. graphic variants) of the same underlying unit. Variations in the phonetic shape of a PHONEME are called allophones (such as different pronunciations of the phoneme /p/ at the beginning and end of the word *pup*). Variations in the form of a MORPHEME are called allomorphs (such as the different forms of the plural ending in *cats, dogs*, and *horses*). Several other allo-terms have been invented. D.C.

allochronic speciation, see under SPECIATION.

allomorph, see under MORPHEME.

allopathy. A term used to describe the conventional medical system of treatment which is contrasted with HOMOEOPATHY. Allopathic treatment is said to be effective as a result of suppressing a symptom. The rise of allopathic medicine is linked to the development of PHARMACOLOGY and anaesthesia in the late 19th and early 20th centuries. The criticisms levelled against an allopathic approach by the homoeopaths is that the incidence of side-effects of the drugs used is high and the body's own defence system against illness and disease is not enhanced and indeed may well be jeopardized. Homoeopaths would add that allopathic treatment focuses on the diseased part and does not address the 'whole patient' and thus cannot bring about a cure (see HOLISTIC MEDICINE). P.C.P.

allopatric speciation, see under SPECIATION.

allophone, see under PHONEME.

alpha particle. A very stable association of two PROTONS and two NEUTRONS, which is emitted during radioactive decay (see RADIOACTIVITY), and which also constitutes the NUCLEUS of the helium ATOM. See also PARTICLE. M.V.B.

alternative architecture. Omnibus term for a number of architectural ideas of around the end of the 1960s mainly to do with self-build architecture based on earth, geodesic and similar structures (see GEODESY; EARTH SHELTERS). They were made from cheap, often recycled materials – sheet metal, plywood, tin cans, tree trunks, lumber and the like. A mainly American phenomenon, alternative architecture tapped a deep-rooted tradition of self-reliance in American culture. Intellectual support was to be provided by several passages in linguistic STRUCTURALIST literature, then fashionable in architectural theory, which made admiring reference to *bricolage* – the act of creation via *ad hoc* piecing together of elements which happened to be at hand – rather than deliberate, knowing, engineering design. S.L.

alternative energy. Because of the large consumption of fossil fuels involved in the production of electric power, and fear about the resulting ecological impacts (e.g. air POLLUTION, ACID RAIN, greenhouse gas emissions (see GREENHOUSE EFFECT), ground subsidence, groundwater contamination), interest has grown in means of generating alternative sources of energy. Likewise there has been a growth in opposition to nuclear power generation because of a perceived risk of a nuclear accident, of RADIATION, and of the uncertainties associated with the decommissioning of nuclear plant and of nuclear waste disposal.

The most important source of alternative energy is that created by harnessing the energy of flowing water (hydroelectric power or HEP). Other alternative energy sources are solar power, windmills and wind turbines, tidal and wave power, geothermal energy (as, for example, in volcanic areas) and biogas (produced by the aerobic digestion of organic materials such as sewage sludge, animal wastes, or landfill waste). As yet, with the exception of HEP, alternative energy sources have not led to any very great reduction in reliance upon traditional power sources in most parts of the world.

A.S.G.

alternative medicine, see under COMPLEMENTARY MEDICINE.

alternative society, see under UNDERGROUND.

alternative theatre. The term which is now most commonly applied to theatre presented outside the REPERTORY or regional theatres and the commercial West End, Broadway or boulevard theatres (see BOULEVARD COMEDY). It has largely replaced such definitions as FRINGE, OFF-BROADWAY, ANTI-THEATRE and even experimental theatre. Although there have been companies devoted to experiment and innovation throughout the 20th century (see THEATRE LIBRE), the contemporary alternative theatre movement blossomed during the intellectual upheavals of the 1960s, when most of the work had a radically political outlook. Nowadays companies are equally likely to be concerned with the exploration of the performers' own creative and technical skills, CELEBRATORY THEATRE, gay and feminist theatre, or the local production of theatre of ethnic and social minorities who are considered culturally deprived. Many alternative theatre companies are short-lived and financially insecure, but others have achieved relatively generous subsidies (see THIRD THEATRE). For further reading: S. Craig (ed.), *Dreams and Deconstructions: Alternative Theatre in Britain* (1980).

M.A.

Althusserianism. The distinctive contribution to contemporary MARXISM of the French philosopher and sociologist Louis Althusser (1918–90). Althusser argued – contrary to most recent interpretations – that Marx did not remain under the spell of Hegel for most of his life. There was, from the late 1840s onwards, a distinct 'epistemological break' (*coupure epistémologique*) in Marx's thinking, whereby he shook off the residual IDEALISM of his youth and embarked on a thoroughly materialistic, scientific SOCIOLOGY. From Marx's later writings Althusser distilled a formal model of the economy and society whose distinctive feature was the absence of the extreme economic determinism which characterized most Marxist theory.

In particular, Althusser reformulated the 'base and SUPERSTRUCTURE' relationship central to traditional Marxism. While the economy – the base – was seen as the determinant 'in the last instance' of other areas of social life, such as politics and IDEOLOGY, the economic base itself depended for its functioning on these other areas: they were 'conditions of existence' of the economy. Thus the political system of the ancient world was the condition of existence of the slave economy, just as RELIGION was the condition of existence of the feudal economy of medieval Europe – even though the slave and feudal economies were 'in the last instance' the determinants of the forms of politics and religion. Althusser allowed for the 'relative autonomy' of the different levels or realms of society – such as politics or culture – to the point where some feel that the distinctively Marxist emphasis on the economic base was in danger of disappearing altogether. He also suggested a degree of overlapping or *overdetermination* of levels of society which further complicated the simple model of an economic base determining a superstructure. Cultural divisions such as those between town and country, particular national or CLASS traditions, and the precise state of international relations at any one time, could all 'act back' on the economic base, inhibiting or reinforcing the primary conflict of classes that took place there. All social phenomena, Althusser suggested, are so 'overdetermined': there is no such thing as 'pure' relations of production. The precise form of overdetermination in any society at any time can make all the difference to such matters as the success or failure of REVOLUTION.

The importance Althusser attached to the superstructure in the operation of the economic base is seen especially in his concept of *ideological state apparatuses*. In order to persist over time, he argued, an economic system such as CAPITALISM must continually 'reproduce' its relations of production, i.e.

the exploitative class relationship arising out of ownership or non-ownership of the means of production. Much of this is done through the work of the ideological state apparatuses, which include TRADE UNIONS and political parties, religious and educational institutions, the FAMILY, the mass media, sport, art and literature (see MASS CULTURE). All these act to integrate individuals into the existing economic system by subjecting them to the HEGEMONY of a DOMINANT IDEOLOGY, a set of ideas and values which ultimately supports the dominance of the capitalist class. Once again this emphasis on the importance of ideology in the functioning of capitalism has led some Marxists to accuse Althusser of substituting a cultural DETERMINISM for the more traditional economic determinism. Certainly there is a nice paradox here, that a thinker who was the foremost advocate of the 'scientific' character of Marxism should at the same time be the principal opponent of straightforward materialist explanations of social life. For further reading: L. Althusser, *For Marx* (1969); L. Althusser, *Lenin and Philosophy, and Other Essays* (1971). K.K.

altruism. Behaviour that is not self-interested. Human altruism has concerned sociobiologists and social psychologists since about 1970 (see SOCIOBIOLOGY; SOCIAL PSYCHOLOGY). No uncontroversial technical definition has been agreed (nor of its supposed opposite, 'selfishness'). Sociobiologists typically state that 'costs' of altruistic acts must outweigh benefits – only to then argue that altruism so conceived is mythical, all apparent altruism covertly benefiting the survival of the actor's GENES. Seeming 'altruism' is thus, oxymoronically, 'reciprocal'. This debate arose because (like Darwin) sociobiologists assume altruism entails selection *against* the fittest (see NATURAL SELECTION), an evolutionary paradox (self-sacrifice of young males in battle being the canonical example). This, however, conflates cases where death is intrinsic to the act with those where it only accompanies failure, while their definition itself makes an act's status dependent on unknown consequences which could fluctuate indefinitely between 'costs' and 'rewards' – whether it is altruistic thereby becoming unknowable.

Social psychologists by contrast have largely ignored such issues, empirically studying the psychological and situational factors facilitating altruism (as commonly understood) and 'pro-social behaviour' in general (including the 'bystander effect' in which individuals are unwilling to intervene in emergency situations when large numbers of people are watching). It is unclear quite why sociobiological-level explanations are needed in addition to these. Biologically, most psychologists would probably see adult altruism as rooted in infant caretaking. There were clear ideological facets to the controversy during the 1970s and 1980s, sociobiology's critics seeing it as rationalizing RIGHT-wing economic policies by collapsing the altruism–selfishness polarity. G.D.R.

ambient music. Term used by the composer Brian Eno to describe some of his compositions which are designed to form an aural background rather than be the centre of the listener's attention. The music is often very simple, repetitive, even minimal (see MINIMAL MUSIC), and played at low volume. This type of music has links with FURNITURE MUSIC and also MUZAK, although its artistic rather than commercial purposes would tend to distance it from the latter. B.CO.

ambiguity. The coexistence in a piece of writing of two or more meanings. William Empson introduced his *Seven Types of Ambiguity* (1930; 2nd ed., 1947) by stating: 'I propose to use the word in an extended sense, and shall think relevant to my subject any verbal nuance, however slight, which gives room for alternative reactions to the same piece of language.' This study, directly influenced by I. A. Richards and Robert Graves, was very much a product of a time excited by T. S. Eliot's poetry and criticism, by the revival of the 17th-century Metaphysical poets, and by Freud. If over-ingenious, *Seven Types of Ambiguity* is a complex and sophisticated work (Empson reminds us that 'if an ambiguity is to be unitary there must be "forces" holding its elements together'), but during the 1930s and 40s 'ambiguity' became so fashionable that many versifiers cultivated it, whether usefully or not, while critics hunted it down indiscriminately, thus denigrating those kinds of literature where they could not find it. Ambiguity is a quality of much fine writing, endowing it with richness, subtlety or surprise, but in itself (like rhyme, onomatopoeia, figures of speech, etc.) it is neither good nor bad. See also PLURISIGNATION. D.J.E.

ambivalence. Term used originally (*as ambivalency*) in ABNORMAL PSYCHOLOGY and PSYCHIATRY, later annexed by literary criticism, to denote the situation in which someone entertains, simultaneously or in alternation, opposed attitudes or feelings or sets of values; the familiar 'love–hate relationship' may be said to exemplify reciprocal ambivalence. Whereas, in general, ambivalence is a potential source of undesirable stress (and in extreme forms is one of the four cardinal symptoms of SCHIZOPHRENIA listed by Eugen Bleuler), in a writer it is widely regarded as a source of strength and desirable TENSION, and in a fictional character as evidence of subtlety in his or her creator. O.S.; M.J.C.

American Dream. Vague yet extremely evocative phrase describing America's self-image as a land of freedom and opportunity for all. While the construct does not appear in Thomas Jefferson's Declaration of Independence of 1776, the idea it expresses is woven into the document, especially in its theory, traceable to the Greeks and familiar to Rousseau, that man is born with inalienable natural rights. Journalist and former Nixon aide William Safire writes that in a 1960 debate about 'national purpose', the poet Archibald MacLeish commented that 'there are those, I know, who will reply that the liberation of humanity, the freedom of man and mind, is nothing but a dream. They are right. It is. It is the American dream.' In post-war literature, the idea that America uniquely embodies freedom and opportunity for all has often invited ridicule. Norman Mailer entitled his lurid novel of wife-killing, alcohol and degradation *An American Dream*. But the power of the phrase resonates beyond such catcalls, at least in the US. 'I say to you today, my friends, that in spite of the difficulties and frustrations of the moment I still have a dream,' the Rev. Martin Luther King said in his historic speech before the Lincoln Memorial in Washington in 1963. 'It is a dream deeply rooted in the American dream', a dream that 'my four little children will one day live in a nation where they will not be judged by the color of their skin but by the content of their character . . . .' R.K.H.

American exceptionalism. The term has two distinct meanings, although they are sometimes mistakenly conflated. The first, and simpler, lies in the belief in the USA as a nation uniquely blessed by some combination of historical circumstance, material abundance, security from invasion, or even divine benevolence, to pursue a more moral and elevated path than other nations. This conceit's history predates the Republic itself, and survived such phenomena as slavery, the virtual destruction of the native population, and the gross inequalities of the industrial age, although it struggled to survive the USA's confrontation with global realities in the COLD WAR years.

The second meaning is more analytic. It is usually traced to Alexis de Tocqueville (1805–59), whose 'Democracy in America' was pervaded by a fascination with the features which he thought distinguished the USA from all European societies, such as its strong individualism and lack of habits of hierarchy and deference. The concept evolved to include emphases on the nation's lack of violent CLASS or ideological conflict (see IDEOLOGY), the persistence of high levels of religious faith in the face of modern pressures towards secularization, and the capacity to absorb great numbers of immigrants without fatal strains.

Disagreement about the utility of this meaning of the term is based partly on doubts as to whether there exists a general, rather than 19th-century European, model of development to which the USA has been 'exceptional', and partly on doubts that the USA's history and modern condition are best understood in terms which stress so heavily such virtues as assimilation, tolerance and consensus. S.R.

American Indian Movement (AIM). The social unrest of the 1960s in the US did not pass by the nation's Indian reservations, which were ripe for change after decades of unwise federal policies that sought to move Indians off reservations and generally ignored abysmal conditions there. The new militancy produced the American Indian Movement, a loosely organized group of activists who in February 1973 engaged in an armed standoff with federal agents on the

Pine Ridge Reservation in South Dakota. AIM gunmen seized control of Wounded Knee, an Indian burial ground that had been turned into a tourist site. On 29 December 1890, soldiers massacred from 150 to 300 Indians – mostly women and children – gathered at Wounded Knee, the last conflict of the 19th-century Indian wars. The 1973 standoff ended with federal agents retaking the area by force. The Pine Ridge reservation remains today one of the poorest places in the US, but some Indian tribes have prospered by passage of a 1988 law that permitted them to open gambling casinos. The advent of casinos, however, has intensified divisions among tribal members who hew to traditional ways, and entrepreneurial Indians who have made millions in recent years from high-stakes bingo, casinos, and the sale of tax-free motor fuels and cigarettes at reservation smoke shops. R.K.H.

Amiens, Charter of, see under SYNDICALISM.

amorphous materials. Solids in which the constituent ATOMS or MOLECULES are not arranged in a perfectly regular pattern as they are in crystals. The most common example of an amorphous material is ordinary glass. There is usually a tendency for many amorphous materials to revert to a crystalline form with time, especially if they are heated, and they generally have to be made by rapidly cooling the molten material to room temperature. The current interest in these materials comes from the SEMICONDUCTOR industry which up to now has relied on very tiny pieces of crystalline silicon or germanium for the fabrication of devices such as TRANSISTORS, etc. However, the exploitation of the properties of semiconductors to produce electrical power from sunlight (solar CELLS) requires large areas of semiconductor so that as much sunlight as possible is trapped, and since it would be very difficult to make these as perfect crystals, it is in principle much easier and cheaper to make them in the amorphous form. It has proved difficult to make amorphous semiconductors with the same electrical properties that crystals have. Nevertheless, amorphous silicon solar cells are now being used to power small calculators and other devices, but their use as power generators on a large scale is still in the development stage. H.M.R.

anal character, see under PSYCHOSEXUAL DEVELOPMENT.

analogue computer. A mechanical device for processing information, used almost exclusively to find numerical solutions to physical problems. Each physical quantity that occurs in the problem is represented by a mechanical displacement or by an electric voltage or current. The various parts of the computer are connected up in such a way that these displacements are related to one another in the same way as the corresponding quantities in the real SYSTEM. The computer thus behaves as a mechanical or electrical analogue of the physical problem. The accuracy of analogue computers is limited, and the time required to set them up for a problem is usually long: as general-purpose computers they are therefore practically obsolete, though the technique they use is sometimes employed in devices dedicated to a particular task (such as navigation systems, or automatic transmission systems). C.S.

analogy.

(1) In historical and comparative work in LINGUISTICS, the process of regularization which affects the exceptional forms in the grammar of a language. Irregular forms tend to become regular – a process which can be heard in early child utterance in such forms as *mans, mouses* and *wented,* which are coined on analogy with regular plurals and past tenses. D.C.

(2) In PHILOSOPHY, likeness or similarity, usually with the implication that the likeness in question is systematic or structural. To argue by analogy is to infer from the fact that one thing is in some respects similar to another that the two things will also correspond in other, as yet unexamined, respects. In LOGIC, reasoning by analogy is a form of non-demonstrative argument which, unlike INDUCTION proper, draws conclusions about the nature of a *single* unknown thing from information about a known thing or things which it to some extent resembles. It is a form of reasoning that is peculiarly liable to yield false conclusions from true premises. A.Q.

analogy tests, see under MENTAL TESTING.

analysis.

(1) In MATHEMATICS, the development of a rigorous basis for the CALCULUS, INFINITE series, standard functions (sine, cosine, logs, etc.), differential equations, etc. – anything involving CONVERGENCE and the real numbers (see NUMBER). Newton and Leibniz started these subjects, but it was only slowly that an appreciation of the underlying problems grew. Indeed, until a satisfactory definition of real numbers was made (by Richard Dedekind in *Continuity and Irrational Numbers*, 1872), mathematicians were guided more by geometric intuition (see GEOMETRY) than by rigour.

There was continued criticism of the arguments used, particularly of the notion of infinitesimals (infinitely small but non-zero quantities) favoured by Leibniz. Although these have at last gained intellectual respectability with the development of Non-standard Analysis, Newton's preference for limiting processes has held the field. This made great strides once Karl Weierstrass (1815–97) invented his ε, δ method. He also discovered a continuous curve on which there is no unique tangent at any point. This and other pathological specimens which mathematicians delight in discovering act as a caution against saying that something is 'obviously true'. N.A.R.

(2) In PHILOSOPHY, the discovery of verbal forms of expression for complex ideas and PROPOSITIONS which make explicit the complexity that is hidden by the more abbreviated character of their usual verbal formulation. As originally conceived by Bertrand Russell and G. E. Moore, it was a kind of defining process, in which the defining terms are more elementary and unproblematic than the terms being defined. Examples are Mill's analysis of 'cause' as 'invariable unconditional antecedent' or the analysis of 'knowledge' as 'justified true BELIEF'. Russell's theory of *descriptions* supplied a technique of analysis that was widely adopted. It showed how sentences with problematic terms in them could be replaced by sentences equivalent in MEANING to them in which the troublesome expressions do not occur. A.Q.

analytic.

(1) In PHILOSOPHY, a term introduced by Kant, who defined an analytic statement as one in which the concept of the predicate is already contained in the concept of the subject. Putative examples are the statements that a triangle has three sides and that a vixen is a female fox. Kant also termed analytic any statement the denial of which is self-contradictory. Those statements that are not analytic – e.g. the statement that there are vixens in Lincolnshire – Kant called SYNTHETIC. More recently, analytic statements have been defined as those that are true in virtue of meaning, or, alternatively, as those which can be shown to be true by definitions and the laws of LOGIC alone. One important consequence of a statement's being analytic is that knowledge of its truth will be knowledge of a peculiarly trivial sort.

The notion of analyticity is particularly important to EMPIRICISM in philosophy. Empiricists take the view that all non-trivial, substantive knowledge is A POSTERIORI. The problem the empiricist immediately confronts is that, on the face of it, we do have knowledge which is both substantive and A PRIORI, e.g. our knowledge of mathematical truths. In order to deal with such putative counter-examples some empiricists have denied that such knowledge is A PRIORI. The majority, however, have instead tried to show that the mathematical and other statements involved are really analytic and thus that our knowledge of their truth is quite trivial after all.

More recently W. V. Quine has argued that we should reject the distinction between analytic and synthetic. There are two prongs to Quine's attack: he argues (i) that the distinction cannot be defined other than circularly; (ii) it depends upon an atomistic conception of meaning that Quine argues should be overturned in favour of a holistic approach (see HOLISM). S.W.L.

(2) In comparative LINGUISTICS, adjective applied to a language (e.g. Vietnamese) in which the word forms are invariable, grammatical relations being indicated primarily by word order and the use of particles, not by inflections or compounding (as in INFLECTING and AGGLUTINATING languages respectively). An alternative term is *isolating*. D.C.

analytic philosophy. The most general term for a wide variety of recent philosophical movements, largely in the English-speaking world, which (1) are sceptical of or hostile to constructive metaphysical speculation (see METAPHYSICS), (2) agree that there is a characteristic method of ANALYSIS with which philosophy alone can arrive at secure results, and (3), for the most part, favour the piecemeal tackling of philosophical problems. The EMPIRICISM of Locke, Hume and Mill was analytical in tendency, seeking to show how the complex IDEAS (e.g. material object, cause, person) with which the mind thinks about the world are composed of simple ideas acquired through the senses. Analytical philosophers of this century have concentrated as a matter of principle, not on ideas in the mind, but on the language in which the mind's thinking is expressed. Bertrand Russell and G. E. Moore inaugurated analytic philosophy in the early years of the century by applying the new LOGIC, to which Russell had so greatly contributed, as an instrument of analysis. Wittgenstein, learning from and influencing Russell, made the practice systematic and emphasized the linguistic character of its proper subject-matter (see LOGICAL ATOMISM). The LOGICAL POSITIVISM of the VIENNA CIRCLE carried the work further, and the earlier suspicion of metaphysics hardened into principled hostility. Wittgenstein later came to question the adequacy of formal logic as the instrument of analysis, and his school, and that of the ordinary-language philosophers of Oxford (see LINGUISTIC PHILOSOPHY) preferred to carry out the analysis of language informally, acknowledging the multiplicity of its uses and the variety and flexibility of the rules that govern it. For further reading: H.-J. Glock (ed.), *The Rise of Analytic Philosophy* (1997). A.Q.

analytic psychology, see under JUNGIAN.

analytical chemistry. The branch of CHEMISTRY concerned with the identification and estimation of ELEMENTS, RADICALS or compounds. *Qualitative analysis* is concerned with the detection of chemical SPECIES and often makes use of chemical reactions which give distinctive products (recognized by colour, solubility, etc.), but characteristic physical properties are often directly investigated. For *quantitative determinations* a wide variety of chemical and physical methods have been developed. Chemical procedures include the precipitation and weighing of an insoluble product, the determination of the oxidizing or reducing properties of a solution, and the measurement of the acid or base strength of a solution. Extensive use is made of physical measurements which may be based on spectroscopic or electrical behaviour (see SPECTROSCOPY), the use of radioactive (see RADIOACTIVITY) ISOTOPES or mass spectrometry. Chromatographic or ION exchange methods may be employed to effect an initial separation of mixtures. B.F.

anaphora. In the field of GRAMMAR, the way in which a linguistic unit refers back to some previously expressed unit of meaning. In the sentence *He did that there*, each word has an 'anaphoric reference', making complete sense only when some previous sentence (such as *John painted this picture in Bermuda*) is known. Anaphora often contrasts with *cataphora*, where the words refer forward, and with *exophora*, where the words refer directly to the extralinguistic situation. D.C.

anaphylactic shock, see under ANAPHYLAXIS.

anaphylaxis. Literally, the opposite of PROPHYLAXIS. In practice its use is confined to an acute form of allergy associated with the introduction of an antigen (see IMMUNITY), particularly a soluble antigen, into an organism that has already made antibodies directed against it. Anaphylaxis may be systemic or local.

(1) *Acute systemic anaphylaxis* occurs (notably in human beings, guinea pigs and dogs) when an antigenic substance enters the bloodstream of an organism containing specific antibodies against it. In severe cases the anaphylactic shock may be associated with rapid shallow breathing, and in extreme cases with waterlogging of the lungs and heart failure. Since the pharmacological agent (see PHARMACOLOGY) of anaphylactic shock is histamine, some protection can be achieved by antihistaminic drugs.

(2) *Local anaphylaxis* is brought about when an antigen, particularly a soluble antigen, is injected into the skin or other tissues of an immune animal. Human beings, guinea pigs and rabbits are specially liable to local anaphylaxis, an intense inflammation,

confined to the area in which the antigen was injected, but causing in extreme cases tissue death. P.M.

anarchism. A political movement advocating the abolition of the state and the replacement of all forms of governmental authority by free association and voluntary co-operation of groups and individuals. Anarchists disagree about what specific relationships the future society is to be based on, and about how it is to be achieved. Contemporary libertarian writers (see LIBERTARIANISM) describe themselves as 'anarchocapitalists' and base their hostility to the STATE on the inviolability of each individual's ownership of himself and his property. Historically, anarchists have been hostile to private property as ordinarily understood. The first English anarchist, William Godwin (1756–1836), was uninterested in political action and wished the 'EUTHANASIA of government' to result from individual moral reformation; more commonly, anarchists have advocated some form of DIRECT ACTION. Their MARXIST critics have complained that this is inimical to good organization and effective tactics. Proudhon (1809–65) and Blanqui (1805–81) divided the allegiances of 19th-century anarchists in France, the former wanting peaceful change, the latter an advocate of spontaneous insurrection. Bakunin led the anarchist wing of the First INTERNATIONAL; his quarrels with Marx and Engels destroyed the organization in 1876. Bakunin's enthusiasm for insurrection and spontaneity degenerated into the romantic and suicidal craze for 'propaganda by the deed' which swept Europe and America at the turn of the century. Johann Moser's obsession with the creative possibilities of dynamite was characteristic of this period, but even Malatesta, Kropotkin and Emma Goldmann were tempted by the thought that assassinating the rich and powerful would lead to a workers' revolt and thence to the anarchist utopia (see UTOPIANISM).

After 1900, anarchism ceased to make much impact on the politics of developed countries. In revolutionary Russia, however, Makhno defied the Bolshevik armies (see BOLSHEVISM) for most of the Civil War, while anarchists held power in Catalonia during the Spanish Civil War. In France, the hold of anarchist ideas on the LEFT has never quite died out; ANARCHO-SYNDICALISM was a powerful force in TRADE UNION circles until after World War I, and in the 'events' of MAY 1968 anarchism rather than orthodox Marxism ruled the day. The TERRORISM which the far left practised during the 1970s was based on an orthodox hatred of CAPITALIST society, but the expectation of insurrection was anarchist. Of much greater intellectual interest has been the continuing revival of INDIVIDUALIST American anarchism associated with writers such as Murray Rothbard and Robert Nozick. For further reading: G. Woodcock, *Anarchism and Anarchists: Essays* (1992). L.L.; A.R.

anarcho-syndicalism. The attempt, which reached its climax at the turn of the century, to unite ANARCHIST and TRADE UNION politics; it began when Bakunin's followers in the Swiss Jura Federation of the First INTERNATIONAL turned away from conspiracy to trade union struggle under the urging of Bakunin's disciple James Guillaume. Trade unions were to provide the spearhead of REVOLUTION as well as a model for economic organization after the revolution. French anarcho-syndicalism developed from the 'revolutionary syndicalism' of Fernand Pelloutier, who had migrated from MARXISM through anarchism to a belief in the revolutionary general strike. Trade unions could abolish CAPITALISM by DIRECT ACTION if they saw the struggle for economic goals as a prelude to the political general strike. Pelloutier's revolutionary syndicalism was emulated elsewhere, but only in Spain did the trade union movement embrace anarchism. In France, the CGT was anarcho-syndicalist before World War I, as was the Industrial Workers of the World (see SYNDICALISM) in America; the better entrenched union movement in Britain and Germany generally shunned anarchism in favour of less violent and more REFORMIST doctrines. Although it vanished after World War I, it left one notable intellectual achievement in Georges Sorel's *Reflections on Violence*, and a non-violent version of syndicalism is discussed with some sympathy in Bertrand Russell's influential *Roads to Freedom* (1919). A.R.

ANC, see AFRICAN NATIONAL CONGRESS.

ancestor worship. Complex of beliefs and

practices which focus upon the veneration of dead ancestors. It involves the recognition of an active relationship between the living and the dead. Ancestors or the spirits of the ancestors can intervene in the social order as Fortes demonstrated in his classic work *Oedipus and Job in West African Religion* (1983). The ancestors provide the legitimation for structures of authority and they have the power to threaten retribution. Ancestor worship is most commonly found in societies with DESCENT groups, and tombs or shrines are an important symbolic focus for the group. Contact may be made with the ancestors at tombs or shrines where offerings and SACRIFICES are made by representatives of the descent group. A.G.

androgyny. From ancient Greek 'andro' (male) and 'gyn' (female). Concept which recognizes both male and female characteristics in human identity. GENDER is not fixed or biologically based, but is fluid. 'Whole' personality is an amalgam of male and female characteristics. Androgyny was a concept developed in the feminist movement (see FEMINISM), particularly by C. Heilbrun (*Towards a Recognition of Androgyny*, 1973), and it represented a movement away from theories of rigid SEX-role or gender stereotyping, i.e. the idea that men and women were forced into the acceptance of separate conventional roles. The solution to sexual oppression was sought through the elimination of gender stereotyping. Androgyny implied that men should develop 'feminine' qualities, women 'masculine' qualities, and thereby dissolve the difference, the source of inequalities, between the sexes. Other feminists, however, have criticized the concept of androgyny for failing to deal with the issue of power and for continuing to recognize conventional male/female traits, if uniting rather than separating them. There has also been some unease in situating the question of sexual oppression in PSYCHOLOGY rather than in material or political spheres. A.G.

Anglicanism. The form of church life characteristic of the Anglican Communion, with about 50 million adherents. This consists of the Church of England (Latin *Ecclesia Anglicana*), which rejected the control of the Pope in the 16th century, and of the Churches outside England which send their bishops to the Lambeth Conference (since 1868 every ten years or so) under the presidency of the Archbishop of Canterbury. In some countries Anglicanism is better known as EPISCOPALISM; its branch in the USA is the Episcopal Church. Because it originated in England's national Church, Anglicanism tries to be comprehensive, reconciling CATHOLICISM with PROTESTANTISM, and also religious LIBERALISM with orthodoxy, in a community united in 'common prayer' and in mutual charity. This example has been an inspiration to the modern ECUMENICAL MOVEMENT. In practice, however, Anglicanism has suffered from the old-fashioned nature of the Church of England, from the declining prestige of England in the world, and from its internal controversies, e.g. those between ANGLO-CATHOLICISM and evangelicalism (see EVANGELICAL). Different 'provinces' (groups of dioceses, each with its own bishop) have made different decisions about the ordination of women as priests, a development which has been extensive in North America. For further reading: S. Neill, *Anglicanism* (1977). D.L.E.

Anglo-Catholicism. A movement within ANGLICANISM, emphasizing the heritage of CATHOLICISM, in contrast with Bible-based evangelicalism (see EVANGELICAL), as well as with modernizing LIBERALISM. D.L.E.

Angry Brigade. A small LEFT-wing group which in the name of the working class mounted sporadic attacks upon various representatives of the ruling class or ESTABLISHMENT. Their claimed successes included the machine-gunning of the US Embassy in London on 20 August 1967 (the first such incident) and the bombing of the UK Minister of Employment's home on 11 January 1971 during the time when he was preparing the controversial Industrial Relations Bill. Like the American WEATHERMEN, the Italian Red Army Faction and the German Baader-Meinhof gang, the activists of the Angry Brigade appeared to be mainly MIDDLE-CLASS ex-students; politically the group appeared to be more ANARCHIST than MARXIST. In 1972 its leaders were tried and imprisoned, and its bombings have been eclipsed by more recent and effective terrorist activities. The Angry Brigade constitutes an early manifestation of European TERRORIST activity from left and right against Western state and private liberal institutions (see LIBERALISM) which is distinguishable from other sources of terror by its lack of nationalist IDEOLOGY and consequent political weakness. P.S.L.

Angst. Variously translated as anxiety, anguish, dread. It was first used in an existential sense (see EXISTENTIALISM) by Søren Kierkegaard in *The Concept of Anxiety* (1844), where he describes the terrifying reality of the state of splitness, indecisiveness and responsibility in front of choice. Heidegger, in *Being and Time* (1927), freely paraphrases Kierkegaard and does not add anything significant to Kierkegaard's analysis. Sartre, in *Being and Nothingness* (1943), again follows Kierkegaard, but adds an element of determinism by making 'anguish' a state of BAD FAITH in which the conscious subject (see SUBJECTIVITY) tries to renege on his inalienable freedom to choose. R.PO.

anima. JUNGIAN term, derived from its original meaning of life force or soul, and referring to the autonomous ARCHETYPE within a man's COLLECTIVE UNCONSCIOUS which symbolizes the feminine side of his nature. In its most basic form this is an inherited collective image of Woman. As with all archetypes, the *anima* is projected onto the world of experience, finding its first incarnation in one's mother; and a similar projection may govern the choice of a wife. The artist's 'muse', with its feminine and creative connotations, is another representation of *anima*. In his later work, Jung introduced the analogous term *animus* to refer to a woman's masculine principle, although the additional functions of *anima* for the male were never fully articulated in his presentation of the female's *animus*. T.Z.C.

animal liberation. The modern animal liberation movement, also known as the animal rights movement, seeks to include nonhuman animals within the sphere of morality in a way that they have not been included previously (see ENVIRONMENTAL ETHICS). The term 'animal liberation' is intended to suggest an analogy with other liberation movements, which have sought equality for BLACKS and women. The equality sought by the animal liberation movement, however, is not equal treatment, but equal consideration of interests. Advocates of animal liberation start from the factual claim that animals have interests – e.g., interests in not suffering, and in being able to fulfil their behavioural needs. They then argue that there is no basis for refusing to take these interests into account, and giving them the same weight as we give to similar interests of human beings.

Central to the animal liberation movement is its rejection of 'speciesism'. The term was coined by Richard Ryder, in the early 1970s, and taken up by Peter Singer in his 1973 essay 'Animal Liberation' and his subsequent book of the same title. Singer describes speciesism as a prejudice or bias against members of species other than one's own. He sees it as analogous to RACISM and SEXISM, in that it is a means by which a more powerful core group justifies its exploitation of less powerful outsiders. Advocates of animal liberation do not deny that there are important differences between normal mature human beings and normal mature members of other species, but they claim that species in itself is not morally significant. The suffering of non-human animals therefore should get the same consideration as we give to the sufferings of human beings at a similar mental level. The animal liberation movement sees our use of animals for food as fundamental to our attitudes to animals, and animal liberationists are generally vegetarian or vegan. The movement also opposes experiments on animals, and the use of animals in entertainment and recreations such as hunting. Some groups within the movement have broken into laboratories and released animals or damaged equipment, but the movement as a whole is strongly against the use of violence towards animals or people. P.A.D.S.

animal rights, see under ANIMAL LIBERATION.

animism. In ANTHROPOLOGY, a term first used by E. B. Tylor (*Primitive Culture*, 1871) for belief based on the universal human experiences of dreams and visions, in 'spiritual beings', comprising the souls of individual creatures and other spirits. In modern anthropology animism as a theory has been criticized, partly because it is concerned with unknowable origins of belief, and partly because it fails to discriminate adequately between concepts of soul and of spirit. The animism debate was revived by Spiro (*Buddhism and Society*, 1970) in his analysis of Burmese religion. Spiro's approach was to draw a distinction between BUDDHISM (the formal, literate tradition) and animism (popular beliefs and practices). Other anthropologists working in Buddhist societies of south-east Asia (e.g. S. J. Tambiah, *Buddhism and the Spirit Cults*, 1970) have addressed this question, but they have disputed the validity of Spiro's concept of animism. M.F.; A.G.

anion, see under ION.

Annales school. A group of historians associated with the journal founded by Lucien Febvre and Marc Bloch in 1929 and now known as *Annales: économies, sociétés, civilisations*. The group stands for a particular style of history. Its members believe that the historian should place less emphasis than is customary on narrative (especially political narrative), on the chronicle of events (*histoire événementielle*), and more emphasis on analysis, on long-term structures and trends (*la longue durée*). They also believe that economic, social, cultural and political history should be integrated into a total history, and that, to do this, historians need to be well acquainted with the SOCIAL SCIENCES. Distinguished living members of the group include Pierre Chaunu, Pierre Goubert and Emmanuel Le Roy Ladurie. An outstanding example of the *Annales* approach translated into English is Fernand Braudel's *The Mediterranean and the Mediterranean World in the Age of Philip II*. See also CONJUNCTURE; SERIAL HISTORY. For further reading: P. Burke, *The French Historical Revolution: The Annales School, 1929–89* (1990). P.B.

anomaly. Literally something which will not fit in with an existing taxonomic order, anomaly can be taken as 'falsifying' accepted theories, and thus, within Karl Popper's view of science (see POPPERIAN), providing the essential trigger to scientific advance. (For Popper science moves on not by establishing truths but by dispelling errors.) Anomaly plays an equally important part in T. S. Kuhn's vision of how the practice of 'normal science' is occasionally interrupted by '*scientific revolutions*'. According to Kuhn, established theories can tolerate a certain build-up of anomalies (which can be accommodated by *ad hoc* hypotheses); beyond a particular threshold, however, anomalies demand rational interpretation in their own right, leading to new scientific GESTALTS or theories (see PARADIGM). Paul Feyerabend, by contrast, has emphasized the degree to which orthodox science clings to, or turns a blind eye to, the anomalies it creates (science is conservative rather than critical). For further reading: T. S. Kuhn, *The Structure of Scientific Revolutions* (1970). R.P.

anomie. A term, resurrected from the Greek (literally, without law) by the French sociologist Émile Durkheim, to denote that condition of society which results from the disintegration of a commonly accepted NORMATIVE code. For Durkheim, industrial CLASS conflict was a symptom of anomie. More loosely, anomie was used in the 1950s and 1960s as a CONCEPT akin to ALIENATION, to describe a condition where an individual had lost his traditional moorings and was prone to disorientation or psychic disorder. D.B.

anonymous Christian. A term used by the Roman Catholic theologian Karl Rahner (1904–84; see CATHOLICISM) to describe the non-Christian who, while not being able or willing to accept identification as a Christian by being named as such in Baptism, responds to God's self-revelation and grace, and obeys his moral law, so far as circumstances permit. Such a person is thought to be promised ultimate salvation by the God revealed by Jesus Christ as the merciful Father of all. This was a development of the teaching of VATICAN COUNCIL II. D.L.E.

anorexia nervosa. Obsessive and chronic dieting (anorexia nervosa) and self-induced vomiting (bulimia nervosa) are now recognized as serious psychological disorders in Western society. They affect mainly girls and young women, though an increasing number of young men are being admitted to clinics for eating disorders. Historically, starvation was and continues to be among some sects a way chosen to mortify the flesh in fervid pursuit of holiness; it is also an expression of passive resistance to injustice, especially to unfair imprisonment. Young anorexics of the Western world, however, are not ostensibly motivated positively: their terror of fatness is so profound and irrational that even after they have starved themselves to skin and bones, they see their reflection in the mirror as 'gross' (their preferred adjective). No doubt the insidious association of thinness with glamour and desirability in Western cultures offers some explanation, or at least an explanation for some cases of anorexia. The rapid loss of curves and the typically symptomatic cessation of menstrual periods combine to make the condition a powerful rejection of sex and destiny, if not of life itself. Refusing food is also a primal insult to parents, particularly mothers who are the original food providers, and it can be seen as symbolic of rebellion against their control. BEHAVIOUR THERAPY is generally applied to anorexics and bulimics, though a growing school of thought believes the condition to be part of a wider psychiatric problem that requires deeper and more subtle treatment. Anorexia is sometimes fatal and rarely fully cured; sufferers often relapse or develop other obsessive-compulsive disorders. For further reading: J. J. Brumberg, *Fasting Girls* (1989). I.K.

anthropic principle. Introduced by the British physicist Brandon Carter to describe a collection of ideas associating the structure of the universe, the constants and the laws of nature with those conditions that are necessary for the evolution and existence of life. The weak anthropic principle is a version of Bayes' Theorem (see BAYESIANISM) of statistical sampling. It is stated by Barrow and Tipler as follows: the observed values of all physical and cosmological quantities are not equally probable but take on values restricted by the requirement that there exist sites where carbon-based life can have evolved and by the requirement that the universe be old enough for it to have already done so. Observed physical quantities (for example, the size of the universe) could not be observed to take on any value with equal probability because observers could only exist in universes in which their values were within a very restricted range. The expansion of the universe requires that universes old enough (more than ten billion years) for the chemical building blocks of human life to have arisen within stars must also be very large (more than ten billion light years in size). This argument was introduced in 1961 by Robert Dicke in a particular form to explain the existence of coincidences between the values of cosmological quantities of very large magnitude. In 1937 Paul Dirac had argued that these coincidences would be explained if the law of gravitation were changing with time, but Dicke pointed out that the observed coincidence was necessary for the existence of chemical life. Our existence places restrictions upon the type of universe we could ever expect to find ourselves observing and investigating. The weak anthropic principle delineates the extent of applicability of the Copernican principle that we do not occupy a special place in the universe. Although we should not expect our position to be special in every way this does not mean it cannot be special in any way because particular conditions must hold for the evolution of life to be possible.

The strong anthropic principle of Carter claims that the universe must have those properties which allow life to develop within it at some stage. This is a speculation that would imply either that the universe was a teleological structure (see TELEOLOGY) designed with life in view, as was believed by natural theologians and scientists in Britain during the 17th to 19th centuries, or that there exists an ensemble of different possible universes and that we inevitably exist in one that contains one of the rare universes whose permutation of physical properties allows life to evolve. The strong anthropic principle suggests in some, as yet unclear, way that observers are necessary to give the universe 'meaning'. It has been suggested that the role played by the observer in the quantum picture of nature may introduce a more precise version of the strong anthropic principle (see QUANTUM MECHANICS). According to the COPENHAGEN INTERPRETATION of quantum mechanics introduced by Niels Bohr, no phenomenon can be said to exist unless it is an 'observed' phenomenon. Observers are necessary to collapse quantum wave functions and bring phenomena into being. John A. Wheeler has suggested a participatory anthropic principle which interprets the Copenhagen interpretation of quantum mechanics as indicating that observers must exist in order to bring the universe into being. This does not require conscious observers to play any special role, but Eugene Wigner has argued that consciousness may be necessary to collapse WAVE FUNCTIONS. Alternatively, the MANY WORLDS HYPOTHESIS suggested by Hugh Everett III is an alternative interpretation of quantum mechanics that predicts that quantum wave functions do not collapse. Instead, physical interactions and observations split reality into disjoint universes, one for each possible outcome of the interaction or observation. Hence, in this interpretation, we would inevitably find ourselves in a member of the special subset of all possible universes which was structured to allow life to evolve successfully. The strong anthropic principle would be tautologically true. A final anthropic principle has been proposed which hypothesizes that information processing can continue indefinitely in the future of the universe.

The anthropic principles play a vital role in the evaluation of any cosmological theory in which there is some randomness in the conception or early history of the universe (see COSMOLOGY). This can be attributable to the intrinsic quantum nature of the initiation of the universe, to quantum gravitational fluctuations which can determine the values of constants of nature, to the inflationary universe which is able to endow the universe with different values of its fundamental constants in different places, or to sudden symmetry breakings occurring at phase transitions during the early stages of the universe. All of these possibilities create the scope for the structure of the universe and the constants of physics to be different from place to place in the universe. Any attempt to evaluate the correctness of fundamental theories which attempt to predict that structure must therefore evaluate not the *a priori* probability that the universe is as observed (which might be low) but the conditional probability that it is observed as it is given that it also satisfies the necessary conditions for the evolution of intelligent agents. For further reading: F. Bertola and U. Curi (eds), *The Anthropic Principle* (1993). J.D.B.

anthropogeography. The study of the distribution of Earth's human communities (see COMMUNITY) in relation to their natural environment. A conceptualization devised in the late 19th century by Friedrich Ratzel in his classic *Anthropogeographie* (1882), it is regarded as a precursor to modern studies of human–environmental interaction. More generally, many geographers use this now somewhat archaic term as a synonym for HUMANISTIC GEOGRAPHY itself (see also GEOGRAPHY). P.O.M.

anthropological linguistics. A branch of LINGUISTICS which studies language variation and use in relation to the cultural patterns and beliefs of man, e.g. the way in which linguistic features may identify a member of a community with a social, religious, occupational or kinship group. See also ETHNOLINGUISTICS; SOCIOLINGUISTICS. D.C.

anthropology. From 'anthropos', the study of man.

(1) *Early phase*. The history of anthropology is part of the history of European thought, but it did not become established as an independent discipline until the late 19th century. It began with the explorers and travellers of earlier centuries (Columbus, Marco Polo), who broadened the area of the known world and increasingly uncovered the diversity of mankind, even if some of their 'discoveries' were not entirely based upon observation. The people they wrote about in their journals (often dog-headed and with tails) interested the Renaissance philosophers (Montaigne and, later, Vico, Rousseau and Montesquieu) in their speculations on the nature of man. 'Primitive' man was established as the OTHER by the philosophers of Europe. He represented either savagery and barbarism in contrast to the civilization of Europe, or innocence and childishness in contrast with European depravity.

(2) *Nineteenth-century evolutionists*. Ideas of RACE and EVOLUTION were important in late 19th-century thinking and anthropology developed as a discipline in this intellectual mould. It was also tied to colonial expansion and could provide justification for the 'civilizing' process of colonial peoples. Primitive man was understood by Morgan, McLennan and Maine to be a 'survival', a representation of earlier stages of mankind. The 1898 Torres Straits expedition (members included Haddon, Rivers, Wilkin, Seligman, Myers and McDougall) was an important landmark

in the development of anthropology. It was an early exercise in FIELDWORK and did much to establish anthropology's empirical base. Anthropology at this time, however, was still an amalgam of different subjects (LINGUISTICS, material culture [see HISTORY OF MATERIAL CULTURE], social custom, physiological typologies). By the beginning of the 20th century the various subdisciplines had begun to develop independently (in particular social, cultural and physical anthropology) and today they are quite separate subjects. *Physical anthropology* is concerned with the physical evolution of the human species and is a matter for geneticists (see GENETICS/GENOMICS) and physiologists. *Cultural anthropology* developed in the United States under the influence of Tylor and Boas. It became a very broad subject, concerned with CULTURE, but often broken down into specialist areas: linguistics, culture and personality studies, primitive art, etc. By contrast, anthropologists in Britain concentrated upon social systems and drew on the work of Durkheim and Weber to establish the independent discipline of *social anthropology*.

(3) *The functionalists*. Malinowski transformed social anthropology by his introduction of fieldwork methodology. It was henceforth founded not upon armchair speculation and conjecture, but upon first-hand participant observation. Malinowski also broke with evolutionary theories and interpreted his Trobriand material within a FUNCTIONALIST framework. Structural-functionalism (see STRUCTURAL-FUNCTIONAL THEORY) was a later development associated with Radcliffe-Brown. This approach moved away from Malinowski's concern with the individual and his needs to the question of SOCIAL STRUCTURE and its continuity over time. Social anthropology expanded in Britain during the 1930s and 1940s. It had a very strong empirical base and fieldwork was largely carried out in the colonial areas of Africa and south-east Asia.

(4) *Structuralism*. In 1949 Claude Lévi-Strauss published *Les Structures élémentaires de la parenté* (Eng. trans., *The Elementary Structures of Kinship*, 1969). It had an enormous impact on social anthropology. Lévi-Strauss's work, the attempt to establish a model of the human mind, emerged from a European tradition, one much more concerned with PHILOSOPHY and theory than with empirical method. In Britain STRUCTURALISM was taken up as a method by Leach, Douglas and Needham, but they adapted and modified it in accordance with the ethnographic tradition in which they worked (E. R. Leach, *Lévi-Strauss*, 1970). The American tradition continued to develop independently, and although Margaret Mead and Ruth Benedict gained popular prominence, few anthropologists seriously engaged with their work. One of the important consequences of structuralism was that it drew the different schools in Europe, the US, Canada and Britain into a common debate.

(5) *Crisis of the 1970s*. The interest in MARXIST ideas which emerged in the wake of structuralism represented another attempt to provide social anthropology with a coherent theoretical framework. Again the stimulus originated in France, and Marxist concepts were most fully elaborated by Meillassoux, Terray and Godelier. The publication of *Woman, Culture and Society* (R. Z. Rosaldo and L. Lamphere, eds, 1974) opened FEMINIST debate and subsequent work has steadily expanded anthropological discourse. Ethnographic film increasingly developed as a sophisticated and independent medium (M. Eaton, ed., *Anthropology-Reality-Cinema*, 1979). The crisis in anthropology lay not in the realm of ideas or concepts but in ETHNOGRAPHY, in the geographical areas for investigation. By the 1970s the colonial empires were largely dismantled and anthropologists found that they were no longer welcome in many newly independent countries. Indeed, anthropology was accused from some quarters of being in the service of colonialism (T. Asad, ed., *Anthropology and the Colonial Encounter*, 1973), and the increasing numbers of British and American anthropologists engaged in 'development' work has raised this very question. Other anthropologists have sought out new areas of fieldwork in history, in rural Europe and in the cities of the developed world. This new orientation may have profound consequences for the discipline. There has been a retreat from grand theory and a return to the examination of concepts accepted as cornerstones of social anthropology (e.g., DESCENT, MARRIAGE, DOMESTIC GROUP) but which were developed in the traditional ethnographic areas. For further reading: A. Kuper,

Anthropology and Anthropologists: The Modern British School (1996). A.G.

anthropomorphism. Less an architectural movement of the 1980s than a recognition that the combination of windows and doors and porches in buildings could sometimes be read as faces or parts of the human body. One or two architects actually designed buildings in this form. S.L.

anthroposophy. The term (literally 'wisdom about man') adopted by Rudolf Steiner (1861–1925) to denote his teachings and to distinguish them from the THEOSOPHY whose adherents constituted his first audience. These teachings he claimed to derive from 'spiritual research' based on an exact 'scientific' mode of supersensible PERCEPTION. A central thesis of anthroposophy is that the present intellectual capacities of humanity have evolved from an earlier mode of CONSCIOUSNESS which brought a direct experience of the transcendental (see TRANSCENDENCE) realities of which Steiner spoke. To carry the clarity and objectivity of the intellect now gained into new modes of spiritual perception (which he called Imagination, Inspiration, Intuition) is, according to Steiner, an essential future task for mankind. Such a 'resurrection' of consciousness has become possible, he held, through the deed of Christ in uniting himself with the destiny of man on earth. Steiner accordingly described one of his earliest books, *The Philosophy of Freedom*, as a 'Pauline theory of knowledge'. His work has given rise to many practical endeavours in education (see STEINER SCHOOLS), farming, medicine, the arts, etc. For further reading: R. Steiner, *Knowledge of the Higher Worlds* (1923). J.D.

anti-art. A term used for works of the DADA movement, which used the arts to attack or deride all established institutions, including the very notion of 'art'. Duchamp's READYMADES were an early manifestation. The term was subsequently used by other AVANT-GARDE movements including Gruppe Zero, FLUXUS, and CONCEPTUAL ART. Other radical movements in modern art, such as POP ART and KINETIC ART, were considered to be anti-art in their initial stages but quickly became accepted as legitimate art forms. This fate has also overtaken the original Dada objects. L.M.

antibiotic. A substance which impedes the growth or multiplication of micro-organisms. Examples are penicillin, streptomycin, terramycin. The *spectrum* of an antibiotic is the range of bacteria (see BACTERIOLOGY) over which it exercises its effect. 'Broad spectrum' antibiotics such as terramycin are particularly useful in medical practice. In general, antibiotics are ineffective against viruses (see VIROLOGY). Naturally occurring anti-bacterial substances such as INTERFERON and lysozyme are not normally classified as antibiotics. P.M.

antibody, see under IMMUNITY.

anti-colonialism, see under IMPERIALISM.

anti-form, see under PROCESS ART.

antigen, see under IMMUNITY.

anti-hero. In literature, a figure bearing the same relation to the conventional hero as does the ANTI-NOVEL to the conventional novel. The term was first used in this sense by W. P. Ker in 1897, but the anti-hero as type – foolish, bumbling, boorish, clumsy, immoral – is ancient. He occurs in the Greek 'new comedy', in the picaresque novel, and in the fiction from which the latter originates. The first deliberately devised anti-hero is in Honoré d'Urfé's sensationally successful *Astrée* (1607–27): this is a sentimental romance, but Hylas, with his championship of infidelity, is clearly a satirical foil to the conventional hero, Céladon. In lyrical poetry Edwin Arlington Robinson's Miniver Cheever provides an excellent example, and T. S. Eliot's Prufrock owed much to him. Modern anti-heroes include Hašek's Good Soldier Švejk, Jimmy Porter in John Osborne's *Look Back in Anger*, Jim Dixon in Kingsley Amis's *Lucky Jim*, and numerous spies and go-getters in conventionally structured popular works. By way of contrast, we have the 'positive hero' of Soviet literature. M.S.S.

anti-imperialism, see under IMPERIALISM.

anti-literature. The first, it seems, of the 'anti-arts' to be so named in English: by

David Gascoyne in 1935. For other (selected) examples of arts, literary genres, etc. that stand previous conventions on their heads, or at least their shoulders, see ANTI-ART; ANTI-HERO; ANTI-NOVEL; ANTI-THEATRE. O.S.

anti-matter. Hypothetical counterpart to matter, composed of anti-particles. Anti-particles have the same mass but opposite electric or magnetic properties to their corresponding PARTICLES. Thus anti-hydrogen would be composed of a POSITRON (the counterpart to the ELECTRON) and an anti-PROTON. The existence of the positron was predicted by Dirac in 1930: on formulating a relativistic equation for the electron, Dirac noticed that, as well as the readily interpretable positive energy solutions, the equation also allowed solutions corresponding to an infinite number of negative energy states. But if electrons are generally found in positive energy states, then on the principle that a particle is expected to occupy the lowest unoccupied energy state, something must stop electrons from falling into the negative states. Given Pauli's EXCLUSION PRINCIPLE, a natural explanation is that the negative states are occupied. Thus there must be an infinite 'sea' of electrons occupying the negative energy states. An electron–positron pair will be created if high-energy RADIATION ejects an electron from a negative energy state, leaving a 'hole': the positron. In the reverse process, electron and positron are mutually annihilated, producing a high-energy PHOTON. It is particularly striking that Dirac's highly theoretical argument should be supported empirically: positrons were detected in 1932 by Anderson, followed by anti-protons in 1955 by Segre and Chamberlain. R.F.H.

anti-natalism, see under MALTHUSIANISM.

anti-naturalism. An approach to PSYCHOLOGY and the SOCIAL SCIENCES which assumes that human beings (and perhaps intelligent animals) are so different from the subject-matter of the NATURAL SCIENCES that quite different approaches are needed for their study. Thus, in studying human beings, one can communicate with them, and attempt to understand the meanings of their words and deeds, whereas a physicist cannot in the same way communicate with the physical substances and mechanisms that he studies. A related view is that human behaviour and mental processes cannot be explained in terms of the physical and chemical, or physiological, processes in the human body (see REDUCTION), and that no amount of study of the structure of the human brain and the processes that occur in it can explain the way people think, decide, act, feel, etc. The opposite view is NATURALISM (sense 3). An intermediate position is that, although human social systems have a kind of complexity unmatched by other physical systems, so that quite new theoretical frameworks and experimental methods are required for their study, nevertheless they are a fit topic for an objective scientific study, albeit a study that is unlike PHYSICS. Cognitive science would be such a study (see MENTALISM). A.S.

antinomianism. The rejection of any element of 'law' (Greek *nomos*) in ETHICS, especially in Christian MORAL THEOLOGY, on the grounds that no detailed code of behaviour has been laid down by God. A Protestant sect (see PROTESTANTISM) arising in Germany in 1535 was so named. In the 20th century, while most Christians have accepted that some rules are needed, most have put first the element usually contrasted with 'law' in this debate: love. Christians are believed to be essentially free to act as they think best in the light of love. See also SITUATION ETHICS. D.L.E.

antinomy. A contradiction between two assertions for each of which there seem to be adequate grounds. It should be distinguished from a *dilemma*, which is a form of argument designed to show that something, usually unpleasant, will follow either if a given assumption is true or if it is false, and also from a PARADOX, which is a single, unacceptable and often self-contradictory conclusion for which there are seemingly irresistible grounds. A.Q.

anti-novel. A compendious label for any novel that protests, explicitly or implicitly, against some other novel or novels regarded as unduly popular or influential. Although Charles Sorel described the 1633 edition of his *Le Berger extravagant* (1627), in part a satire on d'Urfé's *Astrée*, as an *anti-roman*, the first thoroughgoing anti-novel is

Cervantes's *Don Quixote* (1605): devised partly as a protest against popular chivalric fiction, it grew into a tragic masterpiece. It is a paradigm of the true anti-novel: it revolts against conventional form, on the grounds that the latter lulls the reader into a sense of unreality, into an avoidance of (in contemporary EXISTENTIALIST parlance) his own AUTHENTICITY, and itself jerks the reader, by a series of shocks, into awareness of his own predicament. The first English anti-novel is Sterne's *Tristram Shandy* (1759), which continually confronts the reader with what he does not expect from fiction. The anti-novel was revived in the 20th century (especially in France in the form of the NEW NOVEL), though not always successfully, being often either too self-consciously or too dully and philosophically expressed. The contemporary revival was much influenced by the PHENOMENOLOGY of Husserl, if only because this is exclusively concerned with subjective experience. For further reading: N. Sarraute, *Tropisms and the Age of Suspicion* (1963). M.S.S.

anti-particles, see under ANTI-MATTER.

antiphoton, see under ELEMENTARY PARTICLES.

anti-psychiatry. A movement in therapeutic practice, associated in Britain above all with R. D. Laing, and in the USA principally with Thomas S. Szasz, which rejects conventional PSYCHIATRY (in particular, in its public and institutional guises), and argues that the concept of mental illness is both stigmatizing and unscientific. Laing argued in the 1960s that the mentally ill were essentially the victims of intolerable pressures exerted against them by society and in particular the family; and saw the flight into mental illness as at least understandable, and increasingly as a healthy response to a sick society. Laing eventually argued that what was conventionally labelled SCHIZOPHRENIA might be regarded as a particularly sane and insightful condition. Consequential upon this diagnosis was an attack upon psychiatric institutions as coercive and conducive to creating rather than relieving mental illness. Drug and mechanical therapies and PSYCHOSURGERY were especially rejected. Above all, Szasz questioned the ontological status of mental illness, contending that the category of 'illness' should apply properly only to physical, somatic conditions. 'Mental illness' was a dangerous metaphor. For further reading: R. Boyers and R. Orrill (eds), *R. D. Laing and Anti-Psychiatry* (1972). R.P.

anti-quark, see under QUARK.

anti-realism. Theory which holds that we cannot (or should not) make claims about truth or reality beyond whatever is borne out by empirical evidence. Some philosophers adopt an anti-REALIST stance with regard to certain SUBATOMIC PARTICLES, entities which play an explanatory role in the best current theories of PHYSICS, but which cannot (as yet) be detected or observed. On this view there is simply no need or justification for supposing those particles to be real – or actually to exist – just so long as the theory is empirically adequate, i.e. well supported by other kinds of evidence or by the measure of predictive success. This position is also known as *instrumentalism* and has lately received a powerful restatement (under the title 'constructive empiricism') by Bas van Fraassen.

Others, Michael Dummett among them, have adopted a verificationist position according to which statements can be meaningful (i.e. have a definite truth-value) only in so far as we possess some adequate proof-procedure or means of checking them out. Thus, for instance, in mathematics there may be certain theorems – such as Goldbach's famous conjecture that every even number is the sum of two primes – which, according to Dummett, are neither true nor false since they cannot be conclusively proven despite their strong intuitive claims and their having been tested right up to the limit of existing computational techniques.

Dummett himself has expressed concern with regard to its implication that the 'reality' of past events may be in some sense a product of our present-day (knowledge-constitutive) interests. Nevertheless he feels compelled to adopt an anti-realist position – and to accept at least some of these awkward consequences – on logical as well as on epistemological grounds. For further reading: M. Dummett, *Truth and Other Enigmas* (1978). C.C.N.

antisemitism. Discrimination against Jews

on the grounds of RACE, RELIGION or both (see RACISM). In the 20th century antisemitism reached its peak between 1941 and 1944 when Germany devised and carried out the Final Solution, a policy of GENOCIDE towards European Jewry, which resulted in the HOLOCAUST in which six million Jews were systematically murdered or worked to death as slave labour.

The history of antisemitism is almost as old as JUDAISM itself. During the 1st century BC, Jews were resented by the pagan peoples of the ancient world because their monotheism implicitly challenged pagan polytheism. Later, Jews would find themselves persecuted in the Roman Empire because they did not subscribe to the cult of emperor worship. As CHRISTIANITY grew in influence, so did antisemitism; Jews were popularly regarded as Christ-killers. When Christianity became the dominant religious influence and a main force for social and political cohesion in medieval Europe, Jews were excluded from mainstream society and their rights were curtailed. From that period until the early 20th century, Jews were segregated in GHETTOS in most European countries. In the 12th century Jews in many parts of eastern Europe were forced to wear a yellow star on their clothing – the Nazis revived the practice in the 20th century.

Jews were also denied access to the professions (see PROFESSIONALIZATION) and to public life in medieval Europe, with the consequence that many turned to commerce – trade and banking – for their livelihoods. The expansion of trade during the late medieval period and the Renaissance meant that some Jews prospered, arousing envy. Between the 13th and 16th centuries, western European countries began to expel Jews, driving them into eastern Europe. There, they were subject to periodic massacres and POGROMS.

During the 18th century, the effects of the Enlightenment and the French Revolution brought about an atmosphere more conducive to civil rights for Jews. In France and other countries Jews began to assimilate. But the emergence of NATIONALISM in 19th-century Europe again led to widespread antisemitism and in 1894 the DREYFUS CASE in France was both an indicator of – and an occasion for – a revival of resentment against Jews. Dreyfus was a high-ranking officer in the French Army, falsely accused of treason. His name was eventually cleared; but the allegations showed to what extent the institutions of French society and the press were tainted by antisemitism.

The economic misery of post-World War I Europe only exacerbated feeling against the Jews; and in the 1930s, Hitler's rise to power in Germany provided a focus for the anti-Jewish feeling that would lead to the Holocaust.

The Jewish state of Israel was created in 1948, but anti-Jewish sentiment continued throughout the remainder of the 20th century, the lessons of the Holocaust notwithstanding. Indeed, the task of organized antisemitism in the last decade of the century has been the establishment of Holocaust REVISIONISM – the denial that the Holocaust occurred. The electoral success of Jean-Marie Le Pen's RIGHT-wing National Front party in France (which commands the support of 15 per cent of voters) is largely based on its racist policies. In the post-World War II period, antisemitic feeling continued in many parts of eastern Europe, and with GERMAN REUNIFICATION there has been a marked increase in the public display of antisemitism from neo-Nazi and other extreme right-wing groups. For further reading: L. Steiman, *Paths to Genocide: Antisemitism in Western History* (1997). S.T.

anti-theatre. Imprecise journalistic term generally used to denote any type of theatre that does not conform to the familiar patterns of NATURALISM. Coined in the 1950s at the same time as ANTI-NOVEL (and cf. the cult of the ANTI-HERO), it may cover anything from the plays of Ionesco and Beckett (see THEATRE OF THE ABSURD) to the wildest form of experiment. In general parlance it has now been overtaken by the more neutral term ALTERNATIVE THEATRE. M.BI.

antithesis, see under SYNTHESIS.

anti-trust (or **monopoly**) **policy.** The name given to legislation and policies designed to protect the consumer against the exploitation of their market power by MONOPOLIES or 'trusts', as they were known in the 19th century. While there may be powerful reasons for the development of a monopoly situation in certain industries, economic theory suggests that under a monopoly prices tend to be higher and output smaller than would otherwise be the case. This restriction of output reduces ECONOMIC EFFICIENCY and may represent a loss in SOCIAL WELFARE. Monopolies may offer ECONOMIES OF SCALE and give rise to greater technical progress. Thus, monopolies may or may not give rise to net losses in social welfare. In the UK, in order to act against a monopoly or merger, the government has to prove a net economic cost to society of the existence of the monopoly or merger. The underlying assumption in US anti-trust legislation is that monopoly works against the public interest. D.E.; J.P.

anti-utopia (or **dystopia**). A variety of thinking developed to counter what is seen as the false and dangerous optimism of UTOPIANISM. It uses the form of utopian fiction to present future society as a nightmare of oppression and sterility. Taking its lead partly from older satires such as Swift's *Gulliver's Travels*, it has been particularly influenced by the fears explored in Mary Shelley's *Frankenstein* (1816) and Feodor Dostoyevsky's 'Legend of the Grand Inquisitor' from *The Brothers Karamazov* (1880). Science and SOCIALISM, the great hopes of the modern utopia, are its principal antagonists and targets. In this century the most influential anti-utopias have been Evgeny Zamyatin's *We* (1924), Aldous Huxley's *Brave New World* (1932) and George Orwell's *Nineteen Eighty-Four* (1949). Since the 1950s, the function of the literary anti-utopia has been largely taken over by science-fiction films spelling out messages of doom and destruction at the hands of atomic weapons, environmental decay and strange new diseases unleashed by scientific hubris. But some literary anti-utopias have had considerable impact, such as Kurt Vonnegut's *Player Piano* (1952), F. Pohl and C. M. Kornbluth's *The Space Merchants* (1953), Anthony Burgess's *A Clockwork Orange* (1962), and William Burroughs's *Nova Express* (1964). The short stories and novels of the science-fiction writer J. G. Ballard – e.g. *The Terminal Beach* (1964), *The Disaster Area* (1967) – contain some of the most powerful anti-utopian imagery of recent times. Latterly indeed the anti-utopia has abandoned the precise social and political criticism of writers such as Huxley and Orwell. It traffics now in apocalyptic images of doom and disaster on a cosmic scale. K.K.

antivivisection, see under ANIMAL LIBERATION.

anxiety. In ABNORMAL PSYCHOLOGY and PSYCHIATRY, a term used to refer both (1) to an emotional state (see EMOTION) and (2) to a trait of character. As (1) it is often used synonymously with 'fear', and, more specifically, with fears whose object is not known, as in the *anxiety state*, a NEUROSIS characterized by feelings of fear for which the patient can give no reason; within learning theory, it refers to the emotional state elicited by signals of impending punishment. As (2) it describes different degrees of susceptibility to fear. According to H. J. Eysenck, this trait is not unitary, but a composite of neuroticism and INTROVERSION, highly anxious people being neurotic introverts. As such, it is more prominent in women than in men, while women are also more prone to psychiatric disturbances involving anxiety in sense (1). J.A.G.

apartheid. Afrikaans word meaning literally 'apart-ness'; applied to the system of policies maintaining the domination of South Africa's white majority over the non-white populations until the introduction of universal suffrage in 1993/94. The system built on existing patterns of segregation and was established after the election in 1948 of the National Party. Various euphemisms have been offered by apartheid's apologists, including 'separate development' and later the yet more disingenuous 'co-operative co-existence'. In reality the system comprehensively institutionalized the superior status of whites in economic, political and social matters. Among its principal mechanisms were the 'homelands' or *Bantustans* policy, which sought to divide and restrict blacks to ten 'tribal homelands', themselves anthropological fictions. Its purpose was to maintain the supply of black labour to the South African economy while inhibiting the full development of black communities in white-dominated towns and cities, and ultimately to create an alternative basis of citizenship which would deny South African citizenship to its blacks.

The PASS LAWS were a vital support of this system. The legal requirement that blacks carry a 'pass' or document proving their presence in an area legal has a history almost as long as that of white settlement of the region. It was codified and more rigorously applied after 1948. The laws' function, effect and symbolic power made them a major target for resistance, culminating in pressure (particularly from the South African Congress of Trade Unions) which forced their abandonment in 1986. The replacement system requiring members of all races to carry an identity document did not satisfy many blacks.

The remaining legal structure which sustained apartheid was vast, ranging from measures maintaining the segregated and subordinate status of blacks and other non-whites to restrictions on the civil liberties of all South Africans. Apartheid was an unsustainable policy which finally crashed under a period of 'emergency' in South Africa. The release of African National Congress leader Nelson Mandela in 1990 paved the way for the dismantling of apartheid and elections based on one-man-one-vote. For further reading: N. Mandela, *The Long Walk to Freedom* (1994); P. Waldmeir, *Anatomy of a Miracle: The End of Apartheid and the Birth of the New South Africa* (1997). S.R.

aphasia, see under NEUROPSYCHOLOGY.

Apocalypse, see under NEW APOCALYPSE.

Apollonian and **Dionysian cultures.** Terms used by Ruth Benedict to distinguish two 'patterns' of CULTURE. Rooted in the school of cultural ANTHROPOLOGY of Franz Boas, she regarded cultures, especially of the simpler societies, as consistent and enduring patterns of behaviour, thought and action; systems of INSTITUTIONS and psychological orientations with attendant PERSONALITY TYPES. Deriving the terms from Nietzsche (in his discussion of Greek drama; see NIETZSCHEAN) and Oswald Spengler, Benedict used Dionysian to denote a pattern of culture engendering and encouraging emotional abandonment in social responses, and Apollonian to denote one producing order and control. In the burial of the dead, for example, the Zuni Indians (Apollonian) controlled and contained their grief; the Kwakiutl Indians (Dionysian) abandoned themselves in a demonstrative orgy of wailing. Evans-Pritchard called this 'the rustling-of-the-wind-in-the-palm-trees' kind of anthropology. See also FOLK CULTURE; SUBCULTURE. For further reading: R. Benedict, *Patterns of Culture* (1934). R.F.

aporia, apory. Derived from the Greek: 'obstacle', 'blocked passage', 'unpassable path'. Term used mainly by classical logicians and rhetoricians to signify some PARADOX, ANTINOMY or insoluble problem encountered in the course of reasoning on various topics. This usage had its origin in the thinking of the Presocratic philosophers – among them Zeno, Parmenides, Heraclitus and Anaxagoras – who raised far-reaching speculative questions and found themselves regularly driven to paradoxical (aporetic) conclusions. The aporias of motion, for example, were most graphically expressed in Zeno's famous series of paradoxes, including those of the arrow that would never reach its target, and Achilles, who would never overtake the tortoise since there would always be some fraction of the distance between them yet to be covered. In the case of matter it seemed both necessary and impossible that there should exist certain ELEMENTARY PARTICLES (ATOMS) which could not be yet further decomposed into smaller, more basic constituent parts.

Later philosophers – most notably Kant – sought to avert these aporias by various ways and means. Thus, according to Kant, they resulted from the tendency of pure reason to overreach the limits of human understanding – where sensory intuitions must be 'brought under' adequate concepts – and thence to produce all manner of speculative puzzles and paradoxes. This tendency could best be held in check by doing what the Presocratics so conspicuously failed to do, that is, by drawing a clear distinction between epistemological and ontological issues, or those that fell within the bounds of humanly attainable knowledge and those that lay beyond its utmost cognitive grasp. Nevertheless, such aporias have continued to arise and create periodic bouts of vexation despite the best efforts of philosophers to legislate them out of existence. For further reading: J. Derrida, *Of Grammatology* (1976). C.C.N.

appeasement. A term first employed in political contexts in the 1920s, when it meant the removal by mutual agreement of the grievances arising out of the 1919 peace settlement. After the appointment, on 30 January 1933, of Adolf Hitler as Chancellor in Germany, the word was applied to the (unsuccessful) policy pursued by the British and French governments of trying to avoid war with Germany by injudicious, frequently dishonourable and inevitably unrequited concessions, weakening to those who made them and often made at the expense of third parties. The epitome of the policy of appeasement was the MUNICH agreement of 30 September 1938. D.C.W.

apperception. The mental state of PERCEPTION when it is self-conscious, when the perceiver is aware of the fact that he is perceiving as well as of the object perceived. The term was introduced into PHILOSOPHY by Leibniz as a means of distinguishing what had hitherto been supposed inseparable: the mind's activities of perception and its awareness of those activities. Leibniz's view was that it is possible for a mind to perceive something without being aware that it is doing so. A persuasive argument he gave for this conclusion is that we can be surprised by the cessation of a noise, such as the ticking of a clock, which we had not been conscious of perceiving during the time before it stopped. A.Q.

applied geography. The systematic field of GEOGRAPHY that involves the practical application of geographical concepts and techniques to help resolve society's problems. These efforts most often occur in the arena of urban and regional planning undertaken by public-sector agencies. The latter widely embrace the contributions of geographers, who have successfully applied the knowledge of many branches of physical and human geography as well as statistical, cartographic, and GIS techniques. For further reading: M. E. C. Sant, *Applied Geography: Practice, Problems, and Prospects* (1982). P.O.M.

applied mathematics. Strictly, all those branches of MATHEMATICS developed to assist deductive reasoning in the physical and NATURAL SCIENCES. In the UK the term is often used in a more specialized sense to refer to the mathematical techniques useful in CLASSICAL PHYSICS. M.V.B.

applied psychology. The examination of specific practical problems of human life, using the methods and criteria of academic PSYCHOLOGY. In contrast to applied physical sciences, this area of activity can only rarely make use of generalizations which are well established by theoretical work and require merely to be related to the problem. Rather, the practical situation may often reveal new and unsuspected aspects of human nature, whose understanding is a gain to general knowledge as well as to the solution of the particular problem. Occasionally the applied psychologist may differ from the intelligent layman by knowledge of some fact, such as the likely effects of line thickness upon the visibility of illuminated signs seen at night. More usually, he differs only by the habit of seeking some specific breakdown of function behind an undesired action; e.g. multiple accidents on high-speed roads lead psychologists to suspect failures of perception of speed and distance, and of anticipation of likely delays in the driver's own response, and these failures in turn can be traced to the particular visual and other information given to the driver.

Some fields of application are now so highly developed that they are usually distinguished under their own name. Thus applications to mental health are normally termed *clinical psychology*; those to learning and adjustment at school, EDUCATIONAL PSYCHOLOGY; those to the wellbeing and efficiency of people engaged in industry, INDUSTRIAL PSYCHOLOGY. In most fields of application, however, there are related problems, including the construction of methods for assessing the past performance of people, whether schoolchildren, industrial managers or some other category; the attempt to predict which people will be able to meet some situation adequately in the future, as by aircrew selection tests or clinical prognosis; and the comparison of different detailed systems of presenting information and required action, as in the EVALUATION of teaching machines, of different keyboards for telephones, or of different phrasings of public notices of pension entitlement. The physical ENVIRONMENT is also a common problem, as in the effects of airport noise or school lighting; and so is the social or human environment, as in the effects of family background on school performance, or of PARTICIPATION upon the self-respect of an industrial worker.

In many of these areas the applied psychologist has had an influence, which is retrospectively seen to have been salutary, upon general attitudes to human beings. Thus the problems of assessment and prediction forced a respect for individual differences upon academic psychology; the problems of work design in complex semi-automatic systems made it clear that the mind performs highly sophisticated operations upon the stimuli reaching it, rather than simply associating them; and the problem of the social environment, while complicating response to persuasion on food habits or RACE relations, helped to establish the importance of the cultural matrix of individual behaviour. Thus far, however, the output of applied psychology has consisted of verbal analyses and recommendations, which can be accepted or rejected like any others. More recently, tentative techniques have been explored for changing human behaviour directly: advertising, conditioning techniques (see, e.g., BEHAVIOUR THERAPY), or the participation by psychologists in GROUP sessions in a business with the aim of producing an altered organization. These techniques are likely to raise ethical questions among practitioners, as well as complaints of manipulation among those affected; but if successful they may well provide intellectual and practical gains substantially greater than those of the past.

D.E.B.

appropriate technologies. Methods of production that use resources and inputs that are compatible with those available in the economy – in particular, a developing economy – and produce products which are suited to the economy. The appropriate technology movement originated from the view that the technologies used in developing countries are often inappropriate and should be changed to be more labour-intensive, to make more use of local labour, skills and materials and to produce products that are useful to a low-income country. Appropriate technologies can be established by adapting the technologies existing in developed countries or by improving the traditional technologies used in developing countries. As appropriate technologies make better use of the available resources and labour, they may well be more efficient (see ECONOMIC EFFICIENCY). Through using more labour, they may give a more desirable distribution of income, though statements of the latter type require a VALUE-JUDGEMENT. J.P.

apraxia, see under NEUROPSYCHOLOGY.

aptitude tests, see under MENTAL TESTING.

aquaculture. The production of food from aquatic HABITATS. Sites for aquaculture include both natural and man-made bodies of water. Rearing fish in ponds has an ancient history in Africa and Asia. Aquaculture, in contrast to harvesting from the wild, is responsible for an ever-increasing percentage of global consumption of fish and shellfish.

Among the species reared in captivity are shrimp, clams, mussels, lobsters, salmon and Tilapia. Marine species are generally raised in pens placed in natural bodies of water. Freshwater species are often raised in tanks or ponds. There is concern that intensive 'fish farming', which requires the use of antibiotics, prepared feeds and particular strains of the cultivated ORGANISMS, may have significant negative environmental impacts. W.G.R.

Arab nationalism. A political emotion of shared identity based on a common language, past glory, territory and RELIGION which has acquired much of its strength and RHETORIC from opposition to foreign rule. Its origins are found in an Arab renaissance under the Ottomans dating from 1875. In both ideas and action Arab nationalism has fluctuated between loyalty to the Arab nation as a whole (the *umma* or Islamic community) and to a part of the nation territorially defined (the *watan*), so that it has found expression in Hashimite nationalism (based on Jordan and Iraq), Syrian and Egyptian nationalism. In general Arab nationalism proved resistant to attempts at alliance by Britain and America but embraced European ideas, including CONSTITUTIONALISM and then SOCIALISM. As imperial influence has declined and the machinery of independent Arab states has entrenched itself, Arab nationalism has transferred its outward hostility to Israel and exists in uneasy alliance with the resurgence of ISLAM. For further reading: P. Mansfield, *The Arabs* (1985). W.K.

archaeology. The technique of studying man's past using material remains as a primary source. In *text-free archaeology* material remains are the sole evidence, the study being known as PREHISTORY. When texts are available the term PROTOHISTORY is often used. Specialist branches proliferate: *classical archaeology, medieval archaeology, post-medieval archaeology* and INDUSTRIAL ARCHAEOLOGY are now accepted as individual disciplines, while FIELD ARCHAEOLOGY refers to an approach used by all. *Landscape archaeology* is now used to describe the study of visible traces of the past, usually over large tracts of countryside. *Environmental archaeology* uses recent advances, particularly in prehistory, to emphasize man's dynamic relationship with his ENVIRONMENT. In this way it is possible to study man through his effects on the ECOSYSTEM even when artifacts are absent. Many specialist techniques contribute to archaeology, e.g. LINGUISTICS, PALAEOBOTANY, PALAEOPATHOLOGY, palaeoserology, etc. History can, loosely speaking, be regarded as a technique used to augment the most recent fraction of the time span studied by the archaeologist. For further reading: R. Silverberg (ed.), *Great Adventures in Archaeology* (1997). B.C.

archaeomagnetism. The study of residual or *remanent* (in full, *thermo-remanent*) MAGNETISM, usually in an artifact or structure of baked clay. It is based on the principle that magnetite, an oxide of iron, when heated above a certain point (the *Curie point*), loses its magnetism, taking on the qualities of the earth's magnetic FIELD as it cools. The magnetite remains fossilized unless heat is again applied. Thus an *in situ* structure (e.g. a hearth or kiln) retains the magnetic characteristics of its location at the time of its use. For purposes of DATING, the remanent magnetism of the sample is measured for direction (a horizontal component known as *declination* or *D*, and a vertical one known as *inclination* or *I* or *dip*) and intensity. These factors are compared with the pattern of known changes in the earth's field. The dating method is not absolute, since before *c.* AD 1500 calibration data must be acquired by measuring samples of known date. A wide margin of error is often encountered. B.C.

archetype. A JUNGIAN term for any of a number of prototypic phenomena (e.g. the wise old man, the great mother) which form the content of the COLLECTIVE UNCONSCIOUS (and therefore of any given individual's unconscious), and which are assumed to reflect universal human thought found in all CULTURES. W.Z.

archigram. A seminal AVANT-GARDE British architectural group of the 1960s which intermittently published an architectural magazine. Archigram's designs were predicated on impermanence, the deployment of leading-edge electronic and structural technology, plus the general notion that architecture was to do with creating pleasure and entertainment for people. S.L.

architecture. Until the Enlightenment, definitions of Western architecture derived from the formulation of Vitruvius, writing in the first century AD, that architecture has 'commodity, firmness and delight'. Thus architecture related only to those buildings where these three conditions obtained, and hence showed a tendency to gratify luxury in the service of power. Now architecture's range is so broad and complex that its more sophisticated practitioners have taken to using POST-STRUCTURALIST terms, e.g. Foucault's concept of DISCOURSE. During the Enlightenment two contrasting but not completely separate themes took architecture beyond Vitruvius. They loosely followed the division between French RATIONALISM and German IDEALISM. The former architecture to include buildings which aimed at social control without necessarily being delightful, while the latter imbued architecture with intellectual content which might require means of expression other than buildings. German ROMANTICISM, with its adulation of nature and concern with freedom, also fed a critique of industrial production. If architecture should follow nature, it had to show the flaws and imperfections arising from its creators' personalities: i.e. remain craft-based. European MODERNIST architects like Le Corbusier and Mies van der Rohe outwardly overcame the dislike of industry, but retained traces of the other two themes. The combination of the three themes took a particular twist in the USA, where the confrontation with nature was rawer, and the experience of industrialism in some ways more intense. Taking their inspiration on the one hand from the transcendentalists, and on the other from technical successes such as the elevator and the steel frame, American theorists began to formulate original and important ideas in the late 19th century, which came to fruition in the architecture of Louis Sullivan, Frank Lloyd Wright and the ideas of Lewis Mumford, which began to free American architecture from its European shackles.

Architectural thought was long dominated by the search for the 'modern'; a journey which first appeared to find resolution in the white, purist architecture of the 1920s, most consummately achieved by Le Corbusier. When this was introduced to America, however (by Henry-Russell Hitchcock and Philip Johnson), it surprised architects like Frank Lloyd Wright, who thought they had been 'modern' all along, even though their work looked different. That Hitchcock and Johnson described Corbusier *et al* as the INTERNATIONAL STYLE further fuelled Wright's antipathy, although it did not stop the adoption of this idiom as the favoured architectural expression for corporate America after 1945.

Criticisms of Corbusian modernism grew in the 1960s. Europeans tended to expose its social pretensions as sham or undesirable, taken to the greatest extreme in Cedric Price's dictum that an architectural solution need not be a building (but might lie in social policy or practice). American critics coerced the term POST-MODERNISM to be an opposite to 'modernism'; in the hands of Robert Venturi and Robert Stern, it meant complex compositions which often referred to the classical tradition.

In Britain, even leading architects like Norman Foster and Richard Rogers remain fixated with Price-like ideas and their technological expression. But Dutchman Rem Koolhaas and Americans Frank Gehry and Daniel Libeskind have moved the debate forward, designing extraordinarily convoluted forms whose structure defies conventional logic. Dependent on huge computing power, and often on a very large scale, their work of necessity starts to redefine urban, as well as architectural, form. In effect this closes the gap between modernist obsessions with inventing form and the way of understanding modern urban life as a series of incomplete fragments which stems from Georg Simmel and Walter Benjamin, and which commentators like Frederic Jamieson define as 'post-modern'. Architecture thus becomes an analogue of modern life, and its complexity leads to the adoption of aspects of post-structuralism in architectural thought. For further reading: D. Watkin, *A History of Western Architecture* (1996).

J.E.M.

architecture autre. Omnibus term for a range of architectural ideas of the 1960s including biomorphism (see BIOMORPHIC), ad hocism, Bowellism. These and a small number of other *isms* were self-consciously architectural. But they sought to create new forms and spaces from unconventional and new HIGH TECHnology materials as various as sprayed CONCRETE, plastic foam, handcrafted timber, glass fibre, plastics and steel. These materials enabled young designers to experiment with easily built, mouldable three-dimensional forms difficult or impossible to create using orthodox, largely rectilinear building materials. Because of the necessarily idiosyncratic nature of their design, buildings in either group were not readily resellable in the real estate market and the phase remains an interesting sidetrack in the history of architectural experiment.

S.L.

area studies. SOCIAL SCIENCE term for interdisciplinary scholarship focused on the peoples and other geographical contents of a major world region (such as South America or sub-Saharan Africa). In recent decades, this tradition has been overshadowed by more prominent theoretical movements in GEOGRAPHY and the other social sciences. In the 1990s, however, area studies began to rebound, no doubt triggered by momentous geopolitical changes on the world map. The revival of scholarly interest in eastern Europe, following the unexpected demise of the Soviet Union, is an outstanding example.

P.O.M.

areal linguistics. In LINGUISTICS, the study of the linguistic forms found in any geographically defined region – their present-day distinctiveness and their historical antecedents. Particular groups of languages would be established in an *areal classification* (such as the Scandinavian languages, or the British dialects influenced by the speech of London). D.C.

arithmetic, higher, see under NUMBER THEORY.

Armory Show. A landmark in the history of modern art in America, this 'International Exhibition of Modern Art' opened in February 1913 in the 69th Regimental Armory in New York and was later shown in Boston and Chicago. It contained over 1,000 works by some 300 artists, from Ingres to Marcel Duchamp. Cézanne, Gauguin, Redon, the FAUVES and Augustus John were well represented, German EXPRESSIONISM scarcely, and FUTURISM not at all. It attracted the subsequent DADA artist Francis Picabia to the USA, and thus laid the foundation of his and Duchamp's activity there. J.W.

arms control. Restraint intentionally exercised by one or more powers upon the level, characteristics, deployment or use of their armaments in order to promote stability, reduce the danger of WAR, limit its consequences, or otherwise minimize the hazards inherent in the existence or future development of modern weapons. The term is a broad one and includes measures of DISARMAMENT, inter-state agreements on mutual restraint, and unilateral policies (normally of the great powers). The term originated in the American strategic literature in the later 1950s, and the CONCEPT derives partly from economic theory that STATES, like firms (see FIRM, THEORIES OF), can decide to preclude activities that are mutually injurious without abandoning their general competitive or adversary stance; the term and the policy gained acceptance in the early 1960s as the need to control certain military activities (e.g. the atmospheric testing of NUCLEAR WEAPONS) and to limit the number of nuclear-weapon states became palpable while the prospects of negotiated multilateral disarmament (see MULTILATERALISM) remained unpromising. Recent arms control agreements include that on the non-militarization of Antarctica (1959), the Atmospheric Test Ban Treaty (1963), the Non-PROLIFERATION Treaty (1968), and the Soviet–American agreements of 1972 (SALT 1) on the permanent limitation of anti-ballistic missiles (see ABM) in each country and on a five-year standstill on levels of deployed MISSILES. Measures to control the build-up of strategic nuclear weapons were discussed in the 1976 (SALT 2) talks. An example of a unilateral arms control measure was the decision of the USA (and other governments) in 1969 to suspend research on biological weapons and to destroy stocks of them. For subsequent developments, see NUCLEAR WEAPONS, LIMITATION AND CONTROL. A.F.B.

arms race. The continuous accretion of military power by two or more states, based upon the conviction that only by retaining an advantage in such power can they ensure their national security or supremacy. Arms races have a quantitative and a qualitative aspect; but a contemporary distinction has emerged between arms races among minor powers (e.g. Israel and the Arab states), where both aspects are of significance, and among the great (i.e. NUCLEAR WEAPON) powers where the qualitative aspect – improvements in the explosive power, accuracy, penetration, or invulnerability of long-range weapons – is the more significant. Hence the concentration of modern ARMS CONTROL policy as much on the characteristics of weapons as on their numbers. See also NUCLEAR WEAPONS, LIMITATION AND CONTROL. For further reading: D. Carlton and C. Schaerf (eds), *The Arms Race in an Era of Negotiations* (1991). A.F.B.

***art autre*,** see under ABSTRACT ART.

***art brut*.** The casual, often jarring, spontaneous graphic products of non-professionals, whether they be psychotics (see PSYCHOSIS), children, or graffiti-writers; or art which imitates these. *Art brut* ('raw art') was christened, adopted and promoted by Jean Dubuffet, whose own paintings and assemblages of waste materials (see COLLAGE) owe much to the untutored scrawlings which he regards as truly creative reflections of the UNCONSCIOUS mind. P.C.

art history. Art history is a study of art practice. Although many artists regard it as irrelevant, without its insights they could not innovate. Since 1973, when T. J. Clark published his study of Courbet, *The Image of the People*, art history has been predominantly written as SOCIAL HISTORY. The study of contexts led to a democratization of the concept of visual culture and research; writing and exhibitions began to demonstrate connections between high and low culture, ADVERTISING, design and art. Instead of the older élite tradition of connoisseurship, new approaches to art emphasize understanding the CODES and conventions of GENRES and periods and allow art to be read as a system of signs and meanings which can be interpreted (see SIGNIFIER; SAUSSURIAN; STRUCTURALISM; POST-STRUCTURALISM). It is the critical and interpretive aspect of the discipline that appears in daily newspapers and magazines as art criticism.

Art history has developed specific fields of study, such as American and Australian art history. This development was a result of the critique of a dominant mainstream art history centred in Paris, New York or London which had been shaped by institutions such as the Warburg and Courtauld Institute, or the Museum of Modern Art in New York. FEMINIST interventions in the history of art involved much more than adding new materials – namely, women and their history – to existing categories and methods. Griselda Pollock, Mary Garrard and Norma Broude have shown that it led to an art history that made visible the social construction of sexual difference (see GENDER; SEXUALITY), and the ways in which it worked in visual representation. Similarly, the concept of POST-COLONIALISM has resulted in new insights about the representation of non-Europeans, and other cultures in Western art. The growth of art history in universities, museums and even television provided the opportunities for change in the discipline. Despite this, most art history publication still tends to be divided between museum catalogues and monographs on artists for the general public, and more specialized critical research published by the academic presses.

Most art historians pride themselves on their vast personal memory bank of images and sources which enables them to identify and read visual meaning or ICONOGRAPHY. Nevertheless, most critics and historians would admit that they are challenged, and even speechless, when it comes to interpreting hybrid cultural forms, especially those being produced in video and multimedia from Asia: they form a whole new visual language. For further reading: G. Pollock, *Vision and Difference* (1997).

A.V.D.B.

Art-Language, see under CONCEPTUAL ART.

art music. A term used loosely to categorize a composition defined by the intention and method of its composer. He does not write primarily for money, though he usually insists on being paid, and will gladly compose to a commission. He does not despise popular success, but will not modify or simplify his style to achieve it; nor, probably, will he deny that his audience is an ÉLITE. He uses accepted methods of composition, with a high degree of technical sophistication; according to fashion, this might be academic ingenuity or controlled chaos (see ALEATORY). He writes in conventional notation, unlike the composer-performer of FOLK MUSIC, whose work is perpetuated by oral tradition. Folk music is, however, always heard, whereas art music includes academic exercises doomed to eternal silence.

The passing of time and change of taste can recategorize a composition: Mozart's dance music, for example, is now regarded as art music, whereas a jazzed-up version of his 40th symphony would not be. The label 'art music' does not, in any case, imply high artistic worth, nor does the withholding of the label imply the absence of such worth. To dress up a simple expressive folk tune in the trappings of a symphony is to degrade it; and a JAZZ band may exhibit a vitality and imagination well beyond the capacity of many a composer of string quartets and symphonies. To this extent, the term 'art music' has fallen into disrepute. B.K.

art nouveau. An artistic movement based on the use of linear flowing forms which emerged in the early 1890s in Europe and the USA and was probably strongly influenced by the introduction of Japanese art objects to the West. Named after a Paris shop, it was known in Germany as *Jugendstil* (after the satirical paper *Jugend*) and in Italy as *Stile Liberty* (after the London department store). In Austria it became associated with the Vienna SEZESSION started in 1897. The sinuous interweaving forms which became current in painting had their first major architectural application in the interior of the Auditorium Building in Chicago (1888) by Louis Sullivan and a house in Brussels (1893) by Victor Horta. These were attempts to define a new, vigorous style free of academicism and capable of unifying the arts. The notion of 'structural and dynamographic ornamentation' was developed largely by the Belgian architect Henry van de Velde, who was prominent in the WERKBUND and directed the Weimar Design School which developed into the BAUHAUS.

Art nouveau had a strong impact on the applied arts and is most visible in architecture where these meet – the furniture and decorations of the Tea Rooms in Glasgow by Charles Rennie Mackintosh, the ironwork outside his Glasgow School of Art, and that of Hector Guimard for the entrances of the Paris Métro. A full, plastic and often polychromatic expression was achieved by Antonio Gaudi in a number of buildings in Barcelona. Art nouveau declined soon after 1900 and remained out of favour until the late 1950s, when a search for more varied and richer forms (see, e.g., PSYCHEDELIC ART) appeared to make it relevant. For further reading: L.-V. Masini, *Art Nouveau* (1984). M.BR.

art of the real, see MINIMAL ART.

art sacré, l'. French movement for the renewal of religious art in the light of modern painting and the example of the BEURON school in Germany. It dates from the foundation of the *ateliers d'art sacré* by Desvallières in 1919. In 1935 the magazine *L'Art sacré* was started, and after World War II an annual *salon d'art sacré* in Paris. From about 1950 (completion of the church of Notre-Dame at Assy in Savoie) a number of remarkable individual or collective works were created, quite often by unbelievers, under the influence of this movement, with wide international repercussions (e.g. on the decoration of the new cathedrals at Coventry and Liverpool). In particular, Matisse at Vence and Le Corbusier at Ronchamp produced world-famous masterpieces, while outside the movement proper the EX-FAUVE Georges Rouault devoted much of his life to religious art. J.W.

arte povera (impoverished art). Term coined in 1969 by Italian critic Germano Celant to describe the art of his compatriots Michelangelo Pistoletto, Giuseppe Penone, Giovanni Anselmo and others. *Arte povera* concentrated on 'facts and actions' rather than the formal aesthetic qualities of more traditional art, and used a wide range of common materials including, on occasion, live animals. It was 'almost a rediscovery of aesthetic tautology: the sea is water, a room is a perimeter of air, cotton is cotton, an angle is a convergence of three coordinates, life is a series of actions'. There were close affinities with post-minimal process art (see MINIMAL ART; PROCESS ART) in the US, although the matter-of-fact presentation of materials was tempered by a continuing sense of their historical and poetic significance. M.G.A.

artificial insemination. The insemination of a female (human or animal) by other means than sexual intercourse. Semen is collected from the male – by masturbation or in the case of animals by an artificial vagina – and injected into the cervix (neck of the womb).

In animal breeding, especially cattle breeding, artificial insemination is now widely used. Centres exist for the collection of semen from high-quality males which is then directly injected into the females or cooled, preserved and despatched to recipient animals anywhere. Since more semen is produced at a single ejaculation than is necessary to inseminate one female, artificial insemination has the advantage that several females can be inseminated from a semen sample of one male.

In humans a distinction is drawn between artificial insemination by the husband (AIH) and by a donor (AID) whose identity is usually unknown to the couple. AIH is used when, because of difficulty with intercourse or, rarely, anatomical deformity, natural insemination is impossible; AID is used – in an unknown but probably small number of cases – where the male is sterile and the female fertile. There has been controversy about AID between those who object on moral, legal and even genetic grounds (see GENETICS/GENOMICS) and those who feel that, provided certain safeguards are observed, it should be available to married couples who prefer it to adoption. See WARNOCK REPORT. D.A.P.

artificial intelligence (AI). Often defined as a branch of COMPUTER science or computer engineering aimed at making computers do what previously only humans and other animals could do. However, the work done in AI labs, and reported in AI conferences and journals, is far more general: it includes basic scientific research concerned with the general study of principles of INTELLIGENCE, whether in animals, humans or machines. Thus the name 'artificial intelligence', originally coined by John McCarthy, is a misnomer.

The field arose out of pioneering work on the development of computers and theories of computation by Alan Turing and others in the mid-20th century (see TURING TEST), but has centuries-old roots in the idea of making a machine that can think (e.g. a 'Golem'). Whether similar principles can be applied to the functioning of animal brains and artificial brains based on computers is an open question, however. Birds and propeller-driven aeroplanes seem to use very different means of flight, yet the same principles of aerodynamics apply: a propeller is simply a wing that propels by rotating instead of flapping. Likewise the demands of tasks and processes like PERCEPTION, learning, motivation, problem-solving, planning, plan execution, reflex action, communication, self-control, self-awareness, self-evaluation may have deep similarities, whether in animals, humans or machines of the future. Understanding the nature of these demands, and the types of mechanisms capable of performing the tasks, is what much AI is about.

Not all AI research is directly concerned with these grand objectives, though. Much work is very practically oriented, and limited to particular tasks, including: the development of EXPERT SYSTEMS, such as financial advisory packages and medical diagnostic aids; or the very task-limited perceptual mechanisms of assembly-line ROBOTS; the simple speech recognition systems that are increasingly being used on automatic telephone answering systems; factory scheduling systems; computer-based games; intelligent 'front ends'; and systems that help to determine the credit worthiness of customers. Many different techniques are used in these applications, including neural nets (see CONNECTIONISM), production systems which are sets of condition-action rules triggered by internal or external events, LOGIC-based mechanisms that derive theorems from axioms, and many special-purpose computer programs designed for specific tasks, such as analysing or generating natural language (see COMPUTATIONAL LINGUISTICS), computer vision systems, and many sorts of robot control mechanisms. Some of these techniques use special-purpose hardware designs, while others use special-purpose software in the form of programs running on general purpose computers.

In the long run, no one can be sure how successful AI will be. Many of the predictions are based on GÖDEL'S THEOREM, which appears to specify theoretical limits to what can be accomplished by consistent formal systems or machines. However, this is an area of great controversy, and writers like Douglas Hofstadter have sought to prove that no limits to AI are implied by the theorem. One extreme position is the 'strong AI' thesis, which asserts that one day suitably designed computer-based robots will have mental states and processes that are identical to those of humans. At the other extreme, many people believe that human brains have capabilities that cannot be matched by computers, and robots will never be able even to act like us, let alone feel what we feel. The 'weak AI' thesis, somewhere in between these two positions, claims that robots will one day act like humans, but will lack consciousness and therefore be akin to zombies. Common to all these positions, however, is the possibility that any dramatic advances in AI will require the invention of entirely new kinds of machine using new physical principles.

A.S.

artificial language. A language which has been invented to serve some particular purpose. Artificial languages include those which have been devised to facilitate international communications (such as Esperanto), programming languages, languages which communicate with computers or robots in artificial intelligence, and simplified languages which are used by people with learning difficulties.

The thought that a language could be devised to solve the 'problem of Babel' has attracted inventors since the 16th century, and was particularly popular towards the end of the 19th century. In the past century, over 100 such auxiliary or universal languages have been devised, including Esperanto, Novial, Ido, Interlingua and Glosa. Even if such a language achieved universal acclaim, however, there would be no guarantee that its use would ensure world peace, as many supporters imagine. The history of civil wars the world over shows that people will fall out despite the existence of a common language; and conversely, a multilingual community can live in peace, as has been seen in Finland and Switzerland. For further reading: A. Large, *The Artificial Language Movement* (1985). D.C.

artificial life. In COMPUTING, artificial life or a-life involves the creation of digital objects that operate independently and appear to undergo one or more of the processes common to living ORGANISMS: they are born, they grow, they feed or fight, they reproduce, they die. Practitioners of 'weak' a-life describe their digital creatures as simulations of some aspects of real life. Practitioners of 'strong' a-life are trying to create things that could reasonably be said to be alive: as 'alive' as viruses, perhaps, or even bacteria. In the longer term, a-life programs in insect-like ROBOT bodies could be useful – they could clean the outside of skyscrapers, or mow lawns – or just possibly become so intelligent and so powerful that they take over the world and only keep humans around as pets. A-life research started with 'cellular automata' such as John Conway's game, Life, described in *Scientific American* in October 1970, where cells (like draughts pieces on an infinite chess-board) follow simple rules. Today, 'genetic algorithms' are evolved in computer-created worlds to 'breed' solutions to problems, and this technique has real commercial promise. Meanwhile, crude simulations of life have already proved commercially successful in the form of 'artificial pets': cats, dogs, fish, birds and the Japanese Tamagotchi 'chicken', sold as a hand-held toy. There is also enormous potential for semi-intelligent 'software agents' (robot-type programs) that can help people to make better use of their personal computers, and perform tasks like booking tickets or finding information on the INTERNET. J.S.

Arts and Crafts Movement. A reaction in England to the Industrial Revolution and its products (especially as seen at the Great Exhibition of 1851) which was given social and intellectual definition in the writings of Ruskin and translated into practical terms by the founding by William Morris in 1861 of Morris, Marshall & Faulkner, Fine Art Workmen in Painting, Carving, Furniture and the Metals. Morris intended to foster an art restoring the dignity of the craftsman and, since 'it is not possible to dissociate art from morality, politics and religion', to establish a form of society that would combine medieval and SOCIALIST features. The movement, and its followers like Walter Crane, though backward-looking and unable to come to terms with machine production, nevertheless exerted a strong influence on the WERKBUND and hence the BAUHAUS.

The fusion of the applied arts of the movement with those in architecture can be seen in the Red House (1859), designed by Philip Webb for Morris. This later influenced Norman Shaw and C. F. Voysey, whose simple, airy houses of the 1890s proved so important to 20th-century architecture, becoming eventually almost a VERNACULAR of much suburban development. M.BR.

***arts déco*.** Abridged name of the Exposition des Arts Décoratifs Modernes (Paris, 1925) used, then and now, for the style predominant there: a jazzy application of a second-hand visual vocabulary, derived from CUBISM, FUTURISM, FUNCTIONALISM and other recent movements, to decorative, fashionable and commercial ends. The architects Robert Mallet-Stevens and Michel Roux-Spitz were among those prominent in this trend, which coincided with the great period of cinema construction and still continues in, e.g., luxury bookbinding. Following a revival (exhibition at the Paris Musée des Arts Décoratifs, 1966), it has been seen by some as the natural sequel to ART NOUVEAU, whose formal inventiveness and social commitments, however, it fails to share. For further reading: B. Hillier, *Art Déco* (1968). J.W.

ASCII. Acronym for American Standard Code for Information Interchange (pronounced 'ass-KEY'), the leading standard for electronically encoding English alphabet. ASCII is older than computers, having been developed for teletypewriters. Extended ASCII added codes for other symbols, such as letters with accent marks. ASCII's appeal rests on its universal availability. ASCII is used whenever people with different systems are likely to use a computer file. For example, E-MAIL uses ASCII codes because nobody can be sure what system will receive the mail. Over time, however, programs tend to abandon ASCII standards. They change partly to represent things not included in ASCII's code – italicized lettering, for example – and partly because proprietary standards help sales leaders control the market. Thus, in 1985 many serious word processing programs used ASCII files, but by 1995 none did. However, ASCII reappears when users find new work for a computer. The rise of the WORLD WIDE WEB brought renewed strength to ASCII because web pages have to be readable by any computer using any BROWSER. Even with the web's large graphic display, the pages depend on ASCII codes. By linking millions of computers, the INTERNET seems to have assured ASCII's survival – and a good thing too, because over the long run only ASCII files remain readable. Anything written in a non-ASCII form requires the survival of the proprietary system. Much of the data written in the 1980s is already inaccessible without specialized equipment. Writers who fantasize about being discovered posthumously should leave their computer files in ASCII form. E.B.B.

ascribed status. A sociological term used to describe a situation in which one's status in society is determined by accident of birth. This can be contrasted with achieved status, status attained through one's own efforts and by virtue of one's abilities and talents. Ascribed status may relate to KINSHIP (e.g. hereditary peerages) or characteristics such as age, GENDER or RACE which cannot be easily changed. M.D.H.

ascription, see under PATTERN VARIABLES.

Ashcan School. Term applied to American painting at the beginning of the 20th century characterized by the naturalistic (see NATURALISM) depiction of scenes from everyday life, especially in the city. It has been used misleadingly as a synonym for *The Eight*, a group of independents who revolted against New York academic painting, but it more appropriately describes the painting of Robert Henri, John Sloan, George Luks and George Bellows. A.K.W.

aspect perception. A visual experience in which something is seen first as one thing, then as another. An example of aspect perception is provided by Jastrow's 'duck-rabbit': we can go from seeing the picture first as a picture of a duck, then as a picture of a rabbit. Other examples include seeing a face in a cloud, and the Necker cube, where an arrangement of lines is seen as representing a cube orientated first one way, then another. Aspect perception is puzzling for it leads us to want to say seemingly contradictory things: we want to say both that what we see has changed, and also that it hasn't changed. Gestalt psychologists and the philosopher Wittgenstein have attempted to solve this puzzle. S.W.L.

assemblage. In ARCHAEOLOGY (for its meaning in art see under COLLAGE), a group of artifacts found together in a closed CONTEXT OF ASSOCIATION, e.g. in a hoard, a grave or a single occupation level, in such a way as to imply that they were likely to have been in use at the same time. In palaeolithic studies an assemblage of tool types is usually referred to as an *industry*, while recurring assemblages can constitute a CULTURE. B.C.

assimilation. In DEVELOPMENTAL PSYCHOLOGY, a PIAGETIAN term for (1) the incorporation of a new situation transformed to fit into an already organized schema of action; (2) more generally, the subordination of the external world to the activity of the self, as in fantasy and play. For a different sense of the word, see under INTEGRATION (sense 2). P.L.H.

Assisted Places Scheme (APS). A scheme established in 1981 in the UK by the Conservative government to provide financial support for academically bright children from low-income families to attend independent, fee-paying secondary schools. In all, 5,000 places were made available but only approximately half of the children accepted onto the scheme came from homes whose income fell below the national average.

Some private schools with large numbers of APS students came to depend heavily on income from the scheme. Critics regarded the scheme as a means of undermining the principle of comprehensive education and for providing direct subsidies to the private education sector. The annual cost of the scheme rose to more than £20m. In 1997 the Conservative government announced its intention to extend the scheme to preparatory schools but the incoming Labour government moved quickly to end the scheme. S.J.B.

association.

(1) In COGNITIVE PSYCHOLOGY, the mental connection between two or more IDEAS or SENSE-DATA (percepts) or memories, such that the presence of one tends to evoke the other(s). These are presumed to mirror the associations that exist in the external world, so that association provides a mechanism whereby the structure of experience reflects 'reality'. The CONCEPT was central to Aristotle's doctrine of mind as well as that of the British EMPIRICISTS. W.Z.

(2) In ARCHAEOLOGY, when artifacts are found together in a closed CONTEXT they are said to be in *close association*, implying contemporaneity of deposition. The term *loose association* is sometimes used in the case of contexts of broader chronological range. Characteristics may be associated on a single artifact. Juxtaposition is not necessarily association. The term is imprecise and much abused in archaeological literature. B.C.

(3) In ANTHROPOLOGY, a term used to describe the process by which an IMMIGRANT becomes part of the host society. It is a flattening process, i.e. assimilation is achieved through the eradication of all distinguishing features (e.g. language and customs) which have been brought by the immigrant to the new country. Assimilation and its desirability were based upon earlier Jewish (see JUDAISM) and Irish settlements which were assumed to have been successfully assimilated or to have 'disappeared' within British society. In the USA, assimilation was characterized by the idea of the 'melting pot', in which differences between immigrant groups would gradually diminish as they became American.

The question of RACE, however, has presented serious problems for this approach. Assimilation was based on the idea that there was a homogenous host culture. It implied that the host culture was 'pure' and in danger of being overwhelmed or swamped by newcomers. INTEGRATION replaced assimilation as the policy formulated to deal with the consequences of post-war migration to Britain, where it has been closely tied to the need for immigration control. In the USA, the melting-pot idea has given way to MULTICULTURALISM, in which ETHNICITY and religious cultures are increasingly guarded and celebrated as separate from the originally dominant white European idea of what it meant to be 'American'. A.G.; S.T.

associationism. The recurring and variously formulated view (in R. S. Woodworth's classification, one of the six main SCHOOLS OF PSYCHOLOGY) that psychological phenomena comprise elements, such as ideas, sensations, feelings, stimuli and responses, which have become associated (see ASSOCIATION) according to some law or laws, such as similarity or frequency of contiguity. I.M.L.H.

asthenosphere. The analysis of earthquake waves passing through the earth has led to a simple threefold division of the interior of the earth. The outermost solid shell, the crust, is of variable thickness, 30 to 75 km in continental areas but some 5 km under the oceans. The crust is succeeded inwards by the still-solid and denser *mantle* which extends to a depth of 2,900 km below the surface. The very high-density and mainly liquid interior of the earth is known as the *core*. In general the strength or, more correctly, the rigidity of the crust and mantle rock material increases with depth. More detailed seismic study has revealed the presence of a relatively weak plastic zone in the upper part of the mantle named the asthenosphere which extends from 100 to 400 km below the surface. The mechanical weakness of the zone is thought to be due to the presence of small quantities of interstitial liquid. The plastic asthenosphere allows the rigid lithosphere above it to move laterally over the surface of the earth (see PLATE TECTONICS). J.L.M.L.

astronomical unit (AU), see under SOLAR SYSTEM.

astronomy. The oldest exact science, in which the heavenly bodies (moon, sun, planets, stars, nebulae, GALAXIES, etc.) are studied. By analysing the RADIATION received from space as visible light and, more recently, X-RAYS, radio waves (see RADIO ASTRONOMY), and MICROWAVES, the following picture of the universe has been built up: the nearly spherical earth is orbited by the moon; together they move in an ORBIT round the sun, as do the planets and their SATELLITES, and the asteroids, all the bodies so far mentioned constituting the SOLAR SYSTEM. The sun in turn is one star among millions, which together with nebulae and sparse interstellar debris make up the *Milky Way*, which is in turn one galaxy among millions whose mutual recession constitutes the EXPANSION OF THE UNIVERSE.

Distances in astronomy are vividly expressed in light-time, using the fact that light travels 186,000 miles per second. From the earth to the moon is 1.4 light-seconds, from the earth to the sun about 8 light-minutes; the whole solar system is a few light-hours across. The nearest star is 4 light-years away, and the Milky Way is about 100,000 light-years across. The nearest galaxy is about two million light-years away. The distance at which the galaxies are receding from us with the speed of light, which on our present understanding represents the limit of the observable universe, is about ten thousand million light-years.

The study of the motion of the heavenly bodies constitutes CELESTIAL MECHANICS, the investigation of their physical nature ASTROPHYSICS. In COSMOLOGY the universe as a whole is studied, and attempts are made to account for its origin in COSMOGONY. Precise observations of the positions of heavenly bodies were used until recently to establish standards of time measurement (see ATOMIC CLOCK), while for millennia these observations have formed the basis for navigation (recently in the air and outer space as well as on the sea), as well as for astrology. For further reading: M. Hoskin (ed.), *The Cambridge Illustrated History of Astronomy* (1997). M.V.B.

astrophysics. A branch of theoretical ASTRONOMY: the study of stars, and the gases between them, in which the laws of PHYSICS established on earth are applied to the electromagnetic RADIATION and COSMIC RAYS received from space. See also BLACK HOLE; CARBON CYCLE; PULSAR; QUASAR; RADIO ASTRONOMY; RADIO TELESCOPE; SPECTROSCOPY. M.V.B.

atavism. The unsubstantiated belief that complete ancestral types can reappear as 'throwbacks' among an otherwise normal family. This concept of atavism, though based on a grain of truth – the fact that in Mendelian (see MENDELISM) heredity (see GENETICS/GENOMICS) grandparental or more remotely ancestral characteristics may reappear unexpectedly among offspring – belongs to the folklore of RACISM (see also RACE); cf. the totally unwarranted name 'mongolism' for a congenital affliction (Down's syndrome) caused by an accidental derangement of the CHROMOSOMES. P.M.

atheism. Conventionally defined as 'disbelief in, or denial of, the existence of a GOD' (*Oxford English Dictionary*), the meaning of 'atheism' is, in reality, context-specific, determined by the dominant forms of religious BELIEF in any particular time and place. In the ancient world, the charge of atheism was levelled against the philosophical and theological opponents of polytheistic orthodoxies, including Jews and Christians, but it is their theism which constitutes the semantic background to most forms of atheism in the modern world.

Some modern atheists identify with traditional critiques of theism, claiming that there is no good reason to believe in God or – perhaps invoking the existence and extent of apparently pointless suffering – that there is good reason not to. For others, however, theism is not so much unbelievable as unintelligible, and therefore incapable of being true or false, or unacceptable, in the sense that God must be denied (or defied) for the sake of humanity. This 'postulatory atheism' is rooted in Feuerbach and 'the masters of suspicion', Marx, Nietzsche and Freud, who reinterpreted the origins and functions of RELIGION in radically naturalistic ways, and expressed in the work of Camus, Sartre and many other 20th-century writers and artists (see MARXISM; FREUDIAN; EXISTENTIALISM). For further reading: M. Martin, *Atheism: A Philosophical Justification* (1990). C.C.

Athens Charter, see under CIAM.

atmospheric chemistry. The study of the chemical composition of and reactions in the earth's atmosphere. Although constituted primarily from the gases oxygen and nitrogen, the atmosphere also contains a wide variety of trace constituents, both natural and derived from human activities. Chief among these are carbon dioxide and water vapour, but other important trace constituents include nitrogen oxides and sulphur oxides, ozone, methane and free radicals such as hydroxyl. Although present in only very small amounts, these trace gases can have pronounced influences on the environment. Carbon dioxide, water, methane and nitrous oxide absorb infrared RADIATION from the earth's surface and so contribute to the GREENHOUSE EFFECT, which makes the planet around 30 degrees warmer than it would be in their absence. Sulphur and nitrogen oxides contribute to the phenomenon of ACID RAIN, and chlorofluorocarbons (CFCs), used for a variety of industrial purposes, are broken down in the stratosphere to substances that react with the earth's OZONE LAYER. Recognized as a distinct discipline only since the 1960s, atmospheric chemistry has benefited enormously from the invention of instruments that can detect very small concentrations of gases, allowing the discipline to develop and test quantitative models of the chemical processes that take place in the atmosphere. P.C.B.

atom. The smallest unit of a chemical ELEMENT. The idea that matter, which appears continuous to our gross senses, may in fact consist of tiny discrete PARTICLES which cannot be further subdivided seems to stem from Democritus (*c.* 400 BC). But it was only in the late 19th century that accumulating evidence (e.g. the BROWNIAN MOTION) led to the general acceptance of the *atomic theory* among scientists. The entities which we call atoms today are only one of several 'smallest units' at the microscopic level of nature; MOLECULES are the structural units involved in chemical processes, while atoms themselves have a complicated structure (see ATOMIC PHYSICS) of which the ELEMENTARY PARTICLES represent the fundamental units. M.V.B.

atomic clock. A device for counting the vibrations of ATOMS. Because of their extreme regularity, these vibrations are used to define the standard for the measurement of time (1 second = 9,192,631,770 cycles of a certain vibration of the Caesium atom); this is expected to be consistent to about one second in a thousand years (a previous standard, based on the earth's rotation, was accurate only to about one second in one year). M.V.B.

atomic energy. ENERGY obtained from the atomic NUCLEUS during a CHAIN REACTION, which may either be controlled, as in a NUCLEAR REACTOR, or uncontrolled, as in nuclear weapons. See also FISSION; FUSION; MASS-ENERGY EQUATION. M.V.B.

atomic number (of an ELEMENT). The number of PROTONS in the atomic NUCLEUS. It is equal to the number of ELECTRONS in a neutral ATOM, and the ordinal number of the element on a scale of increasing atomic weights. No elements whose atomic number exceeds 92 (uranium) occur naturally; nuclei of the TRANSURANIC ELEMENTS are unstable because the disruptive effect of the ELECTROSTATIC repulsion between the protons outweighs the attraction due to the shorter-ranged STRONG INTERACTION. See also ISOTOPES. M.V.B.

atomic physics. The branch of PHYSICS devoted to studying the structure of ATOMS. The atom is an open structure about a ten-thousand-millionth of a metre across, consisting of a positively charged NUCLEUS about ten thousand times smaller across, whose attraction binds a number of negatively charged orbiting ELECTRONS; this number is equal to the ATOMIC NUMBER if the atom is neutral, but higher or lower if the atom is an ION. It is often helpful to compare the atom with the solar system of sun and planets, but this is not a strict analogy because electrons obey the laws of QUANTUM MECHANICS, not of NEWTONIAN MECHANICS (see WAVE-PARTICLE DUALITY; BOHR THEORY). The weakly bound outer electrons are detached and exchanged during the chemical reactions which may occur when atoms are close together. Transition of electrons from one ORBIT to another, with a change of QUANTUM NUMBER, involves an emission or absorption of ENERGY in the form of PHOTONS, either of visible light (outer electrons) or X-RAYS (inner electrons).

See also ELECTRON SHELL; ENERGY LEVEL; SPECTROSCOPY. M.V.B.

atomic pile, see NUCLEAR REACTOR.

atomic weight. Building upon Lavoisier's pragmatic definition of element (as a substance never yet reduced to any simpler components), John Dalton argued that distinct chemical elements were characterized by being composed of PARTICLES of different (relative) atomic weights. Dalton published his first list of relative weights in 1803, and his idea found widespread acceptance, though it was not until the 1860s that these values were internationally standardized. Belief in a stable, atomic composition of the elements provided the crucial foundations for chemistry's rapid development as a coherent science from the mid-19th century onwards, leading to VALENCE theory, the triumphs of the kinetic theory of gases, and the PERIODIC TABLE of the elements, which predicted the existence of other ELEMENTS not yet discovered. Despite 20th-century investigations of the fine structure of particles, the theory of atomic weights remains the basis of practical CHEMISTRY. R.P.

atonal music. Music divorced from the concept of *tonality* which dominated Western musical thought for more than three centuries. Traditionally, a composer selected one of the 24 tonal families – 12 major and 12 minor – each of which is spelled out by a *scale* and known as a *key*, one note being the *tonic* towards which the others gravitate. It was common practice for the opening phrase of a work to establish the key unequivocally by stating its essential notes in melodic or harmonic terms; similarly it was virtually an unbroken rule that the final cadence (sequence of chords) should confirm the tonality. In the latter part of the 19th century, however, the increasingly free use, notably by Wagner and Liszt, of chromatic notes (those not belonging to the key of the work) led to a gradual erosion of tonality. The process was continued by Debussy (see IMPRESSIONISM; WHOLE-TONE SCALE), Scriabin and particularly Schoenberg, and culminated in *atonalism*. Atonalism is the deliberate avoidance of key; *atonality* is the term used to designate a state of atonalism.

The largest problem in atonal music is to overcome the natural tendency of certain basic intervals such as the fifth and the third to establish a tonality of sorts, however temporary. It is for this reason that atonal music is largely dissonant, since only by avoiding traditional consonances can the implications of tonality be avoided; similarly the melodic lines are harder for the average listener to absorb, since they are often characterized by angularity and wide-spaced intervals. Much, but not all, atonal music is composed according to the serial principles (see SERIAL MUSIC) evolved around 1920 by Schoenberg. A.H.

attachment. In ETHOLOGY, the initial 'bonding' of mother and infant of various species, during which many crucial response mechanisms in the growing infant have been found to depend upon an adequate relationship with the mother. In DEVELOPMENTAL PSYCHOLOGY, the concept was developed by English psychiatrist John Bowlby in his seminal work *Attachment and Loss* (1969; 1982). The development of an infant's personality is very dependent on the quality of its early interaction with the primary caregiver, usually the mother (though of course the father and other adults who interact with the infant can be targets of attachment). When an infant's demands are met regularly, appropriately and predictably, attachment to the adult caregiver occurs. Much of the individual's adult personality is determined during infancy, and the quality of attachment is crucial in human development. By playing with the infant, calming its fears and encouraging its curiosity, the caregiver nurtures a human being who is likely to be personally secure and socially outgoing in adult life. See also IMPRINTING. S.T.

attitude theory. Theories about the nature of social 'attitudes'. Previously referring to physical posture, 'attitude' acquired its psychological meaning in US SOCIAL PSYCHOLOGY during the 1920s. The topic then largely dominated US social psychology until the 1960s, with individuals' attitudes towards particular topics, issues or 'attitude objects' being (it was assumed) major determinants of their social behaviour. Such theorizing developed alongside the devising of attitude-measurement techniques, usually in questionnaire form (pioneered in the late 1920s and early 1930s by Thurstone, Likert and Gutmann). Attitude structure, functions and change all received copious attention, but consensus was never reached. MARKET RESEARCH and opinion polling derive their methods largely from this source.

The attitude–behaviour relationship has always been problematic, since it became evident early on that expressed attitudes did not always correlate highly with actual behaviour (nor is it always clear which behaviour an attitude actually entails). Theoretical approaches adopted ranged from BEHAVIOURISM to the FREUDIAN-influenced AUTHORITARIAN PERSONALITY account, while numerous 'balance', 'congruity' and cognitive dissonance models of attitude-change were proposed. Racial and ethnic attitudes were a prominent theme from the outset (see RACE; RACISM). While leaving a permanent technical legacy, classical attitude theory foundered after 1970 due to irresolvable theoretical difficulties, the topic thereafter becoming assimilated under the new SOCIAL COGNITION paradigm. Radical social psychologists now challenge the very reality of the phenomenon as conventionally conceived. G.D.R.

attribution theory. Theorizing concerning how people ascribe causes to behaviour and events. Originating in post-World War II work by Fritz Heider, this topic became prominent in SOCIAL PSYCHOLOGY post-1970 as a major component of the rising concern with SOCIAL COGNITION. While some findings are fairly settled (e.g. we tend to explain other people's behaviour by internal causes but our own by circumstances), the large number of factors now identified as involved in determining attributions renders generalizable conclusions elusive. These include stability of behaviour over time, controllability of behaviour and circumstances, how typical behaviour is, and individual personality traits. At least seven theoretical approaches can be identified, although most (but not quite all) view individuals as amateur scientists striving to predict and control events by identifying 'causes' in an intuitive statistical fashion, seeking 'correlations' between different 'variables'. There are also overlaps with earlier cognitive dissonance and locus of control theories. Some practical applications have emerged, particularly in clinical psychology (see APPLIED PSYCHOLOGY) and counselling, where clients' problems may be related to erroneous attributions, linking attitude theory to COGNITIVE THERAPY. G.D.R.

AU (astronomical unit), see under SOLAR SYSTEM.

autarky. A national policy of economic self-sufficiency, for example in food, energy and TECHNOLOGY. Such policies tend to be associated with controls and other interferences with free economic exchange across national frontiers and to be contrasted with such post-war ideals as free trade (see PROTECTIONISM), the free exchange of a country's currency for other countries' currencies, and multilateralism (see BILATERALISM). The high period of autarkic policies was between the two world wars, when the USA inclined to ISOLATIONISM, Britain looked to a system of imperial preference and the STERLING AREA to assure its markets and raw materials, Japan tried to construct its Greater East Asia Co-Prosperity Sphere, and Hitler's Central Bank Governor, Dr Schacht, constructed his notorious Schachtian system of controls designed to insulate Germany from the world DEPRESSION while promoting a massive armaments programme at home. More recent examples of autarkic states have been Albania, Tanzania and China; though the latter two have, since the mid-1970s, become more outward looking. P.J.; J.P.

auteur. Term used analogously to its literary sense of 'author' by the French film critics whose theoretical writing precipitated the *nouvelle vague* (NEW WAVE) to distinguish between a film-maker responsible for the entire conception of his films and one who merely stages scripts written by another artist. These future film-makers believed that a true *auteur* both writes and directs his films; but since they admired above all else Hollywood directors who, like the old-guard French film-makers they were trying to displace, often worked from ready-made scripts imposed by studio chiefs, the critical debate (usually referred to as the *politique des auteurs*) centred on the argument that great film-makers or *auteurs* (e.g. Hitchcock, Hawks) transformed the scripts given to them by imposing, visually, their own preoccupations and continuing themes. Often misunderstood, and sometimes abused to attempt to prove that a director is an *auteur* because his work reveals persistent concerns and mannerisms, or that an *auteur*'s subsequent work must be good because he is an *auteur*, the argument has been adopted by English and American critics as the '*auteur* theory'. For further reading: P. Graham (ed.), *The New Wave* (1968). T.C.C.M.

authenticity. In the work of Jean-Paul Sartre, the opposite of BAD FAITH. It is a coincidence of the consciousness of the subject (*pour-soi*) with its own objective reality (*en soi*). If this can be overcome, authenticity is the achieved coincidence of the two. The difficulties in this human enterprise, which are enormous, are sharply presented in Sartre's early novels *La Nausée* (1938) and *L'Age de raison* (1945). For further reading: J.-P. Sartre, *Being and Nothingness* (1957). R.PO.

authoritarian personality. A PERSONALITY TYPE characterized by extreme obedience and unquestioning respect for authority. These defining characteristics are usually accompanied by rigidity, conventionality, prejudice and intolerance of weakness or ambiguity. W.Z.

authoritarianism. The theory and practice of forms of government in which subjects have few or no rights against their rulers and their rulers' authority is of indefinite scope. Among authoritarian theories of politics one may mention Plato's defence of a philosophical dictatorship, Edmund Burke's defence of tradition and divine right against the French Revolution's appeal to the rights of man, Lenin's appeal to the authority of a 'vanguard' party and Hitler's irrationalist appeal to the 'Fuhrerprinzip' or 'leadership principle'. The concept of the AUTHORITARIAN PERSONALITY was explored by German social philosopher Theodor Adorno and his colleagues in *The Authoritarian Personality* (1950). A.R.

authority, see under CHARISMA; POWER.

autism. Term derived from the Greek *autos*, self, and used to describe behavioural patterns which suggest to observers that the individual in question is absorbed exclusively in his or her own interior experiences. Early infantile autism is a syndrome characterized by Leo Kanner as combining 'extreme self-isolation and the obsessive insistence on the preservation of sameness'. The term is loosely used to describe any non-communicating behaviour, especially in children. C.O.

autochthony. Word used by K. C. Wheare in his *Constitutional Structure of the Commonwealth* (1960), and by others since, to designate a characteristic of constitutions to which some countries of the British COMMONWEALTH attached great importance when they achieved independence. They wished not only to have a constitution independent of the Parliament of the UK, to which they had formerly been subject, but to demonstrate that the status of the new constitution as law was not derived from any legislation of the UK, and, like the constitution of other independent sovereign states, had a 'home-grown' or autochthonous quality. H.L.A.H.

auto-destructive. A term used of any artifact designed to damage itself – though generally with a little help from outside. Celebrated examples are the Swiss sculptor Jean Tinguely's machines which dismantled themselves (e.g. 'Study no. 2 for an End of the World', detonated in the Nevada desert), and Gustav Metzger's nylon cloth which he destroyed with hydrochloric acid. Metzger described this as simultaneously 'autocreative', on the tenuous grounds that the work of art (and not simply the artist) had a measure of 'initiative' in transforming itself. Some auto-destructive art has been intended as a reflection on the built-in obsolescence of CONSUMERS' GOODS, or on the suicidal tendencies of military powers. P.C.

autogestion. Literally, 'self-management'. The term was adopted in the 1960s by the French LEFT-wing *Parti Socialiste Unifié* (PSU, led by Michel Rocard) as a means of distinguishing its anti-statist IDEOLOGY and policies from those of traditional SOCIALISM. Autogestion was defined by the PSU in terms of decentralization of responsibility and greater citizen participation in all spheres of life, but especially in the workplace and local government. During the

1970s groups within the French Socialist and COMMUNIST Parties also began to advocate autogestion, and it was a central theme of the Socialist Party's 1981 election manifesto. S.M.

autogolpe. The term – also referred to as a 'palace coup' – is used in Latin America to describe those circumstances under which the executive temporarily suspends constitutional guarantees as well as the legislature (see CONSTITUTIONAL GOVERNMENT; CONSTITUTIONALISM). The executive then either rules by decree or referenda, rewrites the constitution or calls new legislative elections, often to obtain popular legitimacy for a strengthened executive. There have been autogolpes in Peru (1992) under President Alberto Fujimori, which had popular support and therefore strengthened his position in the 1995 elections, and in Guatemala (1993) under President Jorge Elías Serrano, which was short-lived, highly unpopular and which led to his downfall soon after. Both heads of state sought to neuter increasingly hostile and difficult-to-manage parliaments in their respective countries. For further reading: P. Manceri, *State under Siege: Development and Policy-making in Peru* (1996). M.A.P.

autological, see under HETEROLOGICAL.

automatic stabilizers. Mechanisms within the economy which act counter-cyclically (i.e. against the prevailing economic TRADE OR BUSINESS CYCLE) without specific intervention by the authorities. An example is a progressive income-tax system, i.e. one which takes an increasing share of increasing personal incomes and a decreasing share of decreasing ones, thus acting, respectively, to restrain the growth of AGGREGATE DEMAND or to moderate its decline. D.E.

automation. A word introduced by Delmar S. Harder in 1948 for the automatic control of the manufacture of a product through a number of successive stages. It is now generally used for the control of machines by machines with human intervention reduced to a minimum; examples are an automatic pilot, a COMPUTER-controlled assembly line or a ROBOT. Automation is an emotionally charged word since it is frequently used to mean the use of machines to replace human labour. According to some, it merely continues a process of technical change (MECHANIZATION) which is at least as old as the INDUSTRIAL REVOLUTION. In industrialized societies the increase in per capita productivity during the past two centuries is largely the consequence of the increase in quantity and the improvement in quality of the machines and tools with which human workers co-operate. For the alarmists, however, automation is qualitatively different, and threatens vast technological UNEMPLOYMENT as growing numbers of skills are rendered obsolete. Thus far the gradualists have had the better of the argument, but the matter is far from settled. C.S.; R.L.

automatism. In modern English criminal law, involuntary conduct where, owing to a lack of normal control over his bodily movements, a person does an act which would, but for such lack of control, constitute an offence. The chief importance for the law of identifying such cases of automatism is that, even where an offence is one of strict liability (see STRICT OR ABSOLUTE LIABILITY), an accused person will not be criminally responsible for the consequences of his uncontrolled bodily movements unless the loss of control arose from his own failure to take reasonable precautions. The forms of uncontrolled conduct which lawyers now describe as automatism were formerly referred to as cases where there was 'no act' or 'no volition' on the part of the accused. H.L.A.H.

autopoiesis. In CYBERNETICS, a term coined by Humberto Maturana for a special case of HOMOEOSTASIS in which the critical variable of the system that is held constant is that system's own organization. S.BE.

autoradiograph. The image of a radioactive object (see RADIOACTIVITY) obtained photographically by using the RADIATION emitted during the decay process. The distribution of radioactive material is mapped directly on a photographic plate placed in close contact with the object. Autoradiography is an important technique in PHYSIOLOGY and BIOCHEMISTRY. It can be used to follow the diffusion of a radioactive TRACER and in this way has revealed details of the internal boundaries of metals and the permeability of membranes. B.F.

autosome. A CHROMOSOME other than a SEX CHROMOSOME. J.M.S.

auto-suggestion. A therapeutic technique whereby an individual attempts to induce a desired effect by self-instruction and self-encouragement; first made popular by Coué (*Self-Mastery through Conscious Auto-Suggestion*, 1922). W.Z.

autotelic writing. An appropriately new term, in the NEW CRITICISM, for the old notion that a work of art exists for and within itself. The modern origins of this idea are found in the writings of the 18th-century Swiss critics J. J. Bodmer and J. J. Breitinger. Bodmer wrote that from the poet the reader should demand 'only poetry; in this we shall be satisfied with the probability and the reason which lies in its coherence with itself'. This led into 'art for art's sake', and declined into romantic preciosity or elegant wit (e.g. Oscar Wilde's dictum that life seeks to imitate art). The idea appears again in the 20th century in two scarcely related forms: in the work of certain poets (e.g. the 'creationism' of the Chilean Vicente Huidobro and the Frenchman Pierre Revendy) and fiction-writers, notably Borges; and in the New Criticism, where it serves to turn attention away from irrelevancies of neo-romantic criticism and towards the text. It is not often seriously suggested that literature has no place in life, but only that it must first be studied as if it had not. M.S.-S.

***avant-garde*.** French military term used before 1848 for any politically advanced republican or SOCIALIST group, later for the assumption that 'advanced' art must occupy a similar position of leadership in the fight against the bourgeoisie (see BOURGEOIS), and finally in all countries after about 1910 to denote those cultural innovators, whatever their political associations, who appeared most inaccessible to public understanding. Though still able to fire the less sceptical creative artists, middlemen and critics with a fruitful sense of minority cohesion, it is now an anachronism, since many kinds of art, music and literature associated with it are widely accepted and officially supported. J.W.

avant-garde dance. Term largely related to the work of Cunningham (see CUNNINGHAM TECHNIQUE) and the subsequent development of the POST-MODERN DANCE movement and JUDSON DANCE THEATER which emerged in the 1960s in the USA. L.A.

avant-garde music. Term frequently used in connection with certain European composers in the 1950s (see POST-WEBERN SCHOOL). B.CO.

avatar, see under VIRTUAL REALITY.

aversion therapy, see under BEHAVIOUR THERAPY.

avoidance behaviour. A behaviour pattern enabling an animal to avoid some noxious stimulus. The behavioural responses may or may not be learned. The unicellular organism *Paramecium*, for example, responds to a bubble of carbon dioxide in its water by reversing the direction of its swimming for a short distance, turning a small angle, and then swimming on; the response, if repeated, will get it past any obstacle. Higher animals can learn that a stimulus has to be avoided. Rats, for example, will initially eat a small sample of almost anything; but if what they eat makes them sick they avoid eating it again. This kind of 'one-trial' learning is important in the life of an animal with so flexible a diet as the rat. Avoidance learning is a major area of study in the PSYCHOLOGY of learning. See BEHAVIOUR THERAPY. M.R.

axiology. The philosophical theory of value in general, embracing ETHICS or the philosophical theory of morality, but extending far beyond it to include AESTHETIC, technical, prudential, hedonic and other forms of value. Any field of human discourse in which the general value-terms 'good' and 'ought' figure falls within the range of axiology, even that of SCIENTIFIC METHOD with its principles about the degree of belief one *ought* to give to a hypothesis in the light of a given body of evidence. See also VALUE-JUDGEMENT. A.Q.

axiom of choice. The principle (first noted by G. Peano in 1890) that if we have a collection of sets (see SET), we can make a new set by taking one element from each of the sets. This is obviously true in a finite context (and seems so in INFINITE ones), so it has been freely used, and is essential in proving general results such as 'every FIELD has an algebraically closed extension' (see ALGEBRA). But it is known to have some surprising consequences such as the bizarre result (Banach and Tarski, 1925) that a solid sphere of radius one can be divided into five highly interpenetrating subsets, which can then be manoeuvred, without distortion, to form two such spheres. (Clearly the usual notions of volume and weight cannot apply here.)

Then there are the results of Gödel (see GÖDEL'S THEOREM) and Cohen which show that although this axiom (see AXIOMATIC METHOD) is consistent with the rest of MATHEMATICS and set theory, so is its denial. So scrupulous mathematicians are careful to note which of their results are not tainted by the use of the axiom. N.A.R.

axiomatic method. Before the second half of the 19th century mathematicians studied MATHEMATICAL STRUCTURES which were based on practical experience. Proofs were justified, explicitly or implicitly, by an appeal to intuitions (sometimes quite sophisticated) abstracted from that experience. For GEOMETRY Euclid had attempted, with considerable but not complete success, to codify the intuitions in axioms; the theorems should be deduced from these by purely logical arguments. By 1900 AXIOMATICS had become a flourishing industry. The investigations which led to satisfactory sets of axioms for the familiar structures (natural, real and complex NUMBERS, Euclidean geometry) provoked interest in those seemingly counter-intuitive structures which can be characterized by modifying the familiar axioms in a more or less arbitrary way (e.g. non-Euclidean geometries and number systems, such as the quaternions, whose multiplication does not obey the commutative law). Nowadays the axiomatic method predominates. Axioms for the objects to be studied are no longer presented as codifying intuitions, but simply as rules of a game; Russell's dictum that in mathematics we do not know what we are talking about, nor care whether what we say is true, is taken literally.

The great advantages of the axiomatic method are that it liberates MATHEMATICS from the study of the traditional structures (Cantor wanted pure mathematics to be called 'free mathematics'), and that it concentrates the attention on what is essential to the proof of a particular theorem, which can then be applied to *any* objects that satisfy the axioms used in the proof (see BOURBAKI, NICOLAS). But it may lead to sterile ingenuity, and – as in much contemporary teaching and textbook writing – to the suppression of qualities (in particular, intuition and the appreciation of significance) that are essential to good mathematics. R.G.

axiomatics. The branch of logical investigation (see LOGIC) concerned with axiomatic systems, that is to say with systems of assertions in which a handful of initial PROPOSITIONS is laid down as true (the axioms) or postulated (hence the phrase *postulational method*), and further propositions (the *theorems*) are then deduced from them by means of specified rules of INFERENCE (sometimes called *transformation-rules*). To be set out completely an axiom system should also contain a *vocabulary*, in which the terms of the system are enumerated, and a SYNTAX or set of *formation-rules*, determining which combinations of terms of the system constitute well-formed, or significant, assertions. The model for all later axiom systems is Euclid's geometry (imitated in PHILOSOPHY, for example, in Spinoza's *Ethics*). The axiomatization of other branches of MATHEMATICS was carried out extensively towards the end of the 19th century. Soon techniques for the logical study of axiom systems were developed: techniques for determining the consistency of the members of a SET of axioms with each other, their logical *independence* of each other, and the *completeness* of the set, i.e. its adequacy as a basis for the deduction of all the truths statable in the vocabulary of the system. Modern formal logic, as inaugurated by the great treatises of Frege and of Whitehead and Russell, has mostly been expounded in an axiomatic form. For further reading: R. Blanché, *Axiomatics* (1962). A.Q.

Axis. Term invented by Mussolini in a speech of 1 November 1936 to describe the relationship between Nazi Germany and Fascist Italy, after the conclusion of Italo-German agreements (the Berchtesgaden protocols) on international policies; it has been extended to cover other bilateral relationships in which states agree to follow common policies on specific questions. In practice the appearance of joint action and support which the Axis provided was significantly belied by the realities; but it was of some advantage to its adherents so long as active involvement in crisis or war was not in question. D.C.W.

B

Babouvism, see under EGALITARIANISM.

back propagation, see under CONNECTIONISM.

backlash, see under THIRD WAVE FEMINISM.

bacteriology. The science that deals with the structure, properties and behaviour of bacteria, particularly as disease-causing agents.

Bacteria are a highly heterogeneous group, and attempts to classify them according to the full nomenclatural hierarchy appropriate to larger ORGANISMS have not met with the general sympathy of biologists (see BIOLOGY). Nevertheless, a first crude division may be made on the basis of shape and habit of growth. Thus, *cocci* are spherical; *bacilli* are generally rod-shaped; *staphylococci* form clusters like grape bunches; *streptococci* form chains; *vibrios* are rod-shaped with a helical twist. A taxonomic distinction of greater functional significance is between 'gram-positive' and 'gram-negative' bacteria. The distinction is based upon the degree of retentiveness with which the organisms bind the stain crystal violet during their preparation for microscopy. Most bacteria (the leprosy bacteria are a notable exception) can be cultivated in simple media outside the body. Some bacteria ('strict' or 'obligate' *aerobes*) can grow only in the presence of oxygen, others (*anaerobes*) only in its absence.

Bacteria increase their number by fission. After a so-called 'lag phase' multiplication is characteristically of the exponential or compound-interest type, though greater or lesser departures from this norm occur as a result of changes in the growth medium produced by the bacteria themselves, e.g. the using up of nutrients and the accumulation of waste-products. Genetic information in bacteria resides in a NUCLEIC ACID system, and the processes of coding, transcription and translation are essentially the same in bacteria as in higher organisms. Indeed, the study of heredity in bacteria, notably *Escherichia coli* (probably the most deeply understood of all organisms), has thrown very great light on the processes of heredity in higher organisms.

Bacteria are highly mutable organisms, as evidenced by the readiness with which they can eventually utilize new substrates (see ENZYMES) or develop resistance towards newly devised ANTIBIOTICS. These examples of adaptation were at one time known under the comprehensive heading of 'training'. This is a misleading description, however, because it obscures the essential point that all such processes of training are strictly GENE-dependent and selective in character. Under conditions unfavourable for continued growth or even for life, many bacteria have the power to form highly resistant spores. Spores normally resist desiccation and many ordinary procedures of disinfection. Bacteria and spores are, however, killed by the use of the *autoclave* in which objects to be sterilized are exposed to steam under high pressure and at temperatures as high as 120–130°C. Bacteria are pathogenic by reason of the direct effects of their multiplication or because they contain or liberate toxic substances (*endotoxins* or *exotoxins* respectively). Bacterial infections are cured through the action of antibodies (see IMMUNITY) or of natural or artificial antibacterials including antibiotics. The formation of antibodies may be excited either by structural constituents of the bacteria themselves or by the toxins they liberate.

Sexual reproduction – essentially a genetic intermixture – has been described in certain bacilli. In addition a number of 'parasexual' processes may lead to genetic interchange. The most famous of these processes is the TRANSFORMATION of *pneumococci* first described in 1928 by F. Griffith. In this process a mixture of dead and living bacteria of different types leads to the acquirement by the living type of some of the properties of the dead bacteria. In Griffith's example the transforming agent was deoxyribonucleic acid (DNA). This observation was the start of all that is now known about the genetic functions of the nucleic acids. For further reading: G. S. Wilson and A. A. Miles, *Topley and Wilson's Principles of Bacteriology and Immunity* (8th ed. 1990). P.M.

bad faith (*mauvaise foi*). A condition described in Sartre's *Being and Nothingness*

(1943). Bad faith comes about as the result of anguish in front of choice, and represents the subject's attempt to deceive himself about the nature of reality. Bad faith is a direct consequence of the radical and inalienable freedom of the subject to choose himself authentically (see AUTHENTICITY), and of his own attempts to deny, escape or obscure this freedom and duty. Bad faith can take many forms, some of which involve the power of nihilating reality, or of conferring absence upon reality, i.e. the power to conceive, and to insist upon, what is not the case. The worst form of bad faith is that self-deception which allows a subject to believe that he is not free to change things, or that things could not be otherwise. R.PO.

Bahai. A religious movement, originating in ISLAM and stressing the spiritual unity of mankind under God. It was established by Mirza Husein Ali the *Baha-ullah* ('Glory of God') after the founder, Ali Muhammad the *Bab* ('Door'), had been executed in Persia in 1850 for alleged blasphemy. It has attracted adherents, not very numerous but widely distributed, by its support of modern idealistic movements (such as equality between the sexes), its receptivity towards scientific ideas, and its simple, personal forms of prayer. For further reading: W. S. Hatcher and J. D. Martin, *The Bahai Faith* (1986). D.L.E.

Bakhtinian. An approach to cultural history, and especially literature, in the style of the Russian critic Mikhail Bakhtin (1895–1975), best known for his *Problems of Dostoyevsky's Poetics* (1929) and *Rabelais and His World* (presented as a thesis in 1940 but not published until 1965). His work is most famous for its concern with unofficial and popular elements in the oeuvres of great writers, with CARNIVALIZATION as a means of subversion or UNCROWNING, and with the interaction of dialogue between different points of view or languages (HETEROGLOSSIA). For further reading: K. Clark and M. Holquist, *Mikhail Bakhtin* (1984). P.B.

balance of nature. Term sometimes used for the relationship between the various parts of the BIOSPHERE which makes this, in the absence of human intervention, a self-renewing system. It is the well-founded fear of many ecologists (see ECOLOGY) that this balance is being upset by INDUSTRIALIZATION and the reckless exploitation of the ENVIRONMENT. P.M.

balance of payments.

(1) The difference between certain credits and debits in the accounts recording the flow of transactions in a specified period of one nation (sometimes region or group of nations) with others, usually with the rest of the world.

(2) The accounts themselves. The *balance on current account* is the difference between payments and receipts for goods and services, including interest, dividends and profits, and (usually) transfers, e.g. migrants' REMITTANCES and aid. The surplus on the current account represents the country's net acquisition of foreign assets. The *balance of trade* is that part of the current account that relates to goods, i.e. it excludes services. The balance on the capital account is the difference between the sales by domestic residents of real and financial assets to foreigners and the purchase by domestic residents of real and financial assets from foreigners. The sum of the current and capital accounts is the difference between the demand and supply (see SUPPLY AND DEMAND), from traders and investors, for the domestic currency. This difference is accounted for by changes in the official foreign exchange reserves and official borrowing. The change in the latter minus the change in the former is the official financing. By definition, the current account, the capital account and official financing must be seen to be zero. However, errors, omissions and delays in recording transactions mean that it is necessary to include a balancing item to ensure this equality. The balancing item and revisions of balance of payments statistics are often sizeable. Balance of payments problems arise when there is a persistent tendency for a deficit (or surplus) to occur on the current plus capital account. Such a problem represents running down (or accumulation) of a country's foreign assets. The problem can be solved by DEVALUATION (or appreciation) of the EXCHANGE RATE, deflation (or reflation), EXCHANGE CONTROLS or an increase (decrease) in the interest rate. These measures may have undesirable effects on INFLATION, ECONOMIC GROWTH and real income. For further reading: J. C. Pool *et al*,

The ABCs of International Finance (1991).
M.FG.S.; J.P.

balance of power. Described by Martin Wight as the 'political counterpart of Newton's physics' for the period between 1701 and 1914, balance of power is the central 'realist' concept for the preservation of international order. At its height in the 19th-century Concert of Europe, the concept dominated the foreign policies of the great powers, to become discredited after 1914, a view also espoused by liberals (see LIBERALISM) and MARXISTS before 1914. I. Clark (see below) defines balance of power as an acceptance of the role of legitimate force to create or maintain equilibrium by states. He also sees nuclear deterrence (see BALANCE OF TERROR) theory as a 'subset of the general balance of power school'. The term generally implies a 'balancer' state which acts as principal guarantor of the system. For further reading: I. Clark, *Reform and Resistance in the International Order* (1980).
A.W.

balance of terror. A rhetorical term describing a state of equilibrium or of mutual DETERRENCE between nuclear powers, based on the possession of weapons which allow either side to deal a mortal blow to the other. Probably coined by Lester Pearson ('the balance of terror has replaced the balance of power') in June 1955, at the 10th anniversary of the signing of the UN Charter (see UN), and based on Winston Churchill's remark 'it may well be that safety shall be the sturdy child of terror . . .'
A.F.B.

balance of trade, see BALANCE OF PAYMENTS.

balance theory. A view of interpersonal relations that has as its starting-point the situation where the subject's cognitive view of the people he is in contact with accords with his EMOTIONS about them. If either his ideas or his feelings concerning them are altered, the balance is disturbed and stress may be introduced.
H.L.

Balfour Declaration. A British government statement in the form of a letter, dated 2 November 1917, signed by the Foreign Secretary, A. J. Balfour (1848–1930), and addressed to Lord Rothschild, expressing 'sympathy with Jewish ZIONIST aspirations' and viewing 'with favour the establishment in Palestine of a National Home for the Jewish People'. Palestine was then under Turkish occupation but became a British mandate under the LEAGUE OF NATIONS (1922). Thereafter the British government wrestled with the intractable problem of reconciling the Balfour Declaration with the proviso, contained in the same letter, that 'nothing shall be done which may prejudice the civil and religious rights of existing non-Jewish communities in Palestine'. From this followed the chain of events leading to the breakdown of Arab–Jewish relations, the establishment of the state of Israel, and the MIDDLE EAST WARS. For further reading: L. Stein, *The Balfour Declaration* (1961).
A.L.C.B.

balkanization. The fragmentation of a geographical region into smaller, frequently hostile units. This kind of politico-territorial subdivision has been occurring for millennia, most prominently following the break-up of empires that had conquered peoples of diverse nationalities. Contemporary usage of this term derives from the chaos that arose in south-eastern Europe's Balkan Peninsula, early in the 20th century, following the dissolution of the Austro-Hungarian Empire. Modern YUGOSLAVIA was formed in 1919 out of a crazy-quilt ethnic mosaic, and its mainly totalitarian regimes (see TOTALITARIANISM) forcibly held the country together until the early 1990s. After 1991, however, disintegrating Yugoslavia swiftly returned to its earlier state of ethnic and political chaos, giving rise to armed conflicts, GENOCIDE in the form of ETHNIC CLEANSING, and five newly independent states – Serbia-Montenegro, Bosnia-Herzegovina, Croatia, Slovenia, and Macedonia.
P.O.M.

ballet, see under CLASSICAL BALLET.

ballistic missiles, see under MISSILES.

ballistics. The application of NEWTONIAN MECHANICS to the calculation of trajectories of MISSILES influenced by GRAVITATION and air resistance. The early development of ballistics in the 17th century marked the beginning of the application of modern science to warfare. M.V.B.

bamboo curtain. Phrase coined by American publicists in the 1950s, by analogy with IRON CURTAIN, to describe the controls imposed by the Chinese COMMUNIST regime on the free movement of ideas and individuals across China's borders. D.C.W.

Band Aid. A popular cultural (see POPULAR CULTURE) response to the Western media coverage of the Ethiopian famine of 1984, initiated primarily by ROCK MUSICian Bob Geldof, whose aim was to supplement the existing structures of aid and the established famine relief agencies by mobilizing a massive new constituency of donors in the most affluent nations. The means chosen for this mobilization were those characteristic of rock music – electronic communication, youth-oriented, participative and international. The success of Geldof's three successive ventures – Band Aid (an amalgam of musicians brought together in late 1984 to produce the hit single 'Do They Know It's Christmas?'), Live Aid (simultaneous concerts in London, Philadelphia and other venues all drawing on the telephone pledge system, in July 1985) and Sport Aid (sponsored marathon runs in dozens of locations in April 1986) – had significant results in different areas. First, a phenomenal amount of money was raised – £100,000,000. Secondly, the political socialization dimension was important – the values of self-interest, autonomy and pursuit of gain characteristic of the moral agenda of REAGANISM and THATCHERISM were challenged by feelings of compassion, charity and interdependence shared by millions of young people. Thirdly, Band Aid and Geldof responded to the logistical and administrative blockages in delivering supplies to those in need by adopting a new style – publicly chastizing politicians and bureaucrats for their temerity and sluggishness, and by organizing land, sea and air delivery systems on an unprecedented scale. Fourthly, the voluntaristic nature of the entire exercise spawned a series of analogous fund-raising events in higher cultural forms – Opera Aid, Fashion Aid, etc.

Responding to criticism from both older aid agencies and more radical sources, the Band Aid Trust has modified its short-term emphasis and now stresses the importance of long-term development projects that lead to self-sufficiency. Ironically, the very ESTABLISHMENT that prompted Geldof's ire saw fit to reward him for his efforts, and he received an honorary knighthood for services to FAMINE relief in June 1986. P.S.L.

band width. see under INFORMATION THEORY.

Bandung Conference. The first Afro-Asian conference, meeting in Bandung, Indonesia, from 18 to 24 April 1955, with representatives of 29 states of Asia and Africa (including the People's Republic of China). The main motivation of the conference was dissatisfaction with the domination of international politics by the quarrel between the American and Soviet blocs, and concern at the risk of war between the USA and China. See also NON-ALIGNMENT. D.C.W.

bank rate. The rate of interest charged by a central bank on loans it makes to the banking system. Most financial institutions borrow short and lend long. This allows central banking to exert some control over financial matters by acting as a lender of last resort to the commercial banks, which permits the latter to preserve their LIQUIDITY. In the UK the bank rate was previously an announced minimum lending rate, which was above that offered on treasury bills or bonds. The present system does not have a formal announced rate, but reflects the Bank of England's desire to affect interest rates. In the US the bank rate is called the discount rate and serves a similar purpose. M.V.P.

Bantustan, see under APARTHEID.

Baptist. A member of a Protestant denomination (see PROTESTANTISM) which believes that Baptism should be confined to adults after a personal confession of faith. (Other Christian Churches [see CHRISTIANITY] allow the baptism of infants, while asking that these should be the children of Christians and should also be sponsored by godparents.) The first Baptist congregation was founded in 1609; today the denomination is worldwide. Congregations maintain their independence in many matters, and Baptists vary greatly in the conservatism or radicalism of their THEOLOGY and politics. The

'Southern' Baptists in the USA (mainly in the Southern states), and also the Baptist groups in Europe including Russia, are strongly conservative see RELIGIOUS RIGHT. For further reading: R. G. Torbet, *A History of the Baptists* (1966). D.L.E.

Barmen Declaration, see under BARTHIAN.

barrier to entry. An aspect of the structure of a market or industry that makes it difficult for a new firm to enter the industry or imposes an additional cost. Important examples are ECONOMIES OF SCALE, absolute cost advantages held by existing firms, control of the supply of inputs to production, control of retail outlets, preferences of consumers for the goods and services of existing firms, and the threat of a price war on the entry of a new firm. They are an important element of STRUCTURE-CONDUCT-PERFORMANCE THEORY, as the firms in industries with high barriers would be expected to make larger-than-average profits and, because of the lack of competitive (see COMPETITION) pressure, they may not be efficient. J.P.

Barthian. Adjective applied to a style in Christian THEOLOGY associated with Karl Barth (1886–1968), a Protestant (see PROTESTANTISM) who was a professor at Bonn and Basle (see CHRISTIANITY). Barth attempted to deduce all his doctrines from the Bible, without going so far as FUNDAMENTALISM in rejecting HIGHER CRITICISM. Disillusioned by World War I, in a commentary on St Paul's Epistle to the Romans (1919) he attacked Protestant LIBERALISM's belief that man could reach religious understanding by his own reason and develop nobly by his own power. He stressed the corruptions of sin, as did other leaders of CRISIS THEOLOGY. But on this narrower basis he built an elaborate system of DOGMATICS marked by a joyous confidence in the TRANSCENDENCE or majestic 'otherness', and in the graciousness, of the God revealed in Jesus Christ (see OTHER, THE). He extolled Jesus Christ as the 'Risen Lord' and as the one Saviour, and (unlike other CALVINISTS) maintained that God had predestined all to heaven. He took the lead in drawing up the *Barmen Declaration* (1934) against the pseudo-religious claims of NAZISM. The influence of the NEO-ORTHODOXY to which he gave eloquent expression helped many Protestants to regard the Bible as the Word of God powerfully confronting the calamities of the 1930s and 1940s. In the 1950s and 1960s his prestige among Protestant preachers was at a peak, but the influence of his theology declined because it was thought not to be sufficiently in touch with modern AGNOSTICISM. For further reading: E. Busch, *Karl Barth* (1976). D.L.E.

Bartolozzi sounds. Term derived from Bruno Bartolozzi's book *New Sounds for Woodwind* (1967), and frequently applied to new ways of playing woodwind (flute, oboe, clarinet, bassoon) which produce, among other things, chords from these traditionally melodic instruments. J.G.R.

baryon. Member of a class of ELEMENTARY PARTICLES, including the NEUTRON and the PROTON, that take part in strong interactions and possess half-integral spin. They are fermions (see QUANTUM STATISTICS). A QUANTUM NUMBER, termed *baryon number*, is assigned to each baryon taking the value +1 for baryons and −1 for their antiparticles, all other particles having zero. In all known physical interactions the total of the baryon numbers of the participating particles remains unchanged. This is called baryon conservation or conservation of baryon number. It means that protons are stable particles which do not decay. However, it is not believed that baryon number is conserved at very high energies. Theories incorporating the concept of GRAND UNIFICATION require the existence of processes in which that baryon number is not conserved. Attempts are in progress to detect the decay of protons at the very slow rates predicted. The *baryon asymmetry of the universe* refers to the observational fact that the universe is composed primarily of baryons rather than antibaryons. For further reading: P. C. W. Davies, *The Forces of Nature* (1979). J.D.B.

baryon number/baryon asymmetry of the universe, see under BARYON.

base component, see under GENERATIVE GRAMMAR.

basic communities. A translation of the Spanish *comunidades de base*, referring to groups of Christians in Latin America meeting for Bible study and other adult education and discussing their problems and possible action in the light of their faith. Many bishops of the Roman Catholic Church (see CATHOLICISM) have encouraged this widespread movement, although others are cautious, since even when a priest is present in these meetings he is not fully in charge, and even when the main emphasis is on personal spirituality, radical, possibly MARXIST, views on politics and economics tend to be expressed in response to daily experience of a society with enormous disparities between the classes. The success of the movement has been due in part to the shortage of priests in a continent where Catholic faith is still widespread, and in part to the shortage of politicians with the will and the freedom to speak for the poor. The contrast is great with previous movements such as Catholic Action which were closely controlled by the clergy (it was claimed in order to avoid controversial politics) and which tended to accept middle-class values despite the existence of some 'Christian' TRADE UNIONS. These communities have inspired, and been inspired by, LIBERATION THEOLOGY. For further reading: J. Sobrino, *The True Church of the Poor* (1985). D.L.E.

Bauhaus. A school of design, art and ARCHITECTURE based on the ideas of the WERKBUND and founded as a development of the Weimar Applied Art School in 1919. It moved to Dessau in 1925 and remained there for its most fruitful years until 1932. It was dissolved by the Nazis (see NAZISM) in 1933. From 1919 to 1928 it was headed by the architect Walter Gropius, who attempted to implement the demands, voiced in his manifesto of April 1919, for a unity of all the creative arts under the primacy of architecture, and for a reconsideration of the crafts by the artist.

Many major figures of modern art and architecture – Klee, Kandinsky, Moholy-Nagy, Schlemmer, Breuer, Hannes Meyer, Mies van der Rohe – taught at the Bauhaus, though they often disagreed, especially over the relative roles of art, TECHNOLOGY and politics (see MODERNISM). Their innovatory notions as regards form, materials and the need for teamwork became the hallmark of the INTERNATIONAL STYLE in architecture and were evident in the extremely simple geometric forms of Bauhaus-inspired industrial design. These ideas eventually, however, hardened into another academic tradition, not least because they focused too much on a formal vocabulary derived from predilection for pure geometric shapes and too little on problems of use. Something like the Bauhaus *Vorkurs*, an introductory course aimed at creating, through practical work, an awareness of the nature of materials and of simple perceptual relationships, continued to be taught at many schools of architecture and design until well into the 1960s. See also MACHINE AESTHETIC; STIJL, DE. For further reading: H. M. Wingler, *The Bauhaus* (1969). M.BR.

Bay of Pigs. A site on the north-east coast of CUBA where on 17 April 1961 approximately 1,400 Cuban exiles, organized and clandestinely supported by the CIA, attempted an invasion with the purpose of overthrowing the revolutionary regime established in 1959 by Fidel Castro (see CASTROISM). The invaders were crushed and American complicity revealed. President Kennedy's responses were publicly to accept personal responsibility for the affair and covertly to endorse other secret efforts to destabilize the Cuban regime, including plans to assassinate Castro. For further reading: P. Wyden, *Bay of Pigs* (1979). S.R.

Bayesianism. An account, based on PROBABILITY THEORY, of how to update opinion in the light of incoming evidence. Opinion is represented as the assignment of probabilities to propositions, with prior probabilities (priors) giving way to posterior probabilities in a process that is governed by Bayes' Theorem. Bayesianism is distinguished from other models of hypothesis-testing in STATISTICS and philosophy of science by its outcome: the assignment of posterior probabilities to hypotheses, rather than their acceptance or rejection (see SCIENCE, PHILOSOPHY OF). Bayesians fall into two groups. Classical (or objective) Bayesians require priors to be governed by *a priori* constraints such as the Principle of Indifference: in the absence of information to the contrary, assign equal probabilities to different possibilities. The difficulty is to state such principles without generating paradoxes. For personalist (see PERSONALISM Bayesians, the priors are legitimately subjective (see SUBJECTIVITY): OBJECTIVITY emerges in the convergence of opinion as incoming evidence 'swamps' the priors. Within philosophy of science, Bayesian methods have been criticized for the artificiality of their examples, and the implausibility of the idea that every agent is able to assign a probability to every proposition. For further reading: C. Howson and P. Urbach, *Scientific Reasoning: The Bayesian Approach* (1993). R.F.H.

beam splitter, see under NON-LINEAR OPTICS.

Beat. Term coined by the American novelist Jack Kerouac, in the reported phrase 'this is a beat generation', to denote a certain section of American society that emerged in the late 1940s and more particularly the 1950s. Kerouac, who saw the Beats as saintly beings in a pagan world, later connected the word with 'beatific' or 'beatitude' (a related pun turned the wanderers from New York to San Francisco into *Franciscans*); but others preferred the original connotations of weariness and defeat. *Beatnik* was the slightly pejorative generic term coined by an American columnist to denote the followers and hangers-on of the Beats; in time the two words, and the phrase *beat generation*, became interchangeable. Kerouac and his friends Allen Ginsberg, Neil Cassady, Gregory Corso and others between them exemplified, in a manner deliberately anti-literary, the various trends: rootlessness, rejection of the AFFLUENT SOCIETY and indeed of all social values, a predilection for modern JAZZ, resort to ill-assimilated oriental religions (e.g. ZEN) and to DRUGS, pseudo-relaxation ('coolness'), and free sexuality. (Ginsberg was later self-critical with regard to his attitude to drugs.) The phenomenon represented a sudden coalescence of INTELLECTUAL or sensitive people with the *lumpen* elements that exist in all urban societies. The spiritual fathers of the Beats were Walt Whitman and Henry Miller; mentors and spokesmen included Paul Goodman, Norman Mailer and Kenneth Rexroth (who later became disillusioned). The chief *beat poets* were Ginsberg, Corso and Lawrence Ferlinghetti; those influenced include Robert Creeley, Gary Snyder and Michael Rumaker. Other beat or beat-influenced figures include the writers William Burroughs and Alan Watts, the painter Jackson Pollock, and the jazz musician Thelonius Monk. In so far as beat literature is intelligible at all (it set out to defy intelligibility), it represents self-indulgence as a means of self-knowledge, and a hatred of injustice that was often sincere and passionate, even if its expression was immature and over-extravagant. Politically, the Beats found expression in pacifist and anti-nuclear-bomb movements. In appearance, they were distinguished by the wearing of sandals, black roll-neck sweaters, blue jeans and a straggly beard or pale make-up, and made the same type of sartorial impression upon the 1950s that was later made by the HIPPIES, who owed them numerous cultural and behavioural debts. For further reading: J. Kerouac, *On the Road* (1958). P.S.L.; M.S.-S.

beatnik, see under BEAT.

beaux arts. In architecture, a term used to describe a form of rigid, highly composed and usually symmetrical design based on classical architecture and academic in character. It is associated with the teaching of the École des Beaux Arts in Paris, and hence (since that school, founded in 1671, has been in frequent opposition to contemporary trends) often used pejoratively. M.BR.

bebop. Originally just one of the casual store of JAZZ vocal phrases used onomatopoeically to suggest the character of a melody, by the early 1940s bebop had become a code word (also known as rebop and later shortened to bop) for the revolutionary jazz form that overthrew the kingdom of SWING. Compared to earlier jazz, its rhythms were subtler and more complex, its solo lines longer, its harmonic sequences unprecedentedly challenging. The talent of its leading players – the alto saxophonist Charlie 'Bird' Parker and the trumpeter Dizzy Gillespie were regarded as co-principals – was undeniable, and their new orientation made customary jazz practice *passé* overnight. Older musicians were bemused; some opponents of bebop counter-attacked with the deliberately archaic style known as TRAD. The general public found bop tantalizingly abstruse, and the personal eccentricities of its leading players gave the movement a certain cult status, which subsequently inspired subcultures like the BEAT generation. The music itself has unquestionably remained the basic language of modern jazz. GE.S.

behaviour modification, see under BEHAVIOUR THERAPY.

behaviour therapy. In PSYCHIATRY, the treatment of behavioural disorders by a group of procedures based mainly on learning theory and BEHAVIOURISM. The principles derive from the experimental work of Pavlov (see PAVLOVIAN), Watson, Hull, Skinner and other experimental psychologists. The procedures, which are used increasingly often, include *desensitization*, an effective treatment for PHOBIAS, the principle being for the patient to re-enter the feared situation gradually and repeatedly, while ANXIETY is neutralized by relaxation; the contrasted (and less widely used) *aversion therapy*, in which an unpleasant stimulus is repeatedly coupled with an undesired behaviour in order to eliminate the latter; and OPERANT CONDITIONING. Behaviour therapy differs from traditional PSYCHOTHERAPY in not drawing on PSYCHODYNAMIC theory such as Freud's, and in putting more emphasis on changing outward behaviour than on subjective factors. The two approaches are, however, not conflicting but complementary.

The term *behaviour modification*, though used in many ways and often loosely, has two main applications. First, it is sometimes used synonymously with behaviour therapy as defined above. Second, it may be applied in a more restricted sense to B. F. Skinner's techniques of treating disorders of behaviour by operant conditioning, in which rewards are made contingent upon the subject's own behaviour. The latter methods are, for example, sometimes used to enhance the social behaviour of withdrawn schizophrenic patients (see SCHIZOPHRENIA) or the mentally handicapped (see MENTAL RETARDATION). Relaxation forms one therapeutic technique. Another is *aversion therapy*, based upon the association of an unpleasant stimulus used as a conditioning mechanism. This has been extensively used in dealing with sexual offenders, alcoholics and other difficult cases. In ALCOHOLISM, e.g., vomit-inducing drugs such as apomorphine have been injected at the same time as alcohol is taken, in order to produce associations of nausea. Early hopes for aversion therapy have not been fulfilled. When applied to the modification of total social systems this approach is sometimes called SOCIAL BEHAVIOURISM. For further reading: G. L. Thorpe, *Behavior Therapy* (1997). D.H.G.; R.P.

behavioural engineering, see under SOCIAL ENGINEERING.

behavioural sciences. Those sciences which study the behaviour of men and animals, e.g. PSYCHOLOGY and the SOCIAL SCIENCES (including social ANTHROPOLOGY). Some practitioners of these sciences believe that it is unscientific to study mental processes and other phenomena which are not directly observable and measurable, and they therefore concentrate on the attempt to describe and explain *outward manifestations* of such phenomena, namely observable behaviour (like pressing buttons, eating, running through mazes, making noises) and the relations of such behaviour to external stimuli. The attempt to study men and animals on the basis that they do not have minds, but only patterns of behaviour, is called the *behavioural approach*, or sometimes BEHAVIOURISM. Behaviourism contrasts with MENTALISM. For further reading: B. F. Skinner, *Verbal Behavior* (1957). A.S.

behaviourism.

(1) The SCHOOL OF PSYCHOLOGY (in R. S. Woodworth's classification one of the six main such) that studies only unambiguously observable, and preferably measurable, behaviour. It leaves out of account CONSCIOUSNESS and introspection, and its theoretical frames of reference avoid subjective notions such as 'imaging' or 'focus of attention'. In Russia it was closely identified with PHYSIOLOGY and 'reflexes of the brain' as studied by, notably, Ivan Pavlov (see PAVLOVIAN). In America it was launched in 1913 by J. B. Watson, and was represented at its distinctive best by Clark Hull and B. F. Skinner (see also SOCIAL BEHAVIOURISM and, for an opposed view, MENTALISM). American behaviourism attracted, from the start, psychologists with certain kinds of interests, and the word *behaviouristic* came,

by association, to refer to these interests, notably environmental control of behaviour under laboratory conditions which force the 'subject' into a rather passive role with limited freedom of choice (see FREE WILL; DETERMINISM); conditioned-response techniques (see CONDITIONED REFLEX); laboratory learning in animals such as rats and pigeons; elementaristic theory involving stimuli, responses and their objective interrelations (see OPERANT CONDITIONING). This cluster of interests is typically criticized as an elegant but superficial pursuit of trivial problems couched in arid language and too artificial to have relevance for 'real life' problems of either animals or people. Behaviourists typically counter by pointing to the objectivity of their work and stressing that it is only the start of a vastly ambitious enterprise that promises to yield completely general laws of behaviour. Whatever the eventual verdict of history, the deliberate study of objective behaviour has made great strides, and even the 'behaviouristic' approach has contributed much to mainstream PSYCHOLOGY by way of factual discoveries, new ideas and new methods of enquiry, as well as techniques in BEHAVIOUR THERAPY. For further reading: B. F. Skinner, *Beyond Freedom and Dignity* (1971).

I.M.L.H.

(2) In PHILOSOPHY, the view that mental states are nothing but dispositions to engage in certain sorts of behaviour in certain kinds of circumstances. Its leading exponent was Gilbert Ryle (*The Concept of Mind*, 1949). A behaviourist might hold, for instance, that the BELIEF that toadstools are inedible is just a disposition to avoid eating toadstools when one encounters them. The problem with this is that even someone who believes that toadstools are inedible may nonetheless eat them if, for example, he desires to do himself harm. There is no distinctive behaviour which someone who holds such a belief is typically disposed to exhibit. Rather, how someone with a given belief behaves in given circumstances depends in part upon what other mental states that person possesses. Behaviourism, born of a suspicion that the privacy of mental states makes them illicit objects of reference, has now given way to FUNCTIONALISM, which identifies mental states in terms of the causal roles they play in the genesis of behaviour. The demise of philosophical behaviourism has more or less coincided with that of behaviourism as a methodological principle (see METHODOLOGY) in empirical psychology, maintaining that psychology, as an empirical science, should avoid appeal to introspective claims about subjective mental states and study instead publicly observable relationships between environmental stimuli and the behavioural responses of ORGANISMS (see SUBJECTIVITY).

E.J.L.

Being. The fundamental category of EXISTENTIALIST thought. It was Søren Kierkegaard (1813–55), in his struggle to defeat Hegelian abstraction, who first existentialized the notion of human Being, giving a full description of its various possible modes. In early 20th-century thought, with Heidegger, Jaspers, Marcel, Unamuno, and later Sartre, Camus and Merleau-Ponty, the concept of Being was given full existential status. It is the fundamental term in Heidegger's *Being and Time* (1927). Being is more original and fundamental than any series of actually existing beings or objects, and is the ontologically guaranteeing condition for these (see ONTOLOGY). It precedes its various modes of appearance, and thus takes on a quasi-mystical status. Heidegger's presentation of Being has been enormously influential in PHENOMENOLOGY, PSYCHIATRY and HERMENEUTICS, particularly in the work of Hans-Georg Gadamer. Human Being in Heidegger, called *Dasein*, is subsidiary to Being. In Sartre's *Being and Nothingness* (1943) Being is described phenomenologically in three modes, Being-in-Itself, Being-for-Itself and Being-for-Others. These correspond very roughly to brute material existence, without consciousness; self-consciousness set over against the world of brute material existence, yet divided and split in itself and unable fully to coincide with its Being-in-Itself; and a consciousness in the subject that he takes part in, modifies and partly creates the lived existential projects of other people. In this shared world of inauthentic complicity (see AUTHENTICITY), Sartre gives many of his famous examples of love and hate, MASOCHISM and SADISM, in their struggle to establish dominance over the Being-for-Itself of the OTHER. In its Sartrian form, this struggle between CONSCIOUSNESS and world is visibly part of the traditional problematic of Descartes and forms a continuation of it, until the power of the alternative tradition of thought, Hegelian-MARXIST, pulls it under and destroys it. For further reading: S. Kierkegaard, *Either/Or* (1944); M. Heidegger, *Being and Time* (1962); J.-P. Sartre, *Being and Nothingness* (1957). R.PO.

belief. The acknowledgement that a proposition is true (see TRUTH) in the absence of demonstrable PROOF as required by SCIENTIFIC METHOD. Belief is often religious (see RELIGION), as in belief in GOD, MIRACLES or other supernatural phenomena. Belief (or disbelief) is often used to contest what has been demonstrated as true by some authoritative body or process, i.e. many people believe that O. J. SIMPSON is guilty of two murders despite having been found not guilty by a jury. Belief is a popular phenomenon that has historically dogged knowledge (see EPISTEMOLOGY; SOCIOLOGY). Historically, belief can be a stage in the genesis of a particular piece of knowledge, where belief has waited for a METHODOLOGY of adequate sophistication to valorize it as knowledge (i.e. many hypotheses can be classified as beliefs prior to proof). In some CULTURES, beliefs can present themselves systematically so that they constitute a coherent and organizing force. Requiring beliefs to meet standards of truth may cause an observer to overlook defining aspects of the culture or individual being studied. See DESIRE and RATIONALITY. S.T.

bell curve, see under RACE.

Bell's theorem. A mathematical theorem proved by John Bell in 1964. It places constraints upon the interpretations of quantum mechanical reality (see QUANTUM MECHANICS). It shows that no matter what steps are taken to replace the uncertainty of QUANTUM THEORY by hidden deterministic variables the resulting theory must always contain non-local (that is, non-causal) elements. These non-causal elements cannot be employed for faster-than-light transmission of information. Bell's theorem applies to all interpretations of quantum mechanics except for the MANY WORLDS HYPOTHESIS. The theorem results in the deduction of a quantity that must be measured positive if a theory of the quantum world is to be local and causal. Quantum mechanics results in a negative value. These results have been demonstrated in a famous series of experiments performed by Alain Aspect and collaborators (see COPENHAGEN INTERPRETATION). For further reading: J. A. Wheeler and W. Zurek (eds), *Quantum Theory and Measurement* (1983). J.D.B.

Benesh system, see under CHOREOLOGY.

Berlin blockade/airlift. After World War II, jurisdiction of the city of Berlin was divided into sectors under the control of the USA, UK, France and the USSR. In March 1948 the Western Allied powers decided to unite their sectors in a single economic entity. The currency would be the Deutschmark, newly launched with American backing. The Soviets viewed the Deutschmark as a threat to the East German currency. On the day it was introduced, they mounted a blockade which cut Berlin off from all communications with the West. It was a key move in the developing COLD WAR.

The USA and UK responded by organizing an airlift of essential supplies. Over a period of 11 months, Allied planes flew into Berlin, and left carrying German industrial exports to help bolster her economy. The Western Allies prepared for war against the Soviet Union, but the threat did not materialize. The Allies were successful in interfering with East German communications, and placed an embargo on their exports. These measures brought an end to the blockade. See also BERLIN WALL. S.T.

Berlin Wall. After Germany's defeat in 1945, no other part of the divided country was more affected by the strained relations between the Soviet Union and the Western Allies than Berlin. A divided city, deep in the Soviet zone of occupation, with token forces from the three other powers, its population was inevitably involved in the manoeuvres between them. The introduction of the new Deutschmark on 29 June 1948 led to the crisis known as the BERLIN BLOCKADE/AIRLIFT, one of the first confrontations of the COLD WAR.

Eleven months later the Russians abandoned this blockade, and both sides moved to set up separate states, the Federal Republic in the West and, five months later, the German Democratic Republic in the East. The future of Berlin, however, remained unresolved.

After Soviet tanks suppressed a workers' strike by force in 1953, disillusionment with the COMMUNIST regime led 1.5 million people in the next eight years to take advantage of the open frontier between East and West Berlin and 'vote with their feet'. The growing stream of emigrants forced the Communist government to build a fortified concrete wall to seal off East Berlin.

The Berlin Wall lasted for 28 years with the contrast between Berlin East and Berlin West growing steadily. What transformed the situation was radical changes in the Soviet Union itself, where Mikhail Gorbachev came to power in 1985, urging the countries of the Eastern Bloc to find their own solutions to their economic and political problems and withdrawing the Soviet armed forces which had effectively blocked changes. In the autumn of 1989 an irresistible wave of revolution swept across the countries of the Soviet bloc, including the GDR (East Germany) as well as Poland and Czechoslovakia. On 9 November restrictions on travel between East and West Germany were removed; huge crowds swarmed over the Wall and started to pull it to pieces in a wild night of celebration.

The rushed process by which the unification of the two Germanies was carried out has come in for bitter criticism from the people of the former East Germany, but it was completed by 3 October 1990, with a united Germany once again, no Berlin Wall, a larger population than any other European nation, and the once-ruined Berlin as its capital. See also GERMAN REUNIFICATION. For further reading: A. Tusa, *The Last Division: Berlin and the Wall* (1996). A.L.C.B.

***béton brut*,** see under CONCRETE.

Beuron. Influential school of religious painting at the South German Benedictine abbey of that name. It was founded by Didier (Fr Desiderius) Lenz with the aim of evolving an art comparable with plain-song and based on a canon of sacred measurements inspired by those of ancient Egypt. Its principal work was the decoration, 1877–1910, of the mother abbey at Monte Cassino in Italy. Through Denis and Sérusier of the NABIS, the school helped form French ART SACRÉ, while other mystically inclined artists in touch with it include Émile Bernard of PONT-AVEN, Alexei Jawlensky of the NEUE KÜNSTLERVEREINIGUNG, and the BAUHAUS master Johannes Itten. J.W.

Bhopal. In December 1984 the night-time leak of a toxic gas from a tank at a Union Carbide pesticide manufacturing facility in Bhopal, India, resulted in the world's worst industrial disaster. Over 4,000 people were killed, and tens of thousands injured. An International Medical Commission visited Bhopal in 1994 and concluded that as many as 50,000 survivors had permanent disabilities.

The gas was methyl-isocyanate, used in the manufacture of the PESTICIDE Carbaryl (also known as Sevin). The event provoked a storm of protest and litigation. Union Carbide claimed that a disgruntled employee caused the leak but this was never substantiated. Although Union Carbide withdrew from India and paid a fine and some restitution, many felt that the Indian government was not demanding enough in its claims against the company. See also EXXON VALDEZ. W.G.R.

biased galaxy formation, see under BIASING.

biasing (or **biased galaxy formation**). Name given to the theory that the distribution of luminous galaxies (see GALAXY) in the universe is not representative of mass in the universe (see DARK MATTER). It is sometimes used to describe a mechanism which might give rise to such a state of affairs, most notably the possibility that galaxy formation can only occur in regions of the universe where the density of matter exceeds some critical level. This process could give rise to VOIDS in space. J.D.B.

Bible Belt. Term coined in 1925 by the American humorist H. L. Mencken to designate the southern and rural midwestern parts of the US, in which FUNDAMENTALISTS who believed in the literal accuracy of the Bible attempted to impose their values on public life. Over time the term has kept its directly religious connotations, as these areas provide much of the support for the RELIGIOUS RIGHT, but it is also more generally used to evoke images of their resistance to most modern cultural, social and moral forms associated with more liberal (see LIBERALISM) and secular values. S.R.

biblical criticism. The application of a family of modern critical methods to the study of the Jewish and Christian scriptures. In the course of the past two centuries, biblical critics have appropriated a series of methods used in the analysis of non-biblical texts, and developed a few of their own, in the interests of establishing the various stages of the development of a text, its historical reliability, its original meaning, and so on. In consequence, the study of the Bible now involves techniques such as TEXTUAL CRITICISM, source criticism, tradition criticism, form criticism and redaction criticism, which are sometimes described collectively as 'historical criticism', as their aim is to recover the past. The hegemony of the historical-critical approach has been forcefully challenged by many developments in the theory and practice of interpretation (see HERMENEUTICS), and in particular by the proliferation of new modes of reading generated by contextual theologies. For further reading: S. Prickett, *Reading the Text: Biblical Criticism and Literary Theory* (1940). C.C.

biblical theology. The attempt of BARTHIAN and other 20th-century theologians (see THEOLOGY) to develop Christian doctrine afresh by studying the Bible instead of relying on DOGMAS. The movement has produced much enthusiasm among Roman Catholics (see CATHOLICISM), and the decrees of VATICAN COUNCIL II appealed to the Bible more than to tradition. Biblical theology is opposed both to FUNDAMENTALISM (because it accepts the HIGHER CRITICISM of the Bible) and to religious LIBERALISM (because it denies the ability of modern man to reach religious truth without learning humbly from God's self-revelation in the events and teachings recorded in the Bible). Because of the desire to understand the Old and New Testaments without importing modern ideas, special attention is paid to the original meaning of biblical words in Hebrew or Greek. The main criticism of this movement has concerned its tendency to exaggerate the unity of the Bible. For further reading: G. B. Caird, *The Language and Imagery of the Bible* (1980). D.L.E.

bidialectalism (bidialectism). In SOCIOLINGUISTICS, the ability to use two dialects of a language, and thus any educational policy which recognizes the need to develop this ability in children. The notion emerges most commonly in relation to the teaching of non-standard alongside standard English, especially in relation to the abilities of different ethnic groups. D.C.

big band. As standardized during the SWING era, an orchestra of about 15 musicians divided into brass, reed and rhythm sections, playing arranged JAZZ and popular music for dancing. The genre was jazz-inspired, with most groups utilizing the 'call and response' interplay pioneered by black bandleader Fletcher Henderson, in which brass and reeds tossed rhythmic phrases ('riffs') back and forth in an atmosphere of mounting excitement. The bands' actual jazz content varied widely, from the syncopated flavouring of Glenn Miller to the unalloyed masterpieces of Duke Ellington and Count Basie. Though the contrast was not absolute, Ellington and Basie illustrate the poles of big-band jazz, the former favouring sophisticated, polychrome arrangements, the latter loose frameworks for soloists known as 'head arrangements' because they were never written down. Musically their groups made the most enduring contributions in the form, though white bandleaders like Miller, Benny Goodman, Artie Shaw and Tommy Dorsey claimed the lion's share of popularity. GE.S.

big bang theory. A mathematical theory describing the present and past structure of the astronomical universe. The term was coined by Sir Fred Hoyle in a BBC radio broadcast in 1950. It captures the fact that the universe is observed to be expanding; that is, distant clusters of GALAXIES are receding away from each other with a speed that is proportional to their separations (a trend known as Hubble's Law). If this expansion is traced backwards in time, it suggests that the expansion began at a finite time (about 13 billion years) in the past from a state of infinite density and temperature. However, the mathematical theory (Einstein's theory of general RELATIVITY) which is used successfully to describe the expansion of the universe predicts that it must break down and be superseded by a new quantum cosmological theory before this apparent initial state is reached (see COS-

MOLOGY). It is unknown whether the universe began at a finite time in the past. Sometimes the term 'big bang' is used more specifically to describe that hypothetical starting state of infinite density (also known as the 'initial singularity'). More commonly the term is used by astronomers to characterize any theoretical picture of the universe in which it expands from a past state of great density and temperature.

During the period 1948–64, the STEADY-STATE HYPOTHESIS of the universe offered an alternative cosmological picture, in which matter was continually created and the universe would have no beginning or end but always presented the same average appearance. This theory was a rival to the big bang theory during this period and was usually contrasted with it. Hoyle invented the term 'big bang theory' as a pejorative description of the rival to his steady-state theory. The steady-state theory has been decisively disproved by the discovery of the relic RADIATION and the associated nuclear reaction products expected to be left over from the first few minutes of the universe's expansion, with the values predicted by the big bang theory. The INFLATIONARY UNIVERSE THEORY, developed by the American physicist Alan Guth, is a modification to the rate of expansion of the universe that endows the present-day universe with a number of its observed properties. It is also a big bang theory in the sense of espousing an expanding universe that had a hot, dense past, but which did not necessarily begin at a finite moment in the past. For further reading: J. D. Barrow, *The Origin of the Universe* (1994). J.D.B.

Big Brother, see under ORWELLIAN.

big science. An expression coined by Derek de Solla Price in *Little Science, Big Science* (1963) for the changes that science underwent once the successful US atomic bomb project became the exemplar for organized research. Since then, investment in equipment and personnel has been the prime determinant of scientific productivity, as would be expected of an industrial enterprise. While granting the possibly pathological consequences of this tendency (e.g. to think 'more = better' science), Price believed that big science would ultimately experience diminishing returns (see DIMINISHING PRODUCTIVITY OF A FACTOR; SCIENCE, ECONOMICS OF). Reduced funding for high-energy PHYSICS would vindicate Price, if the money saved were not often shifted to the more popular big science of MOLECULAR BIOLOGY. Moreover, it is easy to forget that the first big science projects were actually launched in Germany in the 1890s via the Kaiser Wilhelm Gesellschaften (now known as the Max Planck Institutes), which were modelled on the combination of state, industrial and academic investments that made the 19th century the Golden Age of chemistry. S.F.

bilateral/cognatic descent. Tracing of DESCENT from an ancestor through both male and female lines. An individual is a member of as many groups as ancestors through whom descent is traced. Bilateral descent is most commonly found in western Europe. The formation of the unilineal descent group is impossible in bilateral societies as an individual is a member of several different groups at one time. Bilateral descent groups may be established on the basis of residence, for example, but they are not exclusive and rarely permanent. If tied to property, bilateral descent groups may develop PATRILINEAL features which ensure that property is transmitted through a single line and is not therefore dispersed, or place emphasis upon endogamous marriage (see ENDOGAMY). For further reading: J. Goody, *The Development of the Family and Marriage in Europe* (1983). A.G.

bilateralism and **multilateralism.**

(1) Bilateralism denotes international trade without discrimination between two countries, though trade with the rest of the world may involve discrimination. It contrasts with multilateralism, which is international trade without discrimination between three or more countries. The *most favoured nation clause* in international trade agreements, which is Article 1 of GATT, requires that any tariff concession made by one member country to another must immediately be given to all other members, and so is essentially multilateral. Multilateralism requires the convertibility of currencies and, thus, a country does not have to balance its payments with each country it trades with (see BALANCE OF PAYMENTS).

(2) The meaning of bilateral has changed

over time and now refers to trade between two countries and, in particular, where trade agreements have been negotiated. For example, a number of south-east Asian countries often tie the decision to import a good to the supplier's acceptance of the country's exports as payment in kind.

(3) Aid is termed bilateral or multilateral depending on whether it is given by a donor directly to a country or through an international agency. M.FG.S.; J.P.

Bildungsroman. German term, literally 'formation-novel', for the type of novel in which the (generally youthful) hero is seen developing through exposure to life; his story is often accompanied by an account of the forms of contemporary society. Variant terms are *Erziehungsroman* ('education novel') and *Entwicklungsroman* ('development novel'). The genre is held to originate with Goethe's *Wilhelm Meister's Apprenticeship* (1775) and includes Novalis's *Heinrich von Ofterdingen* (1799), Gottfried Keller's *Green Henry* (1855), Hermann Hesse's *Demian* (1919), and Thomas Mann's *The Magic Mountain* (1924). The British are less given to classification but, with varying degrees of appropriateness, Fielding's *Tom Jones* (1749), Jane Austen's *Emma* (1816), Dickens's *David Copperfield* (1849–50), Samuel Butler's *The Way of All Flesh* (1903) and James Joyce's *A Portrait of the Artist as a Young Man* (1914–15) could be ascribed to this genre, though the Germans would rather consider the last named a *Künstlerroman* ('artist-novel'). D.J.E.

bilingualism. Bilingualism refers to languages in contact, whether in society (societal bilingualism) or in the individual (bilinguality). Societal bilingualism does not necessarily imply that all members are bilingual, as is the case when the languages are territorially separated (Belgium, Switzerland, Quebec *v.* rest of Canada). Bilingualism is a worldwide phenomenon, since an estimated 5,000 languages are used in fewer than 200 STATES and a majority of the world's population know more than one language. In multilingual communities a range, or repertoire, of languages is available to speakers who use all or only some of them to perform a variety of social roles. The different languages do not have equal status: their relative importance depends upon the POWER relations holding between the groups that use them. In order to ensure efficient national and international communication the dominant group will impose one official language through language planning. This need not be an indigenous language, as in former colonized countries where the colonizer's language has been adopted (English, French, Spanish in Africa, Asia and America). If two or more languages coexist in the same speech community, each with a complementary range of functions, we have a situation of diglossic bilingualism, one language being usually reserved for daily spoken communication, the other for formal (e.g. written) uses. A presumed link has been found between multilingualism and UNDERDEVELOPMENT, but this is because many THIRD WORLD countries are former colonies whose borders were artificially drawn up without regard for linguistic boundaries. It is noteworthy that the languages adopted as official languages in multilingual states have high communicativity, that is, they often serve as lingua francas (China's Putonghua, Malaysia's and Indonesia's Standard Malay, Tanzania's Swahili); moreover, many of today's more dynamic countries and cities are multilingual (Canada, Australia, Hong Kong, Singapore, New York). In any case, where many languages are used, people learn each other's languages: in other words, individual bilingualism compensates for linguistic diversity.

Individual bilingualism (bilinguality) has been defined as 'the psychological state of the individual who has access to more than one linguistic code'. This access varies along a number of dimensions, such as relative competence in each of the languages (balanced bilinguality refers to an equal development in both); age and context of acquisition; presence or absence of the languages in the community; relative status of the languages. If both languages are highly valued the child will derive maximum benefit from the bilingual experience, with a secure cultural identity and enhanced linguistic and cognitive development (additive bilinguality). In the case of minority linguistic groups (e.g. immigrants), whose first language is usually devalued, development may be delayed or impaired (subtractive bilinguality). To turn a subtractive into a neutral or additive bilinguality, it is necessary to value the first language and develop it for cognitive functions. This has profound implications for bilingual education. For further reading: J. F. Hamers and M. Blanc, *Bilinguality and Bilingualism* (1989). M.H.A.B.

bill of rights. A formal declaration of civil or NATURAL RIGHTS. A bill of rights may be constitutional, legal or purely political. In the US, the first 10 amendments to the constitution form a bill of rights which is both legal and constitutional. It guarantees such rights as freedom of speech and religion. The 'Bill of Rights' in the UK, however, is purely legal. It can therefore be amended more readily. Other bills of rights, like the UN Declaration of HUMAN RIGHTS, may be purely political if they cannot be enforced by judicial proceedings. M.S.P.

binary nerve gases. Conventional nerve gases, like those developed by German scientists during World War II, are stored in liquid form, which often vaporizes on contact with the atmosphere. Any spillage or accidental discharge is highly toxic. This has meant that the chemical agents are stored under secure conditions, and sometimes far from the battle front, to minimize the danger of unintentional discharge. Binary gases operate on a different principle. They consist of two chemicals which are inert until mixed. Consequently, they are 'safe' weapons, from the user's point of view. The development of binary weapon has revolutionized the possible uses for nerve gas. They are ideally suited for dispersal by gas shells, bombs or even mines. Even gas hand grenades are a practical proposition. Indeed, the many potential uses of binary weapons have given impetus to negotiations for the control and possible abolition of biological weapons. However, because each part of a binary weapon can be manufactured in different locations, the problem of verification of any agreement becomes more difficult. A.J.M.W.

binary pulsar, see under PULSAR.

binary scale. A method of writing numbers (see NUMBER) based on powers of 2, just as our normal method is based on 10, where 298 means $2 \times 10^2 + 9 \times 10^1 + 8$. In decimal notation we use the digits 0 to 9, so in binary we use 0 to 1: this is what makes it so useful in computers, radio and electronic data transmission (see INFORMATION THEORY) – we only need two different signals (for 0 and 1) which could even be ON and OFF in a simple circuit.

Here 11011 means $1 \times 2^4 + 1 \times 2^3 + 0 \times 2^2 + 1 \times 2^1 + 1$ (the total in this case is 27) and binary numbers get very long quite easily. N.A.R.

binary star. One of a pair of stars held together by GRAVITATION, and revolving about their common centre of gravity. Such pairs are very common: about one-third of all stars occur in binaries. M.V.B.

binding. An approach developed in GENERATIVE GRAMMAR of the late 1970s which focuses on the conditions which formally relate, or 'bind', elements of a sentence together. The binding relationships obtain within certain structures, known as 'governing categories' (such as a noun phrase, or a sentence), and the approach as a whole is thus often referred to as the theory of 'government and binding'. D.C.

binding energy. The ENERGY which must be added to an atomic NUCLEUS to break the bonds between its component NUCLEONS, analogous to the energy needed to separate two pieces of wood which have previously been glued together. This energy is released during nuclear FUSION. M.V.B.

biochemistry. The CHEMISTRY of living matter. The older biochemistry was largely compositional in its interests, concerned with the chemical composition of the principal ingredients of the body – PROTEINS, carbohydrates and fats – and with the composition of the body's material input and output. The new biochemistry is above all else a chemistry of bodily processes, i.e. the chemistry of metabolism at both the bodily and cellular level (see CELL). See also BIOPHYSICS. P.M.

bioclimatology. The study of the relationships between the climate, life and health of man. One of its principal objects is to determine the range of climatic conditions most favourable to human habitation and to define the areas where such climates exist. M.L.

bio-cybernetics, see under CYBERNETICS.

biodegradable. This term refers to substances which can be broken down by biological processes such as bacterial action (see BACTERIOLOGY). The decay of leaf litter and logs on the forest floor is perhaps the most conspicuous example of this. Bacteria and fungi in the soil secrete ENZYMES which convert the cellulose, PROTEIN and other complex organic MOLECULES into their simpler components, thereby serving as a source of energy and nutrients for these ORGANISMS.

Whereas nature has evolved enzymes to degrade biological materials, many synthetic molecules are resistant to enzymatic attack. Such materials, including most plastics and synthetic fibres, are thus relatively immune to biological breakdown and are termed non-biodegradable. Synthetic materials may be broken down slowly by purely physical processes such as ultraviolet irradiation or acid hydrolysis, but they persist in the environment much longer than do biodegradable materials and thereby contribute significantly to solid waste disposal and other problems. Incineration may be precluded because their combustion products are often toxic. W.G.R.

biodiversity. The term is a contraction of 'biological diversity' and refers to the vast variety of ORGANISMS, and communities of organisms, that constitute the BIOSPHERE. This diversity of life forms is most frequently thought of in terms of the number of SPECIES that have been described (about 3.5 million), or the total number of species in existence (estimated at 5–50 million). The number of species is but one of three levels of biological organization at which biodiversity is manifest, the others being genetic diversity and ecological diversity (see GENETICS/GENOMICS; ECOLOGY). Genetic diversity refers to the heritable differences between individuals belonging to the same species. The many different associations or communities of organisms (ecosystems) are the expression of biodiversity at the ecological level.

The term biodiversity emerged at the 1986 National Forum on BioDiversity in Washington D.C., co-sponsored by the US National Academy of Sciences and the Smithsonian Institution. Together, the Forum and the published papers (a volume entitled *Biodiversity*) put the term and the concept into the language and onto the priority list of global environmental concerns.

The overall importance of biodiversity, and the rationale for its protection, has several components, with little consensus about their relative importance. Instrumental or economic values include known or potential sources of foods, fuels, raw materials and medicines. While the relationship between the amount of biodiversity of an ECOSYSTEM and its stability is not well understood, it appears that more biodiverse systems are generally more stable and resistant to environmental stress.

Many argue that biodiversity has an aesthetic value, and should be preserved and protected for its contribution to the quality of human life. Another perspective is moral or religious, whereby the human species is seen as the steward of biodiversity, which is GOD's creation. W.G.R.

bio-energetics, see under REICHIAN.

bio-engineering. A scientific or paramedical discipline concerned with:

(1) the devising of mechanical substitutes for parts or organs of the body, e.g. the artificial kidney, in which the patient's blood is conducted through thin wall tubing immersed in a blood-like fluid, thus making possible a process of filtration analogous to that which occurs in the kidneys;

(2) the designing of artificial limbs and other such artificial devices;

(3) the analysis of bodily structure and function along engineering or physical lines, whether structurally (as in evaluating the mechanical properties of bone) or functionally (as in thermodynamic calculations relating to the body). See also BIONICS. P.M.

bioethics. The branch of ETHICS that addresses questions of value and behaviour relating to BIOLOGY. Problems in medical bioethics include life prolongation and EUTHANASIA, organ transplantation, psychoactive drug use, the use of animals in biomedical research, and CONTRACEPTION and ABORTION. Of increasing prominence as areas of bioethical concern are environmental problems such as resource depletion and conservation of natural resources, and the relation between lifestyle and environmental protection, global population growth (see POPULATION PRESSURE) and sustainability. W.G.R.

biofeedback. Therapeutic technique used to provide the patient with some *visual* or auditory feedback to an internal or external physiological process. The patient is usually attached to a machine that will monitor and signal in some way changes in skin resistance, finger temperature, muscle contractility or brain-wave activity. It is used most commonly in the treatment of migraine, where there appears to be an association with peripheral constriction of the blood vessels, affecting skin temperature, and the onset of an attack of migraine. The fingers are attached to a thermometer which is seen by the patient. The patient is taught breathing and relaxation techniques, or some form of autogenic training, which induces a reduction in the constriction of the muscles around the blood vessels. This induced state of relaxation, both of the voluntary and involuntary muscles, has been shown both to prevent and reduce an attack of migraine. Biofeedback has been used for pain-control, reduction of general ANXIETY states and PHOBIAS and hypertension. P.C.P.

biogenesis. The law of biogenesis – *omne vivum ex vivo* – states that all living things are descended from previously existing living things, i.e. that no such phenomenon as 'spontaneous generation' occurs. Not only living CELLS, but also some of their constituents like mitochondria (see CYTOLOGY), are biogenetic in character; thus no mitochondrion is formed except from a precursor mitochondrion. Louis Pasteur's famous experiments may be said to have disproved the notion of spontaneous generation by showing that bacterial contamination of a sterilized nutrient fluid would only occur if it was re-exposed to air. Claims made for spontaneous generation are now attributed to an innocent form of self-deception, perhaps especially to the confusion created by 'myelin forms' which sometimes simulate amoeboid movement quite closely. P.M.

biogeochemical cycles. Unlike radiant energy, which is constantly entering the biosphere from the sun, the chemical elements essential for life must be continually recycled between living ORGANISMS and the environment. Thus carbon, the basic constituent of all living things, is drawn from the reservoir of carbon dioxide in the atmosphere and dissolved in the earth's waters. The carbon is 'fixed' as organic matter by solar energy driving PHOTOSYNTHESIS, and released back into the environment by respiration, which releases the stored energy for life processes. Non-photosynthesizing organisms such as bacteria (see BACTERIOLOGY) and fungi derive their energy from the breakdown of dead organic matter. The burning of fossil fuels also releases fixed carbon back to the atmosphere.

Nitrogen, the second-most abundant chemical constituent of living organisms and a component of amino acids, PROTEINS and numerous other CELL constituents, cycles through the BIOSPHERE along complex pathways. The nitrogen reservoir is the atmosphere, 80 per cent of which consists of the diatomic and relatively unreactive molecule N2. This molecule is converted by lightning or by the action of nitrogen-fixing bacteria into nitrate, NO2, a form that can be used by plants to make amino acids and other nitrogen-containing MOLECULES essential to living organisms. The cycle is completed by denitrifying bacteria which release molecular nitrogen back to the atmosphere.

Water, essential for life, moves between the vapour, liquid and solid states – condensing from the atmosphere and evaporating back into it, freezing and melting, in a *hydrologic cycle*. Plants act like wicks, constantly absorbing water from the soil and evaporating it into the atmosphere. Over the tropical rainforests this process, transpiration, is a significant factor in the hydrologic cycle, and deforestation therefore perturbs weather patterns. W.G.R.

biogeography. The study of global patterns in the distribution of SPECIES. Such patterns were recognized as long ago as the time of Aristotle, who distinguished boreal, temperate and tropical life zones. From the late 19th century into more recent times the distributional patterns have been refined and elaborated to currently include the concept of *biotic provinces*, each of which is a region populated by a characteristic set of taxa (taxonomic groups of species, genera, families), isolated from other provinces by geographical barriers such as mountain ranges and oceans.

The geographical isolation, a consequence of movement of the earth's crust in a geological time frame (see GEOGRAPHY; PALAEONTOLOGY), results in the EVOLUTION of distinctive groups of ORGANISMS characteristic of similar ecological niches (see ECOLOGY) in each province. Divergent evolution results in the mammals of each realm being more closely related to each other than to those in other realms. W.G.R.

bioinorganic chemistry. The study of the role of inorganic ELEMENTS (primarily metals) in BIOLOGY. Many metals, such as sodium, potassium, calcium, iron and magnesium, are essential for life. Some act as carriers of electrical signals – sodium, potassium and calcium, for instance, are responsible for nerve impulses – and many others carry out particular chemical functions within PROTEIN molecules, such as CATALYSIS and the binding of small MOLECULES. Iron binds oxygen in haemoglobin, and magnesium sits at the heart of the light-harvesting centre of CHLOROPHYLL. A major part of bioinorganic chemistry involves the study of these metals in proteins and other biomolecules. Another strand of the discipline focuses on synthetic compounds containing metals and other inorganic elements that interact with biomolecules in useful ways – for example, acting as probes or drugs. P.C.B.

biolinguistics (or **biological linguistics**). A developing branch of LINGUISTICS which studies the biological preconditions for language development and use in man. For further reading: S. Pinker, *The Language Instinct* (1994). D.C.

biological control. The use of living things to control pests. Because of the fears caused by extensive use of synthetic biocides (herbicides and pesticides), biological control is a favoured method for controlling organisms. It involves the use of predators and disease-producing organisms instead of chemicals. It is especially important in cases where a particular organism has spread explosively into a new environment where the natural controls on that organism are not present. An example would be the need to control prickly pear, a native of the Americas, which has invaded large tracts of Australia; or the need to control rabbits, which have also been introduced with disastrous effects into Australia in the last two centuries. A.S.G.

biological linguistics, see BIOLINGUISTICS.

biological rhythm. A periodicity of behaviour associated with a natural subdivision of time such as a day, month or season. Biological rhythms include exactly or approximately circadian (24-hour) rhythms, oestrus and menstrual cycles, the recurrence of breeding seasons, etc. Many such rhythms are deeply grounded physiologically and are by no means totally obscured when animals are removed to an ENVIRONMENT in which the cycles conducive to rhythmic behaviour – e.g. the manifest alternation of night and day – are no longer present. (See also CHRONOBIOLOGY.) P.M.

biology. The collective name for the *biological sciences* (or, as they are increasingly called in America, *life sciences*), i.e. those NATURAL SCIENCES which deal with the classification, structure or performance of living beings. By convention, the biological sciences include ZOOLOGY, BOTANY, anatomy, PHYSIOLOGY, MICROBIOLOGY, biosystematics (see TAXONOMY), BIOPHYSICS, BIOCHEMISTRY and, in general, all sciences whose titles incorporate the prefix 'bio-' or the word 'biology' itself (see, for example, DEVELOPMENTAL BIOLOGY; POPULATION BIOLOGY; SOCIAL BIOLOGY). Present convention allocates ANTHROPOLOGY and PSYCHOLOGY to the SOCIAL SCIENCES, but ETHOLOGY is distinctively a biological science. P.M.

biometry/biometrics.

(1) The use of mensuration, enumeration, STATISTICS and quantitative methods generally in the study of BIOLOGY. In the post-Darwinian era many botanists and zoologists became preoccupied with qualitative descriptions of organisms which were intended to disclose their evolutionary credentials (see EVOLUTION). In reaction a number of scientists – notably Karl Pearson, W. F. R. Weldon and D'Arcy Thompson – insisted upon the importance of measurement and numeration in the study of all

biological phenomena which include an important quantitative or – as in MENDELISM – random element. Among the striking accomplishments of biometry may be mentioned D'Arcy Thompson's and J. S. Huxley's studies of differential growth, the techniques and usages of small-sample statistics introduced by R. A. Fisher, the whole of POPULATION GENETICS, and so much of modern biology that it is hard to think of any branch in which mensuration and numeration are not extremely important. For further reading: J. Maynard Smith, *Mathematical Ideas in Biology* (1968). P.M.

(2) In COMPUTING, biometrics is applied loosely to the measurement of biological, behavioural or other distinctive human data, usually for security purposes. The aim is to enable computer systems to identify or authenticate individuals without them having to remember PINs (personal identification numbers) or passwords, which are notoriously insecure, or carry an identity card. Common approaches include face recognition, iris scanning, electronic fingerprinting, hand checking, vein checking (usually the veins on the back of one hand), voice verification, dynamic signature verification, and facial thermography. Typical applications include operating automated tellers (cash machines), where iris scanning shows promise, and controlling access to buildings, where hand and fingerprint checking have been tried. Dynamic signature verification – where the speed and pressure of the signing are added to the visual appearance – enables contracts to be signed remotely via LCD screens. Some PC users already use face recognition systems to control access to their personal computers. In each case the 'biometrics' are measured and compared with values that have been stored previously, either in a computer database or on a smartcard carried by the user. The main drawbacks are that biometric systems are expensive to install and sometimes cumbersome to use. They may also meet with user resistance: do you really want your fingerprints stored on a bus pass? The advantage is increased security, though once the hackers and crackers have had a few years to find the loopholes, biometrics may not prove to be as secure as was thought. J.S.

biomorphic. Term used in ABSTRACT ART and SURREALISM for non-geometrical forms based on natural shapes, i.e. mainly curves, blobs and bulges. It is associated primarily with the abstract paintings and sculptures of Hans Arp, who consistently used such forms from 1915 on, and secondarily with the work of such Surrealists as Yves Tanguy and Joan Miró. Similar characteristics in the work of Henry Moore are sometimes termed *organic*. Before these labels had come into use, however, much the same approach was applied, with great refinement, in ART NOUVEAU and the designs of William Morris. J.W.

bionics. A portmanteau word (BIOlogical electroNICSs) coined by Dr Hans L. Oestreicher of Wright-Patterson Air Force Base, Ohio, and meaning the application of biological processes, especially of control, to TECHNOLOGY. It is the part of CYBERNETICS (hence sometimes called *biocybernetics*) which is concerned with taking over 'design principles' seen in biological organisms, to create novel technological devices. (Another word closely related in meaning is BIOENGINEERING.) Current emphasis in bionics has moved away from principles of control to the question of how novelty or intelligence may be simulated (see SIMULATION) or produced by machines – see ARTIFICIAL INTELLIGENCE. R.L.G.

bionomics, see under ECOLOGY.

biophysics. The scientific discipline concerned with the study of living things by the application of physical methods, e.g. *ultracentrifugation* (see SEDIMENTATION); filtering through ordinary plane filters of different porosities or through gels with more or less closely spaced lattice works (*gel filtration*); ELECTROPHORESIS, in which MOLECULES can be separated by reason of inequalities of electrical charge – a most important technique with such fragile and unstable molecules as those of PROTEINS. University departments of biophysics are often given the responsibility for (1) supervising the general use of physical methods in BIOLOGY, particularly the use of TRACER techniques using radioactive compounds or other ISOTOPES; (2) ULTRASONICS; and (3) therapeutic or investigative techniques turning upon irradiation. By far the most important part of biophysics is MOLECULAR BIOLOGY, the interpretation of biological structures and performances in molecular terms. P.M.

biorheology, see under HAEMORHEOLOGY.

biosystematics, see under TAXONOMY.

biotic provinces, see under BIOGEOGRAPHY.

biotechnology. A term comprehending all applications of biological knowledge (see BIOLOGY) to industry. Examples are:

(1) industrial fermentation (including brewing, wine-making, and in some countries the accelerated maturation of wines by the addition of ENZYMES);

(2) the preparation of leather and of so-called 'biological detergents', the active ingredients of which are enzymes extracted from heat-adapted bacteria (see BACTERIOLOGY). Much of the food industry, especially as it relates to pre-prepared foods, rests on biological know-how and comes, therefore, under the heading of biotechnology; P.M.

(3) GENETIC ENGINEERING to cause bacterial cells or cultured animal or plant cells to synthesize medicinally important substances, such as insulin, thus avoiding the more costly practice of synthesizing such molecules or isolating them from natural sources such as animal glands. W.G.R.

bipolarity. An intellectual MODEL of the world powers as divided ('polarized') into two main blocs of powers each led by a 'super-power' (the USA or former USSR). As a simplified model of international relations, especially in the field of control of nuclear armaments, it seduced many American policy advisers during the 1950s by its facile answers to some of their problems. The concept lost its attraction when it became obvious that the leadership of the 'super-powers' was never as absolute as the model required, and that this lack offered many opportunities to Soviet and Western anti-American propagandists. Compare MULTIPOLARITY. D.C.W.

birth rate. In general, the number of births in a population divided by the number of individuals in the same population. Demographers distinguish between 'age-specific birth rates' and the 'crude birth rate'. The former term refers to birth rates in distinct age groups, while the latter refers to the birth rate for the population as a whole. J.R.W.

birth trauma. In PSYCHOANALYSIS, a TRAUMA postulated by Otto Rank (one of Freud's early associates), who argued that being born is a deeply disturbing experience, out of which develops the fundamental human conflict: between the wish to return to the embryonic bliss of the womb and the fear of doing so, because the womb is also associated with the fact of birth. This notion has not been widely accepted, even among psychoanalysts. B.A.F.

BIS (Bank for International Settlements). 'The central bankers' central bank', set up in 1930 (in the wake of the 1929 crash) by the central banks of Britain, Belgium, Germany, Italy, Japan and France, with the USA represented by a commercial bank, and with other European central banks, including most in eastern Europe, taking shareholdings which they have retained to this day. Membership has since expanded; and the US Federal Reserve Board is invariably represented, although the USA has never formally taken up the seat on the board still reserved for it. The board of directors includes the central bank governors of the main western European countries ('the Basle Club'), as well as representatives of the private business communities. The bank acts as the agent for central banks in conducting certain operations in financial and currency markets, most notably over the last two decades in the Euro-money markets. The BIS has responsibility for many of the technical aspects of the operations of the various European financial systems, e.g. the European Monetary System. P.J.; J.P.

bitonality. In music, the mixing together of two *tonalities* (see under ATONAL MUSIC) by the simultaneous use of, e.g., two lines of melody or two blocks of harmony, each in a different key. The conflict of tonalities produces an arresting effect which is more likely to be immediately comprehensible than random dissonance, since each part in itself is based on traditional concepts of key. Bitonality was much used at the start of the century, notably by Stravinsky, Holst (in the Fugal Concerto) and Bartók, and in the

1920s by Milhaud. See also PANTONAL MUSIC; POLYTONALITY. A.H.

bivalence, principle of. In PHILOSOPHY, the principle that every sentence in a given class of sentences is either true or false, with 'truth' and 'falsity' as the only possible alternatives. It is a SEMANTIC principle, that is, it relates to the interpretation (establishing the meaning) of sentences in a language. The logical principle to which it corresponds is the law of excluded middle, which states either *A* or not-*A*. The semantic and logical principles are related in that acceptance of the former usually entails acceptance of the latter, but not vice versa. This is because the law of excluded middle depends upon a reading of 'not' which has it that if *A* is true, not-*A* is false, and vice versa, from which it follows that not-not-*A* is equivalent to *A*. This is called the 'classical' reading of negation. However, if one reads 'not' differently, for example as 'not provable', then the law of excluded middle ceases to hold, since in this case not-not-*A* and *A* are not equivalent (to assert 'it is not provable that it is not provable that *A*' is not to assert 'it is provable that *A*'). This is the 'intuitionistic' reading of negation. If one does not accept the principle of bivalence one is thereby rejecting the classical reading of negation and with it the law of excluded middle. However, acceptance of that law does not oblige commitment to bivalence, so the relationship is not symmetrical. The principle of bivalence is associated with REALISM in the philosophy of language. See ANTI-REALISM. For further reading: M. A. E. Dummett, *Truth and Other Enigmas* (1978). A.C.G.

black. Term used to make a political statement. It does not strictly refer to physical or racial attributes (see RACE) but generally includes people who identify themselves on the basis of a common political experience. The notion of blackness and its development as a political symbol began with Marcus Garvey and his Back to Africa movement. Black became part of everyday vocabulary in the wake of the American civil rights and BLACK POWER movements (see CIVIL RIGHTS MOVEMENT) of the 1960s. Black in Britain has become a point of mobilization for postwar migrants (from Asia and the West Indies in particular) and subsequent generations. A.G.

black arts movement. A movement in the 1960s in the USA by a group of BLACK artists led by Imamu Baraka, Hoyt Fuller and Addison Gayle. A basic tenet of this movement was that art should inspire, educate, delight and move people to action. The principal figures in the movement were black nationalists who urged the development of black institutions. The institutions that were established were primarily cultural. The Black Arts Repertory Theater and School established in Harlem was a prime example.

Black institutions were seen as a necessary first step in any effort to liberate and uplift people of African descent. By necessity these institutions had to have economic and political components, but if they were to be successful, the leaders felt, the cultural component could not be ignored. Baraka and other members of the movement believed it was easier to get people to a state of black power consciousness by use of an emotional example rather than a dialectical (see DIALECTIC) argument. For this reason, they used art and music to raise the consciousness of black people and to inspire them to act.

Needless to say, the movement had its critics. Some, both black and white, criticized the movement for having been exclusionary. The black nationalist IDEOLOGY was offensive to many liberal (see LIBERALISM) and progressive thinkers. Others criticized the movement for placing too much emphasis on the cultural and not enough emphasis on the economic and political. In the end, institutions like the Black Repertory Theater and School were not able to maintain the independence that they deemed necessary because they had to depend upon federally funded POVERTY programs for their economic survival. H.M.

black-body radiation. A black body absorbs all radiant energy falling upon it. Black-body radiation is the profile of frequencies emitted by such a body, and is a function of temperature alone. Empirical and theoretical problems afflicted derivations of this function within CLASSICAL PHYSICS. In 1900 Planck derived a theoretically sound and empirically adequate formula, but more important than this formula was the assumption – ENERGY quantization – that he used to derive it. Matter interacting with RADIATION is modelled using an array of resonators oscillating at different frequencies. Planck allowed the black-body resonators to take on only a discrete range of energy values, instead of the CONTINUUM of values previously assumed available (see QUANTUM THEORY). Within the old quantum theory (1900–25), the restriction of energy (or other dynamical quantities) to discrete values was repeated in accounts of a wide range of phenomena, most famously by Einstein (the photoelectric effect) and Bohr (see BOHR THEORY). R.F.H.

black-box theory. A theory that attempts to relate input to output in a SYSTEM by a formal description of the *transformation rules* (see AXIOMATICS) that link the two, but without stating the nature of the process that embodies or gives realization to these rules. N. Chomsky's description of language acquisition and B. F. Skinner's theory of learning may both be considered black-box theories, since they avoid the description of the mechanisms involved. J.S.N.

black comedy (or **dark comedy**). Drama which, although it observes many of the conventions of comedy, either presents a sombre or despairing view of the world or else includes themes traditionally excluded from the genre on account of their painful nature. The use of this style in the modern period relates to the widely held belief that tragedy is an inappropriate genre for an age which has lost religious faith and a sense of the heroic. Although the two terms are to some extent interchangcable, *dark comedy* refers rather to the tragicomic form in which laughter and despair are inextricably mingled, in the style perfected by Anton Chekhov (1860–1904), while *black comedy*, exemplified at its most extreme in the plays of Joe Orton, seeks to unsettle its audiences by laughing at pain, suffering or serious emotion (and thus has an affinity with *sick jokes* and the THEATRE OF THE ABSURD). The term 'black comedy' (*comédie noire*) derives from Jean Anouilh, who divided his plays of the 1930s and 1940s into *pièces roses* and *pièces noires*, and perhaps also from *Anthologie de l'humeur noir*, the title of a volume (1940) in which André Breton illustrated the long-standing SURREALIST interest in the humorous treatment of the macabre or the shocking to indicate 'the superior rebellion of the mind'; the term 'dark comedy' was coined by the critic J. L. Styan in 1962. For further reading: J. L. Styan, *The Dark Comedy* (1968).

M.A.; J.G.W.

black consciousness. This refers both to BLACK perspectives on modern society and black realization of the existential and political reality of black people in the modern world. The roots of black consciousness as a form of resistance reside in black nationalism and PAN-AFRICANISM. The most enduring and influential theoretical formulation of black consciousness is, however, Du Bois's notion of black consciousness as a *double* consciousness of being an insider and an outsider of Western civilization. For some commentators, this duality has situated black consciousness as a perspective that could only have emerged in the modern era, wherein black people were required to assimilate into Western civilization while being condemned as unassimilable. Many formulations of black consciousness appealed, as well, to a racial notion of black genius (HARLEM RENAISSANCE) and black essence and values (NEGRITUDE). In the 1960s, black consciousness took the form of BLACK POWER, wherein black consciousness is politically asserted as solidarity among blacks and encourages the development of ideas and institutions to fortify that solidarity globally to eradicate European colonialism and conquest (see POST-COLONIALISM; IMPERIALISM). Moreover, the history of slavery and stratification of the majority of black populations in the peasantry, the WORKING CLASS and unemployed created an embellished MARXISM as black consciousness of the racial dimensions of capitalistic exploitation (see CAPITALISM). This version was influential in most 20th-century black consciousness movements except for conservative nationalists (see CONSERVATISM; NATIONALISM). Today, the discussion of black consciousness is almost entirely dominated by debates on its status as a racial versus cultural concept (see RACE; CULTURE), although there is a growing existential-phenomenological discussion of it as both (see EXISTENTIALISM; PHENOMENOLOGY). With the growing influence of 'cultural studies' in British and American universities, the sensibilities of black POPULAR CULTURES have taken centre stage, which signals the contemporary dominance of the perspectival conception of black consciousness. L.R.G.

black conservatism. BLACK conservatives (see CONSERVATISM), like their white conservative counterparts, champion the free market and the idea of limited government. The principal figures in the contemporary black conservative movement in the United States include Glenn Loury, Thomas Sowell and Walter Williams. However, unlike their white counterparts, they spend a great deal of time addressing the problem of RACISM. They admit that racism has not totally disappeared from the American landscape, but they deny that this means that there are few, if any, opportunities for people of colour.

They argue that what holds racial MINORITIES back in the USA today are factors like a 'culture of poverty' and a 'victim mentality'. By a culture of POVERTY, they mean that there are good cultural values and bad cultural values and that bad cultural values produce unsuccessful individuals and groups. According to this view, African-Americans who do not succeed fail to do so because of poor values. A victim's mentality is said to be a state of mind that causes racial minorities, especially African-Americans, to be helpless in the face of opportunities. This state of mind is not due to genetic make-up, but brought on by preoccupation with the past history of injustices like American slavery and the Jim Crow system. Black conservatives believe that people are responsible for their own fates. Success or failure is not determined by society, but by the individual. Of course, these claims have been roundly criticized by liberal (see LIBERALISM) and PROGRESSIVE thinkers. H.M.

black economy. That part of economic activity that takes place outside the tax system and which is illegal. The illicit nature of the black economy means that it is difficult to estimate its size. The loss of tax revenue from the black economy is of concern to governments and has become a political issue in many countries. J.P.

Black English, see under EBONICS.

black feminisim. SECOND WAVE FEMINISM of the 1970s was largely based in the experiences and aspirations of white, educated women in Western democracies (see DEMOCRACY). As such, it was open to the criticism that it had little to say to women, both inside and outside those societies, who did not belong to privileged and dominant GROUPS and share their expectations and aspirations. By the end of the 1970s a critical literature had emerged which accused 'white' feminism of blindness to the situation of non-white women in Western cultures and a refusal of the links between the wealth and relative prosperity of those cultures and the poverty and EXPLOITATION of women in the South. Crucial to the development of BLACK feminism was a recovery of the history of black women in the United States, and the novels of Maya Angelou, Alice Walker and Toni Morrison played a central part in articulating an account of a culture which had hitherto been either hidden or marginalized. The identification of black women within the United States with black, and non-white, women in other countries has provided a crucial link between women in diverse cultures and the basis for a radical form of political thinking. For further reading: b. hooks, *Outlaw Culture* (1994). M.S.E.

black hole. A hypothetical astronomical system. When a star near the end of its history contracts under GRAVITATION and becomes smaller than a certain *critical radius* (proportional to the star's mass), then, according to Einstein's theory of RELATIVITY, no RADIATION can escape from it; as far as the rest of the universe is concerned it becomes unobservable – its ESCAPE VELOCITY exceeds the speed of light. Such a black hole would still exert gravitational force, so that its existence could be inferred from the motion of neighbouring bodies; several black holes have been tentatively identified in this way. What happens to the matter falling into a black hole? Does it collapse to a point of infinite density, or is this prevented by QUANTUM MECHANICS, or does the matter re-explode, appearing as a 'white hole' in another universe? These are unsolved problems in theoretical PHYSICS. The sun is in no immediate danger of becoming a black hole within the next few hundred million years, because it is about half a million times larger than its critical radius, which is about 2 miles. See also HERTZSPRUNG-RUSSELL DIAGRAM. M.V.B.

Black Mountain. Black Mountain College, a PROGRESSIVE education institution in North Carolina founded by J. A. Rice in 1933. At first the emphasis was on practical education and painting (the art teachers included Josef Albers, formerly of the BAUHAUS), but in the early 1950s it became a centre of a new, or newly stated, American POETICS, and a place for poets: the connotation of Black Mountain is now almost exclusively literary, referring to the Black Mountain school of poets. This is one of two latter-day manifestations of an American revolt against conventional and academic poetics which began with Ezra Pound and William Carlos Williams – the other being the group of poets which crystallized round Robert Bly's more mythologically and surrealistically orientated Fifties/Sixties/Seventies Press. The key to the Black Mountain poetics is to be found in American PRAGMATISM as exemplified by John Dewey, with its accompanying blind optimism. Its mentor was Charles Olson (1910–70), Rector of the college from 1951 until 1956, during which period he was joined by other Black Mountain poets (e.g. Robert Creeley, Robert Duncan), as students and as instructors. Olson's makeshift poetics (or anti-poetics) is expressed, in a mixture of baseball instructor's and jocose professional slang, in *Projective Verse* (1950), which has been widely reprinted. It is unscholarly, bloody-minded and derivative (mostly from Williams), and raises a host of unanswered questions. But it is important as a summing-up of the attitudes of a somewhat younger generation of American poets, and as a specifically American pragmatic reaction, arising out of what has been called 'intelligent philistinism', to lifeless academicism. Olson's demands had already been fulfilled more humbly by the OBJECTIVIST minor American poets of the early 1930s, with whom Williams and Pound were briefly associated. His disciples do not really fulfil these demands, which are unfulfillable; but they believe that they are doing so. The poet is to concentrate on his own breathing, on the syllable (see SYLLABICS) rather than on metre or rhyme; he is to perform on the typewriter because this spaces more precisely than writing does; syntax, in as much as it hampers the dynamic energy supplied by breath, is to go. There is much emphasis on public readings. And the prime reason for all this is that the old, 'closed' method, as then allegedly practised by such much-loathed poets as Robert Frost, interposed the 'poet's ego' between himself and his audience. In Black Mountain poetry, the (Deweyan) sense of *use* is not actually carried beyond the simple act of creation, and neither Olson nor his chief disciple Creeley give the least indication, outside or inside their poetry, of why they do what they do. The magazine *Origin* (1951–56), edited by Cid Corman, first printed many of the Black Mountain poets. *Black Mountain Review* (1954–57), edited by Creeley, is also relevant. The claim made in one reference book that the Black Mountain poets 'have long since become a major part of 20th-century literature' was decidedly overoptimistic. But they remain a minor part of the history of American poetry. For further reading: M. L. Rosenthal, *The New Poets* (1967). M.S.-S.

Black Muslims, see under NATION OF ISLAM

Black Panthers, see under BLACK POWER.

black power. A slogan first used by radical African-American political activists in the mid-1960s: generally thought to have been coined by Stokely Carmichael of the Student Nonviolent Coordinating Committee. It designated the various aims and values of BLACKS seeking control of the political and economic institutions affecting their lives, and was accompanied by a vigorous emphasis on racial pride. Several organizations, including the Black Panthers, the NATION OF ISLAM and parts of the more disaffected, radical fragments of the CIVIL RIGHTS MOVEMENT articulated versions of the Black Power message. These varied in strategic and tactical detail: some activists included a SOCIALIST perspective, others stressed long-term racial SEPARATISM, while opinions varied over the use of political violence. It is questionable whether the term denotes a single movement or a collection of tendencies, organizations and political styles, although it can be located within a longer black tradition of arguments stressing autonomy and separatism rather than racial integration. However, the phenomenon had a considerable short-term impact. It raised black political consciousness, particularly outside the South (the initial arena for the civil rights movement), polarized white opinion and attracted repressive governmental responses. Its longer-term effects include the continuing influence of the life and writings of Malcolm X (1925–65), increasingly revered by many black Americans as a leader of comparable political vision and spiritual force to Martin Luther King Jr. S.R.

black psychology. US movement of African-American psychologists dissatisfied with PSYCHOLOGY'S handling of RACE issues, formally dating from 1968 when the Association of Black Psychologists was founded under C. W. Thomas. While having roots in the late 1930s, BLACK psychology marked a clear break with the past. African-American psychologists had hitherto worked in alliance with white liberal sympathizers (see LIBERALISM), but it became painfully obvious that these had, unwittingly, largely only replaced older racist images with an equally negative 'damaged negro' stereotype. The 1969 reignition of the dormant 'race and IQ' controversy, following publication of a paper by Arthur Jensen, promptly brought things to a head in a highly fraught cultural climate. As well as rejecting the 'damaged negro' stereotype, black psychology challenged such notions as the pathological nature of the matriarchal (see MATRIARCHY) black FAMILY and the assumption that 'negro' identity was determined solely by relationships with whites. More positively, W. Cross proposed a controversial 'nigrescence' theory of the stages in the African-American person's psychological maturation. Since 1970 black psychology has addressed an expanding range of practical and theoretical issues, black women psychologists becoming increasingly prominent after 1980. Psychology's engagements with race-related topics has, however, become more multi-national and multi-faceted, moving beyond black psychology's initial, more tightly focused concerns. For further reading: R. L. Jones (ed.), *Black Psychology* (1980). G.D.R.

Black Theatre. A movement dedicated to the creation of a drama reflecting the consciousness of BLACK Americans. Lorraine Hansberry's *A Raisin in the Sun* (1959) was the first major success by a black dramatist; in the 1960s, in plays by James Baldwin, Ed Bullins and LeRoi Jones, black drama became progressively more radical (see RADICALISM) until, influenced by the militancy of the BLACK POWER movement at the end of the decade, Black Theatre groups sought to sever their connection with the white American theatre and perform solely for black audiences. Outside the USA, theatre groups in Jamaica and England (comprising West Indians and expatriate Americans) have been influenced by the Black Theatre movement; the work of West African dramatists, of whom the most powerful is the Nigerian Wole Soyinka, represents a complex fusion of indigenous and ex-colonial traditions; in the French-speaking world the plays of the Martinique-born poet and dramatist Aimé Césaire have made an important contribution to the expression of black identity (see NEGRITUDE). M.A.

black theology. A movement in late 20th-century THEOLOGY which reflects on the African-American experience and seeks to promote the social, political, economic and cultural liberation of all African Americans. It is related to Latin American LIBERATION THEOLOGY (see CONTEXTUAL THEOLOGIES), but arose independently in the 1960s as the BLACK CONSCIOUSNESS movement compelled the BLACK Churches to reflect on the historical and contemporary experience of the African-American people. Black theology makes this experience the key to interpreting the Bible and the Christian tradition, drawing on the spiritual, cultural and theological resources of black RELIGION in America and in Africa. Becoming a major theological movement through the work of James Cone and others, black theology continues to develop, especially in dialogue with FEMINIST THEOLOGY and other contextual theologies. A second tradition of black theology arose independently in South Africa, and some understandings of black theology are sufficiently broad that they include many African theologies. For further reading: J. Cone, *Black Theology and Black Power* (1997). C.C.

Black Wednesday. The day on which the British pound (sterling) was ejected from the Exchange Rate Mechanism (ERM) on 17 September 1992. In an awesome display of financial firepower the speculators, including the New York bear trader George Soros, pitted themselves against John Major's government and the Bank of England and won. None of the traditional defence weapons, including raising INTEREST RATES to 15 per cent (five points in one day) and heavy spending of the reserves, worked and the pound was forced out of the ERM. It was a devastating blow to John Major's Conservative administration from which it was never to recover. For further reading: P. Stephens, *Politics and the Pound* (1996). A.BR.

Blast. The 'review of the Great English Vortex', published in London in two issues, June 1914 and July 1915, under the editorship of Wyndham Lewis. Pre-eminently a VORTICIST manifesto, presenting its attitude to the contemporary scene in a Marinetti-like display of 'Blesses' and 'Blasts', it was the most conspicuous expression of this post-Imagist (see IMAGISM) movement in British literature and the arts. Ezra Pound was active in its compilation; there were contributions by T. S. Eliot, Francis Hueffer, etc. But these typographically exciting documents are primarily fascinating as statements of an important theory about the kinetic potential of the MODERNIST arts, and as a synthetic 'projection of a world art'. M.S.BR.

blending inheritance. Inheritance by children of characteristics which are a more or less equitable blend between those of their parents or, in respect of quantitative characteristics, midway between them. Although such a blending is a natural enough presumption, the great lesson of MENDELISM is that it does not occur. If it did so, GENETIC variance would be extinguished in a few generations, whereas in point of fact genetic variance tends to be indefinitely conserved. This is because the determinants of heredity maintain their integrity generation by generation. So far from being a blend between their two parents, children display a novel and possibly a unique recombination of the genetic determinants transmitted to them by their parents. See also MENDEL'S LAWS. P.M.

blitzkrieg. A German concept describing a style of, literally, 'lightning war'. It involved the use of armour, and motorized infantry, and was used to great effect in Poland in 1939 and against France in 1940. It depended for its effect on the shock wave produced by a deep offensive, which disrupted an enemy's planned resistance. Crucial additional elements were the use of tactical airpower, and the psychological effect of a seemingly 'irresistible' attack. A.J.M.W.

blood and soil (*Blut und Boden*). A quasi-mystical Nazi catch-phrase (see NAZISM) intended to glorify the literature and emotions of the peasant as the embodiment of the two qualities from which the high quality of the German race was supposed to stem, German blood and German soil. D.C.W.

Bloomfieldian. Characteristic of, or a follower of, the linguistic approach of Leonard Bloomfield, as exemplified in his book *Language*, published in 1933. *Bloomfieldianism* refers particularly to the school of thought which developed between the mid-1930s and 1950s, especially in America, and which was a formative influence on structural LINGUISTICS. It was especially characterized by its behaviouristic principles (see BEHAVIOURISM) for the study of meaning, and its insistence on rigorous DISCOVERY PROCEDURES. A reaction against Bloomfieldian tenets was a powerful force in producing GENERATIVE GRAMMAR. Though Bloomfieldianism is no longer fashionable, some of its methods are still widely used in field studies. D.C.

Bloom's taxonomy. This theory from the educationist of that name has been applied to the planning and development of the curriculum. It maintains that education should have three objectives: the cognitive (i.e. knowledge and the application of knowledge), the affective (i.e. dealing with the emotions and with values) and the pyschomotor (i.e. dealing with physical skills). The late Sir Alec Clegg, who for many years was chief education officer for the West Riding of Yorkshire, divided education into only two objectives and called them 'the loaves and hyacinths': the loaves being the cognitive (the facts needed to know how to, say, dance the Highland fling), the hyacinths representing the emotions (the verve and passion with which to dance it). J.I.

Bloomsbury Group. A circle of friends without formal membership, rules or common doctrine consisting of Lytton Strachey, Virginia and Leonard Woolf, Clive and Vanessa Bell, Maynard Keynes, Duncan Grant, Saxon Sydney-Turner and (see also OMEGA WORKSHOPS) Roger Fry. Closely associated with this group were E. M. Forster, Gerald Shove, James and Marjorie Strachey, David Garnett, Francis Birrell, Adrian and Thoby Stephen. The group came into existence in 1905, when Thoby Stephen and his sisters, Virginia and Vanessa, then living in Bloomsbury, London, continued friendships begun at Cambridge. Its members were united by a belief in the importance of the arts; they were all sceptical and tolerant, particularly in sexual matters. Beyond this it would be difficult to find any opinion or attitude shared by all. In so far as the group ever had any kind of corporate existence, it began to decline after the death of Lytton Strachey in 1931 and had ceased to exist by 1940. For further reading: L. Edel, *Bloomsbury: A House of Lions* (1979). Q.B.

blue beat, see under REGGAE.

blue notes. One of the purest and oldest features of BLUES and JAZZ, the blue notes are the lowered third and seventh (and sometimes the fifth) degrees of what would otherwise be a major scale. The resulting tension between 'major' and 'minor' – though the blue notes are actually neither – produces the characteristic quality of the blues, a potent mixture of sorrow, defiance and affirmation. Like other jazz elements, the blue notes were incorporated into the vocabulary not only of popular music but classical music as well (see SYMPHONIC JAZZ). GE.S.

blue shift. A displacement towards the blue of the spectral lines of some stars. The shift arises from the DOPPLER EFFECT, and indicates that these stars are approaching us. Because of the overall EXPANSION OF THE UNIVERSE, blue shifts are rare in comparison with RED SHIFTS. M.V.B.

bluegrass, see under FOLK MUSIC.

blues. A specific musical form and one of the most influential musical genres of the century. To a blues singer or JAZZ musician, the blues at its most basic is a twelve-bar structure (occasionally sixteen) consisting of four bars of the tonic chord, two of the subdominant, two of the tonic and two of the dominant with a return to the tonic for a final two bars. When performed vocally, a classic blues verse divides the twelve bars into three four-bar sections, in each of which a single line is sung, the second of which is a repeat of the first. Despite the form's simplicity, its economy and dramatic power have inspired some of the most memorable performances in jazz. Throughout jazz history, the fundamental importance of the blues has never been in doubt, though its harmonic structure has sometimes been elaborately altered. As a musical genre distinct from jazz, the blues has carried on its own development from the 1920s, primarily though not exclusively as a vocal style, with more emphasis on directness of communication than sophistication. Its various forms, urban and country, group or solo, have at times been lumped together under the heading of RHYTHM AND BLUES to distinguish them from jazz. Under any rubric its special qualities remain and have contributed incalculably to rock and roll (see also ROCK MUSIC; BLUE NOTES). GE.S.

body. The body has been at the centre of cultural theory and art practice in the last 20 years partly because it had been previously represented and viewed through a set of assumptions that took no account of social, historical and cultural change. Furthermore, POST-STRUCTURALIST theory has influenced our understanding that representations and cultural inscriptions are active in the constitution of the body and not separate from the physical body, posited by natural science and medicine. Maurice Merleau-Ponty's PHENOMENOLOGY looked at the ways in which physical and psychological PERCEPTIONS are made conscious in the embodied mind through the modes of sensory relations. Jean-Paul Sartre and Simone de Beauvoir shared an existential concept of the body as biologically determined and fundamentally alien to cultural and intellectual achievement, stressing the distinction between a sexually neutral mind and the facticity and mortality of a body which may limit the individual's existence and potential for transcendence (see EXISTENTIALISM).

However, the question of sexual difference in the writing of Jacques Lacan (see LACANIAN), Jacques Derrida, Julie Kristeva and Luce Irigaray has now become one of the most important theories of representation to be explored by artists. The concept of difference, especially the concept of the OTHER, has also been linked to cultural, and by implication racial, difference in ways which offer more complex critical interpretations of representations of the body. For further reading: E. Grosz, *Volatile Bodies: Toward a Corporeal Feminism* (1994). A.V.D.B.

body art, see under CONCEPTUAL ART.

body, history of, see under HISTORY OF THE BODY.

body image. According to Paul Schilder, whose work on the image of the body extended previous psychological and psychiatric work in this area into the domain of PSYCHOANALYSIS, the image of the body and the image of the world, together with a zone of indifference between them, are none of them natural or immediate, but the result of a process of construction dependent on the relations between the individual's perceptual experience and his emotional and libidinal life (see LIBIDO). The body image is originally incomplete and fragmented, and is only given a definite form by persistent effort. New structure is added to the image by a drive to build up a total libidinous structure, always in conflict with a tendency to the cessation of effort leading to the dissolution of the image. Even objects separate from the body, such as semen, blood, breath, voice and surrounding space, are seen as part of the body image. Erogenic zones play a central role in its construction, as do the complexes of dismemberment and body-unity, of castration and the OEDIPUS COMPLEX. Schilder, however, believes that an emotional unity will be achieved when full OBJECT RELATIONS have been developed. This last claim is contested by Jacques Lacan, whose work on the MIRROR PHASE and the IMAGINARY developed these themes of the relation of body and image. For further reading: P. Schilder, *The Image and Appearance of the Human Body* (1935); J. Lacan, *The Ego in Freud's Theory and the Technique of Psychoanalysis* (1987). B.BU.

body popping, see under POPULAR DANCE.

Bohr interpretation, see under COPENHAGEN INTERPRETATION.

Bohr theory. An explanation, devised in 1913 by the physicist Niels Bohr, of the radiation emitted by atomic hydrogen. The theory is based on NEWTONIAN MECHANICS, with the addition of simple rules which appeared arbitrary at first but which were later explained by the more fundamental QUANTUM MECHANICS. See also ATOMIC PHYSICS; ENERGY LEVEL; SPECTROSCOPY. M.V.B.

Bolshevism. The term Bolshevism refers to a political tendency founded by Lenin (see LENINISM). It originated at the second congress of the Russian Social Democratic Labour Party where delegates divided into two factions on the question of conditions for party membership. Lenin and his supporters favoured a membership strictly confined to committed activists whereas Martov and his supporters wanted a looser definition which could incorporate TRADE UNIONS. When the party split on this issue Lenin and his followers took the name Bolshevik from the Russian word meaning 'majority' in contrast to the MENSHEVIKS or 'minoritarians'. The name Bolshevik was not used in the party title until April 1917; it ceased to be employed in 1925 when the name was changed to the All-Union COMMUNIST Party (Bolsheviks) and finally in 1952 to the Communist Party of the USSR.

The central principle of Bolshevism is that, in its struggle against oppressive ruling groups, the WORKING CLASS needs to be led by a disciplined party of full-time, committed revolutionaries. This 'vanguard' party would be able to take the initiative in revolutionary strategy and develop a revolutionary theory to which the working class could not attain if left to its own devices. The party's organizational basis is in DEMOCRATIC CENTRALISM whereby members participate in electing leaders and formulating policy but thereafter show absolute loyalty to policies and leadership.

The success of the Bolsheviks in 1917 led to the extension of their organizational principles to the international SOCIALIST movement and the abiding division between social democratic parties (see SOCIAL

DEMOCRACY) and the newly founded communist parties which were organized on the Bolshevik model. With the ascendancy of STALINISM in the Soviet Union, Bolshevism became closely associated with his policies. As the international communist movement became more diverse, different forms of Bolshevism emerged, such as TROTSKYISM and MAOISM. And more recently the suitability of Bolshevik principles in more liberal Western societies (see LIBERALISM) has been questioned by the Eurocommunist tendency. For further reading: P. Corrigan *et al*, *Socialist Construction and Marxist Theory: Bolshevism and Its Critique* (1978). D.T.M.

bond, chemical. The forces which hold ATOMS together in a MOLECULE or solid. In some molecules, such as gaseous sodium chloride (or ionic solids), the bond arises mainly because of the electrostatic attraction between IONS of opposite charge. Bonds between atoms where the electrons are shared – covalent bonds – are much more difficult to explain, and the modern understanding of bonding in molecules such as hydrogen, water and benzine represents the most important success for the application of QUANTUM MECHANICS in CHEMISTRY. There are two main theoretical MODELS: the VALENCE bond model which considers interaction between individual atoms, and the now more widely used molecular orbital treatment in which the NUCLEI (or charged atomic cores) form a framework of the molecule, which is enveloped by ELECTRONS in discrete ORBITALS of definite ENERGY. Both theoretical models show how electron density builds up nuclei in the formation of a bond. The orbital picture of a molecule is conceptually attractive but it is still an approximation and, except for very simple molecules, directly calculated energies are not very accurate. B.F.

boogie-woogie. A style of JAZZ piano characterized by infectious rolling bass patterns, energetically repeated (it was also sometimes known as 'eight-beat'). It evolved from the work of primitive BLUES pianists in the American South and was officially named in Pine Top Smith's 1928 recording 'Pine Top's Boogie-woogie'. Generally, it retained its blues connections, particularly in the work of its most noted practitioners, Meade Lux Lewis, Albert Ammons and Pete Johnson, who became stars when the genre became a national craze in the late 1930s. Though its limitations were obvious, its happy simplicity made it appealing, and all over America teenagers hammered out boogie-woogie versions of everything from 'Flight of the Bumblebee' to 'Jingle Bells'. GE.S.

book, history of, see HISTORY OF THE BOOK.

Boolean algebra. George Boole (1815–64) believed that LOGIC could be treated by algebraic methods (see ALGEBRA). He treated combinations of sets by using + to denote SET union and × to denote set intersection. He used x' to denote the set of objects not in x (and 0 to denote the empty set, and 1 the Universe). So that a combination (such as $x + x'$) looks like an algebraic expression. He developed the basic rules of manipulation, some of which (e.g. $x + x = x$, $xx' = 0$) are not like ordinary algebra – this gave an early example of a new algebraic system. Any system obeying these rules is called a Boolean algebra. Boole realized that (what we now call) PROPOSITIONAL CALCULUS is one such. By following the rules, logical truths can be proved. Boole showed that there is a DECISION PROCEDURE for deciding if an equation is true.

These methods at once found a use in PROBABILITY THEORY, but, with the arrival of computers (see COMPUTING) and integrated circuits, they were the ideal tool for designing circuits to switch on and off in a specified way. N.A.R.

borderline. A sub-type of personality disorder, with symptoms and behaviour that suggest an individual intermittently crossing the 'border' into brief episodes of PSYCHOSIS. Typically there is a mixture of low self-esteem, emotional lability, limited impulse control and disrupted interpersonal relationships. Suicidal urges in the form of repeated overdoses or self-laceration are common forms of presentation. Controversial as a diagnosis, being much more common in younger women, 'borderlines' are likely to provoke rejection among relatives and healthcare workers. Prisons and hospitals are accustomed to such individuals repeatedly passing through in states of legal or psychiatric distress. Critics of the concept adduce childhood abuse, GENDER prejudice and unempathic clinical attitudes as causative. Causation, pathology and definition remain elusive, but the category has usefully linked psychotherapeutic insight to practical nursing. Within FREUDIAN parlance it is contended that such adults retain 'primitive NARCISSISM', reacting with frustration to the loss of OBJECT RELATIONS. The attempt to see 'borderline' PSYCHOPATHOLOGY in behaviours considered hysterical, childish or manipulative by lay observers continues to undermine psychiatry's popular and scientific acceptance. For further reading: World Health Organization, *The ICD-10 Classification of Mental and Behavioural Disorders* (1992). T.T.

born again. It is reported on the basis of public opinion polls that about a third of the citizens of the US say that they have been 'born again'. The term became most popular in the 1970s during the presidency of Jimmy Carter, who was one such. It means that a person has made a definite, adult decision to be a Christian, experiencing the forgiveness of sins and release from their power. In the tradition of evangelicalism (see EVANGELICAL) this experience has often been called 'conversion' and has been seen as the decisive stage in a process which involves both 'justification' (the acquittal by God of the penitent sinner who relies on the merits of Christ the Saviour) and 'sanctification' (the much slower receipt of the holiness which is the 'fruit' of God the Holy Spirit in the Christian's life). Faith makes all this possible. It is therefore essential, although it must be 'worked out' in love. But particularly since the SECULARIZATION of a land which used to be nominally Christian means that Baptism as an infant cannot be relied on to be the real beginning of life as a Christian, other Christian traditions including Roman CATHOLICISM are increasingly stressing the need to be converted as an adult. This emphasis, with some use of the American phrase, is now found throughout worldwide Christianity. For further reading: J. I. Parker *et al*, *Here We Stand: Justification by Faith Today* (1986). D.L.E.

Bose-Einstein statistics. The QUANTUM STATISTICS that apply to PARTICLES for which the QUANTUM NUMBER describing SPIN is an integer. M.V.B.

bosons, see under QUANTUM STATISTICS.

bossa nova. Jazz has contained Afro-Cuban elements from the beginning, and the bossa nova emerged from Brazil to sweep the world in the early 1960s. The phrase literally means 'new bag', and its novelty lay in the subtle floating rhythm which perfectly suited the image of beautiful young people enjoying idyllic days on the beach. Its melodic and harmonic content owed much to the COOL jazz of the American West Coast; Brazilian innovators Joao Gilberto and Antonio Carlos Jobim admired such stars as tenor saxophonist Stan Getz. Appropriately, Getz's hit album *Jazz Samba* introduced the music to America in 1962, and his recording of 'The Girl from Ipanema', with a distinctively airy vocal by Astrud Gilberto (wife of Joao), popularly defined the bossa nova sound. Bossa nova still survives as a gently infectious rhythm which can be added to almost any tune, the essence of 'light Latin'. GE.S.

botany. The scientific study of plants. The science was founded by Theophrastus, Aristotle's student, and continues to thrive, although it is often disguised under the more modern-sounding term 'the plant sciences'. Botany consists of all the methods and ideas of BIOLOGY in their application to plants. Botanists seek to understand the structure, physiological functioning, embryological development, EVOLUTION and classification (see TAXONOMY) of plants. The subject-matter of botany is made up of the approximately 280,000 living species of plants that have been described so far, together with the yet-to-be-described forms. The described species are formally classified into 10 main divisions; but are conveniently grouped into more inclusive, though probably not evolutionary (see CLADISM), groups. Thus, a grand division separates plants into non-vascular (liverworts and mosses) and vascular forms (all the rest). Vascular plants in turn divide into the seedless (ferns) and those with seeds. Gymnosperms and angiosperms (flowering plants) are the main modern groups of seed-producers. Angiosperms are by far the largest group of plants; about 235,000 species have been described. Plants are economically important in horticulture and agriculture. *Applied botanists* contribute here both by studying the factors that control the germination, growth and form of plants and by breeding improved varieties for cultivation. Botanical discoveries in this way recurrently alter the course of human history in the direction of progress. For further reading: P. H. Raven *et al*, *Biology of Plants* (1986). M.R.

boulevard comedy (*boulevard theatre*, etc.). Theatrical entertainment of a frankly commercial nature, appealing to middle-class or BOURGEOIS audiences without challenging social or artistic conventions. The term derives from the Parisian boulevards whose theatres dominated this form of entertainment in the 19th and early 20th centuries; 'Broadway' and 'Shaftesbury Avenue' carry similar connotations. For a contrasted type of theatre see FRINGE, THE; OFF-BROADWAY; ALTERNATIVE THEATRE. M.A.

bound form, see under MORPHEME.

boundary, see under TOPOLOGY.

bounded rationality. Standard RATIONAL CHOICE THEORY believes individuals have coherent preferences, and are able to work out the consequences of their actions so as to maximize utility with regard to those preferences. The American social scientist and 1978 Nobel laureate for economics Herbert Simon argues that individuals are not able to work out the consequences of all their actions because of limited computational abilities and uncertainty over the future. Thus bounds are placed upon individual rationality and people cannot be expected to maximize their utility; rather, they attempt to satisfy. They choose actions which will satisfy their preferences rather than trying to maximize them. This has important consequences for the very basis of the standard theory, since it suggests that individuals may not have coherent preferences. Because we cannot be sure of the consequences of our actions, and choice is an action, we cannot be sure that if we think we prefer one object to another, we do in fact prefer that object to the other. Our bounded rationality means we cannot be sure about our attitudes to the very objects we want to satisfy. (See RATIONALITY.) For further reading: O. E. Williamson, *Markets and Hierarchies* (1985). K.M.D.

Bourbaki, Nicolas. The pseudonym of a gradually changing group of mathematicians centred in Paris which since 1939 has been producing an encyclopaedic work on the basic MATHEMATICAL STRUCTURES (so far some 20 volumes have appeared). The work has been very influential, both as a paradigm of the AXIOMATIC METHOD, and in its insistence that every important theorem has a correct context which may be different from that in which it was first discovered. R.G.

bourgeois. In the medieval period, a member of a free city or bourg, being neither a peasant nor a lord; in the 17th and 18th centuries, the master or employer in relation to the journeyman or worker, or the merchant in relation to the artisan. Thus bourgeois became synonymous with the MIDDLE CLASS.

Since the 19th century, a contradictory and paradoxical set of judgements has been applied to the bourgeoisie. Economically and politically, the bourgeoisie was regarded as open, adventurous and revolutionary; thus Marx, in the *Communist Manifesto*, writes: 'The bourgeoisie, historically, has played a most revolutionary part . . . The bourgeoisie cannot exist without constantly revolutionizing the instruments of production . . . and with them the whole relations of society.' The political revolutions effected by the bourgeoisie, particularly the French Revolution, ended privileges based on birth, and stressed individualism and achievement as the criteria of place and position in society. Culturally, however, the bourgeoisie has been regarded, from Molière to Balzac, as mean, avaricious, tasteless, REACTIONARY and rapacious, having no sense of values other than the acquisition of money and objects.

The two attitudes derive from different historical perspectives. Most economic and political historians (e.g. Werner Sombart) have seen the bourgeois CLASS as tearing up the roots of traditional society and its fixed ways. Cultural historians and moralists, on the other hand, have tended to write from an aristocratic point of view and to decry the breakdown of standards when all culture becomes a commodity. (See ADMASS; MASS CULTURE.) In the late 19th and early 20th centuries a distinction was increasingly made between the *haute* or *grande* bourgeoisie, who had learned to use their wealth for purposes of refinement, and the petite (or petty) bourgeoisie (see PETIT BOURGEOIS), who were regarded as mean-spirited and niggardly. In recent usage, 'bourgeois' has become associated less with monetary acquisitiveness than with conventional attitudes to sexual conduct. For further reading: C. Morazé, *The Triumph of the Middle Classes* (1966). D.B.

bourgeois hegemony, see under HEGEMONY.

Bradleyan.

(1) In Shakespearean criticism, adjective used to characterize A. C. Bradley's 'Romantic' tendency (in *Shakespearean Tragedy*, 1904) to treat Shakespeare's characters as if they were real people in real life, thus ignoring stage conventions. The best Shakespearean criticism of the 1930s was formed in reaction against Bradley, taking a cooler and more comprehensive view of the play's ingredients and of conditions in the Elizabethan theatre. Yet Bradley's 'closet' commentary, if sometimes lush, is centrally human and preferable to some later critics' REDUCTION of Shakespeare to symbol, MYTH and pattern. D.J.E.

(2) In PHILOSOPHY, adjective applied to the ideas, style, etc. of the IDEALIST philosopher F. H. Bradley (1846–1924). A.Q.

brainwashing. A proselytizing and interrogation technique that aims at the systematic erosion and reversal of a person's habits or convictions, usually with political motive and by the use of prolonged stress. H.L.

brand image. Every product, or service, has an image, whether by intention or by default. That image derives from understood, visible and appreciated intrinsic qualities, and the halo that is achieved through association, presentation and environment. The combination of intrinsic and extrinsic perceived values contrives to produce a GESTALT that, properly worked on, should be unique to any particular product or service. T.S.

brave new world. Originally a phrase used by Shakespeare's Miranda in *The Tempest*: 'O brave new world/That has such people in't'. This is ironic, as some of the people she first sees are in fact scoundrels; but it also affirms her own purity of vision. Aldous Huxley's *Brave New World* (1932) tells of a future state where utopian ideals have turned into nightmare dehumanization; and the contemporary use of the phrase alludes to this rather than to Shakespeare. M.S.-S.

break dancing, see under POPULAR DANCE.

Brechtian. Drama critics' term for anything recalling the work of the German poet, playwright and theatrical director Bertolt Brecht, a leading proponent of ALIENATION (see especially last paragraph) and the EPIC THEATRE, and artistic director, 1949—56, of the Berliner Ensemble. His main concern was with clear dialectical exposition, intelligible language and the concentration of every theatrical means on putting over, with humour and elegance, a plebeian point of view – anarchic, cynical, revolutionary or reflective. The term is, however, most commonly identified with grey colours, drab, realistic costumes, brilliant lighting, slow episodic narration interrupted by projected scene titles, and the direct addressing of the audience by interpolated songs. J.W.

breeder reactor, see under NUCLEAR REACTOR.

Bretton Woods (New Hampshire, USA). In 1944, the scene of the final meetings between the American, British and other Allied finance ministers who set up the International Monetary Fund (IMF) and the World Bank (initially known as the International Bank for Reconstruction and Development).

The IMF's original purpose was to provide a basis of monetary and currency stability for growing world trade and expanding national economies. Members were expected to declare fixed EXCHANGE RATES (see PARITY) which should only be changed in the event of 'fundamental disequilibrium', thus avoiding the pre-World War II evil of unstable exchange rates, including competitive DEVALUATIONS. To help countries deal with temporary BALANCE OF PAYMENTS problems without exchange-rate adjustment, the Fund was empowered to provide short- to medium-term credits to governments. With the suspension of the dollar's convertibility to gold on 15 August 1971, the first devaluation of the dollar in December 1971, and subsequent moves to *floating rates* by a number of major currencies, the Bretton Woods system collapsed and the IMF's role of lending to and stabilizing key-currency economies was much diminished. Since the early 1970s the IMF has accepted the need for flexible exchange rates, although trying, with limited success, to facilitate negotiations between governments and CENTRAL BANKS to reduce currency fluctuations.

The World Bank was created with European reconstruction in mind, but by the 1960s it had become the world's leading international development agency, lending at near-commercial terms; its concessional window for low-income countries, the International Development Association (IDA), became a leading aid agency, loaning at near-zero interest rates for an extended period, with a 10-year grace period.

Since the early 1980s, the IMF, as lender of last resort, and the World Bank have become the major sources of policy lending for developing countries. Fund and Bank conditions, a quid pro quo for borrowing, includes the borrower's adopting economic policies to attain a viable external payments situation – a necessity for preserving the revolving nature of the Bretton Woods institutions' resources. These policies often require that the government reduce budget deficits through increasing tax revenues and cutting back social spending, limit credit creation, achieve market-clearing prices, restrain wage contracts, devalue currency, eliminate price controls, and privatize state enterprises. The World Bank, IDA, donor governments, multilateral agencies and commercial banks usually require an IMF 'seal of approval' before providing loans or grants to a developing country. For further reading: P. B Kenen, *The International Economy* (1994).

E.W.N.; R.H.; P.J.; I.M.D.L; J.P.

***bricolage*.** French word for which there exists no handy English equivalent; perhaps best rendered as 'the art, skill or knack of constructing useful gadgets from whatever bits and pieces come readily to hand'. (The nearest equivalent is the adjectival term 'Heath-Robinson', referring to the British cartoonist who specialized in weird and wonderful contraptions of just that sort.) *Bricolage* has more recently entered the vocabulary of the human and social sciences through its use by the French structural anthropologist Claude Lévi-Strauss. Thus myths and other forms of collective symbolic expression are typified by the *bricolage*-like way in which they put together all sorts of ready-made materials – motifs, allusions, narrative predicaments, stock characters, etc. – and yet manage to produce a seemingly endless range of 'new' stories in response to various localized interests, values and concerns. For this reason they require a STRUCTURALIST mode of analysis which looks beyond their bewildering surface variety in order to identify the underlying logic – the narrative depth-grammar – which they all have in common despite and across such differences of cultural context. For further reading: C. Lévi-Strauss, *The Savage Mind* (1966). C.C.N.

bridewealth. A form of MARRIAGE payment. It involves the transmission of property at marriage from the groom's kin to the male kin of the bride. It symbolizes the movement in the opposite direction of rights over the reproductive powers of the bride. If the marriage is dissolved, payments usually have to be refunded, and this acts as a pressure against divorce. The transference of reproductive rights to the husband's male kin through a bridewealth transaction may give rise to the institution of *levirate*. Levirate is the custom whereby a younger brother of the groom 'inherits' the wife and children of his older brother should he die. The amount of bridewealth paid at marriage varies between societies and it is linked to the extent of the rights transferred from the bride's kin to the groom's kin.

Bridewealth is made up of both perishable and non-perishable goods. Livestock, particularly cattle, is an important part of the payment. The bridewealth received may be used to acquire wives or additional wives (POLYGYNY) by the bride's male kin. Wealth in this way is kept in circulation and is part of a system of exchange.

Bridewealth is found largely in Africa, and work by Goody (*Production and Reproduction*, 1976) has linked its existence with the general economic features of the continent. He has contrasted it with DOWRY, the form of marriage payment associated with

Eurasian societies. For further reading: A. Kuper, *Wives for Cattle* (1982). A.G.

brinkmanship. A term coined by Professor T. C. Schelling (*The Strategy of Conflict*, 1963), and based on a remark of John Foster Dulles in January 1956 about the art of going 'to the brink' of WAR. 'Brinkmanship is thus the deliberate creation of a recognizable risk of war, a risk that one does not completely control. It is the tactic of deliberately letting the situation get out of hand, just because its being out of hand may be intolerable to the other party and force his accommodation.' A.F.B.

British Commonwealth, see under COMMONWEALTH.

broker. In ANTHROPOLOGY, an intermediary who links different NETWORKS. A broker functions at the point where networks intersect. Boissevain draws a distinction between patrons (see PATRONAGE) and brokers. Patrons offer access to what has been called 'first-order resources' (jobs, land, funds, etc.) while brokers deal in second-order resources, making strategic contacts between people. The resources of patrons are limited, those of brokers unlimited. Strategic gains resulting from the manipulation of relationships can be converted by brokers into first-order resources. Brokerage has been developed as a concept by those using network theory to analyse social data from very different areas (see CLIENT). A.G.

Brownian motion. The ceaseless irregular motion of dust PARTICLES which is observed in liquids and gases (and is an example of a STOCHASTIC PROCESS). It provided the earliest evidence for the random heat motion of the underlying MOLECULES, which occurs on a much finer scale. M.V.B.

brownlash. A variant of backlash, brownlash is an emerging term for opposition to stringent environmental protection laws and regulations encouraged by the growth of conservative politics (see CONSERVATISM) and free market policies in the US, UK and other countries. Brown is intended to represent an alternative to the green or environmental movement that advocates strong environmental protection by governments. The term implies that in the absence of legal protections the plant-filled green world will turn brown and dead. W.G.R.

browser. A computer program for finding and reading electronic documents. Developed to display pages from the WORLD WIDE WEB, they have become the display medium in some MULTIMEDIA packages. Some programmers hope to make browsers the principal tool for examining the documents and running the programs found on individual computers. The browser transformed the INTERNET from a specialist's tool to a global phenomenon by making it something for people without technical skills or curiosity. Its simplicity and effects were similar to the GUI systems that increased the personal computer's potential user base. For the first time, television viewers could move to computers without sacrificing their couch-potato status. E.B.B.

Brücke, die ('the Bridge'). Group of young painters active in Dresden, 1905–11, and Berlin, 1911–13. Influenced by the FAUVES and Edvard Munch, they were led by Erich Heckel, E. L. Kirchner and Karl Schmidt-Rottluff, and included at various times Max Pechstein, Emil Nolde and Otto Müller. They formed the nucleus of EXPRESSIONISM in the visual arts, giving it its dominant character of modified CUBIST distortion and great graphic virtuosity, particularly in the woodcut medium. J.W.

bruitisme. The art of noise, as propounded in a manifesto of 1913 by Luigi Russolo, one of FUTURISM's two principal musicians, and featured by DADA. J.W.

Brundtland Report. Report of the World Commission on Environment and Development, released in 1987, and named after Gro Harlem Brundtland, Prime Minister of Norway and Chairman of the Commission. The Commission was created by the UN after the UN Conference on the Human Environment, held in Stockholm, in 1972. The Brundtland Report expounded the concept of sustainability, or sustainable development – practices and policies designed to protect resources and the environment so that future generations will have a quality environment and access to natural resources. W.G.R.

brut, see under ART BRUT; CONCRETE.

brutalism. A movement in architecture that asserted the primacy of architectural elements – space, structure and materials displayed in their untrammelled form – against the visual enfeeblement of the modern movement which had occurred in the late 1940s. It inched mainstream modern from the abstract to the expressive.

Le Corbusier's Unité d'Habitation in Marseilles (1948–54), which turned the use of bare concrete patterned by its rough timber shuttering (see CONCRETE) into a virtuoso performance, showed the potentialities of the vivid expression of materials suggested by economic necessity. His later Maisons Jaoul at Neuilly (1956) extended the vocabulary and provided an idiom capable of imitation. The first building to be labelled 'new brutalist' was the school at Hunstanton, England, by Peter and Alison Smithson (1949). This had an exposed steel frame, unplastered brickwork, exposed floor beams and service runs, and was designed with an austerity derived from Mies van der Rohe. For further reading: R. Banham, *The New Brutalism; Ethic or Aesthetic?* (1966). M.BR.

Bubnovy Valet, see KNAVE OF DIAMONDS.

Buckminsterfullerene (*and* **fullerene**). A form of pure carbon consisting of molecules of 60 carbon atoms joined together in a hollow, approximately spherical cage. The cage is in fact a polyhedron called a truncated icosahedron, and contains 12 pentagonal faces (made from rings of five carbon ATOMS) and 20 hexagonal faces (made from six carbon atoms). The existence of a carbon molecule with this structure was proposed in the 1970s, but was not synthesized until 1985. A technique for its production in large quantities was devised in 1990, leading to the rapid growth of research on its chemical and physical properties. Other, larger carbon cages have also been identified and isolated, collectively known as fullerenes. All possess exactly 12 pentagonal rings, since exactly this number is required to enable a system of connected hexagons to curl into a closed shell. This principle, first deduced by the Swiss mathematician Leonhard Euler, was exploited by the American architect Richard Buckminster Fuller in his geodesic dome structures. Buckminster Fuller's designs provided the inspiration that helped the discoverers of buckminsterfullerene to guess its structure, and so they named the molecule accordingly. For further reading: J. Baggott, *Perfect Symmetry* (1996). P.C.B.

Buddhism. The RELIGION, covering much of Asia, which venerates Gautama the Buddha (or 'Enlightened'), who taught in India during the 5th century BC. Its goal is 'Nirvana' or liberation from 'becoming' things or selves; this has usually been conceived as liberation from an endless cycle of reincarnations or rebirths in different bodies. Its self-discipline is aimed at achieving detachment and an inward peace, and in the end enlightenment. It emphasizes compassion, but mainly in the sense of spreading such peace. It avoids the intellectualism of Christian THEOLOGY, and emphasizes its practical applications – in traditionally Buddhist countries such as Sri Lanka, Thailand and Burma, everyday life is still profoundly influenced by the teaching and example of the monks. In offering a state of mind – enlightenment – rather than elaborate theological theorics, it can be regarded as compatible both with a scientific world-view (see WELTANSCHAUUNG) excluding belief in GOD and with a religious tradition. Indeed, disagreements have grown between the *Theravada* (Little Vehicle) in Ceylon, Burma, Thailand, etc., and the *Mahayana* (Great Vehicle) in Japan, Korea, China, Tibet and Nepal, which is more elaborately developed (and closer to CHRISTIANITY, although very little influenced by it). The difference between these two types of Buddhism can amount, in Western terms, to the difference between AGNOSTICISM or PANTHEISM and a THEISM based on belief in divine 'grace' and therefore in the value of petitionary prayer.

Buddhism has made a considerable impact in the West, partly because it does not have a METAPHYSICS of GOD, partly because of its apparent consonance with science, and partly because of its leaning towards tolerance. ZEN is specially respected. There is also much interest in Buddhist art. Some Westerners have become Buddhists, and many more have admired, and even envied, Buddhism as a way of life.

In the latter part of the 20th century,

Buddhist societies in Asia have undergone vicissitudes. The plight of Tibetans has been well publicized by its exiled spiritual and political leader, the Dalai Lama. But Cambodia has suffered too, at the hands of the KHMER ROUGE, Burma has undergone an isolationist military regime, VIETNAM and Laos have suffered war and oppression, and Sri Lanka has had a bitter and protracted civil war. As Buddhists are driven out of these countries, it may be that the West's interest in Buddhism provides one key to its future as a world religion. See also TANTRA. For further reading: T. Berry, *Religions of India* (1996). D.L.E.; N.SM.

budget deficit, see under PSBR.

buffer state. In political GEOGRAPHY, a small independent STATE lying between two or more larger and potentially hostile states and thus reducing the likelihood of border friction between them. Belgium might be thought to have served as a buffer state in respect of France and Germany. P.H.

building society. Mutual institution owned by the members who borrow from and save with it. They are largely responsible for financing private housing in Britain, performing many of the same tasks as the SAVINGS & LOANS in the US. With the deregulation of financial markets in the UK under THATCHERISM, the mutuals gained new freedoms competing with the banks on the high street with a range of financial services including insurance, PENSIONS, consumer credit and travellers' cheques. The expansion into new areas increased the gap between members and management. Many of the biggest and more successful societies, starting with the Abbey National in 1989 and including the largest in the marketplace (the Halifax) in 1997, have converted into public limited companies providing their members with 'windfall' payouts in the shape of quoted shares. The remaining mutuals led by the Nationwide are fighting to preserve their current status as part of a movement which has preached prudence since its foundation in Victorian times. They offer members advantageous savings rates and cheaper home loans rates in an effort to retain their loyalty. But the commercial pressures in the marketplace could see many of them absorbed by larger financial institutions. For further reading: N. Lawson, *The View from No. 11* (1992). A.BR.

bulimia nervosa, see under ANOREXIA NERVOSA.

Bullock Report. Reports of two separate committees of inquiry set up by the British government (the first by a Conservative, the second by a Labour government) under the chairmanship of the historian and former Vice-Chancellor of Oxford University, Alan (now Lord) Bullock.

The first, *A Language for Life*, published in 1975, was an inquiry into the teaching of reading and the other uses of English in English schools. Its 333 recommendations for improving these, although largely ignored by government, have had a major impact on practice in the schools and on the education of teachers.

The second, *Industrial Democracy*, published in 1977, was an inquiry into the best means of achieving a radical extension of industrial democracy in the control of companies by means of employee representation on boards of directors, to the principle of which the Labour government was committed. The report's recommendations, which proposed the appointment of employee representatives to the boards of all companies with more than 2,000 workers, were rejected by the industrialist members of the committee as by management in general, and aroused widespread controversy. After 18 months' discussion, a Cabinet committee set up by the Labour Prime Minister, James Callaghan, produced a modified version of the report's proposals, which were incorporated in the Labour Party's programme for the 1979 election. Labour's defeat, however, and the advent of Mrs Thatcher, removed industrial democracy from the political agenda. A.L.C.B.

Bureau International de Surréalisme Révolutionnaire, see under COBRA.

bureaucracy. 'Power, influence of the heads and staff of government bureaux' (definition of *bureaucratie* in the Dictionary of the French Academy, 1789 supplement). The modern theory of bureaucracy derives largely from the German sociologist Max Weber, who saw it as the formal codification of the idea of rational organization. A bureaucracy is characterized by legal rules, a salaried administrative staff, the specialization of function, the authority of the (non-hereditary) office, not the person, and the keeping of written records and documents. For Weber, the rational bureaucracy was the major element in the rationalization of the modern world.

Yet, from the start, popular writers have seen bureaucracy as an irrational force, dominating the lives of people, while political theorists have seen it as an independent force tending to swallow all of society in its maw. Balzac popularized the word in his 1836 novel, *Les Employés*, calling bureaucracy 'the giant power wielded by pigmies . . . a government as fussy and meddlesome . . . as a small shopkeeper's wife'. Dickens, in *Little Dorrit* (1857), summarized 'the Whole Science of Government' in his representation of the bureaucracy as 'the Circumlocution Office'. John Stuart Mill, in *On Liberty* (1859) and *Considerations on Representative Government* (1861), contrasted bureaucracy with DEMOCRACY, and saw the former as a threat to representative government and to liberty. And Gaetano Mosca, in *The Ruling Class* (English edition, 1939), described the modern state as essentially a bureaucratic state ruled, inevitably, by a minority.

In contemporary theory, interest in bureaucracy focuses on two aspects. Sociological theorists tend to see bureaucracy as one modal type of organization, wherein the formal dimensions of rule and administration are paramount. Political writers have concentrated on the question of whether the bureaucracy, in modern society, becomes a 'new CLASS' which takes over political rule – as, according to Milovan Djilas, happened in the former USSR. Indeed, though Marx paid little attention to this aspect of the question, it has been the central issue regarding the characterization of Soviet society. Thus Trotsky regarded bureaucracy as indicating the betrayal of the revolutionary ideals (see REVOLUTION) by a new class; while SOCIALIST writers have characterized the former USSR as a new form of 'bureaucratic COLLECTIVISM'. For further reading: M. Albrow, *Bureaucracy* (1970). D.B.

business cycle, see TRADE OR BUSINESS CYCLE.

Business Roundtable. An élite INTEREST GROUP formed in the US in November 1972, essentially devoted to curtailing the influence and bargaining power of labour unions. It was enlarged in membership and scope in June 1973, and grew quickly to consist of about 130 chief executive officers of major corporations. The Roundtable may be seen as an organized response to the series of defeats inflicted on big business by environmental, consumer and PUBLIC INTEREST groups from the late 1960s onwards, and to the more general distrust of corporations amplified by political finance scandals and WATERGATE. The organization attempts to forge some consensus on political issues between different individual and sectoral business interests; to gain high-level access to government; and to encourage members' corporations towards greater political awareness and activity. Its tactics include the orchestration of co-operative campaigns with bodies such as the National Association of Manufacturers and the national Chamber of Commerce, the funding of pro-business think-tanks, and the use of the political 'clout' of its individual members. The influence of the Roundtable is hard to estimate precisely. Observers credit it with a major role in the defeat of liberal (see LIBERALISM) consumer-protection and full-employment legislation, in the attack on unionism since 1974, and in promoting the increasing sophistication of other business lobbying efforts. For further reading: M. Useem, *The Inner Circle* (1984). S.R.

busing. American term for the transfer by bus of children from their own neighbourhood to school in another. The practice evolved in the attempt in the late 1960s to achieve the DESEGREGATION of schools required, but seldom accomplished, since a major Supreme Court decision in 1954 (see SUPREME COURT OF THE UNITED STATES). Busing provoked some vigorous white resistance and slow compliance, and was complicated by successive judicial decisions and changes of government. It nevertheless gained momentum until the late 1970s, after which the Reagan administration brought a substantial reversal of government sympathy for mandatory busing. Debate over the merits of maintaining and extending busing continue. Proponents argue that it improves BLACK educational performance and promotes interracial harmony, thus helping progress from desegregation to INTEGRATION. Conservative critics argue that it does neither to any significant extent, while destroying the valued character of neighbourhood schools. Radical critiques claim that its effects are negligible compared to the deleterious consequences of residential segregation and economic inequality, and are sometimes counter-productive as wealthier white parents react by sending children to private schools. S.R.

buto dance. Term originated from the Japanese *ankokubuto*, meaning dark soul dance. Buto-Buto-Butôh is a Japanese modern dance movement which developed in the 1950s and 1960s under the leadership of Tatsumi Hijikata (1928–86) and Kazuo Ohno. Buto is not a formal technique or academic style but an individual form of expressive movement (or 'fighting form' – Hijikata), appropriate to post-war AVANT-GARDE Japanese theatre. It finds its roots from within Japanese tradition and uses a recognizable restraint to create a paradoxically surrealistic approach to DANCE THEATRE. The buto dancer wears the white face and body paint traditional to Japanese culture in direct contrast to the physical form of the dance. Today more than 30 buto companies exist in Japan. L.A.

Butskellism, see under CONSENSUS POLITICS.

C

C3I, see COMMAND, CONTROL, COMMUNICATIONS AND INTELLIGENCE.

CACM, see CENTRAL AMERICAN COMMON MARKET.

cacogenic, see under DYSGENIC.

CAD, see COMPUTER-AIDED DESIGN.

Caffe Lena, see under FOLK MUSIC.

***Cahiers du Cinéma*,** see under NEW WAVE.

calculus. This means 'rules for calculation', but usually refers to the procedures for finding exact tangents to curves (differentiation), and finding the exact area underneath curves on a graph (integration). The discoveries of Newton and Leibniz (in the 17th century) solved both these problems. The proof that these two procedures are linked is called 'the Fundamental Theorem of the Calculus'.

These techniques turned out to be extremely powerful when applied to planetary motion and, indeed, in every branch of PHYSICS involving change and movement. N.A.R.

calculus of finite differences, see under NUMERICAL ANALYSIS.

calligramme. A poem written and printed in a specific shape. The modern revival of this age-old device was pioneered under the influence of CUBISM by Guillaume Apollinaire, a volume of whose *Calligrammes* appeared in 1918. In their simplest and most light-hearted form these consist of words describing rain, or a motor-car. At their most difficult they seek, as a critic explained, to oblige the reader to understand 'syntheticoideologically' instead of 'analyticodiscursively'. They push experimentation as far as Apollinaire ever pushed it, and influenced CONCRETE POETRY. M.S.-S.

Calvinism. The Christian tradition founded by John Calvin (1509–64) in Geneva, and flourishing especially in Scotland and in New England. It has developed PROTESTANTISM by rejecting every doctrine not found in the Bible, and by finding in the Bible its own doctrines, notably the 'predestination' by God of the 'elect' to heaven and of the rest to hell. The tradition is still creative theologically (see BARTHIAN). A strict and sometimes intolerant morality is associated (see PROTESTANT ETHIC), as is the Presbyterian (see PRESBYTERIANISM) form of Church government. D.L.E.

Camden Town Group. A society of artists founded in 1911; in 1913 it merged with the LONDON GROUP. Of the 16 members, those who may best be described as 'Camden Town' (a district of north London) were: Spencer Gore (President), Harold Gilman, Robert Bevan, Malcolm Drummond and William Ratcliffe, painters who were deeply affected by the opposing influences of Walter Sickert and the POST-IMPRESSIONISTS. Q.B.

Campaign for Nuclear Disarmament, see under PEACE MOVEMENT.

cancer. A new growth in any tissue or organ that behaves as if it had escaped the surveillance of the growth-controlling processes that operate in the other tissues of the body. Cancers are described as more or less malignant in proportion as they are more or less rapidly growing and invasive. Cancer CELLS may escape from their site of origin and set up daughter colonies (*metastases*) in normal tissues elsewhere. Cancers are crudely subdivided into tumours of epithelial tissues (*carcinomas*) and tumours of cells belonging to the connective tissue and bony families (*sarcomas*).

Some industrial chemicals and food additives are known to be cancer-producing (*oncogenic*). Public-health authorities are acutely aware of these dangers, and the use of such chemicals is under very close surveillance. Many causes of cancer are known – e.g. the polycyclic hydrocarbons that are the active ingredients of coal tar, or viruses (see VIROLOGY) such as the Rous virus in chicks, polyoma virus. Although there is a strong and growing presumption that viruses are a cause of human cancers, particularly some of those of the cervix and liver, it is only in the case of the rare blood cancer, adult T-cell leukaemia, that the evidence of a viral cause is compelling.

The branch of medical science concerned with cancer is known as ONCOLOGY. Cancer research is devoted to the earliest possible diagnosis of malignant changes, to analysing ever more deeply the properties of the malignant cell itself, and to the clinical trial of the theoretically or empirically justifiable curative procedures, notably the use of *anti-proliferative* drugs (drugs that suppress cell division, e.g. nitrogen mustards) in the leukaemias, the use of X-irradiation, and, wherever possible, the intensification of the immunological response (see IMMUNITY) which represents the body's natural defence. In addition, hormone-dependent tumours may sometimes be controlled by the artificial administration or deprivation of hormones (see ENDOCRINOLOGY). SURGERY and X-irradiation nevertheless remain the bulwarks of cancer treatment throughout the world.

Analysis of malignant cells has revealed many differences between them and healthy cells, but it continues to be difficult to gauge which of the differences are the cause and which the result of malignancy. A current focus of attention is ONCOGENES, GENES which in their normal form are essential for the normal controlled growth of cells but which, if mutated, may result in the uncontrolled growth that is characteristic of malignant cells. There is, however, still no evidence that oncogenes contribute to the cause of the most frequent types of human cancer. P.M.; P.N.

cannabis, see MARIJUANA.

canned music, see under MUZAK.

canonical conjugates, see under UNCERTAINTY PRINCIPLE.

CAP (Common Agricultural Policy). A web of policies designed to stabilize agricultural markets across Europe and guarantee supplies through farm support mechanisms. The objectives of the Common Agricultural Policy are outlined in the Treaty of Rome, which includes among its goals the maintenance of reasonable prices for consumers. But it has seldom worked like that. It is generally seen as a producers' charter, with the annual Farm Price Review setting minimum prices for most farm products during the coming year, the price set in green currency, the mechanism used to translate the European Currency Unit (Ecu) into national currencies. Among the results of the CAP has been the build-up of surplus food mountains and wine lakes as a result of artificially inflated prices. This has led critics to describe the CAP as a policy which takes cash from EUROPEAN UNION (EU) taxpayers and uses it to make the food consumers buy more expensive products. The complexities of the CAP are among the reasons that EU enlargement to eastern Europe, where food production is so much cheaper, has proved such a substantial problem. A.BR.

capital.

(1) Those assets that are used in the production of goods and services. The assets may belong to producers (e.g. factories and machines), consumers (e.g. houses) or the community (e.g. public buildings and roads). *Capital goods* are those goods used to produce other goods and services. *Working capital* is the MONEY used by a business to conduct its transactions. *Human capital* is the ability, skill and knowledge of individuals which is used to produce goods and services. Capital may be valued at its historic cost, i.e. the past expenditure to purchase it, or at its current cost, which will reflect the discounted (see DISCOUNTING) value of the income it is expected to yield. For most purposes, the latter valuation has the most economic meaning. Capital's ability to producc goods and services declines with age and, in valuing capital, it is important and usual to allow for this depreciation.

(2) The capital of a person, firm, institution, etc. is the money value of real and financial assets. This usage of the term emphasizes the money value of assets rather than their ability to produce goods and services, though the former is usually related to the latter. See also SOCIAL CAPITAL. J.P.

capital punishment. The death sentence. In the West, only the US continues to practise capital punishment. It is a significant feature of criminal and military justice in China, in numerous African countries, and in Islamic countries. It has not been a feature of western European criminal justice systems for nearly a quarter of a century, although the UK Privy Council hears capital appeals from those Caribbean countries – notably Jamaica and Trinidad – which remain part of the COMMONWEALTH.

There are more than 3,500 people on death row in the United States. All of these were convicted post-1976, following a four-year moratorium on the death penalty, which the US supreme court (see SUPREME COURT OF THE UNITED STATES) had found, for that brief period, unconstitutional. In 1977, Gary Gilmore was, famously, the first American to be executed under the newly constitutional death penalty statute in Utah. As of February 1998, a further 439 Americans had been put to death. In the US, 38 states have the death penalty, in addition to the military and the federal government.

In modern times, the US has had the death penalty for RAPE and murder, but presently the law only applies to first-degree murder. The death penalty has been shown to be disproportionately applied to BLACKS; and statistics show that the RACE of the victim, not the killer, is more influential in bringing in a death sentence (especially so if the killer is black and the victim white).

In the US five methods are employed in capital punishment: hanging; shooting by firing squad; the electric chair; the gas chamber; and lethal injection. Since the beginning of the 20th century, execution methods have been driven by technological innovation and a questionable desire on the part of governments to make them more 'humane'. The rope was largely replaced by the electric chair – the invention of a dentist – at the turn of the century after New York State adopted it over the proposed guillotine. An army surgeon invented the gas chamber, meant to be a further humane refinement of execution technology, in the 1920s. But the preferred method of execution in the US is now lethal injection. A series of three drugs is administered – either manually or through a machine – which render the condemned person unconscious before stopping his heart, then lungs. Lethal injection has helped to make capital punishment more palatable to a larger number of Americans, since it does not involve grotesque mutilation of the condemned person, such as often happens with the electric chair. Latest polls show that nearly 80 per cent of Americans favour the death penalty.

Appeals against death sentences are guaranteed in the Bill of Rights of the US Constitution. However, recent legislation ('habeas reform') has limited appellants' right to the petition of habeas corpus in the highest court, and federal funds have been withdrawn from specialized capital punishment resource centres which, in the majority of cases, are condemned inmates' only source of legal assistance. For further reading: S. Trombley, *The Execution Protocol* (1992).

S.T.

capitalism. Often called the 'market system' or the 'free enterprise system', capitalism is unquestionably the most important mode of economic organization in our time. It is also the most unusual. Capitalism is distinguished from all other economic orders, past and present, by three properties. The first is its continuous effort to expand wealth, exercised both by private enterprise and individuals. What is remarkable about this drive is that over most of history, acquisitiveness has been regarded as an unworthy motivation: the Bible calls the love of money 'the root of all evil' (Timothy VI, 10). Although capitalism has not rid the drive for riches of its historic repute, it has put its energizing effects to previously unknown useful purposes.

Second, capitalism is co-ordinated by a network of markets, rather than by the determinations of kings and local lords, the principal means of economic co-ordination from ancient Egypt until the decline of feudalism in the 15th century. If the drive for expansion gives capitalism its dynamism, markets are the source of its unprecedented adaptability.

Third, capitalism is uniquely characterized by a dual system of power. Rather than answering to a single political authority, capitalism has a private sector dominated by the decisions of business enterprise and the judgements of consumers, and a public sector in which government exercises its traditional powers as well as a limited but important regulatory influence over the private sector.

During its three centuries, capitalism has often suffered dangerous economic malfunctions, as in the Great Depression of the 1930s, but its expansive thrust has nonetheless changed material life out of all recognition. Although clearly dominant today,

capitalism faces powerful new challenges – the GLOBALIZATION of modern production to low-wage parts of the world and looming ecological dangers from the emission of industrial gases. These are not the first challenges that capitalism has encountered, but they are of sufficient magnitude that we can expect considerable changes in its organization during the decades ahead, probably mainly in the protective role played by the public sphere. For further reading: J. Boswell, *Capitalism in Contention* (1997).
R.HE.

capitalist state, the. A concept within contemporary MARXISM that attempts to come to terms with the evident fact of the massive presence of the STATE within 20th-century CAPITALISM. It is meant to suggest a new form of state, replacing the limited 'nightwatchman state' of 19th-century capitalism. In the era of 'managed' or 'monopoly' capitalism, the state is seen as increasingly necessary to the preservation of the capitalist system through the public provision of a complex economic INFRASTRUCTURE – transport and communications, subsidies and market regulation, cheap and guaranteed supplies of energy and power – as well as a SOCIAL WELFARE system that stabilizes the social order and absorbs costs – e.g. of education and training – that would otherwise have to be borne by private capitalists. For further reading: B. Jessop, *The Capitalist State* (1982).
K.K.

capitulationism, see under DEVIATIONISM.

capture theory, see under ECONOMIC REGULATION.

carbon cycle. In PHYSICS (for its meaning in BIOLOGY see LIFE CYCLE), a sequence of NUCLEAR REACTIONS thought to occur inside stars, in which a mass of hydrogen NUCLEI at extremely high temperatures is converted into a smaller mass of helium nuclei in the presence of carbon nuclei; the resulting energy leaves the star as RADIATION which is observed by us as starlight or sunshine. See also BINDING ENERGY; MASS-ENERGY EQUATION.
M.V.B.

carbon dating, see RADIOCARBON DATING.

carcinomas, see under CANCER.

cardinal numbers. These are numbers (see NUMBER) which denote the size of a SET of objects. They start with the familiar 0, 1, 2, 3, . . . Georg Cantor (1845–1918), in a series of papers starting in 1874 (the year of his marriage), created the serious study of INFINITE cardinals. Two sets are of the same size (have the same cardinal) if their elements can be paired off, one by one. So an infinite set can be the same size as part of itself, unlike a finite set (the set of natural numbers 1, 2, 3, 4, . . . is the same size as the set of even numbers 2, 4, 6, 8, . . .). Cantor proved that the set of real numbers is bigger than the set of natural numbers, and conjectured (the 'continuum hypothesis') that there is no set with cardinal between the two. He also proved that for every set there is a larger set, which leads to the PARADOX that 'the set of all sets' looks like the largest possible set, but cannot be.

This, and other aspects of his work, led to heated controversy, and some found it appropriate that he died in a mental institution.
N.A.R.

cardiology. The study of diseases of the heart and circulation. These include congenital heart disease, valvular heart disease, ischaemic heart disease (angina pectoris and myocardial infarction), cardiomyopathies, hypertension, arrhythmias and cardiopulmonary disease.
L.J.F.

care in the community, see COMMUNITY CARE.

cargo cults. A variety of MILLENARIANISM found in New Guinea. Its adherents believe that the valued material goods of Western civilization (the 'cargo') are about to be delivered by miraculous means, arriving with the spirits of the dead and ushering in the millennium. The cargo is clearly symbolic of a desired change in the social position of those who await it, and the cults are concerned with POWER and STATUS, not merely with the magical acquisition of material things. The term has also been applied more loosely to a number of anti-Western nativistic movements in the Melanesian region. For further reading: I. C. Jarvis, *Rationality and Relativism* (1984).
M.F.

carnivalization. Term coined by the Russian critic Mikhail Bakhtin (see BAKHTINIAN) to describe the penetration of carnival into everyday life and language and into literature. Sociologists and anthropologists of the Durkheimian school suggest that the function of rituals of reversal (in which what is normally low becomes high and what is normally forbidden, compulsory) is to act as a 'safety-valve' for the release of tension and thus to maintain the social and political structure. Bakhtin, in contrast, saw the medieval 'culture of folk humour' and carnival in particular as profoundly subversive of official institutions and hierarchies, and he suggested that Rabelais, Dostoevsky and other writers drew on the grotesque bodily imagery of carnival for this purpose. P.B.

Carnot cycle. In THERMODYNAMICS, a particular sequence of operations involving the transfer of ENERGY to and from a system. At the end of the cycle the system has returned to its original state. The Carnot cycle is of theoretical importance, since no other cycle can convert heat into work more efficiently. Petrol and diesel engines employ cycles closely related to Carnot's. M.V.B.

carrying capacity. The maximum population of a SPECIES that can be supported by an ECOSYSTEM OF HABITAT without damaging that habitat's ability to support that population in the future. The earth's carrying capacity for the human species is unknown but is believed by many to have already been exceeded. Certainly the loss of topsoil, forests and BIODIVERSITY, and the depletion of fisheries and other natural resources, strongly suggest that the earth's carrying capacity for Homo sapiens is being reduced by that species' activities. See also SUSTAINABILITY. W.G.R.

cartel. A union of sellers of a good or service who raise the price (or other conditions of sale), and the rewards to its own members, to a higher level than would prevail in a FREE MARKET. In order to control the price, a cartel needs to restrict output, and this is usually done by agreeing on quotas for each member's production. If output is not restricted, a fixed price would provide an incentive to existing sellers to sell more output. This would lower the price, reduce the rewards to the members and, perhaps, completely undermine the cartel. Similarly, the interests of the members of a cartel are affected adversely by the entry of new sellers. Thus, cartels are interested in erecting BARRIERS TO ENTRY. Cartels are most easily formed and durable when there are only a few members with similar interests. They are usually regarded as undesirable, because COMPETITION is reduced and there are no offsetting gains. By comparison, MONOPOLIES may be justified by the existence of ECONOMIES OF SCALE. Cartels may actually be formed with the intention of saving the weaker members from destruction (cartels flourished in the Great Depression of the 1930s). Most governments have made cartels and most of their activities illegal. The most important modern cartel is OPEC. S.BR.; J.P.

Cartel. An informal but influential alliance of the four leading independent Paris theatre directors between 1926 and World War II; known for its fresh approach to the classics, its support of such moderns as Pirandello, Chekhov and Giraudoux, and its dislike of NATIONALISM and commercialism. It was formed to carry on the ideas of Jacques Copeau, director of the Vieux-Colombier 1913–24, and consisted of Charles Dullin (Théâtre de l'Atelier), Louis Jouvet (Comédie des Champs-Elysées, later the Athénée), Gaston Baty (Chimère and Théâtre de Montparnasse), and Georges Pitoeff (no fixed theatre). J.W.

Carter doctrine. This was developed by President Carter in January 1980 in response to the Soviet Union's invasion of AFGHANISTAN, which began in late December 1979. Its main element was an indication that the US would contemplate a military response if the Soviet Union threatened the oil-fields of the Persian Gulf, and it was followed by promises of aid to Afghan resistance. More generally, it represented a shift in policy towards the Soviet Union which included Carter's withdrawal of the SALT 2 Treaty from Congress, embargoes on the export to the USSR of American grain and sophisticated electronic equipment, US withdrawal from the 1980 Moscow Olympics, and increases in the defence budget. S.R.

cartography. The science and art of map-making. Cartography today is strongly influenced by evolving methods of information collection (such as satellite remote sensing), by increasingly sophisticated data processing and manipulation (particularly through the use of Geographical Information Systems [GIS]), and by developments in the printing and reproduction of maps. For further reading: A. H. Robinson *et al*, *Elements of Cartography* (1995). P.O.M.

cascade diffusion, see under DIFFUSION.

case grammar. An approach to linguistic analysis developed in the 1960s which saw the basic structure of sentences as consisting of a verb plus one or more noun phrases which relate to it in defined ways. The syntactic MEANING-RELATIONS were called cases (a term covering more than in TRADITIONAL GRAMMAR, where it was restricted to describing certain systems of word-endings). For example, in the sentence *John opened the door with the key, John* is 'agentive' case, *the door* 'objective', and *with the key* 'instrumental'. This approach, first formulated by Charles Fillmore in 1968, has since developed variant forms, and has exercised considerable influence in contemporary LINGUISTICS. D.C.

case method. A distinctive feature of American legal education, developed by Christopher Langdell, dean of the Harvard Law School, beginning in 1870. The standard pedagogical technique in most American law schools today, the case method uses a question and answer format and relies on case opinions as its primary source material. By encouraging students to analyse the application of law rather than legal rules in general, the case method reflects the pragmatic, fact-oriented approach of American lawyers generally, and exemplifies the triumph of SOCIOLOGICAL JURISPRUDENCE in the American legal system. M.S.P.

Casimir effect, see under VIRTUAL PARTICLES.

caste. The name (Portuguese: *casta*) for the traditional hierarchical divisions of Hindu society (see HINDUISM): (1) A hierarchy of purity, the fourfold *varna* division: Brahmin, Kshatriya, Vaisya, Sudra (priests, warriors/rulers, merchants, servants) which is assumed to embrace the whole of society except the scheduled castes (Untouchables/Harijans); (2) The numerous *jati*, local endogamous groups (see ENDOGAMY) arranged hierarchically which compose the society of any area of the country.

Caste is a relative concept; that is, to discuss caste is to discuss intercaste relationships. Caste is both a form of social organization and a system of values. Ideas of purity and POLLUTION keep different castes apart (L. Dumont, *Homo Hierarchicus*, 1970). Endogamous MARRIAGE is an important mechanism for preserving caste integrity. In reality, however, the situation is much more complex and there are different kinds of cross-caste exchange. For example, various marriage strategies (hypergamy and hypogamy; see DOWRY) reveal the fluidity of caste boundaries. Beyond Hindu society caste is to be found in other societies directly influenced by Hindu culture (e.g., Sri Lanka, Bali and among Muslims in the Indian subcontinent). The question of whether caste may be used generally as a concept to describe a system of SOCIAL STRATIFICATION or is culturally specific (i.e. restricted to Hindu society) has been much debated by anthropologists (E. R. Leach, ed., *Aspects of Caste*, 1960). M.F.; A.G.

castration. In 1997, four American states passed legislation allowing for the castration of convicted sex offenders. There are two types of castration: *surgical*, and so-called *chemical* castration. Surgical castration involves an operation known as an orchidectomy in which a small slit is made in the testicles, and the testes removed. The testes produce testosterone, the male sex hormone. Stopping the production of testosterone lowers the sex drive. Supporters of the measure believe that, with a reduced sex drive, criminals may be less likely to reoffend. Unlike surgical castration, so-called 'chemical castration' is a temporary measure in which a testosterone-inhibiting drug such as Depo-Provera is administered by regular injection. Supporters of castration for sex offenders believe that it may reduce prison costs. Opponents – including many rape victims – argue that, since many sex crimes are about POWER rather than SEX, castrated rapists may resort to even more violent means of assault, including the use of substitutional objects instead of a penis; mutilation; and murder. S.T.

castration anxiety. In psychoanalytic theory (see PSYCHOANALYSIS), the allegedly universal fear of castration felt by boys at a certain stage of their PSYCHOSEXUAL DEVELOPMENT; its origin in the OEDIPUS COMPLEX lies in fear of retaliation by the father for the child's feelings of sexuality towards the mother and of hostility towards the competing father. Girls were also said to suffer castration anxiety originating in the ELECTRA COMPLEX; but this view has been largely abandoned. J.S.B.

Castroism. This term is used to refer to the versions of MARXISM drawing their inspiration from the Cuban revolution of 1959, led by Fidel Castro, and further articulated by his colleagues Che Guevara and Regis Debray (see CUBA). These theories emphasize the importance of isolated GUERRILLA foci, or bases, as creating the preconditions for REVOLUTION in Central and South America. The guerrilla force would be the nucleus of a future political party and not the other way round. This involved the elevation of the military above the political in a manner quite uncharacteristic of mainstream Marxism, and an overestimation of the extent to which the social and political structure of Latin America was ripe for revolution. Although severely tested by the US economic embargo, in place since 1962, and the fall of the east European SOCIALIST bloc and the Soviet Union (see USSR), the Castroist revolution has maintained the one-party system and the main tenets of its IDEOLOGY. However, in response to a deteriorating economic situation, some compromises, particularly on economic policy, have been made. Limited private-sector activity is now legal and the government is seeking to promote joint business ventures with Western companies, although these have been hampered by the extra-territorial nature of the 1996 Helms-Burton Law, which tightened the US embargo against Cuba. For further reading: M. A. Centeno and M. Font (eds), *Toward a New Cuba?* (1997). M.A.P.

CAT (CT), see under RADIOLOGY.

catachresis. In critical theory, a trope (see TROPISM) in which a sign which already stands for one thing is applied to another thing which has had no expression. *Head of lettuce* is a prosaic example. The importance of catachresis is that, because there is no substitution of a figurative expression for a literal one, it calls into question the claim that METAPHOR arises from a contrast between the literal and the figurative. For further reading: J. Culler, *The Pursuit of Signs* (1981). S.T.

catalysis. An alteration, usually an increase, in the rate of a chemical reaction. The substance causing this increase is a *catalyst*. Chemical SPECIES usually require a certain amount of extra energy, the ACTIVATION ENERGY, before they react. Normally this energy is provided internally by the collision of ATOMS or MOLECULES, with the required excess ENERGY, but the number of such collisions may be small, and the rate of reaction slow. A *heterogeneous* catalyst speeds up the reactions by providing a surface on which the chemical reaction can proceed with lower activation energy. A *homogeneous* catalyst operates in the same phase and accelerates the reaction by participating in reaction intermediates. Catalysts play an important role in many industrial processes; the most effective are ENZYMES, which facilitate physiologically important reactions. B.F.

catalytic war, see under WAR.

catastrophe theory. Any system can be regarded as a black box (i.e. a mechanism of whose internal workings we may be totally ignorant; see BLACK-BOX THEORY) with an input and an output. Generally, if the input is changed by a small amount, then the output changes by a small amount (the output depends continuously on the input). However, there are often certain critical values of the input where a small change produces a very large change in the output – a catastrophe. Catastrophe theory is a mathematical model conceived in the 1960s by René Thom which describes these phenomena. It is principally qualitative and provides a very useful framework for understanding these discontinuities. For further reading: R. Thom, *Mathematical Models of Morphogenesis* (1983). J.M.

catastrophism. The theory that certain phenomena in world history, notably in GEOLOGY and BIOLOGY, have been strongly affected by catastrophes of various sorts. 'Catastrophe' is a term of ancient Greek drama, for the change in the plot leading up to the conclusion. Used later of any sudden change, the word was appropriated by the geologists to denote any cataclysm or convulsion of the earth's surface. Catastrophism is a doctrine, often associated with the French naturalist Baron Georges Cuvier (1769–1832), explaining the differences in fossil forms found at different stratigraphic levels in terms of repeated cataclysms followed by new creations. The idea took support from scripture (Noah's flood) and contemporary ZOOLOGY. In 1837 the Swiss zoologist and palaeontologist Louis Agassiz (see PALAEONTOLOGY) strengthened the theory with evidence for 'ice ages', and glaciation reaching as far as the Mediterranean. Early catastrophism was opposed by *uniformitarianism* (a word coined in 1832 by William Whewell), the theory that natural agents affecting the Earth uniformly over very long periods are still operating. Most geologists now acknowledge uniform factors as well as the incidence of catastrophes that affect the earth's landforms and biological EVOLUTION. Cometary and asteroid impact, massive volcanic explosions (e.g. Krakatoa), hurricanes and floods, and the TECTONIC erosion of mountain systems, are now added to the list. Some espouse a catastrophism of sorts that explains geological history in terms of cycles of mountain building, the transgression and regression of oceans, and the evolution and extinction of living organisms. Some writers with imagination (e.g. I. Velikovsky) have claimed to detect ancient literary evidence for great catastrophes. For further reading: M. J. S. Rudwick, *The Meaning of Fossils* (1985).

J.D.N.

categorical imperative. The supreme principle of morality, according to Kant, by which all such specific moral principles as 'Do not lie' and 'Do not commit suicide' are to be tested. His basic formulation of it is: So act that the maxim of your action can be willed without contradiction as a universal law. Another, loosely connected, formulation enjoins us to treat people always as ends and never merely as means. In everyday terms Kant tells us to ask of any projected action: what would happen if everyone acted like this? A.Q.

category. A term introduced into PHILOSOPHY by Aristotle, in very much its everyday sense of a class or kind, but restricted in its application to LINGUISTIC items, specifically to the descriptive or non-logical words or phrases which figure as the subjects and predicates of PROPOSITIONS. With his classification of terms into 10 categories, Aristotle tried to systematize the restrictions on the possibilities of significant combination that exist for the different kinds of term. Thus the substance-word 'George' in 'George is heavy' can be replaced only by another term of the same category, such as 'this stone', if significance (not necessarily TRUTH) is to be preserved. Among modern philosophers, very much this idea is present in the influential theory of categories put forward by Gilbert Ryle (see also CATEGORY-MISTAKE), who regarded the tracing of the categorical properties of terms as the prime business of philosophy, but did not believe it possible to develop a comprehensive formal theory of categories. Different, although related, is Kant's use of the term to refer to the very general and abstract CONCEPTS, such as SUBSTANCE and cause, with which philosophy has always been centrally concerned; see also A POSTERIORI, A PRIORI. A.Q.

category-mistake. A grammatically well-formed but nevertheless logically unacceptable sentence in which terms from uncombinable CATEGORIES are put together. 'The number 7 is green' is an uncontroversial example; numbers, unlike numerals, are not perceivable objects in space and cannot be significantly said to be of any colour. Ryle, who named this idea, applied it chiefly to mind-body DUALISM (see also MIND-BODY PROBLEM), which he held to be a massive category-mistake in taking mental and physical things and events to exist or occur in two different worlds. A.Q.

category theory. A recent development in MATHEMATICS which concentrates attention not on *particular* MATHEMATICAL STRUCTURES but on the relations between them. It has had a unifying effect in ALGEBRA and TOPOLOGY. Those who like to work on particular, concrete problems refer to it as 'general abstract nonsense'. R.G.

catharsis (Greek word meaning 'purification', 'purgation').

(1) The 'purging' of undesirable emotions through vicarious experience, especially through seeing them represented on the stage; from its application by Aristotle (*Poetics*, ch. 6) to the postulated effect of tragedy in removing, by the 'pity and fear' it excites, (excesses of) 'such emotions' rather than simply stimulating them, as Plato had argued. (Aristotle seems to intend purification *from* excessive emotions rather than purification *of* them, but the latter interpretation has also been influential.) R.W.S.

(2) In ABNORMAL PSYCHOLOGY, very commonly, the release of repressed emotion, irrespective of the nature of the process. B.A.F.

(3) In FREUDIAN theory, the word has a more specific meaning. In 1882 Joseph Breuer hit upon a new method of PSYCHOTHERAPY, which he called 'cathartic'. It consisted in encouraging the patient to speak about the first occasion on which a symptom appeared; whereupon, Breuer claimed, the symptom disappeared. Freud adopted and used this method when he still believed that neurotic states (see NEUROSIS) originated in traumatic episodes (see TRAUMA). Later, however, he modified this view to allow for neurotic states that were the result of conflict; and after he developed the technique of FREE ASSOCIATION the cathartic method was seen to be only one aspect of this. In Freud's PSYCHOLOGY the mind contains charged mental elements, each of which has two aspects, the ideational and the affective (or emotional); and the charged elements are in movement towards CONSCIOUSNESS so as to discharge themselves. During treatment the patient is continually struggling to prevent the emergence of repressed emotion. When he does release it into consciousness, the element is thereby discharged. It is this whole process that is known as catharsis. See also ABREACTION. B.A.F.

cathexis. In psychoanalytic theory (see PSYCHOANALYSIS), (1) the sexual energy (LIBIDO) which an individual 'invests' in another person or object; (2) more generally, a strong attachment to another. W.Z.

Catholicism. Universality, especially in the Christian Church. This is believed to be safeguarded against personal and local errors by acceptance of the Bible, the Apostles' and Nicene Creeds, the ecumenical Councils (see ECUMENICAL MOVEMENT), the sacraments of Baptism and Holy Communion, ordered, corporate worship, and a regularly ordained (i.e. set apart) 'ministry' of bishops, priests and deacons. There has been much disagreement as to the exact nature of these safeguards (see DOGMA), especially about the position of the Pope as the 'vicar' or deputy of Christ entitled to jurisdiction over the whole Church. The Eastern orthodox Churches (see ORTHODOXY, EASTERN), rejecting the papal claims, have been separated from the Western Catholic Church since 1054. During the 16th century the Reformation split the Western Church, although the Protestant Churches (see PROTESTANTISM) organized after this further revolt against the Papacy have all claimed that they remain Catholic in some sense, and ANGLO-CATHOLICISM claims it strongly. In modern usage, the word usually refers to *Roman Catholicism*, which obeys the Pope, although often in the modern spirit of AGGIORNAMENTO. While Christians who are Roman Catholics in one sense or another cannot be counted accurately, they certainly outnumber Christians who are not by many hundreds of millions. See also MODERNISM; ULTRAMONTANISM. For further reading: J. L. McKenzie, *The Roman Catholic Church* (1969). D.L.E.

causal explanation, see under EXPLANATION.

causality (or **causation).** The relation between two events or states of affairs in which one brings the other about or produces it. Hume took the CONCEPT to be a complex one, its components being the priority in time of cause to effect, their contiguity in space and time, and what he problematically described as their *necessary connection*. Although it seems inconceivable that a cause should follow its effect, it seems possible that the two should be simultaneous. The phenomenon of GRAVITATION is an apparent exception to the requirement of contiguity; that of interaction between mind and body, if the mind is taken to be non-spatial, is another (see MIND-BODY PROBLEM). The 'necessary connection', however, seems indispensable. EMPIRICISTS follow Hume in identifying it with constant conjunction: that event is the cause of this one if events like that are regularly succeeded, in circumstances like these, by events like this. It follows from this that every singular-looking causal PROPOSITION is really general, since it implies a universal law, and it can be justified only by INDUCTION, which Hume took to be unjustifiable, although natural to us. There is no one standard alternative to this view. Some take causal laws to be *a priori* truths (see A POSTERIORI, A PRIORI), discoverable by reason without the aid of experience; others that we can somehow perceive or intellectually apprehend the causal relation between a pair of particular events, most plausibly, perhaps, in the case where one's will brings about a movement of one's body. We have a practical interest in knowledge of causes since we can apply it to produce or prevent occurrences through the production or prevention of other, causally related events that are within our direct control. We have a theoretical interest too: knowledge of causes enables us to explain what has happened and predict what will happen. Many verbs (kill, lift, throw) and many words of other kinds (victim, author, father) are implicitly causal. For further reading: J. L. Mackie, *The Cement of the Universe: a Study of Causation* (1974). A.Q.

celebratory theatre. The idea that theatre may be employed, not to interpret reality, dramatize personal conflict or criticize social conditions, but rather to offer audiences a glimpse, by theatrical means, of some alternative and possibly utopian existence, arises from a study of those societies in which drama forms part of the ceremonial or festive life of the community. It is prefigured in J. G. Frazer's account of myth and ritual in *The Golden Bough* (1890–1915). The BAKHTINIAN notion of CARNIVALIZATION and P. Toschi's study of popular dramatic forms in Italy (*Le origini del teatro italiano*, 1955) point to the same conclusion. But most contemporary practitioners of festive or celebratory theatre would probably claim to be more directly influenced by surviving traditions of popular entertainment. Perhaps the most impressive example of contemporary celebratory theatre has been Le Théâtre du Soleil's *1789*, created collectively under the inspiration of Ariane Mnouchkine (1938–) in 1970, in which the events of the French Revolution are presented from the viewpoint of the common people. Equally influential was Peter Brook's (1925–) Royal Shakespeare Company production of *A Midsummer Night's Dream* (1970), using techniques and imagery drawn from the circus; the Greek director Karolos Koun's productions of Aristophanes in the 1960s should also be mentioned. A different type of celebratory theatre is found in the creation of specially performed pieces to mark particular events or calendar dates: The Welfare State, a British group founded in 1968, produced many examples. M.A.

celebrity. The condition of famousness or notoriety; the phenomenon of fame; or, most commonly, the famous or notorious person. Originally entering usage in the 19th century, 'celebrity' has come in contemporary times to denote a peculiarly empty, artificial, questionable sort of fame. As Daniel Boorstin put it in *The Image* (1961), the celebrity is one who is well known for his or her well-knownness, a 'human pseudo-event'. Typically contrasted to the 'hero' or 'star', whose fame is earned through admirable action or extraordinary qualities, the celebrity is a product of the mass media, garnering attention in large part through 'artificial' means. Because no unique, meritorious conduct or quality is required for celebrity, and because the opportunities for media attention have increased so dramatically with the expansion of mass communications, contemporary celebrity also appears especially democratic – hence Andy Warhol's declaration that 'in the future everyone will be world-famous for fifteen minutes'. Although in *The Frenzy of Renown* (1986), Leo Braudy has shown that the oppositions between pure, 'real' fame and inauthentic, 'artificial' celebrity, and between an aristocracy of the deservedly famous and a democracy of the merely notorious, do not hold up historically, such distinctions are central to the contemporary meaning of 'celebrity'. For further reading: J. Gamson, *Celebrity in Contemporary America* (1994). J.P.G.

celestial mechanics. The study of the ORBITS, or trajectories, of stars, planets, spacecraft, etc. The form of the orbits arises from the force of GRAVITATION, and calculations are based on NEWTONIAN MECHANICS. Celestial mechanics is characterized by great precision (it is the original 'exact science'); the motion of the moon, for example, can be calculated to within a fraction of a second many years in advance. M.V.B.

cell. The smallest viable functional and structural unit of a tissue or organ. The *cell theory*, associated with the name of Theodor Schwann (1810–82), declares that all tissues and organs including the nervous system (see NEURON) are cellular in intimate structure. The process whereby cells multiply is known as *cell division.* See also CELL BIOLOGY; CYTOLOGY. P.M.

cell biology. A branch of BIOLOGY (to be distinguished from CYTOLOGY) that came to the fore after World War II, and of which the ambition is, wherever appropriate, to interpret physiological performances in terms of the behaviour of individual CELLS. Cell biology has played a specially prominent part in immunology (see IMMUNITY), in which every endeavour is made to interpret antibody formation and the aggressive actions of lymphocytes (one of the white blood corpuscles) in cellular terms. Indeed, that branch of immunology which deals with cell-mediated immune reactions is to quite a large extent a natural history of lymphocytes. P.M.

cellular automata. In MATHEMATICS, a technique for constructing or modelling very complicated SYSTEMS or structures from a large number of identical single elements. These elements are allowed to develop according to a set of prescribed rules in which the development of a particular element is controlled by the behaviour of its neighbours. An everyday example is the growth of a snowflake or other crystal. This starts from a small NUCLEUS and its structure extends by the deposition of more water molecules whose position and orientation depend on the precise pattern of molecules which have already been condensed. The ideas of cellular automata have been applied to biological systems, FRACTAL patterns, complex non-linear phenomena such as turbulence, as well as to more abstract fields in mathematics, computation (see COMPUTING) and formal language theory (see NOTIONAL AND FORMAL). H.M.R.

census. A complete enumeration of a population, including detailed information about the distribution of the population by age, sex, occupation, housing, and so forth. The earliest known censuses were conducted during the ancient civilizations of Egypt, Babylonia, China, Palestine and Rome, mainly for purposes of tax collection. Modern censuses, taken for scientific as well as administrative purposes, date from the middle of the 18th century. In the US, for example, a full census of the population has been conducted every 10 years since 1790. It is estimated that only about 17 per cent of the world's population had been counted by the middle of the 19th century. Since the end of World War II, the UN has promoted a worldwide effort to conduct national censuses. Between 1975 and 1984, 96 per cent of the world's population was counted in a census. The difficulties of obtaining a complete and accurate account of a population and its characteristics are enormous, however. Beyond the technical difficulties, some groups have been known to refuse participation in a census out of fear that the information might be used for undesirable political purposes. In recent decades, US censuses have missed approximately 2 per cent of the total population, although the magnitude of this undercount has typically been larger for minority populations and for young men. The political implications of the census undercount in the US are enormous, since many government resources and political representatives are distributed on the basis of population estimates. J.R.W.

Central American Common Market (CACM). Set up in 1960 as part of a broader movement towards regional integration, the CACM aimed to promote development through import-substitution INDUSTRIALIZATION by expanding the market through the abolition of local PROTECTIONIST measures and taking advantage of ECONOMIES OF SCALE. The members were EL SALVADOR, Guatemala, Honduras and Nicaragua; and shortly after, Costa Rica, which joined in 1962. For several years this strategy produced impressive growth rates, especially in Guatemala and El Salvador. However, these were largely attributable to outside investment, and indigenous manufacturing capacity did not significantly increase. The organization was drastically weakened by the 1969 war between Honduras and El

Salvador, after which the two countries refused to trade with each other. Saturation of the small regional market, followed by the 1979 OIL CRISIS and subsequent world recession, plunged the CACM into crisis, and during the 1980s intra-regional trade fell dramatically. In 1993, the members – excluding Costa Rica – set up new agreements to reduce import tariffs, creating the Central American Free Trade Zone. N.M.

central bank. The institution charged with maintaining price stability and acting as lender of last resort in most Western countries. In recent decades the tendency has been towards increasingly independent central banks on the model of the German Bundesbank and the US FEDERAL RESERVE SYSTEM. The removal of control over the MONEY SUPPLY and INTEREST RATES to an independent central bank is seen as critical in the battle against INFLATION and ensuring longer-term stability in economic policy. Such considerations have led both the French government and the Blair government in Britain to give increasing operational independence to their central banks. In Europe an independent central bank is among the conditions required if a country is to qualify for the SINGLE CURRENCY, an important factor particularly in the case of the Banque de France. Advocates argue that independence puts an important policy tool beyond the manipulation of politicians for short-term political gain. But it may also introduce a deflationary bias into policy-making and lead to a democratic deficit if there is insufficient supervision of the bank. In cases of severe financial instability like the October 1987 stock market crash, the central bank makes credit available to prevent a liquidity crisis. For further reading: S. K. Beckner, *Back from the Brink* (1996). A.BR.

Central Intelligence Agency, see CIA.

central limit theorem, see under PROBABILITY THEORY.

central place. A geographical term for villages, towns and cities (see URBANIZATION) that provide centralized wholesale, retail, service and administrative functions for surrounding, tributary regions. Central-place theory specifies the relationships between urban settlements serving such central functions, with special emphasis on their number, size, activity structure and hierarchical spatial organization. The first formal statement of the theory was made by the German geographer Walter Christaller in his classic 1933 work *The Central Places of Southern Germany*. Modern mathematical work has been concerned with generalizing Christaller's and August Lösch's early models to accommodate a wide range of regional variations and to introduce dynamic and evolutionary dimensions to central-place theory. For further reading: B. J. L. Berry, J. B. Parr *et al*, *Market Centers and Retail Location: Theory and Applications* (1988). P.H.; P.O.M.

centralism, democratic, see DEMOCRATIC CENTRALISM.

centrality, see under CENTRAL PLACE.

centre, the. If there are RIGHT and LEFT wings in politics, it follows that there must be a centre between them unless the politics of the country in question is polarized between extreme positions. The centre is the name for moderate, middle-of-the-road parties and politics, scorned by the doctrinaire and idealist, and more concerned with finding compromises that will enable government to be carried on than with the pursuit of ideas to their logical conclusions.

A similar function is fulfilled by the centre group in many political parties, holding together those of more radical views (see RADICALISM) on the one hand and those with more conservative views (see CONSERVATISM) on the other. The centre provides a convenient point on the political spectrum by which to place politicians and policies as 'left of centre' or 'right of centre'. The term 'party of the extreme centre' was coined to make the point that those who believe in moderation and the virtues of toleration and compromise may have a commitment quite as intense and quite as much based on principle as those who believe in intolerance and violence. A.L.C.B.

***centres dramatiques*.** Theatres, sometimes with attached drama schools, set up in various French provincial towns and on the outskirts of Paris, from 1945 onwards, in an attempt to decentralize theatrical culture and bring the theatre to WORKING-CLASS and lower-MIDDLE-CLASS audiences. After 1960, in some localities, the *centres dramatiques* were combined with the new *maisons de la culture* introduced by André Malraux as Minister for Cultural Affairs. Despite conflicts with local authorities (who supply part of the finance) and the upheavals of May 1968 (most of the directors belong to the LEFT), some of the *centres* have achieved notable, if temporary, success, e.g. Grenier de Toulouse, Centre Dramatique de l'Est (now Théâtre National de Strasbourg), Théâtre de la Cité (Villeurbanne) under Roger Planchon, and Comédie de Saint-Étienne under Jean Dasté. J.G.W.

centrifugal/centripetal forces. Complementary concepts in POLITICAL GEOGRAPHY that are useful in providing a qualitative picture of how strongly a NATION-STATE is held together. Centrifugal forces are disunifying and divisive to a political system, while centripetal forces unify and strengthen it. Both forces operate simultaneously in every country, and the challenge to the central government is to maintain a net positive balance of binding forces. Common cultural ties, such as the relatively uniform distribution of language and religion throughout Poland, certainly help. But when these traits are marked by strong divisions, such as the linguistic split between Quebec and the rest of Canada or the clash between Protestants and Roman Catholics in Northern Ireland, the stability of the overarching political system is seriously undermined. Today the nation-state is besieged by the spectre of DEVOLUTION in every corner of the world, and in each instance intensifying centrifugal forces play a central role. Since 1990, these forces have not only reached dangerous levels in many countries but have contributed directly to the break-up of the former USSR, YUGOSLAVIA, Czechoslovakia and Ethiopia. P.O.M.

centripetal/centrifugal forces, see CENTRIFUGAL/CENTRIPETAL FORCES.

centrography. In GEOGRAPHY, the determination and study of the central points of spatial distributions, e.g. changes in the centre of gravity of the United States population. Centrography developed most rapidly during the 1920s and 1930s in the Soviet Union when attempts were made to define optimal centres for REGIONAL PLANNING purposes. P.H.

cephalic index. In physical ANTHROPOLOGY, the index used for recording the shape of the human skull. The index expresses the maximum width as a percentage of the maximum length measured from just above the eyebrow ridges. Where the index is below 75, the skull is described as *dolichocephalic* (long-headed); above 80 as *brachycephalic* (round-headed). A.L.C.B.

cepheid variable. A class of yellow and orange supergiant stars of considerable importance in the determination of astronomical distances. They are named after the prototype, Delta Cephei, discovered in 1784. Polaris (sometimes called the Pole or North Star) is the nearest cepheid to the earth. They pulsate with regular periods of variation from 1 to 50 days, during which they vary continuously in colour, size and brightness by up to about 20 per cent. There exists a characteristic relationship between the period of pulsation and the variation of light intensity which was first deduced by Henrietta Leavitt during the period 1908–12. It uniquely distinguishes cepheids from other variable stars. In 1917 Harlow Shapley established a systematic relationship between the intrinsic brightness and the period of variation of a cepheid variable. Walter Baade divided cepheids into Populations I and II according to their period-luminosity relations. Type I are usually found in relatively young galactic star clusters while type II are found among old stars in globular star clusters. Distances to nearby star clusters containing cepheids can be obtained by studying the systematic relationship between the colour and the brightness of the stars within the cluster. In recent years a revolution in the accuracy with which these measurements can be made has been brought about by the observational programme of the Hipparcos Satellite. For further reading: K. Croswell, *Searching for Meaning in the Milky Way* (1996). J.D.B.

cerebral dominance, see under NEUROPSYCHOLOGY.

cerebrotonia, see under PERSONALITY TYPES.

Cerenkov radiation. The cone of light or other electromagnetic RADIATION emitted by charged PARTICLES travelling through a transparent material faster than the speed of light in that material. Cerenkov radiation is impossible in empty space because, according to RELATIVITY theory, particles cannot travel faster than light *in vacuo*. It is analogous to the sonic boom and to the water-wave pattern behind ships. M.V.B.

CERN. European Organization for Nuclear Research (formerly Conseil Européen pour la Recherche Nucléaire), set up in 1954. The world's largest centre, situated in Geneva, for the experimental (using ACCELERATORS) and theoretical study of ELEMENTARY PARTICLES. M.V.B.

CFC (chlorofluorocarbon), see under GREENHOUSE EFFECT.

CGT (*Confédération Générale du Travail*). French TRADE UNION movement established in 1895 at Limoges, brought together with other trades union organizations in 1902 at Montpellier. It operated both on issues of wage, salary and working conditions and on political matters; in 1906 it was captured by revolutionary SYNDICALISTS who relied on the general STRIKE as their main weapon. The consequent collisions with state power weakened its impetus, and in 1921 the revolutionary wing under COMMUNIST leadership set up a separate organization. Reunited under the slogan of the POPULAR FRONT in 1936, it was dissolved in 1940. Reconstituted in 1946, it came under communist control, its non-communist elements seceding in 1947 to form the Confédération Générale du Travail-Force Ouvrière. While its influence in the service and tertiary sectors is weak, it has traditionally dominated crafts and heavy industries. It has a close, albeit often troubled, relationship with the Communist Party; its leadership is dominated by members of the Communist Party hierarchy. D.C.W.; S.M.

chain index, see under INDEX NUMBER.

chain reaction. Any chemical or nuclear process where each reaction produces PARTICLES which cause a chain of further similar reactions. The process may be unstable, as in explosions (conventional or nuclear), or controlled, as in NUCLEAR REACTORS. See also FISSION; FUSION; NUCLEAR REACTION. M.V.B.

chamber tomb. General term for an artificially constructed burial place designed for use on more than one occasion. Chamber tombs may be cut out of rock (megalithic) or constructed of dry-stone work. This type of burial place was common in western Europe throughout the third millennium BC, but occurs in many parts of the world at different times. B.C.

Chamberlin-Moulton hypothesis. Popular in the 19th century was the so-called nebular hypothesis, which attributed the origins of the planets to the condensation of the supposedly nebulous material which had once been the sun's atmosphere. This in turn was largely discredited at the end of the 19th century by a theory devised by the American geologist T. C. Chamberlin (1843–1928) and the astronomer F. R. Moulton (1872–1952) which claimed that a close encounter between the sun and a passing star would best account for the genesis of the planets and their orbits. The gravitational pull of the star had drawn material away from the sun, which in time formed into 'planetesimals', which had cooled, and, orbiting the sun, had gathered together into the present planets. The hypothesis enjoyed popularity especially in America, before being discredited in the 1930s as part of a rising general scepticism towards theories of stellar collision and catastrophe. For further reading: O. Struve and V. Zerbergs, *Astronomy of the Twentieth Century* (1962). R.P.

chaos. In PHYSICS and MATHEMATICS there are phenomena and expressions for which it is not possible to predict how the situation or the calculation is going to develop when the starting conditions change only very slightly. A simple example is the uncertainty in the result of spinning a coin. A more complex problem is the development of turbulence in a fast-flowing fluid in which the behaviour depends very critically on the shape of the channel or on how the flow was initiated. In mathematics there are expressions which when evaluated give results which vary in an unpredictable way when the value of one of the initial quantities is changed even by a very small amount. These are all examples of chaotic behaviour. Chaotic processes can be simulated by electronic circuits, and these are being used to investigate the behaviour of these complex situations which can be quite unwieldy and time-consuming if they are evaluated with a COMPUTER. H.M.R.

Chappaquiddick. A resort island off the coast of the American state of Massachusetts where in July 1969 US Senator Edward M. Kennedy, the troubled youngest brother of John and Robert, drove his car off a wooden bridge and into a channel, drowning his passenger Mary Jo Kopechne, with whom he had attended a party that evening. Despite considerable evidence that Kennedy contributed to her slow death by not summoning help, he emerged remarkably unscathed from the incident. He was allowed to plead guilty to a charge of leaving the scene of a fatal accident, and given a two-month suspended sentence. He immediately sought to put the crash in the context of what was known as the Kennedy family curse, saying he hoped he would 'be able to put this most recent tragedy behind me'. That proved an impossibility. His apparent complicity in her death put an end to any chance that he could run for President and win, and forever tarnished his name. For further reading: J. Lange, *Chappaquiddick: The Real Story* (1993). R.K.H.

characterology. A pseudo-science of diagnosing personality traits from such evidence as GRAPHOLOGY or the study of handwriting, formulated and practised by the Munich philosopher Ludwig Klages (1872–1956), and sometimes denounced (e.g. by Georg Lukács) for its contribution to the IDEOLOGY of NAZISM. It became pertinent once more after World War II with the rise of quasi-calligraphic painting and with ABSTRACT EXPRESSIONISM's concern with GESTURAL significance. It also relates to Rorschach's system of PSYCHODIAGNOSTICS. J.W.

charisma. A term derived from New Testament Greek (meaning the gift of grace) and introduced into SOCIOLOGY by Max Weber (1864–1920) to denote an 'extraordinary quality' possessed by persons or objects, which is thought to give them a unique, magical quality. Weber distinguished between *individual* charisma, which arises out of the personal qualities of the individual, and the charisma of *office*, which derives from the sacred nature of the position.

Weber carried the CONCEPT over into a general theory of *authority*, in which he distinguished between three types of legitimacy – traditional, charismatic and legal-rational (see LEGAL-RATIONAL AUTHORITY) – and into a rudimentary theory of social change. For where religions or societies are hidebound, or ruled by customs sanctified by the past, the only way such authority can usually be challenged is by some *charismatic* leader whose legitimacy resides in his personal qualities. To that extent, charisma is a great revolutionary force. But once the charismatic leader has achieved his aim, he has to set about creating rational, administrative rules; secondary individuals have to be endowed with the authority of the leader, SYMBOLS replace the person, and there ensues the 'routinization of charisma'.

Among English-speaking sociologists, the concept has been seen primarily in political terms, and has been applied to men like Nkrumah in Ghana, Sukarno in Indonesia, and Nehru in India, whose personal appeal was the source of authority in these nations. It has also been applied, by journalists and others, to all kinds of individuals and phenomena that seemed to have a special, magical ability to evoke an immediate, personal assent from the masses. For further reading: H. H. Gerth and C. W. Mills (eds), *From Max Weber: Essays in Sociology* (1984). D.B.

charismatic movement, see under PENTECOSTALISM.

Charter 77. The movement established in the former Czechoslovakia in 1977 to campaign for the observance of HUMAN RIGHTS by the government. Named after a charter initially signed by 243 people, it urged the authorities to abide by the country's existing laws and international declarations agreed to by the government, such as the Helsinki Final Act (see HELSINKI 1975). It demanded freedoms of expression and religious belief and the observance of the right to education, irrespective of political affiliation. It stressed that it was not forming an opposition and it had no political programme, claiming that it operated within the constitution. It hoped to engage in dialogue with the government, but was accused of being a subversive organization, and many of its members were arrested and punished or forced to emigrate. Its membership consisted mainly of intellectuals of diverse political backgrounds, ranging from the former reformist COMMUNIST Jiri Hajek, to the non-communist playwright Vaclav Havel. For further reading: H. Gordon Skilling, *Charter 77 and Human Rights in Czechoslovakia* (1981). D.PR.

chauvinism. Excessive and unreasonable NATIONALISM mingled with XENOPHOBIA. The word is derived from the name of Nicolas Chauvin, a Napoleonic soldier famous for his simple-minded devotion to Napoleon, and applied by analogy to all extreme intellectual positions held by defenders of a particular set of interests, e.g. 'male chauvinism' (see SEXISM). D.C.W.

chelate. Term, derived from the Greek word for claw, which describes a chemical SPECIES with more than one ATOM capable of bonding (see BOND, CHEMICAL) to a central metal atom or ION. Chelating agents, more usually referred to as *polydentate ligands*, frequently form more stable complexes with a metal atom than similar monodentate groups. They find considerable use in industrial and ANALYTICAL CHEMISTRY – particularly in extraction processes. Metal ions in biological systems are often bound to chelates. B.F.

chemical and biological warfare, see under WAR.

chemical bond, see BOND, CHEMICAL.

chemical equilibrium, see under EQUILIBRIUM.

chemical physics, see PHYSICAL CHEMISTRY.

chemical warfare, see under WAR.

chemiosmosis. The mechanism by which energy is harnessed by mitochondria (see CYTOLOGY), chloroplasts and bacteria. In the process, high-energy ELECTRONS, which are either present in foodstuffs or generated by PHOTOSYNTHESIS, are used to set up a gradient of PROTONS across a biological membrane. The energy generated by the gradient is harnessed in a variety of ways. P.N.

chemistry. The scientific discipline concerned with the investigation and rationalization of the properties of the many thousands of substances which exist in nature or can be made artificially (see SYNTHETIC CHEMISTRY). Traditionally it is subdivided into PHYSICAL CHEMISTRY, which is concerned with the physical laws governing chemical behaviour and includes the specialized branches ELECTROCHEMISTRY, PHOTOCHEMISTRY and STEREOCHEMISTRY as well as studies involving SPECTROSCOPY and THERMODYNAMICS (including THERMOCHEMISTRY); ORGANIC CHEMISTRY, which involves the study of substances containing carbon; and INORGANIC CHEMISTRY, which deals with substances containing the remaining elements. THEORETICAL CHEMISTRY is concerned particularly with the applications of QUANTUM MECHANICS and STATISTICAL MECHANICS to chemistry. The detection and estimation of chemical SPECIES is the sphere of ANALYTICAL CHEMISTRY and (where minute amounts are involved) MICROCHEMISTRY. The distribution of elements in the earth's crust and atmosphere constitutes the study of GEOCHEMISTRY. A good deal of modern chemistry involves interdisciplinary study, especially in conjunction with PHYSICS, BIOCHEMISTRY and METALLURGY. For further reading: M. F. C. Ladd, *Introduction to Physical Chemistry* (1997). B.F.

chemotaxis, see under TROPISM.

chemotherapy. The treatment of diseases by chemicals whose composition is known. Chemotherapy is usually attributed to Ehrlich's use of salvarsan for syphilis in 1910 after Schaudinn described the spirochete in 1905. Previously diseases, whose causes were generally unknown, were treated by a variety of non-specific remedies of varying and obscure composition. With the clearer definition of diseases in the last century, and the recognition of the microbial origin of many of them, it became possible to develop more rational treatment. The two greatest recent advances in chemotherapy have been the discovery in the 1930s of the sulphonamide group of drugs, and the introduction about 10 years later of penicillin and other ANTIBIOTICS – although, strictly speaking, penicillin treatment was not chemotherapy since penicillin, an extract from a mould, was not then a compound of known chemical composition. D.A.P.

chemotropism, see under TROPISM.

Chernobyl. The Ukrainian town where the world's most serious accident involving a NUCLEAR REACTOR occurred on 25 April 1986. The nuclear fall-out produced contamination throughout Europe and the disaster led to increased opposition to the use of nuclear power all over the world. The accident appears to have been caused by human error rather than through any design fault. The Soviet government was subjected to considerable criticism by those nations affected by the fall-out, first for refusing to make the accident public until RADIOACTIVITY was discovered in Sweden, and then for failing to provide adequate information on its extent. It was alleged that the Soviet leadership's newly declared policy of greater 'openness' in making information available to the public was not being implemented. However, since the immediate aftermath of the nuclear leak, the Soviet Union has been more willing to allow international experts to examine the circumstances of the disaster. For further reading: A. Roche, *Children of Chernobyl* (1996). D.PR.

chi, see under ACUPUNCTURE.

Chicago. JAZZ'S second city, following chronologically after NEW ORLEANS. It attracted great New Orleans musicians like King Oliver (soon joined by the young Louis Armstrong) and Jelly Roll Morton, and the teenage white Chicagoans who crowded to hear them were soon imitating and experimenting. Influenced as well by white bands like the New Orleans Rhythm Kings, the resulting Chicago style was rough and enthusiastic, featuring solos more than the New Orleans players did, and also unlike them employing ensemble passages worked out in advance. The Chicagoans thus laid some of the groundwork for the BIG BAND formulas of the SWING era; correspondingly, Chicago players like Dave Tough, Bud Freeman and, above all, Benny Goodman went on to become its stars. GE.S.

Chicago Boys. The term is used to describe a group of mostly Chilean neo-liberal economists (see NEO-LIBERALISM) educated at the University of Chicago in the late 1950s and 1960s who became the dominant ideological expression of the Chilean military government (1973–90), following the coup which overthrew the democratically elected LEFT-wing government of Salvador Allende in September 1973 (see IDEOLOGY; DEMOCRACY). The origin of the Chicago Boys lies in the debate during the 1950s and 1960s between structuralists and monetarists on the developmental problems facing Latin America (see MONETARISM; DEVELOPING COUNTRIES). In response to concerns about the influence of STRUCTURALISM among policy-makers in the region, the University of Chicago's School of Economics – where RIGHT-wing thinkers such as Milton Friedman were highly influential – initiated a counter-attack by establishing a postgraduate programme for economists from Chile, where the UN Economic Commission for Latin America – considered to be the most influential exponent of structuralism in the region – had its headquarters. During the military regime, the Chicago Boys developed and implemented a neo-liberal economic project without any of the constraints normally associated with democratic governments, while combining it with a social and political theory whose function became to strengthen and legitimize the MODEL. The Chicago Boys' agenda was subsequently imitated by other countries in both Latin America and the rest of the world, notably in the UK under Prime Minister Margaret Thatcher. For further reading: J. G. Valdes, *Pinochet's Economists: the Chicago School in Chile* (1995). M.A.P.

Chicago school.

(1) In SOCIOLOGY the work and school of thought associated with the sociology department of the University of Chicago, particularly in the period 1915–40, though sometimes used to refer to later periods as well. Founded in 1892 by Albion Small, it was the first sociology department in the USA. It produced the first American sociological journal, the *American Journal of*

Sociology, and its first sociology textbook, Robert Park and Ernest Burgess's *Introduction to the Science of Sociology* (1921), popularly known as the 'green bible'. The school adopted no single approach but helped to establish a number of different methods and traditions which have influenced sociology worldwide. All the approaches emphasized the importance of using empirical research (see EMPIRICISM) to develop theory. The rapidly growing city of Chicago was used as a kind of natural social laboratory in much of the school's empirical work. Qualitative research methods involving the use of in-depth interviews and documentary sources such as letters were developed in W. I. Thomas and F. Znaniecki's *The Polish Peasant in Europe and America* (1919). However, members of the department also developed quantitative methods such as those used in social surveys. Robert Park pioneered human ECOLOGY in analysing areas of the city in terms of biological processes. The University of Chicago also had very important PHILOSOPHY and SOCIAL PSYCHOLOGY departments. The former is associated with the development of PRAGMATISM which influenced the work of George Herbert Mead, who is widely seen as the founder of symbolic interactionism (see SYMBOLIC INTERACTION). Herbert Blumer, a student of Mead's at Chicago, was largely responsible for developing symbolic interactionism into a sociological perspective which remains influential today. For further reading: M. Blumer, *The Chicago School of Sociology* (1984). M.D.H.

(2) In ARCHITECTURE, a movement rooted in the rapid development of Chicago following the Great Fire of 1871 and continuing up to about 1925. It had two facets: the erection of mainly commercial buildings in the business district of the Loop in the form of SKYSCRAPERS, and the development of freely planned single- or two-storey houses in the suburbs by Frank Lloyd Wright, Louis Sullivan, and their followers. It is the evolution of the skyscraper which is most frequently associated with the achievements of the Chicago school. Both aspects were neglected by historians, and it was not until the publication of Giedion's *Bauen in Frankreich* (1926) and its English-language sequel, *Space, Time and Architecture* (1941), that international interest was revived. This was reinforced by Mies van der Rohe, who had gone to Chicago in 1938 and who demonstrated the validity of its tradition; technical innovation and pure form even in commercial buildings could create architecture of a high order. For further reading: C. W. Condit, *The Chicago School of Architecture* (1964). M.BR.

(3) In ECONOMICS, a term used to describe an influential movement based at the University of Chicago (see CHICAGO BOYS).

child-centred education. Education based on the interests, needs and developmental growth of the child and on a knowledge of child development, as contrasted with an education that emphasizes academic features, the curriculum content, standards of achievement and teaching methods. Originating in a psychological approach, child-centred education has acquired what is sometimes called a philosophy, and is associated with PROGRESSIVE education, and with such names as Rousseau, Froebel, Pestalozzi, Montessori and A.S. Neill (see FROEBEL METHOD; MONTESSORI METHOD). W.A.C.S.

child psychiatry, see under PSYCHIATRY.

child psychology, see under DEVELOPMENTAL PSYCHOLOGY.

childbirth techniques. There has recently been a strong lobby in favour of *natural childbirth*, the delivery of the child by maternal effort in the position and way the mother chooses, without medical interference and sometimes away from medical care altogether. This is a reaction against the increased use of TECHNOLOGY and what is seen as a lack of care and sensitivity by obstetricians and midwives. Grantly Dick Read in 1933 advocated education about labour and childbirth to reduce fear, anxiety and tension which may adversely affect labour. Techniques for teaching relaxation to be practised during labour, including controlled breathing (*psychoprophylaxis*), were developed and, perhaps by competition, reduced the comprehension of pain. Other methods of pain relief include ACUPUNCTURE, HYPNOSIS, transcutaneous nerve stimulation, the use of analgesics such as pethidine and anaesthetics such as nitrous oxide and epidural nerve block. Frederick Leboyer, a French obstetrician, became convinced in the 1960s that birth needed to be much gentler in the interests of the mother and particularly of the baby, and he advocated quiet and low-lit surroundings with very gentle handling of the baby and contact with its mother. Since then Michel Odent, another Frenchman, has developed other techniques designed to increase maternal enjoyment of the birth and the chances of normal delivery. The active birth movement is an even more recent approach. There is widespread acceptance of the need to consider the emotional wellbeing of the parents (for too long the father was excluded from the delivery) and to establish the true place of technology in obstetrics. A balance is required between the desire of a woman to choose how and where she delivers and the reality that labour and delivery are unpredictable, and serious complications can occur without warning. For further reading: F. Leboyer, *Birth without Violence* (1975). S.J.S.

childhood, history of, see HISTORY OF CHILDHOOD.

children, value of, see VALUE OF CHILDREN.

chiliastic, see under MILLENARIANISM.

chlamydia. *Chlamydia trachomatis* is a bacterium which causes many human diseases. Some strains cause trachoma, a severe and potentially blinding eye disease very common in the Middle East and North Africa. Other strains are sexually transmitted (see SEXUALLY TRANSMITTED DISEASE) and cause genital infections. In men, the commonest is non-gonococcal urethritis, which can be complicated by epididymitis, a painful swelling of the testicles which may lead to INFERTILITY. In women, *C. trachomatis* infects the cervix (neck of the womb), and may then spread to cause inflammation of the fallopian tubes (salpingitis) and subsequent infertility. During delivery, the infection may be transmitted from a mother to her baby, and cause conjunctivitis, middle ear disease and pneumonia. In industrialized societies genital chlamydial infection and its complications have reached epidemic proportions. Reliable diagnostic tests are available, and treatment with the tetracycline antibiotics is curative. Control of these infections will require a major effort to examine sex partners of infected individuals, together with screening of high-risk groups. For further reading: J. D. Oriel and G. L. Ridgway, *Genital Chlamydial Infection* (1982). J.D.O.

chlorofluorocarbon (CFC), see under GREENHOUSE EFFECT.

chlorophyll. Any of a number of green pigments which occur in plants and a few animals and are the cause of the greenness of grass, of the leaves of trees, and of the countryside generally. Chlorophyll plays an essential part in PHOTOSYNTHESIS. These pigments have also been said to act as deodorants and have been included in toothpaste, though they are probably useless against halitosis. K.M.

chloroplasts. see under PHOTOSYNTHESIS.

choice, axiom of, see AXIOM OF CHOICE.

Chomskyan. Characteristic of, or a follower of, the linguistic principles of Avram Noam Chomsky, Professor of Modern Languages and Linguistics at the Massachusetts Institute of Technology. His book *Syntactic Structures* (1957) was the first to outline and justify a generative (see GENERATIVE GRAMMAR) conception of language, still the most widely held view. Apart from his technical contributions within LINGUISTICS, he has written at length on the philosophical and psychological implications of a generative theory of language, in particular developing a view of the integral relationship between language and the human mind, and it is this which has made such an impact on disciplines outside linguistics (see, e.g., INNATENESS HYPOTHESIS). These ideas were further developed by Steven Pinker in *The Language Instinct* (1994) and *How the Mind Works* (1997). Chomsky has also made a powerful impression on the American and, to a lesser extent, the British public through his extensive critical writings on political issues in the US. For further reading: J. Lyons, *Chomsky* (1991). D.C.

chordate, see under ZOOLOGY.

choreography. Although originally meaning the writing down of dance steps, with the developments in DANCE NOTATION and CHOREOLOGY the word has now come to mean the art of composing all forms of dance from CLASSICAL BALLET and MODERN DANCE to show dancing. The choreographer is the author of the choreography and arranges material using an individual process to present an end product for performance. Choreographers are responsible for the total visual imagery and expect to negotiate with musicians and costume, set and lighting designers. For further reading: P. Van Praagh and P. Brinson, *The Choreographic Art* (1963). L.A.

choreology. Term coined by Rudolph and Joan Benesh to mean the study of dance forms using notation. In 1962 they founded the Institute of Choreology in London, where choreologists are trained to analyse scores and develop DANCE NOTATION skills (in particular the *Benesh system*), and formed a library of choreographic scores from folk dance to ballet. Choreologists are employed largely by CLASSICAL BALLET companies to record and reconstruct ballets. For further reading: R. and J. Benesh, *An Introduction to Benesh Notation* (1956). L.A.

chosism. Term imported from France ('thingism') for the occurrence, in the writers associated with the NEW NOVEL, and especially in Alain Robbe-Grillet, of obsessively detailed descriptions of trivial objects (cigar boxes, tomatoes, etc.). Some critics consider it 'arid' and ultimately pointless; others regard it as an important means of drawing attention to the tragically anthropomorphic attitude of human beings towards an indifferent ENVIRONMENT. The craze for *choses* quickly passed and things returned to what they used to be. M.S.-S.

Christian atheism, see under DEATH OF GOD THEOLOGY.

Christian Democracy. Political IDEOLOGY associated with political parties allied with Christian Churches (see CHRISTIANITY), usually the Catholic Church. In the 19th century such parties were usually anti-CAPITALIST, anti-SOCIALIST, and often ANTISEMITIC. Their sometimes troubled relations with the Vatican turn on the papacy of Leo XIII, when the movement began to assume a social character which betrayed some parties (as in Austria) into a COLLECTIVIST, co-operativist view, labelled clerico-fascism by their opponents. Since 1945, Christian Democratic parties, having broken out of these traditions, have played a major role in west European politics, notably in West Germany, Italy, France (in the Fourth Republic), Belgium, Austria, Switzerland and the Netherlands. The three basic principles of Christian Democratic ideology are: commitment to liberal democracy (reinforced by anti-COMMUNISM and anti-FASCISM); belief in the SOCIAL MARKET economy; commitment to integration in the dual sense of CLASS reconciliation (through 'non-ideological' mass parties) and transnational integration (manifested through strong support for European integration). The West German Christlich-Demokratische Union/Christlich-Soziale Union (CDU/CSU) held power between 1949 and 1969 and returned to government from 1983 to 1999. The Italian Democrazia Cristiana (DC), less RIGHT-wing than its West German counterpart, provided the backbone of every post-war government up to the early 1990s, in the process acquiring considerable expertise at keeping the communists out of power, by manipulating coalitions and forming an HISTORIC COMPROMISE with the Partito Comunista Italiano (PCI). However, the DC, along with other traditional Italian parties, was dramatically exposed as corrupt by the judges of 'operation clean hands' (see TANGENTOPOLI). It lost public support, to the extent that it had to be disbanded, the rump forming the new Partito Popolare (PP). At the European level, the Christian Democrats established a transnational European People's Party in 1976, which has constituted the second largest group in the European Parliament. V.L.

Christian name politics, see under COMMUNITY POLITICS.

Christian Science. The name adopted by a religious body founded by Mrs Mary Baker Eddy (1821–1910), whose *Science and Health* has run into many editions in and since 1875. Its headquarters are in Boston, Mass., where the First Church of Christ, Scientist (the 'Mother Church') was reorganized on a permanent basis in the 1890s, and it is active throughout the English-speaking world. Its principal interest is in increasing health and curing disease by a faith which affirms that matter, the source of sin and suffering, is not a God-created substance, but a mode of human perception. Cure comes from a yielding of the self to God. The low estimate of matter in this doctrine is usually condemned both by the Churches and by agnostics (see AGNOSTICISM), but a daily newspaper, the *Christian Science Monitor*, is widely respected. Much of the religious and ethical teaching of the movement is shared in common with the Churches, although the unique deity of Christ is denied. For further reading: R. Peel, *Mary Baker Eddy* (3 vols, 1966–77). D.L.E.

Christian socialism. Term for a variety of movements which combine the ethical precepts of CHRISTIANITY with the COLLECTIVIST precepts of SOCIALISM. Originating in Britain, and strongest in the 19th century when F. D. Maurice and Edward Carpenter were well-known propagandists for the cause, it has experienced various 20th-century revivals when undoctrinal socialists have attempted to enlist Christ in the service of socialism. Such movements have been prominent in the Protestant churches of France, Germany, Switzerland, Scandinavia and the United States. Distinguished adherents of Christian socialism have included Paul Tillich, Reinhold Niebuhr and R. H. Tawney. Very different, though spurred by the same impulse, has been the movement of 'LIBERATION THEOLOGY' which has been influential in Latin America, though frowned on by the Vatican. For further reading: C. Rowland, *Radical Christianity* (1987). D.C.W.; A.R.

Christianity. The RELIGION which focuses on the figure of Jesus Christ (*c.* 4 BC–AD 30), and of which in the modern world the main forms are Eastern orthodoxy (see ORTHODOXY, EASTERN), CATHOLICISM and PROTESTANTISM. Christ is regarded as divine, and through his death on the cross and resurrection, he is believed to overcome death and save humankind.

Among important strands of thought in the last half-century of Christian thought (see THEOLOGY) are the following: BARTHIAN theology, based on the work of Karl Barth (1886–1968), who devised a biblically based but non-FUNDAMENTALIST world-view (see WELTANSCHAUUNG) attractive to many after the Nazi disaster; LIBERATION THEOLOGY, combining MARXIST analysis and mostly Catholic themes and especially influential in Latin America; INDIGENOUS THEOLOGY, emphasizing THIRD WORLD themes and traditions, and therefore clothing Christian thought in concepts familiar to poor or previously colonized countries or to underprivileged peoples (BLACK, Native American, African, South Asian, etc.); FEMINIST THEOLOGY; and ecumenical theology (see ECUMENICAL MOVEMENT).

While on the whole Christians accept the compatibility of doctrines of creation and modern cosmology and in general of faith and modern science, fundamentalists usually reject the theory of EVOLUTION. A problem concerns life on other worlds: the vast scale of the universe might suggest that rational beings like ourselves might exist in many other regions of the vast cosmos, and this could query Christ's uniqueness as redeemer. Christianity has initiated a number of dialogues with other major world religions, in part in relation to indigenous theology. On the whole, the uniqueness of the faith is stressed. But Christianity takes very seriously the HOLOCAUST and its own partial responsibility, and stresses too the importance of maintaining good relations with ISLAM, despite a past history of some hostility between the religions. A vigorous dialogue with BUDDHISM is in process, and important exchanges with other religions. Around the more orthodox forms of Christianity there have grown up variants including the MORMONS (the Church of Jesus Christ of Latter-Day Saints), CHRISTIAN SCIENCE, the Unification Church, a large number of African Independent Churches, among them the Nazarite Church of the Prophet Isaiah Shembe and the Church of Jesus Christ on Earth through the Prophet Simon Kimbangu, blends such as Vodun (Voodoo) in Haiti and Condomble in Brazil incorporating Catholic and African motifs. Many of these represent attempts to blend classical and Christian values. For further reading: D. Barrett, *World Christian Encyclopedia* (1982). N.SM.

Christology. That part of THEOLOGY which is concerned with doctrines about the person and work of Jesus Christ. See also DOGMA. D.L.E.

chromatography. A family of chemical separation techniques. The original method, described by Tsvett in 1903, referred to the separation of coloured substances (hence the name), but this is not an essential requirement. All chromatographic methods involve a stationary PHASE (a liquid or solid) and a mobile phase (liquid or gas). Separation depends on individual components of the mixture having different distributions between the two phases, so that they move at varying rates in the mobile phase. Closely similar SPECIES can be separated (e.g. ISOTOPES), and the detection of very small quantities is possible. See also GAS CHROMATOGRAPHY. B.F.

chromosomes. Thread-like structures present in the NUCLEI of all CELLS; they are the carriers of the hereditary factors known as GENES. See also CROSSING OVER; GENETICS/GENOMICS. J.M.S.

chronobiology. The study of how biological processes are controlled through time. Chronobiology is particularly concerned with periodic biological processes. Processes, such as movement, migration, feeding, sleeping and breeding often occur periodically, at intervals of years, months, days or minutes. The periodicity may depend on environmental cues, but in some cases it will persist if the cue is experimentally removed. The periodicity must then be due to the animal's internal clock (see BIOLOGICAL RHYTHM); the physiological mechanisms of internal clocks are little understood. M.R.

Church's thesis, see under RECURSIVE FUNCTION THEORY.

CIA (Central Intelligence Agency). The official American intelligence organization established in 1947 by the National Security Act to co-ordinate the government's overall intelligence efforts. It has persistently combined intelligence-gathering and political warfare with a more extensive role as a covert agent of US policy, including active subversion, GUERRILLA warfare and sabotage. Throughout the COLD WAR such activities were frequently directed at nations governed or influenced by COMMUNISM, and at some which were seen to threaten US economic rather than geopolitical interests. The lengthy catalogue of CIA activity includes the overthrow of governments in Guatemala and Iran in 1954; the BAY OF PIGS incident in Cuba in 1961; the destruction of the Allende government in Chile in 1973; efforts to destabilize the government of Nicaragua in the 1980s. Since the end of the cold war the Agency has suffered from a series of revelations concerning defections, mismanagement and abuse of its powers, and from the difficulty of maintaining morale and recruitment when its role is diminished and uncertain. S.R.

CIAM (*Congrès Internationaux d'Architecture Moderne*). A series of attempts, from 1928 onwards, to solve collectively some of the dominant problems of modern architecture which were at first seen as moral rather than stylistic: CIAM's first manifesto emphasized the need to put 'architecture back on its real plane, the economic and sociological plane'. Most of the great figures of the modern movement attended its meetings and Le Corbusier dominated several of these. A number of national sub-groups were formed, that in Britain being known as MARS (Modern Architectural Research Society). CIAM's most widely known document, the *Athens Charter*, stemmed from its 4th Congress in 1933 and dealt with what were considered the four primary functions of the city: dwelling, recreation, work and transportation. The 10th and last congress, held in Dubrovnik in 1956, saw the introduction of the notion of CLUSTER PLANNING. For further reading: J. L. Sert, *Can Our Cities Survive?* (1944). M.BR.

cinéma vérité. Sometimes known as *cinéma-direct*, from direct, as opposed to post-synchronized, sound recording, the term is derived from the Russian slogan *kino-pravda* applied by Dziga Vertov to his own work in the Soviet silent cinema, and used by Jean Rouch to describe the documentary movement in the early 1960s which in part revived Vertov's kino-eye principles (the camera sees truth; the film-maker should not intervene except in his MONTAGE of what the camera records). It is associated chiefly with the work of Richard Leacock and the Maysles brothers, who attempted to present an objective record of actuality (reconstructed or otherwise), but relegated montage to a subordinate role because new technical developments (lightweight cameras and recording equipment) enabled them to film their subjects unobtrusively and uninterruptedly. Rouch himself subsequently argued that the selectivity of the film-maker's eye negated the supposed objectivity of the camera, and turned increasingly to fiction as a basis for his films, though retaining the element of fact through his approach and his use of non-actors. For further reading: G. R. Levin (ed.), *Documentary Explorations* (1971). T.C.C.M.

CinemaScope. A wide-screen process involving an anamorphic lens (*L'Hypergonar*), demonstrated by Professor Henri Chrétien in 1927 and used by Claude Autant-Lara in an experimental short film, *Construire du Feu*, in 1928, but not developed commercially until bought and copyrighted as CinemaScope by Twentieth Century-Fox in 1952 in an attempt to combat the threat of television by producing bigger images. The first CinemaScope film was *The Robe*, 1953. The standard screen, in use since the earliest days of cinema, is a 4 × 3 rectangle; CinemaScope, using the anamorphic lens in filming to compress the image onto a standard 35mm frame, with a complementary lens to expand it again during projection, offered a 2.5 × 1 rectangle. Other Hollywood and foreign film companies followed suit after the success of CinemaScope with variations on this wide-screen process known as Warnerscope, Superscope, VistaVision, Dyaliscope, Tohoscope, Technirama, etc.

Analogous attempts to extend the cinema screen include *Cinerama*, a development of the triple screen used by Abel Gance in his *Napoléon* in 1927: marketed in 1952, Cinerama originally employed three separate projectors on a curved screen, but later used only one. Subsequent processes (Todd-AO, Panavision 70) dispensed with the anamorphic lens by using 70mm film, double the width of the standard 35mm frame. Seventy-millimetre film had been used for a few films in the early days of sound cinema, the first being *The Big Trail* and *Billy the Kid* (both 1930). T.C.C.M.

cinémathèque. French term coined (on the analogy of *bibliothèque*, library) to describe a film museum or library. The Cinémathèque de la Ville de Paris, founded in 1919, preserved only films which were considered important as historical documents or for teaching purposes. The Cinémathèque Française, founded by Henri Langlois, Georges Franju and Jean Mitry in 1936 (three years after the British Film Institute, its sister organization in London which incorporates the National Film Archive), considers film as an end in itself rather than as a means to education: it collects, preserves and displays not only entertainment films as well as documentaries, but film stills, designs, scripts, models, costumes and optical toys. T.C.C.M.

cinematic address. A concept in film theory that refers to the specific qualities of enunciation in cinema. In the context of structural linguistics, the term enunciation describes the aspect of an utterance, or SPEECH ACT, which addresses and positions its recipients. Enunciation operates in two registers, *discours* and *histoire*: the former inscribing both a speaker (e.g. 'I') and an addressee (e.g. 'you'); the latter being a mode of address – characteristic of narrations of past events – in which no addresser/addressee is implied. Christian Metz has argued that cinematic address operates largely within the register of *histoire*. Cinematic enunciation does not, he suggests, normally identify itself as proceeding from any particular source: a film seems simply to be 'there', unfolding itself before the spectator's eyes. To this extent, cinematic language conceals the marks of its own enunciation, constructing an omniscient, impersonal 'narrating instance'. For further reading: C. Metz, *Psychoanalysis and Cinema: The Imaginary Signifier* (1982). A.KU.

cinematic apparatus. A concept used in psychoanalytically informed film theory to refer to the conditions under which meaning is produced through the interaction of film text and spectator. The cinematic apparatus is comprised of the context in which films are consumed – darkened auditorium, projection system, shadows on the screen – together with the spectator's psychic positioning within this context. It has been suggested that this apparatus structures the spectator's subjectivity in ways identical to the developmental processes in which the human subject is formed. Such arguments tend to stress the UNCONSCIOUS element of spectator-text relations in cinema: cinematic 'speech', for example, is regarded as analogous to the rhetoric of unconscious language; while the 'cinematic state' or the 'filmic condition' is held to be like the dream-state, or in some other sense evocative of regressive, pre-linguistic states of subjectivity. It is useful for its suggestion that the moment of reception is crucial to meaning-production in cinema. A.KU.

Cinerama, see under CINEMASCOPE.

Citizen's Charter. A programme introduced by the UK Conservative government of John Major in July 1991 to improve the quality of public service. The Charter forces service providers, such as government departments, executive agencies, local authorities and the privatized utilities, to provide greater information, choice and value for money, to measure their performance against published targets, and offer redress to the public in the event of failure. It attempts to apply the market-driven strictures of the private sector to the provision of public services. Traditional forms of political accountability to elected bodies have thus been partly replaced by direct, quasi-contractual relationships between service providers and consumers, a development which has attracted much criticism. For further reading: J. A. Chandler, *The Citizen's Charter* (1996). N.O.

citizenship. Aristotle's *Politics* defined the ideal of citizenship – the conduct of civic affairs by all free men in the polis – for the ancient world, and it continued to exert great force down to the 18th century and beyond. The exercise of citizenship, in this view, was the supreme human activity, and was accordingly limited to those who had the leisure to take its requirements seriously. But increasingly the modern industrial world demanded more than the purely political rights and obligations of citizenship. From the time of the French Revolution onwards it was declared that political citizenship was meaningless without the addition of social citizenship: the empowerment of members of the community as agents with sufficient social and economic resources to participate fully in social and political life. This broadening of the ideal of citizenship made it possible for many groups, hitherto excluded from active participation in society, to strive for full membership. These included women, foreigners, ethnic and religious MINORITIES and even, most recently, children. There has also, since the time of the Enlightenment, been the idea of cosmopolitan or world citizenship. With the development of the EUROPEAN UNION (EU) and other supranational organizations, such ideas have achieved a new degree of practical realization, although for most people citizenship remains a strictly national affair, and states have indeed come to exercise their diminishing powers most stringently in restrictive policies of citizenship. But there seems a distinct tendency for citizenship to continue to widen its arc, encompassing not just human society but the whole realm of nature, so that animals can now be endowed with rights and 'planetary citizenship' can refer to rights and obligations relating to the natural world as a whole. Whether such an extension can do more than heighten awareness is a moot point. It seems impossible to imagine citizenship without a corresponding set of social and political institutions. But citizenship undoubtedly retains considerable power as a rallying-cry and a goal, as was vividly demonstrated in the movements that brought down COMMUNISM in eastern Europe and that continue to struggle for political rights in other parts of the world. K.K.

city, see under URBANIZATION.

city technology colleges. Announced in 1986 by UK Secretary of State for Education Kenneth Baker, CTCs were to be innovative, inner-city, specialist colleges jointly funded by central government and industrial sponsors. They were to be independent schools run by educational trusts. Sponsors were to meet a substantial part of the costs of the buildings and equipment necessary to provide a highly technological curriculum. The initiatives were controversial and few sponsors were forthcoming. The first to open was Kingshurst in Solihull. A total of 16 such colleges was eventually established, but most of the capital and running costs have been borne by central government.

Among the 16 are a Christian school and the BRIT school of performing arts. In the early 1990s the Conservative government introduced schemes, again involving industrial sponsorship, to turn existing GRANT MAINTAINED SCHOOLS into specialist schools in the fields of technology, music, languages and sport. S.J.B.

City, the. The name given to the square mile of London which has traditionally housed one of the world's major financial centres. A residue of Britain's era of commercial and industrial supremacy, it has proved itself more adaptable to changing world conditions than most other parts of the British economy. Among its leading financial institutions are the Stock Exchange, the money markets, the insurance institutions (including Lloyd's), commercial and merchant banks, and the various commodity exchanges. It is a major source of Britain's overseas earnings and has become progressively and proportionately more important to Britain's BALANCE OF PAYMENTS. Nevertheless its channelling of British INVESTMENT overseas rather than into British industry became a contentious domestic issue in Britain in the 1970s. As an international financial centre its only major rivals are WALL STREET and Tokyo. In the 1980s, the City was affected by a number of financial scandals. These, and the need to compete with other financial centres, have led to changes in the ECONOMIC REGULATION of the different parts of the City. For example, fixed commissions on dealings in shares have been abolished; and the institutional distinction between those firms buying and selling shares, and those firms advising clients on dealings in shares, has been abolished. D.E.; J.P.

civil disobedience. The strategy of securing political goals by non-violent refusal to co-operate with the agents of the government; most famously, the strategy which Mahatma Gandhi persuaded the Indian National Congress to adopt in April 1930, which envisaged the disruption of British government in India by the mass ceremonial performance of illegal actions. The aim of such mass action is to overload the police and the courts and so to impair the CREDIBILITY of the government. In insisting so strongly on non-violence (see NON-VIOLENT RESISTANCE), the strategy makes great demands on the self-control and patience of its adherents. This was one of its merits in Gandhi's eyes. Interest in civil disobedience has been revived both by those who advocate a non-violent defence strategy as an alternative to nuclear DETERRENCE and by those who adopted civil disobedience in the attempt to alter American policy towards and military involvement in VIETNAM. For further reading: M. K. Gandhi, *Non-Violent Resistance* (1961). A.R.

civil religion. Although known in a general sense to the ancients, it was Jean-Jacques Rousseau who in *The Social Contract* (1762) introduced the term to modern thought to express the core values that must be sustained by the modern state in the absence of the BELIEF in revealed RELIGION. He believed that there was a 'natural religion' common to all humanity, and that its content could be expressed in a few simple dogmas, such as the existence of an intelligent and beneficent Deity, the happiness of the just and the punishment of the wicked, the sanctity of the SOCIAL CONTRACT and the laws, and the inviolability of conscience. The term was revived, with a shift of emphasis, by the American sociologist Robert Bellah in 1967 to describe the idea of a special, divinely ordained mission for a nation which was inscribed in the general beliefs of the nation. Although Bellah confined his discussion to American civil religion, and the belief that America was founded as a 'City Upon a Hill' to act as a shining example to the rest of mankind, other thinkers have generalized the concept to make it refer to a number of belief-systems in the modern world. Prominent among these have been NATIONALISM and MARXISM – especially, in the latter case, in its institutionalization as Marxism-Leninism in the communist societies of eastern Europe. The danger with these extensions is the tendency to make the concept of civil religion fit all and every instance of modern secular IDEOLOGIES. It seems best to stick to some version of Rousseau's original meaning, and to make civil religion stand for some set of fundamental dogmas, involving belief in a transcendental reality and agency, by which a society seeks to live and to understand its role in the world. K.K.

civil rights movement. The campaign for legal enforcement of rights guaranteed to American BLACKS as citizens under the US constitution. It developed in the late 1950s as earlier efforts by groups such as the National Association for the Advancement of Colored People (founded 1910) and the National Urban League (1911) became increasingly regarded as too gradualist and unsuited to overcome Southern white resistance to change. The movement was a coalition of organizations including the Southern Christian Leadership Conference led by Dr Martin Luther King Jr, the Student Non-Violent Coordinating Committee, and the Congress on Racial Equality. Its tactics included various forms of DIRECT ACTION, such as boycotts, sit-ins and marches; in the face of great provocation it tried to adhere to non-violence (see NON-VIOLENT RESISTANCE) and the principles of CIVIL DISOBEDIENCE, and to incorporate the support of white liberals. The movement achieved some successes, such as the Civil Rights Act of 1964 and Voting Rights Act of 1965; it became increasingly disunited as some elements extended their claims from liberal demands for formal civil rights and electoral participation to a more radical prospectus for economic equality both within and outside the South. The fracturing of the movement's identity and the growth of more militant BLACK POWER organizations occurred in 1965–66. For further reading: H. Sitkoff, *The Struggle for Black Equality 1945–80* (1981). S.R.

civil society. A sphere of society lying between the private sphere of the FAMILY and the official sphere of the STATE. As developed especially by the German philosopher G. W. F. Hegel (see HEGELIANISM), it refers usually to the array of voluntary organizations and civic associations – parties, TRADE UNIONS, religious organizations, cultural and educational bodies – that are to be found in modern liberal societies (see LIBERALISM). A key aspect of these bodies is that, though public, they are not official or governmental. They enable individuals to discuss matters of public concern and to participate in the life of society without direction by the state. Civil society has therefore often been seen, as for instance by the French thinker Alexis de Tocqueville, as the bulwark of liberties in free societies. Its absence in the former COMMUNIST states of eastern Europe was widely regarded as the most serious obstacle to a vigorous public life. It was indeed around the slogan 'the revival of civil society' that much of the opposition to communism developed, especially in its later years. Fired by the enthusiasm of east Europeans, Western commentators have in recent years also begun to re-examine the institutions of civil society in their own societies, and have been alarmed at what they have seen as a serious condition of decline. Much social and political thought is currently concerned with the efforts to reinvigorate civil society. K.K.

cladism. Method of classification in BIOLOGY (see TAXONOMY) in which SPECIES are classified together strictly according to the order of their evolutionary branching (see EVOLUTION). (Cladism comes from the Greek *klados*, branch.) Alternatively, species might be grouped according to their similarity of appearance; which is called phenetic classification. Generally, cladistic and phenetic classifications are similar, but not always. For example, crocodiles are more similar in appearance to lizards than either are to birds, and in phenetic classification crocodiles and lizards are grouped together as reptiles, separate from birds. However, crocodiles share a more recent common ancestor with birds than with lizards, and the cladist therefore classifies crocodiles with birds and the group 'Reptilia' ceases to exist in formal classification. Cladism was particularly advocated by the German entomologist Willi Hennig. Cladism can be preferred to phenetic classification on the grounds that evolutionary relations (once known) are unambiguous, whereas phenetic similarity is an ambiguous criterion which depends on the taxonomists' points of view. Cladism may be criticized on the grounds that it produces strange novelties (such as the abolition of reptiles) and is unnecessary. For further reading: M. Ridley, *Evolution and Classification* (1986). M.R.

clairvoyance, see under ESP.

clan. Groups recruited on the basis of common DESCENT, but the ties with an ancestor are assumed rather than demonstrated. If descent is claimed through the male line, the group is known as a *patri-clan*; through the female line, a *matri-clan*. Clans are larger and looser groupings than descent groups. However, even if members are widely dispersed and lack a corporate structure, MARRIAGE for clan members is usually exogamous (see EXOGAMY), i.e. marriage outside the clan. For further reading: J. Goody, *The Development of the Family and Marriage in Europe* (1983).

A.G.

class.

(1) In MATHEMATICS and LOGIC, a synonym for SET.

(2) In SOCIOLOGY, a CONCEPT which denotes different social strata in society. Many sociologists, such as Ralf Dahrendorf, distinguish between the 'estate' systems of feudal and pre-industrial society – in which distinctions were primarily of *rank*, resting on tradition and an intricate system of age-old, often codified rights and duties – and the true class system which emerged when CAPITALISM and the INDUSTRIAL REVOLUTION substituted for these criteria the external criterion of material possessions. In the *Communist Manifesto* Marx identified classes in relation to the means of production, and thus generalized the concept of class to all societies where such distinctions could be made. (See also SOCIAL STRATIFICATION.)

Economic class. For Marx, the criterion of class was economic. However, he never specifically defined 'economic', and at various points in his writings he laid down several quite different criteria for the identification of classes. Moreover, it is difficult to find a single unambiguous criterion, whether it be OCCUPATION or a common standing in the processes of production, that does not encounter logical difficulties in classification. (If, for example, one takes the production process as the criterion, how does one classify those who stand outside production?)

For Max Weber, class is an analytical term which identifies individuals who have similar 'life chances' in the opportunities for gaining income; market assets include skill as well as property. He sees the major historical class struggle as being between creditors and debtors, with the conflict under capitalism between employers and workers as merely a special case.

Social class. For Marx, this was determined by, and coterminous with, economic class. Other sociologists see social class as a more complex variable which includes STATUS, prestige, family lineage and other criteria. In the USA, W. Lloyd Warner was the leading American theorist of class, working at the University of Chicago from 1939 to 1959. He established a six-grade ranking system defined simply by a dichotomous division within the upper, middle and lower classes.

Class conflict. Marx predicted, under capitalism, an increasing POLARIZATION of society, increased exploitation of the worker, and ever sharper conflict between the two classes, leading ultimately to the social REVOLUTION. Social development for the West has belied that prediction. Real wages of the WORKING CLASS have risen, the working class has gained increasing social and political rights, and class conflict, though not eliminated, has become regulated (i.e. subject to legal rules) and institutionally isolated (i.e. there is little carry-over from industrial conflicts into other areas of life). In many industrial societies, moreover, other forms of conflict cut across class lines and divide, say, Irish Protestant from Irish Catholic workers rather than workers from bosses.

Class consciousness. Marx assumed that such consciousness would develop in a class struggle created by the crises of the capitalist system. Lenin, however, regarded the working class, unaided, as able to develop only 'TRADE UNION consciousness'; and to this extent the creation of 'socialist consciousness' is the task of the INTELLECTUALS. In that case the MARXIST notion that 'existence determines consciousness', and the relation between social position and IDEOLOGY, cannot easily be maintained. This is a conundrum from which Marxist theory has not yet extricated itself. For further reading: P. Calvert, *The Concept of Class* (1982). D.B.

classical ballet. Term derived from the Italian *ballare* meaning to dance. Classical ballet strictly means theatre entertainment employing a codified academic dance form called the *danse d'école* (classical school). With the cross-fertilization of dance techniques, the term ballet is often applied to choreographic works performed by MODERN DANCE companies. Classical ballet is based on the fundamental five positions laid down by Pierre Beauchamps in 1650 and built on the principle of outwardness or turnout (i.e. the rotation of the legs in the hip socket) and the codified romantic classical ballet vocabulary established by Carlo Blasis in 1820. The technique aims to produce virtuosity from seemingly effortless execution through disciplined training in body alignment. The classical ballet aesthetic strives for nobility rather than serviceability; the ballerina representing the graceful, ethereal, unattainable romantic female ideal, further enhancing beauty of line and expression by wearing pointed shoes, and the male assuming a steadfast, vital and vigorous authority. Classical ballet is built on a hierarchical system in direct contrast to modern dance, from the prima ballerina down to the corps de ballet. The historical development ranges from a diversion for the nobility in the 17th century, to the romantic era of the 19th century, through Diaghilev's revitalization in the early 20th century, to its worldwide popularity today. For further reading: R. Copeland and M. Cohen (eds), *What Is Dance?* (1983). L.A.

classical conditioning (also known as PAVLOVIAN or respondent conditioning). A form of CONDITIONED REFLEX; after an arbitrary stimulus has been repeatedly paired with the eliciting stimulus of a reflex, the previously neutral stimulus comes to elicit the reflex response even in the absence of the characteristic elicitor. The traditional example is the Russian physiologist I. P. Pavlov's experiment (1906), in which, after the ringing of a bell (the *conditioned stimulus*) had repeatedly been accompanied by the provision of meat (the *unconditioned stimulus*), it was found that the ringing of the bell caused dogs to salivate (the *conditioned response*) even if no meat was produced. Interest in the objective and precise Russian studies was a major influence on the BEHAVIOURIST revolution in America. However, many modern psychologists believe that classical conditioning is merely a special case of OPERANT CONDITIONING: since the conditioned response prepares the organism for the appearance of the unconditioned stimulus, it seems more parsimonious to view the unconditioned stimulus as an operant reinforcer than to regard classical conditioning as an independent kind of learning. Procedures developed from classical-conditioning paradigms, especially *aversion therapy* and *desensitization*, are described under BEHAVIOUR THERAPY. D.H.

classical economic theory. The system of economic theory which was included in Adam Smith's *Wealth of Nations* (1776) and developed during the period ending about 1870. It was based on the assumption that the individual was usually the best judge of his own interests. The conclusion that under a freely competitive economic system the individual pursuit of economic self-interest would result in the economic benefit of the community depended on the analysis of the functioning of the PRICE MECHANISM in allocating resources in response to the supplies and demands for goods and services. When combined with the analysis of the role of the DIVISION OF LABOUR and the INVESTMENT OF CAPITAL in promoting ECONOMIC GROWTH, this led to the further conclusion of the desirability of freedom in international trade and freedom of economic activity, generally, from government intervention. The classical economists generally accepted the QUANTITY THEORY OF MONEY.

There were, however, numerous differences of view among writers of this school, particularly with respect to the theories of value (see VALUE, THEORY OF), wages, rent, population, under-consumption, banking policy and the functions of government. One of the best-known and for a short time most influential MODELS based on classical economic theory is the *Ricardian*. This incorporated the Malthusian (see MALTHUSIANISM) theory of population, the Ricardian theory of rent based on the law of diminishing returns to land (see DIMINISHING PRODUCTIVITY OF A FACTOR), and Ricardo's variant of the LABOUR THEORY OF VALUE. An important conclusion derived from this model was that economic growth was doomed to come to an end owing to the increasing difficulty of producing sufficient food as population increases. See NEO-CLASSICAL ECONOMIC THEORY. For further reading: M. Blaug, *Economic Theory in Retrospect* (1985). M.E.A.B.

classical physics. Group of physical theories encompassing NEWTONIAN MECHANICS, electromagnetic theory (see ELECTROMAGNETISM), thermodynamics and STATISTICAL MECHANICS that reached full flower in the 19th century. 'Classical' is often used as a contrastive term, to describe features that are shared by this group of theories, but which distinguish them from either QUANTUM MECHANICS OR RELATIVITY. It is often said that the classical theories were 'refuted' and replaced by their 20th-century successors, and that both quantum mechanics and relativity, in their different ways, 'reduce to' classical mechanics under certain conditions: classical physics is valid only as an 'approximation', over a limited range. However, correspondences between the classical and non-classical theories are merely quantitative, and are based on limiting-case convergences: a quantum-mechanical or relativistic system can never *be* a classical system, although its behaviour can be brought arbitrarily close. In addition, only classical calculations are both sufficiently detailed and mathematically tractable to be predictive for many physical situations. The quantum-mechanical or relativistic versions are either mathematically intractable, or simply not available. Thus classical calculations continue to be performed alongside applications of relativity and quantum mechanics at the heart of modern PHYSICS. R.F.H.

clear cutting. A forestry practice whereby all harvestable trees are removed from a site at the same time; the result is local DEFORESTATION, loss of HABITAT for the plants and animals of the forest, and soil degradation and erosion (see SOIL EROSION). The erosion resulting from clear cutting carries sediment into streams, thereby degrading that environment. Alternatives to clear cutting include strip cutting or selective cutting, practices which preserve some of the forest habitat and provide a reservoir of SPECIES which may encourage reforestation of the harvested areas. W.G.R.

cleavage, see under EMBRYOLOGY.

client. In ANTHROPOLOGY, an individual in a relationship with a patron (see PATRONAGE) through whom he gains access to resources. In return a client may pledge his support, vote or solidarity to his patron. Patrons often compete for clients and try to enhance their standing by extending their networks of influence. Clients themselves, however, can exercise checks on the power of patrons either through the invocation of quasi-KINSHIP ties or personal obligations or by threatening to leave one patron for another. Clientilism is frequently relative since relationships are part of an extended chain: a client at one level may be a patron to individuals at another. It can have either political or economic (see ECONOMICS) functions, or both at the same time. For further reading: S. N. Eisenstadt and L. Roniger, *Patrons, Clients and Friends* (1984). M.H.

climatology. The study of average temperature, rainfall, humidity and sunshine in different localities over long periods of time (at least 30 years), as contrasted with METEOROLOGY, which studies short-term changes. It is hoped that long-term climatic changes such as ice ages (as revealed by fossil vegetation, for example) may be explained by changes in the composition of the atmosphere. M.V.B.

climax. In ECOLOGY, a final or culminating state of an undisturbed vegetational COMMUNITY. A distinction is usually drawn between an EQUILIBRIUM achieved with respect to climate (*climatic climax*) and to soil (*edaphic climax*). P.H.

clinical linguistics. The application of the theories, methods and descriptive findings of LINGUISTICS to the analysis of spoken or written language handicap, such as aphasia (see NEUROPSYCHOLOGY), language delay or pronunciation disorders. For further reading: D. Crystal, *Clinical Linguistics* (1989). D.C.

clinical psychology, see under APPLIED PSYCHOLOGY.

cliometrics, see under ECONOMIC HISTORY.

clock paradox. The prediction of Einstein's theory of RELATIVITY that clocks and other temporal processes run more slowly as seen by an observer moving relatively to them than similar clocks and processes in his own FRAME OF REFERENCE. This effect (which is only appreciable when the moving clock travels almost as fast as light) does not violate the principle of CAUSALITY or the rules of LOGIC. Indeed, it has been confirmed experimentally by the discovery that swiftly moving MESONS in the atmosphere are observed by us to live much longer before decaying than slower-moving mesons produced in the laboratory; the meson decays according to its internal 'clock', which runs slow as seen by us.

Despite this, the clock paradox has occasioned lively controversy for over 50 years, particularly in the sharpened form of the *twin paradox*, in which a traveller is imagined to leave the earth at high speed and then, after some years, to turn round and come back; his twin, who has stayed behind, will have aged, while the traveller (whose clocks have run slow relative to those on earth) will still be young. The paradox is this: since each twin has been moving relative to the other, might one not equally well look at the situation from the traveller's point of view, in which case the twins' roles and ageing processes will be reversed? It is resolved by the fact that the twins are not in symmetrical situations: when turning around, the traveller must accelerate, and accelerating frames of reference are not dealt with in special relativity; a full analysis requires the general theory of relativity. Einstein's position has been vindicated by the recent experiments of J. C. Hafele and R. E. Keating, who measured small differences, compatible with the predictions of relativity theory, between the times indicated by clocks that had been flown round the world and clocks that had remained in the laboratory. For further reading: L. Marder, *Time and the Space Traveller* (1971). M.V.B.

cloisonnisme**,** see under SYNTHETISM.

cloning. A type of GENETIC ENGINEERING that leads to replication of an ORGANISM without the need for fertilization of a female egg by a male sperm. In the most dramatic example to date, a team in Scotland led by Dr Ian Wimsatt cloned a lamb (which they named 'Dolly') by nuclear transplantation. This technique involves inserting the NUCLEUS of one CELL taken from a ewe into an egg cell (derived from another ewe) from which the nucleus has been removed. The resulting egg, containing the unique genetic material (see GENETICS/GENOMICS) of the donor sheep, was implanted into yet another ewe, who eventually gave birth to a fully developed lamb.

Nuclear transplantation, or some variant of it, could be used to clone multiple copies of a particularly valuable line of livestock such as sheep or cattle. Using genetic material from only one organism would avoid the chance production of unexpected features that normally occur as a result of the mixing of maternal and paternal genetic lines, as is usual in sexual reproduction.

The prospect of using cloning to replicate livestock breeds is significantly less troublesome for most people than the possibility that cloning could lead to the selective replication of human beings. In order to avoid this eventuality, several countries have already banned research that might lead to human cloning.

The term cloning is also used to describe the replication of specific genes via a laboratory process called polymerase chain reaction (PCR). For further reading: K. Drlica, *Understanding DNA and Gene Cloning: A Guide for the Curious* (1997). P.A.L.

closed class, see under WORD CLASS.

closed shop. The restriction of employment in a workplace to members of a particular TRADE UNION, or unions. In the *pre-entry closed shop* only those who are already union members can be engaged. In the *union shop* (USA) or *agency shop* (UK) non-members may be engaged, but can keep their jobs only if they become members (or alternatively, in the UK, contribute the amount of union dues) within a reasonable time. All forms of closed shop meet the feeling of unionists that no one working alongside them should benefit from the activity of their union without paying dues to it. The authority of the union over dissidents is greatly increased when those who leave the union or are deprived of membership are thereby deprived of their jobs too. Some employers have found the closed shop advantageous in this last respect, and many have had no alternative but to accept it; but for an employer to dismiss a satisfactory worker only because he has fallen out with the union is embarrassing, and may be actionable as unfair dismissal. To have to maintain union membership under penalty of losing his job restricts the worker's freedom. In the USA the Taft-Hartley Act, 1947, made it unlawful for employers and unions to enforce the closed shop, but not the union shop. In the UK, since 1971, there have been several Acts of Parliament which have altered the rules governing the operation of the closed shop. In 1987 the closed shop was still legal, although the Conservative government (see CONSERVATISM) issued a green paper (a paper containing proposals to be discussed by Parliament) in that year with the proposal that the closed shop should be made illegal. A.B.E.; E.H.P.B.

cloud chamber. A device invented by C. T. R. Wilson in 1911, and used to study NUCLEAR REACTIONS and ELEMENTARY PARTICLES. It is based on the fact that a fast charged PARTICLE leaves a record of its path, in the form of a trail of droplets, centred on IONS, when it traverses a vapour kept just below its condensation temperature. M.V.B.

Club of Rome, see under LIMITS TO GROWTH.

cluster (in music), see under TONE-CLUSTER.

cluster analysis. A form of FACTOR ANALYSIS in which multivariate measurements or observations on a number of individual entities are statistically analysed, usually with the aid of a COMPUTER, to try to identify internal structure, e.g. the chronological ordering of archaeological objects, or the grouping of a set of manuscripts by authorship. M.S.BA.

cluster planning. Policies which cluster and mix shops, employment, facilities, schools and other land uses within the local area due to a resurgence of interest in more environmentally sustainable (see SUSTAINABLE URBAN DEVELOPMENT) and socially equitable means of neighbourhood planning. Such principles are strongly espoused by European-wide women's town planning groups, who, in the wake of increasing 'Americanization' of their cities, are pressing for 'the city of everyday life' in which local shops and facilities, employment opportunities and social amenities are accessibly located in local areas, within walking distance of homes, rather than being decentralized to remote out-of-town locations. With the support of environmental groups, such ideas are now being taken on board by progressive European government agencies (for example, see Ministry of Environment, *Manual for Alternative Urban Planning*, Oslo, Norway, 1993; and OECD, *Women in the City*, 1994). C.G.

CMEA, see under COMECON.

CND, see under PEACE MOVEMENT.

COBRA. A group of artists that flourished between 1948 and 1951. Its name combines the initial letters of the capital cities where the founder-members worked: Copenhagen, Brussels, Amsterdam. The association inherited the ideas (and many of the members) of three groups, the Dutch *Experimentele Groep*, the Danish *Spiralen group* and the Belgian *Bureau International de Surréalisme Révolutionnaire*. Its leading figures were Asger Jorn, Karel Appel, Christian Dotremont, Pierre Alechinsky, Constant Nieuwenhuys and Cornelis van Beverloo Corneille. In their exhibitions and publications they sought to express, spontaneously and/or unconsciously, profound psychic forces, and their images are often primitive, violent and fantastic. COBRA may be seen as a European variant of ACTION PAINTING and ABSTRACT EXPRESSIONISM. P.C.

cobweb theory (or **model**).

(1) In international relations, a theory developed by J. W. Burton as an alternative to the state-centric approach. Some American scholars were simultaneously applying SYSTEMS concepts and theories, and elaborating the WORLD SOCIETY THEORY. Burton's model sees society as comprising millions of 'cobwebs', each representing a system, not as a distinct territorial unit, but as a set of dynamic social relations, constantly growing in complexity as a result of increased functional interdependence and channelling values and expectations of communities and individuals. Critics have attacked the MODEL for failing to allow sufficiently for the roles of STATES and their foreign policies and interactions, and for being so diffuse and unmanageable that it is of negligible value in developing a general theory of international relations. For further reading: J. W. Burton, *World Society* (1972). P.W.

(2) In ECONOMICS, a model of how a market may behave when production of a good takes a period of time. The decision about how much to produce must be based

on the expectation (see RATIONAL EXPECTATIONS) of the price at the time the output is supplied to the market. In this model, the lag between production and supply is taken as one period and producers assume that the next period's price will be equal to the present price. This means that the present price determines the level of current production and thus how much is supplied to the market in the next period. In the next period, price adjusts to ensure that all that is supplied is demanded. If demand at the expected price is not equal to the amount supplied, i.e. the market is not in EQUILIBRIUM, future prices and production will vary. J.P.

code. In SOCIOLINGUISTICS, a term loosely applied to the language system of a community or to a particular *variety* within a language, e.g. Bernstein's characterization of the different linguistic capabilities of middle- and working-class children in terms of elaborated and restricted codes. D.C.

code-switching. In SOCIOLINGUISTICS, the way bilingual or bidialectal (see BIDIALECTALISM) speakers change from the use of one language or dialect to another, depending on who they are talking to, where they are, and other contextual factors. The amount of code-switching which takes place in everyday conversation between bilinguals has been much underestimated, and is often misinterpreted as illustrating uncertainty or confusion on the part of the speakers. The current view is that the alternations reflect systematically the social and psychological factors involved in the interaction. D.C.

co-dependency. An aspect of ADDICTION, and a term most often used to describe a person's relation to their partner's addiction. It is a vague and imprecise term which usually means anything its user wants it to mean. One can, e.g., be co-dependent on alcohol and nicotine or other addictive substances, co-dependent on substances and people, co-dependent in one's relationship with an addict, or co-dependent as a result of abuse and abandonment from one's parents, thereby setting off one's own progress towards addiction. The concept of co-dependency can be responsible for fuelling self-pity and blame together with a lack of responsibility for self; it can enable therapists of the 'deep and mysterious' persuasion to become even more so; and it can be useful in persuading insurance companies to medicalize a personal or social problem. The co-dependency movement seeks to nurture the 'inner child' and gain understanding and acceptance. For further reading: J. Rice, *A Disease of One's Own* (1996). R.M.H.L.

co-determination, see under PARTICIPATION.

coding.

(1) In INFORMATION THEORY, the representation of data for transmission or storage. Coding theory concerns itself with such questions as 'Is this the shortest representation of the data?'; 'How likely is this datum to be confused with other data if the representation is corrupted?' and with the measurement of REDUNDANCY. It is the basis of the design of encoders and decoders. R.M.N.

(2) In COMPUTING, the final stage in preparing a problem for a COMPUTER (the others being SYSTEMS ANALYSIS and programming). It involves writing exhaustive instructions to make a computer carry out the tasks which have been specified in the previous stages. Typically, coders write their instructions in assembly language – a very lengthy and largely mechanical process in which they are prone to error. It is difficult for anyone who has not experienced it to realize the degree of detail required in coding. This is similar to that required in a knitting pattern (English, not Continental, style), and coding corresponds to constructing such a detailed pattern, given the dimensions of the garment and the basic stitch pattern. Coding can be eliminated by the use of an appropriate high-level programming language. C.S.

codomain (in MATHEMATICS), see under FUNCTION.

coercion. Although all commentators agree that the bank clerk reluctantly handing money to the armed robber is a victim of coercion, there is little agreement on the boundaries between what is and what is not a coercive relationship. Some claim that apparently 'free' bargains are in fact coercive; the employer who offers a starving man a badly paid job may be said to be forcing him to work rather than merely offering him a free choice between working and not working. MARXISTS, who hold that relations between capitalists and workers are coercive rather than a matter of freely reached agreement, point to the origins of CAPITALISM in the forced expropriation of small farmers and the like. Others point to the implausibility of describing bargains struck between participants of very unequal bargaining power as 'free' bargains. Others point to the difference between relationships in which both parties expect to benefit and those in which one party extracts a disproportionate share of the benefits of agreement by his ability to impose worse terms on the other party in the event of their proving recalcitrant – the bank clerk would rather not hand over the money demanded by the robber, but the robber can impose the option of death or injury. Whether this is definitive of coercion or only a symptom of it is another question, and one to which no answer is entirely persuasive. A.R.

co-evolution. A significant component of evolutionary thought (see EVOLUTION) focuses on the reality that SPECIES do not evolve in isolation. The term co-evolution is used to describe instances in which two ORGANISMS evolve to become uniquely adapted to each other. An often-cited example is flower shape and colour and the birds or insects that pollinate them while gathering their nectar; hummingbirds, for example, can see the colour red – and they gather nectar from red flowers. Additionally, the nectar is found at the base of a flower whose petals form a long, narrow tube. The hummingbirds have long, narrow beaks that enable them to reach the nectar. In some instances co-evolution leads to a closely coupled obligatory interdependence termed SYMBIOSIS. W.G.R.

coffee house, see under FOLK MUSIC.

cognatic descent, see BILATERAL/COGNATIC DESCENT.

cognitive archaeology. Also called symbolic or structural archaeology, cognitive archaeology is the study of the mind of past human beings – i.e. their ways of thinking and their symbolic structure – based on the material remains they left behind, together with ancient art and, for historical periods, writing. It incorporates such topics as archaeoastronomy, symbols of authority or power, CULT practices, units of length and weight, etc. For further reading: C. Renfrew and E. B. W. Zubrow (eds), *The Ancient Mind: Elements of Cognitive Archaeology* (1994). P.G.B.

cognitive grammar. In LINGUISTICS, a theory which sees language as an integral part of cognition, a means whereby cognitive content is given structure. The basic function of language is to symbolize conceptualization by means of PHONOLOGY. GRAMMAR is seen as an inherently meaningful (or 'symbolic') component of the theory, linking SEMANTICS and phonology. This pairing of forms and meanings sets up connections between established patterns of neurological activity, and these serve as templates for categorizing expressions. The patterns, or units, each correspond to an aspect of linguistic structure, and sequences of units are used to construct the well-formed expressions in the language. For further reading: R. Asher (ed.), *The Encyclopedia of Language and Linguistics* (1993). D.C.

cognitive metaphor. In LINGUISTICS, a theory in which METAPHOR is viewed as performing an essential role in human language and cognition, encoding world-views in all forms of linguistic activity, including everyday conversation ('conceptual metaphors'). Higher-level concepts such as causality, time and the emotions are seen to be semantically grounded in lower-level domains of physical experience, as in such expressions as 'life is a journey'. 'Poetic metaphors' are seen as extensions or novel combinations of everyday metaphors. This approach thus contrasts with the traditional account of metaphor (with its distinction between literal and figurative meaning, and its focus on rhetorical and literary contexts), which is felt to be of limited relevance to a fully linguistic account of grammatical and semantic structure (see SEMANTICS). For further reading: G. Lakoff and M. Johnson, *Metaphors We Live By* (1980). D.C.

cognitive psychology. A branch of PSYCHOLOGY defined partly by its subject-matter, i.e. cognition, partly by its point of view. With respect to point of view, its main PRESUPPOSITION is that any interaction between an organism and its ENVIRONMENT changes not only its overt behaviour or physiological condition, but also its knowledge of or information about the environment, and that this latter change may affect not only present response but also future orientation to the environment. Historically speaking, cognitive psychology arose out of a combination of Enlightenment psychological SENSATIONALISM and associationist (see ASSOCIATIONISM) EPISTEMOLOGY, grounded in individual and social learning theories and philosophies of educability and CONDITIONING. American psychologist E. C. Tolman (1886–1959), characterizing the difference between the BEHAVIOURIST theory of *stimulus* and *response* and cognitive approaches to the study of learning, applied to the former the image of a telephone switchboard in which incoming stimuli came by practice to be connected to responses, and to the latter that of a maproom where the incoming stimuli were put together into 'cognitive maps' by the use of which responses were constructed to achieve intended outcomes. While the distinction is no longer so clear, thanks to the greater sophistication of the modern CONNECTIONIST's view of 'switch-boards', Tolman's distinction highlights the emphasis of cognitive psychology on those mediating 'knowledge processes' that affect the complex relation between input in the form of stimulation and output in the form of response. Within the last generation, the metaphorical MODELS of cognitive psychology have been transformed by the rise of ARTIFICIAL INTELLIGENCE and computer-based concepts of learning systems. How far COMPUTERS themselves can be understood within the categories of cognitive psychology now forms an important philosophical and practical debate.

Perhaps the main contribution of cognitive studies to the great debates in psychology has been to redress the imbalance created by the radical behaviourism introduced in the 1920s. The new emphasis was undoubtedly given great support by new approaches to information processing in CYBERNETICS, INFORMATION THEORY and COMPUTING. For further reading: C. French and A. Colman (eds), *Cognitive Psychology* (1995). J.S.B.; R.P.

cognitive therapy. A form of psychotherapy based on the theories of Aaron Beck, whereby disordered cognitions are seen as the core of psychiatric disorders. Thus depressive patients are considered to have a distorted view of themselves, the world around them and their future, constantly reinforcing these cognitions ('acts of knowing') by interpreting every event in a negative light. Therapy focuses on generating alternative automatic thoughts that break up this pattern and impose novel and positive ways of viewing problems. The process uses established measurements of symptom intensity, both self-reported and objective, and relatively brief (eight to ten sessions is typical) programmes of treatment. Some successful results in the treatment of obsessional, ANXIETY and depressive disorders (see DEPRESSION) have enhanced cognitive therapy's acceptance in terms of both the healthcare market and evidence-based medicine.

Its popularity also derives from the synthesis of learning theory, BEHAVIOURISM and an interpersonal approach, its avoidance of the verbal complexities of PSYCHOANALYSIS, and its applicability to numerous other problems in living. By employing the reorganization of thinking to treat emotional disorders, it also challenges the accepted dichotomy of logic/feeling in our understanding of how the mind works. Like many popular (because non-biological) approaches to mental disorder, it is at risk of over-extending its claims. For further reading: K. Hawton *et al*, *Cognitive Behaviour Therapy for Psychiatric Problems: A Practical Guide* (1989). T.T.

***cohabitation*.** A term coined to describe the new constitutional situation which emerged in France after the legislative elections of March 1986. The French constitution divides power ambiguously between the President, who is head of state and who is directly elected for a seven-year period, and a prime minister, who is directly elected every five years. Hitherto, the two had always held similar political outlooks, and the President had traditionally exercised considerable influence over the prime minister. Following the victory of the RIGHT-wing coalition in the 1986 elections, the SOCIALIST François Mitterrand became the first President of the Fifth Republic to face a hostile parliamentary majority, having to cohabit with the Gaullist Prime Minister Jacques Chirac. This he negotiated skilfully, wielding considerable influence over events in France. Ironically, following the 1997 elections, there was a reversal of roles: the RIGHT-wing President Jacques Chirac having to cohabit with the SOCIALIST Prime Minister Lionel Jospin, the surprise victor of a snap election called by Chirac. V.L.

coherent light. When light is emitted from a surface the waves that emanate from the different ATOMS in the surface are generally out of PHASE with each other in random fashion. But it is possible to generate light waves in such a way that the same phase of wave is emitted from all parts of the source. The reinforcement of each wave on each of the others produces light with very different properties from that of ordinary light. For example, a beam of coherent light has the power to cut through thick steel plate. The RADIATION has great powers of penetration and persistence and can be bounced off very distant objects such as the moon. It is invaluable as a phase reference in the process known as HOLOGRAPHY. One method of generating coherent light is by passing ordinary light through a hole in an opaque sheet, the hole being so small that only one PHOTON of light can pass through at a time. But the light scrambles itself again within a few millimetres' distance. The first persistent source of coherent light was obtained by irradiating a ruby crystal. Later it was found possible to stimulate a rarefied gas in such a way as to cause it to emit coherent light. Medically it is now used to seal internal haemorrhages, to fix detached eye retinas and perform other similar beneficial functions. E.R.L.

cohesion, see under SPECIES.

cohort. A group of persons who experience a significant event during the same period of time. For example, all babies born in 1990 form the birth cohort for that year, while all individuals marrying in the 1990s make up the marriage cohort for that decade. In DEMOGRAPHY, the cohort is, conceptually, the fundamental unit of analysis. Demographic indices such as LIFE EXPECTANCY or the TOTAL FERTILITY RATE, or broader summaries such as the LIFE TABLE, may refer to actual cohorts with shared life histories. However, these terms may also refer to the experience of a hypothetical cohort whose life history mimics the demographic conditions of a particular time period across the age range. For example, life expectancy for the cohort of 1995 equals the average age at death for all persons born in that year and cannot be computed with certainty until all members of the cohort have died; on the other hand, life expectancy for the period of 1995 equals the average age at death for all persons born in that year on the condition that the death rates by age observed in 1995 do not change in the future. In common practice, demographic indices refer to periods rather than cohorts, since the former can be computed with readily available data. This difference between 'cohorts' and 'periods' (or 'synthetic cohorts') is a fundamental distinction in the quantitative analysis of population change (including not only demographic events such as birth, death or MARRIAGE, but also social, economic and biomedical transitions such as education, employment or illness). Studies taking either cohorts or periods as their unit of temporal analysis are also referred to as 'longitudinal' or 'cross-sectional', respectively. J.R.W.

cold, see under HOT AND COLD.

cold fusion. Although attempts to conduct nuclear FUSION at non-extreme ('cold') temperatures have a respectable history, cold fusion is usually held to refer to the claim by chemists at the University of Utah in 1989 to have achieved this in an electrochemical process (see ELECTROCHEMISTRY). They claimed to have observed a heat output from an electrochemical cell in excess of that which could be explained by a purely chemical process, and subsequently the detection of neutrons characteristic of the fusion process. The process involved ELECTROLYSIS of heavy water at palladium electrodes. Controversial from the outset, these claims are now generally regarded as discredited. P.C.B.

cold war. The generic term which describes the global competition and confrontation short of all-out WAR between the two superpowers, the United States and the former

USSR, together with their allies and proxies, which lasted from 1945 to 1989. Its origins are generally ascribed to the breakdown of co-operation in the wartime alliance, growing Western concerns over Stalin's expansionist policies, and the onset of an 'iron curtain' dividing Europe. Over the ensuing four decades the global struggle between the 'free world' and the 'COMMUNIST bloc' embraced competing ideological, political and economic policies, and intensified with the emergence in the 1950s of a strategic ARMS RACE between the US and the Soviet Union involving NUCLEAR WEAPONS. Possible nuclear war was only narrowly averted during the Cuban missile crisis of October 1962 (see CUBA). Made dramatically aware of the nuclear peril, the US and the Soviet Union throughout the 1970s developed a political mechanism to constrain the build-up of strategic weapons. The result was the first agreement on 'strategic arms limitation' (SALT) in 1972, accompanied by a limited Soviet–American DÉtente (see NUCLEAR WEAPONS, LIMITATION AND CONTROL).

The precarious Soviet–American *détente* of the 1970s was succeeded by the 'new cold war' of the 1980s, precipitated by President Reagan's STRATEGIC DEFENCE INITIATIVE, 'Star Wars'. This ushered in a resurgent American military programme and a technological competition which the Soviet Union could not match. Gorbachev admitted as much in December 1988, retreating from the ARMS RACE and virtually calling off the cold war.

The fall of the BERLIN WALL in November 1989 was both a symbol and a physical manifestation of the collapse of cold war structures. Historians have yet to account fully for the cold war. Martin Walker, *The Cold War* (1993), and John Lewis Gaddis, *We Know Now: Rethinking Cold War History* (1997), are relevant attempts thus far. For further reading: R. E. Powaski, *The Cold War: The United States and the Soviet Union, 1917–1991* (1998). J.E.

collage. Internationally current French term for the sticking together of disparate elements to make a picture. The modern use of this technique, now an artistic and educational commonplace, stems from (a) the traditional scrapbook, (b) *trompe l'oeil* effects in painting, and (c) such house-painter's techniques as marbling and graining. In 1912 the CUBISTS began incorporating scraps of wallpaper, print, etc. in their pictures; a year later Picasso applied similar principles to the construction of three-dimensional reliefs; and thereafter such methods became adopted by FUTURISM (Soffici and Carrà), DADA (Grosz), Russian CUBO-FUTURISM (Tatlin's reliefs), MERZ with its use of rubbish, and, in the mid-1920s, SURREALISM with its incongruous cutting-up of old engravings.

New terms emerged during the collage boom of the 1950s and early 1960s, which accompanied the Dada revival and the rise of POP ART: *combine-painting* (Robert Rauschenberg's use of three-dimensional components), tableau-piège (Daniel Spoerri's ditto) and assemblage (embracing both these), while DÉCOLLAGE came to signify the reverse process. Examples of collage also occurred in other arts, e.g. the 'cut-ups' of the novelist William Burroughs. The real extension of this concept, however, lay in the MONTAGE practised in the 1920s, a much wider artistic principle subsuming photomontage and all other forms of collage. For further reading: H. Janis and R. Blesh, *Collage* (1962). J.W.

collective bargaining. The central job of a TRADE UNION is to undertake collective bargaining on behalf of its members. Members decide what they wish to claim from a management, or what response they might take to a management initiative, and the union bargains on their behalf, given that decision. The collective nature of the bargaining is needed because it is realized that an individual is at a disadvantage when confronting a corporate entity. Collective bargaining is an attempt to equalize the advantages which accrue to either side of the bargaining table. In the last resort the right of management to hire and fire is matched by the ability of each employee to remove his own labour, along with his colleagues. If this sanction is known by an employer to be totally impracticable then employees bargain from a moral position only. Free collective bargaining is a euphemism for a lack of central government controls over pay bargaining, generally expressed as an INCOMES POLICY. This is rapidly becoming more unrealistic as the percentage of workers paid directly and indirectly by central government grows. Many European countries use highly centralized wage bargaining, but in the USA collective bargaining, once a potent force, is in retreat because of the rise of the post-industrial economy, corporate DOWNSIZING and, most importantly, changes in government policies that favour management. A notable example was the mass firing by President Reagan in 1981 of 16,000 members of the Professional Air Traffic Controllers Organization; the wholesale dismissal of union members engaged in an illegal strike and the hiring of replacement workers set a standard for subsequent labour–management negotiations that still applies today. Collective bargaining is no longer just about pay. Redundancies, technological and job changes have become as important. Other non-basic wage elements of the terms and conditions of employment have come to the fore in collective bargaining in recent years. Mortgages, productivity payments, pensions, healthcare, cars, allowances of all descriptions, equal pay, profit sharing, holidays, shorter hours, leisure provisions and health and safety matters are now collectively bargained. For further reading: A. Sloane, *Labor Relations* (1997). B.D.S.

collective consciousness. A term used by Durkheim (in *The Rules of Sociological Method*, 1938) when trying to clarify his conception of SOCIAL (or associational) FACTS. It denotes not the mere sum total of given elements in all the individual consciousnesses in a society, but the engendering, through associative activities within the constraints of specific collective conditions, of new elements of human experience, knowledge, value, will and behaviour. These elements are termed by Durkheim 'collective REPRESENTATIONS': distinguishable sentiments and values (e.g. the British sense of 'justice and fair play') associated with shared cultural SYMBOLS (e.g., in this instance, the perpetuated traditions of the legal profession, courts, schools, games, and patterns of education and upbringing). In their totality, these 'collective representations' make up the 'social heritage', the framework of the distinctive collective life of a community. See also CULTURE; FOLKWAYS; SOCIAL FACT; SOCIAL STRUCTURE; SUB-CULTURE. R.F.

collective farm, see under COLLECTIVIZATION.

collective leadership. The principle, enunciated in the rules of the COMMUNIST Party of the former USSR, that the power to make decisions should be shared by the leadership rather than concentrated in the hands of one person. According to these rules, collective leadership should operate at all levels of the Party. However, the principle is normally applied to the relationship between the general secretary of the Party and other members of the POLITBURO. After Stalin's death in 1953, his successors emphasized the idea of collective leadership, opposing it to the PERSONALITY CULT and the dictatorial methods of STALINISM. A collective leadership actually existed after 1953, but it was marked by serious rivalries between the leaders, and after N. Khrushchev had defeated his colleagues, G. Malenkov and L. Beria, he became supreme leader in 1956. Khrushchev was in his turn accused of establishing a cult of the individual, and collective leadership was restored by L. Brezhnev, elected general secretary of the Party, and A. Kosygin, elected Chairman of the Council of Ministers, after Khrushchev's resignation in 1964. For further reading: D. Lane, *State and Politics in the Soviet Union* (1985). D.PR.

collective security. The principle of maintaining international peace by the concerted efforts of the nations, especially by the efforts of international organizations such as the LEAGUE OF NATIONS and the UN. The concept was introduced into the Covenant of the League of Nations on British initiative and embodied the ancient Anglo-Saxon idea of a crime against civil peace being answered by the 'hue and cry' against the transgressor to which all citizens were bound to respond. During the 1930s, however, many people in the UK deceived themselves and others into believing that by support for the slogan of collective security (with little consideration of how it was to be enforced) they could avoid the hard choices of national foreign and defence policy. It was left to Japan, Italy and Germany to show how little substance was in collective security when put to the test. Great efforts were made after World War II to embody these lessons in the machinery of the UN, whose action in calling on its members to contribute forces for the Korean War (see KOREA) in 1950 was the first example of collective security involving military SANCTIONS. The split between the great powers, however, and the rival alliance systems (NATO, Warsaw Pact) have reduced the UN to a marginal role in preserving peace. A.L.C.B.

collective unconscious. JUNGIAN term for the past experience of the human species, which has been built into the inherited brain structure, and which manifests itself in the recurrent phenomena of the ARCHETYPES. Jung argued that an individual's functioning is the product of this collective unconscious as well as of a personal unconscious whose contents are forgotten, repressed, subliminally perceived, thought and felt matter of every kind, and which, therefore, is not to be equated with the UNCONSCIOUS of FREUDIAN theory. B.A.F.

collectivism. A politico-economic theory advocating that the means of production and/or distribution should be collectively owned or controlled, or both, and not left to the actions of individuals pursuing their self-interest; also a system based on such collective control. SOCIALISM, COMMUNISM and other collectivist IDEOLOGIES proclaim the desirability of such control through public ownership in the interest of the community as a whole. Forms of collective ownership range from state property to a variety of co-operative institutions (see CO-OPERATIVES), with varying degrees of control by members over decisions affecting their lives. Collectivism has a different significance in the context of an Israeli KIBBUTZ, the 'Kolkhoz' (group of farms) of the former Soviet Union (see USSR, THE FORMER), and a Chinese commune. State ownership in itself does not signify collective control. The question of who controls the state and the collective institutions existing in it has been raised by many critics of collectivism as well as by some of its advocates, who have tried to tackle such problems by advocating forms of collectivism which would provide for workers' PARTICIPATION in economic decision-making, e.g. GUILD SOCIALISM and various forms of workers' control. L.L.

collectivization. A conversion, usually compulsory, of individually owned agricultural holdings into large collective farms; the system of agriculture which predominated in most COMMUNIST states, with the exception of Poland and the former Yugoslavia, and which, with certain local variations, derives from the system set up in the former USSR in the early 1930s. In the USSR collectivization was imposed in 1930 by draconian methods which met bitter peasant resistance: millions starved or were arrested and deported. Collectivization in the east European communist countries was not so brutally enforced, and in Poland and Yugoslavia was stopped, the peasants being allowed to adhere or revert to individual farming.

In the USSR the *kolkhoz*, the collective farm, was to be distinguished from the *sovkhoz*, the state farm, in which the peasants were employees of the state. The *kolkhozy* were, legally speaking, the joint property of their members, who received payment in accordance with the particular farm's profits. The original 'COMMUNE' form of *kolkhoz* was early abandoned, for the most part in favour of the less rigorous *artel*, in which the peasant was permitted a small private plot and the odd cow or two. One of the reasons for this change was the decline in agricultural output: the peasants were more productive, cultivating their own plots. For further reading: M. Lewin, *Russian Peasants and Soviet Power* (1968). L.L.; R.C.

collocation. In LINGUISTICS, a term, primarily FIRTHIAN, applied to the regular occurrence together of lexical items in a language, e.g. *bar* is said to collocate with such items as *steel, soap, harbour, public*. See also LEXICON. D.C.

colonialism, see under IMPERIALISM.

colour field painting, see under ABSTRACT EXPRESSIONISM.

combat fatigue, see under POST-TRAUMATIC STRESS DISORDER.

combinatorial chemistry. An approach to chemical synthesis (see CHEMISTRY) that involves the random or systematic assembly of a number of constituent molecular units into a library of related MOLECULES, each with a different structure – akin to a series of shuffled card decks. Combinatorial chemistry stands in contrast to rational synthesis, in which a particular molecular structure is targeted and assembled by standard chemical methods. Because there is still incomplete understanding of how molecular structure determines biochemical function, the effectiveness of rational design for chemotherapeutic drugs remains limited (see BIOCHEMISTRY). The combinatorial alternative is one of trial and error, involving the assembly of a great many molecular variations on a theme and the subsequent use of a diagnostic screening procedure for trawling through the resulting molecular library for one that has the required function. This monkey-with-typewriter approach can be successful simply because of the astronomical numbers of different permutations of the components, even for relatively small molecules – among these huge libraries, there is a good chance that one or two molecules will have the right structure to carry out the task at hand.

The success of combinatorial methods depends on the development of efficient ways of screening through the libraries to find the good products. Typically this might involve the selective binding of the molecules to a particular biochemical target through MOLECULAR RECOGNITION. To this extent the technique resembles the way in which cells of the immune system make antibodies to bind to foreign molecules in the body. Often the number of product molecules is potentially so vast that some degree of rational pre-selection is needed to explore only those permutations that seem likely to produce a good result. Combinatorial methods are commonly conducted using amino acids or nucleotides as the constituent parts; these are assembled to make synthetic PEPTIDES and NUCLEIC ACIDS respectively. This is because biotechnological methods have been developed for combining, isolating and multiplying these compounds, whose natural counterparts are PROTEINS and DNA and RNA. Combinatorial methods are now being explored in other areas of the chemical sciences, for example in the search for new solid-state materials, such as superconductors or phosphors, with complex elemental compositions (see SOLID-STATE PHYSICS; SUPERCONDUCTIVITY). P.C.B.

combine-painting, see under COLLAGE.

COMECON (or **CMA: Council for Mutual Economic Assistance).** A Soviet-sponsored economic organization, set up in January 1949 in reply to the successful working of the MARSHALL PLAN. Originally comprising only states of the SOCIALIST bloc in eastern Europe, it grew to 10 members, including VIETNAM, CUBA and Mongolia. For further reading: G. Schiavone, *The Institutions of Comecon* (1981). D.C.W.; D.PR.

***comédie noire*,** see BLACK COMEDY.

comedy of menace. A dramatic style which emerged in the British theatre of the late 1950s, in which the reaction of one or more characters to some terrifying and often obscure threat to their security is treated as a subject for comedy. The term was first used by David Campton as a subtitle to his four playlets *The Lunatic View* (1957), but was soon applied more widely by critics, in particular to the early work of Harold Pinter. See also BLACK COMEDY; THEATRE OF THE ABSURD. M.A.

Comintern. Abbreviation for the communist (see COMMUNISM) INTERNATIONAL, established in March 1919 at a meeting in Moscow. As an association of revolutionary MARXIST parties of the world rejecting REFORMISM, it was to replace the SOCIALIST International. From the outset its policies were dominated by the Russian Bolsheviks (see BOLSHEVISM), who imposed on it their own LENINIST principles of organization through the *21 Conditions of Admission* (which included the subordination of the member parties to the authority of the Executive Committee of the Comintern). This meant in effect the subordination of the national sections (i.e. parties) to Soviet control of their policies (see USSR, THE FORMER).

At the 2nd Congress of the Comintern in the summer of 1920, when the Bolshevik leaders thought that Europe was on the verge of a proletarian revolution (see PROLETARIAT), they promoted an intransigent revolutionary strategy; they repudiated 'bourgeois democracy' (see BOURGEOIS; DEMOCRACY), and denounced both moderate and radical (see RADICALISM) socialist leaders. When Bolshevik hopes of the imminent REVOLUTION in Europe collapsed, the Comintern leaders proclaimed a 'temporary stabilization of CAPITALISM' and developed various forms of united front tactics.

Beginning with the 5th Congress in 1924, the Comintern reflected the internal factional struggles in the Soviet Communist Party: the elimination from it of Trotsky, Zinoviev, Bukharin and their followers led to corresponding purges in the leadership and the national sections of the Comintern. Its 6th Congress in 1928 inaugurated the 'CLASS against class' policy aimed at the 'radicalization of the masses'. But the disastrous result of communist policy in Germany (where Stalin's denunciation of socialists as 'social FASCISTS' facilitated Hitler's victory in 1933) led to the adoption of POPULAR FRONT tactics at the 7th Congress of the Comintern in 1935. Soon after, most of the leaders of the Comintern, Russian and foreign, were liquidated during the Great Purge (1936–38; see YEZHOVSHCHINA).

Stalin transformed the Comintern into an obedient instrument of Soviet foreign policy. When he concluded the pact with Hitler in August 1939, Comintern propaganda which for years had inveighed against the Nazi menace was peremptorily switched to an anti-Western line. It changed again after Hitler's attack on the Soviet Union in 1941. In 1943 the Comintern was dissolved, presumably as a gesture to the Western allies. It was, however, temporarily resurrected as the Cominform. For further reading: K. McDermott, *The Comintern* (1996). L.L.

Command, Control, Communications and Intelligence (C3I). The management of force in WAR has always depended upon the combination of intelligence, which guides a commander as to how force may best be used, and the transmission of orders based on intelligence. With the ramification of transmission systems since the introduction of the telegraph, armed forces have increasingly recognized the need to integrate command and intelligence systems and rationalize their operation. They also recognize that the management of signal systems is itself a military speciality, as is the administration or control of units and weapons systems not actually deployed or in contact with the enemy. This complex of systems has become known as Command, Control, Communications and Intelligence or C3I. Of particular importance in the management of nuclear strike forces during the COLD WAR, it has taken on a new dimension with the introduction of guided and self-targeting weapons for conventional operations. Permanent SATELLITE and airborne surveillance provides 'real time' intelligence of a duality never before made available to commanders, while data processing and visual display permits, in theory, a rapidity and effectiveness of decision-taking equivalent to that available to the eye-witness. C3I has become C4ISR, or Command, Control, Communications, Intelligence, Surveillance and Computers, and is the basis for what enthusiasts hail as a 'revolution in military affairs' (RMA). Doubters point out that the speed of decision-taking is still that of the human mind and that efforts to accelerate it by by-passing the commander's responsibility to judge wisely is likely to have regrettable, even disastrous results. See also DIGITAL ARMY. J.K.

commensalism, see under SYMBIOSIS.

commercial agriculture. Any agricultural activity that is undertaken for the purpose of earning a profit from the surplus (see SURPLUS VALUE) food or fibre products that result. It is the opposite of SUBSISTENCE AGRICULTURE, which is undertaken to produce only enough food or fibre to sustain a family or at most a small COMMUNITY. Commercial agriculture is associated with the world's higher-income countries and their tropical plantation outposts in the poorer countries. For further reading: D. B. Grigg, *An Introduction to Agricultural Geography* (1995). P.O.M.

commitment. A term the widespread use of which (as of ENGAGÉ, committed) in recent years derives from the position of Jean-Paul Sartre, most succinctly presented in *L'Existentialisme est un humanisme* (1946). Sartre affirms his ATHEISM and his belief in free will; concedes that he cannot be confident of 'human goodness', or of the socially just outcome of the Russian Revolution, which he nonetheless admires because 'the PROLETARIAT plays a part in Russia which it has attained in no other nation'. 'Does that', he asks, 'mean that I should abandon myself to Quietism?' The answer is: 'No . . . one need not hope in order to undertake one's work . . . people reproach us with . . . the sternness of our optimism . . . What counts is total commitment (engagement), and it is not by a particular case or . . . action that you are committed altogether.' 'Commitment' *tout court* is usually assumed to be LEFT-wing, usually quasi-MARXIST; other brands are usually given a specific label, e.g. *Catholic commitment* ('eternal vigilance'). M.S.-S.

commodification. Commodification refers to the artwork's dual role as object and bearer of meaning. The artwork's role as a commodity causes a conflict between its aesthetic and financial value. An awareness of the commodification of the artwork has been heightened by artists, beginning with Marcel Duchamp, who have emphasized the conceptual role of the art object, by separating the creative act from the painting or fabrication of an object. Many forms of art since 1950, such as FLUXUS, MINIMALISM, CONCEPTUAL ART and PERFORMANCE ART, have attempted to resist the commodification of the object by producing art objects which have little intrinsic value. At the same time the increased financial and social investment in art (especially painting) has intensified the tendency for the artwork to become more of a commodity than ever before. Pierre Bourdieu's *Distinction* (1984) has shown how the consumption of works of art is central to the maintenance of social distinctions, and how the exercise of taste becomes a means of acquiring 'cultural capital'. Corporate sponsorship of culture for advertising has intensified this tendency. A.V.D.B.

commodity economy. Since 1978 China has moved away from the typical command economy of COMMUNIST Party states and adopted a commodity economy. The allocation of goods and resources is no longer dependent on central planning, but responds to the effects of market forces. However, this does not mean that central planning and commands no longer exist, merely that more notice is paid to forces of supply and demand in the formulation of economic policy (see DENGISM; FOUR MODERNIZATIONS). S.B.

commodity fetishism. Term used (with sardonic reference to FETISHISM) by Marx in *Das Kapital* in maintaining that though commodities appear to be simple *objects*, they are, in fact, bundles of social relationships, transcendentals, with a life of their own once they enter the sphere of market exchange and values. According to Marx, the apparent 'object' (a table, for example) 'abounds in metaphysical and theological niceties'. In defining the treatment of commodities in CAPITALIST production and exchange, we must therefore, he adds, 'have recourse to the mist-enveloped regions of the religious world'. R.F.

Common Agricultural Policy, see CAP.

common law. Term used in three different and distinct ways. (1) Originally the rules developed by the ordinary courts of England from the Middle Ages as opposed to those applied by the Lord Chancellor's Court of Chancery, which were called equity and which formed a supplement to or gloss on the common law, especially in the field of property. (2) Later came to be used as a description for all law, even including equity, derived from decisions of courts and not laid down by Acts of Parliament as an Act can override or alter any previous law (see SOVEREIGNTY), and as Parliament in modern times has enacted a great volume of legislation, the areas still covered by pure common law in this sense have progressively shrunk. Today statute regulates most law, or provides for its enactment by means of statutory instruments, but the courts must still apply law in individual cases and in doing so exercise considerable authority over the development of the law by way of interpretation of statutes and statutory instruments: and the common law still covers much of the area of private relations, e.g. CONTRACT, TORTS, and some parts of criminal law. (3) More generally common law is used to mean a court-based system of law on the English model in contrast with Continental code-based systems. In this sense common law covers not only the whole of English law, including equity and statute law, but also the laws of most other COMMONWEALTH countries and of the USA. For further reading: W. Geldart, *Introduction to English Law* (1984). D.C.M.Y.

Common Market, see under CUSTOMS UNION; EUROPEAN UNION.

Commonwealth. The loose and flexible association of independent countries, most of which have at an earlier period been within the now defunct British Empire. The Commonwealth evolved, from the late 19th century, as the British Parliament gradually conferred self-government and then full independence upon the great majority of its overseas territories. By the Statute of Westminster (1931), the Dominions of Australia, Canada, the Irish Free State, New Zealand and South Africa effectively became sovereign states and members of the Commonwealth: a voluntary association of self-governing states united in a common allegiance to the British Crown. After World War II, many more colonies joined the Commonwealth on achieving independence, although Burma remained outside in 1948 and Eire withdrew in 1949. In the same year, India renegotiated its membership on becoming a republic. There are no overt rules governing the Commonwealth, and its existence seems to depend on mutual interest and co-operation, and not law. Formally, it is only united by the recognition of the Queen as Head of the Commonwealth. Among its members are a few states which are not former colonies, such as Brunei, Western Samoa and the former South African satellite Namibia, which was admitted in 1990. Britain's 14 remaining dependent territories such as the Falkland Islands (see FALKLANDS WAR), St Helena and Pitcairn Island are not independent members of the Commonwealth. In 1997, the Commonwealth consisted of 51 independent states and their dependencies. Its members' heads of government meet every two years for discussions, although it is rare to find them speaking with a single voice. From the 1960s to the 1990s, the Commonwealth was bitterly divided over the appropriate response to be made to South African apartheid. The relevance of the Commonwealth to UK foreign policy has been in steady decline, especially since the UK joined the European Economic Community in 1973. For further reading: N. Mansergh, *The Commonwealth Experience* (1982).

N.O.; D.C.M.Y.

communalism. A KINSHIP-oriented social formation characteristic of many African societies. It is a system of social relations in which the individual is situated at the centre of concentric circles of duties and obligations revolving around levels of kinship bonds irradiating from household 'blood' connections through lineage membership to the wider circumference of CLAN identity. At its outermost reaches this body of blood relations may add up to a substantial COMMUNITY. Moreover, the entire community of a nation and, indeed, of the comity of nations, is seen on the analogy of this familial construct. What makes existence in a social setting of this kind the very opposite of a life of unrelieved drudgery of duties is that the multifarious obligations are more than matched by an equally multifaceted array of reciprocal rights and privileges, including, most pivotally, the right to land, which was held in common among a lineage. Philosophically, the idea underlying this system is that individuality is to be defined in terms of society rather than the other way round. K.W.

commune. The form of organization of life and work in a collective (see COLLECTIVISM) in which the members hold no private property, share equally the results of their labour, and usually make joint decisions by democratic means which attach little importance to leaders or hierarchies but stress each member's equal right to PARTICIPATION. Early communes were founded under the influence of utopian socialists (see UTOPIANISM; SOCIALISM) such as Proudhon, Fourier, Owen and Cabet, but soon disintegrated. The Paris Commune of 1871 also included elements of Jacobin thought (see JACOBINISM) and was celebrated by Marx. During the period of War COMMUNISM (1917–21) in the former USSR, agricultural communes were formed, but were dissolved by the NEW ECONOMIC POLICY (NEP) or transformed by the COLLECTIVIZATION of Soviet agriculture. During the GREAT LEAP FORWARD in China (1958–61) large rural communes were organized; political pressure and propaganda replaced economic incentives and the strategy was unsuccessfully promoted as a short cut to full-scale communist society. Since the renewed diversification of left-wing thought, the rise of the counter-culture (see UNDERGROUND) and the spread of critiques of industrial

CAPITALISM and political centralization in the 1960s, communes of various idiosyncratic kinds have enjoyed a modest revival. They have only a marginal impact in societies fundamentally wedded to large-scale, highly interdependent economic units and elaborate, bureaucratized political arrangements. L.L.; S.R.

communication, ethnography of. Phrase coined by the American social anthropologist Dell Hymes to refer to the extension to other media of an approach which he calls 'the ETHNOGRAPHY of speaking' and others 'the SOCIOLOGY of language', SOCIOLINGUISTICS or ETHNOLINGUISTICS. Imagery, RITUAL, gesture and even silence (particularly eloquent in the case of the American Indians studied by Hymes) are analysed as forms of language with their own rules. A key concept in the ethnography of communication is that of CODE or register, in other words the variety of language used by a particular speaker (more generally, 'sender') to communicate with particular listeners ('receivers') in particular situations or about particular subjects ('domains'). It has been pointed out, for example, that in a number of cultures women are more careful to obey the rules of grammar than men are, and that when a conversation turns to religion, the code is 'switched' from a lower or more colloquial variety of language to a 'higher' or more literary one. For further reading: M. Saville-Troike, *The Ethnography of Communication* (1982). P.B.

communication, fallacy of. Allen Tate's term, in the context of the NEW CRITICISM, for what he regards as the false belief that literature can communicate non-poetic (e.g. political) ideas. Contrast COMMITMENT. M.S.-S.

communication, heresy of. Cleanth Brooks's term, occasionally employed in the NEW CRITICISM, for what he regards as the mistaken belief that a poem consists of two components which are separable: an 'idea' and a 'form' which ornaments it. To any new critic, a successful poem is an organic whole. M.S.-S.

communications. A traditional term used in GEOGRAPHY and cartography to cover all modes of transportation, including road, rail, air and water, by which people can make contact with others. Today, the term also applies more broadly to any medium that facilitates spatial interaction, including TELECOMMUNICATIONS and COMPUTER networks. P.O.M.

communicative competence. In LINGUISTICS, the speaker's awareness of the way language use is appropriate to social situations (identified in terms of formality, class background, occupation and so on). The notion contrasts with the original sense of COMPETENCE, as introduced in GENERATIVE GRAMMAR, where it was seen as a purely formal notion, referring to the speaker's awareness of the grammatical system of a language. D.C.

communism. A term denoting:

(1) A set of ideas and the ideological tradition (see IDEOLOGY) connected with them. Historically the point of reference for communist ideas is the principle of communal ownership of all property. Thus primitive communism refers to non-literate societies, in which basic economic resources (such as land, boats, etc.) belong to the community as a whole and not to individuals or families. Religious groups (such as early Christians or medieval monasteries) based on communal sharing of property are referred to as examples of communist organization; so are historical societies, such as Sparta, the Münster Anabaptists or the Jesuit Paraguay republic, as well as theoretical schemes for ideal societies, such as Plato's *Republic*, Sir Thomas More's *Utopia*, or Campanella's *City of the Sun*.

Modern communism is specifically linked with the ideas of Karl Marx and the concept of a classless society (see MARXISM; CLASS) based on common ownership of the means of production. Such a society should, according to Marx and his followers, emerge after the transitional period of the DICTATORSHIP OF THE PROLETARIAT and the preparatory stage of SOCIALISM. In a full communist society the state will 'wither away', differences between manual and intellectual labour and between urban and rural life will disappear, there will be no limits to the development of individual human potentialities and of productive forces, and social relations will be regulated by the principle 'from each according to his ability, to each according to his needs'.

(2) Movements, parties and governments deriving their support and legitimation from the claim that they are implementing such ideas. See BOLSHEVISM; CASTROISM; COMINTERN; LENINISM; MAOISM; MARXISM; MARXISM-LENINISM; NEO-MARXISM; REVISIONISM; STALINISM; TITOISM; TROTSKYISM.

(3) Distinctive methods used by such movements, parties and governments, and institutions emerging historically as a result of their actions. See COLLECTIVIZATION; COMMUNE; DEMOCRATIC CENTRALISM; FORCED LABOUR; FRONT ORGANIZATION; GREAT PROLETARIAN CULTURAL REVOLUTION; KGB; KULAK; LYSENKOISM; POLITBURO; POPULAR FRONT; REVOLUTION; SAMIZDAT; SHOW TRIALS; STAKHANOVISM; YEZHOVSHCHINA; ZHDANOVSHCHINA. For further reading: V. Lenin, *Imperialism: The State and Revolution* (1926); A. Westoby, *The Evolution of Communism* (1987). L.L.

communitarianism. A social philosophy that focuses on societal formulations of the good. A central premise is that communities (and societies) legitimately define that which is virtuous. Communitarianism is often contrasted with classical LIBERALISM, a philosophical position that insists the good should be formulated privately by individuals. Communitarians are concerned with both the sources of values (HISTORY, culture and moral dialogues), as well as the social institutions (families, schools and communities) that sustain them.

Communitarian elements can be found to varying degrees in both Old and New Testaments, ancient Greek PHILOSOPHY, Catholic teachings (see CATHOLICISM) and SOCIALIST doctrine. The term was first coined during the mid-19th century. Various kinds of communitarians differ in the degree to which they are also mindful of individual rights. Early communitarians like Ferdinand Tonnies and Robert Nisbet focused on concepts like authority and the social fabric. Asian communitarians are especially concerned about things like social harmony and order.

In the 1980s, Robert Bellah, Charles Taylor, Michael Sandel and Michael Walzer criticized the excessive individualism of classical liberalism, America under President Reagan and Britain under Prime Minister Thatcher (see REAGANISM; THATCHERISM). In the 1990s, responsive communitarians such as Amitai Etzioni, Philip Selznick and William Galston began stressing the need to balance commitment to the social good with respect for individual rights, as well as to ensure that strong communities do not oppress. They formed a platform, a quarterly and a communitarian network often credited with having influenced leaders in a number of Western countries.

Responsive communitarians have worked to develop specific concepts and policies. They tend to favour peer marriages (in which mothers and fathers have equal rights and responsibilities); schools that build character rather than merely teach; and community justice, in which offenders, victims and members of the community work together to find appropriate punishments and reach reconciliation. Communitarians are inclined to support devolution of state power and the formation of communities of communities. For further reading: S. Mulhall and A. Swift, *Liberals and Communitarians* (1996). A.E.

community. This abused and ill-defined term refers to associations of individuals bound together by a shared local environment, rather than by conscious interests or by links defined by a single characteristic such as CLASS or ETHNICITY. Its exact boundaries are unclear, but set by scale and accidents of geography rather than by choice. A community is held to be a source of IDENTITY beyond family and close personal life, but with greater intimacy and more subtle obligations and rewards than those of national identity.

Given the extent of its contemporary usage, the term has a surprisingly thin history as a SOCIAL SCIENCE concept. Following the work of Ferdinand Tonnies (1855–1935), community can be distinguished from society by its more fundamental and 'natural' centrality to human life. Society may be seen as involving a conscious contract among its members, or as a relatively mechanical set of structures. Community is a more primal, organic phenomenon. The difficulties of such contrasting definitions are numerous: suffice to say that they have little bearing on modern, and particularly American, fascination with community except that the contemporary appeal of community seems partly a response to isolating or 'mechanical' qualities of modern life – in suburbs, in large and impersonal companies, in an age of mobility and fragmented families. Most notably, the term is asked by both RIGHT- and LEFT-wing writers and politicians to bear an improbable weight as an ill-defined alternative to numerous contemporary ills. For the PROGRESSIVE, it represents mutuality, tolerance, resistance to overbearing political and economic institutions; for the conservative, it is more rooted in notions of property and security, connoting a haven from interventionist governments and offering an ideal which implausibly combines individualism and reciprocity, autonomy and conformity. S.R.

community architecture. An approach to architectural practice advocated by socially aware architects, especially in the UK. Its intention is to provide architectural skills and services to poor and run-down communities, often providing development and finance-finding skills as well. It is predicated on the active consent and participation of the community whose buildings are to be rehabilitated – which may be as small as a section of a street or as large as a local area. Community architects set up their drawing boards in the locality and many live there while the regeneration programme is in progress. It is practised both in the PUBLIC and PRIVATE SECTORS. In the latter case architects sometimes also operate as builders and developers taking small fees – and options on property whose value increases dramatically when the local improvements are completed. Community architects effectively ignore the traditional stylistic and ideological preoccupations of architecture. S.L.

community care/care in the community. The health and social care of individuals in the community rather than in institutions. Two groups of patients are particularly involved: the mentally ill and the elderly. The early intellectual antecedents to this approach include the work of Erving Goffman, a sociologist whose work *Asylums: Essays on the Social Situation of Mental Patients and Other Inmates* (1961) pointed out the dangers of prolonged institutionalization. During the 1950s and 1960s, views of mental illness began to change, in part owing to new psychiatric drugs which controlled the more extreme symptoms of psychotic patients. Many countries, including the UK, the US and Italy, began closing asylums and moving psychiatric patients into the community. This approach continues to be generally accepted, although some areas have been particularly problematic: the lack of adequate funds and of well-organized staff to care for severely mentally ill patients outside hospital, the failure to recognize that some patients can never cope outside institutions, and the danger to the public of potentially violent unsupervised patients. With regard to the elderly, there has been a similar concern in the UK that their long-term care was too often in institutions. A number of policy reports and initiatives, culminating in the 1990 NHS and Community Care Act, attempted to address the problem. Funding was made available for community care, together with an attempt to encourage private and voluntary rather than state-funded options. As in the case of the mentally ill, a continuing problem has been the distance between rhetoric and reality in terms of the level of funding available to this group, wherever their care is provided. D.F.

community planning. Attempts to plan for the creation and support of community. A community is a group of people who have something in common. A group may constitute a 'community of interest' because its members pursue a shared activity or they may form a 'community of place' because its members all live in the same NEIGHBOURHOOD. Post-war British planners placed great importance upon creating a sense of 'community' among NEW TOWN residents. They sought to engender a sense of community by manipulating the DENSITY and layout of housing areas (see ENVIRONMENTAL DETERMINISM). Nowadays, with mass car ownership, residents are less likely to be limited to their immediate physical locality in choosing their community, friends and interests (C. Bell and H. Newby, *Community Studies*, 1971). Community is also used by town planners in describing residents' groups and grass-roots pressure groups in existing urban areas, especially INNER CITY locations. Studies abound of 'working class communities' within the inner city, and 'ethnic minority communities', on both sides of the Atlantic, such as M. Young and P. Willmott, *Family and Kinship in East London* (1957), and see M. Bulmer, *The Chicago School of Sociology* (1984). Communities, nowadays, expect to be fully involved in the planning process. It is generally the women members of local communities who are the more likely to get involved in community action, public PARTICIPATION activities, and local grass-roots politics. The GEOGRAPHY OF GENDER movement has demanded a more balanced approach to urban community planning research and policy as discussed in J. Little, *Gender, Planning and the Policy Process* (1994). (See also GEMEINSCHAFT AND GESELLSCHAFT.) C.G.

community politics. A term which found widespread currency in Britain during the revival of Liberal Party fortunes after 1972. It first denoted a tactical stress on local issues and grievances as the material for party growth in urban and suburban constituencies. It has acquired a more elaborate meaning; it connotes a distrust of central government and national ÉLITES, and an emphasis on reform initiatives from the 'grass roots'. The approach has been criticized as suited only to an opposition party which profits from the airing of grievances and exposure of government failings. For further reading: P. Hain, *The Democratic Alternative* (1984). S.R.

community psychiatry, see under PSYCHIATRY.

comparatist. A follower of the COMPARATIVE METHOD in LINGUISTICS or literature. Comparative philology began in the 18th century; it involved the hypothetical reconstruction of parent languages (e.g. 'Indo-European'), based on a multiplicity of examples from known languages. The work of Ferdinand de Saussure (see SAUSSURIAN) in linguistics grew out of his involvement with comparative philology, as did his view of language 'as a system of mutually defining entities'. This has had a crucial influence on later developments. Comparative methods in literature embrace such things as the habit (exemplified by Sacheverell Sitwell) of comparing literary works with paintings, architecture and music, as well as the comparison of different literatures. Comparative literature is far more widely taught in the USA than in Britain. For further reading: R. Wellek and A. Warren, *Theory of Literature* (1966). M.S.-S.

comparative education. The branch of educational theory concerned with analysing and interpreting policies and practices in different countries. Despite problems of METHODOLOGY, factors like language, SOCIAL STRUCTURE, political system, IDEOLOGY, geography (e.g. mountains or jungles producing isolated communities) all provide differences which can be studied comparatively, in addition to administrative structures and economic factors. W.A.C.S.

comparative history. Although the ambitious studies of Spengler and Toynbee are both comparative and historical, the term is not normally used to refer to that kind of book. It refers to more modest attempts to compare two or three societies, often neighbours but sometimes as remote from one another as France and Japan. The comparative historian is usually interested in a specific problem, such as the nature of FEUDALISM or of absolute monarchy; tends to emphasize the differences as well as the parallels between the societies he studies; and resorts to comparison not to produce general laws but to understand particular situations. P.B.

comparative law. A misleading but established name for the systematic comparison of laws of different systems. It is a method of legal study and research, and not as the name suggests a distinct branch of the law or body of legal rules. Many studies in comparative law have been inspired by various practical aims, such as the establishment of uniformity in commercial law and in private international law. For further reading: H. C. Gutteridge, *Comparative Law* (1949). H.L.A.H.

comparative linguistics, see under LINGUISTICS.

comparative method. Frequently used in the simple sense of comparing one set of facts with another (for examples, see other headings beginning with COMPARATIVE). In SOCIOLOGY the term is of central importance as referring to sociology's only alternative to controlled experiment. It is the sociological method *par excellence* for the formulation of definitive theories, including the specification of conditions for the crucial testing of hypotheses. What experiment is in the NATURAL SCIENCES, the comparative method is in the SOCIAL SCIENCES. (See also SOCIAL THEORY.)

At least four distinct conceptions have been employed: (1) that of classifying societies according to some criterion (e.g. the nature of the 'social bond'), thus forming a clear framework for amassing and arranging factual information and uncovering connections between social INSTITUTIONS (Spencer, Hobhouse, etc.); (2) that of constructing a TYPOLOGY on the basis of some hypothesis (e.g. Comte's 'Law of the Three States', Spencer's 'military-industrial' polarity, Tönnies' contrast between GEMEINSCHAFT AND GESELLSCHAFT, and Marx's distinctive stages of 'productive forces'), and then comparing it with actual historical societies, to see how far it illuminates them, and to test its reliability; (3) that of comparing specific sets of SOCIAL FACTS (e.g. the rate of suicide and the degree of integration within specific groups – familial, religious, etc.) in order to test theories about their 'constant concomitance'; (4) that of constructing a MODEL in order to understand one particular 'cultural configuration' (e.g. of the rise of industrial CAPITALISM in western Europe) and comparing other similar configurations with it, in order to test the correctness and sufficiency of the interpretation (Weber). For further reading: I. Vallier (ed.), *Comparative Methods in Sociology* (1971). R.F.

comparative psychology. The rapidly developing branch of PSYCHOLOGY whose focus of interest is the similarities and differences between animal SPECIES, including man, especially where these can be understood in relation to the species' BIOLOGY and way of life or to their phylogenetic relationships (see PHYLOGENY). The comparative psychologist – who often prefers to call himself a psychologist *tout court*, or an ethologist (see ETHOLOGY), or just a student of animal behaviour – may study animals because they are simpler than man in their behaviour or brain structure and therefore easier to investigate; or because they represent in some sense an earlier evolutionary stage in man's history, with the implication that the behaviour of a fish or a monkey may tell us something of the fish or monkey stage of man's EVOLUTION. It is, of course, questionable whether the behaviour of such ancestors bore much resemblance to that of the fishes and monkeys alive today; and in any case the various monkey species today show substantial differences in behaviour, so that it is difficult to generalize about *the* monkey. Despite these difficulties it has been possible to investigate some of the animal precursors of human abilities such as INTELLIGENCE, learning skills and language.

Although comparative psychology's interest in animals is by tradition anthropocentric, problems in animals' PERCEPTION or learning or motivation or development are also studied for their own sake. Field studies of animals in their natural environments, by zoologists and psychologists, have given a great impetus to such work, and have shown how the particular psychological and behavioural characteristics of each species are often closely adapted to their everyday needs. The emergence of SOCIOBIOLOGY in the 1970s added a new dimension and a new controversial edge to the field. Hard-line advocates of the new discipline argued for the comprehensive interpretation of patterns of human social behaviour and culture in terms of adaptive evolutionary processes designed to enhance survival prospects. Such facets of human behaviour as aggression or GENDER inequality, which mirror patterns in the animal world, have been newly argued to be not culturally contingent, the product of nurture, but 'natural' and genetically transmitted. The degree to which extrapolation of animal ethology to human society is legitimate remains deeply unclear and contentious. For further reading: D. Dewsbury, *Comparative Psychology in the Twentieth Century* (1984). J.M.C.; R.P.

compatibilism. The philosophical theory stating that although human beings are subject to causal laws (see DETERMINISM) they have FREE WILL and are morally responsible for their actions. The compatibility of freedom with causal determinism is defended by Hume and others, who argue that it is not causal determinism but constraint or compulsion which is the antithesis of freedom. A.C.G.

competence (in BIOLOGY), see under ORGANIZER.

competence and **performance.** A distinction which is central to GENERATIVE GRAMMAR, and has become widely used in LINGUISTICS as a whole. Competence refers to a person's knowledge of his language, the system of rules which he has mastered so that he is able to produce and understand an indefinite number of sentences, and to recognize grammatical mistakes and ambiguities. Performance refers to specific utterances, containing features foreign to the basic rule system (e.g. hesitations, unfinished sentences). According to Chomsky, linguistics before generative grammar had been preoccupied with performance in a corpus, instead of with the underlying competence involved (see ADEQUACY, sense 1). The validity of the distinction has, however, been questioned (e.g. are intonation, STYLISTICS, DISCOURSE matters of competence or performance?). See also LANGUE. For further reading: D. Crystal, *Linguistics* (1985). D.C.

competition. In ECONOMICS, firms compete when they attempt to gain profits at the expense of other firms (by comparison, see CARTEL). Competition will, in certain circumstances, efficiently co-ordinate the demand and supply for goods, services and inputs (see PERFECT COMPETITION). More generally, competition is regarded as a means of making markets operate more efficiently. The Austrian school emphasizes that competition takes place in price, the characteristics of the product, ADVERTISING, research, etc. Successful firms acquire (temporary) MONOPOLY positions and the associated level of profits is a necessary reward and incentive. This view is one of dynamic FREE MARKETS, as compared to the NEO-CLASSICAL ECONOMIC THEORY notion of competition as a static EQUILIBRIUM and the possibility of MARKET FAILURES. The MARXIST view of competition emphasizes the deliberate attempt to acquire and maintain a monopoly position through collusion, growth and takeover. The modern corporate view of competition is that the notion is largely redundant, as large interdependent firms have replaced the competitive market and they can only be analysed in the context of their technological, social and political environment (see FIRM, THEORIES OF). For further reading: M. Waterson, *The Economic Theory of the Industry* (1984). J.P.

competitive equilibrium. An equilibrium of the economy in which, given prices, wages and the initial distribution of resources, no firm or consumer can improve their position. It is an important theoretical concept in ECONOMICS (see EQUILIBRIUM; CORE; PERFECT COMPETITION). J.P.

complementarity principle. A general principle of EPISTEMOLOGY enunciated by Niels Bohr as part of the COPENHAGEN INTERPRETATION of QUANTUM MECHANICS. Bohr's experience with the breakdown of the old quantum theory (see also BOHR THEORY) convinced him that a quantum-mechanical world could not be understood in terms of the easily visualizable pictures in space and time associated with CLASSICAL PHYSICS. Classical physics bequeathed to quantum physics a number of mutually incompatible MODELS in terms of which phenomena are to be understood, including the (continuous) wave, and the (discrete) PARTICLE models. Classical pictures break down because the behaviour of ELECTRONS (for instance) cannot universally be understood in terms of just *one* of these models: different experimental situations require different models (see WAVE-PARTICLE DUALITY). Neither wave nor particle model is sufficient for a full understanding: each half of the mutually exclusive pair is required (wave and particle form just one of many different pairs of complementary concepts). The epistemological part of Bohr's position comes with the claim that we are doomed to attempt to understand the non-classical world in terms of these classical concepts. For further reading: D. Murdoch, *Niels Bohr's Philosophy of Physics* (1987). R.F.H.

complementary distribution, see under DISTRIBUTION (sense 2).

complementary filiation, see under DESCENT.

complementary medicine. Term used to describe approaches to healthcare not normally taught at conventional medical schools. The term encompasses (1) *Systems of healing*, e.g. HOMOEOPATHY, ACUPUNCTURE, osteopathy, chiropractic and herbal medicine; (2) *diagnostic practices*, e.g. hair analysis, muscle testing, iridology, Kirlian photography; (3) *therapeutic skills*, e.g. massage, reflexology, HYPNOSIS; (4) *self-help skills*, e.g. relaxation techniques, meditation, autogenic training. Many of these therapies and practices stem from cultures and philosophies which challenge the Cartesian notion of duality of mind and body. Many posit the notion that man has an 'energetic' base to his being and function; they thus link back to the notion of VITALISM. A further common element lies in their ability to catalyse the self-healing potential present in all humans. They thus lay emphasis on the notion of both internal and external homoeostasis. There is great variety in the education and training offered to complementary practitioners, and as yet no unified system of registration or code of ethics exists. Research into the effectiveness of complementary medicine is sparse but there is growing interest among the public and the scientific community. P.C.P.

complementation. In GENETICS, the process whereby the effects of a defective GENE inherited from one parent can be masked by a functional gene from the other. If the two genes in an individual concerned with a particular function are both defective, they cannot complement one another, even if the defects are in different parts of the gene; this fact can be used to decide whether defective MUTATIONS are situated in the same functional unit. J.M.S.

complex. In psychoanalytic theory (see PSYCHOANALYSIS), a word with no single precise meaning; most often, a nexus of repressed ideas (see REPRESSION) and related EMOTION that plays a distinct role in human development and in the genesis of neurotic disorders (see NEUROSIS). Examples are the OEDIPUS COMPLEX, the ELECTRA COMPLEX and the INFERIORITY COMPLEX. In popular usage, the term is loosely used as a synonym for OBSESSION, also in a popular sense. B.A.F.

complex adaptive systems. Complex behaviour is often created by a process of EVOLUTION through many steps in which small changes occur and are sifted by the environment so that those which are more advantageous to future survival will preferentially survive. This behaviour is characteristic of living things but it has become a branch of scientific study in its own right. Artificial forms of 'life' have been created using computer programmes which simulate challenging environments and random mutations which lead to a process of adaptation (see ARTIFICIAL INTELLIGENCE). The resulting complex SYSTEMS are more than the sum of their individual parts. They possess their overall behaviour as a consequence of the way that parts are interconnected. Such 'complex adaptive systems' have the ability to change and adapt to the environment in which they are located. A particularly important example is provided by the sub-class exhibiting a phenomenon known as SELF-ORGANIZED CRITICALITY. A simple example is provided by a pile of sand on a table. As sand is added to the pile, the slope of the sand pile steepens until it attains a critical slope. Falling sand drops off the edge of the table. It then gets no steeper. This 'critical' slope is maintained by avalanches of sand of all sizes. Although the fall of each grain of sand onto the pile is chaotically unpredictable the overall structure of the pile self-organizes into a stable pattern. Each addition of sand produces avalanches of all sizes, but these local instabilities maintain the overall balance of the pile. Here, the infalling sand produces many possible behaviours, but the force of gravity acts so as to select and organize the structure. This model for the development of a critical state has been applied to many natural problems; for example, the maintenance of pressure balance in the earth's crust by volcanic and seismic activity; the ecological stability of environments by extinctions and new SPECIES; the stability of economies; and the behaviour of traffic systems in large cities. All these are examples of complex systems which organize themselves by a sequence of adaptations to small changes which lead to improvements until a critical or optimal state of organization is reached. For further reading: P. Bak, *How Nature Works* (1996). J.D.B.

complex numbers. Having accustomed themselves to natural numbers, and rational and real numbers (see NUMBER), mathematicians asked 'Can there be more?' With trembling steps they took on board negative numbers. They were then worried that the equation $x^2 = -1$ seemed to have no solution. They imagined that there was a new number i (nowadays often called j) such that $i^2 = -1$. This was combined with ordinary numbers to form mixed (or complex) numbers of the form $a + ib$ (e.g. $2 + i$).

A rich theory developed. Fortunately in 1831 Carl Friedrich Gauss put it on a secure basis by regarding a complex number as a pair of real numbers, with i as the pair (0,1). Gauss also proved that every algebraic equation has a solution if we allow complex numbers (the 'fundamental theorem of ALGEBRA').

When electricity arrived it turned out that complex numbers were the ideal tool for discussing alternating current. This also applies to hi-fi systems, since music signals are combined alternating currents. N.A.R.

complexity theory. The study of how complex an ALGORITHM is, which reflects how long it takes to run, and thus how expensive it will be. The complexity of a sequence of symbols is closely related to the amount of information it contains. It can be defined as the length of (= number of symbols used in) the shortest algorithm which will produce that sequence. For example, a random sequence can only be produced by an algorithm which is essentially as long as the sequence itself, so it has a very high complexity. At the other extreme, a sequence consisting of only one symbol repeated many times can be specified by a much shorter algorithm (whose length is approximately the logarithm of the length of the sequence, at least for long sequences), and so has a very low complexity. J.M.

componential analysis. In SEMANTICS, a method of specifying word-meanings by establishing common components of sense, e.g. *man, woman, child, bull, cow, calf* can be distinguished semantically by setting up the components *human/animal, male/female*, and *adult/young* – the sense of *man* being a combination of the notions *humans, male* and *adult*. Theoretical discussion continues over the psychological reality of the semantic components, and over the extent to which words in different languages can be analysed into the same components.

The term should be distinguished from the general term 'component', referring to a section of a GENERATIVE GRAMMAR. D.C.

composite particle approach, see under ELEMENTARY PARTICLES.

composition (in MATHEMATICS), see under FUNCTION.

compulsion. In ABNORMAL PSYCHOLOGY and PSYCHIATRY, a force or drive or impulse within the individual to do or think or say something or other, a force which he finds difficult to resist. It is a prominent feature in obsessional disorders (see OBSESSION). B.A.F.

computability, see under RECURSIVE FUNCTION THEORY.

computation, see under COMPUTING.

computational linguistics. A branch of LINGUISTICS which studies computer simulation of human linguistic behaviour, especially such applications as machine translation and SPEECH SYNTHESIS. The subject has made great progress since the 1980s, with increasingly sophisticated computers and software permitting the investigation of more complex issues, such as in text processing, NATURAL LANGUAGE PROCESSING, and corpus analysis. For further reading: C. S. Butler (ed.), *Computers and Written Texts* (1992). D.C.

computed tomography, see under RADIOLOGY.

computer. A device for processing information. Although the earliest computers were ANALOGUE COMPUTERS, nowadays the word 'computer' refers almost always to the digital computer, which operates by logical rules on a string of digits, generally on the binary scale. They work by manipulating symbols, making them equally capable of operation on non-numerical information such as text. The importance of the modern digital computer is its ability to carry out computations involving many steps – often millions – at high speed and without human intervention. Giant supercomputers are used by scientists and engineers to solve calculations that would take humans many thousands of years to complete; personal computers are commonplace in the households and workplaces of the USA and Europe; embedded systems are used to control MICROWAVE ovens and airplanes; and global computer networks provide communications and information services, through, e.g., the WORLD WIDE WEB.

Although computers have no innate INTELLIGENCE, and only carry out a series of steps specified in a program, the combination of enormous speed, massive data storage, and programming methods that simulate learning has led some scientists to believe that ARTIFICIAL INTELLIGENCE might one day emerge. In the meantime, computers perform ever more 'intelligent' tasks, such as the victory in 1997 by the computer Deep Blue over Garry Kasparov, the world chess champion.

Although computers have greatly enhanced many aspects of human life, they also carry dangers. Computer surveillance and DATABASES have the power to dramatically erode our privacy if they are not regulated. As more and more aspects of individuals' lives are recorded on computer – from financial information to their medical records – care must be taken to maintain confidentiality. In addition, replacing human workers with computers carries implications for society – both for the workers who must retrain and adapt themselves to the changing conditions, and for consumers who find that contact between people is increasingly replaced by interactions with computers. The challenge of computing is to preserve the impressive benefits and reduce the impact of the problems. S.BA.

computer-aided design. The use of a COMPUTER, typically associated with a visual display, in such a way that a designer can see his design immediately and the consequences of changing it, while remaining free to exercise the unprogrammable qualities of taste and judgement. This might involve showing a perspective view of a complicated three-dimensional object; often the point of view can be moved, giving the impression that the object is being rotated. More sophisticated systems allow for binocular vision, and the designer may even get the impression of walking about inside his proposed design. It is now an important part of engineering practice in many areas, including architecture, automobile design and electronics. C.S.; J.E.S.

computer ethics. Ethical (see ETHICS) issues related to the design and use of computer SYSTEMS. Privacy and safety are key areas of ethical concern for the computer professionals who design and implement systems. The professional has special knowledge and expertise to judge the quality, impact and safety of computerized systems, from DATABASES storing vast quantities of personal data, such as credit bureau or tax agency records, to computerized medical devices and factory ROBOTS. The public, generally, does not have the knowledge or the ability to control how they and their data are affected. Thus the professional has a responsibility to design and test systems well, to describe the weaknesses of a system honestly, and to ensure that privacy and safety are not unreasonably at risk. Some issues are particularly relevant for people in business and government who make decisions about how to use computers. How should personal information be protected? Should computer programs be relied upon totally for decisions such as granting loans or diagnosing diseases? When is it appropriate for an employer to monitor the E-MAIL of its employees? A more fundamental issue is whether or not to develop particular computer technologies or applications in the first place. Are computer-controlled airplanes and automobiles too risky? Should computer-controlled machines fight wars? Are the creators of software to control INTERNET access by children responsible when oppressive governments use the same software to block access to political discussion? Should an application be developed if it will eliminate a large number of jobs? Will ARTIFICIAL INTELLIGENCE diminish the value of human INTELLIGENCE? For further reading: S. Baase, *A Gift of Fire: Social, Legal and Ethical Issues in Computing* (1997). S.BA.

computer virus. A computer program, or a segment of computer code, that inserts a copy of itself, or a modified ('mutated') copy of itself, in other programs. When 'infected' programs are executed, the virus spreads. Like biological viruses (see VIROLOGY), computer viruses can be relatively benign or extremely harmful. The virus code might simply display a funny message on the computer screen, or it might destroy files on the disk. A virus in a medical record system or an emergency services computer can threaten lives. Unlike biological viruses, computer viruses are created and released intentionally by people as acts of vandalism or sabotage. Computer viruses first spread among personal computers via diskettes containing software, but now spread even faster when infected programs are downloaded from the Internet. In response, programmers have developed anti-virus programs to search a computer's disk for known viruses and remove them. 'Worms' and 'Trojan Horses' are examples of other destructive computer programs. For further reading: P. J. Denning (ed.), *Computers Under Attack* (1990). S.BA.

computing. The use of an organized set of planned steps to accomplish a goal. Thousands of years ago, when a man planned how to go down to the river to catch some fish and return home without being attacked by a bear, he was computing. Today computing means the myriad uses of electronic computers, including supercomputers that perform extensive calculations for scientists and engineers, personal computers we use for writing plays and playing games, embedded SYSTEMS that control MICROWAVE ovens and airplanes, global computer networks that provide communications and information services, and transmitters embedded in objects for navigation and tracking. In the 1940s and 1950s, computing meant, primarily, calculation and data processing for large businesses and government. Now, in applications like COMPUTER-AIDED DESIGN, computation is in the background and the user focuses on solving problems. In applications such as searching the WORLD WIDE WEB for information, communications and search technologies predominate. Computers have no innate INTELLIGENCE and only carry out a series of steps specified in a program. However, the combination of enormous speed, massive data storage and programming methods that simulate learning allows computers to accomplish tasks that we associate with intelligence, such as beating the world chess champion. Computing has multiplied our power to do good, to do wrong and to make mistakes. Personal computers and the World Wide Web (see INTERNET have 'empowered' ordinary people and small businesses by providing access to information that used to be easily available only to experts and by providing audiences that once were available only to large publishing and broadcasting corporations. Computing provides increased convenience and time savings. It saves energy by replacing physical travel with communications and by replacing bulky mechanical control systems with microprocessors. Computerized medical instruments, emergency response systems and tools for the disabled save and enhance lives. On the other hand, decision makers sometimes rely on incorrect information in DATABASES, assuming the computer is always right. Poor design, software errors and inadequate testing can lead to disruption of communications or financial systems and deadly failures of medical instruments or aircraft auto-pilot systems. Computer surveillance and databases erode our privacy. Criminals reap huge rewards from computer fraud and embezzlement. The speed at which computing technology advances, eliminating some jobs and requiring retraining for others, can cause social and personal difficulties. Replacing contact between people by interactions with computers is often frustrating and sometimes dehumanizing. S.BA.

concentration. In urban GEOGRAPHY, a term used in the description of the population pattern of an urban area. The *density gradient*, i.e. rate of change of density per unit distance measured from the centre to the edge, is used as a measure of the concentration of a town's population. In contrast to this its *central density*, i.e. number of people per unit area, is used as a measure of its *congestion*. See also DENSITY. M.L.

concentration camps. A term originally used to describe internment centres set up in the Cuban rebellion of 1895 by the Spanish military and in the Boer War (1901–02) by the British military in an attempt to pacify rebels by depriving them of civilian support in their areas of operation.

Since the 1930s, however, the term has been used to describe the prison camps characteristic of totalitarian states, notably

Nazi Germany and the Soviet Union (see TOTALITARIANISM; NAZISM; FORCED LABOUR) staffed by the secret police (the SS in Germany; the NKVD/KGB in Russia) and used for the imprisonment, torture and frequently execution of those whom the regime regards as opponents or sets out to eliminate on the grounds of RACE or CLASS.

The first German concentration camps were established in 1933 and used mainly for the 'protective custody' of political prisoners (COMMUNISTS and Social Democrats); the number of such prisoners was reduced to around 7,500 in winter 1936/37. With the territorial expansion of Germany in 1938 (Austria; Sudetenland) the numbers of camps and prisoners began to grow under the overall control of Himmler as *Reichsführer SS*. The number of Germans imprisoned, other than German Jews, fell, and the great majority of the prisoners, in addition to Jews, were nationals of occupied territories suspected of resistance. From 1941 to 1942 the camps were increasingly used to provide forced labour for the German war effort. In a mass expansion, millions of Poles, Russians, Jews and other east and central European nationals were rounded up under appalling conditions in which an average of 60 per cent of the inmates were literally worked to death. The most notorious of all were the extermination or death camps (Auschwitz, Maidanek and Treblinka in Poland, Buchenwald in Germany) in which the mass slaughter of Jews and others was systematically organized, by shooting, medical experimentation and (the largest number) by the use of gas chambers. The number of Jews known to have perished is between 5 and 6 millions; the total number of those who were killed or died from ill-treatment in Nazi concentration camps (including the Jews) has been estimated as at least 10–12 million, possibly as high as 20 million. For further reading: E. Aroneanu (ed.), *Inside the Concentration Camps: Eyewitness Accounts of Life in Hitler's Death Camps* (1996). A.L.C.B.

concept. Variously used by philosophers to indicate, among other things, the meaning of a word, a constituent of thought, and a way of thinking about an object (see PHILOSOPHY). Traditionally, philosophers have tended to think of concept possession in terms of the possession of a private mental object of some sort, perhaps even a mental image. More recently, however, this view has largely been rejected. Philosophers now tend towards thinking of concept possession in terms of what we can *do*. To possess a given concept involves, among other things, being able to recognize instances under which that concept falls, being able to engage in appropriate inferences involving that concept, and so on. It is in the possession of such abilities that possession of the concept is said to consist.

A central question concerning concepts is: to what extent can we possess concepts independently of possessing a language? On the inner-object model of concept possession sketched above, language acquisition essentially involves learning to associate each public word with its corresponding mental item. But then there seems no reason in principle why an individual should not possess the same concepts as you and I yet lack a public language: they may possess all the relevant inner objects but lack knowledge of any correlated words. However, on the view that concept possession consists in what we can do it is no longer so clear that concept possession is essentially language-independent. Arguably, possession of many concepts (especially more sophisticated ones such as that of INFLATION) involves possession of a range of abilities essentially dependent upon language mastery. Thus we cannot have the concepts without the language. S.W.L.

conceptual architecture. An attempt in the early 1970s to establish an architectural parallel with CONCEPTUAL ART. Some sort of authority existed in a passage in the writings of the Renaissance architect Alberti, itself loosely based on the Platonic theory of Forms (see PLATONISM), and in the designs of French pre-Revolutionary architects based loosely on the Platonic or Phileban solids which symbolized the four elements. The co-existing architectural interest in STRUCTURALISM seemed to offer the possibility of establishing ultimate architecture Forms. Of necessity no conceptual architecture was ever built. S.L.

conceptual art. A deviant movement in the visual arts which employs unprepared, eccentric materials (e.g. earth, fat, refuse) and everyday media (e.g. snapshots, typescripts, video, human and animal bodies) in serial or ALEATORY 'installations', 'environments', performances, lists of instructions, and documentary displays, for the deliberately banal or paradoxical presentation of concepts drawn from PHILOSOPHY, LINGUISTICS, art criticism and ordinary life. Legitimized by exhibition in museums and galleries and reproduction in the art press, yet radically violating traditional canons of artistic production, form and (to a lesser extent) content, conceptual works hold the spectator's normal modes of interpretation and appreciation at bay. Highly self-referential, they seek thus to stimulate scepticism about conventional aesthetic communication, and above all to open out or explode the concept 'art' and its cognates, which are perceived as tainted by élitism, commodification and materialism inherent in the art world. Deriving from DADA, Duchamp and Magritte, and with more recent analogies in the 1950s neo-Dada of Piero Manzoni and Yves Klein, conceptualism (as it is alternatively called) arose by reaction out of MINIMAL ART in the early 1960s (the term 'concept art' being first published by Henry Flynt in 1961) and flourished till the late 1970s. International, loose-knit and diverse, the movement still has many adherents (including Joseph Beuys, Sol Lewitt and Richard Long) who frequently reject the label 'conceptual'. Though accepted by sections of the commercial and official art establishment, its works cause continuing puzzlement and unease. Hence conceptual art has been both dismissed as aesthetic NIHILISM producing a meretricious ANTI-ART, and hailed as the heroic vanguard of an alternative aesthetic. For further reading: L. R. Lippard, *Six Years: The Dematerialization of the Art Object from 1966 to 1972* (1973). B.M-H.

conceptual scheme. In PHILOSOPHY, the BELIEFS, assumptions, science, morality, traditions and general outlook of some community, taken together as a loosely knit inclusive theory in terms of which the community's members explain and interpret their empirical and/or moral experience. By 'community' may be meant a particular society or sub-group in society, or all humans, or even all intelligent beings (including gods and Martians, if any exist); but usually either of the two last. On the grounds that thought (possession and manipulation of CONCEPTS) is not possible above a rudimentary level without language, conceptual schemes are sometimes identified with languages or sets of intertranslatable languages. According to this view, to learn language is to acquire the conceptual scheme it embodies. It has been said that one task of philosophy is to investigate the structure of such schemes, tracing connections within them, identifying the most fundamental concepts, and investigating the inconsistencies which, given their amorphous and historically cumulative character, they may be expected to contain. A major question concerning them is whether there is only one possible conceptual scheme, or many; if the latter, the problem of RELATIVISM arises. For further reading: D. Davidson, *Truth and Interpretation* (1984). A.C.G.

conceptualism.

(1) A philosophic theory of UNIVERSALS which takes them to be CONCEPTS in the minds of those who understand the general word (whether verb, adjective or common noun) whose MEANING the universal is. To the extent that a concept is defined as the meaning common to all of a set of synonymous words, this theory is a truism, since whatever else a universal may be it is the meaning of a general word. What is controversial is the contention that a concept is something mental and proprietary to a particular mind: for if I am to understand what you say I must attach the same meaning to your words as you do. A variant form of conceptualism takes a universal or concept to be a mental image. Here the difficulty is to see how one could have an image of economic inflation or negative electric charge or the conscience. Furthermore, a specific, particular image is ambiguously representative: a mental picture of a particular dog could represent retriever, dog, left-hand surface of an animal, loyalty, chestnut colour, life, or hair. For further reading: H. H. Price, *Thinking and Experience* (1969). A.Q.

(2) A vice of legal reasoning, attributed to some lawyers and legal theorists, which consists in treating the general terms and CATEGORIES used in the formulation of legal rules as having an invariant and completely determinate meaning, so that their applica-

tion to particular cases is regarded as a simple exercise in syllogistic reasoning. According to such a view, which has been stigmatized as *mechanical jurisprudence* or the *jurisprudence of concepts*, it would be possible, simply by consulting the definition or analysis of general terms and categories, to determine whether any real or imaginary case fell within the scope of a legal rule. Legal conceptualism has been regarded as an obstacle to the judicial adaptation of the law to social change and sometimes as a cause of unreasonable or even unjust decisions. For further reading: J. Stone, *Social Dimensions of Law and Justice* (1966). H.L.A.H.

Concertación, the. The Concertación de los Partidos para la Democracia (more commonly known as the Concertación) is a coalition made up of Chile's four principal centre-LEFT parties, which has governed the country since the return to DEMOCRACY in March 1990. It has its origin in the Democratic Alliance, which grouped together centre-left and centre-RIGHT opponents of the military regime (1973–90). The Alliance sought to force the resignation of General Augusto Pinochet and to establish a constituent assembly, through the use of street protests and mass mobilizations. The Concertación, then representing some 17 parties across the political spectrum, first emerged as a movement in 1988 to co-ordinate the successful 'no' campaign in the plebiscite organized by the military government to legitimize a further eight-year term for General Pinochet. The Concertación nominated a single presidential candidate and a joint parliamentary slate against the Right in both the December 1989 election, held as a result of Pinochet's defeat in the 1988 referendum, and the December 1993 poll. The political role of the Concertación and its predecessor, the Democratic Alliance, was critical in ensuring the success of the country's negotiated transition to democracy. For further reading: P. W. Drake and I. Jaksic (eds), *The Struggle for Democracy in Chile, 1982–1990* (1991). M.A.P.

concessional loan, see under ECONOMIC AID.

conciliarity. A term used in CATHOLICISM to express the belief, strengthened by the experience and teaching of VATICAN COUNCIL II, that there should be harmony after consultation between the Pope and the bishops; between the bishops of the worldwide Church and of a nation; and between the bishop, clergy and laity in a diocese. (See AGGIORNAMENTO.) This belief has encouraged hopes in the ECUMENICAL MOVEMENT that the way to greater Christian unity may be found through such meetings involving Christians who are not Roman Catholics, rather than through submission to an 'hierarchical' authority able to dictate. Such hopes have been strengthened by the experience of the World Council of Churches, formed in 1948 and including representatives of Eastern Orthodoxy (see ORTHODOXY, EASTERN), although not of Roman Catholicism. But the extent to which the actual power exercised by the Pope or the bishop should be sacrificed remains a matter of uncertainty. See also INFALLIBILITY. D.L.E.

concrete. Along with steel and glass, one of the signature materials of 20th-century ARCHITECTURE. It is used in construction either (a) as *mass concrete*, a mixture of cement, sand and aggregate with water, where only compressive strength is required; or (b), more usually, as *reinforced concrete*, i.e. combined with steel in the form of bars or wires to create a material able to take both tensile and compressive forces. While the material is setting it is held in place, and its ultimate shape and surface texture determined, by *shuttering*, which may be timber boarding, plywood, steel sheeting or moulded plastic; this process can occur either *in situ* or during *precasting* on special beds.

A patent for reinforced concrete was taken out by Coignet in 1855, and Hennebique showed a highly developed system of columns, beams and floors in 1892. Reinforced concrete has since been used and highly refined by engineers such as Maillart in various spectacular bridges in Switzerland, by Nervi in exhibition halls and sports palaces, and Freyssinet in bridges and hangars, and by such architects as, e.g., Auguste Perret. A new plasticity was given to the material by Le Corbusier, who also pioneered *béton brut*, the use of unplaned timber shuttering to create a rough boarded finish often seen in BRUTALIST architecture. A method of inducing compressive forces in the concrete by stressing the reinforcement before it has to take its normal loads was developed by Freyssinet from *c.* 1926 and is now known as *prestressing*.

Many of the characteristic shapes of civil engineering (curved dams, elevated motorways) and of modern architecture (thin slab floors on columns, curved shells) owe their forms to the use of reinforced concrete, commonplace in all but the smallest buildings. See also PREFABRICATION. For further reading: P. Collins, *Concrete* (1959). M.BR.

concrete art. Term used in the Abstraction-Création group from *c.* 1930 when Hans Arp was calling his sculptures 'concretions' and Van Doesburg of De Stijl (see STIJL, DE) began editing the short-lived *Art Concret*. Associated above all with Max Bill, the Swiss BAUHAUS-trained artist whose strongly geometrical art is based on mathematical reasoning, it signifies the materialization of an intellectual CONCEPT. In 1944 Bill organized an International Exhibition of Concrete Art at Basel, and thereafter the movement spread to Argentina, Italy and Brazil. The work of Joseph Albers in the USA also relates. J.W.

concrete music, see MUSIQUE CONCRÈTE.

concrete operation. In DEVELOPMENTAL PSYCHOLOGY, a PIAGETIAN term for a mental operation involved in the classification, seriation and enumeration of objects. The notion is applied to the mental operations governing the organization of real (concrete) objects but not the organization of imagined possibilities. Such operations are mastered by children in the middle stage of intellectual development. P.L.H.

concrete poetry. A CONCEPT formulated under the influence of Max Bill and Eugen Gomringer, and launched at the São Paulo exhibition of CONCRETE ART in 1956 by a group of Brazilian poets and designers. According to the 'Pilot Plan' in their review *Noigandres* 4 (1958), the concrete poem is an object 'in and by itself', consciously using graphic space in its structure along lines foreshadowed by Mallarmé and Guillaume Apollinaire. Subdivisions of their movement, as it spread across the world in the 1960s, were *semiotic poetry* using symbols, *emergent poetry* exploiting quasi-cryptographic juggling of letters, the related kinetic poetry (see KINETIC ART) with its serial methods and PERMUTATIONS, the *logograms* of the Brazilian Pedro Xisto, and *phonetic* or sound poetry. This last was not in the 'Pilot Plan' but shares its concern with what Max Bense calls 'materiality, verbal, visual, or vocal', though deriving more from the *Lautgedichte* of MERZ and the noises made by FUTURISM and DADA. With this one exception concrete poetry is essentially visual or typographic, and thus emerges in a much larger (and older) confluence of the verbal, visual and printer's arts to which LETTRISM, spatialism (see SPACE) and POP ART contribute also. For further reading: E. Williams (ed.), *An Anthology of Concrete Poetry* (1967). J.W.

concrete universal.

(1) In PHILOSOPHY, a term used by absolute IDEALISTS to describe individual things of a more substantial kind (see SUBSTANCE); 'concrete' aims to emphasize the thing's individuality, 'universal' the rationally systematic coherence which such philosophers take to be the hallmark of the true individual. The only wholly genuine individual for these philosophers is the absolute, or Spirit, or the totality of what there really is. But its pre-eminently substantial individuality is approximated to by finite minds or personalities and by such articulated systems of persons or persistent social groups as nations, professions and CLASSES. A.Q.

(2) In literature, an abstraction developed by W. K. Wimsatt in *The Verbal Icon* (1954) and much used in the NEW CRITICISM. Wimsatt over-optimistically sought, on HEGELIAN lines, to erect a holistic (see HOLISM) POETICS in which the 'particulars' of a 'successful' poem would coalesce into a totality that is its 'own' universal. Another New Critic, John Crowe Ransom, accepted the term – but on condition that it should be understood in a 'Kantian' rather than in a Hegelian sense. He felt that Wimsatt left no room for Kantian 'natural beauty': man needs a 'double vision', so that he may see both the rose itself, *and* (then) its 'idea'. For further reading: J. C. Ransom, *Poems and Essays* (1955). M.S.-S.

condensation. In Freud's analysis of the dream-work, condensation and DISPLACE-

MENT are two of the means by which the 'dream-thoughts' or 'latent content' are transformed into the 'manifest content' of the dream. The much richer, longer and more complex text of the dream-thoughts is 'condensed' as it is filtered through the dream-work, and the dream as remembered may be 'brief, meagre and laconic'. Not only that, but the work of displacement will also have contributed to the 'scrambling' of the dream-thoughts in their passage to the text of the dream. Condensation and displacement, then, are two rhetorical transformations which the repressing 'censor' will have imposed on the dream in its passage from latent to manifest form, and the task of the psychoanalyst (see PSYCHOANALYSIS) will be to interpret these transformations in an attempt to find the deeper or earlier 'text'. Roman Jakobson's 1956 essay on METAPHOR and METONYMY threw a different light on not only Saussure's but also Freud's theories. Metaphor, it seems, is like condensation in its activity, while metonymy is like displacement. Freud's discovery has been interpreted, in the light of Jakobson's distinction, to great effect in the work of Lévi-Strauss, Lacan (see LACANIAN), Barthes and most STRUCTURALIST and POST-STRUCTURALIST literary theory. For further reading: S. Freud, *The Interpretation of Dreams* (1899). R.PO.

condensed-matter physics. The branch of PHYSICS that deals with the behaviour of matter in condensed (primarily liquid and solid) states (see SOLID-STATE PHYSICS). This discipline is commonly interested in the collective behaviour of large groups of ATOMS or MOLECULES, in distinction from atomic or high-energy physics which probes the properties of individual atoms or of fundamental SUBATOMIC PARTICLES (see ATOMIC PHYSICS). Condensed-matter physics has a strong applied element – it is in large part concerned with the electronic and magnetic properties of solid-state materials, which has ramifications for electronic technology. Another predominant theme in condensed-matter physics is the behaviour of surfaces and interfaces, which is relevant to engineering and microelectronic fabrication technologies. P.C.B.

conditioned reflex. The customary translation (more accurately, 'conditional reflex') of the Russian term for a connection established by a CLASSICAL CONDITIONING procedure between an arbitrary stimulus and a reflex response. Pavlov's work (see PAVLOVIAN) suggested to early BEHAVIOURISTS an analysis of all behaviour in terms of involuntary stimulus-response bonds, thus removing the necessity for mental CONSTRUCTS such as 'will', 'motive' and 'intention'. However, conditional reflexes in the Pavlovian paradigm can be clearly established only in physiological systems served by the autonomic nervous system; the conditioning of voluntary behaviour seems to require reward (*reinforcement*). So, although learned emotional reactions may be analysed as conditioned reflexes, most voluntary behaviour must be conditioned by operant rather than classical procedures (see OPERANT CONDITIONING). D.H.

conditioning. The deliberate and systematic attempt to control some aspect of human or animal behaviour, either, in CLASSICAL CONDITIONING (also known as PAVLOVIAN or *respondent* conditioning), by establishing a CONDITIONED REFLEX, or, in OPERANT CONDITIONING (also known as *instrumental* conditioning), by controlling the consequences of behaviour. D.H.

confidence building measures (CBM). Term first used in the Conference on Security and Co-operation in Europe (CSCE) in Helsinki in 1975 (see HELSINKI 1975) to refer to measures designed to reduce tension by increasing the flow of information and increasing the possibility for each side to verify the military intentions and activities of the other. CBMs include the notification of military manoeuvres and the presence of observers at such manoeuvres. Fairly wide-ranging measures were agreed at the 1985 Stockholm CSCE. For further reading: W. G. Baudissin (ed.), *From Distrust to Confidence* (1983). A.W.I.

configuration. An English alternative to the German word GESTALT. I.M.L.H.

confirmation.

(1) The support given to a hypothesis by evidence: the fundamental relation between premise and conclusion in INDUCTION. The fact that every known *A* is *B* confirms the hypothesis that every *A* whatever is *B*, but

does not establish it conclusively, since it is possible that some as yet undiscovered *A* is not *B*, and thus that the unrestricted generalization is false. If evidence confirms a hypothesis, then it confers some probability on it. Some broad principles of confirmation are intuitively acceptable, i.e. those which hold it to increase with the bulk and variety of the evidence. Attempts have been made, most elaborately by Carnap, to develop comprehensive formal theories of confirmation on the basis of such principles. See also FREQUENCY THEORY. For further reading: R. Swinburne, *An Introduction to Confirmation Theory* (1973). A.Q.

(2) In the work of anti-psychiatrist R. D. Laing (1927–89), the response of the OTHER to a person who presents his SUBJECTIVITY in the *lebenswelt*, or 'lived world'. Madness can arise from the lack of meaning which ensues for the person whose subjectivity is 'disconfirmed' by the other – i.e. his experience of the world is regarded as being without significance. For further reading: R. D. Laing, *The Divided Self* (1960). S.T.

conflict theory. A term loosely applied to the work of a number of sociological theorists who have mounted critiques of STRUCTURAL-FUNCTIONAL THEORY on the grounds that it neglects the empirical fact that conflicts of value and interest are inherent in all forms of human society; or, at best, treats conflict as a phenomenon of only secondary interest by taking the very existence of an ongoing society as in itself evidence that some fundamental consensus must prevail. Consequently, it is held, exponents of structural-functional theory underestimate the degree to which the coordination of social activities and the stability of societies derive from the direct or indirect COERCION of less powerful by more powerful groups. Some versions of conflict theory are of a MARXIST character; others, however, reflect a political philosophy of PLURALISM. For further reading: J. Rex, *Social Conflict: a Conceptual and Theoretical Analysis* (1981). J.H.G.

confrontation. Term employed, originally by former Indonesian President Sukarno in the 1960s against Malaysia, to describe a conflict in which a direct attack or declaration of war is avoided and techniques of subversion, propaganda and GUERRILLA raids are employed. It also plays upon the fears of international conflict entertained by the allies and associates of the opposing power in order to cause them to intervene and bring diplomatic pressure to bear. More loosely, any conflict in the stage before a declaration of war or outbreak of general hostilities. D.C.W.

Confucianism. The ruling PHILOSOPHY, over much of its life, of the Chinese Empire, as expressed in the writings edited by and attributed to Confucius and other Confucian scholars. Confucianism developed into a complex philosophy involving a supreme being, or Great Ultimate, who governs the universe according to the rhythm of the male principle (yang) and the female principle (yin). It also relates to the practice of the reverence of ancestors, including that of Confucius himself. A central concept for Confucius (551–479 BC) was *li* or right behaviour, including ritual. The literary works of the tradition were set for the imperial examinations until 1905, when the examinations were abolished. Though attempts at a reformed Confucianism for modern times were undertaken, notably by K'ang Yu-wei (1858–1927), they were not effective. When the COMMUNISTS took over, they suppressed traditions and values from the old order, and during the GREAT PROLETARIAN CULTURAL REVOLUTION it was particularly harshly put down. But outside China, and now to some extent inside, it is undergoing a revival, especially in Singapore and among the Chinese diaspora. For further reading: D. Nivison, *The Ways of Confucianism* (1996). N.SM.

conglomerate. A firm operating in more than one distinct industry; its activities are said to be diversified. Such firms may obtain ECONOMIES OF SCALE in the actual production of each good and service and, more importantly, they may obtain economies across the range of their activities, e.g. raising finance, planning investment, RESEARCH AND DEVELOPMENT and MARKETING. A more vague and common justification for their existence is that it allows a superior management to operate across a wider range of activities. However, the size of conglomerates and their ability to cross-subsidize their products may be used to reduce COMPETITION in each of the industries it operates in. The growth of conglomerates, particularly through mergers, may represent a managerial desire for growth (see FIRM, THEORIES OF) rather than an activity that is of benefit to society. The political, economic and social power of conglomerates has also been of concern. For further reading: D. A. Hay and D. J. Morris, *Industrial Economics: Theory and Evidence* (1979). J.P.

Congrès Internationaux d'Architecture Moderne, see CIAM.

conjuncture. A term derived from the French *conjoncture* (German *Konjunktur*), meaning 'the state of the economy' or 'the way the economic situation is developing'. Economists making short-term economic forecasts (see FORECASTING) use the word as shorthand for 'the complex trends in employment, output, prices, the BALANCE OF PAYMENTS, and other key economic variables'. Analysis of the conjuncture is closely related to the theory of economic fluctuations and business cycles (see TRADE CYCLE). A.C.

connectionism.

(1) A name for a brand of ARTIFICIAL INTELLIGENCE that makes use of artificial NEURAL NETWORKS, more or less loosely inspired by theories of how animal brains work. Connectionist networks consist of a number of interconnected processing units (NEURONS) whose level of activation varies according to incoming excitatory and inhibitory signals from other neurons, and whose outputs to other neurons depend on the level of excitation. Some neurons receive inputs from external sources (e.g. sensors) and some send their output signals to external mechanisms (e.g. other networks, or muscles, or motors).

By carefully adjusting the way in which the neurons respond to stimuli, it is possible to adjust the performance of the whole network, to perform a variety of tasks such as recognition, classification, pattern completion or on-line control. It is also possible for such systems to modify their own performance by changing their weights, e.g. by 'back propagation', which uses a measure of discrepancy between actual output and required output to send adjustment signals back through the network.

Since neural nets use complex non-linear feedback mechanisms, the MATHEMATICS required to MODEL and predict their behaviour can become very complex. Even so, artificial neural nets remain grossly oversimplified compared with real animal brains.

Some who work on neural nets see them as opposed to ARTIFICIAL INTELLIGENCE mechanisms. More broad-minded researchers see them as complementary. A.S.

(2) American psychologist Edward Thorndike's (1874–1949) term for his analysis of psychological phenomena in terms of ASSOCIATION between, not ideas, but situations and responses. 'Learning', he wrote in 1931, 'is connecting. The mind is man's connection system.' I.M.L.H.

conscientization. An understanding of education, developed in the context of literacy programmes for adults in the 1960s by the Brazilian educationalist Paulo Freire, as an instrument for the transformation of the social order. Freire interprets the educational process as a PRAXIS – a 'practice' in which theory and action are dialectically related to one another (see DIALECTIC). Conscientization, therefore, is a theoretical-practical phenomenon which exists in and for the struggle for liberation from all kinds of oppression. Advocates of LIBERATION THEOLOGY have used the term since the late 1960s, as part of their analysis of the theological task in Latin American societies. C.C.

consciousness. The state of an individual when his faculties of seeing, hearing, feeling, thinking, etc., are functioning normally. It contrasts (1) with his state when he goes into a coma, or dead faint, or is deeply hypnotized (see HYPNOSIS), or is asleep dreamlessly; and (2) with his state when, e.g., instead of feeling a pin-prick as he would normally do, he is unconscious of it – either because he has been locally anaesthetized, or because, unconsciously, he does not wish to feel it, or because AUTO-SUGGESTION has successfully enabled him to avoid feeling it, or because he has been mildly hypnotized, or for some other reason. In these latter cases, the content of his STREAM OF CONSCIOUSNESS is somewhat restricted in character. In the case of a man blind from birth, the content is greatly and permanently restricted, since he lacks one of our normal faculties.

At present we do not know what constitutes the full set of necessary and sufficient neuro-physiological conditions (see NECESSARY AND SUFFICIENT CONDITIONS) for the normal functioning of any one of our perceptual and cognitive faculties. *A fortiori* we do not know what constitutes this set of conditions for our conscious functioning in general. Moreover, although consciousness is under constant and widespread investigation under the guise, in particular, of studies in PERCEPTION and cognition, there are deep conceptual conflicts about the CONCEPT of consciousness embedded in our CULTURE, including the SUB-CULTURE of scientists. Thus, how far down the phylogenetic scale (see PHYLOGENY) is it correct to ascribe conscious functioning? Many would ascribe it to a monkey reaching for a banana, or a dog running to greet its master. But what about a rat learning a new maze? If we say 'yes' here, then we will also be obliged to ascribe it to an earthworm learning a maze, and we resist this ascription. If we say 'no' to the rat, our refusal and doubts at once spread upwards to embrace the dog and the monkey. Our scepticism is strengthened by current attempts in PSYCHOLOGY to explain the behaviour of the rat without postulating conscious functioning. It is all too evident, therefore, that we are really quite unclear what we are saying when we ascribe consciousness to an animal or to ourselves.

One solution has been to suggest that our conscious functioning consists in a complex and continuous process of conceptualizing input from within and without the organism. This suggestion is promising and its HEURISTIC value has not yet been fully tapped, let alone exhausted. However, it will probably turn out to have the consequence of restricting conscious functioning to ourselves and to the higher animals for parts of their daily waking lives. This, in turn, has the logical consequence that the lower animals cannot feel pain. Equally serious, this solution by itself leaves unresolved the central problem of consciousness. If we say, e.g., that, when the clamour of the church bells strikes my ears, all I do (relevantly) is to conceptualize input, then (it has been argued) we leave out of account the sensuous and phenomenal features of my auditory experience and consciousness at the time. This, in turn, suggests that there are constituents or aspects of our consciousness that cannot be brought within the order of natural events and the scope of science. So our concept of consciousness seems to commit us to a DUALISM (see also MIND-BODY PROBLEM).

There have been various attempts to remove this dualism, or make it more palatable; e.g. it has been argued that, when I hear the clamour of the bells, the bodily processes and events involved are contingently identical with those that are my hearing the bells. Though this proposal may remove the dualism of events, it leaves us with a dualism of properties, or qualities, that is just as baffling. Again, it can be argued that, in the sense that matters, it is a mistake to claim that there is any sensuous and phenomenal manifold over and above the conceptualizing I perform in hearing the bells. This is a profound contention stemming in part from Wittgenstein. But it is also a very difficult one to grasp, and it has not been as widely appreciated as, perhaps, it deserves to be. One of the reasons for this may be that Wittgenstein's solution appears to commit us to changing our concept of consciousness (and cognate ones) in such a way that it is no longer correct and tempting for us to speak of a sensuous and phenomenal manifold over and above our conceptualizing activity. If this conceptual change were to occur, then the traditional dualism of consciousness would disappear. One of the factors helping to bring this change about is the development of science. The more psychology, and related disciplines, can show how our conscious functioning consists in conceptualizing activity, the weaker will be our resistance to the conceptual changes that will remove the problem, and so bring the phenomena of consciousness fully within the order of nature. For further reading: J. R. Searle, *The Mystery of Consciousness* (1997). B.A.F.

consciousness-raising. Means for making women more aware of their situation, the objective conditions of sexual oppression or PATRIARCHY and their experiences within it. Consciousness-raising groups emerged as an important element in the women's movement of the 1960s. They were usually small (6–12 members), women only, and they were not hierarchically organized or focused on a group leader. Within these groups women could express and explore themselves with other women. Not only did women learn more about the objective state of male dominance, but they also became aware of the more subtle, hidden, unconscious (often repressed) elements of sexual oppression. Consciousness-raising groups validated women's knowledge and experience, and linked the personal to the political. Male consciousness-raising groups are now appearing. These have been established to enable men to reflect upon the politics of their own personal relationships and their place within a patriarchal society. (See also FEMINISM.) For further reading: S. Jackson and J. Jones (eds), *Contemporary Feminist Theories* (1998). A.G.

Conseil Européen pour la Recherche Nucléaire, see CERN.

consensus politics. A term popularized in the 1960s and since used with increasing imprecision to characterize the alleged character of successive Labour and Conservative governments in Britain from 1951 to 1979. It denotes, with some exaggeration, the extent to which they shared a commitment to similar policies which commanded broad popular support across party lines. These included an economy of mixed public and private ownership, limited and selective economic intervention by government, and the maintenance of an extended WELFARE STATE. The approach depended on both parties subduing their more radical elements and on levels of national prosperity which were increasingly hard to achieve. The phrase disguises the extent to which governments of this era preferred ÉLITE to popular opinion on other issues such as immigration, law and order, and questions of morality. The term was a development of 'Butskellism', coined from the names of the moderate Conservative and Labour Chancellors of the Exchequer, R. A. Butler and Hugh Gaitskell. It was notably disdained by Margaret Thatcher, who on becoming Prime Minister in 1979 declared herself to be a 'conviction politician'. For further reading: K. Middlemas, *Politics in an Industrial Society* (1979). S.R.

consequentialism, see TELEOLOGY.

conservation.

(1) In ECOLOGY, the use of natural resources (hence often, explicitly, *resource conservation*; see RESOURCES, NATURAL) in a manner such as to prevent their unnecessary waste or spoliation. Conservation implies use (as distinct from preservation), but for the benefit of mankind on a long-term rather than a short-term basis; in the words of Gifford Pinchot, first head of the US Forest Service, 'conservation means the greatest good for the greatest numbers and that for the longest time'. It may be achieved by positive steps through change in TECHNOLOGY (e.g. stubble-mulching to conserve soil from wind erosion) or ownership (e.g. creation of National Parks for conserving areas of outstanding natural beauty), or by negative steps such as legislation to arrest wasteful practices (e.g. limitations on the size of fish catches). See also RECYCLING. P.H.

(2) In DEVELOPMENTAL PSYCHOLOGY, a PIAGETIAN term for the principle that quantity does not vary across transformations in its EMBODIMENT. Thus a given number of objects remains constant whatever their grouping, and the volume of liquid remains constant whatever the shape of the vessel in which it is contained. The child is said by Piaget to lack this principle as a conceptual formulation until approximately seven years of age. P.L.H.

conservation laws. Principles of great generality and power in PHYSICS, which state that the values of certain quantities characterizing an isolated system do not alter as the system evolves. Thus, in a power station, chemical ENERGY in coal is changed into an equal amount of electrical energy plus heat energy, and in a NUCLEAR REACTION the various colliding PARTICLES may change their electric charge but the total charge is the same before and after. Many more recondite 'conserved quantities' exist, such as the PARITY of the WAVE FUNCTION in QUANTUM MECHANICS during STRONG INTERACTIONS. At a deeper level, some conservation laws follow from SYMMETRY or homogeneity principles involving space and time. Thus the deeply rooted view that space is homogeneous – that 'one place is as good as another', so that an isolated system will behave identically in different places – leads to the conservation of MOMENTUM, and the homogeneity of time leads to energy conservation. Conserved quantities are often called *invariants*. See also MASS-ENERGY EQUATION; TRANSFORMATION. M.V.B.

conservatism/conservative. Conservatism has two distinct senses today. As the doctrine of Conservative parties in Britain, Europe and North America, it combines an enthusiasm for CAPITALISM and the free enterprise economy which is best described as 'neo-liberal' (see NEO-LIBERALISM) with an appeal to the patriotic sentiments of the electorate and an emphasis on social order and moral discipline which is more in tune with traditional conservative values. As a philosophical doctrine, conservatism emphasizes 'the politics of imperfection'. Philosophical conservatism emphasizes tradition, authority, law and order, and the impossibility of achieving anything resembling the utopias (see UTOPIANISM) which radicals have longed for. Human nature, in the eyes of most conservatives, is too imperfect to allow society to dispense with the guidance of tradition and the government of firm authority. Mankind is too short-sighted and too passionate to agree on one answer to the question how best to order our social and political affairs, let alone to do everything that it would demand. It is better to emphasize known duties, to accommodate individual diversity by letting individuals use their own property in the ways they see fit, to preserve the authority of the STATE by limiting its role to national defence and the policing of the marketplace, and to strengthen institutions such as the family, schools and Churches as a means of securing a sound public morality. Many conservatives have objected to attempts to elicit a 'philosophy' of conservatism on the ground that conservatism is not a creed but a disposition, and that the conservative differs from radicals and INTELLECTUALS precisely because he is willing to change his mind and abandon any particular doctrine or any particular goal for the sake of conserving the vital interests of his society. Whether or not this is true, some distinguished philosophers have written in defence of conservatism during the past two decades. For further reading: Roger Scruton, *The Meaning of Conservatism* (1984). A.R.

consociation. The action or fact of associating together. In the 17th and 18th centuries it was widely used to denote an association of churches. In international relations it covers a whole spectrum of associations between states, ranging from the vaguest alliance to the full-scale confederation. It stops short of full-scale federation because consociation implies entirely voluntary participation. More recently the term has been adopted in the study of domestic politics. A. Lijphart, in a seminal article (1968), outlined his influential model of 'Consociational Democracy' in which ethnic, religious and CLASS conflicts are managed, and stability maintained, through a process of mutual adjustment and concession. But this method requires a rare degree of political will and capacity for compromise among all parties to the conflict if it is to succeed. P.W.

conspicuous consumption. A term heavily used by Thorstein Veblen in his *Theory of the Leisure Class* (1899) for the extravagant use of expensive goods or services in order to demonstrate STATUS (sense 2) and wealth. Such ostentatious displays of purchasing power have led in many countries to the situation where a large proportion of economic resources is allocated to the production of luxury goods and so-called CONSUMER DURABLES which need periodic replacement. Consumption patterns which are used to reinforce or emphasize one's resources and status form one of the essential features of ADMASS. P.S.L.

conspiracy theory. The paranoid belief that there exists a gigantic and sinister conspiracy dedicated to, or responsible for, the subversion and ultimate destruction of a way of life. The historian Richard Hofstader has noted that what distinguishes the paranoid type of conspiracy is that its proponents see a vast plot as the *motive force* in historical events. For the paranoid, history itself becomes a conspiracy, initiated by evil forces of transcendent power. Those inclined to accept conspiracies often view them in apocalyptic terms, trafficking, in Hofstader's phrase, 'in the birth and death of whole worlds, whole political orders, whole systems of human values'. Plots can flow into other paranoid plots, generating ever-larger invisible machinations – a paranoid circle that can readily degenerate into

TERRORISM against real and perceived enemies. A susceptibility to conspiracy theories is often a symptom of political weakness, rooted in the feeling that one is powerless to influence one's own life. J.T.M.

constancy phenomenon. In PERCEPTION, the process whereby an object maintains an apparent size, shape or colour that conforms to its 'real' properties rather than to its retinal projection. Thus a circle held obliquely to the line of regard looks 'more circular' than warranted by its oval retinal projection shape, and white paper standing in shadow looks whiter than a piece of black coal in sunlight, though the latter is reflecting more light to the eye. When objects are isolated from their surroundings, as when viewed through a pinhole, constancy is destroyed. For further reading: M. D. Vernon, *Visual Perception* (1937). J.S.B.

constants of nature, see FUNDAMENTAL CONSTANTS.

constituent analysis. In LINGUISTICS, the analysis of a sentence into its *constituents*, i.e. identifiable elements. Any complex constituent may itself be analysed into other constituents; and sentences thus come to be viewed as consisting of 'layers' of constituents. Thus the sentence *The boys are sleeping* consists of two main constituents. *The boys* and *are sleeping*; each of these has two constituents, *the* and *boys, are* and *sleeping*; and of these, two may be split further: *boy* + *s* (the marker of plurality), and *sleep* + *ing* (the marker of continuity). Brackets are often used to indicate constituent structure, e.g. {[The ((boy)s)] [are ((sleep)ing)]}. Such sentence analysis is generally referred to, following Bloomfield, as *immediate constituent* (IC) analysis, and the 'immediate' constituents in which the analysis results are distinguished from the residual, unanalysable *ultimate constituents* (UCs). D.C.

constitutional government. A system of limited government according to clearly articulated principles. These principles are usually set out in a written constitution (as in the US) and occasionally in an 'unwritten' constitution (as in the UK). Examples of written constitutions include the US Constitution and its Bill of Rights, and the French Declaration of the Rights of Man and of the Citizen. Constitutions set out the powers of the various organs of government and the standards for determining the legality of their actions. The success of constitutional government depends on its adaptibility. Constitutional change usually results from JUDICIAL REVIEW, and less frequently by amendment of the original document. Constitutional law is therefore found only partly in the written constitution; most American constitutional law, for example, is found in judicial decisions (see SUPREME COURT OF THE UNITED STATES). M.S.P.

constitutionalism. The doctrine that governments must act within the constraints of a known constitution, whether this is written or in part a matter of unwritten convention. The doctrine dates from the 17th-century conflicts between kings asserting their absolute authority, usually by divine right, and parliaments and the judiciary asserting the ultimate authority of a system of law stemming from something other than royal decree. In the 20th century, constitutionalists have seen the rule of law as a bulwark against extreme LEFT-wing governments inclined to substitute the divine right of the people or the party for that of the monarch or the czar, but reformers in the US have advanced the cause of BLACK Americans, women and the poor by appealing to the constitutional protection of the equal rights of all citizens, too. See also EQUAL PROTECTION and EQUAL RIGHTS AMENDMENT. For further reading: G. M. Marshall, *Constitutional Theory* (1983). A.R.

constraint, developmental. Any restriction or bias in the production of heritable phenotypic VARIATION caused by the nature of embryonic development (see EMBRYOLOGY; GENOTYPE). NATURAL SELECTION can only act on the heritable phenotypic variation caused by the effects of spontaneous changes in the GENETIC material. Hence any restriction in the effects of MUTATIONS on the phenotype constrains what natural selection can 'choose' from. Therefore these biases are called constraints. An example is the mode of mollusc shell development (i.e. the shells of snails, clams, etc.), which involves growth at the rim of the shell only. This mode of skeletal development constrains the evolution of the mollusc exoskeletons to a limited array of shapes, which is much more restricted than the range of shapes realized by the exoskeleton of arthropods (insects, crawfish, centipedes, etc.). This concept plays an important role in explaining the pattern of organic diversity (see BIODIVERSITY), in particular explaining differences among SPECIES which cannot be attributed to adaptation. G.P.W.

construct (or *logical construct*, or *logical construction*, or *hypothetical construct*). Names given to a term or CONCEPT to which it is thought that there is nothing corresponding in reality, so that it is merely a useful fiction. It may be useful for summarizing masses of detailed facts, or formulating explanatory theories. Thus, if a historian or social scientist talks about 'the mood of a nation', this is a construct summarizing, and perhaps slightly distorting, the attitudes and behaviour of millions of people. Some would argue that the theoretical terms of science (e.g. ELECTRON, GRAVITATION, FIELD, GENE, SUPEREGO) are all constructs. Others would argue that even familiar terms of everyday language (e.g. table, tree, house) are constructs. Usually the alleged construct is contrasted with something else which 'really' exists, as opposed to being a useful fiction. However, it is very difficult to formulate and defend any precise analysis of the distinction between real existents and useful fictions. See also ONTOLOGY; REDUCTION; SOCIAL CONSTRUCT. For further reading: R. Harré, *Theories and Things* (1961). A.S.

constructivism. Internationally influential Soviet art movement, most active in the 1920s, which explored the use of movement and machine-age materials in sculpture and had a considerable influence on modern art and architecture. It applied a three-dimensional CUBIST vision, inspired by the sculptor Alexander Archipenko and by Picasso's reliefs of 1912–14, first to wholly abstract non-objective 'constructions' with a kinetic element (1914–20; see ABSTRACT ART; KINETIC ART) and thereafter to the new social demands and industrial tasks of the time. It was thus made up of two threads: (1) the concern with space and rhythm expressed in Anton Pevsner and Naum Gabo's *Realist Manifesto* (1920), and (2) a tussle within the Education Commissariat between such supporters of 'pure' art and a more socially oriented group headed by Alexei Gan, Alexander Rodchenko and his wife Varvara Stepanova, who wanted this art to be absorbed in industrial production. Though all these people shared much the same constructivist vision, as did Vladimir Tatlin, whose model rotating tower for the Third INTERNATIONAL was its classic realization, there was a split when Pevsner and Gabo emigrated in 1922, leaving the newly christened movement to develop on socially utilitarian lines (see UTILITARIANISM). As the *productivist* majority went into typography, photography, industrial and theatre design, it gained the support of the Proletkult and of the 'Left Front' of art in Vladimir Mayakovsky's magazine *Lef* (1923–28), becoming also a dominant influence in the modern Soviet architectural group OSA. Through El Lissitzky's contacts with DADA, De STIJL, MERZ, and the Hungarian László Moholy-Nagy, the movement spread after 1922 to the BAUHAUS, thence to be carried everywhere as part of that school's ever widening influence in design and basic art education.

In its 'pure' form it was later assimilated in the Abstraction-Création wing of international abstract art, making a particular impression on such English artists as Ben Nicholson, Barbara Hepworth, and, after 1950, Victor Pasmore. In Russia, meanwhile, both sides of the movement alike became identified with FORMALISM, leading to its virtual suppression between the early 1930s and the thaw of the mid-1950s, after which there was a tentative rehabilitation of the productivist branch and its contributions to architecture and book design. For further reading: C. Lodder, *Russian Constructivism* (1983). J.W.

consumer durables. CONSUMERS' GOODS that are also multiple-use assets, i.e. assets which, when used, are not used up at once but rather gradually over a period of time. Obvious examples are houses, cars, washing-machines, dish-washers, refrigerators, vacuum cleaners, furniture, clothes, etc. It is not so much the fact that they are durable instead of perishable that distinguishes consumer durables from other consumers' goods, but rather their multiple-use character as against the single-use character of the other consumers' goods; e.g. tinned fish is durable and it is a consumers' good, but it is not a consumer durable. In the case of particularly long-lasting and expensive items of consumer durables it is advisable to count the services they render rather than these goods themselves as entering into consumption. This in fact is the treatment that in the NATIONAL ACCOUNTING is applied to owner-occupied houses. G.S.

consumer price index.

(1) In the UK, an index comparing the current cost of all goods and services purchased by all consumers with the cost of the same commodities if they could have been bought at the prices prevailing in the base year. This current-weighted price index is implied in and can readily be obtained from NATIONAL ACCOUNTING estimates of consumers' expenditure at current prices and the corresponding estimates at constant (i.e. base-year) prices.

(2) In the US, what in the UK is called cost-of-living index. G.S.

consumer society. A society that sets an inordinate value on CONSUMERS' GOODS, which it tends to regard not merely as 'the ultimate aim of all economic activity' but as the ultimate good. See also ADMASS; CONSPICUOUS CONSUMPTION. O.S.

consumerism. Manipulation of the behaviour of consumers, through every aspect of MARKETING communication, from pricing to packaging, and point-of-sale presentation to ADVERTISING, has led to increasing concern about its economic effect and its morality. There has, therefore, been a rise in consumerist resistance. In America, Ralph Nader has been credited with achieving the greatest early influence in this movement, with his criticism of, particularly, the car industry. But most countries now embody consumer protection legislation within their legal framework. The majority of people accept, however, that the law can only marginally influence the behaviour of marketing companies and the strength of consumer response to them. Ultimately, as any marketing textbook will claim, the consumer is sovereign (so long as he can organize himself in sufficient strength to ensure that his feelings are understood and appreciated). In an age when multi-national corporations have assets as large as some of the twenty most powerful nations on earth, and derive their strength from manipulation of their consumers, but derive their management control from a self-electing oligarchy who carefully divide and manage their shareholders, the strength of consumerism may be felt to be inadequate. T.S.

consumers' goods. The ultimate aim of all economic activity is the satisfaction of human wants by means of the consumption of goods and services. It is these goods and services that are referred to as consumers' goods. All goods at earlier stages in the production process, that is before they pass into the hands of consumers, are called *producers' goods*. G.S.

contact improvisation. A dance form created by Steve Paxton in 1972 during GRAND UNION residencies in America. It combines elements of the martial arts (particularly Tai Chi, Aikido, Capoeira), gymnastics and RELEASE DANCE techniques. Contact improvisation is an organic and continuous process between partners involving touch, balance and taking weight. Trust, spontaneity and wordless communication signal the structure of the dance, while detail is left to improvisation. In performance the presentation is casual, clothing is functional and the content unedited. L.A.

contagious diffusion, see under DIFFUSION (sense 3).

containment. In politics (for its sense in PHYSICS see under MAGNETOHYDRODYNAMICS), a policy towards the former USSR originally advocated by the US diplomatist and head of the State Department's policy planning staff George Kennan, writing under the pseudonym 'X' in the American quarterly magazine *Foreign Affairs*, July 1947, on 'The Sources of Soviet Conduct'. The policy assumed the current antagonism displayed by the leadership of the Soviet Union towards the Western democracies to be inherent in the internal system of power in the Soviet Union, and called for a 'long-term, patient but firm and vigilant containment of Russian expansionist tendencies'. Kennan's recommendations became thereafter the basis of American policy towards the Soviet Union, a policy aimed at accommodation, not war, and expressed in economic and technical aid to non-communist countries as well as through diplomacy. Kennan himself, however, subsequently maintained that the policy of ringing the Soviet Union's frontiers with collective security organizations (NATO, CENTO, SEATO) and bilateral military agreements misconceived the nature of the containment for which he had called. For further reading: G. Kennan, *Memoirs 1925–1950* (1968). D.C.W.

contemporary dance. See MODERN DANCE. Contemporary dance is a term most associated with modern dance in Britain, i.e. London Contemporary Dance Theatre. L.A.

contemporary history. Like the serious academic study of the subject, the term goes back to about 1950. It is usually employed to refer to the history of the last 70 years or so, though in France it may refer to history since 1789. The validity of the subject is still challenged by some historians, on the grounds that it is impossible to obtain crucial documents and impossible to see recent events in perspective. It is more reasonable to regard it as a valid field of historical study with its own problems and its own methods; as one useful way, among others, of approaching the events and trends of the contemporary world. See also ORAL TRADITION. For further reading: G. Barraclough, *An Introduction to Contemporary History* (1965). P.B.

content word, see under WORD CLASS.

context. In ARCHAEOLOGY, a term frequently employed to define the exact location of an artifact or structure. A *closed context* is one in which the ASSOCIATION of artifacts is not likely to have been disturbed. A statement of the context of an object or feature involves an assessment of the STRATIGRAPHY of the site. See also PROVENANCE. B.C.

context-free and **context-sensitive** (or *context-dependent* or *context-restricted*). In GENERATIVE GRAMMAR, terms used to distinguish between rules which apply regardless of the grammatical context, and rules specifying grammatical conditions which limit their applicability. Grammars containing context-sensitive rules are called *context-sensitive grammars*. It is claimed that they provide more accurate and economical descriptions of sentence structure than do *context-free grammars*. D.C.

context of situation. In LINGUISTICS, a term applied by FIRTHIAN linguists to the non-linguistic environment of utterances. Meaning is seen as a complex of relations operating between linguistic features of utterances (e.g. sounds, words) and features of the social situation in which utterances occur (e.g. the occupation of the speaker, the number of listeners present). Contexts of situation are a means of specifying and classifying those situational features that are necessary in order to understand the full meaning of utterances. Firth, and the anthropologist Malinowski, made various suggestions for the analysis of relevant contextual categories, but there have been few detailed studies. (See PHATIC LANGUAGE.)

The term is also used, with a similar meaning, outside Firthian linguistics, though *situational context*, or just *context*, is more common. D.C.

context-sensitive, see under CONTEXT-FREE.

contextual definition. In general, a means of defining words or phrases by showing how they are used; definition by giving an example of use in context. This method is employed as a supplement or alternative to other kinds of definition; for example, it is often used when standard *lexical definitions* (providing synonymous or near-synonymous words or phrases) are inadequate or unavailable. In particular, the method is used to define the functional expressions of LOGIC. Contextual definition is sometimes called *implicit definition*. A.C.G.

contextual theologies. A collective name for a family of movements in contemporary THEOLOGY which attempt to construct theology in and through the particularities of their specific cultural context. Many theologians claim that theology has always reflected a specific cultural context but has failed to recognize it, and has, therefore, marginalized all those whose experience of the world is not represented in the supposedly universal statements about 'human nature' and so on with which theology traditionally operates. The term 'liberation theologies' has often been used to describe theologies which, like LIBERATION THEOLOGY, BLACK THEOLOGY and FEMINIST THEOLOGY, identify themselves with the interests of a specific group of people, whose experience becomes the methodological basis of a new theological enterprise. In other theologies, including many African and Asian theologies, the context in which Christian IDENTITY is reconstructed is religiously pluralistic, with methodological consequences that warrant the use of a more inclusive term. For further reading: S. Bevans, *Models of Contextual Theology* (1992). C.C.

contextualism. A somewhat pompous architectural term developed in the 1980s to describe a well-developed and widely agreed belief that buildings and building developments should be in context with their settings. Contextualism goes beyond the small-scale visual arguments of TOWNSCAPE and seeks to embrace the cultural, social and historical context of a work of architecture. Because of the many possibilities of interpretation of existing contexts most claims for contextualism in individual designs have a rather *post hoc* ring. S.L.

contextuality. Whereas most social theories and SOCIAL SCIENCES seek to establish *logical* relationships between structural categories – such as person, CLASS, economy, politics and STATE – plucked somewhat arbitrarily from the hat of all possible categories, a number of voices are now beginning to argue that this compositional approach should be supplemented by a *contextual* approach sensitive to the essentially contingent relationships binding together diverse structural categories in specific times and specific places. This argument is perhaps best developed in GEOGRAPHY, a discipline that has always been centrally concerned with the ways in which all manner of natural and human phenomena interact to produce the unique 'character' of particular localities and regions (see REGIONALISM) – the hallmark of *regional geography* – and a discipline that is currently striving to produce a more theoretically informed account of why this project is so important. A wide variety of theoretical and substantive materials are being mobilized in the process, but of especial note is the difficult but illuminating fusion of what has become known as 'time-geography' with the complex 'structuration theory' developed by the sociologist Anthony Giddens. Although some commentators fear that this development is returning geography to a 'non-scientific' concern with uniqueness, and is thereby denying the claims of geography as SPATIAL SCIENCE, this is to miss the way in which a 'reconstructed' regional geography is deliberately seeking to synthesize long-standing geographical traditions with newer ideas – chiefly those introduced into the discipline by HUMANISTIC GEOGRAPHY and RADICAL GEOGRAPHY – that explicitly attack spatial science for employing a model of 'science' incapable of dealing adequately with either creative human agency or overarching economic and social structures, and incapable of dealing with the intricate interweaving of these different realities in particular temporal and spatial contexts. C.P.

continental drift. A theory originally suggested in the 17th century but only comprehensively stated by A. Wegener in 1911. Wegener based his theory very largely on the remarkably similar shape of the facing coastlines of Africa and South America and on close geological similarities between the two continents. He extended this evidence to propose that the earth, until some 200 million years ago, consisted of a single huge continent, which he called Pangea, surrounded by ocean. The present distribution of the continents had resulted from the breaking up of Pangea followed by a drifting apart of the continental masses. The theory required the continental segments of the crust to move freely through the mantle and oceanic crust. However, geophysical evidence indicated that the mantle and oceanic crust were stronger (more rigid) than the continental crust, and since there were no known forces of sufficient magnitude to move continents the theory lost support. Recently evidence of sea-floor spreading indicates that the continents have moved relative to one other as part of the thicker lithospheric plates (see LITHOSPHERE). Horizontally directed convection currents in the ASTHENOSPHERE dragging mantle material against the base of the plates are a plausible driving force. See also PLATE TECTONICS.

For further reading: J. Shea, *Continental Drift* (1985). J.L.M.L.

continentalism, see under ISOLATIONISM.

contingency.

(1) In PHILOSOPHY, the property of PROPOSITIONS or states of affairs which neither have to be true or obtain nor have to be false or not obtain. A contingent proposition may be true and may equally be false; the matter is contingent on factors external to the proposition itself. Likewise a contingent state of affairs may obtain but may equally not obtain. That there are four apples in this bowl is contingent; that there are four apples in a bowl containing two pairs of apples is necessary. A.Q.

(2) In THEOLOGY, the state of affairs in which each and every existing person or thing might not have existed, all creation being contingent or dependent on the will of the Creator. D.L.E.

contingency planning, see under FORECASTING.

continuing education, see ADULT EDUCATION.

continuous assessment. A mode of replacing formal examinations at the end of a year or a course by a running check on achievement throughout the course. This cumulative testing is seen as part of the current work, a cross-check and not a ritual ordeal; thus the distorting effect of examinations is thought to be removed from the curriculum and the student relieved of much anxiety. Critics of continuous assessment point to the element of strain present in perpetual judgement, and to the lack of an incentive which a final examination provides to sum up and reflect on the course as a whole. This criticism would not apply to a combination of continuous assessment and terminal examination. W.A.C.S.

continuous creation, see under STEADY-STATE HYPOTHESIS.

continuum.

(1) In PHYSICS, the SET of values of a quantity which can vary continuously. Thus, the points on a line form a one-dimensional continuum, and the points on a surface form a two-dimensional continuum. By contrast, the points on a crystal LATTICE, whose atomic positions vary discontinuously, do not form a continuum. M.V.B.

(2) In MATHEMATICS, the continuum is the set of real NUMBERS; other sorts of continuum have been characterized in TOPOLOGY. Cantor's *continuum hypothesis* is that the cardinal of the continuum is the least cardinal greater than aleph zero (see CARDINAL NUMBERS). This remains an open problem of SET THEORY; it can neither be proved nor disproved from the standard axioms. R.G.

contraception. The limitation of FERTILITY by a range of methods. One of the oldest methods of contraception, which also provides protection from SEXUALLY TRANSMITTED DISEASES, is the condom, a rubber sheath worn on the penis which prevents sperm from entering the vagina. The 'Dutch' cap was advocated by early pioneers of contraception such as Marie Stopes and Margaret Sanger. This is a rubber device worn by the woman which covers the entrance to the womb and prevents sperm from entering. This is often used in conjunction with a spermicidal cream. More recent developments have been the intra-uterine device (or IUD), which is semi-permanently implanted in the womb. Use of this form of contraception has declined following research which associates it with a range of side-effects, including cervical CANCER. From the late 1960s, a popular choice of contraceptive was 'the pill' – steroid hormones which inhibit ovulation. These too have recently fallen out of favour with many women as their use has been shown to be associated with unwanted side-effects. A miscarriage-inducing 'morning after' pill is currently in development, and a female condom reached the market towards the end of the 1990s.

Less reliable 'natural' methods of contraception include the 'rhythm method', advocated by the Catholic Church (which forbids the use of any other form of contraception), in which intercourse is restricted to a 'safe' period during the menstrual cycle when no ovum is present to be fertilized. *Coitus interruptus*, in which the male withdraws prior to ejaculation, is an ancient but unreliable method.

In the 1970s and 1980s Depo-Provera

(DMPA), an injectable progestogen, began to be employed by FAMILY PLANNING agencies in THIRD WORLD countries, despite the fact that most first world doctors reject it because of its side-effects. One of the most widely practised forms of contraception worldwide is STERILIZATION – the ultimate contraceptive. But sterilization can be coercive and is sometimes associated with covert eugenic population policies (see EUGENICS). For further reading: G. Greer, *Sex and Destiny* (1984). S.T.

contract. The basis of enforceable legal relations in England between those who make a bargain (see TORTS). Essential elements are an offer by one party, unequivocally accepted by the offeree, the mutual intention to enter into legal relations, and the provision by each of some valuable consideration, i.e. an act or forbearance, or the promise of some act or forbearance, in return for the other party's promise. Thus, in a sale of goods, the supply of the goods or the promise to supply them will be consideration for the promise to pay; and the promise to pay or actual payment is consideration for the promise to supply them. Alternatively a contract will be binding if made by way of deed under seal, even if there is no consideration. Mistakes or misrepresentations may vitiate a contract, as does fraud. Any failure to perform what is promised is a breach of contract which gives the injured party the right to bring legal proceedings for the recovery of damages, i.e. a financial award by the court based upon the loss suffered, or exceptionally for specific performance of the contract. For further reading: H. S. Fifoot and M. P. Furmston, *The Law of Contract* (1986). D.C.M.Y.

contract theory. The SOCIAL CONTRACT was used by innumerable political theorists of the 17th and 18th centuries to explain the origins of government and to justify the doctrine that governments had limited powers over their subjects. But Hobbes, Locke and Rousseau were accused by their critics of trying to explain the origins of government and its authority over us by a contract which nobody had ever signed, and which, anyway, would have bound nobody except its original signatories. A contract which was simultaneously non-existent and inadequate to its purpose naturally fell into philosophical disfavour. However, in recent years contract theory has seen a striking revival. In John Rawls's masterpiece *A Theory of Justice* (1971), the political and economic principles appropriate to a modern democratic state are derived from a 'hypothetical contract', that is to say, from reflection on the principles which rational, moderately self-interested individuals facing an uncertain future would have agreed to as the principles best suited to frame their political and economic affairs if they had made that agreement under conditions which prevented them from taking advantage of each other. Such an agreement would yield a government constrained by CONSTITUTIONALIST principles about the rule of law and individual civil rights, and an economic order devoted to the achievement of social justice. For further reading: M. Lessnoff, *Social Contract* (1986). A.R.

Contract with America. The name given to the innovative campaign document that helped Republicans led by Georgia Congressman Newt Gingrich gain control of the US House of Representatives in 1994, the biggest turnover of Congressional political power in 40 years. The 10-point plan, subsequently expanded to 15 sections, included WELFARE reform, tax cuts, ending Congressional exemption from certain laws, a balanced-budget amendment to the US Constitution, making it easier to use evidence in court against criminal defendants, expanding private-property rights, cutting government regulations, and other perennial conservative issues. Flush with victory, Gingrich proclaimed himself a 'transformational figure', and fawning news accounts portrayed him as a shadow President. But the success was short-lived. Stung by ETHICS charges, criticism over accepting a $4.5 million book advance from Rupert Murdoch, and negative public reaction to his pronouncements (such as suggesting Democratic permissiveness was to blame for the case of a woman who drowned her two sons in a South Carolina lake), Gingrich's star dimmed. R.K.H.

contraction hypothesis. A long-standing theory which attempts to explain the formation of major structures of the earth, such as mountain chains, by crustal shortening. A major prop for the theory is the observation that the earth is losing heat and may therefore be cooling and contracting overall. The most rapid rate of cooling and contraction is assumed to be in a zone a few hundred kilometres below the surface. The outer crust, which is assumed not to be cooling nor contracting to any extent, has therefore crumpled and thickened to fit a smaller surface area. The simplest picture of the crust in this condition would be the skin on a dried apple. Apart from the fact that it is not known whether the earth is cooling down or heating up (radiogenic heat is probably the principal source of heat within the earth), crustal shortening does not explain vertical displacement of rocks nor the major lateral movements of the crust (as part of the LITHOSPHERE) implied in PLATE TECTONICS theory. J.L.M.L.

Contras. Between 1981 and 1990 NICARAGUA was subject to attacks by the Contras, armed groups recruited and financed by the CIA whose aim was to overthrow the SANDINISTA National Liberation Front (FSLN) government and who pursued it by GUERRILLA warfare tactics of hit-and-run raids on civilian and military targets. Brutality was a feature of these attacks, which were carried out from within Honduras into Nicaragua's economically crucial northern coffee-growing regions, or from Costa Rica. The majority of the Contras – particularly within the command structure – were ex-Somocista National Guards, who were renowned for HUMAN RIGHTS abuses. The Contras failed to spark off an uprising against the FSLN and their limited popular support was confined to poor and isolated peasants in the north. Following the defeat of the FSLN in the 1990 elections, the Contras agreed to end their armed struggle. However, it has proved difficult to reintegrate them and former members of the Sandinista army into civil society, and it is estimated that some 33 armed units from both sides, consisting of some 500 fighters, are still active in the north of the country. For further reading: G. Prevost and H. E. Vanden (eds), *The Undermining of the Sandinista Revolution* (1997). M.A.P.

control engineering. The branch of ENGINEERING that deals with the adjustment of apparatus and SYSTEMS, whether or not a human operator is involved. It therefore embraces the subject of AUTOMATION and is concerned with closed-loop systems of control. The detection of an error, and the use of this information to correct the error, is often termed a FEEDBACK system. It involves the use of measuring instruments (detectors), amplifiers and power units. Control engineering, which began experimentally, developed fairly rapidly into a mathematical discipline whose theoretical aspects are closely allied to those of computing. E.R.L.

control group. In scientific research, a group of subjects matched as evenly as possible with a second group (the *experimental group*), and submitted to the same test but without prior exposure to the factor – practice, fatigue, DRUGS or whatever – whose effects are under investigation. If the groups perform differently, the difference (the *dependent variable*) is presumed to be due to that factor (the *independent variable*). Ideally, those conducting the test and analysing the results should be unaware of which subjects are in which group. J.S.B.

control theory, see under CONTROL ENGINEERING; CYBERNETICS.

conurbation. In GEOGRAPHY, a single, continuous urban region formed by the coalescence of two or more previously separate urban centres. A conurbation normally extends across several administrative divisions. The term was first used by Patrick Geddes and C. B. Fawcett in the first quarter of the 20th century in describing English city regions, and officially incorporated into the British census in 1951. P.H.

conventional war, see under WAR.

conventionalism.

(1) In the theory of MEANING, the doctrine that all the truths of LOGIC and MATHEMATICS, traditionally thought to be necessary and A PRIORI, are merely the products of freely chosen LINGUISTIC convention and only justifiable, if at all, on purely pragmatic grounds (see PRAGMATISM). One strength of the doctrine is that it can accommodate the manifest plurality of logico-mathematical systems – for instance, the various forms of non-Euclidean GEOMETRY

and the various non-classical systems of propositional logic. It can also explain our knowledge of logical and mathematical truths without appeal to mysterious powers of *a priori* intuition. However, thoroughgoing conventionalism has now largely fallen out of favour, because it appears to be self-defeating. Clearly, not every logico-mathematical truth can be the individual product of linguistic convention, not least because there are infinitely many such truths. At most it can be held that certain basic principles of logic and mathematics are established by convention and that all other logico-mathematical truths follow from these principles. But then we have to ask in virtue of what these other truths follow from the principles. That they do so cannot itself be a matter of convention. Hence it must be conceded that not the whole of logic can be the product of convention. E.J.L.

(2) The theory that, since the meaning of linguistic expressions is assigned to them by convention, analytic propositions (see ANALYTIC; PROPOSITIONS) owe their TRUTH to the conventions of language. A.Q.

convergence.
(1) The view, developed especially by several Western sociologists in the 1950s and 1960s, that whatever their origins, IDEOLOGIES or historical traditions, all industrial societies will eventually converge on a common pattern of political, economic and cultural institutions. The 'logic of industrialism', it is held, compels all modern societies to adopt certain 'core' practices as functional requirements of an industrial system. These include the specialized DIVISION OF LABOUR, industrial work discipline, co-ordinated planning and management, relatively free labour mobility, and relatively high levels of education and WELFARE. Although largely based on Western experience, convergence theories predict important developments in both CAPITALIST and COMMUNIST countries. Capitalist societies will increasingly be marked by significant areas of STATE enterprise and planning, while for their part communist societies will be increasingly forced to relax state direction and to allow in particular a significant degree of managerial autonomy in the industrial sector. In this fine disregard for formal ideological differences, and in their emphasis on the technical requirements of industrial societies, the original convergence theorists were evidently in tune with those who proclaimed 'the end of ideology'.

The theory has been overtaken by events with the collapse of communism in the former Soviet Union (see USSR, THE FORMER) and eastern Europe. For further reading: C. Kerr *et al*, *Industrialism and Industrial Man* (1973). K.K.; M.D.H.

(2) Arguably a defining feature of modernity is the accelerated pace of GLOBALIZATION. Within the media, COMMUNICATIONS and cultural industries, this has resulted in a further concentration or convergence of ownership to the point where a handful of MULTINATIONAL COMPANIES own and control large tranches of the operations which make up this sector, from newspaper publishing and running leisure complexes to film-making and broadcasting. The flow of cultural artifacts produced around the globe emanates mostly from Western countries, where most of these conglomerates are based – particularly from the USA – to the rest of the world. In tandem with this development is increased technological convergence, which many predict will be advanced by the further development of digital technology and the INTERNET and the consequent possibility of a global information exchange. Digital terrestrial television, e.g., has the capacity to provide hundreds of channels to viewers. With the development of an effective interface between broadcasting, computers and information technology, the television set has the potential to become a very sophisticated, multi-functional piece of communicative hardware enabling its users not only to send and receive messages pertinent to many more areas of their everyday lives, but also to increasingly participate in communicative activities on an international scale, to take part in what Al Gore has described as a 'global conversation', and some would argue to fulfil Marshall McLuhan's prophecy of a global village. The debate about whether these trends will also result in transcultural convergence is both complex and lively, and can be seen as a continuation of that surrounding the thesis of cultural IMPERIALISM. For further reading: J. Lull, *Media Communication, Culture: A Global Approach* (1995). A.P.HI.

(3) In MATHEMATICS, convergence forms a large part of ANALYSIS. The sequence of

NUMBERS ½, ¾, ⅞, 15⁄16, . . . has the property that, once you are well down the sequence, you are extremely close to 1. We say that the sequence converges (or tends) to 1, or has the limit 1. The words 'well down' and 'extremely close' need careful definition: this was undertaken by Weierstrass (in his δ,ε method) and, more recently, topological ideas have been used (see TOPOLOGY).

Convergence is basic to finding derivatives (see CALCULUS), and also to INFINITE series: consider the infinite series ½ + ¼ + ⅛ + 1⁄16 + . . . As we add more and more terms we get the sequence ½, ¾, ⅞, 15⁄16, . . . which tends to 1. So we say that the series converges to 1. Early mathematicians (see MATHEMATICS) believed that, for a series to converge, it is enough for the terms to become small, but the sum of 1 + ½ + ⅓ + ¼ + . . . grows without limit. They also played around with them freely, like finite sums, but certain facts induced caution: it is possible to rearrange the terms of 1 + (–½) + ⅓ + (–¼) +. . . so that it converges to any limit you care to name. N.A.R.

convergence criteria. The tough conditions required to be met by EUROPEAN UNION (EU) members if their currencies are to qualify for EMU (see SINGLE CURRENCY). The convergence of levels of NATIONAL DEBT, annual budget deficits, central banking systems, rates of price INFLATION and national EXCHANGE RATES is crucial if there is to be a durable single currency, recognized by the foreign exchange markets as a 'hard' currency more akin to the German mark than the Italian lira. Since the criteria were first spelled out at MAASTRICHT there has been remarkable progress among all EU members in moving towards qualification, with some of the most profligate governments, such as that of Greece, ratcheting down budget deficits. For the single currency to have any credibility the two largest economies of Europe, Germany and France, will have to be involved, and this has meant squeezing the public finances in both cases. The Benelux countries also will qualify along with Ireland. The position of the Club Med countries of Italy, Spain and Portugal is seen as more tenuous. Critics of the convergence criteria argue than they are too financial in their structure and need to take note of conditions in the real economy like UNEMPLOYMENT. A.BR.

convergers ***and divergers*****.** Two contrasted PERSONALITY TYPES postulated by Liam Hudson, who had observed two distinct patterns of intellectual style within a group of ably working children. *Convergers* are those who do better at conventional intelligence tests; *divergers* are those who do better at open-ended tests, without fixed limits or single correct responses. The distinction is a measure of bias, not of level of ability. Hudson suggests that students of the physical sciences are on the whole convergers, while students of arts subjects are divergers. See also INTELLIGENCE; VERTICAL AND LATERAL THINKING. For further reading: L. Hudson, *Contrary Imaginations* (1966). M.BE.

conversation analysis. In LINGUISTICS and associated fields, a method of studying the structure and coherence of conversations, usually employing the techniques of ETHNOMETHODOLOGY. The approach studies recordings of real conversations, to establish what properties are used in a systematic way when people interact using language. It is basically an empirical, inductive study, which is often seen in contrast with the deductive procedures characteristic of DISCOURSE analysis. D.C.

conversion. In psychoanalytic theory (see PSYCHOANALYSIS), the translation of repressed material into overt symptomatic behaviour, frequently in the form of *conversion hysteria*, a nervous disorder characterized by memory lapse, hallucination and loss of control of various sensory and motor processes. W.Z.

convertibility, see under BILATERALISM AND MULTILATERALISM.

cool. In JAZZ, both a code of behaviour and a musical style that appeared in the late 1940s. The style was specifically launched with records made by a band led by Miles Davis, which featured a controlled, aloof, rather pastel sound instead of the daring impetuosity of BEBOP or the hearty extroversion of SWING and the earlier styles. As a mode of personal and musical conduct, cool superseded HOT as the attitude most appropriate to jazz, signifying artistic *savoir-faire* and a certain ironic detachment instead of old-fashioned attempts to engage the public.

The forefather of cool might well be considered to be Lester Young, whose light, lithe tenor saxophone sound and arch, slightly otherworldly demeanour were imitated by scores of musicians. This was especially true on the West Coast of America, which became synonymous with cool jazz in the early 1950s, while bebop smouldered in the east. GE.S.

co-operative principle. In LINGUISTICS, a notion, derived from the philosopher H. P. Grice, which is often used as part of the study of the structure of conversation. The principle states that speakers try to co-operate with each other when communicating – more specifically, that they will attempt to be informative, truthful, relevant and clear (see MAXIMS OF CONVERSATION). Listeners will normally assume that a speaker is following these criteria. It is of course possible to break these maxims (in lying, sarcasm, etc.), but conversation proceeds on the assumption that speakers do not generally do so. For further reading: S. Levinson, *Pragmatics* (1983). D.C.

co-operatives. Voluntary associations created for mutual economic assistance. They are owned and run by their members, who are workers and/or customers, rather than investors. In most co-operatives, the members receive a share of the net earnings. The co-operative movement grew from the 19th-century ideas of Robert Owen in Britain and Charles Fourier in France. Co-operatives have been set up all over the world and include farming co-operatives (for selling, MARKETING, processing and purchasing), wholesale co-operatives, mutual insurance companies, credit and banking co-operatives, shops and health schemes. For further reading: A. Clayre, *The Political Economy of Co-operatives and Participation* (1980). D.E.; J.P.

co-partnership, see under PROFIT-SHARING.

Copenhagen interpretation. An interpretation of the theory of QUANTUM MECHANICS developed by the Danish physicist Niels Bohr (1885–1962) in the 1920s, sometimes called the Bohr interpretation. It arises from the fact that quantum mechanical experiments contradict the expectations of naïve REALISM. It ascribes reality only to observed phenomena, and these phenomena are viewed as being partially created by the act of measurement. Crucial to this view is Bohr's notion of complementarity (see COMPLEMENTARITY PRINCIPLE). Complementary variables cannot be measured simultaneously with complete accuracy. Position and momentum are complementary variables as are time and ENERGY. Bohr argued that quantum mechanical uncertainty is not just a failure to be able to measure complementary quantities with high accuracy. The complementary aspects cannot exist simultaneously in the quantum world except as an approximation. The Copenhagen interpretation maintains that QUANTUM THEORY does not describe the measurement process. The measurement process is described by an instantaneous collapse of the quantum WAVE FUNCTION. This is the interpretation of quantum mechanics usually adopted by applied scientists. For further reading: J. A. Wheeler and W. Zurek (eds), *Quantum Theory and Measurement* (1983). J.D.B.

copyright. An intellectual property right providing protection for the physical manifestation of intellectual endeavour. Copyright is 'a right to stop others from doing something, not a positive right to do it oneself' (Laddie, Prescott and Vitoria, *Modern Law of Copyright and Designs*, 1995). It does not protect 'ideas' but their physical manifestations; literary, dramatic and musical works must be recorded in writing or in some other form before they are capable of protection. Given that it is an intellectual property right, the owner, through having the right to stop others copying the work, can accordingly authorize its use for economic gain. Although the protection afforded by copyright is governed by the laws of the author's country or state, international treaties have extended the protection to most parts of the world. Copyright laws have had to adapt to meet technological advances, and cover not only traditional literary, musical and artistic works (including ARCHITECTURE and sculpture), but also sound recordings, films, computer programs, broadcasts and cable programmes. In some countries (including the greater part of Europe) the original authors of the copyright works have 'moral rights' (*droit moral*), which cannot be transferred, and enable authors to exercise negative controls even though they have assigned their rights and no longer have any economic interests in the copyright work. M.J.

core (of an economy). A concept used to describe certain distributions of goods and services within an economy. There are countless ways to distribute goods and services between members of a large society, but a given distribution will be in the core if no group of people can trade between themselves to make each of them better off. If, however, the distribution is such that there are people who would – if given the chance – still trade between themselves to their mutual benefit, then it will not be in the core. Distributions which are not in the core are economically inefficient, since there will be unfulfilled possibilities for trade. Command economies tend to be so rigid that not all trading possibilities are exhausted. But even the most unregulated FREE MARKETS may not lead to a core distribution – there are many possible MARKET FAILURES, e.g. MONOPOLIES, ECONOMIES OF SCALE and CARTELS. The concept of the core was first used in GAME THEORY. For further reading: E. R. Weintraub, *General Equilibrium* (1975). J.A.M.; J.P.; A.A.L.

core (of the earth), see under ASTHENOSPHERE.

core area. Geographical term that refers to the heartland of a country. Politically, this is strongest territorial expression of a NATION-STATE, its power centre which contains the capital city. Historically, this is the region of richest national heritage, the greatest concentration of revered places, and the crucible within which society took root and expanded to dominate the nation-state. Demographically (see DEMOGRAPHY), this is the most densely populated part of a country. Economically, this is the most productive zone, the focus of the national transport and COMMUNICATIONS networks, the innovator that has traditionally led the country in the accumulation of national wealth. Examples include the Paris Basin in Europe, the Moscow region in Russia, the North China Plain around Beijing, and the Argentine Pampa surrounding Buenos Aires. P.O.M.

core curriculum. The subjects that form or should form the most essential part of a pupil's learning. At school, such a core might well comprise the mother tongue, a foreign language, MATHEMATICS, a science and the HUMANITIES. Clearly, there are permutations, and successive British governments have tried to lay down clearer definitions of a core. Thus, at primary level, the Three Rs and a science might form such a core, while more advanced syllabuses could be laid down at secondary level. Teachers, who have jealously guarded their autonomy for years, now fear that any directive from the centre on what should be taught will erode that freedom. In fact, the only two subjects on an English school's timetable by law are religious education and physical education. J.I.

core grammar. In recent GENERATIVE GRAMMAR, the set of principles which characterize all the basic trends in grammatical structure found in the world's languages. D.C.

core values, see under PARSONIAN.

corporal punishment. Physical punishment usually inflicted by a cane, a slipper, a tawse (Scotland) or a paddle (US). In 1986 the UK became the last country in Europe (and one of the last in the world) to outlaw corporal punishment from schools thanks to a decision by the House of Lords to amend a Conservative government's Education Bill to this effect. A ruling in the EUROPEAN COURT OF HUMAN RIGHTS a year earlier had implied that parents ought to have the choice of whether their child should or should not be physically punished. This was considered highly confusing since schools would need to differentiate between the two kinds of children. At one stage consideration was given to allotting pupils labels of the 'you may – or may not – cane me' variety. Until the change in law (which does not affect independent schools) the teacher, who is considered *in loco parentis*, was able to administer corporal punishment of the kind that a caring parent might also give. Each punishment had to be entered in a book, kept by the head teacher or school secretary, containing the name of the child concerned, the reason for and date of punishment, and the number of strokes applied. J.I.

corporate crime. 'Crime' committed by or on behalf of a legal corporation in pursuit of its interests (hence distinct from WHITE COLLAR CRIME). In practice, the term is used even where there has been no actual or proven violation of criminal law (CRIME), but where financial, social, moral or other harms have been the consequences of corporate misconduct. Competitors, investors, consumers, the wider general public or the environment may be victims (VICTIMOLOGY), but not the corporation itself. Wilful intent or negligence may account for corporate crime (e.g. illegal price-fixing or health and safety violations), but assigning responsibility and prosecuting individual representatives of corporations or 'corporations as legal bodies' are difficult. Even where corporations have been officially censured for misdeeds, ensuring future compliance with regulations and law remains problematic. N.S.

corporate state. A STATE based on the theory that the political community is composed of numerous economic and other functional groups whose importance in the life of the state and the individual is so overwhelming that they, rather than localities or individual suffrage, should form the basis of political representation. Theoretically, the doctrine looks back to medieval 'estates' and 'guilds' for a model of corporate representation. In practice the doctrine of the corporate state has been tainted by its association with FASCISM, although fascist practice rendered all institutions powerless in the process of transferring all power to the party and its leader. For all that, many writers have claimed that the modern industrial state must *de facto* be a corporate state to govern effectively; a state which fails to incorporate business organizations and organized labour is doomed to impotence because it will be unable to manage the modern economy without acceptance of its policies on pay, prices, investment and public services by these groups. Those who remain hostile to corporatism point out that corporate representation leaves the unincorporated unrepresented, and that these characteristically include the weakest and most vulnerable members of society. For further reading: K. Middlemas, *Politics in an Industrial Society* (1979). D.C.W.; A.R.

corporate strategy. The statement of the long-term objectives of a company and the plans which allow these objectives to be achieved. The development of corporate strategies involves the identification of these objectives and the evaluation of alternative strategies. Corporate strategies emphasize the overall objectives of the company, though this necessarily involves consideration of all of the activities of the organization, e.g. production, finance, sales and research. R.I.T.; J.P.

corporate welfare. A term acquiring some currency in the USA, referring to the irony by which the conventional WELFARE STATE, providing for individuals in need, is being weakened while a range of government supports for business corporations continues to grow at a huge cost to the taxpayer and, arguably, to an economy constrained by subsidized inefficiency. Forms of corporate welfare include direct subsidies to industrial and large agricultural producers, tax breaks which have in recent decades massively reduced the overall proportion of government revenues from corporations rather than individuals, and large research and development grants which bring questionable, but largely unquestioned, results. Critics suggest that the 1997 federal Budget agreement gave particularly extensive evidence of a close relationship between corporations' donations to election campaigns and their ability to obtain these and numerous other benefits. S.R.

corporatism (or **neo-corporatism).** A revival of the theory of the CORPORATE STATE, popular in the 1920s and 1930s. Developments in the 1960s and 1970s in all Western societies suggested that public decision-making was increasingly becoming a tripartite affair of bargaining between the STATE, employers' associations and TRADE UNIONS. Corporate bodies, representing functional interests, were being incorporated in the machinery of state, complementing and to some extent replacing formally representative bodies such as parliament. In return for a share in the making of political decisions, the non-state organizations were expected to be able to discipline their members and to 'deliver' them in support of the agreed policies.

During the 1970s, British governments of

different parties set great store by the SOCIAL CONTRACT with the trade unions. The evident failure of such a strategy, due largely to the inability of the Trades Union Council to control its member unions – and of individual unions to control their own members – led to its rejection by most parties by the end of the decade. But corporatism has continued to be pursued with considerable success in the Scandinavian countries, notably Sweden, and is still strong in Germany and Austria. Some thinkers believe it is the natural form of political rule in complex INDUSTRIAL SOCIETIES, given the insufficiency of the system of representative DEMOCRACY, especially where technical matters of economic management are concerned. They believe that, despite set-backs, corporatism must sooner or later be fully institutionalized. For further reading: T. Smith, *The Politics of the Corporate Economy* (1979). K.K.

corpuscular theory. A theory in OPTICS in which light is treated as a stream of PARTICLES. Because of the great authority of Newton, the corpuscular theory survived until 1820, even though it could not account for wave effects such as DIFFRACTION. In the present century the theory has been partially revived because of the discovery that light is emitted and absorbed in discrete PHOTONS. See also WAVE-PARTICLE DUALITY. M.V.B.

corrasion. In GEOLOGY, a process of erosion in which the principal action is abrasion. Rock particles carried along by running water, wind or glaciers are rubbed against adjacent bedrock, and in doing so are themselves broken down into smaller particles. They are thus more easily carried away. The bed of a river is partly worn away by corrasive action, and potholes are developed in the solid rock of the bed by pebbles and boulders swirling around in eddy currents. The sea erodes the shore and cliffs of the coast in part by this process: waves pick up pebbles and sand from the beach, batter the cliffs, and wash backwards and forwards across the shore. J.L.M.L.

correlation. In STATISTICS it is common to make two or more observations simultaneously, e.g. to measure both a man's height and his weight. If neither of these observations gives any information about the other they are *independent*. If (as with height and weight) they tend to increase or decrease together, they are *positively correlated*; if the tendency is for one to decrease as the other increases, they are *negatively correlated*. If changes in one variable are proportional (whether positively or negatively) to changes in the other (as with the lengths and breadths of leaves from a tree), the correlation is *linear*; otherwise (as with the leaves' lengths and areas) it is *non-linear*. The usual type of correlation coefficient measures linear correlation, and is often misused in circumstances where the dependence is non-linear. R.SI.

correspondence, see under TRUTH.

correspondence principle. Correspondence theory was formulated by Niels Bohr (1885–1962) to cope with a fundamental problem area within the philosophy of science (see SCIENCE, PHILOSOPHY OF), revealed by the development of quantum physics. The correspondence principle postulated that, within problematic areas of science such as those addressed by QUANTUM THEORY, the behaviour of micro-particles (e.g., atoms) should be seen as that predicted by the laws of classical PHYSICS, in so far as that was intelligible. In other words, wherever possible, the explanations offered by new scientific theories (such as quantum theory) should be congruent with the expectations of traditional theories (e.g. NEWTONIAN MECHANICS). The principle thus stressed the relative continuities of a sequence of scientific theories (contrast Kuhn's later notion that science advances by a succession of 'revolutions'), and also provided *ad hoc* support for quantum theory, by allowing it to explain a particular range of phenomena, while invoking classical mechanics to account for others. For further reading: K. Hannabuss, *An Introduction to Quantum Theory* (1997). R.P.

cosmic background radiation. According to the BIG BANG THEORY, the first ten-thousandth of the universe's history was dominated by RADIATION. Because of the EXPANSION OF THE UNIVERSE, this primordial BLACK-BODY RADIATION should by now have cooled to a pale remnant, in the form of MICROWAVES, with a temperature a few degrees above ABSOLUTE ZERO. Its observation in 1965 by A. A. Penzias and R. W. Wilson has, more than anything else, contributed to the wide acceptance of the big-bang hypothesis among cosmologists. M.V.B.

cosmic radio waves, see under INVISIBLE ASTRONOMY.

cosmic rays. Very fast PARTICLES (mainly PROTONS) arriving from space from largely unknown sources. Collisions between particles and ATOMS in the upper atmosphere produce cosmic ray showers made up of a variety of ELEMENTARY PARTICLES, which are detected at ground level by devices such as geiger counters. M.V.B.

cosmogony. Any scientific theory, religious doctrine or MYTH about the origins of the universe (particularly the heavenly bodies). In the West the most famous cosmogony is that presented in Genesis at the beginning of the Old Testament, but this is generally regarded even by religious believers as needing to be DEMYTHOLOGIZED. Currently, the BIG BANG THEORY, based on the discovery of the COSMIC BACKGROUND RADIATION, is widely accepted. See also COSMOLOGY; THEISM. For further reading: J. D. North, *The Measure of the Universe* (1990). D.L.E.; M.V.B.

cosmological constant. A new constant of nature introduced by Einstein in 1916 in order to obtain a MODEL of the universe which was static rather than in a state of expansion or contraction. Einstein later referred to its introduction as the 'biggest blunder of my life'. Subsequently it was found that there existed expanding universe models with a cosmological constant included. The effect of the cosmological constant upon the Newtonian inverse-square law of GRAVITATION is to add to it another force directly proportional to distance.

Of all the physical quantities that can be measured or constrained by measurement, none is restricted to be so close to zero as the cosmological constant. For this reason many cosmologists believe that it is probably exactly equal to zero for some fundamental but as yet unknown reason. The ANTHROPIC PRINCIPLE requires that its value be very small. Since 1981 interest in the cosmological constant has grown with the discovery that in the first moments following the Big Bang (see BIG BANG THEORY) it was possible for matter and RADIATION to behave under the influence of gravity so as to cause the universe to expand for a brief period in the way that it would if there existed a cosmological constant. This type of induced temporary effect is termed an *effective cosmological constant*, and would be responsible for the period of accelerated expansion INFLATION which has been suggested as a resolution of a variety of problems concerning the structure of the universe. In recent years it has become conventional to interpret the cosmological constant as a form of matter with a particular relation between pressure and density rather than as a new constant of gravitation. (The ratio of the pressure and the density of this matter field is equal to minus the square of the velocity of light.) The stress exerted by this type of matter has the unique property of looking the same to all observers no matter how they are in relevant motion. For this reason the cosmological constant has been interpreted as representing the lowest energy state, or vacuum state/energy, of the universe. For further reading: J. D. Barrow and J. Silk, *The Left Hand of Creation: The Origin and Evolution of the Expanding Universe* (1983). J.D.B.

cosmology. The study of the structure and evolution of the universe as a whole or that part of it which is observable in principle (sometimes called the 'observable universe' or the 'visible universe'). The modern study of cosmology is based upon the discovery by Edwin Hubble in 1929 that the universe is expanding. Observations of heat radiation and the products of nuclear reactions throughout the universe demonstrate that the universe was once billions of times hotter than it is today. This picture of a universe expanding from a hot, dense past of high temperature is called the BIG BANG THEORY (a description first coined by Fred Hoyle in 1950). The study of cosmology is concerned with reconstructing the past history of the universe, explaining why GALAXIES exist and why they cluster in the patterns observed, explaining the age, the shape and the expansion rate of the universe by using Einstein's theory of gravitation (general RELATIVITY) and other physical theories.

For further reading: J. D. Barrow, *The Origin of the Universe* (1994). J.D.B.

cosmopolitanism. Soviet term first used by *Pravda* in 1949 in denigration of a few pro-Western theatre critics and extended during the ZHDANOVSHCHINA to mean any reflection of Western influences in, or application of international standards in criticism of, the Soviet arts (see USSR, THE FORMER). Regarded, like FORMALISM, as an offence against the official SOCIALIST REALIST canon, cosmopolitanism became difficult to disentangle from its overtones of ANTISEMITISM. For further reading: H. Swayze, *Political Control of Literature in the USSR, 1949–1959* (1962). J.W.

cost benefit analysis (CBA). A means of setting out the social costs and benefits of an investment project and evaluating whether or not the project should be undertaken. The analysis first quantifies the inputs used in the project and the effects of the project; in many cases, this is a difficult task. For example, a new motorway will require resources to build it, will have effects on the ENVIRONMENT, alter travelling times, and will have an effect on the pattern of the economy. Secondly, the different aspects of the project have to be valued in a common unit: MONEY. It is often very difficult, if not impossible, to value certain effects, e.g. loss of life. These valuations can sometimes be obtained from markets, e.g. how much people are willing to pay to reduce the probability of death. These monetary values are then discounted appropriately (see DISCOUNTING). Finally, the difference of the suitably discounted social benefits and costs of the project, i.e. the net present value (see DISCOUNTED CASH FLOW), is calculated. That set of INVESTMENTS which gives the highest total net present value should be proceeded with. This implies that certain investments with positive and high net present values may not be recommended. This can occur because such investments preclude other investments with a higher net present value or because investment funds may be limited. Cost benefit analysis is rarely used as the sole basis on which to make a decision. Political considerations are not included in the analysis and it is difficult to allow for changes in the distribution of income. The valuations of the social costs and benefits are often only poor estimates and the net present values may vary crucially with different valuations, in particular when different discount rates are used.

Cost benefit analysis differs from financial appraisal, as social cost and benefits are estimated, rather than the costs and benefits affecting an individual firm or person. It differs from cost-effectiveness in that the latter considers the most efficient means of achieving a particular objective. For further reading: R. Sugden and A. Williams, *The Principles of Practical Cost Benefit Analysis* (1978). J.P.

cost-push, see under INFLATION.

Council for Mutual Economic Assistance, see COMECON.

Council of Europe. An organization set up on 5 May 1949 by a statute signed by representatives of Britain, France, Belgium, the Netherlands, Luxembourg, Denmark, Eire, Italy, Norway and Sweden. Six other states (including West Germany) joined later. The Council consists of (1) a Committee of Ministers and (2) a Consultative Assembly, with a permanent secretariat meeting at Strasbourg. To these was added a EUROPEAN COURT OF HUMAN RIGHTS. Opposition on the part of governments, notably the British, drastically limited the powers of the Council, but the meetings of the Assembly have provided a forum for public discussion of matters of common interest. The Council is organizationally separate from the institutions of the EUROPEAN UNION (EU). D.C.W.

Council of Ministers, see under EUROPEAN UNION.

counter-culture, see under UNDERGROUND.

counterfactual (or **counterfactual statement** or **counterfactual proposition).** A statement concerned with a hypothetical event, process or state of affairs that runs counter to the facts, i.e. has not occurred or does not exist. A *counterfactual conditional* (statement) says what would have happened if something had been the case, e.g. 'If the American Civil War had been averted, the South would have abolished Negro slavery in an orderly fashion within one generation.'

A *counterfactual question* asks what would have happened in some state of affairs known not to exist, e.g. 'If the American Civil War had not occurred, would slavery have persisted for the rest of the century?' There are considerable difficulties in clarifying the procedures appropriate for testing such assertions or answering such questions, especially when the counterfactual assumptions depart far from reality, or when the connection between the assumptions and the question or alleged consequent is remote, as in 'If people had wings all nations would be more prosperous'. Counterfactuals are widely employed by practitioners of econometric history (see ECONOMIC HISTORY). Opponents of the method claim that counterfactuals are not history and cannot be verified (see VERIFICATION). Supporters reply that all historical judgements involve implicit counterfactuals and that they can be tested indirectly. A.S.; P.B.

counter-force capability, see under STRATEGIC CAPABILITY.

countertransference. In PSYCHOANALYSIS, a term used to refer to the analyst's UNCONSCIOUS emotional response to the patient. Freud regarded this as an aspect of the analyst's own NEUROSIS, interfering with the analytic work by distorting the analyst's response to the patient's transference. In KLEINIAN psychoanalysis, however, countertransference has become central to the therapeutic process. Here, the unconscious response of the analyst to the patient's PROJECTIONS is a guide to the patient's emotional state. Through reflection on his or her countertransference responses, the analyst becomes attuned to the patient's needs, expressed in the moment-to-moment shifts in quality of the analytic interaction. This MODEL of countertransference, taken from an image of the mother as capable of reflection on her infant's unconscious feelings, has increased the tendency of contemporary psychoanalysis to be intersubjective and focused on the workings of the unconscious in the 'here-and-now' (see INTERSUBJECTIVITY; SUBJECTIVITY). S.J.F.

countervailing power. A term used to describe the forces which generally arise in MIXED ECONOMIES to counterbalance the bargaining power of large buyers and sellers. A class example of countervailing power in the US economy, for instance, is the large labour unions which, by their influence on the wages that the great corporations must pay, partially counterbalance the monopolistic power (see MONOPOLY) of big business. Similarly, the large retail chains, by their influence on the purchasing policies of major manufacturing companies, partly dictate the price the manufacturer receives. Critics of the theory claim its influence on OLIGOPOLIES is marginal. For further reading: J. K. Galbraith, *American Capitalism: the Concept of Countervailing Power* (1952). D.E.

country and western, see under FOLK MUSIC.

***Coup de Prague*,** see under PRAGUE (2).

Court of Justice of the European Communities. Set up under Article 4 of the Treaty of Rome establishing the European Economic Community (see EUROPEAN UNION) in 1957. It has assumed all the functions of the Court of Justice of the European Coal and Steel Community, which had existed since 1952. The court, which sits in Luxembourg, serves all three European Communities (the European Coal and Steel Community, the European Economic Community, and the European Atomic Energy Community).

The court consists of ten judges appointed for terms of six years by member STATES acting in common agreement. The court has several types of competence regarding the interpretation and application of the treaties establishing the three communities. First, it may hear appeals for annulment of decisions taken by the executive organs of the communities. The right to challenge the legality of those decisions is open to the member states, to the executive organs of each community and, to some extent, to people or companies. Secondly, the court has general jurisdiction to hear appeals against sanctions and penalties ordered by the executive organs. In such cases the aggrieved state or individual could petition the court for a JUDICIAL REVIEW of the order in question. In addition to this, proceedings may be initiated with a view to enforcing the contractual and non-contractual liability of the community. Thirdly, the court has administrative jurisdiction to hear appeals by staff members against decisions of the administration of the three communities. Fourthly, the competence of the court extends to preliminary questions raised before municipal tribunals. Fifthly, appeals may be lodged against a member state by an organ of the community or by other member states when breach of obligations is alleged. Although there is no effective means of enforcing judgements of the courts against states, judgements against natural or artificial persons are enforceable by the municipal courts through their normal judicial processes. For further reading: P. Mathijsen, *A Guide to European Community Law* (1985). O.Y.E.

covering law theory. A theory about the logical character (see LOGIC) of the EXPLANATION of singular events or states of affairs. It holds that in order to explain an event (e.g. the breaking of a string) the statement reporting it must be deduced from a description of the *initial conditions* ('this string was loaded with a 10-lb weight') together with a PROPOSITION or law ('the breaking-point of this type of string is 6lb'). Although it is widely regarded as an adequate account of explanation in the NATURAL SCIENCES, its application to HISTORY has been much contested. Its opponents argue that there are no universal historical laws, that human actions are explained by reference to motives, and that these are not causes; they insist (to use the language of the entry on EXPLANATION) that *purposive explanation* is not a special case of *deductive explanation* in the way that *causal explanation* is commonly held to be. A.Q.

creation/creationism.

(1) The word may be held to imply the more or less literal acceptance of the stories of the origins of the world and of mankind recorded in the first two chapters of Genesis in the Hebrew scriptures inherited also by Christians. 'Creationism' of this kind remains fairly strong in the US. But the term is more commonly used by believers in God who reject FUNDAMENTALISM. It is often held that the really fundamental religious attitude is that God is the source, ground and goal of all that exists or is possible in the universe – which can now be truly described by modern sciences. Some support is lent to this degree of LIBERALISM in theology by the facts that two stories, of different origins and incompatible in some details, are given in Genesis, while other ancient Hebrew creation MYTHS are referred to in the Psalms and the Book of Job. Most scholars agree that Genesis was never intended as an account to rival scientific or other knowledge of nature. The term, being traditional, is also used as an alternative to 'nature' by people whose religious beliefs incline to AGNOSTICISM or ATHEISM. For further reading: H. Montefiore, *The Probability of God* (1985). D.L.E.

(2) Creationism is the theory that living species have separate origins, rather than having evolved from a common ancestor (see EVOLUTION). Creationism can take on secular forms, but always has religious inspiration; its source is the biblical book of Genesis, according to which the different species of living things were separately created by God. Scientific evidence points against the separate creation of species, but creationism is rejected by scientists more because it contradicts the scientific worldview, as it introduces a supernatural agency, than because of any evidence. Creationism is particularly promulgated by Southern fundamentalists in the US who have made various legal attempts to enforce the teaching of creationism alongside evolution in BIOLOGY lessons. It is thus as much a social movement as a 'scientific' theory. M.R.

creative destruction. Joseph Schumpeter's expression for the role of innovation in the CAPITALIST marketplace, coined in *Capitalism, Socialism and Democracy* (1942). For Schumpeter, the success of the automobile was due not to material necessity but to the entrepreneurship of Henry Ford, an inveterate risk-seeker confident in his ability to create new wants that would displace the demand for existing modes of transport. Schumpeter used the essential unpredictability of creative destruction to explain why capitalist economies combine long-term growth with boom-and-bust cycles. However, WELFARE STATE capitalism spells the end of creative destruction, as periodically disrupted markets come to be seen as unaffordable. Recently the idea has been revived by economic historians, who nevertheless miss the Schumpeterian irony that the ENTREPRENEUR is ultimately a victim of his own success. In its new guise, creative destruction is not an unusual personal quality but a periodically expressed property of the economic system, which unwittingly recalls Schumpeter's post-entrepreneurial view of innovation as carefully calculated state changes. S.F.

credentialism. The tendency in modern society to demand educational qualifications for every type and manner of work, whether or not the gaining of the qualification actually fits one for the work in question. A cognate term is 'the diploma disease'. Not only does this distort the educational system by forcing it to appear to have mainly a training function, it also disguises the extent to which the system, especially at the level of higher education, is a screen for perpetuating the privileges of the wealthier classes, who tend to possess the necessary CULTURAL CAPITAL for succeeding in the system. The educational system can then appear as a means for restricting access to the more highly paid and respected occupations, such as the professions. For further reading: R. P. Dore, *The Diploma Disease* (1976). K.K.

credibility. The degree to which factors associated with an undertaking create in the minds of others the expectation that it will be carried out if the contingency to which it is addressed should arise; failure to create such an expectation is sometimes known as a *credibility gap*. The term originated in American strategic analysis in the 1950s as a component of an effective strategy of DETERRENCE vis-à-vis the USSR and China in relation to the security of the territorial USA and to the American alliance commitments in Europe and Asia. It is accepted as having (a) a *quantitative* aspect – enough long-range nuclear weapons to inflict unacceptable damage upon a potential adversary; (b) a *technological aspect* – weapons accurate and dependable enough to achieve this purpose and invulnerable enough to prevent an adversary's first strike being a wholly disarming one; (c) a *political and social* aspect – the decision-making structure and the demonstrable national will to engage in a strategic conflict. To this was added another element as Soviet long-striking power grew in the 1950s and early 1960s, namely (d) *local defences*, especially in Europe, adequate to deter minor pressure or blackmail for which the USA (or any other guarantor power) was palpably unprepared to risk nuclear WAR.

The concept of credibility is of particular relevance to the stance of allies who do not themselves possess NUCLEAR WEAPONS. Hence the saying that 'it takes only 5 per cent of American nuclear weapons to deter the Russians, and the other 95 per cent to reassure the NATO allies'. The term is now used increasingly widely to assess political promises or undertakings of any kind. For further reading: T. C. Schelling, *Arms and Influence* (1966). A.F.B.

credit creation, see under MONEY CREATION.

creole. In SOCIOLINGUISTICS, a PIDGIN language which has become the mother tongue of a speech community, as in the case of Jamaica, Haiti and many other parts of the world. The process of development, in which the structural and stylistic range of the pidgin is expanded, is known as *creolization*. D.C.

Cretaceous-Tertiary boundary. The point in time and in the rock record at which the Cretaceous Period of the earth's geological history ended and the Tertiary Period began, about 65 million years ago (see GEOLOGICAL TIME CHART). The Cretaceous-Tertiary boundary is no different in principle from the boundary between any two other geological periods, but it has become the focus of considerable attention in recent years because it coincides in time with the demise of the dinosaurs and numerous other species, a MASS EXTINCTION event for which a revolutionary hypothesis has been proposed. In 1980 L. W. Alvarez and colleagues at the University of California suggested that the extinctions were the result of an impact upon the earth of an asteroid with a diameter of about 10 km. There is no question of the asteroid having hit the organisms directly on their collective heads; rather, the impacting body would have disintegrated and thrown up masses of dust, cutting out sunlight, impeding PHOTOSYNTHESIS, and producing breaks in vital FOOD CHAINS. The chief evidence for the impact comes from the abnormally high concentrations of the elements iridium and osmium in sediments at the Cretaceous-Tertiary boundary, a phenomenon that has since been confirmed at scores of sites around the world. The concentrations are significantly higher than those found generally in the earth's crust but are not uncharacteristic of meteorites, from which comparison Alvarez and his co-workers concluded that the extra iridium/osmium must indeed have come from extraterrestrial sources. However, there has since appeared a rival hypothesis that attributes the high levels of iridium/osmium to a particularly intense episode of explosive volcanism (see VOLCANOLOGY), possibly in India. Volcanoes raise material from the earth's mantle where the levels of iridium/osmium could well be as high as in extraterrestrial bodies. This issue will take some time to resolve, if indeed it is ever resolved. P.J.S.

crime. A crime may be formally defined, as in law, with emphasis upon an act as a 'fact'; or viewed as a behaviour or event to which a socially constructed category of criminality or negative label (LABELLING THEORY) has been applied. To have committed a crime usually means that some form of legal rule or PROHIBITION has been broken. In advanced societies, a legal definition will imply an accompanying system of criminal justice for the detection and control (POLICING), prosecution and PUNISHMENT of criminal offenders. Conscious intent (*mens rea*, literally 'guilty mind') is usually regarded as necessary for the attribution of criminal responsibility; where this is not evident (e.g. in the case of children or insanity) this must be taken into account. Less developed societies may have less well-defined criminal codes and less elaborate criminal justice systems; for tribal societies, social anthropologists (see ANTHROPOLOGY) have recorded the importance of RELIGION, RITUAL, WITCHCRAFT, sexual relationships and economic transactions among sources of definition of TABOOS, 'crime' and offending.

Not all crime is detected or reported. Furthermore, there will not always be universal agreement as to which behaviours and activities are legitimately definable as 'crime'. Who defines 'crime' and who becomes 'criminal' are questions at the heart of several fundamental debates within the SOCIOLOGY of deviance and CRIMINOLOGY. The definition of crime is also a highly relative matter, differing across cultures, periods of history and political contexts (e.g. consider US capitalism, USSR state COMMUNISM and Germany's National Socialism during the 1930s).

Awareness of the incidence of crime in society is socially constructed, dependent upon what enters into the frameworks of official and media reporting, and may seriously underestimate or neglect the incidence of various hidden crimes. These may occur in the home, e.g. domestic violence; or in the workplace (ORGANIZATIONAL CRIME). What some term 'crimes without victims' (e.g. involving drugs, prostitution, illegal gambling) are unlikely to be reported as they are consensual. In recent years, the use of crime surveys to provide information on hidden crimes, and more accurate reports on victimization rates (VICTIMOLOGY), have been a major development. For further reading: M. Maguire, R. Morgan and R. Reiner (eds), *The Oxford Handbook of Criminology* (1997). N.S.

crimes against humanity, see WAR CRIMES.

criminology. The study of CRIME and criminal behaviour. Relatedly: the prevention and deterrence of crime; treatment and PUNISHMENT of offenders (PENOLOGY); victimization and the experiences of victims (VICTIMOLOGY). Traditionally seen as rooted in classicism and positivism (as defined below). The former is associated with the work of Cesare Beccaria (1738–94), reflecting principles of 18th-century philosophy, viewing criminality and the administration of criminal justice as premised upon rationality, responsibility and deterrence. The latter emphasizes the physical, moral, genetic or psychological make-up of criminals. Its earliest statements are associated with Cesare Lombroso (*L'Uomo Delinquente*, 1876) and others of the 'Italian school' of positivism, who claimed a link between dispositions towards criminality and certain physical stigmata. Subsequent works and 20th-century neo-positivism have added acknowledgement of other factors (e.g. socialization, intelligence quotient) as determining influences, and remain influential.

The variety of perspectives within modern criminology is wide, primarily sociological but also embracing approaches from law, PSYCHOLOGY, ECONOMICS and other fields. The orthodoxy of neo-positivist (see POSITIVISM) criminology was challenged and the subject transformed by the impact of LABELLING THEORIES in the 1960s which stimulated a new field of the 'sociology of deviance'. From the early 1970s, various critical criminologies (neo-MARXIST, ABOLITIONIST and others) developed. Recently, both conservative and LEFT-social democratic commentators on crime have sought to influence policy-making through a 'realist' approach. Since the 1970s, FEMINISM has criticized the masculine bias in much criminological work as well as in areas of the criminal justice system. Influenced by the impact of POSTMODERNISM on the social sciences, some commentators now see criminology as 'fragmenting', increasingly merging with other disciplinary fields. Arguably, however, such developments will revitalize the subject. For further reading: M. Maguire, R. Morgan and R. Reiner (eds), *The Oxford Handbook of Criminology* (1997). N.S.

crisis management. Phrase coined after the Cuban missile crisis (see CUBA; MISSILES) of November 1962, by Robert McNamara, then US Secretary of Defense, who remarked: 'There is no longer any such thing as strategy, only crisis management.' The term implies a somewhat mechanistic view of the relations between states as a system which needs to be managed by its chief members so that crises in their relations with one another may be prevented from turning into courses which could only lead to mutual destruction. For further reading: C. Bell, *The Conventions of Crisis* (1971). D.C.W.

crisis theology. A movement in 20th-century Protestant THEOLOGY, precipitated by World War I and the failure of many liberal theologians to resist the militarism and IMPERIALISM which provoked it (see PROTESTANTISM). This 'crisis' focused Karl Barth's criticism of his theological predecessors (see BARTHIAN), but properly speaking it is his emphasis on GOD's judgement – in Greek, *krisis* – which gave the movement its name. This judgement was seen as a negation of all human attempts to know God (see NATURAL THEOLOGY), indeed of RELIGION itself, but simultaneously as an affirmation, and this kind of determination to maintain oppositions without resolution helps to explain the alternative name of the movement, 'dialectical theology'. By the end of the 1920s, the intellectual instability of this style of theology forced its exponents in different directions. Some, like Rudolf Bultmann, moved towards a more explicit existentialist theology; others, like Karl Barth himself, returned to dogmatic theology and initiated neo-orthodoxy. C.C.

criterion.

(1) Most generally, any standard by which somebody or something is judged.

(2) More specifically, a ground for judging that something is the case which is not a logically NECESSARY AND SUFFICIENT CONDITION of the truth of the judgement but is rather a thoroughly reliable contingent indication (see CONTINGENCY) of its truth; e.g. the height of the mercury in a thermometer is a criterion of the temperature of the environment. Criterion in this sense is contrasted with the defining characteristics which are, as a matter of LOGIC, the severally necessary and jointly sufficient conditions of its presence. Thus coherence has been said to be a criterion, but not a definition, of TRUTH.

(3) More specifically still, in the later PHILOSOPHY of Wittgenstein, a special sense is given to the term, according to which the connection between the criterion and what it indicates is logical but nevertheless incomplete, in that its satisfaction does not entail, nor its non-satisfaction logically preclude, the presence of what it indicates. In regarding *behaviour* as the criterion of inward feeling, Wittgenstein's interpreters take him to say that behaviour is, as a matter of logic, not-wholly-conclusive evidence for the judgement that the behaver is in a certain mental state. Wittgenstein's view is that sentences about mental events could have a publicly intelligible significance only if logically linked to what can be publicly observed. What differentiates his position from straightforward BEHAVIOURISM is that the logical linkage in question is one of CONFIRMATION, not entailment. For further reading: J. Pollock, *Knowledge and Justification* (1974). A.Q.

Criterion, The. A quarterly – for a brief period, monthly – review of art and letters edited from London by T. S. Eliot between

1922 and 1939. Its international importance is suggested by the fact that Volume 1 contained Eliot's 'The Waste Land', cantos by Pound, Valéry Larbaud on *Ulysses*, and contributions by Virginia Woolf, Paul Valéry, W. B. Yeats and E. M. Forster. Concerned with 'the autonomy and disinterestedness of literature', it carried such writers as Joyce, Lawrence, Proust, Gertrude Stein, Archibald MacLeish, Hart Crane and, in the 1930s, Auden, Spender, MacNeice, Empson, Allen Tate and Dylan Thomas. It maintained a 'classicist', and later a religious, NEO-THOMIST, position against the 'ROMANTICISM' of Middleton Murry's *Adelphi*. M.S.BR.

criterion referenced test (CRT). Test that measures the ability of a candidate against that of another. In other words, it enables the examiner to see whether the pupil/student has reached a required criterion. This differs from the principle often adopted in examinations, where the result reflects not so much the candidate's knowledge as his/her placing in a league table of grades. Thus, if, for argument's sake, all candidates manage to score over 90 per cent in an examination, those getting 90 to 92 per cent might well be placed in the 'fail' category while only those with more than 98 per cent, say, will receive Grade A. This would be known as a *norm referenced test* (NRT). With a CRT all the candidates would be considered of Grade A standard since they are likely to have reached (and surpassed) the given criterion. See also PSYCHOMETRICS. J.I.

critical ethnography, see under CRITICAL SOCIAL SCIENCE.

critical linguistics. An approach that aims to reveal hidden power relations and ideological processes (see IDEOLOGY) at work in speech or writing. For example, *critical discourse analysis* studies the relationship between discourse events and sociopolitical and cultural factors, especially the way discourse is ideologically influenced by and can itself influence power relations in society (see also DISCOURSE; DISCOURSE OF POWER). The subject emerged in the 1980s, reflecting some linguists' concern that mainstream linguistics was too preoccupied with formalist concerns, lacked adequate social explanations, and obscured ideological and political issues. It thus focused on the social contexts of texts (e.g. in ADVERTISING, journalism, news broadcasts, government statements), and raised previously neglected questions of language policy and planning. It has attracted some criticism from those who feel that the subject as currently expounded may be overly influenced by a LEFT-wing political agenda. For further reading: N. Fairclough (ed.), *Critical Language Awareness* (1992). D.C.

critical mass. The minimum quantity of radioactive material (see RADIOACTIVITY) which will enable a CHAIN REACTION to proceed by means of nuclear FISSION. Although the critical mass for the atomic bomb is not hard to estimate, its value was one of the 'secrets' of the COLD WAR. M.V.B.

critical path analysis. A NETWORK ANALYSIS technique whose main application is to provide optimally efficient scheduling of different phases of some complicated task. Suppose, for example, that a house is to be built by conventional methods. Certain phases – constructing foundations, building walls, fitting roof timbers, tiling – have a natural sequence, and the next cannot be started until the last is complete. Other phases – making joinery, inserting piping and wiring – fit into this scheme more flexibly, although not with complete freedom. It is usually not difficult to work out the time each phase will take, which phases must precede it, and which must follow it. Critical path analysis then provides a technique for scheduling the phases so as to complete the job as quickly as possible. When this scheduling is done it is found that some phases have the property that a small delay in them will cause changes in the schedule as a whole – these phases form the *critical path*. Other phases have a certain amount of slack, and it may be possible to take longer over them, e.g. by using a smaller work-force, without delaying completion of the job as a whole. R.SI.

critical period. In ETHOLOGY, a short period in the early life of organisms when they are susceptible to IMPRINTING or ATTACHMENT to another organism. J.S.B.

critical realism, see REALISM, CRITICAL.

critical social science. Any approach in social science which has a central concern with critically evaluating society for the purpose of improving it. It involves digging beneath the surface of social phenomena and questioning the assumptions on which common-sense knowledge of society is based. There is an emphasis on POWER, inequality, EXPLOITATION and oppression and a belief that PRAXIS should be linked to research. Critical social scientists (see SOCIAL SCIENCE) reject the idea that social scientists should pursue value-freedom and advocate understanding the social world from the perspective of the exploited. Critical ETHNOGRAPHY constructs descriptions of different SITES in the social world through researchers studying the lives of oppressed groups and working with them to understand their oppression. Varieties of critical social science include MARXISM, FEMINISM, anti-RACISM and ANTI-PSYCHIATRY. Critical social scientists are sometimes accused of producing research findings which simply reflect their ideologies (see IDEOLOGY), but there have been attempts in recent years to develop a convincing EPISTEMOLOGY for this approach based upon critical realism (see REALISM, CRITICAL). Critical social science is a broader term than CRITICAL THEORY and encompasses a much larger group of social scientists than the FRANKFURT SCHOOL. For further reading: L. Harvey, *Critical Social Research* (1990).

M.D.H.

critical sociology. A form of contemporary social theory inspired largely by the FRANKFURT SCHOOL. It opposes much traditional sociological theory, such as FUNCTIONALISM and PLURALISM, on the grounds that this is largely an apologia for existing institutions and practices in CAPITALIST societies. By contrast critical SOCIOLOGY sees its task largely as one of 'unmasking' – showing in particular the discrepancy between the formal values and goals of contemporary institutions and their actual practices. Thus the market is formally 'free', bureaucracy formally 'rational', and the political system formally 'democratic'. But in no case do any of these institutions truly live up to the promise of their formal principles. Critical sociology shares with MARXISM a concern for social change. But it does not pin its hopes on any particular agency, such as the PROLETARIAT. It retains rather a HEGELIAN belief in the critical power of thought *per se*. By constantly subverting society's self-regarding IDEOLOGIES, and repeatedly confronting it with the unpleasant truth about itself, it hopes to stimulate a critical awareness that might lead to the desire for change. For further reading: P. Connerton (ed.), *Critical Sociology* (1976). K.K.

critical states, see under SELF-ORGANIZED CRITICALITY.

critical theory. Broadly MARXIST-inspired approach to the understanding of knowledge identified with the pre-war German FRANKFURT SCHOOL (notably T. Adorno and M. Horkheimer), although the Marxist influence decreased over time. Its most influential post-war exponent is J. Habermas, whose *Theory of Communicative Action* (2 vols, 1984, 1987) offers an ambitious holistic sociological theory (see HOLISM). Recently critical theory has greatly influenced more radical anglophone historians and philosophers of science addressing the social functions and character of science and the nature of theorizing in the human sciences. This has been especially marked among contemporary FEMINIST academics and social constructionists, social constructionism being strongly, if not exclusively, rooted in the Frankfurt School's ideas. There are also connections with the HISTORICAL PSYCHOLOGY school, while the AUTHORITARIAN PERSONALITY research of the 1950s involved Adorno and represented a continuation in exile of the Frankfurt School's earlier research programme. A 'critical' position has become prominent in British social psychology since the late 1980s, although its connections with critical theory in the strict sense are somewhat loose. Critical theorists have particularly considered the 'interests of knowledge' – the reasons why knowledge is sought – as a crucial factor in all scientific endeavour. Despite its popularity, critical theory resists some central features of POST-MODERNIST thought, retaining 'modernist' commitments to logical analysis and the need to provide liberationist struggles with an 'objective' grounding. It thereby retains both its Marxist legacy and (especially in Habermas) the traditional ambitions of the 'modernist' Western Enlightenment project. For further reading:

D. Held, *Introduction to Critical Theory: Horkheimer to Habermas* (1980). G.D.R.

cross-cultural study. An investigation comparing performance in some psychological function (PERCEPTION, memory, INTELLIGENCE, motivation) in two or more different CULTURES in order to determine whether and in what manner it might be affected by differences between the cultures studied. The cultural differences usually investigated are patterns of child-rearing, patterns of motivation (notably achievement motivation), and differences in linguistic structure (cf. the WHORFIAN hypothesis). Earlier emphasis on the cultural RELATIVISM of mental functioning has, in recent years, been replaced by increasing evidence of certain basic universals in functioning that differ principally, between one culture and another, in emphasis and form of realization. See also ETHNOPSYCHOLOGY; PATTERN VARIABLES. For further reading: P. E. Vernon, *Intelligence and Cultural Environment* (1969). J.S.B.

cross-over value, see under CROSSING OVER.

cross-section. In NUCLEAR PHYSICS, the effective area that a target presents to an incident projectile; if the area is large, the probability is high that a collision will occur. The concept originated in nuclear physics as a means of specifying the strength of interaction between colliding NUCLEI or ELEMENTARY PARTICLES. M.V.B.

cross-sectional methods, see under LONGITUDINAL.

crossing over. The process whereby GENES on the same CHROMOSOME (i.e. linked genes; see LINKAGE) can be recombined. Crossing over is important in EVOLUTION because it increases the number of genetically different individuals that can arise in a population. It occurs during MEIOSIS, probably by a process of breakage of two chromosomes and reunion after an exchange of parts. The frequency with which two characteristics recombine, known as their *cross-over value*, is an increasing function of the physical distance between the corresponding genes on the chromosome; this fact is used in 'mapping' the genes on a chromosome. J.M.S.

CRT, see CRITERION REFERENCED TEST.

cruelty, theatre of, see THEATRE OF CRUELTY.

cruise missiles. The cruise missile first entered popular consciousness in the early 1980s. Along with the American Pershing and Soviet SS-20 ballistic missiles, it was one of a new generation of intermediate range NUCLEAR WEAPONS, all based in Europe.

Developing the principles of the German V.1 'flying bomb' of World War II, the cruise missile is a small, very accurate, manoeuvrable, subsonic weapon with an internal guidance system. Several advanced technologies came together to make it possible: reliable, long-endurance rocket motors, compact nuclear warheads and computer mapping and inertial guidance systems. This enables the cruise missile to fly under any land-based RADAR system, recognize and adjust its position in relation to internal maps, and so weave its way to a preprogrammed target. Small, comparatively cheap to manufacture and difficult to intercept, the cruise missile, which can be launched from the ground, air or sea, was one of a new generation of 'smart' weapons.

The first cruise missiles deployed were nuclear-armed, ground-launched and mobile. Their mobility proved to be a mixed blessing. When they ventured out on training exercises from their bases (in Britain, at Greenham Common and Molesworth), they were a gift to protesters. While the women-only peace camp at Greenham Common became a rallying point for regular demonstrations and incursions into the base, other (mixed) protesters were harassing the missiles, which soon had to have large police escorts.

Although the nuclear-armed cruise missiles were withdrawn under the Intermediate Nuclear Forces agreement (see NUCLEAR WEAPONS, LIMITATION AND CONTROL), conventionally armed versions, often launched from surface ships and submarines, were developed, especially by the US, who used them in the Gulf War against Iraq. Although the claims for accuracy and reliability were exaggerated, they established themselves as effective weapons, able to be launched with the minimum of preparation, and avoiding any loss of expensive aircrew. For further reading: A. Karp, *Ballistic Missile Proliferation* (1996). L.T.

cryobiology. A combination of two words, cryo (Greek, *kryos*, cold) and BIOLOGY that implies the biology of very low temperatures (liquid gases range). The term has come broadly to describe the field of science which deals with the behaviour of biological systems at temperatures lower than the normal physiological temperature of warm-blooded animals (approximately 37°C). Low temperatures have a paradoxical effect on biological materials. On one hand they reduce the rate of chemical reaction and can therefore preserve biological materials; on the other hand they disrupt the EVOLUTION-optimized, temperature-dependent chemical pathways of life and can therefore destroy biological materials. These two opposing properties of low temperatures have major applications in biotechnology and medicine in the long-term preservation of biological materials (cryopreservation) and in the controlled destruction of biological tissues (cryosurgery). Cryobiology can be divided into the study of phenomena occurring above and below the freezing temperature of water. In both temperature ranges cryobiology deals primarily with: (a) understanding how biological systems have evolved to survive low temperatures and freezing; (b) developing techniques of cryopreservation for such applications as food preservation or medical preservation of biological materials and systems for transplantation (e.g. organs such as the heart, kidney and liver) or implantation (e.g. cells such as embryos, sperm or blood components); (c) developing techniques for cryosurgery of undesirable malignant tissues (tumours) as well as undesirable benign tissues (moles, uterine lining); and (d) developing techniques for using low temperatures to affect the rate of chemical reactions in a biological system (e.g. low-temperature surgery). The first written record of the use of low temperatures in medicine, to treat compound fractures and infected wounds, can be found in an Egyptian papyrus from 2,500 BC (*The Edwin Smith Surgical Papyrus*, vol. 2, plate IV, University of Chicago). Hippocrates (*c.* 460–377 BC) advocated the use of cold to control haemorrhage and reduce swelling. The first scientist systematically to study the effects of low temperatures on animals was Robert Boyle (1627–91). The first physician to use low temperatures in cryosurgery, for the treatment of cancer, was James Arnott (1845). The 1949 *Nature* paper (vol. 164. p. 666) by S. Polge, A. U. Smith and A. S. Parkes, describing cryopreservation of sperm with glycerol protection, is credited with starting the modern field of cryopreservation. The scientific field of cryobiology should not be confused with the field of cryonics, which deals with the scientifically unsubstantiated practice of freezing human beings or animals that have already died in the belief that they can somehow be brought back to life at a future date. B.R.

cryogenics. The branch of PHYSICS which studies the behaviour of matter at abnormally low temperatures. Within the atomistic physics which became dominant during the 17th century, heat was widely regarded as a function of the motion of particles. Cold therefore became associated with their immobilization. Practically, study of the responses of substances at extremely low temperatures was impossible before the development of powerful artificial cooling techniques in the late 19th century. From the 1870s refrigerators were constructed which worked on the principle of the expansion of ammonia, and these proved capable of liquefying air by cooling it below 180K on the absolute temperature scale. Later oxygen was liquefied at 170K, hydrogen at 20.4K and lastly helium at 4.2K. Such successes permitted experimentation upon the behaviour of extremely cold objects. One finding which has proved of major practical application was that below a certain critical temperature, the electrical resistance of many metals (including tin and lead) drops to almost zero. This SUPERCONDUCTIVITY facilitates the construction of highly powerful electromagnets (see ELECTROMAGNETISM) using very little current. See also ABSOLUTE ZERO; THERMODYNAMICS. For further reading: K. Mendelssohn, *The Quest for Absolute Zero* (1977). R.P.

crystallography. The study of the external forms of crystals and the arrangement of ATOMS within them, using X-RAY DIFFRACTION and ELECTRON DIFFRACTION. See also LATTICE; SOLID-STATE PHYSICS. M.V.B.

CT (CAT), see under RADIOLOGY.

Cuba. Caribbean island off the Florida coast in which a COMMUNIST regime was established by Fidel Castro after the overthrow of the repressive government of General Batista on 1 January 1959 (see CASTROISM). The Cuban MISSILE crisis of 1962, in which the USA under Kennedy's leadership forced the Soviet Union to dismantle the rocket sites it was building in Cuba, is believed to have been a decisive factor in Khrushchev's fall from power. For further reading: H. S. Dinerstein, *The Making of a Missile Crisis* (1976). A.L.C.B.

Cubism. An artistic movement often regarded as the most revolutionary and influential of the 20th century. Led by Picasso and Braque, the Cubists, while attempting to represent what the eye sees, aimed to render objects more essential and tangible by means of stylized forms and symbols.

Three phases are commonly distinguished. The first may be dated from the completion early in 1907 of Picasso's *Les Demoiselles d'Avignon*, whose angular, distorted shapes reflected the growing interest in PRIMITIVE sculpture and the work of Cézanne. In the next two years Picasso and Braque depicted familiar objects by means of interlocked geometrical figures, abandoning traditional perspective and chiaroscuro.

The second, 'analytical' phase (1910–12) is notable for the development of the techniques of presenting different facets of an object simultaneously, superimposed or side by side. Guitars, bottles, pipes and written words appear regularly in the paintings of Picasso and Braque at this time. Other artists associated with Cubism included Gris, Léger, Delaunay, Metzinger and Gleizes; the latter two published a theoretical work, *Du Cubisme* (1912), though their own painting tended merely to 'cubify' their subject-matter in harmonious designs, without any radical restructuring.

In May 1912 Picasso included a piece of printed cloth, representing a chair seat, in a painting – a significant moment in the history of COLLAGE; in September of that year Braque incorporated strips of wallpaper in his work, and he, Picasso and Gris soon developed the new medium of *papier collé*, which (they felt) introduced a fresh element of 'reality' into their art. This concern with textures led them to experiment with sculpture: Cubist sculpture, again pioneered by Picasso, was to reach its peak during World War I in the work of Archipenko, Laurens and Lipchitz (forerunners of CONSTRUCTIVISM).

In the final, 'synthetic' phase (1913–14), Cubist painting tended to become more complicated and colourful, employing multiple repetitions of forms and a language of visual signs. But by this time it was less easy to discern a single Cubist school; moreover, the influence of Cubism had spread abroad, affecting EXPRESSIONISM, FUTURISM, DADA, VORTICISM, ORPHISM, SUPREMATISM, De Stijl (see STIJL, DE), etc. The ARMORY SHOW (New York, 1913) included a Cubist contingent. The PURISTS, on the other hand, presently joined by Léger himself, reacted against Cubism in returning to undissected shapes and a severe machine-like precision.

Cubism had affinities with the new European interest in JAZZ; and in 1923 Léger designed Cubist sets for Milhaud's Negro jazz ballet *La Création du Monde*. Indeed, works of art in several other fields have been called 'Cubist', either because they were directly inspired by Cubist painting (as was some of the poetry of Apollinaire and Cendrars) or because of their fragmented, multiple-image structure (Stravinsky's *Petrushka* of 1911, Satie's *Parade* of 1916, Joyce's *Ulysses* of 1922). For further reading: J. Golding, *Cubism: A History and an Analysis, 1907–1914* (1988). P.C.

Cubo-Futurism. Russian name for the modern poetry and art movement of *c.* 1912–18, as imported from France and Italy and identified with the early days of the bolshevik revolution (see BOLSHEVISM). Its component elements were (a) the CUBISM of painters and sculptors – Kasimir Malevich, Nadezhda Udaltsova, Liubov Popova and Ivan Puni (Jean Pougny) – who had studied in Paris; (b) the FUTURIST-influenced RAYONISM of Larionov and Goncharova; and (c) the impact, reflected most strongly in ZAUM and the poetry of Mayakovsky, of Italian Futurism, whose leader Marinetti visited Russia in 1914. It played some part in Soviet aesthetic discussions, but by then had been largely absorbed in SUPREMATISM and CONSTRUCTIVISM. For further reading: V. D. Barooshian, *Russian Cubo-Futurism 1910–30* (1975). J.W.

cult. Organization founded upon the veneration of deity, spirits or a religious or political figure. A cult is a complex of beliefs and practices and members display a high degree of commitment to the organization. It is usually a localized group, but recruitment may be ascribed on the basis of KINSHIP ties (e.g. ANCESTOR WORSHIP) or voluntary (e.g. CARGO CULTS). A cult may emerge spontaneously in opposition to a centre of established authority. These cults have elements of MILLENARIANISM: religious fervour and an anticipation of salvation and deliverance for cult members. The focus of such a cult is a *charismatic* leader, and members are drawn from the dispossessed (in a political rather than an economic sense). In the early stages of development cults are unstable, egalitarian groups (see EGALITARIANISM) perceived to be a threat to social and legitimate order. As time passes, however, a cult becomes 'routinized' and established, and in turn its members view the rise of new cults as potentially subversive. For further reading: S. J. Tambiah, *The Buddhist Saints of the Forest and the Cult of Amulets* (1984).
A.G.

cultural capital. A concept largely developed by the French sociologist Pierre Bourdieu. Bourdieu argues that the BOURGEOIS class in modern society no longer maintains its position by transmitting material property to its children, but more through its transmission of 'cultural capital' to them. By providing a home environment which encourages reading and stimulates an interest in the arts, through foreign travel and study, and by the general inculcation of the values of the educational system, bourgeois parents ensure that their children will perform well in the system, and so acquire the qualifications necessary to secure the best jobs in society. The concept has value in being applicable not just to Western CAPITALIST societies, but also to the COMMUNIST societies of the Far East, whose ÉLITES can similarly ensure that their privileges are transmitted to their own children, despite the absence of private property. For further reading: P. Bourdieu and J.-C. Passeron, *Reproduction in Education, Society and Culture* (1977).
K.K.

cultural deprivation. In the SOCIOLOGY of education the theory advocated by J. W. B. Douglas and others that the WORKING CLASS were disadvantaged in the education system because they lacked the cultural advantages enjoyed by MIDDLE-CLASS and upper-class children. For example, they might be deprived of the parental encouragement, access to books and sophisticated ways of speaking which would make educational success easier to achieve. Some critics of the theory have argued that the differences in working-class and middle-class culture have been greatly exaggerated. Others have claimed that middle- and working-class culture are different but working-class culture is not inferior to middle-class culture, it is simply unfairly devalued by the education system. For further reading: M. Haralambos and M. Holborn, *Sociology: Themes and Perspectives* (1995).
M.D.H.

cultural ecology, see under ECOLOGICAL ANTHROPOLOGY.

cultural geography. The systematic field of GEOGRAPHY that treats the spatial expressions of CULTURE and the interactions between human societies and their natural environments. Cultural geographers focus on six major areas: (1) cultural landscapes, the imprints of human activities successively etched on the natural landscape; (2) culture hearths, source areas from which innovations radiate to the world beyond; (3) cultural DIFFUSION, the mechanisms and channels by which these innovations spread; (4) cultural ecology, the interrelationships between cultures and their habitats; (5) cultural perception, the ways in which ethnic groups perceive their surroundings and behave towards other cultures; and (6) culture regions, the delimitation of a worldwide, hierarchical framework to delineate the spaces occupied by each of the groups that are part of the complex global cultural mosaic. Since 1990, a new research frontier has updated cultural geography and linked it to the latest work in theoretical human geography (see SOCIAL GEOGRAPHY). For further reading: J. S. Duncan and D. Ley (eds), *Place/Culture/Representation* (1993).
P.O.M.

cultural history. Defined by one of its greatest exponents, Johan Huizinga, as the study of 'themes, SYMBOLS, CONCEPTS, ideals (see IDEALISM), styles, and sentiments', it overlaps with the HISTORY OF IDEAS but is also concerned with the HISTORY OF MATERIAL CULTURE and with RITUAL. It is sometimes referred to as *Geistesgeschichte* by those who believe that the art and literature, science and religion of an age are all expressions of the same spirit, that an age is a whole (see HISTORICISM). For those who believe that the 'spirit of an age' (see ZEITGEIST) is an unnecessary entity, cultural history is in danger of fragmenting into such parts as art history and history of science. Cultural history is to be distinguished from *culture history*, a synonym for ETHNOHISTORY. For further reading: J. Huizinga, 'The task of cultural history', in his *Men and Ideas* (1960). P.B.

cultural imperialism, see under IMPERIALISM.

cultural lag. Term coined by W. F. Ogburn (*Social Change*, 1922) for 'the strain that exists between two correlated parts of CULTURE that change at unequal rates of speed' (W. F. Ogburn and M. F. Nimkoff, *A Handbook of Sociology*, 1947). An example is the disjunction that occurs when the organization of the family is considered to be lagging behind other changes in society. The term names an important fact of social life, but does not help to account for it. See also FUNCTIONALISM. M.F.

cultural materialism. A term coined by the literary critic and cultural theorist Raymond Williams (1921–88) to describe 'a theory of the specificities of material cultural and literary production within HISTORICAL MATERIALISM'. Breaking with the mechanistic determinism of vulgar MARXISM, Williams effectively argues that rather than constituting the reflection or effect of the economic base, superstructural activities are themselves both material and productive (see SUPERSTRUCTURE). This means that IDEOLOGY is no longer restricted to serve as a detached system of BELIEFS and ideas, but is regarded as part of a 'whole lived social process'. Williams eventually developed the Gramscian notion of HEGEMONY to encapsulate this broadened definition of a cultural formation, which manifests 'a realized complex of experiences, relationships, and activities, with specific and changing pressures and limits' (*Marxism and Literature*, 1977).

In the course of its emergence during the late 1970s and early 1980s, certain variants of cultural materialism were further revised and enriched by the growing theoretical influence of structuralist and psychoanalytical (see STRUCTURALISM; PSYCHOANALYSIS) variants of MARXISM. Here the work of Louis Althusser and Michel Foucault was to prove especially influential, in its confirmation of the material dimension of ideologies, and its anti-HUMANIST emphasis on a decentred concept of the self. Human SUBJECTIVITY was no longer conceived as a unified or stable given; rather, individual 'selves' were historically and materially constituted by the institutions, ideologies and DISCOURSES OF POWER which continue to regulate and confine subjects within BOURGEOIS culture (see ALTHUSSERIANISM). For further reading: A. Sinfield, *Faultlines: Cultural Materialism and the Politics of Dissident Reading* (1992). J.J.J.

cultural relativism, see under RELATIVISM, CULTURAL.

cultural reterritorialization, see under LOCALIZATION.

Cultural Revolution, see under GREAT PROLETARIAN CULTURAL REVOLUTION.

culturalism. In literary and cultural studies, the approach that emphasizes the importance of the lived experience of human CULTURE. The term is of relatively recent origin and has normally been used only by way of an antithesis with STRUCTURALISM. Where structuralism tends to read culture as a system of texts, situated in relation to wider systems of DISCOURSE or IDEOLOGY, culturalism concentrates on the subjective experience (see SUBJECTIVITY) of making and responding to culture. Culturalist approaches have been especially important in 'history from below', ETHNOGRAPHY, and the kind of literary criticism that attaches a special value to aesthetic experience. Richard Johnson and Stuart Hall used the term to provide retrospective descriptions of the work of the historian E. P. Thompson and the literary critics Richard Hoggart and Raymond Williams. More recent examples of 'culturalism' might include the sociologists Jeremy Seabrook and Paul Willis. Johnson and Hall contrasted culturalism's EMPIRICISM with structuralism's 'theoreticism'. Hall argued that culturalism was prone to elide the distinction between active consciousness and relatively 'given' determinate conditions; and susceptible to an 'experiential pull', which constructs experience as the test of 'authenticity'. More loosely, the term can also be used to refer to a much older, largely 'literary', tradition of speculation about the relationship between culture and society, characterized above all by its anti-UTILITARIANISM. This tradition typically conceived of culture in radically anti-individualist fashion, as an organic whole, and in radically anti-utilitarian fashion, as the repository of values superior to material civilization. The classic account of the history of this British culturalist tradition is Raymond Williams's *Culture and Society 1780–1950* (1958). In some respects, Williams's own work can be read as a late continuation of the 'Culture and Society' tradition. A.J.M.

culture. The subject of a book by T. S. Eliot entitled, with extreme caution, *Notes towards the Definition of Culture* (1948), of one by George Steiner entitled *In Bluebeard's Castle: Notes towards the Redefinition of Culture* (1971), and of *Culture: A Critical Review of Concepts and Definitions* (Papers of the Peabody Museum of American Archaeology and Ethnology, vol. 47, I, 1952). This elusive and emotive word ('When I hear the word culture I reach for my gun,' declared the poet Heinz Johst – not Goering as is generally believed) cannot be comprehensively treated in a work such as this. The following definitions are by an archaeologist and a sociologist respectively. For an anthropologist's use of the word see ANTHROPOLOGY. O.S.

In general archaeological usage, that aspect of social behaviour which can be recognized in the archaeological record. More often it is the material culture that is defined. The assumption has often been made that culture closely reflects social groupings; such a view is now treated with reserve. More precisely, culture has been defined as the consistent recurrence of an ASSEMBLAGE limited in time and space. Here again the assumption is that a culture, thus defined, reflects contemporary social distinctions. The concept was first given prominence by V. G. Childe in 1929 and was of considerable value in the simple ordering of the basic archaeological data; in recent years, however, its limitations have been recognized, and the precise definition is now rapidly declining in use. B.C.

The 'social heritage' of a community: the total body of material artifacts (tools, weapons, houses, places of work, worship, government, recreation, works of art, etc.), of collective mental and spiritual 'artifacts' (systems of SYMBOLS, IDEAS, beliefs, aesthetic perceptions, values, etc.), and of distinctive forms of behaviour (INSTITUTIONS, groupings, RITUALS, modes of organization, etc.) created by a people (sometimes deliberately, sometimes through unforeseen interconnections and consequences) in their ongoing activities within their particular life-conditions, and (though undergoing kinds and degrees of change) transmitted from generation to generation. See also FOLK CULTURE; SUB-CULTURE. R.F.

culture area. Geographical term for a region within which a single CULTURE or similar cultures are found; originally used (*Kulturprovinz*) by the German geographer Ratzel in the last century and given prominence by the American anthropologist A. L. Kroeber in his studies of North American Indians. Thus the Great Plains formed a clearly defined geographical area associated with distinctive Plains Indian material culture, economy and social values. P.H.

culture contact, see under ACCULTURATION.

culture history, see under ETHNOHISTORY.

culture jamming. A term coined by the band Negativland in 1984, 'CULTURE jamming' is the manipulation of the mass media by artists and activists. The intent, in most cases, is to critique the media's manipulation of reality, lampoon consumerism, or question corporate POWER. Culture jamming ranges from 'billboard banditry' – defacing billboards in order to subvert the advertiser's message – to hoaxing the news media into covering bogus stories. Most jammers share the conviction that those who control the mass media – corporate conglomerates, the advertising industry, public relations experts and their ilk – manufacture consent for vested interests. Today, jamming has spread to such an extent that New York's School of Visual Arts offers a course in it. Jamming is part of the secret history of what Greil Marcus calls the 'politics of subversive quotation', in which the signs and symbols of the dominant culture are pried loose from their original contexts and used to tell the stories of the mute and the marginalized. Stuart Ewen, a critic of consumer culture, has suggested that the roots of culture jamming lie in the carnivals of the Middle Ages, in which pigs were baptized, clerics mocked, and the god-given rights of religious power and royal privilege challenged, however briefly. But jamming's immediate progenitor is SITUATIONISM (see CARNIVALIZATION), the French LEFT-wing radical movement of the 1960s whose members monkey-wrenched commodity culture by means of a tactic called *détournement*, defined by Marcus as the 'theft of aesthetic artifacts from their contexts and their diversion into contexts of one's own devise'. The Situationists' détourned comic strips begat today's defaced, 'refaced' billboards. Though only briefly glimpsed, culture jamming's startling vision of a better world, where we are citizens actively engaged in civic life and public discourse rather than passive consumers of media myths, is not easily forgotten. Haunting the commodified images of the good life in our magazines or on our TV screens, it troubles our collective sleep, darkening the dreams that money can buy. M.D.

culture of narcissism. Phrase used as the title and denoting the main thesis of an influential critical analysis of American CULTURE and society by Christopher Lasch. He argued that the US suffered from the increasingly degenerate form of individualism whose characteristics are those of the narcissistic personality (see NARCISSISM) writ large across society. The thesis represents an elaborate attempt to account for a national temper which was widely seen in the 1970s as disturbing and dysfunctional. The alleged trend towards preoccupation with self, a decay of public values and related traits was described by journalist Tom Wolfe as that of the 'Me Decade'. For further reading: C. Lasch, *The Culture of Narcissism* (1979). S.R.

Cunningham technique. A teaching method and movement style based on the work of Merce Cunningham, one of the foremost influences of change in MODERN DANCE, stimulating the POST-MODERN DANCE rebellion (see AVANT-GARDE DANCE). Since his early collaborations with John Cage in 1952 at Black Mountain College, and his experiments with aleatoric form, Merce Cunningham evolved an innovative choreographic process. A former member of the Graham company (see GRAHAM TECHNIQUE), Cunningham rebelled to establish his own choreographic needs and technical demands. He required that dance be its own subject-matter, rejected literary and psychological preoccupations and thematic development, insisted on decentralizing space, ignored stage hierarchies, and worked independently from musical accompaniment and visual design while retaining co-existence with them. Despite such radical changes, Cunningham never dispensed with dance technique, maintaining dance with a traditional appearance while denying its expressive possibilities. However, the content works to destroy logical kinetic phrasing, ignores predetermined positions and preparations, and has no floorwork and set combinations. Collaborations with contemporary artists were an important element of the final CHOREOGRAPHY, e.g. Rauschenberg, Warhol, Johns, Stella, Duchamp, Cage, Tudor and La Monte Young. For further reading: J. Lesschaeve, *The Dancer and the Dance* (1985). L.A.

current fertility, see under FERTILITY.

custom. Expected forms of behaviour which derive legitimacy by reference to tradition. Members of a particular society recognize implicit rules or conventions and are bound by them. Customs introduce elements of regularity, predictability and conformity into social relationships. To break a custom may be TABOO, it may invoke mystical SANCTIONS. This raises the question of the coercive nature of custom. Malinowski (*Crime and Custom in Savage Society*, 1926) took up this issue and examined the binding qualities of custom in societies lacking formal legal machinery. This theme was later explored by anthropologists concerned with political organization and the maintenance of order (particularly Radcliffe Brown and Gluckman). Leach (*Custom, Law and Terrorist Violence*, 1977) broadened the area of analysis beyond small-scale societies and explored the ambiguities and contradictions embodied in the concept of custom. For further reading: E. Leach, *Social Anthropology* (1982). A.G.

customs union. A group of nations between whom trade is free and which apply the same duties and other regulations to trade with non-members. This second provision distinguishes the union from a *free trade area*, whose members can apply different duties and other regulations to trade with non-members. While this latter freedom to differ has its advantages, it may divert imports so that they enter the area through low-duty members and in this and other ways undermine the import-duty structures of the others, an undermining which can be prevented only at some administrative cost. Although they infringe the principle of non-discrimination, both systems are permitted by the GATT. There have been many attempts to form them, but outside Europe few really successful examples exist. A *common market* goes beyond a customs union in permitting free movement of labour, CAPITAL and enterprise, as well as goods. See also EFTA; EUROPEAN UNION; PROTECTIONISM. M.FG.S.

cut-ups, see under COLLAGE.

cybernetics. A subject which dates from 1942 and was named in 1947 by Norbert Wiener and Arturo Rosenbleuth, distinguished mathematician and physician respectively. It was then defined as 'the science of control and communication in the animal and the machine'. This definition indicated (1) that a state of 'in control' depends upon a flow of information, and (2) that the laws governing control are universal, i.e. do not depend on the classical dichotomy between organic and inorganic systems. The name cybernetics derives from the Greek word meaning 'steersman', and was chosen to show that adaptive control is more like steersmanship than DICTATORSHIP. Today, a more general definition of cybernetics might be preferred: *the science of effective organization*.

Always an interdisciplinary subject, cybernetics was seen by its founding fathers moreover as *trans*disciplinary. This perception was followed by the original US workers, and by cyberneticians in the UK, who looked to the science as linking organizational notions in every field, and as specifying quite general principles. Elsewhere in the USA, and in some other countries, notably France, early discoveries about the importance of FEEDBACK and the role of ENTROPY focused the subject on its ENGINEERING aspects, at the expense of its BIOLOGY, its ECONOMICS, its ECOLOGY, and so on. In the USSR, cybernetics was officially treated as an 'imperialist device' until the mid-1950s. At this time, Soviet work in the field, heavily dependent on MATHEMATICS, achieved such importance internationally that the Soviet authorities admitted the science officially.

There remains disagreement about its generality, especially in relation to GENERAL SYSTEMS THEORY, which has objectives identical with those expressed by the founders of cybernetics. Thus, for some, cybernetics and GST are co-extensive, while those could be found who regard either one as a branch of the other. In their origins, at least, they express the same intentions.

Thanks to the academic forces that will always seek to classify in a REDUCTIONIST way, one may hear of *engineering cybernetics* (as above), of *neurocybernetics* (which deals especially with the brain), of *biocybernetics* (also called BIONICS), of COMPUTER cybernetics, of management cybernetics, and so on. A clear perception of cybernetics must accept these distinctions by areas of application, but will not take them as undermining the transdisciplinary unity of cybernetics itself. For further reading: F. H. George, *The Foundations of Cybernetics* (1977). S.BE.

cyberspace. Originally the imaginary spaces where computer simulations occur, but now used more generally for the 'place' where the electronic network links a global community of users. Although contemporary usage often makes it indistinguishable from the INTERNET, its emphasis is on an intangible arena. If, for example, E-MAIL goes undelivered, the phrase 'lost in cyberspace' captures the bewilderment over what happened in a way that 'lost in the Internet' never can. Credit for the coinage generally goes to the American author William

Gibson (1948–) and his 1984 science-fiction novel *Neuromancer*. E.B.B.

cyclogenesis, see under FRONTAL THEORY.

cyclone, see under DEPRESSION (sense 1).

cyclotron. A type of ACCELERATOR. The PARTICLES travel in circular ORBITS under the action of a magnetic FIELD inside two hollow D-shaped electrodes with their straight sides adjacent. Twice during each revolution, when the particles cross the narrow space between the Ds, they are accelerated by an oscillating voltage. When the beam emerges after several thousand revolutions, its ENERGY may reach extremely high levels. M.V.B.

cytogenetics. A term sometimes used in place of GENETICS by those who overestimate the contribution made by CYTOLOGY to our understanding of heredity. It refers especially to the cellular structures and events associated with the hereditary process. J.M.S.

cytology. The biological science which deals with the properties that CELLS enjoy in common. It is usually contrasted with HISTOLOGY, which deals rather with the properties distinctive of each individual tissue and the modifications of cells associated with them, and is to be distinguished also from CELL BIOLOGY. An important branch of cytology (*karyology*) deals especially with the properties and behaviour of the cell NUCLEUS and the CHROMOSOMES contained within it. The 'generalized' animal cell as envisaged in cytology comprises a nucleus which is the seat of genetic information (see GENETIC CODE), and a greater or lesser quantity of CYTOPLASM bounded externally by a plasma membrane. In addition to the plasma membrane, the cells of plants and of bacteria have more or less structurally rigid cell walls. The cytoplasm houses a number of minute structural features known as *organelles* which serve specific cellular functions, e.g. the *mitochondria* which are the seat of oxidative processes, the *ribosomes* (see NUCLEIC ACID) which are the seat of PROTEIN synthesis, the lysosomes, and a number of adventitious fluid-filled spaces or *vacuoles*. There is evidence that mitochondria represent the contemporary record of some deeply ancestral SYMBIOSIS between animal cells and bacteria. P.M.

cytoplasm. The sap of the CELL, excluding the NUCLEUS. P.M.

cytoskeleton. A CONCEPT introduced by the biochemist R. A. Peters to account for the orderly progression of biochemical processes in the CELL and the fact that they need not be disastrously impeded by the stratification of the contents of the cell in the ultracentrifuge (see SEDIMENTATION). The cytoskeleton consists of filaments of PROTEIN arranged in a complex network in the CYTOPLASM of the cell but with attachments to the NUCLEUS, plasma membrane and organelles (see CYTOLOGY). Cell shape, movement and internal organization depend on the cytoskeleton. P.M.; P.N.

Czech Reform Movement. The movement, within the former Czech COMMUNIST Party and outside, which from the early 1960s until 1968 attempted to make the political system more liberal (see LIBERALISM) and democratic and the economic system more flexible. In December 1967, the reformers within the Communist Party were powerful enough to compel the leader, A. Novotný, to resign, and replaced him with Alexander Dubček. In the period before the Soviet invasion, several measures were introduced which provided for DEMOCRACY within the Party, relaxed censorship and allowed associations to be established independent of the Party which could make political demands. Although Czechoslovakia remained a member of the Warsaw Pact, the former USSR and other socialist bloc countries considered that the leading role of the Party was being weakened, and in August 1968 Warsaw Pact troops invaded to put an end to the reforms. The intervention was justified in what has been called the Brezhnev doctrine, in which one socialist country can intervene in another if SOCIALISM is being threatened. For further reading: G. Golan, *Reform Rule in Czechoslovakia* (1971). D.PR.

Czechoslovakia, the former. A former federal state (see FEDERALISM) established on 18 October 1918. The First Czech Republic (1918–38) was a democratic (see DEMOCRACY) state based on parliamentary (see PARLIAMENTARIANISM) government, universal suffrage and the defence of HUMAN RIGHTS. Thereafter the country fell into Nazi (see NAZISM) hands, German troops invading in March 1939. After the war, Czechoslovakia became a COMMUNIST state, a member of COMECON and under the control of the former USSR. The Czechs were never comfortable with Soviet domination, however, and there were attempts by Alexander Dubček and Ludvik Svoboda to introduce reform during the 'Prague Spring' of 1968 (see PRAGUE). The Soviet Union responded by sending tanks into the streets of Prague and installing a more compliant regime led by Gustav Husak. Czechoslovakia remained a Soviet satellite until 1989, when, following the VELVET REVOLUTION, it became an independent pluralist state (see PLURALISM). Czechoslovakia ceased to exist on 1 January 1993, splitting into the independent states of the Czech Republic and Slovakia. V.L.

D

DAC (Development Assistance Committee), see under OECD.

Dada (-ism, -ists). International movement in the arts originating in Zurich in 1916 from a sense of total disillusionment with the art-loving public, the role of the creative artist and, finally, with art as such; famous consequently more for its spirit of artistic flippancy, BOURGEOIS-baiting and NIHILISM than for its purely formal methods, most of which were borrowed from CUBISM and FUTURISM. Its name was 'found in a lexicon – it means nothing. This is the meaningful nothing, where nothing has any meaning.' Its founders were mainly German – the theatre director Hugo Ball, the artist Hans Arp and the poet Richard Hülsenbeck – plus the Romanian Tristan Tzara, while its adherents at one time or another over the next few years included Georg Grosz and John Heartfield (both in Berlin), Max Ernst (Cologne) and Kurt Schwitters (Hanover; see MERZ); the Cuban Francis Picabia and the Frenchman Marcel Duchamp (both of whom had previously experimented in a comparable nihilism in New York; see READYMADES); and finally a literary group centred around André Breton's Paris review *Littérature* (1919–24).

By 1924 the various groups had either stagnated, transferred loyalties, or merged into CONSTRUCTIVISM or SURREALISM; after which the movement's characteristic methods – phonetic poetry (see CONCRETE POETRY), BRUITISME, COLLAGE and nonsense dialogue, as well as its two original contributions, the PHOTOGRAM and photoMONTAGE – were hardly again recognized as such till the publication in New York in 1951 of Robert Motherwell's *The Dada Painters and Poets*, the consequent FLUXUS revival, and the rise of POP ART. In this new context Dada, like its Futurist precursors, became relevant above all for its basic, if unformulated, conception of art as HAPPENING or manifestation, and an exercise in public relations. J.W.

dance notation. The method of recording movement and dance using symbols. Earliest forms of dance notation range from abbreviations, figure illustration, track drawings and stick figures, to current forms of notation practised today, i.e. the analysis of movement based on spatial, anatomical and dynamic principles called *Labanotation*, Eshkol and Wachmann's accurate mathematical description, and Benesh notation based on three-dimensional representation linked to the musical score. Of these systems Benesh and *Labanotation* are the most widely used. *Labanotation* or *kinetography Laban* is appropriate to all forms of movement from ANTHROPOLOGY to PHYSIOTHERAPY as it can record all movement inflections, spatial orientation, movement motivation and dynamics. *Motif* writing is a simpler form of dance notation and was also developed by Laban as a freer, more general indication of basic movement concepts. *Labanotation* is linked to Laban's work on MODERN EDUCATIONAL DANCE, while the Benesh system tends to be used by choreologists (see CHOREOLOGY) employed by CLASSICAL BALLET companies. For further reading: A. Hutchinson, *Labanotation* (1954). L.A.

dance theatre. A synthesis of dance and theatre which aims to present a new form of dance performance with its own language. The term emerged in 1928 in Germany from radical discussion led by Kurt Jooss which denied that dance was an absolute art but rather claimed it to be part of theatre and capable of dramatizing social and political issues. L.A.

dark comedy, see under BLACK COMEDY.

dark matter (*or missing matter*). Observations of the motions of stars and GALAXIES in the universe show that only about one-tenth of the total density of the universe exists in luminous forms. The remainder, termed dark matter or missing matter/mass, and revealed by its gravitational field strength, resides in undetected forms of non-luminous material, and the question of its identity is called the dark matter or missing mass or missing light problem.

There are three parts to the dark matter problem. First, it has been argued, on the basis of the observed motions of stars, since it was first suggested by Jan Oort in 1934, that about 50 per cent of the mass in the disk of the Milky Way in the vicinity of the sun must be in non-luminous form. This dark matter is expected to reside in very faint stars or planetary-sized bodies similar to the planet Jupiter (and hence often referred to collectively as 'Jupiters'). The second dark matter problem is found in spiral galaxies. Measurements of the velocities of stars moving in orbits at different distances (called rotation curves) from the centre in the disks of spiral galaxies reveal that there must exist about 10 times more mass within these galaxies than exists in the form of visible stars, and that the extent of this underlying mass is about 10 times larger than that of the visible galaxy. This unseen material within which the visible parts of spiral galaxies reside is called massive haloes/dark haloes/galaxy haloes. Third, the motions of galaxies within clusters of galaxies have an average speed about eight times larger than that needed to escape the gravitational attraction exerted by all the luminous material within the cluster. It is concluded therefore that there must exist large amounts of non-luminous material within the clusters which contributes additional gravitational attraction. This problem, which first gave rise to the term *missing mass problem*, was first pointed out by the Swiss astronomer Fritz Zwicky in the 1930s. The amount of material necessary to resolve the first dark matter problem associated with the disk of our galaxy falls well short of the amount necessary to resolve the second and third dark matter problems. The dark matter within galaxies and galaxy clusters could also consist of faint stars and 'Jupiters' or BLACK HOLES, but this possibility is strongly constrained by the effect upon the primordial NUCLEOSYNTHESIS of light elements of introducing additional baryonic matter (see BARYON) into the universe. The observed abundances of deuterium, helium and lithium in the universe are in perfect agreement with what would be produced in the Big Bang (see BIG BANG THEORY) if the only baryonic material in the universe was that observed in luminous forms. Because of this it is widely believed that the dark matter in galaxies and clusters consists of weakly interacting massive ELEMENTARY PARTICLES (acronym WIMPS) – for example, NEUTRINOS possessing a small rest mass (about 30 ELECTRON volts) or particles predicted to exist if Nature is supersymmetric (see SUPERSYMMETRY). Underground experiments have been set up in several countries to attempt to detect these particles – if they do actually exist in our own galaxy, the Milky Way, then the earth should be moving through them, making them theoretically detectable.

The total amount of non-luminous material that must be found in order to resolve the three dark matter problems (as they are currently understood) is about five times smaller than that required to ensure that the universe ceases to expand and subsequently recollapses to a high-temperature fate similar to the Big Bang from which it originated. For further reading: L. Smolin, *The Life of the Cosmos* (1997). J.D.B.

Darwinism. The theory of how EVOLUTION might have come about which constitutes the great contribution to science made by Charles Darwin (1809–82). Darwin saw the evolutionary process as a series of adaptations: plants and animals differ one from another in their hereditary endowments, and those variants which equip an organism especially well to cope with the exigencies of the ENVIRONMENT will be preserved in the 'struggle for existence' and will thus become the prevailing type. Darwin used the term NATURAL SELECTION for this process of discrimination, mainly to avoid the lengthy periphrases that would be necessary to avoid its animistic overtones (see ANIMISM), of which he was fully aware. At the turn of the century Darwinism was seriously faulted for its explanatory glibness: 'the natural selection of favourable variations' was a formula that fitted all phenomena too well. In due course Darwinism had to be reformulated in the new language of Mendelian (see MENDELISM) GENETICS, and this revised doctrine, the prevailing one today, is called *neo-Darwinism*.

Neo-Darwinism is still solidly Darwinian in principle. Inheritable variation (no other kind is relevant) is provided for by the recombinations and reassortments of genetic factors which Mendelian heredity allows for, and natural selection becomes now the overall name for inequalities of survival or of reproductive rate, or more generally for inequalities in the contributions made by different organisms to the ancestry of future generations. Those hereditary endowments which increase their representation generation by generation are said to confer *fitness*, and the organisms that possess them to be 'fitter' than those that do not. Thus evolution by natural selection could be represented as the *survival of the fittest*. It is to be noted that although the Mendelian process of shuffling and reshuffling GENES provides the variants upon which natural selection works, yet new genes, i.e. new genetic information (see GENETIC CODE), can arise only by the totally random and unpredictable process of MUTATION. Critics of Darwinism regard this as a deeply objectionable and irreverent element in the process; it is, however, the case. With its emphasis on human and animal inequality and on qualities that are already present because inborn, Darwinism is naturally repugnant to LEFT-wing thought; hence the support lent by a number of British scientists and others, for purely political reasons, to the doctrine known as LYSENKOISM. For further reading: H. Kaye, *The Social Meaning of Modern Biology* (1997). P.M.

Dasein. In Heidegger's *Being and Time* (1927) Dasein is the recognizably human element in the doctrine of BEING. Being itself precedes all beings but many of the modes in which Being appears are modified by being sunk in a human and socialized world. Dasein, literally *Being-There*, is itself a socializing consciousness and exists very much in the condition of *Being-With* and *Being-Towards*. Since *Time and Being* is at once phenomenological and existential, Dasein is described in a series of strikingly original and poetic categories, whose mundanity is unmistakable, such as *Idle Talk*, *Curiosity*, *Ambiguity*, *Falling* and *Thrownness*. But Dasein can also involve the individual in lonely existential exposure to such asocial realities as *Care*, *Conscience* and *Guilt*, and ultimately to the realities of *Being-Towards-Death*. Heidegger's descriptions of the experience of a recognizably 20th-century sensibility under the hold-all term of Dasein have had an immense influence. EXISTENTIALISM, HERMENEUTICS and much deconstructive literary theory (see DECONSTRUCTION) are marked by the peculiarly plangent quality of Heidegger's categorization of Dasein sunk, in a complicit yet helpless way, in the environing absoluteness of Being. For further reading: G. Steiner, *Heidegger* (1978). R.PO.

database. A computer program used to store and display electronic information; the computerized version of a filing cabinet. Databases are probably the most common foundation for a computer program. Chequebook programs, address programs, computer encyclopaedias and spreadsheets all use databases. They are also behind much of what so many people hate about the information age, like junk mail. Databases that can link up separate records are called *relational databases* and they have made it easy for researchers to compile extensive portraits of a person or company's situation. Programmers have long put databases to practical use in managing commercial affairs, although the first attempts revealed many problems. During the 1960s, as billing systems were put under the control of databases, customers had to endure long frustrations when faced with billing errors that seemed impossible to rectify. By the 1990s, however, billing problems could usually be handled quickly, and retail inventory managed a steady supply of merchandise without shortages or backlogs. According to orthodox economists, inventory problems have been the most common trigger of a recession, so a well-functioning database may yield profound social benefits. Perhaps the greatest danger of databases is their need to squeeze facts into narrow slots. In a widely praised essay lamenting the replacement of library card catalogues with electronic databases, Nicholson Baker reminded readers of the 100+ years in which librarians have been writing extra notations by hand. None of that wisdom and insight could be preserved when card information was transferred to a database, so a century and more of intellectual capital was thrown away. E.B.B.

date-rape, see under RAPE.

dating. In GEOLOGY, GEOMORPHOLOGY and ARCHAEOLOGY, the establishing of dates for structures, events and artifacts. In archaeology, until recently, traditional methods such as STRATIGRAPHY and TYPOLOGY were employed to provide a sequence which was then related by various means to historical dates (e.g. the Egyptian King lists). The cross-dating links were often tenuous and the resulting dated sequences were, at best, imprecise. Techniques introduced from the NATURAL SCIENCES began to be used in the 1930s, e.g. DENDROCHRONOLOGY and *varve dating* (the use of sediment sequences formed by melting ice). More recently the techniques of PHYSICS and CHEMISTRY have been employed to provide a wide range of dating methods including ARCHAEOMAGNETISM, THERMOLUMINESCENCE and *obsidian dating*, which involves measurement of the rate of surface hydration. All these are *relative* methods requiring calibration. Other methods are based on measuring the rate of radioactive decay (see RADIOACTIVITY), e.g. RADIOCARBON DATING, *fission track dating* and *potassium-argon dating*. These, theoretically, are capable of providing *absolute dates*. Frequently several techniques are brought to bear on a single problem, thus providing cross-checks. For further reading: J. W. Michels, *Dating Methods in Archaeology* (1973). B.C.

DDT. A powerful and probably the best-known insecticide. A chlorinated hydrocarbon, dichloro-diphenyl-trichloroethane, it acts on most insects, though resistant forms may develop. It plays the major role in anti-malarial spraying but its toxicity has led to restrictions in its use. As far as is known, DDT is harmless to man; the prime case against its widespread use is that it upsets the ecological balance (see ECOLOGY; BALANCE OF NATURE) among insects. But chemical degradation is very slow so that it becomes more concentrated in successive stages of the FOOD CHAIN with, in some cases, demonstrably harmful effects on animal life. B.F.

de Broglie wavelength. The distance between successive crests of the wave which, according to QUANTUM MECHANICS, is associated with every moving PARTICLE. Its value is given by the equation, put forward by Louis de Broglie in 1924, *wavelength* = PLANCK'S CONSTANT ÷ MOMENTUM of *particle*. The motion of the particle may be described by NEWTONIAN MECHANICS to a good approximation only if the wavelength is small in comparison with the range of the forces acting on it; this is true for all systems larger than MOLECULES. See also ELECTRON MICROSCOPE; WAVE-PARTICLE DUALITY. M.V.B.

Dead Sea scrolls. An unprecedented find of ancient manuscripts discovered in 1947–56 in caves in and around Qumran, close to the north-west shores of the Dead Sea in Israel. In all there are some 500 manuscripts, some only fragments, but ten of them perfectly preserved, thanks to their storage in clay jars with lids. Dating from the first centuries BC and AD, they include all the books of the Old Testament except Esther, plus the Apocrypha, and have enabled scholars to push back the date of a stabilized Hebrew Bible to no later than AD 70, as well as to clarify the relationship between early CHRISTIANITY and Jewish religious traditions. The manuscript of Isaiah, a thousand years older than any previously known text, has been placed on display in the specially built Shrine of the Book in Jerusalem.

Other scrolls reflect the life of a devout community, consisting of (or connected with) the Jewish sect known as the Essenes, ending with the Roman suppression of the Jewish revolt in AD 70. Hidden in the wilderness, this community purified itself and prayed in preparation for the coming 'Day of the Lord'. These scrolls are, very roughly, contemporary with the Christian gospels. At some points (e.g. this monastic community's contempt for sinful laymen and for normal daily life) they are very different. They throw more light on John the Baptist than on Jesus. D.L.E.; A.L.C.B.

dealignment, see under REALIGNMENT.

death instinct. In psychoanalytic theory (see PSYCHOANALYSIS), the impulses within a person to bring about his own destruction and death. Most FREUDIANS have not accepted this CONCEPT, and when they have used it they have transformed it into innate AGGRESSION and destructiveness. The death instinct is contrasted with the LIFE INSTINCT. B.A.F.

death of God theology. A radical theological movement of the 1960s associated with William Hamilton and Thomas Altizer. The death of GOD theology, otherwise known as 'Christian atheism', was the radical counterpart to a more liberal secular THEOLOGY (see LIBERALISM) – with which it is often confused – and set itself the task of exploring the possibility of a CHRISTIANITY without BELIEF in God. The death of God (a theme drawn from Nietzsche; see NIETZSCHEAN) was interpreted by some as a cultural process, but for Altizer, influenced by Hegel and the Continental philosophical tradition, it was far more than a METAPHOR, and expressed the secret of the incarnation itself – that God, refusing any other reality, genuinely dies into human life. As a movement, the death of God theology survived only a few years, but its themes continue to resonate in radical POST-MODERN THEOLOGY, represented by the work of Mark C. Taylor and Altizer himself. For further reading: L. Finnegan, *Christian Faith in the American-Death-of-God Theology* (1976). C.C.

death of grand narratives. A concept that owes its precise formulation to the French philosopher Jean-François Lyotard, who announced that in this post-modern age (see POST-MODERNISM) it was impossible any longer to believe in the theories of history and society – 'metanarratives' or 'grand narratives' – constructed in the era of the Enlightenment and later. Such theories depended on concepts of truth and rationality that were matters of faith more than of PROOF. We no longer have the necessary faith, and hence those theories lack all foundations. Lyotard had in mind not just social theories such as MARXISM but all schemes involving the belief in progress and the ability of human beings to exercise an increasing rationality over their common affairs. In place of these grand narratives Lyotard proposed the substitution of 'little narratives' (*petits récits*), forms of 'local knowledge' that were shared by particular communities and which, however 'unscientific', were adequate to their needs. Renouncing any claims to universality, such forms of knowledge could be exchanged between communities in a pragmatic process of give and take. K.K.

death penalty, see under CAPITAL PUNISHMENT.

death rate. The number of deaths in a population divided by the number of individuals in the same population. Demographers distinguish between 'age-specific death rates' and the 'crude death rate'. The former term refers to death rates in distinct age groups, while the latter refers to the death rate for the population as a whole. J.R.W.

death squads, see under STATE TERROR.

debt crisis. A period when the ECONOMIC GROWTH of DEVELOPING COUNTRIES is slowed or reversed by the high ratio of annual interest and principal payments on debt to exports. Debt reaches a crisis when a country has to borrow from a lender of last resort (the International Monetary Fund or World Bank), which sets conditions (reduced government spending, currency DEVALUATION, deregulation, price decontrol) for lending money.

The debt crisis of the 1980s and 1990s, in Africa and Latin America, originated from chronic international goods and services deficits. The deficits increased during the recessions of industrialized countries. Third-world countries contributed to their debt problem by over-borrowing (sometimes lured by interest rates lower than the inflation rate, as in the mid-1970s), inefficiency and poor national economic management, distorted exchange rates (which reduced exports and increased imports), and capital flight.

Perception of the crisis depends on debtor or creditor status. A complete write-off of Latin American debts in the early 1980s would have wiped out many major US commercial banks, which had more exposure to third-world debt than banks in any other country. Yet US exposure declined in the mid-1980s, reducing American interest in the crisis. But the debt overhang still kept standards of living down and limited investment in Africa and a few Latin American countries in the 1990s. For further reading: E. W. Nafziger, *The Debt Crisis in Africa* (1993). E.W.N.

debugging.

(1) The final testing or commissioning of a piece of technological apparatus – an expression that arose in Britain during the 1939–45 war, when unexplained faults in Royal Air Force equipment were blamed on 'gremlins' or 'bugs'.

(2) More recently, the process of finding and removing errors from a COMPUTER program. Detailed and sustained accuracy of the kind required to program correctly is not

within the normal range of human achievement except, perhaps, by the use of more rigorously mathematical techniques than are yet common. It has therefore been necessary to work on the assumption that all programs have errors and to develop techniques for finding and correcting them. These techniques are still very imperfect, time-consuming and costly.

(3) The removal of secret sound-detecting devices. E.R.L.; C.S.; J.E.S.

decadence. In literature, an aspect and offshoot of the 19th-century SYMBOLIST and aesthetic (Art for Art's Sake) movements. Arising from the bohemian protest against BOURGEOIS society in France from the 1840s onward, decadence took and emphasized the febrile, neurasthenic and world-weary element in the Symbolist presumption about the poet, and also dramatized its belief in the essential amoralism of art. As in much Symbolism, it was a subject-matter and an imaginative response enacted as a LIFE-STYLE. Owing much to Flaubert and Rimbaud, the motto of its exponents (known as the *decadents*) was Rimbaud's: 'The poet makes himself a seer by a long, intensive, and reasoned disordering of all the senses.' Intensified by a sense of cultural ANOMIE, a high-style dandyism and a *fin de siècle* despair, it has particular associations with the 1880s and 1890s, e.g. Huysmans's *À Rebours* (1884), and in England Swinburne, Wilde, Aubrey Beardsley (art editor of *The Yellow Book*), Ernest Dowson and Lionel Johnson. With the Wilde/Queensberry trial in 1895 the public display of decadence suffered a setback. However, as a poetic sensibility it has remained important in modern writing. In popular usage, signifying a decline from established artistic and moral standards, decadence is equivalent to DEGENERACY, a CONCEPT first popularized around the same time. See also AESTHETICISM. For further reading: A. E. Carter, *The Idea of Decadence in French Literature, 1830–1900* (1958). M.S.BR.

décalage ('uncoupling, temporal displacement'). In DEVELOPMENTAL PSYCHOLOGY, a PIAGETIAN term for either (*horizontal décalage*) discrepancy in the age or level of intellectual development at which a person can deal with different versions of a problem that are identical when regarded in terms of their formal logical structure; or (*vertical décalage*) a time-gap in his mastery of problems that are different when so regarded. Vertical *décalage* is thus a logical corollary of any theory that posits STAGES OF DEVELOPMENT in the form of intellectual functioning, whereas horizontal *décalage* is in the nature of an anomaly. I.M.L.H.

decarceration. A term popularized by the historical sociologist Andrew Scull to depict the move since World War II to remove people (the mentally ill, criminals, etc.) from exclusive institutional confinement, and to reinstate them within society at large (e.g., within 'community care'). Scull (who has particularly investigated the case of the mentally ill) has put the motivation of this seemingly liberal trend under scrutiny. Alongside the obviously idealistic grounds for this policy, Scull has contended that, in the USA in particular, decarceration represents both a new INDIVIDUALISM of the political RIGHT (the belief that it is not the function of the state to play a paternalistic role) and a financial crisis of WELFARE capitalism. In Britain, policy aims are to reduce institutional confinement for the mentally sick to a minimum, replacing it with community care in various forms (day centres, hospitals, acute units, outpatient clinics and the like). Extensive use of psychotropic (mood-influencing) drugs from the 1950s has guaranteed the safety of such 'deinstitutionalization'. For further reading: A. Scull, *Decarceration* (1984). R.P.

decentration.

(1) In PERCEPTION and thinking, successive shifts of attention which take account of various aspects of a situation and synthesize therefrom a more representative view or interpretation of them than is obtained by centring attention on one aspect only.

(2) PIAGETIAN term for the progress of the child away from an exclusively egocentric view of the world. I.M.L.H.

decision procedure. A routine, ALGORITHM, definite procedure or computer program which will correctly answer 'true' or 'false' when asked a mathematical question. For restricted parts of MATHEMATICS such procedures exist, but there are mathematical questions which we do not know how to begin to answer. In fact, there are many mathematical questions which simply do not have an answer. David Hilbert in 1900 listed 23 questions he thought should be studied, of which number two was to prove the consistency (freedom from contradiction) of arithmetic. His work on this led to a search for a decision procedure for the whole of mathematics. In 1936 Alonzo Church and Alan Turing independently proved that no such procedure could ever be found. Turing's work involved a primitive computer (the Turing Machine), and an amusing by-product of his work was the fact that the halting problem itself can have no decision procedure (the halting problem is to determine, given any program, if the associated calculation will ever come to an end). Lack of decision procedures means that mathematicians need inspiration to solve problems. N.A.R.

decision theory. The context in which the theory of STATISTICS is usually constructed nowadays. The experimenter is faced with a number of possible courses of action and a number of possible states of the real world; in decision theory a cost is associated with each combination of response and reality, and, loosely speaking, the decision on which course of action to adopt is taken so as to minimize the cost. Since the state of the world is usually only known in terms of relative probabilities of different states, a genuine minimal-cost policy is not usually available, and normally policies – *decision procedures* – are constructed so as to minimize the maximum possible cost or the expected cost. The type of policy sought will depend on the experimenter's trade-off between expected cost and cost VARIANCE – a classic economic problem. Most statistical reasoning, whether orthodox or BAYESIAN, can be fitted into the framework of decision theory. Decision theory is often used in the context of MANAGEMENT STUDIES, notably in the form of RISK ANALYSIS. For further reading: H. Raiffa, *Decision Analysis* (1968). R.SI.

decision tree, see under RISK ANALYSIS.

décollage. A technique developed notably by the German graphic artist Wolf Vostell in the late 1950s, by which strips are torn off a COLLAGE to suggest a peeling poster. As these works often involve fragments of words and letters they bear some relation to LETTRISM, as well as to the FLUXUS movement of which Vostell formed part. J.W.

decolonization. The process whereby a country gives up its authority over its dependent territories and grants them the status of sovereign states. It can be seen most clearly in the development following World War II of the former British Empire into the COMMONWEALTH of independent states, or of the French Empire into the Commonauté Française. This represented a triumph for the nationalist movements which had agitated for independence and took over government when the colonial powers withdrew. However, the achievement of national sovereignty and admission to the UN have been followed by controversy over whether decolonization has led to real independence or only neo-colonialism (see IMPERIALISM). This term describes a formal juridical independence accompanied by a *de facto* domination and exploitation by foreign nationals, together with the persistence of many of the features of colonialism: e.g. narrow economic specialization, cultural and educational inferiority. Accordingly, decolonization is now viewed not merely as the transfer of constitutional powers from colonizer to colonized, but as a broader process encompassing, among other things, the ending of financial and trading privileges, the unravelling of military ties and cultural influences, and the demographic and economic shifts which accompanied these processes (see also POST-COLONIALISM. For further reading: J. Darwin, *Britain and Decolonisation: The Retreat from Empire in the Post-War World* (1988). N.O; S.A.; A.L.C.B.

deconstruction. A technique associated with Jacques Derrida, who in 1967 inaugurated the post-structural movement with his book *Of Grammatology*. In a series of astute readings of major philosophical and literary texts, Derrida showed that, by taking the unspoken or unformulated propositions of a text literally, by showing the gaps and *supplements*, the subtle internal self-contradictions, the text can be shown to be saying something quite other than what it appears to be saying. In fact, in a certain sense, the text can be shown not to be 'saying something' at all, but many different things, some of which subtly subvert the conscious intentions of the writer. By throwing into relief the self-betrayal of the text, the effects of the supplement and of *différance*, of *trace* and of *dissemination*, Derrida shows that the text is telling its own story, quite a different story from what the writer imagines he is creating. A new text thus gradually begins to emerge, but this text too is subtly at variance with itself, and the deconstruction continues in what could be an infinite regress of dialectical readings. The main effect of Derrida's deconstructive teaching has been to destroy the naïve assumption that a text has 'a' MEANING, which industry, application and attentive good faith will eventually winnow out – the basic assumption of the old NEW CRITICISM of the 1940s and 1950s. Meaning is not encased or contained in language, but is co-extensive with the play of language itself. Derrida shows that the meanings of a text are 'disseminated' across its entire surface, but are and remain purely linguistic surface features: there is no one guaranteeing 'meaning' which inhabits a text and which constitutes its 'presence'. The link between text and meaning is cut. Authorial intention dissolves in the play of signifiers; the text is seen to subvert its own apparent meaning; and there is no reference from the language of the text to some mystical interior of the text, in which some non-linguistic essence ('meaning') would or could ultimately be found.

Derrida's technique, continued through a series of applied studies of texts, has had an enormous influence, particularly in literary theory in the US. The YALE SCHOOL, comprising Paul de Man, Harold Bloom, J. Hillis Miller and Geoffrey Hartman, dominated American criticism in the 1970s with its deconstructive talent and panache. Deconstruction reached the limits of its enterprise in the early 1980s, and is now in a fallow period, seeking a new theoretical foothold. (See also APORIA; DIFFÉRANCE; LOGOCENTRISM; SUPPLEMENT, LOGIC OF.) For further reading: C. Norris, *Deconstruction* (1982). R.PO.

découpage. Signifying 'cutting up' or 'cutting out' in common French usage, *découpage* has a specific meaning in film terms equivalent to the English 'shooting script': the breakdown, before filming begins, of dialogue and action into shots, scenes of sequences dependent on camera placement, movement of actors, or change of location. By extension, however, *découpage* may be used as a structural concept (as 'shooting script' cannot) referring to the underlying rhythm of a film in terms of spatial and temporal movement. English critical terminology, lacking an equivalent, sometimes borrows *découpage* in this secondary sense. T.C.C.M.

decriminalization. A term employed in several debates about prohibited (see PROHIBITION) and/or illegal activities which have a consensual basis and/or where formal controls are regarded as anachronistic or inappropriate. Examples may include prostitution, soft drug use, gambling or certain types of sexual activity.

Currently, it is most frequently encountered as a proposition in the modern debate about the control of illegal drugs. If drug controls seem to have no effect, drug use continues to rise, and society suffers increasing crime- and health-related problems, then should 'control' be abandoned and 'decriminalization' or 'legalization' be applied? The former would retain the prohibition of drug trafficking, but possession of drugs for personal consumption would no longer be regarded as an offence. The latter would propose the removal of all legal controls in all respects, arguing that these are counter-productive and that it is the illegality of the drug supply system that ensures that high profits may be made by criminal ENTREPRENEURS. If drug supply were legal it could be regulated as a commercial business and taxed, with the revenues supporting health education and services. Drugs would no longer generate criminal activity, thereby saving the criminal justice system money and resources. Crime and violence associated with the illegality of drug use, territorial disputes and trafficking would cease.

Opponents argue that the present system may be imperfect but the proposed changes would be ruinous. They would dramatically increase the population of drug users and hence costs to society, to families and to individual users. Drugs might be legal but would not be free, therefore an increased number of users would still have to find the funds to pay for drugs, which would be likely to increase drug-related crime. Furthermore, increased availability of drugs would have its most destructive effects in those communities of the poor and marginalized already damaged by serious drug problems. The implications of a legalized trade for the THIRD-WORLD nations which are the principal producers of plant drug crops would also need careful thought. N.S.

deduction, see under DEMONSTRATION.

deductive explanation, see under EXPLANATION.

deductivism, see under POPPERIAN.

deep structure ***and surface structure.*** A central theoretical distinction in some models of GENERATIVE GRAMMAR. The surface structure of a sentence is the string of sounds/words that we articulate and hear. Analysing the surface structure of a sentence through CONSTITUENT ANALYSIS is a universal procedure which indicates many important facts about linguistic structure; but it by no means indicates everything, e.g. it cannot explain how we recognize ambiguous sentences which have different surface forms but the same basic meaning (e.g. *cats chase mice* and *mice are chased by cats*). For such reasons, linguists in the late 1950s postulated a deep or 'underlying' structure for sentences – a LEVEL of structural organization in which all the factors determining structural interpretation are defined and interrelated. A grammar was thought to operate by generating a set of abstract deep structures in its phrase-structure rules, subsequently converting these underlying representations into surface structures by applying a set of transformational rules (see TRANSFORMATIONAL GRAMMAR). This two-level conception of grammatical structure has since been largely replaced by other models, but there is no doubting its influence on the development of generative linguistics. D.C.

defamiliarization (*ostranenie*). The central concern of the Russian FORMALISTS was to identify and define what distinguishes a literary work from any other kind of written expression, to define what constitutes LITERARINESS. They settled for *ostranenie*, 'making strange'. Far from reflecting reality in some direct way as 19th-century fiction pretends to do, the literary work tends to upset and disorient readerly expectations, so as to throw into relief the sheerly constructed, arbitrary, written nature of the work of art. AVANT-GARDE literary technique, in particular, by parody, distortion, irreverence, tends to throw into relief the merely conventional nature of precursor works in the same genre. By parodying or undermining previous work in the same genre, the operative assumptions of a genre are 'defamiliarized' and the work's inherence in mere 'literariness' is made self-evident. For further reading: T. Bennett, *Formalism and Marxism* (1979). R.PO.

defeasibility and **incorrigibility.** In PHILOSOPHY, a BELIEF or statement is said to be defeasible when it is vulnerable to refutation by further or future evidence. For example, any of our everyday beliefs, assumptions and expectations may turn out to be wrong and are thus defeasible. The opposite of defeasibility is *incorrigibility*. Beliefs or statements are incorrigible when it is impossible for them to be wrong or for one to be mistaken about them, as for example when they are directly self-verifying. Thus Descartes' 'I exist' is an incorrigible statement since one cannot be mistaken about its truth whenever one utters it. Beliefs and statements about the contents of one's private psychological states, including one's sensory experiences, are said to be incorrigible likewise; their being so is not affected by the fact that they may trivially be misdescribed, as when someone, owing to a slip of the tongue or ignorance, says 'this seems to me red' when to observe convention correctly he should not have used 'red' but 'blue'.

There is a narrower sense of defeasibility in which something, say a CONCEPT or a legal provision, is said to have this property if it only applies when not prevented from doing so by any defeating or obstructing conditions. This is the original legal meaning of the term from which its philosophical use has been adapted. A.C.G.

defects. Topological defects (or defects) are structures that can form when physical systems undergo a change of PHASE. They often consist of lines (STRINGS) or sheets (walls) of energy. Strings (also called 'cosmic strings' to distinguish them from SUPER-

STRINGS) are of particular interest in COSMOLOGY because it is proposed that such structures might have formed naturally in the first moments of the universe's history and then provided the seeds around which ordinary forms of matter congregated and condensed into galaxies and GALAXY clusters billions of years later. Recent simulations of this process by supercomputers have shown that it may be impossible for this sequence of events to have happened without leaving producing patterns in the radiation background in the universe of a sort that are not observed. Defects can also exist in the form of MAGNETIC MONOPOLES. These heavy PARTICLES have never been observed definitively by physicists. Their existence appears inevitable in the big bang theory of the expanding universe. The inflationary universe theory of Alan Guth, in which the expansion of the universe accelerates for a brief period of its early history, was developed in order to show how we can avoid the over-abundance of monopoles in our universe (the so-called 'monopole problem'). For further reading: A. Guth, *The Inflationary Universe* (1997). J.D.B.

defence mechanism. In psychoanalytic theory (see PSYCHOANALYSIS), a FREUDIAN term for any number of unconscious techniques or devices used by the EGO to avoid danger (which is signalled by ANXIETY). There is no single agreed list of defence mechanisms, but these techniques would usually be said to include IDENTIFICATION (sense 2), PROJECTION, RATIONALIZATION and REGRESSION (sense 2). Most of them are unsuccessful defences, i.e. they do not succeed in getting rid of the dangerous impulse. The two best-known successful defences are the destruction of the repressed impulse in the ID, and SUBLIMATION. B.A.F.

deficiency payments. Payments from general exchequer funds to supplement market prices received by farmers with the aim of raising them to some predetermined level. Migration from farming to other occupations over a period tends to reduce the disparity in incomes with those in other sectors of the economy, but not enough to prevent governments from coming under pressure to make farming more prosperous (see AGRICULTURAL POLICY). In consequence, they have introduced a variety of measures, many of them directed towards increasing the prices for farm products above the normal market price. Some of these arrangements raise the level of prices at all stages of the distribution process, e.g. the Common Agricultural Policy (CAP) of the EUROPEAN UNION (EU). Others, e.g. the deficiency payments scheme, introduced first in the UK in the early 1930s, allow the market to operate freely. Typically, a guaranteed price is set in advance, the average actual market price is calculated, and the difference between the two paid direct to the farmer as a deficiency payment. For another method of assisting uneconomic parts of an agricultural industry see STRUCTURAL REFORM. K.E.H.

deficit finance, see under FISCAL POLICY.

deficit hypothesis. In SOCIOLINGUISTICS and EDUCATIONAL LINGUISTICS, the view that some children, especially those belonging to an ethnic minority or with a WORKING-CLASS background, lack a sufficiently wide range of grammatical constructions and vocabulary to be able to express complex ideas, such as will be needed for success in school. An unfashionable hypothesis in today's intellectual climate, it is contrasted with the *difference hypothesis* – the view that the language used by such children is simply different from that found in MIDDLE-CLASS children, though its social standing is lower. The difference hypothesis views all dialects (see DIALECTOLOGY) as intrinsically equal and able to express ideas of any complexity, though children who speak non-standard dialects may not have had the same kind of opportunity or motivation to use their language in demanding educational contexts (see also EBONICS). For further reading: P. Trudgill, *Sociolinguistics* (1983). D.C.

deficit spending, see under FISCAL POLICY.

defining, see under ESSENCE.

deflation, see under INFLATION.

deforestation. Refers to what is believed to be a net decline of forests on a global basis. There is some uncertainty in this conclusion because we have only scanty knowledge of afforestation or deforestation over a long time span. It is well established that some parts of the globe that were once in forest have been largely if not entirely deforested (e.g., England, much of the Near East, Haiti), while other parts, such as the north-eastern United States, have experienced a net increase in forested land in recent decades following extensive deforestation a few centuries ago.

Historically, wood has been harvested from forests for use as fuel, for construction, and to clear land for agriculture. Despite uncertainties regarding past practice it is clear that deforestation is occurring today at unprecedented rates, spurred by POPULATION PRESSURE and the development of cutting and transportation technology. Growing populations create growing demand for wood, and technological developments bring previously inaccessible forests – in the tropics and in mountainous regions – within reach of large corporate foresters.

The deforestation of tropical rainforests in south-east Asia, central Africa and the Amazon river basin of South America, monitored by satellite as well as by ground observation, has been the cause of particular concern. Tropical deforestation exposes shallow soils which are rapidly degraded by rain and depleted by agriculture. Deforestation also causes the extinction of countless members of the forest biota from loss of habitat. Since PHOTOSYNTHESIS in the rainforests absorbs carbon dioxide and produces oxygen, these ECOSYSTEMS have been termed the 'lungs' of the biosphere, and their loss may seriously impair the earth's atmospheric gaseous (as well as its water) balancc and contribute to global climate change. See also: ECOSYSTEM SERVICES; SUSTAINABILITY. W.G.R.

degeneracy. The German term *Entartung* (departure from the Art or 'breed'), as applied to MODERNISM in the arts, derives from a book (1893) of that name by Max Nordau, a doctor and a founder of ZIONISM, who argued that much of the CULTURE of his time was pathologically degenerate. Already potentially racialist (see RACE), this expression became frankly so in the 1920s with the writings of Hans Günther (*Rasse und Stil*, 1926) and the architect Paul Schultze-Naumburg (*Kunst und Rasse*, 1928), to emerge after 1933 as the principal slogan in NAZISM's campaign against modern art. During 1937 the German museums were systematically purged of 'degenerate art', of which a great derisive exhibition was held in Munich; a Degenerate Music show in Düsseldorf followed in 1938. Movements condemned included CUBISM, fauvism (see FAUVES), EXPRESSIONISM, DADA, CONSTRUCTIVISM and SURREALISM, most of IMPRESSIONISM, and all but the MAGIC REALIST wing of NEUE SACHLICHKEIT (Italian FUTURISM was exempted on political grounds); and in music the twelve-note school (see SERIAL MUSIC), GEBRAUCHSMUSIK and JAZZ. Many artists were banned from working or exhibiting; many emigrated, including all the principal teachers of the BAUHAUS. Ironically, degeneracy was largely identified with *Kunstbolschewismus* or 'art BOLSHEVISM' though actually fulfilling much the same role as did FORMALISM in the similar purge conducted simultaneously in the former USSR. For further reading: H. Lehmann-Haupt, *Art under a Dictatorship* (1954). J.W.

degenerationism. Ideas that mankind has declined and decayed from some former Golden Age or Paradisical state have pervaded culture, literature and science ever since biblical and Greek times. Modern scientific ideas of degenerationism take their intellectual ancestry from these roots. But they assumed a new synthesis and power from the mid-19th century. Central to modern degenerationism were medical notions of the progressive manifestation of inherited physical and mental defects, advanced in particular by the French psychiatrist B. A. Morel (syphilis and ALCOHOLISM proved influential models). Such views were supported, perhaps paradoxically, by evolutionary theory (unless society weeded out, rather than protecting, the unfit, mankind would become a declining rather than a progressive species). THERMODYNAMICS also lent a cosmic dimension, with its notions of ENTROPY and the eventual HEAT DEATH OF THE UNIVERSE. Literary bohemianism and the philosophies of Schopenhauer and Nietzsche popularized and even sensationalized *fin de siècle* world-weariness, and the sense of the enervation of liberal and Romantic CULTURE. It remains hotly contested how much 20th-century IRRATIONALIST cults and totalitarian political movements (see TOTALITARIANISM) owe to degenerationist theories (overtly, of course, FASCISM denounced such decadence). At the scientific level, mainstream currents in 20th-century PSYCHIATRY and evolutionary BIOLOGY have rejected degenerationism as speculative and biased. For further reading: J. E. Chamberlin and S. L. Gilman (eds), *Degeneration* (1985). R.P.

dehumanization. The restriction or denial of free play to those qualities, thoughts and activities which are characteristically human. Dehumanization is self-alienation rather than ALIENATION from an external structure or system, although Marx saw it (*Entmenschung*) as an inseparable element of the general alienation of labour in a social system where the worker is obliged to work in order to survive rather than to manifest and develop his individual personality or sensibility. Today the term is widely used in connection with those mechanical, repetitive assembly-line tasks which reduce the performers to the level of components in a machine. P.S.L.

deindustrialization. The decline in the absolute or relative size of the manufacturing sector, where size is measured by output. Correspondingly, the relative sizes of other sectors increase. This decline must be viewed in the context of the characteristic of ECONOMIC DEVELOPMENT that in mature economies the relative level of employment in the manufacturing sector declines. Deindustrialization is important as: (1) the manufacturing sector represents a large proportion of total employment and output, and it may be difficult to switch unemployed resources and labour to other sectors; (2) in developed economies, the manufacturing sector has grown rapidly in terms of output and productivity; (3) if manufacturing and other exports are not able to support the FULL EMPLOYMENT level of imports, NATIONAL INCOME and employment may have to be reduced to balance the current account of the BALANCE OF PAYMENTS.

There are three hypotheses concerning the causes of deindustrialization. (1) The increased share of resources taken by the public sector has crowded out the manufacturing sector (see MONETARISM). (2) The output of the manufacturing sector is particularly affected by a country's and its competitors' abilities to export manufactured goods. Decline in a country's export performance may be caused by an overvalued EXCHANGE RATE, production of types of manufactured goods for which the world demand is only increasing slowly, not producing new types of manufactured goods for which the world demand is increasing rapidly, lack of technical progress, and poor MARKETING. (3) This is really a special case of (2); it is commonly referred to as *Dutch disease*. Countries that begin to export substantial quantities of oil may experience surpluses on the current account of the balance of payments that lead to the exchange rate rising. This reduces the exports of other tradeable goods, particularly manufactures. This can have serious consequences on UNEMPLOYMENT, as, by comparison with oil production, manufacturing is labour-intensive. For further reading: F. Blackaby, *Deindustrialization* (1979). J.P.

deism. The belief that GOD exists but has not revealed himself except in the normal courses of nature and history. Deists have been very cautious about describing God or offering any hope that he will save men from disaster or death. Deism flourished in England, France and the USA in the 18th century, but more recently people so suspicious of personal RELIGION have usually described themselves as agnostics (see AGNOSTICISM), particularly since modern studies have sharply raised the question as to whether God can be known in nature or history. See also THEISM. For further reading: M. Wiles, *God's Action in the World* (1986). D.L.E.

deixis (deictic). In LINGUISTICS, features of language which relate directly to the personal, temporal or locational characteristics of the situation in which an utterance takes place, and whose meaning is thus relative to that situation. Examples include *here/there*, *now/then*, *I/you*, *this/that*. The notion is analogous to that of 'indexical expression' in PHILOSOPHY. D.C.

deliberative democracy. A catchphrase for projects aimed at increasing public participation in political decision-making. The idea has been the basis for experiments using 'citizens' juries' and 'electronic town hall meetings' in Germany, the US and the

UK. Deliberative democracy arose to counteract increasing voter apathy in general elections, as well as long-standing theoretical scepticism to the effect that DEMOCRACY cannot work in culturally diverse, technically complex societies. The experiments have generally shown that a sample of the general public can overcome cultural and technical barriers when told that the results of their deliberations will inform policy. But given the isolated nature of the experiments to date, there has been little opportunity for long-term collective learning, which is needed if deliberative democracy is to raise the average level of political competence. S.F.

delinquency. A fault, misdeed or transgression (Latin *delictum*; *in flagrante delicto* = red-handed) against some written or unwritten law; also the state of being, or tendency to be, a transgressor. In the literature of CRIMINOLOGY the word, whether explicitly or implicitly qualified as *juvenile*, is used with particular reference to children and young offenders, and is almost synonymous with *juvenile crime*, although *juvenile delinquency* is perhaps more likely to imply a theory of the subject. Such theories have been derived from studies of PEER GROUPS (especially in the urban context), while psychiatrists and psychoanalysts maintain that the key to the problem lies in early childhood experiences (see PSYCHIATRY; PSYCHOANALYSIS). Whatever the causes of delinquency, there is today general agreement that juvenile delinquents are less responsible than older offenders, and require special handling in the form of juvenile courts, training institutions, etc. T.M.

delta blues, see under FOLK MUSIC.

demand. In ECONOMICS, the demand for a commodity is the quantity which potential purchasers would like to buy and depends on their preferences, their incomes, the price of other products, and the price of the product in question. When allowance has been made for the other three factors, the dependence of demand on the product's own price is often illustrated by a *demand curve* which shows demand falling as the price rises. Together with supply, demand determines prices in markets (see also SUPPLY AND DEMAND). The total of demands of different people for different products is very important in determining (NATIONAL) INCOME. See also AGGREGATE DEMAND; PRICE MECHANISM. J.S.F.

demand-pull, see under INFLATION.

deme. Originally denoting a township in ancient Attica, and then a COMMUNE in modern Greece, the word has also been used, though not very widely, since 1883 by some biologists to denote an assemblage or AGGREGATION, particularly of single-CELL organisms or even of subcellular bodies such as plastids. Occasionally the term was applied to higher plants and animals, which explains its adoption by some experimental taxonomists (see TAXONOMY) from 1939 onwards as a root, to be used with an appropriate prefix, to denote a group of individuals belonging to a specific taxon or SPECIES, e.g. *gamodeme* (a deme of individuals which can interbreed), *ecodeme* (a deme occurring in a specified HABITAT), *topodeme* (a deme occurring in a specified area), *genodeme* (a deme differing from others genotypically; see GENOTYPE). These uses have, however, only been generally accepted by those associated with the Cambridge (England) school of experimental taxonomy. K.M.

dementia, see under NEUROPSYCHOLOGY.

democracy.

(1) A word originating in the classical Greek city states, and meaning the rule of the *demos*, the citizen body: the right of all to decide what are matters of general concern. The size of modern nation-states has meant that (apart from those which include provision for a referendum in their constitutions) democracy is no longer direct but indirect, i.e. through the election of representatives; hence the term *representative democracy*. The CRITERIA of democracy are therefore: (a) whether such elections are free: i.e. whether they are held frequently and periodically, whether every citizen has the right to vote, whether candidates and parties are free to campaign in opposition to the government of the day, and whether the voter is protected against intimidation by the secrecy of the ballot; (b) whether such elections provide an effective choice:

i.e. whether the choice of the electors is not limited to a single party, and whether a majority vote against the government in power leads to a change of government; (c) whether the elected body of representatives – variously known as parliament, congress, national assembly – has the right of legislation, the right to vote taxes and control the budget (deciding such matters by majority vote), and the right publicly to question, discuss, criticize and oppose government measures without being subject to threats of interference or arrest.

Democracy is based on a belief in the value of the individual human being, and a further criterion is therefore the extent to which certain basic rights are guaranteed (in practice, not just on paper) to every citizen. These are: security against arbitrary arrest and imprisonment; freedom of speech, of the press, and of assembly (i.e. the right to hold public meetings); freedom of petition and of association (i.e. the right to form parties, TRADE UNIONS and other societies); freedom of movement; freedom of RELIGION and of teaching. As a corollary, democracy is held to require the establishment of an independent judiciary and courts to which everyone can have access.

Critics of democracy fall into two groups. The first is opposed to democracy, root and branch, on the grounds that it is the least efficient form of government and one in which the stability of the state is threatened by faction, complex issues are distorted by popular discussion, difficult decisions evaded or put off, and matters of judgement reduced to the lowest common denominator acceptable to a majority of the voters. (See TOTALITARIANISM; FASCISM.) The second, in favour of the *principles* of democracy, argues that these are inadequately realized unless carried further, e.g. by extending equal rights for all citizens from the political and legal to the economic sphere, without which (so it is argued; see SOCIALISM; COMMUNISM) democracy remains at best incomplete, at worst a sham (*formal democracy*) disguising the reality of CLASS rule.

A variant of this type of criticism argues that, with the growth of BUREAUCRACY and the power of governments, decisions are no longer effectively influenced by the view of the government or the elected representatives; hence the demand for greater PARTICIPATION at all levels of decision-making and the problem of how to reconcile this demand with the need for prompt and effective decision on complex and controversial issues. Judged by the criteria set out above, no single-party state (e.g. China, North Korea) can be regarded as democratic since it offers no freedom of choice and little, if any, freedom of expression to its citizens.

(2) The same principles of representative democracy can be applied to other organizations besides the state, e.g. local government councils, trade unions, political parties, Protestant churches, etc. One of the demands of the radical movement of protest in many Western countries since the 1960s has been for democracy to be made more effective in such organizations, as well as in government, by greater participation of the rank-and-file membership in decision-making, and for the extension of democratic procedures to other types of organization, e.g. factories (*industrial democracy*), universities (*student democracy*).

See also SOCIAL DEMOCRACY. For further reading: A. Breton, *Understanding Democracy: Economic and Political Perspectives* (1997); Richard S. Catz, *Democracy and Elections* (1998). A.L.C.B.

democratic centralism. A basic tenet of LENINISM used as the organizational principle in all COMMUNIST parties (see USSR, THE FORMER). It was supposed to combine free political discussion in the Party and free election of its leaders with strict hierarchical discipline in the execution of decisions reached by democratic methods (see DEMOCRACY). Historical evidence suggests that the first part of the formula had nowhere been operative for any length of time and that it had consistently been subordinated to the second. In effect, 'democratic centralism' came to signify the method of autocratic or oligarchic control of the Party through its central apparat. This was made clear in the *21 Conditions of Admission* to the COMINTERN, which declared that 'the Communist Party will be able to fulfil its duty only if its organization is as centralized as possible, if iron discipline prevails, and if the Party centre, upheld by the confidence of the Party membership, has strength and authority and is equipped with the most comprehensive powers'. For further reading: M. Waller, *Democratic Centralism: An Historical Commentary* (1981). L.L.

Democratic Leadership Conference. A group within the US Democratic Party formed by Southern moderates in 1985, following the failed candidacy of Walter Mondale that led to President Ronald Reagan's landslide re-election victory the year before. After that election, the Democratic National Committee commissioned a $250,000 study of 5,000 Southern Democrats who defected to the Republican cause. The report found that many of the so-called Reagan Democrats believed the party had abandoned their interests for blacks, Hispanics and the poor. The DLC was formed in part to help the party recapture the white vote, and in 1988 successfully pushed for holding presidential primaries in the South on the same 'Super Tuesday' to give voters of that region a greater say in selecting the nominee. It did not help in 1988, but the 1992 election of Bill Clinton – a former DLC chairman – vindicated the conference's push to the centre. Still, DLC members were upset by Clinton's adoption of traditional liberal policies in the first two years he held office; a position he quickly abandoned to return to 'New Democratic' policies after the Republican takeover of Congress in 1994. R.K.H.

demographic transition. A gradual shift from the high levels of FERTILITY and MORTALITY characteristic of traditional, agricultural societies to the low levels characteristic of modern, INDUSTRIAL SOCIETIES. Typically, the decline in death rates precedes the fall in birth rates by an interval of at least several decades; during this period, the POPULATION GROWTH RATE is higher than either before or after the transition. The rapid growth of the world population during the last two or three centuries can be directly attributed to the demographic transition. This transition occurred rather slowly in western Europe and the US during the 18th, 19th and early 20th centuries. The transition has been occurring much more rapidly in other parts of the world during the 20th century (and especially since 1950). Currently, all national populations have enjoyed at least a modest decline in death rates and a concomitant rise in life expectancy. The second part of the transition, the fertility decline, is now well advanced in east Asia and in parts of south-east Asia and Latin America. At least moderate fertility declines have now been documented in all regions of the world, including sub-Saharan Africa. The causes of these changes are known to be complex. A dominant factor is the process of INDUSTRIALIZATION, which has contributed to lower mortality through improvements in living conditions (especially better nutrition) and to lower fertility through changes in the relative costs and benefits of raising children (in part due to educational expenses). On its own, however, economic change provides an inadequate explanation of the demographic transition. For example, the decline of mortality was also due to improvements in the scientific understanding of disease, which affected practices in both public health and medicine. Similarly, the decline of fertility has also been driven by the dissemination of knowledge about birth control and by changes in social attitudes concerning sex and reproduction (see also CONTRACEPTION). J.R.W.

demographics. The study of human populations with regard to their current characteristics and short-term trends. The term is also used to refer to the characteristics of a population at some moment with respect to both demographic and economic variables, as in 'the demographics of the baby boom generation'. In the former usage, the term is synonymous with 'applied demography'. Thus, as a field of enquiry, demographics differs from DEMOGRAPHY mainly by its more limited temporal perspective and its emphasis on practical applications (for example, market research, drawing electoral districts, or municipal PLANNING). J.R.W.

demography. The study of human populations in relation to historical changes brought about by the interplay of births, deaths and MIGRATION. More broadly, demography is the study of the dynamic processes that affect the size and composition of human groups or societies (including, for example, patterns of MARRIAGE and divorce, or movements into and out of the labour force). The term is also used to refer to the characteristics of a given population, as in 'the demography of tropical Africa'.

The word was coined by the Belgian statistician Achille Guillard in 1855, although its intellectual roots are much older. A distinction is sometimes made between *pure* or *formal* demography on the one hand, and *population studies* or *social demography* on the other. The former is concerned with the collection and analysis of demographic data and with mathematical MODELS of population dynamics, while the latter implies a broader frame of reference, drawing on work in related fields of study (in particular, SOCIOLOGY, ANTHROPOLOGY and ECONOMICS). J.R.W.

demography, historical, see HISTORICAL DEMOGRAPHY.

demonstratives. In PHILOSOPHY, interest is shown in the demonstrative pronouns 'this' and 'that' because they are guaranteed a reference whenever they occur as the subjects of propositions, for example 'this is red', 'that costs forty pounds', for in every such case there is something at which the speaker might literally point his finger. Therefore no problems arise as they do when use is made of a name or phrase which may fail to refer to anything. For example: there is at present no King of France. If one said 'the present King of France is wise' would one have said something true or false? If one says 'false', does this imply the truth of 'the present King of France is unwise'? Clearly not. The problem here does not concern whether someone is wise or unwise, but the fact that in this case there is no 'someone' of whom wisdom or its opposite can be asserted: the proposition's subject-term, namely 'the present King of France', does not refer to anything. In the course of a famous piece of logical analysis concerning this problem (the *Theory of Descriptions*), Bertrand Russell argued that 'this' and 'that', and their plurals, are the only expressions of ordinary language which are logically acceptable subject-terms in propositions, and that all other expressions which may occupy subject place in the sentences of ordinary language can be 'analysed out' when one inspects their underlying logical structure. Such analysis, he said, shows that whereas the expressions in question may occupy grammatical subject place in sentences, they do not, unlike the demonstratives, also occupy logical subject place in the propositions expressed by those sentences. See ANALYSIS. For further reading: B. Russell, *Logic and Knowledge* (1956). A.C.G.

demythologize. To interpret texts of a mythological character in such a way that their original meaning is recovered and restated in a non-mythological idiom (see MYTH). The concept of demythologization is particularly associated with the work of Rudolf Bultmann, the most important representative of EXISTENTIALIST THEOLOGY, who set out his programme of demythologizing the gospels in his 1941 essay 'New Testament and Mythology'. His aim was not to eliminate the mythological elements of the New Testament world-view (see WELTANSCHAUUNG), as some of his liberal, Protestant predecessors had done (see LIBERALISM; PROTESTANTISM), but to translate it, in the sense that he sought to express in a non-mythological way what the New Testament authors could do only mythologically. The contemporary idiom into which the message of the New Testament was translated was derived from Heidegger's EXISTENTIALIST analysis of SUBJECTIVITY. Once highly controversial, demythologization was overtaken by developments in HERMENEUTICS and the eclipse of existentialist theology after 1970. C.C.

denatured, see under PROTEIN.

dendrochronology. In PALAEOBOTANY, DATING by means of counting the annual growth rings observed in a cross-section through a tree. These rings are affected by climate during the growing season, giving rise to distinctive patterns reflecting local climatic variations. By comparing the tree-ring patterns of isolated timber samples from archaeological CONTEXTS it is possible to construct a sequence in which any ring can be dated relative to any other. If the sequences can be linked to a growing tree or a sample felled at a known time, the floating chronology can be converted into an absolute chronology. The best results are obtained in areas of extreme climatic variation. The classic study was carried out by A. E. Douglass in 1929, using timbers from Pueblo villages in the south-west USA. More recently, extremely long counts covering 6,500 years have been constructed, using the bristlecone pine which grows at high altitudes in California. These sequences have proved an invaluable check to radiocarbon age assessments (see RADIOCARBON DATING). For further reading: D. Eckstein, *Dendrochronological Dating* (1984). B.C.

Dengism. A phrase usually taken to mean the policies adopted in China after Deng Xiaoping (1904–97) consolidated his power at the 3rd plenum of the 11th CCP Central Committee, September 1978. Economically, this led to a radical move away from central planning to a greater role for market forces, and the decentralization of decision-making powers to production-level units; a move towards CAPITALISM which the Chinese prefer to refer to as 'Socialism with Chinese Characteristics'. There has also been a relaxation of controls over literature and freedom of speech, although the arrest of Wei Jingshan for advocating that DEMOCRACY should be the 5th Modernization (see FOUR MODERNIZATIONS), and the banning of certain plays, such as *WM* in 1985, show that the Party's control over society has only been curtailed, not removed. Although Dengism is usually used in reference to the post-1978 period, it is important to note that Deng's policies varied greatly over time, and an overview of his political career shows that his political philosophy was heavily based on PRAGMATISM. For further reading: D. S. G. Goodman *et al*, *The China Challenge* (1986). S.B.

Denishawn. A school established by Ruth St Denis and Ted Shawn from which most American MODERN DANCE originates. Denishawn provided a technical training in all forms of dance including Oriental, Primitive and CLASSICAL BALLET. Students of Denishawn included Martha Graham (see GRAHAM TECHNIQUE), Doris Humphrey and Charles Weidman. Denishawn presented serious concert dance often on the vaudeville stage from 1914 to 1930, appealing to a wide range of audiences across America, Europe and the Orient. Costume, lighting and make-up played a significant role in the glamorous and exotic performances. Denishawn's special interests were religious and philosophical texts, dance tradition and the values of other cultures. Ted Shawn's contribution to modern dance lies in his inspiration to introduce men into dance and to equalize male/female ratios. Graham, Humphrey and Weidman emerged from Denishawn as major choreographic talents who, unlike Denishawn, wished to use dance to communicate change in social and intellectual order and indicate dissatisfaction with the changed IDEOLOGY of the inter-war years. For further reading: J. Sherman, *The Drama of Denishawn* (1979). L.A.

density. Term used by town planners (see TOWN PLANNING) to describe the numbers of houses, buildings or people per square mile or square hectare. Residential densities are measured by the number of habitable dwelling units. There are two main types of density, net and gross. *Net density* is based upon the land taken up by the building plots, while *gross density* also includes land taken up by roads, neighbourhood shops, schools and other ancillary uses in the area. Typically in Britain the average net residential unit is 12 houses to the acre (an acre is 0.405 hectare and a hectare is 2.471 acres). In contrast, in mid-west North America suburban houses may be on one-acre plots, while in Hong Kong up to 100 dwellings per acre is not uncommon.

The formation of thick densities of sedentary populations in ancient times has been held a cause of innovations such as law, government, urban society, the DIVISION OF LABOUR and the keeping of records. High density is now considered undesirable as it leads to crowding and problems of congestion; present planning calls for the lowering of densities whenever possible, although low densities are often recognized as costly, land-consuming and possibly inefficient. (See URBANIZATION; HIGH RISE; URBAN FORM). For further reading: C. Greed, *Introducing Town Planning* (1994). J.G.; C.G.

denudation. A term that embraces all the processes involved in the wearing away and lowering of the land surface. *Weathering*, normally the initial stage in denudation, involves physical and chemical breakdown of the bedrock by various agents, principally ground water, but without any substantial removal of weathered material from the site. All the processes in which a transporting agent, including gravity operating on slopes, is involved are described as *erosion*. Fluvial, glacial and wind erosion each impose a characteristic form on a denuded landscape. See also SOIL EROSION. J.L.M.L.

deontic logic. The branch of LOGIC in which a systematic study of the relations between propositions expressing *obligation* and permission are studied. It is sometimes called 'the logic of obligation', and it is of particular relevance to ETHICS, in which among other things questions arise as to what one *ought* to do and of what one's duties and *obligations* are. Among the principles which deontic logicians seek to clarify and express are 'nothing can be both obligatory and forbidden at once', 'anything obligatory is permissible', and so on. There are close connections between deontic and MODAL LOGIC; the former may be treated as a special case of the latter. For further reading: G. H. von Wright, *An Essay in Modal Logic* (1951). A.C.G.

deontology. Strictly, and as the title of a book allegedly by Jeremy Bentham, the branch of ETHICS which inquires into the nature of moral duty and the rightness of actions; as currently used, the particular ethical theory that takes principles of duty or obligation, those that lay down what men morally ought to do, to be self-evident or self-substantiating and neither to need, nor to be susceptible of, derivation (see DEMONSTRATION) from any supposedly more fundamental moral truths, in particular from propositions or principles about the goodness of the consequences of action. The opposed view, that the rightness or wrongness of actions is determined by the goodness or badness of their consequences (whether actual, predictable or intended), is called TELEOLOGY or consequentialism. 'Let justice be done though the heavens fall' is a deontological slogan. Kant seeks to establish deontology at the outset of his chief ethical treatise by proving that the rightness of an action is unaffected by its having, in a particular case, unfortunate consequences. For further reading: B. Blanshard, *Reason and Goodness* (1961), ch. 4. A.Q.

dependency grammar. In LINGUISTICS, a type of formal grammar, developed in the 1950s (especially by the French linguist Lucien Tesnière, 1893–1954), which established types of dependencies between the elements of a construction as a means of explaining grammatical relationships. Syntactic structure is represented as 'dependency trees' – sets of nodes whose interconnections specify structural relations. D.C.

dependency ratio, see under VALUE OF CHILDREN.

dependency theory. A theory of DEVELOPMENT ECONOMICS developed by neo-Marxists (see NEO-MARXISM) during the 1960s and 1970s. It contends that the POVERTY of the poorer nations of the world results from economic and political domination by richer capitalist (see CAPITALISM) nations which have exploited poorer countries and systematically extracted SURPLUS VALUE from them. From this viewpoint the EXPLOITATION started with colonialism (see IMPERIALISM) and affluent and successful societies (for example, the Aztecs, Incas, India and the civilizations of Ghana and Benin) were impoverished as the colonial powers stole their riches, destroyed their economic and political INFRASTRUCTURES and in some cases enslaved or massacred their populations. UNDERDEVELOPMENT is therefore a key concept in the theory. Since THIRD WORLD countries gained independence, first world countries have been able to continue exploiting them because of their reliance upon first world capital investment, aid, military protection, etc. Dependency theorists argue that significant development will only be possible if third world countries try to isolate themselves from the capitalist world economy and establish autonomous socialist societies (see SOCIALISM). Dependency theory undoubtedly illuminates exploitative aspects of relationships between richer and poorer nations. However, it has fallen out of favour with the collapse of most communist societies (see COMMUNISM) and with the economic success of some formerly poor third world nations (for example, the 'Asian Tiger' economies of Hong Kong, South Korea, Taiwan and Singapore) and with claims that GLOBALIZATION makes autonomous economic development impossible. For further reading: D. Harrison, *The Sociology of Modernization and Development* (1988). M.D.H.

dependent industrialization. A term used by some advocates of a variation on DEPENDENCY THEORY. They are critical of orthodox dependency theory for claiming that development and INDUSTRIALIZATION can never take place in THIRD WORLD countries because they are dominated and exploited by rich capitalist nations (see CAPITALISM). Instead, writers like Cardoso and Faletto (see below) argue that some industrialization is allowed in the poorer countries but they remain dominated by and dependent on richer nations. They are allowed to develop only to a limited extent and in ways which do not fundamentally harm the interests of rich and powerful countries. Whether some development takes place or not depends upon the balance of class forces in third world countries. The idea seems to fit with the presence of industrialization in Latin American countries such as Brazil and Mexico; but some former third world countries, such as Taiwan and South Korea, may have industrialized to the extent that they are much less dependent on countries such as the USA and Japan, and their economic success represents significant competition for the longer-established, successful industrial capitalist nations. For further reading: F. H. Cardoso and E. Faletto, *Dependency and Underdevelopment in Latin America* (1979). M.D.H.

depersonalization. In ABNORMAL PSYCHOLOGY and PSYCHIATRY, a pathological state characterized by loss of the sense of reality of the physical or psychological self. W.Z.

depreciation, see under DEVALUATION.

depression. A term whose many meanings include the following:

(1) In meteorology, an area of low atmospheric pressure with associated weather phenomena. It is formed by a system of air rotating anticlockwise in the northern hemisphere and clockwise in the southern. In the middle latitudes depressions are associated with most of the precipitation and high winds recorded in these areas. The term *cyclone* is sometimes used synonymously with mid-latitude depressions but is usually restricted to severe tropical storms or hurricanes. P.H.

(2) In PSYCHIATRY, a state of malaise (formerly known as *melancholia*) accompanied by lowered mental and physical responsiveness to external stimuli. It may be symptomatic of a serious mental disorder (e.g. MANIC-DEPRESSIVE PSYCHOSIS), but normal depression is also known to be widespread. W.Z.

(3) In ECONOMICS, the period of the TRADE CYCLE when the rate of increase in economic activity is below that which is potentially obtainable over a long period of time. It is usually accompanied by high UNEMPLOYMENT. Economic stabilization policies attempt to flatten out the fluctuations between economic booms and slumps, and maintain a more uniform rate of increase in output (see KEYNESIAN; MONETARISM). A recession has a similar definition, but its duration is shorter. J.P.

depth psychology. The FREUDIAN and other SCHOOLS OF PSYCHOLOGY that place major emphasis on the UNCONSCIOUS aspects of mental functioning and their effects on behaviour. W.Z.

derivation, see under DEMONSTRATION.

dermatology. The science of the skin, the largest organ of the body. The skin consists of a stratified cellular epidermis and an underlying connective tissue dermis. Below the dermis is subcutaneous fat. Human skin may be hairy, possessing hair follicles and sebaceous glands but lacking encapsulated sense organs, or glabrous (hairless), as on palms and soles, possessing such sense organs within the dermis. Signs and symptoms related to the skin may indicate local disease or, less commonly, systemic disease. The work of the dermatologist embraces all aspects of the nature and function of the skin both in health and disease, and includes management of its disorders. Such disorders are common and many present problems particularly to the non-specialist.

Apart from the biology of the skin, its physical and chemical properties are subject to much current research. Research into the causation of atopic dermatitis (atopy indicates an inherited tendency to develop one or more of a related group of conditions including asthma, atopic dermatitis and hay fever) and psoriasis involves many experts and knowledge is increasing in many areas such as wound healing, melanogenesis (production and structure of melanin), inflammation and immunology (see IMMUNITY). The synthetic retinoids (analogues of Vitamin A used in the treatment of severe forms of acne, psoriasis and some congenital disorders) and the antiviral drug acyclovir (an effective treatment for HERPES simplex infections) represent important therapeutic advances. For further reading: A. J. Rook *et al*, *Textbook of Dermatology*, 3 vols. (1986). J.L.V.

desacralization, see under SACRIFICE.

desalination. The process of removing dissolved salts from water (usually sea water). The simplest method is by distillation, but this involves the supply of a large amount of heat ENERGY. Recent developments include the use of ION exchange solids (a similar process to that used in water softeners) and a membrane process which could be described as the reverse of OSMOSIS, in which the water is squeezed through a membrane under pressure. The latter process is useful where the density of salt is of the order of 3 to 5 parts per million, but difficult to apply to sea water, which has about 35 parts salt per million. E.R.L.

descent. In ANTHROPOLOGY, a relationship based on the tracing of a continuous line between an individual and an ancestor. Kin ties based on descent may govern relations between people concerning the inheritance of property and succession to office. Descent may also form the basis for a social group (descent group), the members of which are descended or claim descent from an ancestor (real or mythic). Descent may be traced through a single line, unilineal descent, or through two lines, BILATERAL/COGNATIC DESCENT. Unilineal descent can be further divided into PATRILINEAL (tracing descent exclusively through the male line, also known as agnatic) and MATRILINEAL (tracing descent exclusively through the female line, also known as uterine).

The operation of the principle of unilineal descent allocated individuals to discrete and mutually exclusive units. Societies recognizing the principle of *double unilineal descent* or *double descent* are rare. The Yako of Nigeria is one such example: the inheritance of *movable property* is organized on matrilineal lines, *immovable property* on patrilineal lines. Individuals in this system are still allocated to discrete, exclusive units – members of one patrilineage and of one matrilineage. The case of bilateral or cognatic descent is different. An individual traces common ancestry through both male and female lines. He becomes a member of all the cognatic lineages of his lineal ancestors: two in his parents' generation, four in his grandparents' generation, eight in his great grandparents' generation, and so on. In contrast to the unilineal case, the cognatic system allocates an individual to several, often overlapping, units. Although in theory different societies may be distinguished according to whether they are patrilineal, matrilineal or bilateral, in practice the picture is much less clear cut. All societies have features of the different systems, but one principle is more dominant.

The concept of descent dominated anthropological debate in Britain during the 1950s and 1960s and exercised a profound influence on KINSHIP studies. It was developed particularly by those working in African societies and received its greatest theoretical elaboration in the work of Meyer Fortes. Central to Fortes's work was the idea of descent as a jural institution. Descent groups were identified as corporations, distinct from other groups and existing in perpetuity. They were understood as part of the politico-jural domain and as such one of the fundamental units of social structure. To balance the descent principle, Fortes developed the concept of *complementary filiation*, that is the relationship between an individual and the side of his family through which descent is not traced. Problems in analysis arose when the concept of descent was transferred to other societies, particularly those outside Africa. It also became clear that a distinction had to be made between the *idea* of descent and what it actually meant in practice. For further reading: A. Barnard and A. Good, *Research Practices in the Study of Kinship* (1984). A.G.

de-schooling. A view of schooling and education associated with the names of Ivan Illich, Paul Goodman and Paulo Freire. Illich and Freire speak from experience of the impoverished THIRD WORLD of Latin America, Goodman (who died in 1972) from urban USA. All three men reject CAPITALIST, MATERIALIST society and see the school as at present a perpetuator of exploitation, and a destroyer of education, which ought to be lifelong; education must be separated from the institution of school and operate through 'educational webs', by which is meant the pupil's life experience rather than a curriculum constructed by his teachers. The de-schooling view is partly political and NEO-MARXIST, partly religious, partly anarchistic (see ANARCHISM), wholly radical-reformist (see RADICALISM). For further reading: I. Illich, *Deschooling Society* (1971). W.A.C.S.

descriptions, see under ANALYSIS (sense 2).

descriptions, theory of, see under ANALYSIS (sense 2); DEMONSTRATIVES.

desegregation. The process of ending the provision of separate (i.e. inferior) facilities for recognizably distinct racial or social groups, commonly the American BLACKS. The term was first used in the context of legal action brought by members of the American CIVIL RIGHTS MOVEMENT to end the provision of separate schools and higher education for blacks and non-blacks in the Southern states of the USA, an action pronounced on by the Supreme Court in 1954. As a result orders were issued to the schools and colleges concerned to 'desegregate' and admit blacks to their classes. The term was occasionally employed in discussions relating to APARTHEID in South Africa, particularly the abolition of petty apartheid (mixed race public transport, for instance). See also BUSING. For further reading: G. Orfield, *Dismantling Desegregation* (1996). D.C.W.; S.T.

desensitization, see under BEHAVIOUR THERAPY.

desertification. The spread of desert-like conditions to areas which are not deserts; as a result of either human activities or climatic change or a combination of the two. It is a characteristic of areas with capital-intense agriculture (as in Australia and the USA) and of less developed countries (e.g. in the Sahel). The term was first used in the late 1940s and became a major environmental issue in the 1970s, leading to a UN Conference on Desertification in Nairobi in 1977. Among the phenomena that might be included within desertification are the destruction of vegetation cover, the spread of salinity, sheet erosion and gully formation, dune reactivation and migration, and the generation of dust storms. Although some observers have envisaged desertification as a relentless outward spread of deserts across a wide front, it is more generally to be seen as a rash of land degradation around centres of human population. The causes of desertification have been the subject of debate relating to the relative importance of climatic change (e.g. the dry years in West Africa since the mid-1960s) as opposed to human activities (e.g. overgrazing, deforestation, overcultivation). A.S.G.

design & build. In the UK, a type of building contract made popular during the boom of the 1980s, in which the traditional role of the architect as the leader of the building team is supplanted by that of the building contractor. In some cases, the contractor will engage an architect to create the actual design of the building, but that is not always the case. Clients prefer design and build solutions because they are often cheaper; architects dislike them because they threaten both their workload and their professional status. Design and build contracts are responsible for a large number of deeply uninspired buildings. S.T.

designator, rigid. In PHILOSOPHY, a name or any expression with a naming function is said to designate its bearer. A name does so *rigidly* when it designates the same individual in every situation (in every POSSIBLE WORLD) in which that individual exists. Thus '2 × 2' rigidly designates 4, but 'the most famous student of Plato' does not rigidly designate Aristotle since Aristotle could have studied with someone else. The concept of rigid designation is chiefly associated with the work of Saul Kripke (*Naming and Necessity*, 1980), who, with others, argues that names do not have sense (colloquially, connotation or 'meaning') but only the function of referring to their bearers, a point upon which he insists in opposition to those philosophers who have held that the sense of a name is what a user of it has to know in order to be able to apply it correctly. A.C.G.

desire. The French term 'desire', as it is used in LACANIAN psychoanalysis, takes on a more specific connotation than the English word 'wish'. Whereas in Freud UNCONSCIOUS wishes could be fulfilled, even though only in a distorted way in dreams or in the symptom, through a chain of DISPLACEMENTS and CONDENSATIONS which keeps them repressed, desire is intrinsically unfulfillable, because it is desire for something else which is always missing in us. It is desire for the OTHER (e.g. mother) who will never fill our own lack of being, however hard she might try, but it is also desire of the Other, as all we find in this Other is his or her desire, by which we are captured. Unlike need or demand, which can be partially satisfied by a particular object, the only object of desire is an originally lost object, which Lacan calls OBJECT A. B.BE.

de-skilling. The loss of skill, creativity and control in the work process of industrial societies. Most official occupational censuses suggest the opposite. They show a general rise over time in the skill requirements of jobs in industry, as marked by the higher levels of training and education formally demanded for their performance. Taking its lead from these censuses, post-industrial theory (see POST-INDUSTRIAL SOCIETY) looks forward to a future in which the majority of workers are 'knowledge workers'. De-skilling proponents suggest that the impression of increased skill and knowledge in most jobs is a statistical illusion, created by the tendency to inflate job descriptions, and by the increasing reliance on formal educational qualifications in the allocation of jobs, irrespective of their relevance to the actual work tasks involved (CREDENTIALISM). The actual skill content of most jobs has in fact been declining, as a result of the steady increase in the DIVISION OF LABOUR and the application of the techniques of SCIENTIFIC MANAGEMENT. For further reading: H. Braverman, *Labor and Monopoly Capital: The Degradation of Work in the Twentieth Century* (1974). K.K.

détente. The extensive reduction of tensions between formerly hostile STATES, and consequent reduction of the risk of war. The term is most commonly applied to a phase in US–USSR relations from 1971 to an uncertain point in the late 1970s. The period of détente was marked by both states' asymmetrical and fluctuating interest in establishing a more harmonious relationship. The methods used included attempts at ARMS CONTROL; an increased tolerance of the other state's social and political systems; a less aggressively competitive approach to THIRD WORLD states and to western Europe; the rebuilding or creation of stronger diplomatic, economic and cultural ties. The decay of détente is explained variously as due to the undermining of US policy by divisions in élite and popular opinion and by WATERGATE; the impossibility of genuine accommodation being offered by the USSR; the change in US priorities produced by the election of President Carter in 1976; the over-ambitious attempt to link too many issues, some of which were intractable. For further reading: R. D. Schulzinger, *American Diplomacy in the Twentieth Century* (1984). S.R.

determinant, see under MATRIX.

determination, see under MORPHOGENESIS.

determinism. The theory that the world, or nature, is everywhere subject to causal law (see CAUSALITY), that every event in it has a cause. If it is true, then every event that actually happens has to happen, since it logically follows from a description of the conditions of its occurrence, together with the relevant laws of nature, that it occurs. Likewise any event that does not happen could not have happened. Sometimes the principle of determinism is taken (as by Hume and J. S. Mill) to be the most general and comprehensive of all the laws of nature, and is held to be confirmed by the way in which knowledge of causal laws so often follows the close investigation of a particular field. Sometimes, however, it is held to be a necessary TRUTH: by some because they regard it as self-evident, by others (e.g. Hobbes and Locke) because it seems easy to demonstrate, by others again (particularly Kant) because its truth is held to be a NECESSARY AND SUFFICIENT CONDITION of the possibility of organized and coherent experience. Its necessity would appear to be impugned by the view of the dominant school of quantum physicists (see QUANTUM THEORY) that the ultimate laws of nature are not causally deterministic but assert only the statistical probability (see PROBABILITY THEORY) of occurrences at the subatomic level. If human actions are included in the deterministic system, it follows that no one could ever have acted otherwise than he did, and therefore – though Hume and others have disputed this – that no one is morally responsible for his actions. See also FREE WILL. For further reading: S. Hook (ed.), *Determinism and Freedom in the Age of Science* (1958); K. Popper, *The Open Universe* (1982). A.Q.

deterministic problems, see under DYNAMIC PROGRAMMING.

deterrence. The concept of deterrence, a word whose implications are more accurately conveyed by its French equivalent, *dissuasion*, acquired a largely strategic connotation from the 1930s onwards, by reason of the development of increasingly powerful and long-range means of mass destruction which gradually rendered obsolete older strategies of territorial or maritime defence. Though NUCLEAR WEAPONS are often called 'the deterrent', deterrence essentially involves all acts of STATE policy intended to discourage, by arousing fears of effective counter-action, hostile action by another state. It is thus applicable to general military, economic and political as well as strategic relationships.

In its strategic context different forms of deterrence are distinguished. Thus, by a posture of *active deterrence* (British term) or *extended deterrence* (American term) a state implies that its deterrent power extends to attacks or provocative acts not only against its own territory and nationals, but against those of its allies. Conversely, a policy of *minimum* or *finite deterrence* is intended only to protect the state that exercises it (normally by having only sufficient weapons to destroy the adversary's cities, of which there are a finite number, rather than his forces and bases). By a strategy of *graduated deterrence* a state demonstrates its ability and intention to punish a whole range of hostile actions in proportion to their seriousness, while a situation of *mutual deterrence* is one in which two powers are deterred from attacking each other because of the unacceptable damage that would result from the victim's retaliation. For further reading: C. Bertram (ed.), *Strategic Deterrence in a Changing Environment* (1981). A.F.B.

Deutsches Theater. Berlin theatre associated for three decades with Max Reinhardt, an eclectic perfectionist whose handling of new stage devices (e.g. spotlights, the revolving stage) and power over his actors were decisive in the history of modern theatre and film. Founded in 1893 by Adolf L'Arronge, the theatre was taken over in 1903 by Otto Brahm, whose FREIE BÜHNE society of 1889 had been constituted to perform the new NATURALIST drama, and who presented numerous plays by Ibsen, Hauptmann, Sudermann, Schnitzler and others. In 1905 Reinhardt followed with a programme of naturalist and SYMBOLIST works (notably by Strindberg, whose chief interpreter he became), interspersed with revitalized classics, especially Shakespeare; to EXPRESSIONISM he was less sympathetic. During the 1920s, when Reinhardt increasingly left the Deutsches Theater to be managed by his aides, new staff members included the playwrights Carl Zuckmayer and, in 1924/25, Bertolt Brecht (see BRECHTIAN). In 1933 the Nazis (see NAZISM) took it over; in 1945 it became the main theatre of the Soviet sector of Berlin, under Wolfgang Langhoff's direction, with Brecht's Berliner Ensemble as an offshoot. J.W.

devaluation or **depreciation).** An increase in the number of units of domestic currency required to purchase a unit of foreign currency, i.e. the EXCHANGE RATE is reduced. Devaluation is often suggested as a means of improving the current account of the BALANCE OF PAYMENTS. It reduces the price of exports in terms of foreign currency and increases the prices of imports in terms of the domestic currency. The producers of exports may increase their prices in terms of the domestic currency, but not so far as to increase their prices in terms of the foreign currency. As the price of exports in terms of the foreign currency falls, the demand increases, and as the price of exports in terms of the domestic currency stays the same or increases, the revenue from exports increases (in terms of the domestic currency). Producers of imports may bear some, but not all, of the increase in the price of imports, in terms of the domestic currency. In this case, the demand for imports falls and the revenue, in terms of the domestic currency, increases or decreases, depending on the net effect of the changes in prices and demands. The net effect of a devaluation on the balance-of-payments current account depends on the sum of the beneficial effect on export revenue and the, possibly harmful, effect on import revenues. Initially, a devaluation may worsen a deficit on the current account of the balance of payments, as the domestic expenditure on imports increases and the changes in demands for exports and imports only take place slowly. This effect is known as the *j-curve*. In the long run, the changes in demands may improve the current account.

A devaluation implies a worsening of the TERMS OF TRADE and a consequent reduction in the real NATIONAL INCOME of the country. For the current account to improve, there must be unemployed resources in the economy, which can be used to produce more exports and more substitutes for imports. The use of these unemployed resources will raise the real income of the country and, possibly, offset the effect of the decline in the terms of trade on real income. An improvement in the current account of the balance of payments resulting from a devaluation may be offset by the increase in import prices leading to INFLATION, which reverses the beneficial price effects of the devaluation. The fear of devaluation leads to a flight of CAPITAL, as it will reduce the foreign currency value of domestic holdings of capital. Devaluation may increase confidence in a currency and improve the capital account of the balance of payments, though, if the devaluation is thought to be small, capital may still be moved out of the country. The level of the exchange rate is often linked to national prestige, and governments have often been reluctant to devalue. J.P.

developing countries. Countries with low or middle income (GNP) per person, less than the high-income countries of the West, Japan and the NICs (see NEWLY INDUSTRIALIZING COUNTRIES). The classification of levels of economic development used by the World Bank, *World Development Report* (annual), divides countries into three groups on the basis of per capita GNP. In 1997, these categories were low-income countries (less than $750), middle-income countries ($750–9,000), and high-income countries (more than $9,000). Each year the boundary between categories rises with inflation, but few countries shifted categories between 1975 and 1997.

Developing countries is a euphemism when applied to many in sub-Saharan Africa, which grew (developed) very little during the last quarter of the 20th century. Nevertheless, the term is widely used and usually replaces designations some consider offensive, such as less developed or underdeveloped countries.

Economic interests vary substantially between and within the following types of developing countries: (1) the economies in transition (eastern and central Europe), (2) eight members of OPEC, (3) 46 of the poorest countries, designated as least developed countries (Laos, Bangladesh and most of Africa), and (4) more than 150 other developing countries, which range from upper-middle-income Malaysia to low-income Nigeria. For further reading: E. W. Nafziger, *The Economics of Developing Countries* (1997). E.W.N.

development area. An area designated for special economic assistance, usually because of an above-average level of UNEMPLOYMENT. The assistance can take various forms: financial incentives to firms locating in the area; relaxation of the controls on firms within or moving into the area; and stricter control on expansion of firms outside the area. It has been suggested that the past use of these instruments of REGIONAL PLANNING may not be justified in that the estimated resulting benefits, usually greater employment, are low relative to the costs. J.P.

Development Assistance Committee (DAC), see under OECD.

development economics. The intellectual framework used by policy-makers to promote income growth in DEVELOPING COUNTRIES. For much of the post-World War II period the relationships between the developed and less developed world were based on an enlightened paternalism under which it was assumed that the providers of aid knew best how to raise incomes and relieve poverty in THIRD WORLD countries. This has changed rapidly in recent decades. As DEMOCRACY has spread through the less developed world it has gained a bigger say in its own affairs and it has become clear that grandiose projects like dam building, which disturb the environment and require huge population relocations, are not the answer to development problems. Small-scale development projects aimed at improving health and literacy so that countries have the human CAPITAL to develop have become more important. Moreover, centralized government has been discouraged in favour of open and FREE MARKETS and PRIVATE SECTOR ownership of basic economic structures. The result has been increasingly fast growth rates in Asia and

Latin America and more recently in some countries of Africa, notably Uganda and the Côte d'Ivoire. Economic reforms are now rewarded with relief on existing debt stock which enables countries to invest more heavily in basic services. Africa has continued to fall further behind other less developed regions in the last two decades, partly because of post-colonial political instability (see POST-COLONIALISM) and population growth which has held back per capita income. But in the mid-1990s there were the first signs that even this region can pull out of its secular decline. A.BR.

developmental biology. The study of all aspects of the development of organisms, from the molecular events underlying the differentiation of CELLS to the patterns of multiplication, growth and movement of masses of cells that create tissues and entire organisms. E.O.W.

developmental constraint, see CONSTRAINT, DEVELOPMENTAL.

developmental cycle. Concept developed by Meyer Fortes (*The Developmental Cycle in Domestic Groups*, 1958) to understand the changes which take place within the DOMESTIC GROUP. It provided as a concept the link between the individual and society. Fortes analysed the domestic group as the focus of social reproduction, where members move through a cycle of recognized ROLES at different stages of their lives. The cycle is expressed in spatial or residential arrangements. Fortes identified three phases in the developmental cycle: (1) expansion, the period of marriage, birth and rearing of children; (2) fission, marriage of children, departure from the domestic group and the establishment of a new conjugal unit; (3) replacement, death of parents and birth of children to second generation. Relations between individuals within the domestic group may be reflected in its different stages of development. For example, the tension between father and son over succession may be lessened through the establishment of separate residence. For further reading: A. Barnard and A. Good, *Research Practices in the Study of Kinship* (1984). A.G.

developmental linguistics. A branch of LINGUISTICS which studies the acquisition of language in children; also sometimes known as *developmental psycholinguistics*. The subject involves the application of linguistic theories and techniques of analysis to child language data, in order to provide a precise description of patterns of development, and an explanation of norms and variations encountered, both within individual languages and universally. D.C.

developmental psychology. Also called *life-span psychology*, this is the study of the changes in behaviour which typically take place with age, together with an analysis of their causes. Until the 1950s, it was mainly concerned with the behaviour of children as they grow older (and hence was widely known as *child psychology*); particularly notable were studies based on the observation of infants, and those by Dietrich Tiedemann, Charles Darwin and Jean Piaget still provide some of the basic data on the emotional responses and the changes in SENSORY-MOTOR co-ordination which typically occur in the first few years of life. However, the work of Erik Erikson (1902–94) led to much study in the latter half of the century of the behaviour of adults as they age. Erikson argued that adults pass through several different psychological stages as they grow older, coining the phrase IDENTITY CRISIS to mark the points of transition from one stage to another in the development of adult personality. Nowadays, psychologists study all aspects of human development, not just child development. P.E.B.

developmental theory. Developmental theory owes its greatest debt to the work of Karl Abraham (1877–1925) on the development of the LIBIDO. Although there are many relevant passages in Freud which could be interpreted as asserting the usefulness of such a theory, the bases of the theory were developed by Abraham. The central idea that organizes most varieties of developmental theory is that there is a linear development of successive phases whereby at each phase one particular erotogenic zone dominates the libidinal life of the child, the first two phases being the oral phase and the anal phase. Pathologies can thus be accounted for in terms of a FIXATION at one particular phase of development, or a REGRESSION to such a phase, such that any progression to the supposedly healthy genital stage is blocked, and instead of this, one particular DRIVE seems to freeze the subject at the phase in question. Abraham also stressed how SADISM gets attached to the developmental phases, in such a way that we can view each phase as having two or more substages. Lacan's work, however, has shown the implausibility of the developmental MODEL, particularly in its stress on a linear development, since any serious consideration of what Freud called 'deferred action', the process by which present events give a meaning to past events, would show that the phases in question would take on their values not just synchronically, but at later times in the supposed development of the child. On a more general level, since PSYCHOANALYSIS in the LACANIAN orientation is concerned with structure it is less concerned with the development of the child than with the structural relations between the SUBJECT, the OBJECT A and the signifying chain. D.L.

deviance (or **deviancy).** In SOCIOLOGY, social behaviour that is subjected to social sanctions, including legal sanctions. Deviant behaviour is thus defined in terms of social attitudes rather than intrinsic quality, and includes, as defined at present, not only crime but such things as HOMOSEXUALITY, mental illness, and even deviance from GROUP NORMS that may themselves be deviant from more widely accepted NORMS. The sociology of deviance has developed, as a discipline, partly as a reaction (especially in the USA) against traditional CRIMINOLOGY, with its emphasis on positivistic multicausal theories of crime, and partly against consensus theories of social order. T.M.

deviationism. A tendency within COMMUNIST parties to stray from the official Party line. Such tendencies were branded either as RIGHT or LEFT deviationism, depending on whether they advocated a 'harder' or 'softer' policy. In the former case, it was sometimes branded as *adventurism*; in the latter, as *capitulationism*. In doctrinal terms, deviationists were also often described as displaying *dogmatism* (i.e. sticking to the letter of MARXISM) or REVISIONISM (i.e. violating the spirit of revolutionary theory; see REVOLUTION). The adherence to one worldwide Party line was possible only as long as communism was a unitary movement. With the emergence of communist polycentrism, deviationism remained a political offence leading to factionalism. It was therefore prohibited in accordance with the LENINIST principle of DEMOCRATIC CENTRALISM. Intra-Party polemics went beyond the charges of deviationism and in many cases (particularly in the Sino-Soviet dispute) produced mutual charges of the betrayal of Marxism. L.L.

devolution. The handing down from a higher tier of government to a lower tier, generally on a territorial basis, of powers exercised by ministers or legislators. Unlike the sub-units in a federal system (for example, the American states), which retain authority which the centre may not take away, devolved governments, even if elected, derive their powers ultimately from the higher tier, which may in principle revoke them if it so wishes. In the UK attempts have been made to devolve powers to assemblies in Scotland and Wales. Problems arise when power is devolved to some regions but not others. The most infamous of these is the West Lothian Question, which turns on the role of Scottish MPs at Westminster after devolution. Such MPs must clearly be allowed to attend, since their constituents still pay taxes to support UK (i.e. non-devolved) services. Should they then be allowed to participate in all votes, or only votes on those matters which, in respect of Scotland, have not been devolved? If the former, then Scottish opinion is represented twice on devolved questions, once in Edinburgh and once at Westminster, an obvious unfairness to other parts of the UK. But if the latter solution is adopted, a Westminster government might enjoy a parliamentary majority on UK questions but not on devolved ones. In effect, the rest of the UK would have a devolved assembly too: the Westminster Parliament meeting without Scottish MPs. This problem has led some to favour 'Home Rule All Round', by which power is devolved to assemblies covering all parts of the country. In the UK this proposal has never been attractive because the demand for devolution is not great in England. For further reading: V. Bogdanor, *Devolution* (1979); H. Elcock and M. Keating, *Remaking the Union: Devolution and British Politics in the 1990s* (1998). N.O.

diachronic. Term coined in about 1913 by Ferdinand de Saussure (see SAUSSURIAN) to refer to the study of LINGUISTIC change or evolution, as opposed to *synchronic* which covers 'everything that relates to the static side of our science'. The terms were borrowed by sociologists and anthropologists to distinguish two different approaches in their own fields. Compare the distinction between 'process' and structure made by American sociologists, and that between *conjoncture* and *structure* made by French historians. P.B.

dialect geography, see under DIALECTOLOGY.

dialectic. A theory of the nature of LOGIC which is also a theory of the structure and development of the world. It was devised by the post-Kantian IDEALISTS, starting with Fichte and reaching a culmination in the philosophy of Hegel. It was taken over from Hegel by Marx and put to rather different uses. Kant had distinguished two aspects within logic: (1) analytic, or the logic of understanding, which, applied to the data of sensation, yields knowledge of the natural, phenomenal world; and (2) dialectic, or the logic of reasoning, which operates independently of experience and purports, erroneously, to give knowledge of the transcendent order of *noumena* (or 'things-in-themselves'; see TRANSCENDENCE). Hegel interpreted the dialectic operations of reason, not as concerned with the transcendent, but with reality as a whole, rather than its abstracted, mutilated parts, and thus as giving truer and deeper knowledge than the analytic understanding, which he saw as adequate for NATURAL SCIENCE and the practical concerns of everyday life but not for PHILOSOPHY. Furthermore, taking reality to be of the nature of the mind or spirit, he supposed its activities and development to be of an essentially rational or logical kind. Standard or analytic logic, on this view, is rigid and abstract, a matter of fixed connections and exclusive oppositions. Dialectical logic sees contradictions as fruitful collisions of ideas from which a higher truth may be reached by way of SYNTHESIS. Marx took over the view that dialectical thinking is necessary if true knowledge is to be obtained, and held the process of history to be a dialectical development in which mankind progresses through the clashes of contradictory social systems. For further reading: K. R. Popper, *Conjectures and Refutations* (1969). A.Q.

dialectical materialism. A term which came into prominence in the generation after Marx's death to describe the philosophy of MARXISM as opposed to its historical or political aspects. Marx had applied the DIALECTIC to social and historical processes; it was Engels, in such widely popular works as *Anti-Dühring*, who extended the scope of the dialectic to the natural world and proclaimed a series of completely general scientific laws which governed nature and society alike. These fundamental laws were: the transformation of quantity into quality whereby gradual quantitative change culminated in a revolutionary change of quality; the interpenetration of opposites whereby any entity is constituted by an unstable unity of contradictions; and the negation of the negation whereby any negative force is in its turn negated in a process of historical development which conserves something of the negated elements.

The term dialectical materialism was not itself used by Marx or Engels. It was popularized by Lenin's teacher Plekhanov, and became the official philosophy of the former USSR. Although it appeared to endow Marxist social and economic theories with the growing prestige of natural science, many have thought the assimilation of the methods of natural and social science implied in dialectical materialism to be untrue to the Hegelian and HUMANIST aspects of Marx's thought. For further reading: Z. Jordan, *The Evolution of Dialectical Materialism* (1967). D.T.M.

dialectical theatre, see under EPIC THEATRE.

dialectical theology, see under CRISIS THEOLOGY.

dialectology (or **dialect geography**). A branch of LINGUISTICS which studies local linguistic variation within a language. Dialects are normally defined in geographical terms (*regional* dialects), but the concept has been extended to cover socioeconomic variation (CLASS dialects) and occasionally other types of linguistic variety (e.g. *occu-*

pational dialect). There is therefore some overlap with SOCIOLINGUISTICS. Within dialectology, a distinction is often made between *rural* and *urban* studies. There is also a distinction between the *traditional* dialectology of the early language atlases, with its emphasis on isoglosses, and later studies of systems of dialect contrast, using techniques of structural linguistics, and known as *structural* dialectology. D.C.

diathermy. Local heating from high-frequency current used (1) in treatment of soft-tissue disorders ('muscular rheumatism'), when short-wave diathermy may bring relief of symptoms even when their cause is not fully understood; (2) for chronic deep-seated infections, when the rise of temperature is thought to accelerate healing – since the advent of ANTIBIOTICS this has become a less important method of treatment, but is still valuable, particularly in pelvic infections in women; (3) instead of ligatures, for coagulation of smaller blood vessels in surgical operations. D.A.P.

dictatorship. Originally an office, created in times of emergency by the classical Roman republic, which conferred on a single individual complete authority over the state and the armed forces for a limited period – usually six months. By transfer, the rule of any individual other than a king who enjoys complete authority, unchecked by constitutional limits, over a state. In recent history, dictatorships can be divided into personal tyrannies, usually backed by the armed forces (e.g. in Latin American and Arab countries), and totalitarian regimes (see TOTALITARIANISM), where the dictator is the charismatic leader (see CHARISMA) of a totalitarian movement. For further reading: M. Latey, *Tyranny* (1969). D.C.W.

dictatorship of the proletariat. A MARXIST concept used to refer to the transitional period between the successful proletarian revolution and the advent of a COMMUNIST society. Marx himself mentioned the term only rarely, but seems to have thought (at least at the time) that the Paris Commune of 1871 was an example of such a dictatorship in which direct DEMOCRACY could be ensured by the election, revocability and mandating of all officials whether legislative, executive or judiciary. It should be noted that Marx's notion of dictatorship did not have the contemporary connotation of arbitrary tyranny, but harked back to the classical Roman concept of *dictatura* which was both republican and constitutional. The idea of the DICTATORSHIP of the PROLETARIAT as implementing direct participatory democracy was taken up in Lenin's *State and Revolution* (see below). But circumstances surrounding the birth of the Soviet Union meant that, in practice, the dictatorship of the proletariat came to mean little more than the use of repression by the state over the whole of society in the name of the proletariat. Because of the embarrassing connotations thus acquired, several communist parties in CAPITALIST countries have recently dropped mention of the dictatorship of the proletariat from their programmes. For further reading: V. I. Lenin, *State and Revolution* (tr. with introduction and glossary by Robert Service, 1992); J. Ehrenberg, *The Dictatorship of the Proletariat* (1992). D.T.M.

didactic play, see under LEHRSTÜCK.

diet. People choose to eat only a small section of the range of edible substances available. This choice is dictated by cost as well as taste, but also reflects the rules and regimes of social groups, and the individual's mode of living (the meaning of the word in the original Greek). There are thus descriptive, restrictive and prescriptive aspects of diet. What people actually eat is largely determined by their upbringing, although parental choices may be modified later by external influences including peer pressure, convenience or advertising. The latter is more likely to reflect the forces of marketing or global AGRIBUSINESS in the modern food industry than nutritional benefit for consumers. Among the poor of poor countries, protein, calorie and vitamin deficiencies still cause disease, but if a diet is adequate and reasonably balanced it will provide all that is needed without further modification.

Particular food substances may harm specific individuals who have developed a reaction against them. Thus a diabetic may need to restrict carbohydrates, or someone with a reaction to gluten to avoid wheat flour. Whole populations may develop new conditions related to altered balances in food intake, as is seen in the current epidemic of coronary heart disease among those on Western diets. This is linked among other things both to increased obesity (a result of simple excess of food energy intake) and to increased fat in the average diet. Public health policy aims to reverse these trends. But changes in eating patterns may be responsive to other forces. While religious dietary TABOOS may be on the wane, the concept that a person's diet should reflect his or her values is not. Vegetarianism is increasing and may in some groups become the majority mode, and in some forms of COMPLEMENTARY MEDICINE a correct diet is linked with spiritual wholeness as well as bodily health. Whether such enthusiasms are seen as enlightening or merely fads, they are unlikely to harm: but lives may be altered or threatened by BULIMIA or ANOREXIA as the cult of thinness and youth continues to claim its victims. For further reading: P. Fieldhouse, *Food and Nutrition; Customs and Culture* (1996). R.H.H.

différance. Neologism used by French deconstructionist philosopher Jacques Derrida (1930– ; see DECONSTRUCTION) in his reading of various texts in the Western philosophical and literary tradition. The deviant *a* in the word's last syllable, as Derrida pointedly spells it, is intended as a kind of graphic pun which conjoins the nominalized form of the two French verbs meaning respectively 'to differ' and 'to defer'. His purpose in deploying this portmanteau term is to indicate the process of constant 'differing-deferral' which, according to Derrida, marks every act of language, thought and perception. Thus language is conceived (see SAUSSURIAN) as a structure of purely differential contrasts and oppositions 'without positive terms', a bipolar system of phonetic and semantic relationships that allows of no direct, one-to-one correspondence between signifier and signified, or word and concept. However, Saussure failed to carry this programme through to its ultimate conclusion since he continued to think of spoken language as somehow more natural or proper than writing by virtue of its greater communicative power, its proximity to the sources of authentic meaning or self-present utterer's intent. What emerges from a deconstructive reading of Saussure's text is the fact that his structuralist theory of language *cannot do without* the appeal to writing – to 'graphematic' images, metaphors, heuristic devices, and so forth – in order to make good its cardinal claims about the differential character of *all* language, spoken and written alike. Thus Saussure stands out as a striking example of the deep-laid logocentric prejudice (see LOGOCENTRISM) that has typified the mainstream Western philosophical tradition from Plato to the present day. For further reading: J. Culler, *On Deconstruction* (1983). C.C.N.

differential psychology. The branch of PSYCHOLOGY pioneered by Francis Galton (1822–1911) and greatly developed in this century that studies differences between the psychological characteristics of one person and another, especially by PSYCHOMETRIC techniques designed to yield quantitative measures of such differences. I.M.L.H.

differentiation. In EMBRYOLOGY, the process in the course of which the CELLS derived by MITOSIS from the fertilized egg turn into the various different cells of the body. Differentiation is always a realization of the genetic potentialities of the cells that undergo it. Its detailed mechanism is not yet known. P.M.

diffraction. On passing close to the edge of an opaque object, or through an aperture, and falling on a suitably arranged screen, a beam of light produces a characteristic diffraction pattern of light and dark bands or 'fringes'. The first theoretical investigations of the details of diffraction by Young and Fresnel in the early 19th century led to the conclusion that diffraction phenomena are explicable only by assuming the wave nature of light. The light bands arise from constructive interference between waves (a crest meets a crest, or a trough meets a trough) and the dark bands from destructive interference (crest meets trough, to their mutual cancellation). What is particularly difficult for PARTICLE models of light to account for is the occurrence, under some conditions, of bright spots at the centre of the shadows cast by solid objects. Thus diffraction has become associated with wave phenomena, to the extent that the discovery of X-ray diffraction (see X-RAYS) by von Laue in 1912 was taken to provide evidence for the wave nature of X-rays. Similarly, the discovery in 1927 that electrons also exhibit diffraction (see ELECTRON DIFFRACTION) was interpreted as strong evidence for the WAVE-PARTICLE DUALITY of matter. R.F.H.

diffuseness, see under PATTERN VARIABLES.

diffusion.

(1) In CHEMISTRY, an atomic process by which substances may mix or spread. Thus in gases the MOLECULES move almost independently and diffusive motion is hindered only by random collisions between different molecules. In a solid or liquid, diffusion can only occur when an ATOM or molecule acquires sufficient ENERGY to jump into a nearby position, and eventually these atomic movements can lead to a change in form of the solid (as in sintering) or to a blurring of the interface between two solids or two liquids. In liquids and even gases, mixing may be produced much more efficiently in practice by stirring or convection than by diffusion. B.F.

(2) In ARCHAEOLOGY, the spread of some aspect (whether material or non-material) of a CULTURE from its place of origin into a new area. In the early years of this century *diffusionism* was taken to ludicrous extremes, particularly by W. Perry and Elliot Smith in their support for the BELIEF that all ideas were developed in the East and diffused to the rest of the world. Before the development of RADIOCARBON DATING the validity of diffusionist thought could not easily be tested, but with the appearance of large numbers of absolute dates it is now clear that independent invention was more common in the ancient world than was hitherto thought possible. There is at present a tendency to overreact against diffusion as an explanation for culture change. B.C.

(3) In ANTHROPOLOGY, the idea that cultural features have their origins in a single source. At the beginning of the 20th century diffusionism was an important theory for understanding cultural diversity. Diversity was understood to have resulted from the diffusion of traits from a centre, and this movement was traced in a manner akin to the way ripples may be traced from a stone being dropped into a pool of water. W. H. R. Rivers, a member of the 1898 Torres Straits expedition, was a leading diffusionist. He had fallen under the influence of the ideas of Perry and Elliot Smith and asserted that ancient Egypt was the original source of civilization. Later anthropologists believe that Rivers's increasing insistence upon the idea of diffusion obscured his much more important and original work on KINSHIP. For further reading: I. Langham, *W. H. R. Rivers and His Cambridge Disciples in the Development of Kinship Studies 1898–1931* (1981). A.G.

(4) In GEOGRAPHY, spatial diffusion refers to the dissemination or spreading of an innovation or information across geographical SPACE. Geographers are particularly interested in identifying, mapping and studying the centres (hearths) of innovation, the channels of spread, and the barriers to transmission. Evolving from the seminal work of the Swedish geographer Torsten Hägerstrand, theoretical MODELS have been built that are helpful in the FORECASTING of diffusion patterns, particularly by medical geographers who monitor the spreading of epidemic diseases (see EPIDEMIOLOGY). A distinction is usually drawn between *expansion diffusion*, which occurs within a fixed population, and *relocation diffusion*, which depends on the migration of the carriers. Furthermore, the former is commonly subdivided into *contagious diffusion*, in which the spatial pattern of spread is continuous across a local area, and *hierarchical diffusion*, in which the transmission courses downward (from larger to smaller places) within a network of discrete settlements that constitute a national- or continental-scale urban hierarchy. A large body of practical empirical studies has accumulated, with many applicable to the spatial problems addressed by planners (see PLANNING) and policy-makers. For further reading: L. A. Brown, *Innovation Diffusion: A New Perspective* (1981). P.O.M.

digital army/war. In 1997 the US Army mounted an exercise (code name 'Force 21') to test the application of digital technologies in warfare. The goal of Force 21 was to improve communications and logistics through the application of computer technology generated in the private sector and adapted for military use. The specific aims are to increase awareness of one's own position on the battlefield and to have a clear sense of the enemy's position, in pursuit of the following goals: (1) increased lethality, (2) increased control of the tempo of warfare, (3) the reduction of 'fratricide', or casualties caused by FRIENDLY FIRE. S.T.

digital cash, see under ELECTRONIC COMMERCE.

digital computer, see under COMPUTER.

digital-to-analogue converter. In COMPUTING, a device which changes the representation of a numerical value from a digital encoding (in which it might be manipulated by a digital COMPUTER, for example) to a particular value of some variable physical quantity (usually an electrical potential), as used in analogue computers or to interact with other physical processes (e.g. by regulating part of an industrial plant, or driving a loudspeaker). There are *analogue-to-digital converters*, too. J.E.S.

diglossia. In SOCIOLINGUISTICS, a situation in which two very different varieties of a language co-occur throughout a speech community, each with a distinct range of social functions. Both varieties are standardized to some degree, and have usually been given special names by native speakers. Sociolinguists generally refer to one variety as 'high', the other as 'low', the distinction broadly corresponding to a difference in formality. Diglossic situations can be found in Greek (high: Katharevousa; low: Dhimotiki), Arabic (high: Classical; low: Colloquial), and Swiss German (high: Hochdeutsch; low: Schweizerdeutsch). D.C.

dilemma, see under ANTINOMY.

dilution of labour. The assignment to other workers of parts of the work customarily performed only by skilled workers, or the employment on skilled work of persons who have not passed through the course of training, usually apprenticeship, customarily required for admission to that work; more generally, the assignment to other workers of work previously reserved by custom to a particular category of workers. The issue arose in the UK during World War I, when the shortage of craftsmen relative to the demand in engineering and shipbuilding prompted management to concentrate the time of craftsmen on those parts of their customary work that they alone could perform, and to advance semi-skilled persons to do skilled work. In both world wars it was provided for that the customary lines of demarcation should be restored after the war. In PRODUCTIVITY BARGAINING dilution of labour occurs as tasks are reallocated across customary lines of demarcation.

E.H.P.B.; J.P.

dimension. This is the NUMBER of quantities needed to locate a point in space. On a piece of paper, you need two numbers – distance from the top of the page and distance from the left-hand side are enough to locate any point on the page – so that surface is a two-dimensional space. The world that we experience is a three-dimensional space (or four-dimensional, if you include time as well). A moving object, for example, needs this fourth measure fully to describe its location: unless you say *when* it was in such-and-such a place, it will not be very informative just to give a location in space, since it may no longer be in that place.

There is another meaning, however, which is sometimes used when dealing with FRACTALS. This developed from a curious observation about countries' borders. Different geographical sources often vary quite considerably in their estimates of the length of a given border or coastline. This is because the measurement depends crucially on the way that it is taken. If you used a straight ruler several yards long, and laid it down end to end to measure a coastline, you would arrive at one estimate of its length. If you used a ruler that was several inches long, you would arrive at a much larger estimate, because you would have taken into account many more kinks and bends in the coastline – even individual rocks would have been included in the measurement. In fact, there is a formula which will predict how the measurement will vary – in the case of the coastline, it turns out that if the ruler is reduced in size from 1 metre to 1/k metres, the number of lengths measured will be multiplied by $k^{1.22}$. So the coastline has dimension 1.22. N.A.R.

diminished responsibility. In English law, a mental condition which, since the Homicide Act of 1957, can be pleaded by any person charged with murder, and which in murder cases has largely replaced the old plea of insanity. The Act provides that a person charged with murder can be convicted only of manslaughter if he was 'suffering from such abnormality of mind as substantially impaired his mental responsibility'. This means that he may be considered only for manslaughter although he both knew that he had killed another person and that his act was illegal if his capacity to act in accordance with rational judgement was substantially impaired. H.L.A.H.

diminishing productivity returns of a factor. In ECONOMICS, the circumstances in which equal increases in the use of one FACTOR OF PRODUCTION lead to successively smaller increases in output – the use of all other factors is held constant. This phenomenon is identical to the concept of a declining marginal product of a factor. It is important because, in NEO-CLASSICAL ECONOMIC THEORY, it forms the basis of the MARGINAL PRODUCTIVITY THEORY OF WAGES. It has been enshrined in an ECONOMIC LAW: the law of diminishing returns of a factor. J.P.

Dinge-an-sich, see under NOUMENA.

Dionysian cultures, see under APOLLONIAN AND DIONYSIAN CULTURES.

diophantine equations, see under NUMBER THEORY.

diploid (noun or adjective). A CELL containing two sets of CHROMOSOMES, one set inherited from each parent. The body cells of man and of most higher plants and animals are diploid. Contrasted on the one hand with HAPLOID, on the other with POLYPLOID. J.M.S.

diploma disease. see under CREDENTIALISM.

diplomacy. Has been variously defined as the 'application of intelligence and tact to the conduct of relations between nations' (Satow) and the 'management of international relations by negotiation' (OED and Harold Nicolson). It is carried out generally by diplomats up to ambassadorial level through foreign ministries, and guided by a code of protocol since the Vienna Congress of 1815. Major elements of diplomacy are communication and negotiation, leading to Sir Henry Wotton (1568–1639) describing the diplomat as 'an honest man sent abroad to lie for his country', a remark which cost him his position. Styles of diplomacy vary, with Nicolson dividing diplomats into 'shopkeepers' and 'warriors'. Since 1918 there has been a certain opening up of diplomacy in what was termed the 'new diplomacy', which sees its major expression in multilateral parliamentary diplomacy in the UN. Much of diplomacy is still bilateral, however, and often on economic issues. The diplomat has lost much of his autonomy with the growth of rapid communications and the complexity of much technical negotiation. 'Shuttle' diplomacy, as by Haig in the FALKLANDS WAR, and SUMMIT DIPLOMACY are now often tried to settle particularly difficult and sensitive political issues by leaders themselves. For further reading: H. Nicolson, *Diplomacy* (1939). A.W.

direct action. ANARCHISTS have always advocated unconventional, unconstitutional and non-parliamentary political action of one sort or another. The political general strike of ANARCHO-SYNDICALIST theory was one such form. Non-violent direct action or *satyagraha* was a feature of Gandhi's campaigns of CIVIL DISOBEDIENCE; the same insistence on non-violence marked the American civil rights campaigns of the 1950s and 60s (see CIVIL RIGHTS MOVEMENT), whose techniques of 'sit-downs' and 'sit-ins' were adopted by protesters against the VIETNAM War in later years. Non-violent direct action (see NON-VIOLENT RESISTANCE) is likely to be successful only against authorities who are easily embarrassed by having to resort to force or legal suppression, as the British were in India. This limitation may explain why so many radicals who begin with a commitment to non-violent direct action either drift back into conventional politics or move further towards insurrectionary politics instead. For further reading: A. Carter, *Direct Action and Liberal Democracy* (1973). A.R.

direct marketing. TECHNOLOGY now permits the gathering of a great deal of relevant information, from a large number of diverse sources, about every individual. While this raises the issue of individual rights to privacy, for the MARKETING man the opportunity is a welcome one and, potentially, a cost-effective one for the consumer. By profiling customers, and seeking like characteristics elsewhere, it is now possible to target sales prospects far more efficiently. Responsive television, radio and press ADVERTISING, together with 'piggy-back' mailings, inserts and direct mailing, are all being increasingly utilized in the process of eliminating the middle-man, and affording closer contact with customers. T.S.

direct realism, see under REALISM, NAÏVE.

dirigisme. A policy of STATE intervention in economic affairs, usually associated with post-war France where it has dominated economic policy for much of the period. It does not necessarily involve direct control, as is demonstrated in the French system of 'indicative planning'. It has necessitated, however, control over key economic sectors such as banking. This policy can co-exist with CAPITALISM, SOCIALISM and a variety of systems of property ownership. This approach to the economy has from time to time clashed with ECONOMIC LIBERALISM in other European countries. The French have continued to produce indicative plans, but the dirigiste element in French policy has been watered down in the context of market liberalisation and attempts to meet the MAASTRICHT convergence criteria for monetary union. V.L.

disability politics. The pursuit of equal rights for disabled people, focusing on questions of access and emphasizing the social, rather than the medical, MODEL of disability. The *medical* model stresses the chronic physical condition of the individual; the *social* model emphasizes that sickness and disability are not the same thing and looks at the physical obstacles placed in the way of individuals with disabilities. The example usually given is of a person in a wheelchair confronted by a flight of steps leading up to a public building; the challenge is not to the wheelchair user to do the impossible, but to society to make the building accessible by providing alternative entry.

Disability activists are generally agreed about ends, but argue over the means that should be employed to attain them. There are, so to speak, disability suffragists and suffragettes: those who favour putting their case by means of rational argument and those who chain their wheelchairs and themselves to railings, or block the public highway to demonstrate the inaccessibility of public transport.

The language of disability is a minefield of POLITICAL CORRECTNESS, its strictures ranging from the sensible to the absurd. The expression 'wheelchair-bound' may be offensive to a person for whom a wheelchair is a means of liberation as much as locomotion, but phrases such as 'physically challenged' or 'persons of restricted growth' are both ungainly and unhelpful. As with ETHNICITY, disability RADICAL CHIC takes delight in being shocking, as in Lorenzo Milam's The Cripple Liberation Front Marching Band. T.G.

disappeared, the, see under STATE TERROR.

disarmament. A form of ARMS CONTROL, which may be unilateral, bilateral or multilateral. Implied is the promotion of international security by the reduction of existing military forces and weapons, usually to an agreed minimum. Disarmament treaties usually include provisions for VERIFICATION and enforcement.

A substantial degree of disarmament was forced upon Germany after World War I. In particular, revulsion at the use of gas resulted in a ban on any production of chemical weapons. Under the LEAGUE OF NATIONS, between 1927 and 1934, and later under the UN, there were desultory discussions about general disarmament (applying to all countries) and comprehensive disarmament (covering all categories of weapons), but these came to nothing. Even the prohibitions on chemical weapons broke down as the Italians used gas in Ethiopia, as did Japan in China. After World War II, the losers – Germany, Italy and Japan – were again compulsorily disarmed, although gradual rearmament was later allowed and even encouraged as they took their places in the opposing COLD WAR alliances. Meanwhile moves under the UN towards general and comprehensive disarmament concentrated on NUCLEAR WEAPONS and other weapons of mass destruction. These met with negligible success until the end of the cold war.

Frustration at the failure of traditional multilateral disarmament methods increased as the world's stocks of nuclear weapons grew to an extent devoid of any military sense. This led from the late 1950s to the rise of unilateralism, particularly in Britain, where it is associated with the Campaign for Nuclear Disarmament (CND; see PEACE MOVEMENT). Derided by their opponents as one-sided disarmers, unilateralists held that a disarming act by one side would lead to a series of reciprocal arms cuts – a reversal of the arms race process. This thesis was never fully tested, although there were unilateral moves in the period of East/West détente that followed the 1962 Cuban Missile Crisis (see CUBA) and again at the end of the cold war. However, by then multilateral disarmament negotiations were producing results, and the emphasis of much disarmament campaigning switched to supporting these developments.

Disarmament enforced on the losers by the victors after a WAR or by severe political or economic pressure is likely to be successful in the short term only. After the Gulf War of 1990–91, Iraq was able to hamper the work of UN weapons inspectors by relying on the unwillingness of the West to go to war for a second time, merely for breaches of Iraq's obligations to be open about its weapons programmes. As a result, despite many successes by the UN weapons inspectors, Iraq may have been able to hide substantial reserves of both chemical and biological weapons. Disarmament agreements reached between consenting states are more likely to endure, since even if there is a radical political change by one side, the abrogation of a treaty is a major and very public act, while improvements in verification techniques make successful cheating much less likely. For further reading: L. Wittner, *Resisting the Bomb* (1997). L.T.

discipline history. In the history of science, 'discipline history' draws attention to the fact that knowledge advances not simply through a sequence of abstract, intellectual theories, but through the successive formation and reformation of demarcated bodies of knowledge – that is, the different sciences, such as PHYSICS, CHEMISTRY and, more narrowly, BIOCHEMISTRY or MOLECULAR BIOLOGY. Far from these disciplines being 'timeless', they have their own history. Thus coherent and organized sciences of 'BIOLOGY' and 'GEOLOGY' date only from the beginning of the 19th century. Before then their subject-matters were either comprehended within other disciplinary frameworks (e.g. natural history) or were considered scientifically unimportant. Molecular biology arose as a distinct science only after World War II; GENETIC ENGINEERING is essentially a development of the last decade. Recognition of the importance of disciplinary boundaries as stimuli to scientific development (and, perhaps more frequently, as hindrances to cross-fertilization) involves attention to the structure as much as to the content of science. It requires a grasp both of the wider philosophical allegiances of science and of its socio-economic dimensions. For further reading: B. Barnes, *Interests and the Growth of Knowledge* (1977). R.P.

disco. Discothèques first appeared in France in the 1950s; by the 1960s they sprang up in America, as club-owners appreciated the savings involved in a room where the music was recorded and dancing did not require a live band. But in the 1970s disco became a music and culture all its own, with recordings that emphasized a thumping, synthesized beat and rendered other elements almost superfluous. The streamlined, insistent sound captivated audiences, not just in clubs but on radio and records: the dancing boom was epitomized by the 1977 film *Saturday Night Fever*. Rock fans protested at disco's high-tech impersonality and rap and hip-hop emerged as passionate alternatives. Disco has continued to evolve in the ever more sophisticated forms of 'house' and 'techno', which critics still dismiss as 'just a mindless beat'. GE.S.

discount rate, see under BANK RATE.

discounted cash flow. A method used to assist the management decision-maker in the evaluation of capital investment projects (see CAPITAL; INVESTMENT). Investment opportunities involve the flow of funds: capital payments out and net receipts from the venture in return. Simple comparison between the two gives a rate of return on the investment; but the earlier the return of funds the better. The DCF method takes the timing of funds-flow into account, by calculating the discount rate that is inherent in the expected funds-flow. The *net-present-value* method also takes the timing of the funds-flow into account, but calculates a present value of expected flows, at a standard DISCOUNTING rate, for assessing projects. R.L.T.

discounting. In ECONOMICS, the procedure that values future costs and benefits. As it is usually assumed that individuals and society prefer a unit of consumption in the present, rather than in the future, a benefit or cost in the present is of greater value than if it occurs at a future date. From the viewpoint of the present, it is necessary to adjust, i.e. discount, future costs and benefits; the adjustment depending on when they occur. In order to value these costs and benefits it is necessary to have a common measure: MONEY. The rate of discount that is most frequently used is the interest rate, after it is corrected for the effect of INFLATION. The difference of the suitably discounted benefits and costs is the *net present value*. Net present values are used as a criterion for judging between different investments, e.g. in COST BENEFIT ANALYSIS. The choice of discount rate can make a large difference to net present values and the ranking of investment projects (see INTERNAL RATE OF RETURN). J.P.

discourse.

(1) In LINGUISTICS, a stretch of language larger than the sentence. The term *discourse analysis* is often applied to the study of those linguistic effects – semantic, stylistic, syntactic – whose description needs to take into account sentence sequences as well as sentence structure. D.C.

(2) The term has also become prominent in the work of recent French theorists such as Roland Barthes, Gérard Genette and especially Michel Foucault, whose *The Order of Things* (1966) focused not on texts or authors but on 'fields' such as economics or natural history and the conventions according to which they were classified and represented in particular periods. Major shifts in these conventions were to be excavated by Foucault by his method of 'intellectual archaeology'. The later Foucault placed more stress on relations between discourse and other social practices. P.B.

discourse of power. A phrase associated with the work of Michel Foucault. In a number of brilliantly documented studies after 1961, Foucault analysed the ways in which apparently objective and natural structures in society, which privilege some and punish others for nonconformity, are in fact 'discourses of power'. Studies like *Madness and Civilisation* (1961), *The Order of Things* (1966), *The Birth of the Clinic* (1973) and above all *Discipline and Punish* (1975) elicited the various modes in which the subject is objectified according to the ruling interests of his or her society. Objectification of the subject can take various forms, perhaps the most dramatic being what Foucault called 'dividing practices', the example he gave in 1961 being the isolation of the 'mad' in the very asylums which once housed the lepers; or the way that the criminal, who was tortured to death as a public entertainment in the 18th century, was numbed into conformity by solitary confinement and moral opprobrium in the 19th century, to become at last the object of medical and psychiatric and psychoanalytic expertise in the 20th century (see PSYCHIATRY; PSYCHOANALYSIS), when all guilt has been internalized and the patient is imprisoned in himself. A second mode of objectifying the subject comes about through the classifications and reifications of science and scientific discourse (*Words and Things*, 1966). Finally, in *The History of Sexuality* (1978–88), e.g., Foucault studied the way the subject, in an attempt to come to terms with the dominant POWER structures in his society, attempts to create a meaningful identity for himself. In all this, Foucault's main attention was not so much on the historical facts and contours themselves (though these are impressively vast) but on the discourse which he detected as the real power behind the actual forms of domination. In an interview in 1977, Foucault admitted that he had not, at the time of writing *Madness and Civilisation*, or *Birth of the Clinic*, realized that he was writing about power as such: that was a realization made possible by the events of MAY 1968. Although it is difficult to 'place' Foucault's academic work, his major effect on philosophy, and on the social and human sciences, was at the point where the 'objectivity' of a discipline was most proudly vaunted, or where the hidden nature of its participation in the discourse of power was suddenly made apparent. His brilliant debut in 1961 was an inspiration to EXISTENTIAL PSYCHIATRY in the 1960s and 1970s, when the controlling power of psychiatry as an institution was suddenly seen to be a part of the enforcement machinery of hegemonic rationality (see HEGEMONY). The *Birth of the Clinic*, too, threw into relief the extent to which the patient is turned into an object by the 'medical gaze', and deprived of his SUBJECTIVITY. In his later work, Foucault emphasized again and again that it is only by consistent vigilance and hard intellectual work in examining the hegemonic assumptions of our society that we can come to understand, and to control, our own discourse of power. For further reading: A. Sheridan, Michel Foucault, *The Will to Truth* (1980). R.PO.

discovery procedure. In LINGUISTICS, a set of techniques which enable an investigator to derive the rules of a grammar from a corpus of utterances, with as little reference to intuition as possible. Chomsky criticized BLOOMFIELDIAN linguistics for its preoccupation with discovery procedures at the expense of theoretical questions. D.C.

disease, environmental causes of, see ENVIRONMENTAL CAUSES OF DISEASE.

disease model. A term widely used to depict a particular conception of illness widely held nowadays, particularly among the medical profession. It postulates that sickness is caused by particular pathogenic agents (germs, bacteria, viruses), typically regarded as invading the body from outside. Particular physical organs are attacked and somatic functions impaired. Health in turn is restored largely by physical intervention from outside (e.g. by surgery or drug therapies). The disease model thus regards sickness as essentially a mechanical defect of the body, largely independent of the 'mind' or 'personality' of the sufferer. As such it is to be distinguished from holistic or PSYCHOSOMATIC models of health and sickness (see HOLISTIC MEDICINE), which commonly regard illness as involving an expression of the mental state of the sufferer, as registering a malaise of the whole organism, and as dependent, to some degree, upon the co-operation of the sick person in order to be overcome. The disease MODEL was largely vindicated by the success of scientific medicine in overcoming infectious diseases through drugs such as antibiotics. Controversy still rages as to how far it is the proper way to conceptualize intractable diseases such as cancer. R.P.

disembedding and **re-embedding mechanisms.** According to the British sociologist Anthony Giddens, disembedding is a process in which social relationships become 'lifted out' or separated from local contexts and personal contacts. This usually involves reliance upon symbolic tokens, such as MONEY, which people can use to EXCHANGE goods without knowing anything about the person they are dealing with; or the use of EXPERT SYSTEMS such as the technical features of aviation and the training of pilots. For example, people can entrust their lives to pilots whom they do not know and to machines they do not understand because they can trust the expert systems which produce the plane and pilot. Disembedding is a feature of MODERNITY and contrasts with pre-modern societies where personal relationships and knowledge of others as individuals was the basis of trust. Re-embedding takes place when special efforts are made for people to meet face to face, for example at business meetings or academic conferences, where physically meeting is not strictly necessary. The personal contact helps to anchor trust in other people. For further reading: A. Giddens, *The Consequences of Modernity* (1990). M.D.H.

disengagement. A form of ARMS CONTROL, much discussed in the 1950s by European politicians and strategic writers (e.g. Anthony Eden, Hugh Gaitskell, Adam Rapacki, and the German Social Democratic Party), for reducing international tension in Europe by drawing back all non-indigenous forces or those equipped with NUCLEAR WEAPONS (Soviet, American, British, Canadian) from central Europe while permitting the indigenous states of the area a controlled level of non-nuclear armament. For further reading: E. Hinterhoff, *Disengagement* (1959). A.F.B.

disinflation, see under INFLATION.

disinhibition theory, see under DISPLACEMENT ACTIVITIES.

displacement.

(1) In ETHOLOGY, the elicitation of an

instinctive response by an inappropriate object or event or animal, consequent upon arousal of the INSTINCT to a degree that broadens the range of objects capable of releasing it (see RELEASER; DISPLACEMENT ACTIVITIES). For further reading: I. Eibl-Eibesfeldt, *Ethology* (1970).

(2) In PSYCHOANALYSIS, the implication is of more 'purposeful' displacement, as when feelings of AGGRESSION are aroused by a powerful figure and expressed towards one less powerful in order to avoid retaliation – however unconscious the displacement may be. See also CONDENSATION.

(3) In literary theory, see under CONDENSATION. J.S.B.

displacement activities.

(1) In ETHOLOGY, a term applied to animals' movements which, to the observer who knows their primary function and causation, appear 'out of context'. Thus starlings preen their plumage under two specific and distinct sets of circumstances: (a) when it is wet or out of order, and (b) – the displacement activity – when their aggressive behaviour and withdrawal are elicited at the same time, and neither is shown in full. Displacement activities seem to occur most frequently either (a) when two wholly or partly incompatible behaviour systems are simultaneously elicited (as in the example of the starling), or (b) when a behaviour system is elicited, but is prevented from running its full course by the absence of indispensable stimuli for the later phases or by physical prevention. Human instances of displacement activities include, in certain circumstances, scratching, lighting a cigarette, yawning, pacing up and down.

About the causation of displacement activities there are various theories, not necessarily incompatible. One, the *disinhibition theory*, is based on the fact that when one behaviour system (see INSTINCT) is strongly elicited it suppresses other systems; the theory posits that when two such systems are elicited simultaneously they suppress each other, including the suppressing effect that each normally exerts on third systems, and so allow such a system 'free rein'. Another theory, applicable to movements which belong to the rest-and-sleep systems, argues that the central nervous system compensates for the hyperexcitation caused by conflicting motivations by activating the sleep system with all its subsidiary movements. N.T.

(2) The current popular application of the term to human activities which are 'out of context' merely in the sense that they are undertaken as an escape (conscious or otherwise) from some more urgently needed activity. O.S.

displacement theory. An obsolete term for the theory of CONTINENTAL DRIFT. M.L.

dissipative structures, see under NON-EQUILIBRIUM THERMODYNAMICS.

dissociation.

(1) In chemistry, the spontaneous break-up of a compound in EQUILIBRIUM conditions of temperature and pressure, or in solution. Normally dissociation occurs with an increase in temperature, for example when a gaseous MOLECULE dissociates to give two or more molecules or FREE RADICALS, but it also describes the process by which a neutral molecule forms IONS in solution. B.F.

(2) In PSYCHIATRY, an abnormal mental state in which the subject feels out of step with other subjects and the world in general, where his PERCEPTION of phenomena may differ markedly from that of others. S.T.

dissociation of sensibility. A phrase from T. S. Eliot's essay 'The Metaphysical Poets' (1921). Having described the unity of feeling and thought in the poetry of the Metaphysicals ('A thought to Donne was an experience; it modified his sensibility'), Eliot suggests that after the 17th century 'a dissociation of sensibility set in, from which we have never recovered'. This 'dissociation', aggravated by the powerful examples of Milton and Dryden, manifested itself in a split between 'thinking' and 'feeling' whereby poets 'thought and felt by bits, unbalanced'. The theory defines well the special achievement of the Metaphysicals in their best poems, but should not be regarded as an event as real as the INDUSTRIAL REVOLUTION and as precise in its effects as a lobotomy. The truth is that 'dissociation of sensibility' has always been with us, and that 'unification of sensibility' is a rare phenomenon, not always possible and perhaps not always called for. D.J.E.

distinctive feature, see under PHONEME.

distribution.

(1) In STATISTICS and PROBABILITY THEORY, the set of values taken by a RANDOM VARIABLE, together with the associated probabilities. Thus, the experiment 'toss a fair coin twice' and the random variable 'number of heads' generate a distribution in which the values 0 and 2 each have probability (chance of occurring) equal to ¼ and the value 1 has the probability equal to ½. The *distribution function* is the FUNCTION F such that if x is a value, then $F(x)$ is the probability that the random variable does not exceed x. The *probability density* is the derivative (slope) of F if this exists. Distributions arising empirically arc often described roughly by a measure of location and possibly a measure of dispersion such as the VARIANCE. The *skewness* of a distribution is a measure of its asymmetry. Its range is the separation of its upper and lower extreme values (if meaningful) and the *mid-range* is the mid-point of this interval. The distribution given above is symmetrical about the value 1 and so has zero skewness, and its range is the interval whose endpoints are 0 and 2. Among the most important theoretical distributions are the normal (see NORMAL OR GAUSSIAN DISTRIBUTION) and POISSON DISTRIBUTIONS. See also MODE. R.SI.

(2) In LINGUISTICS, the range of contexts in which a linguistic unit (e.g. a WORD CLASS or PHONEME) can occur. Units which occur in the same set of contexts are said to have an *equivalent* distribution (e.g. the phonemes /h/ and /w/, which in English words occur only initially and medially); units which have no contexts in common are in *complementary* distribution (e.g. prefixes and suffixes). D.C.

distribution map. In ARCHAEOLOGY, a map showing the spatial distribution (or DIFFUSION) of a CULTURE trait, e.g. a distinctive type of axe. It serves as a visual statement of a class of data for which an explanation is then sought. The more valuable distribution maps record both the presence and absence of the trait at every examined location. It has been said that distribution maps often reflect the distribution of field archaeologists. B.C.

distributive justice. A specific form of justice distinguished by Aristotle, which required the burdens and benefits of social life to be distributed among individuals proportionately according to merit and the strength of other prior claims. The expression is now frequently used for standards of fair distribution (not necessarily based on merit or prior claims) which should determine the extent of individual liberties, political rights, opportunities, and ownership of property. Various alternative philosophical bases, some of which, but not all, are utilitarian, have been proposed by social theorists for the principles of distributive justice. For further reading: N. Rescher, *Distributive Justice* (1966). H.L.A.H.

divergence, see under CONVERGENCE (sense 1).

divergers, see under CONVERGERS AND DIVERGERS.

divination. Procedure to discover information about the past, present and future or the means to ascertain the cause of illness and misfortune. It is carried out by an individual specially appointed or trained: an oracle, diviner or medium. Divination may involve communication with the gods and spirits, usually through possession (see SPIRIT POSSESSION). It may concern the ordering of forces that operate in the world (geomancy or horoscope). Divination is usually a RITUAL occasion and in the case of sickness or misfortune it often involves the manipulation of certain objects to discover the cause: the use of oracles, the throwing of dice, the dissection of a chicken. A.G.

division of labour. A concept, akin to specialization, first developed in ECONOMICS and then more generally applied in SOCIOLOGY.

(1) Adam Smith, in the *Wealth of Nations* (1776), demonstrated how the productivity of labour could be enormously improved if tasks previously carried out by a single worker were subdivided into simple, repetitive operations each carried out by separate workers. A man on his own might produce one pin a day; with pin-making divided into eight distinct operations, each performed by 'distinct hands', each pin worker could be

reckoned as producing upwards of 4,800 pins a day. Smith, like Charles Babbage after him, pointed out that not only would such specialization allow the employer to dispense with more skilled, and more expensive, workers, but it would also lead to greater mechanization of production. The division of labour thus carried within it the seeds of a progressive DE-SKILLING of work, leading eventually to total AUTOMATION.

This form of the division of labour is sometimes called the technical or *detailed* division of labour. Understood in the sense that it fragments work and reduces the worker to the status of an appendage of the machine, it was taken over by Karl Marx as a central element of his theory of ALIENATION.

(2) In sociology, the concept is associated especially with Herbert Spencer (1820–1903) and Émile Durkheim (1858–1917), whose *The Division of Labour in Society* (1902) is a seminal text. It is used to refer to the growth in the social division of labour corresponding to the process of social differentiation. As societies progress, they become more complex and achieve an increasing specialization of ROLES and tasks. The 'social organism' here follows the path of the individual organism, as it develops from the simple undifferentiated embryonic form to the complex set of specialized and interdependent structures of the adult organism. For Durkheim, this process was leading to a new principle of the social and moral order in modern societies. The 'mechanical solidarity' of traditional societies, based on unquestioning and automatic obedience of moral and religious norms, was in modern societies replaced by 'organic solidarity', where social integration was achieved by the awareness of the mutual interdependence of specialized parts. In this way, Durkheim thought, modern societies could dispense altogether with the requirements of NORMATIVE consensus. Durkheim later came to think that this was too optimistic a view, and sought increasingly for some secular or 'civil religion' as a substitute for the binding and integrating force of traditional religion.

(3) In more recent use, the concept has come to be applied to the *sexual* division of labour: the division of tasks and roles between men and women.

For further reading: E. Durkheim, *The Division of Labor in Society* (1893; Eng. tr., 1964); A. Giddens, *Capitalism and Modern Social Theory* (1971). K.K.

divisionism, see under NEO-IMPRESSIONISM.

Dixieland. At best, a misleading popular term for all forms of traditional JAZZ. It owes its origin to the Original Dixieland Jazz Band, a white group who brought the music to New York in 1917, when they also made the first jazz recordings. It came to be associated particularly with the white exponents of CHICAGO style to distinguish them from the older generation of NEW ORLEANS players. Nowadays, however, it can mean anything, and usually conjures up an inoffensively jolly, thoroughly derivative jazz, dispensed by an ingratiating band in straw hats and striped blazers. GE.S.

DNA (deoxyribonucleic acid), see under NUCLEIC ACID.

DNA library. For the CLONING of the DNA of, say, liver tissue, the DNA has first to be fragmented by RESTRICTION ENZYMES into pieces small enough for cloning techniques. Since the fragmentation is a random process, the total liver DNA will be represented by numerous cloned fragments. This collection of fragments is known as a liver DNA library or gene library. HYBRIDIZATION with specific DNA or RNA reagents can be used to withdraw particular pieces of DNA from a library if they are present. P.N.

dodecaphonic music, see under SERIAL MUSIC.

dogma. A term in Christian THEOLOGY, meaning a doctrine claiming authority over any private opinion or hesitation in a believer's mind. It is held to be a religious truth established by divine revelation and defined by the Church. If the believer rejects it, he becomes to that extent a heretic. The term is applied specially to the decrees, mainly about CHRISTOLOGY, of the ecumenical Councils of the Church (325–787; see ECUMENICAL MOVEMENT). Roman Catholics accept 14 subsequent Councils. It is also believed that the Pope's *ex cathedra* (solemnly very official) teaching is free of error, according to a dogma defined in 1870 (see INFALLIBILITY). Protestants give greater emphasis to the authority of the Bible (see

DOGMATICS). In RELIGION as in other fields, the term is today mostly used pejoratively, to mean an opinion held on grounds, and propagated by methods, which are unreasonable. For further reading: G. O'Collins, *Has Dogma a Future?* (1975). D.L.E.

dogmatics. The discipline of THEOLOGY concerned with Christian beliefs (see CHRISTIANITY), and therefore distinct from other disciplines like biblical, historical and practical theology, although it is related to each of these in a variety of ways. Methodologically, dogmatics has an analytic and a synthetic dimension, as it attempts to explicate individual doctrines and to relate them to one another as parts of a coherent whole. Not all doctrines, however, are dogmas – normative statements of BELIEF defined in quite specific circumstances – and therefore dogmatics may restrict its operations to certain beliefs authorized by the Churches in creeds and councils. Dogmatic theology, in this sense, would be narrower than systematic theology, but the terms are increasingly synonymous. In the 20th century, a preference for the former (as in the case of neo-orthodoxy) often suggests a distrust of the 'system' in systematics – especially when the system is philosophical in character. C.C.

dollar imperialism, see under IMPERIALISM.

domain (in MATHEMATICS), see under FUNCTION.

domain walls, see under STRINGS.

domestic group. In ANTHROPOLOGY, a general term to describe residential, reproductive and economic units. In rural societies these three units are often coterminous, but in industrial societies they are usually distinct. Domestic group as a concept was developed by anthropologists to replace family, a value-laden term which raised many problems in analysis. External factors, for example demographic and economic, affect the size and composition of domestic groups, but all groups move through phases of expansion and contraction in the DEVELOPMENTAL CYCLE. KINSHIP systems also influence the composition of a domestic group. In MATRILINEAL societies it is usually focused on a woman, her children and brothers. In PATRILINEAL societies it is focused upon a man, his wives and their children. For further reading: R. Netting *et al* (eds), *Households: Comparative and Historical Studies of the Domestic Group* (1984). A.G.

domestic labour. Feminists (see FEMINISM) argue that unpaid work within the home, such as housework and childcare, should not be seen as fundamentally different to paid work or employment. Many feminists believe that domestic labour is devalued (see VALUE, THEORY OF) within patriarchal (see PATRIARCHY) societies because it is predominantly carried out by women and because it is used to justify its low status and lack of material reward. Some Marxist feminists (see MARXISM) emphasize the key role of domestic labour in the reproduction of labour power through women carrying out key maintenance tasks for their male partners in paid work and through reproducing future generations of workers (i.e. their children). Some writers see emotional work (such as the effort involved in worrying about children or keeping their partners happy) as an important part of domestic labour. For further reading: C. Delphy, *Close to Home* (1984). M.D.H.

dominance. The behaviour pattern by which, in social animals, individuals establish the *hierarchy* of the group. In some birds, including domestic fowls, a *pecking order* develops, with one bird dominant to all the rest, and the remainder occupying more or less fixed positions in the chain. Rats and some other mammals behave similarly. Dominance is maintained by aggressive or threatening behaviour on the part of an animal, and by submission on the part of its inferior. In most cases, particularly in the wild, this aggressive behaviour becomes ritualized and ceases when the threatened individual is seen to submit, so violent combat is rare. However, some species (e.g. wild cattle, certain deer) fight to the death for the position of the leader of the group. Extrapolation from animal studies to human behaviour may be misleading, though attempts to dominate others by both men and women are made through ostentation, cunning, and personal sartorial elegance or eccentricity of appearance. In BOTANY, dominance in a plant community is also described (e.g. beech trees in a beech wood, heather on moorland). Here the term is applied to the species which is tallest and most obvious. For further reading: R. Ardrey, *The Territorial Imperative* (1967). K.M.

dominant ideology. 'The ideas of the ruling class', Karl Marx had said in *The German Ideology* (1845), 'are in any age the ruling ideas'. Building on this, certain MARXIST theorists such as Antonio Gramsci (see HEGEMONY) and Louis Althusser have elaborated the notion that the principal mechanism whereby subordinate classes are kept in subjection is through the perpetuation in society at large of a particular set of attitudes, beliefs and values which validate the rule of a particular CLASS, and which together constitute a dominant IDEOLOGY. In traditional societies, religion usually supplies the dominant ideology, acting to reconcile the lower classes to their fate on this earth with the promise of better things to come in the hereafter (cf. Marx: 'religion is the opium of the people'). In modern societies, the dominant ideology is less easy to identify, but is generally thought to include, in the West, the principles of liberal CONSTITUTIONALISM, together with an attachment to the institution of private property, and a widely diffused belief in the beneficence of ECONOMIC GROWTH. COMMUNIST societies share this belief in the virtues of economic growth, but justify both its costs and benefits in terms of a dominant ideology that stresses the advantages of collective ownership and proclaims the end of the kind of class rule that is held to disfigure ECONOMIC DEVELOPMENT in the West. Needless to say, the point of regarding all such beliefs as ideologies is to indicate the discrepancy between the propagated ideals and the actual realities in both East and West. For further reading: N. Abercrombie, S. Hill and B. S. Turner, *The Dominant Ideology Thesis* (1980). K.K.

domino theory. Phrase coined by President Eisenhower in 1954 to describe the belief of successive American administrations since 1947 that the fall of one nation to a COMMUNIST regime would surely lead to the fall of its neighbours. Used by Presidents Kennedy (in 1963) and Nixon (as Vice-President, in 1965) to justify American involvement in VIETNAM, and by other American leaders to justify intervention in Latin America. Subsequent to the US withdrawal from southeast Asia the concept was somewhat devalued by inter-communist disputes (SINO-VIETNAMESE CONFLICT and civil war in Cambodia) and the resistance of other states in the region to communist takeover. For further reading: F. Ninkovich, *Modernity and Power: A History of the Domino Theory in the Twentieth Century* (1994). D.C.W.; A.W.

Donkey's Tail.

(1) Title of an art exhibition in Moscow, 1912, organized by the painter Michel Larionov. In contrast to the KNAVE OF DIAMONDS it contained works in the neo-PRIMITIVE style, influenced by Russian icons, FOLK ART and the East. The provocative title, suggested by a prank in Paris (when brushes were tied to a donkey's tail and the resulting smear exhibited at the Salon des Indépendants), led to the removal of Goncharova's religious works by the police. Other painters taking part included Malevich, Chagall and Tatlin.

(2) An almanac entitled *Donkey's Tail and Target* (Moscow, 1913) contained FUTURIST poetry and the manifesto of RAYONISM. M.C.

Doomwatch. A word popularized through a BBC television series of the early 1970s about a semi-official watchdog agency which monitored developments in all fields of scientific research and acted whenever it felt that human values or social responsibility were being ignored or flouted. It is, therefore, a popular term for social control of the 'mad scientist'. Less sensationally, it can embrace such organizations as the Club of Rome (see LIMITS TO GROWTH) and the Pugwash conferences which periodically extrapolate trends of growth or consumption in order to forecast scarcities of resources, and attempt to avoid potential disasters and irresponsible research. See also TECHNOPOLIS. P.S.L.

doping. The introduction of controlled and usually small amounts of a foreign ATOM to a pure compound, often in the form of a crystal, in order to modify its properties. The addition of dopants is important in determining the electrical characteristics of SEMICONDUCTORS and in the preparation of LASER materials. B.F.

Doppler effect (named after the Austrian physicist Christian Johann Doppler, who discovered it in 1842). The change in the perceived frequency of a wave which results when the observer moves relatively to the source. The frequency is raised when the source and observer are approaching each other, and lowered when they are moving apart. For sound waves the Doppler effect causes the drop in pitch of the whistle of a passing train, and the sonic boom. For light waves, the RED SHIFT in the spectrum of distant GALAXIES is a Doppler effect (see EXPANSION OF THE UNIVERSE). Finally, police RADAR traps are based on the change in frequency of a MICROWAVE signal reflected from a moving vehicle. M.V.B.

double articulation, see under DUALITY OF STRUCTURE.

double-consciousness. In *The Souls of Black Folk* (1961), W. E. B. DuBois describes 'double-consciousness' – a concept that explains the plight and passions of slaves and their descendants. The concept attempts to reveal what it means to live in a black body in a society that is defined by racial strife and oppression (see RACE; RACISM). According to DuBois, 'It is a peculiar sensation, this double-consciousness, this sense of always looking at one's self through the eyes of others, of measuring one's soul by the tape of a world that looks on in amused contempt and pity. One ever feels his two-ness – an American, a Negro; two souls, two thoughts, two unreconciled strivings; two warring ideals in one dark body, whose dogged strength alone keeps it from being torn asunder.'

This condition of double-consciousness is not a phenomenon that is restricted to the experiences of African-Americans in the past. It is also described by contemporary commentators on the African-American experience as a kind of ALIENATION. This form of alienation is said to exist when the self is deeply divided because the hostility of the dominant society forces the self to see itself as loathsome, defective or insignificant. This type of alienation is not estrangement from one's work, but an estrangement from ever becoming a self that is not defined in the hostile terms of the dominant group. H.M.

double descent, see under DESCENT.

double entrenchment, see under ENTRENCHED CLAUSES.

double helix, the. The name given to the crystalline structure of deoxyribonucleic acid (DNA) – see NUCLEIC ACID. Also the title of a well-known book by J. D. Watson describing his discovery of this structure in 1953 in collaboration with F. H. C. Crick. P.M.

double-track systems, see under RECIDIVISM.

double unilineal descent, see under DESCENT.

doublethink, see under ORWELLIAN.

doves and **hawks.** Figures of speech used by the American and, by adoption, European press to distinguish those US politicians who prefer DIPLOMACY and caution (doves) from those who prefer to stress American military strength (hawks) to solve international problems. The terms gained ascendancy during the war of 1812 between Britain and the United States, and acquired a wide currency during the presidencies of Kennedy and Johnson. S.R.

downsizing. The term, called 'rightsizing' by corporations, referring to the mass layoffs of middle managers and supervisors that hit some of the biggest US companies in the early 1990s, as they sought to trim costs and boost their stock prices. The unprecedented lay-offs included 60,000 jobs at IBM, 40,000 at Digital Equipment Corp., and 40,000 at AT&T. 'Our reduction and other actions are absolutely essential if our businesses are to be competitive,' explained AT&T CEO Robert Allen, whose salary at the time was estimated to be in the $5 million range. The lay-offs were fundamentally different from previous workforce reductions, which were part of a business cycle in which all parties assumed many if not all of the jobs would return in better times. This time the jobs were presumed to be made redundant by productivity gains. The estimates of jobs lost from 1989 to 1996 range anywhere from 3 million to 21 million. The long-range economic and political impact of the practice is not yet apparent. R.K.H.

dowry. The transfer of property from parents to daughters at MARRIAGE. The property the bride receives in this way remains in her name and she retains control over it within the marriage. Dowry does not pass to her husband or his kin (as in BRIDEWEALTH). It is a vertical property transmission, between generations, rather than a horizontal redistribution of wealth, which characterizes bridewealth transactions. This has implications for the kind of marriage associated with dowry, usually MONOGAMY. There is normally control over a daughter's marriage if she is property-bearing. Dowry may be used as part of a marriage strategy, to make a good match. In *Bridewealth and Dowry* (1973), Jack Goody and S. J. Tambiah showed that, in India, limited caste mobility is possible through *hypergamy* (a woman marries a man in a higher caste group and the children produced take their father's status), and the role of dowry here is crucial.

Dowry is used to establish a conjugal or familial fund. This will eventually be passed on to the children produced by the marriage. A conjugal fund represents the pooling, but not the merging, of a husband's and wife's resources. If the marriage is dissolved the wife reclaims her dowry portion.

Movable goods, jewellery, money and household items most commonly make up a woman's dowry. It is found particularly in association with marriage in Europe and Asia. It occurs in societies where the principle of bilateral inheritance is recognized (both sons and daughters inherit from parents; see BILATERALCOGNATIC DESCENT). It is, however, a pre-mortem property settlement: once a dowry has been paid, the daughter can make no further claims on the parental estate. Work by Goody (*Production and Reproduction*, 1976) has linked the institution of dowry to certain economic conditions and systems of production in Eurasia. For further reading: U. Sharma, *Women, Work and Property in North West India* (1980). A.G.

Drake equation, see under SEARCH FOR EXTRATERRESTRIAL INTELLIGENCE.

Drancy. A public housing estate in a north-eastern suburb of Paris which was transformed by the French government into a CONCENTRATION CAMP – mainly for Jews (see JUDAISM) – during World War II; 74,500 Jews were deported from France via Drancy to Nazi death camps (see NAZISM). Fewer than 3,000 survived. Drancy was run by French administrators, and *gendarmes* policed the camp. Drancy has become a symbol not only of French collaboration with the Nazis, but of France's active role in the HOLOCAUST. In the post-World War II period, France has been slow to acknowledge the scale of her involvement in the Holocaust – Drancy was one of a system of more than 100 concentration camps there. This is due in part to the fact that former President François Mitterrand had been a minor official in the wartime VICHY government, and that post-war he gave preferment to a number of public figures later implicated in the deportation of Jews. It was only with the election of Jacques Chirac as President in 1996 that France finally admitted the extent of her role in the Holocaust. For further reading: M. Rajfus, *Drancy: un camp de concentration très ordinaire* (1996). S.T.

Dreyfus case. In 1894 Captain Alfred Dreyfus, a French general staff officer of Jewish origins, was condemned to life imprisonment on Devil's Island for betraying secrets to Germany. The evidence was flimsy, and a campaign, in which Clemenceau and Zola played a leading part, was launched to secure a retrial. Fearing the effect of an acquittal on the Army's position as the embodiment of France's national will, senior officers withheld or forged evidence and secured Dreyfus's conviction at a retrial in 1899. President Loubet immediately pardoned him. In 1906 the Court of Appeal quashed the 1894 verdict and Dreyfus was reinstated. For more than a decade *l'affaire Dreyfus* bitterly divided France and dominated French politics: it became a trial of strength between anti-clerical radicals (*Dreyfusards*, including such people as Anatole France, Marcel Proust, Daniel Halévy and Léon Blum) on the one hand and anti-semitic (see ANTISEMITISM), Catholic, conservative defenders of the French officer corps (*anti-Dreyfusards*) on the other. For further reading: D. Johnson, *France and the Dreyfus Affair* (1967); E. Cahm, *The Drey-*

fus Affair in French Society and Politics (1996). A.L.C.B.

drive. In PSYCHOANALYSIS, a translation of Freud's term *trieb*, also translated as 'INSTINCT'. In Freud's usage, this is to be distinguished from the usual meaning of instinct as a biological response tied to external stimuli. Instead, the drive is seen as the 'psychical representative of the stimuli originating from within the organism and reaching the mind' (S. Freud, *Papers on Metapsychology*, 1915) – that is, drives derive from biological urges but are experienced psychologically. In Freud's account, a drive has a source in the BODY, an aim to reduce tension, and an object which is the (contingent) element through which this aim can be achieved (see CONTINGENCY). Various schools of psychoanalysis (for example, EGO-PSYCHOLOGY and OBJECT RELATIONS theory) have differed on the weight to be given to each of these components. Freud's later theory of drives distinguished between the LIFE INSTINCT (Eros) and the DEATH INSTINCT, a distinction which became fundamental to KLEINIAN psychoanalysis. The linguistic and grammatical considerations involved in Freud's discussion of drives also indicate the strongly symbolic aspect of the theory, a point which has been taken up in LACANIAN psychoanalysis. S.J.F.

droit moral, see under COPYRIGHT.

drop-out. Literally one who drops out of, or eschews, the generally accepted behaviour patterns of the society to which he belongs. While society has always had drop-outs in the form of vagrants, hermits, etc., the contemporary drop-out phenomenon was closely associated with DRUGS and with the emergence of HIPPIES and the UNDERGROUND. Dropping out in this context involves a deliberate decision to discontinue some conventionally approved course of action (e.g. higher education, or the use of previously acquired specialist qualifications, or even the earning of a high wage on the assembly line) and to turn elsewhere for fulfilment. Popular choices in the 1960s and 1970s included agriculture (subsistence farming), craft and artisan work, etc., which can be seen as offering an element of individualism against the MASS SOCIETY backdrop, and as a reaction to DEHUMANIZATION. How many of the people who followed Dr Timothy Leary's advice to 'turn on, tune in and drop out' remain engaged in alternative economic activity is a matter for conjecture. Dropping out is not only often a transient activity for individuals but has become a less viable option in an age where high levels of youth unemployment have made vocational training highly desirable. P.S.L.

drugs.

(1) The substances which form the subject-matter of PHARMACOLOGY; see also PSYCHOPHARMACOLOGY.

(2) More narrowly, in colloquial use, those chemical substances which, when taken orally, nasally, by inhalation, hypodermically or intravenously, alter CONSCIOUSNESS, PERCEPTION or mood. There are four groups: (a) *Anaesthetics and sedatives*, such as alcohol, barbiturates, tranquillizers and 'glues' (which are sniffed); these blunt psychic and physical pain; tolerance develops, and with high doses withdrawal causes convulsions or delirium. They have the virtue of not being smoked, but barbiturate injection is particularly damaging; alcohol, fortunately, is often taken for taste or diluted with food (see ALCOHOLISM; ADDICTION). (b) *Opiates*, natural and synthetic, include morphine and heroin; these highly addictive substances are important in medicine for relief of pain, and may produce tolerance and withdrawal symptoms. Of the latter, despite the popular literature, prolonged insomnia may be hardest to deal with. (c) *Stimulants* such as cocaine and amphetamines; cocaine, though possibly the most addictive, generates little tolerance, and only DEPRESSION on withdrawal; but an extraordinary degree of tolerance can arise to amphetamines. (d) *Hallucinogens* such as mescaline, LSD and cannabis (see MARIJUANA); tolerance develops rapidly to LSD, more slowly to cannabis. Cannabis is unique in its cumulative effect and the resultant slow onset of its full action and of recovery from it. Its chemical structure was only recently discovered, as also its effects on sex hormones (see ENDOCRINOLOGY) and CELL development, and on MEMORY and motivation.

Illicit trade in drugs, and drug addiction, was a significant international problem in the late 1960s and early 1970s, growing to epic proportions in the 1980s and 1990s, and culminating in the American WAR ON DRUGS. Authorities in the USA have encouraged many companies to test employees for traces of drugs and to offer counselling. The emergence of 'crack', a cheap and extremely addictive mixture of cocaine and baking soda, has proved a major social problem among the young in the USA and elsewhere. In Britain, heroin addiction, which had been a feature of youth SUB-CULTURE (see also YOUTH CULTURE) in the 1960s, increased during the late 1970s and 1980s, with mass UNEMPLOYMENT and ready availability of cheap supplies cited as contributory causes.

There are probably as many reasons for taking drugs as there are individuals; recurrent themes are availability, curiosity, peer pressure (see PEER GROUP), depression, the avoidance of a problem, boredom and thrill-seeking. Multiple drug use is now common. The great danger is *continued* use, which is why the many psychological, social and physical factors involved in drug dependence and progression to other drugs are important. The death rate for a heroin addict is about 30 times that normal for his or her age, largely from self-neglect or overdose. S.T.; W.D.M.P.

Druze, see under ISLAM.

dual containment. This was announced as official US policy towards Iran and Iraq in May 1993, the idea being to isolate these two countries for their perceived 'rogue' behaviour. It was introduced by the Clinton administration, firstly as a way of 'containing' potential Iraqi and Iranian threats to Western interests in the Persian Gulf and to Western allies – the Gulf Co-operation Council countries. Dual containment's second function was said to be an effective means through which the Arab–Israeli peace process (see MADRID PEACE CONFERENCE) could be insulated from the unstable balance of power of the Persian Gulf, and also an effective way of preventing Iran from derailing the process through its sponsorship of radical Islamic TERRORISM (see ISLAM). Despite criticisms that the strategy would prove unworkable, that the same isolation efforts could not be applied simultaneously to two countries as different as Iran and Iraq (which was already subject to UN sanctions since August 1990), the second Clinton administration continued to uphold this US policy towards the two states. A.EH.

dual organization, see under MOIETIES.

dualism. Any theory which holds that there is, either in the universe at large or in some significant part of it, an ultimate and irreducible distinction of nature between two different kinds of thing. Examples are (1) Plato's *dualism of eternal objects* (forms or UNIVERSALS), of which we can have true knowledge, and temporal objects, which are accessible to the senses, and of which we can at best have opinions; (2) Descartes' *mind-body dualism*, i.e. of mind, as conscious, and of body, as occupying space, the former always infallibly, the latter never more than fallibly, knowable (see also MIND-BODY PROBLEM); (3) *ethical dualism*, which holds, in conformity with the doctrine of the NATURALISTIC FALLACY, that there is an irreducible difference between statements of fact and VALUE-JUDGEMENTS; (4) *explanatory dualism*, which holds that, while natural events, including mere bodily movements, have causes, human actions do not but must be explained by reference to motives or reasons; (5) sometimes called *epistemological dualism* (see also EPISTEMOLOGY), the theory that a distinction must be drawn between the immediate object of PERCEPTION (i.e. the appearance or SENSE-DATA) and the inferred, public, material objects. For further reading: J. A. Passmore, *Philosophical Reasoning* (1970). A.Q.

duality of structure (sometimes referred to as *double articulation*). In LINGUISTICS, a major defining characteristic of human language, which is seen as containing two fundamental LEVELS of structure: (1) a phonological level, at which sounds, themselves meaningless, are organized into (meaningful) combinations (see PHONETICS; PHONOLOGY); (2) a syntactic level, at which the properties of the meaningful expression are studied (in terms of SYNTAX, LEXICON, SEMANTICS). D.C.

duality symmetry, see under GRAND UNIFICATION; SUPERSTRINGS.

due process. A rule of American law, found in the 5th and 14th amendments to the US constitution, to the effect that no person may be deprived of 'life, liberty or property, without due process of law'. Originally intended as a guarantee of fair procedure, the meaning of the phrase was greatly expanded in the late 19th century, and came to encompass guarantees of substantive rights as well. Substantive due process became similar to the idea of natural law, allowing American courts to assess the reasonableness of federal and state laws. Together with the EQUAL PROTECTION clause, due process is the foundation of much modern American constitutional law. M.S.P.

Dumbarton Oaks. Name of the private estate in Washington, DC, at which in August and September 1944 British, American, Soviet and Chinese representatives met to draft a charter for the post-war international security organization to be named the United Nations (see UN). The draft proposed four principal organs, a Security Council, a General Assembly, an INTERNATIONAL COURT OF JUSTICE, and an international secretariat. D.C.W.

dumbing down. The phrase appears to have originated in the early 1930s in Hollywood to describe the process whereby a subtle script could be made less subtle and correspondingly more popular. Later it came to mean deliberately simplifying a school text as a strategy to keep students perceived to have less ability nonetheless passing at desired rates. By the 1980s, especially in the US, the term began to be applied more broadly to a variety of mostly cultural situations in which something valuable would, often with cynical calculation, be downgraded, abridged or mediated in some essential way in order to make it more palatable, more easily accessible; in short, more easily sold. Dumbing down has connections to the MARXIST notion of the CAPITALIST tendency to commodify, or to merchandise ideas, people, institutions – e.g., RELIGION, education, private life, etc. – normally considered too valuable or sacred to be considered for sale.

In his famous essay in *Partisan Review* (1960), 'Masscult & Midcult', American critic Dwight Macdonald astutely discussed this process, whereby high culture, once drawn into the circumstances of mass distribution, is inevitably the loser as it is repackaged for an audience presumed too ignorant to appreciate its intrinsic value. J.F.T.

dumping. Selling in a foreign market at a price below that prevailing in the exporter's home market, or below his cost of production. In comparing prices or costs in the two markets, allowance must be made for differences in terms and conditions of sale and in taxation. The conditions under which dumping is injurious or beneficial to the importing country have been long discussed. The GATT permits countries to levy anti-dumping duties if their industries are or might be injured. M.FG.S.

dust-bowl. In GEOGRAPHY, a type of man-made desert. It is a region subject to low rainfall and occasional severe drought in which arable farming is a hazardous practice. The top soil of the dust-bowl has been removed by wind erosion (see SOIL EROSION), usually because of excessive grazing or ploughing and cultivation of land without the necessary precautions against erosion, and a broad hollow is imposed on the land. The term was originally applied to areas in the western USA, i.e. western Kansas, Oklahoma and Texas, extending into south-eastern Colorado and eastern New Mexico, and is still used mainly in this context. M.L.

Dutch disease. Named when the booming North Seas gas export revenues in the 1970s appreciated the guilder, making Dutch industrial exports more costly in foreign currencies and increasing foreign competition and unemployment. Subsequently, the pathology might better be called Nigerian, Venezuelan (from petroleum), Congolese (copper), or Ghanaian (cocoa) disease, an economic distortion resulting from dependence on one to three booming exports.

These booms have proven a blessing for some countries but a curse for others. Commodity export revenues increase GDP per person, widen employment opportunities, and increase policy options, but they alter incentives, raise expectations, and distort and destabilize output in traditional exports and domestic production, frequently in agriculture.

Still, Dutch disease may seem a mild case of influenza compared to reverse Dutch disease from an oil or primary commodity bust, which a Nigerian economic official compared to winning a lottery, building a castle which cannot be maintained, and then borrowing to move out. For further reading: E. W. Nafziger, *The Economics of Developing Countries* (1997). E.W.N.

dwarf star. A small, faint, hot star of extremely high density. It is possible that dwarf stars are what is left after the explosion of SUPERNOVAE, and therefore represent a late stage in the evolution of stars. See also BLACK HOLE; HERTZSPRUNG-RUSSELL DIAGRAM. M.V.B.

dwarf wheat, see under GREEN REVOLUTION.

dymaxion. A term used by the American engineer Buckminster Fuller (1895–1983) to describe his CONCEPT of the maximum net performance per gross ENERGY input (see BUCKMINSTERFULLERENE). It was applied by him to a factory-produced house (a hexagonal space suspended from a central mast), a bathroom, and a map projection, and is most in evidence in the construction of his *geodesic domes*. These lightweight enclosures are parts of spheres subdivided along lines following Great Circle routes across their surface. Such domes have been airlifted by the US Marine Corps, have housed RADAR equipment in arctic conditions, travelled as exhibition pavilions, and, most notably, housed the US Pavilion at the Montreal Expo in 1967. For further reading: J. Meller (ed.), *The Buckminster Fuller Reader* (1970). M.BR.

dynamic labyrinth, see under ENVIRONMENT (sense 2).

dynamic programming. A technique for attacking optimization problems by choosing the values of the variables sequentially rather than simultaneously. It tends to be particularly appropriate for problems involving time-dependence, such as control problems. The method is expected to provide an *optimal policy*, i.e. a rule for choosing the values of the variables so as to optimize the *criterion function*. Three broad classes of dynamic-programming problems may be distinguished:

(1) In *deterministic problems* all desired information is available at all times and the criterion function can be calculated to discover the effects of any given policy. Many control problems are of this type, e.g. the problem of selecting the minimal-time or minimal-fuel flight-path for an aircraft.

(2) *Learning problems* are deterministic, but the relation between control and effect is *a priori* unknown to the optimizer, who thus has to learn about the behaviour of the criterion function while trying to optimize it. Search procedures (e.g. the classic problem of identifying the broken wire in an unlabelled multi-core cable) are usually of this type.

(3) *Stochastic problems* have the additional feature that the future behaviour of the system is not fully determined by the past and present, knowledge of which merely makes the various future possibilities more or less probable; the best that the optimizer can hope to find is a policy which will maximize the expected value of the criterion function. Among the most important problems in this last class are correction problems for systems without inherent stability, where the policy has to make the best choice between the costs of using an incorrectly set mechanism and the costs of correcting it. R.SL.

dynamic psychology.

(1) A SCHOOL OF PSYCHOLOGY that emphasizes the role of motivation.

(2) More narrowly, the ideas of Freud and other psychoanalytically oriented psychologists (see FREUDIAN; PSYCHOANALYSIS) who, indeed, lay paramount stress on motivation. I.M.L.H.

dysfunctional. The opposite of one of the many meanings of *functional*. In this sense, a process or mechanism within an organism or social system is functional if it serves the interests, needs, aims or purposes of that organism or system, dysfunctional if it interferes with them. A.S.

dysgenic. Term coined in 1915 by Dean W. R. Inge, meaning that which tends to exert a detrimental influence over the genetic quality (see GENETICS/GENOMICS) of the human race – or indeed over smaller units, such as nations or CLASSES. It means the opposite of EUGENIC. For obvious reasons there has been no concerted effort to promote dysgenic policies and therefore no science of dysgenics exists. In 1917 Inge coined a second term, *cacogenic*, which has the same meaning as dysgenic. A.B.E.

dyslexia. The condition of those who experience a difficulty in learning to read which cannot be accounted for by limited ability, usually diagnosed in early childhood. Many dyslexics will have problems with reading and spelling throughout their lives, despite having otherwise normal intelligence and emotional characteristics. The problems can take several different forms, most common being the confusion of one letter for another, or difficulty in ordering some words and letters. The problem is far more common in males than females, and appears to have a hereditary basis, although the precise cause is unknown. Before dyslexia was identified as a specific condition, dyslexic children were simply assumed to be of limited intelligence. Now, however, we know this is not the case. They can respond to intensive instruction in reading, and often their difficulties in this one area are balanced by above-average skills in others. A.A.L.

dystopia, see under ANTI-UTOPIA.

E

early modern. A term which emerged from historical and literary studies during the 1980s and gained wider currency within the work of CULTURAL MATERIALISM and NEW HISTORICISM. Informed by Raymond Williams's sense of the dynamic relationship between the dominant, residual and emergent aspects of the cultural process, and also influenced by Michel Foucault's theorization of the break between historical formations or epistemes, the early modern offered an alternative to the reductive (see REDUCTION) and occlusive epochal connotations of period terms like 'The Renaissance' and implied a more complex understanding of historical transition. Perhaps its most crucial influence was in depriving and displacing *The Elizabethan World Picture* which had been developed in the work of E. M. W. Tillyard (1943) and had proved influential in imposing a nostalgically unified and ordered interpretation of the past. In its contrasting emphasis of the ruptural discontinuity between the premodern or feudal and the emergence of the modern, the early modern sites a liminal zone where the slippage between signifying systems and a fragmentation of any fixed sense of identity seem to mirror and perhaps in part symptomatizes the dislocative uncertainty of POST-MODERNISM. J.J.J.

earth art, see under CONCEPTUAL ART.

earth sciences. In the widest sense, the complete range of the sciences of the solid earth, the oceans and the atmosphere. The origin and motions of the earth as a component of the SOLAR SYSTEM form part of ASTRONOMY; GEOPHYSICS and GEOCHEMISTRY deal, respectively, with the physical and chemical characteristics of the earth and its environs; PALAEONTOLOGY is concerned with the origin and evolution of life on earth; GEOMORPHOLOGY involves the study of surface landforms; OCEANOGRAPHY is the study of the ocean waters and the basins that contain them; meteorology and CLIMATOLOGY cover, respectively, the short-term (weather) and long-term (climate) behaviour of the atmosphere; and GEOLOGY is the study of the nature of earth materials and processes with particular reference to the way in which they have interacted through time to generate the earth's existing features. There is also a host of subsidiary names. SEISMOLOGY deals with earthquakes and seismic waves, VOLCANOLOGY with volcanoes, geomagnetism (see MAGNETISM) with the earth's magnetic field, STRATIGRAPHY with rock strata, and so on.

The boundaries between these disciplines and subdisciplines are highly blurred. Moreover, some words may be used in more than one sense. Geology, for example, is sometimes used in the limited sense above but at other times as a more general term to cover all the sciences of the solid earth (geophysics, geochemistry, palaeontology, etc.). In the latter usage it is synonymous with geological sciences and the solid-earth sciences. Earth sciences, too, is more often than not used in a restricted sense that excludes astronomy, water and air, making it also synonymous with geological sciences and the general form of geology.

An interesting recent development concerns the names given to the study of the moon and planets. Research into the solid bodies of the moon and planets – made possible by satellites, space probes, manned and unmanned lunar missions, and the placing of instrument packages on planetary surfaces – is now considered part of the earth sciences, geological sciences and geology (general). But while no one would ever refer to, say, 'the earth science of Mars' or 'the geological science of Mercury', scientists are quite happy to speak of 'the geology of Venus', even though to do so is etymological nonsense (geo-earth). Terms such as marsology, uranology and (for the moon) selenology are sometimes used, albeit very infrequently, and in any case imply coverage of more than just the solid parts of the relevant bodies. The general term *planetology*, which also covers more than the solid, is rather more common. P.J.S.

earth shelters. Buildings which are dug into the ground and covered with a layer of earth and turf. The interiors are thus very heavily insulated. Insulated windows and doors add to the energy efficiency of this kind of structure. Popular as an idea in the 1960s and early 1970s, particularly in the USA, earth shelters have many real life models in VERNACULAR architecture around the world. Translating those models into a Western real estate culture has not necessarily been easy to achieve. S.L.

Eastern Orthodoxy, see ORTHODOXY, EASTERN.

eating disorder, see under ANOREXIA NERVOSA.

EBCDIC (Extended Binary-Coded Decimal Interchange Code), see under ASCII.

ebonics. A continuum of varieties of English spoken in the US, typically by African-Americans. The academic debate over Black English is at least 25 years old. Scholars have questioned whether the language that some African-Americans speak can be described as a novel version of the English language or whether it should be described as a dialect of Standard English. This debate has focused on the grammatical and syntactical structures of so-called Black English.

The political debate over Black English centres on whether African-American children should be instructed or allowed to communicate in the classroom in Black English. Some critics argue that to instruct children in Black English or to allow them to use this language in the classroom would harm them because to do so would hamper efforts to teach them Standard English. The supporters of Black English maintain that allowing children to communicate in the language spoken at home and in their communities will facilitate the learning process and combat the low self-esteem children will feel if they are told that people who speak like them are not speaking a language. Most of the proponents of Black English believe that it can be used as an effective tool for teaching African-American children Standard English. For further reading: T. Perry and L. Delpit, *The Real Ebonics Debate* (1998). H.M.

EC (European Community), see EUROPEAN UNION.

ECA, see under MARSHALL PLAN.

ecclesiology. That part of Christian THEOLOGY which is concerned with the Church. The modern debate about the Church's essential nature and changing tasks has been stimulated by the ECUMENICAL MOVEMENT and, in CATHOLICISM, by the AGGIORNAMENTO. Sometimes the word refers only to the architecture and furnishings of church buildings. D.L.E.

echo sounding, see under SONAR.

echocardiography. The use of ultrasound (see RADIOLOGY) as a method of investigating the heart non-invasively. The basic principle was derived from the SONAR systems for marine navigation and remote detection of submarines developed during World War II. The echoes from all structures of the heart can be identified from a single ultrasound beam and recorded on photographic strip chart recorders. This is called 'M-Mode' recording. In 1972, Bom and co-workers introduced real-time sector scanning of the heart which allows correct anatomic representation of an entire cardiac cross-section ('cross-sectional' or '2D'). It is a simple and painless method for investigation of heart function. It is especially useful for assessment of abnormalities of the valves and pericardium as well as ventricular performance. New developments include the use of Doppler sound recordings (see DOPPLER EFFECT), which are particularly helpful in quantifying the degree of valvular regurgitation and stenosis. L.J.F.

ecliptic. When we consider the earth as a planet, the *celestial sphere* is that imaginary sphere surrounding the earth infinitely far away on which the earth's equator and poles are projected. The plane of the earth's orbit round the sun is thus a plane passing through the centre of the celestial sphere. Its intersection with the celestial sphere will be a great circle – the ecliptic. The *plane of the ecliptic* is therefore the plane of the earth's orbit round the sun. Since it does not change, the great circle of the ecliptic on the celestial sphere will remain in a fixed position relative to other points (e.g. stars) projected on it. The earth's axis has an inclination from the vertical with respect to the plane of the ecliptic of about 23½° (more accurately 23° 27'). Thus the plane of the ecliptic makes the same angle with the plane of the equator. M.L.

ecodeme, see under DEME.

École de Paris. An expression used confusingly with three overlapping meanings, all relating to the fine arts as practised in Paris during the present century:

(1) Immediately after World War I it referred to a number of artists of non-French origin and predominantly Jewish background: notably the Russians Chagall and Soutine, the Bulgar Jules Pascin, the Czech Coubine, the Japanese Foujita, the Poles Kisling and Zak, and the Italian Modigliani. Sometimes distinguished (first, second École) according to whether they arrived in Paris before or after the war, they formed a distinctive school of FIGURATIVE, easily sentimentalized, more or less EXPRESSIONIST painting which emerged as the main new movement between CUBISM and the extension of SURREALISM to the visual arts.

(2) Later it was extended to include Picasso, Juan Gris and even, by association, Maurice Utrillo and his mother Suzanne Valadon.

(3) Finally, as in the Royal Academy's exhibition in 1951 and the annual shows at the Galérie Charpentier from 1955, it was used for virtually the whole modern art movement centring on Paris. J.W.

ecological anthropology (cultural ecology). A study which focuses on the interrelations between people and their environments and the ideas people hold of these relations. Cultural ecology was founded by the American anthropologist Julian Steward in the mid-20th century on the notion that human social and economic organization is both shaped by and shapes particular environments (*Theory of Culture Change*, 1955). Later proponents argued that culture mediates these processes, as the main means of human adaptation to environmental constraints. In the 1970s cultural ecology was eclipsed by SOCIOBIOLOGY, a new field which claimed that culture was functional to the continuation of individuals' GENES. Recently the trend has been to rethink the nature–society dualism (Descola and Palsson, 1996), a dichotomy that implies that humans CONSTRUCT their worlds from a cognitive blueprint or that they are constructed for humans by environmental or genetic (see GENETICS/GENOMICS) demands. This dualism may neither exist in models outside of Western DISCOURSE, nor may it be an accurate representation of how humans engage with environments. This has led some to argue that environments come into being as people act in them and that persons in turn are constituted by this engagement in the world, thus social life is always ongoing and provisional (for example Ingold, in M. Strathern, *Shifting Contexts*, 1995). For further reading: P. Descola and G. Palsson (eds), *Nature and Society: Anthropological Perspectives* (1996). M.H.

ecological economics. Prevailing economic PARADIGMS – capitalist, socialist, various mixtures (see CAPITALISM; SOCIALISM) – are based on the assumption that continuing economic growth is possible. Resource depletion, pollution and other environmental impacts of economic activity are treated as externalities. In contrast, ecological economics (see ECONOMICS; ECOLOGY), focusing on the uncertainty of the assumption that economic growth is not and will not be constrained by negative ecological impacts, explores the linkages and relationships between ecological and economic systems and the presumed limits to economic growth.

Ecological economics may be said to have achieved formal status as an academic discipline with the appearance in 1989 of *Ecological Economics*, the journal of the International Society for Ecological Economics. See also MALTHUSIANISM. For further reading: H. E. Daly, *Steady-State Economics* (1991). W.G.R.

ecological species, see under SPECIES.

ecological succession. The initial establishment and development of an ECOSYSTEM is termed primary succession. The re-establishment of an ecosystem following a disturbance is secondary succession. Succession is an orderly process, involving recognizable and repeated patterns of change in the flora and fauna of the ecosystem.

Examples of primary succession include the development of ecosystems on emerging volcanic islands and the reforestation of mountain areas on lava and ash following a volcanic eruption. Secondary succession is seen, for example, in abandoned pastures or in forests following fire. In both types of succession early successional plant species, termed pioneers, are generally rapidly growing 'weedy' species, while later stages are characterized by longer-lived, slower-growing species.

Wetland succession as seen in freshwater ponds and bogs may result over time in the accumulation of sediments that may finally obliterate the wetland or pond. Shorelines and sand dunes also undergo typical successional stages. W.G.R.

ecology (also known as *bionomics*).

(1) A term (Greek *oikos*, household or living-place) first used by Ernst Haeckel in 1873 for that branch of BIOLOGY which deals with the interrelationships between organisms and their ENVIRONMENT (sense 1). During the first half of the 20th century the concept spread rapidly, and ecology became an increasingly important part of many university courses. Studies of botanical ecology generally advanced more rapidly than those involving animals, but the subject played an important part in bringing together zoologists and botanists. Within the scientific community there is some division between those who place the greatest emphasis on field observations (the 'muddy-boot ecologists') and those who are more concerned with SYSTEMS analysis, modelling (see MODEL) and COMPUTER simulation of ecological processes (the 'theoretical ecologists'). Ecology is sometimes divided into various subdivisions, i.e. population ecology, evolutionary ecology, community ecology, physiological ecology, and behavioural ecology. Usually these divisions have little validity except to indicate that, possibly in some defined HABITAT, the interrelations of several species are being studied from the point of view of population dynamics, EVOLUTION, and so on. K.M.

(2) The word is also used in a more popular sense to denote concern for the protection of the environment from a wide range of pollutants. Growing awareness of environmental problems during the 1960s and 1970s led to the formation of activist groups, particularly in the USA and western Europe, with the result that governments increasingly introduced legislation to control the release of toxic substances into the environment. Major environmental disasters, such as the release of deadly gas from the Union Carbide plant at Bhopal in India on 3 December 1984 (2,500 dead) and the CHERNOBYL nuclear reactor disaster on 26 April 1986 (36 died immediately; 231 suffered acute radiation sickness; estimates suggest that as many as 34,000 could die over the next 40 years), have placed ecological issues firmly on the political agenda of most countries. 'Green' parties hold significant numbers of seats in some European democracies (see GREEN MOVEMENT). S.T.

ecology, human. An extension of zoological and botanical ECOLOGY to include man. The growth of human ecology is usually associated with sociological writing in the USA in the 1920s; it has since been widely adopted in a number of other SOCIAL SCIENCES. For each discipline, the distinctive character of ecological studies is the attempt to link the structure and organization of a human community to interactions with its localized ENVIRONMENT. For further reading: S. R. Eyre and G. R. J. Jones (eds), *Geography as Human Ecology: Methodology by Example* (1966). P.H.

econometric history, see under ECONOMIC HISTORY.

econometrics. The investigation of economic relationships using mathematical and statistical techniques. The econometric method is to develop a mathematical MODEL that has a basis in economic theory. Using economic data, the strengths of the relationships proposed by the model are estimated and the model is tested statistically. The methods of statistical INFERENCE are used to determine whether the model is an adequate representation of reality. Thus, econometrics in its broadest sense is concerned with the development and testing of economic models and theories. It is also used to construct quantitative models, which are used to forecast the economy. Econometrics suffers from a number of problems. Most economic models are, at best, only approximations to very complex phenomena and are unlikely to be valid in all possible circumstances. The data with which models are tested is rarely measured exactly and does not always directly correspond to the VARIABLES used in the model. The development of models is usually a compromise between what is acceptable in terms of economic theory, the available data, and what is computationally possible. There is little possibility of conducting meaningful economic experiments. The economy is made up of complex interacting systems which are difficult to separate out, model and test statistically; this leads to the problem of IDENTIFICATION. The actual forecasts of economic models may affect the economy, e.g. a forecast of increasing INFLATION may lead to expectations of higher rates of inflation that are self-fulfilling. In economic models, it is usual to assume that non-economic factors are constant. In many cases, this is an unrealistic assumption (e.g. the actions of OPEC). In spite of these problems, the quantitative investigation of the economy is necessary in order to test economic theories and to develop economic policies that are based on valid assumptions, models and forecasts of the economy. For further reading: M. Desai, *Applied Econometrics* (1976).

R.ST.; J.P.

economic aid. Includes development grants or loans made at concessional financial terms by official agencies to developing countries. Military assistance is not part of aid, but technical co-operation is.

A concessional loan, in contrast to one at bankers' standards, has at least a 25 per cent grant element. In the 1990s, the average grant component of bilateral aid of OECD countries to developing countries was more than 90 per cent.

In the 1990s, aid as a percentage of GNP was 0.15 in the US (a steady decline from 1965) and 0.38 in the rest of the OECD (a static percentage). Some OECD aid is channelled through multilateral agencies, such as the World Bank's concessional window, the International Development Association.

OECD leaders, especially in the US, have attacked aid as of little value in strengthening allies, maintaining global stability, and promoting economic development. Yet most research indicates that aid reduces local gaps in skill, food, savings and foreign exchange. For further reading: E. W. Nafziger, *The Economics of Developing Countries* (1997).

E.W.N.

economic anthropology. The study of the organization and processes of human material life. Economic anthropologists (see ECONOMICS; ANTHROPOLOGY) examine both the everyday human arrangements of production, consumption and distribution and the representations people give to these activities. The subdiscipline emerged with the formalist/substantivist (see FORMALISM) debate over MODELS of the economy. Formalists argued that economic concepts (such as profit, credit and CAPITAL) borrowed from neo-classical economics could be abstracted from their social context and be universally applied even to non-CAPITALIST, small-scale economies (Firth, *Primitive Polynesian Economy*, 1939). Substantivists, or institutionalists, inspired by Michael Polanyi (1891–1976), advocated that the economy was not an autonomous sphere, separate from the rest of social life. Instead, they concentrated on the social framework of economies, that is their embeddedness in localized cultural processes and relationships (Sahlins, *Stone Age Economics*, 1972). Contained within this debate is a basic opposition between those theories which emphasize the market (see MARKET ECONOMY) and EXCHANGE as the most important locus for the making of livelihoods and those which give production primacy. Indeed, this DIALECTIC continues to lie at the core of the subject. Since the 1970s other models have emerged. Political economy perspectives in anthropology have analysed historical transformations, and therefore reproduction, and the articulation of non-capitalist economies with the world market system. A core issue here is the value attached to LABOUR in the economic process and how it is organized and controlled (see for example Kahn, *Minangkabau Social Formations*, 1980). More recently Gudeman (*Conversations in Colombia*, 1992) has argued for the distinctively anthropological approach of cultural economics. This model locates all economies in terms of the opposition between the community economy (sustenance and maintenance of a way of life within a locality) and the market economy (accumulation and acquisition across groups). This is an important attempt to integrate ethnographic (see ETHNOGRAPHY) research with serious study of a history of economic ideas. He argues that all economic theories can be explained in terms of this opposition, and counteracts ones which have fetishized market exchanges and neglected the material basis of human renewal. For further reading: S.

Plattner (ed.), *Economic Anthropology* (1989). M.H.

economic development. Economic development is the process of ECONOMIC GROWTH and transformation of poor societies. Economic development is desired as it allows various objectives to be pursued. Until recently, economic development was seen in terms of growth in income per head and the alteration of the structure of production, in which the share of agriculture declines and the shares of the manufacturing and service industries increase. During the 1950s and 1960s, many developing countries experienced rapid growth in income per head, but the results of this economic growth were not considered to be particularly satisfactory. In the 1970s, economic development began to be defined in terms of the elimination or reduction of poverty, inequality and UNEMPLOYMENT. This definition views economic development as a means of meeting the basic needs, i.e. food, shelter, water supply, sanitation, health, education and protection of individuals and social groups. This view was quickly broadened from life-sustenance to include the concept of individuals and societies gaining self-esteem through their own or national prosperity and the freedom from economic servitude and DEPENDENCE on others. Since 1945, there has been a tremendous increase in interest in the study of economic development. Of particular interest have been the large differences in the economic growth of different countries, e.g. the rapid growth of the NEWLY INDUSTRIALIZING COUNTRIES and the dependence between developing and developed countries. There has been considerable dispute about the appropriateness of the concepts and analytical tools of NEO-CLASSICAL ECONOMIC THEORY to the study of developing economies. See also DEVELOPMENT ECONOMICS. For further reading: A. Szirmai, *Economic and Social Development* (1997). J.P.

economic efficiency. This concept is considered in three parts. Firstly, an economy is efficient in production, at a moment in time, if there is no means of using the available inputs to increase the production of one or more goods without reducing the production of one or more other goods. This is sometimes referred to as *X-efficiency*. Secondly, an economy is efficient in exchange if it is not possible to revise the distribution of a set amount of goods and services between people so as to leave one or more persons better off and no person worse off. Finally, there must be efficiency between exchange and production. This exists when, for all possible pairs of goods and services, consumers' willingness to substitute one good for the other is just equal to the economy's ability to switch production from this good or service to the other (see SUBSTITUTION).

Economic efficiency necessarily requires efficiency in investment in technical progress. As the results of such investment are by their very nature uncertain, it is difficult to analyse whether an economy at one moment in time is economically efficient. Uncertainty reduces the usefulness of the concept of economic efficiency. WELFARE ECONOMICS has mainly been concerned with the conditions necessary for economic efficiency. With certain assumptions, both PERFECT COMPETITION and STATE ECONOMIC PLANNING are economically efficient. In evaluating an economy, weight must be given to both its efficiency and distribution of income. The concept of economic efficiency is often applied to the analysis of MARKET FAILURE, e.g. MONOPOLIES, TRADE UNIONS and EXTERNALITIES, and is also used in the theory of COST BENEFIT ANALYSIS. J.P.

economic geography. The systematic field of GEOGRAPHY that is concerned with the ways in which people earn their living, and how the goods and services they produce are spatially expressed and organized. These productive activities are classified as primary (agriculture, mining and other extractive activities), secondary (manufacturing), tertiary (services), and quaternary (information-related), with the last now dominating the labour-force structures of the technologically most advanced countries. The ever greater globalization of the world economy is keenly studied by economic geographers, who today increasingly operate at the international level. For further reading: J. O. Wheeler *et al*, *Economic Geography* (1998). P.O.M.

economic growth. The rate of increase in a country's income (GNP or GDP) per person.

Economists sometimes adjust income for purchasing power for greater accuracy, or use alternative measures, such as the human development index (based on life expectancy, education and living standards), for economic welfare. However, growth is an accessible, though imperfect, indicator of economic progress.

Contributors to growth are knowledge, education, technological innovation, capital formation, social and political institutions (including freedom from arbitrary authority), and financial and trade policies. Rapid, sustained growth began in the late 18th and 19th centuries in the West, due largely to increased CAPITAL and technology and changing institutions associated with CAPITALISM, an economic system where factories and other capital are privately held by persons operating for profit and hiring capital-less workers.

Japan, a latecomer, used 'guided capitalism' for the world's fastest growth from 1867 to 1990. Russia used state planning and control of land and capital to grow rapidly from 1917 to 1971, but soon thereafter exhausted its major growth sources, increases in labour participation, education, and investment rates. Since 1960, Korea, Taiwan, Hong Kong and Singapore (and later Malaysia, Thailand, Indonesia and China) used the state and market for rapid growth up until 1995. However, in most of Africa and South Asia, growth stagnated during the last quarter of the 20th century.

Growth increases people's control over their environment and enhances choice, but also has costs, frequently materialism, rootlessness and social disruption. But given rising expectations, few societies choose stagnation. For further reading: E. W. Nafziger, *The Economics of Developing Countries* (1997). E.W.N.

economic history. The history of economies in the past. The history of agriculture, trade and industry was already flourishing, especially in Germany, in the 19th century, but economic history was recognized as a separate discipline in universities only in the 20th. 'Business history' split off from it in the USA in the 1920s. Since about 1950 economic historians have made greater use of quantitative methods and taken more interest in the MODELS and theories of economists. This *new economic history* (*econometric history* and *cliometrics* are other terms often used) differs from traditional economic history in METHODOLOGY. Instead of building up generalizations gradually as a result of accumulating a large number of facts and reflecting on specific historical cases, very much as any historian might, the exponents of the new method start by framing a hypothesis and collect data with a view to establishing its validity, very much as an applied economist would. Econometric historians also make considerable use of *counterfactual propositions* (see COUNTERFACTUAL; PROPOSITION, TYPES OF). The new methods have made it possible to supplement traditional microeconomic history (the history of specific industries and firms) with macroeconomic history (the measurement of gross national product (see GNP) and ECONOMIC GROWTH in the past). P.B.

economic imperialism, see under IMPERIALISM.

economic law. A proposition in ECONOMICS which is supposed to be of general validity (e.g. GRESHAM'S and SAY'S LAWS). The empirical testing of laws of economics is often less well founded than the testing of laws in the NATURAL SCIENCES (see ECONOMETRICS). For this reason, the laws of economics as propositions of general validity may be less secure. The term is often avoided by modern economists, who are more conscious, perhaps, of the differences between reality and their economic MODELS. R.ST.; J.P.

economic liberalism. The application to ECONOMICS of the doctrines of classical LIBERALISM. It is a preference for competitive markets (see MARKET ECONOMY) and for the use of the PRICE MECHANISM rather than more direct intervention in the economy, e.g. STATE ECONOMIC PLANNING. Economic liberalism is usually considered to differ from LAISSEZ FAIRE, as in the former it is accepted that there is a need for government intervention to deal with EXTERNALITIES, MONOPOLIES and to provide PUBLIC GOODS. Many, but not all, economic liberals favour redistribution of income, preferably in the form of taxes and cash transfer payments, rather than through provision by goods in kind or the regulation of wages and prices. Economic liberals are not necessarily committed to any particular form of property ownership; for example, CO-OPERATIVES are compatible with this economic doctrine. If government intervention is necessary, economic liberalism suggests that it should be implemented through general impersonal rules and not on a piecemeal basis, which allows politicians and officials to make decisions reflecting their own objectives and prejudices. S.BR.; J.P.

economic psychology. The interdisciplinary study of the interface – or sometimes the gap – between ECONOMICS and PSYCHOLOGY. Economic psychologists recognize that (a) the economy powerfully influences the feelings, thoughts and behaviour of individuals; (b) individuals' feelings, thoughts and behaviour are what make up economic life; and (c) there are many problems, both academic and practical, to which both economics and psychology, despite their very different approaches and explanatory styles, can contribute. Examples of such problems include the influence of consumers' attitudes on the behaviour of the economy, the way people take financial decisions involving risk, and the reasons why people save, fail to save, or get into debt. Many more people practise economic psychology than call themselves economic psychologists: very similar approaches are taken under names like behavioural economics, consumer psychology or socio-economics, and also within decision-making or occupational and organizational psychology. S.E.G.L.

economic regulation. The STATE may intervene in markets and industries. Intervention can take the form of legislation, administration, TAXATION and subsidization. There are three theories that attempt to explain the existence and forms of regulation.

(1) The *public interest theory* argues that regulation is an attempt to correct for MARKET FAILURES, such as MONOPOLY, EXTERNALITIES and lack of information. For example, the prices of a natural monopoly may be limited so as to restrict profits and increase output, safety measures may be enforced on airlines and doctors may be licensed to prevent charlatans from treating patients.

(2) This theory suggests that there is a market for regulation. Consumers and producers compete in a political and economic market for regulation. For example, the regulation of airline safety, routes and prices may be in the interest of the airlines, as BARRIERS TO ENTRY are imposed and COMPETITION is reduced. Regulation is regarded as serving the interests of those who are willing to offer the most for the regulation. In this theory, regulation can be purchased through offering political influence and help, and direct financial contributions. Regulation may be regarded as a PUBLIC GOOD, to which the consumer is expected to contribute. The benefit to the individual consumer of an increase in personal expenditure on securing favourable regulation is likely to be small. Thus, though the aggregate benefit to consumers of favourable regulation may be high, as individuals they may not be willing to contribute to the cost of obtaining the regulation. The costs of acquiring information about regulation are also likely to be high. As producers are a smaller group and individual producers stand to gain more from favourable regulation, producers will have more incentive to try to obtain favourable regulation.

(3) *Capture theory* has some similarities to the previous theory, in that it is suggested that producers capture regulatory agencies and control them in their own interests. Capture may occur through regulations being enforced by persons previously employed in the industry, or who hope to be, and holding the same perceptions as the industry. The latter two theories suggest that regulation is made or implemented in the interests of producers rather than the public interest. Thus, it may be in the PUBLIC INTEREST to remove regulations and allow increased competition to reduce costs and prices, and improve the quality of goods and services supplied. This view lies behind the market-orientated policies that have deregulated airlines in Australia and America, and bus and financial services in the UK. Self-regulation is where the industry regulates itself. The advantages of self-regulation are that use is made of the industry's knowledge, the often discretionary nature of the regulations, lower costs of implementation of regulation, and the fact that it often does not require the passing of legislation and recourse to the legal system. The disadvantages are that the regulations may be formed or implemented in favour of the industry rather than the

public interest. See PRIVATIZATION and NATIONALIZATION. J.P.

economic rent. The income of a FACTOR OF PRODUCTION (e.g. land, labour or CAPITAL) may be greater than the amount needed to induce the factor to offer its services. The difference between the former and the latter amounts is the economic rent. The large sums paid to film stars and the best professional footballers are mostly economic rents reflecting the shortage of supply of such persons. In the long run, economic rents provide an incentive for a greater supply of the factor to be provided. Thus, a shortage of land for building houses may lead to higher land prices and a switch of land from other uses. The economic rent rations the limited supply to those most willing to pay for the factor. J.P.

economic theory of imperialism, see under IMPERIALISM.

economic warfare. The disorganization of an enemy's economy so as to prevent him from carrying on war, especially by the denial to him of imports, interference with his exports, and destruction by bombing or sabotage of his industrial centres of production, storage and distribution. In its widest sense (and in official American usage), the term includes all measures against economic activities which directly or indirectly further a belligerent's war effort. In British usage, it covers only measures against an enemy. D.C.W.

economics. The study of methods of allocating scarce resources in production, the distribution of the resulting output, and the effects of this allocation and distribution. This definition differs from the widely quoted and accepted definition of English economist Lionel Robbins (1898–1984) that 'economics is concerned with that aspect of behaviour which arises from the scarcity of means to achieve a given end [and] economics is not concerned with ends as such'. This latter definition considers 'ends' to be the problem of other subjects and economics to be the study of how best to achieve given ends. The attempt to limit economics to value-free investigation (see VALUE-FREEDOM) represented a major move from its progenitor, POLITICAL ECONOMY, and, in its pure form, has few present-day adherents. *Positive economics* is concerned with verifiable propositions, e.g. the level of INVESTMENT is positively related to the interest rate (see MODEL). Normative economics is concerned with what should be done and necessarily involves the use of a VALUE-JUDGEMENT and often uses a positive model, e.g. UNEMPLOYMENT should be reduced by forcing the interest rate down to increase investment and employment. *Microeconomics* is the study of the decisions of individual economic agents, e.g. consumers and firms (see FIRM, THEORIES OF). It is often associated with the economics of prices and SUPPLY AND DEMAND, though it is much broader in scope, e.g. it includes the economics of uncertainty and large parts of MARXIST economics. *Macroeconomics* is the study of the aggregate effects of microeconomic decisions, e.g. NATIONAL INCOME, UNEMPLOYMENT, BALANCE OF PAYMENTS. As such, macroeconomic theory is based upon microeconomic theory.

Marxist economics is, in the words of Oskar Lange (1904–65), 'the social laws governing the production and distribution of the material means of satisfying human needs'. Marxist economics places more emphasis on historical, political and sociological analysis than micro- and macroeconomics. However, Marxist economics can use, and be analysed in terms of, conventional micro- and macroeconomics. Social laws are the product of historical evolution and of the conflict between CLASSES which is the motive force of historical change. The central element of Marxist economics is that labour is the only source of value (see LABOUR THEORY OF VALUE). For further reading: J. Craven, *Introduction to Economics* (1984). R.L.; J.P.

economics of science, see SCIENCE, ECONOMICS OF.

economies of scale. Circumstances that cause the proportionate increase in the total cost of supplying a good or service to be less than the proportionate increase in the amount produced. Economies of scale are usually interpreted as increasing RETURNS TO SCALE with the prices of FACTORS OF PRODUCTION held constant. They are divided into internal economies, which occur as the size of the firm increases, and external economies, which occur as the size of the industry or group of firms increases. Economies occur in the production process (e.g. a more efficient organization of production may be possible at higher levels of output), transport (e.g. it may be relatively cheaper to deliver goods in a geographical area the greater the volume of goods transported), MARKETING, RESEARCH AND DEVELOPMENT (e.g., in the case of the latter three, the associated fixed costs can be spread across a greater level of output). Economies can also be of a dynamic type, e.g. longer production runs and learning by doing. Economies can be real, i.e. they represent a saving in society's use of resources, or pecuniary, in that they are offset by money losses to other firms (e.g. discounts that are extracted by large buyers who threaten to take their business elsewhere), or a mixture of both. J.P.

ecosystem. The system formed by the interaction of all living organisms, plants, animals, bacteria, etc., with the physical and chemical factors of their ENVIRONMENT. The variety of meanings attached to the word by different ecologists (some of whom now doubt its usefulness as a precise term with a rigid definition) reflects the variety of boundaries drawn for 'the environment'. Thus foresters speak of a 'woodland ecosystem' meaning the whole tree-covered area, while an entomologist working in the same wood will restrict the term to a fallen log with its insect fauna and the fungi living on the dead material; such restricted uses have their practical value in helping scientists to define their problem. However, since an ecosystem is usually thought of as occurring within a self-contained and restricted area, and since complete isolation of most areas is impossible, it can be argued that the earth itself is the only real ecosystem. See also ECOLOGY. K.M.

ecosystem services. A term promoted by ecologists (see ECOLOGY) and CONSERVATION biologists to focus attention on some of the functions of natural environments (see ECOSYSTEM). An often-cited example is the role of tropical forests in absorbing carbon dioxide from the atmosphere and the release of oxygen, both through the process of PHOTOSYNTHESIS. Another is the role of wetlands in purifying water by absorbing nutrients and other chemicals.

More obvious examples of ecosystem services include the role of vegetation in protecting soil from erosion by rain and wind, the control by predators of prey populations, and of soil micro-organisms in breaking down and releasing dead organic matter, thus making it available for recycling through the ecosystem. For further reading: Y. Baskin, *The Work of Nature* (1997).

W.G.R.

écriture. Writing. A term thrown into prominence by Roland Barthes in his *Writing Degree Zero* (1953). With his play upon this central term, which makes the act of writing itself distinct both from the writer and from what is written, Barthes ushers in the STRUCTURALIST movement in literary criticism. *Écriture classique*, the convention of writing practised in France from the 17th to the 19th century, relied for its effectiveness upon the unquestionable truths of a social order which it mirrors. But from 1848 each writer has to create his own *écriture*, his own style within style, which enters into the inherited language and literature in order to set itself against these in new 'engaged' hostility to received opinion and literary custom. *Écriture* is thus not only a convention of writing, it is a refusal to go along with what there is, the 'natural', the obvious, the received. *Écriture* is put at the service of demystifying and demythologizing the BOURGEOIS conviction that whatever is, is natural. For further reading: J. Culler, *Structuralist Poetics* (1975). R.PO.

ECSC (European Coal and Steel Community). An organization originating in a proposal (the Schuman Plan, 5 May 1950) by Robert Schuman, then French Foreign Minister, for the creation of a FREE MARKET in coal and steel under a supranational authority. The scheme was seen by the French as the only remaining means of preventing a NATIONALIST revival of West German heavy industry after the establishment the previous year of the West German state. The UK was invited to join, but refused. Signed on 18 April 1951 by representatives of France, West Germany, Italy, the Netherlands, Belgium and Luxembourg, the Charter of the ECSC established a nine-member High Authority with powers to set prices, draw up plans, ensure free COMPETITION, prevent MONOPOLY, and look after the welfare of employees; a common assembly as a watchdog over the Authority; a Council of Ministers and a High Court; all but the Assembly being located in Luxembourg. The ECSC served as a model for the later EEC (see EUROPEAN UNION) into which it was incorporated. D.C.W.

ECT, see ELECTRO-CONVULSIVE THERAPY.

ectomorph, see under PERSONALITY TYPES.

ECU (European Currency Unit), see under INTERNATIONAL LIQUIDITY.

ecumenical movement. 'Ecumenical' (from Greek *oikoumenikos*, 'of the inhabited world') is still sometimes used to refer to the whole of mankind. But its usual usage is Christian, and refers to the Councils of the undivided Church which laid down orthodox CHRISTOLOGY and defined other DOGMAS; to the Ecumenical Patriarch in Constantinople (see ORTHODOXY, EASTERN); or to the modern movement for Christian reunion. This movement began with the World Missionary Conference at Edinburgh in 1910. The formation of the International Missionary Council was accompanied by other world conferences on problems of 'Life and Work' and of 'Faith and Order'. These three streams united in the World Council of Churches, constituted at Amsterdam in 1948. The Roman Catholic Church (see CATHOLICISM) is the only major Christian denomination which is not a member of the WCC, though it participates in many of the latter's activities, and warmer relations with other Christians form an important part of this Church's AGGIORNAMENTO. Discussion about the reunion of the Churches has been active in many countries, and some mergers have been achieved. However, progress in the Churches towards unity has been disappointingly slow, and towards the end of the 1960s a new mood began to grow among Christians, largely ignoring the Churches' problems and hesitations, and concentrating instead on a more informal and radical witness and service in the modern world. This mood restored to the word 'ecumenical' much of its original connection with humanity. For further reading: G. Wainwright, *The Ecumenical Movement* (1983). D.L.E.

edaphology, see under SOIL SCIENCE.

eddy currents. Term originally applied to the irregular flow of fluids past an obstacle or series of obstacles and, as such, generally associated with a swirling motion in liquids. Since the flow of electric current is often likened to fluid flow, the term became associated with electric currents flowing in large sheets or volumes of conductor (as opposed to thin wires), especially when those currents are produced by electromagnetic induction. For further reading: J. Lammeraner and M. Štafl, *Eddy Currents* (1966). E.R.L.

edge of chaos. Complex systems often exhibit behaviour that is chaotically unpredictable (see COMPLEX ADAPTIVE SYSTEMS). That is, the future development of the system is extremely sensitive to small changes in its starting state. They also frequently exhibit organized complexity. Impressive examples of organized complexity often arise when a system is in a state that separates chaotic behaviour from self-organizing behaviour (see SELF-ORGANIZED CRITICALITY). This boundary state is called the edge of chaos. At this state the chaotic unpredictability gives rise to many different variations in its behaviour as a result of small fluctuations and perturbations. These many variations are then organized by the self-organizing processes that arc present. For further reading: S. Kaufmann, *At Home in the Universe* (1995). J.D.B.

EDP (electronic data processing), see under COMPUTING.

educational linguistics. In LINGUISTICS, the application of linguistic theories, methods and descriptive findings to the study of mother-tongue teaching or learning in schools or other educational settings. The subject deals with both spoken and written language (including the development of literacy), and also the range of linguistic varieties (accents, dialects, etc.) available in the community. D.C.

educational psychology. A branch of

APPLIED PSYCHOLOGY concerned with several kinds of activity. The first is with studies of learning and associated forms of PROBLEM-SOLVING as these are revealed in the learning of bodies of knowledge. Closely connected are applications of DEVELOPMENTAL PSYCHOLOGY to the organization of learning and of curricula. More recently, educational psychology has also dealt with the interpersonal and social aspects of classrooms and other less formal learning situations, particularly with the manner in which these affect attitudes as well as the acquisition of knowledge; and moral education has become increasingly a matter of concern in an age of change in cultural NORMS.

A second large area of activity is in testing and EVALUATION, both of INTELLIGENCE and of special abilities such as mathematics, music, spatial capacities (i.e. ability to decipher representational pictures or diagrams of spatial arrays), etc. A principal contribution to this work (notably by Charles Spearman, L. L. Thurstone and Sir Charles Burt) has been the partitioning of intelligence into component abilities and investigation of the extent to which those component abilities are found by FACTOR ANALYSIS to be dependent upon general intelligence – as measured by the common CORRELATION of the components.

Educational psychology has also played an active part in the organizing of school curricula, both in analysing the special problems of learning certain subject-matters, and developing theories of how subjects are learned. An example is the work of J. S. Bruner indicating that central structural CONCEPTS within a field, once learned, aid considerably in mastery of detailed information when such material is shown to be derivable from general principles. Ideas about the structuring of the curriculum have recently been embodied in PROGRAMMED INSTRUCTION.

Finally, educational psychology concerns itself with problems of the SPECIAL EDUCATION of the culturally underprivileged, the mentally retarded (see MENTAL RETARDATION), and those with physical handicaps like deafness and blindness. For further reading: D. Berliner (ed.), *Handbook of Educational Psychology* (1996). J.S.B.

educational sub-normality (ESN), see under LEARNING DISABILITY.

educational tests, see under MENTAL TESTING.

EEG, see ELECTROENCEPHALOGRAPH.

effective cosmological constant, see under COSMOLOGICAL CONSTANT.

EFTA (European Free Trade Association). An association of countries whose main objectives are to bring about free trade between members and with the EUROPEAN UNION (EU). Members have chosen not to join the EEC (see EUROPEAN UNION) as it involves a certain loss of SOVEREIGNTY (see CUSTOMS UNION). Thus free trade agreements between EFTA and the EEC have allowed the creation of a larger free trade area than would have occurred if only membership of the EEC had been available. Austria, Britain, Denmark, Portugal, Sweden and Switzerland formed the association in 1959. For industrial products, free trade was established between members by 1966 and with the EEC by 1977. Britain (1973), Denmark (1973) and Portugal (1984) left EFTA to join the EEC. Finland (1961) has associate membership and Iceland (1970) has also joined. Members are small countries, vary in economic structure and are distributed across Europe. However, they have high average per capita incomes and are generally regarded as having benefited from the free trade area that EFTA helped create. For further reading: European Free Trade Association, *The European Free Trade Association* (1980). J.P.

egalitarianism. A belief in the high value of equality (see EQUALITY, PRINCIPLE OF) among human beings and the desirability of removing inequalities. Such a belief forms part of many religious, political and social movements. In the French Revolution, with its famous slogan of Liberty, Equality, and Fraternity, the second term of the revolutionary trinity took an extreme form in Babeuf's *Conspiracy of Equals* (1796), which bequeathed its legacy to a host of secret organizations in the early 19th century espousing the idea of the universal equality of incomes. 'Babouvism' provided the ground for the emergence of SOCIALIST and COMMUNIST ideas.

Marx (see MARXISM), however, stressed

the paramount importance of CLASS divisions as against individual inequalities and recognized that unequal individual capacities and work will be differentially remunerated in the first stage of building communism. Stalin (see STALINISM) seized this point in his attack on the egalitarian wage structure prevailing in the USSR until 1930 and replaced it with a system of unequal rewards to provide incentives for industrial development. In contrast, Mao Zedong (see MAOISM) favoured a more egalitarian economic policy.

The problems of the egalitarian distribution of goods in society have acquired a new perspective in the 20th century, because historical experience has shown that removal of one kind of inequality can be accompanied by the sharpening of other kinds. While income differences may diminish, differences in POWER within society may increase, since economic, social and political differences do not necessarily change together. Another awkward question is raised by 'equality of opportunity'. Egalitarianism has found it difficult to accept the idea of MERITOCRACY. It also has to face the possibility that 'unequal individual endowment' may be more resilient to social change, because of genetic factors (see GENETICS/GENOMICS), than the ENVIRONMENTALIST beliefs of earlier egalitarians allowed for (see NATURE VERSUS NURTURE). Nonetheless, egalitarianism remains one of the most powerful ideas in modern history. For further reading: R. H. Tawney, *Equality* (1952). L.L.

ego. A psychoanalytic term referring to that part of the mental apparatus in which CONSCIOUSNESS and the system of PERCEPTION resides; but it is also home to UNCONSCIOUS defence mechanisms and hence is more extensive than just what is available to the subject's awareness (see SUBJECTIVITY). The theory of the ego taken up in most contemporary PSYCHOANALYSIS is based on Freud's later work, outlined in *The Ego and the Id* (1927). Here the ego is seen as a precipitate of the ID, formed in two main ways. First, the exigencies of the real world are its province, and the ego's task is to regulate the pleasure-seeking demands of the id in accordance with the REALITY PRINCIPLE. Secondly, the ego is formed by processes of internalization which are modelled on the somatic events with which the infant is familiar. As the growing child has to give up desired sexual objects, the ego takes them on, internalizing them and in the process altering itself. The character of the ego is thus formed along the lines of internalized objects. A substantial reworking of the notion of the ego has come from LACANIAN psychoanalysis. This emphasizes the construction of the ego as a precipitate of IDENTIFICATIONS and hence of something taken in from the 'outside' (see MIRROR PHASE). Since an identification is a form of misunderstanding of who one is, problems of misrecognition and illusion appear. The ego is thus characterized as a system conveying an IMAGINARY sense of integrity and autonomy to the subject. S.J.F.

ego-ideal. A key concept in Lacan's version of PSYCHOANALYSIS. The ideal-functions of the EGO are based on two types of identification: SYMBOLIC and IMAGINARY. The ego-ideal, on the one hand, is based on an attempt to subordinate the psyche to the authority perceived to be operative in the Oedipal triangle, and is constructed through symbolic identification. On the other hand, the IDEAL EGO is an attempt to regain the omnipotence threatened by these Oedipal dynamics, and is based on imaginary identification. The relation of these two forms of identification was worked on by Jacques Lacan in the 1960s, extending his earlier work on the MIRROR PHASE, and developing his theory of the dialectics of DESIRE. The ego-ideal represents an internalized plan of the law; but thc conscience thus generated, being based on identification, represents a misunderstanding of the law. Lacan's variables seek to establish that desire, and the conflict that it enters into, establishes the real structure of the law, which is beyond the scope of the functions of the ego. The ego-ideal works in conjunction with the SUPEREGO, which uses the ego-ideal as a template in the imposition of its morality. For further reading: J. Lacan, *Écrits* (1977). B.BU.

ego-psychology. A school within PSYCHOANALYSIS that originally developed its theses in the 1930s as an attempt to formulate how the problems and theories of psychoanalysis could be developed as a science. Where Freud, and even analysts in some respects fairly close to the ego-psychologists, such as Nunberg, had taken the EGO (see EGO-IDEAL; IDEAL EGO) to be structured by psychical conflict, the leaders of this school (following Heinz Hartmann) postulated the existence of a conflict-free sphere of the ego, a zone whose autonomy was seen as extending to a range of functions including PERCEPTION, thinking and the operations of language. In taking the functioning of the ego as the base where they hoped to establish sufficient cognitive autonomy to be able to construct laws of the mind, their programme flew in the face of Freud's constantly repeated claim that the ego is the locus of illusion and misrecognition. The theories of science, and the associated theories of reality assumed by the ego-psychologists, have been criticized by Jacques Lacan. In terms of analytical practice, ego-psychology aims to orientate the technique of psychoanalysis around the rationality available to the analyst's autonomous ego. By the end of the 1950s this school had come to dominate the main body of psychoanalysis in the US. For further reading: H. Hartmann, *Ego Psychology and the Problem of Adaptation* (1958). B.BU.

Egoist, The. Title from 1914 until its demise in 1919 of a London fortnightly review, the exemplary 'little magazine' of this crucial period and central organ for Anglo-American MODERNISM. Originally the feminist *New Freewoman*, sponsored by Harriet Shaw Weaver, the paper changed title and content after Ezra Pound became literary editor. It included major work, creative and critical, by Pound himself, his editorial successors Richard Aldington, H.D. (Hilda Doolittle) and T. S. Eliot, and such writers as Rémy de Gourmont, James Joyce (including extracts from *Ulysses*), Ford Madox Ford and F. S. Flint. In particular it introduced IMAGISM in England and was the main English outlet for new American poets, including Amy Lowell, Marianne Moore, William Carlos Williams and Robert Frost. M.S.BR.

eidetic image. A vividly clear, detailed mental image of what has previously been seen. It is lifelike, i.e. seen as located outside rather than in the head, and often contains a surprising amount of accurate detail. I.M.L.H.

eidetic reduction. In Edmund Husserl's PHENOMENOLOGY, this is the second of six 'reductions' that are carried out in an effort to purify the APPERCEPTION of a mental phenomenon. Firstly, the entire world of fact, history and nature is eliminated by the famous phenomenological 'bracket' (*epoche*). No reference is to be had to any empirical science. Then, after the 'naturalistic thesis' has been bracketed out, the 'reductions' begin. The first is the 'psychological reduction' which eliminates the idiosyncrasies of the perceiver or analyst himself. Secondly there is the 'eidetic reduction', which sets up the phenomenon as a perceived essence. After the fifth or sixth 'reduction' there is nothing left but the 'pure transcendental EGO', whose apperceptions, just because they have been refined through so many sieves of SUBJECTIVITY, are now purely objective. The 'reductions' are not only very difficult to understand, they also involve a high degree of paradox, which critics of all traditions have not been slow to point out. Nevertheless, it is clear that Husserl was aiming at a breakthrough of some sort with his 'reductions', a freeing of philosophy both from EMPIRICISM and from scientific POSITIVISM. By 'bracketing' the entire world of historical and empirical reality, Husserl believed that acts of INTENTIONALITY could be directed solely and exclusively towards the 'essence' of the bracketed phenomenon in question. He sought for direct access to 'essential' content, an apperception of the essence of a phenomenon which is necessary, complete, objective and unquestionably veridical. Following the work of Hans-Georg Gadamer, Paul Ricoeur has recently queried the usefulness of the initial 'bracketing' out of the real world, and the reality of the ensuing 'reductions', on the grounds that all understanding is necessarily historical, and that HERMENEUTICS has 'ruined' the particularly idealistic interpretation of phenomenology which Husserl gives (see IDEALISM), though it may well have left other, later, kinds intact. For further reading: Q. Lauer, *Phenomenology: Its Genesis and Prospect* (1965). R.PO.

eigenfunction, see under QUANTUM MECHANICS.

Einstellung ('attitude', 'set'). German term

for a habitual procedure for dealing with repeatedly encountered problems of similar type. See also PROBLEM-SOLVING. I.M.L.H.

ekistics. Term coined by the Greek town planner C. A. Doxiadis (see TOWN PLANNING) for the study of human SETTLEMENTS and their problems, by bringing together in an interdisciplinary and international approach experts from such subjects as ECONOMICS, GEOGRAPHY, SOCIOLOGY. For further reading: C. A. Doxiadis, *Ekistics* (1968). A.L.C.B.

El Niño. A perturbation in the ocean circulation system resulting in the development of warm surface waters in the eastern Pacific off the western coast of South America where up-welling of nutrient-rich cold water is the usual pattern. A shift in the pattern of Pacific trade winds, of unknown cause, appears to trigger the perturbation. El Niño was named by fishermen for the Christ child because it appeared, every few years, off the coast of Peru at about Christmas time, disrupting the anchovy fishery. El Niño may produce widespread changes in ocean water circulation, the distribution of fish species, and weather. W.G.R.

El Salvador. The smallest country on the American continental mainland, El Salvador is racially and culturally homogeneous but has a very high population density (5.5 million in 8,259 square miles) which creates enormous pressure on land resources in an economy still largely dependent on primary export crops (coffee, cotton and sugar). A strongly oligarchical society, El Salvador has mostly been ruled by the military, but towards the end of the 1970s the power of this alliance was challenged by the emergence of a GUERRILLA movement, the Farabundo Marti National Liberation Front (FMLN), named after a 1932 COMMUNIST martyr, and its political organization, the Democratic Revolutionary Front (FDR). This plunged the country into civil war, with some parts of the country – mostly in the north – declared 'liberated zones' which were effectively beyond the control of government forces. By 1983 a military stalemate had emerged between the US-aided, -trained and -equipped Salvadoran army and the FMLN, which has evolved into a highly effective rural guerrilla army with substantial support among the peasantry. The US has taken a strong interest in Salvadoran affairs, particularly since the 1979 victory of the Nicaraguan revolution (see NICARAGUA). However, its attempts to promote a centrist solution through the Christian Democrat Party have proved problematic in an atmosphere of extreme polarization between LEFT and RIGHT. Following 1984 presidential and 1985 congressional elections, democracy has been established in El Salvador, and in 1992 the war finally ended. For further reading: M. Lungo, *El Salvador in the Eighties* (1996). N.M.

***élan vital*,** see under VITALISM.

elastic rebound theory. This theory explaining the origin of earthquakes was developed by H. F. Reid after he had studied the effects of the disastrous San Francisco earthquake of 1906. In essence Reid's theory postulates as the immediate cause of earthquakes the sudden movement of rocks of the crust and mantle (see LITHOSPHERE) either side of a pre-existing fracture or fault. This rapid phase is, however, only the culmination of a slow and increasing elastic distortion of the rocks over tens of years. The situation is analogous to pushing one rubber eraser over another. Both will be distorted elastically but only while the frictional resistance of their contacting surfaces is not exceeded. The rubbers 'grip' each other. When the frictional resistance is exceeded each rubber will rebound to its original shape but it will be displaced. Similarly the rocks either side of the potential fault suffer increasing distortion until the frictional resistance of the fault is exceeded. Suddenly, over a period of a few seconds, the fault slips, allowing the distorted rocks to rebound to their original shape. Measured displacements along earthquake faults at the surface range from a few centimetres to several metres. J.L.M.L.

elasticity. In ECONOMICS, a measure of the response of a VARIABLE, e.g. DEMAND or supply (see SUPPLY AND DEMAND), to a change in a determining variable, e.g. price. The measure is the ratio of the relative change in the variable to the relative change in the determining variable. A low elasticity represents a situation in which a moderate relative change in the determining variable gives only a small relative change in the other variable. Elasticities are known to vary between different time periods, prices, incomes, etc. Elasticities depend on the time period over which the changes are considered. Thus, the price elasticity of demand for oil is low in the short run, as people, firms, etc. will not immediately replace oil-burning equipment if the price of oil increases, but they may reduce their consumption slightly. In the long run, the equipment will be replaced and the associated change in the demand for oil will be greater. Though a simple concept, econometric studies (see ECONOMETRICS) of the same elasticity in similar economic circumstances often give quite different estimates. J.P.

electoral behaviour. POLITICAL SCIENCE attempts to construct comprehensive accounts of the determinants of voters' choice in democratic states. Sophisticated models and techniques struggle to encompass diversity and inconsistency of motives, particularly as in many nations, including the USA and the UK, electoral decisions seem decreasingly anchored by strong, continuous factors such as CLASS-based allegiance or firm identification with a political party. The latter often still provides some basis for many voters' choice. It may variously express a sentimental or unreflective attachment, conscious self-interest, or an affiliation formed within the family. However, in recent generations it has become increasingly likely that such bases of allegiance may be displaced by any, or a combination of, several sources of decision. These include issue voting, by which choice is shaped by the congruence of a voter's and a candidate or party's views on a single issue (e.g. ABORTION law in the contemporary USA); retrospective voting, i.e. judging the performance to date of an incumbent candidate or party; prospective assessments of a party or candidate's likely performance in office. Voting choices may also reflect general levels of satisfaction or displeasure at circumstances only partly within a government's control, such as the overall or local state of the economy. It should also be noted that in some countries high levels of abstention also require analysis. In the contemporary USA only about half of the eligible electorate votes in presidential elections. Explanations include restrictive registration laws, the off-putting length of modern campaigns, and high general levels of public cynicism: but most notably, turnout is lowest among the poor and racial minorities, who may feel unlikely to benefit from the election of either major-party candidate, in a system noted less for its ideological breadth than for the influence of strong economic interests. S.R.

Electra complex. In psychoanalytic theory (see PSYCHOANALYSIS), a normal emotional crisis in females resulting, at an early stage of PSYCHOSEXUAL DEVELOPMENT, from sexual impulses towards the father and jealousy of the mother. It is the female counterpart of the OEDIPUS COMPLEX. W.Z.

electrochemistry. The oldest branch of PHYSICAL CHEMISTRY, electrochemistry is the study of solutions of electrolytes (see ELECTROLYSIS) and of the processes occurring at electrodes. It involves investigation of the structure of electrolytes, which are usually (but not necessarily) aqueous, the measurement and formulation of theories of ionic transport, and the kinetics of chemical reactions between IONS. Electrode processes relate to the measurement of THERMODYNAMIC and kinetic properties of reactions taking place at electrodes, to POLAROGRAPHY, and to ionic EQUILIBRIA involving membranes. For further reading: D. Sawyer, *Electrochemistry for Chemists* (1995). B.F.

electro-convulsive therapy (ECT). A technique in PSYCHOSURGERY through which artificial convulsions are induced by means of electric shock, to treat particular mental disorders such as DEPRESSION. At least from the 18th century onwards, shock therapy was used on a purely empirical basis for the relief of melancholy and similar disorders. Its modern application stems largely from the experiments in Rome in the 1930s of Ugo Cerletti, who proceeded from dogs to men, refined his techniques (in terms of the precise quantity of current flowing) and claimed success in relieving epileptics (see EPILEPSY) and gross schizophrenics (see SCHIZOPHRENIA) from 1938 onwards. ECT came to be widely used, though to this day it remains unclear as to precisely how it produces its effects, or indeed as to whether it is truly effective. Most believe that there are temporary gains in excitation but little long-term benefit. Many patients complain of short-term memory loss as an unpleasant side-effect of ECT. For further reading: W. L. Jones, *Ministering to Minds Diseased* (1983). R.P.

electrodynamics. The common ground between MECHANICS and ELECTROMAGNETISM which deals with the motion of charged PARTICLES in an ELECTROMAGNETIC FIELD. Typical electrodynamic effects are VAN ALLEN BELTS and focusing in an ELECTRON MICROSCOPE. For *quantum electrodynamics* see FIELD THEORY; OPTICS. M.V.B.

electroencephalograph (EEG). In NEUROPSYCHOLOGY, (1) an instrument used for recording changes of electric potentials originating in the brain, by means of electrodes applied to the scalp or implanted within the tissues of the brain; (2) the print-out of these electric currents, i.e. records of brain-waves. W.Z.

electroencephalography. The technique of recording and interpreting the electrical activity of the brain on a series of channels (8 or 16 in each hemisphere via electrodes glued to the skin of the scalp) is useful in diagnosing the presence of EPILEPSY. It has now been superseded by modern imaging techniques which more accurately demonstrate the brain's structure (computed tomography and nuclear magnetic resonance: see RADIOLOGY) and function (positron emission tomography). New COMPUTER-assisted electroencephalographic techniques allow more accurate localization of abnormalities. The combination of electroencephalographic recording with visual, auditory and cutaneous stimulation (*evoked potential recordings*) is more useful than simple electroencephalographic recordings. Intraoperative electroencephalographic and evoked potential recordings give early warning of impending damage to the central nervous system structures of patients undergoing operations while under general anaesthesia. A.D.M.

electrolysis. A chemical reaction occurring as the result of the passage of an electric current. Commercially important electrolytic processes include the extraction of metals from their ores, particularly aluminium, and the production of hydrogen and chlorine from brine. B.F.

electromagnetic field. The FIELD whose sources are charges, currents and magnets. Combinations of electric and magnetic fields whose strengths vary with time constitute RADIATION; they may travel great distances from their sources. The existence of an electromagnetic field in a region is indicated by forces exerted on test charges, currents and magnets. See also ELECTROMAGNETISM; ELECTROSTATICS; MAGNETISM. M.V.B.

electromagnetism (or **electromagnetic theory**). One of the main branches of PHYSICS, linking the phenomena of ELECTROSTATICS, electric currents, MAGNETISM and OPTICS into a single conceptual framework. The final form of the theory was devised by Maxwell and is one of the triumphs of 19th-century science. One of Maxwell's earliest predictions was the existence of radio waves, and his equations are fundamental throughout modern TELECOMMUNICATIONS. See also RADAR; RADIATION. M.V.B.

electron. The first ELEMENTARY PARTICLE to be discovered (in the late 19th century). The electron is negatively charged, stable, and about 2,000 times lighter than the hydrogen ATOM. Its importance for science as a whole stems largely from its occurrence as a relatively mobile constituent of atoms; thus it participates in the emission of light (see ATOMIC PHYSICS) and in electric conduction (see SOLID-STATE PHYSICS). M.V.B.

electron diffraction. The DIFFRACTION of a beam of ELECTRONS by matter in the form of a crystal LATTICE. The successful observation of electron diffraction led to the general acceptance of the WAVE-PARTICLE DUALITY. See also CRYSTALLOGRAPHY. M.V.B.

electron gun. An arrangement for producing a beam of ELECTRONS which may be focused and deflected at will, for use in, e.g., cathode ray tubes. See also THERMIONICS. M.V.B.

electron microscope. An instrument invented in 1931 for studying small material structures, such as crystals, micro-organisms and tissues. It is analogous to an ordinary optical microscope with the specimen illuminated by an ELECTRON beam (accelerated by a high voltage) instead of a light beam, and focused by combined electric and magnetic FIELDS instead of glass lenses. The image is displayed on a fluorescent screen (see FLUORESCENCE) instead of being viewed directly. Because of DIFFRACTION, it is impossible in any microscope to resolve objects smaller than the wavelength of the RADIATION used; the very short DE BROGLIE WAVELENGTH of high-voltage electrons (see QUANTUM MECHANICS) has enabled single ATOMS to be discerned – more than a thousand times smaller than can be resolved optically. BIOLOGY has been revolutionized by *electron microscopy*: it has opened up the ultrastructural world of CYTOLOGY and has revealed the anatomical structure of infective PARTICLES such as viruses (see VIROLOGY). M.V.B.; P.M.

electron shell. ELECTRONS in ATOMS can be assigned to different ORBITALS so that, according to the EXCLUSION PRINCIPLE, each has a unique set of QUANTUM NUMBERS. Electrons with the same principal quantum number comprise members of a particular shell; the K shell is closest to the NUCLEUS and has two electrons, the next shell (L) has eight electrons, and so on. Each atom has a characteristic shell structure, but the ENERGIES of electrons in the higher shells overlap and in these cases only electrons in the same sub-shell – i.e. with identical principal and azimuthal quantum numbers – have similar energies. The CHEMISTRY of the ELEMENTS is strongly influenced by the nature and number of electrons in the outer sub-shells. B.F.

electronegativity. A measure of the ability of an ATOM to attract an ELECTRON. There have been several attempts to produce a scale of electronegativity, but the concept cannot be put in a uniquely quantitative way. Pauling devised a method based on bond energies (see BOND, CHEMICAL; ENERGY) which makes fluorine the most electronegative element, followed by oxygen, nitrogen and chlorine. B.F.

electronic banking. The use of the new communications technologies – telephony, information systems and the INTERNET – to conduct financial transactions. This is among the fast-growing areas of personal and commercial banking and allows the consumer or corporation to conduct their business directly through telephone and computer access, rather than the traditional bank teller. Financial firms like Fidelity in the US and Direct Line in Britain have pioneered greater use of electronic banking. However, serious concerns have been raised about the security of electronic banking, particularly when conducted through the Internet. A.BR.

electronic commerce. Business conducted over computer networks (see INTERNET). Electronic commerce includes business/customer interactions such as the sale of products or services (including information services and software), banking on-line (see ON-LINE SERVICE), telecommuting, virtual enterprises, and the negotiation and signing of contracts on-line. Telecommuting means working away from an employer's office, usually at home, using computers and information networks. Virtual enterprises, also called virtual corporations, are short-term arrangements between businesses or individuals, separated geographically, who join together for specific business projects. Virtual enterprises are similar in purpose to joint ventures of large corporations, but are smaller, more flexible, have less administrative overhead, communicate electronically, and focus on information services. Electronic commerce makes conducting business anywhere in the world almost as easy as conducting business in the same town. As a result, the marketplace for products, services and LABOUR becomes global, and the choice of suppliers expands dramatically. On the other hand, the increased base of customers means that businesses are responding to an increased number of inquiries, and automated (see AUTOMATION) systems replace personal service. Strong encryption is essential for electronic commerce. It protects the privacy of, for example, business negotiations and consumer purchases. It prevents fraud by providing a secure way of transmitting payments, whether by credit card numbers or digital cash. Digital cash and the encryption of transactions present challenges for governments trying to maintain two long-time activities: control of the money supply and collection of taxes. Electronic commerce has the potential to reduce the power of national governments and the significance of national borders. S.BA.

electronic democracy. A nebulous concept which tries to encapsulate the political effects of trends in communications technology. Modern politics has often been thought to suffer – particularly in the USA – from the harmful effects of dominant technologies; especially from television's tendency to elevate image and personality over issues and substance. The use of sophisticated opinion polling and political advertising is thought to assist the manipulation of attitudes. Enthusiasts for electronic democracy point instead to the growing possibilities of mass participation via telephone, fax, e-mail and the INTERNET. The latter excites particular optimism as a cheap, potentially universal means of building local, national and transnational political networks and distributing information regardless of government or corporate wishes. The concept's problems lie partly in the sheer novelty of the most relevant part of the Internet, the WORLD WIDE WEB, which makes prediction of its future cost, access and regulation difficult. But the general notion of electronic decision-making, rather than communicating or organizing, also tends to beg questions central to democratic thought, about the relative merits of government by mass sentiment or by representation. S.R.

electronic music. This term can be applied to any music which uses electronic musical instruments. It is, however, more normally used to describe music in which sound sources are manipulated or new sounds are created electronically. Early experiments were made with unusual ways of playing records (speed changing, playing backwards, altering the record grooves, etc.). There was no simple way of recording these experiments until the general availability of the tape recorder after World War II. As well as giving a means of recording sound experiments, the tape recorder provided a whole new series of ways to treat sound (editing, multilayering, etc.). Among the first composers to make substantial use of the tape recorder were those involved with *musique concrète*, who manipulated naturally occurring sounds. Initially this was seen as distinct from the more purist form of electronic music which eschewed natural sounds and constructed its own new sounds from simple electronic test equipment such as sine wave generators, white noise generators, filters, amplifiers, etc. In practice, however, the distinction was quickly lost, and most early electronic music combined the advantages of both methods (the flexibility of pure electronic sound and the diversity of natural sound). Studios were set up in Cologne, Princeton, Milan and elsewhere in the 1950s to produce electronic music, which at this time required months of painstaking work to construct. Experiments were carried out combining live performance (see MUSIC NOTATION) with taped electronic music (e.g. Stockhausen's 'Kontakte'), and also treating live instrumental or vocal performances by amplifying, filtering, ring modulating them, etc. (see also RING MODULATOR; SPATIAL MUSIC).

In the 1960s a new era of electronic music was brought in by the widespread introduction of the synthesizer which was capable of manipulating sound in REAL TIME. Other important developments included computer music and, more recently, sound sampling. The practice of electronic music is now firmly established as an essential branch of musical development, and nearly all universities and colleges have facilities for its study. For further reading: T. B. Holmes, *Electronic and Experimental Music* (1985). B.CO.

electrophoresis. The movement of a charged colloidal PARTICLE under the influence of an electrical FIELD. The effect is similar to the migration of IONS in solution. Because different colloids do not have the same velocity, electrophoresis is widely used in clinical medicine to separate colloids, either as an aid in preparation of a mixture, or prior to chemical analysis. B.F.

electrostatics. The branch of ELECTROMAGNETISM dealing with bodies with an excess of (positive or negative) electric charge. The operation of condensers in alternating-current circuits, and the frictional charging of clouds and aeroplanes, are electrostatic effects. M.V.B.

element. A substance which cannot be broken down into simpler constituents by chemical means, because all its ATOMS have the same ATOMIC NUMBER. The naturally occurring elements range from hydrogen (No. 1) to uranium (No. 92), and about a dozen TRANSURANIC ELEMENTS have been produced artificially. M.V.B.

elementarism. The SCHOOL OF PSYCHOLOGY which holds that experience or behaviour is to be studied by analysing it into its component elements and then discovering how these elements associate together to produce the complex experience or behaviour. For the opposite approach see ORGANISMIC PSYCHOLOGY. I.M.L.H.

elementary particles. The smallest constituents of matter. At present the most elementary constituents of matter are believed to be QUARKS and LEPTONS (the ELECTRON, MUON, tauon and their associated NEUTRINOS and anti-particles; see ANTI-MATTER), the PHOTONS, GLUONS, the W and Z bosons, the GRAVITON and, it is predicted by GRAND UNIFIED THEORIES, a number of very heavy X and Y bosons. These particles are believed to have zero spatial extent and behave as points in scattering experiments. This belief has some experimental support. The electron is known to be at least smaller than 10^{-15} centimetres in diameter.

Protons and NEUTRONS, MESONS and other HADRONS are not truly elementary particles. They are known to possess internal constituents (quarks). These constituents reveal themselves in scattering experiments. There exist theories which endow quarks and leptons with internal constituents called prequarks, preons or rishons, but there exists no experimental evidence for the existence of these more elementary constituents of quarks particles as yet.

Elementary particles possess a variety of properties: MASS, electric charge, lifetimes, SPIN, QUANTUM NUMBERS. These individual properties cannot yet be explained by theories of elementary particles and must be determined by observation. Particles with finite lifetimes are called unstable, the others are denoted stable.

There exist theories which accurately describe the behaviour of different classes of elementary particles (see QUANTUM CHROMODYNAMICS and quantum electrodynamics; see FIELD THEORY). Until recently these theories governed the behaviour of disjoint classes of elementary particles, but progress has been made in merging them together within the framework of an all-embracing theory which gives a unified description of all the different forces and elementary particles of nature. These are called 'grand unified' theories.

Until very recently mathematical theories of elementary particles were invariably quantum field theories, but current interest has moved towards the study of SUPERSTRING theories in which the basic elements are linear strings rather than points. Different elementary particles are envisaged to be the different vibrational excitations of a string of energy.

All elementary particles are believed to possess anti-particles of identical mass and lifetime, but opposite values of all additive quantum numbers like electric charge. In some cases the particle and the anti-particle are identical because the relevant additive quantum numbers are zero (for example, the photon and the anti-photon are identical).

Many physicists believe that there exist a finite number of truly elementary particles from which all the other SUBATOMIC PARTICLES are built up. This is called the *composite particle approach*. Another recurrent idea is that there exists an infinite number of particles of increasing mass and every particle is composed of every other particle. These theories are called *bootstrap* theories, and predict that there exists a maximum temperature in nature. This maximum temperature is sometimes called the *Hagedorn temperature*. They are not currently consistent with experimental evidence unless that maximum temperature is far higher than any yet attained in accelerator experiments.

All successful theories of elementary particles are gauge theories, or gauge invariants. These theories are built upon particular mathematical symmetries which predict which particles do and do not exist and which other particles they will interact with. *Group theory* is used to impose these mathematical symmetries upon theories of elementary particles. Every symmetry of the theory corresponds to a CONSERVATION LAW of nature.

The study of elementary particles is the most extensive area of theoretical PHYSICS and the most expensive area of experimental science. It is carried out using PARTICLE

COLLIDERS and ACCELERATORS which collide subatomic particles together at high speed and monitor the debris of the collisions using sensitive particle tracking devices and computers to identify the constituents revealed in the collision. The most successful accelerators are those at CERN in Geneva, administered by a collective of European nations, and Fermi-Lab in Chicago respectively. The experimental teams involved in the search for a new elementary particle using one of these devices now number many hundreds of individuals. For further reading: S. Weinberg, *The Discovery of Subatomic Particles* (1984). J.D.B.

élite. Collective noun for those who occupy a position (or positions) of superiority within a society or group by virtue of qualities (actual, claimed or presumed) of excellence or distinction. The term's history owes much to the use made of it by V. Pareto (see below) and the observations made by him with regard to (1) the élite as distinguished from the non-élite groups within a social order and (2) the divisions within the élite as between a governing élite and a non-governing élite. Pareto's work and that of others (such as G. Mosca and R. Michels) has generated much debate, e.g. concerning the functions and social supports of *political élites*, the types of such élites found in different societies, their cohesiveness, and their relation to *ruling classes*. Pareto himself sought to establish the psychological basis of élite status, authority and continuity. Within his special conceptual framework and his theory of history as 'the graveyard of aristocracies' he took shifts in that basis as explaining the *circulation of élites* – a cyclical process of élite replacement over a period of time. See also POWER Élite. For further reading: V. Pareto, ed. S. E. Finer, tr. D. Mirfin, *Sociological Writings* (1966). S.J.G.

e-mail. Short for electronic mail; any system for sending messages over a computer network. Almost every office network and ON-LINE SERVICE offers e-mail. It is the INTERNET's most popular service. By the end of the 20th century virtually any two computers with access to a phone line could send messages to one another. Most e-mail software allows users to send and receive pictures and program files as well as plain text. Besides changing the basis of office communications, e-mail has made international communication quick and inexpensive. Because the price of sending e-mail does not vary by distance, it has become, for many, the preferred way of sending documents across borders. Junk e-mail, called 'spamming', differs from the more traditional mass mailings in that it costs no more to send 20,000 copies than it does to send 20. The expense of using the mails ('snailmail') encourages advertisers to pare their lists to the most likely prospects, but that incentive largely disappears with e-mail. Thus, people who would never receive solicitations for, say, PORNOGRAPHY in their postbox may receive plenty of such advertising on-line. Of course, it also costs almost nothing to forward e-mail and many people have signed up to be on mailing lists where everything sent to the service is forwarded to them. This forwarding system creates discussion groups in which members exchange remarks about whatever interests them. Although this practice can create communities of like-minded people around the globe, it can also lead to intense insults known as FLAMING. One change that may eventually matter to historians is the return of written communication to daily life. Biographers often complain that the telephone did away with letter-writing and, hence, documentary evidence of what people said and thought. The rise of e-mail, however, means that people are again setting down their thoughts in readable form and we can recover lost voices of the past. E.B.B.

embodiment. A concept fundamental to contemporary PHENOMENOLOGY. That PERCEPTION and understanding of the world are partly a function of the fact that CONSCIOUSNESS is not 'pure', but exists within a membrane of flesh and blood, has led to a situation in which many of the problems seen as otiose by Descartes have been reintroduced as vital to the understanding of how human beings do in fact perceive or *constitute* their world. In his early work, Edmund Husserl touched on the problem of embodiment in his effort to distinguish *marks* from signs in human communication, but in his revulsion towards all forms of PSYCHOLOGISM he did not allow himself to take up the human body itself into the problem of perception. In fact, he tried more and more strenuously to exclude all human or 'relativistic' factors from his philosophy. However, by the time of *Ideas 2* and *Cartesian Mediations* (1931), Husserl came to see that human embodiment might well be important in the matter of interpreting both one's own perceptions and the perceptions of the OTHER. It was only in the work of the French existentializing phenomenologists, however (e.g. Sartre and Merleau-Ponty), that the fact that the body actually 'lives' a world, and thus projects 'its' values over a world by INTENTIONALITY, was seriously taken into account. Sartre (1943) gave many famous descriptions of how embodiment in its various kinds of BAD FAITH projects its meanings over the world of the Other. Merleau-Ponty's 1945 essay, *The Phenomenology of Perception*, examines embodiment as the fundamental problem in philosophy, the manner in which the world appears to the embodied consciousness and the way in which the world is changed by the projections of embodied consciousness. In 1960, R. D. Laing's *The Divided Self* used the clue of embodiment to take account, as conventional PSYCHIATRY does not, of the subjective or lived quality of the patient's experience. Embodiment, then, represents the subject's own view of his or her body as it has to be lived with subjectively. It represents the exact opposite of one's body as perceived by others in the objective outer world. Sometimes the inner perception of embodiment can be at variance with public perception in a significant and possibly painful way: ANOREXIA NERVOSA is a striking example of this variance, as are many forms of what is lightly called SCHIZOPHRENIA, when the patient's view of his own embodiment is systematically left out of account. In *The Leaves of Spring* (1970) Aaron Esterson showed how the facts of embodiment can render socially intelligible the behaviour of a whole family, and in particular the apparently 'incomprehensible' activities of one member of it. The phenomenological accent on the importance of embodiment as a clue in understanding has enriched EXISTENTIAL PSYCHIATRY in the work of Peter Lomas and David Smail.

Literary theory has also profited from the insight, allowing a new recognition of the importance of a writer's embodiment in the textual DISPLACEMENTS of his or her own literary constructions. The work of Roger Poole, Stephen Trombley and Mark Hussey on Virginia Woolf has shown that no text is innocent of its embodied origins. The fact that the subject's own view of his or her embodiment is just as 'true' for him or for her as the public or outer perception of the body has led to a new questioning of the received understanding of 'objectivity' itself. For further reading: M. Merleau-Ponty, *Phenomenology of Perception* (1962). R.PO.

embourgeoisement. An explanation, popular with MARXISTS since first invented by Friedrich Engels, of the failure of the Western WORKING CLASS to support radical political parties and movements, specifically those committed to full-blooded SOCIALISM. A newfound affluence, it is said, has led workers to adopt middle-class (BOURGEOIS) attitudes and values, so cutting their traditional attachment to working-class institutions and causing a significant minority to transfer their allegiance to political parties of the CENTRE and RIGHT (see also INCORPORATION). For further reading: J. H. Goldthorpe *et al*, *The Affluent Worker in the Class Structure* (1969). K.K.

embryology. The branch of ZOOLOGY that deals with the history and theory of development – in particular the development that begins with a ZYGOTE. (1) In chordate animals development begins with the subdivision (*cleavage* – sometimes called *segmentation*) of the zygote into a number of separate daughter CELLS which rearrange themselves to form a hollow vesicle (*blastula*) or something equivalent to it (e.g. BLASTOCYST). (2) The next major manoeuvre is *gastrulation*, the conversion of this hollow sac into a three-layered larva – the *gastrula*. Then (3) all chordate animals go through a stage called the *neurula* – a slightly elongated embryo with a bulky head and a tapering tail with the elementary nervous system in the form of a hollow tube running from end to end, and under that the notochord or skeletal rod to which the chordates owe their name, both tube and rod being flanked on either side by *somites*, i.e. by muscle blocks arranged segmentally down the length of the body, reminding us that vertebrates are in their origin segmented animals. In chordates the principal body cavity is a *perivisceral coelom*, i.e. a cavity which holds the guts and viscera generally. The kidneys originate in all vertebrates from the narrow connections between the cavities of the segmental muscle blocks and the perivisceral coelom. The eyes of vertebrate animals are formed through the conjunction of an outgrowth from the brain which becomes the retina with a thickening of the ectoderm which becomes the lens. A transverse section through a neurula at this stage looks very much the same in all vertebrates, and only an experienced embryologist can identify the class of vertebrate animal to which a given neurula belongs. It is this fact, that the embryos of related animals resemble each other far more closely than the adults into which they develop (*von Baer's principle*), which contains the germ of truth in the doctrine of RECAPITULATION. In its simplest form this doctrine declares that in development an animal 'climbs up its own family tree'. In the heyday of recapitulation theory it was contended that the gastrula larva represents recapitulation of a very early stage in the EVOLUTION of many-celled animals, namely that stage seen today in hydroids and jellyfish, which are in essentials also simple invaginated two-layered sacs, the single aperture of which serves both as mouth and anus. Embryonic development is guided by instructions contained within the DNA (see NUCLEIC ACID) of the CHROMOSOMES of the zygote. It is only in this sense that the old preformationist theory (see PREFORMATION) is true. The instructions are preformed, but their carrying out is 'epigenctic', i.e. dependent upon the right sequence of stimuli from the ENVIRONMENT and from the cells into which the embryo itself develops. For further reading: W. J. Larsen, *Essentials of Human Embryology* (1998). P.M.

emergent poetry, see under CONCRETE POETRY.

emergent property. A property of some complex whole which cannot be explained in terms of the properties of the parts. Some think the mind is an emergent property of the brain. See also REDUCTION. A.S.

emergent technology. The doctrine that TECHNOLOGY will create a new style and pattern of battle (see WAR). It depends on a belief that warfare can be systematized and controlled by ARTIFICIAL INTELLIGENCE, reducing dependence on large reserves of manpower and crude NUCLEAR WEAPONS. Surveillance by satellite over a huge range of military and economic data will provide a WAR plan which extends the battlefront deep into the enemy's base areas. It is a visionary view of warfare produced as much by the political circumstances of NATO as any realistic assessment of likely developments. The case for emergent technology was advanced in a scheme called 'Battlefield 2000', which resolved all NATO's major problems within a single concept. Its admitted disadvantage was the enormous cost of such a programme. Critics claimed that the 'electromagnetic pulse' emitted by a nuclear explosion high in space would destroy the communications links on which this theory depends. Like the STRATEGIC DEFENCE INITIATIVE, another aspect of emergent technology, its claims remain unproven. A.J.M.W.

emic and **etic.** In LINGUISTICS, terms derived from the contrast between phonemics (see PHONOLOGY) and PHONETICS, and used to characterize opposed approaches to the study of linguistic data. An *etic* approach is one where the physical patterns of language are described with a minimum of reference to their function within the language system, whereas an *emic* approach takes full account of functional relationships, setting up minimal contrastive units as the basis of a description. Thus an etic approach to intonation would describe an utterance's pitch movement as minutely as possible, whereas an emic approach would describe only those features of the pitch pattern which are used to signal meanings. D.C.

Emmert's Law, see under AFTER-IMAGE.

emotion. A word used in ordinary language to refer principally to subjective experience. The Platonic tradition regarded emotion as the enemy of reason, and hence of judgement, truth and morality. From Hume in the mid-18th century onwards, the necessary emotional basis of right conduct and moral philosophy has been repeatedly insisted upon; and many influential 20th-century figures, such as D. H. Lawrence, have elevated the morality of the heart and the healthiness of feeling over the dictates of reason. Such experience is of its nature outside the reach of EXPERIMENTAL PSYCHOLOGY, whose subject-matter, like that of any objective empirical science (see OBJECTIVITY, EMPIRICISM), must contain specifiable experimental operations, empirical observations, and theories formulated to account for such relationships; whereas 'emotion' refers neither to operations nor to observations, and can find a home in the language of experimental psychology only as a theory-word. However, the high tide of BEHAVIOURISM in the 1920s left psychologists reluctant to talk theory at all; rather they preferred stimuli (the psychologist's comprehensive term for experimental operations) and 'responses' (i.e. observations). Nonetheless, the feeling persisted that the layman's term 'emotion' in some way specified a class of behaviour in a specific class of situations. To satisfy this feeling, and yet eschew the dangers of MENTALISM, the vogue arose for studying 'emotional stimuli' and 'emotional responses or behaviour'. In the absence of a theory of emotion, however, such terms are totally undefined, so it is not surprising that they have caused much confusion. One reaction has been to say that there is no unitary class of behaviour which can be distinguished as 'emotional', and that the word should be dropped altogether.

A more useful reaction is to construct an explicit theory of emotion, rather than hiding behind the implicit theory embodied in the stimulus-response formulation. 'Emotion' being a layman's term, one might perhaps begin by attempting to illumine the intuitions behind our ordinary language. This, properly speaking, is the business of the philosopher of language (see LINGUISTIC PHILOSOPHY), but to date PSYCHOLOGY has not drawn much on such work. Nonetheless, at least one current philosophic view of 'emotion' (see EMOTIVISM) – that emotion-words have to do with the appraisal as 'good' or 'bad' of the objects which give rise to emotional states – finds a satisfying echo in recent developments in the psychology of emotion. These developments spring in the main from the theory of learning; in particular, that part which concerns the way subjects (including animals; see also ETHOLOGY) respond to and learn about rewards and punishments. These (the two major forms of *reinforcement*; see OPERANT CONDITIONING) are defined operationally by the changes they produce in the behaviour on which they are contingent. A reward is a stimulus which, when made contingent upon a response, increases the latter's probability of recurrence; a punishment is a stimulus which decreases this probability.

With this in mind, we can define emotion as consisting in the set of states of the organism produced by reinforcing events or by *conditioned stimuli* (see CLASSICAL CONDITIONING) that have in the subject's previous experience been followed by reinforcing events. Put less technically, an emotional state consists in a disposition to act in particular ways, produced by exposure to stimuli which the subject wants to experience or to avoid, or by exposure to signals which predict the imminent occurrence of such stimuli. Such states are, of course, accompanied by changes in neural and hormonal processes, and these have been extensively studied. Signals of the subject's emotional state are also of biological significance for other members of the subject's SPECIES (its *conspecifics*). The study of the way in which one animal communicates to another its current emotional state, thus enabling its conspecifics to predict its likely future behaviour, was first given scientific prominence by Darwin in 1872. Recently, there have been a number of important attempts to apply to the study of emotional expression in man the techniques previously used with animals.

The MODELS proposed by psychologists for an understanding of emotion posit only a few emotional states. Yet in ordinary language there are hundreds of different names of apparently separate emotions. A simple resolution of this discrepancy is to hand. It is clear from experimental work in SOCIAL PSYCHOLOGY that, in ascribing a name to one's current emotional state, one takes into account not only its nature but also the specific circumstances that gave rise to it, and that a multiplicity of names may reflect a multiplicity not of states but only of types of situation giving rise to a single state. For example, the tension felt by someone anticipating a specific painful experience or danger is commonly called 'fear'; the same state is often called 'ANXIETY' when the feared event is unknown or diffuse; and there is experimental evidence that it is this same state which is produced by signals of omission of reward, when one might be described as anticipating 'frustration' or 'disappointment'. For further reading: C. Darwin, *The Expression of the Emotions in Man and Animals* (ed. P. Ekman, 1998); R. A. Hinde (ed.), *Non-Verbal Communication* (1972). J.A.G.; R.P.

emotive and **referential language.** A distinction between two kinds of language popularized by C. K. Ogden and I. A. Richards (*The Meaning of Meaning*, 1923); sometimes expressed as a distinction between CONNOTATION and DENOTATION. Richards, throughout his earlier career, advocated the rights of a complex, organized emotional language – affecting attitudes – against those of the referential language of science, LOGIC OR MATHEMATICS. Poetry was 'the supreme form of emotive language'. The distinction, which crystallized with the advent of ROMANTICISM, is a necessary one; but it requires considerable and subtle refinement, if only because no serious critic could assert that there is an actual split between the emotive and the referential. The NEW CRITICISM is full of such attempted refinements. M.S.-S.

emotivism. In ETHICS, the theory that VALUE-JUDGEMENTS, particularly moral judgements, are expressions of the speaker's emotions about the action, person or situation to which they refer and not, as they grammatically appear to be, statements of fact, true or false. Emotivists emphasize the distinction between utterances that *express* feeling, such as ejaculations or expletives, and utterances that *state* that a certain feeling is being experienced. It is to the former that they assimilate judgements of value. Hinted at by C. K. Ogden and I. A. Richards in the 1920s, emotivism was set out as an explicit theory by A. J. Ayer in the following decade and was developed with great detail and thoroughness in the *Ethics and Language* (1944) of C. L. Stevenson. Its immediate foundation is the apparent irresolubility of much moral disagreement. Indirectly it supplies a need created by the improved version of the doctrine of the NATURALISTIC FALLACY, which holds that value-judgements are quite different in nature from statements of fact. Emotivism's exponents tended to agree, on reflection, that the distinctive feature of value-judgements was that their acceptance by someone committed him to *acting* in a certain way, whereas the acceptance of a statement of fact committed him only to the adoption of the corresponding BELIEF. If this is correct, value-judgements are more like imperatives than merely expressive utterances. As a result emotivism, notably in the influential works of R. M. Hare, has largely given way to *imperativism* or *prescriptivism*. For further reading: J. O. Urmson, *The Emotive Theory of Ethics* (1968). A.Q.

empathy. Projection (not necessarily voluntary) of the self into the feelings of others or, anthropomorphically, into the 'being' of objects or sets of objects; it implies psychological involvement, at once Keats's pain and joy. The word itself was coined by Vernon Lee in 1904, and then employed by the psychologist E. B. Titchener in 1909 as a translation of the German *Einfühlung* ('feeling-into'), the notion of which had been developed in Germany by R. H. Lotze in *Mikrokosmos* (1856–64; tr. 1886); it largely provoked the ALIENATION theories of Brecht in reaction to it. M.S.-S.

empirical theology. A movement in 20th-century THEOLOGY, in the US, distinguished by the way in which it makes experience the primary source of religious knowledge. Our knowledge, for empirical theologians, is derived from the five senses assumed by the philosophers of classical EMPIRICISM, and from a kind of 'sixth sense', which apprehends aesthetic, ethical and religious value. This 'radical' or 'immediate' empiricism is often combined with a PRAGMATIST understanding of TRUTH and a generally naturalistic perspective (see NATURALISM). Anticipated in some respects by pragmatist philosophers like William James and John Dewey, empirical theology as such was practised by Bernard Meland, Henry Wieman and others, and was most influential in the middle decades of the 20th century. Together with PROCESS THEOLOGY, it is one of the classic versions of theological LIBERALISM in the US, and although extensively criticized from various angles it still makes a distinctive contribution to philosophical and theological debate. C.C.

empiricism. The theory (1) that all CON-

CEPTS are derived from experience, i.e. that a linguistic expression can be significant only if it is associated by rule with something that can be experienced, and (2) that all statements claiming to express knowledge depend for their justification on experience. The two aspects of the theory are not inseparable. Many empiricists, moreover, allow some exceptions under both heads. The formal concepts of LOGIC, e.g. those expressed by the words 'not', 'and' and 'all', are widely regarded as being purely syntactical and as having no connection with experience. As for knowledge, empiricists generally agree that there is a class of purely conceptual or analytic propositions (see ANALYTIC; PROPOSITION, TYPES OF) which are necessarily true in virtue of the meanings of the words that express them, even if they stigmatize these propositions as 'trifling' (Locke) or 'merely verbal' (J. S. Mill). The opposite of empiricism is RATIONALISM or, more precisely, apriorism (see A POSTERIORI, A PRIORI). The principle of VERIFICATION is a modern formulation of empiricism. Any statement of the empiricist theory, to be consistent with itself, must be empirical or, if not, analytic. An empirical basis for the theory is provided by elementary facts about the way in which the meaning of words is learned. For further reading: W. H. Walsh, *Reason and Experience* (1947). A.Q.

emporiatrics. The science of travellers' health. The term is derived from the Greek *emporos* (a ship's passenger) and *iatriké* (medicine). The new speciality can be justified since travellers are exposed to changes in ENVIRONMENT, altitude and temperature, to the effects of bodily (circadian) rhythms being out of phase in a different time zone and to infectious or exotic diseases in tropical countries. Emporiatrics applies not only to business travellers and tourists, but also to the crews of aeroplanes, ships and land vehicles, as well as to immigrants, refugees and migrant labourers. Dr Myron G. Schultz, formerly of the US Department of Health and Human Services, has observed that the new science of emporiatrics could aid the development of policies which would prevent avoidable suffering in travellers and help trade and tourism. H.L.E.

enclave and **exclave.** Complementary geographical terms for a non-contiguous TERRITORY of a STATE embedded within the territory of another state. Thus, in the region of the former Soviet Union known as Transcaucasia, Nagorno-Karabakh forms an enclave from the viewpoint of Azerbaijan, the state within which the outlier is located, but forms an exclave from the viewpoint of Armenia, the state to which the outlier belongs. Such outliers are now less common than in the past (e.g. Prussia before 1866 consisted of more than 270 disconnected segments of territory), but sometimes retain an important irritant role (e.g. Gibraltar to surrounding Spain). P.H.; P.O.M.

Encounter. Monthly review of 'literature, art, politics', founded in London in 1953 by Stephen Spender and Irving Kristol; among subsequent editors have been Melvin Lasky, Frank Kermode, Nigel Dennis, D. J. Enright and Anthony Thwaite. Sponsored by the Congress of Cultural Freedom, which probably had CIA funding, the magazine was one of an international, US-financed stable (*Der Monat* in Germany was another) which exchanged articles and had contributors in common; it was a symptom both of the Americanization of Europe and of the close alliance of European and American INTELLECTUALS during the COLD WAR phase. *Encounter* nonetheless was the main British literary-intellectual journal of the period, and pursued an independent critical line. The intellectual alliance was productive; *Encounter* published some of the most interesting figures of the time (e.g. Arthur Koestler, Michael Polanyi, Sir Karl Popper), as well as admirable poetry, criticism and, to a lesser extent, fiction. M.S.BR.

encounter group. In GROUP THERAPY, any therapeutic group in which body contact and emotional expression are encouraged more than the traditional purely verbal interaction. The aim of encounter groups is to increase sensitivity to others, including both physical and emotional awareness. They may take many different forms, including marathon sessions (24 to 48 hours without sleep), meeting in warm baths (the *Esalen* group), and the use of special techniques such as soliloquy, ROLE-playing, PSYCHODRAMA, etc. It has been shown that encounter groups, apart from their positive effects, may also cause breakdowns in vulnerable participants. For further reading: I. D. Yalom, *The*

Theory and Practice of Group Psychotherapy (1970). M.J.C.

encryption, see under ELECTRONIC COMMERCE.

enculturation. A term coined by M. J. Herskovits (1948) for the process by which individuals are brought up to be members of their CULTURE or society, i.e. how they are made, by education in the broadest possible sense, to have the culture appropriate to them. The CONCEPT is thus very close to that of SOCIALIZATION, much used in SOCIOLOGY and DEVELOPMENTAL PSYCHOLOGY. M.F.

end of history. The end of history has been pronounced on numerous occasions – not least by St Augustine in the 5th century AD – but it owes its current popularity to the work of an American theorist, Francis Fukuyama. In an article in 1989, Fukuyama argued that the fall of COMMUNISM had ended the conflict of ideologies that had dominated the modern world since the French Revolution. There was now only one reigning IDEOLOGY or system in the world, that of liberal market CAPITALISM or liberal DEMOCRACY (see LIBERALISM; MARKET ECONOMY). With this history had come to an end since, following the view of the German philosopher Hegel, history essentially consisted in the dialectical interplay (see DIALECTIC) and contest of ideas. Fukuyama received the impressive accolade of being attacked equally from the LEFT and the RIGHT, the assaults gaining credibility by misrepresenting Fukuyama as saying that history in the conventional sense of a sequence of events had ended. Despite the ridiculing of the idea, it is noticeable that no one has yet answered the main claim.
K.K.

end stage, see under OPEN STAGE.

endangered species. SPECIES that are at risk of becoming extinct because of declining populations. The threat of extinction may result from hunting, fishing, loss of HABITAT, or the introduction of predators or disease organisms. While the number of species becoming extinct can only be roughly estimated, it is thought that the extinction rate is higher at present than at any time since the end of the 'Dinosaur Age' 65 million years ago.

Some endangered species are protected under national laws (e.g. the US Endangered Species Act) or international treaties (Convention on International Trade in Endangered Species). More recently, attempts to protect endangered species have focused on habitat (or *in situ*) protection. Worldwide, biosphere reserves have been established to protect habitats and the species therein. The protection afforded by these reserves is often inadequate. Global climate change is seen as a potential threat to habitats and the species therein.

Another strategy for preserving endangered species is *ex situ*, whereby the organisms are maintained in zoological or botanical gardens, or their germ plasm (seeds, eggs, sperm) in germ banks. W.G.R.

endocrinology. The branch of medical BIOLOGY that deals with the nature and manner of action of endocrine glands and their secretions. Whereas most glands in the body (*exocrine glands*) communicate through ducts with the regions of the body in which their secretions (e.g. digestive ENZYMES) are to act, the *endocrine glands* are ductless and liberate their secretions (*hormones*) directly into the lymph vessels or the bloodstream. The chief endocrine glands are: the various elements of the pituitary gland, the thyroid, the islet tissue of the pancreas, the thymus, the adrenal gland, and the sex glands of both sexes.

The anterior pituitary gland holds a key position in the endocrine regulation of the body, because its secretions control the activities of the adrenal cortex, the sex glands and other endocrine organs. Its hormones belong to the PROTEIN family and are indeed *polypeptides* (see PEPTIDE); the same is true of INSULIN, secreted in the pancreas. The sex hormones and the secretions of the adrenal cortex are all steroids. Many hormones can now be manufactured synthetically. P.M.

endogamy. Marriage within a designated group (see MARRIAGE). Lévi-Strauss in *The Elementary Structures of Kinship* argues that all societies are exogamous (see EXOGAMY) and endogamous, because rules prohibiting marriage within or across groups (see INCEST), and prescribing marriage to certain types of people, are logically related. He defined two types of endogamy: *functional* (the obligation to marry a spouse related in a specific way) and *true* (the obligation to marry within a group). In both cases he saw endogamy as a negative aspect of either a highly differentiated society, or a rejection of a notion of EXCHANGE across groups. This view has been criticized for defining marriage as exchange only when it is exogamous and for denying endogamy analytical independence. Overing-Kaplan has shown that a principle of exchange, which maintains the group through time, still operates even when marriage is restricted to the group itself in small-scale kinship-based societies. M.H.

endomorph, see under PERSONALITY TYPES.

endorphins. A family of PEPTIDES discovered in the 1970s which regulate pain and other senses in the body. They are produced naturally by the body, and distributed through the brain and nervous system. Their ability to alleviate pain works in a very similar way to morphine – both morphine and endorphins use the same receptors in the brain – and it has been suggested that their production may be stimulated by acupuncture, amongst other things, which might explain the latter's analgesic effect. P.N.

endotoxins, see under BACTERIOLOGY.

energy. The capacity of a physical system for doing mechanical work – i.e. for moving objects against forces. Energy exists in various forms, the most fundamental according to current theory being kinetic energy, matter (see MASS-ENERGY EQUATION) and the potential energies due to GRAVITATION, ELECTROMAGNETIC FIELDS, and forces between ELEMENTARY PARTICLES (e.g. STRONG INTERACTIONS, WEAK INTERACTIONS). Other kinds of energy arise from these in complicated systems; thus, chemical energy is due to electromagnetic forces between ELECTRONS and NUCLEI in ATOMS, and heat energy is the total kinetic energy of random atomic motion. All these energies may be interconverted without loss because of a CONSERVATION LAW whose apparent universality makes energy one of the most important CONCEPTS in PHYSICS. The basic unit of energy is the *joule* – roughly equal to the work done when an apple is lifted through one yard. One kilowatt-hour is 3.6 million joules. M.V.B.

energy crisis. A term whose meaning has changed over the decades from the short-lived supply crisis of the mid-1970s to the long-term global warming crisis that has been emerging through the 1990s.

The energy crisis of the mid-1970s was precipitated by production cuts imposed by the Organization of Petroleum Exporting Countries (OPEC) on its members. The resulting shortage of petrol in the importing countries resulted in long queues at petrol stations and major increases in the price of petrol and of heating and automotive oil.

Underlying the 1970s crisis, and the tensions between importing and exporting nations, is the fact that oil and gas reserves are finite. Oil exploration becomes increasingly costly, dangerous and environmentally damaging as easily accessible deposits are exhausted. Nevertheless, the cost of petroleum products has remained so low that renewable energy technologies have made only modest advances in most of the industrialized nations.

A new energy crisis emerges from the recognition that the carbon dioxide produced by fossil fuel combustion accumulates in the atmosphere, where it blocks the reradiation of solar energy and thereby causes global warming. The effects of this different kind of energy crisis are not yet clear. Because a need for protection of the atmosphere implies a need for governmental regulation, global warming – or at least a human role in its causation – is denied not only by the energy industry but also by some politically conservative scientists (see CONSERVATISM). There is some evidence, however, that the wall of denial is cracking. Some segments of the energy industry, led by British Petroleum, are conceding the reality of the crisis and are committing to developing alternative energy technologies. Segments of the automotive industry are also signalling a willingness to participate in a switch to efficient and renewable technologies, as is the electric industry (see also RENEWABLE ENERGY). W.G.R.

energy level. In microscopic systems such as ATOMS the ENERGY is constrained to take only certain discrete values. The lowest level is called the *ground state* of the system, and higher levels are *excited states*. Transitions from a higher to a lower level must involve a loss of energy, which is usually emitted as PHOTONS of light or other electromagnetic RADIATION, while transitions to higher levels occur by absorption of light. These energy levels may be predicted more or less directly by QUANTUM MECHANICS, whereas in the earlier BOHR THEORY they were the result of apparently arbitrary rules restricting the application of NEWTONIAN MECHANICS (in which the energy normally varies continuously). See also ATOMIC PHYSICS; SPECTROSCOPY. M.V.B.

engineering. The utilization of (1) raw materials, (2) metals and other products from raw materials, (3) natural sources of ENERGY, and (4) the SCIENTIFIC METHOD in order to build machines and structures intended to serve a specific purpose. This purpose is most often utilitarian – transport, communication, water supply – but may also (e.g. in the building of a RADIO TELESCOPE) subserve the ends of the NATURAL SCIENCES, i.e. enhance understanding of the physical world. It is in the use of the scientific method that engineering transcends (though it may incorporate) the traditional manufacturing crafts, and is aligned with TECHNOLOGY, of which indeed it is an important part.

Engineering has been traditionally divided into civil engineering ('civil', as in 'civil service', implying public functions such as are served by roads, bridges, harbours, waterways, etc.) and mechanical engineering (dealing with machines). During the 19th century, however, electrical engineering emerged as a distinct discipline demanding its own training and qualifications; the advent of aircraft brought with it aeronautical engineering; and an ever-growing list of special branches now includes municipal, electronic, radio, gas, mining, production, structural, chemical, fuel, marine and railway engineering. E.R.L.

enkephalins, see under ENDORPHINS.

Enosis. Greek word for union or unification, used in various political contexts, originally by Greek NATIONALISTS intent on the realization of a Greek empire over those areas outside mainland Greece which had been under Greek rule in classical and Byzantine times and still had substantial Greek-speaking populations, a dream known as the *Megale Idea*. From 1930 the word was more particularly invoked by Cypriot Greeks in their long campaign to obtain independence from British rule, a campaign opposed bitterly by the Turkish minority on the island. The achievement of independence in 1960 led to an equally bitter conflict between the advocates of union with Greece and the Cypriot government of Archbishop Makarios. The death in January 1974 of the movement's leader, General Grivas, led to a marked if temporary decline in its activities. In July 1974, however, the military regime in Greece used its forces in Cyprus to support a coup against the Makarios government by pro-Enosis forces. Their action led to communal strife between Greek and Turkish Cypriot communities and to the invasion of Cyprus by Turkish forces. These seized part of the island, into which the Turkish community was evacuated, while Greek Cypriots took refuge in the unoccupied areas. Relations between Greece and Turkey deteriorated so badly that international mediation was unable to secure any agreement. Despite the overthrow of the military regime in Greece, the emotional support there for Enosis was far too strong for the democratic government which succeeded it to accept the truth that the massacres of Greek and Turkish Cypriots during the period of communal strife precluded any restoration of the *status quo ante*. D.C.W.

entitlement programs. Shorthand for the approximately 400 US government programs that, under federal law, guarantee cash benefits to eligible recipients. The two biggest are Social Security and Medicare (see MEDICAID AND MEDICARE). Other entitlement programs include unemployment compensation and such programs as Aid to Families with Dependent Children, the largest welfare program in the US, foster care, and Supplemental Security Income for the blind or otherwise disabled. Entitlement programs, like many other federal programs providing direct cash assistance, have come under scrutiny because of the huge budget deficits run up by the federal government since the 1980s – deficits that many analysts say are traceable to Reagan-era defense spending and tax cutting, rather than spending on entitlement programs. The era of entitlement began with the passage of welfare programs in 1935, during the depths of the Depression. The curtailing of such government largesse was a key issue in the election year of 1996, when President Bill Clinton signed the Personal Responsibility and Work Opportunity Reconciliation Act, which ended the entitlement to cash welfare payments as well as the federal government's guarantee of benefits for needy children. A reduction in Social Security payments to pensioners does not seem likely because of the political influence of the elderly who, unlike children, are eligible to vote. R.K.H.

entomology. The scientific study of insects; it is a division of ZOOLOGY. Entomology consists of all the methods and theories of BIOLOGY in their application to insects. Because about 80 per cent of living species are insects, entomology is deservedly recognized as a major part of biology. Entomologists seek to understand the structure, physiological functioning, embryological development, EVOLUTION and classification (see TAXONOMY) of insects. Insects are divided into two great groups according to the manner of their development. The Exopterygota include among other groups the dragonflies, crickets and bugs (including aphids); in them the wings develop as external wing buds that grow larger with each succeeding moult until the adult stage. In the Endopterygota the wings initially develop internally and only appear externally in their final form in the adult stage, after a major metamorphosis (such as the chrysalis stage of butterflies). Beetles, wasps, flies and moths are all Endopterygote insects. The Exopterygota and Endopterygota are further subdivided into about 26 *orders*. Many insects are agricultural pests or spread disease; applied entomology seeks to understand the life cycles of these insects and to invent techniques to prevent their destructive habits. For further reading: O. W. Richards and R. G. Davies, *Imms General Textbook of Entomology* (1977). M.R.

entrenched clauses. Those clauses of a constitution for the repeal or amendment of which a special legislative process is required in order to protect them from hasty or too-frequent alteration (see CONSTITUTIONALISM). Such protection may take various forms: it may consist of a requirement that legislation amending or repealing the protected clause must be passed by a larger majority than that required for ordinary legislation, or that it must be passed by a majority of two chambers of a legislature (which normally sit separately) sitting together, or that it must be confirmed by a referendum. To give the fullest measure of protection the special procedure must be made applicable not only to the clauses of the constitution which are to be specially protected, but also, by a provision known as *double entrenchment*, to the clauses providing for such special protection. A much-debated question is whether or not it is open to the British Parliament to entrench legislation (e.g. guaranteeing individual liberties) so as to preclude its repeal by the ordinary process of legislation. For further reading: G. Marshall, *Parliamentary Sovereignty in the Commonwealth* (1957). H.L.A.H.

entrenchment. An idea developed in modern philosophy of knowledge by Nelson Goodman (1906–), arising out of the long-standing problems of INDUCTION. We might, empirically, derive CONCEPTS or theories on the basis of the facts available, e.g. we might call it a law of nature that the sun rises every day, because it has been observed to do so regularly in the past (see NATURAL LAW). But, argued Hume and later critics of induction, that affords no sufficient reason for believing that such events will continue to occur, unless, by a leap of faith, we smuggle in a metaphysical principle (see METAPHYSICS) such as the uniformity of nature. Doing this, however, compounded rather than resolved the problem. Goodman spelt out the subtle implications of this dilemma. He stressed that the schemes of words and concepts we use to describe our sense experiences have no special validity. They are merely the ones which, through historical accident, we habitually use: they are, in other words, entrenched. What is commonly seen as privileged rationality is merely habitual entrenchment. For further reading: L. Losee, *An Historical Introduction to the Philosophy of Science* (1980). R.P.

entrepôt. A term in ECONOMIC GEOGRAPHY that refers to a break-of-bulk point at which goods and people in transit are required to change transport media. A port is a classic example, having originated as a suitable interface between land and sea in order to handle the importing, storage and transshipment of commodities (see COMMODITY ECONOMY) moving through its region (see REGIONALISM). Many of the world's great cities (see URBANIZATION) developed and continue to thrive as entrepôts, with many today performing more break-of-bulk activities at their international airports than at their seaports. Some, such as Singapore, are carefully integrating their global-scale seaport/airport operations in order to become the primary entry/exit point between their entire region (south-east Asia) and the rest of the world. P.O.M.

entrepreneur. The individual who perceives the profitability of production of a good or service and organizes its production. The production of a good or service could be achieved by individuals trading their particular parts of the production process in the market. However, market transactions are not costless and it may well be efficient for the entrepreneur to bring together the different parts of production into one firm (see FIRM, THEORIES OF). The entrepreneur directs the operation of the firm and is usually, but not always, considered to be the owner. The reward to the entrepreneur is profit, i.e. the residual after all other FACTORS OF PRODUCTION have been paid out of the firm's revenue. The concept of a single entrepreneur owning and running a firm is a theoretical abstraction and in many cases is not an adequate description of reality, but it may provide accurate predictions of actual behaviour. In many companies, ownership and management are distinct. Ownership is usually spread across many individuals and institutions. This is achieved through the holding of transferable shares, which do not imply liability for the debt of the firm. These characteristics are important and are ignored by the hypothetical construct of the entrepreneur. J.P.

entropy.

(1) In THERMODYNAMICS, a quantity forming (along with ENERGY, temperature, pressure, etc.) part of the specification of the thermal state of a SYSTEM; a typical system is the steam in a boiler. Entropy may be calculated from the heat which must be added to the system to bring it via intermediate states to the state being considered. It is found that the entropy of any closed system never decreases. This is one formulation of the *second law of thermodynamics*, which can be explained by STATISTICAL MECHANICS, where entropy is interpreted as a measure of the *disorder* among the ATOMS making up the system, since an initially ordered state is virtually certain to randomize as time proceeds. See also HEAT DEATH OF UNIVERSE. M.V.B.

(2) In CYBERNETICS, entropy is generalized to measure the tendency of any closed system to move from a less to a more probable state, using the same mathematical apparatus as in (1). If, however, the system is open to information, then this tendency may be arrested. This is because, mathematically speaking, information can be defined precisely as negative entropy (or *negentropy*). S.BE.

Entwicklungsroman, see under BILDUNGSROMAN.

environment.

(1) In ECOLOGY, the sum total of the biological, chemical and physical factors in some circumscribed area, usually an area associated with a particular living ORGANISM. Essentially an environment only exists because it is inhabited by this organism. Thus a field is the environment for a cow, a cow-dung pat is the environment for a dung-beetle, and the exoskeleton of the dung-beetle is the environment of a parasitic mite. Therefore the field comprises an infinity of overlapping environments. 'Environment' is also used in the sense of HABITAT or ECOSYSTEM. K.M.

(2) In ARCHITECTURE, theatre and the visual arts, the current use of this term, dating from the late 1950s, seems confined to the English language; there is no French or German equivalent. It combines three main concepts: (a) the notion of the all-embracing three-dimensional work of art as evolved by the American Allan Kaprow in 1958 and featured in the '*Dylaby*' (dynamic labyrinth) show (Amsterdam, 1962) by Rauschenberg, Jean Tinguely and others, with Schwitters's Hanover MERZbau of the 1920s as its forerunner; (b) the HAPPENING, which developed from Kaprow's and Claes Oldenburg's work in that direction; (c) the use of such works and events, together with

more orthodox and less autonomous aspects of visual art, to shape, enliven, embellish and improve our surroundings. Hence such new notions as 'environmental art', 'environmental design' (covering anything from landscape gardening to the colour of bus shelters), environmental control, POLLUTION of the environment, and finally, in 1970, as one of the Heath government's innovations, a Ministry of the Environment to deal with town planning and CONSERVATION. J.W.

environmental archaeology. A subdiscipline combining archaeology and the natural sciences with the aim of reconstructing past environments, how human societies have adapted to changing environmental conditions, how humans have exploited plant and animal resources, and how they have both affected and been affected by their natural surroundings. For further reading: J. G. Evans, *An Introduction to Environmental Archaeology* (1978). P.G.B.

environmental areas, see under TRANSPORTATION PLANNING.

environmental causes of disease. In the 19th century, physicians divided the causes of disease into two groups, 'nature' and 'nurture' (see DISEASE MODEL). Nowadays, this is expressed by grouping causative agents as either a genetic effect (see GENETICS/GENOMICS) or some influence of the ENVIRONMENT. The two are not mutually exclusive. For example, a person genetically programmed to produce certain immunoglobulins and subject to hay fever or asthma may thereby show increased sensitivity to certain environmental contaminants such as dusts or pollens. The human environment comprises four components: chemical, physical, microbiological (see MICROBIOLOGY) and psychosocial. In recent years, particularly with regard to the chemical and physical environments, there has been a tendency towards subdivision into the macroenvironment, over which the individual generally has little control (air pollution is an example), and the microenvironment (the environment which immediately surrounds the individual and over which he may exert greater control, as in the case of cigarette smoking). Microbiological diseases such as tuberculosis or cholera are now no longer 'acts of God' but regarded as controllable as we learn to regulate our environment and the way we behave in it. Time will show whether AIDS comes to be regarded in the same light, although control will involve influencing the psychosocial environment. Similarly, cancer of the female cervix is now believed to be due to an infection received from male partners. The chances of infection increase both with the number and promiscuity of such partners. Should the disease be regarded, therefore, as environmental? Current interest in stress in the inner cities, and at work, and stress caused by poverty, acknowledges the influence of the psychosocial environment. It is the physical and chemical factors of the environment which are frequently in mind when talk is of environmental causes of disease. The physical causes include such diverse factors as cigarette and chimney smoke, noise, heat and cold, increased barometric pressure (deep diving), reduced atmospheric pressure (high-altitude flying), ionizing radiation (see RADIATION BIOLOGY and RADIATION GENETICS), and non-ionizing radiation (such as LASERS and microwaves). Dusts which may cause disease (asbestos and silica) are included among the physical hazards. From antiquity, many chemicals, of which lead is a well-known example, have been known to cause disease. Newer processes may release newer chemicals into the workplace or the general environment, either in well-publicized accidental releases or continuously in smaller quantities. ACID RAIN and mercury compounds provide examples of the latter. The control of environmental hazards depends on whether the exposure of a population is voluntary or involuntary. For the latter, exposure may be regulated by legislation and inspection through, e.g., clean air acts, radiation protection and the provision of wholesome drinking water. When exposure is voluntary, as in the case of smoking, alcohol, inappropriate DIETS or sexual behaviour, then we find increasing emphasis on programmes of health education which attempt to influence the individual to reduce his or her own exposure. W.R.L.

environmental determinism. Seeking to determine the nature of human behaviour by the nature of the environment, particularly through architectural design and TOWN

PLANNING. Urban planners have frequently been criticized for 'playing God', in going beyond mere physical planning and attempting to control people's behaviour through the nature of the layout and design of the built environment (see NEW TOWN). The design of the buildings has frequently been blamed for high levels of crime and vandalism in HIGH RISE social housing projects. For further reading: M. Broady, *Planning for People* (1968). C.G.

environmental ethics. Human interaction with the natural environment raises normative issues which form the central question of environmental ethics: how should we govern our relationship with nature?

Often gaining encouragement from holistic accounts (see HOLISM) of evolutionary BIOLOGY and ECOLOGY, ethicists (see ETHICS) have argued for an expansion of the moral COMMUNITY to include non-human life. A celebrated example is that of Aldo Leopold's 'Land Ethic' put forward in his *Sand County Almanac* (1949). The processes of environmental destruction publicized in the 1960s and 1970s gave impetus to such demands for an ethical reassessment of humanity's relationship with the rest of nature.

Environmental ethicists are divided as to what ought to be the subject of moral concern. This disagreement has been formalized as that between 'shallow' and 'deep' ecologies; whereas 'shallow' approaches concern themselves with the effect of environmental despoliation on human welfare, 'deep' ecologies promote preservation on the grounds that all, or parts, of nature have a value which is independent of its usefulness.

Many of the concerns of environmental ethics have consequences which extend far into the future (for example, impacts of nuclear energy generation), meaning that the temporal extent of its reasoning often goes beyond that of traditional ethics. Not only are the interests of present generations of humans and non-humans significant, but so equally are those of future generations (see SUSTAINABILITY). More recently environmental ethicists have also begun to identify the need to combine ethical concern for nature with concern for social justice. C.T.

environmental geography. A relatively new subfield of GEOGRAPHY that focuses on the spatial dimensions of global environmental quality, particularly the degradation of HABITATS caused by human activities. Most practitioners integrate the work of several of geography's subdisciplines, including physical geography, HUMANISTIC GEOGRAPHY, ECONOMIC GEOGRAPHY, and regional geography. Much of their research is applied and focuses on pressing environmental issues, such as air and water pollution, deforestation and land denudation resulting from destructive agricultural and mining practices. Environmental geographers also engage in policy-related studies, especially those aimed at improving land utilization, and many have become involved as grass-roots activists to eliminate environmental abuses in their own communities.
P.O.M.

environmental law. The body of law – international, regional, national and local – designed to protect the environment from damage by human activities (see PUBLIC INTERNATIONAL LAW). The earliest environmental laws were probably local, such as those regulating the burning of wood or coal to protect against smog (a product of the interaction of smoke and fog) or other types of air pollution.

Regional environmental laws include those enacted by OPEC, the EUROPEAN UNION (EU) and bylaws to the North American Free Trade Agreement (NAFTA). At the national level, most countries now have laws intended to protect the environment, although these vary greatly in effectiveness and in the degree to which they are enforced, with the strictest and most comprehensive laws generally found in the most industrialised nations (see INDUSTRIAL SOCIETY).

International environmental laws or conventions are binding only upon those nations that ratify them; examples include Convention on International Trade in Endangered Species (CITES), International Law of the Sea, and the Montreal Protocols. W.G.R.

Environmental Protection Agency (EPA). An American federal agency created in 1970 by the amalgamation of 15 existing agencies. Its role was to enforce federal environmental laws and to work with state and local authorities to reduce environmental pollution and land degradation. It became responsible for carrying out federal programmes in such areas as Environmental Impact Assessment (EIA), the setting of radiation standards, pesticide registration, waste disposal and the control of toxic substances. A.S.G.

environmental studies. Term used to cover almost all activities in schools, colleges and universities which are aimed at making pupils more aware of, and critical of, the conditions in the world in which they live, and of the interrelationships between man, his CULTURE and his living and non-living surroundings. Environmental studies includes, at different levels, natural history, ECOLOGY, POLLUTION, meteorology, ARCHITECTURE, and much that is normally included in GEOGRAPHY. Environmental education is intended to give these topics more coherence. K.M.

environmentalism. Geographical term for the philosophical doctrine that stresses the influence of the ENVIRONMENT on man's activities. (Environment is here usually defined in terms of the physical factors, e.g. climatic conditions.) In its more extreme form it is termed *environmental determinism* or *geographical determinism*. The doctrine was enunciated by Hippocrates in the 5th century BC and reached its peak in the mid-19th century. Modern workers tend to acknowledge the importance of the natural environment but see it operating through a complex network of psychological, social and economic channels which may dampen or accentuate different properties of the environment for different groups, or for the same group at different points in time. P.H.

enzymes. Complex organic catalysts which mediate nearly all material TRANSFORMATIONS in the body. The substance an enzyme acts upon is known as its substrate, and in biochemical terminology an enzyme is named by adding the suffix -ase to the (truncated) name of the substrate; thus *proteases* are PROTEIN-splitting enzymes, etc. Compounds like proteins which are formed by the 'condensation' of their smaller structural units accompanied by the elimination of the elements of water are broken down by the opposite process of *hydrolysis*, involving the release of water. Thus most digestive enzymes are hydrolytic – among them pepsin, formed in the walls of the stomach and liberated into the stomach cavity; trypsin, formed in the pancreas and working in the duodenum; and the carbohydrase ptyalin, a starch-splitting enzyme present in the saliva. P.M.

epic theatre. Originally a German expression, used in contrast to 'dramatic' theatre. 'Epic' in this sense means essentially narrative, defying the Aristotelian unities: i.e. presenting a story step by step (as in *Antony and Cleopatra*) rather than tying it together in a self-contained 'plot' (as in *The Tempest*). Its current use, originating in the NEUE SACHLICHKEIT phase in Berlin, is due particularly to Erwin Piscator and Bertolt Brecht.

Starting with the production of Alfons Paquet's *Fahnen* (1924), a 'dramatic novel' subtitled 'epic', Piscator developed the use of projected texts, film, the treadmill stage and other devices to make a new kind of documentary drama. Brecht took up this concept in 1926 (before working with Piscator), summarized it in his *Mahagonny* notes (1930), and made it for some 20 years the keystone of his thinking. Though he also (see BRECHTIAN) saw it as an aid to tackling new social and economic themes in the theatre, and as subsuming the new technical devices, the essential, for him, lay rather in linear narration ('each scene for itself'), stimulating the audience's reason as against its EMPATHY, and presenting the events as if quoting something already seen and heard. Though he came to call this kind of theatre 'non-Aristotelian', fusing it with his later formula of ALIENATION, he decided in the 1950s that 'epic' was too formal a concept, and thought of replacing it by the more MARXIST-sounding phrase *dialectical theatre*, meaning in effect epic theatre in a changed society. For further reading: B. Brecht, tr. and ed. J. Willett, *Brecht on Theatre* (1964). J.W.

epidemiologic transition. A characteristic shift in disease patterns as the mortality of a population declines in the course of the DEMOGRAPHIC TRANSITION. In its early stages most of the decline in mortality results from a reduction in deaths due to acute, infectious diseases (e.g. cholera, tuberculosis, smallpox, measles, typhoid, tetanus, diphtheria). As individuals live longer, however, they become more likely to suffer and die from chronic, degenerative diseases (e.g. heart disease, stroke, cancer, Alzheimer's dementia). Therefore, the distribution of diseases in the population, and its needs and priorities in terms of medicine and public health, are slowly transformed. J.R.W.

epidemiology. The study of infectious and other diseases which appear in groups or communities. Epidemiologists try to discover the ways in which diseases develop and spread, linking their occurrence with environmental factors and with the demographic characteristics – race, age, sex, occupation – of populations affected. In the past, epidemiology was mostly concerned with infectious diseases: a classical example was John Snow's identification of the Broad Street pump as the source of a virulent outbreak of cholera in 1854. Today, epidemiological method is also applied to non-infectious diseases, for example the relation of DIET and exercise to cardiovascular disease and of smoking to lung CANCER. Epidemiology plays a crucial role in the *etiology* (the study of the causes of disease) and control of many diseases; there are academic departments in the subject at many universities. J.D.O.

epigenesis, see under PREFORMATION.

epigraphy. The study of inscriptions carved or otherwise written on durable material, such as stone or metal, and placed on buildings, tombs, etc. to indicate their name or purpose. Epigraphy provides one of the main sources for our knowledge of the ancient world. A.L.C.B.

epilepsy. Known to the Greeks as the 'sacred disease', epilepsy has often been associated with notions of the divine or transcendental nature of sickness, and of special powers possessed by sufferers (Dostoievsky, for example, was a victim). In the Middle Ages, epileptics were often shunned, and during the 19th century they were frequently confined in lunatic asylums (without it necessarily being believed that epilepsy was a 'mental disease'). Modern scientific research into epilepsy effectively dates from the latter part of the 19th century, with the work of Charles Edward Brown-Sequard, John Hughlings-Jackson and Paul Broca, who conducted experimentation upon the localization of functions in the brain and pioneered brain SURGERY. In a celebrated innovative operation in 1884, Victor Horsley removed a brain tumour and relieved focal epilepsy. In the present century attention has shifted to drug treatments. Replacing 19th-century bromides, phenobarbitol was introduced in 1912 as an effective suppressant; it has been supplemented by dilantin and primidone. No complete cure has yet been found. For further reading: Owsei Temkin, *The Falling Sickness* (1971). R.P.

epiphany. In the Christian religion the Epiphany, celebrated on 6 January, commemorates Christ's first manifestation to the Gentiles, in the form of the Magi. James Joyce was responsible for its introduction as a critical term: Stephen Hero (*Stephen Hero*, 1944) is passing through Eccles Street when he overhears a colloquy: a 'triviality' that makes him 'think of collecting many such moments together in a book of epiphanies'. By epiphany he means 'sudden spiritual manifestation[s]', 'the most delicate and evanescent of such [memorable] focusing moments'. Joyce was concerned to recapture, from the commonplace, the 'radiance', the 'whatness' – as Stephen puts it to Lynch in his conversation with him in *Portrait of the Artist as a Young Man* (1916), the 'enchantment of the heart'. He was anticipated, e.g. by Pater's phrase 'exquisite pauses in time'. It is now often used to mean, less precisely, 'sudden, precious insight'. M.S.-S.

epiphenomenalism. A theory about the nature of the causal relations between mental and bodily events (see MIND-BODY PROBLEM), where these are understood, in accordance with DUALISM, as radically different in nature. It holds that mental events are the effects of physical happenings in the organism, particularly in the brain and nervous system, but that they do not themselves exert any causal influence on the body. In T. H. Huxley's phrase epiphenomenalism conceives mental life as 'the steam above the factory'. Epiphenomenalism follows from the assumptions that mental and bodily events are, though distinct in nature, regularly correlated, and that all bodily events are fully explainable as parts of the inclusive deterministic system of physical nature (see DETERMINISM), which leaves no room for causal intrusion from the domain of the mental. For further reading: K. Campbell, *Body and Mind* (1971). A.Q.

episcopalism. The BELIEF that episcopacy, i.e. the government of the Church by bishops (Greek *episkopes*, overseer), is best, or essential to CATHOLICISM, especially in ANGLICANISM. Those who hold this belief are Episcopalians. D.L.E.

episome. A GENE or group of genes which can reproduce independently of CHROMOSOME reproduction, but which can also be incorporated into and reproduced with the chromosome. Known only from bacteria (see BACTERIOLOGY). See also PLASMAGENE. J.M.S.

epistasis. The phenomenon whereby the effects of GENES at one LOCUS are altered or masked by those at another. Thus the genes in a mouse which determine whether its hair pigment will be black or brown have no effect if the mouse is a genetic albino because of a defect at another gene locus. J.M.S.

epistemics. Word coined at Edinburgh University in 1969 with the foundation of the School of Epistemics. It signifies the scientific study of knowledge, as opposed to the philosophical theory of knowledge, which is known as EPISTEMOLOGY. A more extended definition of epistemics is 'the construction of formal MODELS of the processes – perceptual, intellectual, and linguistic – by which knowledge and understanding are achieved and communicated'. C.L.-H.

epistemological realism, see under REALISM.

epistemology. The philosophical theory of knowledge, which seeks to define it, distinguish its principal varieties, identify its sources, and establish its limits. On the topic of *definition*, it has been recognized since the time of Plato that knowledge involves true BELIEF but goes beyond it. The specification of this residual element is still a matter of controversy. One view is that what distinguishes genuine knowledge from a lucky guess is justification; another is that the causation of the belief by the fact verifies it. One way of distinguishing *kinds* of knowledge is into practical knowledge-how, propositional knowledge-that, and knowledge-of (cf. French *connaître* and German *kennen*). However, the various sorts of knowledge-of seem reducible either to knowledge-how (e.g. knowing Italian) or to knowing-that (e.g. knowing the date of the Battle of Waterloo). Within knowledge-that, the prime concern of epistemologists, empirical and *a priori* knowledge (see EMPIRICISM; A POSTERIORI, A PRIORI) are distinguished and, within each of these realms, the basic or intuitive items of knowledge are distinguished from the derived or inferred ones. *A priori* knowledge is derived from its self-evident axiomatic bases (see AXIOMATICS) by *deduction*; empirical knowledge from uninferred observation-statements by INDUCTION. The usually acknowledged sources of empirical knowledge are sense-perception (see PERCEPTION; SENSE-DATUM) and introspection, while *a priori* knowledge is said to come from reason. The determination of the *limits* of knowledge is a matter of continuing controversy, particularly about the inclusion within the realm of the knowable of morality (see ETHICS), THEOLOGY and METAPHYSICS. For further reading: J. Dancy, *Introduction to Contemporary Epistemology* (1976). A.Q.

epoche, see under EIDETIC REDUCTION.

EPR paradox. An argument presented by Albert Einstein, Boris Podolsky and Nathan Rosen, intended to show that QUANTUM MECHANICS can provide only an incomplete description of reality. It is possible to produce pairs of PARTICLES whose states are correlated in such a way that the state of one can be deduced from a measurement on the other: two ELECTRONS, say, may be such that if the SPIN of one (A) is found to be 'spin-up' (or 'down') then the other (B) must be 'spin-down' (or 'up'). Before measurement on either A or B, each is in a SUPERPOSITION of spin states, and so according to quantum mechanics neither 'possesses' a spin value. However, after measurement on one (for instance A, yielding the value 'spin-up') it can, given the correlation between the two particles, be predicted with certainty that measurement on B will yield 'spin-down'. Einstein, Podolsky and Rosen argued that if the outcome of a measurement can be predicted with certainty, then the outcome-value must be possessed by the measured system prior to measurement. Thus it would seem that the spin-state of B has been affected by a spin measurement on A, since B had no determinate spin value prior to the measurement on A, but does possess one afterwards. But this is unreasonable since A and B could be arbitrarily far apart at the time of the measurement on A. Alternatively, both A and B might possess determinate spin values all along (see HIDDEN VARIABLES), in which case quantum mechanics must be incomplete, since it explicitly rules out such states (see also BELL'S THEOREM). R.F.H.

equal protection. Principle of American constitutional law which provides that people in similar circumstances must be treated in a similar way. It has been one of the most important ideas in the US for the protection of civil liberties, and has been applied in a variety of settings, including housing, transportation, employment, education and voting rights. The doctrine is now applied primarily to racial matters, where it has had far-reaching effects. Its best-known application was in the 1954 school DESEGREGATION case, *Brown v. Board of Education of Topeka*. M.S.P.

Equal Rights Amendment (ERA). A proposed amendment to the constitution of the US which in its most important modern version sought to enshrine the principle that 'Equality of rights under the law shall not be denied or abridged by the United States or by any State on account of sex', and thus assist in the reduction of economic and other forms of discrimination against women. A similar amendment was first produced in the early 1920s by women's organizations which had recently succeeded in winning female suffrage. The issue was revived in the 1940s and raised sporadically and unsuccessfully until it profited from the modern growth in support for FEMINIST causes. The ERA was passed by Congress in March 1972; after a spectacular rate of ratification by some 30 states within a year, it made inadequate headway in the others until the available period ended on 30 June 1982. Its failure was in part due to the successful organization of opposing groups, in part to tactical and organizational weaknesses of pro-ERA groups. For further reading: J. J. Mansbridge, *Why We Lost the E.R.A.* (1986). S.R.

equality, principle of. An assertion made most commonly in this conditional form: that in public matters all persons should be treated identically, except in contexts where sufficient reasons exist for treating particular individuals or groups differently. Such prescriptions for treating men equally (a matter as much of equity as of equality) have, however, been too readily assimilated with assertions that all men *are* equal – assertions which ignore important measurable discrepancies between individuals, e.g. in mental or physical ability. Egalitarian assumptions (see EGALITARIANISM) are, indeed, no more self-evidently 'natural' than inegalitarian ones; and utterances of the kind 'All men are born equal' are best viewed as moral exhortations to allow, at the very least, that by virtue of their shared humanity men should enjoy equal satisfaction of certain basic common rights and needs.

All this leaves vast room for disagreement, especially about the extent of basic rights and needs, and about the criteria for assessing whether a particular instance of differential treatment is justified. Further difficulties arise not only over conflicts between equality and other possible social goals, such as maximal freedom of action for the individual, but even over the relationship between various kinds of equality itself: equal political rights do not necessarily imply identical shares in wealth, and equality of opportunity scarcely ends inequality of condition.

For at least 300 years much of Western political debate has focused on equality, and the drive to implement various interpretations of it has been a major force of the 20th century. Despite conceptual muddle over its positive content, the principle of equality has been negatively of great value in placing the onus of justification firmly on its opponents. For further reading: J. Rees, *Equality* (1971). M.D.B.

equilibrium.

(1) In general, a state of affairs that has no inherent tendency to change while circumstances remain the same. The idea is

used in many different sciences, e.g. PHYSICS, CHEMISTRY, ECONOMICS (see also below), PSYCHOLOGY, ECOLOGY. The equilibrium may be *static* or *dynamic*. In *static equilibrium* there is no change occurring (of interest to the science in question); e.g. the equilibrium of balanced scales. In *dynamic equilibrium* something is changing in a steady way (e.g. planets moving in a fixed orbit; a chemical reaction in a closed system proceeding as fast in one direction as the other, so that the concentrations of the reactants remain constant; or incomes rising at a fixed rate), but there are forces tending to change some aspect of the process (e.g. GRAVITATION tending to draw a planet nearer the sun, or advertisements creating increased consumption and therefore increasing wage claims), and other opposing forces which tend to produce the opposite effect and so prevent the disturbance from occurring. Other categories of equilibrium are as follows. In *unstable equilibrium*, the slightest external disturbance will alter the state radically (e.g. a pencil balanced on its point). In *metastable equilibrium* a state may persist for a long time before changing radically (e.g. a radioactive nucleus (see RADIOACTIVITY) before its decay, or the liquid in a bubble chamber). In *neutral equilibrium* the state may be altered gradually by external influences (e.g. a car at rest with its brakes off on a level road). In *stable equilibrium* the system responds to small influences by returning to its original state (e.g. a cone resting on its base, or an ATOM in its lowest ENERGY LEVEL). A.S.; M.V.B.

(2) In ECONOMICS, a state of the economy in which for every good and service (other than goods whose price is zero), total demand and supply are exactly equal. Equilibrium is usually considered to be a hypothetical state, but the economy may be thought of as moving towards an equilibrium or moving towards different equilibria. The concept of equilibrium is complicated by the KEYNESIAN distinction between effective and notional DEMAND. The most commonly used concept of equilibrium is that of COMPETITIVE EQUILIBRIUM. The existence and uniqueness of an equilibrium are important considerations. The behaviour of economies out of equilibrium may not always be movement in the direction of equilibrium and is complicated to analyse. The actual behaviour of an economy out of equilibrium may affect the demand and supply functions, e.g. the incomes of consumers may change and this affects demand, and also in the long run equilibrium. The economic study of equilibrium has investigated such effects, the role of expectations, the costs of market transactions, the use of cost of information, RISK and GAME THEORY. For further reading: E. R. Weintraub, *General Equilibrium* (1975). J.P.

equity capital. The class of CAPITAL in a company that represents the basic ownership of the company. The remuneration it receives is that income left after deducting, from total revenue, all the costs of production, payments of interest and the principal of outstanding debt, the dividends to preferred shares, taxes and retained profits. If a company is wound up, the value of equity is determined by what is left after all costs, debts, taxes and other forms of capital have been paid. Equity capital in a company is exposed to a greater risk than other forms of capital, but there is the possibility of greater returns. J.P.

ERA, see EQUAL RIGHTS AMENDMENT.

Erastianism. The belief, named after Thomas Erastus (1524–83), that the state ought to have control over the Church even in ecclesiastical matters. D.L.E.

ergonomics. The study of physical relationships between machines and the users of machines, with the object of reducing strain, discomfort and fatigue in the former and improving overall efficiency. Applications include the layout of controls on a machine tool, the design of a suitable driving seat, and the positioning of dials in an aircraft. R.I.T.

eros, see under LIFE INSTINCT.

erosion, see under DENUDATION; SOIL EROSION.

ERP (European Recovery Plan), see under MARSHALL PLAN.

error analysis.

(1) In applied LINGUISTICS, a technique for identifying, classifying and systematically interpreting the unacceptable forms

produced by someone learning a language. Errors are assumed to reflect, in a systematic way, the level of COMPETENCE achieved by a learner. D.C.

(2) In STATISTICS, especially in REGRESSION analysis, it is often assumed that an observed value is a combination of a determinate true value together with an *error term* which is randomly distributed, e.g. has a normal DISTRIBUTION. *Error analysis* is a name often applied to simple estimation techniques which make assumptions of this type, especially in the experimental sciences. R.SI.

Erziehungsroman, see under BILDUNGSROMAN.

escalation. The process whereby each side in turn increases the scope of an international crisis or the violence of an international conflict, in the hope that its adversary's self-imposed limits will be reached before its own. Escalation is thus an aspect of DETERRENCE and of CRISIS MANAGEMENT. (See also BRINKMANSHIP.) President Kennedy's decision in the Cuban MISSILE crisis of 1962 to impose a naval blockade on the incoming Soviet missile-carrying ships deliberately escalated the crisis to a point where any further escalation was judged, correctly, to be above the self-imposed limits of the former USSR. The Kennedy administration also developed an explicit doctrine of controlled escalation to give CREDIBILITY to its posture of extended deterrence in western Europe, by making clear that a Soviet attack on the European NATO powers would incur, as it grew heavier, an increasing level of first tactical and then strategic nuclear riposte. Soviet strategic doctrine came to embrace a broadly similar concept in relation to a NATO attack on the Warsaw Pact states.

Like other strategic terms, escalation is increasingly used in general political contexts, and has conceptual affinities with bargaining theory. For further reading: H. Kahn, *On Escalation* (1965). A.F.B.

escape velocity. The speed with which an object must be projected upwards from the surface of a heavenly body in order to escape, without further propulsion, from the gravitational field (see GRAVITATION) of the body. For the earth, the escape velocity is about 25,000 m.p.h.; for the moon, the escape velocity is only about 5,000 m.p.h., which explains the lack of any lunar atmosphere: any gas MOLECULES would tend to leak away, since their random heat motion is faster than the escape velocity. M.V.B.

ESN (educational sub-normality), see under LEARNING DISABILITY.

ESP (extra-sensory perception). In PARAPSYCHOLOGY, PERCEPTION or knowledge of something achieved without using sense-organs or sensory information. In *clairvoyance*, that something is an object or event; in *telepathy*, another person's thoughts; and when clairvoyance or telepathy concerns something in the future it constitutes PRECOGNITION. The main question is: does ESP exist? Anecdotal instances are open to the criticism of biased selection; e.g. premonitions of disaster are remembered when a disaster follows but forgotten when it doesn't. To avoid this bias, experiments have been undertaken asking people to guess at an event or thought about which they could have no possible sensory information. Some experiments have seemed to validate ESP, but others have been criticized on the grounds of either trickery or failure to eliminate subtle but helpful clues of which neither experimenter nor 'subject' need be consciously aware. The history of these experiments demonstrates that, at best, ESP is not robustly producible under the conditions of scientific experiment.

Another important consideration arises from the logic of scientific enquiry (see METHODOLOGY). It is held in science that a negative hypothesis can never be proved conclusively true; yet ESP is, by definition, a negative hypothesis, since it can be proved true only if all possible alternative assumptions are disproved. Thus the alleged phenomena of ESP pose both practical and logical difficulties for scientific study. At present, the conclusion is that ESP is, from a scientific viewpoint, not proven. For further reading: H. L. Edge *et al*, *Foundations of Parapsychology* (1986). I.M.L.H.

ESS, see EVOLUTIONARILY STABLE STRATEGY.

essence. The set of properties of a thing or of instances of a kind of thing which that thing or those instances *must* possess if it is to be that particular thing or they are to be instances of that particular kind. The essence can also be said to be the *defining properties* of a thing or a kind. It is, thus, part of the essence of a ship that it is designed to float on water; but its having sails rather than an engine or carrying cargo rather than passengers is accidental or *contingent* (see CONTINGENCY). Any consistent set of properties defines an essence, but it is always a further question as to whether the kind has any instances, whether anything with just that set of properties exists. The ontological proof (see ONTOLOGY) of God's existence holds that in his case alone existence is included in essence. Critics of the proof argue that existence, not being a genuine property, cannot be part of any essence. A.Q.

essential contestability. The doctrine that many morally and politically important concepts are not susceptible of 'neutral' definition or explication but are 'contestable' in the sense that rival definitions embody different and undecidable social and political allegiances. So it is held that what morality *is* cannot be agreed outside some agreement on what sort of society is morally acceptable; SOCIALIST and LIBERAL definitions of morality are so deeply involved in socialist and liberal theories of social and political organization that only by agreeing on the whole theoretical position can we expect to agree on the particular concept of morality. Similarly, it has been said that POWER and freedom are essentially contested concepts. Our view that one actor has exercised power over another or that a man or a people is free implies an extended theory of society and human nature so that two observers who hold different views about these will be unable to agree on the application of these narrower concepts too. For further reading: W. E. Connolly, *Concepts in Political Theory* (1980). A.R.

essentialism. Most generally, the theory that there are ESSENCES. More specifically it is applied to the following, quite distinct, beliefs:

(1) that particular things have essences which serve to identify them as the particular things that they are;

(2) that abstract entities or UNIVERSALS exist as well as the instances or exemplifications of them that we meet with in space and time, i.e. Platonic REALISM;

(3) a thesis (sketched by Locke) in the philosophy of science (see SCIENCE, PHILOSOPHY OF) that objects have real essences which are distinct from, but capable of explaining, their observable properties, and that discovery of these real essences is the ultimate goal of scientific investigation. For further reading: S. Kripke, *Naming and Necessity* (1980). A.Q.

essentialist humanism. A term frequently associated with CULTURAL MATERIALISM and in particular with the work of Jonathan Dollimore, who deploys it in order to critique the tendency of idealist literary criticism to assume that the essential truth of literature is at one with a transhistorical and untheorized conception of human nature. Resisting the tendency to posit the human condition as universally valid and indivisible, cultural materialism adopts the philosophical anti-humanism that was a feature of post-structuralist thinking and emphasizes a decentred and divided sense of the self, which is culturally differentiated and historically and socially constituted. For further reading: J. Dollimore, *Radical Tragedy: Religion, Ideology and Power in the Drama of Shakespeare and His Contemporaries* (1989). J.J.J.

Establishment, the. A term, usually pejorative, for an ill-defined amalgam of those INSTITUTIONS, social CLASSES and forces which represent authority, legitimacy, tradition and the status quo. The term was popularized by Henry Fairlie in a 1955 *Spectator* article, and in Britain the phenomenon is regarded, with varying degrees of consensus and justice, as comprising the Monarchy, Parliament, the Civil Service (and the Foreign Office *par excellence*), the Church of England, the Armed Forces, the Law, the professions generally, the CITY, the BBC, certain newspapers, Oxford and Cambridge universities, the PUBLIC SCHOOLS, the landed gentry, and public opinion and individual behaviour patterns as moulded by these. (An oft-cited element of the American 'Establishment' is WASPs, or White Anglo-Saxon Protestants.) Its precise composition, however, tends to reflect the nature and extent of the changes desired, and the sources of opposition or hostility encountered or expected, by the person using the term. It is thus likely to mean very different things on the lips of, say, a self-made millionaire, a radical (see RADICALISM) politician, a HIPPIE and a member of the ANGRY BRIGADE. At its least precise it may merely mean everyone richer or more powerful than the speaker. O.S.

estates, see under CORPORATE STATE.

esthetics, see AESTHETICS.

eternal return. Zarathustra, Friedrich Nietzsche's fictional character (see NIETZSCHEAN), teaches a doctrine borrowed from pre-Socratic PHILOSOPHY: 'Everything goes, everything comes back; eternally rolls the wheel of being'. Given Nietzsche's deep scepticism, he probably did not view Eternal Return as a law of nature. Perhaps he thought it a sign of health to act *as if* one's life would recur endlessly. To believe in Eternal Return was also a way to 'impress the character of being on becoming' – a sign of 'the highest will to POWER'. Finally, Nietzsche may have revived this MYTH as an alternative to TELEOLOGY, especially optimistic Christian teleology. For further reading: P. Sedgwick (ed.), *Nietzsche: A Critical Reader* (1995). P.LE.

eternal sentence. A sentence free of *indexicals*, that is, expressions like 'now', 'here', 'you'. Indexicals relativize sentences to particular times, places, persons or things, so that in order to determine whether or not a given sentence containing indexicals is true one has to know which time, place, etc. is meant. For example, the sentence 'I had a headache yesterday' is dependent for its truth or falsity on when it is said and by whom: it may be true if I say it now but not if you do; it may be true for me today but not tomorrow. By contrast, an indexical-free or eternal sentence is completely explicit in all its temporal, spatial and other references, for example 'Elizabeth I of England died in 1603', and therefore does not change its TRUTH-VALUE according to when, where or by whom it is asserted. A.C.G.

ether. Because light is known to consist of waves, it used to be thought that an underlying, all-pervasive medium must exist to support the undulations, by analogy with air (which supports sound waves) and water (sea waves). This hypothetical medium was called the ether, and its properties provoked much speculation among 19th-century physicists. However, the MICHELSON-MORLEY EXPERIMENT (which led to the theory of RELATIVITY) showed that if the ether existed it could not be observed; furthermore, other kinds of wave (matter waves; see WAVE-PARTICLE DUALITY) are now known which do not have 'ethers' associated with them. M.V.B.

ethical neutrality, see VALUE-FREEDOM.

ethics. The branch of PHILOSOPHY that investigates morality and, in particular, the varieties of thinking by which human conduct is guided and may be appraised. Its special concern is with the MEANING and justification of utterances about the rightness and wrongness of actions, the virtue or vice of the motives which prompt them, the praiseworthiness or blameworthiness of the agents who perform them, and the goodness or badness of the consequences to which they give rise. A fundamental problem is whether moral utterances are really the statements of fact, true or false, that they grammatically appear to be. If they are not statements of fact, as adherents of the doctrine of the NATURALISTIC FALLACY and, in particular, emotivists, believe, how should moral utterances be interpreted: as exclamations or commands? If they are statements of fact, are they empirical statements about such observable characteristics as conduciveness to the general happiness, as ethical NATURALISTS maintain, or can they be known *a priori*, as ethical rationalists argue? A further range of problems concerns the relation of moral CONCEPTS to each other. Is the rightness of actions inferable from the goodness of their consequences? Is the virtuousness of a motive to be inferred from the rightness of the actions that it typically prompts? Next, there is the problem of distinguishing moral value from values of other kinds (see AXIOLOGY). Is the distinguishing mark the factual nature of the ends by reference to which moral injunctions are justified, such as the happiness of mankind in general, or is it the formal character of the injunctions themselves? Finally there is the problem of the conditions under which moral judgements are properly applicable to conduct. To be morally responsible, to be liable to the sanctions of blame and punishment, must an agent be free in the sense that his actions are uncaused, or is it enough that what he did was not wholly caused by factors that sanctions cannot influence? For further reading: D. E. Cooper (ed), *Ethics: The Classic Readings. (Philosophy: The Classic Readings)* (1997). A.Q.

ethnic cleansing. A euphemism for the particular style of GENOCIDE practised during the period 1992–95 in the former YUGOSLAVIA where, under the leadership of the Bosnian Serb Radovan Karadzic, tens of thousands of Muslims and other non-Serbs were killed, tortured, raped and driven from their homes in Serb-dominated regions of Bosnia. Karadzic's lieutenants in this genocidal policy were the Serbian president Slobodan Milosevic and General Ratko Mladic. In 1995 Karadzic and Mladic were indicted for WAR CRIMES by the UN International Criminal Tribunal in The Hague. The charges include genocide, murder and rape. Despite the fact that United Nations (UN) PEACEKEEPING forces were monitoring the daily movements of both men, by 1998 neither had been arrested. For further reading: J. W. Honig and N. Both, *Srebrenica: Record of a War Crime* (1997). S.T.

ethnicity. A relatively new CONCEPT of group association (the term first appears in the 1972 Supplement of the Oxford English Dictionary) which can refer to a whole range (and frequently a combination) of communal characteristics: lingual, ancestral, regional, religious, etc., which are seen to be the basis of distinctive identity. Ethnicity appears to be a new phenomenon as well as a newly recognized one. Especially in nations formed by immigration (e.g. the US, Brazil, Australia), ethnic characteristics were at first seen as survivals from preceding generations which would more or less quickly disappear, or else persist as sentimental associations of no substantive content. Thus the IDEOLOGY of the 'melting pot', which at least in the US was seized upon as a form of reassurance that the CULTURE of the old immigrants would not be overwhelmed.

In the *Communist Manifesto*, Marx and Engels forecast that all pre-industrial distinctions of an ethnic character would disappear with the emergence of a worldwide industrial PROLETARIAT united by a perceived common condition and shared interest. The Workers of the World belief, central to MARXISM, is increasingly presented as central to the falsification of Marxist prediction. (In 1907 the socialist Otto Bauer depicted the nationalist conflicts in the Austro-Hungarian empire as a form of class conflict. Marxism could not readily account for this.)

Twentieth-century nations frequently display a mixture of ethnic and social class stratification, often with the one serving as a surrogate for the other. Ethnicity, combining interest with affect, recurrently proves the stronger attachment and the most volatile source of domestic violence. This tendency appears to intensify as modern communications bring dispersed groups in contact with one another, and inform one and all of victories, defeats and especially of atrocities. Ethnic conflict within the former Soviet empire is likely to prove a major element in 21st-century world politics. In the meantime Walker Connor estimates that nearly half of the independent countries of the world have in recent years experienced some degree of 'ethnically inspired dissonance'. For further reading: N. Glazer and D. P. Moynihan, *Ethnicity, Theory and Practice* (1975).

N.G.; D.P.M.

ethnoarchaeology. Archaeological techniques used to study past communities but within constraints imposed by anthropological concepts. Usually used to study peoples whose direct ancestors are still alive. Thus the true interface between ARCHAEOLOGY and ANTHROPOLOGY. Not to be confused with the sport, popular with some archaeologists, of using ethnographic analogy to 'explain' archaeological observation. For further reading: C. Kramer (ed.), *Ethnoarchaeology* (1979). B.C.

ethnocentrism. Term coined by W. G. Sumner (*Folkways*, 1906), and nearly always used pejoratively, for the attitudes which uncritically presuppose the superiority of one's own group or CULTURE. Such attitudes may be found not only among the members of a tribe or nation who despise other tribes or nations about them, but among anthropologists (sociologists, etc.) if they evaluate the culture or behaviour of members of another society by the light of their own culture. The question of ethnocentrism in ANTHROPOLOGY cannot be avoided. It is inherent in many of the debates concerning the interpretation of beliefs and practices found in other societies. Investigations of European WITCHCRAFT have also revealed that ethnocentrism is a problem in historical understanding as much as in contemporary study. For further reading: J. Overing (ed.), *Reason and Morality* (1985). M.F.; A.G.

ethnography. Term which refers to the descriptive and analytical results of FIELDWORK and anthropological theory (see ANTHROPOLOGY). It is both a product, a concrete text occurring within a genre of writing, and a process of gathering and thinking about data in relation to certain issues. Ethnographies are the testing grounds for theoretical developments, but they could also be the building blocks. Stephen Gudeman and Alberto Rivera argue in *Conversations in Colombia* (1992) that ethnography is a dialogic product involving colleagues, informants, friends and past theorists. The recent trend has been to consider the literary and political nature of ethnographic writing, how the real world fashions the ethnographic enterprise as much as ethnographies construct worlds. For example, to what use does the author put literary techniques in the writing of ethnography? The contextualization of anthropological work in world processes has indicated how fieldworkers often follow trails other than intellectual ones, such as the opening of political frontiers. Another recent development is the freeing of ethnography from its traditional occupation of the study of people in one geographical space. Multiple-site fieldwork studies of migrants and their families has broken locality boundedness, as has the analysis of global cultural processes. For further reading: J. Clifford and G. Marcus, *Writing Culture: The Poetics and Politics of Ethnography* (1987). M.H.

ethnography of communication, see under ETHNOLINGUISTICS; COMMUNICATION, ETHNOGRAPHY OF.

ethnohistory. A term which came into use in the 1940s to describe the history of non-literate peoples, a subject which had been neglected both by anthropologists (because it was concerned with the past; see ANTHROPOLOGY) and by historians (because written documents were lacking). Ethnohistorians need to combine the skills of the archaeologist (see ARCHAEOLOGY), the social anthropologist (to interpret ORAL TRADITION), and the conventional historian (to deal with documents produced by conquerors and missionaries). Their results are likely to be more reliable when they reconstruct CULTURAL HISTORY and SOCIAL HISTORY than when the attempt is made to produce a narrative of events. P.B.

ethnolinguistics. A branch of LINGUISTICS which studies language in relation to the investigation of ethnic types and behaviour. It often overlaps with ANTHROPOLOGICAL LINGUISTICS and SOCIOLINGUISTICS, and the phrase ethnography of communication (see COMMUNICATION, ETHNOGRAPHY OF) has been applied by sociolinguists to the study of language in relation to the entire range of extra-linguistic variables. D.C.

ethnology, see under ETHNOGRAPHY.

ethnomethodology. A term coined, misleadingly (since the first element bears no relation to its usual meaning), by Harold Garfinkel for an activity which he inaugurated: the sociological study of everyday activities, however trivial, concentrating on the methods used by individuals to report their commonsense practical actions to others in acceptable rational terms. This process of imposing a *rational* scheme onto what are essentially *practical* activities is referred to in the shorthand terminology of the ethnomethodological language as 'practical reasoning'. Ethnomethodology, with its interest in how the individual experiences and makes sense of social interaction, is directly and controversially opposed to sociological theories (e.g. those of Marx, Weber and Durkheim) that concentrate on the larger questions of SOCIAL STRUCTURE. It is therefore nearer to SOCIAL PSYCHOLOGY than sociological theory proper, as is also true of the two previous theories from which it has derived the most: G. H. Mead's SYMBOLIC INTERACTION theory and, more importantly, Alfred Schutz's PHENOMENOLOGY. Its critics insist that a preoccupation with trivialities is not a virtue, and that trivial exchanges like 'Hi' – 'Hi' are neither illuminated nor rendered less trivial by such pronouncements as (an actual example from the first book listed below) 'A basic rule of adjacency pair operation is: given the recognizable production of a first pair part, on its first possible completion its speaker should stop and a next speaker should start and produce a second pair part from the pair type the first is recognizably a member of'. For further reading: R. Turner (ed.), *Ethnomethodology* (1974); E. Livingston, *Making Sense of Ethnomethodology* (1987). B.A.

ethnomusicology. The study of all categories of music (including FOLK MUSIC) other than Western ART MUSIC. Although the English word dates only from 1959, the subject, under its earlier name of 'comparative MUSICOLOGY', evolved at the beginning of the 20th century, in Germany, where a predominantly musicological approach was favoured, and later in the USA, where anthropological methods were preferred. The two traditions were to some extent amalgamated with the foundation in 1955 of the international Society for Ethnomusicology, whose activities focus attention upon (1) the collection of data from (a) tangible materials (e.g. excavated instruments, early manuscripts) and (b) oral traditions (e.g. songs and dances); (2) transcription from tape-recordings, structural analysis (aided by mechanical and electronic devices) of *what* is performed, and detailed description of *how* it is performed; (3) collation of findings with general cultural phenomena. British universities have been conspicuously cautious in extending to the subject the recognition it has gained elsewhere. For further reading: B. Nettl, *Theory and Method in Ethnomusicology* (1964). A.K.

ethnopsychology. The branch of PSYCHOLOGY that studies the psychological characteristics of people considered as members of cultural, social, religious or national groups. See also CROSS-CULTURAL STUDY; RELATIVISM; CULTURE. I.M.L.H.

ethology. The name now generally accepted for a type of behavioural study that began as a branch of ZOOLOGY, and attained prominence in the early 1930s with the work of Konrad Lorenz of Vienna. Emphasis was laid on the need to observe and describe the behaviour of as many SPECIES as possible, and there was a tendency to interpret behaviour as the result of EVOLUTION moulded by NATURAL SELECTION. Historical circumstances, e.g. the over-emphasis in PSYCHOLOGY on learning, made ethologists emphasize the non-learned aspects of animal, and even of human, behaviour; much work was also concentrated (mainly under the influence of Heinroth in Germany and J. S. Huxley in Britain) on vertebrates, especially birds. Ethology was at first ignored, later severely (and in part justifiably) criticized, by psychologists and physiologists (see PHYSIOLOGY), while ecologists (see ECOLOGY) were on the whole receptive. Since the war ethology, psychology and neurophysiology (see NEUROPSYCHOLOGY) have come closer together, and there are signs that a more unified, more biologically oriented science of behaviour is emerging.

The importance of ethology for the understanding of human behaviour is beginning to be recognized, and the works of Lorenz and Desmond Morris have aroused worldwide interest, though many students of human behaviour (psychologists, psychopathologists, anthropologists; see PSYCHOPATHOLOGY; ANTHROPOLOGY) have found them over-assertive. There is a growing consensus that, although facts and conclusions about animal behaviour cannot be generalized and applied to human behaviour, certain methods are equally suitable to the study of either. The fact that human behaviour is the result of accumulative non-genetic transfer (see GENETICS/GENOMICS) or individually acquired modifications from one generation to the next can no longer be denied. This 'cultural' or 'psychosocial' EVOLUTION, however, must not be allowed to obscure the effects of the genetic evolution which preceded it, and which still determines the direction, and the limitations, of human behaviour. For further reading: R. A. Hinde, *Ethology* (1982). N.T.

etic, see under EMIC AND ETIC.

etiology (or **aetiology),** see under EPIDEMIOLOGY.

etymological fallacy. The view, criticized in LINGUISTICS, that an earlier (or the oldest) meaning of a word is the correct one, e.g. that *history* 'really' means 'investigation', because this was the meaning the word had in Classical Greek. Linguists, by contrast, emphasize that the meaning of a word can be determined only by an analysis of its current use. D.C.

EU, see EUROPEAN UNION.

Eucharistic theology. The discussion of doctrines about the Eucharist (from the Greek for 'thanksgiving') or Holy Communion, the most ancient and important act of Christian worship. The modern LITURGICAL MOVEMENT has stimulated both rethinking and fresh agreement about the meaning of the Eucharist. For further reading: E. L. Mascall, *Corpus Christi* (1965). D.L.E.

Euclidean geometry, see under GEOMETRY.

eugenics. Term coined in 1883 by Francis Galton (1822–1911), Charles Darwin's cousin, meaning literally 'well-born', but used to describe the science of improving humankind through selective breeding. Eugenic ideas go back at least as far as Plato, but only received systematic elucidation after Darwin's *Origin of Species* (1859) (see DARWINISM) located humankind in the context of a natural process of EVOLUTION. Eugenics is often divided into a positive and negative variety. *Positive eugenics* encourages the reproduction of allegedly superior human beings (e.g. by means of financial incentives to potential parents), while *negative eugenics* attempts to prevent procreation by those with allegedly undesirable traits (e.g. by means of sexual STERILIZATION or segregation from society). Those who advocate eugenics see it as a science based on GENETICS, but the element of objective scientific thinking behind eugenics typically is small. This spurious appeal to 'science' has been used to legitimize a variety of social prejudices, especially those of RACE and CLASS. In fairness, some eugenic decisions can be unprejudiced, when taken voluntarily and concerning conditions with a known hereditary mechanism (e.g. an individual with a family history of Huntington's chorea may decide not to procreate). But more typically eugenicists attempt to coerce or force others to reproduce (or not), while they confuse cultural 'inheritance' (see CULTURE) with genetic inheritance, and mistakenly ascribe a variety of social characteristics to genetic factors (see GENETICISM).

Eugenics first became a popular social movement in Britain. It was largely a professional MIDDLE-CLASS preoccupation, stimulated by the fear that Britain's slow progress in the Boer War was the consequence of the degeneration of the imperial race. By 1906 eugenics was considered one of the four main branches of SOCIOLOGY in Britain. British eugenic writings spawned popular eugenic movements and centres for eugenic study in the US, in Russia and in many European countries. In the US, unlike in Britain, negative eugenic laws were enacted. By 1943, 30 states in the US allowed the sterilization of individuals deemed genetically 'unfit' – particularly the inmates of mental institutions. Most of these laws permitted compulsion when necessary.

As a consequence of Nazi (see NAZISM) involvement in eugenics, it has been viewed with suspicion since World War II. But eugenic ideas survive in all but name and influence attitudes to immigration, the right of the mentally ill and handicapped to procreate, etc. Nazi espousal of eugenic ideas has also obscured the fact that eugenics was and is as much a LEFT-wing preoccupation as that of the RIGHT. Indeed, some of the most enthusiastic early eugenicists were the Fabians (see FABIANISM) in Britain and PROGRESSIVE states like California in the US. Today eugenics tends not to be institutionalized, but influences the decisions of individual bureaucrats and doctors. A notable exception is the Singapore of Lee Kuan Yew, where positive eugenic thinking still shapes government social policy. See also EUTHENICS; DYSGENIC. For further reading: S. Trombley, *The Right to Reproduce* (1988). A.B.E.

eukaryote. A fundamental division of living things, made up of organisms whose CELLS contain a separate nucleus. All living things are either eukaryotes or PROKARYOTES, according to their cellular structure. In eukaryotes, cells have greater internal distinction than in prokaryotes. Eukaryotic cells have a separate nucleus, which contains the cell's DNA (see NUCLEIC ACID), surrounded by a nuclear membrane; they also have other internal organelles, such as mitochondria (see CYTOLOGY). Fungi, plants and animals are all eukaryotes; bacteria are prokaryotes. Eukaryotes probably evolved from prokaryotic ancestors, some time between 1,000 and 2,000 million years ago. It is a matter of controversy whether eukaryotes evolved by the internal DIFFERENTIATION of the prokaryotic cell, or by the symbiotic union of several kinds of prokaryote (see SYMBIOSIS). M.R.

euro, see under SINGLE CURRENCY.

eurocurrency, see under EURODOLLARS.

eurodollars. Deposits held in US dollars at banks located outside the US, though not necessarily in Europe, e.g. there are 'eurodollar markets' in south-east Asia. Other *eurocurrency* markets exist, but the eurodollar market has been and is the most important. The holders of eurodollars may be of any nationality. The deposits and corresponding loans are usually short-term. The eurodollar market exists because of the official restrictions on US banks that allow Euro-banks to offer better rates to lenders and borrowers. In its search for preferred interest rates and currencies, CAPITAL has become internationally mobile and eurodollar markets have greatly increased this mobility, which has reduced US control over its interest rates and monetary system and, it has been suggested, affected the US BALANCE OF PAYMENTS. It has also had important effects on INTERNATIONAL LIQUIDITY and the world money supply. In the mid-1970s, the eurocurrency markets recycled to oil importers a considerable portion of OPEC's surplus oil revenues and so prevented a larger shock to the world economic system. These markets were put under great strain to find short-term borrowers to match the often very short-term nature of these new deposits (see DEBT CRISIS). For further reading: R. B. Johnston, *Economics of the Euro-Market* (1983). J.P.

European Commission, see under EUROPEAN UNION.

European Community (EC), see under EUROPEAN UNION.

European Court of Human Rights. This court, which sits in Strasbourg, was established on 3 September 1958 in accordance with the provisions of the European Convention for the Protection of Human Rights and Fundamental Freedoms of 1950 (The Convention). It is stipulated there that the court shall consist of 'a number of judges equal to that of the Members of the Council of Europe'. The members of the court are elected by the Consultative Assembly for a period of nine years. Article 48 of the Convention provides that the following may bring a case before the court: (a) the Commission; (b) a high contracting party (country) whose national is alleged to be a victim; (c) a high contracting party that referred the case to the Commission; and (d) a high contracting party against which the complaint has been lodged. The conclusion to be inferred from this provision is that an individual who has petitioned the Commission for an alleged violation of the Convention can never bring his case before the court himself. As to the position of respondents, proceedings may be commenced before the court only against a contracting STATE which has either signed the declaration of recognition provided for in Article 46 of the Convention or has consented to reference being made to the court in a particular matter. Once a case has been brought before the court, the latter must decide whether or not there has been a violation of the Convention. If it is satisfied that a violation of the Convention by a contracting state has taken place, its decision may afford just satisfaction to the injured party. The decision of the court, which is binding on the parties to the case, is final. Its execution is supervised by the Committee of Ministers of the Council of Europe. See also HUMAN RIGHTS. For further reading: J. E. S. Fawcett, *The Application of the European Convention on Human Rights* (1969). O.Y.E.

European Court of Justice, see COURT OF JUSTICE OF THE EUROPEAN COMMUNITIES.

European Currency Unit, see under INTERNATIONAL LIQUIDITY.

European Economic Community, see under EUROPEAN UNION.

European Recovery Program (ERP), see under MARSHALL PLAN.

European Steel and Coal Community, see under EUROPEAN UNION.

European Union. (EU). The major vehicle for the process of European integration in the post-war period, the European Economic Community developed from the European Coal and Steel Community (ECSC, created by the Treaty of Paris in 1950). The impetus for its establishment was the desire to prevent further hostilities between France and Germany and to exploit the economic benefits of market integration within a free market framework. Its founding fathers are often considered to be Jean Monnet and Robert Schuman. The EEC was established by the Treaty of Rome of 1957 between West Germany, France, Italy, Belgium, Luxembourg and the Netherlands. This created a CUSTOMS UNION between the six, with free internal trade and a common external trade policy. It also provided the legal basis for an internal common market, in which LABOUR and CAPITAL would be free to circulate, as well as goods and services. The EEC also provided for the establishment of common policies in a number of areas, the most important being agriculture, which has since been run by the Common Agricultural Policy (CAP). There were also significant political and institutional arrangements, with the creation of the European Commission and the Council of Ministers to act as the main decision-making body. Britain refused to join the original EEC, preferring to establish its own trading block in the shape of the European Free Trade Area. When the UK eventually decided to seek membership, its application was vetoed by the French President, General de Gaulle. The UK eventually joined in 1973, along with the Republic of Ireland and Denmark, to form the European Community (EC) nine, which expanded to the south in the early 1980s to include Spain, Portugal and Greece and become the EC 12. The EC was then subsumed into the present European Union (EU), following the MAASTRICHT Treaty signed in 1991. This now has 15 members, with the former European Free Trade Area states of Sweden, Austria and Finland joining in January 1995 (Norway and Switzerland declined to join). It is expected that Poland, Hungary, the Czech Republic, Slovenia and Cyprus will become members as well in the foreseeable future. The aims of the original EEC have been greatly expanded to include integration in a wide political and economic sphere, including the establishment of a SINGLE CURRENCY for qualifying members of the EU. V.L.

eurythmics (or **eurhythmics).** The art of interpreting music through body movements; specifically, the system of rhythmical gymnastics taught by the Swiss composer and educationist Émile Jacques-Dalcroze (1865–1950) in order to develop his students' physical, intellectual and aesthetic sense of musical forms and rhythms; to increase their capacity to analyse musical structure; to give them musical 'experience' rather than musical 'knowledge'. B.L.B.

eurythmy (or **eurhythmy).** An art form evolved by Rudolf Steiner (1861–1925), the founder of ANTHROPOSOPHY. It aims to make visible certain qualities of movement, feeling and character which are held to be inherent in the sounds of speech or music. Stage performances present interpretations of music, poetry and prose by groups or soloists. It is also used educationally for adults and children (notably in STEINER SCHOOLS), and therapeutically, as *curative eurythmy*, under the direction of anthroposophical doctors. J.D.

Euston Road Group. A group of painters associated with The School of Drawing and Painting which was established in 1937, at first in Charlotte Street, then, from 1938 to 1939, at 314–316 Euston Road, London; more particularly, Graham Bell, William Coldstream, Lawrence Gowing, Victor Pasmore and Claude Rogers. The work of these painters was at that time marked by an insistence upon objective drawing, tonality and realistic subject-matter. Q.B.

euthanasia. Literally, death without suffering. Used to describe the 'mercy killing' by a medical practitioner of an incurably ill patient. In the adult, this implies the administration of a drug (or drugs) deliberately and specifically to precipitate or accelerate death. Theoretically, euthanasia can be either *voluntary* or *involuntary* (compulsory). In no country is either form legal, though there is *de facto* acceptance of voluntary euthanasia in Holland. Voluntary euthanasia, requested by the sufferer, has also been described as assisted suicide or homicide by request. Involuntary euthanasia implies a decision by society (or by an individual) to end the life of a sufferer who cannot signify volition; for example, the severely handicapped infant or the demented. Discussion relating to euthanasia has been complicated by the use of the term '*passive* euthanasia'. This is defined as withholding treatment that might lengthen the lives of the incurably sick. However, as it does not involve the deliberate administration of a drug to accelerate death, it should not be described as euthanasia. The use of the term derives from a failure to distinguish between acute and terminal illness. The two are distinct biological entities, and what is appropriate for one may be inappropriate for the other. For example, intravenous infusions, ANTIBIOTICS, respirators and cardiac resuscitation are all supportive measures for use in acute or recurrent illnesses to assist a patient through a critical period towards recovery. Generally, to use these measures in the terminally ill, with no expectation of a return to health, is inappropriate and, therefore, bad medicine. A doctor clearly has a duty to sustain life where life is sustainable; he has no duty – legal or ethical – to prolong the distress of a dying patient. The term '*indirect* euthanasia' has been used to describe the administration of morphine to cancer patients in pain. This is incorrect; giving a drug to lessen pain cannot be equated with giving an overdose deliberately to end life. Should life be marginally shortened by the use of morphine or related drugs, this is an acceptable risk in the circumstances. Correctly used, however, such drugs are much safer than commonly supposed. There is circumstantial evidence that those whose pain is relieved may outlive those whose nutrition and rest continue to be disturbed by persistent pain. For further reading: J. W. Walters (ed.), *Choosing Who's to Live: Ethics and Aging* (1996).

R.G.T.

euthenics. From the Greek 'to thrive' or 'flourish', euthenics is the art or science of improving the wellbeing of humankind through the betterment of the conditions of life. Euthenics is totally at odds with EUGENICS in that it seeks to improve 'nurture' (e.g. by the provision of better housing, sanitation, education, etc.). Eugenicists see these efforts as at best ephemeral and argue for policies to improve 'nature' (e.g. through the sexual STERILIZATION of individuals who are, allegedly, of genetically [see GENETICS/GENOMICS] inferior stock). The term euthenics, unlike eugenics, is little used today. But the debate continues between those who see nature and those who see nurture as pre-eminent in determining the quality of society and the abilities of individuals. See also NATURE VERSUS NURTURE.

A.B.E.

eutrophication. An increase in the nutrient content of a body of water resulting in increased growth of micro-organisms and a consequent upset of the naturally occurring biotic composition of that body. While eutrophication can occur from natural processes, it can have serious environmental impacts when caused by human activities.

Run-off from fertilized agricultural lands and discharges from sewage treatment plants introduce nitrogen, phosphorus and other essential nutrients into lakes, streams and coastal marine waters. The added nutrients may stimulate the growth of microscopic algae, which can turn the water turbid, preventing light from reaching bottom-growing aquatic plants. As the algal 'blooms' eventually die, bacteria (see BACTERIOLOGY) multiply and consume the dissolved oxygen, creating an environment in which fish and other oxygen-requiring organisms cannot survive.

W.G.R.

evaluation. In education, the process of obtaining information, usually for administrators and teachers, about the effects and values of educational activities. As a systematic pursuit, evaluation is typically associated with programmes of educational reform, particularly with the Anglo-American curriculum development movement of the 1960s and 1970s. The initial theoretical framework (R. W. Tyler, *Constructing Achievement Tests*, 1934) stressed the PSYCHOMETRIC assessment of learning objectives, but during the 1960s the SOCIAL ENGINEERING assumptions of this MODEL were challenged, and the field is currently characterized by a proliferation of theory. A major conventional division is that of M. Scriven (1967) between *formative* evaluation, designed to improve a programme, and *summative* evaluation, designed to judge its worth.

Evaluations are typically commissioned by executive branches of central government, both as a CYBERNETIC aid to interventionist management and as a form of public reassurance that central initiatives are subject to disinterested assessment. Much of the diversity evident in the theory and practice of evaluation can be explained in terms of their underlying potential LOGIC. The crucial issue in such an analysis is the impact of evaluation on the distribution of POWER, particularly where, as is now increasingly the norm, government-backed programmes embody technocratic values. Especially in England, attempts to democratize the process of evaluation have led its practitioners to take risks with both bureaucratic convenience and scientific respectability in order to stimulate and inform a broader public discourse about educational change. Given that sponsored independence is a *sine qua non* of such developments, and that more docile and technicist alternatives are readily available, the future of evaluation is likely to reflect government definitions of the need and the right to know. For further reading: E. R. House, *Evaluating with Validity* (1980). B.M.

evaluation procedure. In LINGUISTICS, a set of techniques which enable a linguist to judge which of two GRAMMARS is the better account of a language. The importance of this notion was first pointed out by Chomsky, and there has since been considerable discussion of evaluation CRITERIA (e.g. the economy of a description) for particular areas of language, especially PHONOLOGY. D.C.

evaluative, see under NORMATIVE.

Evangelical. A term sometimes used as another word for Protestant (see PROTESTANTISM). It is applied, e.g., to LUTHERANISM or to BARTHIAN theology. But its most common use in the English-speaking world has been in the description of Protestants who take a conservative view of the authority of the Bible; of the necessity and sufficiency of acceptance by faith of the salvation won by the sacrifice of Christ on the cross; and of the indispensable importance of miracles including Christ's virgin birth, physical resurrection and (in the future) visible return to earth in glory. The decision to accept Christ as Saviour in this sense can be described as being 'born again'. This movement reacts against LIBERALISM in THEOLOGY and has often been identified with FUNDAMENTALISM. But in the 20th century there has been much debate within it about the character of the truth or trustworthiness of the Bible. While probably most Evangelicals still accept the Bible's INFALLIBILITY or 'inerrancy' with few qualifications or none, some have argued that the Bible is the Word of God in what it teaches when taken as a whole, not in everything in poetry, history or science which it touches, and there has been a cautious acceptance of biblical criticism and HERMENEUTICS. Similarly there has been greater sophistication in handling what the Bible affirms in relation to modern questions in ETHICS and other fields. In the 1970s it became clear that this movement, for all its internal tensions, was the most lively feature of religion in the US (see BORN AGAIN) and was gaining influence wherever in the world the style of evangelists from the US (the most famous being Billy Graham) was an acceptable model. See also RELIGIOUS RIGHT. For further reading: C. Catherwood, *Five Evangelical Leaders* (1984). D.L.E.

events, see HAPPENINGS AND EVENTS.

Everett (*or* **Everett-Wheeler interpretation,** see under MANY WORLDS HYPOTHESIS.

everyday, the. A kind of crossroads of new approaches in SOCIOLOGY, ANTHROPOLOGY, PHILOSOPHY and HISTORY. The MARXISTS are naturally as concerned with the everyday as they are with ordinary people, a concern visible in the attempt to write HISTORY FROM BELOW by Edward Thompson and others, and the work of the philosophers Henri Lefebvre and Agnes Heller. At the same time, the phenomenologist (see PHENOMENOLOGY) Alfred Schutz was pursuing his study of what he called the principles of 'commonsense knowledge'. In sociology and anthropology the so-called 'ethnomethodologists' (see ETHNOMETHODOLOGY) such as Harold Garfinkel (who acknowledges a debt to Schutz), Pierre

Bourdieu (in his work on 'theoretical practice') and Erving Goffman (author of *The Presentation of Self in Everyday Life*) have all been concerned to make the commonplace problematic, or more exactly, to show that what is taken for granted in one society is perceived as obviously false or foolish in another. In their different ways, Michel Foucault and the feminists (see FEMINISM) have directed attention to what is sometimes called the 'politics of the everyday', the power relations concealed or revealed in everyday transactions at home, at work, in school, and so on. These theorists are now having some impact on the practice of social historians (see SOCIAL HISTORY), transforming a few of them into historical anthropologists (see HISTORICAL ANTHROPOLOGY). The pursuit of the everyday has challenged a good many traditional assumptions. It has alerted us to what might be called the importance of the trivial in the understanding of society. Nevertheless, the central concept is more elusive than it may seem. The everyday refers at once to attitudes (or mentalities; see HISTORY OF MENTALITIES), to actions (especially to routine), and to material culture (see HISTORY OF MATERIAL CULTURE). The everyday is sometimes opposed to RITUAL (which marks special occasions), yet daily life may be described as a kind of ritual. The idea of everyday knowledge is linked to the notion of cultural rules, but the concept of 'rule' is itself in need of further clarification. For further reading: M. Douglas (ed.), *Rules and Meanings: the Anthropology of Everyday Knowledge* (1973). P.B.

evidentialism. In the philosophy of religion (see RELIGION, PHILOSOPHY OF), the position of those who assume that the rationality of religious BELIEF is a function of the degree to which it is supported by some body of evidence. This position, found in THEISM and ATHEISM alike, presupposes the epistemological framework of FOUNDATIONALISM, according to which a set of 'basic' or 'foundational' beliefs must provide the justification for the 'superstructural' beliefs which do not meet the conditions for 'proper basicality' (see EPISTEMOLOGY). Evidentialism, together with the foundationalism it presupposes, has been identified and criticized by philosophers in several traditions, including 'Reformed Epistemologists' and (much more radically) Wittgensteinians. C.C.

evolution. The theory that the existing varieties of plant and animal, so far from having existed more or less unmodified from the beginning of biological time, have come into being through a progressive diversification that has accompanied their biogenetic descent (see BIOGENESIS) from their ancestors. Although the theory had been adumbrated very many times before the publication in 1859 of Darwin's *The Origin of Species*, it was Darwin's ability to propound an acceptable theory (DARWINISM) of how evolution might have come about which brought the subject into public discussion and intensive enquiry. It is naïve to suppose that the acceptance of evolution theory depends upon the evidence of a number of so-called 'proofs'; it depends rather upon the fact that the evolutionary theory permeates and supports every branch of biological science, much as the notion of the roundness of the earth underlies all GEODESY and all cosmological theories on which the shape of the earth has a bearing. Thus anti-evolutionism is of the same stature as flat-earthism. Biologists therefore do not argue about whether evolution has taken place, but many details of how evolution proceeds are still matters of controversy. See LAMARCKISM; MASS EXTINCTION; MOLECULAR CLOCK; PUNCTUATED EQUILIBRIUM; CLADISM. For further reading: A. Grafen (ed.), *Evolution and Its Influence* (1989). P.M.; M.R.

evolution, social and cultural. Although ideas about the regular development of human CULTURE and society antedate Darwin, the second half of the 19th century was the great period of evolutionary theory in the SOCIAL SCIENCES. It depended on the assumption, now abandoned, that surviving PRIMITIVE peoples represent earlier stages in the development of modern society. In one form, evolutionary theory keeps close to BIOLOGY in speaking of increasing complexity and differentiation; in another, a series of phases or stages of development is posited, although not all societies are expected to go through all of them. Evolutionary thinking is now of secondary importance in Anglo-American and western European social and cultural ANTHROPOL-

OGY, but plays a central role in countries adhering to MARXISM, although not under the name of evolution. See also DIFFUSION; EVOLUTION; STRUCTURALISM. For further reading: M. Augé, *The Anthropological Circle* (1982). M.F.

evolutionarily stable strategy (ESS). In DARWINISM, a strategy which is stable against invasion by any other specified strategy. A 'strategy' here generally refers to a behaviour pattern of an animal, but the theory applies to anything that can evolve by NATURAL SELECTION. Biologists seeking to understand why animals behave in the way they do ask whether the behaviour pattern could be bettered by any alternative behaviour pattern (strategy). If it could not, it is an evolutionarily stable strategy (ESS). Natural selection should give rise to animals that behave according to an ESS. The idea is an application of GAME THEORY to BIOLOGY. The term was coined, and the theory largely developed, by John Maynard Smith. For further reading: J. Maynard Smith, *Evolution Now* (1982). M.R.

evolutionary humanism. A sort of secular RELIGION or religion surrogate founded upon the deeply held conviction that EVOLUTION is the fundamental modality of all change in the universe, so that all agencies that provoke change and all that retard it can be described as 'good' or 'bad' respectively. Sometimes evolutionary humanism is taken for the belief that the human moral sense is itself a product of evolutionary change as opposed to a faculty indwelling in man through the mediation of some supernatural agency. In none of these forms has evolutionary humanism (though its exponents have included T. H. Huxley and Sir Julian Huxley) found for itself a significant following from moralists or theologians. P.M.

evolutionary novelty, see NOVELTY, EVOLUTIONARY.

evolutionary psychology. The study of human psychological evolution, this term having ousted the briefly used coinage palaeopsychology. It was rooted in Victorian evolutionary speculations, and serious and sustained attention emerged only in the 1980s, coalescing from the 1970s revival of interest in the origins of language, the rise of SOCIOBIOLOGY, the expansion of ethological studies (see ETHOLOGY) of higher primate behaviour, and FEMINIST challenges to the male-centredness of traditional speculations. J. Jaynes's stimulating but idiosyncratic 1976 best-seller *The Origins of Consciousness in the Breakdown of the Bicameral Mind* had also helped reawaken academic interest. Given that it is a multidisciplinary field, a variety of approaches have been adopted, e.g. T. Wynn's broadly PIAGETIAN research on stone tools, A. Whiten and R. Byrne's comparative primatological explorations of the evolution of INTELLIGENCE (centring on the notion of deliberate deception), T. Ingold's pioneering MUTUALIST perspective, and K. MacDonald's wide-ranging synthesis of sociobiological and psychological perspectives. Topics studied include language and intelligence, tool use, GENDER roles, AGGRESSION, brain functioning and ALTRUISM. While remaining, necessarily, somewhat speculative and riven with controversy, conceptualization of such issues has improved enormously and many long-orthodox myths (e.g. regarding the evolution of gender roles and the initial functions of language) have fallen by the wayside. One underlying difficulty, however, is that the story's plot depends on how the present is viewed. Traditionally a 'rise' plot was unchallenged, but it might now be argued that the task is rather to diagnose the roots of humanity's disastrous flaws than those of its triumphant successes. Current writers rarely ascribe humanity's uniqueness to a single discrete factor such as bipedalism or language, as was once commonplace. For further reading: K. R. Gibson and T. Ingold (eds), *Tools, Language and Cognition in Human Evolution* (1993); S. Pinker, *How the Mind Works* (1997). G.D.R.

evolutionism. A doctrine especially associated with the names of Herbert Spencer (1820–1903) and Teilhard de Chardin (1881–1955) according to which evolution is the fundamental mode of change, both organic and inorganic, in the universe. Evolutionism is normally associated with a belief in the inevitability of progress. In the writings of Teilhard de Chardin this assumes an extravagant metaphysical form. P.M.

exchange. Relationships established between individuals in which goods and services are exchanged. NETWORKS of relationships are based on the notion of indebtedness and they are sustained by the debts not being fully discharged. If a debt between two people is paid off, the relationship is terminated. The theory of GIFT exchange was developed by Marcel Mauss, and his *Essai sur le Don* (1924) has become one of the central texts of *social* ANTHROPOLOGY. Mauss drew on Malinowski's work on the KULA of the Trobriand Islands and material collected by Boas relating to the POTLATCH of the Kwatiutl Indians. He understood gift exchange in terms of the social relations it established between people and the binding nature of the principle of reciprocity. Exchange was more than an economic transaction, and particularly in non-monetary societies it formed the basis for social solidarity.

Mauss's work exercised an important influence upon Lévi-Strauss. The theory of exchange became central to Lévi-Strauss's work (*The Elementary Structures of Kinship*, 1949), but in this case it was not founded on the exchange of gifts, rather the exchange of women through systems of marriage. Lévi-Strauss distinguished between complex (found in European-type societies) and elementary (found in non-European societies) exchange. He further divided the elementary system into generalized and restricted exchange. Exchange has continued to be an important concept for anthropologists. Attention has focused on the distinctions between gift and commodity exchange, and it has become clear that they are rarely absolute distinctions. The designation of goods and transformations in their status highlights the complex system of social classification. For further reading: J. W. Leach and E. Leach (eds), *The Kula: New Perspectives on Massim Exchange* (1983). A.G.

exchange control. Restriction on the right of a citizen of one country to make a payment to a person not resident in the country. The main purpose of exchange control is to limit the ability to convert home assets into foreign assets, though sometimes they are used to reduce the inflow of unwanted financial assets from abroad. The possibility of adverse movements in the EXCHANGE RATE may lead to holders of home assets converting them into assets denominated in a currency whose value is likely to be maintained or increase. Individuals or firms may wish to acquire foreign financial or physical assets, and hence need to obtain foreign currency with which to make the foreign INVESTMENT. In both these cases, the foreign exchange reserves of the home country are reduced (see BALANCE OF PAYMENTS) and downward pressure is put on the exchange rate. Exchange controls can be used to control the outflow of foreign exchange. With freely floating exchange rates, the demand for and supply of foreign exchange should be balanced, which implies that exchange controls are unnecessary. However, it has been argued that exchange controls can be used to force MULTINATIONAL COMPANIES to invest their profits within the country in which they were made. Similarly, exchange controls may be used to make overseas investment more expensive or difficult and, thus, provide a relative incentive for investment within the country. In October 1979, the UK abolished exchange controls. M.V.P.; J.P.

exchange energy. A stabilizing ENERGY ascribed in QUANTUM MECHANICS terms to ELECTRONS with the same SPIN in an ATOM or MOLECULE. In order not to violate the EXCLUSION PRINCIPLE the electrons must be present in different ORBITALS, and the energy can be thought of as arising from the indistinguishability of electrons with identical spin. The exchange energy is not predominant in chemical bondings (see BOND, CHEMICAL) but it has some influence on chemical reactivity, and there are important consequences in SPECTROSCOPY and for the magnetic properties of compounds. B.F.

exchange models. In SOCIOLOGY, MODELS, associated with George Homans and Peter Blau, that concentrate on elementary social processes in which human groups are seen as formed and held together by exchanges of rewards, satisfactions, esteem, and the creation of common sentiments. Whereas the STRUCTURAL-FUNCTIONAL THEORY deals with whole societies (*macrostructures*), exchange theory tends to concentrate on small groups (*microstructures*). D.B.

exchange particle, see under GLUON.

exchange rate. The British definition is the

foreign currency price of one unit of the domestic currency. The American definition is the domestic currency price of one unit of the foreign currency, i.e. both America and Britain quote the dollar price of sterling as the exchange rate. The exchange rate determines the domestic prices of a country's imports. It is important in determining the demand for a country's exports and its demand for imports. The current account of the BALANCE OF PAYMENTS depends on the exchange rate. A change in the exchange rate alters the foreign currency value of a domestic asset. Expectations of changes in the exchange rate will affect the flows of CAPITAL into and out of a country, i.e. the capital account of the balance of payments. A net surplus/deficit on the combined current and capital account implies an excess demand/supply for the domestic currency. This will put pressure on the exchange rate to rise/fall, unless the CENTRAL BANK acts to alleviate this pressure. The central bank can buy and sell foreign exchange and alter interest rates. From the BRETTON WOODS conference in 1944 to late 1971, nearly all countries had fixed exchange rates. Since 1973, many countries, including the UK, have adopted a policy of a managed float. This policy allows the exchange rate to be determined by the demand and supply for the domestic currency, but the government may intervene on occasions to influence the level and speed of adjustment of the exchange rate. Most member countries of the EUROPEAN UNION (EU) have followed a different policy in the European Monetary System, in which they have agreed to maintain the same exchange rates against each other, within certain bounds. These bounds can be changed, and the member countries have access to funds which can be used to defend the set exchange rate. All these policies are a reaction to the rapid and unstable movements in exchange rates that have occurred since the early 1970s. This instability in the movements of exchange rates has mainly been caused by increases in the international mobility of capital and the majority of foreign exchange transactions being for speculative purposes. However, in the long term, countries' exchange rates are likely to be determined by their relative performance in foreign trade. In the short and medium term, the international mobility of capital poses serious problems for ECONOMIC DEVELOPMENT and ECONOMIC GROWTH. It may be necessary to maintain very high interest rates to induce internationally mobile capital to remain in a country whose exchange rate is expected to fall, because of high rates of domestic INFLATION and a poor foreign trade performance (see DEVALUATION; DEBT CRISIS). For further reading: R. E. Caves and R. W. Jones, *World Trade and Payments* (1985). J.P.

Exchange Rate Mechanism (ERM). The precursor to EMU (see SINGLE CURRENCY) which was designed to stabilize EXCHANGE RATES among European Community – renamed EUROPEAN UNION (EU) – members. During the 1980s the ERM achieved a degree of success in stabilizing the relationships among the key European countries, notably that of France and Germany. The ERM was a voluntary scheme and all members held a portion of their reserves in the European Currency Unit (ECU) which was also used to measure the currencies of ERM members on a common basis. Currencies inside the ERM fluctuated within a band 2.25 per cent above or below the central value. The situation inside the ERM remained relatively smooth until Britain was taken into the ERM by the then Chancellor of the Exchequer, John Major, in 1990. This changed the balance within the ERM and it quickly became clear that Britain had entered the ERM at an unrealistically high central rate. Speculators began a prolonged assault on the pound which reached its peak in September 1992, when unprecedented pressure on the foreign exchanges caused the UK to drop out, effectively devaluing its currency by 17 per cent (see DEVALUATION). Two other weaker currencies, the Spanish pesata and the Italian lira, were forced out with the pound. A second wave of speculation against the French franc, in August 1993, almost destroyed the system, which was reconstituted with 12.5 per cent fluctuation bands. The unhappy history of the ERM in the period 1990–93 underlined the need to make the euro rules as tough as possible (see CONVERGENCE CRITERIA). For further reading: P. Stephens, *Politics and the Pound* (1996).
A.BR.

excited states (in PHYSICS), see under ENERGY LEVEL.

exclave, see under ENCLAVE AND EXCLAVE.

excluded middle, law of the, see under INTUITIONISM.

exclusion principle. A constraint on the assignment of quantum states to some elementary PARTICLES (fermions: see QUANTUM STATISTICS), according to which no two particles of the same kind can occupy identical states. Formulated by Pauli in 1924 to explain the anomalous Zeeman effect in SPECTROSCOPY, the principle can be expressed alternatively as the requirement that many-particle states be anti-symmetric under exchange of particle labels. Applied to the electronic structure of ATOMS, the exclusion principle stipulates that no two ELECTRONS may share all four quantum numbers. The principle helps to explain the complex electronic structures of atoms, with electrons occupying higher orbitals where lower-energy orbitals are full. Otherwise, every electron would be expected to enter the same state, of lowest energy. By explaining electronic structure, the exclusion principle helps to account for atomic line spectra (see SPECTROSCOPY); chemical periodicity; VALENCE and FERROMAGNETISM in crystals. Even at the time he formulated it, Pauli was worried about the theoretical foundation of the principle: it appears to be an *ad hoc* constraint on possible states. Although it has a natural expression in quantum statistics, it is debatable whether this constitutes an explanation. R.F.H.

exclusive economic zones, see under LAW OF THE SEA.

existential psychiatry. A psychiatric movement which took inspiration from existential philosophy (see EXISTENTIALISM). The Swiss psychiatrist L. Binswanger's existential analysis (*Daseinsanalyse*) represented a synthesis of psychoanalytical, phenomenological (see PHENOMENOLOGY) and existential concepts applied to his new clinical approach: a reconstruction of the inner world of experience of his patients, a construction of an 'authentic science of persons' based on Heidegger's work on the structure of human existence. He was critical of some mechanical aspects of Freud's descriptions of the human mind (see FREUDIAN) and favoured the technique of the 'encounter' rather than that of TRANSFERENCE. The Scottish psychiatrist R. D. Laing (see ANTI-PSYCHIATRY) also refused to view the patient as a kind of mechanism, and emphasized the existential concept of 'ontological insecurity' (see ONTOLOGY) of the human state, which he described through the pathological disorders of the 'divided self'. The American psychoanalyst Rollo May's endeavour is to establish a working science of man by uniting science and ontology, and thereby to go beyond the traditional distinction between subject and object: man is understood as experiencing the world in a uniquely human way. In this perspective, May denounces the dehumanizing tendencies in traditional psychotherapeutic approaches, and in the industrial system as a whole. The Viennese psychiatrist Viktor E. Frankl adds a stress on meaning to his existential clinical approach which he calls 'logotherapy'. The American psychiatrist and psychoanalyst Tomasz Szasz gives a further development to the theoretical and clinical framework of the existential approach, by connecting it both to his own socio-historical insights, and to Goffman's ROLE theories. For further reading: R. D. Laing, *The Divided Self* (1960). B.BE.

existential psychology. A SCHOOL OF PSYCHOLOGY which emphasizes that each individual is constantly making choices, great and small, which cumulatively determine the kind of person he becomes (see EXISTENTIALISM). Represented by Rollo May, Abraham Maslow (associated also with HUMANISTIC PSYCHOLOGY) and Carl Rogers, it is concerned with the individual's attempts to discover a satisfying sense of his personal identity and to give meaning to his life (see also EXISTENTIAL PSYCHIATRY). For further reading: R. May, *Love and Will* (1970). I.M.L.H.

existentialism. A body of philosophical doctrine that dramatically emphasizes the contrast between human existence and the kind of existence possessed by natural objects. Men, endowed with will and CONSCIOUSNESS, find themselves in an alien world of objects which have neither (see DETERMINISM; FREE WILL). Existentialism was inaugurated by the Danish philosopher Søren Kierkegaard (1813–55) in a violent reaction against the all-encompassing absolute IDEALISM of Hegel. For Hegel, God is the impersonal absolute; finite human personalities are insubstantial fragments of this engulfing spiritual unity, and everything that happens, including human actions, can be rationally explained as a necessary element in the total scheme of things. Seminal works by Kierkegaard include *Either/Or* and *Fear and Trembling*, both published in 1843. Kierkegaard insisted on the utter distinctness of God and man and on the inexplicability (or 'absurdity') of the relations between them, and of their actions. As developed in this century by Heidegger and Sartre, and by contrast with Christian existentialism, existentialism is atheistic (see ATHEISM) and draws on the PHENOMENOLOGY of Husserl as a method for investigating the peculiarities of the human situation. Man, these later existentialists contend, is a self-creating being who is not initially endowed with a character and goals but must choose them by acts of pure decision, existential 'leaps' analogous to that seen by Kierkegaard in the reason-transcending decision to believe in God. For Heidegger, man is a temporal being, conscious, through his will, of a future whose only certainty is his own death. To live authentically is to live in the light of this bleak and unrationalizable fact, in full awareness of *le* néant (see NOTHINGNESS), both as one's own ultimate destiny and as one's own nature, until one has chosen a character for oneself (see AUTHENTICITY). Sartre's particular interest is in what he sees as the paradoxical relations between one human existence and another. For further reading: W. Barrett, *Irrational Man* (1961). A.Q.

existentialist theology. A movement in 20th-century theology exemplified in the work of Rudolf Bultmann and other Protestant theologians. EXISTENTIALISM has rightly been characterized as 'a reaction of the PHILOSOPHY of man against the excesses of the philosophy of ideas and the philosophy of things' (Emmanuel Mounier), a restoration of that which IDEALISM and REALISM had neglected – the living experience of the individual subject. It originated in the writings of the 19th-century Christian philosopher Søren Kierkegaard (1813–1855), especially *Philosophical Fragments* and *The Concept of Dread*, both published in 1844. Although existentialist theology is often assumed to be inherently atheistic, as Jean-Paul Sartre argued, its proponents have included many religious philosophers (see ATHEISM). Existentialist theology as such, anticipated by CRISIS THEOLOGY in the 1920s, came about through Bultmann's appropriation of ideas from the work of Martin Heidegger, which he employed in his attempt to demythologize the New Testament. Influential from the 1940s to the 1960s, it was ultimately displaced by socio-political criticism and the rise of CONTEXTUAL THEOLOGIES. For further reading: J. Macquarrie, *An Existentialist Theology: A Comparison of Heidegger and Bultmann* (1973). C.C.

exobiology. The branch of BIOLOGY that deals with the search for extraterrestrial life (see PANSPERMIA; SEARCH FOR EXTRATERRESTRIAL INTELLIGENCE). P.N.

exocrine glands, see under ENDOCRINOLOGY.

exogamy. Term developed by McLennan (*Primitive Marriage*, 1865) to describe a set of rules relating to MARRIAGE. They specify out-marriage. Exogamy regulates marriage and is distinct from INCEST prohibitions, regulations concerning sex. Exogamy prohibits marriage within a group; an individual must marry out. Corporate groups, for example DESCENT groups, are usually exogamous, and rules relating to marriage establish links or alliances between different groups. The role of exogamy and the establishment of marriage alliances have been central to Lévi-Strauss's work on kinship (*The Elementary Structures of Kinship*, 1949). In societies without descent groups, for example bilateral societies (see BILATERAL/COGNATIC DESCENT), rules of exogamy are EGO-focused: an individual is prohibited from marrying within a certain range of kin. (See ENDOGAMY; KINSHIP.) For further reading: J. Goody, *The Development of the Family and Marriage in Europe* (1983). A.G.

exon, see under SPLIT GENE.

exotic species. SPECIES which are not native (indigenous) to a particular HABITAT but instead have been deliberately or accidentally introduced. For centuries, domesticated plants and animals have been carried by settlers to new habitats, primarily to provide food.

Lacking natural enemies (predators or pathogens), exotics are often able to proliferate rapidly and may crowd out native species in the process. Deliberate introductions include the mongoose to the Caribbean to control rats. A recent dramatic example of an accidental introduction is the zebra mussel, carried to North America from Eurasia in ballast water and now clogging water intake pipes in the Great Lakes and elsewhere.

The pace of introduction of exotic species has increased with long-distance travel. The brown tree snake, brought to previously snake-free Guam from the Solomon Islands shortly after World War II, has decimated the populations of both native and non-native birds. W.G.R.

exotoxins, see under BACTERIOLOGY.

expansion of the universe. A theory formulated by Hubble in 1923. It is observed that the light from faint (and therefore presumably distant) GALAXIES is reddened. This RED SHIFT is interpreted as a DOPPLER EFFECT, so that the galaxies are believed to be receding from us, and from each other, like spots on the surface of a balloon as it is blown up; the farther the galaxy, the greater is its speed of recession. This is measured by *Hubble's constant*, defined as the ratio *distance of galaxy* ÷ *speed of recession*; its value is about 10 thousand million years. The expansion of the universe is a basic phenomenon which any theory of COSMOLOGY (e.g. the BIG BANG THEORY or the STEADY-STATE HYPOTHESIS) must explain. Galaxies 10 thousand million light-years away are receding from us at the speed of light. More distant objects are receding faster than this so that their light can never reach us. Thus the *observable* universe accessible to ASTRONOMY seems to be finite in extent. See also COSMIC BACKGROUND RADIATION. M.V.B.

expected utility theory. A theory of how decisions that are subject to RISK are or should be made. The decision-maker is *assumed* to consider each course of action and weight the utility (see UTILITY THEORY) of each possible outcome by the associated probability. The sum of the weighted utility values gives the expected utility of the course of action. After an exhaustive consideration of all possible courses of action, that action giving the highest expected utility is chosen. This theory has been considered and widely used in ECONOMICS, ENGINEERING, MANAGEMENT STUDIES, PSYCHOLOGY and PHILOSOPHY. However, the evidence of empirical tests systematically contradicts the predictions of the theory. Unfortunately, no alternative model of decision-making subject to risk has yet been offered which is both theoretically and empirically satisfactory. For further reading: J. Hey, *Uncertainty in Economics* (1979). J.P.

experiment. The manipulation of natural phenomena to answer practical or theoretical questions. In the philosophy of science, experiment has often been viewed as subordinate to theory, and an unproblematic source of objectivity in science (see SCIENCE, PHILOSOPHY OF). However, in detailed studies of past and present experimental practice, historians and sociologists of science (see SCIENCE, SOCIOLOGY OF) have argued that it is an activity with aims and assumptions different to those of theorizing. The experimenter seeks to construct a device that will reliably display a given (and perhaps novel) kind of behaviour. Since new experiments often involve new technology that is itself only partially understood, supposedly unequivocal experimental results may legitimately be subject to disagreement: consensus is reached only as the result of social processes. Some philosophers have responded by constructing detailed models of rational reasoning under experimental uncertainty. For further reading: H. M. Collins and T. Pinch, *The Golem: What Everyone Should Know about Science* (1993). R.F.H.

experimental archaeology. The study of past TECHNOLOGY and behaviour through experimental reconstruction and controlled replication. The experiments produce hypotheses that can be tested against archaeological data. They can range from the simple reproduction of all kinds of ancient tools (to learn about their processes of manufacture, use and discard) to the construction of buildings or whole villages, and long-term experiments involving ancient subsistence practices. For further reading: J. M. Coles, *Experimental Archaeology* (1979). P.G.B.

experimental group, see under CONTROL GROUP.

experimental music. Used mostly in connection with a type of music which became prominent in America in the 1950s and which broke with musical traditions in a more fundamental way than the contemporary European development of AVANT-GARDE MUSIC. In this music John Cage and others sought to weaken the composer-dominated hierarchy of classical music and give more freedom to the performer, the audience and in a way to sound itself (see ALEATORY; INDETERMINACY; MOBILE FORM; TIME NOTATION). For further reading: M. Nyman, *Experimental Music: Cage and Beyond* (1974). B.CO.

experimental psychology. The branch of PSYCHOLOGY that is based on the use of experimental methods. The psychologist's fundamental interest lies in the description, classification, prediction and EXPLANATION of the behaviour of living organisms. He gains access to this behaviour by a variety of techniques. Sometimes he makes his observations in the 'natural' setting, as when the animal psychologist studies the wild animal in its natural ENVIRONMENT (see ETHOLOGY) and the industrial psychologist observes 'man at work' on the factory floor (see INDUSTRIAL PSYCHOLOGY). Increasingly, however, psychological phenomena (e.g. the effect of sleep deprivation on vigilance) have been brought under scrutiny in carefully controlled experimental situations where, ideally, one is able to identify all the significant factors and uncover correlational and cause-effect relationships. The experimental approach to psychological problems was first adopted principally to investigate 'sensory' phenomena (e.g. PERCEPTION), and a whole range of elegant methods was invented to tackle such questions as just how sensitive the human being is to changes in level of sound, light and pressure. As a result a number of principles were formulated that expressed relationships – universal under certain limited conditions – between measurable levels of stimulation and of human sensation. The use of experimental methods is continually expanding, and the 'higher mental processes' listed under COGNITIVE PSYCHOLOGY have come increasingly under experimental scrutiny.

The experimental psychologist's ideal, like that of any other experimental investigator, is to control all the factors that might affect the phenomenon under study. Usually, one or a small number of factors (the *independent variables*) is systematically varied, and aspects (the *dependent variables*) of the subject's performance in response to these variables are tabulated. These dependent variables may be relatively simple and observable responses such as a verbal reply to a question, or they may be much more complex and covert, as with many physiological responses (e.g. changes in brain-waves) to different conditions of stimulation. The ideal of complete control is seldom if ever achieved, however, because of the numerous extraneous and uncontrolled factors – the temperature of the room, time of day, the subject's idea of the experiment, etc. – that may affect the dependent variable; a familiar device for overcoming this problem is the use of a CONTROL GROUP. To assess the significance of the results of any test, the experimental psychologist also needs a sound understanding of STATISTICS. Although the experimental approach has its critics, there seems little doubt that it will continue to play an increasingly vital role in psychological enquiry. For further reading: P. Harris, *Designing and Reporting Experiments* (1986). D.J.W.

Experimentele Groep, see under COBRA.

expert system. An ARTIFICIAL INTELLIGENCE computer program for performing tasks requiring expertise but no great insight or originality. The focus of much commercial interest, expert systems are particularly suited to problems where many possibilities must be considered at once. Some of the domains handled by expert systems include: analysing oil drilling information, offering financial planning advice, and assisting in medical diagnosis. It is a prime example of an *intelligent knowledge-based system* (IKBS).

Most expert systems do not deal with problems that can be reduced to one ALGORITHM, but rather ones where different bodies of information need to be applied in a flexible way. The major difficulty in constructing an expert system is *eliciting* knowledge from a human expert and recording it in a knowledge base in a form suitable for use by the computer. The expert's knowledge is rarely fully articulated, and it is not yet known how knowledge is best represented to a computer. The knowledge base often consists of rules of the form 'If [conditions] then [do, or conclude something]'. The expert system works as a *production system* matching information it has against the conditions of these rules, which causes the system to request or infer further information which may match the conditions of further rules. HEURISTIC rules may determine which rules are most likely to prove helpful in certain circumstances. (See also PROBLEM-SOLVING.) R.S.C.

explanation. The process or end-product of explaining something. The word and its meaning are, of course, perfectly familiar; less so, perhaps, are some related terms and the varieties of explanation that have been distinguished in philosophical analyses of scientific explanations. The thing to be explained is often called the *explanandum* or *conclusion*, henceforth called *C*. *C* may be a fact about some particular event, e.g. 'This apple fell from the tree', or a generalization or law, e.g. 'Unsupported apples fall'. When *C* is explained by means of a set of statements, they are said to constitute the *explanans* or the *premises* of the explanation. Some of the statements in the explanans may themselves express laws, generalizations or regularities, e.g. 'All bodies attract one another', and the SET of such statements will henceforth be called *L*. Other statements in the explanans, e.g. 'A wind was blowing', 'The branch was rotten', may refer to particular events or states of affairs. These are said to specify *initial conditions*, and the set of such statements will henceforth be called *I*. *I* or *L* may, in special cases, be empty, i.e. there may be no such statements. The types of explanation that can be distinguished include the following; they are illustrated with some oversimplified examples.

(1) *Deductive explanations*. In these the truth of the conclusion *C* follows logically, or deductively, from *I* and *L* together, e.g. 'The apple fell because (*I*) it was unsupported and (*L*) unsupported objects fall'. A major dispute in PHILOSOPHY concerns whether deductive (sometimes called deductive nomological) explanations are the only truly adequate scientific explanations, and whether all other kinds are really disguised versions of this kind.

(2) *Probabilistic* or *statistical explanations*. In these, the truth of the conclusion cannot be inferred logically from *I* and *L*: at most one can infer that it is more probable that *C* is true than that it is false, e.g. 'Tom has cancer because (*I*) Tom smokes, and (*L*) 90 per cent of those who smoke get cancer'. Here *L* and *I* together only make Tom's having cancer *highly probable*; it does not follow logically from them that he will have cancer. Many explanations in PSYCHOLOGY and in SOCIAL SCIENCES have this structure.

(3) *Causal explanations*. Here *C* describes some event, and the statements in *I* describe *causes* of the event, e.g. 'The butter melted because (*I*) the temperature rose'. But what does it mean to say that one thing causes another? One answer is that there is some law (e.g. of PHYSICS, CHEMISTRY or other branches of science) which provides a basis for inferring that, if the first thing occurs or had occurred, the second will or would have. On this analysis, causal explanations are simply a special case of deductive explanations, possibly with the relevant laws (*L*) left out, either because they are too well known, or else because it is not yet known what they are.

(4) *Functional explanations*. These – which some prefer to regard as descriptions – answer questions of the form 'What is such-and-such for?' They should not be treated as an explanation of why the such-and-such exists. Thus to say that animals have stomachs because the stomach plays a certain role in keeping the animal alive and well does not explain how it came about that animals have stomachs, unless the explanation is enlarged to include some additional hypotheses about an evolutionary mechanism (see EVOLUTION) which ensures that organisms evolve what they need. Functional explanations are often confused with *purposive explanations*.

(5) *Purposive explanations*. These answer questions about why an agent (which may be a person, an animal or a corporate body such as a committee) performed some action or took some decision, by describing

the agent's intention, motive, purpose, aims, likes, fears, etc., and relating them to what the agent thought would be the consequences of the various alternatives open, e.g. 'He stole the money because he wanted to buy food'. Purposive explanations are common in everyday life and law courts, but also in some of the social sciences and psychology, though some scientists regard them as unscientific, e.g. because the explanations refer to mental events or states.

(6) *Teleological explanations*. This is simply a blanket term used to cover both functional and purposive explanations since these are often not clearly distinguishable.

(7) *Genetic explanations*. These consist of more-or-less lengthy accounts of a sequence of events leading up to the occurrence or existence of the fact to be explained. They are common in HISTORY, GEOLOGY, BIOLOGY and novels. The account generally mentions only a series of particular facts, so that *I* (the initial conditions) may be a large set of statements, whereas *L* may be empty, if no laws are explicitly mentioned. Often such an explanation simply amounts to a sequence of causal and purposive explanations. It is sometimes argued that a genetic explanation is always an abbreviated and sketchy version of a sequence of deductive or probabilistic explanations, where the laws are not stated explicitly because they are sufficiently well known to be taken for granted. A.S.

exploitation. The payment to the owner of a FACTOR OF PRODUCTION of a sum less than the value of its product. In NEO-CLASSICAL ECONOMIC THEORY, exploitation occurs if the owner of a factor of production is paid less than the value of the marginal product of the factor (see MARGINAL PRODUCTIVITY THEORY OF WAGES). The marginal product of a factor is the extra output produced by using one more unit of the factor, while keeping the use of all other factors constant (see MARGINAL ANALYSIS). The value of the marginal product is the price of output multiplied by the marginal product. Only in PERFECT COMPETITION will a factor be paid the value of its marginal product. If it is assumed that an employer attempts to maximize profits, it can be shown that exploitation occurs if the employer has the market power to influence the price of the factor or product, through variation in the quantity of the factor demanded or output supplied. In MARXIST economics, labour is assumed to be the only source of value, as land and other natural resources are taken as free gifts and CAPITAL is the product of past labour. Ownership of capital, land and natural resources is regarded as appropriation of the product of past labour and free gifts. This appropriation allows the owners of these factors, i.e. the CAPITALISTS and resource owners, to receive part of the output produced by labour. Thus, labour is exploited because their work is the only source of value and they do not receive the full value of their production (see VALUE, THEORY OF and LABOUR THEORY OF VALUE). For further reading: J. Craven, *Introduction to Economics* (1984). J.P.

exploitation movie. Initially a derogatory term applied to films whose purpose was to titillate through sex, violence or nudity, in particular the cheap programme-fillers turned out by independent producers during the 1950s when the major Hollywood studios, in an attempt to combat the threat of television, elected to devote their resources to long, costly wide-screen epics. Aimed primarily at teenage audiences and the drive-in cinema market, exploitation movies often revealed an unusual vitality in their devotion to the principle of fast-moving action, while the work of a talented director like Roger Corman demonstrated that such films could also incorporate skill and intelligence. As an independent producer willing to take risks because of the relatively low costs involved, Corman has effectively turned the exploitation movie into a forcing ground for new talent. Among the now noted film-makers who received their first chance to direct in exploitation movies produced by Corman are Francis Ford Coppola, Martin Scorsese, Peter Bogdanovich, John Milius and Jonathan Kaplan. T.C.C.M.

explosive nucleosynthesis, see under NUCLEOSYNTHESIS.

exponential smoothing. In management, an adaptive method of FORECASTING that is ideally suited to computer operation. The basis of the method is that in obtaining a forecast more weight is given to the most recent information. The weights (see INDEX

NUMBER) which are assigned die away exponentially; hence the name by which the method is usually known. H.TH.

exponential time. An ALGORITHM will apply to a collection of similar problems of differing size, *N*, e.g. the 'salesman problem', where a salesman has to visit *N* towns, the problem being to find the shortest route. Of course, the larger *N* is the longer the algorithm takes. An algorithm takes exponential time if the time taken increases as an exponential function of *N*. This is to be contrasted with polynomial time, where the time taken only increases as a power of *N* (which, at least for large values of *N*, is much quicker). The only known algorithms for the salesman problem are all exponential (see COMPLEXITY THEORY). J.M.

Expressionism. Widely applicable term used since 1910 of all the arts, in three main senses:

(1) A quality of expressive emphasis or distortion, to be found in works of any period, country or medium, e.g. in Dostoevsky's novels, Strindberg's plays and El Greco's or van Gogh's paintings.

(2) Virtually the whole modern movement in the arts in Germany and Austro-Hungary between 1910 and about 1924, subsuming all local manifestations of Fauvism (see FAUVES), CUBISM and FUTURISM, and constituting the origins of DADA and NEUE SACHLICHKEIT. Though subsequently extended backwards to cover, e.g., the paintings of the Norwegian Edvard Munch or the early work of the BRÜCKE, the formula 'Expressionism' entered Germany from France in 1910 and thereafter was used to describe the German movements first in art, then in literature, the theatre (from 1918), music, architecture and the cinema. Its hallmarks accordingly were theirs: distortion, fragmentation and the communication of violent or overstressed emotion.

With *Der* STURM and *Die Aktion* as its organs, it embraced (a) in painting, the Brücke and the Blaue Reiter; (b) in literature, the poetry of Georg Heym, Georg Trakl and Franz Werfel, and the prose of Alfred Döblin and Franz Kafka; (c) in the theatre, the plays of Georg Kaiser and Ernst Toller; (d) in music, the early works of Arnold Schönberg and Alban Berg; (e) in ARCHITECTURE, Erich Mendelsohn's Einstein Tower and the UTOPIAN projects of Bruno Taut; (f) in the cinema, Robert Wiene's *The Cabinet of Dr Caligari* (1920).

German Expressionism's predominantly PACIFIST and SOCIALIST political aims, crystallizing in the wartime movement of ACTIVISM, were frustrated by such post-war developments as the suppression of the SPARTACISTS and the Munich SOVIET; and it was superseded by the more pragmatic NEUE SACHLICHKEIT – on which, as on the BAUHAUS, it left a distinctive mark. Though NAZISM suppressed all three movements as degenerate (see DEGENERACY), it was again influential in the revival of the arts in Germany after 1945.

(3) 20th-century works of art in other countries or continents which reflect the influence of German Expressionism or show similar characteristics, e.g. the Flemish Expressionism foreshadowed by Laethem-Saint-Martin, certain works of the ÉCOLE DE PARIS, and the ABSTRACT EXPRESSIONISM of such New York artists as Pollock and de Kooning in the 1950s. For further reading: J. Willett, *Expressionism* (1971). J.W.

expressive form, fallacy of. A prescriptive term, adopted by the critic R. P. Blackmur from Yvor Winters (*The Function of Criticism*, 1957), for the 'dogma that once material becomes words it is its own best form'. Winters called this the 'heresy of expressive form'. He was referring to the belief, in his view mistaken, that disintegration (of belief, of civilization) could most effectively be expressed in a chaotic form. He saw Joyce's *Ulysses* as 'disintegrated': it should have been 'disciplined'. But he was answered by critics who pointed out that *Ulysses*, or the poetry of T. S. Eliot, was not really 'chaotic': it only *looked* as though it were. Winters was attacking, essentially, Coleridge's idea of organic form. Blackmur used the notion to try – unsuccessfully – to dispose of the poetry of D. H. Lawrence and Carl Sandburg, but was not dedicated to it as a theory. For further reading: S. E. Hyman, *The Armed Vision* (1947). M.S.-S.

extended family, see under NUCLEAR FAMILY.

extended standard theory. The name given to a MODEL of GENERATIVE GRAMMAR which developed in the 1970s out of that expounded by Noam Chomsky (see CHOMSKYAN) in his *Aspects of the Theory of Syntax* (1965), which was known as the standard theory. The 'extension' was primarily due to the way in which additional factors (other than the traditional notion of DEEP STRUCTURE) were introduced to account for the way in which a sentence's meaning was to be analysed. Further developments of the approach in the mid-1970s became known as the *revised extended standard theory*. For further reading: A. Radford, *Transformational Syntax* (1981). D.C.

extensionality *and* **intensionality.** Properties of compound PROPOSITIONS, defined by the relation between the compounds as wholes and the elementary propositions of which they are composed. A compound is *extensional* if its TRUTH or falsity is unequivocally determined by the truth or falsity of its components; it is *intensional* if it is not. Thus 'it is cold and it is wet' is extensional since it is true if both components are true and false in the other three possible cases. 'I believe that it is Thursday' is, however, intensional since the whole belief-statement can be true or false whether it is Thursday or not. The two leading kinds of intensional compound are (1) those in which the main verb refers to a 'propositional attitude' such as belief, knowledge, hope, fear, etc., and (2) modal statements of the form 'It is necessary that *p*' or 'It is possible that *p*'. Standard modern LOGIC is resolutely extensional and uses an extensional notion of material implication which differs in MEANING from the intensional connection asserted in the conditional statements of ordinary language. LOGICAL POSITIVISTS and LOGICAL EMPIRICISTS have attempted to find ANALYSES in extensional terms of apparently intensional statements about propositional attitudes or involving modal concepts. Thus '*A* believes that *p*' is analysed into 'There is some sentence "s" which means the same as "p" to which *A* is disposed to assent'. 'It is possible that it is raining' becomes 'The sentence "it is raining" is contingent' (see CONTINGENCY). A.Q.

externalities. In ECONOMICS, the effects of consumers' or producers' actions on others which do not occur through the operation of an economic market. External economies are those that benefit other consumers or producers, e.g. the construction of a beautiful house or an invention. External diseconomies are harmful to other consumers or producers, e.g. pollution and congestion. It is often argued that there is insufficient incentive for the generation of external economies and insufficient discouragement of external diseconomies. If the benefits and costs can be roughly measured, it is usually suggested that external economies should be subsidized and external diseconomies taxed. If the externalities are unspecified and unquantified, care should be taken over calls for subsidization and TAXATION. Externalities are an important, but not the only, reason why the prices of goods, services and inputs differ from the social benefits and costs of their consumption and use (see COST BENEFIT ANALYSIS). J.P.

extinction, see under REINFORCEMENT.

extinction spasm. While extinction is thought to be ongoing at relatively low rates, the relatively abrupt disappearance of the dinosaurs at the end of the Pleistocene era, and the current loss of numerous species, are termed extinction spasms. In past geological eras (see GEOLOGY; PALAEONTOLOGY) such spasms are believed to have been caused by large-scale catastrophic events (e.g. meteor collisions with the earth, volcanic eruptions) causing global climate changes. In contrast, the current spasm is being caused by human activities. W.G.R.

extra-sensory perception, see ESP.

extraterrestrial intelligence, search for, see SEARCH FOR EXTRATERRESTRIAL INTELLIGENCE.

extraterrestrial radio waves, see under INVISIBLE ASTRONOMY.

extroversion. A term current in PSYCHOLOGY that was used by Jung (see JUNGIAN) to denote a process whereby a person who has experienced pain or conflict through being sensitive to his own feelings invests his attention and concern in others; his rapidity ('Hail, fellow, well met') in establishing interpersonal relations tends to be matched by the superficiality of such relations. This process was later reified (see REIFICATION) and generalized to refer to a PERSONALITY TYPE, the *extrovert*, much of whose life seemed to be characterized by these processes and behaviours. Although this usage makes the extrovert and the introvert seem to stand for opposed personality types, the oft-drawn contrast between extroversion and INTROVERSION is entirely superficial, their underlying causes and mechanisms being divergent but in no sense opposites, and frequently united in one personality. T.Z.C.

Exxon Valdez. This 'supertanker', loaded with approximately 1.2 million barrels of crude oil, ran aground in Prince William Sound, Alaska, in March 1989. The oil, from the north slope fields of northern Alaska, had been transported via the Alaska pipeline to transfer to a tanker at the port of Valdez. Approximately 0.25 million barrels (11 million US gallons) entered the Sound's pristine and ecologically rich marine environment before the spill was controlled by transferring the rest of the cargo to another tanker. Spilled oil travelled hundreds of miles to the south in the Gulf of Alaska, contaminating the shoreline and coastal waters and causing extensive damage to the biota. Over $2.5 billion has been spent on the ensuing clean-up, and many millions more on litigation, fines and indemnification of injured parties. The environmental impact of the spill continues to be studied, and clean-up techniques debated.

Perhaps the first tanker spill to attract wide attention was that from the Torrey Canyon, off the west coast of England in 1967, when about 119,000 gallons were lost.

Spills can also result from accidents associated with offshore oil exploration and extraction. Oil pollution of the land can also occur from exploration and drilling mishaps; but perhaps the most troubling and widespread source is leakage from corroded underground storage tanks. In these cases it is gasoline (petrol) rather than unrefined crude oil which enters the terrestrial environment. For further reading: D. Botkin and E. Keller, *Environmental Science* (1995). W.G.R.

F

Fabianism. An approach to the problems of implementing SOCIALIST ideas developed by the Fabian Society (established in London in 1884). Its members put their hopes in the 'permeation' of the existing INSTITUTIONS and the 'inevitability of gradualness' – hence the name, taken from the Roman general Fabius Cunctator, who won his campaigns by avoiding pitched battles and instead wearing the enemy down. Fabian ideas were eclectic rather than synthetic. They concentrated on practical detailed reforms ('gas and water socialism') and shunned grandiose theoretical speculations. They rejected the doctrine of economic LAISSEZ FAIRE and stressed the need for state action to ensure greater equality (see EGALITARIANISM) and the elimination of POVERTY. By accepting a constitutional approach, they helped to make socialist ideas respectable in Britain. Prominent members, such as Sydney and Beatrice Webb, H. G. Wells, George Bernard Shaw and Graham Wallas, are remembered for their individual achievements, rather than for their activities in the Fabian Society. Its direct influence was not very great (its membership was 640 in 1893 and under 3,000 in 1914), but it established a mode of approach to social questions, based on socialist ideas and a study of social problems, which has had a lasting impact on politics in Great Britain. For further reading: B. Pimlott (ed.), *Fabian Essays in Social Thought* (1984). L.L.

fabula. *Fabula* (story) was distinguished from *sjuzhet* (plot, telling technique, narrative style, authorial intention) in the work of the Russian FORMALISTS. Any theory of narrative requires that a distinction be made between the mere narrative, the story, and the way that the narrative or story is told. 'Yes – oh dear yes – the novel tells a story,' said E. M. Forster, pointing up precisely this difference. Various substitute terms for this pair of terms are to be found through STRUCTURALIST theory, but the distinction remains the same. The formalist category of LITERARINESS covers or includes the interrelation of these two aspects in any literary work. For further reading: J. Culler, *The Pursuit of Signs* (1981). R.PO.

factor analysis. Charles Spearman (1904) founded this subject in a study of the examination scores of 33 children in six subjects. He noted that those who did well in one subject tended to do well in others (he calculated the correlations). He noted that one could attach a number to each child (which might be called 'ability' or 'intelligence'), and a number to each subject (which might be called 'difficulty'), and that these numbers (together with a little random fluctuation) accounted for the observed scores.

A general technique developed using fancy MATRIX methods, which computers have now tamed, whereby the scores of a series of people in a number of tests can be related to certain underlying numbers (the 'factors'). Their interpretation is open to discussion. N.A.R.

factors of production. Those inputs used in production, e.g. different types of labour, CAPITAL, land, energy and raw materials. J.P.

factory farming. Systems of livestock production in which farm animals are kept throughout the greater part of their lives indoors under conditions in which movement is severely restricted. Pigs, laying hens, chickens for meat production ('broilers') and calves for veal production are the animals most commonly kept under this type of intensive production. The systems are closely standardized, particularly for pigs and poultry, making possible large-scale production, with a high density of animals per unit area. Many people believe, however, that such systems are unacceptable on humane grounds. K.E.H.

faculty psychology. The attempt to list classes of things performed by the mind, e.g. remembering, willing. Although descriptively useful, such classifications have sometimes led to the incorrect assumption that to each faculty there must correspond one distinct mental operation. The resulting confusion is well illustrated by PHRENOLOGY. I.M.L.H.

Falange. Spanish FASCIST party founded in 1933 by José Antonio Primo de Rivera, son of the former Spanish dictator, to capture the Spanish WORKING CLASS for an authoritarian (see AUTHORITARIANISM), socially radical NATIONALISM, and to overcome individualism and SOCIALISM as forces divisive of the nation. The Falange's failure to capture the working class confined its main strength to university students, though other RIGHT-wing forces were alarmed into supporting it by the victory of the POPULAR FRONT in the elections of February 1936. In 1937 the Spanish military leader, General Franco, took over the Falange, disciplined its leadership, and established his brother-in-law, Ramon Serrano Suner, at its head. It was to remain firmly under Franco's control thereafter, its social RADICALISM a matter solely of rhetoric. For further reading: H. Thomas, *The Spanish Civil War* (1977). D.C.W.

Falklands War. The Falklands (Malvinas) are a small group of islands off the south-east coast of Argentina with an economy devoted almost exclusively to sheep farming, SOVEREIGNTY over which is disputed by Argentina and Great Britain. British settlers have been in continuous occupation since 1833, but the islands are named in a series of earlier treaties between England and Spain, involving maritime access to the area, which leave the issue unresolved in international law (see PUBLIC INTERNATIONAL LAW). In 1964, Argentina formally reasserted its claim to the islands before the United Nations (UN), and the following year the General Assembly adopted a resolution inviting Britain and Argentina to enter into negotiations. Britain has consistently refused to discuss the issue of sovereignty, maintaining that the wishes of the islanders (who overwhelmingly want to remain under British jurisdiction) were paramount. Negotiations from 1968 to 1977 concentrated on the possibility of securing Argentine economic co-operation in the islands, and in 1972 Argentina began a weekly air service for essential supplies. In 1980, a British government initiative consulting the islanders about their future resulted in the unilateral announcement of a 25-year freeze on sovereignty negotiations. Subsidiary discussions continued, but were broken off in March 1982 in an atmosphere of great tension. The armed conflict between Argentina and the UK was precipitated by the Argentine military government's need for a popular victory, its sense that the UK attached little importance to the islands, and by the UK government's determination, once challenged, to defend its interests. The war began with the Argentine invasion of the islands on 2 April 1982; the UK responded by despatching an armed 'task force' which, while diplomatic efforts to find a peaceful settlement failed, repossessed the islands. The Argentine surrender took place at Port Stanley on 14 June 1982. The war hastened the demise of the Argentine JUNTA, and had a markedly beneficial effect on the popularity of the government in Britain and of its Prime Minister, Margaret Thatcher. Diplomatic relations between the UK and Argentina were restored in February 1990, while co-operation between the two countries, especially on issues relating to fishing and oil exploration, has resumed. However, the UK refuses to negotiate on the sovereignty issue, while the 1994 Argentine constitution reasserted the country's ownership of the Falklands, therefore ensuring that the vexed question of sovereignty will continue to be a source of tension between the two sides. For further reading: M. Hastings and S. Jenkins, *The Battle for the Falklands* (1983). M.A.P.

fallibilism. In EPISTEMOLOGY, the view that it is not necessary in science or in everyday life for the factual beliefs that compose the one and guide the other to be established as certain beyond the possibility of doubt. According to this view it is sufficient, and perhaps all that is possible, for our beliefs to be reasonably well supported or justified. Fallibilism, of which C. S. Peirce (1839–1914) was the first thoroughgoing exponent, can be seen as a reasonable compromise between scepticism and dogmatism (or, in one of its senses, INTUITIONISM). For further reading: A. Quinton, *The Nature of Things* (1973). A.Q.

false memory syndrome (FMS). The recall, often in detail, of an event that never happened, yet one its narrator utterly and innocently believes and can swear to in a court of law. FMS generally centres on SEXUAL ABUSE in childhood or adolescence. Modern PSYCHOTHERAPY has tended to give easy credence to recollections in maturity of childhood abuse, perhaps to atone for earlier practitioners who dismissed all such claims

– generally from women – as hysterical fabrications. In Western societies of the 1990s, therapists, social workers, medical doctors, even advice columnists, lawyers and similar professions, accustomed to seeing the worst of human behaviour (or with a vested interest in it), began reporting their clients' 'recovered memories' – some under hypnotic regression – to such a degree that False Memory Syndrome Foundations had to be set up in the USA and Britain to help confused and unhappy men *and* women falsely and publicly accused of child abuse. Today, therapeutic opinion is polarized: some see FMS as a desire to please badgering authority figures not merely by telling them what they appear to want to hear, but by genuinely believing it; others fear that if FMS is generally derided, exposed sex abusers will be able to get away with their crimes. The psychology of MEMORY holds many mysteries; FMS is one that ultimately transcends opinion and politics. For further reading: R. Baker, *Child Sexual Abuse and False Memory Syndrome* (1998). I.K.

falsifiability, see under POPPERIAN.

family. The family as an institution is as old as humanity itself; the family as an object of thought and a focus of concern is much more recent, going back perhaps no further than the Industrial Revolution of the last century. INDUSTRIALIZATION seemed to many to threaten the existence of the family by uprooting it from its traditional community setting and splitting up its members, especially through the rigours of factory work and the atomization produced by life in the big cities (see URBANIZATION). In the event historical and sociological work showed the modern nuclear family to have survived the effects of industrialization remarkably well. What in more recent years has attracted attention is the view of the nuclear family as the arena of acute personal tensions and conflicts, leading in the opinion of some radical theorists to severe mental illness and other forms of dysfunctional IDENTITY. The pressures have seemed particularly severe on women, causing many feminists to declare the modern family 'patriarchal' (see FEMINISM; PATRIARCHY). But though several attempts have been made to imagine and even to practise alternatives to the nuclear family – for instance in the Israeli *kibbutzim* (see KIBBUTZ) – none has so far commanded sufficient general appeal to have had more than a marginal effect on the institution of the family. K.K.

family, extended, see under NUCLEAR FAMILY.

family, history of the, see HISTORY OF THE FAMILY.

family, nuclear, see NUCLEAR FAMILY.

family law. The legal principles governing the relations between married persons, the rights of parents, guardians and children (including the unborn). It covers the law of marriage and the legal consequences of certain types of cohabitation; also nullity and divorce, property rights, trusts, wills and intestacy, legitimacy and illegitimacy. For further reading: S. M. Cretney, *Principles of Family Law* (1984). D.C.M.Y.

family planning (planned parenthood). The use of CONTRACEPTION to limit fertility. Family planning may be an individual decision, taken by a woman who seeks out contraception in order to control her own FERTILITY; or it may be a social policy, implemented by governments or non-governmental organizations to control the population of a particular country or region, often for political or economic reasons. The family planning movement stems from the campaigns for contraception led in the early years of the 20th century by Marie Stopes in Britain and Margaret Sanger in the USA. It is largely as a result of their work that contraception became readily available to most women in developed countries by the middle of the 20th century. But their work also had a crusading quality, based on the premise that, in the first world, there was a danger of an increasing number of births of the 'unfit'; and that developing countries were quickly becoming 'overpopulated'. The extension of family planning services to developing countries (sometimes paid for by corporations with business interests in the target country) has not always been on a voluntary basis, as is evidenced by the mass sterilization programmes carried out in India during the 1970s (coercion continues to be a feature of family planning programmes in other developing countries).

When family planning services are offered on a wholly consensual basis and with sensitivity to cultural context, they are an important aspect of women's healthcare and self-determination. Key promoters of family planning include the United Nations Fund for Population Activities (UNFPA); the World Bank; and the International Planned Parenthood Federation. See also STERILIZATION; EUGENICS. For further reading: G. Greer, *Sex and Destiny* (1984). S.T.

family reconstitution. A technique for reconstructing the demographic history of a population based on information about the vital events of individuals. The technique requires a method for linking records of these events for related persons in order to reconstruct the life histories of individuals, families and entire populations. Like genealogy, family reconstitution requires the collection of information about births, deaths and marriages of all known members of a given family. Unlike genealogists, however, demographers reconstruct families not for their own sake but in order to calculate demographic indices such as LIFE EXPECTANCY, mean age at marriage, the TOTAL FERTILITY RATE, the INFANT MORTALITY RATE, and the POPULATION GROWTH RATE. Although sometimes based on data from vital registration systems (see CENSUS), the majority of family reconstitution studies rely on the parish registers of historical Europe and North America. In populations with minimal mobility and where parish records covering long periods have survived, it has been possible to reconstruct extremely detailed descriptions of a population's history. J.R.W.

family responsibility system, see under HOUSEHOLD RESPONSIBILITY SYSTEM.

family therapy. A form of treatment for psychiatric or interpersonal problems (see PSYCHIATRY) arising in a family setting (e.g. behaviour disorders and NEUROSIS in children, PSYCHOSIS in the adolescent son of a depressed mother). The technique was pioneered by J. Bowlby (in England) and J. E. Bell (in the USA), and involves interviews of the whole family together. Similar conjoint interview techniques are used for couples with marital and sexual problems. Family therapists' theoretical roots are in PSYCHOANALYSIS, SYSTEMS theory or BEHAVIOURISM, and there is a wide variation from short-term, active approaches to long-term, interpretative and insight-giving ones. There is some evidence of efficacy, at least for the behavioural and systems-based approaches. M.J.C.

family values. A term gaining increasing currency in the USA since the 1980s, referring imprecisely to a range of social, moral and implicitly political values said by the term's conservative popularizers (see CONSERVATISM) to represent the core of American standards, which are seen as undermined by forces of MODERNISM and secularization, and by the failure of 'liberals' (see LIBERALISM) to defend moral values in the face of social change.

Family values are taken to be those implied by a particular reading of the nation's Judaeo-Christian tradition: they include an emphasis on the two-parent, heterosexual family structure; on education which inculcates conformity to strong moral norms; on an ethic of personal responsibility within the authoritative framework of essentially patriarchal MARRIAGE.

The 'family values movement' derives partly from the impact of the RELIGIOUS RIGHT; partly from concerns that such phenomena as drug abuse, juvenile crime and illegitimacy rates are explained not by, e.g., social disadvantage, but by a lack of firm moral values and conventional family structures. As such it offers a meeting ground for populist and intellectual conservatives, and for secular and religious elements of the RIGHT: as seen in the web of affiliations between the right wing of the Republican Party, think tanks such as the Heritage Foundation, and lobbying groups such as the Family Research Council. Moderate Democrats have been drawn to mimic parts of the movement's stance, as seen for example in Hillary Clinton's writings on the role of family and local community. The movement's critics emphasize its overt or implicit antagonism to homosexuals, its attribution of economic disadvantage (particularly among BLACK Americans) to inadequate family structures, and its resistance to FEMINIST arguments, including those favouring ABORTION. For further reading: O. Kelly, *Family Values* (1997). S.R.

famine. Famine is an extreme lack of food affecting part or all of a population. It was once considered a principal cause of the periods of unusually high MORTALITY that characterized pre-modern populations; but more recent research suggests that disease was the more common cause of mortality. In modern times, the global incidence of famine has been reduced considerably owing primarily to the expansion of agricultural production (which has outpaced the growth of human population for more than two centuries) and to improvements in transporation networks (which allow for the rapid transport of food supplies in times of local shortage). However, although there is no lack of available food worldwide, famine has not been eradicated, since economic and political pressures can cause acute food shortages in specific regions. In 1984, e.g., Ethiopia continued to export grain and fruit to other countries despite suffering a terrible famine. In 1998, a southern region of Sudan suffered severe food shortages, but because there was a civil war in the country, the government refused either to help or to allow aid agencies to help. J.R.W.

fanzine. A shoestring-budget magazine focusing on a particular aspect of popular culture. Fanzines are produced by enthusiasts for enthusiasts, generally on a non-profit-making basis. The number and range of fanzines is such that they are collectively regarded as a form of alternative or underground press (see UNDERGROUND) which provides an alternative channel for debate and discussion to mainstream commercial publications and other related forms of mass media. Subjects covered by fanzines are varied – they will most typically deal with topics relating to popular music, film or sport, although an increasing specialization in recent years has resulted in fanzines devoted to issues as varied as cult TV programmes and ufology. During the 1960s and 1970s, the DIY appearance of fanzines – low-quality paper and grainy appearance of reproduced photos, etc. – was regarded as an essential part of their counter-hegemonic, underground appeal, an exemplary case in point being the late 1970s punk fanzine *Sniffin' Glue*. In recent years the increasing availability of cheap word-processing equipment, desktop publishing and picture-scanning facilities has prompted a new generation of fanzines which, although retaining an underground significance, sometimes approximate commercially produced magazines in terms of appearance and quality of presentation. A.BEN.

FAO (Food and Agriculture Organization). A specialized agency of the UN set up by an international conference meeting at Quebec in October 1945. FAO, with its headquarters in Rome, had forerunners in the international Institute of Agriculture established in Paris in 1905, and took its own origin from the American-sponsored conference held at Hot Springs, Virginia, in 1943. Its original responsibility was seen as the feeding of the population of countries whose economies had been disturbed by the war of 1939–45, but it soon evolved into handling the basic problems of world distribution of food between areas of crop surplus and areas of endemic food deficiency. D.C.W.

Fascism.

(1) Specifically, the Fascist Movement formed in 1919 which Mussolini led to power in Italy (1922–45). The Italian word, *fascismo*, is derived from the fasces, the bundle of rods with a projecting axe-head which was carried before the consuls as the insignia of state authority in ancient Rome.

(2) Generically, similar authoritarian movements (see AUTHORITARIANISM) in other countries, such as NAZISM in Germany, the FALANGE in Franco's Spain, the Iron Guard in Romania, and Sir Oswald Mosley's British Union of Fascists. Fascism was a product of the deep-seated social and economic crisis in Europe which followed World War I. It produced no coherent system of ideas comparable with MARXISM, and the various Fascist movements reflected the very different national backgrounds of the countries in which they developed. Nonetheless, there were a number of common traits. All were strongly NATIONALIST, violently anti-COMMUNIST and anti-Marxist; all hated LIBERALISM, DEMOCRACY and parliamentary parties, which they sought to replace by a new authoritarian state in which there would be only one party, their own, with a monopoly of power, and a single leader with charismatic qualities (see CHARISMA) and dictatorial powers. Although strongly opposed to democracy, the Fascists, unlike traditional right-wing parties, aimed

to mobilize the masses with a populist appeal, as a prelude to the seizure of power. In their political campaigns they relied heavily on propaganda and TERRORISM; where they attained power they liquidated their rivals without regard to the law. All shared a cult of violence and action, exalted war, and with their uniforms, ranks, salutes and rallies, gave their parties a paramilitary character. RACISM and ANTISEMITISM were strongly marked features of some Fascist movements (e.g. the German) but not all (e.g. the Italian). Fascist movements made a strong appeal to many ex-officers and NCOs resentful of the results of World War I and unwilling to return to civilian life (the 'front' generation); to various groups in the middle and lower MIDDLE CLASSES who felt their position in society threatened by INFLATION, economic DEPRESSION, the organized WORKING-CLASS movements, and the spectre of REVOLUTION; and to youth attracted by the cult of action and the denunciation of 'the system'. Their nationalism and anti-Marxism won them sympathy and sometimes support from the traditional parties of the RIGHT and the army. Originally radical in many of their demands, they shed most of these when they came to power, though they represented a new ÉLITE drawn from social groups very different from the old ruling classes.

(3) The product of World War I and the social upheaval and economic depression which followed the war, Fascism was discredited by the total defeat of the Fascist states in World War II. A number of NEO-FASCIST parties have appeared in Europe since the war, though without achieving any real success. This has been underlined by the failure of the Falange and the Spanish Right to prevent the replacement of Franco's regime by a democratic constitutional monarchy. Regimes with features borrowed from Fascism have appeared in other continents, e.g. PERONISM in Argentina, but in circumstances better understood in the context of their own national histories than in those of inter-war Europe.

(4) Apart from its historical use, the term 'Fascist' was kept alive by the communists who, both before and after World War II, used it as a label to discredit their opponents, whether genuinely Fascist, conservatives or social democrats (see CONSERVATISM; SOCIAL DEMOCRACY), and to promote their tactics of building up anti-Fascist coalitions under communist leadership. For further reading: W. Laqueur (ed.), *Fascism* (1979).

A.L.C.B.

fatalism. The theory that every future event is already necessarily determined and inevitable. It seems to be a necessary consequence of DETERMINISM, but, in its usual form, where it asserts not merely that what will happen will happen in conformity with an all-inclusive system of laws of nature, but that what will happen will happen *whatever anybody does*, it is not (see NATURAL LAW; FREE WILL). Determinism is fully compatible with the view that human action is causally effective and that in its absence events will occur which otherwise would not have occurred. But it does imply that every human action is fully determined by the laws of nature together with the conditions of its occurrence (which will include the character and desires of the agent). For further reading: G. Ryle, *Dilemmas* (1954).

A.Q.

Fauves. A loosely knit group of French figurative painters distinguished by their use of strong, simple colour and energetic execution. In 1905 the organizer of the Salon d'Automne chose to hang the most violently coloured works in the same room: the painters concerned were Derain, Manguin, Marquet, Matisse, Puy, Valtat and Vlaminck, whom the critic Louis Vauxcelles termed *les fauves* (the wild beasts) – referring probably to their rejection of orthodox notions of draughtsmanship, perspective and light effects, but possibly also to Matisse's hairy overcoat. Gauguin and van Gogh were among their heroes; the IMPRESSIONISTS were not, although many of the Fauves (among whom one may also include Camoin, Rouault and van Dongen) had themselves been through an Impressionist phase.

Typically *fauve* painting consisted of flat patterns of familiar forms, simply and freely outlined and unpredictably coloured; supposedly 'background' colours were often as vivid as 'foreground'. But by 1908 the Fauves' colour-schemes were generally more subdued. Braque, after a brief *fauve* phase, had turned to CUBISM, Friesz and Vlaminck to Cézanne, and Derain to something between the two. Dufy entered a short period of geometrical severity, and then returned to lively colouring, but in a witty, idiosyncratic style; of the leading figures, only Matisse continued to paint in a recognizably *fauve* idiom.

In Dresden the BRÜCKE painters shared with the French group an admiration for Gauguin, van Gogh, Negro sculpture, and spectacular unorthodoxy. Many Brücke canvases of 1910–12 are comparable in colouring and outline to the French *fauve* works of the preceding years. The Russian artists Kandinsky and Jawlensky also underwent *fauve* periods after visiting France. The academy organized by Matisse from 1907 to 1911 was attended by an international group of painters who spread Matisse's principles in Scandinavia, North America, eastern Europe, and even (in the case of Matthew Smith) in England. For further reading: J. P. Crespelle, tr. A. Brookner, *The Fauves* (1963). P.C.

FDR, see under EL SALVADOR.

fecundity, see FERTILITY.

Federal Arts Project, see under WPA.

Federal Reserve System. The CENTRAL BANK of the USA, as established in 1913. There are 12 Regional Federal Reserve Banks, covering the whole of the USA; and a Board of Governors of the whole system, whose chairman is essentially the managing director of the Central Bank. The US President appoints all members of the Board of Governors. The Federal Reserve System operates in the open market through the New York Federal Reserve Bank, and controls the banking system through open-market operations, variations in its discount rates, and changes in the legal reserve ratios of the member banks. These member banks (about 6,000) are the main banking houses in the USA. M.V.P.

Federal Theater Project, see under WPA.

Federal Writers Project, see under WPA.

federalism. A system of government in which central and regional authorities are linked in an interdependent political relationship, in which powers and functions are distributed to achieve a substantial degree of autonomy and integrity in the regional units. In theory, a federal system seeks to maintain a balance such that neither level of government becomes sufficiently dominant to dictate the decisions of the other, unlike in a unitary system, in which the central authorities hold primacy to the extent even of redesigning or abolishing regional and local units of government at will.

The origins of federalism may be remotely discerned in FEUDALISM; more clearly in such systems as the defence leagues of medieval commercial cities, in the Swiss confederation, and in the United Provinces of the Netherlands. They may be most clearly seen in 18th-century thought and in the formation of the USA. The American experience, as that of the Federal Republic of Germany, Canada, Australia and other federal states, shows that political practice may depart substantially from theory, and that interdependence rather than true separation of function tends to characterize federalism in action.

For much of the 20th century observers of the American model tended to believe that the balance between central and subnational authorities (i.e. the 50 states) moved inexorably in favour of the former, driven by modern communications, the growth of a more fully integrated national economy, and political pressures for uniform policies. Since the 1980s this view has been increasingly questioned, as successive attempts at a 'new federalism' and a mounting distrust of the federal government's capacity and integrity cumulatively produce a significant revival in the role of state governments. In Europe arguments over the development of the EUROPEAN UNION (EU) reveal the tensions and ambiguities within the concept of federalism, especially when applied to a growing union of existing nation-states. The concept may usefully be distinguished from that of federation, which tends to describe a political system in which a central authority is created for limited purposes, without disturbing the general primacy in other spheres of the constituent governments. S.R.

feedback. The return of part of a SYSTEM's output to change its input. *Positive feedback* increases the input, *negative feedback* decreases it. Hence, if feedback is used (as it is in all regulatory systems) in comparing output with some standard to be approached, negative feedback is inherently stabilizing (because it decreases the error) while positive feedback is inherently destabilizing (and the error gains explosively in magnitude). The classic example of negative feedback is the Watt steam governor, in which a pair of weights attached to the engine shaft fly outward (by centrifugal force) if the engine tends to race, which movement operates a valve to reduce the supply of fuel. An example of positive feedback is a 'growth economy' in which increased profitability is ploughed back further to increase profitability, a process which indeed becomes destabilizing in the limit. The casual use of 'feedback' to mean 'response to a stimulus' is incorrect. S.BE.

FEKS, see under FEX.

Feldenkrais Method. An 'awareness through movement' re-education programme which proposes that students voluntarily change their unconscious and habitual movement patterns through recognition and observation. The method was pioneered by Moshe Feldenkrais in the 1940s, and involves relearning through simple and gentle movements in a non-competitive and non-stressful environment. This method of facilitating movement potential involves understanding how to: achieve and maintain correct alignment, eliminate effort and unnecessary muscular stress, control movement and balance, and link an uninterrupted breathing pattern to movement. Through re-educating counter-productive movement patterns, students of the Feldenkrais Method find increased neuromuscular co-ordination, improvement in body posture, and ability to achieve relaxation and extend the range of movements in the joints. Thus the Feldenkrais Method benefits a wide range of individuals including singers, actors and musicians, as well as people with neuromuscular disturbances. Dancers and particularly those involved in NEW DANCE, often study awareness through movement techniques such as Feldenkrais Method, RELEASE DANCE and ALEXANDER TECHNIQUE, in order to become more in touch with the body centre and senses which can lead to a more organic and exploratory approach to movement (see CONTACT IMPROVISATION). For further reading: M. Feldenkrais, *Awareness through Movement* (1972). G.N.; L.A.

felicific calculus. A method, devised by British philosopher Jeremy Bentham (1748–1832), for the quantitative comparison of the amounts of pleasure and pain which will occur as the consequences of alternative courses of action. Some such technique is needed by any utilitarian ethical theory (see ETHICS; UTILITARIANISM) that defines the rightness and wrongness of alternative possible actions in terms of the amounts of pleasure and pain that they produce. Bentham enumerated a number of 'dimensions' of pleasure and pain: intensity, duration, certainty, propinquity, purity, fecundity and extent. Most of these factors should be taken into account in any appraisal of the consequences of action that aims to be rational and thorough. But Bentham's idea that a fixed amount of intensity is equal in value to a fixed amount of duration rests on a false ANALOGY with spatial measurement, where an inch is the same length in every dimension. For further reading: J. P. Griffin, *Wellbeing* (1986). A.Q.

felicity conditions. In LINGUISTICS, a term used in the theory of SPEECH ACTS to refer to the criteria which must be satisfied if the speech act is to achieve its purpose. For example, before a person is entitled to perform the speech act of baptizing, certain 'preparatory conditions' must be present (e.g. the person must be invested with the appropriate authority). Or, at a more everyday level, the utterance of a request would be 'infelicitous' if the speaker knew that circumstances would not permit the request being carried out (e.g. asking for a window to be opened in a room with no windows). For further reading: S. Levinson, *Pragmatics* (1983). D.C.

fellow-traveller. Originally a Russian term ('*poputchik*') coined by Trotsky to depict the vacillating intellectual supporters of the young Soviet regime (see USSR). When STALINISM established a firmer grip on the expression of opinion, the term disappeared in the former USSR. It was adopted in the West to describe strong sympathizers with the Soviet Union who stopped short of COMMUNIST Party membership. L.L.; S.R.

feminine sexuality. One of the most debated and obscure topics in psychoanalytical theory, as well as in FEMINIST thought (see PSYCHOANALYSIS; SEX; SEXUALITY; GENDER). The debate can broadly be described by two opposed theoretical tendencies. First, an ESSENTIALIST theory, which postulates an innate factor as the essence of femininity. Even though this classical conception has been overtaken by a new constructionalist view of femininity as being socially and historically determined, some contemporary women PSYCHOANALYSTS, such as L. Irigaray and J. Kristeva, have revived the idea of a feminine essence, but as repressed and oppressed by the phallic order of contemporary culture. This approach has appealed to those feminists who do not wish to reassess male values, but seek to reveal what has been hidden and deformed about an original feminine essence. This ambiguity between femininity as an ESSENCE and femininity as a deformation has been stressed since Freud; he discovered the original bisexuality in all human beings, men and women, but he also claimed that the sexual energy, that is the LIBIDO, is masculine only. It was the task of other analysts after Freud, such as Deutsch, Jones and Horney, to make up for this inconsistency. They all claim that as there is only one masculine libido, feminine sexuality must be a deviation from this source, that is, femininity is explained mainly as a perversion in as much as it characterizes the detour of feminine MASOCHISM. According to these authors, this detour is natural, as it obeys an anatomical and biological reality: the female situation of being castrated, copulated with, and giving birth. This sexual destiny is never easily accepted by women, and results in an underlying UNCONSCIOUS penis envy. Like the boy, the little girl establishes her sexual identity at the oedipus stage (see OEDIPUS COMPLEX), taking her father as her love object, and other men as his future substitutes, from whom she expects to receive the Phallus, that is, the representative of paternal authority, in the form of the penis, and babies. An attempt to overcome this dichotomy between anatomical and psychical realities was carried out by the French psychoanalyst J. Lacan (see LACANIAN), who dismissed both the idea of a feminine essence, and the idea of woman as socially constructed: Lacan considered her as symbolically differentiated in relation to the Phallus. This means that the sexual difference would be neither a natural one, nor a made-up one, but rather positional; that is, relative to the place one is given in the Oedipal structure, whether or not in concomitance with one's own anatomical sex. This entails that the value we attribute to sexual difference is not anatomical, but SYMBOLIC, and women have always shown their regret for the subordinate position that the symbolic order assigns to them (see PENIS ENVY; NEUROSIS; LESBIANISM; FEMINISM). But if the woman, because of her position, is deprived of phallic enjoyment (see JOUISSANCE), she does nevertheless achieve another kind of enjoyment because of this very position. This JOUISSANCE is not phallic in quality but, on the contrary, arises from the possible abandonment of ego-boundaries, and the pleasure of surrendering rather than mastering; that is why it has been compared in its quality to mystical states of ecstasy. For further reading: J. Lacan, *On Feminine Sexuality* (1998). B.BE.

feminism. Its broad meaning is the advocacy of the rights of women. There is no single accepted definition and feminism encompasses agitation for political and legal rights, equal opportunities, sexual autonomy, and the right of self-determination (see ABORTION; CONTRACEPTION). The feminist movement stemmed from the recognition of the subordination of women, from the existence of discrimination and inequality based on SEX. Feminism is a set of ideas linked to a social movement for change. The relationship between the ideas and the movement is shifting. Feminism has never been a single unified movement, but it has been made up of different elements which may unite behind a single campaign (e.g. women's suffrage; see SUFFRAGETTE). Its history is one of fission and fusion. Different phases of the feminist movement have gone under different labels: suffragette, women's emancipation, women's liberation, women's movement, feminism, social feminism, radical feminism.

The tension that has run throughout feminism has concerned the advocacy of the rights of women on the basis of similarity (i.e. women are human beings like men and therefore ought to be granted equal rights) or on the basis of difference (i.e. women are different from men and therefore ought to be granted the right to represent themselves).

The origins of feminism cannot be traced to a single source but are located in a number of traditions. In medieval Europe there were early defenders of women's 'nature': Jean de Meung (thirteenth century), Christine de Pisan (fourteenth), Marie de Gournay, Aphra Behn and Mary Astell (seventeenth). The period 1790–1860 marks the beginning of the feminist movement. It was dominated by Enlightenment ideas: the rights of man, reason, NATURAL LAW and equal rights. Both the French and American revolutions raised issues relevant to women's rights, and in this atmosphere Mary Wollstonecraft wrote an important feminist document, *A Vindication of the Rights of Women* (1792, see FIRST WAVE FEMINISM). In both the US and Britain early activists (e.g. Elizabeth Cady Stanton, Margaret Fuller, Lucretia Mott, the Langham Place group) were concerned with securing legal rights for women (in MARRIAGE, education and employment). Feminism was also associated with the 19th-century anti-slavery and evangelical movements (e.g. temperance), and was an important element in Unitarian and Quaker traditions. In contrast to this BOURGEOIS or INDIVIDUALIST feminism was the growing importance of SOCIALIST feminism. It drew its ideas from the early socialist or communitarian movement (of Saint-Simon, Fourier and Robert Owen; see COMMUNITARIANISM).

The suffragette movement (1860–1930) united women of very different backgrounds. In the context of the struggle for votes, feminism developed with great speed. The campaign for female suffrage was an important landmark: women realized that they could not rely on political parties or the organized labour movement for support, and that they themselves would have to fight themselves for equality and justice.

Until Freud, debates concerning the rights of women were conducted in terms of fixed, biologically based categories of male and female (see FREUDIAN; SEX; SEXUALITY; FEMININE SEXUALITY; GENDER). Freud opened up a new area: one of process. His discovery of the UNCONSCIOUS shifted and expanded the discussion of sexuality from surface appearance to what lay beneath. Freud strove to understand the formation of the human subject, the complex process involved in the construction of sexuality (see SUBJECTIVITY). He did not seek to understand what a woman is, but how she comes into being. His discussion of sexuality raised fundamental questions about the foundations of civilization, and more specifically women's oppression under PATRIARCHY. Freud's ideas have been subject to much criticism by feminists but continue to be influential in France.

The women's liberation movement of the 1960s grew out of widespread radical protest by students, workers, blacks and women, especially in France and the US. Women responded to their relegation to a secondary role in protest activity by establishing their own (often women-only) CONSCIOUSNESS-RAISING groups. The motivating force was an idea of sisterhood, women united with little recognition of RACE or CLASS difference. Feminist activity was also stimulated by the work of MIDDLE-CLASS writers, particularly Simone de Beauvoir (*Le Deuxième Sexe*, 1949, Eng. tr. 1953), Betty Friedan (*The Feminine Mystique*, 1963), Kate Millett (*Sexual Politics*, 1969) and Germaine Greer (*The Female Eunuch*, 1970). For the first time a vast range of issues was debated by women: from experiences at work to those in the marriage bed. The personal became the political.

Radical feminism and reaction. The 1970s and 1980s were the decades of the DECONSTRUCTION of woman, expressed in the fission of the feminist movement. Fragmentation into different groups resulted from the recognition of the complexity of women's experience. The universalist claims of the 1960s were increasingly challenged by WORKING-CLASS, THIRD WORLD and BLACK women. In the Anglo-American feminist tradition there has been a growth of *radical lesbianism* ('radical' distinguished from 'liberal' or 'socialist' feminist in seeing sexual oppression as primary and fundamental; see LIBERALISM; SOCIALISM). This strand of feminism has advocated separatism, but the problem of sexuality and power has returned in the form of the debate over lesbian SADOMASOCHISM. The SEPARATIST movement has some parallels with the French *féministes révolutionnaires*. In France, however, important feminist ideas have emerged from work in PSYCHOANALYSIS associated with Lacan, Kristeva, Cixous and the *groupe politique et psychoanalyse*.

The French tradition has explored questions of language, the construction of sexuality, the articulation of sex and DESIRE in the text. It has opposed the notion of a coherent subject, central to the work of bourgeois or HUMANIST feminism.

A disillusionment with the rate and direction of change has seen a retreat from sexual politics by two of the early influential writers: Friedan (*The Second Stages*, 1981) and Greer (*Sex and Destiny*, 1984). This retreat has been held as representative of the 'post-feminist' era. The centre of gravity in feminism may have shifted, its ideas and forms developed beyond the horizons of the 1960s, but the movement is far from dead. For further reading: J. Mitchell and A. Oakley (eds), *What Is Feminism?* (1986). A.G.

feminist criticism. Criticism concerned with both women as writers and women as readers (of male and female texts). Notable feminist critics include bell hooks and Gayatri Spivak. It is an activity which raises questions of AESTHETICS and politics, and of the relationship of women to language. Feminist criticism (see FEMINISM) has recovered lost or neglected writers and highlighted the obstacles facing women as authors (the pertinence of Woolf's essay *A Room of One's Own*, 1929). It has also established the importance for women of having their own space in which to speak and express themselves freely. The feminist movement of the 1960s resulted in an explosion of magazines by and for women (e.g. *Ms*, *Spare Rib*, *Questions féministes*, *Le torchon brûle*, *Signs*) and the foundation of feminist publishing houses (Virago, Women's Press, Des femmes). Women as readers or feminist reading can be divided into Anglo-American (author-centred) and French (text-centred) traditions. In the case of the former, Millett's *Sexual Politics* (1969) was an early challenge to the authority of the author: it questioned, it represented a 'reading against the grain'. Other Anglo-American critics have been uneasy with theory (a male discourse). They have sought to establish the authenticity of the female writer's voice (e.g. Showalter on Virginia Woolf in *A Literature of Their Own*, 1977) and to expose the sexual IDEOLOGY in the work of male and female authors. The French tradition, in contrast, has always been more theoretical and influenced by PSYCHOANALYSIS, STRUCTURALISM and DECONSTRUCTION. It has situated the text (rather than the author) at the heart of critical practice. French feminist criticism (e.g. the work of Cixous, Irigaray and Kristeva) has explored the construction of SEXUALITY through the text and questioned the very existence of a fixed (male or female) human subject. For further reading: M. Eagleton, *Feminist Literary Criticism* (1996). A.G.

feminist geography. The systematic field of GEOGRAPHY that, according to McDowell, is concerned with questions of GENDER inequality and the oppression of women in most spheres of life. Such 'hiding of women from geography' via the discipline's traditional focus on 'man-environment' issues has been compounded by an emphasis on broad-brush research METHODOLOGIES focusing on the sphere of production (the 'public') and on classical MARXIST class inequalities (see RADICAL GEOGRAPHY), rather than on the spheres of consumption and reproduction (the 'private'), which have been ideologically constructed as 'women's place'. In recent years, a movement to redress this imbalance has gained strength, led by the scholarly activities of the 'Women and Geography' Study Group of the Institute of British Geographers and the 'Geographic Perspectives on Women' Specialty Group of the Association of American Geographers. Among key research findings is the recognition that urban spatial form has differential implications for women concerning their access to public facilities and employment, and that the concentration of women in low-skilled, repetitive jobs is a result of the social construction of gender rather than any biologically determined SEX differences. Most work in this subdiscipline is dominated by the assumption that the unequal POWER relations between men and women are essential to an understanding of geography and gender. For further reading: L. McDowell and J. P. Sharp (eds), *Space Gender Knowledge: A Reader for Feminist Geographers* (1997). M.LO.; P.O.M.

feminist history (herstory). An integral part of the feminist movement (see FEMINISM) which grew out of a need to develop an historical perspective which could inform contemporary debate. Feminist history charted the development of the women's movement and the direction in which it was unfolding. It has recovered the lives of women from obscurity, not just the early writers and activists, but ordinary women's lives – those hitherto 'hidden from history' (S. Rowbotham, *Dreams and Dilemmas*, 1973). Feminist history has revealed the complexity of the category 'woman'. BLACK women's history (particularly in the US) is a developed strand, exploring the ORAL TRADITION to link the present to the past. Feminist history has not only provided new information about women, but also about men, the FAMILY, MARRIAGE, production, reproduction (mothering), and the articulation of private and public domains. In this way it has overlapped with social or labour history and has contributed to the expansion of historical discourse as a whole. By recovering herstory, the feminist movement has challenged history as formal, official and literally his-story, a male narrative. For further reading: A. Walker, *In Search of Our Mothers' Gardens* (1984). A.G.

feminist psychoanalysis. The founder of PSYCHOANALYSIS, Sigmund Freud (see FREUDIAN), was intensely aware of sexual difference. However, his interpretations of the impact of what he described as the 'anatomical distinctions' between the sexes (see SEX; SEXUALITY) have been the subject of considerable debate and discussion from the earliest days of psychoanalysis. Women analysts (most particularly Melanie Klein and Karen Horney) challenged Freud's emphasis on the centrality of the father (and the phallus) to human development and argued that it is the child's mother (see MOTHERING) who constitutes the crucial relationship. These debates nevertheless build upon Freud's theory of the UNCONSCIOUS and accept his thesis about the symbolic role of BIOLOGY in human existence. This view – in which female envy of the penis (see PENIS ENVY) and the thesis about fear of CASTRATION on the part of men are central – led to enormous hostility to Freud and psychoanalysis by feminists (see FEMINISM) such as Simone de Beauvoir and Kate Millett. Indeed, the feminist consensus of the 1970s was that Freud had constructed an entirely misogynist theory of human development. Juliet Mitchell's *Psychoanalysis and Feminism* (1974) defended Freud against these criticism and in doing so initiated and encouraged a reading and understanding of Freud which has allowed feminism to come to terms with psychoanalysis in a way which has been enormously influential in the study of literature and the visual arts. For further reading: J. Sayers, *Mothering Psychoanalysis* (1991). M.S.E.

feminist psychology. The study of PSYCHOLOGY from FEMINIST perspectives. It seeks to redress GENDER imbalances in the approach of traditional psychology, which is criticized for various reasons: first, on empirical grounds, e.g. that studies are often conducted on all-male groups of subjects, even when the conclusions are intended to apply to both men and women; second, on conceptual grounds, in particular the failure to properly understand the importance of social factors. An example is the study of POST-NATAL DEPRESSION, which feminist psychologists argue has characterized depressed mothers as deviant and sought explanations in their body chemistry changes, when the cause may actually be, e.g., the stress of giving up a career for motherhood, or a lack of support. There has also been important work on the DEVELOPMENTAL PSYCHOLOGY of women, who were previously not studied enough in their own right. For further reading: L. M. Brown, C. Gilligan, *Meeting at the Crossroads* (1992). A.A.L.

feminist theology. A movement which has antecedents in the 19th century but which began to make an impact on Christian THEOLOGY after VATICAN COUNCIL II. Fundamentally it is a movement for greater justice for women within the Christian Church, whose SYMBOLISM, texts, traditions and fracture have been and remain ambivalent for women. FEMINISTS, male or female, want theology to be clear of traces of the devaluation of women, not least as expressed in the conviction, characteristic of Christianity until very recently, that women are subordinate, because inferior to men. There are likely to be limits to what can be made of Christian scripture, though some outstanding work has been produced which enables a different reading of some texts, with potential both for transforming relationships between men and women, and for symbolizing God. Thus Phyllis Trible's *God and the Rhetoric of Sexuality* (1978) challenges convictions about women's inferiority by fresh attention to Genesis 2 and 3, and tracks down overlooked female/feminine-related imagery for God, as in the book of Isaiah. Elisabeth S. Fiorenza's *In Memory of Her: A Feminist Theological Reconstruction of Christian Origins* (1983) argues that the women's Church may claim Jesus and the PRAXIS of the earliest Church as a prototype of their own history, open to future transformation. The two outstanding works of non-biblical feminist theology to have been produced are Rosemary Radford Ruether's *Sexism and God-Talk* (1983) and Elizabeth A. Johnson's *She Who Is: the Mystery of God in Feminist Theological Discourse* (1992). Feminist theology necessarily pays detailed attention to the way in which GENDER affects how religious traditions work, the symbolism they use, the characteristics of roles within them, and the way religious traditions reflect social assumptions and shape and reshape these (see, e.g., Elaine Graham, *Making the Difference: Gender, Personhood and Theology* [1995]). Because certain gender constructions do not reflect the reality of all women's lives in the way assumed in feminist theology written by educated/Western/white feminist theologians, there now exists African-American 'womanist' theology, Hispanic 'mujerista' theology, Far East Asian feminist LIBERATION THEOLOGY, and a number of other forms. Feminism may in time have an impact on all major religious traditions. Those who think that all such traditions have failed women to date may come to devise new forms of religion and spirituality, as, e.g., post-Christian feminist theology. Whether the Christian tradition can come to terms with feminism is at this stage an open question. A.L.L.

feminization. The 20th century has long been labelled as the century of MODERNISM, and an impact of this form of cultural transformation is the thesis that a crucial part of modernism is feminization. The thesis suggest that as traditional forms of authority (see AUTHORITARIANISM) (in particular the Church and the patriarchal family) lost their control over individual lives and institutions, women were able to claim a greater space for specifically female interests and a more fully articulated female voice. Although this voice acquired classic status in the work of such writers as Virginia Woolf, femininity in print (as Ann Douglas suggests in *The Feminization of American Culture*, 1977) was also preoccupied with NARCISSISM and the trivial. However, despite these negative possibilities to the feminization of culture in the 20th century, a consensus has emerged that for women, children and large numbers of men, a cultural shift towards interests and values which are located in personal and family life has had profoundly positive effects on aspects of individual experience. Assessment of the thesis must also involve a discussion of the consistent domination by men of public institutional (see INSTITUTIONS) POWER and a critical review of pre-modern cultures. For further reading: E. Showalter, *Sexual Anarchy: Gender and Culture at the Fin de Siècle* (1992). M.S.E.

Fenians, see under REPUBLICANISM (IRISH); IRISH REPUBLICAN ARMY.

Fermat's Last Theorem (until recently only a conjecture). We can find whole numbers (see NUMBER) such that $x^2 + y^2 = z^2$ (e.g. 3, 4, 5), but no positive whole numbers have been found that work in $x^3 + y^3 = z^3$, or $x^4 + y^4 = z^4$, or $x^5 + y^5 = z^5$, or for any higher powers. Pierre de Fermat (1601–65) wrote in a margin that he had a PROOF, too long for the margin, of his 'Last Theorem': that no numbers could be found in any of these cases. Later attempts to find a proof stimulated important mathematics, and computers helped to show that, if such numbers existed, the power involved was at least 25,000.

Paul Wolfskehl was saved from suicide by a book on the Theorem. In gratitude he left (1908) 100,000 marks to Göttingen University to found a prize for a proof before 2007. 'Proofs' poured in: none survived scrutiny. On 23 June 1993, Andrew Wiles said in Cambridge that he had the final substantial jigsaw piece.

Germans and Japanese had linked the Theorem to so-called elliptic equations and modular forms – if one could prove the 'Taniyama-Shimura conjecture' then the Theorem followed. Wiles thought he could prove this conjecture, but scrutiny revealed a serious gap. Helped by his former pupil, Richard Taylor, he plugged the gap and the work was published (some 130 pages) in May 1995.

On 27 June 1997 Andrew Wiles received the Wolfskehl prize – despite inflation still worth $50,000. N.A.R.

Fermat's principle of least time, see under LEAST-ACTION PRINCIPLE.

Fermi-Dirac statistics. The QUANTUM STATISTICS that applies to PARTICLES for which the QUANTUM NUMBER describing SPIN is a half-integer. M.V.B.

Fermi paradox. Named after the Italian physicist Enrico Fermi (1901–54) (see SEARCH FOR EXTRATERRESTRIAL INTELLIGENCE).

fermions, see under QUANTUM STATISTICS; SUPERSYMMETRY.

ferrimagnetism. A relatively weak type of MAGNETISM often found in ceramics, in which successive elementary atomic magnets (see SPIN) point in opposite directions. The phenomenon is useful in TELECOMMUNICATIONS because most 'ferrites' are electrical insulators and make sensitive aerials for TRANSISTOR sets. M.V.B.

ferromagnetism. The strong MAGNETISM which can be produced in the metals iron, cobalt and nickel, where it is possible to align all the elementary atomic magnets (see SPIN) in the same direction. Ferromagnetism often occurs naturally, induced by the magnetic field of the earth. Most common horseshoe and bar magnets are ferromagnetic. M.V.B.

fertility. In DEMOGRAPHY, the process whereby births occur in a population. Demographers distinguish between fecundity, which is the physical ability to reproduce, and fertility, which refers to actual reproduction. (In medical and everyday language, the term 'fertility' is often used in both contexts.) The level of fertility in a society is measured by the TOTAL FERTILITY RATE or the NET REPRODUCTION RATE. *Replacement fertility* refers to the level of childbearing necessary to replace the current generation of potential parents; in low-mortality populations, a total fertility rate of about 2.1 ensures replacement. *Natural fertility* refers to a situation in which there is no (or little) deliberate control of fertility; in these settings, fertility varies between populations only (or primarily) as a result of differences in marriage practices, breastfeeding, or traditional behaviours (such as post-partum abstinence) that diminish the exposure to intercourse for women of reproductive age. J.R.W.

festive theatre, see under CELEBRATORY THEATRE.

fetish; fetishism. E. B. Tylor (*Primitive Culture*, 1871) adopted into ANTHROPOLOGY the word fetish, long current in English, to mean an object in which a spirit is embodied, to which it is attached, or through which it conveys magical influence; he applied the term fetishism to the worship, shading into idolatry, of such an object. Influenced by Marx's ideas (*Capital* vol. 1, 1867), anthropologists have taken up the idea of the fetishism of commodities (see MARXISM). It has become an important concept in the discussion of the nature of goods and the qualities or facets they develop in different contexts. The meaning of goods lies beyond the narrow economic sphere and is situated in a much wider social context. Tambiah has recently expanded the debate in anthropology by considering the Weberian concept of CHARISMA in relation to goods and the fetishism of goods. For further reading: S. J. Tambiah, *The Buddhist Saints of the Forest and the Cult of Amulets* (1984). E.G.; A.G.

feud. State of dispute or latent hostility between two parties over an offence, insult or injury. Feud is a private matter, but it follows established rules and conventions. If an individual commits theft or homicide, a group mobilizes around the victim to demand reparation or compensation from the offender's group. Recruitment to feuding groups is usually on the basis of KINSHIP ties. Feud is often not just an isolated incident, but may be a long-term state of affairs between different groups. Feud is essentially a relationship between groups and implies a roughly equal distribution of POWER and STATUS in society. It is a common feature of egalitarian communities without centralized political organization (e.g. the Nuer of East Africa; see EGALITARIANISM) and it is also found in areas of the Mediterranean and Middle East (among the Bedo of Cyrenaica).

For further reading: J. Black-Michaud, *Cohesive Force: Feud in the Mediterranean and Middle East* (1975). A.G.

feudal; feudalism. Terms used since the 18th century to describe the social and military organization prevalent in Europe during the Middle Ages, and also other social systems with similar features in, e.g., China and Japan where it continued down to the 19th century. There have been many varieties of feudalism but it commonly involved a social hierarchy based on the tenure of land, jurisdiction by landlords over their tenants, and the granting of land and offices in return for a vassal's loyalty and services, particularly military service, to the king or lord from whom the land or office was held.

More generally the word 'feudal' is used to characterize (1) any social system in which great landowners or hereditary overlords exact revenue from the land, and exercise the functions of government in their domains (e.g. the Prussian Junker class east of the Elbe); and (2) any society or social group which the writer wishes to condemn as anachronistic and which is based upon inequality and the privileged position of a social, political or economic dynasty (e.g. the phrase *industrial feudalism* often used in histories of 19th-century America). For further reading: M. Bloch, *Feudal Society* (1961). A.L.C.B.

FEX (Factory of the Eccentric Actor). Initially a theatre, then a film studio, organized in Petrograd in 1921 by the young directors Kozintsev and Trauberg ('the fexes'). They sought to revolutionize the theatre on principles of 'eccentricity' imported from the circus and vaudeville, and to replace its obsolete methods by the more dynamic 'lower' genres: street shows, slapstick comedy, and sport. In the cinema the fexes extolled American comedies and gangster films. Their early films tried to convey revolutionary propaganda through grotesque and fantastic imagery, shocking juxtapositions, and circus tricks. In later years their style changed considerably under the influence of Eisenstein and German EXPRESSIONIST cinema. The 'eccentric' tendency gradually gave way to more realistic themes and methods.

The Kozintsev–Trauberg collaboration ended in 1946. Their best-known films were the trilogy *The Youth of Maxim* (1935), *The Return of Maxim* (1937), and *The Vyborg Side* (1939). Kozintsev subsequently reached Western audiences with his *Hamlet* (1964) and *King Lear* (1971). For further reading: J. Leyda, *Kino* (1973). M.E.

fibre optics. Ordinary glass is not a particularly good transmitter of light, a few centimetres being sufficient to absorb over 50 per cent of any incident light. This is entirely due to the impurities in the glass. When such impurities have been dissolved away chemically and the spaces which are left are filled with pure glass, the whole can then be heated and drawn out into long, thin fibres which are capable of transmitting light, virtually without loss of intensity over very long distances (several kilometres). Fibre optics have many applications. In medicine, for example, they are used to illuminate and make optically examinable interior parts of the body without the use of SURGERY. By a similar technique but using coherent RADIATION from a LASER, they can seal haemorrhages in the stomach and other internal organs. They are used in TELECOMMUNICATIONS to replace wires, and hundreds of 'light messages' can be transmitted simultaneously down a single fibre. They also feature in decorative displays for advertising and in the home. E.R.L.

fideism. In the philosophy of religion (see RELIGION, PHILOSOPHY OF), the position of those who maintain that natural theology is neither possible nor desirable, and that religious belief does not require the support of reason. There are several degrees of fideism, according to its critics, which correspond with different views of the nature of the conflict between reason and faith: some, for example, assert that theism is not rationally justified, while others assert that it is not so much as intelligible. The fact that Wittgensteinian and Reformed critics of EVIDENTIALISM are routinely dismissed as fideists, however, brings the usefulness of the concept into question. C.C.

field.

(1) A SET of objects with two methods of combination, usually called + and ×, possessing the usual algebraic (see ALGEBRA) properties (extending to subtraction and division). Familiar examples are the rational

numbers (see NUMBER), the real numbers and the complex numbers. These are infinite, but an 11-hour clock (labelled from zero to ten) gives a finite field ($3 + 4 = 7$, $3 + 8 = 0$, $3 \times 4 = 1$, etc.).

As with groups (see GROUP THEORY), a hunt began to find all the finite fields – it started later, in 1910, but the answer was simpler: for any prime number p and whole number n there is just one field with pn elements (and that's the lot).

These are called the Galois Fields. They are used to construct finite geometries (having only a finite number of points) which in turn lead to designs (used in wheat-growing trials for efficient statistical analysis). They are also used to construct efficient error-correcting codes. N.A.R.

(2) The systems considered in PHYSICS often consist of PARTICLES moving under the action of their mutual forces of attraction or repulsion, according to the laws of NEWTONIAN MECHANICS or QUANTUM MECHANICS. It frequently simplifies the analysis of such systems if some of the particles are considered as the sources of an influence – a *field* – which exists throughout space even when the other particles are not there to feel it. A field is thus basically a matter of conceptual convenience, the carrier of interactions between particles, avoiding the intuitively awkward notion of 'action at a distance' (but see FIELD THEORY). For example: the ELECTRONS constituting the current in the transmitting aerial of a TELECOMMUNICATIONS system produce an ELECTROMAGNETIC FIELD spreading out in space, which then exerts forces on the electrons in any receiving aerial within range; it would be needlessly complicated to consider the electron–electron interactions between the transmitter and each separate receiver.

More generally, any physical quantity varying continuously in space and time is referred to as a field (e.g. the temperature in an aircraft wing, or the pressure in a sound wave). M.V.B.

field archaeology. That aspect of ARCHAEOLOGY which deals with the recognition and planning of ancient landscapes. The techniques used include air photography, RESISTIVITY SURVEYING, surface searching ('field walking'), and survey; some archaeologists would include excavation. The importance of field archaeology was emphasized and demonstrated by O. G. S. Crawford during his employment by the Ordnance Survey. For further reading: M. Aston, *Interpreting the Landscape* (1985). B.C.

field painting, see under ABSTRACT EXPRESSIONISM.

field theory. The attempt to unify the basic laws of PHYSICS by deriving them from the interactions between FIELDS. These fields would become the basic entities of physics, and ELEMENTARY PARTICLES would, hopefully, appear as a result of applying the laws of QUANTUM MECHANICS. This programme is in its infancy, the most successful field theories being the general theory of RELATIVITY (incorporating GRAVITATION into MECHANICS) and *quantum electrodynamics* (incorporating ELECTROMAGNETISM into quantum mechanics). M.V.B.

fieldwork. Method of obtaining information about a particular society through first-hand intensive observation or participant observation. It has become the central and distinguishing feature of social ANTHROPOLOGY. Fieldwork for anthropologists is their RITE DE PASSAGE into the discipline. Expeditions at the end of the 19th century, particularly the famous 1898 Torres Straits expedition, represented a movement away from the armchair speculations of James Frazer and others. Face-to-face contact with the people being studied was established.

It was Malinowski, however, who developed the method of fieldwork which was to distinguish anthropology. Between 1915 and 1918 he lived among the Trobriand Islanders of New Guinea. He participated in their social activity, he learned the local language and kept a detailed record of the daily minutiae of their lives.

For many years anthropologists presented the material they gathered in the form of objective monographs. The relationship between the observer and the observed was rarely, if ever, discussed. Anthropology was pursued as a science, and elaborate methods of collection and classification of data were developed by those working in the field (E. R. Leach, *Rethinking Anthropology*, 1961). The question of the objectivity of social anthropology is now much debated. The posthumous publication of the very personal diary kept by Malinowski while he was in the Trobriand Islands (*A Diary in the Strict Sense of the Term*, 1967) did much to open this debate. Subsequent anthropologists have been more willing to recognize themselves as part of the material collected, but they have continued to publish what they regard as scholarly and personal aspects of fieldwork as separate accounts (e.g. N. Barley, *The Innocent Anthropologist*, 1983). For further reading: G. W. Stocking Jr, *Observers Observed* (1983). A.G.

fifth column. A term coined in October 1936 during the Spanish Civil War by a Nationalist General, Emilio Mola, to denote the underground supporters who, he claimed, were ready to rise within Madrid as four Nationalist columns converged on the city. The term was adopted during World War II to describe secret sympathizers of NAZISM in unoccupied parts of western Europe, then extended to denote any hidden group of enemies within a state, society or organization. S.R.

figurative. Adjective applied (as distinct from 'non-figurative' or abstract (see ABSTRACT ART) to works of visual art involving the portrayal, however allusive or distorted, of elements of the visible world. Hence also 'figuration'. J.W.

figure-ground phenomenon. The characteristic organization of PERCEPTION into a figure that 'stands out' against an undifferentiated background, e.g. a printed word against a background page. What is figural at any one moment depends on patterns of sensory stimulation and on the momentary interests of the perceiver. See also GESTALT. I.M.L.H.

film noir. Generic term originally applied by French critics to a group of markedly pessimistic American films (*c.* 1944–54) reflecting a darkening national mood as World War II drew to a close with chords of uncertainty struck by the death of President Roosevelt, the dropping of the first atomic bombs, the problematic social reintegration of returning servicemen, the formation of the House Un-American Activities Committee, and – by no means least importantly because closest to Hollywood and home – the series of violent labour disputes which had been simmering during the war years within the enormously wealthy film industry. Channelled into plots frequently drawn from pulp writers of the hard-boiled Dashiell Hammett school, often directed by émigré film-makers like Fritz Lang, Billy Wilder, Robert Siodmak and John Brahm who had been schooled in the expressionist ANGST of the German cinema of the 1920s, these doubts and fears emerged transformed into a series of dark, despairing thrillers, redolent of perversity, violence, betrayal, obsession and persecution, and haunted by an indefinable sense of menace. *Film noir* was coined by analogy with *La Série Noire*, a French paperback series which specialized in hard-boiled thrillers, often translated, from Dashiell Hammett, James M. Cain, Raymond Chandler, David Goodis, Cornell Woolrich, Dorothy B. Hughes and other writers regularly adapted by *films noir*. The term is often now used more loosely to describe a film of any period meeting the requirements of mood. For further reading: A. Silver and E. Ward, *Film Noir* (1980). T.C.C.M.

filtration, see under BIOPHYSICS.

final anthropic principle, see under ANTHROPIC PRINCIPLE.

Final Solution, see under HOLOCAUST, THE.

finitism, see under INTUITIONISM (3).

Finlandization. The indirect but total control of a small country by a large and powerful neighbour. It is drawn from the relationship which was supposed to have obtained between Finland and the former USSR, and has become a term of political abuse in the West. While such arrangements do exist between large and small states, it did not accurately describe the position of Finland. Finland, which until 1917 was a province of Imperial Russia, learned how to co-exist with her large, dictatorial neighbour. The Finns had demonstrated their capacity to fight against the Russians three times in this century. At the end of World War II, Finland was not annexed like those other former provinces, Latvia, Lithuania and Estonia, but allowed to remain independent. The arrangement persisted because it was advantageous to both sides. It provided the Soviet Union with a point of contact with the outside world, while the Finns learned those matters over which it was unwise to provoke the Soviet Union. The consequence was a nation with a very high standard of living, a continuing sense of Finnish nationality, and a high degree of practical, if limited, freedom. For further reading: G. Ginsburg and A. Z. Rubenstein (eds), *Soviet Foreign Policy towards Western Europe* (1978). A.J.M.W.

firm, theories of. The economic activities of production, transportation, MARKETING, research, development and decision-making are all included in the theory of the firm. The first theories assumed that firms operated purely in the interests of their owners and attempted to maximize profits. Firms may be forced to maximize profits by the owner-managers pursuing their own interests, managers being concerned about their performance being monitored by shareholders, and by the fear of takeovers and MERGERS. The assumption of profit maximization is a convenient analytical tool and has led to many predictions and theories (see STRUCTURE-CONDUCT-PERFORMANCE THEORY). However, the recognition of an increasing separation between management and ownership of firms led to the development of managerial theories that propose that managers are capable of maximizing their own objectives such as growth, security, salaries and discretionary non-productive expenditure, e.g. luxurious offices. The predictions of managerial theories sometimes differ from those of profit-maximizing theories. For example, managerial theories predict that there will be more mergers and takeovers than can be justified by gains in future efficiency or profitability; these acquisitions are a consequence of managers' desire for growth and security from being taken over themselves. If firms operate in an environment characterized by uncertainty, it is not clear that it is possible to maximize any objective. An alternative theory is based on the suggestion that firms are composed of groups and individuals pursuing different objectives. The firm reconciles the different interests and aspirations by negotiation and setting of targets. The firm sets targets by using rules that have given satisfactory results in the past – this behaviour is called *satisficing*. If the targets cannot be met, they are either reassessed or greater efforts are made to achieve them. These theories have variously been termed *behavioural, bargaining, coalition* and satisficing models. They have been criticized for being mere descriptions of actual behaviour and not providing scope for analysis and prediction. The different theories of the firm are not necessarily competing models, as they can be of analytical, descriptive and prescriptive use for different types of problems. For further reading: M. C. Sawyer, *Theories of the Firm* (1979). J.P.

first-strike capability, see under STRATEGIC CAPABILITY.

first wave feminism. The European Enlightenment of the 18th century created intense debates about the nature of CITIZENSHIP and the centrality of education to an ordered and civilized society. It was recognized by many women that these debates largely excluded women, and assumed a public space which was the preserve of men. Thus 'first wave' feminists (see FEMINISM) – of whom the most well known was Mary Wollstonecraft – were intensely concerned with ensuring that the new CODE and language of citizenship were not ones which excluded women. Wollstonecraft, in *A Vindication of the Rights of Woman* (1792), argued passionately for a concept and process of education which included women in the public world as much as it did not exclude men from the private sphere. That first priority – allowing women access to the world of public POWER and politics – has always received attention, but the second of Wollstonecraft's demands is of equal significance. Nevertheless, first wave feminists in both North America and Europe were primarily concerned with issues relating to the public world: the campaign for enfranchisement was the definitive campaign of first wave feminism. Among other issues which involved women in first wave feminist campaigns were rights of access to education (particularly higher education), the professions (see PROFESSIONALIZATION) and autonomy in the control of FERTILITY. For further reading: K. Rogers, *Feminism in Eighteenth Century England* (1982). M.S.E.

first world. Term for states regarded as developed CAPITALIST countries, high-income market economies, in which capital and land are owned privately. In 1997, high-income countries were those with a GNP per person of more than $9,000 (World Bank, *World Development Report*). These include most OECD countries and NEWLY INDUSTRIALIZING COUNTRIES.

Initially the first world was differentiated from the second world, high-income SOCIALIST countries or centrally planned countries, where the government owns the means of production. The term second world is rarely used now, especially since 1989–91, when eastern Europe, the former USSR, Mongolia, China and VIETNAM have been moving, albeit haltingly, towards the market and (sometimes) private ownership. Ironically, not only are many former second world countries no longer considered socialist countries, but new evidence indicates that virtually none were high-income countries in the 20th century. Countries formerly considered in the second world are, at present, labelled economies of transition, implying a passage to the market; some, such as Poland, are expected to attain high-income status during the early years of the 21st century.

Both first world and second world, for developed countries, have been used in contrast to the THIRD WORLD or DEVELOPING COUNTRIES. For further reading: E. W. Nafziger, *The Economics of Developing Countries* (1997). E.W.N.

Firthian. Characteristic of, or a follower of, the linguistic principles of J. R. Firth (1890–1960), Professor of General Linguistics in the University of London (1944–56), and the formative influence on the development of LINGUISTICS in Great Britain. A central notion is *polysystemicism*, an approach to linguistic analysis based on the view that language patterns cannot be accounted for in terms of a single system of analytic principles and categories (*monosystemic* linguistics), but that different systems may need to be set up at different places within a description; for other features see COLLOCATION, CONTEXT OF SITUATION and PROSODIC FEATURE. Relatively little of Firth's teaching was published, but many of his ideas have been developed by a *neo-Firthian* group of scholars, whose main theoretician is M. A. K. Halliday, Professor of General Linguistics at University College London from 1965 to 1970 (see SCALE-AND-CATEGORY GRAMMAR; SYSTEMIC GRAMMAR). For further reading: J. R. Firth, *Papers in Linguistics 1934–1951* (1957). D.C.

fiscal drag. The deflationary impulse (see INFLATION) generated through the budget when rising money incomes cause government revenues to expand (at unchanged rates of tax) while public expenditure lags behind. This withdrawal of purchasing power may arise because of the increase in real output and incomes which overflows into additional tax revenue and acts as a drag on further growth unless offsetting action is taken to increase government expenditure or reduce TAXATION. A similar effect may be produced by inflation if, for example, rising money incomes are tapped by progressive taxation so that tax revenues expand faster than government expenditures. A.C.

fiscal policy. The policy of a government in controlling its own expenditure and TAXATION, which together make up its budget. The term usually refers to transactions of the central government, but, depending partly on a country's political structure, may also extend to other parts of the PUBLIC SECTOR, namely state or local governments and public enterprise.

Fiscal policy has several functions. One is to regulate, together with MONETARY POLICY and *exchange rate policy*, the level of economic activity, the price level, and the BALANCE OF PAYMENTS. Another is to determine the allocation of productive resources between the public and PRIVATE SECTORS, and among the different parts of the public sector. A third is to influence the distribution of income and wealth, both through taxation and through social expenditures. The size of the public sector and the distribution of wealth are also affected by moves to extend or restrict public ownership, but this is not part of fiscal policy as such.

The government budget in a particular year is said to be in surplus, balance or deficit according as tax receipts exceed, equal or fall short of expenditure. Spending in excess of tax receipts is called *deficit spending*. This term is sometimes applied more narrowly to an excess of government spending on current account alone – rather than of total spending, which includes capital items – over total tax receipts. The budget position is of key importance in connection with the regulation of economic activity and prices. This function of fiscal policy is closely related to KEYNESIAN economic theory, but the MONETARIST view suggests that fiscal policy has little, or perhaps even a harmful, effect on economic activity. An increase in the budget deficit (or reduction in the surplus) boosts AGGREGATE DEMAND; a narrowing of the deficit restricts it. The budget position is affected not only by government decisions to alter taxation or expenditure, but also by fluctuations in economic activity itself. In the upswing, as employment and incomes rise, the budget is strengthened by accelerated tax receipts and a slowdown of social security outlays; in the downswing the movement is reversed. Since a tighter budget helps to curb the boom and an easier budget to limit the recession, the fiscal mechanism thus provides some degree of automatic stabilization (see AUTOMATIC STABILIZERS) to the economy. The fiscal stance of a government is measured by the FULL EMPLOYMENT SURPLUS.

Deficit finance is the finance for deficit spending, and is normally provided by borrowing against the issue of government securities (bonds or Treasury bills), thus adding to the NATIONAL DEBT. A budget deficit may also be financed directly by MONEY CREATION. Conversely, a budget surplus may be used to redeem debt and reduce the money supply. Fiscal policy and national-debt management have important implications for monetary policy. Newly issued government debt, which is used to finance a deficit, may be taken up by (a) the banking system, (b) other domestic residents, or (c) foreign residents. In (a) the quantity of money expands, unless bank credit to the private sector is simultaneously reduced. In (b) the money stock is unchanged; a rise in interest rates may be necessary to induce the public to buy the new debt. In (c) the money stock again remains unchanged if the government's overseas borrowing serves to finance a balance of payments deficit; otherwise it increases, as the central bank creates domestic currency in exchange for the foreign currency which foreigners sell in order to acquire the government debt in question. For further reading: R. A. Musgrave and P. B. Musgrave, *Public Finance in Theory and Practice* (1980).

P.M.O.; J.P.

fission.

(1) In PHYSICS, the splitting of an atomic NUCLEUS, usually by free NEUTRONS during a CHAIN REACTION. For heavy elements the total mass of the fission fragments is less than that of the original nucleus + neutrons, so that large amounts of ENERGY are released (see MASS-ENERGY EQUATION). The atomic bomb, and NUCLEAR REACTORS, derive their energy from fission. See also MODERATOR; QUANTUM MECHANICS; THERMAL NEUTRON. M.V.B.

(2) (in ANTHROPOLOGY), see under LINEAGE.

fission track dating, see under DATING.

fitness, see under DARWINISM.

fixation. In psychoanalytic theory (see PSYCHOANALYSIS), a NEUROSIS consisting of the arrestation of PSYCHOSEXUAL DEVELOPMENT in one of its immature stages (e.g. anal, phallic). W.Z.

flaming. The vituperative insults and personal attacks common to E-MAIL and NEWSGROUPS. Personal abuse of an intensity that is extremely rare in face-to-face confrontations is a regular feature of INTERNET communications, making it difficult to swallow wholly the vision of utopians (see UTOPIANISM) who hope the Internet is creating a global community. Although flames can take any form, a frequent theme is 'I'm right and you are a fool'. E.B.B.

flâneur. A French word meaning stroller, particularly someone who strolls around urban areas. The idea of the flâneur was particularly developed by Walter Benjamin in *Charles Baudelaire: A Lyric Poet in the Era of High Capitalism* (1969). In Baudelaire's work it was originally applied to 19th-century Paris but is now used more generally. The flâneur strolls the streets observing metropolitan life but at the same time being part of the spectacle of the city (see URBANIZATION) himself; he (flâneurs tend to be portrayed as men) wants to be seen as well as seeing others. The significance of flâneurs is ambiguous. They can be seen as detectives and philosophers who interpret the meaning of street life or as rather sad figures who can only feel fulfilled through being part of the transitory and shallow spectacle of urban life. For further reading: K. Tester (ed.), *The Flâneur* (1994). M.D.H.

flat/round characters. Terms coined by E. M. Forster (*Aspects of the Novel*, 1927), and used in criticism of novels, plays and films to distinguish between, at one extreme, characters 'constructed round a single idea or quality' and, at the other, highly complex characters 'capable of surprising in a convincing way'. Flat characters, though usually 'best when they are comic', are not necessarily the product of lesser artistry than round ones: Dickens's characters, for example, are mostly flat. O.S.

flexible firm. According to the British economist John Atkinson there has been a trend, starting in the 1970s, towards firms (see FIRM, THEORIES OF) becoming more flexible. This flexibility takes two forms. Firstly, functional flexibility involves the ability of managers to redeploy skilled key or core workers between a variety of tasks. Secondly, numerical flexibility involves firms being able rapidly to increase or reduce the number of workers directly or indirectly employed by them. These peripheral workers are not employed full-time by the flexible firm but may be self-employed, on short-term contracts or employed by companies to which work has been subcontracted. Flexible firms are seen as well adapted to an era in which consumer tastes change rapidly and GLOBALIZATION makes it difficult for firms to predict demand for their products. The theory is closely linked to the concept of POST-FORDISM. For further reading: F. Atkinson, 'The Changing Corporation' in D. Clutterbuck (ed.), *New Patterns of Work* (1985). M.D.H.

FLN (Front de Liberation Nationale), see under ALGERIAN WAR OF INDEPENDENCE.

floodplain. The flat area adjacent to streams or rivers that has been formed by the erosion and sedimentation caused by periodic flooding over time, and by lateral migration of meander streams. The deposition of sediment combined with flat topography make floodplains fertile and attractive sites for agriculture, as well as for human settlements. POPULATION PRESSURE often results in continuing residential or urban development, which drives prime agricultural land from production, forcing farming onto less fertile, more erosion-prone sites.

When dikes and levees are constructed to prevent flooding, the enrichment of the floodplain by sediment deposition is also prevented, and flood waters, rather than being dissipated on the floodplain, are transferred downstream where they may cause more severe flooding. W.G.R.

flotation process. The process which brings to the surface fine PARTICLES dispersed in a liquid, usually water. A SURFACTANT absorbed in the surface of the particle makes it water-repellent, thus encouraging the particle to remain at the air–water interface. Mainly used for the enrichment of ores, surfactants are also used to effect a differential separation of the suspended mixture of particles. B.F.

flow chart.

(1) In general, any sequential diagrammatic representation of the movements of materials or people.

(2) In computing, an informal method of representing an ALGORITHM or a computer program. It is not suitable for all types of program and is most often used in commercial data-processing. It is intended for use by human beings, and the amount of detail included can vary widely. Even the most detailed flow chart has ultimately to be expressed in a formal programming language – a process known as CODING. C.S.

fluidics. The TECHNOLOGY of small fluid devices, e.g. pipes, joints, elbows in pipes, etc., used as substitutes for electronic circuits. Thus, a Y-shaped junction behaves as a two-state device analogous to an electronic flip-flop circuit: the supply fluid entering by the vertical member is directed into one or other of the branches by means of a small pilot jet or vane. For some control systems (see CONTROL ENGINEERING) fluidic devices are cheaper and more robust than their electronic counterparts. E.R.L.

fluidized bed. A bed of solid particles, e.g. sand, which is given the properties of a liquid by blowing air through the particles. The principle can be applied to the improvement of coal combustion where powdered coal is 'fluidized' by air within the combustion chamber. E.R.L.

fluorescence. The absorption of light at one wavelength and its subsequent emission at a different wavelength, as when the coating of the tube in a fluorescent lamp absorbs ultraviolet light produced by mercury vapour in the tube, and emits visible light. See also RADIATION. M.V.B.

fluoridation. The addition of minute quantities of fluoride IONS to drinking water to reduce the incidence of dental caries. The mechanism is obscure but the fluoride ions probably exchange with some of the hydroxyl ions in the bone mineral apatite, which forms part of the hard tissues of the teeth. The medical profession is united in recommending fluoridation as a public-health measure, but action is often blocked politically by INTEREST GROUPS who object to what they see as government interference with a resource as essential as drinking water. B.F.

Fluxus. Latin word for 'flux' applied by George Maciunas in 1962 to an iconoclastic group of artists, primarily American and West German, of which he was the chief spokesman and organizer. A form of DADA revival, this short-lived movement manifested itself in HAPPENINGS (beginning with a performance in Wiesbaden in 1962) and publications. Associated with Fluxus were Wolf Vostell, Allan Kaprow and the publisher Dick Higgins, while a major influence was the composer John Cage. See also ALEATORY. For further reading: A. Kaprow, *Assemblage, Environments and Happenings* (1966). A.K.W.

flying pickets, see under PICKETING.

FM, see FREQUENCY MODULATION.

FMLN, see under EL SALVADOR.

FMS, see FALSE MEMORY SYNDROME.

folk. An age-old and familiar word which in comparatively recent years has become the first element in an ever-growing list (see, for example, the *Supplement* to the *Oxford English Dictionary*) of compound nouns and phrases, a few of which are treated separately below. The common element in all these terms is that the phenomenon in question is regarded as springing from, or intimately associated with, the 'folk' in the sense of the common people, the PRIMITIVE or less-educated elements of society. 'Folk' in this sense (as against POP) carries connotations of traditionalism, collective wisdom, anonymity, spontaneity, simplicity and sincerity, and is something of a rallying cry with those people (within a wide spectrum of political views) who value such qualities, particularly in opposition to sophistication, flamboyant INDIVIDUALISM, commercialism, MODERNISM, COSMOPOLITANISM and DECADENCE. The adjective *folksy*, on the other hand, is used mostly in a pejorative sense, by those who feel that there is a lack of discrimination, and in some cases an element of self-consciousness, among 'folk' enthusiasts. O.S.

folk art. A category of art that acquired distinctive status (unsophisticated or PRIMITIVE art has always existed) during the latter half of the 19th century, thanks (a) to the development of ANTHROPOLOGY; (b) to the early writings on popular imagery etc. by, most notably, Champfleury, and (c) to the drive for popular awareness of the arts which followed the institution of compulsory education and the writings of William Morris, Tolstoy and others. Today the concept has been somewhat tarnished by its abuse in Nazi (see NAZISM) and Soviet art policy and by its association elsewhere with nostalgia for a pre-industrial society. POP art is another matter. J.W.

folk culture. The social heritage – the INSTITUTIONS, CUSTOMS, conventions, values, skills, arts, modes of living – of a group of people feeling themselves members of a closely bound COMMUNITY, and sharing a deep-rooted attachment and allegiance to it. A folk culture is distinguished from more complex CULTURES in that it is predominantly *non-literate*, and so closely knit as to be transmitted from generation to generation by oral means and by RITUAL and behavioural habituation. See also SUBCULTURE. For further reading: R. Redfield, *Peasant Society and Culture* (1956). R.F.

folk literature. Term loosely applied to oral-traditional works of literary value (in the sense that they have invigorated and even been the prime inspiration of literary works, e.g. Homer) that entertain or have entertained and, to an (arguable) extent, originate from 'the FOLK'. The origins of folk literature (which embraces folk-song, folk-tales, ballads, riddles, proverbs and folk-drama) are mysterious, as are those of PRIMITIVE art, and they approximate in important respects to the untrained, unsophisticated, naïve component in all literature. Thus the greatest writers – Dante, Cervantes, Shakespeare, Goethe – all incorporate much folk material in their work. Important examples of folk literature are: the early epics (the Elder Edda, the East Karelian narrative folk-songs from which Lonnrot compiled the *Kalevala*, etc.), the ballads, the folk-songs, the folk-drama (for example, the dramatic treatment of traditional themes, usually at religious festivals, from which the ancient Greek drama developed), the earlier layers of Homeric epic, and the fairy tales. M.S.-S.

folk model, see under LINEAGE.

folk music. As the term suggests, music *of the people*. Folk music is a very broad concept (though not so portmanteau as its cousin, WORLD MUSIC) which can include music generated mainly in rural areas, from antiquity to the present, often composed by untrained musicians and often non-existent in written form. It is most often used to refer to the mainly acoustic music of America and Great Britain exemplified by 20th-century artists as diverse as Woodie Guthrie, the Carter family, Bob Dylan, John Renbourne, Jacqui McShee and others. Folk music often carries a political message, with songs that tell of the trials and tribulations of the poor and disenfranchised in the face of unsympathetic employers, disaster or STATE abuses of POWER. In the UK, the contemporary folk tradition derives from sources as diverse as sea shanties and the songs of agricultural workers. In the US, folk music draws from the experience of Americans of all colours and conditions. Its tradition includes the *delta blues* of artists like Mississippi John Hurt, singing of rural hardship and joy in the post-slavery era; *bluegrass*, a fiddle-, guitar- and banjo-based music often played at breakneck speed; and *country and western* music which, in its purest form, is a kind of 'white blues' (Willie Nelson), but is often sold as an overproduced confection by Nashville producers.

Folk music enjoyed an enormous revival in the US during the early 1960s (the 'great folk music scare'), and many folk musicians congregated and played in New York City's GREENWICH VILLAGE. Prominent among these was David van Ronk, who would become the guitar teacher of Bob Dylan and, later, of a new generation of folk performers like Rory Block, who combined traditional folk, blues and GOSPEL elements to keep the tradition alive during the 1990s.

Folk music, and the new BEAT culture, found a new type of venue for theatre, music, poetry and conversation: the *coffee house* – a HIP revival of an idea made fashionable in 18th-century London. The oldest continuously operating coffee house in America is *Caffe Lena*, located 150 miles north of New York City in the town of Saratoga Springs. S.T.

folklore. A word coined by W. J. Thoms in 1846 for a central part of FOLK CULTURE: the collective 'wisdom' or 'learning' of the 'FOLK', as embodied in customs, beliefs, RITUALS, games, dances, songs, legends, MYTHS, tales, proverbs, 'sayings', etc. (see FOLK LITERATURE; FOLK MUSIC), all passed on by word of mouth. The term, and the collection by numerous folklore societies and by scholars like Max Müller, Andrew Lang and G. L. Gomme of stories, poems and songs not yet committed to paper, originated in the 19th century. In current popular usage it often means merely a corpus of erroneous but widely held beliefs. For further reading: R. M. Dorson, *The British Folklorists* (1968). R.F.

folkways. Term used by the American sociologist and SOCIAL DARWINIST W. G. Sumner for all those ways of doing things (from technical tasks to religious observances) which, within a COMMUNITY whose members share the same 'life-conditions', gradually come to be not only established, but also sanctioned and obligatory. Sumner believed that in every society an initial body of such folkways underlay all subsequent developments of doctrines, *mores*, law and reflective morality. They were the distinguishing foundation of all human societies; the bedrock on which all else came to be erected. For further reading: W. G. Sumner, *Folkways* (1907). R.F.

food chain. A series of ORGANISMS which eat those lower in the chain, and are eaten by those higher up. A simple food chain is grass–bullock–man. Simple food chains are rare, and the term *food web* is preferable, as this recognizes that most plants are eaten by many different herbivores (e.g. caterpillars, slugs, voles and cattle all eat grass), and that most predators consume a variety of prey. The concept of the food web also includes the breakdown, partly by bacterial decomposition, of dead animals and plants, the incorporation of the nutrients from their tissues into the soil, and the subsequent take-up of the same nutrients by a new generation of plants.

A food chain usually takes the form of a pyramid. The broad base, e.g. grass, contains a great deal of material, in which a smaller mass of herbivores subsist. Higher up come the carnivores, less numerous and containing fewer materials. The pyramidal structure reflects the inefficiency with which the nutrient elements are used. As well as nutrients, toxic substances (e.g. DDT) pass up food chains from prey to predator, and may be retained in the greatest concentration by the organism highest in the chain. K.M.

food policy. A commonly used phrase to describe a set of policy measures, mainly in a THIRD WORLD context, to improve the production and distribution of food, to provide early warning of FAMINE, and to secure international assistance. Though necessarily closely related to AGRICULTURAL POLICY, the emphasis is switched from the farm sector *per se* to the total population with the aim of promoting food security. International action is promoted by a number of agencies such as FAO, the 1980 Food Aid Convention, and the IMF (see BRETTON WOODS) through its food facility established in 1981 as an extension of the compensatory finance facility. Following the problems in Africa in the 1980s, the adequacy of the measures available is strongly debated. G.H.P.

force, see under POWER.

force de frappe. Literally, 'striking force'. This is the popular term for the French independent Strategic Nuclear Force (SNF) developed in the 1960s. The *force de frappe* was a central plank of Gaullist defence policy which was NATIONALIST and anti-Atlanticist in character. Maintenance and development of the SNF is supported by all major political parties in France. S.M.

force ouvrière**,** see under CGT.

forced labour.

(1) During the Nazis' wartime domination of Europe (see NAZISM), millions of workers were forcibly deported from the defeated and occupied countries to provide labour for German factories and farms. In many cases they were treated as no more than slaves, and recruiting and employing forced labour was one of the WAR CRIMES with which the defendants at the NUREMBERG TRIALS were charged. See also CONCENTRATION CAMPS.

(2) Forced labour camps were established in the former USSR as early as 1918 as penal colonies to which millions of Soviet citizens who were regarded with suspicion by the authorities were sent for 'correction', and where most of them died. A great expansion took place during Stalin's campaign, 1928–32, to collectivize (see COLLECTIVIZATION) Russian agriculture and destroy the resistance of the peasants. The total of those arrested in the period 1930–37 who died in camps is estimated at 3.5 million (in addition to the 11 million peasants estimated to have died in the countryside, the great majority from famine). The Stalinist purges of 1936–38 produced further waves of arrests and imprisonment to which must be added those incarcerated after the Soviet occupation of Poland and the Baltic states, German POWs, and Russian POWs returning to the USSR after the war.

The total number at any given time has never been disclosed but has been estimated as reaching a peak of 12–15 million. The huge complex of camps, estimated at the end of the Stalin era (1950) at around 200 scattered throughout Siberia, the Arctic and the Far East, was placed under the Central Camps Administration (see GULAG), a subdivision of the KGB, which exercised an economic as well as a political function by providing forced labour for logging, mining and the construction of such major projects as the White Sea–Baltic canal, particularly in areas with harsh climatic conditions.

Taking the whole period of the Stalin regime, 1930–53, it has been estimated that the number of those who died from hunger, cold and maltreatment, or were executed, exceeded 20 million, and may have been considerably higher. The inhuman regime in the camps improved somewhat after 1950, but it was only after Stalin's death, when a series of strikes and revolts took place, that the government began to reduce their population. Some camps were dismantled, others were transformed into milder 'corrective labour colonies'. However, a number of labour camps with an especially harsh regime were retained. For further reading: E. L. Homze, *Foreign Labor in Nazi Germany* (1967); Alexander Solzhenitsyn, *The Gulag Archipelago* (1974). L.L.; A.L.C.B.

Fordism. A term coined in the 1930s by the Italian MARXIST Antonio Gramsci to refer to the intent and accomplishments of the American car manufacturer Henry Ford in his Detroit plant at the beginning of the century. Ford's pioneering mechanization and AUTOMATION of car production, his employment of the techniques of 'scientific management' in work practices, and his far-sightedness in paying higher than average wages to his employees in return for industrial peace, were seen as representative of capitalist industrial civilization at a particular point in its evolution (see CAPITALISM; INDUSTRIAL SOCIETY; INDUSTRIALIZATION). Fordism came to be associated with the mass production of standardized items by largely unskilled workers in large factories. It is the image of industrial society most often evoked in the popular mind – for instance, in Charlie Chaplin's film *Modern Times* (1936) – even though the majority of workers in industrial societies have never been factory workers. In the 1960s and 1970s, as this form of mass production came under challenge from new forms of work and production, theorists revived the Gramscian concept of Fordism, largely to contrast it with the emerging theory and practice of POST-FORDISM. K.K.

forecasting. In ECONOMICS (but see also TECHNOLOGICAL FORECASTING), the prediction of the future using analytical methods and techniques. Forecasts are required for the development of plans and for evaluating the effects of different policies. Forecasting requires a MODEL of how certain VARIABLES are determined by other variables. These variables are termed endogenous and exogenous respectively. The model has to be tested in some manner and validated as an adequate representation of reality. In order to use the model in forecasting, it is necessary to make forecasts of the exogenous variables. In many cases, trying to set these variables simply raises new problems of forecasting. As the future is uncertain, it is appropriate to prepare a range of forecasts and test plans and policies for different contingencies. This requires some indication of the probabilities (see PROBABILITY THEORY) of the different futures occurring. However, this is a very difficult task owing to the nature of UNCERTAINTY. There are many different forecasting techniques (see ECONOMETRICS). For further reading: S. Makridakis and S. C. Wheelwright, *Forecasting Methods and Applications* (1978). J.P.

foreclosure. In PSYCHOANALYSIS, a term (*Verwerfung*) to which Freud makes a small number of references (see FREUDIAN). In Lacan's work this concept is elaborated, and given an important place within the psychoanalytic theory of the PSYCHOSES (see LACANIAN). REPRESSION, for both Freud and Lacan, was an operation on a SIGNIFIER, something that one was only aware of through its return in the signifying chain in, for example, a slip of the tongue, or a joke. What is foreclosed, however, does not return in the signifying chain, but returns in the real, in the form of, for example, visual and auditory hallucinations. It thus testifies to an impairment of the standard neurotic structure of repression, that is, signifying substitution, and Lacan saw it as involving, more precisely, the foreclosure of the NAME-OF-THE-FATHER, that is, the operator which allows the SUBJECT to symbolize and localize JOUISSANCE in the phallic function. In its absence, then, the subject is left open to the invasions of jouissance which characterize psychotic states (see PSYCHOSIS). D.L.

foregrounding. In STYLISTICS, and associated fields, any deviation from a linguistic or socially accepted norm. The analogy is of a figure seen against a background. A 'foregrounded' feature in English poetry would be the use of alliteration or rhyme. D.C.

foreign-body reaction, see under TRAUMA.

forensic linguistics. The use of linguistic techniques to investigate crimes in which language data form part of the evidence, such as in the use of grammatical or lexical criteria to authenticate police statements. The field of forensic phonetics is often distinguished as a separate domain, dealing with such matters as speaker identification, voice line-ups, speaker profiling, tape enhancement, tape authentication, and the decoding of disputed utterances. Forensic linguistic enquiries have been involved in several famous investigations: an analysis of the grammatical and lexical patterns of police statements played a role in demonstrating the innocence of Timothy Evans (the Christie murders), and forensic phoneticians were involved in the analysis of the regional accent on the tape sent to the police by the supposed Yorkshire Ripper. For further reading: R. W. Shuy, *Language Crimes* (1993). D.C.

forensic medicine. The interface between medicine and the law, also called 'legal medicine' or 'medical jurisprudence'. There are a number of specialist aspects, the best known being forensic PATHOLOGY, where post-mortem examinations of obscure, suspicious or criminal deaths assist the law enforcement agencies and the courts in the investigation of crime. The forensic pathologist often visits the scene of death to attempt to determine the time of death and the identity of the deceased where necessary, then performs an autopsy (post-mortem) to discover the cause of death and the extent of injuries or natural disease. His expertise can interpret such matters as the range and direction of gunshot wounds, the type of head injuries, the nature of stab wounds, and many other factors. As well as assisting in criminal cases, the forensic pathologist contributes to the knowledge of fatal traffic, domestic and industrial accidents and thus to their prevention; for example, motor-cycle crash-helmets and car seat-belts were developed as a result of forensic recommendations. Poisoning, environmental hazards, cot deaths and many natural diseases causing sudden unexpected death are also the province of the forensic pathologist. Other forensic specialists include the forensic odontologist (who applies dental techniques to legal problems); forensic physicians (who carry out legal examinations on living persons, such as drunken drivers, rape victims, abused children and persons in custody); forensic serologists (who deal with blood groups as well as being concerned with bloodstained weapons and clothing); and forensic psychiatrists (who deal with the mental state of accused and convicted persons, mainly in relation to criminal responsibility). See also PSYCHIATRY. B.H.K.

form. In LINGUISTICS, a term used in a variety of technical senses, of which the most important are:

(1) any linguistic element, or combination of elements, especially when studied without reference to their syntactic function;

(2) a variant of a linguistic element in a given context (e.g. the forms of a noun);

(3) the phonetic/phonological/grammatical (see PHONETICS; PHONOLOGY; GRAMMAR) characteristic of a linguistic element or unit, as opposed to its MEANING (e.g. the active form of a sentence). See also MORPHEME; UNIVERSAL; WORD CLASS. For further reading: D. Crystal, *A Dictionary of Linguistics and Phonetics* (1996). D.C.

form class, see under WORD CLASS.

form criticism, see under HIGHER CRITICISM.

form word, see under WORD CLASS.

formal (in LINGUISTICS), see under NOTIONAL.

formal operation. In DEVELOPMENTAL PSYCHOLOGY, a PIAGETIAN term for a mental operation involving the manipulation of PROPOSITIONS. For example, given the statements: X is taller than Z; X is shorter than Y, the subject can infer who is the tallest. According to Piaget such INFERENCES about propositions (as opposed to concrete objects) emerge during adolescence and characterize the final stage of intellectual development. P.L.H.

formal sociology. An approach in SOCIOLOGY founded by the German sociologist Georg Simmel, who tried to establish a 'geometry of social life' by identifying universal forms which could be found in social life at any place and time. The forms he identified included social roles (such as the stranger), different sizes of social groups (individuals, dyads, triads) and different types of interaction such as COMPETITION and conflict (see CONFLICT THEORY). While the content of social life varies with place and time, the role of, e.g., the stranger always has some common elements. Triads are always different to dyads (e.g. triads can have a mediator role whereas dyads cannot), and so on. There is no sociological perspective based solely or mainly upon Simmel's formal sociology but it did influence the CHICAGO SCHOOL and Erving Goffman (see, e.g., STIGMA and TOTAL INSTITUTION). It remains unclear whether formal sociology has much potential for explaining social phenomena or whether it merely provides some basic concepts for sociologists. For further reading: L. Ray (ed.), *Formal Sociology: The Sociology of Georg Simmel* (1991). M.D.H.

formalism. Any school or doctrine that emphasizes, any emphasis on or preoccupation with, form or forms or formal elements in any sphere: of thought, conduct, religion, art, literature, drama, music, etc. Specific uses include the following: O.S.

(1) The view of MATHEMATICS, developed by David Hilbert (1862–1943), that treats mathematical theories as pure deductive systems, no meaning being ascribed to the expressions of the system other than that implicitly assigned to them by its *formation-rules*, which regulate the possibilities of their combination in well-formed formulae (see AXIOMATICS). Bertrand Russell (1872–1970) objected that formalism takes no adequate account of the application of mathematics to the world (most elementarily in the use of arithmetic for counting), and other opponents have described it as 'a game with meaningless marks'. For further reading: R. L. Wilder, *Introduction to the Foundations of Mathematics* (1952). A.Q.

(2) A school of literary theory which flourished in the decade after 1917 in Russia. Its members included Viktor Schlovsky, Roman Jakobson, Boris Eichenbaum, Osip Brik, Jurii Tynyanov and Boris Tomashevsky. These theorists were concerned with what distinguishes a literary work from any other kind of written expression, and took as their object of study the purely formal, artificial and technical aspects of literature. One of their main contentions was that LITERARINESS is mainly achieved through the effect of DEFAMILIARIZATION. For further reading: T. Bennett, *Formalism and Marxism* (1979). R.PO.

(3) In music, the use of traditional forms such as the pavane, passacaglia or gavotte to give formal structure to ATONAL MUSIC, as in Berg's opera *Wozzeck*. A.H.

Fortress America. A term used loosely and widely to characterize an American withdrawal from complex international involvements to an ISOLATIONIST position in which it would rely on its military strength and (mythical) economic independence to resist attacks on its national territory. America's global commitments are so intricate that the phrase should be laid to rest. S.R.

foundationalism. In philosophical discussions of knowledge and belief (see EPISTEMOLOGY) the theory that our BELIEFS form an edifice resting upon a set of basic or *foundational* beliefs which provide the ultimate source of justification for the rest of the belief system. Any belief other than a basic one will, if it is justified, be so because it is immediately supported by a foundational belief or can be inferred from other beliefs so supported. Foundational beliefs themselves are required to be self-justifying, self-evident, or in some other way not themselves in need of justification. A theory which expressly rejects foundationalism is the coherence theory, which states that the justification of beliefs arises from relations of mutual support between them, no belief counting as any more 'basic' than any other. For further reading: K. Lehrer, *Knowledge* (1974). A.C.G.

founder effect, see under SPECIATION.

foundherentism. Theory of the justification of empirical beliefs, intermediate between the traditionally rival theories (see BELIEF; OBJECTIVITY). Foundherentism allows the relevance of a subject's experience, as foundationalism does, but without requiring any beliefs justified by experience alone and ultimately justifying all other justified beliefs. It allows pervasive mutual support, as coherentism does, but without making empirical justification a matter of relations among beliefs alone. What a person's evidence is for a belief is specified by reference to what causes that belief of his; how good his evidence is a quasi-logical matter. Justification is personal, and yet objective.

The foundherentist MODEL of the structure of evidence is a crossword puzzle; the clues are the analogue of experiential evidence, already completed intersecting entries of background beliefs, reasons. As the analogy suggests, degree of justification depends on how well a belief is supported by the subject's experiential evidence and reasons; how justified those reasons are, independent of the belief in question; and how much of the relevant evidence his evidence includes. Because of the qualification, 'independent of the belief in question', there is no vicious circle; because experiential evidence, unlike reasons, needs no justification, there is no infinite regress. For further reading: S. Haack, *Evidence and Inquiry: Towards Reconstruction in Epistemology* (1993). S.W.H.

four-colour conjecture. A mathematical hypothesis stating that if a plane be divided into regions (countries) then it is possible to colour them with at most four colours so that no two countries with a common frontier have the same colour. A fallacious proof (by A. B. Kempe in 1879) was accepted as correct for a decade. Despite intensive research and the development of special techniques, no counter-example was found. Finally, in July 1976, two mathematicians at Urbana, Illinois, claimed to have proved the conjecture by breaking it down into many thousands of cases and using a COMPUTER to check each one. The proof is nearly 1,000 pages long and has now been generally accepted as correct. For further reading: W. W. Rouse Ball, rev. H. S. M. Coxeter, *Mathematical Recreations and Essays* (1939). R.G.

Four Modernizations. A term used in China to refer to the modernization of Industry, Agriculture, Science and Technology and National Defence. Although the term has come to be associated with the economic policies pursued by Deng Xiaoping after 1978 (see DENGISM), it originated with Mao Zedong and was first proclaimed by Zhou Enlai in 1964, and the same four strategic areas for modernization were outlined by Lin Biao in his introduction to the *Quotations of Chairman Mao* (*The Little Red Book*). Deng took great pains to emphasize these precedents in a speech immediately prior to his establishment as leader of the Party at the 3rd Plenum of the 11th Central Committee of the Chinese Communist Party. The term is thus used to grant historical legitimacy to Deng's actions, and as a millenarian (see MILLENARIANISM) slogan to the masses who see achieving the Four Modernizations as the path to economic wellbeing and personal wealth. For further reading: J. Prybyla, *The Chinese Economy* (1978). S.B.

Fourier analysis/series. Baron Jean-Baptiste-Joseph Fourier (1768–1830), in the course of his studies of the transmission of heat, discovered that any graph (see GEOMETRY) in MATHEMATICS can be regarded as the combination of (perhaps infinitely many) simple oscillations (sine-waves) – specifying these oscillations is called Fourier analysis, and the resulting expression is a Fourier series. This is of fundamental importance in modern electronics, hi-fi systems, vibration of bridges, etc.: if one knows how such a system responds to a stimulus which is a simple oscillation, then one can deduce the effect of any more complex stimulus.

Nineteenth-century mathematicians (see MATHEMATICS) found his result disturbing – it stated that a formula could be found for a freehand-drawn graph, perhaps with kinks in it and other unpleasantnesses. They believed that formulae produced only nice smooth graphs.

Fourier, although trained as a mathematician, enjoyed a varied career: he received his barony from Napoleon for his work on the antiquities in Egypt, and he passed many years as a government administrator in Grenoble, draining swamps. N.A.R.

Fourteen Points. During World War I, these were contained in an address by President Woodrow Wilson to the US Congress on 8 January 1918. Despite objections from Britain and France, who had not been consulted, they became the basis of the Armistice with Germany of 11 November 1918, as a result of the Germans invoking them as the basis for an armistice in a note to President Wilson of 4 October 1918. They included: (1) 'Open covenants of peace openly arrived at' instead of secret diplomacy; (2) 'absolute freedom of navigation upon the seas . . . alike in peace and war'; (3) the removal of all trade barriers; (4) general disarmament; (5) impartial settlement of all colonial claims; (6, 7, 8) evacuation and restoration of territory in Russia, Belgium and France (including the return of Alsace-Lorraine); (9) readjustment of Italian frontiers; (10, 12) self-determination for peoples of the Habsburg and Ottoman empires; (11) restoration of territory of Romania, Montenegro and Serbia; (13) creation of an independent Poland with access to the Baltic; (14) establishment of a LEAGUE OF NATIONS. D.C.W.

fourth dimension. When locating an event, it is not sufficient to specify its position in ordinary three-dimensional space. The *time* at which the event occurred must also be known, and the term 'fourth dimension' emphasizes this property of time. See also SPACE-TIME. M.V.B.

fourth world, see under THIRD WORLD.

fractals. In PHYSICS, MATHEMATICS and in nature there are shapes and structures which, although they appear to be irregular and random, nevertheless have a special pattern of regularity in their 'randomness'. This regularity, called *self-similarity*, derives from the fact that at whatever magnification these systems are viewed they still look much the same. The term was invented by the Polish-born mathematician Benoit Mandelbrot (*Objets Fractals*, 1975). An example of a fractal is the shape of a coastline of a country with its inlets, bays, peninsulas, etc. This looks much the same from a high-flying aircraft, from the top of a cliff or close to the seashore and, unless there is a person or a building in the picture to give some idea of size, it is not possible to deduce the scale. If we draw a triangle and on each of its sides we draw a smaller triangle and on each side of these we draw a still smaller one – and so on – we have a figure which exhibits self-similarity and hence is a fractal. There are certain mathematical FUNCTIONS which when plotted out never produce smooth curves even over a very small range, and these, too, are fractal. It has been suggested that the arrangement of molecules in some AMORPHOUS MATERIALS is fractal, and this has led to the development of new mathematical techniques for treating systems with irregular structures. The concept of fractals is now being applied to many other areas where there is a pattern of irregularity – in fields as widely different as GEOLOGY, electrical noise, music and chaotic behaviour (see CHAOS). H.M.R.

fractionation. The separation of chemical substances by a repetitive process. For example, boiling gives a vapour enriched in the more volatile constituent, and successive condensations and reboiling in a specially designed column can effect complete separation. Fractional distillation is widely used in laboratories and industry to separate volatile liquids, and fractional crystallization to separate compounds in solution. B.F.

frame of reference. The context, viewpoint or set of PRESUPPOSITIONS or of evaluative CRITERIA within which a person's PERCEPTION and thinking seem always to occur, and which constrains selectively the course and outcome of these activities. I.M.L.H.

Frankfurt School. The persons and ideas associated with the Institute for Social Research, founded and affiliated to the University of Frankfurt in 1923 under the direction of Carl Grünberg. Exiled to New York during the era of NAZISM, the Institute returned home in 1949. Leading figures have included Max Horkheimer (Director, 1931–58), Walter Benjamin, Theodor Adorno and Herbert Marcuse. The school agreed on the necessity of providing a *critical theory* of MARXISM. This opposed all forms of POSITIVISM (especially those stressing the possibility of VALUE-FREEDOM in SOCIAL SCIENCE) and all interpretations of Marxism afflicted, like Stalin's, with crude MATERIALISM and immutable dogma. In the school's view, only an open-ended and continuously self-critical approach could avoid paralysis in the theory, and therefore also in the practice, of social transformation. Reinvigoration depended on greater appreciation of Marx's early writings, which became generally available only in the 1930s; they encouraged study particularly of Marxism's debt to certain features of Hegel, whose IDEALIST concern with consciousness as moulder of the world had been undervalued by the economic determinism of later orthodoxy (see HISTORICAL MATERIALISM). Consequently the school devoted more attention to areas that had become regarded as merely superstructural (see SUPERSTRUCTURE) and, especially through its treatment of the AESTHETICS of a MASS SOCIETY, sought to rescue Marxist cultural criticism from sterility. The school's leading contemporary figure, Jürgen Habermas (1929–), is notable particularly for his efforts to relate the conditions of rationality to the SOCIAL STRUCTURE of language use.

Though its writings have been more invoked than read, the Frankfurt School has made an important contribution to rehabilitating the libertarian aspect of Marx's thought (see LIBERTARIANISM). It has influenced such radical (see RADICALISM) movements as the NEW LEFT, which have been attracted by its rejection of modern technocratic society (see TECHNOCRACY) whether CAPITALIST or Soviet, and by its conviction that some satisfactory clear alternative can emerge only during the actual practice of REVOLUTION. For many opponents this latter point exemplifies most clearly an evasiveness which is deemed to reflect certain irrational inconsistencies in the school's whole approach to the CRITERIA of TRUTH. For further reading: A. Arato and E. Gebhardt (eds), *The Essential Frankfurt School Reader* (1978). M.D.B.

fraternal polyandry, see under POLYANDRY.

free agent. In October 1969, St Louis Cardinals centerfielder Curt Flood was told he had been traded to the Philadelphia Phillies baseball club. He refused to report as ordered, and thus inaugurated the modern era of professional sports – and multimillion-dollar salaries – in the US. By refusing to follow orders, Flood challenged baseball's reserve clause, which gave the wealthy owners of baseball teams ownership of a player until he was traded or sold to another team. 'After 12 years in the major leagues I do not feel that I am a piece of property to be bought and sold irrespective of my wishes,' Flood wrote to Baseball Commissioner Bowie Kuhn. Flood (paid $90,000 a year in 1969) lost his case before the US supreme court (see SUPREME COURT OF THE UNITED STATES), which ruled that the reserve clause was an 'aberration' but one which Congress and not the courts should rectify. The issue was rendered moot when an arbitrator overturned the reserve clause in 1975. Flood's career was over when he refused to be traded. He died in January 1997. 'Like most pioneers, Curt Flood wound up with an arrow in his back,' said team-mate Lou Brock. R.K.H.

free association.

(1) In PSYCHOTHERAPY, a technique which requires the patient to say at once, and to go on saying at once, whatever comes to mind. The chief idea behind free association is that, by using it in the benign and supportive situation of psychotherapy, the patient will be able slowly to approach and face the ANXIETY producing UNCONSCIOUS material that he cannot face at the beginning, and which is at the centre of his personal difficulties. B.A.F.

(2) In literature, a comparable process whereby one word or image derives spontaneously from another by association of ideas or sounds. The dangers of the method are suggested by the poet and critic L. A. G. Strong (*The Sacred River: An Approach to James Joyce*, 1949). Strong wrote of James Joyce's *Finnegans Wake*: 'The two processes, from association to object, from object to association, seldom harmonize, and often create serious confusion.' In art, spontaneity is no guarantee of profundity or even of interesting sense, and T. S. Eliot's remark on FREE VERSE could be adapted to read 'No association is free for the man who wants to do a good job'. See also STREAM OF CONSCIOUSNESS. D.J.E.

free economy, see under MARKET ECONOMY.

free energy. A THERMODYNAMIC property which represents the maximum amount of work obtainable from a mechanical or chemical process. The *Helmholtz free energy* and the *Gibbs free energy* differ only in that the latter includes work done against surrounding atmosphere. The free energy is related to the internal ENERGY or heat content and the ENTROPY of the substance. Each chemical substance under particular conditions has an associated free energy, but when chemical reactions occur spontaneously there is always a decrease in total free energy. For a chemical reaction in equilibrium the driving forces associated with the changes in heat content and entropy are balanced and no change in free energy is possible. B.F.

free enterprise, see under MARKET ECONOMY.

free form, see under MORPHEME.

free jazz. Despite the exceptional case of TRAD, the direction of JAZZ has customarily been forward and further out, with soloists striving to free themselves from old formulas and expand their expressive language. BEBOP took jazz to a new height of complexity, and, in the late 1960s, with free jazz, the music seemingly went as far out as it could go. Fired by the modal experiments of John Coltrane and the idiosyncratic style of Ornette Coleman, young musicians rejected artificial notions like harmony and rhythm, subscribing whole-heartedly to Coleman's basic creed of 'expressing our minds and our emotions'. Structural principles were minimal; intensity was supposed to generate its own coherence. In fact, to many listeners the results were simple anarchy. The larger result was an identity crisis in jazz, exacerbated by the new, vast popularity of ROCK MUSIC which absorbed the audience alienated by jazz's experimental frenzy. Retrenchment began in the 1970s and continues today, with young jazz players re-examining the roots of older jazz for inspiration, seeking direction by going in rather than out (see FUSION). GE.S.

free market. A market which is not impeded by any form of government intervention. If there are many firms in the free market, it may approximate to PERFECT COMPETITION. The resulting operation of the PRICE MECHANISM is often regarded as beneficial since, in certain circumstances, it will result in ECONOMIC EFFICIENCY.

However, free markets may not give a socially desirable distribution of income; they cannot cope with the existence of EXTERNALITIES; they may fail to supply PUBLIC GOODS and they may not be particularly close to the ideal of perfect competition. J.P.

free port. An area where goods can be imported, processed and exported without payment of any customs duties. The economic benefits from additional trade and economic activity can offset the loss of revenue from customs duties. Singapore is an important example of the economic benefits that can accrue from being a free port. J.P.

free radical. An uncharged RADICAL of abnormal VALENCE, which can have an independent existence. The first free radical (triphenylmethane), discovered in 1900, has trivalent instead of the usual tetravalent carbon. Since then numerous free radicals have been studied, including ATOMS of hydrogen and chlorine. Although they usually have only a transient existence free radicals play an important role in propagating chemical reactions. Living organisms have evolved systems for inactivating free radicals before they cause damage. B.F.; P.N.

free trade, see under PROTECTIONISM; TRADE THEORY.

Free Trade Area of the Americas (FTAA). At the Miami Summit in December 1994, Western hemisphere leaders endorsed the establishment of a Free Trade Area of the Americas (FTAA) by 2005. Negotiations over how best to proceed have led to tensions between the two principal hemispheric trade blocs, the South American Common Market (MERCOSUR, led by Brazil, and the North American Free Trade Agreement (NAFTA), which includes Canada, Mexico and the US. Future negotiations on a hemisphere-wide free trade area may be hampered by opposition from US producers threatened by cheaper imports from Latin America, as well as by continuing tension over the unilateralism of US foreign policy on issues such as drugs trafficking and immigration (see WAR ON DRUGS). For further reading: S. Weintraub, *Institutional Requirements for Western Hemisphere Free Trade* (1996). M.A.P.

free variation. In LINGUISTICS, the relationship between linguistic units having the same DISTRIBUTION which are different in FORM (sense 3) but not thereby different in meaning, i.e. the units do not contrast. The concept is most widely used in PHONOLOGY, referring to variant pronunciations of a word; but it may be used in GRAMMAR, and also in SEMANTICS (where it is called *synonymy*). D.C.

free verse (or ***vers libre***)**.** Verse that lacks regular metre, rhyme and other formal devices, relying in its search for 'organic form' on rhythms natural to speech which should also be 'natural' to the theme and feeling of the poem. Though by no means a modern invention, free verse became prominent with the advent of MODERNISM, and constituted a revolt against the set forms of 19th-century poetry. The easiest verse to write badly, free verse is possibly the most difficult to write well, since no external shaping aids are available. As T. S. Eliot remarked, 'no verse is free for the man who wants to do a good job' ('Reflections on *Vers Libre*', 1917). D.J.E.

free will. We ordinarily think of ourselves as having the freedom to choose our actions. This idea of free will ties in with that of moral responsibility – the idea that our actions are morally evaluable, deserving of reward and punishment, etc. For an individual can only be held morally responsible for an action where he is free not to so act.

Causal DETERMINISM, the thesis that the state of the physical universe at any given time is necessitated by its earlier states plus the laws of nature, raises a fundamental philosophical problem for free will. For determinism and free will seem, on the face of it, to be incompatible. If all our actions are determined, then surely we never act freely. Moreover, if we never act freely, then we cannot legitimately be held morally responsible for our actions.

Two positions are open to those who accept that free will and determinism are incompatible: hard determinists give up free will; libertarians (see LIBERTARIANISM) reject determinism. Compatibilists, on the other hand, argue that the incompatibility is illusory (see COMPATIBILISM).

Compatibilists typically seek to show how free will and determinism are compatible by distinguishing two senses of 'free'. One might point out, for example, that an action can be free in the sense that the agent is not compelled or constrained but chooses so to act, or in the sense that requires that the action not be causally determined. It might then be argued that free will and moral responsibility require only that our actions be 'free' in the first sense not the second, and that our having the first kind of 'freedom' is compatible with our not having the second. One problem with this suggestion is that given that our choices are also causally determined, it is hard to see how we can legitimately be held morally responsible for doing even those things we choose to do.

It has been argued that our possession of free will is introspectively manifest: we are directly aware of the fact that we could have acted otherwise. However, the philosopher John Stuart Mill (1806–73) denied that we have any such awareness. Mill argued that the impression that we are acting freely is generated by a false inference. We remember that while on some similar occasions in the past we did sometimes act in the same way, on other similar occasions we did not. We then mistakenly infer that we could have acted differently on this occasion. Mill argued, however, that on all these previous occasions our action was determined, for we always acted according to our strongest motive.

Some libertarians look to contemporary PHYSICS for help. For physicists now claim that when we look at the subatomic world (see SUBATOMIC PARTICLE) we find a degree of randomness and indeterminacy. Unfortunately, this sort of randomness appears no more compatible with free will than does determinism. Presumably, a random, chance event is no more something that we can be said to have control over or held responsible for than is a determined one. S.W.L.

***Freie Bühne*.** A play-producing organization founded in Berlin by Otto Brahm in 1889 to pioneer the new naturalistic drama (see NATURALISM). It had no permanent ensemble or theatre and played only at Sunday matinées. But it gave high-quality private performances of work banned by the German censors, including Ibsen's *Ghosts*, Zola's *Thérèse Raquin* and Hauptmann's *Die Weber*. And although in 1894 it was affiliated to the more established DEUTSCHES THEATER it was largely responsible for introducing many key modern works into the regular German repertoire. For further reading: J. L. Styan, *Modern Drama in Theory and Practice*, vol. 1 (1981). M.BI.

French Community; French Union. The French Union was set up in 1946 to unite the French Republic with its overseas territories in a union all of whose citizens enjoyed French CITIZENSHIP and political representation in the National Assembly. The French Community was set up by General de Gaulle in 1958, following the loss from the Union of Indo-China, Tunisia, Morocco and Algeria. The Community united members in a free-franc zone, highly dependent on France for trade, investment and aid (some of it military). Membership was based on self-determination in individual states on the basis of universal suffrage, and was extended to former French African colonies and the Malagasy Republic, while Guinea chose to be independent. Members became associated with the EEC (see EUROPEAN UNION) through the Yaounde and Lomé trade and aid agreements. V.L.

French Union, see under FRENCH COMMUNITY.

frequency, see under STATISTICAL REGULARITY.

frequency modulation (FM).

(1) A technique in radio transmission whereby audio frequency signals are made to vary or modulate (see MODULATION) the frequency of a carrier wave of radio frequency. Broadcasts on the radio VHF band employ frequency modulation, which ensures almost total freedom from interference and distortion, at the price of using a greater frequency range for each transmission. M.V.B.

(2) In music, a method of producing complex sound waves by allowing the frequency of a simpler wave (e.g. a sine wave) to be modulated by another waveform. This technique was developed by John Chowning as a simple way of producing musical tones with a complexity approaching that of real musical instruments and is the basis of several new types of synthesizer. B.CO.

frequency theory. A system whereby the probability (see PROBABILITY THEORY) of a single event is assigned a numerical value, between 0 and 1, according to the inductively established (see INDUCTION) proportion of situations like that of the event in question in which events of that kind occur. Thus the probability that John will survive until he is 70 will be ½ if 50 per cent of men like John have been found to do so. A problem arises about specifying the relevant situation (or *reference class*): should John be regarded as a man, as an Englishman, as an English postman, as a cigarette-smoking English postman, or what? Usually the STATISTICS will differ as between such alternatives. If all John's characteristics are taken into consideration he may turn out to be the sole instance of the class or SET, so that no statistics are available at all. The requirements of a closely fitting reference class and of copious and thus more reliable statistical evidence pull in opposite directions, and judgement has to be used in reconciling them, a judgement that can be assisted by the theory of statistical significance. It is generally held that not all probability is frequency, although the identification of the two has been attempted. The crucial point is that the statements of the statistical evidence from which frequency judgements are derived are *inductive* and thus only *confirmed* (see CONFIRMATION) as probable, and not certified, by the grounds on which they rest. For further reading: A. Pap, *An Introduction to the Philosophy of Science* (1963). A.Q.

Freudian. In strict usage, an adjective referring to a tradition or school of psychoanalytic thought and practice (see PSYCHOANALYSIS), namely the one connected with the work of Sigmund Freud (1856–1939); the word can also be used as a substantive, meaning a member of this school. More loosely, the adjective refers to any view popularly associated with the name of Freud, especially any view that picks on the sexual origins and character of thought, motives, feelings or conduct.

Freudian psychoanalysis has three aspects: it is a general theory of PSYCHOLOGY, a therapy, and a method of enquiry or research. The psychology looks on the mind of the adult individual as a system of elements, each carrying a charge of energy. Any one element (e.g. Smith's love for his father) may be capable of entering CONSCIOUSNESS; but where entry into consciousness is liable to raise the excitation of the system beyond the limits of what it can tolerate (as might happen with the element of Smith's hatred of his father), energy is redistributed in such a way that the threatening element cannot enter consciousness and remains UNCONSCIOUS. The energy of the system takes two fundamental forms. In the early version of the theory, the energy was either sexual or self-preservative in character (see LIFE INSTINCT); in the later version it took either a loving or an aggressive and destructive form (see DEATH INSTINCT).

An overriding aim of the system, therefore, is to preserve its psychic equilibrium in the face of the energy distribution, and of threats generated from within and from without. It achieves this aim, in general, by taking defensive action (see DEFENCE MECHANISM) of one sort or another; e.g. RATIONALIZATION, SUBLIMATION, PROJECTION, REGRESSION. To enable it to do this, the mental system of the infant and child develops an internal structure: the ID (the source of energy supply), the EGO (the part of the system that enables it to face reality), and the SUPEREGO (the part that embodies the self-controls of conscience). The child also goes through certain stages in its development to maturity, e.g. the Oedipal period (see OEDIPUS COMPLEX). If this development has been unsatisfactory (such that energy remains tied up, or bound, at some early STAGE (or stages) OF DEVELOPMENT), then the adult person will be disposed to exhibit pathological conduct (see ABNORMAL PSYCHOLOGY) and to experience difficulties of related sorts. When the defences which were erected early in life to keep the dangerous elements at bay break down, then neurotic conflict ensues, and his pathology becomes manifest (see NEUROSIS; PSYCHOSIS).

As a therapy, Freudian psychoanalysis is based on the rule of FREE ASSOCIATION for the patient, and on rules for the analyst that make him play the role of an anonymous figure who cannot be faulted by the patient. One important consequence of these rules is to produce a special relationship between patient and analyst, which encourages the rapid growth of a subtle emotional involvement with the analyst known as TRANSFERENCE. Freudian analysis relies heavily on this emotional involvement.

It was the use of Freudian analysis, in particular, that led many analysts, psychiatrists and others to speak of 'Freud's great discoveries'. But to speak like this presupposes that Freudian psychoanalysis is a valid method of enquiry or research: one which, consequently, uncovers the truth about human nature. This PRESUPPOSITION is so beset by difficulties that it is hardly acceptable:

(1) It can be argued that Freudian practice does not merely 'uncover the facts', but helps to manufacture them, and in ways that go to confirm the Freudian theory used in the practice. In short, it is to some degree a self-confirmatory procedure.

(2) When we try to pinpoint Freud's great discoveries, it is difficult to do so in a way that is generally acceptable, even to analysts in the Freudian tradition.

(3) When we do look at some likely candidate, e.g. the Freudian generalization about the stages of libidinal development (see PSYCHOSEXUAL DEVELOPMENT), it is far from clear what we would have to do to falsify it. (For the principle of falsifiability see POPPERIAN.) For LIBIDO is a theoretical notion, whose observable manifestations are not clear.

(4) When we examine the general psychology that Freudian analysis has erected upon the material produced by the practice, it is evident that it does not embody a 'scientific' theory, in the dominant current sense of this adjective. Its logical relations to science are uncertain, and its whole status controversial.

Unlike that of Darwin, therefore, Freud's theoretical contribution has not yet been incorporated into science. Nevertheless, his work has revolutionized the popular view of human nature in the West (rather as Marx has changed our view of society); and it has penetrated into almost every nook and cranny of our CULTURE. It is this fact, perhaps, that has led many people to rank Freud as a figure of towering genius. Whether, however, he really turns out to be a Darwin of the human mind, or only someone who, like a Ptolemy or a Mesmer, has led us up an interesting and important dead end, is a matter which the future of science will have to decide.

For a modification of Freudian theory see NEO-FREUDIAN. For the development of Freud's theories within the school of Jacques Lacan, see LACANIAN. For other research developments within the Freudian tradition see BODY IMAGE. For further reading: B. A. Farrell, *The Standing of Psychoanalysis* (1981). B.A.F.

Freudian slip. In psychoanalytic theory (see FREUDIAN; PSYCHOANALYSIS), a momentary and transient breakdown in the defensive position of the person, as a result of which he gives unintended expression in speech to repressed (see REPRESSION) thoughts and feelings. W.Z.

friendly fire. The effect of military action directed against the enemy that inadvertently harms one's own side has become known, since the VIETNAM War, as 'friendly fire'. It is as old as man's use of weapons. Archaeological evidence reveals that Stone Age hunters sometimes wounded each other in their struggle to kill their prey. Inadvertent wounding of friends was a recognized feature of warfare with edged weapons, hand-held as well as missile. It became more prevalent with the development of gunpowder and, later, high-explosive missiles. As effective ranges increased, the difficulty of distinguishing between friend and foe increased also. Common occurrences are the bombardment of advancing infantry by their own supporting artillery and firefights between units which fail to recognize each other as friendly. Accidents are particularly likely in engagements between air-defence weapons and aircraft, and the likelihood prompted during World War II the development of IFF (identification friend or foe) transmitters, which were also beneficial in aerial combat. No certain method of averting friendly fire has yet been perfected, however, and it is likely to remain a regrettable feature of military operations. J.K.

Friends of the Earth, see under GREEN MOVEMENT.

Fringe, the. British term (the US equivalent being OFF-BROADWAY) for activities, almost exclusively theatrical – notably of SURREALIST, unconventional, unorthodox, anti-ESTABLISHMENT, obscene, AVANT-GARDE or pseudo-*avant-garde* type – that take place away from the main popular centres of entertainment. First used in the late 1950s of events on the periphery of the Edinburgh Festival, it now embraces the highly conventionalized products of the mediocre and ageing, as well as the genuinely zestful activities of students and other young artists. M.S.-S.

Froebel method. An educational method associated with Friedrich Froebel (1782–1852), who sought to adapt the child-centred principles (see CHILD-CENTRED EDUCATION) of Rousseau and Pestalozzi to infant education in Germany. He founded the Kindergarten where children could grow through play, using nature work, games, toys, handicraft, music, stories, drawing and geometrical shapes (cubes, spheres) which he called 'gifts' – the kind of approach now common in most infant schools. Froebel had an obvious influence on Montessori (see MONTESSORI METHOD), Cizek, and the whole nursery and infant school movement. For further reading: F. Froebel, ed. I. M. Lilley, *Friedrich Froebel* (1967). W.A.C.S.

Front de Libération Nationale (FLN), see under ALGERIAN WAR OF INDEPENDENCE.

Front National (FN; National Front, France). The political party, Le Front National (FN), was founded in 1972 by its present leader, Jean-Marie Le Pen. Like the British National Front, it is an extreme RIGHT-wing party which is anti-IMMIGRANT and racist in outlook. The twin themes of immigration and 'insecurity' occupy a central position in the rhetoric of the FN while the Party's policies include restoration of capital punishment, a ban on ABORTION and the repatriation of immigrants from France. Public support for the FN has grown rapidly since 1980: in the French general election of March 1986 the FN won 9.65 per cent of the vote; and in 1996, more than 15 per cent. After the 1998 elections, the FN held 275 regional seats, and had captured the mayories of Marignane, Noyon and Toulon. S.M.

front organization. An organization that serves as cover for aims and activities other than its professed ones; in particular, an ostensibly non-COMMUNIST organization with liberal (see LIBERALISM), religious or other public men of goodwill as the leading figures, but in fact controlled by the communists. Front organizations in the latter sense were devised in the 1930s by the COMINTERN's propaganda genius, Willi Münzenberg, with aims such as supporting the

Spanish Republic, justifying the MOSCOW TRIALS, and (in England in 1940) advocating peace with Germany. R.C.

frontal theory. Air masses are bodies of air with constant physical properties such as temperature and humidity usually formed in characteristic locations such as polar or tropical regions. The realization that marked changes in the weather often occurred on the boundaries between air masses led to many of the major developments of 20th-century weather forecasting. A group of Norwegian meteorologists working during World War I proposed the term 'front' for these zones of conflict between air masses of different origin. Fronts are often characterized by pronounced temperature gradients, strong vertical motion and rainfall. The term *frontogenesis* is used to describe the formation of frontal zones. This tends to occur in well-defined regions where air masses are likely to clash. As a result of instabilities, waves often form on air mass boundaries and these can rapidly develop into depressions (cyclones). This process is known as *cyclogenesis*. It is these weather systems, depressions and the fronts associated with them which are responsible for much of the character of the weather in middle latitudes. Frontal systems also occur in the tropics but they are weaker and less well defined. For further reading: R. G. Barry and R. J. Chorley, *Atmosphere, Weather and Climate* (1968). P.M.K.

frontier. The boundary line or zone delimiting two contiguous but different countries or cultural domains. The specialists have long debated whether the frontier is a line or a zone of transition. In American usage the latter meaning predominates. In *The Frontier in American History* (1920), the American historian Frederick Jackson Turner stressed the role of the westward march of the frontier in American history, but recognized that, in the sense of the zone of transition to another civilization, the American frontier shifted after 1910 to the large cities. Metaphorical usages in which frontier means 'new opportunities' include President John F. Kennedy's characterization, in 1960–63, of his political programmes as 'the new frontier', and such phrases as 'the frontiers of science'. For further reading: J. R. V. Prescott, *The Geography of Frontiers and Boundaries* (1965). J.G.

frontogenesis, see under FRONTAL THEORY.

FSLN, see under NICARAGUA; SANDINISTA; CONTRAS.

FSP, see FUNCTIONAL SENTENCE PERSPECTIVE.

fuel cell. A chemical CELL in which two fuel substances (such as hydrogen and oxygen) react to produce electrical ENERGY *directly*. The process is the exact opposite to the decomposition of water by ELECTROLYSIS, for hydrogen is fed to cover one platinum electrode while oxygen is fed to the other. No gas escapes, water is continually produced, and an electric current can be driven through an external circuit connected to the electrodes. Invented by the British scientist William R. Grove in 1840, the fuel cell received little attention until recently; today much research is being stimulated by the possible advantages of cells which may compete with other sources of energy without polluting the atmosphere (see POLLUTION). E.R.L.

fuel element. That part of a NUCLEAR REACTOR core which contains fissionable material (see FISSION). E.R.L.

fuelwood crisis. Particularly in developing countries, fuelwood is often the only source of domestic energy supply for cooking and heating. It may also be used for manufacturing charcoal, baking bricks, and other low-technology industrial processes. In some areas the harvesting of fuelwood exceeds sustainable rates of replenishment, while elsewhere land-cover changes (e.g. the spread of agriculture, commercial logging, or pasture) may reduce the extent of available woodland or scrub. Fuelwood collection can be a major cause of DEFORESTATION and can promote serious land degradation (e.g. soil erosion and DESERTIFICATION). A.S.G.

***Führerprinzip*.** Nazi German term (see NAZISM) for the principle of leadership, i.e. the establishment of a national leader and the devolution of sovereign authority and POWER, by decision of the leader, to a recognized hierarchy of subordinates; the entrustment of governmental powers to such leadership rather than to decision by majority in parliament. Hitler's definition was 'unrestricted authority downwards, unrestricted responsibility upwards'. D.C.W.

full employment. Employment of a country's available manpower to the fullest extent likely to be sustainable. Since it is not possible to manage the economy so that there is an exact match between job opportunities and the number of those who want jobs, full employment is consistent with some residual UNEMPLOYMENT. Published figures of unemployment are not, however, a completely reliable indicator of the margin of available manpower. They usually exclude housewives and others who would be willing to take paid employment but do not register for it. The figures may change their significance over time, e.g. because of new regulations as to unemployment benefits. There is also room for debate as to the precise level of employment that can be sustained, since the more closely full employment is approached the harder it becomes to reconcile it with other economic objectives such as the avoidance of INFLATION and a deficit in the BALANCE OF PAYMENTS. A.C.

full employment surplus. The hypothetical surplus (or deficit) on the budget, if, with unchanged government policies, employment rose to the FULL EMPLOYMENT level. Such an increase in employment would affect both tax revenues and government expenditure. Changes in the full employment surplus are a more reliable measure of the development of a government's fiscal stance (see FISCAL POLICY) than movements in the realized budget surplus, since the latter are affected by the actual level of UNEMPLOYMENT and output. J.P.

full recovery cost, see under MARGINAL COSTING.

fullerene, see BUCKMINSTERFULLERENE.

function. In MATHEMATICS, this may be thought of as a 'black box' (see BLACK-BOX THEORY): one drops a NUMBER in, turns a handle, and out comes a (probably different) number. One way of organizing this is to supply a formula, such as $x^2 + 2x$ – we pop in a value such as $x = 3$ and out pops the value of the function, 15 ($= 3^2 + 2 \times 3$). In former times it was insisted that there had to be a formula – nowadays the black box is all we ask for (it could operate, e.g., by referring to a graph [see GEOMETRY]). The concept is extended in various ways – we could pop in more than one number (using, e.g., the formula $x + 2y$), or substitute other things for numbers: differentiation is in fact a function – one pops in a formula (x^2, say) and out pops its derivative ($2x$ here). See also TRANSFORMATION. N.A.R.

function word, see under WORD CLASS.

functional analysis, see under ANALYSIS.

functional explanation, see under EXPLANATION.

functional fixedness, see under PROBLEM-SOLVING.

functional flexibility, see under FLEXIBLE FIRM.

functional grammar. In LINGUISTICS, an approach to grammatical analysis which is based on the pragmatic rules that govern social interaction, the formal rules of PHONOLOGY, SYNTAX and SEMANTICS being seen as secondary. Functional approaches, in various models, developed in the 1970s as an alternative to the abstract, formalized view of language presented by transformational grammar. For further reading: M. A. K. Halliday, *An Introduction to Functional Grammar* (1985). D.C.

functional sentence perspective (FSP). In LINGUISTICS, a theory associated with the modern exponents of the PRAGUE SCHOOL. It refers to an analysis of utterances or texts in terms of the information they contain, the role of each utterance element being evaluated for its semantic contribution to the whole. The different levels of contribution involved result in the notion of the 'communicative dynamism' of an utterance. The main structural elements of this theory are known as 'rheme' (the element in an utterance which adds new meaning to what has been communicated already) and 'theme' (the element which adds little or no new meaning). For further reading: G. C. Lepschy, *A Survey of Structural Linguistics* (1982). D.C.

functionalism.

(1) In PHILOSOPHY, specifically in the philosophy of mind (see MIND, PHILOSOPHY OF and MIND-BODY PROBLEM), the theory that the nature of mental attributes can be specified by means of a description of the causal role or function of those attributes in the mental life and general behaviour of the subject. It states further that mental attributes are 'supervenient' upon brain states, that is, a subject's brain states and activity determine what mental states he is in. A given brain state corresponds to a given mental state just when the causal role played by both is identical. Functionalism counts among those theories whose premise is that mind has a physical basis. A.C.G.

(2) In ANTHROPOLOGY, a group of theories associated above all with the names of B. Malinowski (1884–1942) and A. R. Radcliffe-Brown (1881–1955), although they are perhaps more appropriately, if less agreeably, described as structural-functionalist. In one version, great store is set by the putative human needs, both biological and social, that every society must satisfy. In another (see STRUCTURAL-FUNCTIONAL THEORY), a CULTURE or society is seen as an entity, all the parts of which function to maintain one another and the totality, the disruption of one part provoking readjustment among others. Many anthropologists still describe themselves as functionalists in some sense, but none would accept the common criticism that his functionalism precludes an interest in social change and the study of SYSTEMS over time. See also EVOLUTION, SOCIAL AND CULTURAL; STRUCTURALISM. For further reading: E. R. Leach, *Social Anthropology* (1982). M.F.

(3) In PSYCHOLOGY, a point of view (one of the six main SCHOOLS OF PSYCHOLOGY as classified by R. S. Woodworth) that sees mental phenomena as activities rather than as states or structures. It assumes that function produces structure (as in anatomy, where the shape of an organ system reflects the demands of its function), and attempts to explain the nature of phenomena completely in terms of the use they fulfil. In American psychology, the notion that no response occurs without implicit or explicit *reinforcement* (see OPERANT CONDITIONING) exemplifies a kind of utilitarian functionalism. Efforts to understand PERCEPTION in terms of function performed, as in E. Brunswik's 'probabilistic functionalism' where perception is given a predictive role, are still current. For further reading: R. S. Woodworth, *Contemporary Schools of Psychology* (1965). J.S.B.

(4) In ARCHITECTURE, the theory embodied in Louis Sullivan's dictum 'form follows function', i.e. that the form of a building can be derived from a full knowledge of the purposes it is to serve (see MODERNISM). It derives from such 19th-century architectural writers as Viollet-le-Duc demanding the expression of each of the elements of a building and especially its structure. The theory had a further extension in the 1920s and 1930s in the view that the form which most closely follows function, as apparent in ships or aeroplanes, is also the most beautiful. See also INTERNATIONAL STYLE; MACHINE AESTHETIC; NEUE SACHLICHKEIT. M.BR.

fundamental constants. Quantities appearing in laws of nature as proportionality constants which determine the intrinsic strengths of the fundamental forces of nature, the masses of the most elementary PARTICLES, and various other of their intrinsic properties. They are chosen because they should not vary in space or time and are found to be constant in this way to high precision. As yet these quantities can only be determined by measurement. Current grand unified theories (see GRAND UNIFICATION) and theories of SUPERSTRINGS aim to calculate these quantities numerically or show that they are interrelated. The principal goal of fundamental PHYSICS is to arrive at an understanding of why these constants have the numerical values they do. A number of coincidences between values of combinations of fundamental constants led to the formulation of the ANTHROPIC PRINCIPLES. Precise measurements of these constants are also employed to define the standard units of mass, length and time. They are also termed 'constants of nature'. J.D.B.

fundamental particle, see ELEMENTARY PARTICLE.

fundamentalism. The belief that the Bible possesses complete INFALLIBILITY because every word in it is the Word of God. The term is derived from a series of tracts, *The Fundamentals*, published in the USA in 1909. Other doctrines defended (on the basis of this literal acceptance of passages in the Bible) include the interpretation of the death of Jesus as a 'substitutionary' sacrifice to the just wrath of God on mankind's sins; the virgin birth, physical resurrection and 'Second Coming' of Jesus; and eternal punishment in hell. Fundamentalism is strongest among some American Protestants (see PROTESTANTISM), and is usually accompanied by the condemnation both of the Roman Catholic Church (see CATHOLICISM) and of modern thought. See also ISLAM. For further reading: J. Barr, *Escaping from Fundamentalism* (1984). D.L.E.

Fundamentalism, Islamic. In general, Islamic fundamentalism refers to a wide range of political and ideological movements, from conservative (see CONSERVATISM) to extremist, in different Muslim societies which consider that a revived and politicized ISLAM will offer practical solutions to various political, cultural and even economic problems of the modern world (see IDEOLOGY). Although throughout Islamic history there have been periodic attempts to return to the fundamental tenets of RELIGION in order to revive it as a dynamic force, contemporary fundamentalism is essentially a modern phenomenon and, unlike its medieval counterparts, it has been less engaged in THEOLOGY or PHILOSOPHY and more concerned with IDEOLOGY, politics and cultural representations (such as social typology, cultural forms and relations with the West). Though there are a variety of groups and agendas encompassed by the term fundamentalist, they tend to share the premise that the encounter with the Western world and its projected modernity has been detrimental to the interests of the Muslim peoples. One determining factor in judging whether a government is fundamentalist or not is to examine the extent to which it tends to incorporate the Islamic law (or Shari'a) into its daily practices. Other doctrinal hallmarks include a revision of some modernization measures, and the demarcation of the society along ideological and cultural lines. However, it is misleading to suppose that fundamentalism is necessarily traditionalist or conservative. A major defining attribute of modern fundamentalism has been its political dimension, and most contemporary fundamentalist movements are committed to social and political change. With the exception of groups like the Taliban in Afghanistan, contemporary fundamentalism has tried to find ways to incorporate modernity rather than negate it as such. For example, this tendency can be seen in a variety of practices ranging from an overall interest in the mass media and information technology to the use of modernist styles, GENRES and imagery in the production of a new kind of doctrinaire literature. At times there has also been a commitment to parliamentary politics. However, it may be argued that contemporary fundamentalism has thus far maintained a selective, if not superficial, approach towards the adoption of modern forms and symbols while the more philosophical underpinnings of modernity have been absent from it. Nevertheless, the process as a whole provides a significant step not only towards further identification with modernity, but also towards a willingness to induce recognition and reciprocity. A.GH.

funk. Historically a term for a pungent odour, funk has a particular significance in the history of JAZZ. Buddy Bolden (1868–1931), a key figure in the genesis of the music in NEW ORLEANS, played a rough establishment popularly known as Funky Butt Hall; whether or not there is a direct connection, funk has always stood for music of uninhibited emotion and physicality. Word and concept came into special prominence in the 1950s, when the BEBOP and COOL schools had brought a new complexity to jazz, somewhat at the expense of its roots in the BLUES. Funk, often linked with SOUL, aimed to redress the balance in favour of visceral feelings. Ultimately, funk became a musical genre of its own, marked by a heavy, rock-style beat and amplification (see ROCK MUSIC), but with a distinctive bluesy sonority. For BLACK people it became a full-blown cultural attitude in the work of groups like Sly and the Family Stone, whose psychedelic light shows, outrageous fashions and plangent rhythms gave rise to the funk slogan 'One Nation under a Groove'. GE.S.

furniture music (*musique d'ameublement*).

A type of music envisaged by the composer Erik Satie (1866–1925) that would not draw attention to itself but by its presence simply make the environment more pleasant. This concept of music as some form of aural background, rather like musical wallpaper, is an important precursor of both MUZAK and AMBIENT MUSIC. For further reading: J. Harding, *Erik Satie* (1975). B.CO.

fusion.

(1) In PHYSICS, the production of an atomic NUCLEUS by the union of two lighter nuclei in a NUCLEAR REACTION. Being positively charged, the two original nuclei repel one another, and considerable kinetic energy (i.e. a high operating temperature) is necessary to get the reaction to proceed. But the amount of ENERGY released can be much greater, because the resulting nucleus is often less massive than its constituents (see MASS-ENERGY EQUATION), and a CHAIN REACTION may occur. The power of the hydrogen bomb, and the warmth and light of sunshine, are derived from fusion. M.V.B.

(2) In music, a prime product of the musical and social turbulence of the 1960s, fusion attempted to marry the genres of ROCK MUSIC and JAZZ. The most famous convert to fusion (or jazz rock or crossover, as it was variously called) was Miles Davis (1926–1991), whose *Bitches Brew* album in 1970 defined the mode. The highly praised young trumpeter Wynton Marsalis (1961–) regards jazz as a superior art and has declared 'there is no such thing as fusion'. GE.S.

(3) In ANTHROPOLOGY, see under LINEAGE.

future shock. A phrase coined, on the analogy of culture shock, by Alvin Toffler to describe 'a new and profoundly upsetting psychological disease' caused in Western POST-INDUSTRIAL SOCIETY by 'a rising rate of change that makes reality seem, sometimes, like a kaleidoscope run wild. Change is avalanching upon our heads and most people are grotesquely unprepared to cope with it.' For further reading: A. Toffler, *Future Shock* (1970). O.S.

futures markets. Exchanges where derivative products ranging from pork belly futures in Chicago to interest rate swaps in the City of London are dealt. The development of futures markets was one of the most significant developments in global finance (see GLOBALIZATION) in the 1990s, and the value of transactions conducted now exceeds those conducted on their physical counterparts several times over. Such markets were developed to hedge against future risk, like a bad harvest for oranges or a drop in the EXCHANGE RATE. But over the last decade they have become increasingly sophisticated and mathematical, covering every kind of financial risk and involving countless new products – including outcomes of the Superbowl – which are dealt through exchanges like LIFFE in London or the Chicago Options Exchange, or between individual parties in over-the-counter deals. Such markets make for more efficient transactions and enable end users to protect themselves against all manner of risks. But the size, scope and international scale of these exchanges have made them extraordinarily difficult to regulate and a real problem for global policy-makers. This was brought home sharply in February 1995 when a single trader at the UK merchant bank Barings Brothers in Singapore ran up a bet of £900 million on future movements in the Japanese stock market, leading to the bank's closure as an independent institution. The policing of futures markets has been devolved to the Bank of International Settlements in Basle. For further reading: J. Gapper and N. Denton, *All that Glitters: The Fall of Barings* (1996). A.BR.

Futurism. Italian movement in the arts, originating as a purely literary doctrine with F. T. Marinetti's 'Futurist Manifesto' in *Le Figaro*, Paris, on 20 February 1909; subsequently extended to the other arts, then after 1922 partly assimilated in the official IDEOLOGY of FASCISM, to peter out in the mid-1930s. Its principles, asserted in a forceful succession of manifestos, were dynamism, the cult of speed and the machine, rejection of the past, and the glorification of patriotism and war. Techniques put forward and practised to these ends included (1) in literature, FREE VERSE, phonetic poetry (see CONCRETE POETRY), and a telegraphic language without adjectives or adverbs or much syntax ('words in liberty'); (2) in the visual arts, NEO-IMPRESSIONISM, pictorial dynamism ('lines of force'), simultaneity, and the interpenetration of planes;

(3) in music, a BRUITISME evolved by Francesco Pratella and Luigi Russolo, and based on the noises of the modern industrialized world; instruments were also to be made which would divide the octave into 50 equal MICROTONES.

These largely new methods were demonstrated and tested by, e.g., the painter-sculptor Umberto Boccioni, the painter Ardengo Soffici, and the architect Antonio Sant'Elia (notably in his 1914 series of architectural drawings, *Città Nuova*), while the movement's shows and lecture-demonstrations from 1912 to 1914 had some influence in France (on Apollinaire, Léger and Delaunay), England (VORTICISM), and the USA, making a real contribution in Russia (RAYONISM, Ego-Futurism and CUBO-FUTURISM) and affecting German EXPRESSIONISM via *Der* STURM. Its impact on DADA from 1916 on was even more profound, not only through the new techniques, but still more by Futurism's blurring of the frontiers between different arts, and its conscious exploitation of the mass media's power to publicize any adroitly staged piece of cultural provocation. It thus paved the way both for such artistic developments as concrete poetry, concrete music (see MUSIQUE CONCRÈTE), and KINETIC ART, and for the concept of art as a more or less sensational event. For further reading: M. W. Martin, *Futurist Art and Theory, 1909–1915* (1968). J.W.; A.H.

futurology. A term coined by the German historian Ossip K. Flechtheim in 1949 to designate a 'new science' of prognosis. It has been applied to various efforts, beginning in 1965, to carry out long-range FORECASTING in a wide range of political, sociological, economic, ecological and other fields. Most practitioners reject the idea of a 'new science' and cavil even at the word futurology. Three terms are often distinguished: a *conjecture* or intellectually disciplined speculation; a *forecast*, which is based either on a continuing trend or on some defined probabilities of occurrences; and a *prediction*, which is a prognosis of a specific event. Most practitioners agree that one cannot formalize rules for prediction but argue that the compilation of fuller data and the use of new methods (e.g. computer simulation, stochastic techniques; see STOCHASTIC PROCESS) will allow them to do better forecasting. For further reading: O. K. Flechtheim, *History and Futurology* (1965). D.B.

fuzzy logic. In the broad sense, a term that refers to fuzzy sets and the entire field of mathematical operations which has developed to operate on them. A fuzzy SET is a collection of elements which have varying degrees of membership in the set. This contrasts with a classical set, whose elements are all equally part of the set. For example, a classical set might be persons with a height greater than six feet: a given person is either a member of this set or they are not. A fuzzy set, however, might be that of tall persons: a given person might be 'very' tall, or 'a bit' tall, or 'not at all' tall. Their membership of the set of tall persons is represented by a number, which can lie anywhere between zero – if they are very short – and one – if they are undeniably tall. Fuzzy logic uses these sets to replicate human reasoning in a better way than classical LOGIC. At the end of the 19th century, Lukasiewicz, the Polish logician, suggested a three-level logic which was extended by Zadeh, in 1965, to become an infinite-level logic. Under this system, a completely false proposition has a value of zero, a partial truth takes a value of between zero and one, and a true proposition takes a value of one. Logical rules can then be applied to these propositions. For example, one might have the following rule for a machine: If 'temperature is low' and 'pressure is high', then 'set throttle at medium'. This could be understood easily by humans and fuzzy logic systems, but classical logic systems would have difficulty because the rule is so imprecise. M.JA.

G

G7. The group of seven richest industrial nations, the US, Japan, Germany, France, Italy, the UK and Canada, which acts as a steering group for the global economy. The main focus of the G7 has been to encourage non-inflationary growth and co-ordinate EXCHANGE RATES in an effort to create more stability. The G7 has also taken an active interest in international monetary reform, acting through the IMF, the World Bank and the Bank for International Settlements in Basle (see BRETTON WOODS). The group's exclusivity has been a source of tension with DEVELOPING COUNTRIES. At the Denver G7 summit in 1997 Russia was able to join critical discussions. For further reading: Y. Funabashi, *Managing the Dollar* (1988). A.BR.

Gaia hypothesis. The Gaia hypothesis originated with James E. Lovelock, whose studies of the possibility of life on Mars led him to question the basis of life on earth. The hypothesis (*Gaia: A New Look at Life on Earth*, 1979) suggests that all living things on the planet should be considered as part of a single living being which can alter the planetary ENVIRONMENT as necessary in order to survive. More a way of thinking than a strict scientific hypothesis, Gaia focuses attention on the FEEDBACK systems, often biological in nature, which regulate and control the environment, maintaining the conditions that support life (see SUSTAINABILITY). For example, the composition of the atmosphere has stayed stable over much of geological time, ensuring – and as a result of – the EVOLUTION of life. Carbon dioxide (see GREENHOUSE EFFECT) levels have been maintained by a delicate balance between the biosphere, the oceans and the atmosphere over much of the current interglacial. Gaia also highlights the dangers that lie in perturbing the system and the responsibility that humanity must accept for the state of the global environment (see ECOLOGY; GREEN MOVEMENT). The carbon dioxide cycle is being profoundly disturbed by the destruction of the world's forests and the combustion of fossil fuels. Humankind may have to take a more active role in rational management of the planetary environment if large-scale climatic change results. For further reading: N. Myers (ed.), *Gaia: An Atlas of Planet Management* (1984). P.M.K.

galactic clusters (open clusters). Collections of as few as about 10 or as many as 1,000 stars. More than 1,000 such aggregates of stars are known and several, e.g. the Pleiades, are visible to the naked eye. They lie close to the plane of the Milky Way and consist of relatively young stars, the brightest of which are blue or RED GIANTS. They are only loosely held together as aggregates by the gravitational attraction of their components and are gradually dispersed by the effect of external perturbations. Galactic clusters should not be confused with GALAXY CLUSTERS. For further reading: B. J. Bok and P. F. Bok, *The Milky Way* (1974). J.D.B.

galactic rotation. Since the 18th century a fundamental problem of ASTRONOMY has been the nature of our GALAXY. Once the Milky Way had been resolved into myriads of individual stars (the sun being one of them) apparently related to each other, 18th- and 19th-century astronomy set about the task of mapping the galaxy, assessing its extent and judging its motion. One obvious possibility was that our galaxy might be similar to the spiral nebulae visible through telescopes. How precisely the sun related to other stars in the galaxy remained equally controversial. A major breakthrough came with J. C. Kapteyn's (1851–1922) theory of galactic rotation. Rejecting the traditional view that stars moved essentially randomly through the heavens, Kapteyn claimed that they move systematically in two main directions (star streams). Why this should be so remained unclear until Bertil Lindblad (1895–1965) argued that the galaxy was best considered as made up of a number of sub-systems, each with a different speed of rotation around a common rotational axis. Lindblad's hypothesis was verified by J. H. Oort (1900–) by observational techniques. For further reading: R. W. Smith, *The Expanding Universe* (1982). R.P.

galaxy. One of the collections of stars and gas into which the matter of the universe has been condensed by GRAVITATION. Galaxies usually rotate, resulting in a discus-shaped structure with spiral arms. The earth and sun are situated about halfway out from the centre of our own galaxy, the Milky Way, which is about 30,000 parsecs across. See also EXPANSION OF THE UNIVERSE. M.V.B.

galaxy clusters. Aggregates of GALAXIES, containing as few as about 20 members, as in the case of the local group of galaxies to which the Milky Way belongs, to as many as several thousand member galaxies. The nearest large galaxy cluster to us is the Virgo Cluster. The larger clusters, containing the densest concentration of galaxies, are usually of spherical appearance and predominantly consist of elliptical (rather than spiral) galaxies. Irregularly shaped clusters lack a central concentration of galaxies and contain all types of galaxy. The most prominent and richly populated clusters are called *rich clusters* or *Abell clusters*, and several thousand were catalogued by George Abell. Extensive catalogues of galaxies and galaxy clusters have been compiled, most notably the Zwicky, Shane-Wirtanen and Harvard Center for Astrophysics surveys. These surveys of the distribution of galaxies have been supplemented by surveys which estimate the distance at which the galaxies lie by measuring their red shifts. Work by M. Geller and J. Huchra showed that, when seen in 3-D like this, galaxy clustering occurs in filamentary chains which overlap to create a cobweb network in the universe. One characteristic of this picture is the expectation that there exist large VOID regions in which there are no visible galaxies. DARK MATTER is known to exist in large quantities within galaxy clusters. The brightest member galaxies of rich clusters have very similar luminosities and are usually very powerful radio sources. Large amounts of hot gas, at temperatures of several million degrees Kelvin at which X-rays are emitted, have also been found to exist in between galaxies in rich clusters. Galaxy clusters are themselves often found to be aggregated into *superclusters* of irregular shape. These are believed to be the largest structures in the universe.

The existence of galaxy clusters is believed to be an inevitable consequence of the attractive nature of gravity, which tends to make a slightly non-uniform distribution of MASS become distributed in a progressively non-uniform fashion. For further reading: J. Cornell (ed.), *Bubbles, Voids and Bumps in Time: The New Cosmology* (1989). J.D.B.

Galilean moons. The moons (sometimes termed 'satellites', following Kepler) Callisto, Europa, Ganymede and Io orbiting the planet Jupiter which were discovered by the Italian scientist Galileo Galilei (1564–1642) in 1610 using the first astronomical telescope which he had invented in 1609. Their orbits lie close to the plane through the equator of Jupiter. They were first photographed by the Pioneer space missions in 1973 and 1974 and were spectacularly filmed by the Voyager space probes in 1979. Io was found to have volcanic activity on its surface; the surfaces of Ganymede and Callisto were found to be heavily cratered by impacts of small bodies; Ganymede is known to possess an atmosphere probably of ammonia and methane gases. J.D.B.

Galois theory, see under ALGEBRA.

galvanic skin response (GSR). A change in the electrical resistance of the skin occurring in moments of strong EMOTION; measurements of this change are used in lie detector tests. Galvanic skin response is also called psychogalvanic response (PGR). C.E.D.

game theory. A method of analysing the strategic behaviour of actors in situations of potential co-operation and/or conflict (see CONFLICT THEORY). A game is any set of interactions governed by a set of rules specifying the moves that each participant may make and a set of outcomes for each possible set of moves. Agents act to achieve the outcomes they prefer given others' actions. Adherents hope to produce a complete theory and explanation of the social world in terms of such interactions. Game theory was first developed by John von Neumann and Oskar Morgenstern in the 1940s for two-person zero-sum games (where one person's loss is another's gain). They proposed an equilibrium – maximin – where each person chooses a strategy to maximize the minimum payoff the other can impose on him. A solution must exist if mixed strategies (strategies where actions are chosen at random with probabilities [see PROBABILITY

THEORY] attached to each possible outcome) are adopted. Positive-sum games allow individuals the possibility of co-operation for mutual benefit. Co-ordination games allow mutual benefit as long as individuals can co-ordinate their actions. Games of conflict and co-operation, such as PRISONER'S DILEMMA and Chicken, are positive-sum but include the possibility of conflict. N-person games allow for the generation of coalitions. Iterated games consist of simple games played over and again. Game theory is usually described in two forms. Non-cooperative game theory explains co-operation where there are no enforceable agreements. Co-operative game theory allows for outside enforcement of contracts. Game theory has flourished in the last 15 years and is coming to the fore in ECONOMICS, as well as having important applications in POLITICAL SCIENCE and SOCIOLOGY. It is being applied to all aspects of human endeavour, from market relations to the behaviour of political parties, the development of trust between people, and even relationships within the household. For further reading: J. von Neumann, *Theory of Games and Economic Behavior* (1944); S. P. Hargreaves Heap and Y. Varoufakis, *Game Theory: A Critical Introduction* (1995). K.M.D.

gamma ray bursts. In the 1960s American military satellites began detecting bursts of gamma radiation (see GAMMA RAYS). By 1973 it had been determined that these bursts were of natural, rather than man-made, origin, and the satellite data was declassified. The origin of these bursts has remained a major astronomical mystery. There are two theories: one that they are of 'local' origin with our own Milky Way GALAXY, and arose from quakes or activity on the surfaces of old NEUTRON stars; the other is that they are 'cosmological' in origin and come from sources much farther away than our own galaxy. Modern data favour the cosmological hypothesis for their origin. This is because the observed bursts are random and show no correlation with the shape of the Milky Way or the stars and neutron stars within it. Recently it has been possible to pinpoint some sources of gamma rays by observing them with other instruments. The cosmological hypothesis requires gamma ray sources in the universe to give out bursts of enormous energy (because they are so much farther away) for a few milliseconds and then fade out. The source of this energy is still unknown. The favourite option is a pair of coalescing neutron stars, or a neutron star and a BLACK HOLE. These mergers are expected to occur every 100,000 years. Since there are more than a billion galaxies in the visible universe, this easily accounts for the observed rate of gamma ray bursts of one per day. For further reading: M. Begelman and M. J. Rees, *Gravity's Fatal Attraction* (1996). J.D.B.

gamma rays. Electromagnetic RADIATION emitted in the form of PHOTONS during radioactive decay (see RADIOACTIVITY). The wavelength is about the same as the size of an atomic NUCLEUS (see ATOMIC PHYSICS) or smaller. M.V.B.

gamodeme, see under DEME.

Gang of Four. A group in Chinese politics comprising of Yao Wenyuan, Zhang Chunqiao, Wang Hongwen and Jiang Qing. Originally all from Shanghai, they rapidly rose to positions of power during the cultural revolution (see GREAT PROLETARIAN CULTURAL REVOLUTION), largely due to the influence that one-time actress Jiang Qing exerted over her husband, Chairman Mao (see MAOISM). After Mao's death, a power struggle emerged between the Jiang Qing clique and the self-proclaimed successor to Chairman Mao, Hua Guofeng, which culminated in Hua teaming up with army factions opposed to the policies of the Cultural Revolution, and the subsequent arrest of the Gang of Four on 6 October 1976. From November 1980 to January 1981, the four were tried along with six members of the so-called 'Lin Biao Clique' for crimes committed under the cover of the Cultural Revolution; death sentences passed on Jiang and Zhang were later commuted to life imprisonment, with Wang also facing a life term, and Yao being sentenced to 20 years. By blaming the Gang of Four for the destructive excesses of the mobs, and the deaths of prominent figures during the period of 'Politics in Command', the new leadership could repudiate the policies of the Cultural Revolution without directly attacking Mao himself. For further reading:

J. Gardner, *Chinese Politics and the Succession to Mao* (1982). S.B.

garden cities. Low-density satellite cities based on traditional village-style housing with gardens, and extensive areas of open space, parkland and trees, reflecting a reaction against the overcrowding of industrial cities. Ebenezer Howard (the grandfather of British town planning) put forward these ideals in 1898 in *Tomorrow: A Peaceful Path to Real Reform* (later published as *Garden Cities of Tomorrow*). He sought to combine the best of the modern town and INDUSTRIAL SOCIETY with the best of the countryside and traditional rural way of life in the 'town-country' or 'garden-city'. A range of model towns, garden cities and garden suburbs were built at the end of the century by philanthropic factory owners. These include Lever's Port Sunlight near Liverpool; Rowntree's New Earswick near York; Cadbury's Bourneville in Birmingham; and Letchworth, near London, by Howard. The 1946 New Towns Act took on board many of his ideas, not least by establishing a ring of satellite 'countermagnet' NEW TOWNS around London (see SATELLITE TOWN). For further reading: G. Cherry (ed.), *Pioneers in British Town Planning* (1981). C.G.

gas bearing. A simple bearing in which a cylindrical shaft rotates in a cylindrical hole of slightly larger diameter. The space between shaft and cylinder is filled with gas at high pressure whose viscosity is such that when rotating at speed there is no metal-to-metal contact between shaft and cylinder. The frictional drag in such bearings is very much less than in, say, a ball race. E.R.L.

gas chromatography. A chromatographic method (see CHROMATOGRAPHY) of chemical separation in which a gas or vapour is passed through a stationary PHASE, usually in a heated column, of high surface area. The technique employs either solids or more commonly a liquid phase, e.g. a high-boiling-point hydrocarbon on a solid support. Extensively used since the early 1950s, its main application is in the separation and analysis of mixtures of volatile organic compounds. Quantities less than 109^{-10} grams may often be detected. B.F.

gastroenterology. The sub-speciality of medicine devoted to the study of diseases of the gastrointestinal system. Included are conditions affecting the oesophagus, stomach, duodenum, liver, gall bladder, pancreas, small intestine, colon, rectum and anal canal. The term embraces all aspects of disease, i.e. causation (aetiology), diagnosis and treatment, and incorporates the study of such common disorders as peptic ulcer, CANCER of the stomach and colon, gall stones, diverticular disease, colitis and bowel infections. Disorders of the gastrointestinal system are common and account for approximately 10 per cent of morbidity in the population generally. The cause of many gastrointestinal disorders remains unknown, but dietary and other environmental factors are assuming a more important role than was hitherto given credence. Although SURGERY remains an important diagnostic and therapeutic option, many gastrointestinal disorders can now be controlled if not cured by modern drug therapy. Hopefully, with a better understanding of the causation of disease, the spectrum of gastrointestinal disorders amenable to drug therapy will increase and the need for patients to be submitted to excision of various parts of the gastrointestinal tract gradually reduced. R.H.S.

gastrulation, see under EMBRYOLOGY.

Gate Theatre.

(1) A London theatre devoted to the performance of new and experimental drama from 1925 until its closure in 1940. Under Peter Godfrey, later under Norman Marshall, the Gate introduced English audiences to the work of Toller, Cocteau, Eugene O'Neill, Elmer Rice and Maxwell Anderson, evading the restrictions of censorship by operating as a club theatre; Godfrey was the first English director to be influenced by EXPRESSIONISM. In its later years the Gate became famous for a series of intimate revues.

(2) A Dublin theatre founded in 1928 by Hilton Edwards and Micheál Mac Liammóir, devoted to the performance of world classics as well as contemporary Irish drama. M.A.

GATT (General Agreement on Tariffs and Trade). An international agreement, between countries accounting for over 80 per cent of world trade, covering levels of tariffs (i.e. import duties) and a code of behaviour for governments in international trade. The GATT secretariat is in Geneva. As a result of seven rounds of multilateral negotiations (see BILATERALISM AND MULTILATERALISM), starting in 1947 and ending in 1967, tariffs on manufactures imported by the developed countries have been very substantially reduced. There has been less success in freeing trade in agricultural products, and various *non-tariff barriers* in trade, in general outlawed by the GATT, are attracting more attention. Developing countries (see UNDERDEVELOPMENT) are absolved from making reciprocal concessions, and many impose severe restrictions on trade. M.FG.S.

gauge invariant, see under ELEMENTARY PARTICLES.

Gaullism. A major political movement and IDEOLOGY in France, directly associated with the personality and political ideas of General Charles de Gaulle, President of France between 1958 and 1969. The ideology of Gaullism was based on the following: the primacy of national unity and the denial of the MARXIST notion of CLASS war; the need for order and authority in all branches of public life; the defence of a powerful state and strong executive authority; state participation in the creation of a modern industrial economy; and the assertion of national independence in foreign and European affairs (see FORCE DE FRAPPE). In 1976 the Gaullist party changed its name to the Rassemblement Pour la République (RPR), and elected Jacques Chirac to the presidency of a reformed party with better organization and greater concentration of power in the party leader. Between 1981 and 1986 Gaullism underwent a significant change. The new Gaullisme Chiraquien is POPULIST, neo-liberal (see NEO-LIBERALISM) and NATIONALIST in outlook. Since then the Party has been influential in the process of French government. After the 1986 elections it was the dominant partner in a RIGHT-wing coalition government and Jacques Chirac became Prime Minister. This involved a COHABITATION with the socialist President Mitterrand. Jacques Chirac was elected President in 1995 in succession to Mitterrand, but the fortunes of the Gaullists have waned, as an ill-judged snap election in 1997 handed the position of prime minister to the socialist Lionel Jospin, with whom Jacques Chirac was forced to cohabit. V.L.

Gaussian distribution, see NORMAL OR GAUSSIAN DISTRIBUTION.

gay, see under HOMOSEXUALITY.

gay politics. A theoretical analysis and/or ACTIVIST practice intended to correct perceived injustices in historical and current attitudes towards homosexual acts and homosexuals (see HOMOSEXUALITY). Used loosely, the phrase should be understood to refer both to lesbian politics and to gay men's politics. These are far from identical in their concerns and priorities, though there is overlap both in shared ideas and in co-operative work in post-1969 'gay movement' creations such as information switchboards staffed by volunteers (e.g. London Lesbian and Gay Switchboard, which is the world's largest, taking a quarter of a million calls a year), newspapers and periodicals (though gay men's greater purchasing power has tended to prohibit 50/50 editorial coverage); AIDS counselling and information services (e.g. Gay Men's Health Crisis in New York; Terrence Higgins Trust and Scottish Aids Monitor in the UK) and non-commercial social venues (e.g. London Lesbian and Gay Centre, originally funded from 1985 to 1986 by the Greater London Council, 42 per cent of whose membership was women). Though rooted in 19th-century western European and American speculations *about* homosexuals and self-description and speculation by homosexuals, gay politics is for historical purposes considered to have its start in the Gay Liberation Front (GLF) which emerged after the 'Stonewall Riots' in New York in the days immediately following 27 June 1969. Patrons of a gay bar named the Stonewall had fought back against a routine raid by police. A movement without membership, GLF spread rapidly to Australasia, through the West generally, and in some degree in the Eastern Bloc. As a specific political movement and/or organization, GLF largely disappeared by about 1972. It is most notable as having expressed vociferously and publicly (hitherto almost unprecedented) anger by homosexuals of both sexes at the stigmas of 'illness', 'perversion' and 'criminality' imposed by medicine, PSYCHIATRY, RELIGION, statute law, and in the general CULTURE and media. Rebelliousness against generally contemptuous attitudes within earlier liberation movements of the 1960s, such as the BLACK civil rights (see CIVIL RIGHTS MOVEMENT) and women's organizations – in which homosexuals had played significant but at the time unacknowledged roles – also played a vital part in the emergence of gay politics. From *c.* 1982, initially in the US, gay politics globally has overwhelmingly had to concentrate on a response to the vulnerability of gay men to the AIDS virus, and to the homosexual role in its transmission – pioneering, e.g., the concept of 'safer sex' now encouraged among all sectors of the population and addressing revived religious condemnation of any sexual conduct outside marriage.

A.L.

gaze. Term that refers to the importance of seeing in DESIRE. In Freud's writing, SEXUALITY lies less in the content of what is seen than in the SUBJECTIVITY of the viewer, in the relationship between what is looked at and the developing sexual knowledge of the child (see FREUDIAN; PSYCHOANALYSIS). The relationship between viewer and scene is always one of fracture, partial IDENTIFICATION, pleasure and distrust. Jacques Lacan (see LACANIAN) introduced the concept of the MIRROR PHASE as central to sexuality and subjectivity but embodying a misrecognition or fantasy (1936). FEMINIST theorists such as Jacqueline Rose have argued that women are meant to look perfect, presenting a seamless image to the world so that the man, in confrontation with difference, can avoid any apprehension of lack. The gaze has assumed a central role in the theory of art in relation to the nude and in film and media theory in relation to the camera as a vehicle of masculine desire, creating a problematic relationship with the female subject and spectator. For further reading: J. Mitchell and J. Rose, *Feminine Sexuality: Jacques Lacan and the École Freudienne* (1982).

A.V.D.B.

GCD (general and comprehensive disarmament), see under DISARMAMENT.

Gdansk Agreement. Signed on 31 August 1980 by Lech Walesa, the leader of the newly established independent trade union SOLIDARITY, and representatives of the Polish government, the Gdansk Agreement stipulated that the government should implement a wide range of political and economic reforms. It recognized the need to create new TRADE UNIONS free of control by official institutions, and it forced the government to accept the right to STRIKE. A wage increase for all workers and the introduction of a five-day week were also agreed. Other economic provisions were egalitarian (see EGALITARIANISM) in character and included a number of improvements in welfare and an economic reform which involved self-management and workers' democracy. Management and other administrative personnel were to be appointed on merit rather than because of loyalty to the COMMUNIST Party, a measure which the Party subsequently saw as challenging its leading role in society. In addition, political reforms were proposed in the agreement, such as a restriction of censorship and of police activities. The agreement was never fully implemented by the government, and it was revoked after the suppression of Solidarity in 1981. For further reading: N. Ascherson, *The Polish August* (1981).

D.PR.

GDP (gross domestic product). The output produced within an economy during a specified time period. GDP measures the contribution to economic welfare made by private and public supply of goods and services for consumption, and INVESTMENT, which is needed in order to maintain or improve the future supply of goods and services. As it is a 'gross' figure, the depreciation of the CAPITAL stock is excluded. *Net domestic product* is GDP adjusted for depreciation of the capital stock. GDP can be measured in three different ways, all of which, in principle, give the same result. (1) The expenditure method measures the value of the expenditure necessary to purchase output; (2) the income method measures the incomes generated in producing the output; (3) the value-added method measures and adds together the value of the net addition to output made at every stage of production. In all these methods, in theory, there is no double-counting of the production of intermediate products that are used as the inputs of other products. The output of many publicly supplied goods and services has to be valued at their cost, rather than at their value, as they are not sold in a market. Among economists there are some, but not major, differences of opinion about what constitutes GDP, and NATIONAL ACCOUNTING conventions sometimes differ between countries. (See also GNP.) J.P.

gearing ratio. In ECONOMICS, the ratio of a firm's borrowing to the total value of money raised by the firm from shares and borrowing. As interest has to be paid on debt when the rate of return on CAPITAL is less than the interest rate, shareholders of firms with higher gearing ratios receive lower returns on their equity (see EQUITY CAPITAL), and such firms are more likely to become bankrupt. However, when the return on capital is greater than the interest rate, the shareholders of firms with higher gearing ratios will receive a greater return on their equity. J.P.

***Geistesgeschichte*,** see under CULTURAL HISTORY.

***Geisteswissenschaften*.** Literally, 'sciences of the spirit'. The disciplines that investigate man, society and history; broadly speaking, HISTORY, PSYCHOLOGY and the SOCIAL SCIENCES (SOCIOLOGY, ANTHROPOLOGY, POLITICAL SCIENCE, ECONOMICS). The great development of the human and social sciences in the 19th century had been speculatively reflected in Hegel's philosophy of Spirit, which treated human nature, social INSTITUTIONS and the aspects of high CULTURE (art, RELIGION and PHILOSOPHY) as constituting an autonomous realm, superior to, as well as distinct from, that of the material world. By the end of the century the idea was widely held that quite different methods of enquiry were appropriate to the domains of nature and spirit. Nature is to be *explained*, positivistically (see POSITIVISM), by the subsumption of its events under universal laws, inductively arrived at (see INDUCTION); spirit, the field of the *Geisteswissenschaften*, requires *understanding*, i.e. the sympathetic apprehension of the unique individuality of the persons, institutions and events of which it is composed. The methodological (see METHODOLOGY) distinctness between the NATURAL SCIENCES and the human and social sciences is still an issue of vigorous controversy. For further reading: G. H. von Wright, *Explanation and Understanding* (1971). A.Q.

gel filtration, see under BIOPHYSICS.

***Gemeinschaft* and *Gesellschaft*.** Two common German words ('community' and 'society') which were used by the sociologist (see SOCIOLOGY) Ferdinand Tönnies in 1887 to contrast a social relationship of solidarity between individuals based on affection, KINSHIP or membership of a COMMUNITY such as a family or group of friends (*Gemeinschaft*) with one based upon the DIVISION OF LABOUR and contractual relations between isolated individuals consulting only their own self-interest (*Gesellschaft*). Both terms are used as mental CONSTRUCTS or IDEAL TYPES which, though they do not correspond to any existing society, together provide a pair of contrasting hypotheses that can be used in investigating any system of social relationship. For further reading: C. P. Loomis and J. A. Beagle, *Rural Sociology* (1957). A.L.C.B.

gender. Social construction of male/female identity which is distinguished from SEX, the biologically based distinction between men and women. Gender is an integral part of the process of social classification and organization. It is both a set of ideas (a way of thinking about relations, of influencing behaviour, a set of symbols) and a principle of social organization (allocation to ROLES, DIVISION OF LABOUR). Gender is also an idiom for talking about the relationship between nature and CULTURE. Gender has to be understood within a social context. Although the characteristics associated with male-ness (masculinity: active/rational) and female-ness (femininity: passive/emotional) give the impression of being 'natural' or biologically founded, they are in fact culturally constructed and variable, as early work in ANTHROPOLOGY indicated (M. Mead, *Sex and Temperament in Three Primitive Societies*, 1935). The working of the concept of gender has been important in FEMINIST analyses of patriarchal societies (see PATRIARCHY). In particular, gender has been examined as an ideological mechanism in the subordination of women (i.e. the association of women with 'natural' activities like childbearing which confine them as homemakers to private/domestic space). The family has been understood as an important site for the inculcation of gender roles (see also FEMININE SEXUALITY; SEXUAL POLITICS; SEXUALITY). For further reading: C. MacCormack and M. Strathern (eds), *Nature, Culture and Gender* (1980). A.G.

gender bending. The term GENDER bending is derived from popular culture and the experiments in cross-dressing of singers such as Boy George and David Bowie. Nevertheless, the history of cross-dressing and trans-sexual identity is far older than contemporary popular culture, and critics such as Marjorie Apter (see below) have demonstrated the tradition of experimentation with the limits and boundaries of gender identity which have been a long-standing part of Western culture. Historical evidence about these negotiations with conventional forms of gender identity have formed the supporting material for theoretical accounts of gender identity (most significantly that of Judith Butler in *Gender Trouble*, 1990) in which it is argued that we construct and *perform* our gender identity. This thesis is not an argument for ANDROGYNY, rather the suggestion that what is taken for granted about masculinity and femininity is learned and performed rather than natural and innate. For further reading: M. Apter, *Vested Interests: Cross Dressing and Cultural Anxiety* (1993). M.S.E.

gender gap. A term describing the increasing tendency in the USA since about 1980 for electoral behaviour and public opinion to reveal a difference in political attitudes between men and women, transcending differences of CLASS, RACE or education. The 'gap' has favoured the Democratic Party, which now struggles to attract a majority of male voters in presidential elections and often depends crucially on women's votes in other contests. Women tend more to favour lower defence budgets, greater public spending on WELFARE and public services, and more state intervention on behalf of MINORITIES and the disadvantaged. Above all, they are more likely to favour freedom of choice regarding ABORTION, which has been a fiercely divisive issue in American politics in the 1990s. S.R.

genderquake. A word which encapsulates the social disruption which has occurred as FEMINIST ideas have intersected with rapid social, demographic, economic and technological change. Drawing on the imagery of the earthquake, we sense the inevitability of this social revolution, and appreciate the tensions and fault lines which have come in its wake. The American feminist Naomi Wolf first popularized the word in her book *Fire with Fire: the new female power and how it will change the 21st century* (1994). She describes a fundamental and irreversible shift in power from men to women. H.W.

gene. Originally (Johannsen, 1909) the atom or unit of heredity, corresponding to Mendel's factors; today the functional unit is known to be made of NUCLEIC ACID and to specify, via the GENETIC CODE, a single gene product that is a PROTEIN. Generally there is a single primary gene product, as in the hypothesis 'one gene – one ENZYME', or 'one gene – one antigen' (see IMMUNITY), but gene SPLICING can result in alternative products. For each primary function it is typically the case that an individual receives one gene from each parent, each situated at a particular place or LOCUS on the corresponding CHROMOSOMES. The two genes at a locus may differ, in which case they are said to be different alleles (or *allelomorphs*). An individual with two identical genes at a locus is a *homozygote*; one with two different alleles is a *heterozygote*. In a heterozygote, it is often the case that only one of the two alleles produces an observed effect. In such cases the allele which produces an effect is said to be *dominant*, the other *recessive*. The recessive allele produces an observed effect only in a homozygote. The superior fitness (see DARWINISM) of a heterozygote to a homozygote is known as *heterosis*, and is important as a cause of variability in natural populations, and of the decline in vigour caused by inbreeding. See also GENETICS/GENOMICS. For further reading: B. Alberts *et al*, *Molecular Biology of the Cell* (1983). J.M.S.; P.N.

gene bank.

(1) A collection of genetic material, such as seeds or sperm.

(2) A synonym for gene library (see DNA LIBRARY). P.N.

gene library, see under DNA LIBRARY.

gene splicing. The production of recombinant DNA (see SPLICING; GENETIC ENGINEERING). P.N.

genealogical method, see under KINSHIP.

General Agreement on Tariffs and Trade, see GATT.

General Systems Theory (GST). A movement in scientific theory which originated from developments in the 1940s and 1950s. It has influenced almost every scientific discipline, including the SOCIAL SCIENCES, and was a reaction against the atomistic and fragmented acquisition of knowledge resulting from excessive specialization. One major source of impetus towards a more holistic approach arose in the biological sciences (see HOLISM). In studying living organisms' interactions with their ENVIRONMENT it was found rewarding to study the whole ecological system (see ECOLOGY) as a single unit, and the processes by which living organisms maintain homeostasis or metabolic EQUILIBRIUM while adapting to changes in their environment. Other important influences were the growth of CYBERNETICS and information science, particularly such aspects as FEEDBACK, automatic control and ARTIFICIAL INTELLIGENCE. The General Systems Theory movement went much further than simply seeking to avoid reductionism (see REDUCTION) and analysing complex interactions. It sought to discover general patterns, trends and structural characteristics in all types of system – natural, social and technological – and on this basis to develop a unifying General Systems Theory of universal applicability. As the extreme difficulty of this ambitious task became clear in the 1960s and 1970s, the confidence of this movement has faltered, even in the biological and applied sciences. Its application to the social sciences was extremely problematic from the outset. For example, the anarchical and decentralized character of international relations and the weaknesses and irrationalities of decision-making by STATES make them particularly intractable for the scientific systems theorist. It is hence not surprising to find that many of the GST regional and global models are impoverished by serious neglect or inadequacy of the political dimensions, national and international. The only major area of international relations in which systems analysis has been of major practical value has been in the field of defence policy-making, where it is a proven tool for weapons evaluation, procurement and logistical planning. For further reading: L. von Bertalanffy, *General Systems Theory* (1969). P.W.

generalized phrase structure grammar (GPSG). In LINGUISTICS, a theory developed in the late 1970s as an alternative to accounts of language which rely on the notion of syntactic transformations (see TRANSFORMATIONAL GRAMMAR). In GPSG there are no transformations at all, and the syntactic structure of a sentence is represented by a single tree diagram of its phrase structure. For further reading: G. Gazdar *et al*, *Generalized Phrase Structure Grammar* (1985). D.C.

generation X, see under GRUNGE.

generative grammar. A CONCEPT developed by Noam Chomsky in *Syntactic Structures* (1957) which makes it possible, by the application of a finite number of *rewrite rules*, to predict ('generate') the infinite number of sentences in a language and to specify their structure. Of several possible MODELS of generative grammar he discusses three:

(1) *Finite-state* grammars generate by working through a sentence 'from left to right'; an initial element is selected, and thereafter the possibilities of occurrence of all other elements are wholly determined by the nature of the elements preceding them; Chomsky shows how this extremely simple kind of GRAMMAR is incapable of accounting for many important processes of sentence formation.

(2) *Phrase-structure* grammars contain ordered rules which are capable not only of generating strings of linguistic elements, but also of providing a CONSTITUENT ANALYSIS of these strings, and hence more information about sentence formation.

(3) *Transformational* grammars are in Chomsky's view the most powerful of all, in that very many sentence types can be economically derived by supplementing the constituent analysis rules of phrase-structure

grammars with rules for transforming one sentence into another. Thus a rule for 'passivization' would take an active sentence and reorder its elements so as to produce a passive sentence – a procedure both simpler and intuitively more satisfactory than generating active and passive sentences separately in the same grammar. In later years the role of transformations was questioned, and alternative approaches devised (e.g. GENERALIZED PHRASE STRUCTURE GRAMMAR). In the so-called 'standard' theory of the 1960s, a transformational-generative grammar consists of (a) a *syntactic component*, comprising a basic set of phrase-structure rules (sometimes called the *base component*) which provide the DEEP STRUCTURE information about the sentences of a language, and a set of transformational rules for generating *surface structures*; (b) a *phonological component*, which provides for converting strings of syntactic elements into pronounceable utterance; and (c) a *semantic component*, which provides information about the meaning of the lexical items to be used in sentences (see LEXICON). Later developments (in the 1970s) became known as the EXTENDED STANDARD THEORY and the revised extended standard theory, and the approach has since provided the frame of reference for several linguistic models. See BINDING; PRINCIPLES AND PARAMETERS. For further reading: A. N. Chomsky, *Knowledge of Language* (1986). D.C.

genetic assimilation. Term coined by C. H. Waddington (1953) for a process which mimics Lamarckian inheritance (see LAMARCKISM) without involving directed MUTATION. If those members of a population which respond to an environmental stimulus in a particular way are selected, naturally or artificially, this will result in the accumulation of GENES which favour the response, until the response appears without the environmental stimulus. J.M.S.

genetic code. The 'dictionary' relating the sequence of nucleotides in a DNA MOLECULE (see NUCLEIC ACID) with the amino acids whose nature and order of assembly into a PROTEIN they specify. An amino acid is specified not by a single nucleotide but by a triplet of nucleotides; thus uracil-uracil-uracil specifies the amino acid phenylalanine. Some triplets are either nonsensical, in the sense that they do not specify or code for any amino acid, or are 'punctuation marks' marking the beginning or the end of a certain stretch of genetic information. A consensus of scientists considers that the complex of discoveries comprising the discovery of the genetic functions of DNA, the genetic code, and the mechanism of *transcription* and *translation*, constitute the greatest intellectual achievement of modern science (see GENOME). P.M.; J.M.S.; P.N.

genetic discrimination. The exclusion of a person from rights or services because of their GENOTYPE. Most common in the US, genetic discrimination typically takes the form of an individual being denied health or life insurance or being refused employment because they have a genetic predisposition to a certain disease (i.e. they carry a gene which makes them more likely to contract that disease in the future than the average person is). The motives of insurers are financial – if a person carries a large risk of contracting a disease, a health or life insurer faces larger costs. However, the consequences for the individual are particularly severe in a country like America, where there is no nationalized healthcare provision. Though precise estimates of the scale of the problem have been difficult to obtain, many thousands of people seem to have been affected so far. And as the HUMAN GENOME PROJECT finds ways to diagnose even more diseases in advance, that number is likely to rise unless there is preventative legislation. Though the rapid advances in genetic science offer many advantages, genetic discrimination represents one of the disadvantages of this knowledge. Unless it is properly regulated, it may be abused to the detriment of sections of society who carry certain genes. A.A.L.

genetic drift. Changes occurring in GENE frequency in a population as a result of random processes rather than selection, MUTATION or migration. Drift becomes important only when population size is small, so that sampling error occurs when genes are transmitted from one generation to the next (see SAMPLE). This happens if a population is small and remains so (e.g. on an island), if the population size fluctuates markedly (e.g. varying with a seasonal food supply), or if a new population is founded by a small group leaving an established population. For further reading: J. S. Gale, *Population Genetics* (1980). A.CL.

genetic engineering. The process of artificially combining genetic material (see GENETICS/GENOMICS) to produce new varieties of plants or animals, to alter the characteristics of existing organisms, or to create new life forms. Early attempts at genetic engineering produced bacteria that could digest oil (see BACTERIOLOGY), and tomatoes that grew in shapes convenient for packing and transport. Combinations of the gene that produced human insulin with the common e-coli bacteria allowed for inexpensive production of medication for the treatment of diabetes. More recent experiments in genetic engineering have yielded trans-genic animals such as mice that carry human genetic material.

The notion that specific human characteristics could be 'engineered' genetically has become controversial. It is already possible to terminate pregnancies after a genetic test reveals characteristics or diseases parents find undesirable. 'Genetic therapy', the potential to manipulate the genetic make-up of an unborn child to treat a genetically based disease, is still at the early experimental stages. It is not yet possible to choose such characteristics as the eye colour or height of children before they are born, but the prospect of such developments has already engendered significant opposition to many types of human genetic manipulation, particularly engineering involving embryos. P.A.L.

genetic epistemology. In DEVELOPMENTAL PSYCHOLOGY, a somewhat idiosyncratic PIAGETIAN coinage which appears to serve as an umbrella term for the theoretical ideas informing his own work on the development of knowledge and understanding in the growing child – a development which he regarded, to a considerable extent, as being genetically pre-programmed. For further reading: J. Piaget, *Psychology and Epistemology* (1972). C.L.-H.

genetic explanation, see under EXPLANATION.

genetic linkage. The tendency for different characteristics to be inherited together. The experiments of Gregor Mendel (1822–84) had led him to propose that such characteristics are inherited independently of each other, but William Bateson and others reported in 1905 that certain traits of the sweet pea flower appeared in the parental combinations more often than expected when different strains were crossed. These traits were coupled, or linked. A linkage group consists of all the traits in an organism that tend to be co-inherited with any other member of the group: the physical basis of such a group is the CHROMOSOME. The more closely that any two GENES are located on a chromosome, the less often will they be separated by recombination events at which genetic information is exchanged between members of a chromosome pair. Thus, the more tightly will the genes be linked. Of great importance is the determination of an organism's sex by its chromosomal constitution; traits inherited on a sex chromosome will be transmitted unequally to offspring of the two sexes. For further reading: H. L. K. Whitehouse, *Towards an Understanding of the Mechanism of Heredity* (1973). A.CL.

genetic memory. A phrase sometimes employed by nature-philosophers, e.g. Ewald Hering, for the endowment by which, for example, a frog's egg 'remembers' to grow up into a frog. There is, however, no property of genetic memory that is not explicable in terms of ordinary GENETICS and heredity. Genetic memory therefore belongs to the strange philosophical museum that also contains racial memory, *élan vital* (see VITALISM), and entelechy. P.M.

genetic method. Not so much a precise method as an approach, marked by interest in origins and evolution, which dominated historical studies in the 19th century. More recently, historians have been turning away from the 'idol of origins' (as Marc Bloch [1886–1944] called it) – the tendency to explain recent events in terms of the remote past. The genetic approach has been most successful in biography, and most dangerous, perhaps, when applied to the history of INSTITUTIONS. See also HISTORICISM. P.B.

genetic psychology. A term used in the 1930s and 1940s to cover COMPARATIVE PSYCHOLOGY and DEVELOPMENTAL PSYCHOLOGY.

It meant the phylogenetic and ontogenetic development (see PHYLOGENY; ONTOGENY) of human adult behaviour. This general approach persists and is still a valid one. The term itself, however, seems to have been dropped, probably to avoid confusion with behavioural GENETICS. P.E.B.

genetic system.

(1) The reproductive and hereditary processes of a population;

(2) more generally, the totality of factors that control the flow of genetic information from one generation to the next. J.M.S.

genetic testing. New technologies developed in conjunction with the HUMAN GENOME PROJECT allow scientists to analyse human blood or tissue for a variety of purposes. These analyses are generally described as 'genetic testing'; they focus on identifying particular characteristics of an individual's genetic make-up (see GENETICS/GENOMICS).

Numerous genetic tests are done for medical reasons. For certain cancers, a test might suggest an inherited predisposition to fall victim to the disease. For other conditions, like Huntington's disease, a positive test provides near-conclusive evidence that the tested person will develop the disease, if he lives long enough. Genetic testing is also done to diagnose genetic diseases in foetuses. Among the hundreds of other diseases for which genetic tests have already been developed are cystic fibrosis, Tay Sachs disease and sickle cell anaemia.

Because every person has a unique genetic make-up, genetic testing is also used to determine identity (genetic 'fingerprinting' or DNA evidence; see NUCLEIC ACID). A blood or tissue sample can provide evidence that is useful in the legal context. Tests are now routinely done to prove the biological link between parents and children in paternity contests and to generate evidence of an accused person's guilt or innocence in a criminal trial. Critics of genetic screening as a policy point to its use by some employers to exclude workers from the job market; by some insurance companies to deny coverage to those who test positive for genetic conditions; and by STATES or firms (see FIRM, THEORIES OF) that may wish to pursue EUGENIC policies. Many persons object to genetic testing because it can lead to medical counselling advocating abortion. P.A.L.; S.T.

geneticism. A word coined in 1959 by P. B. Medawar on the MODEL of EVOLUTIONISM, SCIENTISM and HISTORICISM to refer to a scheme of thought which extravagantly overestimates the explanatory power of genetical ideas. The pretended explanation on genetic lines of every aspect of human character and every nuance of personality, and the interpretation of the rise and fall of nations along genetic lines, may all be said to belong to geneticism, which has the ill effect of bringing GENETICS into undeserved discredit. P.M.

genetics/genomics. Genetics is the science of biological variation, or more specifically it is the study of the inheritance of biological variation. Without variation there can, strictly speaking, be no genetics. Mendel (1822–84) gave the earliest clear statement of the rules of inheritance, in the 1860s (see MENDEL'S LAWS; MENDELISM). The term genetics was not introduced, however, until 1905 (by William Bateson) and the term GENE even later, by Wilhelm Johannsen in 1909. CHROMOSOMES were discovered by Flemming in 1877 and so named by Waldeyer in 1888.

Genomics is the study of genomes. Genome is a hybrid word formed by the elision of 'gene' and 'chromosome', and that is what the term means: the set of chromosomes and the genes they contain in each cell of an ORGANISM. One speaks also of the haploid genome (one chromosome from each pair as found in sperm and eggs) and of the diploid genome (present in the body CELLS). The haploid genome of the human contains approximately 80,000 genes distributed over 23 chromosomes (actually 24 types of chromosomes: the 22 autosomes, or non-sex chromosomes, and the sex chromosomes X and Y).

The original importance of genetics was that it provided a law of heredity which was the missing element in Darwin's theory of EVOLUTION by NATURAL SELECTION. (See also DARWINISM.) Today genetics can claim to be the central discipline of BIOLOGY. The discovery of the chemical constitution of genes by Watson, Crick and Wilkins in 1952 revealed in its essentials the process whereby like begets like. This property of heredity, together with the properties of multiplication and variation, provides the necessary conditions for evolution by natural selection, and is therefore the most important property differentiating living from non-living things.

The term genome was first used by H. Winkler in 1920. The term genomics was proposed by Thomas H. Roderick in 1986 to designate the process and discipline involved in 'mapping and sequencing the human genome'. With the HUMAN GENOME PROJECT, genomics has become an established discipline and the term is widely used. The Human Genome Project is a multinational effort first proposed formally in 1985, initiated in 1990 and expected to take 15 years to complete. The end product will be structural genomics; functional genomics is the process of deriving information on function from the sequence. When the structural genomics is completed, we will not know the function of all the genes, their variation between individuals and across populations, and the relationship between varying structure and varying function. That will occupy biologists and physicians for many decades to come.

Genomics permits recognition of the precise DNA change (MUTATION) responsible for the many disorders that are inherited in a simple Mendelian manner, such as cystic fibrosis, muscular dystrophy and Marfan syndrome (see GENETIC TESTING). But it also has the potential of identifying the DNA variation responsible for susceptibility or resistance to 'complex traits' such as cancer, asthma, hypertension and mental illness. Thus, diagnosis and preventive medicine will become increasingly specific and effective.

Knowledge of the genome carries the philosophical risks of reductionism (the thought that once the full sequence is known, we will know everything it means to be human; see REDUCTION) and genetic determinism (the thought that a direct and unavoidable relationship exists between the genome and what we are). Also, genomics widens the gap between what we can diagnose and what we can treat, as in late-onset disorders such as Huntington's disease, thereby creating potential psychological and sociological problems. It also runs the risk of widening the gap between what we know and what we think we know. For instance, an association between a particular genomic structure and a particular trait or ability, good or bad, may be suggested. Some of these associations will prove to be spurious; others will be valid but weak and their significance may be exaggerated, to the detriment of individuals and groups.

The variability in the human genome is the strength of the species. Variability is important in a complex society. Genetic differences should be celebrated, not made the basis of stigmatization or discrimination. For further reading: S. Jones, *The Language of the Genes* (1994). V.A.M.; J.M.S.

Geneva conventions. International agreements designed to alleviate suffering in time of war and to provide for the safety and welfare of prisoners-of-war, non-combatants and innocent victims of hostilities. The first was signed at Geneva in 1864, the year after the foundation of the RED CROSS movement, and was the product of a common humanitarian impulse. It required signatories to care for the wounded who fell into their hands, to treat doctors and nurses as non-combatants, and to spare medical facilities from attack. The first convention was greatly strengthened in 1929, when common rules for the treatment of prisoners were agreed, and again in 1949, when four conventions codified the international law relating to the wounded on land, the wounded and shipwrecked at sea, prisoners and civilians. By 1989, the conventions had been signed, and in most cases ratified, by 165 states, and more have since signed. The conventions have therefore come to have the form of universal law, breach of which is criminal. Protocols were added to the conventions in 1977, providing for the protection of human rights in both international and civil war, and extending, controversially, protection to members of non-state forces in certain circumstances. See also WAR CRIMES. J.K.

genocide. Term coined by American jurist Raphael Lemkin in 1944 to denote the physical destruction of a national, racial, religious or ethnic population (see NATIONALISM; RACE; RACISM). The term genocide was included in the indictment at the NUREMBERG TRIALS of German war criminals accused of involvement in the Nazi attempt to exterminate European Jewry (see

NAZISM; HOLOCAUST, THE; CONCENTRATION CAMPS). It acquired still wider currency in a United Nations (UN) Resolution of 11 December 1946 and UN Convention of 9 December 1948 which sought to make genocide a crime under international law (see PUBLIC INTERNATIONAL LAW). As defined by the Convention, 'genocide means any of the following acts committed with intent to destroy, in whole or in part, a national, ethnic, racial or religious group such as: (a) killing members of the group, (b) causing serious bodily or mental harm to members of the group, (c) deliberately inflicting on the group conditions of life calculated to bring about its physical destruction in whole or in part, (d) imposing measures intended to prevent births within the group (see EUGENICS; STERILIZATION), (e) forcibly transferring children of the group to another group.' In usage, genocide differs from POGROM in that the term was coined after World War II, in a period when destruction of groups occurred on an industrial scale and under the explicit direction of the STATE, as opposed to the more piecemeal and random occurrences of pre-war pogroms, which tended to be carried out by mobs (often with the implicit approval of the authorities, but not officially organized and carried out by the authorities). In practice genocide does not differ from ETHNIC CLEANSING, a euphemism for genocide which was coined during the war in the former YUGOSLAVIA. For further reading: G. J. Andreopoulos, *Genocide: Conceptual and Historical Dimensions* (1994). S.T.

genodeme, see under DEME.

genome. The genetic apparatus (see GENETICS/GENOMICS) of an organism considered as a whole and as characteristic of it, e.g. 'the human genome' referring to the chromosomal make-up (see CHROMOSOMES) characteristic of human beings and to the sum total of the genetic information which it embodies and imparts. P.M.

genotype. The genetic constitution of an individual, as deduced from ancestry or breeding performance, in contrast to its *phenotype*, the characteristics which are manifested in the individual. The distinction is important because it is the genotype, not the phenotype, which is reproduced and can be transmitted to future generations. J.M.S.

genre. In LINGUISTICS, any variety of speech or writing that has achieved a level of general recognition, such as commercial ADVERTISING, jokes and sermons. A genre imposes several identifiable characteristics on a use of language, notably in relation to subject-matter, purpose (e.g. narrative, allegory, satire), textual structure, form of argumentation, and level of formality. Sub-genres can also be identified, as with types of novel or types of news story. The analysis can go into considerable depth, involving a detailed account of the vocabulary and grammatical patterns used, as well as (in the case of spoken texts) such matters as sounds, intonation and rhythm, and (in the case of written texts) spelling, typography and graphic design. For further reading: V. K. Bhatia, *Analysing Genre* (1993). D.C.

gentrification. Term describing middle-class families moving back into run-down inner city areas, refurbishing existing older residential property. This leads to an increase in property values and the exodus of the previous low-income social groups. Gentrification in Britain is often associated with the designation of conservation areas (see URBAN CONSERVATION; URBAN RENEWAL; TOWNSCAPE). For further reading: N. Smith and P. Williams, *Gentrification of the City* (1986). C.G.

gentry controversy. A controversy which began in 1941 when R. H. Tawney published an article on 'The Rise of the Gentry', arguing that the English Revolution of the mid-17th century resulted from the rise of a group of entrepreneur landlords between 1540 and 1640, and that political power followed economic. He was violently attacked by H. R. Trevor-Roper, who suggested that during this period the gentry were in fact in economic decline. Many historians joined in, finer distinctions were drawn, and both literary and statistical evidence received more careful scrutiny than they had first been given. In the course of this 20-year controversy, English SOCIAL HISTORY came of age. For further reading: J. H. Hexter, 'Storm over the Gentry', in his *Reappraisals in History* (1963). P.B.

geochemistry. The description of the CHEMISTRY of the earth. Traditionally it involves the study of the abundance and distribution of ELEMENTS and their ISOTOPES, mainly in the LITHOSPHERE, but also in the seas and the earth's atmosphere. Modern geochemistry is increasingly concerned with understanding the way in which the earth and SOLAR SYSTEM have evolved by means of a combined chemical and geological (see GEOLOGY) approach. For further reading: W. S. Fyfe, *Geochemistry* (1974). B.F.

geochronology. Term used in ARCHAEOLOGY to cover all DATING methods which are based on measurable changes in natural substances. They include ARCHAEOMAGNETISM, DENDROCHRONOLOGY, RADIOCARBON DATING, THERMOLUMINESCENCE, varve dating, and other techniques based on PHYSICS and CHEMISTRY. B.C.

geodesic dome, see under DYMAXION.

geodesy. The observation and measurement of the size and external shape of the earth and the variations in terrestrial gravity (see GRAVITATION). Geodetic surveys based on geometric methods are only considered to be accurate for relatively small areas. Local surveys are referred to a worldwide reference surface, the *geoid*, which coincides with the mean-sea-level surface and its theoretical extension into the continental areas. The shape of the geoid, like the surface of the oceans, is determined by the gravitational attraction of the earth's mass. Since the earth is inhomogeneous, with an irregular distribution of mass (see ISOSTASY), the geoid is also an irregular surface. The precise tracking of artificial satellites has enabled this surface to be more accurately contoured. J.L.M.L.

geographical determinism, see under ENVIRONMENTALISM.

Geographical Information Systems, see GIS.

geography. The academic discipline whose body of knowledge is organized around a number of broad themes: the interrelationship between human societies and their natural environments; the processes that shape the spatial distributions exhibited by all manner of natural and human phenomena; and the resulting similarities and differences – both natural and humanly created – among the diverse parts of the world. One feature common to almost all geographical studies has been their use of the map as a device for classifying, describing and explaining the phenomena under investigation. Underlying these broad themes and features, however, a number of competing theoretical, methodological (see METHODOLOGY) and substantive orientations have led the discipline into recurrent crises of identity and self-doubt. Nonetheless, in practice much of the research conducted by geographers has succeeded in being imaginative, bold in scope, sensitive to the very real problems faced by particular people, places and environments, and consistently open to the ideas of neighbouring disciplines and the wider intellectual debates of philosophers and social theorists.

Despite the efforts of many geographers to tackle the intersection of the natural and human worlds, the discipline continues to straddle two different bodies of knowledge: PHYSICAL GEOGRAPHY and HUMAN GEOGRAPHY (which mirror the broader differences between NATURAL SCIENCE and SOCIAL SCIENCE). In physical geography there has been an accelerating shift in emphasis over the past half-century from descriptively examining the evolution of regional landscape complexes to employing much more rigorous analytical techniques to study the environmental processes that systematically shape the natural landscape. In developing this contemporary approach, physical geographers have drawn upon – and have themselves contributed to – such specializations as earth systems science, CLIMATOLOGY, GEOMORPHOLOGY and hydrology.

In human geography a similar shift in emphasis also occurred, in that the older concern with the uniqueness of particular peoples and places was replaced, in the 1960s, by a more scientific approach focused on the discovery of universal laws supposedly governing human spatial behavior and the spatial organization of human activities. This PARADIGM shift called for a more rigorous theorization of the processes that shape the location of such phenomena as towns, factories, shops, transport routes and political boundaries (see LOCATION THEORY), and one consequence of researchers focusing their attention on the patterns exhibited by these various human productions was the heightened fragmentation of human geography into such systematic components as urban geography, ECONOMIC GEOGRAPHY, transportation geography and POLITICAL GEOGRAPHY. (Note, however, that terms such as 'urban geography' were in use before the advent of geography as spatial science, and note too that these terms are still employed as convenient shorthands by current researchers who in many cases would wish to distance themselves from the spatial scientific approach.) Whereas this reformulation of geographical inquiry generated some important findings, it has itself been criticized, most notably by proponents of HUMANISTIC GEOGRAPHY – who stress the ways in which individual human agents both experience and creatively transform their local surroundings – and by proponents of RADICAL GEOGRAPHY – who stress the ways in which spatial distributions (and particularly geographically uneven distributions of wealth, welfare and resources) are embedded within the workings of complex economic, social and political structures. Thus, while spatial science has continued to be an important part of the discipline (and has turned to increasingly sophisticated quantitative techniques), both the humanistic (see HUMANISM) and radical approaches have gained ground since 1980, the result being a new division within human geography that today involves much philosophical and social-theoretical debate over what certain commentators term the 'spatiality' of the world. At the same time, researchers have displayed an increasing appreciation of both history (see HISTORICAL GEOGRAPHY) and social issues such as CLASS, RACE and GENDER (see FEMINIST GEOGRAPHY).

In both physical and human geography, it can also be argued that since 1990 there has been a rediscovery and restatement of the unique nature of particular places and regions. In physical geography it is increasingly realized that, although geomorphological processes (see GEOMORPHOLOGY) must ultimately obey the invariant laws of PHYSICS and CHEMISTRY, it is impossible to predict from these laws the precise manner in which the components of a particular drainage basin, glacial valley, wetland, etc. are put together. Similarly, in human geography it is increasingly supposed that, whereas it may be possible to identify general tendencies present in the workings of advanced capitalist, socialist and developing societies (see CAPITALISM; SOCIALISM; DEVELOPING COUNTRIES), these tendencies are always played out in quite different ways in different places, seemingly in reflection of the specific manner in which local economies, social structures and political systems are constituted. Accordingly, a number of geographers now draw on philosophical and social-theoretical perspectives to capture the importance of how both natural and human processes come together in specific ways in specific places. For further reading: R. J. Johnston, *Geography and Geographers: Anglo-American Human Geography Since 1945* (1997). C.P.; P.O.M.

geography of gender. Traditionally women have been 'hidden from geography', as is evident from the discipline's conventional concentration upon issues such as 'man's habitat' and 'man and environment'. This omission has been compounded by an emphasis on broad-brush research methodologies focusing on the sphere of production (the 'public') and on classical Marxist class inequalities (see MARXISM; RADICAL GEOGRAPHY), rather than on the spheres of consumption and reproduction (the 'private'), which have been ideologically constructed as 'women's place'. There has recently been some attempt to redress the balance, especially from the 'Women and Geography' Study Group of the Institute of British Geographers. For example, it has been noted that urban spatial form has differential implications for women concerning their access to public facilities, employment, transport, retailing, and so on. Women have, in addition, made up a large proportion of the workforce, and in recent years CAPITALISM has been able to 'take advantage' of the socially constructed separations between men and women and between public and private (see above). The concentration of women in low-skilled, dull, repetitive jobs is a result of the social construction of GENDER (as differences between males and females) rather than any biologically determined SEX differences, and it is for this reason that a geography of gender – rather than of sex – is preferable. Gender, it must be stressed, includes men, and a study of the unequal POWER relations between men and women (PATRIARCHY) is essential to an understanding of geography and gender. For further reading: Institute of British Geographers, Women in Geography Study Group, *Geography and Gender* (1984). M.LO.

geoid, see under GEODESY.

geological time chart. The chronological arrangement of the geological events which are recorded in the most complete succession of rocks exposed on the earth's surface. A purely relative chronology of geological age has been constructed and is usually presented in the form of a stratigraphic column in which the fossiliferous rocks formed since the beginning of the Cambrian period (i.e. from about 600 million years ago) are arranged in vertical succession upwards. Radiometric methods (see RADIOCARBON DATING) give a reasonably accurate DATING, usually recorded in millions of years, of rocks, so that the time chart will also indicate the duration of the periods of known geological age. This method has been applied to the metamorphic rocks of pre-Cambrian age which are almost entirely devoid of fossils. The oldest rock of the continents has been dated by this method as 3,500 million years old. J.L.M.L.

geology. The scientific study of the earth and of other bodies in the SOLAR SYSTEM (e.g. the moon) which may provide evidence relating to its origin and to the evolution of life. The main activities of geology have been to map and classify the rocks exposed on the earth's surface and those accessible underground, and to explain their origin and distribution. The most important economic applications of geology are concerned with the discovery and exploitation of ore deposits, fossil fuels, construction materials and underground water. J.L.M.L.

geomagnetism, see under MAGNETISM.

geometric art, see under ABSTRACT ART.

geometry. Literally the study of measuring the earth. Euclid (*c.* 300 BC) in his *Elements* showed how the properties of triangles, circles, parallel lines, etc. could be deduced from ten axioms (see AXIOMATIC METHOD). His approach dominated the subject for centuries and was applied to such things as the five regular solids, and the conic sections (the shapes made by cutting through a solid cone).

A completely new approach came from the invention of co-ordinates by René Descartes in 1637: most geometric shapes can be represented by an equation in x and y, so that geometric results can be found using ALGEBRA. Indeed, this trend has so developed that it is almost true to say that geometry is now a language for discussing algebra.

Early in the 19th century it was realized that some of Euclid's axioms could be changed. This led to *elliptic geometry*, where there are no parallel lines (just as there are none on the surface of the earth, where the angle sum of a triangle always exceeds 180°). Further loosenings led to four- (and higher) dimensional (see DIMENSION), projective and finite geometries, and a large offshoot, TOPOLOGY, developed. N.A.R.

geomorphology. The study of the nature and evolution of the surface features of the earth, particularly those landscapes produced by sub-aerial erosion. All landscapes owe their form to a balance between constructional processes – such as volcanic eruption and mountain-building, and destructional processes – erosion by the agents water, ice and wind. Geomorphological research has made it possible to identify distinctive landforms resulting from the predominating action of one of the agents of erosion, even when it has ceased to operate. The present landscape of northern Europe and North America, for example, retains the essential features of the glaciated landscape formed during the Pleistocene epoch, even though the glaciers retreated some 15,000 years ago. J.L.M.L.

geophysics. An interdisciplinary science where the theories and techniques of PHYSICS are applied to the atmosphere, surface and interior of the earth. In recent decades the study of earthquake waves and rock magnetism has led to the abandonment of the notion of a rigid earth ('*terra firma*'), and its replacement by theories involving the slow flow of rocks over geological time. See also CONTINENTAL DRIFT; PLATE TEC-

TONICS; SEISMOLOGY. For further reading: N. Calder, *Restless Earth* (1972). M.V.B.

geopolitics. A long-established area of geographical inquiry which considers SPACE to be important in making sense of the world political order. Its scholarly usage should not be confused with *Geopolitik*, a German school of thought which, in developing Darwinian notions (see DARWINISM) such as Lebensraum ('living space'), provided spurious intellectual justification for national 'paranoia', territorial claims and geopolitical objectives in Germany during the 1930s. *Geopolitik* saw STATES as highly individual organisms engaged in perpetual struggle one with another, and in which and through which all nationals are bound spiritually into one organic 'oneness'. In contrast, the intellectual origins of geopolitics can be traced back to the early 20th-century works of Halford Mackinder. In his 1904 'heartland thesis', which is one of the most widely read and influential of geopolitical expositions, Mackinder interpreted European history as a record of struggle to achieve and prevent control over the pivotal area of the Eurasian land mass, and this thesis was to provide inspiration for much post-war US foreign policy thinking, particularly in the shape of Spykman's 'rimland' theory (the attempt to create a 'buffer zone' around the former USSR with a string of neutral states). Recent geopolitical approaches focus on (a) the hierarchical and regional structuring of state power; (b) the role of the geographical imagination in forming state IDEOLOGIES which justify specific territorial actions; and (c) the POLITICAL ECONOMY of state behaviour, in which the links between the processes of CAPITAL accumulation, resource competition and foreign policies are analysed as part of a singular and interdependent global system. For further reading: D. Pepper and A. Jenkins (eds), *The Geography of Peace and War* (1985). GR.S.

Geopolitik, see under GEOPOLITICS.

geotaxis, see under TROPISM.

geotropism, see under TROPISM.

geriatrics. The branch of medicine that deals with the special medical problems of the aged. As the diseases of youth and middle age yield to medical treatment, so the diseases of the elderly become relatively more important. Geriatrics bears the same relationship to GERONTOLOGY as PSYCHIATRY bears to PSYCHOLOGY. P.M.

germ plasm. Term used by August Weismann (1834–1914) for the reproductive CELLS and tissues of the body as contrasted with the 'ordinary' parts of the body – the SOMA. Weismann's *germ plasm theory* is the theory that the cells destined to become reproductive cells are segregated very early in development and are thus untouched by influences from the ENVIRONMENT or from elsewhere in the body. This theory, even if it is not in all cases literally true, is now admitted to be effectively true, because the genetic information (see GENETICS/GENOMICS) contained in the germ cells is indeed totally unaffected by what goes on around them in the body or in the environment. P.M.

German reunification. The process by which Germany was reunited in 1990. Germany had been divided after World War II into West Germany, a capitalist pluralist democracy (see CAPITALISM; PLURALISM; DEMOCRACY), and East Germany, a communist state (see COMMUNISM) under Soviet domination. In the late 1980s the former Soviet satellite states in eastern and central Europe began to obtain their independence, and German reunification became a possibility. The idea was championed by the West German Chancellor Helmut Kohl, and the two Germanies merged their financial and political systems in 1990. Berlin was named as the new capital of the united Germany. Unification has not proved a smooth process, since the East was economically underdeveloped, and the new monetary union was established on an equal basis between the two currencies. This has necessitated huge transfers from West to East, higher taxes and higher interest rates, which contributed to the European recession of the early 1990s. V.L.

gerontology. The branch of BIOLOGY that deals with the nature of ageing. Its central problem is whether the ageing process is an epiphenomenon of life or whether it is innate or genetically programmed in the sense that it will occur irrespective of the vicissitudes to which the organism is exposed in the course of its ordinary lifetime. There is nothing paradoxical about the idea of a genetically programmed ageing process, because the post-reproductive period of life is beyond the direct reach of the forces of NATURAL SELECTION. Among the epiphenomenal theories of ageing is Mechnikov's conjecture, now discredited, that ageing is caused by a progressive auto-intoxication through the assimilation of toxins liberated by an unsatisfactory bacterial population of the gut. Another is Orgel's theory according to which ageing is the consequence of a series of accumulated errors of transcription in the processes by which the genetic information residing in the germinal DNA (see NUCLEIC ACID) is mapped into specific structural PROTEINS or ENZYMES. Experimental evidence lends some support to the latter view. If it is true, the ageing process could not be remedied by any form of physical intervention since it would be largely random in origin. P.M.

Gesamtkunstwerk ('complete-art-work'). The concept, most closely associated with Richard Wagner (1813–83), of a total integration of music, drama and spectacle in which the arts involved are so interdependent that none shall dominate to the detriment of the others. Theoretically, since music, text and theatrical concept should all emanate from the same mind, a perfect balance should be achieved; in practice, this is rarely so, since the chance of one person possessing equally imaginative gifts in three spheres is remote. After Wagner, musical landmarks in the welding of different artistic media into a synaesthetic experience (see SYNAESTHESIA) include Schoenberg's *Die Glückliche Hand* and Scriabin's *Prometheus*. In recent times, the new resources of ELECTRONIC MUSIC, coupled with immense advances in lighting techniques, back-projection, amplification, etc., have made the concept of *Gesamtkunstwerk* more likely to be achieved, though the ultimate gain in artistic terms may be less than Wagner predicted. A.H.

Gesellschaft, see under GEMEINSCHAFT.

Gestalt. German word for a configuration, pattern or organized whole with qualities different from those of its components separately considered; e.g. a melody, since its quality does not inhere in any particular notes as such. Such whole qualities have always been recognized and commented upon, but their explicit experimental study came into prominence in Germany when, in 1910, the self-styled *Gestalt psychologists* began studying the PHI-PHENOMENON. Here was a perceived movement corresponding neither to actual physical movement nor to elementary stimulus events but to several stimulus events in interaction. The founders of Gestalt psychology (in R. S. Woodworth's classification, one of the six main SCHOOLS OF PSYCHOLOGY) were Max Wertheimer, Kurt Koffka and Wolfgang Köhler. Their key argument was that the nature of the parts is determined by, and secondary to, the whole. They saw this argument as applying to every field of PSYCHOLOGY and, indeed, of PHILOSOPHY, science and art. They insisted that inquiry proceed from-above-down rather than from-below-up, i.e. one must not start with supposed elements and try to synthesize these into wholes, but rather examine the whole to discover what its natural parts are. The three founders, who migrated to the USA in the 1930s, applied their approach fruitfully to the concrete understanding of a wide range of phenomena in PERCEPTION, learning and thinking processes, and inspired others to undertake Gestalt-flavoured studies of personality, SOCIAL PSYCHOLOGY and AESTHETICS. In its early years Gestalt psychology seemed revolutionary and aroused much controversy, but by mid-century it had ceased to represent a self-conscious school. While many of its fundamental problems about organized complexities remained unsolved, its main lessons and factual discoveries were absorbed profitably into the mainstream of psychology. For further reading: K. Koffka, *Principles of Gestalt Psychology* (1935). I.M.L.H.

gestalt therapy. A form of PSYCHOTHERAPY predicated upon a holistic concept of mind/body (see HOLISM), owing much to the philosophical influence of Klaus Conrad and Karl Jaspers. As popularized in the USA from the 1960s, gestalt therapy stressed the value of immediate, authentic experience (as distinct from the FREUDIAN emphasis upon recovering fundamentally formative repressed childhood experiences). The individual components of emotional response and behaviour are analysed, with particular stress upon appearance and body presentation (the meaning of breathing, of gesture and suchlike). GROUP THERAPY has been developed, especially under Fritz Perls, and the figure of the 'guru' is valued. Overall, the stress in gestalt therapy is upon the value of feeling over thinking. For further reading: A. Clare, *Let's Talk about Me* (1981). R.P.

Gestapo. German acronym for *Geheime Staatspolizei*, Secret State Police. The term was originally applied to the Prussian plain-clothes political police force evolved during the troubled times preceding the appointment of Adolf Hitler as Chancellor of Germany, but was extended under his chancellorship to the whole machinery of terror and informants untrammelled by any legal constraint which was used by the Nazi state (see NAZISM) against anyone suspected of political deviation or opposition. It is now freely applied as an adjective of an opprobrious kind – 'Gestapo tactics' – to all police operations, whether open or covert, extra-legal or not, directed to the restraint of illegal actions for which political motives can be adduced. For further reading: K. Bracher, *The German Dictatorship* (1973). D.C.W.

gestural. In art criticism, an adjective suggesting conspicuous brushwork, and movement of the body in the painting process. It is particularly relevant to ACTION PAINTING. A.K.W.

***Gestus*.** A German term used by Gotthold Lessing (1729–81) in his dramatic notes of 1767 to mean something distinct from 'gesture', and adopted in BRECHTIAN parlance around 1930 to convey much the same as the old English 'gest' (bearing, carriage, mien), i.e. a mixture of gesture and gist, attitude and point. In Brecht's view there was a 'basic gest' to any play or scene, while everything in it was to be conveyed by a succession of gests, each dictating its own expression in terms of language, music, grouping, etc. For such expression to be 'gestic' it must communicate not merely the meaning but also the speaker's attitude to his listeners and to what he is saying. J.W.

ghetto. Originally applied to the Jewish quarters of medieval Italian cities, the term came to be used of the Jewish quarters of all European cities, especially those of central and eastern Europe. Since World War II, it has achieved a wider sociological currency to refer to any urban area which is inhabited by a group segregated on the basis of ETHNICITY, colour or RELIGION, thus the 'black ghettos' of American cities, the 'Catholic ghettos' (see CATHOLICISM) of Ulster towns, the 'Asian ghettos' of London and Bradford. While ghettos are often deprived areas, the term does not, unlike concepts such as INTERNAL COLONIALISM, necessarily imply a condition of EXPLOITATION or struggle with other groups; it rather suggests a degree of permanency and co-existence. K.K.

gift. In anthropological usage, largely based upon M. Mauss's pioneer study 'Essai sur le don' (*Année Sociologique*, 1923–24), a gift is above all something given in the expectation of reciprocation. Gift-giving in all societies is interested: by means of gifts people and groups create, vary and maintain relationships among themselves, while, in societies lacking markets and a system of MONEY, gift-giving is likely to be a chief mechanism by which EXCHANGES are effected. For further reading: M. Mauss, tr. I. Cunnison, *The Gift* (1954). M.F.

GIFT, see under INFERTILITY.

gift exchange, see under EXCHANGE.

GIS (Geographical Information Systems). Computer systems which can display maps of different geological or geographical features on the screen at the same time. When confined to rolls of paper, maps showing different kinds of features – e.g. rock types or water tables – were awkward to compare with one another. Now, computer technology allows them to be viewed simultaneously, which has led to great advances in CARTOGRAPHY. In addition, satellite technology has meant that the most remote parts of the earth can be mapped relatively cheaply and very accurately, improving maps still further. A.A.L.

glaciology. The study of all forms of natural ice including the study of glaciers, snow, the ice cover of water and subterranean ice, and the interaction of these forms with the atmosphere, HYDROSPHERE and LITHOSPHERE. To the geologist the principal branch of glaciology is that which deals with the behaviour of ice (principally in the form of ice-sheets and glaciers) on the earth's surface, since this provides information which can be applied to the study of ancient glaciations. J.L.M.L.

glasnost. A Russian term, literally meaning 'openness', which refers to the policy of the former USSR of promoting public debate on subjects previously considered too sensitive to discuss. It particularly aimed to widen the area of permitted criticism of Soviet society and its administration. It also involved a greater responsiveness to public opinion and the airing of a greater diversity of views before the population, both in the media and in literature and the arts. The concept was not a new one, but the need for *glasnost* was stressed by the leadership of Mikhail Gorbachev, elected General Secretary of the COMMUNIST Party in 1985, and its scope increased under his leadership. After his election, more attention was given in the media to problems within Soviet society, and failures were reported more candidly: prominent examples are the nuclear accident at CHERNOBYL, which after initial secrecy was widely publicized, and the NATIONALIST disturbances in Kazakhstan in December 1986. The aim of *glasnost* was not to introduce complete freedom of information and criticism. Instead the leadership hoped that it would lead to the correction of faults in policy and its implementation by making them public, and that it would encourage widespread involvement in the political and economic reforms which were introduced between 1985 and 1987. D.PR.

glia, see under NEURON.

global gauge field theory, see under SUPERSYMMETRY.

globalization.

(1) In SOCIOLOGY, the term given to the process whereby information, commodities and images, having been produced in a particular nation or region of the world, enter into a global flow facilitated, for example, by the growth of transnational companies, satellite television and, more recently, the INTERNET. Prime examples of global products include MTV, the soft drink Coca-Cola, McDonald's fast food restaurants, Nike training shoes and Disney films. Certain theorists argue that the overall effect of globalization is to decrease or 'flatten out' the cultural differences between nations as individuals within these nations are subsumed into a single global culture. In noting the dominant flow of commodities and information from Western, or Westernized, industrialized nations to DEVELOPING COUNTRIES, some observers have suggested that globalization is being driven by an uncompromising cultural IMPERIALISM which shows little regard for the traditional cultural ways of life which are being abandoned as individuals strive to attain Western goods and adopt the sensibilities of Western CONSUMER SOCIETIES. Other theorists, however, take a more optimistic view, suggesting that globalization rather highlights the cultural diversity of different nations, the cultural MEANINGS and forms of significance attached to Western products being formulated on the basis of local knowledge and sensibilities (see LOCALIZATION). For further reading: M. Featherstone (ed.), *Global Culture: Nationalism, Globalization and Modernity* (1992). A.BEN.

(2) In economics, the process by which the perceived advantages of Western-style CAPITALISM have been shared with an ever-widening group of DEVELOPING COUNTRIES. The political origins of the process can be traced to the end of the COLD WAR and the spread of more democratic (see DEMOCRACY) political systems to Latin America, eastern Europe, South Africa, the Far East and parts of the world previously untouched by FREE MARKET economics. The NEW WORLD ORDER brought with it a creed of lower trade barriers; an end to exchange controls; freer movement of investment capital; and the displacement of PUBLIC SECTOR capital by the PRIVATE SECTOR. As a result there have been huge movements of CAPITAL from the richer industrial democracies to the developing countries, with private capital flows reaching some $250 billions in 1996 alone. The benefits in terms of new fast-growing markets for financial services have been enormous for global financial institutions like the American investment banks J. P. Morgan and Merrill

Lynch. But there have also been collateral benefits for developing countries which have seen rapid growth, particularly in the Far East and Latin America, and more latterly in eastern Europe. However, globalization has brought with it nasty side-effects including a degree of corruption, a widening of the gap between the haves and have-nots in some developing countries, and on occasions a greater degree of financial instability. In late 1994 a financial crisis in Mexico threatened to spread to other emerging market economies, forcing the Clinton administration in Washington to marshal the biggest rescue operation in financial history. A.BR.

glossematics. An approach to language adopted primarily by Louis Hjelmslev and associates at the Linguistic Circle of Copenhagen in the mid-1930s. The circle aimed to develop a theory applicable, not just to language, but to the HUMANITIES in general. Language, in this view, was seen as merely one kind of symbolic system, the distinctive features of which would be clarified only when it was compared with other, non-linguistic symbolic systems (e.g. LOGIC, dancing). The study of LINGUISTICS would lead on to the more general study of SEMIOTICS. For further reading: L. Hjelmslev, tr. F. J. Whitfield, *Prolegomena to a Theory of Language* (1961). D.C.

glossolalia. In LINGUISTICS, the term used to refer to the religious phenomenon of 'speaking in tongues'. D.C.

glottochronology. In LINGUISTICS, the QUANTIFICATION of the extent to which languages have diverged from a common source. Using a technique known as *lexicostatistics*, one studies the extent to which the hypothetically related languages share certain basic words (*cognates*) and deduces from this the distance in time since the languages separated. The theory and methods involved are not widely used, and are highly controversial. D.C.

gluino, see under SUPERSYMMETRY.

gluon. An ELEMENTARY PARTICLE possessing one unit of quantum mechanical spin (see QUANTUM MECHANICS) which is responsible for mediating the strong interaction between QUARKS. There are eight varieties of gluon in the standard theory of QUANTUM CHROMODYNAMICS. They are sometimes therefore called exchange particles. This interaction is also termed the colour force because it occurs between particles (quarks and gluons) which carry the attribute of 'colour'. Gluons are massive particles and do not possess electric charge. Their collective name refers to the fact that they bind quarks together to create the observed HADRONS like the PROTON and NEUTRON. For further reading: H. Pagels, *Perfect Symmetry* (1985). J.D.B.

Gnostics. In the early centuries of CHRISTIANITY, until about AD 300, various Gnostic sects were the chief religious rivals to orthodox Christianity. Their doctrines were very varied, but in essence taught that men and women had a divine spark in them but had fallen into the material world ruled by fate, birth and death. The divine element in humanity could, however, be reawakened through esoteric knowledge (for which *gnosis* is the Greek word), enabling those who achieved mastery of it to be reunited with the realm of the spirit. Denounced by the Church fathers as heretics, the Gnostics' importance in the development of Christianity was in forcing the early Church to settle the canon of the scriptures; to establish a theological creed; and to set up an episcopal organization in defence of orthodox beliefs.

In the modern world considerable interest in Gnostic ideas has been shown by the JUNGIAN school of PSYCHOANALYSIS with its interest in mythology and theory of ARCHETYPES. FEMINIST writers have also been attracted, e.g. by the feminine figure of Sophia, the goddess repressed by the patriarchal Judaeo-Christian tradition (see PATRIARCHY). For further reading: H. Jones, *The Gnostic Religion* (1958). A.L.C.B.

GNP (gross national product). The output produced by the residents of a country. It differs from GDP by the addition of net wages, interest, profit and dividends earned from abroad. Thus, GNP represents the total income accruing to residents of a country from economic activity within and outside the country. The *net national product* (NNP) is GNP adjusted for the depreciation of the capital stock held by the residents of the country. J.P.

God. In the West, God is usually defined as the Supreme Being, the eternal, infinite and benevolent source of all existence. But Western CHRISTIANITY evolved differently from the other monotheistic traditions that worship the same God. JUDAISM, ISLAM and Eastern Orthodox Christianity all insisted that it was impossible and could even be blasphemous to define (a word that literally means 'to set limits upon') a reality that must transcend all human words and concepts. All our ideas about God could only be symbolic, partial and provisional (see SYMBOLISM). But from an early date, Western Christians fell into the habit of thinking that their doctrines about God corresponded accurately to an objective reality, whose existence could be defined and demonstrated like all other phenomena (see BELIEF; SCIENTIFIC METHOD). This tendency increased as the Western scientific revolution got under way, and became still more prominent after the Enlightenment.

This tendency to interpret the truths of RELIGION as though they were literal facts has made the notion of God vulnerable in the 20th century, as cosmologists (see COSMOLOGY) find no room for God in the physical universe, as the horrors of human life make the idea of a wholly compassionate and omnipotent deity impossible, and as the so-called 'proofs' of God's existence increasingly fail to convince. This loss of faith in the God-concept has been expressed in various ways. Friedrich Nietzsche proclaimed that God was dead (see DEATH OF GOD THEOLOGY; NIETZSCHEAN) in *The Gay Science* (1882). J.-P. Sartre (1856–1939) spoke of a god-shaped hole in modern CONSCIOUSNESS: even if God existed, it would be necessary to reject him because such a coercive being negated our freedom. LOGICAL POSITIVISTS, such as A. J. Ayer (1910–91), argued that the idea of God was meaningless, since it could neither be verified nor shown to be false. The Jewish writer Elie Wiesel (1928–) believed that the all-powerful and wholly compassionate God of Western classical THEISM died in Auschwitz (see HOLOCAUST, THE).

In the 1960s, radical theologians followed Nietzsche in proclaiming that God was dead. Thomas J. Altizer (*The Gospel of Christian Atheism*, 1969) wrote that old conceptions of divinity must die before a theology suited to modern conditions could be born. For William Hamilton (*Radical Theology and the Death of God*, 1966), modern men and women did not need God: they could find salvation and ultimate meaning in the secular world of technology, power and finance.

But others still find meaning in the God-idea, even though they insist that it must be reinterpreted. Paul Tillich (1868–1965) was convinced that the personal God of Western theism had lost its symbolic force; instead we should identify God as transpersonal, a dimension that pervades our normal experience as the ground of all being. The Jesuit Pierre Teilhard de Chardin (1881–1955) saw God as the ultimate end of the evolutionary process, as immanent and incarnate in the physical world. The process theology of A. N. Whitehead (1861–1947) or Daniel Day Williams (1910–) also saw God as inseparable from mundane reality, rather than enclosed in a supernatural order: God could be seen as participating in the ongoing life of the earth, sharing the suffering of humanity and manifest in the 'behaviour' of the world.

As we approach the new millennium, religious people in the West are sharply divided about God. FUNDAMENTALISTS insist on an ultra-literal interpretation of the Bible and its personal God. At the other extreme, Don Cupitt (*After God*, 1997) argues that God is a purely human invention that must now be discarded: religion is less an IDEOLOGY than an art-form, which enhances our spiritual lives through its rituals and practices in much the same way as a great painting or poem. The idea and experience of God has constantly changed during the last 4,000 years, and it may be worth recalling that historically the word 'atheism' has always meant the denial of a particular conception of God, especially at times of religious transition: at an early stage of their history, Jews, Christians and Muslims were all called 'atheists' by their pagan contemporaries because their notion of the divine was so revolutionary that it seemed blasphemous. Perhaps modern Western atheism heralds a new and major religious change. For further reading: K. Armstrong, *A History of God* (1994).

K.A.A.

Gödel's theorem. States that in any formal SYSTEM which contains the arithmetic of natural NUMBERS there is a formula which, if the system is consistent, can neither be proved nor disproved, neither it nor its negation being deducible from the axioms (see AXIOMATIC METHOD). It follows from this that it is impossible to prove the consistency of a formal system of this kind within the system itself. A generally accepted consequence of this startling discovery is that the ambition of Frege and Russell to create a unitary deductive system in which all mathematical truths could be deduced from a handful of axioms (see LOGICISM) cannot be realized. Gödel's results are comparably destructive of Hilbert's programme of demonstrating the consistency of all mathematical theories using no more than the resources of elementary LOGIC (see FORMALISM). Much more speculative is the INFERENCE of the falsity of any theory which takes the human mind to be a mechanical, deterministic system. For further reading: E. Nagel and J. R. Newman, *Gödel's Proof* (1959). A.Q.

gold standard. A state of affairs in which citizens hold their MONEY in the form of gold coins or in the form of bank deposits or notes that are convertible by their banks into gold on demand. A *gold exchange standard* is a state of affairs in which citizens cannot obtain gold on demand in exchange for their deposits, etc., but can obtain on demand the currency of some other country which is on a full gold standard. The classical example of a gold standard country before 1914 was the United Kingdom; that of a gold exchange standard country was India. R.H.

Goldbach's conjecture, see under NUMBER THEORY.

golden number. This is $\tau = \frac{1+\sqrt{5}}{2} = 1.6180$ ... In the ancient world it was derived as the length of the diagonal of a regular pentagon of side 1. The number satisfies $\tau^2 = \tau + 1$. Experiment has shown that if people are shown a line, say 1 metre long, and asked to divide it into two portions, they tend to make these approximately in the ratio $\tau : 1$.

Keen scholars such as Christopher Cornford have surveyed and measured buildings and works of art and noted the ratios involved often close to τ. In the Parthenon the ratio of width to height (up to the top of the pediment) is close to τ, and τ can be found in medieval cathedrals. Luca Pacioli in 'Divina Proportione' (1509) hymned τ, and Le Corbusier (1887–1965) based his Modulor on it. Victorian architects (see ARCHITECTURE) could buy a set square to give a 'golden rectangle', and τ is widely found in, e.g., Truro Cathedral, designed in 1880 by J. L. Pearson. It is found in Vermeer and Mondrian, and Georges Seurat used it in constructing his paintings.

Why this ratio is so satisfying is presumably a matter for psychologists rather than mathematicians (see PSYCHOLOGY; MATHEMATICS). N.A.R.

golpe. Spanish equivalent of coup d'état, i.e. the seizure of POWER, by force, by an organized group within the polity (in Latin America the term usually, but not invariably, refers to action by the military). A wave of military *golpes* overtook the Southern Cone countries in the second half of the 20th century, all of which have had far-reaching implications for political and ECONOMIC DEVELOPMENT. The most important took place in Brazil in 1964 (instigating over two decades of military rule), in Uruguay in 1973, in Chile in 1973 (overthrowing the Popular Unity attempt to build a 'peaceful road to SOCIALISM' and bringing General Pinochet to power), and in Argentina in 1976, which paved the way for the anti-COMMUNIST 'dirty war' and its associated disappearances (see STATE TERROR). N.M.

gospel. A 20th-century development of the great tradition of African-American spirituals, gospel music was largely created by Thomas A. Dorsey (1905–56). A one-time JAZZ and BLUES pianist, he turned to religion in the 1920s and began to write songs which gave the scriptural message a personal, popular form. Such tunes as 'If You See My Saviour' became huge hits, carrying the beat and emotion which had hitherto been the province of the blues into BLACK homes and churches, with worshippers 'singing and dancing in anguish and rejoicing'. The great black singer Mahalia Jackson spread gospel throughout the world. In an intriguing turnabout, performers who grew up singing the music in churches – such as James Brown, Aretha Franklin and Ray Charles – took its ecstatic character back into the popular realm as the key ingredient of SOUL and RHYTHM AND BLUES. GE.S.

GPS (General Problem Solver), see under PROBLEM-SOLVING.

GPSG, see GENERALIZED PHRASE STRUCTURE GRAMMAR.

GPU, see under KGB.

gradient methods. Optimization methods which represent the mathematical equivalent of climbing a hill by always following the steepest path up it. The simplest form of gradient method for maximizing a FUNCTION causes the search process to take a step in the direction of steepest slope, then compare the direction of steepest slope at the new point with that at the old; comparison provides guidance for the choice of the next step-length. A carefully designed process of this kind works fast and efficiently except at the very last stages of the search for the optimum. More sophisticated methods allow the step-length to be chosen in the light of the rate of change of the gradient, and may also suggest a step-direction not exactly along the line of steepest slope; the *Newton-Raphson method* is of this type. Such methods are more laborious per step but usually need fewer steps than the more naïve methods. The methods most widely used in current practice are the *variable-metric methods* developed in the 1960s and based on the work of Davidon, Fletcher and Powell. R.SI.

gradualism. In evolutionary BIOLOGY, (1) the uncontroversial doctrine that complex organs (such as the vertebrate eye) must have evolved in many small stages rather than by a single mutation; (2) the controversial (see PUNCTUATED EQUILIBRIUM; MOLECULAR CLOCK) theory that evolutionary change proceeds at a relatively constant rate. For further reading: R. Dawkins, *The Blind Watch-Maker* (1986). M.R.

Graham technique. A teaching method and movement style based on the work of Martha Graham (1894–1991), who as a founder of MODERN DANCE in the USA and a former member of DENISHAWN rebelled to explore a more serious social message and dramatic form of dance while striving for intellectual respectability. 'Lamentation' (1930), a solo piece, was a landmark in defining Graham's new personal approach to modern dance which has developed into a recognizable technique worldwide. The technique retains traditional lines and the five positions of CLASSICAL BALLET, but is innovative as all movement emanates from the lower back or solar plexus. The technique is dramatic, uniquely expressive and has its own clear identity in the floorwork. Characteristics of Graham CHOREOGRAPHY are dramatic female roles, percussive earth-bound dynamics, an episodic choreographic content which intersperses group dynamics with the solo form, distinctive use of full costume, and collaboration with artists. Graham is most associated with the rise of CONTEMPORARY DANCE in Britain. For further reading: M. Graham, *The Notebooks of Martha Graham* (1973). L.A.

grammar. A central CONCEPT in contemporary LINGUISTICS, traditionally referring to an independent LEVEL of linguistic organization in which words, or their component parts (MORPHEMES), are brought together in the formation of sentences or DISCOURSES. (See MORPHOLOGY; SYNTAX.) In GENERATIVE GRAMMAR, however, and increasingly in other linguistic theories, the word means, more broadly, the entire system of structural relationships in a language, viewed as a set of rules for the generation of sentences. In this sense, the study of grammar subsumes PHONOLOGY and SEMANTICS, traditionally regarded as separate levels. A systematic account of a language's grammar (in either of the above senses) is known as '*a* grammar'. See also CASE GRAMMAR; SCALE-AND-CATEGORY GRAMMAR; SYSTEMIC GRAMMAR; TAGMEMIC GRAMMAR; TRADITIONAL GRAMMAR; CORE GRAMMAR; DEPENDENCY GRAMMAR; FUNCTIONAL GRAMMAR; GENERALIZED PHRASE STRUCTURE GRAMMAR; LEXICAL FUNCTIONAL GRAMMAR; METAGRAMMAR; MONTAGUE GRAMMAR; NETWORK GRAMMAR; REALISTIC GRAMMAR; RELATIONAL GRAMMAR; TRANSFORMATIONAL GRAMMAR. For further reading: F. Palmer, *Grammar* (1984).

In Wittgenstein's later PHILOSOPHY the 'grammar' of a language is constituted by the rules governing that language. These rules include not just the syntactic ones but those governing meaning too. For example, according to Wittgenstein's view, while the sentence 'This is a hand' can be used to make an empirical claim (e.g. on an archaeological dig), it can also be used to give the meaning of the word 'hand', and, in so doing, to express a grammatical rule. In Wittgenstein's philosophy the notion of grammar is closely tied to that of use. It is because a sentence is used to lay down a norm, a standard of correctness, that it expresses a grammatical rule. Such rules determine what constitutes correct and incorrect usage, and thus what it does and does not make sense to say. According to Wittgenstein, it is always our failure to attend sufficiently to the subtleties of use and grammar – e.g. failure to note that a sentence is being used to express a grammatical rule rather than to make an empirical claim – that generates philosophical problems (see LANGUAGE GAME; MEANING IS USE; RULE-FOLLOWING PARADOX).

D.C.; S.W.L.

grammatical word, see under WORD CLASS.

grammaticality. In LINGUISTICS, the conformity of a sentence (or part of a sentence) to the rules defined by a specific GRAMMAR of a language. A preceding asterisk (see STARRED FORMS) is commonly used to indicate that a sentence is ungrammatical, i.e. incapable of being generated by the rules of a grammar. D.C.

grand unification, grand unified theories. Also known by the acronym GUTS. Refers to a class of theories of elementary PARTICLES which aims to unify the different theories of the weak, strong and electromagnetic forces. This unification can occur at very high energies (1015 GeV) and predicts that BARYON number is not conserved in nature and that the PROTON is unstable with an average lifetime of more than 1,033 years. This decay is at least ten times too slow to have been detected. The unification of the weak and electromagnetic interaction is well established and tested by experiment. This theory is known as the Weinberg-Salam theory. When the strong interaction is added to the unification the theories are called 'grand unified' theories. None includes the gravitational interaction, and there are at present many candidate theories built upon different unifying symmetries. Grand unified theories have been extended to incorporate supersymmetry. Such extensions are known by the acronym SUSY GUTS.

These theories have many important cosmological consequences and give a natural explanation for the observed preponderance of matter over ANTI-MATTER in the universe (see COSMOLOGY). Since the mid-1980s there has been a focus of interest on SUPERSTRING theories which offer a means of unifying all four fundamental forces together into a so-called 'Theory of Everything'. Until very recently it appeared that there existed a number of logically self-consistent Theories of Everything of the superstring sort. However, it has recently been shown that these are all different mathematical ways of looking at a single underlying theory, now called M-theory, which has yet to be isolated. The interrelationships are mediated by a deep symmetry of these theories, known as duality symmetry, which links the behaviour of the world on small and large scales. For further reading: J. D. Barrow, *Theories of Everything* (1991).

J.D.B.

Grand Union. An anarchistic collective of dancers/choreographers (see CHOREOGRAPHY) emerging from the JUDSON DANCE THEATER in the 1970s in America, in which improvisation and investigation played a significant role. Initiated by Yvonne Rainer, members included Steve Paxton, Trisha Brown, David Gordon and others. During Grand Union residencies in 1972, Paxton began to explore duet improvisation with student athletes and CONTACT IMPROVISATION emerged as a new dance form. Grand Union disbanded in 1976. For further reading: S. Banes, *Terpsichore in Sneakers* (1980). L.A.

grant maintained school. A status and category of school established in England and Wales by the 1988 Education Reform Act. A GM school is funded directly by the Funding Agency for Schools rather than its Local Education Authority (LEA) and as a result receives an approximate 15 per cent addition to its annual budget. Such a school is no longer accountable to its LEA and has various additional forms of autonomy compared with LEA schools. S.J.B.

graphic design. Design intended for printing, generally with a commercial purpose. As well as creating images and patterns, the graphic designer may be responsible for the layout, titling, scale and colouring of magazines, books, posters and film and television programmes. Graphic design plays an increasingly influential part in societies dominated by mass media and susceptible to skilful packaging. Pioneers of 20th-century graphic design include William Morris, El Lissitsky and the BAUHAUS; today any of a variety of media may be employed, including relief, intaglio and surface printing, screen printing, photographic processes and computer graphics. P.C.

graphic score. A musical score which uses pictures and graphic symbols instead of or as well as conventional MUSIC NOTATION. In some works (e.g. György Ligeti's 'Volumina') graphic scores are used to give an element of performance freedom to the music (see INDETERMINACY). In some cases, such as some works of Sylvano Bussotti, the elements of conventional notation virtually disappear and the music becomes very ambiguous. Many graphic scores have an intrinsic visual beauty independent of their musical value. For further reading: R. Smith Brindle, *The New Music* (1975). B.CO.

graphology.

(1) The study of handwriting as a means of making inferences about the psychological characteristics of the writer.

(2) A term applied by some linguists to a branch of LINGUISTICS that describes the properties of a language's orthographic system (spelling, punctuation). Graphology in this sense is analogous to PHONOLOGY in the spoken medium. I.M.L.H.; D.C.

gravitation (or **gravity**). The force of attraction between PARTICLES which arises from their MASS. Gravity is responsible for the fall of objects towards the centre of the earth, the ORBITS of the moon round the earth and the planets round the sun, and the condensation of the matter in the universe into stars and GALAXIES. The importance of gravitation diminishes as the scale of phenomena is reduced: the life of small insects is dominated by the inter-molecular forces of viscosity and surface tension, while in ATOMIC PHYSICS and NUCLEAR PHYSICS gravity is completely overwhelmed by the vastly more powerful ELECTROMAGNETIC FIELDS, STRONG INTERACTIONS and WEAK INTERACTIONS.

Gravity is in fact the weakest force known in PHYSICS, but it is also the only force which is both (1) long-range in its effects (unlike, e.g., molecular and nuclear forces, which are only appreciable very near their sources) and (2) always attractive (unlike, e.g., electric forces, which may also be repulsive, so that for large masses, where there are generally equal numbers of positive and negative charges, their effects add up to zero). Thus gravity dominates the behaviour of large systems, and is of central importance in COSMOLOGY.

In NEWTONIAN MECHANICS gravitation had the status of an ordinary force, in the same class as, say, MAGNETISM or friction, but in Einstein's general theory of RELATIVITY it is incorporated into the basic structure of MECHANICS from the start (see also MACH'S PRINCIPLE). M.V.B.

gravitational lensing. The presence of a massive body between ourselves and a distant astronomical object can create two identical images of the distant object. The massive object is said to behave as a gravitational lens because it deflects the paths of light rays from the source to create two images of it. The process is called 'gravitational lensing' or 'lensing'. A number of cases are known in which duplicate images of distant quasars have been observed close to each other. The intervening object has not been seen and may be a very massive BLACK HOLE. The existence of lensing allows limits to be placed on the amount of some types of DARK MATTER in space.

The possibility that the gravitational pull of very massive objects can make them behave as lenses by bending the light rays to produce multiple images was predicted by Albert Einstein. In recent years this phenomenon has been spectacularly observed by the Hubble space telescope and has created an entirely new perspective on the universe. GALAXY clusters are seen to create many images of galaxies in the background. These images have distorted shapes according to their position relative to the line of sight to the lens. They allow us to deduce the total masses of the galaxy clusters, including both dark and luminous matter. Gravitational lensing has also been observed more locally in the search for MACHOS around our own galaxy, and is also responsible for multiple images of some QUASARS. For further reading: M. Begelman and M. J. Rees, *Gravity's Fatal Attraction* (1996). J.D.B.

gravitational wave/radiation. Einstein's theory of gravitation (the general theory of RELATIVITY) predicts that the influence of gravity propagates by means of waves, called gravitational waves. The theory views space as a malleable sheet which is curved by the presence of mass and energy. It can be viewed like a rubber sheet on which masses are placed. Any change in a configuration of mass or energy which is not perfectly spherical will create ripples in the 'rubber sheet' of space which will propagate outwards at the speed of light. These waves have been observed indirectly in the binary pulsar system, where the orbit of the visible PULSAR is changing at precisely the rate predicted if the system is losing energy in the form of gravitational waves (see BINARY STAR). Terrestrial detectors are being built in many countries in an international effort to detect gravitational waves directly from cataclysmic astronomical events like SUPERNOVAE, and merging BLACK HOLES and neutron stars. These instruments are the most sensitive detectors ever built. If successful they will launch a new era of gravitational wave astronomy. For further reading: C. Will, *Was Einstein Right? Putting General Relativity to the Test* (1993). J.D.B.

gravitino, see under SUPERSYMMETRY.

graviton. A hypothetical PARTICLE which is predicted to be associated with the FIELD of GRAVITATION in the same way as a PHOTON is associated with the ELECTROMAGNETIC FIELD. See also SUPERSYMMETRY. M.V.B.

gravity, see under GRAVITATION.

Great Chain of Being. All world views and scientific theories require major classificatory systems to map experience. One of the most potent of these ordering devices, handed down from antiquity and integrated into modern thought, was the Great Chain of Being. This postulated that all natural or created things could be arranged into a single vertical line or chain, with each ascending link progressively one degree superior in its attributes to the former. In gross terms, objects in the mineral kingdom possessed only the attribute of existence. Plants had life in addition; animals possessed the qualities of will and mobility; human beings had powers of reason and CONSCIOUSNESS; above men, spiritual beings such as angels were not even encumbered by gross fleshly bodies. Within CHRISTIANITY, God lay at the head of the ladder of being, as its creator. The theory of the chain was capable of infinite sophistication and inflection. Although formally exploded as a scientific scheme as a consequence of Linnaeus's taxonomy, its ghost continues to underpin the evolutionary vision that all living beings are fundamentally connected, forming an ultimate unity. The chain was also used to justify the Romantic notion that every being gloried in its own individuality, as well as later being evoked to support RACIST forms of ANTHROPOLOGY, which argued for a natural hierarchy of the different races of man, Negroes at the bottom being adjacent to the other higher primates. For further reading: A. O. Lovejoy, *The Great Chain of Being* (1960). R.P.

Great Leap Forward. The period in China between 1958 and 1960 when the orthodox Soviet (see USSR, THE FORMER) method of organization and production was abandoned in an attempt dramatically to increase output, and move the social REVOLUTION forward. A decentralization of industry took place as Mao tried to decrease the stultifying power of the party and STATE bureaucracy in an attempt to surpass Britain's industrial and agricultural output within 15 years (see MAOISM). Political mobilization was seen as the key to solving economic problems, with the political and ideological fervour so intense that targets were repeatedly adjusted in an attempt to speed up the movement; for example, it took just two months to create 24,000 Rural People's Communes as the deadlines for the radical COLLECTIVIZATION of the rural population became shorter and shorter. Although there were spectacular increases in production in the short run, the need to satisfy unrealistic production quotas led to a sacrificing of quality to the extent that much of the steel produced in new 'back yard furnaces' was totally useless. By 1960 the economy had seriously overstretched itself, and the appalling harvests of 1959–61 and ensuing famine led to the Great Leap being reined in by Chen Yun and a loss of face and power for the architect of the Great Leap, Mao Zedong. For further reading: S. R. Schram, *Authority, Participation, and Cultural Revolution in China* (1973); R. MacFarquhar, *The Politics of China: The Eras of Mao and Deng* (1997). S.B.

Great Proletarian Cultural Revolution. In 1966, with Mao's *de facto* control of Chinese politics eroded by the command of the party and STATE system passing into the hands of Liu Shaoqi and Deng Xiaoping after the disasters of the GREAT LEAP FORWARD, Mao launched a movement aimed at attacking BOURGEOIS influence and CAPITALIST roaders in the party (see MAOISM). He bypassed the party system to appeal directly to the masses to attack bureaucratic rightist tendencies within the Party (see BUREAUCRACY) in order to restore revolutionary ideals into the system. What followed was a three-year period of mob rule and violence, as teams of RED GUARDS set about attacking anything that was deemed to be 'rightist'. With the Party and state system under attack, society became uncontrollable, and Mao had to call in the Red Guard leaders to halt the near civil war, and ordered the army to step in to restore order in the provinces. By April 1969, the destructive phase of the Cultural Revolution was over, but the term is often used to describe the whole period up to the death of Mao in 1976. For further reading: T. Saich, *China: Politics and Government* (1981); R. MacFarquhar, *The Politics of China: The Eras of Mao and Deng* (1997). S.B.

Great Purge, see under YEZHOVSHCHINA.

Great Society. A phrase provided by speechwriter Richard Goodwin and first used on 23 April 1964 by US President Lyndon B. Johnson. It became the slogan characterizing a rapid, multifaceted burst of liberal, reformist policies from 1964 until 1967 (see LIBERALISM; REFORMISM). These were an extension of the WELFARE STATE principles of the NEW DEAL, with a new emphasis on the economic and political condition of BLACK Americans, and on the deterioration of inner cities.

The programmes of the Great Society have been condemned from the LEFT as attempts to disguise deep-rooted problems with cosmetic measures, and attacked from the RIGHT as costly, ill conceived and as at once excessively bureaucratic yet designed to radicalize blacks and the poor. More accurately, the Great Society may be seen as an attempt to offer greater equality of opportunity to the disadvantaged (through programmes such as the 'Head Start' education policy), and to extend the 'safety net' of WELFARE rights. There was no serious attempt at major redistribution of wealth, for which legislative or popular support would not have existed. The Great Society suffered from the hasty construction of policies, from Congressional tendencies to mistranslate governmental intentions, and above all from the impact of the VIETNAM War, which accelerated inflation and consumed governmental resources and the energies of the Johnson administration. For further reading: E. Ginzberg and R. M. Solow, *The Great Society: Lessons for the Future* (1974). S.R.

green belt. Green belts are protected circular zones around cities. Their purpose is to control urban sprawl, but development has often 'leapfrogged' the green belt, creating an outer ring of ex-urban development. Green belts are also intended to have a beneficial function as the 'green lungs' of the city, providing space for leisure and recreation. There is tremendous pressure for development within green belts where motorways cut across them, and on their inner edge for housing development. For further reading: B. Cullingworth and V. Nadin, *Town and Country Planning in Britain* (1996). C.G.

Green Movement. A broad political movement in many industrial DEMOCRACIES engendered by the growing attention to environmental and ecological questions in the 1960s and 1970s. It expresses alarm at the unprecedented assault on the natural environment by world industrialism (see INDUSTRIALIZATION): its concerns include the depletion of irreplaceable resources (e.g. fossil fuels), the extinction of species, the effects of POLLUTION by industrial processes, the use of nuclear power, and the testing of NUCLEAR WEAPONS. The Green Movement contains some international organizations such as Friends of the Earth and Greenpeace; the latter particularly favours DIRECT ACTION to attract media attention. Several countries possess 'green' political parties and groups. The German green party, *die Grünen*, has been the most visible in Europe – in 1998, it was invited to govern in a coalition government with the Social Democrats. But during the 1990s, Green Party politicians had also joined coalition governments in Finland, Italy and France. It has also found success through other channels. In commerce, particularly, the movement continues to grow and to make itself felt. Thus in response to consumer demand many companies present themselves as environmentally responsible, and some new ones have made environmental friendliness their *raison d'être*.

In the US, for example, several mail order companies (e.g. Seventh Generation, Real Goods) feature, exclusively, items made of recycled materials, energy-efficient light bulbs and electrical appliances, and solar-powered products. In the UK and the US The Body Shop chain of retail stores boasts that its products not only contain organic constituents but that they are obtained in ways and from sources that avoid damage to the environment or to native cultures.

Efforts to use consumer power to hold corporations (see MULTINATIONAL COMPANY) environmentally accountable have inspired boycotts and demonstrations against offenders and their products. Some mutual funds and other financial programmes provide investors with portfolios of securities only of businesses that pursue environmentally benign practices.

The World Bank (see BRETTON WOODS) and other international development agencies, both governmental and non-governmental, have come under increasing pressure to avoid supporting projects which are seen as environmentally destructive. It is questionable, however, whether international development efforts have become significantly 'greener' as a result. See also ORGANIC. For further reading: J. Porritt, *Seeing Green* (1985). W.G.R.

green pound, see under CAP.

green revolution. The dramatic increase in grain production per hectare (and farm worker) in some DEVELOPING COUNTRIES from the packages of high-yielding grain varieties, fertilizers, pesticides, irrigation, and improved transport. In Mexico, India, Pakistan and the Philippines, the revolution reduced food prices and increased wage rates for farm labour and sometimes small-farmer incomes. However, the revolution has made little progress in Africa, which lacks an agrarian INFRASTRUCTURE.

The new seeds are mainly the work of an international network of agricultural research centres (such as Mexico's International Centre for the Improvement of Maize and Wheat and the Philippines' International Rice Research Institute) scattered throughout many ecological zones and co-operating with national research institutes.

Network critics charge that research projects emphasize wheat and rice varieties that benefit large commercial farmers. Also some crop scientists contend that, as in Indonesia, the adverse environmental effects of pesticides, a foundation of the revolution, call into question its long-term sustainability and continuing yield growth. The alternative to pesticides, integrated pest management, using crop rotation, multiculture planting, field sanitation and biological control through natural predators, requires substantial investment in research and technology. For further reading: E. W. Nafziger, *The Economics of Developing Countries* (1997). E.W.N.

Greenham Common, see under PEACE MOVEMENT.

greenhouse effect. The absorption of some solar RADIATION by the earth's atmosphere (see ATMOSPHERIC CHEMISTRY), resulting in atmospheric warming. The gases that absorb the radiation prompt the atmosphere to act like the glass of a greenhouse, preventing the loss of a portion of the incoming solar energy by reradiation, causing the earth and its atmosphere to be warmer than the surrounding space, and hence capable of supporting life. Gases which can absorb a portion of the infrared (heat) portion of the solar spectrum include carbon dioxide and methane.

Atmospheric carbon dioxide, produced by biological oxidation and by the burning of fossil fuels, is increasing at a rate which, it is predicted by computer models, will result in the doubling of its atmospheric concentration by the mid-21st century, leading to an increase in global atmospheric temperature of between two and six degrees centigrade.

Other greenhouse gases are water vapour and methane, the latter produced by microbial action in ruminants and termites, and by microbial activity in rice paddies. Synthetic chemicals such as the CFCs (chlorofluorocarbons) used in refrigeration and air-conditioning also act as greenhouse gases. CFCs are also important because they cause the destruction of atmospheric ozone, which shields the earth's surface from biologically harmful concentrations of solar ultraviolet radiation (see OZONE LAYER).

Some argue that a global warming trend has not been established – that the computer models are inadequate, or that warming may be the result of fluctuations in the sun's energy output. However, the Intergovernmental Panel on Climate Change (IPCC), convened by the United Nations (UN), has concluded after several years of data analysis that global warming is indeed under way and that human activities may be making a significant contribution. W.G.R.

Greenpeace, see under GREEN MOVEMENT.

Greenwich Village. An area of New York City whose name reflects its early origins, and which has traditionally had bohemian and literary connections. In the 1950s and 1960s it became the backdrop to the BEAT and UNDERGROUND movements. Latterly it has provided a focus for the gay community (see HOMOSEXUALITY).

The coffee-houses of the 1950s and 1960s were meeting-places where creative artists, writers and singers could present their work to a small but influential public. Kerouac, Ginsberg, Jackson Pollock and Bob Dylan were among the artists who lived and worked in the Village. P.S.L.

Gresham's Law. Term in ECONOMICS. A coin whose face value is less than its value as a metal will be taken out of circulation and melted down, leaving coins whose face values are greater than their metal values. This effect has been described by the law *bad money drives out good money from circulation*. Artificial currencies such as European Currency Units (ECU) and Special Drawing Rights (SDR; see INTERNATIONAL LIQUIDITY) have shown the limitations of this law as individuals, firms and governments prefer to be paid in more readily acceptable forms of money, e.g. in ECUs rather than in SDRs. This could be interpreted as good money driving out bad money. J.P.

grey dollar. Earlier retirements, improved life expectancy and stronger occupational PENSIONS provision mean that senior citizens in the Western industrial democracies enjoy unprecedented spending power. Much of this cash is concentrated in retirement communities in warmer climates ranging from Arizona to Florida in the US and on the South Coast in Britain. The presence of elderly people has led to the development of strong healthcare and leisure services in the areas concerned. A.BR.

grid-group analysis. A major contribution to the sociology of knowledge (see KNOWLEDGE, SOCIOLOGY OF) derived from ANTHROPOLOGY which attempts to demonstrate how knowledge is shaped and ordered by particular kinds of SOCIAL STRUCTURE. 'Grid' is taken as an internal measure of differentiation within a structure, relating to matters of STATUS, ROLE, rank, etc. 'Group' is a term defining degrees of differentiation between one body of people and another, and relating to their boundaries. An egalitarian society (see EGALITARIANISM) would be 'low group', a GHETTO 'high group'; an army or BUREAUCRACY would be 'high grid', market relations 'low grid'. The combination of grid and group factors determines a person's or a body of people's social position. This in turn is said to correlate with the shaping of CONSCIOUSNESS. Grid-group analysis has mainly been applied to the structure of religious beliefs, but could be applicable to any field of consciousness in which questions of openness and closedness, of boundaries and bridges, of inclusion and exclusion, were to the fore. For further reading: M. Douglas, *Cultural Bias* (1978). R.P.

gridlock. A term used increasingly since the 1970s to connote an American political system which many observers see as increasingly ill equipped to address major policy problems. The USA's system is classically described as one of 'separation of powers', but in fact demands a high level of co-operation and interdependence between branches if it is to avoid a paralysis of effective decision-making. Modern changes in Congressional organization, the proliferation of INTEREST GROUPS, and the post-1968 tendency towards a division of control of Congress and the presidency between different parties are usually cited as the main culprits. Some studies, however, suggest that at least the latter is irrelevant, given that conflicts are often as strong within as between parties, and that party discipline is weak. Such analyses tend to stress the first two factors, but also note the effects on policy-makers of an electoral system which gives them little protection from the narrow and conflicting interests of financial donors, and the sheer difficulty of meeting public demands when economic circumstances and popular attitudes no longer sustain the rough consensus in favour of 'big government' policies which characterized much of post-war politics. S.R.

gross domestic/national product, see GDP; GNP.

ground state (in PHYSICS), see under ENERGY LEVEL.

ground truthing, see under REMOTE SENSING.

group. In Sartre's *Critique de la raison dialectique* (1960) the group is the achieved socialized community of CONSCIOUSNESS which is enforced after the condition of self-interested SERIALITY has been annulled. The group sees to it that the aim of each selfish individual is transformed into the aim of all. Individuals are subject to an 'oath' of allegiance, which allows no criticism of its policies and decisions, nor any departure from them. The oath is enforced by terror and, ultimately, 'lynching'. This ferocious social ideal of Sartre's, which has been called a 'humanism of terror' by Raymond Aron, shows the ultimate impossibility of trying to unify MARXISM and EXISTENTIALISM. For further reading: M. Warnock, *The Philosophy of Sartre* (1965). R.PO.

Group, the. In London in the late 1950s, an attempt to organize a conservative movement in poetry, by means of weekly meetings at which poets read and discussed their work. The Group, initiated by Edward Lucie-Smith, included for a time Ted Hughes and Peter Redgrove, whose similar groups at the University of Cambridge inspired the notion in the first place. The quality of its work may be judged by Lucie-Smith's and Philip Hobsbaum's *A Group Anthology* (1963). Later the Group, by now a spent force, fell into the hands of amateurs, and became known as *Poetry Workshop*. For further reading: M. L. Rosenthal, *The New Poets* (1967). M.S.-S.

group dynamics, see under GROUP PSYCHOLOGY.

group norms. The formation of NORMS within a group of people – a phenomenon widely confirmed by observation as occurring in both natural and experimental groups. Such norms, whether they comprise agreement about mode of dress (teenage groups; see also YOUTH CULTURE), saluting (military groups), meal-times (family groups), opinions (political groups), or perceptions (experimental groups), tend to act as a cohesive influence in the group, and to increase the number of things the group can take for granted, thus improving its efficiency in task performance. Newcomers to a group that they value may begin by merely complying with its norms, but later they may 'internalize' them. Individual members may reject the norms, either through incompatible external norms, through strong personality needs, through original thinking, or simply through a wish to challenge the leader. Such rejection, or DEVIANCE, is dealt with by the leader, or by more conformist group members, through frowns or other non-verbal signals, through verbal explanation ('not the done thing', etc.), or through punishment and, in the last resort, rejection. There is characteristically more conformity to group norms in public than in private acts; and particularly high degrees of conformity on the part of subjects with an AUTHORITARIAN PERSONALITY, and towards REFERENCE GROUPS with which the subject feels an important need to identify. For further reading: M. Argyle, *Social Interaction* (1969). M.J.C.

group psychology. The branch of SOCIAL PSYCHOLOGY concerned with the behaviour of an individual when exposed to the influence of a group of which he is a member, and with the means (the *group process*) by which the group seeks to overcome any resistance to this influence. The subject is also known as *group dynamics*, though this term is more frequently used for the forces of interaction studied than for the study of them. Particularly focused on are the changing patterns of intra-group tensions, conflicts, adjustment and cohesion, and the shifts in these relationships within a group and between one group and another. See also GROUP NORMS. For further reading: M. Shaw, *Group Dynamics* (1983). M.BE.

Group Theatre.

(1) A proselytizing New York theatre company, lasting from 1931 to 1941, that aimed to reflect the social conditions of the time as accurately as possible and to prove that all theatrical technique has to be founded on 'life values'. Run by a fractious triumvirate of Lee Strasberg, Harold Clurman and Cheryl Crawford, it produced some notable plays, including Clifford Odets's *Waiting for Lefty* (1935), Robert Ardrey's *Thunder Rock* (1939), and William Saroyan's *My Heart's in the Highlands* (1939). It also nurtured such impressive actors as Lee J. Cobb and Franchot Tone. Ultimately it collapsed through shortage of funds and division of purpose. But it represented a major attempt to counteract the commercialism of Broadway and to provide America with the kind of ensemble spirit familiar in Europe; and its influence can still be seen in the realistic tradition of modern American drama and in the teaching work of Lee Strasberg at the New York Actors' Studio (see METHOD, THE).

(2) A private play-producing society founded in 1932 at the Westminster Theatre, London. Its policy was never clearly defined but its chief importance lay in persuading major contemporary poets to write for it: Auden and Isherwood's *The Dog beneath the Skin* (1936), *The Ascent of F6* (1937) and *On the Frontier* (1939), T. S. Eliot's *Sweeney Agonistes* (1935), and Stephen Spender's *Trial of a Judge* (1938) were its major productions. Its bare-stage style of presentation also gave writers a valuable geographical freedom and anticipated the scenic austerity of later years. But when it was wound up in 1953 it had long ceased to be an active or influential body. For further reading: M. Sidnell, *Dances of Death: The Group Theatre of London in the Thirties* (1984). M.BI.

group theory. A group is a rather abstract mathematical concept consisting of a SET of objects (which could be numbers, for example), and an operation that is performed on them (e.g., 'plus'). There are certain mathematical criteria which determine whether or not a given group of objects and an operation actually *are* a group – many will not be.

What is interesting is the enormous range of applications that this concept has had. It has been tremendously important in pure mathematics. But most surprising of all, perhaps, was the recent way in which this centuries-old mathematical invention predicted the existence of an ELEMENTARY PARTICLE in PHYSICS. Mathematicians noticed that the list of known elementary particles could *almost* be transformed by a number of symmetries that made up a group. It needed one more particle to make it work. They predicted the existence of this particle, and shortly afterwards physicists found it. Why nature should comply so neatly with group theory is an interesting question.

Finite (see INFINITE) groups are built up from certain 'simple' groups, and enormous effort has gone into finding all of them. In 1981 the last was found ('The Monster') with some 8×10^{53} elements. But the PROOF that the list is now complete takes several thousand pages. N.A.R.

group therapy. Classically, a form of PSYCHOTHERAPY in which clients, preferably strangers to each other, meet as a group with a trained therapist or therapists. Some therapists see the only advantage over individual therapy as being one of relative cheapness for the client, whereas others believe that a group process takes place which brings additional benefits. Groups can be used with hospitalized patients, although here the more disturbed patients need a more supportive kind of therapy. Recent advances in group techniques include ENCOUNTER GROUPS, PSYCHODRAMA, *sensitivity training*, *social competence training*, etc., with a wide variety of techniques and of training for the therapists. Some of these group techniques are also used in non-therapeutic contexts (see, e.g., ORGANIZATION THEORY). For further reading: B. Barnes, S. Ernst and K. Hyde, *Introduction to Groupwork* (1999). M.J.C.

groupthink theory. Term coined by Irving Janis at Yale University and used as the title of a book on foreign policy 'decisions and fiascoes' (1972, 2nd edn 1982). Janis drew on psychological, historical and political studies of the BAY OF PIGS invasion, Pearl Harbor and the VIETNAM war to show the dangers of group conformity. 'Deviant' individuals, i.e. those who disagree with (unwise) group decisions, are excluded for 'violating GROUP NORMS'. Opponents of 'appeasement' in the 1930s and the French belittling of the importance of the German Schlieffen Plan in 1914 are taken as good examples of detrimental groupthink. The management of the Cuban missile crisis (see CUBA) and the MARSHALL PLAN by the US are taken as 'counterpoint' examples of how to avoid it. For further reading: I. L. Janis, *Groupthink: Psychological Studies of Policy Decisions and Fiascoes* (1982). A.W.

Grünen, die, see under GREEN MOVEMENT.

grunge. Hybrid PUNK–heavy metal musical genre and (predominantly young, white) subcultures (see YOUTH CULTURE) emerging from the US Pacific Northwest in late 1980s and early 1990s and spreading globally. As resistance against American fiscal and moral CONSERVATISM during the Reagan–Bush years, grunge articulates a generation politics expressing the socio-economic concerns of 'Generation X', Americans born after 1964; a politics of business as grunge acts record and distribute their music through small, independent record labels maintaining profit and artistic control; a politics of fashion, wearing dishevelled clothes demonstrating dissatisfaction with 'high fashion' and/or allegiance with marginalized social groups; and SEXUAL POLITICS challenging male, heterosexual dominance. P.L.

Gruppe 47. Informal group of mainly LEFT-wing German writers meeting annually in West Germany for readings and mutual criticism between 1947 and 1967. Their prize, awarded only when a work was felt to need publicizing, was won by (among others) Heinrich Böll in 1951, Günter Grass in 1958, and Johannes Bobrowski in 1962. Others associated with what soon became the most serious and influential movement in post-World War II German literature included Paul Celan, Uwe Johnson, H. M. Enzensberger, Erich Fried, the critics Walter Jens and Hans Mayer, and the group's founder, Hans Werner Richter. J.W.

GSR, see GALVANIC SKIN RESPONSE.

GST, see GENERAL SYSTEMS THEORY.

Guam Doctrine, see under NIXON DOCTRINE.

Guanxi. A Chinese word which directly translated means 'relations' or 'relationship' but is used in a political context to describe the strong personal ties between people who attended the same educational establishment, were brought up in the same place, or who share some similar common background. Guanxi places firm, unbreakable and mutual obligations on people who share the special relationship, which traditionally overrides all other imperatives and directives in the decision-making process. Accordingly, Deng Xiaoping's relationship with Liu Shaoqi would be said to be based not on shared aims or philosophies, but on their mutual background as students in France. For further reading: L. Pye, *The Dynamics of Chinese Politics* (1981). S.B.

guerrilla. Spanish word for irregular warfare (see WAR) by independent or autonomous units; as used in English, a member of such a unit. Guerrilla warfare is age-old, but only in the 20th century did it come to be seen not just as an auxiliary method but as a road to the victory of revolution. Its theory was developed by its major practitioners: Mao Zedong (see MAOISM), the Vietnamese general Vo Nguyen Giap (see VIETCONG), and Che Guevara (see CASTROISM), all of whom considered it as part of the doctrine of 'people's war'. This doctrine was an extension of LENINIST ideas about 'colonial revolutions' and the 'anti-Imperialist struggle' (see IMPERIALISM). Communists in economically backward countries (see COMMUNISM; DEVELOPING COUNTRIES; UNDERDEVELOPMENT) found that their revolutionary chances depended on the successful exploitation of local

NATIONALISM and peasant grievances. Guerrillas could operate effectively only in favourable surroundings (like 'fish in water'), and this provided the perspective for the wars of 'national liberation'. In such 'people's wars', Mao concluded, 'the seizure of power by armed force, the settlement of the issue by war, is the central task and the highest form of revolution'. The military implications of this doctrine – and even more of the Chinese revolutionary experience – were elaborated further by General Giap, who not only postulated the transformation of guerrilla warfare into a regular war, but also introduced a psychological element designed to shorten Mao's 'protracted war' in a single stroke – like Dien Bien Phu or the Tet offensive – making the enemy lose his will and give up the struggle (see VIETNAM). Other adherents of guerrilla revolution went even further beyond Lenin's 'objective' conditions for a 'revolutionary situation'. Che Guevara, Régis Debray and the Brazilian revolutionary Carlos Marighella addressed themselves to the question of how to conduct guerrilla warfare in places where Mao's 'support of the people' was lacking. Guevara concluded that 'it is not necessary to wait until all conditions for making revolution exist; the insurrection can create them'. Debray elaborated this by stressing the ideas of *foco insurrecional* (insurrectional furnace) and of the guerrilla force as the political vanguard, 'the Party in embryo'. Carlos Marighella (killed in 1969) advocated guerrilla action in the cities. During the 1960s and 1970s, Latin American urban guerrillas engaged in TERRORISM, political kidnapping and hijacking, but with no more success in 'arousing the masses' than anarchists in the past with their 'propaganda by deed' (see ANARCHISM). Although urban guerrilla groups have largely disappeared from the region, rural-based armed movements are still active, notably in Peru, Colombia and Mexico. They still pose a threat to the rule of law, especially in Colombia, where the Revolutionary Armed Forces (FARC) control large swathes of the country. However, the experience of revolutionary guerrilla struggles – rural or urban – suggests that it is the political and not the military side of their strategy that is paramount. Initially they hope to elicit indiscriminate repression, which will 'alienate the masses' and assure their increasing support, thus creating revolutionary conditions which did not exist before. However, the fulfilment or otherwise of this hope does not depend on guerrillas alone. For further reading: T. P. Wickham-Crowley, *Guerrillas and Revolution in Latin America* (1992). M.A.P.

GUI. Acronym for graphical user interface (pronounced 'gooey') – the name for computer displays that are controlled through the use of pictures. GUIs were a central development in making personal computers popular with untrained users. Anybody who has ever seen a four-year-old master a Macintosh computer in a few minutes will admit the system works. A typical GUI uses a pointing device (called a mouse) to move an arrow around the screen. The user can point the arrow at a particular picture and then click a button to trigger a computer operation. The personal computer market grew much larger after GUIs were introduced – the main versions being the Macintosh system from Apple Computer and the Windows system from the Microsoft Corporation. (GUIs were invented by Xerox researchers, but the Xerox Star computer [1981] was too expensive and had no impact on the market.) Established computer users were originally scandalized by the way GUIs needed so much extra computing power to do what a non-graphic computer could already do, and GUIs were also far slower. It took years for GUI word processors, DATABASES and spreadsheets to match their non-GUI rivals; however, GUIs made some kinds of computing simpler – notably design work. It is easier to lay out a printed page, to draw a picture or to retouch a photograph on a GUI machine (see COMPUTER-AIDED DESIGN). Small businesses and home hobbyists can now publish newsletters and brochures that once were available only to large corporations. Schoolchildren design their own letterhead and boast of having a 'favourite font'. Because of GUI, many people who once never thought about design now have opinions and experience in it. In this way the GUI machines have done more than simply broaden computer appeal. E.B.B.

Guild Socialism. A movement within the British labour movement between 1906 and 1923 advocating the achievement of SOCIAL-

ISM through the transformation of the TRADE UNIONS into monopolistic producers' guilds controlling and administering their branches of industry. A parallel movement to SYNDICALISM in France, it was less militant and tried to make a synthesis of socialist and syndicalist ideas. Guild Socialist ideas were formulated by A. J. Penty in his *Restoration of the Guild System* (1906), by R. A. Orage, editor of *New Age*, and by S. G. Hobson, author of *National Guilds*. Guild Socialists were antagonistic both to parliamentary politics and to the state, the proper role of which was seen as that of an arbiter in case of conflict rather than an administrative instrument. In contrast to the Fabians (see FABIANISM), Guild Socialism was hostile to state BUREAUCRACY.

After an unsuccessful attempt to capture the Fabian Society, Guild Socialists established their own National Guilds League. This split after the Bolshevik Revolution (see BOLSHEVISM), and many members (e.g. R. Page Arnot, R. Palme Dutt, William Gallagher and Maurice Dobb) joined the newly founded COMMUNIST Party of Great Britain. In 1923 the NGL broke up and its organ, the *Guild Socialist*, ceased publication. For further reading: A. W. Wright and G. D. H. Cole, *Socialist Democracy* (1979). L.L.

guilt culture, see under SHAME CULTURE.

GULAG. Russian acronym for the Main Administration of Corrective Labour Camps – the department of the Soviet Secret Police responsible for administering the FORCED LABOUR system. Alexander Solzhenitsyn's *The Gulag Archipelago* – publication of which abroad was the immediate occasion of his expulsion in February 1974 – is a metaphorical expression for the huge scattered 'islands' of Gulag territory existing throughout the Soviet Union. See also CONCENTRATION CAMPS. R.C.

gun control. As citizens of a nation that was born in armed rebellion and consolidated its present borders with blood shed by armed frontiersmen, and whose constitution contains the 'right to bear arms', many Americans view with suspicion government restriction of the right to own and use guns. Apart from a 1934 statute restricting the sale and purchase of machineguns and sawn-off shotguns, a national gun control act was not passed until 1968, and even then its main component was to bar the import of cheap foreign-made weapons. Today there are few restrictions on owning guns in many communities, and gun laws are a patchwork of statutes that vary from place to place. Washington, DC, where it is illegal to own a handgun, leads the nation in the percentage of gun murders, in part because guns are readily available in the border states of Virginia and Maryland. In 1993, President Clinton signed into law the Brady Bill, named after James Brady, the Reagan White House press secretary who was gravely injured in the 1981 assassination attempt on the President. The law requires a five-day waiting period for gun purchases. The bill had been pending before Congress since 1987, prompting Clinton to note that more than 150,000 Americans had been killed by handguns in that time. Federal officials reported in 1991 that 211 million guns – including 71 million pistols – had been manufactured in the USA since the turn of the century. R.K.H.

In the UK, gun control was introduced in 1996 with a total ban on all handguns (including sporting guns in shooting clubs). The move was in response to two incidents: in 1987 a gunman shot dead 14 people in the English town of Hungerford; and the so-called Dunblane Massacre of 1996, when 16 primary school pupils and their teacher were shot to death by a gunman in Scotland. Critics of the UK gun control law argue that handguns are not often used in violent crime in their country. In the USA, the murder rate is 9 per 1,000, most of which are committed using guns; in the UK, the murder rate is around 1 per 1,000. S.T.

GUTS, see GRAND UNIFICATION, GRAND UNIFIED THEORIES.

gynaecology. Literally diseases peculiar to women as opposed to men. Modern gynaecology embraces the broader concept of the medical and surgical care of women and children, including physical and psychological health, health education, FAMILY PLANNING, screening for disease and psychosexual problems, as well as those disorders traditionally the responsibility of the gynaecologist. Further changes have resulted from greater knowledge of reproductive ENDOCRINOLOGY, use of hormones and other therapeutic substances affecting endocrine function, and the control of FERTILITY. Preventative medicine and screening for disease for asymptomatic women include examination of breasts, pelvic examination, and the taking of cervical smears to detect dysplasia, which may be a precursor of carcinoma (see CANCER). Hormone replacement therapy is a term used for the treatment of women who are suffering or may suffer later from lack of oestrogen due to ovarian failure at the menopause, to absence or removal of the ovaries, or to inactive ovaries. For further reading: S. J. Steele, *Gynaecology, Obstetrics and the Neonate* (1985). S.J.S.

gyroscope (*or gyro*). A rotating wheel so mounted on a shaft that either or both of its basic properties can be used to advantage. The first of these properties is that the wheel tends to maintain the direction of its axis of spin in space, not being influenced by the earth or by any other object in the universe, so far as is known. The second property is that, if a twisting force (torque) is applied to the shaft so as to try to rotate the shaft about an axis perpendicular to the shaft, the resulting motion will be a rotation of the shaft about an axis which is at right angles both to the shaft and to the axis of the torque. Such motion is known as *precession*.

Gyroscopic properties are of great importance in the design of vehicles, including the bicycle, on account of the torques applied to the wheels during cornering. Gyroscopes are used in navigational instruments for ships, aircraft and spacecraft; also in conjunction with a magnetic compass, for direction-finding and for the control of automatic pilots. Large gyros have been used to assist the stabilization of ships in rough seas.

A gyroscope may also consist of a vibrating mass rather than a spinning wheel, and in this form it is common in living creatures such as the common crane fly ('daddy-long-legs'). E.R.L.

H

Habimah (Hebrew for 'stage'). A theatre company founded in Moscow in 1917 to perform plays in Hebrew. Stanislavsky (1865–1938) arranged for the actors, mostly from Polish theatres, to be trained by Yevgeny Vaktangov; the first performances were immensely successful, and the company visited America and Palestine (1928). Resident in Palestine since 1931, Habimah became Israel's official National Theatre (with a dramatic school and library) in 1953. M.S.-S.

habitat. In GEOGRAPHY, a term used to denote the natural ENVIRONMENT of a plant or animal. It may be expressed as one of the main natural regions (see REGIONALISM) which are recognized in the subject, such as tropical rainforests or temperate grasslands, or as one of their subdivisions, such as chalk grassland or beech woodland. M.L.

habituation. In CONDITIONING, the process of adjustment to a frequent or constant stimulus, whereby a minimal response is produced, or none at all. H.L.

hacker. A computer enthusiast who has not been technically trained and/or does not work professionally with computers. For most people, the word connotes a kind of vandal or criminal who takes control of computers to alter or copy information. Computer professionals understand the word more benignly, as denoting hobbyists or students who enjoy making computers do their bidding. Hackers created many of the breakthrough programs and ideas (including spreadsheets and BROWSERS) that opened computers to ordinary users. E.B.B.

hadron. Any ELEMENTARY PARTICLE that reacts or decays with STRONG INTERACTIONS (e.g. the PROTON, the NEUTRON). M.V.B.

haematology. The science of the blood – its formation, composition, function and diseases. In the US and Europe most hospitals now have a department of haematology staffed by pathologists, physicians and laboratory technicians. Their function is to provide a diagnostic service, to advance knowledge of their speciality and to be responsible for the care of patients with blood diseases. The department will also be responsible for the hospital's blood transfusion service.

Treatment of blood diseases depends upon understanding their cause. Deficiencies of nutrients necessary for the development of blood cells, such as iron, vitamin B12 and folic acid, can be easily remedied. When there is failure of blood cell formation, blood transfusion can be life-saving. However, donated blood has only a limited lifespan, up to three to four months at the most for red cells and only a matter of days for white cells and platelets. (The blood groups of the donor and recipient have to be compatible.) Leukaemias are difficult to treat although much progress has been made. Powerful drugs are available (chemotherapy); a limitation in their use is their effect on normal blood cells and other tissues as well as on leukaemic cells. The same applies to irradiation. Bone marrow transplantation is valuable in some cases. The donated marrow has to be as compatible as possible with the recipient's tissues. In practice, transplantation is usually restricted to between identical twins (rarely possible) or siblings (brothers and sisters). The procedure is easily carried out: marrow cells are aspirated from the hip bones of the donor and given in suspension into one of the recipient's veins. The marrow cells then 'home' to the recipient's marrow. In exchange transfusion large volumes of the patient's blood are replaced by normal blood. It has been used with particular benefit in infants with haemolytic disease of the newborn. Plasmapheresis involves bleeding a donor of a large volume of blood and returning to him the red cells while retaining the plasma. The technique is used when the plasma of the donor is the blood component required rather than the red cells. J.V.D.

haemorheology. Term coined by A. L. Copley in 1951, as 'a branch of biomedical sciences, concerned with deformation and flow properties of cellular and plasmatic components of blood in macroscopic, microscopic and submicroscopic dimensions, and with the rheological properties of vessel structures, with which blood comes into direct contact'. Theoretical and experimental haemorheology study the complex behaviour of blood (or components thereof) in 'in vitro' systems, such as whole blood and plasma viscosity, viscoelasticity, blood cell deformability and aggregation, blood flow and distribution in narrow channels or branches, etc. Clinical haemorheology deals with medical aspects studying the role of blood RHEOLOGY in haematological (polcythaemia in adults and neonates, leukaemias, red cell dyscrasias, paraproteinaemias) and ischemic (peripheral, myocardial, cerebral) diseases. Its other important aspect is the therapeutical correction of pathological flow properties, as by haemodilution (lowering haematocrit), defibrinogenation, plasmapheresis (exchanging plasma with another fluid), and drug therapy. For further reading: S. Chien *et al*, *Clinical Hemorheology* (1986). E.E.

Hagana, see under IRGUN ZVAI LEUMI.

Hagedorn temperature, see under ELEMENTARY PARTICLES.

half-life. In RADIOACTIVITY, the average time which must elapse for half the nuclei (see NUCLEUS) in a large sample to decay (and which also gives the *probability* of decay in any time interval). More generally, an average time characterizing processes in any large population, e.g. the time taken to sell half the items in a given consignment of goods (the 'shelf-life'). M.V.B.

Hall effect. Discovered by E. H. Hall in 1880, and observed when an electric current is passed along a conductor which itself is in a magnetic field at right angles to the direction of the current. The magnetic field deflects the current so that some of the current carriers (e.g. ELECTRONS) strike the side of the conductor. The build-up of charge thus produced gives rise to a voltage, the Hall voltage, across the conductor in a direction which is perpendicular to the applied magnetic field. Measurements of the Hall effect are very useful because the size of the Hall voltage is a measure of the concentration of the charge carriers in the sample. This is very important in SEMICONDUCTOR technology where the number of charge carriers is very sensitive to small traces of impurity (DOPING) and this can materially affect the operation of a device such as a TRANSISTOR. (See also QUANTUM HALL EFFECT.) H.M.R.

Hall voltage, see under HALL EFFECT.

haploid (noun or adjective). A CELL containing only a single set of CHROMOSOMES. Contrasted with DIPLOID; POLYPLOID. J.M.S.

happenings and **events.** Performances juxtaposing a variety of aural and visual material in a non-representational manner, with the aim of moving the spectator at an unconscious rather than a rational level. The genre owes its origin to the pieces combining music with other media developed by John Cage at BLACK MOUNTAIN College in the 1950s; the term 'happening' was first used by the painter Allan Kaprow (1959). In the work of Kaprow and Claes Oldenburg (1929–) in New York, happenings were associated with the POP ART movement of the early 1960s, particularly in the construction of ENVIRONMENTS. Throughout the 1960s the term was applied to pieces presented in Europe and the USA by artists (e.g. the German graphic artist Wolf Vostell) as well as theatre and dance groups, drawing eclectically upon a variety of traditions from FUTURISM and DADA to the THEATRE OF CRUELTY. In formal terms a happening contains several actions presented sequentially, while an event contains one action (which may be repeated). For further reading: A. Henri, *Environments and Happenings* (1974). M.A.

hard-edge. A phrase coined by the Los Angeles critic Jules Lansner in 1958 to describe the painting of several local abstract artists (see ABSTRACT ART), including John McLaughlin, characterized by (a) flat forms rimmed by hard, clean edges presented in uniform colours, and (b) an overall unity in which colour and shape (or form) are one and the same entity. His term appeared in an introduction to the exhibition 'Four Abstract Classicists', but when in 1960 the show travelled to the Institute of Contemporary Arts in London it was retitled 'West Coast Hard-Edge'. The term has been loosely used since to describe any art that tends towards the geometric. A.K.W.

hard X-rays, see under X-RAY ASTRONOMY.

Harlem Renaissance. The Harlem Renaissance occurred between 1920 and 1940 in Harlem, New York. A group of black artists, authors, musicians and poets practised their crafts as individual artists who attempted to express their diverse experiences in America through their art. Unlike writers like Frederick Douglass and W. E. B. DuBois, the Renaissance writers did not overtly pursue political objectives in their work. Their works had a political dimension, but it was left to be interpreted by individual observers. The idea was to use art and literature to lay bare black values and lifestyles that were being ignored or distorted in the works of white artists and writers (see AFROCENTRICITY). Key figures included novelist James Weldon Johnson and the poet Countee Cullen.

However, some commentators have criticized the movement for portraying stereotypical attitudes and lifestyles of African-Americans. These critics also question the so-called black values upon which the movement was said to be based. Finally, critics have charged that the Harlem Renaissance artists and writers romanticized some questionable aspects of black life, and used their depictions of black life to launch careers that would not have been possible in the more general arena of American arts and letters. For further reading: A. Singh *et al*, *The Harlem Renaissance* (1989).

H.M.

hawks, see under DOVES AND HAWKS.

Hawthorne effect. In INDUSTRIAL PSYCHOLOGY, a result extrapolated from experiments conducted in the Hawthorne works of the Western Electric Company, near Chicago, between 1924 and 1936. It was found that increased productivity depended not so much on any particular incentives as on workers interpreting any change as provisional evidence of management's interest and goodwill. A Hawthorne effect, then, is initial improvement in performance following a newly introduced change. For further reading: F. J. Roethlisberger, *Management and the Worker* (1939). H.L.

health foods. An undefined and broad group of foods which are promoted as being particularly healthy. Their popularity arises from the widespread perception that much of the food we eat has suffered as a result of the production methods involved, whether it be, e.g., due to chemical fertilizers on vegetables, poor-quality feed given to livestock, or artificial additives which prolong the life of the food and alter its characteristics. Health foods include a range of VITAMINS, mineral salts and amino acids as well as supplements such as kelp, lecithin, cider vinegar, bees' royal jelly, and RNA (see NUCLEIC ACID), and also 'organic' vegetables (see ORGANIC FOODS) grown without the use of agricultural chemicals and animals reared on natural foodstuffs. Although many doctors and nutritionists would still maintain that health foods are unnecessary, there is a growing body of opinion supporting their use. A.E.B.; A.A.L.

health promotion. The prevention of disease and the maintenance of good health, including physical, mental and social well-being. Health promotion comprises three essential components – prevention of disease (e.g. screening or immunization), health education (e.g. poster campaigns advising against smoking) and health protection (legal and fiscal measures such as taxation on tobacco, control of alcohol sales or road safety measures). The interest in health promotion stems in part from the realization that health services are only a minor determinant of health. More important factors, and thus legitimate targets for health promotion, are lifestyle and environmental and social factors. Health promotion has been attractive to those concerned with the rising cost of health services, but hard evidence for the view that prevention is cheaper than cure is scant. Scientific evidence for the effectiveness of much health promotion is also lacking, as long-term changes in complex lifestyle choices and behaviours are both difficult to achieve and to demonstrate. The World Health Organization has been prominent in the health promotion movement. Its 1977 'Health For All' strategy, 1978 Alma Ata declaration and 1986 Ottawa Charter have encouraged governments to focus on health promotion, particularly in less-developed countries. They have stressed multidisciplinary collaboration, community participation, healthy public policy and PRIMARY CARE as the key elements of health promotion. D.F.

heartland. Geographical term for the central part of the Eurasian land mass. It was first used by Sir Halford Mackinder (1861–1947) to describe those parts of Eurasia not accessible from the sea and therefore presumed to be immune from attack by a maritime power. P.H.

heat death of universe. The hypothetical situation when the disordering tendency expressed by the second law of THERMODYNAMICS, acting over aeons of future time, results in the absence anywhere in the universe of ENERGY in a form which can be converted into work by organisms or machines of a type familiar to us. The second law may not, however, apply to the universe as a whole, perhaps because of the long-range ordering influence of GRAVITATION. See also STATISTICAL MECHANICS. M.V.B.

heat exchanger. Apparatus for the transfer of heat to a substance which can be used directly in a piece of equipment requiring heat from one which cannot do so for reasons inherent in the system which generated the heat. Thus, the heat energy in radioactive fluid (see RADIOACTIVITY) from a NUCLEAR REACTOR can be used, after passing through a heat exchanger incorporating a radioactive shield, to heat water in another vessel which can then be fed to a steam turbine. E.R.L.

heavy metals. The elements antimony, arsenic, beryllium, cadmium, chromium, cobalt, copper, germanium, lead, mercury, molybdenum, nickel, selenium and zinc. A key ingredient in various industrial processes, heavy metals may contaminate the environment and lead to human health problems if not subject to adequate controls. S.T.

heavy water. Water in which one or both of the normal hydrogen atoms in each MOLECULE is replaced by deuterium. It is similar to ordinary water except for its ability to slow down NEUTRONS without reacting with them, and for this reason heavy water is used in NUCLEAR REACTORS as a MODERATOR. M.V.B.

hedonism. The theory that pleasure is the only thing that is intrinsically good, pain the only thing intrinsically bad. Other things, for the hedonist, are good or bad only instrumentally, to the extent that they are productive of pleasure or pain. What distinguishes hedonism as a philosophical theory from what is colloquially understood by the same name is that it works with a much more inclusive conception of pleasure and pain. It takes pleasure to be, not just immediate bodily gratification, but the satisfaction of any desire whatever, enjoyment or gratification of any kind; pain, similarly, is not just bodily anguish, but any form of suffering or distress. The usual form of hedonist ETHICS, UTILITARIANISM, takes the pleasure and pain of everyone affected by it to be the CRITERION of an action's rightness, and is associated with a psychological version of hedonism which holds that human actions are motivated primarily by a search for pleasure and the avoidance of pain. For further reading: J. Gosling, *Pleasure and Desire* (1969). A.Q.

Hegelianism. In PHILOSOPHY, the idealistic (see IDEALISM) system of G. W. F. Hegel (1770–1831) in which the method of DIALECTIC is used to systematize and complete all aspects of knowledge and experience and weld them into an inclusive whole. Philosophy, for Hegel, is the highest, or absolute, form of human knowledge, and all other forms must submit to its critical modifications. Hegel concludes that reality as a whole, or the absolute, is of the nature of a mind, and that it presents itself to reflection first as a system of CONCEPTS, then as nature, and last, and most satisfactorily, as mind. For further reading: R. Plant, *Hegel* (1973). A.Q.

hegemony (from Greek *hegemon*, meaning leader or ruler).

(1) Since the 19th century a term that has been used especially to describe the predominance of one state over others, e.g. the French hegemony over Europe in the time of Napoleon. By extension, *hegemonism* is used to describe 'great power' policies aimed at establishing such a preponderance, a use close to one of the meanings of IMPERIALISM.

(2) In the writings of some 20th-century MARXISTS (especially the Italian Gramsci) it

is used to denote the predominance of one social CLASS over others, e.g. in the term *bourgeois hegemony*. The feature which this usage stresses is not only the political and economic control exercised by a dominant class but its success in projecting its own particular way of seeing the world, human and social relationships, so that this is accepted as 'common sense' and part of the natural order by those who are in fact subordinated to it. From this it follows that REVOLUTION is seen not only as the transfer of political and economic POWER but as the creation of an alternative hegemony through new forms of experience and CONSCIOUSNESS. This is different from the more familiar Marxist view that change in the economic base is what matters and that change in the SUPERSTRUCTURE is a reflection of this; instead, the struggle for hegemony is seen as a primary and even decisive factor in radical change, including change in the economic base itself. A.L.C.B.

Heisenberg's uncertainty principle, see UNCERTAINTY PRINCIPLE.

helix, double, see DOUBLE HELIX, THE.

helminthology. The branch of ZOOLOGY concerned with the *helminthes*, i.e. parasitic worms. The word is, however, now generally confined to the study of those internally parasitic flat worms (*platyhelminthes*) which include the flukes and such dangerous human parasites as *schistosoma* (or *bilharzia*). Schistosomiasis is one of the gravest and most intractable diseases of tropical Africa. The intermediate host is a water-snail, and most attempts at eradication or control are concentrated upon it. P.M.

Helsinki 1975. The name given to the Conference on Security and Co-operation in Europe at Helsinki on 1 August 1975, attended by 35 nations both non-aligned (see NON-ALIGNMENT) and neutral and belonging to the Warsaw Pact and NATO. In the Final Act of the Conference the NATO countries agreed to the demand of the former USSR that the Western powers officially recognize the *de facto* borders established after World War II and the consequent division of Europe. In return for this concession the Soviet Union accepted a declaration on the observance of HUMAN RIGHTS in its sphere of influence, and on a freer flow of information and freer travel between the two halves of Europe. Subscquently the Soviet Union has been embarrassed by this declaration, as groups were set up throughout eastern Europe to monitor the implementation of the Helsinki agreements (see CHARTER 77). It was also criticized by Western nations at the conferences held to review the execution of the Helsinki accords for ignoring provisions on human rights. However, the conference did help to engender a spirit of co-operation and marked the high point of DÉTENTE between the Eastern and Western blocs. Greater contacts between East and West Germany were permitted, and a large number of Jews were allowed to emigrate as a result of the treaty. For further reading: R. Edmonds, *Soviet Foreign Policy: The Brezhnev Years* (1983). D.PR.

hemispheres of the brain, see under TWO HEMISPHERES, THE.

Herbartian psychology. The SCHOOL OF PSYCHOLOGY based on the ideas of Johann Herbart (1776–1841), German philosopher, psychologist and educationist. He viewed mind as an organized, unitary and dynamic interplay of ideas which actively attracted and repelled each other and struggled for a place in CONSCIOUSNESS. I.M.L.H.

heredity, see under GENETICS/GENOMICS.

heresy. In Christian (see CHRISTIANITY) THEOLOGY, the attitude that makes a personal choice (Greek *hairesis*) rather than accepting the doctrines of CATHOLICISM. To a large extent modern thought rests on independent thinking, so that in modern times the term is seldom used pejoratively. D.L.E.

heritability. That part of the variability of a population which arises from genetic (see GENETICS/GENOMICS) rather than environmental causes. J.M.S.

hermeneutics.

(1) The art or science of the interpretation of texts and works of art. In the 19th century, Wilhelm Dilthey (1833–1911) brought the term from theology into philosophy, elaborating it, in the words of Hans-Georg Gadamer (1900–98), 'into a system

which made it the basis of all the human sciences'. Heidegger (1889–1976) developed philosophical hermeneutics with his insistence that meaning is historical, created always from a particular perspective. Gadamer, following Heidegger, argued that we must free ourselves from the 'prejudices' of *Geistsgeschichte* (CULTURAL HISTORY), the discipline founded by Dilthey. In *Truth and Method* (1975), Gadamer argues that interpretation is always situational and that, therefore, a text's meanings are limitless: there can be no objective, transcendent meaning. 'It is to the development of historical consciousness', writes Gadamer, 'that hermeneutics owes its central function within the human sciences.' To believe that the original historical circumstances in which a work was created can be reconstructed is the illusion of an earlier hermeneutic practice such as that of Friedrich Schleiermacher (1768–1834), whom Gadamer criticizes. Heidegger, Gadamer and their followers' insistence on the historical nature of meaning has been criticized by E. D. Hirsch as leading to complete relativism.

A process of hermeneutics is the 'hermeneutic circle', which refers to the notion that any part of a text cannot be understood until the whole is understood, and that the whole cannot be understood until the parts are understood.

A development of Gadamerian hermeneutics is reception theory. Also, Stephen Toulmin has recently argued that 'the general categories of hermeneutics can be applied as well to the natural sciences as to the humanities'. For further reading: K. Mueller-Vollmer, *The Hermeneutics Reader* (1985). M.F.H.

(2) More generally, the art, skill or theory of interpretation, of understanding the significance of human actions, utterances, products and INSTITUTIONS. In this sense the term was brought into PHILOSOPHY from theology by Dilthey (see above) in the late 19th century to refer to the fundamental discipline that is concerned with the special methods of the human studies or GEISTESWISSENSCHAFTEN which do not merely order the raw deliverances of sensation but must seek an understanding (VERSTEHEN) of their essentially meaningful subject-matter. The term has since been more broadly applied by Heidegger to emphasize the general metaphysical purport (see METAPHYSICS) of his investigations into the nature of human existence. A.Q.

hermetic. Adjective derived from the name of the Greek god Hermes Trismegistus (identified by the Greeks with the Egyptian Thoth, supposed author of mystical works and inventor of a magically airtight container). In literary contexts, it is applied, generally, to poetry of a Platonic, esoteric, recondite or occult kind; or, more specifically, to a movement in contemporary Italian poetry: *poesia ermetica*. The term was coined, and its subject-matter traced, defined and criticized, by Francesco Flora in *La poesia ermetica* (1936). The theoretical pioneer was Arturo Onofri, who carried over DECADENT and SYMBOLIST notions of 'pure poetry' from French to Italian, and who was influenced by Rudolf Steiner's ANTHROPOSOPHY. Onofri advocated (1925) a 'naked poetry', from which all logical elements would be eliminated and which would concentrate on the magic of the single word, on silences and (on the page) blankness. His programme was meanwhile being fulfilled by Giuseppe Ungaretti (1888–1970). Ungaretti sought to purge his poetry of rhetoric, and to restore the 'pristine' meanings to words by approaching them with the utmost simplicity: 'All the emphasis was on the word itself, each word, its sound, meaning, resonance, and the space it could be made to fill.' Ungaretti's successors, Eugenio Montale and Salvatore Quasimodo, were of a very different temperament, and neither had been through a period of enthusiasm for Mussolini, as Ungaretti had. Since it was necessary for genuine poets to write 'over the heads' of the FASCIST censors, the motives for writing 'hermetically' were enhanced. But both Montale and Quasimodo sought to rid poetry of rhetorical embellishment. Montale added to hermetic poetry a musicality, Quasimodo a Greek purity of diction. Both achieved an underlying HUMANISM at odds with fascism. This simplicity of approach involved a subjectivity which some critics found excessively difficult; but *poesia ermetica* is now seen as a pioneering phase in Italian poetry. Other poets classed as hermetic include Mario Luzi, Alfonso Gatto and Vittorio Sereni. The inclination still exists in Italian poetry. M.S.-S.

heroic materialism, see under ZEITGEIST.

herpes. Herpes simplex virus has two types. Type 1 most often affects the mouth, causing 'cold sores', which are usually contracted in childhood. Type 2 usually affects the genitals, is sexually transmitted (see SEXUALLY TRANSMITTED DISEASE) and is of epidemic proportions in the West, particularly in the USA. Shallow painful ulcers appear on the penis, vulva, cervix or anus, which heal in one to two weeks. After a first attack of genital herpes the virus disappears from the skin but becomes latent in adjacent nerve ganglia. Reactivation leads to further attacks of herpes at variable intervals, a sequence which persists indefinitely. During an attack, a person with genital herpes can transmit it sexually to others. It is possible for a woman who has an attack of herpes during labour to infect her baby, but this can be avoided by Caesarian section. There is no permanent cure for genital herpes, but antiviral drugs can shorten and mitigate the attacks. Immunization may be possible in the future, but no safe and effective vaccine is currently available. For further reading: J. K. Oates, *Herpes* (1983). J.D.O.

herstory, see under FEMINIST HISTORY.

Hertzsprung-Russell diagram. An important graph in ASTROPHYSICS, where the total ENERGY radiated by a star (its 'brightness') is plotted against wavelength (i.e. colour). The positions of the majority of stars on this graph lie near a diagonal line, along which, it is believed, typical 'main-sequence' stars progress in the course of their evolution from blue-bright (hot) to red-dim (cool). See also BLACK HOLE; NOVA; RED GIANT; SUPERNOVA. M.V.B.

Hessen thesis. The HISTORICAL MATERIALIST theory of the determination of CONSCIOUSNESS by social being has always found science difficult to place. In the 1930s, official Soviet MARXISM seemingly stated categorically that the Scientific Revolution, as it had developed from the 17th century, was an expression of BOURGEOIS ideology, responding to the needs of CAPITALIST society. In 1931, Boris Hessen argued that Isaac Newton's *Mathematical Principles of Natural Philosophy* (1687) could best be explained as formulated to resolve crucial bottlenecks encountered by industry and TECHNOLOGY in a commercial society. For example, its ASTRONOMY would lead to the advance in navigation required by transoceanic trade. Additionally, Hessen argued that, as an ideologue of the ruling order, Newton chose to retain a place for God in the natural system, rejecting the MATERIALISM which had been espoused by radicals in the Civil War. Though few of Hessen's specific interpretations seem well supported, his analysis of scientific theory as hidden IDEOLOGY has been fruitfully deployed. R.P.

heteroglossia (*raznorecie*). A term coined (like 'polyphony') by the Russian critic Mikhail Bakhtin (see BAKHTINIAN) to describe the diversity of languages or 'social voices' in literature and more especially in the novel. He contrasted the epic, well-defined and official, with the novel, 'one of the most fluid of genres', associated with unofficial ideas, with parody, diversity, and the propensity for dialogue and the confrontation of different views of the world. These possibilities, which he regarded as in some sense built into the genre, were, according to Bakhtin, most fully realized in two of his favourite authors, Rabelais and Dostoyevsky, whose work presents not the viewpoint of the author but the dialogue between different characters, such as Pantagruel and Panurge, or even as in the case of Golyadkin in Dostoyevsky's *The Double* (1866), the 'internal dialogue' of a single character. For further reading: M. Bakhtin, *Problems of Dostoevsky's Poetics* (1929; 1984). P.B.

heterokaryote, see under NUCLEUS.

heterological. This was a word invented to show that there were paradoxes in language as well as in MATHEMATICS, and that seemingly reasonable definitions may contain traps:

'Heterological' is an adjective used of adjectives and means that the adjective does not apply to itself. Thus 'big' is not big, so 'big' is heterological, but 'English' is English and so is not.

We now ask the question 'Is ''heterological'' heterological?' If the answer is 'yes' then it applies to itself and so is not heterological, contrary to what it says. Similarly the answer 'no' is also impossible. Thus here we have a seemingly factual question which cannot be answered 'yes' and cannot be answered 'no'. The solution is to reject the definition and insist that, in defining a new adjective, it can only refer to adjectives already in existence. N.A.R.

heterosexism, see under HOMOSEXUALITY.

heterosis, see under GENE.

heterostructure, see under SUPERLATTICE.

heterozygote, see under GENE; MENDEL'S LAWS.

heuristic.

(1) (adjective) Concerned with ways of finding things out or solving problems. Also (noun) a contraction of *heuristic method*: a procedure for searching out an *unknown* goal by incremental exploration, according to some guiding principle which reduces the amount of searching required (e.g. to reach the top of an unfamiliar hill in fog, a useful heuristic would be to make every step an upward one rather than trying steps in all directions). An important concept in CYBERNETICS and ARTIFICIAL INTELLIGENCE. S.BE.

(2) In SOCIAL SCIENCE, the term is used especially to characterize conceptual devices such as IDEAL TYPES, MODELS and working hypotheses which are not intended to describe or explain the facts, but to suggest possible explanations or eliminate others. For further reading: S. Beer, *Brain of the Firm* (1972). J.R.T.

hidden curriculum. Subjects that are not on a school timetable but are nevertheless taught as part of the total syllabus: social awareness and racial tolerance are examples. J.I.

hidden economy, see under BLACK ECONOMY.

hidden variables. Physical quantities whose determinate values underlie the WAVE FUNCTION of QUANTUM MECHANICS. On a hidden-variables interpretation, a system in a quantum mechanical SUPERPOSITION does in fact possess determinate values of all relevant dynamical variables, contrary to the COPENHAGEN INTERPRETATION. This claim invites a detailed account of the nature and evolution of these hidden-variable states: an alternative theory to quantum mechanics, rather than a conservative extension of it. The best-known hidden-variables approach, developed by Bohm, is related to de Broglie's 'pilot-wave' interpretation of quantum mechanics. According to Bohm's theory, a PARTICLE possesses a determinate position at all times. Its motion is determined by a mathematical entity related to the quantum-mechanical wave function, and it is through this quantity that the peculiar quantum-mechanical behaviour of particles is reproduced (see WAVE-PARTICLE DUALITY; DIFFRACTION; EPR PARADOX). Although von Neumann presented a proof that no hidden-variable theory could be predictively consistent with quantum mechanics, the result was shown to apply only to a restricted class of such theories. However, BELL'S THEOREM does force a choice between determinism and locality (no instantaneous action-at-a-distance) on all hidden-variable theories. Bohm's theory embraces the non-locality horn of this dilemma. For further reading: J. T. Cushing, *Quantum Mechanics: Historical Contingency and the Copenhagen Hegemony* (1994). R.F.H.

Higgsino, see under SUPERSYMMETRY.

high culture, see under MASS CULTURE.

high rise. A residential or office building over ten storeys. The development of the electric elevator and steel-framed building structures in the US enabled architects to expand cities vertically. Le Corbusier (1877–1965), a French-Swiss architect, believed the solution to urban congestion was to pile everyone up into mile-high skyscrapers, thus freeing the ground surface below, creating vertical neighbourhoods and cities. He expressed his ideas in *The City of Tomorrow* (1928) and *The Radiant City* (1930). The high-rise approach to architecture and planning remains popular internationally, albeit associated with problems in the West when utilized in social housing projects. In 1996 the Petronas Building in Kuala Lumpur, Malaysia became the tallest building in the world at 452 metres (1,483 feet), consisting of 18 million square feet of floor space, incorporating offices, shops, apartments and mosques. For further reading: R. Banham, *Megastructures: Urban Futures of the Recent Past* (1976). C.G.

high tech. A distinctive late 20th-century architectural style which places high visual valuation on the deployment of industrial forms and imagery both outside and inside. It derives from one of the MODERN MOVEMENT's architectural beliefs: that buildings should frankly express the materials from which they are constructed, the way in which they are constructed, and should express in some way the new machine culture of the 20th century. It was not until the 1970s that this was realized in any startling way in the form of buildings such as the Centre Pompidou in Paris. Like BRUTALISM, high tech architecture makes aesthetic capital of the building's functional elements – especially mechanical equipment such as air-conditioning ducts, window-cleaning apparatus and dramatic structures. In contrast to brutalism, the preferred materials of high tech are lightweight, reinforcing another strand in high tech to do with the idea of buildings as essentially temporary, flexible structures. Materials include glass, plain sheet materials, especially sheet metal, often highly polished or coloured and often perforated or profiled. Steel is the preferred structural material, often wire-braced and in dramatic configurations which in engineering terms are frequently redundant. S.L.

higher arithmetic, see under NUMBER THEORY.

higher criticism. The objective and exact study of the sources and methods used by the authors of the Bible. The pioneers of this scientific approach were almost all 19th-century scholars in German universities. In a book of 1881, by W. R. Smith, who was one of the British pioneers, the attempt to get behind the text to the actual history was contrasted with 'lower' criticism, i.e. with the study of manuscripts and other evidence in order to get at the text as originally written (see also TEXTUAL CRITICISM). In the 20th century, literary *source criticism* has been supplemented by *form criticism* (i.e. the attempt to discern the form taken by a story or teaching in order to make it more easily memorable, or more impressive, as it was passed on in ORAL TRADITION), and also by *redaction criticism* (i.e. the attempt to recover the theological motive of those redactors or editors who gathered these stories or teachings into the books we have). For further reading: W. G. Kümmel, *The New Testament: the History of the Investigation of its Problems* (1973) and *Introduction to the New Testament* (1975). D.L.E.

Hilbert space. A CONCEPT introduced by David Hilbert (1862–1943) in his investigation of integral equations. The characteristic feature of it and its generalizations is the application of geometric terminology and of methods which had been developed in the study of finite-dimensional (see DIMENSION) vector spaces to 'spaces' of FUNCTIONS which are infinite-dimensional (e.g. by the use of FOURIER ANALYSIS). It is a fundamental concept of functional ANALYSIS and of QUANTUM MECHANICS. R.G.

Hinduism. The RELIGION of most Indians. It has a rich variety, ranging from popular worship of gods in temples and homes, with petitions and celebrations, through devotional THEISM which sees these gods merely as expressions of the One God (e.g. as incarnations of Vishnu), to an austere MYSTICISM which suspects all religious images and seeks the absorption of the individual in the impersonal World-Spirit (the *Brahman*) through enlightenment. This religion has been spread by Indians in many countries and has impressed many disillusioned or bored Christians (see CHRISTIANITY) by its tolerance, its profusion of religious emotion, its imaginative PHILOSOPHY, its methods of self-mastery (especially in YOGA), and its power to give stability to a vast nation. Special admiration has been felt for the *Upanishads* (probably *c.* 800 BC) or ancient meditations on the position of man in a universe he did not make, and for the more warmly personal religion expressed in a later scripture, the *Bhagavad Gita* (probably *c.* 300 BC). The best-known Hindu of this century was Mahatma Gandhi (1869–1948), a saintly lawyer and political leader especially notable for the success of his advocacy of NON-VIOLENT RESISTANCE in ending British imperial rule. But it is difficult for those not born Indians to enter Hinduism's heritage. It is also difficult to reconcile some of its doctrines (e.g. the belief in the reincarnation of the self in successive bodies better or worse according to one's merits) with modern thought; and some of its traditional practices with modern convictions about human EQUALITY. In particular, the caste system – which fixes one's status in society at birth – has been controversial. Though it was outlawed by the Indian government, those who are born into the lowest caste, called *dalat* or 'untouchable', remain stigmatized, considered fit for only the most degrading work.

In the 1990s, there has also been significant unrest in India as various NATIONALIST and RIGHT-wing political parties have argued against Hinduism's traditional tolerance of other religions. The Hindu temple at Ayodhya, which had been supplanted by an Islamic mosque, became the focus of agitation in 1990, culminating in riotous destruction in 1992. For further reading: N. Smart, *Doctrine and Argument in Indian Philosophy* (1982). D.L.E.; N.SM.

hinterland. The German word *Hinterland* or 'back country' originally referred to the inland territory beyond the occupied coastal districts over which a colonial power claimed jurisdiction; thus it was applied in the late 19th century to parts of Africa. The word has been adapted by geographers to mean the land which lies behind a seaport and supplies the bulk of its exports, and in which most of its imports are distributed. In urban GEOGRAPHY the term is also used with reference to other centres of population, e.g. market towns. M.L.

hip. Of mysterious derivation, the term has come to signify fashionable awareness and sophistication. It can also connote an offhand superiority rather like COOL, with which it is often paired. Both words come ultimately from the argot of JAZZ, though hip has had a curious passage, beginning as 'hep' in the 1930s. In the 1940s this evolved into hip and created the 'hipster', a camp follower of modern jazz. By the 1960s, hipsters had metamorphosed into 'hippies' who were identified with ROCK MUSIC. What is hip now is whatever upmarket culture currently deems the latest thing. Though the word is occasionally used ironically, it still retains its prescriptive force. GE.S.

hip-hop. A term for the larger culture which developed around RAP music in black American neighbourhoods in the 1980s. One of its chief elements was acrobatic breakdancing (which included spinning – turning rapidly on head, back or hands – and pop-locking, a stiff-jointed style later identified with Michael Jackson), accompanied by rap singers and DJs. Graffiti artists were also part of an urban assertion of identity despite impoverishment. The name may have come from a rapper's chant: 'hip-hop, you don't stop/that makes your body rock'. Like so many BLACK forms, hip-hop was quickly co-opted by international pop culture. GE.S.

hippies. Term coined in California in 1966–67 to denote the mainly young people participating in the birth of the UNDERGROUND. As with their precursors the BEATS, the hippies' etymology is contentious; the most plausible derivation is from the Negro slang word 'hep' or 'hip' meaning to be knowledgeable, to have experience. Hippiedom in this first instance involved a 'philosophy' of Peace and Love together with a rejection of things material, a devotion to MARIJUANA and lysergic acid (LSD) as instruments of enlightenment and pleasure, a propensity for communal LIFESTYLES and libertarian (see LIBERTARIANISM) sexual behaviour, and a style of dress which included beads, bells and long hair. This original conception of the hippie did not last in its pure form for longer than two years, the originators themselves staging a 'Death of Hippie' parade in San Francisco in 1968. The era of 'love-ins', 'flower-power' and 'beautiful vibes' soon degenerated, largely by over-exposure in the mass media, into commercialism, violence and widespread drug abuse (see DRUGS). Over the intervening period the term hippie was widely, if incorrectly, used to denote any young, long-haired person suspected of unconventional standards. Youthful nonconformity to social conventions, however, has changed in style so that hippies have become a cultural anachronism in the changed economic and sociopolitical circumstances of the late 20th century. (See also DROP-OUT.) P.S.L.

Hiroshima. The Japanese city selected as target for the first atomic bomb dropped by the US Air Force, on 6 August 1945. Over 78,000 were killed, a further 70,000 badly injured, and two-thirds of the city destroyed. Most of the surviving population suffered long-term consequences of radiation. On 9 August a second bomb was dropped on Nagasaki; their combined effect was the surrender of Japan. The decision to use the bomb was primarily governed by the wish to avoid a full-scale invasion of Japan and the consequent heavy losses to the US. It has also been suggested that America wished to end the war quickly to prevent the USSR pressing claims on China or participating in the invasion and occupation of Japan. For further reading: M. Hogan (ed.), *Hiroshima in History and Memory* (1996). S.R.

histogram. In STATISTICS, a simple representational technique for giving an idea of the shape of an empirical DISTRIBUTION. The range of values of the random variable is divided into (usually equal) intervals and a block is drawn on each interval whose area is proportional to the number of observations falling in that interval, or to the proportion of the distribution lying in it. A typical example of the use of a histogram would be to represent the distribution of heights in a SAMPLE of adult men on a centimetre-by-centimetre basis – the size of the block on the interval between, say, 175 cm and 176 cm would be proportional to the number of men of height at least 175 cm but less than 176 cm. R.SI.

histoire du livre, see HISTORY OF THE BOOK.

histoire événementielle, see under ANNALES SCHOOL.

histoire sérielle, see SERIAL HISTORY.

historic compromise (Italy). The eurocommunist strategy of the Italian Communist Party (PCI) developed by the Party leader, Enrico Berlinguer, during the 1960s aimed at establishing an historic compromise with other major political parties. Given the dominance of the Christian Democratic Party (DC; see CHRISTIAN DEMOCRACY), the PCI's aim was to introduce gradually elements of SOCIALISM into government policies through PCI support for Christian Democratic governments. Following the legislative elections in August 1976 the PCI gave parliamentary support to the DC government which, in turn, consulted the PCI (which did not participate directly in the government) over policy. The historic compromise lasted for three years from August 1976 until the elections in June 1979. The strategy was subsequently criticized by many PCI supporters who felt that its strategy had achieved few if any of the Party's objectives. (See ITALIANIZATION.) S.M.

historical anthropology. A term used to describe the work of those historians (e.g. Emmanuel Le Roy Ladurie) who, despite the necessary differences in sources and methods between the two disciplines, share the anthropologists' concern with interpreting the NORMS and categories of other CULTURES, and their view of space, time, GENDER, illness, and other basic concepts as social 'constructions' which vary from period to period as well as from one region to another. These historians believe that 'the past is a foreign country'. This belief informs much current historical work on the EVERYDAY. P.B.

historical demography. The statistical study of populations in the past, concerned in particular with measuring the rates of birth, marriage and death at different periods. The subject grew up in about 1950. Demographers began to study the period before 1800 (when reliable national statistics begin) and historians began to interest themselves in population movements. At first their emphasis was on the idea of a demographic 'old regime' in pre-industrial Europe, with regular crises as population pressed on the means of subsistence. More recently the stress has been on the regional variations in birth, marriage and death rates. See also FAMILY RECONSTITUTION; DEMOGRAPHY. For further reading: E. A. Wrigley, *Population and History* (1969). P.B.

historical geography. A subfield of HUMANISTIC GEOGRAPHY concerned with the reconstruction and interpretation of spatial patterns of the past, and their significance for understanding contemporary human landscapes. Historical geographers have considered a wide range of phenomena – medieval villages, field systems, town plans and urban problems, the spatial DIFFUSION of agricultural and industrial innovations, ways of seeing and representing nature, the formation and struggle of social classes – and in consequence they are united, not so much by their subject-matter or by the METHODOLOGY of their inquiries, as by a common belief that conventional studies in SOCIAL HISTORY and ECONOMIC HISTORY neglect the non-accidental association of most historical phenomena with specific places, environments and landscapes. Not surprisingly, historical geography has periodically experienced definitional disputes as its practitioners have sought either to separate or to reconcile history and temporal modes of explanation with geography and spatial modes of explanation. In recent years, the growing realization that today's geographical distributions cannot be understood without reference to past distributions – or without reference to the dynamic restructuring processes binding the former to the latter – has resulted in a lessening of these definitional disputes. For further reading: R. Butlin, *Historical Geography: Through the Gates of Space and Time* (1993). C.P.; P.O.M.

historical materialism. A shorthand term for the MATERIALIST view of history, the cornerstone of Marx's theory of history. He expressed it most concisely in his preface to *A Contribution to the Critique of Political Economy* (1859): 'The MODE OF PRODUCTION in material life determines the general character of the social, political, and spiritual processes of life. It is not the CONSCIOUSNESS of men that determines their existence, but on the contrary, it is their social existence which determines their consciousness . . . In the social production which men carry on they enter into definite relations which are indispensable and independent of their will . . . The sum total of these relations of production constitutes the economic structure of society – the real basis, on which rises a legal and political SUPERSTRUCTURE and to which correspond definite forms of social consciousness. The mode of production determines the social, political, and intellectual life processes in general.'

This theory (and the concepts used in it) has been subject to myriad different interpretations, ranging from those which present the materialist conception of history as a monistic (see MONISM) *economic* (or technological) *determination* to those emphasizing the interaction between the 'economic basis' and the 'political superstructure'.

Engels (1820–95), like Marx, repeatedly affirmed that their theory 'explains all historical events and ideas, all politics, philosophy, and religion, from the material, economic conditions of life of the historical period in question'. But towards the end of his life he shifted the emphasis and stressed (in a letter to J. Bloch, 21 September 1890) that neither he nor Marx ever subscribed to an unqualified economic determinism which would reduce all historical development to economic causes alone. He wrote that they assert themselves historically only 'in the last resort': 'The economic situation is the basis, but the various elements of superstructure . . . also exercise their influence upon the course of the historical struggle and in many cases preponderate in determining their form. There is an interaction of all these elements . . .'

However, as Eduard Bernstein (1850–1932; see REVISIONISM) noticed, once historical necessity is made dependent on economic causation only 'in the final analysis', there is no way of predicting the historical development of concrete societies, and SOCIALISM ceases to be 'scientific' in the sense attributed to it by Engels. With the MARXIST-LENINIST stress on political VOLUNTARISM, the original theoretical substance of historical materialism has fallen into disregard, and the MAOIST interpretation of it, e.g., goes so far as to include a condemnation of 'the reactionary theory of productive forces . . . [which] describes social development as a natural outcome of the development of productive forces only, especially the development of the tools of production'. For further reading: M. Rader, *Marx's Interpretation of History* (1979). L.L.

historical psychology. A deliberately ambiguous term in that it covers both the study of HISTORY from psychological perspectives and the history of PSYCHOLOGY (the discipline) as a way of illuminating this, centrally assuming that psychological phenomena change over time. While related to PSYCHOHISTORY (which applies a primarily FREUDIAN framework to the study of history), historical psychology is theoretically diverse, although primarily social constructionist in character and conscious of REFLEXIVITY issues. Emerging, mainly in Germany and the Netherlands, since 1980, it has had a growing impact on anglophone historians of psychology. Its complex roots include the German CRITICAL THEORY tradition, the French approaches of Canguilhem and Foucault, and social constructionist social psychology. Anglophone representatives of this school currently include K. Danziger, J. Morawski, M. Ash and K. Gergen, although its character as a 'school' remains largely uncrystallized. For further reading: C. W. Tolman and W. Maiers (eds), *Critical Psychology: Contributions to an Historical Science of the Subject* (1991). G.D.R.

historicism.

(1) (or *historism*: from German *Historismus*). A word which at different times has been applied to two diametrically opposed approaches to history: (a) Originally, in the late 19th century, it meant an approach which emphasized the uniqueness of all historical phenomena and maintained that each age should be interpreted in terms of its own ideas and principles, or, negatively, that the actions of men in the past should not be explained by reference to the beliefs, motives and valuations of the historian's own epoch. Particularly popular in Germany, this approach went with an emphasis on the function of VERSTEHEN in historical method, and with a rejection of the SOCIAL SCIENCES. (b) The term was more recently used by the Austrian-born British philosopher Karl Popper (1902–94) in an entirely different sense, which is now at least as commonly intended as the original one. To Popper, historicism was the belief in large-scale laws of historical development of the kind to be found in speculative systems of history, whether linear or cyclic, such as those of Hegel, Marx, Comte, Spengler and Toynbee. Hostile to them as representing the intellectual foundations of totalitarian IDEOLOGIES, he argued that the course of history was radically affected by the growth of knowledge and that future acquisitions of knowledge could not be predicted. Historicism, in this sense, however, is not associated exclusively with TOTALITARIANISM; most liberals (see LIBERALISM) in the 18th and 19th centuries believed in a law of inevitable progress. For further reading: K. R. Popper, *The Poverty of Historicism* (1957; 1960). P.B.; A.Q.

(2) In ARCHITECTURE, a term of mild abuse for contemporary architecture that deliberately imitates the modes and styles of architecture of the past. Distinguished from the various 'historical' post-modern styles by its deadly seriousness of intention and its attempt to reproduce exactly the forms and detailing of its original models. See also POST-MODERN CLASSICISM. S.L.

historiography. The history of historical writing. At least as old as La Popelinière's *L'Histoire des histoires* (1599), historiography has become a popular subject of research only in the last 30 years. This awakening of interest in history's past goes with an increased self-consciousness on the part of historians, and a rejection of the idea that they can produce an 'objective' description, uncontaminated by their own attitudes and values, of what actually happened. For further reading: E. Breisach, *Historiography: Ancient, Medieval and Modern* (1983). P.B.

historism, see under HISTORICISM (1).

history. Contemporary historical study involves MODELS of social-scientific explanation and interpretative understanding. This contrast co-exists, however, within a broader consensus. Historians no longer treat their diverse topics as autonomous, no longer are content with writing the HISTORY OF IDEAS, and assess research largely in terms of its factual completeness and accuracy. Also, historical research has begun to incorporate modern statistical techniques of sampling (see SAMPLE) and analysis as well as devices such as ECONOMETRICS, DECISION THEORY and public opinion polling in expanding its conception of data.

Two central questions have accompanied these modern conceptions. First, what is an historical explanation? Assuming it is a causal explanation, then causes at the individual and structural levels need to be distinguished. Further, such explanations must consider whether the collective level preempts the individual level in producing events. Second, if the aim is not explanation, what is the alternative of historical understanding?

This contrast, however, is somewhat misleading since interpretation and causal explanation could be compatible. For example, an influential account of historical explanation is the COVERING LAW THEORY of German-born American philosopher Carl Hempel. Explanations are presented as resting upon a logical relation between universal, hypothetical laws or principles and sets of initial conditions directing inquiry towards whatever evidence is relevant given those guiding hypotheses. But the model does not preclude interpretative techniques of EMPATHY, understanding and conceptual analysis in arriving at the hypothetical conditional making such an explanation possible. More radical interpretationists, as will be noted, reject any explanatory aim.

There are two characteristic challenges to the model of history as social-scientific explanation. Is a science of history even possible? Are there genuine historical laws? Wilhelm Dilthey (1833–1911), early in the century, argued that since the sciences were themselves objects of historical study, they were not also the standard for judging history, and because history is the study of the past it could not proceed empirically. HISTORICISM, as some called his view, encouraged historical scepticism and RELATIVISM. Benedetto Croce (1866–1952), also a critic of the idea of a science of history, sought nevertheless to counter such scepticism. He specified that historical explanations were not about the non-existent, past events, but about the existing documentary records. His modification did not, however, rectify historicism's basic confusion. The position claims historical evidence that knowledge, including the sciences, is historically conditioned. But this relativist conclusion, then, applies to the previous historical evidence cited in its defence.

While historians had long claimed to discover and use historical laws, the modern conception of a scientific law requires a distinction between generalizations and laws or between rule-governed and law-like cases. Karl Popper (see POPPERIAN) criticized the prediction of historical events through laws by arguing that any possible historical laws were trivial and thus historical explanations were no more than extrapolations of the LOGIC of social institutions.

Given such objections, the influence of the strict covering law model waned. Subsequently, historians have adopted two broad strategies. The social-scientific model is retained but with greater flexibility. Historians produce, at best, commonsense explanations postulating causal mechanisms embodied in social institutions or practices. While these coarse-grained analyses admit of no historical laws, they do not require any mysterious historical TELEOLOGIES.

On the other hand, radical interpretationists forgo causal explanations entirely. The aim of 'thick description', a phrase associated with the anthropologist Clifford Geertz (1923–), is offered as an alternative. Studies of the rhetorical, literary aspect of historical writing, such as those of Hayden White (*Metahistory*, 1973), stress the conceptual distinction between narration and explanation. Applying the techniques of literary criticism to history is now called POST-MODERNISM. This approach is often identified with the work of Michel Foucault (1926–84) and his opposition to interpretative and explanatory orthodoxies. Foucault, like Croce, identified 'discursive formations' found in archives as history's proper object. But Foucault's 'genealogical model of history' was finally unclear as to whether archival documentation constitutes a type of evidence anyway, and whether discursive analyses are simply preparatory for further explanation or comprehension.

Post-modernism also claims that historical study amounts in the end to a struggle against or justification of political POWER. Such a claim, however, is as reductive as the scientism it disputes. In neither case is the evidence appropriate to historical study nor are the broadest aims of research clarified and retained. R.D.

history from below. A phrase coined by those who believe that historians have for too long been content to present the past from the perspective of the ruling classes, and that ordinary people also have a point of view and a CULTURE of their own, 'POPULAR CULTURE'. In Britain, E. P. Thompson's *Making of the English Working Class* (1963) did much to launch the movement, but the most important single influence on it has probably been that of Antonio Gramsci (1891–1937). As research has progressed, the difficulties inherent in the notion of 'people' have become ever more apparent. Are the people the poor? The powerless? The 'uneducated'? What is the relationship between the attitudes of ordinary men and women, or between the people and the ÉLITE? For further reading: C. Mukerji and M. Schudson (eds), *Rethinking Popular Culture* (1991). P.B.

history of childhood. Systematic interest in the subject goes back to the publication in 1960 of a study by the French 'Sunday historian' Philippe Ariès, which argued that before the 17th century the 'sense of childhood' did not exist, in other words that children – as we see them – were viewed either as animals or as miniature adults. Since then the literature on the subject has been increasing at an almost exponential rate, and the methods as well as the conclusions of Ariès have been challenged by many scholars. On the other hand, the idea that 'childhood' is a cultural construct with a history has become widely accepted. For further reading: P. Ariès, *Centuries of Childhood* (1960, tr. 1962). P.B.

history of ideas. A term popularized, and a discipline founded, by Arthur Lovejoy in the USA in the 1920s. Lovejoy opposed the fragmentation of the historical study of ideas into the histories of philosophy, literature, science, etc., and suggested an interdisciplinary approach which focused on individual concepts like 'nature' and 'primitivism' and on the changes in their meaning and associations. The focus on individual ideas was a reaction against German *Geistesgeschichte* (see CULTURAL HISTORY), with its emphasis on the unity of systems of thought. Lovejoy's approach ran the risk of personifying ideas. Hence some of his successors use the term *intellectual history*, and place more emphasis on thinking men. A more recent German approach, *Begriffsgeschichte*, is concerned with language and its changing uses in different social situations. See also HISTORY OF MENTALITIES. For further reading: A. O. Lovejoy, *Essays in the History of Ideas* (1948). P.B.

history of language. Intellectual and social historians have been taking an increasing interest in language. Some historians of political thought, such as J. G. A. Pocock, regard their subject as the history of the changing language (or as followers of Foucault would say, the DISCOURSE) of politics. Some social historians (see SOCIAL HISTORY), inspired by sociolinguists and ethnographers of communication (see SOCIOLINGUISTICS; COMMUNICATION, ETHNOGRAPHY OF), are paying attention to the different 'speech codes' of different social groups (from aristocrats to beggars), and the different ways in which an individual speaks or writes in different social situations or 'speech domains'. There is greater awareness than there used to be of the influence of linguistic conventions on the historians' 'sources'. For further reading: P. Burke and R. Porter (eds), *The Social History of Language* (1987). P.B.

history of material culture. The history of material objects, from cathedrals to washbasins, from forks to tanks, including the analysis of their various uses in a given society. An expanding area of study on which art historians (no longer confined to 'works of art'), and archaeologists (no longer satisfied with 'PREHISTORY'), as well as economic and social historians (see ECONOMIC HISTORY; SOCIAL HISTORY) are converging. The Marxists entered the field early (the Polish *Quarterly for the History of Material Culture* goes back to 1952). Fernand Braudel (1902–85) produced a brilliant, provocative synthesis in 1967, concentrating on food, clothing and shelter in the early modern world as examples of *civilisation matérielle*. Since then, social historians have learned from social anthropologists and art historians alike to pay more attention to symbolism than Braudel did, noting, e.g., that the preference for white rather than brown bread in early modern Europe symbolized the STATUS (or even the purity) of those who could afford to eat it, or that a particular choice of clothing or housing expressed or helped to create a particular social identity. For further reading: F. Braudel, *The Structures of Everyday Life* (1967; rev. tr. 1981). P.B.

history of mentalities (*mentalités collectives*). An approach to what American scholars call the HISTORY OF IDEAS and PSYCHOHISTORY, developed in France in the 1930s, notably by Lucien Febvre and Georges Lefebvre. It is concerned with everyone's ideas, with peasants' as well as philosophers'; with sensibility as well as with concepts; and, in particular, with basic mental structures. Thus Febvre, writing about 16th-century France, suggested that men had an imprecise sense of time and space; lacked any sense of the impossible; and perceived the world more through the ear than through the eye. His conclusions are still debated, but French historians continue to use his methods. See also ANNALES SCHOOL. P.B.

history of the body. A new phrase for a fairly new kind of history, at the point of convergence between the history of medicine (itself a rapidly expanding field), food, GENDER, hygiene and sexuality, an approach probably influenced as much by movements for gay (see HOMOSEXUALITY) and women's liberation as by aspirations towards a 'total history'. The most important contribution so far to the history of the body is surely Michel Foucault's *Discipline and Punish* (see below), concerned with the relationship between POWER and the body and more especially with the idea of bodily 'discipline' in prisons, armies, schools, factories and elsewhere. Historians and others cultivating this field also owe considerable debts to Mikhail Bakhtin (see BAKHTINIAN) on grotesque images of the body and to Norbert Elias (1897–1990) on the place of bodily control in the 'civilizing process'. For further reading: M. Foucault, *Discipline and Punish* (1975; tr. 1978). P.B.

history of the book. A growing area of research between bibliographers and sociocultural historians and first developed in France (hence the continued popularity of the French term *histoire du livre*). The interests of historians of the book include the organization of libraries; the technology of printing and the production of manuscripts; methods of information retrieval; the economics of the book trade; and the attempts by religious and political authorities to control what was published. Their central concern, however, is with the place of the book in social life. Inventories of private libraries are studied, numbers of editions are counted, and marginalia in individual copies of books are scrutinized in order to discover who read what where and when, and how they interpreted or were influenced by what they read. P.B.

history of the family. Specialization in SOCIAL HISTORY concerned with family relations and family forms, which grew out of interest in HISTORICAL DEMOGRAPHY and SOCIAL STRUCTURE. Much of the initial enthusiasm in the 1960s derived from the work of Peter Laslett on household and family structures, especially the NUCLEAR FAMILY, and from the work of the ANNALES SCHOOL. While much of that early research was quantitative and concerned with the size and structure of families and households, the subject has become a diverse one. One major field of study is the economic relationships within and between families; including those between husband and wife, and parent and child – labour as well as money is included in these calculations; and also the structure of property inheritance and membership in a wider family context. Another major field of study looks at the content and meaning of family relations, such as the nature of the relationships between family members, and the attitudes to such things as sex, discipline and privacy. As with allied interests such as the HISTORY OF CHILDHOOD, there has been considerable debate about the nature and direction of historical change in family forms and relationships. For further reading: David Elkind, *Ties that Stress: The New Family Imbalance* (1995). D.S.

HIV, see under AIDS.

Hohfeldian. Adjective formed from the name of the American jurist W. N. Hohfeld (1879–1918), whose study *Some Fundamental Legal Conceptions as Applied in Judicial Reasoning* (first version, 1917) represented a major clarification of the concept of a legal right. Hohfeld distinguished four basic elements for each of which the expression 'legal right' had been loosely used by lawyers and others, sometimes without an appreciation of the difference between them. Hohfeld used in a special technical sense the four expressions: *claim-right*, *liberty* (or *privilege*), *power* and *immunity* to distinguish these four elements. The distinctions drawn in this Hohfeldian analytical scheme have served to clarify not only the concept of a legal right, but also more complex notions such as that of ownership. For further reading: W. N. Hohfeld, ed. W. W. Cook, *Fundamental Legal Con-*

ceptions as Applied in Judicial Reasoning (1974). H.L.A.H.

holism. The thesis that wholes, or some wholes, are more than the sums of their parts in the sense that the wholes in question have characteristics that cannot be explained in terms of the properties and relations to one another of their constituents. ORGANICISM is a particular version of holism, which is founded on the analogy of complex systems in general with what are literally organisms, whose parts lose their nature, function, significance and even existence when removed from their organic interconnection with the rest of the organism. Holism is central to IDEALIST theories of the STATE and other social INSTITUTIONS, to many accounts of the special unity and integrity of works of art, and to the theory of science advanced by American philosopher William Quine, according to which science is not an assemblage of isolable bits of belief but an interconnected system which is adjusted as a whole to the deliverances of experience. Holism is hostile to the philosophical technique of ANALYSIS, which it conceives to be a falsifying mutilation of what it is applied to. See also METHODOLOGICAL INDIVIDUALISM; METHODOLOGICAL HOLISM. For further reading: E. Nagel, *The Structure of Science* (1961). A.Q.

holistic medicine. Term used to describe an approach to healthcare which spans both the conventional medical model and COMPLEMENTARY (alternative) MEDICINE. The word *holos* stems from the Greek meaning whole, complete – the 'w' is a late-14th-century addition to the spelling. The word *holism* was first used by Smuts (1928) in his book *Holism and Evolution* to describe the philosophical systems that looked on whole systems rather than parts (reductionism; see REDUCTION). The following basic principles govern the approach to holistic practice. (1) *The whole is greater than the sum of its parts*. It is necessary when examining a part, e.g. heart, to be aware of how the whole person (EMOTIONS, thoughts, aspirations, breathing patterns, DIET and exercise practices, family, social CLASS, CULTURE, ENVIRONMENT) impinges on the function of that part. Holism challenges the notion of linear cause and effect and draws on SYSTEMS theory for its explanations. (2) *The use of a wide range of interventions*. This may include conventional medical therapies (drugs, SURGERY, RADIOTHERAPY), alternative therapies (ACUPUNCTURE, HOMOEOPATHY), self-help skills (relaxation techniques, meditation). (3) *Involving the patient/client in his care*. There is an emphasis in holistic practice on encouraging and facilitating the patient to take some responsibility for his own recovery process. (4) '*Physician heal thyself*.' An holistic approach suggests that the health (physical, psychological, spiritual) of the practitioner is an important component in the outcome of the interaction between doctor and patient, therapist and client. P.C.P.

Holocaust, the. Name given to the complex of events in which Germany, under Hitler, systematically killed six million Jews and other 'undesirables' including gypsies and opponents of NAZISM during World War II. The Holocaust had its roots in the German concept of 'race biology', a development of the pseudo-science of EUGENICS. Race biologists advocated increased procreation among the 'fittest' members of society, and restrictions on the fertility of the 'unfit': the congenitally ill or diseased, inebriates and other social misfits. The first law that Hitler enacted after coming to power in 1933 was a eugenic STERILIZATION law whose text was influenced by American eugenic legislation that had been constitutionally tested in the US SUPREME COURT.

In 1935, the NUREMBERG LAWS defined who was a Jew, and imposed grave restrictions on their rights as citizens. In November 1938, in an event known as *Kristallnacht*, Nazi thugs and their supporters vandalized Jewish homes, synagogues and businesses, beating and killing Jews at random. After the invasion of Poland in 1939, Germany began a systematic programme of GENOCIDE in Europe. At first, Jews and other 'enemies' were rounded up and shot. A network of CONCENTRATION CAMPS was built in Germany and eastern Europe, and as successive countries fell to the Germans, Jews were deported to them. In the camps, they were used as slave labour and worked to death. Many were tortured and murdered.

From 1942, CONCENTRATION CAMPS like Auschwitz, Treblinka, Sobibor and others were transformed into centres for mass extermination (see DRANCY). The Germans built gas chambers and large crematoria and practised genocide on an industrial scale. Their intention, referred to as the Final Solution, was to exterminate completely the Jews within the borders of the countries they occupied. Horrifying evidence of the Holocaust was presented at the NUREMBERG TRIALS.

The Holocaust is a defining moment in the 20th century because it raises the fundamental question of how an apparently civilized nation could have committed an act of such gross magnitude. In recent years, neo-Nazis and Holocaust 'revisionists' have sought to argue that the Holocaust never occurred, and is a myth propounded by 'world Jewry'. For further reading: Martin Gilbert, *The Holocaust* (1985). S.T.

holography. A type of photography producing three-dimensional images, which was developed by the engineer-physicist Dennis Gabor in 1947. In conventional photography based on lenses, etc., only the straight-line propagation of light is utilized (see OPTICS) and wave effects constitute a nuisance. Holography, however, relies essentially on wave properties: the PHASE of the wave reflected from an object is revealed by interference resulting from the addition of a 'reference wave', the pattern produced by the combination of the two waves being recorded on an ordinary photographic film negative. When this *hologram* is illuminated by the reference wave alone, there results an image of the original object which is fully three-dimensional (i.e. it shows perspective, etc.). Since the light sources must have a high degree of coherence, LASERS are almost universally used. M.V.B.

homepage. The introductory display of an information provider on the WORLD WIDE WEB. For a large provider, the homepage may be no more than the equivalent of a table of contents or even the cover of a book. But most providers on the Web are small and the homepage is their main page. Thus, a 'homepage' has come to be synonymous for a display on the Web. E.B.B.

homoeomorphism, see under TOPOLOGY.

homoeomorphy, see under PHYLUM.

homoeopathy. A system of therapeutics (treatment) using 'remedies' rather than pharmacologically active drugs. It was developed and established by Hahnemann, a 19th-century German physician. The fundamental principle of homoeopathy is that 'like cures like'. By this is meant that instead of suppressing a symptom or killing bacteria (as modern drugs do), cure is achieved by stimulating the body's own healing powers. This is done by giving a 'remedy' which in much greater doses would *produce* the symptoms the patient is complaining about. These remedies contain minute levels of extracts which have no chemical effect on the body. In homoeopathy it is believed the more dilute the extract or remedy the more potent is its effect. Homoeopathy has a long and traditional history in Britain, having been the preferred approach to treatment among many members of the Royal Family. The majority of homoeopaths are doctors who have gone on to receive further training. It is the one branch of COMPLEMENTARY MEDICINE that is available on the National Health Service in Britain. Conventional doctors are still unconvinced that it has a part to play in the treatment of disease, but there is little doubt that homoeopathy is a safe method of treatment and that in several conditions it appears to have a dramatic effect. P.C.P.

homoeostasis.

(1) The widespread disposition of living beings, including people, to maintain a state of EQUILIBRIUM in the face of changing conditions, whether physical, chemical or psychological. This disposition is often used as an explanatory principle in BIOLOGY and PSYCHOLOGY. See also ADAPTATION. For further reading: W. B. Cannon, *The Wisdom of the Body* (1939). I.M.L.H.

(2) In CYBERNETICS, this disposition is generalized mathematically to include all (not only biological) systems that maintain critical variables within limits acceptable to their own structure in the face of unexpected disturbance. See also AUTOPOIESIS; ULTRASTABILITY. For further reading: W. R. Ashby, *Design for a Brain* (1960). S.BE.

homoerotic. Arousing a homosexual response (see HOMOSEXUALITY); or – of activities, or works of literature, art or POPULAR CULTURE – believed to be expressive of or derived from homosexual affections.

A compound term created from the Greek *homo* (same) and *eros* (sexual love). It has been found useful for critical reappraisals of paintings and novels or poetry whose subject-matter and/or authors may or may not have been overtly homosexual. For example, the homoerotic content and well-springs of Michelangelo and Leonardo da Vinci's work have been extensively analysed, as has the tradition of homoerotic ICONOGRAPHY from classical times into the Renaissance to which they and other painters referred, viz in successive painterly uses of the 'Ganymede myth' of the youth abducted to heaven by Zeus. Social organizations such as the military, single-sex boarding schools and religious orders are sometimes analysed as resulting from or leading to homoerotic 'bonding', without any necessary presumption of homosexual acts. The term is applicable to either sex. A.L.

homology. The relationship among corresponding parts or characteristics of different ORGANISMS. Examples are the limb of a dog and the limb of a monkey. In spite of obvious differences they nevertheless share the same basic 'plan'. The concept can be applied to traits at all levels of complexity. The presence of homologous traits in different SPECIES is explained by inheritance from a common ancestor. Homology is an important conceptual tool for the reconstruction of phylogenetic relationships, because the presence of homologous traits indicates that the species had a common ancestor with the same trait. Methods for recognizing and testing homology are based on character complexity (more complex characters are more likely to be homologous than simple ones), and character congruence (the more putative homologies imply the same phylogenetic relationships the more likely they are true homologies). Recently a biological homology concept has been developed to explain homology in terms of shared developmental genetic 'information'. The objective of this research programme is to identify the parts of the developmental programme which are responsible for the similarity of homologous traits. G.P.W.

homology theory, see under TOPOLOGY.

homosexuality. The state or practice of desire between members of the same sex. Term invented in 1869 by Hungarian writer Benkert as compound of Greek *homo* (same) and Latin *sexus* (sex); to be distinguished from *hetero* (other) sexuality, the state or practice of desire between members of different sexes; and *bi* (two) sexuality, desire for either sex. Entered universal as distinct from specialist usage from late 19th/early 20th century. The word and concept homosexuality (hence homosexual, adjectivally and as a noun) marked a break with a Western tradition commonly called Judaeo-Christian which defined homosexual acts as optional 'wilful' departures from a (God-given) heterosexual nature common to all. The notion that people can 'be' homosexual rather than 'be' heterosexual, regardless of whether they engage in any homosexual acts – which may be fiercely disapproved of – at present commands general acceptance, including from the Churches and among the medical and psychiatric professions. Inquiry into causation, however, has not yielded any results commanding general assent: neither genetic inheritance (see GENETICS/GENOMICS) of a homosexual disposition (like blue eyes) nor unconscious environmental influence ('strong' or 'weak' father or mother, depending on gender of child) has been proved. Originally designed to refer equally to women or men, homosexual (as noun) has largely been co-opted to refer to men. Accordingly, homosexual women have increasingly preferred to be referred to as lesbians, from Lesbos (Mytilene), home of 6th-century BC poet Sappho. From *c.* 1969, beginning in the US, homosexual men (and, loosely, homosexual women) have preferred the self-description gay, asserting an intention of being guilt-free (having self-respect) and open (declining self-concealment) – hence glad to be gay and out. A further term evolved from Benkert's original innovation is heterosexism (entered usage *c.* 1980), intended to describe words or acts of overt heterosexual hostility towards lesbians or gays, i.e. homosexuals of either sex. A.L.

homotopy theory, see under TOPOLOGY.

homozygote, see under GENE.

horizon.

(1) In ECOLOGY, a distinctive stratum, assumed to have been originally horizontal,

which extends over a wide area and can be used to establish a regional stratigraphy.

(2) In PEDOLOGY, an important morphological character exhibited by a soil when inspected in a vertical section known as the *soil profile*. The soil horizons, which occur in layers roughly parallel to the surface, can be distinguished from each other, and from parent rock material at the base of the profile, on the basis of properties such as colour, texture, and amount of organic matter. A number of processes interact to produce soil horizons: the addition and decomposition of organic material, weathering of the parent rock material, and the movement of soluble and suspended constituents by the movement of soil water. The study of the soil profile is basic to the scientific study of soil since it provides a means of identification and classification, and also data relating to soil evolution. J.L.M.L.

(3) 'Horizon' and 'merging of horizons' are terms important in the HERMENEUTICS of Hans-Georg Gadamer (1900–). Gadamer borrows the term 'horizon' from Husserl (1859–1938) in order to give a figure for our historical situatedness and limitation in our world. We inherit our cultural and personal horizons and have to seek for meaning in terms of them. Gadamer insists that the only understanding one can have of one's world, and of the texts which make up its literature, is a historically aware understanding. Grasping the necessity of this involves *effective-historical consciousness* (*Wirkungs-geschichtliches Bewusstsein*). The 'effective-historical' is the recognition of the modifying power of the horizons we inherit. Understanding is a function of the language that one speaks, the history of that language, and the historical-philosophical situatedness in which the hermeneut finds himself. Understanding is achieved when one's own personal horizon 'fuses' or 'merges' with the historical horizon (*Horizontverschmelzung*). Hans Robert Jauss, a leading member of the RECEPTION THEORY school at Konstanz, has used the figure of the 'horizon of expectations' within which any given literary work is actually read or understood. Opposed to Gadamer's is the position of Jürgen Habermas (1929–). Habermas insists that understanding not only can be, but also ought to be, in some sense trans-historical, and can belong in some way to universal reason, however inflected that must be by the influence of local political-economic 'interests'. The debate between Gadamer and Habermas in the late 1960s and early 1970s was intense and influential. It is being continued in the 1980s as the POST-MODERNISM of Lyotard and such American relativists as Richard Rorty struggles with the 'legitimization' demands of Habermas's thought. Christopher Norris's *The Contest of Faculties* (1984) has recently tried to propose a satisfactory position on this issue. For further reading: M. Mueller-Vollmer, *The Hermeneutics Reader* (1986). R.PO.

Horizon. A monthly review of literature and art edited by Cyril Connolly and Peter Watson from London, 1940–50, and displaying a remarkable, eclectic range of talents. Early numbers drew heavily on such writers of the 1930s as MacNeice, Day Lewis, Spender, Auden and Geoffrey Grigson. But it also maintained close contacts with France, and in the post-war period with the USA, printing Malraux, Sartre, Camus, Lionel Trilling, Marianne Moore, Wallace Stevens, e. e. cummings, etc., in addition to such British writers as Evelyn Waugh (whose *Unconditional Surrender*, 1961, includes some satirical remarks about *Horizon*), George Orwell and Angus Wilson (whom it 'discovered'). It also, in Connolly's view, marked the end of the Modern Movement in literature, and ended in 1950 in some desperation as Connolly noted a decline in the aesthetic, AVANT-GARDE impulse he favoured. M.S.BR.

hormic psychology. William McDougall's (1871–1938) term for his form of purposive psychology (see PURPOSIVISM). Human action is governed, in this view, not by a rational search for hedonistic ends, but by primitive urges that have been largely neglected by students of man's social life. For further reading: W. McDougall, *An Introduction to Social Psychology* (1936). I.M.L.H.

hormone, see under ENDOCRINOLOGY.

hot. One of the earliest figurative descriptions of JAZZ, as when King Oliver declared his CHICAGO band of 1922 was 'hotter than a .45!'. It is particularly appropriate for the music's first incarnation, with its extrovert appeal, emphasis on lively syncopation and broad, exciting effects. In the 1940s, however, as jazz became more complex after BEBOP, a more thoughtful, intellectual quality appeared and the up-to-date attitude became COOL. However, it could be said that any jazz is impossible without a distinct degree of emotional pressure, so that coolness is very much a relative concept, and hotness, however banked the fires, will always be present. GE.S.

hot and **cold.** Terms drawn from JAZZ idiom (see HOT) by Marshall McLuhan (*The Gutenberg Galaxy*, 1962), in the course of establishing his thesis that the spoken word is the fullest means of human communication, since its context (intonation, facial expression, gesture, etc.) offers the most reliable means of transmitting a mental state. On this basis, hearing is 'hotter' than seeing or feeling or tasting. The television image, however, is (from a technical standpoint) poorly defined, and is therefore 'cold' (the poor definition demands – McLuhan claims – an effort from the viewer, thus *involving* him). Before the invention of printing, man was 'aural', 'hot', more 'tribal' than subsequently: his emotions lay near the surface of his personality. 'Hot' is not a precise term; Jonathan Miller's definition 'intrinsically richer' (i.e. involving more of the 'plural and voluminous' nature of human experience) is perhaps as near as it is possible to get. Since McLuhan's death, the terms have fallen into disuse. M.S.-S.

household responsibility system. Term used in connection with changes in the Chinese agricultural system dating from 1978 in which communal operation gave way to increased scope for farming by individual households on a contract basis. Some communal activity is retained (e.g. in the provision of irrigation facilities), but land can be leased to households under strict conditions to allow for the development of increasing initiative. The change is widely believed to have provoked considerable improvement in total output. Further changes in 1985 removed some state control over agricultural prices. (See also DENGISM.) G.H.P.

Hubble's constant, see under EXPANSION OF THE UNIVERSE.

Hullian. Relating to the version of learning theory developed by US psychologist Clark L. Hull from the late 1930s to the 1950s. In contrast to the parsimonious SKINNERIAN approach, Hull attempted to formulate a rigorous and complex 'hypothetico-deductive' theory. When fully elaborated this assumed a highly algebraicized and quantified form along with an awesome technical vocabulary (e.g. 'generalized inhibitory potential', 'fractional anticipatory goal-response'). In opposition to classical BEHAVIOURISM (and Skinner's approach), Hull hypothesized numerous internal processes underlying overt behaviour. Some of his simpler algebraic expressions and terminology gained a wider circulation within psychology, but the almost baroque nature of the theory appeared to many as a vast superstructure unsustainable by the rat-learning experiments on which it was erected. Hullian learning theory's appeal rapidly declined as COGNITIVE PSYCHOLOGY emerged during the 1960s. Of all the varieties of learning theory inspired by behaviourism, Hull's remains the most self-consciously ambitious, and if, in hindsight, appearing a little bizarre, it exerted considerable influence on his contemporaries in the field. For further reading: C. L. Hull, *A Behavior System* (1952). G.D.R.

Hubble's law, see under BIG BANG THEORY.

human capital, see under CAPITAL.

human function curve. A MODEL that provides a SYSTEMS APPROACH to medical problems by relating the condition of health to arousal and performance. The condition of health is seen as a continuum ranging from healthy function through fatigue, exhaustion and ill-health to breakdown. This continuum is drawn as an inverted 'U' on a graph starting with healthy function and healthy fatigue on the upslope, exhaustion and the subsequent degradation of human function on the downslope. The horizontal axis represents arousal, the general 'drive' state of the individual determined by his efforts of coping, adapting to change and handling information from both the external environment and the internal milieu. The vertical axis is performance, the accomplishment of action and work and the discharge of one's functions. The representation of healthy function by an upslope indicates that the individual can call upon reserves of energy and information for the enhancement of performance up to a point, beyond which exhaustion sets in and the curve turns downwards. Further effort is self-defeating. Maladaptive behaviour patterns are adopted. Sleep is disturbed, and the metabolism shifts from an anabolic to a catabolic mode when energy and information-handling ability are no longer adequate for the maintenance of a stable and orderly internal milieu. Habituation is impaired and entropy increased. The consequent degradation of the internal milieu presents as ill-health or breakdown from dysfunction of major systems, e.g. hypertension, coronary heart disease, diabetes mellitus and gout (neuroendocrine system); increased vulnerability to infection and neoplasm, and distortion of immune function (neuro-immune system); and loss of stamina and dominance associated with sexual and reproductive morbidity (pituitary – sex steroid system). The model enables medical problems to be examined not only in a reductionist or mechanistic fashion (Is there a disease? What is it?), but also in relation to the individual's coping and adapting ability, behavioural patterns and psychosocial burdens, needs for energy and information, and the integrity of his homoeostatic mechanisms (the holistic [see HOLISM] or biopsychosocial approach). It enables the therapist to integrate modern technology with information, education and communication, in order to serve the patient and enable him to make the best possible use of his resources for self-organization and self-regulation (HOMOEOSTASIS) in recovering from illness and adapting to handicap. P.G.F.N.

human genome project. The United States National Institutes of Health, in collaboration with other governments, is undertaking the mapping of the entire human genome, i.e. the mapping and sequencing of every GENE on every human CHROMOSOME. This massive task, expected to take many years, has been made possible by the development of automated (see AUTOMATION) procedures for determining the nucleotide sequence of each gene (see NUCLEIC ACID; NUCLEON; NUCLEOSYNTHESIS). It is anticipated that the information gained from this undertaking will contribute to the understanding of developmental processes and of the genetic basis of many diseases.

The genomes of other organisms, including invertebrates and bacteria, are also being characterized. The first organism to have its genome completely mapped is a tiny Nematode, *Caenorhabditis elegans*.

Some researchers view this totally reductionist approach (see REDUCTION) as naïve and incapable of contributing significantly to understanding organismal development, claiming that knowledge of the properties of parts (genes and chromosomes) will not reveal properties and processes that emerge from the interactions of the parts. They argue for a more holistic approach. (See HOLISM) W.G.R.

human rights. That there are human rights is a contemporary form of the doctrine of natural rights, first clearly formulated by Locke (1632–1704) and later expressed in terms of the rights of man. Natural or human rights are those which men are conceived to have by virtue of their humanity and not by virtue of human fiat or law or convention. Such rights have therefore been frequently invoked in the criticism of laws and social arrangements. In 1948 the General Assembly of the UN adopted a Universal Declaration of Human Rights, which formulated in detail a number of rights, economic and cultural, as well as political, to form a standard of human rights. This is not a legally binding instrument, but it was followed by a number of international covenants and conventions, including the European Convention for the Protection of Human Rights and Fundamental Freedoms, which have influenced national legislation and provided some machinery for international enforcement. For further reading: J. J. Waldron (ed.), *Theories of Rights* (1984). H.L.A.H.

humanism.

(1) A term invented by a German educationalist, F. J. Niethammer, in 1808 to describe the study of the Greek and Latin classics, *literae humaniores*, 'humane letters', the revival of which had been one of the distinguishing features of the Italian Renaissance, later spreading to the rest of Europe as 'the New Learning'. Part of the attraction of classical studies was the fact that they are man- rather than God-centred (as Cicero said, Socrates brought PHILOS-

OPHY down from heaven to earth), studying the works and thought of Man as revealed in HISTORY, literature and art (the 'HUMANITIES').

(2) Subsequently the use of the term has been widened to signify theories or doctrines, however varied their conclusions, which take human experience as the starting point for man's knowledge of himself and the work of God and Nature. Thus the critical, rational methods of scientific inquiry, which Newton (1642–1727) had applied so successfully to the natural order and which the *philosophes* of the Enlightenment sought to extend to the systematic study of man and society, produced a *secular humanism*, directed from the time of Voltaire (1694–1778) and Hume (1711–76) against the dogmatic claims of orthodox CHRISTIANITY. This was powerfully reinforced by the advancement of science at the expense of revealed RELIGION in the 19th century, and the growing SECULARIZATION of Western society. See AGNOSTICISM, a term invented by T. H. Huxley (1825–95), the champion of Darwin's views on EVOLUTION. See also POSITIVISM and SCIENTISM as expressions of the belief, frequently known as *scientific humanism*, that the SCIENTIFIC METHOD is the sole source of knowledge and that the NATURAL SCIENCES and human sciences alone can (and, in time, will) provide a comprehensive, rational explanation of the universe and human life, replacing the incomplete and misleading earlier accounts offered by MYTH and RELIGION.

(3) Human experience, however, is varied; William James, for example, wrote a classic study of the *Varieties of Religious Experience* (1902). In the 20th century, which no longer shares the robust confidence of the 19th in the identification of science and progress, there has been a reaction against the claim (sometimes made by both secularists and their FUNDAMENTALIST opponents) that the term humanism can be identified with the secular, scientific version of it – any more than religion can be monopolized by fundamentalism.

According to this view, humanism is to be considered as a broad tendency, a dimension of thought and belief within which are found very different ideas, held together not by a unified structure but by certain shared assumptions. The two most important of these are: (i) The belief that human beings have a potential value in themselves, and that it is respect for this which is the source of all other human values and rights. This value is based upon the possibility, which human beings possess to a unique extent, of creating and communicating (language, human relations, the arts, science, institutions) – latent powers which, once liberated (e.g. by education), enable men and women to exercise a degree of freedom of choice and action in shaping their lives. (ii) The rejection of any system of thought which (a) despairs of man and denies any meaning to human life (see NIHILISM) or (b) treats him as a depraved, worthless creature who can only be saved by divine grace (see CALVINISM) or (c) is DETERMINIST or REDUCTIONIST in its view of human CONSCIOUSNESS (see MATERIALISM; BEHAVIOURISM) or (d) regards men and women as having no value as anything more than expendable raw material for use or exploitation by political or economic systems (see TOTALITARIANISM; ALIENATION).

See also LIBERALISM (1) and (2); EXISTENTIALISM; PROCESS THEOLOGY; NEO-MARXISM; POST-MODERNISM; NEW HUMANISM. For further reading: A. Bullock, *The Humanist Tradition in the West* (1985).

A.L.C.B.

humanism, evolutionary, see EVOLUTIONARY HUMANISM.

humanistic geography. A perspective which insists that the world's human GEOGRAPHY can only be properly understood by placing the human being explicitly at the centre of geographical inquiry. Whereas the tendency of geography as SPATIAL SCIENCE during the 1960s was to reduce people to little more than automata rushing around geometric landscapes in response to iron laws of spatial behaviour, in recent years the inherent BEHAVIOURISM of this tendency has been criticized – and in part replaced – by studies concerned to elucidate the subjectively held emotions, meanings and values through which people strive to interpret and act upon their surrounding PLACES, ENVIRONMENTS and landscapes. In attempting to counter the philosophy of POSITIVISM underlying much spatial science, these humanistic studies have drawn inspiration from philosophies as diverse as PHENOMENOLOGY, EXISTENTIALISM, IDEAL-

ISM and PRAGMATISM, although this has sometimes led to a mismatch between formal philosophical claims and the more immediate objectives of research in progress. Influential and revealing as this perspective has been, however, it has itself been criticized – notably by proponents of a RADICAL GEOGRAPHY – for slipping into a VOLUNTARISM blind to economic, social and political realities that can both constitute and seriously constrain human thoughts and actions. See also HUMANISM and SUBJECTIVISM. For further reading: D. Ley and M. S. Samuels (eds), *Humanistic Geography: Prospects and Problems* (1978). C.P.

humanistic psychology. A recent SCHOOL OF PSYCHOLOGY founded mainly by Abraham Maslow (1908–70). It seeks to increase the relevance of PSYCHOLOGY to the lives of individual people, regarded from an existential viewpoint (see EXISTENTIALISM). It is critical of researches that seem trivial, ahuman and even dehumanizing because of a preoccupation with STATISTICS, elegant experimentation, white rats, COMPUTERS, and other 'side-issues' of human psychology proper. For further reading: C. S. Hall and G. Lindzey, *Theories of Personality* (1978). I.M.L.H.

humanities. A term used in Europe and the USA to distinguish literature, languages, PHILOSOPHY, HISTORY, art, THEOLOGY and music from the SOCIAL SCIENCES and the NATURAL SCIENCES. The term originated in Renaissance times, when *litterae humaniores* (a name still in use at Oxford) signified the more humane 'letters' of the revived Latin and Greek authors in contrast to the theological 'letters' of the medieval schoolmen. W.A.C.S.

Hundred Flowers. Campaign of intellectual liberalization launched by Mao Zedong in communist China in 1956 (see MAOISM). Based on the ancient adage 'let a hundred flowers bloom and a thousand schools of thought contend', Mao tried to win the support of the INTELLECTUALS by encouraging their comments and criticisms. He firmly believed that the Party would not be attacked, but the campaign soon got out of hand as existing policies and personalities were bitterly criticized. The Party's response was to brand all those who had expressed criticism as 'rightists', and launch an anti-rightist RECTIFICATION campaign. The term Hundred Flowers was supposed to be a by-word for liberalization, but it became tainted by (and was often used to refer to) the anti-rightist movement that it spurred, although the original meaning of the term re-emerged in the post-Mao era. For further reading: R. McFarquhar (ed.), *The Hundred Flowers* (1960). D.C.W.; S.B.

Hungary 1956. Term referring to the crisis of October 1956 when troops of the former USSR invaded Hungary to suppress a popular uprising. Soviet forces in the country fired on demonstrations in Budapest which followed the overthrow of the STALINIST government in Poland. Revolutionary Councils were set up throughout Hungary and a national government was established under Imre Nagy, a moderate COMMUNIST. It announced radical political reforms, such as the introduction of a multiparty system and the withdrawal of Hungary from the Warsaw Pact, demanding its recognition as a neutral country. The Soviet Union responded by sending troops, who had withdrawn to the borders during the first phase of the fighting, back into the country in greater numbers. After serious fighting during which about 25,000 were killed, the revolutionary forces were defeated. Subsequently Nagy and others were tried in secret and then executed. This episode led to a significant weakening of support for the Soviet Union outside Russia, particularly among the LEFT in western Europe. For further reading: M. Molnár, *Budapest 1956: A History of the Hungarian Revolution* (1971). D.C.W.; D.PR.

hunter-gatherers. Foraging societies which are characterized by extreme technological simplicity, mobility and a distinctive egalitarian structure (see EGALITARIANISM). There is usually considerable flexibility in membership with individuals moving at will between different hunter-gatherer groups. The recognition of individuality is combined, however, with a high degree of cooperation between members within a particular group. The mobility and adaptability of hunter-gatherers are preserved through a lack of emphasis upon accumulation. Production is geared largely to immediate consumption. For further reading: E.

Leacock and R. Lee (eds), *Politics and History in Band Societies* (1982). A.G.

hybridization.

(1) In the BIOLOGY of whole organisms, it is the breeding together of two SPECIES. Different species normally do not interbreed, but they can in some cases be forced to under unnatural conditions. The mule, for example, is the hybrid of a he-ass and a mare; mules are sterile, which suggests why NATURAL SELECTION prevents hybridization in nature. Hybridization is important in BOTANY, because many plant species have originated in the hybridization by accident of two other species. Many horticultural and agricultural species have been artificially produced by the hybridization of species.

(2) In MOLECULAR BIOLOGY, it is the joining together of separate MOLECULES of DNA (or of RNA and DNA: see NUCLEIC ACID). DNA molecules, under appropriate experimental conditions, will join together at a rate proportional to the similarity of sequence of the two molecules. Hybridized DNA and non-hybridized DNA can be distinguished by *ultracentrifugation* (see SEDIMENTATION). Hybridization can be used to measure how similar different DNA molecules (e.g., from different species) are. It can also be used to 'map' GENES. If the DNA (or RNA) of a particular gene has been isolated, it can be put with the whole GENOME of the organism and the isolated gene will then hybridize at that place in the genome where the gene is normally located. Such hybridization, usually with RNA molecules, is the first step in isolating a gene for CLONING. M.R.

hydraulic civilizations. Term coined by German-born American historian Karl Wittfogel to refer to urban or rural SETTLEMENTS based on the establishment of large productive waterworks for irrigation, flood control and hydro-electric power. The type of economy on which they rely is termed by Wittfogel *hydraulic agriculture* to distinguish it from traditional rainfall farming. For further reading: K. Wittfogel, *Oriental Despotism* (1957). M.L.

hydrobiology, see under LIMNOLOGY.

hydrogen bond. A relatively weak chemical bond between a hydrogen ATOM and an electronegative atom (see ELECTRONEGATIVITY), most often oxygen or nitrogen. Hydrogen bonds are some ten times weaker than typical covalent bonds (see BOND, CHEMICAL), but nevertheless they are strong enough to perform some extremely important structural roles in chemistry. For example, hydrogen bonds bind together water molecules in ice, they hold together the two strands of the DOUBLE HELIX in DNA (see NUCLEIC ACID), and they help to determine the shapes of protein molecules (see PROTEIN; MOLECULE). P.C.B.

hydrologic cycle, see under BIOGEOCHEMICAL CYCLES.

hydrolysis, see under ENZYMES.

hydroponics. The cultivation of plants without soil, using instead water containing a balanced mixture of salts and a supporting substratum such as sand or plastic granules. Very heavy crops can be produced in a small area, and the world's food production, needed to feed the growing population, might be substantially increased by the wider use of this technique. At present high costs make the method unsuitable except for luxury products such as cut flowers. K.M.

hydrosphere. The three major realms of the earth are the LITHOSPHERE, the hydrosphere and the atmosphere, respectively solid, liquid and gaseous. The hydrosphere includes all the surface waters of the earth, liquid or solid, in the oceans, and on the continents, together with soil and ground water. J.L.M.L.

hydrothermal vent. A fissure in the floor of the axial zone of an OCEANIC RIDGE from which mineral-laden fluids emerge. Because the axial valleys of oceanic ridges are sites at which molten rock is being forced up from the earth's interior, they are very hot and highly fractured. Seawater enters the fractures, circulates within the molten rock, becomes heated (sometimes above 350°C), dissolves minerals from the rock, and finally emerges from fissures which thus become known as hydrothermal (i.e. hot-water) vents. When the hot water pours out into the cold, the mixing produces dense black or white plumes ('black smokers' or 'white smokers') depending upon the precise mineral content; and metals such as manganese, zinc, cobalt, copper, iron, lead and silver are deposited, often as sulphides or oxides. The minerals form crusts on the surrounding rocks and, if present in sufficient profusion, build columns ('chimneys') up to 30 metres high. The existence of hydrothermal vents, discovered only during the 1970s, has profoundly altered understanding of the ocean waters. Previously it had been thought that all the minerals dissolved in the oceans had been washed down from the land by rivers. But it is now clear that the entire volume of the oceans circulates through the crust at ridge axes once every 10 million years and thus acquires dissolved minerals in a major way not before envisaged. The first scientists to visit hydrothermal vents (in submersibles) also discovered life forms not before envisaged. Where they never expected to find life at all, they came across previously unknown species of tube worms, clams and bacteria that evidently thrive on sulphides. P.J.S.

hyperbolic geometry, see under GEOMETRY.

hypergamy, see under DOWRY.

hypergraphy, see under LETTRISM.

hyperinflation, see under INFLATION.

hyper-reality. A concept from the vocabulary of post-modern thought (see POST-MODERNISM). Owing especially to the electronic media, it is argued, our world has become so saturated with images and symbols that a new 'electronic reality' has been created, whose effect is to obliterate any sense of an objective reality lying behind the images and symbols. In this 'simulated' world, images *become* objects, rather than reflecting or representing them; reality becomes hyper-reality. In hyper-reality it is no longer possible to distinguish the imaginary from the real, the sign from its referent (see SIGNIFIER/SIGNIFIED), the true from the false. It is a world of *simulacra* or images, but images or copies 'of which the originals have been lost', as described by the French theorist Jean Baudrillard. The MODELS of our future, according to this view, are to be found in such examples of Americana as Disneyland and the Hearst Castle in California, or cities such as Las Vegas and Los Angeles: fantasy worlds, says Umberto Eco, that are hyper-real, 'more real than reality'. K.K.

hypersonic, see under MACH NUMBER.

hypertext. In COMPUTING, hypertext is multilayered text displayed on a computer screen, with links to take the reader from one level to another. In its most basic form, hypertext is the computerized equivalent of an index that points to particular references. In hypertext, a user can click an index entry and a computer automatically displays the reference. A slightly more sophisticated use makes definitions available at an instant. A sentence might say, 'Charles Dickens loved the word locofoco, and made it a prominent part of his portrait of America.' Readers familiar with the locofocos can read on without pause. Others can use a hypertext link to check its meaning. Sometimes this technique is called 'hypermedia', since the same procedure is used to call up digital images or sounds instead of words.

Ted Nelson was the first to use the word: in 1965, he defined hypertext as 'non-sequential writing', with the idea that readers could make their own ways through texts by the process of branching. Nelson railed against the fact that computers were used to 'simulate paper in stupefying detail' via word-processing programs: 'paper is a crutch, an old-fashioned idea that is holding us back', he wrote.

Very large hypertext documents can encourage random jumping from entry to entry, giving the users a sensation similar to changing television channels with a remote control. The WORLD WIDE WEB is, essentially, one large piece of hypertext in which every page is linked, eventually, to every other page. The result of this jumping can be either a quick and efficient means of discovering what the reader wants to know, or an infinite 'channel surfing' in which nothing serious is accomplished. E.B.B.; J.S.

hypnosis. The induction of a trance-like state by one person in another. The characteristics of the state come under three main heads. (1) The subject suffers a loss of initiative. He will submit to the hypnotist's authority, and he often shows inertia and extreme reluctance to perform complex tasks of which he is perfectly capable. His attention is subject to redistribution, in particular to increased selectivity resulting from the hypnotist's demands. (2) The subject may achieve extremely vivid recall of fantasies and past memories; even to the point when he believes he is actually reliving his past. Because of the hypnotist's inducement of calm and detachment, he is often less persistent in verifying his experience than he would normally be, and he will accept gross and continued distortions of reality. In addition, post-hypnotic amnesia frequently occurs: he 'wakes' completely forgetful of what has taken place in the trance. The hypnotist, however, is usually capable of restoring the subject's memory by means of a simple command or gesture. (3) The subject may lose his inhibitions, and lend himself enthusiastically to the acting out of ROLES unusual for him, an aspect exploited for entertainment.

The most important factor in hypnosis is suggestibility, and degree of suggestibility determines the subject's suitability for hypnosis. It is a poorly understood trait. Post-hypnotic suggestion, the carrying out of the hypnotist's commands after the session, has both the most promising (for PSYCHIATRY) and the most sinister implications because it constitutes control of a person's normal waking perceptions, behaviour and beliefs without his knowledge. This control, however, is not absolute even after the deepest trance, and not even the most suggestible hypnotic subjects will respond to post-hypnotic suggestion that runs very strongly counter to their beliefs and inhibitions. For further reading: E. R. Hilgard, *Hypnotic Susceptibility* (1965). H.L.

hypostatization. The attribution of real existence to abstractions, i.e. to entities which have no definite, or at least no continuous, location in space and time. Platonic REALISM, according to its critics, hypostatizes UNIVERSALS (properties, relations, numbers). HOLISM, likewise, is criticized for hypostatizing social INSTITUTIONS, such as nations or CLASSES, social movements and forces, and large-scale historical events (e.g. ROMANTICISM, INDUSTRIALIZATION, the Renaissance). Resolute nominalists (see NOMINALISM) regard as hypostatization all attributions of substantial existence (see SUBSTANCE) to things other than definitely and continuously located SPATIO-TEMPORAL objects, including human beings. Philosophical ANALYSIS is typically used to unmask hypostatizations. A.Q.

hypothetico-deductive method, see under POPPERIAN; SCIENCE, PHILOSOPHY OF.

hysteresis. The lag of an effect behind its cause in physical systems undergoing cyclic change. For example, an elastic solid will stretch when pulled, but it will frequently not return to quite its original length when the pulling force is reduced back to zero; similar behaviour occurs in the magnetization of ferromagnets (see FERROMAGNETISM). M.V.B.

hysteria, see under NEUROSIS.

I

I Ching, see under ALEATORY.

iatrogenesis. A term popularized in the analysis of modern medicine developed by the social critic Ivan Illich. Taken from Greek roots meaning 'doctor originated', iatrogenesis describes the (allegedly increasing) phenomenon of disease caused by medicine and the medical profession. Illich, a critic of modern medicine (which he condemns for allegedly 'expropriating' the people's health), diagnosed three modes of iatrogenesis. (1) Clinical, the tendency of malpractice and incompetence among surgeons and the pharmaceutical industry to cause disease in individuals. (2) Social, the process by which organized professional medicine has taken charge of the nation's health, more for its own than for the public benefit. (3) Cultural. Here Illich refers to raised expectations about the prolongation of life and health, put about by the medical profession and widely accepted, leading to doctor-induced medical dependence and a consequent inability to face pain and death. Illich argues that, despite all its promises, scientific medicine has done little to promote health. Though the evidence has been much contested, these notions have been influential in the critique of modern medicine. For further reading: I. Illich, *Limits to Medicine* (1976). R.P.

IBRD. International Bank for Reconstruction and Development, the official name for the World Bank (see BRETTON WOODS). C.E.D.

IC (immediate constituent), see under CONSTITUENT ANALYSIS.

ICBM (inter-continental ballistic missiles), see under MISSILES.

iconography. Term used in art history for the study of the meaning of images, a visual HERMENEUTICS. An iconographical school of art historians grew up *c.* 1900 in reaction against the stress, in the art criticism of the later 19th century, on form as opposed to content. Pioneers of the new approach were Émile Mâle and Aby Warburg. Some art historians, notably Erwin Panofsky, distinguish *iconography* from iconology, defining the latter as the study through art of 'the basic attitude' of 'a nation, a period, a class, a religious or philosophical persuasion', i.e. the HISTORY OF MENTALITIES from visual sources. A reaction against the speculations of some iconographers and their emphasis on the content of paintings is now manifesting itself. For further reading: E. Panofsky, *Meaning in the Visual Arts* (1955). P.B.

id. In psychoanalytic theory (see PSYCHOANALYSIS), a FREUDIAN term for the UNCONSCIOUS system of personality that acts to reduce pain and enhance pleasure, by giving free rein to primitive impulses. Its PLEASURE PRINCIPLE is assumed to collide with the REALITY PRINCIPLE of the EGO, and with the censorious demands of the SUPEREGO, thus setting the stage for inner conflict. W.Z.

IDA (International Development Associates), see under BRETTON WOODS.

idea. The smallest unit of thought or MEANING, the elementary constituent of BELIEFS or assertions. In contemporary PHILOSOPHY the word CONCEPT is widely preferred because (1) in traditional EMPIRICISM 'idea' was used both in the sense given above and at the same time to mean the same as 'image', since the empiricists took thought to be a matter of operating with images; (2) Locke and Berkeley also used 'idea' to mean sense-impression or SENSE-DATUM, using it to refer to the items of immediate experience of which images are copies; (3) in the philosophy of Plato, an Idea is a UNIVERSAL, conceived, in the manner of REALISM, as existing substantially in a world of timeless ESSENCES. A.Q.

ideal ego. In contradistinction to the EGO-PSYCHOLOGY school of PSYCHOANALYSIS, which looked for naturalistic explanations of psychic functioning, the French school of analysts sought to define the subject's experience of the world in terms of the variables of PHANTASY, ideal and DESIRE. They were thus led to take seriously the distinction between ideal ego and EGO-IDEAL, first stressed by Nunberg in 1932. Freud had in various ways distinguished these notions between 1914 and 1933: the basic problem is that of separating narcissistic types of IDENTIFICATION from what Lacan would later formulate as SYMBOLIC identification. Thus the ideal ego seeks to model itself on omnipotence; it rejects everything which displeases, and accepts everything that pleases; it represents an IMAGINARY mode of identification that ascribes to the ego heroic qualities and glamorous attributes. However sharply this distinguishes it from the ego-ideal, some authors equate the two notions. B.BU.

ideal types. Term used by Max Weber (1864–1920) to denote entities (including, e.g., types of 'action' society, or INSTITUTION) as constructed 'hypothetically' by an investigator from component elements with a view to making comparisons and to developing theoretical EXPLANATIONS; the components out of which a 'type' is constructed being empirically observable or historically recognized. Thus Weber used ideal types in his studies of types of action, of religion, economy and authority – distinguishing, e.g., between ideal types of *traditional*, *rational-legal* and *charismatic* (see CHARISMA) authority. The word 'ideal' does not carry with it any NORMATIVE load – it relates rather to what Morris Ginsberg (*On the Diversity of Morals*, London, 1956) called 'HEURISTIC constructions . . . not definitions and averages . . .' that emphasize 'certain characteristics of a group of occurrences, and by linking up with others . . .' are 'so combined by us as to form a coherent or unitary whole'. For further reading: W. G. Runciman, *A Critique of Max Weber's Philosophy of Social Science* (1972). S.J.G.

idealism. The philosophical theory that the only things which really exist are minds or mental states or both. (The distinction between the two is rejected by those, like Hume, who take a mind to be no more than a related series of mental states, and also by those, like Berkeley, who hold that a mental state is inconceivable except as part of the history of some mind.) Berkeley's philosophy is perhaps the simplest version of idealism. For him the world consists of the infinite mind of God, the finite minds that he has created, and, dependently on them, the ideas possessed or experienced by these minds. For Berkeley there are no material things that exist independently of minds: common objects are collections of ideas, in finite minds to the extent that they are observed by them, in the mind of God to the extent that they are not.

Berkeley's brand of idealism, misnamed *subjective idealism* by adherents of Hegel's *objective idealism*, is in fact as objective as the latter. It is not a form of SOLIPSISM, for it acknowledges that much exists over and above my mind and its ideas, namely the minds and ideas of other people and of God. Where Hegel's idealism differs from Berkeley's is in holding that there is only one true mind, the absolute, or Spirit, of which finite minds are dependent fragments, not, as in Berkeley, entities created by the infinite mind with a separate existence of their own. Some idealists of Hegelian inspiration (see HEGELIANISM) hold that in this respect Hegel went too far; see PERSONALISM.

A third type of idealism is found in the philosophy of Plato, in which only IDEAS, in his special sense of the term, are objects of knowledge, and therefore they alone truly exist. Of the changing particulars met with in space and time we can have only opinions, and he infers that these have only a secondary brand of existence. A.Q.

ideas, history of, see HISTORY OF IDEAS.

identification.

(1) In PSYCHOANALYSIS, a process in which the subject is transformed, in whole or part, through taking in aspects of the other (see SUBJECTIVITY). Freud sets out three forms of IDENTIFICATION: *oral identification* in which the other is 'incorporated' as a primitive mode of relationship; *regressive identification* whereby identification appears instead of object choice (see NARCISSISM); and *hysterical identification* based on the desire to assume the other's DESIRE. Of most significance, however, is the developmental role given to identification in the OEDIPUS COMPLEX. As the child renounces sexual DESIRE for one parent, so identification with the other takes its place, creating a new internal psychic structure. Identification, in the sense of building up the inner world on the basis of internalized representations of external 'objects', thus becomes a major mechanism of personality formation. In applications of psychoanalysis, the LACAN-

IAN gloss on identification has been influential. This focuses on the means through which the EGO in the MIRROR PHASE is constructed by identification with an external image; hence, what is felt to be a central aspect of the self is actually something 'other'. Lacanians use this idea to claim that identification makes identity, in the sense of self-identity, impossible. S.J.F.

(2) In SOCIAL PSYCHOLOGY, the process of associating oneself closely with other individuals of REFERENCE GROUPS to the extent that one comes to adopt their goals and values and to share vicariously in their experiences. See also PEER GROUP. W.Z.

(3) In ECONOMETRICS, it is often only possible to measure and estimate MODELS of the actual consequences of underlying economic relationships. An econometric model is identified if it is possible to estimate the relationships underlying the model. The conditions permitting identification are complicated. It is usually assumed that the underlying economic relationships can be represented by linear equations. If it is possible to distinguish a linear equation from any linear combination of the remaining linear equations of the model, then the equation is identified and it is possible to estimate its parameters. A linear equation representing an economic relationship is *underidentified*, or not identifiable, when it is not possible to distinguish it from a linear combination of the remaining linear equations. In this case it is impossible to estimate the parameters of this linear equation. *Overidentification* of an equation occurs when all the linear combinations of other equations always contain more explanatory VARIABLES than the original equation. R.ST.; J.P.

identification friend or foe (IFF), see under FRIENDLY FIRE.

identity. Traditionally, a term used to convey the relatively stable and enduring sense that a person has of himself. PSYCHOANALYSIS postulates that the original source of identity is based on BODY IMAGE; subsequently, IDENTIFICATION with parents and others leads to more complex and elaborate experiences of identity in a variety of contexts. Particular attention is given in contemporary theory to GENDER identity (the experience of oneself as masculine or feminine), sexual identity (as homosexual, bisexual, heterosexual), ethnic identity and (social) CLASS identity. Recent sociological and psychological theory has stressed that a person's 'identity' is in fact something multiple and potentially fluid, constructed through experience and linguistically coded. In developing their identities, people draw on culturally available resources in their immediate social networks and in society as a whole. The process of identity-construction is therefore one upon which the contradictions and dispositions of the surrounding socio-cultural environment have a powerful impact. This is one reason why an individual may find it difficult to describe the sources and nature of his various identities. See also SEXUALITY; GENDER; HOMOSEXUALITY. S.J.F.

identity crisis. A crisis that occurs when the integrity of a person's SELF-IMAGE (see also IDENTITY) is threatened, disrupted or destroyed, usually in a conflict of loyalties or aspirations. See DEVELOPMENTAL PSYCHOLOGY. For further reading: E. H. Erikson, *Childhood and Society* (1951). H.L.

identity politics. An orientation to SOCIAL THEORY and political practice that emerged in response to the declining ability of democratic nation-states to represent adequately the interests of large segments of their constituencies. It is organized around categories not officially recognized in political DISCOURSE, but which contradict the universalistic pretensions of the state's purview. When RACE and GENDER appear as the main organizing principles, identity politics is readily seen as picking up the pieces of the failed SOCIALIST project. Yet religious FUNDAMENTALISM has been an equally important source of identity politics in Iran, India and the USA. In all these cases, the identities in question are social constructions based on mythical portrayals of a collective past attached to symbols of ongoing subordination in the larger society. Advocates differ over whether these constructions should be regarded purely as statements of resistance to the status quo or expressions of essential characteristics possessed by the subaltern groups. Generally speaking, academics prefer the former route, activists the latter. Debate on this point is especially heated among those most susceptible to the charge of possessing 'merely constructed' identities: afrocentrists (see AFROCENTRICITY) and queers (see HOMOSEXUALITY). However, the choice is increasingly blurred by the spread of computer-based information and communicaton technologies, which, so to speak, enable the oppressed to appropriate the tools of the oppressors in the cause of self-representation. Two frequently cited examples in this vein are the success of Christian evangelism on American television and the Mexican Zapatista movement's use of the INTERNET to project a sympathetic image of its activities on the world stage. One would be hard pressed to say what was 'natural' and 'artificial' in the construction of their identities. For further reading: M. Castells, *The Power of Identity* (1997). S.F.

identity theory. The view that the apparently private (see PRIVACY) mental states that each person is conscious of are literally identical with certain states of the brain and nervous system that are accessible in principle to public, scientific observation. The identity in question is held to be *contingent* (see CONTINGENCY) or *empirical*, as is that of a visible flash of lightning and an electrical discharge at the same place and time, and not a matter of logical necessity, i.e. of the MEANING of the terms used to report observations of the two kinds in question. If true, it provides a more satisfactory account of the mind and conscious mental life from the point of view of MATERIALISM, since it neither denies self-consciousness nor asserts an entirely implausible synonymy of mental and neural terms. For further reading: D. M. Armstrong, *A Materialist Theory of the Mind*, vol. 1 (1968). A.Q.

Ideological State Apparatus, see under ALTHUSSERIANISM.

ideology. A word coined by the French philosopher Destutt de Tracy (*Éléments d'idéologie*, 1801–05) to denote the 'science of ideas' which would reveal to men the source of their biases and prejudices. De Tracy believed only in trusting sense impressions and was thus in sympathy with the impulses of English EMPIRICISM. After a period of disuse the word was revived with the publication in 1927 of Marx's previously unpublished *The German Ideology*, and in 1929 (translated 1936) of Karl Mannheim's *Ideology and Utopia*, which brought the sociology of knowledge (see KNOWLEDGE, SOCIOLOGY OF) into contemporary concerns.

The word has been variously used to characterize IDEAS, ideals, BELIEFS, passions, values, WELTANSCHAUUNGEN, RELIGIONS, political philosophies, and moral justifications.

It may be employed, as Marx employed it in *The German Ideology*, to deride the PROPOSITION that ideas are autonomous or the belief in the power of ideas to shape or determine reality; or to argue that all ideas are socially determined. Ideologies may be seen as justifications which mask some specific set of interests. Or – a widely held viewpoint – they may be regarded as 'social formulas', as belief systems which can be used to mobilize people for actions; it is in this sense that the COMMUNIST nations talk of 'ideological combat' or 'ideological competition'.

Within contemporary SOCIOLOGY, Mannheim identifies ideologies as different 'styles of thought' and distinguishes betwcen 'particular' ideologies (the self-interests of specific groups, such as the 'ideology of a small businessman') and 'total' ideologies (*Weltanschauungen* or complete commitments to a way of life). In the 1950s and 1960s a group of sociologists, notably Raymond Aron, Edward Shils, Daniel Bell and S. M. Lipset, applied this concept of ideology as a 'secular religion' to the judgement of an 'end of ideology', or the decline of apocalyptic beliefs in the Western industrial societies.

American sociologist Talcott Parsons (1902–79) defined ideology as an interpretative scheme used by social groups to make the world more intelligible to themselves. Both the MARXISTS and the central sociological tradition see ideology as a 'distortion' of reality, the Marxist contrasting ideology with 'true consciousness', the sociologist with SOCIAL SCIENCE. A later group of writers, notably the anthropologist Clifford Geertz (1923–), see ideology in more neutral terms as one kind of SYMBOL system among other cultural symbol systems such as the religious, the aesthetic, or the scientific. For further reading: D. McClellan, *Ideology* (1986). D.B.

idiographic and **nomothetic.** Adjectives

applied to contrasted types of study: *idiographic* to the study of particular cases (e.g. persons, social groups, works of art), nomothetic to the search for general laws or theories which will cover whole classes of cases. Thus HISTORY and GEOGRAPHY, in so far as they are concerned with the study of particular events, persons and PLACES, are idiographic subjects, whereas some economists would claim that, since they formulate ECONOMIC LAWS, ECONOMICS is a nomothetic science. The word *idiographic* is not to be confused with *ideographic*, which is the adjective formed from *ideogram*. A.S.

idiolect. In LINGUISTICS, the speech habits constituting the language system of an individual. D.C.

IFF (identification friend or foe), see under FRIENDLY FIRE.

illocutionary. In LINGUISTICS, used in the theory of SPEECH ACTS to refer to an act which is performed by the speaker once an utterance has been produced. Examples of *illocutionary* acts include promising, commanding, requesting, baptizing, etc. The term is contrasted with *locutionary* acts (the act of 'saying') and *perlocutionary* acts (where the act is defined by reference to the effect it has on the hearer). D.C.

ILO, see INTERNATIONAL LABOUR ORGANIZATION.

imaginary. Lacan's term (see LACANIAN), like all his other contributions to psychoanalytic theory, is subject to a continual reformulation throughout his work. Initially, it indicates the subject's relation to an image exterior to him, e.g., the visual image in a mirror, or a counterpart. By assuming such an image of wholeness, the child is able to master, to an extent, his motor functions, but such an IDENTIFICATION has a number of consequences. Firstly, the register of aggressiveness is set into motion, since if the child identifies with his counterpart, the introduction of some object will produce a situation of rivalry. Likewise, the assumption of an exterior form will alienate the child – he will always be somewhere else. It is this structure which constitutes the EGO for Lacan, and gives the matrix of images of wholeness and completeness which, we could say, characterize traditional geometry. In 1955, Lacan extended this theorization of the imaginary to include the idea of signification, thus demonstrating that the imaginary is at play in language, and not simply in the specular register. We could point out a continuity in the fact that both the specular image and the category of signification are, strictly speaking, lures, to the extent that they trap the subject in an illusory ideal of completeness: for the former the completeness of the image, for the latter, the completeness of communication. For further reading: B. Benvenuto and R. Kennedy, *The Works of Jacques Lacan* (1986). D.L.

imaginary museum (*musée imaginaire*). Also translated as 'museum without walls', a phrase coined by André Malraux in the first volume of his *La Psychologie de l'Art* (1947) to convey the vast and increasing repertoire of more or less faithful photographic reproductions which now makes it possible to discuss works of art without having been to the actual museums containing them. The implications of this were pointed out much earlier by W. Martin Conway in *The Domain of Art* (1901). J.W.

imaginary number, see under COMPLEX NUMBERS.

imagineering. Term first coined by Walt Disney to define the skills needed to design Disneyland (1955). Disney defined imagineering as the collaboration of designers, engineers, artists, writers, architects, electronic and computer specialists, among others, in the service of making his celluloid creations come alive as a physical 'theme park'. 'Disneyland' established a direct link between television (*The Wonderful World of Disney*) and architecture.

In fact imagineers, as a multidisciplinary team honed to service a particular corporate identity (now including composers, special effects teams, event managers, public relations teams, project managers, etc.), challenge the traditional lofty autonomy of independent professional institutions in the management of the built environment (see also DESIGN & BUILD; THEMED ENVIRONMENT; URBAN VILLAGE; CYBERSPACE). For further reading: M. Elliot, *Walt Disney, Hollywood's Dark Prince* (1994). P.J.D.

Imagism. A brief, central episode in the development of English-language poetry that represented the latter's clearest point of transition into MODERNISM. As a movement it dates from 1912, when Ezra Pound collaborated with F. S. Flint on a manifesto and a list of poetic prescriptions printed in POETRY (CHICAGO) and reprinted in the English *New Freewoman* (later the EGOIST). In 1914 came the first Imagist anthology, *Des Imagistes*, containing H.D. (Hilda Doolittle), Richard Aldington, William Carlos Williams, Ford Madox Ford, James Joyce, and Amy Lowell, who was to take over the anthology side of the movement. It was Pound who enunciated the three primary principles ('direct treatment of the "thing", whether subjective or objective . . . to use absolutely no word that did not contribute to the presentation . . . as regarding rhythm, to compose in the sequence of the musical phrase') and defined the idea of the image as 'a verbal concentration generating energy'. Many of these principles were derivations, especially from the activities of a poetic group centred on T. E. Hulme which met at the Eiffel Tower restaurant, London, around 1909. There was also a derivation from SYMBOLISM, though Imagism is distinguished by its concentration on the hard, verbally created image rather than the translucent symbol. Much subsequent poetry in England, and even more in the USA, was influenced by Imagist lore and practice (e.g. Williams, Stevens). Imagism was not merely an aesthetic, but a campaign in the politics of poetry. It transformed an entire climate and, though its concentration was on the short poem, Eliot's *Waste Land*, Pound's *Cantos*, Williams's *Paterson*, and much other modern poetry is inconceivable without it. Pound moved on from Imagism to VORTICISM, which emphasized a harder, more kinetic view of the image; Amy Lowell took over the popularization of a rather Impressionist form of Imagism in the USA, where it was long especially influential. For further reading: S. K. Coffman, *Imagism* (1951). M.S.BR.

imago. In psychoanalytic theory (see PSYCHOANALYSIS), an idealized or fantasized figure from childhood, often a parent, whose standards the individual incorporates and uses as a model for his own behaviour in later life. W.Z.

IMF (International Monetary Fund), see under BRETTON WOODS.

immanence, see under TRANSCENDENCE.

immediate constituent, see under CONSTITUENT ANALYSIS.

immersion course. A system tried successfully in California and Canada, where English-, Spanish- or French-speaking pupils are 'immersed' in a language other than their mother tongue. In California, English-speaking children would attend lessons given entirely in Spanish and gradually become bilingual. Spanish children would attend lessons totally in English with the same results. J.I.

immigrant. An individual who moves from his homeland to a new country. In a narrow sense the term refers to an individual who migrates in search of work, usually from a rural background to an urban context. The move is voluntary, unlike that of the *refugee*, for whom movement is forced. 'Immigrant' or 'guest worker' indicate the status of the individual in the host country and are used to distinguish him from the indigenous population. These terms imply temporary residence. 'Immigrant' has increasingly developed a pejorative meaning, that is, it identifies someone as an 'outsider', as 'not belonging' or as having only limited rights (see BLACK; INTEGRATION). For further reading: D. Levison and M. Ember (eds), *American Immigrant Cultures* (1997). A.G.

immoveable property, see under DESCENT.

immunity.

(1) In its original and narrower sense, a state of resistance or refractoriness to infection by micro-organisms that might otherwise cause infectious illness. Immunity in this sense can be acquired either 'actively' by direct exposure of the subject to an infectious organism, or 'passively' by the infusion of body fluids containing the protective substances or other agents responsible for the immune state – e.g. those of newborn mammals and chicks, passively acquired from the mother via the placenta or the yolk as the case may be.

(2) In the wider sense now universally adopted, any state of resistance or refractori-

ness caused by an adaptive reaction of the body to invasion by foreign substances including pollen grains, foreign organic matter, and grafts from different members of the same SPECIES. Examples include: allergy towards pollen grains or fur; the rejection of a foreign graft; dermatitis excited by industrial chemicals; anaphylactic shock (see ANAPHYLAXIS); hypersensitivity to drugs such as penicillin. Haemolytic disease of the newborn is an immunological disease caused by accidental leakage of *rhesus positive* (see below) blood from an unborn child into a *rhesus negative* mother.

Substances that excite immunological reactions and thus lead to states of immunity of one sort or another are called *antigens*. The chief offending antigen in haemolytic disease of the newborn is antigen *D* of the rhesus series. The rhesus antigens owe their name to the fact that they were first discovered by injecting the blood of rhesus monkeys into rabbits, a process leading to the formation of antibodies which will react upon the red blood corpuscles of approximately 85 per cent of human beings.

Immunity reactions are put into effect by, or mediated through, (a) *antibodies*, or (b) *Lymphocytes*. (a) Antibodies are PROTEIN constituents of the blood, are formed in response to an antigenic stimulus, and have the power to agglutinate, precipitate, disrupt or otherwise destroy or sequester the offending antigen or the vehicle that carries the antigen, often a living CELL. (b) Lymphocytes are a species of white blood corpuscle, and it is the action of sensitized lymphocytes that brings about the rejection of foreign grafts and the reactions that manifest themselves as bacterial allergies and drug allergies; see also CELL BIOLOGY.

An important and almost a defining characteristic of immunity reactions is their specificity, i.e. the very exact one-to-one matching of antigen and antibody or antigen and particular immunological response. Thus the immunological reaction excited by antigen *A* is visited upon *A* alone, and has no effect at all upon antigens *B*, *C* and *D*.
P.M.

immunoassay. A method of measuring the quantity of a substance, using an antibody against the substance to capture it. Immunoassays are frequently used to measure the quantity of a hormone (see ENDOCRINOLOGY) in the blood and are the basis of many pregnancy tests that rely on measurements of hormones in the urine. P.N.

immunotoxin. A combination of an antibody and a toxin, of potential use in CANCER therapy. The toxin kills CELLS but indiscriminately; the antibody is supposed to recognize MOLECULES that are concentrated on, or even unique to, the cancer cells. Therefore the antibody part of an immunotoxin should ensure that the toxin part is delivered largely, or only, to cancer cells. Immunotoxins have also found a use in the removal from bone marrow of the cells that are most prone to cause rejection of the transplant (see SURGERY). P.N.

imperativism, see under EMOTIVISM.

imperfect competition. The state of affairs in which the conditions required for PERFECT COMPETITION are not met and, in particular, when firms (see FIRM, THEORIES OF) cannot sell as much as they wish at the market price. COMPETITION is in this technical sense generally imperfect but may be intensive and effective nevertheless. G.B.R.

imperial presidency. A term applied to the US presidency in the early 1970s by commentators who believed that the powers of the office had expanded so much, and the standards of their use had fallen so far, that the nation's constitutional system was threatened. Most distinctively, Arthur Schlesinger Jr blamed the presidential abuse of war-making and foreign policy powers, which bred a climate of secrecy, a tolerance of illegality, and a failure to distinguish national and personal interests, all of which spilled over into domestic politics. Other commentators emphasized the growth of the modern state since the NEW DEAL of the 1930s, and the rise of the vast national security apparatus of the COLD WAR, both headed by the President as chief executive.

Reactions to the VIETNAM war and to the 'imperial' excesses of the Nixon presidency (1968–74) included attempts to reassert Congressional authority. Since then the prefix 'imperial' has been applied, with even less rigour or justification, to that branch and to the judiciary. Certainly the contemporary presidency is better characterized by stressing the numerous constraints which surround it than by emphasizing its powers, which can seldom be effectively exercised without the co-operation of other institutions and the careful construction of often fragile coalitions, under the eye of a press which no longer affords the office such great deference. S.R.

imperialism.

(1) In general, the extension of the power of a STATE through the acquisition, usually by conquest, of other TERRITORIES; the subjugation of their inhabitants to an alien rule imposed on them by force, and their economic and financial exploitation by the imperial power. Imperialism in this general sense of 'empire' is as old as history.

(2) More specifically, as a development from the older term 'empire', the word 'imperialism' was adopted in England in the 1890s by the advocates of a major effort (led by Joseph Chamberlain) to develop and extend the British Empire in opposition to the policy of concentrating on home development, the supporters of which the imperialists contemptuously dismissed as 'Little Englanders'. The word was rapidly taken into other languages to describe the contest between rival European powers to secure colonies and spheres of influence in Africa and elsewhere, a contest which dominated international politics from the 1880s to 1914 and caused this period to be named the Age of Imperialism. Both British and continental imperialists justified their policies by claiming that they were extending the benefits of 'civilization', based upon the racial, material and cultural superiority of the white RACES, to the inferior peoples of backward lands (see RACISM; SOCIAL DARWINISM). After World War I their ideas were incorporated into the IDEOLOGIES of FASCISM and NAZISM.

The first systematic critique of modern imperialism was provided by the English radical J. A. Hobson, whose *Imperialism* (1902) gave it a primarily economic interpretation. Taken up and developed by Lenin in *Imperialism as the Highest Stage of Capitalism* (1915), this became the *economic theory of imperialism*. According to Lenin the natural tendency of CAPITAL to accumulate leads to falling profits, and this in turn to the growth of MONOPOLIES as a self-protective device to keep the profit rate up. But this is only a palliative, and the monopoly capitalists are driven to search for profits by INVESTMENT abroad, using the control which they have acquired over government to direct foreign policy towards the acquisition of empire with a view to securing markets, raw materials, and above all opportunities for investing their surplus capital. This, however, is the last stage of CAPITALISM, for competing imperialisms lead to WAR, war brings REVOLUTION, and revolution will finally overthrow capitalism and imperialism together. Besides providing an explanation of imperialism, Lenin's theory, it will be noticed, also traced the origin of war, or at least of 'imperialist' wars, to the inexorable workings of the capitalist system.

No one today would question that economic factors played a large part in modern imperialism; but critics of the Marxist-Leninist theory (see MARXISM-LENINISM) have not found it difficult to show that it provides an oversimplified account even of the economic facts, and that it ignores a whole range of non-economic motives – NATIONALISM, racism, the pursuit of national power – which, as in the case of Fascism and Nazism, combine with but are not reducible to the pursuit of economic advantage. The economic interpretation of imperialism, however, as expounded by Lenin, remains one of the most important elements in contemporary MARXIST theory, with the advantage, for propaganda purposes, that by definition only non-COMMUNIST states can be accused of imperialism and communists can always claim to be on the side of anti-imperialist and anti-colonial movements (for which see below, final paragraph).

Colonialism is a form of imperialism based on maintaining a sharp and fundamental distinction (expressed often in law as well as in fact) between the ruling nation and the subordinate (colonial) populations. Such an arrangement arises most naturally in consequence of the conquest of a remote territory with a population of a conspicuously different physique and CULTURE. These, however, are not necessary conditions – witness Nazi colonialism in eastern Europe, bolstered by a pseudo-racialism based on fictitious racial differences. Colonialism always entails unequal rights. The British and the Dutch empires of the last century provide the purest examples: LIBERALISM, DEMOCRACY and the attrition of

CLASS barriers in the metropolitan country, bureaucratic (see BUREAUCRACY) AUTHORITARIANISM and the colour bar in the colonies. Another fundamental feature of colonialism has been the policy of perpetuating the economic differentiation between the colonies and the METROPOLIS, with the former supplying the raw materials while the latter remains the chief source of manufactures.

Decolonization is the process whereby a metropolitan country gives up its authority over its dependent territories and grants them the status of sovereign states. It can be seen most clearly in the development following World War II of the former British Empire into the COMMONWEALTH of independent states, or the French Empire into the Communauté Française. This represented a triumph for the nationalist movements which had agitated for independence and took over power when the colonial powers withdrew. In many cases, however, the achievement of national SOVEREIGNTY and admission to the UN have been followed by controversy over whether decolonization has led to real independence or only to *neo-colonialism*. This term describes a formal juridical independence accompanied by a *de facto* domination and exploitation by foreign nationals, together with the retention of many features of the traditional colonial situation, e.g. narrow economic specialization, cultural and educational inferiority.

Neo-imperialism, of which neo-colonialism is a form, describes a situation in which an independent country suffers from and resents intervention and control by a foreign government and its nationals, but not necessarily as the result of a previous colonial relationship. In some parts of the world (e.g. Latin America) the synonymous term *economic imperialism* (or, more specifically, *dollar imperialism*) is often preferred. The use of such terms is, of course, coloured by the user's political views: what is 'economic imperialism' to one man is 'aid' to another.

Cultural imperialism may be defined as the use of political and economic power to exalt and spread the values and habits of a foreign culture at the expense of a native culture. A familiar example from an earlier period is the export of American films. Although cultural imperialism may be pursued for its own sake it frequently operates as an auxiliary of economic imperialism – as when American films create a demand for American products.

Anti-colonialism and *anti-imperialism* appear to be self-explanatory. The former is rightly used to describe any movement (e.g. the various African national movements) aimed at ending the subordination of a people to colonial rule. The latter means, more broadly, opposition to any form of imperialism anywhere. Anti-imperialism, however, like anti-Fascism, is a term frequently twisted for propaganda purposes and selectively applied. If it was used with any regard for objectivity or logical consistency, opposition to the Soviet control of eastern Europe or the Chinese conquest of Tibet or the Nigerian subjugation of Biafra would be called anti-imperialist. In current usage, however, the term is commonly restricted to groups hostile to the USA or the countries of western Europe. (See also POST-COLONIALISM.) For further reading: F. Cooper and A. Stoler (eds), *Tensions of Empire* (1997). S.A.; A.L.C.B.

implicature. In LINGUISTICS, a term derived from the philosopher H. P. Grice and now used as part of the study of conversational structure. *Conversational implicatures* refer to the implications which can be deduced from the form of an utterance on the basis of our general understanding about the efficiency and acceptability of conversations. For example, in a school classroom, the sentence 'There's some chalk on the floor' spoken by the teacher would imply that someone should pick the chalk up. For further reading: S. Levinson, *Pragmatics* (1983). D.C.

impoverished art, see ARTE POVERA.

Impressionism.

(1) Movement in French painting originating in the 1860s and so called after the first exhibition, in 1874, of a group including Edgar Degas, Claude Monet, Berthe Morisot, Auguste Renoir, Camille Pissarro, Alfred Sisley, Paul Cézanne, and Armand Guillaumin. One of Monet's pictures there, *Impression – soleil levant* (now in the Musée Marmottan, Paris), suggested the name to the critics, though Léon Lagrange ten years earlier had already heard 'Impression roar-

ing at the gates, with Realism joining in the chorus'. Anticipated in the work of Boudin, Chintreuil, Corot and Turner, the movement was characterized above all by its concern with fleeting effects of light and motion, its disregard of outlines and distaste for sombre colours, its original angles of vision, and its general aura of delicate yet mundane gaiety. In its subject-matter and attitude it was at the same time a product of the REALISM of Courbet and Manet and of the open-air landscape of the Barbizon school; Degas actually conceived of its exhibitions, which continued for 12 years, as a 'realist Salon'.

Virtually every major development in 20th-century art is traceable to the Impressionists. Thus it was at their 1880 exhibition that Gauguin began showing, in his pre-SYNTHETIST vein, while the eighth and last exhibition in 1886 saw the début of the NEO-IMPRESSIONIST Georges Seurat. Through van Gogh the movement influenced EXPRESSIONISM, through Cézanne the CUBISTS. Meanwhile Monet, whose late works were to be important for ABSTRACT EXPRESSIONISM in the 1950s, continued till his death in 1926 as the prototypical Impressionist, while the movement began to spread across the globe, affecting e.g. the NEW ENGLISH ART CLUB and the Berlin SEZESSION, captivating wealthier collectors everywhere, and selling in millions of colour reproductions. For further reading: P. Pool, *Impressionism* (1967). J.W.

(2) In music, by analogy, a style of composition in which the composer evokes a scene in a manner which is undramatic; hence, although there is nearly always a title, the music is descriptive rather than programmatic (see PROGRAMME MUSIC). Its greatest exponent was Debussy, whose *Prélude à l'après-midi d'un faune* (1892) first dramatically established the style. It is marked by a tendency to use sound as colour, to employ shapes of a deliberately nebulous character, to avoid clear-cut rhythm or harmony, and to eschew the dramatic dynamism shown by, e.g., Beethoven. Debussy, Ravel, Delius, Bax, Albéniz and Respighi are typical examples. The SYMBOLIST poets Verlaine, Baudelaire and especially Mallarmé were as potent an influence as the Impressionist painters, and that influence has extended in recent years to Boulez, making him seem in certain ways a follower of Debussy, although his music is more consciously directed by the intellect than by emotion. A.H.

(3) In literature, Impressionism means, in the most general sense, subjectivism: the work attempts to convey the author's own impression (mood, state of mind) rather than an objective description. STREAM OF CONSCIOUSNESS writing is impressionistic – provided that it avoids the deliberate distortions of Expressionism. M.S.-S.

imprinting. In ETHOLOGY, a learning process which leads to an extremely rapid CONDITIONING, and consequent narrowing-down of the situation that elicits a response. The best-known and extreme examples are found in goslings and ducklings, which are normally led by the parents from the nest to the feeding-grounds, almost immediately after hatching and drying. When hatched in an incubator, and shown any moving object, even a matchbox or a large balloon, they will follow this, and will later continue to do so even when offered a choice between this object and their own parents. Although the phenomenon had been reported earlier by Spalding and Heinroth, it was Konrad Lorenz (1903–89) who first emphasized its peculiar nature, and compared it with INDUCTION (as then known) in EMBRYOLOGY. It seems likely that imprinting is an extreme case of conditioning linked by intermediate phenomena to CLASSICAL CONDITIONING. See also ATTACHMENT; CRITICAL PERIOD. For further reading: N. Tinbergen, *The Study of Instinct* (1951). N.T.

improvisation. The art of making music spontaneously without some form of written notation was not used to much extent in Western serious music in the first half of the century, although it plays a fundamental part in JAZZ. More recent developments in 20th-century music have often tended to give the performers greater freedom, sometimes to the extent of improvisation (see ALEATORY; GRAPHIC SCORE; INDETERMINACY). B.CO.

impurity, see under PURITY.

in vitro fertilization, see under INFERTILITY.

incest. Illicit sexual relations among persons

closely related by KINSHIP or MARRIAGE. Each society defines that range of sexually forbidden kinsmen and affines for itself, and societies differ greatly among themselves in the SANCTIONS they apply to offenders. The 'horror of incest' is not in fact universal, although there is probably no society which would tolerate sexual relations between a woman and her son. So great are the variations from society to society that some anthropologists deny the existence of a single universal phenomenon which can be called 'incest'. Incest rules and rules of EXOGAMY are related, not identical. For further reading: J. Renvoize, *Incest: A Family Pattern* (1982). M.F.

incomes policy. A policy which is intended to restrict incomes (i.e. wages, salaries, dividends and rents) in order to reduce INFLATION, particularly through its effects on cost-inflation and inflationary expectations. Many different governments and countries have used incomes policies. After World War II, incomes policies were regarded as necessary because of the declared objective of governments to achieve FULL EMPLOYMENT. This, it was thought, would encourage all forms of labour to bargain for increases in incomes greater than the rate of increase in productivity and, thus, cause inflation. Incomes policies may be mere exhortations or, more commonly, may be backed up by legislation. They are usually accompanied by price controls. The control of wages and prices represents an attempt to interfere with the PRICE MECHANISM and reduces its effectiveness. Restrictions on incomes may result in evasion and, thus, the eventual collapse of incomes policies. J.P.

incommensurability. EMPIRICIST and POSITIVIST views of scientific development have always presupposed that facts in some sense speak for themselves. Theories are derivative from them, and the best theory is that which explains the largest body of facts without ANOMALY. Many modern philosophies of science (see SCIENCE, PHILOSOPHY OF), by contrast, deny any such fundamental disjunction between fact and theory. Facts themselves are recognized only through already existing conceptual and linguistic schemes; they are 'theory-bound'. Appeal to the facts alone, therefore, can never decide which is the better of two rival scientific theories, because each theory makes sense of the facts within its own interpretative framework. This insight lies at the core of the notion of the incompatibility of PARADIGMS, or theories, as advanced in T. S. Kuhn's *The Structure of Scientific Revolutions* (see below). Scientific revolutions occur by the sudden replacement of one theory by another. At that revolutionary moment, it is impossible to appeal to any so-called objective body of facts to adjudicate the claims of rival theories; the theories are INCOMMENSURABLE. Thus, at some level, the theory switch is 'irrational'. Kuhn's holistic view obviously finds support from GESTALT psychology and from studies of visual PERCEPTION, as well as corresponding to the experience of many scientists. For further reading: T. S. Kuhn, *The Structure of Scientific Revolutions* (1970). R.P.

incommensurable. Two theories or sets of beliefs are held to be incommensurable if there is no means of interpreting or understanding one in terms of the other or of comparing them. For example, American Indian theories about how and why rain dances cause rainfall, and meteorological theories about how and why chemical seeding of clouds causes rainfall, are said to be incommensurable. The notion is associated with RELATIVISM. It can take a strong form: e.g., some relativists argue that changes in the meanings of theoretical terms in science entail that early 20th-century theories of atomic structure are incommensurable with theories about the ATOM in the late 20th century. For further reading: P. Feyerabend, *Against Method* (1977). A.C.G.

incorporating (in LINGUISTICS), see under POLYSYNTHETIC.

incorporation. The new industrial WORKING CLASS of the 19th century was widely held to be *in* society but not of it. Incorporation refers to the process over the past century whereby the workers themselves, together with many of their institutions and practices, have been brought into the existing institutional order and made a regular part of its working. Working-class voters, LEFT-wing political parties, TRADE UNIONS and strike activities, at first excluded and often forcibly suppressed, have become legitimate parts of the political and economic system of 20th-century societies. For some sociologists, such as T. H. Marshall and Reinhard Bendix, this represents the achievement of social and political 'citizenship' by the working class, enabling full and effective participation in the life of society. For MARXISTS such as Herbert Marcuse (1898–1979), incorporation rather refers to the loss by the working class of a distinctive radical and 'oppositional' culture, and its accommodation to the values and institutions of BOURGEOIS society. As such, it contributes to the 'deradicalization' of the working class. See also EMBOURGEOISEMENT; DOMINANT IDEOLOGY. For further reading: H. Marcuse, *One-Dimensional Man* (1964). K.K.

incorrigibility, see under DEFEASIBILITY AND INCORRIGIBILITY.

independence (in STATISTICS), see under CORRELATION.

independent assortment, see under MENDEL'S LAWS.

Independent Theatre, see THÉÂTRE LIBRE.

indeterminacy.

(1) In music, the practice of not completely specifying the end results of a composition. Indeterminate music relies on chance (see ALEATORY) or performer interpretation to complete a version of the piece which will thus exist in as many forms as it has performances. This abdication by the composer of some of his control over the final outcome of his music has been championed by John Cage (1912–1992) (see also MOMENT FORM; MOBILE FORM; GRAPHIC SCORE; EXPERIMENTAL MUSIC). For further reading: R. Kostelanetz, *John Cage* (1971). B.CO.

(2) In PHYSICS, see under UNCERTAINTY PRINCIPLE.

indeterminacy principle, see UNCERTAINTY PRINCIPLE.

indeterminism. The opposite of DETERMINISM.

index number. A single measure of the change in a particular characteristic, e.g. price, of a group of entities such as goods. Index numbers measure the change in the characteristic from the base to the current period or from one region to another. The most commonly used indices are for prices and quantities. In measuring, e.g., the change in the prices of a group of goods consumed by a group of consumers in two different years, an index has to allow for the different changes in the prices of the different goods. This could be done by multiplying each price by the quantity consumed of the good – these quantities are called *weights*. These products are summed and the index number is the ratio of the sum for the current period to the sum for the base period. The same quantities are used as weights in both periods, though an important choice has to be made as to whether to use base- or current-period quantities as weights. The index number is usually expressed by multiplying the ratio by 100. Indices of the increase in output, consumption, standard of living, etc. (i.e. quantity indices) can be constructed in a similar manner to price indices, but using prices as weights. An alternative means of constructing a price index is to multiply the relative increase in the price of each good by the good's share in total expenditure and summing. The index number problem is that, as a measure, it is only an approximation, and the closeness of the approximation depends on how different the weights are in the base and current periods. For example, as the relative structures of consumption in the 19th and 20th centuries are very different, the two different sets of weights that could be used to construct an index of the change in prices between the two centuries could give very different estimates of the change. The index number problem has no theoretical solution. For further reading: R. G. D. Allen, *The Theory and Practice of Index Numbers* (1975). J.P.

indicator, see under ECONOMIES OF SCALE.

indifference curves. In ECONOMICS, the term used to denote a collection of different patterns of consumption between which an individual consumer is indifferent. Each indifference curve is associated with a particular level of utility (see UTILITY THEORY). In microeconomics (see ECONOMICS) it is usually assumed that the objective of a consumer is to maximize utility within the constraints of the prices of goods and services and the consumer's income. This can be represented by the consumer attempting to reach, given the budget constraint and prices, the indifference curve with the highest level of utility (see SUBSTITUTION). J.P.

indigenization, see under CONVERGENCE.

indigenous theology. Since the 1960s the determination to study Christian THEOLOGY, and to give training to clergy and laity in styles which are not imported from Europe or the US, has grown. The most flourishing example of what can be achieved is the LIBERATION THEOLOGY of Latin America, but BLACK THEOLOGY has exposed the traditions and aspirations of Christians with roots in Africa, and India has been the scene of a sustained attempt to restate Christianity in terms easily understood by inquirers more familiar with the rich spiritual heritage of HINDUISM. Theologians of the Caribbean islands, of the Chinese world, of Japan, of the South Pacific and of Australia have also taken pioneering steps to break free of their dependence on imports. Since 1976 the Ecumenical Association of THIRD WORLD theologians has provided a platform in its periodic conferences and publications, but the largest initiatives have often come from intellectuals who remain more or less loyal to Roman CATHOLICISM. For further reading: D. L. Edwards, *The Future of Christianity* (1987). D.L.E.

indirect euthanasia, see under EUTHANASIA.

individual psychology. A theory of personality originated by Alfred Adler (1870–1937), whose essential principle was that human behaviour is an attempt to compensate for feelings of inferiority caused by physical, psychological or social deficiencies. The basic human drive is the striving towards superiority which is expressed as a yearning towards perfection. Individual psychology emphasizes the subjective nature of the individual's goal-striving, the innate creativity of psychological adaptation, and the unity of personality. Healthy goals are largely social in orientation and centre on co-operation with others. This view is one of the earliest psychoanalytic theories (see PSYCHOANALYSIS) emphasizing the importance of environmental factors in personality. For further reading: H. L. Ansbacher and R. R. Ansbacher, *The Individual Psychology of Alfred Adler* (1967). R.P.-S.

individualism.

(1) In political theory, a term both of praise and dispraise. LIBERALISM is founded on a belief in the sanctity of the individual and the individual conscience, which in time bred a more romantic and less Puritan enthusiasm for the diversity of individual character and a belief in the value of each person 'doing their own thing'. This has always been attacked by conservatives (see CONSERVATISM), who emphasize the need for social cohesion and for authority rather than individual liberty; more recently, it has been attacked by socialists (see SOCIALISM) as a doctrine which encourages selfishness and social conflict. Liberals retort that they are concerned to defend individual rights rather than selfishness.

(2) In social analysis, individualism is the doctrine that explanation must be rooted in the beliefs and desires of individuals and not in 'holistic' (see HOLISM) concepts such as 'national spirit' or 'the destiny of the proletariat'. It thus suggests that classical and neo-classical economics (see NEO-CLASSICAL ECONOMIC THEORY) is the proper model for the other SOCIAL SCIENCES to follow, a claim as widely resisted as it is accepted. For further reading: S. M. Lukes, *Individualism* (1966). A.R.

individualism, methodological, see METHODOLOGICAL INDIVIDUALISM.

individuation. In PHILOSOPHY a principle of individuation is a means of uniquely distinguishing or identifying particular items or individuals. To say of something *x* that it can be individuated is to say that it can be picked out or separated from other particulars *y* and *z*. It provides not only a criterion for discriminating among particulars but for counting them. A.C.G.

induction.

(1) In LOGIC, a form of reasoning that usually involves generalization, i.e. the INFERENCE from an instance or repeated

instances of some conjunction of characteristics that the conjunction obtains universally. But the term is often used for any inference whose premises do not entail its conclusions, i.e. they support it but do not, if true, logically exclude the possibility that it is false. The justification of induction has been a persistent problem. It seems to presuppose an inductive principle of the form: 'For any *A* and *B*, if all known *A*s are *B*, then all *A*s whatever are *B*.' So stated, however, the principle is obviously false, as is shown by the discovery of black swans in Australia at a time when all known swans were white. A currently favoured position is to contend that the PROPOSITION 'If all known *A*s are *B*, then *probably* all *A*s whatever are B' is ANALYTIC, and that it implicitly defines the CONCEPT of probability in the sense of CONFIRMATION. A.Q.

(2) In MATHEMATICS, see under MATHEMATICAL INDUCTION.

(3) In classical EMBRYOLOGY, the process whereby a certain stimulus, such as a pinprick or exposure to a particular chemical, initiates the formation of new tissues or organs from pre-existing CELLS. E.O.W.

(4) In BIOCHEMISTRY, the process whereby the addition of a particular substance (the inducer) causes CELLS to produce the ENZYMES required to accelerate the chemical transformation of the substance. For example, when the bacterium *E. coli* encounters lactose (the inducer), it rapidly manufactures the three enzymes required to absorb the lactose into the cell and to hydrolyse it to glucose and galactose. E.O.W.

industrial action. Industrial actions may be taken as a sanction against an employer in the course of COLLECTIVE BARGAINING. A STRIKE is the most dramatic and visible of these actions. Such actions are generally a sign that collective bargaining has broken down. There are, however, many other industrial actions which may have as profound an effect as a strike. Many of these have been developed over the past 20 years. Marches and demonstrations are most often used as a weapon against a government. When they are associated with the cessation of work, for however short a period, they become an industrial action. French and Italian unions use this weapon more often than most other union movements. Actions short of a strike include: the banning of overtime; strict adherence to working rule books; boycotts; refusing to cover for absent colleagues (teachers in 1986); non-cooperation with management; the 'blacking' of goods or services; and working without enthusiasm. Other actions are newer. In the UK the Upper Clyde Shipbuilders workers 'worked in' in 1971 and this became an established tactic in redundancy situations. Sit-ins and occupations, pioneered in the late 1960s by students in the US, France and Germany, were taken up by trade unions in the 1970 and 1980s. Under the government of Margaret Thatcher (see THATCHERISM) during that period, the power of trade unions was severely curtailed – a policy continued under the so-called New Labour government of Tony Blair from 1997. See also SYNDICALISM. B.D.S.; S.T.

industrial archaeology. Term coined in the 1950s, originally to refer to the study of the INDUSTRIAL REVOLUTION in England, Germany, Belgium, the USA and elsewhere from the evidence of material remains such as coal mines, textile mills, railways, etc. Industrial archaeology has been slow to establish itself as a serious academic subject, whether among archaeologists (most of them concerned with much more remote periods) or historians (accustomed to working with documentary evidence). It has, however, benefited from amateur enthusiasms for steam trains, LOCAL HISTORY, etc., and has become associated with conservation movements. In Britain, a Register of Industrial Monuments has been compiled and there is an Association for Industrial Archaeology and also a *Review*. In the last few years the scope of this subdiscipline has widened, both chronologically and thematically. Some industrial archaeologists now concern themselves with the artifacts and monuments of the second industrial revolution – aeroplanes, radios, cinemas, typewriters, etc. – while widening their scope to include the entire material culture (see MATERIAL CULTURE, HISTORY OF) of INDUSTRIAL SOCIETIES. As they do so they are coming into closer contact with social historians (see SOCIAL HISTORY). For further reading: K. Hudson, *World Industrial Archaeology* (1979). P.B.

industrial democracy, see under DEMOCRACY; PARTICIPATION.

industrial dynamics, see under SYSTEMS.

industrial psychology. A branch of APPLIED PSYCHOLOGY covering applications of PSYCHOLOGY in the industrial field. Topics now classed under this title may be grouped thus: (1) fatigue, safety, accident-proneness and mental health, all of which were originally matters of medical concern; (2) vocational guidance, selection, training and appraisal, where there are strong links to work in education; (3) personal relations, relations within groups, and relations within the structure of organizations, all of which have links with SOCIAL PSYCHOLOGY and SOCIOLOGY (industrial relations and conflict, which clearly involve psychological considerations, are, curiously enough, seldom treated in depth in works on industrial psychology); (4) interactions between human beings, machines and the ENVIRONMENT constitute a special subject, usually called ERGONOMICS in the UK and *engineering psychology* in the USA; (5) in so far as matters in (3) and (4) lead to the study of control SYSTEMS they also come under the heading of CYBERNETICS.

The term 'industrial psychology' only appears after 1900, and the subject was at first concerned primarily with the efficiency and wellbeing of individual workers. Academically and in practice, its development in Britain came with the setting up of the Health of Munition Workers Committee in 1915. Important later studies were concerned with industrial fatigue. The development of psychological techniques for testing, selection and appraisal contributed in the 1920s to the growth of *personnel work*. Over the same period industrial psychology was affected by ideas of SCIENTIFIC MANAGEMENT and time and motion studies of work processes aimed at increasing efficiency. These had successes, but also met opposition, and increasing interest in social psychology led during the 1930s to a heightened concern with human relations. Since 1945 the scope of the subject has widened again to take into account the contributions of managers and management to the wellbeing and effectiveness of organizations. In these developments industrial psychology overlaps sociology. For further reading: P. E. Spector, *Industrial and Organizational Psychology* (1996). B.B.S.

industrial revolution. General term for the process of the rapid onset of continued economic change and advancement through the application of industrial techniques to traditional forms of manufacture, the divorce of an economy from a restricted resource and agricultural base, and a sustained increase in general living standards and in urbanization. The term was first used by French observers in the 1820s (in an analogy with the French revolution), as a description of the process in which Britain in the late 18th and early 19th centuries became the first industrial nation. The first English use was by Engels (1820–95) and then, more widely, by Toynbee (1852–83). The British experience was then to be followed by other western European nations and the USA, eastern Europe and Japan. The pathway of the industrial revolution was held to be one which economies would follow as they reached a certain stage of ECONOMIC DEVELOPMENT (a view particularly associated with the American economist W. W. Rostow, an assumption akin to that which underwrote the idea of the DEMOGRAPHIC TRANSITION. Recent work on the English (and first) industrial revolution has rejected many of the older certainties about the direction of causality and speed of change, placing emphasis on random factors and the slow and piecemeal character of change, and pointing to inconsistencies between indices of change and the onset of full-scale INDUSTRIALIZATION making the general lessons less applicable to other circumstances. The classic industrial revolution was accompanied by a shift from human and animal power to mechanical power (steam, and later gas and electricity). Commentators now talk of a second industrial revolution, with the advent of widespread computerization, and of a post-industrial (see POST-INDUSTRIAL SOCIETY) service-based (rather than manufacturing-based) economy. For further reading: J. Hoppit and E. A. Wrigley (eds), *The Industrial Revolution In Britain* (1994). D.S.

industrial society. The type of society produced by INDUSTRIALIZATION. In social theory the term has rarely been neutral. FUNCTIONALISTS, taking their lead from Herbert Spencer (1820–1903) and Émile Durkheim (1858–1917), have taken the optimistic view that industrial society tends towards social equilibrium and the orderly integration of its parts. After the initial disruption of the INDUSTRIAL REVOLUTION, and the creation of new CLASSES such as the industrial WORKING CLASS, industrial society gradually elaborated a new stable order based on an extensive DIVISION OF LABOUR. For some theorists, such as the American sociologist Talcott Parsons (1902–79; see SOCIOLOGY), industrial society also generates a new NORMATIVE consensus, based on such values as achievement, equality of opportunity, and legal-rational procedures (see LEGAL-RATIONAL AUTHORITY). MARXISTS on the other hand see industrial society as tending towards greater conflict and eventual breakdown. For them the chief feature of industrialism is its capitalistic character. Industrial society is a system of EXPLOITATION, giving rise to an inevitable conflict of classes which will ultimately lead to the overthrow of its CAPITALIST form and the substitution of a SOCIALIST order. The so-called COMMUNIST societies of eastern Europe and Cuba were not, for most Marxists, proper examples of the new order. These were relatively backward and semi-developed societies when their 'socialist' revolutions occurred. Socialism can only come about when capitalist industrialism has been developed to its fullest extent, on a world scale. See also POST-INDUSTRIAL SOCIETY. For further reading: K. Kumar, *From Post-Industrial to Post-Modern Society* (1995). K.K.

industrialization. A broad CONCEPT, generally thought of as a massive development of CAPITALISM, as the latter came to harness the new knowledge of science by means of MECHANIZATION in new processes of factory production. It entailed new relations between owners of CAPITAL, entrepreneurs, management and wage-labourers; and new physical concentrations both of industry and of population (see URBANIZATION). After early years of uncontrolled development, with many inhumanities, subsequent efforts of reform and political policy have been to *tame* industrialization and to control it for the increase of human welfare. It has thus been regarded as the central set of economic and attendant social features which first appeared with the INDUSTRIAL REVOLUTION in Britain in the late 18th and early 19th centuries, spread to other countries, and marks 'the modern world' off from all earlier periods of history. See also INDUSTRIAL SOCIETY; POST-INDUSTRIAL SOCIETY. For further reading: K. Kumar, *Prophecy and Progress* (1978). R.F.

infallibility. The inability to err. This happy condition has been popularly ascribed to a number of politicians, scientists, etc., but is chiefly associated with the DOGMA of the Roman Catholic Church (1870; see CATHOLICISM) that the Pope is infallible when teaching *ex cathedra* (in full official solemnity), and with the FUNDAMENTALISM of some Protestants (see PROTESTANTISM). The number of occasions on which Popes have so taught, and the exact nature of the truth in the Bible, are matters debated even by those who accept such infallibility. For further reading: F. A. Sullivan, *Magisterium: Teaching Authority in the Catholic Church* (1983). D.L.E.

infant mortality rate. The number of deaths in the first year of life divided by the number of live births. Typically, the infant mortality rate is computed as the ratio of infant deaths in some time period to births that occurred during the same interval. Several additional distinctions are made according to the age at death of an infant or foetus. The 'neonatal mortality rate' is defined as deaths in the first month (28 days) of life divided by live births. Similarly, deaths after the first month of life are described by the 'post-neonatal mortality rate', and deaths around the time of birth (after 20 or 28 weeks of gestation through to the first week of life) by the 'perinatal mortality rate'. J.R.W.

inference. The process or product of reasoning or argument. In a piece of reasoning or an argument a *conclusion* is inferred or derived from a *premise* or premises; it is asserted as true, or probable, on the assumption of the truth of the premise or premises. Thus the connected sequence of assertions 'All men are mortal, Socrates is a man, so Socrates is mortal' is an inference in the sense of process of reasoning; 'Socrates is mortal' is an inference in the sense of product of reasoning. In a valid *deductive* inference the premises entail the conclusion, which thus cannot be false if they are true. In a sound *inductive* inference (see INDUCTION) the premises only *support* the conclusion, or render it probable. An inference of either kind can have both its premises and conclusions true and yet be invalid or unsound. A.Q.

inferiority complex. A term developed by the Austrian-American psychiatrist Alfred Adler (1870–1937) to describe feelings of resentment at being inferior. Adler was deeply influenced by Nietzsche's concept of a WILL TO POWER (see NIETZSCHEAN). Seeing people as aggressive and competitive, Adler saw suspicion, PARANOIA and an excessive focusing upon alleged slights as a functionally adaptive device to enable people to cope with 'underachievement'. The ambiguities of power thus played a role equivalent to sexuality in Freudian PSYCHOANALYSIS. Adler emphasized how such character traits as timidity, indecision, insecurity, shyness, cowardice and submissive obedience could be explained as responses to innate drives to power. R.P.

infertility. Literally, the inability to conceive, though it is interpreted as failure to have a child or children. It may be voluntary, due to coital abstinence or CONTRACEPTION. Involuntary infertility occurs in 10–15 per cent of couples and may be due to problems in either partner or with coitus. Many individuals and couples are really subfertile rather than infertile. In the male, infertility may be caused by genetic (see GENETICS/GENOMICS) or endocrine disorders affecting the development of the testes, by testicular failure or removal, blockage of the vas, and disorders of erection or ejaculation. In the female, causes include infrequent, irregular or absent ovulation (the release of an egg), blockage of the fallopian tubes, abnormalities of the uterus or cervix, and inability to have intercourse. General disease, obesity, poor nutrition, stress, smoking and alcohol can affect fertility adversely. Investigation of the couple is best conducted in a specialized infertility clinic where the history and examination are supported by investigations which include examination of the semen, mucus from the uterine cervix after intercourse (post-coital test), tests for ovulation and tubal patency. Ultrasound enables the ovaries and ripening eggs to be watched, and the operations of laparoscopy and hysteroscopy allow the surgeon to inspect the interior of the pelvis and uterus respectively. Treatment to induce ovulation is often successful, but tubal surgery to open or reconstruct blocked tubes is less so. Treatment of male infertility is generally less successful than of the female. ARTIFICIAL INSEMINATION by donor (AID) is acceptable to some couples when the male is infertile. *In vitro fertilization* (IVF), where eggs are obtained from the ovary, fertilized outside the body by sperm, and then replaced in the uterus, is now an established method. This technique was introduced for women who had badly damaged tubes and those who had suffered surgical removal of the tubes, but is now also used for women with other problems and unexplained infertility. New methods are being developed, including the placing of egg and sperm in the tube (GIFT). The chance of a pregnancy is about 1 in 10 overall and 1 in 3 to 4 where fertilized eggs are actually placed in the uterus. The possibility of egg donation for those who have lost their ovaries, and surrogate pregnancy (another woman 'carrying' the pregnancy) where the woman has had a hysterectomy, have raised the hopes of some as well as posing major ethical issues, including the question of ownership of sperm, eggs and fertilized eggs. (See also WARNOCK REPORT.) For further reading: M. Seibel, *Infertility: A Comprehensive Text* (1997). S.J.S.

infinite; infinity. Our imagination readily transcends the strictly finite. We can see that the sequence 0, 1, 2, 3, . . . can be continued indefinitely, without limit. But the problem of harnessing this insight to MATHEMATICS is not easy and has not been finally resolved. Throughout the history of the subject two opposed tendencies are manifest. One, akin to NOMINALISM and IDEALISM, finds its expression today in *finitism* and INTUITIONISM. Abstract objects such as numbers are considered as creations of the human mind. Hence, although the law describing the above sequence can be grasped, and the members up to a given point can be constructed, the sequence itself must always remain uncompleted. Infinity is only *potential*. Because each real NUMBER is defined by an infinite sequence or SET, this view requires a radical reworking of ANALYSIS; standard theorems are replaced by more sophisticated, less intuitive, counterparts. It is not surprising, therefore, that most mathematicians follow the other tendency, which is akin to REALISM or PLATONISM. Here it is supposed that the *completed* sequence does, in some mysterious way, exist and so can be treated as an object; the infinite is actual. If care is taken to avoid PARADOXES and inconsistencies, one can treat infinite sets rather as if they were finite. The word *transfinite* is used to indicate this extension (e.g. transfinite arithmetic). This view is given a plausible, though partial, expression in the axioms of SET THEORY.

Cantor (1845–1918) first showed that some sets are more infinite than others (see CARDINAL NUMBER). In set theory there is an infinite hierarchy of orders of infinity. Recently many new *axioms of infinity* have been contrived which extend this hierarchy. They have interesting consequences, but stretch intuition to breaking point. For further reading: R. Rucker, *Infinity and the Mind* (1982). R.G.

infinitesimals, see under ANALYSIS.

inflatables, see under PNEUMATIC STRUCTURES.

inflation. In ECONOMICS, a term used to denote an increase in the level of prices or, more commonly, a significant and persistent increase in prices. Over history, there have been periods of falling prices, e.g. the Great DEPRESSION, as well as periods of inflation. Periods of inflation imply a decline in the purchasing power of the unit of MONEY. In theory, if the economy adjusts immediately and costlessly to inflation, no harm is caused. In reality, inflation does have a number of harmful effects. The informational content of prices is reduced as the change in the price of one product has to be seen in the context of changes in the prices of all other products. Information on the latter is likely to be limited and costly to acquire. Thus, decisions may be based on incomplete information and persons may make different decisions than if they were in possession of complete and certain information. The greater level of uncertainty about prices may lead to less INVESTMENT and ECONOMIC GROWTH. For such reasons, there are likely to be greater problems for firms in maintaining sufficient LIQUIDITY. Money rates of interest may not adjust for increased inflation and the real interest rate, i.e. the money rate minus the inflation rate, may be reduced. Previous legal commitments or MONEY ILLUSION may lead to the lending of money at lower real interest rates than at the previous rate of inflation. This would redistribute income from lenders to borrowers. The effect of inflation on saving may be to reduce it, because of the lower real interest rate and uncertainty about the real interest rate, or increase it, because people wish to have more reserves to protect them against future uncertainty. The ability of different groups to adjust to inflation varies, and this may lead to a redistribution of income, e.g. away from those on fixed money incomes. Changes in relative prices are often greater in periods of high inflation. Those consumers who consume relatively more of products whose prices have risen most quickly will suffer most from inflation, unless their incomes increase to compensate them. Thus, the different rates of price increases have consequences on the distribution of income.

Inflation implies a need for a greater quantity of money or higher velocity of circulation (see QUANTITY THEORY OF MONEY) to maintain FULL EMPLOYMENT. The velocity of circulation may increase as the economy adapts, e.g. the emergence of credit facilities outside the banking system and a shortening of the average period for which money is held. The ability of the velocity of circulation to change in the short run is likely to be limited. Thus, in times of inflation, it is necessary to increase the MONEY SUPPLY in order to maintain full employment. Inflation represents a tax on holdings of money that accrues to the government through the supply of money being increased. Monetarists (see MONETARISM) regard inflation as a consequence of inappropriate MONETARY POLICY. KEYNESIANS regard inflation as being caused by cost-push and demand-pull factors (see PHILLIPS CURVE). The latter occurs when AGGREGATE DEMAND is allowed to exceed the productive potential of the economy. The former is caused by a struggle over the distribution of NATIONAL INCOME, especially between different forms of labour, and rises in import prices. In this Keynesian view, accommodating monetary policy increases the supply of money to ensure full employment and is not itself the cause of inflation. An associated view is that the government should control the fixing of wages and prices through INCOMES POLICIES and, thus, secure price stability. Monetarists believe that, at best, incomes policies have only a short-term effect and that inflation should be cured by the government not allowing the money supply to grow more quickly than is warranted by the growth in the productive potential of the economy. Eventually, the wage-setting process will adjust to the government's monetary stance and inflation will be reduced and the economy will return to full employment. However, in the intervening period, which may be very long, serious and persistent UNEMPLOYMENT may occur. The eradication of inflation is made more difficult by people holding expectations (see RATIONAL EXPECTATIONS) of continuing and even increasing inflation.

The term *disinflation* means the reduction in the rate of inflation. This may be brought about through deflationary monetary and FISCAL POLICIES that reduce a high level of aggregate demand which is responsible for the wage and price increases. *Reflation* is the use of expansionary monetary and fiscal policies to increase the level of aggregate demand and is intended to bring the economy back to full employment. *Stagflation* occurs when there is high inflation but a low level of economic activity and high unemployment. It is likely to occur when cost pressures and inflationary expectations force prices up, but the level of aggregate demand is low. Inflation is called *hyperinflation* when prices increase extremely quickly, e.g. the inflation of over 50 per cent per day that occurred in Germany in 1923. It is different in *scale* but not in *kind* to inflation. For further reading: J. Trevithick, *Inflation* (1980). P.M.O.; J.P.

inflationary universe theory/scenario. Phenomenon predicted by theoretical cosmologists to have occurred during the first moments of the universe's expansion from the big bang (see BIG BANG THEORY; COSMOLOGY). The refinement of the big bang cosmological theory including this idea is called the inflationary universe theory/scenario. If matter behaves in a particular fashion that is consistent with but not demanded by current theories of GRAND UNIFICATION and ELEMENTARY PARTICLES during the first 10^{-35} seconds after the beginning of the universe, its expansion can experience a short period during which it is rapidly accelerated. During this period the universe behaves as though there exists a positive COSMOLOGICAL CONSTANT. If inflation occurs it offers a natural explanation as to why the universe is so uniform and similar in its properties from one direction to another. This idea and the term 'inflation' were first introduced by Alan Guth in 1981. The theory was subsequently refined to exclude some undesirable features by several other cosmologists, notably Andrei Linde. It is not yet known whether the theory is true or false. It predicts that our universe must have a total density within one part in 10,000 of the critical level that must be exceeded if it is to recollapse in the future. It does not predict on which side of this critical dividing line the density lies. It is not known whether there does exist as much matter in the universe as is predicted by the inflationary theory, but the issue is uncertain because of the possible existence of very large quantities of DARK MATTER. The theory makes other much more detailed predictions about the pattern of small fluctuations that should be found in the background radiation in the universe. These predictions are consistent with observations made by the COBE satellite. They will be tested in exquisite detail by two future satellite missions (MAP in 2000 and Planck Explorer in 2005). These satellites will be able to confirm or rule out the theory of inflation as the explanation for the overall structure of the universe and the patterns of fluctuations it contains. For further reading: A. H. Guth, A. P. Lightman, *The Inflationary Universe* (1997). J.D.B.

inflecting (or fusional). In comparative LINGUISTICS, adjectives applied to a language (e.g. Latin) in which grammatical relations are expressed primarily by means of changes within the forms of words (the *inflections*). The term *fusional* implies a characteristic, generally absent from AGGLUTINATING languages, namely that different grammatical meanings are often combined within a single affix, e.g. in Latin *bonus* the *us* simultaneously marks nominative, masculine and singular. D.C.

infopreneur. A contraction of 'information

ENTREPRENEUR', used by information scientists and INTELLECTUAL PROPERTY lawyers to refer to someone who makes a living by combining written materials from disparate sources and then distributing them to users whom the original authors would not have otherwise reached. The rise of infopreneurship reflects the new incapacities and capacities created by the INFORMATION SOCIETY. On the one hand, the surfeit of available texts often makes it difficult to access exactly what one needs to know without expert guidance; on the other hand, the ease with which texts can be either photocopied or 'cut and pasted' in CYBERSPACE has removed most of the material obstacles to customizing information to users' needs. One common and legally contested form of infopreneurship is the 'course pack' that university instructors compile to provide students with selected chapters from recent books. Despite the tendency to see infopreneurs as parasites, it is worth recalling that before ROMANTICISM, authorship was based more on authoritativeness than originality, much as we think of editorship today. S.F.

information processing, see under COMPUTING.

information society. One of the varieties of post-industrial thought (see POST-INDUSTRIAL SOCIETY), associated especially with the American sociologist Daniel Bell. Bell argues that the new information technologies, particularly the computer, have so transformed economic and social life that the peoples in the advanced industrial world (see INDUSTRIAL SOCIETY; INDUSTRIALIZATION) now live in societies the main business of which is the production and distribution of information. Most workers are information workers, most products information products. Manufacturing activities have largely been exported to the less-developed parts of the world ('de-industrialization'). While Bell himself is cautious about extending the economic analysis to other spheres of society, other theorists have been bolder in claiming that the informational economy is simply one part of a broader pattern of 'informationalization' that is transforming every aspect of social, cultural and political life. Work, education, family life and politics are, it is argued, all responding to the possibilities opened up by the enormous expansion in the quantity of information, as well as the speed and subtlety of its processing. Home banking, home shopping, home education, home working and vastly expanded home entertainment are all indices of the change. So too is the increasingly precarious hold of the NATION-STATE on the lives of its citizens. In this broader sense, the idea of the information society links up with theories of POST-FORDISM and post-modernity (see POST-MODERNISM). K.K.

information theory. This deals with sending binary-coded (see BINARY SCALE) messages from one point to another. The fundamental theory is due to Claude E. Shannon (1948) of the Bell Telephone Company, and concentrates on how to detect errors in transmission. If one transmits extra digits it may be possible to detect that an error has occurred, and even correct it (see REDUNDANCY). Efficient error-correcting and error-detecting codes exist to cut down the number of digits required. Error-detecting codes tell the receiver that there is an error in a segment of the message – he can then request retransmission. Error-correcting codes make it possible to read the original message provided there is not too much noise. They are used by space probes radioing back to earth, and in CDs whose surface may have imperfections. N.A.R.

informed consent, see under NUREMBERG CODE.

infra-red. Electromagnetic RADIATION whose wavelength can range from 8 ten-millionths of a metre to about 1 millimetre, i.e. just longer than visible light, but shorter than radio frequency waves. Bodies less than red-hot emit infra-red radiation, so that photographic film sensitive to infra-red reveals 'hot spots' such as vehicle exhausts, even at night when there is no visible light. Infra-red radiation penetrates haze because it suffers less than visible light from DIFFRACTION by the small PARTICLES. M.V.B.

infrastructure. The roads, transport systems, communications, sewage facilities, etc. that are necessary to the functioning of the economy and which are not usually supplied in sufficient quantities by the PRI-

VATE SECTOR. These goods and services are really examples of PUBLIC GOODS and, thus, there is an implication that the state should supply them. J.P.

Ingsoc, see under ORWELLIAN.

inheritance of acquired characters. Most evolutionary theories before Charles Darwin's *Origin of Species* (1859) invoked the inheritance of acquired characters as the major mechanism for transformation of species. Lamarck's account, set out in his *Philosophie zoologique* (1809), is the most celebrated. Lamarck claimed that creatures had the capacity to adapt themselves during their lifetimes to environmental challenges (the lengthening neck of the giraffe forms the classic illustration), and that such modifications were passed on to their offspring. There could thus be cumulative improvement down the generations, eventually leading to the appearance of whole new SPECIES. Darwin did not reject the theory, but it played a relatively small part in his explanatory mechanism of species change (which depended fundamentally upon the NATURAL SELECTION of chance genetic variations). Debates between Lamarckians and Darwinians continued to rage long after Darwin's death, in the absence of any experimentally grounded science of GENETICS which would explain the laws of inheritance. This situation was changed by the rediscovery at the beginning of this century of Mendel's HYBRIDIZATION experiments, which demonstrated that the genetic material contained in CHROMOSOMES was fixed and quite independent of any modifications brought about during the life history of the individual plant or animal. The eventual triumph of Mendelian genetics effectively spelt the demise of the theory of acquired characters. See also DARWINISM; LAMARCKISM; MENDEL'S LAWS. For further reading: G. Allen, *Life Science in the Twentieth Century* (1978). R.P.

inhibition, see under PAVLOVIAN.

initial singularity, see under BIG BANG THEORY.

innateness hypothesis. In LINGUISTICS, the view, particularly found in GENERATIVE GRAMMAR, that the rapid and complex development of children's grammatical COMPETENCE can be explained only on the hypothesis that they are born with an innate knowledge of at least some of the universal structural principles of human language. Influentially advocated by Noam Chomsky in *Syntactic Structures* (1957), the hypothesis has had a considerable impact in other fields, notably PSYCHOLOGY and BIOLOGY, though it is not accepted by everyone, even within linguistics. D.C.

inner city. An area skirting the central business district characterized by low rents (but potential threat of redevelopment), poor social infrastructure, and high levels of poverty, UNEMPLOYMENT, crime, and generally a high representation of ethnic minority groups (see MINORITIES), single-parent families and impoverished elderly citizens. In Britain, various government initiatives to revitalize and renew the inner city have tended to move the problem and create new prosperous areas of gentrification, rather than eliminate the inner-city syndrome. For further reading: P. Lawless, *Britain's Inner Cities: Problems and Policies* (1981). C.G.

inner direction, see under OTHER-DIRECTION.

inorganic chemistry. The branch of CHEMISTRY concerned with the study of compounds based on ELEMENTS other than carbon. It embraces the preparation of new compounds, the elucidation of reaction mechanisms, and the measurement and rationalization of the physical and chemical properties of inorganic systems. Compounds containing carbon fall within the scope of the subject when interest is centred on another element or elements, and they are actively investigated, notably in *organometallic chemistry*. Certain areas of study interact with BIOCHEMISTRY, METALLURGY and SOLID-STATE PHYSICS. For further reading: F. A. Cotton and G. Wilkinson, *Advanced Inorganic Chemistry* (1980). B.K.

insider trading. The use of privileged information, obtained in advance, to profit from movements on the financial markets. Those responsible for the regulation of financial markets regard this practice as perhaps the most serious threat to their integrity. In recent years the insiders have focused their activities on FUTURES MARKETS where transactions are more difficult to decipher. The most notorious insider trading case of recent times was brought by the US authorities against the Wall Street trader Ivan Boesky in 1987 after it was discovered that his fortune had built on such trading. It was information provided to the authorities by Boesky in the US which eventually led to the celebrated prosecution of the 'Guinness Four' in Britain. A.BR.

installation. A type of aesthetic experience in which the art object is presented as part of the space it inhabits (as opposed to being exhibited in the space). Following a trend towards marrying the experience of a work of art with that of its physical surroundings, installations may be permanent or temporary, indoors or out, dependent on the availability of empty existing buildings or facilities to install things in/on. Owing much to the CONCEPTUAL ART practice of the early 1970s, installations can be seen as critical of the autonomy of the art piece, and of the white, prestigious, flexible, multivalent, yet institutionalized exhibition spaces of galleries. Walter de Maria's *Earth Room* and *Broken Kilometre* in Manhattan are splendid original examples. Galleries now host installations of their own (Richard Wilson's *Oil Slick* in the Saatchi Collection is memorable). Essentially installations removed a divide between art and architecture. P.J.D.; S.T.S.B.

instinct. A term used in too many different senses to be of further use in the present stage of the BEHAVIOURAL SCIENCES. Derived from the Latin *instinguere* (to drive or incite), it has been applied (1) to the (presumed) internal system that controls complex behaviour even in the absence of proper external stimulation; (2) to the faculty governing behaviour that is 'not learned'. Modern analysis of both the short-term control of adult behaviour and of the development of the control systems during the growth of the individual has invalidated these uses of the word by showing (a) that most, if not all, behaviour patterns are at any moment steered jointly by internal and external determinants, and (b) that they develop partly under the influence of genetic (see GENETICS/GENOMICS) instructions (which limit the range of possible behaviour) and partly by complex interactions with the ENVIRONMENT.

It is also used to denote (3) a major, functionally unitary behaviour system such as feeding, sexual behaviour, etc., and (4) the mere absence of premeditation ('I braked instinctively') – a condition which has so far defied scientific analysis. For further reading: R. A. Hinde, *Ethology* (1982). N.T.

institutionalism, see under ECONOMIC ANTHROPOLOGY.

institutions. In SOCIOLOGY, activities which are repeated or continuous within a regularized pattern that is normatively (see NORMATIVE) sanctioned. Sociologists usually speak of four major complexes of institutions. *Political institutions* regulate the competition for POWER. *Economic institutions* are concerned with the production and distribution of goods and services. *Cultural institutions* deal with the religious, artistic and expressive activities and traditions in the society. *Kinship institutions* focus on questions of marriage and the family and the rearing of the young. Institutions are studied comparatively in order to see how different societies organize their political or religious life. Or a set of related institutions within a society may be studied as a social system in order to see how they affect each other. D.B.

instrumental conditioning, see under OPERANT CONDITIONING.

instrumentalism, see under ANTI-REALISM.

insulin. The hormone (see ENDOCRINOLOGY) secreted by the pancreas, the partial or complete lack of which results in diabetes; its discovery in 1921, by Frederick Banting and Charles Best in Toronto, has saved the lives of millions who would otherwise have died in diabetic coma. It is a *polypeptide* (see PEPTIDE) consisting of two chains, respectively of 21 and 30 amino acids linked together by sulphur ATOMS. Its chemical formula was discovered in 1955 by F. Sanger of Cambridge, and its spatial configuration was worked out in 1970 by Dorothy Hodgkin of Oxford. It is formed in the body from a precursor, *proinsulin*, a fact discovered in 1968 by Donald Steiner of Chicago.

In medical practice insulin is given by injection; it cannot be given by mouth as it is destroyed in the stomach. If too much insulin is given, the blood sugar level falls too low, producing symptoms which if untreated can culminate in unconsciousness and convulsions; but when the dose is properly adjusted, and a satisfactory DIET given, the diabetic's blood sugar can be kept near normal values, and he can lead an almost normal life. D.A.P.

insurgency, see under WAR.

integer, see under NUMBER.

integration. In social contexts, a term having three related, but distinguishable, meanings: (a) A situation of cohesion, deriving from consent rather than coercion, between the parts of a community sufficient to make it a workable whole. The conditions for this were the object of pioneering study by the French sociologist Émile Durkheim (1858–1917). (b) The process whereby any minority group (see MINORITIES), especially a racial one (see RACE), adapts itself to a majority society and is accorded by the latter equality of rights and treatment (see EQUALITY, PRINCIPLE OF). If such a process reaches the point of obliterating the minority's separate cultural identity, a preferable term is *assimilation.* (c) In American usage, the opposite of SEGREGATION; i.e. the process of combining into a single system any educational or other public facilities previously available only on a racially selective basis. M.D.B.

intellectual. The word, as a noun (with which in its plural form *intelligentsia* is synonymous), emerged largely in the 19th century, first in Russia in the 1860s, to designate that section of the university-educated youth who were 'critically thinking personalities' (Pisarev's phrase) or 'nihilists' (Turgenev's term), those who questioned all traditional values in the name of reason and progress. In France it was used, pejoratively or proudly, of and by the Dreyfusards (see DREYFUS CASE). The resultant association of the category *intellectual* with the LEFT was reinforced by such views as those of Alexis de Tocqueville and of Marx who, in the *Communist Manifesto*, described the intellectuals as a section of the BOURGEOISIE who attached themselves to the WORKING CLASS with the function of shaping their ideas (see MARXISM).

Yet if one defines intellectuals as the culture-bearers of their society, then the majority, until World War II, were not of the Left, while many were on the RIGHT, e.g. Maurras, Bernanos, Mauriac; Stefan George, Junger, Gottfried Benn; D'Annunzio, Pirandello; Wyndham Lewis, Pound, Lawrence, Yeats. And if one sees the intellectuals as the defenders of humanist values, then the majority have been of the *clerisy* (Coleridge's term), the upholders of tradition and learning against the popular passions and politics of the day; Julien Benda's *La Trahison des Clercs* (1927, translated as *The Betrayal of the Intellectuals*), with its attack on the intellectuals as seeking to 'govern the world', is a major statement of that position.

In general, one can say that the intellectuals are the custodians of the tradition of creative and critical thinking about the NORMATIVE problems of their society and the effort of men to relate themselves to symbols of meaning outside their immediate self-interest and experience. In social fact, however, an intellectual is often one who simply identifies himself as an intellectual, participates with other intellectuals in discussion of questions that are deemed intellectual, and is confirmed in that STATUS by those who are recognized, informally, as the leaders of the intellectual world. Indeed, with the expansion of higher education in almost all INDUSTRIAL SOCIETIES, and the growth of the cultural sectors (publishing, television, the arts), the intellectuals today constitute a distinct social CLASS. How this ROLE affects their 'historic function' (howsoever defined) is an unresolved problem. For further reading: A. Gouldner, *The Future of Intellectuals and the Rise of the New Class* (1982). D.B.

intellectual history, see under HISTORY OF IDEAS.

intellectual property. The branch of the law traditionally concerned with the assignment of PATENTS to inventions, copyrights to written materials, and trademarks to commercial products. Its importance has increased as the status of knowledge has shifted from that of PUBLIC GOOD to that of commodity. The shift is the natural outcome of the PRIVATIZATION of education and research, not to mention the ease with which knowledge is readily conceptualized in proprietary terms as 'domains'. The extent of this shift can be seen in the following three products and processes for which restrictive property rights have recently been granted in several court rulings: (1) human genetic information; (2) the computer program of an EXPERT SYSTEM; (3) the actual computer needed to execute the proof of a difficult mathematical theorem. These new cases raise issues that go beyond the law's original concern with protecting achievement while promoting effort in creative endeavours. Specifically, intellectual property law must now consider third-party impacts, which in the above cases potentially include (1) HUMAN RIGHTS violations; (2) deprofessionalization and deskilling; (3) economic restrictions of academic freedom. In this respect, an expanded sense of intellectual property threatens to cannibalize other areas of the law. For further reading: V. Weil and J. Snapper (eds), *Owning Scientific and Technical Information* (1991). S.F.

intelligence. The capacity or potential to solve problems, and/or adapt to a changing environment. Like many concepts in PSYCHOLOGY, intelligence has a long past but a short history. Darwin's pioneering work on the EVOLUTION of mind inspired many armchair efforts to rank ORGANISMS within and across species in terms of their intellectual power (see DARWINISM). At the turn of the last century, these efforts culminated in the devising of the first tests of intelligence by the French psychologist Alfred Binet and the British psychometrician Charles Spearman.

Most tests of intelligence are short-answer instruments that assess knowledge of vocabulary, solution of analogies, memory for isolated words or connected text, logical problem-solving, and/or elementary mathematical and spatial capacities. IQ (intelligence quotient) scores on such measures have been used in school placement (including programmes for gifted or retarded students), military recruitment, and vocational placement (see MENTAL RETARDATION; LEARNING DISABILITY). In recent years, the British psychologist Hans Eysenck and the American psychometrician Arthur Jensen have claimed that intelligence reflects neural efficiency which can be gauged by electrophysiological measures (see PSYCHOMETRICS).

Almost since its inception, the study of intelligence has been surrounded by controversy. Among the principal controversies:

(1) Is intelligence inborn or acquired (see INHERITANCE OF ACQUIRED CHARACTERS)? Studies of the heritability of intelligence have generally allocated at least one-half of the variance in intelligence to genetic (inborn) factors (see GENETICS/GENOMICS). Yet critics have stressed the problems entailed in behavioural genetic studies of human beings (e.g. what inferences can legitimately be drawn from the comparison of identical twins reared together and reared apart) as well as the considerable variation in results from such studies.

(2) Is there a single intelligence or multiple intelligences? The presence of positive CORRELATIONS among different factors of intelligence points to a single 'general factor' of intelligence. Even those who favour a single intelligence recognize second-order factors (such as spatial or verbal intelligence). Critics challenge the statistical basis of a single intelligence and question instruments that yield positive correlations among measures of putatively independent intellectual factors.

(3) Are tests of intelligence biased? Early tests were marred by items that clearly reflected cultural or social bias (see RACE; RACISM). Considerable efforts have been evinced to eliminate such items. Yet the actual conditions of testing (the layout of the test paper, testers who behave or dress in certain ways, the very name of the test) may introduce biases that are more difficult to eradicate.

Following a century of domination by the heirs of Darwin, Spearman and Binet, the study of intelligence has been invigorated in recent years. The comparative strengths and operations of human intelligence and ARTIFICIAL INTELLIGENCE are now debated. New forms of testing, ranging from computer-administered instruments to those that probe creativity or 'emotional intelligence', are being used. Certain enigmas, such as the worldwide rise in measured intelligence over the decades, and the greater within-family similarity of intelligence levels during the later years of life, are stimulating investigation. The second century of the study of intelligence promises to be at least as interesting and controversial as the first. For further reading: H. Gardner, *Frames of Mind* (1993). H.G.

Intelligence Quotient (IQ), see under INTELLIGENCE.

intelligent knowledge-based system (IKBS), see under EXPERT SYSTEM.

intelligentsia, see under INTELLECTUAL.

intentional fallacy. Term proposed by W. K. Wimsatt and Monroe C. Beardsley (*The Verbal Icon*, 1954) to denote the converse of the AFFECTIVE FALLACY. Conceding that there is an 'intended' meaning to a literary work, Wimsatt and Beardsley nonetheless separate this from the 'actual' meaning – which is independent of the author (as from all the work's effects). The author's intention, according to this view, may be taken as *evidence* in determining its 'actual', independent meaning; but it should not be confused with it; such evidence is 'external'. The theory is stimulating but not easy to accept: the work's meaning is in one important sense inseparable from the author's whole (no doubt largely subliminal) intention; it is impossible to pretend that we read, say, Keats's work without our own (perhaps unconscious) reference to what we know about his life or to what he thought he wanted to do; and any evidence of an author's intention is nearer to the 'actual' meaning than anything else available, certainly nearer to it than a critic's interpretation. The argument about this became increasingly over-sophisticated and sterile; but Wimsatt and Beardsley eventually failed to convince even the academic world that their primary motive was not extra-critical: to separate writers finally from their works, and to have no further truck with biography. M.S.-S.

intentionality. The central concept in the PHENOMENOLOGY of Edmund Husserl (1859–1938), the specifically phenomenological act of the mind by which the ESSENCE of a mental phenomenon is constituted. The medieval Schoolmen had argued for the 'intentional inexistence of an object' as being characteristic of mental phenomena, and Franz Brentano (1838–1917) had developed this concept, assuming the existence of an individual subject thinking, but it was Husserl who gave a quite new importance to the idea, making it in fact the founding characteristic of phenomenological reflection. In Husserl's version, a series of up to six 'reductions' are carried out, and with each one there is a reduction of the specificity of the phenomenon in question, and an increase in 'pure', that is to say non-individual, SUBJECTIVITY. The act of intentionality is presented, in *Ideas* I (1913), as co-extensive with the whole scope of phenomenology itself. Of this *intentional* act, one can say that it is active, not passive, thus replacing the passive *tabula rasa* MODEL of PERCEPTION dominant since Locke by a model which takes account of the intending, selecting, choosing and ordering capacities of the mind in the act of perception. One can also say of the intentional act that it is an *entry into* the mental phenomenon, an act of decision, creating pattern, context and interrelation for any perceived phenomenon, not merely noting its brute and isolated existence. Thirdly, it seems to involve deciding what value or meaning to attribute within an overarching structure or intersubjective map of meaning (see INTERSUBJECTIVITY). In Anglo-Saxon terms, the act of intentionality could be compared to what E. M. Forster is desiderating with his 'Only connect! Only connect the prose and the passion', that is to say, the intentional act is one which carries the full responsibility for the act of knowing along with it, and the responsibility in particular for deciding on a *context of meaning* which is to be attributed to the observed phenomenon. The intentional act is, fourthly, participatory, entering into the being and nature of what is attended to. Thus an entire phenomenology of emotional states is allowed for, admitted and taken account of in the intentional act: perceiving, judging, valuing and wishing (*Ideas*, para. 84) enter into the judgement, and by extension, there could be a phenomenology of love and hate, desire and fear, etc. – this possibility having been developed not by Husserl himself, but by some of his French, British and American successors. It is obvious that intentionality as an account of perception and analysis submits the concept of an 'objectively' available knowledge to a fundamental critique, though of course Husserl himself asserted that each of the 'reductions' brought the judgement nearer to objective truth, though, since this is achieved by a six-fold multiplication of essential subjectivity, his position is obviously paradoxical and needs close attention before it can be understood. Nevertheless, Heidegger, Sartre and Merleau-Ponty, and in Britain R. D. Laing, chose to understand the Husserlian position as one that could be developed existentially, and the suggestion that it is the subject himself who finally decides on what status to accord to what he experiences or analyses, and that this is, in some ultimate sense, a 'true' decision, has been one of the most fertile in 20th-century thought. See EIDETIC REDUCTION. For further reading: E. Pivčević, *Husserl and Phenomenology* (1970). R.PO.

interactional sociolinguistics. The study of speech in face-to-face communication. The approach deals chiefly with the norms and strategies of everyday conversation, and is characterized by detailed transcriptions of taped interactions, with particular reference to features which have been traditionally neglected in the analysis of conversation, such as prosody, facial expression, silence, and rhythmical patterns of behaviour between the participants. Particular attention is paid to the social factors which help to shape the interaction, such as the desire by the participants to maintain politeness or to recognize mutual rights and obligations. For further reading: J. J. Gumperz, *Discourse Strategies* (1982). D.C.

interactionism, see under MIND-BODY PROBLEM.

interactor, see under UNIT OF SELECTION.

intercontinental ballistic missiles (ICBM), see under MISSILES.

interdependence. Term widely used to describe the increased multiple channels of contact between STATES and non-state actors in the international system. This has led to demands for a new approach to international political analysis from such writers as Burton and Keohane and Nye. The target for attack has been the predominant realist paradigm which is considered too state-centric and POWER-oriented. Keohane and Nye posit that interdependence should be accepted as a necessary corrective to realism, Burton that it should supersede it with what he terms a 'world society/cobweb model' (see WORLD SOCIETY THEORY; COBWEB THEORY). A.W.

interest group/pressure group. POLITICAL SCIENCE terms which may be taken as synonymous, as distinctions drawn between the two are unsatisfactory. They describe associations formed to promote a particular interest by influencing government. Interest groups may be distinguished from political parties by their relatively narrow range of concerns, and more clearly by their uninterest in electing their own candidates to public office and seeking direct control of government. They tend to flourish in states whose political organization allows multiple points of access, and where government activity touches on a wide range of social and economic interests. However, generalizations about their character, roles and tactics tend to founder on variety. They are a crucial unit of the pluralist analysis of politics (see PLURALISM); more generally, they are often regarded as a useful supplement to the representative mechanisms of parties and elections. Some critics, however, are concerned about inequalities of influence between groups of differing resources, with the fate of the unorganized in systems favouring interest-group politics, or with the fragmentation of political decision-making which their presence may encourage. For further reading: T. Moe, *The Organisation of Interests* (1980). S.R.

interest rates. The mechanism used by policy-makers to regulate the MONEY SUPPLY, the level of INFLATION and DEMAND in the economy. When interest rates are raised, the cost of credit is increased and consumption and industrial demand, in the shape of INVESTMENT, cut off. When rates are lowered money becomes cheaper and demand picks up. Following the OIL CRISIS which gave rise to high inflation in the main Western economies, the supply of money and therefore the setting of interest rates have been seen by economists as the key to controlling inflation. Much of the modern intellectual underpinning is contained in the works of the US economist Milton Friedman and his Chicago school (see CHICAGO BOYS) which determined that inflation is always a monetary phenomenon (see MONETARISM). Governments also raise interest rates to support the value of their currencies when they come under pressure on the foreign exchanges (see EXCHANGE RATE). Higher interest rates mean a higher yield to investors, making a particular currency more attractive. For further reading: J. E. Stiglitz, *Economics* (1993). A.BR.

interests, theory of. The concept of an interest is much employed in political debate, especially when individuals or groups are asked to subordinate self-interest to the PUBLIC INTEREST; nonetheless, it is a term whose analysis has caused much difficulty. It cannot mean 'what an individual or group wants', since we often want what is not in our interests; but it must be connected to our wants, for the pursuit of ideals is not always in our interests, whether or not we ought to pursue ideals as well as interests. A plausible view is that what is in our interest is what will enlarge our chances of getting what we want; solicitors, for instance, look after our interests by securing the *means* to whatever we may want, not by doing what we want at the moment. Governments look after the public interest by securing the means which people at large can use for whatever individual purposes they have in mind, not by doing whatever the public wants. See also INTEREST GROUP. A.R.

interface. In technical contexts, the connection between two pieces of equipment. The word is mainly used, in electronics, of equipment handling information (e.g. TELECOMMUNICATION equipment or parts of a computer); the requirement that the behaviour of the various strands in the connection should satisfy fairly complicated overall conventions makes it useful to consider the whole connection as an entity. By analogy, the word is increasingly used in other contexts, e.g. that of intercommunication between various social groups. J.E.S.

interference (in EDUCATIONAL PSYCHOLOGY), see under TRANSFER.

interferons. A family of PROTEINS which were discovered by virtue of their ability to hinder the multiplication of viruses. It is known that in addition to being part of the body's defence against viruses, interferons can also suppress the multiplication of some CELLS. The original difficulties of producing interferon in sufficient quantities to test its clinical value have been overcome by GENETIC ENGINEERING and BIOTECHNOLOGY, and some limited uses of interferons in CANCER and viral therapy are emerging. See also VIROLOGY. P.N.

interior monologue, see under STREAM OF CONSCIOUSNESS.

interlanguage. The linguistic system (see LINGUISTICS) created by someone in the course of learning a foreign language, different from either the speaker's first language or the target language being acquired. It reflects the learner's evolving system of rules, and results from a variety of processes, including the influence of the first language ('transfer'), contrastive interference from the target language, and the over-generalization of newly encountered rules. For example, it is a common experience of English speakers learning French that they fail to recognize the different ways of expressing past time with different types of verbs: in trying to say 'I have gone/eaten/jumped . . .' they use the 'straightforward' translation of the auxiliary verb *have* (French *avoir*), without recognizing that different French verbs require different auxiliaries. If the verb is *go* (*aller*), one must say *je suis allé*, using a form of the auxiliary verb *être*, and not *j'ai allé*, using a form of *avoir*. Those who fail to appreciate this rule, and who regularly use *avoir* instead of *être*, would have the error as part of their interlanguage – it is neither English nor French, but something in between. For further reading: B. McLaughlin, *Theories of Second Language Acquisition* (1987). D.C.

intermediate nuclear forces. MISSILE systems with a range of up to 5,500 miles. In practice these consisted of the Tomahawk (Cruise) and Pershing weapons deployed by NATO, and the SS20 missiles used by the former USSR. The intermediate missile systems were deployed by NATO in response to the Soviet deployment of the SS20, but, equally, in an attempt to lock the

US more tightly into the defence of Europe. The theory advanced for the deployment was that if the Soviet Union could be induced to renounce its intermediate missiles, then NATO could do the same (see NUCLEAR WEAPONS, LIMITATION AND CONTROL). See also CRUISE MISSILES. A.J.M.W.

intermestic affairs. The term refers to the growing interconnection of domestic and foreign policy issues in American politics. It draws a strong contrast with the years from World War II to the late 1970s, during which the imperatives of the COLD WAR, the relative self-sufficiency of the US economy, and the concession of foreign policy responsibilities to the presidency tended to divide the two policy areas. Initial challenges to that division, such as the steep rise in oil prices in the 1970s, were massively compounded as the end of the cold war brought great uncertainty about the USA's international role – anxiety compounded by the late 1980s obsession with a relative decline in US economic performance. Many major issues, such as those involving trade, issues of conscience, or the interests of 'ethnic Americans', are now hard to categorize as domestic or foreign, and are therefore more liable to political conflict and to inconsistent or partial resolution. S.R.

internal clock, see under CHRONOBIOLOGY; BIOLOGICAL RHYTHM.

internal colonialism. A term which suggests that the relation between dominant and subordinate groups, or dominant and subordinate regions (see REGIONALISM), within a nation, can best be understood by analogy with the relationship between the metropolitan POWER and its colonies in an empire. First applied by MARXISTS such as Lenin and Gramsci in the analysis of regional inequalities within societies, it was later more generally applied to social inequalities of various kinds that had a distinctive regional basis. The general idea is that, as in a colonial empire, the dominant groups exist in relation to subordinate groups as 'core' to 'periphery'. Specifically, the analogy is meant to suggest (1) that the relationship between dominant and subordinate groups and regions is inherently exploitative, involving an unequal exchange between 'core' and 'peripheral' regions and groups; (2) that the exploited groups and regions, like colonial peoples, will generally be marked by easily identifiable differences, such as those of colour, language or religion, from the dominant groups, and that these will be used to screen them out in the allocation of positions of prestige and power; and (3) that there will never be equality between regions, nor full civic integration of all groups, because regional inequality is a necessary feature of industrial development and a condition of the maintenance of the existing social order. In recent times, the concept of internal colonialism has been used with considerable effect to analyse the relations between England and the Celtic regions – Wales, Scotland and Northern Ireland – in the context of British national development. Its limitations, however, became apparent when applied to such cases as Quebec in Canada and the Basque and Catalan regions of Spain, all of which cry 'oppression' but none of which fits at all clearly the exploited 'colonial' role. See also SOCIOLOGY OF DEVELOPMENT. For further reading: M. Hechter, *Internal Colonialism: the Celtic Fringe in British National Development* (1975). K.K.

internal rate of return. That rate of interest which when used in the DISCOUNTING of an INVESTMENT gives a net present value (see DISCOUNTED CASH FLOW) of zero. It is a measure of the profitability of an investment. If it exceeds the actual interest rate, it is usually considered to be profitable to proceed with the investment. It has been noted that there may be more than one internal rate of return, in which case the usefulness of the concept as a criterion for investment is limited. However, this problem is usually regarded as a theoretical rather than a practical one. A related but more substantial problem is that internal rates of return may well give a ranking of the desirability of investment projects different from that given by the net present values of the projects. J.P.

internal relations. Those relations of a thing to other things which are essential to it, which it logically cannot cease to have without ceasing to be the thing that it is. Being the square of 4 is essential to 16, or 'being the square of' internally relates 4 to 16, since any number that was not the square of 4 could not be 16. Hegelian idealists (see IDEALISM) subscribe to a general doctrine about the internality of relations, according to which the type of abstract, analytic thinking (see ANALYSIS) used in science and everyday life ('understanding') apprehends the relations between things, inadequately, as external, while a higher, philosophical type of thinking ('reason') apprehends all relations as internal, a thesis foreshadowed in the philosophy of Spinoza (1632–77). Idealists infer from this doctrine that what appear, and are commonly taken, to be complex pluralities, such as a nation or a work of art or the multitude of finite minds, are really unanalysable wholes or systematic unities (see HOLISM). A.Q.

internalization. The process whereby an individual learns and comes to regard as binding the values and NORMS of his social group, or of the wider society as a whole. It is the central psychological mechanism in SOCIALIZATION. Sociologists (see SOCIOLOGY), unlike psychologists, have tended to see it as relatively unproblematic, and have often made it the basis of their shaky concepts of social order or social consensus. For this, they have sometimes been accused of holding to an 'over-socialized' conception of man. K.K.

International, the. Term applied historically to a succession of federations of working-class SOCIALIST parties and organizations. History distinguishes: the *First International*, the international Working Men's Association, founded in London in 1864 with the support of Karl Marx, which in 1872 split into followers of Marx and those who preferred Mikhail Bakunin's brand of ANARCHISM, and in 1876 was dissolved; the *Second International*, founded in Paris in 1889 as a loose federation, which failed to survive the conflict of socialist and NATIONALIST loyalties revealed by the outbreak of World War I in 1914; the *Third International*, or COMINTERN, founded in Moscow in 1919, which, it quickly became apparent, was open only to socialist parties that accepted the discipline and leadership of the Russian COMMUNIST Party, and was dissolved by Russian fiat in May 1943; the *Fourth International*, formed in 1938 by the followers of Trotsky (see TROTSKYISM); the *Labour and Socialist International*, which, recreated in 1923 from the surviving democratic socialist parties (see SOCIAL DEMOCRACY) of the Second International, ceased to function after the Nazi conquest (see NAZISM) of continental Europe; and the *Socialist International*, founded in Frankfurt in 1951, with headquarters in London and a membership of 40 democratic socialist parties. For further reading: G. D. H. Cole, *A History of Socialist Thought*, vols 2–5 (1954–60). D.C.W.

International Bank for Reconstruction and Development, see under BRETTON WOODS.

International Court of Justice. This court, whose seat is at The Hague, was established by the charter of the United Nations (see UN) in 1945. Its organization is governed by Articles 2–23 of the Statute of the Court and by Articles 1–18 and 32–37 of the Rules of the Court. The court subsumed all the functions of its predecessor, the Permanent Court of International Justice. The present court consists of 15 judges who are elected by the General Assembly and the Security Council for terms of nine years and are eligible for re-election. Furthermore, the parties to a dispute before the court are entitled to appoint *ad hoc* judges who sit only in the particular case for which they have been chosen.

The court has jurisdiction to hear contentious cases. Only STATES falling within any of the following three categories may be parties to litigation before the court: members of the UN who are *ipso facto* parties to the Statute of the Court; certain states which are not members of the UN but which have become parties to the Statute in accordance with Article 93 (2) of the Charter; and certain states which are not parties to the Statute of the Court but comply with the conditions laid down by the Security Council Resolution of 15 October 1946. Although to all appearances the court is virtually accessible to all states, no state is necessarily obliged to take its disputes with other states to the court. This is because its jurisdiction in contentious cases depends upon the consent of the parties. Such consent may be expressed in a special agreement; or by accepting the court's jurisdiction in a treaty; or by undertaking in accordance with Article 36 (2) of the Statute to accept as compulsory, in relation to any other state accepting the same obligation, the jurisdiction of the court in all legal disputes concerning (1) the interpretation of a treaty; (2) any question of international law (see PUBLIC INTERNATIONAL LAW); (3) the existence of any fact which, if established, would constitute a breach of an international obligation; (4) the nature or extent of the preparation to be made for the breach of an international obligation. When the court is seized of a dispute it applies, in accordance with Article 38 of the Statute, international treaties and conventions, international custom, the general principles of law recognized by civilized nations and judicial decisions, and the teaching of the most highly qualified publicists as subsidiary means for the determination of the rules of law. Furthermore, the court may determine a case *ex aequo et bono* (i.e. according to the principles of equity) if the parties agree thereto. Apart from its jurisdiction to deal with contentious cases, the court has the competence to give advisory opinions on any legal question, at the request of the General Assembly of the UN, the Security Council or other organs authorized to do so. For further reading: I. Brownlie, *Principles of Public International Law* (1979). O.Y.E.

International Development Association (IDA). An organization set up in 1960 to provide low-interest loans to developing countries. It is part of the World Bank Group (see BRETTON WOODS). C.E.D.

International Labour Organization (ILO). A body set up in 1919 by the Treaty of Versailles (in 1946 it became an agency of the UN) with the object of promoting social justice by associating not only the governments but also the TRADE UNIONS and employers' organizations of member states in an endeavour to establish and raise common standards in the employment of labour. These standards it has embodied in conventions dealing with such matters as the limitation of child labour, the provision of social insurance, minimum wage rates for unorganized workers, freedom of association, and equal pay. Member governments, which now number over 100, are invited to ratify these conventions. The annual conferences of the ILO provide a forum for the discussion of labour questions by delegates from each country's government, trade unions and employers. The office in Geneva, besides its administrative functions, conducts many inquiries – e.g. into the manpower and employment problems of developing countries – on which it issues reports. Since 1945 the ILO has developed technical assistance to the developing countries as a major part of its work. Its continuous activity since 1919 testifies to its independence and its usefulness in the eyes of its members, especially to the developing countries among them, in raising whose standards of labour law and administration it has probably made its main contribution. E.H.P.B.

international law, see under PUBLIC INTERNATIONAL LAW.

international liquidity. Those assets available to governments for settling debts between themselves and limited to the kinds of money held in the official reserves of nations, which are usually deposited with the CENTRAL BANK (see LIQUIDITY). Since World War II the main forms of international liquidity have been gold, reserves of acceptable foreign currencies (which have varied over this period), and *Special Drawing Rights*. At the time of the BRETTON WOODS negotiations in 1944, the economist John Maynard Keynes (1883–1946) suggested that a new international currency (*bancor*) be distributed by a new world central bank. Instead, in 1969, the IMF invented the Special Drawing Right, a new form of interest-bearing deposit held at the IMF. The rules and regulations concerning Special Drawing Rights have varied: at the moment, IMF member and non-member countries can hold them and they can be exchanged for foreign currency; they are valued against a basket of five different currencies; the interest they bear is an average of five different interest rates; and there are various rules about minimum holdings and the transactions they can be used for. Special Drawing Rights were invented because of fears that international liquidity was increasing less quickly than world trade. Until their invention, international liquidity depended on the production of gold and holdings of acceptable foreign currencies. However, Special Drawing Rights account for less than 5 per cent of world international liquidity.

Members of the European Monetary System deposit a proportion of their international foreign exchange reserves with the system. These deposits entitle members to draw funds from the system that are measured in European Currency Units. The European Currency Unit is a weighted sum of the different EUROPEAN UNION (EU) currencies (see EXCHANGE RATE). Though the European Currency Unit is a theoretical unit, it is used as the unit of account in many of the transactions between European central banks and certain European financial and business transactions. For further reading: R. E. Caves and R. W. Jones, *World Trade and Payments* (1985). J.P.

International Monetary Fund, see under BRETTON WOODS.

International Phonetic Alphabet, see IPA.

International School of Theatre Anthropology (ISTA), see under THIRD THEATRE.

international style. The title of a book by Henry-Russell Hitchcock and Philip Johnson published in New York in 1932, and now applied to the mainstream of modern ARCHITECTURE. The label covers the functional architecture derived from De STIJL, influenced by the BAUHAUS, and characterized by a simple rectangular geometry of defined planes; it was to have been a style expressive of contemporary TECHNOLOGY and social programmes (see MODERN MOVEMENT). Its chief exponents during its most vital period, the second quarter of the century, were Mies van der Rohe, Walter Gropius, Le Corbusier, and other more local figures, such as G. T. Rietveld in Holland or Skidmore, Owings & Merrill in the USA, who ensured the wide diffusion of the style. It continued into the late 20th century. Though much criticized as an oversimplified solution and easily debased when used by lesser practitioners, the post-modern style (see POST-MODERNISM) which has become more fashionable may prove to be less enduring. See also CIAM; FUNCTIONALISM; MACHINE AESTHETIC; ORGANIC. For further reading: J. M. Richards, *An Introduction to Modern Architecture* (1940). M.BR.

Internationals, see INTERNATIONAL, THE.

Internet. An international computer network that links other computer networks and even personal computers. Like the telephone system which connects every phone in the world, the Internet can join any two computers. The Internet has many distinct services. The most popular feature – electronic mail, or E-MAIL – is also its simplest; it allows people to send notes and documents. A slightly more complex technological use is in the NEWSGROUPS which post messages about topics and get discussions going. The TELNET system allows users to control a distant computer network, such as a library's card catalogue. The most highly publicized feature is the WORLD WIDE WEB, a system that provides rapid access to any of millions of special displays. The Internet's most distinctive feature is its international – or nonnational – character. Although distance can slow down contact, it is easy to link the US and New Zealand. Even more amazingly, it costs a user no more to contact the opposite side of the globe than it does the other side of town. And much to the annoyance of governments, the Internet's borderless quality makes it difficult to police. It is now common for political exiles to establish newsgroups that discuss events back home, and for dissidents to post pages on the World Wide Web that display proscribed information. Exiles have long been a part of the political scene, but during Lenin's exile provocateurs had to smuggle their illegal newspapers past the police. Nowadays treason comes on-line. The Internet's elusiveness was built in from the start, in 1969, when the US Department of Defense launched the ARPANET (Advanced Research Projects Agency Network) that was designed to withstand nuclear attack. Developers hoped that any surviving computers could contact one another through a greatly decentralized system. Twenty-five years later, when civilians suddenly gained access *en masse* to the system, governments noticed that decentralization robbed them of much enforcement power. The duel between Internet independence and governance appears likely to persist deep into the 21st century. E.B.B.

interpretation. In PSYCHOANALYSIS, the procedure by which an analyst communicates to a patient the UNCONSCIOUS meaning of his actions and words. This is a central aspect not just of therapeutic activity, but of the psychoanalytic world-view (see WELTANSCHAUUNG). At root, psychoanalysis is formulated as a discipline and practice of uncovering latent meanings, of reaching below the surface of action and CONSCIOUSNESS to reveal the disturbing elements of unconscious life. In different formulations, this can be seen as a mode of causal truth-seeking (identifying the TRAUMA, FIXATION or DRIVE constituting the wish and its necessary REPRESSION), or as a hermeneutic enterprise (uncovering the network of unconscious meanings which can be accessed through analysis of the confused patterns of emotion and thought experienced by the person; see HERMENEUTICS). In recent psychoanalytic work, stress has been laid on the interpersonal elements of interpretation, with particular reference to TRANSFERENCE. Where psychoanalytic interpretation differs from many other forms is in its transformative intent: as the interpretation occurs, so the thing in need of interpretation (e.g., the symptom or transference emotion) is modified. S.J.F.

interpretative sociology. Any sociological theory (see SOCIOLOGY) or approach which emphasizes that humans give meaning to social reality before deciding how they are going to act. These meanings must therefore be interpreted before social actions can be explained. Interpretative sociologists are opposed to the claim of POSITIVISM that social life can be explained through an examination of observable regularities without any reference to the subjective states of social actors. As well as studying social actions, interpretative sociology can also examine the meaning of texts and other cultural artifacts. ETHNOMETHODOLOGY, HERMENEUTICS, PHENOMENOLOGY, SEMIOLOGY, SYMBOLIC INTERACTION and the sociology of Max Weber are all varieties of interpretative sociology. For further reading: M. Haralambos and M. Holborn, *Sociology: Themes and Perspectives* (1995). M.D.H.

intersubjectivity. A major concept in PHENOMENOLOGY, where the importance of SUBJECTIVITY is so pronounced. The creation of meaning is an active process, the result of INTENTIONALITY, and each individual proposes his own interpretation of the world, through his language and actions, to a world of countersubjects. Thus a world of intersubjectivity is continuously built up and held in being. An individual's 'intentional hypotheses' are 'fulfilled' if the world confirms or endorses them, and remain 'unfulfilled' if refused. Intersubjectivity is thus very much a local cultural creation, and thinkers following Weber, like Alfred Schutz (see below), have tried to describe the modes of interpretation we need to grasp the conventions of intersubjective understanding. See also PHYSICALISM. For further reading: R. Frie, *Subjectivity and Intersubjectivity in Modern Philosophy and Psychoanalysis* (1997). R.PO.

intertextuality. A term coined by Julia Kristeva in an essay of 1966 to describe the necessary interdependence that any literary text has with a mass of others which preceded it. A literary text is not an isolated phenomenon, it is 'constructed from a mosaic of quotations; any text is the absorption and transformation of another'. In this essay, Julia Kristeva was trying to describe to a French audience the nature and importance of the literary theory of Mikhail Bakhtin (1895–1975), then virtually unknown in the West. Bakhtin's sense of the 'dialogical' nature of the novel led Kristeva to coin a term which had an immense effect in founding a properly STRUCTURALIST literary vocabulary. She herself, and the contributors to *tel quel*, took intertextuality to represent a new freedom from univocity, ESSENTIALISM and all forms of non-political critique. Kristeva was quick to insist, also, that intertextuality simply replaces the phenomenological-BOURGEOIS notion of INTERSUBJECTIVITY, thus doing away at one stroke both with any theory of SUBJECTIVITY and any theory of an INDIVIDUALIST cast. Intertextuality is also, of course, both linguistic and semiotic (see SEMIOTICS), and hence recuperable by PSYCHOANALYSIS and by her own new theory of semanalysis. For further reading: J. Kristeva, *Desire in Language* (1980). R.PO.

interval estimation. In STATISTICS, a way of summarizing experimental evidence about the value of a PARAMETER by calculating from the data an interval with a given fairly high probability of containing the true parameter value. The interval is a *confidence interval*. It is important to remember that the true value of the parameter is a fixed quantity and the interval is a data-dependent (and hence randomly varying) object, and not vice versa. The probability that the (random) interval contains the (fixed) parameter value is the degree of confidence or confidence level. One speaks, for example, of a '95 per cent confidence interval' as a contracted form of 'confidence interval at the 95 per cent confidence level'. A common rule-of-thumb is to take sample ± 2 × sample standard deviation (see VARIANCE) as a 95 per cent confidence interval for the true MEAN. R.SI.

intifadah. The spontaneous Palestinian uprising against Israeli (see JUDAISM; ZIONISM) occupation of Arab territories captured in the Six Day War of 1967, which erupted on 9 December 1987. It was seen as marking the most important phase in the Palestinian resistance. The intifadah gave birth to a Unified National Leadership of the Uprising (UNLU), a coalition of Palestinian local leaders, invariably young, which declared its existence by means of a leaflet dated 10 January 1988. UNLU soon developed links with the PLO (see PALESTINIAN AUTHORITY), which was headquartered in Tunis. The intifadah leaflets became a crucial means of co-ordinating and orchestrating the uprising, with each edition issuing a set of concrete and precise demands and guidelines to the population, from strike hours, the nature and types of strikes, to a boycott of Israeli products. The intifadah provided the impetus for Palestinian institution-building in the Occupied Territories. Crucially, from Communiqué No. 33 (22 January 1989) the letterhead of the leaflets had become 'The PLO–The Unified National Leadership of the Uprising, the State of Palestine'. The intifadah forced changes in Arab–Israeli DIPLOMACY and in the policies of the main participants. The most dramatic changes involved Jordan and the PLO. The former announced the severance of all administrative and legal ties between Jordan and the West Bank (thus far claimed by the Hashemites) on 31 July 1988, and the latter proclaimed the establishment of the State of Palestine on 15 November 1988, at the 19th Palestinian National Council session held in Algiers. For further reading: F. R. Hunter, *The Palestinian Uprising: A War by Other Means* (1991). A.EH.

intimism. Term applied to the work of those late-19th-century painters who concentrated on domestic scenes, somewhat in the genre of Henri Fantin-Latour's early work, e.g. Georges Lemmen and such NABIS as Maurice Denis and Édouard Vuillard. J.W.

intron, see under SPLIT GENE.

introversion. In PSYCHOLOGY, a term introduced by Jung (see JUNGIAN) to denote a process whereby an individual frustrated in his attempts to develop relationships with others withdraws his concern and LIBIDO from them and turns it towards his own fantasies. In protecting his withdrawal, the individual develops behavioural means to defend himself from the enticements to establish relations with others. This process is somewhat similar to that underlying NARCISSISM. Later the process was reified (see REIFICATION) and generalized to refer to a PERSONALITY TYPE, the *introvert*, much of whose life seemed to be characterized by these processes and behaviours. Introversion is not a true opposite of EXTROVERSION, and frequently both co-exist as distinct phases of the same person. T.Z.C.

intuitionism.

(1) In ETHICS, the theory that the fundamental moral TRUTHS are directly apprehended as true by a special faculty of moral knowledge. It takes two main forms, corresponding to two different conceptions of the nature of the fundamental moral truths. According to the first of these, which may be called particular or, less politely, unphilosophical intuitionism, my moral faculty apprehends PROPOSITIONS to the effect that something is my, or some particular person's, duty on a particular occasion, by ANALOGY with the way in which the faculty of sense-PERCEPTION apprehends particular empirical facts. This is roughly the view of Bishop Butler (1692–1752). According to the second, which may be called general or philosophical intuitionism, the moral faculty, here conceived as an aspect of the capacity to apprehend *a priori* truths, such as the propositions of LOGIC and MATHE-

MATICS, apprehends general principles of duty, e.g. that promises ought to be kept or that lies ought not to be told. Most ethical intuitionists are adherents of DEONTOLOGY, but some hold that moral intuition apprehends the goodness or badness of the consequences of action, either in particular cases (G. E. Moore) or in the form of general principles such as that pleasure is good (Rashdall).

(2) In EPISTEMOLOGY, any theory of knowledge which holds that there are (or must be if scepticism is to be repelled) some items of absolutely certain, self-evident and incorrigible knowledge. Peirce criticized the epistemology of Descartes for its intuitionism and defended FALLIBILISM against it.

(3) The philosophy of MATHEMATICS, developed by L. E. J. Brouwer (1881–1966), which is *finitist* (see INFINITE) in that it does not assume there is a totality of NUMBERS but arrives at conclusions about all numbers by MATHEMATICAL INDUCTION, and is 'constructivist' in that it rejects indirect proofs of mathematical existence by *reductio ad absurdum* and acknowledges only such mathematical entities as can be constructed from the natural numbers by intuitively acceptable procedures. In denying that the derivation of a contradiction from 'no number has the property *P*' entails that there is a number with the property *P*, which he holds to be true only if such a number can be positively constructed, the intuitionist has to reject the universal validity of the *law of the excluded middle* (that every proposition is either true or false) and admit a third TRUTH-VALUE, possessed by a class of propositions whose members are, in default of adequate proof, undecidable. For further reading: A. Quinton, *The Nature of Things* (1973). A.Q.

invariant, see under CONSERVATION LAWS; TRANSFORMATION.

inverse power law, see under SELF-ORGANIZED CRITICALITY.

investment.

(1) The creation of CAPITAL which is capable of producing other goods and services. As capital depreciates, there is a distinction between gross investment and net investment (the latter being the actual increase in the stock of capital). Investment can be carried out by either the private or public sector. Positive net investment increases the productive potential of an economy. In KEYNESIAN economic theory, gross investment is an important part of AGGREGATE DEMAND and thus plays an important role in determining NATIONAL INCOME.

(2) The purchase of an asset (e.g. shares in a company) that represents existing or new capital. J.P.

invincible ignorance. A term used in Roman Catholic THEOLOGY to describe the condition of those who because of their heredity, upbringing or environment cannot see a religious or moral truth, e.g. the truth of CATHOLICISM, whatever efforts they may make, and who are therefore not to blame. The term, although apparently offensive, expresses the charitable attitude, now happily characteristic of Roman Catholics, towards both sinners and non-Catholics. D.L.E.

invisibility. In his important existential (see EXISTENTIALISM) first novel, *The Invisible Man* (1952), Ralph Ellison reveals what it is like to not be recognized by the dominant society as a person. According to Wright, African-Americans live in a society that causes them to face the existential question 'Who am I?' in a way that is qualitatively different from the experience of members of the dominant group (see AFROCENTRICITY; DOUBLE-CONSCIOUSNESS). This qualitative difference can be traced to the historical assault on the humanity and citizenship of African-Americans. Ellison's concept of invisibility reveals the psychological and political struggles that African-Americans experience in their attempts to combat stereotypical perceptions of them which serve to undermine their humanity.

Although African-Americans have had significant influence on American culture, they have often not been recognized for their contributions, which are still denied and devalued by a society that is still struggling with the legacy of WHITE SUPREMACY. One important function of African studies is its attempt to address these omissions. Becoming aware of them is seen as a necessary first step in addressing the invisibility so vividly described by Ellison. H.M.

invisible astronomy. There have been two remarkable leaps forward in man's ability to discern the contents of the heavens. One came in the 17th century with the invention of the telescope. The other occurred in the 1930s when astronomers' traditional total reliance upon optical wavelengths for the observation of celestial bodies was supplemented by the use of cosmic radio waves. This was thanks to the discovery by the radio engineer Karl Jansky (1905–50) of extraterrestrial radio waves. RADIO ASTRONOMY, however, was quite slow to develop (it was given a big spur by studies of RADAR during World War II). From 1946 onwards, radio astronomers made increasing finds of radio stars (the first was found in Cygnus by T. S. Hey's team in Britain). Vast radio dishes came to be constructed at Arecibo (Puerto Rico), the Max Planck Institute in Bonn, Jodrell Bank, Cheshire, Goldstone, California, and Parkes, New South Wales. Extra-galactic finds have been central to the role of radio astronomy as an instrument of discovery, but finds within the GALAXY have been important too, including the discovery of QUASARS and PULSARS by the Cambridge team in the 1960s. For further reading: F. G. Smith, *Radio Astronomy* (1974). R.P.

invisibles. That component of a country's BALANCE OF PAYMENTS on current account which comprises receipts and payments for services (as distinct from 'visible' goods); cash gifts, legacies, and other transfers for which no service is rendered; and the two-way flow of interest, profits and dividends between home and abroad. All these items, which may be on government or private account, make up the *invisible balance*. The phrase *invisible exports* and imports, however, is usually restricted to travel, financial and other services such as sea transport, civil aviation, insurance, banking, merchanting, brokerage, etc. These items are also included, with visible trade, in the concept of 'exports and imports of goods and services'. Fuller definitions and figures for recent years are set out in the annual volume entitled *United Kingdom Balance of Payments*. P.J.

involuntary euthanasia, see under EUTHANASIA.

ion. An ATOM OR MOLECULE which is electrically charged because of an excess or deficiency of ELECTRONS (see ATOMIC PHYSICS); excess of electrons results in a negatively charged *anion*, deficiency in a positively charged *cation*. Ions produced by fast charged particles form the basis of several detectors used in ELEMENTARY PARTICLE physics (e.g. the bubble chamber, CLOUD CHAMBER and geiger counter). Ions of chemical salts and acids in solution provide the source of current in many electrical CELLS. Because of its conceptual simplicity, the ionic MODEL is a very useful way of viewing many solids and solutions, but since electrons are at least partially shared between neighbouring atoms it is at best a good approximation. See also IONOSPHERE. M.V.B.; B.F.

ionosphere. The radio-reflecting layers in the atmosphere, on which over-the-horizon radio transmission depends. At heights above about 100 km, positive IONS are produced from ATOMS in the air by short-wave RADIATION from the sun; the resulting free ELECTRONS give rise to the radio reflections. See also PLASMA PHYSICS. M.V.B.

IPA (International Phonetic Alphabet). The most widely used system for transcribing the sounds of a language, originally drawn up in 1889, but subsequently modified and expanded at various times by the International Phonetics Association. See also PHONETICS. D.C.

IRA, see IRISH REPUBLICAN ARMY.

Iran-contra affair. A US foreign-policy scandal during President Reagan's second term (1985–89) that involved the secret sale of arms to Iran in hopes of gaining the release of US hostages held in the Middle East, and the illegal diversion of resulting profits to rebel forces seeking to overthrow the SANDINISTA government of Nicaragua. In 1986, Reagan acknowledged that such an arrangement had been put into place without his knowledge. The disclosure outraged many, given Iran's pariah status and Congress's explicit prohibition against any American aid to the contra rebels. Investigations into the deal painted an unflattering picture of Reagan as detached from policy-making and ignored or misled by his highest aides. The scandal also showed the determination of Reagan's men to topple the Sandinistas. A number of top Reagan aides were convicted on charges as a result of the scandal, most notably Marine Lt-Colonel Oliver North, a gung-ho White House aide who emerged as a conservative icon, later losing a US Senate race in Virginia. On Christmas Eve 1992, a month after losing his re-election bid, President Bush pardoned all the main figures of the scandal, including former Secretary of Defense Caspar Weinberger, who was awaiting trial on charges of lying to Congress. Special Prosecutor Lawrence Walsh put out his own report in 1994 chastizing Reagan and Bush for their role in the scandal, but charged neither with breaking any laws. For further reading: L. Walsh, *Iran-Contra: The Final Report* (1994). R.K.H.

Iran–Iraq War. Originated with an Iraqi attack on Iran in September 1980 and a debilitating phase of secular ideological, political and territorial conflict between Persian Iran and Arab Iraq. Iraqi motives were defensive, to counter the expansion of the Iranian revolution, and offensive, aiming to recover the Shatt al-Arab frontier ceded to Iran in 1975 and to achieve paramountcy in the Gulf region. Expectations of a quick victory over Iranian forces divided by the revolution and attacked in the rear by the Arab populations of Khuzistan proved illusory. The war became a stalemate, confirmed by the failure of a massive Iranian offensive in 1984, with Iraq ready to settle for a return to the status quo, but Iran, for whom the war was an essential part of the revolutionary ideal, insisting that the 'godless' Iraqi Ba'ath regime change. The war was sometimes represented as advantageous to all but the combatants since it neutralized the two main rivals for Gulf supremacy and reduced the supply of oil to a glutted market. But the heavy loss of life and resources, the Iraqi use of gas and anxieties lest the war spread down the Gulf came to outweigh the more optimistic calculations of REALPOLITIK. The war ended in July/August 1988, when Iran too accepted United Nations Security Council Resolution 598, demanding a ceasefire in the war. For further reading: D. Hiro, *The Longest War: The Iran–Iraq Military Conflict* (1989). W.K.; A.EH.

Iranian revolution. The Iranian REVOLUTION of 1979, also known as the Islamic revolution (see ISLAM), marked the end of one of the world's oldest monarchies, dating back over 2,000 years. Iran's revolutionary movement, relying on extensive mass support, started in 1977 and culminated in the ruling (Pahlavi) monarch's downfall on 16 January 1979, ending nearly a century of struggle between the secular-leaning forces and the powerful Shia clerical establishment. The Iranian revolution was unique for being led by a cleric, Ayatollah Ruhollah Khomeini. The revolution set a new pattern in revolutionary politics by its reliance on religious symbols (see RELIGION) and IDEOLOGY, and its rejection of secularist liberation ideologies (see SECULARIZATION). It also prided itself on overturning the MARXIST, MATERIALIST revolutionary agenda of the modern world with a spiritualist, religious one. Finally, the revolution cleared the way for the founding of the Muslim world's first revolutionary-Islamic republic (which was declared on 1 April 1979), in which the clerics emerged as the dominant political élite. A new form of governance, the Velayat-e Faqih (or 'rule of jurist consult') system, was also adopted. The Iranian revolution has left an indelible mark on the modern world, particularly in the Middle East region, where it has inspired and provided moral and material support for other Islamic movements. The revolution, in its efforts to 'export' its message, was increasingly perceived as a mortal threat to neighbouring countries. Such fears caused new tensions between non-Arab Iran and its Arab neighbours, culminating in Iraq's invasion of Iranian territory in September 1980 (see IRAN–IRAQ war). Also, the revolutionary regime presented itself as an alternative to hereditary rule in the Muslim world, thus challenging the legitimacy of other traditional Arab rulers in the area. For further reading: M. M. Milani, *The Making of Iran's Islamic Revolution* (1994). A.EH.

IRBM (intermediate-range ballistic missiles), see under MISSILES.

Irgun Zvai Leumi (Hebrew for 'National Military Organization'). An armed extremist Jewish underground organization founded in 1937 by ZIONISTS in secession from the main Palestinian Jewish self-defence organization, the Hagana. It engaged first in anti-Arab, then in anti-British activities, until the outbreak of war in Europe in September 1939. Remaining inactive until January 1944, it then resumed anti-British sabotage and TERRORIST activities. Irgun Zvai Leumi, acting independently of Hagana, was responsible for blowing up British offices in the King David Hotel, Jerusalem, in 1946 and for the massacre of Arab villagers at Deir Yasin in 1948. It was forcibly disbanded by the Israeli government in September 1948. D.C.W.

Irish National Liberation Army (INLA). A violently militant splinter group of the official IRA, the INLA has since 1973 carried out a campaign of assassination and violence in Ulster, Britain and, in concert with other TERRORIST groups, mainland Europe. It was responsible for the killing of Airey Neave, MP, by a car bomb on 30 March 1979. For further reading: T. P. Coogan, *The IRA* (1987). M.W.

Irish Republican Army (IRA). The Irish Republican Army is a NATIONALIST paramilitary organization dedicated to the unification of Ireland into a single autonomous republic. It is a lineal descendant of the anti-British, revolutionary Fenian movement begun in 1858, reorganized as the Irish Republican Brotherhood (IRB) in 1873, and linked to the Fenian Brotherhood in the US. Defeated in the Easter Rising against British rule in 1916, the IRB and its paramilitary arm, the Irish Volunteer Force, evolved into the IRA in 1919. It fought against British occupation forces, rejected the Anglo-Irish agreement of 6 December 1921 which maintained British SOVEREIGNTY over the six counties of Ulster, and rebelled against the government of the newly formed Irish Free State which accepted that partition. It became an underground and marginal organization, involved in sporadic campaigns of bombing in Britain and raids into Ulster until the mid-1950s, and promoting the 'Border Campaign' of 1956–62.

In 1969 the violent Ulster Unionist response to the CIVIL RIGHTS MOVEMENT revived the IRA's standing in the North. The Belfast-based northern leadership broke with the Dublin-based Army High Command in January 1970 to form the Provisional IRA (PIRA). After a short internecine struggle it dominated the Republican cause in Ulster, while the rump of the official IRA lapsed into insignificance.

Since 1970 the PIRA's fortunes and tactics have fluctuated. Until 1981 it relied largely on terrorist tactics in the attempt to force British withdrawal from Ulster. In that year, in concert with its political wing, Provisional Sinn Fein, it adopted a strategy combining selective violence with conventional political activity – denoted by the phrase of PSF publicist Danny Morrison, 'a ballot paper in this hand and an Armalite in this hand'. Many took the IRA ceasefire from 1994 to 1996 to be a calculated extension of this policy; attempting to win further concessions by claiming an interest in peace. However, some did see the ceasefire as representing the beginning of a genuine commitment to peaceful settlement by the IRA. In 1998, though, the Irish town of Omagh was bombed by an IRA splinter group called the 'Real IRA', and although the IRA itself and Sinn Fein distanced themselves from the bombing, many believe that they have links to the 'Real IRA'. Whether Irish republicanism (see REPUBLICANISM, IRISH) can ever be an entirely peaceful and democratic movement is still an open question. For further reading: P. Taylor, *The Provos, the IRA and Sinn Fein* (1997). S.R.; M.W.

iron curtain. A phrase used to describe the enforced isolation of areas under the political domination of the former USSR from the rest of the non-Soviet world. Often used in German by the Nazi propaganda minister Goebbels, it was adopted in English by Churchill and popularized in his Fulton speech of March 1946. D.C.W.

irradiation, see under PAVLOVIAN.

irrationalism. The view either that the conduct of men *is* not or that it *should* not be guided by reason. On the whole the two views are sharply opposed, and the two parties could be called, respectively, *descriptive* and NORMATIVE irrationalists. (1) The descriptive irrationalists are, for the most part, rather disillusioned or sceptical social theorists. Mild examples are Bagehot and Graham Wallas; a more scornful one is Pareto. Marx and Freud, both themselves dedicated to rationality, can be regarded without distortion as descriptive irrationalists:

Marx for his theory of the false consciousness of men in an alienating social system (see MARXISM; ALIENATION), Freud for his view that the fundamental determinants of belief and conduct are UNCONSCIOUS and irrational (see FREUDIAN). Any theory (like the last two, or like Mannheim's sociology of knowledge; see KNOWLEDGE, SOCIOLOGY OF) which implies that all human thinking is irrational has a self-refuting tendency. (2) Among normative irrationalists may be included Rousseau for his emphasis on sentiment and natural impulse and his hostility to civilized sophistication; D. H. Lawrence for his glorification of primal instinct as against BOURGEOIS prudence and calculation; Kierkegaard for his insistence on the absurdity of the human situation; and, perhaps above all, Nietzsche (see NIETZSCHEAN). Normative irrationalism began and has continued as a protest against the consequences of INDUSTRIALIZATION. A.Q.

irredentism. Politico-geographical term denoting the behaviour of a concerned government towards a COMMUNITY of its nationals who constitute a minority group in a neighbouring state. Frequently this concern escalates from a desire to protect the interests of the cross-border community to an aggressive policy of cultural extension and perhaps even political expansion. The concept originated in the efforts of the Rome government at the turn of the century to annex an adjacent portion of Italian-speaking Austria (South Tyrol), which the Italians regarded as *Italia Irredenta* ('Unredeemed Italy'). Irredentism today is common throughout the ethnic mosaic of south-eastern Europe, where the cultural boundaries of national groups rarely coincide with international political boundaries. The large Hungarian community in south-westernmost Slovakia, located just to the north of the Danube boundary with Hungary, is one of many such trouble spots in this conflict-bedevilled region. P.O.M.

Islam. Literally 'surrender' or 'submission' to God; the religion founded by the prophet Muhammad (*c.* 570–632) in Mecca and Medina in eastern Arabia. The profession of faith which all Muslims must make is the *shahada*: 'there is no God but God, and Muhammad is the Prophet of God'. In addition pious Muslims should pray five times a day, give alms (*zakat*), fast from dawn to dusk during the holy month of Ramadan, and if possible make the pilgrimage to Mecca (the *hajj*) at least once. These four rituals, with the *shahada*, are the five pillars of Islam. Muslims reject the epithet Muhammadan as implying a submission to the prophet which is rightfully owed only to God. The scripture of Islam is the Koran (or Quran), believed to be literally the word of God and the most perfect revelation of God to man. *Shari'a* is Islamic Holy Law, based on the Koran and the sayings and actions of Muhammad and his early companions (the *hadith*). The written word is thus central to Islam, but many pious Muslims, generally known as Sufis, have also sought God through MYSTICISM and have formed religious orders to do so.

The most important sectarian division in Islam emerged within 50 years of the death of the prophet and concerned the succession to the leadership, and its nature. For most Muslims – Sunnis – leadership passed to the first four 'orthodox' Caliphs and then to the Omayyad and Abbasid Caliphates. These successors to the prophet exercised only temporal power. Shi'is believe that the prophet's son-in-law, Ali (the fourth orthodox Caliph), was Muhammad's direct successor and established a line of succession, of which the twelfth leader (Imam) did not die but disappeared, retaining final authority until his eventual return; until then there can be no truly legitimate leader on earth. Shi'is generally have therefore an enduring suspicion of political authority, and this is no doubt strengthened by their minority position (see MINORITIES). Of about 700 million Muslims in the world about 87 million are Shi'is. Only in Iran is Shi'ism the official religion, although Shi'is are a majority in Iraq and a majority of the Muslims in Lebanon. Conflict between Sunnis and Shi'is stems more from NATIONALIST and communal feeling than theological difference. Like CHRISTIANITY, Islam has many minority SECTS. The most important for late 20th-century politics are the Alawites, a Shi'i sect which, although representing only 10 per cent of the population, captured power through the Ba'ath Party and the army, and the more eccentric Druze (believing in reincarnation) in Lebanon, Syria and Israel. Wahhabis, named from their 18th-century founder, are puritanical and fundamentalist, form an essential part of the government, and retain great influence in Saudi Arabia. The BAHAI religion departed from Islam and is regarded as heretical by Muslims and therefore subject to persecution, especially in Iran, where it originated in the mid-19th century.

Islam responded to the expansion of the West first by a movement of reform (the *tanzimat*) originating in the 19th-century Ottoman Empire, and by a movement called pan-Islam – a largely Western concept denoting Islamic resistance to the divisions imposed on Islam by imperial rule. The late 20th century has seen a resurgence of Islam, differing from the reform movement of the 19th century in its emphasis on Muslim fundamentalism. Its political content is not new since Islam has always been concerned with political organization; Muhammad was not only a prophet but a consummate politician who built a community in Medina. The most important fundamentalist organization, the Muslim Brotherhood, was founded in Egypt by Hasan al-Banna in 1928 and survived suppression by Nasser. The proliferation of Muslim groups can, however, be dated from the Egyptian defeat in the MIDDLE EAST WAR of 1967 which discredited 'Arab SOCIALISM' borrowed from the West. In a sense all ACTIVIST Muslim groups look for a return to the Shari'a, since Muslim law gives rules for personal STATUS and conduct as well as for political behaviour. The weakness of Shari'a is that it lacks rules to govern modern political and economic organization, so that neither Libya nor Iran have dispensed with legal systems adopted from the West, and Saudi Arabia has added Western codes to the Shari'a. The diversity of activist Muslim groups is immense, and while some are egalitarian (see EGALITARIANISM) others are conservative (see CONSERVATISM) in economic doctrine. Of key importance are the lengths to which any one group will go in denying the legitimacy of a government. A purifying mission has always been part of the ethos of the Muslim Brotherhood, who tried to assassinate Nasser and from whom a splinter group assassinated Sadat. Other groups merely demonstrate for the adoption of Shari'a as STATE law or are content with strict personal behaviour and dress. Governments of Muslim countries, especially Arab governments alarmed by the added impact of the Iranian revolution, have tried to reinforce their legitimacy by stricter observance of Islam, especially in inessentials such as the banning of alcohol. Arab rulers have also made appeal to the idea of *jihad*, conventionally translated as 'holy war' but originally meaning 'effort'. It was in this sense that so secular a ruler as President Bourguiba called for a jihad of ECONOMIC DEVELOPMENT when Tunisia became independent. King Fahd called for a jihad against Israel when Begin claimed Jerusalem as its capital, but this had no military sequel. Khomeini has invoked jihad against the government of Iraq whom he distinguishes from the Iraqi people since jihad cannot be waged against fellow Muslims. For further reading: B. Walker, *The Foundations of Islam* (1997).

W.K.

isolating (in LINGUISTICS), see under ANALYTIC (2).

isolationism. The doctrine that a nation's interests are best served by abstaining from intervention in the main issues or institutions of international politics. Variously practised in Imperial China, Czarist Russia and arguably in late Victorian Britain ('splendid isolation'), it more specifically applies to American attitudes to the world of great-power politics before 1941, particularly after the US Senate's rejection of the Versailles Treaty and the LEAGUE OF NATIONS. In fact the USA was historically inclined more to a hemispheric than global isolationism, which combined a detachment from European affairs with a lively conviction of its right to order those of the Americas – both attitudes given a common rhetorical justification by appealing to the nation's sense of moral virtue and mission. Since the end of the COLD WAR, American conservatives have revived isolationist arguments which combine a rejection of international institutions such as the United Nations (see UN), an emphasis on the need to attend to the country's own economic problems, and a reluctance to act as a 'global policeman' without due regard for the human or material cost to the nation. Their arguments do not prevail in determining policy, but act as a considerable constraint, particularly on the use of US military force in any situation which does not seriously threaten US interests. For further reading:

E. Nordlinger, *Isolationism Reconfigured* (1995). S.R.

isomorphism. Two mathematical systems are said to be isomorphic if each is, in some precise way, a picture of the other. Certain methods of PROOF may work only in one system, but any properties found will then automatically be mirrored in the other system. Thus the COMPLEX NUMBERS are isomorphic to a certain set of matrices (see MATRIX): all the basic algebraic properties (see ALGEBRA) of those matrices then automatically apply to the complex numbers. The complex numbers are also isomorphic to the points on a piece of (infinite) graph paper, with addition and multiplication corresponding to certain geometrical operations (see GEOMETRY). Many results about these points and operations can be established by purely geometrical arguments, and then results automatically transfer back to the complex numbers. Mathematicians tend (except when being very scrupulous) to regard isomorphic systems as being the same – they say, e.g., 'there is only one group with five elements' when they mean 'all the groups with five elements are isomorphic to each other'. N.A.R.

isoquant. In ECONOMICS, the set of different combinations of inputs of production that can be used to give the same level of output of a product. There is an isoquant for each level of output. The use of the inputs is assumed to be efficient in that the level of output associated with each combination is the maximum possible. In microeconomics it is assumed that the objective of the firm (see FIRM, THEORIES OF) is to minimize the costs of producing a given level of output, and this can be represented on a diagram of isoquants (see SUBSTITUTION). J.P.

isorhythm. The application of a single and reiterated rhythmic pattern to differing melodic shapes. The term was originally applied by F. Ludwig in 1902 to rhythmic patterns that recur in 14th-century motets. Recently isorhythmic patterns have been much exploited by contemporary composers, in particular Messiaen. A.H.

isostasy. Term proposed in 1889 by C. E. Dutton for the principle that the surface features of the earth will tend towards an ideal condition of gravitational EQUILIBRIUM; the *isostatic theory* proposes that balance is achieved by sub-surface inequalities of mass and implies that there is horizontal transfer of mantle material at depth. It is known that the earth's crust is less dense than the underlying mantle (see ASTHENOSPHERE), so that the situation can be likened to blocks of wood floating on water. The bigger the block of wood, the higher it sticks out of the water, and the deeper it sinks underneath. Similarly the increasingly higher blocks of the earth's crust above sea-level are balanced by greater thicknesses of crust below sea-level. The flow of the mantle is very slow, so that the attainment of isostatic equilibrium lags behind the more rapid changes of mass caused by certain geological processes operating on the earth's surface. This is why those parts of the earth's surface that were depressed under the load of the Pleistocene ice-sheets are still rising, even though the ice melted some 15,000 years ago. J.L.M.L.

isotope geochemistry. The study of naturally occurring ISOTOPES with a view to obtaining information on the origin and evolution of the earth's rocks and minerals, and hence ultimately of the earth itself. The most prominent use of isotopes in the EARTH SCIENCES – in this case of RADIO ISOTOPES – is for the DATING of rocks. Because the decay characteristics of radioactive isotopes are known, it is easy to measure the relative proportions of the still-decaying isotopes and the decay products in a rock or rock mineral, and hence extrapolate back to determine the time at which the decay process began. This is taken to be the time at which the rock formed and thus defines the rock's age. The first decay series to be so used, in the early 20th century, was uranium to lead, but the chief series in use today for rocks more than a few tens of thousands of years old are potassium to argon and rubidium to strontium. For younger rocks containing organic remains, and in ARCHAEOLOGY, RADIOCARBON DATING may be used.

Stable isotopes of the lighter elements are not always uniform in nature, their precise distribution being the result of numerous natural processes and of the temperatures at which these processes took place. The isotopic compositions of certain rocks and minerals may therefore be used to deduce the thermal histories of both rocks and natural waters. For example, the ratio of the isotopes oxygen-18 and oxygen-16 in the calcium carbonate shells of ancient organisms provides the temperature at which the carbonate formed and hence of the seawater in which it formed. Isotopes are important in studies of the earth's internal temperature. Radio isotopes emit heat when they decay. Much, though not all, of the earth's internal heat is thought to have been generated in this way throughout the planet's 4,600 million years of history – a figure derived from the analysis of radio isotopes in both the earth and meteorites. P.J.S.

isotopes. ATOMS of the same chemical ELEMENT, having the same ATOMIC NUMBER, but differing from each other in respect of the number of NEUTRONS in the NUCLEUS; e.g. deuterium is an isotope of hydrogen. M.V.B.

Israel, see under JUDAISM; ZIONISM.

issue networks. Term coined in 1978 by political scientist Hugh Heclo to represent his conceptualization of policy-making in the USA. Heclo regarded an older concept of 'iron triangles' – close, mutually supportive and continuous relationships between INTEREST GROUPS, executive bureaux and Congressional committees – as a poor guide to a changed political environment. The changes included a proliferation of increasingly resourceful interest groups, the devolution of Congressional power to subcommittees and staff, and the growth of more complex intergovernmental, academic, partisan and quasi-governmental sources of knowledge and influence. The result is a growth in large, amorphous policy communities or 'issue networks' composed of numerous individuals and institutions competing for influence in an environment made unstable and uncertain by the range and type of participants involved. The term has acquired widespread usage, although it is arguably more evocative than analytic of a complex political system in which the alleged diffusion and unpredictability of influence may be greater in some areas (e.g. consumer law) than others (i.e. defence policy). S.R.

Italianization. Term used in connection with west European COMMUNIST parties. It refers to the ideological and strategic development of the Italian Communist Party during the 1960s and 1970s. In particular, the PCI's support for eurocommunism and its decision to seek an HISTORIC COMPROMISE with other major political parties. S.M.

IZL, see IRGUN ZVAI LEUMI.

J

Jack of Diamonds, see KNAVE OR JACK OF DIAMONDS.

Jacobinism. The Jacobins were the most radical of the French Revolutionaries, and their intransigent commitment to the cause of the REVOLUTION inspired many subsequent radicals; Lenin explicitly compared his Bolsheviks (see BOLSHEVISM) with the Jacobins and the MENSHEVIKS with the more moderate Girondins. Although the Jacobins were in principle committed to some kind of popular DEMOCRACY, the impact of Robespierre's personality and the exigencies of the time led them inexorably to embrace DICTATORSHIP and terror. The 'English Jacobins' of the 1790s never followed them in this, and were, in fact, notably non-violent in their RADICALISM. After the French Revolution, 'Jacobinism' became a non-specific label for any kind of radicalism which put its trust in insurrection and leadership rather than in parliamentary methods and persuasion. A.R.

James-Lange theory. The theory of EMOTION proposed principally by William James (*Principles of Psychology*, 1890) and resting upon the premise that emotion is the perception of bodily changes that occur when we respond to an emotion-arousing situation. That is, we are afraid 'because' we flee rather than fleeing 'because' we are afraid. James elevated the original idea of C. G. Lange (1834–1900) that emotion was a change in the cardiovascular system and gave it the elaboration here noted to account for the distinctive quality of different emotions. J.S.B.

Japanization. A term used by some commentators to refer to the spread of Japanese production techniques to the industries of other countries. These include: teamworking, quality circles which allow staff at all levels to contribute to improvements in production, JIT (just-in-time) systems which deliver components to the place of production as they are needed (saving on the costs of maintaining a stock of components), an emphasis on quality control and continuous innovation and improvements in production, and a corporate culture which emphasizes loyalty to the firm (see FIRM, THEORIES OF). Japanization has been encouraged both through foreign direct investment by Japanese corporations and through the imitation of Japanese methods. Some aspects of POST-FORDISM and of flexible firms fit well with the idea of Japanization, but the extent to which it has taken place is controversial. It has affected different parts of the world to different extents, and some aspects of Japanese practices have proved more popular than others. For further reading: T. Elger and C. Smith, *Global Japanization?* (1994). M.D.H.

jazz. A few key certainties can be distilled out of the misty speculations surrounding the origins of the music (the actual name almost certainly had something to do with sex). Without question it was a unique product of the enforced wedding of African and European musical cultures in the American South. Deprived of everything else, the blacks enslaved on Southern plantations brought with them their musical traditions. The work songs and spirituals they evolved showed characteristics of their African heritage: a rhythmic sophistication and flexibility unknown in European music, a more supple sense of pitch and ornamentation, and a free, emotional style of delivery that reflected the need for their music to express and relieve great care. The work song especially informed the compact, deeply felt declamation of the BLUES. Influcnced heavily by the emerging blues form, jazz also made crucial use of the forms and materials of European music particularly available in the rich culture of NEW ORLEANS, where the African elements mixed with marches, dances like the quadrille and even popular airs from operas. Such cross-fertilization exposed black music to harmonic structures which African music largely lacked. The process intensified in the later 19th century as blacks gained access to orchestral instruments, particularly those of brass bands, which they adapted to their own expressive needs. Certainly by 1890 a kind of proto-jazz had appeared in New Orleans, a blend of all these elements, identified especially by strong but flexible rhythm and improvisation. New Orleans remained the matrix of jazz into the 1920s, by which time the music had established itself not just in America but in Europe as well.

The subsequent development and growing sophistication of jazz increased debate as to its basic nature and identity. By the 1950s, the term encompassed the complexity of bebop, the defiant simplicity of trad, the relaxed maturity of mainstream, and their warring partisans. Factionalism intensified in the 1960s with the onset of free jazz and culminated in a kind of commercial meltdown, in which jazz largely lost its audience to rock. Jazz-rock fusion was one response. Another, after 1980, was spearheaded by a band of brilliant young players led by the trumpeter Wynton Marsalis (1961–), who was determined to reassert the old jazz fundamentals of SWING and blues, condemning both FUSION and free jazz as aberrations. Equally gifted as player, organizer and polemicist, Marsalis has remained a centre of controversy, hailed by some as the saviour of jazz, decried by others as a neo-conservative reactionary bent on cutting the music off from contemporary culture and stifling the variety which has been its strength. Similarly, jazz lovers have mixed feelings about the booming popularity of the music as an academic subject and the rise of repertory bands, dedicated to recreating past achievements rather than inspiring new ones. Indeed, some critics maintain that jazz is a spent creative force, while others insist it will continue to grow in new directions, involving classical, HIP-HOP or WORLD MUSIC. (See also CHICAGO; RAGTIME; SWING; BEBOP; MAINSTREAM; FREE JAZZ; RHYTHM AND BLUES; BOOGIE-WOOGIE.) GE.S.

jazz age. A term used, mainly with reference to the USA, for the decade between the end of World War I and the Great Crash (1929). The white DIXIELAND version of black JAZZ which formed the base of the period's characteristic dance style reflected the general atmosphere of excitement and confidence of the era, created by a popular faith in lasting peace and prosperity. Social, sexual and cultural values were permanently altered by the social and material changes of this first period of mass-consumption, which made available silent movies, radios, cars and other consumer goods. The flamboyance and economic confidence of the period is portrayed particularly well by Scott Fitzgerald, notably in *Tales of the Jazz Age* (1922), including 'The Diamond as Big as the Ritz', and *The Great Gatsby* (1925). The jazz age was also, however, an age of hysteria over 'BOLSHEVISM' (e.g. the execution of Sacco and Vanzetti, 1927), gangster economics (e.g. the Teapot Dome scandal, 1923–24), a *prohibition* of alcohol which was everywhere defied (with pervasive attendant crime), and of intellectual anachronisms like the Scopes Monkey Trial, in which a schoolteacher was arraigned for the teaching of EVOLUTION. P.S.L.

jazz poetry. Poetry designed to be read with JAZZ accompaniment. In the 1960s it had a considerable vogue in Britain and parts of the USA, with Christopher Logue and Kenneth Rexroth, respectively, as leading exponents. M.S.-S.

j-curve, see under DEVALUATION.

Jehovah's Witnesses. A basically American religious body, also called the 'Watch Tower Bible and Tract Society'. Founded by C. T. Russell and by J. F. ('Judge') Rutherford (1869–1941), it attacks the Christian Churches and calls on its adherents to reject military service and blood transfusion. It prophesies that 144,000 Jehovah's Witnesses will form the elect in heaven at the imminent end of the world, and will rule over the 'Jonadabs' or resurrected people of goodwill inhabiting a new earth. The Witnesses are more active than welcome in door-to-door evangelism (see EVANGELICAL). For further reading: H. H. Stroup, *The Jehovah's Witnesses* (1945). D.L.E.

jihad ('holy war'), see under ISLAM.

JIT (just-in-time) systems, see under JAPANIZATION.

jouissance. A French, as well as an archaic English, word for enjoyment. In spite of its stronger sexual connotation in French, it has taken on a wider significance in psychoanalytical theory. In LACANIAN thought, it defines what lies beyond the FREUDIAN pleasure principle, and what escapes the EGO's censorship (see SUPEREGO). When this censorship breaks down, as in nightmares or psychotic states, jouissance manifests itself as unpleasure, in the form of the symptom. It is experienced as pleasurable only in a limited number of cases, as in the form of mystical ecstasy and in some forms of feminine sexual enjoyment (see FEMININE SEXUALITY). B.BE.

Judaism. The RELIGION of the Jews. This is based on interpretations of Jewish history, notably the exodus from Egypt, the foundation and development of Israel and Judah, the exile in Babylon, the fall of the Second Temple in Jerusalem, and the diaspora of the Jews across the Roman world and beyond. Many of these vicissitudes are recorded in the Hebrew Bible (called by Christians the Old Testament). In the time after the destruction of the Temple the religion was significantly carried on by the tradition of the Rabbis, and they studied the Torah as a living, developing entity, summed up above all in the Talmud. The medieval Christian period saw the confinement of Jews to GHETTOS and to substantial tracts of land in eastern Europe and Russia. In the 18th and 19th centuries, the Jews were released from such confinement to a considerable extent, and this saw new forms of the faith emerging: notably reform Judaism, which eschewed the more rigorous interpretations of the Torah; and conservative Judaism, which combined orthodox and modernizing tendencies, and was founded by Solomon Sonlechter (1847–1915). Both these movements were influential in North America.

The foundation of ZIONISM just before the beginning of the 20th century was followed by Chaim Weizmann's (1874–1952) powerful argument for the foundation of a Jewish nation in Israel. That might have foundered but for the horrors of the HOLOCAUST. Israel brought a new dimension into Judaism, not merely because orthodox Rabbis had control over rituals related to the STATE; but also because the old images of Jerusalem and Zion were given a new realistic vividness. The famous greeting 'next year in Jerusalem' could now be interpreted literally. Meanwhile SECULARIZATION developed: many Jews in America, e.g., and in Israel, do not practise or believe in the religion. Others have drifted off into other religions (notably BUDDHISM). New FUNDAMENTALIST groupings have occurred in Israel, committed to a greater or more aggressive stance, such as the Gush Emunim. While reform Judaism tends to play down the ritual aspect of the faith, much of the religion is devoted to ritual – the requirements of the Torah, the celebration of the festivals and high holy days, the ceremonials of family life, and the life of the synagogue. This side of Jewish life is not always thoroughly understood outside the religion. For further reading: N. Solomon, *Judaism: A Very Short Introduction* (1996). N.SM.

judicial review. The power of a court to pass on the validity of legislative or administrative actions. In the US, it is the basis for the power of the US Supreme Court (see SUPREME COURT OF THE UNITED STATES) and its authority to declare state and federal laws void as unconstitutional. The principle was established in the then controversial decision Marbury v. Madison in 1803, but it gradually became the accepted view of judicial power in the US. The doctrine led to a great expansion of judicial power and activism in the late 19th century and throughout this century, and continues to be controversial among supporters of STATES' rights. M.S.P.

Judson Dance Theater. Co-founded by Robert Dunn, Steve Paxton and Yvonne Rainer. It was established as a weekly meeting at the Judson Memorial Church, New York, in 1962. It was a focus for experimental work founded in the POST-MODERN DANCE aesthetic and acted as a forum and catalyst for collaborative projects between artists. The focus of the work corresponded with the MODERNIST movement in that the arts sought to free themselves from convention. The informal and flexible nature of the Judson Dance Theater permitted 'non-dancers' to dance and choreograph, furthering the demystification of dance. Until 1968 it acted as a platform, educating and challenging audience expectations by providing free concerts for the community. For further reading: S. Banes, *Democracy's Body: Judson Dance Theater 1962–1964* (1980). L.A.

Jugendstil, see under ART NOUVEAU.

July 20th. The date in 1944 of an abortive *coup d'état* in Nazi Germany directed at the overthrow of Hitler. Involved in the conspiracy were anti-Nazis in the armed forces and the Prussian aristocracy, together with former diplomats, clergy, civil servants and trade unionists. The *putsch* failed when Hitler escaped with his life, but it achieved considerable momentary success in Paris and Vienna. The German resistance suffered from the fact that, unlike the resistance movement in occupied countries, it ran in the face of national feeling in a time of war, and (particularly when the plot failed) was open to the charge of treason. The conspirators were hunted down and executed, often after being tortured. Their moral courage in risking their lives in protest against the Nazi regime has seemed more important subsequently than their failure to overthrow it. For further reading: M. Thomsett, *The German Opposition to Hitler* (1997). A.L.C.B.

jumping gene, see under TRANSPOSABLE ELEMENT.

Jungian. Adjective applied to a theory of personality put forward by Carl Gustav Jung (1875–1961) as an alternative to the FREUDIAN view, and rejecting the latter's emphasis on the centrality of sexual instincts. Jung left the psychoanalytical movement (see PSYCHOANALYSIS) in 1913 to practise *analytic psychology*, according to which man's behaviour is determined not only by the conflicts already present in his individual and racial history (the personal and COLLECTIVE UNCONSCIOUS), but also by his aims and aspirations. The character and indeed even the quality of dreams suggest the striving towards individuation; according to analytic psychology, man seeks creative development, wholeness and completion. The individual personality contains memories, known as ARCHETYPES, of its ancestral history which can be studied through MYTHS. Jung postulated two basic PERSONALITY TYPES, characterized respectively by EXTROVERSION and INTROVERSION. For further reading: A. Samuels, *Jung and the PostJungians* (1985). R.P.-S.

junk DNA, see under SELFISH DNA.

junta. Although the term literally means an 'executive council' or 'board', it has generally been used to describe the military councils which exercised *de facto* control of the state in a number of Latin American countries, most notably between the 1950s and 1980s, although the first juntas were established in the 19th century during the independence struggles against Spain. In some cases, as in Venezuela during the period known as the 'Trienio', between 1945 and 1948, executive power was shared through a joint civilian-military junta. However, in most cases military governments in the region exercised control through a three-member junta consisting of the commanders-in-chief of the army, air force and navy (as in Argentina in 1955, 1966 and 1976) or a four-member junta (in which the commander of the paramilitary police would also participate), as in Chile in 1973–90. Military juntas were also in power in Bolivia, Ecuador, El Salvador, Guatemala and Peru. In many cases, the army representative on the junta would also act as the country's president. For further reading: A. F. Lowenthal and J. Samuel Fitch (eds), *Armies and Politics in Latin America* (1986). M.A.P.

jurisprudence of concepts, see under CONCEPTUALISM (2).

just-in-time (JIT) systems, see under JAPANIZATION.

justice. Said by many writers to be the first of social virtues, justice has been the subject of intense argument in the last two decades. Recent discussion has centred on the work of John Rawls, Robert Nozick and Friedrich von Hayek. John Rawls's *A Theory of Justice* (1971) argued that recent political theory had been too utilitarian (see UTILITARIANISM), too unconcerned with individual rights; by asking the question 'What rules would mankind contract to obey if they were to establish a social order in conditions where none of them could take advantage of their fellows?' he hoped to arrive at an account of justice which any dispassionate reader would accept. Rawls's view is that justice demands 'maximum equal liberty' and a distribution of economic benefits which makes the least-favoured person as well off as possible – the so-called 'maximin' conception of justice, which concentrates on maximizing the minimum benefit. This view has been attacked both by Robert Nozick and F. A. von Hayek. In their view, justice is not a matter of how benefits are distributed, but a matter of protecting individual rights to resources. Hayek has argued that 'social justice' is a chimera, and that appeals to social justice imply that some authority or other, notably the STATE, has the right and the duty to distribute goods and opportunities as it sees fit. But this is incompatible with individual liberty, which requires that we should be able to use what is ours as we choose. Similarly Nozick denies that there is such a thing as 'DISTRIBUTIVE JUSTICE'. The concept implies an agency entitled to achieve it, but when we look closely, we can see that everything worth distributing already belongs to some owner or other. All the rights over goods and opportunities that there are, are in the hands of single individuals. The state cannot lay hands on any of these things without violating those individual rights. Goods and opportunities are justly distributed when they are in the hands of their rightful owners. Any egalitarian (see EGALITARIANISM) claim for further redistribution is a reflection of the 'politics of envy', not of justice. For further reading: R. Nozick, *Anarchy, State and Utopia* (1974). A.R.

justicialismo, see under PERONISM.

K

Kafkaesque. Adjective applied to situations and atmospheres, whether real or fictional, that recall the writing of Franz Kafka (1883–1924), particularly *The Trial* (1925, tr. 1937) and its sequel *The Castle* (1926, tr. 1937). The essential ingredient is a nightmarish sense of having lost one's IDENTITY, and of bewildered helplessness against a vast, sinister, impersonal BUREAUCRACY which is intuitively felt to be evil, yet which appears to have a crazy kind of transcendent logic on its side. O.S.

Kansas City. One of the proudest JAZZ cities and centre of the music in the American south-west. In the late 1920s and early 1930s, the region evolved the style with which Kansas City is synonymous, an amalgam of the BLUES, a new and deceptive level of technical accomplishment, and a loose, driving beat. It was more sophisticated than NEW ORLEANS, freer than New York. Developed in BIG BANDS like those of Walter Page and Bennie Moten, the music reached its irresistible acme in the Count Basie band, which took America by storm in the SWING era. The light, propulsively swinging feel of his superb rhythm section was quintessentially Kansas City, as were the long, inventive lines of soloists like Lester Young. Both the subtlety of the beat and the freedom it encouraged became key ingredients in the rise of BEBOP (one of its greatest pioneers, Charlie Parker, was from Kansas City). The style itself is one of the main currents in MAINSTREAM jazz. GE.S.

Karmarkar's method. An ALGORITHM for linear programming problems invented by N. Karmarkar in 1985. It is a substantial improvement on the standard simplex method, taking only polynomial time rather than EXPONENTIAL TIME. Each iteration of the algorithm takes longer but the total number of steps is drastically reduced. J.M.

karyology, see under CYTOLOGY.

Katyn. The name of a wood near Smolensk where in April 1943 the Germans announced that they had discovered several thousand bodies of Polish officers and others who, they claimed, had been murdered by the Russians in 1940. The Soviet government at once announced that these men (captured during the Soviet invasion of Poland in 1939) had fallen into German hands in 1941 and that the Germans had murdered them. Previously it had disclaimed all knowledge of some 15,000 Polish officers not among those released after the German invasion of Russia in 1941 and allowed to go to the Middle East to form a new Polish Army. Yet the 5,000 bodies found at Katyn were in the great majority men on the lists the Poles had submitted to the Russians. (The other 10,000 have never been accounted for.)

The Germans allowed a forensic commission (see FORENSIC MEDICINE) including prominent neutral experts to supervise part of the exhumation, which representatives of the Polish underground were permitted, and senior Allied officer prisoners compelled, to attend. All reported that the German story was clearly true; forensic, documentary and other evidence showed that the massacre had taken place in April 1940. The facts, though accepted everywhere else, were never admitted by the former USSR. For further reading: General W. Anders (intr.), *The Crime of Katyn* (1965). R.C.

keratins, see under PROTEIN.

Keynesian. Description of the economic theories resulting from the ideas and writings of John Maynard Keynes (1883–1946). NEO-CLASSICAL ECONOMIC THEORY proposes that the flexibility of wages and prices is sufficient to ensure FULL EMPLOYMENT. Keynes argued that money wages might not fall, because of the actions of TRADE UNIONS, and that, even if money wages fell, full employment would not be obtained. The latter proposition is based on the effects of a fall in money wages: producers may hire more labour and output increases; this increase in output generates an equal increase in NATIONAL INCOME; not all of the increase in national income is consumed, some is saved; this means that AGGREGATE DEMAND increases by less than the increase in output; the unsold output results in prices, output and employment being reduced and a downward spiral of falling wages, prices, output and employment is initiated. In the money market, Keynes noted that, if wages and then prices fall, the real value of the MONEY SUPPLY increases and the interest rate would have to fall to induce people into holding the existing supply of money. Keynes proposed that there is a lower limit below which the interest rate cannot fall and, furthermore, that INVESTMENT was not responsive to reductions in the interest rate. Therefore, a fall in money wages and the consequent reduction in the interest rate cannot be relied upon to increase aggregate demand and move the economy to full employment.

During the 1970s and 1980s, Keynes's work was reinterpreted and given more fundamental theoretical importance. This reinterpretation involved considering the response of the economy to the existence of involuntary UNEMPLOYMENT. The involuntarily unemployed have a notional demand for goods and services, but this demand is not effective, as they have little or no income to pay for the notionally demanded goods and services. For a firm to hire more labour requires an increase in the demand for the firm's product. If all firms simultaneously hire more labour, the notional demand of the involuntarily unemployed is made effective – though some of the demand may be for consumption at a later date – and used to purchase the increase in output. However, an individual firm has no incentive to hire more labour, as such an action has a negligible effect on the demand for the firm's output. Consequently, if there is involuntary unemployment in the economy, it is not necessarily true that the economy will move towards full employment. For the labour market to move towards full employment, the notional demand of the involuntarily unemployed has to be backed up by actual income. In both interpretations of Keynes's work, involuntary unemployment persists because of deficient aggregate demand, and it is the duty of the government to increase aggregate demand. Keynesian and MONETARIST theories are often considered as alternative views of the economy, and they have been extensively contrasted and compared. See MULTIPLIER EFFECT and ACCELERATOR (2). For further reading: P. Arestis and M. Sawyer, *The Relevance of Keynesian Economic Policies Today* (1997). J.P.

KGB (Committee for State Security). The name, since 1953–54, of the secret police of the former USSR, one of the two organizations, the other being MVD, which shared, with somewhat fluctuating lines of demarcation, responsibility for order and security. Roughly speaking, the KGB – like its predecessors Cheka, Vcheka, GPU, OGPU, NKVD, NKGB, MGB, several of which have been bywords for brutality (see, especially, YEZHOVSHCHINA) – was responsible for security troops, counter-espionage, counter-subversion, loyalty supervision among the administrative, political and military ÉLITES, and such features as trials of writers and others. Its other major role was organizing the greater part of the Soviet espionage and subversion effort abroad. Today, KGB personnel co-operate openly with the CIA and other Western security services. For further reading: J. Barron, *The KGB* (1974); D. Murphy, *Battleground Berlin: CIA vs. KGB in the Cold War* (1997). R.C.

Khmer Rouge. COMMUNIST group led by Pol Pot, who ruled Cambodia (Kampuchea) between 1975 and 1979. The Khmer Rouge came to power after the civil war in a coalition with Prince Norodom Sihanouk in 1975, but Sihanouk was soon replaced as head of state by Khieu Samphan and the country was renamed Democratic Kampuchea. Once in power, the Khmer Rouge set about implementing policies of extreme reform: abolishing money and private property, outlawing religion, forcibly removing the entire urban population to the countryside, and wiping out intellectuals and the old MIDDLE CLASSES through mass executions by death squads (see STATE TERROR). A total of 2,700,000 Cambodians are estimated to have been killed before the Vietnamese ousted the Khmer Rouge government in 1979 (see VIETNAM). The remnants of Pol Pot's supporters have since allied themselves with non-communist groups led by Sihanouk and Son Sann, and now profess to pursue non-communist policies in the struggle to oust the Vietnamese. For further reading: B. Kiernan, *The Pol Pot Regime* (1996). S.B.

kibbutz. A form of collective settlement which has played a key role in the creation of modern Israel. The first kibbutz was founded in 1909 by a group of pioneers from Russia. By 1965 there were 230, some of them up to a thousand strong. Allowing for individual variations, the kibbutz combines three functions: (1) *economic*, cultivation of the land, often with some industrial production as well; (2) *social*, providing communities in which SOCIALIST ideals can be put into practice, e.g. equality (see EGALITARIANISM), common property, communal living (including the rearing of children), and collective decision-making; (3) *military*, acting as watch posts, and in times of trouble as strongpoints with their own garrison. There are now over 100,000 Israelis living permanently in kibbutzim. This is less than 5 per cent of the population, but their contribution to the formation of Israel has been much greater than these figures suggest. For further reading: H. Near, *The Kibbutz Movement: A History* (1992). A.L.C.B.

kinematics. One of the two branches of MECHANICS. M.V.B.

kinesics, see under SEMIOTICS.

kinetic art. The extension of the traditionally static arts of painting and sculpture to incorporate an element of motion (a) by making them mobile, (b) by a shifting sequence of static variations, or (c) by exploiting the spectator's movement around a static work so as to give it changing aspects. Though efforts in this direction have been made since the earliest times, the modern history of kineticism really starts with FUTURISM and its use of overlapping 'simultaneous' images and 'lines of force'. Other early attempts were Tatlin's tower (1919–20) and other CONSTRUCTIVIST works, Marcel Duchamp's rotating discs (1920), and László Moholy-Nagy's 'Lichtrequisit' (1930). The real breakthrough, however, came with the American Alexander Calder's invention (*c.* 1931–32) of the *mobile*, a balanced contraption of brightly coloured weights swinging from wires.

By the 1950s many artists (and advertising agencies) were trying their hands at mobiles, and a widespread kinetic trend set in, with Nicolas Schöffer, proponent of 'spatiodynamism' (1948) and 'luminodynamism' (1957), as its most ambitious exemplar, and the Paris *Mouvement* exhibition at the Galérie Denise Renée (1955) as its first collective manifestation. Sub-groups have included the German *Gruppe Zero* (from 1958), the Paris *Groupe de Recherche d'Art Visuel* (1960–68), the Italian groups 'T' and 'N', the 'programmed art' of Bruno Munari, and the Soviet *Dvizhenie* collective led by Lev Nusberg.

Today virtually any practitioner of ABSTRACT ART is liable to include some element of motion or permutation (see PERMUTATIONAL) in his work, the latter particularly if it is of a geometrical or OP ART kind. CONCRETE POETRY reflects a similar concern, and certain writers, mainly English and German, have produced 'kinetic' poems where the movement consists in the calculated (or 'programmed') shifting of words and letters, line by line or page by page. There is also a quasi-cinematic or psychedelic branch of the art (see PSYCHEDELIC ART) in the light show, which bears some relation to Moholy-Nagy's and Schöffer's researches as well as to earlier experiments in SYNAESTHESIA. For further reading: G. Brett, *Kinetic Art* (1968). J.W.

kinetography Laban, see under DANCE NOTATION.

Kinsey Report. A questionnaire-based study of sexual attitudes and behaviour, compiled by the American zoologist Alfred Kinsey (1894–1956) and others, and published in two volumes in 1948–53. By showing that many practices (e.g. *fellatio*) commonly regarded as perversions were actually widespread, it was influential in increasing sexual PERMISSIVENESS. It also indicated CORRELATIONS of social CLASS with sexual habits. It has been criticized for faults in interviewing and SAMPLING techniques, as well as for its title, *Sexual Behavior in the Human Male/Female*, since only mid-20th-century North Americans are actually considered. H.L.

kinship. The study of relations between people based on consanguinity (blood or descent ties), affinity (MARRIAGE and alliance between groups) and 'fictive kinship' (such as godparenthood and adoption). Anthropologists (see ANTHROPOLOGY) have assumed that kinship is universally established through the social significance given to the natural processes of engendering and bearing children, i.e. there is something presocial which gives such ties exceptional social importance. Morgan (*Systems of consanguinity and affinity of the human family*, 1871) argued that native kinship terms held the key to understanding the evolution of family systems. The understanding that kinship is based on natural facts and is a separate domain of social life has been challenged from a number of perspectives. Lévi-Strauss's *Elementary structures of kinship* (1949) developed the notion of alliance, by arguing that the essential dynamic of kinship systems was based on the exchange of women in marriage by men across groups, thus redressing the balance British anthropologists had put on blood ties and the stability of the group. The separation of kinship from other domains has been criticized by a subsequent generation of anthropologists, best represented by M. Strathern and David Schneider. They argue that anthropologists had inflated Western conceptualizations to the status of universal facts. For Schneider the study of kinship was a product of METHODOLOGY (principally the genealogical grid), not the cultural construction of relatedness in the society in question. For the new generation of feminist-inspired analysts (see FEMINISM), the general interest was to show how the study of kinship cannot be separated from GENDER, the economy, social reproduction, and more recently notions of the person and IDENTITY. For further reading: L. Holy, *Anthropological Perspectives on Kinship* (1996). M.H.

Kirkpatrick theory. The theory of political development espoused by Georgetown University professor Jeane Kirkpatrick (1926–), adviser to the Reagan administration and former US Ambassador to the UN. Drawing on the ideas of 17th-century British political philosopher Thomas Hobbes, Kirkpatrick argues that order is the fundamental value of any political system, absence of which precludes the enjoyment of any other values. Adhering to the theories of social modernization developed in the 1960s by Samuel Huntington in *Political Order in Changing Societies*, Kirkpatrick contends that stability can be found either in traditional societies or in modern social systems, but not in the transitional stage. In weak STATES, where governments lack true decision-making POWER and are confronted by fragmented and conflicting civilian interests, political stalemate arises, leading to prolonged instability and consequent vulnerability to externally backed 'TERRORIST' threats to order. Applying the analysis to Central America, Kirkpatrick advocates that US policy give priority to the reconstruction of a stable order in the area, even if this has to be imposed by means of authoritarian models (see AUTHORITARIANISM). N.M.

kitchen sink drama. Pejorative term for those English plays written from the late 1950s onwards (see THEATRE WORKSHOP) whose distinguishing feature was a portrayal of working- or lower-middle-class characters surrounded, in the view of their critics, by an undue degree of domestic squalor. 'The kitchen sink school' was a term applied first to the SOCIAL REALIST paintings of John Bratby (1928–92) and others showing at the Beaux Arts Gallery in London in the early 1950s, but has achieved lasting currency in relation to the theatre. M.A.

klangfarbenmelodie. A term used by Schoenberg in his 'Harmonielehre' (1911) to denote a melody where the sense of shape is given by different tone-colours (e.g. a clarinet and a violin playing the same note have a different musical colour) rather than different pitches as in a conventional melody. Schoenberg used the technique in the third of his 'Five Orchestral Pieces Op. 16' (1909), and the technique was used by his pupils Alban Berg ('Wozzeck') and, to a much greater extent, Anton Webern. The technique is symptomatic of a general heightening of awareness of tone-colour in 20th-century music from Debussy through to ELECTRONIC MUSIC. B.CO.

Kleinian. This term refers to the theoretical and clinical set of psychoanalytic ideas introduced by Melanie Klein (1882–1960), who greatly influenced the approach of British PSYCHOANALYSIS. Klein's theoretical results derive from her pioneering work with children under three years of age, based on her newly introduced play technique. The infantile psychic apparatus is dominated at the oral stage by cannibalistic drives, sadistic in relation to the breast, which become the prototype of all one's future relationships to objects. These aggressive instincts have, as one of their consequences, the arousing of primitive anxieties, as the infant fears both that the breast will be destroyed by its sadistic attacks, and that the breast has powers of retaliation. The breast is then split into a 'bad' retaliating breast, and a 'good' one which the SUBJECT tends to introject to soothe its anxiety. This mechanism of splitting will invest all possible objects of the infantile world, and will remain a tendency throughout all adult life in the form of denial and idealization. Objects will be split into external and internal objects, into bad and good ones, so that the object is never whole, but rather partial (see PARTIAL OBJECT). Klein drew on Ferenczi's concepts of introjection and projection to establish the process by which the splitting and fragmentation of the infantile world occurs: this is introjective and projective identification (see PROJECTIVE/INTROJECTIVE IDENTIFICATION), where parts of the self or of the object (that is, of the internal and external world) are introjected or projected in a pathological exchange of roles. This is the paranoid-schizoid position, which is followed by the depressive position when the child develops a more correct relationship to its object (see OBJECT RELATIONS), where it can perceive it as a whole object, separated from itself. This gives rise to a sense of guilt about one's own AGGRESSION as well as to the major function of the reparative tendency, the expression of the life instinct struggling with the destructive impulses of the DEATH INSTINCT. The Kleinian approach is applied to adults, as insanity is viewed in this perspective as linked to the same phenomena that occur in infancy, where the adult world finds its roots. For further reading: M. Klein, *Love, Guilt, and Reparation, and Other Works* (1975). B.BE.

Knave (or **Jack**) **of Diamonds** (Russian *Bubnovy Valet*). Originally the title of an art exhibition organized by the painter Michel Larionov in Moscow, December 1910, including David Burliuk, Goncharova, Exter, Falk, Kandinsky, Konchalovsky, Lentulov, Malevich, Mashkov, Survage, and the French painters Gleizes, Le Fauconnier, and L.-A. Moreau. An album of 18 reproductions was published with a cover by Goncharova. She and Larionov subsequently left the group in protest against its hardening into a formal society and its French orientation; the remaining artists held a second show, with more French participation, in 1912, and continued to exist as a group till 1916. A retrospective exhibition was held at the Tretiakov Gallery in 1927. For further reading: V. Markov, *Russian Futurism* (1969). M.C.

knot theory. A knot in three dimensions is a closed loop of string – perhaps just a circle, or intertwined in some way. An initial problem is how to describe it, if it is not one of the standard knots such as the trefoil. The main problem (which links us into TOPOLOGY) is whether one knot can be pulled about (without cutting) to produce another specified one: can the trefoil be manoeuvred into the circle?

J. W. Alexander (1928) showed how to associate each knot with part of an algebraic formula, and then demonstrated that, if the knot is pulled about, the formula does not change. The trefoil and the circle have different formulae, so the trefoil cannot be changed into the circle. But the trefoil and its mirror image have the same 'Alexander polynomial', as it is known. Can one then be changed to the other?

In 1984, Vaughan Jones discovered another (invariant) polynomial. The trefoil and its mirror image have different Jones polynomials – so one cannot be manoeuvred into the other. Most surprisingly, the Jones polynomial links the knot curve with the quantum theory of the movement of particles. N.A.R.

knowledge, sociology of. The study of how styles of expression and the character of IDEAS or systems of thought are related to different social contexts. Thus Marx, from whom the contemporary impetus to the sociology of knowledge largely derives, sought to relate art and ideas to particular historical circumstances and the kinds of CLASS systems prevailing at the time; and Max Weber (1864–1920; see WEBERIAN), in *The Sociology of Religion* (1963), analysed the way in which different kinds of religions were the creation largely of specific social groups (e.g. the relation of Confucianism to the Chinese literati and BUREAUCRACY). The effort to broaden the use of sociology of knowledge as a general scheme for the analysis of all ideas is, however, associated largely with three writers: Karl Mannheim (1893–1947), who relativized Marx's ideas to all thought, including MARXISM itself;

Max Scheler (1874–1928), who divided the influences on thought into 'real factors' (different at different historical moments) and 'ideal factors' (a realm of timeless ESSENCES which constituted an absolute order of TRUTH); and Émile Durkheim (1858–1917), who argued that the basic rhythms of social life experienced by a society – its sense of space and time – were a function of its kind of social organization.

Objectors to the sociology of knowledge claim that it attaches insufficient importance to the *content* of knowledge, or to the truth or otherwise of a PROPOSITION; that a cultural SUPERSTRUCTURE, once created, retains a life of its own, and becomes part of the permanent cultural repertoire of mankind; that ideas and works of imagination are alike multivalent and it is crudely reductionist (see REDUCTION) to associate a set of ideas only with a particular political position (e.g. MATERIALISM with RADICALISM, and IDEALISM with CONSERVATISM), or to equate as 'BOURGEOIS' the contrasting work of Flaubert, Zola, Mann, Joyce and Proust; and that art forms and ideas may unfold 'immanently', i.e. out of their inner logic and as a reflection on and extension of previous forms. See also IDEOLOGY. For further reading: J. C. Curtis and J. W. Petras (eds), *The Sociology of Knowledge* (1979). D.B.

kolkhoz (*kollektivnoe khozyaystvo*), see under COLLECTIVIZATION.

Kolyma. The most notorious of Stalin's FORCED LABOUR camp areas, consisting of a large tract round the valley of the River Kolyma down to the Arctic Ocean. Its main product was gold. It is believed that during the period 1937–53 up to four million prisoners died there, mainly of hunger and overwork. See also GULAG. For further reading: R. Conquest, *Kolyma* (1978). R.C.

Korea. The name of one of the historic civilizations of east Asia, frequently used as a shorthand term for the Korean War of 1950–53. Having long lived under Chinese suzerainty, Korea was annexed by the Japanese in 1910, and after the defeat of the Japanese in World War II (1945) was divided between a COMMUNIST state under the patronage of the former USSR in the North and the American-supported regime of Syngman Rhee in the South. After the withdrawal of American forces in 1949, the Soviet-equipped armies of North Korea crossed the partition line and launched a full-scale invasion of the South (25 June 1950). UN forces, largely American and under American command, came to the support of the South. When they in turn carried the war north of the partition line (the 38th parallel) they were met by Chinese communist forces. An armistice, concluded in July 1953, redivided the country along a line close to that of the original partition. The motivation for the original North Korean attack is unclear, but suspicions that it had been instigated by the Soviet authorities played a considerable part in inspiring the collective defence of western Europe by NATO. For further reading: D. Rees, *Korea: the Limited War* (1964). A.L.C.B.

Kremlinology. Strictly, the study of the politics of the former USSR at the higher levels, i.e. of the struggle for POWER and over policy between the leading members of the POLITBURO, who normally met in the Kremlin in Moscow; loosely, any study of Soviet affairs. It implied deduction of what was or had been going on from such clues as emerged from behind the conventional façade of 'monolithic unity' among the leadership. For further reading: R. Conquest, *Power and Policy in the USSR* (1961). R.C.

Kristallnacht, see under HOLOCAUST, THE.

Ku Klux Klan. Name given to post-Civil War secret societies in the US dedicated to WHITE SUPREMACY and, later, nativism. Offshoots of original societies are still active on the fringes of American society and on the INTERNET. The original Klan was organized by former soldiers of the Confederate States of America in Pulaski, Tennessee, in December 1865 to oppose Reconstruction, the name given to the effort to restore civil government in the Southern states. Playing upon the fears and superstitions of freed slaves, the Klan was widely organized by 1867, about the same time as the US Congress passed the Reconstruction Act, which divided the South into military districts ruled by the army. The organization was ordered to disband by 1869, but remained a powerful force, terrorizing blacks and keeping them away from polling places. A second Klan was founded in Stone Mountain,

Georgia, in 1915, adding ANTISEMITISM, anti-Catholicism and anti-immigrant themes to its concerns. This second incarnation was phenomenally successful throughout the Southern and northern states, helped in part by D. W. Griffith's 1915 silent film *The Birth of a Nation*, which beside being a classic of world cinema is a shameless glorification of the KKK. R.K.H.

kula. An elaborate system of gift EXCHANGE which links together different islands in New Guinea. The kula was studied by Bronislaw Malinowski (1884–1942), and his book *Argonauts of the Western Pacific* (1922) was used by Marcel Mauss (1872–1950) in the development of a general theory of gift exchange. Different groups in the Trobriand islands are linked in a circuit of exchange. Two sets of objects, long red necklaces (*soulava*) and white shell bracelets (*mwali*), circulate in opposite directions. At the different points where these objects meet they are exchanged according to fixed rules and conventions. One partner makes his GIFT and the recipient is bound to make a return gift at the next meeting. The kula is a system of ceremonial exchange. The goods involved have no commercial value, but confer prestige. However, *soulava* and *mwali* are constantly in movement and no individual can hold on to an item for any length of time. Relationships established between partners in the kula ring are long-term and bind together different groups through a complex system of exchange (see POTLATCH). For further reading: J. W. Leach and E. R. Leach (eds), *The Kula: New Perspectives on Massim Exchange* (1983). A.G.

kulak ('fist'). Originally a general Russian term for a grasping peasant, later defined as a peasant who employed labour. The COMMUNIST Party of the former USSR was concerned from early days to destroy this element of the peasantry, with the aid of the 'middle peasant', and the village poor. The COLLECTIVIZATION campaign of 1930–33 led to the elimination, by famine or in FORCED LABOUR camps, of about 10 million peasants defined officially as *kulaks*, though later Soviet figures show that many of them were in fact 'middle peasants'. R.C.

Kunstgewerbeschule. Any 'School of Applied Art'; usually that at Vienna, an outstanding training-place for designers of all sorts in the opening years of this century, when the teachers included Josef Hoffmann, founder of the Wiener Werkstätte, and Koloman Moser; Oskar Kokoschka was one of the students. J.W.

L

Labanotation, see under DANCE NOTATION.

labelling theory. An influential approach in the SOCIOLOGY of deviance. It argues that there is no behaviour that can be seen as intrinsically deviant: deviant behaviour is that which has been successfully defined or 'labelled' as such by those social groups with the POWER to make and enforce these definitions. Thus deviance does not inhere in the act itself, but in the response of others to the act. But once so labelled by the reaction of others, the deviant is likely to be led on a career of further deviance. He develops a deviant SELF-IMAGE or self-conception based on the social reaction, and many come to be locked more or less permanently in a deviant ROLE. So for instance the individual whose behaviour comes to be labelled schizophrenic (see SCHIZOPHRENIA), and treated as such, is likely to adapt to the requirements of the role of a mental patient, and to intensify the 'schizophrenic' behaviour in such a way as continually to require treatment.

The humane impulse behind labelling theory is evident. Its radical rejection, however, of the possibility of physiological causes of deviance, and its antagonism – which does not follow logically from the theory – to any form of imprisonment or specialized medical therapy, has sometimes made its position seem naïve if not outrightly callous. For further reading: W. R. Gove, *The Labeling of Deviance: Evaluating a Perspective* (1975). K.K.

Labour and Socialist International, see INTERNATIONAL, THE.

labour, dilution of, see DILUTION OF LABOUR.

labour, forced, see FORCED LABOUR.

labour hoarding. The practice adopted by some companies, during a decline in DEMAND, of retaining their labour force intact, thus reducing the productivity of labour and raising the average variable cost per unit of output. Though widely decried, this practice has a twofold rationale: in any subsequent recovery in demand it avoids (1) problems of attracting sufficient labour back into the industry, and (2) CAPITAL costs associated with the training of a new workforce. D.E.

labour law. Since the inception of TRADE UNIONS in the 19th century, there have been attempts to control them by legal means. These have varied widely in different countries. Unions, being organizations of workers, can be seen as a threat by some regimes which cannot countenance opposition. Labour legislation in such circumstances is highly restrictive, and often punitive; examples are common in Latin America and Africa. In the UK labour legislation has been changed many times. From the early Combination Acts (virtually outlawing unions), through the Taff Vale judgement giving unions rights, to the 1927 restrictive legislation and then on to the years since 1971 in which there have been rapidly changing laws, trade unions have been affected by specific legislation. The 1971 Industrial Relations Act attempted to manufacture specific legal instruments for unions, but only the Industrial Tribunals have remained. The 1974 Employment Protection Act attempted to give collective rights to workers, but of these, only the conciliation body, the Advisory, Conciliation and Arbitration Service (ACAS), remains. The Act ran into the problem that in traditional liberal British law the individual is paramount, but unions are collective organizations. Labour courts are accepted in the US and Australia but failed in the UK.

In addition to specific laws, unions are bound by the general laws of their countries. These may affect PICKETING, demonstrations, STRIKES, the ability to undertake political action, or even prevent a union representing certain types of members. However different labour legislation may be, every country in the world has found it necessary to introduce it, and subsequently change it from time to time, and only rarely have these changes been to give trade union members greater rights. For further reading: K. Wedderburn *et al*, *Labour Law and Industrial Relations* (1983). B.D.S.

labour theory of value. The theory, proposed by Adam Smith (1723–90) and David Ricardo (1772–1823), and adapted by Marx, that any two products will exchange against one another in proportion to the amounts of labour necessary to make them. Thus, only labour can contribute to the value of a product. The part played by CAPITAL in production is allowed for, either by assuming that the same amount of capital is used per unit of labour in making every product, or by treating capital equipment as the product of past labour. By contrast, NEO-CLASSICAL ECONOMIC THEORY allows the value of a good to be determined by its value in consumption (see UTILITY THEORY) and goods exchange at a rate determined by their relative use-values. The labour theory of value has difficulties in dealing with use-values, the interest rate, the value of natural resources, and reducing different types of labour to a common unit. Even in COMMUNIST countries STATE ECONOMIC PLANNING does not adhere exclusively to a labour theory of value, though this theory remains central to communist and MARXIST ideology (see VALUE, THEORY OF). E.H.P.B.; J.P.

Lacanian. Term referring to the branch of PSYCHOANALYSIS developed by the French analyst Jacques Lacan (1901–81). Lacan was a controversial figure in psychoanalysis from the 1930s. He was heavily indebted to SURREALISM, DADAISM and STRUCTURALISM, and in turn influenced thought in those areas. An important example here is that of Althusser (1918–90), who promoted a Lacanian reading of Freud in advancing the claims of psychoanalysis to political significance. Not surprisingly, the amenability of Althusserian Marxism (see ALTHUSSERIANISM) to psychoanalysis was through the issue of IDEOLOGY – the way in which experience is represented (see MARXISM). The novelty here was to theorize representation in terms of the UNCONSCIOUS – the penetration of the human SUBJECT by the structures of sociality, through to the core. What is the subject if not a *social* subject? Lacan's major contribution here has been in the area of what might loosely be termed 'cultural studies': politics, FEMINISM, literature – those areas in which the operations of representation and imagination are crucial, and where the limits of what can be thought are a live issue. Lacanian psychoanalysis is part of this, in its clinical and in its applied, theoretical form. It is particularly opposed to American EGO-PSYCHOLOGY and other attempts to 'domesticate' psychoanalysis into a mode of adaptation.

Lacan introduced a variety of productive concepts into psychoanalysis, some of them with specific developmental aspects (see IMAGINARY; SYMBOLIC). He placed particular emphasis on language as central to consciousness. Lacan was aided in this promotion of language as a causal entity by the use or abuse of SAUSSURIAN linguistics. He employed the notion that the site of language is not in the consciousness of the individual subject, but is given from the outside – a structure through which thought is organized. He also employed to powerful effect the Saussurian emphasis on the arbitrary nature of the sign (there is no essential connection between a sign and the thing to which it refers) and the division of the sign into SIGNIFIER (its form) and signified (the concept to which it gives rise). Meaning is created through the play of signifiers, the enunciation of the differences between them; nothing has an absolute meaning, but rather it is marked out as a series of shifting forms, with meaning arising from the gap. In the psychoanalytic situation, this gap and the meanings evoked by it are the focus of activity: what is speaking in the subject when the subject articulates an 'I'? Truth shifts constantly, in every context of enunciation and exploration, in every intersubjective moment: there is only what we create as we go along (see INTERSUBJECTIVITY). Being a subject of language has a further meaning, confusingly close to the notion of ALIENATION. If I project myself into language, nominating myself as the personal pronoun 'I', I am already risking the loss of something else, at the boundaries of or beyond language – something which is called by Lacanians the Real. Language calls us into being as human, social subjects; it positions us in DISCOURSE and hence can be seen as causal; it 'structures' the unconscious ('the unconscious is structured like a language' is perhaps the most famous Lacanian slogan of all), partly because the unconscious is held by Lacan to be organized as a language itself (a difference from Freud's view), but also because language separates out that which can be communicated from that which cannot. Although what defines the subject as human is entry into the register of the symbolic, there is always something left over – the cause of DESIRE, signified in Lacanian thought as the 'objet *a*'.

Lacan was the originator of at least one contentious technical innovation in psychoanalytic practice: the variable-length session, developed as an enactment of the Lacanian appreciation of the effects of aggressivity. He was at the source of schisms and CULTS, which he seems to have played on as part of his engagement with 'style' and with the issues of mastery and authority. Importantly, he represents a link in a primarily oral tradition of 'teaching' in which the 'master' passes on what he knows through testing and informing his pupils. Thus, his preferred and most important forum for communication was not the written word, but the seminar – relatively open and unstructured, a theatre in which the 'effect of Lacan' can be felt in the round, not held down on a page and inspected in its minutiae. Lacan as a master of 'style' constructed his teaching around the idea that it is in the full, untameable impact of the presence of the OTHER that learning takes place. For further reading: E. Roudinesco, *Jacques Lacan* (1997). S.J.F.

Laffer Curve, see under SUPPLY-SIDE ECONOMICS.

laissez faire. A term used to describe an economy in which the activities of the government are kept to an absolute minimum. See MARKET ECONOMY. R.H.

Lamarckism. The conventional interpretation of the views on EVOLUTION held by the great French zoologist Jean Baptiste Pierre Antoine de Monet, le Chevalier de Lamarck (1744–1829) – the doctrine inadequately summarized as that of the 'inheritance of *acquired characteristics*'. In DARWINISM the heritable variations that are the subject of NATURAL SELECTION arise either spontaneously or not at all. Thus genetic information (see GENETICS/GENOMICS) is self-engendered as part of the responding system. In Lamarckism the motive forces for evolutionary change are an animal's needs and the activities it undertakes in order to satisfy them. Thus, in the traditional example, a giraffe acquired the genetic specification for a long neck through generations of browsing upon the upper foliage of trees. A more sophisticated example is the ADAPTATION of micro-organisms which enables them to use new sources of nutriment or to combat a new ANTIBIOTIC. Lamarckism has a great inherent plausibility, because social evolution is so obviously Lamarckian in character – we learn generation by generation and can propagate our learning to the next generation. Nevertheless, whenever Lamarckism in a purely biological context has been exposed to a critical test it has been faulted. Indeed, according to our modern notions of PROTEIN synthesis (see NUCLEIC ACID), there is no known method by which any modification brought about in a living organism during its own lifetime can be imprinted (see IMPRINTING) upon the genetic mechanism.

Lamarckism, like Darwinism, lends itself to political prejudices. If it were true that all human beings were born equal and that a man was what his environment and upbringing made him, then evolution could proceed only in the Lamarckian manner. It is therefore understandable that an extreme radical form of Lamarckism, bearing the same relationship to it as CALVINISM bears to Puritanism, was advocated in the Soviet Union by the agriculturalist Trofim Lysenko (1898–1976), after whom it has become known as LYSENKOISM. Lysenko's teaching became official doctrine in the COMMUNIST Party, and destroyed genetics in the Soviet Union, as well as many of its practitioners. Considered as an evolutionary procedure, Lamarckism is completely at odds with the central dogma of MOLECULAR BIOLOGY that genetic information flows only from NUCLEIC ACID towards protein or other products, and never the other way about. NEO-LAMARCKISM is the name given to an emphatic reiteration of Lamarckian beliefs by Nature-philosophers. For further reading: L. J. Jordanova, *Lamarck* (1984). P.M.

Lamb shift. A small observed difference between energy levels in the hydrogen ATOM, named after W. Lamb, American physicist (1913–). This difference is predicted to exist by quantum electrodynamics (QED; see FIELD THEORY) and arises because the single ELECTRON orbiting the PROTON which constitutes the hydrogen NUCLEUS interacts with the RADIATION field surrounding the atom to surround the nucleus by VIRTUAL PARTICLE pairs. This effect was first measured by Lamb. For further reading: R. Feynman, *QED* (1986). J.D.B.

land art. Term applied to projects, often large in scale, undertaken by several US artists since the later 1960s. Key works were Robert Smithson's *Spiral Jetty* (1970), built out into Great Salt Lake, and Walter de Maria's *Lightning Field* (1971–77), constructed in a remote area of New Mexico. Also used with reference to the work of British artists Richard Long and Hamish Fulton, who began walking in, and photographing, a variety of more or less isolated landscapes at around the same time. Some of Long's work involved taking materials – driftwood, stones, pine needles – from a particular place and arranging them in simple shapes on the gallery floor. On occasion, Smithson also removed rocks, etc., to the gallery, and it was he who developed the most articulate theory of the relationship between the 'site' where the artist worked and the gallery, or 'non-site', where his maps, texts, drawings and other evidence were exhibited. Since the 1970s the term's application has broadened to encompass a wide range of artistic interventions in the landscape, many of them particularly concerned with issues of conservation. M.G.A.

land reform. The reform of systems of land tenure to break up large estates and distribute ownership as widely as possible, with the consolidation of small holdings. Land reform has been a necessary development where large-scale ownership has been combined with small-scale tenant farming (often on a share-cropping basis) to produce a stationary system of agricultural management. It has been much employed by reformist regimes (see REFORMISM), and also by revolutionary regimes as a necessary intermediary step towards COLLECTIVIZATION and breaking the power of the peasants. For further reading: R. King, *Land Reform: a World Survey* (1977). D.C.W.

land use planning. Provision for the use of land in accordance with a considered policy. The term is used mainly in connection with policies for the national and regional use of land, e.g. for agricultural and non-agricultural uses and, within the latter, for housing, industrial, recreational or other use. Provision must necessarily be made also for multi-purpose uses, e.g. for recreation and forestry. The criteria for decisions and the administrative machinery for carrying decisions into practice differ between countries and over time. K.E.H.

landlocked state. Geographical term for a country in the interior of a continent that does not have a coastline. This often means economic disadvantage as a result of inferior accessibility to international trade routes. Switzerland, however, is one of the few exceptions on the world map, its people having developed trade and manufacturing skills to achieve major economic success despite the difficulties of functioning in their largely Alpine environment. Political history contains many examples of interior countries that have aggressively sought to expand towards seacoasts, most notably Russia, which gained a window on the Baltic Sea during the regime of Peter the Great and later a foothold on the warm waters of the Black Sea, and thereby access to the Mediterranean Sea, under Catherine the Great. In recent times, Saddam Hussein's 1990 invasion of Kuwait was at least in part driven by Iraq's desire to enlarge its tenuous outlet to the Persian Gulf via the narrow corridor lining the Shatt al-Arab waterway which drains the Tigris–Euphrates river system. P.O.M.

landmines. These are explosive devices, usually buried just beneath the surface of the soil and pressure-activated, designed to damage or destroy enemy vehicles or to wound or kill enemy troops. The first landmines, developed early in World War II, were used to blow off tank tracks or penetrate the thinner armour of a tank's belly. Later in the war, anti-personnel mines were introduced, more often intended to wound than kill, since wounding achieved the double effect of disabling a soldier who then became a medical liability. Much effort was devoted to developing devices to locate and lift mines, but miniaturization and non-metallic construction have frustrated countermeasures. International laws restricting the use of anti-personnel mines having proved ineffective; a comprehensive anti-mine convention was adopted by most sovereign states in 1997 but has not yet been universally ratified. J.K.

landscape archaeology, see under ARCHAEOLOGY.

Langmuir-Blodgett (L-B) films. American chemist Irving Langmuir (1881–1957) exploited the fact that when a small quantity of oil or fatty acid is floated on a liquid (e.g. water) it spreads out to a very thin film that is only one MOLECULE thick. The molecules in the film are ordered so they are parallel to one another, and by compressing the film to reduce its area and bring the molecules closer together (with a piston device) it can become solid. He found that such a film could be transferred onto a base material, such as a piece of glass, by slowly dipping the material into the liquid through the film and then withdrawing it. Katherine Blodgett then showed that by repeating this dipping process one could make multilayered films, either of the same or of different materials, in which each layer is ordered with respect to its neighbours – thus the technique is sometimes referred to as *molecular engineering*. The term L-B films is now applied to these multilayered structures in which there has recently been a great resurgence of interest since they can be made to have novel optical, magnetic or electrical properties. Possible applications are acoustic detectors, new TRANSISTORS and other electronic devices, and very high-definition integrated circuits (see SUPERLATTICE). For further reading: I. Langmuir & K. Blodgett, *A Mathematical Investigation of Water Droplet Trajectories* (1946). H.M.R.

language awareness. In the UK, one of the consequences of the NATIONAL CURRICULUM in English, introduced during the 1990s, has been the introduction of a series of targets to do with spelling, grammar, vocabulary and other aspects of language structure and use, spread across the whole age-range of the curriculum. A corresponding fresh emphasis on English language studies has also emerged at higher levels, where the numbers of students opting for A-level English language dramatically increased in the UK during the 1990s. D.C.

language game. In his later PHILOSOPHY, Ludwig Wittgenstein (1889–1951) develops an analogy between using a language and playing a game, an analogy he finds highly instructive. In particular, Wittgenstein uses the analogy in order to stress just how *unlike* calculi (see CALCULUS) natural languages are, to stress that the rules governing natural language do not take the form of a precise, rigid system.

A 'language game' is a simple, primitive form of language. An example can be found in the opening sections of Wittgenstein's *Philosophical Investigations* (1953), where builders develop a simple language consisting initially of just four words: 'block', 'pillar', 'beam' and 'slab'. Wittgenstein uses such examples to draw our attention to the differences with our language. For example, in the builder's language game, all the words stand for kinds of thing, whereas in our language this is not so. Wittgenstein also uses such examples to illustrate the *diversity* of language: the endlessly varied ways in which linguistic practices can evolve and develop. S.W.L.

language, history of, see HISTORY OF LANGUAGE.

***langue* and *parole*.** Terms introduced into LINGUISTICS by Ferdinand de Saussure (see SAUSSURIAN) to distinguish between language viewed as a complete system of forms and contrasts represented in the brains of the language-users, and language viewed as the act of speaking by an individual at a given time. It is similar to Chomsky's distinction between COMPETENCE and performance. See also IDIOLECT. D.C.

Large Hadron Collider (LHC). A device currently under construction by CERN at the foot of the Jura mountains on the French–Swiss border. The project is an international collaboration of particle physicists and engineers from many countries. It will collide PROTONS at energies of 14 TeV, greater than ever before achieved by terrestrial machines. It will study the behaviour of matter at these high energies and search for new ELEMENTARY PARTICLES of matter which have been predicted by theories of high-energy physics. Its prime goals are to find the Higgs boson (see QUANTUM STATISTICS), a particle that plays a key role in producing masses for elementary particles, and to find evidence for the existence of SUPER-

SYMMETRY in nature. If supersymmetry exists in nature then it must give rise to many new varieties of elementary particle at the energies accessible to the LHC. All known elementary particles will possess a superpartner of different mass. The energies created in the LHC also permit us to simulate conditions in the early stages of the universe when it was one thousand billionth of a second old (10^{-12} second). This will advance our understanding of the first moments of the history of the universe and further our understanding of the particles and fluctuations that were present long before stars and GALAXIES ever formed. For further reading: L. Lederman and D. Teresi, *The God Particle* (1993). J.D.B.

large numbers, laws of, see under PROBABILITY THEORY; STATISTICAL REGULARITY.

laser (Light Amplification by Stimulated Emission of Radiation). A device invented in 1960 for producing an intense beam of light with a high degree of coherence, by making all the ATOMS in a material emit light in PHASE. The system is prepared by illuminating it with a flash of light which raises all the atoms into the same *excited state* (see ENERGY LEVEL). When one of the atoms falls back into its *ground state* the light emitted stimulates a small fraction of the other atoms to radiate in sympathy, their light being in phase with that from the first atom. This weak coherent pulse is not allowed to escape but reflects back and forth between carefully spaced mirrors at each end of the specimen until all the atoms have been stimulated to radiate. One mirror is only partially reflecting, however, so that all the light eventually leaks out. The energy in the original illuminating flash (which is incoherent) has been converted into coherent light.

Laser light is used wherever coherence is necessary, e.g. in HOLOGRAPHY and METROLOGY, and wherever a highly localized source of ENERGY (obtained by focusing the beam) is required, e.g. in delicate surgical operations such as welding the cornea of the human eye. M.V.B.

last man. Friedrich Nietzsche's (see NIETZSCHEAN) name for a type of NIHILIST, the 'most contemptible man', who has become so tolerant of all cultures and values that he cannot grasp any BELIEFS as real or important. Under these circumstances, 'Who still wants to rule? Who obey? Both are too much of a burden'. The result: 'No herdsman and ONE herd!' In the age of the last man, 'Everyone wants the same thing, everyone is the same: whoever thinks otherwise goes voluntarily into the madhouse'. The Last Man prevents the affirmation of new values by forgetting how to string the arrow of human longing. For further reading: P. Sedgwick (ed.), *Nietzsche: A Critical Reader* (1995). P.LE.

late modernism. Condescending term used by POST-MODERNISTS for ARCHITECTURE of the last three decades of the 20th century which is of interesting and high design quality but which does not conform with the post-modern canon. As the name suggests, it particularly applies to design which ultimately derives from MODERN MOVEMENT ideology, such as HIGH TECH. (See also MODERNISM.) S.L.

latency period. In psychoanalytic theory (see PSYCHOANALYSIS), the stage of PSYCHOSEXUAL DEVELOPMENT that begins at the age of about five (in the resolution of the OEDIPUS COMPLEX or ELECTRA COMPLEX) and lasts until puberty. During this time sexual tensions are repressed or sublimated (see REPRESSION; SUBLIMATION) into other less conflictive activities. Cultural RELATIVISM in the expression of this phenomenon has been sufficiently emphasized by anthropologists to bring its universality into considerable doubt. W.Z.

lateral thinking, see VERTICAL AND LATERAL THINKING.

laterization, see under RAINFOREST.

lattice. A regular arrangement of lines or points. The ATOMS in a crystal lie approximately at points on a lattice, but the regularity is upset by (1) vibrations of the atoms about the lattice points (see SOLID-STATE PHYSICS), and (2) crystal DEFECTS such as dislocations. M.V.B.

***Lautgedichte*,** see under CONCRETE POETRY.

law and order. An expression used to refer

to (1) social conditions in which there is general conformity to law, especially to the criminal law prohibiting such crimes as violence, theft and disturbance of the peace, and to the firm administration of penalties imposed for breaches of the law; or (2) the conformity by law enforcement agencies themselves to the laws conferring and limiting their powers; or (3) respect for the rule of law (see LAW, THE RULE OF). All three senses of the term have developed as essential campaigning issues for conservative political parties in the West. For further reading: W. J. Chambliss and R. B. Seidman, *Law, Order and Power* (1971).

H.L.A.H.

Law Commission. A commission set up by the Law Commission Act of 1965 to consider reforms of the law and make proposals to the British government for the examination and reform of the laws. Various programmes have been laid by the Commission before the Lord Chancellor for the examination of different branches of the law, and some of these have been undertaken by the Commission itself or by other bodies. The Commission publishes informative annual reports of its activities and proposals and is also responsible for preparing legislation to provide for consolidation and revision of statute law. H.L.A.H.

law, comparative, see COMPARATIVE LAW.

law of averages, see under STATISTICAL REGULARITY.

Law of the Sea. This branch of PUBLIC INTERNATIONAL LAW embraces the rules governing relations between STATES in maritime matters. Its main sources are: (1) *multilateral treaties*, e.g. the 1958 Geneva Conventions: on the territorial and contiguous zone; on the high seas; on the continental shelf; and on the fishing and conservation of living resources of the high seas. The 1982 Convention on the Law of the Sea, signed by 159 states but ratified by only 19, is unlikely to enter into force within the foreseeable future. Nonetheless, some of its articles restate those provisions of the Geneva Conventions representing customary law. Its provisions on the exclusive economic zone reflect the customary law as it had existed before its completion in 1982. (2) *Customary international law*, e.g. the customary law rule that had evolved by the late 1950s recognizing coastal states; ownership over the resources of their continental shelf. (3) *General principles of international law*, e.g. the rule providing for exclusive jurisdiction of the flag state over ships on the high seas.

It is accepted that every coastal state enjoys SOVEREIGNTY over its *territorial sea* (3 to 12 miles), including the airspace over it as well as its bed and subsoil. This sovereignty is subject to the obligation to allow a right of innocent passage to all foreign ships. By contrast, in the area known as the continental shelf, the coastal state can exercise only *sovereign rights* for the purpose of exploring the continental shelf and exploiting its natural resources without prejudice to freedom of navigation and overflight. A similar principle applies, *mutatis mutandis*, to claims by coastal states for exclusive *economic zones*. As regards the high seas, they are open to all nations; hence no state has a right to subject any part of them to its sovereignty. Coastal and non-coastal states alike are entitled to enjoy the freedom of the high seas, viz. navigation, fishing, laying submarine cables and pipelines and flying over such waters. For further reading: R. Churchill and A. Lowe, *The Law of the Sea* (1983). O.Y.E.

law, pure theory of. *Pure Theory of Law* is the title of a major contribution by Hans Kelsen (1881–1973) to the philosophy of law and the theory of the STATE. First published in 1911, it presents a comprehensive account of the distinctive logical or formal structure of laws and legal systems, for the description of which it furnishes new concepts, of which the most novel and important is the concept of a *basic norm*. Kelsen called his theory 'pure' to mark its value-free character (see VALUE-FREEDOM) and independence of moral or other evaluative judgement of the content of the law, and also to mark the distinction between this form of analytical study of the structure of the law and sociological studies of the law which are designed to furnish causal explanations or to establish other empirical relations between law and other phenomena.

The basic norm is introduced into the Pure Theory in order to explain both the systematic unity and the NORMATIVE character of law. It is not to be identified with the legal constitution of any state, or with any other form of positive law or social practice. It is, according to Kelsen, 'a juristic presumption or postulate implicit in legal thinking' prescribing that one ought to behave in the manner stipulated by the constitution and by the laws whose creation is authorized by the constitution. Kelsen believed that without such a presupposition or postulate only a sociological description and not a normative description could be given of the law, and there could be nothing to unify separate laws into a single system. Hence, in Kelsen's view, the presupposition of the basic norm is implicit in the legal thought and the language commonly used by lawyers to describe the law. For further reading: H. Kelsen, tr. M. Knight, *Pure Theory of Law* (1967). H.L.A.H.

law, the rule of. Various meanings have been given to this phrase, and it has sometimes been conceived as a factual summary of the basic principles of the British Constitution and sometimes as a statement of an ideal only partly embodied in actual constitutional practices. It was used by A. V. Dicey in his *Law of the Constitution*, first published in 1885, for three principles, which he thought desirable and which in his view underlay the British Constitution. These principles require (1) that a citizen's legal duties and his liability to punishment should be determined by the 'regular law', and not by the arbitrary fiat of officials or the exercise of wide discretionary powers; (2) that disputes between a private citizen and an official should be subject to the jurisdiction of the ordinary courts; and (3) that the fundamental rights of the citizen should not rest on a special guarantee by the Constitution but should arise from the ordinary law.

Contemporary versions of the rule of law stress the importance of two principles: (1) that the exercise of discretionary powers of rule-making and adjudication should be controlled by impartial tribunals in the light of stated general principles designed to ensure that the power should be exercised fairly and within the limits prescribed by law; and (2) that as large an area of the law as possible and of the criminal law in particular should afford clear guidance to the citizen as to his rights and duties, and that he should be liable to punishment for breach of the law only if he has the capacity and a fair opportunity to conform his conduct to it. For further reading: A. V. Dicey, *Introduction to the Study of the Law of the Constitution* (1885; 1985). H.L.A.H.

laws of physics, see under MODEL.

Le Chatelier's principle. Name given to the tendency of the environment to exert restoring forces on a system disturbed slightly away from stable, static or dynamic EQUILIBRIUM. M.V.B.

***le fantastique*.** A term used in French film criticism which has no direct equivalent in English, usefully encompassing not only horror films but fantasy (everything from SCIENCE FICTION to *Alice in Wonderland*), and even films basically realistic in theme which may have strange, dreamlike or seemingly supernatural elements. French film criticism is also inclined to categorize such films, the latter group in particular, as either *onirique* (meaning dreamlike, now frequently borrowed by English critics as *oneiric*) or *insolite* (unwonted, unusual, weird). T.C.C.M.

leaching. The removal of material in dissolved form from one place to another. Rainwater passing through a soil profile will dissolve and carry away certain ions, thereby being a major cause of soil development. Soil fertility can be reduced if key nutrients are removed by this process. Through leaching, harmful substances in liquids escaping from mines, landfills and other sources may pollute the environment. Groundwater contamination may be prevented by the use of appropriate barriers. A.S.G.

League of Nations. An international security organization created by covenant of the victors of World War I as part of the Treaty of Versailles, and established at Geneva in 1920. Its proposed method of maintaining peace was the application of economic and/or military SANCTIONS by member states against any nation committing aggression and ignoring the various procedures for the peaceful settlement of international disputes. The League's organs included a Council (with five permanent and four elected member powers) and an Assembly. The USA never joined it; Germany did not join until 1926 and withdrew in 1933; Japan withdrew in 1933; the Soviet Union joined in 1934 and was expelled in 1940.

During the 1920s the League enjoyed considerable authority and dealt successfully with a number of disputes. It also administered mandates and made some progress in developing various auxiliary international organizations such as the ILO (see INTERNATIONAL LABOUR ORGANIZATION) and the Court of International Justice. During the 1930s, however, it failed to secure the support of the major powers in the face of Japanese, Italian and German aggression that it was powerless to prevent, and did not survive World War II. At the end of that war it was replaced by the United Nations (see UN). For further reading: G. Scott, *The Rise and Fall of the League of Nations* (1974). D.C.W.

learning curve. Expression derived from experimental studies of learning, in which learning rate is depicted as a graph showing rate of success against number of trials. The resulting 'curve' is steep in cases of rapid learning and shallow in cases of slow learning. In the 1980s the expression entered everyday usage (e.g. 'I may be new at the job but I'm on a steep learning curve.') The popularity of the term is probably related to the wide cultural airing which SKINNERIAN learning theory enjoyed during the 1960s and 1970s. G.D.R.

learning disability. A disorder of the brain in which specific cognitive abilities are impaired, although the individual may have normal or above-normal abilities in other areas, particularly those associated with creativity. Common learning disabilities include dyslexia, which causes difficulties in understanding words or sentences, dyscalculia, which causes difficulties in using mathematical symbols, and dysgraphia, which causes difficulties in writing. They are not to be confused with MENTAL RETARDATION, in which overall intelligence is impaired. Although there is no cure for learning disabilities, early diagnosis and extra help with the specific weaknesses can allow sufferers to overcome many of their difficulties. It is estimated by the National Institutes of Health that learning disabilities affect one in seven people in the United States, although many of those will remain undiagnosed. For further reading: J. Lerner, *Learning Disabilities* (1993). A.A.L.

learning problems, see under DYNAMIC PROGRAMMING.

least-action principle. An alternative formulation of NEWTONIAN MECHANICS, which states that of all the conceivable paths along which a body may move between two points the path actually taken is such that a certain readily calculated property of the paths – the 'action' – is a minimum. A similar law in OPTICS (*Fermat's principle of least time*) governs the bending of light rays.

In the 18th century these principles were often regarded as indicating a 'desire for economy' on the part of nature, which made objects 'choose' the minimal paths. However, this interpretation is untenable, because (1) a wide range of conceivable physical laws, including many known to be false, may be transformed mathematically into minimum principles, and (2) the action may occasionally be not a minimum but a *maximum* (when the paths or light rays have been through a focus). Least-action principles are useful in theoretical studies, such as the connection between Newtonian and QUANTUM MECHANICS. M.V.B.

Leavisite. Adjective or noun formed from the name of the British literary critic F. R. Leavis (1895–1978) – and of his wife, Q. D. Leavis, whose *Fiction and the Reading Public* (1932) can perhaps be regarded as her most notable contribution to their working partnership. Between the 1930s and the 1960s Leavis had been, probably, the most powerful single influence on English studies: as a teacher at Cambridge University (and especially at Downing College), as founder and editor of *Scrutiny* (1932–53), and as the author of such books as *New Bearings in Poetry* (1932), *Culture and Environment* (with Denys Thompson, 1933), *Revaluation* (1936), and *The Great Tradition* (1949). An outstanding exponent of the *practical criticism* (i.e. criticism based on close analysis of the text) pioneered by I. A. Richards (1893–1979), Leavis regarded the study of English as a unique opportunity for developing a general 'critical awareness'. His own critical awareness, however, too often led to critical and even personal acerbity, as in the TWO CULTURES controversy. The term 'Leavisite' is applied, pejoratively, not to Leavis himself nor to such former *Scrutiny* associates as L. C. Knights or D. J. Enright, but (as a noun) to his more dogmatic disciples, and (as an adjective) to the type of criticism or teaching which is concerned with the accurate 'placing' of literature (within Leavis's framework) at the expense of enjoyment. For further reading: E. Bentley (ed.), *The Importance of Scrutiny* (1948). O.S.

Lebensraum ('living room'). Term of biological origin meaning the area inhabited or habitable by a particular life-form (biosphere). It was introduced into political usage by German publicists after 1870 to justify Germany's territorial expansion. A central concept after 1919 in German ultra-NATIONALIST writing, including the propaganda literature of the Nazis (see NAZISM), it looked in particular to an expansion of Germany into eastern Europe, justifying this by the need for agricultural land to maintain the favourable balance between peasant and city-dweller on which the moral health of the German nation was supposed to rest. This was the ideological justification for Hitler's attack on Russia in 1941. See also GEOPOLITICS. For further reading: N. Rich, *Hitler's War Aims* (1974). D.C.W.

Lebenswelt (Lifeworld). An important concept in the later philosophy of Edmund Husserl (1859–1938). During the period 1934–38 he worked on a text we know as *The Crisis of European Sciences*, in which, dismayed by the current political débâcle and the complicity of science in it, Husserl sketched out a theory of a 'Lifeworld' in which men and women historically exist, and which has its own *telos* and ethical reality. Individual epochs do more or less well in their responsibility towards the Lifeworld. In Husserl's view, the present epoch was, or was about to be, the most irresponsible ever. The telos of science and philosophy set up by the Greeks had been abandoned completely, and an ethical concern for the future of the Lifeworld had dropped to virtually zero. The Lifeworld is both part of, and yet distinct from, the physical world around us. It is partly constituted by intellectual, political and ethical INTENTIONALITY, a membrane of INTERSUBJECTIVITY and responsibility in which we encounter the OTHER, and with him, carry on, or fail to carry on, the ethical project which the Lifeworld is. So far as Husserl writing in the late 1930s could see, the very continuation of the Lifeworld as a human project was in danger. For further reading: E. Husserl, *The Crisis of European Sciences* (1970). R.PO.

Leboyer method of childbirth, see under CHILDBIRTH TECHNIQUES.

lect. In SOCIOLINGUISTICS, any collection of linguistic phenomena which has a functional identity within a speech community, such as a regional dialect, or a social variety. A continuum of varieties is recognized, e.g. distinguishing between a variety which has the greatest prestige within a community (the 'acrolect') and that which is furthest away from this norm (the 'basilect'). For further reading: D. Bickerton, *Dynamics of a Creole System* (1975). D.C.

Left, the. Label applied to a range of radical political views (see RADICALISM) and to those holding them. It came into being as a metaphorical extension of the seating plan of the French Estates General in 1789, where the nobility sat on the King's right and the 'Third Estate' on his left. The division of opinion crystallized in the debates on the royal veto, with the more revolutionary deputies opposing it, the conservative ones favouring it, and those in the CENTRE proposing a compromise.

This perception of politics as a continuum in which the body politic is consistently divided by attitudes towards social change and social order resulted in the identification of the Left (or left wing) as the parties of change and of the RIGHT (or right wing) as the forces of the status quo. The left–right dichotomy was that of EGALITARIANISM v. inequalities, of reform (or REVOLUTION) v. tradition, of RADICALISM v. CONSERVATISM, of economic interventionism (see STATE ECONOMIC PLANNING) v. LAISSEZ FAIRE, of internationalism v. patriotism.

However, after World War I political attitudes no longer clustered so consistently along the old left–right division. Although the two terms continue to be used, they have undergone many shifts of meaning; and some of the old contradictory tendencies have appeared in new combinations. The Left could not be defined any more by its attitude to equality *and* change (see EQUALITY, PRINCIPLE OF): the two were sometimes divergent. The Right was no longer necessarily an epitome of conservation and of the defence of the status quo; it could be radical, or even revolutionary like NAZISM. Nor was the Left necessarily internationalist; the emergence of national versions of COMMUNISM testified to this. Even inside the parties internal divisions were no longer always best described in terms of left and right. The Polish REVISIONISTS considered themselves to be to the left of Gomulka, whereas he denounced them as a rightist deviation (see DEVIATIONISM). The MAOIST Chinese similarly denounced Soviet 'revisionism' as a right-wing betrayal of communism, while Soviet communists castigated the Maoists as 'leftist adventurers *and* PETIT BOURGEOIS nationalists'.

The emergence of the NEW LEFT contributed even more to the confusion and shifts in the meaning of the terms right and left. The perception of politics as a spectrum became more difficult, and a definition of 'the Left' in terms of traditional and consistent attitudes even more so. The label continues to be applied because it still helps to describe persistent divisions, but it often contributes more to the obfuscation of political realities than to the clarification of political issues. For further reading: W. Thompson, *The Left in History* (1997). L.L.

Left Book Club. A London publishing venture, founded early in 1936, which epitomized LEFT attitudes during the POPULAR FRONT period. Its publisher was Victor Gollancz and its co-founders were John Strachey and Professor Harold Laski; its editorial director was a communist INTELLECTUAL, John Lewis. Starting with some 10,000 members, within three years it increased five-fold. Although not all of its books were written by COMMUNISTS or FELLOW-TRAVELLERS, most of them were strongly pro-Soviet, and none was in any way critical of Stalin's Russia at the time of the Great Purge (see YEZHOVSHCHINA) and the MOSCOW TRIALS. The Club's success was interrupted by the 1939 Nazi-Soviet Pact, which was denounced by some of the Club's leaders, including Victor Gollancz. Its membership fell rapidly, and in 1948 it was dissolved. For further reading: J. Symons, *The Thirties* (1960; 1975). L.L.

legal positivism. A theory about the nature of law which defines it in a purely descriptive way in terms of the commands, or other *ex officio* pronouncements, of a sovereign or generally recognized authority, and without reference to moral considerations. It was first fully expounded by the 19th-century legal theorist, John Austin (1790–1859), who based his position on the ideas of Hobbes and Bentham. More recent developments of the doctrine have adjusted it to take account of the facts that not all laws are straightforwardly imperative in form and that not all constitutions contain so simply identifiable an ultimate source of law as that of Britain, whose legal system was Austin's prime example. For further reading: H. L. A. Hart, *The Concept of Law* (1961). A.Q.

legal professional ethics. Regulations concerning the conduct of lawyers in their professional capacity. In England, where there are two legal professions, these regulations are for the most part laid down by the Law Society for solicitors and the Senate of the Inns of Court and the General Council of the Bar for barristers, though certain overall provisions are made by Act of Parliament, e.g. concerning complaints about the Law Society's handling of complaints against solicitors. Ethics cover such matters as the conduct of counsel or solicitor advocates in court, fees, ADVERTISING (which is permitted in a limited way for solicitors, but not for barristers), training (including provision for articled clerkships for intending solicitors and pupillage for barristers), and arrangements for partnerships between solicitors. Firms of solicitors may not be incorporated, and barristers may not enter into partnerships of any kind, though they practise from sets of chambers which they share with other barristers, and in which they share a clerk or clerks. A lawyer offending against his profession's ethics will be disciplined by the Law Society or the Bar Council which, in serious cases, may strike a solicitor from the rolls or disbar a barrister. For further reading: R. J. Walker, *The English Legal System* (1985). D.C.M.Y.

legal-rational authority. A term associated

particularly with the German sociologist Max Weber (1864–1920; see SOCIOLOGY). It refers to an IDEAL TYPE of authority dependent not on tradition, as in the rule of elders or leaders in tribal and peasant societies, nor on personal CHARISMA, as with the authority of kings or religious prophets, but on the acceptance of certain formal rules and procedures as rationally valid and legally binding. For Weber, it is the form of authority increasingly characteristic of a modern INDUSTRIAL SOCIETY. Its principal agent and exponent is modern BUREAUCRACY, although Weber was well aware that in practice bureaucracy was quite capable of highly 'irrational' as well as flagrantly illegal behaviour. K.K.

legal realism. A theory about the nature of law which, like LEGAL POSITIVISM, seeks to define it without reference to moral considerations, but goes even further in interpreting statements about legal *rights* and *duties* in a straightforward factual way. It defines a person's legal rights as whatever, as a matter of fact, the courts will decide that he should be allowed to do, his legal duties as whatever the courts will decide he is required to do. A common objection to this self-consciously hard-headed theory is that it can give no intelligible account of the reasoning of judges. A judge asking himself 'What are this man's legal rights?' is really, according to legal realism, asking 'What, in fact, am I going to say he should be allowed to do?' A.Q.

legionnaires' disease. This form of pneumonia achieved notoriety from an outbreak among a group of American ex-servicemen (legionnaires) attending a convention at a hotel in Philadelphia in 1976. Twenty-nine out of about 180 cases died, and it was only after some months of intensive work that the investigators succeeded in finding and growing the bacterium responsible. Had the outbreak affected not the legionnaires but some other convention, this section might have been titled candlemakers' disease or even Eucharistic Congress Syndrome.

The disease is caused by the bacterium *Legionella pneumophila*, which was hitherto unrecognized as it was difficult to grow in the laboratory. It is now generally diagnosed by the finding of a rise in the concentration of antibodies (see IMMUNITY) in the patient's blood. The rise is sought in successive blood samples taken several days apart. About 150 to 200 cases are recognized every year in the UK, and although the bacterium is sensitive to certain ANTIBIOTICS the disease still has a case fatality ratio of about 12.5 per cent. About a third of British cases have become infected abroad, usually in southern Europe, although that distribution possibly reflects the distribution of susceptible travellers. About 70 per cent of the patients are more than 50 years old and most are male. While sporadic cases are found, outbreaks seem to occur in hotels, hospitals and other large institutions where the organism is found to be infecting water systems such as those in air-conditioning or shower heads, from both of which it is inhaled as an aerosol. Some water systems may be found to be infected on routine inspection, and it is not yet clear why explosive outbreaks suddenly arise. W.R.L.

legitimacy. An interest in governmental legitimacy has two bases, either a sociological interest (see SOCIOLOGY) in a government's *de facto* ability to have its word pass for law, or a moral interest in the grounds on which governments ought to have their word pass for law. The first topic has come back into vogue because of a persistent anxiety as to whether modern STATES overstretch themselves in trying to provide 'cradle to grave' WELFARE for their subjects; the second has always exercised political philosophers since subjects first challenged their rulers' authority. Recently, a widespread concern for HUMAN RIGHTS has provoked the thought that if governments possess authority only in virtue of protecting their subjects' rights, few governments are wholly legitimate. (See POWER.) For further reading: J. Habermas, *Legitimation Crisis* (1980). A.R.

Lehrstück ('didactic play'). German term of the 1920s for a form of MUSIC THEATRE designed to instruct the performers rather than entertain an audience. The genre was introduced, apparently as a development of Hindemith's *Gemeinschaftsmusik*, or communual music intended for amateurs, at the 1929 Baden-Baden chamber music festival, when Brecht, Hindemith and Kurt Weill produced the *Badener Lehrstück vom Einverständnis* and the 'radio *Lehrstück*' *Flug* *der Lindberghs* or *Lindberghflug* (later renamed *Der Ozeanflug*). The term was virtually annexed by Brecht, whose model appears to have been the Japanese No drama, which henceforward became an important constituent of his EPIC THEATRE. With Weill and Hanns Eisler, he wrote, in 1930–34, further didactic works, some with an expressly COMMUNIST message, for performance by children or amateurs. For further reading: G. Skelton, *Paul Hindemith* (1975). J.W.

Leicester school, see under AGRARIAN HISTORY.

leisure class. A term coined, with a characteristic degree of irony, by the American social critic Thorstein Veblen in 1899. The leisure CLASS is made up of all those – aristocrats, clergy, BOURGEOIS, *nouveaux riches* – who regard manual labour, and industrial occupations generally, as beneath them, and who devote themselves to government, warfare, religion and sport. Though the values and lifestyles of the leisure class are derived largely from the upper class of FEUDAL Europe, they have persisted in the outlook of the wealthier classes of INDUSTRIAL SOCIETY, and have even been strengthened by the vast private fortunes made possible by industrialism. The leisure class is not, however, interested in riches as such; it is concerned with its social standing in society, and hence indulges heavily in CONSPICUOUS CONSUMPTION. For Veblen this meant a misdirection of industrial effort, in the production of luxury goods for display purposes; though many economists argue that this is a necessary and beneficial stage of ECONOMIC GROWTH above the level of primary accumulation. Some critics today think that Britain is too heavily permeated by the values of the leisure class, leading to an aversion to industrial pursuits and a preference for the professions and public life. For further reading: M. Wiener, *English Culture and the Decline of the Industrial Spirit 1850–1980* (1981). K.K.

lend-lease. An Act of the US Congress, signed by President Roosevelt on 11 March 1941, while the USA was still neutral, to allow the supply of arms and general supplies to Britain and subsequently to other states at war with the AXIS powers. Its basic principle was the leasing of arms and armaments in return for undertakings to return their value after the war was over. The Act did not allow for any extension once hostilities had ended, and its operations were abruptly terminated in 1945 by order of President Truman. For further reading: R. Dallek, *Franklin D. Roosevelt and American Foreign Policy, 1932–45* (1979). D.C.W.

Leninism. The term refers to the version of MARXIST thought which accepts the validity of the major theoretical contributions made by Vladimir Ilyich Lenin (1870–1924) to revolutionary Marxism. These contributions fall into two main groups. Central to the first was the conception of the revolutionary party as the vanguard of the PROLETARIAT. The workers, if left to their own devices, would concentrate on purely economic issues and not attain full political CLASS consciousness, and therefore the revolutionary seizure of power needed the leadership of committed Marxist activists (see ACTIVISM) to provide the appropriate theoretical and tactical guidelines. The role of the Party was thus to be a 'vanguard' in the revolutionary struggle which would culminate in the overthrow of the CAPITALIST STATE and the establishment of a DICTATORSHIP OF THE PROLETARIAT under the HEGEMONY of the Party.

The second major theoretical contribution made by Lenin was to draw the political consequences from an analysis of CAPITALISM as both international and imperialist. The phenomenon of IMPERIALISM divided the world between advanced industrial nations and the colonies they were exploiting. This situation was inherently unstable and led to war between capitalist nations, thus creating favourable conditions for REVOLUTION. For Lenin, the 'weakest link' in the capitalist chain was to be found in underdeveloped (see UNDERDEVELOPMENT) regions of the world economy such as Russia, where the indigenous bourgeoisie (see BOURGEOIS) was comparatively weak, but where there had been enough INDUSTRIALIZATION to create a class-conscious proletariat. The idea of worldwide SOCIALIST revolution beginning in relatively backward countries led to the inclusion of the peasantry as important revolutionary actors affording essential support to the proletariat in establishing a socialist order. Such socialist revolutions in underdeveloped countries would exacerbate the contradictions inherent in advanced capitalist economies and thus lead to the advent of socialism on a world scale.

As compared with the ideas of Marx and Engels, Leninism gives more emphasis to the leading role of the Party, to backward or semi-colonial countries as the initial site of revolution, and to the peasantry as potential revolutionary agents. With the success of the Bolshevik revolution in 1917 (see BOLSHEVISM), Leninism became the dominant version of Marxism and the official IDEOLOGY of the former USSR. Lenin's analysis of imperialism and his idea of the 'weakest link' also made his version of Marxism appealing to emerging ÉLITES in the THIRD WORLD. In the West, however, while Leninist principles are maintained by the small Trotskyist parties, many adherents of eurocommunism have begun to ask how far Leninist ideas reflected specifically Russian circumstances and should therefore be modified to fit the conditions of advanced capitalist societies. For further reading: N. Harding, *Leninism* (1996). D.T.M.

lensing, see under GRAVITATIONAL LENSING.

lepton. Any ELEMENTARY PARTICLE that does not react or decay with STRONG INTERACTIONS, but instead displays only the WEAK INTERACTION or interactions via the ELECTROMAGNETIC FIELD (e.g. the ELECTRON, the NEUTRINO). M.V.B.

lesbianism. Sexual relations between women are a part of all cultures and societies; what differs between societies is the degree of recognition and toleration of these relationships. Female HOMOSEXUALITY, as lesbianism is sometimes described, has seldom attracted the social odium and explicit persecution accorded to male homosexuality, nor has it been systematically criminalized. Nevertheless, the stereotype of the masculine woman, the 'butch' or the 'dyke', is one which is associated with lesbianism and has brought with it stigmatization.

Recent writing on lesbianism – while decrying the marginalization of lesbians – has developed three themes in its discussion: the difficulty of distinguishing between close female friendships and 'lesbianism'; the long tradition in literature and the arts of female associations and relationships; and the distance between stereotypes of lesbian women and the reality. As the value of female friendship has acquired a central place in second-wave FEMINISM, so definitions of lesbianism have become, to different authors, both more exclusive (in that lesbianism is only identified in terms of sexual relations between women) and more inclusive (in that close female friendships, such as that suggested between Jane Austen and her sister, became named as lesbian). For further reading: S. Jeffreys, *The Lesbian Heresy: A Feminist Perspective on the Lesbian Sexual Revolution* (1994). M.S.E.

lethal injection, see under CAPITAL PUNISHMENT.

lettrism. Parisian literary movement founded in 1946, based on a poetic and pictorial concern with letters and signs, and identified particularly with Isidore Isou and Maurice Lemaître. Its works, generally regarded as inferior to comparable exercises in CONCRETE POETRY and by allied artists of a calligraphic bent, take the form of phonetic poetry, picture-writing (*hypergraphy*), and quasi-semiotic painting (see SEMIOTICS). For further reading: I. Isou, *Introduction à une nouvelle poésie* (1947). J.W.

leucotomy (or **lobotomy).** Operation involving cutting the white matter of the brain. In its most drastic form, the *prefrontal leucotomy*, a cut is made in the front part of the brain to divide connecting tracts between the frontal lobes and the thalamus.

Prefrontal leucotomy was introduced when it was noticed (and confirmed by experiments with animals) that injuries to the frontal lobes resulted in a blunting of the EMOTIONS – particularly AGGRESSION and ANXIETY. It was widely practised in the late 1940s and early 1950s, and brought undoubted relief to a number of patients with PSYCHOSIS or severe emotional disorders, but its exact value was never generally agreed, and it is now performed much less often, since reversible, controllable and less drastic results can be achieved by treatment with drugs. For further reading: W. L. Jones, *Ministering to Minds Diseased* (1983). D.A.P.

level. In LINGUISTICS, a fundamental theoretical term which is used in a number of senses, in particular (1) to denote an aspect of the structure of language regarded as susceptible of independent study; three levels (PHONETICS, SYNTAX, SEMANTICS) are generally recognized (but see also DUALITY OF STRUCTURE; FORM); (2) in GENERATIVE GRAMMAR, to characterize the distinction between DEEP STRUCTURE AND SURFACE STRUCTURE ('varying levels of depth'); (3) especially by some American linguists, in the sense of RANK. D.C.

levirate, see under BRIDEWEALTH.

lexeme. A term used by some linguists (see LINGUISTICS) to describe the basic abstract lexical unit which underlies the different inflectional forms of a word, e.g. *sleep*, *slept*, *sleeps*, *sleeping* are variants of a single lexeme, *sleep*. D.C.

lexical functional grammar. In LINGUISTICS, a grammatical theory that developed in the 1970s, in which grammatical relations are represented by means of a 'functional' analysis of sentence structure, and the LEXICON is assigned a more important role than it held in earlier models of TRANSFORMATIONAL GRAMMAR. D.C.

lexical word, see under WORD CLASS.

lexicography, see under LEXICON.

lexicology, see under LEXICON.

lexicometry, see under QUANTITATIVE HISTORY.

lexicon. The dictionary component of a linguistic analysis, in which all information about the meaning and use of individual lexical items in a language is listed. It is particularly used with reference to the semantic component (see SEMANTICS) of a GENERATIVE GRAMMAR. The study of the properties of the lexicon is sometimes called *lexis*, sometimes *lexicology*. The latter must be distinguished from *lexicography*, the principles and practice of dictionary-making. In neo-Firthian (see FIRTHIAN) LINGUISTICS, lexis has a more restricted sense, referring only to the formal, not the semantic, characteristics of the lexicon. In PSYCHOLINGUISTICS, the mental lexicon is the stored mental representation of what we know about the lexical items in our language. D.C.

lexicostatistics, see under GLOTTOCHRONOLOGY.

lexis, see under LEXICON.

liberal feminism. Western FEMINISM is universally associated with the European Enlightenment, and the particular tradition which dates from that period is that of liberal feminism. The author who marks the starting point for discussion within this tradition is Mary Wollstonecraft (1759–97) with her work *A Vindication of the Rights of Woman* (1792), in which she argued for the integration of women into civil society and put the case for the education of women. The two themes – the right of women to full participation in liberal democracy and the right of women to both elementary and higher education – have dominated the history of the struggle for women's rights in Western democracies. The majority of these societies gave women the vote in the early 20th century, although access to higher education had occurred rather earlier. The integration of women into civil society became a mark of a 'modern society'; e.g., in the peace settlement imposed upon Japan by the United States in 1945 the enfranchisement of woman was a key theme.

Liberal feminism has thus traditionally been associated with questions of *access* to existing structures of politics or education. Within liberal feminism there has generally been limited discussion of the structures to which women have sought access: hence liberal feminism is identified with the interests of white, MIDDLE CLASS women for whom participation in formal and/or hierarchical structures is an expectation of an ethic of individual achievement. Nevertheless, in its emphasis on individual rights liberal feminism has made possible shifts in contexts such as medicine and the control of FERTILITY, where an ideal of autonomy and individual choice has significantly enhanced the collective empowerment of women. For further reading: B. Friedan, *The Feminine Mystique* (1963). M.S.E.

liberalism/liberal. A political PHILOSOPHY

whose origins lie in the Renaissance and the Reformation, and which acquired firmer roots in the 18th century and its greatest coherence in the 19th. It then remained a massive influence on the development of increasingly democratic societies, generally in a close marriage with CAPITALIST economic systems. In many nations liberalism lost ground after the severe economic DEPRESSION of the 1930s, the growth of stronger WORKING CLASS parties and TRADE UNIONS, and the post-1945 growth of social democratic movements (see SOCIAL DEMOCRACY). However, in recent years doubts about, e.g., the fiscal and social consequences of extensive WELFARE STATES and the effects of public ownership or wholesale economic regulation have seen a revival. Liberalism's long history and adaptive character have made it somewhat protean in nature, to the confusing extent that its revival, at least in the economic sphere, was largely stimulated by the Conservative Party led by Margaret Thatcher (see THATCHERISM), while in the USA (arguably the nation which had least strayed from liberal values), conservatives (see CONSERVATISM) often use the term as one of opprobrium, to connote social and moral decay and excessive governmental intervention.

Liberalism essentially springs from a vision of society as crucially composed of individuals (rather than, e.g., classes) in a voluntary, contractual relationship with government. It stresses their liberty as the primary social good. This liberty is to be defended in such rights as those to free political institutions, religious practice, intellectual and artistic expression, to equal standing before the law, and to private property. It implies a distrust of the right or efficiency of a state which interferes with such freedoms and with the workings of economic markets.

In the 20th century liberalism has been challenged by doctrines such as FASCISM and variants of MARXISM, respectively stressing the principles of state POWER and equality (see EQUALITY, PRINCIPLE OF). The IDEOLOGY adapted to such threats or influences, and to changing patterns of economic organization, often by accepting the state as a positive influence in alleviating inequalities and protecting minority rights – as in the USA during the NEW DEAL and GREAT SOCIETY eras. The term's flexibility, and its internationally varied forms of adaptation, have led to it also often connoting more loosely such values as tolerance (including, increasingly, in matters of sexual mores), rationality, privacy, minority rights (see MINORITIES), PARTICIPATION.

The fading of COMMUNISM and consequent spread of essentially liberal-capitalist ideas have led some observers to see liberalism as *en route* to becoming the world's unifying ideology. Critics suggest instead, e.g., that many of its elements clash with theocratic systems such as ISLAM, or that its individualism and marriage to capitalism render it unable to address major global concerns such as great international inequalities of wealth, or environmental dangers. For further reading: P. Neal, *Liberalism and Its Discontents* (1997). S.R.

liberalism, economic, see ECONOMIC LIBERALISM.

liberation theology. A movement in late 20th-century THEOLOGY which conceives of theology as a form of critical reflection upon the struggle for liberation from social, political and economic oppression. Principally but not exclusively Roman Catholic (see CATHOLICISM), it originated in Latin America in the late 1960s, in conjunction with the resolution of the Latin American Episcopal Conference at Medellin in 1968 to make 'liberation' (rather than 'development') the centre of its thought. Liberation theologians such as Gustavo Gutierrez are committed to interpreting the Bible and the Christian tradition from the specific perspective of the poor and marginalized. C.C.

libertarianism.

(1) The doctrine that no STATE can be legitimate which sets out to do more than enforce individuals' rights; extreme libertarians hold that no state whatever can be legitimate, and that we are not obliged to obey any authority to which we have not given our actual, and not merely our hypothetical, consent. Unlike orthodox conservatives (see CONSERVATISM), libertarians believe it is no part of the state's duties to enforce private morality; prostitution, drug-taking (see DRUGS) and sexual perversion not involving harm to others are all within the individual's right to do what he chooses with his own resources. Conversely, liber-

tarians are sceptical of the nation-state's tendency to possess large military forces and to spend huge sums on so-called defence. Libertarians differ from 20th-century liberals (see LIBERALISM) in disbelieving in social justice and in thinking that the WELFARE STATE is simply robbery under the cover of law. The intellectual charms of libertarian doctrine are greater than its impact on practical politics has thus far been. For further reading: M. Rothbard, *For a New Liberty* (1974). A.R.

(2) A theory, opposed to DETERMINISM, about the nature of human action which holds that some human actions, those for which it is correct to hold the agent in question morally responsible, are not causally explicable, or not wholly so. A.Q.

libido.

(1) In early psychoanalytic theory (see PSYCHOANALYSIS), a FREUDIAN term for specifically sexual energies.

(2) Later, all psychic energies employed in the service of the LIFE INSTINCT. W.Z.

life chances. A term devised by the German sociologist (see SOCIOLOGY) Max Weber (1864–1920) to refer to the chances of individuals from different social groups achieving those things a society defines as desirable and avoiding those things defined as undesirable. Life chances might therefore include the odds on people from different social CLASSES or ethnic groups achieving high levels of education, avoiding early death, owning particular consumer goods or avoiding UNEMPLOYMENT. Studies of life chances in INDUSTRIAL SOCIETIES show that marked inequalities persist between those from different social groups. For example, studies of health inequalities in Britain and other countries show that those from manual WORKING CLASS backgrounds continue to die younger than those from professional and managerial backgrounds. For further reading: I. Reid, *Social Class Differences in Modern Britain* (1989). M.D.H.

life cycle. One or other of the regenerative processes in the biosphere; examples are the *nitrogen cycle*, the *carbon cycle* and the *oxygen cycle*. The elementary constituents of the biosphere – carbon, hydrogen, oxygen, nitrogen, phosphorus, sulphur – enter into compounds which so far from being static undergo continuous cycles of use and reuse, synthesis and degradation. Nitrogen compounds are essential for living organisms and are probably the most important limiting factor in regulating their abundance. Yet in spite of its enormous abundance (about 80 per cent of the atmosphere) very few organisms have the power to make use of nitrogen directly. For this reason the artificial fixation of gaseous nitrogen is the most important and biologically influential technological innovation since the INDUSTRIAL REVOLUTION. The amounts of nitrogen fixed in industrial processes for the manufacture of fertilizers are of the order of tens of millions of tons per annum, and are probably on the same scale as the natural fixation of atmospheric nitrogen by marine micro-organisms and by the micro-organisms that live in SYMBIOSIS with leguminous plants. The fixation of nitrogen has to compete with the denitrifying processes which in the latest stages of organic breakdown return nitrogen to the atmosphere, and with the wastage produced by the dissipation or misuse of sewage, which is normally rich in nitrogen compounds.

The carbon cycle, closely intertwined with the oxygen cycle, begins and ends with atmospheric carbon dioxide. Although living organisms are compounds of carbon, very much more carbon is locked up in the form of coal and other fossil fuels than in living organisms themselves. The crucial TRANSFORMATION in both the carbon cycle and the oxygen cycle is PHOTOSYNTHESIS. The chief agents fixing atmospheric carbon are terrestrial forests and marine phytoplankton. Carbon dioxide is returned to the air by respiration, by the combustion of fossil fuels, and as a terminal stage of the decomposition of organic matter. In both carbon and oxygen cycles an annual rhythm is superimposed upon a circadian rhythm. P.M.

life expectancy. The average number of additional years of life for individuals of a given age. Thus defined, life expectancy is most easily understood with reference to a specific COHORT of individuals. More commonly, however, life expectancy describes the MORTALITY conditions of a specific time period; in this case, it gives the average number of additional years of life if the mortality experience of some (hypothetical) group of individuals were characterized by the age-specific DEATH RATES of that particular time. Thus, life expectancy at birth in a particular year gives the average length of life for babies born in that year if current mortality conditions (as measured by age-specific death rates) do not change in the future. Conceptually, life expectancy at birth in studies of mortality is analogous to the TOTAL FERTILITY RATE in studies of FERTILITY. J.R.W.

life force, see under VITALISM.

life instinct (*or* ***Eros***). In psychoanalytic theory (see PSYCHOANALYSIS), a FREUDIAN term for the supposed source of all the impulses and drives that serve the individual in self-preservation and reproduction. It is contrasted with the DEATH INSTINCT. See also LIBIDO. W.Z.

life sciences, see under BIOLOGY.

life space. In the TOPOLOGICAL PSYCHOLOGY of Kurt Lewin (1890–1947), the spatial representation of the entire psychological ENVIRONMENT as it exists for an individual person and within which he behaves according to interactions among various needs, values, obstacles, social pressures, aspirations, etc. I.M.L.H.

life-span psychology, see DEVELOPMENTAL PSYCHOLOGY.

life table. A detailed description of the MORTALITY pattern in a population, giving the probability of death and various other statistics at each age. A life table may describe the mortality experience of a specific COHORT over its lifetime. More commonly, however, a life table depicts the mortality conditions in a population during some period of time; in this case, it supplies statistical indicators of the probabilities of death and survival for a (hypothetical) group of individuals whose mortality experience is characterized by the age-specific DEATH RATES observed at that particular time. Perhaps the most important purpose of the life table is to permit the calculation of LIFE EXPECTANCY at birth. The first life table was constructed by John Graunt in London in 1662. J.R.W.

lifestyle. Originally developed by classical sociologists (see SOCIOLOGY) such as Weber and Simmel as a means of exploring the effects of industrialization and concomitant rise of consumerism upon social IDENTITY, lifestyle was subsequently to become a term more readily identifiable with MARKET RESEARCH where it was used as a means of attempting to map taste patterns and predict demand for particular consumer products (see CONSUMER SOCIETY). In more recent years there has been a resurgence of interest in lifestyles among sociologists and cultural theorists. This has in part been prompted by the deindustrialization of Western countries and the increasing importance of leisure. Lifestyle refers to all the observable characteristics of a person, e.g. his manner of speaking, personal appearance, taste in music, choice of leisure pursuits, domestic habits and choice of friends. In the context of late modern consumer-orientated society, it is argued, all of these characteristics are a matter of personal choice rather than fixed attributes. Thus, it is maintained, there is a fundamental difference between a lifestyle and a way of life, the latter being more readily associated with pre- or early industrial society. For further reading: D. Chaney, *Lifestyles* (1996). A.BEN.

Lifeworld, see under LEBENSWELT.

light amplifier, see under NON-LINEAR OPTICS.

lightquantum. A concentration of radiant energy, basic to the quantum conception of the 'free radiation' of light, in contradistinction to the traditional wave theory of light propagation. QUANTUM THEORY proposes that light is emitted by a finite number of lightquanta. Such a view of the behaviour of light gained support from J. J. Thomson's (1856–1940) investigation of X-ray ionization, but it took decisive shape in Einstein's perception that under certain conditions light acted in ways thermodynamically equivalent to the behaviour of a molecular gas. The idea of lightquantum initially met considerable resistance from most physicists, however, for whom it failed to explain DIFFRACTION and interference as well as the traditional wave theory. It received powerful support in the 1920s, however, through the experimental work of Arthur Compton and Peter

Debye, and it was to prove highly influential in the development of later wave mechanics (see QUANTUM MECHANICS), at the hands of Heisenberg and Schrödinger. For further reading: W. Wilson, *A Hundred Years of Physics* (1950). R.P.

liminality, see under RITE DE PASSAGE.

limited war. WAR with limited aims. It can be contrasted with *total war*, which is aimed at the complete destruction of the enemy. The FALKLANDS WAR (1982) was an archetypal case: Argentina and Britain limited themselves to fighting for control of the islands, and refrained from attacks on each other's homeland; prisoners of war were humanely treated and speedily repatriated; and there were no deliberate attacks on the civilian population. Some limited wars have been characterized by particularly ruthless fanaticism, but even these have remained non-nuclear, have avoided a direct clash of arms between the superpowers, and have been limited in geographical extent. Some limited wars continue to defy international efforts at peaceful resolution, and carry ever-increasing risks of escalation. P.W.

limits to growth. A concept popularized by the *Club of Rome*, an international group of philanthropic businessmen, scientists and educationists who since 1968 have been intent on alerting the world to the looming crisis posed by rapid growth in many areas – population, industrial TECHNOLOGY, energy use, consumption of natural resources. Although stressing the interdependencc of social and technical factors, the group has become particularly associated with the stress on the *physical* limits to growth. Sophisticated COMPUTER-based calculations carried out for the Club of Rome suggest that on current and projected rates of population and ECONOMIC GROWTH, the world's natural resources will be badly depleted by the early part of the next century. They also point to environmental destruction on a massive scale, together with intensifying international conflict as states struggle to increase their share of the world's diminishing resources.

A later contribution to the debate, associated especially with the economist Fred Hirsch (*Social Limits to Growth*, 1976), has stressed the *social* limits to growth. Beyond a certain level of economic growth, Hirsch argued, competition for scarce material goods is replaced or reinforced by competition for even scarcer 'positional' goods, such as clean air, open space, personal privacy, and satisfying work. Hirsch predicted an intensifying and, in the nature of things, self-defeating struggle between individuals and groups for such 'positional' goods. Only the development of a new social ethic, he thought, backed by public intervention and regulation, could prevent an authoritarian (see AUTHORITARIANISM), Hobbesian resolution of the predicament. For further reading: D. H. Meadows *et al*, *The Limits to Growth* (1972). K.K.

limnology. The science which deals with the interrelationships between the BIOLOGY, CHEMISTRY and PHYSICS of inland water, including lakes, rivers and marshes. The word derives from the Greek *limnē* (marshy lake), and some naturalists with a classical education prefer the term to be restricted to studies of muddy waters and bogs rather than clear lakes and rivers. Generally, however, it is synonymous with *hydrobiology* or *freshwater biology*. K.M.

line and **staff,** see under MANAGEMENT STUDIES.

lineage. Line of DESCENT traced from a common ancestor. If the line is traced exclusively through the male, it is called PATRILINEAL; if traced exclusively through females, MATRILINEAL. A lineage may function as a group to which individuals are recruited on the basis of descent. Lineage and descent group are often used interchangeably as terms by anthropologists. Lineage may, however, be used to describe the total number of groups which may be traced from a single ancestor, but through the process of segmentation these groups may exist on the ground as separate units.

The term *segmentary lineage systems* was developed to describe the process of *fission* and *fusion*. For example, in a patrilineal society, a brother may establish a new lineage segment by moving out from his elder brother's compound with his wives and children (fission). However, in the context of a FEUD, the two segments headed by sons of the same father would fuse to form a single unit (fusion).

The model of segmentary lineage systems was developed by anthropologists working in Africa (particularly by Evans-Pritchard and Meyer Fortes in *African Political Systems*, 1940) to understand political relations in ACEPHALOUS societies, that is those without centralized or state organization. The Nuer were a classic example. The notion of segmentary lineage systems has been criticized as a model developed by observers which does not correspond to ethnographic (see ETHNOGRAPHY) reality. It also does not represent a *folk model*, that is the model held by the actors of their own society. For further reading: L. Holy and M. Stuchlik, *Actions, Norms and Representations* (1983). A.G.

Linear A and B. Name given to two scripts used in Crete and Greece in the Bronze Age. Both are syllabic. They were first recognized on Crete by Sir Arthur Evans (1851–1941), who proposed the name to distinguish them from the earlier hieroglyphic script. Linear B was deciphered in 1952 by Michael Ventris (1922–56), who showed the language used to be an early form of Greek. The subject-matter of the tablets so far translated is restricted to inventories. Linear A has not yet been deciphered. For further reading: J. Chadwick, *The Decipherment of Linear B* (1963). B.C.

linear accelerator. A type of ACCELERATOR for IONS, which travel along a straight line down the common axis of hollow cylindrical electrodes. The acceleration is produced in the gaps between adjacent electrodes by means of oscillating voltages. See also RADIOTHERAPY. M.V.B.

linear planning. The development of elongated urban settlements. This may occur naturally in the case of communities forming within a valley, e.g. the coal-mining settlements which developed in the Rhondda Valley in South Wales in the 19th century. In the early 20th century a range of idealized city plans were developed based along mechanized fixed-track forms of transport, such as the Soria y Mata proposal for a linear city running from Cadiz in Spain to St Petersburg in Russia. In practice, linear development has generally taken the form of suburban linear expansions to existing cities, and occasional high-tech monorail and light-railway schemes. The linear form can also be joined up to form the 'ring' or 'annular' city, or turned in on itself to form a figure-of-eight as in Runcorn New Town, near Liverpool, built in the 1960s. For further reading: P. Hall, *Urban and Regional Planning* (1994). C.G.

linguistic philosophy. A form of ANALYTIC PHILOSOPHY, the historical successor to LOGICAL ATOMISM and LOGICAL POSITIVISM, first practised by G. E. Moore (1873–1958) in a methodically unselfconscious way and developed as an explicit philosophical method by Wittgenstein from about 1930 and, later, by Gilbert Ryle and J. L. Austin. Like logical positivism, it is hostile to METAPHYSICS, but for a different reason: for the linguistic philosopher, the hallmark of a metaphysical PROPOSITION is its incompatibility with the commonsense view of the world, and he conceives his task to be that of unveiling the mistaken assumptions about the actual use of language on which the persuasiveness of metaphysical argumentation depends. Philosophical problems, according to this view, require not solution but dissolution. Wittgenstein's style of linguistic philosophy has been reasonably described as 'therapeutic', for his concern with the rules of ordinary language extended only so far as was needed to dispel philosophical puzzlement. The Oxford philosophers of ordinary language approached it more systematically. Linguistic philosophers are generally suspicious of formal LOGIC, at least in the role of ANALYTIC instrument in which it was cast by their positivist predecessors. Sometimes the phrase 'linguistic philosophy' is applied to all varieties of analytic philosophy, but the narrower application described above is more usual among philosophers. For further reading: C. W. K. Mundle, *A Critique of Linguistic Philosophy* (1970). A.Q.

linguistics. The scientific study of language. As an academic discipline, the development of this subject, which became particularly widely known and taught in the 1960s, has been recent and rapid. This reflects partly an increased popular and specialist interest in the study of language and communication in relation to human beliefs and behaviour (e.g. in THEOLOGY, PHILOSOPHY, INFORMATION THEORY, literary criticism), and the realization of the need for a separate discipline to deal adequately with the range and complexity of linguistic phenomena; partly the impact of the subject's own internal development at this time, arising largely out of the work of Chomsky (see CHOMSKYAN) and his associates, whose more sophisticated analytic techniques and more powerful theoretical claims gave linguistics an unprecedented scope and applicability.

Different branches may be distinguished according to the linguist's focus and range of interest. A major distinction, introduced by Ferdinand de Saussure (see SAUSSURIAN), is between *diachronic* and *synchronic* linguistics, the former referring to the study of language change (also called *historical* linguistics), the latter to the study of the state of language at any given point in time. In so far as the subject attempts to establish general principles for the study of all languages, and to determine the characteristics of human language as a phenomenon, it may be called *general* linguistics. When it concentrates on establishing the facts of a particular language system, it is called *descriptive* linguistics. When its purpose is to focus on the differences between languages, especially in a language-teaching context, it is called *contrastive* linguistics. When its purpose is primarily to identify the common characteristics of different languages or language families, the subject goes under the heading of *comparative* (or *typological*) linguistics. (See also AGGLUTINATING; INFLECTING; ANALYTIC (2); POLYSYNTHETIC.)

When the emphasis in linguistics is wholly or largely historical, the subject is traditionally referred to as *comparative philology* (or simply *philology*), though in many parts of the world 'philologists' and 'historical linguists' are people with very different backgrounds and temperaments. The term *structural* linguistics is widely used, sometimes in an extremely specific sense, referring to the particular approaches to SYNTAX and PHONOLOGY current in the 1940s and 1950s, with their emphasis on providing DISCOVERY PROCEDURES for the analysis of a language's surface structure (see DEEP STRUCTURE); sometimes in a more general sense, referring to any system of linguistic analysis that attempts to establish explicit systems of relations between linguistic units in surface structure. When the emphasis in language study is on the classification of the structures and units, without reference to such notions as deep structure, some linguists, particularly within GENERATIVE GRAMMAR, talk pejoratively of *taxonomic* linguistics.

The overlapping interests of linguistics and other disciplines have led to the setting up of new branches of the subject, such as ANTHROPOLOGICAL LINGUISTICS, BIOLINGUISTICS, COMPUTATIONAL LINGUISTICS, ETHNOLINGUISTICS, MATHEMATICAL LINGUISTICS, NEUROLINGUISTICS, PSYCHOLINGUISTICS, SOCIOLINGUISTICS. When the subject's findings, methods or theoretical principles are applied to the study of problems from other areas of experience, one talks of *applied* linguistics; but this term is often restricted to the study of the theory and methodology of foreign-language teaching. For further reading: R. E. Asher (ed.), *The Encyclopedia of Language and Linguistics* (1993). D.C.

linkage.
(1) In GENETICS, see GENETIC LINKAGE.
(2) In SYSTEMS ANALYSIS, any recurrent sequence of behaviour which originates in one system and produces a reaction in another. A.L.C.B.

linkage politics. A method for the analysis of international relations, based on the notion of LINKAGE (2) – in this case the interaction between international and domestic policies. Three major types of linkage politics are distinguished: (1) the *penetrative*, e.g. 'the penetration' of West Germany and Japan by the USA after World War II; (2) the *reactive*, e.g. an increase in the defence budget of one country in reaction to increased armament in another country which is felt to be unfriendly; (3) the *emulative*, e.g. the spread of SOCIAL WELFARE measures in Western countries, or of the demand for independence in colonial countries, as a result of seeing and emulating what their neighbours are doing. It is claimed that this method of analysis has the advantage of neither denying nor exaggerating the relevance of national boundaries. For further reading: J. N. Rosenau (ed.), *Linkage Politics* (1969). A.L.C.B.

liquid crystal. A substance that shares both liquid-like and crystal-like properties. The

MOLECULES of a liquid crystal are free to flow but, unlike normal liquids, they also have a degree of order, being on average orientated in a particular direction. Many liquid crystals are comprised of rod-like molecules, which may become orientated like floating logs in a log-jam. Other liquid crystals contain disc-shaped molecules which have a tendency to become stacked like plates. Because of this orientation, liquid crystals are *anisotropic* – they do not look the same from all directions. The possibility of controlling the alignment of liquid crystals using electric fields leads to their use in display devices, e.g. in digital watches and portable computer screens, in which changes in the alignment direction alter the material's transparency to polarized light. P.C.B.

liquidity. In ECONOMICS, the possession of or the ability to realize quickly adequate supplies of MONEY, relative to commitments. An asset is regarded as liquid when it can be used as money or can be changed into money at short notice and at a predictable price. An economy, or part of it, is liquid if it has sufficient level of liquid assets (see INTERNATIONAL LIQUIDITY). J.P.

literariness. The central concept of the Russian FORMALISTS. Roman Jakobson, one of the founder members of the school, wrote in 1919: 'The real field of literary science is not literature but *literariness*; in other words, that which makes a specific work literary.' Literariness is closely connected with the distinguishing quality of DEFAMILIARIZATION. For further reading: T. Bennett, *Formalism and Marxism* (1979). R.PO.

literature and ideology. A traditional concern of MARXIST criticism which has resurfaced as an important issue of debate amidst the transformation of leftist literary criticism (see LEFT, THE; CRITICAL THEORY) over the last 30 years. The critique of literature's relationship to IDEOLOGY was reinvigorated by CULTURAL MATERIALISM, which pushed for a notion of 'literature' that was historically determined and which unmasked its role in the productive process that naturalizes a divisive and class-dominated (see CLASS) education system. In disclosing literature's implication in the 'civilizing mission' of English, cultural materialism succeeded in dislodging many of the complacent assumptions of IDEALIST literary criticism. Yet critics have complained that in its assimilation of the productive model of ideology influenced by variants of Althusserian Marxism, such a rereading of English tends to reduce the significance of literature to its 'instrumental goal' as a mere function of ideology. Most recently, some variants of a new aestheticism on the Left have argued for reconceptualizing an approach to literature which is not restricted to the question of ideology but which opens instead onto alternative levels of 'knowledge and expression'. For further reading: A. Bowie, *From Romanticism to Critical Theory* (1997). J.J.J.

lithosphere. Prior to the theory of PLATE TECTONICS, the terms lithosphere and *crust* were used synonymously for the outermost rock shell of the earth which is succeeded inwards by the mantle (see ASTHENOSPHERE). The term lithosphere is now used within the framework of plate tectonic theory for the relatively rigid outer zone of the earth, some 100 km thick, which includes the rock shell and part of the upper mantle. Thus only the term 'crust' is used for the rock shell. The boundary between the crust and the mantle is defined by an important seismological discontinuity, the *Mohorovicic discontinuity* (*Moho* for short). J.L.M.L.

***Little Review*.** An American literary magazine, founded in Chicago by Margaret Anderson in 1914 as a rival to Harriet Monroe's journal *Poetry*. It began by printing many early American radical poets and writers and importing new European ideas; after Ezra Pound took over the foreign editorship, it acquired Joyce's *Ulysses* as well as verse and prose by Eliot, Wyndham Lewis, Hart Crane, and others. After a shift to New York it moved, in 1922, to Paris and took in DADA and SURREALISM, and various French and American expatriate writers. It folded in 1929. For further reading: M. Anderson, *My Thirty Years' War* (1930). M.S.BR.

Liturgical Movement. The movement to restore to the laity an active and intelligent part in the 'liturgy' (Greek *leitourgia*, people's work) or public worship of God by the Church, especially in Holy Communion. Originating in the French monastery of Solesmes under Abbot Guéranger (1805–75), this movement received the most authoritative expression and blessing in the 'Constitution of the Sacred Liturgy' of VATICAN COUNCIL II (1963), and has been the most conspicuously successful part of the AGGIORNAMENTO in the Roman Catholic Church (see CATHOLICISM). It has also influenced other Churches, particularly ANGLICANISM. For further reading: C. Jones *et al*, *The Study of Liturgy* (1978). D.L.E.

Liverpool Poets. A group of writers from that city who coalesced in the early 1960s as a product of the Anglo-American JAZZ POETRY movement and the local POP music wave which threw up the Beatles. Strongly impregnated with local references, yet rooted in the wider modern movement, the work of Adrian Henri, Roger McGough and Brian Patten was designed mainly for public performance, with or without music, and appealed to a largely pop audience. It was brought to the critics' somewhat disdainful attention by Edward Lucie-Smith's anthology *The Liverpool Scene* (London, 1967) and by Penguin Modern Poets No. 10, *The Mersey Sound* (1967). J.W.

Living Newspaper. A form of didactic political drama which uses journalistic techniques to present an account of a contemporary issue, usually in a satirical or agitational context. The Living Newspaper was developed as a form of agitprop drama by the Red Army during the Russian Revolution to reach a mass and largely illiterate audience (cf. the 'factory-wall newspaper'); in the USA the Federal Theater Project (see WPA) established a Living Newspaper unit in 1935; in England, the UNITY THEATRE presented the first of a number of Living Newspaper productions in 1938. For further reading: J. O'Connor and L. Brown (eds), *The Federal Theater Project* (1980). M.A.

Living Theater. A radical AVANT-GARDE troupe founded by Julian Beck and his wife, Judith Malina, in New York in 1947 and remaining in more or less nomadic but continuous existence until Beck's death in 1985. Beginning with poetic drama (Brecht, Eliot, Lorca), the group moved into improvisational REALISM with work like Kenneth Brown's *The Brig* (1965), set in a US Marines detention cell. The Becks later moved the company to Europe where its members lived in communal poverty and became avowedly ANARCHIST. The group's aim was 'to increase conscious awareness, to stress the sacredness of life, to break down the walls'. The calculated AGGRESSION and audience-harassment of shows like *Paradise Now* (1968) suggested that barriers were being erected rather than broken down, although later pieces like *Prometheus* (1978) aimed at participation rather than confrontation with audiences; but they never wavered in their rejection of AUTHORITARIANISM. Living Theater productions were invariably exciting experiences; but the break-up of the group surprised no one. For further reading: T. Shank, *American Alternative Theatre* (1982). M.BI.

lobotomy, see LEUCOTOMY.

local history. This includes the history of a village, a town, a country, or even a province, and can involve the study of the landscape as well as the study of documentary evidence. Long the preserve of amateurs and antiquarians, local history has been invaded in the last generation by problem-oriented professional historians for whom the regional monograph is the obvious means of testing generalizations. This new local history flourishes most in France. In England there is a group of local historians associated with the University of Leicester and concerned in particular with AGRARIAN HISTORY. For further reading: W. G. Hoskins, *Local History in England* (1984). P.B.

localization. An increasingly popular term in sociology and cultural theory when studying the effects of GLOBALIZATION as goods and services produced by particular nations, typically the USA, are sold to other nations around the world. Taking issue with the notion of a single global culture, such theorists suggest that globalization further enhances the 'local' differences between CULTURES. Thus, it is argued, when appropriating global products individuals inscribe social MEANING in such products based upon the 'reality' of their everyday experiences. For example, while US rap music may be used as a means of addressing Afro-

American GHETTO life, its commercialization and consequent 'global' status has brought it into contact with a range of other national YOUTH CULTURES who each rework the genre into a localized mode of collective expression. This is the case, e.g., in Italy, where rap music is being used as a means of protest against the resurgence of FASCISM. The concept of localization is central to Lull's notion of *cultural reterritorialization* (see below). Lull uses this term as a means of illustrating the way in which global products are ascribed new meanings based upon what is local and close to home. For further reading: J. Lull, *Media, Communication, Culture: A Global Approach* (1995).A.BEN.

location theory. A conceptual device used by economic geographers (see ECONOMIC GEOGRAPHY) which seeks to explain logically the locational pattern of an economic activity and the manner in which its component producing regions are interrelated. These analytical frameworks are associated with the LOGICAL POSITIVIST approach to the discipline, and evolved from the classical location theories devised by Johann Heinrich von Thünen for agriculture (1826), Alfred Weber for manufacturing (1909), and Walter Christaller for urban service centres or CENTRAL PLACES (1933). The METHODOLOGY that accompanies the derivation and application of location theories is almost always rooted in *locational analysis*, which rigorously seeks to answer the question 'Why is this productive activity located where it is?' Researchers are usually concerned with the relative spatial qualities of proximity, concentration and dispersion, as well as the optimization of spatial arrangements. Their studies can become theoretically abstract, and many employ sophisticated mathematical MODELS and/or statistical techniques (see STATISTICS). For further reading: P. Haggett *et al*, *Locational Analysis in Human Geography* (1977).

P.O.M.

Lockheed scandal. Japan's biggest corruption scandal of recent times, involving Kakuei Tanaka (Prime Minister, 1972–74) and a number of other leading politicians, as well as some business executives and an unsavoury ultra-rightist named Yoshio Kodama. The scandal broke in 1976, during the prime ministership of Takeo Miki, as a result of Congressional testimony in Washington by a leading executive of the Lockheed Corporation. Allegations were made that Tanaka had received large sums of money several years previously from Lockheed for the promotion of its Tristar airbuses in Japan. The affair convulsed the political world in Japan throughout 1976. Miki was unwilling to authorize a cover-up, top executives of the Marubeni Corporation and of All Nippon Airways were arrested, and in July Tanaka himself was briefly taken into custody and charged with violations of the Foreign Exchange and Trade Control Law. After a lengthy trial involving Tanaka and several other defendants, in October 1983 Tanaka was sentenced to four years' imprisonment and a fine of Y500,000,000, though he was freed pending appeal. Although forced to resign from the Liberal Democratic Party in 1976, Tanaka continued to exercise great influence within the party as leader of the Tanaka faction, and was in effect 'king-maker' to three successive prime ministers – Ohira, Suzuki and Nakasone. His influence declined, however, after he suffered a stroke early in 1985. Despite many predictions in the late 1970s, the party survived the scandal and has gone from strength to strength. J.A.A.S.

locus (plural *loci*). Position on a CHROMOSOME occupied by one of a set of allelomorphic GENES. J.M.S.

logic. The study of INFERENCE. Logic does not simply describe the kinds or patterns of inference that are actually used; it is concerned with the rules of *valid* inference (see VALIDITY), by which those inferences whose premises really entail their conclusions may be distinguished from those whose premises do not. Logicians, however, are not concerned with particular entailments except as examples, even though for each particular entailment ('This is red' entails 'This is coloured') there is a corresponding rule of valid inference (from 'This is red' infer 'This is coloured'), which can be applied on an indefinitely large number of occasions.

In the first place logic is *formal*. There are abstract patterns of inference of which an indefinite number of particular inferences, all of the same logical form, are instances (e.g., from 'No *A* is *B*' infer 'No *B* is *A*'). Logic may be said to have begun with the formulation of individual rules of this kind. Secondly, logic aims to be *systematic*. The first great logical systematizer was Aristotle (384–322 BC), whose theory of the SYLLOGISM set out in a reasonably systematic (although not yet axiomatic – see AXIOMATICS) way all the rules for valid inference from two premises. The thoroughness of Aristotle's achievement obstructed the further development of the discipline, and its systematic elaboration caused it to be regarded as finally authoritative for more than 2,000 years and overshadowed logical discoveries in fields outside the range of his treatment. In the mid-19th century, however, Boole and De Morgan set out in mathematical form (see MATHEMATICAL LOGIC) an ALGEBRA of CLASSES closely related to Aristotle's logic of predicative terms. De Morgan also started the logical study of *relational predicates*, traditional logic having restricted itself to *attributive predicates*; an attributive predicate is a quality, a relational predicate is a relation, or, in some people's usage, the word for a quality (e.g. an adjective) and the word for a relation (e.g. a transitive verb or a preposition) respectively. The major achievement of the modern period has been the mathematically rigorous system of Friedrich Frege (1848–1925). The structurally similar, but less rigorous, system set out by Whitehead and Russell in *Principia Mathematica* (1910 onwards) had the advantage of a simple notation, and the really fertile period in modern logic may be dated from its publication. The main ingredients of logic, as currently conceived, are (1) the logic of compound PROPOSITION or PROPOSITIONAL CALCULUS or TRUTH-FUNCTION theory and (2) the logic of predicates or PREDICATE CALCULUS or QUANTIFICATION theory. The logic of classes of SET THEORY is now generally viewed as the fundamental discipline of mathematics rather than as a part of logic proper. See also MODAL LOGIC; OBJECTIVITY. For further reading: I. M. Copi, *Introduction to Logic* (1982). A.Q.

logical atomism. A theory about the nature of the facts that constitute reality, devised by Russell (in *Philosophy of Logical Atomism*, 1918) and Wittgenstein (in *Tractatus Logico-Philosophicus*, 1922) and associated with the technique of philosophical ANALYSIS. That technique shows that some PROPOSITIONS can be analysed into others and so may be seen as theoretically dispensable abbreviations for them. The propositions in which analysis terminates reveal the actual structure of the facts which, if they obtain, make the propositions true. Wittgenstein, when a logical atomist, held that 'all propositions are TRUTH-FUNCTIONS of elementary propositions', in other words that *atomic* propositions, which are singular, affirmative and categorical and consist of logically proper names of simple entities together with an attributive or relational predicate, directly picture their verifying facts, while *non-atomic* propositions conceal them. Analysis, then, reveals the structure of the world by exhibiting every kind of true or significant proposition as being an atomic proposition, or some assemblage of atomic propositions, in which only unanalysable words for simple individuals and properties occur. Russell's logical atomism was less thoroughgoing than Wittgenstein's, since he doubted the reducibility (see REDUCTION) to strictly atomic form of negative and universal propositions and also of apparently intensional propositions (see EXTENSIONALITY) about beliefs. The LOGICAL POSITIVISTS accepted the idea of a terminal class of propositions, constituting the part of language that is in direct contact with the world (calling them *protocol* or *basic*, rather than atomic, propositions) but saw them as direct, non-inferential reports of experience, rather than as pictures of fact. See also OBJECTIVITY. For further reading: D. F. Pears, *Bertrand Russell and the British Tradition in Philosophy* (1967). A.Q.

logical construction, see under REDUCTION.

logical empiricism. The philosophical school which, mainly in the USA, immediately succeeded LOGICAL POSITIVISM as a result of the migration to that country, after Hitler came to power, of several leading members of the VIENNA CIRCLE, in particular Rudolf Carnap (1891–1970). The change of name had a more than merely geographical point; it also signified some change of doctrine, most notably a remission of the anti-metaphysical (see METAPHYSICS) fervour of the original logical positivists and a less polemical concentration on the task of articulating or reconstructing in a logically explicit and rigorous form the CONCEPTS and theories of various forms of discourse, above all MATHEMATICS and NATURAL SCIENCE. See also OBJECTIVITY. For further reading: J. Joergensen, *The Development of Logical Empiricism* (1951). A.Q.

logical form, see under PROPOSITION, TYPES OF.

logical positivism. A body of philosophical doctrine developed from the later 1920s by the VIENNA CIRCLE under the leadership of Moritz Schlick (1882–1936) and Rudolf Carnap (1891–1970). It asserted the meaninglessness of METAPHYSICS, which it held to consist of all PROPOSITIONS that are neither verifiable (see VERIFICATION) by empirical observation nor demonstrable as ANALYTIC, and conceived PHILOSOPHY as consisting purely of ANALYSIS, conducted with the assistance of formal LOGIC with a view to the logical reconstruction of mathematical and scientific discourse. Most logical positivists regarded religious and moral utterances as metaphysical and thus as meaningless. There was disagreement within the school (1) as to whether the basic propositions in which philosophical analysis terminates (see LOGICAL ATOMISM) refer to immediate experience (the majority view) or to material objects (see PHYSICALISM); (2) as to whether probability should be interpreted in terms of CONFIRMATION or frequency or both; and (3) as to whether TRUTH is a relation of correspondence between propositions and extra-linguistic reality or one of coherence between propositions. Logical positivism dissolved as a school at the end of the 1930s, but was continued in the USA in the slightly different form of LOGICAL EMPIRICISM. For further reading: V. Kraft, *The Vienna Circle* (1953). A.Q.

logical realism, see under REALISM.

logical syntax (or **syntactics).** The discussion of the logical properties and significance of linguistic expressions in terms that refer only to the expressions themselves and not to their relations to extra-linguistic reality. Exaggerated claims on its behalf by Rudolf Carnap (1891–1970) were abandoned after the successful development of logical SEMANTICS, primarily by Alfred Tarski (1902–83), in the mid-1930s. For further reading: R. Carnap, *The Logical Syntax of Language* (1937). A.Q.

logical types, theory of. A theory devised by Bertrand Russell (1872–1970) to avoid the logical PARADOXES or ANTINOMIES which arise from *self-reference.* (For example, the statement 'This statement is false', if taken to refer to itself, is false if true and true if false. Likewise the class of classes that are not members of themselves is a member of itself if it is not and is not if it is.) The theory of types lays down that a class must always be of a higher type than its members and thus that to say of a class that it either is or is not one of its own members is meaningless. The conclusion that grammatically well-formed sentences may be neither true nor false but meaningless, that there are logical as well as grammatical restrictions on the possibilities of significant combination of words, has been widely influential. It lent force to the attack of the LOGICAL POSITIVISTS, with the VERIFICATION principle, on METAPHYSICS, and it has inspired broader, informal investigations into the possibilities of significant combination of words, investigations that have issued in modern theories of CATEGORIES. A.Q.

logicism. The school of MATHEMATICS which maintains that the fundamental CONCEPTS of mathematics can be defined in terms of the concepts, and its fundamental laws can be deduced from the laws, of LOGIC. It was the principal aim of both Frege and of Whitehead and Russell in *Principia Mathematica* to establish this point. The crucial phase of the project is the definition of NUMBER in terms of the logical notion of class. A natural number, for logicism, is the class of all classes which are 'similar' in the sense of being equinumerous. The number 2 is the class of all pairs and the statement 'There are two chairs in this room' means the same as 'The class of chairs-in-this-room is a member of the class of pairs'. GÖDEL'S THEOREM that in any system containing arithmetic there must be truths that cannot be proved within the system undermined the project of deriving all of pure mathematics from logic. A.Q.

logistics. All the activities and methods connected with supplying armed forces, including storage, transport, and distribution of ammunition, petrol, food, and so on. The term is of American origin and came into general use during and after World War II by reason of the dominant position of the USA in both the wartime and post-war alliances. The word is now acquiring a more general use to connote the supply organization of non-military field operations such as mountaineering expeditions or famine relief organizations. A.F.B.

logocentrism. Term used by French deconstructionist philosopher Jacques Derrida (1930– ; see DECONSTRUCTION) to signify a certain predominant way of thinking about issues of truth, reason, consciousness and language that has characterized the Western 'metaphysical' tradition from Plato to the present.

Derrida argues that *speech* (not writing) has always claimed to be the PARADIGM case of what language ought to be – or what all communication should properly aspire to – when concerned with issues of meaning and TRUTH. For in the act of speech, so this tradition maintains, there is a privileged access to expressive intentions or ideas-in-the-mind which helps to ensure that we attain genuine self-knowledge, that we communicate this knowledge effectively, and that others are able to interpret our words with the least risk of misunderstanding or the least opportunity for wilful distortion. In the case of writing, conversely, we have to do with what Plato denounced in his dialogue the *Phaedrus* as a bad mnemotechnic device; what Aristotle classically defined as merely 'the sign of a sign', that is, graphic symbols for spoken sounds, themselves symbols of pre-existing concepts or ideas; and what Rousseau thought of as a 'bad supplement', one that inherently corrupted and denatured the character of authentic self-present speech. Derrida's point, in brief, is that all these texts 'self-deconstruct', or undermine their own major premise, by appealing to certain predicates of written language (such as permanence, transmissibility, the capacity to signify or communicate meaning from one context to another in the absence of the speaker or lacking any appeal to the self-present utterer's intent) which necessarily apply to language in general, i.e. both written *and* spoken language.

To 'deconstruct' that logocentric prejudice is *not* to declare that we should henceforth abandon all notions of interpretative truth or fidelity to the speaker or author's intentions. Rather it is to say that those intentions are always 'inscribed' in a larger, more complicated logic of conflicting senses and priorities which neither they nor we can fully comprehend or reduce to an order of plain, self-evident, straightforwardly 'authorized' truth. (See also APORIA; DIFFÉRANCE; SUPPLEMENT, LOGIC OF.) For further reading: C. Norris, *Derrida* (1987). C.N.

logograms, see under CONCRETE POETRY.

logotherapy. Psychotherapeutic approach developed by Austrian psychoanalyst Viktor E. Frankl after he had survived the Auschwitz and Dachau CONCENTRATION CAMPS in World War II (see PSYCHOTHERAPY; PSYCHOANALYSIS; HOLOCAUST, THE). Influenced by EXISTENTIALISM, Frankl identified the 'quest for meaning' as more fundamental than those for pleasure, POWER or self-actualization, and termed his approach 'logotherapy', seeing this, however, as a necessary supplementary perspective on, rather than a replacement for, orthodox psychotherapy. Although initiating some distinctive techniques, such as 'paradoxical intention' (when the patient is required to wish, if but momentarily, for the very thing most feared), logotherapy was methodologically orthodox. Frankl's enduring legacy lies in his wise and insightful writings rather than with a specific school of followers. For further reading: V. E. Frankl, *Psychotherapy and Existentialism. Selected Papers on Logotherapy* (1973). G.D.R.

Lolita syndrome. A syndrome named after the eponymous heroine of Vladimir Nabokov's *Lolita* (1955), the theme of which is the unreasoning and self-destructive passion of a middle-aged man for a teenage 'nymphet'. The condition is anticipated, in a psychologically more convincing manner, in the Chilean Vicente Huidobro's untranslated *Satyr, o el poder de las palabras* (1939). M.S.-S.

Lomé conventions. A series of trade agreements between the EUROPEAN UNION (EU) and 66 developing countries from Africa, the Caribbean and the Pacific (ACP). These agreements were implemented in 1975, 1980, 1985 and 1989 (revised in 1995, expiring in 2000). While members no longer view Lomé as an important step towards a NEW INTERNATIONAL ECONOMIC ORDER, they see it as a framework for north–south co-operation that embodies principles of equal partnership. The conventions allow freer access to the EU for many ACP products, provide mechanisms for stabilizing foreign exchange earnings from certain commodities and minerals, and a channel for EU aid. J.P.; E.W.N.

London Group. An association of British artists, founded in November 1913, incorporating the CAMDEN TOWN GROUP and certain smaller groups. Its first president was Harold Gilman; Sickert was a prime influence; the original members included Wyndham Lewis and other leading VORTICISTS. They tended to admire the POST-IMPRESSIONISTS, notably Gauguin, van Gogh and Cézanne, but in later years their sympathies became more diverse and in many cases more conservative. The group is still extant. P.C.

Long March. The epic year-long 6,000-mile journey made by Chinese COMMUNIST forces after the Kuomintang's fifth encirclement campaign dislodged them from their power base in Kiangxi province. During the course of the journey, Mao Zedong established himself as leader of the Party by becoming chairman of the ruling Revolutionary Military Council at the Zunyi Conference, January 1935 (see MAOISM). Under constant attack from NATIONALIST forces, the depleted communist forces arrived in northern Shaanxi province in October 1935. However, the success of the Long March in merely surviving ensured the communists of a base from which to expand later. Swelled by the arrival of groups from other areas, a new Soviet base area was set up in Yan'an, which became the centre for anti-KMT GUERRILLA activities, and the model for post-1949 emulation. For further reading: H. Salisbury, *The Long March* (1985). S.B.

long-range planning, see CORPORATE STRATEGY.

longitudinal. In PSYCHOMETRICS, an adjective applied to a method or type of investigation in which selected variables are studied over time in the same sample of subjects, in contrast to *cross-sectional* methods, where similar variables are studied at different ages, but on different subjects at each age. H.L.

Look, The. In film theory, this concept draws on both FREUDIAN and LACANIAN psychoanalysis to explain aspects of the relationship between film text and spectator (see CINEMATIC APPARATUS). Film theorists argue that looking in cinema involves not only voyeurism (in that the screen image, the object of the spectator's gaze, is distanced from him in such a way that a return of the look is impossible) but also NARCISSISM (in that the spectator recognizes and identifies with the human figure on the screen). The concept of The Look has been taken up by feminist film theory (see FEMINISM) in the argument that the female figure on the cinema screen is constructed pre-eminently as an object of looking, in a spectator–text relation which constructs a 'masculine' subject position from the spectator, regardless of his or her GENDER. For further reading: A. Kuhn, *Women's Pictures: Feminism and Cinema* (1982). A.KU.

loyalism (Northern Ireland). This is a vaguer and more unstable concept that either REPUBLICANISM or UNIONISM. Its meaning was originally almost synonymous with unionism, and fully synonymous with the more militant form of unionism. After the IRISH REPUBLICAN ARMY offensive began in the late 1960s, the paramilitary counter-offensive from the unionist side came to be designated as 'loyalist'. A number of paramilitary groups came to be covered by this designation. Several of these have been no less ferocious in their methods than the IRA, and sometimes more so. In 1998, the two leading loyalist paramilitary groups were represented at the 'peace talks' by their political and propaganda wings, a relationship closely comparable to the relationship between the IRA and it's political wing, Sinn Fein. Unlike Sinn Fein-IRA, which has drawn significant financial and other support from Irish people in some American cities, loyalists have little outside support except from some in the Scottish cities. Inside

Northern Ireland, the loyalist paramilitaries appear to have less support from within the Protestant population (see PROTESTANTISM) – their sole recruiting ground – than Sinn Fein-IRA has from within the Catholic population (see CATHOLICISM), *their* recruiting ground. The loyalist paramilitaries have imitated the tactics of their republican counterparts but have been less sophisticated in their tactics. They are, however, still formidable. C.C.O'B.

LSD, see under DRUGS; HIPPIES.

Lubyanka. The headquarters of the secret police of the former USSR (see KGB), on Dzerzhinsky Square, Moscow, containing the famous prison in which many of the leading 'State criminals' of the Soviet period have been held, and in whose basement they have been executed. It has become synonymous with the whole apparatus of interrogation, confession and liquidation. R.C.

luminodynamism, see under KINETIC ART.

Lumpenproletariat. Term coined by Karl Marx for the fluctuating antisocial elements within the poor of big cities from whom no CLASS identification or solidarity could be expected. D.C.W.

Lutheranism. The Christian tradition begun when Martin Luther (1483–1546) inaugurated PROTESTANTISM. The Lutheran World Federation, mainly German, Scandinavian and American, was formed in 1947. In these self-governing national or regional Churches some Catholic practices (see CATHOLICISM), e.g. leadership by bishops, may be retained, but the dominating feature is the sermon, intended to proclaim God's grace. Luther's experience (much studied by modern scholars) convinced him that no one could become righteous before God through his own efforts; it was necessary to be 'justified' (accounted and then made righteous) by God's grace received through faith. This conviction has been at the heart of German Protestant THEOLOGY, which has thereby been liberated to embark on many intellectual adventures. Although European interest in God has diminished in the 20th century, the Lutheran form of CHRISTIANITY has flourished in the US and Africa. In the 1980s it has about 65 million adherents. For further reading: J. Pelikan, *From Luther to Kierkegaard* (1950). D.L.E.

Luxembourg Compromise. In 1965 the European Commission announced a 'package deal' linking farm price increases to two further measures designed to increase the powers of the European Commission and European Assembly vis-à-vis member states. The French government objected to the measures, removed its permanent representative from Brussels, and for the next seven months boycotted the Community – the so-called 'empty chair' policy. The conflict centred upon the supranational aspirations of the Commission and the proposed extension of majority voting in the Council of Ministers. The crisis was resolved in 1966 by the Luxembourg Compromise, which shifted the institutional balance of power away from the Commission in favour of the Council of Ministers (and by implication, national governments). While the Commission's right to initiate policy was confirmed, it was agreed that it should consult more closely with member states' governments in drafting proposals. With regard to majority voting in the Council of Ministers it was agreed that if a member state has very important interests at stake, the Council will endeavour to reach a unanimous decision. In practice, the Luxembourg Compromise enables a single member state to veto a Community policy. This has seriously hampered Community policy-making (see EUROPEAN UNION). For further reading: A. Daltrop, *Politics and the European Community* (1984). S.M.

Lysenkoism. The Soviet version of LAMARCKISM; named after Trofim Lysenko (1898–1976), whose views became dominant in Soviet BIOLOGY, and especially agricultural science, in the mid-1930s. Many adherents of Mendelian (see MENDELISM) GENETICS were dismissed and liquidated at this time, in particular Nikolai Vavilov, Russia's leading biologist. However, Lysenkoism only gained a complete monopoly in 1948, when the Central Committee officially decreed its correctness. Some criticisms of it were permitted during Stalin's last months, but it was reimposed under Khrushchev and it was only in 1964, and particularly after Khrushchev's fall, that it became totally discredited – though a number of Lysenkoist 'scientists' continue to hold research posts. For further reading: Z. A. Medvedev, *The Rise and Fall of T. D. Lysenko* (1969). R.C.

M

Maastricht. Treaty which amended the 1957 Treaty of Rome and created the EUROPEAN UNION (EU). Signed in 1991 and subsequently ratified, sometimes amid some controversy, in member states, the Treaty also provides a blueprint for a monetary union in Europe. The Maastricht Treaty constitutes a wide-ranging reform of the previous European Community (EC) and a significant step forward for European integration on a number of fronts. Its principal feature is the Treaty on European Union, but there are also 17 assorted protocols (additional agreements not signed by all members) as well as 33 Declarations (guidelines on the interpretation and implementation of the Treaty, which, however, are not legally binding). The Treaty of European Union comprises five aspects:

(1) The European Union, based primarily on the EC and its institutions, but also on a common inter-governmental foreign and security policy, a common home affairs and justice policy (conducted on an inter-governmental basis), and a number of common policies in areas such as education, training, youth, public health, the labour market, industrial policy, communications, research and development, regional policy, environmental policy and development policy.

(2) SUBSIDIARITY.

(3) A Committee of the Regions.

(4) Economic and Monetary Union (EMU).

(5) European Citizenship, which gives European citizens the right to stand for election and vote in local and European elections in all EU states, to be represented by the consuls of all EU states, and to complain to the European Ombudsman about deficiencies in EU institutions.

This is supplemented by some limited institutional reform granting a little more power to the European Parliament, some provisions for tackling fraud and ensuring financial rectitude (the Court of Auditors has become a full EC institution), and an enhancement in the powers of the European Court of Justice to improve the implementation of EU legislation. Finally there is the Social Chapter, a separate protocol outlining basic employment rights to which the UK has not adhered. The UK and Denmark also have the right to 'opt out' of the provisions for EMU. For further reading: C. H. Church and D. Phinnemore, *European Union and European Community* (1994). V.L.

Mach number. The speed of a body flying through the atmosphere, divided by the local speed of sound. The Mach number (named after Ernst Mach, 1838–1916) is less than 1 for *subsonic* speeds, greater than 1 for *supersonic* speeds, and greater than 5 for *hypersonic* speeds. Conventional aircraft like the Boeing 747 fly subsonically, but the Anglo-French Concorde flies at Mach 2.1. Considerable ENERGY is required to 'break the sound barrier' at Mach 1, because of the shock wave which must be created. M.V.B.

Mach's principle. The laws of NEWTONIAN MECHANICS are valid only if events are referred to certain special FRAMES OF REFERENCE. Observations show that these 'inertial frames' are those relative to which the distant matter of the universe is, on the average, not accelerating. In 1872 Ernst Mach (1838–1916) suggested that the distant matter actually determines the inertial frames, by forces related to GRAVITATION; this principle was later given precise expression by Einstein in his general theory of RELATIVITY. M.V.B.

machine aesthetic. A theory about the appearance of objects derived from a belief in how machine-made objects should look. The expression probably originated in a statement by Theo van Doesburg (1883–1931), the Dutch artist who was founder of the de STIJL movement: 'The new possibilities of the machine have created an aesthetic expressive of our time, that I once [in 1921] called "The Mechanical Aesthetic".' Objects were to look like machines (somewhat as in the paintings of Léger) and to look as if they were made by machines – which was taken to mean being made up from undecorated geometric solids such as the sphere, cube, cylinder, etc., even though this did not necessarily correspond with efficient machine production. See also BAUHAUS; FUNCTIONALISM. For further reading:

R. Banham, *Machine Aesthetic* (1955).
M.B.R.

machine intelligence, see ARTIFICIAL INTELLIGENCE.

machismo. Literally, maleness. The cult of virility in Latin America, especially Mexico, identified with a bull-like masculine aggressiveness, invulnerable and indifferent to the attacks of others, above all intransigent, withdrawn, inner-directed (see OTHER-DIRECTION), authoritarian (see AUTHORITARIANISM), absolutist; more loosely, a pejorative term applied by its adversaries to the advocacy of an active, military, interventionist US foreign policy (e.g. in VIETNAM).
D.C.W.

MACHO (massive compact halo object). Astronomers use this term to refer to a particular class of candidates for the DARK MATTER (sometimes referred to as 'missing mass') in the universe. They are objects like dead stars or dense planetary-sized bodies which have small size and high density. These objects are required to be distributed within and outside the distribution of light in our galaxies and others. This extended distribution of dark mass is called the 'halo' of a GALAXY. The acronym was created as a foil for the alternative candidate to explain this dark mass, WIMPs, or weakly interacting massive particles (see WEAK INTERACTION). Unlike MACHOs, WIMPs are ELEMENTARY PARTICLES like heavy NEUTRINOS which have survived from the early stages of the universe's history. In recent years some MACHO candidates in the Large Magellanic Cloud have been detected by the phenomenon of GRAVITATIONAL LENSING. An unseen MACHO moves past background stars and its gravity bends the rays of starlight to produce a temporary enhancement in brightness of the background stars that is the same in each colour band (unlike a variable star's natural changes in brightness). This programme to monitor the brightnesses of millions of stars is called the MACHO Project. For further reading: L. Krauss, *The Fifth Essence* (1994).
J.D.B.

Machtpolitik, see POWER POLITICS.

macrobiotics. Term coined by Georges Ohsawa (1893–1966) to denote a dietary system in which all foods are either *yin* or *yang* or both ('yin', the shadow, is the passive, feminine principle of life; 'yang', the sun, is the active, masculine principle). The diet, which is generally abstemious and loosely vegetarian, prescribes an equal balance of 'yin' and 'yang' components, thus ensuring that the body of the consumer is in harmony with the mystical unity of the cosmos. Most foods contain both 'yin' and 'yang', so complicated cutting is necessary to preserve the balance: an onion is 'yin' at the top and 'yang' at the bottom; it therefore has to be cut vertically rather than horizontally. Fish are supposed to be eaten whole (so as to include their 'yang' heads and tails), and the term wholefood, which is common to many spiritually inclined vegetarian DIETS, is a macrobiotic keyword, indicating the correct, equipoised balance between 'yin' and 'yang'. More loosely, macrobiotics relates to dietary theories of the superior wholesomeness of vegetable food, and conforms to long-standing Western traditions of vegetarianism.
J.R.

macroeconomics, see under ECONOMICS.

macrolinguistics, see under MICROLINGUISTICS.

macroregion, see under REGIONALISM.

MAD, see MUTUALLY ASSURED DESTRUCTION.

Madrid peace conference. The October 1991 Madrid conference, co-sponsored by the US and the former USSR, emerged from the ashes of the second war in the Persian Gulf. The conference initiated nine rounds of direct bilateral and multilateral negotiations between Israeli and Arab representatives between 1991 and 1993, culminating in two peace agreements between two Arab parties (the Palestinians and Jordan) and Israel (see JUDAISM; ZIONISM) in 1993 and 1994 respectively. Despite many Middle East peace initiatives since the 1970s, the Madrid talks were dubbed as 'historic' in that they marked the first occasion at which Israeli and Arab officials and representatives willingly engaged in direct and face-to-face talks about the conflict and their respective fears and aspirations. It was seen as the last, and best, chance to end one of the 20th century's most intractable conflicts. For further reading: C. D. Smith, *Palestinians and the Arab–Israeli Conflict* (1996). A.EH.

Maekawa report. Faced by mounting international criticism of Japan's balance of payments surpluses, the Nakasone government (see NAKASONE'S REFORMS) set up the Advisory Group on Economic Structural Adjustment for International Harmony in October 1985, under the chairmanship of Haruo Maekawa, a former governor of the Bank of Japan. The Group, reporting in April 1986, recommended radical changes in economic management with a view to eliminating the current-account surplus in the medium to long term. The Maekawa Group argued for shifting the thrust of ECONOMIC GROWTH away from exports into domestic demand by increasing wages, shortening the working week, reducing taxes, and improving the social INFRASTRUCTURE. It also recommended encouragement for foreign INVESTMENT, both by Japan overseas and by foreigners into Japan, radical agricultural adjustment, further promotion of manufactured goods imports into Japan, promotion of EXCHANGE RATE stability at realistic rates, liberalization of financial and capital markets, and a variety of policy changes involving improved policies towards less-developed countries (see UNDERDEVELOPMENT). J.A.A.S.

Mafia. The Sicilian word for a clandestine criminal organization so deeply rooted in Sicilian rural society as to amount to a counter-government administering its own law and justice. Established among the Italian immigrant community in the USA, the Mafia became the basis of various organized crime syndicates operating according to the same alternative code as in Sicily, the code of *omerta*, the Italian word for 'connivance'. J. Farrell, *Understanding the Mafia* (1997). D.C.W.

magic. Form of activity in which different elements and forces, physical, supernatural and verbal, are manipulated in order to bring about certain results. The symbolic (see SYMBOL) or RITUAL component of magic sets it apart from merely technical activity. James Frazer (*The Golden Bough*, 1911) described magic as founded upon a mistaken theory of causation. He and later writers (for example Lévy-Bruhl) understood it as an expression of a form of primitive science. Malinowski interpreted the importance of magic for the Trobriand Islanders as fulfilling an emotional need, the need for certainty and order in natural and social events. Later anthropologists (see ANTHROPOLOGY) pursued different levels of inquiry, less functional in analysis: what actually happens in magic (its internal structure), what beliefs underlie its practice (questions of rationality and irrationality), and its place in a particular society. The Victorian division between science and magic has been criticized, since it has been pointed out that very few people in modern societies fully understand technological phenomena. Instead most people believe in such things in a manner similar to that which has been described for so-called primitive cultures using magic. This has led some anthropologists to study the nature and basis of knowledge of the world in terms of universal cognitive structures. For further reading: C. Lévi-Strauss, *The Savage Mind* (1976). M.H.

magic number. The numbers of NEUTRONS OR PROTONS in an atomic (see ATOM) NUCLEUS that is highly stable against radioactive decay (see RADIOACTIVITY). The magic numbers are 2, 8, 20, 28, 50, 82 and 126, and the stability arises from the filling of complete shells (see ELECTRON SHELL) of nuclear ENERGY LEVELS, in a similar manner to the chemical stability of the inert gases. See also PERIODIC TABLE. M.V.B.

magic realism. Term coined by Franz Roh in 1924 to describe certain works of the NEUE SACHLICHKEIT artists, particularly their Munich wing. The still, smoothly painted pictures of figures and objects, with their mildly disquieting SURREALISM-and-water impact, are akin to the neoclassical art of certain Italians (e.g. Felice Casorati) in the metaphysical wake (see METAPHYSICAL PAINTING), as well as to that of the Royal Academy. Among its practitioners were the former member of the NEUE KÜNSTLERVEREINIGUNG, Alexander Kanoldt, and the subsequent president of the Nazi (see NAZISM) Kunstkammer, Adolf Ziegler. Though the names sound similar, the gay and decorative

Peinture de la Réalité poétique associated with Maurice Brianchon and others is a very different affair. More recently, the term has been applied to a group of Latin American authors, the best known of whom is Gabriel García Márquez. J.W.

magnetic monopole. A PARTICLE predicted to exist in nature by Paul Dirac in 1931. It carries an isolated north (positive) or south (negative) magnetic charge. The existence of such a particle in nature would explain why electric charge comes in discrete fractions of the fundamental ELECTRON charge. It has yet to be detected experimentally, although there were claims in 1972 and 1982 that a magnetic monopole had been observed. These observations have not been repeated with the same results and are controversial. GRAND UNIFICATION predicts that the process of grand unification at very high ENERGY must be accompanied by the production of stable magnetic monopoles with a MASS roughly equivalent to the energy at which grand unification occurs. (These are sometimes called Polyakov-t 'Hooft monopoles.) This corresponds to a mass of about 10^8 gms and is 10^{16} times the mass of an atomic NUCLEUS. Until 1981 this property was regarded as a major argument against such theories of their existence because too many monopoles would be formed in the first moments of the universe's expansion from the big bang (see BIG BANG THEORY). The idea of inflation (see INFLATIONARY UNIVERSE THEORY) suggested by A. Guth in 1981 resolves this problem. The presence of magnetic monopoles in space would have adverse effects upon any cosmic magnetic fields. Such fields would be drained away, using their energies to accelerate monopoles. The existence of magnetic fields in planets, stars and interstellar space is therefore evidence against the existence of a significant population of monopoles in the universe. For further reading: J. Trefil, *The Moment of Creation* (1983). J.D.B.

magnetic reconnexion. In PLASMA PHYSICS and COSMOLOGY, this phenomenon occurs when two plasmas interact with one another. An electric plasma always has a magnetic field associated with it. In principle such fields avoid one another and this prevents the two plasmas from interacting. It now appears that the magnetic fields of one plasma are able to link up with those of another, and this is called reconnexion. This is important because when it occurs it is possible for one plasma to affect the behaviour of another plasma. For example, the magnetic field due to the solar wind (from the sun's plasma) can influence the earth's magnetic field. The effect can also be observed in laboratory experiments such as in a TOKOMAK machine. H.M.R.

magnetic resonance. When a system is magnetized, the ENERGY LEVELS associated with the SPINS of its ATOMS and NUCLEI split into a finely spaced sequence. If an electromagnetic wave (see ELECTROMAGNETISM) of radio frequency is applied, its ENERGY will be strongly absorbed by the system whenever the frequency is such that the wave is in RESONANCE with two energy levels. The pattern of resonances as the frequency varies is a valuable tool giving detailed information about the structure of matter. M.V.B.

magnetism. The branch of ELECTROMAGNETISM concerned with magnetic materials and their interaction with electric currents. Magnetic FIELDS are produced by moving electric charges, e.g. the current in the windings of an electromagnet. Thus the magnetism of solid matter arises from the orbital motion and SPIN of atomic (see ATOM) ELECTRONS, while the earth's magnetism (*geomagnetism*) is thought to be due to currents in its rotating liquid core. The smallest magnetic entities are spinning ELEMENTARY PARTICLES; these are dipoles, and no isolated north or south poles have been found. See also ARCHAEOMAGNETISM. For further reading: E. W. Lee, *Magnetism* (1970). M.V.B.

magnetohydrodynamics (MHD). The ELECTRODYNAMICS of free ELECTRONS or IONS in a fluid (e.g. the IONOSPHERE). Motion of charges in the fluid can be produced by magnetic FIELDS, but it is not yet known whether a complete and stable *containment* can be achieved in this way. The problem of containment is of tremendous technological importance, because, if the ENERGY of nuclear FUSION is ever to be tamed for peaceful purposes, the reacting substances must be kept together at temperatures so high that walls of any conventional material would vaporize. See also PLASMA PHYSICS. M.V.B.

magneto-optics. In the 1840s, Michael Faraday discovered that, when placed in a magnetic field, the plane of polarized light rotates. In subsequent experiments, Faraday sought to disturb light magnetically, an endeavour later supported by Lord Kelvin's notion that the magnetic FIELD was a vortex within the ether. Experimentation and theorizing from H. A. Lorentz to J. J. Thomson began to reveal the particulate structure of light emissions, and the crucial role of ELECTRONS. Precise elucidation of magneto-optical phenomena, however, long defied physicists involved in the dilemmas of QUANTUM MECHANICS. The most important breakthrough was made in the 1920s by Wolfgang Pauli, who succeeded in explaining anomalies in the behaviour of electrons in terms of an 'EXCLUSION PRINCIPLE', which drew upon the concept of electron SPIN. Magneto-optics remains an area in which quantum explanations have proved superior to CLASSICAL PHYSICS. For further reading: M. Jammer, *The Conceptual Development of Quantum Mechanics* (1966). R.P.

magnetotaxis, see under TROPISM.

magnetotropism, see under TROPISM.

***magnitizdat*,** see under SAMIZDAT.

Mahayana, see under BUDDHISM.

mainstream. In jazz, a critical term coined in the late 1950s to designate a style neither self-consciously conservative, like TRAD, nor committedly advanced and advancing, like the forms that followed BEBOP. Mainstream players are generally associated with the SWING era, in the middle of jazz's evolution – in fact the French term for the school is 'middle jazz'. By any name, the music exudes a timeless, mature appeal, a relaxed and confident energy. For once, a label performed a valuable service, by returning to public attention a large group of musicians – men like Roy Eldridge, Ben Webster and Jo Jones – who were still at the height of their powers, but who did not fit into the easy dichotomy of ancients v. moderns. Indeed, today it is to such players that musicians are turning for insight into the real meaning of jazz tradition. GE.S.

***maisons de la culture*,** see under CENTRES DRAMATIQUES.

maladministration. Administrative fault, whether illegal or legal. The term has no significance for purposes of litigation in courts or other tribunals, but it is of prime importance in relation to extra-judicial remedies provided by ombudsmen, whose function is to investigate and report on complaints of injustice caused by the maladministration of administrative authorities in the process or procedure leading to an act or determination. It is only rarely defined in legislation governing the powers of ombudsmen throughout the world, and no UK legislation defines it for ombudsmen within the kingdom. This has been intentional because Parliament believes that ombudsmen should have a wide discretion to build up their own case-law. Some maladministration involves conscious wrongdoing or turpitude, e.g. bias, perversity, intentional delay, but in practice most cases found are faults of inadvertence, e.g. inattention, unwitting delay, ineptitude, failure to follow procedures already laid down, or failure to establish proper procedures where their need has been established. For further reading: K. C. Wheare, *Maladministration and Its Remedies* (1973). D.C.M.Y.

male chauvinism, see under SEXISM.

malnutrition. Wrong nutrition caused either by a deficiency of a nutrient or an excess of food. Deficiency diseases which have historically assumed epidemic proportions include scurvy (lack of vitamin C), beri-beri (lack of vitamin B1) and rickets (lack of vitamin D). Kwashiorkor and marasmus (lack of PROTEIN and energy) and iron-deficiency anaemia are common in developing countries. Obesity is included in the definition of malnutrition. See also FAMINE. For further reading: A. E. and D.A. Bender, *Nutrition for Medical Students* (1982). A.E.B.

Malthusianism/antinatalism. An intellectual and political perspective asserting the desirability of limiting the growth of human populations. This theory of population originated with the writings of Thomas Robert Malthus (1766–1834), who claimed that while population tends to increase at a geometric rate (e.g., 1, 2, 4, 8, 16, 32 . . .), the means of subsistence can increase at only an arithmetic rate (1, 2, 3, 4, 5, 6 . . .), resulting in an inadequate supply of the goods (mainly food) needed to support life. In his *Essay on the Principle of Population* (six editions, 1797–1826), Malthus denied the possibility of rapid population increase over the long term, asserting that population size would inevitably be limited through some combination of POSITIVE and PREVENTIVE *checks*. Positive checks refer to means of population limitation that operate through the death rate (famine, war, epidemic disease); preventive checks, on the other hand, operate through the birth rate (CONTRACEPTION, ABORTION, abstinence, late marriage, HOMOSEXUALITY). In order to avoid the positive checks, Malthus advocated a reliance on those preventive checks that he considered morally acceptable: abstinence and late marriage. Despite Malthus's aversion to contraception and abortion, Malthusian principles were upheld later in the 19th century by advocates of birth control in both Europe and America. Thus, the position that combines Malthus's original analysis of the impossibility of unlimited population increase with an advocacy of birth control is referred to as 'neo-Malthusianism'. Malthusianism has been widely criticized as being both scientifically invalid and ethically unsound. Contrary to Malthus's predictions, the food supply has increased faster than human population for the past two centuries and has continued to do so during recent decades. Karl Marx called Malthus 'a shameless sycophant of the ruling classes', because Marx believed that the ills of CAPITALISM should not be blamed on population growth, but rather on social inequalities (see MARXISM). In today's debate about human population growth, Malthusianism has taken on a much broader meaning, and the future availability of food is only one topic in this discussion. For example, even if it is possible to feed a growing population, many observers are concerned about the large-scale changes being imposed upon the global environment owing to the growth of human numbers and consumption. For further reading: G. Gilbert (ed.), *Malthus: Critical Responses* (1997). J.R.W.

Malvinas, see under FALKLANDS WAR.

management studies. Studies related to management. Management has, of course, been practised for as long as men have worked together to accomplish common tasks and have needed to make decisions about scarce resources in uncertain situations. Only in the 20th century, however, has it been made a subject for serious study.

The measurement of work on the factory floor marked the beginning of so-called SCIENTIFIC MANAGEMENT. Soon after, the foundations of the classical, or traditional, school of management thought were laid in the 1920s, seeing management in hierarchical terms with responsibility and authority delegated and subsequent accountability for performance expected. Classical thinking is reflected in the *organization chart* which pictures the hierarchical chain of command.

Such ideas lie behind much of today's management practice and provide the conceptual underpinning of most management control systems. However, by the mid-20th century it had become apparent that management studied only as a set of functional activities was incomplete. Managers achieved their results through people. There followed a proliferation of ideas about the importance, for successful management, of understanding people, both as individuals and in groups. Many of these viewpoints are referred to as *behavioural* approaches and classified as ORGANIZATION THEORY. Other sets of insights into the process of management have been developed, however, e.g. the SYSTEMS approach, which focuses on the use of information in decision-making. In recent times, managerial theories have sought ways in which to make workers feel more included in the decision processes, and to give them a stake in the success of the firm. In Japan, e.g., a culture evolved in some large companies whereby workers at all levels were encouraged to give suggestions for improving efficiency. For further reading: J. Sheldrake, *Management Theory* (1998). R.I.T.

managerial revolution. Phrase popularized by the ex-Trotskyite James Burnham in a book of that title (1941) predicting the rise of a new social CLASS, 'the managers', which would supplant the old capitalist class. Burnham saw Nazi Germany, the

Soviet Union and the NEW DEAL in the USA as variants of this new type, and declared that 'the war of 1939 is the first great war of managerial society' as 'the war of 1914 was the last great war of capitalist society'. His class of managers was never precisely defined, but included production managers, administrative engineers (but not finance executives of corporations), government bureau heads, and the like. The prediction of the collapse of CAPITALISM was wrong. The 'theory' was highly simplified, and in the scope elaborated by Burnham it has been largely abandoned.

In a more restricted sense, however, the managerial revolution may be understood, in the usage of A. A. Berle and Gardiner Means (*The Modern Corporation and Private Property*, 1933), as the shift *within* the modern corporation from the owner to the professional manager as the key figure in the enterprise. This is associated with a parallel change from 'ownership' to 'control' and with the decline of the importance of private property in contemporary capitalism. See also FIRM, THEORIES OF. For further reading: J. Scott, *Corporations, Classes and Capitalism* (1979). D.B.

manic-depressive psychosis. A PSYCHOSIS in which an individual's behaviour alternates between extremes of mood. The manic phase is characterized by hyperactivity and occasionally by violent outbursts; in the depressive phase feelings of inadequacy, sadness and lack of physical co-ordination are manifested. W.Z.

manifest function *and* **latent function.** Contrasted terms applied to the purpose served by a practice, custom or institution (see INSTITUTIONS) in a society. The two poles are not always quite the same, and in some cases only the context may determine whether the intended distinction is (1) between a manifest function of which the society's members are aware and a latent function of which they are not aware, or (2) between a proclaimed (manifest) and a real (latent) function. A.S.

manifold, see under GEOMETRY.

manpower planning, see under CORPORATE STRATEGY.

mantle convection. Large-scale motion of the material comprising the earth's mantle, the region between the planet's outer shell (LITHOSPHERE) and the core (see ASTHENOSPHERE). When the theory of CONTINENTAL DRIFT was proposed by Alfred Wegener early this century it attracted little support, largely because there seemed to be no mechanism by which moving continents could plough their way through the earth's solid surface. With the discovery of CREEP, however, it became clear that the solid mantle beneath the continents might be able to flow slowly under high pressure and over long periods of time, carrying the overlying continents along with it. When, during the 1960s, evidence from the MAGNETISM of rocks proved beyond doubt that the continents are indeed drifting (and that the oceanic lithosphere is spreading), mantle flow, or convection, became a necessity, although there is no direct proof that it actually exists. Some scientists no longer regard mantle convection as the engine driving the moving continents and ocean floors above; rather, they see sliding of the oceanic lithosphere under gravity as requiring compensating flows in the mantle below. Either way, the mantle must be able to move. P.J.S.

manufacture of madness. A term coined by the leading American 'anti-psychiatrist' (see ANTI-PSYCHIATRY) Thomas Szasz (1920–) to describe the process whereby modern societies have allegedly chosen to designate sizable minorities of their populations insane as ways of isolating, labelling and scapegoating deviant individuals. Historically speaking, Szasz argues, the category of the insane has come to fulfil a role equivalent to that of lepers and witches in earlier centuries. This labelling depends upon a bogus concept of 'mental illness', illegitimately constructed by analogy with the somatic reality, physical illness. The notion of 'mental illness' masquerades as sympathetic, but in reality it functions as a stigma rather like the traditional category of sin. The rise of the psychiatric profession, the emergence of the asylum, and the passing of legislation depriving the mad of legal rights and personal freedoms are the sociolegal means whereby this 'manufacture' is accomplished. Szasz's case is not an argument against PSYCHIATRY as such, but against its abuse (as he sees it) by STATE and society. For further reading: Thomas S. Szasz, *The Manufacture of Madness* (1973). R.P.

many worlds hypothesis. An interpretation of the theory of QUANTUM MECHANICS proposed by H. Everett III in 1957 under the title of 'The Relative State Formulation of Quantum Mechanics'. It is sometimes called the *Everett* or *Everett-Wheeler interpretation* of quantum mechanics. Unlike the COPENHAGEN INTERPRETATION it proposes that the WAVE FUNCTION never collapses and the quantum formalism describes the measurement process as well as the evolution of the wave function. This requires that the observer splits each time a measurement is made. The number of splittings is equal to the number of possible outcomes of the measurement. All the sequences of events that are logically possible do actually occur in reality. These many worlds are believed to be causally disjoint and so we will only experience one of them. D. Deutsch has recently suggested that the development of quantum COMPUTERS could allow the existence of the parallel worlds to be tested by experiment. The many worlds interpretation of QUANTUM THEORY must be adopted by cosmologists attempting to create a quantum theoretical description of the entire universe because there is assumed to be no observer who could collapse the wave function of the entire universe as required in the Copenhagen interpretation. Most subscribers to the many worlds interpretation tend therefore to be cosmologists. (See also BELL'S THEOREM; COSMOLOGY; ANTHROPIC PRINCIPLE.) For further reading: P. C. W. Davies, *Other Worlds* (1983). J.D.B.

Maoism. The political philosophy of Mao Zedong (1893–1976). The adaptation of MARXIST-LENINIST theory to suit the practical requirements of Chinese conditions, or as Mao himself put it in 1938, 'The Signification of Marxism'. Maoism conflicts with orthodox MARXIST thought on fundamental levels, such as on the way to solve contradictions in society, definitions of the consistency of the bourgeoisie (see BOURGEOIS) and the peasantry, and the ability to have a successful SOCIALIST revolution in a peasant-based agrarian society. In fact, while Maoism owes a lot to Lenin's *Theory of Imperialism* (1919), the importance of pure Marxist theory in the evolution of Mao's thought is not as important as the GUERRILLA heritage and the lessons learnt during the long struggle for POWER (see LONG MARCH). Because concrete conditions in China have changed over time, Maoism has also changed, to the extent that it has negated itself in many fields, such as the need or otherwise for decentralization. Despite this essentially pragmatic side of Maoism, certain ideas, such as the belief in the ability of political mobilization and storming tactics to solve economic problems, remained important for Mao, but on the whole, while the goal remained the same, the means by which that goal could be achieved depended heavily on Chinese PRAGMATISM. For further reading: D. Wilson (ed.), *Mao Tse-tung in the Scales of History* (1977). S.B.

mapping (in MATHEMATICS), see under FUNCTION.

marginal analysis. A marginal effect is the change in one VARIABLE caused by a small change in another. This concept is often encapsulated in the ratio of the two variables, e.g. marginal cost is the ratio of the additional cost of producing a small increase in the output of a product to the actual increase in output. The rigorous application of the concept of this ratio involves differential calculus. Marginal analysis is used extensively in ECONOMICS, engineering and business. It provides a means of obtaining a maximum or minimum value of a variable (e.g. profit or costs) that depends on some factor that can be controlled. For example, a FIRM may wish to maximize profits, and this is achieved by increasing output if the marginal revenue accruing from an increase in output exceeds its marginal cost. This process continues until the two marginal values are equal, i.e. when profit is at a maximum. J.P.

marginal cost pricing. The setting of price equal to the marginal cost of production. Marginal cost is the additional cost of producing an extra unit of output (see MARGINAL ANALYSIS). If a consumer is rational (see RATIONALITY), a pattern of consumption is chosen such that the additional utility (see UTILITY THEORY) – called the marginal utility – from an additional unit of consumption of a good is just equal to the loss in utility from the decrease in the consumption of other goods necessary to finance the additional consumption. If it is more/less, the rational consumer should increase/decrease consumption of this good and decrease/increase consumption of the other goods. Thus, for rational consumers prices affect the marginal utility of the consumption of different goods. If prices are equal to marginal costs, consumers will implicitly make decisions about their pattern of consumption on the basis of their individual preferences and the marginal costs of supplying extra output. If all prices are equal to the marginal costs, this is often taken as implying ECONOMIC EFFICIENCY. For further reading: R. Rees, *Public Enterprise Economics* (1984). J.P.

marginal costing. In management, a comparison of costs based on the *marginal cost*, i.e. on the expenditure actually incurred by producing the next unit of a product or service; or, conversely, actually saved by not producing it. By contrast, *full recovery cost*, or *absorption cost*, includes both the direct expenditure incurred on the product (such as materials used and labour employed), which will vary directly with the volume produced, and an appropriate share of the overhead or fixed costs (such as staff salaries), which are constant for a period, irrespective of the level of activity or output. R.I.T.

marginal efficiency of capital. The INTERNAL RATE OF RETURN on the least-productive piece of CAPITAL. Nct INVESTMENT will occur up until the point where the interest rate is equal to the marginal efficiency of capital. In this way, with the interest rate and the price of capital goods, it determines the return on capital, the rate of investment, and quantity of capital employed. J.P.

marginal productivity theory of wages. Theory which states that labour is paid a sum equal to the value of the output produced by employing an extra worker, keeping the use of all other FACTORS OF PRODUCTION constant (see MARGINAL ANALYSIS). The theory is often used with the assumption of PERFECT COMPETITION. Profit maximization implies that a firm employs labour up until the point where the additional revenue from employing an extra worker falls equal to the cost of an additional worker. As a perfectly competitive firm can employ as much labour as it wishes at the market wage, this latter cost is the wage. The additional revenue generated by an extra worker is given by the additional output produced by the worker, i.e. the marginal product, multiplied by the price of output, as the perfectly competitive firm can sell as much output as it wishes at the market price. This is equal to the value of the marginal product and, according to the law of diminishing returns (see DIMINISHING PRODUCTIVITY OF A FACTOR), it must fall as more labour is employed. For further reading: J. Craven, *Introduction to Economics* (1984). J.P.

marginal rate of substitution, see under SUBSTITUTION.

marginal utility. The UTILITY or value yielded by the marginal, i.e. last, unit of consumption. The concept is important in DEMAND theory, since an individual consumption of a good will be determined by its marginal utility relative to other goods and its price relative to other goods. D.E.

marijuana. A flowering plant, *Cannabis sativa*, whose leaves and flower buds contain a psychoactive agent, tetrahydrocannabinol (THC). The leaves and/or flower buds are usually smoked in pipes, or rolled in paper to make 'joints'. Inhalation of the smoke produces a mild euphoria.

THC is absent from the cannabis varieties cultivated for hemp fibres, which are used to make fabrics, cordage, and other fibre products. The cultivation of cannabis for fibre, and for medicinal and pleasurable applications, dates back thousands of years in China and throughout the Near and Far East. While the cultivation and use of cannabis is generally tolerated in DEVELOPING COUNTRIES, in industrialized countries these practices are usually illegal.

In the US prohibition of marijuana in 1937 was preceded by its demonization, which began during the period of alcohol PROHIBITION. In spite of the beneficial effects attributed to marijuana (reduction intraocular pressure in glaucoma; restoration of appetite and relief from nausea in AIDS patients and others receiving CHEMOTHERAPY), and in spite of the absence of evidence of negative health effects, marijuana continues to be branded as a dangerous material, the consumption of which will contribute to antisocial behaviour. Although marijuana is not addictive, based on questionable evidence it is also indicted as a 'gateway' drug whose use will lead to ADDICTION to 'hard' drugs such as heroin.

The severity of the laws and the rigour with which they are enforced vary widely from country to country and, in the US, from state to state. In spite of legal deterrents and negative propaganda, since the 1960s counter-cultural revolution marijuana has been popular among youth. It is cultivated indoors under artificial light, as well as outside. Efforts to legalize or decriminalize marijuana continue, but so does the hapless WAR ON DRUGS, with marijuana a continuing target. W.G.R.

marine geography. The systematic field of GEOGRAPHY that treats the 71 per cent of the earth's surface covered by water. Much of it is concerned with PHYSICAL GEOGRAPHY, including such topics as the configuration of surface currents and the terrain of the sea floor in each of the world's ocean basins. The HUMAN GEOGRAPHY of marine environments is a growing subfield today, ranging from studies of coastal development to water POLLUTION impacts to the exploitation of undersea mineral and biotic resources. The POLITICAL GEOGRAPHY of the oceans is a particularly active part of marine geography, and focuses on such pressing international issues as conflicting territorial claims, offshore boundary-making, resolving fisheries disputes, and implementing the policies of conferences on the Law of the Sea which include the establishment of Exclusive Economic Zones by the world's coastal countries. P.O.M.

markedness. An analytical principle in LINGUISTICS whereby pairs of linguistic features, seen as oppositions, are given different values of positive ('marked') and neutral or negative ('unmarked'). For example, in English there is a formal feature (adding an ending, usually *s*) which marks the plural of nouns: the plural is therefore the marked form, and the singular is the unmarked form. In recent GENERATIVE GRAMMAR, a theory of markedness has been proposed: here, an unmarked property is one which accords with the general tendencies found in all languages, whereas a marked property is one which goes against these tendencies. For further reading: V. J. Cook and M. Newson (eds), *Chomsky's Universal Grammar* (1996). D.C.

marker, see under CONSTITUENT ANALYSIS.

market economy. A term synonymous with a free economy and free enterprise. Under certain conditions (see PERFECT COMPETITION), a market economy is economically efficient (see ECONOMIC EFFICIENCY). J.P.

market failure (*or* **imperfection).** A market in which one or more of the assumptions of PERFECT COMPETITION is not valid. There is usually a presumption that a market failure is undesirable, e.g. in the case of external diseconomies (see EXTERNALITIES) and BARRIERS TO ENTRY. However, some market failure may be desirable, e.g. PATENTS and MONOPOLIES can lead to greater technical progress. J.P.

market research. Developing or tailoring a product or service, its packaging, presentation and MARKETING, requires a considerable insight into human habits and motivations in general, and those that directly affect a propensity to buy in particular. Market research is undertaken, at all levels, the better to understand realized and unrealized customer wants and needs, in order to adjust all elements of the 'marketing mix' to achieve optimum effect. Clearly, the research process, in entering the realms of unrealized needs, is necessarily deeply invasive at one level. In the past, market research, particularly qualitative research, was not a highly developed process in Japan, because it was considered impolite to wonder what went on in someone else's mind. There will still be those who view with deep concern, and perhaps with justification, the use to which all forms of research may be put. T.S.

market socialism. A compromise between SOCIALISM and CAPITALISM whereby the means of production are owned publicly, but goods are made and sold in FREE MARKETS. Thus the forces of supply and demand, rather than the government, determine output. In the 1960s, President Tito (1892–1980) introduced a form of market socialism into Yugoslavia (see TITOISM), and Hungary followed suit soon after. A.A.L.

marketing. Now widely held to be the most important of industrial and commercial disciplines. In theory, before development, manufacturing or the organization to provide a service is undertaken, the establishment of the nature and scale of consumer demand, and the price consumers are prepared to pay, is regarded as a prerequisite. In practice, development is often undertaken in isolation, or manufacturing is embarked upon without regard to the marketplace. Or overseas suppliers and manufacturers seek the cost efficiencies of scale. Under such circumstances, marketing practitioners are called upon to develop levels of demand at profitable prices from the marketplace. It is widely believed that it is this retroactive practice of marketing that leads to pricing being the key distributive and competitive determinant. The result is, invariably, lack of profitability. Through the process of marketing come the functions of (1) marketing organization – the recruitment, training and structuring of the individuals or team also will, in concert, orchestrate a marketing programme; and (2) MARKET RESEARCH – the process of probing and evaluating and predicting the market's response to all stages of product work, from concept to death, and of the impact of the environment and the marketplace, especially competitive activity. Thus, marketing people, replete with information and an understanding of the market's predictable or observable response to quality, content, pricing, packaging, presentation, distribution and service, manage the process of optimizing investment and return. So complex is the marketing process, and so essential to it a grasp of human nature and behaviour, that it can only be regarded as an art, rather than a science. T.S.

Markov process, see under STOCHASTIC PROCESS.

marriage. A union established between the sexes which may be singular (MONOGAMY) or plural (POLYGYNY and POLYANDRY). It is governed by rules of ENDOGAMY and EXOGAMY – who one may or may not marry. Marriage has been described as 'a bundle of rights', and as an institution it serves different functions: it establishes legal rights between spouses and the legitimacy of their children; it establishes a domestic group; and it links different social groups through relations of affinity. The ceremony of marriage is a RITE DE PASSAGE, marking the change in social STATUS. The GIFTS and property exchanged at marriage symbolize the transfer of rights from one set of kin to another. Marriage presentations are usually in the form of BRIDEWEALTH or DOWRY. Marriage is not a universal institution. In *The Origins of English Individualism* (1978) Macfarlane's researches in HISTORICAL ANTHROPOLOGY established that in western Europe a certain proportion of men and women have always remained unmarried (spinsters, bachelors, maiden aunts, etc.). The unmarried or celibate individual was socially recognized and accepted. Marriage has been the cornerstone of the alliance theorists – anthropologists who, in following Lévi-Strauss, have stressed the EXCHANGE of women as the critical element in KINSHIP systems. This approach understands primary recruitment to groups not on the basis of DESCENT, but as a result of marriage, or the establishment of links or alliances between social groups. In *The Elementary Structures of Kinship* (1949), Lévi-Strauss distinguished systems as elementary (characterized by a positive marriage rule; rules lay down who one should marry) and complex (without a positive marriage rule; there are rules on who one may not marry, but not on who one *should* marry). For further reading: A. Barnard and A. Good, *Research Practices in the Study of Kinship* (1984). A.G.

MARS (Modern Architectural Research Society), see under CIAM.

Marshall Plan *or* **European Recovery Programme** (ERP). An American plan for aid to European economic recovery after World War II; first publicly proposed in a speech at Harvard on 5 June 1947 by George Marshall, US Secretary of State. The plan offered aid to all European nations, and demanded that they request assistance and act in concert. It reflected American fears that economically dislocated countries (e.g.

France, Italy, West Germany) might fall to COMMUNIST movements, and placed the onus for east European non-involvement on the Soviet Union. Under Anglo-French leadership, plans were developed which led in 1948 to the launching of the ERP, and linked the US Economic Co-operation Administration (ECA) with the Organization for European Economic Co-operation in its implementation. For further reading: S. Hoffmann *et al*, *The Marshall Plan: A Retrospective* (1984). S.R.

Marxism. Refers to the economic, social and political theory and practice of Karl Marx (1818–83) and its subsequent elaboration by his various followers. Although there is considerable dispute as to what Marxism is and what it is not, there is general agreement that most varieties of Marxism typically contain three main strands. Firstly, and most importantly, there is an explanation and critique of present and past societies. The explanation consists in according some privilege to the economic factor over other factors in accounting for social change and development. More specifically, prime importance is given to the forces of production (the tools and instruments that are at the disposal of human beings at any given time) and the relations of production (the way in which human beings organize themselves in order to use the same forces of production) as shaping the political and cultural arrangements in any given society. This view, known as HISTORICAL MATERIALISM, is often jejunely formulated in the proposition that the economic base determines the political and ideological SUPERSTRUCTURE. Although it is accepted that the political and ideological elements can influence the economic structure, it is the development of the latter which produces social change: at a certain stage of their evolution the forces of production develop as far as they can under the existing economic and political organization of society, which then becomes a barrier to their further development, and a period of social REVOLUTION starts in which new economic and political relationships, corresponding to the expanded forces of production, are established. In accordance with this latter, it is possible to pick out the Asiatic, ancient, FEUDAL and modern bourgeois MODES OF PRODUCTION as progressive epochs in the economic formation of society. The critical component in this first strand consists in the view that in these successive modes of production the crucial element in society – the forces of production – have been controlled by a minority who have used their economic power in order to exploit the mass of the population by appropriating the economic surplus for their own benefit. This inherently conflictual situation gives rise to a CLASS struggle which centres around the ownership and control of the means of production. All political INSTITUTIONS and cultural beliefs are shaped by the economic arrangements and those with economic power – the ruling class – so as effectively to bolster the unequal distribution of resources. This yields the Marxist concept of IDEOLOGY as a set of beliefs and practices which serve to maintain an asymmetrical allocation of economic and political power.

The second strand of Marxist thought is the notion of an alternative to a society based on exploitation and divided along class lines. In Marx's view this can only consist of a society based on the common ownership of the means of production in which the human potential stunted by the DIVISION OF LABOUR characteristic of class societies will be enabled freely to develop its manifold facets. Such a society will have no classes and therefore no need for a state apparatus defined as an instrument of class domination. In an initial stage, generally known as SOCIALISM, distribution of goods will be made in the first instance according to the contribution of each individual; later it will be possible to move to a COMMUNIST organization of society which will allow the famous principle of 'from each according to their ability and to each according to their needs' to be implemented. Any detailed description of such a society is bound, on Marxist assumptions, to be highly speculative.

The third strand is some account of how to move from the first to the second. Clearly the materialist conception of history outlined in the first strand comprises the view that the CAPITALIST mode of production is as transitory as all previous ones. Marxists have disagreed over the exact mechanism – whether, e.g., it is the tendency of the rate of profit to fall or the growth of underconsumption – but there is general agreement that the capitalist system is inherently unstable, crisis-ridden and will inevitably collapse. However, socialism will also be the result of the revolutionary activity of those whom capitalist society is producing as its own grave-diggers – the WORKING CLASS whose growing numbers and relative impoverishment will drive them to revolt. Following a revolutionary upheaval, there will have to be a transitional period known as the DICTATORSHIP OF THE PROLETARIAT before a fully communist society can be inaugurated. The relationship of any Marxist-inspired party to the class it represents is subject to more varying accounts than any other aspect of Marxism. Since the era of the mass party only arrived after Marx's death, he himself did not have to cope with this problem and anyone – from a LENINIST proposing a highly centralized 'vanguard' party to lead workers (who would otherwise have the most inadequate views about politics) to a LIBERTARIAN socialist who believes that political POWER should be vested directly in workers' assemblies – can claim, without fear of refutation, that they are in the true Marxist tradition. Since the collapse of the USSR, there have been new interpretations of Marxist thought, broadly referred to as post-Marxism. See also NEO-MARXISM. For further reading: D. McLellan, *Marxism after Marx* (1980). D.T.M.

Marxism-Leninism. Term that originated in the debates and struggle for power in the former USSR following Lenin's death and culminating in the ascendancy of Stalin. It thus came to mean the theory and practice of Marx and Lenin as narrowly defined by Stalin, and was used as a yardstick of orthodoxy to refute all opposition and became part of the official self-description of the Soviet Union. Marxism-Leninism was taken up by the Chinese Communists under Mao as a description and justification of their policies. Currently the term Marxism-Leninism tends to be used by any Marxist party which has retained some sympathy for the policies of Stalin or Mao. See MARXISM; LENINISM; STALINISM; MAOISM. For further reading: L. Schapiro, *The Communist Party of the Soviet Union* (1970). D.T.M.

maser (Microwave Amplification by Stimulated Emission of Radiation). A device producing high levels of power at precisely defined frequencies in the MICROWAVE region. The basic principle is that of the LASER, but the lower frequency means that the ENERGY LEVELS of MOLECULES as well as ATOMS can be used. Masers are used as oscillators in RADAR, and as amplifiers. M.V.B.

masochism. Sexual pleasure derived from being subjected to pain, either self-inflicted or inflicted by another. It was named by Richard Krafft-Ebing (1840–1902) after Baron Sacher-Masoch, who described it in VENUS IN FURS (tr. G. Warner, 1925). W.Z.

mass. A fundamental quantity in PHYSICS. In NEWTONIAN MECHANICS, the mass of a body is a measure of its ability to resist acceleration when acted on by forces. Mass is also a measure of a body's ability to attract other bodies by GRAVITATION. The scientific unit of mass is the kilogram, and masses are measured by comparison with the standard, which is kept near Paris. Einstein's MASS-ENERGY EQUATION shows that mass is not indestructible. M.V.B.

mass culture. This concept started life with decidedly pejorative connotations, moved on to express something approaching approbation, and is now on the point of disappearance altogether. Often linked to the concept of mass society, its use became common in cultural criticism from the 1930s to the 1950s to describe the typical products of the commercially-driven mass communications industries – film, radio, records, advertising, the popular press and television. These were offensive to old-style democrats on the grounds that they debased the authentic FOLK CULTURE produced by the people themselves; they were offensive to conservatives and traditionalists on the grounds that they violated the canons of 'high' art and CULTURE; and they were offensive to LEFT-wing critics because they appeared to be weapons in the armoury of CAPITALIST civilization intent on brainwashing the mass of the people and so preventing them from attaining a true consciousness of the reality of their life in a capitalist society. But already in the 1950s, writers such as Richard Hoggart (*The Uses of Literacy*, 1957) were arguing that WORKING-CLASS culture had a resilience and vitality that enabled it not only to resist the blandishments of mass culture but to turn it to its own use. In the 1960s and 1970s the theorists of POP culture argued that contemporary popular culture had an energy and creativity equal to the now defunct high culture, and was poised to replace it. And the POST-MODERN theorists of the 1980s and 1990s completed the rout with their insistence that all distinctions of 'high' and 'low' were irrelevant and invalid in the new global culture of PLURALISM and hybridity. Even if the post-modernists do not win the day, it seems unlikely that 'mass culture' will ever be resuscitated, at least with anything like its original meaning. For further reading: Simon During (ed.), *The Cultural Studies Reader* (1993). K.K.

mass-energy equation. The famous EQUATION $E = mc^2$ deduced by Einstein from his theory of RELATIVITY. According to this theory matter is one of the many forms of ENERGY, and the equation predicts the amount of energy (E) that is released when a MASS (m) is annihilated (c is the speed of light in empty space). Conversion of mass takes place during NUCLEAR REACTIONS, such as FUSION and FISSION; it is responsible for the light of stars and the sun, and the power from NUCLEAR REACTORS and NUCLEAR WEAPONS. Only a small fraction of the mass involved disappears in these processes; if *all* the mass could be used up, the energy release would be far greater (e.g. the 'burning' of 1 kilogram every second would provide power at the rate of about 100,000 megawatts). M.V.B.

mass extinction. An occasion in the history of life when an exceptionally large number of SPECIES became extinct. The best-known mass extinction took place at the end of the Cretaceous Period about 65 million years ago, and included the dinosaurs. The mass extinction at the end of the Permian Period, about 225 million years ago, is the earliest well-documented mass extinction, and in it as many as 96 per cent of species may have become extinct. The total number of mass extinctions in the history of life is uncertain, but there may have been as many as nine between the Permian and the present, at approximately 26-million-year intervals. Four of these are reasonably well documented. It is unclear whether mass extinctions are the extreme of a continuum of extinction rates, or whether they differ in kind from a normal rate of extinction. The cause, or causes, of mass extinctions is controversial. The discovery, by Luis Alvarez (1911–88), that rocks at the CRETACEOUS-TERTIARY BOUNDARY have a high concentration of the RARE EARTH element iridium, led him to suggest that extinction was caused by a catastrophic meteor impact, because iridium is found in particularly high concentrations in meteors. Other explanations of the iridium anomaly are possible, such as volcanism (see VOLCANOLOGY). Many other hypotheses have been put forward to explain mass extinctions. Humans are probably causing a mass extinction at present, by the destruction of the tropical rainforests. M.R.

mass picketing, see under PICKETING.

mass society. A society in which similar tastes, habits, opinions and activities are shared by the majority of the population who accordingly become less differentiated either as individuals or in terms of social CLASS. In political terms, mass society is seen as a result of the processes of INDUSTRIALIZATION, the extension of suffrage, and the erosion of SOCIAL STRATIFICATION. Some observers argue that the emergent order of mass society threatens a new volatility – of masses responsive to the direct manipulation of despots and tyrants or, vice versa, of governing ÉLITES unable to resist the whims of popular opinion. Among the claimed characteristics of mass society are an extensive BUREAUCRACY, powerful media, a tendency to conformity, mediocrity and ALIENATION. Such an interpretation was central to the mass cultural critique of the FRANKFURT SCHOOL whose members argued that mass society acts to erode the CLASS CONSCIOUSNESS of the WORKING CLASS while simultaneously imposing new forms of social control facilitated by the omnipresent nature of the mass media and the latter's ability to influence public opinion via the careful channelling of information. In recent years, a number of theorists have begun to adopt a more positive view of massification, pointing to enlarged areas of public participation and increased consensus over societal ends and means. With regard to the social influence of mass entertainment or popular culture, this more liberal interpretation of mass society has also given rise to the notion of an active audience whose conferred meanings are deemed an inextricable part of the overall social and cultural significance of given texts, styles or genres. A.BEN.

massive compact halo object, see MACHO.

massive retaliation. A strategy envisaging a strategic riposte to all identifiable provocations or attacks. The term was adapted from a phrase in a speech by US Secretary of State John Foster Dulles on 12 January 1954 in which he said that 'the way to deter aggression is for the free communities to be willing and able to respond vigorously at places and with means of our own choosing'. This phrase was subject to contemporary misinterpretation, for American strategy never envisaged any form of automatic nuclear riposte; the message Dulles was trying to signal to the communist powers was (a) that they could not hope to hide behind aggression by proxy; (b) that they could not expect to limit any ensuing conflict to thresholds chosen by themselves; and (c) that any attack on the United States would involve reprisals against their homeland. The substance of this policy was NATO doctrine from 1954 until 1966 when it was modified in favour of *flexible response*. It remains, however, official French strategic doctrine. See DETERRENCE. A.F.B.

master morality/slave morality. In Friedrich Nietzsche's thought (see NIETZSCHEAN), master morality is an opposition between good and bad (*gut* and *schlecht*), where the former means 'noble', 'strong' and 'beautiful', and the latter means 'common', 'weak' and 'ugly'. Slave morality, on the other hand, is an opposition between good and evil (*gut* and *böse*), where 'holy', 'poor' and 'friend' became honorifics, and 'rich', 'godless', 'violent' and 'physical' become synonyms for 'evil' (*Beyond Good and Evil*, 1886). Masters are vigorous, self-confident but unsophisticated; slaves are resentful and defensive, but they sometimes produce lasting accomplishments. 'While every aristocratic morality develops by saying a triumphant Yes to itself, the slave morality is from the beginning a No to something "outside", something "other", something "not itself": and this No is its creative act' (*Genealogy of Morals*, 1887). JUDAISM was the first 'slave revolt' that achieved a 'reversal of values'; its fruits include CHRISTIANITY, DEMOCRACY and SOCIALISM. Nietzsche writes favourably of master morality, but his preference is deliberately ambiguous. His main goal is to undermine modern values by implying that any system of NORMS is only the self-image of the ruling group. For further reading: P. Sedgwick (ed.), *Nietzsche: A Critical Reader* (1995). P.LE.

material culture, history of, see HISTORY OF MATERIAL CULTURE.

materialism. In ONTOLOGY, the theory that everything that really exists is material in nature, by which is meant, at least, that it occupies some volume of space at any time and, usually, that it continues in existence for some period of time and is either accessible to PERCEPTION by sight and touch or is analogous in its causal properties (see CAUSALITY) to what is so accessible. This denies substantial existence (1) to minds and mental states, unless these are identified with states of the brain and nervous system, and (2), ordinarily, in the style of NOMINALISM, to abstract entities of UNIVERSALS. The first of these denials is the more crucial and controversial. It is generally agreed that statements about mental events are not equivalent in MEANING to statements about physical events in the brain. Yet the obviously close correlation between brain and mind suggests that the event that is described in mental language as experiencing a pain may be the very same event, under a non-equivalent description, as some event in the brain. EPIPHENOMENALISM is a kind of diluted materialism inspired, like the stronger form, by the intimations of complete DETERMINISM in the material world which, if true, would deprive mental events (conceived, in the manner of DUALISM, as radically non-material) of any causal efficacy.

The DIALECTICAL MATERIALISM of Marx and Engels repudiates the mechanistic account of the relations between events given by standard materialism and allows, as do other, biologically inspired forms of emergent EVOLUTIONISM, that mind, while originating in matter, is distinct in nature from it. Materialism excludes the possibility of disembodied minds, whether of God or of the dead. Materialists, from the time of

Democritus to the present, have usually been NATURALISTS in ETHICS, but that does not commit them to materialism in the colloquial sense of an overriding interest in the acquisition of material goods and bodily satisfactions. For further reading: K. Campbell, *Body and Mind* (1971). A.Q.

materialism, heroic, see under ZEITGEIST.

materialist conception of history, see HISTORICAL MATERIALISM.

materials science. The systematic study of matter in bulk, unifying the disciplines of METALLURGY, POLYMER science, RHEOLOGY and SOLID-STATE PHYSICS, and techniques such as CRYSTALLOGRAPHY, electron microscopy (see ELECTRON MICROSCOPE) and X-RAY DIFFRACTION, in an attempt to understand matter and develop useful new materials such as carbon fibres. M.V.B.

mathematical economics, see under ECONOMETRICS.

mathematical induction. In MATHEMATICS, a particular scheme of PROOF for properties of the natural numbers (see NUMBER), which was used as far back as the 16th century (but was given its name by Augustus de Morgan in 1838). If one wants to prove a certain property one establishes two things: (1) a certain starting number – for example, the number 1 – has this property; (2) if all the numbers below any number n have the property, then so does n.

Then it follows that all whole numbers, from the starting number upwards, have the property. For example, to prove that any number above 1 is either prime or is the product of primes: (a) note that 2 is prime; (b) if all numbers below n have the property, then either n is prime or it is $a \times b$ where a and b are smaller than n. So they are prime or the product of primes, and then so is n. N.A.R.

mathematical linguistics. A branch of LINGUISTICS which studies the mathematical properties of language, usually employing CONCEPTS of a statistical or algebraic kind (see STATISTICS; ALGEBRA). D.C.

mathematical logic (also known as *symbolic logic*). A term that covers a range of interconnected disciplines. Traditional LOGIC, because of its concern with logical form (see PROPOSITION), has from the earliest times used symbols to replace words. Leibniz (1646–1716) proposed that logical arguments could be reduced to algebraic manipulations; for traditional logic (in particular for SYLLOGISMS) this was accomplished by De Morgan and Boole in the mid-19th century (see BOOLEAN ALGEBRA). However, as the work of Frege (1848–1925) clearly showed, traditional logic does not suffice for mathematical argument. To support the thesis of LOGICISM he developed QUANTIFICATION theory and the theory of SETS (classes) and gave them an axiomatic formulation (see AXIOMATICS). Russell's PARADOX showed that the logic of classes needed a more mathematically sophisticated formulation (see SET THEORY). Up to this point the development of the subject-matter and the development of the symbolism for it went hand in hand, but since then the distinction between the SYNTAX and the SEMANTICS of formal languages has become of crucial importance. Hilbert (1862–1943), in his version of FORMALISM, developed *proof theory*; through the study of formal proofs, considered simply as strings of symbols, he hoped to defend classical MATHEMATICS against the criticisms of INTUITIONISM by demonstrating that no proof would lead to a contradiction. GÖDEL'S THEOREM shows that such a demonstration must use new principles which are not formalizable in the system studied. Proof theory has thus become a recondite branch of mathematics; it is closely connected with RECURSIVE FUNCTION THEORY. The study of the semantics of formal languages, begun by Tarski in 1936, has blossomed into *model theory*. Here one pushes the AXIOMATIC METHOD to its limit by studying *all* possible interpretations (MODELS) of a given formal language or system of axioms. The results are particularly valuable for abstract ALGEBRA. For further reading: J. N. Crossley *et al*, *What Is Mathematical Logic?* (1972). R.G.; A.Q.

mathematical psychology. A branch of PSYCHOLOGY concerned with devising statistical procedures (see STATISTICS) for extracting information from psychology data, and with constructing COMPUTER or mathematical MODELS that seek to simulate or represent human behaviour. For further reading: G. A. Miller, *Mathematics and Psychology* (1964). J.S.B.

mathematical structure. Before the 19th century MATHEMATICS dealt with objects that belonged to a limited variety of well-defined species (e.g. geometric points, whole NUMBERS, real numbers) whose fundamental laws were given by intuition. Where intuition was lacking (e.g. COMPLEX NUMBERS) the 'objects' were treated with suspicion. In the 19th and 20th centuries there has been an enormous enrichment of mathematical imagination. New objects and new species were introduced, sometimes by formal postulates (e.g. non-Euclidean GEOMETRIES, quaternions), sometimes by construction (GROUPS were first introduced as sets of permutations), sometimes by new intuitions (e.g. the sets of Cantorian SET THEORY), often by a combination of these approaches. Gradually the AXIOMATIC METHOD emerged as the preferred way of handling the multitude of notions, each of which is seen as a particular case of the general CONCEPT (due to BOURBAKI) of mathematical structure. A *first-order structure* is defined by specifying a SET *A* of *elements* (e.g. the points of a line, the natural numbers) together with certain relations (e.g. betweenness) and/or certain FUNCTIONS (e.g. addition). For *higher-order structures* one specifies in addition certain relations of relations, functions of functions, and so on. What is significant to the pure mathematician is the pattern formed by the specified relations, functions, etc. All isomorphic structures (see ISOMORPHISM) will exhibit the same pattern; so one defines the corresponding *abstract mathematical structure*. Here the elements are colourless, structureless individuals, and the specified relations, etc. are defined purely extensionally – by means of (possibly INFINITE) lists and tables. This means that totally arbitrary or chaotic patterns of relations, etc. are counted as structures. Mathematically significant structures are singled out by imposing axioms which the relations, etc. are required to satisfy. The axioms may determine a unique abstract structure; more often they determine a whole family of similar structures (for examples see GROUPS). Such a family may itself be treated as a structure; see CATEGORY THEORY. For further reading: N. W. Gowar, *Basic Mathematical Structures* (1973). R.G.

mathematics. Until the mid-19th century the subject was correctly described as the science of NUMBER and quantity (including the dimensional quantities of GEOMETRY). The thesis of LOGICISM and the introduction of the unifying CONCEPT of MATHEMATICAL STRUCTURE suggested a redefinition: the study of SETS and relations. The rise of the AXIOMATIC METHOD and of FORMALISM led some to describe it as the drawing of correct INFERENCES from axioms. Both of these last views (which have been influential in the new mathematics) are disastrously misleading because they emphasize trivial facets and conceal what is important. Significant structures and difficult theorems are not discovered by playing around with relations and formal inferences. They are found by using imagination, intuition and experience, and are often, initially, logically incoherent; logical packaging comes later. (A good mathematician once said: 'Test of good mathematician – how many bad proofs.') The standards of precision and rigour today are high, but this is not what makes 20th-century mathematics a supreme achievement of the human intellect.

Mathematics arises from trying to solve problems. The problems come from three primary directions: (1) from the external world – the source of GEOMETRY, CALCULUS and parts of TOPOLOGY; (2) from intellectual playfulness – from this comes NUMBER THEORY, PROBABILITY THEORY, much of ALGEBRA and combinatorial mathematics (see FOUR-COLOUR CONJECTURE), some of topology (see MÖBIUS BAND); (3) from reflecting on the power and the limitations of our intellect – see MATHEMATICAL LOGIC, INFINITY, GÖDEL'S THEOREM, RECURSIVE FUNCTION THEORY. The efforts to solve these primary problems produce not only manipulative techniques (such as ALGEBRA and the use of differential equations, vectors, MATRICES, BOOLEAN ALGEBRA) but also new concepts and patterns of thought (for examples see GEOMETRY, GROUP, SET THEORY, TOPOLOGY), which in turn produce new problems. It is these new patterns of thought, at one remove from the primary problems, which form the rich and intricate heart of mathematics. Because these patterns have been formed by *our* intellect, and so are conformable to our understanding, they modify or even revolutionize our view and knowledge of the external world. The theory of groups was invented to solve problems of pure algebra; it is now a part of the physicist's view of nature (see TRANSFORMATION; PARITY). For further reading: P. J. Davis and R. Hersh, *The Mathematical Experience* (1983); J. Gullberg, *Mathematics: From the Birth of Numbers* (1997). R.G.

matheme. A term in Lacan's version of PSYCHOANALYSIS (see LACANIAN). Lacan's clinical practice led him to formulate what he called the REAL, a limit both to the SYMBOLIC and to the IMAGINARY, and thus a stranger, strictly speaking, to the orders of representation, visualization and signification. The matheme was Lacan's response to the problem of theorizing the real without falling into the traps characteristic of imaginary and intuitive representation, since the symbolic writing that constitutes a matheme is both devoid of a univocal signification and bars access to intuitive representation. Hence the mathemes are not to be understood, but to be used; the imaginary connotations carried by the idea of understanding are eliminated by a procedure that produces multiple effects of sense while allowing for a formalization of many aspects of psychoanalysis. For further reading: J. Lacan, *Écrits* (1966, tr. 1977). D.L.

matriarchy. In a limited sense the term means authority exercised by women over men (in contrast to PATRIARCHY, where men exercise power over women). Matriarchy, however, is frequently used more loosely to refer to female autonomy, mother-right, recognition of female principle, worship of goddess, matrilineage, women-centred social organization, etc. Matriarchy was of particular interest to writers at the end of the 19th century in their investigations of the evolution of society. An original state of matriarchy was postulated by Bachofen (*Das Mutterrecht*, 1861) and it became an important stage in the evolutionary schema of Morgan (*Ancient Society*, 1877) and Engels (*The Origin of the Family, Private Property and the State*, 1884). More recently the concept of matriarchy has been important in attempts to understand the origins of sexual oppression. A number of feminists (see FEMINISM) have drawn upon 19th-century and other historical accounts to discover early matriarchal (or gynocentric) organizations (e.g. E. Gould Davis, *The First Sex*, 1971). Those feminists working within an anthropological tradition have also considered the question of matriarchy. They have rejected evolutionary speculation, but investigated the nature of women's power (or lack of it) in contemporary societies (e.g. R. Reiter, *Towards an Anthropology of Women*, 1975). For the feminist movement the potential existence of matriarchy (in history or contemporary society) is important evidence to refute the notion that patriarchy is universal, fundamental and inevitable. It suggests the possibility of dissolving or bringing to an end the state of male domination. For further reading: K. Millett, *Sexual Politics* (1983). A.G.

matri-clan, see under CLAN.

matrilineal. Tracing of DESCENT through a single female line from an ancestor. As with other forms of descent, it may act as a principle governing relations between individuals over the inheritance of property or succession to office. It may also be the organizing principle of a social group, and the basis of membership of a specific matrilineal descent group. Audrey Richards' study of the Bemba of Central Africa (*Land, Labour and Diet in Northern Rhodesia*, 1939) showed them to be a classic example.

Typically, a matrilineal descent group is organized around resident women: mothers and sisters descended from a common ancestress. However, although the line of descent runs through women, the line of authority runs through men. Thus the relationship between a woman and her brother is central. But brothers cannot impregnate their sisters to perpetuate the lineage and thus men are brought from outside as husbands: *matrilocal marriage*. A husband acquires through MARRIAGE rights over the sexual and domestic services of his wife, but not over her reproductive powers. They remain part of her matrilineage under the control of her brother. Children of the marriage are similarly members of their mother's matrilineage and subject to the authority of her brother rather than her husband. Men as husbands are marginal, but as brothers they are central to a matrilineal descent group (see BRIDEWEALTH). For further reading: L. Holy, *Strategies and Norms in a Changing Matrilineal Society* (1985). A.G.

matrilocal marriage, see under MATRILINEAL.

matrix. A rectangular array of numbers (see NUMBER). We can define the addition of two matrices of the same shape (just add them element by element), and also the multiplication of two suitably shaped matrices. With these definitions come a number of algebraic properties (see ALGEBRA).

Matrices proved to be the ideal tool for, e.g., input-output analysis in ECONOMICS, and vibrating systems in MECHANICS. They are used in QUANTUM MECHANICS, and FACTOR ANALYSIS in STATISTICS. Any finite GROUP can be represented by a set of matrices.

With the advent of computers the handling and manipulating of large matrices, such as the matrix by which the Treasury represents the British economy (some 180 × 180 terms), hold no terrors. N.A.R.

matrix mechanics. An alternative formulation of QUANTUM MECHANICS which does not involve a WAVE FUNCTION, devised by Werner Heisenberg in 1925. A dynamical quantity (e.g. MOMENTUM or SPIN) is represented mathematically by a MATRIX, instead of a number as in NEWTONIAN MECHANICS. These matrices form the basis of calculations aimed at predicting experimentally measurable quantities, such as the intensities of lines in SPECTROSCOPY, the HALF-LIVES of radioactive decay (see RADIOACTIVITY), and the ENERGY LEVELS of ATOMS. M.V.B.

matrix organization, see under ORGANIZATION THEORY.

mature/developed socialism. A term used in later Soviet IDEOLOGY (see USSR, THE FORMER) to describe the stage which the Soviet Union had reached in its progress from SOCIALISM to COMMUNISM. Leonid Brezhnev first defined it at the XXIV Congress of the Communist Party in 1971, although the idea had gained some currency earlier, and it featured as an important concept in the Constitution of 1977. It was intended to take into account the ECONOMIC GROWTH achieved since 1936, when Stalin announced that socialism had been created, while putting off the advent of communism to the distant future. The main feature of this stage of socialism was modernization, and particularly the scientific and technical revolution, the encouragement of which would allow socialism to develop further and would create the conditions for the establishment of communism. Another characteristic of developed socialism was the achievement of a large measure of unity among the Soviet people which allowed the Communist Party to become the vanguard of the people, not just of the PROLETARIAT as was the case under the DICTATORSHIP OF THE PROLETARIAT. This accords with the doctrine of the ALL PEOPLE'S STATE. For further reading: N. Harding (ed.), *The State in Socialist Society* (1984). D.PR.

Mavayana, see under BUDDHISM.

maximin, see under GAME THEORY.

maxims of conversation. Notions derived from the work of the philosopher H. P. Grice (*Studies in the Way of Words*, 1989) which are widely cited in research in PRAGMATICS. The maxims are general principles which are thought to underlie the efficient use of language, and which together identify a general CO-OPERATIVE PRINCIPLE. Four basic maxims are identified. The *maxim of quality* states that speakers' contributions ought to be true. The *maxim of quantity* states that the contribution should contain more information than is neccssary for the needs of the exchange. The *maxim of relevance* states that contributions should relate clearly to the purpose of the exchange. And the *maxim of manner* states that the contributions should be perspicuous – especially avoiding obscurity and ambiguity. For further reading: S. Levinson, *Pragmatics* (1983). D.C.

May 1968. The 'events' of May 1968 in France began with student protests in Paris about university conditions and proposed reforms. Violent clashes between students and police were accompanied by student occupations throughout the capital and in some provincial universities. By mid-May factory workers as well as some professional groups, supported by the major TRADE UNIONS, had joined the students; there was a general strike and factory occupations in support of AUTOGESTION. The crisis was resolved in early June 1968 by the government's promise to consult the students over university reforms and the *Grenelle* agreements, which provided workers with a high minimum wage, a shorter working week and an extra week's paid holiday. Although the events of May 1968 were at the time interpreted by many people as a revolutionary threat to the Fifth Republic, the GAULLIST government quickly re-established order, and in the general election of June 1968 was re-elected with an overwhelming majority. Although student protests were the immediate cause of the events, the rapid escalation of the crisis suggests that there was widespread discontent in France at the time with the somewhat illiberal (albeit constitutional) nature of the Gaullist regime. For further reading: K. Reader, *The May 1968 Events in France* (1993). S.M.

McCarthyism. The name, attributed to cartoonist Herbert Block (Herblock), for a brief but lurid phase in US history from 1950 to 1954, in which Senator Joseph McCarthy led an hysterical and mendacious campaign against alleged COMMUNISTS in the US government and other institutions. Although McCarthy's own main motive was self-promotion and his methods crude, his campaign enlarged an existing mood and attracted both substantial popular support and the tacit encouragement of Republican Party ÉLITES. By association, the term now denotes any attempt to persecute members of an organization by innuendo, implication of guilt by association, the suspension of usual rules of evidence and procedure, etc. For further reading: D. Caute, *The Great Fear* (1978). S.R.

McDonaldization. Term introduced by the American sociologist George Ritzer to describe a process in which the methods of organization typical of fast-food outlets such as McDonald's spread to other areas of society including education, work, leisure politics and the FAMILY. It combines elements of the rationality (see RATIONALISM) of bureaucracy, the principles of assembly-line production and SCIENTIFIC MANAGEMENT. For further reading: G. Ritzer, *The McDonaldization of Society* (1996). M.D.H.

mean. The mean of a SET of values is a further value calculated from them as a typical or representative value for the set; the word 'average' is sometimes used as a synonym. The most important type is the *arithmetic mean*, given by adding the values together and dividing the sum by the number n of summands. The *geometric mean* is the nth root of the product of the values, and the *harmonic mean* is the reciprocal of the arithmetic mean of the reciprocals; geometric and harmonic means are useful only when all the values involved are positive. In any technical context 'mean' (unqualified) denotes arithmetic mean: thus in STATISTICS the *sample mean* is the arithmetic mean of the observations making up the SAMPLE. A *weighted arithmetic mean* is obtained by multiplying each value by some non-negative *weight* before summation and then dividing the sum of the products by the sum of the weights. R.SI.

mean deviation. In STATISTICS, the expected absolute value of the difference between the observed value of a RANDOM VARIABLE and a measure of its location. R.SI.

meaning. Either the sense (or intension) of a linguistic expression (see LINGUISTICS) or, alternatively, its reference (or extension). According to Friedrich Frege's (1848–1925) influential theory, the reference of an expression is the item it denotes, while its sense is its mode of presentation of that item. Thus the reference of the name 'Aristotle' is Aristotle himself, and its sense is captured by some description which speakers associate uniquely with the bearer of that name, such as, perhaps, 'the most famous pupil of Plato'. For Frege, sense determines reference; the sense of a whole sentence is the thought it expresses and is determined by the senses of its component expressions; and its reference is its truth-value. Frege's theory has been challenged by Saul Kripke (1940–), who holds that names refer 'directly', without the mediation of senses. According to Kripke, what links a name to its bearer is a causal chain of social practice, as one speaker passes the name on to another following an initial event of 'baptism'. Linguistic or non-natural meaning is distinct from natural meaning: the sense in which 'cloud' means *cloud* is different from that in which clouds mean rain. Both are also distinct from meaning in the sense of *intending*. However, another influential approach to linguistic meaning, due to H. P. Grice, links such meaning with the intentions of speakers to induce appropriate beliefs in their audience. For further reading: M. Platts, *Ways of Meaning* (1979). E.J.L.

meaning is use. A slogan associated with the later PHILOSOPHY of Ludwig Wittgenstein (1889–1951), who said: 'For a *large* class of cases – though not for all – in which we employ the word "meaning" it can be defined thus: the meaning of a word is its use in the language'. Wittgenstein rejects what he calls the Augustinian picture of language in which the role of any linguistic expression is to stand for an object. In Wittgenstein's view, an expression has meaning through having a rule-governed *use* in a language, and these uses are multifarious. In particular, the role of most expressions in our language is not to stand for some object. And even where that is the expression's role, the absence of any corresponding object does not render the expression meaningless, just so long as it has an established use. There are problems with the straightforward identification of meaning with use. For example, some expressions have a use but no meaning, e.g. 'abracadabra', and some have the same meaning while differing in use, e.g. 'cops' and 'the police'. S.W.L.

meaning-relation (also called *sense relation* or *semantic relation*). In LINGUISTICS, (1) a specific semantic association regularly interrelating sets of words in the LEXICON of a language, e.g. synonymy, antonymy (see SEMANTICS, SEMANTIC-FIELD THEORY); (2) the semantically relevant interrelationships between grammatical classes and structures, as well as between single words, e.g. the relations postulated by CASE GRAMMAR. D.C.

mechanical jurisprudence, see under CONCEPTUALISM.

mechanics. The branch of PHYSICS dealing with the motion of matter. The subject is divided into two parts: *kinematics*, consisting of the precise geometrical description of position, velocity, acceleration, ORBITS, etc.; and *dynamics*, where the causes of motion are analysed in terms of forces, interactions between objects, etc.

There are three main theories of mechanics in current use: NEWTONIAN MECHANICS is valid for systems which are large in comparison with ATOMS, moving slowly in comparison with light, and not subjected to very strong gravitational fields (such as those near BLACK HOLES; see GRAVITATION). RELATIVITY mechanics includes Newtonian mechanics as a special case, and is also valid near the speed of light and for objects strongly attracted by gravity; it breaks down on the atomic scale. QUANTUM MECHANICS also includes Newtonian mechanics, but remains valid for atomic and nuclear systems. A completely satisfactory fusion of relativity and quantum mechanics has not yet been achieved. Sometimes the term mechanics is used in a restricted sense, to refer to the purely Newtonian theory required for ASTRONOMY (planetary orbits, etc.) and ENGINEERING (bridges, machines, vehicles, etc.). For further reading: R. H. March, *Physics for Poets* (1970). M.V.B.

mechanism. The theory that all causation (see CAUSALITY) is, in Aristotle's terminology, *efficient*, i.e. that for an event to be caused is for its occurrence to be deducible from the antecedent (in some cases contemporaneous) condition in which it occurs, together with the relevant universal laws of nature. The traditional opponent of mechanism is TELEOLOGY, the view that some, perhaps all, events must be explained in terms of the purposes which they serve, and thus that the present is determined by the future rather than by the past. Other views opposed to mechanism are ORGANICISM, the biological doctrines of emergence and VITALISM, and the position of the dominant school of quantum physicists (see QUANTUM MECHANICS). A.Q.

mechanical and **organic solidarity.** Terms used by the French sociologist Émile Durkheim (1858–1917; see SOCIOLOGY) to describe the ways in which different types of society cohered and remained stable. Simple, agricultural societies were characterized by mechanical solidarity in which there was little DIVISION OF LABOUR and the similarity of individuals made it easy for them to identify the interests of society as a whole with their own interests. In such societies RELIGION was particularly important for achieving solidarity by helping to create a collective consciousness in society. In INDUSTRIAL SOCIETIES, with a much greater division of labour, solidarity was based upon the complementary differences and interdependence between individuals in different social roles. Solidarity was weaker than in simple societies but could be encouraged through the education system. Durkheim's concepts remain useful for analysing the problems industrial societies may have in securing the allegiance and conformity of some of their members. For further reading: E. Durkheim, *The Division of Labour in Society* (1893, 1947). M.D.H.

mechanization. The central technological feature of INDUSTRIALIZATION. Men have always sought to enhance their power and lighten their labour by mechanical means (levers, wheels, pulleys, etc.) and by harnessing natural energies (windmills, watermills, etc.). In the 18th century, however, technological developments, notably in METALLURGY, made it possible to harness *hidden* energies (steam, gas, electricity) and thus to power machines capable of performing certain routine skills automatically and much more rapidly than was possible by hand. Over the greater part of industry, mechanization replaced the craftsman by the 'operative', thus transforming the nature of work, attitudes to work, and a wide range of human relationships. Blake, William Morris and D. H. Lawrence are among those writers who in different ways have emphasized the dehumanizing effects of mechanization (see DEHUMANIZATION); to their fears have been added that of massive UNEMPLOYMENT resulting from AUTOMATION. See also TECHNOLOGY. R.F.

media studies. Media studies is a relatively new subject located, like film studies, in the wider locus of the study of communication. It also draws upon the theoretical and methodological approaches (see METHODOLOGY) from a number of other disciplines, including SOCIOLOGY, PSYCHOLOGY, LINGUISTICS, HISTORY, politics, ECONOMICS and cultural studies. The number of those reading media and communication studies in a range of different courses has risen dramatically over the last decade.

The focus of media studies is the generation and exchange of meaning through the channels of the mass media. An investigation of this process requires analysis of a number of key areas of activity: the history and contemporary structure of the institutions which organize the sending of mass media messages, e.g. the BBC and News International, and the relationships which may exist between them in terms of ownership and control; the impact that technological development has had and may have on the conveying of such messages and how such developments may affect the form, content and reception of messages; the various forms of communication used to send mass media messages, e.g. still and moving images, music, verbal and non-verbal signs, and the contribution they make to the construction of meaning (see NON-VERBAL COMMUNICATION; DECONSTRUCTION); the CODES and conventions used in sending, or encoding, these messages, e.g. language; an analysis of the texts into which the messages are structured, e.g. a television programme; the nature of the messages conveyed; the practices of those working in the media industries; the audiences at which these messages are directed and the factors which affect their reading, or decoding, of the messages, and ways by which their responses, or feedback, may be gained and utilized; the relationship between the mass media and other key national or international institutions, e.g. governments and transnational corporations; and the place of the media within other cultural activities and the nature of its relationship to them.

Some of the current issues within research include: the concentration of ownership and control within the media and cultural industries; the role of the media in constructing personal, GENDER, ethnic and global IDENTITIES; and the relationship between the media and national and international POWER structures. Media studies courses often include the development of both theoretical analysis and of practical skills involved in activities such as photography; desktop publishing; film, television and video production; radio and print journalism. For further reading: J. Watson, *Media Communication: An Introduction* (1998). A.P.HI.

Medicaid and **Medicare.** The US healthcare programmes for the poor and the elderly, respectively. Both were passed by

Congress in 1965 as part of President Johnson's Great Society programme to replace a jerry-rigged system of government and private charitable programmes that mostly provided emergency care. In the 1990s, with pressure to cut welfare programmes and projections that Medicare will be bankrupt by 2002, both programmes have found themselves under intense pressure from policymakers trying to trim federal budget deficits and spending growth. Medicaid, which provides care for about 36 million low-income people, is a joint federal-state-local programme funded by tax revenues whose major achievement has been a significant decline in the infant mortality rate in the US. Before Medicaid, the mortality rate from birth to age one was 93 per 1,000 live births. By 1992, the figure had been reduced to 34. Medicaid now pays for about a third of all deliveries. Medicare, which is available to all those over 65 regardless of income or assets, is financed by a combination of payroll taxes, premiums and tax revenues. It provides help in paying hospital and doctor bills for those over 65, and in 1972 was expanded to include some disabled people and kidney disease patients younger than 65. Before Medicare, less than half of elderly Americans had healthcare coverage and had to pay their own bills or be treated as charity cases. Now, Medicare accounts for about half the heathcare for the elderly in the US, as well as for about one-quarter of all payments to hospitals and physicians. Since the programme's creation, life expectancy has increased from 70 to nearly 76 years in the US. R.K.H.

medical ethics. May be considered under two headings – traditional, and critical or philosophical medical ETHICS. Traditional medical ethics concerns the moral obligations governing the practice of medicine and has been a central concern of the medical profession for at least 2,500 years. The Hippocratic oath required doctors to benefit their patients, and avoid harming them by, among other things, eschewing 'deadly medicines', ABORTION and the seduction of patients and their families, and by keeping secret whatever 'ought not to be spoken of abroad'. The profession has updated its codes of ethics, especially following medical atrocities in World War II. The World Medical Association has promulgated a series of ethical declarations on such topics as medical research, terminal illness, death and organ transplantation, abortion, and medical participation in torture (categorically forbidden). Regulation of professional standards varies in different countries. In Britain it is vested in the General Medical Council (GMC), established by the Medical Act of 1858 and modified in the Medical Act of 1983. The Council, mostly doctors but including non-medical members appointed by the Crown, is empowered to censure doctors and to remove or suspend them from medical practice. Advice on professional ethics is also provided by the British Medical Association (the main professional association or trade union) and to some extent by the medical protection societies, which in effect insure doctors against malpractice claims. There is a growing trend, which started in America in the 1970s, towards the teaching of critical or philosophical medical ethics in which medicomoral claims and their justifications are exposed to critical analysis in the light of counter-arguments. For further reading: E. A. Murphy, *Underpinnings of Medical Ethics* (1997). R.GI.

medical geography. The systematic field of GEOGRAPHY that focuses on the spatial dimensions of human health. Many medical geographers concentrate on the spatial analysis of morbidity and mortality, identifying environmental conditions and hazards in the source areas of various diseases (see EPIDEMIOLOGY), and mapping the DIFFUSION routes of the epidemics and pandemics that often result. These contributions to epidemiology are represented by a number of major atlases of disease distributions as well as case studies of geographical processes that shape the spread of epidemics, including AIDS. Medical geography has expanded its domain in recent years to include the provision and delivery of healthcare, emphasizing the spatial organization of health services and the optimal distribution of healthcare facilities. For further reading: G. Moon and K. Jones, *Health, Disease, and Society: An Introduction to Medical Geography* (1988). P.O.M.

medicalization. The tendency, increasingly marked in the US but also shown elsewhere, as in the former USSR, to treat all socially

undesirable or deviant behaviour as the fit object of medical science and medical treatment (for the opposite view, see LABELLING THEORY). Drugs are invented to treat children diagnosed as 'hyperactive'. Mental patients and prison inmates with particularly intractable problems of behaviour are diagnosed as suffering from constitutional conditions of insanity or AGGRESSION, and given the appropriate drug therapy. Political dissidents are seen as temperamentally disturbed and in need of medical 'correction'. The view is that most if not all social problems – violent crime, vandalism, ALCOHOLISM, HOMOSEXUALITY, political or moral dissidence – are the result of clinically identifiable 'diseases', which can be cured provided the medical profession is given the care of them. Critics of the medicalization of social problems, such as Ivan Illich, not unnaturally see in it an unwarranted extension of the POWER of the medical profession. More seriously, they see danger in the extension of the 'medical model' to problems with complex social causes, for which drugs appear a highly unsuitable form of treatment. For further reading: P. Conrad and J. W. Schneider, *Deviance and Medicalization: From Badness to Sickness* (1980).
K.K.

Medicare, see under MEDICAID.

Megale Idea, see under ENOSIS.

megalopolis. Ancient Greek word for 'great city', revived since 1957 by Jean Gottmann to describe the American urban complex stretching from Boston to Washington. It has been accepted as meaning huge urban regions formed by chains of metropolitan areas. Gottmann saw in it a new pattern in the organization of inhabited space, a vast and dense concentration due to the evolution of society towards white-collar and transactional work and to the gregarious nature of people seeking opportunity. Other megalopolitan regions have been described in Japan, in north-west Europe, and along the Great Lakes. For further reading: J. Gottmann, *Megalopolis* (1961). J.G.

megastructure. In ARCHITECTURE, a large, multi-storey framework, normally in dense urban situations, which would embrace different kinds of activities and allow different spaces to take on a variety of forms, changing while the megastructure remained. Such notions were put forward in the 1960s by the Archigram Group in England, by Yona Friedman in France, and by the Metabolist Group in Japan. They are an enlargement and extension of Le Corbusier's original project of 1947–48 for the *Unité d'Habitation* at Marseilles where 'bottles' (dwellings) were to fit within a 'bin' (structural framework). Their enormous financial cost and likely high social cost have so far prevented any from being built. M.BR.

Meissner effect, see under STRINGS.

melancholia, see DEPRESSION (2).

membrane structures. Generally very thin-skinned flexible structures supported by masts or props and stabilized by cables. Guyed tents and boat sails are a crude form of this kind of structure which can now achieve remarkable spans and very dramatic configurations. In recent years, when membrane structures have become the subject of detailed COMPUTER analysis, they have almost exclusively been made from new-technology fabrics such as coated glass fibre. Flexible Teflon coatings have provided an answer to the problem of cleaning. The term also embraces PNEUMATIC STRUCTURES where the structural support is a combination of pressurized air and the shape of the enclosing structure. Because membrane structures are inherently flexible they are most commonly used only as roofing, detached from whatever enclosing structure is to be found underneath. S.L.

meme. A cultural unit of replication, passed between individuals and across generations. Examples include songs and recipes. The term was proposed by Richard Dawkins (1941–), who derived it from the Greek 'mimeme', meaning 'likeness'. The similarity to the term GENE is intentional. Like a gene, a meme can 'mutate' (see MUTATION), e.g. through accidental miscommunication or learning errors. However, it need not have any direct genetic basis (see GENETICS/GENOMICS). Given a brain capable of learning and complex communication, memes can exist as a consequence. Although the concept is primarily applied to human culture, there are examples for other animals, such as the social transmission of foraging techniques in some birds, cetaceans and non-human primates. The analogy with genes is useful, but limited. The ORGANISM (in this case, the brain) can actively change the idea (meme) through invention, innovation, or even malice. It is also an imperfect measure of cultural evolution, which depends on forces in addition to imitation, such as reason and synthesis. However, Dawkins himself states that his purpose was to 'cut the gene down to size' and not to 'sculpt a grand theory of human culture'. A.R.H.

memory.
(1) The ability of the mind to store and recall previous thoughts and experiences. Very little of human experience – from our self-awareness to the ability to reason – would be possible without our ability to remember. Conversely, it is thought that the tendency of the mind to selectively forget information that does not seem important is equally useful, in freeing us to concentrate on more essential matters. Opinion is divided on the mechanisms of memory: some believe that there is a single store of data into which everything is placed; but most believe that there are different systems, such as *short-term memory*, which retains information for only a few seconds, and *long-term memory*, which retains information for perhaps many years. Evidence for the latter theory is provided by victims of certain kinds of brain damage or amnesia, who are capable of short-term memory but have difficulties in either creating or retrieving long-term memories. Various methods have been devised to improve long-term memory, the most well known being 'mnemonics', which are rules for encoding new information into a form more easily remembered. A.A.L.

(2) Scholars in a number of disciplines are becoming increasingly interested in the process by which different cultures shape the memories of their members, or their views of the past, which can be seen as a kind of collective memory. A pioneer in this field was the French sociologist Maurice Halbwachs, author of *Les cadres sociaux de la mémoire* (1925). Since his day anthropologists and historians have been concerning themselves with the reliability of ORAL TRADITION, while social psychologists and literary critics have analysed the manner in which experience is stereotyped and mythologized as it is recalled. Most recently, historians have become interested in the ways in which societies commemorate the past, studying festivals, museums, war memorials, STATUS, etc., as so many forms of institutionalized collective memory with a crucial part to play in the formation of social identity (national, ethnic, religious, professional, etc.). Like the opposition between 'genuine' and 'invented' tradition, the contrast between spontaneous 'memory' and self-conscious REPRESENTATION now appears increasingly difficult to maintain. P.B.

Mendel's laws. In GENETICS, the laws of inheritance, specifically for inheritance in DIPLOID organisms in the absence of LINKAGE. Mendel did not himself formulate his discovery (1865) in one or a series of laws, but today his findings are often summed up in two laws: of SEGREGATION, by which a hybrid or *heterozygote* transmits unchanged to each gamete one or other of the two factors in respect of which its parental gametes differed; and of *independent assortment*, according to which factors concerned with different characteristics are recombined at random in the gametes. Mendel's laws are now known to follow from the way in which CHROMOSOMES and therefore genetic factors are apportioned to gametes and therefore the next generation. In bisexual organisms the chromosomes are present in pairs (in man, 23 pairs); within each pair one member has derived from each parent. In the formation of gametes these pairs are separated, and each gamete contains only one chromosome from each pair (e.g. a human gamete contains 23 instead of 46 chromosomes). Since segregation is entirely random, the chromosomes in any gamete may be anything from 100 per cent paternally derived to 100 per cent maternally derived. The number of gametes bearing a preponderance of paternally derived chromosomes must, however, be equal to the number bearing a preponderance of maternally derived chromosomes. For further reading: C. Stern and E. R. Sherwood (eds), *The Origin of Genetics* (1966). J.M.S.; P.M.

Mendelism. The branch of GENETICS dealing with the SEGREGATION of characters in sexual crosses of DIPLOID organisms; by extension, the theory of heredity deriving originally from the work of Gregor Mendel (1865). See also MENDEL'S LAWS. J.M.S.

Mensheviks. Between 1903 and 1917, a political faction of the Russian Social Democratic Workers' Party; it constituted itself as a political party in August 1917. After the split between the Mensheviks and the Bolsheviks (for the origin of the names see BOLSHEVISM) a formal reunion occurred in 1906, but the struggle for the domination of the RSDWP continued. The Mensheviks, of whom the most important were Plekhanov, Axelrod and Martov, took the orthodox MARXIST view of Russia's development and rejected Lenin's view of the role of the Party (see LENINISM). The split was further complicated by issues such as underground versus legal forms of struggle, national defence versus revolutionary defeatism (see REVOLUTION), etc., which caused divisions among the Mensheviks themselves. Broadly speaking, however, the Mensheviks were 'softer' than the Bolsheviks and more ready to collaborate with other parties, including non-SOCIALIST ones, in the struggle for a democratic constitution (see DEMOCRACY) and against Czarist autocracy. Following the February 1917 revolution, the Mensheviks had a majority in most SOVIETS. After the Bolsheviks' seizure of power in October 1917, the Mensheviks tried to become a legal opposition, but the dissolution of the Constituent Assembly was followed by repressive measures against their party, culminating in its suppression in 1922. In 1931 Stalin mounted a SHOW TRIAL against the Mensheviks in Moscow (only one of the accused was in fact a Menshevik). The Party maintained its existence abroad, and its leaders, such as F. I. Dan and R. A. Abramovich, continued until the late 1960s to publish commentaries on Soviet developments in the monthly *Sotsialisticheskiy Vestnik* (*Socialist Courier*). For further reading: A. Ascher (ed.), *The Mensheviks in the Russian Revolution* (1976). L.L.

mental age. The level of mental development in a child, expressed in years and months, based on age norms for mental tests (see MENTAL TESTING) designed to measure INTELLIGENCE. See also LEARNING DISABILITY. H.L.

mental deficiency, see under LEARNING DISABILITY.

mental handicap, see under LEARNING DISABILITY.

mental retardation. No longer a politically correct term (see POLITICAL CORRECTNESS), but one that has been used for most of the 20th century to describe those individuals placed, in respect of cognitive attainments, in the bottom 2–3 per cent of their age-group. Some 'mental retardates', however, particularly borderline cases, are so classified more on the basis of social than cognitive competence. Indeed, it has been suggested that in the British Mental Deficiency Act of 1913 (superseded in 1958) mental deficiency was defined almost exclusively in terms of social competence.

The study of 'idiots' goes back to antiquity. Over the last few centuries emergent PSYCHIATRY and PSYCHOLOGY came to distinguish clearly between the disturbed and the defective, and particular attention was vested in so-called 'idiot boys' or 'wild boys', feral children, whose educability could be put experimentally to the test. Mass education brought the problem of retardation to public attention in the late 19th century. For most of the 20th century the major contribution of psychologists to the scientific study of mental retardation has been in the area of techniques of cognitive assessment, and, to a lesser extent, the assessment of social and emotional maturity. In the first decade of this century, A. Binet and T. Simon in Paris developed a MENTAL AGE scale for the more systematic appraisal of judgement and reasoning in schoolchildren. Adapted and expanded forms of this scale, notably L. M. Terman's 1916 revision (known as the *Stanford-Binet test* – a later version being known as the *Terman-Merrill revision*), allied with the CONCEPT of INTELLIGENCE and 'innate mental ability' (C. Burt, 1921), served to condemn children and adults thus 'diagnosed' to society's passive acceptance of their so-called condition. The establishment of special schools (see SPECIAL EDUCATION) and subnormality hospitals had the effect of maintaining and supporting professional and public assumptions, since the inmates not only conformed to expectations but exceeded them in that there was evidence of 'deterioration'.

In educational terms, retarded children were until comparatively recently distinguished in terms of whether they were 'educable' or merely 'trainable'. In Britain, this was a crucial distinction until 1971, since those considered 'ineducable' were excluded from the educational system. For these children the distinction was based mainly on the results of an intelligence test (see MENTAL TESTING), the approximate borderline being an IQ of 50. Children in the IQ category of approximately 50–70 were considered educationally subnormal, a term which now applies to all retarded children; in the USA a distinction is still made between 'educable' and 'trainable' mental retardates, although changes in thinking and educational practice have blurred the division.

Important changes in psychological thinking and practice with regard to mental retardation have become increasingly apparent since the early 1950s – although the implications of new findings, and, more importantly, new ways of thinking, have yet to be absorbed by the relevant professions, let alone society at large. In Britain, pioneer work was done by A. D. B. Clarke (1953) at the Manor Hospital in Surrey; he demonstrated the effectiveness of task analysis and training schedules in teaching adult retardates quite complex skills. Although intelligence testing remains an active process (the fourth revision of the Stanford-Binet Intelligence Scale was published as recently as 1985), an educational revolution has overtaken assumptions about what IQ implies. There is now a large body of empirical evidence which demonstrates that low IQ is not necessarily a barrier to learning of 'academic' skills such as literacy and numeracy if systematic instruction is given. Gillham (1986) suggests that mental handicap should be construed as a function of the degree of dependence on instruction. Helping the mentally handicapped to acquire skills typical of the population at large is part of the wider process of normalization. The recognition of special needs does not imply different goals for the handicapped. For further reading: S. A. Richardson, *Twenty-Two Years: Causes and Consequences of Mental Retardation* (1996).

W.E.C.G.; R.P.

mental testing. The measurement, by means of reliable and validated tests, of mental differences between individuals or groups, or the different responses of the same individuals on separate occasions. The tests can be used clinically, as an aid to psychological diagnosis, and vocationally to help in appropriate work placement. Assessment by means of mental testing is used not only by psychologists, doctors, paramedical professionals, teachers and speech therapists, but also increasingly in the industrial and military fields in order to establish and select criteria of competency for particular tasks. All mental testing involves the interpretation of information about a person and his situation, and the prediction of his behaviour in new situations.

Mental testing may take many forms. *Analogy tests*, which involve the form of verbal reasoning 'A is to B as C is to D', are most commonly used in the assessment of INTELLIGENCE. *Aptitude tests* are designed to measure particular skills possessed by the subject, in order to predict what he might attain with specialized training. *Educational tests* are used to assess basic skills such as reading, arithmetic, spelling, and language comprehension. *Performance tests* measure skill in arranging or otherwise manipulating material (e.g. block designs, mazes) which is visually and spatially presented. *Personality tests* may be *unstructured* as in *story-* or *sentence-completion* (see also RORSCHACH TEST), or structured as in the *Eysenck Personality Inventory*, in which statements about feelings and ideas are presented to the subject for sorting or ticking; his responses can be interpreted to provide insight into his EMOTIONS, and his personal and social relationships.

Mental testing began with the work of A. Binet in 1905. It has been developed by Wechsler, Spearman, Cattell, Thurstone, and many others. Today it is attacked on social and political grounds: on the one hand by those (e.g. Szasz) who fear the misuse of the *results* by an arbitrary authority (such as the state or an institution) or a malignant individual, and on the other by those, mostly egalitarians (see EGALITARIANISM), who believe that the whole CONCEPT of mental testing is contaminated with unacceptable principles (see, e.g., ÉLITE; MERITOCRACY; RACE). For further reading: P. Mittler (ed.),

The Psychological Assessment of Mental and Physical Handicaps (1978). M.BE.

mentalese. In LINGUISTICS, the concepts, and combinations of concepts, postulated as a 'language of thought' (LOT), differing in various ways from the GRAMMAR of natural language. A thought, in this context, is conceived as an intentional state of mind representing something about the world, including the various beliefs, hopes and other PROPOSITIONAL ATTITUDES held by the thinker. The approach is of special relevance in COMPUTATIONAL LINGUISTICS, where mental processes can be modelled as sequences of mental states and transitions. For further reading: S. Pinker, *The Language Instinct* (1994). D.C.

mentalism. The doctrine which holds that mental states and processes exist independently of their manifestations in behaviour and can explain behaviour. It is thus opposed to BEHAVIOURISM and to the application of the latter known as SOCIAL BEHAVIOURISM. Its best-known proponent is A. N. Chomsky (1928–). For further reading: J. A. Fodor, *The Language of Thought* (1975). A.S.

mentalities, history of (*mentalités collectives*), see HISTORY OF MENTALITIES.

mercantilism. A school of economic thought that arose in the 16th and 17th centuries and was interested in the relation between a nation's wealth, primarily measured by its reserves of gold and silver, and the balance of foreign trade. It was believed that the STATE was powerful and should intervene to discourage imports, through imposition of tariffs and other measures, and encourage exports through providing subsidies. A surplus on the balance of foreign trade would lead to a net inflow of precious metals, either directly or because of the relation between these metals and money. This inflow would, it was argued, increase the nation's wealth. In 1776, Adam Smith conducted a largely successful attack on mercantilism (see CLASSICAL ECONOMIC THEORY). Most modern economists disagree with mercantilism, but such ideas have often reappeared, e.g. in the Great Depression, and underlie some of the calls for restrictions on imports and more incentives for exports (see PROTECTIONISM and NEO-MERCANTILISM). For further reading: W. E. Kuhn, *The Evolution of Economic Thought* (1970). R.L.; J.P.

MERCOSUR. Mercado Común del Sur, the South American Common Market, has its origins in the Treaty of Asunción signed by Argentina, Brazil, Paraguay and Uruguay in March 1991. Customs tariffs between the four countries were eliminated and a common external tariff introduced in January 1995. MERCOSUR is today the most important trading bloc in South America and the world's fourth-largest economic group. The four member states, led by Brazil – the largest economy in South America – are seeking to enlarge and deepen the CUSTOMS UNION, as well as establish a South American free trade area (SAFTA), partly to strengthen their negotiating position in talks with the US over a FTAA (see FREE TRADE AREA OF THE AMERICAS) to be established by 2005. A more powerful MERCOSUR would also strengthen Brazil's regional superpower status in the face of competition from the US. For further reading: M. R. Soares de Lima, *Brazil's Response to New Regionalism* (1996). M.A.P.

mercury poisoning, see under MINAMATA DISEASE.

mereology. In PHILOSOPHY, the theory of part-whole relationships, prompted by such questions as 'is a whole something more than the sum of its parts, or not?' Answers depend upon what kinds of entity the whole and its parts are. The chief puzzle is that many wholes are indeed something more than the sum of their parts, in that they have properties the nature of which is not deducible from knowledge of the parts alone; and this requires explanation. A.C.G.

merger. The coming together of two or more firms to form one new firm (see FIRM, THEORIES OF). The term is often used to encompass *takeovers*, where one firm acquires another firm. Mergers can have harmful effects in that they can increase MONOPOLY power, which is used to restrict output and raise prices. A beneficial effect of mergers is that they may give rise to ECONOMIES OF SCALE. However, such effects are likely to be economies in management, planning, RESEARCH AND DEVELOPMENT and MARKETING, as the existing CAPITAL equipment of the merging firms may not be capable of being restructured to give economies in actual production. Larger firms may find it easier to carry the risk and costs of research and development. Thus, they may invest more in R&D. However, the decrease in COMPETITION resulting from a merger may reduce the incentive to produce inventions and innovations. Most countries operate a mergers policy to deter and prevent those mergers that are regarded, on balance, as harmful. Mergers can be *horizontal*, between firms in the same industry; *vertical*, between firms at different stages of the production process; and *diversifying*, between firms in different industries (see CONGLOMERATE). For further reading: M. C. Sawyer, *The Economics of Firms and Industries* (1981). J.P.

meritocracy. A word coined by Michael Young (*The Rise of the Meritocracy*, 1958) for government by those regarded as possessing merit; merit is equated with INTELLIGENCE-plus-effort, its possessors are identified at an early age and selected for an appropriate intensive education, and there is an obsession with QUANTIFICATION, test-scoring and qualifications. Egalitarians (see EGALITARIANISM) often apply the word to any élitist (see ÉLITE) system of education or government, without necessarily attributing to it the particular grisly features or ultimately self-destroying character of Young's apocalyptic vision. O.S.

Mertonian thesis, the. The MARXIST claim that CONSCIOUSNESS is determined by social being has defined the terms of debate for the sociology of knowledge (see KNOWLEDGE, SOCIOLOGY OF) during this century. Against Marx, Max Weber (see WEBERIAN) contended that ideas could be seen as shaping economic structures no less than the other way around. Specifically, PROTESTANTISM was a crucial factor in the growth of the 'spirit of CAPITALISM'. Weber's analysis was taken up, in the field of the history of science, by the American sociologist R. K. Merton (1910–), who contended that the scientific movement of the 17th century was a response not primarily to socio-economic need but to the stimulus of Protestant THEOLOGY. CALVINISM and Puritanism in particular would lead believers to reject the dead-weight of authority and rely on personal experience and experiment. The Calvinist VOLUNTARIST conception of God would encourage scientists to seek His ways in nature, and would foster the notion of a scientific 'calling', encouraging utilitarian (see UTILITARIANISM) ideas of the application of scientific knowledge for human improvement, not just personal glory. Merton postulated a high statistical connection between Protestants and scientists in the 17th century. In their specific form, Merton's hypotheses have hardly stood the test of time, but his work has stimulated a lasting interest in the links between modern science and RELIGION. For further reading: R. K. Merton, *Science, Technology and Society in Seventeenth Century England* (1930; 1970). R.P.

Merz. Name given by the painter, poet and typographer Kurt Schwitters (1887–1948) to his one-man DADA splinter movement in Hanover in the 1920s. Recalling the French term *merde* and the German *ausmerzen* (to extirpate), it supposedly derived from a fragment of the word *Kommerz* (commerce) on one of his COLLAGES of 1919. Thereafter he produced *Merz* 'pictures' (assemblages of rubbish), a magazine *Merz* (1923–32), to which Lissitzky, van Doesburg and Hans Arp all contributed, *Merz* poems, *Merz* evenings with performances of his phonetic poem *Lautgedichte*, three *Merzbaus* (or environmental sculptures; see ENVIRONMENT), a *Merz* stage, a new alphabet or *Systemschrift*, rubber-stamp pictures (*Stempelbilder*), and some virtually concrete 'picture poems' or *Bildgedichte* (see CONCRETE POETRY). All these shared in the revival of Dada in the 1950s. For further reading: W. Schmalenbach, *Kurt Schwitters* (1970). J.W.

mesomorph, see under PERSONALITY TYPES.

meson. A class of ELEMENTARY PARTICLE. Mesons are exchanged during the STRONG INTERACTION of NUCLEONS, and provide the 'glue' holding the atomic NUCLEUS together against the mutual repulsion of the PROTONS in it. This behaviour resembles that of ELECTRONS whose exchange forces hold molecules together, but mesons are unstable, and decay in less than a ten-millionth of a second into electrons, NEUTRINOS and GAMMA RAYS. Mesons have masses ranging from 100 to 500 times that of the electron, and may occur with positive, negative or zero electric charge. M.V.B.

messenger RNA, see under NUCLEIC ACID.

messianism. Belief in the salvation of mankind – or, more often, of the particular group which holds the belief – through the appearance of an individual saviour or redeemer. The word is derived from the Hebrew Messiah, a king of the line of David, who was to deliver the Jewish people from bondage and restore the golden age. The adjective *messianic* is frequently used to describe thinkers who (like Marx) foretell with prophetic power that human history is predestined to lead up to an apocalyptic dénouement in which the contradictions and injustices of the present order will be swept away and Utopia, the New Jerusalem, the classless society, established. See also MILLENARIANISM; UTOPIANISM. For further reading: J. L. Talmon, *Political Messianism: the Romantic Phase* (1960). A.L.C.B.

metagrammar. In LINGUISTICS, some linguists use this term to refer to a GENERATIVE GRAMMAR which contains a set of *metarules*, i.e. rules which define the properties of other rules on the basis of information already present in the grammar. D.C.

metahistory. A synonym for the philosophy of history, in its double sense of reflection on the pattern of the past and the methods of historians. More recently, however, the term has been used by Northrop Frye and Hayden White to refer to the narrative structure of histories, which according to them are of four kinds, tragi-comic, tragic, romantic and satirical, whether the writers are aware that they have 'emplotted' their history in this way or not. For further reading: H. White, *Metahistory* (1973). P.B.

metalanguage. In LINGUISTICS, any technical language devised to describe the properties of language. D.C.

metallurgy. The branch of science and TECHNOLOGY which deals with metals and their alloys. Its existence as a distinct field of study (though it draws heavily on PHYSICS and CHEMISTRY) illustrates the importance of metals (particularly steel, aluminium and copper) in everyday life. It is concerned with the extraction of metals from their ores; with the understanding of their properties in terms of electronic and crystalline structure (see CRYSTALLOGRAPHY); with devising new alloys or new methods of treatment to meet particular needs. Metallurgy grew up as a practical, nearly empirical technology but is nowadays given academic respectability as a branch of MATERIALS SCIENCE. For further reading: A. C. Street and W. O. Alexander, *Metals in the Service of Man* (1976). B.F.

metamathematics. The logical investigation (see LOGIC) of the properties of axiomatically formulated mathematical systems (see AXIOMATICS), introduced by David Hilbert (1862–1943) and associated by him with a FORMALIST interpretation of the nature of MATHEMATICS. It is concerned to establish the consistency, independence and completeness of the axioms (see AXIOMATICS) of formalized deductive systems, that is the compatibility of the axioms with each other, the impossibility of deducing any one of them from the rest, and the deducibility from them of all the TRUTHS expressible in the vocabulary of the system. GÖDEL's theorem proves the incompletability of any system that contains arithmetic. A.Q.

metaphor. It was Roman Jakobson who, in a major essay published in 1956, made a seminal distinction between metaphor and *metonymy*. Jakobson was concerned primarily with a study of aphasia (see NEUROPSYCHOLOGY), and distinguished two types of aphasia, one whose 'major deficiency lies in selection or substitution, with relative stability of combination and contexture'; and the other whose major deficiency lies in 'combination and contexture, with relative retention of normal selection and substitution'. It seemed to Jakobson that this led to a conclusion about language itself, and that metaphor and metonymy are actually *opposed*, because they are generated from antithetical principles. Metaphor belongs, it would seem, to the selection axis of language, allowing of the possibility of *substitution*. Metonymy, however, belongs to the combination axis of language, allowing for the perception of *contexture*. These oppositions correspond to the distinctions made by Saussure between the paradigmatic and the SYNTAGMATIC. Jakobson demonstrates the difference between the two types of thought-process by invoking literature, art and film. Lyrical song, Romantic (see ROMANTICISM) and SYMBOLIST poetry and the films of Charlie Chaplin, e.g., clearly operate according to the principle of metaphor, while the REALIST novel, such as Tolstoy's, demonstrates the metonymic principle of selection in full activity, along with the associated trope of synecdoche, as do the films of D. W. Griffith. The principle that the two forms of language are actually opposed both in principle and in origin had a galvanizing effect upon French STRUCTURALISM. Lévi-Strauss took Jakobson's distinction as one of the bases of his own binary METHODOLOGY, and Lacan, Barthes and the writers round *Tel Quel* all made great play with it. For further reading: R. Jakobson and M. Halle, *Fundamentals of Language* (1956). R.PO.

metaphysical painting (*pittura metafisica*). An Italian movement so named by the artists Giorgio de Chirico and Carlo Carrà at Ferrara in World War I, and later joined by Giorgio Morandi. The mysterious, inhuman calmness of their pictures of empty city spaces, tailor's dummies, and banal 'ordinary things' – of which Chirico's dated largely from before the war – was influential in the development of pictorial SURREALISM, as well as having a muted echo in German MAGIC REALISM. Itself largely a reaction against FUTURISM and a re-evocation of Giotto and other Florentine masters, the movement largely petered out after about 1920, as both Chirico and Carrà became increasingly traditionalist. J.W.

metaphysics. The investigation of the world, or of what really exists, generally by means of rational argument rather than by direct or mystical intuition. It may be either *transcendent* (see TRANSCENDENCE), in that it holds that what really exists lies beyond the reach of ordinary experience (as in the picture of the world supplied by supernatural RELIGION), or *immanent*, in that it takes reality to consist exclusively of the objects of experience. Kant and the LOGICAL POSITIVISTS both denied the legitimacy of transcendent metaphysics, Kant on the ground that the *a priori* elements in thought (see A POSTERIORI, A PRIORI) yield knowledge only if applied to the data of experience, the logical positivists on the ground that sentences ostensibly about the world are not even significant unless susceptible of empirical VERIFICATION. The primary component of metaphysics is ONTOLOGY, in which metaphysicians ascribe existence to, or withhold it from, three major classes of things: (1) the concrete occupants of space and time, (2) minds and their states, conceived in the manner of DUALISM as in time but not space, and (3) abstract entities or UNIVERSALS. A further ontological issue is the number of real existences there are of the preferred kind: is there just one real SUBSTANCE, as MONISTS like Spinoza and Hegel believe, or many? Metaphysicians also propound theories about the overall structure of the world. Is it a mechanical or deterministic system or does it contain chance events or the causally inexplicable emergence of novelty? For further reading: K. Campbell, *Metaphysics* (1976); M. Loux, *Metaphysics: A Contemporary Introduction* (1998). A.Q.

metapsychology. Considerations about PSYCHOLOGY with regard to its definition, purposes, PRESUPPOSITIONS, METHODOLOGY and limitations, its status as a contribution to knowledge, and its relations to other disciplines. I.M.L.H.

metastable, see under EQUILIBRIUM.

metastases, see under CANCER.

metasystem. A system 'over and beyond' a system of lower logical order, and therefore capable of deciding propositions (see PROPOSITION, TYPES OF), discussing criteria (see CRITERION), or exercising REGULATION (3) for systems that are themselves logically incapable of such decisions, such discussions, or of *self*-regulation. This is a CONCEPT used in CYBERNETICS and the SYSTEMS approach, and derives from theoretical MATHEMATICS. The emphasis is on *logical* order, not on 'seniority' in the sense of command. For example, one may observe a system in which playing-cards are dealt to a group of people who proceed to dispose of them according to a set of fixed rules which can be ascertained, and which completely determine winners and losers. Over and beyond this system is a metasystem which is expressed in entirely different terms: money. If the observer failed to understand the metasystem he would not appreciate what the game of poker is actually about. See also ALGEDONIC. S.BE.

metatheory. The set of assumptions presupposed (see PRESUPPOSITION) by any more or less formalized body of assertions, in particular the CONCEPTS implied by the vocabulary in which it is expressed and the rules of INFERENCE by means of which one assertion in the system is derived from another. The idea is a generalization of that involved in the selection of features of deductive systems for investigation that is characteristic of AXIOMATICS or METAMATHEMATICS. A.Q.

method, the. A system of training and rehearsal for actors which bases a performance upon inner emotional experience, discovered largely through the medium of improvisation, rather than upon the teaching or transmission of technical expertise. Based on the theory and practice of Konstantin Stanislavsky (1863–1938) at the Moscow Arts Theatre, it was developed by the American director Lee Strasberg who, in 1947, with Cheryl Crawford and Elia Kazan, founded the *Actors' Studio* in New York as a partial successor to the GROUP THEATRE. For some 15 years the Studio had a profound influence upon American film and theatre, in the work of actors including Marlon Brando, James Dean and Paul Newman. For further reading: R. H. Hethmon (ed.), *Strasberg at the Actors' Studio* (1966). M.A.

Methodism. A Christian denomination active throughout the English-speaking world, with about 26 million adherents. Founded by John Wesley (1707–91), it was originally so nicknamed because of its claim to be methodical in observing the devotional requirements of ANGLICANISM, but was organized as a virtually independent Protestant (see PROTESTANTISM) Church in Wesley's lifetime. It has stressed its warm fellowship, its strict morality, its interest in social problems, and its keen evangelism (see EVANGELICAL). It is well organized – in the USA under bishops. Theologically it is optimistic, believing that all men can be saved, can know that they are saved, and can reach moral perfection, but it has been criticized for a lack of sophistication and of intellectual liveliness. Recently it has been much influenced by the ECUMENICAL MOVEMENT for Christian reunion. For further reading: R. E. Davies, *Methodism* (1963). D.L.E.

methodological individualism and **methodological holism.** Two contrasted approaches to the METHODOLOGY of the SOCIAL SCIENCES. They differ in their answers to such questions as the following: Is it necessary, or even relevant, to mention the BELIEFS, attitudes, decisions or actions of individual people in attempting to describe and explain social, political or economic phenomena? Is it necessary to postulate the existence of SOCIAL WHOLES which have purposes or functions or needs, or which cause events to occur; or are all mentions of such things really abbreviated references to the individual persons in the society concerned (e.g. can a nation or committee be said to have a mind of its own?)? Do SOCIAL STRUCTURES and social processes influence the attitudes, beliefs, decisions, etc. of individuals, or are all such influences to be explained simply in terms of person-to-person interaction? Is the study of society necessarily based on the study of its members, or is there some other means of observing or measuring social entities, like the will of the nation, perhaps through the study of large-scale historical processes?

In answering such questions, *methodological individualists* tend to discount the importance or scientific status of social wholes, while *methodological holists* tend to discount the influence of individuals on social phenomena. It can be argued that the whole dispute is as futile as a dispute between engineers as to whether what is important in a building or mechanism is its structure or the materials or components used. Clearly both are important, but in different ways. See also HOLISM. For further reading: A. Ryan, *The Philosophy of the Social Sciences* (1971). A.S.

methodology. In the narrowest sense, the study or description of the methods or procedures used in some activity. The word is normally used in a wider sense to include a general investigation of the aims, CONCEPTS

and principles of reasoning of some discipline, and the relationships between its subdisciplines. Thus the methodology of science includes attempts to analyse and criticize its aims, its main concepts (e.g. EXPLANATION, CAUSALITY, *experiment*, *probable*), the methods used to achieve these aims, the subdivision of science into various branches, the relations between these branches (see REDUCTION), and so on. Some scientists use the word merely as a more impressive-sounding synonym for method. For further reading: K. R. Popper, *The Logic of Scientific Discovery* (1968).
A.S.

metonymy, see under METAPHOR.

metrology. The precise establishment and comparison of the standard units of measurement. See also ATOMIC CLOCK; SI UNITS.
M.V.B.

metropolis. A Greek word for mother-city which has long meant the main city or largest centre of activity in a region or country. With modern URBANIZATION many cities grew very big, while suburbs and SATELLITE TOWNS sprawled around them. Metropolitan regions are thus formed around many large centres. The use of the term has spread with the phenomenon. 'Metropolitan' government, police, transport, encompassing the metropolis and the region in its orbit, are common concepts, while the term *metropolitanization* has been used to describe certain trends in the USA and other countries where the greater part of the population live in metropolitan areas. The term is also used in the sense of a city recognized as a major market for a certain category of goods or services. For further reading: S. R. Miles (ed.), *Metropolitan Problems* (1970).
J.G.

***mezzo-giorno*.** An economically underdeveloped area (see UNDERDEVELOPMENT) comprising the southern Italian mainland regions of Abruzzi, Molise, Campania, Puglia, Basilicata and Calabria, together with the islands Sicily and Sardinia. The Italian term *mezzo-giorno* means 'midday', and southern Italy is so called because of the intensity of the midday sun. Per capita income in the *mezzo-giorno* lags behind that of northern Italy. Agriculture is the main form of employment; olive oil, fruit and vegetables are the main crops. ECONOMIC DEVELOPMENT programmes for the *mezzo-giorno* are assisted by the European Investment Bank and the Italian government. Economic planners have favoured bringing heavy industries (iron, steel, petrochemicals, car manufacture) into the region.
S.M.

MGB, see under KGB.

MHD, see MAGNETOHYDRODYNAMICS.

MI (Military Intelligence). The gathering of information, by clandestine as well as overt means, about the intentions of enemies or potential enemies and the means at their disposal to effect their intentions. In Britain MI has become in addition a cover name for the Security Service (MI5) and the Secret Intelligence Service (MI6), both civilian forces, the first operating purely on British territory and answerable on security problems through the Home Secretary to the Prime Minister, the other operating outside British territory and therefore answerable to the Foreign Secretary. Both intelligence services have found themselves at the centre of political rows in Britain, particularly when in 1986–87 the Thatcher government attempted to stop the publication of former MI5 officer Peter Wright's memoirs in a notorious court case in Australia. For further reading: P. Knightley, *The Second Oldest Profession* (1986).
D.C.W.; S.T.

Michelson-Morley experiment. It was believed in the late 19th century that the earth must be moving relative to the ETHER which was thought to support light waves; and that because the speed of light would be constant relative to the ether, its speed relative to the earth should vary with direction. In 1888 the American scientists Albert Michelson (1852–1931) and Edward Morley (1838–1923) tried to measure this difference in velocity for light travelling in different directions, but no effect could be detected. A large number of subsequent, more accurate experiments all confirmed this result, except for that of Miller in 1924, who claimed to detect a tiny positive effect; but this was later shown to be due to an identifiable experimental error. It was concluded that the speed of light in a vacuum is independent of the relative motion of source and observer, and this result became one of the postulates of RELATIVITY theory. M.V.B.

microbiology. The discipline concerned with bacteria and viruses in their wider aspects which grew up when it came to be realized, during the past 20 or 30 years, that BACTERIOLOGY and VIROLOGY were important not merely for their own sakes, but also because they might provide MODELS of such phenomena occurring in higher organisms as heredity (see GENETICS/GENOMICS), development and DIFFERENTIATION. P.M.

microchemistry. The branch of CHEMISTRY which deals with the manipulation and estimation of chemical substances in minute quantities. Microanalytical techniques typically allow one ten-thousandth of a gram of material to be determined with an accuracy of 1 or 2 per cent. B.F.

microclimatology. The branch of CLIMATOLOGY concerned with small-scale atmospheric phenomena near the surface of the earth. For further reading: R. Geiger, tr. from 4th German ed., *The Climate Near the Ground* (1965). P.H.

microeconomics, see under ECONOMICS.

microenterprises. Small (often one- or two-person) business firms. THIRD-WORLD poor and small enterprises rarely succeed in business, as they lack money for equipment and working CAPITAL. Moreover, traditional government credit for small business has been limited. People with few assets can rarely raise collateral, which even public agencies require.

Group lending can provide credit for the poor. Under such schemes, similar to that of the Grameen Bank of Bangladesh (1983), peer borrowing groups of five or so people with joint liability approve loans to other members as a substitute for the bank's screening. The group discusses all loan requests, scrutinizes the borrower's investment plan and creditworthiness, and saves an established percentage of the loan. Failure to repay by any member jeopardizes the group's access to future credit. Banks providing credit for microenterprises have sprung up in South Asia, Latin America and the United States, often replicating or modifying the Grameen model. For further reading: E. W. Nafziger, *The Economics of Developing Countries* (1997). E.W.N.

microhistory. This term, first employed in Italian, is coming into use to describe a cluster of books on social and cultural history which attempt to see the world in a grain of sand and concentrate on a small community (like the village of Montaillou in Languedoc, studied by Emmanuel Le Roy Ladurie) or even an individual (like Menocchio Scandella, the miller hero of Carlo Ginzburg's *The Cheese and the Worms*, 1980), in an attempt to reconstitute the experience of life in the past, which according to these scholars is lacking in quantitative 'macrohistorical' studies. The approach has become fashionable, is producing diminishing intellectual returns and sometimes degenerates into anecdote. However, at its best the microhistorical method can reveal the weaknesses and challenge the conclusions of traditional SOCIAL HISTORY and CULTURAL HISTORY. How to link the two approaches is the current problem. For further reading: E. Le Roy Ladurie, *Montaillou* (1975; tr. 1978). P.B.

microlinguistics. A term used by some linguists (see LINGUISTICS) for the study of the phonological and morphological LEVELS (sense 1) of language; but also used in a general sense for any analysis or point of view which concentrates on describing the details of linguistic behaviour as against general trends or patterns (to which the term *macrolinguistics* is sometimes applied). D.C.

micronutrients, see TRACE ELEMENT.

microregion, see under REGIONALISM.

microsome. A small cellular particle consisting mainly of ribonucleoprotein, identified in the 1930s by Albert Claude using the ultracentrifuge (see SEDIMENTATION). For a long time its real existence was in doubt, but now it is thought that microsomes represent a cellular element known as *ribosomes*. See also CYTOLOGY; NUCLEIC ACID. P.M.

microstructure, see under EXCHANGE MODELS.

microsurgery, see under SURGERY.

microteaching. A technique in the training of teachers first used at Stanford University in the USA in 1960. A teacher takes a specially constructed lesson lasting from, say, 10 to 30 minutes with a class of about 5–10 pupils. The lesson is evaluated (under such headings as aims, content and vocabulary) by an observer, the pupils and the teacher; it is then reconstructed, represented and re-evaluated. Videotape is often used and the representation is given to a different group of pupils. For further reading: J. L. Olivero, *Microteaching* (1970). W.A.C.S.

microtone. A fraction of a tone smaller than a semitone. Normally in Western music the octave is divided into 12 equal parts or semitones. It has been argued that a division into 24 quarter-tones would provide greater variety; in 1907, the Italian composer Ferruccio Busoni suggested three divisions to a semitone, making a scale of 36 chromatic notes, while the Czech composer Alois Haba has experimented with sixth- and even twelfth-tones. From the point of view of sheer geographical distribution, microtonal music was, indeed, for centuries the predominant idiom. Chinese, Japanese, Indian, Polynesian, Greek, Arabic, Bulgarian, Hungarian and Andalusian music have this common factor. Yet attempts to introduce microtones into Western concert music have so far met with limited success. It is likely, however, that the infinite variability of pitch obtainable through electronics (see ELECTRONIC MUSIC) and the simultaneous breakaway from traditional tone-colours may hasten their acceptance. A.H.

microwaves. The shortest radio waves, with wavelengths less than about 30 cm and frequencies greater than 1,000 megahertz (1 hertz = 1 complete vibration cycle per second; 1 megahertz = 1 million hertz). Microwaves are generated by oscillating electric circuits or MASERS, and used in RADAR and TELECOMMUNICATION systems. M.V.B.

MIDAS (Missile Defence Alarm System), see under MISSILES.

middle class. Until recently there would have been little to distinguish this term from its Continental synonym, BOURGEOIS, although the English term was always less value-laden, carried less of the pejorative overtones that went with the borrowed foreign term. Increasingly in the 20th century, however, there has been a growth of distinctively middling ranks between the old middle class, the bourgeoisie proper, and the WORKING CLASS. As a result especially of the enormous expansion of private and public bureaucracies, there is now a white-collar salariat, a middle-level, middle-income 'service class' which differs markedly in outlook and prospects from the professional and proprietary middle class – better now thought of as decidedly *upper*-middle class. At the same time the new middle class is very different from the old petite bourgeoisie (see PETIT BOURGEOIS) or lower-middle class of small farmers, small businessmen and artisans. Since the new middle class currently amounts to over one-third of the employed population, and is likely to be about a half by the turn of the century, its attitudes and interests are bound to be increasingly represented in social and political life. What precisely these attitudes and interests are no one seems very sure of, and that includes the middle class itself; but it is already clear that neither the traditional RIGHT nor the traditional LEFT has much to offer it. The struggle for the soul, and the votes, of the middle class is likely to be central to the politics of the coming decades. For further reading: R. M. Glassman, *The New Middle Class and Democracy in Global Perspective* (1997). K.K.

Middle East Wars. Generated from 1948 to 1973 by hostility between Israel and the Arab states, complicated by the interests of the great powers. The wars of 1948–49 arose from Arab refusal to accept the creation of the state of Israel in May 1948. The Arab defeat left Israel with more territory than the UN partition plan for Palestine had recommended, and Jerusalem was divided between Israel and Jordan. The armistice lines which thus became Israeli borders invited Arab infiltration and made Israel strategically vulnerable. At the same time it was cut off from navigation to the south.

The SUEZ war, October–November 1956, originated because of President Nasser's NATIONALIZATION of the Suez Canal which the British government saw as a threat to their world power and the French to their imperial interests in Algeria. Israeli interest in securing the south by an occupation of Sinai produced a loosely jointed alliance and an invasion of Egypt, first by Israel, then by Britain and France under the pretext of a 'police action'. The war was a turning point for all participants. In Britain it was a *cause célèbre* because the government deceived Parliament as to the alliance with Israel; it confirmed the loss of British world power as the Suez action was opposed by the US. In France the Israeli alliance was uncontroversial but the eventual independence of Algeria was taken a step further (see ALGERIAN WAR OF INDEPENDENCE). Israel, under unique pressure from the US, withdrew from all occupied territory and abandoned war as a means of changing the BALANCE OF POWER until 1982. President Nasser won prestige in the Arab world as well as Egypt and was confirmed in his anti-IMPERIALIST Arab policies.

The complex origins of the Six-Day War (June 1967) can best be summarized as an attempt by Nasser to recoup the losses of the Yemen war and a faltering economy by challenging Israel and winning a limited political-military victory. Instead Israel responded to Egyptian moves, including the withdrawal of consent to the UN force in Sinai and a blockade of the straits of Aqaba, by a brilliant air strike which effectively decided the battle with Egypt. This was followed by the occupation of Sinai, and counter-attacks on Jordan and Syria, leaving Israel in occupation of the Sinai, the Gaza Strip, the West Bank and the Golan Heights. Possible Russian support for Egypt was held off by the US.

The October War (1973), known, from its timing, as the Yom Kippur War in Israel and the war of Ramadan in Egypt, was initiated by President Sadat in alliance with Syria and with the support of the Arab oil producers as part of a strategy to recover the Sinai. A successful penetration of the Israeli line on the Suez Canal was followed by an Israeli recovery. The Soviet Union and the US resupplied their clients, Egypt and Israel respectively, and US forces were put on full alert against possible direct Russian intervention. Arab use of the OIL WEAPON had no direct effect on the war but heightened US interest in the region. US Secretary of State Henry Kissinger's shuttle DIPLOMACY then led to disengagement agreements between Israel and Egypt and Israel and Syria. The October War was a prelude to the Egypt–Israel peace treaty of 1979. For further reading: P. Mansfield, *The Arabs* (1985); J. N. Westwood, *The History of the Middle East Wars* (1984). W.K.

middle range, theories of the. Term introduced by Robert K. Merton (1949) for theories, especially in SOCIOLOGY, which aim to integrate observed empirical regularities and specific hypotheses within a relatively limited problem-area – as opposed to either entirely *ad hoc* explanation or attempts at a quite general theory of SOCIAL ACTION or SOCIAL STRUCTURE as in, e.g., STRUCTURAL-FUNCTIONAL THEORY or CONFLICT THEORY. J.H.G.

mid-oceanic ridge, see under OCEANIC RIDGE.

mid-range, see under DISTRIBUTION.

migration. The interdisciplinary study of population redistribution in geographical SPACE, whose participants make changes in their residence that are intended to be permanent. On the map migrants often form 'streams' of relocating people, who simultaneously respond to 'push' factors that drive them out of their place of origin and 'pull' factors that attract them to their new destination. Perceived economic opportunities play a major role, but push and pull factors can also include political, cultural and environmental forces. Many classifications of population movements have been devised by geographers, demographers, historians and other scholars. Some of the common distinctions include international versus internal migrations and voluntary versus forced migrations. Substantial work has also been undertaken at the metropolitan scale, where much of the world's migration takes place as short-distance moves within or among urban neighbourhoods as upwardly mobile people seek better housing conditions as their economic circumstances improve. P.O.M.

migration rate. The net increase in a population due to MIGRATION (immigrants – emigrants) divided by the number of individuals in the same population. Demographers also refer to this quantity as the 'crude net migration rate'. J.R.W.

militancy, see under ACTIVISM (sense 2).

military-industrial complex. A phrase coined by speechwriters for President Eisenhower's farewell address to the American electorate in 1960, in which he warned of the growing influence on economic and foreign policy of the armaments industries and the military establishment, which shared a common interest in constantly growing defence budgets and a militaristic approach to international relations. The theme was surprisingly close to the thoughts of the American LEFT, who adopted the phrase with relish. It survives, denoting more elaborate arguments, in MARXIST and élitist critiques of American government. For further reading: P. Koistinen, *The Military-Industrial Complex: A Historical Perspective* (1980). S.R.

Military Intelligence, see MI.

militia movement. A loosely organized anti-government movement which surfaced in the US in the 1990s following the end of the COLD WAR. Today, militias – small armed groups that train for some unspecified future military action and who share anti-government, pro-gun and, in some instances, virulently racist and ANTISEMITIC views (see ANTISEMITISM) – are active in a majority of the 50 states, where they hold meetings, and on the INTERNET. The novel *The Turner Diaries* is considered to be the Bible of the movement. The book, which admiringly describes how armed GUERRILLAS spark a bloody race war in the US and opens with the destruction of FBI headquarters, was said to have inspired the April 1995 bombing of the federal building in Oklahoma City, which came two years to the day after the federal government's assault on the heavily armed members of the Branch Davidian SECT in Waco, Texas, who espoused an apocalyptic world-view. The militia movement has been associated with the antisemitic Christian Identity movement, but its most unifying belief may be opposition to GUN CONTROL. Movement supporters point to the Second Amendment of the US Constitution, which states that 'a well regulated Militia, being necessary to the security of a free State, the right of the people to keep and bear Arms, shall not be infringed'. R.K.H.

millenarianism or **millennialism.** The belief and practices of those who seek, by way of a religious and/or political movement, to secure a comprehensive, salvationary solution for social, personal and political predicaments. The term has been used by historians and social scientists as a comparative focus for the study of many movements in many parts of the world which have developed sectarian or messianic or salvationary programmes of social transformation (see, e.g., CARGO CULTS). There has been much controversy about the psychological or economic roots of such programmes, their links in specific cases with magical practices, and their utility for the diverse societies in which (or in relation to which) they have been promoted. The term originated – like the related term *chiliastic* – in the myth of Christ's return after 'a thousand years', but the idea has pre-Christian roots and is reflected in Jewish and Islamic thought. For further reading: N. Cohn, *The Pursuit of the Millennium* (1970). S.J.G.

mimicry. In BIOLOGY, similarity of form or behaviour of one SPECIES to another. For example, the viceroy butterfly, which is not poisonous to birds, is almost identical in appearance to the gold-and-black-coloured monarch butterfly, which is poisonous. The two species inhabit similar regions of the southern US. The viceroy gains protection from birds by mimicking the monarch. Cases of mimicry in which one species (the model) is poisonous and the other (the mimic) is not are called *Batesian mimicry*. In other cases, both species may be poisonous; these are called Müllerian mimicry. Other types of mimicry are also known. M.R.

Minamata disease. Poisoning caused by the consumption of fish contaminated with mercury dumped by a chemical company into Minamata Bay on the Japanese island of Kyushu in the 1950s (see POLLUTION). Although symptoms of central nervous system damage were first noticed in the mid-1950s, the link to mercury pollution was not officially acknowledged until the mid-1960s. W.G.R.

mind, philosophy of. The philosophical investigation of minds and their states and our knowledge of them. Starting traditionally from the DUALIST assumption that the mental is radically distinct in nature from the physical, it was principally concerned with the apparent causal relations between mind and body: PERCEPTION in one direction and the operations of the will in the other. More recently the main problem has been that of our knowledge of the minds of others, to whose states we have no direct, introspective access but which we must infer from their perceptible manifestations in speech and behaviour (see BEHAVIOURISM). A persistent problem is whether the mind is a substantial entity, distinct from the thoughts and experiences that make up its history, or whether it is simply the related totality of its experiences. Increasingly, biochemical research is demonstrating organic substrates for 'mental acts'. It remains unclear precisely how brain activity and CONSCIOUSNESS should be conceptually related. A connected issue is that of personal identity. Are two experiences those of the same person by reason of association with a persisting mental substance, or with the same human body, or because of some special relation between the two, e.g. that the later contains a memory, or the possibility of a memory, of the earlier one? A further problem concerns the question of whether the mind is pre-programmed. Chomsky's LINGUISTICS claimed that the use of language was not learned but innate, suggesting a revival of the basic Cartesian notion of an innate human rationality distinct from the conditioned responses postulated by behaviourists. See also MIND-BODY PROBLEM; CHOMSKYAN. For further reading: J. Shaffer, *Philosophy of Mind* (1968). A.Q.; R.P.

mind-body problem. The set of issues that have emerged from the human tendency to postulate a fundamental difference between the realm of mind on the one hand and physical nature on the other. It is generally accepted that any attitude towards the dichotomy creates major, perhaps insoluble, problems of philosophical ANALYSIS. Traditionally, there have been four main attitudes: (1) *Physical monism* (see also MONISM) is probably the most widely accepted among natural scientists, assuming as it does that all phenomena of mind and of nature can be reduced to the laws of PHYSICS and BIOLOGY. (2) *Neutral monism* (or *mental monism*) holds that all is mind, and that the CONCEPT of nature is itself a CONSTRUCT of mind that can only be known through hypotheses tested by reference to experience. This view, which received its contemporary expression in the late 19th century from Ernst Mach (1838–1916), is today expressed as a methodological principle (see METHODOLOGY), based on the premise that, since nature cannot be known directly but only by the mediation of a human observer, one defines nature and mind alike by the kinds of observations one makes and the nature of the INFERENCES one draws – whether these refer to a postulated 'external' system of physical nature, or to the 'internal' system called mind. (3) *Interactionism* (see also PSYCHOSOMATIC) holds that there are two interacting spheres, mind and body: a view that received its first definitive elaboration in the writings of Descartes. The issue of how the two spheres interact without each destroying the self-sufficiency of the other's body of principles remains moot. (4) The classical doctrine of *psychophysical parallelism*, usually attributed to Leibniz, is the view that physical and psychical events run a parallel course without affecting each other. For a fifth, less widespread, view see EPIPHENOMENALISM.

The modern development of the notion has been deeply affected by Darwinian evolutionism (see EVOLUTION), which stressed the ultimate unity and continuity between animal existence and emergent CONSCIOUSNESS. In particular, William James and other American FUNCTIONALISTS around the turn of this century postulated an adaptive functionalism which treated mind rather like other organic faculties. C. Lloyd Morgan argued that the evolution of organized complexity produced a qualitatively distinct level of being, while the school of Pavlov (see PAVLOVIAN) in the former USSR stressed the evolutionary interaction between conscious action and environmental determination (see ENVIRONMENTAL DETERMINISM). Scientifically speaking, classic mind/body dualism cannot survive the implications of evolutionism. For further reading: D. A. Oakley, *Brain and Mind* (1985). J.S.B.; R.P.

miners' strike. The term usually refers to the bitter industrial dispute between the National Union of Mineworkers (NUM) and the British government and National Coal Board (NCB), from March 1984 until March 1985. The strike is widely regarded as the most significant in post-war Britain, raising questions about DEMOCRACY in TRADE UNIONS, the government's capacity to impose its vision of economic modernization, and acceptable techniques of policing industrial disputes. Views as to its origins vary widely. Some critics assert that the government not only prepared for but keenly sought a strike to break the power of a union whose strength and activity in the 1970s was abhorrent to THATCHERISM. Others claim that the NUM was drawn without adequate consultation into untenable positions by a leadership committed to a longer and deeper revolutionary struggle. Neither view is complete or adequate; the strike's beginnings and evolution require detailed assessment. For further reading: G. Goodman, *The Miners' Strike* (1985). S.R.

minimal art (or ABC art, art of the real). A term which came into use in the 1960s to describe art in which all elements of expressiveness and illusion are minimized, and which thus encroaches on the territory of what is (or was thereto) regarded as ANTI-ART. In painting, this movement has been identified with *post-painterly abstraction*, exemplified by the flat colour fields and uncomplicated geometry of Barnett Newman and Ellsworth Kelly; forerunners include Rodchenko and Malevich. But minimalists have turned increasingly to sculpture in their quest for the inexpressive. Donald Judd, Robert Morris and others in the later 1960s produced arrangements of large, fairly regular coloured forms, or *primary structures*, often designed to be seen in relation to a particular ENVIRONMENT. A well-publicized example is Carl Andre's *120 Fire-Bricks* at the Tate Gallery. Still more 'minimal' exhibits have consisted of piles of earth and photographs of simple natural features. For further reading: G. Battcock (ed.), *Minimal Art* (1969). P.C.

minimal music. Type of music arising in America in the 1960s, probably in reaction to the extreme complexities of AVANT-GARDE MUSIC. Minimal music uses in contrast very simple harmonic and melodic progressions which are usually tonal or modal (see ATONAL MUSIC) and frequently involves large amounts of repetition of small phrases (e.g. Terry Riley's 'In C'). See also PHASE SHIFTING; PROCESS MUSIC. For further reading: M. Nyman, *Experimental Music: Cage and Beyond* (1974). B.CO.

minimalism. First popular in art and sculpture in the 1960s (see MINIMAL ART), minimalism as an architectural movement owes much to the patronage of the advertising and fashion industries. Where ARCHITECTURE of the MODERN MOVEMENT pursued its taste for abstract stylistic restraint and an enthusiasm for 'honest' bare plaster or concrete with few covering or masking materials, the minimal environment includes spiritual exhortations to 'voluntary poverty' amid conspicuous consumption and LIFESTYLE choices from scent to settee. Minimalist interiors find materials left self-finished, in their raw industrially produced state. Wallpaper and varnish are rarely used, the sole application being flat areas of paint most often white. It is desirable to alter a material as little as possible, using modular sizes and avoiding cutting. In junctions between materials the appearance of simplicity prevails over the expression of any jointing practicalities. Minimalists may draw inspiration from MODERNISM, but save for a quasi-religious aspect minimalism does not share the social programmes inherent to the Modern Movement in architecture, demanding a private, deeply aesthetic and almost monastic appreciation. For further reading: J. Pawson, *Minimum* (1996). S.T.S.B.; P.J.D.

minimalist programme. A recent development in GENERATIVE GRAMMAR which aims to make statements about language as simple and general as possible. All analytical procedures should be economical, in terms of the number of devices proposed to account for language phenomena (the *principle of economy*). There should be no redundant or superfluous elements in the representation of sentence structure: each element must play a role and must be interpreted (the *principle of full interpretation*).

For further reading: V. J. Cook and M. Newson, *Chomsky's Universal Grammar* (1996).
D.C.

minimax, see under GAME THEORY.

minimum lending rate, see BANK RATE.

minimum wage. The effort by national governments to set a wage level below which it is illegal to employ people. The main argument against a minimum wage, which has been tried and practised in the US, is that it will discourage employers from taking on new workers because the marginal cost (see MARGINAL COST PRICING) will be too high. Small firms may even find themselves shedding employees. Advocates of the minimum wage point out that it is an issue of fairness and social justice that people should receive a recognized payment for services performed. Potentially a minimum wage can be job-creating if it attracts people off the WELFARE and social security rolls into employment.
A.BR.

minorities. Groups distinguished by common ties of DESCENT, RACE, GENDER, physical appearance, language, CULTURE or RELIGION, by virtue of which they feel or are regarded as different from the majority of the population in a society. In modern usage the term tends to connote real, threatened or perceived discrimination against minorities, although in exceptional cases (e.g. South Africa under APARTHEID) a minority may hold power over a majority. Before the 19th century, the only minorities to play any role in national or international politics were religious. With the growth of national consciousness (see NATIONALISM), national minorities acquired significance. Thus in domestic politics national minorities protested their grievances (e.g. Czechs in the Habsburg Empire), while in international affairs the existence of minorities provided grounds for one nation to claim to interfere in the affairs of another (e.g. Hitler's use of German-speaking minorities to put pressure on the Czechoslovak and Polish states). In the 20th century minorities distinguished by other characteristics such as race, ethnic identity as immigrants, gender or sexual preference have joined the range of groups pressing political claims for equality of treatment with that accorded the majority (see AFFIRMATIVE ACTION). For further reading: G. Kinloch, *The Sociology of Minority Group Relations* (1979).
A.L.C.B.; P.B.M.; S.R.

miracle. Traditionally in Christian THEOLOGY, as in many non-Christian religious traditions, a miracle was an event so clearly different from normal events that it revealed divine power. The supreme miracle of this sort was the human life of Jesus, God the Son (the 'second person' of the Holy Trinity), beginning in conception by the power of the Holy Spirit without a father's intervention, continuing in many miraculous acts, and climaxing in the resurrection, when the tomb was empty because the body had been 'raised' gloriously. But in modern times many Christians have become sceptical about miracles including these, either because it is thought that science has revealed unbreakable 'laws' or at least regularities in the 'order' of nature, with convincing explanations of phenomena previously regarded as supernatural, or because particular accounts of miracles seem to be MYTHS or at least to be of dubious historical value (see BIBLICAL CRITICISM). Some Christians have therefore opted for a consistently non-miraculous religion (see DEISM). Others have thought that belief in THEISM necessarily involves the acceptance of God's ability to perform some miracles but that stories about them should be assessed for their probability on the basis of the evidence. Others, however, have continued to trust the Bible or the Church's tradition entirely (see FUNDAMENTALISM). Often it has been agreed that an event can be explained either in scientific language (e.g. 'healing miracles' may be a result of the faithful mind's influence over the body) or in religious terms as something wonderful and therefore specially able to disclose God. The Latin for 'object of wonder' is *miraculum*. Similar modern debates have taken place in JUDAISM and, to a much lesser extent, in other religions. For further reading: R. Swinburne, *The Concept of Miracle* (1970).
D.L.E.

mirror phase. In LACANIAN psychoanalysis, the mirror phase is Lacan's formulation of the structure of imaginary IDENTIFICATIONS, in which he captures something of the contemporary sense of being 'misrecognized'. In this phase, the child assumes an imaginary unity with its BODY IMAGE, inaugurating a permanent tendency whereby the SUBJECT seeks imaginary wholeness to paper over conflict and lack. In contrast to Winnicott, who made the concerned mother's accurate reflection of her child's needs central to healthy development, Lacan emphasizes the impossibility of identity as related to a 'true' self. In his view, the EGO is used to create an armour or shell supporting the psyche, which is otherwise experienced as in fragments. Lacan emphasizes the *exteriority* of this process – that which appears to us as our 'self' is in fact given from the outside as a refuge, an IDEAL EGO. One consequence of the ego's determination by such narcissistic forms (see NARCISSISM) is the generation of the ego-functions of jealousy and aggressivity. The relation of the Oedipal drama to the mirroring ego was described by Lacan in terms of the relationship of the SYMBOLIC to the IMAGINARY (see OEDIPUS COMPLEX). S.J.F.

MIRV, see under MULTIPLE INDEPENDENTLY TARGETED RE-ENTRY VEHICLE; MISSILES.

mise-en-scène. Term originally employed in theatre to designate the contents of the stage and their arrangement, and adopted by cinema critics to refer to the content of the film frame. This includes the arrangement of the profilmic event (elements of the 'real world' which are set up for the camera, or which the camera captures – persons, settings, costumes, props). *Mise-en-scène* also refers more broadly to what the spectator actually sees on the screen – lighting, composition and iconographic features of the cinematic image; and to the relationship between on-screen space and off-screen space created by the framing of the image, in particular through the 'mobile framing' produced by the deployment of telescopic (zoom) lenses or camera movements such as tracking and panning. For further reading: D. Bordwell and K. Thompson, *Film Art: An Introduction* (1979). A.KU.

missiles. Self-propelled projectiles employed in WAR and carrying explosive warheads. In *short-range* missiles, employed against tanks or low-flying aircraft, the warhead consists of ordinary explosive. In *medium-range* (MRBM), *intermediate-range* (IRBM), *intercontinental* (ICBM) and *anti-ballistic* missiles (see ABM) the warhead is nuclear. Missiles may be ground-to-ground, ground-to-air, sea-to-air, or air-to-ground, and may be fired from ground platforms, from under the sea (see TRIDENT), or from an airborne platform, although in this latter category development costs and technical problems have combined to prevent the development of all but short-range 'stand-off' missiles (i.e. missiles whose range enables them to be launched from aircraft flying out of range of conventional anti-aircraft defences). Certain ballistic missiles, including *submarine-launched ballistic missiles* (SLBM), may be equipped with *multiple, independently targetable re-entry vehicles* (MIRV). (A ballistic missile is one which, although initially powered by rockets, completes its trajectory in free-fall.) In this case, there are a number of warheads to the missile, each of which may be targeted independently in succession, and delivered from the outer atmosphere. Mention should also be made of the CRUISE MISSILE, a flat-trajectory missile, comparable in speed and performance to pilotless aircraft, launchable from any kind of platform from torpedo tube to aeroplane, and adaptable to all tactical and strategical purposes. See also NUCLEAR WEAPONS. D.C.W.

missing link. In the popular mind, the 'missing link' is a SPECIES intermediate between *homo sapiens* and the apes, the discovery of which would finally demonstrate the truth of evolutionary theory (see EVOLUTION). (The continuing 'missingness' of the link is sometimes, by contrast, argued by anti-evolutionary creationists [see CREATION/CREATIONISM] as evidence against DARWINIAN theory.) Evolutionary scientists do not expect to find, within the fossil record, links of that kind (apparent finds are characteristically elaborate hoaxes). For Darwinians, true missing links found in fossilized condition are species intermediate between present beings and their own distant forebears. Thus finds of 'prehistoric' man would be expected to have more affinities with the precursors of other modern primates than with the current primates themselves – as in fact has been demonstrated by major anthropoid finds over the last half-century, in particular in East Africa. In previous centuries, belief in the GREAT CHAIN OF BEING, a continuous graded series of creations leading from God, through mankind and down to the merely inanimate stone, encouraged the notion that each species was 'linked' to the next species above and below in the 'chain'. No species could be truly missing, or that would constitute a 'gap' in creation. For further reading: A. O. Lovejoy, *The Great Chain of Being* (1936). R.P.

missing mass problem, see under DARK MATTER.

missing matter, see under DARK MATTER.

MIT school. In LINGUISTICS, those scholars who, following A. N. Chomsky, Professor of Linguistics at the Massachusetts Institute of Technology, adopt a generative conception of language; see CHOMSKYAN; GENERATIVE GRAMMAR. D.C.

mitochondria, see under CYTOLOGY; SYMBIOSIS.

mitosis. In CELL BIOLOGY, the usual process by which the NUCLEUS divides during CELL division. Each CHROMOSOME splits into two, one of the resulting duplicates passing to each of the daughter cells. The process is important in ensuring that the daughter nuclei have identical sets of chromosomes, and hence of GENES. J.M.S.

mixed economy. An economy in which a substantial number, though by no means all, of the activities of production, distribution and exchange are undertaken by the government, and there is more interference by the STATE than there would be in a MARKET ECONOMY. A mixed economy thus combines some of the characteristics of both CAPITALISM and SOCIALISM. See PUBLIC SECTOR; PUBLIC GOOD. R.H.

mixed strategy, see under GAME THEORY; NASH EQUILIBRIUM.

MNC, see MULTINATIONAL COMPANY.

mobile form. In music, the structure of a piece which is composed of sections whose order or relationship to each other is not completely specified by the composer but left to the performer or to chance. The music may therefore be different each time it is performed, and this variety has something of the qualities of the mobile sculptures (see MOBILES) of Alexander Calder (1898–1976). An important pioneer of this form is the composer Earle Brown (1926–), and both Boulez and Stockhausen have used a similar technique (see MOMENT FORM; EXPERIMENTAL MUSIC). B.CO.

mobiles, see under KINETIC ART.

mobility, social, see SOCIAL MOBILITY.

Möbius band. A simple object which prepares one for the fact that in TOPOLOGY things may be far from obvious. Take a strip of paper (e.g. 30 cm by 4 cm). Twist it once and glue the ends together, forming a loop. Despite appearances it has only one edge and one side (surface). Choose a point A on the edge and let a caterpillar crawl from A round the edge – it will eventually reach the edge opposite A, showing that this is part of the edge containing A. Similarly, a spider put on the band can crawl to all points of 'both sides' without crossing the edge, so that 'both surfaces' form a single region. It is amusing to try to guess what will happen if the band is cut round the middle. N.A.R.

modal logic. The part, or kind, of LOGIC concerned with INFERENCES whose constituent PROPOSITIONS embody the CONCEPTS of necessity and possibility and their opposites, CONTINGENCY and impossibility. These four concepts are interdefinable, with the aid of the concepts of negation and disjunction: thus, '*p* is possible' means the same as 'It is not necessary that not-*p*'; '*p* is impossible' as 'It is necessary that not-*p*'; and '*p* is contingent' as 'It is not necessary either that *p* or that not-*p*'. Modern modal logic was initiated by the American philosopher C. I. Lewis (1883–1964) because of his dissatisfaction with the concept of implication found in the standard propositional logic of Russell. But it has developed into an addition to, rather than an improvement upon, extensional logic (see EXTENSIONALITY), using material implication. For further reading: G. E. Hughes and M. J. Cresswell, *Introductions to Modal Logic* (1968). A.Q.

mode. In STATISTICS and PROBABILITY THEORY, (1) the most probable value in a

DISTRIBUTION; in this sense it is sometimes used as a measure of location; (2) more generally, a value which is more probable than any *nearby* value. A distribution having more than one mode is called *bimodal* or *multimodal*, as appropriate, and often arises as the result of mixing simpler *unimodal* distributions. R.SI.

mode of production. A CONCEPT of central importance in MARXISM, though now widely employed by non-Marxist sociologists as well (see SOCIOLOGY). The mode of production encapsulates the relationship between the forces or means of production – TECHNOLOGY, natural resources, human labour, economic instruments such as banking and insurance – and the social relations of production – essentially CLASS or property relations – which determine the pattern and direction of the development of the productive forces. The forces of production, for Marx, are never found in a 'natural', neutral or random state. They are always organized and developed by particular groups – classes – in their own interest. These groups use their possession and control of the means of production to dominate other groups, on whose labour, however, they depend for their superior wealth and POWER.

This is the general form of the relationship between the forces and the relations of production. The precise form varies over time. Thus, according to Marx, in the modern capitalist mode of production (see CAPITALISM) the bourgeoisie (see BOURGEOIS), the owners of land, factories, machinery, and so on, directly dominate and exploit the PROLETARIAT, who own nothing but their labour power which they must sell to the capitalist in return for wages. The proletariat are, however, formally and legally free, unlike the slaves in the slave mode of production of the ancient world, where the slave-owners had legal rights over the bodies of the slaves. In the FEUDAL mode of production, typical of the European Middle Ages, the landowning ruling class did not have direct control of the substantial forces of production – land, cattle, tools – left in the hands of the peasantry; it did, however, have ultimate control of the land through its control of the type of tenure, and it controlled the distribution of the peasants' produce. Finally Marx distinguished the 'Asiatic' mode of production, the form characteristic for many millennia in the ancient empires of Asia, as well as certain parts of eastern Europe and the Near East. Here the STATE – monarch, emperor or BUREAUCRACY – controls the means of production, generally land but also certain crucial economic instruments such as irrigation systems. So far as the West is concerned, Marx discerned an historical succession of modes of production, through 'primitive communism', slavery, feudalism and capitalism. The next and final mode of production would be SOCIALISM, where the 'associated producers' – the proletariat acting as a collectivity on behalf of the whole society – would own and control the means of production, dispensing for ever with the need for a subordinate exploited class. So far this has happened nowhere in the West; and in contemplating those places, such as the former Soviet Union (see USSR, THE FORMER) and China, where socialist REVOLUTIONS were alleged to have occurred, the suspicion must remain that modern socialism runs the real danger of reviving, at a vastly higher and more effective level, the ancient mode of ORIENTAL DESPOTISM – the 18th-century term for what Marx called the Asiatic mode of production. See also ALTHUSSERIANISM. For further reading: B. Hindness and P. Q. Hirst, *Precapitalist Modes of Production* (1975). K.K.

model. A representation of something else, designed for a special purpose. This representation may take many forms, depending upon the purpose in hand. A familiar purpose is to remind ourselves of something we already know about. Thus a model aeroplane, a model of Shakespeare's birthplace, or a photograph all represent an original; they recall to our minds what that original looks like. But the purpose may be discovery. Thus a model aeroplane placed in the controlled environment of a wind tunnel may be used for experiments that will predict how a real aeroplane built to this design would behave in the sky. A third purpose for a model is explanation, e.g. when the solar system is proposed as a model of the ATOM. Again, the model need not necessarily 'look like' whatever it represents. A system of gravitational equations can model the behaviour of the planets as they move around the sun. Such a model is usually called a *theoretical* model.

All models have one characteristic in common, whatever their purpose. This characteristic is the *mapping* of elements in the system modelled onto the model. It is possible for every relevant element to be mapped, in which case the model is an absolute replica (e.g. a paste copy of a piece of precious jewellery). Such a model is the result of an isomorphic mapping (see ISOMORPHISM), and the ordinary person cannot distinguish the fake from the real thing. But an expert knows the difference, because he investigates the stones at a level of abstraction where the mapping is no longer isomorphic. More usually, models openly lose in complexity compared with the original. But if this loss of detail is irrelevant to the purpose in hand, the model is still effective. We may not need every rivet in the model aeroplane to be mapped in order either to recognize the plane, or even to experiment with it in a wind tunnel. When complexity is deliberately sacrificed in the modelling process, according to definite scientific rules set up to govern the TRANSFORMATION, the mapping is called *homomorphic*.

The steps in building a *theoretical model* can be outlined as follows: (1) The variables to be used in characterizing and understanding the process must be specified. (2) The forms of the relationships connecting these variables must be specified. (3) Ignorance and the need for simplicity will ensure that all relationships other than identities are subject to error and so, for purposes of efficient statistical estimation, these *error terms* must be specified. (4) The PARAMETERS of the model must be estimated and the extent of its IDENTIFICATION ascertained; if this is inadequate, the model must be reformulated. (5) Finally, the model must be kept up to date and used, so that an impression can be formed of its robustness and reliability.

Theoretical models are of many kinds: static or dynamic; partial or complete; aggregated or disaggregated (see AGGREGATION); deterministic (see DETERMINISM) or stochastic; descriptive or optimizing. In PHYSICS, when models are well established they are formalized as *laws of physics* and their use for prediction and design becomes a part of ENGINEERING. In ECONOMICS, although the position is rapidly changing, models have usually been static, partial, aggregated, deterministic and descriptive. Despite the limitations of such models, this experience has enabled model-builders to walk; and it is fortunate for economics that they have consistently ignored the arguments of those who claim that if one cannot run it is pointless to be able to walk.

Nevertheless, partly because they tackle much more complicated situations, as compared with physical models, economic and social models tend to be mathematically more naïve and to lack experimental verification. In the less exact SOCIAL SCIENCES, moreover, the term 'model' is often used of the results of step (1), or at most steps (1) and (2), as numbered above, and these results may not be expressed in mathematical form. In SOCIOLOGY, especially, 'model' may be almost interchangeable with IDEAL TYPE.

In interdisciplinary studies (such as operational research or CYBERNETICS), processes that are well understood in one scientific context may be used to investigate the properties of some other system altogether. This often looks as though analogies are being drawn; but a formal model involving homomorphic mapping is something more potent than an analogy. Since mappings are, strictly speaking, mathematical transformations, models are frequently expressed in mathematical notation. This accounts for the popular misconception that the models used in science are necessarily mathematical models.

The use of COMPUTERS has increased the complexity of models that can be handled, but complexity provides no guarantee of validity. Experience shows that simple and apparently reasonable rules often have remote consequences which are extravagant and that 'mid-course correction' (or FEEDBACK) is necessary to produce an acceptable result. Unfortunately feedback of this sort is very difficult to incorporate in a model.

S.BE.; C.S.; R.ST.; J.R.T.

model minority. A term often and sometimes thoughtlessly applied to all or some of the strikingly diverse parts of the US population with Asian origins. It attempts to highlight the rate at which Asian-Americans have succeeded in business and education, and emphasizes their allegedly high commitment to a strong work ethic, FAMILY VALUES and a simultaneous stress on personal and communal responsibility. The term tends to be used most by conservative politicians and commentators (see CONSERVATISM), not least to deflect accusations that American society is intrinsically weighted against racial MINORITIES and to draw crude contrasts with African-Americans' and Hispanic-Americans' socio-economic position, which is thereby viewed as a result of the groups' rather than the society's shortcomings. The 'model minority' view is a caricature: it ignores the considerable variations in the experience of Asian immigrants to the USA, both since the 1880s and since the modern influx which began after reforms of immigration law in 1965, and suggests that variables such as access to capital, linguistic fluency, urban backgrounds and the possession of marketable skills before arrival in the USA are more measurably important determinants of success than are alleged cultural values.

S.R.

model theory, see under MATHEMATICAL LOGIC.

moderator. Any material which slows down NEUTRONS without absorbing them. Moderators such as HEAVY WATER are used in NUCLEAR REACTORS, because CHAIN REACTIONS based on FISSION proceed more efficiently with slow THERMAL NEUTRONS.

M.V.B.

Modern Churchmen. The name taken by a group of liberal theologians (see LIBERALISM) within ANGLICANISM, perhaps most influential in the 1920s. Leaders included H. D. A. Major and W. R. Inge. See also MODERNISM. For further reading: A. M. G. Stevenson, *The Rise and Decline of English Modernism* (1984).

D.L.E.

modern dance. A broad term used to describe a variety of CONTEMPORARY DANCE styles whose vocabulary is not rooted in CLASSICAL BALLET, entertainment revue or musical theatre. Modern dance originated in the USA and Germany in the early 20th century. The work of pioneering modern dancers Loie Fuller, Isadora Duncan and Ruth St Denis arose from a desire for female emancipation and individual expression, and demanded a new dance aesthetic which informed, provoked and enlightened its audience. Leaning heavily on subjective content, in direct contrast to the narrative characteristic of ballet, each first-generation modern dancer devised a system of movement relevant to their thematic concerns and movement theories. Fuller exaggerated costume and light to make performance not performer the central focus; Duncan danced barefoot, demonstrating her rejection of the academic restraints imposed on dance in classical ballet; and Ruth St Denis made exotic and extravagant dances and provided a disciplined, intensive performance training, with her husband Ted Shawn later establishing the DENISHAWN school. In the 1920s Martha Graham (see GRAHAM TECHNIQUE), Doris Humphrey and Charles Weidman rejected Denishawn, concerning themselves with creating serious works of social significance and developing personal techniques. This second generation brought more percussive, forceful expression into their work, e.g. Graham's *Contraction and Release*, and Humphrey/Weidman's *Fall and Recovery*. European modern dance emerged from the German Expressionist Dance (*Austrucktanz*) led by Mary Wigman, and reflected the cultural and political upheaval in Europe, employing expressive gesture as an emotional response, and a particular use of space and improvisation. Wigman, former student of Rudolph von Laban (see MODERN EDUCATIONAL DANCE) and Dalcroze (see EURYTHMICS), established a school in New York (directed by Hanya Holm). Third-generation modern dancers in the USA generally accepted principles laid down by the second generation, except the more AVANT-GARDE DANCE artist Merce Cunningham, who spawned rebellion, culminating in the POST-MODERN DANCE movement. In Britain the influence of Graham gave rise to the Place School and this in turn provoked change giving rise to NEW DANCE. For further reading: J. Morrison Brown (ed.), *The Vision of Modern Dance* (1980).

L.A.

modern educational dance. Based on Rudolph von Laban's (1879–1958) analysis of movement, and introduced by Lisa Ullman into the physical education curriculum of primary and secondary schools in the 1950s. It is used as a means of developing the child's self-expression through the creative use of a self-discovered movement vocabulary, thus encouraging the child to be both creative and interpretive. For further reading: R. Laban, *Modern Educational Dance* (1948). L.A.

Modern Movement. Portmanteau term recalling architects Le Corbusier, Mies van der Rohe, Walter Gropius, Alvar Aalto, J. J. P. Oud and Gerrit Rietveld, but extending to groups such as the Russian CONSTRUCTIVISTS and Mars Group. Principally a movement of between the wars, centred on the BAUHAUS academy, characterized by an enthusiasm for new technology, new considerations of space (often borrowed from modern art) and a new image for life. Driven by the possibilities of rebuilding cities in a modern form and celebrating the opportunities (but not always the practicalities) of mass production on an industrial scale, the architecture is conspicuously ordered, geometric and white. Fundamentally the Modern Movement conjugated an aesthetic with a moral objective, in the midst of a circumstantial alignment of the hygienic with the social. Many of the finest examples are prototypes, or rhetorical models proclaiming a utopian (see UTOPIANISM) ideal (see 'Pavillon Suisse', Paris, by Le Corbusier, 1930).

Unrepentantly bourgeois in origin, the main protagonists found their political sympathies tested with the onset of unsympathetic Nazi (see NAZISM) and STALINIST regimes, as well as sympathetic Italian FASCISM. After World War II, the charm of the aesthetic faded with the realities of mass construction, while there was horror at the capabilities of the MILITARY-INDUSTRIAL COMPLEX. However, the legacy continued to fashion the image of the architect long after the Bauhaus had closed. In Europe, it is a style best preserved in the form of health clinics, schools, swimming pools and private (second) homes. The Modern Movement largely lost its social imperative once it emigrated to the USA, where it might usually be referred to, appropriately enough given its origins, as the International Style. For further reading: Le Corbusier, *Towards a New Architecture* (1927). P.J.D.

modernism.

(1) Although the adjective 'modern' has (see AVANT-GARDE) been applied to many different phenomena at different times, 'modernism' (or the Modern Movement) has by now acquired stability as the comprehensive term for an international tendency, arising in the poetry, fiction, drama, music, painting, ARCHITECTURE and other arts of the West in the last years of the 19th century and subsequently affecting the character of most 20th-century art. The tendency is usually held to have reached its peak just before or soon after World War I, and there has for some time been uncertainty about whether it has ended. Orwell and Cyril Connolly were pronouncing its demise during World War II, but the *avant-garde* events of the post-war period require explanation. Frank Kermode has argued for continuity, suggesting 'a useful rough distinction between two phases of modernism': *palaeo-modernism* and *neomodernism*, the former being the earlier developments, the latter being SURREALIST and post-surrealist developments. Others, especially in America (Ihab Hassan, Leslie Fiedler, etc.), have proposed a sharp distinction, a new *post-modernist* style amounting to a reaction against modernist FORMALISM, a choric, global village art, the product of a 'post-cultural' age, emphasizing developments dealt with here under ALEATORY, ANTI-ART, ANTI-LITERATURE, AUTO-DESTRUCTIVE art, POST-MODERNISM and NEW NOVEL.

As a stylistic term, modernism contains and conceals a wide variety of different, smaller movements, usually reckoned to be those post-dating NATURALISM and characterized by the anti-positivistic (see POSITIVISM) and anti-representational leanings of many late-19th-century artists and thinkers. It would thus include the tendencies of SYMBOLISM, IMPRESSIONISM and DECADENCE around the turn of the century; Fauvism (see FAUVES), CUBISM, POST-IMPRESSIONIST, FUTURISM, CONSTRUCTIVISM, IMAGISM and VORTICISM in the period up to and during World War I; and EXPRESSIONISM, DADA and SURREALISM during and after that war. A number of these movements contain large theoretical differences among themselves, but certain stylistic similarities. Thus atonalism in music (see ATONAL MUSIC), anti-representationalism in painting (see ABSTRACT ART), VERS LIBRE in poetry (see FREE VERSE), fragmentation and STREAM OF CONSCIOUSNESS presentation in the novel, FUNCTIONALISM in architecture, and in general the use of spatial (see SPACE) or COLLAGE as opposed to linear or representational forms, are recurrent features. Another common characteristic noted by critics is the presence of an element of, in Frank Kermode's word, 'decreation' – of technical introversion, or an often ironic self-awareness – in modernist forms. A rough cycle from the late ROMANTICISM of Symbolism and Impressionism through the 'hard', 'classical' or 'impersonal' image and then to the modern psychological romanticism of Surrealism also seems visible in literature and visual forms.

Modernism stretched across the European capitals, reaching a peak of activity and achievement in different countries at different times: in Russia in the immediately pre-Revolutionary years, in Germany in the 1890s and again just before World War I, in England in the pre-war years from about 1908, in America after 1912; in France it is a plateau rather than a peak – though sloping off after about 1939. There was great cross-fertilization between countries and also among the different arts: a complicated interaction between the merging of forms – poetry becoming like music, etc. – and intense specialized exploration within the forms ensued. Modernism had a high aesthetic and formal constituent, and can often be seen as a movement attempting to preserve the aesthetic realm against intellectual, social and historical forces threatening it. But it has been seen as a change larger than simply formal. Its relation to modern thought and modern PLURALISM, to the military, political and ideological (see IDEOLOGY) dislocations of the century, is considerable. Indeed, its forms, with their element of fragmentation, introversion and crisis, have sometimes been held to register the collapse of the entire tradition of the arts in human history. They can be seen either as a last-ditch stand on behalf of the aesthetic in the face of barbarism (as in much Symbolism), or as a probe towards something new. What is clear is that, presentationally and in attitude and belief, modernism does represent a radical shift in the social STATUS and function of the artist, of his art, and of form; that it is the style of a changed SPACE-TIME continuum; and that hence the modernist arts require, for their comprehension, criteria different from those appropriate to earlier art. For further reading: M. Bradbury and J. McFarlane (eds), *Modernism: 1890–1930* (1976). M.S.BR.

(2) In THEOLOGY, the movement to modernize doctrine by taking into account the results of HIGHER CRITICISM and scientific discovery, and the conditions of modern CULTURE. In England and the USA the term has been used for the MODERN CHURCHMEN and other advocates of religious LIBERALISM, but its chief use has been as a label for the outlook of a group of Roman Catholic thinkers (see CATHOLICISM). This group was given both its public identity and its death sentence by the encyclical *Pascendi* issued by Pope Pius X in 1907. Its leaders were Alfred Loisy (1857–1940) and George Tyrrell (1861–1909), priests who felt challenged by critical studies of Christianity's origins. They rejected the call of Liberal PROTESTANTISM to return to the 'pure' origins, and welcomed the development of Christianity in history. They regarded Roman Catholic DOGMAS and devotions as valuable, because helpful, symbols of faith and spiritual life, but believed that a fuller Catholicism was being born. The Pope condemned them as heretics, and the later Roman Catholic AGGIORNAMENTO had to take care not to be identified with them. For further reading: A. R. Vidler, *A Variety of Catholic Modernists* (1970). D.L.E.

modernity. A term sometimes used to refer simply to recent times but increasingly denoting a phase in societal development. Modernity is sometimes seen as dating from the Enlightenment of 17th- and 18th-century Europe, sometimes from the development of industrial society in the 19th century. One of the most influential characterizations of modernity is that of the German sociologist (see SOCIOLOGY) Max Weber (1864–1920), who sees its main feature as an emphasis on RATIONALITY (see BUREAUCRACY). Linked to the emphasis on rationality in modernity is a belief that it is impossible to improve, and perhaps perfect, human society through planned intervention in the social world. Some advocates of POST-MODERNISM (particularly Jean-François Lyotard) argue that modernity has ended or is in the process of ending, and believe that attempts to perfect the social world will only lead to tyranny. Other social scientists, such as Jürgen Habermas, deny that contemporary societies have moved beyond modernity and argue that the pursuit of planned improvements in human societies remains essential. For further reading: A. Giddens, *The Consequences of Modernity* (1990). M.D.H.

modulation. In PHYSICS, any variation in the properties of a high-frequency wave (e.g. a radio wave or a LASER beam), produced by a signal of a much lower frequency. Broadcasting relies on the amplitude modulation or FREQUENCY MODULATION of a carrier wave. M.V.B.

module. In ARCHITECTURE, a standard unit of measurement used in order to create proportional relationships between parts and the whole (as in the Classical Orders and Le Corbusier's Modulor), and to control building design, and thus the manufacture and assembly of building elements. An imaginary grid to which length and thicknesses relate is used to define the position of these elements. Buildings planned on the basis of the module are described as *modular*. The need, common to virtually all building, for some form of dimensional co-ordination becomes acute in PREFABRICATION, for which the use of the modular principle is particularly appropriate. M.BR.

moho (Mohorovicic discontinuity), see under LITHOSPHERE.

moieties. 'Halves', paired social groups. Moieties are similar to CLANS in that recruitment is based loosely on DESCENT, and they are higher-order social groupings. Moieties are usually named after places of origin or natural phenomena. Identity is expressed through a totem (see TOTEMISM) or common SYMBOL. Societies with moieties are usually described as having features of *dual organization*.

Among certain groups in East Africa (e.g. the Turkana) moieties are an important feature of social organization. According to Gulliver (*Social Control in an African Kingdom*, 1963) all Turkana men are divided into two moieties, stones and leopards, and the division extends between and within generations. A man is always in the opposite moiety of his father. The moiety division is expressed at feasts when stones and leopards sit separately to eat, but each serves meat to the other group.

Moieties have long interested anthropologists as exogamous (see EXOGAMY) and RITUAL groups. Early studies of Australian KINSHIP systems identified the importance of dual organization: in particular moieties functioned as marriage or exogamous groups. Alfred Radcliffe-Brown (1881–1955) built on this early work, but the principle of dual organization was most fully investigated by Lévi-Strauss (*Structural Anthropology*, 1963). For further reading: I. Langham, *The Building of British Social Anthropology: W. H. R. Rivers and His Cambridge Disciples in the Development of Kinship Studies 1898–1931* (1981). A.G.

moiré effect. An illusory effect of shimmering movement, produced by superimposing one configuration of multiple lines or dots upon another very similar to it, so that the two do not quite coincide. An effect of this kind may be seen in everyday objects, such as sets of railings, or finely threaded materials (*soie moirée*, watered silk); in the 1960s moiré patterns were cultivated by op and kinetic artists (see OP ART; KINETIC ART), and employed in computer graphics. For further reading: J. Tovey, *The Technique of Kinetic Art* (1971). P.C.

molecular biology. A branch of BIOPHYSICS of which the purpose is to interpret biological structures and functions in explicit molecular terms. Thus much of immunology and BIOCHEMISTRY is now interpretable on a molecular basis. Molecular biology is the basis of GENETIC ENGINEERING and protein engineering. The techniques of molecular biology have added a new dimension to such diverse studies as biosystematics (see TAXONOMY), ENDOCRINOLOGY and molecular medicine. Molecular biology can be divided into two main streams of thought, which correspond fairly exactly to the British and the American traditions of research. The British tradition of molecular biology is predominantly structural; it may be said to have begun with W. T. Astbury's demonstration in the 1940s of an essentially crystalline and therefore molecular orderliness in the structures of, e.g., hairs, feathers and PROTEIN fibres, and to have culminated in the elucidation by Crick and Watson (1953) of the crystalline structure of NUCLEIC ACID and the interpretation by Perutz and Kendrew (1957) of the structure of myoglobin. These achievements rest upon the use of X-RAY DIFFRACTION analysis, pioneered from 1912 onwards by Laue and W. and L. Bragg. The

two traditions of research overlap considerably and converge in the elucidation of the GENETIC CODE, the 'dictionary' relating to the sequence of nucleotides in nucleic acids (DNA and RNA) with the amino acids whose nature and order of assembly into polypeptides (see PEPTIDES) or proteins they specify. The central dogma of molecular biology is that coded information can pass only from DNA to protein and never the other way about; and this irreversibility of information flow is the reason for the falsity of Lamarck's idea (see LAMARCKISM) of the INHERITANCE OF ACQUIRED CHARACTERS. For further reading: T. A. Scott and E. I. Mercer (eds), *Concise Encyclopedia of Biochemistry and Molecular Biology* (1997).
P.M.; P.N.

molecular clock. The theory that EVOLUTION, at the molecular level, proceeds at a relatively constant rate. With the development of techniques for the high-speed sequencing of PROTEINS in the 1960s, it became possible to compare the protein sequences of different SPECIES. Cytochrome-c was one of the earliest proteins to be thoroughly studied in this way. The degree of difference between the cytochrome-c structure of different species was found to be almost exactly proportional to the time since the two species had split from a common ancestor. For species whose evolutionary relationships are not known, the degree of molecular difference can therefore be used to measure their evolutionary relations (see TAXONOMY). How accurately the molecular clock ticks is a matter of controversy. In 1968 the Japanese geneticist Motoo Kimura argued that the constancy of molecular evolution is incompatible with NATURAL SELECTION, and that evolution at the molecular level must take place by chance changes: this is called the neutral theory of molecular evolution. M.R.

molecular ecology. A relatively new discipline based on the application of molecular biological METHODOLOGY (see MOLECULAR BIOLOGY) to problems in ECOLOGY and POPULATION BIOLOGY. In general, it is about the interaction between ORGANISMS and their environment in an evolutionary context (see EVOLUTION). As the field has evolved, it has become much more about molecular genetic applications (see GENETICS/GENOMICS) than about the study of biological molecules and their role in the environment. In practical terms, much of the work has involved the assessment of the level and pattern of genetic diversity within and between natural populations (see BIODIVERSITY), and the impact of aspects of ecology on patterns of KINSHIP over several hierarchical levels, from paternity testing (e.g. to assess reproductive strategy) to the analysis of large-scale patterns of PHYLOGENY. A.R.H.

molecular engineering, see under LANGMUIR-BLODGETT FILMS.

molecular genetics, see under GENETICS/GENOMICS.

molecular recognition. A binding interaction between two or more molecules in which selectivity – the binding of one molecule but not others that differ in composition or structure – is achieved by some kind of structural complementarity in the participants. For example, ENZYMES exhibit molecular recognition of certain target MOLECULES, binding them selectively before effecting their chemical transformation, by virtue of a binding pocket with a shape that matches that of the target. The idea of geometric complementarity, like a lock and key, was advanced by Emil Fischer in 1895 as the basis for enzyme action; but it is clear that chemical complementarity – the juxtaposition in the enzyme and target of chemical groups that interact favourably – is also among the factors that enable molecular recognition. These same principles are now being exploited in synthetic molecular systems with a view to developing new molecular catalysts as well as other complex assemblies that bind reversibly and carry out particular processes such as sensing (see CATALYSIS). P.C.B.

molecule. The smallest structural unit of a material which can participate in a chemical reaction. Molecules consist of ATOMS held together by chemical BONDS arising from exchange forces. See also EXCHANGE ENERGY. M.V.B.

moment form. Musical term used by Karlheinz Stockhausen (1928–) with reference to certain of his works where he feels that the listener's attention may concentrate on the actual musical event happening at that instant ('moment') rather than on the progression and relationships of events over the duration of the whole piece of music. With this relaxed view of structure, Stockhausen allows the performer to rearrange the 'moments' or short sections of the piece in a manner similar to that in MOBILE FORM. The concept of moment form is full of inherent contradictions that Stockhausen has never fully resolved. For further reading: R. Maconie, *The Works of Karlheinz Stockhausen* (1976). B.CO.

momentum. A measure of the ability of a moving body to resist forces acting on it. For a single PARTICLE obeying NEWTONIAN MECHANICS, momentum = MASS × velocity. This is, mathematically, a vector quantity because the velocity of a body is directed along its line of motion. For a system that is isolated (i.e. not acted on by forces from outside), momentum obeys a CONSERVATION LAW which is very useful in analysing the motion of interacting parts of the system. In a NUCLEAR REACTION, e.g., the total momentum before a collision (of incident particle + target) is the same as the total momentum afterwards (of all the reaction products), whatever the interactions during impact. Conservation of momentum is the basis of the motion of rockets. M.V.B.

monads. According to the PHILOSOPHY of Gottfried Leibniz (1646–1716), the ultimate substantial constituents of the world. Leibniz argued that everything complex must be made of simple and indivisible parts and that, since everything extended is divisible, the ultimate simples must be unextended and so mental or spiritual in nature. But while monads are all CONSCIOUSNESSES, they need not be self-conscious or endowed with APPERCEPTION, although some are. God and human souls, according to Leibniz, are monads; and everything that exists that is not a monad, such as a material object, is a collection of monads. For further reading: B. Russell, *A Critical Exposition of the Philosophy of Leibniz* (1900). A.Q.

monetarism. An economic theory that is based on the view that economic markets operate most effectively without government intervention. For example, labour markets will always operate so as to move the economy towards FULL EMPLOYMENT. In the monetarist view production and prices in markets respond quickly to changes in the economy and, consequently, the economy moves quickly towards EQUILIBRIUM. From this assumption, various monetarist propositions have been derived. This has resulted in confusion over what the term monetarist means, especially as what constitutes a monetarist view of the working of the economy has varied considerably between different economists, over time and across countries. The different monetarist views can be explained as follows.

(1) It is considered that the most important reason for holding MONEY is for its use in economic transactions. Starting from equilibrium in the whole economy, an increase in the MONEY SUPPLY will increase holdings of money and this will cause people to spend more. At full employment the effect of this extra expenditure is not to bring forth extra output, but to increase prices. This increase in prices reduces the real value of the money supply; this process continues until the increase in prices is equal to the initial increase in the money supply. At this point, the real value of the money supply has returned to its original level. The increase in the supply of money has had no effect on the equilibrium values of employment, output and the interest rate. The QUANTITY THEORY OF MONEY states that the price level increases at the same rate as the money supply and, in particular, the level of employment remains the same.

(2) As monetarism assumes that the economy is at or moving towards full employment, FISCAL POLICY can have little or no effect on the level of employment and real output. An increase in government expenditure financed by an increase in the money supply will, according to the first monetarist view, have little or no effect on the level of employment and real output. Government expenditure financed by greater borrowing will increase the interest rate and *crowd out*, i.e. replace, INVESTMENT in the rest of the economy. The level of AGGREGATE DEMAND and, thus, output remains unchanged, though as investment has fallen (assuming the increase in government expenditure is not investment) the productive potential of the economy has been reduced. Monetarist theories have been developed to incorporate expectations about

prices (see RATIONAL EXPECTATIONS). If the economy is in equilibrium, an upward shift in aggregate demand – e.g., because of an increase in government expenditure – will increase only prices as output is, by monetarist assumption, at the full employment level. Firms (see FIRM, THEORIES OF) react to higher prices by increasing output through hiring more labour at higher money wages. Labour may not realize that this increase in money wages should be adjusted for the increase in prices, i.e. they may suffer from MONEY ILLUSION. If this adjustment does not occur, the increased money wages attract a larger supply of labour and employment increases. However, as labour adjusts for the increase in prices, the supply of labour is reduced and employment falls. If these expectations of inflation continue to be held, but aggregate demand shifts back, unemployment will rise as labour perceives real wages to be lower than they actually are. This unemployment will persist until expectations adjust to the true value of INFLATION.

(3) The use of fiscal and monetary policies to stabilize the economy is unlikely to be successful, as too little is known about the working of the economy, especially with regard to the lags in the effects of economic policies. The government should attempt to balance the budget and increases in the money supply should be consistent with stable prices.

(4) There are a number of monetarist views about the operation of the economy which have crucial implications for economic policy. The monetarist view is that these relationships are such that markets will always return to equilibrium. Monetarism is often discussed as the major alternative economic theory to KEYNESIAN economics. For further reading: B. Morgan, *Monetarists and Keynesians* (1978). J.P.

monetary policy. The policy of a government or CENTRAL BANK in varying the quantity of money in circulation, the cost and availability of credit, and the composition of NATIONAL DEBT. The classical instruments used for this purpose are discount policy (changes in the central bank's lending rate) and open-market operations (purchases or sales of government debt by the central bank designed to put more or less money in circulation). Other instruments of monetary policy include government control over bank lending, directly or indirectly, and regulation of the rates of interest to be charged by banks and other financial institutions. Economists differ as to the importance of monetary policy (in comparison, e.g., with FISCAL POLICY) in regulating the level of economic activity. As government's budget deficits have to be financed by borrowing or the creation of MONEY, monetary policy is closely linked to the level of the budget deficit, i.e. fiscal policy. For further reading: D. Begg *et al*, *Economics* (1984). A.C.; J.P.

money. Any thing which is generally acceptable as a medium of exchange. Money must be a store of wealth and thus be durable; otherwise people would not want to hold it. In times of very rapid INFLATION (hyperinflation) money loses its value and people avoid holding it. Money is also a unit of account, as it is convenient to express all prices and financial instruments in terms of the same money unit. Money is useful in that it simplifies economic transactions, as the double coincidence of wants necessary for barter is avoided (see MONEY SUPPLY; MONEY CREATION). J.P.

money creation. A bank can create MONEY by lending out money that is deposited with the bank. The ability of banks to create money is limited by their need to maintain sufficient liquid reserves and for them to comply with official regulations concerning the holding of reserve assets. Changes in these regulations can be used to control the MONEY SUPPLY. In this and other ways (see MONETARY POLICY) the government can create money. J.P.

money illusion. The failure to distinguish between real and MONEY income. For example, an individual who experiences a 10 per cent rise in both prices and money income and feels better, or worse, off is said to suffer from money illusion. J.P.

money supply. The amount of MONEY in the economy. As it is possible to finance payments in a variety of notes and coins, bank cheques and BUILDING SOCIETY cheques, similarly it is possible to define money in a variety of ways. The wider the definition of money, the less readily accepted the forms of money that are included in the definition. A fairly wide definition of money is sterling M3, but not the widest; it includes notes and coins in circulation and private (see PRIVATE SECTOR) and PUBLIC SECTOR sterling current and deposit bank accounts (see MONEY CREATION). J.P.

monism. In PHILOSOPHY, (1) the theory that there is only one truly substantial thing in the universe, as in Spinoza's doctrine of SUBSTANCE, also described as Godor-Nature (*deus sive natura*), and Hegel's doctrine of the *absolute idea* (see IDEA); this kind of monism is a limiting case of HOLISM; its opposite is *pluralism.* (2) The theory that there is really only one fundamental *kind* of thing in the universe, whether it be material as in MATERIALISM, mental as in IDEALISM, or abstract as in Platonic REALISM. The two forms of monism are variously combinable; Spinoza held that his Substance had thought and extension as attributes, as well as other unknown ones, whereas Hegel, as an idealist, was a monist in both senses. Materialists ordinarily acknowledge a plurality of individual things or substances, but Parmenides, in the 6th century BC, did not. See also MIND-BODY PROBLEM; NEUTRAL MONISM. A.Q.

monoculture. An agricultural system, such as is used for sugar cane and continuous wheat production, in which the same crop is planted successively on the same land, in contrast to systems in which a sequence of crops is planted in rotation. Some users of the term are particularly concerned to emphasize the extension of such simplified cropping over large areas of countryside, and occasionally it has been applied to all systems except those in which several crops are grown mixed together on the same fields on farms where livestock are an integral part of the system. The simplicity of monocultural systems makes for economy in certain production costs, but they tend to break down because of the build-up of pests and diseases or the deterioration of the soil, with consequent reduction in yields. K.E.H.

monogamy. A form of MARRIAGE in which each partner has only one spouse, a rule which can also prevent remarriage after the death of one spouse. The practice of monogamy has been associated with certain economic conditions and forms of property inheritance. It is particularly found in societies where property is transmitted bilaterally and DOWRY is the common form of marriage payment. Monogamy has been linked to societies based upon intensive or plough agriculture, where land is scarce and intensively worked. Landholding is a crucial element in social differentiation and wealth is carefully preserved between generations. Each partner brings property to marriage, and with the establishment of a single conjugal union fund, monogamy acts for its concentration and against the dispersal of wealth. However, monogamy does not necessarily involve a lifelong relationship with one spouse and can be linked to other factors. In North America and western Europe, the phenomenon of serial monogamy is increasingly common, where one partner may take a number of spouses over a lifetime. In addition, the growth of new REPRODUCTIVE TECHNOLOGIES –in particular the donation of either sperm or egg cell from a third party – has challenged the traditional notion of a monogamous conjugal union. For further reading: J. Goody, *Production and Reproduction* (1976). M.H.

monogenesis. In LINGUISTICS, the hypothesis that all human languages originate from a single source; contrasting with polygenesis, where language is thought to have emerged more or less spontaneously in several places. The terms are also used in discussing the similarities among PIDGINS: monogenetic theories assume the diffusion of a single pidgin to other areas via migration; polygenetic theories assume that the development of a pidgin in one community is independent of the development of a pidgin in another. For further reading: W. Bright (ed.), *International Encyclopedia of Linguistics* vol. 2 (1992). D.C.

monopoly. The only firm (see FIRM, THEORIES OF) producing a certain good or service. A monopolist can restrict output and, thus, charge a higher price than would be obtained in PERFECT COMPETITION. The restriction of output below an efficient level results in a loss of SOCIAL WELFARE, compared with that which can be obtained in perfect competition. The power to restrict output and raise the price, and the definition of a monopoly, depend on the number and closeness of substitutes for the product of the monopoly and BARRIERS TO ENTRY. A legal monopoly is one derived from a privilege conferred by government. A natural monopoly exists when ECONOMIES OF SCALE make it inefficient for there to be more than one firm and, if they exist, the smaller and more inefficient firms will go out of business. It has been argued that monopolies have beneficial effects, as they are more likely to invest in RESEARCH AND DEVELOPMENT and generate technical progress. A monopoly may have a greater incentive to invest in research and development, as the results of such effort are less likely to be imitated because of its monopoly position. Monopolies may have readier access to finance, find it easier to carry the burden of risk and cost of investments and obtain economies of scale in carrying out research and development. Alternatively the lack of rivals may mean that monopolies have no spur to invent and innovate and develop, and that the most favourable industrial structure for technical progress is one of a few large, rival firms (see OLIGOPOLY). The lack of rivals may also result in monopolies not minimizing costs of production (see COMPETITION). For further reading: M. C. Sawyer, *The Economics of Industries and Firms* (1982). G.B.R.; J.P.

monopoly policy, see ANTI-TRUST OR MONOPOLY POLICY.

monosystemic, see under FIRTHIAN.

monotheism, see under THEISM.

Monroe Doctrine. A political doctrine of hemispheric influence, first enunciated in a message to the US Congress by President James Monroe on 2 December 1823. It had four elements: two aimed at restricting the activities of European powers, two those of the US. The former were: (1) The American continents were not to be considered as subjects for annexation by European states; (2) any interference by such states in the affairs of the Americans would be taken as threatening to US interests and security. The latter were: (1) The US would not interfere with existing European colonies in the American continents; (2) nor would she intervene in 'the wars of the European powers in matters relating to themselves'. Although the latter have been largely redundant since US entry into World War I in 1917, the former give the Doctrine continuing relevance in that it is still invoked in attempts to justify a US monopoly of external influence in Central and South America. As such it is widely regarded in those regions as a symbol of US domination. For further reading: G. Smith, *The Last Years of the Monroe Doctrine, 1945–1993* (1994). D.C.W.; S.R.

montage. French term for the assembling and erection of mechanical apparatus. Used internationally in the arts:

(1) For the technique of *photomontage* devised by the Berlin DADA group *c.* 1918 and practised mainly by Raoul Hausmann, Hannah Höch and John Heartfield. This was an application of COLLAGE to photographic and other illustrative material, which Heartfield later adapted to political caricature. Countless designers have come to use it for large-scale display and decorative schemes.

(2) In the cinema, as the ordinary term for editing (the placing of one shot or scene next to another to make a narrative or thematic point). The early Soviet film-makers, influenced by D. W. Griffith's development of *parallel montage* (the simultaneous conduct of two or more narrative themes) in *Intolerance*, gradually developed complex intellectual theories of montage through the experiments first of Kuleshov from 1917, then of Dziga Vertov in his *Kino-Pravda* documentaries from 1922 on, until Eisenstein, elaborating his theory of the *montage of attractions* (the juxtaposition by cutting of seemingly disparate shots to produce a shock or 'attraction'), not only gave montage pride of place in the art of film-making, but raised it into what was to prove a cumbersome mystique.

(3) More loosely, for almost any type of compilation made up of disparate elements, particularly where there is a mechanical quality about the work. J.W.; T.C.C.M.

Montague grammar. A movement in LINGUISTICS in the mid-1970s which owed its impetus to the thinking of the American logician Richard Montague (1930–70). The approach uses a conceptual apparatus derived from the study of the SEMANTICS of formal (logical) languages, and applies it to the study of natural languages. For further reading: D. T. Dowty *et al*, *Introduction to Montague Semantics* (1981). D.C.

Monte Carlo methods. Many problems in applied probability are too difficult to treat theoretically, e.g. for traffic arriving randomly at a crossroads with a given traffic-light sequence: what sort of queues will build up? With a lavish supply of RANDOM NUMBERS we can simulate the situation repeatedly and get a fair estimate of the behaviour. A famous use of the method was at Los Alamos by von Neumann and Ulam in the development of the atom bomb (see NUCLEAR WEAPONS); nowadays computers make the method relatively easy to apply. N.A.R.

Montessori method. Educational method associated with Maria Montessori (1870–1952). After qualifying in 1894 as Italy's first woman doctor, she worked in Rome, first with feeble-minded children, later with normal children aged between three and seven. Influenced by the FROEBEL METHOD – with its emphasis on the importance of play – her specially designed auto-didactic apparatus and furniture provided a challenging environment which exercised the child's physical mechanisms and his discrimination of length, size, weight, texture, shape, and colour. The Montessori method and classroom were commended by progressives as both 'scientific' and sensitive, and many of today's puzzles and educational tools for young children are derived from her ideas. W.A.C.S.

moral panic. A term generally used in relation to the creation of a certain kind of social hysteria by the mass media in modern society. The mass media, it is claimed, in the indulgence of the sensationalism which is one of their principal values, exaggerate relatively trivial acts of violence or misbehaviour to the proportions of a major social or moral crisis. This perception is then taken over by various individuals and institutions of authority – the police, the law courts, community workers, Churches, schools, parents – who are often themselves prisoners of the media in their understanding of society. Acting on these media images, these individuals and institutions seek to stamp out the particular activities which have been highlighted, thus confirming their reputation as grave social evils while at the same time paradoxically enhancing their appeal to other so far unaffected individuals who are attracted by their notoriety. Thus in the 1960s in Britain, the media built up a moral panic over the relatively harmless activities of certain youth groups, such as the 'Mods' and 'Rockers', leading to a glamorization of their cultural styles, and occasioning pitched battles – staged sometimes for, or by, the media – between rival groups on public holidays at seaside resorts on the south coast. These violent incidents then became the fuel for alarmist speeches by politicians and churchmen, and the imposition of tough penalties by magistrates. This in turn stimulated defiant responses from the young, amplifying the behaviour first complained of.

Similar moral panics have been created over 'mugging' – the media suggesting a problem of American proportions – and teenage promiscuity. While the mass media continue to be regarded as the primary producers of moral panics, the term is now used of any kind of collective social or moral hysteria that is artificially, sometimes deliberately, generated. See also LABELLING THEORY. For further reading: S. Cohen, *Folk Devils and Moral Panics* (1972). K.K.

moral theology. A term, more familiar in CATHOLICISM than in PROTESTANTISM, covering the discussion of the relevance of religious, especially Christian, belief to ethical problems (see ETHICS). Most of the discussion has been about a minimum standard of conduct for Christians who do not aspire to the heights of sanctity, and has sometimes resulted in a semi-legal, even hair-splitting, code listing possible concessions to human appetites. This is pejoratively called 'casuistry', a word which can, however, have the nobler meaning of applying moral philosophy to particular cases. See also ANTINOMIANISM; SITUATION ETHICS. D.L.E.

Mormons. A basically American religious body properly called 'The Church of Jesus Christ of the Latter-Day Saints'. Founded by Joseph Smith and Brigham Young, it attracted attention by its establishment, around Salt Lake City, of the State of Utah (1847, admitted into the USA in 1895), by the bizarre nature of its holy book (the *Book of Mormon*), and by its practice of POLYGYNY (now abandoned). In the 20th century it has become well known for its worldwide evangelism. It is now respected for its moral purity, if not for its THEOLOGY. For further reading: L. J. Arrington and D. Bitton, *The Mormon Experience* (1979). D.L.E.

morpheme. In LINGUISTICS, the minimal unit of grammatical analysis, i.e. the smallest functioning unit out of which words are composed. Morphemes are commonly classified into *free forms* (morphemes which can occur as separate words) and *bound forms* (morphemes which cannot so occur – traditionally called *affixes*); thus *unselfish* consists of the three morphemes *un*, *self* and *ish*, of which *self* is a free form, *un-* and *-ish* bound forms. Morphemes are generally regarded as abstract units; when realized in speech, they are called *morphs*. Some morphemes are represented by more than one morph according to their position in a word or sentence, such alternative morphs being called *allomorphs*. Thus the morpheme of plurality represented orthographically by the *-s* in, e.g., *cots*, *digs* and *forces* has the allomorphs represented phonetically by [s], [z] and [iz] respectively; in this instance the allomorphs result from the phonetic influence of the sounds with which the singular forms of the words terminate. See also MORPHOLOGY (3). D.C.

morphogenesis. The sum of the processes by which an animal or plant develops its distinctive form. These processes are: (1) determination, in which the fate of certain CELLS or tissues is determined; (2) DIFFERENTIATION, in which various cells or tissues undergo diverging courses of development; and (3) growth, in which cells enlarge, multiply or both. See also EMBRYOLOGY. E.O.W.

morphology.

(1) In BIOLOGY, a term introduced by Goethe (1749–1832) to denote a science dealing with the very essences of forms – and so distinguished from workaday descriptive sciences like anatomy. In Goethe's mind the word probably had a slightly mystical neo-Platonic significance. P.M.

(2) In GEOGRAPHY and GEOLOGY, a term used to denote the form of landscapes or elements of the natural landscape. Thus the American cartographer Erwin Raisz (1893–1968) defined and standardized symbols for 40 'morphologic types' such as cone volcanoes, scarplands and plains, and added a further 10 based on natural vegetation to diversify the category of plains. More recently the term *urban morphology* has been used, with reference to urban landscapes, to differentiate different parts of a town according to form and structure. M.L.

(3) A branch of LINGUISTICS, traditionally defined as the study of word structure, but now more usually as the study of the properties of MORPHEMES and their combinations. For further reading: P. H. Matthews, *Morphology* (1974). D.C.

morphophonology (sometimes called *morphonology* and, especially in American linguistic work, *morphophonemics*). In LINGUISTICS, the analysis and classification of the different phonological shapes available in a language for the representation of MORPHEMES. D.C.

mortality. In DEMOGRAPHY, the study of deaths in a population. John Graunt's study of the Bills of Mortality in London in 1662 was the first systematic analysis of human DEATH RATES. The mortality conditions of a given population are described by a LIFE TABLE. A life table is derived from age-specific death rates and contains values for the INFANT MORTALITY RATE and LIFE EXPECTANCY at birth, which are the two most commonly used indicators of the health of a population. J.R.W.

Moscow trials. The three great Soviet SHOW TRIALS whose leading victims were Zinoviev, Kamenev and others (August 1936); Pyatakov, Radek and others (January 1937); and Bukharin, Yagoda and others (March 1938). The term is sometimes used to include earlier public trials in the former USSR such as the Shakhty Trial of 1928, the 'Industrial Party' Trial of 1930, the Menshevik Trial of 1931, and the 'Metro-Vickers' Trial of 1933 (when the main accused were British engineers). The principle of these rigged trials was that of public confession by the accused, though some of the earlier ones named were not wholly successful in this respect. See also YEZHOVSHCHINA. For further reading: R. Conquest, *The Great Terror* (1971). R.C.

Moslem, see under ISLAM.

Moslem Brotherhood, see under ISLAM.

Mössbauer effect. Discovered by Rudolf Ludwig Mössbauer in 1958. The emission of GAMMA RAYS with very precisely defined frequencies by an atomic NUCLEUS in a solid. The nuclear velocities, whose DOPPLER EFFECTS broaden the range of frequencies in a gas, may be reduced virtually to zero in a solid, because the MOMENTUM due to recoil and random heat motion is absorbed by the whole crystal LATTICE.

Very small frequency shifts can be measured with these Mössbauer gamma rays; this has led to many applications of the effect in SOLID-STATE PHYSICS, and to a successful test of the prediction from the theory of RELATIVITY that GRAVITATION will cause a RED SHIFT in the frequency of PHOTONS. M.V.B.

most favoured nation clause, see under BILATERALISM AND MULTILATERALISM.

mothering. The high symbolic (see SYMBOL) value that is attached to motherhood is socially universal. In Judeo-Christian (see JUDAISM; CHRISTIANITY) traditions the mother is given an iconographic status and the visual representation of mother and child (as the Virgin Mary and Jesus Christ) is a major theme of Western art. However, the visual and religious (see RELIGION) valorization of motherhood is not, as feminists (see FEMINISM) have pointed out, necessarily accompanied by social support and assistance to mothers or an account of motherhood which regards it as more than an inevitable consequence of heterosexual intercourse. Motherhood and marriage have long been assumed, in many cultures, to have a close – and desirable – association; again this relationship has been challenged in the last 30 years by arguments which have stressed the essential link between mother and child, and not mother, child and father, and have questioned both the construction of the responsibilities of the mother and the situations in which motherhood is regarded as socially acceptable. 'Mothering', or more particularly the quality of mothering, has, since the work of Anna Freud, Melanie Klein *et al*, come to be regarded as a crucial factor in human development, and this recognition has ensured that movements critical of the traditional social organization of mothering have united with those that stress its importance to produce a general social awareness of the need to examine closely the apparently 'natural' condition of being a mother. For further reading: N. Chodorow, *The Reproduction of Mothering* (1978). M.S.E.

motif writing, see under DANCE NOTATION.

moveable property, see under DESCENT.

Movement, the. Name originally given in the mid-1950s to a conservative and anti-romantic tendency then manifesting itself in British poetry. The term is misleading in that there was never any 'movement'; Robert Conquest's *New Lines* (1956), which included poetry by Donald Davie, Kingsley Amis, Philip Larkin, John Wain, Elizabeth Jennings, Thom Gunn, and others, was programmatically retrospective, and very soon after this some British poets, including Gunn himself, Edwin Morgan and Iain Crichton Smith, came under such very different influences as Robert Lowell's 'confessionalism' (a writing of one's own life story by way of the strictly clinical facts), EXISTENTIALISM, and the 'POST-SURREALISM' of John Ashberry. The Movement's tendency – traditionalism in form, irony, 'robustness', distrust of CULTURE, an empirical approach – is most characteristically seen in Philip Larkin, arguably Britain's best post-war poet. The Movement was a reaction against the NEW APOCALYPSE and similarly loose British poetry of the 1940s, a response to the ingenuity of William Empson, and a belated, partial recognition of the achievement of Robert Graves and of (this has been less well acknowledged) Norman Cameron, who in the 1930s and 1940s had been overshadowed by Auden and Eliot. Beyond this it amounted to nothing, and it should be noted only as a tendency. For further reading: M. L. Rosenthal, *The New Poets* (1967). M.S.-S.

MRBM (medium-range ballistic missiles), see under MISSILES.

M-theory, see under GRAND UNIFICATION; SUPERSTRINGS.

Mujahedin, see under AFGHANISTAN.

multiculturalism.

(1) In politics and law, an approach that stresses the existence of a plurality of CULTURES within any given society. Logically, the term can be used to apply to almost all forms of cultural diversity, whether established along the lines of age or social CLASS, GENDER or SEXUALITY. In practice, however, the term is mainly used to denote cultural differentiation according to RACE, ETHNICITY and language. Descriptively, multiculturalism is little more than a truism: virtually all late-capitalist (see CAPITALISM) societies include substantial 'ethnic' MINORITIES. Prescriptively, it recommends that such minority cultures be accorded a respect traditionally reserved only for the dominant cultural forms. In Britain and the US, multiculturalism has overwhelmingly referred to 'race', in Australia to ethnicity, in Canada to language.

(2) In literary and cultural studies, a type of POST-STRUCTURALISM that aims to deconstruct (see DECONSTRUCTION) unitary national narratives so as to decentre (see DECENTRATION) the dominant culture. Multicultural theory commences from a critique of the RHETORIC of cultural dominance, rather than from a celebration of subordinate IDENTITY. Such celebration is normally precluded by the logic of post-structuralism, which insists that there can be no extra-discursively 'real' ethnic identity, to which a multiculturalist politics might appeal for validation. A.J.M.

multi-factor analysis, see under FACTOR ANALYSIS; MULTIVARIATE ANALYSIS.

multilateralism.

(1) The doctrine advanced against *unilateralism*, that DISARMAMENT should be undertaken by all nuclear powers at the same time, and in concert. The two conflicting approaches to disarmament are not particular to NUCLEAR WEAPONS, but emerged in the debates over disarmament in the 1930s. Multilateralism is the traditional diplomatic approach (see DIPLOMACY), based on mutual concession and advantage, subject to control and verification. It is the professional's choice: no STATE possessing nuclear weapons has taken up a unilateralist stance. By contrast, unilateralism appeals to a popular constituency, though some nations, e.g. New Zealand, refuse to allow nuclear weapons on their territory. Unilateralism proved most popular in the UK in the 1980s, through the Campaign for Nuclear Disarmament (see PEACE MOVEMENT). However, the British Labour Party's endorsement of CND in the 1980s was widely perceived to diminish its electoral credibility, and today neither the public nor any mainstream political party supports the idea of unilateral disarmament. For further reading: D. Frei, *Assumptions and Perceptions in Disarmament* (1984). A.J.M.W.

(2) In international trade, see under BILATERALISM AND MULTILATERALISM.

multimedia. Among computer users, refers to the addition of pictures and sound to a computer display, particularly as part of a game or educational program. Multimedia began as a theatrical term for mixing stage action with filmed or taped images and sounds. Computerized multimedia uses only one medium (the computer) but simulates a mix of sources. For example, a multimedia guide to movie history might include texts, film clips, sound tracks and lectures. Central to computerized multimedia is the notion of 'interactivity', meaning the user can control what happens on the screen. Multimedia's backers believe interactivity is ultimately more appealing than passive forms of entertainment like sitting before a television. Others, noting that TV-induced passivity is as bewitching as it is distressing, doubt that multimedia will dominate 21st-century entertainment, although most observers agree that it will be a familiar element. E.B.B.

multinational company (MNC). Business firms with a parent company in one country and subsidiary operations in other countries. MNC foreign production accounts for about one-fifth of world output and MNC intrafirm trade for one-third of international trade.

The largest MNCs, with hundreds of affiliates throughout the world, have an output comparable to the DEVELOPING COUNTRIES with which they bargain. MNCs can reduce shortages of CAPITAL, management and technology and generate tax revenue, but they can increase technological dependence and concentration, expand UNEMPLOYMENT from unsuitable technology, hamper local entrepreneurship (see ENTREPRENEUR), and exacerbate income inequality.

The markets MNCs operate in are often OLIGOPOLIES. MNCs benefit from MONOPOLY advantages, such as patents, technical knowledge, superior managerial and marketing skills, better access to capital markets, and ECONOMIES OF SCALE and VERTICAL INTEGRATION.

In the late 1990s, the US had both the largest inward and outward flows of MNC investment, while China ranked second in inward flows. For further reading: UNCTAD, *World Investment Report* (annual). E.W.N.

multi-party politics. The operation of a nation's party system by many significant parties. The point at which a party system should be regarded as 'multi-party' was much debated by political scientists in the 1970s, largely because multi-party systems were believed to work in distinctive ways. In particular, they were thought to be characterized by instability. This was partly because government formation depended upon protracted periods of coalition bargaining in which a party's bargaining power might be out of all proportion to its level of electoral support. In extreme cases, party competition in multi-party systems might become centrifugal, with parties outbidding each other in their extremism. The politics of Weimar Germany (1918–33), the French Fourth Republic (1946–58) and post-war Italy were much-cited examples. However, with work on other multi-party democracies, the stability of multi-party systems came to be seen as a more complex matter, in which constitutional norms and the nature of ideological and societal divisions were as important as the number of parties. For further reading: P. Mair (ed.), *The West European Party System* (1990). N.O.

multiphonics. In music the use of unusual fingering and breathing techniques to produce two or more notes simultaneously (chords) from a single wind instrument. An important pioneer in the development of these techniques is the composer Bruno Bartolozzi, who has developed series of finger positions to produce not only chords but MICROTONE scales and unusual tone colourings from woodwind instruments. For further reading: B. Bartolozzi, *New Sounds for Woodwind* (1967). B.CO.

multiple independently targeted re-entry vehicle (MIRV). A MISSILE that has several warheads, each one being directed to different enemy targets. MIRV can also refer to any one of the warheads. C.E.D.

multiple personality disorder (MPD). Term formally adopted in the US in 1980 for a PERSONALITY DISORDER, once termed 'DISSOCIATION of personality', in which an individual apparently possesses more than one personality. Such sub-personalities ('alters') may or may not be aware of each other. About 28 per cent of sufferers report so-called 'demonic possession'. The first fully reported cases were 'Miss Beauchamp' (by Morton Prince) and 'Hannah' (by Sidis & Goodhart), both in 1905. 'Eve' (1957) and 'Sybil' (1973) were later well-publicized cases. Originally rare and usually involving only two to four alters, after 1980 the US saw a dramatic increase in both the incidence of MPD and the numbers of alters reported – averaging 24 (in adolescent cases) by 1990 but occasionally over 100, with one 1991 case purportedly exceeding 1,000. Controversy now surrounds the entire issue: the authenticity of more extreme cases, and even of MPD itself, being challenged; psychotherapists being accused of unwittingly creating the condition; and problems regarding sufferer responsibility emerging in several court cases. Reasons for this US 'epidemic' and why most cases are female remain obscure. Most advocates of its legitimacy now consider MPD a form of POST-TRAUMATIC STRESS DISORDER produced by extreme childhood sexual or physical abuse. For further reading: C. S. North *et al*, *Multiple Personalities, Multiple Disorders: Psychiatric Classification and Media Influence* (1993). G.D.R.

multiplicative axiom, see AXIOM OF CHOICE.

multiplier effect. The effect on final NATIONAL INCOME of a change in a component of AGGREGATE DEMAND. The multiplier itself is the ratio of the change in final national income to a change in aggregate demand – changes in the different components of aggregate demand give rise to different multipliers. For example, starting from the whole economy being in EQUILIBRIUM, an increase in INVESTMENT will result in an increase in payments to the owners of those domestic FACTORS OF PRODUCTION, e.g. labour and CAPITAL, used in the additional investment. A portion of this latter increase in national income will be spent on domestically produced goods and services. This additional expenditure will find its way to those domestic factors of production used in producing the extra output that is consumed. A portion of *this* increase in national income will be spent on domestically produced goods and services, and so on. At each stage of this process, not all of the increase in national income is spent on domestically produced goods and services. The remaining portion is saved, used to pay taxes or to purchase foreign goods and services. At each step, the size of the increase in national income gets smaller and is eventually negligible. At this point a new final and higher level of equilibrium national income has been established (see ACCELERATOR and KEYNESIAN). For further reading: J. Craven, *Introduction to Economics* (1984). J.P.

multipolarity. An intellectual MODEL of the international political system which claims that political power is likely to become effectively concentrated and exercised by several major world powers, a process known as *multipolarization.* Like BIPOLARITY in the 1950s and 1960s, multipolarity in the 1970s played a role in determining US foreign policy, having arisen to accommodate the resurgence of China, Japan and western Europe as world powers. Whereas the two 'superpowers' were set apart from the rest by the possession of nuclear capability, the determining factor in the recent evolution of several world powers has been an aggregation of economic strength. D.E.

multivariate analysis. The statistical analysis of data involving more than one type of measurement or observation. Various subdivisions may be distinguished. Thus the CORRELATION or REGRESSION relation of a single variable (e.g. a person's weight) with several other variables (e.g. age, sex, social class) is known as a *multiple correlation* or *regression analysis*. The term multivariate analysis is often restricted to problems where more than one such dependent variable (e.g. both height and weight) are being analysed simultaneously. In some problems no external variables (such as age or sex) with which to correlate are available; and the correlation structure may be expressed in terms of an internal set of hypothetical components or *factors* (see FACTOR ANALYSIS; CLUSTER ANALYSIS). M.S.BA.

multiversity. A word coined by Clark Kerr (see below), former President of the University of California at Berkeley, to indicate the enormous variety of purposes in a university like California set down on about 100 campuses, many of which are universities in themselves. In a university in Newman's sense (*The Idea of a University*, 1852) the parts are those of an organism. In a multiversity, on the other hand, many parts can be added or subtracted with little effect on the whole. For further reading: C. Kerr, *The Uses of the University* (1963). W.A.C.S.

Munich. The capital city of Bavaria, which became the symbol of APPEASEMENT after the 'summit' conference of 29–30 September 1938 attended by Hitler (Germany), Mussolini (Italy), Chamberlain (Britain), and Daladier (France). Acting under the German threat of war, the conference (without Czech participation) awarded to Germany the fortified frontier areas of Czechoslovakia inhabited by the Sudeten-German minority. 'Munich' has since become synonymous with any ill-judged, pusillanimous and self-defeating attempt to buy off would-be aggressors at the expense of third parties under the cloak of 'satisfying their legitimate claims'. For further reading: J. W. Wheeler-Bennett, *Munich; Prologue to Tragedy* (1966). D.C.W.

muon. An ELEMENTARY PARTICLE in the MESON family. M.V.B.

musée imaginaire (museum without walls), see IMAGINARY MUSEUM.

museology. A discipline which studies the research, concepts and methods in the collection and exhibition practices of museums. The museum has changed from its 19th-century model of departments, categorization and display to modern interdisciplinary, often interactive, practices in relation to the audience. Museology began to emphasize the role of the audience through increased services and public facilities often resulting in major architectural changes in museums. There are differences between the display of the permanent collection in purpose-built areas and the provision of large flexible spaces for travelling exhibitions. Museums have developed special heritage sites and buildings for the display of particular collections to replicate original environments and uses, and numerous small specialized museums have developed. By 1970 curators of objects and exhibitions were less influential than directors of museums, who were responsible to governments, foundations and corporations for funding and sponsorship. The emphasis on maximizing audiences has resulted in an increased emphasis on imported blockbuster exhibitions, and international loans of objects, while the exhibiting and cataloguing of permanent collections have often received less attention. For further reading: I. Karp and S. D. Lavine, *Exhibiting Cultures: The Poetics and Politics of Museum Display* (1991). A.V.D.B.

music notation. Various developments in notation have taken place to deal with new ideas in 20th-century music. Paradoxically some of these are related to giving the performer greater freedom (see GRAPHIC SCORE; TIME NOTATION; SPRECHSTIMME) while others relate to music which is much more detailed and exact (see PARAMETERS; MULTIPHONICS; MICROTONE). A whole new area of music notation deals with ELECTRONIC MUSIC and computer music. For electronic music which appears as finished tape recordings the idea of a score may seem redundant, but composers of electronic music have continued to produce them for various reasons including copyright, analysis, visual aids and, most importantly, as guides in electronic works which combine tape and live performance. The special qualities of electronic music (unpitched notes, complex colourings, supercomplex or random rhythms, etc.) are often outside the scope of conventional music notation and composers have used a wide variety of new graphic symbols on the one hand and complex mathematical and acoustical details on the other to try to represent the music. Only rarely, however, are these electronic scores produced for the purpose of the re-creation of the music. For further reading: K. Stone, *Music Notation in the Twentieth Century* (1980). B.CO.

music theatre. Originally, as used by the composers György Ligeti (1923–) and Mauricio Kagel (1931–), a form of musical performance that takes place on a stage, with some theatrical aids such as props and costumes. In London in 1956 Alexander Goehr and John Cox formed their 'Music Theatre Ensemble' which extended this concept to cover the performance of works by Schönberg, Kurt Weill, Goehr, Maxwell Davies, and others, some of them involving a dramatically significant text. It is to be distinguished from opera, but like opera is on the whole of musical rather than theatrical interest. J.W.

musicology. The academic study of music, with particular reference to its history and to questions of authenticity and AESTHETICS. Although musicologists often disagree about the interpretation of points of historical detail, their combined researches have opened up vast areas of music which were previously unexplored or neglected. For many years such research was treated with indifference or derision by the average concert performer; but since about 1950 the validity of the musicological contribution to the actual performance of early music has been widely accepted. While complete authenticity is a chimera (since we cannot hear, e.g., 17th-century music with 17th-century ears and minds), the search for it is always stimulating and revealing to the performer. Notable musicologists include Arnold Dolmetsch, Albert Schweitzer, Otto Deutsch, Alfred Einstein, Oliver Strunk, Egon Wellesz, the composer Peter Warlock (Philip Heseltine), Thurston Dart, and Robbins Landon. A.H.

musique concrète. A form of music, first developed by the Frenchman Pierre Schaeffer in 1948, involving sounds of all types (musical, natural, human, mechanical, etc.) which, recorded on tape, are filtered or manipulated so as to disguise their origin. The music so produced is sometimes powerful and evocative, though often needing a balletic or theatrical interpretation to make its full effect. Maurice Béjart (1927–) has used *musique concrète* in a number of ballets. The composition of concrete music, though slow and laborious, has attracted composers of the stature of Boulez, Messiaen and Sauguet in France, the Greek Xenakis, and the veteran Franco-American Varèse. See also BRUITISME; ELECTRONIC MUSIC; FUTURISM. A.H.

musique d'ameublement, see FURNITURE MUSIC.

Muslim, see under ISLAM.

Muslim Brotherhood, see under ISLAM.

mutation. A change in GENE, or in the structure or number of CHROMOSOMES. Mutation is important in the study of EVOLUTION, because it is the ultimate origin of all new inheritable variation. J.M.S.

mutualism. A British school of thought which, moving beyond social constructionism (see SOCIAL CONSTRUCT), sees psychological realities as constituted by a thoroughgoing *mutual* interaction between (and indeed interpenetration of) individuals and their environments (both social and physical). Inspired by the US PRAGMATIST tradition of John Dewey and J. J. Gibson's 'ecological' approach to perception (though to some extent distancing itself from the 'ecological' position as being over-'REALIST' in character), it has been developed by A. Costall, J. Good and A. Still, and is closely related to the position being developed by the anthropologist T. Ingold. It is argued that such an approach, as well as providing a more sophisticated account than mainstream COGNITIVE PSYCHOLOGY, also avoids the difficulties associated with, and limitations imposed by, the 'construction' metaphor's unidirectional and somewhat mechanistic character. G.D.R.

mutually assured destruction (MAD). The principle of symmetry in nuclear relationships, by virtue of which nuclear aggression by one STATE will bring massive and inevitable retaliation. It depends on both sides having a balance of defensive and offensive forces. Often known as the BALANCE OF TERROR, or by its rather unfortunate acronym MAD, mutually assured destruction successfully underpinned Soviet–US strategic relationships in the period between the 1960s and the collapse of the former USSR in 1990. But it offers no alternative to an escalating ARMS RACE, in an area where both sides had a massive oversupply of offensive weapons. Any sudden rush to change the shape of the nuclear equation was seen as destabilizing and therefore dangerous, so all efforts at limitation and control were limited and cautious. Many attempts were undertaken to make the doctrine of mutually assured destruction more adaptable to new requirements and new technology, but with no striking success. Indeed, the concept is inherent in the politics which surround NUCLEAR WEAPONS, since they are designed to deter rather than to be used. The logic of mutually assured destruction has been reinforced by recent theories concerning the NUCLEAR WINTER which suggest that the use of nuclear weapons would interrupt the FOOD CHAIN and cause a global catastrophe. For further reading: D. Carlton (ed.), *The Dynamics of the Arms Race* (1985). A.J.M.W.

Muzak. Muzak is actually a proprietary name but without a capital letter it has gradually become synonymous with *piped* or *canned music*. This is music, generally bland arrangements of light classical and popular tunes, which is played in lifts, supermarkets and factories. Scientific studies have been done that would seem to show that the correct timing of different speeds and types of music can subconsciously increase the listener's work output. Objections to this type of music have been made on the grounds that the listeners have no choice as to whether they hear the music or not, but presumably many people welcome this form of aural background and feel that it adds warmth and colour to certain environments. For an early anticipation of muzak see FURNITURE MUSIC, and for a contemporary interpretation see AMBIENT MUSIC. B.CO.

My Lai. Complex of villages in South VIETNAM where in 1968 US troops massacred the entire population. (The soldiers mistook the villagers for supporters of the VIETCONG, and thought that the village was a Vietcong stronghold.) In 1971 Lieutenant William

Calley and his immediate superior, Captain Ernest Medina, were court-martialled in the USA, the former being sentenced to 20 years, the latter acquitted. The incident did much to polarize American opinion on the issue of patriotism versus justice, as it did to publicize the decline in morale and discipline of the US Army in Vietnam. For further reading: W. Peers, *The My Lai Inquiry* (1979). D.C.W.

Myers-Briggs Type Indicator. First developed in the 1960s, this questionnaire-format personality test has become among the most widely used such instruments. Based on JUNGIAN theory, it claims to identify the subject's 'personality type' among 16 possibilities. These constitute permutations of basic 'focus of attention' style (extrovert versus introvert) with 'mode of acquiring information' (sensation versus intuition, the 'irrational faculties' in Jung's original system) and 'mode of decision making' (thinking versus feeling, the 'rational' ones). Each individual is assumed to be dominantly 'rational' or 'irrational' with an opposite subordinate faculty. Numerous traits, aptitudes and concerns allegedly characterize each type. It is the only orthodox PSYCHOMETRIC instrument to have emerged from the Jungian 'typological' tradition, and its use is by no means confined to Jungians. G.D.R.

mysterians, see under QUALIA.

mysticism. The term is typically used of an inner religious experience, said to be ineffable and joyful, and for the contemplative practice which surrounds it. The experience delineated by Rudolf Otto in *The Idea of the Holy* (1917) typically involves an awareness of some person or entity external to the perceiver, e.g. the vision of Isaiah in the Temple or Paul's conversion on the road to Damascus. There are other kinds of religious experience, such as the *panenhenio* vision in which one feels a unity with nature; and SHAMANISM, often involving a sensation of spiritual travel. But usually the contemplative inner state involves a feeling of losing the distinction between subject and object; or of somehow uniting them. In much of HINDUISM, JUDAISM, ISLAM and CHRISTIANITY the underlying theism means that the mystical experience is thought to bring about a union with the Divine. In the Catholic (see CATHOLICISM) and Orthodox (see ORTHODOXY, EASTERN) faiths particularly there is at periods a strong emphasis on mysticism, often centred on the monastic life; and from time to time there have been mystical movements within PROTESTANTISM, though there is more stress on devotional piety.

It is attractive to some to postulate an underlying agreement between faiths, and the notion of identifying this with a spiritual experience lying beyond dogmas also is seductive. Whether mysticism is everywhere basically the same, despite wide differences of interpretation, is open to question, and has been debated in recent years, though it is likely in that the experience is described in hauntingly similar basic terms. But this does not mean that all RELIGIONS are the same, since the contemplative way is one among a number and subject to divergences of revealed and other doctrines. For further reading: B. McGinn, *The Foundations of Mysticism* (1991). N.SM.

myth. A 'sacred' narrative, from which legends and fairy tales are not always clearly distinguishable. In a common tradition of analysis, myth is above all explanatory (how something came to be as it is). In the anthropological tradition (see ANTHROPOLOGY) best represented by B. Malinowski (1884–1942), myths are seen as justifications ('charters') of INSTITUTIONS, rights, etc. But the most recent anthropological discussions have been conducted with reference to Lévi-Strauss's thesis that the meaning of a myth lies below the narrative surface, being detectable by a close analysis of the individual incidents and items in the narrative, by their regrouping, and by their study in the context of the transformations they undergo in all versions of the myth. They then reveal an endless struggle to overcome 'contradictions'. The anthropological study of myth links with psychological, literary and classical studies, and with POLITICAL SCIENCE and SOCIOLOGY. In the latter, myth is often no longer a 'sacred' narrative but, so to say, a whole value-bestowing area of belief. See also STRUCTURALISM. For further reading: E. R. Leach and A. Laycock, *Structuralist Interpretations of Biblical Myth* (1983). M.F.

mythopoeia. Deliberate and conscious MYTH-making; a writer's return to the PRIMITIVE habit of non-logical anthropomorphization and ritualization. Some artists, reacting against the sophistications of DEISM, RATIONALISM and ATHEISM, have set out to remythologize the material of their experience, to rediscover 'belief', but in personal and diverse ways. Thus, Blake's mythopoeic system is a response to the thinking of the Enlightenment, Yeats's to the loss of Christian faith; all contemporary mythopoeic activities may be described as responses to the sense of existential disappointment (see EXISTENTIALISM) generated by godless TECHNOCRACIES. M.S.-S.

N

Nabis, les. French artists' group, formed in 1888 under the impact of Gauguin's PONT-AVEN pictures, with Pierre Bonnard, Édouard Vuillard, Maurice Denis, Paul Sérusier, and the sculptors Georges Lacombe and Aristide Maillol as leading members. Their term 'Nabi', deriving from a Hebrew word for prophet, suggests the MYSTICISM tinged with THEOSOPHY that later turned Denis and (at BEURON) Jan Verkade into religious painters. But the main feature of their work in the 15 years of the group's activity was the application of Gauguin's flat surfaces (SYNTHETISM) and bright colours to calmer, more domestic or intimate subjects. Unlike their IMPRESSIONIST precursors, they also ventured into theatre design, book and magazine illustration, posters, screens, and other aspects of applied art. In painting, however, they became overshadowed by the FAUVES, who made more spectacular use of much the same pictorial language. For further reading: C. Chassé, tr. M. Bullock, *The Nabis and Their Period* (1969). J.W.

Nachträglichkeit. Freud's 'theory of deferred action', in which the memory of past events is reconstituted in conformity with the present intentions, fears and DESIRES of the SUBJECT. The past is not recalled 'as it was', but in a form and context which is useful to the subject *now*. It is thus an act of INTENTIONALITY and is part of the life-project of the subject, since the way the past is recalled is operative in forming the way that the future is intended. The concept has been of importance in the theorizing of Lacan (see LACANIAN). For further reading: A. Wilden, *System and Structure* (1972). R.PO.

NAFTA (North American Free Trade Area). The result of a deal signed between the US and Canada in 1989 and extended to Mexico in 1994. The goal of the agreements is the creation of a tariff-free zone in the trade in goods and services across North America, tying the countries closer together economically and creating a free trade area similar to that of the 15 countries of the EUROPEAN UNION (EU). NAFTA has been criticized in Canada because of concern that it could be culturally swamped by its economically more powerful southern neighbour. In the US it is opposed by labour unions, who fear the export of manufacturing jobs to Mexico. Concern has been expressed that a proliferation of regional free trade blocs could undermine the global process of lowering trade barriers (see GLOBALIZATION). A.BR.

NAIRU (non-accelerating rate of unemployment). The level of UNEMPLOYMENT below which it is assumed that the rate of joblessness cannot fall without leading to an accelerating level of INFLATION. In recent times NAIRU has become one of the most powerful influences on economic policy in the major industrial countries. The concept is derived from Professor Milton Friedman's (1912–) notion of the 'natural rate of unemployment'. It provides a counterpoint to the short-term trade-off between unemployment and inflation described by the PHILLIPS CURVE, named after the New Zealand economist A. W. Phillips. In the NAIRU view resort to higher public spending or lower INTEREST RATES to bring down unemployment can only lead to an ever more rapidly rising rate of inflation. Many economists believe that the NAIRU rate of unemployment is in the order of 6–7 per cent. However, the US Federal Reserve demonstrated in the 1990s that it was possible to lower NAIRU below this level by maintaining low interest rates, without leading to a take-off in prices. This has meant fuller employment in the US than seemed possible a decade ago. For further reading: R. Layard *et al*, *The Unemployment Crisis* (1994). A.BR.

naïve art, see under PRIMITIVE (2).

naïve realism, see REALISM, NAÏVE.

Nakasone's reforms. After a decade of short-term prime ministerships, the coming to power in 1982 of Yasuhiro Nakasone ushered in a period of more determined and radical leadership in Japan. Nakasone was a leader with serious reservations about the post-war settlement imposed on Japan by the American occupation, and frequently spoke of a 'settling of accounts with the post-war period'. The reforming efforts of his government focused principally on the PUBLIC SECTOR, finance, trade, TAXATION, education and defence. Inheriting from his predecessor a commission on administrative reform, he strove to cut back the public sector and in particular promoted PRIVATIZATION of the Japan National Railways, which were seriously in deficit. In the interests of 'internationalizing' the economy, he encouraged liberalization of the financial system and promoted a more open trading regime (see MAEKAWA REPORT). He sought taxation reform to eliminate a serious budget deficit and to reduce tax loopholes and abuses.

His government set up a commission on education with a wide brief to recommend educational reform. His major concerns in this field were alleged lack of discipline in schools, the influence of the MARXIST-influenced Japanese Teachers Union, and the need to promote creativity in a system characterized by mass uniformity and an egalitarian ethic (see EGALITARIANISM). Concerning defence, Nakasone sought to reduce inhibitions against military spending inherited from the post-war period, and to strengthen and expand the security relationship with the US. In all these areas of reform a limited degree of success was obtained. J.A.A.S.

Name-of-the-Father. Term adopted by the French psychoanalyst Jacques Lacan (see LACANIAN) for its echoes of the religious invocation 'in the Name of the Father'. It emphasizes the SYMBOLIC function of the father as representative of law and authority. The attribution of procreation to a real father is not self-evident; the father gives his name in order to function as a paternal authority. Freud had already come to realize the importance of the paternal function in the Oedipal triangle of mother–father–child in his work with neurotics (see OEDIPUS COMPLEX). The father who intervenes, as the prohibitor of INCEST, to separate mother and child from their symbiotic and devouring relation, becomes for the UNCONSCIOUS the father-to-be-killed, and after that, the dead father. This unconscious father is the symbolic father who ties the SUBJECT to the law. But if in the neurotic there is always a flaw in relation to the Name-of-the-Father, in the psychotic the paternal function has not worked as a principle of separation from the mother – it is *foreclosed*. The father represents in the Oedipal stage the third term which prohibits the arbitrariness of the mother–child relation, thus changing the structure of infantile reality. The Name-of-the-Father, by introducing the prohibition of incest as a primordial law, replaces the order of nature by the order of CULTURE. B.BE.

nanotechnology. A diverse collection of scientific and engineering disciplines that attempt to construct devices on the scale of nanometres. At this scale, devices will consist of just a few dozen to a few hundred ATOMS. Nanotechnology began to evolve into a practical discipline in the 1980s as a result of several different technological developments. First, the miniaturization of microelectronics provided a major impetus: standard lithographic techniques reached below the micrometre scale to produce components hundreds of nanometres in dimension. Second, the SCANNING TUNNELLING MICROSCOPE provided a tool for imaging arbitrary structures with atomic resolution, and later for moving atoms around one by one. Third, CHEMISTRY began to concern itself not just with the creation of individual MOLECULES but with the self-assembly and self-organization of many molecules into well-defined structures (see SUPRAMOLECULAR CHEMISTRY). Advances in the ability to manipulate matter at the atomic and molecular scale made it possible to envisage a 'bottom-up' approach to nanotechnology, abandoning conventional attempts to make tiny devices by carving them lithographically out of larger blocks of material and instead assembling them from smaller (single-molecule) component parts. Atomic manipulation with the scanning tunnelling microscope provides a major focus for nanotechnology, but this is still an embryonic discipline. P.C.B.

narcissism. In PSYCHOANALYSIS, a term with a range of meaning converging on the idea of an investment of LIBIDO in the self. A common distinction is between PRIMARY and SECONDARY *narcissism*, the former referring to the initial (object-less) absorption of the infant in itself, and the latter to the installing of lost love objects in the EGO (see IDENTIFICATION). In contemporary psychoanalytic theory, narcissistic states are connected with fragility of selfhood and impoverished OBJECT RELATIONS. Narcissism has been one of the psychoanalytic concepts with considerable impact on wider social thought. It has been used, controversially, in descriptions of HOMOSEXUALITY and creativity, and also, famously, by Christopher Lasch to characterize specific features of the late-modern or post-modern (see POST-MODERNISM) fascination with surfaces and images (see CULTURE OF NARCISSISM). S.J.F.

narcodemocracy. Term used by some commentators to describe those countries where DRUGS trafficking has taken such a pervasive hold over the political and economic system that democratic institutions are threatened (see DEMOCRACY). Colombia, the world's largest producer of cocaine, and Mexico, the main source for narcotics entering the US, have been cited as examples of narcodemocracies in Latin America. Drugs-related corruption in both countries is rife, with all sectors of society implicated, from high-ranking military and police officers to guerrilla organizations and members of the legislature, the judiciary and the executive, including presidents and former heads of state. Moreover, the economies of both countries, especially Colombia, are highly dependent on the drugs trade, which makes it difficult to switch to alternative forms of production. Latin American governments have often criticized the US for its punitive stance on drugs trafficking, which they claim fails to recognize the responsibility of consumer countries (see WAR ON DRUGS). As a result of this policy, Washington has barred current and former presidents from entering the US owing to their alleged links with the drugs trade, and has withdrawn financial assistance to a number of Latin American countries. For further reading: E. Joyce and C. Malamud (eds), *Latin America and the Multinational Drug Trade* (1997). M.A.P.

narrative theology. A collective name for a series of developments in theology in the 1970s and 1980s, rather than a movement as such, in which the category of 'narrative' is central. The conviction that narrative forms and sustains the identity of individuals, communities and traditions is common in contemporary thought, not least in theology, where it has generated new interpretations of the Bible and new understandings of the nature of theology itself. While much of the initial enthusiasm for 'theology as story' has evaporated, as awareness of complex issues in hermeneutics and in literary theory has increased, thinking about narrative has yielded significant results in ethics – where theologian Stanley Hauerwas has explored the same issues of narrative, community and character that have concerned major philosophical ethicists like Alasdair MacIntyre and Martha Nussbaum – and in some other fields. It is arguable, however, that narrative theology has achieved greater impact through its contribution to the 'post-critical' or 'post-liberal' dimension of post-modern theology than it could ever have hoped for had it become an independent theological movement. For further reading: G. Loughlin, *Telling God's Story: Bible, Church and Narrative Theology* (1996). C.C.

Nash equilibrium. A CONCEPT in GAME THEORY which has been used in ECONOMICS. A number of individuals or firms, with possibly conflicting interests, are in a Nash equilibrium if each of them is following the best STRATEGY they can, given the strategies being followed by others. American mathematician J. F. Nash showed in 1950 that such an EQUILIBRIUM exists generally if *mixed strategies* (i.e. strategies involving a random choice of action) are allowed. However, the concept allows no role for the formation of coalitions, or agreements to make side-payments. For further reading: M. Waterson, *Economic Theory of the Industry* (1984). J.A.M.

Nation of Islam. The term now tends to refer to the dominant branch, led by Louis Farrakhan, of a movement founded by W. D. Fard in Detroit in the 1930s which has evolved through numerous internal schisms and shifts of identity and coherence. Its origins lie in a mixture of BLACK supremacism, elements of Sunni ISLAM, and then a unique and bizarre THEOLOGY sustaining the notion of blacks' moral superiority. The movement grew during the 1950s and early 1960s while revealing a divided emphasis between spiritual and secular matters, increasingly personified by the tense relations between its formal leader, Elijah Muhammad, and the charismatic Malcolm X, whose departure from the movement and growing stature as an independent and more coherently political voice was ended with his assassination by a Black Muslim in 1965. The movement remained a small sect until the former's death in 1975, after which competition to claim his inheritance as leader led to its fragmentation. The mantle was most effectively claimed by Farrakhan in the early 1980s. The relationship between politics and RELIGION is still often unclear, and followers variously pursue conventional or unorthodox Islamic beliefs. Nevertheless, the movement has acquired size and influence, although estimates of its active membership vary wildly from some 10,000 to about 100,000.

Minister Farrakhan has attracted widespread criticism for alleged ANTISEMITISM, for accepting economic aid from states hostile to the US such as Libya, for a deeply conservative (see CONSERVATISM) and repressive view of the role of black women, and for a rhetoric which seems to veer from black separatism to anti-white RACISM. Nevertheless, he is a forceful voice for many black Americans (disproportionately the young, urban and disadvantaged), and in 1995 won support from far outside the movement for the 'Million Man March' in Washington, DC, organized with Benjamin Chavez, former director of the more moderate and conventional National Association for the Advancement of Colored People. The March celebrated black unity and called for black men to accept their responsibilities to their families and communities. For further reading: M. Gardell, *In the Name of Elijah Muhammad: Louis Farrakhan and the Nation of Islam* (1996). S.R.

nation-state. Term used by social scientists (see SOCIAL SCIENCE) to refer to a substantial political unit whose territory is sharply delineated and is inhabited by a tightly bound population that considers itself to constitute a nation. Such a politico-geographical entity is often called the 'European state model', and countries throughout the rest of the world still seek to emulate it by striving to forge national states out of divided peoples, insecure territories, and embryonic systems of economic and political organization. The 1990s, however, saw the rise of a major threat to the continued success of the nation-state in the form of DEVOLUTION, which, when carried to its extreme, led to the break-up of such countries as the USSR, Czechoslovakia and Ethiopia. P.O.M.

national accounting. The statistics of the NATIONAL INCOME, e.g. private and public consumption and INVESTMENT, saving, exports and imports. These variables are related to each other by various identities (see GDP and GNP). They provide a statistical description of the economy. However, the definitions and conventions used in national accounting raise many problems, e.g. the statistics for the national income of a country take no account of the (dis)advantages conferred by a lack/abundance of natural resources. J.P.

National Bolshevism. A polemical term in use in Germany between the wars to describe a policy of NATIONALIST resistance to the Treaty of Versailles and the West based on alliance with the other 'pariah power', Bolshevik Russia, against their common enemies. The idea was first mooted by Karl Radek in 1919; its paradoxical appeal attracted groups on both extremes of the political spectrum – nationalists on the RIGHT (like Reventlow and Moeller van den Bruck) and dissident COMMUNISTS and SOCIALISTS on the LEFT. It did not survive the Nazi (see NAZISM) seizure of power. A.L.C.B.

National Curriculum. The National Curriculum in England and Wales was established by the 1988 Education Reform Act. In its initial version it consisted of three core subjects (English, Mathematics and Science) and eight other foundation subjects, with assessment at ages 7, 11, 14 and 16. The Curriculum was revised in 1995. The prescription of content for non-core subjects was 'slimmed down', freeing up to one day a week for discretionary use by schools; the number of attainment targets was reduced; the amounts of monitoring and testing required of teachers were also reduced; and greater flexibility of options for 14–16-year-olds was introduced, to allow for the development of a vocational pathway which would enhance motivation for many students who were not getting adequate benefit from school. S.J.B.

national debt (or **public debt).** The interest-bearing debt of a central government, sometimes extended to include the debt of state or local governments and public enterprises. The debt instruments may be marketable (bonds and Treasury bills) or non-marketable (deposits at savings banks and the like) and of varying maturity, from deposits withdrawable at sight to irredeemable bonds. The composition is influenced by MONETARY POLICY. The debt is accumulated through government borrowing (see FISCAL POLICY), and may be held by either home or foreign residents. The interest on the debt is paid by tax or other government receipts. Where the debt is partly held by foreign residents, the payment of interest and the principal has to be in foreign exchange and represents a debit on the BALANCE OF PAYMENTS. Except in this sense, the national debt does not constitute a burden on the economy. For further reading: J. Craven, *Introduction to Economics* (1984). P.M.O.

National Health Service (NHS). The delivery of healthcare organized by the state in the UK, founded in 1948 by Minister of Health Aneurin Bevan (1897–1960). The key features were the provision of universal medical care to the whole population, free at the point of delivery and funded through central taxation. The development of the NHS was accompanied by improvements in the population's health, but also by a continuous increase in demands on the service. The UK spends relatively less on the NHS than is spent on health in comparable countries, but during the 1980s and 1990s financial pressures led to successive changes and reorganizations. Increased user charges were introduced for areas such as payments for medicines. The free availability of other areas of healthcare, some (such as optical and dental care) previously considered part of the NHS, was limited, a phenomenon known as the RATIONING of healthcare. Attempts to control costs by introducing competitive principles led to the creation of an internal market. Providers of healthcare (such as hospitals) were separated organizationally from purchasers of healthcare (health authorities and general practitioners). As a result NHS care could be provided by private hospitals, redefining the old boundaries of the NHS. A particular development was fundholding, whereby general practitioners were given budgets to buy services on behalf of their patients. Although fundholding is being abolished by the Labour government elected in 1997, the model by which general practitioners are given a prominent role in deciding on health services locally is continuing in the latest incarnation of the service, the PRIMARY-CARE-led NHS. For further reading: R. Loveridge and K. Starkey (eds), *Continuity and Crisis in the NHS* (1992). D.F.

national income. The income generated, in a given period of time, by the economic activity of the residents of a country. The term is used so as to correspond to either GNP or net national product, i.e. the value of economic activity after deduction of the depreciation of CAPITAL. The latter usage is the more meaningful, as it refers to the income available for spending on goods and services after allowance is made for keeping capital intact. Incomes are included in national income only in so far as they arise from production, i.e. it does not include transfer payments such as welfare benefits. J.P.

National Socialism, see NAZISM.

nationalism.

(1) The feeling of belonging to a group united by common racial, linguistic and historical ties, and usually identified with a particular territory.

(2) A corresponding IDEOLOGY which exalts the NATION-STATE as the ideal form of political organization with an overriding claim on the loyalty of its citizens.

Developing first in western Europe with the consolidation of nation-states, nationalism brought about the reorganization of Europe in the 19th and 20th centuries and has been the prime force in the political awakening of Asia and Africa. In the first half of the 19th century it was associated with DEMOCRACY and LIBERALISM; its greatest prophet, Giuseppe Mazzini (1805–72), gave a generous interpretation of the 'principle of nationality', seeing the individual nations as subdivisions of a larger world society which ought to live together in peace. In the later 19th century, however, nationalism assumed aggressive, intolerant forms (*integrative nationalism*) identified with military and trade rivalries, national expansion at the expense of other peoples, and IMPERIALISM. In the 20th century it has been an essential element in FASCISM and other totalitarian movements (see TOTALITARIANISM), but also a moving force in the rebellion and liberation of colonial peoples and in the resistance of nations and national MINORITIES threatened with subjugation by more powerful states.

In its African and Asian manifestations, nationalism has assumed three analytically distinct forms which sometimes conflict and at other times are interwoven. (a) Territorial nationalism sustains the states created by decolonization which often contain different ethnic groups, e.g. Zambia, Kenya, Uganda, Malaysia, India. (b) Ethnic nationalism expresses the wishes of such groups to revise national boundaries to form ethnically homogeneous states, e.g. the Tamil, Kurdish, Ibo or Kikuyu peoples. (c) There is also the 'pan' or 'superstate' variant, which seeks to unify a number of culturally similar or geographically contiguous states into a larger state or confederation of states (see PAN-AFRICANISM; pan-ISLAM). In many Western countries, the ethnic nationalisms of regionally concentrated cultural or linguistic groups have challenged their nation-state and sought a weaker or independent relationship, as in Canada, France, Spain and Britain.

Nationalism has been a powerful source of inspiration in the arts; it formed one of the dynamic elements of ROMANTICISM in 19th-century Europe and has more recently shaped artistic expression in the 'new nations' of Africa and Asia. Despite the rival claims of CLASS war on the one hand and internationalism on the other, nationalism as a mass emotion has been the most powerful political force in the history of the world. For further reading: E. Gellner, *Nations and Nationalism* (1983). A.L.C.B.; S.R.

nationalization. The acquisition by the government of property held by private persons or companies to form nationalized industries. Nationalization may be accompanied by compensation, paid in money or government bonds to the previous owners, or it may be by expropriation. Nationalization may be for the direct political purpose of SOCIALISM or it may be for the more limited objective of increasing the government's control of the economy. There are economic arguments for the STATE providing PUBLIC GOODS, correcting for EXTERNALITIES and controlling natural MONOPOLIES. The degree of control governments exert over nationalized industries varies between industries and countries. In western Europe, since World War II, most countries have had nationalized railways and electricity supply systems, and coal mines and steel firms have sometimes been nationalized. In France and Italy, certain motor car firms are in the PUBLIC SECTOR. For many years, nationalization has been an important political issue, e.g. ownership of the gas industry in Britain has passed from private into public ownership and back again (see PRIVATIZATION). For further reading: R. Rees, *Public Enterprise Economics* (1984). M.V.P.; J.P.

nationalized industries, see under NATIONALIZATION.

nativism. In DEVELOPMENTAL PSYCHOLOGY, the theory that perceptual (see PERCEPTION) or other faculties are innate and not dependent on experiential stimuli or REINFORCEMENT for their development. See also NATURE VERSUS NURTURE. H.L.

NATO (North Atlantic Treaty Organization). The alliance was set up by the Treaty of Washington, signed on 4 April 1949, between Belgium, Canada, Denmark, France, Iceland, Italy, Luxembourg, the Netherlands, Norway, Portugal, the UK and the US; Greece and Turkey were admitted on 18 February 1952 and West Germany on 9 May 1955. Spain became a member in May 1975. The purpose of NATO, as originally established, was to defend western Europe against Soviet aggression following the failure to arrange a comprehensive political settlement of the continent's future after the end of World War II. It is a permanent mutual-assistance alliance, the key article of its terms of association being the fifth, which declares an attack on any one member state to be an attack on all. Since its foundation, the post of Supreme Military Commander has always been held by an American, that of Secretary-General by a European. Dissatisfaction with the command structure led France to withdraw from military (though not political) membership in May 1966, when the headquarters were moved to Mons, in Belgium. Greece temporarily followed suit in August 1974, in protest at the Turkish invasion of Cyprus. NATO is often described as the most successful military alliance in history, having assured the security of western Europe for over 40 years, a period culminating in the withdrawal of Soviet forces from eastern Europe after the collapse of the German Democratic Republic in 1989 and the subsequent dissolution of the Warsaw Pact (see BERLIN WALL; GERMAN REUNIFICATION). Subsequently NATO has attempted to act as a medium of PEACEKEEPING in the former YUGOSLAVIA, though with less success. It is expected that Poland, Hungary and the Czech Republic will be admitted to membership in the near future. Most other former Soviet-bloc states also seek to join. For further reading: C. Clemens, *Nato and the Quest For Post-Cold War Security* (1997). J.K.

natural childbirth, see under CHILDBIRTH TECHNIQUES.

natural justice. The practical application by the English courts of NATURAL LAW theories in the form of two basic presumptions to be enforced unless in any instance there is express statutory provision to the contrary. They are (1) that no man may be a judge in his own cause; and (2) that no man is to be condemned unheard. Actions or decisions which, in the absence of express statutory authority, breach either presumption are void. Accordingly a court will quash the decision of an administrative authority if any member of the authority had a personal interest in the issue, unless this is expressly permitted by an Act of Parliament. Similarly an office-holder may not be validly dismissed from office unless he has first been adequately informed of the charge against him, and then been heard in his own defence and permitted to bring witnesses or produce evidence. These presumptions have in recent years become the basic judicial test of fair dealing by the administration. For further reading: P. Jackson, *Natural Justice* (1979). D.C.M.Y.

natural kinds. In PHILOSOPHY, an expression used to denote those kinds which are, as Locke put it, 'made by nature' as opposed to those made by ourselves. For example, one might suggest that when we group together animals into SPECIES or substances into chemical kinds we are, as it were, carving nature at the joints, marking boundaries that are already there in nature, whereas when we group together e.g. plants as being either flowers or weeds, or bits of rock (by size) into boulders, rocks and stones, the boundaries we mark are entirely man-made. Note that 'natural kind' does not mean naturally *occurring* kind. Some naturally occurring kinds are not natural kinds (e.g. the pebble, the weed), and some artificially produced kinds are natural kinds (e.g. polythene, californium).

The philosophical dispute over whether there really are natural kinds has been confused by the failure of philosophers to be clear about what they mean by a 'natural kind'. Some philosophers reject the claim that there are natural kinds on the grounds that it involves a commitment to the contentious metaphysical thesis (see METAPHYSICS) that the world comes, as it were, with *essence* 'built in'; others, however, seem to use the term 'natural kind' in such a way that to claim that there are natural kinds is merely to state a relatively uncontentious scientific truth. S.W.L.

natural language processing. In LINGUISTICS, the computational processing of textual materials in natural human languages. The aim is to devise techniques which will automatically analyse large quantities of spoken (transcribed) or written text in ways which are broadly parallel to what happens when humans carry out this task. The field emerged out of machine translation in the 1950s – when computers were first set to the task of translating one natural language into another – and came to be much influenced by research in ARTIFICIAL INTELLIGENCE. Recent work has concentrated on devising 'intelligent programs' (or 'expert systems') (see INTELLIGENCE) which will simulate aspects of human behaviour, such as the way people use their knowledge of the world and their ability to draw inferences in order to make interpretations and reach conclusions. For further reading: W. Bright (ed.), *International Encyclopedia of Linguistics* vol. 3 (1992). D.C.

natural law. Rules of law laid down by nature. Though many theorists through the ages have recognized the importance of natural law, and have often argued that human law is subordinate to it, they have interpreted what it is and how it has been derived in many different ways. Aristotle believed that natural laws were universally recognized, e.g. the law of murder, and never changed. The Stoic philosophers considered natural law to be based on rational thought. St Thomas Aquinas argued that it was the reflection of divine wisdom in human beings, and many Christian philosophers have asserted that human laws and even national sovereigns are subordinate to the law of God. International law (see PUBLIC INTERNATIONAL LAW), regulating relations between independent states, has been much influenced by natural law theories. Locke based his ideas of life, liberty and estate upon NATURAL RIGHTS, which also influenced the French Declaration of Rights, 1789, and the United States Declaration of Independence, 1776, and Bill of Rights, 1791. The effect of natural law theories upon practical English law is seen in the development of equity by the Court of Chancery, the doctrine of unreasonableness as the test of negligence (see COMMON LAW and TORTS), parental rights in FAMILY LAW, the rules of natural justice, and civil liberties (see HUMAN RIGHTS). Natural law ideas are often about an ideal, e.g. the Universal Declaration of Human Rights. The English jurist H. L. A. Hart believes there is a minimum content of natural law, but few today think that natural law is immutable. For further reading: J. Finnis, *Natural Law and Natural Rights* (1980).
D.C.M.Y.

natural monopoly, see under MONOPOLY.

natural product. An organic MOLECULE produced by a living ORGANISM. Although in principle this term could be applied to any biological molecule, it is commonly reserved for non-PROTEIN and non-NUCLEIC-ACID molecules based on a carbon backbone, such as certain hormones and toxins. Many natural products, particularly those from plants, have physiological effects that are important pharmaceutically, and so a prominent strand in ORGANIC CHEMISTRY involves attempts to synthesize natural products from simpler commercially available compounds, with the aim of developing a synthetic source of the drug or of making more efficacious variants. P.C.B.

natural rights. Declared by Jeremy Bentham (1748–1832) to be 'nonsense on stilts', the doctrine of natural rights has enjoyed something of a revival in recent years, though under the label of 'human' rather than 'natural' rights. The most extravagant versions of the doctrine that 'nature' endows us with natural and inalienable rights to life, liberty and the pursuit of happiness have fallen into disrepute along with a faith in reason and reason's dictates. On the other hand the view that no government is lawful which fails to secure the rights of its citizens is widely held, and is supported by the United Nations Universal Declaration of Human Rights. These rights are, evidently, more fundamental than rights which merely happen to be enshrined in the local law, and are, in that sense, natural rights. In spite of Bentham's scepticism about rights which were nowhere spelled out by their creator, the 20th century has felt a great need for a doctrine which will justify the view that governments exist in order to enforce rights which governments did not create and are not entitled to abrogate. For further reading: M. Cranston, *What Are Human Rights?* (1953). A.R.

natural sciences. Roughly speaking, those branches of organized knowledge concerned with the material aspects of existence. But the CONCEPT of 'Nature' is so all-embracing, historically variable and dependent upon metaphysical assumptions (see METAPHYSICS), that it cannot be given an *a priori* definition. Traditionally, the natural world was contrasted with the 'supernatural' realm of THEOLOGY, but the modern convention is to draw a distinction between the natural sciences and the SOCIAL SCIENCES and/or BEHAVIOURAL SCIENCES, related perhaps to the elements of CONSCIOUSNESS and choice in the sphere of human relations. The core disciplines of PHYSICS and CHEMISTRY (once called *natural philosophy*), GEOLOGY and BIOLOGY (*natural history*) encroach on PHILOSOPHY through MATHEMATICS and spread vaguely into PSYCHOLOGY. This categorization has no practical significance, but is a convenient classification scheme for academic purposes (e.g. the Natural Sciences Tripos, an examination curriculum at Cambridge University). J.Z.

natural selection. The mechanism of evolutionary change, suggested simultaneously by Darwin and Wallace in 1858. The theory asserts that EVOLUTION occurs because those individuals of a SPECIES whose characteristics best fit them for survival are the ones which contribute most offspring to the next generation. These offspring will tend to have the characteristics by virtue of which their parents survived, and in this way the adaptation of the species to its ENVIRONMENT will gradually be improved. It is now generally accepted that natural selection, acting on MUTATIONS which are in their origin non-adaptive, is the primary cause of evolution. (See also DARWINISM.) For further reading: C. Darwin, *On the Origin of Species* (1859). J.M.S.

natural theology. The traditional theological term for the knowledge of God which is available to the 'natural reason', as distinct from the knowledge of God which is made possible by revelation. The scope and status of natural theology have been subjects of controversy for many centuries, and Protestant suspicions about the very possibility of natural theology were revived and intensified in 20th-century movements such as crisis theology and neo-orthodoxy. Natural theology, however, has kept evolving, and contemporary theologians have reinterpreted the concept of 'the natural knowledge of God' in a variety of ways. A more restricted understanding of natural theology, as the analysis of arguments for and against the existence of God, is increasingly rare among theologians but still common in the philosophy of religion, where 'natural theology' is opposed by the 'natural atheology' of those who argue that atheism, and not theism, is justified by the evidence of the world (see EVIDENTIALISM). For further reading: E. Long (ed.), *Prospects for Natural Theology* (1992). C.C.

natural unit of time, see under PLANCK TIME/ERA.

naturalism.

(1) In ETHICS, the doctrine that the CRITERION of right action is some empirical feature of the natural world, such as the happiness of sentient beings or the self-preservation of an individual, group or SPECIES. Agreeing that moral utterances are genuine PROPOSITIONS, which can be known to be true or false, it maintains that the facts that verify them (see VERIFICATION) are of an ordinary empirical kind and not of a supernatural character (as in MORAL THEOLOGY) or constituents of an autonomous realm of moral values, accessible only to a special moral faculty (as in INTUITIONISM). It is this doctrine, in the first instance, that G. E. Moore (1873–1958) taxed with committing the NATURALISTIC FALLACY.

(2) More generally, any PHILOSOPHY which sees mind as dependent upon, included within, or emergent from material nature, and not as being prior to or in some way more real than it. Its direct opposite is not *supernaturalism*, which holds that the realm of the divine is the only or primary reality, but ANTI-NATURALISM. IDEALISM is anti-naturalistic but is not always supernaturalistic. A.Q

(3) An approach to PSYCHOLOGY and SOCIAL SCIENCE which assumes that human beings are essentially physicochemical SYSTEMS, and can be studied in exactly the same way as the rest of the physical world. For the opposite view, and for an intermediate position, see ANTI-NATURALISM. A.S.

(4) In literature and drama, a tendency – consequent on but distinguishable from REALISM – influential in western Europe from the 1870s to the 1890s and in the USA and Russia from the 1890s. A form of literary POSITIVISM, naturalism is basically post-Darwinian and inclined towards an environmentalist and often evolutionary explanation of life (see ENVIRONMENT; EVOLUTION); it often takes the form of close reportage and documentation and involves systematized views of connection and CAUSALITY; and it is disposed to regard the literary act as an 'experiment' on the scientific model. This last analogy is established by Zola in the most explicit book on the subject, *Le roman expérimental* (1880); his own Rougon-Macquart series of novels exemplifies classic naturalism, based on intensive research into social conditions and forces and on physiological and evolutionary principles. In the theatre the leading naturalist was Henrik Ibsen (1828–1906), whose influence spread massively over Europe in

the last two decades of the 19th century. In America the delayed reaction to naturalism was perhaps the result of neglecting the vast forces for social change and the moral and social problems that arose in American society at its high point of INDUSTRIALIZATION; but with Frank Norris, Stephen Crane and Hamlin Garland in the 1890s a tradition developed which has been remarkably persistent. By this date naturalism in Europe was giving way to a new AESTHETICISM and SYMBOLISM: August Strindberg (1849–1912) was overtaking Ibsen, and the impressionistic (see IMPRESSIONISM) element in naturalism was pushing through to create the uncertain surface of much MODERNIST writing and painting. Naturalism was the transition point at the end of an era in Europe; in some countries and in some writers it has persisted significantly into the new century. For further reading: L. R. Furst and P. N. Skrine, *Naturalism* (1971). M.S.BR.

(5) In French painting, an analogous movement which derived from mid-19th-century REALISM, and to conservative eyes soon seemed a safer alternative to the Impressionism which was springing from the same roots at the same time. Its prophet was the critic Castagnary; its product the stock art of the Third Republic, as exemplified by the former Musée du Luxembourg.

In senses (4) and (5), the term was used pejoratively by COMMUNIST critics, who tended to see naturalism as the dispassionate, more or less detailed photographic rendering of a non-tendentious scene, and compared it unfavourably with realism, and even more with SOCIALIST REALISM. The latter, however, in Western eyes, is often extremely naturalistic. J.W.

(6) In the philosophy of science, naturalism is the view that there is no prior standpoint in EPISTEMOLOGY from which to assess scientific claims, no justification of scientific knowledge that is external to the theories and practice of science itself (see SCIENCE, PHILOSOPHY OF). Questions about the correct SCIENTIFIC METHOD are construed as empirical questions concerning the most reliable way to achieve one's cognitive ends. Empirical questions require empirical answers, so naturalistic theories of scientific method take into account practices that have successfully been applied by past scientists, and the results of psychological investigations into learning (see PSYCHOLOGISM). According to the non-naturalist view, in contrast, it would be circular to appeal to the results of empirical investigation in giving an account of scientific method, because it would have to be assumed that the particular methods employed in that investigation were legitimate. Naturalists reply that this is to seek what is not available: foundations for knowledge that are external to science (see FOUNDATIONALISM). For further reading: H. Kornblith (ed.), *Naturalizing Epistemology* (1994). R.F.H.

naturalistic fallacy. In ETHICS, a term coined by G. E. Moore (1873–1958) for the alleged mistake of defining 'good' in terms of ordinary empirical expressions such as 'pleasant' or 'desired' or, indeed, of giving any ANALYSIS of 'good', that is to say any definition intended to elucidate its MEANING. Moore branded ethical NATURALISM, which involves such analyses or definitions, as fallacious, and defended ethical INTUITIONISM, taking goodness to be a characteristic of states of affairs that cannot be discerned by ordinary empirical observation but only by an autonomous moral faculty. The phrase has come to be applied to any account of ethical terms or utterances which identifies them in meaning with any terms or utterances of a factual or descriptive kind and, in particular, with any INFERENCE that purports to derive a NORMATIVE conclusion from purely factual premises, any passage in reasoning from 'is' to 'ought'. In this form it is the negative starting-point of EMOTIVISM and all other ethical theories which classify VALUE-JUDGEMENTS as some form of discourse that is not propositional (see PROPOSITION). For further reading: G. E. Moore, *Principia Ethica* (1903). A.Q.

nature versus nurture. In DEVELOPMENTAL PSYCHOLOGY, the controversy over ascribing due weight to genetic facts on the one hand (see GENETICS/GENOMICS) and ENVIRONMENTAL ones on the other as factors responsible for the characteristics of an organism. See also NATIVISM. H.L.

Nazism. Term formed from the abbreviation for National Socialist German Workers' Party, a political movement founded in 1919 and taken over by Adolf Hitler (1889–1945) in the early 1920s to become the basis on which he established his 12-year DICTATORSHIP (1933–45) in Germany. Nazism originated as a movement of protest against the surrender of 1918 and the Treaty of Versailles (and the WEIMAR REPUBLIC, which Hitler held to blame for both), but it was only in 1930, with the economic DEPRESSION and mass UNEMPLOYMENT, that the Nazis succeeded in attracting mass support. Taken into partnership by a RIGHT-wing coalition in January 1933, Hitler rapidly disposed of his partners, liquidated the opposition parties, and established a totalitarian regime (see TOTALITARIANISM) based on monopoly of power by the Nazi Party.

Nazism shared many of the features of FASCISM in other countries. Its special characteristics were (1) the Nazi Party, which proved capable of matching the success of the WORKING-CLASS movement (COMMUNISTS and social democrats; see SOCIAL DEMOCRACY) in mobilizing a mass following in a highly industrialized state, and the methods used to achieve this; (2) a racist IDEOLOGY which proclaimed the racial superiority of the 'Aryan' RACE and specifically of its best exemplar, the German people, a 'master race' (*Herrenvolk*) with an inalienable claim to LEBENSRAUM at the expense of other inferior races such as the Slavs in central and eastern Europe; (3) a virulent ANTISEMITISM that denounced the Jews as the mortal enemies of the German people and found expression before World War II in the NUREMBERG LAWS and during the war in the Final Solution, a plan, largely carried into effect, for the extermination of the Jewish population of Europe; (4) the creation of the SS as an instrument of arbitrary power responsible solely to Hitler to put the ideological commitments of (2) and (3) into effect without regard to the traditional institutions of the state and the legal system; (5) the realization of German ambitions, backed by German military power, to establish its HEGEMONY over Europe, which was a principal cause of World War II; and (6) the personality of Adolf Hitler, who as Führer (Leader) of the German people showed a ruthlessness, only equalled by Stalin, in carrying out the programme contained in (2), (3) and (5) above, and a determination to see Germany destroyed rather than admit defeat. For further reading: J. Noakes and G. Pridham, *Nazism 1919–1945: A Documentary Reader* (1998). A.L.C.B.

NDP (net domestic product), see under GDP.

NEAC, see NEW ENGLISH ART CLUB.

néant, le, see under NOTHINGNESS.

necessary *and* **sufficient conditions.** PROPOSITION A is a *necessary condition* of proposition B if B's truth and A's falsity are incompatible; proposition A is a *sufficient condition* of proposition B if B's falsity and A's truth are incompatible. I.M.D.L.

necessary truth. By a 'necessary truth' philosophers usually mean a truth that could not have been false. The contrast is with a contingent truth: what is only contingently true *might* have been false. Putative examples of necessary truths include: 5 + 7 = 12; a vixen is a female fox; every surface is extended; no surface can be both red and blue all over simultaneously. On the other hand, it is only contingently true that there are vixens in Lincolnshire or that leaves are green in the spring.

One should not confuse this sort of necessity with *natural* necessity. It is perhaps a matter of natural necessity that every action is accompanied by an equal and opposite reaction, but it is *not* usually supposed to be a necessary truth in the above sense. For, arguably, the laws of nature might have been different.

Many philosophers have held that every necessary truth is knowable A PRIORI if knowable at all (some have also held that they are all ANALYTIC). However, Saul Kripke (1940–) has made a strong case for there being necessary truths that are only establishable A POSTERIORI. Kripke argues, for example, that it is an *a posteriori* necessary truth that gold has the atomic number 79. For more on this see RIGID DESIGNATOR.

A necessary truth is sometimes said to be true with respect to every POSSIBLE WORLD. For further reading: S. Kripke, *Naming and Necessity* (1980). S.W.L.

Needham thesis. Joseph Needham (1900–95), a biochemist by training, became deeply involved in the study of Chinese science while on duty in China during World War II. For Needham, Chinese science posed a fundamental dilemma to the historian. Until the 15th century it had easily outstripped Western science and TECHNOLOGY in both its theoretical and applied dimensions. Thereafter, Chinese science had fallen relatively stagnant at precisely the time when European science underwent its most fundamental revolution. Why? A Marxist, Needham attributed it to China's failure to undergo a parallel bourgeois REVOLUTION to that in the West, ushering in a CAPITALIST economy which would act as a spur to scientific and technological change. The centralized authority of the Emperor valued intellectual orthodoxy above innovation, and the mandarinate bureaucratized knowledge. Scholars remain divided as to whether Needham's stress upon what China failed to achieve is a fruitful approach to understanding the true nature of Chinese science. For further reading: J. Needham, *Science and Civilization in China* (1954). R.P.

negative income tax. A tax system that guarantees a minimum income and applies a high rate of tax on all other incomes up until a break-even point, at which the tax paid is equal to the minimum guaranteed income. The tax rate above this point is lower. This high initial tax rate is necessary to recoup the costs of guaranteeing a minimum income and to target the benefits, as much as possible, at the poorest households. This high rate of tax gives rise to a POVERTY TRAP. With a reasonable guaranteed minimum income and even a high initial tax rate, the break-even point is quite high. This implies that the scheme is costly and that not all the benefits go to the poorest households. See SOCIAL DIVIDEND. For further reading: M. J. Artis, *The UK Economy* (1986). J.P.

negative population growth (NPG). Applies to a population in which the number of births plus immigrants is less than the number of deaths plus emigrants. Singapore is an example of a country in which disincentives to FERTILITY have resulted in negative population growth. S.T.

negentropy, see under ENTROPY (2).

negritude. A literary movement for the upliftment of the black RACE inaugurated in the 1930s by Aimé Césaire, a poet from Martinique, and now mostly associated with the name of Leopold Senghor, poet, philosopher and ex-President of Senegal. Initially a reaction against the colonialist denigration of African culture, it inspired significant literary output from poets and novelists from Senegal, Cameroon, the Congo and Madagascar (see POST-COLONIALISM). With Senghor, it later became a PHILOSOPHY and IDEOLOGY for post-colonial social reconstruction. Negritude, according to him, embraces (and celebrates) 'the whole complex of civilized values . . . that characterizes black peoples'. Of particular interest to him was what he regarded as the emotional, synthesizing rationality of black people (as opposed to the 'analytical' rationality of the West), which led, in cognition, to an empathy with the whole of creation and, in politics, to a 'collective' society in which, through a judicious combination of 'communal' and individual ownership of economic resources, no one was left in indigence or isolation. In his own country Senghor's attempt to capture this historic COMMUNALISM in a modern form of AFRICAN SOCIALISM, academically aware of MARXISM and other currents of thought, seems to have met with debatable results. Though literary or philosophical affirmations of negritude are now no longer a prominent feature of black intellectual production, interest in it is still alive, and defences of it are heard from time to time. K.W.

neighbourhood. Term embodying the idea of a recognizable physical unit which is also a social unit. The idea has been highly influential in urban PLANNING, and especially in the post-war NEW TOWNS. It stems from a view of the medieval small town as an ideal entity which requires re-creation if the anonymity of the METROPOLIS is to be avoided. Such neighbourhoods have as a rule been taken as equivalent to the catchment area of a primary school. It has, however, been argued that the real social contacts of a mobile PLURALIST society are not so geographically circumscribed. M.BR.

neighbourhood planning. The subdivision of urban settlements, especially NEW TOWNS, into smaller residential units, usually of around 5,000 population, replete with local facilities, shops and school. The term 'neighbourhood unit' was coined by Clarence Perry (1872–1944), who was responsible for planning new residential areas in New York State in the 1930s. Perry's work was linked with that of Stein and Wright in Radburn, New Jersey (see RADBURN PRINCIPLE) and was subsequently copied in the British new towns (see COMMUNITY). For further reading: C. Greed, *Introducing Town Planning* (1994). C.G.

neo-classical economic theory. A school of economic thought based on the view that markets function efficiently and, in particular, adjust to EQUILIBRIUM. The theoretical justification for this view is that markets satisfy the assumptions of PERFECT COMPETITION and adjust to a COMPETITIVE EQUILIBRIUM. This theory is associated with MARGINAL ANALYSIS and has dominated much of economic thought and analysis for the last century. In content, it has similarities to the schools of economic thought associated with ECONOMIC LIBERALISM, FREE MARKETS, MONETARISM, LAISSEZ-FAIRE and SUPPLY-SIDE ECONOMICS. Many forms of economic analysis are based on its assumptions, e.g. TRADE THEORY, or on situations when the assumptions do not hold, e.g. when dealing with EXTERNALITIES and PUBLIC GOODS. For further reading: M. Blaug, *Economic Theory in Retrospect* (1985). J.P.

neo-classicism.

(1) In ARCHITECTURE, a movement between 1750 and 1850 which became the first international style, ranging from St Petersburg to Virginia, and strongly influencing the MODERN MOVEMENT, both intellectually and visually. It was inspired by the recent archaeological discoveries in Greece and Rome, by the rational ideas of the Enlightenment and the resulting notions of 'apparent utility' developed by Laugier, and by the rejection of baroque and rococo forms in favour of simple geometric, largely rectilinear shapes derived from antique sources. Neo-classicism was strongest in France and Germany and its influence on such 20th-century architects as Mies van der Rohe can be traced directly back through Behrens to Schinkel (1781–1841). A perverted form was associated with totalitarian Germany, Italy and the former USSR during the 1930s (see TOTALITARIANISM). For further reading: H. Honour, *Neo-Classicism* (1968). M.BR.

(2) In painting and sculpture, the evocation of the 'noble simplicity and calm grandeur' declared by Johann Winckelmann (1717–68) to characterize the art of the Ancients. The style spread rapidly from the mid-18th century: Canova, David and Flaxman, then Ingres and Thorwaldsen, were leading exponents.

More recently Picasso displayed a thoroughly neo-classical style, especially in his line-drawings of the 1920s, sometimes even taking classical subjects. The term has also been applied (though more obscurely) to various works of the same period: the Ingres-inspired paintings of Matisse, the METAPHYSICAL PAINTING of de Chirico and Carrà, and the serene still-lifes of Morandi. Just as 18th-century neo-classicism had supplanted the exuberance of baroque, so did these productions of the 1920s represent a return to passivity and restraint after the turbulent experiments of the preceding decade. P.C.

(3) In music, a 20th-century reaction against the emotional extremes of Wagner and his immediate followers, a conscious rejection of ROMANTICISM, and a harking back to 18th-century models. This postulated a certain detachment from the musical material and a suppression of personal involvement on the part of the composer. Paradoxically it was Stravinsky, whose *Rite of Spring* had revolutionized musical thought, who in turn became an anti-revolutionary, reverting to 18th-century patterns and textures in the bulk of the compositions he wrote between about 1920 and 1950. Of these, *Pulcinella* (1919, based on music by Pergolesi, with actual quotations), the Octet for Wind Instruments, the Piano Concerto, the Symphony in C, the ballet *Apollo*, and *The Rake's Progress* are notable examples of the neo-classical style. Hindemith, Casella, Malipiero and to a lesser extent Bartók are other composers who tried to find a satisfactory contemporary equivalent to classical ideals. A.H.

neo-colonialism, see under IMPERIALISM.

neo-conservatism.

(1) A modern American term applied to a loose coterie of intellectuals and politicians who neither claim allegiance to the organic

CONSERVATISM of European tradition nor to what they see as the mixture of morally relativist, egalitarian, statist and internationalist values which they believe has perverted the development of the USA's core liberal consensus (see LIBERALISM). The movement is represented in the works of intellectuals such as Irving Kristol and Norman Podhoretz, in publications such as *The Public Interest* and *Commentary*, and in 'think-tanks' such as the American Enterprise Institute.

Neo-conservatives differ over many issues, and disagree as to whether they share an IDEOLOGY or merely a temperament. Many are former left-wing radicals, often from Jewish (see JUDAISM) or Catholic (see CATHOLICISM) backgrounds, who became disillusioned by the Stalinist model of COMMUNISM or by their revulsion at cultural shifts in America in the 1960s and 1970s. They tend to see themselves as sophisticated realists with an informed pessimism about the limitations of human nature, and the dangers of concentrating authority in the hands of the STATE. Although not primarily concerned with economic affairs, they tend to defend CAPITALISM as an imperfect but manageable system which promotes or at least allows democratic forms. They claim to value the defence of liberty over the pursuit of equality – a frequent source of conflict in the USA's system of proclaimed values. Consequently they tend to distrust the WELFARE STATE, and to challenge government action on behalf of minority groups (see MINORITIES) as a breach of an American commitment to the individual. In recent years the expanding list of those considered neo-conservative includes some who also emphasize most strongly the necessity for a strong sense of collective national identity as the nation absorbs great numbers of immigrants; a firm moral consensus which tolerates but does not unduly encourage variety; and the place of religion and family as sources of social stability.

In foreign policy the collapse of the communist system has left them without a clear focus of agreement, although while seldom ISOLATIONIST they tend towards a distrust of international institutions and to see the use of US military force as justifiable by strong criteria of direct American interest. For further reading: R. Kroes (ed.), *Neoconservatism: Its Emergence in the USA and Europe* (1984). S.R.

(2) A term which some commentators apply to a body of conservative thought which has developed in Britain since the mid-1970s. It is distinct from the New RIGHT in that it attempts to reinstate supposedly conservative values rather than to smuggle elements of 19th-century liberalism into conservative ideology. As such it probably does not deserve the prefix 'neo'; its emphasis lies on familiar themes of social cohesion and stability, national integrity and purpose. Its voice on concrete policy issues is heard most in such areas as immigration and RACE relations, education and the family. For further reading: R. Scruton, *The Meaning of Conservatism* (1984). S.R.

neo-dada. First used in 1958 in reference to US art made between ABSTRACT EXPRESSIONISM and POP by artists becoming increasingly familiar with and influenced by the work of Marcel Duchamp (1887–1968). The example of composer John Cage's use of chance and his teaching at BLACK MOUNTAIN College was an important factor in the development of a tendency notable for Robert Rauschenberg's 'Combine' paintings, incorporating discarded junk, and Jasper Johns' borrowing of the American flag and other READYMADE patterns for his painting. Related to HAPPENINGS and NOUVEAU RÉALISME and feeding the development of FLUXUS, the major expression of the alternatively termed 'junk culture' was 'The Art of Assemblage' at New York's Museum of Modern Art, 1961. M.G.A.

neo-Darwinism. A term introduced in the 1890s to denote a theory of EVOLUTION in which NATURAL SELECTION is the only driving force. At the time, DARWINISM meant simply 'evolutionism' – even Charles Darwin, the discoverer of the principle of natural selection, had accepted a role for other mechanisms. By the 1940s a synthesis of natural selection and genetics allowed neo-Darwinism to become the PARADIGM of scientific evolutionists. Genetic MUTATION creates random variation in the population, and those variants which are adapted to the environment survive and breed – what Herbert Spencer called the 'survival of the fittest'.

Modern neo-Darwinists such as Richard Dawkins claim that the selection of random variations can explain the production of every organic character. Many still doubt that it can account for the social behaviour of human beings. There has always been opposition to neo-Darwinism from those who feel that something more purposeful than trial and error must be involved. Samuel Butler called natural selection a 'nightmare of waste and death', while Bernard Shaw wrote that if neo-Darwinism were true 'only fools and rascals could bear to live'. Neo-Darwinism survives because its opponents cannot translate their distaste into a workable scientific theory. P.J.B.

neo-expressionism. Painting, particularly German, of the late 1970s and early 1980s characterized by large figurative canvases executed with loose handling of the paint. Although there were, in general, echoes of EXPRESSIONIST technique, the many artists associated with the term remained widely divergent in intention and style. Markus Lüpertz used a transformed SURREALISM in painting his 'dithyrambs'. Georg Baselitz painted his images upside down from 1970 onwards so that the viewer would first see the paint rather than what it represented. Jörg Immendorff's 'Café Deutschland' series explored art-world politics in the context of Germany's social conditions. Anselm Kiefer questioned the redemptive possibilities in art while addressing Germany's recent history and its mythological and folkloric traditions. The tendency was identified by some as part of the TRANSAVANTGARDE. M.G.A.

neo-fascism. A term characterizing the values, aims and methods of political groups or movements reminiscent of and sometimes explicitly based upon those of pre-1945 FASCISM. It is applied to such cases as the Movimento Sociale Italiano (MSI) in Italy and the FRONT NATIONAL in France, and more loosely in political rhetoric directed at extreme RIGHT-wing factions everywhere. S.R.

neo-Firthian, see under FIRTHIAN.

neo-Freudian. Adjective used to describe several schools of PSYCHOANALYSIS which modified the view of Freud and his followers that the individual is motivated by instinctual drives which control the psychic energy, called LIBIDO, behind all human action. The neo-Freudians expanded the motivating forces to include both maturation and environmental factors, thereby rejecting the concept of libido with its link to the Eros instinct (see LIFE INSTINCT). The neo-Freudians are so called because they broke away from classical pyschoanalysis during Freud's lifetime; those who altered his views after his death in 1939 are generally known as ego-psychologists (see EGO-PSYCHOLOGY). The most influential of the neo-Freudians is Erik Erikson (1902–94), who achieved recognition well beyond psychoanalytic circles for his specification of the epigenetic stages through which the personality develops throughout life. For Erikson, the fundamental personality problem is the adjustment of the individual to the external, social world. At each period of the life cycle, from infancy through old age, the individual faces particular EGO crises concerned with the sense of identity. Resolution of the crisis leads to the acquisition of ego strengths which in turn enable the ego to master the demands from both the inner and the external world associated with subsequent stages of the life cycle. In this way Erikson depicts the ego from a psychosocial perspective. Other prominent neo-Freudians include Karen Horney, Heinz Hartmann and Erich Fromm. For further reading: C. Monte, *Beneath the Mask: An Introduction to Theories of Personality* (1980). R.P.-S.

neo-geo. Abbreviation of neo-geometric. In general a reference to a range of abstract painting of the later 1980s, notably in New York. Ross Bleckner, Philip Taaffe and Peter Schuyff recreated OP ART patterns. Making art by copying the most vacuous modernist style (see MODERNISM) they could find was in part a refusal to succumb to feelings of helplessness in the face of the impact of AIDS on the New York art community at the time. Peter Halley's day-glo blocks of colour linked by lines he called 'conduits' reflected his interest in Jean Baudrillard's theory of hyper-reality. Sherrie Levine's checkerboard patterns were derived from the chessboard, and were part of a reinterpretation of Marcel Duchamp's work. The term was also applied around the same time to the painting of Helmut Federle, Olivier Mosset and other Austrian and Swiss artists. M.G.A.

neo-Hegelianism. A revival of the philosophical IDEALISM of Hegel (1770–1831). Prominent neo-Hegelians have been, in Britain, the school of T. H. Green (1836–82) and F. H. Bradley (1846–1924), whose most loyal (if idiosyncratic) member was J. E. McTaggart (1866–1925) and most recent R. G. Collingwood (1889–1943); in France, Léon Brunschvicg (1869–1944); in Italy, Benedetto Croce (1891–1970). A.Q.

neo-imperialism, see under IMPERIALISM.

neo-Impressionism. French school of painting deriving from IMPRESSIONISM but based on the more scientific approach of Georges Seurat (1859–91), whose readings in SPECTROSCOPY led him to elaborate two techniques of rendering effects of light, both laborious by comparison with the Impressionist sketch: (1) *divisionism*, or the splitting of the spectrum into dabs of pure primary colour, and (2) *pointillisme*, or the reduction of those dabs to small dots. The term neo-Impressionism was coined by the critic Félix Fénéon in the Brussels magazine *L'Art moderne* on 19 September 1886, the year when Seurat's masterpiece *Un Dimanche d'été à la Grande Jatte* (now in the Art Institute of Chicago) was shown at the last Impressionist Exhibition. Among its adherents were Camille Pissarro and his son Lucien, Paul Signac, H. E. Cross and Maximilien Luce; van Gogh too was influenced during his last few years in France. The school was ANARCHIST or SOCIALIST in its sympathies; this was sometimes reflected in the choice of subjects, especially Luce's. Outside France it embraced the Belgians Théo van Rysselberghe and Henri van de Velde (the subsequent ART NOUVEAU designer and architect), the Dutchman Jan Tooroop, the Italians Giovanni Segantini and Gaetano Previati, and through them the FUTURIST painters, who included a form of divisionism in their 'Technical Manifesto' of 1910. For further reading: R. L. Herbert, *Neo-Impressionism* (1968). J.W.

neo-Kantianism. A school of German philosophers in the late 19th century, inaugurated by Liebmann's invocation of 1865: 'back to Kant'. In effect it was a revival of aprioristic (see A POSTERIORI, A PRIORI) EPISTEMOLOGY encouraged by the failure of METAPHYSICS, as expounded by Hegel and subsequent speculative thinkers, to do justice to developments in MATHEMATICS and the NATURAL SCIENCES. Leading neo-Kantians were Lange, Cohen, Natorp and Cassirer in Germany, Renouvier in France, Adamson in Britain. For further reading: T. E. Willey, *Back to Kant* (1978). A.Q.

neo-Lamarckism. Neo-Lamarckism built upon the fundamental evolutionary concept advanced by Lamarck in his *Philosophie Zoologique* (1809), that species change was largely the product of the INHERITANCE OF ACQUIRED CHARACTERS. It flourished in the late 19th century and early 20th century, most prominently in France, in an attempt to formulate a theory free from the apparent defects of Darwin's theory of EVOLUTION by the NATURAL SELECTION of chance variations. To many natural historians, Darwin's random and tiny variations could not provide a credible basis for the appearance of wholly new SPECIES. Adaptive, purposive, unidirectional change must surely be required for the establishment of new species, for which the inheritance of modifications undergone during a creature's life span (e.g., for Lamarck the stretching of a giraffe's neck to gain access to high leaves) seemed the best explanation. Darwin's accent upon accident also seemed morally unacceptable. Neo-Lamarckism's stress upon acquired characters restored a place within evolution to purpose. In France, neo-Lamarckism was closely linked to philosophical movements, such as Bergson's VITALISM. In the USA, by contrast, it was the favoured theory of palaeontologists such as Alpheus Packard and E. D. Cope, seeking to make sense of the complex historical interaction of organism and ENVIRONMENT as revealed by the fossil record. Nowadays few scientists look to neo-Lamarckism to resolve the residual problems of DARWINISM. See also LAMARCKISM. For further reading: P. J. Bowler, *The Eclipse of Darwinism* (1983). R.P.

neo-liberalism. An American hybrid of uncertain character, which may be more a label attached to a package of politically expedient positions than any important revision of liberal thought (see LIBERALISM). The term was coined by Charles Peters, editor of the *Washington Monthly*, to encompass the ideas developed since the mid-1970s by a diverse group of INTELLECTUALS and politicians. Neo-liberalism rejects some of the orthodoxies which characterized American liberalism in its NEW DEAL and GREAT SOCIETY phases. It rejects a KEYNESIAN role for the state in the economy, accepts elements of conservative critiques of the WELFARE STATE, and seeks to detach the Democratic Party from uncritical endorsement of trade unionism (see TRADE UNIONS). It purports to favour selective state intervention in the economy, mainly to assist the restructuring of production towards new industries and services, and to find forms of WELFARE provision which are neither excessively bureaucratic nor conducive to welfare dependence. Neo-liberalism demonstrates a concern for social PLURALISM and tolerance which represents less of a break with the liberalism of the 1960s. Its ambiguous foreign policy perspective tends to be masked by an emphasis on defence issues, in which the movement stresses the need for military reform and urges a greater reliance on conventional armaments and EMERGENT TECHNOLOGY to complement reductions in nuclear arms. S.R.

neolithic, see under THREE-AGE SYSTEM.

neo-Malthusianism, see under MALTHUSIANISM.

neo-Marxism. A term used to refer to mainly post-war developments in MARXIST thought, particularly in the West, which considerably revise the classical Marxist tradition. Two strong early influences on neo-Marxism were the young György Lukács (1885–1971) and Antonio Gramsci (1891–1937). Lukács laid emphasis on the Hegelian aspects of Marx's thought (see HEGELIANISM) and developed a striking critique of the BOURGEOIS world-view as reified – that is, unacceptably static, fragmented and objective. Gramsci re-evaluated the role of the SUPERSTRUCTURE in Marxist theory by stressing the role of INTELLECTUALS in politics and discussing the importance of HEGEMONY in the sense of the process by which the PROLETARIAT gained leadership over all the forces opposed to CAPITALISM and welded them into a new political bloc capable of resisting and eventually overthrowing the hegemony of the bourgeoisie.

Whereas both Lukács and Gramsci were political activists, neo-Marxism as it emerged from World War II was much more academic. It has been characterized by two opposite tendencies, both of which sought to rejuvenate Marxism with the aid of some more contemporary philosophy. The first, largely embodied in the FRANKFURT SCHOOL and the later Sartre, stressed the subjective side of Marxism. Whereas Sartre attempted to combine a form of Marxism with his own version of EXISTENTIALISM, the Frankfurt School was most influenced by PSYCHOANALYSIS, and their work tended to move from the traditional Marxist version of politics and economics to a more general critique of bourgeois culture. The second trend was influenced by STRUCTURALIST ideas and conceived of Marxism as a science. The work of the most prominent of these Marxists, Louis Althusser (see ALTHUSSERIAN), in particular his concept of the problematic and his insistence on the relative autonomy of the sciences, was a good antidote both to all types of REDUCTIONISM and to extreme forms of Hegelian Marxism. Nevertheless, neo-structuralist Marxism, too, was cut off from the influence of the conditions of social production and ultimately appeared as the preserve of an intellectual ÉLITE disconnected from the revolutionary activity of the WORKING CLASS. As the influence of structuralism has declined there have been recently, and particularly in the Anglo-Saxon world, some interesting attempts to re-examine Marxist concepts with the aid of linguistic analysis and GAME THEORY. For further reading: D. McLellan, *Marxism after Marx* (1980). D.T.M.

neo-mercantilism. A term coined by the economist Harry Johnson (see below) for modern rationalizations of policies designed to protect home producers from overseas competition, or to subsidize exporters, especially by indirect and selective methods. Old-fashioned MERCANTILISM was based on the belief that a country's wealth consists of its stocks of precious metals, which should be increased by securing a favourable balance of trade. Mercantilism gained a second wind with the Great Depression of the 1930s, when countries tried to export their UNEMPLOYMENT by trade restrictions and competitive DEVALUATIONS. This beggar-my-neighbour approach to employment policies has not disappeared from popular political debate. But an attempt has been made to give PROTECTIONIST policies a new respectability by the cult of 'technologically advanced industries' (which very often do not pay commercially) as the key to growth, and by the argument that CUSTOMS UNIONS such as the EUROPEAN UNION (EU) must be held together by highly protectionist farm policies. For further reading: H. G. Johnson (ed.), *The New Mercantilism* (1974). S.BR.

neo-modernism, see under MODERNISM.

neonatology. The paediatric care of newborn babies is now part of everyday PAEDIATRICS. It entails the routine supervision of mature healthy babies and those who are born prematurely or are of low birth weight. They may require treatment in Special Baby Care Units. Such babies require specialized skilled nursing in conjunction with specialized paediatric management. During the lying-in period the paediatrician can detect early changes which, if recognized and treated promptly, can avoid serious harm to the baby's growth and development: jaundice and a fall in the blood sugar are two of the commonest such happenings. D.M.

neo-orthodoxy. A movement in 20th-century Protestant theology (see PROTESTANTISM; THEOLOGY), represented by Karl Barth, Emil Brunner, Reinhold Niebuhr and H. Richard Niebuhr. The movement grew out of CRISIS THEOLOGY, with which it shared an emphasis on divine transcendence and the impossibility of any knowledge of GOD outside God's own self-revelation; but by drawing out the consequences of accepting that Christ is the self-revealing word of God, it sought to go beyond the paradoxes of crisis theology in order to develop a new style of systematic theology (see DOGMATICS). The way in which Karl Barth and others reinterpreted the themes of the Reformation, and, in particular, employed the resources of later orthodox theologies, forged the idea of neo-orthodoxy, and, under this name, it was influential – not least ecumenically – until the 1960s. The theology of Barth, however, influenced SECULAR THEOLOGY and NARRATIVE THEOLOGY, and continues to inform the development of some post-modern theology (see POST-MODERNISM). C.C.

neo-plasticism, see under STIJL, DE.

neo-Prague school, see under PRAGUE SCHOOL.

neo-rationalism. In ARCHITECTURE of the 1970s and later more commonly known as rationalism. An entirely European movement, its protagonists were nicknamed Rats in the English-speaking world. The Rationalists, arguing from a somewhat MARXIST standpoint, were in line with POST-MODERNISM in rejecting the visual formulae of the Modern Movement – but detested the elements in post-modernism which celebrated the visual vernacular of CAPITALISM. Their argument was that the true architectural model was a stripped-back version of classical buildings. In practice their built designs often have the appearance of the stripped classicism of the interwar years – leading their opponents to link the movement with the architecture of the totalitarian regimes of those times (see TOTALITARIANISM). S.L.

neo-realism. Term originally used by Umberto Barbaro in 1943 to define the poetic REALISM characteristic of the pre-war French cinema, in particular the Carné Prévert films, which he held up as an object lesson to Italian film-makers at a time when Visconti's *Ossessione* (1942 – a raw, uncompromisingly honest adaptation of James Cain's *The Postman Always Rings Twice*) had finally broken the stranglehold of MIDDLE-CLASS gentility so dominant in FASCIST cinema. The great days of Italian neo-realism began in 1945 with Rossellini's *Rome, Open City*, continued with films by Rossellini, De Sica, Visconti, Lattuada and De Santis, and ended some five years later under opposition (financially expressed) from Church and state. A product of political and social circumstances (the legacy of Fascism and World War II), the movement was essentially a bitter outcry against widespread poverty and injustice. Though the Italian neo-realist films were disparate in approach and method, the term is now usually applied to films (of any nationality) following the guidelines laid down by Cesare Zavattini, scriptwriter and theorist of the movement: 'real' people, not professional actors, human situation rather than plot, humble setting (peasant, slum, outcast society), social indignation. Neo-realism is not to be confused with NOUVEAU RÉALISME. For further reading: P. Leprohon, tr. R. Greaves and O. Stallybrass, *The Italian Cinema* (1972). T.C.C.M.

neo-scholasticism, see under NEO-THOMISM.

neoteny. An evolutionary process (see EVOLUTION) in consequence of which organisms become sexually mature and therefore in effect adult at a stage corresponding to the embryonic or foetal stage of their ancestors. Neoteny has, unquestionably, been a most important evolutionary stratagem, making possible what has been described as an 'escape from specialization'. The chordates themselves (see ZOOLOGY) probably arose neotenously from animals akin to sea-urchins. Again, the ostrich has some characteristics reminiscent of a foetal bird, and human beings have some characteristics of foetal apes – e.g. the relatively enormous size of the brain. In the latter context neoteny has been referred to as foetalization. P.M.

neo-thermal period, see under POLLEN ANALYSIS.

neo-Thomism. A movement in 19th- and 20th-century Roman CATHOLICISM concerned with the recovery and reappropriation of the PHILOSOPHY and THEOLOGY of St Thomas Aquinas (1225–74). Sometimes identified with 'neo-scholasticism', it is, in fact, simply one dimension of that general revival of medieval thought, although more important than any other for the history of 20th-century theology. Following the official endorsement of Thomistic philosophy and theology by Pope Leo XIII in 1879, Roman Catholic thought was dominated by neo-Thomism up until the Second Vatican Council, of 1962–65, which created the conditions for a new methodological PLURALISM in both philosophical and theological studies. C.C.

neo-vernacular. Originally in the mid-1970s a British critics' term of abuse for housing design which imitated vernacular building. The word neo-vernacular has now begun to lose its pejorative sense as more and more architects, housing speculators and local authorities in the UK erect this kind of housing. The essential ingredients are pitched roofs, brick walls, porches and, latterly, tile hanging, harling, dormers, strapwork, and leaded window glass. Neo-vernacular estate developments normally have picturesque, winding layouts, and an attempt is normally made in more expensive developments to enhance the appearance of village rusticity by varying the mixture of decoration applied to the façades. S.L.

NEP, see NEW ECONOMIC POLICY.

nephanalysis. Meteorological term for the analysis of cloud patterns, e.g. in the interpretation of synoptic conditions. Its use is now generally reserved for the study of global weather by SATELLITE monitoring where nephanalysis may provide early warning indication of hurricane centres. See also REMOTE SENSING. For further reading: E. C. Barrett, *Viewing Weather from Space* (1967). P.H.

net barter terms of trade, see under TERMS OF TRADE.

net domestic product (NDP), see under GDP.

net national product (NNP), see under GNP.

net present value, see under DISCOUNTED CASH FLOW; DISCOUNTING.

net reproduction rate (NRR). In DEMOGRAPHY, the average number of daughters born per woman, taking into account the levels of both FERTILITY and MORTALITY in a population. Thus, the NRR represents the ratio of live female births in successive generations. For example, a value of 1.0 for the NRR indicates that fertility and mortality are precisely balanced, so that a population will exactly replace itself from one generation to the next. Like the TOTAL FERTILITY

RATE, the NRR may refer to a COHORT of individuals or to a period of time. J.R.W.

network. In ANTHROPOLOGY, a concept elaborated by J. A. Barnes (*Class and Community in a Norwegian Island Parish*, 1954) as a means for studying the internal dynamics of society. As an analytical tool, a network cuts across the divisions drawn between rural/urban and simple/complex societies. A network comprises a field of social relations. It may be analysed as a personal or ego-focused network (ties which radiate from an individual) using interactional criteria, or as a general network (an abstract MODEL in which society as a whole is understood as being made up of different elements linked through multiplex relationships) using structural criteria.

In the case of a personal network a number of critical features have been identified for study. They concern the nature of links: the diversity of ties between an individual and others, the content of transactions between individuals, the direction in which goods and services move, the frequency, duration and intensity of interaction. It may be difficult, however, to specify the limit of a personal network, and the total number of networks focusing on an individual may not have been activated at the time of analysis. The structural aspects of a general network refer to the patterning of the total number of links within a society: the size, density and connectedness of networks. Anthropologists have particularly utilized network analysis in the study of the system of PATRONAGE widespread in Mediterranean societies (see POLITICAL ANTHROPOLOGY; EXCHANGE; BROKER; CLIENT). For further reading: J. Boissevain, *Friends of Friends* (1974). A.G.

network analysis. In operational research, the use of a MODEL designed to represent a SYSTEM as a concatenation of connected points to depict a special sort of relationship between them. For a particular type of network analysis see CRITICAL PATH ANALYSIS. S.BE.

network grammar. A class of grammars which have developed out of the concerns of COMPUTATIONAL LINGUISTICS and ARTIFICIAL INTELLIGENCE to show how language understanding can be simulated. A 'network' is a certain way of representing the structure of a sentence – a series of *states* (points at which alternative grammatical possibilities exist, in analysing a construction) and *paths* (the points of transition between states). The grammatical analysis of a text is known as a *parse*. D.C.

Neue Künstlervereinigung (New Association of Artists). A Munich-based group of artists formed in 1909 under the chairmanship of Vasily Kandinsky (1866–1944) as a breakaway from the local SEZESSION. It included the Russian Alexei Jawlensky as well as such Germans as Adolf Erbslöh and Alexander Kanoldt. Its main achievement was to introduce Germany to the work (in its 1910 exhibition) of Picasso, Braque, Rouault, and other French contemporaries. It evolved into the *Blaue Reiter*, a similarly informal group which exhibited works between 1911 and 1914, formed by Kandinsky and Franz Marc. J.W.

Neue Sachlichkeit. New Objectivity, or New Matter-of-Factness. A German term for architectural FUNCTIONALISM, used also in the other arts, where it came to stand for much of the reaction against EXPRESSIONISM during the 1920s. Thus (1) in painting it was popularized by G. F. Hartlaub, who defined it as 'the new realism bearing a socialistic flavour' and in 1925 used it as the title of an exhibition at the Mannheim Kunsthalle which featured coolly and impersonally representational pictures by Max Beckmann, Otto Dix and the ex-DADAISTS Grosz and Schlichter, besides a group of MAGIC REALIST works. These latter apart, its main characteristics were hardness of outline, smoothness of finish, a bald but often distorted or caricatured literalism, and a choice of subjects that concentrated on modern technical apparatus and the less cheerful aspects of the big cities and their inhabitants. Differing from Soviet SOCIALIST REALISM in its debt to other modern movements, it easily merged into the 'proletarian' art (see PROLETARIAT) favoured by the German COMMUNISTS from 1928 to 1933. (2) By extension the same label was applied in literature, where it described the socially critical fiction and documentary reportage of Ludwig Renn, Hans Fallada and Egon Erwin Kisch, and the satirical verse of Erich Kästner and Kurt Tucholsky; again, a 'proletarian' school of writing developed from this. (3) Where the remaining arts adopted a similarly cool approach – as with the music of Hindemith and Kurt Weill, the theatre of Brecht and Erich Engel, or the typography of Jan Tschichold – the term was again often used, as was the related idea of 'utility' or GEBRAUCHS (*-musik, -lyrik, -grafik*). For further reading: J. Willett, *The New Sobriety: Art and Politics in the Weimar Period, 1917 – 33* (1978). J.W.

***Neue Sezession*,** see under SEZESSION.

neural networks. A class of ALGORITHMS which allow COMPUTERS to adapt to perform new tasks through learning by example. Originally inspired by studies of information-processing in mammalian nervous systems, they are sometimes called artificial neural networks to distinguish them from networks of biological neurons. Interest in neural networks grew significantly during the 1980s following the perceived failure of conventional approaches to ARTIFICIAL INTELLIGENCE. A typical neural network model consists of a mathematical function (see MATHEMATICS) which takes a set of input values and transforms them into a set of output values. The form of this function is governed by a number of adjustable parameters called *weights*, whose values are adapted during a learning, or training, phase. The most widely used neural network algorithms employ 'supervised learning' in which the network is presented with many examples of a task (considered as inputs to the network) together with the corresponding desired solutions (representing targets for the outputs of the network). For instance, a network may be presented with images of handwritten digits and be told which digit each image represents. After a period of training the network can be presented with a new image at its inputs and will then produce a corresponding assessment of the identity of the digit at its outputs. Although there has been some interest in implementing neural networks in special-purpose hardware, most neural network models are currently simulated in software running on standard computers. Neural networks have found numerous applications, mainly in areas falling under the general heading of pattern recognition. Examples include learning to play backgammon, automatic screening of cervical smears, and fault diagnosis in turbo-machinery. C.M.B.

neurasthenia. One of the most commonly diagnosed psychiatric conditions between the 1880s and the 1930s, although the term is rarely deployed nowadays. The diagnosis was developed by the American psychologist G. M. Beard, who characterized it as a state of abnormal tiredness or nervous prostration, associating it with a particular PERSONALITY TYPE and appearance (thin, infantile looks, flaccid). It was most commonly diagnosed as a female complaint, and psychiatrists often saw it as symptomatic of the 'new woman', and frequently blamed intellectual overstimulation. For further reading: S. P. Fullinwider, *Technicians of the Finite* (1982). R.P.

neuroanatomy, see under NEUROPSYCHOLOGY.

neurocybernetics, see under CYBERNETICS.

neuroendocrinology. The branch of ENDOCRINOLOGY that is concerned with the action of NEURONS and their secretions, including the neuropeptides. P.N.

neuroglia, see under NEURON.

neurolinguistics. A new and developing branch of LINGUISTICS, sometimes called *neurological linguistics*, which studies the neurological (see NEUROLOGY) preconditions for language development and use in man. D.C.

neurology. The branch of medicine that deals with disorders of the nervous system. Because it has to do with physical abnormalities of the brain and peripheral nervous system, neurology is to be distinguished from PSYCHOLOGY and PSYCHIATRY. For the application to psychology of knowledge derived from neurology, see NEUROPSYCHOLOGY. P.M.

neuron (or neurone). The cellular element of the nervous system. In terms of CYTOLOGY, the conducting element of the nervous system consists of neurons and a number of supporting CELLS which are known collectively as the *glia* or *neuroglia*. Although neurons do not undergo cell division, they are typical cells in that they consist of a cell body (perikaryon) out of which grow long cytoplasmic extensions – axons or dendrites, known collectively as 'nerve fibres', along the surfaces of which the nerve impulse is propagated. P.M.

neuropathology. Disorders of the nervous system; also the study of such disorders. Neuropathology (in the first sense) can take one of two forms – inactivation of a neural control mechanism or its inappropriate action. It may result from flawed genetic instruction (see GENETIC CODE), mechanical damage, inflammation, deprivation of blood supply, or replacement or compression of NEURONS by tumour tissue. It can be investigated by clinical neurological examination (see NEUROLOGY), by electrical recording from neural tissue, by radiological techniques (see RADIOLOGY), by MAGNETIC RESONANCE imaging, and by microscopic and chemical analysis of neural tissue and surrounding fluids. Samples may be obtained during life (biopsy) or after death (autopsy). For further reading: J. G. Greenfield *et al*, *Greenfield's Pathology* (1985). M.K.

neurophysiology, see under NEUROPSYCHOLOGY.

neuropsychology. The study of changes in behaviour that result from alteration in the physical state of the brain. These behavioural changes are not only of scientific interest by virtue of their implications for knowledge of the way the brain is organized; they also have clinical diagnostic interest as indicators of the location of brain disease, and clinical rehabilitative interest in that they reveal the mechanism of the difficulty the patient is experiencing.

The nature of brain organization is inferred from brain-behaviour relationships. Damage to particular areas of the brain induces characteristic and recognizable changes in behaviour. It is then inferred that the affected area of brain was necessary to the integrity of the processes that normally underlie the behaviour in question. Thus damage to the most complex and evolutionarily recent area of brain, the paired cerebral hemispheres (see TWO HEMISPHERES, THE), is apt to disturb higher mental functioning, which includes PERCEPTION, memory, language, reasoning, and motor skill. Different localized cerebral areas are implicated by damage underlying disordered perception (*agnosia*), memory (*amnesia*), language (*aphasia*), and motor skill (*apraxia*); widespread diffuse cerebral damage degrades the ability to reason (*dementia*). This localization of function within the cerebral hemispheres goes further, and each of the disorders mentioned can take a variety of specific forms according to the precise location of the damage.

The mental functions so far discussed involve the analysis of external events and the programming of specific responses. These functions tend to be represented in the left cerebral hemisphere of right-handed subjects, and are said to manifest left *cerebral dominance*. The right hemisphere also has its characteristic responsibility, namely for the ability to orient the body in space and to articulate input into an immediate and a remembered spatial framework. Thus it lends context to the precise and focused activities of the left hemisphere. In a few left-handers, cerebral dominance may be less marked or even reversed. In children, delays in the development of lateralized cognitive processes may be correlated with delayed language development, or in older children with delayed availability of reading skills (DYSLEXIA). Certain mental processes are represented in both hemispheres, and only suffer when damage is bilateral. Bilateral injuries may cause pathological forgetting (*amnesia*); its victim can neither remember events from the recent past nor learn new information. Still other forms of brain damage change the patient's emotional make-up, e.g. they may produce apathy and lessened motivation to act.

In animals, brain-behaviour relationships can be studied by inflicting operative damage on pre-selected areas of the brain and observing the behavioural results. In man, opportunities for such observations arise through naturally occurring disease and operative remedial efforts. The neuropsychologist requires expertise in relation both to behaviour and to brain structure (*neuroanatomy*) and function (*neurophysiology*) if he is to make full use of the opportunity his science offers to elucidate the organization of those processes that outstandingly characterize the human species. See also NEUROLOGY. M.K.

neurosis (or **psychoneurosis).** In PSYCHIATRY and ABNORMAL PSYCHOLOGY in the West, a term used for one of the main classes of mental illness. Though there is no generally accepted way of defining the class (for the relationship between the neuroses and the psychoses see PSYCHOSIS), it is helpful to say that they are states of mental conflict, which, in different ways, represent exaggerations of our normal difficulties, and our normal impulses, feelings, etc. They include a wide range of states that have traditionally been subdivided (in part) as follows:

(1) *Anxiety states*, including PHOBIAS. The ANXIETY is beyond normal limits in intensity, and is unwarranted by the objective situation.

(2) *Obsessional states* (see OBSESSION), including compulsive states (see COMPULSION). In these the person develops ideas or impulses which he wishes to resist as distasteful, but from which he cannot free himself, and which often drive him into ritualistic conduct (e.g. compulsive body-washing) that can be time-consuming and exhausting.

(3) *Hysteria*. The person's functioning, in some respect or other (e.g. eyesight, digestive system, sexual functioning, motor abilities), is upset and unable to work satisfactorily. The disorder cannot be accounted for organically, and may run quite counter to what is known about the way the body works. But the symptoms enable the person to play the role of someone who is ill, and this in turn brings him certain immediate advantages in his particular situation (e.g. the battle-weary soldier who develops leg trouble).

The establishment in psychiatry of the neuroses was the outcome, in particular, of the work of the psychotherapists, e.g. Janet and Freud (see FREUDIAN). The generally recommended method of treatment is PSYCHOTHERAPY, though other methods (e.g. OPERANT CONDITIONING) have been developed. Prognosis depends on the severity of the condition, but there seem to be factors at work in these states that contribute slowly to spontaneous improvement and recovery. This fact makes it particularly difficult to establish the effectiveness of the therapy employed. For further reading: M. Gelder *et al*, *Oxford Textbook of Psychiatry* (1983). B.A.F.

neurosurgery. The clinical practice of SURGERY of the central nervous system includes operative procedures on the brain, the spinal cord, their coverings (the meninges) and their adjacent bone and ligamentous structures. Benign tumours (meningioma, acoustic neuroma) can be totally removed using modern operative techniques which include the operating microscope, the ultrasonic scalpel (see ULTRASONICS) and LASER beams. Haemorrhage from Berry aneurysms and arteriovenous malformations is prevented by operative removal of these lesions, with the prospect of total cure. *Stereotaxic surgery* permits biopsy of other tumours, and the selective production of lesions to relieve pain and disorders of movement. The insertion of drainage tubes will relieve raised intracranial pressure from hydrocephalus (accumulation of abnormal quantities of cerebrospinal fluid in the ventricular system of the brain). Management of head-injured patients (approximately 1 million attend hospitals in Britain per year) is directed towards the early detection and removal of blood clots which compress the brain. Correction of spinal cord and nerve compression by disc protrusions, bone abnormalities and tumours may alleviate pain and relieve disabling paralysis. The development of computer tomography (see RADIOLOGY) and nuclear MAGNETIC RESONANCE imaging has improved the accuracy of diagnosis in neurosurgery. Research into the mechanisms of brain damage by compression, raised intracranial pressure, reduced cerebral blood flow and brain swelling promises hope to patients suffering from severe head injury, stroke and intracranial haemorrhage. Controversy exists regarding operative procedures for relief of narrowing and occlusion of arteries. Similar controversy surrounds the removal of hormone-secreting tumours of the pituitary gland (see ENDOCRINOLOGY) and the timing of surgery for ruptured aneurysms. There is very little to offer to patients with metastatic CANCER of the central nervous system and to patients with intrinsic tumours of the glial cells of the brain (gliomas). For further reading: G. Tindall *et al* (eds), *The Practice of Neurosurgery* (1996). A.D.M.

neutral monism. The theory that the ultimate constituents of the world are individual momentary experiences, in themselves neither mental nor physical but of which, differently arranged, both minds and material things are composed. The ground for the theory is that such experiences are the sole direct object of empirical knowledge. It is, above all, the philosophy of Ernst Mach (1838–1916) and his British allies, Clifford and Pearson, but was first called 'neutral monism' by William James (1842–1910), who took it to be the ontological consequences (see ONTOLOGY) of his 'radical EMPIRICISM'. It was adopted by Bertrand Russell, largely under James's influence, around 1914. In broad terms it extends PHENOMENALISM from material objects to minds, conceiving them too, in the manner of Hume, as no more than ordered collections of experiences. For further reading: B. Russell, *Our Knowledge of the External World* (1926). A.Q.

neutrality. Foreign policy option open to a STATE, enforced by acceptance in treaty form (e.g. Switzerland and the guarantee of its neutrality by the Treaty of Vienna in 1815). A difficult option in that it relies on the respect of great powers, and is often abused, as with Belgium in 1914 and Poland in 1939. Some states, such as Switzerland, have opted for an 'armed neutrality' based on a militia army of some strength. Such states have been used by powers as useful 'neutral' territory for contact with their opponents, as with Switzerland and Sweden in World War II. Often referred to in the 20th century as neutralism. A.W.

neutrality, affective, see under PATTERN VARIABLES.

neutrino. A type of stable ELEMENTARY PARTICLE emitted during the decay of NEUTRONS and MESONS. Neutrinos are difficult to detect because they have zero MASS and are electrically neutral, and hardly interact at all with measuring apparatus. The original prediction of their existence was a triumph of pure reason: it was necessary to postulate 'carriers' of MOMENTUM, ENERGY and SPIN in order to satisfy the CONSERVATION LAWS for these quantities during neutron decay. Neutrinos differ from PHOTONS in that their quantum for spin is ½ instead of 1. See also SUPERSYMMETRY. M.V.B.

neutron. An electrically neutral ELEMENTARY PARTICLE (discovered by James Chadwick in 1932) which is one of the two components of an atomic NUCLEUS, the other being the PROTON. In isolation, a neutron is unstable, and undergoes radioactive decay (see RADIOACTIVITY), with a HALF-LIFE of about 12 minutes, into a proton, an ELECTRON and a NEUTRINO. A neutron is slightly heavier than a proton. M.V.B.

neutron bomb. Nuclear explosions are a cocktail of different mixes of RADIATION: NEUTRONS, GAMMA RAYS, alpha and beta particles (see ALPHA PARTICLE). These, plus blast and heat, create the various lethal effects of atomic weapons. The ideal battlefield nuclear device is one which kills the enemy forces, but does not produce long-lasting radiation or great physical damage from blast or heat. The aim of enhanced radiation weapons, usually known as the neutron bomb, is to achieve just that effect.

These weapons are engineered to produce the maximum short-term radiation emission over a limited distance. This radiation can penetrate armour plate and kill tank crews, leaving the vehicle unharmed. Often these devices are intended for delivery by battlefield NUCLEAR WEAPONS, and at present they can be designed to have a limited killing radius of about 2 km. In theory, therefore, they make the nuclear battlefield a more plausible option for strategists, all part of the concept of a 'winnable' nuclear encounter. As such, they have been attacked as destabilizing the current nuclear balance, and the US has postponed development and deployment. But they involve no technical breakthrough, nor even much alteration to current production systems, so the neutron bomb can confidently be expected in the arsenal, although perhaps secretly rather than openly, given the political cost of opting for 'dirtier' nuclear weapons. A.J.M.W.

neutron star, see under PULSAR.

new age music. A MARKETING concept rather than a musical one, this catalogue of music, originating in America in the 1980s, embraces a diverse range of styles including classical, non-Western and ELECTRONIC MUSIC. Some of its common features, however, are immaculate glossy presentation (records often using digital music recordings), instrumental music rather than vocal music, and a tendency to avoid extremes. This music is therefore very suitable as a sophisticated form of background music (see AMBIENT MUSIC; MUZAK). B.CO.

New Age, The. A London-based weekly review taken over in 1907 by A. R. Orage, and brilliantly edited by him until 1922, *The New Age* was a central literary, cultural and political clearing-house of GUILD SOCIALIST political bias, carrying the work of G. B. Shaw, Arnold Bennett, H. G. Wells, F. S. Flint, Ezra Pound, T. E. Hulme, Wyndham Lewis, Katherine Mansfield, Marinetti, and other important radical (see RADICALISM) or new writers. It is a superb atmospheric record of a tempestuous period, displaying, e.g., the changing response from REALIST to post-realist and POST-IMPRESSIONIST developments in literature and the general impact of European MODERNISM, strongly supporting the idea of a literary 'Risorgimento', and carrying many novel works and manifestos. M.S.BR.

New Apocalypse. A short-lived, youthfully grandiloquent and undisciplined movement in British poetry during World War II. The name comes from the first of three anthologies of this 'new Romantic tendency, whose most obvious elements are love, death, an adherence to myth and an awareness of war': *The New Apocalypse* (1940). This was edited by J. F. Hendry; the other two, *The White Horseman* (1941) and *The Crown and the Sickle* (1945), were edited by him and Henry Treece. Of the many poets (e.g. Hendry himself, Vernon Watkins, G. S. Fraser, Norman MacCaig) who contributed to the anthologies, few deserve to be described as 'new apocalyptics'. They held that one of their members, the forgotten poet Nicholas Moore, was 'greater than Blake'. The group introduced into British poetry an awareness of contemporary American verse. M.S.-S.

New Association of Artists, see NEUE KÜNSTLERVEREINIGUNG.

New Christian Right, see RELIGIOUS RIGHT.

New Criticism. An ill-defined term generally taken as referring to 20th-century literary criticism's self-purification: to the reaction against the view of criticism as the mere expression of personal preferences, and to the belief that precision, method and some theory are required. When J. E. Spingarn first coined the term (1910) he used it to describe a new trend in scholarship and the application of extraliterary, statistical, stylometric devices (see STYLOMETRY). On this basis, Caroline Spurgeon's work on Shakespeare's imagery was 'old criticism' so far as her inferences were concerned; but her statistical METHODOLOGY was entirely 'new'. The names – predominantly American – of those most frequently designated 'new critics' are I. A. Richards, Allen Tate, Cleanth Brooks, John Crowe Ransom, Kenneth Burke, William Empson, R. P. Blackmur, and Yvor Winters. Ransom's *The New Criticism* (1941) found fault with Richards, T. S. Eliot, Empson, and Winters, and suggested that it was time for a new 'ontological' critic to appear. This demonstrates how little – scholarship and philosophical overscrupulosity apart – the new critics had in common; and this variegated movement later diversified itself still further into: proponents of pure aesthetic theory (Wimsatt, Beardsley, Krieger); would-be scientific bibliographers (Fredson Bowers); and more eclectic critics who write from a particular point of view, though with due care and attention to the text. Several important critics (e.g. Lionel Trilling, Northrop Frye) were never considered as 'new' in this specific sense. The New Criticism has long given way to, first, STRUCTURALISM and then to DECONSTRUCTION. However, since it is difficult to produce truly readable criticism of individual authors along the lines laid down by these theories, the New Criticism is still largely practised, if sometimes with perfunctory bows to them. For further reading: M. Winchell, *Cleanth Brooks and the Rise of Modern Criticism* (1996). M.S.-S.

new dance. A term referring to a new style of British MODERN DANCE which emerged in the early 1970s both in performance and studio work. The new dance aesthetic is somewhat akin to POST-MODERN DANCE in that it was initiated from a desire to remove oppressive characteristics of dance training and return to the basics of movement and stillness. Influences include CONTACT IMPROVISATION, tai chi, RELEASE DANCE and alignment work. L.A.

New Deal. A phrase of contested genesis which occurred in Franklin D. Roosevelt's acceptance speech at the 1932 Democratic Party nominating convention, and became the label for the main features of domestic policy in Roosevelt's presidency from 1933 to World War II. The New Deal was characterized by policies designed to rescue the economy from the Great Depression, to exert greater regulatory control over economic activity (see ECONOMIC REGULATION), and to extend the state's responsibilities for the WELFARE of its citizens – especially the elderly and unemployed. Its methods were experimental and results patchy; World War II rather than the New Deal restored employment levels, while its WELFARE STATE framework was limited by a long-standing American intolerance of state remedies for poverty. Nevertheless, it averted greater social unrest and more violent class conflict, and laid the foundations for post-war LIBERALISM. Among its effects (not all intended) were the incorporation of labour unions into a more legitimate role in industrial relations and politics; a shift in the balance of governmental authority from state to federal level; and an elevation of the presidency to a more central position as the major source of policy initiatives. It may also be said to have created a fragmented style of politics in which organized interests (see INTEREST GROUPS) developed comfortable relations with the relevant parts of the governmental apparatus, rendering difficult the imposition of electoral choice or the representation of unorganized interests. For further reading: J. Braeman *et al* (eds), *The New Deal*, 2 vols (1975). S.R.

new economic history, see under ECONOMIC HISTORY.

New Economic Policy (NEP). A policy introduced by the former USSR in March 1921 after the 10th Congress of the Bolshevik Party (see BOLSHEVISM). Ending the policy of 'war communism' (see COMMUNISM), it aimed at restoring the economy by concessions to private trade and industry and by abandoning the pressure on peasant smallholders. Before NEP these were forced to provide the state with compulsory deliveries of agricultural products and were considered to be the natural enemies of SOCIALISM. But although under NEP the state retained control over the 'commanding heights' of the economy – heavy industry and foreign trade – the new policy encountered opposition inside the Party from radical elements (see RADICALISM), who considered it a betrayal of the workers in the interests of the peasant and of socialism for the sake of state CAPITALISM.

The economic consequences of NEP were beneficial, and the country recovered economically, reaching in 1927 the production level of 1913. Politically, NEP produced a relaxation in internal Soviet policies, but at the same time Party discipline was strengthened by the elimination of the RIGHT to factional disagreement, and the Party increased its hold over the state. By the time NEP was abandoned by Stalin in 1929 the Party was well on the way to monolithic STALINISM, with oppositionists defeated and the resistance from the Party right (led by Bukharin) to compulsory COLLECTIVIZATION and forcible INDUSTRIALIZATION neither organized nor effective. The new policies which replaced NEP after 1929 amounted in effect to a 'second revolution', this time implemented 'from above'. NEP thus proved to be an interval, a tactical retreat, perhaps shorter than Lenin envisaged when he introduced it. For further reading: E. H. Carr, *The Bolshevik Revolution, 1917–23*, vols 2, 3 (1952–53). L.L.

New English Art Club (NEAC). A society of artists founded in 1885 whose members were critical of the Royal Academy and the traditions which it fostered. Augustus John, Wilson Steer and Walter Sickert were all members at some time. Many of these artists looked to France for artistic inspiration: they tempered their own work with a little mild IMPRESSIONISM. By 1910, however, the NEAC itself seemed old-fashioned to those artists who formed the CAMDEN TOWN GROUP. P.C.

new frontier. A key phrase associated with John F. Kennedy's brief tenure (less than three years) as 35th President of the US. He introduced the phrase to great acclaim at the 1960 Democratic National Convention in Chicago, where he was nominated on the first ballot with Lyndon B. Johnson, who had also sought the presidential nomination, as his running mate. 'We stand today on the edge of a New Frontier,' Kennedy said in his acceptance speech. Thus, New Frontier became synonymous with his governmental programme. As the youngest man ever elected President, at the age of 43, and the first Roman Catholic to hold the office, Kennedy did embody a new era for the US. Besides pushing the space programme ahead, his term was notable for the signing of a nuclear test ban treaty between the US, the Soviet Union (see USSR, THE FORMER) and Great Britain in August 1963, the first slowing of the arms race since the beginning of the COLD WAR. R.K.H.

new historicism. A contextualist (see CONTEXTUALITY) approach to the study of literature. The new historicism emerged in America during the 1980s and gained initial prominence in the area of EARLY MODERN or Renaissance studies. In contrast to an older historicism, 'new' historicism dispenses with the reductive (see REDUCTIONISM) distinction which formerly separated the study of HISTORY as background from the interpretation of literature as an independently 'privileged' foreground, in order to explore the potential intertextual relations which obtain between literature and history (see INTERTEXTUALITY). Early practitioners of new historicism, like the literary critic Stephen Greenblatt, were clearly influenced by the linguistic turn of much post-structuralist theory, but also by American antecedents such as Hayden White, who had emphasized the importance of relocating history as a form of narrative and representation. Generally speaking, new historicists display a self-reflexive awareness concerning the interpretative strategies they adopt, and this 'post-modern perspectivism' (see POST-MODERNISM) marks a distinct break with more traditional forms of historical practice. Rather than attempting to produce an objective description of the past or to impose a unilinear sense of history as a form of speculative 'grand narrative', new historicism argues instead for a sense of history which is more discontinuous and complex – its concern is with histories rather than History (see HISTORICISM). For further reading: P. Hamilton, *Historicism* (1996). J.J.J.

new humanism. Humanism, the Renaissance movement that focused on the value or dignity of the human being in the organization of intellectual, religious, aesthetic and political life, has undergone several 20th-century permutations under the rubric of 'new humanism'. Early 20th-century new humanism attempted to found this ascension in science and the various philosophical developments of the times. It focused on the centrality of human action and its role in the achievement of human potential. EXISTENTIALISM was the most overtly humanistic in this regard. Jean-Paul Sartre (1905–80), e.g., claimed that, in its focus on human reality as the locus of freedom and responsibility, existentialism *is* a humanism. By the middle of the 20th century, STRUCTURALISM, POST-STRUCTURALISM and the intellectual resources of the NEW LEFT began to articulate a critique of prior humanisms, the effect of which was a new set of intellectual icons by the 1960s and 1970s. These thinkers set the stage for a philosophical centring of 'man' that was attuned to the limitations of the modern and 19th-century formulations, whose humanism was misanthropic for all but a small sector of humankind. Particularly striking was this humanism's focus on the analysis of CULTURE. Its proponents argued that human potential cannot be realized without an understanding of the relative shifts in the location and understanding of the human in different societies and the impact of Europe's history of colonization and conquest of the rest of humankind. In the 1980s and 1990s, new humanism offers a critique of racial essences and RACISM. The most recent manifestation of humanism – the 'newest' new humanism – focuses on the need for a human minimum with which to adjudicate tensions raised by cultural difference and increased global dependence. The liberal version of this new humanism (see LIBERALISM) usually articulates itself as 'cosmopolitan liberalism', where liberalism is wedded to a theory that recognizes cultural differences across national boundaries but rejects differences that appeal to social 'essences'. This liberalism is usually supported by a cultural and political reformulation of SOCIAL CONTRACT theories or consensus models of politics. The Left version of this recent new humanism is usually wedded to Fanonian analyses of the importance of the relation between a new formulation of the human and a new way of living or being human. L.R.G.

new international division of labour. A

post-1985 borderless system of trade and investment organized by multinational companies in Japan, the US and other advanced economies, with a highly specialized division of knowledge and function, replacing an older division of final primary and manufacturing production. The Japanese system selects sophisticated activities, including R&D-intensive industries (see RESEARCH AND DEVELOPMENT), for the NEWLY INDUSTRIALIZING COUNTRIES (NICs), while assigning standardized labour-intensive production to China and the ASEAN four (Indonesia, Malaysia, the Philippines and Thailand).

This system necessitates little ownership by the Japanese corporation that has technology, loan, exclusive-agency, contractual or purchase arrangements with foreign firms (see FIRM, THEORIES OF). Thus Sony has factories for audio and video products in the NICs and ASEAN, the major distribution warehouse in Singapore, and a global linkage of these units on-line with subsidiaries and co-operating firms.

This division, however, widens the gap between modern and traditional industries within ASEAN, which lacks the NICs' ability to innovate but is less peripheral to labour division than Africa and South Asia, with little INFRASTRUCTURE. For further reading: S. Tokunaga (ed.), *Japan's Foreign Investment and Asian Economic Interdependence* (1992). E.W.N.

New International Economic Order (NIEO). The new order comprises all economic relations and institutions that link people from different nations, including the World Bank (see BRETTON WOODS), which lends capital to developing countries; the IMF, which provides credit to ease short-term international payment imbalances; the World Trade Organization, which administers rules of conduct in international trade; bilateral and multilateral trade, aid, banking services, currency rates, capital movements, and technological transfers; and international commodity stabilization agreements. Since the 1970s, there have been two NIEO visions: that of the Group of 77 (G-77) DEVELOPING COUNTRIES (adopted by the UN General Assembly, 1974) and the ECONOMIC LIBERALISM of the rich countries.

The G-77 wanted more policy influence in international institutions and more control over international economic relations. The UN resolution asked for increased (especially food and agricultural) aid, more transfer of science and technology, the strengthening of G-77 technical INFRASTRUCTURE, the redeployment of protected industries to the G-77, trade policies conducive to G-77 export expansion, and increased export stability.

For many rich countries, the NIEO implied vague intentions, not implementation, which required painstaking negotiations. Moreover, industrialized countries, led by the US, opposed much of the NIEO agenda, replacing this with market-friendly policies enforced by the Bretton Woods institutions they dominated. These policies, introduced during the erosion of G-77 bargaining power with the DEBT CRISIS of the 1980s, included monetary and fiscal contraction, wage restraint, price and EXCHANGE RATE decontrol, deregulation, and PRIVATIZATION. For further reading: E. W. Nafziger, *The Economics of Developing Countries* (1997). E.W.N.

New Left. A political tendency which emerged in several countries in the late 1950s and 1960s through disenchantment with the conventional LEFT. Its idealism was generally more intense; it was partly based on a new emphasis on the MARXIST concept of ALIENATION and on other aspects of NEO-MARXIST thought. It also came to embrace elements of ANARCHISM, SYNDICALISM, TROTSKYISM, MAOISM and CASTROISM. In Britain the New Left's emergence was stimulated by the disillusionment of many British COMMUNISTS with the Soviet Union (see STALINISM), by changes in Marxist analysis, and by non-communist radicals. These strands came together in the founding of the *New Left Review* in 1960. In the US the origins of the New Left are usually traced to the Port Huron Statement, a manifesto issued in 1962 by Students for a Democratic Society (SDS), an organization which became a key component of the New Left. More generally the movement's impetus came from radicalizing effects of the CIVIL RIGHTS MOVEMENT, campus revolts against the university system, and the war in VIETNAM. In France, West Germany and Japan the New Left of the 1960s was also a predominantly student and MIDDLE-CLASS phenomenon. It stimulated the events of

MAY 1968 in Paris, widespread unrest in universities, and such TERRORIST splinter groups as the Baader-Meinhof group in Germany and the Japanese RED ARMY Faction. By the end of the decade the movement had fragmented; in varying proportions in each country, ACTIVISTS entered more conventional Left politics, fringe terrorist organizations, or tendencies such as the GREEN MOVEMENT or radical FEMINISM, while others withdrew from politics. The more sophisticated elements of New Left thought have retained some currency in intellectual debate. For further reading: A. Matusow, *The Unraveling of America* (1984).
L.L.; S.R.

new novel (*nouveau roman*). The name given to a new kind of ANTI-NOVEL, i.e. to the kind of work produced by a group of French novelists (notably Alain Robbe-Grillet, Nathalie Sarraute and Michel Butor) who tried deliberately to adapt the technique of novel-writing to what they considered to be the requirement of mid-20th-century sensibilities. Although they were not, and did not claim to be, a school, they all rejected such features of the traditional novel as character-drawing, linear narrative, and obtrusive social or political content. Instead, they offered elaborate, and often apparently gratuitous, structures, as well as minute notation of psychological and physical detail. All were strongly avant-gardist (see AVANT-GARDE), i.e. they believed that each new generation of artists must reveal fresh aspects of reality, and were convinced of the inseparability of form and content. They can be seen both as following on from EXISTENTIAL PSYCHOLOGY and PHENOMENOLOGY, and as reacting against Sartre's theory of COMMITMENT, which was the prevailing literary doctrine when Robbe-Grillet, the most prominent member of the group, first emerged in the mid-1950s. Typical novels are Robbe-Grillet's *La Jalousie* (1957), Sarraute's *Les Fruits d'or* (1963), and Butor's *L'Emploi du temps* (1957), and the two major theoretical statements *Pour un nouveau roman* (1963) by Robbe-Grillet and *L'Ere du soupçon* (1956) by Sarraute. This wave of experimentalism was important mainly in France, though there have been echoes elsewhere, e.g. Uwe Johnson in Germany, Susan Sontag in America, Christine Brooke-Rose and Rayner Heppenstall in England. For further reading: J. Sturrock, *The French New Novel* (1969). J.G.W.

New Orleans. The traditional birthplace of JAZZ, and home to a jazz style which still possesses much of its original character. Compounded of BLUES, marches, RAGTIME and dances like the quadrille, it emerged in the 1890s in black dance halls and social clubs, performed customarily by a three-man front line, which roughly but exuberantly filled the basic musical functions: trumpet or cornet played a strong lead supported by the trombone, while a clarinet spun upper-register embroidery. Below them, piano, string bass or tuba and banjo provided the firm rhythmic pulse. Indeed, all the instruments contributed to the warm, throbbing pulse which is still the music's stamp. In its classic form, individual virtuosity mattered less than the ensemble effect, and, except for short breaks, solos were relatively rare. All that would be changed, however, by New Orleans's most famous son and jazz's first genius, Louis Armstrong (*c.* 1898–1971). GE.S.

new/processual archaeology. A development of the 1960s which aimed to make ARCHAEOLOGY less intuitive and subjective, and hence more scientific, by stating its assumptions, testing its hypotheses, and using specific scientific procedures derived from POSITIVISM; some practitioners even believed that laws of human behaviour could be attained by using the correct METHODOLOGY. Its emphasis was on studying the processes (hence the name) of culture change through the relationship between social and economic aspects of culture and the environment. For further reading: L. R. Binford, *In Pursuit of the Past* (1983).
P.G.B.

new religious movements (NRMs). Also referred to as 'alternative religions' (or as SECTS OR CULTS), they tend to be new in so far as they became visible in their present form after World War II, and religious in so far as they offer answers to the ultimate questions traditionally addressed by mainstream RELIGIONS.

Of course, all religions were new at some time, but the current wave of NRMs is unique in its sheer abundance and diversity. Numbers depend upon the precise definition used, but it has been estimated that there are around 2,000–3,000 movements in the West, 10,000 in Africa, and several thousands more in Japan and elsewhere. The number of adherents is, however, relatively small; even the better-known movements, such as the Unification Church (Moonies), Hare Krishna and The Family have no more than a few hundred core members in any one country at any one time.

NRMs differ radically from each other. They may come from the traditions of CHRISTIANITY, HINDUISM, BUDDHISM, ISLAM or Paganism; they may draw on a host of alternative ideologies (see IDEOLOGY) and philosophies. Their practices, lifestyles and legal and financial status also exhibit wide variations. However, they usually share, at least initially, the characteristics of a membership of first-generation converts (who typically exhibit far greater enthusiasms than those born into a religion), and a founder who frequently wields a charismatic authority (see CHARISMA; PERSONALITY CULT; AUTHORITARIANISM). Furthermore, by promoting alternatives to mainstream beliefs and practices, they are commonly treated with suspicion and hostility by the rest of society. E.V.B.

new riddle of induction. INDUCTION is that form of reasoning in which the premises are supposed to support the conclusion drawn while not actually entailing that conclusion. An example would be: All observed emeralds are green; therefore: all emeralds are green. Inductive reasoning allows us to draw conclusions about what we haven't observed on the basis of what we have observed. Hume raised the classic problem of induction: such reasoning appears to depend on the background assumption that nature is uniform, and it seems this assumption can be justified neither by experience nor by reason. It appears, then, that reasoning inductively is irrational.

The philosopher Nelson Goodman presents a new riddle concerning induction. Let the predicate 'grue' apply to an object just in case it is green and observed before midnight tonight, or else blue and not observed before midnight tonight. Then all observed emeralds are grue. Yet we would not consider ourselves justified in concluding that all emeralds are grue (because, of course, that would commit us to the unobserved ones being blue). The problem is to say why, on the basis of those emeralds we have observed, we are justified in concluding that all emeralds are green, but not justified in concluding that all emeralds are grue. What makes the former piece of inductive reasoning legitimate, and the latter not? One obvious strategy would be to come up with a way of distinguishing between those predicates like 'green' which are acceptable for the purposes of inductive reasoning, and those predicates like 'grue' which are not (Goodman calls this the problem of distinguishing between 'projectible' and 'non-projectible' predicates). However, it is not obvious how this distinction should be made. S.W.L.

new town. Term generally taken to refer to development of green-field, government-funded, mass housing settlements built mid-century in both the US and the UK. However, there is a much longer tradition of utopian new town building (D. Hayden, *Seven American Utopias: The architecture of communitarian socialism*, 1976).

Under the 1946 New Towns Act SATELLITE TOWNS of 30,000–50,000 population were built outside the London GREEN BELT, incorporating GARDEN CITY principles, and divided into neighbourhood units (see NEIGHBOURHOOD PLANNING). In the 1960s and 1970s under the Labour government a subsequent phase of new town building was developed as regional growth magnets in the North and the Midlands. Nowadays greater emphasis is put upon URBAN RENEWAL of existing towns. For further reading: M. Aldridge, *The British New Towns* (1979). C.G.

new vocationalism. A term used to describe a shift in emphasis in British educational policies from the late 1970s onwards, particularly under Conservative governments (see CONSERVATISM) between 1979 and 1997, though also under New Labour. The new policies placed much less emphasis on EGALITARIANISM and the liberal-humanist ideal (see HUMANISM; LIBERALISM) of using education to develop individual potential for its own sake and much more on improving levels of attainment and training in the workforce to facilitate growth of the economy. New policies included allowing schools to decide to opt out of local authority control to become centrally funded, encouraging diversity in schools and competition between them, introducing new vocational qualifications and an emphasis on traditional teaching methods. Critics question the assumption, on which such policies were based, that educational standards had been declining. Some see the real purpose of the policies as strengthening central government control over education and reintroducing a two-tier education system to the benefit of predominantly middle-class children in the more successful schools. For further reading: S. Ball, *Politics and Policy-Making in Education* (1990). M.D.H.

new wave (*nouvelle vague*). Loose journalistic term to define the sudden influx of new talent into the French cinema in 1959–60, when 67 new directors embarked on their first feature films. It was coined on the analogy of the 'new look' (clothing styles introduced by Christian Dior in the late 1940s) and the NEW NOVEL (*nouveau roman*). Spearheading the movement were the *Cahiers du Cinéma* group of critics (François Truffaut, Jean-Luc Godard, Claude Chabrol, Eric Rohmer, Jacques Rivette). The commercial and artistic success of their first films, made very quickly, cheaply, and without established stars, revolutionized production in the French film industry. But the methods characteristic of the early *nouvelle vague* films – improvisation, hand-held cameras, location shooting, minimum technical crews – were exigencies of economy rather than a matter of principle. The only real unifying principle behind the movement, which included documentarists (Alain Resnais, Chris Marker) and young film-makers from within the industry (Louis Malle, Roger Vadim), was the belief, constantly reiterated by the *Cahiers du Cinéma* critics, that a film should be the conception of one man, the AUTEUR, rather than a commercial package arbitrarily put together by a studio or a producer. In its English form, the term has subsequently been applied to any sudden creative surge in the cinema, e.g. in Britain immediately after the French *nouvelle vague*, or in Australia in the 1970s and 1980s. For further reading: P. Graham (ed.), *The New Wave* (1968). T.C.C.M.

new wave (in popular music), see under PUNK.

new working class, see under WORKING CLASS.

new world order. The phrase popularized by US President George Bush as he sought to build support for the Gulf War of 1991. The phrase was in long use – and echoed by both Hitler's 'New Order' and the Latin phrase *novus ordo seclorum* which appears on the American dollar bill – before appearing in a Bush speech just a few months before the Iraqi invasion of Kuwait. It found its definitive usage by Bush on 11 September 1990, in an address to the US Congress, when he declared that an international effort to help Kuwait and create 'the new world order' was one of the objectives of the war effort. Bush may have picked up the term from Soviet leader Mikhail Gorbachev, who used it at the United Nations (UN) in 1988 to describe the post-cold war landscape. Whatever the origin, elements of the far Right and Christian fundamentalists feared that the phrase was a code word for a UN-led one-world government or even the coming of the Antichrist. But Bush had a more prosaic interpretation in his speech months before Saddam's invasion: 'Time and time again in this century, the political map of the world was transformed. And in each instance a new world order came about through the advent of a new tyrant or its end.' R.K.H.

New Writing**.** A bi-annual founded in London by John Lehmann in 1936 to give voice to younger writers 'conscious of the great social, political and moral changes going on round them', rally anti-FASCIST voices, and emphasize the international dimension of this entire tendency. The venture – retitled *Folios of New Writing* (1940–41) and *New Writing and Daylight* (1942) – carried many major writers of its period: Spender, Auden, Isherwood, Edward Upward, William Sansom, Rex Warner, Orwell, Pasternak, Silone, and André Chamson, as well as a good number of working-class authors. An important extension was *Penguin New Writing* (1940–50), which through the war years carried much important writing, including valuable reportage and documentary, and a broad interest in all the arts, to a wide audience. M.S.BR.

New York School. A general term applied

to artists working in New York City in the 1940s and 1950s, primarily in the ABSTRACT EXPRESSIONIST style. School in this case connotes no more than a sense of community, energy and ambition among artists as diverse as Jackson Pollock, Arshile Gorky, Franz Kline, Adolph Gottlieb, Willem de Kooning, Hans Hofmann, and Barnett Newman. It is now used, analogously with ÉCOLE DE PARIS, to encompass subsequent artistic styles with an American flavour. See also ACTION PAINTING. For further reading: D. Ashton, *The New York School. A Cultural Reckoning* (1973).

A.K.W.

newly industrializing countries (NICs). Late-coming high-income and upper-middle-income countries that have experienced rapid ECONOMIC GROWTH and a rapid increase in the shares of manufacturing in their national output and exports since the 1950s. These increases have usually been matched by declines in the shares of agriculture and primary exports. Most economists regard these transformations in the structure of their economies as the cause of their rapid economic growth (see ECONOMIC DEVELOPMENT). This process of industrialization is usually attributed to countries' policies of promoting manufactured exports. FREE MARKET policies and state guidance are both important in explaining these countries' economic success. NICs include high-income South Korea, Taiwan, Hong Kong and Singapore; and perhaps upper-middle-income countries Brazil and Malaysia. For further reading: E. W. Nafziger, *The Economics of Developing Countries* (1997).

J.P.; E.W.N.

newsgroups. An INTERNET service comparable to membership of a global discussion club or salon. The name implies they are news outlets, but they exchange more opinions and history than news. Visitors can read or post comments. Thousands of these groups exist and discuss every known kind of fetish, philosophy, science, political theory, sport and disease. Newsgroups are perhaps the strongest example of the electronic world's ability to unite people of shared interest, no matter how much space separates them.

E.B.B.

Newspeak, see under ORWELLIAN.

Newton-Raphson method, see under GRADIENT METHODS.

Newtonian mechanics. One of the three great theories of MECHANICS. The basic principle is that the forces exerted on a material system by its interaction with other matter produce an acceleration of the system – i.e. a *change* in its velocity or MOMENTUM. The precise law is: *acceleration = force ÷ mass* (see MASS). This means that if there is no force acting on a system its acceleration is zero, and the system persists unaltered in its state of rest or motion. (By contrast, in an earlier mechanics deriving mainly from Aristotle, it was believed that force was necessary to maintain motion itself, so that a body far from all others would come to rest.)

Newtonian mechanics is prevented from being a tautology by a series of 'laws of force' which state the various ways in which systems can interact. Fortunately there appears to be only a small number of basically different forces in nature: GRAVITATION, ELECTROMAGNETISM, STRONG INTERACTIONS, and WEAK INTERACTIONS. Other forces such as friction can be explained in terms of these.

When dealing with the interactions between the parts of a composite system, it is necessary to add a further postulate: the force on body *A* exerted by body *B* is equal in magnitude but opposite in direction to that on body *B* exerted by body *A* (i.e. 'action and reaction are equal').

Abundant verifications of Newtonian mechanics are provided by experiments and observations ranging from the motion of the heavenly bodies (see CELESTIAL MECHANICS) to the CONTINUUM systems studied in RHEOLOGY. For systems of atomic dimensions Newtonian mechanics no longer holds, and must be replaced by QUANTUM MECHANICS, while for systems moving near the speed of light or in enormous gravitational fields it must be replaced by RELATIVITY. See also MACH'S PRINCIPLE; PHYSICS. For further reading: P. Harman, *Metaphysics and Natural Philosophy* (1982).

M.V.B.

'next steps' agencies. Executive agencies established in the UK as a product of the reform of the civil service since 1988. The 'next steps' reforms envisaged the splitting of the civil service into a core of policy advisers and a network of agencies dedicated to delivering the services and day-to-day operations. Agencies enjoy a high degree of autonomy over questions of recruitment, pay, grading and internal organization. They work within 'framework documents' negotiated with their sponsoring departments, which set out their performance targets, including not merely financial indicators but also measures of service quality. By 1997, 77 per cent of permanent civil servants worked in agencies. The advantages of the scheme are held to be greater efficiency in management and flexibility and diversity in civil service organization. However, difficulties have emerged, especially in politically controversial areas such as prison administration and benefit provision. It has not proved easy to demarcate 'policy' and 'operations', which has led to accusations that the work of agencies is both too subject to ministerial interference and also insufficiently accountable to Parliament. Critics have also argued that the reforms have damaged the integration of the civil service and its traditional values of impartiality and public service. For further reading: K. Dowding, *The Civil Service* (1995). N.O.

NGOs (non-government organizations). NGOs have no governmental status or function, are not created by governments, nor are their agendas set by governments. NGOs may be local, national or international; the range of their concerns and objectives is almost infinite.

The NGOs which have given the term currency are largely concerned with issues relating to the environment, development, human population, reproduction, health, food and housing – all of which are perceived as global as well as national problems. NGOs organized around these themes and issues may be supported by foundation grants, gifts and bequests, and by general membership fees and fund drives. These NGOs devote their efforts to the development of policies in the areas of concern, and to influencing policy-makers at various levels of government, and the public, regarding these issues and relevant policies and laws.

While NGOs have long been active in some of the developed countries their visibility and effectiveness concerning controversial issues may depend on the availability of legal protections and the respect and protections afforded by governments.

International NGOs are usually confederations of national organizations – examples are the World Wildlife Fund, Greenpeace, Friends of the Earth, and the Rainforest Alliance. With the development of the United Nations (UN) and its agencies, and the emergence of environmental and other problems of global dimensions, NGOs have gained international prominence and influence. At major national and international conferences on topics of interest to them but in which they are not participants, NGOs may organize concurrent conferences. This is particularly the case regarding UN agencies such as UNEP (United Nations Environment Programme). W.G.R.

NHS, see NATIONAL HEALTH SERVICE.

NICs, see NEWLY INDUSTRIALIZING COUNTRIES.

Nicaragua. Central American republic with an economy based on primary export crops, mainly coffee, cotton and sugar. Subject to repeated invasions by the US in the first quarter of the 20th century, Nicaragua was occupied by US Marines from 1927 until 1934. Washington withdrew its troops under Franklin D. Roosevelt's Good Neighbor Policy, but left behind a surrogate force in the Nicaraguan National Guard, which supported 45 years of dictatorship by the Somoza family (1934–79). *Somocismo* was characterized by extreme centralization of power, corruption and wide-scale HUMAN RIGHTS abuses. Anastasio Somoza Debayle was overthrown in July 1979 by a popular uprising led by the Sandinista National Liberation Front (FSLN), after a prolonged civil war which claimed over 50,000 lives. (See SANDINISTA; CONTRAS; REAGAN DOCTRINE.) For further reading: G. Black, *Triumph of the People* (1981). N.M.

NIEO, see NEW INTERNATIONAL ECONOMIC ORDER.

Nietzschean. Ideas derived from or resembling the writings of the German philosopher Friedrich Nietzsche (1844–1900). Most famous for repudiating Christianity during his lifetime and for being used to justify fascist IDEOLOGY (see FASCISM his death, Nietzsche's work was notable for its stylistic virtuosity, and heavy use of irony, humour and exaggeration, which has contributed to the difficulties in interpreting it. He is still an influential figure today, as many see his fragmented style and distrust of truth as anticipating POST-MODERNISM. He originated many important concepts, including APOLLONIAN AND DIONYSIAN CULTURES, ETERNAL RETURN, LAST MAN, MASTER MORALITY, ÜBERMENSCH, and WILL TO POWER. For further reading: P. Sedgwick, *Nietzsche: A Critical Reader* (1995). A.A.L.

Night of the Long Knives. The dramatic events of the weekend of 29 June–2 July 1934 in Germany when, on the orders of Hitler, Ernst Roehm and the leadership of the brown-shirted SA were liquidated. The SA Stormtroopers had been an indispensable element in the Nazis' rise to power (see NAZISM) but had become a major embarrassment in Hitler's relations with the German Army, which were the key to his succeeding the dying Hindenburg as head of state and Commander-in-Chief as well as Chancellor. Goering and Himmler (whose black-shirted SS carried out the executions) were the moving spirits in organizing the killings. Hitler was apparently convinced by the argument that the SA leaders were plotting a second and more radical REVOLUTION; but the smoothness with which the operation was carried out and the absence of any resistance suggested that this was a pretext with little substance. Among the 150–200 estimated to have been killed were a number (such as Gregor Strasser and General von Scheicher) who had no connection with the SA but were victims of earlier feuds. The events were the turning-point of the Nazi regime: they opened the way to Hitler's succession to Hindenburg with the approval of the army. At the same time Hitler's assumption of personal responsibility for the executions, carried out without any pretence of a trial, made clear the ruthless character of the regime, and the role played by the SS laid the foundation for their supremacy among its instruments of power. For further reading: M. Gallo, *The Night of the Long Knives* (1973). A.L.C.B.

nihilism. An attitude or viewpoint denying all traditional values and even moral truths. The word was invented by Turgenev in his novel *Fathers and Sons* (1861) to describe that part of the radical Russian intelligentsia (see RADICALISM; INTELLECTUAL) which, disillusioned with the slow pace of reform (see REFORMISM), abandoned the liberal faith of their predecessors (see LIBERALISM) and embraced the belief that the destruction of existing conditions in Russia justified the use of any means. The chief ideologist of revolutionary UTILITARIANISM in politics, ETHICS and AESTHETICS was D. I. Pisarev (1840–68), who was portrayed as Bazarov in Turgenev's novel and who proudly accepted the new label. Many members of subsequent generations of the Russian intelligentsia adopted nihilistic postures, from P. G. Zaichnevsky, who summoned his contemporaries 'to the axe', to Sergei Nechaev, author of a *Revolutionary Catechism*, who was portrayed as the unscrupulous Peter Verkhovensky in the novel by Dostoyevsky variously translated as *The Devils* or *The Possessed*. The term has subsequently been applied to various radical movements outside Russia: the Nazi (see NAZISM) victory in Germany in the 1930s was described as a 'REVOLUTION of nihilism'. For further reading: J. Gouldsblom, *Nihilism and Culture* (1980). L.L.

nitrogen cycle, see under LIFE CYCLE.

Nixon doctrine. Also known as the *Guam Doctrine* after its enunciation at Guam in 1970 to the press and then to American client President Marcos in the Philippines. The doctrine was contained in a speech made by President Nixon on 3 November 1969. It reflected the belief, prompted by the increasingly unpopular entanglement of the US in VIETNAM, that the nation should not readily involve itself in another land war on behalf of an allied or client state. The doctrine's propositions were that the US would keep its treaty commitments; would 'provide a shield' to protect allies or states whose survival mattered to US interests against threat from a nuclear power; and would deal with other types of aggression towards such states by providing economic aid, military advice and material, but not troops. Thus the US signalled its preference for using smaller states as surrogates to execute anti-communist policy, such as the military regimes of Central and South America, of the Shah in Iran, and Marcos in the Philippines. The doctrine eschewed any judgement of regimes' characteristics except for their resistance to COMMUNISM, stability, and disposition towards the US. For further reading: S. Hoffmann, *Primacy or World Order* (1978). S.R.

NKGB, see under KGB.

NKVD, see under KGB.

NNP (net national product), see under GNP.

no boundary condition. A proposal to characterize the initial state of the universe, introduced by Stephen Hawking and James Hartle. The idea was widely publicized in Hawking's book *A Brief History of Time* (1988). The proposal combines the assumption that as we follow the universe back towards its apparent beginning we will find that the combination of QUANTUM THEORY and gravitation will ultimately lead to time becoming another dimension of space. The universe can then be viewed as a four-dimensional version of a ball. The surface of such a ball is finite but has no boundary. This leads to a quantum cosmological theory in which the universe is imagined to come into being out of 'nothing' as a quantum event. It begins expanding and as it gets larger the time dimension becomes more and more significant. The fact that we observe the universe to possess a clear notion of time is a reflection of the fact that the universe is now very large and old, and is far from the extremes of temperature and density in which quantum gravitational effects predominate. This is not the only proposal for a special initial state for the universe but it has proved of particular interest to cosmologists because it seems to require a minimal amount of information to specify it. So far, there are no observational tests to confirm or refute the no boundary condition. For further reading: H. Price, *Time's Arrow and Archimedes Point: New Directions for the Physics of Time* (1996). J.D.B.

no first use. A declaration that a STATE will never be the first to use NUCLEAR WEAPONS: in effect, the renunciation of the use of nuclear weapons for offensive purposes. Although some Western experts argue that NATO defence should not be so dependent on a nuclear strike, NATO has always refused to make such a declaration. It argues that the uncertainty created by the possibility of a nuclear 'first strike' deters not only conventional warfare, but also biological and chemical attacks upon it. A.J.M.W.

noise pollution. Any sound that is not wanted by a recipient. Excessive noise may lead to mental stress and/or hearing disorders. To deal with the problem some authorities establish noise-abatement zones as part of planning procedures, while noise control legislation is widely applied to limit, e.g., noise from vehicles or aircraft. Noise levels are measured in decibels, a logarithmic scale in which a sound of 0 is just audible to a person with good hearing and 120 causes pain. An increase of 10 units means that the noise perceived by a listener has about doubled in loudness. A.S.G.

Nolan Report. The colloquial name given to the UK's First Report of the Committee on Standards in Public Life, published in May 1995. The Report investigated the potential conflict between an MP's parliamentary duties and his outside interests. It asserted the priority of constituency and national duties over an MP's private interests and recommended clearer rules to control paid advocacy. It led to the establishment of a Parliamentary Commissioner for Standards and tighter rules governing the disclosure of legislators' interests. For further reading: F. F. Ridley and A. Doig (eds), *Sleaze: Politicians, Private Interests and Public Reaction* (1995). N.O.

nomadism. Anthropological term for the LIFESTYLE in which human groups follow a wandering life. It is usually restricted to livestock-keeping groups whose movements are directly related to the search for pasture. Examples of such pastoral nomadism are increasingly rare; the Lapps of northern Scandinavia and the Kirghiz of Turkestan come nearest to the model. See also TRANSHUMANCE. P.H.

nominalism. A denial of the existence of abstract entities of any kind, including NUMBERS, SETS, properties and PROPOSITIONS. Abstract entities are those which cannot be accommodated within the natural world of concrete things existing in space and time and subject to CAUSALITY. Denial of their existence is motivated both by doubts as to how we, as members of the natural world ourselves, could have knowledge of them, and by doubts as to how the existence of such causally inert entities could have any relevance to facts about the natural world. It has been argued by realists that MATHEMATICS is indispensable to scientific theories of the natural world and therefore that science is committed to the existence of such abstract objects as numbers and sets. But against this nominalists claim that mathematics is at most a useful fiction and that reference to mathematical objects can always in principle be eliminated from scientific theories. More narrowly, nominalism is the doctrine that UNIVERSALS – i.e. common properties, such as redness or roundness – do not exist and that all that two red things, e.g., have in common is either a certain resemblance to each other or else, according to more extreme nominalists, just the name 'red'. Since universals, if they exist, are abstract entities, nominalist arguments against their existence are similar to those against the existence of mathematical objects. For further reading: H. Field, *Science without Numbers* (1980). E.J.L.

nomothetic, see under IDIOGRAPHIC.

non-accelerating rate of unemployment, see NAIRU.

non-alignment. The refusal of states to take sides with one or other of two principal opposed groups of powers such as existed at the time of the COLD WAR. Non-alignment was less ISOLATIONIST than the neutralism which it superseded, and was associated with the concept of positive NEUTRALITY, i.e. of collective intervention to prevent BIPOLARITY from degenerating into open military conflict; as in the conference of non-aligned powers held at Belgrade in 1961 in which some 35 Mediterranean and Afro-Asian powers took part. Subsequent conferences have demonstrated a common belief in the need for a NEW INTERNATIONAL ECONOMIC ORDER and the Non-Aligned Movement was a principal influence on the setting up of UNCTAD, the UN forum for the discussion of THIRD WORLD economic development. They also demonstrated (especially at Havana, 1979) ideological splits about the role of 'brother states' such as the former USSR, with CUBA a leading proponent of a more active anti-US stance. For further reading: L. Mates, *Non-Alignment: Theory and Current Policy* (1972). D.C.W.; A.WI.

non-Euclidean geometry, see under GEOMETRY.

non-equilibrium thermodynamics. The THERMODYNAMICS of systems that are not at EQUILIBRIUM. Processes that are irreversible evolve towards an equilibrium state that has a greater ENTROPY than the initial state; when equilibrium is reached, the rate of entropy production is zero. If a system is constantly supplied with matter or energy, it can be maintained in a non-equilibrium state in which entropy is continually generated. It was thought by the originators of thermodynamic theory that non-equilibrium states would be disorderly, but observations show that they can find highly ordered structures, such as the hexagonal pattern of convection cells first seen by Henri Bénard in 1900. Other examples of ordered non-equilibrium states include the chemical patterns predicted by Alan Turing in 1952. These ordered non-equilibrium states are called dissipative structures, since they must dissipate energy in order to persist. Their existence is counter-intuitive, because the generation of entropy would be expected to engender disorder in the system. As most natural processes, such as the functioning of CELLS and the circulation of the atmosphere and oceans, operate away from equilibrium, the importance of understanding non-equilibrium structures is clear. P.C.B.

non-figurative art, see under ABSTRACT ART.

non-government organization, see NGO.

non-intervention. The opposite view to the right of intervention maintained by the great powers of the 19th century as an accepted part of international law (see PUBLIC INTERNATIONAL LAW). According to the then accepted view, one STATE was within its rights in intervening (if necessary by force) in the affairs of another state where the second state's government was unable or incompetent to exercise sovereign powers (see SOVEREIGNTY), particularly in the protection of the rights, property and persons of nationals of the first state. This view was challenged by the Argentinian jurist Carlos Calvo, who in 1868 maintained that all sovereign states enjoyed absolute equality. The MONROE DOCTRINE denied *European* rights to intervene in the Americas; the Calvo doctrine and that put forward by the Argentinian, Dr Louis Drago, in 1903, and embodied in part of Article I of the second Hague Convention of 1907, were directed to prevent *US* intervention. After the Bolshevik revolution (see BOLSHEVISM), the doctrine became an integral part of the treaties negotiated by the former USSR with its non-Soviet neighbours. In times of civil war, as in the Spanish Civil War, the major powers have adopted non-intervention as a kind of self-denying ordinance intended to avoid ESCALATION into international conflict, but usually (as in the case of Spain) with very unequal results. D.C.W.

non-linear optics. When an intense beam of light – an electromagnetic wave (see ELECTROMAGNETISM) – passes through certain materials (e.g. lithium niobate) their ATOMS OR MOLECULES do not respond to the light linearly, i.e. in a manner directly proportional to the strength of the electromagnetic wave. Instead their response is greater than this and is termed non-linear. The effect is to modify the character of the transmitted light in ways similar to that in which electronic circuits can affect radio waves. For example, frequency doubling can occur so that a red beam can emerge with part of it changed to blue. The difference frequency between two incident beams can be generated and in this way certain INFRA-RED frequencies can be produced which are not within the range of conventional LASERS. Non-linear devices can be designed to provide *light amplifiers*, *beam splitters* and guides and the MODULATION of light beams by speech and other signals. All these are essential in the technology of FIBRE OPTIC communications. H.M.R.

non-linear phonology. In PHONOLOGY, any model which avoids a linear representation of the sounds present within a word – representing them as a series of segments occurring in a strict horizontal sequence. These approaches cannot handle features of sound which extend over domains greater than an individual segment (e.g. certain properties of tones, or vowel harmony). In the 1980s, several non-linear models were developed to handle these phenomena. For further reading: J. A. Goldsmith (ed.), *The Handbook of Phonological Theory* (1995). D.C.

non-nuclear defence. The use of conventional forces, enhanced by technologically advanced weapons systems, to resist attack by a superior enemy. Where NUCLEAR WEAPONS conventionally provide the margin of superiority, advanced but non-nuclear weapons will perform the same function. Another approach is to use battlefield nuclear weapons, but these carry the potential risk of wider nuclear war which a non-nuclear defence does not. A third approach, involving renunciation of nuclear weapons (see MULTILATERALISM) without making the investment in advanced TECHNOLOGY and other resources, is not held to be militarily credible. See also EMERGENT TECHNOLOGY. A.J.M.W.

non-objectivism. Russian ABSTRACT ART movement led by Alexander Rodchenko (1891–1956) during World War I. J.W.

non-proliferation, see under PROLIFERATION.

non-representational art, see under ABSTRACT ART.

non-theistic religion. RELIGION not involving belief in God or gods. Although in the Western world religion is usually thought to imply such belief (see THEISM), this is not true historically (see BUDDHISM; CONFUCIANISM; PANTHEISM). Many modern agnostics (see AGNOSTICISM) value teachings traditionally associated with religion, notably reverence for nature and for other people, self-discipline, and the spirit of service to society. See also DEATH OF GOD THEOLOGY; HUMANISM. D.L.E.

non-verbal communication. The larger interpersonal context within which all verbal communications take place. All human actions are suffused with meaning. Hence all actions communicate meanings. How I reach for, hold and drink from my teacup is a communicative act as well as an instrumental act. As one speaks, one's tone, speed, pause structure, gestures, facial expression and degree of proximity to one's auditor modulate the meaning of the communication. These latter activities are the nonverbal context in which speech is embedded. Without such a context, all speech would be ambiguous. An important stimulus to the concept lies in social philosopher Michael Polanyi's (1891–1976) idea of TACIT KNOWLEDGE, the acquisition and communication of wisdom through the fingers and other body organs. For further reading: R. A. Hinde, *Non-Verbal Communication* (1972). T.Z.C.

non-violent resistance. A strategy or policy of resisting an adversary's attack or an occupation of one's country by non-violent means; the appeal to world opinion, political resistance, or CIVIL DISOBEDIENCE. Recent examples are Gandhi's organization of resistance to the British Raj during its final decades, the prevailing policy of the Norwegian resistance movement in World War II, and the decision of the Czechs to offer no military resistance to the Soviet invasion of their country in August 1968, but to rely on civil disobedience and global publicity. A recent example of domestic civil disobedience is, in the USA, the National Association for the Advancement of Colored People's campaign for civil rights (see CIVIL RIGHTS MOVEMENT). For further reading: A. Roberts (ed.), *The Strategy of Civilian Defence* (1967). A.F.B.

norm. Established and expected form of social behaviour. Norms are sets of implicit social rules, MODELS of what should happen. Émile Durkheim (1858–1917) developed the notion of norms in his analysis of SOCIAL FACT, i.e. the conventions of behaviour and standards of value which exist independently of individuals and which exercise a coercive influence. Breaches of norms can result in the imposition of SANCTIONS (sense 2). It is important to draw a distinction between social norms (what individuals think ought to happen) and statistical norms (what actually happens). For further reading: L. Holy and M. Stuchlik, *Actions, Norms and Representations: Foundations of Anthropological Inquiry* (1983). A.G.

norm-referenced, see under PSYCHOMETRICS.

norm-referenced test, see under CRITERION REFERENCED TEST.

normal or **Gaussian distribution.** When a number of objects are measured, in the resulting list of measurements most values cluster around some central point, with progressively fewer as one moves away from that point – the graph looks like a bell curve. For example, if one measured the heights of a large sample of men, most of the heights would be within a few inches of each other, with relatively few men being over six feet tall, or under five feet. If, however, one measured their ages instead, you would not find a bell curve – ages do not, in general, cluster around any particular value.

It has been noticed by mathematicians that a very large number of attributes turn out to provide bell curves when they are measured, from IQs to salaries, and that these bell curves are close to a set of mathematical curves known as the normal distribution. This tendency is accentuated if one takes measurements not from individuals, but from small samples of a population, combining the measurements of, e.g., six men to give a single number each time. Even ages will provide a normal distribution, if you add up six people's ages to get each measurement. The 'central limit theorem', finally proved by Andrei Markov at the beginning of the century, states that regardless of the attribute being measured, such combined measurements will always approximate a normal distribution. N.A.R.

normalization. Already current in the sense of (industrial) standardization, the word was used in post-1945 European contexts to signify a return to friendly relations between STATES, ruling parties, etc. (as after the Moscow–Belgrade breach); then specifically of Gustáv Husák's counter-REFORMIST policy in Czechoslavakia from 1969, with restoration of complete control by pro-Soviet leaders and reintegration into the Soviet bloc in all aspects. See USSR, THE FORMER. D.V.

normative. In general, concerned with

rules, recommendations or proposals, as contrasted with mere description or the statement of matters of fact. The words *evaluative* and *prescriptive* are used in much the same way, though 'normative', unlike the other two, tends to imply (see NORM) that the standards or values involved are those of some social group rather than of an individual. Specific applications include the following. A.S.

(1) In PHILOSOPHY, the label is applied to VALUE-JUDGEMENTS by EMOTIVISTS and other adherents of the doctrine of the NATURALISTIC FALLACY, who conclude that the TRUTH or falsity of value-judgements cannot be assessed. LOGIC, likewise, is sometimes called a normative science because it does not simply classify forms of INFERENCE that are actually followed but critically selects, and by implication recommends, those it regards as valid (see VALIDITY). A valid inference, after all, is one whose conclusion *ought* to be accepted if its premises are. A.Q.

(2) In LINGUISTICS, the adjectives *normative* and *prescriptive* are applied interchangeably to the largely outmoded view that there are absolute standards of correctness in language, and that the aim of linguistic analysis is to formulate rules of usage in conformity with them. This attitude is opposed to the aims of *descriptive* linguistics, which emphasizes the need to describe the *facts* of linguistic usage – how people actually speak (or write), not how they (or the grammarians) feel they ought to speak. D.C.

North American Free Trade Area, see NAFTA.

North Atlantic Treaty Organization, see NATO.

north–south dialogue. A dialogue concerning the nature of the NEW INTERNATIONAL ECONOMIC ORDER and the possible mutual benefits to be gained from the transformation of the political and economic relationships between developed and developing countries. The rich countries have exerted military, political and economic POWER over developing countries and the cessation of such aggressive acts would have many benefits for individual countries and the world. Those supporting a north–south dialogue stress the moral imperative for action to promote ECONOMIC GROWTH and development in DEVELOPING COUNTRIES and the effects of such action on economic growth in developed countries, through increased demand for their goods and services. For further reading: E. W. Nafziger, *The Economics of Developing Countries* (1997). J.P.; E.W.N.

nothingness (*le néant*). In Sartre's *Being and Nothingness* (1943) nothingness is the polar opposite of BEING. Being is primordial, but *being-for-itself*, i.e. the consciousness possessed by an individual being, is capable of conferring nothingness, negation or absence upon the world, which is a uniquely human property, and only possible because of the activities of the imagination. In Sartre's famous example, he enters the café looking for his friend Pierre, but Pierre is *not there*. The searching glance decides on the absence of Pierre, and imposes 'inhalation' upon an apparently real and full world. When nothingness is used as an activity in BAD FAITH, the subject decides to accord reality to what is not the case, thus reneging on his own freedom. For further reading: M. Warnock, *The Philosophy of Sartre* (1965). R.PO.

notional and **formal.** Adjectives applied respectively to grammatical analysis which does, and does not, assume a set of undefined extra-linguistic notions as its basis. 'Notional' often has a pejorative force for linguists reacting against the widespread notionalism of TRADITIONAL GRAMMAR. D.C.

noumena (or **things-in-themselves;** German *Dinge-an-sich*). Terms used by Immanuel Kant (1724–1804) to refer to the things that underlie our experience both of the physical world and of our own mental states (called by him the phenomena of outer and inner sense) and that are not themselves objects of possible experience. A.Q.

nouveau réalisme. A phrase (literally, 'new realism', but bearing no relationship to either REALISM or NEO-REALISM) coined by the French critic Pierre Restany to describe artists' work in Paris in the late 1950s and early 1960s which incorporated junk and common objects into assemblage and COLLAGE forms. The French artist Arman is the figure most associated with this style, which is akin to POP and *assemblage* art. Yves Klein, Jean Tinguely, Daniel Spoerri and Martial Raysse can also be counted within this movement. For further reading: H. Martin, *Arman* (1973). A.K.W.

***nouveau roman*,** see NEW NOVEL.

***nouvelle vague*,** see NEW WAVE.

nova. A star whose brightness suddenly increases by up to 10,000 times through the ejection from it of incandescent gases. M.V.B.

novelty, evolutionary. Any evolutionary change which permanently alters the dynamics of EVOLUTION by NATURAL SELECTION. Examples are the origin of multi-cellular life forms (plants and animals) from single-celled ancestors (see CELL; CELL BIOLOGY). This event shifted the level of selection from the single cell to aggregates of cells, i.e. the multi-cellular ORGANISM. Other examples are the acquisition of a new character or organ like the tetrapod limb, or the evolution of language in the human lineage. A multiplicity of mechanisms have been proposed to explain evolutionary novelties, among them selection for co-operation and developmental side-effects of other evolutionary changes. The origin of novelties in evolution represents a third class of evolutionary processes besides adaptation (improvement by natural selection) and SPECIATION (the origin of an independent lineage). G.P.W.

NPG (NEGATIVE POPULATION GROWTH), see under ZERO POPULATION GROWTH.

NPV (net present value), see under DISCOUNTED CASH FLOW; DISCOUNTING.

NRT, see under CRITERION REFERENCED TEST.

nuclear disarmament, see under PEACE MOVEMENT; NUCLEAR WEAPONS, LIMITATION AND CONTROL; MULTILATERALISM.

nuclear family. A co-resident domestic group of husband, wife and children (see MARRIAGE; KINSHIP). This simple FAMILY structure contrasts with the *extended family*, to which kin are added extending the group laterally (kin of the same generation) or vertically (another generation). Most developed INDUSTRIAL SOCIETIES have the nuclear family as the dominant IDEAL TYPE, while many other parts of the world are characterized by various extended family forms. SOCIAL MOBILITY and geographical mobility are stronger features of the nuclear family than other family systems, while the instrumental importance of kinship relations is likely to be weaker. The belief that the nuclear family is a product of modern industrial society is a tenacious one, but is belied by much historical evidence. Before the INDUSTRIAL REVOLUTION in much of western Europe, and in England in particular, the nuclear family was frequently the norm. This undermines theories which place emphasis on the structure and interaction of the nuclear family in itself as producing tension and stress, divorce, delinquency, and the weakening of cultural transmission. Particularly through the growth of divorce and consensual unions, by the mid-1980s only about a third of all households in Britain conformed to the nuclear family ideal type, but its powerful symbolism is evident in its ubiquitous use in ADVERTISING and consumer images. For further reading: R. Wall *et al* (eds), *Family Forms in Historic Europe* (1982). P.S.L.; D.S.

nuclear fission, see under FISSION.

nuclear fusion, see under FUSION.

nuclear physics. The study of the atomic NUCLEUS and its constituent NUCLEONS, and the NUCLEAR REACTIONS between nuclei. See also QUANTUM MECHANICS. M.V.B.

nuclear reaction. In NUCLEAR PHYSICS, any process resulting in structural changes in an atomic NUCLEUS. Generally the ATOMIC NUMBER alters so that it is possible to transmute small amounts of one ELEMENT into another, thus fulfilling the dream of the medieval alchemists; this could not be achieved in any purely chemical reaction since only the outer ELECTRONS are involved (see ATOMIC PHYSICS). FUSION reactions are responsible for starlight and the operation of the hydrogen bomb, and FISSION reactions are involved in RADIOACTIVITY, NUCLEAR REACTORS and the atomic bomb. See also QUANTUM MECHANICS. M.V.B.

nuclear reactor (originally called atomic pile). A device (of which the prototype was completed in 1942 under the direction of Enrico Fermi) in which a controlled CHAIN REACTION is set up, based on nuclear FISSION. It contains a core of fissile materials, which when bombarded by NEUTRONS yields up a portion of its ATOMIC ENERGY as heat. This heat is then transported out of the fissile core by a variety of methods. The material undergoing fission (usually an ISOTOPE of uranium) is normally mixed with a MODERATOR to increase the efficiency of the neutrons. The speed of the reaction is controlled by adjusting rods of neutron-absorbing material such as cadmium. Nuclear reactors generate (1) ENERGY, which is used to drive turbines, which in turn drive electric generators; and (2) RADIOACTIVITY, which is used in the production of isotopes (e.g. TRACE ELEMENTS) for industry and medicine.

Nuclear reactors are classified in a variety of ways, and the types mentioned in the following sentences are selected from several classifications. A *breeder* reactor is one in which fissile material is produced in greater quantities than it is consumed, so that even if part of the final product is used in the same reactor there will still be a surplus for use elsewhere. A *fast reactor* is one in which no moderator is used, but this absence is compensated by a high concentration of core material. A *thermal reactor* is one in which the bombarding agents are THERMAL NEUTRONS. A *pressurized-water reactor* is one in which water under pressure (of the order of 2,000 lbs per square inch) is used both as moderator and coolant. In a *boiling-water reactor* water acts as a coolant only. In a *gas-cooled reactor* (in which graphite is used to slow the neutrons) the heat is carried away by a gas (originally carbon dioxide, later helium) which can be used at very high temperatures (up to 1,000°C) and can then operate directly on the blades of a gas turbine. M.V.B.; E.R.L.

nuclear testing. The first test of a NUCLEAR WEAPON by the US in 1945 was rapidly succeeded by the dropping of atomic bombs on HIROSHIMA and Nagasaki. Both occasions had many of the characteristics of a test. A series of atmospheric and underwater tests followed, particularly at Bikini Atoll in the Pacific. These were designed firstly to produce reliable and controllable nuclear weapons and then to establish the effects, immediate and long-term, of a nuclear explosion on both people and military machinery, and the extent to which troops could fight effectively on a nuclear battleground. Surplus warships were anchored in the blast zone, animals were staked out and – a little further away but dangerously close – thousands of military personnel watched.

After the US, the former USSR (1949), Britain (1952), France (1960) and China (1964) developed and began to test their own nuclear weapons. The cumulative environmental effects of testing attracted growing concern. The 1963 Partial Test Ban Treaty (PTBT) banned tests in the atmosphere, under water and in space. The US, Britain and the Soviet Union, followed by France (1974) and China (1980), moved their tests underground.

Spasmodic attempts to conclude a Comprehensive Test Ban Treaty (CTBT) were bedevilled by COLD WAR politics, but after final and much-protested-against French and Chinese testing programmes, a CTBT was agreed in 1996.

Some problems remained. India and Pakistan refused to sign. Under the terms of the treaty this prevents its coming into force, and so limits the setting up of VERIFICATION systems. Nor was the development of new nuclear weapons entirely stopped, since computer simulation, laboratory and non-explosive testing were not banned. For further reading: A. Karp, *Ballistic Missile Proliferation* (1996). L.T.

nuclear war, see under WAR.

nuclear weapons. Arms which depend on the principles of nuclear fission to produce an awesome explosive force and RADIOACTIVE fallout (see RADIOACTIVITY). The explosion comprises a blast effect, a fire storm with winds of several hundred mph and temperatures rising to 1,000°C. Longer-lasting and more widespread effects come from the scattering of fallout, causing RADIATION sickness and long-term diseases including a range of cancers. The power of these weapons is expressed in kilotons (one kiloton = one thousand tons of TNT) or with the later and more powerful weapons megatons (one million tons of TNT).

Fallout effects depend both on the size of the weapon and whether it is exploded on or above the ground. Radioactive contamination can be carried on the wind over great distances: that from the nuclear power station accident at CHERNOBYL in the Ukraine in 1986 spread over most of western Europe.

Nuclear weapons can be dropped from aircraft as free-fall bombs, fired in missiles from planes and ships, including submerged submarines, and from the ground. These can be short-range (tactical) and long-range (strategic), extending to 8,000-mile+ intercontinental weapons. During the COLD WAR there was a proliferation not only of nuclear weapons but of categories, often very precise and each with an arcane doctrine attached to it. Most of these are now regarded as meaningless – such as Graduated Response, the theory that two sides in a nuclear confrontation could intially fire small missiles at each other, only gradually escalating to all-out nuclear WAR.

All tactical nuclear weapons were withdrawn from Europe, east and west, in the mid-1990s. The intermediate-range cruise (see CRUISE MISSILES), Pershing and SS-20 missiles were withdrawn under the 1987 Intermediate Nuclear Forces agreement. Strategic weapons, deployed by the US, Russia, Britain, France and China, remain, although under the START 1 & 2 treaties American and Russian numbers are being cut (see also NUCLEAR WEAPONS, LIMITATION AND CONTROL). L.T.

nuclear weapons, limitation and control. It is axiomatic that states with nuclear weapons (NWS) wish to prevent other states acquiring them. However what they have, they want to keep – and indeed improve. States without nuclear weapons are reluctant to give up their right to them unless the NWS in turn promise some degree of nuclear DISARMAMENT.

This dichotomy underlies and has frequently frustrated all general attempts at nuclear arms control. Thus the 1968 nuclear Non-Proliferation Treaty (NPT) which divides signatories into NWS or non-NWS, each with different obligations, includes a clause on disarmament which the NWS prefer to ignore. This non-compliance in turn caused considerable problems during both the NPT extension and the Comprehensive Test Ban Treaty negotiations (see NUCLEAR TESTING).

However, bilateral agreements such as the Intermediate Nuclear Forces (INF) and Strategic Arms Reduction Treaties (START 1 & 2) between the US and the former USSR/Russia have proved easier to achieve, particularly with the end of the COLD WAR. Under the INF, for the first time, a whole class of nuclear weapons (including the US CRUISE MISSILES) was scrapped. In addition practical VERIFICATION systems, including reciprocal on-site inspections, were set up. This in turn made easier the START 1 & 2 and the Chemical Weapons Conventions negotiations.

The break-up of the Soviet Union temporarily resulted in a further three NWS by inheritance (Belarus, Kazakhstan and the Ukraine). This delayed ratification of START 1 until the three agreed to get rid of their nuclear weapons and sign the NPT as non-NWS. Russia then ratified. That these complexities could be overcome by goodwill (aided by some application of US aid to the Ukraine) was encouraging. Unfortunately the eastward expansion of NATO soured the atmosphere in Moscow and the Russian parliament protested by refusing to ratify START 2.

After START 2, pressure increased on Britain, France and China to enter their own nuclear weapons into future negotiations, while a series of practical, step-by-step plans for total nuclear DISARMAMENT began to be put forward by various international commissions, who often included senior military and diplomatic figures. For further reading: A. Karp, *Ballistic Missile Proliferation* (1996). L.T.

nuclear winter. The term 'nuclear winter' was coined to describe the potential climatic effects of nuclear WAR, but it is also a useful metaphor for the acute disruption of global civilization that would result from nuclear war and the cumulative threat to life on earth that is posed by the existence of NUCLEAR WEAPONS. In the early 1980s, the atmospheric chemists Paul Crutzen and John Birks realized that the smoke and debris thrown up into the atmosphere by nuclear blasts and fires may be sufficient to generate a substantial climatic change. Later work, by the pioneering TTAPS group (Turco, Toon, Ackerman, Pollack and Sagan) and other climate modellers, confirmed that temperatures could fall by tens of degrees Celsius, turning summer into nuclear winter. A major investigation undertaken by SCOPE (the Scientific Committee on Problems of the Environment, a standing committee of the International Council of Scientific Unions) concluded that the sensitivity of the biosphere is such that even minor environmental stress, coupled with the loss of industrial production in the nuclear nations, international trade, aid and other aspects of modern civilization, would result in global famine. Nuclear winter highlighted the need to consider the long-term consequences of the use of nuclear weapons. For further reading: O. Greene *et al*, *Nuclear Winter: the Evidence and the Risk* (1985). P.M.K.

nucleic acid. Nucleic acids are of crucial importance in all living organisms and in viruses (see VIROLOGY) as the sole vectors of genetic information. They are giant polymeric (see POLYMER) MOLECULES of which the structural unit is a nucleotide, a compound built up of (1) a sugar, either ribose (in ribonucleic acid, RNA) or deoxyribose (in deoxyribonucleic acid, DNA), (2) a nitrogen-containing base, and (3) a phosphoric acid. These nucleotides are joined together linearly to form a *polynucleotide* through the combination of the phosphoric acid of one nucleotide with the sugar constituent in its neighbour, and so on. In DNA the nitrogenous bases are adenine, thymine, guanine and cytosine; in RNA uracil substitutes for thymine. Each such base defines a distinct nucleotide, and these are the symbols of the GENETIC CODE by means of which genetic information is embodied and transmitted. It was shown by Watson and Crick (1953) that DNA has a binary structure: each molecule consists of two strands aligned to each other in such a way that adenine is linked non-covalently with thymine, and guanine with cytosine. The two strands have a helical twist – which gives them the form of the famous DOUBLE HELIX. The first crucial piece of information demonstrating that nucleic acids are the vectors of genetic information came from the work of Avery and his colleagues (1944), showing that the agent responsible for bacterial TRANSFORMATIONS was indeed DNA itself. PROTEINS are synthesized according to information coded in DNA. The flow of information from DNA into protein begins with the 'transcription' of the DNA into a single-stranded RNA. *Splicing* of the RNA removes any *introns*. The result is *messenger* RNA, the information in which is 'translated' according to the genetic code through the mediation of *transfer* RNA which assembles individual AMINO ACIDS into *polypeptides* (see PEPTIDES) and proteins. Although under special circumstances reverse transcription can occur, translation is irreversible, and there is no known mechanism by which information can flow from protein into nucleic acid. This is the central dogma of MOLECULAR BIOLOGY. See also GENOME. For further reading: B. Lewin, *Genes II* (1985). P.M.; P.N.

nucleon. A generic term for either of the two types of ELEMENTARY PARTICLE, i.e. PROTONS and nucleons, which form the NUCLEUS of an ATOM, and which may be regarded as different states of the same PARTICLE. M.V.B.

nucleonics. Engineering based on NUCLEAR PHYSICS. M.V.B.

nucleoprotein, see under NUCLEUS.

nucleosynthesis. The production of atomic NUCLEI by a sequence of NUCLEAR REACTIONS. The end products may be the result of breaking up heavy nuclei by nuclear FISSION or amalgamating light nuclei by nuclear FUSION. *Primordial nucleosynthesis* is the sequence of nuclear fusion reactions which occurred during the first three minutes of the universe's history. The BIG BANG THEORY of the universe's early history and primordial nucleosynthesis correctly predicts the abundances of hydrogen, helium-3, helium-4, deuterium and lithium in the universe. This is one of the principal pieces of evidence for the big bang COSMOLOGY.

Nuclei heavier than helium-4 are not produced in significant abundance by primordial nucleosynthesis. They are produced by *stellar/explosive nucleosynthesis* – nuclear reactions within the interiors of stars, and in SUPERNOVAE. The detailed results of this process were first calculated by W. Fowler, F. Hoyle and G. and M. Burbidge in 1957, and explain the relative abundances in the universe of those atomic nuclei not produced by primordial nucleosynthesis. For further reading: S. Weinberg, *The First Three Minutes* (1983). J.D.B.

nucleotide, see under NUCLEIC ACID.

nucleus.

(1) In ATOMIC PHYSICS, the tiny central core (discovered by Ernest Rutherford in 1912) containing most of the mass of an ATOM. The nucleus is composed of PROTONS and NEUTRONS, held together by STRONG INTERACTIONS resulting from the exchange of MESONS. (The sole exception is hydrogen, which consists of a single proton.) Most ISOTOPES found in nature are stable, but some are unstable, and their nuclei undergo radioactive decay (see RADIOACTIVITY). Nuclei of the TRANSURANIC ELEMENTS are all unstable because the number of protons is sufficient for their long-range ELECTROSTATIC repulsion to overcome the strong interactions. See also QUANTUM MECHANICS. M.V.B.

(2) In CYTOLOGY, the administrative centre of the CELL. The nucleus, which with rare exceptions (e.g. the red blood corpuscles of mammals) is possessed by all plant and animal cells, is separated from the main bulk of the CYTOPLASM by a membrane of its own, distinct from the outer cell membrane. It is the repository of all the cell's genetic information and of all the information, therefore, that specifies in exact detail the synthesis of the PROTEINS of the cell. Whenever the division of the nucleus is not accompanied by a division of the cytoplasm a binucleate cell results. By special experimental methods, particularly the use of ultraviolet-inactivated Sendai virus (see VIROLOGY), two different cells can be fused in such a way that two nuclei of different origins may be housed within one cell body. Such a cell is called a *heterokaryote*, and its study can throw light upon, e.g., the properties of a CANCER cell which are responsible for its malignancy. Nuclei are composed mainly of *nucleoprotein*, which is a salt-like compound of deoxyribonucleic acid (see NUCLEIC ACID) and a basic protein such as a histone or protamine; and virtually all the DNA of the cell is housed within the nucleus. If a cell such as a ZYGOTE is deprived of its own nucleus and its place is taken by a nucleus from a cell of some other type from a later embryo, the zygote may nevertheless develop with a fair approximation to normality – an experiment which demonstrates that the GENOME of all cells in the body derived by MITOSIS from the zygote is the same. Thus DIFFERENTIATION must consist in some process by which genetic potentialities of the cell are realized in different ways in different cells. P.M.

null hypothesis. This is the theory, mainly used in statistical analyses, that all things are equal – or, at least, that there is no vital difference between them. Thus an analysis may start from a level base. If one is testing two or more separate groups for their standards in a subject, be it reading, mathematics or whatever, one would test each group, making sure that they comprise large samples, are evenly distributed and do not show any notable differences. Differences, if any, will show up once the test answers have been analysed. J.I.

number. In MATHEMATICS, a term with several distinct meanings:

(1) The *natural numbers* $\{0, 1, 2, 3, \ldots\}$ (with or without 0) come first; according to Leopold Kroenecker (1823–91) they come from God, all else being the work of man. They may be thought of as the finite CARDINAL NUMBERS or ORDINAL NUMBERS, or as a MATHEMATICAL STRUCTURE satisfying axioms which were first clearly stated by Giuseppe Peano in 1889. The simplest, if impractical, system of *notation* is to represent the number n by n successive strokes. The Greeks and Romans used various combinations of letters, inadequate for representing arbitrary large numbers. The decimal system, derived from Babylonia, India and the Arabs, can be generalized to an arbitrary *base* b. The choice of b is pragmatic. The decimal system ($b = 10$) seems well suited to the human brain; $b = 8$ and $b = 12$ have also been used. The BINARY SCALE is suitable for COMPUTERS or other devices whose components may be in either of two states ('on' or 'off').

(2) The *integers* $(0, \pm 1, \pm 2, \ldots)$.

(3) The *rational numbers*: all (proper and improper) factions of the form p/q where p and q are integers and q 0, with the identification $p/q = rp/rq$ for any integer r 0.

(4) The *real numbers*. As early as the 6th century BC it was known to the Pythagoreans that *incommensurable ratios*, or *irrational* numbers, exist: e.g. $\sqrt{2}$. Intuitively, once an origin and a unit of measurement have been fixed there is a one-to-one correspondence between the real numbers and the points of a straight line; for this reason the set of real numbers is called the CONTINUUM. Despite a brilliant attempt in Euclid, book 5, it was not until about 1870 that Cantor and Dedekind gave satisfactory definitions. The easiest definition to convey (though not to theorize with) is to say that every real number can be expressed as an infinite decimal: $\pm\ n.a_0a_1a_2\ldots$ where n is a natural number and $a_0, a_1, a_2\ldots$ is an *arbitrary* sequence of decimal digits. Observe that there is still an appeal to intuition for the understanding of 'arbitrary'; for further discussion see SET. Not all real numbers are the roots of algebraic equations (see ALGEBRA). Those which are not (e.g. e and π) are *transcendental*.

(5) The COMPLEX NUMBERS; the algebraic numbers form a subset of these.

(6) 'Number' used also to be applied to the elements of other mathematical structures occurring in algebra; but it is nowadays confined to (1)–(5) above. For further reading: R. L. Wilder, *Evolution of Mathematical Concepts* (1978). R.G.

number theory. This is the study of the natural numbers (1, 2, 3, . . .; see NUMBER) and has enjoyed wide interest because most people can understand the questions raised (even if the solutions may be hard). Are there infinitely many prime numbers? Is there an infinity of primes p such that $p + 2$ is also prime? Is every even number (above 4) the sum of two primes? (These last two problems are unsolved.)

Then there is 'additive number theory': which numbers are the sum of two squares (e.g. $3^2 + 5^2 = 34$)? Show that all numbers are the sum of at most four squares (proved by Joseph Louis Lagrange in 1770). Also 'Diophantine equations': solving equations such as Pell's equation $x^2 - 2y^2 = 1$, where x and y are whole numbers. See also FERMAT'S LAST THEOREM. Number theory, for all its fascination, has few practical uses, so it is gratifying that it led to Public Key Crypto Systems, which coded messages mathematically, and which has been used by secret services around the world. N.A.R.

numerical analysis. In general, the science and art of computing approximate solutions to problems formulated in mathematical terms. The numerical analyst must not only use ingenuity and skill in choosing methods which will yield approximations that converge rapidly towards the true solution (see CONVERGENCE), but must also investigate with complete rigour the degree of error involved. The advent of high-speed digital COMPUTERS has greatly enhanced the importance (and the difficulty) of the subject. For further reading: A. Graham, *Numerical Analysis* (1973). R.G.

numerical flexibility, see under FLEXIBLE FIRM.

nuptiality. The frequency of MARRIAGE (or more generally, consensual unions) in a population. Attention in research is usually focused on the formation of unions, especially first marriages which have considerable implications for FERTILITY. Important statistics include those showing the mean average age when first married, and the proportion of the population which never marries at all. But with many developed societies having rising rates of divorce or the dissolution of unions, there is now considerable demographic and sociological interest in the process whereby unions end and re-form. For further reading: H. S. Shryock *et al*, *The Methods and Materials of Demography* (condensed ed.) (1976).

E.G.; D.S.

Nuremberg Code. At the close of the Nuremberg Medical Trial in 1947 (see NUREMBERG TRIALS), the US judges pronounced a set of ten guiding principles for medical experiments on humans. A key innovation was that of informed and voluntary consent. Called the Nuremberg Code, this became a landmark in the ethics of clinical research, even though it has been criticized and revised.

The Code had an international impact. In 1947 the UN Commission on Human Rights accepted the principle that 'no one shall be subjected without his free consent to medical or scientific experimentation', arising from a British proposal that no person shall be subjected to 'medical or scientific experimentation against his will'. French and Israeli proposals altered the phrasing to informed consent in 1948–49. The Code has gained increasing acceptance, while undergoing modification, as at Helsinki in 1964 for cases where the subject is incapable of consent. The Code is still criticized as too permissive and as difficult to enforce. For further reading: G. J. Annas and M. A. Grodin, *The Nazi Doctors and the Nuremberg Code* (1992). P.J.W.

Nuremberg Laws. A series of antisemitic decrees (see ANTISEMITISM) promulgated by Hitler at the Nazi Party conference in Nuremberg on 15 September 1935. These defined Jews as those with three Jewish grandparents, those practising JUDAISM, and those married to Jews. The Nuremberg Laws denied them any rights of state or local citizenship, and forbade marriage, and any sexual relations, between 'Jews' and 'non-Jews'. Other decrees excluded Jews or half-Jews from public office; from owning businesses, economic enterprises or land; and from practising as doctors, lawyers, writers, journalists, teachers in schools and universities, etc. The Nuremberg Laws, reducing the Jews to the status of second-class citizens, were the beginning of a process which led to the Final Solution and thc ensuing HOLOCAUST. For further reading: M. Gilbert, *The Holocaust* (1985). D.C.W.

Nuremberg Trials. The trial at the end of World War II of 24 former Nazi leaders (see NAZISM), and the 12 subsequent trials of major war criminals from the army, the ministries, the legal community, the medical profession, business, etc., on charges of crimes committed before and during the war. These included the planning and waging of aggressive war, GENOCIDE, the ill-treatment of prisoners of war and deportees, crimes against humanity, the use of FORCED LABOUR, and general breaches of the laws of war. The legal justification for such trials of the vanquished by the victors has been a matter of subsequent dispute among jurists. Of the 177 men indicted, 25 were sentenced to death, 20 to life imprisonment, and 25 acquitted. For further reading: B. F. Smith, *Reaching Judgment at Nuremberg* (1971). D.C.W.

O

OAS, see ORGANIZATION OF AMERICAN STATES.

OAU, see under ORGANIZATION OF AFRICAN UNITY; PAN-AFRICANISM.

object (a). A term used by the French psychoanalyst Lacan (see PSYCHOANALYSIS; LACANIAN), who regarded the object (a) as his most important contribution to analytical theory: the object, says Lacan, falls, and each particular object (a) (breast, faeces, look, voice) has its own time of falling. By falling, we can understand the idea of remainder, or waste product, such that when the SUBJECT takes on signifiers in the OTHER, there is a remainder which cannot be taken up into the signifying chain (see SYMBOLIC). This remainder signifies all that is left of the living nature of the subject, since the signifying chain, with its autonomous structure of repetition, is in a sense 'beyond' life – it carries on regardless of the contingencies of human activity, and thus Lacan could equate it with the death drive. On the other hand, where life is to be found is on the side of what is cut off by the signifying chain, i.e. the object. This object (a) is what is offered as a response to the DESIRE of the Other, and thus comes to function as the cause of desire. For further reading: J. Lacan, *The Four Fundamental Concepts of Psychoanalysis* (1977). D.L.

object relations. In PSYCHOANALYSIS, a post-FREUDIAN emphasis on the interrelation between subject and object, rather than on the study of the SUBJECT only. This theory derives from Freud's description of the development of the libidinal stages, but whereas he viewed the object as secondary in relation to the subject's problems of libidinal attachment, many post-Freudians saw the object as an integral part of the subject's psychic development, which starts from PARTIAL OBJECTS such as the breast, and then leads on to the whole person perceived as another subject. Michael Balint stressed the necessity of looking at the subject as interacting with others, and as being determined by this process, so that clinical work as a consequence should concentrate on a person-to-person relationship, on the modes of the original mother–child dual relation.

The KLEINIAN theory of object relations is based on the infant's relation to his primary perceptions of the external object as part of himself and the ensuing frustrations at having to perceive it as separated and independent of his instinctual demands. The object is then split into 'bad' unaffording parts, and 'good' parts colluding with the baby's satisfaction. In this way the object is endowed with moral and pragmatic qualities: it is not only good or bad, but it acts upon the subject by persecuting or reassuring him. The object relation process functions, for Klein, as an assessment of the subjective stage of psychic development and integration.

The Freudian oral, anal and genital stages of libidinal development are applicable to the object relations theory; starting from sadistic and persecuting oral and anal stages, where the objects and the self are split into pieces (paranoid-schizoid position), the infant has to develop a relation to a whole, independent but not persecuting object. This passage from a partial to a whole relation to the object is called the depressive position, whose overcoming in turn introduces the child to the genital stage. These various modes of relation to the object can overlap, alternate or combine with each other. The difficulty of this approach is in sorting out the ambiguity of the status of the object: whether it is as a real object that it determines the infantile phantasized relation, or whether it is as a PHANTASY object that it operates. B.BE.

objective correlative. Term coined by T. S. Eliot in his essay 'Hamlet' (1919): 'The only way of expressing emotion in the form of art is by finding an "objective correlative": in other words, a set of objects, a situation, a chain of events which shall be the formula of that *particular* emotion; such that when the external facts, which must terminate in sensory experience, are given, the emotion is immediately evoked.' Eliot maintains that Hamlet is dominated by an emotion which is 'in excess of the facts as they appear'. As with DISSOCIATION OF SENSIBILITY, Eliot's dictum cannot be made into a universal law (and has been disputed in its application to

Hamlet), but it provides an excellent description of the sort of immature writing where intense emotions remain inexplicable and unengaging because they lack a context which will evoke and define them. D.J.E.

objective idealism, see under IDEALISM.

objectivism. An American poetic movement of the early 1930s, short-lived but influential. According to William Carlos Williams, whose *Collected Poems 1921–1931* was published by the Objectivist Press in 1934: 'Objectivism looks at the poem with a special eye to its structural aspect, how it has been constructed . . . It arose as an aftermath of IMAGISM, which the Objectivists felt was not specific enough, and applied to any image that might be conceived.' Other poets associated with the movement were George Oppen, who founded the Objectivist Press (originally TO: The Objectivists); Carl Rakosi; Louis Zukofsky, who edited *An Objectivist's Anthology*; and Charles Reznikoff. Ezra Pound gave postal encouragement. M.S.-S.

objectivity. The CONCEPT that there exists a 'pure' type of description – or even knowledge – that is untainted by the problem of perspective arising from the human condition of SUBJECTIVITY and EMBODIMENT. Objectivity is a concept studied (and employed) by philosophers and scientists, but it also has great significance in everyday life. For instance, we demand that the judiciary, the news media and those with whom we have even the smallest transactions be 'objective', by which we mean fair, impartial, unbiased.

Science requires objectivity because SCIENTIFIC METHOD itself wants to be objective. One aim of science is the accurate description of phenomena in the world: the search for 'facts' which we all can agree are 'true'. From these basic building blocks of agreed fact, science can proceed with its processes of hypothesis, experimentation and conclusion. The methods employed are those of EMPIRICISM, REDUCTIONISM and POSITIVISM.

In PHILOSOPHY, objectivity is the goal of LOGICAL POSITIVISTS for whom all knowledge must be verifiable in a scientific sense. This tradition, which dominated in British and some American universities during the second half of the 20th century, derives from the work of the VIENNA CIRCLE and was created to contradict the WELTANSCHAUUNG put forward by METAPHYSICS. To put it bluntly, positivists believe that if you can't touch 'it' or see it, it doesn't exist in any meaningful way. For many, this tradition has impoverished philosophical investigation and the study of philosophy as a university subject.

The metaphysical tradition descends into the 20th century via Edmund Husserl (1859–1938), the father of PHENOMENOLOGY, who brought a new rigour to the study of ONTOLOGY and EPISTEMOLOGY, while including human subjectivity as part of the knowledge equation. Phenomenology developed via Martin Heidegger (1889–1976) through Jean-Paul Sartre (1905–80) as EXISTENTIALISM – a way of doing philosophy and a way of viewing the world and man's relation to it that stands in defiance of logical positivism. Perhaps the problem of objectivity was best stated by the French phenomenologist Maurice Merleau-Ponty (1908–61), who observed that objectivity required a multitude of simultaneous perspectives. He held that in order for us to have a truly objective view, instead of being limited by the perspective that is possible as a result of our embodiment as subjects (derived not only from our physical location and condition, but also from our experience), we would have to be everywhere at once – but only GOD can be everywhere at once. S.T.

objet trouvé (found object). Any strange, romantic or comic bit of stone, wood or manufactured bric-à-brac which is presented by the finder as an art object. The term was much used by the SURREALISTS to whom such objects, whether found or fabricated, became from the late 1920s onwards as significant as their pictures or sculptures. J.W.

obsession. In ABNORMAL PSYCHOLOGY and PSYCHIATRY, a form of NEUROSIS marked primarily by an emotionally charged idea that may persistently impose itself on the subject's conscious awareness; in this sense, the phrase obsessional disorder is widely used. In popular usage, any excessive preoccupation. W.Z.

obsidian dating, see under DATING.

occultism. The occult is the mysterious that lies below the surface of things; occultism is the exercise of magical procedures to influence this, by a knowledge of it. Elements of MAGIC, WITCHCRAFT, etc., have persisted in all civilizations; anthropologists insist that these features may be present in the RITUALS of all types of society (modern as well as PRIMITIVE), and they have not been dissipated by modern science. With the supposed 'flight from reason' during recent decades, occultism has enjoyed a popular revival. The Society for Psychical Research was founded in Britain in 1882, and in recent years a growing literature has examined telepathy, hypnotism, clairvoyance, the evidence for survival beyond death, and, in general, those supranormal faculties of man which still seem to lie beyond the range of testable knowledge. R.F.

occupation. The ways in which men obtain their livelihood are commonly divided into: (1) *primary occupations*: the production or extraction of raw materials, e.g. agriculture, fishing, hunting, lumbering and mining; (2) *secondary occupations*: the production of man-made goods or the processing of raw materials. The growth of secondary at the expense of primary occupations is a feature of the early stages of INDUSTRIALIZATION; (3) *tertiary occupations*: the provision of services (see SERVICE INDUSTRY) rather than the production of goods. Some expansion of tertiary as well as secondary occupations takes place in the early stages of industrialization, but the marked growth of tertiary at the expense of both primary and secondary occupations is one of the distinguishing characteristics of advanced INDUSTRIAL SOCIETIES. A.L.C.B.

occupational therapy. In medical practice, the treatment of physical or mental disability by purposive occupation. Originally activities like farming helped to combat the apathy of long-stay patients in mental hospitals. Later, handicrafts provided soothing diversions for the physically or mentally sick. Modern occupational therapy is much more actively therapeutic, aiming to foster interest and self-confidence, to overcome disability, and to develop fresh skills enabling patients to perform a useful function in the community. Activities are tailored to the needs of individual patients, and range from games to typing, domestic science, and light industrial work supervised by technical instructors. Group activities are emphasized as a means of encouraging social interaction. Occupational therapy now forms an integral part of the treatment of many illnesses, particularly chronic physical or mental handicap, whether in hospital or not. For further reading: E. M. MacDonald (ed.), *Occupational Therapy in Rehabilitation* (1975). D.H.G.

oceanic ridge (mid-oceanic ridge). Any section of the more or less linked system of rugged mountain ranges that rise from the floors of all the world's major oceans. The system has no single name; in the central and south Atlantic it is called the mid-Atlantic ridge, in the north Atlantic to the south-west of Iceland it is the Reykjanes ridge, in the Pacific it is the east Pacific rise, and so on. It is about 80,000 km long overall, has an average width of about 1,000 km, rises to 2–3 km above the ocean floors on average (but with individual peaks rising to 5 km and some even breaking the surface to form islands, e.g. Bouvet Island, Jan Mayen Island), and has a rift valley along the axis for much of its length. It is the earth's largest and longest mountain chain. The oceanic ridge system is a crucial element in PLATE TECTONICS. The central rift valleys are the sites at which molten material rises continuously from the ASTHENOSPHERE below, cools, solidifies and becomes new oceanic LITHOSPHERE, which then spreads away from the ridges in both directions. Oceanic ridges are thus the chief manifestations of the earth's volcanism, in comparison with which the conventional, land-based conical volcanoes are as almost nothing. Detailed examination of rift valleys from submersibles has revealed the presence of current tectonic activity in the form of fresh lavas, active fissures, high heat flow and HYDROTHERMAL VENTS (see SUBDUCTION ZONE). P.J.S.

oceanography. Scientific study of the phenomena associated with the ocean waters that cover 70 per cent of the earth's surface. The main branches are *physical oceanography* (concerned with waves, ocean currents, tides and circulation systems); *chemical oceanography* (e.g. analyses of the constituents of ocean water); *biological* *oceanography* (e.g. study of marine fauna), and *geological oceanography* (e.g. study of ocean basins, MORPHOLOGY of the sea bottom, oceanic sediments). Scientific oceanography dates from the mid-19th century with growing interest in deep-sea biology, marked by the establishment of research centres such as the Stazione Zoologica in Naples, founded in 1872. The *Challenger* voyages in the 1870s are an early landmark in the development of special research exploration voyages. Current interest in oceanography is widening its scope to include broader issues of a legal, economic and ecological nature (see ECOLOGY). Leading centres for oceanography include the Scripps Institution of Oceanography at La Jolla, California, the Woods Hole Oceanographic Institute in Massachusetts, and the National Institute for Oceanography at Wormley, England. For further reading: W. A. Anikouchine and R. W. Sternberg, *The World Ocean: An Introduction to Oceanography* (1981). P.H.

OCR. Acronym for optical character recognition, computer software that can read printed or handwritten text. One of the most pressing tasks of the information age has been transferring printed data to computers. The development of OCR software to translate print into machine-usable text has made the Bible, the classics, great dictionaries and encyclopedias, and many more ordinary documents available electronically. It has been a task as ambitious, and perhaps even as important, as the ancient world's setting the oral classics in writing. E.B.B.

October War, see under MIDDLE EAST WARS.

OECD (Organization for Economic Cooperation and Development). An intergovernmental organization which was established in a convention of 1961 comprising the 20 original members of the Organization for European Economic Cooperation (OEEC), and subsequently including Yugoslavia (1961), Japan (1964), Finland (1969), Australia (1971), and New Zealand (1973). The objectives of the convention are to promote policies that encourage ECONOMIC GROWTH and employment in member countries and the rest of the world, and which contribute to world ECONOMIC DEVELOPMENT and the expansion of world trade. The OECD is also interested in science, education, social affairs and the relations between developed and developing countries. It is based in Paris, and the reports and forecasts of its economic secretariat are widely reported and influential in the formation of opinions. W.B.; J.P.

Oedipus complex. In psychoanalytic theory (see PSYCHOANALYSIS), the normal emotional crisis brought about, at an early stage of PSYCHOSEXUAL DEVELOPMENT, by the sexual impulses of a boy towards his mother and jealousy of his father. Resultant guilt feelings precipitate the development of the SUPEREGO (conscience). Its female counterpart is the ELECTRA COMPLEX. W.Z.

Off-Broadway. A collection of some 30 theatres surrounding New York's Broadway on all sides but the west, best known for the development of new dramatists such as Edward Albee and Jack Gelber, and the revival of old masters like Eugene O'Neill. The movement and the term date back to 1915 when the PROVINCETOWN PLAYERS and the *Washington Square Players* established themselves in Greenwich Village. Dedicated to good production of good plays in intimate surroundings, the movement acquired a new lease of life in 1952 with a notable revival of Tennessee Williams's Broadway failure, *Summer and Smoke*. But, despite much excellent work in the 1950s and 1960s, soaring costs and the desire for commercial success gradually turned Off-Broadway into a replica of Broadway itself, and the really experimental work began to take place off Off-Broadway in coffee houses, cabarets, churches and warehouses. See also ALTERNATIVE THEATRE and, for a British equivalent, FRINGE, THE. For further reading: M. Gottfried, *A Theater Divided: the Postwar American Stage* (1969). M.BI.

OGPU, see under KGB.

oil crisis. Precipitated by OPEC's substantial increases in the price of oil in 1974 and 1979. The use of oil is crucial to most economies, as the substitution of other forms of energy for oil is difficult or can only take place over a long time span. These price increases raised awareness about the use and exhaustion of finite reserves of fossil fuels (see ENERGY CRISIS). They also contributed to the world economic recession and the steep rise in inflation during the 1970s. The funding of increased oil import bills has been an important cause of the DEBT CRISIS. For further reading: P. R. Odell, *Oil and World Power* (1986). J.P.

oil weapon. Used by the Arab states during the October War (see MIDDLE EAST WARS) in 1973, it consisted of a monthly percentage reduction (5 per cent) and an embargo on oil exports to the US and the Netherlands. Led by Saudi Arabia and based on a decision of the Organization of Arab Petroleum Exporting Countries (OPEC), it was too short-lived (from October 1973 to March 1974) to have a direct effect on events. But the unusual unanimity of the Arab states and the subsequent fourfold increase in the price of oil agreed by OPEC gave a sense of euphoria to the Arab producers and caused a corresponding sense of alarm among consumers. Neither the political cohesion nor the market conditions necessary for a renewed use of the oil weapon have so far recurred. W.K.

O. J. Simpson, trial of. The trial of celebrity athlete O. J. Simpson in 1995, for the alleged double-murder of his ex-wife, Nicole Brown Simpson, and her friend, Ronald Lyle Goldman, in Los Angeles on 12 June 1994. It is generally considered a recent low point of American justice because of judicial ineptitude, police misconduct, prosecutorial incompetence, and the willingness of Simpson's legal 'dream team' to use racial issues to win Simpson's acquittal. Despite convincing evidence of guilt, a predominantly black jury found the celebrity athlete not guilty as charged on 3 October 1995. Much of the trial was carried live on television, and the verdict exposed a deep split between whites who believed Simpson was guilty and blacks who rejoiced at his acquittal. In 1997, Goldman's survivors won a huge civil judgement in a wrongful death suit naming Simpson as the defendant. R.K.H.

oligarchy. A new application, for our times, of the old theory that rule can only be by the few, never by the many. It has been developed especially in relation to the institutions of modern mass DEMOCRACIES, such as political parties and TRADE UNIONS. As Robert Michels (1876–1936) was among the first to point out in 1911, formally democratic organizations with large memberships face a constant tension between efficiency and democratic control. In seeking to survive and to prosper, they tend to produce oligarchies of full-time officials. These have the expertise and experience to control the life of the organization, and can generally smother, head off, or ignore the views of dissident and usually disunited members. They can also usually modify the IDEOLOGY and formal goals of the organization, according to their perception of its long-term interests. 'Who says organization', said Michels, 'says oligarchy.' The 'iron law of oligarchy' has been shown at work in a host of modern organizations, with striking effect in the case of those formally committed to radical or democratic goals and procedures, such as SOCIALIST parties and trade unions. It is one explanation of the 'de-radicalization' of working-class political parties. Michels has been accused of a Machiavellian cynicism (or detachment), as have proponents of similar élitist views such as Gaetano Mosca (1858–1941) and Vilfredo Pareto (1848–1923). But so far it has proved difficult to show how large-scale organizations can function adequately if subject to constant intervention by the mass membership. Co-operative, decentralized enterprises (see CO-OPERATIVES), such as that of Mondragon in the Spanish Basque provinces, seem to be successful only where there is a strong local tradition of communal self-help. For further reading: T. B. Bottomore, *Élites and Society* (1966). K.K.

oligopeptide, see under PEPTIDE.

oligopoly. An industry in which a good or service is provided by only a few firms (see FIRM, THEORIES OF), which implies that the actions of any one of them affect the circumstances of the other firms. Oligopoly is often thought to be close to the reality of much of manufacturing business. A firm's choice of strategies will be influenced by its view of how rivals will react to its actions. Firms may collude and attempt to act as a MONOPOLY. Collusion will be more difficult the larger the number of sellers and the more different the interests of the sellers. Collusion may be difficult to arrange and, in practice, may take the form of price leadership and tacit rules of behaviour, e.g. not encroaching on other firms' territories. Explicit or tacit collusion will be limited by the possibility of entry of new firms into the industry (see BARRIER TO ENTRY and GAME THEORY). For further reading: J. Craven, *Introduction to Economics* (1984). G.B.R.; J.P.

ombudsman. A state official entrusted by the legislature with very wide powers enabling him to intervene in the bureaucratic and administrative process in the interests of individual citizens whose complaints he investigates. The institution originated in Swedish practice as early as 1809, and has since been copied in civilian matters by Finland (1919), Israel (1950), Denmark (1953), Norway (1962), New Zealand (1962), and Britain (1967). In military matters Norway and West Germany have similar officials. The successful operation of the institution depends on the extent of the official's powers and on his capacity for initiative, two elements notably restricted in the British case. For further reading: R. Gregory and P. Hutchesson, *The Parliamentary Ombudsman* (1975). D.C.W.

Omega Workshops. Established in London by Roger Fry in 1913 to provide a livelihood for young artists. For a small weekly wage, the members anonymously decorated furniture, pottery and other functional objects. Adversely affected by the war, the Omega was dissolved in 1919. Q.B.

on-line service. A company that provides access to the INTERNET or other network. These businesses show that hardware, expertise and support form an indispensable trinity for every electronic information service. Although they can use established phone systems, they need computers to serve their customers. Programming expertise gives their customers software for contacting the service. They must be ready with technical assistance for customers as problems arise. These elements come even before information's content, which may be why so much modern information reveals more technique than meaning. E.B.B.

oncogene. A GENE that contributes to tumour formation. The most convincing examples of oncogenes are those in tumour viruses; if the oncogene of such a virus is experimentally removed, the virus no longer causes tumours. From the notion that the oncogenes of such viruses had their origins in the animals that are the target for the viruses came the discovery of what are presumed to be the progenitors of oncogenes. Since, in healthy animals, these progenitor genes direct the production of PROTEINS that are important for normal CELL growth – particularly hormone-like substances (see ENDOCRINOLOGY) or their RECEPTORS – it is misleading to call them oncogenes. Instead the term *proto-oncogene*, which indicates their potential subversion, is often used. It is possible to detect oncogenes in some human tumours, where it is reasonable to suppose that, e.g., a carcinogen has directly or indirectly converted a proto-oncogene into an oncogene. But the relative importance of oncogenes in the development of human tumours is by no means clear. See also CANCER. P.N.

oncology. The branch of medical science concerned with CANCER. The prefix onco (from a Greek word meaning 'mass' or 'bulk') denotes something to do with a tumour; thus *oncoviruses* are tumour-causing viruses (see VIROLOGY), an oncogen (or carcinogen) is an agent giving rise to tumours, and an ONCOGENE is a gene that has a role in cancer. P.M.; P.N.

ondes martenot (*ondes musicales*). An electrophonic instrument invented by Maurice Martenot in 1928 and similar to the THEREMIN, having a keyboard and a capacity for glissandi. It now generally replaces the theremin and has solo roles in major works of Messiaen, notably *Turangalîla*. J.G.R.

one-sided disarmers, see under DISARMAMENT.

ontogeny. The course of growth within the lifetime of a single member of a SPECIES. It is contrasted with PHYLOGENY. J.S.B.

ontology. The theory of existence or, more narrowly, of what really exists, as opposed to that which appears to exist but does not, or to that which can properly be said to exist but only if conceived as some complex whose constituents are the things that really exist. It is the primary element in METAPHYSICS. Some ontologists have argued that many things exist that are not commonly acknowledged to do so, such as (1) abstract *entities* and (2) NOUMENA (Kant's 'things-in-themselves') inaccessible to empirical observation; others have argued that many things commonly thought to exist do not, e.g. material things, the theoretical entities of NATURAL SCIENCE, mental states conceived as something other than dispositions to behaviour, and objective value-properties. The ontology of a theory or body of assertions is the SET of things to which that theory ascribes existence by referring to them in a way that cannot be eliminated or analysed out (see ANALYSIS) by REDUCTION. See BELIEF; OBJECTIVITY. For further reading: A. Quinton, *The Nature of Things* (1973). A.Q.

op art. A scientifically oriented ABSTRACT ART movement in the 1960s concerned with perceptual dynamics and retinal stimulation. Geometric forms, colour dissonance and kinetic elements (see KINETIC ART) were used to achieve optical effects, illusions, afterimages, and moiré patterning (see MOIRÉ effect), and to stress the act of perception as the central meaning. Artists involved in this somewhat *passé* movement were: Julio Le Parc, founder of the Groupe de Recherche d'Art Visuel in Paris in 1960; Victor Vasarely in Paris; Bridget Riley in England; and Richard Anuszkiewicz in New York. Its more romantic counterpart was PSYCHEDELIC ART. For further reading: F. Popper, *Origins and Development of Kinetic Art*. (1969). A.K.W.

opacity, referential. In philosophical discussions of reference, a term is said to be 'referentially opaque' when it is not being used in a straightforward way to refer to some object. For example, in 'Tom is happy' the name 'Tom' is being used simply to refer to a given individual. This is shown by the fact that if Tom has a second name, say 'Philip', then one can substitute 'Philip' for 'Tom' in the sentence 'Tom is happy' and its TRUTH-VALUE will remain unaffected. Here, therefore, 'Tom' is being used in a 'referentially transparent' way. But this is not the case in 'I believe that Tom is happy'. Suppose that I do not know that Tom's other name is 'Philip'. Then, although I believe that Tom is happy, I do not believe that Philip is happy; substituting 'Philip' for 'Tom' will therefore change the truth-value of the sentence. Thus 'Tom' is here occurring in a referentially opaque context. Opaque contexts are generated in other ways too; e.g., referring terms falling within the scope of the modal adverbs 'necessarily' and 'possibly' (see MODAL LOGIC) also suffer from referential opacity. For further reading: L. Linsky, *Reference and Modality* (1971). A.C.G.

OPEC (Organization of Petroleum Exporting Countries). Formed in 1960 by Venezuela, Saudi Arabia, Iran, Iraq and Kuwait, OPEC was a response to the major oil companies reducing payments to host countries for crude oil. In the early 1970s, a toughening in the attitude of the organization and, in particular, Libya and Algeria revealed its potential power as a CARTEL. In October 1973 OPEC began the first of a series of dramatic rises in the price of oil, which would ultimately lead to the price escalating to $30 a barrel by 1980, having been $3 in early 1973. Since this peak, the price has fallen, however, and the strength of the coalition has been diminished. Western industrialized countries reacted to the high prices of oil by exploiting their own reserves, e.g. in the North Sea, and by developing alternative sources of energy such as coal and nuclear power. Meanwhile, the unity of the member countries of OPEC has been compromised by the wars Iraq has fought against both Iran and Kuwait. See OIL CRISIS; OIL WEAPON; ENERGY CRISIS; DEBT CRISIS. For further reading: D. Yergin, *The Prize: The Quest for Oil, Money and Power* (1991). J.P.; A.A.L.

Open Cities and **Special Economic Zones.** Areas of low TAXATION and high INVESTMENT designed to act as a window into China, and attract vital foreign currency and TECHNOLOGY into the country in an attempt to stimulate ECONOMIC GROWTH. There are 18 open cities and four special economic zones, the most famous being Shenzhen on the China–Hong Kong border, and Xiamen (Amoy). Bearing a more than passing resemblance to the much-hated treaty ports of the pre-liberation era, their job was to stimulate international interest in trading with China, and also to facilitate the return of Hong Kong by showing that China was prepared to tolerate areas of CAPITALISM within her jurisdiction. Recently, their importance has declined with the extension of the right to make trade arrangements with foreign companies being extended to all units of production without their first having to seek government approval. For further reading: H. Harding (ed.), *China's Foreign Relations in the 1980s* (1984). S.B.

open court reading plan. A reading method used in many American schools where children are taught the sounds of letters by breath and touch. For instance, the sound for 'h' in reality cannot be 'aitch' or even 'huh'. Children 'breathe' the soundless 'h' onto their hands or arms, thus 'feeling' it properly. The method proved highly successful and children were found to read at a level well beyond their norm. J.I.

open door policies. A term relating to the conditions of confinement within mental hospitals. The legal framework within which lunatic asylums developed in the 19th century was that of compulsory confinement. Only those certified by due legal process were to be admitted as patients. This strict legalism was enacted in order to prevent the occurrence of detention as a form of psychiatric abuse. Increasingly, this situation was found psychiatrically counterproductive. The precise requirements of certification too often meant that patients were not admitted until their PSYCHOSES had become severe; moreover, discharge was an equally cumbersome process. The English Mental Treatment Act of 1930 effectively changed this situation, encouraging voluntary admissions (and hence a greater right of self-discharge) and thus greater 'permeability' between asylum and community. This open door policy was greatly extended by an Act of 1959, as a consequence of which the majority of patients attending mental hospitals are voluntary. For further reading: T. Butler, *Mental Health, Social Policy and the Law* (1985). R.P.

open government. A policy to make the proceedings of government more visible to the governed. A degree of openness in government is clearly necessary on grounds of accountability, so that voters possess sufficient information to make democratic choices properly. But governments have felt obliged to withhold information that might be prejudicial to national security, or which might inhibit the free discussion of sensitive issues by ministers and civil servants. There are, of course, also self-interested reasons for governments to suppress information that might embarrass them. In practice, 'open government' measures normally go no further than 'Freedom of Information' Acts to give citizens the legal right to gain access to selected material, the progressive release of official records, the institution of governmental watchdogs (such as ombudsmen), and the use of consultative forums such as public inquiries to widen public participation in the policy process. For further reading: R. Chapman, *Open Government* (1989). N.O.

open plan. An arrangement of spaces, usually in domestic or office ARCHITECTURE, where the division between areas is implied by screens, columns, changes of level, or different ceiling heights, rather than defined by walls. It was largely developed by Frank Lloyd Wright in his house plans from the mid-1890s onwards and owes something to his familiarity with the traditional Japanese house. A variant, *le plan libre*, was practised by Le Corbusier, taking advantage of skeletal construction. Its acceptance is largely due to the emergence of efficient heating systems and the great reduction in the number of household servants; in the case of offices it allows the regrouping of work areas with the least disturbance. M.BR.

open-plan schools. Schools where the ARCHITECTURE provides for minimal or no visual and acoustic separation between teaching-stations. Commonly between two and eight teachers and their pupils share a large teaching-space to which one or more quiet rooms or learning-bays may be connected. Teachers necessarily work in view and hearing of one another; effective teaching therefore requires them to co-operate in decisions about deployment of groups of children, scheduling, curriculum, teaching and learning problems. The focus of decision-making is typically shifted from the individual teacher to the team, and vertical grouping is facilitated. Some pupils and teachers thrive in the atmosphere of an open-plan school, but others feel lost and insecure and would be happier and better cared for in self-contained classrooms. A prime target for criticism in open-plan schools is the noise level, and adequate soundproofing is of great importance. E.L.-S.

open prison (or **prison without bars**). An establishment with minimal or token security, and in general a less restrictive regime than that of an ordinary prison; a feature of prison systems in Britain, the USA and Scandinavia since the 1930s. Inmates are selected, for short sentences or the latter part of long ones, on the basis of their constituting negligible escape risks. There is little evidence to suggest that open prisons have more than humanitarian value. T.M.

open society. Sir Karl Popper's (see POPPERIAN) term for the free society, where all are able to criticize effectively those who hold authority in it. Popper quotes and approves of Pericles: 'Although only a few may originate a policy, we are all able to judge it.' This entails a forthright attack on totalitarian doctrines (see TOTALITARIANISM); on 'closed' hierarchies of social and political organization which do not allow individuals to rise according to merit; on indoctrination in education; on HISTORICIST social theories which predict the destiny of human society on the basis of 'unalterable laws' of historical development; and on totalitarian programmes for the reform of 'society as a whole' – which can easily replace one AUTHORITARIANISM by another. See also SOCIAL ENGINEERING. For further reading: K. R. Popper, *The Open Society and Its Enemies* (1967). R.F.

open stage. A term first used by Richard Southern (1953) to denote any form of staging in which the actor is not separated from the audience by a proscenium arch. The move towards open staging in this century is part of the reaction against NATURALISM which, in the theatre, is associated with realistic stage setting seen through the 'picture frame' or 'fourth wall' of the proscenium opening. The techniques of the open stage were developed in the first half of this century in productions by William Poel, Max Reinhardt, Jacques Copeau, Vsevolod Meyerhold, and Nikolai Okhlopkov, and in the design of Walter Gropius's unrealized TOTAL THEATRE project for Erwin Piscator (1927). The principles of open staging have been increasingly incorporated in theatre architecture since the 1940s.

The principal forms of open stage are *thrust stage*, in which an acting area with a scenic or architectural background is surrounded on three sides by an audience; *end stage*, in which an audience faces the stage in a rectangular auditorium; *transverse stage*, in which an audience is seated on two opposite sides of a performing area; and *theatre in the round* (see THEATRE ANTHROPOLOGY). An adaptable theatre is one designed to allow a variety of forms. For further reading: R. and H. Leacroft, *Theatre and Playhouse* (1984). M.A.

Open University. Originally called the *University of the Air*, the Open University (headquarters at Milton Keynes in Buckinghamshire) offers degree courses (and a variety of non-degree courses) to people who do not have the qualifications required for ordinary university entrance. Founded in 1971, it now has over 160,000 people registered on courses, most working from their own homes for degrees on a cumulative course credit system, normally over at least four years. The teaching is provided through specially prepared books and book lists, weekly television and radio programmes (broadcast by the British Broadcasting Corporation), regionally organized study centres, written work on a correspondence basis, local counsellors and tutors recruited regionally, and full-time summer courses in university centres. W.A.C.S.

operant (or **instrumental**) **conditioning**. A form of CONDITIONING in which behaviour is controlled through systematic manipulation of the consequences of previous behaviour; a sophisticated branch of American BEHAVIOURIST psychology developed by B. F. Skinner (see SKINNERIAN). A central idea is that of REINFORCEMENT. Knowledge of (or control over) the delivery of reinforcements in a given situation is both A NECESSARY AND A SUFFICIENT CONDITION for the prediction (or control) of behaviour.

Although Skinner's ideas originated in studies of rats and pigeons in restricted experimental ENVIRONMENTS (see SKINNER BOX), he extended his conceptual analysis to human behaviour, including language.

Techniques derived from operant conditioning have proved useful in PSYCHIATRY, EDUCATIONAL PSYCHOLOGY and INDUSTRIAL PSYCHOLOGY. For further reading: B. F. Skinner, *The Behaviour of Organisms* (1938). D.H.

operationalism. A theory that defines scientific CONCEPTS in terms of the actual experimental procedures used to establish their applicability. Expounded by Percy Bridgman in 1927, it identifies length, e.g., with the set of operations by which length is measured. It is a radically EMPIRICIST doctrine and very close to that version of the VERIFICATION principle which defines the meaning of a PROPOSITION as 'the method of its verification'. Einstein's famous rejection of the concept of absolute simultaneity, on the ground that the simultaneity of events is always relative to the FRAME OF REFERENCE of the observer who is assessing it, is operationalist in spirit. For further reading: P. W. Bridgman, *The Logic of Modern Physics* (1927). A.Q.

operator.

(1) In MATHEMATICS, a synonym for FUNCTION, often used when the arguments are non-numerical or themselves functions.

(2) In QUANTUM MECHANICS, the representation of a physical quantity. R.G.

operon. A group of GENES brought into action simultaneously. The concept is based on studies of gene action in bacteria (see BACTERIOLOGY) by Jacob and Monod (Nobel Prize, 1965). J.M.S.

opportunity cost. In ECONOMICS, that which is forgone by taking a particular action, e.g. a decision to invest in a particular project prevents the associated resources being used elsewhere in the economy. It is measured by considering the consequences of the best alternative use of the resources, e.g. the best alternative INVESTMENT project. The alternative forgone is not necessarily financial, but it is usual to measure opportunity cost in terms of money. The concept is fundamental to the definition of ECONOMIC EFFICIENCY. In PERFECT COMPETITION, price represents the opportunity cost to the consumer of the purchase of a good and the opportunity cost of producing the good (see MARGINAL COST PRICING). In COST BENEFIT ANALYSIS and applied economics, it is often necessary to value goods and inputs for which there are no directly observable markets. This can be done by considering the opportunity cost involved in the consumption of the good or use of the input (see SHADOW PRICE). For further reading: J. Craven, *Introduction to Economics* (1984). J.S.F.; J.P.

optical character recognition, see OCR.

optics. The branch of PHYSICS devoted to the study of light. There are four conceptual levels, appropriate to different phenomena: (1) *Geometrical optics*, where light is considered as rays travelling according to the laws of refraction and reflection. This is sufficient for the understanding of lenses and mirrors in cameras, telescopes, etc. (2) *Physical optics*, where the interference and DIFFRACTION effects due to the wave nature of light are taken into account – in order to explain, e.g., the limit to the fine detail that can be discerned even with a perfect lens, or the operation of HOLOGRAPHY. (3) ELECTROMAGNETISM, where the *physical nature* of light waves as undulating ELECTROMAGNETIC FIELDS is studied. Thus light is seen in a new perspective, as just one frequency band in the spectrum of electromagnetic RADIATION. (4) *Quantum electrodynamics*, where the application of QUANTUM MECHANICS to the electromagnetic field explains the parcelling of light ENERGY into discrete PHOTONS which are most easily discernible at very low levels of illumination. For further reading: A. C. S. van Heel and C. H. F. Velzel, *What Is Light?* (1968). M.V.B.

optimal foraging. The theory that animals adjust their behaviour in searching for and exploiting food in such a way as to maximize their rate of intake of energy. When feeding, animals have to decide (presumably unconsciously) by what method to search for food, how long to spend searching, and (once a patch of food has been found) how long to spend exploiting a patch before moving on to search for another. When exploiting a food resource, the animal should also decide which food items to eat and which to leave. The mathematics of *optimality theory* have been used to predict how these decisions should be taken in a specified set of circumstances of food distribution and abundance. The predictions have been extensively tested by experiment, especially on birds. John Krebs has been a leader in this research. The theory assumes that the behaviour of animals has evolved under NATURAL SELECTION. M.R.

optimal policy, see under DYNAMIC PROGRAMMING.

optoelectronics. A hybrid of electronic and optical (light-based) technologies for handling information (see OPTICS). Optical data handling (PHOTONICS) offers potential advantages over the currently predominant electronic technologies, but at present only a limited range of processes (primarily data transmission) can be managed optically. Typically, data is transmitted through optical fibres using LASER light pulses, but is converted back to electronic form for data processing. This hybrid technology remains rather cumbersome, but there are attempts to combine optical devices (such as photodetectors and lasers) with electronic devices (such as TRANSISTORS) on single microchips. P.C.B.

oracy. A word formed by analogy with 'literacy' (the ability to read and write) and meaning mastery of the skills of speaking and listening. It was coined by Andrew Wilkinson in the 1960s to draw attention to the neglect of the oral skills in education despite the fact, confirmed by research, that the ability to communicate in speech is a necessary precondition of learning to read and write and an essential stage in human development. Like numeracy, oracy has proved a convenient coinage that has now come into general use. For further reading: J. Britton, *Language and Learning* (1970). A.L.C.B.

oral character, see under PSYCHOSEXUAL DEVELOPMENT.

oral history. The gathering and preserving of historical information in spoken form. The credit for the modern practice of oral history is given to Allen Nevins, who wrote in his 1938 volume, *Gateway to History*, that some organization was needed which would make 'a systematic attempt to obtain, from the lips and papers of living Americans who had led significant lives, a fuller record of their participation in the political, economic and cultural life of the past 60 years'.

The principal rationale for oral history is to preserve and collect human memories that might otherwise be lost. Until the invention of the tape recorder and videotape, these memories were written down. The recording of the memories and reflections of the actual participants in events is thought to enhance the scholarly knowledge of the event. At first most oral history projects centred on the lives of prominent and famous persons. In recent years, the focus of the oral historian has broadened to include the memories and reflections of 'ordinary' people or persons involved in little-known or extraordinary professions, e.g. jazz musicians or coal miners.

Oral history is seen as a way to get into the real lives of the participants of an event. There is nevertheless debate among historians about how to test the validity of oral reports. The Oral History Association is attempting to codify certain principles, rights and obligations for the creation of source material that is authentic, useful and reliable. For further reading: D. Dunaway and W. Baum (eds), *Oral History: An Interdisciplinary Anthology* (1984). B.E.L.

oral tradition. Defined by Vansina (see below) as 'oral testimony transmitted verbally from one generation to the next one or more'. Oral tradition is one of the basic sources for the study of ETHNOHISTORY. Its reliability is still controversial. The conventional wisdom of historians has been that oral tradition is valueless or that it is impossible to determine its value. This view has been challenged by historians working on African societies that paid great attention to the correct transmission of their traditions.

It is convenient to reserve the term *oral history* for the study of CONTEMPORARY HISTORY through interviews, often tape-recorded, with eye-witnesses. For further reading: J. Vansina, *Oral Tradition as History* (1985). P.B.

orbit. The path or trajectory along which an object travels in space according to NEWTONIAN MECHANICS. For example, the nearly circular orbit of the moon around the earth arises because the attracting force of

GRAVITATION produces an inward acceleration i.e. the tangential velocity of the moon constantly changes in direction by bending inwards, while remaining constant in magnitude. See also BALLISTICS; CELESTIAL MECHANICS. M.V.B.

orbital. In the quantum description of the ATOM, Niels Bohr (in 1911) introduced the concept of an orbit in which the ELECTRONS followed planet-like motions around the NUCLEUS. Modern wave-mechanical treatments (see QUANTUM MECHANICS) do not allow the path of the electron to be pinpointed (see UNCERTAINTY PRINCIPLE), but there is a relation between the WAVE FUNCTION used to describe an electron in an atom or MOLECULE and its spatial distribution. The region within which there is a reasonable (say 95 per cent) probability of finding an electron is termed an orbital. B.F.

ordinal numbers. NUMBERS are used to denote the size of a collection of objects (cardinal numbers), but also to denote position in a series (1st, 2nd, 3rd, . . .): then called ordinal numbers. With a finite SET (of objects) there is basically only one pattern of arrangement in a line, but with INFINITE sets things are more complicated (and interesting). Georg Cantor (1845–1918) focused on the 'well-orderings': these have the property that if you make any selection of the objects in your line then one of your selected objects comes before all the others (the whole numbers, in their natural order, have this property – the positive fractions do not, for some selections).

The first infinite ordinal is ω, represented by 1, 2, 3, 4, . . . in their natural order. To get $\omega + 1$ we remove 1 from the start and place it at the end after all the others. Similarly for $\omega + 2$, $\omega + 3$, etc. Then 2ω is represented by 1, 3, 5, 7 . . . 2, 4, 6, 8, . . . And ω^2 by 2, 4, 8, 16, . . . 3, 9, 27, . . ., 5, 25, 125, . . . where we use all the powers of all the prime numbers. They are used in mathematical logic (see MATHEMATICS; LOGIC) in a process called transfinite induction. N.A.R.

ordinary language philosophy, see LINGUISTIC PHILOSOPHY.

organic. In ARCHITECTURE (for its meaning in art see BIOMORPHIC), adjective used (1) principally by Frank Lloyd Wright (1869–1959) as a term of approval for certain buildings, including his own, which were usually asymmetrical and integrated closely with the particular features of the site; in this sense the term is opposed both to 'classical' and to the INTERNATIONAL STYLE; (2) often in its more literal sense of being abstracted from the forms of nature, especially in the case of ornaments such as the arabesque; (3) occasionally to describe buildings, or parts of buildings, organized on a direct biological analogy such as that of the human body. See also FUNCTIONALISM. For further reading: F. L. Wright, *The Future of Architecture* (1963). M.BR.

organic chemistry. One of the main branches of CHEMISTRY. Originally defined as the chemistry of substances formed by living matter, but since 1828, when it was shown that organic chemicals could be produced from inanimate material, better described as the chemistry of compounds containing carbon (except for some compounds containing metal IONS). Over half a million organic compounds have been described, including petroleum products, rubber, plastics, synthetic fibres, dyes, explosives, perfumes, insecticides, fertilizers, ANTIBIOTICS, VITAMINS, alkaloids, hormones (see ENDOCRINOLOGY), sugars, and PROTEINS. The organic chemist is concerned with the extraction and identification of naturally occurring materials, the synthesis and study of a wide range of compounds, and the relationship between molecular structure and physiological action. For further reading: J. D. Roberts and M. C. Caserio, *Modern Organic Chemistry* (1977). B.F.

organic foods/organic farming. Food production without the use of inorganic fertilizers but relying on manure or compost, including both organic vegetables and also livestock reared on organic vegetables. Since it yields less food per acre and is more labour intensive than normal Western farming methods, organic produce is more expensive than non-organic alternatives. However, it has nevertheless become commonplace in supermarkets, and is growing in popularity. Though there is some dispute, many consider it to be both tastier and healthier than non-organic food, since it is free of artificial chemicals. It has also been suggested as a useful aid in reducing European food surpluses. (See also HEALTH FOODS.) For further reading: E. Trimmer, *The Good Health Food Guide* (1994).

A.E.B.; A.A.L.

organic labour state. The model formulated by the British commentator Neil Harding (see below) to characterize the nature of Soviet-type STATES (see USSR, THE FORMER). It suggests that in these systems the maximization of production is considered to be the main objective of both the state and society, which are organically linked and neither of which has a separate identity. Society is regarded as 'an organically developing system of production relations' which only the state can co-ordinate. As a result the state controls the main forces of production and grants rewards and rights to its citizens dependent on their contribution to production. A single political party puts forward policies which will lead to the realization of economic goals. As these goals are in the interests of all members of society, any opposition to the Party is considered unacceptable. This model has been criticized by some analysts for failing to take account of the diverse interests which have some influence on state authorities, and for over-emphasizing the state's economic objectives at the expense of political concerns such as ensuring the conformity of the population. For further reading: N. Harding (ed.), *The State in Socialist Society* (1984).

D.PR.

organicism. In PHILOSOPHY, the theory that some, or all, complex wholes have the kind of systematic unity characteristic of what are literally organisms. An organism is held to differ from a mere mechanism or aggregate by reason of the dependence of the nature and existence of its parts on their position in the whole. A hand is, or remains, a hand only if united to a living body. The notion has been applied to social INSTITUTIONS and to the universe at large (e.g., in the philosophy of Alfred Whitehead, 1861–1947). The organic analogy implies not only that the parts of the whole are unified by INTERNAL RELATIONS but that the whole has a characteristic LIFE CYCLE or course of development as organisms typically do.

A.Q.

organism. In modern biological theory (see BIOLOGY) the organism concept refers (i) to the organized structure of interdependent parts of any individual animal, plant or microbe and (ii) to a functionally integrated biological entity characterized by all relevant biological functions specific to a living being in its environment or ecological niche. The organism concept is also closely related to the problem of individuality in nature, the question concerned with establishing the individual boundaries of biological entities. Ecological communities (see ECOLOGY) or colonies of individuals have often been referred to as superorganisms. Another dimension of the organism concept is to fulfil an integrative role for many biological theories that deal with specialized functions of biological individuals such as reproduction, development or ADAPTATION. As such the organism concept is central to a recent research programme in organismal biology established in part as a counterpart to the reductionistic tendencies (see REDUCTIONISM) inherent in MOLECULAR BIOLOGY where biological processes are investigated on the molecular level. Another challenge to the standard organism concept comes from research in artificial life. Here the question arises as to whether organisms are bound to their organic material nature (carbon-based molecules) or whether they can also be characterized by a representation of their functional properties within a computer program (see ARTIFICIAL INTELLIGENCE; ARTIFICIAL LIFE).

M.D.L.

organismic psychology. Any approach to PSYCHOLOGY which emphasizes that an organism, in developing from the single-CELL egg onwards, functions as a complex and many-sided but essentially unitary psychobiological whole which must be studied by proceeding from this whole to its parts rather than vice versa. For the opposite approach see ELEMENTARISM. For further reading: K. Goldstein, *The Organism* (1939).

I.M.L.H.

organization man. Term used by William H. Whyte in *The Organization Man* (1956) to denote a character-type encountered in modern bureaucratized social systems – that of individuals who work for large-scale organizations, primarily in managerial roles within American corporate business enterprises, but also within scientific establishments; and who in various senses 'belong' to such organizations. They are dominated by a SOCIAL ETHIC rather than the PROTESTANT ETHIC. This fact or self-perception of 'belonging' or 'togetherness' affects the LIFESTYLE and wider social aspirations of such individuals – influencing, via education and ideological pressures (see IDEOLOGY), the way in which they see themselves and their societies, and including a level of standardized mediocrity and conformity. S.J.G.

Organization of African Unity (OAU). An association of African states, established in 1963 to fight colonialism and promote unity among African nations. C.E.D.

Organization of American States (OAS). Consultative body of Latin American nations and the US, established at the Ninth Pan-American Conference held in Bogota in 1948. The OAS set up an institutional and legal framework for the hemisphere, based on the guidelines of the UN Charter, in the belief that there existed a community of interests between North and South America. The OAS endorsed the CIA-instigated overthrow of the leftist Arbenz government in Guatemala in 1954, suspended the Cuban government's participation in the organization in 1962, following alleged Cuban interference in the internal affairs of Venezuela, and supported the US 1962 trade embargo on CUBA until 1975. It also backed the US 1965 invasion of the Dominican Republic. In 1979, however, the OAS rejected a US motion to introduce an OAS PEACEKEEPING force to prevent a revolutionary victory in NICARAGUA (see REVOLUTION). The organization was relatively moribund during the 1980s and early 1990s, but is today playing an active role in the negotiations for a FREE TRADE AREA OF THE AMERICAS (FTAA). For further reading: G. Pope Atkins, *Latin America in the International Political System* (1995). M.A.P.

organization theory. The study of the functions, structure, relationships and behaviour of organizations and their relationships with the external environment. There are many different aspects to this broad subject: (1) the effect of management's interest in workers' problems (see HAWTHORNE EFFECT); (2) the effect of a bureaucratic form (see BUREAUCRACY), in the sociological, Weberian sense, on the structure, relationships, behaviour and efficiency of an organization; (3) the implications of managers who see work as being performed in response to their commands and managers who see work as being a potential source of satisfaction and self-fulfilment; (4) different techniques of management that can be used in organizations; (5) the effects of an organization's TECHNOLOGY, size, range of products and geographical spread; (6) the *matrix* of relationships crossing the traditional organizational structure, e.g. the setting up of a project team with members drawn from different parts of the organization; (7) the motivations and systems of learning and perception of individuals and groups that may be established in the organization; (8) the reaction of organizations to external and/or unpredictable events. For further reading: D. S. Pugh (ed.), *Organization Theory* (1984). R.I.T.; J.P.

organizational crime. Various forms of CRIME have organizational dimensions. Probably most familiar is the term 'organized crime', which describes vertical and horizontal arrangements in which criminals are brought together to participate in continuing criminal enterprises. The classic image is of a Mafia-type organization, seen as an association of criminal 'families' with a hierarchical chain of command from the apex of the pyramid to the 'foot-soldiers' on the street. Organized crime structures undoubtedly co-operate, and the growth of the international DRUGS trade has been a major stimulus to this. Nonetheless, many commentators have challenged popular images of organized crime as ethnically based conspiracies threatening the fabric of society.

Crime also has organizational dimensions in the sense of being committed by legal organizations (CORPORATE CRIME) or within and against them (WHITE COLLAR CRIME; or blue collar crime, involving theft, fiddles, 'perks', at the expense of employers, albeit sometimes with their collusion as part of unofficial reward structures).

Much work on criminal organizations has highlighted the features they share with legitimate commerce, e.g. entrepreneurialism, risk-taking and rule-breaking in pursuit of profit-maximization, specialist division of labour, investment strategies. Some work takes this further, pointing to examples of symbiosis between corporate enterprises and criminal organizations (e.g. in the gambling industries, the arms trade, and the toxic-waste disposal business). N.S.

organizer. A term in EMBRYOLOGY. All animals belonging to the chordate line of descent (see ZOOLOGY) undergo, early in development, a fundamental metamorphosis known as *gastrulation*. The effect of *gastrulation* or of an equivalent process is to form an embryo which in addition to an outermost layer or ectoderm contains inside it an *archenteron* or rudimentary gut. The central nervous system begins as a median dorsal tubular formation in the ectoderm overlying the roof of this primitive gut. In a number of classical experiments the German embryologist Hans Spemann (1869–1941) showed by operations on amphibian embryos that the primitive central nervous system or nerve tube arises in response to some influence emanating from the roof of the archenteron. To this important region of the embryo he accordingly gave the name *organizer*. The nature of the influence emanating from this organization centre is not yet known. A region equivalent to the organizer of amphibian embryos is found in other vertebrate embryos. It is generally agreed that one element in the action of the organizer is a purely evocative chemical stimulus which realizes the potential of the overlying ectoderm to roll up into a nerve tube. The other element in its action is more strictly an organizational one, i.e. one which imposes a pattern. The ectoderm responds to the action of the organizer only when it is in a state of so-called *competence* – a condition of reactivity which is soon lost in the course of development. P.M.

organometallic chemistry, see under INORGANIC CHEMISTRY.

oriental despotism. A term common in the political vocabulary of the 18th century, and employed with particular effect in Montesquieu's *Spirit of the Laws* (1748), to compare and contrast the arbitrary and despotic political regimes of the eastern hemisphere with the constitutional republics and limited monarchies of the West. In current usage the term has largely been superseded by or subsumed under the MARXIST concept of the 'Asiatic' MODE OF PRODUCTION. It has, however, been partly revived to suggest a fundamental continuity between the political system of the old oriental empires and that of COMMUNIST states such as the former Soviet Union and China. For further reading: K. A. Wittfogel, *Oriental Despotism* (1957). K.K.

orientalism.

(1) The process by which Western writers have since antiquity created an image of the 'Orient' as the binary opposite of the 'Occident' through various discourses that elaborate stereotypical fictions rather than describe any actual person or place. Among such stereotypes are the 'mysterious East', the 'lustful Turk', and 'Asian inscrutability'. 'Oriental' has for centuries been used by writers in a wide variety of fields to designate not merely a geographic location but also supposed moral, cultural and intellectual attributes. For example, Herodotus frequently contrasts the rationality of the Greek with the irrationality of the Asiatic Xerxes. In *Orientalism* (1978), Edward Said has delineated the structures of the discourse of orientalism. More recently, the term has come to describe generally the activity by which a hegemonic discourse represents the 'other'.

(2) An older meaning refers to the academic study of the Orient, the origin of which was the establishment by the Church Council of Vienna in 1312 of a series of chairs at Paris, Bologna, Avignon and Salamanca to study Arabic, Greek, Hebrew and Syriac. For further reading: E. Said, *Orientalism* (1978). M.F.H.

origin of species, see under EVOLUTION.

ornament. Until recently Western architects have taken the view that buildings should be undecorated – that any deviation from plainness should derive directly from the shape or colour of materials or the building's structural system, as opposed to being merely applied to a building. Various attempts have been made to establish a terminological distinction between the two, between ornament and decoration. But with the abandonment of the basic MODERN MOVEMENT aesthetic rules the difference has become redundant. S.L.

orogeny (orogenesis). The processes by which the world's major mountain ranges, or orogenic belts, are formed (e.g. the Alps, Himalayas and Andes). Strictly speaking, an orogeny is a period of mountain building (which may last for tens of millions of years) and orogenesis refers to the processes involved; but the distinction has largely been lost by lax usage, and only pedants now insist upon it. Orogenic belts are exceptionally thick accumulations of sedimentary (see SEDIMENTATION) and volcanic rocks. They are also structurally extremely complex, comprising a highly compressed, deformed and metamorphosed (altered by high pressures and temperatures) mixture of continental crust and marine sediments together with oceanic crust and even bits of the earth's mantle. The complexity, composition and huge mass of mountain belts long presented geologists with their greatest problem, the most popular, but not entirely convincing, explanation being that the ranges were the 'crinkles' on the surface of an earth that was cooling and contracting. When independent evidence for contraction failed to appear, the true solution had to await the discovery of PLATE TECTONICS during the 1960s.

The details are poorly understood even now, but the key to mountain building is undoubtedly the motion of the plates of the earth's LITHOSPHERE. Oceanic lithosphere, created continuously at OCEANIC RIDGES and gradually forced sideways, ultimately plunges back into the earth's interior at SUBDUCTION ZONES along the edges of certain continents (e.g. South America). Where subduction and continent meet there is intense deformation, volcanic activity and uplift, resulting in an orogenic belt of the Andean type. When a moving ocean floor brings a continent into the subduction area, however, there is an even greater confrontation, for continental material is too light to subduct. As the continents collide and are inexorably forced into coalescence (e.g. India with the main body of Asia) there is even greater deformation and uplift, converting the orogenic belt into one of the Alpine-Himalayan type.

Ranges such as the Himalayas, Alps and Andes are still being formed; but older, extinct orogenic belts (e.g. the Urals and Appalachians) also exist in various states of erosion, suggesting that plate tectonic processes of some sort must have operated on the earth for at least 2,000 million years. P.J.S.

Orphism (or **Orphic Cubism).** In 1913 the paintings of Delaunay, Duchamp, Léger and Picabia were described by Apollinaire as 'orphic', in the sense that they were more abstract (see ABSTRACT ART) and offered a more purely abstract aesthetic pleasure than did other CUBISTS; but the artist to whom this epithet has clung most firmly is Robert Delaunay (1885–1941), with his lyrical, non-representational colour formations of 1910–14. He was joined by Sonia Terk (whom he married) and František Kupka; and his geometrical patterns influenced the work of Kandinsky, Marc and Klee. The inheritors of his theories of the primacy of colour were the Americans Stanton Macdonald-Wright and Morgan Russell, who were followers of Delaunay in Paris in 1912, and who have been regarded as the initiators of the first distinctively American art movement, *synchromism.* P.C.

Orthodoxy, Eastern. The faith of the ancient Christian Churches of Russia, Greece and the Middle East, with their modern offshoots in the USA and elsewhere, all of which are in communion with the Ecumenical Patriarch of Constantinople. These Churches are self-governing and reject the Pope's claims. In general they are conservative although not uniform, and the secret of their survival despite some persecution (e.g. in the former Soviet Union) is their Eucharistic worship (see EUCHARISTIC THEOLOGY), which feeds a spiritual life that can be profound. Some smaller Eastern Churches, e.g. the Nestorians, are not 'orthodox' because they do not accept the decisions of the Ecumenical Councils about CHRISTOLOGY; but the most important causes of these continuing divisions are sociological. In the 1980s Orthodox Christians in the world appear to number about 170 million, although exact numbers, especially in the former Soviet Union, are difficult to ascertain. See also CATHOLICISM; ECUMENICAL MOVEMENT. For further reading: T. R. Ware, *The Orthodox Church* (1963). D.L.E.

Orwellian. Characteristic or reminiscent of the writings of George Orwell (1903–50) – though the word is mainly used with reference to a not particularly characteristic work: his nightmarish vision, published in 1949, of the year *Nineteen Eighty-Four*. In this novel the world is divided into three totalitarian superstates (see TOTALITARIANISM), each permanently at war with one or both of the others. Life in the state known as Oceania includes such features as *Big Brother*, whose black-moustached face gazes down from a million posters; the *Thought Police*, who make good the boast that 'Big Brother is watching you'; and the *Newspeak* language, 'designed to meet the ideological needs of *Ingsoc*, or English Socialism'. The vocabulary of Newspeak shrinks every year, the ultimate object being to make heretical thoughts (*crime-think*) 'literally unthinkable'; meanwhile *Oldspeak* (i.e. English) has borrowed from it such deliberately unlovely words as *prolefeed* ('rubbishy entertainment and fictitious news' for the submerged masses or *proles*), *doublethink* ('the power of holding two contradictory beliefs in one's mind simultaneously, and accepting both of them'), and *unperson*. The best-known Orwellian *mot*, however, comes from his fable of COMMUNISM in the former USSR, *Animal Farm* (1945): 'All animals are equal but some animals are more equal than others'. O.S.

oscillating universe, see under PULSATING UNIVERSE.

Oslo Accords. The September 1993 peace agreement between Israel (see JUDAISM; ZIONISM) and the Palestinians emerged from the so-called Oslo Accords. This is because for some time, from December 1992 to August 1993, some Palestinian and Israeli representatives had used the good offices of the Norwegian Foreign Ministry in Oslo to initiate secret bilateral discussions about resolving the Palestinian–Israeli conflict. The Accords produced two documents: the Declaration of Principles and the Letters of Mutual Recognition. The latter were an important aspect of the accords, whereby Chairman Arafat recognized Israel's right to exist in security and peace, and Prime Minister Rabin recognized the role of the Palestine Liberation Organization (PLO) in representing the Palestinian people in all negotiations. The Accords resulted in the development of elaborate plans for the transfer of some administrative, bureaucratic, security and political powers to the to-be-established Palestinian Interim Self-Governing Authority (see PALESTINIAN AUTHORITY), and provided the basis for Israeli troop withdrawals from designated parts of the Occupied Territories and redeployment of Israeli forces. The Accords also finalized the procedures and timetables for future negotiations, elections in the 'liberated' territories, and for the implementation of the other aspects of the declaration of principles signed in Washington, DC, on 13 September 1993. For further reading: D. Makovsky, *Making Peace with the PLO: The Rabin Government's Road to the Oslo Accord* (1996). A.EH.

osmosis. The process whereby, when a volume of, e.g., cane sugar solution is separated from a volume of pure water by a membrane which is permeable by water but not by sugar, water enters the sugar-containing compartment to dilute the solution and increase its volume. Very high *osmotic pressures* may be developed in this way. Osmosis plays a most important part in all biological transactions involving water transport or water imbibition in plants and animals. With reference to some chosen standard, solutions having an equal, higher or lower osmotic pressure are referred to as *isotonic*, *hypertonic* and *hypotonic* respectively. Osmotic pressure may sometimes be a disruptive force. Thus the red blood corpuscles soon swell up and burst in hypotonic solutions, and shrivel up and crinkle ('crenate') in hypertonic ones. P.M.

ostensive. A term applied to definitions which correlate words, not to other linguistic expressions (as in the verbal definitions of a dictionary), but to actual things that are representative instances of the correct application of the word. Every verbal definition of the form '*A* means the same as *B*' has to presume that *B* is already understood if it is to explain the meaning of *A*. It is usually argued that there must therefore be some verbally undefinable, or at least undefined, terms (the colour words are a favourite example) where meaning is explained in some non-verbal (see NON-VERBAL COMMUNICATION) or ostensive way so that the process of verbal definition has a stock of already understood terms to start from. See also PARADIGM CASE. A.Q.

Other, the (*autrui*). In PHENOMENOLOGY the Other is a constituting factor in the self-image that a subject builds up. In Husserl's fifth *Cartesian Meditation*, in the work of Sartre and of Merleau-Ponty, and notably in later existential psychiatric usage (see EXISTENTIAL PSYCHIATRY) such as R. D. Laing's, the Other is the perceiving, conscious, meaning-conferring other person who helps, or forces, the conscious SUBJECT to define his own world-picture and his own view of his place in it (see WELTANSCHAUUNG). Knowledge, as defined in phenomenological description, is thus precisely not SOLIPSISM, as is often averred, but precisely the opposite. Knowledge is a world-picture built up, partly through the instrumentality of other people in the world in INTERSUBJECTIVITY, and is thus a social, socializing and socialized process through and through. The Other socializes and intersubjectivizes PERCEPTION because of the fact of EMBODIMENT. R.PO.

other-direction. A quality ascribed by David Riesman in *The Lonely Crowd* (1950) to persons (or their characters) predominantly influenced by a 'need for approval and direction from others'. Riesman emphasizes (1) orientation towards the individual's contemporaries ('either those known to him or those with whom he is indirectly acquainted through friends or the mass media') and (2) a capacity for 'a superficial intimacy with and response to everyone'. Other-direction is contrasted with *tradition direction* and *inner direction*. S.J.G.

otherness. Term often used in radical philosophical DISCOURSE to describe a subject's condition of non-conformity to social NORMS or of disenfranchisement through the activities of the STATE or other institutions in which POWER is vested (e.g. the professions). The other in this usage becomes marginalized, alienated. S.T.

outsider. Word given currency for a few years by Colin Wilson's study of pseudo-NIETZSCHEAN and other ideas in *The Outsider* (1956). His 'outsiders' included Kierkegaard, Nietzsche, T. E. Lawrence, Kafka and Hemingway – an oddly disparate group. In this sense the word admits of no precise definition; all that can be said is that the term as used by E. M. Forster ('the artist will tend to be an outsider') is here given a superman flavour (see ÜBERMENSCH): the artist should not merely stand apart from society to concentrate upon his own function within it, but should raise himself above it and become a superior being. Essentially this was a reprehensible and mischievous misunderstanding of Nietzsche's conception of the 'overman'. M.S.-S.

outsider art. Work recognized as art but which is produced by people who have no connection with the art world, and who do not necessarily think of themselves as artists, or of what they do as art. Although it has some connection with traditions of naïve art and FOLK ART, the term is primarily associated with the art of the mentally ill. Walter Morgenthaler's 'Ein Geisteskranker als Kunstler: Adolf Wølfli' (1921) and Hans Prinzhorn's 'Bildnerei des Geisteskranken' (1922), along with his collection of the art of the mentally ill, laid the ground for the study more recently continued by the Austrian analyst Leo Navratil. The concept was also strongly influenced by Jean Dubuffet's *art brut*, 'work produced by people immune to artistic culture in which there is little or no trace of mimicry'. M.G.A.

overdetermination, see under ALTHUSSERIANISM.

overheating. In ECONOMICS, the inflationary consequences (see INFLATION) of excessive pressure on resources during a period of expansion in demand. So long as there are idle resources such an expansion usually leads first to increased employment and output, and it is only at a later stage, as shortages and bottle-necks develop, that the pressure expends itself increasingly in higher prices. A.C.

overidentification, see under IDENTIFICATION.

overkill. A polemic term of the COLD WAR period, used primarily by advocates of minimum DETERRENCE who argued that both the USA and the former USSR already possessed a nuclear capability far exceeding that which was necessary for mutually assured destruction. It is also used in non-military contexts, e.g. of the excessive use of chemical poisons in dealing with agricultural pests. For further reading: R. Lapp, *Kill and Overkill* (1963). A.F.B.

Overman, see ÜBERMENSCH.

overpopulation. A situation in which a population (of humans or other SPECIES) is too large relative to the resources available and necessary for its maintenance. In its original Malthusian meaning (see MALTHUSIANISM), the term refers to an excess of population relative to the food supply. In common usage, the term also refers to an excess of human beings relative to various resources (land, energy, minerals, etc.), or relative to the earth's ability to withstand the effects of environmental changes associated with human activity (pollution, deforestation, atmospheric change, etc.). J.R.W.

ownership and **possession.** It is difficult to give a precise and consistent meaning in English law to the concept of property, which is a patchwork of different 'estates' and 'interests' denoting shades of proprietary right. Nevertheless, ownership denotes the right of a person in the fullest degree to the use and enjoyment of land or goods, including their disposition or destruction, though it remains subject to rules of law protecting the rights of others, and in the case of land to rules imposed by statute concerning, e.g., planning control and powers of compulsory acquisition. The ownership of land may also be subject to rights of the public or of a neighbour to cross it by, e.g., a footpath. Whereas ownership is essentially a right, albeit not absolute, possession is primarily a matter of fact, of physical occupation of land or retention of custody of goods. The owner of land need not necessarily be in current possession of it, and his ultimate right may be subject to current occupation by someone else: even a squatter may enjoy some limited legal protection. A thief of goods will have current possession of them, though unlawfully, and the owner's right to recover them is not thereby diminished. For further reading: G. C. Cheshire and E. H. Burn, *Modern Law of Real Property* (1982). D.C.M.Y.

oxygen cycle, see under LIFE CYCLE.

ozone hole, see under OZONE LAYER.

ozone layer. Ozone is a MOLECULE consisting of three ATOMS of oxygen. It is found in the upper atmosphere, at altitudes of 12–25 km and in concentrations of only a few parts per million. Ozone is the only atmospheric gas that absorbs ultraviolet solar RADIATION, thus preventing it from reaching the earth in amounts that would kill or severely damage living ORGANISMS.

In 1985 British scientists reported that a thinning of the ozone layer over Antarctica had been occurring every year since 1979. This so-called ozone hole is caused by a class of industrial chemicals called chlorofluorocarbons (CFCs), widely used in air-conditioning. By 1988 it was concluded that the ozone layer was depleting rapidly over the entire globe. W.G.R.

P

pacifism. The belief and, consequently, conduct of those who believe that WAR and the employment of organized armed force are unjustifiable. Until the 20th century this was a view held only by such minority Christian groups as the QUAKERS and the PLYMOUTH BRETHREN. The word 'pacifism' first came into use at the beginning of the 20th century to describe movements advocating the settlement of disputes by arbitration and the reduction of armaments. Efforts to influence national policy in favour of the unilateral (see BILATERALISM AND MULTILATERALISM) renunciation of war have continued (e.g. CND, Campaign for Nuclear Disarmament; see PEACE MOVEMENT), in the face of the objection that a nation which adopted such a policy would be more likely to encourage than discourage aggressive action. From the time of World War I, the word has also been used to describe the refusal of individuals, on grounds of conscience, to undertake military service, whatever the consequences to themselves. States have varied a great deal in their treatment of such a refusal. In only a small number of countries has the right to conscientious objection been recognized; in the majority it is treated as a breach of the law and often harshly punished. See also NON-VIOLENT RESISTANCE. A.L.C.B.

paediatrics. The medical care of ill children has become a speciality in the UK in the last 50 years, in contrast to the previous care of ill children by family doctors and adult physicians. Whereas the main work is still diagnosis and treatment, it now also involves the promotion and maintenance of health, the earliest possible detection of deviations from health, and their correction and rehabilitation after treatment. The fall in the number of infectious diseases and the overall improvement in children's health have been reflected in a dramatic drop in the numbers of those with rickets, tuberculosis and gastro-enteritis. Involvement in the care of the newborn infant is now widespread, and entails care of premature and low-birth-weight babies in special units. There has also been a growth of interest in the psychological and emotional wellbeing of children, exemplified in the more humane care of children in hospital, with unrestricted visiting for parents. Children with special needs have attracted more interest, as have those taken into care, those suffering non-accidental injury and SEXUAL ABUSE. Preventive and developmental paediatrics involving the school health services provide for regular supervision of children's dental health and auditory and visual monitoring. Speciality within paediatrics has grown apace in the last ten years, and kidney and heart transplants (see SURGERY) have become a part of hospital paediatrics, with considerable team involvement. D.M.

pair bonding. The habit of forming a sexual pair for purposes of breeding. Pair bonding is rare among animals considered as a whole, but is found in a few shrimps, insects and fish, several species of mammals, and the majority (over 95 per cent) of species of birds. Pair bonding is usually associated with the co-operative rearing of young, and is probably found in species in which the young can only survive if looked after by two parents. Pair bonds are formed after a prolonged period of courtship. Once formed, they are maintained by a variety of behaviour patterns. In some birds, pairs sing duets. Mammalian pairs may mark their partners; male tupaid tree shrews, e.g., spray urine on their mates. The duration of a pair bond may be for a single breeding cycle or longer; or, as in kittiwakes, e.g., it may depend on the pair's breeding success – successful pairs tend to stay together, unsuccessful pairs to split up. M.R.

palaeobotany. The study of the floral remains of the past, encompassing POLLEN ANALYSIS, DENDROCHRONOLOGY, and the identification of wood, charcoal, cultivated grain, weed seeds and fibres. One rapidly expanding branch, *palaeoethnobotany*, is concerned with the evolution of cultivated plants. For further reading: J. M. Renfrew, *Palaeoethnobotany* (1973). B.C.

palaeoclimatology. The study of the climates of the past – a study which depends on many branches of science, mainly GEOLOGY but also CLIMATOLOGY and meteorology. The basic data have been principally geological, derived in particular from PALAEOBOTANY, whereas explanations are presented in an astronomical or meteorological framework. Evidence of climates of the past is drawn from three main sources: BIOLOGY (e.g. the restricted HABITAT of corals), lithology (e.g. evaporites), and GEOMORPHOLOGY (e.g. glacial landforms). J.L.M.L.

palaeodemography. The study of the population dynamics of communities living in the distant past. Attempted by archaeologists with untestable degrees of success. For further reading: F. A. Hassan, *Demographic Archaeology* (1981). B.C.

palaeoethnobotany, see under PALAEOBOTANY.

palaeogeography. The reconstruction of the GEOGRAPHY of a given region (see REGIONALISM), essentially the distribution of land and sea, at a particular time in the past. Palaeogeography is an exercise in STRATIGRAPHY, using the biological and lithological characters which are determined by the depositional ENVIRONMENT preserved in the sedimentary rocks of a particular period. It is assumed that depositional environments of the past, certainly from Cambrian times (see under GEOLOGICAL TIME CHART), were similar to those of today. J.L.M.L.

palaeolithic, see under THREE-AGE SYSTEM.

palaeo-modernism, see under MODERNISM.

palaeontology. The science which deals with the fossil remains (*palaios* is the Greek word for 'ancient') of animals and plants found buried in rocks. The term, in practice, is restricted to the study of animal remains; fossil plants are dealt with by PALAEOBOTANY. Fossils are of importance to geologists (see GEOLOGY) as time-markers which help to establish the succession of strata in the earth's crust. They also throw light on the geographical conditions under which rocks were laid down and on the PALAEOGEOGRAPHY and PALAEOCLIMATOLOGY of the world as a whole. Any succession of fossil-bearing rocks shows a fossil succession which corresponds to the biological process of EVOLUTION and adds greatly to the understanding of this. Finally, palaeontology is of value to ARCHAEOLOGY for the evidence fossil remains afford of the early domestication of animals and of other local environmental conditions of archaeological sites. A.L.C.B.

palaeopathology. The use of ancient human remains for the study of disease, injury and nutrition. Normally only skeletal material is available, but occasionally (as in the case of the Danish bog burials, the bodies preserved in permafrost conditions in the Altai Mountains, and mummified remains) hair, skin, flesh and entrails survive for scrutiny. For further reading: D. R. Brothwell, *Digging Up Bones* (1981). B.C.

palaeozoology. The branch of PALAEONTOLOGY which deals with fossil animals and the historical record they embody. For most practical purposes the record begins in Cambrian times (see GEOLOGICAL TIME CHART). Until the acceptance of the theory of EVOLUTION, fossil remains made very little sense – Georges Cuvier (1769–1832), the leading zoologist of his day, could describe a fossil ichthyosaur as *homo diluvii testis* (man witness of the Flood). The fossil record is biased in as much as soft-bodied animals normally leave no fossil traces. P.M.

Palestinian Authority (PA). The establishment of a Palestinian authority in the Occupied Territories was one of the requirements of the OSLO ACCORDS. Less than a year after the signing of the Oslo accords, on 1 July 1994, Chairman of the Palestine Liberation Organization (PLO), Yasser Arafat, returned to his homeland, hoping to establish Palestinian authority and rule over as much of Palestinian territory and population of the Occupied Territories (OT) as possible. At first, he and his team were only able to extend their control and authority over two relatively small pieces of land: Jericho (on the West Bank) and Gaza. Most Palestinians were hopeful, however, that within a relatively short period of time the PA would be able to extend its authority over the largest Palestinian population centres and to put in motion the plans for founding the State of Palestine in the OT. The PA has grown in size, now boasting of a substantial security and civilian bureaucracy, displaying all the features and trappings of an independent state (ministries, parliament, uniformed police and security forces, an airline, etc). The PA now represents, and rules over, many Palestinians in parts of the Occupied Territories, but for many complex reasons it has been unable to conquer the final summit, and found the Palestinian state with its capital in East Jerusalem – this being the main national aspiration of the Palestinian people. A.EH.

palynology. The study of pollen, especially of fossil pollen grains, for which see POLLEN ANALYSIS. K.M.

pan-Africanism. Less a movement for a united Africa than a quasi-NATIONALIST set of beliefs in the uniqueness and spiritual unity of BLACK Africans, beginning among American and West Indian blacks returning to Africa from the 1850s on, and linked with the cultivation of cultural NEGRITUDE among black Africans from French African colonies. Pan-African conferences met in London, Paris and New York in 1900, 1919, 1921, 1923 and 1927, and in Manchester in 1945. The first to be held in Africa met in Accra in 1958. Since the attainment of independence by most African states, pan-Africanism has expressed itself through the ORGANIZATION OF AFRICAN UNITY. For further reading: C. Legum, *Pan-Africanism* (1962). D.C.W.; S.R.

Panama Canal Treaty. A treaty governing the operation and defence of the Panama Canal, signed by the US and Panama in September 1979 and entering into force in October 1979. It replaces the 1903 treaty which established the US-owned Panama Canal Company and the US-administered Panama Canal Zone. By the provisions of the new treaty Panama will gain full SOVEREIGNTY rights over the former Canal Zone and is to accept control of the Canal itself by the year 2000. A second part commits the US and Panama jointly to maintaining the permanent neutrality of the Canal. Congressional amendments have given the US leeway to intervene militarily to reopen the Canal (if its operations were to be interrupted) even after the end of 1999. There is increasing concern in Panama over the economic repercussions of a US withdrawal, and domestic public opinion appears to favour the continued presence of American troops in the Panama Canal Zone. The US has also expressed an interest in maintaining a minimal military presence, especially to oversee anti-narcotics operations in Central and South America. For further reading: D. N. Farnsworth and J. W. McKenney, *US–Panamanian Relations 1903–1978: A Study in Linkage Politics* (1983). M.A.P.

pan-Arabism, see under ISLAM.

Panch Shila. 'Five Principles' publicly adhered to by Jawaharlal Nehru, Prime Minister of India, and Chou En-lai, Premier of the People's Republic of China, in 1954: NON-INTERVENTION in the internal affairs of other states, mutual respect for territorial integrity and SOVEREIGNTY, mutual non-aggression, mutual aid, and peaceful co-existence. The same principles were adopted by the states attending the BANDUNG CONFERENCE the following year. D.C.W.

panentheism, see under PANTHEISM.

pangenesis. Now obsolete theory of heredity (see GENETICS/GENOMICS) according to which particles travelled from all parts of the body to the gonads, where they were incorporated into the gametes. It was suggested by Darwin (1868) to account for the supposed INHERITANCE OF ACQUIRED CHARACTERS. J.M.S.

pan-Germanism. A late-19th-century and early-20th-century movement aiming at the union of all German-speaking peoples into a single state, strengthened by racial theory on the one hand, HISTORICIST and geopolitical arguments on the other (see GEOPOLITICS; RACE; RACISM; GERMAN REUNIFICATION). It was embodied as a political movement, the *Alldeutscher Verband*, in 1894, and was at first mainly confined to academics, INTELLECTUALS and publicists. It captured the imagination of the German High Command during World War I and was embodied into the doctrines of the RIGHT, both parliamentary and anti-parliamentary, under the WEIMAR REPUBLIC, emerging as an essential element in NAZISM. For further reading: G. A. Craig, *Germany, 1866–1945* (1981). D.C.W.

panic, theatre of, see THEATRE OF PANIC.

pan-Islam, see under ISLAM.

panspermia. The theory that life on earth originated on another planet. Whether life exists on other planets is unknown (see EXOBIOLOGY), but if it does, it could conceivably have been transported here, and have seeded life on earth. The transport could have been deliberate and active, by means of a rocket, or passive, if, e.g., small organisms travelled here on comets. The difficulties for the theory are: (1) the small chance of successful transport, and (2) the small chance that life evolved on another planet would be appropriately built for life on earth (see ADAPTATION). The appeal of the theory is that it makes less improbable the origin of life from inorganic systems, by multiplying the number of places where it could have happened. For further reading: F. Crick, *Life Itself* (1981). M.R.

pantheism. Any belief which identifies GOD as identical to parts or all of the world, either by interpreting God in terms of nature or interpreting nature in terms of God. 'Pantheism' and its cognates were invented in the early 18th century, but pantheistic PHILOSOPHY and THEOLOGY are at least as old as some of the principal religious traditions of India. In Christianity and other monotheistic religions, God's immanence and transcendence with respect to the world are both affirmed in such ways that the possibility of pantheism is excluded. Pantheistic tendencies have been detected in various philosophical-theological schools (such as Christian Neoplatonism), but the single most important Western pantheist was the 17th-century philosopher Baruch Spinoza (1632–77), who claimed that there was only one substance and that this substance was necessarily divine. Many of the literary and philosophical products of early ROMANTICISM were pantheistic, explicitly or implicitly, and the pantheistic vision has continued to appeal to many artists. Pantheism should be distinguished from *panentheism*, which is the belief that everything exists in God, but that God's existence exceeds that of the world. This ultra-immanentist theology is particularly associated with PROCESS THEOLOGY, but to a greater or lesser extent it can be found in many contemporary theological movements, especially those associated with FEMINISM and ecological concerns. C.C.

pantonal music. Music whose component parts are at times identifiable in terms of various conventional 'keys', without any one key being established as predominant. It is thus intermediate between polytonal (see POLYTONALITY) and ATONAL MUSIC, with borderlines so uncertain and subjective that Schoenberg sometimes applied the adjective 'pantonal' to music that is normally called atonal. A.H.

paper architecture. Architectural designs which are destined never to be built. The motive for creating such ARCHITECTURE is most often an enchantment with the concepts of deconstruction. Ideas shaping paper architecture include: (1) advances in reprographic technology and publishing, which increasingly define architecture in terms of images; (2) a literal borrowing from mathematics (fractal geometries; see FRACTALS) and of philosophical terms (*The Fold* from philosopher Leibniz via Jaques Deleuze) to authenticate twisted and folded schemes – they have won commissions and become some of the most striking architecture of the 1990s (Daniel Libeskind, Jewish Museum, Berlin); (3) a great tradition of competition-winning, dramatic, beautifully drawn, AVANT-GARDE, high-minded 20th-century architecture that has proved unpopular with either the conservative public or reactionary commissioning bodies, and hence remains literally on paper (Zaha Hadid, Cardiff Bay Opera House). For further reading: G. Broadbent, *Deconstruction; A Student Guide* (1991). P.J.D.; S.T.S.B.

par values, see under PARITY.

paradigm. A term given a technical meaning within the philosophy of science (see SCIENCE, PHILOSOPHY OF) by T. S. Kuhn (1922–96) in his book *The Structure of Scientific Revolutions*. Countering standard EMPIRICIST versions of the growth of scientific knowledge, Kuhn denied that hypotheses or theories were simple products of INDUCTION from sense experience. A more 'holistic' (see HOLISM) notion of visual and intellectual perception applied: theories were comprehensive orderings of reality, in which the whole was in some sense prior to its parts and made sense of its individual components. Theories gave meaning to facts rather than, in any simple sense, arising out of them. All scientific thinking and practices operated within theoretical frameworks, or, as Kuhn termed them, paradigms. Kuhn's conception of paradigm-bound science was widely criticized on two grounds. First, the notion of paradigm was itself too vague (the term seemed to be used to describe both whole sciences and individual concepts within them). Second, by viewing the development of science as a succession of self-contained paradigms (e.g. Ptolemaic ASTRONOMY, Copernican astronomy), Kuhn was committing the RELATIVIST fallacy, and denying that science approximated ever nearer to a true account of reality. See OBJECTIVITY. For further reading: T. S. Kuhn, *The Structure of Scientific Revolutions* (1996). R.P.

paradigm case. A representative instance of a CONCEPT, used to provide an OSTENSIVE definition of it. In so far as some concepts must be ostensively defined for the process of verbal definition to have a starting-point, it follows that if any word is to have MEANING at all some must truly apply to actual things. This argument from paradigm cases was introduced by the philosopher G. E. Moore (1873–1958) to rebut comprehensive sceptical theories, such as that no proposition is certain or that no material object is known to exist. How, he asked, could the word 'certain' or words for material objects have meaning at all unless there are actual instances for them to be ostensively learned from? The argument assumes, questionably, that some particular words must be ostensive (a stronger claim than that there must be some ostensive words), that it is possible to establish which they are, and that 'certain' and words for material objects are among them. A.Q.

paradigmatic, see under SYNTAGMATIC.

paradox. A statement which appears acceptable but which has unacceptable or contradictory consequences. Three kinds of paradox have proved important in the development of LOGIC and MATHEMATICS. (1) Paradoxes of the INFINITE. Zeno of Elea argued thus: space is infinitely divisible; so an arrow must pass through infinitely many points in its flight; therefore it can never reach the target. This (like many variants) is resolved by the theory of CONVERGENCE to a limit: an *infinite* sequence can have a *finite* limit. (2) SEMANTIC paradoxes. Epimenides the Cretan said (and was believed by Saint Paul): 'The Cretans are always liars.' If true, the statement would have made the speaker an invariable liar, and would therefore have been false. Therefore it must be false. (For another example see HETEROLOGICAL.) (3) Paradoxes of SET THEORY. Bertrand Russell considered the class (or SET) R which consists of just those classes that do not belong to themselves. Then R belongs to itself if and only if it does not.

Paradoxes of types (2) and (3) are said to involve *self-reference*. Following a suggestion of Poincaré, Russell proposed the resolution of paradoxes on the *vicious-circle principle*: an object (such as a PROPOSITION, predicate or class) is illegitimate if its definition involves a totality to which itself belongs. Thus Epimenides' saying refers to *all* statements by Cretans, itself included, and so is not a proposition, does not express anything. The proposal was worked out in great detail as the *ramified theory of types* of Russell and Whitehead in *Principia Mathematica* (1910–13); but the theory has proved unsatisfactory from almost every point of view. It is now customary to distinguish sharply between (2) and (3). The semantic paradoxes are resolved by distinguishing levels of language: Epimenides' saying is at a higher level, it is *metalinguistic* (see METALANGUAGE); the lies it refers to are those of ordinary discourse, and so it does not apply to itself and may therefore be true. The set-theoretic paradoxes are avoided in axiomatic set theory; another solution is provided by the *simple theory of types*. In this theory, individuals are of type 0, sets (or predicates) of individuals are of type 1, sets of sets of individuals are of type 2, and so on. Sentences like 'an individual is equal to a set' or 'a set of type 2 belongs to a set of type 1' are regarded not as false but as ungrammatical, meaningless. A paradox should be distinguished from an ANTINOMY. See also CLOCK PARADOX. For further reading: E. P. Northrop, *Riddles in Mathematics* (1945). R.G.

paralanguage. In suprasegmental PHONOLOGY, a range of vocal effects (e.g. giggle, whisper) that contribute to the tones of voice a speaker may use in communicating meaning. They are less susceptible of systematic description than the other areas of phonology, and are considered by many linguists to be marginal to the sound system of the language. For some scholars, the term also subsumes kinesic phenomena (see SEMIOTICS). D.C.

parameter.

(1) In MATHEMATICS, originally a particular auxiliary co-ordinate used in describing *conic sections*; the term is still used for an auxiliary VARIABLE in terms of which others are expressed by *parametric* equations. R.G.

(2) In its modern usage in mathematics and its applications, particularly in ECONOMICS, it denotes a quantity that is constant in the MODEL or circumstances under consideration. This quantity may take a different value in other models or circumstances. For example, the marginal propensity to consume (see MARGINAL ANALYSIS) is thought to increase with income, though over small enough ranges it may be assumed to be a constant, i.e. it is a parameter. D.E.; J.P.

(3) In STATISTICS, a summary measure such as the MEAN of a characteristic of members of a population. R.G.

(4) In music, a term often used since 1950 to denote the different aspects of a musical sound (e.g. duration, loudness, pitch, tone colour, attack, spatial location, etc.). B.CO.

paranoia. In ABNORMAL PSYCHOLOGY and PSYCHIATRY, a type of PSYCHOSIS in which the individual experiences delusions, typically of persecution and/or grandeur. It is often accompanied by hallucinations. W.Z.

parapatric speciation, see under SPECIATION.

paraphilia. A term that came to replace 'sexual deviation' in the clinical literature of PSYCHIATRY and its therapies during the final decade of the 20th century. Most practitioners in the field differentiate between paraphilias which are defined by (1) arousal by an unusual (usually inappropriate, often illegal) sex *object*, and (2) those in which the choice of sexual *act* determines the nature of the disorder.

Object-defined paraphilias include *paedophilia*, where an adult can only achieve sexual arousal and satisfaction by thinking about, or engaging in, sexual activity with children. Other paraphilias include *zoophilia* (or bestiality, where the sex object is an animal); *necrophilia* (sexual activity with a corpse); *fetishism* (sexual arousal obtained through inanimate objects); and *transvestism* (sexual pleasure obtained through wearing clothes of the opposite sex).

Act-defined paraphilias cover a very wide range of sexual behaviours, some legal, some not. They include *sadism* (pleasure derived from inflicting pain on others); MASOCHISM (pleasure derived from the activities of a sadist); SADOMASOCHISM (where one partner agrees to be 'dominated' by another); *voyeurism* (the observing of others engaged in sexual activity); *exhibitionism* (exposing one's sex organs to a stranger, often in a public place). Sadomasochistic sex is often engaged in by mutually consenting parties. Act-defined paraphilias involving non-consenting partners are criminal offences, and are often part of the complex of behaviours exhibited in RAPE. For further reading: J. Money, *Lovemaps* (1986). S.T.

parapsychology (or *psychical research*). The scientific study of actual or alleged paranormal phenomena (such as ESP and PSYCHOKINESIS). For further reading: H. L. Edge *et al*, *Foundations of Parapsychology* (1986). I.M.L.H.

parasitology. The scientific study of parasites. Parasites are organisms that live and feed on organisms of other species. Some such parasites live on humans and cause disease. For example, perhaps 200 to 300 million people are suffering at present from schistosomiasis, a disease caused by infestation by a genus of blood fluke; and parasites are so ubiquitous and dangerous that the biologist J. B. S. Haldane (1892–1964) once suggested they were the main influence in human evolution.

Parasites may be simple one-celled organisms or complex multi-celled structures. PROTOZOA are the simplest organisms in the animal kingdom, consisting of a single nucleated CELL. Malaria, amoebic dysentery, sleeping sickness, giardiasis and trichomoniasis are all caused by protozoa. Although insects and bugs (arthropods) such as mosquitoes, lice and fleas are primarily vectors of pathogens, some can be directly injurious to man (see VECTORS OF DISEASE). They can cause pain, allergy and psychological problems such as entomophobia and delusionary parasitosis. The third group of parasites are complex multi-cellular worms such as threadworms, hookworms, tapeworms, filaria, schistosomes and guinea worms. Many of these, such as tapeworms and hookworms, live and breed in the intestines, but others such as filaria live in blood vessels, muscles and the brain. Parasitic diseases require specialist attention. Some, like malaria, sleeping sickness and schistosomiasis, can be fatal. Unlike many bacterial and viral infections, parasitic infections do not lead to immunity from further infection with the same parasite, and repeated infections are common.

The most important part of parasitology is its medical application, which seeks to control human parasites. Parasitologists study the often complex and multi-staged LIFE CYCLES of parasites, how they are transferred between hosts, and the factors affecting their abundance. This knowledge can be put to use in controlling the parasite. M.R.; A.P.H.

parental choice. A mainstay of educational reforms in many countries since the mid-1980s. Restrictions on access to schools are removed to allow parents to select the school they see as best suited to the needs of their child. In many parts of the USA and Israel 'controlled choice' schemes are operated to produce social mixing. Choice reforms are typically part of the introduction of the 'market form' into state provision of education, whereby schools are funded according to their recruitment and 'weak' schools are identified by their unpopularity among parents. S.J.B.

Pareto optimum. The formal conditions, named after the Italian sociologist and economist Vilfredo Pareto (1848–1923), under which general ECONOMIC EFFICIENCY is obtained. The condition is said to exist when there is no reorganization of the economy which makes one or more persons better off without making one or more others worse off. This concept of efficiency is fundamental to much of microeconomic theory and normative economics. Though a Pareto optimum is efficient, the resulting distribution of income may be undesirable. In particular, there may be other Pareto optima that entail a greater SOCIAL WELFARE. R.L.; J.P.

parity.

(1) In PHYSICS, a precise mathematical description of left–right symmetry or 'handedness'. For systems of atomic size or larger, nature makes no fundamental distinction between left and right, so that an object and its mirror image are equally compatible with the laws of physics. (Left- and right-handed systems need not actually occur *equally often* in nature: by an accident of EVOLUTION, almost everybody's heart is on his left side, but the reverse occasionally occurs with no ill effects.)

A perfectly symmetrical isolated system has a value of the parity which can be calculated from the WAVE FUNCTION; as the system evolves it remains symmetrical, and the parity does not alter – it is an *invariant* (see CONSERVATION LAWS). For the WEAK INTERACTIONS between ELEMENTARY PARTICLES, however, parity is not conserved, e.g. an apparently symmetrical NEUTRON decays into components with a definite 'handedness'; on this level it appears that nature does know left from right. For further reading: M. Gardner, *The New Ambidextrous Universe* (1991). M.V.B.

(2) In ECONOMICS, the word has at least two distinct meanings:

(a) *Par values* of the BRETTON WOODS currency system are the fixed EXCHANGE RATES between currencies and the internationally accepted standard of value, the dollar. This system of fixed exchange rates collapsed in the early 1970s.

(b) The *purchasing power parity theory* states that exchange rates are mainly determined by the relative price levels in different countries. As not all goods and services are traded, it is the price levels of tradables that are relevant to determining exchange rates. The prices at which trade actually takes place depend on subsidies, taxes and transport costs. Exchange rates are also affected by relative interest rates and inflows and outflows on the CAPITAL, as well as the current account of the BALANCE OF PAYMENTS. For further reading: D. Begg *et al*, *Economics* (1986). J.P.

Parkinson's Law. A principle formulated by the British political scientist C. Northcote Parkinson (*Parkinson's Law*, 1958) to the effect that 'work expands so as to fill the time available for its completion'. As a corollary Parkinson states that 'a perfection of planned layout is achieved only by institutions on the verge of collapse'. *Parkinson's Law* and similar popular studies such as *The Peter Principle* (which states that employees tend to be promoted above the level at which they are efficient) serve to counteract the tendency for management to take itself too seriously. P.S.L.

parliamentarianism. The view that the best form of government is a parliamentary form, conforming more or less to the 'Westminster model'. By association, the idea that reform and social change should take place only by means of legislative measures agreed on by an elected parliamentary government, as opposed to being pushed through by the rulers of a one-party system or on a dictator's unsupported say-so. A.R.

parole. In PENOLOGY (for its meaning in LINGUISTICS see under LANGUE), a shorthand term applied to the premature release of a convicted prisoner on expiry of part of his sentence, with provision for recall if he violates the parole terms; thus to be distinguished from *remission*, which cannot be revoked once the prisoner is released. Originating in the 19th-century 'tickets of leave' system for transported convicts, parole has always been widely used in the USA, in combination with indeterminate sentences. In Britain, it was introduced only in 1967 by the Criminal Justice Act, but by 1998 some 130,000 offenders were supervised in the community by the probation services, roughly twice the number remanded in prisons at that time. T.M.

parsing. In traditional grammar, the process of labelling the grammatical elements of sentences, e.g. subject, singular noun. Several different approaches to parsing have now been developed within linguistics, and the notion has proved to be central to work in computational linguistics, especially NATURAL LANGUAGE PROCESSING. For further reading: W. Bright (ed.), *International Encyclopedia of Linguistics*, vol. 3 (1992). D.C.

Parsonian. Derived from or resembling the sociological theories of Talcott Parsons. Parsons (1902–79), professor of SOCIOLOGY at Harvard for most of his life, became the leading American sociological theorist of his generation. His approach, a type of STRUCTURAL-FUNCTIONAL THEORY, was most influential in the 1950s. Though his ideas changed continuously, four main themes emerged. (1) Individual personalities, societies and CULTURES can all be analysed as self-equilibrating SYSTEMS and described in terms of a common conceptual framework, that of *action systems*. (2) Action systems contain four *subsystems*, performing functions of pattern maintenance, integration, goal-attainment, and adaptation. (3) As SOCIAL ACTION systems, societies evolve towards greater functional specialization of structure: e.g. modern political and economic INSTITUTIONS largely correspond with the analytical subsystems 'polity' and 'economy' which perform the goal-attainment and adaptation functions. (4) SOCIAL STRUCTURE is analysable into four components (values, NORMS, collectivities, ROLES), and the institutionalization of certain *core values*, through the NORMATIVE regulation of collective activities and individual role performances, primarily determines the stability and functioning of societies. Critics of Parsonian theory have asserted that it contains only verbal categorizations from which no testable PROPOSITIONS follow; or that it can (perhaps) explain stability but not change; or even that it merely expresses a conservative preference for a society devoid of significant disagreements over values. Although it has inspired much empirical research, its claim to be scientific is not yet established. For further reading: W. C. Mitchell, *Sociological Analysis and Politics: the Theories of Talcott Parsons* (1967). J.R.T.

partial object. In psychoanalysis, a concept which refers to the predominance in the infantile psychic world of parts of whole objects, such as the breast and faeces. Taking up Karl Abraham's ideas about partial love, Melanie Klein developed her theory of OBJECT RELATIONS, which develop in connection with the different psychosexual stages (see KLEINIAN; DEVELOPMENTAL THEORY), and the evolution of the relation to the object as a whole. She introduced the concept of 'part-object' as central in her theory of object relations. Even though partial, the infantile objects have the uppermost power in the infant's psychic world; they are endowed with threatening or reassuring qualities, and they are split according to their moral qualities into 'good' or 'bad' objects in the same sense as one would ascribe these properties to individuals. A massive SPLITTING mechanism characterizes the primitive oral and anal stages, which will persist throughout all adult life, in spite of the development of the third, genital stage, which introduces the establishment of a relation to whole objects. B.BE.

participation. A slogan which came into widespread use in the 1960s to express what the EUROPEAN UNION (EU) calls 'the democratic imperative', defined as the principle that 'those who will be substantially affected by decisions made by social and political institutions must be involved in the making of those decisions'. It is argued that the size and complexity of modern MASS SOCIETIES, the centralization of political POWER, the growth of BUREAUCRACY, and the concentration of economic power all mean that the traditional guarantees of DEMOCRACY need to be strengthened and extended in order to check the tendency for more and more decisions affecting people's lives to be made in secret by small groups which are often remote and not easily identified or called to account, since they act in the name of the STATE, of a local authority, or of some large, impersonal business corporation.

So far as politics is concerned, the principle is as old as democracy itself. Thc problem is how to implement it – a problem likewise as old as democracy itself, but made vastly more difficult by the scale and comprehensiveness of modern government and by the need for clear-cut and rapid decisions, failure to produce which is no less a matter for protest on the part of those who demand greater participation. The new feature in the period since World War II is the proposal to extend participation to fields other than politics, e.g. to higher education, where it was the major demand of all student protests in the late 1960s and early 1970s, and, of much greater importance, to industry and business. The practice (*Mitbestimmung* or *codetermination*) by which employees take a part in management decisions was introduced by the Federal Government of Germany in 1952, has spread in various forms to other countries in western Europe, and has been adopted as an objective by the EU. In the UK the 1977 BULLOCK REPORT, *Industrial Democracy*, proposing a variant of the German system, was rejected by employers. Since then the TRADE UNIONS have resolutely failed to agree on a common policy. Other forms of participation, notably the growth of interest in CO-OPERATIVES and PROFIT-SHARING and share ownership schemes, have superseded the EU initiative. In the US, progress was started when Doug Fraser of the Auto Workers Union became a member of the Chrysler Corporation board, but the example has not been repeated. Within the EU structures the concept of 'social partners' has attempted to provide a platform for participation from the top down. A.L.C.B.; B.D.S.

particle. A relative term, in common use throughout PHYSICS, denoting any object which may be considered as a moving point, characterized by a few simple properties such as MASS and SPIN. The concept is an idealization, valid whenever the internal structure, size and shape of the object are irrelevant to the phenomenon being considered. Thus, e.g., such a complicated system as the earth may be treated as a particle for many purposes of ASTRONOMY, and it is sufficient to treat ATOMS as particles in order to explain much of the behaviour of matter in bulk. Particles interact with one another via FIELDS. See also ATOMIC PHYSICS; ELEMENTARY PARTICLE; WAVE-PARTICLE DUALITY. M.V.B.

particle collider. Device for accelerating ELEMENTARY PARTICLES to very high energies and colliding them together in a region surrounded by sensitive detection instruments. New elementary particles are sought in the debris of the collisions. (See also ACCELERATOR and LARGE HADRON COLLIDER.) J.D.B.

particular, see under UNIVERSAL.

particularism, see under PATTERN VARIABLES.

partisan dealignment. A concept used by some British psephologists (see PSEPHOL-

OGY), particularly Ivor Crewe, to describe a situation in which people no longer have strong, loyal attachments to political parties. Most individuals no longer identify strongly with one party and they are less likely to vote for the same party in election after election. It is closely associated with the idea that the influence of social CLASS on voting patterns has declined since the 1970s. It is also used to explain the increasing volatility of the electorate in Britain, which appears more willing to shift allegiance from one election to the next. Although some psephologists have questioned the view that the influence of class on voting has declined, most accept the more general claim for increased volatility and a decline in partisanship. The enormous swing away from the Conservative Party in the 1997 election gave further credence to the theory. For further reading: B. Sarlvick and I. Crewe, *Decade of Dealignment* (1983). M.D.H.

pass laws. Under the former APARTHEID system in South Africa, a term denoting the body of South African law requiring blacks to carry at all times passes permitting their movement within the nation. Their abolition was successfully demanded in 1985 by the newly formed Confederation of South African Trade Unions, although the replacement measure of identity cards to be carried by members of all races did not satisfy many opponents of the regime. S.R.

passive euthanasia, see under EUTHANASIA.

Past and Present. A journal founded in 1952 by a group of young MARXIST historians (including its first editor John Morris, Christopher Hill, Eric Hobsbawm) to challenge the dominance of political history and western European history in more orthodox periodicals. Under the editorship of the late Trevor Aston it became one of the best-known historical journals in the English-speaking world, associated with a greater variety of approaches to history than before but continuing to emphasize SOCIAL HISTORY and the history of the world outside Europe. P.B.

pastiche, see under POST-MODERNISM.

patent. An exclusive legal right to the use of an invention or innovation. The information embodied in an invention or innovation may be regarded as a PUBLIC GOOD whose use should not be artificially restricted. If the use of this information cannot be restricted, imitation occurs. Imitation reduces the economic rewards to invention and innovation and, thus, the incentive to invent and innovate. A restriction on imitation is justified, if the costs of a legal MONOPOLY are more than offset by the technical progress following from the greater incentives for successful invention and innovation. For further reading: P. Stoneman, *The Economics of Technological Change* (1983). J.P.

pathology. The study in all its aspects of departures from normality in respect of health and bodily function. Since all illnesses represent departures from normality it could be said, and by pathologists has been said, that pathology comprehends all medicine. Pathology is subdivided into a number of branches, notably *pathological* (gross) *anatomy*, such as is laid bare on the post-mortem slab; HISTOPATHOLOGY, dealing with structural abnormalities at the tissue level; *cellular pathology*, comprehending any attempt to interpret abnormalities of form or function at a cellular structural level; and *chemical pathology*, which has to do with diagnosis and interpretation of disease at a biochemical level (see BIOCHEMISTRY) – thus it is the chemical pathology laboratory which undertakes the analysis of blood samples for evidence of impaired liver function, or tests urine samples for evidence of impaired kidney function or metabolic abnormalities, including the 'inborn errors of metabolism' (e.g. phenylketonuria, alkaptonuria and galactosaemia) first recognized and defined by Sir Archibald Garrod (1857–1936). In these disorders a defective genetical programming has the consequence that some ENZYME necessary for metabolism is missing so that intermediate metabolites, some of which may be toxic, accumulate in the body, or some biochemical function is missing altogether. The consequences of these single enzyme defects are often widespread throughout the body: thus both phenylketonuria and galactosaemia may have secondary effects on the central nervous system leading to an impairment of mental function, while galactosaemia may be associated with cataract. In many modern departments of pathology the experimental approach is supplanting the merely descriptive. For further reading: I. A. R. More, *General Pathology* (1994). P.M.

patriarchalism. In the writings of historians of political thought, it refers to the 17th-century doctrine that the authority of kings over their subjects is of the same kind as that of fathers over their children, and in both cases is absolute and arbitrary. The political theory of John Locke (1632–1704) was a wholesale refutation of this doctrine and therefore a justification of the 'Glorious Revolution' of 1688. For further reading: G. Schochet, *Patriarchalism in Political Thought* (1975). A.R.

patriarchy. Derived from the Greek 'rule of the father'. The term describes authority and control exercised by men over women. Patriarchy is used as a concept by feminists (see FEMINISM) to refer to what is perceived to be a fundamental and universal state of male dominance. Patriarchy is both a state of affairs (i.e. men control social institutions) and an IDEOLOGY (embedded in languages). Kate Millett's *Sexual Politics* (1969) was a landmark in the study of patriarchy. Questions of GENDER, the nature of the family and the process of socialization were highlighted in understanding the nature of male supremacy. For Millett, the political relationship between the sexes was central to patriarchy, and male power was expressed and contained in the sexual act itself. Other feminists have pursued the question of male power in studies of PORNOGRAPHY and RAPE (e.g. A. Dworkin, *Pornography*, 1981, and S. Brownmiller, *Against Our Will*, 1975). The examination of the material bases of patriarchy (rather than the ideological or pyschological) has focused upon the place of women in public (in the workplace) and in private (in the home). One strand of this debate has drawn on the work of Engels (*The Origin of the Family, Private Property and the State*, 1884) to locate the origins of patriarchy within a particular MODE OF PRODUCTION. Firestone has taken Engels's MATERIALIST interpretation in a new direction. Patriarchy is understood to have its foundations in biological MATERIALISM, establishing the primacy of SEX class over economic CLASS (S. Firestone, *The Dialectic of Sex*, 1970). Other writers have avoided revolutionary speculations and biological materialism. Patriarchy is understood as historically variable and as stemming from a complex of factors, particularly from the articulation of public and private domains. For further reading: H. Eisenstein, *Contemporary Feminist Thought* (1984). A.G.

patri-clan, see under CLAN.

patrilineal. Refers to the tracing of DESCENT through a single line from an ancestor, the male line. Patrilineality may act as a principle governing relations between people in terms of the inheritance of property or succession to office. It may also be the basis for the recruitment to a social group, a patrilineal descent group. A society may be described as patrilineal, but need not necessarily have patrilineal descent groups. A patrilineal descent group consists of the male descendants of a particular ancestor, his brothers and sons. The degree of corporateness may vary, but usually the women – sisters and daughters – marry out of the LINEAGE. The men bring in women as wives. Husbands pay BRIDEWEALTH and thereby acquire rights over the domestic, sexual and reproductive powers of their wives. This MARRIAGE arrangement is called *patrilocal* (men stay put, women move). POLYGYNY is common in patrilineal societies, and the wives perpetuate the lineage of their husbands by bearing children. ANCESTOR WORSHIP may be found in association with a patrilineal descent group. For further reading: R. S. Watson, *Inequality among Brothers: Class and Kinship in South China* (1985). A.G.

patrilocal marriage, see under PATRILINEAL.

patronage. NETWORK of strategic links through which individuals gain access to resources. It is a system founded upon an unequal distribution of POWER. The patron has standing, wealth, contacts, and in entering into a relationship with him a CLIENT is offered access to the sources of power. The relationship between patron and client is complex and involves a diversity of transactions. It is usually long-term and cast in terms of quasi or spiritual KINSHIP. There is a strong element of personal loyalty and essentially the relationship is voluntary rather than contractual. It is closely linked with the concept of honour. Systems or networks of patronage most commonly involve relationships between individuals (not corporate groups).

It has been suggested that patronage is a feature of societies where at the local level there is little corporate sense or group solidarity, e.g. the bilateral (see BILATERAL-COGNATIC DESCENT) societies of the Mediterranean. There is very limited autonomous access to sources of power except through structures of mediation. A number of writers have also understood certain forms of religious practice as an integral part of this particular social configuration. For example, CATHOLICISM has been linked to systems of patronage. In Catholicism access to spiritual power is through the mediation of a priesthood or hierarchy of saints. For further reading: S. N. Eisenstadt and L. Roniger, *Patrons, Clients and Friends* (1984). A.G.

pattern variables. In PARSONIAN theory, a set of paired terms specifying the ranges of variability within which persons engaging in social interaction orient themselves to one another. They were originally formulated as (1) *affectivity v. affective neutrality* (does the relationship involve EMOTION, or not?); (2) *self-orientation v. collectivity-orientation* (is the other person to be appraised in relation to my personal goals, or to those of some larger group?); (3) *universalism v. particularism* (does the other person represent a category, or something unique?); (4) *achievement v. ascription* (does the other's STATUS depend on his achievements, or on attributes beyond his control?); (5) *specificity v. diffuseness* (is the other's participation based on some specialized interest or qualification, or not?). For the most part, people assume and adjust orientations without reflection or conscious effort, because standardized expectations about behaviour in social ROLES are learned, as more or less habitual responses, in the form of NORMATIVE 'patterns'. There is only a limited number of such patterns culturally available to a society. Any pattern is in principle capable of description in terms of the five variables. This is the simplest version; in later work Parsons modified this scheme in order to integrate it with other parts of his theory. For further reading: T. Parsons and E. A. Shils (eds), *Toward a General Theory of Action* (1959). J.R.T.

Pauli principle, see under EXCLUSION PRINCIPLE.

Pavlovian. Relating to the work or views of the Russian physiologist I. P. Pavlov (1849–1936). Studying in Petersburg University, Pavlov developed a lasting passion for nervous PHYSIOLOGY. His major contribution to science came in the fields of the circulation of the blood, the physiology of digestion (for which he was awarded a Nobel Prize) and the physiology of the brain (his most famous work).

Pavlov maintained that the nervous system controls all physiological activity, and saw its function as being, in addition to the conduction of nervous impulses, one of setting up patterns of excitation for the control of functions and also of inhibiting impulse patterns once they had been started in the nervous system. Above all, however, he conceived of the nervous system as being involved in making connections between neural patterns so that associations in the nervous system could be set up which mirrored associations between stimuli in the external world, as well as between incoming stimuli and responses that had been made to them in the past. The principal result of this form of connecting activity in the nervous system, known as CLASSICAL CONDITIONING, shows that the nervous system is adaptive, permitting the organism to anticipate crucial events by virtue of their being signalled by those events which precede them, thus also permitting the organism to respond in advance with an appropriate reaction. Pavlov considered the importance of the CONDITIONED REFLEX to be its role in the general organization of higher nervous systems. This organization he saw as the basis for the formation of human temperament. In his later writings, Pavlov distinguished between classical conditioning and the SECOND-SIGNAL SYSTEM.

Pavlov also emphasized the adaptive value of *inhibition*, the process by which it was possible for the organism to withhold response in the nervous system initially to protect it from firing too intensely, and which later provided a means of delay in response appropriate to the nature of the situation. He extended this notion of the adaptive function of inhibition by suggesting that sleep was itself an extension of inhibition which allowed the nervous system to recover. Pavlov was also much interested in the problem of generalization of response to an array of stimuli. This problem he attempted to solve by the doctrine of *irradiation*, a process whereby responses would be made not only to the stimuli to which they had initially been conditioned, but also to a range of similar stimuli. He extended the concept of irradiation well beyond its original meaning, and talked about the irradiation of inhibition and excitation to account for certain general response tendencies important to the development of temperament and character. Towards the end of his life Pavlov's interest moved increasingly towards PSYCHIATRY. His lasting importance lay partly in directing neurophysiological research increasingly in the direction of the study of animal behaviour, and came partly through showing the crucial significance of conditioned reflex activity within a largely vitalist (see VITALISM) framework. For further reading: J. A. Gray, *Pavlov* (1979). G.M.; J.S.B.; R.P.

pax Americana. The concept of a peace imposed by North American rule or, more broadly, the settlement of conflict on US terms and in accordance with US interests. A variation on the term *pax romana*, it has been used in recent years primarily with reference to crises in Central America. N.M.

peace movement. The umbrella term given to diverse groups, organizations and movements in several countries since the late 1950s. The term is arguably a misnomer since the movement has been less concerned with international frameworks for peace and more with a series of specific objectives, particularly the abolition of NUCLEAR WEAPONS and other weapons of mass destruction.

In Britain, the Campaign for Nuclear disarmament (CND), bringing together a number of earlier, often PACIFIST groups, was established as a mass movement in opposition to the spread of nuclear weapons and of NUCLEAR TESTING. From the mid-1960s the US peace movement was principally concerned with opposing the US role in the VIETNAM War.

Mass peace movements wax and wane, often rapidly, in response to outside events, in particular WARS and rumours of wars. CND reached a first peak in 1961–62, diminished in the 1970s and then grew again from 1979 when the deployment of new nuclear weapons in Europe was accompanied by an alarming degree of warlike rhetoric by politicians in the US and Britain. In recent years, however, its influence has considerably diminished.

The peace movement also reached mass proportions in a number of western European states, including West Germany and Holland. All were opposed to their governments' policies, but in eastern Europe most states had 'official' peace movements that were generally controlled by their government. Unofficial groups such as Swords & Ploughshares in East Germany and CHARTER 77 in Czechoslovakia were severely harassed. By comparison, harassment in Britain was largely confined to infiltration by the security services, counter-propaganda from the government, and occasionally heavy-handed treatment of demonstrators. L.T.

peacekeeping. The impartial role of a force composed of outside military contingents, typically from several countries, in aiding the implementation of a ceasefire or peace settlement in an area of conflict. The functions of peacekeeping bodies include interposition along armistice lines; observing disengagement and disarmament; collecting surrendered weapons; mediating in disputes; assisting delivery of humanitarian aid; and monitoring elections. Peacekeeping forces (which sometimes include civilian and police components as well) are usually lightly armed: they are typically mandated to use weapons in self-defence, but not to impose a particular outcome by force.

In the post-1945 period the UN has been the main provider: although peacekeeping forces are not mentioned in its Charter, by February 1997 the UN had set up 42 peacekeeping and observer missions.

While peacekeeping and observer missions have helped in the transition to peace in many countries – including Namibia in 1989–90 and El Salvador in 1991–95 – their role has often been controversial. Sometimes, as in Cyprus from 1964 onwards, their presence seemed to freeze a conflict, not resolve it. Their dependence on the consent of the warring parties meant that they could not stay when one party ordered them out, as Egypt did in 1967 before the outbreak of the Arab–Israeli war that year. They were sometimes passive in the face of atrocities and ceasefire violations. Events in Bosnia in 1992–95 exposed the difficulties in inserting a peacekeeping force in the midst of an ongoing war, and in combining peacekeeping with the protection of humanitarian assistance. For further reading: A. Parsons, *From Cold War to Hot Peace: UN Interventions 1947–1995* (1995). E.A.R.

Peano's fifth postulate, see under MATHEMATICAL INDUCTION.

pecking order, see under DOMINANCE.

pedestrianization. The separation of pedestrians from cars for the purposes of road safety and to achieve unimpeded traffic flow. The concept has its roots in the Radburn superblock (see RADBURN PRINCIPLE) and was developed further in Britain by Colin Buchanon (see below) as the 'environmental area' (see TRANSPORTATION PLANNING). In the 1960s Britain was obsessed with 'planning for the motor car', as epitomized in the Bull Ring Development in the centre of Birmingham where the whole of the central shopping and business district was cut off by a ring road and pedestrian access could only be gained by underpasses which proved particularly problematic for women. Nowadays emphasis upon ACCESSIBLE ENVIRONMENTS and SUSTAINABLE URBAN DEVELOPMENT has led to greater control of the motor car in favour of the pedestrian, and the introduction of traffic calming. For further reading: C. Buchanon, *Traffic in Towns* (1963). C.G.

pedology. A component part of SOIL SCIENCE concerned with the study of soils as naturally occurring phenomena, particularly their MORPHOLOGY (see also HORIZON), classification, and distribution on the land surface. The aims of pedology are to describe the properties of soils and to identify the processes which have produced particular soils. The subject has suffered from the lack of a universal system of soil classification. J.L.M.L.

peer group. A group of people who regard themselves, or who are regarded, as of approximately equal standing in the larger society to which they belong; standing can be defined in terms of a very wide range of criteria (see CRITERION). M.BE.

***Peinture de la realité poétique*,** see under MAGIC REALISM.

penetrance. In GENETICS, the frequency with which a dominant GENE (or a recessive gene in a homozygote) manifests itself in the phenotype (see GENOTYPE). The fact that penetrance is not always 100 per cent implies that some genes require a particular environment before they are expressed. J.M.S.

penis envy. In FREUDIAN theory, the female desire to possess male genitals; a desire arising initially out of the small girl's assumption that because she lacks a penis she must at some stage have been castrated (see CASTRATION ANXIETY). Postulated as universal by Freud, the phenomenon has been challenged on theoretical grounds by some psychoanalysts (see PSYCHOANALYSIS) and psychologists, and on experiential grounds by some women. W.Z.

penology. Rooted in the Greek for PUNISHMENT, the term first appeared in 1838; penology developed as the 'science of punishment', involving reformers and lawyers concerned to civilize punishment, replacing its retributive emphasis with ideals of rehabilitation and deterrence. Today, it is a branch of CRIMINOLOGY concerned with: the study of punishment; the administration of prisons and the experience of imprisonment; penal codes; sentencing, its principles and effectiveness or otherwise. Generally, the ideals of prison reform have not materialized, prisons being commonly criticized as 'human warehouses' and 'universities of crime', unsuccessful at rehabilitating criminals, at reducing RECIDIVISM, and at providing for the reintegration of released prisoners back into society. In this view, 'prisons do not work'. Nonetheless, in recent years the eagerness of politicians to support imprisonment as a measure of being 'tough on crime and criminals' has been based on a claim that prisons 'do work', if only by removing offenders from society for a period of time. N.S.

pensions. The greying of populations in the industrial democracies (see GREY DOLLAR) together with pressures on the public finances has made the provision of state pensions for retirement an expensive luxury. In Britain the post-war Beveridge consensus on protection from cradle to grave has been eroded, and state pensions are now largely seen as a safety net supported by special benefits for the most needy; while in the US a more generous social security system has been groaning under the pressure of the shifting age profile of the populace, and real benefits are being cut. In the UK some 70 per cent of the population is already covered by occupational pension schemes and private pensions plans, giving it a considerable advantage in pensions funding for the future. State pensions will gradually be phased out and replaced by 'stakeholder' pensions under which individuals have ownership of their own pensions account into which they will compulsorily contribute on a regular basis: these funds will be managed in the private rather than the public sector. In the US there has already been considerable success in persuading the public of the need to provide pensions for themselves through self-administered pension plans offered by employers. These schemes have proved hugely popular and have contributed to a strong flow of LIQUIDITY into equity markets (see EQUITY CAPITAL) in New York and globally. A.BR.

Pentagon Papers. The name given to the 7,000-page top-secret US government report that constituted a history of the origins and escalation of the VIETNAM War. A summary of the contents, given to the newspaper by Daniel J. Ellsberg, a disillusioned former National Security Council defense analyst, was published by the *New York Times* in instalments, beginning on 13 June 1971. Its publication was a turning-point in the relationship between press and government in America and a landmark First Amendment case, with the Supreme Court (see SUPREME COURT OF THE UNITED STATES) turning down the White House's bid to stop it. The publication led President Nixon to create the 'plumbers', a team of covert White House operatives charged with plugging leaks of classified information. The team burgled the office of Ellsberg's psychiatrist and, on 17 June 1972, was arrested for breaking into Democratic National Committee headquarters at the Watergate hotel. R.K.H.

pentecostalism. The gift of the Holy Spirit is described in the Bible (Acts 2) as having descended on the 50th day (Greek *pentekoste*) after the Jewish Passover festival, with extraordinary resultant phenomena. In the 20th century many Christians have claimed to experience the same gift (in Greek, CHARISMA) and phenomena, and are referred to as the *Charismatic Movement*. Some have remained in the historic Churches but many have organized themselves in Pentecostal Churches, specially in the USA and Latin America, with a strong emphasis on informality, confidence and joy, and a THEOLOGY mostly FUNDAMENTALIST. The largest such Church is the 'Assemblies of God, USA'. The rapidly spreading 'independent' Churches in Africa, which are free from Western control and influence, have many similar characteristics. See also QUAKERS. For further reading: W. W. J. Hollenweger, *The Pentecostals* (1972). D.L.E.

people's democracy. A COMMUNIST euphemism for regimes which display the machinery of public participation in government while denying the electorate any real choice between political parties. Such regimes are usually distinguished by the absence of those legal and constitutional restraints on the use of the power of the state which are essential to DEMOCRACY or to any genuine PARTICIPATION by 'the people' in the processes of government. For further reading: F. Fejtö, *A History of the People's Democracies* (1971). D.C.W.

peptide. A relatively simple polymeric molecule formed by the conjunction of amino acids (see POLYMER; MOLECULE). The simple or short-chain peptides are called *oligopeptides* and include many biological effectors such as hormones (see ENDOCRINOLOGY) – e.g. oxytocin and vasopressin – whereas the larger, long-chain *polypeptides* grade directly into PROTEINS which are essentially polypeptides, e.g. the trophic hormones of the anterior pituitary, INSULIN, etc. P.M.

percept, see SENSE-DATUM.

perception. In general, awareness or appreciation of objects or situations, usually by the senses. Historically, perception was a branch of OPTICS. Till the 17th century it was commonly assumed that vision depended upon rays issuing forth from the eye, rather than emitted from the object and striking the eye. From the 18th century, perception became embodied within emergent SENSATIONALIST psychology. Specific technical meanings are related to the many theories of perception still extant in PHILOSOPHY, PSYCHOLOGY and PHYSIOLOGY. It is a theory-laden word, and so changes its meanings and implications across rival theories. There are, in particular, two essentially different theories of perception:

(1) That perceptions are *selections of reality*: i.e. they are essentially like, and made of the same stuff as, objects of the external world. This notion has a strong appeal to philosophers wishing to accept perceptions as the unquestionable basis of empirical TRUTH (see OBJECTIVITY). Errors of perception – illusions and hallucinations – are clearly embarrassing for such a theory; and indeed the *argument from illusion* claims to disprove it. How can we know that a perception is true, if we have reason to believe that other perceptions appearing just as sound are illusory?

(2) That perceptions are not any kind of selection of reality, but are rather *accounts*, *descriptions* or, most interesting, *hypotheses* of the object world. According to this view perception is only indirectly related to reality, and there is no difficulty over illusions. But, correspondingly, it offers no guarantee that any particular perception can be relied upon as true. Thus all knowledge based on perceptions is essentially uncertain; perceptions must be checked before they can be relied upon, and even then perhaps no set of perceptions can be *completely* trusted as true. It is generally accepted that this holds also for all scientific observations, instrument readings, or signals.

The status of perception may be very like that of scientific hypotheses. What we see is affected by what is likely; and we can be driven into error by following assumptions which are not appropriate for the available sensory data. This is a development of the notion of German physiologist Hermann von Helmholtz (1821–94) that perceptions are unconscious inferences from sensory and memory data. Some illusions may be fallacies of perceptual inference. Furthermore there has been considerable dispute as to the status of perception. One school (essentially EMPIRICIST) stresses that perceptions are built up through slow, gradual, complex, acquired learning processes. Another (the GESTALT) sees perceptual organization as more innate and holistic. For further reading: M. Merleau-Ponty, *The Phenomenology of Perception* (1962); R. L. Gregory, *Eye and Brain* (1978). R.L.G.; R.P.

perceptual defence. A process of unconscious 'censorship' that prevents PERCEPTION of unacceptable events, objects, words, etc., as when TABOO words presented briefly in a *tachistoscope* are 'normalized' into an acceptable form. It is usually contrasted with *perceptual vigilance*, a state of increased sensitivity to threatening or unacceptable events. For further reading: F. H. Allport, *Theories of Perception and the Concept of Structure* (1955). J.S.B.

perceptual realism, see under REALISM.

perestroika. Russian, literally 'reconstruction, reorganization'. The programme M. S. Gorbachev expounded in *Perestroika: New Thinking for Our Country and the World* (1987) embracing wide-ranging economic reform of the Soviet system, measures of political democratization, and greater freedom for the Soviet media (see USSR, THE FORMER). Political and economic reform were judged inseparable, necessitating a 'profound transformation' in the economy and the 'entire system of social relations' to banish 'stagnation, apathy and self-glorification'. An important corollary of *perestroika* was GLASNOST, 'openness', 'wide, prompt and frank information'.

Perestroika twinned with *glasnost* fell victim to the concepts' internal contradictions. The attempt to liberalize parts of the Soviet system weakened its internal cohesion. *Glasnost*, frank disclosures of shortcomings and failures, undermined official IDEOLOGY, removing coherence from policy. Gorbachev himself was the source of incongruity. He maintained that the 'SOCIALIST option' was irreversible. Yet in pursuing 'democratization' he fatally weakened the COMMUNIST Party structures on which the 'socialist option' depended for its survival. J.E.

perfect competition. A hypothetical state referring to a market or the economy as a whole. The conditions of such a state are: (1) within each industry, each firm produces an identical product; (2) each firm and individual consumers pursue their own material objectives; (3) there is no restriction on what persons or firms can buy or sell; (4) each firm and person is small and has no effect on the prices at which goods, services and inputs are traded; (5) there is perfect information (this assumption can be relaxed); (6) there are no EXTERNALITIES. A COMPETITIVE EQUILIBRIUM is an equilibrium of a perfectly competitive economy. A competitive equilibrium is economically efficient (see ECONOMIC EFFICIENCY) and, thus, is usually considered as desirable. The desirability of the PRICE MECHANISM, COMPETITION and FREE MARKETS is based on this view. However, the distribution of income in a perfectly competitive economy is not necessarily desirable. In economic markets that most closely resemble perfect competition, e.g. certain markets for agricultural produce, there have been examples of chronic and wasteful instability. Though the above assumptions are unrealistic, perfect competition is often used as a MODEL of markets and the economy. For further reading: J. Craven, *Introduction to Economics* (1984). J.P.

perfect equilibrium. A concept in ECONOMICS and GAME THEORY, introduced by Reinhard Selten. It disallows threats or plans that are not credible. As in a NASH EQUILIBRIUM, each player (competing firm, negotiator or combatant) does what best serves his own interests, given the strategies of others. The special feature is that these strategies should never require actions that are not best for the player at the time when they are to be taken. For example, it is inadmissible to attempt deterrence by threatening actions that would not, in the event, be rational, once the past must be taken as given. The concept provides a powerful theory of bargaining. If accepted, it also means that reputation and nuclear DETERRENCE can be explained only by supposing that each participant thinks there is some chance that others would irrationally adhere to unenforceable commitments. For further reading: K. G. Binmore and P. S. Dasgupta, *Bargaining* (1986). J.A.M.

performance art. A kind of art which in its purest form would claim to be a branch of the visual arts differing from painting or sculpture only in its use of live performers as material and, as a consequence, having only a temporary existence within finite limits of time. Many of the HAPPENINGS AND EVENTS of the 1960s and 1970s were of this kind. However, the introduction of language, music and the technical skills of actors and dancers tends to enlarge the aesthetic response evoked by performance art and place it in a theatrical context. Some performance groups, notably the People Show (founded 1966) in its early years, owed their disruptive effects to the aesthetics of DADA and Artaud's THEATRE OF CRUELTY. For further reading: J. Nuttall, *Performance Art* (1979). M.A.

performance tests, see under MENTAL TESTING.

performative. In LINGUISTICS, deriving from the work of the philosopher J. L. Austin (1911—60), a type of sentence where an action is 'performed' by virtue of a sentence having been uttered, e.g. *I apologize . . ., I promise . . ., I baptize you* . . . Performative verbs have a particular significance in SPEECH ACT theory, as they mark the ILLOCUTIONARY force of an utterance in an explicit way. Performative utterances are usually contrasted with *constative* utterances: the latter are descriptive statements which, unlike performatives, can be analysed in terms of TRUTH-VALUES. For further reading: S. Levinson, *Pragmatics* (1983). D.C.

period-luminosity relation. A fundamental problem of ASTRONOMY has been the nature of *variable stars*, i.e. stars whose brightness changes. They were first discovered in the 16th century. By the end of the 18th century, thanks largely to the observations of Delta Cephei by John Goodricke (1764–86), the regularities of their variations had been ascertained. The introduction of photography into astronomy in the 1840s vastly increased the number of variable stars (or cepheids; see CEPHEID VARIABLE) identified: some 19,000 variable stars are known to exist today. The major problem with such stars has been establishing the relation between observed brightness and real luminosity; for this, the work of Ejnar Hertzsprung (1873–1967) and Henry Norris Russell (1877–1957) towards the understanding of their periodicity has been crucial. On this basis, Edwin Hubble (1889–1953) was able to demonstrate that spiral nebulae were external GALAXIES, and Walter Baade (1893–1960) further built upon Hubble's findings to show that the galaxies were about twice as distant as previously thought. For further reading: R. Smith, *The Expanding Universe* (1982). R.P.

periodic table. An arrangement of the chemical ELEMENTS into rows and columns; it was formulated by the Russian chemist Dmitri Mendeleyev in 1869. The ATOMIC NUMBER increases across each row and from one row to the next, while the chemical properties (e.g. VALENCE) of the elements in each column are similar (e.g. the 'inert gases' helium, neon, argon, etc., lie in the same column). The physical basis of the periodic table is explained by ATOMIC PHYSICS: elements in a given column contain the same number of ELECTRONS in the unfilled outer ELECTRON SHELL, while elements in a given row have the same number of filled shells. M.V.B.

permanent revolution. An expression first used by Marx in his *Address to the Communist League* (1850), but mostly associated with Trotsky, who between 1904 and 1906 developed it into a theory which put Russia potentially at the forefront of world REVOLUTION. The argument rested on the idea that it was possible to have a SOCIALIST revolution in an economically backward country. Trotsky held that in Russia the bourgeoisie (see BOURGEOIS) was too weak to oppose the Tsarist autocracy in its own interests and envisaged a direct revolutionary confrontation between the autocracy and the PROLETARIAT. While the proletariat might begin by demanding merely liberal reforms (see LIBERALISM), it could only retain power by making the revolution 'permanent' and immediately proceeding to implement socialist policies – a viewpoint to which Lenin himself was converted during the course of 1917. A second element in the notion of permanent revolution was that the establishment of socialism in the Soviet Union could only be successful if the revolution were to spread to the more advanced CAPITALIST countries – a viewpoint originally shared by all the Bolsheviks (see BOLSHEVISM), but later contested by Stalin with his slogan of 'socialism in one country'. Permanent revolution is thus the central concept of what came to be known as TROTSKYISM. For further reading: L. Trotsky, *Permanent Revolution* (1962). D.T.M.

permissiveness. The view that the individual's pursuit of pleasure should, provided no harm is done to others, be unrestricted by external factors such as laws or by internal guilt arising from social conventions. The 'permissive society', a cliché of the late 1960s, was exemplified by the decline of stage and film censorship, by public acquiescence in the relaxation of certain moral and social conventions, and by a series of legislative derestrictions on HOMOSEXUALITY between consenting adults, ABORTION, divorce, etc. Although legislation of this type indicates toleration rather than endorsement, there has subsequently been a public reaction which seeks a return to more rigid moral and social conventions and prescriptions. There have recently been attempts to trace the sources of endemic social problems back to 1960s permissiveness, but this narrowly political reaction appears not to be widespread. P.S.L.

permutational. Adjective applied to works of art where a prescribed set of elements, rules or dimensions is subjected to variation, whether controlled by the artist or of an ALEATORY kind. Essential to music (especially SERIAL MUSIC), such treatment may also occur in the visual arts (notably in OP ART), in writing (as in anagrams and word-games and some kinds of CONCRETE POETRY), and in photography and film. It can also lead to the production of subtly varied multiples, particularly when guided by a COMPUTER as in computer graphics; the art then lies in the structure and sequence of the data fed to the machine. J.W.

Peronism. An IDEOLOGY – also known as *justicialismo* – associated with Juan Perón

(1895–1974), elected ruler of Argentina (1946–55 and 1973–74), and his wife Eva (Evita). In domestic affairs it involved the mass demagogic organization of the WORKING CLASS in labour unions (see TRADE UNIONS) and a workers' militia against the upper MIDDLE-CLASS élites; an organization backed by mass social security (see SOCIAL WELFARE) and other redistributive methods on the one hand, and repression on the other; and in foreign affairs, the espousal of the so-called 'Third Position', whereby Argentina was to steer a middle course between CAPITALISM (the US) and COMMUNISM (the USSR); the inflammation of Argentine national feelings against the US and the claim that Argentina should lead Latin America. Perón proved unable to solve the economic problems facing his country and lost much support after Evita's death in 1952, but his prestige was such that it brought him back to the presidency by popular acclaim in 1973. On his death in 1974, the Peronist cause was briefly led by his second wife and successor as President, but foundered with the revelations of incompetence and corruption that followed her 1976 overthrow by the military. The Peronists were returned to office in 1989 with Carlos Menem as President. The Menem administration has abandoned almost all the principal tenets of traditional Peronism. It has instead opted to pursue a pro-privatizing (see PRIVATIZATION) and anti-labour free market agenda. This has led to increasing tensions within the Peronist movement and with the powerful Peronist trade unions. For further reading: F. C. Turner and J. E. Miguens (eds), *Juan Perón and the Reshaping of Argentina* (1983). M.A.P.

personal idealism, see under PERSONALISM.

personalism. A form of IDEALISM which holds that everything real is a person or an element in the experience of some person. Inspired more by Berkeley than by Leibniz (whose MONADS, although described as souls, are too simple to count as persons), it is generally opposed to the absolute idealism of Hegel in which all finite persons are absorbed into an absolute which transcends personality (see TRANSCENDENCE). The *personal idealism* of such dissenters from absolute idealism as McTaggart and Rashdall around the turn of the century is perhaps the most philosophically significant form of personalism, but it has been more recently exemplified in modern French NEO-THOMISM, and there has been a continuing tradition of personalism in the USA with a strong theistic tendency (see THEISM). A.Q.

personalistic psychology. An approach to PSYCHOLOGY that takes as its FRAME OF REFERENCE the individual person as a unique, unitary being, and relates fractional studies of PERCEPTION, learning and the like to this personal frame of reference. For further reading: W. Stern, *Psychology of Early Childhood* (1930). I.M.L.H.

personality cult. The formula employed in the former USSR by Soviet advocates of COLLECTIVE LEADERSHIP against any of their number who seemed to be accumulating too much personal power and consequent public adulation. It was first employed after Stalin's death in 1953 to discredit those who attempted to capitalize on his memory, and was one of the central themes of Khrushchev's denunciation of the STALINIST era in his 'secret speech' to the 20th Congress of the Soviet Communist Party (25 February 1956). The accusation was subsequently employed to discredit Khrushchev himself after his resignation in 1964. It was also used in China by the successors of Mao Zedong to criticize his methods of leadership. For further reading: R. Conquest, *Power and Policy in the USSR* (1961). D.C.W.; D.PR.

personality disorder. The current psychiatric term to describe a pattern of abnormal behaviour and temperament, apparent from childhood, that usually sets one apart from social NORMS (see PSYCHIATRY; ABNORMAL PSYCHOLOGY). The term 'psychopathic disorder' is used in the 1983 UK Mental Health Act, and defined as 'deeply ingrained maladaptive patterns of behaviour'. Unfortunately the concept has created as much dissent as coherence, its use as a diagnosis being controversial, given the circularity of defining a disease by bad habits and vice versa. A number of sub-categories have been derived, based on clusters of symptoms and behaviours, including 'avoidant', BORDERLINE, 'emotionally unstable', and 'antisocial'. The characteristics of impulsivity, criminality and irritability, associated with drug and alcohol abuse and a persistent failure in enduring relationships, indicate the social alienation of such disorders. There is no established physical basis, but improvement with age is usual. Many deem the term to be a 'dustbin' for disposing of the socially deviant; thus 'sociopath' has been used in the American literature.

There has been a long-standing uncertainty as to the relationship between a moral analysis and disease classification, deriving from the 19th-century category 'moral insanity' (see DISEASE MODEL). Exhaustively debated by generations of lawyers and psychiatrists in the search for diagnostic clarity and jurisprudential culpability, its elusive nature reflects the difficulty of defining 'personality'. Treatment is often ineffective, despite imaginative psychotherapeutic approaches – thus the popular resort to institutional or economic segregation (see PSYCHOTHERAPY; PSYCHOANALYSIS). For further reading: World Health Organization, *The ICD-10 Classification of Mental and Behavioural Disorders* (1992). T.T.

personality tests, see under MENTAL TESTING.

personality types. Idealized descriptions of personality derived either by statistical procedures (e.g. FACTOR ANALYSIS) or by theoretical postulation or by some more or less skilful combination of the two. Historically and in contemporary practice, types are based upon differences in physiological hormonal functioning (see ENDOCRINOLOGY) which reflects itself in temperament, as in the classification by Galen of the *phlegmatic*, the *choleric*, the *melancholic*, and the *sanguine* – the outward manifestations of the so-called bodily humours. One of the most successful efforts to describe personality types in relation to body type is William H. Sheldon's. By careful anthropomorphic measurement, he has been able to distinguish three basic physical types (most individual subjects appearing as a mix): the round, soft *endomorph*, the square, muscular *mesomorph*, and the long, thin *ectomorph*. By the use of personality tests (see MENTAL TESTING), Sheldon established temperamental qualities associated with these. With endomorphy goes *viscerotonia*, a certain passivity and pleasure in sensation; with mesomorphy, *somatotonia*, a pleasure in physical activity; with ectomorphy, *cerebrotonia*, a pleasure in the exercise of cognitive activities. Another attempt was made by Jung, in his postulation not only of the well-known types characterized by INTROVERSION and EXTROVERSION, but also of types contrasted in terms of orientation towards the world: sensation-oriented v. thought-oriented, feeling-oriented v. instinct-oriented. The isolating of *function types* that may be mixed in any given individual is most closely associated with Hans Jurgen Eysenck (1916–97). Work on *value types*, represented principally by the Allport-Vernon-Lindzey *Study of Values* (1951), is aimed at establishing dominant value orientations (i.e. political, aesthetic, social, religious, theoretical) and has achieved considerable predictive success. See also CONVERGERS AND DIVERGERS. J.S.B.

perspectivism. In PHILOSOPHY, the theory that there are alternative systems of CONCEPTS and assumptions, not equivalent to each other, in whose terms the world may be interpreted and as between which there is no authoritative external way of making a choice. It is to be found in the philosophy of Nietzsche (see NIETZSCHEAN), for whom belief systems are instruments serving the impulse to survive and succeed, and, in a less passionate and more domesticated form, in Ortega y Gasset. Broadly analogous conclusions have been reached by Ajdukiewicz and Quine (the latter under WHORFIAN inspiration). They maintain that there are, or can be, different languages which are not translatable into each other and which supply their speakers with quite different pictures of the world. Like other sceptical hypotheses of comparable generality, perspectivism invites the question: is it not itself just one perspective on thought and language among others, with no greater claim to validity than they have? A.Q.

pesticide. Pesticides are chemicals or chemical mixtures used to kill pests, be they plant (herbicide), insect (insecticide) or rodent (rodenticide). Some pesticides are naturally occurring, but the vast majority of those in commerce are synthetic, and are not found in nature. The latter are particularly potent because organisms lack chemical defences to them. Pesticides owe their efficacy to the fact that the target organism is more sensitive to them than other organisms. For example, weeds are often broad-leafed plants (dicotyledons), which are more sensitive to many herbicides than are the narrow-leafed grains and lawn grasses (monocotyledons). Many synthetic pesticides have caused unanticipated damage to non-target SPECIES and to the environment, and the cumulative effects to humans and other species of exposure to low levels of numerous pesticides in foods and from other sources are largely unstudied. Consequently there is a growing desire in the public for 'organic' foods, raised without exposure to synthetic pesticides. W.G.R.

Peter Principle, see under PARKINSON'S LAW.

petit bourgeois. A member of the French *petite bourgeoisie*, as opposed to the *haute bourgeoisie* (see BOURGEOIS). The *petite bourgeoisie* were men of small-scale wealth and property, owners of individual shops, single houses, small plots of urban land, small workshops and factories, etc. The limited scale of their wealth was widely regarded as being paralleled by their limited horizons, narrow minds, and obscurantist attitude to art and culture. Hence the hyphenated adjective *petit-bourgeois* is most often used pejoratively – a connotation emphasized by the common anglicization of *petit* (or *petite*) as petty. See also POUJADISM. D.C.W.

petrography. A division of PETROLOGY concerned with the description and classification of rocks. Most rocks are aggregates of mineral grains, and an important part of the subject is the investigation of the texture of rocks, i.e. the shape and relationship of their constituent grains. J.L.M.L.

petrology. The study of rocks, their composition (see PETROGRAPHY), occurrence and genesis. Three main classes of rocks are recognized: igneous, sedimentary and metamorphic. *Igneous* rocks are those which have solidified from hot molten material called magma which is generated below the earth's crust (see LITHOSPHERE) and rises to cool on or just below the surface; *sedimentary* rocks are formed on the earth's surface, mainly on the sea floor, by the deposition of mineral matter weathered and transported from rocks on the land surface; *metamorphic* rocks are produced by the deep-seated alteration of pre-existing rocks due to the action of heat and pressure. Petrology is one of the few branches of GEOLOGY in which observation and analysis are supported by experimental work. J.L.M.L.

PFI (private finance initiative). Seeks to bring the financing techniques used in business to PUBLIC SECTOR projects. In the UK the initiative first launched by John Major's Conservative administration (see CONSERVATISM) had a bumpy start largely because of the opposition of UK Treasury officials, who for decades have adhered to a fundamentalist position for NATIONAL ACCOUNTING which frowns upon the mixing of private and public finance. This contrasts with the position in the US, where successive administrations using institutions such as the Small Business Administration and the Tennessee Valley Authority have used loan guarantees to support the development of smaller enterprises, rural electrification and major power projects such as dam-building. In the UK, among the major projects being handled through the PFI are the second Avon crossing to South Wales and the Channel Tunnel rail link from Folkestone to St Pancras. The 1997 Labour government has sought to breathe some life into the initiative, in the hope of shifting investment projects from the public to the private sector, with the appointment of a special minister responsible for the PFI. A.BR.

PGR (psychogalvanic response), see under GALVANIC SKIN RESPONSE.

phagocytes. CELLS which can nourish themselves by the direct entrapment and engulfment of solid particles, which are taken into the CYTOPLASM and digested by hydrolytic ENZYMES. *Phagocytosis*, the name given to this process of ingestion by cells, was discovered by the Russian zoologist Ilya Mechnikov (1845–1916), who may have attached undue importance to its role in bodily defences. Phagocytosis occurs in the amoeboid PROTOZOA and also among white blood corpuscles, particularly the monocytes, polymorphs, and the cells lining lymphatic sinuses. In the living organism phagocytosis of bacteria (see BACTERI-

OLOGY) is greatly promoted by the action of antibodies (see IMMUNITY). Thus bacteria which would not be phagocytized in their native state may come to be so if they are coated by an antibody. P.M.

phallic character, see under PSYCHOSEXUAL DEVELOPMENT.

phallus. In LACANIAN theory, a term preferred to the Freudian 'penis' in order to emphasize psychoanalytic concern with fantasy rather than with biological 'reality' (see PSYCHOANALYSIS). The Lacanian phallus is neither a physical organ nor a specific fantasy, but it is a SIGNIFIER with a particular function: it guarantees the existence of symbolic meaning. It is generative and connecting, possessed of an aura of procreation and sexual linkage. On the other hand, it also specifically signifies a cancellation in that neither the male nor the female infant can become or wholly possess the phallus, but rather are subject to CASTRATION ANXIETY. The phallus, therefore, is not to be thought of as something positive and full of potency, but as a kind of negativity which can be known only through its effects. It is in this mode that the phallus as a concept has had an impact on wider feminist and cultural studies (see FEMINISM). The phallus cannot be taken literally; it only works if it is not seen, its message being that there is no centre to POWER, just the emanation of some remarkable effects (see DECENTRATION). The phallus is a function, something that happens and makes things happen; it is often related to in the IMAGINARY register as a fantasy, like the fantasy of mastery. S.J.F.

phantasy. In KLEINIAN psychoanalysis, this term refers to UNCONSCIOUS mental representations of the (biological) DRIVES or 'instincts'. Phantasies are held to exist from birth and to be the dominant component of mental life. At first they derive directly from bodily sensations, but gradually they become more autonomous and symbolizable. It is through phantasy that the drive is linked with an object, as the infant experiences bodily pressure and conjures up an object to which that pressure relates. The importance of this concept is that it makes problematic any idea of 'correct' perception of reality, instead emphasizing the active unconscious process through which experience is constructed. This contrasts with the LACANIAN view of phantasy as something fixed and static, a defence against castration and a way of dealing with the enigma of the DESIRE of the OTHER. For classical FREUDIANS, the Kleinian notion of phantasy assumes the existence of complex mental processes too early in an infant's life. S.J.F.

pharmacology. The branch of BIOLOGY that deals with the properties and mode of action of DRUGS and other biological effectors, particularly those of external origin and thus conventionally excluding hormones, the subject-matter of ENDROCRINOLOGY. Pharmacology consists partly of a taxonomy or functional classification of drugs (particularly in relation to chemical structure), partly of a study of their fate in the body and their metabolic transformations, and partly of an investigation of their mode of action, particularly at a cellular level; this investigation involves the identification of special drug receptors on the CELL surface and a detailed analysis of how the drug alters the cell's behaviour. It includes the study of anaesthetics, antidotes to drugs, and drug ADDICTION. (The measuring, dispensing and formulation of drugs is the subject-matter of *pharmacy*.) Among the biological agents that are not drugs in the conventional sense but come under the study of pharmacology are the ANTIBIOTICS. A most important branch of pharmacology is that which has to do with the standardization and testing of drugs – procedures especially necessary for those drugs which, being of biological origin, are often not chemically characterized and therefore not open to ordinary chemical methods of measurement and potency testing. Safety control is another important – sometimes vitally important – procedure associated with the preparation, marketing and medical use of agents of biological origin such as hormones, antibodies (see IMMUNITY) and antibiotics. For further reading: H. Kalant and W. Roschlau (eds), *Principles of Medical Pharmacology* (1998). P.M.

phase.

(1) In PHYSICS, an angle specifying position along a wave, or the extent to which two waves are 'in register'. One complete cycle (crest + trough) corresponds to 360°.

Thus waves which are a quarter wavelength out of step have a phase difference of 90°, while waves whose phase difference is 180° are half a wave out of step, and still interfere destructively if superimposed, because the crests cancel the troughs.

(2) One of the chemically identical but physically different states of the same system; e.g. ice, water and steam, or graphite and diamond. M.V.B.

phase conjugate mirror. In PHYSICS, an optical device which reverses the PHASE of any light which it reflects. The most striking result of this is that, irrespective of the angle of the beam of light to the mirror, it is always reflected back along its original path, whereas with an ordinary mirror this would only occur if the light struck the mirror at right angles. The effect of phase conjugation goes much further than this, however, since any distortion produced in the wave before it enters the mirror will be reversed on reflection, and the net result is that distortion-free effects can be produced. Some examples are (1) an image of a picture or a diagram can be projected with complete faithfulness – this is being developed to produce microcircuits containing very fine detail. (2) A point source of light, say from a LASER, can be focused back to a point (rather than to a tiny blob) – a property which is being exploited in the development of laser FUSION for power generation. (3) In fundamental physics the mirror is used in SPECTROSCOPY to produce and study lines of atomic spectra without the usual broadening which is introduced by atomic motion and collisions. The mirror effect is actually produced by the interference of beams of light in a non-linear optical medium (see NON-LINEAR OPTICS). A hologram (see HOLOGRAPHY) is produced in the medium which when illuminated by another beam of light 'undoes' any distortion which was present in the beam that originally produced the hologram. H.M.R.

phase shifting. The technique frequently used by American composer Steve Reich of moving the emphasis or the starting point of a repeating musical phrase often against a solid rhythmic background or against itself. This change in the aspect of a musical phrase often makes the listener misinterpret what is basically a very simple technique with the result that he frequently hears countermelodies in the music that were not specifically intended by the composer. The technique often produces a hypnotic effect and forms an important part of PROCESS MUSIC. Phase shifting is also sometimes used to denote the electronic technique of slightly moving the phase or orientation of a soundwave against itself, thus producing a richer sound. For further reading: S. Reich, *Writing about Music* (1974). B.CO.

phase transition. An abrupt change in the state of a SYSTEM, e.g. the melting of ice, the freezing and boiling of water. Phase transitions are induced by changes in some control parameter, typically temperature. Whereas the physical properties of a system alter only slowly with changing conditions away from a phase transition, at the transition this change is abrupt and the system has qualitatively different characteristics, e.g. switching from a liquid to a solid. Phase transitions were first recognized within the context of THERMODYNAMICS, where they are seen to be accompanied by an abrupt change in the thermodynamic variables such as density. But phase transitions are now recognized as a central feature of all modern PHYSICS: the appearance of SUPERCONDUCTIVITY in a cooled metal is the result of a phase transition, as is the splitting of a primeval force into the four fundamental forces of nature in unified theories of the origin of the universe (see GRAND UNIFICATION). Phase transitions exhibit the property of universality, whereby transitions in apparently very different systems (such as the onset of magnetic ordering in iron and the quenching of a SUPERCRITICAL FLUID to a liquid and a gas) share the same general mathematical features. P.C.B.

phatic language. In LINGUISTICS, a term deriving from the anthropologist Malinowski's (1884–1942) phrase *phatic communion*, and applied to language used (as in comments on the weather or enquiries about health) for establishing an atmosphere rather than for exchanging information or ideas. D.C.

phenology. Study of the times of recurring natural phenomena. Used primarily within BIOLOGY for study of seasonal variations, e.g. in plant flowering times or bird migration. P.H.

phenomena (in PHILOSOPHY), see under NOUMENA.

phenomenalism. The theory, propounded by J. S. Mill (1806–73), that material things are 'permanent possibilities of sensation'. It has been elaborately developed by analytic philosophers (see ANALYTIC PHILOSOPHY) in this century, expressed in a more linguistic idiom as the (REDUCTIONIST) theory that statements about material things are equivalent in meaning to statements about actual and possible SENSE-DATA, the sense-data that an observer would have if certain conditions were satisfied. It seems an irresistible consequence of a radically EMPIRICIST theory of meaning together with the widespread philosophical assumption, created by the *argument from illusion*, that material objects are not directly perceived (the *sense-datum theory*). But both of those premises are open to question. For further reading: A. J. Ayer, *The Foundations of Empirical Knowledge* (1940). A.Q.

phenomenology.

(1) In PHILOSOPHY, a method of enquiry elaborated by Edmund Husserl (1859-1938) as a development of his teacher Franz Brentano's conception of 'descriptive', as opposed to 'genetic', PSYCHOLOGY. It takes philosophy to begin from an exact, attentive inspection of one's mental, particularly intellectual, processes in which all assumptions about the causes, consequences and wider significance of the mental process under inspection are eliminated ('bracketed'). Husserl was insistent that phenomenology is not an empirical technique. It is an a priori (see A POSTERIORI, A PRIORI) investigation or scrutiny of ESSENCES or meanings, the objective logical elements in thought that are common to different minds. This much it shares with Descartes' famous thought-experiment, i.e. suspending every item of commonsense or everyday belief that might conceivably be open to doubt, and thereby arriving at a truth self-evident to reason. (*Cogito ergo sum*: 'I think, therefore I am.') However, Husserl claims to go further than Descartes in both the sceptical rigour and the reconstructive scope of his enterprise. Starting out from a standpoint of radical doubt, he will then rebuild the entire edifice of human knowledge on new and secure foundations.

This is why Husserl devoted much attention to issues in the philosophy of LOGIC, MATHEMATICS, GEOMETRY and the NATURAL SCIENCES. These disciplines were under threat – he argued – from two directions: on the one hand from an outlook of uncritical or unreflective scientific POSITIVISM, and on the other from a sceptical-relativist or irrationalist backlash represented by Nietzsche and his latter-day progeny (see NIETZSCHEAN). Hence what Husserl diagnosed (writing in the early 1930s) as a looming 'crisis' of the European sciences, a crisis that could only be averted by re-examining the very grounds – the conditions of possibility – for PERCEPTION, thought, knowledge and experience in general. What is not so clear is the order of priority between these various modes of human understanding. Husserl's early work on the foundations of arithmetic was criticized by the logician Gottlob Frege (1848–1925) on account of its supposed PSYCHOLOGISM, i.e. its lack of objectivity or logical rigour. Husserl took this criticism to heart and strove – in subsequent writings – to practise a form of *transcendental phenomenology* that would concern itself solely with 'absolute ideal objectivities', and hence avoid any such charge. However, he later came to think that the 'crisis' in contemporary thought was a long-term result of precisely that objectifying outlook – that detachment from the LEBENSWELDT, or Lifeworld, of communal experience – brought about by the mathematization of the natural sciences from Galileo on. So it was now more a matter of recalling attention to those background contexts of lived or intuitive knowledge from which the sciences had first taken rise and in the absence of which they would lose all sense of humanly intelligible meaning and purpose.

These shifts of emphasis in Husserl's thinking are reflected in the history of varying responses to his work among philosophers, sociologists and cultural theorists. The phenomenological method has been applied by others, notably Max Scheler, to less austerely intellectual subject-matter, and Husserl's pupil Heidegger used it for the investigation of the extreme states of mind in which, according to EXISTENTIALISM, the situation of man in the world is most authentically revealed. For further reading: D. Bell, *Husserl* (1990). A.Q.; C.C.N.

(2) In the PSYCHOLOGY of PERCEPTION, a doctrine or school which postulates that the significant role of SENSE-DATA lies in the form of the object as perceived, however erroneously or distorted, by the individual, and not in the object itself nor in material descriptions, locations or identifications of the object that follow the rules of physical science. For further reading: M. Merleau-Ponty, *Phenomenology of Perception* (1962). H.L.

(3) In SOCIOLOGY, Husserl's method (see 1, above) was adapted by Alfred Schutz (1899–1959) to investigate the assumptions involved in everyday social life. In the sociology of knowledge (see KNOWLEDGE, SOCIOLOGY OF), phenomenologists have concentrated on the way in which commonsense knowledge about society feeds back, through SOCIAL ACTION, into the moulding of society itself. Other developments range from highly generalized descriptions of how people in different types of society think and feel about the world and their place in it, to analyses, in ETHNOMETHODOLOGY, of the unconscious routines by which people manage their interpersonal contacts. Critics of phenomenological sociology mistrust its aprioristic tendencies (see A POSTERIORI, A PRIORI), and are impatient with its preference for description and uncontrolled hypothesis over EXPLANATION. When explanations are offered, it is claimed, they are disappointingly trite. For further reading: A. Schutz, *The Phenomenology of the Social World* (1967). J.R.T.

phenotype, see under GENOTYPE.

pheromone. A chemical scent that is released by one organism and produces a specific response in another organism. Female moths, e.g., attract their mates by releasing pheromones; when the male senses its species' pheromone it flies upwind, which brings it to the female. The full importance of pheromones in the lives of animals is unknown, because they are difficult for humans to detect. They are, however, used by all the main kinds of animals, to mediate all the main kinds of behaviour. The use of pheromones is probably most strongly developed in ants, which use different pheromones to co-ordinate all the behaviour patterns of their complex social lives – ants use, e.g., a variety of 'recruitment' pheromones in exploiting food, 'propaganda substances' in battles between colonies, and 'alarm' pheromones to warn of danger. M.R.

Phillips curve. A negative relationship between UNEMPLOYMENT and INFLATION that was proposed and given sound empirical justification by British economist A. W. Phillips in 1958. The downward slope of the convex Phillips curve implies that as unemployment declines, the rate of change in wages and prices rises; the convexity implies that to obtain equal decrements in unemployment requires successively larger increases in inflation. The curve was explained by the proposition that an excess demand for labour forced up money wages (and thus prices), and excess demand for labour is associated with low levels of unemployment. The shape of the curve was explained by the downward inflexibility of wages at low or negative levels of excess demand for labour and the flexibility of wages at higher levels of excess demand. Until the late 1960s the Phillips curve was seen as an important economic policy MODEL which demonstrated a widely accepted and used trade-off between unemployment and inflation. However, although there is no doubt that unemployment and inflation are closely related, the precise relationship between the two depends on many other factors, and when both of them began to rise at the same time in Britain in the 1970s, it became clear that the Phillips curve was a very limited economic model. For further reading: J. Craven, *Introduction to Economics* (1984). R.L.; J.P.

philology, see under LINGUISTICS.

philosophical linguistics. A branch of LINGUISTICS which studies (a) the role of language in relation to the understanding and elucidation of philosophical concepts, and (b) the philosophical status of linguistic theories, methods and observations. For further reading: R. Harris, *The Language Connection* (1996). D.C.

philosophical theology. Sometimes used as a synonym for the philosophy of religion (see RELIGION, PHILOSOPHY OF), 'philosophical theology' is, in fact, a discipline of THEOLOGY, rather than of PHILOSOPHY, which is distinguished by its systematic use of philosophical methods and concepts in the theological context. The philosophy of religion is a product of the Enlightenment, but something like philosophical theology has always been part of Christian theology, especially when it has been argued that beliefs concerning the existence and nature of GOD can be justified by reason independently of any revelation (see NATURAL THEOLOGY). Philosophical theology is often reckoned to coincide with FUNDAMENTAL THEOLOGY, the study of the foundations of belief, which precedes 'systematic theology' or DOGMATICS, particularly in theologies which have reinterpreted the tradition through the categories of philosophers from Plato and Aristotle to Hegel and Heidegger. Recently, however, the remit of philosophical theology has been more narrowly defined in the philosophy of RELIGION, in terms of the philosophical analysis of the divine attributes, divine action and specifically Christian doctrines such as incarnation and atonement. See also CHRISTIANITY. For further reading: P. Van Inwagen, *God, Knowledge and Mystery: Essays in Philosophical Theology* (1995). C.C.

philosophy. A term that cannot be uncontroversially defined in a single formula, used to cover a wide variety of intellectual undertakings all of which combine a high degree of generality with more or less exclusive reliance on reasoning rather than observation and experience to justify their claims. The chief agreed constituents of philosophy are EPISTEMOLOGY, or the theory of knowledge, METAPHYSICS and ETHICS. There is a philosophy of every major form of intellectual activity of less than wholly general scope: science (see SCIENCE, PHILOSOPHY OF), HISTORY (see METAHISTORY), RELIGION (see RELIGION, PHILOSOPHY OF), art (see AESTHETICS), and others. These departmental philosophies are either epistemologies of the type of knowledge involved or metaphysical accounts of the domain of objects which that knowledge concerns. (The distinction is often marked as that between the critical and the speculative philosophy of whatever it may be.) Until fairly recent times LOGIC was so closely associated with philosophy as, in effect, to form part of it; but today logic is as often taken to be a part, a very fundamental part, of MATHEMATICS. The philosophical theory of logic, however, that is to say SEMANTICS, in a wide sense, or the theory of MEANING, is very much part of philosophy and, to a large extent, has replaced epistemology as the fundamental philosophical discipline. In the colloquial sense of the word, philosophy is a set or system of ultimate values. This is rather the subject-matter of than identical with ethics. The rational pursuit of such a value-system must rest on a general conception of the nature of the world in which values are sought, the goal of metaphysics. Metaphysics, in its turn, presupposes a critical investigation of the various sorts of knowledge-claim and methods of thinking from and by which a general picture of the world (or WELTANSCHAUUNG) might be constituted, in other words epistemology. The main preoccupations of technical or academic philosophy are all to be found in the writings of Plato and Aristotle and, less comprehensively, in the work of their ancient Greek predecessors, and a continuous tradition of philosophical discussion derives from them. If a single short formula is insisted on, the least objectionable is that philosophy is *thought about thought*; this distinguishes philosophy from those various kinds of first-order thinking about particular parts or aspects of what there is (i.e. science, history, etc.) whose ideas, methods and findings constitute the subject-matter of philosophy. For further reading: M. Hollis, *Invitation to Philosophy* (1997). A.Q.

philosophy of history, see METAHISTORY.

philosophy of mind, see MIND, PHILOSOPHY OF.

philosophy of religion, see RELIGION, PHILOSOPHY OF.

philosophy of science, see SCIENCE, PHILOSOPHY OF.

phi-phenomenon. A type of illusory perceptual impression of movement produced when, e.g., two stationary, spatially separated lights are flashed in brief succession. 'Phi' refers specifically to an impression of pure movement dissociated from PERCEP-

TION of an object. See also GESTALT. I.M.L.H.

phlebology. A field of medicine dealing with the diseases of veins. Veins transport the blood to the heart and contain 70 per cent of the blood volume, taking part in the regulation of cardiac output, hydrostatic pressure in the microcirculation, and body heat exchange. Composed of muscle fibres, collagen and some elastic tissue, veins have valves which are folds of the intimal layer, functionally important for the 'venous muscle pump'. Numerous collateral veins are preformed in the extremities. Common venous diseases are varicosis (a malfunction of valves), thrombosis (the obstruction by a blood clot) and the post-thrombotic syndrome. Thrombosis occurring in deep veins can result in fatal pulmonary embolism. Its risk factors are heart disease, SURGERY, malignancy, trauma, clotting abnormalities, pregnancy, obesity and oral contraceptives. Varicosis supposes a genetical predisposition. Treatment of venous diseases depends on the individual case and is applied by specialists from various fields. It can consist of drugs, physical therapy or surgery. Therefore the definition of phlebology differs slightly depending on the school of thought concerned. E.E.

phobia. An ANXIETY state (see also NEUROSIS) marked primarily by an intense fear out of proportion to the actual danger present in the feared situation or object. Phobias are diagnosed also by their intractability to the effects of direct experience with the relevant situations or objects. W.Z.

phonaesthetics; phonesthetics. In LINGUISTICS, the study of the aesthetic properties of sound, especially the sound symbolism attributable to individual sounds (such as the *ee* of teeny, *wee*, etc., suggestive of smallness). D.C.

phoneme. In LINGUISTICS, the minimal unit of phonological analysis (see PHONOLOGY), i.e. the smallest unit in the sound-system capable of indicating contrasts in meaning; thus in the word *pit* there are three phonemes, /p/, /i/, /t/, each of which differs from phonemes in other words, such as *bit*, *pet* and *pin*. Phonemes are abstractions, the particular phonetic shape they take depending on many factors, especially their position in relation to other sounds in the sentence. These variants are called allophones, e.g. the /t/ phoneme has (among others) both an alveolar allophone (the sound made with the tongue contacting the alveolar ridge above and behind the teeth, as in *eight*) and a dental allophone (the sound made with the tongue further forward, against the teeth, as in *eighth*, because of the influence of the *th* sound which follows).

In GENERATIVE GRAMMAR, this concept of the phoneme is not used: the sound features themselves (e.g. alveolar, nasal), referred to as *distinctive features*, are considered to be the most important minimal units of phonological analysis. In the 1990s, the way these features are identified and organized became a central part of phonological theory. For further reading: P. Hawkins, *Introducing Phonology* (1984). D.C.

phonemics, see under PHONOLOGY.

phonetic poetry, see under CONCRETE POETRY.

phonetics. A branch of LINGUISTICS which studies the characteristics of human sound-making; normally divided into *articulatory* phonetics (the processes of sound articulation by the vocal organs), *acoustic* phonetics (the transmission of vocal sound through the air, often referred to as acoustics), and *auditory* phonetics (the perceptual response to human sound). The term *instrumental* phonetics is used for the study and development of mechanical aids for the analysis of any of these aspects. The name *general* phonetics is often used to indicate the aim of making phonetic principles and categories as universal as possible. See also IPA; PHONOLOGY. For further reading: J. Laver, *Principles of Phonetics* (1994). D.C.

phonology. A branch of LINGUISTICS, sometimes called *phonemics*, which studies the sound-systems of languages. It is normally divided into *segmental* and *suprasegmental* (or *non-segmental*) phonology: the former analyses the properties of vowels, consonants and syllables, the latter analyses those features of pronunciation which vary independently of the segmental structure of a sentence, e.g. intonation, rhythm, PARALANGUAGE. See also PROSODIC FEATURE. For further reading: R. Lass, *Phonology* (1984). D.C.

phonon. An elementary vibration in a crystal. Heat is conducted by an incoherent superposition of short-wave phonons, while sound in solids is a coherent superposition of phonons whose wavelength is much longer than the distance between neighbouring ATOMS in the crystal LATTICE. M.V.B.

photino, see under SUPERSYMMETRY.

photobiology. The branch of BIOLOGY that deals with the influence of light on various biological performances. It includes PHOTOSYNTHESIS, the deposition of melanin in the skin through the action of sunlight, the emission of light by such organisms as glow-worms, and the behavioural responses towards sources of light of organisms such as moths and beetles. P.M.

photochemistry. The study of chemical reactions induced by light. It was recognized early in the 19th century that only the light absorbed by a MOLECULE produces a photochemical change (the first law of photochemistry). Stark and Einstein (1912) were responsible for the second law, which states that, when a molecule is activated and caused to react, one quantum of light has been absorbed. Photochemical reactions are of great importance; they include PHOTOSYNTHESIS, production of the OZONE LAYER in the upper atmosphere, photochemical oxidation (e.g. the fading of dyes in light), photographic processes, and the chemistry of vision. B.F.

photoelectric cell. A device for detecting the presence of light and measuring its intensity, as in a photographer's light meter. PHOTONS arriving at the surface of a suitable material (e.g. selenium) interact with ELECTRONS in it, thus producing measurable electrical effects. M.V.B.

photogram. Abstract or near-abstract photograph produced without a camera by the action of light and shade on sensitized paper. A DADAIST technique first employed by Christian Schad in Geneva in the winter of 1919–20 and subsequently by Man Ray in Paris; hence the alternative names *schadograph* or *rayograph*. J.W.

photolysis. The decomposition of a MOLECULE by light (see PHOTOCHEMISTRY). B.F.

photomontage, see under MONTAGE.

photon. The ELEMENTARY PARTICLE OF 'quantum' of ENERGY in which light or other electromagnetic RADIATION is emitted or absorbed when an ELECTRON, in an ATOM (see ATOMIC PHYSICS) or MOLECULE, changes its ENERGY LEVEL. The energy of a photon is equal to its frequency multiplied by PLANCK'S CONSTANT. Between emission and absorption, when the light is travelling through space, the intensity is usually so high that many photons are present, and classical OPTICS based on ELECTROMAGNETISM provides a sufficiently accurate description; this is an example of the WAVE-PARTICLE DUALITY. A burst of light containing no more than a few photons is detectable by the naked eye. M.V.B.

photonics. An information technology in which all processes – data transmission, processing and storage – are carried out using light pulses rather than electricity. Photonic technology offers potentially higher transmission capacities, processing speeds and storage densities than electronic technology. At present, only photonic data transmission (using fibre optic cables) is well developed. Prototype optical-based storage systems, particularly involving HOLOGRAPHY, do exist, but few are marketed commercially. Photonic data processing, meanwhile, remains embryonic. P.C.B.

photosynthesis. A highly complex oxidative-reduction reaction between carbon dioxide and water which takes place in the presence of CHLOROPHYLL and involves the absorption of solar energy. In plants photosynthesis takes place in *chloroplasts*, small organelles within plant cells. The reaction results in the production of glucose and of higher carbohydrates which provide the food (and thus the energy) required by animals. In addition, the oxygen in the atmosphere is renewed by photosynthesis, so the whole LIFE CYCLE of the earth ultimately depends upon this reaction. K.M.

phototaxis; phototropism, see under TROPISM.

phrase-structure grammar, see under GENERATIVE GRAMMAR.

phrenology. A would-be science with some popularity in the 19th century but now completely discredited by the findings of NEUROPSYCHOLOGY. It supposed that mental faculties were located in distinct parts of the brain and could be investigated by feeling bumps on the outside of the head. I.M.L.H.

phylogeny. The evolutionary (see EVOLUTION) history of a taxonomic group or lineage (see TAXONOMY). Phylogenetic relationships can be interpreted from a variety of character types, from morphological (see MORPHOLOGY) to molecular (see MOLECULE). These are measured in terms of the similarity of characters on some quantifiable scale which can be either discrete or continuous. Molecular phylogenies (based on changes in DNA; see NUCLEIC ACID) can be based on distance measures (e.g. the proportion of shared bases of DNA at a GENE), or on 'character' measures (a series of discrete variables). In either case, there can be numerous trees that are equally viable, given the set of measurements used. For this reason, among others, phylogenetic histories can be difficult to interpret. The accuracy of a phylogeny also depends on certain assumptions about the characters used to generate the trees (such as a constant rate of change), which may not strictly apply. A.R.H.

phylum. A group of organisms united by basic similarity (or *homeomorphy*) of ground plan. Thus the chordates (see ZOOLOGY) form a phylum because all pass through a *neurula* stage (see EMBRYOLOGY) in which the basic layout is essentially similar throughout. P.M.

physical chemistry. A major branch of CHEMISTRY concerned with the measurement and understanding of chemical processes. It deals with chemical THERMODYNAMICS, in particular the position of chemical EQUILIBRIUM and the forces between chemical SPECIES (ATOMS, IONS or MOLECULES) in the gaseous, liquid and solid states. The rates of chemical reaction and their mechanisms are a central study. Other major areas are the determination of molecular structure and the investigation of the allowed ENERGY LEVELS for chemical species in different environments. Since many of these topics might equally well be studied by physicists, there is practically no distinction, except academic convention, between physical chemistry and *chemical physics*. For further reading: W. J. Moore, *Physical Chemistry* (1972). B.F.

physicalism. The theory that all significant empirical statements can be formulated as statements referring to *publicly* observable physical objects. LOGICAL POSITIVISM, in its early stages, combined the desire to legitimize scientific statements as the paradigm of what is significant and knowable with a commitment to the view that the empirical basis of MEANING and knowledge is *private* sense-experience (see PRIVACY; SENSE-DATUM). Otto Neurath, a member of the Vienna Circle, held that the scientific requirement of *intersubjectivity* (i.e. of being publicly observable) must extend to its foundations – he converted Rudolf Carnap, another member, from his previous 'methodological SOLIPSISM'. Neurath saw physicalism as establishing the unity of science, contending that there is no difference of method or, fundamentally, of subject-matter between the NATURAL SCIENCES and the SOCIAL SCIENCES. In its original form physicalism interpreted statements about mental events in a behaviouristic way (see BEHAVIOURISM) as statements about the dispositions of living human bodies to behaviour of various kinds. The doctrine has been revived by exponents of the IDENTITY THEORY of mind and body (see also MIND-BODY PROBLEM), notably J. J. C. Smart (see below), for whom mental events are in fact events occurring in the brain and nervous system. For further reading: J. J. C. Smart, *Philosophy and Scientific Realism* (1963). A.Q.

physics. The study of fundamental forces of matter, the laws governing them, and the outcomes of those laws. There are four fundamental forces: the electromagnetic, strong, weak, and gravitational forces (see ELECTROMAGNETISM; GRAVITATION). The mathematical theories describing them are at present, respectively, quantum electrodynamics (QED; see FIELD THEORY), QUANTUM CHROMODYNAMICS (QCD), the Weinberg-Salam theory, and general RELA-

TIVITY. When velocities are small compared with that of light, gravitational fields are weak, and the sizes of objects are much larger than their quantum wavelengths, then QED and general relativity reduce to the classical theories of Maxwell and Newton respectively (see CLASSICAL PHYSICS). Physics is divided into many subdisciplines according to the forces of nature under study and the arena of their application, e.g. ASTROPHYSICS, BIOPHYSICS, GEOPHYSICS, chemical physics. Within the mainstream subject area it divides into sub-branches devoted to the study of condensed-matter physics, OPTICS and laser physics, ATOMIC PHYSICS, NUCLEAR PHYSICS and particle physics. J.D.B.

physiology. The branch of BIOLOGY that deals with function rather than structure and constitution. There are as many branches of physiology as there are distinct organ and tissue systems, e.g. NEUROLOGY, ENDOCRINOLOGY, etc. P.M.

physiotherapy. A systematic method of assessing musculoskeletal and neurological disorders of function, including pain and those of PSYCHOSOMATIC origin, and dealing with or preventing these problems by natural methods based essentially on movement, manual therapy and physical agencies. Physiotherapy is involved with all problems of function and the ability and mobility of the population from birth to death; from antenatal preparation, through childhood disability, physical and mental handicap, accidents and illness to dealing with the problems of elderly people. C.J.; D.L.W.

phytogeography. The branch of BIOGEOGRAPHY which studies the geographical distribution of plants. Over a limited area plant distribution depends mainly on the soil type, determined by the GEOLOGY of the underlying rock. The other main factors are climatic (see CLIMATOLOGY). Agriculture has now changed the plant cover of the whole landscape in developed countries, and man, by burning the bush, for instance, has affected other, less developed areas. This means that stable natural vegetation is becoming increasingly rare, and many of the original CONCEPTS of phytogeography cannot now be easily demonstrated. For further reading: M. I. Newbigin, *Plant and Animal Geography* (1957). K.M.

phytopathology. The study of the diseases of plants; alternatively, the study of diseases caused by vegetable organisms, such as fungi. K.M.

Piagetian. An adjective referring to Jean Piaget (1896–1980) and his theory of intellectual development. The theory is distinguished by an account of intellectual development as a universal sequence of mental stages (see STAGE OF DEVELOPMENT). The order of the stages is invariant, the later incorporating and resynthesizing the earlier. Development is divided into three broad stages: the SENSORY-MOTOR period (from birth to 18 months), in which the infant constructs a picture of a stable world divided into objects which retain their identity through space and time; the CONCRETE OPERATIONS period (from 2 to 11), in which the young child acquires classificatory principles of number, class and quantity for organizing such objects; and the FORMAL OPERATIONS period (from 12 onwards), in which the adolescent acquires the ability systematically to co-ordinate his own classificatory principles.

Piaget took a characteristic position over various central psychological controversies. INTELLIGENCE is seen neither as a resonance to the external world (EMPIRICISM) nor as the unfolding of a predetermined system (NATIVISM), but as the progressive co-ordination between an organized intellectual system and the external world, beginning with the initial co-ordination between reflex and stimuli. Nor is intellectual development guided by cultural and social tools such as language. Instead, Piaget argued that intellectual development guides the usage of those tools.

The theory has contributed to the recent growth of COGNITIVE PSYCHOLOGY and contemporary interest in mental operations as opposed to observable behaviour (see BEHAVIOURISM). Nonetheless, even within cognitive psychology, Piaget remained distinctive. First, he adopted a developmental approach to cognition, and second, he concerned himself with epistemological categories (see EPISTEMOLOGY) and issues such as the nature of space (see SPACE PERCEPTION), quantity and causality, rather than with psychological categories such as short-term memory, attention and retrieval, etc. See also ACCOMMODATION; ASSIMILATION; CONSERVATION; DEVELOPMENTAL PSYCHOLOGY. For further reading: J. Piaget, *The Origin of Intelligence in the Child* (1963). P.L.H.

picketing. Picketing is the practice of the posting of strikers or their agents to intercept non-strikers and/or third parties to the dispute and to persuade them not to cross the 'picket-line', thereby adding to the effectiveness of the strike. The persuasion and the interception should be peaceful. In the UK picketing is constrained by two sets of laws, one specific to picketing (viz pickets must only be placed at the place of work of the strikers; only strikers may picket, etc.) and COMMON LAW (viz laws of obstruction, trespass and riot; see LABOUR LAW). Since individual police discretion is required, these laws are applied inconsistently.

Historically, picketing has also been used as a human barrier to prevent the movement of people or supplies into or out of a plant or office. In the US in the 1920s and 1930s in the car and steel industries, these tactics led to violence and deaths. In the UK *mass picketing* came to prominence in the 1973/74 miners' strike at the Saltley coke works and at the photographic printers Grunwick in 1976. In more recent times the 1984/85 miners' strike and the 1986/87 mass picket outside News International in Wapping have both seen violence, notwithstanding massive police presences.

Flying pickets are a variation on the mass pickets. They consist of workers who are prepared to travel speedily, and in considerable strength, to picket at a workplace where they themselves do not work. This tactic was pioneered in 1972 in the construction industry dispute and in 1974 in the miners' dispute. It is now illegal in the UK. *Secondary picketing*, that is a picket at a place of work not directly involved in the dispute, is also illegal. B.D.S.

picture-writing, see under LETTRISM.

pidgin. In SOCIOLINGUISTICS, a language with a markedly reduced GRAMMAR, LEXICON and stylistic range, which is the native language of no one. Pidgin languages are formed when people from two different speech communities try to communicate (e.g. for trading purposes) without the aid of an interpreter. These languages flourish in areas of economic development, as in the pidgins based on English, French, Spanish and Portuguese in the East and West Indies, Africa and the Americas. Pidgins develop into CREOLES when they become the mother-tongue of a community. For further reading: P. Trudgill, *Sociolinguistics* (1984). D.C.

piezoelectrics, see under SMART MATERIAL.

pink dollar. Term reflecting the recognition by commercial organizations in Britain and the US that the spending power of the gay movement is an economic force worth harnessing. Since many gay households comprise two adults in upper-income professions, without children, they enjoy unusually high levels of disposable income which are much prized by MARKETING men. Trade exhibitions specifically aimed at capturing the pink dollar/pound are held annually at Olympia in London. There is also a recognition that the pink dollar is contributing to economic growth, particularly in the creative professions. A.BR.

pioneers, see under ECOLOGICAL SUCCESSION.

piped music, see under MUZAK.

PK, see PSYCHOKINESIS.

place. Although the term 'place' is routinely used to identify a specific location or portion of worldly space, whether this be a room in a house or the TERRITORY of a whole country, it has also acquired a particular pertinence for a perspective within human GEOGRAPHY known as HUMANISTIC GEOGRAPHY. In this context place – or, to be more precise, 'sense of place' – connotes the myriad values, beliefs, feelings, hopes and fears that human beings attach both individually and collectively to certain settlements, regions, environments and landscapes. Distance from a place is hence to be measured, not simply in terms of physical distance, but in terms of the extent to which people feel that they belong to or are 'at home in' this place. And, similarly, attention needs to be paid to whether people perceive places as 'authentic' – as rooted in a set of time-honoured local traditions and customs – or as 'inauthentic' – as littered with buildings, institutions and suchlike that are somehow alien, perhaps through being manifestations of a curiously 'placeless' modern Western CULTURE. (For a rather different treatment of place by geographers, see CENTRAL PLACE.) For further reading: E. Relph, *Place and Placelessness* (1976). C.P.

Planck time/era. A unit of time obtained from combining three fundamental constants of nature: the velocity of light, Newton's constant of gravitation, and Planck's quantum of action. It has a value of 10^{-43} seconds. It was first derived by German physicist Max Planck in 1900 (although a similar quantity had been computed by George Johnstone Stoney in 1874). The Planck time is the earliest time in the history of the universe to which our current scientific theories are believed to apply. The interval of cosmic history beginning at the big bang (assumed to be the start of time; see BIG BANG THEORY) and lasting for the Planck time is called the Planck era by cosmologists (see COSMOLOGY). During this period no known theory of nature remains consistent. The structure of the material universe during this epoch is sometimes called space-time foam. Before the Planck time the entire universe behaves as a quantum wave of probability rather than as a classical physical entity (see QUANTUM MECHANICS; CLASSICAL PHYSICS).

The Planck time is an example of a natural unit of time; i.e., it is not defined in terms of man-made artifacts but by reference to the fundamental constants of nature. There also exist related standards of mass and length called the Planck mass (10^{-5} grammes) and Planck length (10^{-33} centimetres). For further reading: J. D. Barrow, *The World within the World* (1988). J.D.B.

Planck's constant. A universal constant (generally written *h*) first introduced by German physicist Max Planck in 1900, which relates the mechanical properties of matter to its wave properties (see WAVE-PARTICLE DUALITY). The ENERGY of a PARTICLE determines its frequency according to the equation *frequency* = *energy* ÷ *h*, while the MOMENTUM of a particle determines its DE BROGLIE WAVELENGTH. The extreme smallness of Planck's constant makes NEWTONIAN MECHANICS an excellent approximation to QUANTUM MECHANICS in normal circumstances. M.V.B.

plan-séquence. A term in French film vocabulary signifying an entire sequence or segment of a film shot in one unbroken take, where otherwise a cut might be used to indicate a displacement from one viewpoint to another. Sometimes rendered in English as *sequence shot*, but the looser term 'long take' (briefly made fashionable as 'the ten-minute take' by Alfred Hitchcock's experiment with the technique in *Rope*, 1948) remains in more current usage. Film theorists, notably the French critic André Bazin, have attempted somewhat simplistically to divide film-makers into two broad groups: those who followed the principles of MONTAGE to heighten reality, and those who attempted to let the camera record reality by refusing to cut away from it. T.C.C.M.

plane of the ecliptic, see under ECLIPTIC.

planetary rings. Systems of small rocks and PARTICLES observed orbiting around the planets Saturn, Jupiter and Uranus. Saturn's rings were first discovered by Galileo in 1610. The rings are probably no more than 5 km thick and appear to consist of constituent particles between 1 mm and tens of metres in size. They may have arisen when material failed to condense into moons (see GALILEAN MOONS) during the formation process of the central planet. Six principal rings of Saturn (A, B, C, D, E and F) are known. The most recently discovered is the F (or 'braided') ring. There may exist other fainter rings. All these rings exhibit complicated internal structure and constituent ringlets. J.D.B.

planetesimal theory. One of a number of hypotheses proposed for the origin of the SOLAR SYSTEM which have as a common starting-point the disruption of the primitive sun by an external force. Thomas C. Chamberlin and Forest R. Moulton proposed that planetesimals, fragments which aggregated to form the planets, were derived from the break-up of the primitive sun and another star, on their close approach to each other. There are, however, serious physical and chemical objections to all theories involving disruption of the sun. Chemical evidence alone suggests that it is very unlikely that the planets were formed from the interior of the sun. J.L.M.L.

planetology, see under EARTH SCIENCES.

planned parenthood, see FAMILY PLANNING.

planning. In POLITICAL ECONOMY, the mode of thinking which stresses the advantages of a central planning authority to co-ordinate the development of the national economy, or, more loosely, of government intervention in some form (as opposed to a LAISSEZ FAIRE approach). In the wake of the CAPITALIST chaos of the 1930s, the Soviet example of planning, and especially its emphasis on heavy industry, exercised considerable intellectual appeal. By the post-war period, not only had the former USSR, eastern Europe and China all adopted rigorous central planning, but the majority of the THIRD WORLD countries also favoured a planned approach. Meanwhile most Western industrial countries have adopted MIXED ECONOMIES of varying shades. See also STATE ECONOMIC PLANNING. D.E.

planning gain. Agreements made between local authorities and developers to get a higher level of social provision in a development than is required by TOWN PLANNING law, in return for a more satisfactory planning permission. For example, under what is known in Britain as a Section 106 agreement, in return for a slightly higher density the developer may be persuaded to improve the level of facilities and access for minority groups. Likewise the system of 'zoning bonusing' (and inclusionary zoning) in some American states operates in a similar manner. Provision under such agreements might include crèche and childcare provision (day-care) as part of the development; improved public facilities; and environmental improvements. For further reading: P. Ambrose, *Whatever Happened to Planning?* (1986). C.G.

plasma physics. The study of fluids containing a large number of free negative and positive electric charges, e.g. the IONOSPHERE or the gases in which a FUSION reaction is occurring. Such systems are strongly affected by electric and magnetic forces, so that their complicated motions must be interpreted within MAGNETOHYDRODYNAMICS. M.V.B.

plasmagene. A GENE or group of genes not incorporated into a CHROMOSOME. It once seemed that the presence in CELLS of structures such as mitochondria (see CYTOLOGY; SYMBIOSIS) and chloroplasts (see PHOTOSYNTHESIS), which arise only from pre-existing structures of the same kind, indicated the existence of a hereditary mechanism profoundly different from the Mendelian one (see MENDELISM). These structures are now known to contain DNA (see NUCLEIC ACID), and it seems that the difference concerns the way in which DNA is transmitted from cell to cell rather than the process of self-replication upon which heredity (see GENETICS/GENOMICS) depends. See also EPISOME. J.M.S.

plasmid, see under CLONING.

plastic (reconstructive) surgery. SURGERY to restore or reconstruct damaged, diseased or congenitally malformed tissue to normal form. This is achieved by the transfer of similar living tissue from adjacent or more distant parts of the body, or by the reshaping of the malformed tissue itself. The major part of plastic surgery involves the treatment of head, neck and skin cancers, injuries of the soft tissues of the face, hands and legs, burns, and of birth deformity such as cleft lip and palate, birthmarks and deformed hands. Tissue transfer and repair have been developed from skin grafting to the transfer of composite tissue such as muscle and bone and, more recently, whole limbs using suture of individual arteries, veins and nerves under the operating microscope. The origins of the art are recorded in Egyptian writings of 2000 BC (case histories of treatment of a fractured, deformed nose), and in Indian scripts of 600 BC (describing how cheek skin could be cut to repair deformities of ears and face). During the 17th and 18th centuries successful surgical experiments were made transferring tissue from undamaged to mutilated parts, but the advent of anaesthesia in the 1840s allowed the surgeon the time to carry out the more intricate procedures previously denied. Early skin grafting for burns was introduced in the USA in 1905. World War I trench injuries provided the impetus for Harold Gillies (1882–1960) and Pomfret Kilner (1890–1964) to set up plastic surgery units within hospitals where specialist care could be provided. Specialist provision for victims of burns injuries became available during and after World War II at the instigation of Archibald McIndoe (1900–60), though the first burns unit in Britain had been set up a hundred years before in Edinburgh. For further reading: I. A. McGregor, *Fundamental Techniques of Plastic Surgery and Their Surgical Applications* (1980). J.V.H.K.

plate tectonics. A hypothesis of global TECTONICS which postulates large-scale horizontal movements of the rigid outer shell of the earth, termed the LITHOSPHERE, over a plastic layer of the upper mantle, the ASTHENOSPHERE. The theory has developed as a result of recent discoveries of patterns of remanent magnetism of the ocean floor which make it virtually certain that oceanic crust is being continually created by upwelling of mantle material along a worldwide mid-ocean fracture system (see OCEANIC RIDGE). The oceanic lithosphere so created spreads laterally at a rate of a few centimetres a year, moving in opposite directions on either side of the mid-oceanic fracture system, and eventually sinks down to be reabsorbed in the mantle under certain continental margins. The major zone of sinking is the circum-Pacific region from the Philippines to Chile. Six major plates of the lithosphere, five of them carrying continental crust, are moving relative to each other across the earth's surface away from the mid-ocean fracture, and in doing so they seem to determine the major tectonic features of the earth. See also CONTINENTAL DRIFT. J.L.M.L.

Platonic realism, see under REALISM.

Platonism. The theory that abstract entities or UNIVERSALS really exist, outside space and time, in an autonomous world of timeless ESSENCES. (Plato, indeed, held that such Ideas or Forms are the *only* things that really or wholly exist, on the ground that it is only of them that we have absolutely certain knowledge, namely in MATHEMATICS.) One argument for the existence of universals is that there are statements, known to be true, which refer to them. Critics object that such references can be eliminated by ANALYSIS: 'Honesty is the best policy', with its apparent implication of the existence of honesty-in-general, is just an idiomatic abbreviation for 'Anyone who acts honestly acts prudently'. But it has been argued by William Quine that any language mathematically rich enough for the needs of science must contain irreducible references to classes (see SET THEORY), and that classes are abstract entities. If *a priori* knowledge (see A POSTERIORI, A PRIORI) is conceived by ANALOGY with PERCEPTION, abstract entities provide suitable objects for acts of rational insight or intellectual intuition. For further reading: B. Russell, *The Problems of Philosophy* (1912), chapters 9, 10. A.Q.

pleasure principle. In psychoanalytic theory (see PSYCHOANALYSIS), a FREUDIAN term for the principle of mental functioning that characterizes UNCONSCIOUS, primitive instincts (the ID), which are driven to gratification without regard to their consequences either socially or for the individual's adaptation. It is usually contrasted with the REALITY PRINCIPLE. W.Z.

pleiotropy. The development of apparently unrelated characteristics under the influence of a single GENE. It is thought that each gene has only one primary function, and that pleiotropic effects arise because a single primary effect can have many consequences. J.M.S.

PLO, see under PALESTINIAN AUTHORITY.

PLR (Public Lending Right). The principle that authors should receive some kind of payment when their works are borrowed from public libraries. Public Lending Right may be operated in various ways; and there are different means of raising the money – e.g. by direct government grant, by a levy on the rates, etc. It exists in Denmark, Sweden and several other countries, but not in the USA. In Britain the idea was pioneered by the novelist and writer John Brophy and then by his daughter Brigid Brophy and an association she formed called Writers Action Group (now dissolved, its aims fulfilled). Legislation to implement it was announced in the Queen's Speeches of 1974 and 1975, and in 1983 it was put into effect. It is based on a loan-sample and has been widely accepted, but is unfair – as is also accepted – to the poverty-stricken authors and editors of reference books. The anomalies – mainly that those least in need get most – cannot be ironed out. M.S.-S.

plural society. A society containing within it two or more communities which are distinct in many (predominantly cultural) respects – colour, belief, RITUAL, practices both institutionalized (e.g. form of marriage and family) and habitual (e.g. preferred food, dress, leisure) – and which in many areas of social behaviour remain substantially unmixed; a society whose elements acknowledge, or are constrained by, an overall political authority, but are strongly disposed to the maintenance of their own traditions and are therefore motivated towards SEPARATISM. In plural societies the problem of preserving order and freedom is especially great; a slender unity easily breaks into warring national, racial or religious groups. All societies other than the very simplest are pluralist in possessing local, regional and CLASS communities, but the concept has come strongly to the fore since World War II when many hitherto subjected and newly immigrant (or refugee) groups feel the right to equal STATUS, and when, with movements of population, many societies (e.g. Britain) now contain distinctive cultural groups. The plural society has created moral, legal and political problems of a new degree of difficulty – from APARTHEID at one extreme to the all-embracing statement of equality (see EQUALITY, PRINCIPLE OF) in the Constitution of the USA at the other – and has rendered any analysis of social co-operation and conflict in terms of the orthodox concepts of SOCIAL STRATIFICATION (slavery, serfdom, CASTE, estate, class) much too simple. The more detailed analysis required has been provided in discussions of the composition of a population by F. H. Giddings (in *The Elements of Sociology*, 1898) and of cultural communities and INTEREST GROUPS by Gustav Ratzenhofer (e.g. as expounded by Albion W. Small in *General Sociology*, 1905). See also CULTURE. For further reading: H. M. Kallen, *Cultural Pluralism and the American Idea* (1956). R.F.

pluralism. In political thought (for its meaning in PHILOSOPHY see MONISM), a term with three meanings, not always clearly distinguished: (a) institutional arrangements for the distribution of political POWER; (b) the doctrine that such arrangements ought to exist; and (c) (a somewhat slipshod usage) pluralist analysis, i.e. the analysis of power distributed in this way. It is frequently used to denote any situation in which no particular political, ideological, cultural or ethnic group is dominant. Such a situation normally involves competition between rival ÉLITES or INTEREST GROUPS, and the PLURAL SOCIETY in which it arises is often contrasted with a society dominated by a single élite where such competition is not free to develop. For further reading: S. Lukes, *Power* (1974). M.BA.

plurisignation. Term introduced by Philip Wheelwright, in *The Burning Fountain* (1954), as a substitute for William Empson's AMBIGUITY, which, in his view, had an irrelevantly pejorative connotation, and was over-restrictive. 'Real plurisignation differs from simply punning or wit-writing .... Empson's use of the term ''ambiguity'' generally refers to the plurisignative character of poetic language; his word is inappropriate, however, since ambiguity implies an ''either-or'' relation, plurisignation a ''both-and''.' 'The plurisign, the poetic symbol, is not merely employed but enjoyed'; 'it is a part of what it means'. The term extends the Empsonian CONCEPT by relating it to the mystico-religious connotation of words. M.S.-S.

plutocracy. Word of Greek origin for the rule of the wealthy, a state in which citizenship or POWER is defined by great wealth. A strict example of such a state is difficult to find; the Venetian republic probably comes closest, while the high property franchise obtaining in France under Louis Philippe (1830–48) and the roles open to the wealthy in American politics in the last decades of the 19th century gave these societies distinctly plutocratic elements. D.C.W.

plutonium. The most important TRANSURANIC ELEMENT. Plutonium (atomic number 94) is produced artificially in a NUCLEAR REACTOR from naturally occurring uranium by a succession of NUCLEAR REACTIONS which follow NEUTRON absorption. Unlike the uranium 238 ISOTOPE, which constitutes

99.3 per cent of natural uranium, the chief isotope of plutonium (atomic weight 239) is a fissionable material which can be used in atomic bombs and to fuel nuclear reactors. Large-scale production of plutonium and separation from uranium began towards the end of World War II, and the first plutonium-containing bomb was exploded in New Mexico in 1945. Fast-breeder reactors produce excess plutonium in addition to generating power. B.F.

Plymouth Brethren. A Christian SECT, originating in 1830 in Plymouth, England, but now widely distributed and vocal, although still not large. Its doctrines are generally FUNDAMENTALIST, and one section, the 'Exclusive' Brethren, interpret biblical passages about the 'holy' people as forbidding marriage or friendship with non-members. The 'Open' Brethren are somewhat more liberal. D.L.E.

PMS, see PREMENSTRUAL SYNDROME.

pneumatic structures. Enclosures in which a membrane is air-supported by means of the difference in pressure between the inside and outside. As a rule air is pumped into such an enclosure through fans, and this air also acts as the mechanical ventilation. To prevent its escape, the membrane is tightly sealed and entrance is through an airlock. The membrane has to be in sufficient tension to withstand wind and snow loads. Much of the technology derives from lighter-than-air balloons and dirigibles.

Pneumatic structures can be erected and dismantled quickly and have thus so far been mostly used for temporary buildings, and in HAPPENINGS, play areas, etc., where they are often called *inflatables*. Some of the most complex examples were seen at Expo '70 in Osaka. Small, totally enclosed forms have been used as furniture. For further reading: R. N. Dent, *Principles of Pneumatic Architecture* (1971). M.BR.

poetics. The theory and/or practice of poetry; alternatively, an exposition of such theory or practice. O.S.

Poetry (Chicago). One of the first and chief of American 'little magazines'. It began in Chicago in October 1912, edited by Harriet Monroe, with Ezra Pound as foreign correspondent, and had much to do with the modern revolution in poetry; it included work by T. S. Eliot, William Carlos Williams, Wallace Stevens and Marianne Moore (all largely via Pound) as well as more 'native', middle-western voices like Vachel Lindsay and Carl Sandburg. Harriet Monroe, basically sympathetic to the latter tradition, finally lost Pound to Margaret Anderson's rival LITTLE REVIEW. Though the early years are the best, the journal's tradition continues, subsequent editors including Morton D. Zabel and Peter de Vries. For further reading: H. Monroe, *A Poet's Life* (1938). M.S.BR.

Poetry Bookshop. A bookshop set up in December 1912 at 35 Devonshire Street, London, by Harold Monro (1879–1932), as an adjunct to his middle-of-the-road *Poetry Review* (succeeded by *Poetry and Drama*). His hope of bringing poetry out of the study and 'back into the street' was hardly realized; but the Poetry Bookshop, housed in a splendid 18th-century mansion, played an important part in bringing poetry to those who really wanted it. There were readings; indigent poets were offered lodgings. Most of the readings and poems were bad; but the poets included Robert Frost, Rupert Brooke, T. E. Hulme, Wilfred Owen, and Conrad Aiken. For further reading: J. Grant, *Harold Monro and the Poetry Bookshop* (1967). M.S.-S.

Poetry Workshop, see under GROUP, THE.

pogrom. In Russian, the literal meaning of pogrom is 'devastation' or 'riot'. Usually, the term applies to attacks on Jews in the Russian Empire from the end of the 19th century and into the early 20th century, in which they were killed or injured, and their property stolen or destroyed. The pogroms differed from the GENOCIDE which characterized the HOLOCAUST in that they were not explicitly sponsored and carried out by the STATE. However, antisemitic policy in Russia (see ANTISEMITISM) allowed mobs to feel that pogroms were justified. The beating and killing of Jews, along with the destruction of their property that occurred on Kristallnacht in Germany in 1939, may be characterized as a pogrom, whereas the Germans' systematic killing of six million Jews from the beginning of the Final Solution in

1942 is properly described as genocide. For further reading: P. Brass (ed.), *Riots and Pogroms* (1996). S.T.

point block, see TOWER BLOCK.

pointillism.

(1) In music, the use of melodic lines so disjointed that the individual notes seem to stand alone and not to refer to each other, sounding rather like points of sound. The music of Anton Webern (see SECOND VIENNESE SCHOOL) is often referred to as pointillist owing to his fragmentation of the musical fabric by the use of silences in between the notes and by his frequent changes of tone colour in a single melody (see KLANGFARBENMELODIE). This fragmentation was taken to even greater extremes in the 1950s by composers of the POST-WEBERN SCHOOL. B.CO.

(2) In fine arts, see under NEO-IMPRESSIONISM.

Poisson distribution. In STATISTICS and PROBABILITY THEORY, a DISTRIBUTION on the non-negative integers which attaches probability $\lambda^n e^{-\lambda}/n!$ to the integer n. Both the MEAN and the VARIANCE of the distribution are equal to the value of the PARAMETER λ. The distribution arises naturally in a number of ways, and is often used in applied probability as a model for the occurrence of a rare event in a large number of trials – e.g., the number of misprints per page in a newspaper has approximately a Poisson distribution. R.SI.

Polaris missile, see under TRIDENT.

polarization.

(1) In OPTICS, the state of affairs in which light or other radiation has different properties in different directions at right angles to the direction of propagation.

(2) The process whereby, when an electric FIELD acts on matter, positive and negative charges separate.

(3) The process whereby a social or political group is divided on, e.g., a political or religious issue into two diametrically opposed sub-groups, with fewer and fewer members of the group remaining indifferent or holding an intermediate position. A.S.

polarography. A method of chemical analysis, invented by Czech chemist Jaroslav Heyrovsky around 1920, involving the measurement of current-voltage curves as mercury, which forms one electrode, drops steadily from a fine capillary through a solution. It can be used to determine dilute concentrations of any metal ION or organic SPECIES which can be reduced at the dropping electrode, as well as to investigate oxidation-reduction chemistry in solution. B.F.

police powers. In the US, the federal government is, in theory, the government of generally delimited powers, while the states retain inherent powers over public health, safety, welfare and morals. These state powers are referred to as the 'police powers'. Federal review of state activities is permitted only to determine whether state actions under their police powers violate a specific constitutional limitation. This distinction between the powers of state and national government is the basis of the American federal system, and also explains why the US is not a complete legal union. M.S.P.

policing. Originally, the notion of 'police' was broadly equated with the good administration of a city or state. Historically, various forms of private, voluntary and co-operative initiatives provided the arrangements for policing. The narrower idea of a civil, professional police force follows from Sir Robert Peel's 1829 Metropolitan Police Act. In a liberal DEMOCRACY, modern policing is regarded as dependent upon consensus, legitimacy and legal authority; such bases are lacking in totalitarian states (see TOTALITARIANISM) which employ police for explicitly political tasks. Policing involves preservation of order, CRIME prevention and detection. Late-20th-century policing has seen the re-emergence of private policing arrangements as well as the increasing specialization of public police. N.S.

Politburo. In the former USSR, the most powerful institution in the Soviet COMMUNIST Party and the main policy-making body of the nation. As the Political Bureau of the Central Committee, it was officially responsible for directing the activities of the Communist Party in between plenary sessions of the Central Committee, which nominally elected it. However, in practice Politburo members were recruited by co-option and had much more say over policy than did the Central Committee. It met once or twice a week and was particularly concerned with foreign and national security affairs, although it also dealt with internal economic questions. Its membership was small: in 1986 it had 12 full members and 7 candidate (non-voting) members. Its most influential member was the General Secretary to the Central Committee. Representatives of important government departments such as the Ministry of Foreign Affairs and much more recently the KGB were usually included in its membership, together with the chiefs of key party regional organizations, such as Moscow, Leningrad and the Ukraine. Having risen to prominence after its establishment in 1919, it lost much of its power under Stalin in the period after the YEZHOVSHCHINA, but was restored to its central position after 1953. For further reading: R. J. Hill and P. Frank, *The Soviet Communist Party* (1981). D.PR.

political action committee. The name for organizations created by TRADE UNIONS, corporations and other INTEREST GROUPS to contribute money – collected voluntarily from individuals – to election campaigns in the US. About 4,000 PACs are active on the federal level, dispensing hundreds of millions of dollars to candidates, including providing nearly half the cash in winning races for the House of Representatives. Restrictions on corporation campaign donations have been in place since 1907, but the modern era of PACs began in World War II with the formation of the National Citizens' Political Action Committee by John L. Lewis, leader of the United Mine Workers of America. Congress had enacted a ban on direct union donations after Franklin D. Roosevelt was elected to a third term in 1940. Lewis formed the PAC to provide money to help FDR win a fourth term in 1944. PACs grew in number as a result of post-WATERGATE reform, when Congress permitted corporations and trade associations to finance the administrative cost of running PACs. While PACs are considered a suspect influence by some, constitutional experts say they are protected under the First Amendment's right of free association guaranteed in the Constitution of the US. R.K.H.

political anthropology. The study of forms and processes of POWER and political organization in both institutional settings and everyday life. It was effectively established as a field with the publication in 1940 of *African Political Systems* edited by Evans-Pritchard and Fortes. The TYPOLOGY the editors drew up was based on the distinction between centralized (state) and uncentralized (acephalous) societies. The work led a strong research agenda for many years into the study of social control, resolution of conflict (see CONFLICT THEORY) and inequality in non-industrial societies. The model came under heavy criticism for being ethnocentric (see ETHNOCENTRISM) and evolutionary (see EVOLUTION), having a MODEL of power derived from Western societies and constituting other societies in accordance with their distance from this baseline. Furthermore it presumed all political power to be coercive (see Clastres, *Society against the State*, 1977). Leach's *Political Systems of Highland Burma* (1954) broke with this model and focused upon political process and the transformations effected at the level of structure. This was a model that the Kachin – a Burmese tribal people – held themselves, but was constantly changing as a result of individuals' choices and power-seeking. The Manchester school under Max Gluckman developed political anthropology in another direction again from the mid-1950s. Gluckman was interested in the role of conflict and the balance of oppositions in the creation of social equilibrium (see *Custom and Conflict in Africa*, 1956). Another leading member of the Manchester school, V. Turner, emphasized the importance of processual and spatial aspects of political life (e.g. *Schism and Continuity in African Society*, 1957). Since the 1960s, political anthropology has been trying to reinvent itself, following third world political struggles and critiques of forms of imperialism and neo-imperialism. More recently another shift was signalled by the influence of Foucault and a revival of Gramsci in SOCIAL THEORY. In terms of the latter's notion of HEGEMONY, attention was drawn to acts of resistance to dominant power holders (see J. Scott, *Weapons of the Weak*, 1985). Foucault's concern with the mechanics of power and the relation of power to knowledge directed political anthropologists to look at how power inheres in everyday practices, and the concrete form taken by relations between the governing and the governed. For further reading: J. Vincent, *Anthropology and Politics* (1990). M.H.

political correctness. The name for a grassroots anti-free speech movement that emerged from the LEFT on American university and college campuses in the 1980s. Its base premise, embraced by advocates of identity politics, was that the everyday use of language and standard academic inquiry tended to uphold harmful group stereotypes, 'dehumanize' people, and encourage homophobia, RACISM and sexism – the three-headed Great Satan of the PC movement. By the early 1990s, many campuses had enacted rules to stamp out 'hate speech', a category broad and vague enough to be used effectively to harass and discredit dissenting views, and encourage self-censorship for the majority. Some institutions de-emphasized the study of standard texts of American literature or books by 'dead white European males', replacing them with lesser works whose protagonists were often victims of Western culture or 'marginalized' by the dominant CULTURE. Any hint that one culture or way of life was superior to another was condemned, unless Western culture, Roman CATHOLICISM or fundamentalist Protestant sects were the ones portrayed as inferior. The movement was noted for such absurdities as the 1992 seizure of snapshots from the History Department at the University of Minnesota in Duluth after a complaint was lodged that the pictures encouraged violence against women. The shots in question showed an ancient historian holding a Roman sword and a military historian with an antique revolver. Ultimately, courts declared that hate-speech sanctions violated the First Amendment right to free speech. As political correctness moved from academia to society at large, it was met with ridicule and parody by many, and acquiescence by others. The movement remains a fact of life at many colleges and universities, and has even spawned a new academic offshoot called 'white studies'. R.K.H.

political culture. A term meant to encompass political values and attitudes wider than intimated by the more formal political system, and to some extent upholding it. A political culture is formed by the practice of politics. It is the sum of the dispositions created by the regular operation of the political system of a particular society. A political culture can encourage participation and involvement by the majority of citizens, as tends to be the case in democratic politics, especially the smaller ones (ancient Athens, 18th-century Geneva). Or it can promote attitudes of passivity and acquiescence, as in authoritarian or totalitarian (see AUTHORITARIANISM; TOTALITARIANISM) political systems (Tsarist Russia, Nazi Germany; see NAZISM).

A political culture is largely formed by the political system, but it depends for its persistence and vitality on the support of other social INSTITUTIONS. In modern societies, there is a complex and sometimes contradictory relation between the attitudes and values developed in formal political practice, and those formed by other institutions such as the family, school, Church and the mass media. Somewhat idealistically, the 'civic culture' of Western DEMOCRACIES is said to exhibit a basic congruence of democratic values and practices across all the major social institutions. What is learned and practised in the family and school matches and confirms the practices of the political system. Elsewhere, the lack of fit between the political system and other institutions can undermine the system. Thus in Germany in the 1920s, the authoritarian tradition still persistent in the German family and educational system is seen as an important cause of the weakness and eventual demise of the democratic WEIMAR REPUBLIC. For further reading: R. E. Dowse and J. A. Hughes, *Political Sociology* (1986). K.K.

political economy. The management of the economy of the STATE. By the end of the 18th century the scope of political economy was limited by a number of writers (Du Pont in France, Verri in Italy, Sir James Steuart and Adam Smith in Great Britain) to problems connected with the *wealth* of a state. Although at this time considerations of the moral, political and social desirability of economic policies and also the administrative problems involved were still included in treatises on political economy, during the early 19th century they were gradually excluded. Throughout that century there were discussions of the definition of political economy and of other methodological issues (see METHODOLOGY). Attempts were made to define the relation between political economy and other SOCIAL SCIENCES, particularly SOCIOLOGY and politics. Distinctions were made between a pure scientific study of economics and the VALUE-JUDGEMENTS that are implied in the political choice of actual economic policies. Towards the end of the century the term political economy was being gradually superseded, in English-speaking countries, by the single word ECONOMICS. This change was partly for convenience, but it also reflected the hope that it would be possible to separate out the positive from the normative aspects of economics. How successful economics has been in making this distinction is a matter of dispute. The change of name may have altered the popular image of economists slightly but it has not abolished the problems or the discussion of scope and method. For further reading: S. Hollander, *The Literature of Political Economy* (1998). M.E.A.B.; J.P.

political geography. The systematic field of GEOGRAPHY that focuses on spatial expressions of political behaviour. This includes a large variety of topics, among them territoriality; the rise of nations, states and NATION-STATES; boundary-making on land and sea; CORE AREAS and capital cities (see URBANIZATION); unitary and federal states (see FEDERALISM); GEOPOLITICS and POWER conflicts; voting patterns; effects of IMPERIALISM; military strategy; and the many spheres of international relations. Political geography in the first half of the 20th century was embroiled in many controversies (none greater than the emergence of *Geopolitik* as a policy tool by the Nazi regime in Germany), and the field declined markedly in the post-war era. A revival has been under way since the 1970s, and political geography today again constitutes a major component of HUMANISTIC GEOGRAPHY. Among its new frontiers is a growing concern with the globalization movement, which is studied from several new perspectives including world-systems analysis. For further reading: R. E. H. Mellor, *Nation, State, and Territory: A Political Geography* (1989). P.O.M.

political science. The study of the organization and conduct of government. This has existed since the time of Aristotle at least. But so long as reflection upon politics remained substantially inseparable from the speculations of 'moral philosophy' about society in general, it could assert no sustained claim to be a discipline in its own right. Only during the later 19th century was its independence adequately established, under British, French and American leadership. Even then, its subject-matter remained uncomfortably ill defined. The new discipline was distinguishable from *political philosophy*, however, in having empirical rather than NORMATIVE interests – i.e. in describing things as they are rather than as they ought to be. The comparative study of governments featured strongly, and was indicative of a dominant concern with INSTITUTIONS. In the second half of this century, however, there has been a considerable shift of emphasis towards behavioural issues (see BEHAVIOURAL SCIENCES). Political scientists now devote much time to probing into the patterns of SOCIAL ACTION and behaviour which underlie the operation of political institutions and which condition such phenomena as the competition for POWER or the making and implementation of public decisions. The consequent involvement in matters of attitude and motivation, value and cognition, suggests the extent of common ground – and the difficulties of demarcation – with, especially, POLITICAL SOCIOLOGY and SOCIAL PSYCHOLOGY. For further reading: A. Finifter (ed.), *Political Science: the State of the Discipline* (1983). M.D.B.

political sociology. A field of study which came into existence to emphasize the sociological dimensions of politics. Major political issues include ÉLITES (see also POWER ÉLITE); LEGITIMACY and effectiveness (e.g. Max Weber's analysis of three types of authority: traditional, charismatic [see CHARISMA], and legal-rational; see LEGAL-RATIONAL AUTHORITY; WEBERIAN); the relation of economic to political development (e.g. Samuel P. Huntington's study of turbulence in the new states created after World War II, *Political Order in Changing Societies*, 1968); DISTRIBUTIVE JUSTICE (see also RELATIVE DEPRIVATION); conditions of DEMOCRACY (attempts to relate effective democracy to the degrees of literacy, PARTICIPATION, the character of voluntary associations, the nature of national character, and the strength of tradition in different societies); TOTALITARIANISM; conditions of REVOLUTIONS; and the political ROLE of social groups, such as the WORKING CLASS or the INTELLECTUALS. Behavioural studies have concentrated in three areas: types of party systems (one-party, two-party, multi-party) and the social bases of parties and political division (e.g. CLASS, RELIGION, RACE); the comparative structure of governments (e.g. centralized and decentralized, presidential and parliamentary); and public opinion. For further reading: R. E. Dowse and J. A. Hughes, *Political Sociology* (1986). D.B.

political theology. A movement in late-20th-century THEOLOGY, characterized by a distinctive critique of the social, political and economic order. It originated in Europe in the 1960s, and is particularly associated with the works of two German theologians, Johann Baptist Metz and Jürgen Moltmann. Like other theologians, they criticized the subjectivist and individualist assumptions of much modern theology, but reinterpreted them as aspects of the 'privatization' of religion under capitalism. Where the political theologians differed from the advocates of secular theology, therefore, was in treating the structures of modern capitalism as part of the problem rather than the solution, and in criticizing these they drew freely on the resources of neo-Marxist thought. Political theology introduced concepts such as 'oppression' and 'liberation' into the theological mainstream, and although, as a movement, it was soon eclipsed by LIBERATION THEOLOGY and other contextual theologies, many of its conclusions are assumed in contemporary theologies. For further reading: O. O'Donovan, *The Desire of the Nations: Rediscovering the Roots of Political Theology* (1996). C.C.

poll tax. A tax levied equally on each citizen. In Britain there have been three attempts to levy such a tax. The first two, in the reign of Richard II, stimulated the Peasants' Revolt of 1381. The third was the 'community charge' which was levied by the local authorities of the UK in the late 1980s. The 'community charge' was a policy disaster. Like its 14th-century predecessors, it was characterized by severe administrative complications, widespread tax evasion and civil disobedience. The tax was widely implicated as a factor in the departure of Mrs Thatcher (see THATCHERISM) as Prime Minister. For further reading: D. Butler *et al*, *Failure in British Government: The Politics of the Poll Tax* (1994). N.O.

pollen analysis. The recognition and counting of pollen grains preserved in a sample of soil or peat. The technique relies on the fact that the exine (outer coat) of pollen is both distinctive as between SPECIES and resistant to decay. The pollen is extracted from a suitable sample and examined under the microscope, the different species being identified and their relative commonness assessed by counting the different grains within a representative area of the microscope slide. There are two principal applications: the establishment of a general pattern of climatic change within the *neothermal period* (following the end of the Ice Age), and the study of local ENVIRONMENTS to assess the effect of man's activities on the flora. The first application has allowed the definition of a number of vegetational zones which have been calibrated by RADIOCARBON DATING methods, thus providing a sequence by means of which associated archaeological material can be dated. The second application has been extensively used to examine the initial effects of forest clearance and the introduction of a food-producing economy on a virgin area. For further reading: K. Faegri and J. Iversen, *Textbook of Pollen Analysis* (1964). B.C.

pollution. The contamination of soil, water or the atmosphere by the introduction of foreign substances in amounts that result in harmful health or environmental effects.

Air, water and ground pollution are usually classified according to their place of origin. *Point source pollution* originates at specific sites, such as smokestacks or waste pipes. *Non-point source pollution* comes from diffuse sources, such as run-off of rainwater which can carry pollutants from farmlands or streets and parking lots into bodies of water or into the soil. *Air pollution* may be gaseous (e.g. carbon monoxide from incomplete burning of fossil fuels) or particulate (e.g. soot from motor vehicle exhausts, wood fires, factories).

Another kind of pollution is caused not

by matter (chemicals or particles) but by sound – compression or pressure waves transmitted thorough the atmosphere. Sound of such an intensity as to cause discomfort is termed noise pollution. Because discomfort levels vary between individuals and among cultures, noise pollution may be difficult to define and to regulate. Evidence that marine mammals, which navigate with the aid of echolocation and communicate through 'song', may be disturbed by sounds generated by humans and transmitted through water (e.g. ship engines) adds new biological dimensions to this kind of pollution. See also ACID RAIN; MINAMATA DISEASE. W.G.R.

polyandry. Term used to describe a form of plural MARRIAGE in which a woman has several husbands. Most commonly, a set of brothers share a single wife: *fraternal* or *adelphic polyandry*. In these cases often only the eldest of the set of brothers undergoes the formal marriage ceremony, the younger brothers becoming husbands *de facto* as they come of age. Sexual access to the wife is on the basis of seniority, but frequently the conditions in which polyandry occurs influence this arrangement. For example, in Ladakh, each household is required to pay labour tribute to the monastery. Brothers take it in turns to perform these services, and while one is absent the one left behind has access to the wife.

Early writers associated polyandry with 'group marriage' and with the existence of MATRIARCHY. It was understood as representing an early stage in the evolution of marriage forms. Later anthropologists have tried to relate its appearance to specific economic conditions. This has been difficult since although polyandry may have superficial cross-cultural similarities, the economic reasons for its appearance in any one society may be quite different. A.G.

polyarchy. A term coined by Robert Dahl (1953) to characterize the working of contemporary American government in which rule by the majority is unfeasible, and DEMOCRACY has come to mean rule by various minorities. Literally, it means 'rule by many' as distinct from what Aristotle feared, namely 'rule by the many'. Dahl's point was that although 'the people' did not and could not govern, nevertheless a lot of people did govern, in contradistinction to dictatorial and totalitarian regimes (see TOTALITARIANISM) where almost everyone was shut out of the corridors of power. For further reading: Robert Dahl, *Polyarchy* (1974). A.R.

polydentate ligand, see under CHELATE.

polygene. When a single characteristic is influenced by GENES at many loci (see LOCUS), its inheritance is said to be polygenic or multifactorial. The genes concerned have sometimes been called polygenes, but they probably differ from other genes only in having a small effect on the characteristic under study. For further reading: D. S. Falconer, *Introduction to Quantitative Genetics* (1960). J.M.S.

polygyny. A form of legitimate plural MARRIAGE (as opposed to illegitimate, i.e. bigamy) in which a man has several wives. Polygyny is occasionally found in Eurasia and it is usually a strategy to provide an heir when an existing wife has failed to produce offspring. It was also practised in the United States by the Mormons until 1890, when federal pressure encouraged them to desist. It is most commonly found in Africa, where approximately 35 per cent of marriages are estimated to be polygynous. A young man would make his first marriage with a woman of a similar age. Later he would acquire other wives through the payment of BRIDEWEALTH and the age differential between the spouses would continue to increase.

Co-wives and their children usually occupy separate huts within the man's compound, but the degree of solidarity between them is very variable. Tensions between co-wives may lead to accusations of WITCHCRAFT. One strategy that reduces hostilities in a polygynous situation is for a man to marry sisters: *sororal polygyny*.

The incidence of polygyny has been linked to certain economic conditions in Africa. It has been suggested that polygyny is associated with extensive or hoe agriculture where labour is the critical factor in production and women play an important role in cultivation. Thus the more wives a man has the greater will be the productivity. Other anthropologists (Goody, *Polygyny, Economy and the Role of Women*, 1973) have linked polygyny not with women as producers, but as reproducers: i.e. their ability to produce children which alleviates labour scarcity and allows expansion in the areas of economic activity. For further reading: D. Parkin, *The Cultural Definition of Political Response: Lineal Destiny Among the Luo* (1978). A.G.

polymer. Any material consisting of macromolecules formed by the linking of many similar chemical units into long chains. Nylon, polythene and many other synthetic plastic substances, as well as PROTEINS and other materials vital to life, are all polymers. Prediction *a priori* (see A POSTERIORI, A PRIORI) of the properties of polymers from the fundamental laws of PHYSICS is very difficult, because of the great structural complexity of these systems. Therefore polymer science is interdisciplinary, and techniques from BIOLOGY, CHEMISTRY and ENGINEERING are being employed to understand, e.g., the physical basis of inheritance (see DNA under NUCLEIC ACID) and the RHEOLOGY of bulk polymers such as wood. M.V.B.

polymorphism. The presence in a single population of more than one genetically distinct type, each at a frequency too high to be explained by repeated MUTATION alone. The study of polymorphism is important for an understanding of EVOLUTION, which depends on populations being variable. J.M.S.

polynomial time, see under EXPONENTIAL TIME.

polynucleotide, see under NUCLEIC ACID.

polypeptide, see undcr PEPTIDE.

polyploid. A CELL containing more than two sets of CHROMOSOMES. In an *autopolyploid* the chromosomes all come from a single SPECIES; in an *allopolyploid* from two or more species. Allopolyploids arise by HYBRIDIZATION between species followed by a doubling of the chromosome number. They are often sexually fertile, even if the DIPLOID hybrid is not. The process has been important in the origin of wild and domestic plant varieties, including wheat and cotton, but is rare or absent in animals. J.M.S.

polyrhythm. The mixture of markedly differing rhythms, effected in such a way as to be a striking feature of the music rather than a mere incidental; in particular, the combination of rhythms based upon different pulses or metres. Dating from the Middle Ages and brought to a point of perfection by the Elizabethan madrigalists, polyrhythm became relatively unimportant in the music of the 18th and 19th centuries, though examples occur in the finale of Mozart's Oboe Quartet and the ballroom scene in *Don Giovanni*. In the 20th century composers as diverse as Charles Ives, Michael Tippett and Olivier Messiaen have been fascinated by the exploration of polyrhythm. A.H.

polysynthetic (*or* **incorporating).** In comparative LINGUISTICS, adjectives sometimes applied to a type of AGGLUTINATING language (e.g. Eskimo) which displays a very high degree of synthesis in its word forms, single words typically containing as much structural information as entire sentences in ISOLATING languages. D.C.

polysystemicism, see under FIRTHIAN.

polytheism, see under PANTHEISM; THEISM.

polytonality. The simultaneous combination of several tonalities, each instrumental line adhering to one key regardless of possible conflict with other lines. Used occasionally in the past for humorous purposes (e.g. Mozart's Musical Joke), it was much exploited in scores by Milhaud (e.g. the Serenade in the 3rd Symphony), Bartók, Stravinsky, Holst (e.g. the Terzetto for Flute, Oboe and Viola) and others. Like BITONALITY, it serves to preserve some of the stability conveyed by traditional tonality, while adding harmonic bite. A.H.

Pont-Aven. School of French painting, centred on the small Breton town of that name, which was much frequented by artists in the late 19th century, notably Gauguin around 1886–89. With a few younger painters, including Émile Bernard and Paul Sérusier, he there established his characteristic way of painting Breton subjects, using simplified outlines, flat two-dimensional surfaces, and clear colours. This SYNTHETISM became, through Sérusier, the launching platform for the NABIS. J.W.

pop. An abbreviation of 'popular' used in the arts since the 1950s to signify work employing aesthetic or symbolic elements calculated to appeal to a modern mass audience. The basis of the calculation is normally commercial, though the use made of the elements is often not. Originating in some measure as an updated and industrialized version of the FOLK concept, it differs in its overtones both from the German *volkstümlich* and from the French *populaire*, and is a purely Anglo-Saxon term which other cultures have had to import. The three main usages are:

(1) *Pop music*. Term used for a broad range of commercial music arising in the 1950s and 1960s in the US and Europe and aimed to a large extent at the growing youth market. Pop music has its roots in the popular song styles of the first half of the century, but has been influenced by rock and roll, country music, ROCK MUSIC, SOUL music, REGGAE, etc. This has led to a diverse range of formats and styles, but dominant among these are the three-minute song, recorded on a single and performed by a vocalist accompanied by electric guitars, electric bass, drums and various other instruments, including more recently electronic musical instruments (see ELECTRONIC MUSIC). Pop music is often criticized for its disposable nature (in contrast to serious music and rock music) and for the massive influence of fashion and commercial interests on its production. These concerns can undoubtedly lead to stagnation and a smothering of other musical styles, but among the vast amount of pop music produced there is an astonishing amount of highly original music. B.CO.

(2) *Pop poetry*. A type of easily intelligible poem, akin to the pop lyric and often appealing to the same age-group, which is written primarily for public reading (often in combination with JAZZ; see JAZZ POETRY) and is associated particularly with the LIVERPOOL POETS, whose rise followed that of the Beatles.

(3) *Pop art*. A term first used in the mid-1950s by the critic Lawrence Alloway to describe such elements as flags, juke-boxes, packaging, comic strips, badges, and chromium-plated radiator grilles, then transferred to the often sophisticated, startling, ironic or nostalgic constructions which high-brow artists began to make out of them. Based largely on the visual trappings of American industry (including the entertainment industry) and contemporary FOLKLORE (from Batman to Marilyn Monroe), much the same symbols served both British (Richard Hamilton, David Hockney, Peter Blake) and American painters (Jim Dine, Andy Warhol, Roy Lichtenstein), who throughout the 1960s used a DADA-like COLLAGE technique and the silk-screen printing process to convey their many-levelled visions. Sometimes isolating the most mundane objects – e.g. the soup tin or the mass-produced hamburger – they were echoed by sculptors like Claes Oldenburg, who made inflated versions of these in all kinds of materials. Lettering and sign-language were further elements which sometimes became dominant. Though the term remained Anglo-American, a similar imagery and approach could be found among Continental artists associated with NOUVEAU RÉALISME, and it also affected the cinema, notably certain films of Jean-Luc Godard and the Beatles' cartoon film *The Yellow Submarine* (1968). Fashion, packaging and GRAPHIC DESIGN quickly conformed, the whole complex sometimes being known as the *pop scene*. For further reading: G. Melly, *Revolt into Style* (1971). J.W.

Popperian. Adjective referring to Sir Karl Popper (1902–94), Professor of Logic and Scientific Method at London University 1949–69, and especially to his views on (1) the nature of scientific procedure and (2) the philosophical foundations for social reform.

(1) Popper's arguments for *deductivism*, or the *hypothetico-deductive method*, are expressed in *The Logic of Scientific Discovery* (1934; English tr. 1959). He contends that a scientific theory can never be accorded more than provisional acceptance, and that even this cannot properly depend upon VERIFICATION of the kind made orthodox by Bacon and Mill. Their *inductivism* (see INDUCTION) suggests that the scientist must accumulate and classify particular observations and thereafter generalize the regularities which these exhibit. Popper retorts that no number of cases of *A* being *B* can establish that all *A*s are *B*. Yet he also notes that such universal statements, though unprovable, remain in principle *disprovable*. According to this principle of *falsifiability*, a theory holds until it is disproved; and falsification, not verification, is the appropriate object of the observational and experimental procedures of science. Enlargement of our

provisional knowledge begins with the conversion of hunches or other imaginative insights into hypotheses. Then, once the conditions for their falsification have been established by the application of deductive LOGIC, such hypotheses must be tested through sustained search for negative instances.

(2) The same distrust of dogmatism pervades Popper's more political writings, such as *The Open Society* (1945) and *The Poverty of Historicism* (1957). He argues that social theories based on mistaken notions of certainty (e.g. 'scientific' MARXISM) breed AUTHORITARIANISM and unrealistic blueprints for total change; they embody a 'holistic' (see HOLISM) insistence that the individual possesses value only in so far as he subserves the needs of the whole. To this Popper opposes his own brand of METHODOLOGICAL INDIVIDUALISM, which seeks to understand 'all collective phenomena as due to the actions, interactions, aims, hopes, and thoughts of individual men, and as due to traditions created and preserved by individual men'. Popper's preference is for programmes of 'piecemeal SOCIAL ENGINEERING', which accord not only with individuals' competing aspirations but also with the spirit of critical self-scrutiny involved in the principle of 'falsification' outlined above. For further reading: J. Shearmur, *The Political Thought of Karl Popper* (1996).

M.D.B.

popular culture. Historically, popular culture refers to the oral, folk or 'little' tradition of the pre-literate mass; this vernacular cultural tradition is usually distinguished from the more esoteric high or 'great' literate culture characterized by its association with objects, texts and scores that are accessible through an extended and developed sense of AESTHETICS. While all have access to popular culture, high culture implies limited ingress. The sensitivity of popular culture to social change contributes to its ephemeral and transient character, and has prompted various conceptualizations and methodological approaches to the phenomenon. In the 1950s Richard Hoggart, Raymond Williams and others extended the serious analysis of CULTURE and the question of aesthetics to include EVERYDAY visual, stylistic and material reflections of the experience of ordinary people and their response to real or imagined structural subordination. Popular culture has since become understood in terms of active processes and practices as well as objects and artifacts, and encompasses a variety of phenomena including mail order catalogues, the design of cars and other consumer durables, clothes, food fashions, football matches, videotapes, Christmas, etc. It has been suggested that popular culture has the capacity to subvert, even invert (Burke cites the historical function of the carnival [see CARNIVALIZATION] to 'turn the world upside down') the established hegemonic order (see HEGEMONY). Cultural élitists have traditionally criticized and attempted to neutralize or improve the culture and LIFESTYLE of the masses.

However, since 'the people' do not constitute an undifferentiated collectivity, their culture will vary according to their structural location and the perceptions that this entails, which has led to sub-cultural analysis (see SUB-CULTURE). Current POST-MODERNIST fascination with popular culture reflects the rediscovery of 'the people' by 18th- and 19th-century European INTELLECTUALS; then as now, the cultural system of the masses was undergoing changes (industrial capitalism, growing literacy, impact of the print media, SECULARIZATION and participatory politics). Contemporary concerns with MASS SOCIETY, the commodification of leisure, identity, etc., under consumer CAPITALISM, have led to an erosion of the distinction between ÉLITE and popular culture, and now cultural SEMIOTICS deconstructs (see DECONSTRUCTION) all REPRESENTATIONS and signs to expose their uniform ideological significance. See also MASS CULTURE; HISTORY FROM BELOW. For further reading: P. Burke, *Popular Culture in Early Modern Europe* (1978).

P.S.L.

popular dance. Sometimes termed social dance, this has its roots in the SOCIAL STRUCTURE of society, in particular interclass relationships, changing attitudes towards women and patterns of social conventions, and the level of TECHNOLOGY. Popular dance therefore reflects the spirit of the age in any particular society, and the term covers all forms of dancing related to recreation and leisure. Historically court dancing and folk dance come into this category, unlike CLASSICAL BALLET or MODERN DANCE. Popular dance plays a significant role in the

general pattern of any society, e.g., in Britain, ballroom dancing in the 19th and early 20th century, rock and roll of the 1950s, the dance crazes of the 1960s like the twist, and free-form dance of the 1970s. Most recent innovations in popular dance have emerged in the street dance of the South Bronx, New York, where *body popping* and *break dancing* have developed into *hip-hop* culture finding expression across all the arts. This form of popular dance clearly exemplifies its social roots, inspired by repetitive drum machine sequences, robotics, and the body-conscious competitive athleticism of the 1980s. For further reading: F. Rust, *Dance in Society* (1969).
L.A.

Popular Front. A COMMUNIST-inspired policy in the 1930s, aimed at bringing about the collaboration of the LEFT and CENTRE parties against RIGHT-wing movements and regimes. It was launched in July 1935 at the 7th Congress of the COMINTERN, after the abandonment of the policy of attacking social democrats (see SOCIAL DEMOCRACY) as 'social FASCISTS', which had contributed to the victory and consolidation of power by the Nazis in Germany (see NAZISM). The new policy of broad Left alliances brought Popular Front governments to power in France and Spain in 1936, and in Chile in 1938. In France the Popular Front government of Léon Blum (which did not include communists, although it was to some extent supported by them) was replaced by that of Daladier after the coalition broke down in April 1938. In Spain the electoral victory of the Popular Front under President Azaña resulted in a CONFRONTATION with the Spanish Right and the civil war which ended in 1939 with the victory of Franco.

Generally, the Popular Front policy came to an end after the conclusion of the Nazi–Soviet pact (August 1939). The new Comintern line, radically changed, lasted until Hitler's attack on the USSR in June 1941. This attack once again led the communists to seek co-operation with other parties in an 'anti-fascist front'.

Since World War II the policy of collaboration with SOCIALIST and 'BOURGEOIS' parties has undergone a variety of modifications, particularly since the emergence of polycentrism. It was abandoned in 1947 with the establishment of the Cominform and a new tough ('Zhdanov') line, but resumed by various communist parties after Stalin's death, and particularly since the Soviet rehabilitation of Tito (see TITOISM) in 1955. This tendency continued. Coalition tactics played an important part in the practice of communist parties, particularly in France, Italy and Spain. For further reading: D. R. Brower, *The New Jacobins: The French Communist Party and the Popular Front* (1968).
L.L.

population ageing. A process of demographic change whereby the distribution of a population by age shifts from the younger to the older age ranges. Typically, this shift is indicated by a rise in the percentage of the elderly, a decline in the percentage of children, and an increase in the mean or median age in the population. Population ageing is an inevitable consequence of the DEMOGRAPHIC TRANSITION and has implications for the fiscal soundness of national pension funds and healthcare systems.
J.R.W.

population biology. The study of all aspects of the structure and function of populations, in so far as they can be distinguished as comprising the unit of organization between the organism and the ECOSYSTEM. The subject includes the discipline of POPULATION GENETICS; population ECOLOGY, including DEMOGRAPHY; and many aspects of SOCIOBIOLOGY.
E.O.W.

population genetics. The study of genetic variation and change in populations; fundamental for an understanding of EVOLUTION, and also of animal and plant breeding. For further reading: J. F. Crow and M. Kimura, *An Introduction to Population Genetics Theory* (1970).
J.M.S.

population geography. The systematic field of GEOGRAPHY that is concerned with the spatial dimensions of DEMOGRAPHY. Population geographers deal with the distribution, composition, growth and movement of people as related to variations in living conditions across the face of our planet. Their work has become quite rigorous in recent years as they cartographically and statistically analyse sets of demographic variables in order to understand the complexities of population clusters and regional patterns. Population geographers all over the world contribute to the design and interpretation of national censuses in their countries, and many are also deeply involved in the demographic planning and policy-making efforts of their governments. (See also MIGRATION.) For further reading: J. L. Newman and G. E. Matzke, *Population: Patterns, Dynamics, and Prospects* (1984). P.O.M.

population growth rate. The net increase in a population due to all sources of demographic change (births – deaths + immigrants – emigrants) divided by the number of individuals in the same population. Thus, the population growth rate equals the BIRTH RATE minus the DEATH RATE plus the MIGRATION RATE. The population growth rate is also referred to as 'Lotka's r' after the mathematician Alfred Lotka, who first developed the theory of stable populations. J.R.W.

population pressure. The tension created by an excess of population (of humans or other species) relative to the resources available and necessary for its maintenance. In other words, population pressure is the tension created by OVERPOPULATION. From a strictly Malthusian perspective (see MALTHUSIANISM), this tension can be relieved only by an increase in the death rate (the 'positive check') or by a decrease in the birth rate (the 'preventive check'). In reality, however, this tension has been resolved by various means (not only by a rising death rate or a falling birth rate, but also by an expansion of the resource base or an increase in rates of out-migration) depending on historical circumstances and choices made by individual members of the population. For example, an excess of population relative to the food supply has led to successful efforts to expand agricultural production during the past two centuries, in both rich and poor countries. Also, population pressure in Europe during the 19th century and in developing countries more recently has served as a catalyst for emigration. J.R.W.

populism. A form of politics which emphasizes the virtues of the uncorrupt and unsophisticated common people against the double-dealing and selfishness to be expected of professional politicians and their intellectual helpers. It can therefore manifest itself in LEFT, RIGHT or centrist forms. On the Left, it flowered in Russia, where the Narodniks believed that Russia might be spared the horrors of CAPITALISM and move directly to a form of SOCIALISM based on the peasant COMMUNE or *mir*. Russian populism had distinguished liberal adherents such as Alexander Herzen, and wilder revolutionary adherents such as Bakunin and Tkachev. In the US, too, populisms have been seen as equally likely to be driven by right-wing fears of social and political change or by left-wing hopes for such change. Senator La Follette's Progressive Party represented the latter, the forces behind Senator Joseph McCarthy (see MCCARTHYISM) the former. Populism in South America in the mid-20th century tended to rely on strong WORKING-CLASS support, yet did not seek a radical transformation of the existing dominant economic and political order: the failure of their economic policies quickly led to loss of popular support. American liberals (see LIBERALISM) such as Edward Shils, Seymour Lipset and Daniel Bell have described all varieties of populism as pathological. Populism flourishes only when orthodox democratic politics does not. For further reading: G. Ionescu and E. Gellner (eds), *Populism* (1969). A.R.; M.A.P.

pornography. The term pornography is generally used to describe the visual or literary representation of the human body in ways which are sexually (see SEX) explicit. However, the distinction between the pornographic and the erotic has often been difficult to maintain, while the meaning of the term can also include any material which is offensive or disruptive of social convention. Nevertheless, the word is most often used in the context of explicit representation of the female body. The way in which women's bodies are displayed in pornography has been described by the critic John Berger as 'the male GAZE', meaning that the image is constructed for male viewers, in a way which makes the woman passive and subject (see SUBJECTIVITY). This widely influential term assumes a heterosexual male gaze, and gay male critics have argued that heterosexual pornography actually reveals not the extent of male control over women but the degree of male fear of women. For further reading: G. Dines, *Pornography: The Production and Consumption of Inequality* (1997). M.S.E.

port-of-trade. Term widely used in ARCHAEOLOGY denoting a defined location on the interface between discrete territories, specializing in the exchange of goods and raw materials between two or more socio-economic systems. B.C.

positional goods. Goods limited not by ECONOMIC GROWTH but by physical and social congestion, so that acquiring these goods depends on advancing relative to others in society. Examples include housing in Manhattan or central London, lake-front property, domestic servants, and goods in fixed supply receiving ECONOMIC RENT (such as a Rembrandt painting). But education as screening for high-status jobs may be the prototypal positional good. Indeed Fred Hirsch, in *Social Limits to Growth* (1977), attributes opposition to integration in the US and Britain as being due not to fears of the reduced quality of superior schools but to their students' loss of edge. The general advance in positional goods is an illusion. E.W.N.

positive economics, see under ECONOMICS.

positive neutrality, see under NON-ALIGNMENT.

positivism. The view that all true knowledge is scientific, in the sense of describing the co-existence and succession of observable phenomena. So named by French philosopher Auguste Comte (1798–1857), it was the leading principle of his comprehensive philosophical system, which took the unsophisticated form, for the most part, of an encyclopedic classification of the findings of scientific inquiry. Positivism is a scientifically oriented form of EMPIRICISM. The word is now most commonly used as an abbreviation for LOGICAL POSITIVISM. In view of its close association with PHENOMENALISM and REDUCTIONISM generally, it is sometimes opposed to REALISM, particularly in the interpretation of the nature of the unobservable theoretical entities that occur in scientific discourse (see OBJECTIVITY). A.Q.

positron. The positively charged anti-particle (see ANTI-MATTER) corresponding to the ELECTRON. M.V.B.

possession, see under OWNERSHIP.

possible worlds. In PHILOSOPHY, situations or states of affairs which are free of internal inconsistency and which therefore do or can exist. The term is standardly employed to denote a situation or 'world' which, whether or not it in fact exists, nevertheless *could* do so. German philosopher Gottfried Leibniz (1646–1716) originated the notion in arguing as follows: God could have created any contradiction-free world he chose. However, his goodness would prompt him to create only the very best such world. Therefore this world – the one we inhabit – must be the best of all possible worlds. In contemporary philosophy the notion is used in attempts to explain the modal concepts 'necessity' and 'contingency'. By means of it *necessary truth* is described as truth in every possible world, and *contingent truth* as truth in at least one possible world. It is claimed to be an important concept for investigating other issues in philosophy and LOGIC besides, but its use is controversial. In its strictest contemporary sense, the concept belongs to the SEMANTIC interpretation of quantified MODAL LOGIC. For further reading: A. Plantinga, *The Nature of Necessity* (1974). A.C.G.

post-capitalist; post-economic, see POST-INDUSTRIAL SOCIETY.

post-colonialism. In literary and cultural studies, a type of cultural theory, often but not always POST-STRUCTURALIST, which seeks to address the cultural conditions characteristic of politically independent societies that until recently formed subordinate parts of larger colonial empires. The term has most commonly been applied to the former British Empire. A controversial extension applies it to all CULTURE affected by the imperial process, from the moment of colonization onwards. The origins of post-colonial theory can be traced to Edward Said's *Orientalism* (1978), a study of the ways in which British and French scholarship constructed the near-Eastern Orient as OTHER. For Said, *Orientalism* was a DISCOURSE, in the sense of the term pioneered by Michel Foucault. Other post-colonial theorists, such as Gayatri Spivak and Homi Bhabha, have made extensive use of post-structuralism, especially the kind of DECONSTRUCTION associated with Jacques Derrida. Spivak is perhaps best known for her advocacy of 'strategic essentialism', which recommends that, whatever deconstruction's theoretical purchase when directed at European HUMANISM, post-colonial theory may need to proceed as if humanism were still valid, whenever it aims to represent insurgent, or 'subaltern', consciousness. Post-colonial theory was originally the work of THIRD WORLD intellectuals: Edward Said is Palestinian, Gayatri Spivak Indian. But recent amendments by Australian and Canadian writers have advanced the controversial argument that these settler colonies are also in some sense analogously post-colonial. A.J.M.

post-communism. The condition of societies that for a greater or lesser period had experienced COMMUNISM, and are now in the process of transition, at least in intent, to liberal market societies (see LIBERALISM; MARKET ECONOMY). The revolutions of 1989 in central and eastern Europe brought down the communist regimes in Poland, Hungary, Czechoslovakia, East Germany, Bulgaria and Romania; by 1991 communism had also gone in Albania, YUGOSLAVIA and the former USSR. In all these countries strenuous efforts are being made, with varying degrees of success, to introduce market economies and PLURALIST systems of DEMOCRACY. This has produced in most cases a new managerial ruling class made up of ex-Party functionaries and a political system with a bewildering number of parties with shallow roots in the population. Post-communist societies face two major problems: the transition from one-party states and command economies to democracy and markets is historically unprecedented, and therefore there are no historical parallels and lessons to guide policy-makers; and secondly, all such societies carry the legacy of between 40 and 70 years of communist rule, which has imbued their populations with certain psychological and social attitudes that create serious obstacles to the introduction of liberal market institutions. What may be even more problematic in the long run is the absence in most of these societies of any tradition of democratic rule, even before the onset of communism, and the weak development of the institutions of civil society. The situation has not been helped by the well-meaning but misguided efforts of some Western advisers to hasten change, especially in the direction of unregulated markets and the private provision of services such as health and education. K.K.

posterior distribution, see under STATISTICS.

post-Fordism. A view of current developments in work and business organizations that suggests that we have moved beyond the era of mass, standardized production – FORDISM – to a system of small-batch, customized production carried on with a flexible workforce using computer-controlled technology that allows for swift and relatively cheap alterations in design and output. The practice of the Italian firm Benetton was one of the earliest indications of the change, and small firms in central and northern Italy – sometimes referred to as the area of the 'Third Italy' – were in general the early leaders in the new forms of work and production. But the changes have not been confined to small firms nor to the Third Italy. Large corporations such as IBM and Olivetti have pushed 'flexible specialization' even further than smaller firms, and areas such as Silicon Valley in the US, the M4 corridor in Britain, and several regions of Germany and Japan have become the forcing-ground of new post-Fordist practices. Whether post-Fordism has comprehensively displaced Fordism is doubtful; the two modes continue to exist happily side by side, in complementary fashion, as is clearest in the case of Japanese industry. But there is no question that it has revolutionized several sectors of production, and it has had particular impact on the 'flexible' workforce that must now expect frequent bouts of retraining and, probably, unemployment. For some theorists, post-Fordism is the core of changes not just in production but in lifestyles and culture generally. It heralds a new kind of society based on a high degree of individual choice, cultural diversity, and decentralized forms of work and organization which to some extent recreate the world of craft production. K.K.

post-Freudians. Those psychologists and therapists of the 1940s to 1960s who, while adopting a broadly FREUDIAN conceptual framework, radically departed from certain central doctrines. Mostly US-based, these typically rejected wholesale UNCONSCIOUS determinism and motivation, reasserting the EGO's capacity for autonomy and the existence of rational motives. They also downplayed, while not rejecting, the role of early infancy in determining adult character, e.g. E. H. Erikson supplemented the five Freudian developmental stages with three others extending throughout adulthood. Karen Horney also offered a less male-centred version as well as rejecting the biologically based universality of Freud's basic model. Other leading post-Freudians included I. H. Hartmann, E. Kris, H. Stack Sullivan and E. Fromm, author of several influential popular diagnoses of the human condition (e.g. *The Fear of Freedom* and *The Sane Society*). Post-Freudians were at one time commonly called 'neo-Freudians', but this term is now usually reserved for those who further developed Freud's original doctrines or gave them a more extreme interpretation (e.g. the British KLEINIAN and the French LACANIAN schools). Post-Freudians by contrast may be considered as having moved in the opposite direction, rendering the theory more optimistic and acceptable in the post-war US cultural climate. For further reading: E. Kurzweil, *The Freudians: A Comparative Perspective* (1989). G.D.R.

post-humanism. In literary and cultural studies, a type of cultural theory that seeks to explore the possibilities of 'post-human' existence. The term seems to have been coined by Ihab Hassan, in 1977, to mark the 'coming to an end' of '500 years of HUMANISM'. In itself, this implied little more than an elaboration of the more generally STRUCTURALIST tendency to explain human SUBJECTIVITY as the effect of structures of DISCOURSE, rather than to see structure as the effect of human agency. However, this theoretical post-humanism has also been complemented by the practical post-humanism of a whole range of new technologies for re-EMBODIMENT and disembodiment. If the 'human' in humanism was by 'nature' neither genetically engineered (see GENETIC ENGINEERING) nor augmented by prosthetics, neither extended by ARTIFICIAL INTELLIGENCE nor into VIRTUAL REALITY, then the users of these kinds of technology might well be considered 'post-human'. Traditionally, the prospects for any such development have been read very negatively, both in humanist high culture and in popular culture. The novelty of recent post-humanist cultural theory, as of some recent PERFORMANCE ART and 'cyberpunk' SCIENCE FICTION, consists in their increasingly positive accounts of what it could mean to be post-human. In performance art, these notions have been explored by Stelarc and Orlan; in science fiction, by William Gibson, Bruce Sterling and Octavia Butler; in cultural theory, by feminist writers such as Donna Haraway and Elizabeth Grosz. A.J.M.

Post-Impressionism. An English term for modern French art from IMPRESSIONISM to World War I. It derived from the Post-Impressionist Exhibitions organized by Roger Fry at the Grafton Gallery, London, in 1910 and 1912, and was used to embrace all the artists revealed there, i.e. the NEO-IMPRESSIONISTS, Gauguin and the PONT-AVEN school, Cézanne, the FAUVES and the early CUBISTS, and also (by adoption) the work of van Gogh. Hence there is no equivalent in German or French. For further reading: J. House and M. A. Stevens (eds), *Post-Impressionism: Cross-currents in European Painting* (1981). J.W.

post-industrial society. A term coined by the American sociologist Daniel Bell (see below) to describe the new SOCIAL STRUCTURES evolving in INDUSTRIAL SOCIETIES in the latter part of the 20th century which (he believes) point the way to the emergence of a new form of society in the USA, Japan, the former USSR and western Europe in the next century. What Bell calls the 'axial principle' of post-industrial society is 'the centrality of theoretical knowledge as the source of innovation and of policy formation for the society'. Economically, it will be marked by the change from a goods-producing to a service economy; occupationally, by the pre-eminence of the professional and technical CLASS; and in decision-making by the creation of new 'intellectual technology'.

The same term has been used by other writers with a different emphasis on the features which they believe will mark post-industrial society, e.g. the search by young people for a world beyond materialism (Kenneth Kenniton, Paul Goodman); or the displacement, as a result of technological change, of the WORKING CLASS from the ROLE assigned to it by MARXISTS as the historic agent of change in society (various NEO-MARXISTS). Other terms which have been used to convey the same idea of the emergence of a new form of society are 'post-economic'; 'post-capitalist' (Ralf Dahrendorf); 'post-maturity' (W. W. Rostow); and 'technetronic' (Z. Brzezinski). For further reading: D. Bell, *The Coming of Post-Industrial Society* (1974). A.L.C.B.

post-Marxism. A loose collection of Western social and political theories that have emerged in the wake of the Soviet bloc's disintegration (see USSR, THE FORMER; MARXISM). Despite its increasing attraction to the LEFT, post-Marxism is nevertheless the most conservative intellectual response to Marxism's declining political fortunes. Post-Marxists typically replace one of the major premises of Marxism and then see how much of the original theoretical edifice remains. The most vulnerable premises concern Marxism's commitments to STRUCTURALISM, DETERMINISM and COLLECTIVISM. However, the results can be strikingly different. At one extreme, Ernesto Laclau and Chantal Mouffe stress the relative autonomy of politics from society's economic infrastructure. They deconstruct the Marxist concept of HEGEMONY, which purports to explain how workers can accept a capitalist ideology (see CAPITALISM; IDEOLOGY) that goes against their class interests (see DECONSTRUCTION). They argue that the desire to participate in a common CULTURE may override sectarian interests, and hence explain, e.g., why workers adhered to Tory political culture in the 1980s, even though few directly benefited from THATCHERITE 'reforms'. At the other extreme, Jon Elster (see below) denies that collective agency exists independently of the combined agency of individuals. Consequently, he explains most of the 'cunning of reason' effects in Marxism as MARKET FAILURES, the unintended consequence of many individuals' activities. While Laclau and Mouffe's post-Marxism gropes towards the sort of civic discourse found in REPUBLICANISM, Elster's version leans towards a LIBERALISM marked by a keen sense of human cognitive limitations. For further reading: J. Elster, *Making Sense of Marx* (1985). S.F.

post-modern classicism. As POST-MODERNISM took over as the reigning AVANT-GARDE architectural stance in the Western world, certain models became more preferred than others. Classical ARCHITECTURE was the main preference – more accurately, the details of classical buildings: keystones, rustication, arches, friezes, fountains, columns, pilasters, domes, vaults, etc. This was partly because the well-defined language of classical architecture was reasonably easily grasped by architects, who all had a cursory training in the history of architecture, partly because clients recognized classicalism from the 19th-century buildings remaining in their cities and believed that they were getting buildings which related to that tradition. Thus designing post-modern classical buildings was a pragmatic response to the market and the fact that other architects would understand the architectural 'jokes'. Increasingly the joke element (never admitted to people outside the closed architectural circle) faded as post-modernists began to regard themselves with great seriousness – including an attempt by some of them to restyle themselves under the heading *symbolic architecture* in which the various details of a building could be explained one by one, providing buildings with a deeper 'meaning' than that given by inventive reuse of formal historical elements. S.L.

post-modern dance. A form of AVANT-GARDE DANCE in the USA that emerged from Cunningham's inspiration (see CUNNINGHAM TECHNIQUE) in the 1960s and broke from the more traditional MODERN DANCE. Post-modern dancers influenced by Anna Halprin, James Waring and Robert Dunn reacted against the expressiveness of modern dance, narrative choreographic content, musical formulae and demands for technical excellence. The post-modern aesthetic proposed changes in structure and performance attitude, and that conceptual development of theories or systems of movement might be a reasonable framework through which to look at movement for its own sake. This aesthetic proposed that dance be akin to real life, using the body in a relaxed, casual and ordinary way, i.e. pedestrian movement; that REAL TIME be used; that attention be deliberately drawn away from skill or virtuosic technique; and that flaws and limitations were not to be hidden from the audience. Since the body was the subject for the dance, it raised direct questions about sexual politics. Analytic post-modern dance used recognizable processes of construction, e.g. accumulation, tasks, systems, aleatoric structure (see ALEATORY), rules, etc., to shape this anti-illusionist approach. For further reading: S. Banes, *Terpsichore in Sneakers* (1980). L.A.

post-modern feminism. A recent development in FEMINIST thinking which seeks to use POST-MODERNIST and POST-STRUCTURALIST theories for feminist ends.

It draws on their analyses of the ubiquitous and fragmentary nature of POWER, and of the role of language in constructing reality, to see language, knowledge and culture both as mechanisms of social control and as arenas of feminist struggle through which hegemonic masculinities can be resisted (see HEGEMONY). It uses post-modern ideas about the impossibility of objective knowledge to reinforce the feminist argument that Western PHILOSOPHY has disguised partial, male perspectives as universal truths. It also builds on post-modernism's critique of stable categories, including the idea of the unified self, to analyse the shifting and fluid nature of GENDER identity and to argue that other feminists have falsely universalized from the experiences of white, middle-class, Western women.

Post-modern feminism is, however, fiercely contested. Critics argue that at best it dresses up good feminist understanding, gained through women's own experiences, in inaccessible philosophical clothes designed by misogynistic men. It is also said to be a deeply conservative philosophy, which seeks to deny women's collective identity and the existence of patriarchal power (see PATRIARCHY). V.A.B.

post-modern theology. A series of movements in theology, at the end of the 20th century, which celebrate the advent of post-modernity in various ways. Since there are many POST-MODERNISMS, there are many post-modern theologies – but what they share is a conviction that the project of the Enlightenment, and all that goes with it in terms of models of SUBJECTIVITY, RATIONALITY, representation, and so on, is now at an end. Some say that post-modern THEOLOGY is anticipated in the work of Karl Barth, or Paul Tillich, in earlier generations, but it owes far more to the giants of French intellectual culture, such as Derrida, Foucault and Lacan, and, through them, to Heidegger and Nietzsche. Different readings of these sources, and of the intellectual and cultural circumstances to which they bear witness, have generated radically different theologies in the 1980s and 1990s. The conflict between them has already become one of the most important debates in contemporary theology, and it is probable that it will move even further up the theological agenda in the years to come. For further reading: D. Griffin *et al*, *Varieties of Postmodern Theology* (1989). C.C.

post-modernism. A now familiar yet still controversial term for defining the overall direction of experimental tendencies in Western arts, ARCHITECTURE, media, etc., since the 1950s, particularly recent developments associated with POST-INDUSTRIAL SOCIETY and cultural GLOBALIZATION. The term holds its own paradox; it suggests MODERNISM is decisively over and a new artistic era has succeeded, yet also implies that successor movements are dependent on it, or in continuous revolt against it. It also suggests a wider historical situation of post-modernity – a post-modern condition, as the French post-structuralist J.-F. Lyotard calls it, a fading of progressive modernity, marked by distinctive ideological, philosophical, cultural, social and technological circumstances, and the end of totalistic explanations or 'grand narratives'. Most modern attempts at definition suggest that the post-modern condition arises from the broad if belated acceptance of modernism and its AVANT-GARDE aspirations as the dominant 20th-century tradition – hence centralizing the AVANT-GARDE, but proposing a later cultural stage in which experience has been transformed by new technologies, typologies and changed world conditions.

In aesthetic terms, this has given the post-1945 artist an unprecedentedly wide, pluricultural range of styles, techniques, technologies, and ranges of reference – and also created distinctive uncertainty about their use and authority. Hence post-modernism is often associated with a revolt against order, representation, narrative, system and signification, and a tendency towards eclecticism, irony, parody, quotation, self-referentiality and indeterminacy. In architecture, post-modernism now refers largely to building design subsequent to the Modern Movement – Mies van der Rohe, etc. – and a move from explicit functionalism towards eclectic quotation and colourful play (e.g. the architecture of Robert Venturi, Richard Rogers, I. M. Pei, Charles Moore). In painting, tendencies from the 1950s acceptance of ABSTRACT EXPRESSIONISM – POP art, CONCEPTUAL ART, body art, video art, the cults of improvisation and installation – have been seen as 'post-modern'. In music, work from Messiaen, Stockhausen, John Cage and John Adams, again marked by amatory qualities, play with techno-sonic effects, and forms of MINIMALISM, have been similarly identified. In literature, the term links a very wide variety of tendencies in fiction, drama and poetry subsequent to James Joyce, and inclining to what John Barth has called 'the literature of exhaustion', a writing at once conscious of the 'usedupedness' of forms and the dying of 'true stories', and of the eclectic possibilities of quotation, pastiche and generic self-consciousness that arise once such notions are accepted. In the novel this ranges among phenomena as diverse as the French NOUVEAU ROMAN, the cut-up novel (William S. Burroughs), the self-reflexive novel (Nabokov, Beckett, Borges, Brooke-Rose), the cybernetic novel (Pynchon, Gaddis, Gibson) and the MAGIC REALIST novel (Marquez, Cortázar, Rushdie, Eco). The general tendency is to render uncertainty, eclecticism and anti-representationalism as the basis of art. Similarly a variety of merged forms – multi-media arts, HAPPENINGS and improvisations, crossovers between high art and kitsch, the hybridization made possible by ever more open access to video, film, digital technologies and editing – can be captured under the heading of post-modernism.

The strongest philosophical context has been that of STUCTURALISM, DECONSTRUCTION and FEMINISM, late-20th-century philosophies of demystification, decanonization and decentring which move beyond humanist notions of subject and object, nature and being, and the 'modern' project of the Enlightenment. Some recent debate – particularly that between the German philosopher Jurgen Habermas and Lyotard – has proposed that post-modernism is the spirit of an age of counter-revolutionary politics, *avant-garde* exhaustion and defeated PROGRESSIVE impulses, in contrast to a stronger, more ideologically conscious modernism. But as modernism contained both the radical and the conservative, so has post-modernism, which has shown a tendency to aesthetic play, but has also owed much to the radical movements of the 1960s, and later feminist and post-colonial critiques of society (see POST-COLONIALISM), identity, NATIONALISM and patriarchalism (see PATRIARCHY). As modernism was a broad church containing many schisms and counter-tendencies, so it is with post-modernism. However, the contrasting strands and tendencies are harder to identify, because they are part of continuing contemporary debate and activity, and because the definition of post-modernism has become ever more wide-ranging and inclusive.

Indeed, according to Charles Jencks, 'In the last ten years post-modernism has become more than a social condition and cultural movement, it has become a world view.' Recent studies have emphasized this, devoting themselves not simply to artistic and cultural phenomena but to the changing PARADIGM of the age, deriving from structures of scientific knowledge, psycho-social notions of the decentring of the subject, medical advances in GENETICS and CLONING, the internationalization of experience in a time of rapid media access to other cultures, and the acceleration of technological change in post-industrial society. Fredric Jameson has it that 'Post-modernism is what you have when the modernization process is complete and nature is gone for good', creating a world of simulacra, commodity FETISHISM, NARCISSISM, affectless eroticism, depthless history, and, in cultural expression, 'the first specifically North American global style'.

Yet, for all the energetic argument, and the dominant sense that the latter half of the 20th century has seen a fundamental cultural change that has accelerated since the collapse of MARXISM, post-modernism remains a catch-all term. It designates a still-amorphous body of cultural trends and directions, marked by eclecticism, pluriculturalism, and a post-industrial, hi-tech, internationalist frame of reference, coupled with a sceptical view of the technical progress which nonetheless enables many of its manifestations. Like structuralism and reconstruction, it appears both to revolt against and seek to recover HUMANISM and some form of historical MATERIALISM. To date, it remains best seen as a complex map of late-20th-century cultural expressions, social directions, fantasies and anxieties, rather than as a clear-cut aesthetic or philosophical ideology. For further reading: J-F. Lyotard, *The Postmodern Condition* (1979; 1984); F. Jameson, *Post-modernism: Or the Cultural Logic of Late Capitalism* (1991); D. L. Marsden, *Post-modernism: A Bibliography. 1926–1994* (1995). M.S.BR.

post-natal depression. The emotional or psychological upset which may occur after childbirth and before the return of normal menstruation. Before the antibiotic era the extreme form of post-natal PSYCHOSIS was usually due to puerperal fever, resulting from infection of the womb and carrying a high death rate. In the 1960s, Dr Brice Pitt did much to emphasize the misery of post-natal blues, in which unexpected, emotional crying occurs during the first two weeks after birth, and also of post-natal depression, which is more severe, lasts longer and occurs in some 10 per cent of all new mothers. Health visitors today are expected to check for post-natal depression at their six-week examination of all new mothers and, if present, either to refer them to their general practitioner or to counsel them. Post-natal depression may result from sociological conditions (single parenthood, lack of support, difficulty in adjustment from a career); it may result from genetic factors; or from the massive fall in placental progesterone which occurs at the moment of birth; or it may herald a psychological disease (SCHIZOPHRENIA; MANIC-DEPRESSIVE PSYCHOSIS). In the severe form of psychosis there is lack of maternal behaviour with rejection of the baby, hallucinations, infanticidal and suicidal fears. K.D.

post-painterly abstraction, see under MINIMAL ART.

post-processual archaeology. A reaction to new or processual archaeology, it rejects most of its tenets, seeing it as reducing the explanation of human behaviour to ecological factors (see ECOLOGY). Instead, post-processualists seek the reasons for change within the cultures themselves, as specific responses to particular conditions, and see culture as a set of symbols that evoke meanings which vary according to context and history. For further reading: I. Hodder, *Reading the Past* (1986). P.G.B.

post-structuralism. A set of extremely influential cultural theories, which share some of the central thematics and much of the theoretical vocabulary of STRUCTURALISM, but which abandon the older structuralist aspiration to scientificity, on the grounds that meaning is ultimately always indeterminate. The three key figures in this movement were Jacques Derrida, Michel Foucault (1926–84) and Jacques Lacan (1901–81). Where structuralism had privileged the linguistic sign (see SIGNIFIER/SIGNIFIED) over the referent, Derrida argued that writing consisted not of signs, but of signifiers. Writing is thus an indefinite referral of signifier to signifier and is thereby infinitely equivocal. Where structuralism had recognized that language is founded on DIFFÉRANCE, Derrida stressed that difference is also always deferral. Derrida's DECONSTRUCTION is a kind of textual analysis designed to uncover these deferred meanings. Foucault's 'genealogy' was concerned with the interconnectedness of DISCOURSE and POWER (see DISCOURSE OF POWER). The theoretical innovation here consisted in the argument that such connectedness was internal to discourse; and in a view of the human BODY as both an object of control and a source of resistance. For Foucault, power had become essentially ubiquitous in modern society, and this rendered it open and indeterminate. Lacan's central proposition was that the UNCONSCIOUS is structured like a language. This led to the notion that language and sexual identity are acquired simultaneously (see SEXUALITY; LACANIAN). He argued that the child originally inhabits a pre-Oedipal (see OEDIPUS COMPLEX) 'IMAGINARY', characterized by speechless identity with the mother, and acquires SUBJECTIVITY only by entering into the symbolic order of language and only at the price of a loss of this imaginary. Thereafter DESIRE moves restlessly from object to object, from signifier to signifier. These ideas have been especially significant in PHILOSOPHY and in literary and cultural studies, in particular those varieties most strongly influenced by FEMINISM and POSTMODERNISM. For further reading: J. Sturrock (ed.), *Structuralism and Since: From Lévi-Strauss to Derrida* (1979). A.J.M.

post-traumatic stress disorder/syndrome. Term accepted by the American Psychiatric Association (1980) for extreme psychological distress following involvement in a traumatic event (abbreviated PTSS or PTSD). The earliest forms recognized appear to have been 'cannon-ball wind' (suffered by early-19th-century soldiers) and 'railway spine' (which afflicted late-19th-century survivors of railway accidents). During World War I, however, the psychological, as opposed to physiological, nature of such distress was first acknowledged by British psychologists such as C. S. Myers and W. H. R. Rivers working with SHELLSHOCK (coined by Myers and later renamed 'combat fatigue'). Only during the 1970s did serious attention begin to be paid to PTSD in civilian contexts. Following a period of some resistance it is now accepted that emergency service workers and survivors can benefit from debriefing and counselling following a disaster or traumatic event, thereby averting or reducing long-term psychological problems. (This development, in Britain at any rate, probably reflects a wider willingness to abandon a traditional 'stiff upper lip' stoical attitude to emotional suffering.) Initiating traumas can be of the most diverse kinds. Symptoms vary widely but typically include flashbacks, guilt, depression, loss of motivation and psychosomatic disorders of many kinds, while traumatic childhood abuse has been controversially linked to MULTIPLE PERSONALITY DISORDER. For further reading: J. R. Freedy and S. E. Hobfoll (eds), *Traumatic Stress from Theory to Practice* (1995). G.D.R.

postulational method, see under AXIOMATICS.

post-Webern school. Collective name given to those composers in the 1950s who were influenced by the work of Anton Webern. The most important of these are Boulez and Stockhausen, and some of the areas they developed were total serialism (see SERIAL MUSIC), POINTILLISM and MOBILE FORM. For further reading: R. Smith Brindle, *The New Music* (1975). B.CO.

potassium-argon dating, see under DATING.

potlatch. 'To give'; potlatch is a form of institutionalized *gift exchange* (see GIFT; EXCHANGE). It was found among the Kwakiutl and other Indian communities of the American north-west. A detailed study of potlatching was made by Franz Boas (*Kwakiutl Ethnography*, 1897) and his work was used by Marcel Mauss (1872–1950) in his development of a theory of gift exchange. A potlatch is a public distribution of goods and the holder of a potlatch makes a claim to STATUS on the basis of his POWER to give. Goods for redistribution may have been accumulated through a cycle of smaller potlatches and from the NETWORK of gifts and loans which bind kin or members of a DESCENT group. In giving the potlatch the holder binds the recipients in a relationship of debt. The system is fiercely competitive, with each holder trying to outdo rivals in generosity.

It has been suggested that the potlatch has a sound economic rationale. It redistributes food from those with surplus to those experiencing temporary shortage. At the same time it allows the holder to convert perishable goods into durable status. On occasions a potlatch may involve a dramatic public destruction of property, and the holder lays down a challenge to his rivals to outbid him in the amount they can destroy. There are a number of similarities between the potlatch system of the Kwakiutl and the kinds of ceremonial exchange, for example the KULA and *moka*, found in New Guinea. A.G.

Potsdam. The site of the last great conference between the USSR, US and Britain of World War II (see also YALTA), held after the German capitulation from 17 July to 2 August 1945. The main actors were Stalin, Truman and Churchill, the latter being replaced by the new Prime Minister, Attlee, during the conference. The three powers attempted to resolve a series of questions including war reparations, the boundaries of Poland, treatment of Germany's European allies, and the post-war political character of Germany. The contemporaneous successful testing in the US of the atomic bomb encouraged President Truman to lead the issue of the Potsdam Declaration, which demanded the unconditional surrender of Japan, whose resistance was met with the decision to drop an atomic bomb on HIROSHIMA. For further reading: A. W. de Porte, *Europe between the Superpowers* (1986). S.R.

Poujadism. A set of attitudes derived from a political movement founded by Pierre Poujade, a French small-town shopkeeper, in 1953. These embodied lower-middle-class, PETIT BOURGEOIS resentment at the increasing interference of the state through taxation, investigation of tax evasion, and other regulatory powers over their economic freedom of action. Poujadism was essentially hostile to the state as anything more than the provider of LAW AND ORDER, and therefore to modernization or any encouragement of large-scale labour or business organization. The Poujadist Association for Defence of Shopkeepers and Artisans won 50 seats and three million votes in the 1956 parliamentary elections, but disintegrated in the political crisis of 1958 with the advent of GAULLISM. D.C.W.

poverty. Poverty is the lack of sufficient income and other resources (including the income roughly equivalent to the use of assets and receipt of goods or services in kind) to enable individuals to exist or subsist from day to day, but also minimally meet their social obligations created by the STATE, employers, market, custom and living in families and COMMUNITIES. There are therefore scientific criteria of need, scale and kind of deprivation, external to income, which have to be specified in determining the level of the 'poverty line' of income appropriate for a society. The level must be set according to uniform criteria, but will vary in practice from country to country.

For many decades there has been a struggle to extricate the concept from political IDEOLOGY – in particular to overcome the prejudice that the poor can make do with money to meet their barest physical but not their social needs, and that standards of need have to be much more generous for rich than for poor countries. There has been a significant breakthrough in the 1990s. In 1995, 117 countries signed a declaration at the Copenhagen World Summit on Social Development agreeing that a two-tier measure of 'absolute' and 'overall' poverty should be applied to every country. In a statement to the European Parliament in March 1997, more than 100 European social scientists urged the adoption of that agreement, so that standards of living in different countries could be better compared, and priorities for remedial action better justified. See also ABSOLUTE POVERTY. For further reading: P. Townsend, *The International Analysis of Poverty* (1993). P.T.

poverty trap. The process by which the less well-off in society become poorer as a result of the workings of the tax and benefits system. In recent years the poverty trap both in Britain and the US has been perceived as a critical problem as changes in the tax system brought about by the Reagan–Thatcher economic revolutions (see REAGANISM; THATCHERISM) served to increase income inequality, trapping up to one-third of the population in Britain in poverty. Once caught in the poverty trap people often find themselves better off claiming WELFARE benefits from the state than re-entering the jobs market, which might give them the opportunity to climb a ladder of opportunity. The combination of the poverty trap and welfare dependency led President Clinton to introduce welfare reforms in the US which have so far taken one million people off the welfare rolls. Similar reforms are being contemplated in the UK in an effort to create an escape route. For further reading: A. Goodman *et al*, *Inequality in the UK* (1997). A.BR.

power. One of the central CONCEPTS of political theory, which sociologists have sought to define by distinguishing it from *authority* on the one hand, and from *force* on the other.

Power is the ability of its holders to exact compliance or obedience of other individuals to their *will*, on whatsoever basis. Yet, as Rousseau observed in *The Social Contract* (1762), 'The strongest man is never strong enough to be always master unless he transforms his power into right and obedience into duty.'

Authority is an attribute of social organization – a family, a corporation, a university, a government – in which command inheres in the recognition of some greater competence lodged either in the person or in the office itself. Relations between states – in the absence of any common framework of law or consensus – are usually power relations. Relations between individuals and groups, if regularized and subject to rules, traditional or legal, tend to be authority relations.

Force is a compulsion, sometimes physical (when it then becomes violence), invoked by wielders of power and authority. Force may be utilized in support of authority, as in the spanking of a child or the imprisonment of a felon. And the threat of force often lies behind the use of power to enforce a power-holder's will. Yet there are examples of the use of power (i.e. will) in history without force, such as Gandhi's *satyagraha* (NON-VIOLENT RESISTANCE) to British authority.

In political theory, the state alone, among modern associations, can make legitimate use of police and military force in the exercise of its authority. In contemporary social theory, the important component in the exercise of authority is LEGITIMACY, the rightful rulc or exercise of power, based on some principle (e.g. consent) jointly accepted by the ruler and the ruled. For further reading: S. Lukes, *Power* (1974). D.B.

power élite. A phrase coined by the American sociologist C. Wright Mills (1916–62) for those who stand at the heads of the major institutional hierarchies of modern society – the corporations, the military and the state – and who, through their pooled interests, become 'an intricate set of overlapping cliques [sharing] decisions having at least national consequences'. The theory has been criticized by MARXISTS for its focus on ÉLITES, rather than on CLASSES, and by liberals (see LIBERALISM) for preaching a conspiracy theory of POWER; for confusing *arenas* of action (e.g. the political system) with INSTITUTIONS; for loosely asserting a shared degree of interests between institutional sectors, rather than organized groups; and for failing to focus on decision-making and decisions, rather than on institutional hierarchies. For further reading: C. W. Mills, *The Power Elite* (1956). D.B.

power politics. An emotive phrase applied to the employment of calculations of comparative POWER and influence made by those responsible for the major powers' conduct of foreign policy, as in the phrase 'playing power politics'. Critics of power politics wish to substitute for it the rule of ETHICS, law and justice in international relations; others hold that, so long as the world is divided into independent sovereign states, there is no alternative to international relations being based upon considerations of power, and that it is self-deception to pretend otherwise. For further reading: M. Wight, *Power Politics* (1977). A.L.C.B.

PR. Abbreviation for either PROPORTIONAL REPRESENTATION or PUBLIC RELATIONS.

practical criticism, see under LEAVISITE.

pragmatics. In LINGUISTICS, the study of language from the viewpoint of the users, especially of the choices they make, the constraints they encounter in using language in social interaction, and the effects their use of language has on the other participants in the act of communication. This field, which deals with such diverse topics as politeness, conversational interaction, DEIXIS, PRESUPPOSITION and SPEECH ACTS, is not as yet capable of clear definition or delimitation from such areas as SEMANTICS and SOCIOLINGUISTICS. For further reading: G. Yule, *Pragmatics* (1996). D.C.

pragmatism. In PHILOSOPHY, a version of EMPIRICISM, developed at the turn of the century in the USA by C. S. Peirce, William James and John Dewey, which interprets the meaning and justification of our beliefs in terms of their 'practical' effects or content. Peirce's pragmatic maxim was a theory of MEANING which identified the content of a PROPOSITION with the experienceable difference between its being true and its being false. James put forward a pragmatic theory of TRUTH as that which it is ultimately satisfying to believe, either because the expectations a true belief excites are actually fulfilled or, in the less empirical case of the propositions of THEOLOGY and METAPHYSICS, because they contribute to the satisfactoriness of, and effectiveness in, the conduct of life. Dewey stressed that aspect of pragmatism which holds knowledge to be an instrument for action, rather than an object of disinterested contemplation. In general, pragmatists emphasize the conventional character of the CONCEPTS and beliefs with which we seek to understand the world as opposed to the 'intellectualism' which sees them as a passive reflection of the fixed, objective structure of things. An incentive to this view has been the idea that mutually inconsistent scientific theories can each be compatible with all the known empirical data so that only non-logical features of simplicity, convenience and utility can provide a reason for selection between them. For further reading: A. Rorty (ed.), *Pragmatic Philosophy* (1966). A.Q.

Prague. The capital of the former CZECHOSLOVAKIA and the scene of three major crises of 20th-century European history, each of which is frequently named after it.

(1) *Prague, 1939*. In March 1939 Hitler ordered the occupation by force of the capital and the rest of Czechoslovakia, which had already been truncated by the MUNICH agreement of 1938. Apart from the consequences for the Czech people, who spent the next six years under German 'protection', this new and undisguised act of aggression ended any illusions that Hitler would be satisfied with the incorporation into the Third Reich of territories with a German-speaking population, and confronted the other powers with the choice between acquiescing in Hitler's domination of Europe or steeling themselves to fight in order to prevent it. A.L.C.B.

(2) *Prague, 1948*. In February 1948 the Czechoslovak COMMUNIST Party, with its adjunct the Slovak Communist Party, seized power and replaced the coalition government, in which they were already the largest single element, with a virtual single-party dictatorship. The coup was achieved by a combination of mass demonstrations and threats, while technically remaining within the forms of the constitution; the term *coup de Prague* has come to be used generally for any quasi-constitutional change backed by street pressures. As in the case of (1), apart from the consequences for the people of Czechoslovakia themselves, Prague 1948 ended illusions in the West that the Soviet Union would be satisfied with anything less than complete control through local communist regimes of the countries within her sphere of influence in eastern and central Europe, and led to an intensification of the COLD WAR. R.C.; A.L.C.B.

(3) *Prague, 1968*, refers to two developments which attracted worldwide attention. The first, known as the *Prague Spring* (from an annual music festival in the capital), was the attempt by reforming elements in the Czechoslovak Communist Party, with growing public support, to liberalize domestic affairs ('SOCIALISM with a human face') and achieve some international freedom of action without abandoning overall Party control or Warsaw Pact membership. Replacement of Antonin Novotný by the more open-minded Slovak Alexander Dubček as Party leader in January earned the backing of Slovak autonomists for a cautious reform programme. The second development was the open intervention of the Soviet Union to suppress the CZECH REFORM MOVEMENT, which led to the invasion of Czechoslovakia by Soviet armed forces in August 1968 and the replacement of Dubček by the conservative Gustáv Husák eight months later. The Party Congress held secretly during the invasion in Prague-Vysoçany was then annulled, censorship reimposed, the ideas of the reformists abjured in favour of so-called NORMALIZATION, and their spokesmen decried as REVISIONIST or counter-revolutionary. For further reading: H. G. Skilling, *Czechoslovakia's Interrupted Revolution* (1976). D.V.

Prague School. A group of linguists (notably R. Jakobson and N. Trubetskoy; see LINGUISTICS) working in and around Prague in the late 1920s and early 1930s. Their primary contribution was the formulation of an influential theory of PHONOLOGY in which sounds were analysed into sets of distinctive oppositions. Later, a *neo-Prague school* concentrated on developing syntactic theory in terms of the SAUSSURIAN notion of functionally contrastive constituents of sentences (see SYNTAGMATIC AND PARADIG-

MATIC): this is known as FUNCTIONAL SENTENCE PERSPECTIVE (FSP). For further reading: J. Vachek (ed.), *A Prague School Reader in Linguistics* (1966). D.C.

Prague Spring, see under PRAGUE (3).

Pravda (*Truth*). Defunct daily newspaper of the former USSR, when it was the official organ of the Soviet COMMUNIST Party – its editorials provided the best indication of the current party line. It was founded in 1912 and published legally in Tsarist Russia until 1914, when it was banned because of its 'revolutionary defeatism'. It reappeared after the 1917 February revolution, and from October 1917 was the leading Soviet journal. However, its readership collapsed as the USSR broke up, and although private investors tried to rescue it, it was finally shut down in 1996. Its editors had included Stalin and Bukharin. L.L.; S.T.

praxis. This Greek term for 'action' or 'practice' was given a special meaning in the early philosophy of Karl Marx (see MARXISM). It refers to the idea of 'the unity of theory and practice'. Thought or theory, Marx claimed, cannot be seen as separate from practice, as some abstract standard or contemplative ideal. It arises out of practice, and is developed and modified by it. Marx considered that the split between 'ideal' and 'reality', between an irrational world and a RATIONALIST critique of it, could only be overcome by the development of a theoretical consciousness among social groups engaged in the practice of changing the real world. The praxis of the PROLETARIAT, therefore, would consist in the growth of a SOCIALIST consciousness arising out of the conditions of life of the proletariat and its attempts to transform them. For further reading: L. Kolakowski, *Main Currents of Marxism*, vol. I (1981). K.K.

prebiotic chemistry. The study of the chemical events that led to the origin of life on earth. Although it has been shown that complex biological MOLECULES can be formed from simple chemicals under the conditions that are thought to have prevailed in prebiotic times, these experiments are far removed from the experimental creation of life, and there is no prospect of that being achieved in the foreseeable future. As a result a few people have been driven to take seriously the concept of PANSPERMIA, even if that simply passes the problem on to another time and place. P.N.

precasting, see under CONCRETE.

precession, see under GYROSCOPE.

Precisionism. A name given to American REALIST painting in the 1920s and 1930s that combined ideas and techniques of photography and CUBISM in its representation of the contemporary industrial landscape. So-called Precisionists Charles Sheeler, Charles Demuth and Preston Dickinson painted machine forms and domestic architecture with dryness, clean detail and sharp focus that occasionally bordered on abstraction (see ABSTRACT ART). For further reading: S. Hunter, *American Art of the 20th Century* (1972). A.K.W.

precognition. The direct awareness of future events, or true prophecy, as contrasted with the rational prediction which derives beliefs about the future, which there is good reason to think true, from the present state of things, together with more or less well-confirmed laws of nature. Memory, as distinct from apparent memory, implies that the event remembered really has happened. Likewise precognition implies that the event precognized really will happen. It can be argued that precognition is impossible in so far as the notion of knowledge that is logically included in it entails that the state of knowing is caused by the fact known. For if there were precognition a future event would have to cause a present one and a cause can never be temporally subsequent to its effect. This, however, is a semantic point. It does not mean that people cannot have true, uninferred beliefs about the future but only that, since this cannot be causally explained, it cannot be called knowledge. A.Q.

preconscious. In psychoanalytic theory (see PSYCHOANALYSIS), a word used in two ways. (1) To refer to thoughts which, although not actually present in CONSCIOUSNESS, are nevertheless capable of being brought into consciousness by ordinary recall and effort. By contrast, UNCONSCIOUS thoughts can be recovered only – if at all – by the aid of technical methods, such as PSYCHOTHERAPY and psychoanalysis (see also REPRESSION). (2) To refer to the part of the mental system, or apparatus, that contains these preconscious thoughts. B.A.F.

predicate calculus. One of the two chief logical calculi, consisting of a formal system of notation, axioms and rules for handling QUANTIFICATION. See also AXIOMATICS. R.G.

pre-emptive strike, see under STRATEGIC CAPABILITY.

prefabrication (*or* **industrialized building).** The manufacture of building elements for subsequent assembly at the site in an attempt to shift the major effort to the controlled conditions of the factory. The factory may be either, e.g., a distant plant making complete bathroom units, or an enclosure on or near the site making cladding panels of precast CONCRETE.

Prefabrication in any serious sense began in the 19th century with the manufacture of cast- and wrought-iron structural members, particularly where these, together with glass, were marketed to provide complete greenhouses. After 1945 systems of industrialized building were developed in which a coordinated range of components could be assembled to provide whole schools or flats. In the former USSR and eastern Europe the method was widely used for housing. Industrialized systems, however, have not yet shown the economic benefits claimed for them, while the visual effect has frequently been undistinguished. For further reading: B. Kelly, *The Prefabrication of Houses* (1951). M.BR.

preference. In ECONOMICS, an international trading arrangement between two countries or more whereby one or both give favourable treatment to the other(s) by removing or lowering its/their existing tariffs. Preferences run counter to an alternative principle in trading arrangements, which argues that they should be entirely non-discriminatory, a principle enshrined in GATT. Preferences have become highly controversial as the expanding EUROPEAN UNION (EU) makes preferential arrangements with an increasing number of countries in the Mediterranean area as well as in Africa. For further reading: B. Sodersten, *International Economics* (1980). D.E.

preformation *and* **epigenesis.** Alternative interpretations, thought in Victorian times to be mutually exclusive, of the development of animals and plants. Preformationists believed that the adult simply enlarges or unfolds from a miniature precursor, e.g. homunculus; epigenesists that development results from the evocative influences of the ENVIRONMENT shaping the germ into its adult form. The truth is now known to lie somewhere between the two: the genetic instructions which are followed in development are certainly preformed – or at all events inherited – but their working out and realization is epigenetic in pattern, i.e. depends upon an interplay between environmental stimuli and the effects of neighbouring CELLS upon the genetic programme built into them. See also EMBRYOLOGY. P.M.

prefrontal leucotomy, see under LEUCOTOMY.

prehistory. The study of the past of a given region before the appearance of written records relevant to that region. See also ARCHAEOLOGY. B.C.

premenstrual syndrome (PMS). The recurrence of symptoms before menstruation – which disappear again after menstruation – severe enough to require medication or severely interfere with work and social life. Tension is the most common symptom and was recognized by Hippocrates, who described the monthly irritability and depression as due to 'agitated blood trying to find an outlet from the woman's body'. With the recognition by Greene and Dalton in 1953 that it is not only psychological symptoms which can occur regularly each month, but also physical symptoms like asthma, headaches, acne or epilepsy, the term premenstrual syndrome was introduced. PMS interferes with all aspects of the woman's life, including mental ability, and for that reason some have advocated changes in education methods in schools and universities, to avoid end-of-course examinations in favour of projects which can be completed when the woman is not in her dull premenstruum. PMS may cause amnesia, uncontrolled behaviour and irritability, which may be accepted in law as a responsible factor in murder, and in mitigation for arson, assault, theft and child negligence, with probation granted subject to effective treatment. It is caused by menstrual hormone changes, relating especially to progesterone, which is only present after ovulation. Symptoms ease during pregnancy when menstruation ceases and the placenta produces massive amounts of progesterone. PMS is an illustration of the theory that psychiatric problems may be due to disorder in brain chemicals rather than life events. For further reading: H. Chihal, *Premenstrual Syndrome: A Clinic Manual* (1990). K.D.

preon, see under ELEMENTARY PARTICLES.

prepared piano. A piano whose timbre is altered by the attachment of a variety of objects (metal, rubber, wood, glass, etc.) to the strings and hammers so as to produce intriguing and unexpected sounds. It resulted from the compositional investigations of the American John Cage. Part of the effect lies in the denial of expectation: seeing a piano, the audience has a preconceived notion of the sound it will make. A.H.

preparedness continuum. In the early 1970s it became apparent to experimental psychologists that innate factors (i.e. level of biological preparedness) affected the ease with which some stimulus-response pairings were learned (see EXPERIMENTAL PSYCHOLOGY). A continuum between 'prepared' and 'contraprepared' was thus proposed. For example, it is virtually impossible to condition wing-preening in pigeons to a food reward (contraprepared). This phenomenon set limits on the applicability of classical learning theory, effectively compelling learning theorists to reincorporate genetic factors (see GENETICS/GENOMICS) and abandon the radical ENVIRONMENTALISM originally characterizing this research tradition. G.D.R.

preppie. An early POPULAR CULTURE manifestation among young people after the 1960s of a return (see PERMISSIVE; HIPPIES) to a more conventional and conformist LIFESTYLE, attitudes and external appearance. Loosely based on folk memories of 1950s élitist East Coast American prep school styles (specific brands of button-down shirts, shoes and trousers and short neat haircuts), its display of 'higher' cultural SYMBOLS reflects a distancing from counter-cultural (see UNDERGROUND) forms. P.S.L.

prequark, see under ELEMENTARY PARTICLES.

Presbyterianism. A system of church government. In the New Testament, an 'elder' (Greek *presbuteros*) is a leader of a Christian congregation. Returning to that system as part of their Calvinist (see CALVINISM) THEOLOGY, Presbyterian churches have been established around the world, including the Church of Scotland. 'Elders' lead a local church; one of them is 'the Minister', who preaches, and representatives gather in a 'Presbytery', which supervises church life in an area. Both EPISCOPALISM and the independence of the congregation are rejected. In the 1980s about 43 million Christians belonged to such churches, and more than five times as many adhered to 'united' churches influenced by this tradition but often having bishops with limited powers. D.L.E.

presence. Presence is a particularly significant term in the early work of Jacques Derrida. Speech has been privileged over writing in Western PHILOSOPHY since Plato, according to Derrida, because both speaker and listener are simultaneously present (in both the temporal and spatial senses) to the spoken word; this gives rise to the notion that writing is a corrupt form of speech, open to misinterpretation due to the absence of the utterer. Being has been determined as presence in Western METAPHYSICS, leading to what Derrida characterizes as the LOGOCENTRISM of Western thought. Derrida argues that 'all the terms related to fundamentals' in Western metaphysics depend upon the notion of constant presence, and thus that the history of that metaphysics rests upon the false premise that words refer to meanings present in their utterance. The premise is false because meaning is created through a play of differences between SIGNIFIER and signified: a sign has no independent meaning for it always contains traces of other, absent signs, whether spoken or written. The present itself, e.g., always contains traces of what it is not, what is absent from it (the past and the future). For further reading: J. Derrida, *Writing and Difference* (1978). M.H.

prescriptive, see under NORMATIVE.

prescriptivism, see under EMOTIVISM.

present-value method, see under DISCOUNTED CASH FLOW.

presidentialism (France). The 1958 Constitution of the Fifth Republic was written by General de Gaulle (President of the Republic 1958–69) and close associates such as Michel Debré (Prime Minister 1958–62). De Gaulle (see GAULLISM) believed that the parliamentary system of government (see PARLIAMENTARIANISM) which had existed during the Fourth Republic (1945–58) had been a major cause of the political instability and eventual collapse of this regime (see CONSTITUTIONAL GOVERNMENT; CONSTITUTIONALISM). The primary objective of the authors of the 1958 Constitution, therefore, was to establish a powerful political executive which would no longer be at the mercy of parliament. This was achieved in two ways: the legislative powers of parliament were substantially reduced; and executive power shared between a prime minister, who is 'in general charge of the work of the government', and a powerful president, elected every seven years, who 'ensures by his arbitration the regular functioning of the organs of government and the continuity of the STATE'. The Constitution is, however, vague on the precise responsibilities of the president. At first, successive presidents sought to increase their power. However, in recent times the experience of COHABITATION has led to presidents involving themselves less in domestic politics, and confining themselves mostly to the traditional presidential role of guiding foreign policy. S.M.

pressure group, see under INTEREST GROUP.

prestige goods economy. Useful concept borrowed by archaeologists from ANTHROPOLOGY. An economy in which social STATUS is maintained by the acquisition and selective distribution of goods acquired from outside the system. For further reading: J. Friedman and M. J. Rowlands, *The Evolution of Social Systems* (1977). B.C.

prestressing, see under CONCRETE.

presupposition.

(1) In PHILOSOPHY, the logically necessary condition (see NECESSARY AND SUFFICIENT CONDITIONS) of some state of affairs which must be satisfied if the state of affairs is to obtain. Thus the uniformity of nature has been held to be a presupposition of the rationality of inductive reasoning (see INDUCTION); the real existence of UNIVERSALS to be a presupposition of our ability to classify things into kinds as we do with predicative general terms; memory, less controversially, to be a presupposition of our having a CONCEPT of the past. Philosophy has sometimes been held, not unreasonably, to be a matter of the pursuit and critical examination of the presuppositions of the varieties of human thinking. Kant's theory of the synthetic *a priori* principles of the understanding (see A POSTERIORI, A PRIORI) is, in effect, an account of the presuppositions of Newtonian PHYSICS; his ethical theory of the CATEGORICAL IMPERATIVE an account of the presuppositions of a particularly rigorous form of Protestant morality. R. G. Collingwood (1889–1943) held that in different ages men conduct their thinking within the framework of different sets of absolute presuppositions, ultimate assumptions about the nature of things which form, for their time, the limits of critical thinking. Presupposition as defined above (P. F. Strawson uses the term somewhat differently) is a species of entailment. A.Q.

(2) In LINGUISTICS, and especially in SEMANTICS and PRAGMATICS, what a speaker assumes in saying a particular sentence, as opposed to what is actually asserted. For further reading: S. Levinson, *Pragmatics* (1983). D.C.

price mechanism. The response of SUPPLY AND DEMAND to prices, which can be used to bring order and co-ordination to a wide range of economic activities. The term can refer either to the spontaneous adjustments of the marketplace or to the deliberate governmental adjustment of prices. On either interpretation, the price mechanism is at least a partial alternative to more direct intervention. In the short run it can be used to prevent shortages and surpluses; in the long run its main use is to adapt the structures of production to consumer requirements. Its successful working depends on the movement of prices *relative to each other*, whereas the containment of INFLATION is concerned with the average movement of *all* prices. Failure to appreciate this distinction has been the source of much confusion. The efficient operation of the price mechanism in the marketplace lies behind the view that markets should be left to operate freely (see FREE MARKET; LAISSEZ FAIRE; ECONOMIC LIBERALISM; PERFECT COMPETITION). For further reading: D. Begg *et al*, *Economics* (1984). S.BR.; J.P.

primal therapy. Psychotherapeutic approach developed by Arthur Janov around 1970 which received wide publicity following the publication of *The Primal Scream* (1973) (see PSYCHOTHERAPY; PSYCHOANALYSIS). Its central feature was REGRESSION of the client to infancy to re-experience the 'primal pain' resulting from repeated emotional rejection. Primal therapy begins with a period of one-to-one therapy during which the client's defences against reconnecting with primal pain are broken down, and moves into a group setting in which regressive behaviour is given a free rein as clients re-experience the long-repressed emotional traumas which underlie all NEUROSES. The primal therapy movement's aspirations became more grandiose over time, particularly the claims Janov's later works made for the 'post-primal' personality, to the detriment of its reputation as a mainstream therapy. In many respects primal therapy embodies the popular image of an alternative therapy involving reconnecting with one's 'inner child' and reverting to infantile behaviour. Janov, an ex-psychoanalyst, saw his work messianically as a revolutionary breakthrough, but by the late 1980s primal therapy's popularity had fallen behind that of rival psychotherapies. G.D.R.

primary care. Or primary healthcare – provided by the first doctor a patient contacts for any illness. In the UK this is most likely to be by a general practitioner, and the terms general practice and primary care are sometimes used interchangeably. Primary care is generally seen as one of the great strengths of the NATIONAL HEALTH SERVICE (NHS). General practitioners act as gatekeepers between patients and more expensive specialist or secondary care services. In recent years general practitioners have increasingly tended to work in groups of several doctors and nurses, forming 'primary healthcare teams'. There has also been extensive discussion about the extent of services which can be provided by primary care doctors. Recent health policy has favoured a shift from secondary care (specialists or hospitals) to primary care, so that services such as minor surgical operations are increasingly provided as part of primary care. Likewise there has been a trend to increase the provision of HEALTH PROMOTION and preventive services in primary care. Since the NHS reforms of the 1990s, the position of primary care doctors has become more prominent, first as fundholders and then as part of the primary-care-led NHS. This gives general practitioners greater powers, e.g. by controlling the distribution of funds to local hospitals. In the US primary care has generally had lower status than in the UK, and patients have had freedom to self-refer to secondary care specialists. However, as a result of the crisis in healthcare funding, there is increasing interest in promoting a system in which primary care doctors with a gatekeeper role decrease the use of secondary care services. The World Health Organization uses the term primary healthcare in a much more wide-ranging way. Its definition includes the full gamut of preventive, curative and rehabilitative health services, as well as basic sanitation, nutrition and housing needs. D.F.

primary occupation, see under OCCUPATION.

primary structures, see under MINIMAL ART.

primary succession, see under ECOLOGICAL SUCCESSION.

prime ministerial government. A term popularized in 1963 by Labour politician R. H. S. Crossman's contention that a series of political changes had undermined Cabinet government in Great Britain, combining to elevate the office of Prime Minister to greater power and authority than that granted by the Constitution (see CONSTITUTIONAL GOVERNMENT; CONSTITUTIONALISM). As the argument was put by Crossman and others, it emphasized the Prime Minister's extensive resources of patronage; power to dissolve Parliament; control over Cabinet agenda, procedure and committees; opportunities for media exposure, etc. The case was at best overstated, neglecting, e.g., a host of constraints on a Prime Minister's actions, the vagaries of individual temperament, and the different environments of Conservative and Labour governments. The argument was, however, revived in the late 1970s by Tony Benn and other Labour Party reformers, whose wish to place tighter restraints on the Prime Minister may have derived less from reverence for the Constitution than from their aim to strengthen the non-parliamentary party at the expense of its parliamentary leadership. For further reading: P. Norton, *The Constitution in Flux* (1982). S.R.

prime mover. In attempting to explain directional change in past societies, archaeologists may seek a single motive force such as population growth, plague, climatic change, while conscious of the dangers of monocausal explanation. B.C.

primitive. Adjective used:

(1) Traditionally, to define the subject-matter of ANTHROPOLOGY. Its use derives from the discipline's evolutionary heritage (see EVOLUTION), and it is often nowadays redefined to try to avoid evolutionary assumptions: thus primitive societies are said to be small in scale, non-literate, and based upon simple technologies; indeed, 'small-scale' (likewise 'tribal'; see TRIBE) is often used as a euphemism corresponding to 'underdeveloped' (see UNDERDEVELOPMENT) and 'developing' in ECONOMICS and POLITICAL SCIENCE. But it is arguable that anthropology, though it has properly eliminated 'savage', will always need 'primitive', from which it should strive to remove the last vestige of cultural and political condescension. All men are 'cultured' by definition; some CULTURES/societies are more complex (less primitive) than others.

By taking primitive forms and manifestations as the centre of its interest, anthropology deals in a special way with many of the problems studied by the various social and human sciences. For example, alongside the work undertaken in economics, political science and jurisprudence, there lie anthropological treatments of primitive economic organization, primitive systems of politics and government, and primitive forms of law. Again, RELIGION, MYTH, music and visual art are all studied in their primitive manifestations by anthropologists, their special treatment sometimes being signalled by the prefix ethno- (as in ETHNOMUSICOLOGY). For further reading: E. R. Leach, *Social Anthropology* (1982). M.F.

(2) In late 19th-century art criticism, to categorize European pre-Renaissance painting, especially of the 14th and 15th centuries; thereafter it acquired a different, alternative sense with the growing appreciation of non-Western and non-academic art. After 1900 this sophisticated interest in exotic or naïve work – e.g. Negro sculpture and Bavarian glass paintings, with their influence respectively on CUBISM and the *Blaue Reiter* – combined with a new approach to child art to create a vogue for untutored contemporary 'primitives' like Henri Rousseau (1844–1910), the retired toll-collector (*douanier*) who became a spare-time or 'Sunday' painter and exhibited with the FAUVES in 1905. Leaders of this trend in France, where it affected the whole École de paris, included Picasso, Apollinaire, and the critic Wilhelm Uhde. There was a wave of international exhibitions of naïve art in the 1960s, which led to the concept becoming greatly extended, covering, e.g., the art of Yugoslav peasants (in the Zagreb Museum of Primitive Art), Eskimos, Haitians, 18th- and 19th-century dilettantes, do-it-yourself architects, and extremely old ladies. Chimpanzee art, which also attracted some attention in that decade, relates more to ACTION PAINTING. For further reading: S. Errington, *The Death of Primitive Art and Other Tales of Progress* (1998). J.W.

primitivism. In RELIGION (for primitivism in art see PRIMITIVE), either the desire to imitate the 'primitive' (i.e. first) Christians or, more commonly, an interest in, usually with an admiration for, the vitality of African, West Indian, etc., tribal religion, in which the supernatural and the natural, the dead and the living, the individual, the family and the TRIBE are all bound together by a corporately accepted system of imagery, RITUAL and behaviour. See also SHAMANISM. For further reading: J. V. Taylor, *The Primal Vision* (1963). D.L.E.

primordial nucleosynthesis, see under NUCLEOSYNTHESIS.

principles *and* **parameters.** In LINGUISTICS, an approach to UNIVERSAL grammar in which the statements are much broader in scope than the rules recognized by previous grammatical models. A specification of the variations that a principle manifests among different languages is known as a parameter; e.g., a parameter would specify the position of the elements of a phrase, allowing the options of adjectives going before or after nouns, or auxiliary verbs going before or after the main verb – options which are taken up differently between languages. For further reading: V. J. Cook and M. Newson, *Chomsky's Universal Grammar* (1996). D.C.

prior distribution, see under STATISTICS.

prisoner's dilemma. A famous scenario in GAME THEORY, which illustrates the potential difficulties in achieving optimal economic distributions of goods (see ECONOMICS). Adam Smith's (1723–90) theory of the 'invisible hand' underpins CAPITALISM: that the self-interested actions of individuals will turn out to be best for society as a whole. The prisoner's dilemma is an example of a situation where self-interest leads to everyone involved being worse off (see ALTRUISM).

It concerns two suspects of a crime, who are interrogated independently. If both confess, they will receive a five-year sentence. If just one of them confesses, he will get a mitigated one-year sentence, while the one who refuses to confess will get a ten-year sentence. If both deny involvement, though, they will escape prosecution for the most serious charge, and each get two-year sentences.

If they could make binding agreements with each other, they would agree to remain silent, and take the two-year sentence together. However, if they act independently, each will receive a lesser sentence by confessing, *whatever the other decides to do*, and so the only sensible action is to confess. Thus both will confess, and serve out five years together. This indicates that there are times when solutions must be imposed collectively, rather than left to the individuals concerned. An example of a prisoner's dilemma might be international pollution: it is in no nation's interest for the world to be over-polluted – but neither is it in any nation's interest to unilaterally penalize itself for polluting. A.A.L.

privacy. In EPISTEMOLOGY, being known to, or knowable by, only one person. It is in this sense that the thoughts and feelings of which a person is introspectively aware within his STREAM OF CONSCIOUSNESS are held to be private. More precisely, a thing is private in this epistemologically important sense if it is knowable *directly* and without INFERENCE by only one person. My smile is, of course, as much mine and no one else's as my feelings are, but this makes it proprietary rather than private and is of little epistemological interest (though my smile, unlike my bicycle, cannot be mine at one time and somebody else's at another). The mental states of another are indeed private in the sense defined, but that does not exclude me from having indirect, inferential knowledge of them. For further reading: A. J. Ayer, *The Concept of a Person* (1963). A.Z.

private finance initiative, see PFI.

private good. The consumption of a private good by one person means that it cannot be consumed by another person. Examples of private goods are food and energy. A distinction is usually made between private and PUBLIC GOODS, though it is difficult to classify certain goods and services in just one of these categories. J.P.

private language. In the PHILOSOPHY of Ludwig Wittgenstein (1889–1951), a language which is intelligible only to its user; e.g., a language whose expressions refer to its user's private sensations and inner psychological states and which is therefore intelligible only to himself. Wittgenstein invented the idea of private language in order to deny that there can be any such thing: he argued that language is essentially public because it is a rule-governed activity, in which learning the rules and subsequently checking that they are being followed correctly requires a shared public context of language use. For further reading: L. Wittgenstein, *Philosophical Investigations* (1953). A.C.G.

private sector. That part of the economy that is not owned and controlled by the government. In terms of output, it includes the economic activity of private firms, charities and non-profit-making organizations. On the expenditure side, it refers to the expenditure of these bodies and also the expenditure of individuals. The economy can be categorized into the private and PUBLIC SECTORS. (See also PRIVATIZATION.) J.P.

privatization. The process of transferring state-owned assets and services from the PUBLIC SECTOR to the PRIVATE SECTOR. Of all the changes wrought by THATCHERISM, this has been the most durable and successful, spreading far beyond the UK to other Western democracies, the DEVELOPING COUNTRIES and eastern Europe. Although the manner in which the process has been carried out has sometimes been questioned, the results have not. In removing commercial enterprises from the control of government, in almost every case, from British Telecom to British Gas, the result has been greater COMPETITION, efficiency, enterprise and technological innovation, and in the end lower prices to the consumer. However, mistakes have been made both in the UK and abroad. In Britain privatization led to the over-enrichment of managers – the so-called 'fat cats' – and there was an insensitivity to effects on the workforce and consumer services as opposed to price. In countries as diverse as Russia and Mexico ill-conceived privatizations increased the level of corruption. In the US privatization has been relatively limited and mainly a means of raising money to reduce the budget deficit. In general it is agreed that the defence of the realm, health and the social safety net should remain in government hands. For further reading: T. Clarke and C. Pitelis, *The Political Economy of Privatisation* (1993). A.BR.

probabilistic explanation, see under EXPLANATION.

probability density, see under DISTRIBUTION.

probability theory. The mathematical theory of processes involving uncertainty; the traditional illustrative cases are those of tossing a coin, rolling a die, and drawing a card from a pack; and it was in the context of gaming odds that early probabilistic calculations were carried out from the 17th century onwards. Proper theorems (as distinct from mere calculations) including versions of the Central Limit Theorem (see below) were proved by Laplace and others, but the subject only began to be taken seriously by pure mathematicians with Kolmogorov's definitive characterization of the theory, around 1930, as a branch of the pure mathematical discipline of measure theory. Although probability theory draws heavily on analysis for its techniques, it has a strong flavour of its own in consequence of its role as a mathematical MODEL for empirical phenomena, and probabilistic methods can on occasion feed ideas and proofs back into analysis. The major results of the theory include a class of theorems known as *Laws of Large Numbers*, which equate the numerical probability of an event with its observed statistical frequency as the experiment is repeated indefinitely. These theorems are enshrined in folklore as the 'law of averages', usually in a highly incorrect form (see STATISTICAL REGULARITY). Another major theorem is the *Central Limit Theorem*, which may be thought of as stating that suitably standardized distributions arising from the summation of large numbers of independent errors converge in the limit to the normal distribution (see NORMAL OR GAUSSIAN DISTRIBUTION). The work of Markov in the early 20th century led to interest in probabilistic systems evolving through time; these are now known as STOCHASTIC PROCESSES. Probability theory forms the foundation on which STATISTICS is built, but in recent years the phrase 'applied probability' has come to mean the study of particular stochastic processes thought to be reasonable mathematical models for such empirical processes as the spread of epidemics, the inheritance of GENES, the interaction of components of a biological environment, and the growth of crystals and POLYMERS. For further reading: I. Hacking. *The Emergence of Probability* (1975). R.SI.

problem-solving. That form of activity in which the organism is faced with a goal to be reached, a gap in the 'route' to the goal, and a set of alternative means, none of which are immediately and obviously suitable. It is studied by psychologists in a variety of forms: circumventing detours, solving puzzles and mathematical problems, finding a common basis of classification for a diverse array, solving chess problems, etc. The most widely held view of the problem-solving process in contemporary PSYCHOLOGY is some variant of what is called *means-end* analysis, illustrated best, perhaps, by the *General Problem Solver* (GPS) program of A. Newell and H. A. Simon (1957), a COMPUTER program designed to simulate a human problem-solver's procedure.

GPS begins by comparing the present state of solution of the problem with the desired outcome and first determines a set of differences in terms of selected outcome attributes; thus, in the well-known cannibals and missionaries example, it notes that there are too many missionaries on one side of the river. The program has available a number of *transformation rules* (see AXIOMATICS) for altering current states in the direction of desired outcomes. The transformation highest on the list is applied; if it does not succeed, GPS then tries out other means of solution, or seeks to change the situation so that other means can be applied. A rule for recognizing dead ends is included so that a stop order can be imposed, after which the next transformation on the list is tried. The notice order for spotting differences between desired outcome and present state, and the order of application of transformations, are HEURISTICS or 'rules of thumb' based on knowledge of how real problem-solvers proceed. It is apparent from this account that such phenomena as *functional fixedness* (being stuck too long with an incorrect hypothesis) and other, human-like errors are committed by the program as a function of its presuppositions, and it is this feature that makes GPS not a 'super-problem-solver' but a recognizably 'human' one.

Current research is concentrated on determining some of the biases inherent in programs designed in this way in order to locate more clearly the nature of the difficulties in human problem-solving. For further reading: A. Newell and H. A. Simon, *Human Problem-Solving* (1972). J.S.B.

process art (or **anti-form**). A term applied to US art of the late 1960s which involved subjecting materials to a variety of simple actions – ripping, piling, placing, scattering, etc. – in the exhibition space. This formal looseness succeeded and contrasted with the simple, engineered forms of MINIMALISM. Robert Morris referred to it as art which 'holds on to [process] as part of the end form of the work'. Richard Serra, Barry Le Va, Alan Saret, Keith Sonnier, Eva Hesse and others were, in addition to Morris, associated with the tendency. Like other contemporaneous trends including CONCEPTUALISM, LAND ART and ARTE POVERA, it stressed the importance of context and of change through time, rejecting the idea that art was a series of objects each containing a straightforward meaning. The New York shows, 'Anti-Form' (1968) and '9 at Castelli' (1969), were its major showcases at the time. M.G.A.

process music. A type of music where certain processes are set in action or followed by the performers. It quite frequently has a certain mechanical inevitability, and the logical resolution produced by the completion of the process (sometimes cyclical) is often an important quality. An important innovator is Steve Reich (e.g. 'Pendulum Music'). For further reading: S. Reich, *Writing and Music* (1974). B.CO.

process theology. A movement in 20th-century theology, primarily in the United States, inspired by the process philosophy of A. N. Whitehead (1861–1947) and Charles Hartshorne. Process thought attempts to unite PHILOSOPHY, science and RELIGION in a METAPHYSICS of 'events' rather than 'substances', privileging 'becoming' over 'being', and to interpret the world dynamically and organically. Correspondingly, process theologians such as Hartshorne himself, John Cobb and Schubert Ogden criticize both classical THEISM and PANTHEISM from a 'panentheistic' perspective, in which GOD includes, but exceeds, the totality of finite processes. Reinterpreting causation in terms of persuasion rather than coercion, process theology denies that God is omnipotent, and has therefore generated significant new approaches to THEODICY and other theological issues. Process theology has been extensively criticized, but it remains the single most important expression of theological LIBERALISM in the US, and it continues to develop as it reflects on the issues raised by movements such as LIBERATION THEOLOGY and FEMINIST THEOLOGY, and by phenomena such as the ecological crisis and religious PLURALISM. For further reading: C. Mesle, *Process Theology: A Basic Introduction* (1993). C.C.

producers' goods, see under CONSUMERS' GOODS.

productivists, see under CONSTRUCTIVISM.

productivity. In LINGUISTICS, a major defining characteristic of human language, the creative capacity of language-users to produce and understand an infinite number of sentences using a finite set of grammatical rules. In this respect, human language is often contrasted with the extremely limited range of signals which constitute the communication systems of animals. D.C.

productivity bargaining. A form of COLLECTIVE BARGAINING, developed in the UK in the early 1960s, in which higher rates of pay are traded against employees' acceptance of changes in inefficient methods of production. The use of machinery that embodies old technology, wasteful working practices, lines of demarcation of tasks between different grades of labour, and contrived overtime are all examples of inefficient production practices. The objective of productivity bargaining is to raise real wages, but reduce average costs by increasing overall productivity. In the UK there have been many notably successful examples of productivity bargaining. For further reading: H. A. Clegg, *The Changing System of Industrial Relations in Great Britain* (1979). J.P.

professionalization. One of the key features of the emergence of 'modern society', it has been claimed, is the transformation of many occupations into professions. This process involves the development of formal entry qualifications based upon education and examinations, the emergence of regulatory bodies with powers to admit and discipline members, and some degree of state-guaranteed monopoly rights. Advocates of professionalization argue that it is a movement which helps protect the public from the hazards of a '*caveat emptor*' marketplace situation, in which their ignorance would put them in jeopardy. Critics by contrast see it as essentially an oligarchic tendency, in which corporate power serves to increase an occupation's leverage against the public through reducing competition or public accountability (see OLIGARCHY). For further reading: W. J. Reader, *Professional Men* (1966). R.P.

Profintern. Red International of Labour Unions founded in Moscow in July 1921 to implement point 10 of the programme adopted by the Second Congress of the COMINTERN in 1920, and to establish a rival to the International Federation of Trades Unions (see USSR, THE FORMER). Initially (1921–28) its main tactic was the capture of national TRADE UNION movements by 'boring from within'. In 1928–35 this was replaced by the formation of competing unions, a policy abandoned in turn in 1935 for that of the POPULAR FRONT. After 1937 the Profintern was moribund. D.C.W.

profit-sharing. Term applied to a number of arrangements under which most of the employees of a firm receive a part of its profits in accordance with an agreed scheme. A common arrangement is for the balance of net profits after payment of a fixed rate of return on share capital to be divided in fixed proportions between shareholders and employees; each eligible employee participates in proportion to his earnings. The transfer to employees may be made in the form of shares. Under *co-partnerhip* employees hold shares and, as shareholders or through consultative bodies, have a voice in the conduct of the business. See also PARTICIPATION. E.H.P.B.

programme music. Music normally without words but directly associated with extra-musical subject-matter such as literature (e.g. Berlioz, *Roméo et Juliette*) or natural phenomena (e.g. Debussy, *La Mer*). The concept is particularly associated with 19th-century ROMANTICISM and the symphonic poem (e.g Liszt, *Les Préludes*), but is much older; its survival in the 20th century, despite being an obvious target for anti-Romantic reaction, suggests that it is a natural form of musical expression. To its forms must now be added 'mechanical romanticism' (Honegger, *Pacific 231*). Extra-musical connotations for instrumental music are implicit even in Stravinsky's preference for *Le Sacre du Printemps* in the concert hall rather than as a ballet. Programme music may be related to the GESAMTKUNSTWERK, although the non-musical elements are usually left to the imagination. On these grounds critic Ernest Newman even argued that the symphonic poem should supersede the music drama. J.G.R.

programmed art, see under KINETIC ART.

progressive. Adjective used to characterize:

(1) Generally, believers in the possibility and desirability of progress, i.e. of a moral and social improvement in the human condition, a view which implies a certain optimism about human nature. A.L.C.B.

(2) The term broadly applies to political parties and movements seeking progress – i.e. what they take to be an improvement in the human condition – by novel rather than established means: thus in the UK 'New Labour' might describe itself as progressive to suggest a wish to innovate and to mark a break with its antecedents. More specifically the term has a particular, if still sometimes imprecise, currency in the USA. The Progressive Movement from about 1900 to World War I pressed for numerous changes in the regulation of an unstable and oligopolistic economy and for state action to alleviate the grosser problems of urban and industrial society. It therefore laid some of the foundations for the NEW DEAL of the 1930s, and now is loosely evoked by diverse elements of the moderate LEFT, within and beyond the Democratic Party. Their assumptions and prescriptions vary, but may be fairly summarized as including a search for a new balance in the relationship between increasingly remote global corporations and the interests of the worker, consumer and environment; for improved means to secure greater equality for women and minorities; for a redistribution of political POWER from corporate capital and from a vast federal government; for a tolerance which embraces the nation's growing ethnic and cultural diversity. S.R.

(3) Generally used in education to describe a school whose ethos or teaching methods are different from the more formal or 'fundamental' schools. Progressive is often interpreted as describing a school which pays little attention to the academic and examinations, but this is a gross oversimplification, although, generally, such schools tend to concentrate more on the happiness of the child than his love for learning. J.I.

prohibition. Broadly, a proclamation by the authorities that certain individual behaviour(s), or social or commercial activities, are socially forbidden and/or outlawed. Examples may include certain sexual practices, gambling in some contexts, drug-taking, or trade in endangered species. More specifically associated with the failed social experiment to totally prohibit use and distribution of alcohol in America, dating from the 1919 ratification of the 18th Amendment to the US Constitution, repealed under the 21st Amendment in 1933. Alcohol prohibition failed in its intentions; involved the criminalization of those who broke an unpopular law; and contributed to the growth of organized CRIME (see ORGANIZATIONAL CRIME) in the United States. Prohibitions regarding alcohol use do exist in other nations, e.g. for reasons of religion (Islamic states), or cultural history in which temperance figures strongly and alcohol availability is controlled (e.g. Finland). N.S.

projection.

(1) In PSYCHOLOGY, the tendency to attribute to others unacceptable impulses and traits that are present in oneself. In extreme cases it may be pathological in nature, though generally it is one of the normal DEFENCE MECHANISMS. J.S.B.

(2) In critiques of RELIGION, the process in which the individual, community or SPECIES unconsciously attributes some aspect of its own reality to a god. Expressed in these terms, the idea is as old as pre-Socratic critiques of anthropomorphic theologies, and these were scarcely atheistic. But 'projection', as such, belongs in the conceptual world of Hegel, Feuerbach and Marx (see MARXISM), with 'objectification' and ALIENATION, and now tends to imply that GOD has no reality other than as a projection of our characteristics, desires or fears. Ludwig Feuerbach's (1804–72) theory of projection is historically definitive, but

others, including Freud (see FREUDIAN), have produced significant new versions. C.C.

projective geometry, see under GEOMETRY.

projective/introjective identification. A term derived from the psychoanalytic concept of PROJECTION: the ejection into the outside world of something which the subject refuses in himself. Melanie Klein (see KLEINIAN) expanded the modalities of this psychic mechanism in her explorations in the field of the analysis of young children. The infant projects outside those parts of the self (see PARTIAL OBJECT) which are defined as 'bad internal objects' in its defence against depressive anxiety due to the psychic process of separation from the mother. Klein coined the term 'projective identification' in connection with the paranoid-schizoid position of the infant in relation to his first object, the maternal breast (see OBJECT RELATIONS). The baby projects split-off parts of the self, or later the whole of its self, into the external object in order to harm and control it. This mechanism corresponds to primitive oral infantile phantasies of sadistic attacks and invasions into the inside of the mother's body. In this way the object, breast or mother's body, is perceived as having acquired the characteristics of the projected 'bad' parts of the self which thereby becomes identified with the object of its own projection. The introjective identification works at the level of a retaliation of the object which was attacked by the projective identification in the first place. Pathological projective identification functions as a result of minute disintegration of the self, whose parts are then projected into the object and disintegrated. This pathological process explains the adult psychotic sense of disintegration (see PSYCHOSIS). For further reading: M. Klein, *The Psychoanalysis of Children* (1932). B.BE.

prokaryote. A fundamental division of living things, made up of CELLS that lack a separate NUCLEUS. All living things are either prokaryotes or EUKARYOTES, according to their cellular structure. Prokaryotic cells have little internal differentiation, and their DNA floats around in the cell rather than (as in eukaryotes) being enclosed in a separate nucleus. The bacteria and archaebacteria are the main kinds of living prokaryotes; they are practically all single-celled. Prokaryotes are probably ancestral to the eukaryotes. M.R.

prolefeed; proles, see under ORWELLIAN.

proletariat. The word first appeared (Latin *proletarius*, from *proles*, offspring) in the Servian constitution of the sixth century BC in which military service and taxes were required of the landowners and other classes. Those who could not serve the state with their property did so with their offspring; hence the idea of service by labour. The term disappeared by the end of the second century of the Christian era but reappeared after the enclosure movements of the 15th and 16th centuries, to designate men made landless and able to live only by selling their labour power. It was central in the *Étude sur l'économie politique* (1837) by the Swiss economist Jean Sismondi, the founder of the underconsumption theory of economic crises. It was used by Proudhon, Cabet, Louis Blanc and other French radicals and was popularized by the German social critic Lorenz von Stein in *Der Sozialismus und Communismus des heutigen Frankreichs* (1842).

The term is, however, associated predominantly with MARXISM. In the *Critique of Hegel's Philosophy of Right* (1843), Marx talks of the proletariat as a 'CLASS in radical chains' and ends with the peroration: 'Philosophy cannot be realized without the abolition of the proletariat, the proletariat cannot abolish itself without realizing philosophy.' And the *Communist Manifesto* (1848) begins with the ringing declaration: 'The history of all human society, past and present, has been the history of class struggle. Freeman and slave, patrician and plebeian, lord and serf . . . the BOURGEOIS age . . . has simplified class antagonisms . . . society is splitting into two great hostile classes . . . bourgeoisie and proletariat.' Yet it also seems likely that he used the term largely for dramatic effect. In *Das Kapital* (1867–94) it appears only infrequently; Marx uses instead the more specific (and in English more familiar) terms 'wage-labourers', 'factory hands', 'the WORKING CLASS'. Nonetheless it became an important concept in the COMMUNIST movement of the 1920s, not least among artists and INTELLECTUALS;

and following the Proletkult a number of 'proletarian' cultural groupings sprang up, particularly in Germany and the former USSR. They were liquidated, for differing reasons, by Hitler and Stalin respectively in the early 1930s. For further reading: J. Ehrenberg, *The Dictatorship of the Proletariat* (1992). D.B.; J.W.

proliferation. In political contexts, an increase in the number of states possessing the technological capacity needed for independent production of and control over NUCLEAR WEAPONS. Thus the treaty of 1968, by which three nuclear powers (the USA, the former USSR and Britain) undertook not to transfer such TECHNOLOGY, and some 100 other signatory states not to develop it, is entitled the Treaty on the Non-Proliferation of Nuclear Weapons. A.F.B.

pro-natalism. An intellectual and political perspective asserting the desirability of promoting the growth of a particular human population. Pro-natalist policies attempt to increase the POPULATION GROWTH RATE by raising the average level of FERTILITY in a population. Throughout history, various groups have supported pro-natalist measures for a variety of reasons. Some religious teachings (in particular, Roman CATHOLICISM) are fundamentally pro-natalist in character (as in the exhortation to 'go forth and multiply'). Most nationalist political movements have advocated pro-natalism out of a concern for military strength (e.g. France during the late 19th and early 20th centuries, Germany and Japan before World War II, the USSR under Stalin, and some DEVELOPING COUNTRIES today). Many European governments have adopted pro-natalist policies in recent decades in response to the fact that their countries' fertility rates have typically fallen below the level necessary for demographic replacement (see FERTILITY). Traditionally, most pro-natalist policies have sought to raise fertility by limiting access to CONTRACEPTION or ABORTION. Today, however, at least in developed countries, they provide financial or other incentives in order to encourage higher fertility without restricting reproductive choices. Such incentives may include government stipends, tax reductions, and housing benefits for families with children, as well as legal requirements for parental leave from employment around the time of birth. J.R.W.

proof. Denotes an attempt to convince people of the truth of what you are saying. But in MATHEMATICS it has historically been a two-way process – even if the methods and details are accepted at first, later generations may come to modify or reject them (as with the CALCULUS). Thales of Miletus (*c.* 635–548 BC) is credited with inventing the idea of formal deduction, and Euclid, in his *Elements of Geometry* (*c.* 300 BC), used it, starting from his axioms (see AXIOMATIC METHOD). In the later 19th century it was realized that he used the notions of 'between' and 'within' without a proper basis, and David Hilbert, in his *Grundlagen der Geometrie* (1899), supplied what was missing.

More fundamentally, there has always been debate about the axioms and rules themselves. In the 20th century some have questioned the AXIOM OF CHOICE, and the intuitionists (see INTUITIONISM) demand to see a construction for any object which is said to exist – for them it is not enough to prove that it is absurd that it should not exist.

And what are we to think of proofs like that of FERMAT'S LAST THEOREM, of which it is said that no one has checked all of it since different parts were covered by different people, or of the FOUR-COLOUR CONJECTURE, for which some 1,000 hours on a computer were necessary to check the 1,936 possibly exceptional cases? N.A.R.

proportional representation. A political principle, often referred to simply as PR, aspired to by most of the world's democratic states, although not by Britain or the US. It refers to the system used to elect legislatures, and requires that a representative body be elected by a method which seeks to reflect as far as possible the exact distribution of voting preferences within the electorate. There are several different kinds of electoral system which are based on PR, of which the commonest are the single transferable vote and additional member (or 'party list') systems. PR has long been opposed by the major parties in Britain, who disguise their main concern that its adoption would disadvantage them behind the claim that it would not produce stable and authoritative governments, but would tend to produce coalitions, which they allege are not liked by the British. For further reading: V. Bogdanor, *What Is Proportional Representation?* (1984). S.R.

proposition, types of. In LOGIC and EPISTEMOLOGY, propositions may be distinguished in respect (1) of their *logical form*, e.g. (a) singular, particular or universal, (b) affirmative or negative, (c) categorical (see CATEGORY), hypothetical or otherwise complex, (d) existential, attributive or relational; (2) of their kind of TRUTH OR VERIFICATION, as *a priori* (see A POSTERIORI, A PRIORI) or empirical (see EMPIRICISM), necessary or contingent (see CONTINGENCY), analytic or synthetic (three distinctions that do not obviously, but may fundamentally, coincide); (3) of their subject-matter, as physical, psychological, experiential, scientific, historical, moral, philosophical, etc.; (4) of their epistemological status as basic or intuitive on the one hand or as inferred or derivative on the other. The first of these classifications is of primary interest to logic; the other three are the concern of epistemology. A.Q.

propositional attitudes. Mental acts of believing, intending, hoping, wishing, fearing and others like them are directed upon a particular mental content which can be represented by a proposition; thus (where 'p' stands for any proposition) we attribute BELIEFS, etc., to someone by saying 'he believes that p', 'hopes that p', 'fears that p', and so on; e.g., 'Tom believes that the earth moves'. Believing and the rest are thus characterizable as *attitudes towards propositions*. Propositional attitudes are important in PHILOSOPHY because among other things they figure in accounts of the nature of mind and in explanations of behaviour, action and mastery of language. The TRUTH-VALUE of a statement ascribing a propositional attitude to someone is independent of the truth-value of the proposition, embedded in the 'that' clause, towards which the given attitude is being taken. For example, it can be true that 'Tom believes that Santa exists' despite the falsity of the proposition 'Santa exists'. For this reason some philosophers say that, unlike 'believing', 'knowing' does not name a propositional attitude because 'Tom knows that p' can only be true if 'p' is true. Attitudes with this property might be called 'cognitive' attitudes to distinguish them from propositional attitudes. A.C.G.

propositional calculus. Developed to formalize logical arguments. We use letters p, q, . . . to stand for sentences – we do not enquire what those sentences are. We combine them using $\rightarrow$ ('implies'), $\sim$ ('not'), & ('and'), and $\vee$ ('and/or'). Thus

$$[p\rightarrow (q\&{\sim}q)]\rightarrow{\sim}p$$

denotes the important method of argument known as *reductio ad absurdum*: if p implies a contradiction (that q and not q are both true), then p is false.

And

$$({\sim}q\rightarrow{\sim}p)\rightarrow (p\rightarrow q)$$

is the equally useful: if not q implies not p, then p implies q.

It can be set up on axiomatic basis (see AXIOMATIC METHOD) (using $\rightarrow$ and $\sim$ as basic symbols and defining $p \vee q$ to be $({\sim}p)\rightarrow q$, and $p\&q$ to be ${\sim}(p\rightarrow{\sim}q)$). We take a handful of axioms and rules of deduction and then produce many results. In fact, propositional calculus is isomorphic (see ISOMORPHISM) to BOOLEAN ALGEBRA, so that results can be swapped between the two systems. N.A.R.

prosodic feature. In PHONOLOGY, any systematic variation in pitch, loudness, speed or rhythm that carries a difference in meaning. In FIRTHIAN linguistics, prosodic features (or *prosodies*) are any features which can be found throughout a sequence of sounds; thus if all the sounds in a word were nasal, the nasality would be considered a prosodic feature. The notion is also prominent in non-linear approaches to phonology (see NON-LINEAR PHONOLOGY). D.C.

prosopography. The study of collective biography, usually but not necessarily the biography of Élites such as peers or Members of Parliament. Prosopography is one of the most important types of QUANTITATIVE HISTORY. The prosopographical method has been employed regularly by historians since about 1930, in particular by political historians such as Sir Lewis Namier (1888–1960), and is increasing in popularity because it lends itself to computerization (see COMPUTERS). The great advantage of the method is that it gives a firm basis to some kind of general statement about groups. It has been criticized for taking the ideas out of history, because it is easier to card-index a man's economic interests or family relationship than his fundamental values. P.B.

proteases, see under ENZYMES; PROTEIN.

protectionism. Government interference in international trade. Free trade is the absence of government interference. Free trade is beneficial since it allows countries to specialize in the production of goods and services that they have a comparative advantage in and, consequently, world production and real income increase (see TRADE THEORY). There are many forms of interference: banning of or quotas on certain imports; regulation of the quality of imports; international agreements limiting the level of a country's exports; tariffs on imports; and subsidies on exports. For the century prior to the 1930s, many countries, but not all, followed free trade policies. The Great Depression led to many countries adopting protectionist policies and world trade declined. Since World War II, many, but not all, of the restrictions on free trade have been removed; this increased freedom has mainly been the result of the efforts and negotiations of GATT. However, there have been a number of cases of protection of particular industries. Protectionist policies may be beneficial to a country, as they can increase employment and output. Tariffs can change the TERMS OF TRADE in favour of a country and, thus, increase its real income. Tariffs raise revenue for the government. An infant industry can be protected in its growing stages and, at a later stage, it may give rise to ECONOMIES OF SCALE and beneficial EXTERNALITIES. Protecting an industry increases the rewards to the owners of those FACTORS OF PRODUCTION employed in the industry and imposes costs on the rest of the economy through higher prices. The protection of industries has often been a political measure, to favour those with interests in the industry. Protected industries may become inefficient because they lack the spur of international competition to force them to minimize costs. It is often argued that any net economic benefits from a protectionist policy occur at the expense of other nations. For further reading: B. Sodersten, *International Economics* (1980). J.P.

protein. Giant polymeric (see POLYMER) MOLECULES, found in all living organisms, and built up of amino acids united to each other by the so-called *peptide bond*, CO-NH. The elementary composition of a protein thus depends directly upon its constitution in terms of amino acids. Proteins contain carbon, hydrogen, oxygen and nitrogen, and most proteins contain also sulphur and phosphorus. In skeletal structure the protein is a giant polypeptide (see PEPTIDE); the first protein of which it could be said that its structure was fully elucidated was myoglobin (by Perutz and Kendrew, 1957). The functions fulfilled by proteins are protean. ENZYMES are proteins, and so are connective tissue fibres including tendons and ligaments, while hairs and nails are formed by insoluble proteins of the class known as *keratins*. When proteins are altered in such a way that they lose their distinctive structures or become insoluble, they are said to be *denatured*. Heating a protein normally causes irreversible coagulation, such as occurs in cooking an egg. The main classes of soluble protein are albumins, globulins and fibrous proteins such as fibrinogen out of which blood clot fibres are formed. In digestion, proteins are broken down by hydrolytic enzymes into raw peptides or individual amino acids. The enzymes that break down proteins are known as *proteases*. Protein synthesis (see NUCLEIC ACID) is directed by information encoded in GENES. Experimental modification of the information results in the synthesis of modified proteins, a procedure known as protein engineering. For further reading: R. Passmore and M. A. Eastwood, *Human Nutrition and Dietetics* (1986).
P.M.; P.N.

Protestant ethic. A phrase deriving from Max Weber's proposition, put forward in 1905–06, that, while CAPITALISM has existed throughout most of history, a particular *spirit* of capitalism, that of methodical accumulation and a rationalistic ethic, is found only in western Europe and after the 16th century, in Protestant countries or among Protestant sects within Catholic countries (see WEBERIAN). Though disputed by a number of writers who have argued that the spread of capitalism in Holland was due primarily to economic causes, or that the rise of capitalism was a general phenomenon whose inhibition in Catholic countries was due largely to the Counter-Reformation, Weber's thesis has been one of the most influential ideas in contemporary SOCIAL SCIENCE. Many writers still assume that the Protestant ethic undergirds contemporary capitalism; but Weber specifically argued that 'victorious capitalism', resting largely on materialist and hedonistic incentives, 'needs [the support of the Protestant ethic] no longer'. The pursuit of wealth, he maintained, had become stripped of its religious and ethical meaning. For further reading: M. Weber, tr. T. Parsons, *The Protestant Ethic and the Spirit of Capitalism* (1930). D.B.

Protestantism. The RELIGION of those who make an EVANGELICAL protest against what are believed to be corruptions in CATHOLICISM, urging a return to a more purely biblical faith; so called from a *Protestatio* issued in 1529 as part of the Lutheran Reformation (see LUTHERANISM). In the 19th and 20th centuries the USA has come to share the leadership of Protestantism with Europe, but Protestantism has experienced a need to redefine its position more positively, both in its attitude to Catholicism and in its adjustment to modern thought (see MODERNISM). Where the Bible is not treated in a FUNDAMENTALIST way, the central problem for Protestantism is authority. If the only real authority is the individual's conscience, it is not clear why a Church is needed at all. For further reading: M. E. Marty, *Protestantism* (1972). D.L.E.

protohistory. The study of the past of a given region at a time when it is referred to, but only sporadically, in written records. Protohistory follows PREHISTORY but precedes the period served by regular written sources sufficient to create a cohesive history. B.C.

proton. A positively charged ELEMENTARY PARTICLE about 2,000 times heavier than the ELECTRON. Protons are stable, and constitute one of the two structural units of the atomic NUCLEUS, the other being NEUTRONS. M.V.B.

proto-oncogene, see under ONCOGENE.

protoplasm. An obsolescent term intended to designate the ingredient of living systems that was truly living – a sort of biological ether that permeated or lay between otherwise inert structures. With the realization that the distinctive characteristics of living things are above all else organizational, the entire conceptual background of 'protoplasm' has collapsed; nevertheless, nature-philosophers, unlike practising scientists, do still confront themselves with questions like 'Are connective tissue fibres really alive?' P.M.

protozoa. A sub-kingdom of single-CELL animals comprising some 30,000 SPECIES of both free-living (e.g. amoeba) and parasitic (e.g. the malaria parasite, plasmodium; trypanosoma) forms. The protozoa also comprehend chlorophyll-bearing autotrophic organisms intermediate between animal and plant cells – the phytomonadines. Marine planktonic protozoa with hard 'skeletons' or shells are an important element in the formation of marine geological deposits. Some protozoa produce what are in effect ANTIBIOTICS. Thus a paramecium belonging to one of the so-called 'killer' races produces an infective particle – in effect a virus which kills members of 'non-killer' races. Susceptibility to this infection (kappa) is under strict genetic control. Because of its sexual process the GENETICS of paramecium is now very thoroughly understood. The protozoa generally are ubiquitous in distribution. P.M.

protozoology. The branch of ZOOLOGY that deals with PROTOZOA. P.M.

Proustian. Adjective formed from the name of Marcel Proust (1871–1922), the author of the outstanding French fictional work of the 20th century, *À la recherche du temps perdu* (1913–27). It may refer to Proust's method of reliving the past in the present by means of memory, and thus purporting to triumph over time; to the long, evocative sentences which constitute his normal style; to his remarkable feeling for nature, works of arts, and historic buildings; or to the characteristic *belle époque* high society of aristocrats, men of fashion and *demi-mondaines* that he describes. J.G.W.

provenance. The place at which something

has been found, or from which it has originated. Provenance is often important in such fields as the attribution of works of art, TEXTUAL CRITICISM and bibliography, and invariably so in ARCHAEOLOGY. In the case of the latter it normally implies only location; it lacks the stratigraphical precision (see STRATIGRAPHY) of CONTEXT. B.C.

Provincetown Players. An American experimental theatre group founded in Provincetown, Mass., in 1915 and active in New York from 1916 to 1929. It was intimately connected with the early work of Eugene O'Neill, whose first play, *Bound East for Cardiff*, it presented in 1916. M.A.

Provos.

(1) *Provokants*. An urban movement of Dutch radical youth of an anti-industrialist, individualist, anti-ESTABLISHMENT kind, distinguished by its members' uniform of white socks, their preference for the bicycle (as 'non-pollutant'; see POLLUTION), and the unconventional humour of their campaigns. In the late 1960s individual provos stood for election to municipalities.

(2) Abbreviation for the 'provisional' faction of the IRISH REPUBLICAN ARMY. D.C.W.

proxemics, see under SEMIOTICS.

Prozac. The trade name for the antidepressant drug Fluoxetine, introduced in 1987 (see DEPRESSION). Thanks to innovative marketing it became the most prescribed psychiatric medication by 1990, and the second-bestselling drug in the world by 1994. Prozac's popularity was due not only to its effectiveness in ameliorating depressive illness, particularly the milder forms. Unlike older antidepressants, with their often unpleasant side-effects, Prozac was associated with mild weight loss and the feeling of being energized or even 'high'.

Its novel action, based on enhancing levels of the brain neurochemical serotonin, is similar to other modern, serotoninergic agents, which are also widely prescribed though less well known in terms of brand name or personal mythology. Particular concern has been expressed as to the notions of a 'legal drug' and 'cosmetic personality psychopharmacology', thus there is a continuing debate as to whether milder forms of depression (also termed dysthymia) are true psychiatric illnesses or natural variations of personality. The current decline in the popularity of PSYCHOANALYSIS has been attributed in part to Prozac and its sister drugs. Why talk expensively through that psychic pain when a pill a day resolves it? It has also been suggested that there is a fashioning of artificial forms of disorder by multinational companies, so as to create a market for their product.

The idea that human individuality and temperamental quirks, variously defined as character or free will or whatever, are at the beck and call of neurochemical modifiers has become a further twist in the long-standing vitalist/mechanist debate as to the basis of human nature (see DETERMINISM; MECHANISM; VITALISM). A more prosaic explanation may be that Prozac is showing us the poor definition of current psychiatric syndromes. For further reading: E. Shorter, *A History of Psychiatry* (1997). T.T.

PSBR (public sector borrowing requirement). The gap between what the government spends on the provision of goods and services and that which it raises by means of taxes and other charges. This gap – known in the US as the budget deficit – has to be filled by means of government borrowing on the financial markets through sales of gilt-edged stock in the UK, or bonds in the US. Among the goals of a SINGLE CURRENCY is that of reducing PSBR levels to below 3 per cent of total wealth. Budget deficits above this level are seen as inflationary (see INFLATION), since a proportion of the debt raised is likely to be financed by short-term instruments which contribute to higher prices. Over the longer haul running big budget deficits is seen as counter-productive since an ever larger proportion of public spending will be spent on meeting interest payments, rather than providing better services. During the Reagan–Bush period in the US (see REAGANISM) from 1980 to 1992 the budget deficit was seen to be the central problem of economic management leading to higher inflation and INTEREST RATES and cuts in public services. Large tax increases put in place in the latter Reagan–Bush years, together with the sustained economic growth seen since President Clinton came to power in 1993, have almost wiped out the budget deficit as a problem. For further reading: C. Johnson and S. Briscoe, *Measuring the Economy* (1995). A.BR.

psephology. The study of elections, voting patterns and electoral behaviour. The word is a recent coinage, being derived as an academic jest from the *psephos* (pebble) deposited in urns by voters in classical Athens. For further reading: I. Maclean, *Elections* (1980). D.C.W.

psichiatria democratica. A movement to reform the care of the mentally ill in Italy, developed from the 1970s above all by Franco Basaglia. It has concentrated on replacing traditional mental hospitals with neighbourhood residences. Fired by a political POPULISM associated with the COMMUNIST Party, Basaglia campaigned in particular against compulsory confinement and custodial restraint, and met success in 1978 when the Italian Parliament abolished all new admissions to mental hospitals, concentrating treatment for acute cases upon special wards of general hospitals. In certain north Italian centres such as Bologna, effective community care units have been established. In other areas, the demise of the public mental hospital has led either to the neglect of disturbed people, or the emergence of a new 'private sector' of specialized mental units. For further reading: P. Sedgwick, *Psycho Politics* (1982). R.P.

psychedelic art. Art primarily concerned with sensory PERCEPTION, distortion and hallucinations similar to those mental states produced by DRUGS such as LSD and mescaline (see HIPPIES). Such art often combines visual, aural and kinetic elements (see KINETIC ART) borrowed from TECHNOLOGY to heighten the spectator's sensory experience. Light and sound ENVIRONMENTS could be considered within this category, but psychedelic art can take so many diverse forms that its association with any one technique or medium is precluded. It has a more sober and more organized equivalent in OP ART. For further reading: D. Davis, *Art and the Future* (1973). A.K.W.

psychiatric society. A term, developed above all by the French psychiatrists Robert and Françoise Castel (see below), to characterize the alleged domination of 20th-century Western polities by the rationales of the 'psy complex' (PSYCHIATRY, PSYCHOANALYSIS, PSYCHOTHERAPY, PSYCHOLOGY, etc). Earlier societies, it is argued, responded punitively to malefactors and deviants (see DEVIANCE). Modern society, following the principle of an economy of coercion, chooses to regulate disturbing elements not punitively but therapeutically, by treatment and mental readjustment. Moreover, whereas the 19th-century psychiatric goal was the asylum, utterly segregated from society, in the present century psychiatry has entered the community, through voluntary therapy, the introduction of psychology into schools and the workplace, and psychiatry into the judicial domain. In this vision, the 'psy complex' can be seen as a hegemonic value system, playing the equivalent role to a new religion. For further reading: Robert Castel *et al*, *The Psychiatric Society* (1981). R.P.

psychiatry. The branch of medicine concerned with the study and treatment of mental illnesses and of other disorders, both behavioural and physical, in which psychological factors are important as causes or clinical features (see DISEASE MODEL). As an independent medical specialism, psychiatry began to develop with the RATIONALIST approaches to 'madness' of the late 18th century. Its emergence was heavily associated with the concomitant rise of the lunatic asylum and mental hospital in the 19th century throughout Europe.

As typically practised, psychiatry has leaned heavily upon its medical bases, making presuppositions about the organic source of mental disturbances, while not abandoning the insights derived from PSYCHOANALYSIS and the various PSYCHOTHERAPIES. A psychiatrist is a medical practitioner (and thus distinguished from a psychologist) with postgraduate training in the treatment of the severe mental illnesses (PSYCHOSES) such as SCHIZOPHRENIA and MANIC-DEPRESSIVE PSYCHOSIS, the less severe NEUROSES and emotional disorders, PSYCHOSOMATIC disorders, and behavioural anomalies such as the ADDICTIONS and sexual deviations (see PARAPHILIA). As a branch of medicine, psychiatry has its foundations in the basic biological sciences (see BIOLOGY); it also derives fundamental CONCEPTS and methods from the behavioural (see BEHAVIOURISM) and SOCIAL SCIENCES, particularly PSYCHOLOGY and SOCIOLOGY, and to a lesser extent ANTHROPOLOGY and ETHOLOGY. In its medical aspects, psychiatry uses modes of investigation derived from anatomy, PHYSIOLOGY, BIOCHEMISTRY, NEUROLOGY and other related sciences; these methods are applicable to a range of psychiatric disorders, especially those associated with demonstrable disease of the brain or with conditions such as EPILEPSY or ALCOHOLISM.

In medical practice, psychiatric principles are playing a growing role in the treatment of physical illnesses, as it is increasingly recognized that psychological factors may determine the manifestations, course and outcome of such disorders. Modern psychiatry extends over a wide range of subspecialities, in some of which the traditional medical model of treatment is less applicable. For example, *child and adolescent psychiatry* is largely but not exclusively concerned with emotional and conduct disorders, and the associated family dynamics, among children; *forensic psychiatry* is concerned with the behavioural deviations and legal complexities of managing delinquents and criminals (see DEVIANCE; DELINQUENCY; CRIMINOLOGY). Psychoanalysis, the FREUDIAN theoretical system and method of treatment, has been influential in the USA; most British psychiatrists, though acknowledging that Freud's contribution has been radical and stimulating, are not psychoanalysts. Sharply contrasted with the individualist approach of psychoanalysis is the recent development of *social and community psychiatry*, which is concerned with the provision and delivery of a co-ordinated programme of mental healthcare to a specified population. This applies particularly in the light of current community care policies, and the closure of many mental institutions.

In the post-war period, much attention was paid to social factors as determinants of psychiatric disorders. *Psychiatric social workers* were trained to deal with occupational, domestic, economic and family problems. Psychosocial research concentrated on economic isolation and SOCIAL MOBILITY, emigration, deprivation and cultural variables, and the extent to which they are correlated with differences in the prevalence and outcome of mental illnesses and abnormal behaviours such as suicide, or attempted suicide. The contributions of psychology should be emphasized. In psychiatry extensive use is made, e.g., of PSYCHOMETRIC techniques and statistical devices applied to the measurement of cognitive functions and personality. Behavioural and cognitive approaches derived from learning-theory principles are being increasingly used in the treatment of neuroses. Group, family and marital therapies using the skills of specialist nurses, psychologists and lay therapists are integral to service delivery.

Psychiatry has in particular had to develop an eclectic approach to the rising tide of mental illness generated by ageing POST-INDUSTRIAL SOCIETIES. This bio-psycho-social model attempts to integrate modern research (e.g. psychopharmacology; molecular GENETICS; brain-scanning techniques) with an understanding of individual experiences (e.g. abuse in childhood; life events) and the social context of personal distress (e.g. UNEMPLOYMENT, cultural differences). As such it remains a bastion of clinical and interpersonal medicine, with a therapeutic potential far beyond its stigmatized past history. For further reading: M. Gelder *et al*, *The Oxford Textbook of Psychiatry* (1996). T.T.

psychic determinism, see under PSYCHOANALYSIS.

psychical research, see PARAPSYCHOLOGY.

psychoanalysis.

(1) The PSYCHOLOGY and the PSYCHOTHERAPY associated with the work of Freud and the FREUDIAN traditions.

(2) More broadly, the whole family of SCHOOLS OF PSYCHOLOGY, stemming from the original work of Breuer and Freud in the 1880s and 1890s.

(In both senses, the word is popularly used to refer *only* to the therapy, and not to the theory on which this is based.) Themes or doctrines common to these traditions include the following:

(a) The doctrine of *psychic determinism.* This amounts to a directive to refuse to accept an item of behaviour (e.g. a slip of the tongue, a casual remark) as a matter of chance, but to look instead for its psychological significance to the individual (see FREUDIAN SLIP).

(b) The doctrine of the UNCONSCIOUS. This amounts to the thesis that there are mental processes which operate outside the realm of an individual's awareness, and which play a key role in his life and in the explanation of his behaviour (whether it be a slip of the tongue or a neurotic collapse).

(c) The doctrine of *goal-directedness*. Human functioning is much more goal-directed than we ordinarily suppose. Hence this doctrine lays stress on the motivation of human thought, behaviour, etc., and prescribes that we look for the unconscious motives that, according to (b) above, go to determine and explain our conduct.

(d) The doctrine of *development*. This emphasizes the importance of experience, and especially early experience, in the development of the individual towards adulthood.

(e) The doctrine of *treatment*. The proper form of treatment for the NEUROSES is psychotherapy. For all other non-organic disorders, psychoanalysts would confess (probably) to having a professional preference for psychotherapy, but (in general) they would not urge that it should always or even generally be adopted in these cases. For they recognize the great practical limitations of psychotherapy and the advantages to be had from using other recognized methods of PSYCHIATRY.

The main psychoanalytic schools stem from the work of Freud, Jung and Adler, and the differences between them centre on their different psychologies (see FREUDIAN; JUNGIAN; ADLERIAN). Thus, Jung rejected Freud's view of the sexual LIBIDO and extended the notion of the individual unconscious to cover that from which the individual CONSCIOUSNESS emerges, i.e. the COLLECTIVE UNCONSCIOUS; and he developed his own view of personality and PERSONALITY TYPES. Adler also rejected Freud's theory of libido, and emphasized the interpersonal relations in the family as a chief source of the LIFESTYLE of the person, which could be unrealistic, and so lead to neurosis. In the POST-FREUDIAN period, there has been a proliferation of different variants of psychoanalysis, all claiming adherence to Freud through acceptance of the doctrines given above. Among the most important of these variants are the KLEINIAN, contemporary Freudian and OBJECT RELATIONS schools in Britain, the ego-psychologists (see EGO-PSYCHOLOGY) and self psychologists in America, and the LACANIANS in France and elsewhere. Among the features that differentiate these variants are the relative emphasis given to DRIVES or object relations, the timing and sequence of developmental phases (especially the weight given to the OEDIPUS COMPLEX), and the understanding of therapeutic mechanisms, particularly TRANSFERENCE.

Psychoanalysis has been employed outside of the treatment situation in the production of accounts of art, literature, culture and politics. A major assumption in all these applications is that INTERPRETATION of phenomena adds materially to the possibility of understanding them. A shared problem is that of validation, whether it be of an interpretation given in therapy or of a social or political event. Debates continue concerning the scientific standing of psychoanalysis, the question of whether its explanations are hermeneutic or causal (see HERMENEUTICS; CAUSALITY), whether it is PROGRESSIVE or REACTIONARY in its applications (e.g. with regard to HOMOSEXUALITY or femininity), and whether or not it is therapeutically effective. For further reading: A. Bateman and J. Holmes, *Introduction to Psychoanalysis* (1995); S. Frosh, *For and Against Psychoanalysis* (1997). S.J.F.

psychoanalytic criticism. Literary criticism influenced by the work of Sigmund Freud or, more recently, Jacques Lacan (see LACANIAN). Early psychoanalytic critics (see PSYCHOANALYSIS) like Marie Bonaparte on Poe or Ernest Jones on *Hamlet* analysed the texts by uncomplicatedly assuming that literary works merely mirror the UNCONSCIOUS obsessions or NEUROSES of the writer, or of the characters themselves in a novel or play; and that in order to establish the nature of these obsessions, they could interpret basic 'FREUDIAN' symbols as if these had an exact and unchanging denotative value. A good deal of freeing conceptual work was achieved by Roman Jakobson's essay on METAPHOR and metonymy of 1956. In the hands of Lévi-Strauss, Lacan and Barthes, this opposition was exploited to achieve a conceptually less naïve view of the relation of representation to reality. The importance of language as a self-subsistent entity in the literary work, the way in which metaphor and metonymy can be seen as homologous with CONDENSATION and *displacement*, the two major techniques at work in Freud's account of dream-work, led eventually to Lacan's extreme outer position, in which language achieves complete independence of the writer and indeed enjoys its own unconscious. Critics writing under the influence of Lacan present the literary text as a set of free-floating 'signifiers' for which no 'signifieds' can be established, and in which there is in no significant sense an originating consciousness, a SUBJECTIVITY, a 'presence'.

Major conceptual innovations in Freudian psychoanalytic criticism have been made in America by Harold Bloom (*The Anxiety of Influence*, 1973) and the YALE SCHOOL; and by Norman Holland (*Five Readers Reading*, 1975), David Bleich (*Subjective Criticism*, 1978) and the 'Buffalo School'. Psychoanalytic criticism has also influenced the reader-response theoreticians (see READER-RESPONSE THEORY). In all these forms of influence, the emphasis has been on the writer, the reader, or the relation between the two. Properly Lacanian criticism, however, seems to have abandoned concern for these relationships, and to have developed a metaphysic (see METAPHYSICS) of its own. In this metaphysic, the text is unknowable and independent, and indifferent both to its writer and its readers. The complex 'philosophy' of Lacan himself is deployed as if it were of use in analysing literature, and his anti-humanistic bias is deployed to justify reading the text as a diagram for everything which we cannot have and everything which is not possible. The Phallus (the principle of reality and exclusion; see REALITY PRINCIPLE) constantly blocks DESIRE and commits human beings to senseless repetition and frustrated 'slippage' from one 'signifier' to another. When applied to literary texts, the formal application of Lacanian theory seems to do nothing but darken counsel. But the attractiveness of Lacan's theories to feminist critics (see FEMINISM) has something of the paradoxical about it, as it is obvious from Lacan's own texts that he is more 'phallocentric' than the patriarch Freud himself. Nevertheless, FEMINIST CRITICISM emanating from France, and including in particular Julia Kristeva, Luce Irigaray and Helene Cixous, has established the Lacanian form of psychoanalytic criticism as the most powerful form of ideological theorizing (see IDEOLOGY) now on offer. In its endless negativity, French Lacanianism has resulted in a kind of SOLIPSISM in which women are locked into a consideration of the physical construction of their own bodies, or the irreparable loss of their mothers, in a way which excludes an analysis of the male psyche altogether. An insistence upon 'sexual difference', partly derived from Lacan and partly from Derrida, has become an entrenched position from which all forms of male presence and activity can be harassed, and in particular all forms of self-deluded belief in male adequacy. It is not clear from this how the political situation will be changed in any way, though their emphasis on 'difference' is often equated, in their writings, with the taking of a 'political', 'radical' or even 'revolutionary' position. For further reading: E. Wright, *Psychoanalytic Criticism* (1984). R.PO.

psychodiagnostics. The assessment of personality characteristics and possible psychiatric disorder through interpretation of either (1) objective behavioural indices such as gait, facial expression and GRAPHOLOGY; or (2) the way in which a person, in terms of his motivational CONSTRUCTS, responds to a series of inkblots (see RORSCHACH TEST). See also MENTAL TESTING. G.M.

psychodrama. In PSYCHOTHERAPY, a technique in which the patient plays out a ROLE in the dramatic enactment of a particular situation, in order to help him understand his subjective and interpersonal feelings. W.Z.

psychodynamic. An adjective, used in PSYCHIATRY and PSYCHOLOGY, for which there is no accepted definition. In one usage it is applied to theories which represent symptomatic behaviour as determined by an interplay of forces within the mind of an individual subject without involving awareness. This is exemplified by FREUDIAN psychoanalytic theory (see PSYCHOANALYSIS), which postulates intrapsychic conflicts between UNCONSCIOUS mental activities, such as primitive sexual and aggressive impulses, and those parts of the mind (EGO and SUPEREGO) concerned with morality. The adjective is also applied, in a wider sense, to behavioural symptoms and indicates that these are regarded as being determined by both intra-psychic and extra-psychic factors, the latter including, e.g., parental influences, family conflicts, occupational and other stresses. D.H.G.

psychogalvanic response (PGR), see under GALVANIC SKIN RESPONSE.

psychogenic, see under PSYCHOSOMATIC.

psychohistory. A term coined in the 1960s to describe an approach to historical subjects which attempts to take into account SUBCONSCIOUS and private elements of human experience studied by psychologists, particularly of the FREUDIAN school. Although attempts have been made to apply this approach to collective experiences (e.g. WITCHCRAFT, Puritanism, MILLENARIANISM), or, by Norbert Elias, to the 'process of civilization', the examples which have attracted most attention have been biographical studies, beginning with E. H. Erikson's *Young Man Luther* (1958). Other examples are biographies of Gandhi (by Erikson) and Newton (by Frank Manuel), and Lyndon Johnson (by Doris Kearns).

The method has been sceptically received by most historians on the ground that the evidence available is insufficient to produce more than conjectural conclusions. On the other hand, to write history, and especially to write biography, without assumptions about PSYCHOLOGY is impossible, and Erikson, e.g., in his study of Luther faced certain crucial problems more seriously than earlier historians had been willing to do. The controversy continues. For further reading: D. Stannard, *Shrinking History* (1980).

A.L.C.B.; P.B.

psychokinesis (PK). In PARAPSYCHOLOGY, movement of physical objects caused by somebody not using physical forces; e.g. making a dice fall in a certain position merely by willing it to do so. PK is probably not involved in movements of divining rods and ouija boards since such movements can, like automatic writing, result from unconscious muscle movements. It is sometimes alleged to be responsible for poltergeist hauntings and for the performances of people, like Uri Geller, who produce movements of and in objects without using any apparent physical force. PK is the kinetic counterpart of ESP and poses the same challenges to scientific investigation. I.M.L.H.

psycholinguistics. A branch of LINGUISTICS which studies variation in linguistic behaviour in relation to psychological notions such as memory, PERCEPTION, attention and learning. D.C.

psychological anthropology. Currently the usual US term for studies of psycholog ical aspects of non-Western cultures, covering topics such as child-rearing (see MOTHERING), personality, NON-VERBAL COMMUNICATION and PERCEPTION (see PSYCHOLOGY, ANTHROPOLOGY). Psychological anthropology differs from European cross-cultural psychology (see CROSS-CULTURAL STUDY) primarily in that the latter has tended to explore the universality of Western psychological theories (see UNIVERSALS), whereas psychological anthropology has closer connections with social anthropology. It has thus been somewhat more RELATIVIST in orientation. The psychological anthropology approach had its immediate origins in the work of the Columbia University-based 'Culture and Personality School' of M. Mead, A. Kardiner, R. Linton and G. Devereux, which flourished from the mid-1930s to *c.* 1960, much of which was heavily influenced by FREUDIAN thought, and a little more distantly in the social anthropology of Franz Boas (1858–1942). For further reading: P. K. Bock, *Continuities In Psychological Anthropology: A Historical Introduction* (1980). G.D.R.

psychological medicine, see under PSYCHOLOGY.

psychological parallelism, see under MIND-BODY PROBLEM.

psychological warfare, see under WAR.

psychologism. The interpretation of philosophical problems as questions of a factual kind to be answered by PSYCHOLOGY. Locke and Hume both explicitly endorsed this conception of philosophical enquiry, although they were not wholly bound by it in practice. Their theory of MEANINGS as images causally dependent on previous sense-experiences, and Hume's account of the associative mechanisms underlying the CONCEPTS of cause and identity, are influential examples of psychologism. Critics have argued that psychologism treats questions of ANALYSIS and justification, which concern the correct use of words and the *right* formation of beliefs, as questions about the actual mental associates of the use of words and the psychological causation of belief, thus misinterpreting what is logically NORMATIVE as if it were psychologically descriptive. Husserl's phenomenological theory of philosophy (see PHENOMENOLOGY) as the intuitive scrutiny of ESSENCES was negatively inspired by a rejection of the psychologism of Mill, particularly about MATHEMATICS. Again, the contemporary philosophy of mind (see MIND, PHILOSOPHY OF) is not a very abstract and general *part* of psychology, but an examination of its PRESUPPOSITIONS. A.Q.

psychology. A word variously defined as the study of mind, the study of behaviour, or the study of man interacting with his social and physical ENVIRONMENT. Historically, psychology was a late emergence as an independent science and discipline, traditionally being variously subsumed within THEOLOGY, LOGIC, PHILOSOPHY and learning theory. In England and France, the lineage from Locke through Condillac to the ideologues put the psychological study of mental operations (such as memory, imagination and judgement) and the validation of knowledge on the map as a science in its own right. The word psychology as such was rarely used until the 19th century.

The definition one prefers has theoretical and methodological consequences (see METHODOLOGY), since it conceptualizes what is central in one's concern about man and predisposes one to study different aspects of human experience and behaviour and their determinants. But, while its 'schools' and their theoretical debates have at times been divisive, the field has taken a fairly definite shape with respect to subject-matter studied, methods used, and professions created. At the same time, psychology has not achieved the degree of organization of its knowledge characterizing such NATURAL SCIENCES as PHYSICS or CHEMISTRY, principally because it still lacks fundamental central CONCEPTS comparable to the CONSERVATION LAWS of the physical sciences.

If one takes the ultimate aim of psychology to be the systematic description and explanation of man at the fullness of his powers, as a thinking, striving, talking, enculturated animal (see ENCULTURATION), it has often proved most advantageous to pursue that aim by comparative study. Psychology typically divides into fields of study based on the comparisons used. When, e.g., one compares man with other organisms at different levels of EVOLUTION, there emerges the set of disciplines known as COMPARATIVE PSYCHOLOGY. Since its tools of analysis must be as manageable when working with animals as with man, much of the work in comparative psychology looks for its explanations in terms of the relation of brain and behaviour, of blood chemistry and the endocrine (see ENDOCRINOLOGY) system of GENETICS, and of the functional ADAPTATION of organisms to their natural environment in response to SELECTION PRESSURES. But although in theory one is looking for direct comparisons, in practice no phenomenon need be excluded, since every phenomenon has its analogue (if not its homologue) elsewhere in the animal kingdom; e.g. communication in bees or dolphins is analogous to human speech; the capacity of a chimpanzee to recognize and differentiate his own image in a mirror from that of another animal is analogous to human self-awareness.

A second comparison, that between adult and child, is the basis of DEVELOPMENTAL PSYCHOLOGY, a field including studies of growth in other species as well as in man. Developmental studies, strongly influenced by the work of Jean Piaget (1896–1980), have centred increasingly in recent years on the growth of adult powers of PERCEPTION, reasoning, memory, language, and moral judgement; but analysis of the factors that may affect these (e.g. the growth and transformation of motives, the role of mother–child interaction and of the family, personality formation) has also continued. The developmental approach has also been used to explore in increasing detail the effects of different CULTURES on the growth of mental processes and motives. Since much of development is strongly affected by formal or informal schooling, the principal application of work in this field is through EDUCATIONAL PSYCHOLOGY and child psychology.

A third comparison is between man operating effectively and man afflicted either by PSYCHOPATHOLOGY or NEUROPATHOLOGY, the two often being difficult to distinguish. This comparison is the basis of ABNORMAL PSYCHOLOGY, and it serves in its applied form as a field ancillary to PSYCHIATRY. A fourth comparison, of human and animal behaviour in different social settings, forms the basis of SOCIAL PSYCHOLOGY, which has recently been freed, by a marked growth in research, from an ETHNOCENTRISM often criticized by ANTHROPOLOGY. Fifth and last, there is a new and fruitful comparative study of the difference between 'natural' man functioning in his 'natural' surroundings and computer-built MODELS of man functioning in hypothesized environments, with programs embodying assumptions about human behaviour and human environments. The assumptions are tested by direct comparison of outcomes. The study of ARTIFICIAL INTELLIGENCE is a good example. There is nowadays massive debate as to how far artificial minds should be understood psychologically, in the same terms as human ones.

But psychology can also be characterized in two other ways: by its choice of processes to be studied, and by its method of analysis. With respect to the processes studied, the distinctions can most easily be made in terms of an input-output metaphor. One part of psychology tends to specialize more on input processes: *sensory processing*, perception, *short-term memory*, and HABITUATION. Generally, the object of such study is to discern the manner in which organisms transduce or transform ENERGY changes in the physical environment, converting them into sensations or percepts. It was in this enterprise that psychology was founded as an experimental science, in research that still continues rigorously in PSYCHOPHYSICS. At the other extreme, psychologists are concerned with the nature of response processes, e.g. with skill, expressive movement, motives and drive states, language, and various forms of social behaviour. Between the two are studies of the processes that mediate between input and output, e.g. attention, the organization of memory and learning, the formation of attitudes, and concepts and rules whereby the organism can regulate response systematically with respect to stimulus changes, in a fashion that is systematic but not a direct reflection of the nature of the stimulation.

It is from work of these three types that psychology derives the processes used to explain the differences and similarities that emerge from its comparative studies. Another important subfield of psychology over the last century has been *psychological medicine*, aiming to understand the cognitive basis of mental dysfunction and the misconstrual of reality. The stress on failures in cognition (memory, etc.) and the attempt to relate these to neurological defects (see NEUROLOGY) retains the distinction between psychological medicine and most departments of psychiatry proper.

With respect to methods of analysis, psychology inevitably uses a variety of approaches (experimental [see EXPERIMENTAL PSYCHOLOGY], observational, clinical, even literary) and tools (field studies, mathematical and computer modelling). Even more striking than its growth as a university subject has been its proliferation as an applied field (see APPLIED PSYCHOLOGY) in industry (see INDUSTRIAL PSYCHOLOGY), education, medicine, ENGINEERING, politics, and the armed forces. See also BEHAVIOURISM; COGNITIVE PSYCHOLOGY; DEPTH PSYCHOLOGY; DIFFERENTIAL PSYCHOLOGY; DYNAMIC PSYCHOLOGY; EXISTENTIAL PSYCHOLOGY; FACULTY PSYCHOLOGY; GENETIC PSYCHOLOGY; GESTALT; GROUP PSYCHOLOGY; HERBARTIAN PSYCHOLOGY; HORMIC PSYCHOLOGY; HUMANISTIC PSYCHOLOGY; INDIVIDUAL PSYCHOLOGY; MATHEMATICAL PSYCHOLOGY; ORGANISMIC PSYCHOLOGY; PERSONALISTIC PSYCHOLOGY; PSYCHOLINGUISTICS; SCHOOLS OF PSYCHOLOGY; STRUCTURAL PSYCHOLOGY; TOPOLOGICAL PSYCHOLOGY. For further reading: G. Butler, *Psychology. A Very Short Introduction* (1998). J.S.B.; R.P.

psychology of religion, see RELIGION, PSYCHOLOGY OF.

psychology of science, see SCIENCE, PSYCHOLOGY OF.

psychometrics. The techniques of quantifying human mental traits, particularly the statistical treatment of MENTAL TESTING. Until recently, these techniques were almost exclusively concerned with sorting people into different categories, especially for educational and vocational placement. QUANTIFICATION is usually accomplished by devising test items that show maximum discrimination between individuals, and by the use of standard test STATISTICS that emphasize the internal consistency of the items to one another. Such tests are *norm-referenced*, i.e. individual scores are determined by reference to the scores achieved by a relevant group, most often a group of the same age.

Psychometrics, and consequently the mental testing movement, were initiated in 1883 by the English eccentric and father of EUGENICS Sir Francis Galton during his investigations into HEREDITY. His statistical methods for the analysis of data on individual differences were developed by his students and their associates, particularly Karl Pearson (1892) and Charles Spearman. Pearson's work on CORRELATION, together with the introduction by Spearman (1904) of the CONCEPT of FACTOR ANALYSIS, was the breakthrough that launched the mental testing movement, pioneered by J. McK. Catell (1890) and E. L. Thorndike (1904) in America, and in Europe by A. Binet and T. Simon (1905), who produced the first influential measures of scholastic aptitude. In Britain Cyril Burt, an associate of Spearman and devotee of Galton, began in 1909 a lifetime's work on the testing of INTELLIGENCE and achievement. His work and much of the tradition it represents were thrown into disrepute in the 1970s when it was discovered that he falsified results.

The development of group testing during World War I (for classifying recruits according to intellectual level) gave additional impetus to a movement which has steadily expanded and proliferated. Today, in most industrialized countries, there are large establishments devoted to the construction, application and interpretation of standardized tests which are widely used for educational and vocational selection, and which play an important part in the determination of life-chances.

In recent years, opposition to mental testing has grown. On the one hand, it is attacked by those who claim that its meritocratic rhetoric masks the perpetuation of existing inequalities in the distribution of power and opportunities (see ÉLITE; RACISM; MERITOCRACY); American psychometricians, e.g., have revealed the loading of most vocabulary tests in favour of whites by devising other such tests which are loaded in favour of blacks, and in which the normal higher white rating is reversed. On the other hand, it is criticized for having failed to evolve new forms to meet changing applications, particularly in the field of education. Here a major effort has been made during the last decade to improve the quality of the curriculum; but appropriate procedures for measuring the efficacy of educational treatments rather than the performance of students have yet to be devised.

Recently there has been a tendency to replace norm-referenced tests by criterion-referenced ones (see CRITERION REFERENCED TEST), whose primary function is to compare individual performance, not with other individual performances, but with a specific criterion, such as how well the subject might need to perform a specified task, or how well he might reasonably be expected to perform if given adequate instruction. Since tests are traditionally validated against how particular groups perform, and since test statistics are based on concepts of individual differences, the classical ways of judging tests through 'validity' and 'reliability' are not suited to criterion-referenced tests. How to judge their quality remains a formidable problem. For further reading: R. L. Thorndike, *Applied Psychometrics* (1981). B.M.

psychoneurosis, see NEUROSIS.

psychopathology. In PSYCHIATRY, the study of abnormal mental states, which especially emerged out of the sustained observation of asylum patients in the 19th and early 20th centuries (see ABNORMAL PSYCHOLOGY). In this context the parallel developments in PATHOLOGY and PHYSIOLOGY, degeneration theory (see DEGENERATIONISM) and the materialist/metaphysical debate stimulated psychiatrists into clarifying the core symptoms of mental illness (see MATERIALISM; METAPHYSICS). Linking emotional and psychological dysfunction to possible biological substrates, as well as the effects of childhood experience, traumatic events, heredity and cognitive processing, psychopathology has been the basis of disease concepts in modern psychiatry (see DISEASE MODEL).

The phenomenological (Husserl, Jaspers; see PHENOMENOLOGY) and psychodynamic (Freud, Jung) approaches have been its major schools, and the PSYCHOSES (especially SCHIZOPHRENIA) its most public area of analysis. Behavioural and learning theory have increasingly challenged the traditional approaches. For further reading: F. Kraupl Taylor, *Psychopathology* (1960). T.T.

psychopharmacology. The study of the behavioural effects of DRUGS (sense 1). It is Janus-like: it may aim principally at the classification of drugs according to the similarity of their effects on behaviour, or at the classification of types of behaviour according to the similarity of their susceptibility to the effects of drugs. The former aim has usually been more prominent, but the latter may eventually prove more important. With regard to the former, the existing pharmacological classifications have proved very unhelpful in predicting effects of drugs on behaviour, while it is often difficult to see any pharmacological similarity between drugs that are indistinguishable in their behavioural effects. Furthermore, drugs that have a relatively precise pharmacological action frequently turn out to have remarkably unspecific behavioural effects, while drugs that have highly specific effects on behaviour have very wide-ranging and unspecific effects on the chemistry of the brain. Thus psychopharmacology is very much a discipline in its own right and not merely an INTERFACE between its two parents, PSYCHOLOGY and PHARMACOLOGY. See also NEUROPSYCHOLOGY. J.A.G.

psychophysics. The study of relations, especially quantitative, between psychological characteristics of perceived properties and physical characteristics of stimuli, e.g. between the heard loudness and pitch of a tone and the intensity and frequency of the acoustic stimulus. Pioneered in Germany around 1850 by G. T. Fechner, psychophysics is a field in which work has continued vigorously. I.M.L.H.

psychoprophylaxis, see under CHILDBIRTH TECHNIQUES.

psychosexual development. The processes whereby human beings reach a mature expression of their sexual impulses, including attitudes and values concerning their sexuality. In Freud's view, psychosexual development included the earliest feelings of affection of the boy for his mother or the girl for her father (see OEDIPUS COMPLEX; ELECTRA COMPLEX) and the development of *erogenous zones* connected with which there was some pleasure or tension created by relations with the mother or foster-mother. The first phase was the *oral phase* related to the child's preoccupation with the intake of food: the child's mouth was conceived of as a centre not only for nutriment but for exploration, and, provided there were no difficulties with feeding, the child was thought to develop expectations concerning gratification. The second phase was the *anal phase*: the crises connected with the bowel movements, and the approval these were given by the mother, were thought to be a focus for the organization of early sexual tendencies. The development of stronger and more direct sexual feelings towards the mother (in boys; the father in girls) were thought, next, to produce CASTRATION ANXIETY, leading to the suppression of sexual feelings during the pre-adolescent LATENCY PERIOD. Adolescence then produced a resurgence of sexuality in the *phallic phase* (a somewhat curious expression for a phenomenon postulated of girls as well as boys), with the emphasis more on expression of sexual feelings as such (e.g. through masturbation) than on sexual relations with a partner, including the sharing of gentler, more tender feelings. Full or 'genital' maturity took the form, finally, of sexuality expressing itself in the context of a mature relationship with a loved partner whose satisfaction and wellbeing also provided an important aspect of sexual gratification.

It was proposed in psychoanalytic theory (see PSYCHOANALYSIS) that either indulgence or frustration at any stage of psychosexual development would lead to FIXATION at that stage with character traits emerging in the adult reflecting unrequited requirements. In consequence one speaks of an *oral character* or an *anal character* or a *phallic character* as reflecting these early fixations.

Studies of sexual development have shown that it follows no fixed course but is highly influenced by the NORMS of the CULTURE or SUB-CULTURE in which the child grows up. The FREUDIAN theory has also been criticized for assuming the invariable presence of castration anxiety and the latency period, as have most theories, including the Freudian, for their inadequacy in describing the course of psychosexual development in women. See also DEVELOPMENTAL THEORY. J.S.B.

psychosis. In PSYCHIATRY and ABNORMAL PSYCHOLOGY in the West, a term used for one of the main classes of mental illness. In the present state of psychiatric knowledge it is not possible to classify the majority of mental illnesses on the basis of causal factors, and modern systems of classification go back to the work of Emil Kraepelin (1856–1926), a German psychiatrist who endeavoured to establish definite psychiatric diseases and to bring order into psychiatric taxonomy. Psychoses are usually distinguished from NEUROSES, personality disorders, PSYCHOSOMATIC disorders, and MENTAL RETARDATION, and are themselves divided into the *organic* and the so-called *functional* psychoses. Within the original terminological framework, psychoses were seen essentially as disturbances of consciousness, without any necessary organic correlate. As such they included functional disorders, and could comprehend the less serious mental complaints. Over the last century, terminological confusion between psychoses and neuroses was common, as is exemplified by Freud's alternative usages of neuropsychosis and psychoneurosis. In organic psychoses, such as general paralysis of the insane and delirium, there is a demonstrable physical abnormality in the brain. In functional psychoses, such as SCHIZOPHRENIA and the affective psychoses, no underlying physical disease has been discovered; but the mental and physical symptoms, together with the results of genetic research (see GENETICS/GENOMICS), are thought by many psychiatrists to indicate underlying morbid endocrine or biochemical changes (see ENDOCRINOLOGY; BIOCHEMISTRY).

Traditionally, much attention has been paid to the time-honoured distinction between psychoses and neuroses. Probably the origins of this distinction were mainly social and historical: psychotic (mad, insane, or lunatic) patients were those whose behaviour was so deranged that they were placed in madhouses or asylums, while neurotics were treated in physicians' consulting-rooms. There is no single characteristic by which psychoses can be defined. Psychoses have been said to be distinctively characterized by greater severity of illness; total dissolution of the personality; lack of insight into the illness; inability to distinguish between subjective experience and reality; the presence of delusions and hallucinations; the occurrence of a marked personality change which cannot be interpreted as an understandable development of the personality or reaction to psychological TRAUMA. Exceptions are readily found to all these criteria. Nevertheless, psychiatrists of similar training can achieve a high level of agreement in classifying patients as neurotic or psychotic.

While most psychiatrists agree that a system of diagnostic classification is necessary, the term psychosis is not of great value in clinical practice. Other, less inclusive diagnostic categories are more useful, and decisions as to treatment and prognosis are based on other considerations. For further reading: P. Buckley (ed.), *Essential Papers on Psychosis* (1988). D.H.G.

psychosomatic. Adjective derived from the Greek words for 'soul' and 'body' and used in medical and psychiatric contexts (see PSYCHIATRY) – it can be applied to a patient or to his disorder – to imply a relationship between mental and physical states of health; *psychosomatics* is the study of this relationship. Historically, the traditional humoral theory of disease made no clear distinction between mind and body and so saw all disease as to some degree psychosomatic. The rise of scientific medicine in the 19th century tended to stress the organic substrate, but the visible presence of such conditions as hysteria (see NEUROSIS) ensured a hearing for psychosomatic interpretations of apparently organic dysfunctions. The adjective is most commonly used in the context of physical conditions, e.g. gastric or duodenal ulcers or severe headaches, that derive from stress states. Most theories of psychosomatic illness offer inadequate explanations both of why some individuals 'somatize' their symptoms of stress while others do not (manifesting ANXIETY OR DEPRESSION instead), and of 'organ choice', i.e. why one person develops ulcers, another chronic fatigue. Contemporary research indicates that in stress there is massive involvement of the adreno-cortical system, and that this can express itself in a variety of physical symptoms by maintaining in the bloodstream high levels of circulating catecholamine which may disrupt different organ systems. Psychosomatic disorders are to be distinguished from *psychogenic* (i.e. those originating exclusively in the mind). See also ABNORMAL PSYCHOLOGY; MIND-BODY PROBLEM.

J.S.B.; R.P.

psychosurgery. The use of surgical means against mental disease (e.g., trepanning the skull to release pressure and tension) has a long history, but became a movement only in the present century with the work of Egas Moniz (1874–1955) in Lisbon. A distinguished neurologist, Moniz believed that functional PSYCHOSES largely stemmed from diseases of the frontal area of the brain. By removing parts of the frontal lobes he expected to provide relief or cure. He performed his first lobotomy (see LEUCOTOMY) in 1935, and the operation spread in the 1940s, finding loud advocates in the USA in particular. It was found that lobotomized patients were less violent, but that many were turned into 'zombies', lacking ambition and energy. Psychosurgery was widely criticized because it was imprecise and irreversible, and since the 1970s its use has been drastically curtailed.

R.P.

psychotherapy. A sub-class of the methods used – either within PSYCHIATRY or outside it – for treating sufferers from mental abnormalities. The sub-class is easier to delimit by giving examples of what it *includes* (e.g. PSYCHOANALYSIS, counselling, ordinary psychiatric interviews, transactional analysis, the non-verbal movement and body therapies) and what it *excludes* (e.g. ELECTRO-CONVULSIVE THERAPY, PSYCHOPHARMACOLOGY, surgical interference with the brain, OPERANT CONDITIONING, the desensitization technique of BEHAVIOUR THERAPY) than by a formal definition. But perhaps the most fruitful way of trying to distinguish between psychotherapy and other methods is in terms of the sort of situation and interaction set up in the former between patient and therapist and deliberately used for therapeutic purposes. This revolves essentially around a special relationship between patient and therapist that is produced and maintained by the rules of operation the particular therapist employs. Thus, a psychoanalyst will operate in accordance with certain rules which will generate a characteristic type of situation and relationship between patient and analyst, in which, e.g., the development of TRANSFERENCE is a key feature. In contrast, a counsellor in the tradition of American psychotherapist Carl Rogers (1902–87) will operate in a different way, and this will produce a different type of situation and relationship, in which transference is minimal and the development of spontaneity in the verbal expression of feeling becomes important.

Historically, psychotherapy became an accepted part of contemporary psychiatry partly or largely as the result of the growth and influence of psychoanalysis. Likewise, the different methods of contemporary psychotherapy are, in large measure, developments out of psychoanalytic practice. In the last three decades, however, many therapists have become increasingly dissatisfied with psychoanalytic practice because of its length and slowness, the few patients who can be reached by it, its great expense, and its rigidities, which (allegedly) restrict its effectiveness. Accordingly, many psychotherapists have struck out in novel directions in attempts to overcome the limitations of traditional psychoanalysis, e.g. by shortening the duration of therapy, and by a variety of group techniques such as GROUP THERAPY and PSYCHODRAMA. About the results of psychotherapy it is very difficult to establish any claims, whether positive or negative, because of the massive complexity of the issue, and the comparative crudities of our current techniques of investigation. At best, perhaps, it can be said that we have some grounds for thinking that psychotherapy can be of use when it is appropriately and skilfully deployed.

Despite the doubts and difficulties that surround it, psychotherapy has had an immense impact on Western culture. Thus, it has greatly affected our ways of thinking about and organizing human relations in various departments of life, e.g. educational practice, prison organization, and the selection and training of business managers. Material produced by psychotherapy has formed the evidential base for a number of theories (FREUDIAN, JUNGIAN, etc.) about human nature which are of great interest, and, if valid, of enormous importance. These theories have stimulated psychologists in their efforts to uncover the hard facts about human nature, and have permeated our thought and attitudes in ways not yet adequately charted. For further reading: C. Feltham (ed.), *Which Psychotherapy?* (1997). B.A.F.

psychotic, see under PSYCHOSIS.

public art. Term which gained currency from the early 1970s onward to refer to art made for an outdoor setting rather than for showing in a gallery. Drawing on the twin examples of the 'art into production' values of the post-revolutionary Soviet Union, and the murals of Diego Rivera and other Mexicans, it was initially a primarily urban phenomenon. A strong impulse was the desire to avoid the perceived élitism and privilege of the gallery system in favour of a more egalitarian and socially useful artistic practice. The scope of the term subsequently broadened to include more mainstream sculpture projects commissioned as part of property developments and urban design schemes. In recent years practitioners have been as concerned with issues of conservation and environmental protection as with countering the effects of urban decay. This has led to a merging with certain developments in LAND ART. M.G.A.

public debt, see NATIONAL DEBT.

public good. The consumption of a public good by some people allows others to consume the same good. The consumption of a pure public good means that all other persons necessarily consume the same quantity of the good. Examples of public goods are clean air, knowledge and defence. Often it is technically difficult or prohibitively expensive to exclude persons from consuming public goods. If private firms cannot force individuals to pay for the consumption of a public good, they will be unwilling to supply them. A function of the state is to supply public goods, the costs of which are covered by taxes. The incidence of this TAXATION and the distribution of the benefits resulting from consumption of public goods can have important redistributive impacts. If the incidence of taxation is according to the estimated benefits derived from consumption, a free-rider problem exists, as the level of supply of the public good is altered only by a negligible amount by an individual's payment of the taxes associated with the stated benefit. Thus, individuals have an incentive to underestimate the strength of their preferences for publicly supplied public goods. If everyone adopted this strategy, there would be no supply of public goods. As taxes are rarely levied in this way, the free-rider problem is unlikely to be of practical importance. However, it remains difficult to ascertain the true demand for public goods. Many public goods, e.g. mass transport systems, have low costs of exclusion and there is considerable economic and political debate as to whether they should be supplied by the private or the public sector (see PRIVATE SECTOR; PUBLIC SECTOR; EXTERNALITIES; PRIVATE GOOD). For further reading: D. Begg *et al*, *Economics* (1984). J.P.

public housing. Dwellings financed directly by governmental agencies and/or local authorities, and rented to tenants. It assumes the provision of housing as a basic social service for those groups unable to compete in the housing market, or as a service to a much wider group, depending on the political outlook of the country. In Britain the ratio between private and public housing built since 1945 has fluctuated around 40:60, with the larger share going to one or other sector according to political control. In the USA the proportion of public housing is very much smaller, in the former USSR very much greater. For further reading: D. V. Donnison, *The Government of Housing* (1967). M.BR.

public interest. A term used in contradistinction to the selfish interests of some individual or group (see INTEREST GROUP). It is of interest to political theorists because of the plausibility of the thought that while individuals and small, well-organized groups can be trusted to promote *their* interests, the unorganized mass of the population cannot be expected to look after the public's interest in the same way – from which the familiar view that it is the task of the state to defend the public interest follows quite naturally. See also INTERESTS, THEORY OF.

For further reading: B. Barry, *Political Argument* (1965). A.R.

public interest immunity. The protection of documents from production in court as evidence by reason of the public interest. In England until 1968 the courts automatically granted this immunity or privilege in respect of all documents or classes of documents for which the Crown, in proper form, claimed that production would be injurious to the public interest. But in that year the House of Lords established the modern rule whereby any such claim must be tested by the court to determine whether or not the public interest in keeping the document confidential should properly outweigh the other public interest that justice be done. Thus 'class claims' to immunity no longer succeed, and all individual claims are examined by the courts on their merits. For further reading: D. C. M. Yardley, *Principles of Administrative Law* (1986). D.C.M.Y.

public interest theory, see under ECONOMIC REGULATION.

public international law. A term used to define a body of rules which are regarded as binding by STATES in their relationship with each other, e.g. state responsibility for breach of international obligations, or observance of diplomatic privileges and immunities. Although it is only states which are subjects of international law, individuals and institutions figure increasingly in the international domain. The sources of international law outlined in Article 38 of the Statute of the INTERNATIONAL COURT OF JUSTICE are: (1) international conventions, whether general or particular, establishing rules expressly recognized by the contesting states; (2) international custom, as evidence of a general practice accepted as law; (3) the general principles of law recognized by civilized nations; and (4) judicial decisions and the teachings of the most highly qualified publicists of the various nations, as subsidiary means for the determination of the rules of law. Where a conflict arises between the rules of international and municipal law, an international tribunal will opt for the former. By contrast, where the conflict arises before a municipal court, it will be resolved on the basis of the constitutional rules of the state in which that court is situated. An apparent defect of the international system is its lack of an effective central organ for the enforcement of legal rights. Nonetheless, due to the role of reciprocity in international relations and the deterrent effect of countermeasures, in practice international law operates efficaciously. For further reading: E. Shaffer and R. Snyder (eds), *Contemporary Practice of Public International Law* (1997). O.Y.E.

Public Lending Right, see PLR.

public relations. Anything enjoys the benefits, or disadvantages, of external perceptions, whether it wants to or not. The management of public relations for a business (or for the product of a business) is, in many ways, more difficult than the management of paid-for communication. Press, television and radio are the main media of public relations. Relationships with the media are often a case of 'damned if you do, damned if you don't'. Historically, many businesses have managed their public relations on the basis of saying nothing, and being prepared to pay to avoid mention – this on the basis that, if all other communication is being carefully managed and controlled, then nothing is left to chance. In the era of investigative and exposé reporting even silence cannot guarantee non-mention, and public relations practitioners have learnt to ride tigers.

Just like the ADVERTISING process, effective management of public relations starts with a clear definition of key target audience(s), and an explanation of consumer benefits. The most effective medium is selected for the communication of benefits to the target, with a due recognition that, to adapt Marshall McLuhan, the medium can affect the message. Then no effort is spared in ensuring that key journalists are the recipients of detailed product information on a regular basis. T.S.

public school.

(1) In the USA, any primary or secondary school supported by public funds.

(2) In Britain, a term paradoxically applied to certain private or independent schools for pupils of, mostly, 13 to 18, the most famous of which, founded in the Middle Ages (e.g. Eton, Winchester), have long been the nurseries of the British

governing CLASS. Variously defined, public schools show, typically, these features: (a) foundation or considerable enlargement during the 19th century, in the heyday of British imperial expansion (see IMPERIALISM); (b) an inherited ethos which stems from Thomas Arnold's declared aim (1828) of turning out 'Christian men' and emphasizes such virtues as 'gentlemanly conduct' (Arnold's phrase), discipline, self-discipline, public service, and the 'team spirit'; (c) a wide range of extra-curricular activities; (d) above-average academic standards and results, helped by (e) an above-average staffing ratio; (f) pupils who are predominantly or exclusively boarders, and (g) of one sex only (though co-education is increasing); (h) very high fees. Their supporters stress (b), (c) and (d); opponents emphasize the unfairness of (e) and (h), the psychological effects of (f) ('an undeveloped heart', according to E. M. Forster), the sexual dangers inherent in (g), and the élitism (see ÉLITE) and social divisiveness of the whole system.
In America the nearest equivalents to the British public schools, found mainly on the East Coast, and today mainly co-educational, are known as *college preparatory schools*; in Britain a *preparatory school* is one that prepares pupils (from, in general, the age of about nine) for the entrance examination of the public schools, many of whose features it shares. O.S.

public sector. That part of economic activity that is owned and controlled by the government, central or local. It includes nationalized industries, public corporations, those firms that are owned by the government but are not directly controlled by them, and those bodies providing services and goods such as education, health, etc. Until recently, the relative size of the public sector has been increasing in most CAPITALIST economies (see AFFLUENT SOCIETY). It has been suggested that such an increase is undesirable (see PRIVATIZATION; NATIONALIZATION). In SOCIALIST countries most of the economic activity takes place in the public sector. J.P.

public sector borrowing requirement, see PSBR.

pulsar. A very regularly pulsating astronomical source of RADIATION. Such sources were observed in 1967 by A. Hewish and J. Bell-Burnell and were for a time suspected of being signals from intelligent extraterrestrials (see SEARCH FOR EXTRATERRESTRIAL INTELLIGENCE). Subsequently they were explained as very rapidly rotating *neutron stars*. They have a mass roughly equal to that of the sun but a diameter similar to that of a planet like the earth. As a result their density is 1,014 times greater than that of water and roughly equal to that inside the atomic NUCLEUS. Radiation is beamed away from a region on the surface of the rotating neutron star which we see every time the neutron star rotates to point the beam in our direction. The effect is similar to that seen when a lighthouse beam rotates. Almost every known pulsar is an isolated star, but there exists a *binary pulsar* which is a very important site for examining the predictions of the general theory of RELATIVITY. In this system the pulsing of the pulsar is regular to a higher precision than can be measured by any terrestrial clock. The binary pulsar has been observed to be losing energy very slowly, revealed by a tiny change in the pulsing frequency. This change is equal to that predicted to occur due to loss of energy by gravitational radiation (see GRAVITATION), according to Einstein's theory of general relativity. The most famous pulsar is that residing at the centre of the Crab nebula, an expanding remnant of an exploding star (SUPERNOVA) first observed in the 11th century. A very large number of pulsars are known with a wide range of pulse periods. They possess large (typically 100 million tesla) magnetic fields and are surrounded by a complex magnetosphere of electrically charged PARTICLES. A detailed theoretical explanation of the source of the pulses has not yet been found and is an active area of study. For further reading: M. Beigelman and M. Rees, *Gravity's Fatal Attraction* (1996). J.D.B.

pulsating universe/oscillating universe. The idea that our universe might be cyclic in time. If it contains enough matter one day to reverse the current state of expansion into contraction, then it is possible that the universe might 'bounce' back into a state of expansion and continue to oscillate in this way for ever. One criticism that has been levelled at this theory is that if the second law of THERMODYNAMICS is respected from cycle to cycle then the ENTROPY of the universe should continue to rise and the cycles will get bigger as time goes on. It is not clear that this is undesirable. Such a feature would explain why our universe is so large and why its entropy is so huge. However, this theory is extremely speculative and does not admit a critical observational test. Barrow and Dabrowski demonstrated in 1995 that if a COSMOLOGICAL CONSTANT exists then the oscillations must eventually end. Other versions of this theory, in which new universes appear on each occasion when stars collapse to a BLACK HOLE, have also been proposed by Smolin. For further reading: J. D. Barrow, *The Origin of the Universe* (1994); L. Smolin, *The Life of the Cosmos* (1997). J.D.B.

punctuated equilibrium. The theory that EVOLUTION proceeds mainly in fits and starts, rather than at a constant rate (GRADUALISM). Evolutionary changes, as seen in the fossil record, often appear to take place in sudden jumps. This had generally been attributed to the gaps in the record, but in 1972 two American palaeontologists, Niles Eldredge and Stephen Gould, argued that the jumps reflect the way evolution normally proceeds. The 'jumps' in the fossil record are on the human time scale rather slow; in one well-documented case among the snails of Lake Turkana, the sudden evolutionary event took 5,000–50,000 years. How generally evolution proceeds in the punctuated or the gradual mode is a matter of factual controversy. Punctuated equilibrium has sometimes been suggested by publicity-hungry biologists and gullible journalists to be anti-Darwinian; however, it is not. M.R.

punishment. The expression of social disapproval of defined acts or behaviours (see CRIME; CRIMINOLOGY; PENOLOGY) through application of fines, confiscation, community service, restraint, imprisonment or pain. Punishment may be absolute (CAPITAL PUNISHMENT); proportionate to the offence; aim to deter the offender and others; to treat and readjust and/or to rehabilitate. Punishment may take place within designated settings (e.g. prison) or in the community, possibly supervised by probation officers. Justifications of the right to punish are debated within PHILOSOPHY and penology. The historical shift from the public exhibition and physical punishment of offenders to the development of prisons and penal discipline has recently attracted considerable attention. N.S.

punk. A British youth sub-cultural movement (see SUB-CULTURE) that rose to prominence in 1976, in many ways created and effectively destroyed by media exposure. (It impinged upon public consciousness by way of the Sex Pistols' – a renowned early punk band – use of bad language on a popular TV programme.) Punk started life as both a style – anti-fashion – and a musical form – fast, aggressive, raw and deliberately unprofessional. Like most youth sub-cultures, it refers simultaneously to a COLLECTIVE CONSCIOUSNESS, an aesthetic, musical innovations and unmistakable stylistic signals, and the punk movement – later transformed into '*new wave*' – stressed cultural rebelliousness, self-parody, NIHILISM, surrealism and iconoclasm. In many respects, punk was a reaction to the classless liberal PERMISSIVENESS of the 1960s. Sixties YOUTH CULTURE reached further up the age and CLASS scale than any previous manifestations, and punk started off by reclaiming lost territory for the young – increasingly workless – WORKING CLASS. Punk music was intended to be open access – anyone can play; no heroes, no leaders – and was a response to the expense and absurdity of megastar and supergroup idolatry that had beset 'progressive' ROCK MUSIC; it was also a reaction to the campness of glitter rock. Punk was symbolically rather than actually violent; despite fears that swastikas and Nazi regalia (see NAZISM) would be taken at face value, punk veered slightly LEFT in terms of political orientation, and the musical commentary on RACISM, UNEMPLOYMENT and urban disorder ranged from radical to anarchic.

The strain of simultaneously carrying cultural criticism, political consciousness, stylistic élan and musical innovation soon began to dilute punk which, as a distinctive mass-based phenomenon, died in the transition from youth sub-culture to diffuse cultural and intellectual movements. Overexposure began to destroy the authenticity of punk to the point where it became an all-encompassing description for a whole range of eclectic youth styles, from the infamous spiky hair, bondage trousers and ripped clothing, through the purple hair streak and studded belt of the suburbanite to the studied coolness of the new wave. Though commentators were quick to label it 'dole queue rock', the phenomenon was as Bohemian as it was proletarian (see PROLETARIAT) and, save for a few latter-day adherents, most young people have reverted to more predictable consumer habits beloved of the commercial interests that dominate the youth market. Art theory and sub-culture had, however, intersected, and post-modern theory (see POST-MODERNISM) was given a tremendous boost. For further reading: R. Bayley *et al*, *Blank Generation Revisited* (1997). P.S.L.

purchasing power parity theory, see under PARITY.

Pure Land Schools, see under BUDDHISM.

pure line. A pure line of organisms is a lineage which has become virtually homozygous (see GENE), so that genetic VARIATION has been extinguished. Pure lines can be achieved in self-pollinating plants and in laboratory animals such as guinea-pigs and mice which have been bred together, parent to offspring or brother to sister, for upwards of 50 successive generations. Sex differences apart, the members of such pure lines resemble each other as closely as if they were identical twins. P.M.

pure theory of law, see LAW, PURE THEORY OF.

purism. An aesthetic movement proposed in 1918 by Amédée Ozenfant and the architect Le Corbusier (Charles-Édouard Jeanneret) in their book *Après le Cubisme* which advocated the restructuring of CUBISM. Reacting to the prettification of Cubism after 1916 by painters such as Braque, and to the NEO-CLASSICISM of Picasso, purism sought to maintain the representation of clearly identifiable objects and forms and a logical composition. No significant school developed, despite the interest of other artists such as Fernand Léger, and some analogies in the work of Giorgio Morandi and certain NEUE SACHLICHKEIT artists. For further reading: A. Ozenfant, *Foundations of Modern Art* (1952). A.K.W.

purity/impurity. Notions particularly developed by English social anthropologists Mary Douglas and Edmund Leach (1910–89). Early work by Franz B. Steiner (*Taboo*, 1956) suggested the existence of objects or states surrounded by restrictions. They were regarded as unclean, polluting and dangerous. Ideas of purity and impurity were more fully elaborated in the wake of Lévi-Strauss and STRUCTURALISM. States of purity/impurity arise from the process of classification. Douglas described pollution or impurity thus: 'dirt is matter out of place' (*Purity and Danger*, 1966). Pollution arises from the disruption of cultural categories or from the area between categories. It is closely associated with POWER. Pollution can be the state of an object or a person, and in this condition they are regarded as contagious and surrounded by restrictions. Objects commonly designated as impure include semen, nail clippings and menstrual blood. Persons who are impure are frequently those in the process of movement between social states in a RITE DE PASSAGE. For further reading: E. R. Leach, *Social Anthropology* (1982). A.G.

purposive explanation, see under EXPLANATION.

purposivism. A label for any approach to PSYCHOLOGY which asserts that man is a purposeful, striving creature who is, in large part, responsible for his own conduct and destiny, e.g. William McDougall's HORMIC PSYCHOLOGY, COGNITIVE PSYCHOLOGY, EXISTENTIAL PSYCHOLOGY, HUMANISTIC PSYCHOLOGY. The opposite assertion is that man's conduct is nothing but the fully determined outcome of his heredity (see GENETICS/GENOMICS), his past experience, and his present ENVIRONMENT. For further reading: M. Wertheimer, *Fundamental Issues in Psychology* (1972). I.M.L.H.

Q

QCD, see QUANTUM CHROMODYNAMICS.

QED (quantum electrodynamics), see under FIELD THEORY.

QSO, see under QUASAR.

***Quadragesimo Anno*.** An encyclical issued by Pope Pius XI in 1931, 40 years after *rerum novarum* had asserted the rights of workers to receive a 'just wage' and to assemble in e.g. trade unions in order to achieve it. The *Quadragesimo Anno* expanded the Roman CATHOLIC teaching on social problems, condemning COMMUNISM and LAISSEZ FAIRE, and implying a preference for GUILD SOCIALISM. D.L.E.

Quakers. Members of a religious body, so nicknamed soon after its foundation by George Fox (1924–91); its official title is the Society of Friends. Dispensing with many of the outward forms of RELIGION such as creeds, professional clergy, and traditional words in worship, the Quakers have commended themselves by their philanthropy, their PACIFISM, and their basis in Christian (see CHRISTIANITY) MYSTICISM. Their nickname was suggested by their trembling or excitement when gripped by religious ecstasy (see PENTECOSTALISM), but nowadays in their worship calm, although spontaneous, words arise from a corporate silence. For further reading: H. Barbour, *The Quakers* (1988). D.L.E.

qualia (singular, 'quale'). The contents of conscious experience, including visual qualia (experienced colours, shapes, textures, movements), auditory qualia (experienced tone qualities, loudness), and thought qualia (what you experience when you are planning, considering, deciding, etc.). Some thinkers equate having CONSCIOUSNESS with having qualia. Many scientists think that brain mechanisms produce qualia, and even suspect that suitably designed machines (see ARTIFICIAL INTELLIGENCE) will have qualia. Others (often dubbed 'mysterians' by their opponents) argue that qualia cannot be explained by brain mechanisms, and claim that a machine with an exact duplicate of our brain might lack qualia, i.e. it might be an unconscious 'zombie' externally indistinguishable from conscious agents. Some (DUALISTS) even think qualia could exist without any physical substrate, e.g. surviving bodily death. Such debates are confused by the difficulties in properly defining these concepts. Perhaps qualia are simply components of VIRTUAL MACHINES. A.S.

quality circle. A management process in which a small group of employees involved in a particular area of an organization is formed into a team with the purpose of finding ways of improving the efficiency of the organization (e.g. the RECYCLING of waste materials from the production process). Quality circles originated in the field of quality control and they have been applied to many other areas of organizations. They are widely used in Japan. For further reading: G. A. Cole, *Management: Theory and Practice* (1982). R.I.T.; J.P.

quango. Acronym for Quasi-Autonomous Non-Government Organization. The term was coined in 1967 by Alan Pifer, President of the Carnegie Corporation, to describe private sector organizations which were financed wholly or largely by government. The term has since undergone a subtle shift in meaning. It is now generally used to refer to organizations which are set up and funded by governments, but which are given a large degree of autonomy to manage their own affairs, subject only to periodic review. Quangos are thus in theory free from day-to-day political pressures and gain the managerial benefits of operating at arm's length from government and close to the private sector. Examples in the UK include the British Broadcasting Corporation and the Commission for Racial Equality. The regulation of quangos has long been a source of concern, since most are not directly accountable to Parliament, but only to ministers. While the quango controls its own staffing and the distribution of its budget, its governing board is normally appointed by the executive, providing a useful source of patronage for government. For further reading: F. F. Ridley and D. Wilson (eds), *The Quango Debate* (1995). N.O.

quantification.

(1) In general, the expression of a property or quality in numerical terms. Properties that can usefully be expressed in these terms are said to be *quantifiable*; descriptions, theories and techniques couched in such terms are said to be *quantitative*. Despite the widespread myth that only quantitative measurements and descriptions are of use to science, many *non-quantifiable* things, i.e. things that cannot be usefully measured on numerical scales, can be given precise objective descriptions that can play a valid role in scientific theories and EXPLANATIONS. Thus linguists (see LINGUISTICS) describe the structures of sentences, chemists (see CHEMISTRY) describe the structures of chemical MOLECULES, COMPUTER scientists describe computational processes, and psychologists (see PSYCHOLOGY) may one day be able to describe the structure of mental processes, using precise mathematical language including *non-numerical* symbols. MENTALIST psychology and ARTIFICIAL INTELLIGENCE have taken the first steps in this direction. It is arguable that much research effort has been wasted – particularly in the SOCIAL SCIENCES, but perhaps also in the NATURAL SCIENCES, e.g. BIOLOGY – in attempting to force non-quantifiable processes into quantitative moulds, instead of searching for more relevant kinds of mathematical representation. A.S.

(2) In LOGIC, the referring aspect of propositions (see PROPOSITION, TYPES OF) which do not refer to a particular, designated individual but to all members or some members of a class (universally and existentially quantified propositions, respectively). In the PREDICATE CALCULUS, or logic of quantified statements, the basic, universally quantified formula 'For all *x*, if *x* is *A* then *x* is *B*' is not quite equivalent in meaning to its counterpart in ordinary language, 'All *A* are *B*'. It is entailed by it, but does not entail it, since the latter is not true unless there are some *A* things (i.e. unless it has 'existential import'), whereas the former is, vacuously, true if there are none. The quantificational interpretation of universally and existentially general statements justifies its deviation from ordinary language by its systematic formal manipulability and by its perspicuousness. On the second part, it makes explicit the ambiguity of 'Everybody loves somebody' which it represents either as 'For any *x* there is some *y* that *x* loves' or as 'There is a *y* that every *x* loves'. Besides 'all' and 'some' and their synonyms, language contains other quantificational expressions: 'most', 'many', 'several', 'a few'. A.Q.

quantitative history. Any serious attempt to present statistical evidence in a work of historical research. Economic historians took the lead in the 1920s with studies of price history. Political historians followed, using the methods of PROSOPOGRAPHY. More recently, quantitative methods have transformed SOCIAL HISTORY and have even made some impact on the HISTORY OF IDEAS, e.g. in the studies of *lexicometry* (the study of the frequency of theme words in a corpus of texts) carried out for 18th-century France. Quantitative historical studies received a great boost in the 1960s, when academics began to get access to COMPUTERS for their research projects. The profession is still divided about the reliability and the significance of the results. See also ECONOMIC HISTORY; SERIAL HISTORY. For further reading: R. Floud, *An Introduction to Quantitative Methods for Historians* (1973). P.B.

quantitative linguistics. A branch of LINGUISTICS which studies the frequency and distribution of linguistic units, using statistical techniques. The subject has both a pure and an applied side: the former aims to establish general principles concerning the statistical regularities governing the way words, sounds, etc., are used in the world's languages; the latter investigates the way statistical techniques can be used to elucidate linguistic problems, such as authorship identity. For further reading: P. Scholfield, *Quantifying Language* (1995). D.C.

quantity theory of money. A theory relating the price level in an economy to the MONEY SUPPLY and the volume of goods produced. Its simplest form is MV = PT, where M is the supply of money, V the velocity of circulation (i.e. the average number of times a unit of money changes hands within the given period), P the price level, and T the quantity of goods produced. This relationship is true by definition, i.e. it is an identity (see IDENTIFICATION, sense 1). Only if the velocity of circulation is assumed to be constant does the theory become of causal importance. Thus, writing the theory in the form P = (MV)/T, with V constant and a fixed level of output, the formula shows that the price level is proportional to the money supply. This theory is one of the basic tenets of MONETARISM. For further reading: J. Craven, *Introduction to Economics* (1984). D.E.; J.P.

quantum chemistry, see under THEORETICAL CHEMISTRY.

quantum chromodynamics (QCD). Quantum FIELD THEORY of QUARKS and GLUONS, so called because these particles possess an attribute called 'colour' which is an analogue of electric charge. QCD describes how quarks and gluons interact together. It possesses the property, called ASYMPTOTIC *freedom*, that interactions between quarks and gluons become weaker at high energies, and these PARTICLES behave as though they were free of any forces at very high energies. The intuitively reasonable converse of this property, called *confinement*, would result in all coloured particles being confined to exist in combinations of zero total colour charge at low energies. This remains unproven but is supported by all the unsuccessful experimental attempts to observe free quarks. PROTONS and NEUTRONS are combinations of three quarks with zero net colour. MESONS are combinations of a quark and an anti-quark with zero net colour. For further reading: F. Close, *The Cosmic Onion* (1984). J.D.B.

quantum dot. A structure so small that its electronic, optical or magnetic properties are strongly influenced by QUANTUM MECHANICS. The energy states of an ELECTRON in a quantum dot are different from those in a much larger piece of the same material. A quantum dot may support discrete energy states that can contain only a few electrons each, and to this extent it acts as a kind of artificial atom with characteristic states that can be altered by changing the dot's size. Because the electron energies influence the way the dot interacts with light, its optical properties (e.g., the colour of its fluorescent light emission) can also be tuned in this way. Thus quantum dots can provide both tools for investigating fundamental physics and structures that might have useful technological properties for high-density memories and light-emitting devices. P.C.B.

quantum electrodynamics, see under FIELD THEORY.

quantum electronics. A branch of engineering devoted to the design and construction of MICROWAVE power generators (e.g. the MASER) whose operation is based on QUANTUM MECHANICS. M.V.B.

quantum fluid. In PHYSICS, the behaviour of individual ATOMS is dictated by QUANTUM MECHANICS, but quantum effects are usually so small that they are not easily detected. As the temperature is reduced, however, the atoms move more slowly, and in two liquids, helium 4 and helium 3, their motions, instead of being quite random, appear to become correlated with one another. The complete assembly of atoms then appears to act as a single unit whose behaviour as a single entity is determined by quantum mechanics. This transition to what is called a quantum fluid occurs at very low temperatures (2.17 K for helium 4 and 0.002 K for helium 3) and is accompanied by a range of properties which are not observed in any other liquid. The most outstanding of these is the phenomenon of *superfluidity* – these liquids appear to have no viscosity and so they are able to flow through extremely fine channels or tubes without any apparent resistance. The term quantum fluid is also applied to the assembly of ELECTRONS in certain materials when they become superconducting (see SUPERCONDUCTIVITY). In this case it is the electrons which, instead of moving independently as they do at high temperature, interact and behave as a single system. This manifests itself in the complete disappearance of the electrical resistance of the material. H.M.R.

quantum Hall effect. Discovered by Klaus von Klitzing (Nobel Prize for physics, 1985). It is an extension of the HALL EFFECT technique when applied to a very thin layer of SEMICONDUCTOR (the active region of a special type of TRANSISTOR, the mosfet, was actually used). In a very high magnetic field at low temperatures the Hall voltage across the sample does not change gradually as the current through the material is increased.

Instead it exhibits a series of regularly spaced quantum jumps or steps whose height is accurately related to the quantity h/e^2, which involves the FUNDAMENTAL CONSTANTS h (PLANCK'S CONSTANT) and e (the charge on the ELECTRON). These steps can be measured with high precision and so the effect can be used to check the value of h/e^2, and also to establish a standard of electrical resistance. H.M.R.

quantum mechanics. System of mechanics originally formulated to account for physical phenomena at the subatomic level (see SUBATOMIC PARTICLE). Historically, quantum mechanics was the product of two distinct developments: the matrix mechanics of Heisenberg, Born and Jordan (a descendant of Bohr's original QUANTUM THEORY of the atom – see BOHR THEORY) and the wave mechanics of Schrödinger. While Heisenberg, Born and Jordan saw their theory as an agnostic attempt to account for the complexity of atomic spectra (see SPECTROSCOPY) without attributing a visualizable atomic structure, Schrödinger self-consciously introduced a theory based on the second-order differential equations that in CLASSICAL PHYSICS were characteristic of wave processes. Despite the clear interpretative and mathematical differences between matrix mechanics and wave mechanics, an intimate theoretical connection between the two theories was established by Schrödinger in 1926. This connection was cemented with their subsumption within more general formulations of quantum mechanics through the efforts of Born, Dirac and von Neumann.

Physical quantities are represented within quantum mechanics by OPERATORS. Associated with each operator is a particular range of functions (its *eigenfunctions*), and with each eigenfunction is associated a characteristic number. If a system is in a state describable by one of the eigenfunctions of the operator that represents a particular quantity (an *eigenstate*), then it can be said to possess the associated number as value for that physical quantity. However, it is a distinctive feature of quantum mechanics that it allows a system also to be in a SUPERPOSITION state, in which no determinate value is possessed. It is a consequence of the theory, in fact, that possession of a determinate value for one quantity (say momentum) may *preclude* a system from possessing a determinate value for another (in this case, position: see UNCERTAINTY PRINCIPLE). In classical physics, in contrast, physical systems are assumed always to possess determinate (although possibly unknown) values for all dynamical variables. This peculiar feature of quantum mechanics has led to a special importance for measurement within the theory, for direct measurements of physical quantities always result in determinate values. How can a system pass from a state (before measurement) in which no determinate value is possessed, to one (after measurement) in which such a determinate value is possessed? The theory itself gives no account of this process, which is sometimes called 'collapse of the wave packet'. One way to 'explain' how a determinate value can result from a measurement on a superposition is to appeal to the observer as cause of the collapse (see SCHRÖdinger's cat).

Quite what it means for a quantum system to be in a superposition has been a central issue in the long-running debates over how best to interpret the theory. According to one view – favoured by Einstein – quantum mechanics provides only incomplete descriptions of physical systems, which possess determinate values for dynamical variables at all times (see HIDDEN VARIABLES). These determinate values are revealed on measurement. Quantum states are not real states of physical systems: rather they express our ignorance of their real (but unknown) states. In another view, the quantum state is a real state of the system, and provides a complete description. In a superposition, the values of physical quantities are objectively 'fuzzy' or 'smeared out' (much like the 'position' of a wave). According to this view, measurement brings about a real physical change in the state of the system measured, which makes it especially difficult to give a response to the EPR PARADOX. In a third view, the COPENHAGEN INTERPRETATION championed by Bohr, it is meaningless to speak of the 'value' of a physical quantity independently of an experiment to measure that quantity. Since experiments to determine (say) position and momentum are mutually exclusive, it is meaningless to speak of the momentum value just when it is meaningful to speak of the position value, and vice versa (see COMPLEMENTARITY PRINCIPLE). For further reading: D. Z.

Albert, *Quantum Mechanics and Experience* (1992). R.F.H.

quantum number. A number used to label the state of a system in QUANTUM MECHANICS. For example, the ENERGY LEVELS of an ELECTRON in an ATOM have the quantum numbers 1, 2, 3, etc. (starting from the *ground state);* two further numbers label the rotational state, and a fourth (half-integral) quantum number describes the SPIN. Whenever the quantum number is an integer, it is equal to the number of oscillations of the WAVE FUNCTION. M.V.B.

quantum statistics. The QUANTUM MECHANICS of systems of identical PARTICLES (e.g. ELEMENTARY PARTICLES). The STATISTICAL MECHANICS of such systems depends on whether or not the particles are *fermions* (e.g. ELECTRONS and NUCLEONS), which obey the EXCLUSION PRINCIPLE, or *bosons* (e.g. MESONS and PHOTONS), which do not. See also BOSE-EINSTEIN STATISTICS; FERMI-DIRAC STATISTICS; SPIN. M.V.B.

quantum theory. A major branch of modern physical theory, developed above all by Max Planck from 1900 onwards, arguing for the emission of light or radiant energy from light-sources in discrete amounts, or 'quanta'. In 1905, Einstein lent his support to the theory by using it to explain photoelectricity (i.e. the ejection of ELECTRONS from metal surfaces). Following on from Planck and Einstein's work, it became necessary to view light as possessing both the qualities of waves and those of PARTICLES. Niels Bohr then extended quantum theory to the field of SUBATOMIC PARTICLES, arguing that electrons could 'jump' from one ORBIT of ENERGY to another, thereby causing the radiation PHOTONS (or light quanta).

This new perception that light sometimes acts like waves and sometimes like particles was subsequently extended to other fields of physics by Schrödinger, Heisenberg and De Broglie, in particular in the development of wave mechanics (see QUANTUM MECHANICS). Though challenging traditional NEWTONIAN MECHANICS, quantum theory is now established as a cornerstone of modern PHYSICS, even though its philosophical problems (concerning reality and causality) remain contentious. For further reading: D. Lindley, *Where Does the Weirdness Go?* (1996). R.P.

quantum wave function, see WAVE FUNCTION.

quark. In PHYSICS, one of three different hypothetical PARTICLES which might be the structural units from which many of the ELEMENTARY PARTICLES are constructed. Quarks have the unusual property that their electric charges are multiples of one-third of the charge on the electron. Despite extensive searches, no free quarks have yet been observed. This is precisely what is expected in the standard model of PARTICLE physics. Quarks are only expected to be manifested as pairs of quarks and anti-quarks (which produce the observed MESONS) and in triplets (which produce the observed HADRONS). All these combinations possess zero net colour charge. The presence of quarks within hadrons can be confirmed by the study of the detailed behaviour of these particles when bombarded by other high-energy particles. At present it is believed that quarks, along with LEPTONS, are indivisible: the most elementary particles of nature. For further reading: F. Close, *The Cosmic Onion* (1983). J.D.B.

quarter-tone, see under MICROTONE.

quasar. Astronomical object which emits enormous quantities of energy, equal to the output of hundreds of galaxies, despite being compact and starlike in appearance. The name arose as a contraction of Quasi-stellar object (or Quasi-stellar radio source) and is abbreviated as QSO. Quasars were first discovered in 1963 by John Bolton and Cyril Hazard, but many hundreds of others have since been identified. They possess very high red shifts of their emitted light, and this is now unanimously interpreted as being indicative of their high recession speeds and hence great distance from us. The greatest measured red shift is currently 5. The fact that their unusual observed light spectra could be simply explained as the red-shifted spectra was first pointed out by M. Schmidt in 1964. The large amounts of energy emanating from very small regions in the quasar have led to a theoretical picture of the quasar phenomenon in which a central BLACK HOLE accretes material which emits large quantities of radiation *en route* to being captured by the black hole (see ACCRETION). The light emission from quasars resembles that from other unusual types of GALAXY (Seyfert galaxies, BL Lacertae objects and radio galaxies – these are known collectively as active galaxies) which emit large quantities of radiation. Some quasars are surrounded by faint material which suggests that they might be the bright central regions of very distant active galaxies whose outer regions are too indistinct to be generally visible. It is believed that quasars are associated with the formation of the very first galaxies in the universe. A number of quasars have been found to possess identical companions near by on photographic images. This is believed to be the result of a very massive intervening object acting as a gravitational lens (see GRAVITATIONAL LENSING) and producing two images of a single object. Some unconventional explanations have been offered for the high red shifts of quasars which do not associate them with high recession velocities and hence argue that they are not at very great astronomical distances from us. These explanations do not seem to be consistent with all known facts about quasars. For further reading: M. Begelman and M. J. Rees, *Gravity's Fatal Attraction* (1996).

J.D.B.

quasi-stellar object, see under QUASAR.

queer theory. A theoretical approach based on analysing societies and cultures from the viewpoints of lesbian, gay, bisexual and transgendered people (see SEXUALITY; GENDER; HOMOSEXUALITY). Queer theory focuses, in particular, on showing how concepts of heterosexuality and masculinity depend on the simultaneous covert desire for, and overt denial of, homosexual attraction.

Queer theory draws together several antecedent ideas from recent philosophical currents and from gay and lesbian movements. Gay liberation (see GAY POLITICS), in its heyday in the early 1970s, posited that 'homosexuality' and 'heterosexuality' are artificial distinctions in the flow of desire which should be overcome in the name of a more 'liberated' sexuality. French post-structuralist theory, most notably the work of Guy Hocquenghem and Michel Foucault, drew attention to the ways in which homosexual identities and peoples had been manufactured through discourses peculiar to 19th-century Europe (see IDENTITY; DISCOURSE; DISCOURSE OF POWER). Social constructionist theory noted the cultural and historical specificity of Western understandings of sexuality, gender and family. Queer Nation, a short-lived spontaneous social movement of the early 1990s, challenged the apparently increasing acceptability and banality of lesbian and gay identity by attempting to disrupt conventional categories of gender and sexuality. Finally, queer theory relies, as well, on camp, the long-standing popular tradition of irony among gay men that punctures pretensions of the heterosexist universe such as gender conformity, machismo, FAMILY VALUES and PATRIARCHY.

One of the most influential statements of queer theory appeared in 1990 in Judith Butler's *Gender Trouble*, which challenged the 'naturalness' of conventional ideas of gender and sexuality, stressing the performative and interdependent aspects of the concepts of male and female, homosexual and heterosexual. Critics of queer theory have found it too oriented towards questions of style and performance, and too little informed by an analysis of the practices of homophobic institutions such as STATES, corporations, FAMILIES and mass media.

B.D.A.

Qumran, see under DEAD SEA SCROLLS.

R

r&b, see RHYTHM AND BLUES.

R&D, see RESEARCH AND DEVELOPMENT.

race. A classificatory term, broadly equivalent to subspecies. Applied most frequently to human beings, it indicates a group characterized by closeness of common descent and usually also by some shared physical distinctiveness such as colour of skin.

Though the concept is a very commonly used one, it has been largely scientifically discredited. The consensus among social scientists today is that race is a social construction, rather than a genuine biological category. They recognize that all humans derive from a common stock and that groups within the SPECIES have migrated and intermarried constantly. Human populations therefore constitute a genetic continuum (see GENETICS/GENOMICS) where racial distinctions are relative, not absolute. It is also acknowledged that visible characteristics, popularly regarded as major racial pointers, are not inherited in any simple package and that they reflect only a small proportion of an individual's genetic make-up.

With the advent of MENTAL TESTING as a means of attempting to measure INTELLIGENCE, the concept of race became more controversial, with some researchers claiming that, because some groups of black children have performed badly on intelligence tests, they are genetically inferior to whites. The most recent version of this claim is popularized by Richard Herrnstein and Charles Murray in their book *The Bell Curve* (1994). Critics of this notion point out that intelligence and other 'mental' tests are designed from a white, middle-class perspective that is skewed towards one group and will inevitably lead to poor performance by the other. They argue that intelligence is not distributed in the population by race, but arises from a combination of genetic and environmental factors. M.D.B.; S.T.

race riots. A term which gained currency in the 1960s, then applied mainly to the dozens of disturbances in American cities beginning in 1964, but worsening and attracting international attention with the riots, based on BLACK economic and political resentments, in the Watts district of Los Angeles in 1965. Three years of urban unrest established common features different from those of earlier American disturbances occasioned by racial tensions, whose history predates the Republic and which until the 'two sided' riots of 1919 were characterized by white attacks on black Americans and their property, to an extent resembling POGROMS. The 1960s pattern instead included the spontaneous response of urban blacks to acts of perceived local injustice or police oppression; the burning and looting of white-owned property; the need for major local, National Guard and federal responses; numerous deaths.

Other Western nations have not been immune to analogous events: notably in 1981 several British cities experienced major clashes between predominantly young blacks and the white authorities, particularly over questions of economic disadvantage and alleged racial biases in policing and the criminal justice system (see RACISM). A more complex pattern emerged in Los Angeles in 1992, when black anger, catalysed by perceptions of a racially unjust court case involving apparent police violence, led not only to anti-white protests but to the looting and burning of stores and businesses owned by Asian-Americans, and sporadically also involving Hispanic-Americans. Lesser but significant 'copycat' events in several other cities further highlighted multiracial tensions and the politically under-recognized problems faced by many urban blacks. S.R.

racial stereotypes. Racial stereotyping occurs when a person commits what the philosopher Alfred N. Whitehead (1861–1947) called the fallacy of misplaced concreteness. Whitehead identified this fallacy in reference to a philosophical analysis of the concepts of mind and matter, but it also has application to our everyday lives. According to Whitehead, this fallacy occurs when one mistakes the abstract for the concrete.

The fallacy occurs in reference to RACE when we assume that a concrete individual (say a BLACK person) has characteristics that are thought to belong to black people in general. We are not warranted in inferring that a specific black person has C from the claim that black people in general have C. Racial stereotyping is thought to involve the improper use of racial generalizations. However, the crucial question is 'When are racial generalizations improper?'

Some theorists argue that racial generalizations are always improper because they have pejorative connotations. According to these theorists, they are harmful even when they are not the result of malevolent motives. Other theorists maintain that some racial generalizations are not pejorative and do not entail any wrongdoing. According to their view, racial generalizations are acceptable if they are based upon good statistical information. H.M.

racism. A dislike, hatred or fear of people belonging to RACES other than one's own, often wedded to the conviction that some races are fundamentally superior to others. Much racism in the 20th century has been justified by dubious appeals to scientific theories; however, mankind's tendency to discriminate on the basis of race has historically depended not on science, but on more primitive impulses and intuitions. Men depict themselves and see one another in terms of groups which, however frail their objective basis, thereby assume social importance.

Psychologists now identify several different forms of racism, ranging from those rooted in the individual personality to cultural and institutional racism. Many consider that defining race prejudice as an individual-level trait – e.g., viewing it as symptomatic of some kind of personal psychopathology – distracts attention from its social and cultural nature. How the phenomenon is conceptualized clearly affects the kinds of countermeasures that will be appropriate for its reduction and prevention.

Institutionalized racism was exemplified by APARTHEID in South Africa, where domestic social and political relations were explicitly structured around race criteria, until 1993. However, race was a major – and still underestimated – theme in the rest of the Western world from at least 1850 until 1945. The term *racialism* applies to the doctrines about the central significance of racial inequality that were developed by Western scientists in that period, which would soon be linked with SOCIAL DARWINISM. They contributed to the ethos of IMPERIALISM, and in Europe to ANTISEMITISM. An early landmark in this literature of racist determinism was A. de Gobineau's *Essay on the Inequality of the Human Races* (1853–55). The theory and practice of NAZISM marked the culmination. Even today, however, the tradition's basic idiom of virtuous purity and vicious blending remains embedded in much popular thinking about race. The suggestion by writers like Hernstein and Murray (*The Bell Curve*, 1994) that there is a correlation between race and intelligence has given new life to these theories.

Attempts, notably in the US, to reverse the effects of past racial discrimination have met with controversy. In 1978, the US Supreme Court (see SUPREME COURT OF THE UNITED STATES) ruled in *Regents of the University of California v. Bakke* that AFFIRMATIVE ACTION was constitutional: they argued it was acceptable to discriminate on grounds of race, if the purpose in doing so was to bring about a more egalitarian society (see EGALITARIANISM). This led to the quota systems – where jobs and university places were specifically set aside for racial minorities – which were vigorously promoted by the Carter administration. However, critics of positive discrimination argue that even if the motives for discriminating are noble, racial discrimination is wrong whatever form it takes; some found it difficult to reconcile the Supreme Court's 1978 judgement with its earlier assertions that the Constitution was 'colour-blind'. For further reading: J. Solomos and L. Black, *Racism and Society* (1996). M.D.B.; G.R.; H.M.

radar (RAdio Detection And Ranging). A system whereby short pulses of MICROWAVES are sent out from an aerial, which may be on land, or on a ship or aircraft. Any objects in the path of the beam cause echoes which are received back at the source. The time delay and nature of these echoes (viewed as a display on a cathode ray tube) give information about the distance and nature of the reflecting object. See also SONAR. M.V.B.

Radburn principle. Developed in Radburn, New Jersey: each Radburn superblock (NEIGHBOURHOOD) was ringed by a peripheral road to take through traffic, while culs de sac provided penetration into the neighbourhood. Pedestrians gained access to the front doors of their houses and could walk to the shops, schools and community centres within the neighbourhood by means of separate landscaped footpaths. Cars gained access to the rear of the houses through the culs de sacs and there were originally no footpaths (sidewalks) alongside the roads. This subsequently caused some confusion and danger for residents when the Radburn concept was imported into British new town schemes, such as Milton Keynes. Women were fearful of using isolated footpaths, while children played in the garage courts and cul de sac areas behind the houses at risk from reversing cars, and nobody quite knew which was 'really' the front and which the back door. For further reading: C. S. Stein, *Towards New Towns for America* (1957). C.G.

radiation. Waves or PARTICLES travelling outwards from a source; also the emission of such waves or particles. The term usually refers to electromagnetic waves (see ELECTROMAGNETIC FIELD). These cover an enormous frequency range (the 'electromagnetic spectrum') of which visible light (see OPTICS) constitutes only a very small part.

The principal kinds of electromagnetic waves, in order of increasing wavelength, are: GAMMA RAYS, X-RAYS, ultraviolet radiation, visible light, INFRA-RED radiation, MICROWAVES, and radio frequency waves. Frequency and wavelength are related by the equation *wavelength × frequency = speed of light in empty space*; the speed of light is 300 million kilometres per second. See also BLACK-BODY RADIATION; QUANTUM MECHANICS; SPECTROCSCOPY. M.V.B.

radiation biology (or **radiobiology).** The branch of BIOLOGY that deals with the immediate and long-term effects of RADIATIONS, particularly ionizing radiations, and the useful purposes which such radiations may be made to serve. Penetrating ionizing radiations such as X-RAYS and GAMMA RAYS have a disruptive effect on DNA (see NUCLEIC ACID) and can therefore lead to MUTATION (see RADIATION GENETICS). They also suppress CELL division – a property that is put to good use in the RADIOTHERAPY of tumours, for it is characteristic of radiation and of radiomimetic drugs (i.e. drugs whose pharmacological actions mimic those of irradiation) that they both cause CANCERS and also, under different conditions of administration, discourage their growth. A characteristic biological effect of radiation and radiomimetic drugs on warm-blooded animals is that of interfering with the manufacture of red blood corpuscles because of the destruction of stem cells. For a cognate reason, such radiations also diminish IMMUNITY (sense 2). In experimental animals the transplantation of bone marrow is a feasible method of repairing radiation injury in so far as it affects the manufacture of red blood corpuscles, but the genetic effects of radiation are cumulative, irreversible and, in general, harmful (see GENETICSGENOMICS).

Radiobiology also includes the preparation and use of radioactively labelled ELEMENTS and compounds to serve as TRACERS in studies of metabolism. The use of radioactive substances (see RADIOACTIVITY) for this purpose needs to be controlled by strict regulations, and the same applies to the use of radioactive substances in painting watch dials, etc. In all civilized countries legislation has been introduced to reduce to a minimum the population's exposure to radioactive substances, whether produced by atomic or NUCLEAR WEAPONS or by atomic power plants (see ATOMIC ENERGY; NUCLEAR REACTOR). P.M.

radiation genetics. A branch both of GENETICS and of RADIATION BIOLOGY that grew up under (1) the influence of American geneticist H. J. Muller's discovery in 1926 that ionizing RADIATIONS can induce MUTATION, and (2) the realization that certain industrial processes and offensive weapons may increase the dosages of radiation to which human beings are exposed. For further reading: P. C. Koller, *Chromosomes and Genes* (1971). P.M.

radical. In CHEMISTRY, a term used since the time of Antoine Lavoisier (1743–94) – though now rarely – to denote a building block in the construction of a chemical compound. A radical is often merely one ATOM, but is frequently a group of atoms which behaves as a single atom or ION. Thus ethane (C_2H_6) can be considered as the combination of two methyl (CH_3) radicals, while the ammonium ion and the sulphate ion are examples of inorganic radicals. B.F.

radical chic. A phrase coined in 1970 by American journalist Tom Wolfe to describe specifically a benefit concert given by Leonard Bernstein for the Black Panthers (see BLACK POWER) and, more generally, the current fashion of adopting radical political causes (see RADICALISM) in New York society. He likened this trendy romanticizing of primitive souls, e.g. American Indians and Chicano grapeworkers, to the French 19th-century phenomenon denoted by the phrase *nostalgie de la boue* (literally, 'hankering after mud'). A.K.W.

radical feminisim. To many people all FEMINISM is radical, in that it questions given structures of social and sexual (see SEXUALITY) organization in which men and masculinity achieve greater public and private power than women. But the generally accepted interpretation of radical feminism is the one which understands the term as a theory of universal male dominance over women.

Radical feminism thus asserts sexual difference as the primary form of social difference, in which relations between women and men are structured in terms of the male oppression of women. Theorists such as Mary Daly, Adrienne Rich and Andrea Dworkin have argued that men have constructed a phallocentric culture in all societies (see SOCIETY), and cite social practices such as foot-binding and clitoridectomy as instances of woman-hating practices which are inspired and tolerated by patriarchal (see PATRIARCHY) cultures.

The practical implications of radical feminism have been many and various, while the powerful political statements by women such as Catherine Mackinnon (on PORNOGRAPHY) have inspired feminist initiatives on a number of issues. Radical feminism is often associated with sexual separation and the articulation and establishment of women-only institutions and associations. The target of radical feminism attack is, however, less men *per se* than masculinity and those cultural practices which seem to endorse and condone masculinist behaviour. The refusal by some radical feminists to tolerate the importance of class and ethnic differences has separated them from liberal and socialist feminism, and this has created intense argument within feminism about the nature and cause of women's oppression. For further reading: S. Jeffreys, *The Idea of Prostitution* (1997). M.S.E.

radical geography. A perspective that asserts that the world's HUMANISTIC GEOGRAPHY can only be properly understood by considering the way in which spatial distributions of all kinds are shaped by the inequitable and socially divisive workings of economy and society. Proponents of this perspective are particularly critical of GEOGRAPHY as spatial science, which is seen as isolating geographical distributions from their socioeconomic context when seeking to 'explain' them by reference to the known laws of GEOMETRY and the hypothesized laws of spatial organization. As one alternative to this type of geographical inquiry, a number of recent studies by radical geographers have adopted a welfare stance that seeks to relate spatial disparities in wealth, welfare and resource ownership to inequalities inherent in regional, national and international social structures. Another alternative has been the adoption of a MARXIST stance, which aims to sharpen these welfare accounts by tracing the links among spatial disparities, social inequalities, and the economic logic of an underlying mode of production (which in most cases is found to be CAPITALISM). There are many difficulties with these radical geographies, such as the danger of slipping into an economic DETERMINISM that is insensitive to the role of human thought and action. But there can be little doubt that they constitute a significant and provocative break from previous traditions of geographical inquiry. For further reading: R. J. Johnston, 'Radical Approaches' in *Geography and Geographers: Anglo-American Human Geography since 1945* (1997). C.P.; P.O.M.

radical lesbianism, see under FEMINISM.

radicalism. A tendency to press political views and actions towards an extreme. Historically, radicalism has always been associated with dissatisfaction with the status quo and an appeal for basic political and social changes. But the meaning of the word has varied in different periods and countries, ranging from the moderate CENTRE, like the

Parti Républicain Radical et Radical Socialiste which was influential in France before 1939, but was neither radical nor SOCIALIST, to the extreme ultra-revolutionary (see REVOLUTION) radicals of the post-war NEW LEFT. Although in some countries, e.g. the USA, 'radicalism' is mostly used with reference to the LEFT (where radicals are clearly distinguished from liberals; see LIBERALISM), it can also be characteristic of the RIGHT; notable examples are FASCISM and NAZISM. The term is also used in the wider sense of a disposition to challenge established views in any field of human endeavour, e.g. in the arts or scholarship. For further reading: M. J. Lasky, *Utopia and Revolution* (1976). L.L.

radio astronomy. A branch of ASTRONOMY, in which RADIO TELESCOPES are used to study electromagnetic RADIATION at radio frequencies emitted by sources outside the earth. Most of the radio sources are GALAXIES, but the sun and the planet Jupiter, as well as PULSARS, QUASARS and SUPERNOVAE, all emit radio waves. Apart from visible light, radio waves (in the 1 cm to 10 metre wavelength band) constitute the only electromagnetic radiation (see ELECTROMAGNETISM) capable of reaching the ground without being absorbed in the atmosphere or reflected by the IONOSPHERE. The revolution in COSMOLOGY in the last two decades has been stimulated largely by the discoveries of radio astronomy, especially the COSMIC BACKGROUND RADIATION. For further reading: M. Beigelman and M. Rees, *Gravity's Fatal Attraction* (1996). M.V.B.

radio isotope. Any ISOTOPE of an ELEMENT which is radioactive (see RADIOACTIVITY). Some radio isotopes occur naturally but others may be produced artificially by NEUTRON irradiation or by bombardment with helium and other light NUCLEI. They are widely used in diverse fields including medicine (e.g. in RADIOTHERAPY), GEOLOGY and ARCHAEOLOGY (see RADIOCARBON DATING), as well as PHYSICS, CHEMISTRY, BIOLOGY and ENGINEERING. Radioactive traces provide information on the mechanism of chemical reactions, diffusion processes, chemical analysis, rates of wear, etc. B.F.

radio stars, see under INVISIBLE ASTRONOMY.

radio telescopes. The 'eyes' of RADIO ASTRONOMY, which receive and locate the direction of radio frequency electromagnetic RADIATION reaching the earth. Because the wavelength of such radiation is thousands of times greater than that of visible light, radio telescopes are gigantic structures. The steerable parabolic dishes which focus the radio waves (in the same way as the mirrors of ordinary telescopes focus light waves) may be hundreds of feet across, while *radio interferometers*, which locate direction by measuring the PHASE difference between the waves reaching different aerials in an array, may extend over several miles. M.V.B.

radioactivity. The spontaneous decay of certain types of atomic NUCLEUS. Decay usually takes place by emission of an ALPHA PARTICLE or by the decay of one of the nuclear NEUTRONS and emission of the resulting beta particle; thus radioactivity generally results in a change in ATOMIC NUMBER. It is not possible to predict the precise moment at which a given unstable nucleus will decay. However, the HALF-LIFE can be calculated by means of QUANTUM MECHANICS.

Most naturally occurring ISOTOPES are stable; the exceptions either have long half-lives (e.g. several thousand million years for uranium) or else are produced continuously by various processes (e.g. radium is a decay product of uranium, and radiocarbon is produced in a NUCLEAR REACTION by COSMIC RAYS – see RADIOCARBON DATING). A great number of short-lived radioisotopes can be produced artificially in NUCLEAR REACTORS (see also TRACE ELEMENT). The health hazards of radioactivity arise from the ENERGY liberated when PARTICLES collide with atomic nuclei in living matter. This causes mechanical damage to tissues, and affects the genetic structure of CELLS, often resulting in MUTATION (see GENETICS/GENOMICS). M.V.B.

radiobiology, see RADIATION BIOLOGY.

radiocarbon dating. In ARCHAEOLOGY, a method of DATING pioneered by American chemist W. F. Libby, who first proposed it in 1946. It is based on the rate of decay of the radioactive (see RADIOACTIVITY) ISOTOPE C^{14} incorporated in organic matter. C^{14} is produced from nitrogen^{14} by cosmic

RADIATION in the upper atmosphere and is absorbed by living matter in the form of carbon dioxide. The proportion of C^{12} to C^{14} remains constant in the atmosphere and in living plants and animals, but as soon as the organism dies, and further absorption of carbon dioxide ceases, the proportion of C^{14} to C^{12} is steadily decreased by the decay of the unstable radioactive isotope. If we know the HALF-LIFE of C^{14} and the ratio of C^{14} to C^{12} in a sample it is, in theory, possible to work out the absolute age at the time of death for a substance which was once alive. The validity of the method as an absolute dating technique rests on two basic assumptions: that the half-life of C^{14} can be accurately determined, and that C^{14} has been produced at a constant rate. Early calculations used a half-life of 5,568 ± 30 years (the 'old half-life'), but recent recalculation suggests that 5,730 is a better approximation (the 'preferred half-life'). Comparison between radiocarbon dates and historical dates (e.g. obtained from dating Egyptian woodwork) has for some time shown a certain lack of CORRELATION. Recent studies involving the radiocarbon dating of tree rings of known age (see DENDROCHRONOLOGY) have confirmed the discrepancy. It is now suggested that the production of C^{14} was not constant throughout time and that it is necessary to recalibrate 'radiocarbon years' against tree-ring dates to arrive at 'real years'.

Dates are always quoted ± x years, representing the standard statistical error; 4300 ± 50 BC means that there is a 2:1 chance of the date lying between 4250 and 4350. Dates are often published BP (before the present), the present being 1950. In the wake of the confusion following the apparent need to recalibrate, some writers have adopted the procedure of quoting the date 'BC' meaning 'radiocarbon years' and offering a recalibrated date 'BC' to represent an approximation to 'real years'. Each data assessment is uniquely numbered according to international agreement. It is accepted that this laboratory number should always be quoted. For further reading: T. Watkins, *Radiocarbon: Calibration and Prehistory* (1975).
B.C.

radiology. The study of the human body by the utilization of X-RAYS, which were discovered by German physicist Wilhelm Conrad Röntgen in 1895. As a beam of X-rays passes through the body it is attenuated to different degrees by different tissues. The pattern of the X-ray beam emitted from the patient is then recorded on photographic film. *Computed tomography* (CT) uses X-rays to produce an image of a thin slice of a patient in cross-section. The machine is designed so that the X-ray source circles the body through 360° and the information obtained is recorded by special detectors. This information is then analysed in a COMPUTER and the image produced is displayed on a television monitor. The advantage of CT over conventional radiology is that very fine differences in the attenuation of X-rays can be delineated and it is possible to identify tissues and abnormalities not visible on a conventional X-ray film. *Ultrasound* has been widely used in medicine since the early 1970s. An ultrasound pulse is produced by a transducer. The pulse penetrates the tissues of the body and produces an echo at tissue interfaces. These echoes are recorded and displayed on a television monitor. Ultrasound is mainly used for examination of abdominal and pelvic organs and is particularly useful for the assessment of pregnancy. Advances in ultrasound have led to the development of transducers which can measure blood flow through major vessels and can record cardiac abnormalities. Nuclear Magnetic Resonance (NMR) is a new development in clinical medicine. The patient is placed in a magnet and hydrogen atoms within the body are excited by a radio frequency pulse. The hydrogen atoms line up in the direction of the magnetic field. The pulse is then switched off and the hydrogen atoms relax, giving up energy as they do so. Different tissues relax at different rates and this information provides the basis of magnetic resonance imaging. The images produced demonstrate anatomy and PATHOLOGY in a similar way to CT, but since they are obtained in a different way, different and sometimes more detailed information is obtained.
J.H.

radiotherapy. The use of ionizing RADIATION in the treatment of CANCER based on the ability of many normal tissues to recover from the CELL-killing effects of radiation more efficiently than malignant tissues. Radiotherapy has a major curative role in cancers which have not spread far from their sites of origin at the time of diagnosis. Ionizing radiations in the form of X-RAYS or GAMMA RAYS are generated by LINEAR ACCELERATORS or produced as decay products of radioactive ISOTOPES such as cobalt 60 or iridium 192. Linear accelerators enable sharply defined beams of X-rays to be directed accurately at deep-seated tumours from different directions, thereby ensuring maximum dose to diseased tissues with minimal exposure of surrounding healthy tissues. Radioactive isotopes in the form of small tubes, needles or wires can be inserted temporarily inside or around diseased organs to treat, e.g., cancers of the uterine cervix, mouth, tongue and breast, resulting in the cure of selected patients without recourse to radical SURGERY. J.R.Y.

ragtime. An ancestor of JAZZ with a firm identity of its own. It began to emerge in the late 19th century in the southern and south-western US, the hotbed of BLACK musical CULTURE, and came to be particularly associated with the towns of St Louis and Sedalia, in Missouri. It blossomed into maturity in the gay nineties as an ideal accompaniment to the ebullient dance of the era, the cakewalk. Ragtime's chief characteristic is snappily syncopated melodies over a regular march-like, 'oompah' bass. Though performed by instrumental combinations, it was and is primarily a piano genre, and its most famous compositions were written for the instrument, like 'Maple Leaf Rag' and the many other works by Scott Joplin (1868–1917), the medium's greatest composer. Though the syncopation is an obvious link, ragtime is a more limited and more formal genre than jazz, lacking the expressive depth supplied by the BLUES, and demanding strict fidelity to the written score. It could be said to have anticipated SYMPHONIC JAZZ, influencing classical composers like Debussy and Stravinsky. GE.S.

rainbow coalition. The term was first applied to the unsuccessful mayoral campaign of BLACK candidate Mel King in Boston, Massachusetts, in 1983, in which King attempted to construct an electoral coalition which united racial and sexual MINORITIES, FEMINISTS, progressive clergy, the PEACE MOVEMENT and LEFT-labour ACTIVISTS. The strategy became, in modified form, that of Jesse Jackson's attempt to win the Democratic Party's presidential nomination in 1984. The movement led by Jackson sought to tilt the balance of power within the party towards its less advantaged and more radical supporters, and to raise issues which the party's 'mainstream' wished to avoid. These included continuing problems of racial inequality; REAGANISM's lack of sympathy for feminist causes and gay rights (see GAY POLITICS); the moral premises of America's foreign and defence policies. The coalition in 1984 failed to develop convincingly from its largely black base, partly because of Jackson's inability to distance himself from Black Muslim (see NATION OF ISLAM) supporters such as Louis Farrakhan. Since 1984 the movement has tried to convert itself into a stable organization, but is still characterized by internal tensions and predominantly black support. For further reading: A. L. Reed Jr, *The Jesse Jackson Phenomenon* (1986). S.R.

rainforest. Not all rainforest is tropical and not all tropical forest is rainforest. Nevertheless, the term rainforest is most often used with reference to the rainforests of the tropics, which lie between the Tropic of Cancer and the Tropic of Capricorn. The largest of these is found in the Amazon river basin of South America, the second-largest in south-east Asia, and the smallest in the Congo river basin of Africa.

Tropical rainforests are characterized by high input of solar energy, frequent (essentially daily) rainfall totalling about 2 metres annually, essentially constant high temperature and humidity, and dense green vegetation throughout the year.

The relentless growth of the global human population (see POPULATION PRESSURE) results in dramatic and continuing losses of tropical rainforest. Growing markets for lumber and meat trigger the felling of the forests, with their replacement by farms and cattle ranches (see DEFORESTATION; CLEAR CUTTING). Because tropical rainforests are singularly rich in plant and animal SPECIES, this deforestation is accompanied by declines in BIODIVERSITY. Tropical rainforest soils are thin and fragile, lacking in organic matter and containing high concentrations of iron and aluminium oxides. When the forest is removed the soil is subject to sun and rain which cause chemical changes leading to the formation of an impervious layer termed laterite. This process of laterization soon renders the soil unfit for agriculture or for reforestation, and may have been the cause of the disappearance of some ancient civilizations, such as the Khmer in Cambodia. Temperate rainforests, such as those of the coast of western Canada and the north-western US, are also undergoing intense deforestation, as are the deciduous dry tropical forests found at higher altitudes in Central America. W.G.R.

ramified theory of types, see under PARADOX.

random number. Everybody thinks they know what is meant by this term, but it is difficult to give a precise definition. To begin with, a single number cannot be random – what we hope is random is the method of choosing the number. It is not enough to say 'every number must be chosen equally often, in the long run': 1, 2, 1, 2, 1, 2, . . . has this property but is not a random sequence. One might say 'there is no way of guessing the next number to be chosen' – but even then there may be a tendency for some numbers to be chosen more frequently (some roulette wheels are made like that!). N.A.R.

random variable. Any way of obtaining a number which describes the outcome of an experiment in PROBABILITY THEORY. Thus with the experiment 'toss a coin 10 times' we might associate the random variables 'number of heads', 'length of longest sequence of heads', etc.; with the experiment 'draw a card', the random variable 'number of pips'. See also DISTRIBUTION. R.SI.

random walk, see under STOCHASTIC PROCESS.

range (in STATISTICS), see under DISTRIBUTION.

rank. A CONCEPT in some theories of LINGUISTICS which suggests that the relationship between linguistic units and structures is best viewed taxonomically in terms of composition, a particular structure being described in terms of units which operate at a 'lower' level or rank. It is an important concept in neo-Firthian (see FIRTHIAN) linguistics, where sentence, clause, group, word and MORPHEME are placed on a *rank scale*. See also LEVEL. D.C.

rank-size relations. The distributions which result when objects in some collection are arranged by rank-size order (i.e. the largest first, the next-largest second, and so on). Rank-size studies have been particularly used by biologists in the study of SPECIES abundance and by urban geographers in the analysis of city sizes by population. For further reading: G. K. Zipf, *Human Behaviour and the Principle of Least Effort* (1965). P.H.

rap. A musical style which first arose in black neighbourhoods in New York in the 1970s. The name itself was 1960s slang for straight talking. The music was based on rhythmic rhymed patter improvised by one or more speakers accompanied by a disc jockey who provided a complex recorded background by sampling bits of different discs on separate turntables and mixing them into a single track. Rap's intensity and variety was a reaction to the glossy artifice of DISCO. Its lyrics also directly reflected black urban experience of privation, anger and despair, qualities which emerged in the 1982 hit 'The Message' by the seminal rap group Grandmaster Flash and the Furious Five. Rap took a more aggressive turn in the Californian style called 'gangsta rap': its lyrics revelled in sex and violence, attacks on police and any other adversary, and actually inspired mini-gang wars, resulting in the deaths of several rap stars. GE.S.

rape. A type of sex offence in which a victim is subjected to a non-consensual sexual act. Laws vary from country to country (and, in the US, from state to state) about precise legal definitions, but the act need not necessarily include penetration of the vagina by a penis – indeed, in a significant number of rape cases, there is no ejaculation. There are a number of types of rape, examples of which include *statutory rape* (sex with a person under the legal age of consent); *opportunistic rape* (committed when the opportunity arises, for instance in the commission of another crime, such as burglary); and *serial rape* (the rape of numerous victims over a period of time, usually conforming to an identifiable pattern).

Rape is a crime of epidemic proportions in the West, and it is difficult to measure its incidence accurately. Only one in ten victims of rape report to the police. The reasons for this are complex, and include shame, police insensitivity and victims' unwillingness to relive their ordeal in a public trial, with all its attendant publicity. The causes of rape are the subject of heated debate, especially among feminists and criminal psychologists. It is traditionally held that rape is a sex crime in the sense that the rapist seeks sexual gratification. Feminists and others – including prosecutors and experienced police investigators – argue that rape is more about POWER than it is about SEX; that rapists are more intent on controlling, humiliating, terrifying and hurting their victims than they are on solely forcing them to have sexual relations. This debate over the causes of rape leads to a discussion of appropriate punishment and/or treatment of rapists. Those in favour of treatment argue that therapy, perhaps in association with CASTRATION, can be effective, while at the same time reducing the cost of imprisonment. Critics of this view argue that incarceration is the correct answer, as rapists have a high rate of recidivism, and that castration may provoke some rapists into attacks of even greater brutality in which substitutional objects (guns, knives) may replace the penis, and in which murder may be the result. For further reading: S. Brownmiller, *Against Our Will* (1986). S.T.

rare earth. Any ELEMENT with ATOMIC NUMBER between 57 and 71. Rare earths are all metals, closely similar in their ELECTRON SHELL structures and chemical properties. M.V.B.

Rastafarianism. A BLACK religious and sociopolitical movement first articulated by Marcus Garvey (1887–1940) in Jamaica during the 1930s, though having roots in the Caribbean's earlier experiences of colonialism. It came to prominence as a specific vehicle for the expression of black identity in white societies such as Britain in the 1970s, while continuing to manifest itself in the West Indies. The conceptual order of the Rastafarian is centred on Ras Tafari (Haile Selassie, Emperor of Ethiopia 1930–74, regarded as divine), the shared identity and interests of all black people, the decadence of white social, political structures and values (known as Babylon), the eventual return to Zion (Africa), and the use of ganja (cannabis) as a sacrament to achieve spiritual enlightenment. The millennial (see MILLENARIANISM) PAN-AFRICANISM of the movement must be seen primarily as a symbolic response to the predicament of deracinated and marginalized blacks in white industrial cultures. It combats low self-esteem, dissolves inferiority and subordination, and fosters a new separatist sense of identity rooted in the past and ordering the future. Two particularly recognizable attributes of (male) Rastafarians are their physical appearance – dreadlock hairstyles (multiple coiled locks of hair), the red, green, black and gold colours – and their predilection for REGGAE music. Female Rastafarians are encouraged to adopt modest dress and a generally supportive stance. Its many youthful adherents bestowed subcultural (see SUB-CULTURE) connotations on the phenomenon, and the struggle to have religious legitimacy conferred upon it continues. For further reading: P. B. Clarke, *Black Paradise: The Rastafarian Movement* (1986). P.S.L.

rational choice theory. Rational choice theory (also known as public choice) attempts to explain political institutions and public policy by modelling the behaviour of rational actors – be they individuals, political parties or other organizations. It uses RATIONALITY assumptions to explain the behaviour of actors and explain political outcomes by the strategic response of actors in given structural and institutional settings. Rational choice theory is often viewed as methodologically individualistic, but by generalizing the preferences of actors and the strategic situation in which they find themselves, it produces structural explanation as much as individualistic. Rational choice theory has been most important in explaining the unintended consequences of human action. This includes, through the 'invisible hand', socially optimal outcomes, despite self-interested action, and, through 'back of the hand' processes, suboptimal outcomes, despite common interests. Rational choice is most famous for these collective active problems. For further read-

ing: J. Elster (ed.), *Rational Choice* (1986); D. C. Mueller, *Public Choice II* (1989).
K.M.D.

rational-emotive therapy. Therapeutic technique developed by Albert Ellis during the 1950s after he had abandoned PSYCHOANALYSIS and POST-FREUDIAN methods as too lengthy and relatively unsuccessful. Fusing a range of contemporary ideas from post-Freudianism, BEHAVIOURISM and COGNITIVE PSYCHOLOGY, Ellis began addressing patients' problems in a more direct and rational fashion, e.g. setting them 'homework' on tasks they found difficult, claiming more rapid outcomes and higher success rates. Ellis saw his task as enabling clients to develop a rational philosophy of life, paying little attention to previous life-history and the childhood origins of their problems. The client has, rather, to actively learn and rethink his view of life. Ellis was especially hostile to the concepts of sin and blame, seeing mental distress as fundamentally a result of rectifiable irrationality. Rational-emotive therapy was thus in marked contrast to the various other new psychotherapies which emerged at around the same time (such as GESTALT, PRIMAL THERAPIES and TRANSACTIONAL ANALYSIS). Ellis's tradition is now generally called COGNITIVE THERAPY, although that has slightly broader connotations. For further reading: A. Freeman, K. M. Simon, L. E. Beutler and H. Arkowitz (eds), *Comprehensive Handbook of Cognitive Therapy* (1989).
G.D.R.

rational expectations. Rational expectations theory suggests that people are not going to continue to use a FORECASTING rule that makes the same systematic mistake. It suggests that usually people will predict the future correctly even if they do not understand the causal processes which led to their prediction. This does not mean that people will always get the future exactly right. Sometimes people will think INFLATION will be higher than it actually proves to be, sometimes they will predict it to be lower; but they will not make systematic errors in the same direction for ever. Only completely unforeseen shocks will lead people's best estimates of the future to go completely astray. (See RATIONALITY and RATIONAL CHOICE THEORY.) For further reading: C. L. F. Attfield *et al*, *Rational Expectations in Economics* (1985).
K.M.D.

rational number, see under NUMBER.

rationalism. Either (1) apriorism (see A POSTERIORI, A PRIORI); or (2) the opposite of IRRATIONALISM, in which sense it denies the acceptability of beliefs founded on anything but experience and reasoning, deductive or inductive (see INDUCTION); or (3), a little datedly, disbelief in the supernatural. In PHILOSOPHY the first meaning is commonest. The 'Rationalists' are the great 17th-century metaphysicians (see METAPHYSICS) Descartes, Spinoza and Leibniz, who believed that the general nature of the world could be established by wholly non-empirical demonstrative reasoning.
A.Q.

rationality. Explaining human behaviour requires understanding individuals' reasons for action. Reasons are composed of DESIRES and BELIEFS. Given any two of the trilogy belief, desire, action, the third can be explained given stringent rationality conditions including connectedness, transitivity and independence. Connectedness says one can relate all possible objects in some preference ordering: i.e., I always know whether I prefer strawberries to raspberries or am indifferent between them. Transitivity says if an individual prefers strawberries to raspberries and raspberries to loganberries then he must prefer strawberries to loganberries. Without transitivity individuals could not choose for they would always be prepared to swap one alternative for another. Independence says my preference between two objects should not depend upon my preference between each and some third independent alternative. Thus if I choose rabbit rather than chicken from the menu, I should not then decide to have the chicken when I am told that duck is also available. Without rationality it is difficult to explain human action. People often break these conditions. When we eat unhealthy food despite wanting to be healthy we break connectedness. Intransitive preferences are revealed in surveys, especially through 'framing effects' where alternatives can be made more attractive through description. Independence is broken in experiments through 'asymmetric dominance'. This occurs when two alternatives (x and y) are rated on two criteria, with *x* preferred to *y* on one criterion and *y* preferred to *x* on the other. If a third alternative *z* is introduced which is worse than *x* on both criteria, but better than *y* on one criterion, experiments show that people are now more likely to choose *x*. Despite such cases where strict rationality breaks down, people generally conform to the rationality assumptions. (See RATIONAL CHOICE THEORY; RATIONAL EXPECTATIONS; BOUNDED RATIONALITY.) For further reading: P. Anand, *Foundations of Rational Choice Under Risk* (1995); S. P. Hargreaves Heap, *Rationality in Economics* (1989). K.M.D.

rationalization. A DEFENCE MECHANISM whereby the individual justifies his behaviour by imposing on it a plausible rational explanation. W.Z.

rationing/prioritizing. The distribution of scarce health resources to populations and individuals. Rationing may occur at different levels – from national decisions on the amount of resources allocated to health, to individual access to treatments. Examples include limiting self-referral to specialist care, excluding certain treatments from healthcare systems, excluding certain categories of patients from treatment (e.g. on the basis of age or medical condition), and the use of waiting lists. During the 1980s concern about the rising cost of health services led governments and health insurance companies in many countries to try to develop fair and explicit ways of rationing healthcare. Unresolved issues include the question of who should decide on health priorities – patients, the public, health professionals or politicians – and the difficulty of comparing benefits or cost-effectiveness across different categories of health interventions ranging from preventive medicine to surgery. A fundamental difficulty has been the relative value of health benefits to different individuals. Some have advocated UTILITARIANISM as the philosophical basis of resource allocation, while others have favoured alternative systems of DISTRIBUTIVE JUSTICE with a greater emphasis on fairness and equity. D.F.

Raumbühne, see under SPACE (2).

rave. One of the defining elements of youth culture since the 1980s, raising the concept of partying to a new level of dedicated intensity. Usually taking place in a venue in the country, a barn or marquee in a field, raves are organized by well-heeled young people who dance to DISCO music at shattering volume, often against a background of disorientating lighting effect. Drugs are a central ingredient of the experience, which aims to create a complete environment. Night-clubs may seek a similar atmosphere, but the true rave occasion must be as self-contained as possible: a world of sensory stimulation all its own. GE.S.

rayograph, see PHOTOGRAM.

rayonism. Method of painting evolved by Michel Larionov in Moscow in 1912 and expounded in his pamphlet *Luchism*, 1913 (Italian tr. *Radiantismo*, 1917). Since the eye sees objects by means of rays of light, the colour relationship and intersection of these can be used in non-objective compositions. Rayonist works by Larionov and Goncharova figured in the Target (*Mishen*) exhibition in Moscow, 1913, and in Paris (1914; also a retrospective exhibition in 1948). The movement, which bears some relationship to FUTURISM and its 'lines of force', was short-lived, and few of the manifesto's other signatories made a name. In the mid-1950s Goncharova again produced some rayonist works. For further reading: W. George, *Larionov* (1966). M.C.

reactionary. Adjective or noun applied to those who not merely resist change but seek to put the clock back and return to some earlier order of society which is seen as having possessed characteristics (discipline, respect for authority and privilege, a hierarchical structure, sense of duty) which the present is felt to lack. The word *reaction* was much used by 19th-century radicals (see RADICALISM) who spoke of the 'forces of reaction' (the Catholic Church, absolutist monarchies and hereditary aristocracies) blocking progress towards a more just, equal and enlightened society. Contemporary radicals would characterize the forces of reaction differently but would have as little doubt as their predecessors that such forces exist and are still bent upon blocking change and annulling reforms already achieved.

The words 'reaction' and 'reactionary'

are commonly regarded as the opposite of 'progress' and PROGRESSIVE. Few people, however, would describe themselves as reactionary, and the term is thus most frequently pejorative. It is employed mainly by the LEFT although both the Nazis (see NAZISM) and the FASCISTS also used it, in their case to describe the resistance of traditional INSTITUTIONS to their RIGHT-wing radicalism. A.L.C.B.

reactor, see NUCLEAR REACTOR.

reader-response theory. An influential school of thought in literary theory, mostly based in America, but influenced by RECEPTION THEORY critics such as Wolfgang Iser. Leading exponents are Norman Holland, Stanley Fish, David Bleich, Walter Benn Michaels, Michael Riffaterre and Jonathan Culler. These critics emphasize the important role of the reader in establishing the 'meaning' of any literary text, thus subverting the emphasis which is traditionally laid upon the text as an 'objective' entity whose nature and meaning are to be established by the self-effacing reconstructions of the reader or critic. Reader-response theory emphasizes, on the contrary, that the 'meaning' any literary work is accorded will depend to a very large degree on the 'subjective' contributions of the reader as he reads, hence the title of one of Norman Holland's most important books, *5 Readers Reading*, where it is the 'identity theme' of the reader which in fact constitutes the meaning of the work being read. This is argued by comparing five different sets of perfectly acceptable responses to a single literary text, Faulkner's story 'A Rose for Emily'. Holland sees himself as writing *transactive criticism*, i.e. a criticism which is a free interchange between subjectively offered text and subjectively constituted reading. Holland's influence on other members of the 'Buffalo School' (e.g. David Bleich's *Subjective Criticism*, 1978) has been pervasive. Drawing on insights in Iser's *The Implied Reader* (1974), reader-response criticism has insisted upon a diminished objectivity of the given text, an insistence which has fitted in harmoniously with the doctrine of DECONSTRUCTION. Instead of an unknowable Kantian DINGE-AN-SICH (see NOUMENA), the literary text now becomes a matter of subjective agreement between 'writer' and 'reader'. Stanley Fish has emphasized the degree to which even the very act of reading, the travelling eye across the line, can set up and constitute properties of the text which the original author had deliberately left in a 'virtual state' – a state which has to be 'fulfilled' by any given reader. This is connected to the phenomenological (see PHENOMENOLOGY) doctrine of INTENTIONALITY, and indeed reader-response criticism, in its insistence upon the MEANING-conferring nature of the act of reading, is phenomenological through and through. This is clearly visible in Iser's second famous book, *The Act of Reading* (1978), which creatively disagrees with the work of Roman Ingarden, Husserl's disciple, without for all that abandoning the basic theoretical assumption that all reading is a phenomenological act, deeply complicit with various kinds of intentionality. For further reading: J. Tomkins, *Reader-Response Criticism* (1980). R.PO.

readymades. Term adopted in the USA by the painter Marcel Duchamp (1887–1968) to describe his DADA-like use, for exhibition and similar purposes, of incongruous manufactured objects such as the porcelain urinal which he submitted to a New York jury in 1917. These continued to feature in his *oeuvre* after his return to Paris in 1919, being put forward, in an ironic-nihilistic spirit, as works of art rendered so by the arbitrary decision of the artist. J.W.

Reagan doctrine. Term used by Karl Krauthammer in the April 1985 edition of *Time* to describe President Reagan's foreign policy. It was seen as a reaction to the 'VIETNAM syndrome' and President Carter's emphasis on US promotion of HUMAN RIGHTS. The US ambassador to the UN expressed its essence by writing that 'the central goal of our foreign policy should be . . . the preservation of civilized conceptions of our own national interest'. This was translated by Reagan into a constant evocation of the Soviet threat – he once described the former USSR as the 'evil Empire' – and a return to the support of authoritarian regimes (see AUTHORITARIANISM) in their suppression of revolutionary movements. The doctrine justifies limited intervention to suppress such movements, but avoiding if possible the use of US combat personnel by engaging local forces to do the job (as with the CONTRAS in NICARAGUA and UNITA in Angola) in what has been termed (by Robert Pfaltzgraff) 'low intensity combat'. Some doubt was shed on the compatibility of such actions with international law (see PUBLIC INTERNATIONAL LAW) and it led to much criticism of US foreign policy towards the THIRD WORLD. A.W.

Reaganism. The term given, mainly by the European media and the LEFT, to the ideological character of the rhetoric and policies of Ronald Reagan's two terms as President of the US (1981–85, 1985–89). The term has an imprecise meaning; Reagan was not noted for depth or clarity of conceptual thought, and the fragmented structure of US government inhibits consistency and coherence in policy-making. It may, however, be seen as a variant of American CONSERVATISM which bears some New RIGHT influences and which rejects many of the premises of NEW DEAL liberalism which dominated American politics from 1932 to the 1970s. Reaganism aimed to reinvigorate the US economy by reducing government regulation of business, taken to stifle innovation and reduce flexibility; and by tax cuts whose rationale was derived from SUPPLY-SIDE ECONOMICS. The economic recovery after 1983 was arguably more the result of massive increases in defence expenditure, and hence was accompanied by an unprecedentedly large budget deficit. Reaganism also claimed a commitment to reducing the size and cost of the federal government, partly by devolving programmes to state level, partly by cuts in WELFARE expenditure. These aims were largely frustrated by the resistance of state governments and Congressional opposition. Reaganism's proclaimed commitment to conservative social values such as the defence of the FAMILY, the protection of religion, and a resistance to FEMINISM, were pursued less through legislation than by more modest tactics such as the appointment of conservatives to the federal judiciary. In foreign policy, some distinctive strands were discernible behind the inconsistencies created by executive-branch disunity and electoral imperatives. Policy was largely shaped by emphasis on East–West relations, to the extent that some observers identified a second COLD WAR. The Soviet Union was regarded with suspicion and, sporadically, open hostility, and it was stressed that any attempt at ARMS CONTROL should be undertaken with caution and from a strong bargaining position (see REAGAN DOCTRINE). For further reading: J. L. Palmer and I. V. Sawhill (eds), *The Reagan Record* (1984). S.R.

real. In PSYCHOANALYSIS, a LACANIAN notion which emerged in the early 1950s as a limit concept in relation to the SYMBOLIC. The real, in one sense, is simply what is excluded from the symbolic, excluded from the network of signifiers which build up the reality of the world, and which is hence impossible to know. Given that a major part of the analytic experience is concerned with this real, Lacan attempted to theorize it using an algebra consisting of what he baptized as MATHEMES: in this way, he thought, it was possible to transmit, through symbolic letters, what otherwise escaped knowledge and, specifically, linguistic representation. D.L.

real number, see under NUMBER.

real time.

(1) In music, the ability of an ELECTRONIC MUSIC or computer music device to react quickly enough to produce music at the speed at which it is performed. Early electronic and computer music often required setting-up and computing time that was longer in duration than the music itself, but recent advances in technology have made real time instruments common, thus facilitating live (as opposed to pre-recorded) electronic music.

Real time composition is also used to refer to a method of programming sequencers and drum machines in contrast to STEP TIME COMPOSITION.

(2) In dance, the performing of an action (e.g. walking) in the amount of time that it would take in real life rather than in some artificial, perhaps music-dominated time scale. Real time is an important facet of POST-MODERN DANCE. B.CO.

realignment. A term of American origin denoting a major shift in the partisan allegiance of substantial blocks of voters, which then becomes the stable base of a new balance of political forces for a long period. In its more formal version, a realignment may develop over several elections or occur at one 'critical' election; it reverses the majority and minority status of parties in a two-party system; is accompanied by a rise in PARTICIPATION, a heightened intensity of debate, and the emergence of new issues in the political arena. Some authorities find the concept more appropriate to the past than the present, believing that the modern US electorate is in a phase of *dealignment*, in which many voters have replaced their former allegiance with great fluidity of choice. Both terms are now applied to other electorates, with variations in precise meaning. For further reading: J. E. Chubb and P. E. Peterson (eds), *The New Direction in American Politics* (1985). S.R.

realism.

(1) In philosophy, the view that statements concerning a given area of discourse are without exception made determinately true or false by mind-independent facts (see TRUTH; BELIEF). Thus, a realist about the past believes that any statement concerning the past, such as 'A dinosaur stood on this spot 70 million years ago', is determinately true or false, whether or not any empirical evidence is now available for or against that statement (see EMPIRICISM). By contrast, an anti-realist about the past holds that there are no 'facts of the matter' which determine the truth or falsehood of such a statement independently of empirical evidence which is available to us now. One may be a realist with regard to one area of discourse, such as talk about the past, while being an anti-realist with regard to another, such as talk about material objects, mental states, or MATHEMATICS. But no one, it seems, could coherently be an anti-realist with regard to every area of DISCOURSE. Anti-realism is usually motivated by considerations to do with MEANING, especially the thought that we cannot intelligibly confer upon a statement a meaning which transcends the empirical possibilities of its verification or falsification. More narrowly, realism in the philosophy of science is a belief in the existence of theoretical entities, such as atomic particles; in METAPHYSICS, realism is a belief in the existence of abstract entities, such as UNIVERSALS. For further reading: M. Dummett, 'Realism', in his *Truth and Other Enigmas* (1978). E.J.L.

(2) In the arts, a key term used to define both a general, recurrent characteristic of nearly all art, and a specific historical movement. Realism in the general sense – what Harry Levin calls the 'willed tendency of art to approximate to reality': to attempt precise imitation of external and historical experience, to make empirical observations, to follow laws of probability, to seem true – has magnetized artists as diverse as Homer, Breughel and Defoe. During the 19th century, however, realism grew from a technique into a powerful theoretical aim: first and foremost in painting, but also in fiction and drama. Reacting against ROMANTICISM and philosophical IDEALISM, suspicious alike of MYTH, RELIGION and abstraction, it concentrated heavily on the here-and-now, and developed new techniques for the detailed, accurate representation of life in all its social and domestic aspects.

In France between 1848 and 1870 it was a key aesthetic movement; it had a political component, was to some extent a child of the 1848 Revolution, and carried radical implications (see RADICALISM). Its primary theoreticians were Champfleury and Duranty; as exemplary artists they took Courbet and Degas, whose 'plebeian' realism contrasted and interacted with Flaubert's 'higher' version. A key line runs from Balzac to Flaubert to the Goncourts, and into NATURALISM. In England, Mrs Gaskell, George Eliot and George Moore are representative; in Russia, Gogol, Turgenev and Tolstoy; in Germany, Raabe, Fontane and early Mann; in the USA, James and W. D. Howells. The realist sensibility embraces arguments as various as George Eliot's view of Dutch genre painting as a model for the novelist; the Goncourts' demand that the novel provide the social history of the lower classes; and Flaubert's claim of 'no lyricism, no beauty, the author's personality absent'.

Both in painting, via Courbet, Manet and Degas, and in literature, realism evolved (a) towards IMPRESSIONISM, stressing the aesthetic and perceptual technique, the new way of setting down what was seen; and (b) towards naturalism, emphasizing the scientific and evolutionary elements that help interpret the subject. Erich Auerbach in *Mimesis* has emphasized, however, the long historical dimension of realism, and its role in attaching art to familiar experience through numerous sceptical techniques. Realism cannot logically be formless, nor beyond form; it is itself an aesthetic and contains certain logical structures. However, one of its triumphs is to limit complex techniques and mannerisms so that (as Spanish philosopher Ortega y Gasset puts it) art becomes 'humanized'. Thus it emphasizes character, controls fantasy and idealism, and insists on experience, fact and the sceptical view in the spirit of Howells's 'Is it true – true to the motives, the impulses, the principles that shape the life of actual men and women?' Today it is usually identified as a BOURGEOIS phase of style, associated with EMPIRICISM and INDIVIDUALISM, but deep-seated concepts of realism persist in forms as varied as SOCIALIST REALISM and CHOSISM. For further reading: E. Auerbach, *Mimesis* (1953). M.S.BR.

realism, critical. A theory of PERCEPTION which denies that the perceiver is ever directly aware of material objects which exist independently of him but holds that he can derive knowledge of independent material things from the appearances or SENSE-DATA which are directly present to perceptual consciousness. Dawes Hicks in Britain, Arthur Lovejoy and George Santayana in the USA, were the chief critical realists so to describe themselves – the doctrine was first advanced in Santayana's book *Essays in Critical Realism* (1920). The word 'realism' marks a contrast with IDEALISM or PHENOMENALISM, which take objects to be wholly constructed out of appearances or ideas; 'critical' indicates a rejection of the naïve realism (see next entry) which takes our perception of material objects to be commonly immediate or direct. A.Q.

realism, naïve (or **direct realism).** The theory that in PERCEPTION we are as a rule directly and non-inferentially (see INFERENCE) aware of material objects which exist independently of us. Its does not imply that we always perceive things as they really are, nor does it imply that we ever perceive more than a small selection of what is true about a material object. It rejects the consequence derived from the *argument from illusion* that what are directly perceived are never material objects, but always private SENSE-DATA or impressions. Its adherents, disliking the derogatory epithet 'naïve', often describe themselves as direct realists. For further reading: D. M. Armstrong, *Perception and the Physical World* (1961). A.Q.

realistic grammar. In LINGUISTICS, an approach to grammatical analysis which aims to be psychologically real, in that it contributes to the explanation of such areas of linguistic behaviour as comprehension and memory. A contrast is intended between this approach and earlier, formal characterizations of GRAMMAR on the basis of intuition alone. The aim is to 'realize' a TRANSFORMATIONAL GRAMMAR within a psychological model of language use, so that the model genuinely represents users' knowledge of their language. For further reading: M. Halle *et al*, *Linguistic Theory and Psychological Reality* (1978). D.C.

***réalités nouvelles*,** see under ABSTRACT ART.

reality principle. In psychoanalytic theory (see PSYCHOANALYSIS), a FREUDIAN term for the principle governing the functioning of the EGO. The reality principle imposes constraints on the PLEASURE PRINCIPLE by delaying gratification until the desired object or state can realistically be achieved and by causing an impulse towards such a goal to be modified into a socially acceptable form. W.Z.

***Realpolitik*.** Term originated by the German publicist Ludwig von Rochau in his *Grundsätze der Realpolitik* (1853), a critique of the lack of realism in the policies followed by the German Liberals during the years 1848–49. The term was particularly applied to Bismarck's policy during and after the years of German unification, and is to be distinguished from a policy of self-interest or from a ruthless reliance on naked power. The phrase has been used, by American theorists of international politics opposed to the ideological elements (see IDEOLOGY) in traditional American foreign policy, to cover the integration of POWER, morality and self-interest into a 'policy of the possible'. For further reading: H. J. Morgenthau, *Politics among Nations* (1967). D.C.W.

Rebel Art Centre, see under VORTICISM.

recapitulation. The notion embodied in the familiar phrase that in development an animal 'climbs up its own family tree' – i.e.

that the development of an individual animal recapitulates its ancestry. In this naïve form *recapitulation theory* is associated with the German naturalist Ernst Haeckel (1834–1919; see also PHYLOGENY) and is entirely discredited. The element of truth in it is the unquestioned fact, sometimes referred to as von Baer's principle (see EMBRYOLOGY), that the embryos of related animals resemble each other more closely than do the corresponding adults. As an animal develops from a ZYGOTE we can determine its affinities with increasing confidence: first the embryo will be recognizable as a chordate (see ZOOLOGY), then as a vertebrate, then as a mammal, then as a primate, and finally, maybe, as a man. P.M.

reception theory (*Rezeptionsästhetik*). A school of literary theory associated with the University of Konstanz and grouped around the journal *Poetik und Hermeneutik* from 1964 onwards. Unlike READER-RESPONSE THEORY, which is made up of a set of independent reflections on the importance of the reader in the act of reading, the Konstanz theory has a certain corporate identity. In America, Wolfgang Iser was a well-known member of the school, but the most famous statement of its aims is Hans Robert Jauss's essay 'Literary History as a Challenge to Literary Theory' (1970). Attempting to avoid the impasses of MARXISM and FORMALISM, neither of which take much account of the reader, Jauss proposes that a literary work should in future be studied in terms of the impact it has upon its contemporaries. In order to establish this impact it is necessary to discover the 'horizon of expectations' that environs the new work. The indebtedness of this concept to Jauss's old teacher Hans-Georg Gadamer, and his own use of the Husserlian concept of *horizon*, is evident. Jauss instances and analyses the differing receptions accorded to Flaubert's *Madame Bovary* and Feydeau's *Fann*, both of which appeared in 1857. For further reading: R. Holub, *Reception Theory* (1984). R.PO.

receptor. Structural or molecular grouping in, or on the surface of, a CELL which has an affinity for a pharmacological or immunological agent (see IMMUNITY; PHARMACOLOGY). Thus in IMMUNOLOGY an *antigen* on a cell surface may be thought of as a receptor for the *antibody* whose formation it may excite if administered in a suitable way. Likewise, cells which are specifically affected by them are presumed to have receptors for various drugs. The same applies to hormones (see ENDOCRINOLOGY) and the cells they act upon, resulting in SIGNAL TRANSDUCTION and RECEPTOR-MEDIATED ENDOCYTOSIS. P.M.; P.N.

receptor-mediated endocytosis. After a hormone (see ENDOCRINOLOGY) or an equivalent signalling MOLECULE binds to its RECEPTOR, one result is SIGNAL TRANSDUCTION. Another is that the complex of hormone and its receptor is removed from the surface of the CELL to the interior within small vesicles. Receptor-mediated endocytosis, as the process is known, ensures that the signal delivered by the hormone is short-lived. The notion survives that the hormone and its receptor can trigger responses within the interior of the cell, but it is more likely that the hormone is simply destroyed there, while the receptor is recycled to the surface of the cell. For further reading: B. Alberts *et al*, *Molecular Biology of the Cell* (1983). P.N.

recession, see under DEPRESSION (3).

recessive, see under GENE.

recidivism. Behaviour of the repeat or 'habitual' offender, serially arrested and/or reconvicted for offences. Usually measured in terms of reconviction within certain time periods (e.g. one, five or ten years). Personal and social problems (e.g. alcohol/drug dependency, homelessness) may be underlying contributory factors. Reconvictions may involve trivial or very serious offences; however, we cannot know how many repeat offences go undetected, hence we do not know the true extent of recidivism. Strategies for dealing with the problem have included experiments in sentencing and community supervision which may also seek to restrict the offender's movement and association within a community. For some, the use of electronic tagging may be considered. N.S.

recombinant DNA, see under GENETIC ENGINEERING.

recombination (in GENETICS), see CROSSING OVER.

***reconciliación*.** The term – which means reconciliation – has become a by-word for the compromises being made in a number of Latin American countries to balance the identification and punishment of those who violated HUMAN RIGHTS during the military regimes of the 1970s and 1980s with the need to ensure a stable and peaceful transition to democratic rule. Following the return to DEMOCRACY in Argentina in 1982, many of those responsible for human rights violations were imprisoned. This was possible owing to the demoralization and weakening of the military following its defeat in the 1982 FALKLANDS WAR, although many were later pardoned by the government of President Carlos Menem. In contrast, in Chile, where the armed forces remain strong, the democratic administration of President Patricio Aylwin set up a Truth and Reconciliation Commission to investigate only those cases of abuse which resulted in death between 1978 and 1990, although most abuses occurred between 1973 and 1978. These are exempt by an Amnesty Law promulgated by the military government in 1978. Very few cases have come to court, and even fewer have resulted in convictions. Although a relatively small number of human rights activists in these countries – and others in Latin America – have sought to keep the issue high on the political agenda, governments have by and large successfully neutralized political conflicts which may have potentially damaged civil–military relations. For further reading: A. B. de Brito, *Human Rights and Democratization in Latin America: Uruguay and Chile* (1997). M.A.P.

reconstructive surgery, see under PLASTIC RECONSTRUCTIVE SURGERY.

recreational geography. The systematic field of GEOGRAPHY devoted to the study of leisure-time activities. Local concerns centre on demands for, and access to, recreational facilities. Where longer-distance travel is involved, *tourism* is a leading concern, particularly its impacts on regional economies, cultural landscapes and natural environments. The geography of sport is a new research focus and connects to parallel work in such cognate fields as HISTORY, ECONOMICS and SOCIOLOGY. For further reading: S. L. J. Smith, *Recreation Geography* (1983). P.O.M.

rectification. A general term used in Chinese politics to refer to campaigns directed against those whose ideas do not conform with the official line, the first one being in Yan'an in 1942 (see LONG MARCH). The idea is to criticize others and, more importantly, to accept criticisms in order to rectify mistakes and realize the errors of one's past. Rectification campaigns have been used often in the latter half of the century. Because of the responsiveness of the masses to the central directives – particularly evident under Mao Zedong (1893–1976) – rectification was used as an opportunity to purge those cadres or leaders whose positions were becoming too powerful. Deng Xiaoping (1904-1997), who was himself the subject of rectification during the GREAT PROLETARIAN CULTURAL REVOLUTION, led the reformers who rehabilitated many political prisoners after Mao died, and carried out their own rectification campaign from 1982 to 1985 to remove those who did not support reform. S.B.

recursion (or recursiveness). In LINGUISTICS, the attribute of rules which may be applied an indefinite number of times in the generation of sentences, e.g. a rule which would introduce an adjective before a noun. D.C.

recursive function theory. The study of what can and what cannot be done by an ideal COMPUTER (limitations of space and time being entirely ignored). Its importance for MATHEMATICS comes through the general acceptance of *Church's thesis*: any effective, or routine or algorithmic process in mathematics (see ALGORITHM) can be performed by an (ideal) computer. The first such 'computer' considered – in 1936, before modern computers existed – was a TURING MACHINE, which was to work in the following manner: Let P be a property of natural NUMBERS or of finite sequences of symbols ('words'); P is *decidable* (or *computable*, or *solvable*) if there is a program for an ideal computer such that when any number n or word W is given as input the computer will (eventually) print 1 if n or W has the property P and 0 otherwise, e.g.

'being prime' is decidable. The most significant from a great range of results are: (1) '*W* is a theorem of the PREDICATE CALCULUS' is undecidable; (2) '*W* is a diophantine equation (see NUMBER THEORY) which has a solution' is undecidable. But, in contrast to (1): (3) '*W* is a correct proof in the predicate calculus' is decidable; (4) '*W* is a theorem of ''elementary'' Euclidean GEOMETRY' is decidable ('elementary' is a technical term; Euclid's theorems all satisfy it). The theory is closely linked with GÖDEL'S THEOREM, and with INTUITIONISM (sense 3). For further reading: D. R. Hofstadter, *Gödel, Escher, Bach* (1980). R.G.

recursiveness, see RECURSION.

recycling.
(1) The recovery of scrap material after use, followed by reprocessing in order to permit of further use, sometimes of a different kind, as when waste paper is used in the manufacture of cardboard. The word has become a battle-cry among those concerned with the POLLUTION of the ENVIRONMENT and with the need for CONSERVATION of the earth's resources. In this context it usually refers to the decomposition of biodegradable materials after use so as to form nutrients for fresh organic growth, this in turn renewing the source of the original materials.

(2) In ECONOMICS, accumulated surpluses on a country's current and/or capital accounts of the BALANCE OF PAYMENTS may be put back into international financial circulation. This recycling can be conducted through the country's CENTRAL BANK, or, as is more common since the early 1970s and the era of freer foreign exchange (see EXCHANGE CONTROL), through the decisions of private individuals, firms and financial institutions. This recycling is important to the growth of world trade and the stability of the world financial system. See DEBT CRISIS; EURODOLLARS; OIL CRISIS. For further reading: R. B. Johnston, *Economics of the Euromarket* (1982). J.P.

Red Army.
(1) Originally, a catch-phrase for the army of the former USSR: the Soviets themselves stopped using the name in 1946.

(2) A terrorist organization (*Sekigun*) of extremist if vague revolutionary views which emerged from the Japanese radical (see RADICALISM) student movement in 1969. It is characterized by (a) its rejection of Japanese CHAUVINISM on the one hand and of NON-VIOLENT RESISTANCE on the other; (b) the elimination of internal disagreement by a willingness to kill dissenting members of the group; (c) the large part played by women in its ranks; and (d) the transference of its activities, following drastic pressure from the Japanese police, to bases and activities in Europe and the Middle East. These include the action at Lod airport in Israel in May 1974 in which 26 were killed and 71 injured by indiscriminate machine-gunning of airport users; the hijacking of airliners to Korea in 1970 and in Amsterdam in 1973; an attack on an oil refinery in Singapore in February 1974; the seizure of the French Embassy at The Hague in September 1974; and the hijacking of an airliner at Dacca in September 1977. Following this last incident the Red Army was heard from less frequently, but it still commits occasional acts of terrorism today, and has never disbanded. D.C.W.; J.A.A.S.

Red Cross. The International Committee of the Red Cross (ICRC) has been entirely Swiss since its foundation in 1863, when it protected the rights of wounded and captured soldiers. Florence Nightingale criticized the organization as legitimating WAR. National Red Cross organizations were affiliated to the ICRC, and from the 1890s increasingly undertook welfare work. Islamic Red Crescent organizations were also affiliated. In 1919 the ICRC opposed a new type of organization, the League of Red Cross Societies, which saw a peacetime role for Red Cross organizations, while wishing to end Swiss control. The ICRC kept its position, seeking to negotiate new agreements to protect soldiers, but failing to secure protection for civilians under occupation. During World War II, the ICRC was compromised by the pro-German bias of the Swiss, when it failed to prevent the atrocities of the Nazi-run (see NAZISM) CONCENTRATION CAMPS and the HOLOCAUST. The ICRC has subsequently taken a more dynamic role in often challenging crisis situations. For further reading: J. F. Hutchinson, *Champions of Charity: War and the Rise of the Red Cross* (1996). P.J.W.

red giant. A very large, relatively cool star near the end of its life (see HERTZSPRUNG-RUSSELL DIAGRAM). Red giants may be hundreds of times larger than the sun in diameter, but their densities are extremely low – some are more tenuous than air.

M.V.B.

Red Guards. A civilian revolutionary (see REVOLUTION) militia formed mainly among students and idealistic youth in China during the period of the GREAT PROLETARIAN CULTURAL REVOLUTION, as a response to Mao Zedong's appeal to maintain revolutionary fervour and attack bureaucratic and administrative inertia. After clashing with the work teams sent into educational establishments by Deng Xiaoping and Liu Shaoqi in order to restore their authority, the Red Guards became noted for their excesses of enthusiasm and vindictiveness against their opponents, and even against rival Red Guard factions. With the country at a standstill and in a state of virtual civil war, the People's Liberation Army stepped in to restore effective control of society, and the students were ordered to return to their studies in November 1967. The name has come to be connected with the indiscriminate destructive excesses of the Cultural Revolution, and the blind loyalty of hot-headed idealistic youth in their support of a party or IDEOLOGY. For further reading: G. A. Bennet and R. N. Montaperto, *Red Guard* (1971). D.C.W.; S.B.

red shift. A displacement towards the red of the spectral lines of distant GALAXIES and some stars. It is usually interpreted as a DOPPLER EFFECT; this implies that the galaxies are receding, and the red shift constitutes the main evidence for the EXPANSION OF THE UNIVERSE. M.V.B.

redaction criticism, see under HIGHER CRITICISM.

reduction; reductionism.

(1) In PHILOSOPHY and related subjects, the process whereby CONCEPTS or statements that apply to one type of entity are redefined in terms of concepts, or analysed in terms of statements, of another kind, normally one regarded as more elementary or epistemologically (see EPISTEMOLOGY) more basic. *Reducible* is the adjective describing a type of entity that is considered susceptible of reduction; *reducibility* is the property of such a type of entity; *reductionism* is the systematic practice of reduction (also the view that reduction constitutes the business of philosophy). If entities of one kind, e.g. nations, are regarded as reducible to entities of another, in this case individual people, they are said to be CONSTRUCTS or *logical constructions* out of the latter.

Reduction is seldom an uncontentious activity, and to list some of the many varieties of reductionism (which may be contrasted with HOLISM) is to list a series of controversies: whether (as in PHENOMENALISM) material objects are reducible to SENSE-DATA; whether mental events and processes are reducible to physiological, physical or chemical events and processes in human brains (see PHYSICALISM; MATERIALISM; BEHAVIOURISM; *physical monism* under MIND-BODY PROBLEM); whether SOCIAL STRUCTURES and social processes are reducible to relationships between and actions of individuals (see METHODOLOGICAL INDIVIDUALISM); whether (as denied by VITALISM) biological organisms are reducible to physical systems; whether (as in LOGICAL POSITIVISM) philosophy is reducible to ANALYSIS; whether (as in LOGICISM) MATHEMATICS is reducible to LOGIC. The reductionist sometimes justifies his activity as a principle of economy in EXPLANATION, a principle that has obviously paid off in science; the anti-reductionist argues the existence of irreducible or EMERGENT PROPERTIES.

Some of the points at issue, however, are more apparent than real, and stem largely from terminological confusion (exacerbated in some cases by plain prejudice). Thus, a *logical construction* (see above) also needs to be distinguished from an aggregate or whole whose constituents are literally parts of it; e.g., the phenomenalist claims, not that a material thing is literally *composed* of sense-data, but merely that everything that can be said about material things can in principle be stated in assertions that refer only to sense-data. Some versions of reductionism, moreover, are purely methodological (see METHODOLOGY), involving only the claim that the study of phenomena of type *A* has to be restricted to the study of evidence provided by class *B*; thus a methodological behaviourist might argue that, although mental events and processes exist, they can only be studied in terms of the behaviour they produce (see MENTALISM). For further reading: A. Koestler and J. R. Smythies (eds), *Beyond Reductionism* (1970).

A.Q.; A.S.; J.S.B.

(2) In CHEMISTRY, the addition, to an ATOM OR MOLECULE, of ELECTRONS or electropositive groups such as hydrogen IONS, or the removal of electrons or electronegative groups such as oxygen ions. The opposite of OXIDATION. M.V.B.

redundancy.

(1) In INFORMATION THEORY, the representation of data by longer strings of symbols than are necessary to distinguish between all the possible different data items in a context. Redundancy is a bad thing if it leads to unnecessary expense in storage or transmission of representations of data, but a good thing if it permits reconstitution of data whose representation has been accidentally corrupted. Compare 19F3 with nineteen sebenty three; each has one character wrong. R.M.N.

(2) In CYBERNETICS, usage (1) is familiar, but the term is also applied to extra channels in a network which are intended to guard a whole system against the failure of an entire channel. It is possible to calculate mathematically how much redundancy is required to reduce the risk of a mistake (getting the message wrong in (1), or failure of the system in (2)) to an *arbitrarily* small degree. For further reading: C. E. Shannon and J. McCarthy (eds), *Automata Studies* (1956). S.BE.

re-embedding mechanisms, see under DISEMBEDDING AND RE-EMBEDDING MECHANISMS.

reference. In LINGUISTICS, the relationship between linguistic forms and the objects, events, etc. (*referents*) in non-linguistic experience to which these forms refer. Most linguists are careful to distinguish reference from *sense*, which is a purely intralinguistic property arising from the MEANING-RELATIONS between words. D.C.

reference class, see under FREQUENCY THEORY.

reference group. Term introduced by Herbert H. Hyman (in *Archives of Psychology*, 1942) for a social collectivity, real or imagined, in relation to which an individual regularly evaluates his own situation or conduct. A *comparative* reference group is one that serves as a standard against which the individual appraises his achievements, social circumstances, life-chances, rewards, etc., and which thus influences the level of his expectations and, in turn, his degree of relative satisfaction or deprivation; thus the structure of comparative reference groups among members of different occupations has been shown to be important in determining the extent to which wage differentials are regarded as legitimate and the level at which wage claims are made. A NORMATIVE reference group is one which the individual perceives as a source of values and GROUP NORMS of which he approves, and with whose members he would wish to identify himself; thus a socially aspiring individual may take the ÉLITE of his local community as a normative reference group, and seek to emulate their LIFESTYLE, manners, tastes, opinions, etc. in the hope of being himself accepted into the élite. For further reading: R. K. Merton, *Social Theory and Social Structure* (2nd ed., 1957). J.H.G.

referential language, see EMOTIVE AND REFERENTIAL LANGUAGE.

reflation, see under INFLATION.

reflex, conditioned, see CONDITIONED REFLEX.

reflexivity. 'Reflexivity' generally refers simply to the phenomenon of self-reference, particularly propositions such as 'this sentence is written in English'. As such it long attracted the attentions of logicians and philosophers (see LOGIC; PHILOSOPHY). More recently, however, reflexivity has been recognized as raising problems for the status of the human sciences, especially PSYCHOLOGY and SOCIOLOGY. These are essentially 'reflexive' because they are generated by, and involved in constituting, their own subject-matters. A psychological theory is itself a psychological phenomenon, a comprehensive psychological theory should be able to explain itself, and 'having a high IQ' is a psychological possibility created by the psychologists who devised intelligence tests.

The discipline of sociology is itself a social institution, and sociological theories provide many of the terms in which social phenomena are understood and acted upon. This contrasts with physical sciences, where it is axiomatic that the subject-matter exists independently of the scientist and that its properties remain unaltered by scientific inquiry. One lesson of this is that sociologists and psychologists are not external 'objective' observers of the social and psychological phenomena they study but active and creative participants in, and contributors to, the social and psychological lives of the societies in which they operate. Reflexivity manifests itself most oddly when an individual, apparently unconsciously, enacts the very thing he is talking about (e.g. turns his gaze in another direction while saying 'look at it another way'), or when, e.g., the word 'dyslexia' is misprinted. This, however, has rarely been discussed in print. For further reading: S. Woolgar (ed.), *Knowledge and Reflexivity: New Frontiers in the Sociology of Knowledge* (1988). G.D.R.

reformism. A policy of social and economic reform by gradual stages rather than by revolutionary change (see REVOLUTION). The term has been applied in particular to a tendency in the SOCIALIST movement to abandon the idea of revolutionary violence and to rely instead on the slow transformation of social INSTITUTIONS through democratic means. It found its expression in British FABIANISM, French *réformisme*, German REVISIONISM, Russian 'economism', etc., but it was only in countries with a parliamentary suffrage that the constitutional framework favoured such a gradualist approach. It eventually became the hallmark of the Socialist INTERNATIONAL. The establishment of the COMMUNIST International reflected the split in the labour movement between the evolutionary and the revolutionary attitudes, a split resting upon fundamental differences of attitude towards DEMOCRACY and MARXISM.

Some socialist parties, like the British Labour Party, never embraced Marxism; some, like the German Social Democrats (see SOCIAL DEMOCRACY), abandoned it later. The further evolution of the socialist movement has produced a growing differentiation between moderate and radical elements (see RADICALISM). The latter have tended to prefer the socialist, the former a social-democratic label. In some countries, like Italy and Japan, this division has led to the establishment of separate socialist and social-democratic parties. In others it tends to create a growing gap between the moderate and LEFT-wing groups in labour and socialist movements. For further reading: L. Johnston, *Marxism, Class Analysis and Socialist Pluralism* (1986). L.L.

refugee, see under IMMIGRANT.

refurbishment. Term used in architecture to describe the rehabilitation and fitting out anew of older buildings. Refurbishment became a major activity of many British architects as land shortages, ultra-conservative planning laws and a widespread public rejection of the work of post-war architects made designing, developing and erecting new buildings a difficult task. With the decline of older industries in the Western world, together with their buildings, combined with an admiration for older industrial buildings, refurbishment of those structures which can be used in new and profitable ways has also been a major factor in retaining snippets of the architectural heritage of many countries. S.L.

reggae. A BLACK musical form with African and American RHYTHM AND BLUES roots which emerged in Jamaica during the 1960s. The immediate antecedents of reggae were *ska/blue beat* and *rock steady*, music and dance styles that share a firm percussive beat counterposed by a bass off-beat. The wider significance of reggae is due to three factors: it constitutes yet another significant black contribution to popular music; it transcended its ethnic dimensions and became a sub-cultural (see SUB-CULTURE) phenomenon (white YOUTH CULTURE adopted reggae in various ways, from the skinheads' approval of street machismo to the *two-tone* phenomenon of deliberately multiracial bands purveying an anti-racist message); it was closely associated with the Rastafarian movement (see RASTAFARIANISM) and the growth of black consciousness during the 1970s.

During the early and mid-1970s reggae became the dominant channel through which Rastafarian ideals were effectively communicated to young blacks in the urban industrial centres of the West. Reggae musicians drew extensively on the Rastafarian conceptual universe for their lyrics, developing a musical style from this source, and imparting a vicarious sense of unity to groups in industrial society who saw themselves as under pressure (this included elements of white youth). The dissemination of this message to a more differentiated and international audience was partially achieved through the emerging superstar status of the most renowned reggae musician, Bob Marley, who died prematurely of cancer in 1981. Though the connotations of black redemption have faded from reggae, it is still a characteristically black genre, and it has spawned more contemporary black cultural and musical forms such as *toasting* and *scratching*, *rapping* and *hip-hop*. P.S.L.

regime theory. An increasingly fashionable way of explaining the relationships in international society as demonstrated by INTERDEPENDENCE. It concentrates on regional and international attempts to show how regimes will form as 'principles, norms, rules and decision-making procedures around which actor expectations converge in a given issue area' (Stephen Krasner, 1982). It retains the state as principal actor in the international system, especially at the stage of regime formation, with the notion of the state 'hegemon' (see HEGEMONY). It can be applied to any area of international politics, from trade to HUMAN RIGHTS. It has been criticized as being an intellectual fad, and as a disguising of objective power relationships. A.W.

regional planning. Planned intervention by central governments to adjust regional inequalities within the state, particularly in relation to economic investment and employment. It also describes intervention by two or more governmental bodies to meet the problems of a shared natural region. This may be between two municipalities or, in respect of global regions such as the Pacific Rim, between adjacent countries. While in the past regional planning was primarily economic in objective, a collaborative approach is increasingly common in respect of environmental and social issues. For further reading: P. Hall, *Urban and Regional Planning* (1994). C.G.

regional science. An interdisciplinary field within the SOCIAL SCIENCES that focuses on the integrated study of economic and social phenomena in a regional setting. The term is particularly associated with Walter Isard's research group at the University of Pennsylvania which draws heavily on mathematical MODELS to frame regional-science theories. See also REGIONALISM. For further reading: W. Isard, *Introduction to Regional Science* (1975). P.H.

regionalism. In its broadest usage, an application based on the geographical (see GEOGRAPHY) term 'region', which refers to a homogeneous area of the earth's surface exhibiting characteristics that make it distinct from all such areas that surround it. The distinction may be based on natural or human-landscape characteristics, or a combination of both. A nested hierarchy of regions exists, ranging from micro-scale regions of local areas up to macro-scale regions of continental proportions; thus Greater London forms a subregion of south-eastern England, which in turn is a subregion of the United Kingdom, which is itself a subregion of the British Isles, which is a subregion of Europe. Moreover, regions possessing common region-wide characteristics (*uniform regions*) are distinguished from those in which the defining characteristics are most strongly discernible at or near the centre of the region and least strongly at the periphery (*nodal regions*).

Used more narrowly by political geographers (see POLITICAL GEOGRAPHY), regionalism refers to a sociopolitical movement that seeks to (1) foster or protect an indigenous culture in a particular region, or (2) decentralize the powers of a central government to an intermediate level between that of the state and the traditional units of local government. The latter, known as DEVOLUTION, has been intensifying throughout the world since 1990. On the European continent, devolution has strongly affected Belgium, Spain, Italy and France, and even led to the break-up of Czechoslovakia in 1993. Since the 1970s, devolution has also affected the political life of the United Kingdom, embodied in the strengthening of the movement for home rule in

Scotland and Wales. For further reading: M. Keating, *Nations against the State: The New Politics of Nationalism in Quebec, Catalonia, and Scotland* (1996). P.O.M.; P.H.

regression.

(1) In STATISTICS, it is common to attempt to explain the variation in some observed quantity as a combination of some simple kind of dependence on values set by the experimenter, together with an error term (see ERROR ANALYSIS). Such a representation is called a *regression*. It is found, e.g., that the rate at which a cicada chirps is linearly related to the difference in the ambient temperature, but any particular observation may as a result of random error fail to lie exactly on this regression line: this example is of *linear regression*. The design of experiments to obtain good estimates of regression coefficients is an important statistical problem. R.SI.

(2) In PSYCHOLOGY, a DEFENCE MECHANISM whereby an individual responds to stresses such as fear, frustration, isolation, etc., by reverting to behaviour characteristic of a less adult, more primitive and impulsive stage of development. In psychoanalytic theory (see PSYCHOANALYSIS) the regression is either to an earlier state of libidinal interest and sexual organization (see LIBIDO; PSYCHOSEXUAL DEVELOPMENT) or to an earlier stage of EGO development. In the former, the person regresses from adult genitality to earlier (pre-genital) oral or anal sexual interests. In the latter, the person deals with the danger threatening him by behaving in a more childlike and generally dependent way. W.Z.; B.A.F.

regression analysis, see under MULTIVARIATE ANALYSIS.

regulation.

(1) In EMBRYOLOGY, the process of CELL reorganization or readjustment that occurs in the restoration of an organic defect or incompleteness; more especially, the phenomenon whereby, if a sea urchin's or starfish's embryo at the two-cell stage is divided into the two separate cells, each one will grow up into a whole organism. This phenomenon was made the basis of very far-reaching philosophical speculations by Hans Driesch (1867–1941). P.M.

(2) In ENGINEERING, a quantity that expresses – unexpectedly, in view of the normal meaning of the word – the degree of imperfection of a device or SYSTEM. Familiar examples are electrical transformers and electrical transmission systems, where the regulation is the amount by which the voltage falls when the appliance or load is connected, and driving motors, where it is the amount by which the speed of the motor falls when its load is coupled to the motor. Both voltage and speed regulation are usually expressed as a percentage of their respective values when no load is connected. E.R.L.

(3) In CYBERNETICS, any systematic behaviour within a system that tends to restrict fluctuations of any variable. This systematic behaviour will be embodied in a set of physical connections, which will need some form of ENERGY to operate them. However, the critical commodity used by any regulator is *information*. All regulators detect discrepancies from some expectation (which may be not a fixed value, but the varying output of some other part of the system) and FEEDBACK information to make adjustments that reduce the discrepancy. S.BE.

(4) In ECONOMICS, see under ECONOMIC REGULATION.

Reichian. Relating to the beliefs or the followers of Wilhelm Reich (1897–1958). Reich's career began in orthodox PSYCHOANALYSIS, but he quickly developed original theories, relating NEUROSIS to sexual frustration and failure to achieve complete orgasm. This led to a complex therapeutic approach called *character analysis* or *bio-energetics*. Reich's interest in sexual energy led to his 'discovery' of the *orgone*, a 'life force' (for Bergson's earlier version of this, see VITALISM) which he found to be blue in colour, and to be present in living and inorganic matter throughout nature and interstellar space. His commitment to the 'Orgone Energy Accumulator' (a metal box which, he claimed, concentrated orgone energy and cured illness) led to his imprisonment in 1955 for selling medical equipment prohibited by the US Food and Drug Laws. The film *Mysteries of the Organism* helped to publicize Reich's views, but it is still not clear whether he was a charlatan or a genius; the truth doubtless lies somewhere between the two. For further reading: W. E. Mann,

Wilhelm Reich: The Man Who Dreamed of Tomorrow (1990). M.J.C.

reification. The act of regarding an abstraction as a material thing.

An analysis of any relationship in a complex world involves a process of simplification through a set of abstractions in which certain aspects of a given phenomenon are selected and stressed for HEURISTIC purposes. These abstracted elements of reality may be reduced to an IDEAL TYPE or a conceptual MODEL. If they are taken as a complete description of the real phenomenon and the resulting abstractions endowed with a material existence of their own, the process exemplifies what philosopher A. N. Whitehead called in his *Science and the Modern World* (1962) 'the fallacy of misplaced concreteness', which is in effect a special case of the fallacy of reification. (See also *reductionism*, under REDUCTION.)

Reification as a CONCEPT with a special meaning was used with particular emphasis by Karl Marx (see MARXISM). For him, reification (*Versachlichung*, *Verdinglichung*) meant that the 'social relation between men ... assumes for them the fantastic form of a relation between things'. In CAPITALIST society, he saw it as the result of ALIENATION (*Entäusserung*) or the estrangement (*Entfremdung*) of labour, a separation of the worker from the product of his work. Marx wrote that 'the general social form of labour appears as the property of a thing' and is 'reified' through the 'FETISHISM of commodities'. This is a social situation which is determined by 'the action of objects which rule the producers instead of being ruled by them'.

Marx's concepts of reification and alienation have been used as key terms by the NEW LEFT. In their popular form alienation was taken to mean the estrangement of man from an oppressive society, reification the treatment of men as objects of manipulation, as things rather than as human beings. In the theoretical writings of the Marxist forerunners of the New Left, such as György Lukács and the philosophers of the FRANKFURT SCHOOL, the concept of reification has been applied to all pre-revolutionary (see REVOLUTION) activities and INSTITUTIONS, including science (which for Max Horkheimer is a 'reified IDEOLOGY'), TECHNOLOGY (which for Herbert Marcuse is a 'vehicle for reification'), and general intellectual concepts (which for Lukács are instances of reification). L.L.

reinforcement. In the context of OPERANT CONDITIONING, the supplying of a consequence for certain behaviour which will *strengthen* that behaviour, i.e. make it more likely to recur in the same situation. In *positive reinforcement*, the behaviour is strengthened by the contingent presentation of a reward (e.g. food); in *negative reinforcement*, the behaviour is strengthened by the contingent removal of an aversive stimulus (e.g. electric shock, loud noise). Sometimes, negative reinforcement is extended to include the case where behaviour is made *less* likely to recur as the result of contingent presentation of an aversive stimulus, an operation properly termed *punishment*. The behaviour may be abolished (*extinguished*) if reinforcement no longer follows it; the abolition procedure is known as *extinction*. The rules that specify when and under what circumstances an operant response should be reinforced are known as *schedules of reinforcement*; such schedules may require, e.g., a minimum time interval between responses, or the occurrence of a set number of unreinforced responses between successive reinforced ones. For further reading: C. B. Ferster and B. F. Skinner, *Schedules of Reinforcement* (1957). D.H.

relational grammar. A development of GENERATIVE GRAMMAR of the mid-1970s which takes as central the notion of grammatical *relations* (such as subject and object) rather than the categorical terms of earlier models (such as noun phrase and verb phrase). For further reading: P. Matthews, *Syntax* (1981). D.C.

relative deprivation. A CONCEPT introduced by the American sociologist S. A. Stouffer in 1949 and based upon the proposition that people's attitudes, aspirations and grievances depend largely upon the FRAME OF REFERENCE in which they are conceived. Thus, when one COMMUNITY observes another comparable community or REFERENCE GROUP to be relatively prosperous, a feeling of deprivation arises which, prior to comparison, did not exist. The concept is a useful reminder of human envy, but fails to establish criteria for determining the point at which deprivation becomes absolute as well as relative. For further reading: W. G. Runciman, *Relative Deprivation and Social Justice* (1966). P.S.L.

relativism. The doctrine that statements in a given area of discourse can be true for one group of people but false for another: e.g., that ethical statements can be true for the members of one SOCIETY or CULTURE but false for those of another. In its most extreme form, relativism reduces to SUBJECTIVISM: the view that whatever is true for anyone else need not be true for me. Many relativists implicitly contradict themselves in stating and defending their views. For example, the ethical relativist may urge that it is wrong for the members of one society to impose its values on those of another, on the ground that there are no UNIVERSAL values which hold true for the members of all societies. But, on the relativist's own principles, to say that this is wrong can only be true relative to the values of some particular society, not universally, so that it is open to someone else to say that this is *not* wrong, relative to his own system of values. Relativists often forget that, according to their own account, what they have to say in defence of their doctrine is only true for them or for some group of which they are members and consequently that their doctrine invites its own rejection by the members of another group. As a consequence, despite the persisting allure of relativist thinking, it fails to instil lasting conviction and sooner or later gives way to some form of objectivism. E.J.L.

relativism, cultural. CULTURES (see ANTHROPOLOGY) are relative in the trivial sense that what is right and good in one society may not be in another. 'Cultural relativism' is usually restricted, however, to an anthropological doctrine most forcefully expounded by American cultural anthropologist Melville J. Herskovits (1895–1963), according to which the values and institutions of any culture must be taken to be self-validating. In so far as this doctrine entails a stance of moral relativism, it is subject to the criticism (among others) that we are often obliged to judge the actions of members of other societies by standards which are not theirs. The question of relativism has been at the heart of much anthropological debate. It concerns fundamentally the unity of man. It has emerged in the form of discussions concerning rationality, 'PRIMITIVE mentality', modes of thought, etc. In ECONOMIC ANTHROPOLOGY it took the form of a debate between formalists and substantivists. Relativism has been most persistent in the attempts to interpret and understand certain practices and beliefs, particularly WITCHCRAFT, SORCERY and MAGIC. For further reading: E. Gellner, *Relativism and the Social Sciences* (1985). M.F.; A.G.

relativity. A system of MECHANICS developed by Einstein early in this century, based on the principle that it must be possible to express the physical laws governing the motion of a body in a manner which is independent of the motion of any observer who may be studying the body. In other words, no absolute FRAME OF REFERENCE exists. Relativity is divided into two parts:

(1) In the *special* (or *restricted*) *theory* (1905), only frames of reference moving relatively to one another with constant velocity are considered. In addition, the status of a basic postulate is given to the result of the MICHELSON-MORLEY EXPERIMENT, i.e. that the speed of light in a vacuum is the same for all observers (a result inconsistent with NEWTONIAN MECHANICS). The principal deductions are: (a) The TRANSFORMATIONS between the position and time of an event as viewed by differently moving observers imply that the separate CONCEPTS of absolute space and absolute time must be replaced by the four-dimensional CONTINUUM of SPACE-TIME. In particular this leads to many surprising predictions such as the CLOCK PARADOX. (b) The MASS of a body increases with its speed, becoming INFINITE at the speed of light (see REST MASS); thus an infinite force would be necessary to 'cross the light barrier', and the speed of light is a natural upper limit in mechanics (but see TACHYON). (c) Matter is a form of ENERGY (see MASS-ENERGY EQUATION). These deductions have all been abundantly verified for ELEMENTARY PARTICLES moving near the speed of light in experiments with ACCELERATORS and in NUCLEAR REACTORS.

(2) The *general theory* (1916) goes on to consider transformation between *any* frame of reference which may have a mutual

acceleration. In addition, the fact that GRAVITATION attracts bodies so that they all fall with the same acceleration (which appears as a coincidence in Newtonian mechanics) is built into the basic structure of the theory. The space-time continuum is not 'flat' (i.e. *Euclidean*) as in the special theory, but 'curved' (i.e. *Riemannian*; for these terms see GEOMETRY). The curvature is produced by matter (see MACH'S PRINCIPLE), and PARTICLES move along 'straight lines', or geodesics (see GEODESY), in this curved space – analogous to the 'great circles' connecting points on the two-dimensional continuum of points on the earth's surface; thus gravitation is explained as geometry.
On the comparatively small scale of the solar system, general relativity predicts that the motion of planets and light rays will differ slightly from that expected in Newtonian mechanics, and these effects have been confirmed – although not as precisely as the predictions of special relativity. The difference between Newtonian mechanics and general relativity is, however, much greater near BLACK HOLES and on the vast scales contemplated in COSMOLOGY. For further reading: F. Close and C. Sutton, *The Particle Explosion* (1987). M.V.B.

relaxation. A general term used in PHYSICS to denote the process whereby a system attains EQUILIBRIUM by neutralizing a disturbing force. For example, when a solid is suddenly stretched, large elastic forces are set up, which gradually relax to zero through 'creep' – the solid flow of a solid under stress, seen e.g. in sagging stone lintels and tombstones. Electric conduction in metals is a relaxation effect: the ELECTRONS neutralize an applied voltage by adjusting the rate at which they collide with IONS. M.V.B.

relaxation time. The time taken for RELAXATION to occur. In RHEOLOGY, solids are characterized by long relaxation times (e.g. about a year for glass), fluids by short relaxation times (e.g. one thousandth of a second for water), while visco-elastic materials occupy an intermediate position (e.g. 'potty putty', whose relaxation time is several seconds, bounces elastically under the sudden force of impact, but flows slowly under the more persistent force of GRAVITATION). M.V.B.

release dance. A movement form which works towards releasing habitual movement conditioning, thereby encouraging an efficient and economic use of the body. In the mid-1930s in the USA, Mabel Ellsworth Todd instigated release work in her study of posture and alignment, movement energy, breathing and relaxation. Dancers, most notably Mary Fulkerson working at Dartington College, Devon, and Joan Skinner and Marsha Paludon, developed release work from this therapeutic approach into a creative form of dance. Fulkerson uses simple early learning patterns, imagery, focus on breathing and qualities of stillness to arrive at an intuitive, kinaesthetically aware and expressive form of dance which de-emphasizes technique and virtuosity, and provides an experience for everyone who wishes to dance. Release dance is not a definitive school but is dependent on individual teachers and shares with ALEXANDER TECHNIQUE general principles of movement re-education. For further reading: M. O'Donnell Fulkerson, *Language of the Axis* (1977). L.A.

releaser.

(1) In ETHOLOGY, a translation of the German *Auslöser*, a term coined by Konrad Lorenz in 1935 to denote those structures, movements, sounds, scents, etc., which act as social signals. Releasers in this narrow sense are intricately adapted, as far as is compatible with other requirements, to their dual function of conspicuousness and unambiguity. The majority are intraspecific, i.e. they serve to ensure co-operation between members of one SPECIES; examples are the breeding colours of many animals, the songs of songbirds, and other mating-calls. Other releasers are used in inter-species relationships, such as SYMBIOSIS on the one hand, and repulsion of predators on the other. Releasers are often structures or behaviour patterns that have originally had another function and have evolved their special signalling properties as a secondary ADAPTATION (*ritualization*) to the need for effective communication.

(2) By extension, the word is often misleadingly applied to *any* external stimulus complex that 'releases' or elicits behaviour. Thus the silvery colour of many pelagic fish may 'release' hunting behaviour in predatory fish such as the pike, even though the

function to which it is adapted is the opposite one of concealment. N.T.

religion. An attitude of awe towards GOD, or gods, or the supernatural, or the mystery of life, accompanied by beliefs and affecting basic patterns of individual and group behaviour. In Latin *religare* means 'to bind', and religion is traditionally what most deeply binds a society, but the 20th century has been, more than any previous age, an age of SECULARIZATION. Paradoxically, the many challenges to inherited patterns of belief and behaviour in religion have made this a fertile age in THEOLOGY, and an unprecedented dialogue between the world's great religious traditions has opened both on the scholarly and the popular levels (see RELIGION, COMPARATIVE STUDY OF). The opinion is growing that none of these faiths will be able to make an adequate response to the secular challenge without learning from each other as well as from modern thought. NATIONALISM too has been a religion in a loose sense. It has also been associated with the revival of traditional religion as the assertion of cherished national values against the influence either of communism (as in eastern Europe) or of the West (as in the Middle East). Certainly religious belief has failed to disappear at the speed expected by many when the modern age began.

D.L.E.

religion, comparative study of. The CROSS-CULTURAL STUDY of RELIGION, mainly in the West: sometimes it involves treating single traditions and sometimes themes across traditions, such as MYSTICISM or sacrifice or devotion. In the latter manifestation it is sometimes called phenomenology of religion (see PHENOMENOLOGY). Mainly it originated in the 19th century, but it has flourished more than at any other time in the latter part of the 20th century. In the guise of 'history of religion' it had great influence in Chicago under the inspiration of Romanian historian Mirca Eliade (1907–86). It is a significant part of RELIGIOUS STUDIES, together with the scientific study of religion. For further reading: N. Smart, *The World's Religions* (1998). N.SM.

religion, philosophy of. The philosophical discipline which reflects on issues arising in connection with religious BELIEFS and practices in general, but usually emphasizing theism, and especially CHRISTIANITY. Intellectually and institutionally a product of the Enlightenment, the philosophy of RELIGION is still concerned with the issues discussed by philosophers like Hume and Kant in the 18th century, but in recent years its agenda has been steadily expanding.

For much of the 20th century, the philosophy of religion has been influenced by a series of 'systems', including IDEALISM, Thomism and process philosophies, and, to a lesser extent, by the alternatives to such metaphysical systems offered by PRAGMATISM, PERSONALISM and EXISTENTIALISM (see EXISTENTIALIST THEOLOGY). Since the 1950s, however, the philosophy of religion has been dominated by questions raised by the revival of EMPIRICISM, and in particular by LOGICAL POSITIVISM and its successors. Rather than investigating whether theistic propositions were true or false, philosophers of religion were forced to investigate whether they were so much as meaningful – given the strict criteria for meaning expressed successively in the principles of 'VERIFICATION' and 'falsification'. The discipline's centre of gravity shifted from the question of justification, involving the analysis of arguments for and against the existence of GOD (see NATURAL THEOLOGY), to the question of intelligibility, and the analysis of religious language occupied many philosophers of religion through the 1960s and 1970s. The influence of Wittgenstein, and of linguistic philosophy in general, helped philosophers of religion to see that the search for a universal criterion of meaning was fundamentally misconceived, and that religious discourse, like other forms of discourse, could be meaningful in a variety of distinctive ways.

The analysis of religious language remains a live issue for the philosophy of religion, as are many traditional questions: the arguments for and against the existence of God, the problem of evil (see THEODICY), faith and reason, revelation, miracles, immortality, religion and science, and religion and ETHICS. But the philosophy of religion continues to reflect the major philosophical debates of its age, and through the 1980s and 1990s its central concerns have included the legitimacy of FOUNDATIONALISM – the assumption that most beliefs, including theistic ones, can only be justified by inference from a set of 'foundational' beliefs, which is presupposed by theistic and atheistic evidentialism but challenged by philosophers in the Reformed and Wittgensteinian traditions – and the conflict between realist and anti-realist interpretations of theism (see ATHEISM; REALISM). Other important contemporary developments include the revival of PHILOSOPHICAL THEOLOGY, the rise of FEMINIST THEOLOGY, and some signs that ANALYTIC PHILOSOPHY of religion is opening up to voices from the Continental philosophical tradition – particularly in questioning assumptions about 'religion', 'reason', and human SUBJECTIVITY, reflecting the origins of the discipline in the Enlightenment. For further reading: P. L. Quinn and C. Taliaferro (eds), *A Companion to Philosophy of Religion* (1997). C.C.

religion, psychology of. The analysis of religious experience (both MYSTICISM and more everyday phenomena), not necessarily admitting or denying its validity but relating it to the rest of PSYCHOLOGY. The main challenge has come from Freud's (see FREUDIAN) treatment of all religious belief as an unhealthy illusion. In contrast, the JUNGIAN approach has been to stress the universality and life-interpreting functions of the basic SYMBOLS used in religion, although this need not mean that the symbols correspond with eternal realities. In addition to these great attempts to make sense (or nonsense) of the whole of religion, there have been many less judgemental case-studies, largely with an American background, of the functions of religious beliefs and customs in personal existence. For further reading: R. H. Thouless, *An Introduction to the Psychology of Religion* (1982). D.L.E.

religion, sociology of. The dispassionate study of the behaviour of groups influenced by religious beliefs. This can involve surveys of the adherents of a religious body in a given area, or may extend to the discussion, inevitably more speculative, of the interaction of social and emotional pressures in the beliefs of a whole society, e.g. the PROTESTANT ETHIC in its relations to the values of CAPITALISM. It may even embrace a general theory of the origins and functions of RELIGION in the life of mankind. The pioneers in these FUNCTIONALIST inquiries were Max Weber (1864–1920), who stressed religion's role as giving 'meaning' to social life; Émile Durkheim (1858–1917), who believed that through religious RITUAL the social group periodically reaffirms its identity and values; and Bronislaw Malinowski (1884–1942), who analysed religion as escape from the stress of powerlessness, e.g. in the face of death. There has been special interest in the role of religious SECTS in protesting against the social order of the day, and in the role of the more 'respectable' Churches in maintaining it, as in Ernst Troeltsch, *The Social Teaching of the Christian Churches* (1912). There is disagreement among sociologists about whether, in view of the central role of religion in the past, society can ever be thoroughly secular (see SECULARIZATION). For further reading: P. L. Berger, *Religion in Sociological Perspective* (1982). D.L.E.

religious right/New Christian Rights. Name given to the American movement of largely EVANGELICAL and FUNDAMENTALIST Christians which, from a strongly conservative standpoint (see CONSERVATISM), sees political involvement as a moral obligation. Although its breadth and organizational variety contain differences of emphasis and tactics, its elements are united in an attempt to redirect the political agenda towards the group's social and political values derived from its members' religious beliefs. It is particularly concerned to prohibit ABORTION, to reintroduce prayer and 'Christian values' to public schools, and to oppose any diversity of sexual mores.

Its precise origins lie in a reaction against US Supreme Court decisions (see SUPREME COURT OF THE UNITED STATES) sustaining the legality of abortion in 1972 and 1973, and in governmental moves in 1978 to remove the tax-exempt status of private religious schools suspected of perpetuating racial segregation (see RACE; RACIAL STEREOTYPES). More generally, the movement is a reaction against what its members see as the dangers of 'secular HUMANISM' – its term for the socially liberal (see LIBERALISM), culturally experimental values of recent decades. Among its early key institutions were the Moral Majority, Christian Voice and the Religious Roundtable, the latter formed in 1979 as an élite network to unite New Christian Right leaders with those of other conservative groups.

The movement's impact on national politics in the 1980s was less than many leaders hoped and critics feared. Its goals were not whole-heartedly adopted by the Reagan or Bush administrations, and its reputation was damaged by a series of sexual and financial scandals. However, in the 1990s it substantially recovered, acquired more mature political strategies to reach a broader constituency, including many conservative Catholics (see CATHOLICISM), successfully infiltrated and sometimes dominated many state Republican parties, and adopted a less fierce rhetoric while broadening its policy agenda. Under the umbrella of Pat Robertson's Christian Broadcasting Network, the Christian Coalition became a particularly sophisticated organization, credited with crucially mobilizing support for Republican candidates in the party's 1994 victories, which gave it control of both houses of Congress. In general the movement continues both to provide support for but also create tensions within the party, while drawing rightwards the political centre of gravity. For further reading: M. Urofsky and M. May (eds), *The New Christian Right* (1996). S.R.

religious studies. The multidisciplinary study of religion, including the history of religions, the HISTORY OF IDEAS, the comparative study of religion (see RELIGION, COMPARATIVE STUDY OF), the SOCIAL SCIENCE of religion, and the PHILOSOPHY of religion. It may include the study of IDEOLOGIES such as NATIONALISM, FASCISM and MARXISM which bear similarities to religion. It typically also includes some treatment of THEOLOGY. It was the IRANIAN REVOLUTION in 1979 that finally persuaded political scientists of the importance of religion, and this has been reinforced by the collapse of the former USSR and the resurgence of religion in that area (including ISLAM in central Asia and BUDDHISM in the Far East).

Religious studies essentially dates from the 1960s. In Britain the first major department was founded in Lancaster University in 1967, and the movement spread fairly rapidly. The feeling was that the old departments of theology, dealing with Christian doctrine and biblical studies, had far too narrow a basis for studying religion. In America, the 1960s saw the opening up of departments in the secular or state universities, involving the separation of Church and state. The presence in so many countries of communities from other cultural areas, including Hindus, Muslims, Sikhs, east Asian Buddhists, Confucianists and others (see HINDUISM; ISLAM; SIKHISM; CONFUCIANISM), as well as classical African and new Churches, means that there is a demand for the study of religions outside those of the Christian West. The rise of cultural studies has been in part due to the example of religious studies.

From the 1970s onwards, FEMINIST approaches to the study of religion have been influential, and a lot of work has been done on the SOCIOLOGY of new religions (see FEMINIST THEOLOGY). As yet the impact of religious studies has been less than it might be, in so far as many other disciplines in the social sciences and humanities have been Westernized; FREUDIAN studies, e.g., has been insufficiently confronted by Buddhism and other traditions that fail to fit in with its tenets. For further reading: N. Smart, *The Phenomenon of Religion* (1973). N.SM.

remission, see under PAROLE.

remittance. Money sent by a migrant working abroad to his family back home. It is usually sent at regular intervals, and in the early days of migration it represented a substantial part of the wage packet. Expenditure in the new country is minimized to allow a greater amount of money to be remitted. Remittances are the expression of the obligations a migrant worker owes to his family. They also symbolize the continuing link between the migrant and the homeland. A migrant who falls behind in payments will not return to the home village and will have brought shame upon the family.

Remittances are spent in different ways by the family: to pay off debts, to buy land and agricultural equipment, to educate children, to pay marriage costs (DOWRY) or to purchase luxury goods. The economic and social STATUS of the family is enhanced by monies received. Whole communities may become dependent upon remittances, and governments in the underdeveloped world rely heavily on this cash inflow from abroad. Remittances usually decline over time, and ties weaken as a migrant community develops in the new country. For further reading: J. L. Watson (ed.), *Between Two Cultures* (1977). A.G.

remote sensing. Observation and data collection at a distance from the object(s) under observation. The most dramatic example of remote sensing is the use of orbiting SATELLITES to collect information about the earth's temperature, vegetation and ocean circulation. Intensity of infra-red radiation (sees INFRA-RED; RADIATION) reflects chlorophyll concentrations in forests and oceans. High-altitude balloons, and aeroplanes, are also used in remote sensing. The verification, on site, of data collected by remote sensing is termed 'ground truthing'. Thus, direct measurement of chlorophyll concentration in samples collected from land or sea sites is used to confirm or correct data collected by remote sensing. W.G.R.

renewable energy. Energy sources that are not depleted through use, particularly energy captured from solar RADIATION which for all practical purposes is infinite in supply. In contrast, both fossil and nuclear energy sources are finite, and some fossil fuel supplies are approaching exhaustion, at least in some regions (e.g. petroleum in the North Sea), or are increasingly remote and thus difficult to recover. Nuclear energy, once touted as 'too cheap to meter', has proved to be more costly than fossil fuel-based electricity, and the problem of safe disposal of spent fuel has defied solution over decades.

Solar energy can be used directly to heat water or enclosed spaces, or can be converted to electricity by making steam to drive turbines. Sunlight can be converted directly to electricity by photovoltaic cells (PVCs). These cells utilize semiconductor materials such as silicon wafers, and solid state electronics. As PVC technology is refined, the cost of solar electricity declines, but in most situations solar is not yet competitive with electricity generated from fossil fuels. An exception is at remote sites where the cost of transmission lines would be prohibitive. Wider use of PVCs for powering vehicles and residences awaits the development of more efficient storage batteries.

Wind is an indirect source of solar energy, as is the falling water that drives turbines in hydroelectric facilities. Wind-driven turbines are a cost-effective source of electricity in some areas with sufficient average wind velocities. Additional sources of renewable energy are tidal water movement and heat escaping from the earth's core through thermal vents. Unlike energy from fossil or nuclear fuels, renewable energy capture and use is relatively free of environmentally unsafe by-products. W.G.R.

reparations. Term used to describe the payments that are demanded by a victorious power from the defeated parties after a conflict, to compensate for the costs of the war. The most noted instance of this concerns the reparations that were imposed on Germany by the victorious Allies after World War I. After the November 1918 armistice, Germany was forced to accept total blame for the war, and a Reparations Commission was set up, which imposed total reparations of 132 billion gold marks ($33 billion). Even though this was never fully paid, it provoked extreme anger and NATIONALISM in Germany, and facilitated the rise of National Socialism (see NAZISM) and the subsequent World War II. V.L.

repertory.

(1) The collection of plays in active production at a theatre in one season, each play taking its turn in a constantly changing programme. Long established on the Continent, the system of playing 'in repertory' is still not widespread in Britain: only the National Theatre, the Royal Shakespeare Company and a handful of regional theatres have adopted the practice.

(2) A British theatrical movement in which plays are mounted by a permanent company for limited runs of anything from one to four weeks (the very opposite of Continental repertory). Initiated by Miss A. E. F. Horniman at the Gaiety Theatre, Manchester, in 1907, the movement has provided an excellent training-ground for actors and directors. With help from the Arts Council, the British repertory movement achieved a flourishing condition, comprising some 60 subventioned theatres scattered throughout the land, but lost some of its vigour in the years of declining public subsidies after 1979.

In the USA the nearest equivalent is *summer stock* (short seasons of interesting plays taking place outside the big cities and often graced by visiting stars), but in New York successive attempts to set up a permanent company have come to grief. For further reading: G. Rowell and A. Jackson, *The Repertory Movement* (1984). M.BI.

replacement theory. In management and ECONOMICS, a theory that provides a method for deciding upon the most economic strategy for replacing equipment. The productivity of equipment may decline over time; there may be more productive alternative types of equipment; and the present equipment may fail or require maintenance. The theory compares the discounted (see DISCOUNTED CASH FLOW; DISCOUNTING) costs incurred under different strategies – it is possible to allow for RISK by discounting expected costs. In making this decision, the relevant variables to consider are the lifetimes of the equipment, initial and operating costs, depreciation, the productivity of different types of equipment, and the likelihood of equipment failures. J.P.

replicator, see under UNIT OF SELECTION.

representationism. In PHILOSOPHY, the theory that our knowledge of material objects is gained through our direct PERCEPTION of the private impressions or SENSE-DATA which they cause us to experience and which, in some way or other, they resemble. In Descartes and Locke the resemblance is held to extend only to the 'primary qualities', i.e. the mathematically measurable, spatial qualities with which PHYSICS is principally concerned. According to this view the secondary qualities of colour, texture, sound, smell and taste are subjective, at least to the extent that there is no similar property in the material objects that cause us to perceive them. The crucial difficulty for the theory is the justification of the thesis that there is a resemblance between objects and our impressions of them, when the first term of the relation is not accessible for purposes of comparison with its perceived effects. The aim of representationism is to show that the sense-datum theory does not imply SOLIPSISM. A.Q.

representations. It is no new idea that art, literature and even the human mind do not mirror reality but represent it according to unconscious or semi-conscious conventions, but it is relatively recently that such representations have become a focus for interdisciplinary research, involving literary critics, social anthropologists, art historians and intellectual historians. The phrase 'collective representations' was a favourite of the French sociologist Émile Durkheim (1858–1917), and corresponded to what some historians now call mentalities (see HISTORY OF MENTALITIES). In early-20th-century Germany, a concern with views or representations of the world was central to the sociology of knowledge (see KNOWLEDGE, SOCIOLOGY OF). More recently, the study of representations has been encouraged and influenced by STRUCTURALISM, with its presentation of cultures as systems of signs. The cultural codes which underlie representations were an abiding concern of Michel Foucault (1926–84), who suggested that these deep structures were a proper subject for 'intellectual archaeology' rather than history. P.B.

repression. In psychoanalytic theory (see PSYCHOANALYSIS), a FREUDIAN term which is used largely to refer to two distinct processes. (1) *Primal repression.* An infant or child defends itself against the threat of excessive tension by attaching energy to some object or activity – which energy functions antithetically, or counter, to the threatening tension. (2) *Actual repression*, or *repression proper*. When an adult is threatened by the excessive tension that might arise if some UNCONSCIOUS wish, or impulse, moved into CONSCIOUSNESS, this danger is signalled by ANXIETY, and is met in various ways, e.g. by withdrawing energy from the idea of the threatening impulse, so that it cannot move into consciousness but remains unconscious. Repression proper is a function of the EGO, and is unconscious in its operation. See also DEFENCE MECHANISM. B.A.F.

repressive tolerance. Term coined by German-born American philosopher Herbert Marcuse (1898–1979) to describe an 'illusion of freedom' which exists in Western democracies such as that of the USA. Influenced by the ideas of Hegel, Freud and Marx, Marcuse believed that MASS CULTURE and MATERIALISM were subtle means of social control that, at best, induced complacency and, at worst, ALIENATION. See

FREUDIAN; MARXISM. For further reading: H. Marcuse, *One-Dimensional Man* (1964). S.T.

repressor. In GENETICS, a substance, produced by a *repressor gene*, which inactivates another GENE or group of genes (OPERON). J.M.S.

reproduction rate. Measures which indicate the extent to which a population is reproducing itself. The gross reproduction rate is the number of daughters a woman would have if throughout her lifetime she were subjected to current age-specific fertility rates; the more revealing net reproduction rate is the number of daughters she would have if subjected to current FERTILITY and MORTALITY (with a value of 1.0 indicating exact replacement). E.G.; D.S.

reproductive technology. During the 1960s and 1970s developments in medical science made possible what has become known as the 'new' reproductive technology. The research was, in part, motivated by the perceived need to assist heterosexual women who were unable to conceive. Nevertheless, despite this humanitarian impetus to the work, reproductive technology has always been surrounded by dissent and controversy from a number of viewpoints. To conservative and Roman Catholic critics, medical intervention in the process of conception raises ethical (see ETHICS) problems about the appropriate limits of human action. Reservations have been voiced by feminists (see FEMINISM), who have criticized the social assumptions underlying innovations in reproductive technology, namely that motherhood (see MOTHERING) is 'natural', a desirable and crucial state for women, and that this state should be encouraged only in women in conventional heterosexual relationships.

Thus reproductive technology – particularly the development of an embryo outside the mother's body rather than *in vitro* fertilization (see INFERTILITY) – has given rise to two fiercely contested debates. One involves the moral legitimacy of the use of artificial means of conception while the second relates to the social control of fertility and the degree to which motherhood (and indeed fatherhood) is a 'natural' right or one which should be limited to those meeting the conventional norms of parenthood. The issue of heterosexuality is crucial here, since a great deal of the debate around ARTIFICIAL INSEMINATION has revolved around the right of lesbian (see LESBIANISM) women to become mothers independent of social and sexual (see SEXUALITY) relationships with men. These debates and discussions have generally resulted in some form of rationing and restriction in the access of women to medically assisted conception – a form of control which has in itself been contentious given the overwhelmingly male domination of the medical hierarchy. During the late 1990s, new legal issues came into being over questions such as who 'owns' frozen embryos, and who has access to them. (A controversial case in the UK involved a petition from a woman whose husband had died to obtain the embryos they had created in order to impregnate herself.) New ethical issues also arose over selection and disposal of frozen embryos, and their use in genetic research. The creation of multiple embryos, and the selection, via GENETIC TESTING, of 'appropriate' ones for implanting, raised the spectre of EUGENICS. Another controversy has surrounded the 'right' of persons with HIV (see AIDS) to demand access to *in vitro* fertilization. For further reading: L. Fenwick, *Private Choices, Public Consequences* (1998). M.S.E.; S.T.

republicanism. A re-emerging political sensibility that promises to rival LIBERALISM and COMMUNITARIANISM for 21st-century affections. In philosophical histories of politics, republicanism appears as a transitional phase between the close-knit communitarianism of agricultural societies and the dispersed liberalism of commercial societies. Exemplary republican societies include classical Athens, pre-imperial Rome, the city-states of Renaissance northern Italy, Whig Britain, the US Constitution's rule by countervailing forces, and Popper's OPEN SOCIETY of science. Republicanism's basic idea is that freedom requires the expression, not merely the toleration, of different opinions. The realization of this idea presupposes certain conditions: (1) that people's opinions might change as a result of hearing an opposing opinion; (2) that people need not fear the consequences of their expressed opinions on their material wellbeing; (3) that there is a PUBLIC INTER-

EST or 'civic ideal' to which people may appeal which transcends specific individual and group interests. Republican policies aim to ensure that all citizens are sufficiently secure in their material circumstances that they are not inhibited from speaking their minds. A guaranteed minimum income is thus the archetypal republican proposal. Republicanism's new lease of life largely reflects the need to find a justification for the state's existence after the decline of SOCIALISM, given that liberalism and communitarianism justify social cohesion in non-statist terms (i.e. self-interest and cultural identity, respectively). For further reading: P. Pettit, *Republicanism* (1997).
S.F.

republicanism (Irish). A term derived from the REPUBLICANISM of the French Revolution following the declaration of the French Republic in 1793. The Irish republicans, whose leader was – or at least is seen retrospectively as – Theobald Wolfe Tone (1763–98), sought to overthrow the British monarchy with aid from the French Republic. After the death of Wolfe Tone, and the extinction of the original French Republic, followers of the movement founded by Tone continued to call themselves republicans. The continuing function of the word was to rule out any possible compromise with the British monarchy, such as more moderate varieties of NATIONALISTS were disposed to entertain. The movement was of little significance – and probably only intermittent existence – during most of the 19th century, but it revived in the 1860s in the form of the secret and oath-bound society known as the Irish Republican Brotherhood, generally known as Fenians. The IRB founded the IRISH REPUBLICAN ARMY (IRA), which is still in being. It was the IRB which determined the execution and timing of what became the Easter Rising of 1916. Later the IRA split into two factions in what became the Irish Civil War of 1922–23. The losing faction in the civil war retained the title IRA, and the modern IRA is the direct descendant of that faction. In recent years it has developed a promising tactic of interspersing its revolutionary war with temporary ceasefires for which it has expected and received political rewards from the British and Irish governments. In 1998, following a fragile political consensus and a referendum, provisions were made to set up an elected chamber in Northern Ireland, but its success will depend on the willingness of extremists to finally lay down their arms.
C.C.O'B.

research and development (R&D). Basic research is the pursuit of scientific knowledge that may or may not have commercial uses. Applied research is the application of scientific knowledge to the discovery or modification of inventions with the direct intention of later commercial gain. Development is the process in which inventions are transformed into new production techniques and products for commercial gain. The economic benefits of research and development are more economically efficient production (see ECONOMIC EFFICIENCY) and new goods and services that satisfy a wider range of wants. It is often suggested that these economic benefits are large, relative to the costs, and there is insufficient INVESTMENT in research and development. Research and development can be costly and subject to UNCERTAINTY, and successful projects may be imitated. These effects may deter private firms from investing in research and development. Basic research may suffer most from these effects, as the commercial opportunities and gains are more uncertain, and most of the benefits accrue to other firms through an increase in the stock of scientific knowledge. As the knowledge from successful research and development has the attributes of a PUBLIC GOOD, it is often suggested that the state should undertake and finance such activities on behalf of society. A problem with this suggestion is that it requires the state to be capable of making decisions about which projects should be funded. For further reading: P. Stoneman, *The Economics of Technological Change* (1983).
J.P.

resistance. In PSYCHOANALYSIS, a term referring to a patient's opposition to progress. Specifically, it denotes the patient's AMBIVALENCE, whereby he might be genuinely seeking therapeutic help yet might also be undermining all attempts to achieve insight into the unconscious source or meaning of his symptoms – hence subverting the therapeutic process. Freud realized early on that resistance is universal in psychoanalytic work, understanding it mainly as the attempt by the EGO to defend itself against disturbing unconscious impulses. As such, resistance is not only an obstacle to analytic progress but also an indication of the areas requiring most careful and thorough INTERPRETATION. Freud also recognized resistance arising from the ID (in the form of 'repetition compulsion') and the SUPEREGO (as feelings of guilt demanding punishment). Resistance has at times become a protean concept, employed to dismiss all opposition to psychoanalysis, whether by patients in treatment or by critics. It is, however, of general significance as a way of indicating how a person might want something (e.g., to change) but not want it at the same time. S.J.F.

resistentialism. A fictitious philosophical school invented by *Observer* columnist Paul Jennings in 1948. Foreshadowed by the 19th-century thinkers Freidegg and Heidansiecker, the school has as its leading luminary Pierre-Marie Ventre. Ventre 'reversed the traditional mechanism of philosophy, which until then had been the consensus of what men think about Things: Resistentialism is concerned with what Things think about men. Briefly, they are Against us (*Les choses sont contre nous*).' Resistentialism crystallizes definitively ideas which have long been in circulation: one's shoelaces are always impossibly tangled into knots when one is in a particular hurry, the better the carpet the more often the toast falls butter-side down, and so on. Harassment of the animate by the inanimate is seen not as the just punishment for hubris, but as an inevitable consequence of the animate/inanimate dichotomy. The absence of any physical basis for resistentialism is more than counterbalanced by its appeal as a psychological theory. R.SI.

resistivity surveying. In ARCHAEOLOGY, a technique for discovering buried features by measuring differences in the resistance of the subsoil. It is based on the principle that man-made disturbances such as a buried ditch or wall retain water in differing degrees as compared with the undisturbed soil. Since resistance depends on water content, where an area containing buried features is surveyed with a resistivity meter disturbances will appear as anomalous readings. Recent improvements include continuous recording on punched tape and COMPUTER plotting. B.C.

resonance. The sympathetic vibrations of a system subjected to an oscillating force whose frequency is close to one of the 'natural frequencies' of the system. Examples: (1) a child on a swing raises it by 'pumping' ENERGY into it at its natural frequency; (2) the tuning of radio receivers is based on 'resonant circuits' which oscillate only when stimulated by electromagnetic RADIATION of the correct radio frequency; (3) a PHOTON can be absorbed by an ATOM only if its frequency corresponds to an energy equal to the difference between two ENERGY LEVELS of the atom. See also MAGNETIC RESONANCE. M.V.B.

resources, natural. That part of the material components of the ENVIRONMENT, including both MASS and ENERGY, physical and biological, that can be used by man. As such, resources are bounded by concepts of utility (see UTILITY THEORY), and resource estimates change with changing technological and socioeconomic conditions. A distinction is conventionally drawn between *non-renewable resources* (sometimes termed *stock resources*), like coal and oil deposits, and *renewable resource* (sometimes termed *flow resources*), like tidal power. See also CONSERVATION. P.H.

respondent conditioning, see CLASSICAL CONDITIONING.

rest mass. The MASS of a system as measured by an observer at rest relative to it. According to the special theory of RELATIVITY, the mass of a body moving relative to the observer is greater, the difference appreciable only near the speed of light. M.V.B.

restoration ecology. A rapidly developing branch of ECOLOGY dedicated to restoring disturbed or destroyed ECOSYSTEMS as nearly as possible to the undisturbed state. Ecologists initially sought to study pristine ecosystems, free of the effects of human activity. As human populations have grown and human impacts have spread, disturbed ecosystems have become more prevalent and pristine ones ever scarcer (see POPULATION PRESSURE).

Perhaps the first ecosystem restoration effort was undertaken by Aldo Leopold at the University of Wisconsin. Leopold wondered whether pastures of farms abandoned in the great DEPRESSION would gradually revert to the tall grass prairie that had occupied the site before farming was introduced. The Leopold prairie at the University Arboretum is now over 50 years old, and has an appearance very similar to native prairie. Leopold found, however, that prairie restoration required considerable human intervention. Non-native SPECIES had to be removed and prairie species introduced and protected until they became established; controlled burning was required, simulating naturally occurring prairie fires of old.

Other ecosystems which have suffered major alterations, and for which restoration is desirable, include wetlands and forests. Wetlands are biologically productive and diverse, but are often drained for highways, agriculture or commercial development. In the US wetlands are partially protected, and in many instances wetland loss to development must be mitigated with 'made' wetlands according to laws stipulating 'no net loss'.

The criteria for designation of wetlands (e.g. permanent or seasonal) are in contention. Also, there is disagreement among restoration ecologists as to how closely restored ecosystems can or should resemble native ecosystems in terms of species distribution and composition. W.G.R.

restriction enzyme. An essential tool of GENETIC ENGINEERING. The natural function of restriction ENZYMES is to protect the bacteria that make them from any invading foreign DNA (see NUCLEIC ACID). Each restriction enzyme recognizes and cuts particular permutations of nucleotides in DNA. P.N.

restrictive practices. Industrial and commercial agreements or arrangements which operate in restraint of free COMPETITION even though they may be valid under the ordinary law of tort or contract. In the UK, since the enactment in 1948 of the MONOPOLIES and Restrictive Practices Act, they have been subjected to various forms of legal control, notably the Restrictive Practices Act of 1956, which created a new judicial tribunal, the Restrictive Practices Court, to investigate agreements or arrangements designed to restrict in various ways the supply of goods and to declare them void if they are found to operate contrary to the PUBLIC INTEREST. Examples of such restrictive practices are agreements regulating the prices to be charged for goods supplied to customers, or the quantities to be supplied, or the conditions of supply. For further reading: R. B. Stevens and B. S. Yamey, *The Restrictive Practices Court* (1965). H.L.A.H.

Resurgence of Islam, see under ISLAM.

retaliation, massive, see MASSIVE RETALIATION.

retardation, mental, see MENTAL RETARDATION.

returns to scale. The relation between a proportionate increase in the use of all the inputs in production of a product and the proportionate increase in output. Returns to scale are increasing/constant/decreasing if the proportionate increase in output is greater than/equal to/less than the proportionate increase in output. It is usually assumed that increasing returns to scale exist over a certain range of output (see ECONOMIES OF SCALE). At higher levels of output the difficulty of managing large organizations may give rise to decreasing returns to scale. At an abstract level, the exact doubling of inputs must give rise to twice as much output. Thus, the returns to scale considered in practice implicitly refer to situations where it is not possible to increase all inputs exactly. For further reading: J. Craven, *Introduction to Economics* (1984). J.P.

reversal theory. A psychological theory formulated by British psychologist Michael Apter in the late 1970s while attempting to clarify the relationship between arousal and 'hedonic state' (i.e. level of pleasure) in a way which integrated the theoretical approaches of BEHAVIOURISM and PHENOMENOLOGY. Apter proposed two fundamental 'metamotivational states'. In the 'telic' state (roughly equivalent to 'work'), high arousal is unpleasant, producing ANXIETY, and low arousal pleasantly relaxing. By contrast, in the 'paratelic state' (roughly equivalent to 'play'), high arousal is pleasantly exciting and low arousal unpleasantly boring. Apter claims that we typically reverse from one state to the other, especially when things become unpleasant. A more comprehensive theory and a PSYCHOMETRIC test (the Telic Dominance Scale) evolved from this core thesis. (For instance, since individuals vary in both dominant metamotivational state and ease of reversal, it extended to personality issues.) Apter now identifies several additional metamotivational pairs (e.g. mastery versus sympathy in interpersonal situations). Applications are being explored in such fields as PSYCHOTHERAPY and health psychology. A current difficulty is that orthodox experimentalists reject the theory's phenomenological character, while dissident social constructionists (see SOCIAL CONSTRUCT) reject its scientific orthodoxy. For further reading: M. Apter, *Reversal Theory: Motivation, Emotion and Personality* (1989). G.D.R.

reverse transcription. The transcription of RNA into DNA (see NUCLEIC ACID).

revisionism.

(1) The most notorious usage, emerging in the late 20th century, is revisionism as it relates to the HOLOCAUST. Holocaust revisionists maintain that the extermination of six million European Jews did not occur; that gas chambers did not exist in Nazi CONCENTRATION CAMPS (see NAZISM); and that the Holocaust is a myth promoted by the Jews to promote the cause of ZIONISM. Leading revisionist historians include David Irving in the UK and Robert Faurisson in France. In the USA Holocaust revisionism is promoted by the extreme RIGHT-wing Institute for Historical Review. For further reading: R. Knoller, *Denial of the Holocaust: A Bibliography* (1992). S.T.

(2) A CONCEPT denoting a critical reinterpretation of MARXIST theories and/or a doctrinal deviation (see DEVIATIONISM) from the official ideological position (see IDEOLOGY) among COMMUNIST factions, parties and states. In communist polemics, the relationship of revisionism to orthodoxy appears to be a secular counterpart to that of HERESY to religious DOGMA. The term dates from the 1890s, when the German Social Democrat (see SOCIAL DEMOCRACY) Eduard Bernstein (1850–1932) attempted to modify Marxist ideas in the light of historical experience. In the communist movement it became a term of opprobrium for any attempt to revise official interpretations of the Marxist canon. It has been invoked particularly since the emergence of communist polycentrism. After the 20th Congress of the Soviet Communist Party (1956), which undermined Party infallibility by admitting Stalin's errors, revisionism became a label frequently used to denounce the ideas, policies and general ideological positions of the opposing communist parties, Soviet and Chinese, Yugoslav and Albanian, all of which claimed to be orthodox. Their own doctrinal innovations they described not as revisions but as 'a creative development of MARXISM-LENINISM' or its application to local conditions. For further reading: L. Labedz (ed.), *Revisionism* (1962). L.L.

(3) A term applied before World War II to the claims of such countries as Germany, Hungary and Bulgaria to the territories which they had lost in World War I. L.L.

(4) A tendency in American HISTORIOGRAPHY in the 1960s and early 1970s to rewrite the history of the COLD WAR and shift the blame for it onto the USA. This trend was strongly reinforced by the faults and failure of US policy in VIETNAM, which revisionist historians argued were not a divergence from but a consequence and illustration of an IMPERIALIST foreign and economic policy followed by the USA from the end of World War II. The revisionists' attack on the orthodox version of US postwar policy represented the second stage in the historiography of the cold war. This in turn has been succeeded by a third stage which offers a more balanced appreciation of the complexities of the situation in the 1940s and represents a synthesis of the first two. For further reading: R. J. Maddox (ed.), *The New Left and the Origins of the Cold War* (1973). A.L.C.B.

revolution. A term (meaning rotation or turn) which was applied by Copernicus to the movement of celestial bodies in his treatise *De Revolutionibus Orbium Coelestium* (1543), and which in the 17th century, after the astronomical revolution, began to be applied metaphorically to political and social upheavals. From this it has developed to mean any fundamental or complete change in the mode of production (the

INDUSTRIAL REVOLUTION, technological revolution, etc.), in the political and social system (the French and Russian Revolutions, etc.), or in some aspect of social, intellectual or cultural life (scientific revolution, the GREAT PROLETARIAN CULTURAL REVOLUTION, etc.). But it is sudden radical changes in the political, social and economic structure of society which form the subject of revolutionary theories and of the theories of revolution. These are concerned not with mere changes of rulers ('palace revolutions'), but with changes of ruling CLASSES, of the methods of rule, and of social INSTITUTIONS, with the revolutionary passions and actions which lead to these changes, and with their consequences.

Revolutionary theories, like MARXISM or LENINISM, not only advocate revolution; they also try to explain how it comes about. The classical Marxist approach looked for the 'causes' of revolution in the development of 'the forces of production' which, by clashing with 'the conditions of production', engender industrial class-struggle to the point of explosion. Leninism shifted the emphasis from 'objective' to 'subjective' conditions for revolution, stressing the role of the revolutionary organization, the Party.

Most contemporary sociological theories (see SOCIOLOGY) focus on the need for modernization as a 'root' cause of modern revolutions; they point to the confluence of the aspirations of the 'advanced intelligentsia' (see INTELLECTUAL) and the miseries of the 'backward peasantry'. However, the theories of revolution concentrating on UNDERDEVELOPMENT fail to explain the absence of revolutionary developments in some backward countries and their presence in some industrial ones. On the other hand, the experience of the 20th century points to the abandonment of Marxian *Gesetzmässigheit*, i.e. of the belief that the stages of social development leading to revolution conform to a system or regular (and predictable) 'laws'. Such a belief cannot survive 'revolutions of underdevelopment' and the decoupling by the NEW LEFT theoreticians of the 'subjective' from the 'objective' conditions for revolution, a separation that goes beyond Leninist VOLUNTARISM (as in the early work of French theorist Régis Debray, and renders the old Marxist debate about the relation between BOURGEOIS and SOCIALIST revolutions obsolete.

Some contemporary analysts of the revolutionary phenomenon go beyond the relation between revolution and ECONOMIC DEVELOPMENT (Marx), underdevelopment (Lenin), and 'over-development' (the New Left), or even the question of 'modernization'. Their view of revolution transcends purely economic causation or even sociological DETERMINISM. They emphasize the recurrence of utopian and millenarian motives in history (see UTOPIANISM; MILLENARIANISM), and look for chiliastic elements in contemporary secular movements (Norman Cohn, Eric Voegelin). In this perspective, the history of the revolutionary idea may throw more light on the phenomenon of revolution than do either the existing revolutionary theories or the existing theories of revolution. See also PERMANENT REVOLUTION. For further reading: E. Voegelin, *From Enlightenment to Revolution* (1975). L.L.

revolutionary science. Classic philosophies of science (see SCIENCE, PHILOSOPHY OF), such as EMPIRICISM and POSITIVISM, argued that science evolved. Facts steadily accumulated, and broader, more comprehensive theories emerged automatically out of them. In some way, science approximated nearer towards the truth. American philosopher T. S. Kuhn's *The Structure of Scientific Revolutions* (1970) aimed to scotch this view. For Kuhn, science operates for long stretches without any fundamental change. This is normal science, within a PARADIGM – a period in which the implications of existing theories are worked out in detail. Kuhn speaks of 'puzzle solving'. Very occasionally, however, science is revolutionized. Within the existing paradigm, ANOMALIES increasingly build up, and eventually a new theory is required, which can incorporate these anomalies. With the catastrophic speed of a REVOLUTION, the new paradigm ousts the old. Kuhn regards this as a revolutionary act, because it is, in his view, an irrational moment in science. The new theory establishes itself not because of any objective, rational superiority but through a leap of faith by the scientific community. The new science does not augment the old; it destroys and buries it. For this reason, Kuhn's critics have accused him of undermining belief in the progressiveness of science, and of retreating into a kind of

RELATIVISM. These are charges which Kuhn has, not completely convincingly, denied. In historic reality the notion of scientific revolutions is quite ambiguous. The period between Copernicus and Newton is often termed 'The Scientific Revolution', but the time-span involved, over 150 years, makes the process sound more like EVOLUTION than revolution. For further reading: T. S. Kuhn, *The Structure of Scientific Revolutions* (1970). R.P.

revolutionary violence. Although revolts against systems of government have existed for over two millennia, the reflective organization of violence for the sake of revolutionary change began primarily with the work of Karl Marx and Friedrich Engels (see REVOLUTION; MARXISM). Although the modern philosophers (Hobbes, Locke, Rousseau, Hume and Kant) reflected on conditions of legitimate violence against governments, the goal of revolution in itself was never defended as a legitimate basis for such violence. Marx was not in fact a defender of violence in itself, but his and Engels's articulation of CLASS struggle and BOURGEOIS conceptions of rights was such that it required a reconsideration of the understanding of violence. Reconsideration was forcefully stated by French social philosopher Georges Sorel's (1847–1922) notion of a global STRIKE. Here, revolution is articulated as affecting the structures of society. Sorel's formulation clearly need not entail physical violence; its 'violent' dimension is, in the end, a conception of force that is social with material consequences. In the 1950s, Jean-Paul Sartre (1905–80) developed an existentialist Marxist theory that explored the SERIALITY of racial and colonial violence and led to a critique of appeals to non-violence in such anti-colonial and anti-racist struggles (see RACISM; IMPERIALISM; NON-VIOLENT RESISTANCE; POST-COLONIALISM). Sartre raised the possibility of the everyday sphere as a violent sphere and the need for social transformation of such practices. For many revolutionaries of colour, the task became the articulation of the revolutionary significance of colonized and conquered peoples. Trinidadian writer C. L. R. James (1901–89) had already argued in the 1930s, e.g., that had the 18th-century Haitian slaves waited for the French to develop a revolutionary consciousness, their condition of slavery would have been maintained. The Haitian slave revolts revealed that the conditions of social transformation were not laws of nature but principles subject to human intervention. In Frantz Fanon's thought (late 1950s), revolutionary violence involves a two-levelled process of human reassertion. The first is the HEURISTIC effect of asserting one's humanity at the risk of death. At best, this stage offers hope of decolonization. The second stage is the heuristic value of ongoing humanizing activity. This stage offers hope of post-coloniality. Both cases appeal to an assertion of agency as a vital dimension of human development. The most influential theorist of revolutionary violence, Fanon's position does not necessitate physical violence, although it does not exclude (and some times encourages) it. It is the transformative activity of asserting the humanity of denigrated peoples. The goal of revolutionary violence is, thus, a humanistic goal. (See HUMANISM; NEW HUMANISM.) L.R.G.

revolving stage. A turntable stage whose earliest recorded use was in Roman theatres in the 1st century BC. The first such device installed as permanent equipment was used in Japanese Kabuki theatre around 1760; its first recorded use in modern Europe was at Munich in 1896. Difficulties in fitting three or more sets into one circle led to the invention of sliding and rising and falling stages. The most elaborate of these were installed in cabaret theatres such as the Pigalle in Paris in the 1920s. But the basic turntable stage is now a standard feature of most large theatres, greatly facilitating changes of scene. For further reading: R. and H. Leacroft, *Theatre and Playhouse* (1984). M.BI.

rewrite rules, see under GENERATIVE GRAMMAR.

***Rezeptionsästhetik*,** see RECEPTION THEORY.

rheology. The branch of NEWTONIAN MECHANICS dealing with the deformation and flow of materials which are neither solid nor completely liquid, such as non-drip paint, bread dough, modelling clay, glacier ice, and lead on roofs. See also RELAXATION; RELAXATION TIME. M.V.B.

rhesus factor, see under IMMUNITY.

rhetoric. In classical approaches to language, the study of effective or persuasive speaking and writing, especially as practised in public oratory. Several hundred rhetorical figures were recognized by classical rhetoricians, classifying the way words could be arranged in order to achieve special stylistic effects, some of which have continued in modern stylistics, such as METAPHOR, simile, personification and PARADOX. The study of rhetoric has been given a new lease of life in modern courses on communication, where the aim is to understand the processes underlying successful argument and persuasion. For further reading: W. Nash, *Rhetoric: The Wit of Persuasion* (1989). D.C.

rhetoric of science, see SCIENCE, RHETORIC OF.

rheumatology. The sub-speciality of internal medicine devoted to the study and management of disorders of the musculoskeletal system. Rheumatic disorders, such as soft tissue rheumatism, osteoarthritis, rheumatoid arthritis and ankylosing spondylitis, are the most common clinical problems within the speciality, but the field is much wider, comprising other inflammatory and immunological disorders which affect muscles and joints, e.g. the so-called 'connective tissue' disorders such as systemic lupus erythematosus, scleroderma, polymyositis, dermatomyositis, overlap connective tissue disease, and vasculitic syndromes such as polyarteritis nodosa, polymyalgia rheumatica, and giant cell arteritis. Many systemic diseases produce locomotor symptoms and signs and so involve the rheumatologist. Gout, a disorder of uric acid metabolism, is perhaps the best known of these, but other metabolic disorders, infections (both bacterial and viral) and inflammatory disorders, such as sarcoidosis, can cause arthritic disease. The causes of the major rheumatological disorders are not known, but the pathology of rheumatoid arthritis and the connective tissue disorders is characterized by inflammatory reaction and disordered immune response, and in ankylosing spondylitis genetic factors play an important role (see GENETICSGENOMICS). Treatment of rheumatological disorders focuses on relieving the symptoms of inflammation with anti-inflammatory and analgesic drugs, suppressing the disordered immune response, and minimizing physical disability with the aid of paramedical specialists such as physiotherapists and occupational therapists (see PHYSIOTHERAPY; OCCUPATIONAL THERAPY). D.D.; D.L.W.

rhythm and blues. Another of the labels applied to BLACK music which the form's determined vitality and variety has dislodged. As a genre, rhythm and blues in the late 1920s and 1930s came to stand for BLUES-based music that was not JAZZ – simpler harmonically and rhythmically, more ruggedly emotional, performed by soloists or duos instead of bands. Recordings of the style were known as 'race records', turned out specifically for black audiences. In fact rhythm and blues was merely a catch-all for the current evolutionary stage of the blues, whether 'city' or 'country', played or sung. By the 1940s 'r&b', as it came to be known, had developed a more concerted version, reflecting the influence of the BIG BANDS of the SWING era; it crossed brass and saxes with its own traditional accessibility to produce a heady mixture of driving, good-time music that defied bodies not to dance. The most widely known of these infectious 'jump bands' was probably Louis Jordan's Tympany Five, though other groups, like that of Junior Parker, had strong local followings. As this strain became identified with r&b, the old guitar and vocal form of the music followed its own course. Less commercial than the jump bands, it claimed a different audience, and, partly as a result of the rise of rock and roll, achieved a vogue of its own. Rock performers of the 1950s, like Bill Haley (see ROCK MUSIC), showed the influence of the jump bands, but gutty, passionate performers like Muddy Waters and B. B. King inspired 1960s groups like the Rolling Stones. Despite some surface similarities, partisans of blues (as the form came simply to be called to distinguish it from commercialized r&b) insisted on the superior authenticity and integrity of their music over rock. But in the late 1960s and 1970s it began to be supplanted by a new metamorphosis of black music: SOUL. GE.S.

ribbon development. In GEOGRAPHY, the extension of a town or village in the cheapest possible way, i.e. next to its main services and thus alongside its main roads. Many industrial towns of Britain, e.g. those of south-west Lancashire, were linked in this way. Post-war development has tended to infill such areas so that building has taken place between the ribbons. In contrast, the Rhondda Valley mining villages in Wales, confined from the start by topography, the position of coal seams, and the practices of the coal-mining industry, are linear in shape but not, strictly speaking, examples of ribbon development since their shape was unavoidable. M.L.

ribosome, see under NUCLEIC ACID.

ribozyme. A type of RNA (see NUCLEIC ACID) that can act as a catalyst. Almost all catalytic reactions in BIOCHEMISTRY are mediated by ENZYMES, which are PROTEIN molecules. But in the 1980s, certain RNA MOLECULES, belonging to the class of biomolecules called nucleic acids, were also found to be capable of CATALYSIS. A wide variety of ribozymes, both natural and synthetic, are now known. Natural ribozymes assist the process of splicing, in which segments of RNA molecules are excised and the ends joined back together before the RNA acts as a template for the synthesis of proteins. Ribozymes that catalyse non-natural reactions can be developed by a biotechnological strategy called *in vitro* evolution, and might find uses as drugs. The discovery of ribozymes has strong implications for theories of the chemical origin of life, since it suggests how complex chemistry could have been conducted in an RNA WORLD before the advent of protein catalysts. P.C.B.

rich clusters, see under GALAXY CLUSTERS.

Right, the. Label applied to a range of political views at the other end of the political spectrum from the LEFT (q.v. for the origin of both terms), and to those holding such views.

(1) Originally, the Right comprised those who defended the monarchical INSTITUTIONS attacked by the French Revolution. During the 19th century the term was associated with authority, patriotism, tradition, strong government, property, the Church, and the army. In France it remained monarchist even after the establishment of the Third Republic, but it was everywhere evolving from its aristocratic affinities towards the protection of CAPITALIST interests against the threat of SOCIALISM. It was now opposed not only to EGALITARIANISM, but also to state intervention in the economy, which the ultra-right French Legitimists and Bismarck had strongly favoured.

But the new Right was concerned not just with economic policies. It became increasingly influenced by the attitudes and ideas of romantic NATIONALISM. After World War I a new radical (see RADICALISM) Right emerged which was sharply different from the traditional conservative Right (see CONSERVATISM). It was no longer preoccupied simply with the defence of the established order, and was often hostile to the interests of the upper classes; its most extreme form was Hitler's National Socialism (see NAZISM). In line with its mystique of the nation and the state, it was hostile to economic LAISSEZ FAIRE and in favour of strong economic controls for its totalitarian (see TOTALITARIANISM) and military aims. L.L.

(2) After World War II the Right remained diverse in values and configuration; in many democratic states its dominant factions accepted the KEYNESIAN approach to economics and the principles of the WELFARE STATE. By the 1970s the perceived inadequacy of such approaches in the face of mounting economic difficulties and social problems prompted a resurgence encapsulated by the term New Right. It is a phrase denoting a number of complex and loosely connected intellectual currents and political tendencies, ranging from elements of LIBERTARIANISM to the AUTHORITARIANISM of its French variant. Components of New Right thought have shaped the character of REAGANISM and THATCHERISM. These include economic theories associated particularly with Friedman and Hayek, often described as neo-liberal (see NEO-LIBERALISM), which exalt capitalism not only for its productive capacity, but claim it to be uniquely conducive to the maintenance of political and social liberty. The New Right thus opposes a strongly interventionist or ownership role for the state in the economy. Its social philosophy is ambiguous; its stress on individual freedom contradicts conventional conservatism's preference for hierarchy and obligation, but shares its con-

cern for the maintenance of law and order. For further reading: N. Bosanquet, *After the New Right* (1983). S.R.

right to choose, see under ABORTION.

right to life, see under ABORTION.

rigid designator. American philosopher Saul Kripke introduced the term 'rigid designator' into PHILOSOPHY to mean an expression that designates the same object with respect to every POSSIBLE WORLD in which that object exists. Most definite descriptions are not rigid designators. For example, 'the Prime Minister of Great Britain during the summer of 1997' designates Tony Blair with respect to the actual world, but other individuals with respect to some other possible worlds – e.g. those in which John Major won the 1997 election. Proper names, on the other hand, are rigid designators, e.g. the name 'Kripke' designates the same person, Kripke, with respect to every possible world (though it is of course true that that person is not *called* 'Kripke' in all those worlds: Kripke might have been called something else).

The notion of rigid designation is philosophically important. In particular the notion plays a key role in one of Kripke's arguments for there being NECESSARY TRUTHS that can only be established A POSTERIORI. Kripke points out that if the terms flanking the 'is' in a true identity statement are both rigid designators, then that statement will be necessary, for there will be no possible world with respect to which the respective designations of the two terms come apart. Thus, e.g., in the true identity statement 'Cliff Richard is Harry Webb', both names are rigid designators, and so it must be a necessary truth that Cliff Richard is Harry Webb. Yet that Cliff Richard is Harry Webb is of course *a posteriori* knowledge, not A PRIORI knowledge. So it is an *a posteriori* necessary truth that Cliff Richard is Harry Webb. For further reading: S. Kripke, *Naming and Necessity* (1980). S.W.L.

ring modulator. An ELECTRONIC MUSIC device which takes in two sounds and adds and subtracts the frequencies of their harmonics. This results in complex sounds that bear strange relationships to the originals: e.g. if one of the sounds is rising in pitch the resultant sound rises (sum) and also falls (subtraction). Frequently a live sound (e.g. piano) and a simple electronic sound are combined in this way, thus producing instantaneous complex sounds usually of a bell-like nature (as in Stockhausen's 'Mantra'). B.CO.

Rio Group. A diplomatic initiative which emerged in 1986 to help resolve the political, economic and social crisis affecting Central America. Its origins lie with the Contadora group created in 1983 by Colombia, Mexico, Panama and Venezuela, and the Group of Eight which brought in Argentina, Brazil, Peru and Uruguay as new members in 1985. These initiatives were set up amid fears of US intervention in El Salvador and Nicaragua, and marked a radical shift from traditional Latin American acquiescence to US foreign policy. Member countries of the Rio Group at present include Argentina, Bolivia, Brazil, Chile, Ecuador, Mexico, Panama, Paraguay, Peru, Uruguay and Venezuela, and represent the principal association for regional political co-ordination. Since the end of civil war in Nicaragua (1990), El Salvador (1992) and Guatemala (1996), the Rio Group has concentrated efforts on issues such as the consolidation of DEMOCRACY and the promotion of regional integration and economic development, as well as co-ordination of foreign policy initiatives. M.A.P.

Rio Treaty. The Inter-American Treaty of Reciprocal Assistance signed by representatives of 18 Latin American countries and of the USA in Rio de Janeiro in August 1947, as a mutual defence alliance against armed aggression and other situations threatening the peace of the American continents. Regular meetings of foreign ministers of the signatories provide a consultative organ. The Treaty became a model for other regional security pacts such as NATO and SEATO. For further reading: G. C. Smith, *The Inter-American System* (1966). D.C.W.

rishon, see under ELEMENTARY PARTICLES.

risk. In ECONOMICS, risk means something slightly different from its everyday meaning: it refers to a situation where there are different possible outcomes, each of which has a known probability of occurring. In real life, it is often impossible to know the exact chances of different outcomes; but for the purposes of economic calculations it is necessary for the probabilities to be precisely quantified. There has been much recent work on risk, and how people deal with it. It is observed that people can be divided into two broad categories, 'risk-loving' and 'risk-averse', depending on how they react to the following choice, between e.g. (a) a guaranteed return of ten dollars, or (b) a 50-50 chance of getting either twenty dollars or nothing at all. It is also observed that people are more willing to take risks when all the outcomes involve a gain of some kind. When they have to choose between different possibilities of loss, they tend to play safe rather than gamble on even small possibilities of very large loss. A.A.L.

risk analysis. An application of DECISION THEORY whereby SIMULATION, introspection and various techniques are used to form *probability density functions* (see DISTRIBUTION; FUNCTION) of the different possible outcomes corresponding to the alternate courses of action. It has been extended to cover decisions which have to be made sequentially. This version of the procedure uses a *decision tree* and is known as *stochastic decision tree analysis*. Risk analysis is used in ECONOMICS, MANAGEMENT and ENGINEERING. See also EXPECTED UTILITY; RISK; UNCERTAINTY. For further reading: H. Raiffa, *Decision Analysis* (1968).

H.TH.; J.P.

***rite de passage*.** Rite of transition, a term developed by French ethnographer Van Gennep (*The Rites of Passage*, 1909; Eng. tr. 1960) to describe the movement of an individual from one state to another. The transition is marked by RITUAL and involves initiation. In this way society recognizes and legitimates change. Examples of *rite de passage* include MARRIAGE, circumcision, coronation and mortuary rituals. Van Gennep identified three elements in *rite de passage*. (1) Rite of separation: temporary removal of an individual from society while preparing for the change. (2) Rite of marginality/*liminality*: moment of transition, initiation. (3) Rite of aggregation: new STATUS affirmed and the individual is reincorporated into society. The middle element or liminal phase is potentially dangerous as the individual is between social ROLES. In this phase the initiate is subject to restrictions and TABOO. For further reading: J. S. La Fontaine, *Initiation: Ritual Drama and Secret Knowledge across the World* (1985).

A.G.

ritual. Formalized behaviour or activity in accordance with rules and procedures specified by society. The 'peculiarity' or 'alerting' quality of ritual sets it apart from other social activity. Ritual may be individual and private (e.g. a sorcerer casting his spells) or social and public (e.g. SACRIFICE). The clarity of the boundary between ritual and non-ritual varies. Certain rituals are very clearly marked off from the rest of social activity. Ritual may have an elaborate internal structure (beginning, middle and end), and this may be seen in RITES DE PASSAGE: circumcision, mortuary rites, etc.

Ritual has both instrumental and expressive aspects: it is an activity (it does something) and it is a statement (it says something). Anthropologists working in the FUNCTIONALIST tradition (Malinowski, Radcliffe Brown, Gluckman) have attempted to understand the *function* of ritual by situating it within a specific social context. Others have focused upon the content of ritual and pursued its meaning rather than its function. These anthropologists are usually subdivided into 'intellectualists' and 'symbolists'. An intellectualist approach (ritual concerned with providing an explanation of the world) may be seen in the work of Stephen Hugh-Jones (*The Palm and the Pleiades*, 1979). The symbolists have highlighted the expressive or emotional content of ritual. V. W. Turner's work (*The Forest of Symbols*, 1967) has been important in establishing this approach. For further reading: M. Bloch, *From Blessing to Violence* (1986).

A.G.

ritualization, see under RELEASER.

RNA (ribonucleic acid), see under NUCLEIC ACID.

RNA world. A hypothesis proposed to explain how the chemical basis of life evolved from primitive replicating molecules to acquire the dualism of DNA and

PROTEINS found in living ORGANISMS today (see NUCLEIC ACIDS). DNA in CELLS can replicate only with the assistance of protein ENZYMES, but these are themselves manufactured from blueprints on DNA. This poses a chicken-and-egg conundrum of which came first. In the scenario of the RNA world, both were preceded by MOLECULES based on RNA, which shares both DNA's ability to replicate and the ability of proteins to facilitate complex chemical transformations by CATALYSIS. The chemical properties of RNA make it a more plausible candidate than DNA for the original 'genetic' data bank. The RNA world hypothesis gained much credibility when catalytic RNA molecules called RIBOZYMES were discovered in the 1980s (see GENETICS/GENOMICS; HUMAN GENOME PROJECT). P.C.B.

robot. A term originally introduced to describe a machine built to resemble a human in appearance and functioning. Later the use of the word was extended to any device which performed a function previously only thought to be possible for a human, e.g. traffic lights which do the job of a policeman on point duty, but which do not resemble a policeman in appearance or action. As more and more mechanical devices were used in conjunction with automatic control systems to replace human operators in factories concerned with mass production or in situations hazardous to humans, the study of these machines became a subject in its own right, known as *robotics*. This embraces the subjects of automatic control, COMPUTERS and microprocessors, as well as many facets of electrical, electronic, mechanical and chemical ENGINEERING. E.R.L.

rock music. The collective name for a diverse range of popular musics coming to prominence in the 1960s with its roots in rock and roll and heavily influenced by SOUL music. Rock music normally uses amplification, electronic instruments (in particular the electric guitar) and drums, and its forms range widely from simple song structures (often BLUES) to long and complex improvisatory forms. The term rock music is often used interchangeably with POP music, but the former is generally held to be less commercially oriented, more diverse and eclectic and aimed at a more knowledgeable audience. Many sub-categories exist within rock music, including *progressive rock* (more experimental, and less song-dominated), *heavy metal* (using extreme volumes, insistent rhythms and giving prominence to electric guitars and drums), *glam rock* (with emphasis on the appearance, make-up and clothes of the performers), etc. Rock music is also frequently linked to other musical types as in *jazz rock* (see FUSION) and *folk rock*. Rock music has been crucial to the development of ELECTRONIC MUSIC and recording techniques, and its links with YOUTH CULTURE, style and politics are also extremely important (see PUNK). For further reading: P. Friedlander, *Rock and Roll: A Social History* (1996). B.CO.

rock steady, see under REGGAE.

Rock the Vote. Public Education and activist initiatives started in the US in 1990 by recording industry personnel, using recording artists to encourage 18–24-year-olds to register to vote through concerts and media appearances (it can claim more than 350,000 new voters). RTV was instrumental in agitating for the National Voter Registration Reform Act (signed by President Clinton in 1993), and also promotes anti-censorship initiatives. In the UK, RTV began as an apolitical charity supported by the Labour, Conservative and Liberal parties and recording industry artists in 1996, and it processed more than 400,000 voter registration cards by April 1997. P.L.

role; role theory. In SOCIAL PSYCHOLOGY, 'role' connotes the bundle of formal and predictable attributes associated with a particular social position, as distinct from the personal characteristics of the individual who occupies that position. The waiter or the doctor, e.g., is called upon to perform a professional role expected of him by his public audience which may be quite at variance with his own inclinations of the moment. Roles as official and publicly recognized as these are frequently supported by uniforms and strict linguistic codes. But most social 'roles' are so inexactly defined that they are barely more than intuitively felt guidelines to the correct behaviour for a particular social situation.

The earliest systematic uses of the term

were in the social psychology of G. H. Mead (1863–1931; see SYMBOLIC INTERACTION), which emphasized the importance of 'taking the role of the other', and the role-playing therapy invented by Jacob Moreno (1892–1974; see SOCIOMETRY; PSYCHODRAMA). Later it became current in social ANTHROPOLOGY, where it lent itself especially to describing the rights and duties associated with positions in KINSHIP systems. Sociological theorists often adopted it, together with STATUS, as a suitable term for the basic elements from which SOCIAL STRUCTURES are built up, and various attempts have been made to use it as an interdisciplinary CONCEPT, bridging the gap between, on the one hand, the treatment of social systems and INSTITUTIONS by sociologists and political scientists and, on the other hand, the experimental study of personality, motivation and group processes by social psychologists. The structural-functional (see STRUCTURAL-FUNCTIONAL THEORY) and NORMATIVE emphasis given to 'role' in PARSONIAN theory was not accepted by all students of standardized behaviour, and prompted a rediscovery of the original dramaturgical metaphor, which had suggested a degree of conscious theatre in EVERYDAY social life, and which had been largely forgotten when the term became part of a technical vocabulary.

It was in this sense that Erving Goffman (1922–82) expanded the term in *The Presentation of Self in Everyday Life* (1956), where he elaborated two key concepts: *role distance* (the extent to which the individual may free himself from the demands of mere adequacy in a given role, and exploit the possibilities of play and improvisation above and beyond the necessities of 'correct' behaviour); and *role conflict* (what happens when the individual finds himself in the position of playing two or more roles at once – when, e.g., the doctor has to minister to a member of his own family, thereby confusing his professional and fatherly roles). Armed with these more subtle and modified terms, Goffman presented a most influential analysis of social behaviour as an elaborately mounted drama, in which virtually no area of human activity, public or private, was excluded from the essentially histrionic demands and conditions of the 'presented' self. From 1960 a great variety of ETHNOMETHODOLOGIES proliferated, all stressing the ritual nature of stylized public performance and the need for an adequate HERMENEUTICS to interpret it.

During the 1960s, the term became part of the commonplace idiom of social workers and political journalists. *Role*, along with other dramaturgical vogue words (notably *scenario*), was used to describe any kind of staged or impersonated performance, especially those in public life. The main problem with the concept of 'role' is its lack of constraint; it is a tearaway word which tends to carry all of human behaviour indiscriminately away with it. For further reading: J. A. Jackson (ed.), *Role* (1972).

J.R.; J.R.T.

roman-fleuve ('river-novel'). French term, used originally perhaps with ironical intent, for the multi-volume novel which attempts to cover a large area of society or to follow the fortunes of a family through more than one generation. (The term *fleuve* has no specific connection with the concept of the STREAM OF CONSCIOUSNESS.) Balzac's *La Comédie humaine* and Zola's *Les Rougon-Macquart* can be classed retrospectively as *romans-fleuves*, but the term appears to have been first used with reference to Romain Rolland's *Jean Christophe* (1906–12). More recent French examples are *Les Thibault* (1922–40) by Roger Martin du Gard, *La Chronique des Pasquier* (1933–44) by Georges Duhamel, and *Les Hommes de bonne volonté* (1932–46) by Jules Romains. English and American examples include Galsworthy's *Forsyte Saga* (1906–21), Anthony Powell's *Dance to the Music of Time* (1951–75), and Upton Sinclair's Lanny Budd series.

J.G.W.

Romanticism.

(1) In the arts generally, and in PHILOSOPHY, an overwhelming international tendency which swept across western Europe and Russia at the end of the 18th and beginning of the 19th centuries, in reaction against earlier NEO-CLASSICISM, MECHANISM and RATIONALISM. Arising in an age of social and internal REVOLUTIONS, involving a new model of being, Romanticism had much the same relationship to the 19th century as MODERNISM has to the 20th. More than simply a return to nature, to the UNCONSCIOUS, the realm of imagination or feeling, it was a synthesizing temper that trans-

formed the entire character of thought, sensibility and art; many of its preoccupations and notions remain central to the modern mind, including interest in the psychological and the expressive, in the childlike, the revolutionary, the nihilistic, the PLEASURE PRINCIPLE. It was a specific revolt against formality and containment in the art, ideas and notions of man, an assertion of the primacy of the perceiver in the world he perceives; hence theories of the imagination as such are central to it. In central Romantic thought, the organic relation of man and nature, of the interior and the transcendent imagination, is proposed; but much Romanticism is about loss of contact and 'dejection', and can lead to the hallucinatory or fantastic as a mode of perceptual redemption. Hence its relation to the tradition of 'romance', and its disposition towards fantasy, MYTH, the picturesque, the Gothic, the Faustian and Promethean. Romanticism takes different forms in different national strands (despite its internationality and its primary interest in the foreign and strange, it contains deep nationalistic and populist assumptions; see NATIONALISM; POPULISM), ranges from strongly individualistic (see INDIVIDUALISM) to revolutionary-collective concerns, and extends from IDEALISM and neo-PLATONISM to an agonized NIHILISM. Hence definitions of it vary widely. In fact, it is as much an international sensibility as a style or a philosophy; and its writing, painting, music, architecture and thought, some of it intensely subjective and solipsistic (see SOLIPSISM), some of it strongly marked by distancing and fantasy, amount to an eclectic new world-view or WELTANSCHAUUNG which shifts the prevailing idea and function of the artist and of man himself and his ROLE in the world.

Romanticism is usually held to have originated in French (especially Rousseau) and German (notably Herder, Kant, Fichte, Schelling) thought; to have strong roots in German *Sturm und Drang* writing of the 1770s; to have spread to England and then America, returned to France somewhat later, and to have shaped or affected all Europe in varying degrees at different times. Clearly related to dislocations in thought and SOCIAL STRUCTURE consequent on three revolutions – the American, the French, and the industrial (see INDUSTRIAL REVOLUTION) – and to the new, self-conscious isolation of the artist or INTELLECTUAL in a post-patronage era, it dominates perhaps three literary generations, from the 1790s to the 1840s. It then splinters, on the one hand towards REALISM, which philosophically amends it, on the other towards latter-day versions like SYMBOLISM and AESTHETICISM. There is now much argument about whether we still live in a Romantic age of style and sensibility; one strand in modernism assaults Romanticism's 'split religion' (T. E. Hulme's phrase), but another (e.g. Symbolism, EXPRESSIONISM) seeks to restore it. Certainly its revolutionary and pre-FREUDIAN overtones affect much modern art and thought. For further reading: H. Honour, *Romanticism* (1979). M.S.BR.

(2) In ARCHITECTURE, a tendency that largely derives from the Picturesque movement of the 18th century, especially as embodied in English landscape practice. In modern architecture it manifests itself not so much as a return to an earlier period as in an emphasis on natural materials and forms. In America it is exemplified by the ORGANIC architecture of Frank Lloyd Wright (1867–1959), which evolved from the work of H. H. Richardson and Louis Sullivan. In Europe, where it was influenced by ART NOUVEAU, it is an alternative tradition to that of the INTERNATIONAL STYLE. The most notable examples come from Alvar Aalto, who dominated Finnish architecture from the 1930s until his death in 1976. His freely and flowingly arranged forms, whether in buildings, furniture or light fittings, have that appearance of being naturally composed which the tenets of the Romantic movement require. For further reading: V. J. Scully, *Modern Architecture* (1961). M.BR.

(3) In music, a movement belonging largely to the first half of the 19th century, and exhibited notably in the works of Beethoven, Weber, Schubert, Schumann, Chopin, Berlioz, Liszt, Verdi, and Wagner. It received its stimulus partly from German literature of the late 18th century (A. W. Schlegel, Tieck, Novalis), and partly from the ideals associated with the French Revolution. It is characterized by a tendency among composers to view music as an expression as much of their psyche as of their craft; through the power of association they sought to embody their own ideals and passions in their music; in so doing they cultivated an extremely personalized and

sometimes exaggerated style. Reflected in their music is a series of opposing forces: between the individual and society; between intimacy and bombast; between the fusion of poetry and music and the pronounced self-sufficiency of instrumental music. Constant is the belief in music's power to translate human experience and to express human ideals. The term is often extended to include late-19th-century NATIONALIST composers (Dvořák, Tchaikovsky, Grieg), and the 'late Romantics' Bruckner, Mahler and Richard Strauss. For reactions against Romanticism see IMPRESSIONISM; NEO-CLASSICISM. For further reading: A. Einstein, *Music in the Romantic Era* (1947). E.H.

Rorschach test. A projective test designed by the Swiss psychiatrist Hermann Rorschach (1884–1922), consisting of ten bilaterally symmetrical inkblots to which the subject is asked to provide associations. Interpretation of the subject's responses is believed by its adherents to yield a description of general personality characteristics as well as UNCONSCIOUS conflicts. Responses are interpreted according to their content, their uniqueness or commonness, and the proportion and particular features (colour, shading, etc.) which have been used in forming the percept. Due to a lack of agreement over what this test measures, its popularity has declined sharply since the 1960s and it is now infrequently used in the diagnosis of mental illness. For further reading: M. Rickers-Ovsiankina, *Rorschach Psychology* (1977). R.P.-S.

round characters, see FLATROUND CHARACTERS.

rule-following paradox. A philosophical paradox (see PHILOSOPHY) developed by Ludwig Wittgenstein (1889–1951) in his book *Philosophical Investigations* (1953). We think of ourselves as following rules, e.g. the rules of the road, the rules governing our language, and arithmetical rules. But how are we to know what to do at any given step? For example, how are we to know that in the series generated by the rule for adding two we should write '1,002' after '1,000' rather than, say, '1,010'? When we look for guidance on how to carry on, e.g. to a formula or a previous segment of the series, we have always to *interpret* such indicators, and they can be interpreted in innumerable different ways. In fact, however we decide to continue there will be a way of interpreting what has gone before in which we are following the rule 'correctly', and also a way of interpreting what went before in which we are following 'incorrectly'. This raises the question: how are we to *know* which interpretation is the right interpretation? and also: what *makes* one particular interpretation the right interpretation? The problem is that whatever we might point to in attempting to answer these two questions (e.g., a second rule that is supposed to determine how the first is to be interpreted) will itself be open to innumerable different interpretations, so what in turn determines which of THESE interpretations is correct? The extraordinary conclusion we seem forced to accept is that while we might think that the rule determines how we should continue, in fact NOTHING makes one way of continuing correct and others incorrect. But that is just to say that there is no rule. This conclusion undermines all rules, including those that give our words meaning, and so renders language meaningless.

Quite how Wittgenstein responds to this paradox is controversial. Some believe Wittgenstein ACCEPTS the conclusion that there can be no such thing as following a rule, at least so far as the individual considered in isolation is concerned, but allows that an individual CAN be said to be carrying on correctly or incorrectly in so far as he respectively either marches or fails to march in step with the other members of a wider community. It is the community which provides us with a way of checking that we are following the rule correctly. According to this interpretation of Wittgenstein, the rule-following paradox forms part of a PRIVATE LANGUAGE argument: because all language involves rule-following, and rule-following must be shared by a community, so all language must be shared by a community.

Others interpret Wittgenstein differently. It has been suggested that it is not Wittgenstein's intention that we should accept the conclusion of the rule-following paradox. Rather, the absurdity of that conclusion is supposed to make us question the assumption upon which the argument for it rests, the assumption that in order to grasp a rule we *have* to *interpret* it. What Wittgenstein uses the paradox to demonstrate is that there must be a way of grasping a rule that does not involve interpreting it. What is less clear, perhaps, is precisely what this other way of grasping a rule is. For further reading: S. Kripke, *Wittgenstein on Rules and Private Language* (1982). S.W.L.

rule of law, see LAW, THE RULE OF.

rule, work to, see WORK TO RULE.

S

sacralization, see under SACRIFICE.

sacrifice. Seeks to establish a relationship, through an intermediary, between society and the supernatural order. Important elements in sacrifice include donor, RITUAL officiant, sacrificial object and recipient. The kind of intermediary is not randomly chosen, but culturally specified, and it is linked symbolically with the donor. Sacrifice has both instrumental aspects (i.e. an intention to bring something about) and expressive aspects (says something about the social and supernatural order). In establishing contact with the 'other world', sacrifice can involve elements of purification, symbolic exchange and communion. The classic work *Sacrifice: Its Nature and Function* (1899) by Hubert and Mauss has exercised an important influence in ANTHROPOLOGY. It represented the movement away from the evolutionary theories of sacrifice developed by Robertson Smith and James Frazer.

Evans-Pritchard in *Nuer Religion* (1956) took over from Hubert and Mauss the concepts of *sacralization* (spirit from gods come to man) and *desacralization* (man gets rid of spirit) and linked them respectively to his distinction between collective and personal sacrifice. Collective sacrifice was connected with changes in social STATUS, confirming a RITE DE PASSAGE. Personal sacrifice was concerned with the warding off of potential dangers. Although Evans-Pritchard concentrated on the reasons for the performance of sacrifice, he did not neglect what actually happened in sacrifice. Other anthropologists (e.g., Leach, *Culture and Communication*, 1976) have particularly taken up this aspect and in utilizing a structural (see STRUCTURALISM) method, they have examined its internal logic. For further reading: L. de Heusch, *Sacrifice in Africa: A Structuralist Approach* (1985). A.G.

sadism. A PARAPHILIA in which sexual pleasure is derived from inflicting pain on others. It was named by German psychiatrist Richard Krafft-Ebing (1840–1902) after the Marquis de Sade, who described its practice in *Justine* (1791) and other works. The word is often used loosely to denote cruelty of any kind. W.Z.

sadomasochism (SM). Sexual practice in which one partner agrees to be dominated by the other. At one extreme, it may involve inflicting severe pain or humiliation upon the submissive partner. At the other, it may involve little more than dressing up and role-playing, or, e.g., spanking.

Many sexual activities that were once considered perverted have become quite normal in recent decades, and glossy magazines celebrating fetishism and body piercing can be found in most bookshops and record stores. Night-clubs such as the Torture Garden in London, or the Vault in New York, are attended by all kinds of people, most of whom do not think of themselves as sexually deviant (see PARAPHILIA).

In the 1990s, several pressure groups have been set up to advocate the legalization of hard-core SM practices: at present, such practices are outlawed in the UK and the USA. One of the most famous groups was the Spanner Trust, which was formed in Britain in 1990. It protested the decision in the House of Lords to uphold the criminal convictions of 16 men who had indulged in extreme, but consensual, SM sex which left some of them with scars. However, in 1997 the European Court of Justice (see COURT OF JUSTICE OF THE EUROPEAN COMMUNITIES) upheld these men's convictions, arguing: 'The protection of private life means the protection of a person's intimacy and dignity, not the protection of his baseness . . .' This decision – which closely mirrors the 1986 US Supreme Court (see SUPREME COURT OF THE US) verdict to allow American states to outlaw sodomy – makes it unlikely that the law will change in the foreseeable future. A.A.L.

salami tactics. The technique whereby one element in a governmental coalition achieves a monopoly of POWER by destroying its allied parties section by section; in particular as employed in eastern Europe after 1945. The phrase derives from a frank account by the Hungarian COMMUNIST leader Mátyás Rákosi (1892–1971) of how the majority Smallholders Party and the

Social Democratic Party (see SOCIAL DEMOCRACY) had each in turn been bullied into 'slicing off' first their RIGHT wing, then their centrist members (see CENTRE, THE), until only close collaborators of the communists remained. R.C.

salinization. The tendency for the concentration of mineral salts in the soils of irrigated lands to increase over time as a result of the evaporation of irrigation water. As salts build up, yields decrease and the land may become useless for cropping. The process is particularly a problem in tropics where heat and low humidity may produce rapid rates of evaporation. This process may have caused the collapse of some early settlements or cultures. To counteract salinization, techniques are sought for efficient application of irrigation water (e.g. pulsed rather than continuous), and for the development of salt-resistant varieties of crop plants. W.G.R.

salsa. The Spanish word means 'sauce'. Musically it stands for a particularly hot and spicy version of the Afro-Cuban tendency in jazz which appeared in New York in the 1970s. An amalgam of MODERNIST invention and an exuberant beat, usually provided by several percussionists, it was taken up internationally by devotees of JAZZ, Latin rhythms and, above all, dancing. GE.S.

SALT (Strategic Arms Limitation Talks), see under NUCLEAR WEAPONS, LIMITATION AND CONTROL.

samizdat ('self-publication'). A Russian coinage, in general use between *c.* 1966 and the collapse of the former USSR in 1990, for the circulation in typescript (including carbons) of literary and political books and articles refused by, or not submitted to, regular publishers. The format is designed to evade legal restrictions on printing and duplicating – though (as many cases have shown) people could later be charged with the possession or circulation of 'anti-Soviet material'. The large and striking literature in *samizdat* ranged from such novels as Solzhenitsyn's *The First Circle* to political analyses such as Academician Andrei Sakharov's *Progress, Coexistence and Intellectual Freedom*, and Ivan Dzyuba's *Internationalism or Russification*, together with much poetry and various periodical publications, notably the *Chronicle of Current Events*. The analogous *tamizdat* ('published there') consisted of work in Russian published in the West and reaching the USSR more or less clandestinely, as did copies of Pasternak's *Dr Zhivago*. *Magnitizdat* refers to such material as dissident songs and poetry (or foreign broadcasts) recorded on tapes which circulated unofficially in the USSR. For further reading: P. Reddaway (ed.), *Uncensored Russia* (1972). R.C.

sample; sampling. In STATISTICS, the data themselves, or the random selection from which they are obtained, are often called the sample; sampling is the process of collecting such data. Thus an experiment to determine the height distribution of adult males in Britain might involve the selection of a random sample of, e.g., 5,000, from a total population of around 20 million. The problem of sampling is to ensure that the sample is in some sense a fair representation of the underlying population; a sample which is not is sometimes said to be *biased*. Ideally selection procedures should be such that every individual has an equal chance of being chosen, but in a population which is known to be divided into sub-populations it may be advantageous to sample from each sub-population in the correct proportions. A *Gallup Poll* is a SURVEY of voting intentions carried out in this manner. R.SI.

sanctions.

(1) In politics, measures taken to secure the target state's fulfilment of international obligations. The term usually refers to non-military measures such as the cessation of trade, cultural or other links. Sanctions may be organized by regional bodies (as with the support given by the ORGANIZATION OF AMERICAN STATES up to 1975 for the US trade embargo against CUBA) or by bodies with a wider membership. The constitutive documents of both the LEAGUE OF NATIONS and the UN provided for the use of sanctions. Throughout the 20th century there has been controversy about the effectiveness of sanctions. Their use against Italy in response to its invasion of Abyssinia (1935–36) notoriously failed to stop fascist advances (see FASCISM), and there were strong doubts about the extent to which UN sanctions

against Rhodesia (1966–79) contributed to the departure of the white minority regime there in 1980. Even in those rare cases where sanctions are effective in stopping international trade, they may still be ineffectual in bringing about the desired change of policy in the target state. The sanctions imposed on Iraq after its seizure of Kuwait in 1990 failed to dislodge it from the territory – force was eventually used, in the Gulf War of 1991 – and their subsequent continuation did not succeed in the objective of inducing Iraq to abandon its weapons of mass destruction. E.A.R.

(2) The response, positive or negative, to modes of behaviour. Anthropologists distinguish between positive sanctions or rewards for socially approved behaviour (prizes, titles, decorations) and negative sanctions, responses to breaches of NORMS. Sanctions support the norms and customs of society. The term sanctions, however, most commonly refers to negative sanctions (i.e. the response to transgressions). They have particularly interested anthropologists who have studied societies without formal legal systems.

In his study of the Trobriand Islanders (*Crime and Custom in Savage Society*, 1926), Bronislaw Malinowski focused upon the importance of social reciprocity, and he understood the threat of its withdrawal as the ultimate sanction against a breach of norms. Radcliffe Brown's approach was more theoretical and had cross-cultural application (see CROSS-CULTURAL STUDY). In *Structure and Function in a Primitive Society* (1952) he constructed a TYPOLOGY of sanctions. He drew a distinction between *organized* (e.g. law) and *diffuse* (e.g. WITCHCRAFT, ostracism) sanctions, and he distinguished between *primary* (actions by the whole community) and *secondary* (private) sanctions (see CUSTOM; FEUD; TABOO). For further reading: E. R. Leach, *Custom, Law and Terrorist Violence* (1977). A.G.

Sandinista. A member or, more loosely, a supporter of the Sandinista National Liberation Front (FSLN), a GUERRILLA organization formed in 1962 with the aim of presenting a coherent political and economic response to *Somocismo*, the 45-year dictatorship of the Somoza family. It is now the vanguard party of the Nicaraguan REVOLUTION. Taking their name from General Augusto Sandino, who led an anti-IMPERIALIST struggle against the 1927–34 occupation, the Sandinistas held power in NICARAGUA from 1979 until 1990, when they lost the democratic elections. FSLN IDEOLOGY draws on three distinct sources: (1) third world NATIONALISM, (2) post-Medellin Conference Latin American CATHOLICISM and (3) MARXISM. During their time in power, the FSLN pursued redistributive policies to attack the extreme concentration of economic resources which characterized Somoza's Nicaragua, but did not seek to eliminate the PRIVATE SECTOR. Education, healthcare and literacy programmes were implemented, and a non-aligned foreign policy pursued (see NON-ALIGNMENT). Though in opposition now, they remain a significant force in Nicaraguan politics. See also CONTRAS. For further reading: G. Prevost and H. Vanden (eds), *The Undermining of the Sandinista Revolution* (1997). N.M.

sarcomas, see under CANCER.

satellite. Any body constrained by GRAVITATION to revolve in a circular ORBIT around a much more massive body. For example, the planets are satellites of the sun, while the moon and all the artificial communications satellites are satellites of the earth. M.V.B.

satellite town. In expanding, a town causes the formation of industrial or residential centres which depend upon it, which are separate from it, and without which its activities cannot be considered. Such a centre is often called a satellite town. V. G. Davidovich has defined a satellite by three characteristics, all of which require that communications between a central town (which may rank as a METROPOLIS) and its satellites are easy and frequent: (1) people living in a satellite town come to work in the central town; (2) the central town guarantees a certain number of services, notably cultural services, for its satellites; (3) the satellites accommodate the town's population for relaxation, e.g. in parks, sports centres and public houses.

J. Beaujeu-Garnier has distinguished between a *consumer satellite* (i.e. a dormitory town) and a *production satellite*, for which the term satellite town should be reserved. Under this classification, the satellite town is one in which some provision is made for the industrial and commercial employment of its inhabitants independently of employment provided by the metropolis, e.g. the NEW TOWNS developed in Britain after World War II as a means of decongesting London. For further reading: V. G. Davidovich and B. S. Khorev (eds), *Satellite Towns* (1962). M.L.

satori**,** see under ZEN.

Saussurian. Characteristic of, or a follower of, the principles of Ferdinand de Saussure (1857–1913), especially as outlined in his posthumous *Cours de linguistique générale* (1916, Eng. tr. 1959). His conception of language as a system of mutually defining entities underlies much of contemporary structural LINGUISTICS. See also the distinctions between synchronic and DIACHRONIC, LANGUE AND PAROLE, SYNTAGMATIC AND PARADIGMATIC; see also COMPARATIST; SEMIOLOGY. For further reading: A. Lubell, *Saussure for Beginners* (1996). D.C.

Savings and Loan scandals. The government deregulation of key US industries that began during the tenure of President Carter reached its nadir with the Savings and Loan disaster of the 1980s. After the election of Ronald Reagan, federal regulators permitted thrift lenders to expand their business of providing home mortgages to include making risky investments in overvalued real estate, shopping centres and other questionable projects. By the time the last S&L was liquidated, the cost to taxpayers was estimated to be nearly $165 billion, with the true cost put by analysts at perhaps four times that figure – the worst financial disaster since the Great Depression in the 1930s. Thousands of investors were swindled out of their life savings by S&L operators whose salesmen convinced depositors to withdraw money from federally insured accounts and buy junk bonds issued by the lending institutions. One of the most reviled S&L figures, Charles Keating, cost taxpayers an estimated $3.4 billion when his Lincoln Savings thrift failed in California. Lincoln bondholders, many of whom were pensioners, lost $288 million. Keating prompted an ethics investigation when it was revealed that he had given $1.3 million to five US senators who agreed to intercede on his behalf with regulators who seized Lincoln in 1989. R.K.H.

Say's Law. An ECONOMIC LAW which is often taken as stating that 'supply creates its own demand' (see SUPPLY AND DEMAND). In an accounting sense, the law must be true as NATIONAL INCOME, output and expenditure are, by definition, equal (see GDP). The law must also be true in a barter economy, as the supply of a good constitutes a demand. If production occurs and is just added to stocks, no extra demand has materialized. Additionally, supply may even fall in the next period. An alternative statement of the law is that the value of the planned supply of all goods equals the value of the planned demand for goods. This interpretation, first given by John Maynard Keynes (1883–1946), is that of an EQUILIBRIUM condition rather than a truism, as is the case in the first definition. The different definitions and interpretations of Say's Law have caused much dispute and confusion. J.P.

scale-and-category grammar. A theory of GRAMMAR developed by Halliday and other neo-FIRTHIAN scholars in the early 1960s, and so named because it analysed grammatical patterns into a small number of theoretical *categories*, interrelating these through the use of *scales* (see, e.g., RANK). The grammatical analysis presupposed a general MODEL of language which distinguishes three basic LEVELS of *substance*, *form* and *context*. D.C.

scale, economies of, see ECONOMIES OF SCALE.

scale, returns to, see RETURNS TO SCALE.

scanning tunnelling microscope (STM). A device invented in the 1980s for imaging the structure of surfaces at the atomic scale. An electrically charged fine needle tip, only a few ATOMS across at its apex, is scanned over the surface, and the ELECTRONS that 'tunnel' between the tip and the surface give rise to a current that provides a sensitive measure of the separation between the two. In this way the corrugations of the surface due to its atomic structure are registered by a rising and falling tunnelling current. The instrument is also used to study the shapes of MOLECULES stuck to the surface, and by careful adjustment of the interaction between the tip and the sample it can pick up, put down and drag around atoms or molecules on the surface. The STM has therefore been proposed as a tool for NANOTECHNOLOGY, enabling manipulation of matter on the atomic (nanometre) scale.

P.C.B.

scat. Since it is based on improvisation, JAZZ has always been a mainly instrumental music, with vocalists' contributions constrained by lyrics and preordained melodic lines. But scat offers an opportunity for a singer to improvise like an instrumentalist. According to jazz mythology, it first appeared in Louis Armstrong's (*c.* 1898–1971) recording of 'Heebie Jeebies', when the trumpeter-singer forgot the lyrics and spontaneously concocted a chorus out of rhythmic syllables like 'skeet' and 'skat'. The serendipitous innovation soon became a technique adopted by singers of all sorts and abilities. Sometimes the results are merely silly, but when employed by a virtuoso like Ella Fitzgerald, scat can be a medium of extraordinary invention and excitement.

GE.S.

scenario, see under ROLE; TECHNOLOGICAL FORECASTING.

***Schadenfreude*.** German term for pleasure derived from the misfortunes of others. In English it tends to be used, more or less jokingly, to describe satisfaction at what is felt to be a just retribution. Its occasional occurrence is thus a perfectly normal feeling; excessive proneness to it indicates an unkind or malicious nature, but is quite distinct from SADISM.

O.S.

schadograph, see PHOTOGRAM.

scheduled territories, see under STERLING AREA.

schedules of reinforcement, see under REINFORCEMENT.

Schenker analysis. The analysis of primarily tonal music using the methods of Heinrich Schenker (1868–1935). Schenker's analytical techniques are based on the extraction of basic harmonic and linear progressions (*urlinie*) from masterpieces of classical tonal music, in particular the music of Beethoven. Schenker breaks the musical work down into layers: the foreground, the actual musical surface; the middle-ground, the music stripped of complexities; the background, the essential essence of the music.

B.CO.

schizoid. In PSYCHIATRY, a term associated with the name of Ernst Kretschmer (1888–1964), who believed that the whole population fell along a normal curve of distribution (see NORMAL DISTRIBUTION) from manic-depressives (see MANIC-DEPRESSIVE PSYCHOSIS) at one end to schizophrenics (see SCHIZOPHRENIA) at the other. The group that was closest to the schizophrenic end of the curve, but not psychotic (see PSYCHOSIS) and therefore not abnormal, was the group he called schizoid.

Today the word is characteristically applied, independently of Kretschmer's theory, to a PERSONALITY TYPE whose main features are aloofness, detachment and a tendency to suppress the outward show of emotion. This usage is imprecise and apt to vary from one clinical worker to another, while the CONCEPT which it reflects is based on the impressionistic judgements of clinicians, and has not yet been satisfactorily validated by objective methods. Some workers, nevertheless, especially some psychoanalysts, find it useful.

B.A.F.

schizophrenia. A psychiatric diagnosis introduced by Swiss psychiatrist Eugen Bleuler (1911), outlining a psychodynamically informed category of PSYCHOSIS. Based on the notion of the splitting of mental functions, and the four key symptoms of AUTISM, AMBIVALENCE, affective disturbance and impaired ASSOCIATIONS, by the 1940s it had largely replaced its predecessor, 'dementia praecox'. Subsequently criticized for its loose definition, schizophrenia became the object of intense research and diagnostic interest when effective anti-psychotic drugs (e.g. Chlorpromazine) emerged in the 1950s and 1960s.

Modern operational definitions of schizophrenia and its variable presentations have established the diagnostic entity. This is based on symptoms such as auditory hallucinations, delusions, passivity experience and formal thought disorder, a given time course and the absence of organic or obviously manic-depressive features (see MANIC-DEPRESSIVE PSYCHOSIS). While GENETICS and perinatal trauma explain only some of its causation, as well as its onset mainly in the 18–30-year age-group, the variable outcome and limited response to medical and psychosocial interventions give it a continuing and intriguing aetiological uncertainty.

New medications and cerebral imaging techniques are reinforming the notion of a complex brain disease possibly intrinsic to the evolution of human consciousness. The misuse of the terms 'schizophrenia' and 'schizophrenic', to mean 'in two minds' *à la* Jekyll and Hyde, is to be decried. For further reading: G. Berrios and R. Porter, *A History of Clinical Psychiatry* (1995). T.T.

scholasticism, see under NEO-THOMISM.

schools of psychology. Psychological issues, being many-sided and complexly interrelated, can be regarded from many viewpoints which, although different, are not necessarily contradictory, and which vary according to the psychological aspect being studied, the method of study, and the theoretical FRAME OF REFERENCE within which the study is set. These diverse approaches can themselves be classified in different ways and are sometimes grouped into so-called schools so as to highlight theoretical similarities and divergences. There is no agreed repertoire of schools but the phrase 'schools of psychology' most often refers to certain groupings that dominated theoretical PSYCHOLOGY, particularly in America, during roughly the first half of this century, when psychology was asserting its independence from other disciplines.

According to R. S. Woodworth (*Contemporary Schools of Psychology*, 1931, revised 1948 and 1964), whose historical interpretation is widely accepted in America, there were six main schools. STRUCTURALISM sought by systematic introspection to discover the elementary contents of CONSCIOUSNESS, while FUNCTIONALISM was concerned with the activities by which the mind worked (see also COGNITIVE PSYCHOLOGY). ASSOCIATIONISM wanted to study isolated psychological elements in their interconnection, while GESTALT psychology asserted the priority of whole-characteristics and resisted segmentation into elements. BEHAVIOURISM insisted that only objective behaviour, and not subjective experience, be studied. PSYCHOANALYSIS attempted in a distinctive way to understand the motivational forces governing conscious and unconscious phenomena. Of these six, only behaviourism and psychoanalysis survived the mid-century as distinctive schools separated from the eclectic, middle-of-the-road orientation of most psychologists who bow to the breadth and diversity of their subject-matter by accepting that no one theory or method or field of specialization has proper monopoly, and that complex problems are profitably approached, even simultaneously, from different viewpoints. I.M.L.H.

Schrödinger's cat. An unfortunate animal introduced into debates over the interpretation of QUANTUM MECHANICS by Austrian physicist Erwin Schrödinger (1887–1961) in 1935 to highlight ambiguities in the COPENHAGEN INTERPRETATION. Schrödinger presented the following thought experiment: a cat is placed in a box with a phial of poison, a small sample of a radioactive substance and a Geiger counter, arranged so that when one of the ATOMS decays, its decay will be detected by the counter, the phial of poison will be broken, and the cat will die. According to the Copenhagen interpretation, argued Schrödinger, quantum mechanics yields only a probability (see PROBABILITY THEORY) that one of the atoms has decayed after the elapse of some given period, and this is all that can be said about the state of the atoms: the atoms are in a SUPERPOSITION of decayed and non-decayed states. Were the box to be opened and inspected, the cat would be found either alive or dead depending on whether or not one of the atoms has decayed. But if the state of the cat depends on the state of the radioactive sample, which is a superposition according to quantum mechanics, the cat *too* must be in a superposition of live and dead states before the box is inspected. Or is the cat itself enough of an 'observer' to collapse the atoms' superposition to a definite outcome state? For further reading: E. Schrödinger, 'The Present Situation in Quantum Mechanics', in J. A. Wheeler and W. H. Zurek (eds), *Quantum Theory and Measurement* (1983). R.F.H.

Schwinger process, see under VIRTUAL PARTICLES.

science, economics of. Currently a growth area of SCIENCE STUDIES, though much longer of interest to PHILOSOPHY than to ECONOMICS. The PRAGMATIST philosopher C. S. Peirce (1839–1914) is often credited with first defining the field in the 1870s as the provision of COST BENEFIT ANALYSES for alternative lines of inquiry. Since the 1960s, under the influence of D. de Solla Price's conception of BIG SCIENCE, considerable attention has been paid to diminishing returns on public investment in basic research. Despite generally agreeing that new technology is the main source of industrial innovation, economists have said relatively little about science as such, since their own classification of knowledge as a PUBLIC GOOD precluded it from any straightforward economic analysis. However, as public sector spending in science declines, economists have become more willing to equate the economics of science and technology, thereby subordinating the utilities of science to those of industry. Virtually all economic analyses of science to date have aimed to represent or improve science's productivity, assuming that 'more is better'. What is lacking is a WELFARE ECONOMICS of science. For further reading: P. Mirowski and E.-M. Sent (eds), *The New Economics of Science*, 2 vols (1998). S.F.

science fiction. Unsatisfactory but firmly established term for an Anglo-American literary genre that shows average human beings confronted by some novelty, usually daunting: an invasion from another planet, a plague, space travel, time travel, a non-human civilization, a society ruled by machines, etc. There are anticipations in tales of wonder from the 17th century onwards, and notably in the works of Jules Verne, but the first and still the greatest true exponent was H. G. Wells (1866–1946) in *The Time Machine* (1895), *The War of the Worlds* (1898), etc. Until about 1940 most stories involved gadgetry, simple menace, or fantastic adventure. The next 25 years widened the range to include political, economic, technological and psychological speculation. In the later 1960s the so-called New Wave imitated the stylistic and presentational trickery of the ANTI-NOVEL, but this has passed and the genre has returned to its traditional themes, though with an added emphasis on the potentialities of the mind and on philosophical questions. Often ostensibly concerned with the future, science fiction at its best throws a fresh light on the present. Notable post-war exponents of the genre include Brian W. Aldiss, Isaac Asimov, J. G. Ballard, Arthur C. Clarke, Philip K. Dick, Harry Harrison, Damon Knight, Ursula Le Guin, Frederik Pohl, and Robert Silverberg. The abbreviations SF and sf are approved by practitioners and connoisseurs; sci-fic and sci-fi are not. For further reading: B. W. Aldiss, *Billion-Year Spree* (1973). K.A.

science indicators. One goal of science has been to create a 'science of science', enabling the study of its own development and history to be put upon a quantitative basis. At the same time, society has increasingly needed reliable ways to judge the performance of science itself, particularly as science has demanded ever greater state funding. To meet these needs, science indicators have been devised. These focus upon statistical measures of the resources allocated to science, scientific output and productivity, measured in terms of publications, conferences, citations of papers, patent registrations, employment expansion, capacity to win support from industry, etc. Their deeper value remains in doubt, however, because science may choose to orient itself precisely in directions that score well among the indicators. In any case the measure of qualitative worth remains unfathomable. For further reading: Y. Elkana *et al*, *Toward a Metric of Science* (1978). R.P.

science, philosophy of. This has included a number of distinct traditions of thought. Within neo-Kantian German culture in particular (see NEO-KANTIANISM), it has set about answering the question: what makes the universe intelligible? and has focused upon the status of such concepts as time and space. Anglo-Saxon philosophy of science over the last century, by contrast, has been preoccupied with investigating and confirming the validity of scientific knowledge, above all with showing that NATURAL SCIENCE forms the normal, even the only, mode of true knowledge (as distinct from received authority or mere subjective assertion). As a discipline, the philosophy of science has wavered between description (being an account of what scientists actually do) and prescription (what scientists ought to do to advance truth).

An older view, much touted by Victorian scientists, championed the use of INDUCTION as recommended by Francis Bacon. The business of science was to maximize facts; in due course scientific laws would emerge, almost spontaneously, from the sheer weight of data. The attraction of this idea lay in minimizing the risk of being misled by false theories. Eventually, simple induction was accepted as being unrealistic. Popular in the middle of this century was *hypothetico-deductivism*, the notion that facts should lead to hypotheses which would guide further investigation leading to the testing of hypotheses, and so forth, in a progressive manner. Sir Karl Popper's 'falsificationism' formed a radical variant on this (see POPPERIAN). Science could only be truly critical if investigators systematically strove to *disprove* every theory advanced: or, in other words, science could never prove any theory correct, merely falsify all the untrue theories. Popper's sceptical perception that science could never be sure it had obtained truth was underlined by T. S. Kuhn's idea that science proceeds through a series of 'revolutions' which successively destroy old theories (PARADIGMS), replacing them with new ones (see REVOLUTIONARY SCIENCE). New theories form radical discontinuities, involving new perceptions (GESTALTS). Old and new theories are incommensurable. Scientific progress is thus unprovable, and science possibly thus appears as relativistic (see RELATIVISM) as other modes of knowledge. The implication that science is unavoidably subjective has been carried further by sociological philosophies, which have stressed that scientific language is itself contaminated by everyday associations, and that scientific reasoning contains elements of rationalization tainted with personal interests and IDEOLOGY. Defenders of a more sophisticated version of scientific objectivity such as Lakatos and Laudan have countered with appeals to the long-term capacity of science to sift truth from error through experimental testing. Ironically, these rival philosophies have revealed that the metaphysical bases of science are far more dubious than ever imagined.

Since the Popper–Kuhn era, therefore, philosophy of science has offered less ambitious accounts of science, with fewer theories of scientific method that claim to cover *all* scientific epochs, and *every* different 'scientific' activity. Also problematic is the question of what method to apply in deciding which scientific method is the 'correct' one, given the historical evidence. Recent studies in the history and sociology of science meet with different kinds of response: attempts to construct accounts of scientific objectivity that engage with historical and sociological insights (see SCIENCE, SOCIOLOGY OF); retreat into the rational citadels of abstract confirmation theory. In addition, there are detailed investigations of specific scientific activities (theory construction, experiment), and studies in the foundations of specific disciplines (especially BIOLOGY and PHYSICS). For further reading: D. Papineau (ed.), *Philosophy of Science* (1996). R.P.; R.F.H.

science, psychology of. The branch of SCIENCE STUDIES that is most sympathetic to natural scientific modes of inquiry. Most work in this field has studied scientific reasoning in experimental settings. Nevertheless, it has proved nearly as controversial as other branches of science studies because: (1) subjects in the PSYCHOLOGY experiments are not usually mature scientists but rather students performing scientific tasks; (2) when scientists are used as subjects in such tasks, they often do not perform much better than non-scientists; (3) the complex and creative aspects of science, though often expressed in experimental settings, may be stifled if the setting is artificially created, as in a psychology lab. However, to take these objections too seriously would call into question the existence of a SCIENTIFIC METHOD that transcends the specific activities of professional scientists. One robust finding is that PROBLEM-SOLVING ability is greatly affected by group organization. For further reading: W. Shadish and S. Fuller (eds), *The Social Psychology of Science* (1994). S.F.

science, rhetoric of. A branch of SCIENCE STUDIES that applies the tools of classical rhetoric and literary criticism to texts and communication patterns in the natural and social sciences. The field is motivated by two sets of concerns. On the one hand, most scientific communication is conducted by texts that make claims which very few readers can confirm for themselves. On the other hand, disciplinary jargons, while a mark of scientific specialization, also make scientific claims difficult to understand and assess. In both cases, the rhetorician is concerned with how the scientific author establishes credibility with various audiences. Although distinguished social scientists such as economist Donald McCloskey and psychologist Kenneth Gergen have embraced the field as a means of making their home disciplines more publicly accountable, many rhetoricians of science exhibit a POPULIST distrust of expertise which is fuelled by growing public scepticism in science. Significantly, the field developed out of technical writing courses that are routinely required of science and engineering students. S.F.

science, sociology of. Perhaps the most controversial branch of SOCIOLOGY today, mainly because it reflexively applies sociology's critical gaze to the discipline's own basis for authority, namely science as a way of knowing (see EPISTEMOLOGY). Karl Mannheim (1893–1947) excluded science from his original formulation of the sociology of knowledge (see KNOWLEDGE, SOCIOLOGY OF) in the 1920s, partly for this reason and partly because he held that the validity of scientific knowledge transcends its specific cultural origins. Over the next 50 years, several versions of the sociology of science were developed within Mannheim's strictures. Among the most influential were those proposed by Robert Merton and Joseph Ben-David. Merton systematized the normative pronouncements of famous scientists and epistemologists from the past, while Ben-David identified the social roles and institutional settings that enabled these NORMS to be enforced. However, in the 1970s Mannheim's strictures were overthrown by the self-styled 'Strong Programme in the Sociology of Scientific Knowledge', led by David Bloor's 'Edinburgh School'. They compared their predecessors' work to a sociology of RELIGION that relied exclusively on the testimony of priests and theologians without any first-hand empirical investigation of 'science in action' (see EMPIRICISM). By the late 1980s, the followers of the Strong Programme had redressed the balance, turning the sociology of science into a research hotbed that now provides much of the empirical and theoretical core of SCIENCE STUDIES. For further reading: D. Bloor, *Knowledge and Social Imagery* (1991). S.F.

science studies. An umbrella expression for a growing number of overlapping fields in the humanities and SOCIAL SCIENCES whose object of inquiry is science, technology and/or medicine.

Increasingly, 'science studies' is a name given to academic units and degree programmes, signalling the emergence of a new discipline. (In this context, it is often called 'Science & Technology Studies', or 'STS'.) The core of science studies is HISTORY, PHILOSOPHY and the sociology of science (see SCIENCE, SOCIOLOGY OF). Recent additions include ECONOMICS, PSYCHOLOGY and the rhetoric of science (see SCIENCE, RHETORIC OF). Most SOCIAL EPISTEMOLOGIES as well as FEMINIST and MULTICULTURALIST critiques of science would also be covered by this rubric. Much of the excitement and controversy surrounding science studies stems from its core methodological assumption that the special qualities of scientific knowledge – especially its objectivity and RATIONALITY – can be explained as one would any other social or cultural phenomenon (see CULTURE), i.e. without invoking the concept of TRUTH (see BELIEF; METHODOLOGY). For further reading: D. Hess, *Science Studies: An Advanced Introduction* (1997). S.F.

scientific law. A general statement of fact, methodically established by INDUCTION, on the basis of observation and experiment, and usually, though not necessarily, expressed in mathematical form. In so far as it is empirical, a scientific law is not a necessary, demonstrable truth; in so far as it is methodically derived from intentionally acquired evidence, however, it differs from everyday commonsensical generalization. Ideally, scientific laws are strictly universal or deterministic (see DETERMINISM) in form, asserting something about all members of a certain class of things, but they may also be 'probabilistic' or statistical and assert something about a methodically estimated proportion of the class of things in question. There is a problem about the distinction of laws from 'accidental' generalization, statements that just happen to be true about all the things there are of the kind to which they relate. The distinction is marked, but not explained, by the fact that laws do, but accidental generalizations do not, imply COUNTERFACTUAL conditionals. Only if 'All *A* are *B*' is a law does it imply that if this thing, which is actually not *A*, had been *A*, it would have been *B*. This logical peculiarity lends some support to the view that scientific laws do not just describe universally pervasive regularities but assert some necessary connection between the kinds of properties mentioned in them. A.Q.

scientific management. Term coined by Frederick Winslow Taylor in 1911 to describe the techniques he adopted to increase the output of workers. Close observation of factory workers led to what became known as time and motion studies, which sought ways to make their movements as efficient and simple as possible, so that output could be increased. Controversial at the time (it was the subject of a Congressional hearing in 1912), the approach is today seen as mechanistic and anachronistic. R.I.T.

scientific method. The procedure by which, as a matter of definition, SCIENTIFIC LAWS, as contrasted with other kinds of general statement, are established. The orthodox view is that this procedure is inductive (see INDUCTION), but several philosophers of science have criticized *inductivism* (see POPPERIAN) as misrepresenting the actual procedure of scientists. Two phases of scientific activity need to be distinguished: the initial formulation of hypotheses, which seems mainly, as the anti-inductivists maintain, to be a business of inspired guessing that cannot be mechanized, and the CONFIRMATION of hypotheses thus formulated, which does appear to be a comparatively pedestrian and rule-governed undertaking. For further reading: K. R. Popper, *The Logic of Scientific Discovery* (1959). A.Q.

scientific revolutions, see under ANOMALY; REVOLUTIONARY SCIENCE.

scientism. The view that the characteristic inductive methods (see INDUCTION) of the NATURAL SCIENCES are the only source of genuine factual knowledge and, in particular, that they alone can yield true knowledge about man and society. This stands in contrast with the explanatory version of DUALISM which insists that the human and social subject-matter of history and the SOCIAL SCIENCES (the GEISTESWISSENSCHAFTEN) can be fruitfully investigated only by a method, involving sympathetic intuition of human states of mind, that is proprietary to these disciplines. A.Q.

Scott Report. Colloquial term for the Report of the Inquiry into the Export of Defence Equipment and Dual-Use Goods to Iraq and Related Prosecutions which was published in the UK in February 1996. The Inquiry, under Lord Justice Scott, was set up in November 1992 after the revelation that the arms manufacturers Matrix Churchill, three of whose executives were undergoing trial for breach of export regulations, had been acting in accordance with government guidelines which had been modified without Parliament's knowledge. In his lengthy report, Scott found that ministers had failed to give a full account to Parliament and that some inaccurate and misleading replies had been made deliberately. He also criticized ministerial use of the defence of 'public interest' to conceal government information from the trial judge. He recommended that Parliament should play a greater role in monitoring export policy, restrictions on the deployment of 'public interest immunity' certificates, and a tightening of the rules governing ministers' duties to Parliament. Despite these criticisms, no minister resigned and the government claimed to have been vindicated. For most commentators, the Report exposed the inadequacies of parliamentary scrutiny of the executive and the doctrine of ministerial responsibility. For further reading: B. Thompson and F. F. Ridley (eds), *Under the Scott-Light: British Government as Seen through the Scott Report* (1997). N.O.

scratching, see under REGGAE.

***Scrutiny*,** see under LEAVISITE.

SDI, see STRATEGIC DEFENCE INITIATIVE.

SDRs (Special Drawing Rights), see under INTERNATIONAL LIQUIDITY.

SDS (Students for a Democratic Society). A radical (see RADICALISM) American student organization which was a key element in the NEW LEFT of the 1960s. It was formed in 1960 from the residues of the nearly moribund student branch of the League for Industrial Democracy, and grew through its attempts to unify disparate protests against such matters as the ARMS RACE, nuclear testing, restraints on freedom of speech, and the denial of CIVIL RIGHTS to BLACK Americans. In 1962 its Port Huron Statement provided a manifesto for a burgeoning movement, although its emphasis on HUMANIST themes and participatory DEMOCRACY was soon transcended. The SDS became committed to supporting the more radical elements in black politics, to opposing the VIETNAM War as a manifestation of American IMPERIALISM, and to protesting against universities as agents of a repressive system of quasi-liberal (see LIBERALISM), PRO-CAPITALIST values. Its attempts to construct a coherent IDEOLOGY out of numerous fragments are variously seen as innovative or incoherent, and accentuated schismatic tendencies which fatally divided the organization by 1969. Of its remaining functions, the WEATHERMEN were most significant. For further reading: K. Sale, *SDS* (1973). S.R.

search for extraterrestrial intelligence (SETI). Searches for signals from intelligent extraterrestrial life were first made by Frank Drake's Osma Project (1960), which listened for radio signals from Epsilon Eridani and Tau Ceti, the two nearest stars resembling our sun. No signals were detected. Other search strategies have since been suggested. A continuing listening channel is employed using the 'Haystack' radio telescope in the US. Freeman Dyson pointed out that the waste heat from advanced technological civilizations might be visible as infra-red radiation. A search has also been made at special frequencies (for example 21 cm radio waves) which are associated with universal properties of nature likely to be known to any scientifically advanced civilization. A programme to transmit signals from earth has also been initiated using similar principles. NASA space probes to the outer planets, which will eventually be pointed out into deep space, carried information and pictures aimed at informing inhabitants of other planets of our own existence, location, physical characteristics and cultural development. Any form of communication with extraterrestrials is constrained by the enormous distances involved. Each signal to a nearby star would take many years to travel between there and the earth at the speed of light. Theoretical estimates of the likelihood of making contact with extraterrestrial intelligence are extremely uncertain. The most famous attempt is the Drake equation. This gives the probability that intelligent life which eventually attempts interstellar communication will evolve in a star system as the product of the probability that a star will possess planets, the number of habitable planets in a SOLAR SYSTEM possessing planets, the probability that life evolves on a habitable planet, and the probability that an intelligent species will attempt interstellar communication in a reasonable time. The evaluation of estimates for these probabilities requires knowledge of exobiology, the range of living systems that are possible in non-terrestrial environments.

A common argument against the likely success of SETI is the Fermi paradox, which argues that advanced life forms could so easily have made contact with us that we must conclude that they do not exist. A counter-argument called the zoo hypothesis, posited by J. A. Ball in 1973, suggests that a very advanced life form might choose to leave us undisturbed as an object for study. At present there exists no positive evidence for the existence of any intelligent extraterrestrial life form. However, in recent years there has been a resurgence of interest in this project following the discovery of planetary systems around a number of nearby stars. These planets are large Jupiter-like bodies, but they confirm that planet formation is a common process in the universe. Interest has also been stimulated by the speculative possibility that protobacteria had been carried to earth in meteoritic material expelled from the surface of Mars. For further reading: D. Goldsmith, *Worlds Unnumbered: the search for extrasolar planets* (1997); D. Goldsmith, *The Hunt for Life on Mars* (1997). J.D.B.

searching-instinct. According to the work of Imre Hermann (1889–1984), the instinct for grasping plays a particularly privileged role in the development of the human mind. The associated searching-instinct comes into operation whenever the grasping-instinct finds itself without an object; the frustration of the instinct for grasping thus repeatedly produces the joint operation of this pair of antagonistic instincts acting as a couple. Hermann's analysis of the process of thinking takes place within the field of these two variables, since thinking includes within it this function of seeking. Hermann claims that there is a *parallelism* – an identity of structure – between forms of thinking, and the possible forms of instinctual conflict. He does not hope to reduce thinking to a PSYCHOPATHOLOGY, but by establishing structures common to bodies of theory and the formation of the UNCONSCIOUS, to show how each domain in turn is able to explain problems in the field of the other.

In particular, Hermann claimed that the developments introduced into the psyche by the generation of language structure (PRECONSCIOUS word-representations), by idealization, and by love based on the admission of separation, are best described by the type of spatial structure known as a hyperbolic non-Euclidean GEOMETRY; that the structure of the SUPEREGO is best described by the restricted space of an elliptical non-Euclidean geometry (which in Jacques Lacan's work in this field is represented as a 'cross-cap'; see LACANIAN); and that the transition from the first geometry to the second is represented clinically by the depressive moment – and the reverse transition by the hypermanic moment – of certain psychotic states. His psychobiographies of creative mathematicians attempted to present their work as struggling with the mental conflicts whose structure was congruent with the themes of their work; he was in this way able to extend this class of results to the problem of the creation of the mathematical theory of sets (see SET THEORY), and to MATHEMATICAL LOGIC. B.BU.

second-order theorizing. Making theories about theories. The term has no unique field of application, but two typical kinds of second-order theorizing can be broadly distinguished: (1) epistemological, logical, mathematical, etc., theories about the formal properties of other theories, e.g. demonstrating their structural similarity, justifying their claims to validity, or explicating their assumptions (see METATHEORY); (2) sociological, psychological, historical, etc., theories about how theories come into being, persist or change. The first-order theories which compose the subject-matter of second-order theorizing are perhaps most commonly those of the NATURAL SCIENCES and SOCIAL SCIENCES. For further reading: T. S. Kuhn, *The Structure of Scientific Revolutions* (1970). J.R.T.

second-signal system. In PSYCHOLOGY, a PAVLOVIAN term used to differentiate a physical stimulus that was directly conditioned and linked to a response (see CONDITIONED REFLEX) from one that has been categorized in language and can thus be associated by meaning with a range of other similarly coded stimuli. Pavlov aimed to distinguish CONDITIONING in animals from learning in man, in which the ordinary laws of conditioning were superseded by linguistic association. J.S.B.

second-strike capability, see under STRATEGIC CAPABILITY.

second Viennese school. The collective name sometimes given to the composer Arnold Schoenberg (1874–1951) and his two most famous pupils, Anton Webern and Alban Berg, owing to their connections with Vienna (the first Viennese school being Mozart, Haydn and Beethoven). Among the important developments in the work of these three composers are atonality (see ATONAL MUSIC) and SERIAL MUSIC. For further reading: O. Neighbour *et al*, *Second Viennese School* (1980). B.CO.

second wave feminism. The late 1960s saw the revitalization of FEMINISM in countries in North America and western Europe. Feminism had never been absent from these societies, but the political and social movements of this period gave rise to new interpretations and constructions of feminism – crucial to the changes that took place was an emphasis on what was described as 'personal politics', and a much-cited slogan of second wave was 'the personal is political'. The slogan explicitly challenged the division between the private and the public which had previously been assumed in Western societies. The challenge allowed questions to be asked about issues of SEXUALITY, POWER and the division of labour in marriage, all of which were crucial terms of an analysis which identified PATRIARCHY and patriarchal values as central determinants of social experience.

The intellectual and social energy of second wave feminism gave it a lasting place in the history of the contemporary world. Although the roots of the movement lay in Anglo-Saxon and industrialized countries, the implications of a radical rethinking of the social position of women were rapidly developed by women in other countries, and from cultures other than the white MIDDLE CLASS. Thus second wave feminism became a global phenomenon involving the experiences of diverse communities (see COMMUNITY) of women. For further reading: S. Rowbotham, *Women in Movement: Feminism and Social Action* (1997). M.S.E.

second world, see under THEORY OF THREE WORLDS.

secondary occupation, see under OCCUPATION.

secondary picketing, see under PICKETING.

secondary succession, see under ECOLOGICAL SUCCESSION.

sect. Term used to describe an exclusive social group which has mobilized around a charismatic religious or political leader. Boundaries are usually clear and separate those who are members of the sect from those who are not. Membership is voluntary, but usually involves total commitment to the sect. The term was developed by Ernst Troeltsch (1865–1923) in his studies of CHRISTIANITY. Following his work, sect was often employed as a concept in opposition to Church. Sect represents HERESY, unorthodoxy and opposition in contrast to an official legitimate authority. For further reading: Bryan Wilson, *Religion in Sociological Perspective* (1982). A.G.

secular theology. A movement in late-20th-century Protestant THEOLOGY, which is distinguished by its determination to celebrate the process of secularization. Evolving in the 1960s, secular theology intensified the critique of 'RELIGION' which characterized crisis theology and neo-orthodoxy, but its principal debt was to Dietrich Bonhoeffer, a German theologian executed by the Nazis (see NAZISM) in 1945, who in his final letters from prison wrote of the need for a 'religionless CHRISTIANITY' for a world which, quite rightly, was growing out of the ways of thinking that Christianity had taken for granted. Whatever Bonhoeffer meant by this, it inspired theologians such as Harvey Cox to celebrate the process of secularization as the fulfilment of the biblical witness to the desacralization of the world and its institutions. Essentially liberal (see LIBERALISM), where DEATH OF GOD THEOLOGY was radical (see RADICALISM), secular theology lasted longer, but its enthusiasm for 'technocratic CAPITALISM' has been decisively criticized by LIBERATION THEOLOGY. For further reading: C. West, *The Power to Be Human: Toward a Secular Theology* (1971). C.C.

secularization. The decline of RELIGION. This has been more marked in the 20th century than in any previous period of recorded history, and the concentration on this age (Latin *saeculum*) instead of on the divine has become the real orthodoxy of the modern ESTABLISHMENT. At its minimum, secularization means the decline of the prestige and POWER of religious teachers. It involves the ending of state support for religious bodies; of religious teaching in national schools; of religious tests for public office or civil rights; of legislative protection for religious doctrines (e.g. the prohibition of CONTRACEPTION); and of the censorship or control of literature, science and other intellectual activities in order to safeguard religion. Individuals are then free to deviate openly from religious DOGMAS and ETHICS. In all or most of these senses, secularization now seems desirable to many religious believers as well as to all agnostics (see AGNOSTICISM; SECULAR THEOLOGY). In the USA, e.g., Church and state are strictly separate, although most Americans are personally attached to one or other of the Christian churches; and the Republic of India is officially 'secular', although most Indians are devout Hindus (see HINDUISM).

The term can, however, also mean the decline of widespread interest in religious traditions, so that the religious bodies no longer attract many practising supporters or enjoy popular respect. Most industrial workers suspect religion of being 'opium for the people' to keep them quiet under injustice, while the influence of religion has also been blamed for the stagnation of rural life. INTELLECTUALS tend to resent religion's record of interference with freedom of opinion and behaviour, preferring HUMANISM. In COMMUNIST countries such as the former Soviet Union and China there have been systematic, official attempts to suppress religion as antisocial. At its maximum, secularization would mean the end of all interest in religious questions and attitudes, including MYSTICISM. There is, however, little evidence that the 20th century has reached this last stage. On the contrary, both communism and the worldwide YOUTH CULTURE seem to owe some of their popularity to the inclusion (in secular form) of religious features such as idealism, uniformity of dogma, and hero-worship. See also RELIGION, SOCIOLOGY OF. For further reading: D. L. Edwards, *The Future of Christianity* (1987). D.L.E.

sedimentation. The slow natural settling of substances under the influence of gravity (see GRAVITATION) – especially the formation of sedimentary rocks, such as chalk, slate and shales, by the compacted calciferous or siliceous skeletons of myriads of minute sea animals, especially PROTOZOA. The term normally refers to the settling out of particulate matter (see PARTICLE). It can also, however, be extended to the sedimentation of MOLECULES – a process normally impeded by BROWNIAN MOTION.

Sedimentation is enormously speeded up by increasing gravitational forces – achieved in laboratories by the use of the *centrifuge*, an apparatus which enables most precipitates formed in chemical reactions to be thrown down as a sediment in a matter of minutes where otherwise they might take hours to undergo natural sedimentation. By this means, blood is separated into red blood CELLS (the lowest stratum), white blood cells (the next above), and plasma. Svedberg's *ultra-centrifuge* is widely used to separate particulate suspensions in suspending media differing from them only very slightly in density. In this apparatus centrifugal forces up to 100,000 times that of gravity can be achieved as a matter of routine. Large molecules, particularly of the larger PROTEINS, can also be thrown down by such strong centrifugal forces. P.M.

seduction theory. As long as PSYCHOANALYSIS was a traumatogenic theory of neurosis (i.e. human misery – aka the neuroses – caused by traumas), pride of place belonged to sexual trauma. For several years between 1895 and 1900 Freud (see FREUDIAN) believed that the neuroses were caused primarily by a 'seduction' (early on he preferred the more accurate terms RAPE, abuse and sexual assault) and claimed that virtually *all* of the patients he had seen, both men and women, were victims of such assaults early in their lives. The seduction theory thus posited the reality of sexual abuse in early life and its serious consequences. These early 'scenes' were repressed (see REPRESSION) and could only be remembered through therapy. For reasons that remain somewhat mysterious (the Freudians claim that Freud realized he was wrong, others think that he caved in to societal pressure), Freud abandoned this position in the early years of the century and claimed that in the vast majority of cases women (men soon disappeared from the discussion) were imagining or fantasizing these events under the pressure of Oedipal yearnings (see OEDIPUS COMPLEX) they could not acknowledge. The only first-hand information we have about this period of Freud's development comes from the letters he wrote to his best friend, Wilhelm Fliess, between 1887 and 1904. For years we were restricted to those letters Freud's daughter, Anna Freud, chose to include in her edition of the letters, called *The Origins of Psychoanalysis*. A fuller picture, and a most complex one, has emerged with the publication of the complete letters in 1986. The matter is of more than arcane or purely scholarly interest. Our modern world is deeply affected by the different positions staked out by feminists (see FEMINISM), therapists, their critics and cultural historians (see CULTURAL HISTORY). Controversy still rages over Freud's motives, over the reality and extent of SEXUAL ABUSE in childhood, over whether repression is real, and over whether therapy helps uncover the abuse or fabricates it. For further reading: J. Masson, *The Assault on Truth: Freud's Suppression of the Seduction Theory* (1985). J.MA.

segmentary lineage system, see under LINEAGE.

segmentation, see under EMBRYOLOGY.

segregation.

(1) In GENETICS, the apportioning out of CHROMOSOMES to gametes, and thereby of genetic factors to the next generation; see MENDEL'S LAWS. P.M.

(2) The establishment by law or custom of separate (and inferior) facilities for social or (the most usual sense) racial (see RACE; RACISM) and ethnic groups, as in the 'Jim Crow' legislation of the Southern states of the USA providing separate educational, recreational and other facilities for whites and blacks. Segregation inevitably results in discrimination in favour of one group over the other or others. The word has been extended to cover a whole range of discriminatory practices including the denial of employment and voting rights and prohibition against intermarriage. In South Africa the term APARTHEID was used; see also DESEGREGATION.

(3) In SOCIOLOGY, the process by which individuals and groups settle in those areas of a community already occupied by people of similar social characteristics or activities. D.C.W.

seismology. A subject that began as the study of earthquakes but has widened its field to cover all the movements of the solid earth. The types of earth movement range from fast vibrations due to earthquake body-waves, with a period of one second, to diurnal earth tides caused by the attraction of the sun and moon. The bulk of our knowledge about the interior of the earth has depended on seismic studies. For further reading: R. H. Tucker *et al*, *Global Geophysics* (1970). J.L.M.L.

Sekigun see RED ARMY (2).

selection pressure. A figurative expression of the magnitude of the force of NATURAL SELECTION. One of the conundrums of pre-Mendelian DARWINISM was to devise some means of measuring this force. The problem was solved independently and in slightly different ways by J. B. S. Haldane (1892–1964) and R. A. Fisher (1890–1962). Common to both is the principle that selection pressure is measured by the rate at which one ALLELE replaces another in the course of EVOLUTION. Fisher's system is modelled closely on demographic practice (see DEMOGRAPHY) and amounts to allocating a NET REPRODUCTION RATE to the possessors of a particular GENE or GENOTYPE. P.M.

self. In PSYCHOANALYSIS, a term used to refer either to the whole of the person or just to the symbolized, consciously reflective parts. It is conventionally distinguished from the EGO because of its closer relationship to experience. It has come to represent in some psychoanalytic work an opposition to the more mechanistic tendencies of traditional psychoanalysis. In British OBJECT RELATIONS theory it has been used particularly to communicate a sense of inherent human integrity. Disorders of the self thus relate closely to relationship disturbances. Donald Winnicott's (1896–1971) distinction between the 'true self' connected with the actual needs of each SUBJECT, and the conformist and inauthentic 'false self' which arises defensively out of the failure of the environment to support the true self, has become influential in some recent social theory (see AUTHENTICITY). This concept offers a bridge between psychoanalysis and HUMANISTIC PSYCHOLOGY. It should be noted that some branches of psychoanalysis do not use the term 'self' at all, and others argue that it is an alienating fiction (see LACANIAN). S.J.F.

self-actualization. In EXISTENTIAL PSYCHOLOGY, a term used by Abraham Maslow (1908–70) for the processes whereby an individual comes to understand himself and thereby develops his talents and capacities with acceptance of his limitations. W.Z.

self-assembly. Within CHEMISTRY, the programmed association of MOLECULES into a complex but well-defined structure. Self-assembly is displayed abundantly in biomolecular systems, whose component molecules contain all the information needed to allow them to come together into multi-molecular protein ENZYMES, cell membranes, tissues, composite materials like bone, etc. The discipline of SUPRAMOLECULAR CHEMISTRY is largely concerned with learning how to effect self-assembly among synthetic molecules to make large multi-molecule structures with predetermined shapes or features. The key to this goal is molecular information: the components are given the 'information' required for their spontaneous assembly, in the form of the apposite positioning of chemical groups that will bind to one another selectively (e.g., through MOLECULAR RECOGNITION). P.C.B.

self-determination. Originally the right of the subjects of a state to choose their own government or form of government (a concept embodied both in the American Declaration of Independence of 1776 and in the French revolutionary Declaration of the Rights of Man of 1789). From this, by way of the nationalist assumption that the state must reflect the national group, self-determination came to encompass additionally the idea of national groups seceding from multinational states and empires in order to set up their own national state. (See NATIONALISM; SEPARATISM.) As such it played an important part in Allied propaganda during World Wars I and II (e.g. in the FOURTEEN POINTS), was embodied at various points in the Charter of the UN, and became the main basis for anti-IMPERIALISM. D.C.W.

self-image. The impression an individual has of himself, which may differ greatly from the impression he gives others. See IDENTITY. W.Z.

self-organization. The property of a system that can spontaneously arrange its component parts into a non-random distribution in space or time, without the aid of an external agency. The lipid MOLECULES that constitute CELL membranes, e.g., will under appropriate conditions aggregate from solution into double-layered sheets in which all of the molecules are aligned. Similarly, the molecules of liquid crystals align themselves spontaneously even though they remain as mobile as those in a liquid. Self-organized regular patterns of different chemical composition, such as spots or stripes, appear in certain chemical reactions according to a mechanism proposed by English mathematician Alan Turing in 1952; in developmental biology these patterns may be responsible for animal pelt markings. Self-organizing systems stand in contrast to a microelectronic silicon chip, in which the circuitry is carved into the semiconducting material using the external means of lithography, ultimately guided by a human agency. Self-organization is being explored as an alternative for making certain kinds of chip microstructure that will build themselves. P.C.B.

self-organized criticality. A property of certain SYSTEMS that adopt a steady state away from thermodynamic EQUILIBRIUM. In a self-organized critical state, fluctuations in the distribution of the system's components happen at all accessible scales. This is in contrast to the random thermal fluctuations that a system undergoes at equilibrium, which have a characteristic size dependent on the temperature. In this sense, self-organized critical states are said to be scale-invariant. The canonical model example is a pile of sand. Once it has grown to its maximum stable slope, the pile can undergo avalanches of any size when a single grain is dropped into it. The probability of a fluctuation (an avalanche) of a certain size decreases as the fluctuation gets bigger; this probability distribution is described mathematically by an inverse power law, which is a characteristic feature of self-organized criticality.

Critical states with scale-invariant fluctuations and power-law relationships are found in equilibrium thermodynamics, e.g. at the critical point of a fluid where the distinction between liquid and gas vanishes. But these critical states are unstable, in the same sense as a needle balanced on its tip. Self-organized critical states, in contrast, are robust – if perturbed, the system will adjust its configuration back to the critical state.

Whether real sand piles are self-organized critical states is still unclear. But self-organized criticality has been advanced as a MODEL for a tremendous variety of out-of-equilibrium systems, from forest fires to earthquakes, ecosystems, solar flares and the large-scale structure of the universe. For further reading: P. Bak, *How Nature Works* (1997). P.C.B.

self-orientation, see under PATTERN VARIABLES.

self-reliance. Calls for self-reliance followed the growing dissatisfaction of THIRD WORLD governments and INTELLECTUALS from north and south with prevailing patterns of development (see UNDERDEVELOPMENT). The idea was conceived as a response to ties of 'DEPENDENCE' and articulated at the international level mainly in the United Nations Conference on Trade and Development (UNCTAD), which was set up in 1964 to provide a forum for the discussion of third world economic development. Self-reliance was first formulated by Mao Zedong as 'regeneration by our own efforts' in 1945, according to Johan Galtung (see below), but can be dated back to Soviet ideas of AUTARKY in the 1920s. It draws its inspiration from Marxist (see MARXISM) STRUCTURALIST ideas in its present form, particularly centre-periphery analysis. Key dates in its recent development are the Arusha Declaration of 1967 and the NEW INTERNATIONAL ECONOMIC ORDER of 1974. Has led to calls for 'south–south' trade which have not to date led to any noticeable shifts in world trade patterns. For further reading: Galtung, O'Brien and Preiswerk (eds), *Self-Reliance: A Strategy for Development* (1980). A.W.

self-similarity, see under FRACTALS.

self theory. An American development within PSYCHOANALYSIS, based particularly on the work of Heinz Kohut (1913–81) and concerned with recasting classical analytic theory into a more interpersonal mode. The focus of the theory is on the development of the SELF as an active centre of psychological experience, with an emphasis on the conditions for the formation of healthy selfhood, the structure of the self, and the sources of narcissistic pathology. Kohut refers to the formative 'objects' (people) in the child's life as 'selfobjects', emphasizing the way selfhood develops as a process of internalization of self–other relationships. For Kohut, NARCISSISM, with its grandiose and idealizing tendencies, is a normal developmental phase necessary for the foundation of a secure self. However, when these tendencies are not negotiated successfully, the self grows in a distorted or partial way, with damaged objects and narcissistic rage.

Self theory has had a powerful impact on American psychoanalysis; it is also close in many of its concerns to British OBJECT RELATIONS theory, particularly the work of Donald Winnicott. S.J.F.

selfish DNA. Defined by Orgel and Crick in 1980 as DNA sequences (see NUCLEIC ACID) that spread within the genome (see GENETICS/GENOMICS) without making any positive contribution to the phenotype of the organism (see GENOTYPE). It is a fundamentally REDUCTIONIST interpretation of the Darwinian concept of 'survival of the fittest' (see DARWINISM). Orgel and Crick suggest an analogy with 'the spread of a not-too-harmful parasite within its host' (see PARASITOLOGY). Part of the inspiration for the idea (originating with Richard Dawkins several years earlier) is the observation that there is an abundance of DNA for which there is no known function (sometimes called 'junk DNA'). There are various mechanisms whereby 'excess' DNA is generated. Some DNA segments can copy themselves to another part of the genome (called 'transposable elements'). These are especially good candidates for 'selfish DNA'. Other expanses of DNA are made up of repetitive sequences, often generated as an error in the normal processes of copying DNA and the interaction between DNA strands, and expanded by chance. A.R.H.

selfish gene. The selfish gene is DARWINISM in sharper form. It is a restatement of EVOLUTION by NATURAL SELECTION at the level of the GENE, rather than the more traditional level of the individual. Natural selection will always favour genes that are 'selfish', that is genes which have effects that promote their own survival at the expense of alternative competing genes. Most gene survival is achieved by building a body that is good at surviving and reproducing, and of acting in its own self-interest – i.e. a selfish individual. However, gene survival may also be enhanced by the individual acting altruistically. This will be the case if the individual directs his altruism at others who share copies of the gene for altruism which are identical by descent (kin selection), or if there is a high chance that altruism will be reciprocated at a later date (reciprocal altruism). Using these arguments, British ethologist Richard Dawkins's book *The Selfish Gene* (1976) showed that group selection explanations of altruism – that altruism had evolved for the good of the group or SPECIES – were highly implausible. Genes are replicators, entities that produce copies of themselves with the occasional error; individuals and groups are only vehicles, entities through which replicators influence their own survival. Dawkins further developed these ideas in *The Extended Phenotype* (1982). A.P.

semantic-field theory. In LINGUISTICS, the view that the vocabulary of a language is not simply a listing of independent items (as the headwords in a dictionary would suggest), but is organized into areas, or *fields*, within which words interrelate and define each other in various ways. The words denoting colour are often cited as an example of a semantic field: the precise meaning of a colour word can only be understood by placing it in relation to the other terms which occur with it in demarcating the colour spectrum. D.C.

semantic relation, see MEANING-RELATION.

semantics.

(1) The branch of LINGUISTICS that studies MEANING in language (and sometimes in other symbolic systems of communication). Much neglected by early linguists, it is now the central focus of theoretical interest, though no adequate semantic theory has yet been developed. One influential approach is that of *structural* semantics, the application of the principles of structural linguistics to the study of meaning through the notion of MEANING-RELATIONS. See also COMPONENTIAL ANALYSIS. For further reading: F. R. Palmer, *Semantics* (1981). D.C.

(2) In PHILOSOPHY and LOGIC, (a) the study of the relations between linguistic expressions and the objects in the world to which they refer or which it is their function to describe. This discipline was inaugurated by the Polish logician Alfred Tarski in the 1930s as the field in which lay his own influential investigations into the CONCEPT of TRUTH, in opposition to the view that all logical and philosophical problems about the MEANING of linguistic expressions could and should be treated within (logical) SYNTAX, namely the study of the relations of linguistic expressions to each other; (b) more generally, the philosophical theory of meaning as a whole, in which to semantics narrowly conceived as in sense (a) are added both syntax and *pragmatics*, the study of the dependence of the meaning of linguistic expressions on their users, and on the circumstances in which and the purposes for which they are used. Rudolf Carnap employed the word SEMIOTICS in this sense to bring these three disciplines together, but in this sense it has not caught on. For further reading: C. Morris, *Foundations of the Theory of Signs* (1938). A.Q.

semeiology, see SEMIOLOGY.

semiconductor. A material that is normally an electrical insulator but becomes a conductor either when the temperature is raised ('intrinsic semiconductor') or when 'doped' (see DOPING) with a small number of 'impurity' ATOMS of another ELEMENT ('extrinsic semiconductor'; see also SOLID-STATE PHYSICS).

The ease with which their electrical characteristics can be adjusted accounts for the importance of semiconductors in TECHNOLOGY, the principal application being the TRANSISTOR. The elements germanium and silicon are commonly used intrinsic semiconductors; almost any atoms may be used as impurities, provided their VALENCE differs from that of the bulk. M.V.B.

semiology (or **semeiology).** The general (if tentative) science of signs: systems of signification, means by which human beings – individually or in groups – communicate or attempt to communicate by signal: gestures, advertisements, language itself, food, objects, clothes, music, and the many other things that qualify. The subject was proposed by the linguist Ferdinand de Saussure (see SAUSSURIAN), but influentially developed by the French writer Roland Barthes (1915–80). Barthes's complex Gallic METHODOLOGY has seemed over-recondite or obscure to some Anglo-Saxons; but the value of many of his insights, if not of his system, is undisputed. For further reading: R. Barthes, tr. A. Lavers and C.

Smith, *Elements of Semiology* (1968). M.S.-S.

semiotic poetry, see under CONCRETE POETRY.

semiotics. The study of patterned human behaviour in communication in all its modes. The most important mode is the auditory/vocal, which constitutes the primary subject of LINGUISTICS. The study of the visual mode – of systematic facial expressions and body gestures – is generally referred to as *kinesics*. The study of the tactile mode – e.g. interpersonal movement and touch activity – is sometimes called *proxemics*. Semiotics can also mean the study of sign and symbol systems in general; for which an alternative term is SEMIOLOGY. A similar approach to animal communication is called *zoosemiotics*. For further reading: T. A. Sebeok, A. S. Hayes and M. C. Bateson (eds), *Approaches to Semiotics* (1964). D.C.

sensationalism. In PHILOSOPHY, the theory that the only things which ultimately and irreducibly exist, and to which everything else that exists is reducible, are sensations. It has close affinities with NEUTRAL MONISM and differs from it only in describing the elements of reality as mental rather than as neither mental nor physical. Ernst Mach was a sensationalist, as, with some qualification, were David Hume and J. S. Mill. If all factual knowledge comes from PERCEPTION and, as the SENSE-DATUM theory maintains, only sensations or sense-impressions are perceived, it seems to follow that we can know nothing to exist apart from sensations (and what can be constructed from them). A.Q.

sense-datum. The private impression or appearance which has generally been held by philosophers to be the direct and immediate object of PERCEPTION. When looking at, e.g., a chair, what one sees – so the argument goes – is not the chair itself, but patches of colour on one's retina, from which the presence of the chair is inferred. These patches of colour are the sense-data, and can also occur even if the chair is not there, e.g. if one is hallucinating. Sense-data have also been called sensations, sensa, presentations, representations, percepts, and (by Locke and Berkeley) IDEAS. A visual sense-datum is commonly taken to be the colours that make up the visual field; a tactual sense-datum is a felt, textured, resistant surface. The sense-datum theory is presupposed by REPRESENTATIONISM and PHENOMENALISM, which seek to avoid SOLIPSISM by explaining how belief in an external world can be rationally grounded in direct knowledge confined to sense-data. However, if one accepts that only sense-data can be directly perceived, it is very difficult to avoid the conclusion that we can be certain of nothing about the external world. For thousands of years, philosophers have agonized over the possibility that their entire life is but a dream. For further reading: S. Blackburn, *Spreading the Word* (1984). A.Q.

sense-relation, see MEANING-RELATION.

sensory deprivation. The condition produced by cutting off all patterned stimulation from the visual, auditory, tactual and other sensory systems (including those activated from within the organism) by such devices as diffusing goggles, white noise, padded gloves and clothing, and flotation in a liquid medium. Its effect is to produce feelings of unreality and loss of identity, together with a marked decline in such intellectual operations as reasoning, comparison and learning. Beyond a certain duration, subjects may report quasi-psychotic symptoms (see PSYCHOSIS). The work on this phenomenon has underlined the necessity of continuous sensory activity for the maintenance of effective functioning. Sensory deprivation is not to be confused with BRAINWASHING, with which it is sometimes associated in science fiction. See also NEUROPSYCHOLOGY. For further reading: P. Solomon *et al* (eds), *Sensory Deprivation* (1961). J.S.B.

sensory-motor. In DEVELOPMENTAL PSYCHOLOGY, an adjective applied to the period of early infancy (from birth to 18 months) when many co-ordinations of PERCEPTION and action emerge. See also PIAGETIAN. P.L.H.

sensum, see SENSE-DATUM.

separation of powers. The doctrine that the agencies through which the three basic and essential functions of the government of an independent country (legislative, executive and judicial) are exercised should be quite separate from each other. It is put into practice as far as possible in the USA, under the Constitution of which the federal legislative power is conferred on Congress, the executive power on the President, and the judicial power on the courts, but there are some overlaps both in the Constitution itself (e.g. the President's power to veto bills passed by Congress; presidential nomination of judges for the Supreme Court, subject to confirmation by the Senate) and in its practical application (e.g. the executive's participation in the creation of subordinate legislation; the courts' power to judge the constitutionality or otherwise of actions of the President and acts of Congress). In the UK there is no attempt to keep the three agencies separate. Thus ministers are or will become members of one or other Houses of Parliament; most judges are appointed by the Queen on the advice of the Lord Chancellor, who is himself a Cabinet minister, Speaker of the House of Lords and president of the Judicial Committee of the House of Lords, which is the ultimate court of appeal, and whose members are all members of the upper House of Parliament; and the supreme legislative authority of Parliament (see SOVEREIGNTY) may always override or alter the powers or functions of other agencies. The virtue of the doctrine lies nevertheless in bringing attention to the undesirability of too much power being vested in any one person or INSTITUTION, and to this end it is a valuable constitutional guide. See CONSTITUTIONAL GOVERNMENT; CONSTITUTIONALISM. For further reading: D. C. M. Yardley, *Introduction to British Constitutional Law* (1984). D.C.M.Y.

separatism.

(1) The demand of a particular group or area to separate from the territorial and political SOVEREIGNTY of the state of which it forms a part, e.g. the desire of Basques in Spain for an independent Basque state, or the demand of French-speaking nationalists in Quebec for their own state. See also NATIONALISM; SELF-DETERMINATION. D.C.W.

(2) A feminist strategy of not engaging at all with men. It grew out of *radical lesbianism* (see FEMINISM), women who sought freedom from heterosexual commitments through women-focused relationships. Lesbianism is not merely a personal orientation, but also a political statement. Lesbian separatists, in establishing relationships exclusively with women, have attempted to escape from PATRIARCHY, male definitions and male POWER. For lesbian separatists heterosexuality is one of the pillars of male authority. Their position is founded on the idea that women are only able to develop fully on their own terms in relationships with other women: authentic relationships are between women.

Universalism (i.e. claiming to speak for all women) has been inherent in many statements by lesbian separatists, and their neglect of the differences of RACE and CLASS has drawn criticism (e.g. 'Many Voices One Chant', *Feminist Review*, Autumn 1984). Other sections of the women's movement have been critical of the utopian implications (see UTOPIANISM) of lesbian separatism and its spurning of political activity. For further reading: C. Bunch, *Building Feminist Theory* (1981). A.G.

(3) In BLACK politics, a policy of pursuing a separate development from whites – a kind of apartheid or segregation in reverse. It was most famously advocated by Malcolm X (1925–65), leader of the NATION OF ISLAM. S.T.

Serapion Brothers. A Russian literary group named after German writer E. T. A. Hoffmann's hero. It was formed in Petrograd in 1921 by the young writers Fedin, Kaverin, Lunts, Ivanov, Zoshchenko, Nikitin, Slonimsky, Gruzdev, Tikhonov, Elizaveta Polonskaya, and Pozner, most of whom were to become leading Soviet writers and literary critics (see USSR, THE FORMER). Their literary work was initially guided by Zamyatin and the novelist, literary critic and leading FORMALIST theoretician Victor Shklovsky.

The Serapions stood for creative freedom, and in their writings shunned any form of political partisanship or UTILITARIANISM. They had no formal organization and no common aesthetic platform or literary tradition, being united mainly by their concern for literary craftsmanship. Along with other writers of moderate political outlook who wrote about the Revolution and Civil War, the Serapions were dubbed by Trotsky

FELLOW-TRAVELLERS of the Revolution. For further reading: M. Slonim, *Soviet Russian Literature* (1964). M.E.

serial history (*l'histoire sérielle*). Term current in France from about 1960 among the ANNALES SCHOOL for attempts to study long-term trends rigorously as continuities and discontinuities within a series. What is needed for this approach to be fruitful is a long sequence of relatively homogeneous data. Wheat prices, births and Easter communicants have all been studied in this way. As these examples suggest, 'serial history' is a new term for an older practice: it is one kind of QUANTITATIVE HISTORY. P.B.

serial music. Music organized according to a system devised by Schoenberg and later extended by Webern, Boulez, Stockhausen and others. Around 1910 disillusionment with the lines of development established in the last two decades of the 19th century seems to have set in, and Stravinsky with *Le Sacre du Printemps* and Schoenberg with *Pierrot Lunaire* broke completely new ground. Stravinsky, however, was not to turn to serialism until after 1950; it was Schoenberg who consciously grasped the problems raised by the break-up of tonality (see ATONAL MUSIC). The latter between 1910 and 1920 devised the *serial* method of composing. Serial music is not, however, necessarily atonal; certain composers, e.g. Alban Berg (notably in his Violin Concerto), Frank Martin, Humphrey Searle and Karl Blomdahl, have employed serial techniques within a recognizably tonal framework.

Serialism is a PERMUTATIONAL method rather than a style. Every serial composition is based on the concept of a *tone-row*, a sequence that uses, normally but not invariably, all twelve notes of the chromatic (semitone) scale in an order which is chosen for the purpose, and which varies from work to work. (The term *twelve-note* – or *dodecaphonic* – applies only to works which follow this norm, not to works – e.g. Stravinsky's *In Memoriam Dylan Thomas*, based entirely on a five-note row – where the series is of more or fewer than 12 notes.) Normally no note may reappear in the row after its initial appearance, lest it should assume the characteristics of a tonal centre, and establish a sense of traditional key. Initially, the row is conceived in four guises: (a) the row itself; (b) its *inversion* (i.e. with falling intervals replacing rising ones and vice versa); (c) its back-to-front or *retrograde* form; and (d) the inversion thereof. To add to his resources, the composer may also transpose the whole series so that it begins on any one of the 12 semitones. There are thus 48 possible permutations of the original row.

Serial method is a discipline that concerns the composer alone, and not his audience. In no sense is it a complex extension of a traditional form such as fugue. It is simply a new grammar and syntax for handling a new concept of musical language. A later development, of around 1950 and associated with Messiaen, Boulez and Stockhausen, was *total serialization*, i.e. the strict organization of rhythm, silences and even dynamics (gradations of volume and timbre). It was doubtless in reaction against this that the drift towards ALEATORY music began. A.H.

seriality. In Sartre's *Critique de la dialectique* (1960) this is the condition under which selfishly motivated individuals live in an alienated society (see ALIENATION). A bus queue, e.g., consists of a collectivity of individuals, united in their desire to catch a bus, but each wanting to catch the bus for his own selfish reasons. The collectivity of seriality is thus illusory. The condition can be transcended by establishing a *group* which has common goals and where the aim of each is the aim of all. Naturally, in this group the individual will have been subject to an 'oath' of allegiance, which is enforced by 'terror' and, ultimately, 'lynching'. For further reading: R. D. Laing and D. Cooper, *Reason and Violence* (1964). R.PO.

service industry. An industry that provides customers with services rather than tangible objects. Service industries range from coach tours and retailing to the banking facilities of the CITY of London and teaching or broadcasting. The view that they are unproductive is sheer superstition, although the productivity of some service industries is inherently much more difficult to measure than that of, say, CONSUMER DURABLES. (What is the productivity of a teacher, and is it reduced if the numbers in his class go down?) See also OCCUPATION; QUANTIFICATION. S.BR.

set. In MATHEMATICS and LOGIC, a collection of objects, itself considered as a single abstract object. Except in *axiomatic set theory* (see AXIOMATIC METHOD; SET THEORY), 'set' and 'class' are synonymous. Two sets are identical if they have the same members. (It is convenient also to admit a unique *empty set*: unique because the set of unicorns and the set of centaurs each have, in their negative way, the same members.) Sets are to be distinguished (1) from the predicates signifying the properties that define them (the predicates 'featherless biped' and 'man' differ in meaning but define the same class); (2) from mere assemblages. Thus, the United Nations is a set whose 180-odd members are nations; each nation can in turn be considered as a set of people, but these individuals are not members of the UN. Similarly, to each object *A* (e.g. a person) there corresponds its *unit class* whose only member is *A* and which is distinct from *A* (it is a set, not a person). As with FUNCTIONS, mathematicians no longer think that a set must be defined by an expressly stated property; it is determined by its members and these can be chosen at random. (In fact functions can be defined in terms of sets, and sets in terms of functions, so that it is a matter of convenience which notion is taken as primary.)

Some useful notions concerning sets are now familiar to every schoolchild who learns the new mathematics, so it is appropriate to give them here. A *subset A* of a set *B* is a set which is included in *B*; every member of *A* is a member of *B*. Conventionally the empty set and *B* itself are counted as subsets of *B*. If *A* and *B* are sets, then the *union* of *A* and *B* consists of the members of either, the *intersection* of *A* and *B* consists of members of both (it is empty if *A* and *B* are *disjoint*), and the complement of *A* in *B* consists of those members of *B* which are not members of *A*. Under these operations the subsets of a given set form a BOOLEAN ALGEBRA. For further reading: R. L. Wilder, *Evolution of Mathematical Concepts* (1978). R.G.; A.Q.

set theory. SETS (or classes) occur naturally in MATHEMATICS, but their importance was only appreciated after G. Cantor (1845–1918) had developed the theory of INFINITE sets. His ideas formed the basis for the LOGICISM of Frege and Russell. The discovery of various PARADOXES showed that the naïve theory of classes is contradictory. Cantor himself made a distinction between collections (such as the totality of *all* abstract objects), which are too all-embracing to be treated as wholes, and smaller totalities (such as the set of all real NUMBERS) which can be regarded as single objects; nowadays the former are called *proper classes*, the latter are called *sets*. On this basis modern *axiomatic set theories* (see AXIOMATIC METHOD) have been erected. They provide a foundation for contemporary mathematics and are apparently free from contradiction. The various theories differ in strength; e.g., the AXIOM OF CHOICE may be included or rejected. All of them are incomplete; i.e. there are important questions concerning infinite sets which cannot be decided on the basis of the axioms (e.g. the CONTINUUM hypothesis). This reflects an inadequacy of contemporary intuition. Opinions differ as to how far this inadequacy may eventually be overcome. For further reading: W. S. Hatcher, *Foundations of Mathematics* (1968). R.G.

SETI, see SEARCH FOR EXTRATERRESTRIAL INTELLIGENCE.

settlement. The forms and processes of population distribution over the land. Settlement may be classified as urban, rural, suburban, or pioneer. Settlement policies, redistributing people within a territory, are needed in case of migration or rapid population change. Such problems as overpopulation, resettlement, decentralization, and planning of new towns have usually been controversial. See also DENSITY; EKISTICS; URBANIZATION. J.G.

settlement geography. The systematic field of GEOGRAPHY devoted to the study of the facilities people build in the process of occupying an area. Research in this field has been marked by a strong historical dimension, expressed in a central concern for the role that human settlements have played in the evolution of cultural landscapes. Although settlement geographers pay attention to architectural and other characteristics of individual dwellings and non-residential structures, much of their work has focused on the spatial form and layout of urban population clusters, ranging in scale from the tiniest hamlets and villages to the largest metropolitan AGGLOMERATIONS. Not surprisingly, settlement geography is closely tied to related fields of HUMANISTIC GEOGRAPHY, including CULTURAL GEOGRAPHY, SOCIAL GEOGRAPHY and urban geography. Some settlement geographers specialize in studying the contents of the rural landscape, particularly the composition and layout of farms, and their work also contributes to the field of agricultural geography. P.O.M.

sex. The anatomical differences between women and men define individual biological (see BIOLOGY) sexual (see SEXUALITY) identity, but as is now widely accepted in many cultures, biological sexual difference is not necessarily the same as sexual identity. The naturalistic (see NATURALISM) – and in many societies the traditional – assumption that sexual relations will always be conducted with members of the opposite sex has been superseded by more pluralistic (see PLURALISM) accounts of sexual activity and sexual identity which rely heavily on constructionist theories of human development. Thus 'sex', in the late 20th century, is interpreted both in terms of conventional heterosexuality (in the majority of societies still the only legally recognized form of marriage) and in other, more diverse, forms. What has become widely recognized is that although the institutional (see INSTITUTIONS) organization of sex is still largely limited to heterosexual sexual and social practice, the actual range of human sexual activity is much more diverse and less consistent. There is considerable historical evidence to suggest that this was always the case, and that what has changed is little about the practice of sex, but a great deal about its discussion and recognition. For further reading: D. Richardson (ed.), *Theorising Heterosexuality* (1996). M.S.E.

sex chromosomes. CHROMOSOMES that differ in number or structure between the sexes. The commonest pattern is that found in man and other mammals, in which females have two large chromosomes, the X chromosomes, and males have one X chromosome and a smaller Y chromosome. Spermatozoa bearing X and Y chromosomes are produced in approximately equal numbers, and the sex of the new individual is determined at the time of fertilization by the type of sperm fertilizing the X-bearing egg.

Characteristics determined by GENES on the X chromosome are inherited differently from those determined by other genes. Such characteristics are said to show SEX LINKAGE. Examples in man are haemophilia and red-green colour blindness. There are few or no genes on the human Y chromosome other than those determining maleness. J.M.S.

sex linkage. A form of LINKAGE that arises when more than one genetic determinant is present on a SEX CHROMOSOME, particularly the X chromosome. With a sex-linked recessive (see GENE) disease such as haemophilia (at least in one of its forms), the condition can be inherited only through females. On average, half the sons of a maternal carrier of the haemophilia gene will be afflicted and half her daughters will be carriers like herself. P.M.

sex ratio. The ratio of males to females at birth or at any other age. We may take it that the norm for bisexual organisms is unity (1 to 1) over the reproductive period, but in large industrial populations and wherever there is adequate provision for antenatal, maternal and infant welfare the ratio exceeds unity, and in Europe and America is about 1.06 (106 male births to 100 female births). Later in life the ratio falls below unity because females have a better life expectancy at all ages and women therefore preponderate in the most senior age groups: by the age of 70, there will be just 60 to 65 males for every 100 females. It has been repeatedly observed that the sex ratio rises at or towards the end of major wars. The exact causes of this are not known but it is not helpful to describe it as 'nature's way of making good' the disproportionate loss of male lives. P.M.

sexism. A word coined, on the analogy of RACISM (see RACE), for a deep-rooted, often unconscious system of beliefs, attitudes, behaviour and INSTITUTIONS in which distinctions between people's intrinsic worth are made on the grounds of their biological sex and GENDER roles. Whether consciously or not, the sexist sees woman (or man) as suffering from innately inferior capacity in areas of performance deemed significant, and behaves accordingly. As with racism, the term, though not the phenomenon, tends in practice to be restricted to one-way attitudes only, i.e. to male sexism. In the aggressive form of sexism known as 'male chauvinism', the paradigm is one of an assumed innate male supremacy in all the most important areas of activity (with the possible exception of child-rearing), accompanied by a predisposition to treat women as anonymous objects for male sexual pleasure and material wellbeing. For a female response to male sexism, see FEMINISM.

P.S.L.

sexual abuse. The term has a long history in PSYCHOANALYSIS and is still a highly controversial topic in our modern world. Originally sexual abuse was used by Freud to refer to the sexual traumas that children suffered at the hands of unscrupulous adults, often close relatives. These ranged from touching of the genitals to full penetration or even anal RAPE. The consequences, according to Freud, were devastating, leading to lifelong emotional debility (NEUROSES) ranging from hysteria all the way to a full-blown PSYCHOSIS. Remembering the full event, and then 'working through' it in long-term psychoanalytic therapy (using dreams, FREE ASSOCIATION and analysis of the TRANSFERENCE), was the only way to undo the harm. It was irrelevant to Freud, initially, whether children took sexual pleasure in the events or even encouraged them. Later, however, he came to believe, for reasons that have never been clarified, that when his female patients implicated their own fathers in such sexual acts, there could be no truth in the matter: they were lying to themselves (he called it 'hysterical mendacity') under the pressure of sexual wishes, desires and impulses they had for their father which they could not acknowledge. This gave rise to the Oedipal theory (see OEDIPUS COMPLEX) of the neuroses, the eventual cornerstone of the entire foundation of psychoanalysis. The problem is that modern research, particularly by feminists (see FEMINISM), has shown beyond any shadow of a doubt that sexual abuse (unwanted sexual advances of any kind on the part of an adult towards a child) is real and is common. *How* common is still disputed, but the most highly regarded research, that by Diana Russell, a British sociologist (see below), indicates the figure to be about 38 per cent of women before the age of 18 in the US. This figure has been replicated in several other studies and in different countries. Although the psychological profession (see PSYCHOLOGY) in general was very reluctant to admit the reality and the prevalence of sexual abuse (no doubt because it had been instrumental in denying its reality for so many decades), recently many therapists have embraced the feminist position and are offering, only too eagerly, to open up their practice to victims (also called 'survivors') of sexual abuse. A much smaller, but no less vocal, school of critics (headed by a professor of English, Frederick Crews), taking the position that the majority of claims of sexual abuse are simply fabricated, with the willing assistance of therapists eager for financial gain or professional advance, blame Freud's theory of REPRESSION for the spate of claims of belated memories of abuse. In response feminists and others point out that many women have always remembered the abuse, having had recourse neither to repression nor to PSYCHOTHERAPY. Moreover, as Sándor Ferenczi (1873–1933), one of Freud's earliest and most beloved disciples, pointed out as early as 1932, some men in analysis confessed to being the perpetrators of the abuse, thereby casting the theory of fabrication into the dustbin of history at least in those cases. For further reading: D. Russell, *The Secret Trauma: Incestuous Abuse of Women and Girls* (1986).

J.MA.

sexual politics. Term made popular by the FEMINIST writer Kate Millett in her book of the same name (1969). Widely adopted, the CONCEPT of sexual politics is based on the notion that issues of SEX and GENDER exist in a broad political realm rather than a narrow personal one. This politicization of relations between the sexes, and of women in relation to patriarchal structures of POWER (see PATRIARCHY), emerged during the 1970s in CONSCIOUSNESS-RAISING groups, where women were encouraged to consider every aspect of their lives including the distribution of responsibilities inside the FAMILY (such as housework), control over their own fertility (see CONTRACEPTION), and the possibility of professional lives in spheres formerly closed to them (latterly, as executives in corporations, or even as soldiers), as political issues demanding clear enunciation and practical, legislative measures (see EQUAL RIGHTS AMENDMENT).

S.T.

sexuality. The term 'sexuality' is generally understood in terms of the different forms and practices of sexual relationship (see SEX) between human beings. To speak of 'sexuality' in the singular implies a single MODEL of sexual practice, but there has been a general recognition in the last 30 years of sexualities, i.e. a wide range of human sexuality. The most influential writer on sex and sexuality in this period was the French historian Michel Foucault (1926–84); in his work he argued that post-Enlightenment Europe attempted (and largely succeeded in achieving) the theoretical organization and codification (see CODE) of human sexuality, with the result that sexual practice became the subject of legislation and the creation of rigid sexual identities (see IDENTITY) (particularly that of the male homosexual). Foucault's work has had a considerable impact on writing in sexuality, and his reinterpretation of the HISTORY of sexuality has led to the revision of orthodox assumptions about the 'repression' of sexuality and the definition of sexual activity and sexual pleasure. In particular, Foucault (in common with other writers) has proposed the separation of sexual practice and sexuality from morality. For further reading: M. Foucault, *The History of Sexuality* (1990). M.S.E.

sexuality, feminine, see FEMININE SEXUALITY.

sexually transmitted disease (STD). An infectious disease contracted only through sexual intercourse. In the UK a Royal Commission, reporting in 1916, designated syphilis, gonorrhoea and chancroid as the *venereal diseases*; the first two of these can be transmitted to babies during pregnancy or delivery. Since then it has become clear that there are many other sexually transmissible diseases. In some (e.g. genital HERPES, chlamydial infection; see CHLAMYDIA) this is the route of infection in the great majority of cases, but in others (e.g. AIDS, hepatitis B, genital yeast infection) sexual contact is one of several ways in which infection can be acquired. Because of the difficulty of categorizing many conditions in this 'all or nothing' way, the term venereal disease (which in any case has an inescapable stigma) is less used today. In England, the following are reportable as sexually transmitted diseases from hospital clinics: syphilis, gonorrhoea, chancroid, donovanosis (granuloma inguinale), lymphogranuloma venereum, non-specific urethritis, trichomoniasis, genital candidosis (yeast infection), scabies, pubic lice, genital herpes and genital warts. To this day, only syphilis, gonorrhoea and chancroid are statutory sexually transmitted diseases. J.D.O.

Sezession. Name given in the German-speaking countries to a number of art organizations seceding from the official academies around 1900, to start their own exhibitions. The first was that in Munich (1892), the most important that in Vienna (1897), which gave the name 'Sezession' to the Austrian ART NOUVEAU style and is associated particularly with the paintings of Gustav Klimt, its president from 1898 to 1903. In 1900 a Berlin Sezession was formed, with the IMPRESSIONIST Max Liebermann as its first president and Ernst Barlach and Max Beckmann among the early exhibitors. A *Neue Sezession* which split off in 1910, with the BRÜCKE painters and others, lasted only two years. J.W.

SF, see SCIENCE FICTION.

shadow economy, see BLACK ECONOMY.

shadow matter, see under SUPERSTRINGS.

shadow prices. In ECONOMICS, estimates of the marginal social costs or benefits of goods, services and inputs. In general, prices emerge from the interaction of SUPPLY AND DEMAND in markets. In the case of PERFECT COMPETITION, prices can be taken as measures of the marginal social value of the associated good, service or input. However, markets do not exist for many goods, services and inputs. In many markets, prices do not indicate the marginal social value of the good, service or input, i.e. there are MARKET FAILURES. In these two cases, economic analysis may require the estimation of shadow prices. In the case of an unknown social marginal benefit or cost, the concept of OPPORTUNITY COST implies a fairly direct means of calculating the shadow price. If a directly observable market for a good or service does not exist, shadow prices can be calculated from other markets where a similar product is consumed. For example, the value of time can be estimated by

investigating the trade-off between the time spent in making the same journey by different modes of travel and the cost of the different modes. In the case of market imperfections, the existing price can be corrected for the imperfections. The concept of shadow prices originated in linear programming. Shadow prices are used extensively in applied economic analysis and COST BENEFIT ANALYSIS. For further reading: R. Sugden and A. Williams, *The Principles of Practical Cost-Benefit Analysis* (1978).
J.S.F.; J.P.

shadow world, see under SUPERSTRINGS.

shamanism. A variety of RELIGION which reveres the ability of the tribal priest-doctor (Russian *shaman*) to influence the good and evil spirits controlling life. It is found among various peoples of northern Asia, and also among Native American, especially in the north-west. See also PRIMITIVISM. For further reading: M. Eliade, *Shamanism* (1964).
D.L.E.

shame culture and **guilt culture.** Terms apparently introduced into ANTHROPOLOGY by Ruth Benedict in *The Chrysanthemum and the Sword* (1946) to distinguish between CULTURES which rely, respectively, 'on external sanctions for good behaviour' and 'on an internalized conviction of sin'. Societies differ, no doubt, in the extent to which individuals are expected to consult their own consciences and monitor their own behaviour; but no society could dispense either with the internalization of NORMS (how otherwise could men influence one another?) or with the systematic surveillance of an individual's conduct by his fellows. The terms spring from a phase in the development of psychological anthropology and now have little currency.
M.F.

Shanghai Communiqué. The document signed by Chinese Premier Zhou Enlai and US President Richard Nixon on 27 February 1972, at the end of the President's historic visit to China. The communiqué consisted of seven major parts: (1) a formal statement of the visit; (2) a joint appreciation of the contacts made; (3) a US declaration on foreign policy; (4) a Chinese declaration on its alliances with North Korea and North VIETNAM; (5) a joint statement about the principles of foreign policy held by both sides; (6) a summary of differing points of view on the Taiwan issue; (7) a joint declaration on expanding cultural and political relations between the two nations. Although the communiqué expressed more differences than common ground between the two, and full diplomatic relations were another six years in coming, it marked a new thrust in Chinese foreign policy, and signalled a much wider international acceptance of China as an important power in world affairs. For further reading: G. Segal, *The Great Power Triangle* (1982).
S.B.

Shari'a, see under ISLAM.

Sharpeville. A town in South Africa where on 21 March 1960 the South African police fired on African demonstrators against the PASS LAWS, killing 67 and wounding 186, including 48 women and children. The catch-phrase 'Remember Sharpeville' was much used by advocates of international action to force South Africa to abandon APARTHEID.
D.C.W.

Shavian. Characteristic or reminiscent of the writings of George Bernard Shaw (1856–1950). Nouns to which the adjective is frequently applied are wit, irreverence, paradox, ebullience, insouciance.
O.S.

shell structure of atoms and nuclei, see under ELECTRON SHELL; MAGIC NUMBER.

shellshock. A psychiatric disorder that first became apparent during World War I when soldiers in large numbers developed paralysis in the face of battle. Whereas some traditional military authorities regarded it as malingering and cowardice and urged court-martials, medical opinion tended to view shellshock as akin to the grand hysteria (see NEUROSIS) with which they were familiar in their practices with female patients. Electric shock treatment (faradization) was commonly used, though more enlightened doctors attempted psychotherapeutic means to restore courage. It was considered essential for the victim's own morale and manliness, as well as for the nation's war effort, to restore him to the front. The term is now out of date in a clinical sense, having been replaced during World War II by the term combat fatigue and, after the VIETNAM war, POST-TRAUMATIC STRESS DISORDER. R.P.; S.T.

shiggs, see under SUPERSYMMETRY.

Shi'i Muslims, see under ISLAM.

Shinto. The Way of the Gods: it is the indigenous Japanese RELIGION, which places a strong emphasis on purity and on nature spirits. It believes in a variety of spirits, or *Kwami*, who are headed by the goddess Amaterasu. In the Meiji period, during the modernization of Japan, it became an expression of the Japanese patriotic spirit and was forcibly separated from BUDDHISM (with which it had lived in symbiosis). It was something whose rites all Japanese should attend to; but it was declared not to be a religion, since the constitution decreed a separation of religion and the state. It was associated with the rituals surrounding the Emperor. The goddess Amaterasu was not merely the sun goddess but was the founder of Japan. During the occupation after World War II, the Emperor was demystified, though not entirely freed from Shinto ritual. For further reading: D. Holton, *The National Faith of Japan: A Study in Modern Shinto* (1995). N.SM.

shock therapy.

(1) See ELECTRO-CONVULSIVE THERAPY (ECT).

(2) An economic strategy advocating an enormous jolt in price decontrol, market creation, reduced government spending, monetary restrictions, deregulation, legal changes, and privatization as the former communist countries of eastern and central Europe and the Soviet Union make the transition to CAPITALISM. The strategy is associated with Jeffrey Sachs, an adviser to the governments of Solidarity leader Lech Walesa in Poland and later Boris Yeltsin in Russia in their market reforms. Howard Wachtel, an evolutionist, who emphasizes the gradual building of institutions, contends that shock therapy downplays the creation of a small-scale private sector, small independent banks, market reforms in agriculture, and funds for a 'safety net' for social programmes and full employment for the population. By the mid-1990s, electorates in Poland, Russia and Hungary, disillusioned with market reforms, voted the former Communist Party (see COMMUNISM), often reincarnated as democratic socialists (see SOCIALISM), to a parliamentary plurality in place of the party of economic reform. In response to critics, Sachs argues that production was in decline, INFLATION rates were surging, and the black-market value of the rouble was falling in the immediate years before Yeltsin came into power in late 1991. Moreover, Sachs charges that the US and IMF aid to Russia was disbursed too slowly, and that shock therapy could not have failed because it was never tried. For further reading: J. Sachs, *Poland's Jump to the Market Economy* (1993). E.W.N.

show trials. Trials run on the principles of the MOSCOW TRIALS, e.g. in eastern Europe in the 1940s and 1950s: the trials of László Rajk and others in Hungary (1949), of Traicho Kostov and others in Bulgaria (1949), and of Rudolf Slánsky and others in Czechoslovakia (1952). R.C.

shuttering, see under CONCRETE.

shuttle diplomacy, see under DIPLOMACY.

SI units (*Système Internationale d'Unités*). The system of units used at present for scientific work. SI units are built on the MKS system, an earlier set of fundamental units based on the length of the metre, the mass of the kilogram, and the time of the second. However, SI also includes electric current, temperature, luminosity, and molecular weight. M.V.B.

sick jokes, see under BLACK COMEDY.

signal transduction. The CELLS of a tissue or organ respond to many external signals, frequently hormones in a fluid that bathes them. Since cells are surrounded by a membrane that is not permeable to large MOLECULES, hormones instead bind to a RECEPTOR on the cell membrane. The consequence is signal transduction, in which an internal response is generated to the external signal. The internal response involves one or more second messengers – small molecules that mediate the first stages of the internal response. It remains uncertain whether the process of RECEPTOR-MEDIATED ENDOCYTOSIS contributes to the ultimate internal response of the cell. (See also ENDOCRINOLOGY.) For further reading: B. Alberts *et al*, *Molecular Biology of the Cell* (1983). P.N.

significance (in STATISTICS), see under STATISTICAL TEST.

significant form. A term coined by English critic Clive Bell in 1913 to describe the essential quality of a work of art, that which (he believed) evoked a special 'aesthetic emotion'. It was supposed to consist of certain forms and relations of forms, including colour. The theory of significant form was briefly influential in English AESTHETICS, especially as it coincided with the rise of the POST-IMPRESSIONISTS. For further reading: A. C. H. Bell, *Art* (1914). P.C.

signifier/signified. In his *Course in General Linguistics* (1916), the French linguist Ferdinand de Saussure (1857–1913; see SAUSSURIAN) described the unit of language (the SIGN) as being composed of a mental component (or CONCEPT) which he called the signified, and a sound-image or written form, which he called the signifier. Thus, the signifier 'tree' will call into the mind of one who hears or reads it the concept 'tree'. His crucial point was that there is no necessary relationship, no natural connection, between a signifier and the signified: what is 'tree' in one language is 'arbre' in another. Saussure predicted that the consequences of this insight were 'numberless', and indeed they have been, beginning with attempts by anthropologists to analyse the structural principles of hundreds of natural languages. Several influential 20th-century European thinkers have taken Saussure's insights as their point of departure: Claude Lévi-Strauss, Michel Foucault, Roland Barthes, Jacques Lacan (see LACANIAN), and Jacques Derrida. Lacan's 'return to Freud' (see FREUDIAN) by way of structuralist linguistics (see STRUCTURALISM), and Derrida's description of the 'freeplay' between signifier and signified, and of language as a 'play' of signifiers endlessly deferring meaning, are two particularly infamous examples of Saussure's progeny. For further reading: J. Sturrock, *The Structuralist Controversy* (1979). M.F.H.

Sikhism. The faith that goes back to Nanak (1469—1539) and the succeeding nine Gurus, culminating in Guru Gobind Singh (*d.* 1708). Though originally based in Punjab, it has now spread widely across the world. Nanak emphasized the essential oneness of Hindu *bhakti* (devotional) piety and Islamic worship. However, later in its development the Sikh community was harassed by the Mughal dynasty and formed a more militant organization under Gobind Singh. He abolished CASTE distinctions and laid down various badges, known as the five Ks (keeping the beard and hair uncut and so typically wearing turbans; carrying a comb; wearing breeches, then soldiers' dress; wearing a bangle; and a short sword or dagger). They were forbidden alcohol and tobacco and meat butchered in the Muslim style. Doctrinally, the Sikhs (whose name means 'disciples') emphasized the unity of God and his formlessness. In the 19th century they achieved dominance in the Punjab, but were defeated by the British, and were incorporated into the Raj. In the Partition in 1947 most Sikhs joined India. Many later migrated to Britain, Canada and elsewhere, and this helped to strengthen a militant movement in the Punjab devoted to a separate Sikh state (Khalistan). In June 1984, separatists occupying the Golden Temple were driven out by the Indian Army: a consequence was the assassination of premier Indira Gandhi in October, and murderous rioting against the Sikhs. On the whole they are a prosperous and well-knit community. For further reading: W. Owen Cole, *The Sikhs* (1986). N.SM.

silicones. A group of synthetic silicon-containing compounds in which the silicon ATOMS are held together by bonds (see BOND, CHEMICAL) to oxygen atoms acting as 'bridges'. Each silicon atom is attached to at least one organic RADICAL. Apart from simple compounds (strictly called *siloxanes*), silicon and oxygen can be linked in branched or unbranched chains to generate oils and POLYMERS which find use as water-repellents, lubricants and rubbers. They are more resistant to heat than carbon-linked polymers, and the viscosity of the oils changes little over a wide temperature range. B.F.

simulation. A technique of applied PROBABILITY THEORY (and hence of operations research) used to compare a stochastic model (see STOCHASTIC PROCESS) with reality by actually generating particular random results from the MODEL. RANDOM NUMBERS are usually used to produce the simulation, commonly on a computer. R.SI.

single currency. A system designed to link the MONETARY POLICY of the qualifying members of the EUROPEAN UNION (EU) by means of a common currency known as the euro. The architecture of European Monetary Union (EMU) was established by the MAASTRICHT Treaty of 1992 under which all members of the EU agreed to strive to meet the strict conditions (see STABILITY PACT) attached to joining the single currency by January 1999: under the terms of the treaty Britain and Denmark were given the option of staying outside the euro area even if the economies of the two countries met the CONVERGENCE CRITERIA. A single currency is seen by proponents as deepening the economic and political co-operation among countries, leading to higher growth and living standards and lower levels of price INFLATION. This is achieved by lowering the cost of cross-border transactions, increasing trade within the single market (see TRADE THEORY), cutting INTEREST RATES and providing a level playing field for COMPETITION among businesses. Opponents fear that it is a back-door route to creating a federal Europe (see FEDERALISM), unpicking centuries of SOVEREIGNTY for Europeans nations. They also argue that there is insufficient economic convergence among the nations concerned, and that the single currency, in which the dominant influence is German monetary policy, will be deflationary, leading to higher UNEMPLOYMENT across the community and the inability of individual countries to adjust their competitiveness through DEVALUATION. Single currencies are not a new idea; much of international trade and investment in the 19th century was conducted under the auspices of the GOLD STANDARD. In the US the dollar was first adopted as the national currency in 1785, but it was not until the creation of the Federal Reserve System of central banks in 1913 that an orderly single currency and monetary policy developed. For further reading: C. Johnson, *In with the Euro Out with the Pound* (1996). A.BR.

Sino-Vietnamese conflict. On 7 February 1979 the Chinese government ordered 75,000–85,000 troops to cross the border with VIETNAM to 'teach Hanoi a lesson' after the Vietnamese had deposed Pol Pot and the KHMER ROUGE in Kampuchea. After suffering high casualty levels and drawing no Vietnamese troops from Kampuchea, the Chinese withdrew, and the hostilities were over by March 1979. The Chinese claim that one of the main reasons for their action was to support the ethnic Chinese who had been heavily persecuted in Vietnam, and indeed, two-thirds of all Vietnamese boat people were ethnically Chinese. At the real crux of the matter, however, was China's disputes with the Soviet Union, who backed Hanoi, and Beijing's subsequent attempt to support its anti-Soviet beachhead in east Asia, namely Pol Pot, who had been deposed by the Vietnamese in January 1979. For further reading: M. Yahuda, *China's Foreign Policy after Mao* (1983). S.B.

site. In archaeology, a place where there is some kind of evidence of human behaviour – such evidence can range from a single artifact to a city. Sites are classified according to their inferred function – e.g. domestic of habitation sites, kill- or butchery-sites, quarry sites, etc. They may contain the material residues of human culture, as well as organic and environmental remains. P.G.B.

site catchment analysis. The study of the interrelationship between a COMMUNITY and the territory which it exploits. The occupants of each SETTLEMENT utilize a tract of land and in doing so create changes within the natural ENVIRONMENT. In site catchment analysis the territory upon which the settlement or community is dependent is defined in terms of the total material needs of the community, and explanations are sought for the processes by which the environment is utilized. The CONCEPT has recently been introduced into ARCHAEOLOGY from GEOGRAPHY. It is of particular value in the early prehistoric period (see PREHISTORY), but its usefulness in periods of complex social organization needs to be demonstrated. For further reading: M. Chisholm, *Rural Settlement and Land Use: An Essay in Location* (1970). B.C.

situation ethics. The insistence, against the legalism characteristic of much conventional morality and MORAL THEOLOGY, that the right solution to any moral problem depends much more on the situation itself than on any general, external code; and that the key to the solution is always love. This position is criticized as leading to ANTINOMIANISM. For further reading: J. Fletcher, *Situation Ethics* (1966). D.L.E.

situational analysis; situational logic. Terms introduced by philosopher Karl Popper (1902–94) in 1945 to denote an approach to the explanation of SOCIAL ACTION in which a detailed reconstruction of the circumstances of action (including both objective conditions and the participants' aims, knowledge, beliefs, values, and subjective 'definitions' of the situation) is taken as a basis for hypothesizing rational courses of action for the individuals involved, through which their observed behaviour may be rendered intelligible; i.e. through which its subjective logic in relating means to ends under given constraints may be appreciated. The approach has a close affinity with that of VERSTEHEN as advocated by Max Weber, but rejects any reliance on intuition as in the HERMENEUTICS of Dilthey or Collingwood. See also BELIEF; OBJECTIVITY; SUBJECTIVITY. For further reading: K. R. Popper, *Objective Knowledge* (1972). J.H.G.

Situationism. The radical philosophy of a group of mainly French social and cultural critics whose views first appeared in an avant-garde magazine, *Internationale Situationniste*, from 1958 onwards. Heavily influenced by SURREALISM and DADAISM, their thinking took on a greater political significance when it emerged as the main influence on the student radicals active in the MAY 1968 events in Paris. The Situationists denounced all conventional LEFT-wing RADICALISM – including MARXISM – as hidebound and anachronistic. Instead of the takeover of the state and economy that was the aim of most revolutionaries, they demanded a 'REVOLUTION of everyday life' that would transform personal relationships and cultural outlooks. Through changes in attitudes to SEX, family life, work, and the urban environment, there would take place a thoroughgoing cultural politicization that would eventually substitute itself for the conventional institutions of politics. The Situationists were the inspiration of many of the best-known graffiti that covered the walls of Paris in MAY 1968: 'demand the impossible'; 'do not adjust your mind, there is a fault with reality'; 'Je suis Marxiste, style Groucho'. For further reading: C. Gray (ed.), *Leaving the 20th Century: The Incomplete Work of the Situationist International* (1974). K.K.

Six, les. A group of six composers, five of them French, brought together by Jean Cocteau (1889–1963) in 1917. Although said to be influenced by and disciples of the French composer Erik Satie (1866–1925), no common aesthetic identity can really be observed except for an occasional and fashionable cynicism. Auric, Milhaud, Poulenc and Germaine Tailleferre were each to develop their own musical styles; Durey's talent soon faded, while the Swiss Honegger felt no particular admiration for Satie. As a significant artistic force their influence proved negligible, their collective name being little more than a convenient label attached by critics to a certain aspect of French 20th-century music that moved in a different direction from the IMPRESSIONISM of Debussy. A.H.

Six-Day War, see under MIDDLE EAST WARS.

ska, see under REGGAE.

skeuomorph. An archaeological term for an object made in a form similar to that which it would have had if it had been made in another material. *Skeuomorphism* – the close copying of form and function in a substitute material – is often well demonstrated by pottery types; e.g. in southern Britain in the sixth century BC a small bowl was produced with a sharply angled shoulder, furrowed decoration, an indented (or omphalos) base, and a surface covering of hematite to give a glossy red-brown appearance. Many of these characteristics are alien to ceramic technique but are evidently adopted to give the pot the appearance of contemporary bronze vessels. A modern plastic bucket still retains skeuomorphic features, reflecting its galvanized iron ancestry. B.C.

skewness, see under DISTRIBUTION.

Skinner box. A device developed by B. F. Skinner (see SKINNERIAN) for training animals to learn appropriate responses. The animal is placed in an isolating box provided with little more than one or more buttons or levers to press. Correct responses produce escape, food, water, etc. Using techniques of AUTOMATION, the investigator can register a cumulative record of response to different conditions of *reinforcement* (see OPERANT CONDITIONING), etc. W.Z.

Skinnerian. In PSYCHOLOGY, an adjective applied to a type of experiment (see also SKINNER BOX) and a type of EXPLANATION associated with the American BEHAVIOURIST B. F. Skinner (1904–90). The typical experiment involves an *operant response* (see OPERANT CONDITIONING), like pressing a button or lever, followed immediately by a REINFORCEMENT that increases the probability of the operant response being repeated. At a theoretical level, the term applies to explanations that eschew any reference to internal mediating or mental processes. For further reading: B. F. Skinner, *The Behaviour of Organisms* (1938). J.S.B.

skyscraper. Term applied since the 1880s to tall multi-storey buildings. Their evolution stemmed from high land values and was made possible by the development of the skeleton frame, the lift, the water closet, and central heating. Early landmarks included W. Le B. Jenney's 10-storey Home Insurance Company, Chicago (1883–95), and the 102-storey Empire State Building, New York (1931). Extremely tall structures are no more efficient to maintain or use than smaller ones, but they are so symbolic of achievement and pre-eminence that cities and large corporations continue to build them. In 1998, the *Times of India* reported that building was due to begin on a 224-storey building in Katangi, India, which would have the capacity to house a working population of up to 60,000 people.
M.BR.; A.A.L.

slash and burn. Originally this term referred to a type of agriculture practised by some so-called primitive peoples in tropical forests (see RAINFOREST). A portion of the forest (usually less than an acre) is partially cleared by machete or other hand-held cutting tool, accompanied by burning. The resulting ash and scorched detritus serves to fertilize the cut area. A large variety of SPECIES of plants is left to grow, or is planted, in this soil which has been enriched with its own ash. In a few years the yield from such a plot will diminish because of nutrient depletion, and the site will be abandoned. The farmer moves on to other sites, which now are similarly prepared and planted. He returns to the abandoned site after a fallow period of several years. Overall the system is sustainable because the abandoned sites revert to forest rapidly, and can be cultivated again later. Although the slash and burn system is one of minimal negative environmental impact, the term has come to mean its very antithesis. Perhaps it is the implied ferocity of the word slash, coupled with the scorched-earth implications of burn, that results in the term slash and burn connoting utter destruction.
W.G.R.

slave morality, see under MASTER MORALITY/SLAVE MORALITY.

SLBM (submarine-launched ballistic missiles), see under MISSILES.

slepton, see under SUPERSYMMETRY.

slice of life. A term originally applied (*tranche de vie*) to the fiction of the French NATURALISTS, particularly Émile Zola (1840–1902), one of whose conscious aims was to present a cross-section of society (usually lower-class) in its actual, unselected totality.
M.S.-S.

slump, see DEPRESSION.

smart material. A material that undergoes pronounced changes in its properties as a result of gradual changes in the conditions to which it is subjected. Smart materials are beginning to replace mechanical devices in sensing and switching technologies – as they have no mechanical parts, they can be more compact and robust. One of the most commercially important classes of smart material is piezoelectrics; piezoelectric materials develop an electric FIELD in response to stress or pressure. Quartz is such a material, and is used to convert regular mechanical vibrations into an oscillating electric signal in watches and clocks. Piezoelectrics are also widely used in microphones and SONAR sensors, and in strain gauges for buildings and bridges. Other smart materials change colour in response to light or heat, or expand or contract substantially when subjected to heat, electric or magnetic fields, chemical signals or light. They afford fine positional control in devices such as microscopes, and are being developed as artificial muscles for robotics (see ROBOT). P.C.B.

smog. In 1905 the founder-president of the British Smoke Abatement Society, Dr H. A. Des Voeux, first used this term to describe a mixture of (sm)oke and f(og) that was characteristic of air pollution at that time. Now, however, the term is applied to almost any mixture of objectionable air pollutants whether or not smoke or fog is involved.

Smogs caused by the action of sunlight on primary pollutants such as nitrogen oxides and hydrocarbons are called photochemical smogs and are characteristic of cities with large emissions of vehicular-derived pollutants. Smog reduces visibility, causes eye irritation, can damage rubber, and may cause damage to vegetation. Smog levels have been reduced in some cities through rigid enforcement of emission standards for vehicles. A.S.G.

SNCC (Student Non-Violent Co-ordinating Committee), see under NEW LEFT.

sneutrino, see under SUPERSYMMETRY.

soap opera. A type of serial fiction originated in the late 1920s by American, mainly female, radio programme-makers, characterized by an emphasis on human relations, domesticity and daily life. Their generic name derived from their early sponsorship by soap manufacturers. Today, popular soaps like *Sunset Beach* in America, and *EastEnders* in the UK, continue to attract huge audiences around the world. Originally ridiculed for their consistently improbable plot-lines – celebrated examples including the revelation that years of *Dallas* had just been a dream of one of the characters, Bobby Ewing – soap opera now attracts serious critical attention. FEMINIST film and TV theorists have written much on the special appeal of the genre to female audiences, pointing to the cultural significance of the unending quality – the 'indefinitely expandable middle' – of soap opera narrative, to the kinds of 'cultural competences' required in order to 'read' soap opera, and to the ways in which viewing soaps slots into work and social relations in home and family. For further reading: Museum of Television and Radio, *Worlds without End: The Art and History of the Soap Opera* (1997).

A.KU.; A.A.L.

social, see under SOCIETAL.

social action. In politics, activity by an interested group aimed at securing some particular reform, or support for a cause. In SOCIOLOGY, the most general term used for the subject-matter of the science: human activity regarded from the point of view of its social context. Theorists have disagreed as to where and how the boundary should be drawn. Some (see WEBERIAN) have distinguished sharply between, on the one hand, natural events and the scientific procedures appropriate to studying them, and, on the other hand, human actions, which can only be identified through the ideas and purposes of conscious agents and which therefore call for different methods of study. Others (e.g. Durkheim) have minimized this difference and aimed to study human actions naturalistically, as SOCIAL FACTS. A further difference is between theorists who regard social action as synonymous with human action (e.g. because it involves conceptual thinking and hence language, a social product) and others who define social action as a sub-class of human actions, involving direct interaction between persons, or a conscious reference to the expectations of others. Talcott Parsons's (see PARSONIAN) synthesis of Weber's and Durkheim's approaches located social action within social systems, treating CULTURE and personality as other types of action system. This synthesis stressed purposive interaction, but proposed a naturalistic and functional analysis in terms of the SYSTEMIC properties of its results. The vogue of Parsonian FUNCTIONALISM provoked a reaction in favour of a more subjective, neo-Weberian 'action approach'. Where functionalists preferred EXPLANATIONS in terms of adaptive responses to social expectations by 'actors' who are presumed to have learned and accepted the NORMS pertaining to their ROLES, action theorists emphasize the agent's own 'definition of the situation', his power of rational choice, and his ability to negotiate interaction or manipulate expected role performances. This approach shares common ground with the theory of SYMBOLIC INTERACTION and with PHENOMENOLOGY. For further reading: T. Parsons, *The Structure of Social Action* (1937). J.R.T.

social anthropology, see under ANTHROPOLOGY.

social area analysis, see under SOCIAL GEOGRAPHY.

social behaviourism. An approach, linked with the name of American psychologist B. F. Skinner (1904–90), to the analysis and modification of social systems within the framework of BEHAVIOURISM (1). It turns directly to the relationship between behaviour and the ENVIRONMENT, and neglects supposed mediating states of mind. It is based upon the idea that behaviour is shaped and maintained by the consequence of previous behaviour, and also that the environment can be manipulated so that preferred responses are rewarded and so reinforced (see OPERANT CONDITIONING). The claim that if properly used it would solve the problems of mankind has been criticized because the direction of the changes in behaviour cannot be derived from the theory. It raises the question of which basic values are to be chosen and inculcated, and by whom. For further reading: B. F. Skinner, *Beyond Freedom and Dignity* (1972). M.BE.

social benefits, see under EXTERNALITIES.

social biology. The study of the application of BIOLOGY to social problems, from food production, POLLUTION, overpopulation, etc., to the long-range goals of social and ecological (see ECOLOGY) planning. To be distinguished from SOCIOBIOLOGY. E.O.W.

social capital. An expression introduced by economist Glenn Loury in the late 1970s to capture the cultural preconditions of wealth production, especially the cognitive and social dispositions that enable individuals to acquire the skills needed for gainful employment. In the 1980s, the idea was popularized by Pierre Bourdieu, who argued that educational systems are mainly devoted to the reproduction of social capital and, by extension, social STATUS. Loury himself stressed the family's role in social capital formation, but Robert Putnam's studies of the political and economic backwardness of southern Italy showed that the family had played too dominant a role, thereby creating the low-TRUST environment epitomized by the MAFIA. Francis Fukuyama has generalized this insight to explain cross-cultural differences in the ease with which people can form long-term associations that are not explicitly self-interested or coerced. Social capital typically diminishes if it is not regularly renewed or replaced. Such depreciation is often marked by the shutdown of places where people spontaneously congregate, e.g. churches, schools, pubs and clubs. S.F.

social chapter. The section of the MAASTRICHT Treaty which seeks to codify basic work rights among the countries of the EUROPEAN UNION (EU). These include the rights to join a TRADE UNION, equal rights for men and women, safety standards in the workplace, and representation of labour on the boardrooms of companies. The chapter has been accepted by all EU members with the exception of Britain, which took the view that such workplace matters should be determined nationally. The Conservatives (see CONSERVATISM) feared that imposing extra costs on commerce would create a less flexible labour market leading to higher UNEMPLOYMENT. Since most of the provisions of the chapter are already enshrined in UK law this is thought to be mythology rather than reality. Following the election of Tony Blair's Labour government in 1997, the UK pledged to sign up to the provisions of the social chapter. A.BR.

social closure. The process by which social groups (see GROUP THERAPY) seek to exclude outsiders from membership of their groups and therefore restrict access to the cultural and economic resources over which they have control. Examples include the way in which members of ÉLITES might tend to recruit the children of other members of the élite to positions, or the way in which PRO-

FESSIONALIZATION may be used to restrict the supply of qualified professionals of a particular type and thereby strengthen the profession's bargaining position. Social closure may also be used by ethnic groups. The concept was first used by the German sociologist (see SOCIOLOGY) Max Weber (1864–1920) and later developed by the British sociologist Frank Parkin. For further reading: F. Parkin, *Marxism and Class Theory: A Bourgeois Critique* (1979).
M.D.H.

social cognition. How people reason about social life, social behaviour and experience. In making this their primary concern following the demise of classical ATTITUDE THEORY around 1970, experimental social psychologists (see SOCIAL PSYCHOLOGY) realigned themselves with COGNITIVE PSYCHOLOGY, then coming to dominate EXPERIMENTAL PSYCHOLOGY. The existence of several older 'cognitivist' approaches, notably COGNITIVE DISSONANCE THEORY and the US GESTALT tradition of Heider and Asch, facilitated this shift. One major component of social cognition theory is ATTRIBUTION THEORY, but more fundamentally it examines how we form our general pictures of the nature of our social worlds and reason about them. Deploying cognitivist concepts like 'schemata' and 'categorization', in some respects social cognition theorists simply apply general cognitivist theories of memory and thinking to more specifically social topics. However, while rejecting thoroughgoing social constructionism (see SOCIAL CONSTRUCT), social cognition theorists do also address the involvement of social processes (such as the role of 'cultural representations' of, e.g., MINORITIES, GENDER roles, etc.) in determining social cognition. It has also proved possible to maintain the study of attitudes under this new dispensation. Social cognition has in fact become a very broad covering term primarily signifying adherence to the mainstream social psychological experimental tradition as distinct from more radical critical and social constructionist positions. For further reading: M. Hewstone *et al* (eds), *Introduction to Social Psychology: A European Perspective* (1996).
G.D.R.

social compact, see under SOCIAL CONTRACT (2).

social construct. A CONSTRUCT devised to aid in the analysis and understanding of social phenomena. It is a deliberate abstraction from reality which focuses on particular aspects and ignores others in order to open up new lines of thought and new areas of investigation. Its function is HEURISTIC, not descriptive. Examples are the CONCEPTS of STATUS and ROLE.
A.L.C.B.

social construction of mental illness. A radical wing of the ANTI-PSYCHIATRY movement since the 1960s has denied the objective reality of insanity as an authentic disease. Instead, it has contended that mental illness is best seen as a subjective category, designed to register and replicate social difference (above all, DEVIANCE). Various types of evidence are adduced to support the case. First, comparative studies of concepts of madness in different CULTURES (East/West, advanced/PRIMITIVE, etc.) indicate no uniform, stable medical categories. Second, historical studies demonstrate massive transformations in what has been designated insane (one age's saint is the next age's madman). Third, CLASS, GENDER and STATUS distinctions often govern diagnosis. 'Social construction' theorists commonly claim that the supposed rise of mental illness over the last two centuries is an illusion, created by the emergence of the psychiatric profession and of institutions (mental hospitals) for housing the insane. Opponents have argued for a real organic substratum of mental disease. They have also contended that the 'social constructionist' analysis, while seeking to sympathize with the insane, actually demeans them. For further reading: P. Sedgwick, *Psycho Politics* (1982).
R.P.

social contract.

(1) An unwritten agreement between the members of a society to behave with reciprocal responsibility in their relationships under the governance of the 'state' which, in *social contract theory* (or CONTRACT THEORY), is presupposed by the existence of that society. The idea is of ancient origin (cf. Plato, Lucretius, etc.), but it was chiefly used as a tool for criticizing established, traditional authority when the modern nation-states were breaking away from Christendom, and seeking both auton-

omy and just internal constitutions. Its chief exponents were Thomas Hobbes (1588–1679), who argued that the social contract *created* mutual obligations which did not exist prior to the constituted state; John Locke (1632–1704), who argued that moral principles and obligations existed before the creation of the state, so that men could change the state if it failed to uphold these principles; and Jean Jacques Rousseau (1712–78), who devoted a famous work to the subject. For further reading: M. Lesnoff, *Social Contract* (1983). R.F.

(2) The name given to the attempt by the 1974–79 Labour government in Britain to secure voluntary TRADE UNION agreement to restrain demands for pay increases, in exchange for an increase in the social wage (via increase in WELFARE provision and social security and restraint on price increases). First described before the government achieved office as the *social compact*, the change of name was intended to evoke an inappropriate comparison with much older, weightier and broader notions of the 'contract' between citizen and state (see above). The policy was only of limited success in 1975–77, after which high levels of INFLATION, the fragmented behaviour of trade unions, and constraints on spending policies imposed by the International Monetary Fund (see BRETTON WOODS) undermined its fragile foundations (see also WINTER OF DISCONTENT). For further reading: J. Palmer, *British Industrial Relations* (1983). S.R.

social costs, see under EXTERNALITIES.

social credit. A theory of economic and social development, largely discredited, which rests on the proposition that modern economies suffer from a deficiency of purchasing power. The remedy for this situation, according to Major C. H. Douglas, who first propounded the theory in the interwar years, was to increase purchasing power by controlling prices and creating 'social credit' which would be distributed to consumers by discounts paid to retailers, and also by 'dividends' paid to citizens for the heritage of earlier generations. Social Credit came to power in Alberta, Canada, in 1935 on a programme of issuing social credits based on the real worth of the land, but never implemented its theory while in office. For further reading: C. H. Douglas, *Social Credit* (1933). D.E.

social dance, see under POPULAR DANCE.

social Darwinism. The application of the concept of EVOLUTION to the historical development of human societies which lays particular emphasis on 'the struggle for existence' and 'the survival of the fittest'. Though not rooted in DARWINISM (the idea preceded publication of the *Origin of Species*), such theories had a great popular vogue in the late 19th and early 20th centuries, when they were applied to the rivalries of the Great Powers and provided a pseudo-biological justification for POWER POLITICS, IMPERIALISM and war. Hitler picked up these ideas in Vienna before 1914 and made them a feature of NAZISM. See also EUGENICS. For further reading: M. Hawkins, *Social Darwinism in European and American Thought, 1860–1945* (1997). R.F.; A.L.C.B.

social democracy. A term whose history is at odds with its present meaning. In the 19th and early 20th centuries, the followers of Marx were 'social democrats', and Lenin's Bolsheviks (see BOLSHEVISM) were members of the Russian social democratic party (see MARXISM). After the split between REFORMIST and revolutionary socialists which began soon after Lenin's seizure of power in the Russian Revolution of October 1917, 'social democrats' were those who insisted that only the parliamentary road to SOCIALISM could achieve socialism without an excessive cost in violence, DICTATORSHIP and political suppression. Among the things that social democrats have insisted on is the value of independent TRADE UNIONS and the indispensability of civil rights (see CIVIL RIGHTS MOVEMENT). Today, social democrats are committed to the maintenance of the WELFARE STATE and a belief in the STATE's role in maintaining prosperity and achieving a more just society than the market alone would do, but have few or no theoretical or ideological commitments (see IDEOLOGY) beyond that. A.R.

social dividend. A tax system that guarantees a minimum income which is free of tax. The minimum income is paid in cash or as a tax credit. All other income is taxed. Thus, there is an income, the break-even income, at which the tax paid is equal to the minimum guaranteed income. Compared to a Negative Income Tax System (NITS), the tax rate below the break-even point is lower. This implies a higher break-even point and a wider distribution of the benefits of the system. This means that a social dividend system is more costly and requires higher tax rates above the break-even point. For further reading: M. J. Artis, *The UK Economy* (1986). J.P.

social drama. Phrase coined by the British social anthropologist Victor Turner (1920–83), who (beginning with his field-work experiences in East African villages, and later widening out and generalizing) analysed social situations, especially situations of conflict, as if they were plays, distinguishing four main phases which he described as the 'breach' of normal social relations; the 'crisis', or widening of the breach; 'redressive action'; and finally the phase of 'reintegration'. This idea was taken up by other anthropologists, by social historians, and finally (bringing the wheel full circle) by students of literature. The metaphor of the world as a stage goes back of course to the ancient Greeks, and it was given a somewhat different twist (comic rather than tragic) by the American sociologist Erving Goffman in his *Presentation of Self in Everyday Life* (1956), at much the same time that Turner was working out his ideas. For further reading: V. Turner, *Dramas, Fields and Metaphors* (1974). P.B.

social dynamics, see under SOCIAL STATICS.

social engineering. The planning of social change according to a blueprint, and the associated TECHNOLOGY of social design and manufacture. The basic idea is as old as Plato's Republic and broad enough to encompass party political manifestos, but the force of the metaphor in modern times derives from a belief in the power of science-based technological thinking to solve social problems. In this respect related terms are *social technology, social intervention, utopianism and* TECHNOCRACY. In its strongest sense the term connotes a belief in the human capacity to invent a future which is discontinuous with the past. In this sense related terms are GENETIC ENGINEERING and behavioural engineering, which is associated with the psychologist B. F. Skinner (1904–90) and explores the possibility of altering individual behaviour through manipulation of the environment, and EUGENICS, which raises in acute form the ethical problems inherent in any approach to social reform that sees it as a technological problem of product specification and design.

The term has also been embedded in a significant political debate related to the nature of historical change, but its usage in this context has been confusing. Sir Karl Popper (1902–94), e.g., in attacking both Plato's élitism and Marx's social physics as enemies of the OPEN SOCIETY, argues for piecemeal social engineering, a label he attaches to an evolutionary process of social experimentation that is essentially indeterminate, akin to his view of SCIENTIFIC METHOD (see POPPERIAN). But this usage conflicts with more common, and arguably more accurate, applications to PROBLEM-SOLVING approaches, like, e.g., normative TECHNOLOGICAL FORECASTING, whose feasibility rests upon closed or authoritarian values determination. Given this confusion, the term may be regarded as a floating resource in ideological discourse. For further reading: K. R. Popper, *The Poverty of Historicism* (1957). B.M.

social epistemology. An intellectual movement of broad cross-disciplinary provenance that attempts to reconstruct the problems of EPISTEMOLOGY once knowledge is regarded as intrinsically social. It is often seen as philosophical science policy or the normative wing of SCIENCE STUDIES. Originating in studies of academic knowledge production, social epistemology has begun to encompass knowledge in multicultural (see MULTICULTURALISM) and public settings, as well as the conversion of knowledge to information technology and INTELLECTUAL PROPERTY. Despite their many internal differences, social epistemologists agree on two points: (1) classical epistemology, philosophy of science and sociology of knowledge (see SCIENCE, PHILOSOPHY OF; KNOWLEDGE, SOCIOLOGY OF) have presupposed an idealized conception of scientific inquiry that is unsupported by the social history of scientific practices; (2) nevertheless, one still needs to articulate normatively appropriate ends and means for science, given science's status as the exemplar of RATIONALITY for society at large. The question for social epistemologists, then, is whether science's actual conduct is worthy of its exalted social status and what political implications follow from one's answer. Those who say 'yes' assume that science is on the right track and offer guidance on whom people should believe from among competing experts, whereas those who say 'no' address the more fundamental issue of determining the sort of knowledge that people need and the conditions under which it ought to be produced and distributed. For further reading: S. Fuller, *Science* (1997). S.F.

social ethic. Term used by W. H. Whyte in *The Organization Man* (1956) to denote 'that contemporary body of thought which makes morally legitimate the pressures of society against the individual. Its major propositions are three: a belief in the group as the source of creativity; a belief in "belongingness" as the ultimate need of the individual; and a belief in the application of science to achieve the belongingness.' Whyte stresses the paradox that though 'practical' in its use within modern corporate INSTITUTIONS, it is, in essence, a 'utopian faith'. See also OTHER-DIRECTION. S.J.G.

social fact. The term used, especially by Émile Durkheim (1858–1917), to make clear the distinctive subject-matter of SOCIOLOGY and to emphasize the psychological creativity of human society. It is not the case, Durkheim argues, that human association is 'sterile' – a mere AGGREGATION of a number of individuals whose mental characteristics already exist, in given, permanent form, before association takes place. On the contrary, association is a *creative* process, producing new experiences, and new levels of experience; without it, indeed, the human 'person' could not come to exist. Social facts are therefore a qualitatively distinct *level* of facts in nature, requiring careful analysis and investigation at this level, and therefore a new and appropriate science – sociology. This, of course, was the essential, initial statement of Auguste Comte, which Durkheim reiterated and emphasized. See also COLLECTIVE CONSCIOUSNESS; CULTURE; FOLKWAYS; SOCIAL STRUCTURE; SUBCULTURE. For further reading: A. Giddens, *Durkheim* (1978). R.F.

social geography. The systematic field of GEOGRAPHY that describes and explains spatial expressions of social phenomena. The roots of social geography lie in the discipline's long-standing human-environment tradition, with its focus on the interaction between societies and their HABITATS. In the late 19th and early 20th centuries, this field was dominated by debates among environmental determinists (see DETERMINISM) and their detractors, with a consensus emerging (around the work of American scholar Carl Sauer [1889–1975] and others) that people mould cultural landscapes from the natural landscape. By the middle of the century, social geography had become largely associated with POPULATION GEOGRAPHY. But the 1960s saw geography's quantitative revolution and the rise of social problems, particularly in large American cities (see CITY), which triggered a new research thrust closely affiliated with urban geography. Sophisticated studies in social area analysis soon appeared, and an increasing concern with policy and welfare issues paved the way towards the contemporary period in which social geography is interwoven with new movements in HUMANISTIC GEOGRAPHY (for examples see RADICAL GEOGRAPHY and FEMINIST GEOGRAPHY). Social geographers believe that social justice is spatial justice, and today many are important contributors to SOCIAL THEORY, critical analysis, and the other discourses that are shaping the frontiers of SOCIAL SCIENCE. For further reading: C. Hamnett (ed.), *Social Geography: A Reader* (1996). P.O.M.

social gospel movement. The attempt of many influential liberal Protestants (see LIBERALISM; PROTESTANTISM), especially in the USA from *c.* 1880 to 1930, to bring 'the Kingdom of God' closer by working for the improvement of society, usually along SOCIALIST and PACIFIST lines. The most influential theologian was Walter Rauschenbusch (1861–1918). The evolutionary optimism involved was later attacked by neo-orthodox thinkers (see NEO-ORTHODOXY) such as Reinhold Niebuhr (1892–1971). But this was not the end of the passionate concern of American Christians to improve and perfect society. For further reading: R. T. Handy (ed.), *The Social Gospel in America* (1966). D.L.E.

social history. A subject at one time left to amateur historians, defined as the history of everyday life, and studied mainly from literary sources. Since about 1950, however, the subject has undergone a revolution. It has become the history of social groups or CLASSES, and of changes in the SOCIAL STRUCTURE, carried out by professional historians or sociologists, using the methods of QUANTITATIVE HISTORY. This revolution has made the traditional term an embarrassment to some, but the alternatives suggested, 'sociological history', 'the history of society', 'societal history', and 'social structural history', have not become generally accepted. See also GENTRY CONTROVERSY; PAST AND PRESENT. P.B.

social intervention, see under SOCIAL ENGINEERING.

social learning. Term used by the American psychologist Albert Bandura as the basis of a psychological theory that emphasizes the role of cognitive (see COGNITIVE PSYCHOLOGY), vicarious and self-regulatory factors in human behaviour. While recognizing that people learn by direct experience, social learning theory stresses that they also learn, with fewer attendant hazards and burdens, by observing the example of others. Theories that portray behaviour as the product of external rewards and punishments alone are criticized as ignoring the part played by self-evaluation. Social learning theory acknowledges three ways in which REINFORCEMENT operates: people regulate their actions on the basis of consequences they experience directly, of those they see happening to others, and of those they create for themselves. Transitory experiences are coded into imaginal, verbal and other symbols for memory representation, and thus have lasting effects, since these internal representations of behaviour patterns and their probable consequences serve as guides for action on later occasions. Social learning theory stresses the reciprocal influence between people and the environment: behaviour is influenced by environmental contingencies, but the contingencies are partly of people's own making. For further reading: A. Bandura, *Social Learning Theory* (1977). A.B.

social market. A social market society is one in which a fundamentally CAPITALIST economy is supported by government provision of WELFARE and educational services which are intended to make it possible for every member of the society to participate fully in the advantages of the MARKET ECONOMY. The concept seems to have been first employed by the German politician Ludwig Erhard (1897–1977), and had some impact on the thinking of the British Social Democrats. A.R.

social mobility. The movement of individuals, families or groups from one social position to another which is usually designated higher or lower on some socially evaluative scale (see SOCIAL STRATIFICATION; STATUS). The idea that each person in a society should have an equal chance to rise, or gain a place commensurate with his talents, is a fruit, largely, of the modern egalitarian idea (see EGALITARIANISM). In modern INDUSTRIAL SOCIETY, social mobility is largely occupational mobility, and education is the chief means of access to a higher (i.e. more skilled) position – though family background and cultural advantages give the children of the upper and MIDDLE CLASSES a better start than children of the WORKING CLASS. The major change in modern society, however, is the status change upward in the entire slope of the occupational structure as the number of unskilled jobs decline under AUTOMATION and the number and proportion of white-collar and office employments expand in the post-industrial phase of society (see POST-INDUSTRIAL SOCIETY). For further reading: A. Heath, *Social Mobility* (1981). D.B.

social overheads. The costs imposed on the public purse by private agents, costs for which they do not necessarily have to pay unless the tax burden is suitably adjusted. The stock examples are the schools, roads, sewage facilities, etc., associated with urban and industrial development. S.BR.

social precedence, see under AGGRESSION.

social psychology. A branch of PSYCHOLOGY, usually defined as the scientific study of human social behaviour. The study as we know it is very much the product of the last 100 years. Drawing to some degree on older studies of mass hysteria (see NEUROSIS), crowd behaviour, panic phenomena and the supposed distinctive dispositions of the different social CLASSES, social psychology developed to a large degree out of McDougall's theory of instincts, Mead's pioneering work on ROLE-playing, and the sympathetic studies of the Freudians Erich Fromm and Karen Horney on the shaping importance of social institutions (see NEO-FREUDIAN).

In order to test its theories and hypotheses, social psychology endeavours to use methods of laboratory experimentation and of controlled research in 'natural' surroundings. Its theories often attempt to explain and systematize the complexities of human social behaviour in terms of wide-ranging generalizations about the individual psychological roots of various aspects of social interaction such as competition, co-operation, conformity, the functioning of small groups, the exercise of social influence, the development of social motives in the individual, relations between human groups, etc. Most of this work has been undertaken in the context of Western societies, but efforts at cross-cultural validation (see cross-cultural study) have also been made.

The need to formulate and empirically test its theories has often led social psychology to look for its data to the study of individual reactions rather than to characterizing the properties or reactions of larger social aggregates. Typical is its emphasis on the study of individual attitudes, their formation and change. Much has been gained in precision by this approach, but there is increasing dissatisfaction with some of its constraints. Social psychology is today in the process of change, characterized by a continuous search for new CONCEPTS and methods capable of bringing present individualistic ideas of man in society nearer to the social complexities of human life and to a more adequate analysis of man as both a creature and a creator of his society. In research methods, this is reflected in the growing influence of ETHOLOGY, and of other attempts to study behaviour in 'natural' settings. In the development of theory, there is much preoccupation with the study of human social communication and with the manner in which social behaviour is determined or affected by the conceptions about his society that each individual assimilates from the CULTURE. There is also increasing suspicion of the value of premature and often disappointing attempts to reduce the complexities of human social behaviour and experience to 'simpler' or 'elementary' laws of functioning.

Nowadays a social psychologist is someone who functions simultaneously as a 'man from Mars' and as a social anthropologist (see ANTHROPOLOGY), the former because he needs to achieve detachment from his material, and be aware of the social origins of his theoretical assumptions, the latter because he cannot hope to study human social conduct unless he relates it to the context of values, NORMS and social expectations by which social action is powerfully affected.

Social psychology's subject-matter lies in the area between the biological (see BIOLOGY) and the SOCIAL SCIENCES. Evolutionary, genetic and physiological perspectives (see EVOLUTION; GENETICSGENOMICS; PHYSIOLOGY) contribute to the understanding of how and why man became the kind of social animal he is; they also define his limitations, particularly in relation to the laws governing his development, both as a SPECIES and as an individual. But, in order to adapt, man has also created much of his ENVIRONMENT, not only social but also physical. He survived as a species because of his flexible ability to construct new modes of existence for himself. The understanding of these modes of adaptation requires a level of analysis that transcends the biological. Obviously, the range of social choices and actions open to individuals is dependent also upon individual psychological processes. In order to study the actual content of human social behaviour, therefore, social psychologists must look at the manner in which individuals perceive and conceptualize social and physical events, and at their motives, values and norms developed in reaction to these idiosyncratic views of the world.

While social psychology is one of the oldest of human preoccupations, its importance for our understanding of the human condition remains to be proved. It is at present widely used in application to studies of consumer habits, voting behaviour (see PSEPHOLOGY), worker morale, and RACE prejudice (see RACISM), and is an established feature of many industrial, political and military organizations. For further reading: M. Gold, *A New Outline of Social Psychology* (1997). H.TA.; R.P.

social realism. Socially concerned yet objectively presented works of REALIST art or literature of several different formal schools. To be distinguished from SOCIALIST REALISM. J.W.

social science. The term 'social science', appearing *c.* 1836, gradually replaced 'moral science' as the modern designation for ECONOMICS, SOCIOLOGY, ANTHROPOLOGY, PSYCHOLOGY, LINGUISTICS and politics. This new usage led to debates as to whether there was a single method for the natural and social sciences, whether social laws were possible, whether social explanations were causally individualistic or collective, and whether social science was value-neutral. Early critics of the idea of a social science thought it somehow inconsistent with freedom of the will (see FREE WILL) and the importance of values in social life.

The modern era has seen a compromise position emerge in which these sciences are thought to pursue causal explanations, but by a method of interpretation not found in the natural sciences. This compromise generates two further issues. First, can the vocabulary of individual beliefs and desires which requires the method of interpretation be eliminated from social explanation? BEHAVIOURISM, e.g., dismissed talk of inner mental states as pseudo-scientific.

The second issue concerns the possibility of social-scientific laws. Social-scientific laws seem too complex to some, while others consider them conceptually impossible. This stronger objection has been called 'anomalous monism' by American philosopher Donald Davidson. Anomalous monism allows that there is causal interaction between the mental and physical and natural-scientific laws, but no strict psychophysical laws. The reason for this limit is that the social or mental vocabulary necessarily involves concepts of RATIONALITY, consistency and coherence not found in any physical vocabulary.

A different response to the above issue is to reject the very idea of social science. If interpretation and explanation are incompatible, then all compromises are ill conceived. Such pessimism about any possible social science is now called POST-STRUCTURALISM. It treats the study of society as more akin to literary criticism than PHYSICS, and thus eschews both causal explanation and value-neutrality. For further reading: H. Settanni, *Five Primers in the Social Sciences* (1995). R.D.

social statics and **social dynamics.** The application to SOCIOLOGY of a distinction, valid for all sciences, which Auguste Comte (1798–1857) made between two types of method: *statics*, which analyses the distinctive nature of the subject-matter (in the case of sociology, the distinctive nature of social systems or societies), and *dynamics*, which applies this analysis to establishing testable knowledge about the varieties of the subject actually existing in the continuing processes of nature and history. A common fallacy is the belief that social statics (and certain schools of theory, such as FUNCTIONALISM) regard society in a static way, studying it at one particular point of time, whereas social dynamics studies societies 'on the move'. Neither Comte nor anyone else held that a human society could ever be *static*; indeed, Comte insisted that one of the distinctive features of societies was their essentially changing, cumulative, historical nature. R.F.

social stratification. The process that occurs when individual inequalities – of physique, strength, wealth, power, etc. – become systematic, are given positive and negative evaluation, and are organized into patterns that are recognized, if not accepted, by most members of a society. There are two general theories of stratification: the FUNCTIONALIST theory, derived from the work of Émile Durkheim and Talcott Parsons, in which every society necessarily grades its activities because some functions are valued more than others; and a contrary theory, derived from Rousseau, Proudhon and Marx, which argues that POWER, not functional necessity, is the basis of stratification. Max Weber accepted, in part, the MARXIST notion that stratification is a manifestation of unequal power in society, but argued that stratification exists along three different dimensions – economic, social and political. Some writers, deriving from the Saint-Simonian tradition, have argued that stratification may exist as a functional necessity, and create levels of command in a society based on technical competence, but these need not be converted into material advantage and into exploitative or power relations; this is the foundation for a theory of a MERITOCRACY. See also CLASS; SOCIAL MOBILITY. D.B.

social structure. The discernible framework, form, shape, pattern, of the interrelationships of men in a society. It is always an outcome both of deliberate purpose in specific activities and of the manifold unforeseen consequences of all activities, and it can be analysed into its major elements, e.g. its political, legal, military, religious, educational, and family organization. All these, however, are interconnected both by INSTITUTIONS (e.g. marriage, which links the family, religion, law, property relations, political authority, etc.) and by groups, within many of which the same individuals have varying functions, ROLES and STATUS. In any society, therefore, the total social structure can be broken down into the specific roles, and sets of roles, which individual persons have to fulfil. See also SUPERSTRUCTURE. For further reading: S. F. Nadel, *The Theory of Social Structure* (1965). R.F.

social studies. The wide variety of studies that concern themselves with urgent social problems (e.g. RACE, DRUGS, poverty), or with areas of social life (e.g. the development of transport, home-making, leisure activities, the mass media). Though supposedly resting on the foundations of the SOCIAL SCIENCES, social studies frequently fail to exercise scientific stringency. Indeed, they may even not attempt to do so, being concerned merely to make people aware of problems, of ways of investigating and discussing them, and of political policies which might be designed to solve them. In schools and colleges they may simply be elementary studies introducing children and young people to methods of analysing their own experience and the world in which they live.

Social studies also enter into courses for the training of social workers. This has led to a conflict of standards between them and the social sciences; but social workers are increasingly turning to social sciences for a more systematic study of the problems with which they are concerned. R.F.

social technology, see under SOCIAL ENGINEERING.

social theory. Used loosely, this term connotes all those areas of thought that concern men and women as social beings. Its more precise, modern use denotes what would more accurately be termed 'sociological theory'. In this usage social theory is to be distinguished (1) from SOCIAL SCIENCE, i.e. speculative and analytic ideas are distinguished from those statements that claim scientific, falsifiable status (see POPPERIAN); (2) from the social INSTITUTIONS or practices it seeks to explain; (3) from economic, political or psychological theory (see ECONOMICS; POLITICAL SCIENCE; PSYCHOLOGY). For further reading: R. Bernstein, *The Restructuring of Social and Political Theory* (1985). M.BA.

social town planning. TOWN PLANNING measures which incorporate a social dimension, particularly in relation to meeting the needs of minority groups, such as women, ethnic MINORITIES, the disabled and elderly, and the needs of those living in the INNER CITY, usually as part of wider equal opportunities policy. Town planning, and related ZONING activities, have been primarily concerned with physical, land use and layout issues, but by default they have often had social and economic ramifications. Many minority groups, WORKING-CLASS representatives, plus a variety of community interest groups, have long argued that planning is not neutral but that it predominantly meets the needs of affluent, young, male, white, middle class, car-driving individuals. Alternatively social planning may be seen as a means of social control through social engineering – ENVIRONMENTAL DETERMINISM. Also it may have connotations of state-led SOCIALIST planning as existed previously in parts of eastern Europe. C.G.

social welfare. In ECONOMICS, the WELFARE of society as a whole (see WELFARE ECONOMICS). Its measurement requires VALUE-JUDGEMENTS, and this raises problems. The welfare of an individual is often taken as the person's UTILITY. Social welfare is usually regarded as being a function of these utilities. Individuals may not make decisions in their own best interests, in which case utility and individual welfare are not the same. As measuring social welfare requires comparing the welfare of different individuals, it is difficult to see how an acceptable consensus can be reached about the relation between social and individual welfare. This negative view has led economists to attempt to distinguish between changes in ECONOMIC EFFICIENCY and changes in the distribution of welfare across individuals. By considering the former, economists have tried to avoid making value-judgements and have restricted their attention to criteria and statements which are value-free (see VALUE-FREEDOM). However, the use of value-judgements appears to be unavoidable and should be made explicitly. For example, the evaluation of NATIONAL INCOME, ECONOMIC GROWTH and different policies using COST BENEFIT ANALYSIS all imply or require value-judgements. Ultimately, the evaluation of social welfare not only relates to choice between alternative economic policies, but requires value-judgements about alternative social systems. For further reading: J. Bonner, *Politics, Economics and Welfare* (1986). J.P.

social whole. Generally, the larger social context within which a particular SOCIAL FACT requires to be seen before it can be sufficiently explained or understood. In sociological analysis, the CONCEPT operates at different levels. Thus, the full significance of a particular form of MARRIAGE can only be understood within its wider context of the family and KINSHIP system; but this in turn can only be understood within the wider context of the property relations, the religious doctrines and RITUAL, the political authority and WELFARE provisions, of the society as a whole. This 'whole society', again, may only be fully understood as part of a wider CULTURE AREA, or as having been fragmented from, or having separated itself from, a wider civilization (e.g. the European nations from medieval Christendom). See also SOCIAL STRUCTURE. R.F.

socialism. A word with a wide variety of meanings, the most common being a social system based on the common ownership of the means of production and distribution. Although the modern origins of socialism go back at least as far as Winstanley and the Diggers in the period of the English Civil War, the term first began to be widely used in the 1830s. It was the combined product of the Enlightenment, of the liberal and egalitarian principles of the French Revolution (see LIBERALISM; EGALITARIANISM), and the impact of industrialism. Although most early socialist thought was utopian (see UTOPIANISM) and of French inspiration, as in such thinkers as Fourier and Saint-Simon, it was the English Chartists who, in the 1830s and 1840s, created the first mass WORKING-CLASS movement to give expression to socialist ideas for DEMOCRACY, equality (see EQUALITY, PRINCIPLE OF) and COLLECTIVISM.

The ideas of Marx and Engels resulted in a more precise version of socialism which attempted to give a historical, MATERIALIST and scientific basis to the socialist project (see MARXISM). Although Marx was quite willing to refer to his ideas as socialist, the success of Lenin and the Bolsheviks (see BOLSHEVISM) in 1917 led to a contrast between COMMUNISM and socialism. In orthodox communist theory, socialism referred to a transitional stage between the proletarian revolution (see PROLETARIAT) and a communist society which still lay in the future. Outside the communist bloc, socialism became associated with the more REFORMIST tendencies of the social democratic parties (see SOCIAL DEMOCRACY).

As an historical phenomenon, therefore, the socialist movement has been essentially confined to the European LEFT. In European countries it has successfully pressed for the extension of universal suffrage, social reforms, improved working conditions, and a greater economic role for the state in controlling the market mechanism and the ravages of an unrestrained CAPITALISM. In the countries of Asia and Africa, socialist movements have been occupied with immediate problems of eradicating illiteracy, improving health standards, and promoting economic, mainly agrarian, development. The extent to which the former Soviet Union (see USSR, THE FORMER) and eastern Europe were ever properly described as socialist is a matter of continuing controversy. More generally it can be said that socialism is currently going through a period of reappraisal. Proponents of a movement originating in the optimistic, PROGRESSIVE climate of the 19th century now have to come to terms with the global scarcity of natural resources, the resistance of many societies to fundamental reform, and the very limited sources of actual socialist projects. Hence, e.g., in 1995 the British Labour Party, traditionally identified as a socialist party, removed from its constitution the commitment to a common ownership of means and productions. Nevertheless, the inability of pure capitalism to live up even to its own principles of liberty and equality should ensure the survival of socialist ideas at least for the foreseeable future. For further reading: M. Beaud, *Socialism in the Crucible of History* (1993). D.T.M.

***Socialist Courier*,** see under MENSHEVIKS.

socialist feminism. The development of a socialist (see SOCIALISM) movement in Europe in the 19th century is often identified with male figures such as Marx (see MARXISM), Engels and Jaurès. Yet from the earliest days of European socialism women involved in socialist movements contested men's definitions of socialism and argued for programmes and analyses which more adequately included the interests of women. The history of women in TRADE UNION and socialist movements is, as historians such as Sheila Rowbotham and Barbara Taylor have pointed out, often a history of a dual struggle: of opposition to entrenched privilege *per se* and of resistance to patriarchal (see PATRIARCHY) ideologies (see IDEOLOGY) which have marginalized the access of women to the public sphere and hence to a part in the transformation of social organization.

A central issue in the history of socialist feminism was the assertion, in Marx and Engels's *Origin of the Family, Private Property and the State* (1884), that the way forward for the emancipation of women lay in women's entry into paid labour. This crucially important idea defined the domestic policies of state socialist societies such as the Soviet Union (see USSR, THE FORMER) and the People's Republic of China. In order to enable women to take part in paid labour, the state provided nurseries and childcare facilities on a scale unknown in the West. Since 1989 much of this infrastructure has disappeared, but even before the disappearance of the Berlin Wall (see GERMAN REUNIFICATION) it had become apparent that women's entry to paid labour was no guarantee of political POWER, and in many ways perpetuated institutional misogyny. Despite the considerable theoretical contribution of women such as Emma Goldmann, Alexandra Kollontai and Rosa Luxemburg to the history of socialist thought, the part played by women in the formal politics of socialism has, until recently, been limited. The gradual shift in some Western societies towards women's fuller participation in socialist movements has occurred in response to the widespread recognition of informal constraints on women's participation in politics. For further reading: B. Taylor, *Eve and the New Jerusalem* (1983). M.S.E.

Socialist International, see INTERNATIONAL, THE.

socialist realism. In the former USSR, the official formula for the COMMUNIST Party's demands of the creative artist, whatever his medium. First proclaimed by Maxim Gorky and the politicians N. Bukharin and A. A. Zhdanov at the Soviet Writers' Congress of 1934, this recipe was never precisely defined, though its essence proved to consist in the harnessing of the late-19th-century REALIST techniques of art (Repin), fiction (Turgenev), and theatre (Stanislavsky) to the portrayal of exemplary Soviet characters (the 'positive hero') and a rosy future (the 'positive conclusion'). Socialist realism was, however, regarded as incompatible not only with any kind of pessimism but also with FORMALISM, COSMOPOLITANISM and other forms of DEGENERACY. While its practical application was modified after the heyday of STALINISM, so that formerly unacceptable innovators like Mayakovsky and Brecht could be posthumously covered by it, this doctrine remained a serious obstacle to the development of the Soviet arts, not least because of the vagueness of its relevance to music and ARCHITECTURE, where for many years it seemed to signify the use (respectively) of FOLK tunes and mock-classical ornamentation, as favoured by the Party leaders. Outside the USSR it was a great embarrassment to many communist parties, particularly the French, so that its interpretation and practical implementation varied widely from country to country.

Socialist realism is to be distinguished from SOCIAL REALISM. For further reading: T. Lahusen, *How Life Writes the Book* (1997). J.W.

socialization. In DEVELOPMENTAL PSYCHOLOGY, the early stages of induction of an infant or child into a CULTURE's values, rules and ways of operating. It is one of the major topics of CROSS-CULTURAL STUDIES. In the early work on socialization, major emphasis was placed on the control of motivation by systems of reward and punishment (see OPERANT CONDITIONING), with special reference to critical stress points in development: early bowel-training, control of AGGRESSION, the transition into adolescent sexuality (an emphasis attributable to FREUDIAN theory). More recent studies have been more concerned with the process whereby children learn underlying rules and properties of the culture, an approach partly influenced by the emergence in ANTHROPOLOGY of STRUCTURALISM, with its insistence upon the connected role patterns characterizing cultures. See also PSYCHOSEXUAL DEVELOPMENT. For further reading: P. H. Mussen (ed.), *Carmichael's Handbook of Child Psychology* (1983). J.S.B.

societal. A term which in current usage functions mostly as a pseudo-scientific and pompous variant of 'social'. Nevertheless, a case for retaining it can be made in view of the exceedingly wide range of meaning of 'social', as in 'social work', 'social event', 'social inadequacy', and 'social revolution'. 'Societal' could be defined as a term which refers to the attributes of society as a whole; its structure or the changes therein. 'Social' would remain a wider term which not only includes 'societal' but can also be applied to interpersonal relations as well as to attributes or acts of an individual which affect other human beings. S.A.

societal history, see SOCIAL HISTORY.

sociobiology. Term created by American biologist E. O. Wilson in 1975. It denotes a theory based upon evolutionary BIOLOGY (see EVOLUTION) which attempts to explain human behaviour in biological terms. Evolutionary selection (see NATURAL SELECTION) is held to lead to behaviour which maximizes the chance of humans passing on their GENES through breeding. It is particularly controversial in explaining human sexual behaviour (see SEXUALITY) and differences in the behaviour of men and women. Some sociobiologists argue that men are bound to tend towards promiscuity because they have the potential to father innumerable children (see MOTHERING). Women, on the other hand, invest much greater effort in producing each offspring and can give birth to only a limited number of children. Women therefore tend to be 'coy' and hold back from SEX until they can mate with the most genetically (see GENETICS/GENOMICS) well-endowed man they can find. Altruistic (see ALTRUISM) behaviour towards kin (see KINSHIP) is explained in terms of protecting those who share genetic characteristics, although other forms of altruism are harder to explain. Sociobiologists also have problems providing convincing explanations for HOMOSEXUALITY and celibacy. Sociobiology has been fiercely criticized by sociologists, anthropologists (see ANTHROPOLOGY) and feminists (see FEMINISM), all of whom argue that human behaviour varies considerably between CULTURES and cannot be reduced to biological DETERMINISM. Feminists see sociobiology as an ideological (see IDEOLOGY) justification for the continuation of PATRIARCHY. Some recent versions of sociobiology pay more attention to cultural influences on human behaviour, but continue to give primary importance to biological influences. For further reading: S. Rose *et al*, *Not in Our Genes* (1984); E. O. Wilson, *Sociobiology: The Abridged Edition* (1980). M.D.H.

sociogram. A presentation in diagrammatic form of the relations among members of a social group. Although originating in the eclectic body of doctrine known as SOCIOMETRY, it is frequently employed without reference to the tenets of that creed. The credibility and informativeness of a sociogram greatly depend on the skill of its author. K.H.

sociolinguistics. A branch of LINGUISTICS that studies the relationship between language and society, e.g. the linguistic identity of social groups, the patterns of national language use. There is some overlap in subject-matter between this branch and

ANTHROPOLOGICAL LINGUISTICS. See also DIALECTOLOGY. For further reading: P. Trudgill, *Sociolinguistics* (1984). D.C.

sociological jurisprudence. An approach to the study of the law which starts from the conviction that no statutes or codes, however detailed, can relieve the courts of the task of choosing between conflicting social interests and considering the weight of different values recognized by the community. Jurists impressed by these facts, e.g. the American jurist Roscoe Pound (1870–1964), have urged the need for a sociological jurisprudence drawing upon all the SOCIAL SCIENCES to provide the courts with an analysis and classification of the various interests which they are called upon to adjust and of the different values which influence the law's development, and a realistic account of the legal system, including the judicial process itself. H.L.A.H.

sociological theory. Today such founders of SOCIOLOGY as Marx, Weber and Durkheim are regarded as 'theorists', though they would be the first to deny the label (see MARXISM). The much-vaunted 'renaissance' in sociological theory refers to the fact that theoretical concerns have become autonomous from empirical ones (see EMPIRICISM) to such an extent that 'theory development' in sociology more often refers to the latest creative combination of the discipline's founding ideas than the elaboration of hypotheses that are testable on some domain of phenomena. This tendency is traceable to Talcott Parsons's *The Structure of Social Action* (1937), though its more immediate causes lie in the collapse of the WELFARE STATE, which had funded much of the original empirical research in sociology. Consequently, sociological theory is now fostered primarily by the textbook industry. Nevertheless, the result has not been all bad. The field provides significant export product for HUMANISTS and social scientists seeking what they hoped, but failed, to find in contemporary PHILOSOPHY: an overarching framework and some 'sensitizing concepts' that can be applied in a variety of interpretive contexts. Because most of these concepts (ANOMIE and BUREAUCRACY are good examples) constitute persuasive definitions of the slice of social life they purport to capture, theoretical discourse can easily reveal sociologists to be either 'priests' or 'prophets', i.e. reinforcers or reformers, of their own societies. In this context, 'social theory' is increasingly the preferred term, as it includes FEMINIST and cultural studies scholars who perform a similar function, though they may not have been formally trained in sociology. For further reading: B. Turner (ed.), *The Blackwell Companion to Social Theory* (1996). S.F.

sociology. The study of societies: both the observation and description of social phenomena, and the articulation and application to these phenomena of a coherent conceptual scheme. In so far as there are several competing schemes, sociology is less fully a discipline than, say, ECONOMICS (with its general EQUILIBRIUM theory), and needs to be considered historically, by reference to the three different streams which one can identify in the rise of modern sociology:

(1) Curiosity about how a society hangs together. The major impulse here is NEWTONIAN MECHANICS, which inspired many efforts (e.g. Malebranche, Berkeley) to create an analogous 'social physics' that would account for, e.g., the distribution of human populations on the basis of some single principle, or (Montesquieu) explain the variations between societies and peoples by reference to climate, soil, numbers, or some combination of these physical attributes. Rousseau contrasted the 'state of nature' with society, and postulated a SOCIAL CONTRACT in which the wills of all are fused into a single personality, the community. Finally, the French Revolution suggested to de Maistre and Bonald the role of common faiths or MYTHS in holding a society together.

(2) A theory of social EVOLUTION which derives either from the Enlightenment belief in progress as developed by Auguste Comte, from the immanent development of consciousness or man's material powers (Hegel and Marx), or from SOCIAL DARWINISM (Herbert Spencer). These three independent skeins of thought together gave a powerful impetus to the idea of SOCIETAL change and a progressive direction of history.

(3) A curiosity about the actual facts of social life which became translated into systematic empirical inquiry. Notable examples are Frédéric Le Play's *Les Ouvriers européens* (2nd ed., 6 vols, 1877–99), the

famous 'blue books' which Marx and Engels used to document their statements about the English WORKING CLASS, and Booth's *Labour and Life of the People in London* (9 vols, 1892–97) with its quantitative data and case studies.

Most of the concerns and problems of contemporary sociology, if not the conceptual structures as well, derive in large measure from four men:

(a) For Karl Marx (1818–83; see MARXISM), all SOCIAL STRUCTURE was CLASS structure, and the history of all societies was the history of class struggles. In his fundamental METHODOLOGY, Marx argued that social existence determines CONSCIOUSNESS, and that IDEOLOGY is merely a SUPERSTRUCTURE, economic relations being the substructure. (See BOURGEOIS; PROLETARIAT.)

(b) Herbert Spencer (1820–1903) saw society in organismic terms and aimed to construct a social MORPHOLOGY of societies in terms of their structure and function. Sociology's fields were the family, political organization, ecclesiastical structures, the system of restraints (i.e. social control), and industry or work; its task was 'to give an account of [how] successive generations of units are produced, reared, and fitted for cooperation'.

(c) For Émile Durkheim (1858–1917), the major focus of sociology was social solidarity, or social cohesion: society consisted of a 'collective conscience', a moral force, at the centre of which was a core of values or beliefs that was considered sacred. (Society is thus the source of RELIGION.) Durkheim saw social change in terms of the breakdown of 'segmentation', i.e. the replacement of isolated social structures by complex and interdependent modern society, with its competition, specialization, and structural differentiation.

(d) For Max Weber (1864–1920; see WEBERIAN) the focus of sociology was on types of action, of which economics and law were the MODELS of rational action, and religion of non-rational action. His encyclopedic work, based on the COMPARATIVE METHOD, covered the great religious systems of the world, the studies of large bureaucratic systems, and the interrelations of economics, law and society. Much of it is definitional, and Weber was concerned to identify the different kinds of authority (traditional, charismatic – see CHARISMA – and rational), the different kinds of POWER (*Macht* or force and *Herrschaft* or coordinated domination), the evolution of BUREAUCRACY (patriarchal – see PATRIARCHY – patrimonial and legal-rational), and the different kinds of rational conduct. He also aimed to unfold the complex process by which rationality, in its various forms, developed in the West rather than other CULTURES. Modern CAPITALISM was defined on the basis of a rationalizing spirit and the creation of large rationalized organizations, and capitalism and SOCIALISM were two variants of a larger, more inclusive entity, bureaucratic society.

Spencer, Durkheim, Weber, and Ferdinand Tönnies (1855–1936) all conceptualized social change in terms of contrasting modal types of societies (roughly speaking, traditional and modern), with sufficient overlap to allow for an assimilation of the terms to one another. In the one kind of society, relations were personal, communal, primary, with strong similarity of attitudes, and in orientation to the past. In the other, relations were impersonal, bureaucratic, differentiated, open and mobile, and men looked to the future. Whereas Marx placed his sequence of societies – FEUDAL, capitalist and socialist – completely within a historical frame, the implicit intention of the other four was to use these historical types as building blocks for the ahistorical analysis of different kinds of social relations in any society.

The most comprehensive effort to use sociological concepts purely as analytical elements, outside historical frameworks, has been made by the American sociologist Talcott Parsons (see PARSONIAN; PATTERN VARIABLES). In the period after World War II Parsons was the dominant figure in American and indeed Western sociology; more recently there has been a reaction against his schemes as being too abstract and a return to historical categories and problems of social change and social conflict.

Among the key *unit-ideas* of sociology, American sociologist Robert Nisbet listed COMMUNITY, authority, STATUS, the sacred, and ALIENATION. To the extent, however, that sociology becomes a discipline, it has to achieve this status through the articulation of a coherent set of interrelated CONCEPTS which can be applied to phenomena and codified as theories, or through the construction of simplifying models which facilitate EXPLANATION. Unlike economics, sociology has no systematic theories which are formalized in mathematical terms. There are, instead, a number of different kinds of models: the *structure-function* model (see STRUCTURAL-FUNCTIONAL THEORY), associated with the work of Talcott Parsons and Robert Merton; EXCHANGE MODELS, associated with George Homans and Peter Blau; *conflict models* (see CONFLICT THEORY); *evolutionary models* (see EVOLUTION; TECHNOLOGY); *ecological models* (see ECOLOGY); and a growing number of *mathematical models*, which seek to formalize the relations or VARIABLES which are stated in the other models. Finally, one can look at sociology not as a scientific discipline, defined by its concepts and methods, but, in a view derived from the humanities, as a mode of consciousness, as a way of observing the subtle and complex ways in which men interact with one another, and of reporting these interactions in their complexity rather than simplifying them as a science necessarily does.

A survey, necessarily brief, cannot take into account the thousands of detailed empirical studies which seek to relate social phenomena (e.g. social class to occupation, crime to migration, family roles to value changes) in systematic inquiry.

As the 20th century draws to a close, the integrity of sociology's domain of inquiry has been increasingly called into question from, so to speak, 'above' and 'below'. From above, WORLD SYSTEMS theory has challenged the idea that societies can be studied in isolation from the larger global processes of capitalism. From below, ETHNOMETHODOLOGY has questioned sociology's ability to identify the unique normative structure of a society, given the often contradictory interpretations that its members impose on their actions. The ultimate source of these challenges is not difficult to discern. Although Weber equated sociology with social science in general, the field has usually followed Durkheim in identifying society with the NATION-STATE.

Unlike introductory textbooks in, e.g., economics or psychology, those in sociology exhibit significant cross-national differences. Moreover, the discourses surrounding such sociological expressions as 'social problems', 'social system' and 'social order' would make little sense if one did not presuppose the nation-state as the unit of analysis. Not surprisingly, empirical sociological research has been most amply funded in the name of the WELFARE STATE, and so it is not unreasonable to suppose that sociology's disciplinary fortunes are tied to the existence of a superindividual agent defined by its responsibility for a geographically delimited population. In that case, the simultaneous emergence of superstates like the EUROPEAN UNION (EU) and devolved regional identities like Scotland and Catalonia may mean that in the 21st century 'sociology' comes to be seen as an atavism, namely the academic ideology corresponding to 19th-century European NATIONALISM. For further reading: I. McIntosh (ed.), *Classical Sociological Theory: A Reader* (1997); I. Wallerstein (ed.), *Open the Social Sciences* (1996). D.B.; S.F.

sociology of development. A branch of the general study of the development of non-industrial or industrializing societies. It shares with MODERNIZATION *theory* a concern with values and INSTITUTIONS going beyond the purely economic, although it accepts that economic changes are at the core of the development process. The early SOCIOLOGY of development tended to assume too readily that development in the THIRD WORLD would follow the pattern of earlier Western development. The process of INDUSTRIALIZATION was taken to be largely a neutral, technical matter, and on the whole beneficial. The more recent view, mainly under MARXIST influence, has been that non-Western development takes place largely in the shadow of Western societies, and under their direction and control. It has emphasized that third world societies have to some extent been 'de-developed' or underdeveloped (see UNDERDEVELOPMENT) in the interests of Western economies, so that, e.g., from being exporters of food, as many traditionally were, they have been converted into net importers. A related perception is that many of the development and aid programmes offered by Western governments, or by such agencies as the World Bank (see BRETTON WOODS) under Western control, have Western assumptions built into them that are not necessarily appropriate to the societies in question, and which work ultimately to the advantage of the West. Overall the sociology of development has been concerned to stress the continuing dependence of non-Western societies on those of the West, despite the attainment in most cases of formal political independence. (See also DEVELOPMENT ECONOMICS.) For further reading: H. Bernstein (ed.), *Underdevelopment and Development* (1976). K.K.

sociology of education, see under CULTURAL DEPRIVATION.

sociology of knowledge, see KNOWLEDGE, SOCIOLOGY OF.

sociology of religion, see RELIGION, SOCIOLOGY OF.

sociology of science, see SCIENCE, SOCIOLOGY OF.

sociometry. The attempt to analyse interpersonal relations in such a way that the results can be plotted in diagrammatic form, on a SOCIOGRAM. Replies to a questionnaire about individual friendship and leadership choices are plotted by means of connecting lines to indicate which members of a particular social group are the effective leaders, the isolates, or the popular 'stars'. This approach to small-group social relations formed part of the idiosyncratic approach to social life adopted by its founder, Jacob Moreno (1892–1974). Although Moreno hoped that his technique would have very wide applicability, it is now seen as merely one of the available methods of obtaining popularity or leadership ratings from members of a social group. For further reading: W. E. Saris and I. N. Gallhofer (eds), *Sociometric Research* (1988). M.BA.

soft money. Following WATERGATE, which unearthed evidence of illegal campaign donations, the US Congress adopted laws to reform the methods by which money was raised for political campaigns. What the reforms ultimately produced was a system that lawyers and campaign specialists proved brilliant at exploiting, especially when it came to soft money. This is the term for unregulated cash from unions, corporations and other special INTEREST GROUPS that is collected by party committees, laundered, then spent on campaign direct mail, TV and radio advertising, and other tools – thus evading regular donation limits. In recent years, Republicans and Democrats have collected tens of millions in soft-money cash. One of the most famous examples came in 1994, when Amway (a home-products sales company whose name is a take-off of the phrase 'the American way') gave $2.5 million in a single donation to the Republican National Committee just weeks before Republicans gained control of the US Congress. President Clinton proved a genius at raising soft money, so much so that his second term was enmeshed in a scandal over his fund-raising methods before the 1996 election. R.K.H.

soft X-rays, see under X-RAY ASTRONOMY.

***soie moirée*,** see under MOIRÉ effect.

soil erosion. The partial or complete removal of the soil of farmland by the action of running water or wind. Rain collecting as surface water can flow down sloping land as a sheet, removing the fertile top soil, or it can concentrate in channels to cut deep gullies. In regions of low rainfall soils are liable to dry to an incohesive state. Strong winds which sweep the coarse soil particles along the surface are capable of carrying the finest dust up into the atmosphere to be deposited hundreds of miles away (see DUST-BOWL).

The basic cause of soil erosion is the unavoidable removal, during harvesting, of much of the vegetative cover, and the consequent exposure of bare soil; overgrazing of grassland by stock can also reduce the plant cover to a point where soil erosion is inevitable. Vegetation protects the soil from the impact of raindrops which break down soil aggregates into smaller and therefore more easily removable individual particles. It also combats wind erosion by reducing wind velocity and by trapping moving soil. J.L.M.L.

soil science (or **agrology).** The study of the soil, embracing PEDOLOGY and also *edaphology*, i.e. the study of the soil as the natural medium in which plants grow. The object of soil science is the utilitarian one of improving plant production through a better understanding of plant/soil relationships. The science is concerned therefore with investigating the reasons for the varying fertility of soils so as to conserve and improve the productivity of land. J.L.M.L.

solar system. Collection of astronomical objects bound to the sun by its gravitational attractive force. It includes the nine known planets (Mercury, Venus, Earth, Mars, Jupiter, Saturn, Uranus, Neptune and Pluto) and a large number of moons (or satellites) of those planets, a large belt of asteroids (sometimes called minor planets or planetoids) lying between the orbits of Mars and Jupiter, numerous comets, meteoroids and rocks. There are only about 200 asteroids larger than 100 km in diameter, but probably tens of thousands smaller than 1 km. These bodies orbit around the sun, and all except the comets orbit in the same direction in trajectories lying in the same plane. Mercury, Venus, Mars and Earth are called inner planets, the others outer planets. The solar system moves as a whole around the centre of the Milky Way GALAXY in a circular orbit at a speed of about 250 km per second.

The astronomical unit (abbreviated AU) is the average distance from the earth to the sun, 149,597,870 km. The planets within the solar system extend to about 50 AU from the sun, but the smaller bodies can move more than 100,000 AU from it. The age of the solar system can be estimated from the age of its oldest constituents. Stony meteorites (carbonaceous chondrites) are known to be as old as 4.6 billion years. There have been various theories for the origin of the solar system: the vortex theory of Descartes (1644), the tidal theory of Buffon (1785), the nebular theory of Kant (1755) and of Laplace (1796). The favoured modern theory is the accumulation theory, in which small planetesimals collide with each other and coalesce, eventually growing to the size of planets. In recent years astronomers have discovered a number of large planetary bodies around other nearby stars. The detection technique is only sensitive enough to see sizable planets, like Jupiter, but the detections show us that planet formation is probably a common process in the universe, and closely linked to the sequence of events that gives rise to stars. For further reading: D. Goldsmith, *Worlds Unnumbered: the search for extrasolar planets* (1997). J.D.B.

solid-state device. In electronic circuits, a unit consisting principally of a piece of semiconducting material connected to electrodes so that the element may be used to control the flow of current. Such devices include TRANSISTORS and THYRISTORS. Among their advantages over electronic and THERMIONIC valves is that they require no heating element. See also SEMICONDUCTOR; SOLID-STATE PHYSICS. E.R.L.

solid-state physics. A branch of PHYSICS whose intense development in recent decades has been stimulated by the demands of TECHNOLOGY and by the understanding of solids made possible by QUANTUM MECHANICS. There are two main parts to the subject:

(1) The study of the crystal LATTICE on which the ATOMS are arranged: DEFECTS in the regularity of this lattice (especially DISLOCATIONS) are responsible for the brittleness, ductility, hardness, etc., of solids, while the random vibrations of atoms about the lattice positions (see PHONON) determine how well solids conduct heat or electricity.

(2) The study of the ELECTRONS in solids: instead of the ENERGY LEVELS characteristic of ATOMIC PHYSICS, the electron states are grouped into 'energy bands', separated by 'energy gaps'. Solids whose most energetic electrons lie at the top of a band are *insulators*, except when the next energy gap is very narrow, in which case the solid is a SEMICONDUCTOR. If the electrons only half fill a band, the solid is a *metal* which conducts electricity to a degree determined by lattice vibrations (see also SUPERCONDUCTIVITY).

In the hi-fi industry, the phrase 'solid state' is used honorifically to denote any apparatus containing TRANSISTORS. For further reading: C. Kittel, *Introduction to Solid State Physics* (1996). M.V.B.

Solidarity. The name of the federation of independent TRADE UNIONS set up in Poland in August 1980 which developed into a mass movement for the reform of the political system. Led by Lech Walesa, an unemployed electrician, and enjoying the support of the Roman Catholic Church (see CATHOLICISM), its membership grew to 10 million, in addition to the 2½ million who joined Rural Solidarity. Its criticism of existing political and economic arrangements became more radical, and at its conference in 1981 it called for the establishment of a 'self-managed republic', an idea with syndicalist connotations which directly challenged the COMMUNIST government. As a result, in December 1981 martial law was imposed by General Wojciech Jaruzelski and Solidarity was driven underground. However, renewed social unrest in 1988 forced the government to legalize Solidarity again, in April 1989, and after success in the free elections held in June, it became part of a coalition government. In the 1990s, its prominence diminished, owing partly to the proliferation of other political parties in Poland. For further reading: A. M. Cirtautas, *The Polish Solidarity Movement* (1996). D.PR.

solipsism. The theory that nothing really exists but me and my mental states. Not surprisingly, philosophers are more frequently accused of being solipsists than ready to admit to being of that opinion. If the ultimate source of all factual knowledge is taken to be introspection or self-awareness, and if immediate experience is held to be the only thing that is directly known, solipsism is a consequence hard to avoid. The usual recourse for doing so, among philosophers committed to some version of the SENSE-DATUM theory, is the causal argument from the involuntary character of sense-experience proper, as contrasted with images. A taint of solipsism, even if it is dismissed as 'methodological' (see METHODOLOGY), attaches to the alternative, phenomenalist (see PHENOMENALISM), way of reconciling the existence of an external world with the sense-datum theory. A.Q.

soliton. A type of wave which can propagate in a non-linear system or medium without ENERGY loss. An everyday example of a soliton is the sharp bow wave from a boat. This is able to maintain its shape and travel a considerable distance before it dies away. Solitons have the property that they are able to pass through one another and then reform without distortion, and hence they can be used to represent various types of PARTICLE. H.M.R.

soma. Name used (1) by August Weismann (1834–1914) for the 'ordinary' parts of the body in contrast to the GERM PLASM; (2) by Aldous Huxley for a harmless but generally elevating DRUG much used by the inhabitants of his BRAVE NEW WORLD (1932). P.M.

somatotonia, see under PERSONALITY TYPES.

***Somocismo*,** see under NICARAGUA; SANDINISTA.

sonar (SOund NAvigation Ranging; also called *echo sounding*). A technique whereby short pulses of *ultrasound* are emitted under water, and the time delay and nature of any echoes are interpreted to yield information about the presence and location of shoals of fish, submarines, the seabed, etc. Sonar was developed because radio waves cannot be transmitted through water, so that RADAR cannot be used. M.V.B.

sorcery. Refers to a technique employed to attain certain aims, based on the principles of MAGIC. Unlike WITCHCRAFT, which is thought to be involuntary or unconscious (a person may be a witch without knowing it), sorcery is conscious and intentional. A sorcerer deliberately employs spells and physical materials to bring about results. The status of sorcery, however, is morally ambiguous: it may be socially beneficial or harmful.

All individuals may use sorcery. They have access to the means, but their STATUS and the purpose to which it is directed define whether sorcery is being used to legitimate or subvert the social order. Sorcery may be used by persons in recognized positions of authority to bring benefits to society (to drive out evil and threatening forces). These same individuals, if they use sorcery for their own ends, will be acting illegitimately as evil sorcerers. Sorcery as a technique may be employed by those without power to challenge or lay claim to established and legitimate positions of authority (see RITUAL). For further reading: L. Holy and M. Stuchlik, *The Structure of Folk Models* (1981). A.G.

sororal polygyny, see under POLYGYNY.

soul. Part musical style, part social attitude, soul became the dominant force in BLACK music in the 1960s. More positive in outlook and more public than the BLUES, its close antecedent is gospel music, the traditional voice of the black community, with its spirit of passionate freedom transferred from the church to the disco. Soul emerged as a force at the same time as that community was declaring its rightful identity in American life: in one of his biggest hits, soul's biggest star, James Brown, exhorted his brothers and sisters to 'say it loud, I'm black and I'm proud'. As a musical genre it was and is urban, aggressive, ecstatic, making equal use of high energy and high tech. The skills of recording engineers and producers (like Motown's Barry Gordy) are as formidable and necessary as those of the performers, and the result is as smooth, polished, potent as a racing car. If the simple individuality of the blues has been lost, many blacks regard the older form as 'slave time' music anyway, with associations better forgotten. For them, soul represents the authentic voice of contemporary black aspiration and deserves all its commercial success. For further reading: P. Garland, *The Sound of Soul* (1969). GE.S.

sound-law. In PHILOLOGY, a term referring to a hypothetical phonetic principle governing regular changes in sounds at different periods in a language's history. Such a hypothetical principle is derived from the analysis of uniform sets of correspondences operating between the sounds at these different periods. D.C.

source criticism, see under HIGHER CRITICISM.

sovereignty. Literally, the possession of ultimate legal authority; a STATE is sovereign when its rulers owe allegiance to no superior power and are themselves supreme within the local legal order; an individual may be said to be 'sovereign over himself' when he need ask permission of no one else to do as he chooses in a given area. The interest of the CONCEPT lies in the theoretical problems it produces; the US, e.g., is plainly a sovereign state, but commentators have never agreed where sovereignty is located within the US – the US Supreme Court (see SUPREME COURT OF THE UNITED STATES) can veto Congressional legislation if it is unconstitutional, but Congress and the states can alter the constitution. No one body possesses supreme authority in all areas – does the US possess a sovereign, then? For further reading: B. de Jouvenel, *Sovereignty* (1957). A.R.

Soviets. Originally workers' councils which first emerged in Russia during the 1905 revolution. In 1917 they appeared again as Soviets of Workers' and Soldiers' Deputies. After General Kornilov's attempt to halt the Revolution (September 1917), many important Soviets switched allegiance and transformed a MENSHEVIK into a Bolshevik majority (see BOLSHEVISM). The Petrograd Soviet, led by Trotsky, established a Military Revolutionary Committee which became an instrument for the Bolshevik seizure of power under the slogan 'All Power to the Soviets'. Subsequently they lost their autonomy, becoming the COMMUNIST Party's 'transmission belts to the masses' and eventually the principal INSTITUTIONS in the formal structure of power. For further reading: J. Hough and M. Fainsod, *How the Soviet Union Is Governed* (1979). L.L.

sovkhoz, see under COLLECTIVIZATION.

Soweto, see under BLACK CONSCIOUSNESS.

space.

(1) In meteorology and ASTRONOMY, space is considered to be the region lying beyond the limit of the earth's atmosphere. M.L.

(2) In the arts, space has become an increasingly important concept with the development of ABSTRACT ART, notably as rationalized by the CONSTRUCTIVISTS. Among the term's uses and abuses are (a) the space-stage, or *Raumbühne*, of Friedrich Kiesler and Karl Heinz Martin in the 1920s; (b) the 'spatio-dynamism' of Nicolas Schöffer's kinetic works (see KINETIC ART); (c) the 'spazialismo' manifesto of the Movimento Spaziale (Milan, 1954); (d) the French 'Espace' movement of 1951; and (e) the poetic 'spatialism' of Pierre Garnier, a freer form of CONCRETE POETRY. J.W.

(3) GEOGRAPHY can be described as the study of how events and phenomena are distributed and linked together across space. Geography before the 1960s was principally concerned with the uniqueness of peoples in specific PLACES, REGIONS and ENVIRONMENTS, and sought to produce regional geo-

graphies. With the rise of geography as a SPATIAL SCIENCE, space came to the fore as the prime organizing CONCEPT. It began to be thought that all geographical distributions, irrespective of their time and place, were governed by – and therefore could be 'explained' in terms of – universal laws of spatial organization and human spatial behaviour, and this introduced an 'absolute' view of space as a distinctive entity possessing its own causal powers (see CAUSALITY). This view has been attacked for its 'spatial fetishism', but that revision is itself under attack for downplaying the role of space. For further reading: R. D. Sack, *Conceptions of Space in Social Thought* (1980). C.P.

space perception. The process in vision whereby we locate the positions, sizes and distances of objects in external space. Problems arise because any size of image in an eye – a retinal image – may be given by a small near object or by a correspondingly larger and more distant object. So the size of retinal images is not sufficient to determine how large or how distant an object is, or appears. The two eyes work together to give *stereoscopic* depth; but this does not function for distant objects, because the 'base line' given by the eye separation is too short, only 2½ inches. The visual world seems to be scaled for size and distance by acceptance of typical features, such as perspective convergence and texture gradients, present in the retinal image as 'clues' to size and distance. This implies that the brain must carry out quite complicated computations to estimate scale. When the available 'clues' are not typical they may mislead PERCEPTION, to produce distortions of visual space, such as some of the well-known visual illusions in perspective drawings. See also GESTALT; VISUAL CLIFF. R.L.G.

space-stage, see under SPACE (2).

space-time. A mathematical CONSTRUCT, representing the arena of events. In NEWTONIAN MECHANICS, the three dimensions of space and the FOURTH DIMENSION of time can be clearly separated; this means that the distance separating two events, and the time interval between them, are independent of the motion of the FRAME OF REFERENCE from which they are studied.

But according to RELATIVITY this absolute separation between space and time cannot be made; *both* the time and the distance between events will vary with the motion of the observer. The only 'absolute' quantity, which can truly be said to belong to the events themselves independently of any observer, is the so-called 'interval', a mathematical analogue of distance in four-dimensional space-time. M.V.B.

space-time foam, see under PLANCK TIMEERA.

spam; spamming, see under E-MAIL.

span of control, see under MANAGEMENT STUDIES.

Spartacists. Anglicization of the *Spartakusbund*, a LEFT-wing revolutionary splinter group (named after the leader of the Roman slaves' revolt of 73–71 BC; see REVOLUTION) which broke away from the German social democratic movement (see SOCIAL DEMOCRACY) in 1917 under the leadership of Rosa Luxemburg and Karl Liebknecht. The Spartacists attacked the continuation of the war, supported the Bolshevik revolution in Russia (see BOLSHEVISM), and called for the overthrow of the government by direct action and a SOCIALIST revolution in Germany to be carried out by setting up workers' and soldiers' SOVIETS. In the period of revolutionary disorder that followed the abdication of the Kaiser (9 November 1918), the Spartacists (who reconstituted themselves as the Communist Party of Germany on 30 December) led a series of mass demonstrations against the compromise policy of Ebert's republican government, and in January 1919 occupied a number of public buildings and newspaper offices in Berlin. They were driven out by force and their two leaders shot by army officers. The murder of Liebknecht and Luxemburg ensured them a place in COMMUNIST hagiography which criticism of Lenin's tactics and their dislike of large-scale organization and party discipline would certainly have denied them had they lived. For further reading: S. Bronner, *Rosa Luxemburg: A Revolutionary for Our Times* (1997). D.C.W.

***Spartakusbund*,** see under SPARTACISTS.

sparticle, see under SUPERSYMMETRY.

spatial diffusion, see under DIFFUSION (3).

spatial music. There are quite a few instances in the history of music of composers taking an interest in the spatial placing of the performers in their music (e.g. Wagner, Ives), but it is only in the last 40 years that an intense interest in this aspect of music has arisen. The main catalyst for this enthusiasm is undoubtedly the use in ELECTRONIC MUSIC of multiple speaker systems which give the composer the ability to place sounds in specific locations around and among the audience, and even to move sounds around in various ways during a performance. Specific architectural environments have even been built to house such works. The use of space has spread to instrumental music such as Stockhausen's 'Gruppen' which uses three orchestras situated around the audience. B.CO.

spatial science. A perspective that surfaced in human GEOGRAPHY during the 1960s, and which attempted to replace the discipline's older focus on the uniqueness of particular peoples and PLACES – the hallmark of *regional geography* – with a desire to discover the universal laws of spatial organization supposedly governing how human beings everywhere and at every time distribute their settlements, farms, factories, shops, roads and other productions across the physical landscape. In addition, this perspective embraced a concern to discover the universal laws of *spatial behaviour* supposedly governing how human beings everywhere and at every time organize their use of these myriad spatial distributions. In searching for universal laws – and in employing statistical, mathematical and modelling techniques as tools vital to this search – geography as spatial science succumbed to both a NATURALISM (sense 3) and a little-examined commitment to the philosophy of POSITIVISM. While many interesting findings have emerged from this 'new' geographical departure, it is now being heavily criticized by advocates of HUMANISTIC GEOGRAPHY and RADICAL GEOGRAPHY for neglecting, respectively, the creative role of human beings and the complex socio-economic contexts in which geographical distributions are always embedded. See also LOCATION THEORY; SPACE. For further reading: R. Abler *et al*, *Spatial Organization: The Geographer's View of the World* (1971). C.P.

spatialism, see under SPACE (2).

spatiodynamism, see under KINETIC ART.

speaker recognition. In PHONETICS and COMPUTATIONAL LINGUISTICS, the acoustic analysis of a speech sample to infer the identity of the speaker (see BIOMETRY/BIOMETRICS). In speaker verification, a sample of speech is acoustically analysed to check a claimed identity against a reference sample stored in a computer. This technique is used, e.g., in such situations as controlling access to buildings. In speaker identification, a speech sample from a known speaker is compared to one obtained from an unknown speaker, to determine whether the same person is involved. For further reading: F. Nolan, *The Phonetic Bases of Speaker Recognition* (1983). D.C.

Spear of the Nation, see under AFRICAN NATIONAL CONGRESS.

Special Drawing Rights (SDRs), see under INTERNATIONAL LIQUIDITY.

Special Economic Zones, see under OPEN CITIES.

special education. As defined in Great Britain, education provided to meet the special needs of pupils with marked disabilities of body or mind (see LEARNING DISABILITY). Such provision is made under the 1944 Education Act and subsequent regulations, the children (from the age of two and upwards) being classified as blind, partially sighted, deaf, partially hearing, delicate (including diabetics, asthmatics, heart cases), educationally sub-normal (ESN), epileptic (see EPILEPSY), maladjusted, physically handicapped, or speech-defective. Special education is provided in many forms: particular arrangements in ordinary schools, special classes, boarding-houses or hostels, hospitals, guidance clinics of many kinds, special schools, and home visiting. Training in the teaching of handicapped children is widely offered in colleges and Institutes of Education, usually in the form of one-year courses for teachers already possessing normal qualifications and school experience.

In the USA the classifications of special educational need are similar to those in Great Britain, although under the heading of the education of exceptional children the intellectually gifted are also included. Special education is administered at federal, state and local levels, funds for training and research coming from federal sources, direct services to children from state and local ones. For further reading: M. Farrell, *The Special Education Handbook* (1997). W.A.C.S.

speciation. The birth of a new SPECIES. The process is typically too slow to detect in the lifetime of an observer, but theoretical expectations can be tested against existing levels and patterns of genetic (see GENETICS/GENOMICS) variation. It is generally agreed that differentiation by chance between geographically isolated populations (*allopatric* speciation) is an important mechanism, and this can be facilitated when a new population is founded by a small number of individuals (known as a *founder effect*). However, a number of other mechanisms have been proposed for specific cases, including the differentiation of contiguous populations (*parapatric* speciation), and the differentiation of populations in the same geographic region (*sympatric* speciation). Sympatric speciation has been further divided into proposed mechanisms such as *allochronic* speciation, where sympatric populations differentiate after acquiring different breeding seasons, and *stasipatric* speciation, where the formation of a new species develops following chromosomal (see CHROMOSOME) rearrangements. A.R.H.

species. In BIOLOGY, a reproducing COMMUNITY of ORGANISMS that defines an evolutionary lineage over time (see EVOLUTION). The phylogenetic (see PHYLOGENY) species concept regards being a distinct evolutionary lineage as necessary and sufficient for being a species. Other species concepts require additional attributes that cause a reproducing population to behave as a lineage before being regarded as a species. For sexual (see SEX) populations, the biological (isolation) species concept defines the boundaries of the reproductive community negatively through intrinsic isolating mechanisms that prevent reproduction with other species. The recognition concept defines the boundaries positively by requiring the sexual organisms to share a common fertilization system. All organisms, both sexual and asexual, live in an ecological context (see ECOLOGY) that defines forces of NATURAL SELECTION which can also delimit the boundaries of an evolutionary lineage (*ecological species concept*). Isolating mechanisms, fertilization systems and selective forces induced by ecological context are not mutually exclusive. Accordingly, the *cohesion species concept* defines a species as a reproducing population of organisms (sexual and/or asexual) that is a distinct evolutionary lineage because of any mixture of isolation, fertilization and/or ecological mechanisms. A.R.T.

speciesism, see under ANIMAL LIBERATION.

specificity, see under PATTERN VARIABLES.

spectrographic analysis. A method of quantitative analysis involving a study of the light emitted when a substance vaporizes. It is based upon the fact that the light produced by each element, when split by a prism, yields a characteristic pattern of black lines crossing its spectrum. In practice a small sample of the substance to be analysed is caused to vaporize between graphite electrodes, the light emitted being recorded, usually on a photographic plate. Since the method requires relatively small quantities of material it is particularly useful in ARCHAEOLOGY for analysing artifacts such as bronze implements and weapons. B.C.

spectroscopy. The analysis of electromagnetic RADIATION emitted by matter. By means of a spectroscope (simply a glass prism in the case of visible light) the different frequencies or colours in the radiation are spread out into a spectrum. Each frequency has been emitted as the result of transitions of ELECTRONS in the source from one ENERGY LEVEL to another. The distribution of energy levels is different for all substances and all states of temperature, pressure, etc., so that the intensities with which the various frequencies occur in the spectrum provide a precise and powerful method for determining the nature of the source. The spectra of the sun and stars consist of continuous coloured bands emitted by the dense hot core, crossed by thousands of sharp dark lines caused by absorption by ATOMS in the tenuous relatively cool atmosphere (see also ASTROPHYSICS). M.V.B.

speech act. In LINGUISTICS, a notion derived from the philosopher J. L. Austin (1911–60) to refer to a theory which analyses the role of utterances in relation to the behaviour of speaker and hearer in interpersonal communication. It is not an 'act of speech', in a purely physical sense, but a communicative activity (a 'locutionary' act), defined with reference to the intentions of the speaker while speaking (the ILLOCUTIONARY force of his utterances) and the effects he achieves on his listener (the 'perlocutionary' effect of the utterances). Several categories of speech acts have been proposed, such as *directives* (e.g. begging, commanding), *commissives* (e.g. guaranteeing, promising), and *expressives* (e.g. welcoming, apologizing). For further reading: S. Levinson, *Pragmatics* (1983). D.C.

speech science. This emphasis on the combination of relevant disciplines is of particular importance in such domains as speech pathology and therapy, where specialists need to take into account a number of related observations from the different subjects. For example, the investigation of the speech patterns produced by a child born with a cleft palate will require a range of data to do with PHYSICS and PHYSIOLOGY of the vocal tract, as well as several kinds of LINGUISTIC analysis. D.C.

speech synthesis. The simulation of human speech by artificial means. Early attempts used mechanical MODELS of the human vocal tract, air being pumped through while the model was manipulated in accordance with the hypothesized processes of articulation. More recently, electronically generated noise has been modified so as to simulate the resonances of the different parts of the vocal tract. It is now possible, using computers, to produce synthesized speech which sounds extremely natural. An important part of speech synthesis is as a technique in experimental PHONETICS for evaluating hypotheses about the perceptual analysis of speech: if a particular acoustic feature is believed to be a significant determinant of a sound's recognizability, this can be tested by synthesizing the sound with the feature present in varying degrees, and rating the products for intelligibility and naturalness. For further reading: J. P. H. van Santen, *Progress in Speech Synthesis* (1996). D.C.

sphere of influence. Geographical term denoting a TERRITORY over which a state is acknowledged to have preferential rights of a political or economic kind but over which it exercises little or no effective government. Spheres of influence may be declared unilaterally as in the MONROE DOCTRINE (1823), in which the USA stated its special interest in the Western hemisphere, or multilaterally, as in the agreement over African territory between France, Germany and Britain in the last quarter of the 19th century. One of the classic cases of bilateral agreement was the Anglo-Russian 1907 agreement dividing Persia into a northern Russian sphere, a southern British sphere, and a neutral sphere between. For further reading: N. J. G. Pounds, *Political Geography* (1963). P.H.

spin. Rotation of a body about an internal axis. In QUANTUM MECHANICS, the term refers to the intrinsic angular momentum of an ELEMENTARY PARTICLE. Quantum-mechanical spin is only distantly related to the classical notion, as it exhibits space quantization: if the direction of an ELECTRON's spin is measured (e.g. in a Stern-Gerlach apparatus), one of only two orientations is found, instead of the continuous range allowed classically. Spin was introduced by Goudsmit and Uhlenbeck in 1925 using spectroscopic arguments (see SPECTROSCOPY), but Pauli had earlier referred to a 'classically indescribable two-valuedness' of electron states, and it was Pauli who later brought spin within quantum mechanics. In 1928, Dirac showed how spin arose naturally within a relativistic quantum mechanics of the electron. The spin states a PARTICLE may exhibit depend on the quantum statistics it obeys: fermions (e.g. electrons, PROTONS and NEUTRONS) have half-integral spin values, while bosons (e.g. PHOTONS) have integral spin values (see also EXCLUSION PRINCIPLE). R.F.H.

spin-doctor. A political adviser with responsibility for managing the presentation of policy, especially to print journalists and television reporters. While press secretaries have long been a feature of most democratic systems, contemporary politicians, especially in the USA, have been forced by the growth of media attention and the increasing speed of modern communications to appoint specialists to advise them about how to tailor their policies and statements to attract favourable media coverage and to control the delivery (the 'spin') of each issue in such a way that the desired image is projected. For further reading: J. Cooney and T. McGarry (eds), *Spin-Doctors: A Threat to Democracy?* (1994). N.O.

spin-off. A useful, usually unplanned, by-product or side-effect of some activity. For instance, spin-off from the space exploration programme includes the improvement of domestic electronic equipment such as radios and television sets. The term is normally restricted to desirable side-effects. Radioactive contamination of the environment by nuclear power stations, e.g., would not normally be described as a spin-off, though perhaps it might if the RADIATION was found to kill off only undesirable people. A.S.

Spinelli initiative. The Italian COMMUNIST, Altiero Spinelli, veteran FEDERALIST and national politician, has campaigned since the war for a federal European Community (see EUROPEAN UNION). Elected to the European Parliament in 1979, in 1981 Spinelli put forward a comprehensive plan for institutional reform of the European Community. His proposals were federalist in nature and involved granting more powers to the supranational institutions (the Commission and the European Parliament) and reducing the policy-making influence of national governments within the Council of Ministers. The Spinelli initiative formed the basis of the Draft Treaty on European Union which was formally endorsed by the European Parliament in February 1984. This Draft Treaty then formed the basis of subsequent discussions on EC institutional reform in the Council of Ministers which culminated in the Single European Act of January 1986. This provided for only minor adjustments in the institutional balance of power within the European Community, and was for that reason criticized by Spinelli. S.M.

Spiralen Group, see under COBRA.

spirit possession. State of dissociation or trance brought about in a person by a spirit entering the body. It involves a dramatic public performance. It may be involuntary and spontaneous possession which can be violent and uncontrolled. Spirit possession may express illness or mental instability, but it can also represent a claim to social recognition. I. M. Lewis suggested (*Ecstatic Religion*, 1971) that it was used by the peripheral or powerless (e.g. women) to attain a social ROLE and STATUS. Those who undergo voluntary and controlled possession are known as spirit mediums or shamans (see SHAMANISM). They may be specially trained and initiated into the role or may have established a relationship with a spirit after spontaneous possession. Spirit mediums can seek the causes of misfortune through contact with the spirits. In entering into a relationship with the spirits, a medium can placate and control their influence in society. For further reading: M. Lambek, *Human Spirits: A Cultural Account of Trance in Mayotte* (1981). A.G.

splicing. The removal of introns (see SPLIT GENE) from RNA (see NUCLEIC ACID). See also GENE SPLICING. P.N.

split-brain. In NEUROPSYCHOLOGY, a separation of the right and left lobes of the cerebral cortex effected by sectioning the great commissure (*corpus callosum*). In man, when such an operation is performed, the result is that the left cortex appears to be dominant and superior in processing information received in linguistic form, the right for dealing with SENSORY-MOTOR messages. For further reading: M. S. Gazzaniga, *The Bisected Brain* (1970). J.S.B.

split gene. While the DNA (see NUCLEIC ACID) of a GENE encodes the instructions for the production of a PROTEIN, most genes of higher organisms, but very few genes of micro-organisms, do not carry the instructions in a continuous stretch of DNA. Instead the genes are split, with *exons*, the stretches of DNA that contain a part of the information, interrupted by *introns* or intervening sequences, stretches that do not encode instructions. After transcription of a split gene into RNA, the introns are removed by GENE SPLICING. The unexpected discovery of split genes in 1977 has profoundly influenced ideas on gene and protein evolution. Exactly why many genes should be split is still a puzzle, but the most likely answer is that it allows and reflects the construction of genes, and hence proteins, in modular fashion. The most advantageous combinations of modules will be selected in the course of EVOLUTION. In addition, variations in gene splicing enable more than one protein to be made from a single gene, overthrowing the long-standing dictum of 'one gene – one protein'. For further reading: B. Alberts *et al*, *Molecular Biology of the Cell* (1983). P.N.

splitting, see under PARTIAL OBJECT.

***sprechstimme/sprechgesang*.** A vocal technique developed by Arnold Schoenberg (1874–1951) which is halfway between talking and singing (literally speech voice/speech song). The singer follows the written rhythm of the melodic line and begins each note on the written pitch and then allows the pitch of the voice to fall as in speech. The most impressive use of *sprechstimme* is in Schoenberg's 'Pierrot Lunaire', and the technique has occasionally been used by other 20th-century composers. For further reading: C. Rosen, *Schoenberg* (1996). B.CO.

sprung rhythm. A term coined by Gerard Manley Hopkins (1844–89): 'One stress makes one foot, no matter how many or how few the syllables', and 'the feet are assumed to be equally long or strong and their seeming inequality is made up by pause or stressing'. Hopkins added, 'it is natural in Sprung Rhythm for the lines to be *rove over*, that is for the scanning of each line immediately to take up that of the one before', so that the stanza is to be scanned as a whole, from beginning to end, and for its full effect the verse should be read aloud. Thus, from 'The Wreck of the Deutschland' (1876):

> Thou hast bóund bónes and véins in
> me, fástened me flésh,
> And áfter it álmost únmade, whát with
> dréad,
> Thy dóing: and dóst thou tóuch me
> afrésh?

Hopkins noted that sprung rhythm can be found at times in old English alliterative verse, the Psalms, Elizabethan plays, and nursery rhymes, and 'it is the rhythm of common speech and of written prose, when rhythm is perceived in them'. It does much to account for the dramatic expressiveness of his own poetry. D.J.E.

squark, see under SUPERSYMMETRY.

St Ives School. Since Whistler and Sickert spent a few weeks painting in the west Cornish fishing village of St Ives early in 1884, artists, mostly of an 'academic' persuasion, have worked there in their hundreds until the present day. The term is unprecise. It is usually applied to the MODERNIST artists of the place (Alfred Wallis, Ben Nicholson, Barbara Hepworth, Naum Gabo, Patrick Heron, Bernard Leach, Roger Hilton and others), though 'St Ives School' is also applied to more traditional artists living there. For further reading: T. Cross, *The Shining Sands* (1994). D.BR.

stabile. Term coined by the American sculptor Alexander Calder (1898–1976) for his static, non-'mobile' works (see KINETIC ART). But a *teatro stabile* is the Italian version of a REPERTORY theatre (sense 2). J.W.

stability pact. A mechanism for keeping the economies of countries which intend to join the SINGLE CURRENCY on the straight and narrow. The German authorities feared that without the discipline provided by the pact (which was agreed at the Dublin summit in 1996) there was a strong danger that downward pressure on budget deficits in individual member countries could slip. This would lead to fiscal (see FISCAL POLICY) and monetary tension (see MONETARY POLICY) within the euro area and could weaken the confidence of foreign exchange markets in the single currency. France, one of the strongest backers of the euro, disliked the idea because it gave too much power to bureaucrats (see BUREAUCRACY) at the European Commission in Brussels and at the European Central Bank (see CENTRAL BANK) in Frankfurt to make critical economic decisions. As a result, greater supervisory powers were granted to the Council of Ministers (see EU). A.BR.

stabilizers, see AUTOMATIC STABILIZERS.

stable population. A population that has an unchanging SEX and age structure, which is closed to migration, and which therefore increases or decreases in size at a constant rate. A stationary population is a special case of a stable population, where births equal deaths and there is ZERO POPULATION GROWTH. The concept of the stable population is in itself an unreal abstraction, but has been an important tool in formal demographic analysis (see DEMOGRAPHY) and in understanding complex demographic interrelationships. For further reading: H. S. Shryock *et al*, *The Methods and Materials of Demography* (condensed ed.) (1976). E.G.; D.S.

stage of development. In DEVELOPMENTAL PSYCHOLOGY, each of successive developmental periods, especially of INTELLIGENCE. Each stage is assumed to be characterized by a relatively stable structure. In PIAGETIAN theory, the sequence of stages is invariant, later stages incorporating and resynthesizing the structures of earlier stages. P.L.H.

stagflation, see under INFLATION.

stakeholder economy. At the broadest level this is the vision of the economy as a COMMUNITY in which everyone is involved. Unless, e.g., the MIDDLE CLASSES can be brought back into state education in the UK they will have no stakeholder's interest in seeing them prosper. Similarly, unless inner-city youth in the US can be persuaded that society has something to offer them they will remain outside, confined to POVERTY and CRIME, with no stake in seeing their cities prosper. Stakeholder ideas of inclusion can be traced back to Thomas Paine and Adam Smith, and were elevated into the public arena by the then Labour Party leader (now Prime Minister) Tony Blair in a speech in Singapore in early 1996. But this alternative to SOCIALISM, cast in language which suited the new middle way adopted by Mr Blair in Britain and President Clinton in the US, was quickly forgotten by Blair when attacked from the RIGHT. A much narrower form of stakeholding which views the public company as an intermeshing series of interests has, however, taken hold in Anglo-Saxon CAPITALISM. Instead of managers simply being the custodian of the interests of shareholders/stockholders alone, the corporation is viewed as representing a much broader array of stakeholders: the workforce, consumers, the environment and the broader public interest. Ultimately, attention to this broader range of players, as seen in companies like Marks & Spencer in the UK and Ben & Jerry's in the US, is seen as operating in the best interests of shareholders too. For further reading: J. Plender, *A Stake in the Future* (1997). A.BR.

Stakhanovism. A movement associated with the name of Alexei Stakhanov (1906–77), a miner in the Ukraine who in 1935 devised a system of increasing his output by the skilled organization of a group of subordinate workers. Others followed him in other industries, and the Stakhanovites became the official heroes of Soviet labour. They were, moreover, paid according to an incentive scheme which put them into the richest section of the community. For this and other reasons they tended to be unpopular with rank-and-file workers. The word has been applied, by extension, to anyone putting in particularly effective and energetic work in any field. R.C.

Stalinism. The policies and methods associated with the rule of Joseph Stalin (1879–1953) and his followers in the Soviet Union. They included bureaucratic (see BUREAUCRACY) terrorism and the propagation for obligatory acceptance, both in Russia and in eastern Europe, of fictions which were accepted as DOGMAS in the COMMUNIST movement while Stalin was alive.

Stalinism emerged when Stalin began to consolidate power during and after his struggle to succeed Lenin (1870–1924). His policy of 'SOCIALISM in one country' meant in effect the enforced COLLECTIVIZATION of agriculture and forcible INDUSTRIALIZATION in the Soviet Union. In implementing these aims, Stalin expanded police controls over the population, using harsher and more ruthless means to achieve his ends. Purges (see YEZHOVSHCHINA), FORCED LABOUR camps, the use of secret police (see KGB), and other totalitarian methods (see TOTALITARIANISM) were combined with the PERSONALITY CULT of Stalin to enforce conformity and present a picture of a benevolent ruler protecting with infinite wisdom his happy and prosperous people from the hostile 'CAPITALIST encirclement'. All the resources of state propaganda, the monopoly of information, SOCIALIST REALISM in literature, the rewriting of history, etc., were used to inculcate this vision of reality internally and to propagate it externally. The victory of the Soviet Union in World War II and its post-war expansion were used to indicate the historical inevitability of its worldwide triumph.

The process of 'de-Stalinization' which began with Khrushchev's 'secret speech' to the 20th Party Congress in 1956, and the repudiation of 'the errors of the personality cult', weakened the Soviet Union's authority in the international communist movement, strengthened the polycentric tendencies in it, and raised the question of Stalinism's role in Soviet history. The attempts to dissociate Stalinism from MARXISM-LENINISM as the basis of ideological (see IDEOLOGY) legitimacy, both internally and externally, during the de-Stalinization period were minimized after the fall of Khrushchev. For further reading: E. Radzinskii, *Stalin* (1996). L.L.

standard deviation, see under VARIANCE.

standard of living. A wide and rather vague concept that refers to the welfare of an individual or society (see WELFARE ECONOMICS). All those factors affecting the welfare of an individual should be taken into account, e.g. consumption of goods and services, leisure, the ENVIRONMENT, health and the political system. The standard of living is often naïvely and incorrectly associated with just the income of an individual or society. It is difficult or impossible to obtain agreement about what should be included in a measure of the standard of living and how the different components should be weighted (see INDEX NUMBER). Additionally, in the case of a society, there is the problem of assigning weights to the standards of living of the different members of society (see SOCIAL WELFARE). J.P.

Stanford-Binet test, see under MENTAL RETARDATION.

star wars, see under STRATEGIC DEFENCE INITIATIVE.

starred forms. In LINGUISTICS, a linguistic FORM (sense 1) preceded by an asterisk to indicate that it is either a historical reconstruction or a deviant utterance in a language or IDIOLECT. D.C.

START (Strategic Arms Reduction Talks), see under NUCLEAR WEAPONS, LIMITATION AND CONTROL.

stasipatric speciation, see under SPECIATION.

state. It is surprisingly difficult to define the state; it is reducible neither to government and administration nor to the nation, yet impossible to detach from both. Insight into the CONCEPT may be gained by asking what leads us to call some societies 'stateless'; it is primarily that they lack a way of changing the rules or NORMS which govern their behaviour and a way of choosing those who are to exercise that POWER. Innumerable theorists have speculated about just what leads to the creation of a state where none existed before – the needs of WAR, economic and technical change, and population pressure have all been offered. MARXISTS and their critics have long debated whether states are the passive victims of economic forces or free agents playing an active role in stimulating and directing economic change. Recently, theorists have been impressed by the paradox that states are increasingly able to wield overwhelming force against the subjects of their and other states, but less able to secure the loyalty of their subjects by managing the domestic economy or supplying the WELFARE services which modern states are expected to supply. For further reading: A. Giddens, *The Nation State and Violence* (1986). A.R.

state economic planning. The STATE's control or intervention in the economy in an organized manner. This planning replaces, either completely or partly, the PRICE MECHANISM as a means of co-ordinating the economy and, thus, contrasts with the LAISSEZ FAIRE approach. This planning requires a large volume of information and a large administration, when compared with the simplicity of the price mechanism in PERFECT COMPETITION. In varying degrees and types, the former USSR, eastern European countries and China use planning to control and direct the economy. Given the rudimentary position of the economies and markets of developing countries, many of them make great use of economic planning, though such a policy has its critics. Most economists accept the need for some state economic planning, even if it concerns only the provision of PUBLIC GOODS, TAXATION and MONOPOLY and MONETARY POLICIES. J.P.

state terror/death squads/the disappeared. The implementation by state security forces of a series of extra-legal operations as part of a clearly defined programme of government, intended to stifle any resistance to the established order by creating a psychosis of terror among the population. Carried out in the name of eliminating 'COMMUNIST subversion', such measures include routine assassinations, political imprisonment (usually involving the use of torture), and summary executions. In countries such as Guatemala and EL SALVADOR death squads were a primary means of applying a policy of state terror. These organizations, which governments claim are beyond official control, in fact have the approval and often the patronage of the government and the army. They hold lists of people suspected of being 'communists' (in practice they tend to target anyone who is involved in local, Church or political organizations which lie outside official control) and systematically kill them. Their characteristic method is to seize victims at night, torture and kill them (often by strangulation), disfigure the bodies by amputation and/or mutilation of face, hands and genitals, and dump them in public places, such as along roadsides, as a 'warning'. Such killings often follow denunciations by neighbours, employers or local security officers, which are a product of the climate of fear created by state terror. A further method used in state terror is the disappearance, a kidnapping of a targeted figure by the security forces, who then deny all knowledge of the victim's whereabouts and refuse to acknowledge that he has been detained by them. The tactic enables the government to avoid abiding by legal provisions for the defence of personal freedom and safety. Typically, victims are seized openly – on the street or at work or home – by small groups of armed but plainclothes men who drive away in unnumbered vehicles. The disappeared are normally tortured and murdered, although a few people have 'reappeared'. The term is most often associated with Argentina, where thousands of people disappeared under the military regime (1976–82), pledged to wage a 'Dirty War' against communism. Although disappearances also occurred under authoritarian regimes in Brazil, Chile, Haiti, Uruguay, El Salvador and Guatemala, the incidence of human rights abuses has dramatically fallen in most of Latin America owing to the consolidation of democratic rule in the 1980s and 1990s. However, right-wing paramilitary groups and rogue police units are still responsible for human rights atrocities in a number of Central American countries, as well as in Brazil, Colombia, Mexico and Peru. For further reading: G. Black, *Garrison Guatemala* (1985). M.A.P.

states' rights. In the USA, the political doctrine that the several states of the Union should enjoy the exclusive exercise of powers not specifically granted to the Federal Government. The advocates of states' rights oppose the steady extension of federal jurisdiction as undesirable and unconstitutional. In 1815 this was the cry of the New England states; but since the 1850s and the Civil War (which ended the claim that states could secede), the argument of states' rights has been characteristic of the southern states, especially since the CIVIL RIGHTS MOVEMENT secured the support of the law and of federal law enforcement agencies for DESEGREGATION by appeal to the Supreme Court (see SUPREME COURT OF THE UNITED STATES) in 1954. There has also, during the 1990s, been a growing mood in the Supreme Court against the use of federal judicial powers to overturn decisions of state courts on appeal. One area in which this has had a dramatic effect is in death penalty appeals (see CAPITAL PUNISHMENT). See also FEDERALISM. For further reading: H. J. Abraham, *Freedom and the Court* (1998).

D.C.W.; S.T.

stationary population, see STABLE POPULATION.

statistical explanation, see under EXPLANATION.

statistical linguistics, see under QUANTITATIVE LINGUISTICS.

statistical mechanics. A basic theory of PHYSICS developed in the 19th century by Boltzmann, Maxwell and Willard Gibbs, in which the behaviour of matter in bulk is explained in terms of forces and collisions between vast numbers of constituent ATOMS and MOLECULES interacting according to the laws of MECHANICS. It would be impossibly complicated to compute the trajectories of all the atoms, and in any case their initial positions and velocities cannot be measured with sufficient precision. Therefore, the laws of mechanics are supplemented by the methods of PROBABILITY THEORY, in order to calculate average values of dynamical quantities. For example, air pressure is calculated from the average MOMENTUM of air molecules continually striking solid surfaces, while temperature is calculated from the average kinetic energy of random molecular heat motion.

The behaviour of bulk matter is *irreversible* – it is easier to demolish a house than to build one – so that the future can always be distinguished from the past; this 'arrow of time' is expressed by the second law of THERMODYNAMICS, according to which ENTROPY always increases. But the laws of mechanics are *reversible*, and any closed system must eventually return approximately to its original state, no matter how highly ordered this was. This apparent contradiction is resolved by statistical mechanics, within which the laws of thermodynamics can be shown to hold with overwhelming probability rather than certainty. The chances of observing a spontaneous return to order are remote, because the average time between such returns far exceeds the age of the universe as at present estimated from COSMOLOGY. The implication that the direction of time is defined only for large-scale systems has caused considerable controversy, still not completely resolved.

Despite a century of intensive development, only relatively simple phenomena can be accurately described by statistical mechanics. A proper statistical theory of melting and boiling is still lacking, as is a detailed atomic explanation of the RHEOLOGY of bulk matter. For further reading: R. Bowley, *Introductory Statistical Mechanics* (1997).

M.V.B.

statistical regularity, or the 'law of averages' in PROBABILITY THEORY and STATISTICS, is correctly viewed as the *laws of large numbers* and other limit theorems in practical operation; if an event of probability p is observed repeatedly and the repetitions are independent, then the observed *frequency* – the number of times the event actually occurs divided by the number of times the experiment is repeated – becomes close to p as the number of repetitions becomes large. There is a common misconception that some form of mysterious compensatory mechanism involving memory is required to bring this convergence about; this sort of mistake is enshrined in the advice to air travellers always to carry a bomb – because the chance that there are *two* bombs on a plane is so small as to be negligible. (Such reasoning is perhaps an illegitimate extension of the doctrines of RESISTENTIALISM.) The gambler's run of good or bad luck is of a similar nature; there is no reason to believe that such runs occur with other than the frequency which probability theory predicts.

R.SI.

statistical test. A rule for deciding from the data whether to retain the initial (*null*) *hypothesis* or whether to reject it in favour of a specified *alternative hypothesis*. For example, if a coin were tossed 100 times and landed heads up 93 times, most experimenters would regard this as good evidence for rejecting the null hypothesis that the coin was fair in favour of the alternative hypothesis that it was biased towards heads. The test in this case might take the form 'reject the null hypothesis if the number of heads is N or more, otherwise retain it', where N is fixed in advance by the experimenter. A large value of N would lead to a small probability of wrongly rejecting the null hypothesis but a large probability of wrongly retaining it; these are called *errors* of the *first* and *second kinds* respectively. Similarly a small value of N would give a small probability of an error of the second kind at the cost of a large probability of an error of the first kind. The probability of an error of the first kind is the *size* or *significance level* of the test, and 1 minus the probability of an error of the second kind is the *power* of the test. Usually the significance level is chosen in advance, typically as 5 per cent, and a test is designed to give the largest possible power at that significance level – there is an extensive theory of the design of such tests, based on the work of J. Neyman and E. S. Pearson. R.SI.

statistics. A word with different meanings for different people, and with different meanings in the singular and plural. To the layman a statistic is a piece of numerical information, often of a singularly useless variety; statistics are a multiplicity of these, often assembled with the intention of baffling or confusing him, or concealing something underhand – witness the familiar slander 'lies, damned lies, and statistics'. To the statistician such information is 'data', which he tends to view in the same jaundiced light as does the layman: statistics is the analysis of such data, usually with a probabilistic MODEL as a background (*classical statistics*); 'statistic' is a technical term for a function of the data; and a statistician is a man who is prepared to estimate the probability that the sun will rise tomorrow in the light of its past performance. Early attempts at statistical reasoning can be traced back to classical antiquity, but it was the work of Karl Pearson and R. A. Fisher around the early years of the 20th century which first gave the subject coherence. Statistical theory has always been noted for deep and acrimonious divisions between various schools of thought, particularly for that between orthodox and Bayesian statisticians (see BAYESIANISM). In recent years DECISION THEORY has tended to unify the subject again by revealing that some of the differences are more apparent than real.

The basic idea of statistics is to regard some repeatable empirical phenomenon (the experiment: e.g. tossing a coin) as being governed by a probabilistic model not all of whose PARAMETERS are known (the probability of landing heads up is the unknown parameter in the coin-tossing experiment). The object of statistical analysis is to use the data obtained from repeated experimentation to provide information about the parameter values. This may take the form of hypothesis testing (STATISTICAL TEST) – failing to reject a null hypothesis (coin fair) or rejecting it in favour of an alternative hypothesis (coin biased); or of *point estimation* – giving a good guess (estimate) for the values of the parameters (e.g., probability of heads is 0.65); or of INTERVAL ESTIMATION – giving an interval for each parameter (confidence interval) (or a region for the set of parameters) in which the value of the parameter is likely to lie (e.g., 0.55 < probability of heads > 0.75); or – the Bayesian approach – of altering the weights (*prior distribution*) attached to the parameter values as degrees of belief so as to obtain a new system of weights (*posterior distribution*). Sometimes a statistic is used simply to summarize information about the data – e.g. the *sample mean* (see MEAN) of a set of observations may be used as a MEASURE OF LOCATION of the distribution, or a HISTOGRAM may be plotted to show it in more detail. For further reading: D. S. Moore, *Introduction to the Practice of Statistics* (1993). R.SI.

status. In SOCIOLOGY, a term used (1) neutrally, to designate a *position* in the SOCIAL STRUCTURE, such as the status of a father, or of a legislator (cf. ROLE, which defines the expectations of conduct assigned to a status); (2) to describe different social *evaluations* – in the form of rank, prestige, etc. – of a person or group. In pre-CAPITALIST society, status was often fixed and recognized by distinctive dress; in modern society, status distinctions are marked by different LIFESTYLES. In pre-modern societies status was often accorded on the basis of birth; in contemporary industrial society prestige is usually associated with the rankings of OCCUPATIONS.

Status as a dimension of SOCIAL STRATIFICATION, rather than a motive, is a feature of the analytical sociology of Max Weber (1864–1920). Weber contrasted status with CLASS on the one hand and POWER on the other, and used the term *status groups* to designate certain segregated groups, e.g. CASTES or ethnic groups, who are marked off by distinct CRITERIA from other social groups in the society. Gerhard Lenski has used the term *status inconsistency* to deal with the common phenomenon of individuals (e.g. blacks with high occupations) being ranked differently on different scales; and the theory of status inconsistency has been applied to discrepancies in political behaviour and RACE and class contact. The opposite of status inconsistency, *status consistency*, is sometimes called *status crystallization*. For further reading: F. Parkin (ed.), *The Social Analysis of Class Structure* (1974). D.B.

status symbol. Any visible sign of a person's social STATUS (sense 2). It may indicate either affluence, as with a Rolls-Royce car or lavish entertaining (see also CONSPICUOUS CONSUMPTION), or non-financial standing, as with the aristocrat's coat of arms, the don's gown, or the barrister's wig. Evidence from ANTHROPOLOGY refutes the widely held misconception that the status symbol is a product of modern CONSUMER SOCIETY. See KULA; POTLATCH; SYMBOL. For further reading: M. Douglas and B. Isherwood, *The World of Goods* (1980). M.BA.

STD, see SEXUALLY TRANSMITTED DISEASE.

steady-state hypothesis. A theory proposed by Hoyle, Bondi and Gold in 1948, in which the observed EXPANSION OF THE UNIVERSE is compensated by a continuous creation of matter throughout space, at a rate which need not exceed 10^{-43} kilograms per cubic metre per second – too low to be directly observable. The theory had the attractive feature of requiring neither an initial moment of creation nor a limit to the extension of space; nevertheless, it has now been superseded by the rival BIG BANG THEORY, both as a result of the latest evidence from RADIO ASTRONOMY, which suggests that the distribution of GALAXIES is evolving rather than being in a steady state, and also because of the discovery of COSMIC BACKGROUND RADIATION. See also COSMOLOGY. M.V.B.

Steiner schools. Schools based on the principles of Rudolph Steiner (1861–1925), the founder of ANTHROPOSOPHY. The first such school was founded by Steiner himself in 1919, in a cigarette factory in Stuttgart; it was closed by the Nazis (see NAZISM) and reopened in 1946. There are now over 600 Steiner schools throughout the world, of which more than 100 are for handicapped children, who are understood and treated against a background of belief in *karma* or reincarnation. Children in Steiner schools do not learn reading or number work until after seven years of age, and much emphasis is given to art, drama, EURYTHMY and music. There is no streaming, and entry to a class is determined by chronological age. For further reading: L. F. Edmunds, *Rudolf Steiner Education* (1992). W.A.C.S.

stellar nucleosynthesis, see under NUCLEOSYNTHESIS.

stellar populations. Once observational ASTRONOMY began the systematic task of mapping out the GALAXY in the 18th century, the nature of the distribution of stars within that wider whole became intensely problematic. Did stars have any relations with their neighbours? Was the galaxy merely a random heap of stellar masses? Most astronomers traditionally assumed that all parts of the galaxy were made up of the same sorts of stars. This view was challenged in the 1940s through the work of Walter Baade (1893–1960), using the 100-inch telescope at Mount Wilson Observatory in America. Baade resolved into stars the Andromeda galaxy and the nucleus of the Andromeda galaxy, and in doing so noticed that the brightest stars of the nucleus were to a remarkable degree fainter than the stars of the outer regions. This was a surprising finding; and on the basis of it, Baade invoked the concept of stellar populations, involving the assumption that different luminosities were possessed by seemingly similar stars in different populations. Baade proposed two different populations (Types I and II), but since his work additional types have had to be introduced. For further reading: R. W. Smith, *The Expanding Universe* (1982). R.P.

stenothermous, see under ZOOGEOGRAPHY.

stereochemistry. The study of shapes of MOLECULES or complex ionic SPECIES. Stereochemistry is particularly concerned with the immediate atomic environment of an ATOM OR ION and is thus intimately connected with descriptions of chemical bonding (see BOND, CHEMICAL). B.F.

stereoscopy. Term, deriving from the invention of the stereoscope by English physicist

Sir Charles Wheatstone in 1838, for the artificially induced illusion of relief in visual PERCEPTION.

(1) In photography, two separate photographs, taken from slightly different points of view corresponding to the position of two human eyes, are mounted side by side on a card. When viewed through the angled prisms of the stereoscope, the two views blend into one, giving the appearance of depth or solidity. The process is very important in aerial photography (both for military and for survey purposes), and in medical photography.

(2) In the cinema, experimental stereoscopic processes have been demonstrated since the early 1930s, most successfully during the Festival of Britain in 1951, but were not developed commercially until 1952 when (for the same reason as the introduction of CINEMASCOPE) the first '3-D' feature film, *Bwana Devil*, was launched in a process called Natural Vision. Combining the use of polaroid glasses and twin projection of superimposed images, the process had a certain success as a novelty, but proved too cumbersome for general commercial dissemination, though it is still occasionally used. In Russia, a process involving a grille of copper wires (later, optical lenses) to split the images thrown by two projectors – thus dispensing with the need for special glasses – was developed. For further reading: N. A. Valyus, tr. H. Asher, *Stereoscopy* (1966). T.C.C.M.

stereotaxic surgery, see under NEUROSURGERY.

stereotypes, racial, see RACIAL STEREOTYPES.

sterilization. The destruction, by surgical or other medical means, of the reproductive capacity of an organism. Since the 1960s, voluntary sterilization of persons has become a much-sought-after form of permanent CONTRACEPTION. However, compulsory or coercive sterilization, particularly of the mentally retarded, social deviants and non-white, multiparous women, has been a major violation of HUMAN RIGHTS in the 20th century. (See also EUGENICS.)

Sterilization is generally effected in women by a surgical operation known as tubal ligation, in which the fallopian tubes are cut and tied. This operation is not reversible. In men, sterilization is normally carried out by means of vasectomy, in which the vas deferens, under a local anaesthetic, is cut. It is occasionally possible to reverse vasectomy. For further reading: S. Trombley, *The Right to Reproduce: A History of Coercive Sterilization* (1988). S.T.

Sterling Area. A term long applied to a group of countries which have used sterling as a reserve currency, and as a trading currency for a substantial part of their transactions. From World War II onwards the grouping became a more formal one for EXCHANGE CONTROL purposes and was known as the *Scheduled Territories.* Since the early 1970s sterling and other EXCHANGE RATES have been allowed to float and only the UK, the Channel Islands, the Isle of Man and Gibraltar remain within this area. The special COMMONWEALTH trading relationships, which originally provided part of the purpose of the Sterling Area (although Sterling Area and Commonwealth were never conterminous), have been overtaken by the progressive liberalization and internationalization of world trade. Other privileges enjoyed by Sterling Area members, such as access to borrowing in the London CAPITAL market, have become less important as international capital transactions have moved increasingly into the EURODOLLAR market. P.J.

Stern gang. This organization, formally known as the Lohamei Herut Israel (or Lehi), was a splinter of the Irgun Zvai Leumi, and one of the most militant ZIONIST paramilitary organizations, in Mandate Palestine. Lehi was led by the anti-British Avrahm Stern (1907–42), and was responsible for the assassination of the British Minister of State for the Middle East in November 1944 and the UN mediator, Count Bernadotte, in September 1948. Its members were also involved in the Deir Yassin massacre of April 1948, in which two-thirds of this Palestinian village's population were killed. The gang was incorporated in the Israeli Defence Force in 1948. A.EH.

stigma. A concept associated especially with the work of the American sociologist Erving Goffman (1922–82; see SOCIOLOGY). A stigma is a personal or social attribute which is discrediting for the individual or group in the eyes of society as a whole. There are stigmas of the body – blemishes or deformities, such as pygmyism; stigmas of character, such as HOMOSEXUALITY or mental illness; and stigmas of social collectivities, such as membership of races or tribes regarded as inferior by the majority social groups. Stigmas are different from other forms of DEVIANCE, such as political deviance, in that usually an attempt is made to conceal them. One technique for doing so is 'passing': i.e. adopting a pose or disguise which hides the stigma in question and allows the individual to 'pass' as a member of normal society or the majority group. Many American BLACKS with light-coloured skins have in this way successfully passed as whites in American society. (See also TOTAL INSTITUTION.) For further reading: E. Goffman, *Stigma: Notes on the Management of Spoiled Identity* (1964). K.K.

Stijl, De. The name (1) of a Dutch magazine first published in June 1917; (2) of the group which founded it; (3) eventually, of a whole movement. The aim of the magazine was 'to make modern man aware of new ideas that have sprung up in the plastic arts', i.e. of a pure form of abstraction (see ABSTRACT ART) which was to be 'the direct expression of the universal' and which they simply labelled 'the style'. It found its clearest expression in the paintings of Piet Mondrian, who called his attempts to paint without reference to any objective reality *neo-plasticism*, and whose rectangular primary-coloured paintings had direct counterparts in the architecture and furniture of Gerrit Rietveld. The group's intellectual leader was Theo van Doesburg, architect, painter, poet and critic, who visited the Weimar BAUHAUS and ensured the introduction there of *De Stijl* ideas. Shortly after his death, the influence of the movement began to decline. This Dutch contribution to modern art left, however, an international legacy of a purity and vividness in abstraction which has been paralleled but hardly equalled. See also INTERNATIONAL STYLE. For further reading: H. L. C. Jaffe, *De Stijl, 1917–1931* (1956). M.BR.

STM, see SCANNING TUNNELLING MICROSCOPE.

stochastic decision tree analysis, see under RISK ANALYSIS.

stochastic music. Term invented by the composer Iannis Xenakis in 1956 for his musical compositions which use mathematical structures, and in particular PROBABILITY THEORY, to organize the sounds. A feature of this music is often the formation of clouds of sound built up from distributions of small individual elements. Xenakis frequently uses computers to help him with the calculations involved in the composition of his music. For further reading: I. Xenakis, *Formalized Music* (1971). B.CO.

stochastic problems, see under DYNAMIC PROGRAMMING.

stochastic process. In PROBABILITY THEORY, a system involving time-dependence. For example, suppose that a 'drunkard's walk' is defined by repeated tosses of a coin: when the coin lands heads up, the drunkard takes a step forward; when tails, backward. This is a stochastic process of a particularly simple kind, in that its future behaviour depends only on its present state and not on the route by which that state was reached – the process has no memory; such a process is called a *Markov process*. The progress of an epidemic, the behaviour of the economy or an ECOSYSTEM, BROWNIAN MOTION, the flow of traffic, and the serving of a queue all represent complicated empirical phenomena for which stochastic processes provide MODELS. R.SI.

strangeness. A property of some of the more exotic ELEMENTARY PARTICLES whose lifetime before decay is millions of times greater than expected. This must arise from some characteristic of their internal structure, corresponding to a 'strangeness QUANTUM NUMBER' which is zero for ordinary particles. M.V.B.

Strategic Arms Limitation Talks (SALT), see under NUCLEAR WEAPONS, LIMITATION AND CONTROL.

Strategic Arms Reduction Talks (START), see under NUCLEAR WEAPONS, LIMITATION AND CONTROL.

strategic capability. The war-making or reprisal capability of those states that possess long-range aircraft or MISSILES has become differentiated according to its technical characteristics. Thus *first-strike capability* characterizes a force which is sufficiently vulnerable (e.g. bombers on airfields) to be destroyed by an enemy strike and which therefore must be employed first in a *pre-emptive strike* if the possessor state is not to be disarmed; an example is the attack on Egyptian airfields by the Israeli Air Force on 5 June 1967. *Second-strike capability* characterizes a force capable, through a combination of RADAR early warning systems and missiles in underground silos or in submarines, of surviving a first strike in sufficient strength to inflict unacceptable damage on the adversary. *Counter-force capability* characterizes a strategic force capable of crippling the adversary's strategic military installations and troop concentrations while leaving a reserve for the destruction of his cities and industries; the USA is thought to have possessed such a capability in relation to the former USSR in the early 1960s, and both probably still possess it in relation to China. Its antithesis, *counter-value capability*, characterizes a force sufficient only to destroy or damage an adversary's cities and industries; the British and French nuclear forces are of this kind. See DETERRENCE. For further reading: H. Kahn, *Thinking about the Unthinkable* (1962). A.F.B.

Strategic Defence Initiative (SDI, or Star Wars). An expensive and ill-fated programme of space-based defensive weapons designed to intercept attacking strategic MISSILES. This plan was announced by US President Ronald Reagan in March 1983. His aim was to replace MUTUALLY ASSURED DESTRUCTION with Mutually Assured Security, by offering to share the TECHNOLOGY of the Strategic Defence Initiative. A budget of $30 billion was allocated to the project, which then attracted wide support from military and industrial interests. The system was to have comprised ground- and space-based surveillance equipment, and destructive weapons mounted in space (X-RAY lasers, which generated their own LASER beams to attack incoming missiles; some versions were reflectors which concentrated rays projected from terrestrial bases; other systems used guided missiles to create a lethal screen which would destroy incoming warheads). After the break-up of the former USSR, the programme was scrapped. For further reading: E. Reiss, *The Strategic Defense Initiative* (1992). A.J.M.W.

Strategic Nuclear Force, see under FORCE DE FRAPPE.

strategic studies. A widely used term first proposed in 1958 to the founders of the Institute of that name in London by its first Director, Alastair Buchan, to connote the scholarly analysis of the role of military and paramilitary force in international relations. The field of strategic studies is considerably wider and more political in character than military or war studies, and embraces not merely problems like defence and DETERRENCE but also ARMS CONTROL and the economic and social consequences of armaments, ARMS RACES and DISARMAMENT. Though the central focus of the field is the reinforcement of international security or peace, 'security' has so many meanings (social security, internal security, national security, personal security, commercial securities, etc.) as to make it valueless as a descriptive term, while 'peace' or 'conflict' studies and research, as evolved in Scandinavia and elsewhere, are either based on behavioural rather than political assumptions or else largely concerned with one aspect of the field, namely disarmament. A.F.B.

stratification, social, see SOCIAL STRATIFICATION.

stratificational grammar. A theory of GRAMMAR developed by S. M. Lamb in the 1960s, the name reflecting his choice of the term 'stratum' to refer to the various interrelated LEVELS of linguistic structure recognized by the theory. D.C.

stratigraphy. The principle used in GEOLOGY and ARCHAEOLOGY which states that a layer must be earlier than the one which *seals* it (i.e. which can be physically demonstrated to lie above it). Stratigraphy is the basis of all modern archaeological excavations. Most sites occupied for any period of time show a superimposition of layers, the careful observation of which provides the raw material for constructing a sequence. Particular attention is paid to the recognition of the surface from which any feature, e.g. a wall footing, post-hole or pit, is cut, since depth alone is not a criterion by which the stratigraphic position of an artifact can be assessed. The position of an artifact or structure in a stratified sequence is referred to as its CONTEXT. A well-stratified site provides a relative chronology which can be calibrated by means of dated artifacts or absolute dating methods (e.g. RADIOCARBON DATING). *Horizontal stratigraphy* is the linear development of a site whose focus gradually shifts. It is particularly appropriate to the study of cemeteries. For further reading: P. Baker, *The Techniques of Archaeological Excavation* (1977). B.C.

stream of consciousness. Phrase coined by William James in his *Principles of Psychology* (1890) to describe the ceaseless, chaotic, multi-levelled flow that characterizes human mental activity: 'let us call it the stream of thought, of CONSCIOUSNESS, or of subjective life'. Henri Bergson's account of the mind (1889) is also much concerned with this, and was highly influential in the development of stream-of-consciousness fiction, which attempts, often by means of *interior monologue*, to capture the exact nature of this flow. Pre-Jamesian examples include Sterne's *Tristram Shandy* (1767) and Édouard Dujardin's *Les Lauriers sont coupés* (1887); modern exponents include James Joyce (Molly Bloom's interior monologue in *Ulysses*), Virginia Woolf, and the less intrinsically important and distinctly more prosaic Dorothy Richardson (*Pilgrimage*, 1916–57). Originally, as in Dujardin, and then Richardson, the stream-of-consciousness technique was an extension of REALISM; it has since taken two forms. In one the author – e.g. Dorothy Richardson – merely attempts to mime or imitate mental activity (the extreme example is the German Arno Holz's '*Sekundenstil*', which tries to represent the passing of seconds). In its other, more fruitful form the author is aware that he can only *simulate* mental activity: he deliberately abandons realistic, descriptive techniques (though of course aiming at a deeper realism) in order to achieve his artful – and artistic – purpose. This form is fundamentally EXPRESSIONIST, although, as in Joyce, it may give the appearance of realism. Virginia Woolf hovers uncertainly between the two forms. Four main techniques of stream-of-consciousness fiction have been noted: soliloquy, omniscient narration of mental processes, and both indirect and direct interior monologue. The most sophisticated and revealing forms of stream-of-consciousness fiction were until recently to be found in the works of Latin Americans: João Guimarães Rosa, Miguel Asturias, Juan Rulfo, and others. But the Latin American novel now tends to parody itself (and the authors their own artistic successes), and the truly vigorous exercise of stream of consciousness is seen only in individual and occasional works. For further reading: R. Humphrey, *Stream of Consciousness in the Modern Novel* (1954). M.S.-S.

street dance, see under POPULAR DANCE.

street furniture, see under TOWNSCAPE.

strict (or **absolute**) **liability.** In English law, as in that of most civilized countries, a person accused of a crime is generally not liable to conviction if he did not intend to do what the law forbids or know that he was doing it, and took reasonable care to avoid doing it. In the case of some offences, however, e.g. breaches of law regarding adulteration of food or drugs and driving offences, most but not all of which carry minor penalties, a man may be liable to conviction without proof of such knowledge, intention, or lack of reasonable care. Such offences are known as offences of strict liability. For further reading: P. A. Jones and R. Card, *Introduction to Criminal Law* (1980).

H.L.A.H.

strike. A strike is defined as a refusal by employees to continue working; a temporary withdrawal of labour or stoppage of work, generally at the behest of a TRADE UNION. A strike is the ultimate weapon that can be used by groups of workers in order to exert pressure on an employer, or a third party, in the course of COLLECTIVE BARGAINING. While thought to be exclusively associated with trade union action, strikes predate trade unions. The Sabine women, Spartacus and his followers, and the 17th-century London apprentices who downed tools to force the reduction of oysters from their diets were all strikers. The term was first used in its present context in the Annual Register of 1768. Indeed, employers can strike: viz the strike of bus *owners* in Chile prior to Allende's deposition. Not all strikes are successful. The Greyhound workers' strike in 1982 and the air traffic controllers in 1980 in the US were both unmitigated disasters for the unions. The British MINERS' STRIKE of 1984–85 was similar.

The right of workers to withdraw their labour is considered to be a basic HUMAN RIGHT. It is enshrined in the legislation, or the constitution, of many industrialized states. It is rarely an untrammelled right. Many groups of workers (viz the military, police, government workers) are forbidden to strike by national legislation in many countries. In addition there are often legal requirements as to balloting of strikers and a minimum notice period before a strike can be called. These requirements change as government policies change. Strikes may be of a limited or an indefinite duration. They may affect workers nationally or locally. It is rare to find a strike which does not have adverse effects on third parties (viz the unburied dead in Liverpool in 1979). For this reason strikes are held to be unpopular by the public at large. However, a strike of telecommunication workers in Australia which gave the public free telephone calls was immensely popular. Strikes may have a political connotation; directly and indirectly. The 'General Strike' in Britain in 1926 was seen as a direct challenge to the government, as was the miners' strike of 1984–85. In 1973 Edward Heath called, and lost, an election over the miners' dispute, and it is widely thought that James Callaghan lost the election in 1979 through the strikes in the 'WINTER OF DISCONTENT'. While the UK and the US have no history of political strikes, France, Italy and Germany all have. Most of these strikes were (are) of a limited duration only. B.D.S.

strings. Linear distributions of mass-energy arising in some theories of ELEMENTARY PARTICLES. Vacuum strings (sometimes called cosmic strings) could arise during a particular type of change in the material state of the universe during the first moments of the universe's expansion from the big bang (see BIG BANG THEORY). They would exist as a network of tubes of energy which gradually become stretched and straightened by the expansion of the universe. An analogous phenomenon is observed to occur when matter is cooled to low temperature, and is termed the Meissner effect. The existence of vacuum strings may explain the clustering patterns of galaxies in the universe, but there is as yet no direct evidence for their existence (see GALAXY). Sheet-like forms of energy (called domain walls) are also possible in principle, but would produce observational effects in the universe which are not seen.

Strings and domain walls arise because underlying symmetries of nature break in disconnected ways in different parts of space, and these linear or sheet-like structures form at the boundaries between regions of different symmetry. They are sometimes called topological defects (see DEFECTS and MAGNETIC MONOPOLE).

Physicists Michael Green and John Schwarz have suggested a new theory of the ultimate nature of matter in which the most fundamental entities are not points, as is usually assumed, but line-like entities called SUPERSTRINGS. The theory of superstrings requires the universe to possess more than three spatial dimensions and offers the first self-consistent approach to combining QUANTUM THEORY and general RELATIVITY into a single unified theory of all physical phenomena (see GRAND UNIFICATION; ELEMENTARY PARTICLES). It is hoped that the masses of all elementary particles and the values of all fundamental constants of nature will ultimately be predicted and explained by superstring theories. Vacuum strings are not superstrings but superstring theories may give rise to vacuum strings. J.D.B.

strong anthropic principle, see under ANTHROPIC PRINCIPLE.

strong interaction. The strongest force known, which is an attraction acting over extremely short distances between NUCLEONS, and thus enabling the atomic NUCLEUS to resist the ELECTROSTATIC mutual repulsion of its PROTONS. Strong interactions are caused by the exchange of MESONS, and are about a million million times stronger than WEAK INTERACTIONS. M.V.B.

structural adjustment. A term used to describe programmes of economic and social change introduced to THIRD WORLD countries by impoverished governments as a condition of securing loans from the World Bank or International Monetary Fund (see BRETTON WOODS). They tend to be based on classical economic theory and MONETARISM. They advocate an emphasis on FREE MARKET economics, a drive to increase exports and impose cuts in government expenditure on subsidies and welfare programmes. In the short term this tends to lead to cuts in domestic living standards, particularly for the poor, a deterioration in welfare services (see WELFARE STATE), and sometimes even to political instability. The longer-term benefits are supposed to be economic growth, but often a substantial proportion of any extra foreign currency earnings simply goes to pay the interest on foreign debts. Structural adjustment programmes have had a major impact on sub-Saharan Africa and Latin America. For further reading: D. Ghai (ed.), *The IMF and the South: The Human Impact of Crisis and Adjustment* (1991). M.D.H.

structural-functional theory (structural-functionalism). A mode of theorizing in SOCIOLOGY (developed from FUNCTIONALISM in social ANTHROPOLOGY) in which societies, or smaller units such as communities or organizations, are conceptualized as SYSTEMS, and the attempt is then made to explain particular features of their SOCIAL STRUCTURE in terms of their contribution – i.e. the function they fulfil – in maintaining the system as a viable entity. Thus RITUAL and ceremonial practices may be explained as serving to reinforce shared beliefs and values and to maintain solidarity among different groups within a society – even though this function may be quite unrecognized in the purposes of those engaging in ritual and ceremony. Structural-functional theory is thus able to treat SOCIAL ACTION from the standpoint of unintended as well as intended consequences. A major problem it faces is that of specifying precise criteria for the viability of social systems, whether in the sense of their 'survival' or of their 'efficiency'. Structural-functional theory has also been criticized by exponents of CONFLICT THEORY for its neglect of the part played by *coercion* in organizing social activities and preserving social stability. See also PARSONIAN. For further reading: A. R. Radcliffe-Brown, *Structure and Function in Primitive Society* (1952). J.H.G.

structural linguistics, see under LINGUISTICS.

structural psychology. A SCHOOL OF PSYCHOLOGY concerned with the systematic, experimental, elementaristic (see ELEMENTARISM) study of conscious experience. By analogy with CHEMISTRY's periodic table, the aim is to isolate and classify the elementary constituents of CONSCIOUSNESS without regard to their function. I.M.L.H.

structural reform. The process of assisting parts of an agricultural industry which are uneconomic (because farms are small or badly laid out or suffer from other deficiencies) to become capable of providing acceptable living conditions. Among the reasons why farm incomes may be low compared with those in other sectors of the economy, or even in other parts of a country's agricultural industry, are the small size of farms, the farmers' lack of business and technical skills, and poor access roads and other elements of the INFRASTRUCTURE. Since they had too little to sell, measures to improve prices of farm products (see DEFICIENCY PAYMENTS) could not solve the problems of these farmers. Consequently various countries, including those in the EU, have introduced measures designed to encourage the early retirement of farmers and the amalgamation and consolidation of farms. For further reading: M. Tracy, *Agriculture in Western Europe* (1982). K.E.H.

structural semantics, see under SEMANTICS.

structural unemployment, see under UNEMPLOYMENT.

structuralism.

(1) In LINGUISTICS, any approach to the analysis of language that pays explicit attention to the way in which linguistic features can be described in terms of structures and SYSTEMS. In the general, SAUSSURIAN sense, structuralist ideas enter into every school of linguistics. Structuralism does, however, have a more restricted definition, referring to the BLOOMFIELDIAN emphasis on the pro-

cesses of segmenting and classifying the physical features of utterances (i.e. on what Noam Chomsky later called surface structures; see DEEP STRUCTURE), with little reference to the abstract, underlying structures (Chomsky's deep structures) of languages or their meaning. It is this emphasis which the CHOMSKYAN approach to language strongly attacked; for generative linguists (see GENERATIVE GRAMMAR), accordingly, the term is often pejorative. For further reading: G. C. Lepschy, *A Survey of Structural Linguistics* (1982). D.C.

(2) In the (other) SOCIAL SCIENCES (but see also SCHOOLS OF PSYCHOLOGY), a movement characterized by a preoccupation not simply with structures but with such structures as can be held to underlie and generate the phenomena that come under observation, or, to use the Chomskyan distinction mentioned in (1), with deep structures rather than with surface structures. The outstanding contributor in the social sciences is Claude Lévi-Strauss (1908–). For him a social structure is not a web of social relationships that may quickly be abstracted from concrete behaviour, but a MODEL. Further, any set of relationships making up a structure must be transformable by systematic change in the relationships. In his first major structuralist work, *Les Structures élémentaires de la parenté* (1949), Lévi-Strauss strove to demonstrate that the wide variety of KINSHIP behaviour and INSTITUTIONS rests ultimately upon a principle of communication that is the driving force behind INCEST prohibitions and the EXCHANGE of women in MARRIAGE. In that study modes of action and modes of thought were treated together, but his later work on TOTEMISM and MYTH has concentrated upon modes of thought. Structures have, of course, to be devised for each body of material selected for study, but in the last analysis they are all referable to basic characteristics of the mind (apparently considered to operate on a binary principle); and it is perhaps this feature of structuralism that distinguishes it most sharply from other movements in contemporary ANTHROPOLOGY. Like them, it starts from cultural variety, but unlike them it busies itself with the ultimate basis from which the variety is generated. See also EVOLUTION, SOCIAL AND CULTURAL; EXOGAMY; FUNCTIONALISM. For further reading: C. Lévi-Strauss, tr. C. Jacobson and B. G. Schoepf, *Structural Anthropology* (1963). M.F.

(3) In ARCHITECTURE: despite the grave doubts of the father of structural anthropology, Claude Lévi-Strauss, a number of architects in the early 1970s believed it possible to transfer its basic METHODOLOGY to architectural thinking and analysis. Sceptical contemporaries highlighted the probability that architects were attracted by the name structuralism and the fact that it sought to give order. The belief by some architectural protagonists that they would eventually grasp the essential and underlying pattern of architecture is not known to have been realized. S.L.

structure/agency. These are two opposed ways of explaining social outcomes, and are the basis of a pervasive DUALISM within the SOCIAL SCIENCES. One can view social life as largely determined by social structures, which predate and therefore condition the behaviour of individuals in that society. Or one can view social life as largely determined by those individuals, or 'agents', without whom there would be no social structures. Early sociologists (see SOCIOLOGY), such as Émile Durkheim (1858–1917), emphasized the priority of structure over agency; WEBERIAN sociology has reversed that emphasis, and shown how structures are created and maintained by human agency. Much subsequent sociology has sought to reconcile this dualism. In particular, Anthony Giddens has been influential in trying to build a synthesis, called STRUCTURATION THEORY. This is a MODEL of social systems in which order emerges as the result of interaction between intelligent individuals (the agency), each of whom is aware of the 'rules' (the structure) that govern their society, but who are also capable of acting contrary to those rules, thereby allowing the possibility of structural change. Though the theory sounds reasonable, just how useful it will be in practice is controversial. I.P.R.; A.A.L.

structure-conduct-performance theory. The view that the structure of an industry is the major determinant of the conduct and, thus, the performance of the industry and firms. *Structure* is defined by such factors as size and number of firms in the industry, BARRIERS TO ENTRY, type of product, existence of substitutes and complements to the industry's products, price and income ELASTICITIES for the product and related products, the supply of inputs, retailing of the product, and the TECHNOLOGY used in production. *Conduct* encompasses the behaviour and objectives of firms and their reactions and attitudes to the behaviour of rivals. *Performance* in defined in terms of such VARIABLES as growth, ECONOMIC EFFICIENCY, technical progress, profitability, employment, exports and ADVERTISING. This theory has been central to the study of the economics of industries. For example, it has been suggested that the industrial structure of MONOPOLY and profit-maximizing behaviour (conduct) leads to the restriction of output and higher prices. This implies higher-than-average profits (performance). The theory has been criticized in that conduct and performance affect industrial structure (e.g. technical progress and advertising may raise new barriers to entry). Also, it is not clear that different industries are sufficiently similar to permit generalizations about structure, conduct and performance. For further reading: M. C. Sawyer, *The Economics of Industries and Firms* (1981). J.P.

structure of feeling. In literary and cultural theory, a term first coined by Welsh critic Raymond Williams (1921–88) during the early 1950s, but not extensively theorized until the 1960s. In *The Long Revolution* (1961), Williams uses it as a mediating concept, between 'art' and CULTURE, to denote the 'deep community' that makes communication possible. A structure of feeling, in this sense, is neither universal nor class-specific, but is 'a very deep and wide possession'. The term was meant to embrace both the immediately experiential and the generationally specific aspects of artistic process. Williams himself used the notion as a key organizing concept in his accounts of both the English novel and modern drama. In *Marxism and Literature* (1971), he reformulated the concept along neo-Gramscian lines. He argued that structures of feeling were social experiences 'in solution' (as distinct from other social semantic formations, which are already precipitated) and were thus closely related to 'emergent' (as distinct from dominant or residual) cultural formations. In this reformulation, the concept refers very precisely to those particular elements within the more general culture which most actively anticipate subsequent mutations in the general culture itself; in short, to those that are quite specifically counter-hegemonic. Terry Eagleton describes the concept as 'vital' in 'examining the articulations between different sign-systems and practices'. Fredric Jameson has toyed with the idea that postmodernism might best be understood as a structure of feeling. Edward Said uses this 'seminal' concept in his analyses of the relationship between culture and IMPERIALISM. See CULTURAL MATERIALISM. A.J.M.

Students For A Democratic Society, see SDS.

***Sturm, Der*.** A complex of Berlin cultural enterprises founded by Herwarth Walden around his magazine of that name (1910–32), which was the chief organ of German EXPRESSIONISM before 1914 and did much to introduce the ideas of the FUTURISTS, CUBISTS and other innovators into Germany. There was a *Sturm* gallery (from 1912), *Sturm* readings featuring the near-phonetic poetry (see CONCRETE POETRY) of August Stramm, a *Sturm* theatre under Lothar Schreyer (later of the BAUHAUS), and even a *Sturm* march composed by the founder. After World War I *Der Sturm* lost ground, its one important new recruit being Kurt Schwitters, whose energies went rather into MERZ. J.W.

stylistics. A branch of LINGUISTICS which studies the characteristics of situationally distinctive uses of language, with particular reference to literary language, and tries to establish principles capable of accounting for the particular choices made by individuals and social groups in their use of language. For further reading: J. J. Weber (ed.), *The Stylistics Reader* (1996). D.C.

stylometry. A specialized branch of STYLISTICS: the methodical study of an author's chronology or development by analysing the proportions of parts of speech to one another in a particular work, his shifting preoccupations of thought or imagery, and other such factors. Such analyses are best made with the aid of COMPUTERS, which, when modestly and properly programmed, can solve many problems of attribution. M.S.-S.

subalternity. A concept within the field of post-colonial studies (see POST-COLONIALISM), and therefore concerned to explore the experience of peoples who have been subject to Western colonialism (see IMPERIALISM). The term, specifically associated with the project in 'subaltern studies' initiated by the Indian historian Ranajit Guha, refers to the search for the authentic voice of those social groups – peasants, illiterate townsmen, members of lower castes, village women – who have normally been 'written out' in the historical accounts given not just by Western scholars but by Western-educated élites in post-colonial societies. In the characteristically over-intellectualized controversies that typify this field, such an endeavour has been seen as yet another falling into the categories of modernist thought (see MODERNISM), with its assumption of an unproblematical subject whose voice can be discovered and given 'permission to speak'. K.K.

subatomic particle. Any PARTICLE smaller than an ATOM, i.e. the atomic NUCLEUS and the ELEMENTARY PARTICLES. M.V.B.

subconscious. A term of popular PSYCHOLOGY used to refer to those mental items and processes that are outside the range of an individual's awareness. Though frequently used as a synonym for unconscious, it is not equivalent to UNCONSCIOUS in FREUDIAN theory, primarily because it blurs the distinction between unconscious and PRECONSCIOUS. Moreover, though apt to be associated rather with the psychology of Jung (see JUNGIAN), it is not equivalent, either, to Jung's CONCEPT of the personal unconscious, since, in his theory, it is used to refer to the part, or aspect, of the personal unconscious which is closer to the COLLECTIVE UNCONSCIOUS, and not to those parts which are closer to CONSCIOUSNESS. B.A.F.

sub-culture. Despite centripetal tendencies, no society has a uniform system of meanings, perceptions or artifacts common to all elements of its population. The location of a social group in relation to POWER, authority, STATUS, its own sense of identity – ethnic, occupational or otherwise – leads to the development of a sub-culture whose function it is to maintain the security and identity of the group in question, and to generate a set of meanings that enable it to tolerate the exigencies of its situation. In a weak sense all recognizable subgroupings in society, from coal miners to executive directors, croupiers to royalty, have their own patois, hierarchy of values and characteristic modes of appearance and behaviour, but this over-extension of sub-culture can lead to its virtual redundancy as an analytical tool. Sub-culture is primarily useful in summarizing visible and symbolic resistance to real or perceived subordination, high levels of ROLE or status ambiguity, etc., and this usage illuminates the ideological (see IDEOLOGY) and material responses of such diverse groups as ethnic MINORITIES, the poor, academic underachievers, youth, women, 'deviants', etc. By far the most extensive usage of the concept has been in relation to YOUTH CULTURE with its series of visibly sub-cultural responses – PUNKS, skinheads, mods, HIPPIES, etc. A problematic element of sub-cultural analysis is the nature of the accommodative relationship between dominant and sub-cultural forms (see POPULAR CULTURE; UNDERGROUND). For further reading: K. Gelder and S. Thornton, *The Subcultures Reader* (1997). P.S.L.

subduction zone. A linear or arcuate region of the earth at which the spreading oceanic LITHOSPHERE bends downwards and re-enters the planet's interior, where it melts and becomes assimilated at depth. The angle of descent, which is usually about 45° (but can be somewhat shallower or steeper in particular cases), is marked by intense earthquake activity, the result of the large stresses induced in the descending lithospheric slab. The surface expression of a subduction zone is often a long trench up to 10 km deep, which compares with the 3–5 km depth of the typical ocean basin. Subduction zones, the most important of which lie around the edge of the Pacific, play a crucial part in PLATE TECTONICS. New lithosphere created at OCEANIC RIDGES spreads away from the ridges and is ultimately 'destroyed' at subduction zones at the same rate at which it was formed (see OROGENY). P.J.S.

subject. In LACANIAN psychoanalytic theory, the focus of psychoanalytic inquiry, replacing the 'SELF', the 'individual' and other such terms. Lacan's idea of the subject, which has its roots in Hegel, is a complex one, slipping between the linguistic notion of the subject of a sentence, the psychological notion of the individual human entity with agency and SUBJECTIVITY, and the social/political notion of being 'subject to' something more extensive than oneself (e.g., the law against INCEST). It developed out of Lacan's polemic with EGO-PSYCHOLOGY, and he formulates it in opposition to the ego, which is the source of resistances. The IMAGINARY register of the ego is what blocks the relation to the OTHER, and it is thus a primary task of analysis to bring the subject into prominence. The Lacanian subject is therefore part of the SYMBOLIC order, the subject of the unconscious.

What is apparent in the Lacanian account is that subjecthood is not pre-given; a process of 'subjectification' occurs as the subject staggers across the boundaries of the imaginary and symbolic orders. S.J.F.

subjective idealism, see under IDEALISM.

subjectivism. In ETHICS, the theory which holds that impersonally formulated VALUE-JUDGEMENTS, such as 'This is good' and 'That ought to be done', are in reality only statements about the likes and dislikes, desires and aversions of the speaker. More generally, any ethical theory which denies the ultimate resolubility in principle of disagreements about questions of value. More generally again, but on a somewhat different tack, any theory which takes private experience to be the sole foundation of factual knowledge is subjectivist, even if it admits that objective knowledge can be derived from this subjective basis. A.Q.

subjectivity. The role that subjectivity plays in philosophical reflection has worried and intrigued philosophers since Plato disagreed with Protagoras. Subjectivity takes on a major role in romantic (see ROMANTICISM) EPISTEMOLOGY, but becomes central to the philosophical enterprise itself in the work of Søren Kierkegaard in the mid-19th century. Kierkegaard insisted that philosophical judgements must be subjective and existential (see EXISTENTIALISM), and implied that the amount of objectivity available to us is vanishingly small and anyway not coextensive with the claims of philosophers or scientists. It is in the PHENOMENOLOGY of Edmund Husserl (1859–1938) that subjectivity is accorded a constitutive role, though Husserl's own understanding of how consciousness achieves ever greater subjective purity as a result of the EIDETIC REDUCTION is a paradoxical one, and he uses the concept of subjectivity in a way that does not refer to the subjectivity of any one experiencing or reflecting individual. Nevertheless, Husserl's inscription of subjectivity into the philosophical programme bore a plentiful harvest in the phenomenological work of Sartre (1943) and Merleau-Ponty (1945), where subjectivity and EMBODIMENT were made matters of fundamental importance for the first time since Descartes had banished them from the proper purlieus of philosophical awareness. The work of the French phenomenologists had a particular impact upon EXISTENTIAL PSYCHIATRY, which has its founding document in R. D. Laing's *The Divided Self* (1960), and upon existential psychotherapy, in the work of Peter Lomas and David Smail.

The effect of this phenomenological tradition has been to point up the degree to which a world constructed by an individual subjectivity is as 'real' and as 'true' to that individual as any reality or truth imposed from outside, and therefore that it is to the subjectively constituted world of meaning that we must attend if we wish to be of any help in the psychiatric situation (see PSYCHIATRY). Psychiatrists of the Laingian school have thrown into doubt the assumed 'objectivity' of the world from which the patient is claimed to have departed, for it is now obvious that social constructs are themselves intersubjectively (see INTERSUBJECTIVITY) created and sustained and are not in any sense necessary or necessarily 'true'. This is the essential contribution of existential phenomenology to psychiatric theory. It makes possible the retrieval of intentional meaning (see INTENTIONALITY) and excuses the analyst from imposing 'objective', 'scientific' or 'medical' hegemonic meanings (see HEGEMONY) over signs and embodiment which plead to be understood in their own terms. R.PO.

sublimation. In psychoanalytic theory (see PSYCHOANALYSIS), a FREUDIAN term for the gratification of instinctual impulses, usually sexual or aggressive in nature, through the substitution of socially acceptable behaviour for prohibited drives. See also DEFENCE MECHANISM; REPRESSION; SUPEREGO. W.Z.

subliminal. Adjective applied to stimulation operating below the threshold (*limen*) of PERCEPTION. There is much concern that subliminally presented messages can alter attitudes, but this has not been borne out by research. H.L.

submarine-launched ballistic missiles, see under MISSILES.

sub-optimization, see under SYSTEMS.

subsidiarity. A principle, often associated with Germany, according to which the various functions of government should be exercised at the lowest level of government (local, national, supranational) which is consistent with the efficient discharge of that function. Now important in the EUROPEAN UNION (EU), since it forms part of the MAASTRICHT Treaty. It was introduced into the Treaty largely to allay the fears in certain quarters (notably Britain) that too much power might be transferred to the EU level. Paradoxically, it might also pave the way for regionalism and the marginalization of the nation-state in the (very) long run. V.L.

subsistence agriculture. Farming intended primarily to supply the food and clothing needs of the farmer and his dependants. Subsistence agriculture accounts for a substantial part of the agricultural industries of many low-income countries. The term is occasionally used in high-income countries to refer to the activities of those who run small farms, which would be uneconomic as business enterprises, largely for the satisfaction of having home-grown foodstuffs and the amenities of country life, while earning their living in other ways. For further reading: C. Clark and M. R. Haswell, *The Economics of Subsistence Agriculture* (1970). K.E.H.

subsonic, see under MACH NUMBER.

substance. In PHILOSOPHY, either (1) a concrete individual thing, to which existence can be attributed in an unqualified way (everything else that exists being reducible to it; see REDUCTION), or (2, sometimes called *substratum*) that which, as distinct from the properties which a concrete thing may share with other things, confers its individuality on it. Substance in the first, Aristotelian, sense is a complex, composed of properties together with an individuating substratum or substance in the second sense. Many philosophers have held that there are no individuating substrata, and thus that a thing is no more than the collection of its properties. Mental substances, the soul or self, is often conceived as the substratum of the series of mental states that make up the biography of a person. See also INTUITIONISM. A.Q.

substantivism, see under ECONOMIC ANTHROPOLOGY.

substitution. In ECONOMICS, substitution is an important element in economic decisions. Rational consumers (see RATIONALITY) will substitute between different goods in order to obtain that pattern of consumption which is most preferred and is feasible, given prices and income. For any two goods, this can be represented by considering the rate at which the goods can be substituted for each other while leaving the consumer at the same level of utility (see UTILITY THEORY; INDIFFERENCE CURVES). This rate is called the marginal rate of substitution and, in achieving the most preferred feasible consumption pattern, the rational consumer should, for each possible pairing of goods, equate the marginal rate of substitution to the ratio of the prices of the two goods. Similarly, firms minimize costs of production by substituting between FACTORS OF PRODUCTION until the marginal rate of substitution between any two factors is equal to the ratio of the prices of the factors (see ISOQUANT). Substitution underlies much of the production and consumer demand theory of microeconomics. J.P.

substrate, see under ENZYMES.

substratum, see under SUBSTANCE.

sub-system, see under SYSTEMS.

subtopia. A term first used by Ian Nairn in the *Architectural Review* to denote certain areas beyond or within suburbs, areas which were 'the world of universal low-density mess' and included such things as 'abandoned aerodromes, fake rusticity, wire fences, traffic roundabouts, gratuitous notice boards, car parks and Things in Fields'. Nairn's campaign aimed to emphasize the distinction between town and country and to preserve the characteristics of each. In its more extreme forms, however, it became an attack on any low-density building in SUBURBIA. For further reading: I. Nairn, *Outrage* (1955). M.BR.

suburbia. The extensive ring of low-density, low-rise housing development circling modern cities. Suburbia may be seen as a pejorative term suggesting that suburban development is somehow inferior to true urban development. 'SUBURBANIZATION' is the term used to describe the process of suburban development and related population movement. The exodus of 'up and outers' from older urban areas has been seen as a contributory factor in urban decline, and social segregation in American cities. Yet nowadays 50 per cent of the population of North America live in suburbia, and so it is 'the norm' rather than a social aberration. Classical models of urban form developed in the US imply that the further out one goes the higher the class of the resident and the larger and more expensive the dwellings. This proves inappropriate to the British situation, where many inner-city areas have experienced GENTRIFICATION. Likewise, in Paris the central *arrondissements* (districts) have always been seen as fashionable neighbourhoods, whereas suburban development has been seen as for the working classes. C.G.

Suez. Term used to denote the international crisis of October/November 1956 and the decline of British power which it is taken to symbolize. The crisis followed the NATIONALIZATION by Egypt of the Suez Canal and the other assets of the Suez Canal Company, the majority of whose shares were owned by the British government and by French private shareholders. The British and French governments used the pretext of an Israeli attack on Egypt, in the planning of which they had colluded, to attempt a forcible occupation of the Canal Zone, ostensibly to ensure its security. Their action attracted widespread international condemnation, including crucially that of the US, and was abandoned in the face of a collapse of international confidence in sterling and a widening breach in Anglo-American relations. The episode is regarded as the last (unsuccessful) attempt by Britain and France to assert great-power status. For further reading: F. S. Northedge, *Descent from Power: British Foreign Policy 1945–73* (1974). S.R.

sufficient condition, see NECESSARY AND SUFFICIENT CONDITIONS.

suffragette. Term applied to women who were members of the suffragist movement, but specifically advocating votes for women. By 1860 the discourse of republicanism and citizenship prevalent in Britain, France and the United States had stimulated the interest of MIDDLE-CLASS women. They began to claim political and civil rights denied to them.

The importance of an historical perspective in contemporary FEMINISM has led to a re-examination of early suffragette activity. There has been a shift, however, in attention from the leaders, e.g. the Pankhursts, to the rank and file or local activists (e.g. Selina Cooper). For further reading: J. Mitchell and A. Oakley (eds), *What Is Feminism?* (1986). A.G.

summer stock, see under REPERTORY (2).

summit diplomacy. Personal negotiations held face to face between heads of state or government of the major powers in the hope of resolving their mutual conflicts. Although the actual practice of such negotiations can be traced back to ancient times, the actual term 'summit diplomacy' appears to have originated with Winston Churchill's call for a 'parley at the summit' in his election speech on 14 February 1950. The idea of summit diplomacy appeals to populations suspicious of traditional diplomatic methods, and especially to liberal internationalists who believe that conflict is due to misunderstanding.

In times of international tension, summit meetings often attract high hopes which are then disappointed. A May 1960 US–Soviet summit in Paris collapsed ignominiously when an American spy plane was shot down over the Soviet Union. In late 1986 the abortive summit at Reykjavik between Gorbachev and Reagan failed because the leaders discussed nuclear disarmament proposals so ambitious that, at least on the US side, they frightened both America's experts and its allies.

Yet summits also have a positive record. Nixon's visit to China in 1972, the Camp David accords of 1979, and some of the other Gorbachev–Reagan meetings resulted in substantive and enduring agreements. Some multilateral summits have also been successful, including the 35-country meeting at Helsinki in 1975 (see HELSINKI 1975) to approve the Final Act of the Conference on European Security and Co-operation. The regular summit meetings of the major economic powers (the G7) have become an international institution. Where such meetings are effective, it is usually in proportion to the amount of advance agreement achieved at preparatory meetings by officials – the 'sherpas' who do the hard work for the 'summiteers' to ratify, and to dignify with high-level political commitment. For further reading: K. Eubank, *The Summit Conferences, 1919–60* (1966); A. Eban, *The New Diplomacy* (1983). E.A.R.

Sunni Muslims, see under ISLAM.

superblock, see under RADBURN PRINCIPLE.

supercluster, see under GALAXY CLUSTERS.

superconductivity. The complete disappearance of electrical resistance observed (first by Dutch physicist Heike Onnes in 1911) when certain materials are cooled below a certain *transition temperature* (generally a few degrees above ABSOLUTE ZERO). An electric current set up in a superconducting circuit will persist undiminished for years without requiring a CELL to drive it around. These 'persistent currents' may be employed as memory elements in COMPUTERS, while on a much larger scale their magnetic FIELDS may power rapid-transit vehicles between cities, levitated above superconducting track. The transition to and from the normally conducting state is sudden, and easily induced by changes of temperature or magnetic field; this has led to 'superconducting switches', applicable to large complex systems like computers where economy of space is important. In these technological applications, promise has so far outstripped performance. M.V.B.

supercritical fluid. A fluid that is heated above its CRITICAL TEMPERATURE, where the distinction between liquid and gas disappears. The density of a supercritical fluid can be altered continuously from liquid-like to gas-like by changing its pressure, whereas below the critical temperature there is an abrupt change in density when the liquid boils and evaporates. Supercritical fluids are now used as solvents for chemical processing, since they may dissolve chemical substances that are insoluble in the corresponding liquid. This enables benign fluids such as water and carbon dioxide to replace environmentally harmful solvents such as volatile organic compounds. P.C.B.

superego.

(1) In FREUDIAN psychoanalytic theory (see PSYCHOANALYSIS), a term for that part of the structure of the mind which is concerned with controlling excitation from the ID and the activity of the EGO. This control is largely UNCONSCIOUS, but manifests itself in CONSCIOUSNESS in the pronouncements of conscience and feelings such as guilt and shame. The superego is developed in the child through subtle and complex identifications with the parents, and by introjecting them as controlling or guiding models, with their corresponding moral attitudes. B.A.F.

(2) In LACANIAN psychoanalytic theory, the incorporation of certain verbal residues, leading to an interiorization of the law. The broken nature of this internalization leads to the establishment of a law unable to represent conflict and DIALECTIC. Despite the claims of the superego to be able to judge, it in fact establishes a tyrannical and merciless system of imperatives; the function of censorship that it introduces has as one of its aims to keep beyond any access the structural relationship of the SYMBOLIC to DESIRE. B.BU.

superfluidity, see under QUANTUM FLUID.

supergravity, see under SUPERSYMMETRY.

superlattice. In PHYSICS new semiconducting materials (see SEMICONDUCTOR) are being made by depositing very thin layers of different materials, only a few tens of ATOMS thick, on top of one another. It is now possible to form each layer in a very perfect crystalline state, and the final assembly of many layers is called a superlattice or *heterostructure*. The different layers couple with each other so that the heterostructure has new properties which are unlike those of its constituent layers. Among the materials which are used are gallium arsenide and alternating silicon/germanium layers. By DOPING with, say, aluminium or indium in the various layers, it is possible to alter the electrical and optical properties in a controlled way so that their characteristics can be tailor-made for the production of devices such as LASERS and light sensors. The term is also used to describe crystals of certain alloys. In general the constituent atoms in such materials are arranged in a random manner on the permitted LATTICE, but sometimes after suitable heat treatment an ordering process can occur so that all the atoms of one type are in one particular position – e.g., at the corners of cubes – while those of the other type of atom are all at another set of regular sites – e.g., at the centres of the cubes. When this occurs the alloy is said to have formed a superlattice. H.M.R.

superman, see under ÜBERMENSCH.

supernova. An exploding star, which may be millions of times brighter than the sun. It is thought that the contraction of a RED GIANT due to the GRAVITATION of its MASS may cause nuclear FUSION reactions which accelerate the contraction, thus producing a catastrophic collapse and the emission of vast amounts of ENERGY. With the naked eye only two supernovae have been observed in the past thousand years, but with the aid of telescopes many have been seen in other GALAXIES. See also DWARF STAR. M.V.B.

super-particle, see under SUPERSYMMETRY.

superposition. In QUANTUM MECHANICS, when a system is in a superposition with respect to some physical quantity, it possesses no definite value for that quantity. Suppose there is an observable property that admits of a range of possible definite values, and let $s_1, s_2, \ldots, s_n$ be the states in which the system possesses those values. Quantum mechanics stipulates that in addition to $s_1, s_2, \ldots, s_n$, there are possible states of the system (combinations of some or all of $s_1, s_2, \ldots, s_n$) in which no definite value for the physical quantity is possessed by the system. However, given the superposition state, it is possible to calculate the probability (see PROBABILITY THEORY) that any particular value corresponding to $s_1, s_2, \ldots, s_n$ will be found on measurement. That quantum mechanics allows physical systems to lack definite values for such basic physical quantities as position, momentum and energy is arguably the most radical difference between quantum and CLASSICAL PHYSICS. Certainly it seems to lie at the heart of many of its counter-intuitive implications (see EPR PARADOX; SCHRÖDINGER'S CAT; UNCERTAINTY PRINCIPLE). R.F.H.

supersonic, see under MACH NUMBER.

superstrings. A new theory of the most elementary structure of the universe proposed by physicists Michael Green and John Schwarz in 1984. Whereas previous theories of elementary particle behaviour are quantum field theories in which the basic entities are 'points' of zero extent, superstring theories possess lines (strings) as the basic elements (see QUANTUM THEORY). These strings possess a tension which collapses them down to points in a low-energy environment. Superstring theories will therefore give rise to the conventional quantum field theories in the low-energy limit. These theories were shown by Green and Schwarz to possess remarkable mathematical properties. Unlike the conventional quantum field theories they do not possess infinities when physical quantities are calculated. They develop an old idea that ELEMENTARY PARTICLES are microscopic strings by the addition of SUPERSYMMETRY. They appear to offer a possible route to combining the general theory of RELATIVITY and quantum theory. It is believed that this theory allows the fundamental constants of nature and the properties of all elementary particles to be calculated mathematically. For this reason the theory is sometimes referred to as a possible theory of everything (and denoted by the acronym TOE). As yet there is no observational evidence for or against superstring theories, and a means of calculating their observational predictions has yet to be found. It is the principal current area of research into elementary PARTICLE physics. Superstring theory appears to predict the existence of an entire population of elementary particles which possess only very weak interactions comparable in strength to gravitational interactions with other bodies. The population is called shadow matter or the shadow world. Until very recently it appeared that there existed a number of logically self-consistent Theories of Everything of the superstring sort. However, it has recently been shown that these are all different mathematical ways of looking at a single underlying theory, now called M-theory. The interrelationships are mediated by a deep symmetry of these theories, known as duality symmetry. For further reading: B. Greene, *The Elegant Universe: Superstrings, Hidden Dimensions and the Quest for the Ultimate Theory* (1999). J.D.B.

superstructure. According to Marx and Engels's theory of HISTORICAL MATERIALISM, the primary reality in the world is matter and its quantitative combinations; the qualitative characteristics of differing natural forms are secondary, emerging from the nature and changes of such combinations. In history, the material structure (basis) of any society (its economic system; its productive forces – including its socioeconomic CLASSES) is the primary reality, and on this rests a qualitative *superstructure* of INSTITUTIONS. This superstructure has two sides, or perhaps layers. First, there are the legal and institutional forms of the social system – the state, the machinery of law, government, and official power; second, there is the IDEOLOGY of the system, the body of ideas and beliefs – moral, political, religious and philosophical – which serve to ratify the society's institutional arrangements, particularly its property system or mode of distributing the fruits of the productive process. Marx's view is that the predominant direction of causal influence is from base to superstructure: major historical change begins in the economic base and leads to a more or less revolutionary transformation of the superstructure. R.F.; A.Q.

supersymmetry. Theoretical idea in ELEMENTARY PARTICLE physics which aims to effect a unification between bosons (which possess integral units of quantum mechanical spin; see QUANTUM MECHANICS; QUANTUM STATISTICS) and fermions (which possess half-integral units of quantum mechanical SPIN) in nature. Supersymmetry transforms bosons into fermions and vice versa. This symmetry requires that there exist a new population of elementary particles: every boson possesses a new superpartner possessing half-integral spin, while every fermion possesses a super-partner with integral spin. For example, the superparticle of the PHOTON is called the photino and that of the NEUTRINO the sneutrino. The other particle-to-super-particle partnerships are as follows: LEPTONS (sleptons), GLUONS (gluinos), W bosons (winos), Z bosons (zinos), gravitons (gravitinos), Higgs boson (Higgsino or shiggs), QUARKS (squarks). The super-particles are termed sparticles. None have yet been observed but they are expected to be too heavy to have shown up in past ACCELERATOR searches. They are being searched for in the current accelerator experiments at CERN in Geneva. SUPERSTRING theories and some GRAND UNIFIED THEORIES possess supersymmetry. Supersymmetry is a global gauge field theory. If the gauge symmetry is made local then the theory encompasses gravity (see GRAVITATION) and is called supergravity. For further reading: H. Pagels, *Perfect Symmetry* (1985). J.D.B.

supervenient. Inseparable from the other properties of something. Two objects may be identical except that one is red and the other not, but they cannot be identical except that one is beautiful and the other not; thus beauty is a supervenient property.

It seems that mental states and processes (including QUALIA) are supervenient on brain states and processes: i.e. no mental change can occur in a person unless there is some physical change in the brain.

However, the exact relationships are not well understood. States and processes in COMPUTER-based VIRTUAL MACHINES like word processors or chess programs are supervenient on the underlying physical machines.

Because the same program can run on physically different computers, we know that artificial virtual machines are capable of being implemented in (i.e. supervenient on) a range of physically different machines. What is not clear is whether human minds are similarly 'implementation independent' as implied by the 'strong' ARTIFICIAL INTELLIGENCE thesis. A further subtlety is that some mental states are described partly in terms of their external relations (e.g. 'Mary loves Paris') and such states are not totally supervenient on brain states: they also depend on relationships with objects in the environment (e.g. the city referred to). A.S.

supplement (logic of). Term used by deconstructionist philosopher Jacques Derrida; see DECONSTRUCTION) to denote a certain form of deviant, anomalous or paradoxical reasoning to be found in various texts, especially those of Jean Jacques Rousseau (1712–78). One example is music: melody *should* be conceived as prior to harmony both in terms of historical development and as regards its intrinsically superior qualities of naturalness, spontaneity, closeness to the origins of passionate speech-song, etc. However, Rousseau is more than once constrained to say just the opposite of this, namely that there cannot be – and historically never was – a melody so pure as to admit no taint of 'supplementary' harmonic structure.

Then again, Rousseau declares: one *should* be able to think of the origins of civil society in terms of an original close-knit organic community which only later became subject to all the bad effects of social division, property laws, delegated authority, specialized skills (such as writing), etc. Yet this is an argument that Rousseau cannot sustain without running up against the sheer *impossibility* of describing a state of social existence that would not *already* have suffered the transition to those kinds of differential structure which contravene his own prescription. Society is born out of those same 'civilized' (i.e. decadent and corrupting) factors which should belong to a late state in its development yet which must be conceived as having existed from the outset. Quite simply, this would *not yet have been* a society – in even the most primitive sense of that term – just as language would *not yet have been* language in the absence of just those constitutive features (articulation, syntax, lexical distinctions, tense-structure, etc.) which for Rousseau mark the beginning of its decline into 'civilized' decadence and artifice. For further reading: C. Norris, *Derrida* (1987). C.N.

supply and demand. The usual term for the market forces governing prices, in the absence of administrative control, output and the distribution of income. These forces make themselves felt through the PRICE MECHANISM, as responses in the quantities offered for sale (supply) or the quantities that consumers are prepared to buy (DEMAND) when the market price changes. Normally the responses are equilibrating since a rise in price tends to enlarge the supply and reduce the demand, and vice versa (the ECONOMIC LAW of supply and demand); but they may at times be disequilibrating (e.g., if a change in price excites expectations of a further change in price in the same direction). Emphasis on supply and demand implies, not that there should be no interference with the price mechanism, but that control dampens market reactions and risks perpetuating a shortage or surplus. The more any form of economic organization relies on market forces, the more freedom it must allow to supply and demand to respond to changes in price. The operation of market forces will, in the case of PERFECT COMPETITION, result in ECONOMIC EFFICIENCY, but there is no reason to suppose that the resulting distribution of income is or is not desirable. Additionally, the operation of the law of supply and demand will not deal efficiently with MARKET FAILURES such as PUBLIC GOODS, EXTERNALITIES, MONOPOLIES, etc. For further reading: J. Craven, *Introduction to Economics* (1984). A.C.; J.P.

supply-side economics. The view that TAXATION has severely reduced the incentives for work and INVESTMENT and that ECONOMIC GROWTH can be increased by large reductions in the taxation of the supply side of the economy. This view contrasts with the KEYNESIAN approach which proposes that the level of AGGREGATE DEMAND is important in determining the level of output and employment. Supply-side economics proposes that a reduction in the taxation of incomes and profits will result in people working harder and investing more. An example of this view is the Laffer Curve, which considers the relation between tax revenue and the rate of tax. A zero tax on, e.g., income would give no tax revenue; increases in the tax rate would take larger proportions of income. According to the Laffer Curve view, as the rate of tax increases the incentive to work is reduced, and people choose to work less hard and earn less income. Thus, as the rate of tax increases, the tax base decreases in size. It is suggested that there is a tax rate at which tax revenue reaches a maximum, and many countries have tax rates beyond this point. If this is true, a reduction in the tax rate would increase income and tax revenue. Most economists believe that actual tax rates are below this point, though taxation may have an effect on the incentive to work. For further reading: E. J. Neil (ed.), *Free Market Conservatism* (1984). J.P.

supposed subject of knowledge. This notion is set at the heart of the theory of TRANSFERENCE elaborated by French analyst Jacques Lacan (1901–81), and presents an immediate difficulty in translation. Although it would seem to indicate a knowledge supposed to a subject, Lacan is careful to point out that what is supposed is not a knowledge (which is already there in the UNCONSCIOUS), but a SUBJECT. Hence, transference love is connected to knowledge, the supposed subject being the analyst, and if the analyst is loved because of this knowledge, we can say that the patient loves the analyst because of what he lacks. The LACANIAN practice of PSYCHOANALYSIS attempts to interpret from a position which would undermine this fiction, however necessary it may be in the transference, of a supposed subject of knowledge, to demonstrate to the subject that there is always an irremediable split between a subject and knowledge, never a union. D.L.

supramolecular chemistry. The synthesis and study of well-defined groups of MOLECULES that interact through chemical forces other than the covalent and ionic bonds (see BOND, CHEMICAL; CHEMISTRY). Supramolecular assemblies are generally bound together by weak interactions such as HYDROGEN BONDS, which enable the individual molecular components to retain their distinct identities, thereby allowing the possibility of reversible association and dissociation. Whereas non-covalent molecular assemblies feature in the traditional discipline of colloid chemistry, supramolecular chemistry usually involves highly specific interactions that dictate a particular size and shape in the assembly. It makes extensive use of MOLECULAR RECOGNITION, the selective binding of two or more molecules through complementarity of shape, charge and other factors. The principles involved in supramolecular assembly are often those exploited by natural biomolecular systems such as DNA (see NUCLEIC ACID) and ENZYMES. Thus the central characteristic of supramolecular chemistry is not 'mere' binding between molecules but 'programmed' binding: the individual molecules are imbued with the information needed to guide them together into an organized assembly. In this way, the power of chemistry is extended beyond the ability to make molecules into the realm of complex molecular systems, which might perform tasks such as CATALYSIS, energy conversion, sensing and even information processing. P.C.B.

suprematism. A form of more or less geometric ABSTRACT ART propounded by the Russian EX-CUBIST Kasimir Malevich (1878–1935) in a manifesto of 1915 and exemplified in his classic painting of a white square on a white background (now in the Museum of Modern Art, New York). Though it influenced Lissitzky, Rodchenko and other CONSTRUCTIVISTS, his movement was virtually stifled by their campaign against pure art and easel painting, only to be revived at the BAUHAUS (which published his book *The Non-Objective World*, 1959) and again in the 1960s, when there were exhibitions of his work in Stockholm and Amsterdam. In his own country it is still held to be FORMALISM, and accordingly unacceptable. J.W.

Supreme Court of the United States. The apex of the American judiciary and a linchpin of the system of 'checks and balances', which sustains the nation's political equilibrium. Regarded by the Founding Fathers as 'the least dangerous branch' of government, compared to the President and Congress, the Court has nevertheless profoundly influenced the character of the federal union (see FEDERALISM), assuring the supremacy of Washington over the fractious states (see STATES' RIGHTS), consolidating a continent-wide single market for interstate commerce, and finely elaborating the civil liberties in the Bill of Rights (see LIBERTARIANISM). Through imaginative interpretation, the Court has enabled a constitution written in the 18th century to remain a vibrant source of fundamental principle (see CONSTITUTIONAL GOVERNMENT; CONSTITUTIONALISM).

Consisting of nine appointees with life tenure, the Court is certainly the least democratic branch (see DEMOCRACY). Its authority to override the majority will, by invalidating legislation, is largely self-proclaimed. Yet this non-elected body has often seized opportunities to make the electoral process more open and equitable, serving as a court of last resort for aggrieved MINORITIES who can obtain no remedy through the ballot box. Gross population disparities among constituencies, e.g., have been held unconstitutional.

Because the Constitution restricts policy options, political issues are often reduced to judicial questions, as French historian de Tocqueville observed early in the 19th century, and brought before the Court. In deciding such cases, the justices have advanced both conservative (see CONSERVATISM) and PROGRESSIVE causes. Until the 1930s, they delayed the advent of the regulatory state by staunchly defending property rights guaranteed in the Fourteenth Amendment. In the 1940s and 1950s, in contrast, the Court dismantled official racial discrimination (see RACISM) by finding SEGREGATION a denial of 'the equal protection of the laws', as mandated by the same amendment. Although nominally bound by precedent, the Court, it has been said, 'follows the election returns', responding to broad shifts in public opinion by revising outmoded doctrine. For further reading: K. L. Hall (ed.), *The Oxford Companion to the Supreme Court of the United States* (1992). R.V.D.

surface-active agent, see under SURFACTANT.

surface structure, see under DEEP STRUCTURE.

surfactant (or **surface-active agent).** A substance (e.g. a detergent) which accumulates at a surface and makes it easier for the surface to spread. This lowering of the surface tension is used to encourage the 'wetting' of a material, and surfactants are also used to assist FLOTATION PROCESSES. B.F.

surgery. A method of treatment, the means whereby wounds can be repaired after injury, organs removed or parts of the body reconstructed on account of injury, disease or deformity. The basic procedures include incision (cutting into) to release infection and tension, or to gain access to parts and organs; excision (cutting out); and suturing (sewing together). As John Hunter (1728–93) demonstrated, advance in surgical knowledge and of the surgeon as an informed professional can only develop against a background of research. This concept reappeared in the 19th century when Lister applied Pasteur's discovery of MICROBIOLOGY to prevent and overcome the infection of wounds which had until then made impossible any technical advance beyond a crude craft. At the same time anaesthetic agents were discovered. Further advances came with World Wars I and II with regard to the treatment of wounds, haemorrhage and shock (blood transfusion). With the arrival of penicillin in World War II surgeons began to operate on chest wounds with increasing confidence. This led to modern thoracic surgery, and with the development of machines to pump oxygenated blood, bypassing heart and lungs, it became possible to stop the heart, open it and repair or replace torn or worn-out valves, to rectify heart deformities in children, and also to bypass, with veins taken from the leg, those obstructions of the coronary arteries which cause angina. Rigorous control of infection enables the surgeon to implant artificial parts, e.g. plates and screws for broken bones, artificial hip joints for arthritis, artificial arteries to replace or bypass those which are obstructed or distended and bursting (aneurysms). The science of immunology has enabled surgeons to *transplant* cooled but living organs from one person to another. Just as blood for transfusion must be matched between donor and recipient, so must organs (tissue typing), and rejection of the graft due to any other differences is suppressed by immunosuppressive drugs. Thus the kidney, heart, liver, lung and pancreas can be transplanted at all ages, with varying results. Developments in PHYSICS contribute significantly to advances in surgery. The operating microscope enables the surgeon to sew together minute vessels and nerves. Severed limbs can be rejoined and special skin and muscle and nerve grafting is possible. *Microsurgery* facilitates eye surgery, e.g. lens removal and artificial lens implantation for cataract. It has advanced surgery on the brain and spinal cord, and operations can extend to the innermost part of the ear for deafness, including the implantation of micro-electrical circuits. So-called 'keyhole' surgery has been developed to allow certain procedures to be carried out without large incisions: a hollow tube is passed up through a bodily passage, which might include a vein, and small instruments inside the tube perform the operation. Other developments in physics include the use of the LASER to replace the scalpel and of *ultrasonic* devices to locate obstructions in arteries, stones in the gall bladder and the kidney, and even to allow destruction of kidney stones without the use of the surgeon's scalpel. Now the space programme is producing new knowledge which can be applied to the healing of wounds and to the production of acceptable CELLS for transplantation, and as compounds which may reduce the need for the surgeon's knife. Strange as it may seem, the surgeon of today works with the scientist towards the means of dispensing with surgical operations, though it has to be remembered that the wounded in particular will always be in need of a well-trained surgeon. See also PLASTIC RECONSTRUCTIVE SURGERY. For further reading: H. Bailey and R. Love, rev. A. Rains and H. Ritchie, *Short Practice of Surgery* (1984). A.J.H.R.

surplus value. A concept in MARXIST theory, specifically related to the LABOUR THEORY OF VALUE. Engels called it Marx's principal 'discovery' in ECONOMICS. It refers to the value remaining when the cost of maintaining the worker – his subsistence costs – has been subtracted from the total value of the product he produces. If a worker has a ten-hour working day, only a part of that day – say eight hours – is needed for him to produce goods equal in value to his subsistence costs. In the remaining two hours, the worker creates surplus value, which is appropriated by the CAPITALIST as profit. The concept of surplus value is hence central to the Marxist theory of EXPLOITATION in capitalist society. Some Marxists, especially those of a TROTSKYIST persuasion, have argued that surplus value may be appropriated, and hence exploitation may continue, even in those economic systems where private ownership of capital has been abolished. In eastern Europe, they say, the state as 'collective capitalist' appropriated the surplus value created by the workers, and distributed it among the political and bureaucratic ÉLITES who control the state. For further reading: A. Gamble and P. Walton, *From Alienation to Surplus Value* (1972). K.K.

Surrealism. French literary movement evolving from the Paris wing of DADA during 1920–23, thereafter establishing itself also in the visual arts, theatre and cinema, to become the last (to date) of this century's great international modern currents. Though the name had been coined in 1917 by Guillaume Apollinaire, the true spiritual ancestors of the movement were Rimbaud, the newly rediscovered poet Lautréamont, the German and other late-18th-century Romantics (including de Sade; see ROMANTICISM), and the SYMBOLISTS. Its animator was the poet André Breton, who in 1919 founded the review *Littérature* with his friends Louis Aragon and Philippe Soupault, joined later that year by Paul Éluard, and there published his first experiments in *automatic writing*: a random stream of words coming from that SUBCONSCIOUS which the movement now deliberately set out to explore. Already aware of the manifestos and activities of Zurich Dada, as well as Tzara's poems, in the winter of 1919/20 Breton joined forces with Picabia and Tzara himself to create a comparable succession of Parisian shocks and scandals, whose aggressive, continually newsworthy tactics thenceforward became an integral part of his movement. In 1924, with Dada outside France effectively dead and his new allies discarded, Breton and his friends formally constituted the Surrealist group. Its manifesto, proclaiming the inferiority of REALISM to 'psychic automatism' and 'previously neglected forms of association' of a magical, irrational, hallucinatory sort, appeared that October; its new, politically tinged review *La Révolution Surréaliste* two months later.

Though visual art was neglected in the manifesto and its place at first far from clear, a distinctive Surrealist art gradually developed. Its main model was the METAPHYSICAL PAINTING of de Chirico, with its disquieting perspectives and poeticizing of the banal, but the more Dadaist work of Arp, Ernst, Duchamp and Picabia also contributed, and some attempt was made to annex Picasso and Paul Klee. In 1923 André Masson began to make 'automatic drawings' (or largely random doodles), influencing the light-hearted BIOMORPHIC art of Joan Miró who, with Arp, represented the more abstract wing of the movement (see ABSTRACT ART). But the surreal poetry of de Chirico's pictures – a blend of strikingly dead subject-matter, at once familiar and improbable, with a smoothly academic technique – was not developed further until the emergence, during the second half of the 1920s, of such artists as Yves Tanguy, the Belgians René Magritte and Paul Delvaux, and finally the Spaniard Salvador Dali, who settled in Paris at the end of 1929. Basing himself on a 'paranoiac-critical method' (delirium tempered by a Meissonier-like meticulousness), Dali depicted soft watches, decomposing human limbs, and other glutinously biomorphic props lost in endless arid landscapes. By a mixture of technical skill and brilliant self-projection, he became, for the public of the next two decades, the quintessential Surrealist.

As a literary movement, Surrealism spread mainly to those areas where French cultural influence was strong, e.g. Latin America, the Middle East, Spain, and eastern Europe, though it had its followers (such as David Gascoyne) in England, while there was an important group in pre-1939 Czechoslovakia. As a political force, dedicated to a concept of REVOLUTION that became increasingly TROTSKYIST, it was always negligible, its pretensions, which were largely those of Breton himself, leading only to disagreements (hence the secession of Aragon and Éluard in 1932 and 1938 respectively) and mystification. In the visual field, however, as also in Antonin Artaud's THEATRE OF CRUELTY and Luis Buñuel's films, it had a worldwide impact, particularly as a result of the London Surrealist Exhibition of June 1936, of Dali's window-dressing and HAPPENINGS in New York of 1939, of the posters of A. M. Cassandre and other epigones, and finally of the arrival in the USA of Breton, Ernst, Masson, Tanguy, and other refugees from German-occupied France. Gimmicks apart – and certainly it had these – Surrealism acted throughout the second quarter of this century as a universally intelligible plea for a revival of the imagination, based on the UNCONSCIOUS as revealed by PSYCHOANALYSIS, together with a new emphasis on magic, accident, irrationality, symbols, and dreams. Not the least of its achievements was that it led to a major revaluation of comparable romantic movements in the past. For further reading: F. Bradley, *Surrealism* (1997). J.W.

survey. A method for estimating characteristics of a population by analysis of a SAMPLE, whose members are so selected that the techniques of STATISTICS may be employed to assess the accuracy with which inferences may be made from sample to population. Its aim is not perfect precision but the control and estimation of random error (see ERROR ANALYSIS). Its preferred techniques of investigation are interviewing, the postal questionnaire, and observation. It contrasts with other methods of empirical social inquiry such as participant observation and the case study in that it typically uses more rigorously standardized procedures for eliciting information, and seeks to minimize the exercise of judgement in the recording of responses. A survey is distinguished from an enumeration or registration by the fact that a respondent or interviewee participates in a representative capacity. The method is at its best in eliciting information by methods which the informant regards as significant but not intrusive, but it can be misleading when it involves assessment of matters remote from his present concerns.

Survey analysis is regarded with suspicion by some because its complex techniques are often not sustained by adequate data, because analysis may be undertaken to give scientific legitimation to a preformed policy or IDEOLOGY, and because the mass media have low standards of reporting both the technical details and the institutional affiliations of survey inquiries. Nevertheless, it remains an indispensable means for investigating the degree of VARIANCE of a characteristic, and the extent to which characteristics co-vary. A non-trivial general proposition about a population can, in strict logic, be established or refuted only by analysis of data which represent that population to a known degree of approximation. Surveys are especially valuable for effecting comparisons and detecting trends. For further reading: C. A. Moser and G. Kalton, *Survey Methods in Social Investigation* (1985). K.H.

survival of the fittest, see under DARWINISM.

sustainability. An emerging concept in the environmental sciences and in the international development community. It refers to management practices that are designed to ensure that the exploitation of resources is conducted in a manner that protects the resource base for use by future generations. Sustainable energy technologies are those that rely on renewable or essentially infinite sources (e.g. solar, hydro, wind) rather than on finite supplies of fossil fuels, and which do not generate environmentally damaging pollutants such as many of the by-products of the combustion of fossil fuels. Sustainable harvests – from forests, farmlands or fisheries – are limited to levels that can be sustained indefinitely without damage to the productivity of the resource itself. See also CARRYING CAPACITY; BRUNDTLAND REPORT. W.G.R.

sustainable urban development. Development that incorporates the principles of SUSTAINABILITY, with particular reference to the environmental movement. Sustainability may be defined as having four elements: to conserve the stock of natural assets; to avoid damaging the regenerative capacity of ECOSYSTEMS; to achieve greater social and economic equality; and to avoid imposing risks and costs on future generations. These principles are embodied in the BRUNDTLAND REPORT. For further reading: A. Blowers (ed.), *Planning for Sustainable Development* (1993). C.G.

SUSY GUTS, see under GRAND UNIFICATION, GRAND UNIFIED THEORIES.

swami. In HINDUISM, a formal title given to a specially honoured spiritual teacher. GURU is a more informal term. D.L.E.

sweet. A term used especially in the SWING era to distinguish between those BIG BANDS that played JAZZ and those that played softly for the customers. Jazz fans sneered at the sweet bands, but for the musicians the relationship was more complex. Given the commercial context of popular music, even HOT bands had to play sweet from time to time – Count Basie recorded a fulsome version of 'Danny Boy' complete with 'Irish' tenor – and jazz stars often admired the technical accomplishment of the better sweet bands as well as envying their audience appeal. In a classic case, the great Louis Armstrong recalled with unfeigned relish the time he sat in with Guy Lombardo and his Royal Canadians, a band that epitomized everything sweet and, to Armstrong lovers, sickening. GE.S.

swing. Variously, a JAZZ style and a jazz essence. As a genre, swing followed NEW ORLEANS and CHICAGO in the course of the music's development. It dominated and named the swing era, which lasted roughly from the mid-1930s to the mid-1940s, and whose typical medium was the BIG BAND, touring the country playing arranged music, interspersed with improvised solos, for dancing. In character, jazz in the swing style was subtler than the earlier forms, though generally still closer to them harmonically and rhythmically than to the music of the BEBOP revolution that followed. At its best, as in the playing of Benny Goodman (known as the King of Swing for the popularity of his band) and men like Lester Young, Coleman Hawkins and Johnny Hodges (to name a very few), it conveys an effortless, timeless maturity, fully justifying its later designation as MAINSTREAM. As a vital quality of jazz, swing refers to its rhythmic aspect, that feeling of lift and drive that makes it unique. To swing is not simply to play rhythmically. RAGTIME does not swing, nor (depending on the particular listener) do the earliest forms of jazz, being too strictly tied to the underlying pulse. Swing in its mature sense depends on a subtle pulling away from the beat, blending tension and relaxation in perfect equilibrium. Describing it in abstract terms is impossible, but it is perceptible immediately, distinguishing the jazz player from any other musician, and jazz from any other music. GE.S.

syllabics (or **syllabic verse**). Name given to a type of prose arranged to look like verse, written in the late 1950s and early 1960s, which was based simply on syllable-count (the number of syllables in the line, irrespective of their duration or accentual value). The verses in question (by, e.g., George Macbeth) were invariably crude or flat or both; but serious experimentation had earlier proved fruitful in the work of genuine poets such as Robert Graves, Herbert Read and Marianne Moore, who did not care to draw attention to the new techniques they were trying out. A fairly cogent if incomplete discussion, by a practising poet, occurs in Roy Fuller's *Owls and Artificers* (1971). The discussion of this subject – though never using the term syllabics – has a long history. There are experiments in English quantitative verse by Edmund Spenser, Tennyson and others; Robert Bridges also gave much thought to the problem, which is essentially one of making quantity (length of syllable) felt in an accentual context. The 'experimenters' of the 1960s thought that they had invented a new kind of verse, but it was chopped-up prose because no distinction between syllables of different lengths was made (or, doubtlessly) noted. This episode was therefore irrelevant. M.S.-S.

syllogism. In LOGIC, a deductive argument in which a *conclusion* is derived from two *premises* and in which each of the three PROPOSITIONS asserts or denies that all or some things of a certain kind are also of another kind. Each of the terms, or kinds, mentioned in the conclusion occurs in only one premise, together with a term (the *middle term*) which occurs in both premises but not in the conclusion. Thus in the syllogism 'All men are mortal, all Greeks are men, so all Greeks are mortal', 'men' is the middle term; 'mortal', the second term in the conclusion, is the *major term*, and the premise in which it occurs the *major premise*; and 'Greeks', the first term of the conclusion, is the *minor term*, and its premise the *minor premise*. The order of terms in the premises can be reversed, jointly or severally. This yields four patterns of term-arrangement or 'figures'. Each of the three propositions may be of any of the four recognized logical forms: all *A* are *B*, no *A* are *B*, some *A* are *B*, some *A* are not *B*. There are thus 256 possible syllogistic forms: 64 possible form-combinations multiplied by the four figures. Of these only 19 are valid. The theory of the syllogism was developed to a high degree of systematic completeness by Aristotle. A.Q.

symbiosis.

(1) The original meaning: in BIOLOGY, the state of affairs in which two often very dissimilar organisms live together in mutual dependence and for mutual benefit, each making up for the other's shortcomings. Thus a lichen is a symbiotic union of fungus and single-celled green alga. The compound organism, unlike a fungus, is AUTOTROPHIC. Symbiosis may have played an important part in EVOLUTION. Thus mitochondria (see CYTOLOGY) may have originated as symbiotic bacteria (see BACTERIOLOGY), and chloroplasts (see PHOTOSYNTHESIS) may have originated in the same way by union of non-CHLOROPHYLL-containing CELLS with single-celled green algae. A phenomenon which may be regarded as a step on the road towards full symbiosis is *commensalism*, in which two organisms 'dine at the same table': thus a sea anemone may grow on the shell which houses a hermit crab, and various little crustacea live within the giant respiratory chambers of, e.g., sea squirt. The field of study dealing with symbiosis is sometimes known as *symbiotics*. P.M.

(2) In SOCIOLOGY, relations of mutual dependence between different groups within a community are described as *symbiotic* when the groups are unlike and the relations complementary; as *commensal* when they are like and the relations are supplementary. A.L.C.B.

symbol. Based upon a relationship of metaphor (X stands for Y), but the relationship is arbitrary. For example, a red rose is a symbol for love. Symbols have the ability to link previously separate areas of conceptual experience and allow the human mind to go beyond what is known or observed. This bridging process opens up an area of connotation which gives symbols their multifaceted, ambiguous qualities.

Anthropologists have pursued the study of symbols along two lines: meaning and function. Those influenced by Claude Lévi-Strauss and the structuralist method (see STRUCTURALISM) have studied symbols and the nature of symbolization as a cognitive process. This approach has considered 'the logic by which symbols are connected'

(Edmund Leach, *Culture and Communication*, 1976). Meaning is generated from the combinations, relationships and transformations of different elements within a symbolic context. The second approach has focused upon the function of symbols for individual expressiveness and social requirements. This has located symbols within a specific social context and highlighted their emotional content. Attempts to link these two lines of inquiry have explained the power and effectiveness of symbols as arising from the dissonance between intellectual and emotional properties. For further reading: M. Augé, *The Anthropological Circle* (1982). A.G.

symbolic. The symbolic is a term introduced into PSYCHOANALYSIS by Jacques Lacan (1901–81), and designates the set of pre-existing structures into which the child is born, e.g. KINSHIP relations, language, and other combinatorial structures. We cannot, however, simply identify the symbolic with language, since the latter involves REAL and IMAGINARY dimensions: if there is a specifically symbolic side to language, it is on the side of the signifier whereby each element takes on its value owing to its difference from other elements in the chain-like structure. D.L.

symbolic interaction. The aspect of human behaviour on which American social psychologist G. H. Mead (1863–1931) based his ROLE THEORY. Mead argued that what distinguishes man from the other animals is the enormous number of symbolic or conventional meanings which his highly complex nervous system and the faculty of language enable him to store in his memory and to express by particular words and actions. These agreed meanings are learned through the process of symbolic interaction, i.e. of seeing yourself as you are seen by others, which is a necessary condition of playing roles; thus as a child you learn the role of bus-passenger-at-a-request-stop by taking the role of the driver, i.e. by imagining him seeing your raised hand, realizing you are trying to attract his attention, and stopping. This account of the learning process is extremely vulnerable to criticism from a SKINNERIAN or BEHAVIOURIST standpoint; while Mead's insistence that the self is merely the sum of the social roles an individual plays can be taxed with failing to take into account genetic (see GENETICS/GENOMICS) or personality factors (see PERSONALITY TYPES). See also CHICAGO SCHOOL (1). For further reading: P. Rock, *The Making of Symbolic Interactionism* (1979). M.BA.

symbolic logic, see MATHEMATICAL LOGIC.

Symbolism. A general literary term and technique; but, specifically, the name of a central late-19th-century movement in the arts which marks the turn from ROMANTICISM to MODERNISM. Historically there are many Symbolist movements and tendencies, but Romanticism opened new possibilities by attaching special value to the imagination, the seer-poet, and the poetic path towards a transcendent world (Blake, Shelley, Poe). France, the 1850s and Charles Baudelaire (1821–67) form the starting-point for fresh developments: the matching of the Swedenborg-type theory of 'correspondences' (connections within the visible, or between the visible and invisible, worlds) with a prime role for the hyper-aesthetic imagination of the poet, who digests the 'storehouse of images and signs' in the visible world and relates them to create 'a new world, the sensation of newness'. Language itself had a transcendent content: thus Baudelaire's sonnet on the vowels. In 1886, Jean Moréas held that Symbolism had replaced all prior movements, and asserted the TRANSCENDENCE of art. In Rimbaud, Verlaine, Gautier, Nerval, Mallarmé and Valéry, these ideas evolve into complex interplays of a subjective, magical poetic vision and the idea of a timeless, epiphanic image (see EPIPHANY) which art pursues and releases by its rhythmic, metaphoric or linguistic action. As in Romanticism, the poet risks his own senses and experience for occult discovery through the imagination: Valéry emphasizes his special 'psychophysiology', Yeats his 'visions'. However, Symbolism emphasized much more than Romanticism the need to *create* form; a high premium is set on the fictionalizing act itself; linguistic mechanisms are stressed; technique becomes an end in itself; the idea of the 'supreme fiction' emerges. The world is seen less as an imaginative power than as a bundle of fragments; when the notion of cultural, historical and linguistic crisis is added, this leads the way to much 20th-century modernist thought.

Hence the 'Symbolist movement' was particularly concentrated in the transitional 1890s: in Paris, with the Mallarmé circle, Huysmans and Valéry; in Britain, with Yeats, Wilde, Symons; not much later in Germany (Stefan George), Austria (Rilke) and Russia (Bely, Blok, etc.). Though strongly focused on the SYNAESTHESIA of poetry, it stressed the relation of all art-forms. It is evident in fiction (late James, Joyce, Proust), drama (Strindberg, Maeterlinck), music (Debussy, Scriabin), painting (Redon, Gauguin), and dance. Critic Edmund Wilson rightly sees Symbolism coming through into familiar modernism (Trakl, Schönberg, Kandinsky). Gradually the transcendent element in Symbolism, its devotion to penetrating the veil beyond time, fades. IMAGISM and SURREALISM are distinguishable from it because the neo-Platonic bias goes. However, much modernist writing is Symbolist in spirit, because of the high value it places on form, holistically conceived (see HOLISM), as against materialistic, realistic, historical or DOCUMENTARY presentation. See also AESTHETICISM; DECADENCE. For further reading: P. G. West (ed.), *Symbolism: an Anthology* (1980). M.S.BR.

symmetry, group, see under GROUP.

sympatric speciation, see under SPECIATION.

symphonic jazz. To some people the name is a contradiction, since the essence of JAZZ is spontaneity and individuality, the opposite of the symphony's massed forces and regimentation. But in fact composers and jazzmen have long been tantalized by the possibility of harnessing the distinctive flavour of jazz to the formal expressiveness of classical music. Among the first attempts were Darius Milhaud's *La Création du Monde* (1923) and George Gershwin's *Rhapsody in Blue* (1924). Action from the other side came in the 1930s with the extended compositions Duke Ellington wrote for his BIG BAND, *Creole Rhapsody* and *Reminiscing in Tempo*, just the first of numerous attempts throughout his career to wed his own improvisatory style to a more substantial structure. A notable product of the 1940s was Igor Stravinsky's *Ebony Concerto*, written for Woody Herman's band, but much more Stravinsky than Herman. By the 1950s, jazz musicians absorbed in serious musical study produced a spate of works employing classical forms that were given the collective label 'third stream'. But in the 1960s, with jazz beginning to suffer an identity crisis under pressure from FREE JAZZ and ROCK MUSIC, such ambitions waned. It may be that mutual awareness and respect for what the two genres have to offer will enrich them both, without some form of self-conscious union. GE.S.

synaesthesia. The experience, whether real or hallucinatory, in which a stimulus applied to one sense elicits a response from one or more others; also, the literary device that corresponds to this experience, as in 'silvery trumpet-note', 'scarlet stench', 'loud, stinking colour'. Synaesthesia (*synesthésie*) occurs in all poetry, but was especially popular among the Romantic (see ROMANTICISM) and SYMBOLIST poets (as in Baudelaire's sonnet 'Correspondances') of the 19th century – mainly because mentally disturbed or drugged people claim to have experienced it. The CONCEPT enjoyed some facile revival in the DRUG-dominated 1960s, as 'sense-overload' and other such journalistic notions. The psychedelic light-show was a practical manifestation. M.S.-S.

synaesthesis. Term coined by James Wood, I. A. Richards and C. K. Ogden in *The Foundations of Aesthetics* (1922) to describe the harmony allegedly achieved by a work of art, which is said to raise the receptor to an awareness of beauty by its equilibrium: its capacity to balance strong emotions. M.S.-S.

synchrocyclotron, see under ACCELERATOR.

synchromism, see under ORPHISM.

synchronic, see under DIACHRONIC; LINGUISTICS.

synchronicity. JUNGIAN term for an acausal connecting principle that would give meaning to series of coincidences (e.g. the frequent recurrence of a particular numeral over a short period of time) not explicable through notions of simple causality, as well as to the experiences labelled déjà vu and

PRECOGNITION. In this CONCEPT, Jung argued against the classical elementaristic view of experience, in favour of a view of events as participants within a structured whole (see STRUCTURALISM). Hence, according to this view, the meaning of events is to be found in terms of their structural relationships, as well as their causal antecedents. Jung's structuralism entails a form of experiential harmony – harmony among events, and a harmony between the structure of our understanding and the event structure. T.Z.C.

synchronism. In ARCHAEOLOGY, to establish a synchronism means to demonstrate, usually by means of TYPOLOGY, the contemporaneity of CULTURES, artifacts or structures. Thus the synchronism of two disparate settlements might be argued on the basis of both containing like ASSEMBLAGES of distinctive tool types. Synchronisms over larger areas may be constructed with reference to the occurrence of characteristic types extensively traded. Until the advent of RADIOCARBON DATING this was one of the few methods available for correlating prehistoric cultures (see PREHISTORY). B.C.

synchronous orbit. The path in space of an artificial SATELLITE which always remains directly above a fixed point on the equator. It is necessary for the ORBIT to be a circle about 22,500 miles above the earth; this figure is calculated from NEWTONIAN MECHANICS, using the MASS and radius of the earth and the fact that the orbit must be traversed in exactly one day. Synchronous satellites are used for intercontinental TELECOMMUNICATIONS. M.V.B.

synchrotron, see under ACCELERATOR.

syncopation. The transference of musical accents onto the subsidiary pulses of a musical measure. Normally, the music has a regular pulse or time, of which three-beat (waltz) and four-beat (march) are the commonest. The natural accentuation falls on the first beat of three, and on the first and (to a lesser degree) third beats of four. In a syncopated rhythm the accent is shifted, although the main pulse continues in the background, even if only by implication. Examples of syncopation can be found as early as the 14th century; it has been a marked feature of much 20th-century music, and in JAZZ is all-pervasive. A.H.

syncretism. Fusion, in PERCEPTION or thought (including dreams), of incompatible elements; e.g. an inchoate dream image of someone who is at once mother and brother, or man and horse. I.M.L.H.

syndicalism. A militant TRADE UNION movement which started in France (*syndicat* is the French word for trade union) in the 1890s, and aimed at transferring the control and ownership of the means of production, not to the state, but to the unions themselves. The movement derived partly from the anti-parliamentary ideas of Proudhon and partly from the reaction of the workers against both the 'parliamentarism' of the SOCIALIST Party and the exclusive emphasis placed on politics by such MARXIST leaders as Jules Guesde. The syndicalists rejected politics, regarding CLASS struggle in the form of INDUSTRIAL ACTION as more effective; the fight on the shop floor was eventually to lead to a 'general STRIKE' (which Georges Sorel later made into the cornerstone of his theory of DIRECT ACTION). Socialist INTELLECTUALS were regarded with suspicion, and the need for workers' solidarity as a precondition of the success of any industrial and trade-union action was stressed in the *Charter of Amiens* (1906) and other texts of the Confédération Générale du Travail, in the pronouncements of the famous British leader of 'industrial unionism', Tom Mann, and in those of the organizers of the American Industrial Workers of the World (the 'Wobblies').

Another factor permeating the syndicalist movement was the Bakuninist ANARCHIST tradition, particularly in France, Switzerland, Italy and Spain, countries where in its early phase syndicalism appeared in its revolutionary form (see REVOLUTION) of ANARCHO-SYNDICALISM. In other countries, syndicalism as a reaction to a still-decentralized economy was seen, in Bertrand Russell's words, as 'the anarchism of the market place'. As an IDEOLOGY legitimizing direct industrial action by the workers, syndicalism has left a strong legacy in their trade-union organizations, but as a political current it disappeared from the scene as an effective force before World War I. For further reading: F. F. Ridley,

Revolutionary Syndicalism in France (1970). L.L.

synergism. In BIOLOGY, the relationship between agents whereby their combined effect is greater than the sum of the effect of each one considered individually. Thus, considered as narcotics, barbituric acid derivatives and alcohol have a greater depressant effect than the sum of the two acting separately. The more general term SYNERGY can also bear this specific meaning. P.M.

synergy. The additional benefit accruing to a number of SYSTEMS should they coalesce to form a larger system. This CONCEPT reflects the classical opinion that 'the whole is greater than the sum of the parts'. In practice, synergy may turn out to be negative, because the totality is ill conceived or ineffectively organized. Synergy is formally studied as a property of systems by CYBERNETICS. In management, synergy is the subject of measurement by operational research, especially where business MERGERS are concerned; but the word is also frequently used in a much looser way in discussions of CORPORATE STRATEGY, simply to indicate general expectations of collaborative benefit. More generally still, the term is applied to the generation of unplanned social benefits (see EXTERNALITIES) among people who unconsciously co-operate in pursuit of their own interests and goals. The term derives from BIOLOGY, where it is an alternative term for SYNERGISM. R.I.T.; S.BE.

synonymy, see under FREE VARIATION.

syntactics, see LOGICAL SYNTAX.

syntagmatic/paradigmatic. In LINGUISTICS, adjectives applied to two kinds of relationship into which all linguistic elements enter. Syntagmatic refers to the linear relationship operating at a given LEVEL between the elements in a sentence; paradigmatic refers to the relationship between an element at a given point within a sentence and an element with which, syntactically, it is interchangeable. For example, in the sentence *He is coming*, the relationship between *He*, *is*, *com-* and *-ing* is syntagmatic (at the level of MORPHOLOGY); the relationship between *He* and *She*, *is* and *will be*, etc., is paradigmatic. D.C.

syntax. In LINGUISTICS, a traditional term for the study of the rules governing the way words are combined to form sentences in a language. An alternative definition (avoiding the concept of *word*) is the study of the interrelationships between elements of sentence structure, and of the rules governing the arrangement of sentences in sequences (see DISCOURSE). See also CONSTITUENT ANALYSIS; DEEP STRUCTURE AND SURFACE STRUCTURE; GRAMMAR. D.C.

synthesis. The final stage, succeeding thesis and antithesis, in a DIALECTIC triad, a phase of the dialectic process. (See also DIALECTICAL MATERIALISM.) First some thought is affirmed; the *thesis*. On reflection this reveals itself as unsatisfactory, incomplete or contradictory, and prompts the affirmation of its opposite: the *antithesis*. But further reflection shows that this too is inadequate and so it, in turn, is contradicted by the *synthesis*. This, however, does not, as in classical LOGIC, where double negation is identical with affirmation, simply reinstate the original thesis. The synthesis is held to embrace or reconcile the more rational and acceptable elements in the conflicting and now superseded thesis and antithesis from which it emerges in a 'higher unity'. A.Q.

synthetic, see under ANALYTIC.

synthetic chemistry. The laboratory or industrial preparation of chemical substances from simpler starting materials. Synthetic methods may be routine or directed to the preparation of new compounds. B.F.

synthetism. One wing of the SYMBOLIST movement in painting, developed mainly by Gauguin and the young Émile Bernard, whose *Pots de grès et pommes* of 1887 was inscribed '*premier essai de synthétisme et de simplification*'. With its use of clearly defined flat areas of colour (sometimes called *cloisonnisme* because of its dependence on *cloisons* or partitions), synthetism was quite different from the more atmospheric, surreal symbolism (see SURREALISM) of Odion Redon and Gustave Moreau. Its adherents, who showed as a group at the Café Volpini in Paris in 1889, were drawn mainly from the PONT-AVEN school. For further reading: H. R. Rookmaaker, *Synthetist Art Theories* (1959). J.W.

system dynamics, see under SYSTEMS.

systematic theology, see DOGMATICS.

systematics, see under TAXONOMY.

***Système Internationale d'Unités*,** see SI UNITS.

systemic grammar. A theory of GRAMMAR which British linguist Michael Halliday developed from his earlier SCALE-AND-CATEGORY GRAMMAR, the new name reflecting his view of language as an organization of *system networks* of contrasts. D.C.

systems; systems approach; systems analysis.

(1) A *system* is a group of related elements organized for a purpose. The nature of systems is studied by the science of CYBERNETICS and by GENERAL SYSTEMS THEORY (GST). A *systems approach* (or *systems analysis*, though this phrase also bears the narrower meaning defined in (2) below) is an approach to the study of physical and social systems which enables complex and dynamic situations to be understood in broad outline. It is a conceptual tool, the user of which may also receive scientific assistance from operational research. The approach is valid whether the topic is a heating system, a postal system, a health or education system, a firm, an economy, or a government.

To identify a system it is necessary to distinguish its boundaries, to be aware of its purposes (whether these are a blueprint for its design or inferred from its behaviour), and to define the level of abstraction at which it is to be treated. Systems may turn out to contain recognizable *sub-systems*, sub-sub-systems, etc. These arrangements are sometimes investigated as hierarchies; but because the arrangement often involves a nesting (in the manner of Chinese boxes) of systems within each other, they may also be defined by RECURSION. One of the discoveries made by the systems approach is the extent to which attempts to improve the performance of a sub-system by its own criteria (*sub-optimization*) may act to the detriment of the total system and even to the defeat of its objectives.

In management contexts, the systems approach concerns itself with growth and stability in the system under a range of possible futures, unpredictable perturbations, and alternative policies. The classic tool for studying these matters is a systems MODEL which is used for purposes of SIMULATION, and whose implications can be explored by means of a digital COMPUTER. *System dynamics* is a term coined by American computer engineer Jay Forrester (1918–) for a style of model-building in which large structures are built which make little use of empirical evidence or previous knowledge of the subject. Forrester has shown how policies, decisions, structure and delayed responses are interrelated to influence growth and stability. First applied to industrial systems, his METHODOLOGY has subsequently been used to study urban and world ecological systems (see ECOLOGY) where the vision of an all-embracing model and its striking conclusions have gained a wide audience. The systems approach to a problem can alert scientists to interactions whose importance they have failed to recognize. However, systems analysis has also been applied to a number of disciplines where its contributions have yet to achieve significant influence. See also METASYSTEM. S.BE.; R.I.T.; J.A.M.; M.A.H.D.

(2) More narrowly, *systems analysis* is the first stage in presenting any large task to a computer (the other stages being programming and CODING). It is performed by a *systems analyst* and consists of analysing the whole task in its setting and deciding in outline how to arrange it for the computer; estimating how much work is involved and hence how powerful a computer will be needed; dividing the process into a number of relatively independent parts; and finally specifying each of these, together with their interconnections, in sufficient detail for a programmer to take over. C.S.

systems engineering, see under CONTROL ENGINEERING; CYBERNETICS; SYSTEMS.

T

TA, see TRANSACTIONAL ANALYSIS.

table of mortality, see LIFE TABLE.

***tableau-piège*,** see under COLLAGE.

taboo. A linguistic legacy to Europe from Polynesia, through Captain Cook. In its homelands the word seemed to mean both that which was holy and that which was prohibited. It is the latter sense upon which English has for the most part seized, and taboo (or tabu) is now, as noun, verb and adjective, employed loosely to mean prohibition/prohibit/prohibited in the vast field of behaviour ranging from etiquette to RELIGION (but usually excluding law). In the SOCIAL SCIENCES, however, the term has taken on technical senses, some of which incorporate the apparent duality of its Polynesian origins. For many anthropologists, taboo means a RITUAL prohibition that may express either the sacredness (holiness) or uncleanness of what is set apart. The thing tabooed is in some fashion dangerous. Anthropologists utilizing Claude Lévi-Strauss's structural method (see STRUCTURALISM) (e.g. Mary Douglas, *Purity and Danger*, 1966) have understood taboo as arising from the process of social classification. The duality is preserved in a different manner in FREUDIAN psychoanalytic theory (see PSYCHOANALYSIS), where taboo prevents people from doing what their unconscious desires impel them towards. INCEST and food taboos are among the commonest of those discussed in the literature. See also PURITY/IMPURITY. For further reading: E. R. Leach, *Social Anthropology* (1982).

M.F.; A.G.

***tachisme*,** see under ACTION PAINTING.

tachyon. A hypothetical PARTICLE travelling faster than light. Because of the 'light barrier' of RELATIVITY theory, tachyons could not be produced by the acceleration of ordinary particles. Tachyons would generate a special kind of electromagnetic RADIATION, but this has not been detected.

M.V.B.

tacit knowledge. An idea formulated by Hungarian-born chemist and social philosopher Michael Polanyi (1891–1976) with wide-ranging implications in many fields of experience, though most commonly discussed in terms of its applicability to scientific knowledge. Polanyi established it as a fact of common PERCEPTION that we are typically aware of certain objects without our attention being fixed upon them. The former kind of perception ('tacit knowledge') was not, he argued, an inferior or irrelevant dimension of CONSCIOUSNESS, interfering with deliberate attention. Rather it was integral to the entirety of our consciousness, forming the background grid which made focused perceptions possible, intelligible and fruitful. Polanyi made the comparison with certain acquired skills (e.g. manual dexterity) through which highly deliberate acts (e.g. composing on the piano) come within our grasp. Polanyi's insight has led others to build upon his work and stress how science itself is largely a 'craft skill', dependent (to a degree which major philosophies of science scarcely recognize; see SCIENCE, PHILOSOPHY OF) upon know-how rather than explicit, formal methodological rules (see METHODOLOGY). For further reading: M. Polanyi, *The Tacit Dimension* (1966).

R.P.

tagmemic grammar. A theory of GRAMMAR developed by American linguist K. L. Pike in the early 1950s. The name reflects the use the theory makes of the CONCEPT of the *tagmeme*, a device for conveying simultaneously formal and functional information about a particular linguistic unit. Thus, in the sentence *The cat sat on the mat*, the formal information that *the cat* is a noun phrase and the functional information that it is the subject of the sentence are combined in a single tagmemic statement, written S: NP. Many of the principles underlying Pike's linguistic theory have since been applied to the analysis of non-linguistic phenomena (see also EMIC), of particular note being his *Language in Relation to a Unified Theory of Human Behaviour* (1967).

D.C.

Tailhook. The US Navy scandal that began when a female lieutenant reported she was sexually abused by drunken fellow officers at a Las Vegas hotel on 7 September 1991, during the annual convention of the Tailhook Association, an unofficial military auxiliary group. The name refers to the part of a jet fighter that catches on wires strung across the deck of an aircraft carrier. Full membership in the group is reserved for aviators who have accomplished such an 'arrested carrier landing'. However, Tailhook – an event of drunken debauchery in which at least 26 women, half of them naval officers, were sexually abused – came to symbolize the US military's difficulties in integrating women into the services. The scandal resulted in the forced resignation of Secretary of the Navy H. Lawrence Garrett III, and was the forerunner of other disclosures of SEXUAL ABUSE, RAPE and harassment of women in the US military. R.K.H.

take-off point. A phrase derived from American economist W. W. Rostow's *Stages of Economic Growth* (1960). The essential idea is that there is a recognizable stage in a country's history, lasting for perhaps 20–30 years, during which the required conditions for sustained and fairly rapid growth are consolidated and beyond which such growth is more or less assured. The characteristic of this stage was defined as an increase in the proportion of NATIONAL INCOME that is saved from a low level to 10 per cent or more. The idea has been seriously criticized by most development economists (see ECONOMIC DEVELOPMENT), but has become part of the language of economic development. I.M.D.L.; J.P.

takeovers, see under MERGER.

***tamizdat*,** see under SAMIZDAT.

***tangentopoli*.** Term, loosely translated as 'bribesville', coined to describe the municipal and other corruption that was uncovered by *Operazione mani pulite* (Operation Clean Hands) in Italy in the early 1990s. The original *tangentopoli* was Milan, where widespread corruption was uncovered in the local authority administered by the Partito Socialista Italiano (PSI), but subsequently comparable or worse levels of corruption were discovered in many government bodies among virtually all the established political parties, with the partial exception of the Partito Democratico di Sinistra (PDS), as well as in a variety of other contexts. Operation Clean Hands effectively discredited the greater part of the political establishment that had ruled Italy since World War II, and led to the emergence of new political parties such as Forza Italia and the Partito Popolare (PP), as well as the renaming of others, such as the PDS and Alleanza Nazionale (AN, the former fascist Movimento Sociale Italiano – MSI). V.L.

Tantra. A discourse imparting doctrines in the tradition of Mahayana BUDDHISM, usually said to have been spoken by a mythical Buddha. Thousands of Tantras have been written from *c.* AD 500 onwards, and some have received new attention as a result of the worldwide interest in Buddhism in the 19th and 20th centuries; most notably the *Tibetan Book of the Dead*, written probably in the 8th century to give guidance to dying persons. D.L.E.

Taoism. A RELIGION of the Chinese. Less official than CONFUCIANISM, it has been essentially a way (Chinese *Tao*) of life through virtue to prosperity, longevity and immortality. Virtue has been seen as conformity to nature without and within man. This way has included both meditation in temples of great beauty and tranquillity, and a more popular traffic in charms and magical formulae, often linked with secret societies. Although the China Taoist Association was formed in 1957 with government permission, on the whole the COMMUNIST rulers of China since 1949 have suppressed Taoism. For further reading: W. Chan, *Religious Trends in Modern China* (1953). D.L.E.

Tarski's theory of truth. The nature of TRUTH is a problem on which 20th-century philosophers, like those of previous ages, have not reached agreement. Certain philosophies (see PRAGMATISM) downgrade the idea of truth altogether; others have contended that truth is largely a formal property (e.g. the coherence of the components of a theory within a rational whole). Perhaps the most elementary and commonly persuasive notion of truth is that it lies in correspondence to the facts (a conception to the fore in the various forms of EMPIRICISM). In the 20th century, that view has been defended in the most subtle way by Alfred Tarski

(1901–83), who pitched the discussion of truth on to a metalinguistic plane (see METALANGUAGE), by stipulating rigid conditions under which 'truth language' would be applicable. Precisely, he argued that a statement such as 'snow is white' is true if, and only if, snow is indeed white. Such a formulation endowed the concept of truth with unambiguous linguistic meaning. Tarski's insight has often been said to provide support for philosophical REALISM. For further reading: R. Harré, *Philosophies of Science* (1972). R.P.

taxation. The transfer of resources from private individuals, institutions, groups and firms to the government. Taxation can be on income, i.e. direct taxation; on wealth, i.e. capital taxation; or on transactions, i.e. indirect taxation. Governments levy taxes in order to cover the costs of providing PUBLIC GOODS and any losses of firms in the PUBLIC SECTOR, to redistribute income and wealth, to subsidize and encourage the consumption of particular goods and services (e.g. education), to control AGGREGATE DEMAND and to pursue various other aims. Taxation necessarily alters prices and incomes that would otherwise obtain in a FREE MARKET and is usually regarded as reducing ECONOMIC EFFICIENCY. The extent to which efficiency is reduced is disputed and of importance (see SUPPLY-SIDE ECONOMICS). A system of taxation should be designed so that while achieving the above aims, the chosen forms of taxation result in the minimum distortion of the economy and loss of economic efficiency (see POVERTY). A tax system is progressive/neutral/regressive, if the average rate of tax increases/stays the same/decreases as people get richer. In assessing the effects of increased public expenditure on the distribution of economic welfare, the distribution of the benefits of the expenditure and the increased tax payments have to be considered. J.P.

taxis, see under TROPISM.

taxonomic linguistics, see under LINGUISTICS.

taxonomy. The classification of living things; also known as *biosystematics*. Biosystematics was founded by Linnaeus, who introduced the familiar binomial nomenclature in which each organism is given a generic (e.g. *Homo*) and a specific name (*Homo sapiens*). The most majestic of taxonomic distinctions is into plant and animal *kingdoms* (the subject-matters of BOTANY and ZOOLOGY respectively). Next in order of rank is the PHYLUM, the members of which are united by a basic similarity of ground plan which may only be apparent at a relatively early stage of development.

A phylum comprises a number of *classes*. Members of a class are united by a somewhat closer degree of similarity than the members of a phylum – extending to points of anatomical detail as well as to ground plan. For example, the phylum Arthropoda includes the classes Insecta and Crustacea, the Insecta being united by having three pairs of legs attached to the thoracic region of the body and respiring by means of *tracheae*; while within the Vertebrates (often accorded the rank of a sub-phylum within the phylum Chordata) fishes, reptiles, amphibians, birds and mammals are all graded as classes.

Next below the class come successively the *order*, the *family*, and the *genus* (plural *genera*). It is not possible to specify the degree of resemblance that unites members of orders, families or genera in a way that will apply to all animals and plants; it may be noted, however, that among mammals the whales and dolphins, the carnivores, the rodents and the primates each form an order. Finally, below the genus comes the SPECIES; thus the great cats belong to the genus Panthera, in which *Panthera leo* (the lion) and *Panthera tigris* (the tiger) are species.

Of the larger taxonomic subdivisions it may be said that all phyla, classes and orders are intended to have the same 'value', i.e. to be of the same rank in the systematic hierarchy. Furthermore, each group within itself is intended to be *monophyletic*, i.e. to be such that the common ancestor of the members of the group is itself a member of the group. (There are exceptions: notoriously, the class Reptilia is polyphyletic in the sense that reptiles are subdivided into two main streams – one leading towards birds and one towards mammals – both of which evolved out of amphibian ancestors.) On the other hand, taxonomic divisions are not intended to be a dossier of evolutionary relationships (see EVOLUTION); the purpose of taxonomy is to *name* reliably and consistently. Nevertheless, the fact of the evolutionary relationship imposes a certain pattern upon classification which is not to be avoided.

Taxonomic characteristics, i.e. those upon which a systematic allocation may be made, are wherever possible structural, since physiological and behavioural criteria are of little use to the museum taxonomist who normally has to handle dead specimens. Similar difficulties restrict the use of immunological criteria (see IMMUNOLOGY) in determining blood relationships. They have, however, helped to show that whales are more nearly akin to pigs than to other mammals that have been alleged to be their relations. P.M.

technetronic society, see under POST-INDUSTRIAL SOCIETY.

technocracy. Term coined in 1919 in California by an engineer, William Henry Smyth, for his proposed 'rule by technicians'. In 1933–34 it was taken over and popularized by Howard Scott, a former associate of Thorstein Veblen (whose book *The Engineers and the Price System*, 1921, was taken as a bible for the idea), and technocracy as a social movement had a brief vogue in the USA during the early Depression years. During the 1960s the term gained wider currency in France, where it was identified with the theories of Saint-Simon (who predicted a society ruled by scientists and engineers) and used by writers such as Jean Meynaud (see below) to argue that 'real power' has shifted from the elected representatives to the technical experts and that there now 'begins a new type of government, neither DEMOCRACY nor BUREAUCRACY but a technocracy'. The power of the technocrats is identified with the rise of economic PLANNING, strategic thinking in defence matters, and the expansion of science and research. Most social analysts agree that in advanced industrial society the role of the expert has been enlarged but doubt that rule by technicians can supplant the political order. For further reading: J. Meynaud, *Technocracy* (1969). D.B.

technological determinism. Although sometimes confused with HISTORICAL MATERIALISM, this is a simpler and cruder theory of social change. It asserts that most major changes in society are the product of changes in tools and techniques. Thus much of the FEUDAL organization of society is traced to changes in medieval warfare made possible by the invention of the stirrup; the invention of printing is held to be responsible for the Protestant Reformation; and the social changes brought about by INDUSTRIALIZATION are attributed to such inventions as the power loom and the steam engine. Today many who probably do not subscribe knowingly to technological determinism are looking to a future society, the 'information society', determined largely by the COMPUTER. MARXISTS – and many others – criticize this view of change as naïve. TECHNOLOGY is not neutral. Its development and applications are governed by social values and social interests – what Marxists call the 'social relations of production' (see MODE OF PRODUCTION). The applications of the computer, they say, are governed by the interest of the government in greater social control, and of the CAPITALISTS in greater profits. Nevertheless, some form of technological determinism remains a popular philosophy. It seems to square very well with our everyday experience of an increasingly mechanized environment. For further reading: L. Winner, *Autonomous Technology* (1977). K.K.

technological forecasting. A range of techniques used, in formulating CORPORATE STRATEGY, to predict potential technological developments. The principal methods are intuitive ones based on individual expectations; the *Delphi technique* (developed by the Rand Corporation), in which experts work together in a laboratory situation to crystallize their reasoning and reach a consensus on likely developments; CORRELATION analysis; and imaginative statements (often called *scenarios*) of possible events and their likely outcomes. For further reading: J. P. Martino, *Technological Forecasting for Decision Making* (1983). R.I.T.

technological unemployment, see under UNEMPLOYMENT.

technology. The systematic study of techniques employed in industry, agriculture, etc. More generally, the term is used for any application of the discoveries of science, or the SCIENTIFIC METHOD, to the problems of man and his environment in peace and war. See also ENGINEERING; METALLURGY. For further reading: A. Pacey, *The Culture of Technology* (1983). M.V.B.

technopolis. A term popularized in 1969 by science writer Nigel Calder to describe a society which is moulded and continuously and drastically altered by scientific and technical innovation; scientific *policy* being either non-existent or concerned with such peripheral issues as efficiency per pound invested, or speed of results, rather than with ultimate direction or moral considerations. For further reading: N. Calder, *Technopolis* (1969). P.S.L.

tectonics. The study of the deformation of rocks, with the principal aim of establishing the extent and exact nature of the deformation and when it occurred. It may be possible to infer from the deformation the orientation of the stresses involved and the mechanism which produced them. Tectonics can be studied on all scales from microscopic distortions of single crystals to the displacement of whole continents (see PLATE TECTONICS). J.L.M.L.

Tel Quel. An influential French literary magazine, founded in 1960 by the novelist and critic Philippe Sollers, and publishing until 1980. Its aims and objects were usefully stated in Sollers' *Logiques* (1968). Influences on the *Tel Quel* school included Bachelard, Ponge, Roussel, Barthes (see also SEMIOLOGY), and the quasi-Marxist existentialism of Sartre. The position of *Tel Quel* was originally aesthetic, but over its first decade this evolved into a complex ACTIVISM. Briefly, the *Tel Quel* school believed that certain writings (e.g. of de Sade, Lautréamont, Mallarmé, Artaud) could transform society for the better, but are ignored by society in various subtle ways. *Tel Quel* aimed to restore to language its 'original revolutionary power', and proposed literature as the prime means of doing this because 'literature is a language made with language'. M.S.-S.

telecommunication. Communication over long distances, based on ELECTROMAGNETISM. In telephony and telegraphy signals are transmitted as electric impulses travelling along wires, while in radio and television the signals are transmitted through space as MODULATIONS of carrier waves of electromagnetic RADIATION. See also FIBRE OPTICS. M.V.B.

telecommuting, see under ELECTRONIC COMMERCE.

teleological explanation, see under EXPLANATION.

teleology (or **consequentialism).** Literally, the study of ends, goals or purposes; more specifically, the theory that events can only be explained, and that evaluation of anything (objects, states of affairs, acts, agents) can only be justified, by consideration of the ends towards which they are directed. Teleologists contend that minds or living organisms can only be explained in a forward-looking way and that mechanistic explanation (see MECHANISM) in terms of efficient causes is inadequate. As an ethical doctrine (see ETHICS) teleology argues, in opposition to DEONTOLOGY, that rightness is not an intrinsic property of actions but is dependent on the goodness or badness of the consequences, whether actual, predictable or expected, to which they give rise. There are, undoubtedly, teleological systems, i.e. complexes of events (e.g. a stock exchange or a cat stalking a bird) which take on a significant order only if seen as all directed towards some outlying purpose. The controversial issue is whether the teleology of the whole can be reduced (see REDUCTION) to the mechanically explicable behaviour of its parts (e.g. by taking the desires of the stockbrokers to buy and sell, or of the cat to kill the bird, as efficient causes). The invention of servo-mechanisms such as thermostats and self-correcting gun-aiming devices encourages the view that such reduction is possible in principle. Darwin's theory of NATURAL SELECTION supplied a mechanistic account of the evolutionary process (see EVOLUTION); the discovery of DNA (see NUCLEIC ACID) did much the same for the special properties of living matter. Kant reasonably described the argument from the evidences of design in the natural world to a supernatural designing intelligence as the teleological proof of God's existence. A.Q.

telepathy, see under ESP.

telnet. An INTERNET service that allows users to use many local computer networks. For example, a researcher in London can sign on to the computer network in Washington, DC, for America's Library of Congress and browse through the library catalogue. The system provides a way of connecting computer networks that were developed before the rise of the WORLD WIDE WEB and the growing standardization of the Internet. E.B.B.

tension. In the NEW CRITICISM, a term defined by American poet Allen Tate (who derives it from the logical terms *ex* tension and *in* tension) as the sum total of meaning in a poem. The poem has a literal MEANING (extension) and a metaphorical one (intension); the simultaneity of these meanings results in tension. New Critics tend to judge poetry by its ability to achieve such tension. M.S.-S.

tensor. In some situations in PHYSICS (such as in a body which is being distorted in a complicated manner) it needs more than the three numbers (see NUMBER) represented by a vector to specify the situation. This gave rise to tensors (which are often given by nine numbers, but there can be 27 of them, or 81, . . .). As with vectors, one tensor equation can represent a multitude of non-tensor ones.

Of importance are the metric tensor (to represent distances on a complicated surface), the curvature tensor (in twisted spaces), and the stress tensor (in twisted solids). Tensors are used in fluid mechanics and QUANTUM THEORY, and, most famously, in Einstein's theory of relativity. N.A.R.

teratogen, see TERATOLOGY.

teratogenesis, see TERATOLOGY.

teratology. Term coined by French zoologist Étienne Geoffroy Saint-Hilaire (1772–1844) in 1822 to describe the study of either cold- or warm-blooded abnormal animals. The word sprang into prominence and common usage, following the thalidomide disaster in 1962, to describe the study of environmental factors responsible for the birth of deformed humans, e.g. X-radiation (see X-RAYS), rubella and some drugs administered to the mother during pregnancy. Although it could be regarded as applicable to genetically induced abnormalities, it is not commonly used in this connexion. Deriving from teratology are *teratogen* (a physical or chemical agent which produces abnormal young when the mother is exposed to its influence during pregnancy), and *teratogenesis* (the process by means of which teratogenic factors exert their deleterious effects). In current practice the word is usually confined to experimentation upon warm-blooded mammals such as rats, mice and rabbits, and on rare occasions, such as the Seveso tragedy of 1976, to the epidemiological effects of a teratogen in the human. Most authorities stress the interplay of genetic (see GENETICS/GENOMICS) and environmental factors in producing malformed mammalian young, including children. For further reading: R. O'Rahilly, *Human Embryology and Teratology* (1996). D.H.M.W.

Terman-Merrill revision, see under MENTAL RETARDATION.

terms of trade. The quantities of goods and services (imports) that can be purchased from the proceeds of the sale of given quantities of goods and services (exports). An INDEX NUMBER measuring changes in the terms of trade is obtained by dividing an index number of prices of sales (exports) by one of prices of purchases (imports), a rise indicating an improvement. The concept may be applied to transactions within a country (e.g. between farmers and the rest of the economy), or between one type of product and another (e.g. between raw materials and manufactures), but is mostly applied to the imports and exports of a nation. Economists call these the *net barter terms of trade*, and have invented other concepts (e.g. 'gross barter', 'income', 'single', and 'double factorial' terms of trade) which have attracted less general interest. M.F.G.S.

territorial imperative. Phrase coined by the American scientific popularizer Robert Ardrey (see below) for the theory that man is a creature whose behaviour in relation to the ownership, protection and expansion of the territory he regards as his or his group's exclusive preserve is analogous to the territorial behaviour of animals (see TERRITORY) and is acquired genetically in the same way.

In accordance with the principles of territorial behaviour, mutual antagonism grows as natural hazards diminish. For further reading: R. Ardrey, *The Territorial Imperative* (1967). D.C.W.

territorial sea, see under LAW OF THE SEA.

territoriality. The process of attempting to affect, influence or control actions by delimiting and asserting control over TERRITORY. Many studies emphasize territoriality as a fundamental human need based on identity, defence and stimulation, although spurious analogies are sometimes drawn between human needs and such animal behaviour as the need for an exclusive preserve for reproduction and security. It is therefore important to envisage human territoriality as conditioned primarily by cultural NORMS and values that vary in structure and function from society to society, and which also vary with the scale of social activity – from the territoriality inherent in the bubble of personal SPACE, through the territoriality which acts as a focus and symbol for group membership and identity (e.g., urban gangs and their 'turfs'), to the territoriality underlying patterns of regional identification. While it has become common practice to envisage political SOVEREIGNTY as crucial to understanding the exercise of state POWER over territory, it is also important to acknowledge that the exercise of such power is invariably bound up with other aspects of territoriality, such as social consent and state LEGITIMACY. G.R.S.

territory.

(1) The portion of geographical SPACE under the jurisdiction of a recognized authority. Territorial claims have often been at the root of political tensions and conflicts; recently these claims have been related more to the resources available within the territory than to its function as shelter. Territorial SOVEREIGNTY extends over adjacent maritime and air spaces, and maritime powers are now widening the breadth of their territorial seas (see LAW OF THE SEA) and claiming control over the contiguous continental shelf. For further reading: J. Gottmann, *The Significance of Territory* (1973). J.G.

(2) In ETHOLOGY, an area in which an organism or a group of individuals is dominant – e.g. the territory within which a male bird will allow no intrusion and towards which he acts in a way distinctly analogous to that of a human being (in most societies) towards his private property, or the 'group territories' of lions, hyenas and some other mammals and birds, which likewise evoke behaviour analogous to human behaviour (see DOMINANCE). This pattern of behaviour is known as TERRITORIALITY. See also TERRITORIAL IMPERATIVE. P.M.

terrorism. The systematic use of coercive intimidation, usually to service political ends. It is used to create and exploit a climate of fear among a wider target group than the immediate victims of the violence, and to publicize a cause, as well as to coerce a target into acceding to the terrorists' aims. Terrorism may be used on its own or as part of a wider unconventional WAR. It can be employed by desperate and weak MINORITIES, by STATES as a tool of domestic and foreign policy, or by belligerents as an accompaniment in all types and stages of warfare. A common feature is that innocent civilians, sometimes foreigners who know nothing of the terrorists' political quarrel, are killed or injured. Typical methods of modern terrorism are explosive and incendiary bombings, shooting attacks and assassinations, hostage-taking and kidnapping, and hijacking. The possibility of terrorists using nuclear, chemical, or bacteriological weapons (see NUCLEAR WEAPONS) cannot be discounted.

One basic distinction is between *state* and *factional* terror. The former has been vastly more lethal and has often been an antecedent to, and a contributory cause of, factional terrorism. Once regimes and factions decide that their ends justify any means or that their opponents' actions justify them in unrestrained retaliation, they tend to become locked in a spiral of terror and counter-terror. *Internal* terrorism is confined within a single state or region while *international* terrorism, in its most obvious manifestation, is an attack carried out across international frontiers or against a foreign target in the terrorists' state of origin. But in reality, most terrorism has international dimensions, as groups look abroad for support, weapons and safe haven.

Terrorism is not a philosophy or a movement: it is a method. But even though we may be able to identify cases where terrorism has been used for causes most liberals (see LIBERALISM) would regard as just, this does not mean that even in such cases the use of terrorism, which by definition threatens the most fundamental rights of innocent civilians, is morally justified. Paradoxically, despite the rapid growth in the incidence of modern terrorism, this method has been remarkably unsuccessful in gaining strategic objectives. The only clear cases are the expulsion of British and French colonial rule from Palestine, Cyprus, Aden and Algeria. The continuing popularity of terrorism among NATIONALIST and ideological and religious extremists must be explained by other factors: the craving for physical expression of hatred and revenge; terrorism's record of success in yielding tactical gains (e.g. massive publicity, release of prisoners and large ransom payments); and the fact that the method is relatively cheap, easy to organize, and carries minimal risk. Regimes of TOTALITARIANISM, such as NAZISM and STALINISM, routinely used mass terror to control and persecute whole populations, and the historical evidence shows that this is a tragically effective way of suppressing opposition and resistance. But when states use international terrorism they invariably seek to disguise their role, plausibly denying responsibility for specific crimes. Another major conducive factor in the growth of modern terrorism has been repeated weakness and APPEASEMENT in national and international reaction to terrorism, despite numerous anti-terrorist laws and conventions and much governmental rhetoric. Early writings on terrorism tended to treat it as a relatively minor threat to law and order and individual HUMAN RIGHTS. Professor Paul Wilkinson, in a series of studies, concluded that major outbreaks of terrorism, because of their capacity to affect public opinion and foreign policy and to trigger civil and international wars, ought to be recognized as a potential danger to the security and wellbeing of afflicted states and a possible threat to international peace. For further reading: W. Laqueur, *The Age of Terrorism* (1997). P.W.

tertiary occupation, see under OCCUPATION.

tetrahedral theory. An extension of the CONTRACTION HYPOTHESIS to explain the distribution of the continents and oceans. If the earth was cooling and contracting, its shape would tend to become tetrahedral, since the tetrahedron is the regular figure with the smallest volume. Though the distribution of continents and oceans is roughly tetrahedral, with the oceans corresponding to the faces, the theory presents a picture which is inconsistent with ISOSTASY and it has therefore been abandoned. J.L.M.L.

tetranucleotide hypothesis. An influential conception in the emergence of modern BIOCHEMISTRY, the tetranucleotide hypothesis postulated that NUCLEIC ACIDS were made up of nucleotides (their basic building blocks) in proportions of equal mass. When first formulated, the theory argued that DNA consisted of just one each of the four nucleotides arranged in a chain. RNA was believed to be similarly composed. This notion was demonstrated to be unacceptable in the 1940s, when it was recognized that the structure of nucleic acids was far more complex. In the process, they ceased to be seen as nucleotides, and came to be reconceptualized as polynucleotides, comprising long chain MOLECULES with fixed sequences. The work of Chargaff and Vischer in particular demonstrated the different base proportions of DNA, posing in a particularly acute form the problem of its structure, which the work of Crick and Watson in the 1950s so spectacularly resolved. For further reading: F. H. Portugal and J. S. Cohen, *A Century of DNA* (1977). R.P.

text, theory of. Term used by the German critic Max Bense and others to convey the 'scientific' analysis of 'text' – chosen as a word free from the VALUE-JUDGEMENTS implicit in terms like 'literature' or 'poetry' – by largely quantitative methods such as STYLOMETRY. J.W.

textual criticism. The part of editing a literary work which deals with the establishment of the text. The need for textual criticism is occasioned by the fact that all texts of every kind tend to become *corrupt* (i.e. falsified) in the normal course of transmission. In many cases different witnesses offer variant readings at particular points, and often there are radically different versions of a work. It is now fairly generally agreed that the ideal of textual criticism is to present the text which the author intended.

Textual criticism was the principal form of literary study, by professionals and amateurs alike, from the time of classical antiquity until the 19th century. The main subjects were the New Testament and the Greek and Latin classical writers; the chief method was *emendation* of words or passages on aesthetic grounds, either by logic or by reference to the readings of other witnesses. The formalization of analysis (with the construction of *stemmata*, i.e. of family trees of witnesses) and the emergence of BIBLIOGRAPHY (as the detailed and systematic study of the printed book) at the end of the 19th century caused the practice of textual criticism to be confined to specialists, who have now brought editing to a laborious, sophisticated and time-consuming level.

The textual critic needs a sound aesthetic (see AESTHETICS), a thorough knowledge of the text under consideration, and access to any authorial or other relevant statements about the text. The five major steps to textual criticism are *collecting* the texts (i.e. the various appearances of the text); *analysing* the differences between the texts; *selecting* the *copy-text* (i.e. the version regarded as most authoritative and therefore used as a basis); *perfecting* the copy-text (i.e. replacing passages known or thought to be corrupt by the introduction, from other sources, of readings known or thought to be authorial); and *explaining* and justifying the editor's procedures and decisions. For further reading: J. Thorpe, *Principles of Textual Criticism* (1972). J.T.

texture. In the NEW CRITICISM, the particular aspect of a poem as distinct from its abstract or universal aspect; just as the smooth or rough texture of a vase may be distinguished from its general design. American poet and critic John Crowe Ransom (1888–1974) has elaborated this: the general design of a poem, its argument, is its structure, while its texture consists of all its 'local' detail, its personal or unique qualities. In poetry, Ransom argues, texture clashes with and modifies structure. Compare TENSION. For further reading: J. C. Ransom, *The World's Body* (1938). M.S.-S.

TG, see TRANSFORMATIONAL GRAMMAR.

Thatcherism. A term used mainly by media commentators and opponents to characterize the dominant political force in Britain since the election in 1979, and re-election in 1983 and 1987, of a Conservative government under the leadership of Prime Minister Margaret Thatcher. In so far as the term denotes a coherent set of values and policies, they may be said to derive in part from the theories of the New RIGHT. Thus Thatcherism sought to substitute market forces for STATE action wherever possible (see PRIVATIZATION); to weaken the influence of TRADE UNIONS and reflect the trend towards CORPORATISM discernible in post-war Britain; and in its early years to use MONETARIST policies to control INFLATION. While reducing the area of state responsibility, it sought to raise the state's capacity to operate within its sphere: Thatcherism combined an increase in the centralization of political authority with a more traditional conservative stress on law and order (see CONSERVATISM). It drew widespread criticism, including from within conservatism, as being negligent of the interests of the more disadvantaged groups and regions of the country, and as inferring a mandate for radical policies from election victories won without popular majorities. In 1990, Thatcher stepped down from the leadership of the Conservative Party, her position having been weakened by widespread discontent with the poll tax legislation and party splits on the matter of political and monetary integration with Europe. While Thatcher is no longer active in politics, some aspects of Thatcherism live on. After the Conservatives finally lost power in the 1997 general election, the Labour Prime Minister Tony Blair surprised many supporters and critics alike by implementing policies such as welfare cuts which seemed to continue a political trend established by Mrs Thatcher. For further reading: E. Evans, *Thatcher and Thatcherism* (1997). S.R.; S.T.

THC (tetrahydrocannabinol), see under MARIJUANA.

The Look, see LOOK, THE.

theatre anthropology, see under THIRD THEATRE.

theatre in the round. Any form of staging in which the acting area is surrounded on all sides by the audience, minimizing the scenic element and concentrating attention upon the figure of the actor. The use of this form is attested for some medieval and primitive drama; in the 20th century its attraction has lain in the sharp contrast it presents to 'picture-frame' NATURALISM (see OPEN STAGE). The first important central stage production of modern times was by Okhlopkov in Moscow (*The Mother*, 1933); the first permanent theatre in this form was the Penthouse Theater, University of Washington, Seattle (1940); the New Victoria Theatre, Stoke on Trent (1986), was Europe's first purpose-built theatre in the round. The form has been used for large-scale, circus-like productions with spectacular effects achieved by movement, costume and mobile stage properties and units, and for small-cast plays where a sense of intimate involvement between actor and audience is required. Few directors, however, have been willing to confine their work exclusively to this form. For further reading: S. Joseph, *Theatre in the Round* (1967). M.A.

Theatre Laboratory. An itinerant and highly influential experimental Polish theatre company directed by Jerzy Grotowski. In Grotowski's theatre the actor became paramount, making use of all the physical and mental powers at his disposal; the emphasis was on austerity, poverty and simplicity, in reaction against the 'wealth' of contemporary theatre; and the texts were mainly Grotowski's own radical adaptations of classic Polish works. The company was founded in 1959, gave its first performance outside Poland in 1966, and had a major influence on figures as diverse as the director Peter Brook and the choreographer Jerome Robbins. Also, Grotowski's notion of a company as a monastic, self-contained troupe became gospel for many of the AVANT-GARDE, e.g. notably the LIVING THEATER and Eugenio Barba's Odin Theatre (see THIRD THEATRE). After *Apocalypsis cum Figuris* (1969), no new theatre pieces were presented, and Grotowski concentrated upon research, teaching and theorizing, often obscurely, upon the nature of performance. The Laboratory Theatre was formally dissolved in 1984. For further reading: Z. Osiński, *Grotowski and His Laboratory* (1986). M.BI.

Théâtre Libre. An experimental Parisian theatre club founded in 1887 by actor-manager André Antoine (1858–1943) which had a profound influence on French playwriting, acting and design. It became a showplace for naturalistic writers (see NATURALISM) like Eugène Brieux dedicated to a theatre aimed at the cure of social evils; but it also staged controversial works by the great European dramatists such as Ibsen, Strindberg, Hauptmann and Verga, and the kind of *comédies rosses* ('cynical comedies') popular in the closing years of the century. At the same time it helped to liberate French acting from sentimental rhetoric and scenic design from artificial prettiness. It also inspired the creation of similar theatres such as Otto Brahm's FREIE BÜHNE in Berlin and J. T. Grein's Independent Theatre in London. It closed in April 1897, largely for economic reasons, but its influence in Europe and beyond was incalculable. For further reading: O. G. Brockett and R. R. Findlay, *Century of Innovation* (1973). M.BI.

Théâtre National Populaire (TNP). A state-financed theatre, established in 1951 in the Palais de Chaillot, under the direction of Jean Vilar, with the express purpose of appealing to a wide popular audience and creating an atmosphere different from that of the commercial BOURGEOIS theatre. The TNP enjoyed a period of exceptional prestige when Gérard Philipe was its resident star, and it did much to familiarize schoolchildren and factory workers with the drama, both French and foreign. In 1963 Vilar was succeeded as director by Georges Wilson, who carried on the same tradition of serious, eclectic theatre. J.G.W.

theatre of cruelty. A form of theatre which seeks to communicate to its audience a sense of pain, suffering and the presence of evil, primarily through non-verbal means. The term was first used by the SURREALIST actor Antonin Artaud in his essay 'Le Théâtre de la cruauté' (1932). He developed his ideas further in a series of essays, letters and manifestos published as *Le Théâtre et son double* (1938). Artaud rejected the Western tradition of theatre, whose emphasis upon

REALISM and psychological character-study he considered trivial, and hoped to re-create theatre at the more universal level that he found in primitive RITUAL and oriental drama. Artaud's writing was visionary rather than practical, and no complete body of theory exists behind it. Outside France, where he had a strong influence upon the director Jean-Louis Barrault, Artaud was little known before the first English translation of his book in 1958. In the 1960s his ideas were widely discussed, and the concept of the theatre of cruelty was explored and developed, most notably in productions by Jerzy Grotowski (see THEATRE LABORATORY), Peter Brook and the LIVING THEATER. See also THEATRE OF THE ABSURD. For further reading: R. Hayman, *Artaud and After* (1977). M.A.

theatre of panic. Term (*théâtre panique*) coined by the Spanish-born French dramatist Fernando Arrabal (1932–) in 1962 to describe the kind of ceremonial theatre he favours. The reference is to the god Pan, a deity combining the attributes of rustic vitality, grotesque fun and holy terror; and Arrabal's concept is a blend of tragedy and a Punch and Judy show, of bad taste and refinement, of sacrilege and the sacred. Heavily influenced by the theories of Antonin Artaud, Arrabal has put his ideas into practice in a number of ritualistic plays including *The Architect and the Emperor of Assyria* (1967) and *And They Handcuffed the Flowers* (1969). Similar ideas are apparent among French AVANT-GARDE companies, most notably Jerome Savory's rowdily picturesque Grand Magic Circus and the Spanish group El Comediants. M.BI.

theatre of the absurd. Term coined in 1961 by the critic Martin Esslin to define a form of theatre which, rejecting NATURALISM as the basis for its presentation of character and action, uses a variety of dramatic techniques defying rational analysis and explanation to express, by implication rather than direct statement, the 'absurdity' of the human condition; Esslin adopts and expands the concept of the absurd employed by the EXISTENTIALIST Albert Camus in *Le Mythe de Sisyphe* (1942). The absurd is not so much a single, identifiable theatrical tradition as a common denominator to be found in the work of a number of 20th-century dramatists, who are individually indebted to a variety of independent traditions from DADA and SURREALISM to the routines of vaudeville and the circus. Some elements of the absurd may be traced back to Alfred Jarry's *Ubu Roi* (1896), and found in plays by Cocteau and Ivan Goll written in the 1920s; but the term is usually associated with writers active after World War II, notably Samuel Beckett, Eugene Ionesco, N. F. Simpson, and Harold Pinter. In its rejection of rational, analytical processes, the genre has some affinities with THEATRE OF CRUELTY. For further reading: M. Esslin, *The Theatre of the Absurd* (1969). M.A.

Theatre Workshop. A theatre company founded, with a policy of COMMITMENT to the LEFT, by Joan Littlewood and Ewan McColl in 1945, and housed after 1953 in the Theatre Royal, Stratford, east London. In the second half of the 1950s it presented work by new dramatists including Brendan Behan, Shelagh Delaney and Frank Norman, all infused with a theatrical vigour that was indebted equally to the writers' WORKING-CLASS backgrounds and to Joan Littlewood's directorial style. In 1963 her production of *Oh What a Lovely War!* helped to inspire a distinctively English form of documentary theatre; beset by financial and other difficulties, Littlewood directed her last production in 1973. The title Theatre Workshop was abandoned in 1978. For further reading: H. Goorney, *The Theatre Workshop Story* (1981). M.A.

theism. Minimally, 'belief in the existence of a God'. This distinguishes theism from atheism, but implies that 'theism', like 'atheism', could mean many different things in different contexts. In the philosophy of religion, however, it is typically defined much more precisely – as in Robert Flint's standard definition of theism as 'the doctrine that the universe owes its existence, and continuation in existence, to the reason and will of a self-existent Being, who is infinitely powerful, wise, and good'. Philosophically, therefore, theism is constituted by a specific set of beliefs concerning God, and God's relationship with the world, which distinguish it not only from atheism but also from a variety of positions which in the minimal sense of the word are 'theistic' – polytheism, deism (which so emphasizes God's transcendence that God's immanence in the world is negated), pantheism (which so emphasizes God's immanence in the world that God and the world are identified with one another), etc. The assumption that theism is a kind of lowest common denominator for Christianity, Judaism and Islam has been extensively criticized, and although theism remains central for mainstream philosophy of religion it is often disowned by contemporary theologians suspicious of 'the god of the philosophers'. C.C.

thematic apperception test (TAT). A projective test (see PROJECTION; MENTAL TESTING) developed by Henry Murray (1893–1988), in which the subject is asked to describe what is happening in a series of standard pictures that are sufficiently vague to permit a variety of interpretations. Interpretations are assumed to reflect *themas* (i.e. themes) that play a major role in the subject's own life. W.Z.

themed environment. In ARCHITECTURE, a usually derogatory term, referring to 'real' (but not 'authentic') environments inspired by POPULAR CULTURE (see IMAGINEERING). The MODERN MOVEMENT's polemic against decoration and story-telling fading, scholars may now recognize pre-modern precedents for an architecture of narrative contriving 'fake' materials into 'scenes' and 'events' on an extraordinary distorted scale for popular amusement from at least Renaissance origins.

The most extreme themed environment today is Las Vegas (where each casino resort models itself on an individual theme from cornice to carpet, from sidewalk to artificial sunset). Themes are now associated with a whole series of enterprises from Harley Davidson motorcycles to the British monarchy, and no longer restricted to theme parks but the general experience of the commercial mall (US) or high street (UK). For further reading: R. Venturi *et al*, *Learning from Las Vegas* (1972). P.J.D.

theodicy. Originally, the division of natural theology concerned with defending belief in God against objections related to the existence and extent of suffering, but now, by extension, the philosophical genre of which all discussions of 'the problem of evil' are a part. The term, from the Greek for 'the justification of God', was coined by Leibniz in the 17th century, but the apparent conflict between the reality of evil and the omnipotence, omniscience and perfect goodness of God has been on the philosophical agenda for at least 2,000 years. Despite disagreements as to the nature of evil, and the nature of the philosophical problem which it presents, the theodicists continue to create variations on the traditional 'free will defence' (see FREE WILL) which makes human freedom – and the kind of environment necessary for its exercise to be genuine – the key to the solution. Whether people, believers and non-believers alike, should be more outraged by the 'solutions' than by the way in which the 'problem' is characteristically defined and discussed remains a mystery. C.C.

theology. Originally, and literally, 'the science of GOD', 'theology' has come to mean a number of different things. With the foundation of the universities, e.g., the meaning of 'theology' was broadened to cover the whole of 'sacred learning' – i.e. everything studied in a faculty of theology rather than in a faculty of law or medicine. Another shift has taken place since the Enlightenment, as 'theology' has, increasingly, come to mean the study of religious BELIEFS rather than of that to which they appear to refer. These semantic shifts have made it possible to call any body of religious beliefs (see RELIGION) a 'theology', even if a specific religious tradition lacks any belief in one or more gods. But scholars of JUDAISM, ISLAM, HINDUISM and BUDDHISM regularly resist this extension of the term, since theology has been a Christian concept for so long that it cannot be applied to other religious traditions without prejudging a wide range of questions. As a result, this article focuses on Christian theology.

Three different meanings of 'theology' may be distinguished without difficulty. First, it is the family of disciplines which is studied in departments or faculties of Theology, in the European universities, and in Divinity Schools in the US and in other countries. Second, it is the theological discipline concerned with beliefs in particular, as opposed to the characteristic concerns of biblical, historical and practical theology.

Third, within this discipline, it names a specific group of beliefs: the doctrine of God. Most of the time, however, 'theology' serves as shorthand for theological studies as a whole, or for theology as the study of beliefs (systematic theology, or DOGMATICS) and of the foundations of belief (fundamental theology).

Theology, in this second sense, has always involved the reinterpretation of tradition in changing intellectual and cultural circumstances. What counts as 'tradition' varies, of course, between different theologians, since Orthodox, Roman Catholic and Protestant theologians (see ORTHODOXY, EASTERN; CATHOLICISM; PROTESTANTISM) inherit different accounts of the classical sources of theological authority – the New Testament, the ecumenical councils, the writings of the early Church Fathers, etc. At the end of the 20th century, however, confessional differences are often much less significant than differences over the degree to which the tradition has to be reinterpreted. These are differences of judgement concerning the nature and the extent of the challenges presented to CHRISTIANITY by the modern world, and they often run across traditional confessional boundaries.

Histories of modern theology used to distinguish between 'conservative', 'mediating' and 'liberal' theologies, which represented a variety of responses to the philosophical challenges of the Enlightenment, and of the post-Enlightenment philosophies of Kant and Hegel in particular. But this typology hardly did justice to Protestant theology in central Europe, lct alone in England, Scotland and the US, and it could not make any real sense of Roman Catholic and Orthodox theological traditions. Even in the 19th century, moreover, many theologians understood that the challenges of modernity were not exclusively philosophical. For further reading: A. E. McGrath, *Christian Theology: An Introduction* (1997). C.C.

theology of hope. The discussion of the meaning of eschatology in Christian THEOLOGY produced, in reaction to Rudolf Bultmann's (1884–1976) proposal to DEMYTHOLOGIZE the biblical images, by interpreting them exclusively in personal terms as understood in Christian EXISTENTIALISM, a proposal that GOD's control over nature and history should be reaffirmed. The promise of God's triumph was derived particularly from belief in the resurrection of Jesus from the dead in a glorified body. This new hopefulness was connected with a new mood of optimism in the 1960s. Jürgen Moltmann's *Theology of Hope* (in German, 1964) was an international influence among readers of theology, although it was criticized as being insufficiently aware of the THIRD WORLD problems which preoccupied LIBERATION THEOLOGY. Later the general mood in Europe and the English-speaking world became less optimistic, and third world Christians were tempted to despair, but there was no going back to existentialism's neglect of public affairs. For further reading: R. Alves, *A Theology of Human Hope* (1969). D.L.E.

theoretical chemistry. An academic discipline in which theoretical PHYSICS is applied to chemical phenomena, such as bonding, reaction rates (see BOND, CHEMICAL; CATALYSIS), etc. Much effort is devoted to mathematical calculations of the properties of theoretical MODELS, using QUANTUM MECHANICS (hence the near-synonym *quantum chemistry*) and STATISTICAL MECHANICS. B.F.

theory ladenness (of observation). Observation of the world and what happens in it, whether or not aided by instruments, is never free of the theories, beliefs, assumptions and expectations brought to the task by the observer himself. In philosophy this is put by saying that both the process of observation and the terms in which what is observed are described are 'theory-laden', i.e. imbued with theoretical content by the observer. There is therefore no neutral or unalloyed access to a realm of pure 'facts', as had been hoped by philosophers in the tradition of EMPIRICISM, including some of the LOGICAL POSITIVISTS to whom the debate about theory ladenness is chiefly owed. A.C.G.

theory of everything, see under SUPERSTRINGS; GRAND UNIFICATION.

theory of three worlds. An expanded and updated version of Mao's 1964 concept of a 'Second Intermediate Zone', delivered by Deng Xiaoping to the 6th Special Session of the UN General Assembly in 1974 (see

MAOISM). The theory suggested that since the COLD WAR there had been increasing collusion between the US and the former USSR in their search for international HEGEMONY. As a response to the creation of this superpower bloc, the Chinese argued that the SOCIALIST camp was no longer in existence, and the COMMUNIST Party states of eastern Europe were now under IMPERIALIST domination. Similarly there had been a disintegration of the Western bloc, which was now seeking greater unity in order to resist the expansion of US hegemony. In essence, the superpowers made up the first world, the developing countries in Asia, Africa and Latin America the third, and the developed nations between the two made up the second world. The suggestion was that China, as a THIRD WORLD country, must increase its ties with other third world nations to try to resist the superpowers' quest for world domination. For further reading: J. Gittings, *The World and China* (1974). S.B.

theosophy. A religious movement founded by Madame H. P. Blavatsky and Annie Besant in India towards the end of the 19th century and subsequently gaining adherents in many countries, especially in Germany, where in turn it gave rise to the ANTHROPOSOPHY taught by Rudolf Steiner. The terms come from the Greek, meaning respectively 'wisdom about God' and 'wisdom about Man'. D.L.E.

therapeutic community. Once the effectiveness of traditional therapies within the lunatic asylum or mental hospital was increasingly challenged from the 1920s, one alternative approach to be developed was the therapeutic community. This was a unit, generally within the hospital, involving up to around 100 patients, in which efforts were made to break down the traditional hierarchy of doctor/patient relations. Instead, both groups were urged to participate in creating a real community environment, and patients were to participate in their own therapy. Often this involved relatively democratic decision-making techniques on the ward, aimed at raising patients' levels of responsibility and group awareness. R.P.

therapeutic state. A notion advanced by the libertarian American psychiatrist Thomas Szasz to depict what he regards as an unholy alliance between public PSYCHIATRY and the powers of the central state. Just as the medieval Church, with its inquisitorial powers, persecuted heretics in the service of social uniformity, so, argued Szasz, today's psychiatric profession polices DEVIANCE in the service of the central state. This occurred most nakedly during the COLD WAR in the abuses of Soviet psychiatry (see USSR, THE FORMER; BRAINWASHING), where departure from the Party line was treated as a form of mental perversion; but the belief that those holding unorthodox views are in need of treatment forms the rationale for a wide range of public medical interventions in Western societies too. Underpinning Szasz's argument is a radical scepticism about the very category of mental illness and a libertarian suspicion of professional power. More neutrally, the aspirations of any WELFARE STATE, aiming to rectify pre-existing deficiencies in health and opportunity, could be described as 'therapeutic'. For further reading: Thomas Szasz, *The Therapeutic State* (1984). R.P.

Theravada, see under BUDDHISM.

theremin. An electronic musical instrument (see ELECTRONIC MUSIC) invented *c.* 1924 by a Russian scientist of that name. Tone is generated by the proximity of the player's hand to a short antenna attached to two oscillators, one operating at a fixed frequency, the other at a variable frequency. The difference between the two frequencies causes a 'beat' effect which is the third 'audio' frequency. The player controls pitch with one hand, volume with the other. A.H.

thermal neutron. A slow NEUTRON, whose kinetic energy is roughly equal to that of the random heat motion in the material through which it is passing. Thermal neutrons produce most of the FISSION reactions in a NUCLEAR REACTOR (see also MODERATOR). M.V.B.

thermal reactor, see under NUCLEAR REACTOR.

thermionics. The design of electronic devices whose operation depends on the emission of ELECTRONS from the surface of a hot metal cathode, e.g. the ELECTRON GUN in a cathode ray tube, and the thermionic valve used in radio receivers and COMPUTERS before the advent of the TRANSISTOR. M.V.B.

thermochemistry. The part of THERMODYNAMICS concerned with the accurate measurement of the heat given out or absorbed during chemical reactions. B.F.

thermodynamics. A branch of PHYSICS developed in the 19th century, dealing with heat and temperature. The subject is based on three laws:

(1) The *first law* connects thermodynamics with MECHANICS by the statement 'Heat is a form of ENERGY'. This implies that no engine can produce work indefinitely without a permanent source of heat, so that 'perpetual motion machines' cannot be made.

(2) The famous *second law* expresses the irreversibility of processes: 'It is impossible to produce work by transferring heat from a cold body to a hot body in any self-sustaining process.' It is of course possible to use the reverse process – heat transfer from hot to cold – to produce work, and this is the basis of the internal combustion engine, the steam engine, and nuclear and conventional power stations. A mathematically equivalent form of the second law is: 'ENTROPY always increases in any closed system not in EQUILIBRIUM, and remains constant for a system which is in equilibrium.'

(3) The *third law* states: 'It is impossible to cool a system right down to the ABSOLUTE ZERO of temperature.'

In addition to their importance in the theory of heat engines and CRYOGENICS, these three laws provide relations between the thermal properties of materials (e.g. the amount of heat necessary to produce a given rise in temperature) and their mechanical properties (e.g. the pressure necessary to produce a given decrease in size). They involve no mention of the underlying atomic structure of matter; the more powerful methods of STATISTICAL MECHANICS enable the laws to be derived, and their significance understood, in terms of atomic motions. M.V.B.

thermoluminescence. In ARCHAEOLOGY, a DATING technique based on the principle that, if a clay body is heated, ALPHA PARTICLES, trapped in the crystal LATTICE, will be released as light ENERGY which can be measured. The light is therefore proportional to the number of trapped alpha particles which in turn are directly related to the degree of flawing of the lattice, the intensity of the radioactive environment (see RADIOACTIVITY) in which the object was buried, and the length of exposure. The first variable can be determined by re-exposing the sample to a source of known strength and measuring the light emitted on reheating; the second can be measured directly. It is thus possible to estimate the length of the exposure, which in terms of baked clay means the time between the last ancient firing (usually the date of manufacture) and the date of testing. The method has value as a means of absolute date assessment. It is also widely used to test the authenticity of artifacts out of CONTEXT. B.C.

thermonuclear reaction. A CHAIN REACTION based on nuclear FUSION. M.V.B.

thermonuclear war, see under WAR.

thesis, see under SYNTHESIS.

things-in-themselves, see NOUMENA.

third age. The third age is, according to Peter Laslett, the age of 'personal fulfillment, the apogee of the lifecourse, or the crown of life'. It comes after the first age of dependence and immaturity and the second age of maturity and responsibility and precedes the fourth age of final dependency and death. It renders the notion of old age obsolete. It is a 20th-century phenomenon originating from the unique mix of conditions that have existed in advanced Western INDUSTRIAL SOCIETIES since the 1950s. The WELFARE STATE brought security in retirement to the population at large. People are also healthier and living longer than ever before. More and more retirees seek a life of fulfilment beyond their working lives and see their twilight years as an opportunity for learning and self-discovery. For further reading: P. Laslett, *A Fresh Map of Life: The Emergence of the Third Age* (1989). H.W.

third sector. The third sector is, according to Jim Joseph, President of the Council on Foundations in the US, 'an intermediary space between business and government where private energy can be . . . deployed for public good'. It has arisen in response to needs that are not being met either by the marketplace or the public sector. In an era of devolved and 'downsized' government it has expanded dramatically and become differentiated as dozens of large service-providing organizations have grown up primarily dependent on government contracts. This has prompted political debate about the coherence of a sector which spans local and community groups through to multi-million-pound businesses. H.W.

third stream. A term coined in the 1950s by composer-critic Gunther Schuller to describe the fusion of jazz and classical music. In fact tendencies in that direction had appeared as long before as the 1920s, in such works as Milhaud's *La Création du Monde* and Gershwin's *Rhapsody in Blue* and *Concerto in F*. The 1950s movement, however, aimed at a thorough integration of the two forms' central characteristics – the improvisation and rhythmic freedom of JAZZ wedded to the formal breadth and structure of classical. Though some interesting pieces were written by such leading musicians as John Lewis of the Modern Jazz Quartet, the two strains resisted ultimate unification. Since then, however, as classical and jazz musicians have learned more about each other's disciplines, less self-conscious connections have occurred, reflecting the general conflation of genres in the late 20th century. GE.S.

third theatre. A term coined in 1976 by Eugenio Barba to describe the nature and work of such groups as his own Odin Teatret (founded in Oslo in 1964) which exist on the margins of official culture, usually suffering from poverty, hardship and critical neglect and often living a nomadic or, as Barba puts it, 'migrant' existence. The allusion, which does not hold good in all particulars, is to the conditions experienced in the THIRD WORLD itself. Early in his career Barba formed an association with Grotowski, the influence of whose THEATRE LABORATORY can be seen in the long gestation period for Odin's theatre pieces accompanied by arduous physical and vocal training for the performers; and like Grotowski, Barba has studied in great detail the performance techniques used in oriental and other theatrical forms outside the realistic Western tradition. Equally important in Barba's thinking is a concern for the vanishing cultural traditions of non-industrial societies in Europe and the third world (he has worked extensively in South America and in southern Italy, where he was born), and he has developed the notion of *barter*, an exchanged demonstration of cultural skills in place of the conventional cash transaction which usually initiates or concludes a performance. Barba and his most sympathetic observer, the Italian scholar F. Taviani, have also speculated interestingly upon the sociology of the actor and his work within such a group. In 1979 Barba founded the International School of Theatre Anthropology (ISTA), a body whose sporadic conferences and training schools are devoted to 'a comparative study of acting techniques in an intercultural perspective'. For further reading: E. Barba, *Beyond the Floating Islands* (1986). M.A.

third wave feminism. Third wave FEMINISM is recognized as the feminist writing which emerged in the wake of the radical and innovative feminism of the 1970s. Notable figures in the movement include Susan Faludi, Kate Roiphe and Natasha Walters. Essentially, third wave feminism has addressed two themes which were of limited relevance to previous writing: one is the issue of cultural and ethnic diversity within societies while the other is a spirited attack on those feminist politics which proposed sexual and political SEPARATISM for women. The diverse voices contributing to third wave feminism came from a range of countries: non-white women condemned what they regarded as the cultural dominance of first and second wave feminism and spoke against what they saw as its imperatives of white middle-class existence. From inside the West, women spoke against feminism *per se*; this 'backlash' against feminism is identified with a number of writers, some of whom have attacked what they see as the implicit moral assumptions of feminism (particularly around issues of sexuality) while others have claimed that feminism is based on a faulty, and entirely misguided, account of relations between the sexes.

In all, third wave feminism contains a multiplicity and diversity of women's writing. Its relationship to previous feminist work is often contentious, but it shares with previous work a continuing engagement with the question of relations between the sexes. For further reading: S. Faludi, *Backlash* (1992). M.S.E.

third world. Collective term of French origin (*le tiers-monde*), taken up by American writers, for those states not regarded or regarding themselves as members of either the developed CAPITALIST or the developed SOCIALIST worlds: they are classified by their state of economic development as 'underdeveloped', 'less developed', or 'developing' states (see UNDERDEVELOPMENT and DEVELOPING COUNTRIES). The third world includes most of the countries of Latin America, Asia and Africa. Many of these share a colonial past and a strong resentment of IMPERIALISM; they are low-income or middle-income countries. In the early post-colonial period, many, following the Indian example, have favoured non-alignment in foreign policy. The third world accounts for the greater part of the membership of the UN and is strongly represented in the United Nations Conference on Trade and Development (UNCTAD), which was set up in 1964 to provide a forum for the discussion of third world economic development.

While the term third world is still used, much of its original meaning has been lost. With the end of the COLD WAR, non-alignment no longer has the same meaning. Moreover, since former second world members have moved towards the market (see FIRST WORLD), people no longer perceive a tripartite world. To complicate terms, some people refer to a fourth world, comprising countries designated by the UN as least-developed countries because of low GNP per person, little industrialization, low adult literacy, and low population. See also THEORY OF THREE WORLDS. For further reading: E. W. Nafziger, *The Economics of Developing Countries* (1997).

A.L.C.B.; E.W.N.

thought police, see under ORWELLIAN.

three-age system. A simple technological MODEL used to order the past. It was introduced in Denmark in 1816–19 by Christian Thomsen (1788–1865), who proposed that the prehistoric period (see PREHISTORY) could be divided into an Age of Stone, an Age of Bronze, and an Age of Iron. His theoretical scheme was soon shown by excavation to be largely valid. With numerous elaborations and subdivisions, including the subdivision of the Stone Age into *palaeolothic* ('Old Stone Age') and *neolithic* ('New Stone Age') periods by Sir John Lubbock in 1865, it was widely adopted in the Old World, but the development of American and African ARCHAEOLOGY showed that it was not universally applicable. It is now regarded as of little further value, although its basic terminology is still used as a convenient shorthand. For further reading: G. Daniel, *The Three Ages* (1943). B.C.

Three-Gorges Dam. Termed the largest hydroelectric project ever attempted anywhere in the world, the plan to dam the Yangtze river is highly controversial. The project is intended to increase China's electrical generating capacity by a ninth, and to aid in flood prevention. The dam will also submerge one of the country's most scenic regions, remove an estimated 100,000 hectares from agricultural production, displace as many as 1.2 million people, and may trigger widespread environmental damage. The project is expected to take 20 years to complete, but with widespread opposition from environmentalists and some international financial institutions its future is problematical even as work proceeds.

W.G.R.

Three Mile Island. The site near Harrisburg, Pennsylvania, of the first serious accident at a commercial nuclear power station (see NUCLEAR REACTOR). The incident began on 28 March 1979 with the minor failure of water pipes and, through a combination of human error and engineering flaws, nearly resulted in a meltdown of the nuclear reactor core – an event that was supposed to have been a one-in-200-million-years occurrence. The partial meltdown prompted the flight of most people living within ten miles of the plant, even though officials counselled residents to stay inside and not use their air-conditioners. After mistakes by both the plant operators and the Nuclear Regulatory Agency, the plant was brought under control on 7 April. No one died in the accident and the release of RADIATION was minimal. But the health effects are still being debated. The catastrophic 1986 explosion of the CHERNOBYL reactor in Belarus, along with public worries about disposal of nuclear wastes (see POLLUTION), cast a pall over the future of nuclear power in Western nations. A second undamaged reactor at Three Mile Island remains in operation, but the destroyed reactor remains under watch until the plant's scheduled closing in 2021. R.K.H.

three worlds theory, see THEORY OF THREE WORLDS.

throwback, see under ATAVISM.

thrust stage, see under OPEN STAGE.

tiger economies. The nation states of east Asia including South Korea, Hong Kong, Singapore, Thailand and Malaysia, which experienced extraordinary and dynamic economic growth in the 1980s and 1990s. A World Bank study attributed this 'miracle' to cultural factors found in Asian societies, including qualities of hard work, thrift, family and entrepreneurship (see ENTREPRENEUR) which are less prominent in other DEVELOPING COUNTRIES. These qualities, together with political stability, attracted large volumes of foreign direct INVESTMENT, particularly from Japan and the USA.

As the economies of the first wave of 'tigers' became more mature, production was being shifted to second wave tigers like the Philippines and Vietnam, where labour costs are lower. The new focus on property, financial services and other non-productive activities among the tigers led to a sharp asset price INFLATION contributing to sharp falls in their currencies, stock markets and property values in 1997–98. New economic and financial plans were put in place by the IMF (see BRETTON WOODS) and World Bank, backed by official credits. The cultural factors which set the tiger economies apart as centres of economic growth have not been so easily produced in more mature economies, with the exception of the immigrant communities on the Pacific coast of the USA. For further reading: J. Fallows, *Looking at the Sun* (1994). A.BR.

time notation. A type of MUSIC NOTATION pioneered by avant-garde composer Earle Brown (also called *time-space notation*) where the durations of the notes are not indicated by conventional rhythmic symbols but by either the distance between the notes on the musical score or by the length of horizontal lines extending from them. This system is much less exact than conventional rhythmic notation and gives the performer more interpretational freedom (see INDETERMINACY). For further reading: M. Nyman, *Experimental Music: Cage and Beyond* (1974). B.CO.

time-space convergence. Concept used in HISTORICAL GEOGRAPHY to denote the space shortening that takes place as breakthroughs in transport technology enable distant places to become nearer to one another. Each technological transformation engenders a revolution in travel time, thereby facilitating the ever wider spatial organization of people and activities. P.O.M.

time-space distanciation. In the social theories of the British sociologist Anthony Giddens (see below) this is a feature of MODERNITY in which particular geographical locations are shaped by forces which may be geographically distant. Space has lost significance because instantaneous communications and the speeding up of travel mean that all parts of the globe can be closely connected to one another. Time-space distanciation is therefore a feature of GLOBALIZATION, and it has led to particular localities losing some of their distinctiveness. Thus even the smallest local shop will contain goods from around the globe. For further reading: A. Giddens, *The Consequences of Modernity* (1990). M.D.H.

time-space notation, see under TIME NOTATION.

tissue engineering. The engineered growth of biological tissues such as skin and tendon, typically on artificial POLYMER scaffolding. At present, damaged tissues in the body are replaced either by grafts or transplants or by synthetic materials such as biocompatible polymers. But the discovery that tissue CELLS can be grown in culture vessels if provided with essential nutrients and a polymer scaffold to guide the growth has led to attempts to regenerate natural tissues, ideally from a patient's own cells to avoid the problem of immune rejection (see IMMUNITY). Artificial skin grown in culture on porous, biodegradable polymer supports seeded with epithelial cells is now marketed for treatment of severe burns; and similar polymer sheets can be surgically grafted onto damaged areas of skin to enable real skin, rather than scar tissue, to regrow. There are ongoing attempts to grow structural tissues such as ligament and tendon, and even functional tissues such as kidney, liver and pancreatic cells. Entire organs might eventually be regenerated in culture on seeded polymer scaffolds and subsequently implanted to replace defective ones. P.C.B.

Titoism. A term invented to characterize the specific political evolution of Yugoslav domestic and foreign policies after President Josip Broz Tito's (1892–1980) break with Stalin in 1948; it has also been applied to the policies of other communist parties displaying similar tendencies towards doctrinal REVISIONISM and national COMMUNISM (see YUGOSLAVIA, THE FORMER; USSR, THE FORMER). Internally, Titoism was marked by some attenuation of the Party's administrative (though not its political) role and of the power exercised by the political police. It permitted a far greater contact with other countries by liberalizing travel, allowing emigration, and developing the tourist industry. It reversed the harsh COLLECTIVIZATION drive in favour of individual small-scale farming. Its most novel policy, which it claims as its doctrinal trademark and the most distinctive characteristic of Yugoslav SOCIALISM, was that of introducing 'workers' self-government' through 'workers' councils', together with the industrial 'self-management' of enterprises in a MARKET SOCIALISM. Political decentralization led to demands for autonomy in federal states on ethnic and economic grounds, and this produced a certain reversal of Tito's policies, a clamp-down on 'anarcho-liberal' tendencies and on Croat and other local NATIONALISM.

Externally, Tito's foreign policy after 1948 became completely independent of the Soviet Union. It achieved this by taking advantage of the BALANCE OF POWER in Europe and by developing special relationships with THIRD WORLD countries on the basis of NON-ALIGNMENT. The resumption of closer relations with the Soviet Union at the Party level did not impair Yugoslavia's jealously guarded independence, which was expressed not only in foreign policy, but also in cordial relations with those communist parties (e.g. the Romanian, Italian and Spanish) which opposed the Soviet Union's attempts to re-establish its doctrinal and political leadership in the communist movement, and to exclude China from it. For further reading: R. West, *Tito and the Rise and Fall of Yugoslavia* (1994). L.L.

TM, see TRANSCENDENTAL MEDITATION.

TNP, see THÉÂTRE NATIONAL POPULAIRE.

toasting, see under REGGAE.

TOE (theory of everything), see under SUPERSTRINGS; GRAND UNIFICATION.

tokomak. A very large piece of experimental equipment first developed in the former USSR which is used to study the conditions in which controlled nuclear FUSION might occur and the manner in which it could be exploited for power generation. Investigations are being undertaken on the behaviour of very dense currents of hydrogen IONS. Unfortunately such currents are usually unstable – they wobble and change shape and they can strike the walls of the confining chamber. A tokomak is an experimental chamber in which these instabilities are studied and removed. It consists basically of a large hollow ring inside which the ion currents circulate. Large coils around the ring produce a magnetic field which acts on the circulating ions in such a direction that their trajectory is stabilized. H.M.R.

tomography. To discover what is inside some closed container, such as your skull or a terrorist's suitcase, X-rays (or NMR, Nuclear Magnetic Resonance) are used. Owing to scattering and interference the direct observations are blurred and confused: tomography is the science of feeding several of these observations into a computer which is then able to produce clear pictures of the contents, as in CAT (Computerized Axial Tomography). N.A.R.

tonality, see under ATONAL MUSIC.

tone-cluster (or *cluster).* A group of adjacent notes, usually played on a keyboard instrument, and not susceptible of conventional harmonic analysis. Tone-clusters may be played with the palm of the hand, the forearm, or a piece of wood or other material of a specified length. First appearing in the music of American AVANT-GARDE composers such as Charles Ives and Henry Cowell, they have now become a routine device and part of the normal vocabulary of music. A.H.

tone-row, see under SERIAL MUSIC.

Tonton Macoute. In Haitian Creole literally: Uncle bagmen. A 10,000-strong paramilitary stormtroop organization, personally recruited from 1959 onwards by Jacques Duvalier, dictator of Haiti, to terrorize (see TERRORISM) political opponents and critics of the regime. Officially entitled *Volontaires de la Securité Nationale*, and untouched by any legal restraint, its members acquired a name for extortion, torture and brutality. In the disorder that followed the fall from power of Duvalier's son Jean-Claude ('Baby-Doc') in 1986, the Macoutes became the target of much vengeful violence. For further reading: R. I. Rotberg, *Haiti: the Politics of Squalor* (1971). S.R.; D.C.W.

topic neutrality. The idea, introduced to PHILOSOPHY by Gilbert Ryle (1900–76), that certain terms may be neutral with respect to a given context of DISCOURSE within which they occur. He defined the notion thus: expressions of, e.g., English are topic-neutral if a foreigner who understood *only* them when reading an English passage could not understand what the passage as a whole is about. It is suggested that the chief examples of topic-neutral words are the 'constants' of LOGIC, such as 'and', 'or', 'if', 'not'. Some philosophers argue that since these terms are fundamental to logic they should be regarded as neutral with respect to different ways of interpreting other logical terms. Ryle argued that any arbitrarily chosen topic-neutral words could serve as the constants of logic. The matter is controversial. For further reading: G. Ryle, *Dilemmas* (1954). A.C.G.

topodeme, see under DEME.

topological defect, see under STRINGS.

topological psychology. A form of PSYCHOLOGY associated with Kurt Lewin who, much influenced by GESTALT psychology, used topological GEOMETRY (i.e. non-metric spatial relations; see TOPOLOGY) to represent and theorize about the field of interacting psychological forces (the LIFE SPACE) within which a person lives and acts. For further reading: K. Lewin, *Principles of Topological Psychology* (1936). I.M.L.H.

topology. This is of necessity something of a ragbag of a subject – it concerns those properties of space not covered by GEOMETRY with its notions of exact lengths and angles, etc. Some branches developed from seemingly trivial problems – the problem of the Königsberg bridges (solved by Leonhard Euler in 1736) led to graph theory. His theorem about polyhedra ('faces plus vertices equals edges plus 2') leads into the Classification of Surfaces (part of the study of those properties which survive the study of those properties that survive distortion – 'rubber sheet geometry' or 'plasticine geometry' – including the FOUR-COLOUR CONJECTURE about map colouring, and KNOT THEORY).

The fixed-point theorems can be used to produce general results in, e.g., MECHANICS and ECONOMICS. One theorem says that if you fit a circle with a piece of rubber, then distort the rubber as much as you like, and put it back within the circle, some bit of rubber will still be in its original position. In the 20th century topology has developed links with ALGEBRA, GROUP THEORY, combinatorial methods, and much else, and has studied problems of great complexity, far removed from its simple beginnings. N.A.R.

torts. Wrongs done to others independent of any contractual relationship, for which the injured party may sue. Whereas the outcome of any action for breach of contract depends upon the terms of the contract concerned (see CONTRACT), tortious liabilities are of widely varying kinds. The commonest tort is negligence, the failure of a defendant to discharge an objectively tested duty of care towards others, albeit inadvertently, unintentionally or even unknowingly. Although the motive with which a tortious act is done is usually immaterial, so that a lawful act does not become unlawful merely because it is done with a bad motive, such as a wish to injure, there are some torts in which malice is an essential ingredient, e.g. fraud, malicious prosecution. Some torts may be directly intentional, e.g. assault, false imprisonment, while others may sometimes be voluntary and at other times involuntary, e.g. defamation, trespass to property, nuisance, interference with contractual relations or trade. The judicial remedy sought in civil proceedings for tort is normally damages, i.e. a sum of money to be paid by the defendant to the plaintiff to recompense him for his injury; but in some cases, e.g. nuisance to a neighbour, the court may grant an injunction ordering that the act complained about must cease. For further reading: H. Street, *The Law of Torts* (1983). D.C.M.Y.

total art. The creation of 'total environments' – walls, rooms, large spaces – usually involving various media, so as to disturb or in some way interest the spectator (or explorer). Examples are the houses, interiors and accumulations (MERZ structures) built by German artist Kurt Schwitters (1887–1948), and more recently the tableaux of American artist Ed Kienholz (1927–94). In its attempt to free the concept of art from its associations with collectors' pieces, and to break down the traditional barriers between 'art' and 'life', total art took inspiration from CONSTRUCTIVISM, SURREALISM and DADA. For further reading: A. Henri, *Environments and Happenings* (1974). P.C.

total fertility rate (TFR). In DEMOGRAPHY, the average number of children born among women who survive until menopause. Thus defined, the TFR is most easily understood with reference to a specific COHORT of individuals; in this case, the quantity measured by the TFR is also referred to as 'completed fertility'. More commonly, however, the TFR describes the FERTILITY conditions of a specific time period; in this case, it gives the average number of children if the entire reproductive experience of some (hypothetical) group of women were characterized by the age-specific BIRTH RATES of that particular time. Conceptually, the TFR in studies of fertility is analogous to LIFE EXPECTANCY at birth in studies of MORTALITY. J.R.W.

total institution. A concept developed by the Chicago sociologist Erving Goffman (1922–82) to designate the special characteristics developed by institutions, such as mental hospitals and prisons, absolutely set apart from society at large, and with RITUALS which totally deny the individual, private existence of its occupants. Such institutions typically have a formal, official, society-oriented rationale (gaols are punitive, asylums are therapeutic). Goffman contended, however, that, by virtue of their isolation, they develop self-regulating systems and rationales of their own, essentially geared to their own internal self-perpetuation. Strategic adjustment among staff and patients alike through internal SUBCULTURES subverts the explicit goals of the institution, produces a survivor mentality, and creates institutional dependence. Goffman's work served as an important critique of classic institution-based reformist strategies. For further reading: E. Goffman, *Asylums* (1968). R.P.

total serialization, see under SERIAL MUSIC.

total theatre. Theatre regarded as primarily a director's medium using the text as only a minor part of an overall theatrical experience of lights, music, movement of all sorts, sets, and costumes. The term was first used in the mid-1920s: an abortive *Totaltheater* planned by Walter Gropius for Erwin Piscator in Berlin; but the concept was first effectively executed by Jean-Louis Barrault in works like Claudel's *Christophe Colombe* (production of 1953) and Barrault's adaptation (with André Gide) of Kafka's *The Trial* (1947). Subsequently it was taken much further by other directors, especially the Italian, Luca Ronconi, in his travelling version of Ariosto's *Orlando Furioso* (1970), in which the peripatetic spectators were constantly engulfed by the action. For further reading: E. T. Kirby (ed.), *Total Theater: A Critical Anthology* (1969). M.BI.

total war, see under LIMITED WAR.

totalitarianism. A theoretical view of NAZISM, FASCISM and former Soviet COMMUNISM which sees them as examples of a political system dominated by a single party and IDEOLOGY in which all political, economic and social activities are absorbed and subsumed and all dissidence suppressed by police TERRORISM. Total monopoly of the ordinary flow of information and public argument is essential to such a system. This view was much current in the 1930s–50s period among dissident MARXIST intellectual commentators on the *Gleichschaltung* (Nazification) of parties, TRADE UNIONS, universities, professional associations, etc., in Nazi Germany and on the degree of central control exercised by the STALINIST dictatorship in the USSR. It owes much to organic theories of the state. Later writers have tended to emphasize the degree to which rivalries for the leadership, factionalism, and the development, in industry, applied science or the armed forces, of separate centres of POWER and influence and of hierarchies parallel to the Party but essential to the state preserve an element of PLURALISM and modify the earlier monolithic image of the totalitarian state. For further reading: S. Tormey, *Making Sense of Tyranny: Interpretations of Totalitarianism* (1995). D.C.W.

totemism. For long regarded as a large and heterogeneous set of religious practices in PRIMITIVE societies in which groups of people associated themselves, usually as DESCENT groups, with natural objects. In the early 1960s French social anthropologist Claude Lévi-Strauss revived interest in the subject by radically changing our vision of it (*Le totémisme aujourd'hui*, 1962, Eng. tr. 1964). He argued that what had hitherto been treated under that head was a mode of thought and a classification of nature in relation to men. The argument sought to strip away both the religious and utilitarian elements that had accumulated in the theoretical writings since the last century. See also STRUCTURALISM. For further reading: S. J. Tambiah, *Culture, Thought and Social Action* (1985). M.F.

tower block. A tall narrow block placed in a city or landscape so that its simple geometry is clearly discernible, as in Le Corbusier's plan (1922) for the centre of a city for three million people. The geometry is usually that of a rectangular block or a cylinder, and not the pyramidal form of so many SKYSCRAPERS. M.BR.

town planning. Town planning, also known as city, urban, community and/or land-use planning, has been defined as 'the art and science of ordering the land uses, and siting the buildings and communication routes, so as to secure the maximum level of economy, convenience and beauty' (Lewis Keeble, *Principles and Practice of Town and Country Planning*, 1969). From a social perspective, one must ask 'for whom?' Those affected are not a unitary group, in terms of CLASS, GENDER, RACE and income (see SOCIAL TOWN PLANNING). Those who have access to a motor car may have a very different view of how a town should be planned from those who are dependent on public transport. Likewise those who are in the compulsory purchase site-line of new urban road development may adopt a NIMBY approach (Not In My Back Yard), but they would, in other circumstances, normally expect the government to build more roads to enable them to travel more speedily.

In Britain, 'town planning' is officially called 'town and country planning' in the relevant legislation because it has always been concerned with planning both town and countryside, and a range of rural planning policies and legislation has developed protecting the countryside from urban expansion. Nowadays rural planning policies are increasingly intertwined with environmental sustainability policies (see SUSTAINABLE URBAN DEVELOPMENT). For further reading: C. Greed, *Introducing Town Planning* (1996). C.G.

townscape. The visual character of the built environment, the sum total of the visual impression created by individual architectural façades, the ambience of the overall urban backcloth, and the effect of street furniture, lighting, vegetation and local topographic features. The current re-emergence of interest in townscape has been linked to the URBAN CONSERVATION movement. The term townscape is considered to have been first used in the *Architectural Review* in the 1950s, but it was the work of Gordon Cullen, *Townscape* (1961) and *The Concise Townscape* (1971), and that of Kevin Lynch, *The Image of the City* (1960), which popularized the concept. On both sides of the Atlantic there is a concern with visual authenticity and awareness of the dangers of creating a stage-set urban reality which is not reflective of user needs and modern urban realities. An entire 'heritage industry' has developed, in Europe particularly, which is strongly linked to tourism. American commentators are concerned with the unreality of newly manufactured heritage townscapes, modelled on an idealized 'Main Street USA' vision of the past (see, e.g., the new town of Celebration, Florida, built by the Disney Corporation). For further reading: A. Madanipour, *Design of Urban Space* (1996). C.G.

toxicology. The science of poisons – identification, mode of action, and antidotes. *Toxins* and *venoms* are poisons of biological origin. In general they are *antigens* and their remedies are *antibodies* (see IMMUNITY). Snake venoms are very often ENZYMES which have profound effects on blood-clotting processes, and for that reason may be used therapeutically, e.g. in haemophilia. The belief that very low doses of poisonous substances – e.g. strychnine – have a stimulatory and thus salutary effect is altogether without foundation. Toxins deprived of their poisonous but not their antigenic properties are described as *toxoids* – e.g. diphtheria or tetanus toxoid. Toxoids excite active immunity, and their use is greatly preferable to that of *antisera*, e.g. anti-tetanus serum. Vast numbers of industrial chemicals are now known to be poisonous substances: thus coal tar and its derivatives are CARCINOGENS, and organic solvents like carbon tetrachloride (used in the dry-cleaning industry) are known to cause grave liver damage. P.M.

trace element. Biologically important substances, also called *micronutrients*, and found, usually in minute amounts, in the soil and in food. Those needed for healthy plant growth are iron, molybdenum, boron, magnesium, copper, chlorine, and cobalt. For animals micronutrients include copper, iron, manganese, cobalt, zinc, molybdenum, iodine, and selenium. Certain animals and plants require specific elements which do not seem essential to most others, e.g. tunicates require vanadium, some plants need barium and strontium. Although needing only small amounts, living organisms concentrate trace elements in their tissues, sometimes having levels many thousand times higher than those found in soil or food. Trace elements are probably important as part of ENZYMES rather than as general tissue constituents. However, there is no rigid division in all animals between major nutrients and micronutrients.

Some soils are naturally deficient in trace elements (e.g. copper in South Australia), and until they are added farming is impossible. Micronutrients are also added to the diet of farm animals, particularly those reared intensively. But care must be taken to avoid overdosing, as trace elements may be very poisonous in excessive quantities. Thus copper in small amounts is needed by plants, but in higher concentrations is used as a fungicide and a weedkiller; and even man is harmed by water containing 10 parts per million. For further reading: G. W. Cooke, *The Control of Soil Fertility* (1967). K.M.

trace theory. In GENERATIVE GRAMMAR since the late 1970s, an approach which provides a formal means of marking the place a grammatical constituent once held in the derivation of a sentence before the constituent was moved to another part of the sentence by a transformational rule. The position from which the constituent was moved is known as a 'trace'. For further reading: A. Radford, *Transformational Syntax* (1981). D.C.

tracer. A distinguishable variant of some common ELEMENT which, being handled by the body in exactly the same way as its normal form, can be used to follow the course of a metabolic reaction in the body as a whole or in CELLS in a test-tube or other artificial environment. Tracer elements are distinguished from their normal counterparts by RADIOACTIVITY or by differences of mass. Tracer techniques represent the most important advance in biochemical METHODOLOGY in the present century, and it is no exaggeration to say that the whole of modern BIOCHEMISTRY and much of immunology (see IMMUNITY) is founded upon their use. An example in medicine is the use of radioactive iodine to examine the functions of the thyroid. Tracer technology is combined with microscopy in the technique known as *autoradiography*, in which a histological section containing radioactive tracers is made, in effect, to take a photograph of itself by applying it to a photographic emulsion (see AUTORADIOGRAPH). P.M.

trad. A conservative movement in JAZZ that swept America and Europe in the 1940s. Partisans of trad (short for 'traditional') declared, usually with great heat, that jazz was real only in its original state. The style of NEW ORLEANS alone was truly pure, though some CHICAGO players were acceptable. SWING, however, was decadent, and BEBOP a godless perversion. By the late 1940s trad bands were flourishing, attempting to keep the true flame alive, imitating the ancient classics with a zealot's passion. In the States the movement received a boost with the discovery of a living ancient, the trumpeter Bunk Johnson, who, given a new set of teeth and a horn, galvanized New Yorkers with his band of New Orleans veterans. To the supporters of bebop, however, trad was a travesty of the principle that jazz must always move forward, and they dismissed trad-lovers as 'mouldy figs'. But even today the music retains a broad appeal, frequently among people who would not otherwise consider themselves jazz fans, though it would not be unfair to say that what is referred to as 'trad' often lacks the real fundamentalist fervour and is inseparable from DIXIELAND. GE.S.

trade/business cycle. Cyclical fluctuations in the level of economic activity, where activity is defined with reference to the degree of utilization of productive resources. There is more UNEMPLOYMENT and underemployment of labour and CAPITAL in the slump than in the boom of the cycle. In the context of ECONOMIC GROWTH, a cyclical recession (see DEPRESSION, sense 3) is usually reflected in a slowing down in the growth of NATIONAL INCOME, rather than an actual contraction. In the definition, it is usual to include only cycles lasting between one and twelve years. Historically, most cycles have been somewhere between three and twelve years in duration. The duration and severity of cycles have varied across time and between countries. The term is usually applied to fluctuations in economic growth that have some uniformity in the cyclical pattern, as distinct from more random changes in the economy. The most common explanation of trade cycles is one of instability. The booms of the cycle are cut off by shortages of FACTORS OF PRODUCTION and by saving increasing as a proportion of income, as income rises, and, thus, AGGREGATE DEMAND failing to increase as quickly as output. These effects push the economy into recession. The economy recovers from this slump through the growth in consumption and government expenditure, and the level of certain forms of investment being relatively stable or increasing, in spite of income only growing slowly or even falling. This process leads to increases in the aggregate demand and brings a return to more rapid economic growth. Since World War II, deliberate government policies, usually related to BALANCE OF PAYMENTS considerations, have been prominent in causing or amplifying cycles in a number of countries, notably the UK. The terms 'trade' and 'business' cycle are respectively British and American. For further reading: M. J. Artis, *The UK Economy* (1986).

R.C.O.M.; R.H.; J.P.

trade theory. The theory of comparative advantage is often used to explain and justify trade between countries. A country is said to have a comparative advantage/disadvantage in production of a good or service if the relative cost of production is low/high (see OPPORTUNITY COST). If resources in countries can be switched from areas of comparative disadvantage to areas of comparative advantage, the combined production of goods and services in all countries can be increased. Trade between countries allows consumers to benefit from the greater production. Specialization in production may be limited by the use of less productive inputs (e.g. land), diseconomies of scale, the difficulty of using resources that have been released from production in areas of comparative disadvantage, and the costs of transport of goods and services to the final consumer. Alternatively, specialization may be encouraged by ECONOMIES OF SCALE. The importing of foreign goods and services increases competition. Foreign trade allows new TECHNOLOGY, ideas, attitudes and institutions to be acquired from abroad. The long-term benefits and losses from trade depend on changes in relative prices and demands for exports and imports, and economies of scale, EXTERNALITIES and technical progress in the production of exports and imports. See PROTECTIONISM; NEW INTERNATIONAL ECONOMIC ORDER; NEWLY INDUSTRIALIZING COUNTRIES. For further reading: R. E. Caves and R. W.

Jones, *World Trade and Payments* (1984). J.P.

trade unions. Trade unions are collections of workers who have freely combined in order to better represent their interests to their employers, or their interests as workers with other persons or bodies. Trade unions emerged from the INDUSTRIAL REVOLUTION in Europe in the late 18th and through the 19th centuries, and were often based on existing professional guilds. The early unions were craft and locally based (viz the Halifax Association of Carders and Tenters), with primarily Friendly Society functions. Only later did unions become industrially or generally based.

Trade unions rely on the collective strength and influence of their members (see COLLECTIVE BARGAINING). The International Labour Organization guarantees workers the right to free trade unions in its Convention 87, adopted in 1948, although not every country has signed this convention. Trade unions are usually perceived as being on the SOCIALIST side of the political spectrum, but there are many Conservative and Christian Democrat unions (see CONSERVATISM; CHRISTIAN DEMOCRACY) around the world, especially in Europe and the less developed countries. In many countries, Germany and Sweden especially but throughout much of Europe, trade unions are regarded as one of the 'Social Partners' (see PARTICIPATION). In general terms unions are tolerated as a necessary evil in democracies and incorporated or treated as actively hostile agents in less democratic socicties. This is true of many DEVELOPING COUNTRIES in Asia, Latin America and Africa.

As the workforce and methods of work change, so the types of union and their membership change too. The major long-term changes affecting all trade unions in industrialized countries are: rising long-term UNEMPLOYMENT; increase in the number of women workers; increase in the number of part-time and temporary workers; the decline of the smoke-stack industries and the rise of the high-technology industries; the increase in technically sophisticated jobs; the growth of the NEWLY INDUSTRIALIZING COUNTRIES and the increase in the use of new technologies. The tendency is for membership to diminish, especially in the USA and the UK, which saw direct confrontations in the 1980s between the government and the trade unions, leaving the unions much weakened. B.D.S.

tradition-direction, see under OTHER-DIRECTION.

traditional grammar. A summarizing (and often pejorative) term in LINGUISTICS, referring to the set of opinions, facts and principles which characterize grammatical analysis not carried out within the perspective of modern linguistics; e.g. the NORMATIVE emphasis of traditional grammar contrasts with the descriptive emphasis within linguistics. D.C.

***trahison des clercs*,** see under INTELLECTUAL.

transactional analysis (TA). In PSYCHOTHERAPY, a theoretical and practical approach developed by Eric Berne, and popularized in his book *Games People Play* (1964). Building on Freud's stress upon infantility and Adler's preoccupation with power strategies and LIFESTYLE, it postulates three positions from which people can communicate (child, adult and parent) and six possible classes of transaction (e.g. work, pastimes, intimacy), of which games are most frequently the focus of transactional analysis. In a typical game, one player pretends to be having an adult–adult relationship with another, but is actually trying to manipulate the other into being a 'parent' to his 'child', and thereby to achieve a goal such as avoiding responsibility for his own actions. The analyst, usually working with a group (see GROUP THERAPY), exposes such games, and encourages more constructive ways of interacting. Transactional analysis (commonly shortened to TA) has become a major popularization of the concepts of unconscious PSYCHIATRY. R.P.; M.J.C.

***transavanguardia internazionale*,** see TRANSAVANTGARDE.

transavantgarde (*transavanguardia internazionale*). Italian critic Achille Bonito Oliva's term for the renewed interest in figurative painting witnessed across Europe and the US in the late 1970s and early 1980s following the apparent dryness of conceptualism in the preceding years. As witnessed in the major exhibitions 'A New Spirit in Painting' (London, 1981) and 'Zeitgeist' (Berlin, 1982), the stylistic diversity among these artists, who included Schnabel, Salle and Rothenberg in the US, Clemente, Chia and Cucchi in Italy, the NEO-EXPRESSIONISTS and *neue wilde* in Germany, and others in France, Spain, the UK and elsewhere, was considerable. What Bonito Oliva saw connecting them was a shared interest in borrowing imagery from many different sources and reworking it in what was often an ironic manner. In so far as these borrowings and pastiches eschewed the sense of progressive development associated with the modernist (see MODERNISM) AVANT-GARDE, the transavantgarde was a quintessentially post-modern phenomenon (see POST-MODERNISM). M.G.A.

transcendence. The state of being beyond the reach or apprehension of experience; its opposite is *immanence*. The THEIST's God, conceived as a creator external to the perceivable world he creates, is *transcendent*; whereas the PANTHEIST's God, who is identified with the perceivable world, or some part of it, is *immanent*. Kant held that the metaphysical (see METAPHYSICS) CONCEPT of the soul, as an unobservable SUBSTANCE underlying the particular mental states that are accessible to INTROSPECTION, is transcendent, as is the conception of nature as a unity or complete whole. There is an important distinction in the philosophy of Kant between the transcendent and the *transcendental*. The former is unknowable by our minds, dependent as they are on the senses for raw material (see SENSE-DATUM). What is transcendental is the logical apparatus of concepts and principles, common to all rational minds, that organizes experience and is thus logically prior to it. The transcendental aspect of the mind's operations can be elicited by a critical philosophy that works out the PRESUPPOSITIONS of our knowledge. A.Q.

transcendental arguments. In PHILOSOPHY, an argument designed to show what must be the case if a certain region of thought or experience is to be possible. Although such arguments have been employed at least since Aristotle, they are chiefly associated with Immanuel Kant (1724–1804), whose use of them is intended to establish that possession and application of certain concepts is indispensable to empirical experience. Since Kant, and particularly in recent philosophy, transcendental arguments have been used in various attempts to refute scepticism. If a sceptic argues that we are not justified in, e.g., believing that there is an external world, he might be refuted by a transcendental argument showing that such a belief is a necessary condition of our discourse and experience (our CONCEPTUAL SCHEME). For further reading: R. C. S. Walker, *Kant* (1978). A.C.G.

transcendental meditation (TM). A technique, based on Hindu traditions (see HINDUISM), for relaxing and refreshing the mind and body through the silent repetition of a mantra. C.E.D.

transcription, see under NUCLEIC ACID.

transfer. In EDUCATIONAL PSYCHOLOGY, the improvement of one type of mental or motor activity by training in another, related one. Identical response elements may be transferred, when the new task has some of the same components as the old one; e.g. learning tennis after learning squash. Or rules may transfer, e.g. from one branch of MATHEMATICS to another. Or transfer may take place when the learning of a specific skill results in a non-specific faculty being trained; e.g. the general logical discipline supposedly gained from chess-playing or learning Latin. Transfer may be positive (helpful) or negative (hindering). Negative transfer results either from *proactive interference* between moderately similar response patterns, each partially learned, where earlier learning of one affects later learning of another, or from *retroactive interference* with mastery of a previously learned skill by the learning of a new one. H.L.

transfer RNA, see under NUCLEIC ACID.

transference. In Freudian PSYCHOANALYSIS, transference is a particular instance of the displacement of affect from one idea to another. It refers to the focusing onto a current interpersonal relationship (notably with the psychoanalyst) of emotions and fantasies which properly belong to other objects from the past – usually the parents. By virtue of the fact that the analyst has been invested with the patient's DESIRES, central themes in the patient's interpersonal relationships recur in the analytic situation. Transference is thus connected to a repetition of affects associated with UNCONSCIOUS ideas, and it is the task of the analyst to channel them towards verbalization. Transference, for Freud, became both the greatest obstacle and the greatest assistance to the analytic cure.

n much POST-FREUDIAN psychoanalysis, particularly of the OBJECT RELATIONS and KLEINIAN variety, transference has become the central point of reference in the interpretative work. Analysts of these schools have come to view transference as an instance of PROJECTION rather than displacement. This produces a reading of the analytic encounter as one in which the patient projects onto the analyst unconscious impulses, wishes, anxieties and aspects of the self (see PROJECTIVE/INTROJECTIVE IDENTIFICATION) which would otherwise be difficult to bear. The task of the analyst is to contain and ameliorate these unconscious elements, understanding them through the COUNTER-TRANSFERENCE and reflecting them back through INTERPRETATION. The analogy here is with the mother's capacity to tolerate her infant's intense feelings and to create a safe setting for growth. This model has been criticized not only by classical Freudians, who argue that the intense fixation upon transference interpretations in Kleinian analysis leads to a disregard of reality, but also by LACANIANS, who posit a third term, the power of language, as the neutralizing factor which changes the previous one-to-one infantile relation to the world. In Lacanian psychoanalysis, transference is based primarily on an attribution to the analyst of a special knowledge and authority – the analyst is thus positioned as 'the SUBJECT supposed to know'. The necessary failure of the analyst to fulfil this expectation opens up a desire for truth. S.J.F.

transfinite, see under INFINITE.

transformation.

(1) In MATHEMATICS and PHYSICS the objects studied are often referred to by using *labels* (usually numerical). Examples: (a) the diagrams in a book are referred to by number; (b) the points in a plane are described by their co-ordinates; (c) vectors are described by their components. A systematic relabelling is called an *alias transformation* (or a *transformation of co-ordinates*). It can be specified by, and it is often identified with, a FUNCTION f given by (1) $a' = f(a)$, where a' is the new label of the object whose old label is a; f is a PERMUTATION of the labels. Note that in example (b) f consists of two real-valued functions, one for each co-ordinate. The result of successive transformations is obtained by composition: if $a'' = g(a')$, then $a'' = g(f(a)) = g.f(a)$. Equation (1) may be interpreted in another way: one regards a' as the (old) label of a different object, into which the object with label a has been sent by the transformation f; f is then called an *alibi transformation*. It represents a movement of the objects.

Any relation between, or function of, objects can be expressed in terms of their labels. In general this expression will change with relabelling. If it remains identically the same under a transformation f, or under all the transformations belonging to some set S, then the corresponding relation or function is said to be an *invariant* of f or S. If f is considered as an alibi transformation, then an invariant represents an unchanging feature of the situation; e.g. the distance between two points of a rigid body is invariant under any rotation of it. There are two classic problems: (1) given certain relations and functions to find the set (actually a GROUP) of all transformations (here called *automorphisms*) under which they are invariant; (2) given a group G of transformations, to find all (or, better, methods for constructing all) the invariants of G. Both problems are of great significance for physics. In the special theory of RELATIVITY it is postulated that light rays (as relations between points of SPACE-TIME) are invariants; the corresponding group is the Lorentz transformations. Knowledge of the invariants of this group (and others) plays an essential role in the theory of the fundamental PARTICLES. See also PARITY. For further reading: J. Singh, *Mathematical Ideas* (1972). R.G.

(2) In BIOLOGY, (a) a change in the genetic make-up of a micro-organism, particularly a bacterium (see BACTERIOLOGY),

brought about by a quasi-infective action of a NUCLEIC ACID. If the nucleic acid is introduced by a vector of some kind, e.g. a virus, the process is spoken of as *transduction*. (b) Scottish zoologist D'Arcy Thompson's (1860–1948) 'method of transformations' was a scheme for showing up similarities and differences between outline drawings of related plants or animals by inscribing them within co-ordinate systems by which one can be shown to be a regular geometric transformation of the other. (c) A change that occurs in some CELLS under long-term tissue culture as a consequence of which they change their appearance and habit of growth and acquire malignant properties. P.M.

transformation-rules, see under AXIOMATICS.

transformational grammar (TG). Any GRAMMAR which operates using the notion of a *transformation*, a formal linguistic operation which alters ('rewrites') one sequence of grammatical symbols as another, according to certain conventions, e.g. 'transforming' active sentences into passive ones. This type of grammar was first discussed by Noam Chomsky (see CHOMSKYAN) in *Syntactic Structures* (1957) as an illustration of a powerful kind of GENERATIVE GRAMMAR. Several models of TG have since been developed, but the theoretical status of transformations has been questioned, and some contemporary approaches do without them (e.g. GENERALIZED PHRASE STRUCTURE GRAMMAR). For further reading: R. Huddleston, *An Introduction to English Transformational Syntax* (1976). D.C.

transgenic animal. An animal that has developed from an *in vitro* fertilized egg (see INFERTILITY) that has had one or more extra GENES (transgenes) added to it. Since the genc is incorporated into the egg it will be present in all tissues of the animal that develops, including the gonads. Therefore, by inbreeding, the gene becomes a permanent part of the GENOME. Transgenic animals have become important in the study of DIFFERENTIATION and in DEVELOPMENTAL BIOLOGY. But they also have considerable agricultural potential. For example, animals provided with extra genes for growth hormone (see ENDOCRINOLOGY) may grow more rapidly and yield more meat; and transgenic animals provided with a gene that has been manipulated so that it is active only in the mammary glands will excrete the product of the gene in their milk, from which it can readily be extracted. P.N.

transhumance. In GEOGRAPHY, regular seasonal cycles of livestock movement, e.g. the Turkana system of cattle movement between mountains and plains or the use of summer Alp pastures in central Europe. The basis of the movement is regular seasonal changes in pasture availability related to seasonal thermal and moisture cycles. Transhumance is more restricted in usage than pastoral NOMADISM, which describes irregular and non-seasonal herding movements. P.H.

transistor. A SOLID-STATE DEVICE (invented 1948), based on the action of junctions between SEMICONDUCTORS with different electrical characteristics, which can be used as an amplifier or rectifier for electrical signals. Because of their small size, robustness and safeness (since they operate at low voltages), transistors have virtually superseded thermionic valves (see THERMIONICS) as the principal electronic components in hi-fi, radio, television and COMPUTERS. They have also rendered practicable medical and surgical apparatus which could not otherwise have existed. M.V.B.

transitional object. A term coined by the British psychoanalyst D. W. Winnicott (1896–1971) referring to those objects such as a teddy bear, a blanket, or any soft or hard toy which some children take to bed in the transition from waking to sleep, and to which the child forms a special attachment. Only by holding it and possessing it is the child helped to withstand frustration, deprivation and changing situations. It designates the intermediate area of experience between the baby's fist-in-mouth and the teddy bear, i.e. between subjective inner reality and shared external life, between me and not-me, and ultimately between oral eroticism and true OBJECT RELATIONS (see DEVELOPMENTAL THEORY). Its function is fundamental as regards the capacity to symbolize, as it constitutes a resting place in the effort to keep internal and external realities separated and yet interrelated. Although it has no symbolical value as such, it allows primary creative activity as the baby apprehends the object as its own creation in the wake of the primary illusion that the mother's breast is part of the infant. It is this illusion – that what the infant creates really exists – which allows for its growing ability to recognize and accept reality. Nevertheless, this illusory experience is retained throughout life in the experiencing that belongs to the arts, religion, and creative or scientific work. On the other hand, if the subject does not develop to a further stage of object relations, its pathological fixation can lead to fetishism in adult sexual life, or other symptoms such as addiction or stealing. B.BE.

transitions to democracy. A concept and a field of studies related to the wave of democratization that occurred in several regions of the world in the 1970s and 1980s (see DEMOCRACY). These included southern Europe (Spain, Greece and Portugal), South America (Argentina, Chile, Brazil), Asia (South Korea, Taiwan, the Philippines, Pakistan), and most spectacularly the COMMUNIST societies of central and eastern Europe (though conspicuously not that of China, which greeted the worldwide move towards democracy with a massacre of demonstrating students in Tiananmen Square, Peking, in June 1989). In all these countries authoritarian or dictatorial rule gave way to various forms of democracy. Scholars were not surprisingly moved to speculate on the reasons for this tidal wave of democratization, and to enquire whether there might not be certain general features associated with the transition to democratic rule. While reasonable doubts have been cast on the assumption that societies of such varying character can be lumped together for this purpose, and even more scepticism displayed towards the emerging field of 'transitology', there have been some stimulating studies produced in response to this undeniably striking political phenomenon. K.K.

translation, see under NUCLEIC ACID.

translocation. In GENETICS, a mutational event (see MUTATION) by which part of one CHROMOSOME becomes attached to or intercalated into another chromosome. Translocations almost invariably have important genetic effects. P.M.

transmutation of elements, see under NUCLEAR REACTION.

transnational company, see under MULTINATIONAL COMPANY.

transnational relations; transnational society. Terms coined by Raymond Aron (*Paix et guerre entre les nations*, 1962) to describe the variety of relationships, activities and organizations which operate across national frontiers and which include, e.g., the Roman Catholic Church; MULTINATIONAL COMPANIES; TRADE UNIONS; professional, scientific and sporting organizations; revolutionary movements (see REVOLUTION). Aron suggested that when such activities flourished, as in Europe before 1914, the freedom of exchange, of movement and of COMMUNICATION, the strength of common beliefs, and the number of non-national organizations created a transnational society. He contrasted this with the period 1946–53, when the COLD WAR was at its height and communication between western and Soviet Europe was reduced to a minimum and conducted solely through governmental channels. For further reading: R. O. Keohane and J. S. Nye (eds), *Transnational Relations and World Politics* (1972). A.L.C.B.

transplants, see under SURGERY.

transportation planning. Planning for the highways infrastructure and the management of traffic therein, in relation to the distribution of the land-uses which the system serves. Nowadays, the concept also embraces the agenda of planning for mobility, public transport, accessibility and sustainability, whereas previously it really meant 'planning for the motor car'. Many would argue, instead, for the 'city of short distances', mixed land-uses and higher densities. Such a radical change may prove more difficult in vast, dispersed American cities, but the installation of rapid transit systems can ameliorate the situation. Also, much is now being made of the role of new technology to render obsolete 'the journey to work', especially the use of modems to enable people to work from home using the

INTERNET and E-MAIL. For further reading: S. Graham and S. Marvin, *Telecommunications and the City* (1995). C.G.

transposable element. A piece of DNA (seldom a GENE, but when so can be called a *jumping gene*) that can move from place to place in the GENOME. Most transposable elements move very infrequently and into a site that is chosen at random. The result may be harmful, beneficial or neutral and will be appropriately selected for or against, making an important contribution to the process of EVOLUTION. Often, instead of a simple move from one place to another, the original transposable element remains in place and it is a copy which is moved elsewhere. SELFISH DNA (see also NUCLEIC ACID) comprises transposable elements that have been copied and spread throughout the genome with little or no harmful effect. For further reading: B. Alberts, *Molecular Biology of the Cell* (1983). P.N.

transuranic element. Any artificially produced ELEMENT whose ATOMIC NUMBER exceeds 92. The atomic NUCLEUS of these elements is unstable and undergoes radioactive decay (see RADIOACTIVITY) or FISSION. About a dozen transuranic elements have been produced (usually in very small quantities) in NUCLEAR REACTORS. M.V.B.

transverse stage, see under OPEN STAGE.

transvestism. The projection of an image and the wearing of clothes usually associated with the opposite sex. The practice is immemorial and, notwithstanding such conventions as the male portrayal of female roles on the Elizabethan stage, usually sexual in its implications. These may range from the overt expression of HOMOSEXUALITY to the widespread latent bisexuality implied by 'unisex' fashion in the late 1960s, as exemplified by such rock artists (see ROCK MUSIC) as David Bowie. Another element, reflected by the pop star Boy George, is the use of transvestism to deny the significance of GENDER ('gender bender'). Transvestism has been popularly accepted as an entertainment form ranging from 'drag' acts in British public houses to Andy Warhol's New York coterie. For further reading: P. Ackroyd, *Dressing Up: Transvestism and Drag, the History of an Obsession* (1979). P.S.L.

trauma. Greek word for 'wound'. A physical injury or emotional shock such as may lead to TRAUMATIC NEUROSIS. In early FREUDIAN terminology the trauma is usually emotional (e.g. BIRTH TRAUMA) and can be specifically sexual (e.g. seduction by a parent). The trauma is supposed to break through the individual's defences, and in the absence of normal ABREACTION to cause a *foreign-body reaction* – the mental equivalent of the process whereby the tissues of the body wall off a foreign body lodged in them. Subsequent emotional arousal may reawaken early traumatic experience, resulting in an attack on DEFENCE MECHANISMS from inside and outside simultaneously. In Freud's later writings the concept of trauma assumes much less importance. Recent theorizing has tended to be focused on the broader concept of the post-traumatic stress disorder. M.J.C.

traumatic neurosis. A NEUROSIS precipitated by extreme shock or TRAUMA, which upsets the previous stability of the person, and leads him (typically) to exhibit uncontrollable EMOTION, or to experience disturbances of sleep with ANXIETY dreams in which the trauma is relived. The precipitating trauma may be primarily emotional (e.g. seduction in childhood or terrifying experiences in battle) or purely physical (e.g. severe concussion leading to the post-concussional syndrome, in which neurotic complaints such as blurred vision or lack of concentration are experienced). B.A.F.; M.J.C.

traumatology. The term is used to describe the study of all aspects of injury to the soft tissues, bones and joints, however caused. When referring to soft tissues this means injury to such structures as muscle, ligaments and tendons. The subject includes the mechanism of injury, its effects (physiological and pathological – see PHYSIOLOGY; PATHOLOGY), the healing process and diagnosis and treatment. N.H.H.

travelgate. The Clinton White House's May 1993 firing of non-partisan White House Travel Office staff, apparently to clear the way for patronage hires and, possibly, a lucrative contract for a Hollywood producer and Clinton friend named Harry Thomason, who owned a travel charter service. The firings in the office, whose job was to make arrangements for the press corps that shadows the President, turned into a true scandal when it was revealed that the White House had misused the FBI to investigate and persecute the hapless office workers and others. Subsequent events showed that Hillary Clinton lied about not having ordered the firings. Office chief Billy Ray Dale, accused of embezzlement for keeping travel office funds in his personal accounts, was acquitted by a federal jury and, he said, financially and professionally ruined by the Clinton-ordered purge. R.K.H.

Treaty of Paris, see under EUROPEAN UNION.

Treaty of Rome, see under EUROPEAN UNION.

tremendismo. A Spanish word not yet naturalized as 'tremendism'. The word *tremendista* was first applied to Camilo José Cela's novel *La Familia de Pascual Duarte* (*The Family of Pascal Duarte*, 1942) because the reader's shock and horror at what is revealed can only be described as 'tremendous'. Cela's Spanish precursors were 'Parmeno' and Emilio Carrere; but fundamentally *tremendismo* is a late, intensive, specifically Spanish development of NATURALISM arising from the horrors of the Civil War, the victory of the RIGHT, and Spain's consequent social backwardness. The savage vein, if not the term itself, continues in Spanish fiction and has been used to describe some Latin American novels of social protest. M.S.-S.

tribe. In ANTHROPOLOGY, a term too vaguely used for political entities, territorially defined, of differing scale. It is applied sometimes to (relatively) independent political entities, in which case it becomes analogous to 'nation' in more complex societies (though a tribe is not necessarily centralized and hierarchical in its organization); sometimes to divisions of such larger entities. A tribe is usually assumed to be culturally and linguistically homogeneous. The term *tribalism* has been applied to expressions and organizations founded upon a common ethnic identity in the cities of the underdeveloped world (e.g., P. Mayer, *Townsmen or Tribesmen*, 1961). Tribe/tribal/tribalism have been used as labels by anthropologists to designate groups regarded as pre-modern, non-literate or PRIMITIVE. Apart from the association of tribe with evolutionary ideas, it has very limited empirical value. The use of the concept of tribe by anthropologists represents the imposition of a non-indigenous concept and one which renders static a complex and fluid ethnographic reality. For further reading: M. Bloch, *Marxism and Anthropology* (1983). M.F.; A.G.

tribology. The science and design of interacting surfaces in relative motion, including the study of such topics as friction and wear and the study and manufacture of bearing metals and lubricants. E.R.L.

Trident. The successor to the American Polaris/Poseidon Submarine-Launched Ballistic Missile (SLBM) system and bought by Britain, the Trident missile has twice the range and greater accuracy. It also has Multiple Independently Targeted Re-entry Vehicle (MIRV) warheads, each of which can be directed to a different target. Similar systems have been developed by the Russians, the French and probably by the Chinese. The nuclear-powered submarines have very long endurance and are very difficult to detect.

Although the missiles could be equipped with conventional warheads, given the expense and complexity of the Trident system this would not be a cost-effective use of what was the ultimate COLD WAR NUCLEAR WEAPON. For further reading: A. Karp, *Ballistic Missile Proliferation* (1996). L.T.

Trojan horse, see under COMPUTER VIRUS.

tropism.

(1) In BIOLOGY, an involuntary directional movement determined by the pattern of incidence of an external stimulus. For most ordinary purposes tropism and *taxis* can be regarded as synonymous. Orientations towards light, gravity and sources of chemical stimuli are known as *photo-*, *geo-* and *chemo-taxis* or *-tropism* respectively. In 1975 MAGNETOTAXIC bacteria were discovered, and there is some evidence that

other SPECIES, including pigeons and bees, can sense the earth's magnetic field. Experiments on human sensitivity to MAGNETISM are inconclusive. P.M.; M.R.

(2) In literary criticism, the word has been popularized by the French novelist Nathalie Sarraute (see NEW NOVEL), who sees mental life as being made up of myriads of infinitesimal responses to stimuli. The problem of REALISM is to translate these movements into words before they have been falsified by the grid of conventional language embodying ossified attitudes and beliefs. J.G.W.

Trotskyism. The version of MARXISM associated with the ideas of Leon Trotsky (1879–1940). The basis of Trotskyism is the concept of PERMANENT REVOLUTION, first formulated in 1906, according to which the uneven development of different countries meant that it was possible to envisage a direct transition to SOCIALISM in Russia provided there was also a rapid progress from the national to the international phase of socialist REVOLUTION. Banished from the former USSR, Trotskyism found its organizational expression in the Fourth INTERNATIONAL established in 1938 to oppose Stalin's COMINTERN. Although unable to develop into a mass movement and much plagued by sectarian in-fighting, from the 1960s Trotskyism played a considerable role in the revival of socialist ideas. It combined an adherence to the original principles of BOLSHEVISM, a sharp rejection of any evolutionary, parliamentary road to socialism, a confidence in the revolutionary potential of the industrial proletariat, and a strong international dimension. For further reading: A. Callinicos, *Trotskyism* (1990). D.T.M.

Truman Doctrine. An important declaration of US foreign policy by President Truman in an address to Congress on 12 March 1947. At a time of growing tension between the Soviet Union and the Western world, Truman went on record as saying that 'it must be the policy of the USA to support free people who are resisting subjection by armed MINORITIES or outside pressures'. At the request of the President, Congress voted $400 million to help Greece and Turkey, and three months later the US Secretary of State made the offer to Europe which became known as the MARSHALL PLAN. The Truman Doctrine is taken by historians to mark an important stage in the COLD WAR, a break with the USA's traditional policy of no commitments in peacetime, and the first of many subsequent US economic and military aid programmes. For further reading: J. L. Gaddis, *The United States and the Origins of the Cold War* (1972). A.L.C.B.

trust. The latest candidate for an all-purpose social glue. In common parlance, 'trust' implies that A forgoes a live option to check B's behaviour as a sign of respect, and B responds by behaving in a manner worthy of A's respect. However, in contemporary SOCIOLOGICAL THEORY, 'trust' is often used to describe what, in earlier times, would have been called a 'mutual protection racket'. Here A has no choice but to trust B, because failure to do so would probably result in dire consequences for A. This state of affairs is associated with the complexity of post-modern societies (see POST-MODERNISM), in which people are forced to delegate much of their thinking to experts. Yet 'trust' in this sense goes against an older strand of social thought, according to which distrust tends to intensify among factions as societies become increasingly complex. Consequently, formal, often quantitative, procedures are introduced to resolve interpersonal differences. Some political scientists and economic historians have recently revived the original sense of trust as a generalized display of respect under the rubric of SOCIAL CAPITAL. S.F.

truth.

(1) The property implicitly ascribed to a PROPOSITION by BELIEF in or assertion of it; the property implicitly ascribed to a proposition by disbelief in or negation of it is *falsity*. There have been many theories of the nature of truth. The most common sees it as a *correspondence* between a proposition and the fact, situation or state of affairs that verifies it (see VERIFICATION). To explain the MEANING of a sentence is to teach someone its truth-conditions, the circumstances under which it is correct to assert it; and, in the simplest cases, this is done by uttering it, in an exemplary way, in circumstances in which it is true. Thus, for someone to have learned the meaning of 'It is raining' is for him to have been trained to believe or be ready to assert it when it

is, in fact, raining. The correspondence may, but need not, be regarded as some sort of natural *similarity* or *resemblance* between proposition and fact.

(2) Some philosophers, holding that all awareness of facts is itself propositional, i.e. that it necessarily involves the assertion of some proposition, maintain that truth is a relation of *coherence* between propositions.

(3) PRAGMATISTS define truth in terms of the *satisfactoriness of belief*, the empirically verifying fulfilment of expectations being only one form of this.

(4) Occasionally truth has been taken to be a *quality* rather than a relation, a view which has some plausibility in connection with ANALYTIC propositions whose truth depends not on something external to them but on the meaning that is intrinsic to them. A.Q.

truth-conditional semantics. An approach to SEMANTICS which maintains that meaning can be defined in terms of the conditions in the real world under which a sentence may be used to make a true statement. It can be distinguished from approaches which define meaning in terms of the conditions on the use of sentences in communication, such as in SPEECH ACT theory. D.C.

truth-function. A compound PROPOSITION whose TRUTH or falsity is unequivocally determined by the truth or falsity of its components for all possible cases. Thus '*p* or *q*' is a truth-function of *p* and *q* since it is false if they are both false, but true if *p* is true or if *q* is true or if they both are. The principle of EXTENSIONALITY states that *all* compound propositions are reducible (see REDUCTION) to truth-functions of their ultimate components. Some compound propositions, however, do not appear to be truth-functional at first glance: '*p* because *q*' cannot be true unless both *p* and *q* are true, but if they are it may be either true or false. See also PROPOSITIONAL CALCULUS. A.Q.

truth-value. In standard or classical 'two-valued' LOGIC, TRUTH *or* falsity. Some logicians, however, have devised systems with more than two truth-values. INTUITIONISTS (sense 3) have contended that there is a third class of undecidable PROPOSITIONS which are neither true nor false, and the formal properties of systems of logic with three or more truth-values have been investigated. A.Q.

tumour virology, see under VIROLOGY.

Turing machine. An abstract, mathematically defined 'machine' introduced by English mathematician Alan Turing in 1936 to make the idea of mechanical computability precise – by reducing it to the properties of a universal Turing machine. Turing machines form a very simple type of COMPUTER. In consequence of this simplicity, the resulting programs are inordinately long. For this reason practical computers are not much like Turing machines. (See also RECURSIVE FUNCTION THEORY.) C.S.

Turing test. Mathematician Alan Turing (1912–54) wrote a paper (in 1950) asking 'Can Machines Think?' He threw the question back as 'How could one tell that a machine was thinking?' and suggested we should apply practical, rather than conceptual, tests. His idea was to link the machine to a distant teleprinter and ask someone to conduct a typed conversation. If the answers from the machine convinced the person that they were coming from another person, then Turing felt it would be reasonable to say that the machine was thinking: it had passed the Turing test – he predicted that within 50 years such machines would exist.

Since 1991, there have been annual Turing tests for new computer programs (see COMPUTING) at the Computer Museum in Cambridge, Massachusetts. At present they are allowed to restrict the topics of conversation (and the enormous cost of development means that we are unlikely to see a general program, for which a prize of $100,000 is offered, soon). In 1991 a program on 'Whimsical Conversation' convinced five of the ten judges that a person was sending the answers (but 'Problems in Romantic Relationships' convinced only two of them). N.A.R.

twelve-note music, see under SERIAL MUSIC.

twin paradox, see under CLOCK PARADOX.

two cultures, the. Term introduced in *The Two Cultures and the Scientific Revolution* (1959) by novelist and physicist C. P. Snow

(Lord Snow) in reviving an old controversy, that of science versus literature and/or religion. This was the Rede Lecture at Cambridge, and it was answered by critic F. R. Leavis (see LEAVISITE) in the Richmond Lecture at Downing College, Cambridge, in 1962. Snow diagnosed society's INTELLECTUALS as divided, unable to speak to each other, having no common language. Each group he called a 'CULTURE'; he maintained that scientists couldn't read and that 'humanists' couldn't understand even simple scientific CONCEPTS such as the second law of THERMODYNAMICS. Leavis's answer was perhaps no more ill mannered and shot with sour irrelevancies than Snow's original lecture, brashly in favour of scientific culture in the interests of human survival, was ill argued. The kernel of the dispute may be found in a civilized form in T. H. Huxley, *A Liberal Education and Where to Find It* (1868) and *Science and Culture* (1881), and in Matthew Arnold's answer, *Literature and Science* (1882). A. N. Whitehead's *Science and the Modern World* (1927) is a brilliant and reconciliatory essay by a truly distinguished mind. For further reading: L. Trilling, *Beyond Culture* (1966). M.S.-S.

two hemispheres, the. Studies of brain damage have suggested that the two halves (hemispheres) of the human brain may perform differing but complementary functions; and American neuroscientist Roger Sperry (1913–94) has shown experimentally in his 'split-brain' experiments that, in cases where the hemispheres had been surgically separated, patients were being controlled by two distinct brains, neither of which 'knew' the recent experiences of the other half. Further investigation confirmed that the left hemisphere, which controls the right-hand side, is largely concerned with logical, sequential and digital processes such as language, whereas the right hemisphere is much more concerned with spatial, musical and pictorial functions. Non-human primates appear not to share this specialization of cerebral function, and it has been suggested that this development in human EVOLUTION was linked with tool use and the emergence of language. The educational and cultural implications of these findings are likely to be great. See also NEUROPSYCHOLOGY. For further reading: J. B. Hellige, *Hemispheric Asymmetry: What's Right and What's Left* (1993). R.A.H.

two-party system. The mode of political organization invented in the United States that took shape at the end of the 18th century as a response to the rise of EGALITARIANISM and the decline of ascriptive class societies, or aristocracies. Even today, the two-party system – where the disputes between internal party factions are often more pronounced than the overall difference between the two organizations – is still the exception rather than the rule in representative democracies. In the USA by the 1790s, committees of correspondence, organizing a network of influential citizens, were active in promoting meetings of 'our friends in your town', especially in Pennsylvania and New York. Such activities troubled George Washington, who warned in his Farewell Address of September 1796 that party spirit would 'enfeeble the Public administration' and create 'ill-founded jealousies and false alarms . . . [and] occasional riot and insurrection'. But when he left office in 1797 the first two-party competition was born between the Federalists and Republicans. In Britain, the rise of modern parties did not happen until the 1832 Reform Act, which extended the suffrage and produced local registration societies. In the 20th century, the two-party system in the USA has been challenged by third-party organizations headed by a populist rabble-rouser, such as Alabama Governor George Wallace. In 1968, the former segregationist ran for President while telling voters there was 'not a dime's worth of difference' between the two parties. More recently, Texas billionaire Ross Perot has used his Reform Party to promote an idiosyncratic populism initially based on opposition to NAFTA. Perot saw his presidential campaigns in 1992 and 1996 falter because of questions about his intentions and fitness for office; his legacy may be the move by both major parties to the political middle and a non-ideology that emphasizes moderation in tax and spending policies and toleration on social issues. (See MULTI-PARTY POLITICS). R.K.H.

two-tone, see under REGGAE.

types, ideal, see IDEAL TYPES.

typological linguistics. An approach in LINGUISTICS which studies the structural similarities between languages, regardless of their history, as part of an attempt to establish a classification (or TYPOLOGY) of languages. D.C.

typology.

(1) Any system for classifying things, people, social groups, languages, etc., by types. Typology has long been a mainstay of ARCHAEOLOGY. The grouping of a series of artifacts according to type, and the arrangement of like types in the form of a type series illustrating change, have in the past been the major preoccupation of some archaeologists, and the basis for detailed chronologies. Many of these are of value, particularly those supported by independent chronological evidence. However, with the advent of absolute DATING methods, the need to construct elaborate typologies has decreased. B.C.

(2) In THEOLOGY and Christian art, the joining of ideas or images in the Old Testament with ideas or images in the New. D.L.E.

U

Übermensch. The Overman (or Superman), a figure from Friedrich Nietzsche's thought (see NIETZSCHEAN), is often misunderstood as an evolutionary advance over *homo sapiens*, a powerful egoist, or a member of some master class. More likely, Nietzsche's *Übermensch* is a person who recognizes the arbitrary and relative nature of all values, yet enthusiastically affirms his own creations. Tyrants are not good examples, because their behaviour is conventional and their cruelty often betrays fear. The best examples are artists. For further reading: P. Sedgwick (ed.), *Nietzsche: A Critical Reader* (1995). P.LE.

ujamaa. A term applied by Julius Nyerere, first President of Tanzania, to his brand of AFRICAN SOCIALISM, signifying the perception of society as a kind of 'extended family'. Of all the African socialists, Nyerere was perhaps the least persuaded of foreign models of SOCIALISM. His study of his own society convinced him that the ideal society was one in which differences in wealth did not reach the level at which some could exploit others. This, in the circumstances of Tanzania, required substantial social control of the means of production and distribution, which, according to him, could only be compatible with socialism if it was instituted by a democratic state (see DEMOCRACY). Tanzania being hampered by the proliferation of scattered and unproductive settlements, a major part of his socialist policy was the resettlement (forcibly, on occasion) of these units in viable magnitudes and on a 'family' MODEL. In the event, the one-party system upon which he settled proved neither kind to the democratic management of these settlements nor conducive to their 'familyhood'. Nyerere's ujamaa system is expounded with unsurpassed clarity in his *Ujamaa: Essays on Socialism* (1968). K.W.

ultracentrifuge, see under SEDIMENTATION.

ultraism. In general, extremism; specifically, a Spanish literary movement (*ultraismo*) that flourished around 1919–23 and is best characterized as Spanish EXPRESSIONISM. The chief theoretician and coiner of the term was Guillermo de Torre; other more important writers (Borges, Lorca, Cernuda, Salinas) were influenced by it. The ultraists' programme involved the purgation of all rhetorical, romantic and anthropomorphic elements from poetic language. Partly SURREALIST, partly HERMETIC, ultraism reflected the peculiarly Spanish awareness of MODERNISM. Borges took ultraism back with him to Argentina, but soon abandoned it. M.S.-S.

ultramontanism (from Latin *ultra montes*, 'beyond the mountains', i.e. the Alps viewed from France). The emphasizing of the doctrinal INFALLIBILITY and practical authority of the Pope, at the expense of the looser and more national organization of the Catholic Church (see CATHOLICISM) as advocated by the French 'Gallicans'. See also VATICAN COUNCIL II. D.L.E.

ultrasonics. The study of waves of the same physical nature as sound, i.e. longitudinal undulations of pressure and density, but whose frequency is so high that the waves are not heard by the human ear. Ultrasonic waves are usually generated by applying electrical oscillations to a quartz crystal transducer, or by a magnetostriction oscillator. In the latter case a rod of ferromagnetic material (see FERROMAGNETISM) is alternately magnetized and demagnetized by means of a coil around it which carries alternating current. This current causes the rod to expand and contract at the same frequency as that of the current. The length of the rod is chosen to 'tune' at the frequency required to obtain increased amplitude of vibration. When one end of the rod is clamped, the acoustic waves are sent out from the opposite end.

Ultrasonic waves are used for non-destructive testing of metal castings which may contain cracks. Medical examination of unborn babies is carried out with *ultrasound*, and the short wavelength (centimetres or millimetres) enables fine detail to be detected. Very high-intensity waves can, however, be destructive and are used for the scaling of boilers and in dentists' drills. In such circumstances the generator is placed near to the surface to be attacked. The action by which the sound waves rip off the surface layer is known as cavitation. High-ENERGY waves are being tested medically for brain surgery without opening the skull, for waves of given frequency can be made to produce cuts at a given depth of penetration in a given position. At lower intensities the waves can shake loose the MOLECULES of air nearest to a surface and not normally movable by convection. This effect is used to improve the heat transfer across a surface, as in boilers.

Many animals (e.g. dogs, bats, dolphins) and insects (mosquitoes, moths) are capable of hearing and in some cases emitting ultrasound below about 100,000 Hz. They use it for sexual communication, 'seeing' in total darkness, and for the detection and evasion of enemies. M.V.B.; E.R.L.

ultrasound, see under RADIOLOGY.

ultrastability. In CYBERNETICS, the capacity of a system in HOMOEOSTASIS to return to an equilibrial state after perturbation by unknown or unanalysed forces (against the intervention of which the system was not explicitly designed). S.BE.

***ultra vires*.** Though of some importance in issues concerning capacity to CONTRACT, its main significance is as the primary ground upon which JUDICIAL REVIEW of administrative action is based, namely that the person or institution concerned acted outside his or its legal powers. Such powers are normally conferred by Act of Parliament, or under the authority granted by statute. Determination whether a decision or action was *intra* (within) or *ultra* (beyond) the *vires* (powers) conferred is therefore largely a matter of statutory interpretation. Varieties of *ultra vires* activity are virtually unlimited, and may be either substantive or procedural. Thus, a power may have been exercised by the wrong institution, or by the right one but excessively, unreasonably, in bad faith, for an improper purpose, or against the wrong person. The institution exercising the power may have been improperly appointed or constituted. Some fact which is a condition precedent to the possession of the power may have been absent. Irrelevant considerations may have been taken into account. In some views an error of law by a deciding body renders the whole determination *ultra vires*. In any of these instances a decision by the court that the act was *ultra vires* means that it was void and of no effect. For further reading: D. C. M. Yardley, *Principles of Administrative Law* (1986).

D.C.M.Y.

Umkhonto we Sizwe, see under AFRICAN NATIONAL CONGRESS.

UN (United Nations). Association of governments of sovereign states established on 24 October 1945. With headquarters in New York, it has several other offices, the largest being in Geneva. As the number of recognized states in the world has increased (owing mainly to European decolonization, and the break-up of the Soviet Union and Yugoslavia) the number of UN member states has progressively risen: from 51 in 1945 to 185 in 1997. No state has ever left the UN, though a few have walked out from some of its bodies temporarily.

The UN Charter, adopted by the representatives of 50 states meeting at San Francisco on 26 June 1945, defines the organization's purposes as: (1) maintaining international peace and security; (2) developing friendly relations among nations based on respect for the principle of equal rights and self-determination of peoples; and (3) achieving international co-operation in solving international problems of an economic, social, cultural, or humanitarian character.

In accord with the Charter, there are six 'principal organs' of the UN: the General Assembly (the 'parliament' of all the members); the Security Council (which at present contains 15 members); the Economic and Social Council (54 members); the Trusteeship Council (which, having superintended the transition to self-government of trust territories, now has no functions); the INTERNATIONAL COURT OF JUSTICE (in The Hague); and the Secretariat (headed by the Secretary-General). The 'UN system' also comprises the 16 specialized agencies which operate under the UN, and many other subsidiary bodies.

The UN's performance in its central task of maintaining international peace and security has been mixed. Under the Charter, there are five permanent members of the Security Council (China, France, Russia – which took over from the former USSR in 1991 – the UK and the USA), any one of which can veto a resolution. The veto was used extensively in the UN's first 45 years: by May 1990, the USSR had vetoed 114 resolutions; the USA 70; the UK 30; France 18; and China 3. Thus during the COLD WAR, the Security Council was not able to take action on most East–West issues, and such international security as existed was due largely to measures taken outside the UN framework. From 1990, the five permanent members operated more co-operatively, only five vetoes being cast in the period from May 1990 to mid-1997.

The Security Council has authorized use of force several times, mostly since 1990: the main cases are KOREA in 1950 (when the Soviet Union had temporarily absented itself from the Security Council), the Gulf in 1990 (following the Iraqi seizure of Kuwait), Somalia in 1992, and Haiti in 1994. In all these cases the UN authorized US-led coalitions rather than managing forces itself. In addition, the Security Council imposed SANCTIONS on a number of states, and initiated numerous PEACEKEEPING operations.

In a few cases when the Security Council has been prevented by veto from acting, it has been the General Assembly rather than the Security Council which has taken action regarding military operations under UN auspices. However, control of peacekeeping and enforcement activities has returned firmly to the Security Council.

The UN and some of its agencies have been criticized on many grounds. They have often been better at airing issues than at taking action. There is a long history of accusations of 'double standards'. In the 1970s and 1980s the US became increasingly critical both of an allegedly bloated bureaucracy, and of what it saw as an anti-Western bias in General Assembly resolutions: it showed its dissatisfaction by becoming the largest of the many defaulters on obligations to pay agreed contributions to the UN budget. In the 1990s the UN proved incapable of developing a clear strategic view of what should be done in conflicts such as those in the former YUGOSLAVIA and Somalia.

Despite its weaknesses and perennial financial crises, the UN has become the first genuinely global international organization, bringing almost all sovereign states together under one set of principles. It has played a significant role in setting international standards in such matters as human rights, sexual equality and environmental protection. Thanks to its assistance in the decolonization process, the UN (which some hoped would limit the excessive powers of sovereign states) has presided over an unparalleled expansion of the number of sovereign states. For further reading: A. Roberts and B. Kingsbury (eds), *United Nations, Divided World* (1993). E.A.R.

uncertainty. In ECONOMICS, a decision or course of action is subject to uncertainty if the probabilities (see PROBABILITY THEORY) of the different possible outcomes are not known. Decision-making under pure uncertainty is difficult to analyse and, in this way, is to be distinguished from RISK. In practice, imprecise views or beliefs are usually held about the likelihoods of the different possible outcomes occurring. For further reading: J. D. Hey, *Uncertainty in Economics* (1979). J.P.

uncertainty principle. A consequence of QUANTUM MECHANICS first derived by German theoretical physicist Werner Heisenberg (1901–76) in 1927. Within quantum mechanics, certain pairs of physical quantities – canonical conjugates – are linked by formal relationships between the *operators* that represent them. Heisenberg deduced that when this relationship holds, the 'spread' or indeterminacy of the two quantities are related as follows: the more determinate or 'sharp' the value of one of the quantities, the *less* determinate (or more 'unsharp') its value for the other quantity. The physical quantities' position and momentum form one of these conjugate pairs, which constitutes one of the most radical differences between quantum mechanics and CLASSICAL PHYSICS. A particle's position and momentum together define its path, or trajectory, but the uncertainty principle implies that sharply defined position and momentum values cannot both be possessed by a quantum-mechanical system (see PARTICLE). The notion of a classical path would therefore seem to be inapplicable. Heisenberg's initial discussion of the uncertainty relations was somewhat misleading, as it suggested that they arise from limits to the possible accuracy of measurements on otherwise determinate states. There may be such limitations to measurement, but they are not especially quantum-mechanical. The uncertainty relations present an *indeterminacy* in the dynamical states of physical systems, one that exists independently of attempts to measure them. For further reading: W. Heisenberg, 'The Physical Content of Quantum Kinematics and Mechanics', in J. A. Wheeler and W. H. Zurek (eds), *Quantum Theory and Measurement* (1983). R.F.H.

unconscious. A familiar word with, in psychoanalytic theory, two meanings: (1) as an adjective applied to thoughts which cannot be brought to CONSCIOUSNESS by ordinary means, but only, if at all, by technical methods such as PSYCHOTHERAPY and PSYCHOANALYSIS (see also PRECONSCIOUS; REPRESSION); (2) as a noun in the expression 'the unconscious', i.e. the part of the mental system or MODEL which contains these unconscious thoughts. To be distinguished from SUBCONSCIOUS. B.A.F.

uncrowning. According to the Russian critic Mikhail Bakhtin (1895–1975), the uncrowning of the mock-king is the central act of carnival and all carnivalesque festivals because it expresses what he called 'the joyful relativity of all structure and order' and the pathos of death and renewal (see CARNIVALIZATION; BAKHTINIAN). P.B.

underclass. Victims of the POVERTY TRAP, largely concentrated in the inner cities of the Western democracies, who have become a downwardly mobile block excluded from the broader benefits of society. In America this group has largely been identified as African-Americans, whereas in the UK the underclass is seen as spread more broadly across the racial divide. The underclass tends to live in high-rise/tower blocks on estates in the poorer sections of cities, the young people attend 'sink schools' from which there is very little chance of escape, and leaving school tends to mean a life on the streets indulging in petty crime and drug activity. In the minds of their critics they are the single parents, or 'welfare queens' of conservative mythology (see CONSERVATISM) in the US.

Whether or not we view the underclass in pejorative terms, the problems still exist. One group maintains that the underclass exists because of bad value-systems. They appeal to the culture of POVERTY thesis and the idea of a victim's mentality to characterize this class. According to this view, the key to improvement lies in changing the values of the members of this CLASS. On the other hand, others argue that in order to solve the underclass problem, American society must focus on the design of economic and social institutions rather than the values of individuals within this class. Thus far, WELFARE reforms in the US and elsewhere have failed to reach the underclass and there is concern that, as benefits are withdrawn, it may find itself even more divorced from mainstream society. For further reading: A. Hacker, *Two Nations* (1992). A.BR.; H.M.

underdevelopment. The state of those countries which have successively and with increasing euphemism been termed backward, underdeveloped, less-developed (LDC), and developing (see also THIRD WORLD; DEVELOPING COUNTRIES). The meaning of the terms development and underdevelopment are imprecise and, thus, there are sometimes differences in the classification of countries by these terms (see ECONOMIC DEVELOPMENT). Underdeveloped countries are usually taken as comprising the majority of independent countries in Central and South America, Africa and Asia, the main exclusions being South Africa, Hong Kong, South Korea, Singapore, mainland China, and Taiwan. Turkey and the poorer countries of southern Europe are sometimes included as underdeveloped. The original meaning, indicating that resources exist which have not been exploited, seems to have vanished. Although the word is now close in meaning to 'poverty', a few 'underdeveloped' countries, especially those with much oil and few people, are very rich in income per head. They may still be regarded as underdeveloped where the quality of INSTITUTIONS, the skills, educational attainments and health of the people are well below those of countries of longer-standing wealth. For further reading: M. P. Todaro, *Economic Development in the Third World* (1985). I.M.D.L.; J.P.

underemployment. Inadequate or precarious employment, such as that arising from an insufficient amount of work (people working fewer hours than they would like), a misallocation of labour, and an imbalance between CAPITAL and labour. Underemployment affects both developed and DEVELOPING COUNTRIES (see International Labour Office, *World Labour Report 1995*, 1995).

Economists used to include in their analyses non-commercial agricultural workers in developing countries who could be removed entirely without a fall in production. However, field investigations indicate virtually no such workers.

In developing countries, urban underemployment is caused by slow ECONOMIC GROWTH, rapid population growth, rural–urban MIGRATION from low PRODUCTIVITY in agriculture, wage rates in excess of market rates, subsidized capital costs, distorted foreign currency rates, unsuitable technology, and unrealistic earnings expectations by educated workers.

While the underemployed are a potential source of social unrest and political discontent, they are difficult to operationalize in surveys. Most figures purporting to measure underemployment are impossible to interpret. E.W.N.

underground.

(1) A word used to describe a range of resistance movements in Europe during World War II. They were secret organizations which specialized in sabotage and a range of other clandestine activities designed to thwart the efforts of the AXIS military powers. S.T.

(2) The name (recalling the resistance movements of World War II) under which in the mid-1960s an emergent movement of HIPPIES and kindred spirits expressed its corporate identity and sense of community in the face of opposition and even organized attack by the ESTABLISHMENT. The phenomenon first occurred in the USA, but also emerged in other highly developed urban-industrial societies. Its LIFESTYLE, which was reminiscent of the BEATS, involved, typically, a tendency towards MYSTICISM, a taste for rock music, the use of DRUGS, ideas of Universal Love expressed partly in terms of sexual PERMISSIVENESS, and a willingness to adopt communal forms of living without great regard for traditional standards. The movement, whose character was anti-technological, anti-materialist, experimental, and INDIVIDUALIST, and was therefore opposed to the tenets, customs and values of MASS SOCIETY, had its own newspapers, films, plays, music, and art, and its own outlets for disseminating them – facts which lend some plausibility to the underground's claim to be regarded as a *counter-culture* or an *alternative society*.

In order to survive and proselytize, the underground required some relatively formal structures, and these developed mainly through pressure from indigenous political elements; the earliest was the underground press, which described the new forms of lifestyle, discussed the problems involved, and debated the strategies to be devised. Generally, however, the Alternative Society has limited its corporate activities to the establishment of self-help organizations which advise and assist DROP-OUTS, those in trouble over drugs, and those with medical, travel or basic survival problems. Alternative living structures have emerged, such as COMMUNES, non-profit shops and entertainment facilities, and, for a brief period, alternative schools. For the majority of the population, however, a real alternative society in terms of parallel structures has yet to emerge. For further reading: T. Roszak, *The Making of a Counter-Culture* (1970). P.S.L.

underidentification, see under IDENTIFICATION.

underlying structure, see under DEEP STRUCTURE.

underwater archaeology. The survey, excavation and analysis of archaeological remains under water – whether the sea, lakes, rivers or pools. In the sea these usually take the form of sunken ships. The technique was first pioneered in the Mediterranean, but is now used in many parts of the world, employing sophisticated high-tech equipment which helps tackle the formidable problems involved in working under water. For further reading: K. Muckelroy, *Maritime Archaeology* (1978). P.G.B.

unemployment. A member of the labour force is unemployed if he does not have a job. There are various different classifications of unemployment. Those persons not wishing to work at the going labour market wage rate are *voluntarily* *unemployed*. Those persons who are willing to work at the going wage rate but cannot find jobs are *involuntarily unemployed*. *Frictional unemployment* occurs as a result of a temporary disequilibrium in the labour market and the adjustment to EQUILIBRIUM not being immediate. Examples of such disequilibria are the entry of new workers into the labour force, the introduction of new production techniques, mismatches in the skills of the labour force and the demand for skilled labour, and changes in demand. If these disequilibria in the labour market persist for some time, the unemployment is referred to as *structural*. *Technological unemployment* in an industry occurs when the introduction of new TECHNOLOGY reduces the use of labour – the unemployment may be frictional or structural. FULL EMPLOYMENT occurs when the labour market is in equilibrium. In a dynamic economy (i.e. with people continuously entering and leaving the labour market) the equilibrium of the labour market necessarily has a certain amount of frictional unemployment, the level of which is termed the natural rate of unemployment. In theory and practice, it is often difficult to distinguish between the different types of unemployment. For further reading: J. Craven, *Introduction to Economics* (1984). J.P.

UNEP (United Nations Environment Programme). Established in 1972 and headquartered in Geneva, UNEP is responsible for the administration of the international conventions relating to environmental issues, including: DESERTIFICATION, BIODIVERSITY, chemicals, international trade in ENDANGERED SPECIES (CITES), migratory species, global climate change, and atmospheric ozone depletion. See OZONE LAYER; BRUNDTLAND REPORT. W.G.R.

unified field theory. Early in his career Albert Einstein (1879–1955) enjoyed extraordinary success in revealing the links between fundamental phenomena of nature – above all, the relations between light, time and space – first in the special theory of RELATIVITY (1905) and then through the general theory of relativity (1916). This led him back to one of science's most fundamental ambitions, the attempt to demonstrate how all of nature's forces derive from one common unity and a single ultimate fundamental law of action. Einstein aspired to link electricity-magnetism, time and space, together with that force which had remained a mystery to Newton: gravity (see GRAVITATION). Einstein's own, largely solitary theorizings were matched by the attempts of others, including Theodor Kaluza, who postulated a five-dimensional GEOMETRY, in which gravity and ELECTROMAGNETISM determined the nature of time and space. Providing any kind of experimental corroboration for such hypotheses remained, however, a great stumbling-block. To the end of his life, Einstein sought the ultimate unified field theory, but it continues to elude science. See also GRAND UNIFICATION. For further reading: J. D. Barrow, *Theories of Everything* (1991). R.P.

unilateralism, see under MULTILATERALISM.

unilineal descent, see under BILATERAL-COGNATIC DESCENT.

unionism. Modern unionism first emerged in 1886, in organized opposition to Gladstone's First Home Rule Bill, perceived as the first serious threat to the (then) Union of Great Britain and Ireland. In the period 1910 to 1914 organized unionist resistance to the Third Home Rule Bill succeeded in getting the then British government to abandon its effort to impose Home Rule on resistant Protestant areas in eastern and central Ulster. In 1920, this led to the creation of Northern Ireland. From 1920 until 1970 there was a unionist government in Northern Ireland, resting on the steadfast support of the Protestant majority in the Province but subordinate to the British Parliament. While dominant in Northern Ireland, unionism died out in the Republic. In the early 1960s a well-organized campaign by the Catholic-dominated (see CATHOLICISM) CIVIL RIGHTS MOVEMENT against real though limited abuses of POWER by unionist governments in Northern Ireland led to the abolition (aka prorogation) of the unionist government in the Province (Stormont). Since then unionists, while still in a majority (about 60 per cent) in Northern Ireland, have generally been on the defensive. Their NATIONALIST adversaries are buoyed up by American support and a weakening of British interest in the Province. Unionists still have in their favour, however, the advantage of their majority status in the Province, and the inherent difficulty of detaching a British province most of whose inhabitants want to remain British. C.C.O'B.

unit of selection. In modern theories of NATURAL SELECTION a unit of selection refers to a specific biological entity that is involved in the process of natural selection in the same way as MOLECULES and ATOMS are involved in processes of chemical transformation. Natural selection itself is a process that entails different sub-processes such as replication of the hereditary material and interaction with the environment in such a way that reproductive success is differential. Similarly, different units of selection exist depending on the different roles they play in the process of EVOLUTION by means of natural selection. Most commonly a *replicator* (a biological entity that passes on its structure directly in replication, such as a GENE) is distinguished from an *interactor* (a biological entity that interacts with its environment, such as an ORGANISM). The question of which biological entities are relevant replicators and interactors constitutes the unit-of-selection debate. M.D.L.

Unitarian. A believer in GOD and in Jesus Christ's supreme goodness who rejects the doctrine of the Trinity, i.e. that God is 'Son' and 'Holy Spirit' as well as 'Father'. Unitarian congregations were first constituted in Europe in the 16th and 17th centuries, but have flourished chiefly in New England and elsewhere in the USA in the 19th and 20th centuries. Some Unitarians accept the authority of the Bible, but others are guided only by reason and conscience. For further reading: C. G. Bolam and H. L. Short, *The English Presbyterians, from Elizabethan Puritanism to Modern Unitarianism* (1968). D.L.E.

United Nations, see UN.

United Nations Environment Programme, see UNEP.

United States Supreme Court, see SUPREME COURT OF THE UNITED STATES.

Unity Theatre. A LEFT-wing, amateur theatre group established in London in 1935 with the object of presenting SOCIALIST and COMMUNIST plays and encouraging WORKING-CLASS dramatists. As well as presenting American, Russian and British plays under the direction of André van Gyseghem, John Allen, Herbert Marshall, and others, it successfully pioneered the LIVING NEWSPAPER in England and produced a series of satirical pantomimes. Unity Theatre groups, most of them short-lived, were founded in a number of cities, and in 1946 it briefly established professional companies in London and Glasgow. M.A.

universal.

(1) In PHILOSOPHY, a term contrasted with *particular*: universals are abstract properties and relations, particulars the concrete things that exemplify them. Redness and fatherhood are universals; an individual tomato is a particular exemplifying the former; the pair of individuals composed of a man and his child are two particulars which, as a pair, exemplify the latter. Particulars are concrete in the sense that they are individuals or objects of reference with a position in time and also, ordinarily, in space. Universals are referred to by abstract nouns derived from verbs (e.g. 'suspicion'), from adjectives (e.g. 'roundness'), from prepositions (e.g. 'betweenness'), and from common nouns (e.g. 'motherhood'). They either have no location in space and time or are indefinitely scattered throughout them (redness, one could say, is all over the place), and, if so, are frequently superimposed within them (a particular lemon, e.g., has a multitude of properties at the same place at the same time). Particulars are ordinarily continuous in time and in space, and each excludes all other particulars, except its parts and the wholes it is a part of, from the spatio-temporal region it occupies. Logical, or Platonic, REALISM ascribes real existence to universals; NOMINALISM denies it to them. Those who deny that there is more to an individual thing than the set of its properties would seem committed to the view that particulars are reducible (see REDUCTION) to universals. A.Q.

(2) In LINGUISTICS, (a) a linguistic feature claimed as an obligatory characteristic of all languages; (b) a type of linguistic rule which is essential for the analysis of any language. Noam Chomsky called the former *substantive* universals, the latter *formal* uni-

versals. The establishment of linguistic universals is of considerable contemporary interest, particularly in relation to the question of how children learn a language. In the 1990s, much attention has been devoted to identifying the properties of *universal* GRAMMAR – the set of characteristics that define the possible form of a human grammar. See also INNATENESS HYPOTHESIS. For further reading: V. J. Cook and M. Newson, *Chomsky's Universal Grammar* (1996). D.C.

Universal Declaration of Human Rights. Adopted by the UN General Assembly in Paris on 10 December 1948, representing the first catalogue of human rights and fundamental freedoms enumerated by the UN. Forty-eight states voted in favour and eight abstained, including South Africa, Saudi Arabia and the Soviet Union. The Declaration proclaims among its 28 Articles that: 'Everyone has the right to life, liberty and security of person' (Article 3), and that 'No-one shall be subjected to torture or cruel, inhuman or degrading treatment or punishment' (Article 5). The juridical status of the Declaration remains a matter of some debate. Arguments have been proposed to the effect that the Declaration does not by itself intend to create binding obligations in international law (see PUBLIC INTERNATIONAL LAW) for the UN's member states, however great its moral or political authority. Support, however, exists for a more radical view that in the years since its adoption the Declaration forms part of customary international law by reason of the consistent practice of states and international institutions. The Declaration was used as a springboard to further treaties, approved as late as 1966: the International Covenant on Civil and Political Rights (ICCPR) and the International Covenant on Economic, Social and Cultural Rights. The delays in approval were derived from the COLD WAR in which the US strongly qualified the nature of its commitment to the Universal Human Rights Movement. The US finally ratified (subject to reservations) the ICCPR on 8 September 1992. Despite the current dichotomy of the US's posturing on human rights and the continuing execution of death row inmates not provided with the most basic and fundamental of the rights enshrined within the Declaration (see CAPITAL PUNISHMENT), it retains the initial burst of idealism and enthusiasm and represents the single most invoked human rights instrument. J.E.O.

universalism, see under PATTERN VARIABLES.

universals. In PSYCHOLOGY 'universals' are features shared by all people as opposed to those specific to particular CULTURES. Their existence and identification have long preoccupied the discipline. Likely candidates include basic grammatical structure (see CHOMSKYAN), certain communicative gestures and facial expressions (see NON-VERBAL COMMUNICATION), and basic emotions. Identification of universals has proved difficult for a number of reasons, not least the great range of linguistic variation in psychological categories. Cross-cultural research after *c.* 1940 seriously challenged the universality of PIAGETIAN and FREUDIAN theories of DEVELOPMENTAL PSYCHOLOGY, while many are now challenging the universality of European concepts of the 'self' and autonomous personal IDENTITY. Within PSYCHOLINGUISTICS the controversy is long-running, extreme RELATIVISM having been proposed by the linguistic anthropologists Benjamin Whorf and Edward Sapir in the 1930s. The issue is also infused with ideological ambiguity. While the existence of universals would confirm the common humanity of all peoples, a belief in them has often seemed to connote ETHNOCENTRISM. Conversely, in practice, proponents of cultural relativism have often been in the forefront of anti-RACISM (see PSYCHOLOGICAL ANTHROPOLOGY). It seems likely that universals exist at the levels of basic sensory functioning, 'deep' grammatical structure and core emotional states, but even these are, necessarily, only knowable in culturally mediated forms. For further reading: D. E. Brown, *Human Universals* (1991). G.D.R.

University of the Air, see OPEN UNIVERSITY.

urban conservation. In Britain and many other European countries large sectors of historic towns are protected by conservation area designation, and individual buildings of historical or architectural significance are listed to prevent demolition or external alteration. In the US there is a growing emphasis upon the designation and protection of buildings of 'heritage' value and of 'landmark sites', and a National Register of Historic Places has been developed. Conservation implies continued use of the buildings as part of the living fabric of the city, for housing or commercial use, e.g., while 'preservation' has the connotation of the property being guarded and kept as a museum. For further reading: B. Cullingworth, *The Political Culture of Planning: American Land Use Planning in Comparative Perspective* (1993). C.G.

urban design, see under TOWNSCAPE.

urban form. The form, character and physical structure of towns and cities, with particular reference to the nature of land-use patterns and related transportation structure. For centuries most cities were based on walking distances and horse and carriage travel, and so they seldom were more than a mile or so in diameter. With the coming of the railways cities could spread out for several miles, but development tended to be fairly disciplined as commuters had to live near to the railway station. The coming of the public omnibus and the private motor car meant that, subject to road-building funds, citizens could live anywhere and travel freely around the city. With changes in technology new forms of urban development emerged, in particular the satellite dormitory town, the garden city, and suburbia (see SATELLITE TOWNS; GARDEN CITIES; SUBURBANIZATION). Not only did new technology enable cities to expand outwards, it enabled architects to expand cities vertically too, leading to the development of the HIGH RISE movement, and its promotion by visionaries such as Le Corbusier. Town planners have sought to address the problems created by continuing urban growth and the related problems of traffic congestion, pollution and development pressures, by a variety of means, including traffic management and restructuring the relationship between land-use zoning and transport infrastructure. In particular there has been a range of policies concerned with the design of the local areas that compose the cell structure of the city at the micro level (see CLUSTER PLANNING) and policies concerned with overall city form and structure at macro level. Nowadays there is an increasing demand for urban containment, and for more intensive environmentally sustainable forms of infill development, in reaction to the continuation of pressure for urban decentralization, dispersal and out-of-town development (see SUSTAINABILITY; SUSTAINABLE URBAN DEVELOPMENT). For further reading: P. Hall, *Urban and Regional Planning* (1994); L. Mumford (ed.), *The City in History* (1996). C.G.

urban guerrilla, see under GUERRILLA.

urban history. The history of towns is a traditional branch of LOCAL HISTORY, but the term 'urban history' or 'the new urban history' came into use in the 1960s to refer to a new approach, practised most of all in the USA. This new urban history is problem-oriented, concerned in particular with ECOLOGY, immigration and SOCIAL MOBILITY. It draws heavily on urban SOCIOLOGY for its concepts and makes considerable use of quantitative methods. For further reading: D. Fraser and A. Sutcliffe (eds), *The Pursuit of Urban History* (1983). P.B.

urban renewal. Policies, strategies and perspectives concerned with the redevelopment, rebuilding and revitalization of run-down INNER CITY areas. Typically these are areas which have declined in the wake of economic restructuring, or which are areas of social deprivation and poor housing. In Britain, the emphasis in the post-war reconstruction period (1940s to 1960s) was upon slum clearance and demolition. Now the pendulum has swung in the other direction towards policies based on provision of housing grants and allowances for modernization and refurbishment of older properties. This has also been the case in the US under HUD (Department of Housing and Urban Development) policies, particularly in relation to black community areas. Emphasis was put upon a holistic approach which tackled housing conditions alongside health, education and employment under the Model Cities Program, Community Action Program, and a range of subsequent initiatives. While such programmes were originally aimed primarily at working-class and ethnic minority residents, increasingly middle-class households have been moving back into renewed inner city areas (see

GENTRIFICATION; URBAN CONSERVATION). For further reading: N. Oatley, 'Regenerating Cities and Modes of Regulation', in C. Greed (ed.), *Investigating Town Planning* (1996). C.G.

urban revolution. Term used to describe the emergence of urban centres in the Middle East. The phrase was introduced into ARCHAEOLOGY by Australian archaeologist V. G. Childe (1892–1957) as part of a broad scheme in which he suggested that man had passed through three great periods of change, the *neolithic revolution*, the *urban revolution*, and the INDUSTRIAL REVOLUTION. During the first he learned to produce food and acquired a static form of existence which paved the way for the second, the development of organized city life. Childe believed that cities developed rapidly in the valleys of the Tigris and Euphrates. Recent discoveries in Palestine and Turkey, however, have shown that the phenomenon was more widespread in time and space. The CONCEPT is now little used among archaeologists, although geographers still seem to find some value in it. B.C.

urban village. A revival of city life characterized by a shift in emphasis from production (factories, warehouses, etc.) to consumption (bars, shops, etc.). Examples would include waterfront developments in Baltimore and St Louis, in the US; and Albert Dock, Liverpool, and Docklands, London, in the UK. These 'villages' have presented a newly diverse array of social arenas defined by lifestyle. The emphasis on the neighbourliness of these groups contrasts with the image of the great metropolis, popular in the 19th century, as the realm of alienation and anonymity. P.J.D.; S.T.S.B.

urbanism.

(1) An alternative term for URBANIZATION.

(2) In America (and cf. French *urbanisme*), an alternative term for town planning.

(3) the urban character or typical condition of the town. The functions of the town should be largely divorced from the rural society surrounding it for this term to be applicable. M.L.

urbanization. The process of people coming together *en masse* to form towns and cities. It is a defining movement of the 20th century. In 1801, 80 per cent of Britain's population lived and worked in the countryside. By 1981, over 80 per cent of the population were urban. *Megalopolis* is an ancient Greek word for 'great city', revived in 1957 by Jean Gottmann (*Megalopolis*, 1961) to describe the American city stretching from Boston to Washington. Likewise Los Angeles may be seen as a megalopolis in Western terms, although nowadays far larger cities exist outside the US. The main thrust of urbanization is in the THIRD WORLD, and according to the UN 45 per cent of the world's population is urbanized. Much of the new urbanization is caused more by push-factors from the countryside, rather than the pull of employment from the towns, and by overall demographic growth. Many of the new urban populations are poor, unemployed and living in large shantytown settlements ringing the cities. The largest city in the world (in 1997) is Mexico City at 25.6 million, the second-largest São Paulo at 22.1 million. Tokyo at 19 million is the third-largest city, Shanghai is fourth at 17.0 million, New York is fifth at 16.8 million, while Los Angeles is ninth at 13.9 million. None of the ten fastest-growing cities, such as Dhaka at 6.5 per cent p.a. and Lagos at 5.5 per cent p.a., is in the northern hemisphere. In fact Chicago (4.9 million) and London (6 million), once renowned for their growth, are now slightly declining in population. The average size of the world's largest 100 cities has grown from 200,000 in 1800 to 5.1 million in 1990. Asia contains three-fifths of the world's population and 44.5 per cent of the world's urban population. Although India remains 70 per cent rural it contains the largest urbanized population in the world, with 15 million inhabitants in Mumbai (Bombay), living at 17,000 persons per square kilometre (the equivalent figure for London is 1,200, which is considered high by Western standards). In such cities traditional Western TOWN PLANNING may be inappropriate, and instead emphasis upon basic sanitation and drainage provision, the establishment of tenure rights in the shanty areas, and overall economic and social reform are more relevant objectives. For further reading: P. Calthorpe, *The Next American Metropolis* (1993). C.G.

USSR, the former. The Union of Soviet Socialist Republics was formed in December 1922 when the several Soviet republics established by the Bolsheviks after their seizure of power in October 1917 united (see SOVIETS; BOLSHEVISM). Communist one-party rule, justified in the name of the DICTATORSHIP OF THE PROLETARIAT, aimed to develop a new form of collectivized society, implement state ownership of the means of production, and occupy a vanguard role in the international struggle of 'the toiling masses' pitted against 'world CAPITALISM'. 'New Soviet man' would shoulder the burden of MODERNIZATION.

The early IDEALISM, even UTOPIANISM, quickly yielded to harsh economic reality and political factionalism. PERMANENT REVOLUTION was displaced in the mid-1920s by 'SOCIALISM in one country', Joseph Stalin's triumph over his opponents (see STALINISM). Communist autocracy replaced Tsarist autocracy. 'One-party rule' quickly became 'one-man rule', Stalin's infamous 'cult of personality'. Modernization meant building heavy industry for which the collectivized peasantry was made to pay (see COLLECTIVIZATION). Stalinist autarchy displaced 'proletarian internationalism'.

The Stalinist regime spawned 'the great terror' of the 1930s but survived the destruction imposed by the Soviet-German war (see GULAG; CONCENTRATION CAMPS). Sadly the price of victory in 1945 proved to be a devastating toll of lives and resources. 'De-Stalinization' after 1953 brought welcome relief from the nightmarish repression, but the economy suffered gross distortion between the insatiable demands of the military and the impoverished civilian sector. Consolidation under Leonid Brezhnev in the 1970s became 'stagnation', preservation of personalized power at the expense of releasing the potential of Soviet society. In the end, which came abruptly in December 1991, the Soviet Union failed to meet the sustained challenge of modernization analysed by T. Von Laue in *Why Lenin? Why Stalin? Why Gorbachev?* (1993). Realization that effective economic reform demanded political democratization came too late. Gorbachev finally understood that saving the system meant first having to destroy it, unassailable proof that the Soviet Union was trapped in one of history's monumental blind alleys. For further reading: B. Fowkes, *The Disintegration of the Soviet Union* (1997). J.E.

utilitarianism. In ETHICS, the theory that takes the ultimate good to be the greatest happiness of the greatest number and defines the rightness of actions in terms of their contribution to the general happiness. It follows that no specific moral principle is absolutely certain and necessary, since the relation between actions and their happy or unhappy consequences varies with the circumstances. Sketched by earlier philosophers, notably David Hume (1711–76), utilitarianism was made fully explicit by Jeremy Bentham (1748–1832) and, in a qualified way, by John Stuart Mill (1806–73). It was widely rejected in their time for its unedifying HEDONISM (which was nevertheless altruistic). In this century it has been criticized for its commission of the supposed NATURALISTIC FALLACY. Its chief opponents are the kind of ethical INTUITIONISM that takes values to be quite distinct in nature from matters of empirical fact, and the DEONTOLOGY (often associated with that view) that holds certain kinds of conduct to be right or wrong intrinsically and quite independently of any consequences they may have. For further reading: A. Quinton, *Utilitarian Ethics* (1973). A.Q.

utility theory. In ECONOMICS, an individual's consumption of goods and services satisfies human wants and, thus, yields utility. The degree to which goods and services satisfy wants is denoted by their utility. It is usually considered impossible to measure utility, but possible to produce a ranking, in order of preference, of different patterns of consumption. With certain assumptions of RATIONALITY, utility is considered as a measure of an individual's preferences for different patterns of consumption. Utility is a function of the goods and services consumed. Thus, to say that the set of goods and services *A* has more utility than the set *B* simply implies that *A* is preferred to *B*. The assumption that individuals make decisions upon consumption in accordance with their preferences is equivalent to assuming that individuals maximize their utility, i.e. they are rational. As the choice of consumption pattern is constrained by prices and income, a consumer will not purchase a further unit of a good unless it gives an addition to utility, which is termed the MARGINAL UTILITY, at least as great as that obtained by spending the same amount of money on some other good. Thus, the price of a good is related to the marginal utility of consumption. This proposition underlies the NEO-CLASSICAL ECONOMIC THEORY of price and is used to justify the working of the PRICE MECHANISM. The concept of utility can be used to derive mathematical FUNCTIONS representing the demand for goods and services. Such derivations ensure that the preferences underlying the demand functions are rational. These demand functions can be estimated by econometric methods (see ECONOMETRICS). Utility theory is the basis of much of WELFARE ECONOMICS, consumer microeconomics and EXPECTED UTILITY THEORY. For further reading: D. Begg *et al*, *Economics* (1984). D.E.; R.ST.; J.P.

utility theory of value, see VALUE, THEORY OF.

utopian ideal. An important strand in the development of planning and architecture based on the ideas of English, French and American utopian reformers such as Robert Owen (1771–1858), Charles Fourier (1772–1837) and Étienne Cabet (1788–1858). Each of these tried to execute social experiments in which the physical disposition of buildings would correct the obvious evils of the industrial city and allow man to flourish fully as a rational and emotionally fulfilled being. Owen's co-operative at New Lanark in Scotland, Fourier's projected Phalanstery, and Cabet's Icarian settlements in the USA were all attempts to create an early form of SOCIALISM and give it visible expression. Each placed his ideal community in a rural setting but tried to provide it with urban facilities. This combination had a marked impact on the GARDEN CITY movement and, through its insistence on the relationship between social wellbeing and buildings, on the whole MODERN MOVEMENT in architecture. M.BR.

utopianism. A form of thinking invented by Sir Thomas More, in his *Utopia* (1516). Utopia is the perfect society that is found nowhere – on earth, at least. In the two centuries after More, utopia functioned as a critical political and moral standard by which to judge the INSTITUTIONS and practices of European societies. In the 19th century, fired by the promise of the Industrial and French revolutions, men strove to realize utopia here on earth, sometimes in their own lifetime. Europe, and even more the new republic of America, was swept by a wave of secular MESSIANISM, of which SOCIALISM was the dominant expression. The socialist utopia took several forms. There were the practical utopian experiments, as in Robert Owen's New Lanark in Scotland and the Owenite New Harmony colony in Indiana. There were the fictional utopias such as Étienne Cabet's Icaria which were converted into actual utopian communities in the New World of America, itself regarded by many in a utopian light. And there were utopian social philosophies, such as those of Saint-Simon, Fourier, Comte and Marx, which confidently looked forward to an end to scarcity and suffering in the impending scientific, socialist society. Even where, as in the United States, utopian communities such as the Shakers and Oneida still took their inspiration from Christian MILLENARIANISM, they tended to adopt the practices and outlook of modern socialism, becoming in the end practically indistinguishable from the secular utopian socialists.

Socialism is still the modern utopia, but far less clearly or confidently so. In the 20th century, assailed by the experience of two world wars, the Great Depression, German NAZISM, Russian STALINISM, and a glimpse of the destructive potential of the atomic bomb, utopia has been on the defensive – it has even been pronounced dead. In the first half of the century it was largely replaced by the ANTI-UTOPIA, a bleakly pessimistic rebuttal of the hope of utopia. But since the 1950s utopia has made something of a recovery, if still not attaining the commanding position it enjoyed in the last century. The 1950s and 1960s produced a stream of NEW LEFT utopias, blending Marx and Freud (see MARXISM; FREUDIAN) in a euphoric message of psychological and political liberation. And more recently, the success of industrialism in raising standards of living worldwide, coupled with the dazzling achievements of TECHNOLOGY – e.g. the revolutions in genetics (see GENETICS/GENOMICS) and COMPUTING – has led to new predictions of technological utopianism that read almost as SCIENCE FICTION. As the millennial year 2000 approaches, it is impossible to say whether hope or despair has the upper hand; but at the very least it is clear that utopia is far from dead. It may even be that, once invented, utopia becomes an existential necessity without which human social life could not be carried on. For further reading: K. Kumar, *Utopia and Anti-Utopia in Modern Times* (1987). K.K.

V

vacuum strings, see under STRINGS.

Vajrayana, see under BUDDHISM.

valence (or **valency).**

(1) In CHEMISTRY, a NUMBER characteristic of a particular ELEMENT describing the number of bonds (see BOND, CHEMICAL) that it makes with other ATOMS in a MOLECULE. Thus, in methane (CH_4), carbon forms four bonds with hydrogen, and is therefore four-valent (or quadrivalent), while hydrogen is univalent. The same element may, however, have different valencies in different compounds – e.g. phosphorus trichloride (PCI_3) and phosphorus pentachloride (PCI_5). The explanation of valency in terms of the sharing of ELECTRONS between adjacent atoms (*covalency*) is one of the major achievements of QUANTUM THEORY. For further reading: C. A. Coulson, *Valence* (1979). B.F.

(2) In LINGUISTICS (especially DEPENDENCY GRAMMAR) a term referring to the number and type of bonds which syntactic elements may form with each other. A valency grammar presents a MODEL of a sentence containing a fundamental element (usually the verb) and a number of dependent elements (valents) whose number and type are determined by the valency attributed to the verb. For example, *vanish* is 'monovalent', as it can only take a subject, whereas *scrutinize* is 'bivalent', as it can take both a subject and an object. For further reading: P. Matthews, *Syntax* (1981). D.C.

validity. The characteristic of an INFERENCE whose conclusion must be true if its premises are (see SYLLOGISM). An inference can be valid and yet have a false conclusion, but only if not all of its premises are true. Equally, an inference can be invalid even though both its premises and its conclusions are true, e.g. *some men are Catholics*, *some Catholics are pipe-smokers*, therefore *some men are pipe-smokers*. (The invalidity of the inference becomes clear if 'women' is substituted for 'pipe-smokers'.) A.Q.

value-added tax, see VAT.

value analysis. The study of a manufactured product in order to identify opportunities for reducing the cost by improving style, shape, function, materials, or method of manufacture. For further reading: L. D. Miles, *Techniques of Value Analysis and Engineering* (1961). R.I.T.

value-freedom. From the German *Wertfreiheit*, the exclusion of value-words and VALUE-JUDGEMENTS from the discussion of human and social affairs. Its adoption in the SOCIAL SCIENCES as a methodological (see METHODOLOGY) ideal (recommended by Max Weber – see WEBERIAN) does not imply that the valuations of the men being studied cannot be discussed, or that the selection of the problem in hand for investigation does not reflect a value-judgement about its interestingness, or that logical evaluations about the strength of evidence and the VALIDITY of INFERENCES will not figure in it. What is excluded is the making by the social scientist of moral and political value-judgements about the people in his field of study. The aim is to minimize possibilities of disagreement by eliminating from scientific work controversial and disputable matter. It reflects a methodological value-judgement that to count as scientific a body of assertions must contain only what can be established objectively as true or reasonable by SCIENTIFIC METHODS. Though there is no inconsistency in that, it is an ideal that is hard to realize in practice. Synonyms for *value-free* are *value-neutral* and *ethically neutral*; its opposite is *value-loaded, evaluative*, or NORMATIVE. A.Q.

value-judgement. An utterance which asserts or implies that some thing, person or situation is good or bad, that some action ought or ought not to be done. Value-judgements need not explicitly contain the pure value-words 'good', 'bad', 'right', 'wrong', 'ought', and their obvious synonyms and cognates. 'That is stealing' is a value-judgement, since 'steal' means the same as 'take wrongly'. On the other hand, the presence of a pure value-word is not an infallible mark of a value-judgement. 'The train ought to have arrived by now', said at a distance from the station and in ignorance of the actual facts, is only vestigially evaluative, meaning simply that it is reasonable to believe that the train has arrived. A.Q.

value of children. Phrase used to encapsulate a variety of cost benefit (see COST BENEFIT ANALYSIS) or social benefit (see EXTERNALITIES) approaches to FERTILITY. The main areas of interest are the cost of rearing children as opposed to the income they can or will bring to the family; the emotional value of children; absolute and relative value of children, depending on the age structure of the population and the *dependency ratio* (the proportion of productive to non-productive members of the society); and, in one telling phrase about modern contracepting societies, fertility decisions regarding 'children as CONSUMER DURABLES'. D.S.

value theory (in PHILOSOPHY), see under AXIOLOGY.

value, theory of/utility theory of value. There are two basic theories of value: the LABOUR THEORY OF VALUE and the UTILITY THEORY of value (although the phrase *theory of value* is often employed as a short way of indicating the *utility theory of value*). In the utility theory of value the relative value of a good is determined by the relative benefit derived from the consumption of an additional unit of the good. Thus, while water is essential to life, it is of little *value* as the benefit of drinking an additional gallon of water is small. If such a valuation of a good is greater than its cost of production, one may expect to find that in the future more resources are devoted to its production. The benefit of the consumption of each additional unit of the good tends to decline with increasing consumption of the good. Thus in the long run one may expect to find the valuation of a good equal to its cost of production. See NEO-CLASSICAL ECONOMIC THEORY. For further reading: M. Blaug, *Economic Theory in Retrospect* (1985). J.P.

Van Allen belts. Two groups of charged PARTICLES (discovered by the American physicist J. A. Van Allen in 1958) whose ORBITS lie just outside the earth. It is thought that the particles come from COSMIC RAYS and from the sun; their motion is influenced by the earth's MAGNETISM rather than by GRAVITATION. M.V.B.

van de Graaf generator. A machine for producing the high voltages needed to accelerate SUBATOMIC PARTICLES (see ACCELERATOR). Electric charge is 'sprayed' onto a moving belt which transfers it to a large hollow metal sphere whose potential may eventually reach millions of volts. M.V.B.

variable. A symbolic device essential in MATHEMATICS; the name, which is misleading, arose in connection with the CALCULUS. The fundamental use of variables is to express FUNCTIONS (e.g. $f(u, v) = u^2 + v^2 + 1$). The letters used for the argument(s) of the function are the *independent* variables; if a letter is used to denote the value of the function it is called the *dependent* variable. Particular values of the function can be computed after assigning values to the variables which occur in its expression (its arguments). If an expression or statement depends on *all* the values of the function, as in '$\int f(x)dx$' or '$f(u, v)$ is positive for all u, v', then the (argument-denoting) variables are said to be *bound* and it makes no sense to substitute values for them. Otherwise they are *free*. Variables may be restricted by implicit or explicit hypotheses or conditions. If the problem is to find values for them which satisfy the conditions they are called *unknowns*. Symbols for constants (e.g. Π) and for PARAMETERS can be thought of as variables which are restricted by more or less permanent hypotheses. When letters are used for purely manipulative purposes, without thought of assigning meaning to them, they are often called *indeterminates*. R.G.

variable-metric methods, see under GRADIENT METHODS.

variable stars, see under PERIOD-LUMINOSITY RELATION.

variance. In STATISTICS, the variance of a DISTRIBUTION is a measure of how scattered it is – a measure of dispersion. The variance is the expected squared difference between the expected value of a RANDOM VARIABLE and its actual value – in mathematical terms it is $E((X - \bar{X})^2)$ where $\bar{X} = E(X)$ is the expected value of X. The variance is often denoted by σ^2, and its square root σ is called the *standard deviation*; it is a root mean square error. For the normal distribution (see NORMAL OR GAUSSIAN DISTRIBUTION) of mean 0 and variance 1 the probability of the interval [–1.96, + 1.96] is 0.95 – hence the rule of thumb that for a bell-shaped density function 95 per cent of the probability lies within 2 standard deviations of the mean.

R.SI.

variance, analysis of. In STATISTICS, a procedure for allocating the variability found in a population to different sources, as in attempting to determine crop yield as a function of fertilizer used, chemical composition of soil, amount of rainfall, etc. It requires a design for analysis that keeps the variables isolated. (Failure in this respect is known as *confounding* – as when a study of the effect of social CLASS on the rate of bodily growth ignores differences in the nutrition enjoyed by the different classes.) Its basic logic is the comparison of the total variability in a population with the variability contributed by each of the sources of variance studied, and its typical test for 'significance' of a source of variability is the ratio of the variance left after all known sources have been extracted.

J.S.B.

variance-reduction methods, see under MONTE CARLO METHODS.

variation. In BIOLOGY, the process that leads to differentiation between the members of a single SPECIES. We may distinguish between (1) *heritable variation*, which is the consequence of genetic differences (see GENETICS/GENOMICS) and may therefore be propagated to the next generation, and (2) *phenotypic variation*, the consequence of differences of ENVIRONMENT or upbringing. Phenotypic variation is not heritable and therefore makes no direct contribution to evolutionary change. See also POLYMORPHISM.

P.M.

varve dating, see under DATING.

VAT (value-added tax). A form of indirect TAXATION imposed on goods and services throughout the EUROPEAN UNION (EU). Governments use VAT both to raise revenues and to make adjustments in economic policy. In contrast to the sales taxes, which it has largely replaced, VAT is levied at every stage of production which makes it cumbersome to operate but does mean that all firms contributing to a taxed product are involved in revenue collection, not just the final seller and the end users. The complication of the tax is also reckoned to have encouraged tax avoidance measures and contributed to the growth of the BLACK ECONOMY. Higher rates of VAT on an ever-widening range of goods and services have allowed governments to reduce direct taxes on income. The switch from direct taxes to VAT is designed to encourage personal enterprise and entrepreneurship by giving people more choice in how they spend or invest their disposable income. But because VAT falls evenly on everyone, whereas direct taxes are graduated on the basis of income, VAT falls more heavily on the less well-off, leading to a wider income gap between the better-off and the poorest in society. In the UK successive governments have sought to minimize the impact of VAT by excluding certain items, including food and children's clothes. For further reading: K. Messere, *Tax Policy in OECD Countries* (1993).

A.BR.

Vatican Council II. The Ecumenical Council (1962–64; see ECUMENICAL MOVEMENT) opened by Pope John XXIII to renew Roman CATHOLICISM. Whereas the First Vatican Council (1869–70) had seen the triumph of ULTRAMONTANISM, this Council did much to authorize a more BIBLICAL THEOLOGY and the aspirations of the AGGIORNAMENTO. For further reading: W. M. Abbott (ed.), *The Documents of Vatican II* (1966).

D.L.E.

Vcheka, see under KGB.

vectors of disease. A vector is an insect or other organism that transmits a pathogenic fungus, virus (see VIROLOGY), bacterium (see BACTERIOLOGY), etc., to a human being. The vector is usually immune to the pathogen (an agent that can cause disease). One of the best examples is the anopheles mosquito. The mosquito bites an infected animal or human and ingests the malaria parasite which reproduces within the insect. It then injects the parasites into another human through its saliva, causing malaria. Occasionally, human beings act as vectors of disease. Some people acquire organisms of diseases such as typhoid or salmonella but do not show any symptoms of the disease. However, they often pass the organism on to others, occasionally causing epidemics. Food handlers, e.g., have been pinpointed as the sources of outbreaks of salmonella and other food poisonings. A.P.H.

Vedanta. A system of beliefs developed by many Indian thinkers (most notably Samkara in the 8th century AD) and based on four of the ancient scriptures of HINDUISM, all having the Sanskrit *veda*, knowledge, in their titles. The emphasis is on the unity of the ultimate *Brahman*, and on the unreality of the world in comparison. For further reading: C. Isherwood (ed.), *Vedanta for the Western World* (1948). D.L.E.

veganism, see under DIET.

vegetarianism, see under DIET.

Velvet Revolution. Term coined to describe the peaceful overthrow of the pro-Soviet Union government in the former CZECHOSLOVAKIA in 1989, and its replacement with a Western-style pluralist democratic state (see PLURALISM; DEMOCRACY). The Czechs had never taken kindly to the Soviet domination to which they had been subjected after World War I, challenging the status quo during the PRAGUE Spring of 1968. Repression of the latter by the Husak regime led to the emergence of a strong underground dissident movement, typified by the CHARTER 77 movement. From 1987 the Soviet empire began to disintegrate, and Czechoslovakia turned itself into an independent state. The communist leader Milos Jakes resigned in November 1989 and began negotiations with the opposition Civic Forum led by the poet Vaclav Havel. The following month a new government took power, with Havel as President, Marian Calfa as Prime Minister, and the former dissident leader Alexander Dubcek chairman of the Federal Assembly. The new government won a substantial majority in the first free elections held in June 1990. V.L.

venereal disease, see under SEXUALLY TRANSMITTED DISEASE.

verification.

(1) The establishment of a BELIEF OR PROPOSITION as true. The chief philosophical employment of the notion is in the verification principle of the LOGICAL POSITIVISTS which requires a proposition, if it is to be significant, to be verifiable by sense-experience (see SENSE-DATUM), or by attention to the MEANING of the words that express it, or, indirectly, by INFERENCE from propositions that are directly verifiable in either of these two ways, i.e. by INDUCTION or demonstration. Formulation of the principle gave much difficulty. Whose experience is relevant? If, as seems reasonable, it is that of the speaker, are propositions about the past or other minds therefore meaningless? Must meaningful propositions be conclusively verifiable? Can the verification principle itself be verified? See also POPPERIAN. A.Q.

(2) A major problem with all ARMS CONTROL treaties has always been that of preventing cheating (see DISARMAMENT; NUCLEAR WEAPONS, LIMITATION AND CONTROL). However, various technological advances from the 1970s largely provided a solution. Satellite photography became so sophisticated that the preparations for NUCLEAR TESTING or the construction of a military site could be spotted. Seismic monitoring equipment, developed for earthquake measurement, could record and identify any underground test while sensors could detect any gases vented by such an explosion.

More contentious was the issue of on-site inspections, especially if these were provoked by information gathered through intelligence work. This is a world dominated by American agencies such as the CIA (not only does the CIA have a less-than-perfect reputation for accuracy and impartiality, but no smaller country has the resources to gather information in the US).

In 1991 it was realized that Iraq, which had signed the Non-Proliferation Treaty as a non-nuclear weapons state, had had for a number of years a major clandestine NUCLEAR WEAPONS programme. The failure to spot this showed up inadequacies in that treaty's verification systems. After the Gulf War, International Atomic Energy Authority (IAEA) teams, under the aegis of the UN, set up a rigorous inspection regime, but this in turn provoked a series of crises. It was belatedly realized that verification systems had to be supported by much tighter international controls on both the trade in arms and in certain areas of high technology such as missile or nuclear power components. L.T.

vernacular. In ARCHITECTURE, adjective applied to an indigenous style of building that is largely untutored, but thought to be of considerable virtue and to some extent associated with a golden past. It is the architecture of the Cotswold village or the Mediterranean hillside town or the adobe settlement of the American Indian. Modern architects have often claimed as one of their aims the establishment of a new vernacular. For further reading: B. Rudofsky, *Architecture without Architects* (1964). M.BR.

vers libre**,** see FREE VERSE.

Verstehen**.** Term used in Germany from the late 19th century to denote understanding from within, by means of EMPATHY, intuition or imagination, as opposed to knowledge from without, by means of observation or calculation. The term was employed in particular by the sociologist Max Weber (1864–1920) and by philosophers of the NEO-KANTIAN school such as Wilhelm Dilthey and Heinrich Rickert (see WEBERIAN). *Verstehen* was thought by some to be characteristic of the SOCIAL SCIENCES as opposed to the NATURAL SCIENCES; by others to be characteristic of history and literature, as opposed to the social sciences. Today, the value of *Verstehen* is debated mostly by sociologists. See also HERMENEUTICS; HISTORICISM. For further reading: W. Outhwaite, *Understanding Social Life* (1975). P.B.

vertical/lateral thinking. Terms coined by British psychologist Edward de Bono for two contrasted but complementary modes of thinking. In PROBLEM-SOLVING, vertical thinking elaborates methods for overcoming obstacles in the chosen line of approach, while lateral thinking tries to bypass them by switching to a radically different approach involving a distinct reformulation of the problem. The two modes of thinking are characteristic of, respectively, CONVERGERS AND DIVERGERS. For further reading: E. de Bono, *Lateral Thinking* (1970). I.M.L.H.

vertical integration. Control by one management of two or more steps in the process of production and distribution of a product, as when a book publisher acquires a printing press or a bookshop, or a firm that slaughters and packs broiler chickens for distribution obtains management control of the production process on farms through agreements with farmers. K.E.H.

Vichy. Town in southern France which was the seat of the country's collaborationist government after capitulation to the Germans in June 1940. The Germans divided the country in two, occupying the northern half and the western coast to the Pyrenees. The remainder of the country, under Vichy control, was the so-called '*zone libre*'. Marechal Henri Philippe Pétain (1856–1951), a World War I hero, was made head of state. His Prime Minister, for part of 1940 and again from April 1942 until September 1944, was Pierre Laval. The Vichy government was eager to please the Germans, devising and enforcing antisemitic laws and, ultimately, participating in the Final Solution by rounding up Jews and holding them in French CONCENTRATION CAMPS (including DRANCY in Paris) before deporting them to German concentration camps and certain death. With the restoration of General de Gaulle's provisional government in 1944, both Pétain and Laval were tried and sentenced to death. Laval was executed; Pétain's sentence was commuted and he died in prison. For further reading: P. Webster, *Pétain's Crime* (1990). S.T.

victimology. A subfield of CRIMINOLOGY, developing as an important area in its own right. The study of the characteristics and experiences of victims of CRIME, of the relationship between victim and offender, and of patterns of victimization. Early studies were concerned with 'victim proneness': the idea that particular types of people may be more prone to victimization than others. In modified ways, this idea remains important in crime prevention campaigns. Studies have also considered 'victim precipitation' – did the behaviour of the victim (style of dress, language, etc.) contribute to their victimization? This approach has been criticized for 'blaming the victim'. In the case of sexual assaults against women, FEMINISTS and others have criticized the assumptions of some victim-centred work and the crime prevention proposals that follow as sexist. Victim precipitation may be less contentious in other cases, e.g. where violence involving young men was preceded by alcohol consumption. The growth of victim surveys has done much to improve awareness of previously hidden rates of victimization in the community and home. N.S.

Vienna Circle (*Wiener Kreis*). A group of philosophers, mathematicians and scientists who came together under the leadership of Moritz Schlick (1882–1936) in the late 1920s to inaugurate the school of LOGICAL POSITIVISM. Leading members were Rudolf Carnap, Friedrich Waismann, Otto Neurath, Herbert Feigl, Hans Hahn, Philipp Frank, Karl Menger, and Kurt Gödel. It was associated with a like-minded group in Berlin, led by Hans Reichenbach, and the two groups jointly published the journal *Erkenntnis* (Knowledge). Schlick's death in 1936 and Hitler's occupation of Austria in 1938 brought the Vienna Circle to an end as an organized group, but its ideas were developed, under the name of LOGICAL EMPIRICISM, by various members who emigrated to the USA and elsewhere. For further reading: V. Kraft, *The Vienna Circle* (1969). A.Q.

Vietcong. A blanket term coined by the government of South VIETNAM to refer to anti-government forces in order to give the impression that all rebels were COMMUNISTS. The successors of the pre-1954 VIETMINH guerrillas, the 'National Liberation Front' was initially an alliance of all opposition forces. From 1958 onwards, however, they became increasingly dependent on support and aid from North Vietnam. Communist cadres increased their influence, and by 1965 the Vietcong was wholly dependent on North Vietnam for any chance of gaining control in the South. For further reading: N. T. Truong, *A Vietcong Memoir* (1985). D.C.W.; S.B.

Vietminh. Abbreviation of the VIETNAM *Duc Lap Dong Minh* (Vietnamese Independence League), founded in China in 1941. It was initially an alliance of COMMUNISTS and NATIONALISTS assisted and aided by the US in the struggle against Japan, but after the Japanese surrender in 1945, it developed into a front organization for the Communist Party of Indo-China (founded by Ho Chi Minh in 1921). It was the Vietminh and Ho Chi Minh who emerged in control of North Vietnam after the defeat of the French in the first Vietnamese War, 1945–54. For further reading: T. L. Hodgkin, *Vietnam: The Revolutionary Path* (1981). D.C.W.; S.B.

Vietnam. A country of south-east Asia under increasingly unstable French colonial rule until 1954, then partitioned, and from 1960 to 1975 the scene of a civil war between the COMMUNIST government of North Vietnam (capital Hanoi) and the US client government of South Vietnam (capital Saigon). The war expanded as American military involvement increased from 1964. It was maintained in the face of mounting criticism within the US and throughout the world, and of fading chances of a resolution satisfactory to the US, until the ceasefire agreement of 23 January 1973 ended active American military participation. The ceasefire was quickly broken; the US continued to support the South's forces until February 1975; the fall of the Southern regime quickly followed US withdrawal of aid. American methods and ultimate failure to secure its objectives did much to damage the country's morale and prestige, and contributed to the fall of non-communist governments in Laos and Cambodia. 'Vietnam' has become a byword for wars in which major powers invest massive resources in local conflicts on dubious moral and strategic grounds. For further reading: G. Kolko, *Anatomy of a War* (1994). S.R.

Village, the, see GREENWICH VILLAGE.

virology. The science that deals with the structure, properties and behaviour of the sub-microscopic infective particles known as viruses, especially as agents of disease. Viruses are not living organisms. They do not grow in the conventional sense, and are not self-reproducing: they subvert the synthetic machinery of the cells which they infect in such a way as to produce more copies of themselves, and have no existence apart from the cells they infect. All viruses contain NUCLEIC ACID (DNA or RNA), and it is this that transforms the metabolism of the affected cell to make it produce more copies of the virus, usually at the cell's expense. (It is conceivable, though, that many other viruses exist which are not recognizable as viruses because they produce no such effects.) Diseases caused by viruses include smallpox, common colds (for which one or more of upwards of 40 'rhinoviruses' may be responsible), influenza, certain types of cancer, and AIDS. ANTIBIOTICS do not act upon viruses, but a naturally occurring agent, INTERFERON, may protect uninfected cells against infection by virus. Recovery or protection from a viral infection depends upon the action of antibodies (see IMMUNITY), and this also forms the basis of preventive methods. P.M.; P.N.

virtual corporations, see under ELECTRONIC COMMERCE.

virtual enterprises, see under ELECTRONIC COMMERCE.

virtual machines. A computer can do quite different things when different programs are running on it: at one moment it contains a word processor, then later a DATABASE, then a chess program, then a compiler, etc. But if you open up the computer you will always find the same physical machine. The word processor, database and chess machine are 'virtual' (or 'abstract') machines.

These operate on non-physical objects, such as numbers, words, sentences or chess positions which exist only in the virtual machines. Transformations of virtual machine objects are not subject to physical laws, but to the laws of the 'virtual world', e.g. the rules of chess or the formatting rules of a document class.

One characteristic of virtual machines is 'circular causality': events in virtual machines can cause events in physical machines, e.g. a robot's program could select a plan which causes its arm to move, and events in physical machines can cause changes in the virtual machine, e.g. sensory input changing a robot's assessments about the environment. Seeing analogies with the structure of human beings, some have suggested that our minds are just virtual machines implemented in brains, just as an operating system is a virtual machine implemented in a computer (see ARTIFICIAL INTELLIGENCE; SUPERVENIENT). A.S.

virtual particles. PARTICLE which exists for a very short period of time and with an energy such that it is unobservable according to Heisenberg's UNCERTAINTY PRINCIPLE (i.e., the act of directly observing such a particle would cause too large a perturbation to its lifetime and ENERGY). This brief existence is maintained in order to allow there to exist an interaction between two other particles. Individual virtual particles are unobservable although their collective effects upon ATOMIC ENERGY levels have been successfully predicted and observed to occur (see LAMB SHIFT.) Virtual particles can be transformed into individually observable (or real) particles by applying an external electric field across a vacuum. The resulting production of particles is called the *Schwinger process*. The existence of virtual particles can be exhibited by placing two parallel plates in a vacuum. Only virtual particles with a quantum wavelength which will fit exactly between the two plates will be present between the plates while all virtual particle wavelengths will be present outside. The greater pressure on the outside of the plates causes them to draw closer. This is called the *Casimir effect*. Grand unified theories (see GRAND UNIFICATION) of ELEMENTARY PARTICLE physics are possible because the effective strengths of the different fundamental forces of nature change with the temperature of the environment in which they are measured. The changes in effective strengths are created by the appearance and effects of virtual particles. These changes are found to be such that the strong (see STRONG INTERACTION), electromagnetic and WEAK INTERACTIONS will have the same strength at some very high temperature. For further reading: R. Feynman, *QED* (1986). J.D.B.

virtual reality (VR). In COMPUTING, virtual reality involves the creation of a three-dimensional simulated world, which may be a simplified version of the real world or an imaginary construct. In the first VR demonstrations, mounted in California by Jaron Lanier of VPL Research, entering the virtual world involved wearing a movement-tracking device and a headset containing two small television sets with LCD screens, one for each eye. However, the term is now commonly applied to 3-D virtual worlds displayed on conventional monitors, where the viewer may be represented by a graphical but not necessarily humanoid figure known as an avatar. Early research into VR was financed partly by NASA (one of Lanier's big customers) and the US military, where VR training offers the same benefits as flight simulators: it can create a real feeling of motion sickness without risk of injury. VR has also been used for entertainment – especially in theme park rides – and for 'virtual meetings'. A few hospitals are already linked via a VR system that enables bedridden children to meet and move around in imaginary worlds. VR requires massive amounts of computer processing power and a 'willing suspension of belief' to achieve moderate effects, though neither is much of a problem in the computer industry, where 'real life' is a tenuous concept at best. The sex industry is also getting excited about the prospect of adding 'touch' or 'force feedback' to VR images, while science fiction writers are confident that we will soon inhabit virtual worlds that are practically indistinguishable from reality, except that no one ever has to do the washing up. J.S.

virus, see under VIROLOGY.

virus, computer, see under COMPUTER VIRUS.

viscerotonia, see under PERSONALITY TYPES.

visual cliff. A device for testing young animals' PERCEPTION of depth. It consists of two identically patterned horizontal surfaces, one well below the other, the upper being extended over the lower by means of a sheet of transparent glass. An animal unwilling to move off the upper surface onto the transparent glass that projects over the lower surface is said to possess *depth perception*. Many SPECIES have been found to possess it at birth. J.S.B.

vital registration, see under CENSUS.

vitalism. A miscellany of beliefs united by the contention that living processes are not to be explained in terms of the material composition and physico-chemical performances of living bodies. Exponents of vitalism include Hans Driesch (1867–1941) and Henri Bergson (1859–1941), according to whom living things are animated by a vital principle such as an ENTELECHY (Driesch's term) or an *élan vital* or *life force* (Bergson's, popularized in England by G. B. Shaw). Dogmatic vitalism is contrasted with MECHANISM, the system of beliefs or lack of beliefs to which modern BIOLOGY and medicine owe all their great triumphs, and which consists, methodologically, of behaving *as if* all vital activities could be adequately explained in terms of material composition and physico-chemical performance. P.M.

vitamins. Originally defined as organic substances which cannot be synthesized in the body and must therefore be provided in small amounts ready-made in the DIET. There are, however, two exceptions to this definition: vitamin D can be made in the skin under the influence of sunlight, and niacin can be made from dietary tryptophan (found in all PROTEINS). Since most vitamins can exist in more than one chemical form (e.g. vitamin A is found preformed as retinol and in plant food as carotene; vitamin B6 exists in three forms), it is current practice to refer to each by its chemical name, e.g. pyridoxine, pyridoxamine or pyridoxol, and to use the term vitamin, in this instance vitamin B6, as a generic descriptor. A severe deficiency of any vitamin gives rise to specific symptoms (vitamin C deficiency – scurvy; vitamin D deficiency – rickets). For further reading: B. M. Barker and D. A. Bender, *Vitamins in Medicine* (1982). A.E.B.

voids. Large regions of intergalactic space found to contain no visible galaxies (see GALAXY CLUSTERS; DARK MATTER). The largest is the Bootes void. These regions may contain large quantities of faint stars or dark matter. J.D.B.

volcanology. The study of volcanoes, their life-history, and their lava, gas and fragmentary constituents. Volcanology is concerned with the study of all volcanoes, active, dormant and extinct, and their distribution in space and time. The monitoring of active volcanoes is an important social aspect of the subject, but one in which long-term predictions of eruptions, though demanded, cannot be produced with any degree of certainty. J.L.M.L.

volition. An act of will or decision, conceived as a mental event immediately antecedent to voluntary bodily movement or action proper, as contrasted with purely reflex or automatic behaviour. English philosopher Gilbert Ryle (1900–76), wishing to deny the existence of inner mental states in the interests of his version of BEHAVIOURISM, declared the concept of volition to be empty or mythical. Certainly not all voluntary action seems to be preceded by introspectible mental preliminaries, but some does. Against the view that the occurrence of volition is a CRITERION of freedom and responsibility in action, Ryle argued that volitions are themselves represented as a species of, admittedly inward, actions about which the question of intention or voluntariness can again be raised, thus generating an infinite regress. For further reading: A. J. Kenny, *Action, Emotion and Will* (1963).
A.Q.

Volksbühne (The People's Stage). A German theatre association founded by Bruno Wille in 1890 which remains the most successful and longest-lived product of the European 'people's theatre' movement around that time. Starting with no theatre of its own, it split on the issue of alignment with the SOCIALIST Party, then reunited 70,000 strong to open its own Berlin theatre in 1914. Here Erwin Piscator (1893–1966), a pioneer of the epic (see EPIC THEATRE) and documentary theatres, became the chief director in 1924, leaving in 1927 to set up his own company with the support of the COMMUNIST section of the membership. Subsequent directors before the Nazi takeover (see NAZISM) included Karl Heinz Martin and Heinz Hilpert. Suppressed under the Nazis, it was reactivated after World War II but soon fell into two halves, one in East Berlin, the other in West. In 1962 the latter was again taken over by Piscator, who introduced the new documentary dramas of Rolf Hochhuth, Peter Weiss and Heinar Kipphardt. Today it continues to stage productions in Berlin.
J.W.

voluntarism.

(1) Any theory that emphasizes the role of the will in mental life, especially thinking and the pursuit of knowledge, or, again, in decisions about conduct. PRAGMATISM is voluntaristic in its conception of knowledge as subservient to action and of our CONCEPTS or beliefs as instruments devised by us for the satisfaction of our desires. The philosophy of Schopenhauer (1788–1860) is a highly generalized form of voluntarism, in which ultimate reality is taken to be of the nature of will.
A.Q.

(2) In historical, political and social theories about the behaviour of man, voluntarism emphasizes the individual choice in decision-making, which it considers as not entirely determined by external conditions. It stands in contrast to the deterministic (see DETERMINISM) MODEL of human behaviour which excludes will and voluntary action as causative factors in individual experience and in society. In politics 'voluntarist' has usually been applied abusively to leaders who overestimate the ability of determined men to conquer circumstances. LENINISM is perhaps the best-known example of a voluntarist political theory and practice, emphasizing the almost limitless possibilities open to a determined leader backed by a devoted party.
L.L.; A.R.

von Baer's principle, see under EMBRYOLOGY.

Vorticism. One of the very few English modern-form movements in the arts, and the one most contemporary with international developments in all the visual arts. Related to CUBISM and FUTURISM in painting, and partly emerging from IMAGISM in literature, it was a unique compound of new theories of energy and form, rare in England, in that it brought painters (e.g. William Roberts) and writers (especially Ezra Pound) together in the 'Great English Vortex'. Wyndham Lewis (1882–1957), its prime founder, was both: he saw the movement visually as 'a mental emotive impulse . . . let loose on a lot of blocks and lines', verbally as a hard, unromantic, external presentation of kinetic forces. Pound, in parallel, dropped the neo-SYMBOLIST bias of Imagism, with which he was disillusioned, and emphasized the hard energy-centre in poetry. The movement, anti-representational, brutalist, an 'arrangement of surfaces', came out of the *Rebel Art Centre*, founded by Lewis, Edward Wadsworth, Christopher Nevinson and others in 1913; associated painters and sculptors included Bomberg, Gaudier-Brzeska and Epstein. A Vorticist exhibition was held at the Doré Gallery in March 1915; the main document of the movement was the visual-verbal manifesto-magazine BLAST. For further reading: R. G. Cork, *Vorticism and Abstract Art in the First Machine Age* (1976). M.S.BR.

vraisemblance. A concept important in early STRUCTURALIST criticism and celebrated in a special number of the journal *Communications* in 1968. It is by *vraisemblance*, which might be loosely translated as 'fittingness', that a literary work is recognized, or recognizable, as inhering 'naturally' in a certain type of DISCOURSE, whose conventions are known in advance. The degrees of conformity or fittingness required for a work to be 'naturally' part of a certain kind of literary discourse vary from having to meet the basic demands of common sense, through various culturally received conventions of likelihood, obviousness, relevance, pertinence, conformity, etc., up through the conventions of given literary genres themselves, up to and including outright parody, where all claims for first-order fittingness are abandoned. *Vraisemblance* is related to the inescapability of what Julia Kristeva calls INTERTEXTUALITY and also to the doctrine of ÉCRITURE as propounded in 1953 by Roland Barthes. For further reading: J. Culler, *Structuralist Poetics* (1975). R.PO.

Vygotskian. Pertaining to the thought of Russian psychologist Lev Vygotsky (1896–1934), whose studies of DEVELOPMENTAL PSYCHOLOGY were conducted in the former USSR during the interwar period. Publication problems and the COLD WAR prevented wide dissemination of his work in the West until the 1970s. Since then it has attracted much attention, its originality and value now being generally recognized. Vygotsky particularly stressed the role of social processes in the child's cognitive development, a topic largely unexamined if not entirely ignored in PIAGETIAN theory, e.g. exposure to others undertaking tasks beyond the present competence of the child provides 'scaffolding' for its own efforts (see COGNITIVE PSYCHOLOGY). In this context he talked of 'the zone of proximal development' (ZPD). Steering between simple BEHAVIOURISM and ideologically suspect IDEALISM, Vygotsky exploited Pavlov's notion of the 'Second Signal System' to address the development of language and CONSCIOUSNESS, while setting this in a subtly MARXIST framework. His accounts of the nature and role of language are currently proving his most influential legacy, while Newman and Holzman (1993) make strong claims for the revolutionary character of his approach. For further reading: F. Newman and L. Holzman, *Lev Vygotsky: Revolutionary Scientist* (1993). G.D.R.

wage restraint, see under INCOMES POLICY.

Wageningen school, see under AGRARIAN HISTORY.

wages policy, see INCOMES POLICY.

Wall Street. The name given to the lower end of Manhattan Island, New York, where the world's most important financial centre – comprising banks, trust companies, insurance companies, exchanges, etc. – is situated, and which also houses the headquarters of most of America's largest business corporations. As a popular term Wall Street, or 'the Street', has become increasingly synonymous with the interests of American CAPITALISM and embraces businesses far removed physically from the area to which it properly refers. D.E.

Walras' Law. In ECONOMICS, this law states that the sum of the demand minus the supply of each good and service multiplied by its price must be equal to zero. This law should be true whether or not the economy is in EQUILIBRIUM. The proof of this law lies in the decision to supply a good or service implying a decision to consume a good or service of equal value. For a barter economy, this law is true by definition. However, when the KEYNESIAN distinction is made between notional and effective demand, it is clear that, for the former type of demand, the law is not true. For further reading: R. Levacic and A. Rebmann, *Macroeconomics* (1982). J.P.

war/warfare). Developments in technological means of destruction in political organization, in the international system, and in analysis of the subject, have led to the classification of different kinds of war. Thus *catalytic war* is conflict between two states brought about by the deliberate actions of a third. COLD WAR is a state of international conflict wherein all measures short of organized military violence are used to achieve national objectives. *Conventional war* is armed conflict between states in which NUCLEAR WEAPONS are not used; *nuclear war* (under which is subsumed *thermonuclear war*) is conflict in which they are. *Chemical warfare* involves the use of incendiary, asphyxiating or otherwise noxious chemicals, *biological warfare* the use of living organisms such as disease germs; the two are often bracketed together as 'CBW' (chemical and biological weapons), although the employment or intended employment of (particularly) the biological component is more often asserted than proved. GUERRILLA war or *insurgency* is conflict conducted by irregular forces within a state and aimed at alienating the mass of the population from the authority of the established government with a view to its final overthrow. LIMITED WAR is military conflict limited either by terrain, the weapons used, or the objectives pursued. *Prolonged* or *protracted wars* extend over one or more decades. A recent example was the VIETNAM War. Success in these conflicts requires considerable social discipline and control. *Psychological warfare* involves the use of propaganda (by radio, agents, etc.) to weaken the morale of an adversary population or army, and to discredit the motives and diminish the authority of an adversary government. For further reading: A. F. Buchan, *War in Modern Society* (1968); W. H. McNeill, *The Pursuit of Power: Technology, Armed Force and Society Since AD 1000* (1983). A.F.B.; A.J.M.W.

war crimes/crimes against humanity. Despite the scale of its slaughter – or perhaps because of it – warfare in the 20th century is bound by rules which have accreted through various international conventions. War crimes are violations of those rules, and are tried under international law (see PUBLIC INTERNATIONAL LAW). The definition of war crimes and the mechanism for dealing with them (through an International Military Tribunal) date from the NUREMBERG TRIALS after World War II, in which German war criminals – ranging from high-ranking soldiers who waged aggressive war to judges who upheld RACIST laws to industrialists who helped arm Hitler for war – were put on trial. At Nuremberg, three types of war crimes were defined: (1) crimes against the peace (the waging of aggressive war); (2) conventional war crimes (murder and harm inflicted upon civilian populations); (3) crimes against humanity.

Conventional war crimes had been committed and punished in the past, but the attempt to define crimes against humanity dates specifically from the Nuremberg Trials. Crimes against humanity may include, in their grossest form, GENOCIDE – the systematic attempt by a government to exterminate a group of people on the basis of their religion, ETHNICITY or political beliefs. But at Nuremberg it was also accepted that crimes against humanity may include various types of persecution of groups which may or may not be a prelude to genocide: e.g., the persecution of a group under the law, as was the case with the NUREMBERG LAWS, under which German Jews were stripped of civil rights. In the post-World War II period, war crimes and crimes against humanity have no doubt been committed, but the only war crimes trial to have been successfully mounted since Nuremberg is the tribunal sitting in The Hague during the late 1990s to judge crimes committed during the war in the former YUGOSLAVIA. For further reading: T. McCormack and G. Simpson, *The Law of War Crimes* (1997).

S.T.

war on drugs. In a 1982 speech, President Reagan declared a 'war on drugs', specifically naming MARIJUANA as the enemy. First Lady Nancy Reagan aided the effort by her much-publicized 'just say no' campaign aimed at discouraging experimentation by children. The war has dragged on since then with no conclusion in sight, except for a growing public sentiment against cocaine, largely because of the crack epidemic of the 1980s. Law enforcement personnel and border agents admit they seize only a fraction of the narcotics smuggled into the US from Mexico and South America. While there is little support for legalizing such DRUGS as heroin and cocaine, the same is not true for marijuana, which some experts say is the largest cash crop in the US. In 1996, California voters approved ballot Proposition 215, the Compassionate Use Act. The controversial law allows 'seriously ill' Californians to obtain marijuana without fear of prosecution if a physician recommends its use. Other states are considering similar medical marijuana laws over the objections of critics who fear an increase in pot use and the precedent of making medical decisions on the basis of referenda. President Clinton, who admitted smoking marijuana without inhaling while at Oxford, was among the opponents of Proposition 215.

R.K.H.

warfare, see WAR.

Warnock Report. Dame Mary Warnock was chairman of the Committee of Inquiry into Human Fertilization and Embryology, which was set up in July 1982 and reported in June 1984. The Committee took evidence from a wide range of interested parties, and reached a consensus view on most topics. A review of services for infertile couples was recommended, and the need for guidance as to what facilities should be available within the NHS. Both ARTIFICIAL INSEMINATION by donor (AID) and *in vitro* fertilization (IVF), it reported, should be legal, but should only be available at centres licensed by a new statutory body. They should be available for the prevention of inherited disease as well as the treatment of INFERTILITY. The law required changes to allow a child conceived in such a fashion to be the legitimate child of the woman who gave birth to him, with her husband as the registered father. In the event of the father's death preceding his child's birth, such a child would be excluded from succession and inheritance unless *in utero* before the death. The donor of semen or egg should have neither rights nor duties towards their biological progeny, and their anonymity must be complete except where a friend or family member was involved. Donors must be examined medically, and be free of inherited and infectious disease as far as could be determined; a central register should be kept to prevent more than ten children being sired by one man, and donors should not stand to make pecuniary gain. Selection of donors on all but a few characteristics (ethnic origin, health) should be avoided. The recommendations concerning surrogacy and embryo research were more controversial, and unanimity was not achieved. Surrogacy, with one woman carrying a foetus for another unable to do so, should not be illegal *per se*. Surrogacy agreements, however, should be illegal contracts, and surrogacy agencies should be banned – whether commercial or charitable. It should be illegal for professionals to promote private surrogacy arrangements in any way. The human embryo (fertilized egg) should be protected in law, and not be allowed to develop beyond the 14-day stage in the laboratory: it could be used for research until then. A.CL.

Warren Commission. The informal name of the commission, appointed by US President Lyndon B. Johnson, to investigate the assassination of his predecessor, John F. Kennedy. The Commission – appointed exactly one week after JFK's shooting in Dallas, Texas, on 22 November 1963 – had as its chairman Earl Warren, the 14th Chief Justice of the United States and a former governor of the state of California. In September 1964, the Commission issued a report that found there was no evidence of a conspiracy to assassinate Kennedy. Commission members, including future President Gerald Ford, concluded that former Marine rifleman Lee Harvey Oswald, who was himself murdered while in police custody, was the gunman. The Commission's conclusion has been supported by independent investigators examining the same evidence, but that has not deterred Kennedy conspiracy theorists. R.K.H.

Washington Square Players, see under OFF-BROADWAY.

waste disposal. Waste can be loosely defined as all unused, unwanted and discarded materials including solids, liquids and gases. Alternatively it can be defined as something for which we have no further use and which we wish to get rid of. Waste is generated in large quantities by humans and its control and disposal is a major environmental issue. In the USA an average city with 250,000 inhabitants has to collect, transport and dispose of 450 tonnes of refuse every day. In general about 2–3 kg of municipal waste and 3–4 kg of industrial waste are produced in the United States per person per day. In the UK, about 137 million tonnes of controlled waste (waste which is either incinerated or disposed of to a landfill) is produced a year. Landfill takes 90–95 per cent of the controlled waste. The relative importance of different methods of disposal varies from country to country so that, e.g., whereas most municipal solid waste in the UK and Australia goes to landfills, in Switzerland nearly half is incinerated and in Japan about two-thirds is incinerated. Landfilling is a cheap means of disposal, and in countries where there are many voids (e.g. old quarries and gravel pits to be filled) it may be a convenient way not only to dispose of waste but also to reclaim such land for other uses. If poorly managed, such sites can produce environmental problems like groundwater pollution.

Incineration can greatly reduce the volume of waste. Incinerators are expensive to construct and may contribute to air pollution; but they can also produce usable energy. Compaction can also reduce waste volume. Waste reduction can be achieved by substitution of durable goods for disposable ones, composting of garden waste, reduction of waste in the production process, reuse of materials and extension of their lives (e.g. use of rechargeable batteries and refillable bottles), recycling of paper, glass, etc., and recovery of materials from waste (e.g. magnetic separation of ferrous metals). A.S.G.

water crisis. Water is a fundamental resource that is integral to all environmental and societal processes. Rivers, lakes and groundwater are increasingly contaminated with biological and chemical wastes, billions of people lack clean sources of drinking water and basic sanitation services, and millions of people die each year from water-related diseases. Demand for water is burgeoning, and fresh water resources are unevenly distributed. Fresh water supplies are susceptible to seasonal inequalities, to longer-term droughts, and to longer-term climatic changes (whether natural or human-induced). As increasing numbers of people live in large urban centres, the problems of reliably supplying sufficient quantities of water of adequate quality are increased. There is fear that, as competition for adequate water resources intensifies, 'water wars' may result. Quarrels over rivers like the Ganges, Indus, Paraná, Rio Grande, Colorado, Euphrates and others in the Middle East produce a highly volatile situation. There is a disturbing trend towards the use of force in water-related disputes. Some nations are willing to use water supply systems as targets and tools of war. There remains little international legal agreement about coping with conflicts over resource disparities or environmental damage. A.S.G.

Watergate. The name is taken from an apartment-hotel-office complex in Washington, DC, in which the Democratic Party's National Committee kept its headquarters for the 1972 presidential election. It refers to the scandal whose roots lay in the burglary on 17 June 1972 by employees of the rival Campaign to Reelect the President, who seemed intent on placing electronic surveillance devices in the headquarters. The whole sequence of events known collectively as Watergate took over two years to unravel (if indeed the whole story can be said to have emerged). It was discovered that some of President Nixon's White House associates had planned the break-in; that they and others had conspired to cover it up, and that the President himself was drawn into the conspiracy. To the last he attempted to disguise his role, giving way only when the Supreme Court compelled him to relinquish tapes revealing his complicity. He finally resigned on 9 August, almost devoid of political support and under threat of impeachment by Congress. The episode also saw the conviction on a rich variety of charges of some 20 members of his circle, including his former Attorney-General and White House Chief of Staff. Its ramifications raised serious questions about the administration's disregard for law and ETHICS, about Nixon's moral and political judgement, and about the adequacy of safeguards against such events. Although Watergate produced a brief sense of crisis, it came to be regarded often in sanguine terms as proof of the political system's self-correcting capacity and as an end to the IMPERIAL PRESIDENCY. For further reading: R. N. Roberts, *From Watergate to Whitewater* (1997). S.R.

wave function. The mathematical representation of the strength of the waves associated with matter according to the WAVE-PARTICLE DUALITY. Each state in QUANTUM MECHANICS is fully described by a wave function which varies from point to point in space. The intensity of this wave at a given point gives the probability that a particle will be found there. For example, the wave function of an ELECTRON in an ENERGY LEVEL of an ATOM is characterized by oscillations in the region where an ORBIT of the same ENERGY would exist if the electron obeyed NEWTONIAN MECHANICS; outside this region, the wave function falls smoothly to zero, so that there is a high probability that the electron will be found somewhere near its Newtonian orbit. M.V.B.

wave function of the universe. A quantity used to describe the state of the universe in QUANTUM THEORIES of COSMOLOGY. The wave function of the universe gives the probability (see PROBABILITY THEORY) that the universe will be found in a particular state. It can also be used more speculatively to give a probability for a universe to exist and to judge the relative likelihoods of universes existing with different sizes, densities and shapes. The wave function of the universe is a solution of a cosmological version of the Schrödinger equation of ordinary QUANTUM MECHANICS, called the Wheeler-de Witt equation. Its solution requires the imposition of a boundary condition to prescribe the initial state of the universe. One favoured candidate is the NO BOUNDARY CONDITION of Hartle and Hawking. The interpretation of the wave function of the universe in such theories is still very controversial. For further reading: S. W. Hawking, *A Brief History of Time* (1988); S. W. Hawking and R. Penrose, *The Nature of Spacetime* (1996). J.D.B.

wave guide. A metal tube used to transmit MICROWAVES for use in RADAR; the electromagnetic equivalent (see ELECTROMAGNETISM) of the old-fashioned 'speaking tube' for sound waves. M.V.B.

wave mechanics, see QUANTUM MECHANICS.

wave-particle duality. The manifestation by a single entity of the seemingly incompatible kinds of behaviour associated with PARTICLES and waves. Although represented in CLASSICAL PHYSICS as an electromagnetic wave (see DIFFRACTION), light exhibits typically particulate behaviour in collision processes (the Compton effect) and in its interactions with matter as discrete packets or quanta of radiation (BLACK-BODY RADIATION, the photoelectric effect). ELECTRONS, on the other hand, were represented classically as discrete particles, but in certain circumstances display typical wave behaviour (ELECTRON DIFFRACTION). In a precursor to QUANTUM MECHANICS, de Broglie (1892–1987) tried to capture the duality by associating, with the motion of particles, so-called 'pilot'-waves that governed the interference effects exhibited in diffraction experiments. In wave mechanics, Erwin Schrödinger (1887–1961) tried to abolish the particle altogether, hoping to identify particles with the 'crests' of relatively localized waves. In his COMPLEMENTARITY PRINCIPLE, Niels Bohr (1885–1962) presented the duality as a consequence of the way different kinds of experiment are conceptualized in terms of the classical wave and particle MODELS (see COPENHAGEN INTERPRETATION). R.F.H.

WEA (Workers' Educational Association), see under ADULT EDUCATION.

weak anthropic principle, see under ANTHROPIC PRINCIPLE.

weak interaction. The force that causes the unstable ELEMENTARY PARTICLES (e.g. NEUTRONS) to decay. PARITY is not conserved during weak interactions, which are about a million million times weaker than the STRONG INTERACTIONS that bind NUCLEONS together. M.V.B.

weakly interacting massive particles (WIMP), see under MACHO.

Weathermen. A radical faction of the American NEW LEFT which issued from the SDS in spring 1969. Its name derived from a manifesto whose title echoed singer Bob Dylan's observation that 'You don't need a weatherman to know which way the wind blows'. The Weathermen flirted unsuccessfully with the notion of alliance with the Black Panthers (see BLACK POWER) and, yet more improbably, with thoughts of stimulating a revolutionary movement of WORKING-CLASS youth. They were then left as a small, intense, self-elected revolutionary ÉLITE employing tactics of sabotage and bombing, mainly of public buildings. The movement faded during the early 1970s, suffering from government countermeasures and its own isolation. For further reading: A. Matusow, *The Unraveling of America* (1984). S.R.

Weberian. An approach to the study of social life influenced by the German historical sociologist Max Weber (1864–1920) (see SOCIOLOGY). Though Weber saw the need to give the SOCIAL SCIENCES a sound methodological basis (see METHODOLOGY), his approach emphasized the distinctive nature of human science as opposed to the NATURAL SCIENCES. In particular, he thought there could be no laws of human behaviour, at the individual or the collective level, as there are laws of molecular behaviour: there is no such thing as historical inevitability. And since he argued that social reality was nothing more than the sum of the individuals in that society, he was suspicious of collective concepts such as the STATE when used as if they represented an entity in their own right. He acknowledged that one must use generalized CONCEPTS, but thought they should be regarded as imperfect, crude expressions of a reality which is actually infinitely complex.

He applied his ideas most significantly to the study of modern INDUSTRIAL SOCIETY, and the increasing role played by large-scale organizations and BUREAUCRACY. He emphasized the effects of these institutions on the individual agents in society who implemented them, arguing that people would become rule-bound and uncreative as they pursued narrow, specialized tasks. Political dogmas which require centralization, such as SOCIALISM, were all the more likely to exacerbate this problem, in Weber's view; and he saw an irony in the fact that although DEMOCRACY had initially represented a great advance on human freedoms, it now tended to stifle them, since individuals were only likely to achieve POWER within large political parties if they compromised their BELIEFS to a greater or lesser extent. A more recent reworking of these themes, within a Weberian framework, is available in George Ritzer's book *The McDonaldization of Society* (1993). I.P.R.; A.A.L.

weights/weighting, see under INDEX NUMBER; MEAN.

Weimar Republic. The first German parliamentary democratic republic established on the abdication of Kaiser Wilhelm II on 9 November 1918, the constitution of which (promulgated 11 August 1919) was drawn up at Weimar, the Thuringian city associated with the memory of Goethe. Burdened by the resentments of the supporters of monarchism and by all the other resentments directed from the RIGHT against the terms of the Treaty of Versailles, challenged by a series of unsuccessful revolutionary outbursts on the LEFT, and under great external pressure from France, the Republic never captured the loyalties of a sufficient proportion of the German people. Its parliamentary government collapsed in 1930, after the onset of the world economic crisis, to be followed by a series of minority governments, acting under the reserve powers of the presidency, until on 30 January 1933 Adolf Hitler, leader of the Nazi Party (see NAZISM), was established as Chancellor. The record of the Weimar Republic was taken by many as fundamental evidence of the German lack of capacity for DEMOCRACY or a democratic tradition, a view now increasingly difficult to maintain. In contrast to its political vicissitudes, the period of the Weimar Republic was marked by a remarkable flowering of the experimental attitude in the arts, a view which has been confirmed in retrospect. For further reading: W. Laqueur, *Weimar* (1975). D.C.W.

welfare. The word 'welfare' in welfare legislation or the WELFARE STATE refers generally to government support for the poor, and particularly to the free or subsidized supply of certain goods or services, e.g. health and education. I.M.D.L.

welfare economics. The study of the desirability of different possible patterns of production and the distribution of the resulting output. This requires some measure and, thus, implicit VALUE-JUDGEMENT of the welfare of each individual. This is normally taken as the utility (see UTILITY THEORY) derived from the individual's consumption of goods and services. This view has been criticized because society often decides that people are not always the best judges of what is in their own best interests, e.g. compulsory education and government provision of goods and services in kind rather than income to purchase them. With a measure of individual welfare, it is possible to use the concept of PARETO OPTIMUM (see ECONOMIC EFFICIENCY), beyond which it is impossible to construct a change that makes one or more persons better off, without making one or more persons worse off. As the Pareto principle cannot distinguish between different Pareto optima, it is necessary to use a value-judgement in comparing different Pareto optima. It is very difficult to construct such a SOCIAL WELFARE function or see where it is going to come from. However, a social welfare function is implicit in most decisions that the government makes, though it is rarely explicitly specified. Welfare economics has not progressed very far from this nihilistic conclusion (see NIHILISM). However, welfare economics includes the study of the useful and important concepts of EXTERNALITIES, PUBLIC GOODS and MARGINAL COST PRICING and encompasses all policy-orientated ECONOMICS. It makes up a large part of economics, and criticisms of its usefulness reflect the difficulty of making statements about the desirability of different social states, rather than any failing on the part of economists. For further reading: J. Bonner, *Politics, Economics and Welfare* (1986). A.K.S.; J.P.

welfare state. A political system assuming STATE responsibility for the protection and promotion of the social security and welfare of its citizens by universal medical care, insurance against sickness and unemployment, old age pensions, family allowances, public housing, etc., on a 'cradle to grave' basis. Social insurance was introduced in Germany in the 1880s and in Britain before 1914, but a comprehensive scheme (and the term 'welfare state') was first adopted by the British Labour government of 1945–50. Similar provision is made by the state in many other countries, e.g. in western Europe, Scandinavia, New Zealand. In recent years the welfare state has been criticized, particularly by the New RIGHT, as destroying the self-reliance of its beneficiaries, and in many countries has met difficulties caused by economic recession which undermines its fiscal base. For further reading: C. Noble, *Welfare as We Knew It: A Political History of the American Welfare State* (1997). D.C.W.; S.R.

welfare to work/workfare. Term given to government attempts to replace the concept of WELFARE payments (e.g. to the unemployed or to single parents of young children) as absolute entitlements with contractual arrangements requiring welfare recipients to undertake paid work, or in some circumstances compulsory education, vocational training and other means thought to help the recipient's future in the labour market (see UNEMPLOYMENT; WELFARE STATE). In the USA the concept's history lies in NEW DEAL programmes, but its modern forms were sketched in the 1970s, filled out in the 1988 Family Support Act, and found their fullest expression in the 1996 Personal Responsibility and Work Opportunity Reconciliation Act. The recent thrust of policy is both to devolve to state governments greater responsibility for welfare and to oblige them increasingly to transfer clients to workfare schemes. Such schemes have generally been advocated by conservatives (see CONSERVATISM) in the face of fragmented and diminishing liberal resistance (see LIBERALISM). They argue from both pragmatic and moral premises, pointing both to the trap of welfare dependency created by older programmes and to the innate virtues of work and self-development (see POVERTY). It is far from clear, however, whether existing workfare schemes provide either an adequate basic income or lead to greater self-sufficiency. Critics also suggest that schemes do not offer conventional workers' rights, and may depress demand for other unskilled workers in the open labour market.

The concept has in very recent years gained considerable ground in the UK, including at senior levels of the Labour government elected in 1997. For further reading: W. Wilson, *When Work Disappears* (1997). S.R.

Weltanschauung (German for 'world-outlook'). General conception of the nature of the world, particularly as containing or implying a system of value-principles. Any total philosophical system may be so styled which derives practical consequences from its theoretical component. It is common for important but comparatively local scientific discoveries or conjectures to be generalized into total systems of this kind, e.g. those of Newton, Darwin, Marx and Freud. A.Q.

Weltschmerz**.** German word ('world-pain') for a feeling of the overwhelming oppressiveness of existence that may colour an individual's entire WELTANSCHAUUNG. W.Z.

Werkbund**.** The *Deutscher Werkbund* was founded in 1907 by the architect and then Superintendent of the Prussian Board of Trade for Schools of Arts and Crafts, Hermann Muthesius (1861–1927), who had been influenced by William Morris and the ARTS AND CRAFTS MOVEMENT. The *Werkbund* attempted to harness the artist to machine production in order to ensure a place for Germany in the growing industrial export market. Its stated aim was to achieve quality through 'not only excellent durable work and the use of flawless, genuine materials, but also the attainment of an organic whole rendered functional, noble and, if you will, artistic by such means'. The idea had considerable diffusion: an Austrian *Werkbund* was started in 1910, a Swiss in 1913; the Design and Industries Association was founded in England in 1915 and a similar Swedish institution by 1917. An important *Werkbund* Exhibition was held at Cologne in 1914 at which Walter Gropius and Adolf Meyer designed a model factory. In 1919 Gropius went to head the BAUHAUS, which continued the ideals shaped by Muthesius. For further reading: N. Pevsner, *Pioneers of Modern Design* (1960). M.BR.

Wertfreiheit**,** see VALUE-FREEDOM.

wetlands. A generic term applied to areas that are submerged for at least a part of the year. Swamps, bogs and salt marshes are perhaps the most common wetland types. Wetlands are highly productive biologically; their flora and fauna are distinctive, and they provide critical ECOSYSTEM services, including HABITATS and spawning grounds for fishes, and feeding grounds for migratory birds. Wetlands store carbon and nutrients, serve as natural filters that purify water, trap sediments, moderate downstream flooding, and recharge groundwater. Coastal wetlands buffer against storm damage.

Historically, wetlands have often fallen prey to draining or filling for agriculture, industry or other development activities. Wetlands have been particularly vulnerable because of the intense POPULATION PRESSURE on coastal regions and on the shores of inland lakes and seas. Recognition of the ecological importance of wetlands has led to efforts to protect and restore this rapidly dwindling resource (see also ECOSYSTEM SERVICES; RESTORATION ECOLOGY). W.G.R.

Whig interpretation of history. Defined by English historian Herbert Butterfield (1900–

79), who coined this somewhat ethnocentric term in 1931 (see ETHNOCENTRISM), as the tendency of historians to see the past as the story of the conflict between PROGRESSIVES and REACTIONARIES, in which the progressives, or Whigs, win and so bring about the modern world. He suggested that this was to overestimate the likenesses between present and past and to assume, fallaciously, that men always intend the consequences of their actions, whereas no one in the past actually willed the present. For further reading: H. Butterfield, *The Whig Interpretation of History* (1951). P.B.

white collar crime. A term formulated by Edwin Sutherland (1883–1950) in the 1940s and recognized as a milestone in the field of CRIMINOLOGY. Criminology and the criminal justice system were/are too narrowly focused on the crimes of the WORKING CLASS, failing to reveal and scrutinize the crimes of the middle and upper classes. Sutherland and others demonstrated that 'respectable' members of society routinely commit crime and that this is particularly significant in that such crimes violate the trust placed in professionals. As or more important than the financial cost of such crime is its contribution to the erosion of ethics and social morale. White collar offences typically include legally defined crimes, e.g. embezzlement and fraud or other injurious actions against employers, partners, competitors and customers (see CORPORATE CRIME). A more radical attempt to extend the concept even further, to include crimes of STATES and governments, has so far met with limited success, despite the examples of the NUREMBERG TRIALS of Nazi leaders (see NAZISM), and the WATERGATE affair in America.

An outstanding feature of white collar crime is that it is not popularly perceived as crime, at least not as serious crime. White collar crime typically does not fit the stereotype of the individual criminal, assaulting or robbing another individual. It is often crime against institutions, not particular individuals. Its effects are frequently diffuse and long-term, making it difficult to be precise about attributing responsibility, and to lay charges against specific individuals. As a consequence judges and juries, fairly reflecting public opinion, tend to be lenient about such crimes. All these features are well illustrated in two famous cases: that of the Ford Motor Company and their Pinto car, whose propensity to explode in rear-end collisions was known to Ford executives; and that of the Distillers Company and their drug thalidomide, which given to pregnant mothers was responsible for congenital deformities in their babies. K.K.; N.S.

white dwarfs. A peculiar type of star came to be identified in the 1920s, typified by a combination of high temperature and low luminosity. This mixture of attributes seemed to suggest that such stars (termed 'white dwarfs') were extremely small, generally no bigger than the earth. It seemed probable therefore that they were possessed of extremely high densities. This characterization of these problem stars was given theoretical credibility by the work of A. S. Eddington (1882–1944) and R. H. Fowler (1889–1944). Fowler's great breakthrough lay in applying to white dwarfs the quantum statistical mechanics (see QUANTUM STATISTICS) which had emerged from the conceptualizations of Pauli, Fermi and Dirac. (Thus the new PHYSICS came to the aid of ASTRONOMY, and astronomy provided an important application of QUANTUM MECHANICS.) Being typified by high density and small size, white dwarfs became an obvious focus of attention for those concerned with the implications of the general theory of RELATIVITY, in particular the phenomenon of the reduction in the frequency of light being emitted from an extremely dense gravitational field (see GRAVITATION). This presumed effect was indeed verified (by Walter Adams in 1924), thus adding a confirmation of Einstein's general theory. For further reading: R. W. Smith, *The Expanding Universe* (1982). R.P.

white supremacy. The belief that there are biological differences between different human groups, resulting in different levels of humanity, with fair-skinned people holding the superior position. This philosophy has been deeply ingrained in Western consciousness since at least the 15th century, and helped the slave trade to flourish in the western hemisphere for 400 years. By the beginning of the 17th century there were at least 500,000 African slaves in the western hemisphere, brought there by Dutch, Spanish and Portuguese traders; by 1776, one in six residents of America was an African held as a slave or in indentured servitude. In Britain, IMPERIALISM produced Kipling's euphemism 'the White Man's burden', in a famous 1899 poem that spoke of the need to subdue 'Your new-caught, sullen peoples,/Half-devil and half-child'. In the 1960s, the US enacted numerous laws guaranteeing civil rights for the descendants of former slaves who had become subject to forcible SEGREGATION and institutionalized discrimination. The changes were met with opposition and violence from white supremacists. In more recent times, the phenomenon has produced unrest in Britain and Europe. In the 1990s, it found a powerful new forum in the INTERNET. R.K.H.

Whitewater. A failed Arkansas land development venture that became a catch-all phrase for a series of hard-to-grasp but persistent scandals and accusations involving US President Bill Clinton and his wife, Hillary Rodham Clinton. A Congressional committee looked at whether Madison Guaranty Savings and Loan (see SAVINGS AND LOAN SCANDALS), a failed Arkansas thrift which had employed Mrs Clinton as a lawyer, illegally diverted federally guaranteed funds to the Whitewater project. Republicans endeavouring to discredit Clinton saw a 'pattern of deception' and 'a web of interconnected scandals' in Whitewater-related events, most famously the mysterious suicide of White House deputy counsel Vincent W. Foster Jr on 20 July 1993. R.K.H.

WHO (World Health Organization). A specialized agency of the UN, whose forerunners were the International Office of Public Health, set up in Paris in 1909, and the Health Office of the LEAGUE OF NATIONS (1923). Its activities include the encouragement of research, the control of epidemic and endemic diseases (e.g. malaria), and aid to strengthen the national programmes of member states in the field of public health. Its headquarters are in Geneva. D.C.W.

whole-tone scale. A musical scale in which the 12 semitones of the octave are divided into two sets of six equal tones, thus producing, e.g., the scale A, B, C sharp, D sharp, F, G, A. It appears a number of times in compositions by Liszt; but it was Debussy who exploited it to the full. Music based on the whole-tone scale gives a curiously nebulous effect, seeming to lack the positive character given by normal tonality (see ATONAL MUSIC). This is partly because there are only two possible 'scales', each employing six of the 12 semitones. The equality of interval precludes the possibility of any other permutation (see PERMUTATIONAL), nor does any note in the 'scale' give the feeling of being a root or 'tonic'. A.H.

wholefood, see under MACROBIOTICS.

Whorfian. In LINGUISTICS, characteristic of, or a follower of, the views of Benjamin Lee Whorf (1897–1941), particularly the 'Sapir-Whorf hypothesis' (also propounded by Edward Sapir) that our conceptual categorization of the world is partly determined by the structure of our native language. The strong form of this hypothesis, that our conceptualization is largely or wholly determined in this way, has been rejected by most linguists. For further reading: B. L. Whorf, J. B. Carroll (eds), *Language, Thought and Reality: Selected Writings* (1956). D.C.

***Wiener Kreis*,** see VIENNA CIRCLE.

will to power. Friedrich Nietzsche (see NIETZSCHEAN) proposed that we consider 'our whole instinctive life', 'all organic functions' and 'all effective force' as Will to Power – then we would behold 'the world seen from the inside' (*Beyond Good and Evil*, 1886). Thus what exists is will, not SUBSTANCE or ESSENCE, and the will's sole end is POWER, not wealth, survival, truth, happiness, or biological reproduction. A will has no goal other than to will powerfully. But Nietzsche describes this theory only as '*my* proposition', reached by pushing certain methodological principles to 'absurdity'. Indeed, the idea that everything is Will to Power *cannot* be true, because it implies that it (like everything else) must have been invented by an arbitrary will. And if we call the Will to Power Nietzsche's personal invention, then we encounter a second paradox, for the idea of a conscious, autonomous self is also a product (says Nietzsche) of the Will to Power. In short, the doctrine is carefully constructed to undermine faith in truth. Its other purpose is to present the world minus some characteristics that Nietzsche considered mere prejudices: personal identity, freedom, conscious motivation, inherent meaning or value, and purpose. For further reading: P. Sedgwick (ed.), *Nietzsche: A Critical Reader* (1995). P.LE.

WIMPS (weakly interacting massive particles), see under DARK MATTER; MACHO.

wino, see under SUPERSYMMETRY.

winter of discontent. A tiresome cliché, maladapted from Shakespeare's *Richard III*, referring to the winter of 1978–79 in the United Kingdom. This period saw the final breakdown of the SOCIAL CONTRACT between TRADE UNIONS and the Labour government, as it attempted a fourth round of controlled pay increases. Numerous STRIKES, particularly among PUBLIC SECTOR workers, fuelled anti-union and anti-government sentiment which contributed to the election of a radical conservative government in 1979 (see CONSERVATISM; THATCHERISM). For further reading: C. Crouch, *The Politics of Industrial Relations* (1982). S.R.

wish-fulfilment. FREUDIAN term for seemingly fortuitous actions, misperceptions, fantasies and dreams that represent fulfilments of a conscious or UNCONSCIOUS wish. Freud claimed that such wish-fulfilment constituted the essence of dreams. I.M.L.H.

witchcraft. In ANTHROPOLOGY, a term usually restricted to mean causing harm to other people and their possessions by the involuntary exercise of extraordinary, mystical powers, and distinguished from SORCERY, which is the intentional practice of rites for this purpose. Unlike sorcery, witchcraft can be known only after its alleged occurrence and by its alleged results. What anthropologists study, therefore, is *accusation* of witchcraft. These accusations are often closely examined in relation to the structure of the society (e.g. to see whether there is a tendency for particular classes of person to be accused, such as women married into patrilineally constituted domestic groups); and ideas of witchcraft are studied in relation to the total system of ideas about moral responsibility, right conduct, and causation. There has been increasing contact between anthropologists and historians in the study of witchcraft. The problems of interpretation raise serious questions concerning rationality, cultural RELATIVISM and ETHNOCENTRISM. For further reading: C. Larner, *Witchcraft and Religion* (1984). M.F.; A.G.

Wobblies, the (American Industrial Workers of the World), see under SYNDICALISM.

women's liberation, see under FEMINISM.

women's studies. The area of academic study which has become known as women's studies grew out of the feminist (see FEMINISM) movement in Europe and the United States in the early 1970s. Feminism within the academy questioned the ways in which knowledge was organized and constructed. Initially, the issue of the absence of women from the curriculum was a priority, but this has given way to a discussion of the more complex issue of the domination of the male human subject (see SUBJECTIVITY). Thus across the range of subjects taught in Western universities feminist academics argued that what existed in all subjects was a GENDER bias – a bias which sometimes simply excluded women or could only include women in terms of a discussion rooted in male experience and understanding. The great theoretical traditions of the West, in particular MARXISM and PSYCHOANALYSIS, were re-examined in terms of a critical standpoint which questioned the implicit association between a constructed objectivity and a taken-for-granted masculinity.

In the 30 years that women's studies has been part of the Western academy there has been a radical re-examination of the subject-matter and the theoretical categories of academic work. Sheila Rowbotham's *Hidden from History* (1973) put the case for the literal absence of women from the academic curriculum; subsequently, authors such as Julia Kristeva and Luce Irigaray have suggested that what is absent from conventional understanding is an acceptance of the feminine in both a literal and a symbolic sense. This thesis has had enormous influence on academic readings of literature and social life: SEXUALITY has been given an explicit place in explanations of the social world and the impact of gender difference on all forms of social organization has acquired a recognized significance. For further reading: M. Evans, *The Woman Question* (1994). M.S.E.

word class. In LINGUISTICS, a class of words that are similar in their formal behaviour (e.g. noun, adjective). Such classifications are made to facilitate the economic statement of grammatical rules, and many different detailed systems have been proposed, the most familiar being the system of *parts of speech*, which uses notional as well as formal criteria (see FORM). Various general classifications have also been used, e.g. the dichotomy between *form* (or *function*, or *grammatical*) *words*, whose primary role is to indicate grammatical relationships, and *content* (or *lexical*) *words*, whose primary role is to provide referential meaning (see REFERENCE); or the distinction between *open classes* of words (i.e. classes whose membership is capable of indefinite extension, e.g. nouns) and *closed classes* (or *systems*) of words (classes containing a small, fixed number of words, e.g. conjunctions). A classification of linguistic forms not restricted to the notion of words is a *form* class. D.C.

Work Projects Administration, see WPA.

work to rule. A form of strike without withdrawal of labour, in which output is reduced by the workers taking the time needed to comply to the fullest extent with requirements of working rules drawn up by management – e.g., the rule that a driver shall satisfy himself that his vehicle is in serviceable condition before he takes it out. Those working to rule are able to place pressure on management, and intensify it at will without losing the pay due for hours worked. The employer has no remedy short of locking the workers out. E.H.P.B.

Workers' Educational Association (WEA), see under ADULT EDUCATION.

workfare, see WELFARE TO WORK.

working class. Often used as a homely synonym for the more specialized Marxist concept of the PROLETARIAT, 'the working class' is both more and less than that. It is less in that it does not, unlike the Marxist concept, look forward to a future society conquered by, and remade in the image of, the working class. It is more in that it includes a range of values and cultural traits that go beyond the narrowly political role assigned to it by MARXISM. Working-class culture is largely defensive and conservative (see CONSERVATISM). It was shaped by the struggle for survival in the cities of the INDUSTRIAL REVOLUTION. In the course of this it elaborated the values of mutual aid, co-operation and community. Working-class communities became largely self-reliant and inward-looking, distrustful of MIDDLE-CLASS philanthropists and middle-class politicians, especially of the radical kind. In Germany, France and Italy, though not in Britain and the US, workers supported SOCIALIST parties but mainly as agencies of social betterment, not as the spearhead of socialist REVOLUTION. The working class has remained cautious and pragmatic, willing to exert its industrial and political muscle only where gains are evident and immediate. It has in this sense developed only what Lenin called a 'TRADE UNION consciousness', and not the radical consciousness expected of it by Marx. While combative in the industrial sphere, it has found no difficulty in reconciling this toughness with a high degree of patriotism and NATIONALISM.

The traditional homogeneity of working-class communities has, since World War II, been declining. Urban redevelopment has broken up the old tightly knit communities of the inner cities. Changes in work, especially with the introduction of new TECHNOLOGY, have produced a new skill hierarchy, cutting off a new skilled working class in the new industries from the unskilled and semi-skilled workers in the old declining 'smokestack' industries of the early Industrial Revolution. Much has been made by certain Marxists of the political potential of this '*new working class*' of skilled technicians. They are seen as a better-educated and more socially confident group who are likely to develop a more sophisticated and more radical CLASS consciousness than the old working class. In practice, as with the new middle class, the new working class has been ambiguous in its CULTURE and politics. It has borrowed from the old working class a pragmatic outlook, and seems prepared to engage in hard bargaining for the best deal it can get from both state and industry, whatever the ideological outlook of their managers (see IDEOLOGY). For further reading: J. Bourke, *Working Class Cultures in Britain, 1890–1960* (1994).

K.K.

working-class conservatism. LEFT-wing thinkers have been puzzled and frustrated by what seems to them an anomaly. A substantial minority – between one-third and two-fifths – of the manual working class in Western democracies has consistently supported conservative parties (see CONSERVATISM), instead of the labour or SOCIALIST parties which are the presumed 'carriers' of their CLASS interest. Early attempts at explanation, drawing on Walter Bagehot and Friedrich Engels, postulated a class of 'deferential workers' who accepted the old status hierarchy and clung to the view that the conservatives, as the party of the old ruling class, were the 'natural' leaders of society. Later theories have rested more on EMBOURGEOISEMENT and the idea of a DOMINANT IDEOLOGY. The problem has been complicated by the general decline of class-based voting in Western societies in recent decades. Working-class conservatives are now really no more anomalous than MIDDLE-CLASS socialists; it may indeed be the working-class Labour voter that is the fast-vanishing species. Voting and party preference show a volatility and instability that are a fair reflection of the more instrumental and calculating mood among voters of all classes of society. For further reading: A. Heath *et al*, *How Britain Votes* (1985).

K.K.

World Bank, see under BRETTON WOODS.

World Community of al-Islam in the West, see under NATION OF ISLAM.

World Health Organization. The LEAGUE OF NATIONS developed an innovative health organization: it prevented epidemics, collated statistics of deaths and diseases, established standard measures for vitamins and pharmaceuticals, and investigated the economic causes of sickness. The UN founded the World Health Organization in 1948, as an agency where medical experts could co-ordinate data on health hazards and diseases, as well as to undertake eradication programmes as for malaria (a failure), or smallpox (a success). In 1978 a shift of strategy to promoting primary healthcare occurred with the aim of 'Health for All by the Year 2000'. This stressed diet, sanitation, immunization and education. The education side further developed with AIDS prevention, although expert programmes have continued. The WHO has been criticized for administrative inertia, and other UN agencies have taken initiatives in preventive medicine, as with UNICEF's vaccination programme.

P.J.W.

world-line. The notion of world-line arises from German mathematician Hermann Minkowski's (1864–1909) conception of SPACE-TIME, itself a reinterpretation of Einstein's special RELATIVITY. Within the unification of space and time implied by Minkowski's concept, world-line is the trajectory plotted by the history of a material point. It is the dimension of temporality; or, put in other terms, the distance between two events differentiated on the world-line is a measure of time. In Minkowski's formulation, the interval along the world-line measures its own proper time. Regarded thus in relation to the world-line, clocks can be said to be unaffected by relative motion. For further reading: C. Weiner (ed.), *History of Twentieth Century Physics* (1977).

R.P.

world music. Not to be confused with ETHNOMUSICOLOGY, world music is largely a product of the 1960s, when notions of universal love inspired crossover experiments in culture. Rock musicians (see ROCK MUSIC) like the Beatles dabbled in Indian music: sitar and drone bass combined attractively with electric guitar and rock's repetitious pulse. Over the years, similarly seductive sounds have been co-opted from ethnic musics – native instruments, folk singing, tribal chants and drumming help brighten the increasingly monochrome character of pop. To its supporters, world music demonstrates an underlying unity between cultures: all musics are one. But its detractors maintain that it merely demonstrates that a rock beat can be added to anything and that what claims to be an exercise in democracy is simply a dilution of the rich particularity of indigenous forms.

GE.S.

world society theory. Conceives of the world as a society of individuals and communities rather than as a patchwork of competing nation-states. This idea has a long history and was reflected, e.g., in medieval aspirations for the unity of Christendom, and later in Kant's idealistic proposals for securing perpetual peace. In addition to utopian schemes to transcend the nation-state (see UTOPIANISM), in the 1970s a group of mainly American scholars began to develop world society models and theories as a means of overcoming what they perceived as the serious limitations of the traditional state-centric approach. Theorists such as R. Keohane and J. S. Nye (1971) emphasized what they termed 'the characteristics of complexity and INTERDEPENDENCE' such as 'multiple channels' linking societies, especially transnational connections. They challenged the assumption that states act as coherent units. One British contributor to this school is J. W. Burton (see COBWEB THEORY). Rather than accord primacy to diplomatic-strategic issues, contemporary world society theorists seek to give equal attention to 'new' global issues such as energy, resources, environment, and the use of the oceans. It is when they address such issues that they tend to smuggle in the NORMATIVE assumption that man's wants must be modified so that they can be more effectively matched with available resources. They have also been criticized for wishful thinking in assuming that the fragmentation of the world into nation-states is already being transcended and that the emergence of a uniform global society and culture would be a desirable development. For further reading: M. Smith, R. Little and M. Shackleton (eds), *Perspectives on World Politics* (1981). P.W.

world systems theory. A theory of UNDERDEVELOPMENT devised by Immanuel Wallerstein in the 1970s, closely related to DEPENDENCY THEORY. It argues that the development of CAPITALISM since 1450 has led to the integration of the world economy into one system. In that system there are three groups of nations: the core (rich, exploiting capitalist [see CAPITALISM] nations), the peripheral (poor and exploited THIRD WORLD countries), and the semi-peripheral (which are exploited by the core but exploit the periphery). Unlike dependency theory it sees some movement within this system as possible: core countries may decline and join the semi-periphery and successful peripheral countries may climb into the semi-periphery. Because of the interdependence of the world economy socialist (see SOCIALISM) REVOLUTIONS will be ineffective in individual states and world revolution is the only way of transforming capitalism. In some ways world systems theory anticipated aspects of GLOBALIZATION theory long before the idea of globalization became fashionable, but it has been criticized for its emphasis on economic factors and the neglect of culture. For further reading: I. Wallerstein, *The Capitalist World Economy* (1979). M.D.H.

World Trade Organization, see WTO.

world-view, see under WELTANSCHAUUNG.

World Wide Web. An INTERNET system, commonly referred to as 'the Web', that takes advantage of many of the most recent features of computers; it uses a series of links, known as HYPERTEXT transfers, to display information, making a computer's physical location invisible to the user. A display might jump from information on a computer in Denver to data from Hong Kong to something in Chile. A single display can show text from San Francisco and images from Seattle. Interest in the Web grew in 1994 with the creation of the first graphical web BROWSER. Its easy point-and-click operation brought the Web to the level computer users had come to expect, and by 1995 curiosity about it had exploded. Sceptics suggested that the Web could suffer the fate of citizen's band (CB) radio. During the mid-1970s there had been extensive interest in CB, but the rage passed. Web investors, however, had deeper pockets than CB fans. Corporations established information displays (called 'Web pages' or HOMEPAGES) and governments were providing extensive information sources as well. Their pages made it easy to check movie reviews, health information, financial data, annual reports, and personal biographies. Retailers provided books, records, PORNOGRAPHY, and anything else that could be sold through mail order. For all the growth and activity, it was still not clear how to make money on the Web. Could Web pages provide the advertising audiences enjoyed by network television or even mass-market magazines?

Retail sales seemed possible, but will mail-order customers really prefer to browse on-line instead of from a printed catalogue? Information can be sold on-line, but how many paying customers are there for the product? Can any on-line entertainment compete seriously with CD music, VCR movies, cable television, or even computer MULTIMEDIA for home entertainment? After several years, even the Web's most ardent proponents could say only that the answers were uncertain. Even without profitability the Web has come to stay. Governments, corporate public relations units, educational institutions, and ordinary people looking to advertise themselves have, within the space of three years, turned the Web into the world's most important source of non-profit information. E.B.B.

worm, see under COMPUTER VIRUS.

Worpswede. North German village near Bremen, centre of an artists' colony (*c.* 1890–1914) whose outstanding figure was the short-lived Paula Modersohn-Becker (1876–1907), a forerunner of EXPRESSIONISM. Other members included Fritz Mackensen, Otto Modersohn, Heinrich Vogeler, and Hans am Ende. An account of the colony was given by Austrian poet Rainer Maria Rilke in his *Worpswede* (1902). J.W.

WPA (Work Projects Administration; later Work Progress Administration). A NEW DEAL organization, set up by President Roosevelt in 1935, with an initial appropriation of $4,880 million, to counter some of the effects of the post-1929 DEPRESSION. WPA, which included the Federal Arts, Theater and Writers Projects (and, until 1939, the National Youth Administration), was killed by Congress long before its official death in 1943. The *Federal Arts Project* was mainly concerned with the rebuilding, redesigning and mural decoration of public offices. The *Federal Theater Project* was the most remarkable in its results, since it implemented its intention to give dramatists and actors a livelihood without inhibiting their creative freedom. The guiding spirit and director was Hallie Flanagan, who inaugurated an experimental LIVING NEWSPAPER (which was edited by Arthur Arent, and from which emerged Joseph Losey and others), put on documentary and original plays, and staged important revivals. The Theater Project was effectually shut down in 1939, soon after Christopher Marlowe, author of one of these revived plays, had been indicted as a communist (see COMMUNISM). The *Federal Writers Project* was run by Henry G. Alsberg. Its most notable achievement was the production of the American Guide Series, a state-by-state portrait of the American people (which in the main they resented). M.S.-S.

WTO (World Trade Organization). The successor organization to GATT. It is the co-ordinating group for world trade discussions and the court of final settlement in national trade disputes. The goal of the WTO is to remove all barriers to trade (see TRADE THEORY) and INVESTMENT among nations, and the WTO seeks to mediate between the interested parties both from the developed and developing world (see DEVELOPING COUNTRIES). The Organization was established in 1995 at the conclusion of the Uruguay trade round at which substantial reductions in the tariffs on manufactured goods were negotiated, along with a phase-out of agricultural subsidies. Future trade rounds will move beyond physical goods to trade in services, investment, telecommunications and labour standards. The lowering of trade and investment barriers among nations is generally considered to make a huge contribution to global growth and prosperity (see GLOBALIZATION), although serious tensions still exist between major players like the US and Japan and the richer Western countries and the less-developed world. A.BR.

X chromosomes, see under SEX CHROMOSOMES.

X-efficiency, see under ECONOMIC EFFICIENCY.

xenophobia. The condition of disliking individuals or groups thought of as foreign. The 'groups' may range in size from an entire continent (as with anti-American or anti-European feeling) to a neighbouring family of IMMIGRANTS (or even of migrants from another part of the country if regarded as intrusive); and the dislike can range in intensity from a normally controlled awareness of preferences to an abnormal state of pathological fear and ANXIETY. It commonly takes an ethnic form (see RACISM; ANTISEMITISM), and in its most extreme and widespread forms of expression may reflect the paranoid, psychotic state (see PARANOIA; PSYCHOSIS) of those in power, as it did with Hitler and Stalin. M.BE.

X-ray astronomy. That branch of ASTRONOMY devoted to the study of celestial bodies beyond our SOLAR SYSTEM which emit X-RAYS. X-radiation is electromagnetic radiation (see ELECTROMAGNETISM) with wavelength in the 0.0025–12 nm range, and so with ENERGY between 0.1 and 500 kv. Low-energy X-rays are called soft X-rays; high-energy X-rays are called hard X-rays. They are produced in the universe wherever fast-moving ELECTRONS collide with matter or move in magnetic fields. This radiation band does not penetrate the earth's lower atmosphere and hence observations of astronomical X-ray sources are made using balloons, rockets and SATELLITES. The first X-ray source to be found (Scorpius X-1) was detected with a rocket-borne detector in 1962. The first X-ray observing satellite, Uhuru (= Swahili for 'Freedom'), was launched in December 1970. Subsequent launches have made surveys of the sky over X-ray wavelengths and found X-ray-emitting binary pairs of stars to be the most common source of X-rays in our GALAXY. The X-ray source Cygnus X-1 is almost certainly a BLACK HOLE accreting material from a companion star. The infalling material emits X-rays (see ACCRETION). Hot intergalactic gas in rich clusters of galaxies (see GALAXY CLUSTERS) emits X-rays. There exists a diffuse low-intensity background of X-rays in the universe, which is believed to be caused by the integrated emission from distant QUASARS and other galaxies. In 1975 bursts of X-rays were discovered from sources within our galaxy. It is believed that they originate from sporadic accretion of material on to condensed WHITE DWARFS and neutron stars (see PULSAR). For further reading: M. Longair, *Our Evolving Universe* (1996). J.D.B.

X-ray diffraction. The DIFFRACTION of X-RAYS by the ATOMS in a crystal LATTICE, which occurs because the wavelength of the X-rays is comparable with the interatomic spacing. X-ray diffraction is a principal tool in CRYSTALLOGRAPHY and BIOCHEMISTRY, where it has made possible the structural analysis of DNA (see NUCLEIC ACID) and other macromolecules associated with life. M.V.B.

X-ray laser, see under STRATEGIC DEFENCE INITIATIVE.

X-rays. Electromagnetic RADIATION (discovered by German physicist Wilhelm Röntgen in 1895) whose wavelength is about 1,000 times smaller than that of visible light, and which is emitted during transitions of the innermost ELECTRONS in an ATOM between low-lying ENERGY LEVELS. X-rays are produced by bombarding a metal target with fast electrons from an ELECTRON GUN. The medical usefulness of X-rays in forming shadow images of bones arises because the absorption of X-rays in a material increases rapidly with its density and ATOMIC NUMBER, and because X-rays can form an image on an ordinary photographic plate. See also X-RAY DIFFRACTION. M.V.B.

Y

Y chromosomes, see under SEX CHROMOSOMES.

Yale School. A group of literary critics influenced by Freud and the DECONSTRUCTION of French philosopher Jacques Derrida. During the 1970s it comprised Harold Bloom, Paul de Man, Geoffrey Hartman, J. Hillis Miller, and Derrida. Since the death of Paul de Man and the removal of J. Hillis Miller and Derrida to California, the 'school' no longer exists. In its heyday it operated under the dual aegis of Paul de Man's *Blindness and Insight* (1971) and Harold Bloom's *The Anxiety of Influence* (1973). Paul de Man, following Derrida, regarded the literary text as a set of opposed possibilities which eventually led to an *aporia*, i.e. when the text enforces a decision between two opposed readings and actually, for internal textual reasons, prohibits the choosing of either of these. This approach is given classical expression in *Allegories of Reading* (1979). Harold Bloom, choosing to regard the writing of poetry not so much as willing submission to the influence of a great 'precursor' as having to face the anguish and guilt of trying to 'replace' him (as a son attempts to 'replace' his father), introduced a heavily FREUDIAN element into a theory of the text that already emphasized reader response (see READER-RESPONSE THEORY) to a very high degree. Bloom's theory of the 'anxiety of influence', an anxiety which leads the poet to try to escape the implication of his own work through six rhetorical 'defence mechanisms', had a galvanizing effect upon literary theory generally. From 1973 literary critics were not able to avoid the implications of rhetorical-deconstructive and of Freudian-rhetorical theorizing. J. Hillis Miller emphasized the rhetorical and formally linguistic, non-referential nature of poetry, and Geoffrey Hartman acted as mediator for the theories of Derrida, while eventually adding a decided theological disclaimer of his own, *Saving the Text* (1981). Meanwhile, Derrida himself moved beyond his own contributions to the Yale School towards a new theory which reinvestigated the PHENOMENOLOGY of the text, and started with a study of *Midrash* contributed to Harman and Budick's *Midrash and Literature* (1986). For further reading: J. Arac *et al* (eds), *The Yale Critics: Deconstruction in America* (1983).

R.PO.

Yalta. A town in the Crimea, the scene (4–11 February 1945) of the second war-time summit conference (see SUMMIT DIPLOMACY) between Churchill, Roosevelt and Stalin. Even more than at Teheran, the conference was marked by President Roosevelt's determination to subordinate every other consideration to winning Soviet goodwill and, a new development, to securing early Soviet participation in the war against Japan. Britain, much more concerned than the USA with the post-war settlement in Europe, secured a postponement (in practice, abandonment) of plans to dismember Germany, and a vote for France in the occupation and control of Germany. On all other issues, notably the post-war frontiers of Poland, the Soviet view was accepted. In the 1950s, Yalta became a point of attack for American RIGHT-wing critics of Roosevelt, who accused him of betraying America's long-term interests to the enemy of American DEMOCRACY. For further reading: H. Freis, *Churchill, Roosevelt, Stalin* (1957).

D.C.W.

yang, see under MACROBIOTICS; ACUPUNCTURE.

Yezhovshchina ('the Yezhov time'). The period of the most intense terror in Russia under Stalin, namely from September 1936 to December 1938, when Nikolai Yezhov (1894–1940) was People's Commissar for Internal Affairs, i.e. head of the secret police. It included the second and third great MOSCOW TRIALS, and the trial and execution of Marshal Tukhachevsky and other leading officers in June 1937. Soviet estimates published later imply that during this period at least seven million people were arrested, 90 per cent of whom – including half the Party membership, three-quarters of the Central Committee, about half of the corps of officers, and several hundred writers, artists and scientists – perished in FORCED LABOUR camps or by execution. After Yezhov's dismissal, he was himself shot. He was succeeded by Lavrenty Beria. For further reading: R. Conquest, *The Great Terror* (1971). R.C.

yin, see under MACROBIOTICS; ACUPUNCTURE.

yoga. The spiritual discipline of the higher forms of HINDUISM, including a carefully planned course of fasting with physical and mental exercises in order to concentrate the mind. In its narrower sense the term refers to a Hindu movement which produced the *Yoga Sutras*, scriptures describing union (Sanskrit *yoga*) with the supreme spirit after much self-sacrifice. As used in the West, the phrase may refer more loosely to exercises for mental and physical fitness, adapted from Indian sources. D.L.E.

Yom Kippur War, see under MIDDLE EAST WARS.

youth culture. A loosely used label which in the 1960s and 1970s was often mistakenly employed as a synonym for counter-culture or alternative society (see UNDERGROUND). Youth culture can best be described as denoting the transient NORMS, values and LIFESTYLES – symbolized by specific modes of dress, language, music and consumption patterns – through which adolescent and young adult communities in advanced INDUSTRIAL SOCIETIES (and increasingly in DEVELOPING COUNTRIES) mark themselves out from the parent CULTURE and the other institutions of the dominant society. During the 1970s and early 1980s the study of youth culture was dominated by the work of the Birmingham Centre for Contemporary Cultural Studies (CCCS), which applied the term *youth sub-culture* (borrowed from the CHICAGO SCHOOL) to post-war British working-class youth cultures such as mods, rockers and skinheads. According to the CCCS, such sub-cultures used style as a means of both expressing and resolving the structural and experiential contradictions of their existence. There are, however, problems associated with the concept of sub-culture, not least of all the fact that it suggests a tight coherent unit when, in reality, youth cultures are typically unstable social categories with fluid boundaries and floating memberships. More recent developments in the cultural sphere of youth have further problematized the concept of sub-culture. The advent of urban dance music forms such as house, techno and jungle (see HIP-HOP) from the late 1980s onwards has resulted in an increasing fragmentation of youth style. The stylistic divisions which separated, e.g., the mods from the rockers during the mid-1960s, or punks from skinheads in the 1970s, have drastically diminished, with youth becoming increasingly eclectic and individualistic in terms of stylistic preference. Some observers suggest that this is an effect of POST-MODERNISM as youth cultures become parodies of themselves. For further reading: K. Gelder and S. Thornton (eds), *The Subcultures Reader* (1997). A.BEN.

Yugoslavia, the former. Former federation of the Slavic states of Serbia, Bosnia and Herzegovina, Croatia, Macedonia, Montenegro and Slovenia in the Balkan Peninsula, which was formed in 1918 and disintegrated amid a bloody civil war in 1991. The history of the Yugoslav state was characterized by conflict between the Serbs who dominated the government and the other ethnic groups who were denied autonomy. The country suffered greatly during World War II, experiencing invasion and partition. It was liberated by partisans led by Marshal Tito, who then ruled the country as premier and President until his death in May 1980. Tito succeeded in mediating the tensions between the various ethnic groups that formed Yugoslavia. Under him the country to an extent became part of the Soviet bloc, but a relatively independent part, experimenting with its own form of economic organization which came to be known as market SOCIALISM, and becoming a member of the group of non-aligned nations. After Tito came economic problems and the re-emergence of ethnic conflict. The ruling League of Communists of Yugoslavia finally surrendered power in 1990, and free elections in that year resulted in strong support for nationalists (see NATIONALISM) in the various Yugoslav states. Slovodan Milosevic came to power in Serbia and embarked on a policy of re-establishing Serbian control of Yugoslavia by force, whereupon the country disintegrated into its various national components. V.L.

Z

Zaum. The Russian word for trans-sense (transrational) language – the arbitrary combination of sounds, or the play with the morphological components (see MORPHOLOGY) of a familiar word practised by Russian Futurist poets (see FUTURISM), notably Kruchenykh and Khlebnikov. *Zaum* stemmed from the Futurists' belief that the word, as the material of poetry, should be emancipated from its 'traditional subservience to meaning' and become a self-sufficient entity, interesting for its outward form, i.e. its graphic and phonic characteristics. It led to the creation of poetic neologisms, or completely non-referential words. M.E.

Zeitgeist. German word meaning literally 'the Spirit of the Time (or Age)'. It is associated with attempts to epitomize the mode of thought or feeling deemed fundamentally characteristic of a particular period, e.g. to interpret the 19th century as an age of '*heroic materialism*' (Kenneth Clark). The term was first regularly employed by the German Romantics (see ROMANTICISM). Tempted always to reduce the past to essences, they often treated the *Zeitgeist* less as a conceptual instrument than as a grandiose historical character in its own right. Most historians handle the term with caution on the grounds that the characteristics of any historical period are more complex than a formulation of a *Zeitgeist* can suggest. See also CULTURAL HISTORY. For further reading: G. W. F. Hegel, *Lectures on the Philosophy of World History* (1975). M.D.B.

Zen. The Japanese version of the Ch'an sect of BUDDHISM in China, noted for its simple austerity, its MYSTICISM leading to personal tranquillity, and its encouragement of education and art. Some of its scriptures and paintings have become widely known and admired in the West; and Aldous Huxley and others in California led something of a cult of Zen, which in the 1960s began appealing to students as a way of having religious experience without DOGMAS or religious INSTITUTIONS. The trouble is, however, that the reality experienced after ecstasy (*satori*) is hard to describe, and the approach to it hard to reconcile with reason. Many of the statements encouraged by the masters of Zen seem deliberately nonsensical – e.g. the idea of a single hand clapping – although they are intended to open the doors of PERCEPTION into a world of wonder. For further reading: A. Watts, *The Way of Zen* (1957). D.L.E.

Zero, Gruppe, see under KINETIC ART.

zero option, see under NUCLEAR WEAPONS, LIMITATION AND CONTROL.

zero point energy. The ENERGY of the motion remaining in a body at ABSOLUTE ZERO of temperature. The body is then in its *ground state* (see ENERGY LEVEL), which according to the UNCERTAINTY PRINCIPLE of QUANTUM MECHANICS cannot correspond to the complete absence of motion. M.V.B.

zero population growth (ZPG)/negative population growth (NPG). Technically, a situation in which a population is not growing (ZPG) or is decreasing in size (NPG). The significance of both terms is as much political as scientific, however, since they have been used as rhetorical devices to advance the Malthusian (see MALTHUSIANISM) view that the POPULATION GROWTH RATE must be reduced to zero or negative values in order to correct the problem of human OVERPOPULATION. J.R.W.

zero-sum game, see under GAME THEORY.

zero tolerance. Associated with the work of Wilson and Kelling (see below) and their 'broken windows' thesis: this suggests that community deterioration follows a developmental sequence – a street or neighbourhood suffers vandalism to empty buildings, incivilities increase, local businesses and respectable families move out, and COMMUNITY order disintegrates. What is required is the reassertion of public order and early intervention to counter the signs of deterioration and intrusion by undesirables. To pursue this, some police forces (most famously in New York City) have recently exercised 'zero tolerance' of the most minor offences, aiming to 'clean up' the streets. Supporters claim considerable success has followed this approach. However, similar improvements in crime reduction have been claimed for other police force areas in the US and elsewhere, which have not adopted this tactic. Critics have objected that zero tolerance is intentionally uncompromising; aggressive in ways that may generate aggression in response; and targets 'people as problems', merely displacing individuals from one location to another. In this view, zero tolerance does nothing to address the social and structural problems that underpin the deterioration of urban communities. For further reading: G. L. Kelling, J. Q. Wilson, *Fixing Broken Windows: Restoring Order and Reducing Crime in Our Communities* (1982). N.S.

Zhdanovshchina ('the Zhdanov time'). The period 1946–48, in which heavy Party pressure was brought to bear in the Soviet cultural field, under the aegis of Andrei Zhdanov, Secretary of the Central Committee in charge of IDEOLOGY. It was marked by attacks on many leading Soviet writers, notably Mikhail Zoshchenko, Anna Akhmatova and Boris Pasternak. See also USSR, THE FORMER. For further reading: H. Swayze, *Political Control of Literature in the USSR, 1946–1959* (1962). R.C.

zino, see under SUPERSYMMETRY.

Zionism. The Jewish national movement to re-establish the Jewish nation in Palestine. Zionism was a secularist and nationalistic (see NATIONALISM) transformation of an aspiration basic to orthodox JUDAISM, in reaction to the Tsarist persecution of Russian and Polish Jewry and to other outbursts of ANTISEMITISM, e.g. during the DREYFUS CASE. Theodor Herzl (1860–1904), the founder of modern Zionism (who reported the Dreyfus trials for an Austrian paper), argued in his book *Der Judenstaat* (1896) that the only alternative to continued persecution was to found a Jewish state, and in 1897 he called the first World Zionist Congress in Basle. It was Chaim Weizmann (1874–1952) who insisted that a Jewish nation could only be re-created in Palestine, a course which became practicable with the BALFOUR DECLARATION of 1917. Since the foundation of the state of Israel in 1948, the term Zionism has a mainly historical meaning. It is still used, however, to describe (1) the organized sympathies and support of Jews in the West, especially in the US, for Israel; (2) the efforts by Soviet Jewry to emigrate to Israel; (3) the continuing promise by Israel to offer a national home to any Jew in the world who seeks it. For further reading: R. Robertson and E. Timms (eds), *Theodor Herzl and the Origins of Zionism* (1997). A.L.C.B.

zone of transition, see under FRONTIER.

zoning (land use planning). The separation of land-uses (e.g. residential from commercial uses) in order to create urban order from what was perceived as the natural chaos of mixed land-uses and unplanned development, and thus to improve the efficiency of the city (particularly in relation to infrastructural provision) and the overall quality of urban life. A major component of TOWN PLANNING, particularly in the US, has been the use of 'zoning' regulation. In reality zoning has often been used to protect property values and has intensified social divisions between classes and racial groups, by means of controlling densities, minimum plot size and household composition, as well as just 'land-use'. The first comprehensive zoning regulations were enacted in the US in 1916. Zoning began to be challenged from the 1970s, as a cause of INNER CITY decline, SUBURBANIZATION and related social polarization. Zoning is increasingly used more positively in encouraging economic revitalization and as a means of social policy (see PLANNING GAIN). It is often said that British town planning is policy-based. But it has a strong element of land-use zoning, as manifest in the 'development plans' for each main urban area (currently under the 1990 Town and Country Planning Act). Nowadays, in the wake of the movement for greater concern with the environment and SUSTAINABLE URBAN DEVELOPMENT, plus considerable pressure and criticism from a range of organizations concerned with what is seen as the socially biased nature of modern town planning policy, there is much pressure for a return to a more human scale based on walking distances, and upon de-zoning and mixing of uses. For further reading: C. Greed, *Introducing Town Planning* (1994). C.G.

zoo hypothesis, see under SEARCH FOR EXTRATERRESTRIAL INTELLIGENCE.

zoogeography. The branch of BIOGEOGRAPHY which studies the geographical distribution of animals. In any region (see REGIONALISM) this is determined by the nature of the vegetation on which the herbivorous animals (the vast majority) depend. Thus forest-inhabiting animals only occur after trees have grown up. On the world scale, climate and EVOLUTION are important. Many species are *stenothermous*, i.e. they exist only over a narrow range of temperature. Isolated areas, e.g. Australia, have seen the evolution and establishment of SPECIES (e.g. kangaroos and other large marsupials) which have been protected from competition with the 'higher' forms dominant elsewhere. For further reading: P. J. Darlington, *Zoogeography* (1957). K.M.

zoology. The science that deals with the classification (see TAXONOMY), structure and functions of animals, including by convention those CHLOROPHYLL-containing PROTOZOA which could equally well be classified as plants. The old-fashioned distinction between vertebrates and invertebrates is not taxonomically useful and makes no kind of sense in terms of PHYLOGENY. There is a tendency nowadays, therefore, to distinguish two main lines of descent among animals:

(1) a *chordate* line of descent including the chordates themselves (animals distinguished by the possession at some stage of their life history of a notochord, and a central nervous system in the form of a median dorsal hollow nerve tube), and certain other phyla (see PHYLUM) related to the chordates by fundamental similarities of early development; these include those phyla of which typical members are sea-urchins, sea-cucumbers and starfish (echinodermata), together with sea-squirts (tunicata), all forming together the chordate line of descent; and

(2) a miscellany of *non-chordate* phyla including the worms strictly so called (annelida) and – wrongly so called – the flatworms (platyhelminthes) and roundworms (nematodes) and one or two other groups of lesser importance. P.M.

zoosemiotics, see under SEMIOTICS.

ZPG, see ZERO POPULATION GROWTH.

zygote. The single CELL that is the product of the fusion between an egg cell and a spermatozoon from which all vertebrate development proceeds. As a result of this fusion, a zygote contains the normal double complement (DIPLOID number) of CHROMOSOMES. P.M.